Brief contents

Contents

Contents

Your complete learning package

Visit www.mylawchamber.co.uk/bainbridgeip to access a wealth of resources to support your studies and teaching.

Self study resources
- Interactive multiple choice questions to test your understanding of each topic
- Practice exam questions with guidance to hone your exam technique
- Weblinks to help you read more widely around the subject and really impress your lecturers
- Legal updates to help you stay up to date with the law and impress examiners
- Legal newsfeed

Teaching support materials
- **PowerPoint** slides with visual support in explaining legal concepts

Also: The regularly maintained mylawchamber site provides the following features:

- Search tool to help locate specific items of content.
- Online help and support to assist with website usage and troubleshooting.

Preface

There have been relatively few legislative changes since the previous edition, though notable are the controversial copyright provisions of the Digital Economy Act 2010 with its copyright infringement reports and initial obligations code. An initial challenge to these provisions was made by BT and TalkTalk Telecom, but this was unsuccessful. It remains to be seen whether this attempt to control online copyright infringement will be effective without being unduly heavy-handed or raising serious privacy concerns.

The Supreme Court replaced the Appellate Committee of the House of Lords in October 2009 as the highest court in the UK. Thus far it has handed down judgments in two important intellectual property cases. The first case is *Lucasfilm* v *Ainsworth* (a case involving the Stormtroopers' helmets in the Star Wars films). The case is important in ruling on the scope of 'sculpture' for copyright purposes and in relation to jurisdictional issues. The second case, *Human Genome Sciences* v *Eli Lilly* is arguably the most important UK case on the meaning of industrial application for the purposes of patent law.

Other important cases from the courts in the UK and the Court of Justice of the European Union include the use of trade marks as internet search engine AdWords, the doctrine of freedom to supply services (relevant to encrypted broadcasts of live football matches), database copyright and the concept of repair under patent law. There has been a further development in the principles applicable to employee compensation where an invention turns out to be of outstanding benefit to the employer. All the above cases are discussed in this new edition as well as a multitude of other recent cases. All parts of the book have been updated to incorporate these cases.

When describing and discussing remedies in terms of each branch of intellectual property law, it is inevitable that there is some overlap as some remedies, such as injunctions and damages are generally available. However, and following a suggestion from a reviewer of the previous edition, for which I am grateful, it was felt that it would be useful to have a separate chapter on remedies. This permits a general discussion on the remedies available under each type of intellectual property law, leaving a more in depth discussion of specific remedies under each part of the book.

Since the cut-off date of the previous edition, the EC Treaty has been replaced by the Treaty on the Functioning of the European Union. The necessary changes have been made as appropriate and reference now is generally to the latter Treaty. However, some references to the old Treaty are made in an attempt to ensure clarity, especially when discussing earlier cases. A table of equivalents setting out the relevant provisions of both Treaties appears in the section on law reports, references, etc. just before the first chapter.

The previous edition noted some of the recommendations made in the *Gowers Review of Intellectual Property*. Since then, a relatively small number of recommendations have been adopted. More recently, the *Hargreaves Report* has reiterated some of these recommendations and made further recommendations. These include the establishment of a digital copyright exchange, provisions easing the use of 'orphan works', format shifting, and dealing with problems in patent law such as patent thickets. Improving IP education and delivering effective IP advice to SMEs are also seen as important matters that should be addressed. Reference is made to both Gowers and Hargreaves in this edition. It has to be said, however, that further legislative changes must be compatible with EU law and the various international IP Conventions and Agreements. Some of the recommendations are already permitted as options under EU copyright Directives, such as format shifting and parody, but which the UK has thus far failed to implement.

As ever, I have enjoyed writing the ninth edition of this book and learnt more about intellectual property whilst doing so. I thank Cheryl Cheasley and all the people at Pearson Education for their help, support and patience and my wife Lorraine for her help and encouragement. I have attempted to state the law as at 1 January 2012.

David Bainbridge

Table of cases

Other national cases

European court of justice and court of first instance (now the general court) cases

European patent office cases

Office for the harmonisation of the internal market (trade marks and designs) cases

European court of human rights cases

Table of legislation

l

Glossary

Terms and phrases common in intellectual property law

Assignment: the transfer of the title in a chose in action. For example, ownership of copyright is transferred by means of an assignment in writing which is signed by or on behalf of the previous owner of the copyright, that is, the assignor. In intellectual property law, an assignment must be distinguished from an exclusive licence, which is similar in many practical respects, but which does not involve the transfer of the title to the right. Strictly speaking a patent is an item of personal property without being a 'thing in action' (section 30(1) of the Patents Act 1977), but transfer of title is still referred to as an assignment.

Character merchandising: this occurs when the owner of the rights in some popular character or personality grants licences to others allowing them to apply drawings, photographs or other representations of the character to goods and articles which those others make or sell. Typically, the character will be a famous fictitious character popularised by television or film. Examples are Mickey Mouse, Bob the Builder, Denis the Menace, Indiana Jones, Harry Potter, etc.

Collecting society: a society that collects revenue in respect of the exploitation of an intellectual property right and distributes that revenue amongst the right owners. In some cases, the owners of the right will assign part of their rights to the collecting society. An important example is the *Performing Right Society* (PRS) which takes an assignment of the performing rights in music, grants blanket licences and distributes the revenue thus earned between the songwriters, composers, and publishers of music. *Phonographic Performance Ltd* (PPL) collects and distributes money on behalf of record companies and performers in respect of public performances of recordings. The *Mechanical Copyright Protection Society* (MCPS) collects and pays royalties where music is copied onto any format, such as CDs and DVDs. Music played in shops, restaurants and other premises to which the public have access usually will need to pay for a PRS and PPL licence and, possibly depending on the circumstances, a MCPS licence. Work premises will also usually need such a licence. There have been moves to integrate the licence provisions of these organisations to simplify matters.

Another important collecting society, the *Copyright Licensing Agency* (CLA), licenses the copying of extracts of books, journals and periodicals on behalf of authors and publishers. Typically Universities hold CLA licences allowing them, for example, to make copies of a journal article or a chapter of a book to distribute to a class of students. The royalties to authors are distributed though the *Authors' Licensing and Collecting Agency* (ALCS), members of which, including the author of this book, are represented by the CLA. Whereas some collecting societies, such as the PRS, take an assignment of the relevant rights others, such as the CLA, do not.

Comptroller of Patents, Designs and Trade Marks: the head of the Patent Office (its operating name is now the UK Intellectual Property Office) with responsibility for the administration and grant of patents, registered designs and trade marks. Under trade mark legislation and design legislation the Comptroller is referred to as the *Registrar*. The Comptroller has other duties. Examples are: the conduct of hearings and proceedings, the production of statistics and an annual report, increasing public awareness of the work of the Patent Office in addition to working with, advising and participating with the European Patent Office, the World Intellectual Property Organisation and the Council of Europe. The Comptroller has the power to make non-binding opinions as to validity (novelty or inventive step) or infringement of patents. In the year ending 31 March 2011, the Patent Office employed 899 persons (as at 31 March 2011) and had a turnover of over £66 million.

Exhaustion of rights: a doctrine emanating from EU law. Basically, the owner of an intellectual property right which relates to articles which have been put into circulation by him or with his consent anywhere within the European Economic Area ('EEA' – the EU Member States, Iceland, Liechtenstein and Norway) cannot exercise that right to prevent the subsequent import, export or sale of those particular articles. The right is said to be exhausted. This will only apply where trade between Member States is likely to be affected. The doctrine does not apply in relation to articles put on the market outside the EEA and imported into the EEA.

Freezing injunction (formerly Mareva injunction): an injunction freezing the assets of a defendant thus preventing him from removing them out of the jurisdiction of the court. Such an injunction is useful where the defendant is not resident within the United Kingdom. Originally named after the case *Mareva Compania Naviera SA* v *International Bulk Carriers SA* [1980] 1 All ER 213.

Get-up: a style, mark, appearance, packaging or form of advertising or marketing used in connection with, or applied to, an undertaking's ('trader's') goods or services which may be or become distinctive in relation to that undertaking and which may give rise to, contribute to, or be associated with, the undertaking's goodwill which is protected by the law of passing off. A particular stylised logo, emblem or other form of insignia may, in appropriate circumstances, be registered as a trade mark.

Infringement: intellectual property law gives rights to the owner of that property permitting him to do certain acts in respect of the thing in which the right subsists. Any person who does one of these acts without the permission or authority of the right-owner is said to infringe the right unless the act concerned is permitted by law or a defence applies. Thus, it is usual to speak of an infringement of copyright or to say that a patent has been infringed.

Licence: a licence is a permission given by the owner of a right (the licensor) to another person (the licensee) allowing that other person to do certain specified things in respect of the subject matter of the right. For example, the owner of the copyright subsisting in a musical work may grant a licence to a publishing company allowing it to print and sell copies of the work in the form of sheet music. Another example is where the proprietor (owner) of a patent grants a licence to another person permitting the working of the invention by that other person. Intellectual property licences are normally contractual in nature and the licensor will usually receive royalties by way of consideration for the permission.

Licences may be exclusive or non-exclusive. An *exclusive licence* is one where the licensee has the exclusive right to do certain things to the exclusion of all others including the licensor. Several *non-exclusive licences* may be granted to different persons in respect of the same work and the same activities. For example, the owner of the copyright in a dramatic work may grant several non-exclusive licences to theatre companies permitting each of them to perform the dramatic work live on stage.

Compulsory licences may be granted under the provisions of an Act of Parliament. For example, the Patents Act 1977 gives the Comptroller of Patents, Designs and Trade Marks the power to grant a compulsory licence to an applicant if, for example, where the invention is a product, demand in the United Kingdom is not being met on reasonable terms. In some cases, licences are available as of right. This may be the ultimate result of a report from the Competition Commission (for example, if a patent or design is not being sufficiently

worked and this is contrary to the public interest), or because of a statutory provision, for example as regards designs subject to the design right during the last five years of the right, or because the owner has volunteered that such licences be available (in the case of a patent, the proprietor may do this and from then on he will only pay half the usual renewal fees).

If there is a defect in an assignment or a misunderstanding as to the ownership of a right, a court might be prepared to imply a licence. For example, if a person commissions the making of a work of copyright and there is no express agreement for the assignment of that copyright, the court might be able to imply a licence so that the commissioner can use the work for certain purposes consistent with the purpose of the commission. Alternatively, the concept of beneficial ownership may be used to similar effect.

Moral rights: the rights that the author of a work of copyright has independent of the economic rights of the copyright owner. The moral rights are: to be identified as the author of the work (or the director of a film) and to be able to object to a derogatory treatment of the work. These rights leave the author with some control over his work even if he does not own the copyright. Any person also has a right, under copyright law, not to have a work falsely attributed to him. Moral rights have also been extended to performers in respect of their live performances and recordings thereof.

Public domain: refers to all material which is available to the public at large (or a portion of it) and which may be freely used and exploited without infringing anyone's intellectual property rights. Material may be in the public domain because: (a) it is commonplace or lacks novelty, (b) it has been put there deliberately by the 'owner', and (c) the intellectual property rights concerning the material have expired or lapsed. It is possible that material has fallen into the public domain through a breach of confidence, in which case only those persons who have come across the material in good faith without notice of the breach of confidence will be free to make use of it. Such cases will be rare.

Reverse engineering: the process where information about the design or construction of an article is determined by an examination of the article itself, frequently after dismantling or measuring the dimensions of the article. Another manufacturer can copy articles by this process without having to inspect drawings and other design documents made for the article. For example, one company copied another's exhaust pipes by removing an exhaust system from a car, examining and taking measurements of it. The protection of spare parts is a controversial area, particularly with respect to spare parts for vehicles. The UK approach is to deny protection to elements of such parts which have to be a particular shape to fit or match a composite article of which they form a part.

Royalty: a payment mechanism, normally calculated on a percentage of the income derived from sales of works or articles subject to an intellectual property right. This is a common method of paying for a licence to exploit an intellectual property right. For example, the author of a literary work may grant a licence to a publisher permitting him to print and sell copies to bookshops. The publisher may then pay the author 10 per cent of the price he receives from the booksellers. Sometimes, royalty figures will have to be agreed by the Comptroller of Patents, Designs and Trade Marks or by the Copyright Tribunal (for example, where a compulsory licence is obtained and the parties cannot agree a royalty). A percentage based on sales is not the only method of payment and a single lump sum or series of sums can be agreed between the parties instead. It is not unusual for writers to be given an advance on royalties.

Search order (formerly Anton Piller order): an order of the High Court permitting the aggrieved party to enter the premises of an alleged wrongdoer and take into safe custody or copy materials that are important evidentially. Originally named after the case of *Anton Piller KG v Manufacturing Processes Ltd* [1976] 1 Ch 55. The order must be executed by a solicitor. The applicant must show, *inter alia*, a strong case. Its purpose is the preservation of evidence, that is, to prevent the destruction or concealment of evidence by an alleged wrongdoer. The order is common in intellectual property cases, for example to allow a copyright owner to take possession of alleged pirate copies of his work to be used in evidence. The successful applicant for a search order usually has to give an undertaking in damages to compensate the other person should the applicant lose the case at trial.

Computer terms and phrases

Assembly language: *see* low-level programming language.

Computer memory: the storage facilities of a computer. Computers can store vast amounts of data. Some of the computer's storage is internal, such as that provided for by integrated circuits and an internal magnetic disk. Other forms of storage are external, for example, magnetic external hard drives, solid state memory, CDs and DVDs. Older forms of external storage include punched cards, paper tape, magnetic tape and disks. Internal computer memory can be classified as being ROM (read only memory) or RAM (random access memory). ROM contains programs such as the start up program and parts of the computer's operating system. ROM cannot be altered; it is permanent. RAM is transient memory;

the contents are alterable. It is used to store application programs in current use and associated data during the operation of a computer program or software suite. When the computer is switched off, the contents of RAM are lost.

Computer program: a series of instructions which control or condition the operation of a computer.

Decompilation and disassembly: disassembly is an operation whereby the object code of a computer program is converted into assembly language (a low-level programming language). This is relatively easy to do using an appropriate computer program. Much more difficult is decompilation. This is where object code is converted into its original form in a high-level language. For this to be feasible, the type and version of the high-level language in which the program was originally written must be known. Quite often the word decompilation is used to describe disassembly (in essence, the process is the same, retrieving a source code program from an object code version). Reverse analysis of computer programs is usually undertaken using a disassembler program.

Under certain circumstances, lawful users of computer program are permitted to decompile that program to achieve 'interoperability' with that or another computer program.

High-level programming language: a language that resembles natural language more closely than machine code (object code) or assembly language. High-level language is relatively remote from the machine language which can be directly 'understood' by the computer's central processing unit (processor). It is easier to write programs using a high-level language. However, for the program to operate, it must be converted permanently (compiled) or temporarily (interpreted) into machine code. Each statement in a high-level language corresponds to several statements in machine code. From reading a listing of a computer program written in a high-level language, it is possible to obtain a good insight into the ideas used and the program's algorithm. Examples of high-level languages are C++, Java, COBOL, BASIC, PASCAL and FORTRAN.

Ideas and principles: generally ideas and principles underlying computer programs and computer programming languages, as such, are not protected by copyright. Lawful users of computer programs are entitled to observe, study and test the operation of a computer program to determine those ideas and principles. This is in line with the general principle that copyright protects expressions of ideas rather than the ideas themselves.

Low-level programming language: (or assembly language) a language which is very close to the machine code directly executable by the computer. Each statement is directly equivalent to a machine code operation. Assembly language is usually written using mnemonics and memory addresses. Programs written in low-level languages have the advantage of being faster than programs written in high-level languages.

Programming language: a set of words, letters and numbers which, according to the particular syntax of the language, describe a computer program, directly or indirectly, to a computer.

Object code: the machine code resulting from compiling a program written in a high-level language. Alternatively, it is produced by 'assembling' a program written in a low-level language. Object code is directly executable by a computer. Object code is not directly intelligible and must be converted by disassembly before it can be understood by humans. Most computer programs are marketed in object code form. It is processed faster and is far less easy to modify than a source code program.

Reverse analysis: this is the computer equivalent of reverse engineering. It is the process where a computer program is analysed by converting object code into assembly language or high-level language to determine features about the program. Reverse analysis can be used to discover interface details, that is information which will enable the writer of another program to make his program (or the files generated by his program) compatible with the other program. Reverse analysis can also be used to determine a program's algorithm and structure and to facilitate the writing of a program which will perform the same task. Hence, the scope and permissibility of reverse analysis are of utmost importance to the computer industry.

Source code: a program in a high-level language which must be converted into object code before it can be executed. *See also,* **object code**.

Internet terms and phrases

AdWord: keywords used by Google advertisers to increase the chances of links to their websites being listed following a search by users. Controversially, advertisers have used trade mark words belonging to other organisations as keywords. This has generated a significant amount of litigation. See Chapter 21 for examples.

Domain name: the unique name that is the address of a website or its URL (Uniform Resource Locator) that describes the location of the site. For example, the author of this book has a number of domain names, including **http://www.davidbainbridge.com**.

Electronic mail (e-mail): a system for sending mail electronically, via computer networks, anywhere in the world, almost instantaneously. Persons using electronic mail have their own e-mail address. This may be supplied by the person's employer or their Internet Service Provider (ISP).

HTML (Hypertext Markup Language): the language used to format content for display on a web Browser. It comprises a set of markers to indicate formatting of text and images, etc. and to link within a web page or to other web pages or other files.

For example, consider the phrase 'The cat sat on the mat'. To display the whole phrase centralised with the word 'cat' underlined and the word 'mat' emboldened, the HTML version would read as follows:

The C<u>AT</u> sat on the **mat**

Internet: a global system of linked telecommunications and computer networks which allows the sending of data or messages from one computer to another anywhere in the world.

Internet Service Provider (ISP): an organisation that provides its subscribers with access to the internet together with other services such as chat rooms, bulletin boards and hosting web pages. Injunctions may be available against ISPs requiring them to block access to material infringing copyright. They may also be required to collect data on and send reports on serial copyright infringers, thereby facilitating legal action against them.

Intranet: a computer network within a single organisation allowing for the transfer of data, e-mail messages and computer documents. For example, a company may have an intranet that serves the head office and all its branch offices, wherever physically located.

Search engine: a system for searching the World Wide Web for sites that best match the query entered by the user. For example, a user looking for websites relating to restaurants in Tewkesbury might enter 'Tewkesbury restaurants' which will return a list of links to eating places in and around Tewkesbury.

World Wide Web (WWW or the web): the collection of resources using the Hypertext Transfer Protocol (HTTP, a protocol of established rules for communication over the internet controlling the transfer of data and information).

Website: a specific location on the World Wide Web. It may contain numerous web pages that link together as well as links to other websites. A website may be controlled and managed by a company or other organisation or by a single individual. The author manages a village website at **www.eckington.info**.

List of bibliographic abbreviations

AC	Appeal Cases	F	Federal Reporter (US)
AIPC	Australian Intellectual Property Cases	FCA	Federal Court of Australia
All ER	All England Reports	FSR	Fleet Street Reports
ALR	Australian Law Reports	F Supp	Federal Supplement (US)
ATPR	Australian Trade Practices Cases	Godbolt	Godbolt's Reports
B & C	Barnewall and Cresswell's King's Bench Reports	Hare	Hare's Chancery Reports
		ICR	Industrial Cases Reports
BCLC	Butterworth's Company Law Cases	IIC	International Review of Industrial Property and Copyright Law
Beav	Beavon's Reports		
BGH	Bundesgerichtshof (Criminal)	IRLR	Industrial Relations Law Reports
BGHZ	Bundesgerichtshof (Civil)	JCPC	Judicial Committee of the Privy Council
Bro PC	Brown's Parliamentary Cases	Jur	The Jurists Report
Burr	Burrow's King's Bench Reports	KB	King's Bench
Ch	Chancery	LJ CH	Law Journal Reports (Chancery)
Ch App	Court of Appeal in Chancery	LT	Law Times Reports
Ch D	Chancery Division	Mac & G	Macnaghten and Gordon's Chancery Reports
CLSR	Computer Law and Security Report		
CMLR	Common Market Law Reports	MacG CC	MacGillivray's Copyright Cases
Co Rep	Coke's Report	MLR	Modern Law Review
CPC	Community Patent Convention	NSWLR	New South Wales Law Reports
Cr App R	Criminal Appeal Reports	NZLR	New Zealand Law Reports
Crim LR	Criminal Law Review	OJ	Official Journal of the European Communities
CTM	Community Trade Mark		
De GJ & S	De Gex, Jones and Smith's Report	OJ EPO	Official Journal of the European Patent Office
ECC	European Commercial Cases	P	Probate
ECDR	European Copyright and Design Reports	Pet	Peter's Supreme Court Reports (US)
ECR	European Court Reports	QB	Queen's Bench
EHRR	European Human Rights Reports	QBD	Queen's Bench Division
EIPR	European Intellectual Property Review	RPC	Reports of Patent, Design and Trade Mark Cases
EMLR	Entertainment and Media Law Reports		
ENPR	European National Patent Reports	Russ & M	Russell and Mylne's Chancery Reports
EPO	European Patent Office	S Ct	Supreme Court
EPOR	European Patent Office Report	SI	Statutory Instrument
Eq	Equity Cases	Stra	Strange
ETMR	European Trade Mark Reports	TLR	Times Law Reports
EWCA Civ	Court of Appeal, Civil Division (England and Wales)	UKHL	House of Lords (United Kingdom)
		USC	United States Code
EWHC	High Court (England and Wales) (with suffix as appropriate, eg (Ch) or (QB))	USPQ	United States Patents Quarterly
		WLR	Weekly Law Reports
EWPCC	Patents County Court	WPC	Webster's Patent Cases

Law reports references, etc.

There have been some changes to the system of referencing for law reports and terminology, as described below. The Treaty on the Functioning of the European Union has replaced the EC Treaty and a table of equivalents is given at the end of this section.

References to law reports

Since the beginning of 2001, some (though by no means all) law reports references have changed their reference system to make them media neutral (particular examples are ETMR, FSR and RPC). The same applies to reports published by the Court Service. This means that a reference will be the same whether the report is published on paper or electronically and, importantly, reference can be made to a particular part in a judgment by paragraph number without using page numbers. Thus, cases in some series of law reports are numbered seriatim, rather than referring to the first page of the report, and a reference to a part of the judgment is made using the paragraph number.

For example, to refer to the case of *British Airways plc v Ryanair Ltd* at the point where Jacob J talks of the defendant's advertising as amounting to no more than 'vulgar abuse', the citation should be *British Airways plc v Ryanair Ltd* [2001] FSR 32 at para. 35. That case was the 32nd reported in the Fleet Street Reports for 2001 – in the report as published on paper, the reference would be [2001] FSR 541 at 554. In this edition of this book, the convention is to use media-neutral referencing, that is, by case number rather than the first page number of the case as printed in paper form. This practice accords with the referencing used by judges.

Availability of law reports and legislation

Apart from subscription services such as the Law Reports, the All ER, FSR, RPC and online subscription services such as LexisNexis and Westlaw, increasing numbers of the full text of judgments are available free of charge by online access. Appendix 2 indicates the website addresses where access to these may be made though at this stage it should be noted that BAILII (British and Irish Legal Information Institute) is particularly good and has a wealth of UK, Court of Justice and General Court of the European Union and foreign cases available, usually uploaded soon after the judgment is available.

Judgments of the Court of Justice of the European Union and the General Court (formerly the Court of First Instance) are available from Europa Eur-Lex and Curia websites. Both give free access to the European Court Reports which may be accessed by means of the year and case number (for example, Year 2000 No 291 in the case of Eur-Lex) or case reference (for example, C-291/00 in the case of Curia). The latter is more up to date than the former but does not carry the ECR reference where available. Consequently, to assist readers in accessing these cases, the case number is given, as is the ECR reference. Many of the Court of Justice rulings and decisions of the General Court are also available in the conventional law reports. Although these have the advantage of a headnote and summary, as with national cases, students will be rewarded by studying the full text of the judgments.

Full text UK legislation is available freely at **www. legislation.gov.uk**. Care should be taken as not all the legislation is fully updated. European Union legislation is available from Europa Eur-Lex and the text of most of the international treaties and conventions is available at the WIPO website. The European Patent Office website gives access to the European Patent Convention and to cases before the Boards of Appeal. The Office for the Harmonisation of the Internal Market (Trade Marks and Designs) also carries decisions of the Divisions and Boards of Appeal.

Terminology

The changes in terminology resulting from the Civil Procedure Rules 1998 are used throughout this book. Verbatim quotations from older cases have not been modified. Thus a judge in an older case will refer to the plaintiff rather than the claimant. (Scotland and Northern Ireland are unaffected.)

The European Court of Justice is now known as the Court of Justice of the European Union (CJEU) and the Court of First Instance is now known as the General Court of the European Union.

Supreme Court, etc.

Note that there have been some changes to the names of the courts. The Supreme Court of England and Wales (Court of Appeal and High Court) is now known as the Senior Courts of England and Wales. Of course, the Court of Appeal (Civil and Criminal Divisions) and the High Court Divisions retain their previous names. The Appellate Committee of the House of Lords is now known as the United Kingdom Supreme Court. The establishment of the Supreme Court marks a constitutional significant change as the justices of that court are now independent of Government and Parliament.

The Treaty on the Functioning of the European Union

The Treaty on the Functioning of the European Union (TFEU) came into force on 1 December 2009 as a result of the Lisbon Treaty. The TFEU replaced the EC Treaty. References in this book are generally to the TFEU with cross-references to the EC Treaty as appropriate. In some cases a reference to the EC Treaty is retained, for example, where a decision of the Court of Justice of the European prior to the TFEU refers to the EC Treaty (again a cross-reference is given if needed for clarity).

The following table sets out the provisions of the TFEU referred to in this book with the equivalent numbering from the old EC Treaty.

Provision	EC Treaty	TFEU
No discrimination on the grounds of nationality	Art 12	Art 18
Quantitative restrictions on imports prohibited	Art 28	Art 34
Quantitative restrictions on exports prohibited	Art 29	Art 35
Exceptions justified on a number of grounds including the protection of industrial property	Art 30	Art 36
No restrictions on the freedom to provide services	Art 49	Art 56
Meaning of 'services'	Art 50	Art 57
Prohibition of anti-competitive agreements, etc.	Art 81	Art 101
Prohibition of abuses of dominant positions	Art 82	Art 102
Approximation of laws of Member States*	Arts 95–97	Arts 114–118
Preliminary rulings by the Court of Justice of the EU	Art 234	Art 267
Binding nature of Regulations, Directives, etc.	Art 249	Art 288
Treaties not to prejudice systems of property ownership	Art 295	Art 345

* The EC Treaty did not have an equivalent of Article 118 which concerned the establishment of EU-wide intellectual property rights (although, of course, the Community trade mark and Community design were previously in existence).

Part One

PRELIMINARY CONSIDERATIONS

Introduction to intellectual property rights 1

This chapter looks at some of the basic principles underlying this area of law, examines the nature of intellectual property law and discusses some cross-cutting themes that transcend boundaries between individual forms of intellectual property rights. Some practical considerations are also dealt with briefly at this stage, such as the essential rationale for intellectual property and its importance in a commercial sense. Finally, the nature of the study of intellectual property is discussed. The purpose of this chapter is to give the reader a feel for intellectual property law and to introduce some of the important issues, laying the foundations for the more detailed study which follows.

What is intellectual property law?

Intellectual property law is that area of law which concerns legal rights associated with creative effort or commercial reputation and goodwill. The subject matter of intellectual property is very wide and includes literary and artistic works, films, computer programs, inventions, designs and marks used by traders for their goods or services. The law deters others from copying or taking unfair advantage of the work or reputation of another and provides remedies should this happen. There are several different forms of rights or areas of law giving rise to rights that together make up intellectual property. They are:

- copyright
- rights in performances
- the law of breach of confidence, especially with respect to technical and commercial information
- patents for inventions
- registered designs
- unregistered design rights
- trade marks
- passing off
- malicious falsehood (trade libel).

This list is not exhaustive and there are other rights, for example, the rights associated with plant and seed varieties protection, but these will not be dealt with in detail in this book.

Taxonomy of intellectual property rights

Obviously, there are many similarities and differences between the various rights that make up intellectual property law. For example, there is common ground between patents and registered designs, as there is between copyright and rights in performances. Some rights give rise to monopolies, while others merely prevent the unfair use by others of an existing work or article. The various rights are not necessarily mutually exclusive and two or more of the rights can co-exist in relation to a certain 'thing'. Sometimes the rights will progressively give protection, one right taking over from another over a period of time during the development of an invention, design or work of copyright.

A practical distinction that can be used to subdivide the various rights is whether there is a requirement for registration; that is, whether the right is dependent upon the completion of formalities, or whether it automatically springs into life at a specified time. Another distinguishing feature is the nature of the right, whether it applies to something which is primarily creative or has to do with goodwill in a wide commercial sense. Creative things can be further subdivided into those that are creative in an artistic or aesthetic sense, such as an oil painting, music or literature, or those that are inventive in an industrial context, such as a new type of machine or engine, or a new way of making a particular product. Before looking further at each type of right, consider Table 1.1, which shows how, somewhat imperfectly, intellectual property rights conform to the above taxonomy. The word 'artistic' is used in an everyday and wide sense and should not be confused with the artistic category of copyright works where the word has a special significance.

Formalities

Some intellectual property rights, in respect of particular ideas, works or things, are secured by the successful completion of a formal application and registration procedure. The necessary formalities are not simply satisfied by depositing details with an appropriate authority because such rights are not granted lightly. They do, after all, put the owner of the right in a privileged position whereby he can restrain others from doing certain things while exploiting the right himself. The rights impinge upon the freedom of action of others. The owner has a form of property which he can use as he likes, subject to some constraints, and he can take legal action either to deter would-be trespassers or to obtain damages against those who have trespassed just as the owner of real property can do.[1]

For those rights that require registration, the applicant will succeed in obtaining such registration only if certain rigorous standards are achieved.[2] The rationale for this is that rights subject to formalities are generally monopolistic in nature. Another distinction is between those rights that are provided for and governed by statute and those that derive

[1] This also extends to other persons having rights under intellectual property law such as an exclusive licensee of a copyright or patent, as it does to lessees and licensees of real property.

[2] However, the examination of trade mark and registered design applications has been relaxed. Patent applications remain subject to a rigorous search and examination process.

Table 1.1 Taxonomy of intellectual property

Whether formalities required	Basic nature of right		
	Creative		Commercial reputation and goodwill
	Artistic	Industrial	
Formalities required		Patents Plant varieties	Registered trade marks
	Registered designs		
Formalities not required	Copyright Rights in performances Database right		Passing off Malicious falsehood
	Unregistered designs		
	Law of breach of confidence		

Table 1.2 Statutory and common law rights

Statute	Common law (or equity)
Copyright	Breach of confidence (equity)
Database right	Passing off
Rights in performances	Malicious falsehood
Patents	
Registered trade marks	
Registered designs	
Unregistered designs	
Plant varieties	

from the common law or equity (although the latter are given statutory recognition). There is no correlation between the need for formalities and whether the area of intellectual property law is rooted in statute, as a comparison of Table 1.1 and Table 1.2 shows.

Industrial property

Traditionally, a number of intellectual property rights were known collectively as industrial property. Such rights include patents, trade marks and designs. This description is used in the Paris Convention for the Protection of Industrial Property 1883. Included in this term by implication are the law of confidence[3] and passing off. When other rights such as copyright and related rights (for example, rights in performances) are added to industrial property the phrase used to describe the entirety of rights is intellectual property and this has become the phrase normally used to describe these individual, and sometimes disparate, rights collectively. Significant moves have been made in terms of the international harmonisation of intellectual property law, but it should be remembered that the early development of copyright, patents and trade mark law in England set the mould that was largely adopted throughout the common law countries of the world. Even before the beginning of the twentieth century, international collaboration and cooperation was well under way, reflecting the worldwide importance of intellectual property.

Before discussing further the nature of intellectual property, it will be useful to describe briefly each right individually using non-technical language.

Copyright

Copyright is a property right which subsists (exists) in various 'works', for example literary works, artistic works, musical works, sound recordings, films and broadcasts. The author of a work is the person who creates it[4] and he (or his employer) is normally the first owner of the copyright, which will last until 70 years after the author's death or 50 years after it was created depending on the type of work.[5] Copyright gives the owner the right to do certain things in relation to the work, which includes making a copy, broadcasting or giving a public performance. Anyone else who does any of these things (known as the acts restricted by copyright) without the permission of the owner, infringes copyright and may be subject to legal action taken by the owner for that infringement. Ownership of a copyright is alienable and it can be transferred to another or a licence may be granted by the owner to another, permitting him to do one or more specified acts with the work in question.

Copyright does not protect ideas, only the expression of an idea (that is, its tangible form), and others are free to create similar, or even identical,[6] works as long as they do so independently and by their own efforts. In other words, copyright does not create a monopoly in a particular work.[7] In addition, certain things may be done in relation to

3 Especially where the information is of a technical or commercial nature.

4 For some types of works, the author is the person by whom the arrangements necessary for the creation of the work are undertaken. Films are usually works of joint authorship, the authors being the principal director and the producer.

5 From the end of the calendar year during which the author died or the work was created, as appropriate. The 50-year period has been raised to 70 years for some forms of works.

6 For example, two photographers may independently take photographs of the same scene which when viewed alongside each other are virtually indistinguishable. Each will have their own copyright in their own photograph.

7 Except perhaps where the creator of the work is the only person with access to the contents or other material from which the work has been created.

a work of copyright without the permission of the copyright owner, such as making a copy of a work, for example for the purposes of non-commercial research, private study, criticism or review. Such acts are known as the 'permitted acts' and limit the scope of copyright protection. Copyright gives rise to three forms of rights:

1 the proprietary or economic rights in the work, for example the right to control copying;
2 moral rights which leave the author (or principal director of a film), who may no longer be the owner of the copyright, with some control over how the work is used or exploited in the future; and
3 an artist's right to a royalty on the resale of his work.[8]

The author (or film director) has a right to be identified as such and has a right to object to a derogatory treatment of the work. The moral rights are independent of the economic rights and hence the importance of the distinction between the author of a work and the owner of the copyright subsisting in it. There are some forms of infringement which can be grouped together as being of a commercial nature, such as importing or dealing with infringing copies, that carry criminal penalties.

International protection of copyright works is effected mainly through two international conventions: the Berne Convention for the Protection of Literary and Artistic Works 1886 and the Universal Copyright Convention 1952, both of which lay down minimum standards of protection to be attained and for reciprocity of protection between those countries that are signatories to the conventions. The conventions have been partly responsible for the measure of harmony that now exists on the world stage, albeit far from complete. The effect is that a foreign national can take legal action in the UK for copyright infringement occurring there as if he was a British subject.[9] The UK is a member of both conventions. Further and significant harmonisation has taken place throughout the European Union as a result of a number of harmonising Directives.

Rights in performances

Live performances give rise to two different sets of rights: the rights of performers and recording rights. Formerly, a performer only had one type of right not dissimilar to the author's moral right in copyright, whilst persons with whom the performer had an exclusive recording contract acquired a right similar to the copyright owner's economic right. However, as a result of the Copyright and Related Rights Regulations 1996,[10] bolstered by the Copyright and Related Rights Regulations 2003,[11] the performer now also has a true property right relating to making copies, the issue of copies and the rental and lending of recordings of his performance. Being property rights, these rights may be assigned or licensed. Performers now also have express moral rights to be identified as the performer and to object to a derogatory treatment of their performances.[12]

The need for specific rights in live performances is that they give the performer, and the person having exclusive recording rights, a means of protecting live performances from persons making illicit ('bootleg') recordings of such performances.[13] Of course, the work being performed may be protected by copyright, but the copyright owner may not wish to take action. These rights are directly enforceable by the performer and the recording company. In some cases, the work on which the performance is based may be an old work in which copyright no longer subsists, such as an operatic aria by Mozart. Rights in performances are not restricted to music and are available in respect of a dramatic performance, the reading or recital of a literary work and the performance of a variety act such as by a juggler.

Rights in performances last for 50 years from the end of the calendar year during which the performance took place.[14] Where a sound recording of a performance is published commercially and is played in public or included in a broadcast or cable programme

8 This right was introduced in the UK in 2006 as a result of an EU Directive. It is described in Chapter 5 on authors' rights.

9 *Hanfstaengl* v *Empire Palace* [1894] 2 Ch 1. All three judges in the Court of Appeal commented on this then novel state of affairs. For a list of countries afforded reciprocal protection see the Copyright and Performances (Application to Other Countries) Order 2008, SI 2008/677, amended to include Bermuda by the Copyright and Performances (Application to Other Countries) (Amendment) Order 2009, SI 2009/2745.

10 SI 1996/2967.

11 SI 2003/2498.

12 By virtue of the Performances (Moral Rights) Regulations 2006, SI 2006/18.

13 Bootleg recordings of performances by Phil Collins and Cliff Richard were the subject of a case before the European Court of Justice in which it was held that German copyright law was contrary to Article 12 of the EC Treaty (now Article 18 of the Treaty on the Functioning of the European Union) in that it discriminated against non-German nationals: Joined Cases C-92/92 and C-326/92 *Collins* v *Imtrat Handelsgesellschaft mbH* [1993] ECR I-5145, [1994] FSR 166.

14 Unless within that 50 years it was 'released', in which case the rights last for 50 years from the end of the calendar year when it was so released.

service, the performer is entitled to an equitable remuneration from the owner of the copyright in the sound recording. This right may not be assigned except to a collecting society, which will enforce the right on behalf of the performer.

The law of breach of confidence

The law of breach of confidence developed in equity as a way of protecting confidential information by preventing its misuse by persons to whom the information has been divulged in confidence or the further disclosure of the information by such persons. A wide variety of types of information is protected, ranging from industrial or trade secrets to details of a personal nature to secrets about the government or defence of the realm. In the context of intellectual property, it is with trade and industrial secrets and confidential commercial information that we are primarily concerned. The rationale of the law of confidence is that it stops a person making wrongful use of information beyond the purposes for which it was disclosed to him. The law of confidence protects ideas and is a useful ally to other intellectual property rights, often being the only form of protection when the subject matter is still in an embryonic state.

Patent law

The rights granted by a patent, because a patent gives its owner a monopoly over his invention, is the form of intellectual property *par excellence*. A patent may be granted in respect of a new and non-obvious invention capable of industrial application and gives a monopoly right that can last for up to 20 years.[15] This very strong form of protection is reserved for inventions that satisfy rigorous standards (for example, novelty and inventive step) and an application for a patent has to be drawn up precisely and accurately stating the scope of the invention and the claims made in respect of it for which protection is sought. A patent may be for a product such as a new type of low energy and longer lasting light source, a new hybrid engine for a motor car or a new pharmaceutical product, or it may be for a new industrial process, for example a new way of making plasma screens or a novel technique for making fibre optic cables.

15 Twenty-five years for certain medicinal and plant products.

Patents can be assigned and licences may be granted in respect of them. The owner of a patent is the person who is registered as the proprietor. A large number of inventions are made by employees and usually, in such cases, the employer will be the proprietor although the inventor will be named as such in the patent as published. If the invention turns out to be of outstanding benefit to the employer, the employee may apply for a compensation award. By their nature, patents usually protect ideas, as expressed in the description and claims, but there are several controls on the monopoly status they confer upon proprietors. For example, compulsory licences may be available after the first three years from the grant of a patent, or it may be indicated on the register of patents that a licence is available as of right. There are other controls over patents resulting from either domestic or EU Competition law. For example, the grant of a compulsory licence, or providing that licences are available as of right, might be appropriate if a patented invention was not being worked at all or if the proprietor was limiting supply of a patented product in order to maintain excessively high prices or refusing to grant licences to work the invention in the UK where the invention represented an important technical advance of considerable economic significance. There is also provision for compulsory licensing of patents relating to the manufacture of pharmaceutical products for export to countries with health problems. This is the result of an EU Regulation.[16]

16 Regulation (EC) No 816/2006 of the European Parliament and of the Council of 17 May 2006 on compulsory licensing of patents relating to the manufacture of pharmaceutical products for export to countries with public health problems, L 157, 09.06.2006, p 1.

The European Patent Convention permits the application for a bundle of patents covering a specified number of Member States including the UK. The administration of the convention, patent applications, patent grant and opposition are within the remit of the European Patent Office, situated in Munich, which has its own Boards of Appeal.[17] This route to obtaining patent protection throughout Europe (not limited to the countries of the EU) has grown in importance and, eventually, it may be possible to obtain a Community-wide patent as is now the case with the Community trade mark and the Community design. Protection in other countries may be obtained through the Patent Cooperation Treaty, a system which facilitates the application procedure where several countries are concerned, including numerous countries outside the EU.

As a result of the European Patent Convention and the Patent Cooperation Treaty, and looking forward to the introduction of a Community Patent Convention, if and when it ever comes into force, a number of the provisions of the UK Patents Act 1977 are framed so as to have, as nearly as practicable, the same effect as the corresponding provisions of the European Patent Convention, the Community Patent Convention (when in force) and the Patent Cooperation Treaty.[18]

The UK has not had a form of intellectual property right known elsewhere as a petty patent or utility model. Such protection is now available in most of the countries of the EU with a few exceptions including the UK. There has been a proposal for an EU Directive to harmonise this form of protection throughout the EU.[19] Progress has been minimal and there have been no plans to introduce a Community-wide utility model form of protection. No real progress has been made thus far. It is arguable that the panoply of other intellectual property rights available in the EU and Member States as they now exist should provide adequate protection for anything that could be protected by a utility model form of protection, whether on a national or European-wide basis.

Design law

A new product or article may be designed which is not sufficiently novel or inventive to satisfy the exacting requirements for the grant of a patent. It may, however, be protected by design law, an area of intellectual property law that has become much more important following harmonisation of registered designs throughout the EU and the introduction of Community-wide design rights.[20] The Community design takes a twin-track approach protecting new designs having an individual character by registration for up to 25 years, or, failing registration, giving protection as an informal right for up to three years. Apart from protection through the Community design, in the UK a design may be protected by means of registration under the Registered Designs Act 1949, as amended, or through the UK's *sui generis*, unregistered design right, which bears little relationship to other forms of protection for designs.

Design law typically protects a wide range of designs of products that may have some eye appeal but the rights under design law are not so limited and they apply to designs that are new and have an 'individual character'. They do not apply generally to the design of products not normally on display during ordinary use but the UK unregistered design right is not limited to designs that are normally seen by eye. It can be argued that, in the UK, any new or unusual design will be protected, whether or not registered, and that UK protection for designs, though arguably diminished from the position before the Copyright, Designs and Patents Act 1988 came into force, has never been so strong.

The protection afforded by registration of a design, whether in the UK or through the Community design, lasts for up to 25 years, initially granted for five years and then subject to renewal every five years. Failure to register can still result in three years' protection through the unregistered version of the Community design or up to a maximum of 15 years through the UK unregistered design right (although reduced effectively to no more than ten years' protection following commercial exploitation). The rules as to first ownership of a design are different to those for copyright and, in the UK, the fact that a design is commissioned may be determinative of first ownership.[21]

17 Applications can also be made through the Patent Office in London. This would be the normal procedure for a UK applicant.

18 Patents Act 1977 s 130(7).

19 Amended proposal for a European Parliament and Council Directive, approximating the legal arrangements for the protection of inventions by utility model, COM (1999) 309 final, OJ C248, 29.8.2000, p 56.

20 Even if the product is subject to patent rights, this does not prevent protection by design rights where the criteria for subsistence or registration are satisfied.

21 The rules on ownership of commissioned designs differs between the UK registered and unregistered designs and the Community design.

Trade marks

Trade marks may not have the glamour of inventions or creative works but they are, nevertheless, of substantial importance in an industrial and commercial sense. Trade marks are closely associated with business image, goodwill and reputation. Goods or services are often requested by reference to a trade mark and the public rely on many marks as indicating quality, value for money and, particularly, the origin of goods or services.

Trade marks are registered in respect of certain classes of goods or services. Registrations for trade marks may be renewed indefinitely. Registration for trade marks began in 1876 and some of the first marks registered (including the very first mark, the Bass Red Triangle label mark) are still in use today. In addition to marks applied to or used with goods or services to indicate a connection in the course of trade, there are also certification marks indicating the origin or quality of the goods, for example the 'wool mark', and collective marks, typically used by members of an association. All registered marks must be used and they can be subject to revocation proceedings if they are not used for five or more years. A basic principle is that a trade mark should be capable of distinguishing goods or services of one 'undertaking'[22] from those of other undertakings. In other words, trade marks should operate as 'badges of origin'. That is their basic function and purpose and they should not be registered if they fail, or are likely to fail, in serving that purpose.

Significant changes to trade mark law were made by a European Directive that attempted to achieve a limited harmonisation of trade mark law throughout the EU and which formed the basis for the Trade Marks Act 1994 which replaced the outdated and obscure Trade Marks Act 1938. In addition to bringing trade mark law up to date, the 1994 Act allowed the UK to ratify the Protocol to the Madrid Convention for the international registration of trade marks. Since then there has been a Community-wide trade mark system in operation under which undertakings can register Community trade marks (CTMs) which apply throughout the EU and have a unitary nature. This system has become very popular and although the requirements for registration, infringement and other aspects are equivalent to or very similar to those for the harmonised trade mark, the CTM has generated a significant amount of case law in its own right as indeed has the Directive harmonising trade mark law throughout Europe.

22 The Trade Marks Act 1994, following the language of the European Directive harmonising trade mark law, uses the term 'undertaking' rather than 'trader'.

Passing off

The tort of passing off is, in effect, a common law version of trade mark law. Indeed, trade mark law developed from passing off, which in turn developed from the tort of deceit. Being common law, passing off can be more flexible than trade mark law, and can protect marks that would not be sufficiently distinctive for registration as a trade mark or are otherwise unregistrable. Passing off protects the goodwill a trader has developed and which is associated with his business. As goodwill is such a vague concept, protection can apply to all manner of aspects of a trader's business operations and activities and advertising and marketing techniques. It is often said that passing off protects a trader's 'get-up'. As with trade mark law, such protection has the secondary effect of protecting the buying public from trade deception. One area of interest is character merchandising, usually a massive commercial activity whereby famous and often fictional characters are used to promote the sale of goods, for example by applying names or images of the characters to the goods, such as 'Peppa Pig' dolls and merchandise and 'Bob the Builder' toys and games.

This area of law has also proved very useful in controlling 'cybersquatting', the registration of internet domain names containing company names or trade mark names by persons hoping to sell the names at grossly inflated prices to the relevant companies or trade mark proprietors. Although most organisations register and police their trade marks, passing off remains important in protecting unregistered trade marks and controlling other forms of unfair competition where the rights under registered trade mark law may not be engaged, for one reason or another. Indeed, the goodwill protected by passing off may be used to challenge the registration of trade marks.

Nature of intellectual property

Intellectual property as property

Intellectual property rights give rise to a form of property that can be dealt with just as with any other property, and which can be assigned, mortgaged and licensed. Table 1.3 shows a classification scheme for property and how intellectual property fits in with this scheme.

Intellectual property is property in a legal sense: it is something that can be owned and dealt with. Statutory forms of intellectual property are declared to be property rights, but even common law forms have been recognised as producing a form of property right.[23] Most forms of intellectual property are akin to 'choses in action', rights that are enforced only by legal action as opposed to possessory rights. Channell J described a chose in action in the following terms in *Torkington* v *Magee*:

> 'Chose in action' is a known legal expression used to describe all personal rights which can only be enforced by action, and not by taking physical possession.[24]

This has implications as regards the transfer of rights (assignment) and the requirement for consideration. In many cases, the assignment of intellectual property rights is expressly governed by statute and, where this is so, assignment requires no consideration.[25] Otherwise, assignment of a chose in action (meaning 'thing in action') is governed, in England and Wales, by the Law of Property Act 1925 s 136, which requires the assignment to be written and signed by the assignor, to be absolute and followed by express notice.[26] However, there is some doubt as to whether intellectual property rights are truly choses in action. Indeed, patents are declared to be personal property without being a thing in action by the Patents Act 1977 s 30(1). In *Colonial Bank* v *Whinney*,[27] Lindley LJ said (at 284) that while debts, money in funds, company shares, copyrights and patents are all incorporeal personal property, care must be taken not to give them a common name which conceals their differences. He held that company shares were not choses in action. He was overruled in the House of Lords.[28] Copyright has been accepted as being a chose in action in a number of cases in the Court of Appeal[29] but the question is not beyond doubt. There remain a number of authors who doubt that it is a chose in action.[30]

23 For example, in the passing off case of *Leather Cloth Co Ltd* v *American Leather Cloth Co Ltd* (1863) 4 De GJ&S 137, the Court of Chancery recognised that the claimant had acquired a property in a trade mark which was valid in equity.

24 [1902] 2 KB 427 at 430.

25 *Re Westerton, Public Trustee* v *Gray* [1919] 2 Ch 104.

26 This has been recognised as extending to equitable choses in action. It is possible to have an equitable assignment of an equitable chose in action.

27 (1885) LR 30 ChD 261.

28 *Colonial Bank* v *Whinney* (1886) LR 11 App Cas 426.

29 For example, *Chaplin* v *Leslie Frewin (Publishers) Ltd* [1966] Ch 71; *Paterson Zochonis & Co Ltd* v *Merfarken Packaging Ltd* [1986] 3 All ER 522; and *London General Holdings Ltd* v *USP plc* [2006] FSR 65.

30 For example, Penner, J.E. (1997) *The Idea of Property in Law*, Oxford University Press, at pp 118–19 cf Groves, P. (1997) *Sourcebook on Intellectual Property Law*, Cavendish Publishing, at p 17.

Table 1.3 Classification of property and examples

Real property		Personal property	
Tangible (immovable)	*Intangible*	*Tangible (movable)*	*Intangible*
Land	Easement Profit à prendre	Car Desk Book Box of chocolates	Cheque Company shares Intellectual property e.g. copyright

Jurisprudential character

Intellectual property gives rise to rights and duties. It establishes property rights, which give the owner the right to do certain things in relation to the subject matter. The rights are negative in nature in that they allow the owner to prevent others carrying out certain specified acts in relation to the subject matter without consent. For example, if the right is a copyright and the subject matter is a piece of music, the owner of the copyright has the exclusive right to make copies of the sheet music, to make an arrangement of the music and to control the performance of the music. However, this exclusive right gives the owner the negative right to prevent others from doing such things in relation to the music. The right can arise automatically, on the creation of the thing to which the right pertains, an example being copyright which springs to life automatically upon the recording of a work.[31] In other cases, the right depends on the completion of an application and registration procedure, patents and trade marks being examples of such rights. In one area of intellectual property, the right comes into existence only after goodwill has been established. This is passing off where one trader is attempting to take unfair advantage of another trader's goodwill. The law can only give remedies here if the aggrieved trader has built up goodwill associated with his business, and this could take several years or just a few days, depending on the circumstances.

We have seen that intellectual property law is concerned with rights. Conversely, it must create duties, for according to the legal theorist Hohfeld, every right has an associated duty – there cannot be one without the other. It is instructive to take the Hohfeldian analysis of legal rules further, particularly in terms of his legal correlatives and oppositions as shown in Figure 1.1.

Rights and duties have a distinct relationship and are called legal correlatives by Hohfeld.[32] In terms of intellectual property, the right is a right to do certain things, such as making copies of a work of copyright, making articles to a design covered by a design right or making products in accordance with a patented invention. The correlative duty is a duty owed by all others not to infringe the right. This duty exists even if the person infringing the right does not know of it.[33] Looking at Hohfeld's scheme again, it can be seen that there are associated privileges and 'no rights'. The right resulting from the operation of intellectual property law gives the owner of that right a corresponding privilege, that is, the privilege to exploit the work. The correlative 'no right' is to the effect that persons other than the owner do not have this privilege, without the owner's consent.

In this overall scheme of things, certain provisos must be added. In the area of intellectual property, the law strives to reach a balance between conflicting interests, to reach a justifiable compromise.[34] Therefore, the duty not to infringe is often curtailed by way of exceptions to infringement. For example, the right given by registration of a design does not extend to features of appearance solely dictated by a product's technical function.[35] Copyright law permits many things to be done that would otherwise infringe, for example, the 'fair dealing' provisions. Infringement in areas of intellectual property provided for by statute is carefully and precisely defined and any act that falls outside can be freely

31 Recording, in this sense, means putting ideas into some tangible form, for example by writing down on paper, recording on magnetic tape or entering into a computer memory.

32 Hohfeld, W.N. *Fundamental Legal Conceptions as Applied in Judicial Reasoning*, 23 Yale Law Journal 16 (1913–1914).

33 Knowledge of the existence of the right may be relevant in terms of the applicability and measure of some of the remedies for infringement. For example, in an action for infringement of copyright, damages are not available against an 'innocent' infringer: Copyright, Designs and Patents Act 1988 s 97(1).

34 Justifiable on the grounds of protecting private interests and promoting investment while providing benefits for society at large in terms of increased wealth, knowledge and employment.

35 Registered Designs Act 1949 s 1C(1).

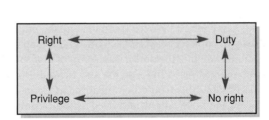

Figure 1.1 Hohfeld's correlations and oppositions

done by anyone, regardless of the right owner's wishes. An example in copyright law is lending a book to a friend; copyright law does not control such an act, however much the author or the publisher may argue that a sale has been lost as a result.

The honest use by a trader of his own name will not infringe a trade mark comprising the same name. Hohfeld's 'no right' is also compromised as it is possible, under certain circumstances, to exploit the intellectual property under a compulsory licence or licence of right even if the owner of the right is vehemently opposed to this. For example, it may be possible to obtain a compulsory licence to exploit a patent irrespective of the proprietor's wishes. The final limitation on intellectual property rights concerns their duration. Most of the rights are limited in time. As a rule of thumb, it can be said that the duration of the right is inversely proportional to its power. For example, a patent gives a monopoly right which is limited to 20 years maximum, but a copyright, which is not a monopoly right, will last for at least 70 years.[36] Some rights may, however, endure for longer.[37] Trade mark rights are of indefinite duration and last as long as the proprietor of the mark is prepared to continue both renewing his registration and using the mark. The law of passing off will give protection to the goodwill of a trader as long as this still exists. The law of breach of confidence will be available to protect the information concerned for as long as it can be kept confidential.

Purchasers' rights and intellectual property

The theoretical nature of intellectual property has many practical ramifications. Of particular interest in the understanding of intellectual property law is the question of what rights a purchaser of an article that embodies an intellectual property right obtains. An examination of this question is best carried out by means of an example, and that following is set in the context of copyright law although some of the principles are relevant to other rights. Consider the situation where a person, Georgina, goes to a bookshop to purchase a copy of a best-selling novel. The text of the novel itself will be protected by copyright as a literary work.[38] Georgina picks up a copy of the novel, takes it across to the sales point and buys it. Georgina has become the owner of the book and she now has legal title to it – or does she? She certainly has legal title to the paper, the cover and the printer's ink which are the physical embodiment of the book. But what are her rights in relation to the literary work expressed in the book – does Georgina own it and can she do with it as she pleases? The answer emphatically is NO: the copyright in the literary work still belongs to the publisher of the novel or the author as the case may be.[39] Georgina can do certain things, such as reading the book, selling it to a second-hand bookseller or she may even destroy it by burning it because none of these acts is controlled by copyright. However, Georgina may not make a copy of the book or translate it into a foreign language (and, in so doing, writing it down or printing it out) because these acts are controlled by copyright.[40]

What if Georgina wishes to lend the novel to her friend John? Non-commercial lending is not a restricted act, so at first sight this would seem to be perfectly lawful. However, if Georgina looks inside the flyleaf of her book she will find a notice stating that certain things cannot be done without the permission of the publisher and lending might be one of them. This brings into question Georgina's status *vis-à-vis* the publisher.[41] The sale of the book was a sale of goods contract between Georgina and the proprietors of the bookshop – there is no privity of contract between Georgina and the publisher. Even if there was, it is extremely doubtful whether the notice was a term of that contract. The only way a contractual link can be forged between Georgina and the publisher would be on the basis of a copyright licence, but this would be unrealistic as Georgina does not need a licence to be able to read the book; she would need a licence only if she intended to perform one of the acts controlled by copyright. Therefore, it would seem that, apart from those parts of the notice that refer to the acts restricted by the copyright, Georgina can

36 In many cases, the period will be significantly longer. However, typographical arrangements of published editions are limited to 25 years' protection.

37 Until 1 August 1989, copyright contemplated perpetual rights in respect of works the copyright in which was vested in the Universities of Oxford and Cambridge and some other colleges.

38 Unless the copyright has expired. Copyright endures for 70 years after the end of the calendar year during which the author dies. The typographical arrangement will also be protected by copyright but this is not considered further in the example.

39 If the author was the first owner of the copyright, he may have retained that ownership and granted an exclusive licence to the publisher or he may have assigned his copyright to the publisher.

40 A translation of a literary work is a form of adaptation, which is within the owner's exclusive rights but an adaptation is not made until it is recorded in writing or otherwise. Simply translating a book in one's mind without recording the translation does not infringe the copyright.

41 Or the author depending upon which of those two owns the copyright.

ignore it and lend the book to her friend.[42] It would be different, however, if the book was an e-book, as reading it would involve making transient copies in the device used to read it and, without the licence of the copyright owner, this would infringe copyright.

Another issue is what remedy Georgina has should the novel turn out to be very poorly written, lacking a good plot. Georgina can do nothing at all unless there has been some misrepresentation by the bookseller concerning the quality of the novel which is sufficient to make the contract between Georgina and the bookseller voidable.[43] Of course, if the tangible matter is defective, for example the printer's ink is poor and has smudged, destroying the legibility of the book, or if the binding is poor and the book falls apart soon after, Georgina may obtain redress from the bookseller as it was not of satisfactory quality: the Sale of Goods Act 1979 s 14(2). However, the absence of a contractual link between Georgina and the publisher robs her of any remedy if the story itself turns out to be very badly written, and it does not appear that the implied terms of satisfactory quality, fitness for purpose and sale by description contained in the Sale of Goods Act 1979 ss 13 and 14 apply to a work of copyright.[44] Lastly, suppose that the book is not a novel but a cookery book and one of the recipes contains a mistake that can lead to serious illness or even poisoning if that recipe is used. If Georgina suffers as a result, can she sue for negligence, and, if so, who? The bookseller might be liable in negligence on the basis of *Donoghue* v *Stevenson*[45] or on the basis of the contract between them,[46] or the publisher might be liable under the product liability provisions of the Consumer Protection Act 1987. However, the definition of 'product' and 'goods' in that Act would appear not to include intellectual property.[47]

These issues are complex and, in the main, largely unresolved. The problems are compounded tenfold where the transaction includes a licence from the right owner in addition to a normal sale or service contract for example, where the contract relates to computer software. The 'sale' of computer software must include a licence because using the software will normally require the performance of an act restricted by copyright, unlike the case of reading a book. The licence may be express, but will otherwise be implied. This may result in a hybrid contract involving a sale of goods contract for the physical items such as floppy disks, together with a licence to use the computer programs included in the package.[48]

The nature of the transaction is far from clear. In Scotland, in the Court of Session, Outer House, Lord Penrose held that a contract for the acquisition of off-the-shelf software was *sui generis*.[49] An Australian case, *Toby Construction Products Pty Ltd* v *Computer Bar (Sales) Pty Ltd*,[50] had been influential in England and Wales in classifying contracts to acquire software as sale of goods contracts. In that case, hardware had been acquired which incorporated defective software. The hardware accounted for most of the overall cost and the court held that the contract was a sale of goods contract with the consequences that entailed, such as the implication of terms relating to quality. In *St Albans City & District Council* v *International Computers Ltd*,[51] at first instance Scott Baker J concluded, *obiter*, that a contract for the writing of computer software was a sale of goods contract, citing *Toby Construction* with approval. However, on appeal, Glidewell LJ accepted that it was not a sale of goods contract as the program was not sold but licensed.[52] Nevertheless, he went on to say that it would be appropriate to imply a term that a program was reasonably capable of achieving its intended purpose.

The better view is that a contract for the acquisition of computer software is or includes a licence between the copyright owner and the person acquiring the software. That licence will be implied if it is not express. If goods are delivered with the software, there may be a collateral sale of goods contract, the importance of which is reflected in the main purpose of the transaction. For example, did the 'buyer' predominantly want to acquire hardware or other things falling in the conventional classification of goods, or were the goods merely the vehicle on which the software was delivered?

42 A restriction on lending 'by way of trade or otherwise' is common. The lending of a copy of, *inter alia*, a literary work to the public is a restricted act: Copyright, Designs and Patents Act 1988 s 18A(1).

43 A publisher who sold a book written by Alastair MacNeill, based on an outline for a story made by the famous novelist, the late Alistair Maclean, was found guilty of offences under the Trade Descriptions Act 1968 because the relative prominence of Alistair Maclean's name compared to the actual author's name was such that the buying public thought that they were acquiring a book *written by Alistair Maclean*. The publisher was fined £6,250: *The Times*, 28 September 1991.

44 By the Sale of Goods Act 1979 s 61(1), 'goods' include all personal chattels other than things in action and money. Copyright is a thing in action and, therefore, outside the provisions of the Act.

45 [1932] AC 562. But is it realistic to expect a bookseller to check the safety of instructions in books which he sells? Even if he wants to check, the bookseller will be ill equipped to validate the integrity of the contents of many books.

46 For example, compare with the latent defect in a catapult giving rise to damages for breach of contract in *Godley* v *Perry* [1960] 1 WLR 9.

47 Consumer Protection Act 1987 s 45(1).

48 For a discussion of the nature of a contract for the acquisition of computer software, *see* Bainbridge, D.I. (2008) *Introduction to Information Technology Law* (6th edn) Longman, Chapter 13.

49 *Beta Computers (Europe) Ltd* v *Adobe Systems (Europe) Ltd* [1996] FSR 367.

50 [1983] 2 NSWLR 48.

51 [1995] FSR 686.

52 [1997] FSR 251 at 266.

As regards liability for defective software, it is now firmly established that the Unfair Contract Terms Act 1977 ss 2–4 apply to the bulk of the terms in software licence agreements and the effect of para 1(c) of Sch 1 to the Act, excluding the operation of those sections in relation to contracts for the creation or transfer of a right or interest in any patent, trade mark, copyright, etc. is very limited.[53] In terms of advice contained in a book or provided by computer software, the law of negligent misstatement is very relevant and, as a result of the Unfair Contract Terms Act 1977, it may be difficult to restrict liability for loss occasioned by defective advice generated by computer software.

53 See, for example, *The Salvage Association* v *CAP Financial Services Ltd* [1995] FSR 654 and *St Albans City & District Council* v *International Computers Ltd* [1997] FSR 251.

Cross-cutting themes

Two particular features or aspects permeate through all or most forms of intellectual property rights. The first is concerned with the control of an abuse of the rights, for example, by the proprietor of a patent who is unfairly manipulating the market to his own advantage by restricting supplies of his patented product to maintain artificially high prices. Obviously, a line will have to be drawn because part of the rationale for intellectual property is that it provides a mechanism for exploiting ideas and the tangible expression of those ideas, but sometimes there is a danger that the exploitation will reach unacceptable levels. The second aspect concerns the international pressures and opportunities presented by intellectual property law, and of particular importance in this respect is competition law both within the UK and the EU.

Abuse of intellectual property

The owner of an important and prominent item protected by intellectual property law might be tempted to use his position to control a market to the disadvantage of competitors and consumers alike. He can prevent or deter potential competitors from developing products similar to his own, and he can charge high prices for the product. To some extent this is to be expected in a capitalistic society; there must be sufficient rewards for the risks of investment in new products and entrepreneurial creation of employment and wealth. Nevertheless, human nature being what it is, some will try to take an 'unfair' advantage of their status as intellectual property right holders. Some rights, such as patents and registered designs, give a monopoly and this can lead to obvious abuse. However, there are provisions in domestic UK patent law and in EU law to control abuse. The Patents Act 1977 s 48 allows any person to apply for a compulsory licence to work the patent after three years of the patent being granted, on the basis of specified grounds, for example when the demand for the product is not being met on reasonable terms. Article 101 of the Treaty on the Functioning of the European Union[54] controls restrictive trade practices and Article 102 prohibits the abuse of a dominant position within the EU where either affects or is likely to affect trade between Member States.[55] There seems to be an irreconcilable conflict between the basic monopoly concept of a patent and Article 102. However, EU law recognises the existence and utility of patents and does not prevent dominant trading situations developing; it only controls abuse of such dominant positions where this affects trade between Member States.

Another way in which the owner of an intellectual property right can abuse his position is to threaten potential competitors with legal action. In some cases the threats may be groundless, but the victim might be prepared to cease the relevant activities or pay a royalty rather than risk the court action and its attendant costs. Litigation can be very expensive, and this may deter the person threatened from challenging the validity of the right concerned or otherwise defending the alleged infringement. UK patent law, design

54 TFEU. This Treaty replaced the former EC Treaty as from 1 December 2009. Article 101 of the TFEU was previously Article 81 of the EC Treaty.

55 There are equivalent controls under the UK Competition Act 1998 which apply where trade within the UK is affected by the prohibited behaviour.

56 Patents Act 1977 s 70, Registered Designs Act 1949 s 26, Copyright, Designs and Patents Act 1988 s 253 and Trade Marks Act 1994 s 21.

57 Trade Marks Act 1994 s 95. There is an equivalent provision for registered designs (Registered Designs Act 1949 s 35). There are offences as regards false representations in respect of patents: Patents Act 1977 ss 110 and 111.

58 Apart from the possibility of applying for a declaration of non-infringement under the court's inherent jurisdiction.

59 *See* Chapter 23.

law and trade mark law contain remedies for groundless threats of infringement proceedings[56] and it is an offence falsely to represent that a trade mark is registered.[57] In the UK, there are equivalent provisions in respect of groundless threats made in relation to the Community design and the Community trade mark and there is an offence of falsely representing that a trade mark is registered as a Community trade mark. There is no control over groundless threats of infringement proceedings with respect to an alleged copyright infringement.[58] Bearing in mind the commercial importance of copyright and the possibility of legal tactics by dominant companies to control the market, this seems a serious omission. However, the tort of malicious falsehood (trade libel) might be available in limited cases to provide a remedy.[59]

The Competition Act 1998 contains provisions equivalent to the controls in the EU Treaty in respect of restrictive trade practices and abuses of a dominant trading position but which apply in relation to the UK rather than in respect of trade between Member States.

European and international considerations

Intellectual property law has long been set upon an international stage, and therefore it is not surprising that the UK's membership of the EU has had a great influence on copyright, patents, trade marks and the like. Three particular issues mark the impact of the EU on intellectual property law:

1 the drive towards greater harmonisation of the laws of individual Member States;
2 the move to Community-wide intellectual property rights;
3 the impact of the Treaty on the Functioning of the European Union (formerly the EC Treaty) on the use and abuse of intellectual property rights.

Each of these aspects is discussed in the context of individual intellectual property rights in the relevant parts of the book. However, a brief overview of basic principles is given below.

Harmonisation

The Internal Market in the EU is reinforced and trade between Member States is facilitated if the intellectual property rights implemented in each Member State are alike. The process of harmonisation of national laws in the field of intellectual property has been proceeding for some time and has not been restricted to the EU. Harmonisation of patent law was effected through the European Patent Convention which has a larger membership than that of the EU. UK patent law was changed on 1 June 1978 as a result of this Convention.[60] European Union Directives[61] have been instrumental in changing domestic laws protecting, *inter alia*, computer programs, semiconductor products, databases, biological inventions, trade marks and registered designs. Other changes have been made to copyright law and rights in performances. A right of artists to a royalty on the resale of their works was introduced into the UK in 2006 as a result of a Directive and there is a proposal for a Directive to harmonise utility model protection though this seems to have lost momentum for the time being.[62]

60 The date that the Patents Act 1977 came into force.

61 Previously European Community Directives: even older ones were known as Council Directives (being the Council to the European Communities).

62 Although a harmonising Directive, this will have the effect of introducing this form of protection into the UK as there previously existed no equivalent protection in the UK.

Community-wide rights

It would be ideal if identical intellectual property rights were recognised and given effect throughout the European Union. Work has been done towards this goal in respect of patent law and trade mark law. A proposal for a Community Patent Convention was first published in 1975.[63] The Community patent differs from a patent under the European Patent Convention in that the Community patent system will be a unitary system, granting patents that will take effect throughout the European Union, whereas a grant obtained under the European Patent Convention presently gives a bundle of national patents. The Community patent will be administered by the European Patent Office. The Patents Act 1977 contains the necessary mechanism for recognition of the Community patent.[64] Interest in the Community patent flares up now and again but it does not seem as if it is likely to come into being in the immediate future. This is a great pity as it could help overcome the difficulties facing a proprietor trying to enforce a number of national patents obtained through the European Patent Convention for the same invention. A proposal for a harmonising Directive on software-related inventions was rejected by a massive majority in the European Parliament during 2005.

There have, however, been some success stories regarding Community-wide rights. The Community trade mark has proved very successful and the Community design seems to be replicating this success, though on a smaller scale. The Office for the Harmonisation of the Internal Market (Trade Marks and Designs) (OHIM) was established at Alicante in Spain and started accepting applications to register Community trade marks on 1 January 1996. The OHIM is also responsible for registering the Community design and started registering Community designs as from 1 April 2003. The introduction of Community-wide rights is a logical part of the process of consolidating the single market.

Enforcement Directive

Accepting that intellectual property is essential for the success of the Internal Market of the EU, a Directive was adopted on the enforcement of intellectual property rights.[65] The Directive recognises the importance of intellectual property rights in promoting innovation and creativity and in developing employment and improving competitiveness. The Directive seeks to strike a balance between providing inventors and creators with the opportunity to realise a legitimate profit and encouraging the widest dissemination of works, ideas and new know-how whilst not hampering freedom of expression, freedom of information and the protection of personal data on the internet. To this end, Member States are required to provide for measures, procedures and remedies necessary to ensure the enforcement of intellectual property rights, those measures, procedures and remedies to be effective, proportionate and dissuasive.[66] The scope of the Directive is wide in that it applies to all intellectual property rights covered by EU provisions in the field and Member States may, if they wish, extend the provisions to their laws relating to unfair competition.[67]

The Enforcement Directive was implemented in the UK by the Intellectual Property (Enforcement, etc) Regulations 2006.[68] The Directive is discussed more fully in Chapter 24 (Part 7) on remedies for infringement of intellectual property rights.

Conflicts with the Treaty on the Functioning of the European Union (TFEU)

The control of abuses of intellectual property rights by provisions in the TFEU has been noted previously. Those provisions are: Articles 34 to 36 which promote the free movement of goods, Article 101 which prohibits restrictive trade practices and Article 102 which is designed to prevent the abuse of a dominant market position.[69] It must be stressed that these controls are relevant only if trade between Member States is affected or is likely to be affected. By their very nature, the rights given by intellectual property law can easily offend against the TFEU. For example, the proprietor of a patent will wish to exploit that patent to its best advantage, and to do this he may be selective about markets and persons to whom licences are granted and this may operate against the free movement of goods.

63 Convention for the European Patent for the Common Market (Community Patent Convention) (76/76/EEC), OJ L401, 30.12.89, p 1.

64 Patents Act 1977 ss 86 and 87.

65 Directive 2004/48/EC of the European Parliament and of the Council on the enforcement of intellectual property rights, OJ L 157, 30.04.2004, p 45.

66 Article 3.

67 Recital 13 to the Directive.

68 SI 2006/1028.

69 Article 18 of the TFEU, which prohibits discrimination on the grounds of nationality, may also be relevant.

70 *See* Chapter 25.

71 This doctrine extends to the States of the European Economic Area which is made up of the Member States of the EU, Iceland, Liechtenstein and Norway by virtue of equivalent provisions in the Agreement on the European Economic Area, OJ L 1, 03.01.1994, p 3, Articles 11 to 13. There are other provisions equivalent to Articles 101 and 102 of the TFEU.

72 As at 17 February 2012.

However, EU law recognises the advantage of intellectual property law and is sufficiently realistic to appreciate the value of licensing arrangements and the like. Article 345 of the TFEU states that nothing in the Treaty shall prejudice the rules in Member States governing the system of property ownership; and, as already mentioned, intellectual property is a form of property. Nevertheless, the worst abuses are struck down without hesitation by the Commission or the Court of Justice and this has sometimes been controversial, as evidenced by opportunistic parallel importing and the doctrine of exhaustion of rights.[70] This doctrine means that the owner of an intellectual property right cannot use that right to prevent the further commercialisation of articles subject to that right which have been placed on the market within the European Economic Area by him or with his consent.[71]

International aspects

On a wider international stage, it is worth mentioning briefly the importance of uniform laws and reciprocal protection. The vast majority of the world's developed nations play a role and are members of one or more of the various international conventions relating to intellectual property rights. Several of these conventions are administered by the World Intellectual Property Organisation (WIPO), which is part of the United Nations. One of the most important and earliest conventions is the Paris Convention for the Protection of Industrial Property 1883, to which there are currently 174 signatories, including the UK.[72] This convention, which is updated and amended occasionally (last revision in 1979), applies to inventions, trade marks, industrial designs, indications of origin and unfair competition. It establishes basic principles for laws in individual countries and reciprocal protection, and also priority rights in respect of patents, trade marks and industrial designs. The WIPO also administers, *inter alia*, the Berne Convention for the Protection of Literary and Artistic Works and the Madrid Agreement for the international registration of trade marks. The UK has ratified the Protocol to this latter agreement. Another important convention on copyright law is the Universal Copyright Convention. Most countries belong to one or both of the copyright conventions and 142 countries are Contracting Parties to the Patent Cooperation Treaty which provides a streamlined method of obtaining a patent internationally.

The Uruguay Round of the GATT (General Agreement on Tariffs and Trade) was concluded on 15 December 1993 with a series of agreements including the 'TRIPs Agreement' (Trade Related Aspects of Intellectual Property Rights), now administered by the World Trade Organisation (WTO). The TRIPs Agreement lays down minimum standards of protection for intellectual property on the basis that adequate and effective protection must be given in such a way that the enforcement of intellectual property rights does not create barriers to legitimate trade. There is an obligation on members to comply with certain parts of the Paris Convention for the Protection of Industrial Property, the Berne Convention for the Protection of Literary and Artistic Works, the Rome Convention for the Protection of Performers, Producers of Phonograms and Broadcasting Organisations and the Washington Treaty on Intellectual Property in Respect of Integrated Circuits. Part II of the Agreement sets out the standards relating to copyright and related rights, trade marks, geographical indications of origin, industrial design, patents, layout designs of integrated circuits, protection of undisclosed information and the control of anti-competitive practices in contractual licences. There are also measures dealing with enforcement and the resolution of disputes, for example, where a member considers a judicial decision affects its rights under the Agreement.

There are transitional provisions notable in that they grant a period of grace in respect of most of the provisions of the Agreement of four years to developing countries and ten years for the least developed countries. The Agreement came into force on 1 January 1995. The TRIPs Agreement is, arguably, the most important international initiative in the field of intellectual property since the Paris Convention of 1883. Of course, much of UK law already complies, but there are differences. However, the TRIPs Agreement is not of direct effect: *Lenzing AG's European Patent (UK)*.[73] In the UK, its effects will be felt through European Union legislation, though it has to be said that there are unlikely to be many changes to domestic law in Europe resulting from the TRIPs Agreement. Members are permitted to grant more extensive protection than that set out in the Agreement provided that it does not conflict with the other provisions of the Agreement. The unregistered design right is an example of such more extensive protection. A submission that it was incompatible with the TRIPs Agreement was unsuccessful in *Azrak-Hamway International Inc's Licence of Right Application*.[74]

73 [1997] RPC 245.

74 [1997] RPC 134.

Practical considerations

Rationale and justification for intellectual property law

Various justifications have been put forward for the existence of intellectual property law and these have usually been set in the context of patents. A more detailed discussion of the justification for intellectual property rights is, therefore, contained in Chapter 11 concerning patent law. The basic reason for intellectual property is that a man should own what he produces, that is, what he brings into being. If what he produces can be taken from him, he is no better than a slave. Intellectual property is, therefore, the most basic form of property because a man uses nothing to produce it other than his mind.[75] It is claimed that investment should be stimulated by the presence and enforcement of strong laws that provide a framework ensuring that the publication of new works and the manufacture of new products will be profitable, assuming, of course, that they are sufficiently meritorious, useful and commercially attractive to attain a viable level of sales. If investment is stimulated this should lead to increased prosperity and employment. Another justification is that the existence of strong laws in this area encourages the publication and dissemination of information and widens the store of available knowledge. For example, details of patents are published and are available for public inspection. In due course, when the patent expires, anyone is free to make the product or use the process, as the case may be. This would seem to be ample vindication for offering a monopoly protection in the case of patents.

75 I am indebted to Professor Bryan Niblett for suggesting this simple but powerful reason.

Another reason is that a person who creates a work or has a good idea which he develops has a right, based partly on morality and partly on the concept of reward, to control the use and exploitation of it, and he should be able to prevent others from taking unfair advantage of his efforts. Why should others be able to save themselves all the time and effort required to create or invent the thing concerned? Surely, on this basis, the law should provide remedies against those who appropriate the ideas of others, and a person who has devoted time and effort to create something has a right to claim the thing as his own and also has a right to obtain some reward for all his work. The tendency in the UK has been to encourage innovation through economic incentives, but in other countries stress has been placed on moral aspects although there have been moves in the UK to afford rights to the creator independent from the ownership of the right.

The grant of formal intellectual property rights has sometimes been explained in terms of a contract between the inventor or designer and the state. For example, in return for the grant of a patent, offering monopoly protection for a limited period of time, the inventor donates his invention to the state. This is the consideration theory and two variants of it were identified by Jacob J, at first instance, in *Philips Electronics NV v Remington Consumer Products Ltd*.[76] An extension of this view of intellectual property rights

76 [1998] RPC 283.

is to argue that a particular invention should no longer be protected by other intellectual property rights once the patent has expired. Jacob J said (at 310):

> I would only add this about the 'it-was-once-patented, or expired right' point. In general there is no rule of law which prevents one type of intellectual property right from running parallel to another. In particular, for instance, it has long been held that in some circumstances a design can also be a trade mark . . . Similarly, patents and designs can coexist . . . and passing off rights can exist in shapes the subject of a patent . . . The notion that there may not be parallel rights seems to be based on two fallacies, or perhaps one expressed in two different ways. One is that by applying for one form of monopoly the applicant is abandoning all others (the 'election theory') . . . The other is that by obtaining such a monopoly for a fixed term the applicant is deemed to dedicate the subject of the monopoly to the public when the monopoly expires (the 'dedication theory').

Jacob J went on to dismiss the 'consideration theory' and said that it had no place in the modern statutory scheme of things and had no application to modern intellectual property law. Of course, there is no reason why a number of different intellectual property rights cannot give protection to the same subject matter. The preferred embodiment of a product invention might possess aesthetic qualities making both patent protection and registered design protection appropriate. The shape of a container might be registrable as a design and as a trade mark. There is a complete absence of statutory provisions bringing one form of right to an end on the expiry of another right in respect of the same invention, design or logo. When a patent expires, it brings to the public the right to work the invention subject to the patent but does not automatically bring a bonus to do other things protected by subsisting intellectual property rights. When a document, which was confidential, is published, that does not bring the copyright subsisting in it to an end also. It would be preposterous if it did and would emasculate copyright protection. The next section in this chapter explores concurrent protection by intellectual property rights.

Other considerations come into the study of the place of intellectual property law in modern society. Counterfeiting is a serious problem which should be attacked, not only to protect the interests of legitimate traders but to protect society from being deceived into buying substandard goods. In some cases, safety is at issue: for example, where the counterfeit is a poorly made toy covered in a paint containing high levels of lead. Furthermore, there are links between organised crime and intellectual property crime.[77] This is one main reason why the maximum penalties for copyright offences and trade mark offences are considerable.

Certain offences under copyright law, rights in performances and trade mark law have been designated as serious offences for the purposes of the Serious Crime Act 2007. This Act provides for serious crime prevention orders which may contain prohibitions, restrictions or requirements or other terms which are considered appropriate by the court for protecting the public by preventing, restricting or disrupting involvement by a person concerned in serious crime.[78] This is a reflection of the seriousness with which some intellectual property offences are now viewed.[79]

Pharmaceutical patents have been controversial where the high cost of drugs and medicines protected by patents can work against public health issues in developing countries, especially where there are serious and widespread health problems. The World Trade Organisation attempted to deal with this issue in the 'Doha Declaration'[80] concerning the possibility, *inter alia*, of using compulsory licensing and parallel importing to cut the cost of pharmaceutical products. Compulsory licences may be available for pharmaceuticals to be exported to countries with health problems under an EU Regulation.[81] The Doha Declaration also postpones the deadline for least developed countries to provide for patents for pharmaceutical products until 1 January 2016. Compulsory licensing may not solve the problem, however, if the country in question does not have the facility to manufacture drugs and other medicines. The issue is a sensitive one requiring a balance

77 *The Gowers Review of Intellectual Property*, HMSO, 2006, at p 97.

78 The orders will be made under s 1 of the Act. These provisions apply to England and Wales and Northern Ireland. In force 6 April 2008.

79 The *Gowers Review*, op cit.

80 Fourth Ministerial Conference at Doha, Qatar, November 2001.

81 Regulation (EC) No 816/2006 of the European Parliament and of the Council of 17 May 2006 on compulsory licensing of patents relating to the manufacture of pharmaceutical products for export to countries with health problems, OJ L 157, 09.06.2006, p 1.

between public health issues and the economic realities of running pharmaceutical companies which are answerable to their shareholders and need to maintain profitability to fund research into new products in order to remain successful.

Combination of intellectual property rights

The lifespan of an invention or a work of copyright can comprise several different and distinct stages, and during these stages different intellectual property rights may afford protection to the invention or work. For example, an idea for an invention will be protected by the law of confidence until such time as a patent application is published. Once a patent has been granted in respect of the invention, patent law takes over. Other rights might be appropriate, such as the law of trade marks or passing off, if a mark or name is applied to the product. Intellectual property rights work together to provide legal protection throughout the life of the product until such time as all the rights have expired for one reason or another. Tables 1.4 and 1.5 give examples of how the various intellectual property rights work together to give continuity of protection.

Table 1.4 The life of an invention

Stage in the life of an invention	Form of intellectual property right				
	Confidence	Copyright	Patent	Trade marks	Passing off
The bare idea, in the inventor's mind only	***				
Discussion with friends and colleagues	Maintain air of confidence				
Idea expressed in tangible form, e.g. in writing, on drawings, in a computer memory		***			
Preliminary negotiations with potential manufacturers	Maintain air of confidence				
Patent application (assumed successful)	Only in respect of things not disclosed in the patent application		*** From priority date		
Further negotiations with potential manufacturers					
Put invention into production and sell articles made to it				*** If applied for	
Establish a reputation associated with the product					***
	Protected for author's life plus 70 years	Up to a maximum of 20 years	For as long as renewed	For as long as reputation associated with article	

***Signifies the commencement of the right.

Table 1.5 The life of a play

| The life of a play | Form of intellectual property right | | | |
| | | Copyright | | |
	Confidence	Dramatic work	Typographical arrangement	Rights in performance
The bare idea for the play in the playwright's mind only	***			
Preliminary negotiations with potential publishers	Maintain air of confidence			
Play is recorded by, e.g., writing, typing or using word processor		***		
Further negotiations with potential publishers	Maintain air of confidence			
Publish play	Idea now in public domain		***	
				***
Performance of play made in public				
		Dramatic works protected for author's life plus 70 years	For 25 years from end of year of first publication	For 50 years from end of year of first performance

*** Signifies the commencement of the right.

Note: rights in performance are for the benefit of the performers and any person with whom they have a recording contract.

Note that, in the first example, copyright protection might be all but exhausted because, under the Copyright, Designs and Patents Act 1988 s 47, documents submitted in a patent application are open to public inspection and may be copied (with the authority of the Comptroller-General of Patents, Designs and Trade Marks). Copyright still provides limited protection to these documents, for example if copied without such permission.

In the tables, solid vertical lines represent the duration of the right, and a broken line signifies that the right still exists but in a weaker form.

The nature of the study of intellectual property

Intellectual property law is a demanding subject, but this is compensated by being one of the most enjoyable and diverse of all substantive law areas. Many aspects of procedural law are also highly relevant. As much as any subject in the study of law, intellectual property law cuts across boundaries and makes the oft-imposed compartmentalisation of legal subjects seem awkward and inappropriate. A study of intellectual property law embraces property law (real and personal), contract law, tort, criminal law, commercial law, competition law, European Union law, evidence, procedure and jurisdiction. An understanding of the subject is enhanced by a knowledge of the basic principles of equity, some legal philosophy and at least a superficial grasp of other disciplines such as economics, sociology and industrial history. A liking for, or sympathy with, science and technology is also helpful. A number of practitioners in the field of intellectual property, including members of the Chancery Bar, solicitors, patent agents and trade mark agents, have science degrees in addition to law degrees or other legal qualifications, and this dual educational background can be very much an advantage in the practice of intellectual property law. A command of one or more foreign languages may also be useful.

Commercial exploitation of intellectual property

Intellectual property is a valuable asset which may be exploited in a number of ways. It may be assigned, whereby the ownership in the whole or part of the right is transferred, or licences may be granted in respect of it. As with assignments, licences may be in respect of the whole or part of the right. For example, the owner of the copyright in a dramatic work might grant a licence to a number of theatre companies to perform the work in public for five years, each company being restricted geographically in terms of where it might make the performance.

Licences may be exclusive or non-exclusive. An exclusive licence grants the rights governed by the licence to the licensee who can perform those rights to the exclusion of everyone else including the owner. For example, the proprietor of a patent may grant an exclusive 'worldwide' licence to a manufacturer to work the invention. A non-exclusive licence is appropriate where the owner of the intellectual property right wishes to grant licences to numerous licensees, a good example being in the case of computer software.[82] Sometimes a sole licence is appropriate. This grants permission to perform the particular acts to only one licensee but, unlike the exclusive licence, the owner retains the right to perform the acts himself.

Other forms of exploiting intellectual property include using it as security for loan, such as by way of a mortgage or other charge. Alternatively, it may be acquired as an investment, by paying a capital sum in return for an assignment; the person acquiring it will hope to receive income from it over a number of years by granting licences. In 1996, Enid Blyton's copyrights were sold for £13 million.[83]

It has already been pointed out in this chapter that intellectual property rights are very diverse in nature. Some are informal and arise automatically whilst others can only be acquired by applying for registration. This distinction leads to some persons collectively describing the informal intellectual property rights as 'soft IP' and those subject to registration as 'hard IP'.

It is important to note that, even in the case of soft IP, certain formalities must be adhered to in many cases to make a transaction effective at law. For example, in the case of an assignment of copyright, it must be in writing and be signed by or on behalf of the person making the assignment, the assignor.[84] An exclusive licence in respect of a copyright must be in writing signed by or on behalf of the copyright owner.[85]

Most types of transactions involving hard IP must also conform to certain statutory requirements. For example, an assignment or mortgage of a patent is void unless it is in writing and signed by or on behalf of the assignor or mortgagor, as appropriate.[86] An assignment of a registered trade mark is not effective unless it is in writing signed by or on behalf of the assignor.[87] To be effective, a licence to use a registered trade mark, whether exclusive, non-exclusive or a sub-licence, must be in writing signed by or on behalf of the grantor.[88] It may take some time before the patent is granted or the trade mark is registered and it is possible to deal with the application for a patent or to register a trade mark and similar formalities apply to applications as well as the granted rights.

A further requirement exists with hard IP. Not only must the fact of registration appear on the appropriate register, but most forms of transactions concerning the right must also

82 In some cases, the licensee of computer software may require an exclusive licence or even an assignment such as where the software has been written for his specific requirements.

83 *The Times*, 24 January 1996. Enid Blyton died in 1968 and her copyrights will endure until the end of the year 2038.

84 Copyright, Designs and Patents Act 1988 s 90(3).

85 Copyright, Designs and Patents Act 1988 s 92(1).

86 Patents Act 1977 s 30(6) as amended by the Regulatory Reform (Patents) Order 2004, SI 2004/2357.

87 Trade Marks Act 1994 s 24(3).

88 Trade Marks Act 1994 s 28(2). References in the Act include sub-licences (s 28(4)).

be notified and placed on the register. Copies of register entries are available to the public on payment of a fee and it is important that the register accurately reflects the fact of proprietorship and what rights have been granted in or under the particular intellectual property. For example, in the case of a patent, the register will include information relating to the proprietor of the patent and, where appropriate, transactions affecting rights in or under the patent such as assignments, the grant or assignment of a licence, sub-licence or mortgage.[89]

Registration of a transaction will be made following application on the appropriate form. For example, for a registrable transaction concerning a patent,[90] Patents Form 21 must be used and include evidence establishing the transaction, instrument or event.[91] Similar provisions apply to trade marks and to registered designs.

Failure to register a registrable transaction may have serious consequences. There are a number of statutory provisions that can fairly be said to have as one of their main purposes the encouragement of the registration of transactions involving hard IP. A person who takes the right under a transaction may acquire the title to the intellectual property as against someone claiming under an earlier transaction if that earlier transaction had not, at the time of the later one, been registered and the person taking under the later transaction did not know of the earlier one.[92]

A defendant in an infringement action in respect of a patent or trade mark will be able to set up a failure to register a relevant transaction as a partial defence so as to negate the remedies of damages or an account of profits. For example, in respect of a patent, costs (expenses in Scotland) are not available unless the relevant and registrable transaction, instrument or event was registered within six months or, if it was not practicable to register within six months,[93] it was registered as soon as practicable thereafter.[94] Originally, this worked to deprive a claimant of damages or an account and was described by Jacob J as being designed to encourage the registration of transactions rather than providing an infringer with a fortuitous defence.[95]

IP in acquisitions and mergers

Often intellectual property will be acquired as part of a transaction which includes all manner of other property. For example, some or all of the assets of a company may be acquired, the assets comprising tangible property such as premises, plant and equipment in addition to intangible property such as intellectual property. Some of the intellectual property is likely to be soft IP such as copyright in engineering drawings and software, whilst other rights might be in relation to hard IP such as patents, registered designs and trade marks. Many of the points discussed below also apply in the case of mergers and de-mergers.

The organisation making the acquisition is likely to have a number of questions in respect of the various intellectual property rights (IPR). These questions will include:

- what the IPR are and how long they will endure, assuming hard IPs are renewed to the maximum extent, and what their territorial scope is;
- whether the IPR are owned outright or jointly;
- whether any of the IPR are licensed in (that is, whether they were being exploited under a licence granted by a third party to the company now selling its assets) and, if so, what the scope of the licences are;
- whether any IPR are licensed out (that is, the company now selling its assets granted licences to third parties enabling them to exploit the IPR) and, if so, what the scope of the licences are;
- whether all registrable transactions were registered in a timely manner, and whether there are any other transactions affecting the IPR;

89 Patents Act 1977 s 32.

90 Registrable transactions, instruments and events are set out in the Patents Act 1977 s 33(3).

91 Patents Rules 2007, SI 2007/3291 r 47.

92 Patents Act 1977 s 33(1), Trade Marks Act 1994 s 25(3).

93 The court or Comptroller-General of Patents would have to be satisfied that it was not practicable to register within six months.

94 Patents Act 1977 s 68.

95 *Coflexip Stena Offshore Ltd's Patent* [1997] RPC 179.

- whether all renewal fees in respect of hard IPR have been paid on time;
- whether there have been challenges to the IPR and, in the case of patents, whether there have been any opinions by the Comptroller of Patents;
- whether the IPR have been infringed and, if so, what the outcome was;
- whether there are any current potential infringements of the IPR and what evidence has been gathered and what preliminary steps have been taken;
- whether there have been any instances where the IPR have infringed or have been alleged to infringe IPR belonging to third parties;
- how much the IPR are worth.

These questions can be answered, at least to some extent, by carrying out an audit. This will involve obtaining up-to-date register entries in respect of hard IP, and asking for some evidence of the date of creation of important soft IP. For example, the company may have carried out a policy of depositing copies of its engineering drawings with an independent third party such as the Stationers' Company. Assignments will be scrutinised for form and validity. Licence agreements will be inspected as well as records of royalty payments. In some respects, the organisation acquiring the intellectual property will have to rely on the company now divesting itself of its assets. It will be sensible in such circumstances for the agreement for the transfer of assets to include appropriate warranties: for example, a warranty that a trade mark has been renewed when due and has been in continuous use.[96]

Some information may require more significant detective work such as determining the history of the IPR as regards litigation, or steps taken preliminary to litigation which did not or has not come to fruition. Another problem may be the existence of equitable rights in relation to the IPR. These are not generally registrable in the case of hard IP[97] and, for all forms of IPR, may arise without any written agreement. In other cases, there may be some written agreement which does not comply with the requirements as to form. There may also be an implied licence which is not supported by any direct documentary evidence. Again, the inclusion of warranties in the agreement to transfer the IPR may help, but is no substitute for actual knowledge of all the rights and interests that might affect the value or exploitation of the IPR. The investigative work which is performed to verify and assess the nature, scope and value of IPR is often referred to as 'due diligence'.

It is not unusual for a contract under which IPR are to be transferred to take effect as an agreement to assign the IPR, the formal assignments of the IPR being executed subsequently. If this is the case, the contract should include a term to the effect that the assignor will do everything necessary, including executing the required agreements and completing and submitting the necessary application forms, to give effect to any assignments or other transactions covered by the agreement and ensure their registration.

Framework for description of rights

In this book, each of the various rights is described, examined and discussed within the following broad framework:

- overview and history
- nature of the right and its subsistence
- ownership of the right and dealings with it
- infringement of the right
- exceptions and defences
- remedies.

96 If a trade mark has not been put to genuine use in the UK during the first five years following completion of the registration procedure, or if such use has been suspended for an uninterrupted period of five years, it will be susceptible to revocation (Trade Marks Act 1994 s 46(1)). Similar provisions apply in relation to the Community trade mark.

97 For example, the Trade Marks Act 1994 states that no notice of any trust (express, implied or constructive) shall be entered in the register: see s 26(1).

There is a separate section on European and international aspects although, of course, the implementation of European Directives and Community-wide rights are dealt with in the appropriate chapters. The above framework is followed wherever possible, although it has been modified for some of the rights. Given the nature of these rights, it is usual to speak of infringement rather than breach. You infringe a right, but breach a duty. Breach is suggestive of a pre-existing contractual or tortious duty owed by and to specific persons (though infringing copyright is a tort). Therefore, a person infringes a copyright, a patent or a trade mark; he is not in breach of copyright, etc. However, many judges talk in terms of breach of copyright and, strictly speaking, this is just as valid an expression. With passing off, it is usual to say that a person has committed the tort of passing off or is guilty of passing off. Breach of confidence is the usual phrase, though it should be noted that this is not a tort as such, as an obligation of confidence is a creature of equity.

Summary

Intellectual property laws protect inventions, creative works, confidential information and trade secrets, designs, trade marks and business goodwill. The nature of intellectual property rights varies considerably. They are intangible rights, distinct from the tangible works or products to which they apply.

Intellectual property rights are either formal or informal:

- formal rights, such as patents, are subject to a formal registration system;
- informal rights, such as copyright, come into being when the subject-matter is created or fixed in some tangible form.

Formal intellectual property rights give monopoly protection whilst the protection afforded by informal rights requires proof of an act in relation to the subject-matter, such as making a copy. Generally, monopoly rights do not last as long as some (though not all) informal rights. To this there are exceptions:

- unregistered design protection has a short lifespan;
- registered trade marks may be renewed indefinitely provided the trade marks continue to be used.

The owner of an intellectual property right has economic rights, being rights of exploitation. For copyright and performance rights, the creator or performer also has moral rights, which primarily are:

- a right to be identified as creator or performer; and
- a right to object to a derogatory treatment of the subject-matter.

Intellectual property rights are true property rights which may be exploited in a number of ways such as by:

- transfer of ownership, in whole or in part;
- the grant of licences to others to allow them to carry out certain acts in relation to the subject-matter of the right;
- the grant of mortgages or otherwise using the rights as security for loans.

Intellectual property rights operate by giving the owner the right to perform certain acts in relation to the subject-matter, such as making a patented product or using a patented process. Any person who carries out such acts without the licence (permission) of the owner will infringe the right. However, there are a number of defences and acts which are permitted without infringing the right.

Intellectual property rights provide for checks and balances to prevent the rights becoming too powerful or extensive and there are a number of controls over the abuse of intellectual property rights, for example:

- copyright law contains numerous 'permitted acts' which may be carried out without infringing copyright;
- compulsory licences may be available, for example, if a patent is not being reasonably exploited because the owner is limiting supply to drive up prices;
- licences of right may be available in some cases;
- competition law may be used to curb the worst excesses of intellectual property rights involving restrictive trade agreements or abuses of dominant positions.

Intellectual property rights are territorial and only apply in the relevant territory. Protection in other countries is afforded by means of international conventions. However, some rights have a unitary nature and apply throughout the EU, examples being the Community trade mark and the Community design. There has also been significant harmonisation of some intellectual property rights throughout the EU.

Intellectual property rights are vital to industry, business and commerce and may be justified on the basis that the protection afforded encourages financial, human and technological investment in the creation of new or improved works, inventions and designs. The rights are not without controversy, however, and there are a number of associated issues, such as the conflict with the desirability of plentiful supplies of inexpensive pharmaceuticals to poor countries with major health problems.

The problem with piracy and counterfeiting and the involvement of organised crime in such activities has been met with increased penalties for criminal offences.

Discussion questions

1 Consider why some intellectual property rights give rise to monopoly protection whilst others do not. Should all forms of intellectual property rights require proof of copying or some other act in relation to the subject matter of the right concerned? Discuss.

2 Different intellectual property rights may apply during the development of a work or product and its exploitation. Discuss how these rights may apply and interact in relation to (a) a logo used to promote a new product and (b) a new means of making a widget which has a different appearance compared with pre-existing widgets.

3 Discuss the justification for intellectual property rights and consider the consequences, if any, if all intellectual property laws were repealed.

Selected further reading

Abbott, F.M. and Reichman, J.H., 'The Doha Round's public health legacy: strategies for the production and diffusion of patented medicines under the amended TRIPs provisions' (2007) 10(4) *Journal of International Economic Law* 921 (considers the implications of an amendment to the TRIPs Agreement aimed at meeting the needs of less developed countries in respect of cheaper medicines).

Ashiq, S., 'EU: trade agreement – counterfeiting' (2008) 19(3) *Ent LR* N21 (considers whether the anti-counterfeiting trade agreement should be extended to other countries including China).

Batchelor, B., 'The fallout from Microsoft: The Court of First Instance leaves critical IT issues unresolved' (2008) 14(1) *Computer and Telecommunications Law Review* 17 (looks at the CFI decision confirming the heavy fine imposed on Microsoft for abuses).

Derclaye, E., 'Patent law's role in the protection of the environment: re-assessing patent law and its justifications in the 21st century' (2009) *International Review of Intellectual Property and Competition Law* 249 (considers the appropriateness of patent law in the context of polluting inventions and whether patent laws should be modified to encourage the use of green inventions and to prohibit polluting inventions).

Helberger, N. *et al.*, 'Never forever: why extending the term of protection for sound recordings is a bad idea' [2008] *EIPR* 174 (considers why extending the term of protection for music and the like is not justified even though some recordings may still have economic value when the existing term of protection ends).

Intellectual Property Office, 'Intellectual Property Explained' (2007) as revised.
Overview of intellectual property rights available at: **http://www.ipo.gov.uk/myip.pdf**.

Other publications and information about intellectual property available at: **http://www.ipo.gov.uk/**.

Visit www.mylawchamber.co.uk/bainbridgeip to access study support resources including interactive multiple choice questions, practice exam questions with guidance, weblinks, legal updates and a legal newsfeed.

Part Two

COPYRIGHT AND RELATED RIGHTS

Background and basic principles

2

What is copyright?

Copyright is a property right that subsists in certain specified types of works as provided for by the Copyright, Designs and Patents Act 1988. Examples of the works in which copyright subsists are original literary and artistic works, films and sound recordings. The owner of the copyright subsisting in a work has the exclusive right to do certain acts in relation to the work, such as making a copy, broadcasting or selling copies to the public. These are examples of the acts restricted by copyright. The owner of the copyright can control the exploitation of the work, for example, by making copies or selling copies to the public or by granting permission to another to do this in return for a payment. A common example is where the owner of the copyright in a work of literature permits a publishing company to print and sell copies of the work in book form in return for royalty payments, usually an agreed percentage of the price the publisher obtains for the books.

If a person performs one of the acts restricted by copyright without the licence (permission) of the copyright owner, the latter can sue for infringement of his copyright and obtain remedies: for example, damages and an injunction. However, there are limits and certain closely drawn exceptions are available, such as fair dealing with the work. An example would be where a person makes a single copy of a few pages of a book in a library for the purpose of private study.[1] Other acts may be carried out in relation to the work if they are not restricted by the copyright: for example, borrowing a book from a friend to read in private.[2]

A broad classification can be made between the various types of copyright work. Some, such as literary, dramatic, musical and artistic works, are required to be original. As will be seen later, this is easily satisfied and the work in question need not be unique in any particular way. It is a question of whether the work originated with the author and can be considered to be an intellectual creation. Generally, the quality of the work is not an issue: copyright protects meritorious works as well as awful ones.[3]

Other works such as sound recordings, broadcasts[4] and typographical arrangements can be described as derivative or entrepreneurial works and there is no requirement for originality: for example, repeat broadcasts each attract their own copyright.[5] Films sit uncomfortably in this grouping as they are treated more like the original works and the term of protection for films is now similar to that for the other original works.

Copyright extends beyond mere literal copying and covers acts such as making a translation of a literary work, performing a work in public and other acts relating to technological developments, such as broadcasting the work or storing it in a computer and transmitting it electronically, for example, by placing the work on a website.

1 Licences may be available from collecting societies allowing certain uses and copying of copyright works which may go beyond the exceptions to infringement.

2 This would not allow copying, for example, an e-book to give to a friend.

3 It would be regrettable if the court became an arbiter of good taste. Things are not so clear though when it comes to works of artistic craftsmanship (a form of artistic work) as we will see in the following chapter.

4 Cable programmes (sent by cable as opposed to being transmitted through the ether) were a separate form of work but, as a result of the Copyright and Related Rights Regulations 2003, they were reclassified as broadcasts, the definition of which was amended accordingly.

5 Under previous copyright legislation, original works were described as Part I works and derivative works were described as Part II works (*see* Copyright Act 1956). The copyright in a repeat broadcast expires at the same time as the copyright in the original broadcast: Copyright, Designs and Patents Act 1988 s 14. However, no copyright arises in a repeat broadcast made after the expiry of copyright in the original broadcast: s 14(5).

31

Fundamentally and conceptually, copyright law should not give rise to monopolies, and it is permissible for any person to produce a work which is similar to a pre-existing work as long as the later work is not taken from the first.[6] It is theoretically possible, if unlikely, for two persons independently to produce identical works. Each will be considered to be the author of his own work for copyright purposes. For example, two photographers may each take a photograph of Nelson's Column within minutes of each other from the same position using similar cameras, lenses and films, after selecting the same exposure times and aperture settings. The two photographs might be indistinguishable from each other but copyright will, nevertheless, subsist in both photographs, separately. The logical reason for this situation is that both of the photographers have used skill and judgment independently in taking their photographs and both should be able to prevent other persons from making copies of their respective photographs.

Another feature of copyright law which limits its potency is that it does not protect ideas; it merely protects the expression of an idea. The late Barbara Cartland did not have a monopoly in romantic novels. Anyone else is free to write a romantic novel, since the concept of a romantic novel is an idea and not protected by copyright. However, writing a romantic novel by taking substantial parts of a Barbara Cartland novel infringes copyright, because the actual text of the novel is the expression of the idea. Just how far back one can go from the expression as formulated in a novel to the ideas underlying the novel is not easy to answer. If a person gleans the detailed plot of a novel and then writes a novel based on that detailed plot, there is an argument that there has been an infringement of copyright even though the text of the original novel has not been referred to further or copied during the process of writing the second novel.[7] A detailed plot, including settings, incidents and the sequence of events can be described as a non-literal or non-textual form of expression. However, the boundary between idea and expression is notoriously difficult to draw.[8] Suffice it to say at this stage that judges have been reluctant to sympathise with a defendant who has taken a short cut to producing his work by making an unfair use of the claimant's work, especially when the two works are likely to compete.

Copyright is also restricted in its lifespan; it is of limited duration, although it must be said that copyright law is rather generous in this respect. For example, copyright in a literary work endures until the end of the period of 70 years from the end of the calendar year in which the author dies.[9] Approximately, therefore, copyright lasts for the life of the author plus 70 years.[10] This temporal generosity can be justified on the basis that copyright law does not lock away the ideas underlying a work.

Ownership of the copyright in a work will often remain with the author of the work, the author being the person who created it or made the arrangements necessary for its creation, depending on the nature of the work. However, if a literary, dramatic, musical or artistic work is created by an employee working in the course of his employment, his employer will be the first owner of the copyright subject to agreement to the contrary. Additionally, copyright, like other forms of property, can be dealt with; it may be assigned;[11] it may pass under a will or intestacy or by operation of law, and licences may be granted in respect of it.

Full acknowledgement of moral rights came into being in the UK on 1 April 1989: the date that most of the provisions of the Copyright, Designs and Patents Act 1988 came into force. Moral rights for authors and film directors was already well established in other European countries,[12] reflecting differences in the historical development and conceptual foundations of copyright between the UK and continental Europe.[13] These moral rights, such as the right to be recognised as the author of a work and the right to object to a derogatory treatment of the work, remain with the author irrespective of subsequent ownership and dealings with the ownership of the copyright. They recognise the creator's contribution, a way of giving legal effect to the fact that the act of producing a work is an

6 In some circumstances, copyright can give an effective monopoly right: for example, where the content of the work is available only to the creator of the work and none other.

7 *Corelli* v *Gray* [1913] TLR 570.

8 For example, in *Nichols* v *Universal Pictures Corporation* (1930) 45 F 2d 119 the eminent US judge Learned Hand said of the boundary between idea and expression: 'Nobody has ever been able to fix that boundary, and nobody ever can' (at 121).

9 This was increased from life plus 50 years by the Duration of Copyright and Rights in Performances Regulations 1995, SI 1995/3297.

10 For some types of works, the period is 50 years or, effectively, 25 years.

11 An assignment is a transfer of ownership.

12 Moral rights were included in the Berne Convention for the Protection of Literary and Artistic Works 1886 by virtue of the Rome revision of 1928. These rights already existed in France and Germany.

13 For a discussion of the continental tradition of moral rights, *see* Cornish, W.R. 'Authors in Law' (1995) 58 MLR 1 at 8.

14 Under the Legal Aid Act 1988, legal aid was not available for defamation actions, but legal aid was possible for an action for false attribution. The Access to Justice Act 1999 continued this prohibition on legal aid for defamation actions but did not rule it out altogether as there was a discretion in exceptional circumstances. In *Steel and Morris* v *United Kingdom* (2005) 41 EHRR 403 (the libel case involving the 'McDonald's Two') the European Court of Human Rights found that the lack of legal aid in defamation actions could render the proceedings unfair and a breach of Article 6.1 (right to a fair trial) of the Council of Europe Convention for the Protection of Human Rights and Fundamental Freedoms 1950 and a breach of the right of freedom of expression (Article 10).

15 The protection of designs by means of the copyright in design documents such as engineering drawings was considerably curtailed by the Copyright, Designs and Patents Act 1988 s 51.

16 However, it has been amended a number of times, largely as a result of EU harmonisation initiatives.

17 For example, in the UK, the Copyright (Computer Software) Amendment Act 1985 (now repealed); in France, 1985 Law, Article 46 (Law No. 85–660 of 3 July 1985); in the Federal Republic of Germany, BGbl 1985 I 1137 amending the Copyright Law of 1965 and, in the United States, Pub. L. No. 96–517, 12 December 1980, 94 Stat 3028, amending the Copyright Act of 1976.

18 Incredibly, in the year AD 567. Apparently, St Columba surreptitiously made a copy of a Psalter in the possession of his teacher Finnian: *see* Bowker, R.R. (1912) *Copyright: Its History and its Law*, Houghton Mifflin, p 9.

act of creation and that the creator has a link or bond with the work which should be preserved regardless of hard economic considerations. The tort of defamation has, of course, long been available and could provide remedies if an author's work were to be distorted or if a work was falsely attributed to someone, depending on the circumstances: for example, if a dreadful musical composition was falsely attributed to a famous and brilliant composer. But the difficulties of suing in defamation and the attendant expense and uncertainty are good reasons for the author–work nexus to be specifically recognised and enforceable under copyright law.[14]

Copyright law adopts a very practical posture and takes under its umbrella many types of works which lack literary or artistic merit and may or may not have commercial importance. Thus, everyday and commonplace items, such as lists of customers, football coupons, drawings for engineering equipment, tables of figures, a personal letter and even a shopping list, can fall within the scope of copyright law.[15] One important reason for protecting such things is that some of them are likely to be of economic value and usually will be the result of investment and a significant amount of work, such as a computer database. Without protection there are many who would freely copy such things without having to take the trouble to create them for themselves and who would be able, as a consequence, to sell the copied items more cheaply than the person who took the trouble to create the original. If this were to happen, the incentive for investment would be severely limited. Neither is copyright generally concerned with the quality or merit of a work, the rationale being that it would be unacceptable for judges to become arbiters of artistic or literary taste or fashion. Copyright implicitly accepts that tastes differ between people and over a period of time. If the converse were true, many *avant-garde* works would be without protection from unauthorised copying and exploitation.

The pace of technological development in recent times has been unprecedented, but copyright law has striven to keep pace and the current legislation, the Copyright, Designs and Patents Act 1988, attempted to provide a framework which would be resilient to future changes.[16] An example of copyright being adapted to prevent the unfair use of works created by or associated with modern technology is the way that many countries extended copyright expressly to include computer programs and computer databases in the fold of copyright works.[17]

Brief history

Dating back almost to the beginnings of civilisation there have been those eager to profit from the work of others. In ancient times, the idea that the author of a work of literature had economic rights to control dissemination and copying was not particularly well established, and yet those who falsely claimed a work were considered contemptible. Most authors were primarily teachers, hence the emphasis on moral rights. The word 'plagiarist', meaning one who copies the work of another and passes it off as his own, is derived from the Latin 'plagiarius' meaning kidnapper. The problems of unauthorised copying of works produced by others stretch back into antiquity.

Copyright law has a relatively long history and its roots can be traced back to before the advent of printing technology, which permitted the printing of multiple copies quickly and at relatively little expense. The first record of a copyright case was *Finnian* v *Columba*.[18] Statutes of the University of Paris in 1223 legalised duplication of texts for use within the university. However, two factors limited the importance of protecting literary works. Before the late fifteenth century, works of literature were mainly religious and were written by scholarly monks who would work painstakingly for considerable periods of time preparing their gloriously illuminated books. Obviously, because of the substantial human labour and skill required to produce such works, plagiarism of books was not usually a viable consideration. Additionally, there was not a market for books due to the general illiteracy of the population at large. The religious books which were produced were made mainly for use within monasteries or churches.

Two inventions in the late fifteenth century changed everything. It could be claimed that printing has had a greater impact on civilisation than any other single invention. Gutenberg invented moveable type, first used in 1455, and Caxton developed the printing press and published Chaucer's *Canterbury Tales* in 1478, the first 'bestseller'. An Act of Richard III in 1483 encouraged the circulation of books from abroad. In 1518, the first printing privilege was issued to Richard Pynson, the Royal Printer, which prohibited the printing, for two years, of a speech by anyone else.[19] A copyright notice was appended to the speech.

19 Bowker, R.R., ibid, p 19.

Until the early sixteenth century, the art of printing was practised freely and England was quickly established as an important centre for printing in Europe.[20] But Henry VIII, desiring to restrict and control the printing of religious and political books, eventually banned the importation of books into England. By an Act of 1529, Henry VIII set up a system of privileges and printing which came to be controlled by the Stationers' Company, originally a craft guild.[21] The Company received a Royal Charter in 1557 which gave them a monopoly in printing and the Company kept a register of all books produced in England. With the backing of the infamous Court of Star Chamber, the government and the Stationers' Company maintained an elite group of printers and regulated publishing. Only registered members of the Stationers' Company could print books, the titles of which had to be entered on the Company's Register before publication. Members of the Company had the right to print their books in perpetuity and this right became known as 'copyright', the right to make copies. The Stationers' Company had powers to enable it to control printing and it could impose fines, award damages and confiscate infringing copies. Following the abolition of the Star Chamber by the Long Parliament in 1640, infringement of copyright was still subject to statutory penalties. For example, in 1649, a penalty of *6s 8d* was imposed for reprinting registered books without permission. Eventually, after the lapse of this system, common law copyright was enforced in the Court of Common Pleas which soon recognised that copyright could be assigned as a property right.

20 As were Germany, France, Venice and Florence.

21 Its full title being the Worshipful Company of Stationers and Newspaper Makers. The Company dates back to 1403 and became known as Stationers because they set up fixed stalls rather than being itinerants.

The system of privileges, registration and control survived, going through phases of varying effectiveness and licensing systems, until its ultimate collapse in 1695; and, following a brief period when piracy of books flourished, the Statute of Anne was passed in 1709.[22] In the period leading up to the Act, many had argued that copyright was a true property right:

22 8 Anne c. 19.

> . . . just the same as houses and other estates and that existing copies [assignments of copyright] had cost at least £50,000, and had been used in marriage settlements and were the subsistence of many widows and orphans.[23]

23 Bowker, R.R., *op cit*, p 23.

It was said that Jonathan Swift, the author of *Gulliver's Travels*, who had himself suffered at the hands of copyright pirates, had a hand in drafting the Statute of Anne.

The effect of wide-scale piracy of books was described in the Act, in words bordering on the emotional, as being '. . . to their [authors and proprietors of books and writings] very great Detriment and too often to the Ruin of them and their Families'. The importance of the law as a means of encouraging the dissemination of information was also recognised in the Preamble which described the Act as being for:

> . . . the Encouragement of Learning by vesting the Copies of Printed Books in the Authors or Purchasers of such Copies.

The Statute of Anne gave 14 years' sole right of printing to authors of new books (books already published by 1710 were given 21 years' protection). At the end of that period, the right returned to the author and, if still alive, he was granted an additional 14 years. Persons infringing copyright were to pay a fine of one penny for every sheet of the infringing book, one moiety of which went to the author, the other to the Crown. This was a considerable fine. In addition, infringing books and parts of books were forfeit to the proprietor who 'shall forthwith damask and make waste paper of them'. A system of registration was still in place and an action could be brought only if the title had been entered in the register book at the Stationers' Company before publication. The 'copy', by the Act, was the 'sole liberty of printing and reprinting' a book and this liberty could be infringed by any person who printed, reprinted or imported the book without consent. The Act was also the first clear acknowledgement of the legal right of authorship. The 1709 Act did not extend to certain universities and libraries, but some doubt about the scope and effectiveness of this was remedied by the Copyright Act of 1775[24] which gave a perpetual copyright to copies belonging to the Universities of Oxford and Cambridge and the Colleges of Eton, Westminster and Winchester. This survived until the Copyright, Designs and Patents Act 1988 which substituted a period of 50 years from the end of 1989, after which such rights expire.[25]

Later, there was some argument as to whether the author had, apart from a statutory copyright, a perpetual common law right to print or publish his work (a right that could be assigned to a publisher in perpetuity). Soon after the expiry of the statutory term for previously published cases, there were challenges to the common law copyright. In *Millar* v *Taylor*[26] the Court of King's Bench held that a perpetual common law copyright existed independent of any statute. That case concerned the copyright to Thomson's *The Seasons* published in four parts from 1726 to 1730.[27] Thomson died in 1748 and his copyright was sold by his executors to Beckett who took legal action against Donaldson, an alleged infringer, obtaining a permanent injunction from the Lord Chancellor. However, the case was appealed to the House of Lords and was heard before 11 Law Lords. In *Donaldson* v *Beckett*,[28] it was held that the author did have common law rights that were potentially perpetual (that is, the right of first printing and publishing), but once the work was published, this common law right was extinguished and the author's rights were to be determined solely from the Statute of Anne 1709. On the latter point, the decision was a majority decision of 6:5; a narrow victory that has not gone without criticism since. For example, Drone points out that many jurists consider that:

> . . . intellectual productions constitute a species of property founded in natural law, recognised by the common law, and neither lost by publication nor taken away by legislation.[29]

The Statute of Anne was copied almost verbatim by the United States when it enacted the US Copyright Act 1790[30] and *Donaldson* v *Beckett* followed in the Supreme Court in *Wheaton* v *Peters*.[31] This explains some of the now limited similarity between the copyright laws of the UK and the US.[32]

The scope of copyright was gradually increased to include other works, such as engravings and prints in 1734–35, lithographs in 1734, sculptures in 1798, dramatic works in 1833 and musical works in 1882.[33] Moves were also made to extend the term of copyright, though these changes did not go unchallenged; for example, the historian Macaulay described copyright as 'a tax on readers for the purpose of giving bounty to writers'.[34]

In the meantime, it was becoming recognised that copyright was important in an international context, and the Berne Convention for the Protection of Literary and Artistic Works 1886[35] was formulated with the purposes of promoting greater uniformity in copyright law and giving copyright owners full protection in all Contracting States. A basic principle was that Contracting States should give the same protection to works originating from other Contracting States as they do their own nationals. Reciprocal protection is based on the place of publication or, failing this, by reference to the nationality of the author. The Berne Convention was remarkable in that it successfully reconciled the

---

24 15 Geo. III c. 53.

25 Copyright, Designs and Patents Act 1988 Sch 1, para 13. The Whitford Committee found that the universities and colleges concerned were not overly anxious to retain perpetual copyright: *Copyright and Design Law*, Cmnd 6732, HMSO, 1977.

26 (1769) 4 Burr 2303.

27 James Thomson was a Scottish poet.

28 (1774) 2 Bro PC 129.

29 Drone, E.S. (1879) *A Treatise on the Law of Property in Intellectual Productions in Great Britain and the United States*, Little, Brown & Co.

30 The first US copyright Act. However, the Act also extended expressly to maps and charts.

31 (1834) 8 Pet 591.

32 There are now, however, some significant differences which compromise the impact of US precedents. Some of the differences can be explained by the fact that the US did not join the Berne Convention until 1989 and, especially, because of the impact of EU harmonisation of copyright and related rights.

33 Musical works were protected earlier though the form of protection was unsatisfactory.

34 Hansard, H.C. Deb vol 56 (5 February 1841). However, he was not arguing for the abolition of copyright, merely against extending it beyond the author's life.

35 Hereinafter, the 'Berne Convention'.

fundamentally different nature of UK copyright law with the French tradition of *droit d'auteur*.[36] In the Berlin revision of 1908 (the Berlin Act), *inter alia*, the term of copyright protection was increased to the life of the author plus 50 years and copyright was extended to cover choreographic works, works of architecture and sound recordings. The revision also introduced the compulsory licence and removed formalities (works still had to be registered in the UK). Works are protected automatically, without formality. Major changes to UK copyright law were introduced by the Copyright Act 1911, heavily influenced by the Berlin revision. The 1911 Act formed the basis of copyright law throughout the British Empire and accounts for similarities in copyright law between the UK and countries such as Australia, New Zealand and South Africa.

Since the Berne Convention and subsequent revisions (and the later Universal Copyright Convention, first promulgated in 1952), and until the drive to harmonise intellectual property rights throughout the EU,[37] the impetus for change in copyright law has been largely the result of the conventions[38] rather than internal national considerations. The 1911 Act was replaced in the UK by the Copyright Act 1956, which added three new forms of works: cinematograph films, broadcasts and the typographical arrangement of published editions. The Performing Right Tribunal was also created.[39] The 1956 Act classified works as being either original works (Part I works – literary, dramatic, musical and artistic works) or Part II works, sometimes known as derivative works or entrepreneurial works (namely sound recordings, cinematograph films, broadcasts and the typographical arrangement of published editions). These works could be described as derivative as they were usually based on a Part I work. For example, a sound recording may be made of the live performance of a musical work. The link was not essential and a Part II work could be subject to copyright protection without an equivalent Part I work: for example, a sound recording of a bird singing could qualify for copyright protection.

Finally, in response to major technological developments, the current Act, the Copyright, Designs and Patents Act 1988, was passed. This Act takes due account of *moral rights*, inalienable rights which belong to the author irrespective of the ownership of copyright.[40] These are equivalent to the *droit moral* of the 1928 Rome revision to the Berne Convention; that is a right to claim authorship of a work and the right to object to any distortion, mutilation or other modification of a work which could be prejudicial to the honour and reputation of the author.[41] This also has the effect of pulling English copyright law closer to that subsisting in other European countries.

Copyright and its relationship to other intellectual property rights

Like other intellectual property rights, copyright does not stand in splendid isolation. The unfair taking or use of the results of the application of human intellect may infringe more than any one single right. An act giving rise to infringement of copyright may be associated with or accompany a breach of confidence. For example, if an employee copies a confidential report belonging to his employer without permission and then passes on the copy to a competitor of the employer, there will be an infringement of copyright by the act of making a copy without permission and a serious breach of confidence by the employee giving the copy to the competitor, and also by the latter if he realises or ought to realise that the report is confidential. Additionally, the employee will be in breach of his contract of employment. The action taken by his employer may depend on the remedies available and, in the example quoted, it is likely that the employer would dismiss the employee (for being in breach of the contract of employment) and an injunction

---

36 Authors' rights.

37 The EU harmonising initiatives take account of the Berne Convention and other treaties, such as the WIPO (World Intellectual Property Organisation) Copyright Treaty, the Performances and Phonograms Treaty and the WTO (World Trade Organisation) Treaty on Trade Related Aspects of Intellectual Property (TRIPs). WIPO is a specialised agency of the United Nations and administers 24 Treaties on intellectual property including the Berne Convention.

38 And, more recently, the European Community.

39 Now replaced by the Copyright Tribunal.

40 Including now the *droit de suite*, the author's right to payment on subsequent sale of his work of art or manuscript: Berne Convention, Article 14[ter]. Introduced into the UK by the Artists' Resale Right Regulations 2006 SI 2006/346 implementing Directive 2001/84/EC of the European Parliament and of the Council of 27 September 2001 on the resale right for the benefit of the author of an original work of art, OJ L 272, 13.10.2001, p 32.

41 Article 6[bis] of the Berne Convention.

would be sought (for breach of confidence) against the competitor, restraining him from using the information and from divulging it further. It is unlikely that there would be much to be gained by suing the employee for infringement of copyright, although this could be a case where 'additional damages' might be appropriate (*see* Chapter 6).

Generally, things that fall within the ambit of copyright law are excluded from the grant of a patent,[42] but preliminary materials such as plans, sketches, specifications, and the like, are likely to be protected by copyright. That is, copyright will subsist in each of these items irrespective of any patent granted for the invention with which the items are concerned.[43] However, there are two limitations to this, the first being where the details of the invention represented in drawings fall within the scope of the UK unregistered design[44] and the second being that copies may be made of patent applications (including the specification) by permission of the Comptroller-General of Patents, Designs and Trade Marks without infringing copyright.[45] Ideas for a new invention, while outside the scope of copyright until such time as they are given some tangible form of expression, will be the subject matter of the law of confidence. There is also a close relationship between copyright and the law of designs, and many articles that are subject to design law will have been prepared from drawings and written specifications. However, any potential overlap between design law and copyright is reduced by the Copyright, Designs and Patents Act 1988.[46]

Changes to UK registered design and the introduction of the Community design (registered and unregistered) has increased the potential overlap between copyright and design law as, for example, typefaces and graphic symbols may be protected by design law in addition to copyright protection. The difference between registered designs and copyright can be important where there is such an overlap as, although copyright gives longer protection, a registered design, whether a UK design or a Community design, gives monopoly protection.

Sometimes, different rights may be relevant at different times during the life of a work. For example, if a musician has an idea for a piece of music, that idea will be protected by the law of confidence, unless it is already in the public domain. When the music is written down, it will be protected by copyright both before and after publication. After publication, of course, confidentiality will be lost. Live performances of the music will be protected under the Copyright, Designs and Patents Act 1988 Part II which deals with rights in performances (replacing the Performers' Protection Act 1963) and any recordings made will be protected as sound recordings and, separately, as a recording of a live performance. If a copy is made of a vinyl record, magnetic tape or compact disc of the music, the copyright both in the sound recording (and 'recording right') and the original music will be infringed. If the music is a song, the lyrics will be independently protected as a literary work. Thus, it can be seen that a single item may be subject to several copyrights. This is essential as different interests may be involved. For example, in the case of a song, the music may have been written by one person, the words by another. The recording company will also require direct protection of the sound recording so that it may take action against anyone making duplicates of the recordings. The performer and, if recorded live, the recording company, also require protection against persons making unauthorised 'bootleg' recordings of the live performance.

Copyright as a means of exploiting a work

Copyright provides a very useful and effective way of exploiting a work economically. It provides a mechanism for allocation of risks and income derived from the sale of the

---

42 Patents Act 1977 s 1(2). But *see* Chapter 12 for instances when a computer program (which is a literary work under copyright law) can indirectly achieve patent protection.

43 The Patents Act 1977 makes provision for the possibility that an employee might be entitled to a patent for an invention but copyright or design rights might belong to his employer: s 39(3).

44 Indirect copying of a drawing of a design by making the article represented does not infringe the copyright in the drawing: Copyright, Designs and Patents Act 1988 s 51(1).

45 Copyright, Designs and Patents Act 1988 s 47.

46 With respect to the unregistered design right, *see* Copyright, Designs and Patents Act 1988 s 236.

work. For example, if a poet compiles an anthology of poems, this will be protected as a literary work even if unpublished. Copyright provides remedies in respect of published and unpublished works. If an unpublished work is copied and sold by someone without the permission of the copyright owner, remedies such as damages, additional damages, accounts of profits and injunctions are available depending on the circumstances. They are, however, available only to the owner of the copyright, an exclusive licensee or a non-exclusive licensee expressly granted the right of action by the copyright owner.

A beneficial owner is one who owns the copyright at equity. It is possible for a copyright to have two owners; one at law and one at equity. This could happen where a work of copyright is created by an author working under a commission. Without any agreement as to the ownership of the copyright, the author will be the first owner of the copyright at law but the commissioner may be the beneficial owner if the circumstances are such that one would have expected him to own the copyright. This could be the case where the commissioner has paid a sum equivalent to what he would have paid to own the copyright outright, rather than the level of payment appropriate for a licence to use the work.

A beneficial owner of the copyright cannot obtain damages or a perpetual injunction without joining the owner of the legal title to the copyright, although a beneficial owner may be able to obtain an interim injunction on his own. If the poet in the example wants his anthology of poems published, he might decide to approach prospective publishers, and, if one agrees to publish, the poet might grant an exclusive licence to the publisher allowing him to print and sell copies of the poems in book form. Alternatively, the poet might agree to assign the copyright to the publisher. In either case, the publisher usually takes the risk – he pays the cost of printing, binding, marketing and distributing. In return, the poet will be paid a fee or a royalty of, say, 15 per cent of the income obtained by the publisher on sales of the anthology.

An added attraction, in the case of an exclusive licence,[47] for example, a licence granting the exclusive rights of publishing the work in the UK, is that the publisher has the right to sue for infringement, and, if the publisher is successful, the poet will be entitled to a share of the damages awarded equivalent to his lost royalties attributable to the infringement.[48] Depending on the terms of the exclusive licence, the poet may be free to make agreements in respect of other modes of expression of the poems, such as a sound recording of the poems being recited by a famous actor. Of course, if the poet assigns the work to the publisher, the publisher will be entitled to sue for infringement as owner of the copyright and the assignment agreement may provide for a division of the damages awarded between the author and the publisher. For the author, a major attraction of granting an exclusive licence,[49] or for that matter an assignment, to a publisher is that copyright actions tend to be fairly expensive and daunting for an individual to pursue, but a reputable publishing company will not hesitate in enforcing its rights under copyright law and, indirectly, the rights of the author.

A copyright can be considered to comprise a bundle of rights, associated with the acts restricted by the copyright. These are the acts that only the copyright owner is allowed to do or authorise. These acts include copying, issuing copies to the public, performing, playing or showing the work in public and broadcasting the work. These can be exploited separately and a copyright owner must be careful not to assign or grant licences for more rights than necessary for the exploitation envisaged. For example, the owner of the copyright in a dramatic work might grant an exclusive right to publish the work in book form to a literary publisher. The owner may then later grant other rights to others, such as the right to perform the work on stage, or even the right to make it into a film. In this way, the income the owner derives from the work can be maximised.

47 Or a non-exclusive licence in which the licensee has been expressly granted a right of action by the copyright owner: s 101A.

48 By the Copyright, Designs and Patents Act 1988 s 102 neither the owner nor the exclusive licensee may proceed without the leave of the court unless the other is joined in the action.

49 Or non-exclusive licence where the licensee has expressly been granted a right of action.

Summary

Copyright is a property right. It provides the owner with the exclusive right to perform certain acts ('restricted acts') in relation to the work that is subject to the copyright. Anyone performing any of these restricted acts, in relation to the whole or a substantial part of the work, without the licence (permission) of the copyright owner will infringe the copyright.

Copyright does not give a monopoly right (unless the owner alone has access to the constituents of the work). This means it is possible for others to create similar works, providing they do not carry out a restricted act, such as copying, all or a large part of the first work.

Particular features of copyright are:

- it protects expression rather than 'ideas';
- it has a long duration, life plus 70 years for the original works and films;
- regardless of ownership, the author may have moral rights which apply to certain types of work in most circumstances.

Copyright developed from a means of controlling printing to a very broad right which protects a wide range of works. Although there was some doubt about this, it became settled that statutory copyright left no room for a common law form of copyright which was potentially perpetual in duration.

Copyright may exist alongside other rights and obligations, such as those under a contract or in respect to confidential material.

Copyright may be exploited directly by its owner or it may be exploited by others by means of:

- an assignment (transfer of ownership);
- an exclusive licence; or
- non-exclusive licences.

Discussion question

1 Originally concerned with the control and protection of books, why do you think copyright developed to protect a wide range of things such as sound recordings, films, artistic works, computer programs and databases? Do you think other new forms of rights should have been introduced to protect these things? If so, consider how new forms of rights might have been formulated to give a balanced and effective protection to these things.

Selected further reading

Berne Convention for the Protection of Literary and Artistic Works 1886, as revised and amended, especially Articles 2, 3, 4, 5 and 6bis. The Convention is available at: **http://www.wipo.int/export/sites/www/treaties/en/ip/berne/pdf/trtdocs_wo001.pdf**

Gowers, A., *Gowers Review of Intellectual Property*, HMSO, December 2006 (sets out, *inter alia*, proposals for changes to IP laws and procedures – useful material on copyright for this and subsequent chapters in Part 2 of the book). Available at: **http://www.official-documents.gov.uk/document/other/0118404830/0118404830.pdf**

Hargreaves, Professor I., *Digital opportunity: a review of intellectual property and growth*, May 2011 (a further review subsequent to the *Gowers Review*, again there is much of interest in relation to copyright). Available at: **http://www.ipo.gov.uk/ipreview-finalreport.pdf**.

Intellectual Property Office, *Copyright: Essential Reading* (2011), available at: **http://www.ipo.gov. uk/c-essential.pdf** (useful overview of copyright to supplement this chapter and a good primer for the remainder of Part 2 of the book).

Note: Lecturers may wish to refer students to appropriate parts of Gowers and Hargreaves as and when relevant to their IP courses.

Visit www.mylawchamber.co.uk/bainbridgeip to access study support resources including interactive multiple choice questions, practice exam questions with guidance, weblinks, legal updates and a legal newsfeed.

Subsistence of copyright 3

Introduction

Fundamentally, copyright law exists to prevent others from taking unfair advantage of a person's creative efforts. The courts have displayed very little sympathy for plagiarists and frequently have demonstrated that copyright law ought to be interpreted in such a way as to protect the interests of the copyright owner. This approach is best summed up in the words of Peterson J in *University of London Press Ltd* v *University Tutorial Press Ltd*, where he said:

> . . . there remains the rough practical test that what is worth copying is prima facie worth protecting.[1]

1 [1916] 2 Ch 601 at 610.

However, this goes too far and, if applied literally, protection would be afforded to works which were not the result of the application of intellect (or skill and judgment). Pumfrey J made this point in *Cantor Fitzgerald International* v *Tradition (UK) Ltd*[2] where he said of the above maxim (at 133):

2 [2000] RPC 95.

> This maxim is open to the criticism that it proves too much. So it is possible that entirely mechanical labour may be saved by copying something produced by entirely mechanical labour, involving no skill.

As we will see later, the test for originality has been relatively easy to satisfy in the past and does not usually present a major obstacle to copyright subsistence. But something more than the expenditure of labour alone in the making of a work should be present in deciding whether or not a work deserves copyright protection. Whilst it might be true that a work having commercial value might be the product of labour or effort only, it is questionable whether such works should be subject to copyright.[3] The modern trend is towards a more transparent approach to the denial of protection to works produced in the absence of skill and judgment and which are the result only of the application of the 'sweat of the brow'.[4] The better view is that the application of the human intellect in the creation of a work is needed, though it might not be a substantial application or the sole contribution.

3 The *sui generis* database right was introduced to protect databases which might fail to meet the requirements for copyright protection but were, nevertheless, the result of a substantial investment.

4 That is, works that are the result of effort only. *See* Chapter 8 for more discussion on this point.

5 In its original form. The Act has been amended on numerous occasions.

The Copyright, Designs and Patents Act 1988 is the legislative source of copyright law. This voluminous Act, comprising 306 sections and eight Schedules,[5] also deals with designs, rights in performances and has miscellaneous provisions concerning patent law and trade mark law. The copyright provisions of the Act came into force on 1 August 1989. Although some significant changes were made to copyright law by the Act, it was not intended to change fundamental copyright principles and much of the case law developed prior to the coming into force of the Act may still be used as an aid to the construction of the Act and for determining whether the previous law has been departed from.[6] Also, copyright provisions under the Act which correspond to provisions under the previous law are not to be taken to depart from previous law merely because of a change of expression.[7]

Some of the primary effects of the 1988 Act in terms of copyright law are that it:

1 takes account of new technology and it attempts to use definitions that will prove to be sufficiently flexible to take future technological developments in its stride;
2 provides more effectively for 'moral rights' for authors, in accordance with the Berne Convention for the Protection of Literary and Artistic Works;
3 removes some of the anomalies under the old law (for example, under the Copyright Act 1956, the author of the copyright in a photograph was the person who owned the film,[8] not the photographer);
4 attempts to rationalise design law and its overlap with copyright.

The Act has been changed on numerous occasions, primarily to comply with Directives harmonising copyright throughout the European Union. Some of these changes have been very significant, such as the extension to the term of copyright, significantly increased rights in performances, the protection of computer programs and databases and the introduction of specific provisions dealing with copyright in the information society. Other changes have been more to do with rationalising some of the aspects of copyright, such as the inclusion of cable programmes as a form of broadcast, ending the distinction between the two forms of work. With these and many other changes, major parts of the Act as it presently is bears only scant resemblance to when it first came into force on 1 August 1989. This makes it very difficult to pin down some of the provisions in the Act and this is made more complex because of the defective implementation of some of the European Directives. An example of the complexity is provided by the duration of copyright in sound recordings for which the following provisions may be relevant (notwithstanding the transitional provisions in Schedule 1 to the 1988 Act and the fact that a film sound track was treated differently to the film):

● Copyright in a sound recording expires 50 years from the end of the calendar year in which it was made or, if released before the end of that period, 50 years from the end of the calendar year in which it was released (s 13(1) of the Act as at Royal Assent and s 13A which along with s 13B substituted the old s 13) (released meant first published, broadcast or included in a cable programme service).
● Copyright in an existing sound recording continues to subsist as calculated under the 1988 Act prior to amendment if longer than the duration calculated under the Act as amended by the Duration of Copyright and Rights in Performances Regulations 1995 (reg 15 of those Regulations).
● Copyright expires 50 years from the end of the calendar year in which it was made or, if published during that period, 50 years from the end of the calendar year in which it was published or, if during that period it was not published but was made available to the public by being played in public or communicated to the public, 50 years from the end of the calendar year in which it was so made available or communicated (new s 13A(2) inserted by the Copyright and Related Rights Regulations 2003).
● Copyright in an existing sound recording shall continue to subsist as determined under reg 15 of the 1995 Regulations if longer than the term under new s 13A(2) inserted by the 2003 Regulations.

There is a strong case for a new consolidating Copyright Act but it is unlikely to be high on any parliamentary wish-list given the volume of primary legislation put before Parliament. Indeed, other domestic IP legislation could be significantly improved and made more transparent by such action, as will be seen when looking at the mess that has been achieved in relation to the UK's registered design legislation.

6 Copyright, Designs and Patents Act 1988 s 172(3). Statutory references in this chapter are to the Copyright, Designs and Patents Act 1988 unless otherwise stated.

7 Section 172(2).

8 Copyright Act 1956 s 48(1).

Moving on to look at the specifics of copyright subsistence, it should be noted that copyright can subsist only in specified descriptions of works. Section 1(1) lists the works in which copyright can subsist, subject to the qualification requirements (discussed later), as being:

(a) original literary, dramatic, musical or artistic works;
(b) sound recordings, films or broadcasts; and
(c) the typographical arrangement of published editions.

Each of these categories is now examined in detail.

Original literary, dramatic, musical or artistic works

All of these must be original and must be 'works'. Over the course of time, the courts have attempted to develop tests for showing whether the subject-matter is an original work. Apart from defining originality and searching for the threshold that brings the status of a 'work', judges have often engaged in more esoteric exercises, particularly in terms of differentiating between unprotectable idea and copyright expression. It should be noted at once that nowhere in the Act does it state expressly that ideas are not protected by copyright. However, by the Copyright, Designs and Patents Act 1988 s 50BA, lawful users of computer programs are permitted to gain access to ideas and principles which underlie any element of the program by carrying out certain acts they are entitled to perform, and Article 2 of the WIPO Copyright Treaty 1996[9] states that copyright protection extends to expressions and not to ideas, procedures, methods of operation or mathematical concepts as such.[10] The US Copyright Act 1980 also states that copyright protection for an original work does not extend to '. . . any idea, procedure, process, system, method of operation, concept, principle or discovery . . .'.[11]

Before looking at each of the original works separately, the basic issues relating to subsistence of copyright are discussed.

Original works and intellectual creations

There is a significant body of case law on the meaning of originality and on what constitutes a work for copyright purposes. Most of it is irrelevant. In the majority of cases, the judges may have reached the 'right conclusion' but not necessarily for the right reasons. The source of modern copyright is undoubtedly the Berne Convention for the Protection of Literary and Artistic Works.[12] The WCT requires Contracting Parties to comply with the substantive parts of Berne[13] as does the TRIPs Agreement.[14] European Directives on copyright refer to Berne and show a general adherence to the Convention. The main impetus behind the seminal British Copyright Act of 1911 was the Berlin Revision to Berne dated 1908. Consequently, it is to the Berne Convention that we should turn to determine the requirements for subsistence of copyright.

The first thing one notices when looking at the Berne Convention is that the list of works covered in Article 2(1) under the term 'literary and artistic works' is very wide and '. . . shall include every production in the literary, artistic and scientific domain, whatever be the mode or form of its expression . . .'. The Article goes on to give numerous examples.[15] There is no mention at this stage of the need for any of these works to be original. However, Article 2(3) states that translations, adaptations, etc. are to be treated as original works without prejudice to the copyright in the original work. Article 2(5) is the key. It states:

9 WIPO is the World Intellectual Property Organization. The Treaty is referred to hereinafter as the WCT.

10 Article 9(2) of the Agreement on Trade-Related Aspects of Intellectual Property 1994 ('TRIPs Agreement') is to the same effect.

11 § 102(b) 17 USC.

12 1886 as revised and amended. The current version includes the Paris Act 1971 and further amendments made in 1979.

13 That is, Articles 1 to 21 and Appendix 1: see Article 1 of the WCT.

14 Article 9 of TRIPs with the exception of moral rights under Article 6[bis] of Berne.

15 Certain types of work are not specifically mentioned such as computer programs and sound recordings but these must fall within the protected works either by interpretation or implication.

> Collections of literary or artistic works such as encyclopaedias and anthologies which, by reason of the selection and arrangement of their contents, **constitute intellectual creations** shall be protected as such, without prejudice to the copyright in each of the works forming part of such collections *(emphasis added)*.

The only plausible explanation for the presence of this test of intellectual creation is that this is inherent or implicit in works generally classified as literary or artistic works. The reason it is express for collections as such is to ensure that collections which result from the expenditure effort alone, lacking intellectual creativity in their making, do not have protection. That being so, it can be assumed that the threshold for copyright protection is that the work in question must be the result of the author's intellectual creation. The Court of Justice confirmed this interpretation in Case C-5/08 *Infopak International A/S v Danske Dagblades Forening*[16] where it said (at para 34):

> It is, moreover, apparent from the general scheme of the Berne Convention, in particular Article 2(5) and (8), that the protection of certain subject-matters as artistic or literary works presupposes that they are intellectual creations.[17]

This observation is reinforced by the express use of the test of a work being the author's own intellectual creation for copyright protection in the Directive on the legal protection of computer programs and the Directive on the legal protection of databases. In the former Directive, a computer program is protected if original in the sense that it is the author's own intellectual creation.[18] For a database to be protected by copyright, it must, by reason of the selection and arrangement of its contents, constitute the author's own intellectual creation.[19]

A football match is not a work as it is not an intellectual creation, though a broadcast of a football match can be a work as a broadcast and include elements such as logos, music and pre-recorded film extracts of past matches can be works in their own right.[20]

Further support is found in the cases such as *Cramp (GA) & Sons Ltd v Frank Smythson Ltd*[21] in which it was held, *inter alia*, that setting out facts in a table was not protected because there was no room for taste or judgment. The same applied to the work of putting together a few pages of information of the sort normally found at the beginning of diaries. In the United States, the Supreme Court denied copyright protection to the White Pages in a Telephone Directory on the basis that it was the result of effort only, lacking in skill and judgment in compiling the entries.[22]

In the UK judges have generally looked for skill and judgment in the creation of one of the 'original works' of copyright. This can be seen as equivalent to the test of intellectual creation. The denial of copyright to trivial or very small things such as a short slogan, title or single word supports this approach to some extent.[23]

In the light of the above discussion, it seems tolerably clear that the test for copyright subsistence is that the work must be the author's own intellectual creation. No other criteria should be used and any reformulation of the test is likely to prove unhelpful. Bearing these things in mind, there now follows a discussion of case law on originality, the meaning of 'work' and the application of the *de minimis* rule.

Originality

One can be excused for believing that the word 'original' requires that the work must be new or innovative in some sense, but in copyright law 'original' does not have its ordinary dictionary meaning and the courts have interpreted the concept very loosely. The work in question does not have to be unique, or even particularly meritorious. Rather, originality is more concerned with the manner in which the work was created and is usually taken to require that the work in question originated from the author, its creator, and that it was not copied from another work. In *Ladbroke (Football) Ltd v William Hill (Football) Ltd*, Lord Pearce said that the word 'original' requires:

16 [2009] ECR I-6569.

17 Article 2(8) of the Berne Convention denies protection to 'news of the day' or 'miscellaneous facts having the character of mere items of press information'.

18 Article 1(3).

19 Article 3(1). The test for protection under the *sui generis* database right is different (*see* Chapter 8).

20 Joined Cases C-403/08 and C-429/08 *Football Association Premier League Ltd v QC Leisure*, Court of Justice of the European Union, 4 October 2011.

21 [1944] AC 329.

22 *Feist Publications Inc v Rural Telephone Service Co Inc* 499 US 340 (1991).

23 As we will see, the word EXXON was denied copyright even though it is arguable that it was the result of intellectual creativity, being decided upon for a new corporate name after considerable market research.

only that the work should not be copied but should originate from the author.[24]

A drawing of an existing object may not be original because the design of the object was not created by the act of drawing. Harman J came to this conclusion in *Duriron Company Inc* v *Hugh Jennings & Co Ltd*[25] in the context of an inaccurate drawing of an existing design of an anode, described as being of the most jejune and simple character. It would be unthinkable if this view of originality were applied to drawings made by artists. The act of drawing a representation of a flower, a wild bird or a scene from nature requires skill and judgment, even if a faithfully accurate reproduction is the purpose. Although the thing drawn already exists, it is in respect of the drawing that the test of originality must be applied. In this respect, the judgment of Harman J is very questionable. It would have been better if he had based his decision on a lack of skill or judgment, or that the drawing was not a 'work'. There is, however, some authority for the proposition that an accurate representation of a pre-existing subject is not an original work for copyright purposes, even if its creation requires skill and judgment. In *Antiquesportfolio.com plc* v *Rodney Fitch & Co Ltd*[26] it was argued that photographs of antiques placed on a website were not works of copyright. Neuberger J considered that a photograph of a three-dimensional object, such as a sofa, could be an original work as there was skill and judgment (albeit of a commercial sense) in positioning the object and choosing the angle at which the photograph was taken,[27] the lighting and focus. He reviewed the views of learned writers on originality and photographs. Where a photograph was taken of a two-dimensional object, such as a painting or an existing photograph, providing some skill has been used by the photographer, for example in respect of angle, lighting, choice of film and filters, then the resulting photograph could be original for copyright purposes. The main test should be whether the photographer intended to make a faithful copy of the original or whether he wanted to imbue the finished photograph with his own flair. Was he trying to make a duplicate, indistinguishable from the original, or was he trying to put his own 'signature' on it? This is particularly relevant nowadays in the context of computer technology and the ways in which images can be modified and manipulated.

Although it may seem difficult to reconcile a refusal of copyright for an attempt to duplicate an existing photograph or painting with an attempt by an artist to create a painting that accurately records a scene from nature, in practice there is such a distinction. In the latter case, the artist is working with a three-dimensional scene and has an almost infinite choice of positioning and angle. He must also decide on the field of view. Simply trying to reproduce an existing photograph in full leaves the photographer none of these choices, regardless of the fact that this may require a significant amount of technical skill. If the motive is to create as exact a duplicate as possible, will copyright be denied?[28] If the photographer's purpose is to stamp his own personality and taste on the finished product, then it may well be a work of copyright. One might ask why the photographer's motive should be relevant. But it is the desire to create something different, something reflecting the photographer's own taste, that gives originality.[29] One only has to think of the work of Andy Warhol or Damien Hirst to see this.

Where the purpose of creating an image is to replicate an original two-dimensional image, there are a number of possibilities:

1 A photographer places the original in a suitable position, arranges artificial lighting to illuminate the image, and then uses a film camera in manual mode, focuses on the image, selects a fast shutter to eliminate blur caused by 'camera shake' and then selects a lens aperture to achieve an appropriate exposure. He then develops the film and makes an enlargement of the negative. This entails choosing the type and grade of the photographic paper, focusing the enlarger lens on the paper, selecting the time of exposure and using tools to prevent blown-out highlights, shadows lacking detail and to hide any dust spots.

24 [1964] 1 WLR 273 at 291.

25 [1984] FSR 1.

26 [2001] FSR 23.

27 Unless, perhaps, the object was a sphere.

28 Though see the discussion of *Hyperion Records Ltd* v *Dr Lionel Sawkins* [2005] RPC 32, below.

29 However, creating a work based on a previous work will bring difficult questions of the scope of protection available for the new work.

2 As 1 above, but the photographer uses a digital camera and processes and manipulates the photograph using a suitable software.

3 A photographer takes the original image outside and ensures it is placed in a vertical position. He then uses a 'point and shoot' digital camera or other digital camera set to fully automatic mode, standing in a position so that the image almost fills the viewfinder or LCD screen at the back of the camera. This allows for the fact that most camera viewfinders or LCD screen show slightly under 100 per cent of the image to be photographed. He then processes and manipulates his photograph using suitable software. This includes slightly cropping the image to remove a small border.

4 As 3 above, but the photographer does not process or manipulate the photograph apart from cropping the border.

5 A person places the original image in a photocopier and takes a copy, trimming off any surplus borders.

Which of these possibilities requires the expenditure of skill and judgment (or, more properly put, which is or are intellectual creations)? In all cases, the objective is to create an image as close as possible to the original. At one end the scale option 1 (and possibly option 2) would seem to come closest, with option 5 being the furthest from being an intellectual creation. If some or even all of the above possibilities are considered to be intellectual creations, are they still to be denied copyright on the ground that they are not original? They have not originated from their authors, being mere copies. But consider again an artist painting a landscape with the intention of making as faithful a representation of the scene. The scene did not originate from the artist – it was already there. Is photography different? Or is the key fact that a landscape, as such, is not a work of copyright. The same applies to a portrait of a person, whether executed in oil paints or by photography. Can it be said that copying an existing work does not create a new copyright in the copy. The problem with this hypothesis is that making a sketch, painting or photograph of a modern building would be denied copyright because the building is itself a work of copyright, being a type of artistic work.

Minor alteration to existing work

Making trivial alterations to an existing work is unlikely to result in a new copyright being brought into existences. In *Interlego AG v Tyco Industries Inc*[30] small modifications made to existing drawings of 'Lego' bricks were held not to give rise to new works independently protected by copyright, even though the modifications were technically significant. To hold otherwise would result in the possibility that copyright in what was essentially the same work could be extended indefinitely. Thus, half a day's work by a draughtsman making a new drawing by tracing over an existing drawing and making some minor alterations was not sufficient to create a new work of copyright. Originality requires something more than competent draughtsmanship. In *Interlego AG v Tyco Industries Inc*[31] Lord Oliver said that producing a good copy of a painting or an enlarged photograph from a negative would not create an original artistic work, even though the copy painting or positive print would require 'great skill, judgment and labour'. Of course, an artist making a faithful representation of, for example, a still life, uses more than his skill in applying paint to canvas. He also uses compositional and lighting skills, and it is in respect of these that copyright is earned. Some photographers might take issue with Lord Oliver's denial of copyright to photographic enlargements taken from negatives unless, as seems likely, he intended to restrict his comment to those cases where there is no selectivity in cropping the photograph and the entire negative is enlarged without any special effects.[32] The point Lord Oliver was making was that simply to produce a copy of an existing work, no matter how much skill and labour went into its making, could not give rise to a new original work of copyright.

30 [1989] 1 AC 217.

31 [1989] 1 AC 217 at 262.

32 Curiously, in an unreported case, *Manners v The Reject Shop*, June 1994, Bow Street Magistrates' Court, a stipendiary magistrate decided that a photocopy (in this case of a design applied to a ceramic tile) could be an original work: *see* Kinnier-Wilson, J. 'Criminal Copyright Offences under Sections 107 and 110 UK CDPA' [1995] 1 EIPR 46.

Preliminary works

A work in respect of which copyright subsistence is in issue may be preceded by preliminary works, such as sketches made prior to a finished drawing or painting. This does not prejudice the originality of the finished work. In *Biotrading and Financing OY v Biohit Ltd*[33] it was held that, where an author makes preliminary drawings before producing a final version, the final version does not lack originality merely because it was preceded by the preliminary drawings.[34] In *LA Gear Ltd v Hi-Tec Sports plc*,[35] the Court of Appeal thought the point so obvious that it needed no authority,[36] whilst in *Macmillan Publishers Ltd v Thomas Reed Publications Ltd*,[37] the court relied on a sequence of 'chartlets' in successive editions of a nautical almanac. The sense of this approach can be seen when one considers the alternative – it would be curious if a rough sketch were protected by copyright yet the finished drawing was not. The same principle should apply to the other original works: for example, where a written plan for a speech precedes the final printed speech.

Whether constituent parts must be original

Peterson J gave the issue of originality detailed consideration in *University of London Press Ltd v University Tutorial Press Ltd*, where he said:

> The word 'original' does not in this connection mean that the work must be an expression of original or inventive thought. Copyright Acts are not concerned with the originality of ideas, but with the expression of thought, and, in the case of a 'literary work', with the expression of thought in print or writing. The originality which is required relates to the expression of thought.[38]

He went on to say that the work must not be copied from another work, but that it should originate from the author. The implication of this is that the constituent parts of the work themselves need not be new in any sense and that the work as a whole can be made up from commonplace and pre-existing materials. In a case concerning a street directory, *Macmillan & Co Ltd v K & J Cooper*,[39] it was held that although many compilations have nothing original in their parts, yet the sum total of the compilation may be original for the purposes of copyright. The basic argument for holding that copyright can subsist in such things is that a reasonable amount of work involving judgment and selection has been used in making the compilation.

Formulae

A formula may be original but its use will not create new works of copyright. In *Bookmakers' Afternoon Greyhound Services Ltd v Wilf Gilbert (Staffordshire) Ltd*[40] Aldous J said that, once a formula has been derived, he did not consider that sufficient skill, labour and judgment is used when calculating, in this case, dividends from starting prices in greyhound races.[41] Aldous J also considered that there was no copyright in a list of 12 such dividends, as it amounted to a mere collocation and not a copyright compilation. There was no skill or judgment and minimal labour in writing them down.

Well-known techniques

Where the author of a work expends considerable labour and skill in creating a work which uses techniques that are well known in the relevant trade, that will not necessarily deprive the finished work of copyright protection. So it was held in *IPC Magazines Ltd v MGN Ltd*.[42] In that case, it was argued that the claimant's 'masthead' logo for *Woman* magazine had been infringed by the defendant. Summary judgment was granted in favour of the claimant. Although the logo made use of common techniques such as the font used, and appeared in white letters on a red background, it was accepted that sufficient time and labour had been spent on the design of the logo. Richard McCombe QC, sitting as deputy High Court judge, said (at 438):

33 [1996] FSR 393.

34 In the Court of Appeal, Aldous LJ said that the question is whether sufficient independent labour, skill and judgment had been expended in the creation and this is a matter of fact and degree. It was confirmed that the final drawings were works of copyright: *Biotrading and Financing OY v Biohit Ltd* [1998] FSR 109. *See also Guild v Eskandar Ltd* [2001] FSR 38 in relation to modifications to existing garment designs.

35 [1992] FSR 121.

36 This point was accepted by Lewison J in *Taylor v Rive Droite Music Ltd* [2004] EWHC 1605 (Ch).

37 [1993] FSR 455.

38 [1916] 2 Ch 601 at 608–609.

39 (1923) 93 LJPC 113.

40 [1994] FSR 723.

41 *Quaere* whether a formula would be deemed *de minimis; see* below.

42 [1998] FSR 431.

Mr Platt-Mills submitted that the logo is 'little more' than the word 'Woman' written in ordinary letters and ordinary manner; he says no great skill and labour is involved. In summary, he submitted, 'I could do that'. Decisively, however, to mind he did *not* do that; Mr Earl did, and indisputably he spent time and labour in doing so. (Original emphasis.)

It is perhaps unfortunate that the phrase 'time and labour' was used. Although, as discussed below, judges have used different phrases in the past, and variations of similar phrases, the better test for originality now is the work must be the author's own intellectual creation or, to use the language traditionally favoured by judges, the author of the work must have expended skill and judgment in its creation.

Finally

We have seen that the test of originality has been applied in a relatively soft manner but the modern trend amongst judges is to look for skill and judgment in the creation of a literary, dramatic, musical or artistic work. The prominence which 'labour' or 'effort' had in the process of creating a work now seems to have faded. That being so, it now seems reasonable to argue that a work is original if it is the author's own intellectual creation and that the two standards are, or should be, one and the same. This is not beyond doubt, however, given the very large body of case law on originality, but it would be regrettable if a different standard applied to computer programs and databases as applied to the other forms of original works of copyright.[43] As noted earlier, the Court of Justice accepted that, under the Berne Convention, a work had to be the author's own intellectual creation in Case C-5/08 *Infopak International A/S v Danske Dagblades Forening*.[44]

Had the Court of Appeal used the standard of the author's own intellectual creation in *Hyperion Records Ltd v Dr Lionel Sawkins*,[45] discussed later, they would have found it far easier than they did to hold that Dr Sawkins' performing edition of Baroque music was original for copyright purposes.

Meaning of 'work'

For copyright to subsist in a literary, dramatic, musical or artistic work, it must qualify as a 'work'. Arguably, this should be satisfied simply by asking whether the subject-matter is the result of the author's own intellectual creation. In the past, judges in the UK have tended to determine whether skill, labour or judgment has gone into its creation.[46] Judges have displayed some inconsistency in the formulae they have used: for example, 'work or skill or expense' *per* Lord Pearce in *Ladbroke (Football) Ltd v William Hill (Football) Ltd*,[47] 'knowledge, labour, judgment or literary skill or taste' *per* Lord Atkinson in *Macmillan & Co Ltd v K & J Cooper & Co Ltd*[48] and 'skill and labour' *per* Lord Templeman in *British Leyland Motor Corp Ltd v Armstrong Patents Co Ltd*.[49] Nevertheless, it is clear that some measure of skill or judgment must have been expended in the production of the work before it can attract copyright protection.[50] In *Baily v Taylor*,[51] a case concerning the copying of tables of values of leases and annuities, a request for an injunction to restrain publication of a work containing the copied tables was refused partly on the ground that any competent person could have recalculated the tables in a few hours.

It is misleading to suggest that the creation of a work of copyright should extend over a significant period of time. After all, the time taken might be quite small as in the case of an artist creating a sketch in a matter of minutes or in taking a photograph. However, *Baily v Taylor* is not authority for saying that there can be no copyright in a work which takes but a short time to create. As the claimant brought his action in the Court of Chancery, the only remedies available to him at that time were an injunction and/or an account of profits. The Court of Chancery did not say that copyright did not subsist in the tables, and the claimant was left to pursue a remedy for damages at law should he wish. What is of greater interest is the position where the information contained in the work is

43 For computer programs and copyright databases, the relevant Directives use the test of the author's own intellectual creation.

44 [2009] ECR I-6569.

45 [2005] RPC 32.

46 Strictly speaking, the exercise of labour alone is not sufficient to bring copyright into existence.

47 [1964] 1 WLR 273 at 291.

48 (1923) 93 LJ PC 113 at 121.

49 [1986] 2 WLR 400 at 419.

50 The author's view is that 'skill or judgment' is equivalent to intellectual creation.

51 (1829) 1 Russ & M 73.

entirely factual such that there is no 'design freedom', as was the case in *Baily* v *Taylor*. Speaking of factual information in a table containing information such as sunrise and sunset times, Viscount Simon said, *obiter*, in *Cramp (GA) & Sons Ltd* v *Frank Smythson Ltd*:[52]

> The sun does in fact rise, and the moon set, at times which have been calculated, and the utmost that a table can do on such a subject is to state the result accurately. There is so far no room for taste or judgment.

The creation of a new table or compilation containing exclusively factual information may require a significant amount of work and effort in deriving that information, for example, by scientific observation and measurement. It seems unduly harsh to deny protection against another wishing to copy the information to save himself the trouble and expense of deriving the same information independently, particularly if his purpose is to produce a competing work. Of course, there may be copyright in the manner in which the information is presented (for example, in the design and layout of the table itself or in annotations), but that does not protect the information.

It may be that the person recording or calculating the information has done so imperfectly. What if the table contains a number of mistakes and someone copies the table without permission? Notwithstanding that the presence of common mistakes may be potent evidence of copying, is there a copyright in mistakes? Another way of looking at the situation where there is no freedom of expression is to argue that the issue is not one of subsistence of copyright, but is rather a matter of evidential value in an infringement action. The fact that two persons create works containing the same information which must, by necessity, be identical is not evidence of copying; something further is needed.

The question is whether the application of labour alone, absent skill or judgment, is sufficient to bestow copyright upon the resulting work. The US Supreme Court held not in *Feist Publications Inc* v *Rural Telephone Service Co Inc*[53] in denying copyright protection to purely factual compilations, laying to rest the 'sweat of the brow' doctrine.[54] In that case it was held that the 'White Pages' in a telephone directory were not protected by copyright because that section of the directory was the result of effort only and did not require the application of skill and judgment. It was basically a question of arranging names in alphabetical order and including addresses and telephone numbers. On the other hand, 'Yellow Pages' in telephone directories could be copyright material because of the skill and judgment expended in selecting the classification system and the fact that other copyright materials such as advertisements were also included.[55]

In another US case, *Southco Inc* v *Kanebridge Corp*,[56] copyright was denied to part numbers used to identify fastening devices known as retractable captive-screw assemblies. Southco, which made the fasteners, derived a system for allocating part numbers comprising nine-digit codes to the fasteners. The Court of Appeals said that short phrases and part numbers were denied copyright protection because they lacked creativity.[57] An example of a part number used by Southco was 47-10-202-10. This lacked any creative spark, being produced by the mechanical application of the numbering system. The fact that thought and conception went into designing and developing the numbering system did not help. The assignment of the part numbers required no human judgment but was based on the properties of the fasteners.

The approach in *Feist* and *Southco* is not necessarily at odds with the position in the UK and Europe and, apart from the woolliness of some judgments on this point, it appears that the same principle applies. For example, in *Cramp (GA) & Sons Ltd* v *Frank Smythson Ltd*,[58] a diary containing the usual information printed in diaries, such as a calendar, tables of weights and measures and postal information, failed to attract copyright in respect of the work of selecting and arranging the information. The reason was that the commonplace nature of the information left no room for taste or judgment in the selection and organisation of the material.

52 [1944] AC 329 at 336.

53 499 US 340 (1991).

54 According to this doctrine, copyright was a reward for the hard work that went into compiling facts.

55 However, *in Bell South Advertising and Publishing Corp* v *Donnelly Information Publishing Inc* 999 F 2d 1436 (11th Cir, 1993), it was held that copying factual information from Yellow Pages did not infringe copyright.

56 324 F 3d 190 (3rd Cir, 2003).

57 The case can also be seen as an example of the application of the *de minimis* principle discussed later.

58 [1944] AC 329.

In *Waterlow Directories Ltd* v *Reed Information Systems Ltd*,[59] the subsistence of copyright in legal directories containing lists of names and addresses of firms of solicitors and barristers was not put in issue. The defendant simply denied infringement. In *Cobbett* v *Woodward*,[60] it was suggested that a Post Office directory which was purchased by the public could be subject to copyright, although it was held that there could be no copyright in a trade catalogue, a fact that must be seriously doubted now. Though there must be some doubt about the copyright status of compilations which require no skill or judgment in their making, as soon as some additional material is included by reason of the application of skill or judgment by the compiler, then copyright will subsist in the compilation. That additional material may be a set of headings for a classification scheme,[61] or a credit rating appended to each client in a database of customers. This approach accords with German copyright law, which requires a work to be a 'personal intellectual creation'[62] and the EU approach and the Court of Justice decision in Case C-5/08 *Infopak International A/S* v *Danske Dagblades Forening*[63] in which the court accepted that works of copyright must be the author's own intellectual creation under the Berne Convention. This also accords with the Directive on the legal protection of computer programs and the copyright provisions of the Directive on the legal protection of databases.

Where the creation of the work itself does not require skill or judgment, it may still attract copyright if there is sufficient skill or judgment expended in the work carried out in preparing for its creation. Aldous J so held in *Microsense Systems Ltd* v *Control Systems Technology*[64] in relation to a list of mnemonics designed to control pelican crossings. He said it was at least arguable that the 'skill and labour' in devising the functions and operations of the controller should be taken into account.

Copyright in completing surviving fragments of old works

Scholars who carry out research into old works are concerned about the copyright status of the results of their research. For example, if a literary scholar, by his research, attempts to piece together the true text of a medieval sonnet, does he gain a copyright in his finished work? It would seem entirely possible, especially if the approach of Aldous J in the *Microsense* case above is accepted as representing the true position. Indeed, in Israel it has been held that a scholar who, by his extensive knowledge of the Hebrew language, history and culture, pieced together fragments of one of the Dead Sea Scrolls, filling in missing pieces based on his research, created a work of copyright.[65] It could be argued that there must be a limit to this approach and the new work must be more than a mere copy of the original. Logically, if a scholar manages to reproduce an old work exactly as it was originally written he can have no copyright. A long-since expired copyright cannot be resurrected.[66] Of course, if the original does not exist in its complete form, it is impossible to tell for certain whether it has been re-created precisely. On the other hand, there should be some reward for the undoubted research, skill and judgment that goes into re-creating old works that no longer exist in their original and complete form.

It would seem likely that, on the basis of skill and judgment, discovering, understanding and translating ancient text in a language not previously understood would attract copyright in the translation: for example, in the case of the Rosetta stone which enabled Jean-François Champollion to decipher ancient Egyptian hieroglyphs by comparing them with the Greek and Demotic script also on the stone.[67] This would, however, not give any rights to prevent the use of the hieroglyphic language by others.

A person who uses his or her expertise to fill in the missing parts of an old work which cannot readily be pieced together from remaining parts and fragments will usually require the expenditure of skill and judgment, sometimes on a substantial scale. In *Hyperion Records Ltd* v *Dr Lionel Sawkins*,[68] the Court of Appeal had to decide whether this could give rise to a new copyright. Dr Lionel Sawkins was a recognised world expert on the work

---

59 [1992] FSR 409.

60 (1872) 14 Eq 407 LR.

61 It was held that there was copyright in a set of headings in a trade catalogue in *Lamb* v *Evans* [1893] 1 Ch 218.

62 German Copyright Act 1965 s 2(2).

63 [2009] ECR I-6569.

64 Unreported, 17 July 1991.

65 *Elisha Kimron* v *Hershel Shanks* [1993] 7 EIPR D-157.

66 Except where the term of copyright is increased by legislative action, as happened under the Copyright Act 1911 and the Duration of Copyright and Rights in Performances Regulations 1995, SI 1995/3297.

67 He deciphered the hieroglyphs in 1822, having to make a number of educated guesses about the meaning of some of the hieroglyphs.

68 [2005] RPC 32.

of a French composer Lalande who lived from 1657 to 1726 and had been court composer to the French monarchy. Relatively little remained of the manuscripts of Lalande's music and Dr Sawkins carried out extensive research that took him to numerous libraries all over the world which had parts of original manuscripts and other materials. Dr Sawkins decided to write new performing editions of a number of Lalande's musical works, carrying out a significant amount of work on what remained of the source material, making additions and corrections. In the case of some works, these were considerable. He also added 'figuring' for the bass parts, absent from much of the original manuscripts and wrote some missing viola parts. Dr Sawkins' admitted intention was to recreate the works as faithfully as possible though he said that whether that was achieved was a matter of guesswork based on his knowledge and experience. At first instance, the judge, Patten J, described the process gone through by Dr Sawkins as combining his 'scholarship and knowledge derived from a long and detailed study of the composer's music with a certain amount of artistic inventiveness'.

The works were to be performed by an orchestra with choir known as *Ex Cathedra* and was to be recorded by Hyperion Records. Dr Sawkins sent copies of the scores to the conductor for the performances and he also registered the works with the Performing Right Society and the Mechanical Copyright Protection Society Limited. Each of the works as registered carried a copyright notice in the name of Dr Sawkins. An agreement was forwarded to Hyperion Records which stated that Dr Sawkins was the copyright owner and imposed restrictions on the use of the scores. Hyperion Records refused to sign this although it was prepared to credit Dr Sawkins as author. However, Hyperion Records had a policy of not paying royalties on works that were out of copyright. Negotiations went on right up to the time the recordings took place and it appeared that Dr Sawkins hoped the copyright issues would be resolved. After Hyperion Records produced and marketed CDs of the recording, Dr Sawkins commenced proceedings for copyright infringement and breach of his moral right to be identified as the author (although he was named on the CDs, it was not as author).

Patten J in the Chancery Division held that Hyperion infringed the copyright in all but one of the works complained of (this was a relatively small work with few changes made by Dr Sawkins). He also held that there had been a breach of the right to be identified as author. The Court of Appeal agreed. As regards originality, the case of *Walter v Lane*[69] was cited with approval. In that case, a reporter attended a speech made by Lord Roseberry and took shorthand notes of it. Later, he wrote a newspaper report which carried the speech. He had written it from his notes, partly working from memory and adding corrections and punctuation. It was held that copyright subsisted in the report which had been copied without consent by the defendant. In *Hyperion v Sawkins*, Mummery LJ said (at para 36):

> . . . on the application of Walter v Lane to this case, the effort, skill and time which the judge found Dr Sawkins spent in making the three performing editions were sufficient to satisfy the requirement that they should be 'original' works in the copyright sense. This is so even though (a) Dr Sawkins worked on the scores of existing musical works composed by another person (Lalande); (b) Lalande's works are out of copyright; and (c) Dr Sawkins had no intention of adding any new notes of music of his own.

Jacob and Mance LJJ agreed. Jacob LJ was of the opinion that *Walter v Lane* was still good law even though it was based on the Copyright Act 1842 before the requirement of originality (this was introduced in the Copyright Act 1911).[70] He was also of the opinion that public policy was in favour of granting protection to works such as the performing editions written by Dr Sawkins as such work should be encouraged and it saves others the time and trouble to re-create old works. It does not give a monopoly and others may make use of the works providing they seek the author's permission. If they choose not to,

69 [1900] AC 539.

70 Probably what Lord Oliver said *obiter* in *Interlego v Tyco*, above, about making faithful copies not attracting copyright, was too widely stated.

there is nothing to prevent them independently going through the same process. Even though their performing editions may be very similar to that of Dr Sawkins they would be the authors of their versions for copyright purposes.

The greater the skill and expertise of the author, the closer one may get to the work as originally written or composed. In *Walter* v *Lane*, the better the reporter was at taking short-hand notes, the nearer to the speech the finished report would be likely to be. But this cannot be a relevant consideration in deciding whether copyright subsists. If the speaker was very eloquent, clearly spoken and unhesitating in his delivery and the reporter very able, it may be that the report would well-nigh be identical to the speech. On the other hand, if the speaker was indistinct and hesitant[71] and the reporter's shorthand skills were poor, the finished report might bear much less resemblance to the exact text of the speech. Should the latter attract copyright because the reporter's contribution to the finished report would have to be greater than in the first case? The answer must be that both cases require the expenditure of skill and judgment. In the first case, it is the skill in taking shorthand notes and then adding appropriate punctuation and splitting the speech into paragraphs. There would still probably be a few gaps to fill in and, possibly, structural changes. In the second case, the skill comes from producing a finished report from a very imperfect set of notes of the speech. This point was made by Lord Davey in *Walter* v *Lane*.

Finally, it can be said that one way of looking at the requirement for skill or judgment to have been used in the creation of a work of copyright is to consider it as an example of the basic principle, as alluded to by Peterson J in the *University of London Press* case, that copyright does not protect ideas, merely the expression of ideas.

Idea/expression

The USA has a well-defined legal principle that copyright protects expression but not ideas; indeed the US Copyright Act of 1976 specifically states that ideas, procedures, processes, systems, methods of operation, concepts, principles and discoveries are excluded from copyright protection.[72] Blank forms for accounts were denied protection by the Supreme Court in *Baker* v *Selden*[73] and the idea/expression dichotomy has been developed to high levels of sophistication by the US courts ever since. The distinction is important in two respects:

1 some things can be expressed only in one way, the expression being dictated by its function or external factors; and
2 if copyright were limited only to the actual words used (in a literary work), it would be too easily circumvented by rewriting the work using different words.

Therefore, as a direct result of these points, some forms of expression are not protected as being ideas (or equivalent to, or dictated by, ideas) and some forms of expression are not directly perceivable (they are non-literal forms of expression).

Internationally, the TRIPs Agreement and the WCT both state that copyright protection extends to expression but not to ideas, principles, methods of operation or mathematical concepts as such. Underlying ideas and principles are denied protection under the Directive on the legal protection of computer programs. The position in the UK should be the same as TRIPs, the WCT and the Directive. The main difficulty is applying such rules in practice.

UK legislation does not explicitly make the distinction between idea and expression, either in legislation or in case law.[74] It has been pointed out that use of the aphorism 'there is no copyright in an idea' is likely to confuse.[75] Indeed, as Lord Hailsham observed in *LB (Plastics) Ltd* v *Swish Products Ltd*, agreeing with the late Professor Joad, it all depends on what you mean by 'ideas'.[76] However, English judges have decided cases in such a way as to produce similar results. In *Page* v *Wisden*[77] (which was cited in *Baker* v *Selden*) it was

71 In *Walter* v *Lane*, Lord Robertson, dissenting, said that some speakers do not speak in sentences but in fragments of sentences, and yet, the following morning, there appears a coherent and grammatical discussion on the subject in a report of the speech. In such cases, as distinct from the facts of *Walter* v *Lane*, the reporter's intellectual and literary contribution may be as great as that of the speaker.

72 United States Copyright Act of 1976, 17 USC § 102(a). Council Directive 91/250/EEC of 14 May 1991 on the legal protection of computer programs, OJ L 122, 17.05.1991, p 42 (replaced by Directive 2009/24/EC of the European Parliament and of the Council of 23 April 2009 on the legal protection of computer programs (codified version), OJ L 111, 05.05.2009, p 16) also adheres to the idea/expression distinction as, by Article 1(2), underlying ideas and principles are not protected by copyright.

73 101 US 99 (1880).

74 Judges may sometimes recognise the principle: for example, Whitford J in *Geo Ward (Moxley) Ltd* v *Sankey* [1988] FSR 66 and Ferris J, applying US authorities, in *John Richardson Computers Ltd* v *Flanders* [1993] FSR 497. The Directive on the legal protection of computer programs denies protection to underlying ideas and principles (*see* Chapter 8).

75 Jacob J in *IBCOS Computers Ltd* v *Barclays Mercantile Highland Finance Ltd* [1994] FSR 275.

76 [1979] RPC 551 at 629.

77 (1869) 20 LT 435.

held that a cricket scoring sheet was not protected by copyright. In *Kenrick* v *Lawrence*[78] effective protection was denied to a drawing showing a hand holding a pen and marking a ballot paper. The intention of the person commissioning the drawing was that it could be used to show persons with poor literacy skills how to vote. It was held that a similar drawing did not infringe because it was inevitable that any person who attempted to produce a drawing to show people how to vote would create a similar drawing. In other words, it was an unprotectable idea.[79] The use of design concepts taken from the common stock of architectural ideas that every one is entitled to use, *per se*, will not infringe the artistic copyright in an architect's plans.[80] However, design concepts and underlying structures and developed ideas may be protected providing they are not too remote from the work as expressed. For example, non-literal expression has been recognised as being within the scope of copyright protection in *Rees* v *Melville*[81] and *Corelli* v *Gray*[82] concerning the plot of a play taken from a novel.

More recently, in *Baigent* v *Random House Group Ltd* (the Da Vinci Code case),[83] the Court of Appeal accepted that expression can extend beyond the language of a work to the original selection, arrangement and compilation or raw research material.[84]

Lord Hoffmann identified two propositions when looking at the idea/expression dichotomy in *Designers Guild Ltd* v *Russell Williams (Textiles) Ltd*.[85] The first was that a work may express ideas that are not protected by copyright because they do not relate to works of copyright, such as an idea for an invention or an inventive concept. The second proposition was that, although the ideas related to a literary, dramatic, musical or artistic work, they are not original or are so commonplace so as not to form a substantial part of the work. In that particular case, he said that the notion of combining stripes and flowers for artwork for a fabric design would not have represented sufficient of the author's skill and labour so as to amount to a substantial part of the work.

The idea/expression rule of subsistence has proved, and will continue to prove, very difficult to apply as the boundary between idea and expression is notoriously difficult to discover.[86] This factor and the idea/expression dichotomy in general, have become highly relevant in terms of computer programs and are discussed at more length in Chapter 8.

De minimis principle

It is clear that it would be ridiculous to afford copyright protection to works that are trivial in the extreme or so small as to be entirely insignificant. However, a line has to be drawn separating works that are the proper subject matter of copyright from those that are not. The courts will sometimes use the principle *de minimis non curat lex*,[87] that is, that the work is insufficiently significant to be afforded copyright protection. For example, in *Sinanide* v *La Maison Kosmeo*,[88] it was held that to quote a bit of a sentence of a literary work was too small a matter on which to base a copyright infringement action. *A fortiori* a name cannot be subject to copyright. For example, the name of the fictional television detective 'Kojak' was not protected by copyright.[89] Nor is there any copyright in a single word such as 'Hitachi'.[90] In the *Sinanide* case, the claimant had used an advertising slogan 'Beauty is a social necessity, not a luxury' and complained about the defendant's use of the phrase 'A youthful appearance is a social necessity'. Generally, copyright will not subsist in advertising slogans and titles because they are usually fairly brief, and the song title 'The Man who Broke the Bank at Monte Carlo' was held to be insufficiently substantial for copyright purposes.[91] Nevertheless, there may be circumstances where a title is of such an extensive nature and important character that it will be the proper subject matter of copyright. The *de minimis* rule also applies in the US and examples of short phrases denied copyright protection include 'most personal sort of deodorant' and 'Good morning Detroit. This is J.P. on JR in the A.M. Have a swell day'.[92]

---

78 (1890) 25 QBD 99.

79 However, the judge went on to say that if the drawing had been an exact duplicate, there would have been an infringement of copyright. Is this true to say that exact copies would infringe but inexact copies would not?

80 *Jones* v *London Borough of Tower Hamlets* [2001] RPC 23. See also *Ultra Marketing (UK) Ltd* v *Universal Components Ltd* [2004] EWHC 468 (Ch).

81 [1911–1916] MacG CC 168.

82 [1913] TLR 570.

83 [2007] FSR 24.

84 See also *Allen* v *Bloomsbury Publishing plc* [2010] ECDR 16 in relation to an allegation that one of the Harry Potter books infringed the copyright in an earlier book about wizards entitled 'Willie the Wizard'.

85 [2001] FSR 11.

86 For an example involving 'Fantasy Football', *see Bleiman* v *News Media (Auckland) Ltd* [1994] 2 NZLR 673, discussed in Brown, B 'The Idea/Expression Dichotomy and the Games that People Play' [1995] 5 EIPR 259.

87 The law does not concern itself with trifles. In *Exxon Corporation* v *Exxon Insurance Consultants International Ltd* [1981] 3 All ER 241, it was held that the word 'EXXON' could not be an 'original literary work' without recourse to the *de minimis* principle.

88 (1928) 139 LT 365.

89 *Tavener Rutledge Ltd* v *Trexapalm Ltd* [1977] RPC 275. Nor is 'ELVIS' protected by copyright; *ELVIS PRESLEY Trade Marks* [1997] RPC 543.

90 *Hitachi Ltd* v *Zafar Auto & Filter House* [1997] FSR 50, Copyright Board, Karachi, Pakistan.

91 *Francis Day & Hunter Ltd* v *Twentieth Century Fox Corporation Ltd* [1940] AC 112.

92 Quoted in *Southco Inc* v *Kanebridge Corp* 324 F 3d 190 (3rd Cir, 2003) Court of Appeals for the Third Circuit in which it was held that nine-digit part numbers were not protected by copyright.

In *Shetland Times Ltd* v *Dr Jonathan Wills*,[93] the Court of Session, Outer House, Scotland, considered that headlines on an internet website could be a literary work. Some of the headlines consisted of eight or more words put together for the purpose of imparting information. This seems to be inconsistent with the line of cases mentioned above, though it should be noted that, in the *Shetland Times* case, the defendant had conceded the point. The basic question should remain – can the subject matter be claimed to be a *work*? It is arguable that a small number of words may so qualify if they are the result of a significant amount of work involving the exercise of skill and judgment. Nevertheless, the Court of Appeal was not attracted by an argument that the considerable amount of market research that had gone into the selection of the word 'EXXON' could, by itself, mean that the word was an original literary work.

If a name or title is represented in a particular way it seems possible that copyright might subsist in it. It was held in *News Group Newspapers Ltd* v *Mirror Group Newspapers (1986) Ltd*[94] that the use by one newspaper in its advertisements of the logo of another newspaper (the *Sun*) gave rise to an arguable case of copyright infringement. Similarly, in *IPC Magazines Ltd* v *MGN Ltd*,[95] it was accepted that a stylised version of the word 'Woman' in white on a red background as part of a magazine masthead was, at least arguably, a work of copyright. Of course, unauthorised use of a name or title in connection with goods or services or other business activity could infringe a trade mark or be actionable as passing off.

Another way of looking at the *de minimis* principle is that it just another tool in determining whether the work in question can be regarded as the author's own intellectual creation. If the work is very small then it is unlikely that it can be so regarded. But even if a significant amount of intellectual work has gone into the creation of the work, as in the *Exxon* case, that alone does not mean it will be afforded protection.[96]

Tangibility

We have seen that copyright does not protect ephemeral things such as an idea for a novel or a play.[97] As such, ideas may have some protection under the law of confidence, depending upon the circumstances. Copyright law is, because of the nature of the drafting of the current Act and previous Acts, directed to the expression of ideas rather than to the ideas themselves.[98] The method used by copyright law is to require that the work has some tangible form. In the case of some works, such as sound recordings and films, their very existence implies tangibility. The same applies to artistic works. For example, according to Lawton LJ in *Merchandising Corp of America* v *Harpbond*[99] a painting is not an idea: it is an object. However, literary, dramatic and musical works clearly can exist without any material form. For example, a person may compose a poem and recite it from memory without ever having written it down. A musician may devise a tune while sitting at a piano keyboard without recording it in some way. Article 2(2) of the Berne Convention states that countries of the Union may prescribe that works in general or in specified categories may not be protected unless they have been fixed in some material form. Therefore, for literary, dramatic and musical works, the Copyright, Designs and Patents Act 1988 declares that copyright does not subsist in such works unless and until they are recorded, in writing or otherwise.[100] 'Writing' is defined in s 178 (the interpretation section)[101] as including any form of notation or code, whether by hand or otherwise and regardless of the method by which, or medium in which, it is recorded. These definitions are deliberately couched in language which should ensure that copyright will not be defeated by technological advances, hence the use of the phrase 'or otherwise'. The requirement for some tangible existence is also important in that it dates the creation of the work, that is, the work is deemed to have been made when it is recorded for the first time.

93 [1997] FSR 604.

94 *The Times*, 27 July 1988.

95 [1998] FSR 431.

96 Discussed later in the section on literary works.

97 Provided that they are not so detailed as to be considered a non-literal form of expression.

98 This distinction is evident in the Berne Convention which protects literary and artistic works '. . . whatever may be the mode or form of their expression . . .': Article 2(1).

99 [1983] FSR 32.

100 Copyright, Designs and Patents Act 1988 s 3(2).

101 Section 178 contains several important definitions, but other definitions are scattered throughout the 1988 Act. However, the Act is very helpful in that an index is provided to assist in the location of definitions: s 179. Other indexes are provided for the parts of the Act dealing with rights in performances and the design right.

Of course, one would expect that the record is made by the author or with the author's permission, but this is not essential, and s 3(3) states that it is immaterial whether the work is recorded by or with the permission of the author. Therefore, if a person delivers an impromptu unscripted speech without having made any notes previously, and a member of the audience records the speech verbatim in writing, then the speaker will be the author of the written work for copyright purposes. If the member of the audience uses skill and judgment in recording the speech, perhaps adding structure and punctuation, then he is likely to be considered to be the author of that record of the speech, as in *Walter v Lane*,[102] where it was held that copyright subsisted in a newspaper report of a speech by Lord Roseberry prepared from a reporter's shorthand notes and that the newspaper for which the reporter worked, *The Times*, owned that copyright.[103]

Section 3(3) goes on to state that nothing in s 3(2) affects the question whether copyright subsists in the record as distinct from the work recorded. This is likely to be relevant in a case where a sound recording is made of a literary, dramatic or musical work that has not previously been recorded in any form. Consider a musician who sits down at a piano and plays an impromptu piece of music which he composes as he plays. He does not make any record of the music. However, as he plays the music, another person makes a sound recording of it. At the time the sound recording is made the work, as a musical work, does not exist for copyright purposes. The person making the sound recording will be the producer of it and, therefore, its author. He will have a copyright in that sound recording as a sound recording. If the musician is able to remember the music and later decides to write it down on paper, using musical notation, it will then exist as a musical work and the musician will be the author of it as such. The effect of the proviso to s 3(3) is to prevent any prejudice to the copyright in the sound recording. However, the impact of rights in performances must be noted and should resolve any potential conflict between the two copyrights, for example, where the sound recording is later played in public without the consent of the musician.

Literary works

The Copyright, Designs and Patents Act 1988 s 3(1) defines a literary work as any work, other than a dramatic or musical work, which is written, spoken or sung, including:

(a) a table or compilation other than a database;
(b) a computer program;
(c) preparatory design material for a computer program; and
(d) a database.[104]

Note that there is no attempt to list exhaustively all the many forms of work which could be considered to be literary works.

It should already be clear that a literary work does not have to be a work of literature, and this is implied by the inclusion of tables, compilations, computer programs, preparatory design material for computer programs and databases in the category of literary works. The courts have long since been prepared to take a very wide view of what constitutes a literary work. For example, Lord Halsbury said, in *Walter v Lane*:

> Although I think in these compositions [the record of the speeches made by the reporter] there is literary merit and intellectual labour, yet the statute seems to me to require neither . . . the right in my view is given by the statute to the first producer of a book, whether that book be wise or foolish, accurate or inaccurate, of literary merit, or of no merit whatever.[105]

In similar vein, Peterson J said in *University of London Press Ltd* v *University Tutorial Press Ltd*:[106]

---

102 [1900] AC 539.

103 At the time of this case there was no requirement for originality. It may depend on whether the person making the record exercises some skill thus bringing some originality to the report: *see Roberton v Lewis* [1976] RPC 169 and Cross J's comments on *Walter v Lane*. In *Express Newspapers plc v News (UK) Ltd* [1990] 1 WLR 1320 it was held that *Walter v Lane* was still undeniably good law. It was applied by the Court of Appeal in *Hyperion Records Ltd v Dr Lionel Sawkins* [2005] RPC 32.

104 Preparatory design material was added by the Copyright (Computer Programs) Regulations 1992, SI 1992/3233 and databases were added by the Copyright and Rights in Databases Regulations 1997, SI 1997/3032 in compliance with the relevant European Directives.

105 [1900] AC 539 at 548. However, it seems clear now that the work must be an intellectual creation.

106 [1916] 2 Ch 601 at 608.

> It may be difficult to define 'literary work' as used in this Act [Copyright Act 1911], but it seems to be plain that it is not confined to 'literary work' in the sense in which that phrase is applied, for instance, to Meredith's novels and the writings of Robert Louis Stevenson . . . In my view the words 'literary work' cover work which is expressed in print or writing, irrespective of the question whether the quality or style is high. The word 'literary' seems to be used in a sense somewhat similar to the use of the word 'literature' in political or electioneering literature and refers to written or printed matter.

This must be expanded nowadays to cover material recorded on modern storage media. For example, a report produced using a word processor is a literary work the moment it is stored on a computer disk because it is then recorded 'in writing or otherwise'.

Examples of works afforded literary copyright are books of telegraphic codes,[107] examination papers,[108] football coupons,[109] consignment notes,[110] headings in a trade directory,[111] business letters,[112] legal forms and precedents[113] and case headnotes and summaries.[114] Tables and compilations expressly fall within the meaning of literary work, examples of tables being railway timetables, company balance sheets, actuarial tables and mileage charts. In the past, compilations included things like lists of customers, directories, listings of television programmes and the 'Top Twenty' bestselling records. Now, with the introduction of databases as a specific form of literary work, provided they are the author's own intellectual creation, most of these things will be protected by copyright as databases, providing they are intellectual creations.

Few examples of compilation copyright may now exist though one example is a compilation of musical performances on CD, expressly excluded from the scope of the database Directive.[115] Compilation copyright may also still be available for collections of materials that are not arranged in a systematic or methodical manner, this being required for databases protected under the Directive.

In the past it was accepted that a compilation can comprise both literary and artistic materials,[116] but a change in terminology in the 1988 Act compared to the previous legislation suggested that there is no copyright protection in a compilation of artistic works only because a literary work must be written, spoken or sung, and it can be argued that artistic works are not written.[117] However, the introduction of database copyright has probably resolved such doubts. Additionally, of course, the artistic works may be protected in their own right.

In *Anacon Corp Ltd v Environmental Research Technology Ltd*,[118] Jacob J was prepared to accept that circuit diagrams from which circuit boards were made, in addition to being artistic works, were also literary works as a circuit diagram has writing on it which is intended to be read rather than simply appreciated by the eye. The writing may be in code: for example, the value of a component. Nevertheless, the written information forms a table or compilation and the fact that it is scattered about and joined by lines does not prevent it being so. The headnote to the law report states that the circuit diagrams were literary works. This goes too far. They are artistic works that contain information protected by literary copyright. The graphic elements such as representations of components and connecting lines are not subject to literary copyright. Laddie J considered this to be the correct view of *Anacon* in *Electronic Techniques (Anglia) Ltd v Critchley Components Ltd*[119] where he dismissed an application for summary judgment. Part of the basis for his decision was that, ignoring the graphic elements of the diagrams, as a literary work the circuit diagram was little more than a list of five or six components. Consequently, the defendant had a significant defence that the diagram was not sufficiently substantial to qualify as an original literary work.

The Copyright, Designs and Patents Act 1988 affords copyright protection to computer programs and preparatory design material for computer programs as literary works. The Act, very wisely, does not attempt to define what a computer program is.[120] In view of the rate of development of computer technology, any precise legal definition could prove to

107 *Ager v Peninsula & Oriental Steam Navigation Company* (1884) 26 ChD 627 and *DP Anderson & Co Ltd v Lieber Code Co* [1917] 2 KB 469.

108 *University of London Press Ltd v University Tutorial Press Ltd* [1916] 2 Ch 601.

109 *Ladbroke (Football) Ltd v William Hill (Football) Ltd* [1964] 1 WLR 273.

110 *Van Oppen & Co Ltd v Van Oppen* (1903) 20 RPC 617.

111 *Lamb v Evans* [1893] 1 Ch 218.

112 *British Oxygen Co Ltd v Liquid Air Ltd* [1925] 1 Ch 383.

113 *USP plc v London General Holdings Ltd* [2006] FSR 6. Of course, where forms and precedents are published for sale to lawyers, there will usually be an implied licence to copy and use the forms and precedents for clients.

114 *Law Society of Upper Canada v CCH Canadian Ltd* [2004] SCC 13.

115 Recital 19 to the Directive. However, the exclusion is not absolute as music CDs are excluded 'as a rule' because they fail to comply with the requirements for copyright and for the *sui generis* database right.

116 For example, *Purefoy Engineering Co Ltd v Sykes Boxall & Co Ltd* (1955) 72 RPC 89, concerning a trade catalogue containing literary and artistic materials.

117 Neither are they spoken or sung. Monotti, A. 'The Extent of Copyright Protection for Compilations of Artistic Works' [1993] 5 EIPR 156.

118 [1994] FSR 659.

119 [1997] FSR 401.

120 Neither does the Computer Misuse Act 1990 define 'computer program'. The Banks Committee described a computer program as 'a series of instructions which control or condition the operation of a data processing machine' (*Committee to Examine the Patent System and Patent Law*, Cmnd 4407, 1970, p 140, para 471). The USA has a statutory definition: being 'a set of statements or instructions to be used directly or indirectly in a computer to bring about a certain result', 17 USC § 101. This gives rise to the question 'what is a computer?'!

be inappropriate in the future or, at least, could unduly inhibit flexibility in the law. Where the Act does contain definitions, they tend to be very widely drawn. The classification of computer programs as a form of literary work follows international developments and is in line with the Directive on the legal protection of computer programs. Computer programs, preparatory design material for computer programs, databases and other items of computer software are considered more fully in Chapter 8.

For a work to be an 'original literary work', it must accord with that phrase taken as a whole. It is not sufficient that a work satisfies each word individually. This is another limitation on the scope of copyright, the effect of which is similar to the *de minimis* principle. In particular, the word 'original' should not be looked at in isolation. In *Exxon Corporation* v *Exxon Insurance Consultants International Ltd*,[121] the claimant was a multinational oil company. It decided to choose a new corporate name, and after considerable research and consultation the word 'Exxon' was decided upon. The claimant contended that the word 'Exxon', being first used by it, was *original*, that it was *literary* because it was expressed in letters and that it was a *work*, being the result of considerable research and effort. Therefore, the claimant argued that the word 'Exxon' was an 'original literary work' within the Copyright Act 1956 s 2(1). However, it was held that the term 'original literary work' was a composite expression denoting a literary work intending to offer information, instruction or pleasure in the form of literary enjoyment.[122] For a word or expression to be within the meaning of 'original literary work', it was not enough that the work could be described as 'original', 'literary' and a 'work'. Although 'Exxon' could be described thus separately, it was not an original literary work because it conveyed no information, provided no instruction and gave no pleasure in the form of literary enjoyment. There was, therefore, no copyright in the word 'Exxon'.[123] However, the requirement for literary enjoyment must be questioned now because of the addition of computer programs to the categories of literary works.

There may be an issue as to the limits of protection by copyright. If copyright subsists in a literary work, for example, to what level of abstraction does copyright extend? In *Baigent* v *Random House Group Ltd*,[124] an allegation had been made that the novel *The Da Vinci Code* infringed the copyright in an earlier work entitled *The Holy Blood and The Holy Grail*. Both works were the result of substantial research. Whilst the latter was described as a work of 'historical conjecture' including material on the Knights Templar and the Merovingian Kings and drawing on writings on the Holy Grail and early Church history, the former book was described as a thriller novel drawing on similar material. Mummery LJ said (at para 156):

> Original expression includes not only the language in which the work is composed but also the original selection, arrangement and compilation of the raw research material. It does not, however, extend to clothing information, facts, ideas, theories and themes with exclusive property rights, so as to enable the claimants to monopolise historical research or knowledge and prevent the legitimate use of historical and biographical material, theories propounded, general arguments deployed, or general hypotheses suggested (whether they are sound or not) or general themes written about.

In other words, copyright subsistence (and hence infringement) may extend to the way in which facts, ideas and theories are expressed by the author but this does not mean that those facts, ideas and theories are themselves the subject matter of copyright. This shows that copyright does not give a monopoly in such aspects of a work and others should be free to use them providing they express them in their own way.

Dramatic works

A dramatic work includes a work of dance or mime.[125] Under previous law, it was possible, theoretically, for a work to be both a dramatic work and a literary work: for example, a

121 [1981] 3 All ER 241.

122 Based on the definition of a literary work given by Davey J in *Hollinrake* v *Truswell* [1894] 3 Ch 420 at 427. This seems to be a narrower definition than that adopted by Peterson J in *University of London Press Ltd* v *University Tutorial Press Ltd* [1916] 2 Ch 601.

123 The word 'Exxon' was registered as a trade mark both within the UK and elsewhere.

124 [2007] FSR 24.

125 Copyright, Designs and Patents Act 1988 s 3(1).

script for a play could fall into both of these categories. This was of no consequence as the rights provided for were identical for both types of work. Under the Copyright, Designs and Patents Act 1988, this sterile overlap was removed and a literary work is defined to exclude a dramatic work. Dramatic works, in common with literary and musical works, must be recorded for copyright to subsist in them. In *Tate v Fullbrook*[126] it was held that a visual skit for a music hall sketch involving the use of a firework was not the subject matter of copyright because it had not been reduced to writing.[127] In *Green v Broadcasting Corporation of New Zealand*,[128] it was held that the dramatic format of a television show had to have some certainty in its subject matter for that format to be entitled to copyright protection. The appellant, Hughie Green, devised the television show *Opportunity Knocks* and claimed copyright in the scripts and dramatic format of the show. The latter comprised catchphrases, the use of a 'clapometer' and sponsors to introduce competitors. Finding for the respondents, Lord Bridge said that the protection which copyright gave was a monopoly, and that there had to be certainty in the subject matter of such a monopoly. However, Lord Bridge erred in this respect because copyright certainly does not give a monopoly, it being free to anyone else to produce a similar work as long as they do so independently.[129] A better rationale is that Mr Green's dramatic format could not be protected either because it lacked certainty for want of material form, or because the respondent had copied only the ideas and not the expression of those ideas. It is difficult to reconcile this case with earlier cases such as *Rees v Melville*[130] concerning the plot of a dramatic work, in which it appears that the plot of the play, in addition to the written expression, may be afforded some protection. It depends on the level of abstraction from the literal expression: the closer it is, the more likely it can be considered to be protected. The further away it is, the more likely it will be considered to be an unprotected idea.[131]

A further problem to protecting a format as a dramatic work is that a dramatic work should be capable of being performed. A dance must be capable of being danced and a work of mime must be capable of being mimed. As Lord Bridge of Harwich said in the *Green* case (at 702):

It seems to their Lordships that a dramatic work must have sufficient unity to be capable of performance.

At first instance, in *Norowzian v Arks Ltd (No 2)*,[132] Rattee J readily accepted this proposition in relation to a dramatic work, recorded on film, which had been made by a process described as 'jump cutting'. The claimant had made such a film of a man dancing to music but recorded on film in such a way that the position of the man suddenly changed in a way that could not be performed. This was done by cutting out parts of the film and joining together the parts before and after the part that had been removed. The film was supposed to show a spectrum of emotions and was called *Joy*. The first defendant was an advertising agency which made a film for the second defendant, Guinness, using a similar technique and which showed a man dancing about impatiently waiting for his pint of Guinness stout to settle. Again, impossible movements were portrayed as the man suddenly changed position. This film was called *Anticipation*. It was held that the work could not be a dramatic work because it could not be performed live before an audience. It was also held that a film could be a recording of a dramatic work but that it could not be a dramatic work itself.

On appeal, the Court of Appeal disagreed with the finding that a film could not, *per se*, be a dramatic work.[133] Nourse LJ said that the definition of dramatic work (the Act states simply that it includes a work of dance or mine) is at large and the term must be given its natural and ordinary meaning. That being so, a dramatic work is a work of action with, or without words or music, which is capable of being performed before an audience. A film is, of course, capable of being performed before an audience. Thus, there is an

---

126 [1908] 1 KB 821.

127 *See* also *Tate v Thomas* [1921] 1 Ch 503.

128 [1989] RPC 700.

129 The only exception is where the copyright owner is also the only source of the information contained in the work; see Joined Cases C-241/91P and C-242/91P *RTE & ITP v EC Commission* [1995] ECR I-743.

130 [1911–1916] MacG CC 168.

131 Legislative action is needed to clarify the protection of the dramatic format of 'game shows'. An opportunity to include suitable measures in the Broadcasting Act 1990 was not taken advantage of.

132 [1999] FSR 79.

133 *Norowzian v Arks Ltd (No 2)* [2000] FSR 363.

overlap between dramatic works and films and three possibilities were identified in that a film could be:

- a dramatic work in itself;
- a recording of a dramatic work and also a dramatic work in itself;
- a recording of something which is not a dramatic work.

The Court of Appeal confirmed that the film *Joy* was a dramatic work in itself, being a work of action which was capable of being performed before an audience.[134] However, it was not a recording of a dramatic work although the unedited version of the film was. Despite finding that *Joy* was a dramatic work, the court went on to hold that it was not infringed by *Anticipation*. There was a striking similarity in terms of styles and editing techniques but that was as far as it went. There is no copyright in style or technique.

The decision of the Court of Appeal makes sense and recognises the use of modern techniques such as digital recording and computer manipulation of images in making dramatic works. Thus, a cartoon film made using images developed on or generated by computer will be protected as both a dramatic work and a film but is not a recording of a dramatic work. It could be said that this was Parliament's intention as the Copyright Act 1956 expressly excluded films from the definition of a dramatic work[135] whereas under the 1988 Act there is no such exclusion. Furthermore, the decision of the Court of Appeal accords with the Berne Convention for the Protection of Literary and Artistic Works which states that cinematographic works should be protected as original works.[136]

It appears that a computer game is not a dramatic work. In *Nova Productions Ltd v Mazooma Games Ltd*,[137] at first instance, it was argued, *inter alia*, that a computer game based on the game of pool was a dramatic work. The judge rejected the argument, referring to Nourse LJ in *Norowzian v Arks Ltd (No 2)*[138] who described a dramatic work as a work of action with or without music, which is capable of being performed before an audience. The game could not be so described, it had no unity of action and the results depended to a large extent on the way in which it is played. According to Kitchen J, features of similarity between the claimant's and defendant's computer games could no more be described as features of a dramatic work than those relied on in *Green v Broadcasting Corporation of New Zealand*.[139] In the subsequent appeal in *Nova v Mazooma*,[140] the dramatic work point was not further argued.

Musical works

A musical work is one consisting of music, exclusive of any words or action intended to be sung, spoken or performed with the music. A song will, therefore, have two copyrights: one in the music and one in the words of the song, the latter being a literary work. This is convenient as it is common for different persons to write the music and the lyrics. Once again, the work must be reduced in writing or otherwise. The Copyright, Designs and Patents Act 1988 gives no guidance as to what a musical work is, but in practice this does not seem to cause any problems; what is beautiful music to one man might be a dreadful cacophony to another. It would seem that a relatively small number of notes and chords are sufficient for copyright protection as a dispute as to the ownership of the copyright in a previous piece of Channel 4 logo music, comprising a four-note theme in an orchestral setting, demonstrated.[141]

Making an arrangement of an existing piece of music may attract its own copyright in addition to, and running alongside, the copyright subsisting in the prior work. For example, a musician who expends a reasonable amount of skill in arranging and adapting a piece of music originally written for a rock group so that it is suitable for a traditional orchestra will have a copyright in the orchestral work.[142] Of course, he could be guilty of

---

134 One slight reservation is that although one normally talks about a live performance, a film is *played* (not performed) before an audience. A distinction is also made between performing, showing or playing a work in public in s 16 setting out the acts restricted by copyright.

135 Copyright Act 1956 s 48(1).

136 Article 14[bis].

137 [2006] RPC 14.

138 [2000] FSR 363 at 366.

139 [1989] RPC 700.

140 *Nova Productions Ltd v Mazooma Games Ltd* [2007] RPC 25.

141 *Lawson v Dundas, The Times*, 13 June 1985.

142 *Wood v Boosey* (1868) LR 3 QB 223.

infringing the copyright in the earlier piece of music, should copyright still subsist in it, if he makes his arrangement without the permission of the copyright owner.[143]

Making a new performing edition of an incomplete old work of music out of copyright may itself be worthy of copyright protection even if few or no new notes are added. In *Hyperion Records Ltd v Dr Lionel Sawkins*,[144] Dr Sawkins wrote new performing editions of some of Lalande's baroque musical compositions. He added a figured bass (numbered guidance to musicians, giving them some flexibility in playing the piece of music) and he also corrected notes that he considered wrong or unsatisfactory. In the Court of Appeal, Mummery LJ rejected Hyperion's argument that Dr Sawkins had not written any new music so his work was not a musical work. Mummery LJ said (at paras 55 and 56):

> In principle, there is no reason for regarding the actual notes of music as the only matter covered by musical copyright, any more than, in the case of a dramatic work, only the words to be spoken by the actors are covered by dramatic copyright. Added stage directions may affect the performance of the play on the stage or on the screen and have an impact on the performance seen by the audience. Stage directions are as much part of a dramatic work as plot, character and dialogue.
>
> It is wrong in principle to single out the notes as uniquely significant for copyright purposes and to proceed to deny copyright to the other elements that make some contribution to the sound of the music when performed, such as performing indications, tempo and performance practice indicators, if they are the product of a person's effort, skill and time . . .

This is a sensible way of looking at what a musical work is. Although 'musical work' is not defined in the Copyright, Designs and Patents Act 1988, it cannot be restricted only to the actual notes to be played. Mummery LJ made the point that a musical work can be infringed even without taking the actual notes.[145] In *Hyperion*, it was clear that the music could not have been played at all without Dr Sawkins' work in creating the performing editions.

Rap music is heavily influenced by the lyrics, although the lyrics are a literary work. They influence (one might say 'dictate') the beat and rhythm of the musical work. However, they are still two distinct forms of work. This needs no confirmation and is a matter that should be beyond doubt. But in *Williamson Music Ltd v The Pearson Partnership Ltd*,[146] Judge Baker QC explained his understanding of the relationship between the lyrics and the music by saying (at 109):

> It is, I think, misleading to think of them in mutually exclusive compartments. The words by themselves are or may be the subject of literary copyright. But those same words when sung are to me part of the music. After all one gets enjoyment from hearing a song sung in a language with which one is totally unfamiliar. The enjoyment could well be diminished if the vocal line were replaced by another instrument, eg, the piano or a flute. I should say, although I do not wish to take up time by going into it in any detail, that I do not myself see anything in section 8(5) of the Copyright Act which depends upon the absolute division between the words and the music.

In the rap music case, *Peter Hayes v Phonogram Ltd*,[147] Blackbourne J sought to explain the above quote by saying that Judge Baker QC could only have meant that the human voice could represent an instrument in the orchestra and he could not have meant to suggest that the lyrics could in some way form part of the musical work. This would be quite wrong, even in a rap song.

Artistic works

The artistic work category is a diverse one and includes several different types of works. It is a category that causes special problems because it overlaps with design law and the

---

143 This falls within the meaning of making an adaptation, one of the acts restricted by copyright: Copyright, Designs and Patents Act 1988 s 21(3)(b).

144 [2005] RPC 32.

145 In *Austin v Columbia Gramophone Co Ltd* [1917–1923] MacG CC 398 it was held that infringement of copyright in music is not a question of note for note comparison but falls to be determined by the ear as well as by the eye. *See* also *Francis Day & Hunter Ltd v Bron* [1963] Ch 587.

146 [1987] FSR 97.

147 [2003] ECDR 11.

relationship between copyright and design law is not at all clear-cut. The Copyright, Designs and Patents Act 1988 s 4(1) defines 'artistic work' as meaning:

(a) graphic work, photograph, sculpture or collage, *irrespective of artistic quality*;
(b) a work of architecture being a building or a model *for* a building; or
(c) a work of artistic craftsmanship. (emphasis added)

According to Jacob LJ in *Nova Productions Ltd* v *Mazooma Games Ltd*,[148] all the things falling within the artistic work category have one thing in common in that they are all static, non-moving. Although a screen display shown during the playing of a computer game is undoubtedly a graphic work, there is no separate copyright in a series of such images. This view is supported by the existence of films as a separate category of copyright work. However, this probably goes too far and it is possible to have a moving sculpture, for example, in the case of some moving water features and fountains. Certainly a series of graphic images cannot be a compilation which, being a literary work, is written, spoken or sung.[149]

As copyright is stated to subsist in the first category irrespective of artistic quality, a painting of coloured rectangles by Mondrian or a Jackson Pollock painting made up of coloured squiggles is as deserving of copyright protection as is a portrait or a landscape painted in a traditional manner. Relatively simple things such as football club badges are works of artistic copyright[150] as are crests applied to porcelain articles and patterns applied to tableware.[151] The formula 'irrespective of artistic quality' ensures that personal taste or preference is no bar to copyright protection, and it also safeguards utilitarian and functional works such as drawings for engineering equipment, photographs made for scientific or record purposes, weather charts and plans for civil engineering and building works. However, it appears that for works falling into the last category of artistic works, that is, works of artistic craftsmanship, some qualitative characteristic is required, as will be discussed later.

The Copyright, Designs and Patents Act 1988 s 4(2) expands on the definitions and states that a graphic work includes:

(a) any painting, drawing, diagram, map, chart or plan; and
(b) any engraving, etching, lithograph, woodcut or similar work.

Like literary, dramatic and musical works, artistic works must be 'original'. However, there is no requirement for them to be recorded as their very existence implies some form of tangibility. With the exception of works of artistic craftsmanship, artistic copyright is very generous in what it can protect and in the scope of the protection. Some fairly simple things have been afforded artistic copyright, such as a bare design of a hand,[152] chartlets (simplified coastal maps), a simple label,[153] a working sketch of machinery,[154] a label for a whisky bottle[155] and an inverted 'R' with a dot in the loop which looked like a rabbit's head.[156]

The scope of some of the artistic works is very difficult to fix with any certainty. This is inevitable given the breathtaking range of things that could potentially fall within this category. Unlike some of the other categories of artistic works, graphic works should cause little difficulty. Where there is an issue of subsistence it will be most likely a question of whether the work in question is the result of sufficient skill or judgment.

Photographs

A photograph means a recording of light or other radiation on any medium on which an image is produced or from which an image may by any means be produced, and which is not part of a film. The definition is media-neutral so, for example, it matters not whether the photograph is captured on celluloid film or on a digital sensor. A still image

148 [2007] RPC 25 at para 16.

149 *See* the definition of literary work in s 3(1).

150 See, for example, *Football Association Premier League Ltd* v *Panini UK Ltd* [2004] 1 WLR 1147.

151 *X Ltd* v *Nowacki (t/a Lynton Porcelain Co)* [2003] EWHC 1928 (Ch).

152 *Hildesheimer and Faulkner* v *Dunn & Co* (1891) 64 LT 452. But see also *Kenrick* v *Lawrence* (1890) 25 QBD 99 involving a simple design of a hand showing voters how to cast their votes.

153 *Charles Walker Ltd* v *British Picker Co Ltd* [1961] RPC 57.

154 *B O Morris Ltd* v *F Gilman (BST) Ltd* (1943) 60 RPC 20.

155 *William Grant & Sons Ltd* v *McDowell & Co Ltd* [1994] FSR 690.

156 *Hutchison Personal Communications Ltd* v *Hook Advertising Ltd (No 2)* [1996] FSR 549.

from a film is not a photograph. Copyright may subsist in a photograph of a painting provided skill and judgment has been expended, for example, by selecting part of the painting only and/or choosing lighting conditions, aperture settings, etc. In *Groves' Case*[157] it was held that copyright subsisted in a photograph of an engraving taken from a picture – three potential copyrights!

Copyright in photographs of paintings, and for that matter other types of work, which are themselves out of copyright can prove valuable commercially. But what is required to confer copyright on such a photograph? Making a slavish copy where there is little of no skill or judgment in its making cannot create a new work of copyright. For example, taking a photograph of a painting with a digital camera using automatic settings where the digital image comprises the whole painting and nothing else would seem to lack skill and judgment unless, perhaps, the photographer made arrangements for the painting to be lit in a particular way. In *Interlego AG v Tyco Industries Inc*,[158] Lord Oliver said (at 262–63): 'skill, labour or judgment merely in the process of copying cannot confer originality'. Making a faithful reproduction of a painting by photography was held not to confer copyright in the photograph regardless of the fact that more skill would be required than in the case of making a photocopy in the US case of *Bridgeman Art Library Ltd v Corel Corp*.[159] The judge applied UK and US copyright law,[160] coming to the same conclusion in both cases. He also rejected an argument that the change in medium was sufficient to confer copyright. In *Bridgeman v Corel* the works in question were photographs of old masters. It has current resonance as the National Portrait Gallery recently complained about the use of images of paintings on Wikimedia Commons.[161] At the present time, all that can be said is that the position of photographs of paintings is unclear. On the other hand, a photograph of a three-dimensional article such as a sculpture carved from stone may have its own copyright because of the skill and judgment in positioning the article, lighting it, selecting angle from which it is to be photographed, lens aperture and shutter speed.[162]

Sculptures

The meaning of 'sculpture' potentially could be particularly wide. It could depend on whether it is intended that sculptures are artistic works in the sense they have been created by 'creative' artists or whether any three-dimensional object can be said to be a sculpture even if the purpose of the object is wholly functional with no aesthetic merit or any intention by its creator or designer that it should have eye-appeal. Section 4(2) provides a non-exhaustive definition stating that sculpture includes a cast or model made for the purpose of sculpture. While a three-dimensional head carved from a block of wood or stone or cast in bronze or a model of a lady in a flowing gown made in clay as a model from which porcelain figures will be made are obviously sculptures, not just any three-dimensional article would qualify. A collection of bricks laid out in an art gallery is a sculpture as it has been made by an artist, but the same cannot be true for a metal casing for a gearbox, a container for bleach or a moulded plastic bath. Things such as these are utilitarian and designed for utilitarian purposes. That does not mean that no consideration is given to appearance and an attractive shape may make a utilitarian product more desirable. What about a moving sculpture such as a 'mobile' or Chinese windcharms? Dictionary definitions of 'sculpture' are suggestive of works of art, but this contradicts the phrase 'irrespective of artistic quality'. If we require the work to have been produced by a sculptor, this is difficult to reconcile with the fact that graphic works are not required to be made by an artist as engineering drawings qualify as artistic works.

There is relatively little case law on sculptures and some of it is unsatisfactory.[163] In *J & S Davis (Holdings) Ltd v Wright Health Group Ltd*[164] Whitford J was held that a cast for making a denture was not a sculpture because it was not made for the purposes of

157 (1869) LR 4 QB 715.

158 [1989] 1 AC 217. A case before the Judicial Committee of the Privy Council.

159 36 F Supp 2d (SD NY 1999).

160 In relation to UK copyright law, the judge was heavily influenced by Lord Oliver in *Interlego v Tyco*.

161 *Amateur Photographer*, 1 August 2009, p 5. Wikimedia Commons is operated by the Wikipedia Foundation.

162 See *Antiquesportfolio.com plc v Rodney Fitch & Co Ltd* [2001] FSR 23, and the discussion on photographs earlier in this chapter in the section on originality.

163 Some of the cases described have been disapproved of in the Star Wars case, at first instance, in the Court of Appeal and in the Supreme Court; *infra*.

164 [1988] RPC 403.

165 [1985] RPC 127.

166 The provisions of the New Zealand Copyright Act 1962 s 2, defining artistic works, were equivalent to those under the UK Copyright Act 1956. An important factor was that the wooden model was made by hand.

167 [1980] RPC 397.

168 [1995] FSR 77.

169 However, in *Lucasfilm Ltd v Ainsworth* [2009] FSR 2, discussed *infra*, Mann J doubted the correctness of the *Wham-O* and *Breville* decisions.

170 [1997] FSR 718.

171 [2002] FSR 16.

sculpture. A very generous view of the meaning of sculpture was taken in the Court of Appeal in New Zealand in *Wham-O Manufacturing Co v Lincoln Industries Ltd*,[165] in which it was held that a wooden model, from which moulds were made in order to produce plastic flying discs known as Frisbees, was a sculpture.[166] The moulds were held to be engravings, following the decision of Judge Paul Baker in *James Arnold & Co Ltd v Miafern Ltd*,[167] in which he said that the term 'engraving' encompassed not only the final image made by the engraved plate but the plate itself. Correspondingly, in *Breville Europe plc v Thorn EMI Domestic Appliances Ltd*[168] plaster shapes made for die-cast moulds for the heating plates of sandwich toasters were held to be sculptures.[169]

This generous application of the artistic copyright in sculptures may owe something to the lack of any requirement for artistic quality. Does the absence of artistic quality as a threshold for protection mean that any person, whether an artist or not, may make an artistic work? Certainly, in the case of a draughtsman preparing an engineering drawing or a plan for a house, that would seem to be the case (even more so perhaps in these days of computer-aided design). Does this mean a sculpture can be made by someone who is not a sculptor in the artistic sense? Is an 'Anglepoise' lamp a sculpture? Or a domestic heating radiator? Or a 'desk tidy' made up of a number of tubes to hold pencils, pens and other bits and pieces? In *Metix (UK) Ltd v GH Maughan (Plastics) Ltd*,[170] Laddie J accepted that it was not possible to say with precision what is and what is not a sculpture. However, he considered that counsel's submission that a sculpture is a three-dimensional work made by an artist's hand was near to the mark. However, this is difficult to reconcile with the requirement that copyright subsists irrespective of artistic quality, as pointed out by Christopher Floyd QC in *Hi-Tech Autoparts Ltd v Towergate Two Ltd (No 2)*[171] involving metal plates for making rubber floor mats for cars having a non-slip underside. It was held that the plates were engravings for copyright purposes. It could hardly be claimed that the person who engraved the plates was an artist even though he used skill and judgment in creating them.

Tests appropriate to sculptures

The test for subsistence of artistic copyright does not seem to be whether the object is permanent or transient, and an ice sculpture is no less a sculpture because it will melt as it gets warm, assuming that a chef is an artist.[172]

172 Laddie J approved of this example in *Metix (UK) Ltd v GH Maughan (Plastics) Ltd* [1997] FSR 718, where he disapproved of Whitford J's distinction between a carved wooden model and a model fashioned in Plasticine in *J & S Davis (Holdings) Ltd v Wright Health Group Ltd* [1988] RPC 403.

173 [1997] EMLR 444. Although the claimant failed to show a sufficiently arguable case on the basis of copyright, an interim injunction was granted on the ground of breach of confidence.

174 [2009] FSR 2 at para 118.

There are, however, limits to what can be a sculpture. An arrangement of objects and people, including a white Rolls-Royce car lowered into a swimming pool, for the purpose of taking a photograph of the scene for the album sleeve for a new recording by the band Oasis, was held not to be a sculpture in *Creation Records Ltd v News Group Newspapers Ltd*.[173] Nor was it a collage. Such a work involved, as an essential element, the sticking of two or more items together. Also, as the arrangement was ephemeral, its continued existence being only as represented in the photograph, it was distinguishable from Carl Andre's bricks in the Tate Modern and installation art generally.

A distinction was made by Mann J in *Lucasfilm Ltd v Ainsworth*[174] between the Tate bricks and an identical pile of bricks left at the end of a drive for a forthcoming building project. The former was a sculpture because an artist made it for artistic purposes whilst the latter was not a sculpture because a builder made it for building purposes. In *Lucasfilm*, Mann J had to decide, *inter alia*, whether the helmets worn by the Imperial Stormtroopers in the Star Wars film were sculptures. The defendant made the Stormtrooper's armour for the film and had retained the tools and moulds from which the armour, including helmets, was made. In 2004 he started selling the helmets and armour to the public, advertising them on his website. The claimants which had made the film and subsequently licensed the relevant intellectual property rights brought proceedings in England for copyright infringement, breach of confidence and passing off.[175] In holding that the helmets were not sculptures, Mann J reviewed the authorities above and set out what he

175 The claimants also sought to enforce a US judgment of infringement of US copyright.

called 'guidance factors' (as opposed to points of principle or rigid requirements) to assist in determining whether a particular thing is a sculpture for the purposes of the Copyright, Designs and Patents Act 1988. They can be summarised accordingly (not wholly verbatim):

(i) Some regard has to be had to the normal use of the word 'sculpture'.

(ii) Nevertheless, the concept can be applicable to things going beyond what would normally be expected to be art in the sense of the sort of things expected to be found in art galleries.

(iii) It is inappropriate to stray too far from what would normally be regarded as sculptures.

(iv) No judgment is to be made about artistic worth.

(v) Not every three-dimensional representation of a concept can be regarded as a sculpture because, otherwise, every three-dimensional construction or fabrication would be a sculpture, and that cannot be right.

(vi) It is of the essence of a sculpture that it should have, as part of its purpose, a visual appeal in the sense that it might be enjoyed for that purpose alone, whether or not it might have another purpose as well. The purpose is that of the creator. This reflects the reference to 'artist's hand' as per Laddie J in *Metix*. An artist (in the realm of the visual arts) creates something because it has visual appeal which he wishes to be enjoyed as such. He may fail, but that does not matter (no judgments are to be made about artistic merit). It is the underlying purpose that is important.

(vii) The fact that the object has some other use does not necessarily disqualify it from being a sculpture, but it still has to have the intrinsic quality of being intended to be enjoyed as a visual thing. It explains why the Frisbee itself should be excluded from the category, along with the moulds in *Metix* and *Davis*.

(viii) The process of fabrication is relevant but not determinative. I do not see why a purely functional item, not intended to be at all decorative, should be treated as a sculpture simply because it is (for example) carved out of wood or stone.

Mann J said that his approach would exclude the wooden model in *Wham-O* and the plaster casts in *Breville*, and he respectfully disagreed with the conclusions reached by the judges in those cases that those things were sculptures. He said that those decisions did not accord with the ordinary view of what a sculpture is. The reason being that there was no intention that the articles in question should have visual appeal for their own sake. There was every intention that they would be purely functional.

Mann J must be right. It is a fallacy to conclude that the absence of a requirement of artistic quality means that the purpose for designing or making the article is question also has nothing to do with art in a wide sense. Artistic purpose must be present whether or not the finished product achieves that purpose, objectively or subjectively. The phrase 'irrespective of artistic quality' must be intended to prevent challenges to copyright subsistence based on a perceived lack of artistic merit rather than an intention to confer copyright protection on three-dimensional articles designed for purely functional or utilitarian purposes. For such articles, there are other forms of protection such as unregistered design law. Strong support for this view is given by the underlying rationale of the Copyright, Designs and Patents Act 1988 and the introduction of shorter term protection for functional designs.

The Court of Appeal[176] agreed with Mann J on the sculpture point as did the Supreme Court.[177] Both the Court of Appeal and the Supreme Court noted that an appellate court should be slow to interfere with a trial judge's finding made after hearing all the evidence from numerous witnesses. Lords Collins and Walker, with whom the other judges agreed on the sculpture point, said (at para 46): 'Long and thorough as [Mann J's] judgment is, he may not have recorded every nuance that contributed to his conclusion. He did not err

176 [2010] FSR 10.

177 [2011] UKSC 39. This case has the distinction of being the first intellectual property case before the Supreme Court.

in law or reach an obviously untenable conclusion . . .'. In the Court of Appeal, there had been a discussion of the situation where a film was made with actors as soldiers wearing twentieth-century military helmets and the fact that this would not accord with the normal use of language to describe such helmets as sculptures. Lords Collins and Walker in the Supreme Court said (at para 44):

> The argument for applying the term [sculpture] to an Imperial Stormtrooper helmet is stronger, because of the imagination that went into the concept of the sinister cloned soldiers dressed in uniform white armour. But it was the Star Wars film that was the work of art that Mr Lucas and his companies created. The helmet was utilitarian in the sense that it was an element in the process of production of the film.

As had the courts below done, the Supreme Court disapproved the decisions in *Wham-O* and *Breville* and these cases must now be taken to be wrongly decided as to the meaning of 'sculpture'. The correct approach now must surely be that accepted by Laddie J in *Metix*. A sculpture, for copyright purposes, is a three-dimensional work made by an artist's hand. Of course, the work may lack merit and the courts are not arbiters of what is or is not artistic. This accounts for the proviso that most of the forms of artistic works are protected by copyright irrespective of artistic quality. Although intellectual property law developed to provide different protection regimes for copyright works and designs, owners of three-dimensional works have attempted to blur the boundaries between the two and extend the meaning of sculpture beyond that understood by the public at large so as to extend the protection for their designs. Absence of a requirement of artistic quality now must be taken to mean, in the case of sculptures at least,[178] that a work lacking merit from a subjective perspective does not mean that any three-dimensional object is an artistic work.

The section 4(1)(a) artistic works (graphic works, photographs, sculptures or collages) must be distinguished from works of architecture which appear to protected, *per se*, assuming they are original and otherwise qualify for protection and works of artistic craftsmanship, which is another difficult category as will be seen below.

Works of architecture

A work of architecture is a building or a model for a building. A building includes any fixed structure, and a part of a building or fixed structure.[179] Buildings effectively have double protection, as works of architecture and through the plans drawn up for the buildings. Models *for* buildings, such as a model made for a proposed building to show to prospective investors and clients, are specifically protected, but models *of* buildings are not. However, if a model made of an existing building is copied, the copyright in the building itself and in the drawings made for the construction of the building will be infringed.

Typefaces

Typefaces are not specifically mentioned among the categories of artistic works in the Copyright, Designs and Patents Act 1988 s 4. Nevertheless, it is beyond doubt that a typeface is an artistic work. Indeed, there are references in the Act to typefaces as a form of artistic work. For example, ss 54 and 55 (permitted acts in relation to typefaces) are stated in terms of the 'copyright in an artistic work consisting of the design of a typeface'. In the past, registered design law was not particularly appropriate to protect typefaces (common features such as a new design of serif might have been registrable) but, following the changes to domestic registered design law (and the introduction of the Community Design), typefaces are expressly mentioned amongst the list of things that fall within the definition of 'product' for the purposes of the UK registered design and the registered and unregistered Community design.

178 The same principles must also apply to photographs, collages and some of the graphic works such as engravings and woodcuts.

179 *MacMillan Publishers Ltd* v *Thomas Reed Publications Ltd* [1993] FSR 455.

Artistic craftsmanship

Works of artistic craftsmanship give rise to the greatest difficulty amongst artistic works. Normally, one might expect this category to include such things as jewellery to a special design, 'designer' goods such as furniture and clothing, and quality hand-made items intended to appear attractive or 'rustic' in some way and as found in craft shops.[180] Certainly, the phrase 'artistic craftsmanship' conjures up items made by hand by skilled workers which are bought because of the quality of workmanship and because of their eye-appeal. Better examples of hand-carved cuckoo clocks made in Switzerland should clearly be works of artistic craftsmanship. But where is the line drawn? What about mass-produced cuckoo clocks which are crudely assembled from machine jigged plywood, incorporating a cheap timepiece and a plastic cuckoo? And what about a mock-up for furniture to be mass-produced, roughly made with a light timber frame held together with nails and covered in upholstery but too flimsy to be able to support a person sitting on it? The case of *George Hensher Ltd* v *Restawhile Upholstery (Lancs) Ltd*[181] concerned such a prototype made for a suite of furniture, described as 'boat-shaped'. The House of Lords held that the prototype was not a work of artistic craftsmanship and that for something to fall into this category it must, in addition to being the result of craftsmanship, have some artistic quality. None of their Lordships seemed able to lay down a workable test for the required artistic quality, but agreed that the work must be viewed in a detached and objective manner. The question of whether a particular item possesses that quality is one of fact and evidence; in particular, expert evidence is an important factor in reaching a decision. Lord Reid said that a work of artistic craftsmanship would have the necessary artistic quality if any substantial section of the public genuinely admired and valued the thing for its appearance even though others may have considered it common or vulgar.

Lords Reid and Kilbrandon considered that the intention of the maker of the article was an important though not conclusive issue. While Viscount Dilhorne considered that mass-produced articles could not be works of artistic craftsmanship, Lord Simon of Glaisdale said that the word 'artistic' was not incompatible with machine production. However, the claim of copyright infringement concerned the appellant's prototype, not the furniture made from it, and the real obstacle standing in the way of copyright protection for it was that the appellant was unable to convince any of their Lordships that the prototype was, in any sense, artistic. It was likely that the design of the mock-up chair would have been accepted for registration under the Registered Designs Act 1949, as the Act then was, because it was new and designed for eye-appeal,[182] albeit somewhat vulgar, and the failure to apply for this relatively inexpensive form of protection against copying reduces the sympathy one can feel for the appellant. Nevertheless, a substantial amount of thought lay behind the design, aimed at reviving falling sales, and the respondent simply copied the appellant's furniture made in accordance with the prototype, saving itself the trouble of designing furniture that would appeal to the public and sell in large numbers. The respondent took unfair advantage and the decision in the House of Lords is difficult to square with Peterson J's oft-quoted dictum that a thing worth copying is worth protecting.[183]

The *Hensher* case did nothing to clarify the meaning of 'artistic craftsmanship', and while items such as Chippendale chairs, hand-crafted jewellery and fashion clothing are clearly within the meaning, utilitarian and mass-produced works are left vulnerable in terms of copyright protection even though they will often be subject to large commercial investment and risk. For once, the pragmatic and commercially sound approach of copyright law founders on the rock of taste, and one might ask why atrocious or feeble paintings and sculptures are protected by copyright law while other things, such as furniture, that have proven visual appeal, fail to attract protection, and why the *Hensher* principles

180 In some cases, an article which might properly be considered to be a work of artistic craftsmanship might also qualify for protection as a sculpture: for example, a three-dimensional wood carving.

181 [1976] AC 64.

182 Eye-appeal is no longer required for registration but the design must be new and have an individual character. The designs of articles normally hidden from view are not registrable.

183 *University of London Press Ltd* v *University Tutorial Press Ltd* [1916] 2 Ch 601 at 610.

have not been discarded by the Copyright, Designs and Patents Act 1988. The one saving grace is that many of the articles that will fail to be classed as works of artistic copyright will be protected either as registered designs or under the unregistered design right.[184] However, the former requires registration and the payment of a fee, and these rights require a standard of novelty or originality, as the case may be, that is probably higher than is the case for copyright.

The question of artistic craftsmanship was considered again later in the High Court in *Merlet* v *Mothercare plc*.[185] Walton J, applying *Hensher*, held that a prototype cape for a baby, called a 'Raincosy', was not a work of artistic craftsmanship. He said that the test was whether the thing itself was a work of art and, consequently, the garment had to be considered by itself and not as worn or containing a baby. The 'Raincosy' was a work of craftsmanship only and not a work of artistic craftsmanship because the garment itself was not aesthetic, although seeing the ensemble of mother, child and garment may have given an onlooker some sense of aesthetic satisfaction. On the issue of the maker's intention, he said that the purpose of the garment was to protect a child from the rigours of the Scottish climate and the claimant had not been concerned with the creation of a work of art.

In the New Zealand case of *Bonz Group (Pty) Ltd* v *Cooke*[186] Tipping J noted that the expression 'artistic craftsmanship' was a composite one. The notion of craftsmanship relates more to the execution of the work rather than its design and, conversely, the requirement that the work be artistic relates more to its design than its execution. Thus, the author of the work must be both an artist and a craftsman, an inconsistently high standard. However, Tipping J did recognise that the author would usually be a single person, but one person could provide the artistic element while another provided the craftsmanship. This decision has been applied in England in *Vermaat and Powell* v *Boncrest Ltd*.[187] That case involved designs for patchwork bedspreads and cushion covers. The designs were set out in drawings having small samples of fabric attached to them indicating the colours of the patches and their arrangement and the colour of the border material. The drawings were sent to a manufacturer in India which made samples made by seamstresses to send back to the designers. Unfortunately, the Indian manufacturer also made other bedspreads and cushion covers to the designs and supplied the defendant with them. It was held that the test of artistic craftsmanship was that the work must derive from an author who is both an artist and a craftsman. Where a number of people combine to design and execute the finished work, it may still qualify as a work of artistic craftsmanship providing the requirements of artistry and craftsmanship are present. In this sense, an artist is someone who has the creative ability to produce something which has aesthetic appeal. A craftsman is someone who takes pride in his workmanship and who makes something in a skilful way. Applying this test to the bedspreads and cushion covers, it was held that they may have been works of craftsmanship, having been made by a seamstress, but they lacked sufficient artistic quality. Although the designs were pleasing to the eye, they did not possess the necessary requirement of creativity. However, it was held that the drawings themselves were graphic works under s 4(1)(a).

In *Merlet*, Walton J distilled the judgments in the House of Lords in *Hensher* and developed what now seems to be the accepted two-stage test for artistic craftsmanship as applied in *Vermaat*. The test is usually set out in what one might think to be reverse order, that is as follows:

1 Did the creation of the work involve an exercise of craftsmanship by a person who exercises skill in its manufacture and who takes a pride in what he creates?
2 Was the work created by an artist such that it has aesthetic appeal?

Logically, conception ought to precede manufacture but the test has a number of other problems. The use of the term 'artist' could set the test too high and, in *Guild* v *Eskandar*

184 Or, under the Community design system.

185 [1986] RPC 115. The case went to the Court of Appeal, but only on the issue of whether there had been an infringement of the copyright in the drawings of the garment concerned.

186 [1994] 3 NZLR 216.

187 [2001] FSR 5, deciding a preliminary issue of copyright subsistence.

Ltd,[188] this possibly led Rimer J into saying that he would have to be satisfied that the garments under consideration were works of art. Another difficulty is whether the test is subjective, that is, whether the intention of the creator is relevant. In *Guild*, Rimer J said it was a matter of evidence but a primary consideration was whether the creator had a conscious purpose of making a work of art. He was happy to contemplate that, if that intention existed, it would be a work of art unless he failed manifestly to bring that purpose to fruition. Another implication of the test is that it seems to make it fairly clear that machine-made articles cannot be works of artistic craftsmanship. In *Guild* v *Eskandar*, the garments were machine-made.[189]

The outcome of all the cases on artistic craftsmanship seems to be that it is very limited in its scope even though there is recognition that two or more people may combine to create such a work. Although this category of works seems out of step with other forms of artistic works, design law steps in to rescue the situation for most works, whether aesthetic or not, which fail to meet the high standards required for copyright as works of artistic craftsmanship. Indeed, in *Guild* v *Eskandar*, it was held that the unregistered design right subsisting in the garments had been infringed.

The distillation of *Hensher* and the above cases now seems fairly predictable in practice. At first instance, in *Lucasfilm Ltd* v *Ainsworth*,[190] Mann J considered that, although the Imperial Stormtroopers helmets and armour were undoubtedly works of craftsmanship, the design had no aesthetic purpose. The helmet design was intended to convey a particular impression in the Star Wars film. Mann J said (at para 134):

> A work of artistic craftsmanship does not have to be something of which William Morris would have been proud, but it is a not wholly irrelevant test in a case like the present to consider whether he would recognise it as having anything at all with what his movement was seeking to do. I do not think he would.

In the present case, the helmets would not stand up to close scrutiny as a work of artistic craftsmanship should. What looked like corrugations of a glass tube were, in fact, painted on. Mann J also held, on similar grounds, that the rest of the Stormtroopers' armour was not a work of artistic craftsmanship. It is arguable that Mann J placed too much emphasis on the Arts and Crafts movement but probably reached the correct conclusion nonetheless.[191]

Sound recordings, films or broadcasts

These are sometimes referred to as derivative works. They are usually based on original literary, dramatic, musical and artistic works: for example, a recording of pop tunes, where the record is protected as a sound recording and each tune will have musical copyright and literary copyright in any lyrics. Sometimes, however, a work in these categories is not based on one of the 'original' works. For example, a recording of the noise of the Flying Scotsman train engine building up steam will be a sound recording but there is no other underlying work. Sound recordings, films and broadcasts need protection so that the investors and entrepreneurs involved in such works can take direct action in case of infringement. The fact that several different original works may be encapsulated in a single film or sound recording makes it much more convenient for the owner of the rights in the latter to sue directly for any infringement. To take an example, consider a musical film such as *South Pacific*; there may be separate copyrights in the music, the lyrics to the songs and the dramatic parts of the film. If a part of the film is copied without permission, the owner of the copyright in the film can sue, otherwise it would be necessary to identify which rights were affected and who owned those rights

188 [2001] FSR 38.

189 It was also held in this case that, for the purposes of assessing whether a garment is a work of artistic craftsmanship, it is acceptable to view the garment both in its unworn state and also as worn by a mannequin.

190 [2009] FSR 2.

191 The designs could have had protection by design law, though that would have expired by now. Mann J's finding that the helmets and armour were not works of artistic craftsmanship was not subject to the appeal to the Court of Appeal and the subsequent appeal to the Supreme Court.

and what the relationships were between those persons and the owner of the film. The situation could become very complex and this could work to the detriment of the film industry, the ensuing confusion making it easier for film piracy to flourish. Of course, if the owner of the copyright in a film successfully sues for infringement of copyright, he may distribute part of the award in damages to the various copyright owners in accordance with pre-existing contractual arrangements. In the case of an award of account of profits in respect of concurrent rights under an exclusive licence, the court will apportion the profit between the licensor and licensee.[192]

Compared to the 'original' works of copyright, these derivative works give rise to far fewer problems relating to the question of copyright subsistence. There is no express requirement that these works be original because many would fail: for example, in a broadcast of a play, the play may be an original dramatic work in the copyright sense, but the broadcast cannot be original in the popular sense.

Sound recordings

Under the Copyright, Designs and Patents Act 1988 s 5A(1), a sound recording is either:

(a) a recording of sounds, from which the sounds may be reproduced; or
(b) a recording of the whole or any part of a literary, dramatic or musical work, from which sounds reproducing the work or part may be produced, regardless of the medium on which the recording is made or the method by which the sounds are reproduced or produced.

Under s 5A(2) copyright does not subsist in a sound recording which is, or to the extent that it is, a copy taken from a previous sound recording.[193]

Note that the language of the Act talks of 'sound' not music, so that recordings of non-musical sounds will come within the definition and a recording of a person reciting a passage from a book or a poem falls within the meaning of a sound recording. The definition is very wide in terms of storage media to take account of changes in technology. There is nothing to prevent several persons making recordings of the same thing at the same time and each having their own copyright. For example, if several persons made a sound recording of the song of a rare bird such as a nightjar, each will own the copyright in their own recording, and can sue for infringement if someone makes a copy of *their* recording without permission.

Films

Films are defined in s 5B(1) and are a recording on any medium from which a moving image may by any means be produced. Again, notice the width of the definition – 'any medium' and 'by any means'. Until 1 January 1996, the definition only referred to the image and a film sound track was not included. Now, however, by s 5B(2), the sound track accompanying a film is treated as part of the film.[194] It may also have a separate copyright as a sound recording.[195] Film copyright can subsist in a series of graphic images produced during the playing of a computer game.[196] Copying an old film does not bring about a new copyright, for, under s 5B(4), copyright does not subsist in a sound recording or film which is, or to the extent that it is, a copy taken from a previous sound recording or film.

Under the 1956 Act, a film could not be a dramatic work[197] but it now appears that there can be an overlap and a film can be a dramatic work in itself or it can be both a dramatic work and a recording of a dramatic work.[198] This can give the owner of the copyright in the film an advantage as there are some differences between dramatic works and films in terms of infringement.

192 Copyright, Designs and Patents Act 1988 s 102(4).

193 Section 5A was inserted by the Duration of Copyright and Rights in Performances Regulations 1995, SI 1995/3297. The definition is identical to the previous one in the old s 5.

194 There are some limitations to this treatment under s 5B(3), for example, references to playing or communicating to the public a sound recording do not include playing or communicating the film sound track to accompany the film.

195 Copyright, Designs and Patents Act 1988 s 5B(5) states that nothing in this section affects any copyright subsisting in a film sound track as a sound recording.

196 This appears to have been accepted without question in *Nova Productions Ltd* v *Mazooma Games Ltd* [2007] RPC 25 but an allegation of infringement of the computer game as a film was not pursued either at first instance or in the Court of Appeal.

197 Copyright Act 1956 s 48(1).

198 *Norowzian* v *Arks Ltd (No 2)* [2000] FSR 363, discussed above.

Broadcasts

Until 31 October 2003, broadcasts and cable programmes were distinct works of copyright, the former being transmitted by wireless means, through the ether, the latter being transmitted by cable. Now broadcasts have been redefined to include cable programmes and 'broadcast' is, under new s 6(1) of the Copyright, Designs and Patents Act 1988:

> an electronic transmission of visual images, sound or other information which –
>
> (a) is transmitted for simultaneous reception by members of the public and is capable of being lawfully received by them, or
> (b) is transmitted at a time determined solely by the person making the transmission for presentation to members of the public;
>
> and which is not excepted by subsection (1A).

Section 6(1A) excludes from the definition most forms of internet transmission – for example, where a person decides to access a website, unless it is:

> (a) a transmission taking place simultaneously on the internet and by other means,
> (b) a concurrent transmission of a live event, or
> (c) a transmission of recorded moving images or sounds forming part of a programme service offered by the person responsible for making the transmission, being a service in which programmes are transmitted at scheduled times determined by that person.

In other words, internet transmissions which are analogous to conventional radio or television broadcasts are within the meaning of 'broadcast'.[199] Under s 6(2), if a transmission is encrypted it is still regarded as capable of being lawfully received by members of the public if decoding equipment has been made available to the public by or with the authority of the person making the transmission or the person providing the contents of the transmission. Under s 6(6), copyright does not subsist in a broadcast which infringes (or to the extent that it infringes) the copyright in another broadcast.

Although wireless broadcasts and cable programmes are now treated collectively as broadcasts, there is still a distinction between the two for certain purposes. The meaning of 'wireless broadcast' is important for this reason and is defined in s 178 as a broadcast by means of wireless telegraphy which itself is defined as the sending of electro-magnetic energy over paths not provided by a material substance constructed or arranged for that purpose, *but does not include the transmission of microwave energy between terrestrial fixed points.*[200]

It is important to know from where a wireless broadcast is made as this will determine whether it attracts UK copyright. This could be an issue where the broadcast is made by satellite; s 6(4) states that a wireless broadcast is made from the place where, under the control and responsibility of the person making the broadcast, the programme-carrying signals are introduced into an uninterrupted chain of communication. Where the transmission is via a satellite, that includes the chain leading to the satellite and down towards earth.[201]

The area of reception of a broadcast, its 'footprint', is likely to overlap national boundaries and further complications arise where a wireless broadcast originates from another country, particularly if it is outside the European Economic Area (EEA).[202] There are some special provisions, inserted by the Copyright and Related Rights Regulations 1996, which are designed to give rights to persons involved in the broadcast who are located in the EEA where the country from which the wireless broadcast originates does not provide adequate protection in terms of broadcast rights, performers' rights and rights of authors of sound recordings and performers to share in a single equitable remuneration in respect of the broadcasting of sound recordings.

These special provisions (termed 'safeguards') are contained in s 6A. Figure 3.1 shows a typical situation covered by the safeguards. The signals are broadcast by wireless telegraphy

199 In *Australian Performing Right Association Ltd* v *Telstra Corp Ltd* [1994] RPC 299, the Federal Court of Australia held that transmissions to mobile telephones from base stations were not broadcasts for the purposes of the Australian Copyright Act 1968.

200 The italicised words were added by the Copyright and Related Rights Regulations 1996, SI 1996/2967 reg 8.

201 This is a slight change in definition made by the Copyright and Related Rights Regulations 1996, SI 1996/2967 reg 5, as from 1 December 1996. These regulations implement, *inter alia*, Council Directive 93/83/EEC of 27 September 1993 on the coordination of certain rules concerning copyright and rights related to copyright applicable to satellite broadcasting and cable retransmission, OJ L 248, 06.10.1993, p 15.

202 Under s 172A(1), the EEA means the European Economic Area and an EEA state is a Member State of the European Economic Community (now EU), Iceland, Liechtenstein and Norway.

from a non-EEA country and are received by a station in an EEA country from where they are transmitted to a satellite to be received in that and/or other countries. That station is known as the uplink station. Where, as in the example, the broadcast is made from a country outside the EEA and which does not afford an adequate level of protection as described above, if the uplink station is located in an EEA state, that state is treated as the place from where the broadcast is made, and the person making the broadcast is deemed to be the person operating the uplink station: s 6A(2). Where the uplink station is not located in an EEA state then, under s 6A(3), a broadcast may still qualify for the protection of the appropriate EEA state if it was commissioned by a person established in an EEA state. The person so established is deemed to be the person making the broadcast, and the place from which the broadcast is treated as having been made is the place in which he has his principal establishment within the EEA. For example, a company registered and established in England commissions a broadcast transmitted from Israel. It is received in Turkey where it is instantaneously re-transmitted to a satellite from where it can be received in a number of EEA states. The English company is deemed to be the maker of the broadcast, and it is deemed to have been made in the UK and subject, therefore, to UK copyright.

Before the revocation of s 7, which used to define cable programmes and cable programme services, it was held that a passive 'website' on the internet could be a cable programme service and items contained within that website could be cable programmes. So it was held in *Shetland Times Ltd* v *Dr Jonathan Wills*[203] in the Court of Session, Outer House in Scotland in granting an interim interdict to the claimant which published a newspaper called the *Shetland Times* and which also made it available on the internet. Even though the information passively awaits access by callers to the website, Lord Hamilton considered that there was an arguable case that the process involved the sending of information as required by s 7(1). Additionally, although the service had an interactive element in that callers to the site could send comments and suggestions, this was not within s 7(2)(a) which excluded from the definition of 'cable programme service' services (or part of a service) an essential feature of which was that while visual images, sound or other information were being conveyed by the person providing the service there will or may be sent from each place of reception, by means of the same system (or same part of it), information (other than signals sent for the operation or control of

203 [1997] FSR 604.

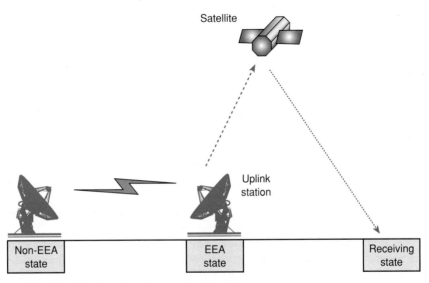

Figure 3.1 Satellite broadcast via uplink station

the service) for reception by the person providing the service or other persons receiving it. In other words, the interactive element has to be an essential feature of the service to be excluded from the definition. Lord Hamilton considered that the interactive element was not an essential feature of the service, the primary purpose of which was to distribute news and other items. In any case, even if it was, it was arguable that it was a severable feature. Changes to copyright law by the Copyright and Related Rights Regulations 2003[204] strengthened the protection of materials made available online and rendered the separate treatment of cable programmes redundant.

Typographical arrangements of published editions

This form of copyright did not exist until provided for by the Copyright Act 1956, largely as a result of pressure from publishers. The purpose of this form of copyright was to protect the skill expended in designing the pages of the publication and the labour and capital in setting up the type and keeping it standing. But publishing has changed since then and computer technology has taken away the skill involved in setting up metal type. Now, the skill and labour in a publication is principally expressed in its overall design. This is particularly so in relation to a newspaper and, in *Newspaper Licensing Agency Ltd* v *Marks & Spencer plc*,[205] it was suggested that the skill and labour used in the creation of the typographical arrangement could not be expressed in anything less than a full page.

The Copyright, Designs and Patents Act 1988 s 8 defines a published edition, in the context of a typographical arrangement of a published edition, as a published edition of the whole or any part of one or more literary, dramatic or musical works. Copyright in the typographical arrangement of published editions gives some protection to the publisher of a work which is itself out of copyright, and also gives some recognition to the skill expended in work such as selection of typestyles, format and typesetting. Artistic works are not included. If a publisher produces a book of a literary work which is still in copyright and a person copies a substantial part of the book, say by photocopying, then both the copyright in the literary work and the copyright in the typographical arrangement will be infringed.[206] If the copyright in the content of the book has expired, for example in the case of a Shakespeare play, copying the book, say by photocopying or scanning into a computer, will infringe the typographical arrangement only.

A number of issues relating to the scope of protection of typographical arrangements of published editions have been resolved in the House of Lords in *Newspaper Licensing Agency Ltd* v *Marks & Spencer plc*.[207] Newspaper publishers assigned their copyrights in the typographical arrangement of their newspapers to the claimant which granted licences allowing licensees to make copies of articles of interest or provide copies of such articles to others. One of the licensees, a press cutting agency, supplied copies of newspaper articles to others. Generally, the articles supplied had been cut from their surrounding articles and rearranged to fit on a blank sheet of A4 paper. The defendant subscribed to the agency and received photocopies of newspaper articles. However, on receiving these copies, the defendant made further copies of some of the articles and other items of interest and distributed these further copies to members of its staff. The claimant's action for infringement of the copyright subsisting in the typographical arrangements was successful at first instance[208] but the defendant successfully appealed to the Court of Appeal.[209] The claimant's appeal to the House of Lords was dismissed.

In the House of Lords, the primary issues were the meaning of 'edition' and the scope of protection of this form of copyright in relation to a newspaper and whether substantiality was to be judged differently to the test applicable to the original works of copyright. It had been argued that each article in a newspaper could be subject to a typographical

204 These Regulations implemented Directive 2001/29/EC of the European Parliament and of the Council of 22 May 2001 on the harmonisation of certain aspects of copyright and related rights in the information society, OJ L 167, 22.06.2001, p 10, discussed in more detail in Chapter 8.

205 [2003] 1 AC 551.

206 However, if the person types the text of the book into a computer, there will be an infringement of the literary work but not of the typographical arrangement. Scanning the book into a computer will infringe, however, as this will create a facsimile copy: s 17(5).

207 [2003] 1 AC 551.

208 *Newspaper Licensing Agency Ltd* v *Marks & Spencer plc* [1999] RPC 536.

209 *Newspaper Licensing Agency Ltd* v *Marks & Spencer plc* [2001] RPC 5.

arrangement and that substantiality should be judged by reference to quantity rather than quality.

The definition of a published edition in the Act is a published edition of the whole or any part of one or more literary, dramatic or musical works.[210] It was held that this confirms that there is no congruence between the concept of an 'edition' and the underlying works contained in it and, in relation to a composite work, such as a newspaper, this means the entire 'between the covers' work.[211] Whilst accepting that literary copyright can subsist in an individual work published as part of a compilation, in addition to a separate literary copyright in the compilation as a whole, this was held not to be the case with published editions. This leads to an apparent paradox. Consider the following scenario: one publisher (publisher 'A') decides to publish a collection of 20 poems in a book. One of those poems is relatively short; say it is called 'Ode to a Butterfly', and is also published by another publisher (publisher 'B').[212] However, publisher 'B' publishes the poem on its own, say in a leaflet comprising one or two pages only. Both publishers have expended skill in designing the layout of their publications. It is beyond doubt that publisher 'B' will have a typographical arrangement copyright in relation to 'Ode to a Butterfly' but this is not so clear in the case of publisher 'A'. The situation is even more bizarre when considering a newspaper article. A single article of, say, 1,000 words and taking up less than one side of A4, if published separately, will enjoy protection through the copyright in the typographical arrangement yet it will not if published along with many other articles and other items in a newspaper. In terms of newspapers, this form of copyright owes more to the overall design of the newspaper than the detail applied to a particular article, such as font size and line-spacing and horizontal and vertical alignment of paragraphs within that article. Particularly in the context of composite works, this form of copyright, therefore, operates on a macro-scale rather than a micro-scale and it is the interrelationship and interaction between the individual items that is paramount.[213]

In spite of this serious limitation to this right, typographical arrangement copyright is increasingly important because of advances in photocopying technology. Of course, if copyright subsists in the individual works in a composite work, an action for infringement of that copyright should be more likely to succeed. It appears, however, that relatively few words may be required to be a typographical arrangement. *X Ltd* v *Nowacki (t/a Lynton Porcelain Co)*[214] concerned, *inter alia*, a dispute regarding copyright in a stamp applied to exclusive porcelain products such as dinner services. An example of the stamp is given below. It carries the crest of the customer, SO, for whom the porcelain was made, together with wording.

[Customer's crest]

SPECIALLY MADE FOR

SO

by

The Claimant

Finest Bone China

MADE IN ENGLAND

Mr Christopher Floyd QC, sitting as deputy judge of the High Court, said that when the crest is put to one side, what is left looks a bit like a typographical arrangement. He also suggested that the choice of different fonts and their use in combination with the crest went further than a mere typographical arrangement and that artistic copyright might subsist in the whole. He admitted being cautious about his suggestions as it had not been fully addressed by counsels' argument. That a stamp applied to porcelain which contains a number of words or phrases can be protected by typographical arrangement copyright is surely wrong. It would be bizarre if a porcelain dinner plate could be described as a published edition. In any case, the judge did not mention any cases on

210 Section 8(1).

211 Approving Wilcox J, at first instance, in the Federal Court of Australia in *Nationwide News Pty Ltd* v *Copyright Agency Ltd* (1995) 128 ALR 285.

212 Assume that neither publisher copies the other's typographical arrangement and that the copyright in the poem has expired or that both publishers have the consent of the owner of the copyright subsisting in the poem.

213 The apparent paradox is answered, according to Lord Hoffmann in the *Newspaper Licensing Agency* case above, by focusing on the issue of substantiality rather than granting overlapping copyrights in typographical arrangements in a composite work.

214 [2003] EWHC 1928 (Ch).

typographical arrangements. Consideration of the *Newspaper Licensing Agency* case above would surely have led him to ignore the possibility that such a copyright could subsist in the stamp.

In order to prevent publishers extending the life of their typographical arrangement copyright indefinitely, copyright is declared not to subsist in the typographical arrangement of a published edition if, or to the extent that, it reproduces the typographical arrangement of a previous edition.

Qualification

For copyright to subsist in a work, under the Copyright, Designs and Patents Act 1988 s 1(3), the qualification requirements must be satisfied. This can be achieved in the following ways: either by reference to the author of the work, or by reference to the country of first publication or, in the case of a broadcast, the country from which the broadcast was made.[215] In most cases, qualification will be easily satisfied, such as where the work is created by a UK citizen (or an individual domiciled or resident in the UK) or is first published in the UK. Also, international copyright conventions will give protection to works that would not otherwise qualify. Basically, these Conventions, of which there are two, afford protection to member countries on the basis of 'national treatment', and most developed countries belong to one or other or both. The UK is a signatory to both the Berne Convention[216] and the Universal Copyright Convention.[217] As a result, if a work is first published in or transmitted from a convention country, or if the author of the work is a citizen of or is domiciled in a convention country, the owner will be able to take action for infringement in the UK. Similarly, works first published or transmitted in the UK, or having an author who is British or is domiciled in the UK will be protected in all the other convention countries.[218]

Qualification by reference to the author

As will be seen in the following chapter, authorship and ownership of copyright are two distinct concepts and it is quite common for copyright to be owned by artificial legal persons, such as corporations. However, it is self-evident that the author of a literary, dramatic, musical or artistic work will be a living (or lately deceased) person. In the case of computer-generated literary, dramatic, musical and artistic works and sound recordings, films and broadcasts, the Copyright, Designs and Patents Act 1988 still defines the author in terms of a 'person', that is the person who makes the arrangements necessary for the creation of the work, makes the work or the broadcast or provides the service, but in relation to these works it would seem that all forms of legal persons, including artificial persons such as corporations, can be the author of the work. The author of the typographical arrangement of a published edition is the publisher and this will often be a corporation such as a limited company. For this reason, the qualification requirements cover the situation where the author is a corporate body.

Under s 154(1) a work will qualify for copyright protection if the author comes within any of the following categories:

(a) a British citizen, a British overseas territories citizen, a British national (Overseas), a British Overseas citizen, a British subject or a British protected person within the meaning of the British Nationality Act 1981;
(b) an individual domiciled or resident in the UK or another country to which the relevant copyright provisions apply;

215 Copyright, Designs and Patents Act 1988 s 153. In relation to Crown Copyright, the qualification requirements are waived in the case of a work made by an officer or servant of the Crown in the course of his duties: s 163(1)(a). Similarly in respect of parliamentary copyright: s 165(1). There are now also provisions in relation to Bills of the Scottish Parliament, Northern Ireland Assembly and the National Assembly of Wales: ss 166A to 166D. Separate provisions also apply in the case of copyright vesting in certain international organisations.

216 The Berne Convention for the Protection of Literary and Artistic Works, 1886.

217 Universal Copyright Convention 1952.

218 *See* Article 5, Berne Convention. Authors from another convention country shall enjoy the same rights which are granted to nationals. The Copyright and Performances (Application to Other Countries) Order 2008, SI 2008/677, makes the necessary legislative provisions. This Order revoked the previous Order and came into force on 6 April 2008. The Order was amended to include Bermuda by the Copyright and Performances (Application to Other Countries) (Amendment) Order 2009, SI 2009/2745. *See also* Article II of the Universal Copyright Convention.

(c) a body incorporated under the law of a part of the UK or another country to which the relevant copyright provisions apply.

219 Copyright, Designs and Patents Act 1988 s 157.

The countries to which these provisions apply can be extended by Order in Council to the Channel Islands, the Isle of Man or any colony.[219] A work also qualifies if at the 'material time' the author was a citizen of or a subject of or domiciled or resident in another country, or if the author was a body incorporated under the law of another country to which the provisions have been extended.[220] Parties to the Berne Convention, the Universal Copyright Convention and countries which otherwise give adequate protection under their law are included.

220 Copyright, Designs and Patents Act 1988 s 159.

The 'material time' is defined in s 154(4) as being, in the case of an unpublished literary, dramatic, musical or artistic work, the time it was made; or, if it was made over a period of time, a substantial part of that period. If published, the material time is the time of first publication. If the author dies before first publication, the material time is the time immediately before the author's death. For sound recordings, films and broadcasts, the material time is the time they were made. For a typographical arrangement of a published edition it is the time when the edition was first published.

A work of joint authorship qualifies for copyright protection if, at the material time, any of the authors satisfy the requirements for qualification by reference to the author, and only those who do satisfy those requirements are to be taken into account for the purpose of first ownership of copyright and duration of copyright.[221]

221 Copyright, Designs and Patents Act 1988 s 154(3).

Qualification by reference to country of first publication or transmission

There is a distinction between broadcasts and all other forms of works. In the case of the latter, under s 155, they qualify for protection if they are first published in the UK or any other country to which the relevant provisions extend or in respect of which an Order has been made under s 159. A publication can still be a first publication even if it is simultaneously published elsewhere, and a period not exceeding 30 days is considered simultaneous. As an example, if a musical work is made by an author who fails to meet the qualification requirements (such as an Iranian living in Tehran) and the work is first published in Iran but is then published in the UK within the following 30 days, the music will attract UK copyright protection under the provisions contained in s 155. The music will be deemed to have been simultaneously published in Iran and the UK.[222]

222 The 30-day rule is a result of Article 3(4) of the Berne Convention.

The meaning of 'publication' is central to these provisions and it is defined in s 175 as being the issue of copies to the public, including by means of electronic retrieval systems in the case of literary, dramatic, musical and artistic works. The construction of a building is equivalent to publication of the work of architecture it represents and any artistic works incorporated in the building.[223] In order to clarify the meaning further, some specified acts are declared not to amount to publication: for example, a performance of a literary, dramatic or musical work, an exhibition of an artistic work, the playing or showing of a sound recording or film in public, or the communication to the public[224] of a literary, dramatic, musical or artistic work or a sound recording or film. Also excluded are the issue to the public of copies of a graphic work (for example, a sketch) representing, or photographs of, a work of architecture in the form of a building or a model for a building, a sculpture or a work of artistic craftsmanship.[225]

223 Copyright, Designs and Patents Act 1988 s 175(3).

224 Communication to the public means communicating to the public by electronic transmission (for example, broadcasting): s 20.

225 Copyright, Designs and Patents Act 1988 s 175(4).

Selling sheet music or video films to the public will be regarded as publication, but selling photographs depicting an original sculpture will not be. Whether the sale of the original sculpture to a member of the public is to be regarded as publication is a moot point and it may be stretching the language of s 175 too far, especially as it talks in terms of the plural. This is reinforced by s 175(5) which excludes publication which is 'merely colourable and not intended to satisfy the reasonable requirements of the public'. This means that a non-qualifying author who intends to sell copies of his work to the public in large numbers in a non-convention country cannot obtain the international benefits of the conventions simply by putting a few copies on sale at the same time in a convention country. However, selling or offering for sale small numbers of copies may still be deemed to be publication if the intention is to satisfy public demand, as in *Francis Day & Hunter Ltd v Feldman & Co*[226] in which the sale of six copies of the song 'You Made Me Love You (I Didn't Want To Do It)' was deemed to be good publication because of the publisher's intention from the outset to satisfy public demand in the UK. Section 175(6) states that no account is to be taken of any unauthorised acts; therefore, publication by a person without the permission of the copyright owner will not have any consequences as regards the qualification requirements for the work involved.

For broadcasts, the qualification requirements are satisfied if they are made from the UK or any country to which the copyright provisions are extended by Order in Council. Qualification is determined by reference to the country from which the broadcast is made and not the country or countries of reception. There is no provision here for dealing with simultaneous broadcasts within a 30-day period.

It can be seen that qualification for copyright protection will rarely be in issue, particularly as a result of the operation of the Berne Convention and the Universal Copyright Convention and the reciprocity they provide for. Under s 160, provisions may be made under an Order in Council to deny protection to citizens or bodies of countries not giving adequate protection to British works. No such Orders have been made.

Duration of copyright

The Copyright, Designs and Patents Act 1988 simplified the provisions relating to the duration of copyright. For example, under the Copyright Act 1956 there were three rules for the duration of copyright in artistic works, depending on which variety of artistic work they were.[227] There were also different rules for works published or unpublished at the time of the author's death.[228] Things are now much clearer, although the transitional arrangements which applied to works in existence at the time when the 1988 Act came into force were not particularly straightforward.[229] The duration of copyright in most of the 'original works' and in films was extended to 'life plus 70 years' by the Duration of Copyright and Rights in Performances Regulations 1995 (the '1995 Regulations').[230] A number of countries outside Europe also extended their term of copyright, notably Australia and the United States. The United States raised the period to life plus 70 years by the Sonny Bono Copyright Term Extension Act 1998. This was challenged as being unconstitutional in *Eldred v Aschcroft*[231] but the challenge was rejected by the US Supreme Court.

The rules for determining the duration of copyright depend on the nature of the work in question but, as a basic rule of thumb, copyright lasts for the life of the author plus 70 years for literary, dramatic, musical and artistic works (the 'original works') and films, and at least 50 years for sound recordings, 50 years for broadcasts and 25 years for typographical arrangements of published editions. Copyright in certain types of artistic works that have been commercially exploited is also limited to 25 years. There are also special rules for the duration of Crown copyright, that is in respect of works of which Her Majesty the Queen is the first owner of the copyright, and parliamentary copyright. Perpetual copyright previously enjoyed by the Universities of Oxford and Cambridge and the Colleges of Eton, Winchester and Westminster in relation to certain works under the Copyright Act 1775 was abolished and such works existing at the time the Copyright,

226 [1914] 2 Ch 728.

227 Copyright Act 1956 s 3.
228 Copyright Act 1956 s 2.

229 *See* Copyright, Designs and Patents Act 1988 Sch 1, para 12.

230 SI 1995/3297, implementing Council Directive 93/98/EEC of 29 October 1993 harmonising the term of copyright and certain related rights, OJ L 290, 29.10.1993, p 9. This Directive has now been replaced by a codified version: Directive 2006/116/EC of the European Parliament and of the Council of 12 December 2006 on the term of protection of copyright and certain related rights, OJ L372, 27.12.2006, p 12.

231 537 US 186 (2003).

232 Copyright, Designs and Patents Act 1988 Sch 1, para 13.

Designs and Patents Act 1988 came into force were given a 50-year copyright, commencing at the end of 1989.[232]

The increase to the duration of copyright in the 'original works' and films had a number of implications, especially in terms of extending the duration of existing copyright and reviving copyright in some works which had fallen into the public domain in the UK. One feature of the modified provisions on duration of copyright is that they are set in the context of the European Economic Area (EEA) and not just the EU.[233] Thus, Iceland, Norway and Liechtenstein are included in the provisions.

233 An EEA state is a state which is a Contracting Party to the EEA Agreement signed at Oporto on 2 May 1992, adjusted by the Protocol signed at Brussels on 17 March 1993: 1995 Regulations reg 2.

Apart from the new rules for determining the duration of copyright for the original works and films, extended and revived copyright and some other aspects of the 1995 Regulations are described towards the end of this chapter.

Literary, dramatic, musical and artistic works

As a rule, the identity of the author of a work will be known and commonly the author will have produced his work on his own, not in collaboration with another author. The copyright in a literary, dramatic, musical or artistic work of known authorship, having a single author, expires at the end of the period of 70 years from the end of the calendar year during which the author dies.[234] Therefore, when the work is made it is impossible to pinpoint the exact time when the copyright will expire; a work created by a relatively young author should have a long copyright, perhaps close to or even exceeding 120 years. If the work is the result of the collaboration of two or more authors and the contribution of each is not distinct from the other or others, it is a work of joint authorship and, under s 12(8), the 70-year period runs from the end of the calendar year during which the last surviving author dies. If the identities of all the authors are not known, the period is calculated by reference to the end of the calendar year during which the last surviving known author dies.

234 Copyright, Designs and Patents Act 1988 s 12(2) (substituted by the Duration of Copyright and Rights in Performances Regulations 1995, SI 1995/3297). Note that there has been some renumbering of the subsections of s 12.

If the country of origin of the work is a non-EEA state and the author is not a national of an EEA state, the duration of copyright is limited to that in the country of origin provided it is not greater than life plus 70 years.[235] Thus, if the country of origin is New Zealand and the author is a citizen of New Zealand, the duration of copyright as far as the countries within the EEA are concerned remains at life plus 50 years, the present term in New Zealand.

235 The meaning of 'country of origin' is described near the end of this chapter in the section on extended and revived copyright.

It is conceivable, though unlikely, that a work might be created by a person unknown.[236] The work may still qualify for protection on the basis of the country of first publication and s 12(3) makes provision for the duration of copyright for works of unknown authorship. Copyright expires at the end of the period of 70 years from the end of the calendar year in which the work was made or, if made available to the public during that period, the 70-year period runs from the end of the calendar year in which the work was first made available to the public.[237] 'Making available to the public' includes, in the case of a literary, dramatic or musical work, a performance in public or communication to the public. For artistic works, it includes public exhibitions, showing a film including the work in public or communication to the public. The definitions are not exhaustive and should also cover acts such as selling or offering to sell to the public copies of the work. In determining whether the work has been made available to the public, no account is taken of any unauthorised act, so that the period of 70 years does not start to run if the work has been performed in public without the permission of the copyright owner. Before the changes made by the 1995 Regulations, copyright in a work of unknown authorship potentially was perpetual, that is if the work was not made available to the public, which seemed to be an anomaly difficult to justify. Even so, the practical effect of this was diluted because, under s 57(1), the copyright in a literary, dramatic, musical or artistic work was not infringed if it was not possible, by reasonable inquiry, to ascertain

236 Of course, there may be situations when, for reasons of his own, the author does not want to be identified and his identity remains a secret between the author and his publisher. In such circumstances, it would appear that the work would be one of unknown authorship for copyright purposes.

237 Copyright, Designs and Patents Act 1988 s 12(3).

the identity of the author and it was reasonable to assume that the copyright had expired or that the author died 50 years or more before the beginning of the calendar year in which the relevant act was done.[238] If the work involved is truly anonymous, there may be considerable difficulties regarding the ownership and enforcement of the copyright, although in such circumstances s 104(4) contains a presumption that the publisher of the work as first published was the owner of the copyright at that time. If the identity of the author becomes known before it would have expired under s 12(3), then the normal rule applies under s 12(2).

The final form of literary, dramatic, musical or artistic work having special provision is where the work is 'computer-generated', being a work generated by computer in circumstances such that there is no human author.[239] Without the life of a human author to measure the term of copyright, the starting date for the 50-year period (which is retained for such works) is sensibly calculated, under s 12(7), from the end of the calendar year in which the work was made.[240] Apart from works of unknown authorship, this is the only form of literary, dramatic, musical or artistic work in which the actual time the work was made is relevant to the duration of copyright.

The duration of protection of certain types of artistic work will be considerably shortened if they are 'commercially' exploited. Under s 52, where an artistic work has been exploited by or with the licence of the copyright owner by making articles which are copies of the work by an industrial process and marketing them, the copyright subsisting in the artistic work will be largely ineffective from the end of the period of 25 years from the end of the calendar year during which the articles were first marketed. The copyright in the artistic work still runs its full course notionally but, after the 25-year period, the work may be copied by making articles of any description or doing anything for making such articles without infringing the copyright. The fine detail was left to the Secretary of State, and by the Copyright (Industrial Processes and Excluded Articles) (No 2) Order 1989[241] an artistic work is deemed to have been exploited for the purposes of s 52 if more than 50 articles have been made or goods manufactured in lengths or pieces not being hand-made have been produced.[242] Certain types of artistic work are excluded from this provision: for example, works of sculpture, wall plaques, medals, medallions and printed matter primarily of a literary or artistic character. Typically, works of artistic craftsmanship will be caught by this reduction in terms of copyright, if exploited. The purpose of these provisions was to prevent artistic works which were to be mass-produced and which were registrable as designs enjoying the longer term of protection under copyright.[243] However, domestic registered design law was changed significantly to comply with a harmonising Directive but neither s 52 nor the 1989 Regulations were modified to reflect the changes to the scope of what can be registered as designs. Consequently, some artistic works that are commercially exploited may enjoy the full term of copyright protection in addition to the monopoly rights given by registration. Examples are designs of computer icons and typefaces. The new system of design law is fully explored in Part Five of the book.

Sound recordings

Until 1 January 1996, both sound recordings and films were governed by the same rules and, for either, the duration of copyright depended on when the work was made or, in some circumstances, when it was released. Now, for sound recordings, under s 13A(2) of the Act, sound recordings are protected for 50 years from the end of the calendar year during which they were made. However, there are two provisos to this and the overall term of copyright in a sound recording can be extended by delaying the time when it is published or, if not published, when it is played or communicated to the public. Thus, if a sound recording is published within 50 years from the end of the calendar year during which it was made, a new 50-year period commences at the end of the calendar year when

238 This presumption still applies but now by reference to the 70-year period: Duration of Copyright and Rights in Performances Regulations 1995, SI 1995/3297 reg 5(2).

239 Copyright, Designs and Patents Act 1988 s 178. Computer-generated works are fully explained and discussed in Chapter 8.

240 Unchanged by SI 1995/3297, though previously this provision was contained in old s 12(3).

241 SI 1989/1070.

242 SI 1989/1070 reg 2.

243 The maximum term of protection as a registered design is 25 years.

it was first published. If, during that first 50-year period, instead of being published,[244] the sound recording is played in public or communicated to the public (for example, by broadcasting), the new 50-year period runs from the end of the calendar year when it was so played or communicated. No account is taken of any unauthorised act in determining duration. Where the author of a sound recording is not a national of an EEA state, the duration is limited to that available in the country of which he is a national providing this is not longer than under s 13A(2) – unless this would be at variance with an international obligation to which the UK became subject prior to 29 October 1993 (the date of the term of copyright Directive), in which case the rule in s 13A(2) applies.

Films

Until 1 January 1996, the duration of copyright in films was as for sound recordings but the changes wrought by the Duration of Copyright and Rights in Performances Regulations 1995 include a similar means of determining copyright in films as applies to the original works, that is, based on life plus 70 years. This reflects the view that certain types of films are more akin to artistic works than derivative works. Indeed, Article 2 of the Berne Convention includes cinematograph works in the literary and artistic work category. A number of different persons who make a creative contribution to the film are used to provide the relevant 'life'. Under s 13B, copyright in a film expires at the end of the period of 70 years from the end of the calendar year during which the death of the last to die of the following occurs:

- the principal director
- the author of the screenplay
- the author of the dialogue
- the composer of music specially created for and used with the film.

In the event that there is no person in the above list (that is, where the film was made without a director, screenplay, dialogue or specially written music) the period is 50 years from the end of the calendar year during which the film was made: s 13B(9). This could be in the case of a film recorded by closed circuit television ('CCTV') or a surveillance camera.

If the identity of the persons referred to above is unknown, under s 13B(4) the duration is 70 years from the end of the calendar year during which it was made. However, if it was made available to the public during that time, a fresh 70-year period commences from the end of the calendar year when it was so made available. Making available to the public means showing in public or communicating to the public (under s 20(2) this means broadcasting or making available by electronic transmission so that members of the public can access the work at a time and place of their choosing: for example, by placing the work on a website). If the identity of any of those persons becomes known before the expiry of copyright under s 13B(4), the normal rules apply.

Where the country of origin is not an EEA state and none of the authors are nationals of an EEA state, the term of protection is limited to that in the country of origin providing it is not longer than under s 13B(2) to (6).

Broadcasts

245 As amended by the Copyright and Related Rights Regulations 2003, SI 2003/2498.

246 For example, see *British Leyland Motor Corp Ltd v Armstrong Patents Co Ltd* [1986] 2 WLR 400 and *Purefoy Engineering Ltd v Sykes Boxall Ltd* (1955) 72 RPC 89.

A period of 50 years from the end of the calendar year during which the broadcast is made is the duration of copyright in broadcast: s 14(2).[245] Copyright is deemed to exist in a repeat broadcast but this expires at the same time as the original, subject to there being no copyright in a repeat broadcast made after the expiry of the copyright in the original: s 14(5). Copyright in repeats may seem unnecessary as the concept of indirect copying has been accepted by the courts for some time[246] and now has statutory effect under s 16(3). At first sight, copyright in repeats might seem useful when no tangible copy is made, such as where a person without permission receives a broadcast and simultaneously relays it to others, but communication to the public (which includes broadcasting) is amongst the acts restricted by copyright.

Section 14(6) states that a repeat broadcast is one which is a repeat of a broadcast previously made. Under s 14(3), where an author of a broadcast is not a national of an EEA state, the duration is that of the relevant state provided it is not greater than that in s 14(2) unless contrary to an international obligation to which the UK became subject before 29 October 1993: s 14(4).

Typographical arrangements of published editions

The copyright in a typographical arrangement of a published edition expires at the end of the period of 25 years from the end of the calendar year in which the edition was first published.[247] Under s 175(1)(a), publication for typographical arrangements of published editions occurs when copies were issued to the public. It does not include making available to the public by means of an electronic retrieval system as this applies only to literary, dramatic, musical or artistic works.

247 Copyright, Designs and Patents Act 1988 s 15.

Crown and parliamentary copyright

Crown copyright subsists in works made by Her Majesty or by an officer or servant of the Crown in the course of his duties. Crown copyright in a literary, dramatic, musical or artistic work lasts until the end of the period of 125 years from the end of the calendar year in which the work was made or, if the work is published commercially before the end of the period of 75 years from the end of the calendar year in which it is made, copyright continues to subsist until the end of the period of 50 years from the end of the calendar year in which it was first published commercially.[248] Therefore, if a work of Crown copyright is published in the first year it was created, it will have copyright protection for only 50 years from the end of that year. Commercial publication in relation to a literary, dramatic, musical or artistic work means, under s 175(2), issuing copies to the public at a time when copies made in advance of the receipt of orders are generally available to the public or when the work is available to the public by means of an electronic retrieval system.

248 Copyright, Designs and Patents Act 1988 s 163(3).

There are no special provisions for Crown copyright as regards the other types of copyright work, so the usual rules will apply. In the case of a work of joint authorship where one or more of the authors, but not all, fall within the requirement for Crown copyright, the provisions in s 163 apply only in relation to those authors and the copyright subsisting by virtue of their contribution to the work.[249] Does this mean that the rights of the other joint author(s) are unaffected by Crown copyright? This could be problematical as s 10(1) provides that, by definition, a work of joint authorship is a collaborative one in which the work of each joint author is not distinct. Taken to its logical conclusion, this could mean that the copyright subsisting in such a work of joint authorship would have, theoretically, two durations, which is a nonsense.

249 Copyright, Designs and Patents Act 1988 s 163(4).

Her Majesty is entitled to copyright in every Act of Parliament, Act of the Scottish Parliament, Measure or Act of the National Assembly for Wales, Act of the Northern Ireland Assembly and Measures of the General Synod of the Church of England which are protected by copyright from Royal Assent until the end of the period of 50 years from the end of the calendar year in which the Act or Measure received the Royal Assent (or, in the case of a Measure of the National Assembly for Wales, 50 years from the end of the calendar year during which the Measure was approved by Her Majesty in Council).[250] No other copyright or right in the nature of copyright subsists in an Act or Measure. Thus, there can be no publication right or database right in relation to Acts and Measures.

250 Copyright, Designs and Patents Act 1988 s 164(2).

Parliamentary copyright applies to works made by or under the direction or control of the House of Commons or the House of Lords. Parliamentary copyright in a literary, dramatic, musical or artistic work continues to subsist until the end of the period of 50 years from the end of the calendar year in which the work was made.[251] Works within this category include reports of select committees. The duration of copyright in sound recordings, films and broadcasts is in accordance with the usual rules. Parliamentary Bills are separately provided for under s 166, and copyright in a Bill expires when the Bill receives the Royal Assent, at which time the copyright in the new Act commences, or, if the Bill does not receive Royal Assent, copyright expires when the Bill is withdrawn or rejected or at the end of the Session. There are similar provisions for Bills of the Scottish Parliament, Northern Ireland Assembly and Measures and Bills of the National Assembly for Wales.[252]

Providing for copyright in Acts of Parliament and other legislative material is a controversial issue, especially as Her Majesty's Stationery Office became more active in enforcing that copyright.[253] It could be argued that such works should be in the public domain, as it is in the public interest that Her Majesty's subjects are aware of the law. No less than Laddie J suggested that such materials should be freely available.[254]

There was a significant relaxation in HMSO's approach to use of Crown copyright material by publishers. A 'Dear Publisher' letter was placed on the internet by HMSO, dated 1 March 1996. It allowed reproduction without permission or charge of Acts of Parliament, Statutory Instruments and Statutory Rules and Orders and certain Press Releases (though not for providing a commercial Crown Press Release Service). This was all subject to the text being 'value-added' (for example, where the publisher has included annotations or comments), the source being acknowledged as Crown copyright and the material being reproduced accurately and in such a way as not to be misleading. Reproduction could be worldwide and by electronic means. Since then, unrestricted copying of certain categories of Crown copyright material is allowed. This includes legislation and court forms and, although copyright still subsists in such material, copyright is waived. The condition that the material is reproduced accurately and not in a misleading context remains and it is still required to acknowledge the work correctly and to identify the source and status of the material.

Peter Pan by *Sir James Matthew Barrie*

As a special concession to the Great Ormond Street Hospital for Sick Children, to which Sir James Barrie donated his copyright in the play *Peter Pan*, a *sui generis* right to continue to receive royalties beyond the life of the copyright was provided for in the Copyright, Designs and Patents Act 1988. This was the result of an amendment moved by Lord Callaghan. The copyright in the play *Peter Pan* expired on midnight 31 December 1987, and under s 301 of and Sch 6 to the Act, royalties are payable to the Hospital for Sick Children, Great Ormond Street, London, in respect of any public performance, commercial publication or communication to the public of the whole or a substantial part of the play or an adaptation of it. The right is not absolute and will come to an end if the hospital ceases to have a separate identity or no longer cares for sick children. However, as a result of the Duration of Copyright and Rights in Performances Regulations 1995,[255] discussed below, it would appear that the copyright in *Peter Pan* was revived and expired in EEA states at the end of the year 2007. Presumably, the above provisions are suspended until that time as the Great Ormond Street Hospital now has full rights of ownership, as any owner of revived copyright, in relation to the work. Indeed, the special jurisdiction of the Copyright Tribunal to determine the royalty in the absence of agreement has been removed by reg 24(2)(b) of the Copyright and Related Rights Regulations 1996.[256] However, as the copyright has been revived, it will be subject to licences as of right following notice and, in the absence of agreement as to royalty, referable to the Copyright

251 Copyright, Designs and Patents Act 1988 s 165.

252 *See* ss 166A to 166D.

253 The Stationery Office Ltd now controls the former HMSO bookshops. A residual HMSO administers Crown copyright.

254 Gibb, F. 'Attack on Copyright', *The Times*, 5 December 1995, p 41.

255 SI 1995/3297.

256 SI 1996/2967.

Tribunal under reg 25 of the 1995 Regulations instead. Although achieved in a different manner, the result is the same.

The position in the United States as regards *Peter Pan* is somewhat doubtful. Great Ormond Street Hospital claims *Peter Pan* is protected by copyright there until the end of 2023 on the basis of a script for the play first published there in 1928.[257]

Extended copyright, revived copyright and other aspects of the 1995 Regulations

The Duration of Copyright and Rights in Performances Regulations 1995[258] increased the term of copyright for original literary, dramatic, musical and artistic works and films.[259] There are some important transitional provisions to deal with cases where existing copyright is extended, for example, as to who will own the extended copyright and the position in respect of pre-existing licences, and where copyright is revived. Before looking at these provisions and other aspects of the 1995 Regulations, it is important to note the appropriate definitions which are contained in regs 12 and 14.

An 'existing work' is one made before commencement of the 1995 Regulations (1 January 1996) and an 'existing copyright work' is one in which copyright subsisted immediately before commencement (that is, 31 December 1995). '1988 provisions' means the provisions of the Copyright, Designs and Patents Act 1988 immediately before commencement of the 1995 Regulations. The 'new provisions' are those of the Act as amended by the 1995 Regulations.

Under reg 15(1), copyright in an existing copyright work will continue to subsist until the date it would have expired under the 1988 provisions if that date is later than provided for under the 1995 Regulations. This preserves the duration of works that were, prior to the Copyright, Designs and Patents Act 1988, works of perpetual copyright or unpublished works or where the work was published after the author's death. For example, perpetual copyright was conferred on works of certain universities and colleges by the Copyright Act 1775 and this was reduced to 50 years from the end of the year of commencement of the 1988 provisions. As regards works published after an author's death, consider an author of a literary work who died in 1958. His work was not published until 1987. Under the Copyright Act 1956, his copyright would not expire until the end of 2037 (50 years after publication).[260] The 1988 provisions maintained this rule with a cut-off from the end of the year of commencement.[261] Under the new provisions, copyright would be based solely on the year of the author's death and would expire at the end of 2028. As a result of the transitional provisions, the copyright will continue until the end of 2037.

Changes to the method of calculating the duration of copyright in sound recordings brought about by reg 29 of the Copyright and Related Rights Regulations 2003 could prejudice the saving in reg 15 of the 1995 Regulations but reg 39 of the 2003 Regulations preserves the effect of reg 15 of the 1995 Regulations if this would result in copyright expiring later than under the changes made by the 2003 Regulations.

Under reg 15(2), there is a saving such that where the above rule applies the provisions in s 57 (assumptions as to expiry of copyright in anonymous or pseudonymous works) are unmodified (that is, where it is reasonable to assume that the author died 50 years ago). The 1995 Regulations increase that period to 70 years in other cases.

The new provisions as to duration, as described earlier, apply to:

- copyright works made after commencement;
- existing works which first qualify for copyright protection after commencement (for example, where the author, being a Taiwanese citizen, created the work in 1992, but the work is first published in the UK after 1 January 1996);
- existing copyright works (subject to reg 15 above);

257 The US Copyright Act 1976 (17 USC) allowed a maximum of 95 years (being made up of 28 and 67 years) to certain pre-existing works: § 304.

258 SI 1995/3297, implementing Council Directive 93/98/EEC of 29 October 1993 harmonising the term of copyright and certain related rights, OJ L 290, 29.10.1993, p 9. This Directive has now been replaced by a codified version Directive 2006/116/EC of the European Parliament and of the Council of 12 December 2006 on the term of protection of copyright and certain related rights, OJ L372, 27.12.2006, p 12.

259 There are some changes in respect of rights in performances also, for which *see* Chapter 9.

260 Copyright Act 1956 s 2(3).

261 Copyright, Designs and Patents Act 1988 Sch 1, para 1.

- existing works in which copyright expired before 31 December 1995 but which, on 1 July 1995, were protected in another EEA state (1 July 1995 is the date that the Directive on harmonising the term of copyright and certain related rights should have been complied with).

Extended and revived copyright

Regulation 17 defines 'extended copyright' and 'revived copyright' as follows:

- extended copyright is any copyright which subsists by virtue of the new provisions after the date on which it would have expired under the 1988 provisions;
- revived copyright is any copyright which subsists by virtue of the new provisions after having expired under the 1988 provisions or any earlier copyright enactment.

Regulation 18 states the rules for determining who the owner of extended copyright is and it is the person owning the copyright immediately before commencement of the new provisions. However, if that person did not own the copyright for the full term under the 1988 provisions, the extended copyright is part of the reversionary interest. For example, if Mary owns the copyright in a literary work and the copyright was to expire at the end of 1999, it will continue to subsist until the end of 2019 and Mary will continue to be its owner. If, on 31 December 1990, Mary assigned the copyright to Jacob for seven calendar years, on 1 January 1998 the copyright will revert to her and she will be the owner of the remaining term of copyright (that is, from 1 January 1998 to 31 December 2019, when it will finally expire).

The owner of revived copyright is, under reg 19, the owner at the time the copyright expired. If the former owner died before commencement of the new provisions (or ceased to exist if a corporation), the revived copyright vests in:

- for films the principal director or his personal representatives;
- for other works the author or his personal representatives.

The personal representatives hold the revived copyright for the benefit of the person who would have been entitled to it had it been part of the director or author's estate immediately before his death and devolved as part of that estate.

There are provisions for prospective ownership of extended or revived copyright which are similar to those applying to prospective ownership of future copyright, as discussed in the following chapter. Under reg 20, where, by an agreement made before commencement of the new provisions, the prospective owner of extended or revived copyright purports to assign that copyright wholly or partly, in writing and signed by the prospective owner, then if on commencement the assignee or person claiming through him would be entitled as against all other persons to require the copyright to be vested in him, the copyright shall so vest in the assignee or successor in title.

Any licence granted by the prospective owner will, as under normal copyright rules, bind every successor in title of his except a purchaser in good faith for valuable consideration without actual or constructive knowledge of the licence. Persons deriving title from such a person will also take free of the licence.

There has to be provision for dealing with pre-existing licences and other rights and obligations. Under reg 21, any copyright licence, term or condition of an agreement relating to the exploitation of a copyright work or waiver or assertion of moral rights will continue to have effect during the extended term of copyright, subject to agreement to the contrary, provided:

- the licence, term, waiver, etc existed immediately before commencement of the new provisions in relation to an existing copyright work; and
- it is not to expire before the end of the copyright period under the 1988 provisions.

There is an equivalent provision regarding licences, terms or conditions imposed by order of the Copyright Tribunal, subject to any further order of the Copyright Tribunal. Revived copyright could cause particular concern. For example, what about a person who, *bona fide*, performs acts within the scope of copyright in relation to a work in which copyright has expired in the UK. Suddenly, that person could be prevented from doing something he was previously doing quite lawfully. Regulation 23 contains some savings to cover such a situation to the effect that:

- no act done before commencement infringes revived copyright;
- it is not an infringement of revived copyright –
  - to do anything after commencement in pursuance of arrangements made before 1 January 1995 at a time copyright did not subsist in the work, or
  - to issue to the public after commencement copies of a work made before 1 July 1995 at a time copyright did not subsist in the work;
- there are equivalent provisions for literary, dramatic, musical, artistic works and films containing copies or adaptations of works in which revived copyright subsists;
- it is not an infringement of revived copyright to do after commencement anything which is a restricted act in relation to the work if the act is done at a time when (or in pursuance of arrangements made at a time when) the name and address of a person entitled to authorise the act cannot by reasonable inquiry be ascertained;
- it is not an infringement of a moral right to do anything which, by the above provisions, does not infringe copyright.

Where these savings do not apply, licences are available as of right in relation to revived copyright (unless a licensing body could have granted the relevant rights) under reg 24. The licence as of right is subject to payment of a reasonable royalty, to be fixed by the Copyright Tribunal in default of agreement. However, the person intending to take advantage of the licence of right provisions must give reasonable notice of his intention to the copyright owner, stating when he intends to begin the acts concerned. Absence of a notice will mean the carrying out of the acts will not be treated as licensed.

Revived copyright could apply in many cases. Before the changes resulting from the Directive on the term of copyright, Germany already granted protection for life plus 70 years.[262] One hypothetical example of revived copyright could be where Hans, a German composer, wrote a piece of music in 1935. He published it both in Germany and in the UK (within a few days of the German publication) during that year, hence gaining German and UK copyright. Hans died in 1944. The UK copyright expired at the end of 1994, but the German copyright was still in existence at 1 July 1995. Therefore, the UK copyright was revived on 1 January 1996 and will continue to subsist until the end of 2014.

Now imagine that the music was created instead by Edward, a British citizen, who also died in 1944. The work was not published in Germany within the 30-day rule,[263] so he had no German copyright. Say that Edward's work was copied without permission in Germany during 1997 and his estate brought an action in Germany on the basis of the Berne Convention for the Protection of Literary and Artistic Works. If the German court held that the action must fail because the UK copyright had expired, this could be deemed to be discrimination on the ground of nationality contrary to Article 18 of the Treaty on the Functioning of the European Union ('TFEU'). The reason is that, had Edward been a German citizen, his copyright would still subsist and be enforceable in Germany. One of the implications of Joined Cases C-92/92 and C-362/92 *Collins* v *Imtrat Handelsgesellschaft mbH*[264] is that such discrimination is not permissible and, on that basis, it is at least arguable that Edward's UK copyright also should be revived. In other words, all works in which copyright expired in the UK between 1 January 1975 and 31 December 1995 should be revived, whether or not they had copyright in another EEA state on 1 July 1995.

262 Spain granted life plus 80 years.

263 Under the Copyright Act 1911 s 35(3), the publication in the other country would have to be within 14 days, not 30 days.

264 [1993] ECR I-5145. This case is discussed further in Chapter 24, *see* p 936.

The utility of revived copyright was seen in *Sweeney* v *MacMillan Publishers Ltd*.[265] The claimants were the trustees of the late James Joyce and the defendant published in 1997 a reader's edition of the James Joyce novel *Ulysses*. Under the Copyright Act 1956, the copyright expired at the end of 1991 as James Joyce died during 1941. However, the copyright was revived as from 1 January 1995, after the work had spent four years in the public domain. The defence in reg 23 was not available as most of the work was done after 1 January 1995 and not during the four-year 'limbo' period and could not properly be said to have been done in pursuance of arrangements made during that period. However, reg 24 applied and the defendants could take a licence of right in return for payment of a reasonable royalty. The only problem for the defendant was that its book contained material from other sources, also administered by the trustees, which were still subject to conventional copyright and, in respect of those parts, the trustees could simply refuse to grant a licence to the defendant.

Other aspects

The country of origin of a work may be important in some cases in the determination of duration of copyright. Basically, if the country of origin is an EEA state, the provisions on duration in the 1995 Regulations will apply. If the country of origin is a non-EEA state, then the duration will be that provided for by the country of origin though not longer than that set out in the 1995 Regulations. The test for determining the country of origin is not a simple one.

Country of origin is defined in the Copyright, Designs and Patents Act 1988 s 15A (inserted by reg 8), as being:

● if first published in a Berne country and not published simultaneously elsewhere, that country;
● if first published simultaneously in two or more countries, one of which is a Berne country, the Berne country is the country of origin;
● if first published simultaneously in two or more Berne countries:
  – if any is an EEA state, that country
  – if none is an EEA state, the country of origin is the Berne country providing the shortest term of protection;
● if first published in a non-Berne country:
  – if a film and the maker has his headquarters or is domiciled in or resident in a Berne country, that country
  – if the work is a work of architecture constructed in a Berne country or an artistic work incorporated in such a building, the Berne country is the country of origin
  – in any other case, the country of origin is the country of which the author is a national.

There is a permitted act in relation to films: the Copyright, Designs and Patents Act 1988 s 66A.[266] The copyright in a film is not infringed if:

● it is not possible by reasonable inquiry to ascertain the identity of any of the persons (by reference to whom duration can be fixed); and
● it is reasonable to assume that copyright has expired or the last of those persons has been dead for 70 years or more before the beginning of the calendar year during which the relevant act was done or arrangements are made.

This is equivalent to s 57 (assumptions on expiry of copyright in anonymous or pseudonymous literary, dramatic, musical or artistic works).

Regulation 13 deals with the case where a film is protected but not as a film. Where a film is protected not as a film, but as an original dramatic work or by virtue of photographs forming part of the film, reference to copyright in a film includes references to other such copyrights.

The sound track of a film is now considered as part of the film and the definition of 'film' is amended accordingly.[267] References in the Act to showing a film now include playing the sound track, though playing a sound recording does not include playing the film sound track to accompany the film.[268] There are some further provisions in terms of moral rights and amendments to the law relating to rights in performances (*see* Chapters 5 and 9).

Appropriate consequential amendments are made to the Copyright, Designs and Patents Act 1988 to account for the new term of copyright and the new definitions.

Publication right

A person may own an old original manuscript which is out of copyright, the author having died more than 70 years ago. Perhaps the manuscript has never been published, but the current owner would like to publish it and sell copies, or grant a licence to a publisher to do so. With no copyright to protect against unauthorised copies being made and sold, the economic incentive to publish would be limited. To overcome this problem, a publication right was introduced by the Copyright and Related Rights Regulations 1996.[269] It has some of the appearances of a copyright and, under reg 16(1), is declared to be a property right equivalent to copyright. The publication right applies where a literary, dramatic, musical or artistic work or a film is, after the expiry of copyright, published for the first time. It then endures for 25 years from the end of the calendar year during which it was first published. Publication includes any making available to the public, in particular:

- the issue of copies to the public;
- making the work available by means of an electronic retrieval system;
- the rental or lending of copies to the public;
- the performance, exhibition or showing in public;
- communicating the work to the public.[270]

Unauthorised acts, being without the consent of the owner of the physical medium in or on which the work is embodied or recorded, are not taken into account. Consequently, the publication right can only belong to a person who makes the publication subject to such consent. As the right cannot arise until there has been first publication (with the consent of the owner of the physical medium), any prior unauthorised act cannot infringe the publication right. There may, however, be other legal remedies, such as breach of confidence, conversion or the criminal offence of theft. Unauthorised copying and publication could be deemed to be an assumption of the rights of the owner and, even if the physical medium is only 'borrowed', the circumstances could be such to be equivalent to an intention permanently to deprive the owner.

As with normal copyright, there are some qualification requirements being that the first publication must take place in the European Economic Area (EEA) and the publisher is, at that time, a national of an EEA state or, in the case of a joint publication, at least one of the joint publishers is. There is no provision for the 30-day period of grace which applies to qualification for copyright protection under the Copyright, Designs and Patents Act 1988 s 155 (simultaneous publication). The right cannot arise in relation to works which were subject to Crown copyright or parliamentary copyright.

Under reg 17, most of the copyright provisions will apply to the publication right as they do to copyright,[271] subject to some omissions and modifications. In particular:

- There are no moral rights in respect of the publication right.
- A small number of the permitted acts do not apply (ss 57, 64 and 66A).
- The presumptions as to the identity of the author, owner, director, producer, etc. in ss 104–106 do not apply.

267 Copyright, Designs and Patents Act 1988, s 5B. Section 5A defines a sound recording which is as before.

268 Copyright, Designs and Patents Act s 5B(3). This now also applies to communicating a sound recording to the public, copying a sound recording or issuing, rental or lending to the public of copies of a sound track. The changes to s 5B(3) were made by the Performances (Moral Rights, etc.) Regulations 2006, SI 2006/18 as from 1 February 2006.

269 SI 1996/2967. The publication right came from Article 4, Council Directive 93/98/EEC of 29 October 1993 harmonising the term of copyright and certain related rights, OJ L 290, 24.11.1993, p 9. This Directive has since been repealed and replaced by Directive 2006/116/EC of the European Parliament and of the Council of 12 December 2006 on the term of protection of copyright and certain related rights (codified version), OJ L372, 27.12.2006, p 12. The equivalent provision is Article 4.

270 SI 1996/2967 reg 16(2).

271 Thus, infringement of the publication right is the same as for copyright.

- The exception to the licensing scheme provisions in Chapter VII (for licences or licensing schemes covering works of more than one author for licences or schemes covering only single collective works or collective works of which the authors are the same, or works made by, or by employees of or commissioned by, a single individual, firm, company or group of companies) does not apply to the publication right.
- The maximum penalty for the offences of making or dealing with infringing articles is only three months and/or a fine not exceeding level five on the standard scale.

Other relevant provisions, including Chapter VIII of the Copyright, Designs and Patents Act 1988 on the Copyright Tribunal, apply *mutatis mutandis*, and other enactments relating to copyright apply in relation to the publication right as they do to copyright, unless the context requires otherwise.

The publication right provisions came into force on 1 December 1996. No act done before this date can infringe the right, nor can anything done in pursuance of an agreement made before 19 November 1992 (the date of adoption of the rental right Directive, which was also implemented by the 1996 Regulations).

The publication right could encourage the greater dissemination of old works where, until now, the owner of the physical medium has declined to publish because of concerns about unauthorised copying or piracy. It could now be worth considering publishing a book of old legal documents such as wills, deeds of conveyance, leases and even copyright assignments. Anyone discovering an old, hitherto unknown, music score by a great composer might similarly be tempted to publish.

Table 3.1 shows the duration of copyright as it applies to the various types of works, including the publication right (this is of course a simplification).

Table 3.1 Duration of copyright

Type of work	Event	Duration: from end of year of event
Literary, dramatic, musical or artistic		
Known author	Author dies	70 years
Unknown author	Work made	70 years
	Or, if made available to the public within that 70 years	70 years from the end of the calendar year during which it was first so made available
Computer-generated work	Work made	50 years
Joint authors	Death of last surviving known author	70 years
Sound recordings	Sound recording made	50 years
	Or, if during that period it is published	50 years from publication
	Or, if during that period it is not published but made available to the public or communicated to the public	50 years from making available or communicating to the public
Films	Last to die among: ● principal director ● author of screenplay ● author of dialogue ● composer of music specially created for and used for the film	70 years
Broadcasts	Broadcast made	50 years
Typographical arrangements of published editions	First publication	25 years

Table 3.1 *cont'd*

Type of work	Event	Duration: from end of year of event
Crown and Parliamentary copyright, etc.		
Literary, dramatic, musical or artistic works	Work made	125 years
	Or, if published commercially within first 75 years	50 years from the end of the calendar year of commercial publication
Acts and Measures	Royal Assent	50 years
Parliamentary copyright	Work made	50 years
Parliamentary Bills[272]	Bill made (presumably)	Until Royal Assent or rejection
Publication right		
Unpublished literary, dramatic, musical or artistic work or a film in which copyright had previously expired	First publication with consent of the owner of the medium containing the work	25 years

272 Including Bills of the Scottish Parliament, National Assembly for Wales and the Northern Ireland Assembly.

Notes:

Duration is measured from the end of the calendar year in which the event occurred.

Copyright subsists before the commencement of the period shown, from the time at which the work is first recorded or made.

In effect, copyright in certain types of artistic works which have been exploited is reduced to 25 years (at least copying articles which are copies of artistic works does not infringe). The types of artistic works covered by this were those which would generally have been registrable as designs (though the changes to design law have somewhat compromised this aim).

Summary

Copyright may subsist in a wide variety of works. These are:

- original literary, dramatic, musical or artistic works;
- sound recordings, films and broadcasts;
- typographical arrangements of published editions.

Further clarification is given as to the meaning of copyright works: for example, literary works include tables, compilations, computer programs, preparatory design material for computer programs and databases. Most definitions are not exhaustive.

The word 'original' does not mean that a work is novel or unique; simply that it is the author's own work and has not been copied from another work. However, for computer programs and copyright databases (which are among the category of original literary works), these are required to be the author's own intellectual creation.

Some principles (perhaps better described as rules of thumb) in determining whether a work is protected as an original work of copyright are:

- a work which is the result of effort only will not be protected by copyright;
- copyright protects the expression of an idea but not the idea itself and a work which is deemed to be an idea will not be protected;
- very small or trivial works are not protected.

Amongst the artistic works category, particular difficulties exist in determining the scope of 'a work of artistic craftsmanship' and a 'sculpture'.

The definitions of sound recordings and films are quite wide. Broadcasts include transmissions over the ether and by cable. They do not generally include material made available online such that persons can access the material at a time and place they decide.

For UK copyright to exist in a work, it must qualify for protection. There are a number of ways this can be satisfied, such as where the author is a British Citizen or the work is first published in the UK (there is a 30-day 'period of grace' for this).

Copyright has a long duration in most cases. The basic rule is the life of the author plus 70 years (copyright expires 70 years from the end of the calendar year during which the author dies). Where the work is one of joint authorship, the 70 years runs from the end of the calendar year during which the last surviving author dies. Different rules apply to some works, for example, computer-generated works, sound recordings, broadcasts, typographical arrangements or works of unknown authorship.

The duration of copyright for the original works (excluding computer-generated works) and films in 1996. This resulted in special provisions for extended and revived copyright.

A publication right exists which applies where a work in which copyright had expired is first published after expiry of copyright. It applies to the original works and films and gives 25 years' protection. It would apply, for example, to old previously unpublished manuscripts, drawings and musical scores (such as a newly discovered concerto written by Mozart).

Discussion questions

1 Should it be a requirement for protection that all the original works of copyright be the author's own intellectual creation?

2 What is the idea/expression dichotomy and consider how this applies under (a) US copyright law, and (b) UK copyright law.

3 Why should a work of artistic craftsmanship require some sort of artistic quality and/or be the result of the hands of a craftsman when most other forms of artistic work are declared to be protected 'irrespective of artistic quality'?

4 Consider the scope of 'sculpture' as a form of artistic work and case law on the meaning of the term. Discuss whether you think the Supreme Court decision in *Lucasfilm* v *Ainsworth* is satisfactory or should there be further modification or clarification of the meaning of 'sculpture'.

5 Under what circumstances are works made available through a website deemed to be broadcasts?

Selected further reading

Arnold, R., 'Reflections on the "Triumph of Music": copyright and performers' rights in music' [2010] *Intellectual Property Quarterly*, 153 (looks at copyright and performers' rights in music; reflects on the meaning of 'music' and authorship; and discusses recent case law such as *Fisher* v *Brooker* and *Beckingham* v *Hodgens* – the part on performers' rights is relevant to Chapter 9).

Rosati, E., 'Originality in US and UK copyright experiences as a springboard for EU-wide reform debate', [2010] *International Review of Intellectual Property and Competition Law*, 524 (looks at EU reform and at originality in the US and UK, including how it has evolved and considers the value of originality in relation to reform and harmonisation).

World Intellectual Property Organization, *'Learn from the past, create the future: the arts and copyright'* (2010 edition) available at: **http://www.wipo.int/freepublications/en/copyright/935/wipo_pub_935.pdf** (a light-hearted and fun look at the basics of copyright from the perspective of artists – also useful for subsequent chapters on copyright).

Lucasfilm Ltd v *Ainsworth* [2011] UKSC 39, available at: **http://www.supremecourt.gov.uk/docs/UKSC_2010_0015_Judgment.pdf** (this case is also important in relation to Chapter 26 IPR and conflict of laws).

Authorship and ownership of copyright 4

Introduction

As copyright is a property right, this raises important questions about ownership and the mechanisms for exploiting copyright. Authorship and ownership are, in relation to copyright, two distinct concepts, each of which attracts its own peculiar rights: the author having moral rights, and the owner of the copyright possessing economic rights. Sometimes, the author of a work will also be the owner of the copyright in the work, but this is not always so, and many works have separate authors and owners as far as copyright is concerned. Ownership flows from authorship; the person who makes the work is normally the first owner of the copyright in the work, provided that he has not created the work in the course of employment, in which case his employer will normally be the first owner of the copyright.[1] The owner of the copyright in a work may decide to exploit the work by the use of one or more contractual methods. He may grant a licence to allow another person to carry out certain acts in relation to the work, such as making copies, in which case he retains the ownership of the copyright. Alternatively, the owner may assign the copyright to another, that is, transfer the ownership of the copyright to a new owner, relinquishing the economic rights under copyright law. One point to bear in mind is that a third party can carry out certain acts in relation to the whole or a part of a work protected by copyright without the permission of the owner of the copyright in the work and without infringing the copyright in the work, for example, by performing one of the acts falling within the fair dealing provisions, or because the act is not restricted by the copyright. There is little that the owner of the copyright can do about these limitations and exceptions to copyright protection apart from denying access to the work itself, for example, by refusing to publish the work.

Consider a single work in which copyright subsists. There may be several relationships and activities connected with the work and the copyright to the work. Figure 4.1 (overleaf) shows the relationships that might exist in relation to a work.

1 The author is the person who has created the work in question.
2 The copyright in the work is owned by a person who might be the author or the author's employer or a person who has become the owner of the copyright because the title to the copyright has been transferred to him.
3 With respect to the work, there are certain acts which are restricted by the copyright. These 'restricted acts' (an example is making a copy of a work) can be carried out only by the owner of the copyright or by someone having the owner's permission, such as a licensee. Otherwise, subject to certain exceptions and limitations, the copyright in the work will be infringed.

1 There are other exceptions: *see* below.

91

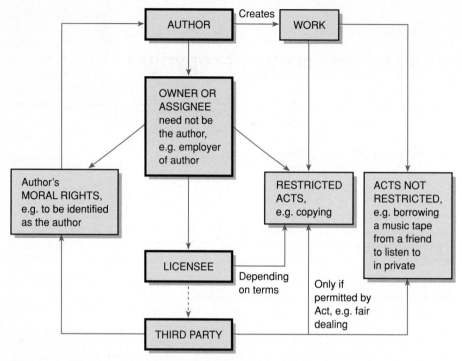

Figure 4.1 Mechanism of copyright

Notes:

1 The third party may be a member of the general public or a sub-licensee.

2 The licensee may also carry out the permitted acts and any acts not restricted by the copyright, subject to the terms of the agreement.

3 A licence may impose obligations on the licensor preventing him from doing certain acts himself.

4 The copyright owner can grant licences in respect of the work which will allow the licensee to do all or some of the restricted acts, in accordance with the terms of the licence. Sometimes, a licensee will be permitted to grant sub-licences to others.

5 The copyright owner and any licensees and sub-licensees, subject to the terms of the licence agreement, will be able to carry out all or some of the restricted acts.

6 A third party, for example, a member of the general public, can carry out a restricted act *only* if it is permitted by copyright law (for example, the permitted acts of fair dealing for criticism or review) or some other defence applies, such as the public interest defence.

7 Any person can carry out acts in relation to the work that are *not* acts restricted by copyright, such as lending to a friend a book or a music CD to listen to in private, or reading a book. There may, however, be contractual restrictions affecting such acts.

8 All persons, including the owner of the copyright, licensees, sub-licensees and members of the public generally, must respect the author's moral rights. The author may be able to enforce his moral rights irrespective of the identity of the present owner of the copyright (provided that the author has asserted his right to be identified as author and has not otherwise waived it).

Authorship

2 Copyright, Designs and Patents Act 1988 s 9(1). Unless otherwise stated, statutory references are to the Copyright, Designs and Patents Act 1988.

3 *Waterlow Publishers Ltd v Rose* [1995] FSR 207, which concerned, *inter alia*, the authorship of *The Solicitors' Diary and Directory.*

4 [1995] FSR 818.

The author of a work is the person who creates it.[2] In terms of some types of works this will be self-evident: for example, the author of a work of literature is the person who writes it; the author of a piece of music is its composer; the author of a photograph is the photographer and so on. The author of a compilation is the person who gathers or organises the material contained within it and who selects, orders and arranges that material.[3] The author does not have to be the person who carries out the physical act of creating the work, such as by putting pencil to paper. An amanuensis taking down dictation is not the author of the resulting work. In *Cala Homes (South) Ltd v Alfred McAlpine Homes East Ltd*,[4] drawings were made by draughtsmen, but another person had told them what features were to be incorporated in the designs for new houses. In some cases, that information was imparted by means of sketches, in other cases, verbally. The person giving the instructions also marked up the preliminary drawings with alterations he required to be incorporated in the finished drawings. Laddie J said that what is protected by copyright is more than just the skill of making marks on paper or some other medium, and that it was wrong to think that only the person who performs the mechanical acts of fixation is the author. He held that the person giving the instructions was a co-author of the drawings and, hence, the claimant, for whom he worked as design director, was a joint owner of the copyright.

5 [1998] FSR 622.

According to Lightman J in *Robin Ray* v *Classic FM plc*,[5] where he reviewed the decision in *Cala Homes* above, the author of a work does not have to exercise penmanship but something akin to penmanship is required. Someone acting as a mere scribe, producing the copyright expression accurately in accordance with instructions, but without making any creative contribution whatsoever, can never be an author or co-author of a work. Lightman J was of the view that there must be that essential creative input, a 'direct responsibility for what actually appears on the paper', to satisfy the test of authorship. Apart from cases of amanuensis, circumstances where a person has not produced the form of expression but is still deemed to be an author or co-author will be rare. In this respect *Cala Homes* was exceptional as the design director gave very detailed instructions to the architects who prepared the plans and could be said to have made a very significant contribution to the finished work.

With some types of works, further explanation of authorship is required and this is furnished by the Copyright, Designs and Patents Act 1988. Under s 9(2), the author of a broadcast is the person making the broadcast, including, in the case of a broadcast relaying another broadcast by reception and immediate re-transmission, the person making that other broadcast. The publisher of the typographical arrangement of a published edition is considered to be its author. If the work is a computer-generated literary, dramatic, musical or artistic work, which is generated by computer in circumstances such that there is no human author, the author is deemed to be the person by whom the arrangements necessary for the creation of the work are undertaken,[6] a formula similar to that for sound recordings.

6 Copyright, Designs and Patents Act 1988 s 9(3).

7 SI 1996/2967.

8 Copyright, Designs and Patents Act 1988 s 9(2)(aa).

9 Copyright, Designs and Patents Act 1988 s 9(2)(ab).

The author of a sound recording or film used to be simply the person by whom the arrangements necessary for its making are undertaken. As a result of the Copyright and Related Rights Regulations 1996,[7] the author of a sound recording is the producer[8] and the joint authors of a film are the producer and principal director.[9] Unless the producer and principal director are one and the same, a film is treated as a work of joint authorship under s 10(1A). The term 'producer' is defined in s 178, in relation to a sound recording or film, as the person by whom the arrangements necessary for the making of the sound recording or film are undertaken. Hence, for sound recordings the result is the same as before, but for films this is a major change. Previously, a film director was not the author or one of the authors, although film directors did enjoy moral rights in respect of their films. This change applied as from 1 December 1996 in relation to films made on or after 1 July 1994. The reason for the latter date is that the European Union Directives on rental and lending rights and on the term of protection of copyright, both of which contained this provision, allowed Member States to choose not to apply it to films made before that date.

Copyright protects only the expression of an idea, so there may be occasions when the originator of the information that forms the basis of the work in question will not be considered to be the author of the work. For example, in *Springfield v Thame*[10] the claimant, a journalist, supplied newspapers with information in the form of an article. The editor of the *Daily Mail*, from that information, composed a paragraph which appeared in the newspaper. It was held that the claimant was not the author of the paragraph as printed in the newspaper. Similarly, a person making a speech in public will not be the author of a report of the speech made by reporters. In *Walter v Lane*,[11] reporters for *The Times* made reports of the speeches of Lord Roseberry which were printed verbatim after they had been corrected and revised. It was held that the reporters were the authors of the reports and, as a result of the terms of the reporters' employment, the copyright in the reports belonged to *The Times*. In the latter case, it can be argued that the reporters had used skill and judgment in making, correcting and revising the reports and adding punctuation and structure. However, as noted above, if a person is simply writing down dictation, the person dictating will be the author for copyright purposes, as the person doing the writing is simply the agent by which the work is made.[12] The distinction is a fine but important one, as authorship will determine first ownership of the copyright.

In principle, there is nothing to prevent a corporate body being the author of a work, as s 154(1)(c) recognises that a work may qualify for copyright protection if the author is a body incorporated under the law of the UK. This may apply in the case of a sound recording, where the work in question is the result of arrangements made by senior officers of a music company or under the direction or delegated powers of such senior officers,[13] in which case the company can be deemed to be the author. If the person who makes the arrangements in practice is lower down in the company hierarchy so that his actions are not automatically deemed to be the actions of the company, the company will probably still *own* the copyright (as opposed to being the author) on the basis of the employer/employee relationship or because of some contractual provision. The identification of the author is important for determining the first ownership of copyright and also for measuring the duration of the copyright. In the case of many of the original works, the copyright expires at the end of the period of 70 years from the end of the calendar year during which the author died.[14]

The Copyright, Designs and Patents Act 1988 recognises that the identity of the author may not always be known. A work is of 'unknown authorship' if the identity of the author is unknown or, in the case of a work of joint authorship, the identity of none of the authors is known. The identity of an author is regarded as unknown if it is not possible for a *person* to ascertain the identity of the author by reasonable inquiry.[15] It is not clear who the 'person' referred to might be. One possibility is that it is the person wishing to copy the work, making the test subjective;[16] on the other hand, it may be the ubiquitous 'reasonable man', an objective test. The work may be truly anonymous or it may be pseudonymous, that is the author does not wish his identity to be disclosed. The Berne Convention for the Protection of Literary and Artistic Works, by Article 15, makes presumptions in the case of anonymous and pseudonymous works and there is no requirement under UK copyright law that the identity of the author be disclosed to ultimate purchasers of material incorporating the copyright work, for example purchasers of books written by the author. This has little significance, other than with respect to the duration of the copyright in the work concerned, and may be relevant in terms of infringement,[17] and evidentially as regards ownership.

10 (1903) 19 TLR 650. Originality would be in issue now.

11 [1900] AC 539.

12 The principle cannot apply when a person at a séance produces a work under the influence of a person long since dead. In *Cummins v Bond* [1927] 1 Ch 167, the medium who had written down the work was the author, not the extraterrestrial psychic being. The judge said he must confine his inquiry to persons alive at the time the work was made.

13 An analogous principle in criminal law is that of corporate liability, where a company can be criminally liable on the basis of acts or omissions of its senior officers who are deemed to be the 'brains' or directing mind of the company. See the judgment of Lord Denning MR in *H L Bolton (Engineering) Co Ltd v T J Graham & Sons Ltd* [1957] 1 QB 159 at 172 and *Tesco Supermarkets Ltd v Nattrass* [1972] AC 153. This might be an issue in relation to whether a failure to renew a patent is the fault of the patentee on the basis of whether the person at fault was the directing mind of the patentee; see *Textron Inc's Patent* [1989] RPC 441, per Lord Oliver and Lord Goff, discussed in Chapter 11 (*see* p 410).

14 Duration of Copyright and Rights in Performances Regulations 1995.

15 *See* Copyright, Designs and Patents Act 1988 s 9(4) and (5). Section 9(5) further states that once the author's identity is known, it cannot subsequently be regarded as unknown.

16 See Merkin, R. (1989) *Copyright, Designs and Patents: The New Law*, Longman, p 50.

17 The Copyright, Designs and Patents Act 1988 s 57(1) provides for permitted acts on the basis of certain assumptions as to the expiry of copyright or death of the author in relation to anonymous and pseudonymous works. *See* Chapter 7.

Frequently, a work will be the result of the efforts of more than one person. Several employees may work together to produce a written report, a team of computer programmers and systems analysts together may produce a computer program, two or more persons may collaborate in the writing of a work of literature, a piece of music or the painting of a landscape in oils. Collaboration between two or more persons will result in a work of joint authorship only if their respective contributions to the finished work are not distinct from each other, under s 10(1); that is, the work cannot be broken down so that each author's contribution can be separately identified. Thus, an abstract oil painting created by two painters applying paint to create an effect previously agreed by them would be a work of joint authorship. A book comprising separate chapters written by different authors is not a work of joint authorship; neither is a song where one person has written the music and another has written the words, as in a Gilbert and Sullivan operetta. In the latter cases, each person involved will be the author of his own distinct work, and, in the case of a song, the person writing the music will be the author of the musical work while the person writing the lyrics will be the author of those lyrics, as a literary work. Two copyrights will exist in the song, each having different authors (and, possibly, different owners) and the duration of the copyright in the music and the lyrics will differ according to the dates when the composer and lyricist die.

There is no requirement that the authors intend to create a work of joint authorship: the question is simply that the authors collaborated and created a work in which their contributions are not separate. In *Hodgens* v *Beckingham*,[18] counsel submitted that there must be an intention to create a work of joint authorship.[19] This was rejected by the Court of Appeal, which confirmed the decision below that an artiste known as Bobby Valentino wrote part of the music for the song 'Young at Heart'. Jonathan Parker LJ said that there was nothing in the statutory wording to require the imposition of such a requirement.[20]

The act of collaboration may involve taking part of an existing work and reworking it so as to make it significantly different. In *Fisher* v *Brooker*[21] the claimant was the organist who played the organ solo in the famous work by Procul Harum known as 'Whiter Shade of Pale'. The part had originally been written for the piano by the first defendant but the claimant reinvented it for the organ. Blackburne J said at para 42:

. . . it is abundantly clear to me that Mr Fisher's instrumental introduction (i.e. the organ solo as heard in the first eight bars of the Work and as repeated) is sufficiently different from what Mr Brooker had composed on the piano to qualify in law, and by a wide margin, as an original contribution to the Work. The result in law is that Mr Fisher qualifies to be regarded as a joint author of the Work and, subject to the points to which I shall next turn, to share in the ownership of the musical copyright in it.

The claimant was awarded a 40 per cent share in the song as a musical work.[22] However, because of his inordinate delay in bringing the action, Mr Fisher was held to have gratuitously licensed the defendants to exploit the work. Blackburne J made the following declarations:

1 [Mr Fisher] is a co-author of . . . 'A Whiter Shade of Pale' as recorded by . . . Procul Harum ('the work') and released as a single on 12 May 1967.
2 [Mr] Fisher is a joint owner in the musical copyright in the work, with a share of 40 per cent.
3 The [defendants'] licence to exploit the work was revoked on 31 May 2005.

On appeal to the Court of Appeal,[23] the majority judges held that defences of acquiescence and laches applied so as to deprive Mr Fisher from a share in the future exploitation of the song. The Court still recognised that he had a 40 per cent share in the copyright. Because of the delay in bringing the claim, the defendants had not suffered any detriment and had received royalties, part of which would have otherwise gone to Mr Fisher. Unlike proprietary estoppel, there is no requirement for detriment. It is not altogether clear whether the organ solo could be considered to be a collaborative work given that the

18 [2003] EMLR 18.

19 This was based on a decision of the Canadian Supreme Court in *Nuedorf (Darryl)* v *Nettwerk Expressions* [2000] RPC 935 where the judge said that there must be an intention to combine the contributions into a unitary whole and each joint owner must have intended the other to be a joint author.

20 This aspect of the case turned on the wording of s 11(3) of the Copyright Act 1956 which was very similar to s 10(1) of the 1988 Act; the only significant difference was that the former said the contributions were not separate whereas the latter said that they were not distinct.

21 [2007] FSR 12.

22 Defences based on estoppel failed; *see* the discussion of this aspect of the case in Chapter 7.

23 *Brooker* v *Fisher* [2008] FSR 26. The defence of impossibility of a fair trial due to the passing of time failed as did the defence of proprietary estoppel. Detriment is an essential element of that defence and the defendants failed to show detriment.

finished organ solo was so different to what had been written by the defendant considering that a work of joint authorship is one where the contribution of each author is not distinct. The House of Lords overturned the Court of Appeal decision and reinstated the declarations of Blackburne J.[24] Lord Neuberger suggested that acquiescence was essentially another form of estoppel as well as being an example of the doctrine of laches. As laches is an equitable doctrine, it cannot apply to a declaration of a statutory right to property. It may be relevant to an application for an injunction, leaving the claimant with a right to damages only. The majority decision in the Court of Appeal recognised that Mr Fisher had a 40 per cent share in the copyright but refused, on equitable grounds, to declare that the right existed. That was clearly wrong in principle.

24 *Fisher* v *Brooker* [2009] FSR 25.

A person may make a significant contribution to the creation or development of a work of copyright and yet may fail to be a joint author. It is a matter of looking at the process of creation of the work and identifying the nature of the contribution. It must be a contribution which relates to bringing about the subsistence of copyright rather than the creation of the subject matter of that copyright. In other words, the joint author must have made a significant contribution in terms of the skill and judgment required to endow copyright on the subject matter. For example, in *Fylde Microsystems Ltd* v *Key Radio Systems Ltd*,[25] the defendant claimed that he was co-author of computer software used in mobile and portable radios of the sort used by security guards. The defendant's contribution was substantial in testing the software and reporting errors and making suggestions as to the cause of some of the faults. The defendant's employees had also been involved in developing the specification for the software. However, the software was entirely written by the claimant's employees. It was held that the defendant was not a joint owner of the copyright subsisting in the software as the contribution made by the defendant's employees did not amount to an act of authorship. Considerable time may have been saved by the efforts of the defendant's employees. Their work, particularly in testing the software, involved skill and judgment but it was not an authorship skill. An analogy between testing software and proofreading a conventional literary work found favour with the judge.

25 [1998] FSR 449.

A person who contributes suggestions, ideas and information to assist the author create a work will not, without more, be a joint author of the finished work. In *Robin Ray* v *Classic FM plc*,[26] the late Robin Ray was a recognised expert on classical music with very extensive knowledge of the subject. He was commissioned by the defendant to advise on its repertoire of classic music to be played on its radio station. He produced and submitted proposals for detailed classifications of musical works in five documents and wrote a catalogue of music. Some information in the catalogue was provided to him by the defendant's employees who also made some suggestions. However, it was accepted by the judge that Robin Ray provided the most important input by his selection of tracks and assessment of the popularity of those tracks. The defendant's contribution was primarily to assist Robin Ray in his work of creating the catalogue. Lightman J said (at 637):

26 [1998] FSR 622.

> . . . the plaintiff was solely responsible as author for the writing of the five documents and the catalogue and the way the ideas were expressed in them. He was not, as submitted by the defendant, 'the team scribe'. The fact that the documents in part (and in fact only in a relatively small, though significant, part) reflect the defendant's representatives' input is totally insufficient to make the defendant joint author.

This reinforces the view that even a significant contribution cannot guarantee co-authorship; it has to be inexorably linked with the creative input required to produce a work of copyright. If a person says to an artist, 'Why don't you go down to the river and paint the arch-bridge with the church spire in the background at sunset?' that does not mean that the person who made that suggestion will be a joint author of the completed painting, even if he helped to carry the artist's canvas and paints and helped to mix the paints. Of course, this does not prevent a person who has not put pen to paper from being a joint author providing the contribution is towards the creation of the work in which copyright subsists.[27] This will apply only in exceptional cases. Changes to a dramatic work made during rehearsals after input by the director of the play were not sufficient to give the director joint authorship. It might have been different if the director and writer had collaborated to develop the plot even if the finished play was written by the writer only.[28]

Refusing to give joint authorship to a person who contributes ideas only is entirely consistent with the principle that copyright protects expression not ideas. Whilst a significant or substantial input into the creative spark that gives rise to copyright is required for joint authorship, it is clear that the contributions of joint authors need not be equal. In determining whether a contribution is significant or substantial, it is suggested that regard ought to be had to the relative quantitative and qualitative contributions of the joint authors.[29]

Joint authorship in terms of films is unlikely to be contentious as the general rule is now that a film is a work of joint authorship. The producer and principal director are joint authors, unless they are one and the same person.[30]

In the case of a broadcast, s 10(2) provides that it will be treated as a work of joint authorship where more than one person is to be taken to be making the broadcast. References to the person making the broadcast or a transmission which is a broadcast are, under s 6(3), to the person transmitting the programme if he has responsibility to any extent for the content of the broadcast and to any person providing the programme who makes, with the person transmitting it, the arrangements necessary for its transmission. References to 'programme' in the context of broadcasting are to any item included in a broadcast.

Ownership

The Copyright, Designs and Patents Act 1988 s 11 states the basic rule that the author of a work is the first owner of the copyright. This will apply in a good number of cases, for example to persons creating works for their own pleasure or amusement, independent persons not employed under a contract of employment and even to employed persons if the work in question has not been created in the course of their employment. However, there are some exceptions to this basic rule, and where a literary, dramatic, musical or artistic work or a film is made by an employee in the course of his employment, his employer is the first owner of the copyright subsisting in the work subject to any agreement to the contrary.[31] It is not required that the agreement to the contrary has to be between the employer and employee, whether express or implied, but can be between the employer and a third party. In *Cyprotex Discovery Ltd* v *University of Sheffield*,[32] an employee of Cyprotex wrote computer programs for Sheffield University under a sponsorship scheme. The agreement to the contrary was between Cyprotex and the University which provided for ownership of intellectual property rights arising from a research project under which the employee worked. An example of an implied term to the contrary between employer and employee is given in *Noah* v *Shuba*[33] where it was held that the copyright in a work created by an employee in the course of his employment could still belong to the employee on the basis of a term implied on the ground of past practice. If the employee's name appears on the work or copies of the work, there is a presumption that the work was not made in the course of employment.[34]

Other exceptions relate to Crown copyright and parliamentary copyright. Her Majesty the Queen is the first owner of the copyright in her own works and in works produced by an officer or servant of the Crown in the course of his duties, and of the copyright subsisting in Acts of Parliament, the Scottish Parliament, Measures and Acts of the National

27 See *Cala Homes (South) Ltd* v *Alfred McAlpine Homes East Ltd* [1995] FSR 818.

28 *Brighton* v *Jones* [2005] FSR 288.

29 *Neudorf (Darryl)* v *Nettwerk Expressions Ltd* [2000] RPC 935, Supreme Court of British Columbia. In *Bamgboye* v *Reed* [2004] EMLR 5 it was held that the claimant was entitled to a one-third share.

30 Copyright, Designs and Patents Act 1988 s 10(1A).

31 Copyright, Designs and Patents Act 1988 s 11(2).

32 [2004] RPC 44.

33 [1991] FSR 14.

34 Copyright, Designs and Patents Act 1988 s 104(2).

Assembly of Wales, Acts of the Northern Ireland Assembly and Measures of the General Synod of the Church of England.[35]

One issue in respect of Crown copyright is whether works created by some types of organisation, such as NHS Trusts, can be regarded as being Crown copyright. Can persons working for such organisations be properly described as officers or servants of the Crown? Under the 1956 Act, the test was wider in that it required the work to be made under the direction or control of the Crown, or was so published.[36] This could have applied to a situation where a body was exercising powers devolved from the appropriate Secretary of State. There seems to be no relevant authority under copyright law, but there are some patent cases. For example, in *Pfizer Corp v Minister of Health*,[37] use of a patented drug to treat patients in an NHS hospital was deemed to be use for the services of the Crown, and in *Dory v Sheffield Health Authority*[38] it was accepted that a health authority was a government department for the purposes of the Patents Act 1977 s 55,[39] exercising powers of the Secretary of State on his behalf. However, the test under patent law is more widely expressed than under the 1988 Act, being in relation to acts done 'for the services of the Crown'. Determination of this issue may be important where an NHS Trust has created a work, for example computer software, for its own purposes, but then realises that it can exploit it commercially, by licensing its use to other NHS Trusts.

If a work is made by or under the direction or control of either or both Houses of Parliament, the first owner of the copyright is the appropriate House or Houses.[40] This includes Bills, public, private and personal. There are equivalent provisions for Bills of the Scottish Parliament and the Northern Ireland Assembly and proposed Measures and Bills of the National Assembly for Wales.[41]

A final exception to the general rule applies to original literary, dramatic, musical or artistic works made by an officer or employee of certain international organisations, or published by the organisation and which do not otherwise qualify for copyright by reference to the author or country of first publication. In such cases, under s 168(1), copyright is declared to subsist in the work and the organisation concerned is deemed to be the first owner of the copyright in the work. The relevant international organisations are designated by Order in Council and include the United Nations and the Organisation for Economic Co-operation and Development. Unlike the position under the Copyright Act 1956, the copyright in certain commissioned works no longer vests in the first instance in the commissioner of the work.[42]

The ownership of the copyright subsisting in anonymous works can present problems, as there is no author available or willing to give evidence as to the ownership. To cope with the evidential difficulties associated with anonymous works, s 104(4) contains a presumption that the publisher of an anonymous work is the owner of the copyright in the work at the time of first publication unless the contrary is proved, provided that the work qualifies for protection by reason of the country of first publication and the name of the publisher appears on copies of the work as first published. In *Warwick Film Productions Ltd v Eisinger*,[43] the claimant failed to rebut the equivalent presumption under the Copyright Act 1956 in relation to an anonymous work, *Oscar Wilde: Three Times Tried*, first published in or around 1911.

If a work is a work of joint authorship, unless the authors are employees acting in the course of employment, the joint authors will automatically become the joint first owners of the copyright in the work.[44] They will own the copyright as tenants in common and not as joint tenants: *Lauri v Renad*.[45] This means that effectively each owner's rights accruing under the copyright are separate from the others, and he can assign his rights to another without requiring the permission of the other owners, and on his death his rights will pass, as part of his estate, to his personal representatives. Where the whole or a part of a copyright is assigned to two or more persons, they will hold as tenants in common, unless the agreement states otherwise. As copyright can be considered as a bundle of rights,

---

35 Copyright, Designs and Patents Act 1988 ss 163 and 164.

36 Copyright Act 1956 s 39.

37 [1965] AC 512.

38 [1991] FSR 221.

39 Use of patented inventions for services of the Crown.

40 Copyright, Designs and Patents Act 1988 s 165.

41 Copyright, Designs and Patents Act 1988 ss 166A to 166D.

42 This applied to commissioned photographs, portraits (painted or drawn) and engravings provided they were made for money or money's worth: Copyright Act 1956 s 4(3).

43 [1967] 3 All ER 367.

44 Subject to other provisions relating to Crown copyright, parliamentary copyright, etc.

45 [1892] 3 Ch 402. However, where the co-owners have some relationship such as husband and wife, it may be reasonable to infer that they hold the copyright as joint tenants and not as tenants in common: *see Mail Newspapers plc v Express Newspapers plc* [1987] FSR 90. On the death of one joint tenant, the other automatically takes the whole copyright.

an assignment might be partial. For example, the owner, C, of a copyright in a dramatic work might assign the right to perform the work in public to new joint owners X and Y, and the right to publish paper copies of the work to W and Z jointly. The original owner, C, will remain the sole owner of the remainder of the copyright which will include, *inter alia*, the right to translate the work. However, simply granting one right to one person and another right to another person does not make them joint owners. Each will be the sole owner of that part of the copyright, for example, where there is an assignment of the paper publication right to X and an assignment of the public performance right to Y.

Contractual agreements providing for ownership of copyright (and other intellectual property rights) can present problems of interpretation, particularly if the performance of the contract is not precisely as envisaged or definitions are imprecise. In *Cyprotex Discovery Ltd v University of Sheffield*,[46] the University had developed computer programs to simulate the effects of new drugs on the human body under the Symcyp Project. The software was not suitable for commercial use and it was decided to write it in a form suitable for a Windows-based environment under a sponsorship deal. The plan was that sponsors would be given royalty-free non-exclusive licences and that the intellectual property rights would belong to the University. A research agreement was drawn up between the University and Cyprotex under which Dr Edwards, an employee of Cyprotex, would carry out the programming work. Before the work was completed, there was a dispute as to the ownership of the copyright. Unlike the position with other sponsors, the University agreed to pay a contribution towards the costs of Cyprotex's programmer. Clause 9(b) of the agreement stated that intellectual property rights resulting from the project conceived or made by employees and agents of the University alone or jointly with employees of the sponsors in relation to the performance of the project ('Resulting IPR') would belong to the University. However, clause 9(d) stated that intellectual property rights made solely by employees of the sponsor ('Sponsor IPR') should belong to the sponsor. The Court of Appeal held that clause 9(d) must be read as subject to clause 9(b) and the work carried out by Dr Edwards fell within clause 9(b) as an agent of the University. Clause 9(d) covered work *related* to the project whereas clause 9(b) concerned the project itself. This gave a commercially sensible result as the other sponsors had provided funding for the project in the expectation that the University would own the rights and grant them royalty-free licences.

Beneficial ownership and implied licences

There may be occasions when the operation of the basic rule regarding first ownership results in an injustice. For example, a consultant may produce a work for a client in circumstances in which the client expects that he will own the copyright in the finished work and pays the consultant accordingly. However, if there is no provision for the assignment of the copyright and the consultant cannot be classed as an employee working in the course of his employment, the consultant will be the first owner of the copyright. The consultant may realise the implications of this position and may decide later either to interfere with the client's exploitation of the work or to deal with the work himself without the client's permission. The first possibility, that is where the consultant attempts to interfere with the client's use or marketing of the work, should be defeated on the basis of non-derogation from grant,[47] or alternatively on the basis of an implied licence. Both the first and second possibility can be overcome if the court is willing to use equitable principles to infer beneficial ownership.[48] This was done in the case of *Warner* v *Gestetner Ltd*,[49] in which Warner, who was an expert in the drawing of cats, agreed orally to produce some drawings to be used by Gestetner to promote a new product at a trade fair. Gestetner subsequently used the drawings for promotional literature, and Warner complained that this went beyond the agreement and infringed his copyright. Warner remained the owner of the copyright in the drawings because it had not been assigned to Gestetner.

46 [2004] RPC 44.

47 See *British Leyland Motor Corp Ltd* v *Armstrong Patent Co Ltd* [1986] 2 WLR 400.

48 If beneficial ownership is found, the courts are likely to order a formal assignment of the legal title to the copyright to the beneficial owner.

49 [1988] EIPR D-89.

However, Whitford J found that he could imply a term granting beneficial ownership of the copyright to Gestetner. Thus, the copyright had two owners, one at law and one at equity, and Gestetner, as beneficial owner, could deal with the work as it wished, Warner's legal interest in the copyright being of little practical significance (although infringement actions are much less effective if brought by a beneficial owner without the legal owner being joined as a party).[50] The concept of two owners, one legal and one beneficial, is used extensively in the law of real property, but there have been other examples of its application to intellectual property law. For example, in *Ironside* v *Attorney-General*[51] it was held that an agreement for the design of the reverse face of coins gave rise to an assignment in equity, or alternatively an implied licence.[52] Of course, to be able to imply beneficial ownership, the creator of the work should have been paid a fixed sum rather than a royalty, as the latter is inconsistent with a transfer of ownership. Both the above cases involved a lump sum payment.

The use of beneficial ownership has to be consistent with the overall tenor of the agreement. *Warner* v *Gestetner* was distinguished in *Saphena Computing Ltd* v *Allied Collection Agencies Ltd*[53] where a software developer had developed new computer software under the agreement. It is common for software developers to license their software to other customers in the future. The grant of non-exclusive licences in respect of computer software, even if written for a particular client, is common and this is inconsistent with beneficial ownership. Furthermore, the Court of Appeal considered that, in order to give the agreement business efficacy, there was no reason to imply a term that beneficial interest should pass to the client. This is not to say that beneficial ownership can never arise in relation to computer software. It depends on the circumstances. If the common intention is that the client will be the only person using the software, such an implied term might be appropriate. For example, in John *Richardson Computers Ltd* v *Flanders*,[54] computer software developed by an ex-employee acting as a consultant to his former employer gave rise to beneficial ownership in favour of the latter.

A less contrived approach than implying beneficial ownership which would, in many cases, have the same effect in practical terms, would be for the court to imply a term to the effect that the commissioner of a work has a licence to continue to use the work. This approach was taken by Lord Denning MR in *Blair* v *Osborne & Tomkins*[55] in which an architect was commissioned to draw building plans for the purpose of obtaining planning permission for some houses. The site for which the plans had been drawn was then sold with the benefit of the planning permission and the plans were transferred to the purchaser, who employed his own surveyors who modified the plans for building regulations approval and put their name on the plans. Eventually, houses were built in accordance with the plans, and the architect sued for infringement of copyright. It was held that the architect owned the copyright in the plans and there had been an infringement by the surveyors who had submitted the plans to the council in their own name, but only nominal damages were appropriate as no harm was suffered by the architect as a result of this.[56] On the issue of the building of houses by the purchaser of the land in accordance with the architect's plans, it was held that the purchaser had an implied licence to use the plans for this purpose. The person who commissioned the architect had such an implied licence which extended to the making of copies of the plans to be used in respect of that site only and not for any other purpose, and this implied licence extended to any purchaser of the site. The rationale for thus deciding this case was that the architect had received his fee once, and failure to imply a licence would have meant that the architect would have been able to charge a second fee to the purchaser of the site without having to carry out any further work. It must be noted that the scope of the licence was limited to building the houses on that site only, and the purchaser would have been prevented from building further houses in accordance with the plans on other sites.

50 Generally, on his own, a beneficial owner will be entitled to interim remedy only. See also *Bookmakers' Afternoon Greyhound Services Ltd* v *Wilf Gilbert (Staffordshire) Ltd* [1994] FSR 723 at 735–37 per Aldous J. In that case, equitable title to copyright in race cards was based on an intention to assign copyright.

51 [1988] RPC 197.

52 See also *Performing Right Society Ltd* v *London Theatre of Varieties Ltd* [1924] AC 1, discussed later.

53 [1995] FSR 616.

54 [1993] FSR 497.

55 [1971] 2 WLR 503.

56 Nowadays, the architect would have an action under the Copyright, Designs and Patents Act 1988 s 77 for infringement of his right to be identified as the author, provided he had asserted this right.

Architects usually operate under a standard form contract that provides that the copyright in the architectural plans remains with the architect. Where, part way through a development, a builder goes into administration, the administrator may wish to sell the partly completed development and pass on the architectural drawings to the buyer. Subject to confidentiality issues, there will not normally be a problem if all that is done is to pass on the drawings for use by the buyer. It is only when copies are made that copyright issues may come into play. In *Thurgood* v *Coyle*,[57] the contract under which the development was being carried out appeared to limit the use of the drawings to works under the contract. Lewison J did not read the contract as having that effect, as a matter of construction and also for practical reasons. For example, the builder would have wanted to be able to continue to use the drawings if the contract was terminated for whatever reason. It was held that the licence was transferable and the buyer would be able to use and reproduce the drawings.

Sometimes a licence may be implied in unexpected circumstances because it is needed to give business efficacy to a contract. In *Taylor* v *Rive Droit Music Ltd*,[58] it was held that a licence would be implied to a song writer to continue working on a song after the copyright in the unfinished draft had vested to a publisher under a publishing agreement. Such a licence would not, however, extend to enable others to collaborate on further work to the song as this could compromise the publisher's ability to exploit the work (for example, by giving the others joint ownership of the copyright in the version they had worked on).[59] This would amount to derogation from grant. A licence was implied in *Brighton* v *Jones*[60] in respect of work done by the defendant on a draft script for a play sent to the defendant by the claimant.

In deciding whether to grant beneficial ownership or an implied licence, a minimalist approach should be used, granting the least rights required to satisfy the commercial reality of the circumstances. There is no justification for granting beneficial ownership when an implied licence will produce a fair and reasonable result that is workable in practice. Perhaps the best analysis of the considerations to be taken into account is that set out by Lightman J in *Robin Ray* v *Classic FM plc*[61] in the context of a contractor (creator of the work) working for a client. What he said is summarised below.

1 The contractor is entitled to ownership subject to any express or implied term to contrary effect.
2 The contract may itself expressly provide for entitlement to ownership.
3 The mere fact that a contractor has been commissioned to create the work in question is insufficient to entitle the client to the copyright.
4 The implication of terms into a contract was firmly established in *Liverpool City Council* v *Irwin*[62] (the term must be reasonable and equitable, must be necessary for business efficacy to the contract and no term will be implied if the contract is effective without it, the term must be so obvious that 'it goes without saying', it must be capable of clear expression and, finally, it must not contradict any express term).
5 Where it is necessary to imply a term to fill some lacuna in the contract, a minimalist approach should be taken in deciding which of the alternatives should be used, implying that which is necessary and no more.
6 If it is necessary to imply some term in respect of a copyright work and either an assignment or the grant of a licence will do, then the grant of a licence only should be implied.
7 Circumstances may exist where an assignment may be appropriate, including where the client needs in addition to the right to use the work, the right to prevent the contractor from using it and the right to enforce it against third parties (for example, where the purpose was to allow the client to make and sell copies of the work in the absence of competition from the contractor or third parties) or where the work is derivative of

57 [2007] EWHC 2696 (Ch).

58 [2004] EWHC 1605 (Ch).

59 However, the Court of Appeal put a different construction on the agreement which meant that there was no need to imply a licence: *Taylor* v *Rive Droit Music Ltd* [2006] EMLR 52.

60 [2005] FSR 288.

61 [1998] FSR 622 at 641ff.

62 [1977] AC 239.

an existing work belonging to the client or where the contractor is part of a team made up of employees of the client to create a composite or joint work in circumstances such as the contractor is unable, or cannot have been intended to be able, to exploit the work for his own benefit (including any distinct contribution of his). Lightman J said '[i]n each case it is necessary to consider the price paid, the impact on the Contractor of assignment of copyright and whether it can sensibly have been intended that the Contractor should retain any copyright as a separate item of property'.

8 If necessity only requires the grant of a licence, the ambit must be the minimum to secure to the client the entitlement to which the parties must have intended. The price paid may be a factor.

9 The licence accordingly is to be limited to what is in the joint contemplation of the parties at the date of the contract, and does not extend to enable the Client to take advantage of a new unexpected profitable opportunity.

Implying beneficial ownership or a licence, as the case may be, may only be made if it is necessary and then only of what is necessary and no more. The test is, therefore, one of strict necessity.[63]

In *Griggs Group Ltd* v *Evans (No 2)*,[64] there was some criticism of point 7 above, particularly where Lightman J asked whether it could be sensibly intended that the contractor should be able to retain the copyright as a separate item of property. This appears to contradict the first point which raises a presumption that it is the contractor who is entitled to the copyright in the absence of any express or implied terms to the contrary. Jacob LJ said (at para 15) that this could be resolved by putting the question another way round, being 'given that Parliament vests the first ownership in the author, is it sensible that the parties intended that to remain the position?' Otherwise, he thought Lightman J's summary of the position masterful.

In *Griggs Group Ltd* v *Evans*, the claimant made and sold boots under the Dr Martens trade mark.[65] It also used its own trade mark 'AirWair' with its boots. Eventually, it decided to combine the two marks and engaged the first defendant, Mr Evans, who worked for a small advertising agency, Irwin Jordan Ltd. He created the combined logo for the claimant in 1988. Irwin Jordan ceased trading but not before it purported to assign the copyright in the combined logo to the claimant, but this was ineffective as Mr Evans was an independent contractor and not an employee. He had been paid £15 per hour by Irwin Jordan for the work in designing the logo. There was no evidence of any agreement as to copyright ownership and it was accepted that Mr Evans was indeed the owner of the legal title to the copyright.

Later, after failed negotiations between the claimant and Mr Evans concerning an assignment of the copyright to the claimant, Mr Evans assigned the copyright to the second defendant and competitor of the claimant, an Australian Footwear Company, called Raben Footwear Pty Ltd.

At first instance,[66] the judge held that the claimant was entitled to beneficial ownership of the copyright subsisting in the logo. It was argued that, adopting Lightman J's minimalist approach, all the claimant needed was an implied licence to use the logo in the UK as it appeared that the parties thought that the logo was to be used only in the UK. Jacob LJ said that this conclusion was fantastic. If the 'officious bystander' was present when the agreement to design the logo was made and asked whether Mr Evans was to retain any rights in the logo and could use it as against the claimant, the answer would surely have been 'of course not'. Jacob LJ also agreed that the judge was right to find that Mr Evans had been paid the proper rate for the job and rejected the notion that he would have charged more had he known about the wider intended use.

An implied licence may be appropriate to cover some prior use and exploitation of a work preceding a decision affecting copyright ownership. This will be quite rare. One example

63 Per Mr Robert Ham QC, as deputy judge of the High Court, applying the 'Robin Ray' guidelines in *Meridian International Services Ltd* v *Richardson* [2007] EWHC 2539 (Ch) at para 60. The term sought to be implied would have assigned copyright in software but, at the relevant time, there was only a draft oral agreement with terms to be negotiated. The Court of Appeal upheld his decision in *Meridian International Services Ltd* v *Richardson* [2008] EWCA Civ 609.

64 [2005] FSR 31.

65 This was under a licence from the successors in title of the German doctors who originally developed the Dr Martens boot.

66 [2004] FSR 48.

67 [2007] FSR 12.

is the case of *Fisher* v *Brooker*[67] in which it was held that the claimant who played the organ solo in 'Whiter Shade of Pale' was a joint author and owner of the copyright in the musical work. It was nearly 40 years before the claimant attempted to establish his claim for joint authorship and, in the meantime, he had 'sat back and permitted two [collecting] societies to account to the defendants for royalties . . .' In the circumstances, Blackburne J held that the claimant must be taken to have gratuitously licensed the exploitation of his copyright. That implied licence lasted until March 2004 when his solicitors first intimated the claim to the defendant. However, in the Court of Appeal, in *Brooker* v *Fisher*,[68] the majority judges held that there was an irrevocable licence in favour of the defendant. An important factor was that, had Mr Fisher been a joint owner of the copyright in the song, he might have been able to prevent its future exploitation by seeking injunctive relief. However, David Richards J, dissenting, said that it would be unconscionable to deprive a person of his property right for the future in a case where he has not agreed, expressly or impliedly, for consideration to give up that right. David Richards J said (at para 139):

68 [2008] FSR 26.

> . . . a property right should not in effect be extinguished without either consideration or detriment, although delay amounting to laches may properly be a bar to equitable remedies such as an injunction. Nor do I consider the result to be unjust. Where the defendants retain all past earnings and have suffered no detriment from Mr Fisher's delay, there is in my view no injustice if his interest in the copyright is now established for the future.

The House of Lords agreed with Blackburne J and the dissenting judgment of David Richards J in the Court of Appeal.[69]

The Limitation Act 1980 has no bearing on late claims to ownership of copyright although, of course, it would bar a claim to past royalties paid more than six years before. The views of the majority judges in *Brooker* v *Fisher* are difficult to reconcile with the notion of inviolability of property rights. Indeed, Article 1 of Protocol 1 to the Council of Europe Convention for the Protection of Human Rights and Fundamental Freedoms states that 'no one shall be deprived of his possessions except in the public interest and subject to the conditions provided for by law and by the general principles of international law'.[70]

69 *Fisher* v *Brooker* [2009] FSR 25.

70 This provision was used in relation to copyright before the European Court of Human Rights in *Balan* v *Moldova* [2009] ECDR 6, discussed in Chapter 6.

71 In *Pasterfield* v *Denham* [1996] FSR 168, it was held that the person who commissioned the work had an equitable interest in the copyright but, even if he did not, he had an implied licence to use the finished work.

72 In *Robin Ray* v *Classic FM plc* [1998] FSR 622, the claimant had been paid around £250,000 to create the works and it was accepted that the implied licence extended to use of the works for the purposes of its broadcasting operations in the UK. It did not, however, extend to the grant of licences by the defendant allowing foreign radio stations to make use of the works in relation to their broadcasts.

73 For a useful description of factors used in deciding whether an assignment of licence is most appropriate, see Lightman J in *Robin Ray* v *Classic FM plc* [1998] FSR 622 at 642.

The courts have some flexibility in whether to decide on an implied or beneficial assignment of copyright or an implied licence to overcome a failure to address ownership or licensing issues in the consultancy agreement.[71] Beneficial ownership is most likely to be appropriate if the justice of the case suggests that the client should have complete control over the restricted acts, even to the exclusion of the consultant who remains the legal owner, and the ability to enforce the copyright against third parties. An implied licence is most appropriate where the circumstances are such that continued exploitation (including the granting of further licences) by the consultant is not incompatible with the use of the work by the client as originally contemplated by the parties. Where a licence is implied it should be the minimum consistent with the original intention of the parties.[72] The price paid by the client is obviously an important factor.[73] Although both beneficial ownership and implied licences are often important retrospectively, for example, to cure some alleged past infringement, they are also useful in terms of future conduct. In such cases, it seems possible that the courts have the power to order specific performance and require that a formal assignment or licence is drawn up between the parties.

Copyright in work created by a fiduciary

74 [2006] EWHC 1678 (Ch).

75 It did not appear that the director was classed as an employee of the company. There was no contract of employment. However, the judge could not decide this issue in the present applications for summary judgment.

Where a person is in a fiduciary relationship to another and creates the work in question in the context of that relationship, then he will hold the copyright in the work on trust for the other. In *Vitof Ltd* v *Altof*,[74] the defendant was a director of the claimant company.[75] He wrote source code for the company's labelling machines. It seems some of the source code was written before the company was formed, though most was written after that event. However, it also appeared that the source code might have infringed the copyright in source code belonging to another company which the defendant had previously worked for. As the defendant was a director of the claimant company, he owed the company fiduciary duties and Richard Arnold QC[76] had no doubt in deciding that he held the source code on trust for the company. Had the defendant been able to retain the source code for himself, this would mean that he would have had a conflict of interests. The fact that a small part had been written prior to the formation of the company did not matter as it was written in contemplation of the formation of the company. As he held the source code on trust for the company as legal owner, the defendant would be required to assign the copyright to the company and it was irrelevant whether it infringed a third party copyright. Where a work infringes a third-party copyright, it might still be a work of copyright itself.[77]

Holding that a person in a fiduciary position is a trustee is common in the case of company directors and other senior officers of companies and other organisations.[78] In *Ultraframe (UK) Ltd* v *Fielding*,[79] the Court of Appeal held that a director with 100 per cent shareholding of the companies he operated through held the design rights in designs he created as trustee for the companies. In *Ball* v *Eden Project Ltd*,[80] a director of the defendant company through which a charitable trust ran the famous Eden Project in Cornwall registered 'The Eden Project' as a trade mark. By doing so, he was clearly in breach of his fiduciary duty to the company. In such cases, it is usual for an order to assign the right in question to the person or body to whom the fiduciary duty is owed.

Employees

The main difficulty with the ownership provisions concerns the employer/employee relationship and the meaning of 'in the course of his employment', or, in the case of Crown copyright, 'in the course of his duties'. There will be many situations where it will be obvious that the work has been made by an employee in the course of his employment, for example a sales manager who, during his normal working hours, writes a report on the last quarter's sales figures for the board of directors of the company he works for. However, difficulties arise if an employee has created the work in his own time, whether or not using his employer's facilities, or if the nature of the work is not that which the employee is normally paid to create. To some extent the expectations of the employee and employer as manifested in the contract of employment are important: for example, the employee's job description and whether the nature of the thing produced sits comfortably with that job description, either expressly or by implication. To take an extreme example, say that a person who is employed as a cleaner writes some music during his own time. He will be the first owner of the copyright in the musical work because he is employed as a cleaner, and not as an author of musical works. Even if our cleaner writes the music during the time he should be performing his employment duties, he still will be the first owner of the copyright, but may have to answer to his employer for this breach of the contract of employment.[81]

The situation changes if the employee is employed under a contract with a very wide job description, for example as a research and development engineer, and he prepares a work of copyright which is useful to his employer's business. The copyright will probably belong to his employer, even if the employee created the work on his own initiative outside normal working hours. A complicating factor may be that the employee's formal job description no longer completely and accurately describes his present duties, in which case the actual type of work carried out by the employee will be relevant. A basic test is whether the skill, effort and judgment expended by the employee in creating the work are part of the employee's normal duties (express or implied) or within any special duties assigned to him by the employer. If the answer is 'no', then the employee will be the first owner of the copyright, even if he has used his employer's facilities or assistance. In

76 Sitting as Deputy High Court Judge.

77 *ZYX Music GmbH* v *King* [1995] FSR 566, at first instance.

78 *See*, for example, *Regal (Hastings) Ltd* v *Gulliver* [1967] 2 AC 134.

79 [2004] RPC 24. This case is discussed at length in Chapter 18 (*see* p 665).

80 [2002] FSR 43, discussed in Chapter 20 (*see* p 735).

81 A soldier in the SAS is not employed to write a book describing his experiences in the Falklands War. However, the Ministry of Defence sought to claim copyright in such a book as a means of preventing publication: Alberge, D. 'MoD Will Claim Copyright on SAS Book if Ban Fails', *The Times*, 5 August 1995, p 3.

82 [1952] RPC 10.

Stephenson Jordan & Harrison Ltd v *MacDonald*,[82] an employed accountant gave some lectures, which he later incorporated into a book. It was held that, even though his employer had provided secretarial help, the copyright in the lectures belonged to the accountant because he was employed as an accountant to advise clients, and not to deliver public lectures. However, part of the book was based on a report that the accountant had written for a client of his employer, so the copyright in this part belonged to his employer.

Employees sometimes perform work which is outside the contract of employment, that is, a contract of service. In such a case, the work is created under a contract for services rather than a contract of service, and the employee will be the first owner of the copyright. The point is illustrated well by Lord Denning in *Stephenson Jordan & Harrison* where he said:

> [In] *Byrne* v *Statist* [1914] 1 KB 622 . . . a man on the regular staff of a newspaper made a translation for the newspaper in his spare time. It was held that the translation was not made under a contract of service but under a contract for services. Other instances occur when a doctor on the staff of a hospital, or a master on the staff of a school, is employed under a contract of service to give lectures or lessons orally to students. If he, for his own convenience, puts the lectures into writing, then his written work is not done under a contract of service. It is most useful as an accessory to his contracted work but it is not really part of it. The copyright is in him and not in his employers.[83]

83 [1952] RPC 10 at 22.

Thus, an academic teacher, such as a university lecturer, will own the copyright in the notes he has prepared for the purpose of presented lectures and will be able to exploit those notes, for example, by granting a licence to a publisher, provided there is not an express term in his contract of employment to the contrary. Presumably, the same can be said in respect of 'handouts' distributed to students during lectures, unless these could be seen as an integral part of the lecturing duties. However, the changing nature of teaching and lecturing duties driven by the greater drive towards improving standards of quality has probably modified Lord Denning's robust view and it is likely that certain written materials produced by teachers and lecturers, such as module outlines, lecture plans and handouts, to be distributed to pupils or students in printed form or electronically, are prepared in the course of employment. The same would not apply to research papers, journal articles and books produced by teachers and lecturers unless specifically covered by the contract of employment. In the main, writing such materials may be encouraged by educational establishments but is not a required part of the teaching or lecturing duties.

If the employer wishes, he may allow the employee to be the first owner of the copyright, as s 11(2) includes the phrase 'subject to any agreement to the contrary'. Normally, transfer of ownership of copyright must be in writing and signed by or on behalf of the copyright owner,[84] but in this case it would appear that a verbal or even implied agreement will suffice because this is not a case of assignment, since the copyright does not exist until the time it has a first owner.[85] On the other hand, if an employee produces a work, the creation of which lies outside his normal duties (that is, it is not created in the course of his employment), any agreement that the employer will be the owner of the copyright must comply with s 90(3) and must be in writing and signed by or on behalf of the employee. The reason is that the employee automatically will be the first owner and the copyright must, therefore, be assigned to the employer. If there is such an agreement, but the formalities are not complied with, the employer may have an implied licence or may be deemed to be the beneficial owner of the copyright.

84 Copyright, Designs and Patents Act 1988 s 90(3).

85 *Noah* v *Shuba* [1991] FSR 14 provides an example of an implied agreement that the employee owned the copyright in a work created during normal working hours.

Freelance workers and consultants may be difficult to classify as employees in the normal sense of the word. Under s 178 'employed', 'employee', 'employer' and 'employment' refer to employment under a contract of service or of apprenticeship. The categorisation of a person as an employee or self-employed person is so crucial to the question of ownership of copyright that it requires further exploration, and employment law may provide some guidance as to how the distinction may be made. A person's status as employee or self-employed is important in employment law as many of the statutory safeguards, such as the right to claim unfair dismissal and the entitlement to redundancy pay, depend upon this question. Although the case law on this subject is far from satisfactory, questions such as who controls the work, whether the person is entitled to sick pay, who provides a pension, the method of payment (for example, weekly or monthly or on the basis of a lump sum for an agreed item of work), whether tax is deducted at source and financial responsibility (for example, for faulty work) may combine to provide an overall test.[86] In *Beloff* v *Pressdram Ltd*[87] the question of ownership of a memorandum written for the editor of the *Observer* newspaper had to be determined. The claimant, the author of the memorandum and who worked for the *Observer*, sued the publisher of *Private Eye* for infringing the copyright in the memorandum. The claimant could sustain the action only if she were the owner of the copyright in the memorandum. She would be the owner only if she was not an employee of the *Observer*.[88] Ungoed-Thomas J referred to a number of indicia which could be used to determine whether the contract was a contract of service (in which case the claimant would be an employee) or a contract for services. He decided that the former was the case.

Factors in favour of the arrangement being a contract of service were that the *Observer* provided the claimant with office space, equipment and resources, including a secretary; she did not use her own capital and her remuneration was not affected by the success or otherwise of the newspaper; deductions from her earnings were made in respect of PAYE and a pension scheme and, finally, the claimant's job was an integral part of the newspaper's business. The fact that the editor did not have full control over her work was not particularly relevant, and the judge pointed out that the greater an employee's skill, the less significant the question of control becomes. Control might be a more important determining factor in the case of employees carrying out lowly tasks under supervision. Lack of supervision and control by the client together with other factors such as working from home at times of his own choosing except when required to attend meetings was indicative of a contract for services in *Robin Ray* v *Classic FM plc*.[89] The agreement between the parties explicitly stated that it was not a relationship of employer and employee but between an independent contractor and the client. However, this is not decisive and the courts will go beyond such statements to look at the substance of the agreement.

None of the factors mentioned above is conclusive as such. In *Hall* v *Lorimer*[90] Mummery J said that the court could not run through a checklist of items pointing one way or the other. He went on to suggest that a whole picture should be painted and viewed from a distance to reach an informed and qualitative decision. Emphasis has been placed on 'mutuality of obligation', described by Kerr LJ in *Nethermere (St Neots) Ltd* v *Taverna*[91] in the following terms:

> [The alleged employees] must be subject to an obligation to accept and perform some minimum, or at least reasonable, amount of work for the alleged employer.

A case which seems to push the boundaries in favour of employers is *King* v *South African Weather Service*[92] before the Supreme Court of Appeal of South Africa. The claimant was employed as a meteorological officer in charge of one of the defendant's offices. The defendant developed an automated weather system using a number of computer programs. The claimant later wrote some computer programs to facilitate his task of collecting meteorological data and transmitting them to the defendant's head office. The claimant's duties varied over time but did not include writing computer programs. At first he wrote the programs mainly after hours or at home but later began to work on the programs during working hours. His claim for ownership of the copyright in the computer programs he had written failed and his appeal to the Supreme Court of Appeal was dismissed.[93] The court accepted that it was not possible to lay down hard and fast rules as to whether a work was created in the course of employment. It was a factual issue to be

---

86 *Market Investigations Ltd* v *Minister of Social Security* [1969] 2 QB 173 at 185 per Cooke J.

87 [1973] 1 All ER 241.

88 A purported assignment of the copyright to the claimant was ineffective.

89 [1998] FSR 622.

90 *The Times*, 4 June 1992.

91 [1984] IRLR 240.

92 [2009] FSR 6.

93 Having refused to hand over the source code, the employee had been subject to a disciplinary hearing and then dismissed.

decided on the basis of the terms of the employment contract and the particular circumstance in which the work was created. Important factors in this case which pointed to the employer being the first owner of the copyright were:

- The programs were integrated into the employer's automated weather system and were of advantage to the employer.
- Although the duties of a meteorologist did not ordinarily include writing computer programs, they had been developed to assist in his duties of collecting and transmitting data – although he may have written the programs to make his job easier, he had done it because of his job.
- There was a close causal connection between the claimant's employment and the creation of the programs – some of the programs had been written for other weather stations at the employer's request. They had not been created for external use and the employer had specified the format of these programs which had to be approved by the employer before implementation and use.
- The job description had not been all-embracing – a later fuller description was issued which stated that a work could be created in the course of employment without having been created in terms of the contract. Furthermore, a contract of employment could change either expressly or by implication.

Some particular facts help explain the decision. King had submitted quarterly reports to his employer in which he stressed his programming activities. In a job evaluation he stated that he was responsible for system development and programming and calibration of the employer's automatic weather station network. He was at that time spending about 50 per cent of his working time on developing the computer programs in question. It would seem that there was a degree of mutual though tacit understanding between employee and employer that program development was part and parcel of his duties even though no mention was made in the express terms of the contract of employment. This case is distinguishable from *Stephenson Jordan & Harrison* on a number of grounds, including the fact that creating the programs was intimately tied up with the meteorologist's duties.

In the United States, the author of a work is generally the first owner of the copyright but were a work is 'made for hire' the situation is that the employer or other person for whom the work was prepared is consider to be the author and will own the copyright subject to an agreement to the contrary.[94] Section 101 of the US Copyright Act 1976 defines a work made for hire as, *inter alia*, a work prepared by an employee within the scope of his or her employment.[95] In determining whether a work is prepared within the scope of employment, the Supreme Court case of *Community for Non-Creative Violence v Reid*[96] which involved a sculpture commissioned to be made by Reid is instructive. The Court applied the general common law of agency and to determine whether a hired party is an employee consideration should be given to:

> the hiring party's right to control the manner and means by which the product is accomplished. Among the other factors relevant to this inquiry are the skill required; the source of the instrumentalities and tools; the location of the work; the duration of the relationship between the parties; whether the hiring party has the right to assign additional projects to the hired party; the extent of the hired party's discretion over when and how long to work; the method of payment; the hired party's role in hiring and paying assistants; whether the work is part of the regular business of the hiring party; whether the hiring party is in business; the provision of employee benefits.

This is not unlike the tests in *Market Investigations Ltd v Minister of Social Security* and *Beloff v Pressdram Ltd*, discussed above (see p 106).

Given the difficulty of predetermining the status of a person carrying out work for another, it is preferable, if there is any doubt whatsoever, to provide contractually for the

94 US Copyright Act 1976, 17 USC 201.

95 Certain specially ordered or commissioned works are also deemed to be works made for hire: s 101(2) of the Copyright Act 1976.

96 490 US 730 (1989).

ownership of copyright subsisting in anything produced by the worker. Certainly, there is a good deal of confusion about the ownership of commissioned works, the commissioner often believing, mistakenly, that he will automatically own the copyright subsisting in the work created.[97] In these situations, the person commissioning the work should insist that the contract contains provisions for the assignment of the future copyright.[98] Of course, in terms of the relationship between employer and employee and between client and consultant, there is the additional factor of the obligation of confidence owed by one to the other.[99] The law of confidence may help the employer or the client prevent the subsequent use of commissioned material by the employee or consultant, regardless of the question of copyright ownership.

Complexity of rights

For the derivative works of copyright there will usually be several rights associated with the work, and the exploitation of works in which numerous rights exist can be fairly complex, although collecting societies such as the Performing Right Society bring some simplification. As an example of the number of rights that can subsist in a work, consider a song which has been recorded as a sound recording. The following rights can exist:

- musical copyright;
- literary copyright;
- copyright in the sound recording;
- rights in a live performance of the song (these are neighbouring rights to copyright – the performers and recording company have rights);
- rental and lending rights;
- the composer's moral rights;
- the lyricist's moral rights.

The exploitation of the sound recording must take account of all these rights by way of assignments, licences or waivers. The rights themselves can be subdivided. For example, in the above case the following cross-cutting rights are important:

- the right to make copies of the sound recording;
- the right to play the sound recording in public;
- the right to permit rental of copies of the sound recording.

A film may be subject to many rights. The screenplay will be a dramatic work and may be based on a novel produced as a book. The novel will have literary copyright which will initially be owned by the novelist. The copyright in the film as a film will be owned, in the first instance, jointly by the producer and the principal director, unless they are employees making the film in the course of employment. Even so they will be joint authors and will consequently have a right to authorise or prohibit rental or lending.[100] Add to this the various rights associated with the sound track, performance rights and moral rights and it becomes clear that lawyers will be kept busy in drawing up all the necessary agreements and consents. Mechanisms for exploiting works of copyright are described in the subsequent sections of this chapter.

Dealing with copyright

As has been previously mentioned, copyright is a property right, and as such the owner of that right can deal with it. He can transfer the right to another, or he can grant licences to others, permitting them to do some or all of the acts restricted by copyright in relation

97 This problem came to light as regards the ownership of the 'Lightman Report' commissioned by the National Union of Mineworkers. A publisher intended to publish the report with the permission of Mr Lightman QC, in the face of strong objection by the Union which believed it owned the copyright in the report – *see The Times*, 1 October 1990, p 3. However, unless there was a signed written assignment of the copyright, the person commissioned, Mr Lightman, would be the first legal owner of the copyright in the report, although the Union might have had some rights as beneficial owner of the copyright in equity.

98 Copyright, Designs and Patents Act 1988 s 91 provides for prospective ownership of copyright.

99 *See* Chapter 10 (pp 368–372) for a discussion of the operation of the law of confidence as regards employees.

100 *See* Dworkin, G. 'Authorship of Films and European Commission Proposals for Harmonising the Term of Copyright' [1993] 5 EIPR 151.

to the work. However, it must be remembered that the author of a work has certain moral rights, and the owner of the copyright and his assignees or licensees, indeed the public in general, must take notice of and respect these moral rights. Therefore, the ultimate owner of a copyright is not entirely free to do as he wishes with the work that is the subject matter of the copyright. Nevertheless, in most cases, respecting the author's moral rights will not be a hindrance to the economic exploitation of copyright.

Why should the owner of a copyright wish to transfer his ownership of the copyright or grant licences in respect of it? Bearing in mind that the author of a work of copyright will often be the owner of the copyright, the owner may not be in the best position to exploit the work commercially. For example, the author of a work of literature such as a romantic story (if he is the first owner of the copyright, as will usually be the case) will find it more advantageous in terms of the balance between financial reward and the degree of risk involved to approach a well-established publisher who will arrange for the printing, marketing and sale of books of the story. Not only that, but the publisher will also be better placed to take legal action against persons infringing the copyright. Similarly, the composer of a piece of music may approach a record company which might arrange for the recording of the music by a well-known orchestra and for the manufacture, distribution and sale of records, cassettes and compact discs on a worldwide scale. Copyright can also be a form of investment. A lump sum can be invested to acquire the copyright in works which will continue to provide income over many years.[101] Alternatively, copyright may be used as security for a loan or other financial transaction. Finally, transfer of ownership of copyright will occur on the death of the owner or a part-owner of the copyright.

Two main ways of dealing with copyright are considered below: by assignment and by licensing. Licences may be exclusive or non-exclusive. In the case of an assignment of copyright or an exclusive licence, the transaction, to be effective, must be in writing and signed by or on behalf of the present copyright owner.[102] Although this can be seen as a safeguard for the copyright owner, who may be negotiating with powerful publishing organisations from an unequal bargaining position, it can lead to difficulties in the case of commissioned works because it clearly means that the commissioner cannot have any legal rights of ownership under copyright law unless a written signed agreement exists.[103] The language of the statute is very clear on this point, so the implication by the courts of terms into the contract for the commissioned work dealing with ownership is unlikely, though not an impossibility.[104]

One co-owner of a copyright may not perform or authorise restricted acts to be done in relation to the work without the permission of his co-owners.[105] Where the copyright is owned by more than one person (or a certain aspect such as the right to perform in public is jointly owned), references in Part I of the Act are to all the owners. In particular, this means that where there are joint owners, the licence of all of them is required. This is because infringement is defined in relation to doing (or authorising another to do) any of the acts restricted by copyright without the licence of the copyright owner under s 16(2). Section 173(2) makes it explicit that, where there are joint owners, the licence of every one is required. It is no answer for one joint owner to argue that he is free to license the performance of a restricted act in the face of objection from another joint owner provided he accounts to that other joint owner for a share in the profits realised from the licence.

As an example, consider the copyright subsisting in a sound recording that has joint owners either because it was created by joint authors, or because the copyright has been assigned to more than one person. The sound recording is to be reproduced and sold commercially and each joint owner will be entitled to an agreed share of the profits arising from the sales. One joint owner may be anxious to obtain some immediate capital. To do this, he will be able to 'sell' his future share of the profits to a third party for a lump sum, assigning his copyright interest to that person. He can do this without having to seek

101 This may be advantageous in terms of tax liabilities. For the tax implications of intellectual property *see* Gallafent, R.J., Eastaway, N.A. and Dauppe, V.A.F. (2003) *Intellectual Property Law and Taxation* (6th edn) Sweet & Maxwell.

102 Copyright, Designs and Patents Act 1988 ss 90(3) and 92(1).

103 However, under s 85(1), the commissioner of a photograph or film made for private and domestic purposes has certain rights: for example, a right not to have the work issued to the public.

104 *See* the discussion above (p 99) on *Warner* v *Gestetner Ltd* [1988] EIPR D-89.

105 *Cescinsky* v *George Routledge & Sons Ltd* [1916] 2 KB 325. This restriction on co-owners should be compared to patent law, where one co-patentee can exploit the patent without the permission of his co-patentees, but cannot license, assign or mortgage his share without the consent of the others: Patents Act 1977 s 36. In the context of copyright, see *Robin Ray* v *Classic FM plc* [1998] FSR 622.

or obtain the permission of the other co-owners. However, the co-owner cannot grant a licence to a third party allowing that third party to make and sell copies of the sound recording without the agreement of all the other co-owners. Another example is where a co-owner of a copyright dies leaving all his property to his widow. In such a case, his copyright interests pass to his widow who will, from then on, be entitled to a share of the royalties or profits accruing from the sale or other commercial exploitation of the work.

Assignment and transmission of copyright

One point that must be made at this stage is that physical possession of an object containing or representing a work of copyright or a copy of such a work does not by itself give any rights under copyright law. For example, mere possession of a book does not give a right to perform any of the restricted acts such as making copies of the book. The same principle applies to a painting, and the sale of a painting, no matter how expensive, does not automatically assign the copyright in it. The purchaser obtains a property right in the physical object but, in the absence of an assignment or licence, no interest in the copyright. This may be inconvenient and the courts will construe any documents, such as a receipt, generously to keep the two forms of property together. For example, in *Savory (EW) Ltd v The World of Golf Ltd*,[106] it was held that a written receipt for card designs 'inclusive of all copyrights' was sufficient to assign the copyright to the purchaser. In *Cray Valley Ltd v Deltech Europe Ltd*,[107] Jacob J confirmed that the written document does not have to expressly refer to copyright and it may be sufficient if it refers to 'assets'. He said (at para 69):

> Of course a word such as 'assets' will take its meaning in any written agreement not from its acontextual or mere dictionary meaning but from its context. In the present case where the evident commercial intention behind the lost agreements was to transfer everything to the assignee I see no reason to suppose if the assignment used the words 'assets' there would or could have been any intention to hold anything, and specifically copyright, back.

There is a convention or custom amongst artists that where an artist creates a work in a medium such that multiple copies may be made and the artist limits the number actually made, such as in a limited edition print, the artist has a right to make and retain or sell up to two additional copies. However, that convention usually applies where an artist sells to purchasers and, in *Danowski v The Henry Moore Foundation*[108] the Court of Appeal declined to imply such a term into a contract of service, between employer and employee. Additionally, referring to Ungoed-Thomas J in *Cunliffe-Owen v Teather & Greenwood*,[109] for a practice to amount to recognised usage, it must be notorious. That was not the case here, nor was the convention certain. Anyway, an implied term based on such a convention would be inconsistent with the express terms of the agreement and its overall tenor.

An assignment of copyright can be thought of as a disposal of the copyright by way of sale. Copyright may also pass under a testamentary disposition or by operation of law. The present owner (the assignor) can assign the copyright to another and, under s 90(3), such an assignment must be in writing signed by or on behalf of the assignor. However, the assignment, and other transmission, of the copyright need not be total and absolute; it can be partial. Under s 90(2), the assignment or other transmission of copyright can be limited either in terms of the things the copyright owner can do, or in terms of the period of subsistence of copyright. As an example, consider a play, a dramatic work, the copyright in which will expire in 40 years' time (William, the author, having died some 30 years ago). The current owner, William's widow Ann (the assignor), may decide to assign the total copyright in the play to another person, Frances. Alternatively, she might decide to assign only the public performance right to Frances for the remainder of the duration of the copyright while retaining the other rights, allowing her to make and issue printed

106 [1914] 2 Ch 566.

107 [2003] EWHC 728 (Ch).

108 [1996] EMLR 364.

109 [1967] 1 WLR 1421.

copies of the play either personally or by granting a licence to Richard to do this. Finally, she might decide to assign all the rights to Frances for a period of five years only, after which the copyright will revert to her.

The agreement under which copyright is assigned may provide for a reversion of the copyright under specified conditions. In *Crosstown Music Company 1 LLC v Rive Droite Music Ltd*,[110] the agreements under which two writers of musical composition assigned their copyright to Rive Droite, to exploit in return for payment of royalties, contained a clause which provided for reversion of the relevant copyrights to the writers should Rive Droite be in material breach of the agreements and fail to remedy such breaches within a specified time of being sent 'cure' notices by the writers. Subsequently to numerous breaches and failures to remedy breaches as set out in the cure notices, Rive Droite purported to assign the copyrights to Crosstown. Mann J noted that s 90(2) allowed for reversion of copyright after a period of time and a reversion clause could provide for that to happen earlier if material breaches were not remedied in accordance with the clause. The Court of Appeal agreed with this interpretation, rejecting an argument that s 90(2) only permitted assignment of a reversion after a fixed, pre-determined term.[111] An automatic 'floating reversion' following some event such as a material breach of contract was within the statute. The Court of Appeal also confirmed that a time limited assignment of copyright did not need to be expressly re-assigned back on reversion.

Assignments limited in time need careful thought as to what happens to any copies of the work that have not been sold at the time of the reversion of the copyright. In *Howitt v Hall*[112] it was held that the defendant who had been assigned the copyright in a book for four years could continue to sell copies printed during those four years after the copyright reverted to the original owner.

If the formalities of the Act are not complied with, it may be that a court will be prepared to infer that there has been an assignment of the copyright in equity only: see *Warner v Gestetner*, above (p 99). In these circumstances, there will be a legal owner of the copyright and an equitable owner, the legal owner being the purported assignor; and he will still be the legal owner because of some defect in the formalities: for example, the written assignment was not signed by him or on his behalf, or the attempted assignment was made orally.[113] Being an owner in equity only does have some disadvantages. In *Performing Right Society Ltd v London Theatre of Varieties Ltd*,[114] it was held that the owner of an equitable interest in the performing rights of a song entitled 'The Devonshire Wedding' could not obtain a perpetual injunction without joining the legal owner of the copyright as a party to the action. This case was applied in *Weddel v JA Pearce & Major*,[115] a bankruptcy case, in which it was held that although an equitable assignee could sue in his own right, he could not obtain damages or a perpetual injunction without joining as a party the assignor in whom the legal title of a chose in action was vested.[116] Normally, joining another party in an action would mean both appearing as co-claimants, but it is sufficient if the other party is the defendant. For example, in *John Richardson Computers Ltd v Flanders*[117] the owner in equity sued the legal owner.

The rationale for the rule that a beneficial owner cannot obtain a permanent injunction or damages is based on the principle of double jeopardy.[118] If the beneficial owner obtained damages without joining the legal owner, the latter could come along subsequently and bring a fresh action for damages. Of course, apart from joining the legal owner in the action, another way around the difficulty is for the beneficial owner to take an assignment of the copyright. It appears that this will be effective at any time before judgment provided the assignment includes preceding rights of action.[119]

Of course, the person who executes the assignment may be acting as the agent of the assignor and the general rules of agency apply. It is in the intended assignee's interests to satisfy himself as to the authority of the agent. The case of *Beloff v Pressdram Ltd*[120] involved the publication of a memorandum written by the claimant (an employee of the

110 [2009] EWHC 600 (Ch).

111 [2011] FSR 5.

112 (1862) 6 LT 348.

113 In some cases, it is possible that equitable ownership may arise in the absence of agreement: *see Massine v de Basil* [1933–1945] MacG CC 223 and Lea, G. 'Expropriation of Business Necessity?' [1994] 10 EIPR 453.

114 [1924] AC 1.

115 [1987] 3 All ER 624.

116 Copyright is, arguably, a chose in action.

117 [1993] FSR 497.

118 *Batjac Productions Inc v Simitar Entertainment (UK) Ltd* [1996] FSR 139.

119 *Weddell v JA Pearce & Major* [1987] 3 All ER 624.

120 [1973] 1 All ER 241.

Observer newspaper) by *Private Eye*. The memorandum referred to a conversation between the claimant and a prominent member of the government, in which the latter said that if the Prime Minister were to run under a bus, he had no doubt that a certain Mr M would take over as Prime Minister. The *Observer* owned the copyright in the memorandum and the editor attempted to assign it to the claimant so that the claimant could sue the publishers of *Private Eye*. However, as the editor had never before executed an assignment on behalf of the *Observer* and had no express authority to do so, the purported assignment was ineffective. Neither could there be any imputed authority because any representation made by the editor that he had authority had not induced the claimant to enter into the assignment or take any relevant step.[121]

Sometimes, there may be an assignment of copyright in a work which has not yet come into existence. Such prospective ownership of copyright and its assignment is provided for under s 91. If an author decides to write a play, he will be the first owner of the copyright in the play when it is written, provided he is not writing the play as an employee in the course of his employment. The author is the prospective owner of the future copyright, and he can deal with that future copyright by assigning it to another. Under s 91(2), 'future copyright' means copyright which will or may come into existence in respect of a future work or class of works or on the occurrence of a future event. The prospective owner can assign the copyright by an agreement signed by him or on his behalf and the actual assignment will take effect automatically when the copyright in the work in question comes into existence. The assignment can be whole or partial. Before the Copyright Act 1956, it was not possible to assign a future copyright, even if in writing and signed by the prospective owner.[122] This was changed by the 1956 Act and in *Chaplin* v *Leslie Frewin (Publishers) Ltd*[123] it was held that a contract for writing an autobiography between the infant son of Charlie Chaplin and a publisher was effective to transfer the copyright in the work when it came into existence.[124]

An assignment may be declared by the court to be unenforceable if it is unconscionable or contrary to public policy being in restraint of trade. In *Schroeder Music Publishing Co Ltd* v *Macaulay*[125] a young and unknown songwriter assigned the worldwide copyright in any musical composition produced by him for five years to a music publishing company. The agreement was very one-sided, the company did not undertake to publish any of the writer's work and could terminate by giving one month's notice. The songwriter could not terminate and was paid only £50 (although he would receive royalties on any of his songs actually published). The House of Lords held that the agreement was unenforceable, being in restraint of trade.[126] It required total commitment from the songwriter, but virtually no obligation was placed upon the company. Lord Diplock said that it was not without significance that successful and established songwriters were not offered the standard form agreement given to the respondent in this case.

It has been common for an assignment to include the formula 'X, as beneficial owner, hereby assigns . . .' The use of the phrase 'beneficial owner' was thought to imply covenants contained in the Law of Property Act 1925 by virtue of s 76.[127] The Law of Property (Miscellaneous Provisions) Act 1994, which came into force on 1 July 1995, made some changes to the content of the implied covenants, repealing s 76 of the 1925 Act. Now, an assignment of copyright (or other intellectual property right) should take account of the new formulae of full title guarantees and limited title guarantees. Under s 8(1) of the 1994 Act, the parties are free to extend or limit the implied covenants. The phrase 'as beneficial owner' should now be replaced by the appropriate title guarantee.[128]

An assignment of UK copyright cannot be defeated by the law of another state which attempts to confiscate that copyright if the agreement is not presented for approval or does not warrant approval. In *Peer International Corp* v *Termidor Music Publishers Ltd*,[129] the claimant music publisher claimed to own the copyright (or alternatively to be exclusive licensees) in music composed by Cuban nationals. Agreements made in the 1930s and

---

121 *Freeman & Lockyer* v *Buckhurst Park Property* [1964] 1 All ER 630 applied.

122 *Performing Right Society Ltd* v *London Theatre of Varieties Ltd* [1924] AC 1. An attempted assignment of a future copyright could take effect in equity only, regardless of the formalities used in practice.

123 [1966] Ch 71.

124 The son was 19 years old at the time, but still classed as an infant for legal purposes. He tried to avoid the contract, fearing passages in the work might be libellous, but it was held that the contract was analogous to a beneficial contract of service and was, therefore, not voidable at the infant's option.

125 [1974] 3 All ER 616.

126 But there are limits to the doctrine, such as where the individual is fully aware and has expert legal advice: *see Panayiotou* v *Sony Music Entertainment (UK) Ltd* [1994] 2 WLR 241, the 'George Michael' case.

127 Anderson, M. 'Applying Traditional Property Laws to Intellectual Property Transactions' [1995] 5 EIPR 237.

128 The assignment is likely to contain express warranties. *See* Stokes, S. 'Covenants for Title in IP Dispositions' [1995] 5 EIPR D-138.

129 [2004] 2 WLR 849.

1950s were supplemented by 'confirmations' and 'addendum' made around 1989 or 1990. Taken together, the Court of Appeal accepted that these were effective to assign the UK copyright in the music to the claimants. However, in 1960, following the revolution, Cuba passed a law (Cuban Law 860) which provided for a Cuban organisation to administer copyright and which forbade certain contracts relating to copyright: for example, where an author assigned the copyright in his future works or where the agreement was of unlimited or more than 10 years' duration. Furthermore, in respect of existing agreements, Decree 10 of Chapter VIII of Law 860 required presentation of those agreements for approval, which could be withheld. If presentation was not made within 60 days or approval was withheld, the rights assigned would be forfeit and the authors would be free to sign new contracts with others in respect of the same rights. Generally, the laws of one state cannot affect the ownership of property situated in another state, unless there are compelling public policy reasons for doing so. In any case, such laws will not be effective in the UK if they are confiscatory in nature. That was the position here in that failure to present agreements or withholding approval of any agreement presented would result in confiscation. Therefore, the claimant was entitled to the UK copyrights and subsequent purported assignments by the Cuban organisation which administered copyright to the defendant were ineffective.

This rule that laws of one state cannot affect the ownership of property situated in another state is not an absolute one. In *Griggs Group Ltd* v *Evans*,[130] the judge, having found the claimant entitled to beneficial ownership of the copyright in a drawing of a logo applied to Doc Marten shoes, ordered the assignment of the copyright from the defendant to the claimant. Although it was not made explicit in the judgment, it became clear that this order affected not just UK copyright but all the other copyrights in the drawing in other jurisdictions. It was submitted that the court did not have jurisdiction to order the assignment of copyrights in other countries in *Griggs Group Ltd* v *Evans (No 2)*.[131] That claim was rejected by Peter Prescott QC sitting as a deputy judge of the High Court. The claimant had an equity in England arising from a contract subject to English law and it was not shown that the laws of foreign countries would extinguish that equity. The alternative would have meant that the claimant would have to bring proceedings in numerous other countries and this could have seriously frustrated or hindered the claimant from exploiting the copyright in countries other than the UK. The decision is a very pragmatic one based on fairness and reason, especially as the second defendant, to whom the first defendant had assigned the copyrights, knew of the facts giving rise to the equity and could not be described as the 'darling of equity'.[132] It is an exception to the basic rule. However, had evidence been adduced that the laws of one country or another would not also have ordered an assignment of copyright, it is likely that the court would have taken account of that and the order would not have extended to those other countries.

Licensing of copyright

A licence is, in essence, a permission granted by the owner of a right or interest to another person allowing him to do something in respect of that right or interest. For example, it may be a licence to enter land for some purpose, such as for accommodation or to take a short cut across a field. Licences may be contractual, in which case they can be enforced in a court of law: for example, the owner of a field allows a neighbour to graze his sheep there in return for an annual fee of £100. In relation to copyright, a licence is an agreement between the owner of the copyright (the licensor) and another person (the licensee) whereby that person is permitted to do certain acts in connection with the work involved that would otherwise infringe the copyright in the work. In return for this arrangement, the licensee will pay the licensor either by way of a lump sum, or by making royalty payments. For example, the owner of the copyright in an artistic work such as an oil-painting might agree with a publisher of art works that the publisher can make and sell prints

130 [2004] FSR 48.

131 [2005] FSR 31.

132 That is, the *bona fide* purchaser for value without notice.

made of the painting, and in return the publisher will pay the copyright owner £5 for each print he sells. Normally making the prints would be an infringement of copyright, being an act restricted by copyright, that is making a copy of the work.[133]

Where a copyright has joint owners, any licence granted under it must have the consent of all the joint owners. This is a consequence of ss 16(2) and 173(2). The former provision states that copyright is infringed by doing, or authorising another to do, any of the acts restricted by the copyright without the licence of the copyright owner. The latter provision states that references to the owner, where there are joint owners, are references to all of them.

Like an assignment of copyright, a licence can be limited in terms of either the scope or the duration, or both. Scope can be limited either in terms of the acts the licensee is permitted to do or territorially. The licence may be for the whole of the remainder of the period during which copyright will continue to subsist in the work, or may be for a shorter period. There will usually be provisions in the licence agreement for its earlier termination: for example, if one of the parties is in breach of an important obligation under the agreement or on the insolvency of one of the parties.

A licence may be exclusive. Under s 92(1), an exclusive licence is a licence in writing signed by or on behalf of the copyright owner authorising the licensee, to the exclusion of all other persons *including the owner*, to exercise a right that would otherwise be exercisable exclusively by the copyright owner. The licensee is exclusively granted rights to do certain things in relation to the work and the owner (licensor) will not grant those equivalent rights to anyone else, or even exercise them himself. For example, the owner of the copyright in a work of literature may grant an exclusive licence to a book publisher for the purpose of publication of the work. The owner of the copyright will not grant the right of publication to anyone else while the exclusive licence is in existence, and indeed, if he attempts to do so, he will be in breach of the exclusive licence. However, although the licence is exclusive, it need not apply to all the acts restricted by copyright and may encompass only one or some of them, such as publishing a book, and the owner will be free to deal with other rights, such as the broadcasting of extracts of the work recited by a famous actor. In the case of a non-exclusive licence, the licensor may make several agreements in respect of the same acts restricted by copyright. For example, the owner of the copyright in a play may allow several theatrical companies to make public performances of the play.

Under s 90(4), a licence granted by a copyright owner is binding on every successor in title to his interest in the copyright, except a purchaser in good faith for valuable consideration without actual or constructive notice and persons deriving title from such a person. So, 'equity's darling', the *bona fide* purchaser for value without notice, is given protection that overrides the interests of licensees, which is one reason why a commercial organisation, such as a publisher, wishing to exploit a work of copyright might prefer to take an assignment of the copyright rather than to operate on the basis of an exclusive licence. However, in practice it would be very difficult for a purchaser of the copyright to show that he did not have constructive notice, especially if the work had already been exploited commercially. Note that only a purchaser of the copyright is protected, and a person who receives the copyright as a gift or on the death of the owner must respect any existing licences covering the work regardless of knowledge.

Although licences are, subject to what has been said above, binding on assignees, care must be taken when assigning copyright to ensure that the assignee can enforce the licence against the licensee. In the Scots case of *Profile Software Ltd* v *Becogent Ltd*[134] the liquidator of a software company granted new and wider software licences to existing licensees of the company and then assigned the intellectual property rights in the software to the pursuer, Profile. The assignment was badly drafted and it was argued that it did not carry the title to sue under the licence agreements which remained with the liquidator. The judge rejected this submission, noting that it would have the effect that the assignee had an interest to sue but no right to do so whilst the liquidator had a right to sue but no interest in doing so.

133 For infringement generally *see* Chapter 6. Making a copy of a literary, dramatic, musical or artistic work is defined as reproducing the work in any material form: Copyright, Designs and Patents Act 1988 s 17(2).

134 [2005] CSOH 28.

Future copyright can be licensed by the prospective owner under s 91(3), but again protection is given to a purchaser in good faith for valuable consideration without actual or constructive notice as against a licensee. Thus, when a work is eventually created that is subject to a previously executed licence agreement, the owner of the copyright will be bound by the terms of the licence. If the owner later dies and, for example, the copyright passes to the surviving spouse, he or she will also be bound. If that person then assigns the copyright to Andrew, a person who knows about the licence, he will be bound. If Andrew then gives the copyright to Bernard who does not know, or could not be expected to know of the licence, Bernard will be bound by the licence because he has not purchased the copyright but has taken it by way of a gift. However, if Bernard then assigns the copyright to Cyril, who acts in good faith and does not know of the licence and could not be expected to know of it, Cyril will take free of the licence. Furthermore, if Cyril later disposes of the copyright to Duncan, who knows of the licence and is acting in bad faith, Duncan can take free of the licence because he has derived his title from a purchaser in good faith. The licence is effectively destroyed by the intervention of the purchaser in good faith for valuable consideration without notice. It may be, however, that the licensee has a remedy against his licensor under the original agreement, as there may be a contractual provision in the agreement requiring successors in title of the owner to be given notice before the copyright is assigned. However, this measure can be really effective only until the chain of notification of the licence between assignors and assignees is broken.

As an example of the exploitation of the various rights associated with the copyright in a particular work, consider the author (and owner of the copyright) of a dramatic play. He decides to deal with the play in terms of its publication, its performance in public and also, because of the popularity of the play, is able to negotiate the making of a film based on the play and the making of sound recordings of famous actors reading the play. Figure 4.2 shows the types of relationships in terms of assignments and licensing that could ensue. In the case of a work such as a computer program, the use of which normally involves a restricted act, the ultimate 'purchaser' of a copy will usually receive a non-exclusive sub-licence.

Differences between assignments and licences

An exclusive licence agreement can appear, at first sight, to look like an assignment and it is sometimes difficult to distinguish between the two.[135] Both an assignment and a

135 The implied covenants under the Law of Property (Miscellaneous Provisions) Act 1994 will not apply to a licence agreement.

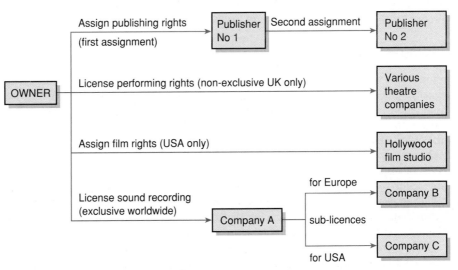

Figure 4.2 Assignment and licensing

licence agreement may provide for the payment of royalties, which might be thought of normally as being associated with a licence. In *Jonathan Cape Ltd* v *Consolidated Press Ltd*,[136] there was an agreement between the author (being the first owner of the copyright) and the claimant publishing company, granting the latter, its successors and assigns 'the exclusive right to print and publish an original work . . . provisionally entitled "A Mouse is Born" in volume form'. The agreement was partial in terms of the copyright acts (printing and publishing) and in the territorial scope (a specified area including Australia). The defendant substantially reproduced the work, but argued that the agreement was a licence and that, as a result, the claimant could not bring an action without joining the author. It was held that the question of whether an agreement was an assignment or a licence was a matter of construction and, in this case, the words used implied that the agreement was a partial assignment of the copyright. Even the use of the words 'licensor' and 'licensee' in an agreement is not conclusive that it is a licence.[137]

The payment of royalties is inconsistent with an assignment and is, therefore, highly suggestive of a licence. Indeed, the owner of a copyright would be foolish to assign that copyright in return for royalty payments. If the copyright is subsequently re-assigned to a third party, the terms providing for royalty payments could be unenforceable against that third party, on the basis of privity of contract.[138] It was held in *Barker* v *Stickney*[139] that a person acquiring a copyright is not bound by mere notice of a personal covenant by a predecessor in title.

In *JHP Ltd* v *BBC Worldwide Ltd*,[140] Norris J had to decide whether an agreement between the late Terry Nation who devised the Dalek characters in the *Dr Who* television series and various books and the predecessor in title to the claimant was an assignment or an exclusive licence. The agreement spoke of the grant of a sole and exclusive right to publish the work in book form. This was highly suggestive of an exclusive licence. The word 'grant' had been used rather than 'assign' or 'transfer'. Even though the agreement had a reverter clause,[141] it was held that it was an exclusive licence rather than an assignment. Furthermore, it would have been highly improbable that Mr Nation would have assigned his rights in the Daleks at that time as he was still actively engaged in the creative development of the Daleks for future television series.

Other differences between assignments and licences are that only the owner has a right to sue (although an exclusive licensee may sue after joining the owner or by leave of the court) and a right to alter,[142] subject to the author's moral rights. In the absence of express provisions to the contrary, an assignment will generally be assignable, but a licence will not be assignable unless expressly provided for. There are also differences as regards the effect of the insolvency of the assignee or licensee.

New forms of exploitation

In time, new ways of exploiting a work of copyright might be discovered and the effect on existing licence agreements may be disputed: for example, whether the new form of exploitation falls within the scope of the licence. It will be a question of construction of the licence on the basis of what was properly regarded as being in the contemplation of the parties when the agreement was made. In *Hospital for Sick Children* v *Walt Disney Productions Inc*[143] the question arose as to whether a licence granted in 1919 by Sir James Barrie in respect of all his literary and dramatic works was limited to silent films or extended to sound films.[144] In the United States of America, Peggy Lee was awarded $3.8 million in respect of her contributions to the Walt Disney cartoon film *The Lady and the Tramp* on the basis that her contract with Walt Disney did not extend to selling videos of the film.[145] The contract was drawn up before video technology existed.

The growing use of information technology may pose problems, for example, where there was an agreement between a copyright owner and a licensee to publish the work in question in paper form but, subsequently, the licensee publishes the work electronically.

---

136 [1954] 3 All ER 253.

137 See, for example, *Messager* v *British Broadcasting Co Ltd* [1929] AC 151.

138 Though now this has to be subject to the effect of the Contracts (Rights of Third Parties) Act 1999. In Scotland, the doctrine of *ius quaesitum tertio* could give enforceable rights under a contract to a third party: *see Beta Computers (Europe) Ltd* v *Adobe Systems (Europe) Ltd* [1996] FSR 367.

139 [1919] 1 KB 121.

140 [2008] FSR 29.

141 In the case of a licence a reverter clause is unnecessary as rights under a licence in relation to the use of a copyright work in question come to an end when it expires or is terminated.

142 *Frisby* v *British Broadcasting Corporation* [1987] Ch 932. A licensee, expressly or by implication, may not be allowed to alter the work.

143 [1966] 1 WLR 1055.

144 The first sound film shown to cinema audiences was *The Jazz Singer* in 1927.

145 *The Times*, 7 October 1992, p 16.

This is a particular issue where works are later included in an online archive. Of course, it is a matter of interpreting the original agreement (and any subsequent binding agreements or representations). Particularly relevant will be the presumed intention of the parties at the time of the agreement. This may be difficult to ascertain where the agreement was oral or based on the conduct of the parties and not reduced to writing.

In *MGN Ltd* v *Grisbrook*,[146] the respondent was a freelance photographer who had supplied the appellant (Mirror Group Newspapers) with large numbers of photographs for inclusion in its newspapers. Where these photographs were used, the photographer was paid a fee. If a photograph was published in a later publication, another though lower fee was paid. Photographs were retained in the MGN's picture library. Although there was no written agreement between MGN and Mr Grisbrook, it was accepted that Mr Grisbrook retained the copyright in his photographs. Eventually, MGN decided to make an archive of MGN's newspapers available to the public online. At first instance, it was held that there was an implied term permitting MGN to retain back issues of its newspapers in a safe and effective way and this extended to storage, for example, in microfiche or electronic form. However, this implied licence did not extend to making back issues of the newspapers widely available to the public. The Court of Appeal differentiated between two forms of publication: delivery by means of hard copy and by means of communication to the public by placing works on a website. Newspapers published on paper are essentially ephemeral and have no long-lasting status.[147] On the other hand, as Sir Andrew Morritt[148] said (at para 38):

> A website operates over a global area, its coverage is greatly in excess of anything MGN could have reached with hard copy newspapers. It enables a member of the public to read it before deciding whether he wants a hard copy and the production of hard copies by the public far in excess of anything MGN could have produced. The extent of the market and the costs incurred in reaching it are quite different to those of the hard copy newspapers of the past. There is no need to emphasise the differences further.

He went on to say that a suggestion that an intention may be imputed whereby Mr Grisbrook and MGN had agreed that MGN should be able to exploit Mr Grisbrook's photographs by inclusion on MGN's website, without further charge, was unacceptable.

Collecting societies

It may be inconvenient for the owner of copyright to agree licences and collect fees, or alternatively the copyright owner may want the backing of a powerful body to help to defend his or her rights in a court of law, if it comes to that. On the other hand, it is much more convenient if a user of copyright material can negotiate a single licence with respect to a range of works rather than having to agree separately with all the individual owners. Therefore, a proprietor of a hairdressing salon can obtain a licence from the Performing Right Society (PRS) and Phonographic Performance Ltd (PPL), to be able to play music to the shop's clients. Of course, there is a danger that bodies such as the PRS and PPL may abuse their positions. The PRS operates by taking an assignment of the copyright in the performance and broadcasting of musical works, administering that copyright, collecting fees and distributing them amongst its members.[149] Normally, the person wishing to play or broadcast musical works will obtain a blanket licence to do so in respect of all the works managed by the PRS. As a result of the very large number of works administered by the PRS, it clearly has a dominant position and might be tempted to try to control the proportion of music played during a broadcast or the relative proportions of live and recorded work, or to charge high fees. To prevent such abuse, the Performing Right

146 [2011] ECDR 4.

147 Except, perhaps, for collectors.

148 The Chancellor of the High Court (a position which replaced the former Vice-Chancellor of the Supreme Court following the Constitutional Reform Act 2005).

149 Other collecting societies include the Copyright Licensing Agency, operating in the field of copying. The need for such a scheme can be equated with developments in the technology of photocopying and other means of copying. The issue of a blanket licence is one way that copyright owners can obtain at least some recompense for the vast amount of reproduction of copyright material that takes place nowadays.

Tribunal was set up by the Copyright Act 1956 to regulate the licensing of performing rights, and this has now become the Copyright Tribunal, having extended jurisdiction and powers in comparison with the Performing Right Tribunal. The Copyright Tribunal may, for example, confirm or vary the terms, including royalty or fees to be paid, in a licence granted by collecting societies.

A collecting society usually operates by owning and enforcing the relevant copyrights. For example, Phonographic Performance Ltd (PPL) takes assignments of rights in sound recordings relevant to performing and broadcasting those sound recordings. Being in such a powerful position, it may be tempting for a collecting society to refuse to grant a licence to someone who has infringed those rights in the past unless they agree to pay for the past infringement (perhaps at a higher than usual royalty) and agree to pay for future use of the copyrights. Such a practice was considered by the Court of Appeal, in *Phonographic Performance Ltd* v *Saibal Maitra*,[150] and the following points were made:

150 [1998] FSR 749.

- Generally, although discretionary, where copyright infringement was established as well as a threat of continued infringement in the future, an injunction would be granted.
- A collecting society, *prima facie*, had the same rights as any ordinary copyright owner and should be treated the same by the court and granted the same relief.
- A copyright owner who exploits his copyright by licensing should be entitled to refuse to grant a licence unless it is granted on his own terms and conditions, including the payment of fees and it is not therefore an abuse to refuse to grant a licence without an appropriate payment being made for past infringement and an agreement to pay for future use.

In the particular case the judge, from whose decision the appeal was brought, stayed the injunctions for 28 days. The Court of Appeal held that this was wrong as it would allow the defendant to continue infringing for a further 28 days. Such further infringement, on the facts, would also constitute a criminal offence. In *Ludlow Music Inc* v *Robbie Williams*,[151] although not a collecting society case, the question of availability of injunctions was considered by Nicholas Strauss QC, sitting as a deputy judge of the High Court in the Chancery Division. He said (at 278):

151 [2001] FSR 19.

> [counsel for the claimant] rightly submits that, in considering whether to grant a permanent injunction, the balance of convenience is irrelevant. Although the remedy is discretionary, in the absence of special circumstances, the law will protect property rights; a person is not to be forced to sell his property for its reasonable market value, and a defendant is not to be permitted to buy the ability to infringe rights by the payment of damages.

However, in distinguishing *Phonographic Performance Ltd* v *Saibal Maitra*,[152] he went on to say that, although a copyright owner was legally entitled to charge whatever he wished, it was arguable that to do so was oppressive if he intended to exploit a defendant's weak position and had not asked for a reasonable payment but made excessive demands.

152 A very different type of case, being brought by a collecting society.

Licensing schemes

The provisions in the Copyright, Designs and Patents Act 1988 concerning licensing schemes are designed to prevent abuse of monopoly powers by copyright owners. The Copyright Tribunal is given control over licensing schemes and over licences granted by licensing bodies. The Tribunal can also grant compulsory licences, discussed later. A *licensing scheme* is, under s 116(1), a scheme setting out the classes of case in which the operator of the scheme, or the person on whose behalf he acts, is willing to grant copyright licences, and the terms on which licences would be granted in those classes of case. That is, it is a scheme concerning the licence fees to be charged in respect of specific types of works, for example a tariff of licence fees to be charged for performing musical works in public. A *licensing body* is a society or other organisation that has as its main object, or one of its main objects, the negotiation or granting of copyright licences, including the granting of such licences covering the works of more than one author. The body will be negotiating or granting licences either as owner or prospective owner of the copyright, or as the agent of the owner or prospective owner.[153]

The provisions for references and applications in respect of licensing schemes apply, under s 117,[154] to schemes operated by licensing bodies covering the work of more than one author (or publisher in relation to the publication right), so far as they relate to licences for:

(a) copying the work;
(b) rental or lending copies of the work to the public;
(c) performing, showing or playing the work in public;
(d) communicating the work to the public.

The copyright licensing provisions apply generally to the publication right as they do to copyright. However, the exception to the licensing provisions in s 116(4) in relation to a single collective work or collective works of which the authors are the same, or certain commissioned works, does not apply to the publication right. Hence, a collective work comprising previously unpublished works of one author which is out of copyright will, on publication, be subject to the publication right and to the licensing provisions of the Act, unlike the case of a collective work of one author which is still in copyright.

Any of the above schemes can be referred to the Copyright Tribunal. In the case of a proposed scheme to be operated by a licensing body, referral to the Tribunal can be made by an organisation claiming to be representative of users of the copyright material to which the scheme would apply under s 118.[155] If a licensing scheme is already in operation and there is a dispute between the operator of the scheme and a person claiming that he requires a licence under the scheme or an organisation representing users, under s 119, that person or organisation may refer the matter to the Tribunal. The Tribunal may, in either case, confirm or vary the scheme (existing or proposed) as the Tribunal thinks reasonable in the circumstances. There are also provisions for reference to the Tribunal if a person has been refused a licence by the operator of the scheme, or the operator has failed to procure a licence for him, for example if the person is seeking a licence for a work that is in a category of case excluded from the scheme.

The Copyright, Designs and Patents Act 1988 ss 124–128 apply to licences such as those in s 117 above granted by a licensing body but otherwise than in pursuance of a licensing scheme: for example, the Copyright Licensing Agency's licence with education authorities. The provisions are very similar to those for licensing schemes in respect of the works covered and the scope of the licences.[156] However, reference must be by a prospective licensee in the case of a proposed licence or, in the case of an existing licence, by the licensee on the ground that it is unreasonable that the licence should cease to be in force: that is, if the licence is due to expire under the terms of the licence. An application by an existing licensee cannot be made until the last three months before the licence is due to expire. The Tribunal may confirm or vary the terms of a proposed licence or may, in the case of an existing licence, extend the licence either for a fixed period or indefinitely. Under s 127, applications may be made by the licensing body or the person entitled to the benefit of the order to the Tribunal asking for it to review the order.

Sections 128A and 128B were inserted into the Act to deal with licensing schemes in relation to excepted sound recordings. However, in practice, the provisions were problematic and of unclear scope. They were repealed by the Copyright, Designs and Patents Act 1988 (Amendment) Regulations 2010.[157]

153 Copyright, Designs and Patents Act 1988 s 116(2).

154 This is a new section substituting the old s 117, by virtue of the Copyright and Related Rights Regulations 1996, SI 1996/2967.

155 See, for example, *British Phonographic Industry Ltd v Mechanical Copyright Protection Society Ltd* (No 2) [1993] EMLR 86.

156 Copyright, Designs and Patents Act 1988 s 124.

157 SI 2010/2694. The regulations came into force on 1 January 2011. For a discussion of the working of ss 128A and 128B, see the 8th edition of this book at pp 113–114.

The Copyright Tribunal has to make its determinations on the basis of what is reasonable in the circumstances, and under s 129 this means that the Tribunal shall have regard to the availability of other schemes, or the granting of licences to other persons in similar circumstances and the terms of those schemes or licences. Furthermore, the Tribunal shall exercise its powers so that there is no unreasonable discrimination between licensees (existing or prospective) under the scheme or licence that is subject to the referral, and licensees under other schemes operated by, or other licences granted by, the same person. Further guidelines relating to specific works or forms of use are given in ss 130–134. For example, s 130 covers the reprographic copying of published literary, dramatic, musical or artistic works or the typographical arrangement of published editions. With respect to such works, the Tribunal shall have regard to the extent to which published editions of the works are available, the proportion of the work to be copied and the nature of the use to which the copies are to be put. Also, for these types of works, under s 137 the Secretary of State can extend a licensing scheme under ss 118–123 operated by a licensing body, or a licence under ss 125–128 to works of a description similar to those covered by the scheme or licence that have been unreasonably excluded from the scheme or licence. This is provided that making them subject to the scheme or licence would not conflict with the normal exploitation of the works or unreasonably prejudice the legitimate interests of the copyright owners. Appeal from s 137 orders lies with the Copyright Tribunal which can confirm, discharge or vary the order.

Section 140 gives the Secretary of State powers of investigation as to the need for a licensing scheme or general licence to authorise educational establishments to make for the purposes of instruction reprographic copies of published literary, dramatic, musical or artistic works or the typographical arrangement of published editions. The Secretary of State may within one year of making a recommendation under s 140 grant a statutory licence free of royalty if provision has not been made in accordance with the recommendation.

Additionally, under s 143, the Secretary of State may certify licensing schemes on application from the person operating or proposing to operate the scheme in question.[158] The Secretary of State shall certify the scheme by way of statutory instrument, if he is satisfied that the scheme enables the works to which it relates to be sufficiently identified by persons likely to require licences, and clearly sets out the terms of the licences and charges payable, if any. Such schemes cover some of the acts permitted under copyright, such as the educational recording of broadcasts, or the making of copies of abstracts of scientific or technical articles, so that, if a certified licensing scheme is in operation, anyone carrying out one of the particular permitted acts included in the certified licensing scheme will infringe copyright, unless covered by the scheme. Some of the permitted acts can thus be nullified by certification.[159]

Most references to the Copyright Tribunal are likely to concern royalty rates set by collecting societies and under the statutory licensing scheme under s 135A permitting inclusion of sound recordings in broadcasts. As noted above, the Tribunal has wide discretion to have regard to all relevant circumstances and determine terms as the Tribunal considers reasonable. In *British Phonographic Industry Ltd* v *Mechanical-Copyright Protection Society Ltd*,[160] the Tribunal reiterated that it had a discretion of the widest and most general form. An important purpose of the Tribunal was to curb any unwarranted gain by virtue of the monopoly collecting societies enjoyed and to strike a balance between copyright owners and users. The Tribunal had to consider licences with numerous bodies offering online and off-line delivery. Webcasting was a particular issue and differed from terrestrial broadcasting where the broadcasters were required to offer a substantial quantity of non-music content. In webcasting, the music had a greater impact on the listener and, consequently, a greater connection with revenue generated by the webcaster.

In *British Sky Broadcasting Ltd* v *Performing Right Society Ltd*,[161] the licensee offered a royalty of £1.9 million per year to broadcast musical works from the repertoire of the PRS

158 For the purposes of ss 35, 60, 66, 74 and 141; an example being the Copyright (Certification of Licensing Schemes for Educational Recording of Broadcasts) (Open University) Order 2003, SI 2003/187.

159 This is acknowledged in the Copyright, Designs and Patents Act 1988 Chapter III, which deals with the permitted acts. *See*, for example, ss 35(2), 60(2) and 66(2).

160 [2008] EMLR 5. The Mechanical-Copyright Protection Society was involved (as well as the Performing Right Society) because downloading music necessarily involves making a copy of the music.

161 [1998] RPC 467.

which wanted some £17 million per year. Looking at comparable licences, under s 129, and all the relevant circumstances, the Tribunal decided £2.75 million per year was a reasonable royalty. The Tribunal considered it was wrong to calculate the royalty on the basis of revenue as the PRS had done. Music was just one component of the licensee's broadcasting operations and was not necessarily linked to the overall revenue.

The comparable licence approach is the most appropriate one to use, if such licences exist, unless there are special circumstances. A profits available approach, in which a collecting society takes a percentage of the profit made by the licensee, is not useful in this context as it leaves the collecting society vulnerable to the choice of a low profit margin by the licensee.[162] Tariffs used by foreign collecting societies may be useful where the licensee operates on an international scale. However, they need to be treated with caution, especially if there are several overlapping collecting societies and licensees are able to drive rates down by playing one off against the other. Apart from other difficulties, a major problem is determining how much the licence is worth to the licensee, especially if his main business is not the provision of entertainment but it is merely ancillary to his business. Both the preceding points would apply to an airline company with many destinations in other jurisdictions, competing with airlines from those other jurisdictions, and which provided in-flight entertainment which not all passengers would want.[163]

Educational establishments make use of licences for multiple copying of materials to be issued to students, such as handouts and resource packs. In *Universities UK* v *Copyright Licensing Agency Ltd*,[164] the Copyright Licensing Agency ('CLA') ran such a scheme covering the making of photocopies of parts of copyright works by staff and students (including copies made to distribute to students) in Universities and other Higher Education Institutions (collectively referred to below as 'HEIs') in return for payment of an annual fee based on the number of full-time educational students ('FTES') at the institution. The licence operated as a blanket licence (the 'Current Licence') and the amount payable for the year 2000/2001 was £3.25 per FTES. The fees collected were distributed by CLA to publishers and authors.

The Current Licence required separate clearance to be obtained for the making of resource packs for distribution to students. These packs were defined in the licence agreement as four or more photocopied extracts from licensed material from one or more sources which exceeded 25 pages, intended to be provided to students with a compilation of materials designed to support the teaching of a course of study and prepared and distributed in advance of or during the course of study either piecemeal or in batches. There were limitations on the proportions of books, etc. from which copies could be made under the scheme. The system for obtaining clearance for course packs was known as 'CLARCS' (Copyright Licensing Agency's Rapid Clearance Service). Not all publishers subscribing to the blanket licence were subject to CLARCS. On giving individual clearance, the CLA would inform the applicant of the fee payable if clearance was available. The system was cumbersome and incurred heavy administrative costs both for the CLA and the HEIs.

The CLA licence excluded separate artistic works from the scope of the licence. Later, the CLA introduced an Artistic Works Protocol which allowed copying under the scheme to extend to artistic works found in licensed material. Universities UK was formerly the Committee of Vice Chancellors and Principals of the United Kingdom. It made a number of references to the Copyright Tribunal for decisions as to certain aspects of the CLA's licensing scheme, concerning matters such as the payment to be made under the scheme, whether there should be a unitary system or two-tier system (a blanket licence plus CLARCS) and the scope of the exclusion relating to artistic works described as 'separate illustrations, diagrams and photographs'.

The Copyright Tribunal held:

- Sections 118 and 119 provide that proposed or current licensing schemes can be referred to the Tribunal which can confirm or vary the scheme as it determines is

162 *AEI Rediffusion Music Ltd* v *Phonographic Performance Ltd* [1998] RPC 335.

163 See *British Airways plc* v *Performing Right Society Ltd* [1998] RPC 581.

164 [2002] RPC 36.

reasonable in the circumstances. Under s 129, the Tribunal is required to look at comparable licensing schemes to ensure that there is no discrimination between licensees under the scheme and licensees under other schemes operated by the same person.

- Section 130 provides guidance in respect of reprographic copying of published literary, dramatic, musical or artistic works. The Tribunal is required to have regard to the extent to which published editions of the works in question are available, the proportion of the works to be copied and the nature of the use to which the copies are likely to be put. The Tribunal must also have regard to all relevant considerations under s 135.

- In deciding what the fee under the blanket licence should be, consideration must be given to the amount of material that could be copied under the permitted acts without infringing copyright. In particular, consideration should be given to copying within the fair dealing provisions under s 29 (which can include, under s 29(3), limited copying by librarians for students).

- It is fair dealing for a student to take an article from a journal or a short passage from a book for purposes associated with his course of study. On the other hand, material provided by staff for distribution to a number of students would not in general amount to fair dealing, nor would it be fair dealing for a lecturer to instruct every member of his class to make copies of the same material (this would not be the case, however, in respect of the mere distribution of a reading list without instructions to copy).

- A comparable licence was that used for schools and, in respect of which, the fees were considerably lower than under the Current Licence. However, the material copied in schools is different to that copied in HEIs and there are economies of scale in terms of publishing for schools, being a much bigger market. Furthermore, school books are cheaper than academic books and very little copying of journals takes place in schools. The differences in the charges for schools and HEIs could be described as being within a reasonable band, though the HEI charges were clearly at the top end of that band. The school licence comparator, therefore, exerted a downward pressure on future royalties for HEIs.

- Comparison with licences for Further Education Institutions lent support to the reasonableness of the Current Licence as such institutions simply adopted what the HEIs had done.

- It was acceptable to take into account other factors such as what the applicant was prepared to offer in negotiations.

- CLARCS, on its own, was not a licensing scheme within the meaning in s 116(1) of the Act. However, this fact alone did not deprive the Tribunal of jurisdiction over CLARCS, nor did the Tribunal believe that bringing the resource packs licensed under CLARCS within the standard blanket licence (the 'Current Licence') meant that the Tribunal was engaging in compulsory licensing. One of the terms in the Current Licence was to the effect that there was a restriction on copying course packs and this meant that the Tribunal had jurisdiction to consider whether that restriction was reasonable in the circumstances.

- The evidence showed that there existed high levels of dissatisfaction with CLARCS. It was unwieldy, expensive to administer, it took a long time to obtain clearances and the system was complex and burdensome. Furthermore, the Tribunal was not persuaded that the provision of resource packs had a significant impact on the level of textbooks sold.

- The Tribunal considered that it would be highly desirable to dispense with the two-tier system and bring an end to CLARCS but the provision of resource packs should give an entitlement to a higher royalty rate compared to other forms of copying.

- The only type of artistic works excluded from the Current Licence were those appearing on separate pages from the text and which were unnecessary for an understanding of the text.

- A formula based on the notional average number of pages copied multiplied by the number of FTES at an institution and a notional cost per page was not appropriate although it was sensible to base the fee payable on the number of FTES.
- The basic fee should be set at £2.75 per FTES with an uplift of £1.20 per FTES for including CLARCS in the basic blanket licence and an uplift of £0.05 per FTES for including artistic works appearing with text. This would give an overall figure of £4.00 per FTES. The new licence would run for five years commencing on 1 August 2001. On each anniversary of that date, the fee would be increased in accordance with the retail price index.
- Universities UK had suggested £0.60 per FTES and the CLA suggested £10.25.

Compulsory licences and licences as of right

Compulsory licences may be granted by order of the Secretary of State in respect of the lending to the public of copies of literary, dramatic, musical or artistic works, sound recordings or films under s 66, unless there exists a certified licensing scheme under s 143. In its previous form, s 66 was restricted to rental to the public of copies of sound recordings, films or computer programs. Should s 66 ever be used, under s 142, the Copyright Tribunal has the power to settle the royalty payable if the parties cannot agree on a royalty.

Licences as of right may become available following a reference to the Competition Commission (previously the Monopolies and Mergers Commission) under s 12(5) of the Competition Act 1980 or under a number of provisions in the Enterprise Act 2002. Under s 144(1) this applies where there are restrictive conditions in licences or where the copyright owner refuses to grant licences on reasonable terms. Such conditions may be cancelled or modified or it may be provided that licences shall be available as of right.[165] The terms of the licence will be settled by the Copyright Tribunal in the absence of agreement. A proviso is that the powers under s 144 may be exercised only if to do so will not contravene the conventions to which the UK is a party, that is the Berne Copyright Convention and the Universal Copyright Convention.

There are provisions under s 144A for the compulsory exercise of rights in literary, dramatic, musical or artistic works, sound recordings or films in respect of cable re-transmission of wireless broadcasts from another EEA state in which the work is included.[166] The right is referred to as the 'cable re-transmission right', and it may be exercised against a cable operator only through a licensing body. If the copyright owner has not acted to transfer this right to the appropriate licensing body, it will be deemed to be transferred, but such a person must claim his rights within three years from the date of the relevant cable re-transmission. A 'cable operator' means a person responsible for cable re-transmission of a wireless broadcast, and 'cable re-transmission' means the reception and immediate re-transmission by cable, including the transmission of microwave energy between terrestrial fixed points of a wireless broadcast.[167]

Sections 135A–135C provide a right to use certain sound recordings in broadcasts, being recordings where the appropriate licence could have been granted by or procured by a licensing body. Either one of two conditions must be present, being (a) refusal to grant or procure a licence at terms acceptable to the person including the recordings (or at terms set by the Copyright Tribunal) and which permits unlimited 'needletime' or such as demanded by that person or (b) where the person holds a licence, but the needletime is limited. There are requirements for the person desiring to include the sound recording in the broadcast to give notice to the licensing body and to the Copyright Tribunal. Section 135D covers applications to the Copyright Tribunal to settle terms of payment and further provisions as to references and applications for review are contained in ss 135E–135G.[168]

165 The powers are exercisable by the Secretary of State, the Office of Fair Trading or the Competition Commission as the case may be.

166 Inserted by the Copyright and Related Rights Regulations 1996, SI 1996/2967 and modified by the Copyright and Related Rights Regulations 2003, SI 2003/2498.

167 Thus, for these purposes wireless broadcasts are treated differently to broadcasts by cable.

168 These provisions were inserted by the Broadcasting Act 1990.

Copyright Tribunal

The Copyright Tribunal is the old Performing Right Tribunal with more powers and a much wider scope of operation, as has been noted above. Section 145 states that the Performing Right Tribunal, which was established under the Copyright Act 1956 s 23 to regulate the licensing of performing rights, is renamed the Copyright Tribunal. The Copyright Tribunal is made up of a chairman and two deputy chairmen appointed by the Lord Chancellor after consulting the Secretary of State, and between two and eight ordinary members appointed by the Secretary of State. A person appointed as chairman or a deputy chairman must have satisfied the judicial-appointment eligibility condition on a five-year basis, be an advocate or solicitor in Scotland of at least five years' standing, be a member of the Northern Ireland Bar or a solicitor of the Supreme Court of Northern Ireland of at least five years' standing or who has held judicial office.[169] The Copyright, Designs and Patents Act 1988 s 146 contains provisions for the resignation or removal of members of the Tribunal and provision is made for the payment of members in s 147, as well as for the appointment of staff for the Tribunal.

The constitution of the Tribunal for the purpose of proceedings is to comprise a chairman, either the chairman or a deputy chairman, and two or more ordinary members.[170] Voting on decisions is by majority, with the chairman having a further casting vote if the votes are otherwise equal. The jurisdiction of the Tribunal is set out in s 149 and includes:

1 the determination of royalty or other remuneration to be paid with respect to re-transmission of a broadcast including the work;
2 applications to determine amount of equitable remuneration where rental right is transferred;[171]
3 applications and references in respect of licensing schemes;
4 applications or references with respect to use as of right of sound recordings in broadcasts;
5 appeals against the coverage of a licensing scheme or licence;
6 applications to settle the terms of copyright licences available as of right;
7 applications under s 135D in respect of the terms of payment for licences of right to include sound recordings in broadcasts.[172]

Other areas of jurisdiction of the Copyright Tribunal are provided for elsewhere: for example, with respect to rights in performances.

The Copyright, Designs and Patents Act 1988 has further provisions as regards the making of procedural rules for the Tribunal[173] and fees to be charged, and, under s 151, the Tribunal can make orders as to costs and, under s 151A, award interest in some cases. Finally, under s 152, appeals may be made to the High Court, or to the Court of Session in Scotland, on any point of law arising from a decision of the Tribunal. It should be noted that the Tribunal is not a proactive body and can only respond to applications and references made to it.

169 Previously, the general period was seven years but this was changed to five years by virtue of the Tribunals, Courts and Enforcement Act 2007, with effect from 21 July 2008.

170 Copyright, Designs and Patents Act 1988 s 148.

171 The basic rule is that the concept of equitable remuneration must be applied uniformly in Member States though models based on a number of factors may be used; Case C-245/00 *Stichting ter Exploitatie van Nabiruge Rechten* v *Nederlandse Omroep Stichting* [2003] ECR I-1251.

172 Copyright, Designs and Patents Act 1988 ss 135A–135G were inserted by the Broadcasting Act 1990 as a result of a Monopolies and Mergers Commission report proposing compulsory licensing of broadcasts of sound recordings and the abolition of the Phonographic Performance Ltd's imposition of restrictions on 'needletime'. In *AIRC* v *PPL and BBC* [1994] RPC 143, the Tribunal set royalty value rates and rejected the rates proposed by PPL. The Tribunal also pointed out that ss 135A–135G had deprived PPL of injunctive relief.

173 Copyright Tribunal Rules 1989, SI 1989/1129, as amended.

Summary

The author of a work of copyright is the person who creates the work. For the original works this is usually self-explanatory but further guidance is given for some works. For example, the author of a sound recording is its producer. In the case of a film, the producer and principal directors are the authors. The author of a computer-generated literary, dramatic, musical or artistic work is the person by whom the arrangements necessary for the creation of the work are undertaken.

A work is one of joint authorship where it is created collaboratively by two or more persons such that the contribution of each is not distinct from the other or others. It is also possible for a work to be one of unknown authorship.

As to ownership, the basic rule is that the author will be the first owner of the copyright. To that simple rule there are exceptions, the main being where the work was created by an employee in the course of his employment in which case, subject to agreement to the contrary, the employer will be the first owner of the copyright. Other exceptions apply in relation to Crown copyright, Parliamentary copyright and in relation to certain international organisations such as the United Nations.

In some cases, for example, where the work was created under a commission (that is, not by an employee in the course of his employment), the person commissioning the work will not be the first owner (unless assigned to him by the author). The courts may overcome the difficulties this may cause by granting beneficial ownership to the person commissioning the work or may imply a licence to allow his continued use. The leading case on the circumstances under which either will be granted are set out in *Robin Ray* v *Classic FM* (subject to some clarification by Jacob LJ in *Griggs* v *Evans*).

Copyright can be dealt with as other property. It may be:

- assigned (transfer of ownership);
- licensed, either:
  - exclusively (no-one else, including the copyright owner, may carry out the relevant acts), or
  - non-exclusively (any number of licences may be granted).

Assignments and licences may be partial. They may grant limited rights in relation to the acts covered by the copyright, such as:

- the right to carry out only some of the acts in relation to the right;
- the right to carry out some or all of the acts but limited to a specified territory;
- the right to carry out some or all of the rights for a limited period of time.

Assignments and exclusive licences are subject to formalities. They must be in writing and signed by or on behalf of the assignor or owner as the case may be. Failure to comply may be remedied by the courts by granting beneficial ownership or by implying an appropriate licence. Although there are no formalities for non-exclusive licences to take effect, it is sensible to have them recorded in writing and, where appropriate, signed by the owner.

Collecting societies exist to collect fees by granting licences for the use of works and to distribute the income amongst copyright owners. Formal licensing schemes may be set up, subject to the powers of the Copyright Tribunal.

Discussion questions

1 Do you think provision should be made in the Act such that a person commissioning the creation of a work of copyright automatically becomes its first owner?

2 Describe the concept of beneficial ownership of copyright and consider the circumstances which a court might take into account in deciding whether it is appropriate.

Selected further reading

Booton, D., 'The informal acquisition of copyright', [2011] *Intellectual Property Quarterly*, 28 (looks at case law on beneficial ownership and considers whether the lack of certainty resulting from the application of equity to ownership of copyright can be justified).

Farmer, S., 'Infection Control Enterprises Ltd v Virrage Industries Ltd: refusal to infer copyright transfer in a software development agreement' [2010] *Computer and Telecommunications Law Review*, 76 (discusses the case and the consequences of failing to properly provide for ownership of copyright in the context of a software development agreement).

Howe, H. R., 'Copyright limitations and the stewardship model of property', [2011] *Intellectual Property Quarterly*, 183 (looks at a liberal model of property and the community interest in relation to copyright and argues for a stewardship model to best serve the community interest; and points to the difficulty of creating derivative or transformative works, such as parodies, without infringing copyright unless further exceptions are developed or changes are made to concepts such as idea/expression or substantiality).

Authors' rights   5

Introduction

This chapter looks at the rights of authors which are independent of the economic rights under copyright law. Some of the rights are known as 'moral rights' and are described as such in the Berne Convention for the Protection of Literary and Artistic Works 1886 (the 'Berne Copyright Convention'), Article 6bis. These are the right to claim authorship and the right to object to modification and derogatory treatment of the author's work. These rights are important in that they give the author some control over his work in the future. This is particularly important where the author no longer has any economic rights in the work enabling him to control how it is used or modified in the future. The categories of moral rights under the UK's Copyright, Designs and Patents Act 1988 includes some other 'rights' under the heading moral rights including a right not to have a work falsely attributed and rights to privacy in certain photographs and films.

This chapter also looks at another right recently introduced which gives authors or works or art and manuscripts a royalty when the work is resold in the future. This right, known as the *droit de suite*, derives from Article 14ter of the Berne Copyright Convention. It has existed in some countries for some time, first introduced in France shortly after the First World War to compensate widows of artists killed during that war. It can be justified on the 'genius in the garret' principle. Many artists sell their works cheaply (reputedly, in some cases, giving them in return for a meal). Later, when they become famous, their earlier works may sell for vast sums of money and it is thought that a modest royalty payable to the artist, or his estate after his death, goes some way to reduce the apparent inequity.

The artists' resale right was brought into the UK as a result of implementing a European Directive. The fact that some Member States, such as the UK, did not have such a right was seen as giving rise to potential discrimination on the grounds of nationality contrary to Article 18 of the Treaty on the Functioning of the European Union.[1] It has to be said, however, that the introduction of the right was not generally welcomed in the UK and auction houses were particularly concerned about the effects that the right might have on their business. The artists' resale right and the Directive are discussed towards the end of this chapter.

1 Formerly Article 12 of the EC Treaty.

Moral rights

2 The Rome Act 1928 added the *droit moral* to the Berne Convention, being the right to claim first authorship of a work and the right to object to any distortion, mutilation or other modification which would be prejudicial to the honour or reputation of the author.

In tardy recognition of parts of the Berne Copyright Convention[2] and in acknowledgement of the importance with which moral rights are regarded in much of the rest of Europe, the Copyright, Designs and Patents Act 1988 gave overt recognition and legal effect to such rights given to the creator of a work in which copyright subsists. UK copyright law has a tradition of emphasising the economic rights associated with copyright, while the French model stresses the author's rights to control and be identified with his work regardless of the ownership of the economic rights. The Copyright, Designs and Patents Act 1988 bundles a collection of rights together under the appellation 'moral rights', even though some might not be thought to fall within this description, an example being the false attribution right and the right to privacy in certain photographs and films. There are four rights within the 'moral right' designation, being:

1 the right to be identified as the author of a work or director of a film, the 'paternity right' (ss 77–79);
2 the right of an author of a work or director of a film to object to derogatory treatment of that work or film, the 'integrity right' (ss 80–83);
3 a general right, that every person has, not to have a work falsely attributed to him (s 84);
4 the commissioner's right of privacy in respect of a photograph or film made for private and domestic purposes (s 85).

Until 1996, a film director had only moral rights and no other rights of authorship.[3] Now, the principal director of a film is a joint author along with the producer unless, of course, they are the same person, in which case the principal director will be the sole author.

In typically half-hearted fashion, these moral rights do not apply globally to all types of copyright work and, additionally, there are many exceptions to the application of the rights. The rights can be waived, or even fail for lack of positive assertion on the part of the author or director. That the rights can be waived at all is unsatisfactory bearing in mind the economic pressure the creator of a work may be subject to. Others may argue that the UK is wise to take a cautious approach to these rights on the basis of experience elsewhere, particularly in France where the exercise of moral rights forced a television channel to complete making a series of programmes against its wishes and where any objectionable treatment of a work is likely to attract a claim that it infringes the integrity right.[4] Although authors seem keen on enforcing their moral rights in France, there has been relatively little activity in the UK.

French copyright law is more robust when it comes to moral rights. The right of an author to enjoy respect for his name, his authorship and his work is perpetual, inalienable and imprescriptible.[5] However, the descendants of Victor Hugo failed to prevent the publication of novels presented as continuations of Victor Hugo's *Les Miserables*: in *Hugo v Plon SA*,[6] an action was commenced against an author who recently wrote a sequel to Hugo's novel. It was Victor Hugo's wish that no sequel be written and, at first instance, the court agreed that his moral rights had been infringed. However, on appeal, the *Cour de Cassation* remitted the case back for reconsideration as the court below failed to properly consider whether, in fact, Victor Hugo's moral rights had been infringed. Eventually, in *La Société des gens de lettres de France (SGDL) and Pierre Hugo v SA Les Éditions Plon and François Cérésa*[7] the *Cour d'Appel* held that Victor Hugo's moral rights had not been infringed. The court said that:

> . . . the author of the continuation is required to remain true to the work that he uses, to respect its spirit, which does not of itself exclude a certain freedom of expression and imagination. It is in the exercise of this freedom that the author of the continuation creates an original work while taking care not to distort the first work. Whether the continuation is in the same genre or a different genre to that of the work on which it is based is of no importance, the same freedom of expression and the same obligation to respect the spirit of the original applying to the author of the continuation in both cases

In contrast with the position under French law, under the UK Act, the rights to be identified as author and to object to a derogatory treatment last only as long as the economic rights.[8]

3 This was a result of changes made by the Copyright and Related Rights Regulations 1996, SI 1996/2967, with effect from 1 December 1996. It applied to films made on or after 1 July 1994.

4 *See* Cornish, W.R. 'Authors in Law' (1995) 58 MLR 1.

5 Article L 121–1 of Law No 92–597 of 1 July 1992 on the Intellectual Property Code, as amended. That moral rights may be perpetual is allowed under the Berne Convention for the Protection of Literary and Artistic Works; Article 6[bis].

6 [2007] ECDR 9.

7 Case RG 07/05821, *Cour d'Appel*, Paris, 19 December 2008.

8 Victor Hugo died in 1885.

To supporters of moral rights, the way in which they have been dealt with in the UK by the Copyright, Designs and Patents Act 1988 seems to be very much a compromise. Often there will be a conflict between a moral right and an economic right, an example being in the case of employee-authors or directors. Bearing in mind that, as regards a literary, dramatic, musical or artistic work made by an employee in the course of his employment, the employer will be the first owner of the copyright under s 11(2), the Act effectively overrides the author's right to be identified as the author in relation to anything done by or with the authority of the copyright owner.[9]

Moral rights were hailed as a novelty in UK copyright law.[10] However, this is not really so – other areas of law could give remedies to the author. A licence agreement or an assignment of copyright can contain terms requiring that the author's name be placed prominently on copies of the work and that the work must not be modified. A treatment of an author's work which is derogatory or the false attribution of a work might give rise to an action in defamation. For example, an eminent and distinguished author, Edward, might write a serious and noble play about love conquering adversity and assign the copyright to a television company. If that television company then rewrites the play and changes it into a smutty farce and broadcasts it, and Edward's name appears in the credits as being associated with the writing of the play, Edward will have an action in defamation on the basis that this would significantly harm his reputation.[11] The same might apply if an inferior and tasteless musical work has been falsely attributed to a celebrated and highly regarded composer with an international reputation.

An author's moral rights can be protected indirectly because the act complained of might also involve a normal infringement of copyright. For example, if another person, without permission of the copyright owner, makes a parody of the work, the author might feel aggrieved and the copyright owner might decide to sue for infringement because the parody contains a substantial part of the original work. However, only the copyright owner could bring a legal action and an author who did not own the copyright in his work would have to stand by helplessly unless the treatment of the work was defamatory.[12] It should be noted that the right to object to a derogatory treatment of the work is likely to be actionable in wider circumstances than would be the case in defamation because it extends to treatment which distorts or mutilates the work without necessarily affecting the author's reputation. In fact, a distortion or mutilation of a work is, from the language of s 80(2)(b), prejudicial to the honour or reputation of the author or director *per se*.

Right to be identified as the author or director of a work (the 'paternity right')

The right to be identified as the author of a literary, dramatic, musical or artistic work, or as the director of a film, was an innovation for UK copyright law. But it is not as wide-ranging as it should be, and there are a number of exceptions to it. Additionally, the author or director must assert the right for it to be effective. The right does not apply to other types of works, such as sound recordings and broadcasts where it would be inappropriate in any case; nor does the right apply to works in which copyright does not subsist – the work must be a 'copyright' work. Furthermore, the right does not apply to all forms of the works included – for example, the right does not apply to computer programs, even though these are literary works.[13]

The Copyright, Designs and Patents Act 1988 s 77(1) states that the right to be identified as author or director applies to literary, dramatic, musical and artistic works, and to films. However, the right is not infringed unless it has been asserted in accordance with

9 The same applied in respect of employee-directors.

10 De Freitas, D. 'The Copyright, Designs and Patents Act 1988 (2)' (1989) 133 *Solicitors Journal* 670 at 675. De Freitas recognises correctly that the right not to have a work falsely attributed to a person is of older vintage: *see* Copyright Act 1956 s 43.

11 That is, it would be likely to lower him in the estimation of right-thinking people generally.

12 Unless the author had asserted his right to be identified and he had not been identified as such.

13 Though the right may apply to copyright databases.

s 78 so as to bind the person who carries out an activity which gives rise to the right to be identified. Under s 78(2), the right may be asserted generally or in relation to specified acts either:

(a) on assignment, by including a statement in the instrument effecting the assignment – for example, a term in the assignment stating that the author or director asserts his moral right to be identified as such (an assignment must, of course, be in writing and signed by or on behalf of the assignor by s 90); or

(b) by written instrument signed by the author or director – for example, by including a suitable term in a licence agreement. However, it may simply be a written notification of the right and not part of some contractual document.

There is no requirement that the right must be asserted before or at the time of any assignment or licence, and it would appear that the right might be asserted at any time even subsequent to the transfer of the economic rights in the work. However, there may be a term in an assignment or licence agreement to the effect that the author or director must not at some future date assert this right. If this is so, the author or director will be in breach of contract if he subsequently asserts the right.[14] The Act does not make clear whether the effect of any written notice is retrospective, that is whether an author or director can make this right apply to things done prior to the assertion. This could be extremely awkward for an assignee or licensee but for the fact that the Act does allow a court to take into account any delay in asserting the right when considering remedies.[15] As s 78(2) refers to signature by the author, it would seem that the right to be identified as author (or director) cannot be brought to life after his death, say by his widow.

Under the transitional arrangements contained in the Copyright, Designs and Patents Act 1988 Sch 1, paras 22–24, the right to be identified as author applies to literary, dramatic, musical and artistic works made before the commencement of the 1988 Act if the author was still alive at that date.[16] Therefore, the right to be identified as author can be asserted in respect of a pre-existing work, by a written instrument signed by the author. There are certain safeguards – for example, nothing done before the commencement date is actionable as an infringement of moral rights, and assignees and licensees may continue to perform acts covered by an assignment or licence granted before the commencement date.

There are additional means of asserting the right to be identified that apply in relation to public exhibitions of artistic works. Under s 78(3), when the author or first owner of copyright parts with possession of the original, or a copy is made under his direction or control, the right may be asserted by identifying the author on the original or copy, or on a frame, mount or other thing to which it is attached. Also, in relation to a public exhibition of an artistic work made in pursuance of a licence agreement, the right may be asserted by including, in a licence authorising the making of copies of the work, a statement to that effect.

It is one thing to assert a right, but quite another to enforce it against third parties, and therefore there must be provisions for determining whether a person is bound by the assertion and whether notice, actual or constructive, is required. In terms of the paternity right, the formula depends on the mode of assertion, and s 78(4) states the circumstances in which assignees, licensees and the like are bound by an assertion of the right to be identified as the author or director. In the case of an assignment, the assignee and anyone claiming through him are bound by the right regardless of notice. For example, if a person takes an assignment of the copyright in a literary work and the agreement includes a statement to the effect that the author asserts his right to be identified as author or director, and that person, the original assignee, subsequently assigns the copyright to a third person, then the latter will be bound by the right even if he has no knowledge of it and could not reasonably be expected to know of its existence. This will apply also to subsequent licensees, and even to a situation where a person obtains ownership of the copyright by

14 It might also be a breach of an express or implied term in respect of quiet enjoyment.

15 Copyright, Designs and Patents Act 1988 s 78(5).

16 The commencement date of the copyright provisions of the Copyright, Designs and Patents Act 1988 is 1 August 1989.

way of a gift. Any person without knowledge of the assertion subsequently obtaining rights in the copyright will be bound even if he is acting in good faith, provided that he derives his right or interest in the copyright through the original assignee. If observing the right to identification is likely to be inconvenient, a person acquiring a licence or assignment of copyright in a literary, dramatic, musical, artistic work or film should, if at all possible, have sight of the original assignment of the rights he now wants to acquire before concluding the agreement.[17]

Where the assertion is other than by assignment, only persons to whom notice of the assertion is brought are bound by it. The plain language of s 78 seems to be to the effect that the notice must be actual notice and that constructive or imputed notice will not suffice to bind the person with respect to the right. It is clear, therefore, that as far as the author or director is concerned, the right to be identified is far better asserted through an assignment than by any other means. Of course, if the author or director is also the first owner of the copyright, he may make contractual provision safeguarding this right, for example by including a term that infringement of the right is to be considered a breach of condition and that sub-licences may not be granted except with the owner's consent and such sub-licences must include a term asserting the right. Least effective of all is the position where the right is asserted by a written and signed non-contractual document.

In relation to public exhibitions of artistic works, terms in licences asserting the right to be identified as author bind everyone, regardless of notice, into whose hands a copy made in pursuance of the licence comes. In the case of identification placed on the original or copy, frame, mount or other thing to which the artistic work is attached, any person into whose hands the original or copy comes is bound even if the identification is no longer present or visible. Therefore, the right is not to be defeated simply because an intermediate possessor of the artistic work deliberately or accidentally removed the identification.

Scope of the right to be identified as the author or director

The right to be identified as the author or director does not apply to every act that can be performed in relation to the work. For example, the right does not apply when a dramatic work is performed privately, say to a group of friends, or in the case of non-commercial publication. The scope of the right varies according to the nature of the work, as is to be expected, and is provided for in s 77. It is interesting to note that the classification of copyright works given in s 1 is not followed precisely and some regrouping is required to make sense of the scope of the right. In particular, a literary work consisting of words intended to be sung or spoken with music is treated the same as a musical work.[18]

In relation to literary works (other than words intended to be sung or spoken with music) and dramatic works, the author has the right to be identified whenever:

(a) the work is published commercially, performed in public or communicated to the public; or
(b) copies of a film or sound recording including the work are issued to the public.[19]

Communicating a work to the public means communication by electronic means and includes broadcasting a work or making available to the public by electronic transmission so that members of the public may access the work from a place and at a time individually chosen by them: s 20(2).[20] The former form of communication can include conventional television or radio broadcasts through the air or by cable and the latter is intended to cover situations where, for example, works are placed on internet websites for access.

The right also applies to these acts in respect of adaptations; that is, the author has the right to be identified as the author of the work from which the adaptation was made. For example, if an author, Florence Smith, writes a story in English and another person later translates the story into German and publishes copies of the German translation

17 Of course, in most circumstances, applying the author's name to copies of the work will not be onerous.

18 Copyright, Designs and Patents Act 1988 s 77(3).

19 Copyright, Designs and Patents Act 1988 s 77(2).

20 Substituted by the Copyright and Related Rights Regulations 2003, SI 2003/2498.

commercially, then, provided that Florence has asserted her right to be identified as author, copies of the German version must contain a clear and reasonably prominent notice to the effect that the story has been translated from the original English version written by Florence Smith.

The author of a musical work or literary work consisting of words intended to be spoken or sung with music, for example the lyrics of a song, has the right to be identified as the author of the work whenever:

(a) the work is published commercially; or

(b) copies of a sound recording of the work are issued to the public; or

(c) a film of which the sound track includes the work is shown in public or copies of such a film are issued to the public.[21]

21 Copyright, Designs and Patents Act 1988 s 77(3).

As with dramatic works and the remainder of literary works, the right also applies to the above events in relation to an adaptation, namely that the original author has the right to be identified as the author of the work from which the adaptation was made.

The author of an artistic work has, under s 77(4), the right to be identified whenever:

(a) the work is published commercially or exhibited in public, or a visual image of it is communicated to the public; or

(b) a film including a visual image of the work is shown in public or copies of such a film are issued to the public; or

(c) in the case of a work of architecture in the form of a building or model for a building, a sculpture or a work of artistic craftsmanship, copies of a graphic work representing it, or of a photograph of it are issued to the public.

Also, under s 77(5), the author of a work of architecture in the form of a building (that is, the architect) has the right to be identified on the building as constructed or, where more than one building is constructed to the design, on the first to be constructed. However, it is unlikely that names of architects will be found on the first example of a mass-produced design, such as on a speculative builder's housing estate, because, as will be seen below, all moral rights can be waived. It is likely that a property developer commissioning an architect will press for a waiver of this moral right unless, of course, the architect is very famous and the fixing at or near the entrance of the finished building of a suitable plaque upon which the architect's name is inscribed would be a good selling point. Alternatively, the fame and reputation of the architect may be such that he is in a strong bargaining position and can insist on exercising his right to be identified. There is no provision for the right in respect of adaptations of artistic works, the reason being that it is not an infringement of an artistic work to make an adaptation of it.[22]

22 *See* Copyright, Designs and Patents Act 1988 s 21.

Section 77(6) gives the director of a film the right to be identified whenever the film is shown in public or communicated to the public or copies of the film are issued to the public. An example of the last would be when video recordings of the film are made available to the public by way of sale or rental.

The Act provides that the right to be identified applies in relation to the whole or any substantial part of the work.[23] For example, if a short extract from a literary work is printed and published commercially, the right still applies provided that the extract represents a substantial part of the whole work. It would be ridiculous if the copying and publication of a short extract would infringe the economic right but not the moral right, and therefore it is to be expected that 'substantial' in the context of moral rights will have the same meaning developed by the courts for economic rights, remembering that under s 16(3)(a) acts restricted by copyright apply in relation to the work as a whole or any substantial part of it. The transitional provisions in Sch 1 confirm this approach in that para 23(3) links infringement of moral rights to infringement of the economic rights under copyright, although this is in the context of things permitted under assignments or

23 Copyright, Designs and Patents Act 1988 s 89(1).

licences. It would seem sensible that infringement of moral rights should be on all fours with the infringement of economic rights concerning the requirement for substantiality.

Method of identification

Having the right to be identified as the author or director would be greatly diluted if there were not also provisions relating to the prominence of the notice containing the identification. Section 77(7) deals with this important matter and requires that the identification must be clear and reasonably prominent. The manner of identification depends to some extent on the nature of the act making the work available. In the case of the commercial publication of the work or the issue to the public of a film or sound recording, the author or director (or both if appropriate) should be identified on each copy or, if that is not appropriate, in some other manner likely to bring his identity to the notice of a person acquiring a copy. Where the identification relates to a building, it should be by appropriate means visible to persons entering or approaching the building: for example, by means of a plaque on the wall adjacent to the entrance. In any other case, the author or director should be identified in such a manner likely to bring his identity to the attention of a person seeing or hearing the performance, exhibition, showing or communication in question. For example, if a play is performed in public, notices, advertisements and the like, and programmes or brochures sold to the audience, should contain the author's name in a prominent place. If there are no written or printed materials, the author's name should be clearly stated to the audience prior to the performance.

Simply naming the author is not sufficient to comply with the right to be identified and the acknowledgement must be to the author *as author*. Under s 77(8), the author or director may specify a pseudonym or initials, or some other form of identification, and if he does that form shall be used as the means of identification. In all other cases, any reasonable form of identification may be used. In *Hyperion Records Ltd v Dr Lionel Sawkins*,[24] the composer of performing editions of old musical works required that a copyright notice be used in the following form:

24 [2005] RPC 32.

© Copyright 2002 by Lionel Sawkins

CDs had been issued to the public which included a booklet carrying the acknowledgement 'With thanks to Dr Lionel Sawkins for his preparation of performance materials for this recording'. The judge at first instance considered that this was insufficient to identify Dr Sawkins as the author and the Court of Appeal agreed. This was hardly a surprising result in the light of the fact that it was Hyperion's case that no new copyright had been created by Dr Sawkins.

Some forms of works may pose serious problems in terms of identifying authors or directors. For example, a multimedia product such as an encyclopaedia on CD-ROM. There may be thousands of authors and directors involved in making such a product. If the credits had to be 'rolled' as is common in the case of a cinematograph film or television drama, this could take several minutes before the person consulting the encyclopaedia could proceed. There are ways of overcoming this problem, the first being to ensure that all moral rights have been waived. Another way is to give the person using the CD-ROM an option to see details of the contributors should he choose to do so. Whether this is likely to bring the identity of the authors and directors to the notice of the person acquiring a copy is debatable, as few may elect to view this information, at least all the way through. It does, however, accord with pragmatism. A further approach might be to include details of contributors in any printed matter supplied with the multi-media product. However, under s 79(6) there is an important exception to the right to be identified where the work has been made for the purpose of publication in, *inter alia*, an encyclopaedia or where it has been made available with the consent of the author for the purposes of such publication. Note: it is the consent of the author and not the owner of the copyright which is important, and the statutory exception does not cover films, presumably because the draughtsman of these provisions was thinking of paper publication only. Therefore, although the exception may be useful, it is not a universal exception in the case of electronic publication.

Exceptions to the right to be identified

The exceptions to the right to be identified as the author or director are contained in s 79. These exceptions have the effect of significantly weakening the right to be identified in respect of certain types of works or as regards authors with a particular status. Coupled with the fact the right must be asserted and that the right, in common with the other moral rights, is capable of being waived by the person entitled to it, this reduces the practical importance of the right to what is, perhaps, a regrettable extent.[25] If an author has been commissioned to create the work, he might be under pressure to waive his moral rights by his paymaster, who may be of the view that moral rights are an undesirable hindrance to the commercial exploitation of the work, or just plain inconvenient.

The exceptions to the right to be identified as the author or director of a relevant work are classified by reference to:

1 *The type of work* (s 79(2)). Computer programs, designs of typefaces and computer-generated works are excluded from the province of the paternity right. This confirms the uncomfortable categorisation of computer programs as literary works. However, other items of computer software such as databases,[26] preparatory design material and other works stored in computers may be subject to moral rights. A typeface includes an ornamental motif used for printing and would normally fall within the graphic work category of artistic works. If justification is required for the first exception, it may be on the basis that a large number of persons could be involved in the design, development and subsequent modification of the program and that it would be inconvenient to allow the right.[27] Another argument could address the fact that computer programs and typefaces are more of a commercial character and less of an 'artistic' nature than the other works to which the right applies. As computer-generated works have no human author by definition (s 178), it seems reasonable that they must be excluded.[28]

2 *The employment status of authors and directors* (s 79(3)). If the first owner of the copyright in the work is the author's or director's employer by virtue of s 11(2), then the right does not apply in respect of acts done by or with the authority of the copyright owner.

3 *The permitted acts*. There are exceptions relating to some specific permitted acts which are:
    (a) s 30, fair dealing to the extent that it relates to the reporting of current events by means of a sound recording, film or broadcast;
    (b) s 31, incidental inclusion of a work in an artistic work, sound recording, film or broadcast. It would obviously be troublesome and difficult to give credits identifying the author or director, for example, if, in a live television news report, some music could be heard playing in the background;
    (c) s 32(3), examination questions. However, it is normal practice for the author of a work quoted in an examination paper to be acknowledged;
    (d) s 45, parliamentary and judicial proceedings, and s 46(1) and (2), Royal Commissions and statutory inquiries. Again, it is unlikely that the author or director would not be acknowledged as a matter of courtesy;
    (e) s 51, permitted acts in relation to design documents and models, and s 52, relating to copyright in artistic works that have been exploited in a commercial sense; and
    (f) s 57 or s 66A, in respect of acts permitted on assumptions as to the expiry of copyright, or the death of the author in the case of anonymous or pseudonymous works.

25 Waiver of moral rights is provided by the Copyright, Designs and Patents Act 1988 s 87.

26 But not in respect of the database right.

27 This could also be true for many works of architecture.

28 A nice conundrum is that a computer-generated work is one created in circumstances such that there is no human author (s 178), yet s 9(3) states that the author for computer-generated works is the person making the arrangements necessary for the creation of the work. This will often be a human being (it could also be an artificial legal person such as a corporation). If the author, so defined, is a human then surely the work cannot, by definition, be computer-generated because it has a human author after all.

4 *Works made for the purpose of reporting current events* (s 79(5)). A matter of convenience again. To some extent, the difficulty in identifying the author depends on the nature of the work involved. In the case of newspaper reports, there should be no real difficulty except in so far as the report has been 'taken' from another source, such as a rival newspaper, or if the original report has been edited and rewritten by one or more other persons. The problem is worse in the case of a television newscast that will include a good number of reports written by different individuals or teams of individuals, and may have been edited or modified by others. While long credits may be acceptable in the case of feature films, it would be burdensome to have to identify all the various authors (and film directors), and the time taken to roll the credits might be nearly as long as the newscast itself.

5 *Publication in various types of publications* (s 79(6)). This exception applies to literary, dramatic, musical and artistic works that are published in newspapers, magazines or other similar periodicals and in an encyclopaedia, dictionary, yearbook or other collective work of reference. However, for the exception to apply, the author must have created the work for the purpose of such publication or have made the work available with the consent of the author for the purposes of such publication. In many works falling into these categories, authors tend to be identified anyway, if only by way of a list of contributors. However, if there are many authors, identifying each would be onerous, especially if their contributions are interleaved in any way. A question arises as to whether this provision is limited to materials published in paper form as many of the works described are available, additionally or alternatively, in electronic form. If it is so limited then presumably the exception will not apply to these things if they are published in electronic form. For example, certain journals are available using the LexisNexis computer-based legal information retrieval system.[29] If the exception extends only to hard copy publications, the author must be identified in the case of works stored electronically, including computer storage, magnetic storage and compact discs, an irrational and absurd result. The exception does not apply to films.

6 *Crown and parliamentary copyright* (s 79(7)). As might be expected, works in which Crown or parliamentary copyright subsists are excepted from the author's or director's right to be identified. Also excluded are works in which the copyright originally vested in an international organisation by virtue of s 168. This exception does not apply if the author or director has previously been identified as such in or on published copies of the work.

29 Some publishers of journals seek the agreement of authors to the inclusion of the author's article in such a computer database.

Right to object to derogatory treatment of the work

In addition to having a right to be identified as author or director (subject to exceptions and conditions), the author of literary, dramatic, musical or artistic work and the director of a film has an 'integrity right', a right to object to derogatory treatment of the author's or director's work. It has always been possible for a copyright owner to limit the extent and nature of alterations that can be made to a work by a licensee. A copyright owner who is also the author can thus provide for the continuing integrity of the work by contractual means. Before the right to object to derogatory treatment existed, in the absence of express or implied terms in a licence agreement, the licensee had the right to make alterations, but this was not necessarily an absolute right and in *Frisby* v *British Broadcasting Corp*[30] it was said that the court would, in appropriate circumstances, limit that right to make alterations.[31]

The integrity right is described in s 80(1) as the right belonging to the author or director not to have the work subjected to derogatory treatment. For the right to apply, the work must be a 'copyright' work, that is a work in which copyright subsists; furthermore, the

30 [1967] Ch 932.

31 The BBC wished to remove words from a script which it considered would be offensive to a large proportion of the viewing public, even though the claimant author considered that the words were important.

right is subject to exceptions and applies only as regards certain acts carried out in relation to the work. As with all other moral rights, the right can be waived with the consent of the person entitled to the right, who might be the author or director, or a person taking the right after the death of the author or director. The integrity right also applies to works which existed prior to the commencement date of the Copyright, Designs and Patents Act 1988, subject to certain conditions.[32]

'Derogatory treatment' is described in s 80(2) as being a treatment which amounts to distortion or mutilation of the work, or is otherwise prejudicial to the honour or reputation of the author or director. The insertion of the word 'otherwise' suggests that a distortion or mutilation, *per se*, is not enough and that there must be prejudice to honour or reputation.

Treatment

'Treatment' is defined as meaning the addition to, deletion from or alteration to or adaptation of the work, but not including a translation of a literary or dramatic work or an arrangement or transcription of a musical work involving no more than a change of key or register. Notice that the meaning of 'treatment' is not the same as the very technical meaning of 'adaptation' given in s 21. In some respects, treatment is wider than adaptation because it includes additions and deletions, but narrower in the sense that translations and arrangements are not included. The definition of 'treatment' is directed towards the activities that could offend the author, whereas a straightforward translation of a literary work should not upset any author. The right to object applies in relation to the whole or any part of the work under s 89(2). There is no stipulation that the part must be substantial and, theoretically, the right could arise in relation to a small part (in terms of quality or quantity), although the smaller the part, the less likely it is that its treatment would be considered to be derogatory.

An important aspect of the integrity right is the question of what amounts to a derogatory treatment of a work. Certainly, reducing the aesthetic content or damaging the literary style of the work by altering it – in other words, reducing the merit or quality of the work – would probably fulfil the requirements; for example, where a parody is made of music intended to be taken seriously, or in the case of a performance of a send-up of a worthy drama. An indication of the meaning can be gleaned from the French case of *Rowe v Walt Disney Productions*,[33] heard in the *Cour d'Appel* in Paris. In this case it was argued that moral rights under French law had been infringed, including the author's right to integrity. The claimant, a citizen of the USA, resident in France, had written a story about an aristocratic family of cats living in one of the better, more elegant areas of Paris, believing that a film would be made using live animals. Eventually, the defendant made a film based on the story, not using live animals but in the form of an animated cartoon, called *The Aristocats*. The claimant, the author of the story, claimed, *inter alia*, damages for the harm done to the integrity of his work.[34] The claimant's various claims failed because of a number of factors, not the least being that the original assignment was subject to English law, and the then current English copyright legislation, the Copyright Act 1956, did not expressly recognise moral rights.[35]

The right to oppose a derogatory treatment of a work can apply where duplicate copies of the original work are poor quality and sold at a derisory price. In *Jacky Boy Music v X*,[36] a French singer, Henri Salvador, recorded songs during the period 1948 to 1952. After the original recording had entered the public domain, the appellant made and sold CDs containing recordings of 18 of the songs. They were reproductions of the originals but of poor sound quality. They were sold in large stores at a price of only €1 each. The *Cour de Cassation* in Paris[37] held that the singer's right to object to a derogatory treatment had been infringed. The merit of the works would be likely to be devalued due the mediocre

32 *See* Copyright, Designs and Patents Act 1988 Sch 1, paras 22–25. The provisions are similar to those for the right to be identified as author or director.

33 [1987] FSR 36.

34 Initially, the author had asked for further payment in respect of his authorship of the story.

35 A citizen of the US resident in France enjoys the same moral rights as French authors. However, the law of the country in which the contract is signed becomes the law of the parties, and neither the Universal Copyright Convention nor any other provisions of international law could give the claimant moral rights afforded by French law which were denied to him under the law of contract. The assignment had been signed in London.

36 [2010] ECC 22.

37 This is the French Supreme Court.

quality of the recordings, the derisory price and the retail outlets from which the CDs were sold, not being dedicated music shops, would all contribute to the likelihood that the singer's reputation would be harmed.[38]

Writing a new edition of a book can be regarded as a treatment. In *Harrison v Harrison*,[39] the claimant was the author of the first edition of a book entitled 'How to avoid paying care charges'. It was published by the first and second defendants, trading as 'Streetwise Publications'. Later, the parties fell out and Streetwise engaged another author, the third defendant, to write a second edition of the book. In the Patents County Court, HH Judge Michael Fysh QC held that this amounted to a treatment of the work. He said (at para 60):

> 'Treatment' of a work is, I think, a broad, general concept; *de minimis* acts apart, it implies a spectrum of possible acts carried out on a work, from the addition of, say, a single word to a poem to the destruction of the entire work.

In the High Court of Delhi, it was accepted in *Sehgal v Union of India*,[40] that destruction of the work in question was a mutilation of the work in the sense used in the Berne Convention. The work was very large bronze mural sculpture which had been removed, and severely damaged in the process of removal, from the building it had first been commissioned to be displayed in.

Derogatory

A treatment of a work is derogatory if it amounts to distortion or mutilation of the work or is otherwise prejudicial to the honour or reputation of the author or director.

In *Confetti Records v Warner Music UK Ltd*,[41] a track called 'Burnin' was composed. In its original form it was described as consisting of an insistent instrumental beat accompanied by the vocal repetition of the word 'Burnin' (or variants of it). It was alleged that a version of the track which had been overlain with a rap containing references to violence and drugs was a derogatory treatment of it. Lewison J said (at paras 150 and 151):

> I hold that the mere fact that a work has been distorted or mutilated gives rise to no claim, unless the distortion or mutilation prejudices the author's honour or reputation. The nub of the original complaint, principally advanced by Mr Pascal, is that the words of the rap (or at least that part contributed by Elephant Man) contained references to violence and drugs. This led to the faintly surreal experience of three gentlemen in horsehair wigs examining the meaning of such phrases as 'mish mish man' and 'shizzle (or sizzle) my nizzle'.

It appeared that the words of the rap were difficult to decipher and this itself tended to militate against a finding that the treatment was derogatory. Another weakness in the case was that there was no evidence of the honour or reputation of the composer of 'Burnin', nor any prejudice to either of them. The judge rejected an invitation to infer prejudice.

Other forms of treatment that could injure the honour or reputation of an author or director could include a situation where, for example, the work is not itself altered but it is placed alongside or between other works which may affect adversely the perception of the work. This could happen where a short but respectable 'nature' film is broadcast among a selection of pornographic film clips or where a poem which happens innocently to contain some potential innuendos is placed on a website amongst a collection of lewd poems. However, such forms of treatment fall outside the provisions and would not give rise to a cause of action because of the relatively narrow definition of 'treatment'.

The right to object to a derogatory treatment is couched in fairly strong terms. It is not enough if the author is simply aggrieved at the treatment of his work. In *Pasterfield v Denham*,[42] the author of an artistic work which included a pictorial representation of a formation of German Second World War bombers used to promote the Plymouth Dome objected to a treatment of his work which included colour changes and a number of omissions and inaccuracies. He alleged that this resulted in a diminution of the 'vibrancy

38 The court seemed to take a wide view of the meaning of 'treatment' compared with the UK statutory definition. However, Article 6bis of the Berne Convention speaks of '. . . distortion, mutilation or other modification of, or other derogatory action in relation to [the work] . . .'.

39 [2010] FSR 25.

40 [2005] FSR 39.

41 [2003] EMLR 35.

42 [1996] FSR 168.

and excitement' of the original work. The judge, at Plymouth County Court, considered that the differences were relatively trivial and could have been the subject of a 'Spot the Difference' competition in a children's comic. Such differences were not a distortion or mutilation of the original work and it would be wrong to elevate such differences to a finding that there had been a derogatory treatment of the original work.

The Berne Convention for the Protection of Literary and Artistic Works uses a slightly different formula for what amounts to a derogatory treatment. Article 6[bis] gives the author the right, *inter alia*, '. . . to object to any distortion, mutilation or other modification of, or other derogatory action in relation to, the said work, which would be prejudicial to his honour or reputation'. Some states seem to take a liberal approach to this and the right can be interpreted as applying to any modification. The fact that a work has been modified without the author's consent seems to be taken to be prejudicial to the author's honour or reputation, *per se*. For example, in *Google Inc v Copiepresse SCRL*,[43] Copiepresse, a copyright management society, brought an action alleging that Google News infringed the copyright in newspaper articles belonging to its members by placing extracts on the Google News website. In addition to finding infringement of copyright, the Court of First Instance in Brussels found that the moral rights of the authors had been infringed. The Court held that an author has a right of respect for his work and this means that he can challenge any modification to it. There is no need to show that the author has suffered any harm. A modification can include a change in the environment of the work, its title or classification.[44] By placing extracts of articles together by theme, the editorial or philosophical approach of the author could be altered.[45]

The nature of the work in question may affect a finding that a treatment has been derogatory. Another factor may the qualitative status of the honour or reputation of the author or film director, as the case may be. In *Harrison v Harrison*,[46] by writing a second edition of the book written by the claimant, there was no allegation that the claimant's work had been distorted or mutilated. For the most part the claimant's allegations amounted to no more than 'omissions of detail rather than error or outright blunder'. It was held that, in the case of a technical work, it was inherently difficult to show that an omission of inessential detail could amount to a prejudicial treatment of the antecedent work. Furthermore, without evidence of honour or reputation, the judge described the claimant's professional honour or reputation as being 'very modest'. The particular complaints made were of a trivial kind and were not prejudicial at all, let alone being such as to affect the claimant's honour or reputation.

Scope of the right to object to derogatory treatment

There are, as might be expected, some similarities in the scope of this right when compared to the right to be identified. However, the scope of this particular right is expressed in terms of a classification of works which is more faithful to that given in s 1. In the case of literary, dramatic and musical works, the right is infringed by a person who:

(a) publishes commercially, performs in public or communicates to the public a derogatory treatment of the work; or

(b) issues to the public copies of a film or sound recording of, or including, a derogatory treatment of the work.[47]

In the case of an artistic work, under s 80(4), the right is infringed by a person who:

(a) publishes commercially or exhibits in public a derogatory treatment of the work, or communicates to the public a visual image of a derogatory treatment of the work;

(b) shows in public a film including a visual image of a derogatory treatment of the work or issues to the public copies of such a film; or

43 [2007] ECDR 5.

44 This would seem to include placing an extract of a work which was published in paper form on the internet.

45 As the authors' names were not mentioned on Google News, there was a further breach of the authors' moral rights.

46 [2010] FSR 25.

47 Copyright, Designs and Patents Act 1988 s 80(3).

(c) in the case of a work of architecture in the *form of a model for a building,* a sculpture or a work of artistic craftsmanship, issues to the public copies of a graphic work representing, or of a photograph of, a derogatory treatment of the work. (emphasis added)

However, unlike the right to be identified, this right does not apply to works of architecture in the *form of a building.*[48] Nevertheless, under s 80(5), where the author is identified on the building and the building is subjected to a derogatory treatment, the author has the right to have the identification removed. Other remedies will not, therefore, be applicable in this latter situation.

As regards films, the right to object to a derogatory treatment is infringed by a person who:

(a) shows in public or communicates to the public a derogatory treatment of the film;

(b) issues to the public copies of a derogatory treatment of the film.[49]

Section 80(7) provides that the right extends to apply to the treatment of parts of a work resulting from a previous treatment by a person other than the author or director, if those parts are attributed to, or are likely to be regarded as, the work of the author or director. Thus, derogatory treatments of versions of the work that have already been altered by a third party are covered by the right. For example, an author, Joe Brown, writes a story in English and assigns the copyright to a publishing company. The story becomes well known. Another person is engaged by the publishing company to translate the story into French. The publishing company grants a licence to a French theatre company permitting the latter to perform the French version in public. The French theatre company decides to perform a parody of the story in the form of a farce. If this treatment is judged to be derogatory and the work is likely to be attributed to him, Joe Brown's moral right has been infringed. Ironically, the enhanced position given to authors and directors by the right to be identified as such increases the possibility that the author or director will have his integrity right infringed. The stronger the association between the author or director and the work, the greater the likelihood of the integrity right, as regards treatments of previous treatments, being infringed, as indeed is the likelihood that a treatment will harm the honour or reputation of the work. Some authors and directors may find it embarrassing to be so clearly identified as such.

Exceptions and qualifications to the right to object to the derogatory treatment of a work

The right is limited in its scope by exceptions and qualifications provided for under ss 81 and 82, respectively. The right to object to derogatory treatment of a work is subject to exceptions as follows:

1 *The right does not apply to computer programs and computer-generated works* (s 81(2)). Although there may be a great deal of creative effort involved in computer programs and, indirectly, in computer-generated works, any right to integrity could be seen as an unwanted potential restriction on the future modification of the work. Nevertheless, professional reputation will be associated with computer programs particularly and it seems anomalous to omit computer programs from the ambit of this right and, indeed, the right to be identified as author. Computer programs are the result of a great deal of skill, judgment and experience and the author-work bond will be as great as with any other form of literary work, and in many cases it will be greater.[50] As regards computer-generated works, it is accepted that the right, at first sight, seems inappropriate. Computer-generated works are defined as being created in circumstances such that there is no human author under s 178, and there should not be a human author to feel aggrieved if the work is subsequently subjected to derogatory treatment. However, under s 9(3), a computer-generated work does have an author, being the person making the arrangements for the creation of the work, who is likely to be a living

48 The consequences of failing to provide for this can be seen in a Swiss case reported in [1994] 10 EIPR D-267.

49 Copyright, Designs and Patents Act s 80(6).

50 Some computer programs and suites of programs are the result of many years of work.

individual and who may feel angry or distressed by the treatment of the work by a subsequent copyright owner or licensee. For example, the work may be subjected to treatment which makes it derisory and this reflects on the author.

2 *The right does not apply in relation to any work made for the purpose of reporting current events* (s 81(3)). As with the right to be identified, this reflects worries expressed by the media during the passage of the Copyright, Designs and Patents Bill through Parliament, that providing for moral rights in such circumstances would be very onerous.

3 Under s 81(4), the right does not apply in relation to the publication of a literary, dramatic, musical or artistic work in:

(a) a newspaper, magazine or other similar periodical, or

(b) an encyclopaedia, dictionary, yearbook or other collective work of reference.

However, for the exception to apply, the author must have made the work for the purposes of such publication, or the work must have been made available with the consent of the author for the purposes of such publication. Furthermore, the right does not apply to any subsequent exploitation elsewhere of such a work without modification of the published version. As the author's work will be one of many in the publication, the purpose of this exception is to facilitate the modification of the works included in the publication and, for example, later storage in a computer database. If only one author could object on the basis of his right to integrity, it could hamper or delay the subsequent publication of the entire work. In many cases, editors of collective works reserve the right to modify the author's original manuscript to produce the finished version for publication. An example of a case in which a single author could hamper publication is where the editor of the compendium work wishes to reduce the length of a submitted article by leaving out a few paragraphs against the wishes of the author. This exception can be seen as recognising the editor's role, his skill and judgment, and allows the editor the discretion he needs to carry out his work.

4 *The right is not infringed by an act which by virtue of ss 57 or 66A would not infringe copyright* (s 81(5)). Section 57 deals with permitted acts based on assumptions as to the expiry of copyright or the death of the author in the case of anonymous or pseudonymous works. Section 66A contains equivalent provisions in respect of films.

5 Under s 81(6), the right is not infringed by anything done for the purpose of:

(a) avoiding the commission of an offence;

(b) complying with a duty imposed by or under an enactment; or

(c) in the case of the British Broadcasting Corporation (BBC), avoiding the inclusion in a programme broadcast by them of anything which offends against good taste or decency, or which is likely to encourage or incite crime, or to lead to disorder or to be offensive to public feeling.

If the author or director is identified at the time of the relevant act or has previously been identified in or on published copies of the work, there must be a sufficient disclaimer. One of the main purposes of this exception is to allow the BBC to censor parts of works which are to be broadcast without falling foul of the integrity right. The last exception applies only to the BBC, therefore the independent television companies, and, for that matter, other broadcasters and, for example, organisations and persons making works available online, must choose whether to run the risk of being sued for infringement of the right if they make cuts, whether to screen the work in full or whether to refuse to use the work at all.[51] A sufficient disclaimer would be to the effect that certain scenes which, for example, would be offensive to many people, have been omitted. Examples of scenes that could fall within this provision are:

- explicit or pornographic sex;
- showing how a terrorist makes bombs;
- violence at a demonstration.

51 Alternatively, the author or director may be asked to waive his integrity rights.

Section 82 is described in the sub-heading as 'qualification of right in certain cases'. It is really just another list of exceptions to the right and applies to employee works (where the first owner of the copyright is the author's or director's employer), Crown and parliamentary copyright and works in which the copyright originally vested in an international organisation under s 168. In respect of these works, the right to object to derogatory treatment does not apply to anything done by or with the authority of the copyright owner unless the author or director:

● is identified at the time of the relevant act; or
● has previously been identified in or on published copies of the work.

In other cases concerning the works included in the provisions of s 82, that is where the right still does apply (for example, if the author is not and has not been identified), the right is not infringed if there is a sufficient disclaimer.

Infringement by possession of or dealing with an infringing article

Almost as a parallel to the secondary infringements of copyright, the right to object to derogatory treatment can be infringed by possessing or dealing with infringing articles. An infringing article is defined under s 83(2) as a work or a copy of a work that has been subjected to derogatory treatment and that has been or is likely to be the subject of any of the acts within the scope of the right in circumstances infringing that right.[52] Under s 83(1), a person also infringes the integrity right if he:

(a) possesses in the course of business, or
(b) sells or lets for hire, or offers or exposes for sale or hire, or
(c) in the course of business exhibits or distributes, or
(d) distributes otherwise than in the course of business so as to affect prejudicially the honour or reputation of the author or director,

an article which is, and which he knows or has reason to believe is, an infringing article.

These activities are the same as or very similar to those relating to some of the secondary infringements of copyright and the associated criminal offences. However, the above activities do not, in terms of the integrity right, give rise to criminal liability, but there is a requirement for knowledge on the part of the person infringing the right. The criminal penalties provided under s 107 are expressed in terms of an 'infringing copy' and it therefore would seem that the criminal penalties do not apply to infringement of the integrity right alone, as this is expressed in terms of an 'infringing article'. An infringing copy is an article, the making of which infringed copyright (or would have done so if made in the UK where it has been or is proposed to import it into the UK). In some circumstances, a copy of a work may be made which is an infringing copy for the purposes of s 107 but which is also an infringing article for the purposes of s 83. For example, the work in question may have been parodied and recorded and the recording may include a substantial part of the work.

52 Note that the definition is different to that for 'infringing copies' as given by the Copyright, Designs and Patents Act 1988 s 27(2) which relates to secondary infringement of copyright.

False attribution of a work

Any person could be angered or distressed if a work of poor quality or a work containing scandalous or outrageous comment were falsely attributed to him. For example, an artist with a high standing in the art world would be likely to object if another person painted a substandard work in the artist's style and tried to pass it off as being made by the artist. Obviously, the artist's reputation could be harmed by this unless the painting was an obvious 'fraud'. Of course, the law of defamation may be available to give some remedy to the person to whom an inferior work is attributed, and substantial damages may be available in appropriate cases.[53] In cases such as the one described, an action in defamation may be the most attractive route to follow for the aggrieved person, especially as such cases tend to attract considerable publicity.

However, the ingredients necessary for an action in defamation may be missing. The work that has been falsely attributed might be of a high standard. The person who has created it may be hoping to 'cash in' on the reputation and standing of a famous person, or may be intending to embarrass some other persons.[54] An example of the latter situation is the work of the exceptionally skilled artist, the late Tom Keating, who produced many paintings in the style of important artists such as Constable, Turner and Palmer. The paintings were not copies of original paintings, but Mr Keating adopted the style used by famous artists and his work was of such a high standard that several reputable art dealers and art collectors were fooled.[55] Mr Keating later appeared in a television series showing how he created his 'masterpieces'.

It is difficult to know whether the 'false attribution right' is a moral right in the true sense, as it does not concern any work created by the person to whom the right accrues. Nevertheless, the Copyright, Designs and Patents Act 1988 places the right firmly amongst the other moral rights, and includes another right which is somewhat out of place in terms of traditional moral rights, that is a right to privacy in relation to certain photographs and films.

The false attribution right is not new and was originally provided for in the Copyright Act 1956 s 43. For example, in *Moore* v *News of the World Ltd*,[56] the claimant, Mrs Edna May Moore (known professionally as Dorothy Squires and one-time wife of Roger Moore who played the lead in *The Saint* television series), alleged that an article which appeared in the *News of the World* falsely attributed authorship to her and was defamatory. The article was entitled 'How My Love For The Saint Went Sour' and was claimed to be by Dorothy Squires talking to a reporter, Weston Taylor. The claimant claimed that the article implied that she was an unprincipled woman who had prepared sensational articles about her private life for substantial payment. The case was heard before a jury which awarded £4,300 for the libel and £100 for false attribution.

Where there is a court action which involves a claim in defamation together with a claim in respect of false attribution, the general rule is that double damages will not be awarded – there can be no duplication of damages, but the jury might properly take the defamation award into account in quantifying damages. In the above case, Lord Denning considered that the jury had decided upon an overall figure of £4,400 and had split this between defamation and false attribution in the proportions £4,300 and £100 respectively.

There must be a 'work' that has been attributed, and in *Noah* v *Shuba*[57] it was held that two short sentences by themselves could not be a work for copyright purposes. The defendant had quoted, with acknowledgement in a magazine article, the whole of a passage from a guide on hygiene and sterilisation procedures with respect to electrolysis (a method of hair removal) written by the claimant. Two sentences in the passage had not been written by the claimant and they gave the impression that the claimant agreed with the defendant's view that, if proper procedures were followed, there would be no risk of viral infections after treatment. It was held that the whole of the quoted passage had been attributed, and because it was not taken verbatim from the claimant's work the *whole of the passage* had been falsely attributed even though the differences were small. Even a slight change in wording can significantly alter the meaning of a written work. The claimant was awarded £250 for the false attribution and a further £7,250 in respect of defamation.[58]

Persons quoting extracts from the works of others must be careful to use verbatim extracts only and check carefully for typographical errors. For example, if the word 'not'

53 Defamation cases usually are heard before a jury and the amount awarded to a successful claimant can be seen as being something of a lottery, as it is the jury which decides the measure of damages.

54 In such circumstances, there may be an action in passing off.

55 Criminal proceedings against Mr Keating in respect of his activities were halted because of his ill-health.

56 [1972] 1 QB 441. The case was notable in that it was the first to come before the UK courts on the question of false attribution.

57 [1991] FSR 14.

58 There was a further award of £100 for copyright infringement. The judge refused to award additional damages in respect of the copyright infringement. A company which has a work falsely attributed to it could, presumably, also have an action in malicious falsehood.

is omitted from a quoted passage and the author's name is acknowledged, it would seem that the whole passage has been falsely attributed. The omission of the word would change the meaning of the passage or part of it and would, therefore, amount to a distortion of the work, making an action on the basis of the integrity right an alternative or additional claim.

A work can be falsely attributed even though the claimant is not mentioned by name. In *Harrison* v *Harrison*,[59] the false attribution claim was based on the second edition of a book, the first edition of which had been written by the claimant. He was expressly mentioned as author of that edition. But he had no involvement in writing the second edition of the book, copies of which carried no author's name. The false attribution came about by association. Persons seeing the second edition might have been familiar with the first edition and assume both editions were by the same author. HH Judge Michael Fysh QC said that the claimant had to establish a single meaning which the work would convey to a notional reasonable reader. He also confirmed that the tort was actionable without proof of damage. In finding for the claimant on the false attribution claim, the judge said (at para 55):

59 [2010] FSR 25.

> We must assume first that a reasonable, interested person of average intelligence has read these four items on the back cover [testimonials]. What message would this material convey to such a person? The encomia obviously refer back to an apparently successful antecedent first edition which must obviously have had an author (or authors) and it matters not that a reader of the back cover of the second edition did not know (or was not then given) the name of that author. The 'single message' to a reader (e.g. a purchaser) from the back cover of what is stated to be a second edition, in my view is this: here is the updated second edition of the excellent first edition of this book. Praise is for the author responsible for its creation and not for Streetwise [the publisher] who produce a slew of books on different subjects. In the absence of any indication to the contrary, the reader of the back cover would, I consider, assume that the author of the title had not changed. But that is of course contrary to the fact. There was also argument about sequential editions of (for example) legal and medical texts and travel guides having unchanging titles, not necessarily being by the same authors. This may be so but one must I think, consider the circumstances of each case.

The false attribution right applies to the same categories of works (original works and films) as do the other moral rights, but there are no exceptions. Therefore, unlike the right to be identified, it applies to computer programs, typefaces and computer-generated works. A 'person', which presumably can also be an artificial legal person, has the right not to have a literary, dramatic, musical or artistic work falsely attributed to him as author, or to have a film falsely attributed to him as director.[60] Attribution means an express or implied statement as to who is the author or director of the work. The right is infringed in a number of circumstances as follows:

60 Copyright, Designs and Patents Act 1988 s 84.

61 The false attribution may be in or on the offending copy of the work.

1 issuing copies of a falsely attributed work to the public (s 84(2)(a));[61]
2 exhibiting a falsely attributed artistic work or copy thereof in public (s 84(2)(b));
3 performing in public or communicating to the public a literary, dramatic or musical work as being the work of a person, knowing or having reason to believe that the attribution is false (s 84(3)(a));
4 showing in public or communicating to the public a film as being directed by a person, knowing or having reason to believe that the attribution is false (s 84(3)(b));
5 with respect to the above acts, issuing to the public or publicly displaying material containing a false attribution (s 84(4)) – this would include publicity materials such as leaflets distributed informing the public of a performance or posters advertising some event;
6 possessing or dealing with a copy of a falsely attributed work (a work with a false attribution in or on it) in the course of business, knowing or having reason to believe

that there is such an attribution and that it is false (s 84(5)). In the case of artistic works, possessing and dealing with the work itself is caught if the relevant knowledge is present. Dealing is defined in s 84(7) as selling or letting for hire, offering or exposing for sale or hire, exhibiting in public, or distributing; or

7 in the case of an artistic work, dealing with a work, which has been altered after the author parted with possession of it, as being the unaltered work of the author or dealing with a copy of such a work as being a copy of the unaltered work of the author, knowing or having reason to believe that this is not the case (s 84(6)). 'Dealing' has the same meaning as above.

The false attribution provisions also apply to adaptations of literary, dramatic and musical works and to copies of artistic works that are falsely represented as being copies made by the author of the artistic work: s 84(8). Under s 89(2), the right of a person not to have a work falsely attributed to him applies in relation to the whole or any part of a work. As regards false attribution before the commencement date of the 1988 Act, the Copyright Act 1956 s 43 applies.[62]

> [62] Copyright, Designs and Patents Act 1988 Sch 1, para 22(2).

As before, it is unlikely that many persons will feel the need to turn to the false attribution provisions except as an alternative or additional cause of action, as in serious cases the law of defamation is more appropriate and, if the false attribution has affected the commercial sales of some article incorporating a copyright work, an action in passing off might be relevant and provide greater recompense.

With the assistance of computer technology it is now possible to re-use and manipulate old film clips and photographs to create 'new' images and film action including deceased persons. For example, it is possible to make a new film starring Marilyn Monroe, or a new television advertisement with Alfred Hitchcock or an advertising hoarding featuring Sid James. Relatives and persons who were friends with such celebrities might feel aggrieved at the use of their images (and voices) in this way. The following points can be made about exploiting the characteristics and appearance of deceased persons:

1 There can be no false attribution right actionable by their personal representatives because there is no work in respect of which authorship is falsely attributed to them.
2 There is no action in defamation as deceased persons cannot be defamed.
3 The photographer or director of the original photographs or film clips used to make the new work could have an action for false attribution if the new work is indeed attributed to either of them.
4 The owner of the copyright, if any, subsisting in the original photograph, film or broadcast may be able to use his economic rights, bearing in mind that a single frame is a substantial part of a film.
5 In some cases, if the original work is a recording of a film or sound recording of a live performance, there will be rights in that performance which last for 50 years from the end of the calendar year during which the performance took place. The person entitled to the performer's rights on his death should be able to obtain injunctive relief and/or damages, as too should the person having an exclusive recording contract with the performer.

In some cases, there will be no way in which close relatives of deceased performers can prevent the making of the new work including images of the deceased person. It is possible that the owner of the economic copyright will be happy to license the use of the original work for such purposes. Of course, the copyright owner may be the person making the new work. It is arguable that a *sui generis* right ought to be introduced to control the use of old images of deceased persons for a substantial period of time after their death. That might entail the introduction of an image right for living persons.[63]

> [63] Certain forms of processing images of persons may invoke individuals' rights under data protection law though these rights only apply to living individuals.

Right to privacy in photographs and films

Prior to the Human Rights Act 1998, English law recognised no general right to privacy. Prior to the 1988 Act, the right to privacy in relation to photographs or films could be achieved only through the application of the economic rights, for example by obtaining an injunction to prevent publication. In *Mail Newspapers plc v Express Newspapers plc*,[64] an injunction was granted to prevent the publication of wedding photographs of a married couple. The wife had suffered a brain haemorrhage when 24 weeks pregnant and was kept on a life-support machine in the hope that the baby could be born alive. The husband had granted exclusive rights to the claimant in respect of the photographs, together with an undertaking that he would pose for photographs with the baby within 24 hours of its birth. The defendants had intimated that they would also publish copies of the couple's wedding photographs.[65]

The inclusion of the right to privacy in photographs and films was considered necessary because of the power of visual media and the danger that photographs and films made for private purposes would later be published against the wishes of the persons who commissioned them, as happened in the case of *Williams v Settle*.[66] One reason this right is required is that the first owner of the copyright in, for example, a commissioned photograph is the photographer and not the commissioner.[67] The first owner of the copyright in a film is the director (and producer if a different person) unless an employee making the film in the course of employment, in which case the employer will be the first owner of the copyright. Therefore, commissioners of films and photographs, in common with other works of copyright, will not be able to control the subsequent use of the work through the medium of ownership. Of course, it is open to the commissioner to make contractual arrangements to protect privacy, or by taking an assignment of the copyright or becoming an exclusive licensee. However, it will often be the case that the person commissioning the photograph or the film gives no thought to this matter. This new right gives him some safeguards to prevent a publication that would be an unwelcome invasion of his privacy or that of the persons appearing in the photograph or film, or at least to provide him with some legal redress.

Under s 85, the right to privacy applies in the case of a copyright photograph or film which has been commissioned for private and domestic purposes. The scope of the right is not to have:

(a) copies of the work issued to the public (here the difficulty with the scope of this phrase is unlikely to be a problem as it will usually be the first issue to the public that causes the complaint);

(b) the work exhibited or shown in public; or

(c) the work communicated to the public.

The right may be infringed indirectly, such as where a person authorises the act complained of. There are some minor exceptions to the application of the right connected with a number of the permitted acts.[68] However, the right does not apply to photographs and films made before the commencement of the 1988 Act. The right does apply in relation to a substantial part of the film or photograph, as well as the whole of it.[69] This will include a single frame from a film.

Joint works

The fact that many works are the result of the effort of joint authors (or joint directors), defined as being collaborative works where the respective contributions of the authors or directors are not distinct from the others,[70] requires that the moral rights provisions in the

64 [1987] FSR 90.

65 The case hinged on whether the husband could grant exclusive rights, as it appeared that the husband and wife were joint owners of the copyright in the wedding photographs. However, it was questionable whether the wife was alive or clinically dead. If the former, her consent would be required for the exclusive licence, but plainly she was not in a position to give it.

66 [1960] 1 WLR 1072. *See* Chapter 6 for a discussion of this case.

67 The Copyright Act 1956 had a different rule. Under s 4(3), a person commissioning a photograph for money or money's worth would be entitled to the copyright.

68 The relevant permitted acts are those under the Copyright, Designs and Patents Act 1988 ss 31, 45, 46, 50 and 57.

69 Copyright, Designs and Patents Act 1988 s 89(1).

70 Copyright, Designs and Patents Act 1988 ss 10 and 88(5).

Act have to contain some rules to be applied in such cases. Not only does the Act have to address infringement of the paternity and integrity rights associated with joint works, but it also has to consider the possibility that a work might be falsely attributed to joint authors or that a photograph or film may be subject to a joint commission. Section 88 deals with joint works and briefly makes the following provisions:

1 For a joint author (or director) to take advantage of the right to be identified, he must assert the right himself. An assertion by one joint author will not benefit the other.
2 The right to object to derogatory treatment applies to each joint author or director individually. The consent of one to the treatment does not prejudice the right of the other.
3 The false attribution right is infringed by any false statement as to the authorship of a work of joint authorship and by falsely attributing joint authorship to a work of sole authorship. Similar provisions apply to film directors.
4 The right to privacy in certain films and photographs applies to each commissioner individually. The consent of one to the relevant act does not prejudice the right of the other.

A principal director of a film is a joint author of the film along with the producer, where the producer is a different person. However, film producers do not have moral rights. Note that, although only principal directors and producers can be authors of films, the duration of copyright in a film is determined by the death of the last to die of the principal director, author of the screenplay, author of the dialogue or composer of music specially created for and used with the film under s 13B(2).

Duration and transmission on death

The duration of moral rights is provided for in a fairly straightforward way by s 86. In all cases except the false attribution right, they endure as long as copyright subsists in the work in question. As the duration of copyright is, in most cases where moral rights are likely to be in issue, the life of the author plus 70 years, this can be seen as fairly generous. However, it could be argued that the right to be identified and the integrity right should have no time limit.[71] Why should a person be able to make a derogatory treatment of a Shakespeare play yet be prevented from doing the same in respect of a work written by an author who is still living or who died not more than 70 years ago? One possible answer is that, given the passage of time, it is less likely that anyone would feel aggrieved personally (others might feel angered simply because the work of a great author was being debased). If the rights were perpetual, eventually it would be difficult to say who had a right of action, that is *locus standi*; it might no longer be clear who could enforce the right. Finally, the law tends to dislike perpetual property rights, as evidenced by the development of technical rules to prevent the tying up of rights in the law of real property, and especially as exhibited in the Act itself which removes perpetual copyright from certain universities and colleges granted under the Copyright Act 1775.[72]

After the author's (or director's, or commissioner's) death, the right to be identified, the integrity right or the right to privacy in relation to certain photographs and films will pass as provided for in the testamentary disposition; or, in the absence of an appropriate direction, the rights pass with the copyright, should it form part of his estate or, failing this, the rights will be exercisable by the author's personal representatives: s 95(1).

Where the copyright is part of the person's estate but is divided, for example, by passing one part to one person and another part to another person, any moral right which passes with the copyright is correspondingly divided under s 95(2). An example is where

71 Indeed, in France there is no time limit and the moral rights are declared to be perpetual and inalienable: Article L 121-1 Law No 92-597 of 1 July 1992, on the Intellectual Property Code, as amended.

72 Copyright, Designs and Patents Act 1988 Sch 1, para 13.

Bernard is the author of and owns the copyright in a dramatic work and he dies leaving the publication rights to Angela and the remaining rights to Claire. Similarly the copyright could be left to two or more persons consecutively, such as where Bernard leaves his entire copyright to Lynne for five years, after which it reverts to his estate. Lynne will be able to enforce the moral rights for the five-year period, following which the rights will be exercisable by whomsoever took under Bernard's estate.

As regards the right not to have a work falsely attributed to a person, this continues to subsist for a period of 20 years after the person's death.[73] Of course, in this case there is no copyright of which the person concerned is the author, in order to measure the duration of the right. It is questionable whether 20 years is sufficient to give the widow or children of the person falsely attributed an action to prevent or claim damages for false attribution. There seems to be no good reason why this right should not endure for a longer period of time, say 50 years, after the person's death.

Any infringement of the false attribution right is, following the person's death, actionable by his personal representatives: s 95(5). Any damages recovered by personal representatives in respect of this and the other moral rights will devolve as part of the person's estate (as at the time of his death): s 95(6).

Consent and waiver

Under s 87(1) it is not an infringement of a moral right to do any act to which the person entitled to the right has consented. Such consent may be implied or the law of estoppel may be relevant.

The major chink in the armour in moral rights in the UK is that they may be waived by the author or director by whom they are owned. It is very likely that copyright owners (unless the owner is the author or director), assignees and licensees will seek to avoid the inconvenience of having to respect the author's or director's moral rights and that pressure may be brought to bear in the hope of obtaining a waiver. Those authors and directors who are in a weak bargaining position may be tempted to acquiesce.

One safeguard for the author or director is that the waiver must be by written instrument signed by the person giving up the right by s 87(2), and the waiver may be conditional or unconditional and may be expressed to be subject to revocation (s 87(3)(b)). The waiver may relate to a specific work or specified description of works or to works generally and may cover existing and future works. For example, an author of plays (dramatic works) may agree in writing to waive his moral rights in:

1   a play entitled *A Long Summer*;
2   all the existing plays in a series written for television;
3   all his works up to 31 December 2008;
4   a play, yet to be written, entitled *A Short Winter*.

If the author or director intends to waive all or some of his moral rights in an assignment or licence agreement, he would be wise to insist on a term to the effect that the waiver is to be revoked if the assignor or licensee commits a breach of the agreement.

If the author has created the work under a commission in circumstances such that the person commissioning the work has beneficial ownership of it or an implied licence to make use of it, this does not automatically mean that the author has waived his moral rights in respect of the work.[74] This confirms that economic rights and moral rights are independent of each other. A waiver of moral rights cannot be implied simply on the basis that a licence in respect of the economic rights has been implied. This reinforces the need to deal with both economic rights and moral rights in respect of commissioned works.

73 This was the period provided for under the Copyright Act 1956 s 43.

74 *Pasterfield v Denham* [1996] FSR 168.

There is a presumption that a waiver, made in favour of the owner or prospective owner of the copyright in the works affected by the waiver, extends to licensees and successors in title unless a contrary intention is expressed. The author or director will be bound, in respect of the waiver, as regards third parties who subsequently acquire economic rights in the work or works involved unless there is a term in the agreement to the contrary effect. If the formalities required for a waiver are imperfect – for example, a written unsigned waiver coupled with an oral agreement – the general law of contract or estoppel may be available. An example would be where the author was the first owner of the copyright and he assigned the copyright to another person who was acting in good faith, and the author orally assured the other that he would waive his moral right to be identified as author. If the author later attempted to exercise that right, he might be estopped by the courts on the basis of his conduct.[75] Generally, a waiver by a joint author or joint director does not affect the moral rights of the others.[76]

Remedies

An infringement of a moral right is actionable as a breach of statutory duty owed to the person entitled to that right.[77] Mandatory injunctions will be relevant, such as where a judge orders that the author's name is added to copies of the work remaining in stock and to future copies, or that an architect's name is placed in a prominent place at or near to the entrance of a building. Prohibitory injunctions may be granted to prevent subsequent infringement of the integrity right and a *quia timet* injunction may be appropriate to prevent the planned publication of, or broadcast of, a derogatory treatment of the work.

Normally damages are available for a breach of a statutory duty, and in the case of infringement of moral rights this would appear to include damages for non-economic loss for the simple fact that moral rights are not economic in nature. Whether aggravated or exemplary damages are available is difficult to say with any certainty. Additional damages were granted in *Williams* v *Settle*,[78] a case involving the publication of a photograph showing a man who had been murdered. Although the effect of the case was to give a remedy for compromising privacy in relation to a photograph, it was done on the basis of an infringement of the economic rights of copyright for which the remedy of additional damages was clearly available, and this remains so under s 97(2).[79] However, the case of *Moore* v *News of the World Ltd*[80] indicates that damages for false attribution may be slight, certainly in comparison with those available for defamation.

It appears that the guidelines for assessing damages under reg 3 of the Intellectual Property (Enforcement, etc.) Regulations 2006[81] also apply to damages for breaches of moral rights. Under reg 3, where the defendant knew or had reason to believe that he engaged in infringing activity, the damages awarded shall be appropriate to the actual prejudice to the claimant and all appropriate aspects are to be taken into account including the moral prejudice suffered by the claimant.

The final point on remedies is that a court has a discretion, in a case involving the alleged infringement of the right to object to derogatory treatment, conditionally to grant a prohibitory injunction requiring that a disclaimer is made dissociating the author or director from the treatment of the work, the disclaimer being in such terms and in such manner as may be approved by the court.[82] This could be appropriate where the copyright owner intends to broadcast a much-abbreviated version of a play and the author objects, complaining that this is a mutilation of his original work. This power is unlikely to be used if the nature of the version subjected to the treatment complained of is such that, despite the disclaimer, the reputation of the author is at some risk, however

75 For examples of the doctrine of promissory estoppel in contract law, *see Central London Property Trust Ltd* v *High Trees House Ltd* [1947] KB 130 and, in the context of a non-exclusive licence in respect of a patented process, *Tool Metal Manufacturing Co Ltd* v *Tungsten Electric Co Ltd* [1955] 2 All ER 657.

76 Copyright, Designs and Patents Act 1988 s 88(3) and (6).

77 Copyright, Designs and Patents Act 1988 s 103(1).

78 [1960] 1 WLR 1072.

79 In principle, exemplary damages are more appropriate for infringement of moral rights than they are in respect of infringements of economic rights.

80 [1972] 1 QB 441.

81 SI 2006/1028. The Regulations implemented, *inter alia*, Directive 2004/48/EC of the European Parliament and of the Council of 29 April 2004 on the enforcement of intellectual property rights, OJ L 157, 30.04.2004, p 45.

82 Copyright, Designs and Patents Act 1988 s 103(2).

small. One reason is that the long-term effectiveness of even a strong disclaimer may be doubtful, and that in years to come the author may be causally linked to the work as so treated.

Moral rights and revived copyright

83 SI 1995/3297, implementing the Council Directive 93/98/EEC harmonising the term of copyright and certain related rights, OJ L 290, 29.10.1993, p 9. This Directive was repealed and effectively replaced by a codified version, Directive 2006/116/EC of the European Parliament and of the Council of 12 December 2006 on the term of copyright and certain related rights, OJ L 372, 27.12.2006, p 12. For the main effects of the Directive, *see* Chapter 3.

In some cases, copyright which had expired in the UK was revived as a result of the Duration of Copyright and Rights in Performances Regulations 1995.[83] The 1995 Regulations contain some provisions as to moral rights in respect of works in which copyright has been revived. The duration of the moral rights to be identified, to object to a derogatory treatment and in respect to privacy of certain photographs and films is declared by the Copyright, Designs and Patents Act 1988 s 86(1) to subsist as long as copyright subsists in the work. In terms of duration, therefore, those moral rights are affected in the same way as copyright and will be revived along with the copyright. However, by reg 22(6), the provisions of paras 23 and 24 in Sch 1 to the Act still apply (no moral rights in respect of which the author died or the film or photograph was made before commencement, 1 August 1989).

By reg 22(3), moral rights are exercisable by the author (or director of a film) in relation to revived copyright, or, if the author or director died before commencement, by his personal representatives. Any waiver or assertion subsisting immediately before the expiry of copyright will continue to have effect during the revived period.

Any damages recovered by personal representatives for infringement after the author's/director's death devolve as part of his estate as if the right of action had subsisted and been vested in him immediately before his death: reg 22(5).

Artists' resale right

84 Formerly Article 12 of the EC Treaty. See Joined Cases C-92/92 and C-326/92 *Collins v Imtrat Handelsgesellschaft mbH* [1993] ECR I-5145.

85 Directive 2001/84/EC of the European Parliament and of the Council of 27 September 2001 on the resale right for the benefit of the author of an original work of art, OJ L 272, 13.10.2001, p 32.

86 SI 2006/346.

Article 14[ter] of the Berne Copyright Convention provides that 'the author, or after his death the persons or institutions authorised by national legislation, shall, with respect to original works of art and original manuscripts of writers and composers, enjoy the inalienable right to an interest in any sale of the work subsequent to the first transfer by the author of the work'. This is expressed in the Convention as being an option for convention countries and the detail of the remuneration and method of collection are left to national legislation.

Some Member States did not have an artists' resale right and this could result in discrimination on the ground of nationality where laws in Member States that provided such a right could deny reciprocal protection to nationals of other Member States contrary to Article 18 of the Treaty on the Functioning of the European Union.[84] A Directive was adopted to prevent such discrimination, which could prejudice the single market, to provide for an artists' resale right throughout the European Union.[85] The Directive was implemented in the UK by the Artist's Resale Right Regulations 2006.[86]

Under Article 1 of the Directive, the author of an original work of art is given an inalienable right, which cannot be waived even in advance, to receive a royalty payable by the seller on the price obtained from any subsequent sale of the work except where the sale is a private sale, being a sale between two private individuals. Sales by professional sellers such as in salerooms, by auctioneers, in art galleries and, in general, by any dealer in works of art are subject to the royalty. Member States may disapply the right where the seller has obtained the work directly from the author less than three years before the resale where the sale price does not exceed €10,000. The UK took advantage of this derogation. The seller is liable to pay except where Member States provide that the buyer, art market professional or art dealer is liable alone or jointly with the seller. Reg 13 of the Artist's Resale Right Regulations 2006 imposes liability jointly and severally on the seller and 'relevant person', being the seller's agent or, where there is no seller's agent, the buyer's agent or, where there are no such agents, the buyer.

The type of works covered are, by Article 2, original works of art, being works of graphic art or 'plastic art'[87] such as pictures, collages, paintings, drawings, engravings, prints, lithographs, sculptures, tapestries, ceramics, glassware and photographs which have been made by the artist himself. Also included are 'copies considered to be original works of art'. Limited edition copies are also included. These are where the artist has made or authorised the production of the copies: for example, limited edition prints made of an original painting. Normally, such copies will be numbered, signed or otherwise duly authorised by the artist. The right does not cover original manuscripts of writers or composers. Article 3 of the Directive allows Member States to set the minimum threshold before the right is triggered, providing it is not more than €3,000. The UK chose to set the threshold at €1,000.

The scale of royalty payment is set out in Article 4 on a sliding scale as in Table 5.1. Note that the royalty is calculated based on the portion of the sale within the relevant price range. Therefore, if the sale price is €250,000, the royalty is:

$$4\% \text{ of } €50,000 + 3\% \text{ of } €150,000 + 1\% \text{ of } €50,000 = €7,000$$

For a sale price of up to €50,000, the royalty will be 4 per cent (Member States were allowed to set this figure at 5 per cent instead if they wish – the UK uses 4 per cent). Where the sale price is over €500,000, the rate is 0.25 per cent subject to a cap of €12,500 maximum royalty.[88] The royalty is net of tax and is payable to the author or, if deceased, to his estate. Royalties may be collectively managed and appropriate arrangements may be made where the author is a national of another Member State. Nationals of third countries have a right to receive the royalty on resale if their country affords reciprocal rights to nationals of EU Member States.

By Article 8, the right to receive the resale royalty endures as long as copyright – that is, life plus 70 years. However, under Article 8(3), Member States which did not previously have a resale right may, by way of derogation, not apply the right for the benefit of the author's estate after his death not later than 1 January 2010.[89] Exceptionally, a further two years may be added on the grounds that it is necessary to enable economic operators in the Member State to adapt gradually to the system while maintaining their economic viability before they apply the right for the benefit of those entitled after the author's death. Where this derogation is taken advantage of, there are provisions for notification, giving reasons and opinions from the Commission. On 18 December 2008, the Secretary of State for Innovation, Universities and Skills wrote to the European Commission setting out that the UK intended to extend its use of the derogation for a further two years because of the current economic climate. This additional derogation was implemented by the Artist's Resale Right (Amendment) Regulations 2009,[90] extending the period to 1 January 2012.

87 The term is not defined in the Directive apart from the examples given.

88 This would be achieved when the sale price is €2,000,000.

89 In relation to rights after the death of the artist. This derogation was implemented in the UK.

90 SI 2009/2792, coming into force on 1 December 2009.

Table 5.1 Resale royalty rates

Sale price	Royalty per cent
Up to €50,000	4.00
€50,000.01 up to €200,000	3.00
€200,000.01 up to €350,000	1.00
€350,000.01 up to €500,000	0.50
Exceeding €500,000	0.25

Authors and persons entitled after the death of the author have a right, up to three years from the sale in question, to obtain information necessary to secure payment of the resale royalty from art market professionals (this also appears to apply to collecting societies where Member States provide that payments shall be made to a collecting society): Article 9. The type of information involved might be confirmation of the sale price and the identity and whereabouts of the person liable to pay.

The European Commission is currently reviewing the scheme, following a consultation period which closed on 11 March 2011, and is expected to publish its report by October 2011. Over 500 responses where submitted to the Commission.

As the Directive contained a number of options and derogations, some particular features of the UK's implementing regulations, the Artist's Resale Right Regulations 2006, are described below.

- For the royalty to be payable the resale must be such that the buyer, seller, or either's agent, if there is one, is acting in the course of business of dealing in works of art: reg 12. So a private sale from one individual to another where neither is operating in the course of business of dealing in works of art is not a resale to which the right applies. However, a sale may be a resale even though the first transfer of ownership of the work of art was not made for consideration: for example, where it passed by testamentary disposition or by way of a gift (although this is not expressly mentioned). There is also a lower threshold of €1,000. If the sale price is less than this figure, the resale right does not apply.
- The threshold of €10,000 applies where the resale takes place by a seller who previously acquired the work of art directly from the author less than three years before the sale.
- The UK has chosen not to use the 5 per cent option where the sale price is under €50,000.
- The right may be enforced by nationals of the EEA and other countries providing reciprocal rights or a 'qualifying body' (generally, a body having charitable status) or, where the right has vested by operation of law, a personal representative or receiver in bankruptcy.
- There is a rebuttable presumption that the name of an artist on a work of art is that of the author: reg 6.
- A work is of joint authorship where two or more authors created the work (there is no requirement that their contributions are not distinct) and joint authors hold the right as owners in common in equal shares: reg 5. Where they choose to hold in unequal shares this must be by written agreement signed by or on behalf of each party.
- The right is not assignable and any charge on it is void. It may be held by a trustee for the benefit of the author (for example, where the author lacks capacity to hold personal property). However, the right may pass by way of testamentary disposition or the rules on intestacy and the person so taking the right may then transfer it to any natural person or to a qualifying body. A qualifying body may subsequently transmit it to another qualifying body. The right may transfer *bona vacantia*.[91] Any purported waiver of the right is void as is any agreement to share or repay resale royalties.
- The seller is liable to pay jointly and severally with the relevant person who is the agent of the seller or, where there is no such agent, the agent of the buyer or, where neither the seller nor the buyer have an agent, the buyer. Liability to pay arises on completion of the sale although it may be withheld pending evidence of entitlement. Where two or more persons are entitled to the royalty as owners in common, the obligation to pay is satisfied by paying the full amount to one of them.
- The right may only be managed through a collecting society to whom holders of resale rights transfer their right of management: reg 14. If holders of resale rights do not transfer the management of their right, the collecting society is mandated to manage it without prejudice to the holder's rights. Where there is more than one collecting

91 That is, pass to the Crown or the Duchies of Cornwall or Lancaster in a situation where there is no person apparently entitled to it: for example, where the author dies intestate with no-one entitled to his estate.

society, the holder can choose to which to transfer his right of management. For the purposes of the resale right, a collecting society is one which has, as its main object, or one of its main objects, the administration of rights on behalf of more than one artist. A fixed fee or percentage of the royalty may be charged by the collecting society. In the UK, most artists use the Design and Artists Copyright Society as their collecting society, At the time of writing, it paid out around £12m in royalties under the artist's resale right since February 2006.

- A request for information should be satisfied within 90 days of the receipt of the request; failure to furnish the information (such as the royalty payable and, where not payable by the person to whom the request was sent, the name and address of the person liable to pay) can be dealt with by application for a court order. Any information provided will be treated as confidential.
- The resale right will apply to sales made on or after commencement of the statutory instrument even if the work was created before.
- Where the author died before commencement, the right cannot be exercised in respect of sales before 1 January 2012.[92] There are provisions for deemed transfer of the right where the author dies before commencement.

92 Extended by two years from 1 January 2010.

93 Graddy, K., Horowitz, N. and Szymanski, S., 'A study into the effect on the UK art market of the introduction of the artist's resale right', Intellectual Property Institute, 2008.

In a study commissioned by the UK Intellectual Property Office, it was found that there was no evidence that the right has not diverted business away from the UK, in spite of initial concerns amongst auction houses.[93] The resale right was considered by some to be likely to be difficult and burdensome to administer and this has been borne out in the report in relation to a significant minority of art market professionals and major auction houses. Furthermore, it was found that the extension of the right in 2012 could increase the overall size of payments under the right by four times. Art market professionals thought that this could damage the UK art market by diverting trade elsewhere. Thus far, however, there does not seem to have been any damage to the UK art market nor any evidence of auctions of valuable works of art being diverted from London to markets in places where the right does not exists, such as New York[94] or Geneva. However, the ceiling on the maximum payable of €12,500 (which will apply to sale prices of €2m and over) is quite modest. Nonetheless, collectors buying works of art directly from artists might need to reflect on the fact that they may have to pay the royalty on any future sale, for example, through an auction house. Even a modest price of £1,000 will attract a royalty of £40, and this is on top of the auctioneer's commission.

94 Although there is not a resale right in the United States generally, there is such a right in California.

Summary

Authors of literary, dramatic, musical or artistic works and directors of films have moral rights (as distinct from economic rights) which are the right:

- to be identified as the author or director;
- to object to a derogatory treatment of the work or film;
- not to have a work or film falsely attributed to him as author or director.

The scope of these moral rights varies depending on the form of the work and there are a number of exceptions. The right endures as long as the copyright with the exception of false attribution which lasts for 20 years after the death of the person to whom the work was falsely attributed. Moral rights may be waived by the author or director and it is not an infringement where the author or director has consented to the act in question.

The right to be identified as author or director must be asserted. Moral rights cannot be assigned but pass on the death of the author or director, for example, under a will.

There is a right to privacy in respect of photographs and films which have been commissioned for private and domestic purposes.

Artists have a resale right, being a right to a royalty on subsequent sales of their works of art. The royalty is calculated on a sliding scale with a maximum amount payable. It is paid to a collecting society for distribution to artists. The resale right cannot be waived.

Discussion questions

1 Do you think moral rights are necessary or are they a hindrance to the economic exploitation of a work of copyright? Furthermore, do moral rights interfere with the right of freedom of expression as provided under Article 10 of the Council of Europe Convention for the Protection of Human Rights and Fundamental Freedoms?

2 The right to object to a derogatory treatment of a work endures, in the UK, as long as the copyright in the work. Do you consider that this is adequate or should the right last for indefinitely or for fixed period longer or shorter than life plus 70 years?

3 Describe the working of the artist's resale right in practice. Do you think it is harming or will harm the art market in the UK by diverting sales of works of art to countries where the right does not exist?

Selected further reading

Blakeney, S., 'The great debate – using artistic licence to resist the artist's resale right', [2011] *Entertainment Law Review*, 22 (considers the impact of the resale right on the art market).

Case Comment: France: Intellectual Property Code, arts. L. 121-1, L. 123-1; New Code of Civil Procedure, art. 700; European Convention on Human Rights, art. 10 – 'Victor Hugo III' [2009] *International Review of Intellectual Property and Competition Law*, 979 (concerns the *Hugo* v *Plon* case on Victor Hugo's moral rights in relation to novels written by authors as sequels to Hugo's novel *Les Miserables*).

Graddy, K., Horowitz, N. and Szymanski, S., 'A study into the effect on the UK art market of the introduction of the artist's resale right', Intellectual Property Institute, 2008, available at: **http://www.ipo.gov.uk/study-droitdesuite.pdf** (looks at the initial impacts of the resale right).

Lui, D., 'The artist has got moral rights and that ain't bad' [2011] *European Intellectual Property Review*, 169 (looks at and justifies moral rights under Chinese copyright law and the relationship between moral rights and economic rights).

Rogerro, C., 'Colourisation and the right to preserve the integrity of a film: a comparative study between civil and common law' [2011] *Entertainment Law Review*, 25 (looks at the right to object to a derogatory treatment of a film in the context of the digital colourisation of an original black and white film and discusses John Houston's 'Asphalt Jungle' case in France).

6 Rights, infringement and remedies

Rights of copyright owners

The Copyright, Designs and Patents Act 1988 marks out the rights of copyright owners by reference to certain acts which only the owner can do or authorise; he is given exclusive rights in respect of these acts. These are the *acts restricted by copyright*. Other activities, which are mainly of a commercial nature, such as dealing with infringing copies of a work, if they are done without the licence of the copyright owner, are described as secondary infringements. Anyone who does one of the acts restricted by the copyright, including the secondary infringements, without the permission or licence of the copyright owner, infringes copyright, unless a defence or any of the exceptions known collectively as the *permitted acts* apply.[1] Strictly speaking, the permitted acts, although so described in the 1988 Act, are better described as exceptions to copyright infringement. This is because any activity in relation to a copyright work which is neither a restricted act nor a secondary infringement of copyright can be performed by anyone without the permission of the copyright owner. For example, lending a book to a friend does not infringe copyright; neither does making an artistic work from a literary work.[2] Therefore, unless there is an issue of infringement, the relevance of the permitted acts does not enter into the equation. If there is no infringement, there is no need to rely on the permitted acts to excuse the particular activity concerned.

Copyright may be infringed vicariously, where a person without the permission of the copyright owner *authorises* another to do a restricted act.[3] Simply playing a major role in selecting material to include in the infringing work is not, by itself, sufficient to make a person liable by authorising infringement.[4] 'Authorise' means to grant or purport to grant to a third person the right to do the act complained of.[5]

As well as giving an aggrieved copyright owner civil remedies for copyright infringement, the Act also provides for criminal offences which generally, though not exactly, mirror some of the secondary infringements of copyright. Offences will normally be dealt with by the Crown Prosecution Service on reference from the police or by Trading Standards Officers. Of course, private prosecutions may be possible, and have been brought by collecting societies as in *Thames & Hudson Ltd* v *Design and Artists Copyright Society Ltd*.[6]

1 *See* Chapter 7.

2 *Brigid Foley Ltd* v *Ellott* [1982] RPC 433. It was held that a literary work comprising the words and numerals in a knitting guide was not infringed by the making of garments by the defendant using the knitting guide. But *see* the section on making an adaptation later in this chapter (pp 180–182).

3 Copyright, Designs and Patents Act 1988 s 16(2). Statutory references in this chapter are, unless otherwise stated, to the Copyright, Designs and Patents Act 1988.

4 *Keays* v *Dempster* [1994] FSR 554.

5 *CBS Songs Ltd* v *Amstrad Consumer Electronics plc* [1988] AC 1013.

6 [1995] FSR 153. In England and Wales, the Director of Public Prosecutions has certain powers in respect of private prosecutions, including a power to intervene and undertake the conduct of proceedings even if the purpose is to offer no evidence and thereby abort those proceedings: Prosecution of Offences Act 1985 s 6.

The acts restricted by copyright

The copyright owner has, under the Copyright, Designs and Patents Act 1988 s 16(1), the exclusive right:

- to copy the work;
- to issue copies of the work to the public;
- to rent or lend the work to the public;
- to perform, show or play the work in public;
- to communicate the work to the public;
- to make an adaptation of the work or do any of the above in relation to an adaptation.

The copyright subsisting in a work is infringed by any person who does or authorises another to do any of these acts restricted by copyright without the licence (that is, without permission, contractual or otherwise) of the copyright owner.[7] Copyright may be infringed if the act complained of relates to only a part of the work for, under s 16(3), the doing of an act restricted by copyright includes doing it to any *substantial* part of the work. The question of substantiality has been taken by the courts as referring to the quality of what has been taken rather than its quantity in proportion to the whole. In *Ladbroke (Football) Ltd v William Hill (Football) Ltd*, Lord Pearce said:

> Whether a part is substantial must be decided by its quality rather than its quantity. The reproduction of a part which by itself has no originality will not normally be a substantial part of the copyright and therefore will not be protected.[8]

However, to speak of the reproduction of a part which has no originality *per se* is misleading. Many works have nothing original, if viewed in terms of their constituent parts, yet it is clear that compilations of commonplace material may still be works of copyright; the rationale is that sufficient skill, effort or judgment has been expended in making the compilation.[9] Therefore, taking part of a compilation of unoriginal material may still be deemed to be a substantial part of the entire work if the part of the compilation reflects a substantial application of skill or judgment on the part of the person creating the compilation.[10]

In *Ladbroke v William Hill*, Lord Evershed alluded to the substantial significance of the part taken and suggested that the question of substantial reproduction is incapable of precise definition but is, rather, a matter of fact and degree.[11] On this basis it is clear that copying a small portion of a work can infringe copyright if that part is important in relation to the whole work. For example, in *Hawkes & Sons (London) Ltd v Paramount Film Service Ltd*,[12] a newsreel contained 28 bars comprising the main melody of the well-known march 'Colonel Bogey'. This portion lasted only 20 seconds, whereas the full march lasted for some four minutes. Nevertheless, the newsreel was held to infringe the copyright in the march. It was said that what is substantial is a matter of fact, and value as well as quantity must be considered. The importance of the part taken to the copyright work as a whole is often taken to be the litmus test for substantiality and judges so often refer to quality in the context of the relative importance of the part taken. For example, in *PCR Ltd v Dow Jones Telerate Ltd*,[13] Lloyd J said that quality was at least as important as quantity and that the defendant had infringed copyright because he had taken the most important and interesting parts of the claimant's reports on the world status of cocoa crops.

Taken to its extreme limits, this emphasis on importance as a way of determining substantiality can deflect consideration from the only valid approach to the question, at least in terms of the original works of copyright. Such works, if they are to merit copyright protection, must be the result of skill or judgment.[14] Substantiality must, therefore, be measured in relation to the skill or judgment expended to create the work of copyright. In other words, has there been an appropriation of sufficient of that skill or judgment to amount to an unwarranted intrusion into the property right which is the copyright which will be regarded as unlawful? This question must require consideration in terms of both quality and quantity. There is a danger that, by concentrating on quality, the courts may

7 Copyright, Designs and Patents Act 1988 s 16(2).

8 [1964] 1 WLR 273 at 293.

9 For example, *see Macmillan & Co Ltd v K & J Cooper* (1923) 93 LJPC 113.

10 It is better nowadays to consider whether the part taken is an intellectual creation, particularly in relation to the original works. This is express in terms of some works (computer programs, databases and photographs) under EU Directives. However, 'intellectual creation' and 'skill and judgment' probably are equivalent to all intents and purposes.

11 The Copyright Act 1956 contained a restricted act of reproducing a work in a material form, broadly equivalent to copying a work under the Copyright, Designs and Patents Act 1988. Indeed, for literary, dramatic, musical and artistic works, copying is defined in s 17(2) as reproducing the work in any material form.

12 [1934] Ch 593.

13 [1998] FSR 170.

14 Some judges still use the term 'labour' as an alternative. This is now questionable.

fall into the trap of looking at the merit of the copyright work. Fortunately, the courts appear to have resisted that temptation.[15]

Another difficulty with deciding substantiality by looking at the importance of the part taken is that it may reflect very little skill or judgment. For example, in *Cantor Fitzgerald International* v *Tradition (UK) Ltd*,[16] an argument that a small part of a computer program could be a substantial part of the program if the program would not work without it or if it was used frequently during the execution of the program was firmly rejected. Taken to its extreme, this argument would mean that a single command or even a single piece of punctuation could be a substantial part of a computer program on the basis that the program would not function correctly without it.

The emphasis on skill or judgment in testing for substantiality was made in *Newspaper Licensing Agency Ltd* v *Marks & Spencer plc*[17] in which the Agency, which took assignments of the copyright in the typographical arrangement of published editions of newspapers, complained of the defendant making further copies of articles and items from newspapers which had been supplied legitimately by a press cutting service. The House of Lords reiterated that substantiality is more a question of quality rather than quantity but it is a matter of looking at what copyright was designed to protect. In the case of typographical arrangements of published editions, it is the 'skill and labour' used in creating the overall design of the edition. It is in that context that substantiality should be decided rather than looking at the proportion of the part taken to the whole of the edition.

Where the defendant has added to the parts of the copyright work he has taken, in evaluating substantiality, the court should focus on the parts of the claimant's work reproduced by the defendant rather than concentrating on the defendant's entire work. In *Spectravest Inc* v *Aperknit Ltd*,[18] Millett J said (at 170):

> In considering whether a substantial part of the claimant's work has been reproduced by the defendant, attention must primarily be directed to the part which is said to have been reproduced, and not to those parts which have not.

The test seems to be, therefore, to identify the parts taken by the defendant, to then isolate them from the remainder of the defendant's work and then, finally, to consider whether those parts represent a substantial part of the claimant's work.[19] That comparison will be based on a test that is, according to Millett J, qualitative and not, or not merely, quantitative.

An alternative and, at first sight, very attractive test is to consider whether the act complained of is likely to harm the copyright owner's economic interests. In *Cooper* v *Stephens*,[20] it was said that copying even a small portion of an author's work would be restrained if used in a work which competed with the author's work or with a work that the author might publish in the future. However, such a test, taken literally, would be very difficult to apply and could mean that copying even a small unimportant part could infringe copyright, which plainly is not the result intended by the Act. Basically, if the part taken is significantly important, regardless of actual size, it is very likely to be detrimental to the copyright owner's interests. Another point is that, in a number of situations, the copyright owner may not wish to exploit the work commercially. For example, the work may have been produced for personal pleasure or interest, such as in the case of a private diary.

Another issue is the extent to which the author of the copyright work has based his work on the common stock of information or ideas that everyone is free to use. Certain 'design features' may be commonplace in a particular profession or business and it would seem to be wrong to consider such aspects of the copyright work in looking at infringement. In *Jones* v *London Borough of Tower Hamlets*,[21] an architect created architectural drawings including floor plans for a proposed housing development. The defendant's housing development had similarities compared to that designed by the claimant. It was held that,

15 *See*, for example, *Ludlow Music Inc* v *Robbie Williams* [2001] FSR 19 (p 271).

16 [2000] RPC 95.

17 [2003] 1 AC 551.

18 [1988] FSR 161.

19 This approach was confirmed by Lord Millett in *Designers Guild Ltd* v *Russell Williams (Textiles) Ltd* [2001] FSR 11 at para 38.

20 [1895] 1 Ch 567.

21 [2001] RPC 23 (p 407).

in considering whether a substantial part of the plans had been copied, account should be taken of the common stock of architectural ideas that anyone was free to use. Infringement was found only in respect of a plan for a bathroom in which the claimant had developed a unique design solution. Although this recognition of the 'public domain' in copyright law is attractive, it should be remembered that copyright can subsist in a compilation of commonplace material. If there is skill or judgment in selecting, arranging or combining elements from the public domain, copyright should subsist and infringement should be found if a substantial part of that skill or judgment has been 'borrowed' by the defendant. However, taking an underlying idea is unlikely to infringe, particularly if it is fairly abstract or simple. This is because abstract and simple ideas are unlikely to be deemed to be a substantial part of the copyright work.[22]

The Copyright, Designs and Patents Act 1988 explicitly provides for indirect infringement of copyright under s 16(3), regardless of whether any intervening acts themselves infringe copyright.[23] This is particularly valuable in the context of articles made to drawings, so that a person making copies of the articles will indirectly infringe the copyright subsisting in the drawings. In *LB (Plastics) Ltd v Swish Products Ltd*,[24] the claimant manufactured a plastic 'knock-down' drawer system of furniture, known as 'Sheer Glide', in accordance with working drawings. The House of Lords upheld the claimant's claim that the copyright subsisting in the drawings had been infringed by the defendant who had copied the drawers. There was some evidence that the defendant had directly used the drawings in question, but the trial judge, Whitford J, based his judgment on indirect copying of the drawings by the defendant's use of the claimant's drawer as a model for making similar drawers, and this approach was affirmed in the House of Lords.

Recalling that copyright subsists in drawings as artistic works irrespective of artistic quality, even functional articles sometimes were afforded protection through their working drawings under the Copyright Act 1956. However, the 1988 Act, while expressly reinforcing the notion of indirect infringement of copyright, reduces its scope because of an overlap with design law.[25] The Copyright, Designs and Patents Act 1988 s 51(1) states that the copyright in a design document (or model recording or embodying a design) is not infringed by making articles to the design unless the design is, itself, an artistic work. A design document is, under s 263, any record of a design, whether in the form of a drawing, a written description, a photograph, data stored in a computer or otherwise.[26]

The individual infringing acts will now be considered in more detail. Sections 17–21 of the 1988 Act expand upon the meaning and scope of the acts restricted by copyright. Infringements of the rights associated with the restricted acts were described in the 1956 Act as 'primary infringements'. They are no longer so called, although the 1988 Act still classifies some activities as secondary infringements and some writers still refer to primary infringements to distinguish them from the secondary infringements. It should be noted at this stage that the scope of the acts restricted by copyright varies according to the nature of the work involved.

Copying

Making a copy of a work is the act which most people think of in terms of copyright infringement: for example, making a photocopy of pages in a book or a recording of music. But 'copying' has a technical meaning which varies depending on the nature of the work in question. Section 17 of the 1988 Act comprehensively deals with the concept of copying and, generally, copying is a restricted act for all categories of copyright works.[27] When considering the definitions of copying, it is essential to recognise that many of the words and terms used are themselves widely defined in the Act.

22 *Designers Guild Ltd v Russell Williams (Textiles) Ltd* [2001] FSR 11 (p 113) at para 26 *per* Lord Hoffmann. But *see* Chapter 8 (p 264) in relation to non-literal copying.

23 An example may be where the intervening act is committed outside the jurisdiction of the UK.

24 [1979] RPC 551.

25 Designs created before 1 August 1989 were still protected through their drawings as a result of the transitional provisions until, at the latest, 1 August 1999. In *Valeo Vision SA v Flexible Lamps Ltd* [1995] RPC 205 it was held that there was an infringement of the copyright subsisting in drawings of vehicle lamp clusters.

26 This definition applies to the Copyright, Designs and Patents Act 1988 Part III which concerns the design right subsisting in original designs.

27 Copyright, Designs and Patents Act 1988 s 17(1).

Section 17(2) defines copying, in relation to a literary, dramatic, musical or artistic work, as reproducing the work in any material form.[28] This does not extend to taking the idea underlying the work. For example, in *Breville Europe plc v Thorn EMI Domestic Appliances Ltd*,[29] it was held that taking the idea of using triangular dividers in a sandwich toaster would not infringe the copyright in the claimant's drawings. The defendant's toaster was created independently and no use was made of the skill, labour and effort expended in creating the drawings.[30]

Reproducing in a material form is stated by s 17(2) to include storing the work in any medium by electronic means. Thus, recording a copy of any of the 'original' works of copyright in modern computer storage media falls within the meaning of copying, acknowledging the fact that a work can be stored electronically in an intangible form and copied without the need for paper. 'Electronic' has an extremely wide meaning going well beyond an engineer's understanding of the word. Under s 178, 'electronic' means actuated by electric, magnetic, electro-magnetic, electro-chemical or electro-mechanical energy. However, s 17(2) is phrased in terms of storing the work *in* any medium rather than storing the work *in* or *on* any medium, although this is unlikely to cause problems in practice because the phrase 'reproducing the work in any material form' should be wide enough in its own right to include any form of storage, given the spirit of the Act.

The inclusion of electronic storage as a means of reproducing a work in a material form means that a musical work recorded on magnetic tape, CD or DVD will infringe unless the recording was made with the copyright owner's licence. In the past, there have been problems with some forms of storing works. For example, in *Boosey v Whight*[31] it was held that the manufacture of a paper roll with perforations in it so that it could be used to play music on a mechanical organ did not infringe the copyright in the music so represented. However, this case was decided under the Copyright Act 1842 s 15, which was in terms of the author's right being to prevent copying sheet music regarded as a book. That is, it envisaged copying sheet music as sheet music. It is submitted that making a 'piano roll' will infringe under the current legislation. By analogy, storing a work on punched card or paper is no different to storing the work as magnetic pulses on a disc. Music generated from a recording on punched tape is reproduced in a material form.

As regards films or broadcasts, copying includes making a photograph of the whole or any substantial part of any image forming part of the film or broadcast.[32] Therefore, taking a single photograph of a substantial part of one frame of a film, or a photograph capturing a substantial part of a momentary display on a television, infringes copyright. In *Spelling-Goldberg Productions Inc v BPC Publishing Ltd*,[33] the claimant made a 'Starsky and Hutch' film and the defendant copied and published a photograph of one frame of the film. It was held that the making of a copy of a single frame of the film was an infringement of the copyright in the film because a single frame was a part of the film within the meaning of the Copyright Act 1956 s 13(10). The same applies to a photograph taken of a screen display of an internet webpage. However, in *Football Association Premier League v QC Leisure (No 2)*,[34] it was held that a frame of a film, not being a photograph, is not a substantial part of a film. Kitchin J said (at para 224) that '. . . four frames [of a film] do not constitute a substantial part of the film works. They occupy a fraction of a second and there is no suggestion that they have any inherent value than as part of the whole.' The frames in question were held not to be photographs because they were still part of a film. This case is distinguishable from *Spelling-Goldberg* as the defendants in *Football Association* had not made photographs of the films or broadcasts in question. However, in Football Association, a number of questions were submitted to the Court of Justice for a preliminary ruling. The ruling has not yet been handed down but the Advocate General's Opinion has been published[35] and he is of the view that the playing of the broadcast, even though only four frames at a time are stored at a time, still fell within the reproduction right under Article 2 of the Directive on copyright in the information

28 Under the 1956 Act, this was held to extend to the display of a work on a television monitor: *Bookmakers' Afternoon Greyhound Services Ltd v Wilf Gilbert (Staffordshire) Ltd* [1994] FSR 723.

29 [1995] FSR 77.

30 However, it was held that the registered design in the claimant's toaster had been infringed.

31 [1900] 1 Ch 122.

32 Copyright, Designs and Patents Act 1988 s 17(4).

33 [1981] RPC 283.

34 [2008] FSR 32.

35 Joined Cases C-403/08 and C-429/08 *Football Association Premier League Ltd v QC Leisure*, 3 February 2011.

society. It is submitted that this is correct and the 'little and often' taking of a copyright work infringes if those small parts are themselves intellectual creations.[36]

Where the work in question is a computer game and the contents of the computer chip through which it is played are not themselves at any given time a substantial part of the game as a whole, the artistic works displayed on screen are a substantial part of the original drawings. The use of the 'pause' button confirms this. In *R v Gilham*,[37] the defendant sold 'modchips' which permitted the playing of counterfeit computer games. The Court of Appeal used, as an example, the Tomb Raider game which 'stars' Lara Croft. Although images of Lara Croft on screen may not have been identical to the original drawings from which the game is made, they were sufficiently similar to be substantial copies of those original drawings. It made no difference if a particular image was only displayed for a brief time as copying extends to making transient copies.

The generous definition of 'photograph' contained in the 1988 Act should be considered in relation to this form of copying and the fact that photographs and films are mutually exclusive.[38] It should also be noted that s 17(4) states that copying includes making a photograph, and that making a film of a film or a film of a broadcast will fall within the act of copying. It is possible in such examples that photographs of some kind may be used in an intermediate process, in which case there will be an infringement in respect of the intermediate copies as, under s 17(6), copying includes the making of copies which are transient or incidental to some other use of the work.[39] A limitation on the act of copying a film is that it appears that it requires that the recording of the film must itself have been copied.[40] It is not enough if a film is 'copied' by making a new film based on the first, for example, by using the same ideas and techniques.

Copying in relation to a typographical arrangement of a published edition simply means making a facsimile copy of the arrangement.[41] Section 178 offers some assistance with the meaning of 'facsimile copy', stating that it includes a copy which is reduced or enlarged in scale. It is reasonable to assume that the word 'facsimile' has its ordinary dictionary meaning, an exact copy or duplicate of something, especially in relation to printed material. This is obviously intended to catch copying by the use of photocopying technology. It will also apply to copies transmitted using 'fax' machines (facsimile transmission machines) and conversion into digital form for storage on computer media so that it may be reproduced faithfully in the future. Not only can the copyright in the typographical arrangement of published editions be infringed by digital storage or the use of a fax machine, but also copyright in other works, especially the original works, may be infringed. For example, a person faxing a drawing will infringe the copyright in the drawing because he has made a copy of it, unless, of course, he has permission from the copyright owner to do this. Facsimile transmission is carried out by the sender's machine scanning a document and converting the data contained in the document into digital codes which are then transmitted over the telecommunications system to the receiving machine, which converts the digital data back to an image. The person receiving a facsimile will obtain a faithful copy of the original although there may be some degradation in print quality.[42]

Care should be taken in framing a claim for copyright infringement in specifying the work alleged to be copied where this is not the entire work in question. For example, where only certain aspects of a work have been taken, it may be tempting to try to identify those aspects collectively as being a work of copyright separate from and independent of the entire work. This is unacceptable and, in such cases, it is far better to base the claim on the entire work and allege that the parts taken represent a substantial part of the whole work.[43] In *Coffey v Warner/Chappel Music Ltd*,[44] the claimant was a songwriter who claimed that a song written by Madonna and another person infringed the copyright in her earlier song. The claim was based not on the song as an entirety but on '. . . an original musical work comprising the combination of vocal expression, pitch contour and syncopation of

36 Case 5/08 *Infopaq International A/S v Danske Dagblades Forening* [2009] ECR I-6569, para 37. Taking single words from separate parts of a literary work will not infringe.

37 [2010] ECDR 5 (p 57).

38 Copyright, Designs and Patents Act 1988 s 4(2) states that a photograph cannot be a part of a film.

39 A transient copy is one that exists for a short duration and is deleted automatically, such as copies made on computer during the acts of browsing or caching: Case 5/08 *Infopaq International A/S v Danske Dagblades Forening* [2009] ECR I-6569. Printing part of a work on paper during a data capture process which depends on a person to later delete it is not a transient copy.

40 *Norowzian v Arks Ltd (No 1)* [1998] FSR 394, at first instance.

41 Copyright, Designs and Patents Act 1988 s 17(5).

42 Similar considerations apply to documents transmitted electronically as e-mail attachments or downloaded from internet sites.

43 However, such an approach might be possible where the entire work is itself made up of individual works of copyright, such as in the case of a compilation or database.

44 [2005] FSR 34 (p 747).

or around the words "does it really matter"'. The defendants applied to strike out the claim on the basis that it stood no reasonable prospect of success. Blackburne J allowed the application and said (at para 10):

> What the copyright work is in any given case is not governed by what the claimant alleging copyright infringement chooses to say that it is. Rather, it is a matter for objective determination by the court.

The claimant had, in effect, embarked upon a cherry-picking exercise, formulating the claim in such a way that the copyright work alleged to have been infringed had been tailored to suit the parts or elements alleged to have been copied.

In an earlier case, Laddie J spoke of the dangers of excision in relation to the formulation of a claim. In *IPC Media Ltd* v *Highbury-Leisure Publishing Ltd*,[45] he said (at para 11):

> Furthermore, it may be necessary to be alert to the possibility of being misled by what may be called similarity by excision. Michelangelo said of one of his sculptures 'I saw the angel in the marble and I carved until I set him free'. In copyright cases, chipping away and ignoring all the bits which are undoubtedly not copied may result in the creation of an illusion of copying in what is left. This is a particular risk during a trial. Inevitably the court will be invited by the claimant to concentrate on the respects in which his work and the alleged infringements are similar. But with sufficient concentration one may lose sight of the differences. They may be just as important in deciding whether copying has taken place. The effect can be explained by an analogy. Two individuals drop similar small quantities of sand on the floor. If one removes all the grains of sand which are not in equivalent positions, all you are left with are those which are in equivalent positions. If you look at those remaining grains it is possible to say that similar patterns of distribution exist. It is even possible to say that these similarities are surprising. But the similarities and the surprise they elicit are an artefact created by the very process of ignoring all the other grains. This type of artefact created by close attention only to the areas of similarity is a risk in any court proceedings.

Despite such sentiments, it is not always an easy matter to determine precisely what the copyright work relied on should be. What about a book? Is it the whole book or each individual chapter? In the case of a film, we have seen that capturing a single frame can infringe. That being so, it might be legitimate to claim copyright in the single frame alleged to have been taken. On the other hand, typographical arrangement copyright infringement looks to the whole of the published edition rather than single articles within it.[46] It is suggested that the test for identifying the work in which copyright is claimed to subsist requires consideration of the following factors:

1 Does the 'work' claimed stand on its own as a discrete item which represents skill and judgment in its own right sufficient for copyright subsistence?
2 An important factor is the type of work. One might expect that, in terms of musical works, it is a single piece of music though, perhaps, in relation to classical music it may be a single movement in, for example, a symphony or concerto.
3 A further factor is the form of infringement and the statutory tests – for example, infringement by copying for films and broadcasts covers making a photograph of a single image, as mentioned above.
4 In the case of non-literal copying, where the allegation is based on the skill and judgment expended in creating and developing the detailed scheme underlying the finished work (this could be described as the ephemeral version of the work prior to its tangible expression) it is important to identify it with some precision. In this respect, reliance on preliminary design materials, sketches and the like might help.[47]

Table 6.1 summarises the scope of the restricted act of copying as it applies to different categories of works. It should be recalled that, generally, copying is a restricted act for all types of work.[48]

45 [2005] FSR 20 (p 434).

46 *Newspaper Licensing Agency Ltd v Marks & Spencer plc* [2003] 1 AC 551.

47 *Electronic Techniques (Anglia) Ltd v Critchley Components Ltd* [1997] FSR 401.

48 There is a limitation in respect to film sound tracks in that references to copying a sound recording does not include copying the film sound track to accompany the film: s 5B(3)(c). There are equivalent limitations for sound recordings in respect of the acts of playing, communication, copying, issuing, rental or lending: s 5B(3).

Table 6.1 The restricted act of copying

Work	Restricted act
Literary, dramatic, musical, artistic: s 17(2)	Reproducing the work in any material form, including storing the work in any medium by electronic means
Artistic (additional): s 17(3)	Includes making a copy in 3-D of a 2-D work and making a copy in 2-D of a 3-D work: for example, making a painting of a sculpture or constructing a building from an architectural drawing
Film, TV broadcast: s 17(4)	Includes making a photograph of the whole or any substantial part
Typographical arrangement of a published edition: s 17(5)	Making a facsimile copy of the arrangement
All works: s 17(6)	Includes the making of copies which are transient or are incidental to some other use of the work

Note: 'Photograph' has the meaning given in s 4(2); 'material form' is not defined but should include invisible means of storage such as on CDs, DVDs, magnetic tape, computer disks and integrated circuits.

Copying – an accumulation of insubstantial taking

A defendant may have taken small parts of a work over a period of time where each small part would not, by itself, be regarded as substantial. In *Cate v Devon & Exeter Constitutional Newspaper Co*,[49] the defendant extracted and reproduced small amounts of material from the claimant's newspaper on a regular and systematic basis. The defendant's purpose was to include the material in his own newspaper. It was held that he had infringed copyright, even though the amount taken each week was small.

The logical problem of holding that the regular taking of insubstantial parts being, eventually, considered to be a substantial taking was highlighted by Laddie J in *Electronic Techniques (Anglia) Ltd v Critchley Components Ltd*[50] where he said, criticising *Cate v Devon* (at 409):

> At its most extreme it could be put this way: a competitor who, because he only took insubstantial amounts, did not infringe yesterday, does not infringe today and will not infringe tomorrow, will be held to infringe if he continues not infringing for long enough.

Laddie J's sentiment holds true where each insubstantial taking is in relation to a different work of copyright, as in *Cate v Devon*. However, in respect of a single work, that approach is flawed. What if, over a period of time, the defendant takes the entire work? A better way to look at an accumulation of insubstantial takings is to consider them as part of a continuing act, as was recognised as a possible explanation by Laddie J in *Electronic Techniques*. That case involved applications for summary judgment only and Laddie J did not come to any firm conclusion on the matter, although he did suggest it might be timely if *Cate v Devon* was reconsidered. A line of authorities, including this case, appears to take the defendant's behaviour into account when determining substantiality. That is, a deliberate and repeated taking of small parts might be held to infringe. However, the language of s 16 of the Act does not suggest any such thing.

The status of an accumulation of the repeated taking of insubstantial parts of a film was considered in *Football Association Premier League v QC Leisure (No 2)*.[51] Some of the defendants were publicans who had obtained unauthorised decoders and showed football matches which had been transmitted in encrypted form by the claimants which owned the relevant copyrights. The decoders only stored a few frames of the films of the football matches at a time. They were held for a very short period of time before being destroyed as the next few frames were processed. Although s 17(6) of the Act extends the meaning of copies to transient copies, Kitchen J considered that, to infringe, a substantial part must be embodied in the transient copy and this did not apply to a series of transient copies which are stored one after the other. He approved of the judgment of Emmett J in

49 As copyright can be infringed indirectly, it may be that such things, if expressed in tangible form, may be deemed to be works of copyright in their own right and infringed by the defendant.

50 (1889) 40 Ch D 500.

51 [2008] FSR 32.

Australian Video Retailers Association Ltd v *Warner Home Video Pty Ltd*,[52] a decision under the Australian Copyright Act of 1968 where he said (at 65):

> It is clear that neither the whole nor any substantial part of a cinematograph film or motion picture is ever embodied in the RAM of a DVD player or personal computer at any given time. The mere fact that, over a period of time, being the time taken to play the motion picture or cinematograph film, tiny parts of it are sequentially stored in the RAM of the DVD player or personal computer does not mean that the motion picture or cinematograph film is embodied in such a device.

There are differences between Australian and UK copyright law but Kitchen J thought this also represented the position under the UK Act. If correct, it has significant implications for the use of computer technology to view and/or listen to films, music and audio-visual works. recordings and copyright works and the control of copyright. It is respectfully submitted that Kitchin J is wrong on this point.[53] Although *Cate* v *Devon* has been subject to criticism, it concerned repeated insubstantial takings from each of a series of publications, not from the same publication. *Football Association* v *QC Leisure* concerned the repeated and systematic taking of insubstantial parts of the same work amounting to the entire work. Criticism of Kitchen J's view is based on three factors:

- Article 9(1) of the Berne Convention for the Protection of Literary and Artistic Works states that 'Authors of literary and artistic works protected by this Convention shall have the exclusive right of authorising the reproduction of these works, *in any manner and form*' (emphasis added). This is very wide and contradicts the very technical approach taken by Kitchen J and, in Australia, Emmet J.
- Article 2 of the Directive on copyright and related rights in the information societ[54] also provides for a reproduction right which is the exclusive right to authorise or prohibit *direct or indirect, temporary or permanent reproduction by any means and in any form, in whole or in part* for, *inter alia*, the producers of the first fixations of films, in respect of the original and copies of their films (again, emphasis added).
- The database Directive[55] contemplates infringement of the database right by the repeated and systematic extraction and/or reutilisation of insubstantial parts of the contents of a database protected by the database right. In Case C-304/07 *Directmedia Publishing GmbH* v *Albert-Ludwigs-Universität Freiburg*[56] the Court of Justice confirmed that, to infringe, the accumulation of individual extractions must be equivalent to a substantial taking. Although not explicit in relation to copyright in databases, it would be unlikely that it was intended that the protection afforded to a copyright database was less extensive in this respect than that available through the database right. An accumulation of repeated acts should infringe copyright if equivalent to a substantial part.

Copyright is concerned, *inter alia*, with securing the economic rights of owners and, consequently, the test for substantiality should be related in some way to the issue of whether the claimant's economic rights have been prejudiced by the defendant's acts. Perhaps more than anything else, that explains why quality has been important in determining substantiality. The systematic taking of small parts can, in some circumstances, injure the claimant's economic advantage in owning the copyright in the work. A computer database is an example. Indeed, reg 16(2) of the Copyright and Rights in Databases Regulations 1997 specifically accepts that the repeated and systematic extraction or re-utilisation of insubstantial parts of a database may amount to the extraction or re-utilisation of a substantial part.[57]

Notwithstanding the above criticism of the approach of Kitchen J to transient copying, the Court of Justice ruled, inter alia, in Joined Cases C-403/08 and C-429/08 *Football Association Premier League* v *QC Leisure*,[58] that the reproduction right under Article 2(a) of

---

52 (2001) 53 IPR 242.

53 However, Kitchen J referred a number of questions to the Court of Justice including questions about the scope of the reproduction right.

54 Directive 2001/29/EC of the European Parliament and of the Council of 22 May 2001 on the harmonisation of certain aspects of copyright and related rights in the information society, OJ L 167, 22.06.2001, p 10.

55 Directive 96/9/EC of the European Parliament and of the Council of 11 March 1996 on the legal protection of databases, OJ L 77, 27.03.1996, p 20.

56 [2008] ECR I-7565; [2009] 1 CMLR 213.

57 An example of this form of infringement is discussed in Chapter 8 in relation to the database right.

58 4 October 2011.

the Directive on copyright and related rights in the information society required that each transient fragment must contain the expression of the author's own intellectual creation if it is to infringe the right.

Copying – dimensional shift

In respect of artistic works, copying is extended to include the making of a copy of a two-dimensional work in three dimensions and vice versa.[59] Thus, making a three-dimensional model from a drawing is copying, as is making a drawing of a three-dimensional sculpture. As mentioned earlier, copyright can be infringed indirectly and this means that the process of 'reverse engineering',[60] copying an article by inspecting it, taking measurements and examining details of its construction and using the knowledge thus gained to make the copies, may infringe the copyright in any original drawings of the article concerned. In *British Leyland Motor Corp Ltd* v *Armstrong Patents Co Ltd*,[61] the claimant designed and made motor cars and also made spare parts for its cars. The claimant also granted licences to other companies permitting them to copy and sell spare parts for the claimant's cars in return for a royalty payment. The defendant refused to obtain a licence and manufactured replacement exhaust pipes for the claimant's cars by copying the shape and dimensions of the exhaust pipes made by the claimant for the Morris Marina car. The defendant simply bought a Morris Marina and removed the exhaust pipe and examined it to see how it was made, what its contours and dimensions were. The claimant claimed that the defendant's exhaust pipes infringed the copyright in the original drawings of the exhaust pipes. It was held that the defendant had infringed the copyright subsisting in the drawings of the exhaust pipes by the process of reverse engineering, but the claimant would not be allowed to assert its rights under copyright law. It was said, in the House of Lords, that car owners have an inherent right to repair their cars in the most economical way possible, and for that purpose it was essential that there was a free market in spare parts. This required the adoption of the non-derogation from grant principle in *Browne* v *Flower*[62] in which Parker J said (at 225):

> the implications usually explained by the maxim that no one can derogate from his own grant do not stop short with easements.

Lord Templeman thought this principle could apply to a car just as easily as to land. He said:

> The principle applied to a motor car manufactured in accordance with engineering drawings and sold with components which are bound to fail during the life of the car prohibits the copyright owner from exercising his copyright powers in such a way as to prevent the car from functioning unless the owner of the car buys replacement parts from the copyright owner or his licensee.[63]

Therefore, although there had been a technical infringement of copyright, the claimant was not allowed to derogate from or interfere with the car owner's right to a free market in spare parts. This case is important because it shows how the courts are prepared to control actual or potential abuse of a copyright, but changes to copyright and design law have removed the possibility of infringing artistic copyright by copying an article made to a drawing if the article is subject to a design right and is not itself an artistic work.[64] However, this did not apply until 1 August 1999 to design documents and models which were created before 1 August 1989.[65] Nevertheless, it is clear that the *British Leyland* defence survived the 1988 Act, both in respect of the transitional provisions[66] and in relation to infringements occurring thereafter: see *Flogates Ltd* v *Refco Ltd*.[67] But it does not appear that the defence will be developed further and, on the contrary, the modern trend seems to be to keep it on a tight leash.

---

59 Copyright, Designs and Patents Act 1988 s 17(3).

60 Sometimes referred to as 'reverse analysis', especially in terms of computer programs. *See* Chapter 8.

61 [1986] 2 WLR 400.

62 [1911] 1 Ch 219.

63 [1986] 2 WLR 400 at 430.

64 *See* Chapter 18 on the design right.

65 *See* the transitional provisions in the Copyright, Designs and Patents Act 1988 Sch 1, para 19(1). An example of the working of these provisions is the case of *Valeo Vision SA* v *Flexible Lamps Ltd* [1995] RPC 205.

66 *See* Copyright, Designs and Patents Act 1988 Sch 1, para 19(9).

67 [1996] FSR 935.

The *British Leyland* principle, that the owner of a complex article which will require replacement parts over its lifetime cannot be deprived of a free market in such parts, can be criticised in that it interferes with and curtails a clear statutory right, particularly as the 1988 Act contains numerous permitted acts, excusing what would otherwise infringe. The principle should be applied, therefore, only sparingly. The Judicial Committee of the Privy Council, indicating that the principle should not be extended in its application and scope, went so far as to direct some criticism at it, saying that it was constitutionally questionable for a judicially declared head of public policy to override or qualify an express statutory provision. In *Canon Kabushiki Kaisha v Green Cartridge Co (Hong Kong) Ltd*,[68] which concerned the spare parts market ('aftermarket') for cartridges for laser printers and photocopiers, it was held that the principle could not be regarded as being founded upon any principle of the law of contract or property, but was based on an overriding public policy. Lord Hoffmann, delivering the judgment of their Lordships, said (at 826):

68 [1997] FSR 817, an appeal from the Court of Appeal in Hong Kong.

> Their Lordships consider that once one departs from the case in which the unfairness to the customer and the anti-competitive nature of the monopoly is as plain and obvious as it appeared to the House in *British Leyland*, the jurisprudential and economic basis for the doctrine becomes extremely fragile.

A number of factors in the *Canon* case distinguish it from *British Leyland*. The toner cartridges would normally be replaced when nothing was wrong with the printer or copier that could be described as requiring repair. It would have simply run out of toner. The cost is more like a normal running cost, such as servicing a car, rather than a repair. The aftermarket itself was different in that the cost of new cartridges was a much higher proportion of the cost of the printer or copier compared with the cost of an exhaust pipe in relation to the cost of a car. Cartridges are replaced much more frequently than exhaust pipes. Basically, the decision is a triumph for market forces. Lord Hoffmann accepted that customers are likely to calculate the lifetime cost of a printer or copier, taking into account the cost of cartridges, in comparing different manufacturers' products. If customers do this, it cannot be said that controlling the aftermarket is anti-competitive[69] and a manufacturer who charges too much for his cartridges is likely to sell fewer machines.

69 There was no evidence of any abuse of the monopoly position.

The Judicial Committee of the Privy Council in *Canon* also directed some criticism at a line of authorities including *Dorling v Honnor Marine Ltd*[70] and *LB (Plastics) Ltd v Swish Products Ltd*[71] on copying by reproducing an article represented in a drawing or other graphic work. The Committee had been invited to depart from these authorities and decide that copying a functional three-dimensional object is not an indirect reproduction of the drawings. Lord Hoffmann said that such cases did not sufficiently distinguish between the reproduction of an artistic work (whether in two-dimensional form or three-dimensional form) and the use of the information contained in an artistic work, such as a drawing together with additional text as the instructions for making a three-dimensional object. Although plainly derived from the drawing, the object does not reproduce the drawing. For example, in *Burke and Margot Burke Ltd v Spicers Dress Designs*[72] it was held that a frock made by the defendant (whether spread out or held up to view) was not a reproduction of the claimant's sketch of the frock. However, as the sketch showed the frock worn by a woman, Clauson J said that there might have been an infringement had the complaint been that the frock had been worn by a woman posing as in the sketch.[73] The Committee declined to depart from previous law, partly because the law had changed and, in *British Leyland*, the House of Lords decided after much consideration to follow the earlier cases.

70 [1965] Ch 1.

71 [1979] RPC 551.

72 [1936] Ch 400.

73 On the basis of *Bradbury, Agnew & Co v Day* (1916) 32 TLR 349, where a *tableau vivant* infringed the copyright in cartoons from *Punch* magazine.

Under previous law, there was a defence under the Copyright Act 1956 s 9(8) to the effect that there was no infringement of artistic copyright by a 'dimensional shift' if the alleged infringing object would not appear to persons, not being experts in relation to such objects, to be a reproduction of the artistic work. In other words, for an infringement, the object copied in a different number of dimensions from an artistic work would have to look like the artistic work in the eyes of the layman. He should have been able to recognise the artistic work in the copy. This test became known as the 'lay recognition test', and was neither easy nor fair to apply as many drawings, particularly engineering drawings, do not appear to be much like the objects they represent in the eyes of a layman.[74] For example, in *Merlet* v *Mothercare plc*[75] the defendant had copied a baby's rain cape designed by the claimant. On the question of infringement of the drawings made by the claimant for the cape, it was held in the Court of Appeal that the s 9(8) defence succeeded because the layman would not recognise the claimant's drawing by comparison with garments made by the defendant. The drawing was in the form of a cutting plan and it was not permissible for the purposes of applying the 'lay recognition test' to unstitch the defendant's garment.[76] However, that test, which limited the strength of protection in relation to three-dimensional articles offered primarily through the medium of drawings, was abandoned by the 1988 Act. The test itself was criticised by senior judges and clearly had failed to achieve its purpose of limiting the scope of copyright. It also provided some indefensible anomalies. For example, simple objects produced from simple drawings would be protected, while complex equipment produced from engineering drawings, difficult for the layman to comprehend, would fail to attract such protection because the notional non-expert would fail to recognise one from the other. Judges had even shown an inclination to fail to take account of differences in scale when applying the test. For example, in *Guildford Kapwood Ltd* v *Embsay Fabrics Ltd*,[77] although the defendant's fabric, greatly magnified, did resemble part of the claimant's lapping diagram, Walton J, regarding himself as the notional non-expert, did not think that the fabric appeared to be a reproduction of the lapping diagram.

The 'lay recognition test' emphasised visual appearance. In *Interlego AG* v *Tyco Industries Inc*[78] it was said that what mattered in relation to artistic works, especially drawings, is that which is visually significant. Indeed, in *Anacon Corp Ltd* v *Environmental Research Technology Ltd*[79] Jacob J held that making a printed circuit board from a circuit diagram did not infringe the artistic copyright in the diagram because the finished board did not look anything like the diagram.[80] However, Jacob J failed to note that, under s 17(2), 'reproducing in a material form' includes storage by electronic means which cannot, by its nature, have any relevant visual significance. It is submitted that, in respect of that part of the judgment, Jacob J was unduly influenced by the 1956 Act.

'Dimensional shift' copying applies only to artistic works. For example, in *Bradbury, Agnew & Co* v *Day*,[81] the claimant owned the copyright in a cartoon in *Punch* magazine. Some actors who enacted the cartoon on stage by dressing up and posing to look like the cartoon were held to have infringed the copyright in the cartoon. The actors formed a three-dimensional representation of a two-dimensional artistic work, that is, the cartoon. However, in *Brigid Foley Ltd* v *Ellott*,[82] it was held that converting a two-dimensional literary work, a knitting pattern, into a three-dimensional object, a woolly jumper, was not an infringement of the copyright subsisting in the knitting pattern, and was not a reproduction in a material form for the purposes of copyright.

Copying and alteration

Significant difficulties may arise in infringement actions if the defendant has produced his work based on a previous original work but has made considerable alterations. Two approaches are possible: first, it is a question of whether the second work is sufficiently the result of skill and labour so that it becomes itself an original work of copyright; second, the distinction between idea and expression may be relevant to this situation. A person might freely admit that he has used another work during the preparation of his own, but may claim that he has not copied the expression of the first work and that his

74 In *Merchant Adventurers v M Grew & Co Ltd* [1971] 2 All ER 657, it was held by Graham J that the test was whether the drawings were such that, after inspecting them, a man of reasonable and average intelligence would be able to understand them to such a degree that he could visualise in his mind what a three-dimensional object made from the drawings would look like.

75 [1986] RPC 115.

76 The claimant also failed to show that the finished garment was a work of artistic craftsmanship.

77 [1983] FSR 567.

78 [1989] 1 AC 217.

79 [1994] FSR 659.

80 Jacob J went on to hold that the circuit diagram was also a literary work because it was intended to be read and, by making a 'net list', a list of components and their interconnections, the defendant had infringed the literary copyright.

81 (1916) 32 TLR 349.

82 [1982] RPC 433. However, in *Autospin (Oil Seals) Ltd v Beehive Spinning* [1995] RPC 683, Laddie J suggested that, in principle, there was no reason why a literary work could not be infringed by making a three-dimensional reproduction of it, in spite of authority to the contrary.

use of it was simply to determine the unprotected ideas contained therein. In other words, he has not made use of the copyrightable elements of the work, but only of the underlying ideas. *Glyn* v *Weston Feature Film Co*[83] provides an example of the former approach, that is whether the second person has used sufficient skill and effort to produce a new and distinct original work of copyright. In that case, a film entitled *Pimple's Three Weeks (without the Option)*, which was a send-up of a risqué play, *Three Weeks*, was held not to infringe copyright in the play because very little of the original remained. It could not be said that the film was a reproduction of a substantial part of the incidents described in the play.

It may be the case that the defendant's work contains a number of similar elements but nothing identical to parts of the claimant's work. In *Designers Guild Ltd* v *Russell Williams (Textiles) Ltd*,[84] the claimant owned the copyright in a fabric design comprising horizontal stripes of irregular thickness with flowers scattered around the design in a manner described as somewhat impressionistic. The defendant created a similar design based on stripes and scattered flowers but, whilst it looked very similar, there were many detailed differences. In such cases, the test for infringement is in two stages, the first being a comparison of the two works, looking at both the similarities and the differences so as to assess whether the second work has been copied from the first. If there is no copying, then there can be no infringement. Once the court is satisfied that there has been copying, the question is then whether the copied parts represent a substantial part of the claimant's work. The focus should then be on similarities rather than differences and whether the parts now accepted to have been copied represent a substantial part of the claimant's work. Where what has been copied is not identical but similar, the court has to decide whether the defendant's work incorporates a substantial part of the skill and labour involved in the creation of the claimant's work and where, as in the present case, there were a number of similarities, the cumulative effect of those similarities ought to be considered.[85]

If all that can be shown to be taken is a basic idea, bearing in mind the oft-used phrase 'copyright protects expression not idea', it is unlikely that infringement will be found. In *Designers Guild*, Lord Hoffmann[86] distinguished two categories of ideas. Some he said were not protected because they had no connection with the literary, dramatic, musical or artistic nature of the work, such as a drawing disclosing an inventive concept. Other ideas, whilst they may be ideas of a literary, dramatic, musical or artistic nature, were not protected if they lacked originality or were so commonplace that they could not be a substantial part of the work, such as the idea underlying a drawing showing illiterate persons how to vote.[87]

Judges are generally unsympathetic to a person who has created a work by making use of a prior work of copyright. It seems wrong in principle that someone can take a short cut to producing his own work by relying on the skill and effort of others. If there is evidence that the defendant has used the claimant's work in some way, judges appear to be reluctant to find for the defendant, regardless of fine distinctions between idea and expression. For example, in *Elanco Products Ltd* v *Mandops (Agrochemical Specialists) Ltd*,[88] the defendant started to sell a herbicide invented by the claimant and called 'Trifluralin' after the expiry of the patent. The defendant sold the herbicide together with a leaflet and label which were partly identical to those used by the claimant. After the claimant complained, the defendant produced a second leaflet using a different format and language. The claimant still complained, and eventually the defendant started using a third version based on the second one, claiming that the information in the claimant's leaflet was in the public domain and that, although copyright protected the expression of language, it did not protect the content of it. As a matter of fact, it was found that most of the information in the defendant's leaflet could be traced to the public domain. Nevertheless, it was held that there was an arguable case of infringement of copyright, although the claimant

83 [1916] 1 Ch 261.

84 [2001] FSR 11 (p 113).

85 The House of Lords reinstated the finding of the judge at first instance that the defendant had copied a substantial part of the claimant's design. There was some criticism of the Court of Appeal decision and the way it had revisited the judge's conclusion as to substantiality, absent an error in principle by the trial judge.

86 At para 25. As regards idea/expression, Lord Hoffmann noted that the TRIPs Agreement states that copyright protection extends to expression and not to ideas.

87 As in *Kenrick* v *Lawrence* (1890) 25 QBD 99. The basic idea of a fabric design comprising stripes and flowers would be an unprotectable idea. The defendant's design in *Designers Guild* went further than this though.

88 [1980] RPC 213, an interim hearing.

was refused an injunction. Plainly, if the defendant had simply taken the trouble to locate and use information in the public domain in the preparation of its leaflet there would have been no infringement. But the fact that the defendant had used the claimant's original leaflet did not help its case and Buckley LJ said that, concerning infringement, the question was whether, by using the claimant's literature, the defendant was making use of the skill and judgment of the claimant.

Of course, if there is a substantial amount of language copying and the same characters and incidents are used, then the fact that the two works may have other differences will not help the defendant's cause. In *Ravenscroft* v *Herbert*,[89] the defendant wrote a work of fiction but had used the claimant's non-fictional work as a source to provide credibility in relation to historical facts. The claimant's work concerned a spear reputed to have been the one used to wound Christ at the crucifixion, and to have been a source of inspiration for Nazi Germany. The spear is part of the Hapsburg treasure in the Hofburg Museum in Vienna. The defendant's claim to have used only historical facts from the claimant's work was rejected on the basis of substantial copying, particularly in terms of language copying, incidents and in the interpretation of events. Altogether, it was held that the infringing part represented only 4 per cent of the defendant's work, but, in assessing damages, that 4 per cent was rated as being worth 15 per cent in terms of its value to the whole of the work.

Copyright owners have occasionally complained about parodies of their works, that is satirical or comic send-ups. A parody usually involves a fair amount of alteration, but the link with the first work is quite blatant since the effect of the parody might largely be lost otherwise. Of particular importance, since the passing of the 1988 Act, in addition to the question of whether a substantial part of the first work has been copied, is that infringement of the author's moral rights may also be a significant issue.[90] In *Joy Music Ltd* v *Sunday Pictorial Newspapers (1920) Ltd*,[91] a song entitled 'Rock-a-Billy' was parodied in another song which used the words 'Rock-a-Philip, Rock' in the chorus but, otherwise, the words of the two songs were different. It was held that the parody did not infringe the copyright in the original song. However, in *Schweppes Ltd* v *Wellingtons Ltd*,[92] the defendant produced a label for a bottle which was very much like the claimant's famous bottle labels, except instead of using the word 'Schweppes' the defendant used the word 'Schlurppes'. Even though it was accepted that the defendant's label was a parody, it was held that the claimant's copyright had been infringed. There is no reason why parodies should be treated any differently to other works which are derived from or based on prior works, although they do seem to have been looked on more kindly by the judiciary. Any difference in treatment runs counter to the Act and confirmation that the same principles apply to parodies as to other copies of works was indicated in *Williamson Music Ltd* v *Pearson Partnership Ltd*,[93] a case involving a parody of the Rodgers and Hammerstein song 'There is Nothin' Like a Dame' for the purpose of advertising a bus company on television. It was held that the test for determining whether a parody amounted to an infringement of the parodied work was whether the parody made substantial use of the expression of the original work. In other words, to find an infringement by the restricted act of copying, the second work must contain a reproduction in a material form of a qualitatively substantial part of the first work. To this must be added the fact that the 'author' of the second work must have made use of the first work in creating the second, that is there must be some causal connection between the works.[94]

In some countries, making a parody of a work does not infringe copyright. For example, in France, once a work has been disclosed, the author may not prohibit the making of a parody, pastiche or caricature of his work providing it is within the rules of the genre.[95] It was proposed to allow this also in the UK. The proposal initially came from the *Gowers Review of Intellectual Property*[96] and a detailed discussion together with suggested proposals are contained in a consultation document.[97] Subsequently, the Hargreaves

89 [1980] RPC 193.

90 Especially the right to object to derogatory treatment and the right not to have a work falsely attributed to the author. Cases on parodies prior to the 1988 Act must be viewed in the light of subsequent strengthening of the author's moral rights.

91 [1920] 2 QB 60.

92 [1984] FSR 210.

93 [1987] FSR 97.

94 For the 'original' works of copyright, the act of copying is defined as reproducing the work in any material form. 'Reproduction' implies some creative relationship between the works, a causal link.

95 Art L 122-5 of Law No 92-957 of 1 July, 1992 on the Intellectual Property Code, as amended.

96 Commissioned by the then Chancellor of the Exchequer, Gordon Brown, HMSO 2006 available at http://www.hm-treasury.gov.uk/media/6/E/pbr06_gowers_report_755.pdf.

97 UK Intellectual Property Office, *Taking Forward the Gowers Review of Intellectual Property: Proposed Changes to Copyright Exceptions*, 2007, pp 31ff, available at http://www.ipo.gov.uk/consult-copyrightexceptions.pdf.

Report also called for the introduction of an exception to infringement to allow the use of a work in parody.[98]

Copying – causal connection

The infringing work must be derived from the claimant's work. There must be a causal connection as independent creation of a similar work does not infringe. In an action for copyright infringement by copying, proof of copying and the question as to which party bears the burden of proof are frequently important issues. Of course, the claimant has the burden of proving that the defendant has copied but, having discharged that burden, it can fairly be said that the burden of proof then shifts to the defendant in that he then is given the opportunity to rebut the inference of copying by offering an alternative explanation of the similarities between his work and the claimant's work.[99] In *Francis, Day & Hunter Ltd v Bron*,[100] it was alleged that the defendant had reproduced the first eight bars of the song 'In a little Spanish Town' in his song 'Why?' ('I'll never let you go/Why? Because I love you'). The case is also of interest because it deals with the possibility of subconsciously infringing copyright. Willmer LJ accepted counsel's submission that in order to constitute reproduction:

1 There must be a sufficient objective similarity between the two works (an objective issue, that is, would the 'reasonable man' consider the two works sufficiently similar).
2 There must also be some causal connection between the two works (a subjective question but not to be presumed as a matter of law merely upon proof of access).

In his judgment, Diplock LJ described the issue of proof of copying in very clear terms:

> The degree of objective similarity is, of course, not merely important, indeed essential, in proving the first element in infringement, namely, that the defendant's work can properly be described as a reproduction or adaptation of the copyright work; it is also very cogent material from which to draw the inference that the defendant has in fact copied, whether consciously or unconsciously, the copyright work. But it is not the only material. Even complete identity of the two works may not be conclusive evidence of copying, for it may be proved that it was impossible for the author of the alleged infringing work to have had access to the copyright work. And, once you have eliminated the impossible (namely, copying), that which remains (namely, coincidence) however improbable is the truth; I quote inaccurately, but not unconsciously, from Sherlock Holmes.[101]

As indicated by Diplock LJ, factual similarity coupled with proof of access does not raise an irrefutable presumption of copying; at most it raises a prima facie case for the defendant to answer. Thus, in such cases, the burden of proof will shift to the defendant who will then have to satisfy the court, on a balance of probabilities, that he had not copied the first work and that any similarity is the result of coincidence, not copying. This approach was later accepted by the House of Lords in *LB (Plastics) Ltd v Swish Products Ltd*[102] where it was held, *inter alia*, that a striking similarity combined with proof of access raised a prima facie case of infringement that the defendant had to answer.

The nature of the similarities is also important. If the information copied is incorrect in its original form, this may be excellent proof of copying. For example, in *Billhöfer Maschinenfabrik GmbH v T H Dixon & Co Ltd*,[103] Hoffmann J said (at 123):

> . . . it is the resemblances in inessentials, the small, redundant, even mistaken elements of the copyright work, which carry the greatest weight. This is because they are least likely to have been the result of independent design. (original emphasis)

This is a very good reason why authors may deliberately include redundant material, mistakes or dummy entries in their work. It will be very hard for a defendant to give a plausible reason for their existence in his work. Unless admitted by the defendant, the

98 Professor I Hargreaves, *Digital opportunity: a review of intellectual property and growth*, May 2011, pp 8 and 50: available at http://www.ipo.gov.uk/ipreview-finalreport.pdf.

99 *Creative Technology Ltd v Aztech Systems Pte Ltd* [1997] FSR 491, Court of Appeal, Singapore.

100 [1963] Ch 587.

101 [1963] Ch 587 at 627.

102 [1979] RPC 551.

103 [1990] FSR 105.

claimant has to prove his work is a work in which copyright subsists, that he is the owner of that copyright (or the exclusive licensee), that the defendant has copied from it and that he has taken a substantial part. The inclusion of a few 'deliberate mistakes' in his work will remove one of those barriers. As subsistence and ownership will not frequently be in issue, the outcome will be determined solely on the issue of whether a substantial part has been taken unless the defendant is relying on a particular defence to infringement. *IBCOS Computers Ltd* v *Barclays Mercantile Highland Finance Ltd*[104] clearly demonstrates the effectiveness of errors and redundant material in proving copying. It also shows that the amount of such material does not have to be great to convince a judge that copying has occurred.

The presence of similarities may raise a presumption of copying, especially where the person creating the alleged offending work has had access to the first work. But differences may also be important in that they may lead to an inference that the second work has been independently created.[105] As Lewison J put it in respect of an inference of copying in *Ultra Marketing (UK) Ltd* v *Universal Components Ltd*[106] (at para 14):

> However, like most evidential presumptions, this evidential presumption is merely a tool. At the end of a trial, once all the evidence has been heard, it is a question of fact whether a drawing has been produced as a result of copying a copyright work or as a result of independent design.

Of the complaint in that case that the defendant had copied the claimant's drawing of extruded aluminium frames incorporating pips, the judge said that what it came down to was not that the drawing had been copied but that the defendant had copied the idea.

The possibility of subconscious copying has already been mentioned above. Musical works are particularly susceptible to this form of copying, where the author of the second piece of music has heard the first music some time before, but has no contemporary conscious recollection of the first piece of music and certainly does not deliberately set out to copy it. This is what was alleged in the *Francis, Day & Hunter Ltd* v *Bron* case, where it was accepted by the judge at first instance that there had been no conscious copying. Nevertheless, the first eight bars of each song were virtually identical (these are reproduced in the law report). Even so, there must be some causal link between the works – truly independent and coincidental similarity is not copyright infringement. In the Court of Appeal, Willmer LJ said (at 614):

> . . . in order to establish liability [on the grounds of subconscious copying] it must be shown that the composer of the offending work was in fact familiar with the work alleged to have been copied.

At first sight, the notion of subconscious copying might appear bizarre, but it appears to be accepted also in the law of breach of confidence.[107] Of course, if the first song has been popular, it will be difficult for a defendant to claim that he has not heard of it and has truly written his work independently in ignorance of it. In terms of music and, to some extent also, computer programs, the author should consider taking deliberate measures to make sure that his work does not appear to be similar to an existing work.

The ultimate safeguard against allegations of subconscious copying is for the author to cut himself off from the rest of society, or that part of society knowledgeable about the particular class of works, and to create his work in a 'clean-room' environment. But, surely, copyright law does not and should not intend that authors should have to take such extreme measures. Nevertheless, proof that the defendant has taken such measures will help his argument that he has not infringed copyright. In *Plix Products Ltd* v *Frank M Winstone (Merchants)*[108] the fact that the defendant had instructed his designer to work alone without talking to others involved in the design of kiwifruit packs and without referring to existing packs showed that there had been no direct copying. However, it was

104 [1994] FSR 275. This case is discussed in Chapter 8.

105 Per Lord Millett in Designers Guild Ltd v Russell Williams (Textiles) Ltd [2001] FSR 11 (p 113).

106 [2004] EWHC 468 (Ch).

107 *Seager* v *Copydex Ltd* [1967] RPC 349.

108 [1986] FSR 63.

held that the defendant had copied through the medium of the New Zealand Kiwifruit Authority's specification for kiwifruit packs which was, in turn, derived from the claimant's design. This New Zealand case is also notable in that it accepts that copyright can be infringed by copying from a verbal description, as is, in principle, also a possibility under UK law as s 16(3)(b) admits infringement by indirect copying.[109]

Giving a design brief to a person engaged to create a work of copyright can itself infringe. It is all a matter of design freedom. For example, if a person after seeing a copyright work instructs another person to create something similar, the first might be guilty of infringement if the design freedom is so limited that the creation of a work substantially similar is almost inevitable. The same might apply if one person instructs another to create a number of works which are somewhat like the copyright work if the first, having knowledge of the copyright work, then selects the one most like the copyright work for commercial exploitation.[110]

Certainly, the restricted act of copying should be construed as being concerned with an intentional act. The remedies available for copyright infringement give some support to this approach because, by s 97(1), the claimant is not entitled to damages if it is shown that the defendant did not know and had no reason to believe that copyright subsisted in the first work at the time of the infringement. The difficulty is that, if the burden of proof shifts to the defendant, he may find it almost impossible to show that he did not base his work on a previous work which has become very well known, even though it was popular several years earlier.

If there is evidence that the defendant has copied in the past, this may be admissible as similar fact evidence. In *Designers Guild Ltd v Russell Williams (Textiles) Ltd*,[111] at first instance, the claimant had evidence that a third party had made an allegation of copying of one of its designs by the defendant. Evidence of copying in one case only is not, *per se*, evidence of copying in another case but may be relevant when judging the truth of any denial of copying or other explanation of the reason for an objective similarity by the defendant. In *Stoddard International plc v William Lomas Carpets Ltd*,[112] the claimant relied, *inter alia*, on similar fact evidence relating to two other instances of producing carpet designs which were lookalikes of carpet designs owned by a third party. However, this evidence was very unsatisfactory and failed to indicate a propensity to copy or produce lookalikes.

Where a defendant has been convicted of a criminal offence in relation to the same acts that give rise to a claim for copyright infringement, s 11(2)(a) of the Civil Evidence Act 1968 states that in civil proceedings evidence of a conviction is proof that a person has committed the offence unless the contrary is proved and s 11(2)(b) makes admissible in evidence the contents of the indictments to identify the facts on which the convictions were based. In *Microsoft Corp v Alibhai*,[113] the defendants had been convicted in 2002 of conspiracy to defraud by distributing and selling counterfeit copies of Microsoft products. They had been sentenced to $4^1/_2$ years' imprisonment. Later in 2002, Microsoft commenced a civil action against them for copyright infringement. The effect of s 11(2) of the Civil Evidence Act 1968 was to establish that the defendants had committed the tort of conspiracy in the absence of any evidence to the contrary adduced by the defendants. The judge granted summary judgment to the claimant but he did decline to make an order for interim payment as the conviction and the indictment provided no evidence of the amount of Microsoft's losses or the profits made by the defendants.[114]

Non-literal copying

It has long been accepted that copyright can be infringed by non-literal copying;[115] that is, where the defendant does not take the literal text (or a substantial part of it) of the work copied but instead uses the skill and judgment expended in non-literal elements of

109 As, at the time, only the claimant's design had been accepted by the Authority (giving the claimant a monopoly in kiwifruit packs), the application of the idea/expression merger doctrine from US copyright law, discussed in Chapter 8, would probably deny copyright protection to the claimant's packs. However, the law of designs and passing off could also apply to this type of situation.

110 *Stoddard International plc v William Lomas Carpets Ltd* [2001] FSR 848.

111 [1998] FSR 803.

112 [2001] FSR 848.

113 [2004] EWHC 3282 (Ch).

114 It appeared that the defendants' activities had brought in £2.2m but Microsoft had claimed nearly £11.8m in damages. The judge did, however, grant an interim costs award of £200,000.

115 *See*, for example, *Corelli v Gray* [1913] TLR 570; *Rees v Melville* [1911–1916] MacG CC 168; *Glyn v Weston Feature Film Co* [1916] 1 Ch 261; and, in the United States, *Nichols v Universal Pictures Co* (1930) 45 F 2d 119.

a copyright work. The principle is not necessarily limited to literary works and should also apply to other forms of works, such as artistic, musical or dramatic work or even films, broadcasts and typographical arrangements of published editions. For example, a person may copy from an existing work of copyright aspects such as a detailed plot of a play, a very particular and unusual theme for a painting, such as *The Scream* by Edvard Munch,[116] or the set of algorithms underlying a complex suite of computer programs.

116 Munch created a number of versions of *The Scream*.

The central question for the court in an allegation of copying at a level of abstraction from the work as expressed is whether what is alleged to have been copied represents sufficient skill and judgment in the creation of the work. A plot for a novel can be expressed at a number of levels of abstraction. For example, at its highest level of abstraction, a novel about a spy might simply be expressed in terms of a secret agent having adventures on the trail of a megalomaniac set on blackmailing a country's government by threatening to set off some incredibly destructive weapon unless he is paid a huge sum of money. That clearly does not go beyond a basic idea not protected by copyright. It cannot represent a substantial part of the skill and judgment that would be expended in writing the finished novel. As copyright is concerned about protecting the skill and judgment used in expression, simply taking that basic idea cannot infringe the copyright in the novel. But what is the position where the plot is taken at a level much closer to the finished text of the novel? Say that the copyist takes the same events in the same sequence with similar characters, intermediate occurrences, outcomes and the same denouement? There has been no copying of the literal text of the novel, any similarities being coincidental only.

Going back to *The Scream*, what would be the position if an artist, having seen the painting, decided to create a painting of a person standing on a bridge or pier, running diagonally from top left to bottom centre, face clasped with his or her hands and with two figures in the background all set at dusk with a dramatic red sunset as a backdrop? No further reference is made in creating the second painting. Ignoring any possibility of subconscious copying, would the second painting infringe the copyright in Munch's painting?[117] One could argue that copyright should protect not only the paint on the canvas as such but the ideas underlying the painting and its composition at a level one step away from the actual execution of the painting, what was in the artist's mind and what he wanted to achieve. Munch could have executed the painting in a number of different ways: for example, in oil paints (as he did), in water-colour paints or coloured pencils or even with charcoal in black and white. That being so, should copyright protection extend not just to the physical painting but also to colourable imitations of it in different forms and in different media? Should such copies infringe because they are substantially similar to the lowest level of abstraction, being that closest to the finished painting, rather than being substantially similar to the physical embodiment of the painting itself? After all, it is the level of abstraction one step removed from the finished work that represents the greatest result of the application of human creativity. From there to completing the work requires skills associated with execution rather than creativity. Although clearly an oversimplification and ignoring editorial and artistic changes made during the application of paint to canvas, it could be argued that the final stage requires little more than the skill of an artisan proficient in applying paint to canvas.

117 As Edvard Munch died in 1944, the copyright in *The Scream* will last until the end of 2014.

The concept of non-literal copying is used mainly in the context of computer programs and is discussed in Chapter 8 in more detail. It does not come up often in relation to other works nowadays though there have been a couple of interesting cases, the first in relation to the layout and overall appearance, or 'look and feel', of glossy magazines. The second case involved a claim of non-textual copyright of the 'plot' of the book *The Holy Blood and the Holy Grail* by the author of *The Da Vinci Code*.

118 [2005] FSR 20 (p 434).

In *IPC Media Ltd* v *Highbury-Leisure Publishing Ltd*,[118] the claimant published the *IDEAL HOME* magazine. The defendant published a rival magazine entitled *HOME*. There was no allegation of direct copying of text or images but it was argued that the defendant was liable for non-literal infringement of copyright on the basis that the defendant had copied the 'look and feel' of *IDEAL HOME*. Particular allegations related to the front covers of the magazines and some internal sections in a number of issues. The defendant said that any similarities were trivial, being no more than 'design tricks' common in glossy magazines. The front cover of *IDEAL HOME* included the logo (being the name of the magazine), the straplines (lines of text immediately above and below the logo) and the hot-spot (so-called because, being just under the logo, it would be visible on racks of magazines for sale and would be important to attract buyers). The background to the cover was a photograph, typically of a room interior.

Laddie J did not accept that there had been copying of each of these elements *per se*. Because of the way the pleadings had been worded and amended, the allegation descended into claims targeted at individual elements of the magazines alleged to have been copied rather than at the overall format. Original claims were directed at the design, subject matter, theme and presentational style of *IDEAL HOME*. Laddie J said (at para 23):

> It may be that a substantial part of the copyright consists of the Design Elements, so that unlicensed copying of them by Highbury would amount to copyright infringement, but the way in which the Re-Amended Particulars of Claim and IPC's evidence have been drafted has the effect of drawing one's attention away from the covers and articles as a whole and concentrating only on the areas of alleged similarity as if those areas were covered by copyright in their own right.

He also said that '. . . copyright is not a legal millefeuille with layers of different artistic copyrights'. However, it does appear from the judgment that Laddie J recognised that copyright can subsist and be infringed in respect of a level of abstraction, though probably a level quite close to the final form of expression. He also quoted from the speech of Lord Hoffmann in *Designers Guild Ltd v Russell Williams (Textiles) Ltd*[119] where he said (at para 25):

119 [2001] FSR 11 (p 113).

> [C]ertain ideas expressed by a copyright work may not be protected because although they are ideas of a literary, dramatic or artistic nature, they are not original, or so commonplace as not to form a substantial part of the work. *Kenrick & Co v Lawrence & Co* (1890) 25 QBD 99, is a well-known example. It is on this ground that the mere notion of combining stripes and flowers would not have amounted to a substantial part of the plaintiff's work. At that level of abstraction, the idea, though expressed in the design, would not have represented sufficient of the author's skill and labour as to attract copyright protection.

On the basis of this impressive authority, it seems fair to say that non-literal copying is a theoretical possibility if a substantial part of the skill and judgment used by the person in the creation of the first work has been taken.[120] Skill and judgment and substantiality must be measured in relation to the finished work only and infringement tested accordingly. On the continuum between idea and expression, the threshold is likely to be towards the expression end of the scale. In other words, it must be perhaps no more than one step removed from the literal text of a literary work or very detailed scheme for other works, perhaps representing the penultimate step before 'putting pen to paper'. Anything at a higher level of abstraction is likely to be too vague or lacking the input of sufficient creativity to warrant protection. Therefore, the dramatic format for a talent show[121] and the business logic for computer software[122] have been held not to be protected by copyright. Although in themselves they may have been the subject of much work and research and the exercise of substantial skill, they are too far removed from the finished work to be considered to be a substantial part of it.

120 Although there have been very few recent examples where claims of non-literal copying have succeeded. One partial success was in *John Richardson Computers Ltd v Flanders* [1993] FSR 497, discussed further in Chapter 8.

121 *Green v Broadcasting Corporation of New Zealand* [1989] RPC 700.

122 *Navitaire Inc v EasyJet Airline Co Ltd* [2006] RPC 3 (p 111).

Allegations of non-literal copying rarely succeed. The reasons are that the non-literal parts taken do not form a substantial part of the work or the detail of the claim is poorly formulated, or both. A good example was given in the case of *Baigent v The Random House Group Ltd*.[123] This concerned an allegation of non-literal copying, referred to by the judge

123 [2006] FSR 44 (p 893).

124 An appropriate description as the work alleged to have been copied was a literary work.

125 At the time of the trial, the defendant also published HBHG. This aroused suspicions that the true reason for the action was to publicise both books.

126 Any textual copying was described as being secondary footprints supporting the allegation of copying the Central Theme.

as 'non-textual',[124] by the author of *The Da Vinci Code* novel ('DVC'), Dan Brown, from an earlier work known as *The Holy Blood and The Holy Grail* ('HBHG'). The claimants were two of the three authors of HBHG and the action was taken against the publisher of DVC.[125] There were few textual similarities between the literal texts of the books and the claimants did not allege copyright infringement in relation to these. Instead they relied on an allegation of copying the 'Central Theme' of HBHG.[126]

The Central Theme itself was broken down into 15 points. They included assertions that Jesus had married Mary Magdalene and had children, and that after the crucifixion, Mary had fled to France with the Royal Blood (that is, Jesus' bloodline). Other assertions were that the bloodline intermarried with the royal line of the Franks and eventually resulted in the Merovingian dynasty. Around the end of the eleventh century Godfroi of Bouillon, Duke of Lorraine, emerged and embarked on the first crusade in 1099 to regain the throne of Palestine, which was his birthright. He had a circle of counsellors, eventually known as the Priory of Sion, who set up the Knights Templar. The Priory used France as its main base and acted as protectors and custodians of the Merovingian bloodline, the Holy Grail. Grandmasters of the Priory were claimed to include Leonardo Da Vinci, Sir Isaac Newton and Victor Hugo. At first instance, Peter Smith J had to decide whether the Central Theme was a work of literary copyright, whether it had been copied by Dan Brown and, if so, whether the part taken represented a substantial part of the Central Theme.[127]

127 Originally, the claims included allegations of copying the structure or architecture of HBHG. These were abandoned.

128 [1980] RPC 193. This case is discussed earlier in this chapter.

Peter Smith J referred to *Ravenscroft* v *Herbert*.[128] In relation to a historical book, as HBHG was claimed to be, it could be argued that the author intended the reader to use the facts imparted in the book. He said (at para 176):

> . . . the facts and the themes and the ideas cannot be protected but how those facts, themes and ideas are put together . . . can be. It follows from this that the Claimants must show that there is a putting together of facts, themes and ideas by them as a result of their efforts and it is that which Mr Brown has copied.

Peter Smith J held that the Central Theme was not a genuine Central Theme of HBHG and was 'an artificial contrivance designed to create an illusion of a Central Theme for the purposes of alleging infringement of a substantial part of HBHG'. He said that if there was a Central Theme to HBHG it was the merger of the Merovingian bloodline with the Royal Bloodline of Mary Magdalene but that was at too general a level of abstraction to be capable of protection under copyright law.[129] It was almost incredible that the claimants could not formulate their own Central Theme which must have been in their minds always when writing HBHG.[130] Consequently, it was held that the DVC did not infringe the copyright in HBHG.

129 *See* also, *Nova Productions Ltd* v *Mazooma Games Ltd* [2007] RPC 25 (p 589), discussed in Chapter 8, where it was held, *inter alia*, that non-literal features of a computer game alleged to have been copied were at too high a level of abstraction.

130 There is a mystery in the judgment in that it appears that Peter Smith J inserted his own code into it. Certain letters are inexplicably italicised. They are, in order (as far as can be made out), 'smithycodeJaeiextost-psacgreamqwfkadpmqzv'.

131 *Baigent* v *The Random House Group Ltd* [2007] FSR 24 (p 579).

The claimants' appeal to the Court of Appeal was dismissed.[131] There was some criticism of the judgment of Peter Smith J which showed some confusion between subsistence of copyright and infringement. These are two distinct issues. The identity of the copyright work was that it was HBHG itself and, per Mummery LJ (at para 132):

> it is wrong to divide up the whole copyright work into parts and to destroy the copyright in the whole by concluding that there is no copyright in the individual segments. Similarly, on the issue of infringement, it is wrong to take the parts of the original copyright work that have been copied in the alleged infringing work, to isolate them from the whole original copyright work and then to conclude that 'a substantial part' of the original copyright work has not been copied because there was no copyright in the copied parts on their own.

It all comes back to the essential copyright questions. First, does copyright subsist in the claimants' work? Only if this is decided in the positive and a relevant act or acts of copying are found, is the question of whether the part or parts taken represent a substantial part of the claimants' work. Thus, in the present case, the issue is not whether the Central Theme or its elements were sufficient to qualify as an original literary work.

Although this form of copying was described as non-textual copying, Mummery LJ was not comfortable with that epithet and said that it could be potentially confusing. Although 'non-textual copying' and 'language copying' do not appear in the Act, the latter may be used to describe word-for-word copying. He gave the example of an anthology of poems which were themselves out of copyright. Word-for-word copying of the poems is not relevant to infringement of the anthology, being a literary compilation. The question is whether the selection and arrangement of the poems has been copied, that selection and arrangement could properly be described as the text of the anthology.

It was accepted that the Central Theme and its elements were important to the claimants, resulting from years of research, discussion and speculation. But they were not in themselves a substantial part of HBHG in a copyright sense 'any more than a fact or theory that took a lifetime to establish, or a discovery that took a fortune to make'.[132] These individual elements were not sufficiently developed to constitute a substantial part of HBHG.[133]

Issuing copies of the work to the public

Under s 18(1), the issue to the public of copies of a work is an act restricted by the copyright in every description of copyright work. Article 4(1) of the Directive on copyright and related rights in the information society[134] provides for a distribution right which is the equivalent to issuing copies to the public. Article 4(1) goes on to say that the exclusive right is to authorise or prohibit any form of distribution to the public by sale or otherwise. The UK Act does not use the phrase 'or otherwise' but its meaning came up for consideration before the Court of Justice in Case 456/06 *Peek & Cloppenburg KG v Cassina SpA*.[135] In that case, which involved furniture placed in a store and in a shop window for display purposes only, it was argued that the reproduction right included distribution by way of possession as well as sale. The Court of Justice referred to the WIPO Copyright Treaty 1996 ('WCT') and the WIPO Performers and Phonogram Treaty 1996 (WPPT). The equivalent provisions in those Treaties refer to distribution by sale or 'other transfer of ownership'.[136] As Article 4 of the Directive on copyright and related rights in the information society was intended to implement the relevant provisions of the Treaties, it was clear that the distribution right must involve a transfer of ownership and not merely possession of the original or copies of the work in question.

The doctrine of exhaustion of rights is concerned with the freedom of movement of goods. Thus, a person who has put his goods into circulation cannot prevent someone, who lawfully acquires them, from reselling them or importing them into another country for resale. His rights to prevent further commercialisation of the goods are said to have been exhausted by the placing of the goods on the market by or with the consent of the owner of the goods. The doctrine is one of the cornerstones of the Common Market. The market would be too easily distorted if a company could sell identical products in different Member States at different prices. Of course, exhaustion of rights should not and does not prejudice the right of a person to put goods into circulation for the first time.

Issuing copies of a work to the public is a restricted act that applies to all categories of works; s 18(1).[137] Under s 18(2) this means (a) the act of putting into circulation in the European Economic Area (EEA)[138] copies not previously put into circulation in the EEA by or with the consent of the copyright owner, or (b) the act of putting into circulation outside the EEA copies not previously put into circulation in the EEA or elsewhere. This does not include any subsequent distribution, sale, hiring or loan of copies previously put into circulation,[139] or any subsequent importation of such copies into the UK or another EEA state except so far as (a) above applies to putting into circulation in the EEA copies previously put into circulation outside the EEA.

The main thrust of these complicated provisions is that the copyright owner can take action against anyone who issues a copy of his work to the public for the first time without

132 *Per* Mummery LJ at para 153.

133 There was no 'architectural' similarity between the works as the 11 elements of the Central Theme found to have been copied were differently expressed, collected, selected, arranged and narrated in DVC.

134 Directive 2001/29/EC of the European Parliament and of the Council of 22 May 2001 on the harmonisation of certain aspects of copyright and related rights in the information society, OJ L 167, 22.06.2001, p 10.

135 [2008] ECR I-2731.

136 Article 6(1) of the WCT and Article 8(1) of the WPPT.

137 Section 18 has been amended on two occasions, most recently by the Copyright and Related Rights Regulations 1996, SI 1996/2967.

138 An EEA state is a state which is a contracting party to the EEA Agreement signed at Oporto 2 May 1992, adjusted by a protocol signed at Brussels 17 March 1993; Copyright and Related Rights Regulations 1996 reg 2. EEA states are the European Union countries plus Norway, Iceland and Liechtenstein.

139 Subject to s 18A: infringement by rental or lending.

his consent. However, as in the exhaustion of rights doctrine, in respect of copies already put into circulation by or with the consent of the owner, he loses effective control over them. He cannot, for example, take action against someone who has lawfully bought copies of his work in France and who now wishes to import them into the UK for the purpose of selling them to the public. The precise application of these provisions depends to some extent on whether the relevant act takes place in the EEA.

Placing a carrier on which a copyright work exists in an overseas postal service for delivery in the EEA is putting it into circulation within the EEA. In *Independiente Ltd v Music Trading Online (HK) Ltd,*[140] a Hong Kong company accepted orders online for CDs and DVDs which had not previously been put into circulation in the EEA. Its website was in English and directed at customers in the UK. It was held that, by posting the CDs and DVDs in Hong Kong for delivery to customers in the UK, the company was putting them in circulation in the EEA within s 18(2). The effect of s 32(4) of the Sale of Goods Act 1979, as amended, was that in a consumer sale, delivery to a carrier was not delivery to the buyer. The CDs and DVDs were, therefore, put into circulation in the UK by the defendant.

It should be noted that this restricted act applies to each and every copy of the work and, under s 18(4), includes the original. Thus, the issue to the public of some copies of a work does not exhaust the right in respect of other copies not yet issued to the public.

As an example of the workings of s 18 consider the following possibilities in respect of 100 copies of a book:

1 if they are infringing copies – issuing them to the public anywhere will infringe under s 18;
2 if they are copies made for the copyright owner, but he has not consented to their sale (expressly or impliedly) – issuing them to the public anywhere will infringe under s 18;
3 if the owner consented to their sale in the UK – the buyer can resell them or export them for resale anywhere within the EEA;
4 if the owner consented to their sale in Norway (an EEA state) – as 3 above;
5 if the owner consented to their sale in the USA – the buyer can resell them or export them anywhere except to an EEA state.

The subsequent acts that can be done include hiring or loan, but this may infringe under s 18A which controls rental or lending.

It can be seen from the examples above that the owner's right to issue to the public is not restricted to the issue of infringing copies, and it is possible to infringe by issuing to the public copies which were authorised by the copyright owner.[141] This will be rare as in most cases the person in possession of the copies will have the copyright owner's express or implied consent to issue the copies to the public: for example, in the case of a publishing agreement. One example where the issue of authorised copies may infringe under s 18 is where copies have been made by a printer on behalf of the copyright owner, but an employee of the printer has stolen and sold some of them.

Rental and lending right

The Copyright and Related Rights Regulations 1996[142] introduced, as from 1 December 1996, comprehensive rental and lending rights in relation to copies of works. Previously, only sound recordings, films and computer programs enjoyed specific protection in relation to rental.

Renting or lending copies of a work to the public is now a restricted act, the scope of which is set out in s 18A. The right applies to the 'original' works of copyright (literary, dramatic, musical or artistic works), films and sound recordings. However, there is an exception as regards some of the artistic works and the right does not apply to works of

140 [2007] FSR 21 (p 525).

141 As noted by Laddie J in *William Nelson v Mark Rye and Cocteau Records Ltd* [1996] FSR 313.

142 SI 1996/2967, implementing, *inter alia*, Council Directive 92/100/EC of 19 November 1992 on rental right and lending right and on certain rights related to copyright in the field of intellectual property, OJ L 346, 27.11.1992, p 61 and Council Directive 93/83/EC of 27 September 1993 on the coordination of certain rules concerning copyright and rights related to copyright applicable to satellite broadcasting and cable re-transmission, OJ L 248, 6.10.1993, p 15. Council Directive 92/100/EEC has been repealed and replaced by codifying Directive 2006/115/EC of the European Parliament and of the Council of 12 December 2006 on rental right and lending right and on certain rights related to copyright in the field of intellectual property, OJ L 376, 27.12.2006, p 28.

architecture in the form of a building or model for a building nor to works of 'applied art'. This latter phrase derives from Article 2(3) of Directive 92/100/EC (no further indication of its meaning is given there either).[143] It is likely to cover those commercially exploited artistic works falling within s 52.

'Rental' and 'lending' are defined in s 18A(2). Rental is 'making a copy of the work available for use, on terms that it will or may be returned, for direct or indirect economic or commercial advantage', and 'lending' is 'making a copy of the work available for use, on terms that it will or may be returned, otherwise than for direct or indirect economic or commercial advantage, through an establishment which is accessible to the public'. There are some exceptions to the definitions. Neither includes making available for the purpose of public performance, playing or showing in public, communication to the public, exhibition in public or for on-the-spot reference use. Furthermore, lending does not cover making available between establishments accessible to the public (for example, where a library obtains a copy of a book from another library although, of course, the ultimate loan to the borrower is still within the meaning of lending). A charge may be made for lending which, provided it does not go beyond the operating costs of the establishment, will not take the transaction out of the meaning of lending. A higher charge will result in the act being considered to be rental. The rights apply to the original work as well as to copies of the original.

Under s 36A lending by educational establishments does not infringe, and s 40A contains an appropriate exception where lending is in respect of a book under the public lending right scheme or lending by prescribed libraries or archives (other than public libraries) which are not conducted for profit.

Films and sound recordings usually include other works of copyright. For example, the dialogue of a film may be based on a novel or have been written as a screenplay. Music may be included in the sound track. Where an author of an original work agrees with a film producer to its inclusion in the film, unless the agreement provides otherwise, there is a presumption that the author has assigned his rental rights in relation to that film under s 93A. The right is replaced by a right to an equitable remuneration on the transfer of the right. However, the presumption does not apply in respect of any dialogue, screenplay or music *specially* created for and used in the film and, in such cases, express assignment would be required. Where the presumed assignment operates, the absence of any signature on the part of the author does not prevent the operation of s 91(1) (purported assignment of future copyright). If a film producer and principal director make an agreement with the author of a pre-existing piece of music to include the music in the film and the agreement is silent on rental rights, and before the film is made the producer and director sign an agreement with a third party assigning to that third party the copyright in the film, the copyright will automatically vest in the third party and include the relevant rental rights in relation to the music.

Section 93B deals with the detail in relation to the right to equitable remuneration. The right arises where there has been a transfer of the rental right concerning a sound recording or film (including presumed transfer in respect of the inclusion of a copy of a work in a film) and applies to authors of original works and the principal director of a film.[144] The right itself may only be assigned to a collecting society, although it is transmissible by testamentary disposition or operation of law as personal property[145] and may then be assigned by the person into whose hands it passes. The restriction on assignment to a collecting society only no longer seems to apply in such cases. The remuneration is payable by the person for the time being entitled to the rental right. Any purported agreement excluding or restricting the right to an equitable remuneration is to that extent of no effect. The Copyright Tribunal is given the power to determine the amount payable in default of agreement and to vary the amount, and its jurisdiction is modified accordingly.[146] Under s 93C(4), a remuneration shall not be considered

143 This provision is now contained in Article 3(2) of Directive 2006/115/EC.

144 Although the producer and the principal director are now considered co-authors of a film, this right does not apply to film producers.

145 In Scotland, moveable property.

146 Copyright, Designs and Patents Act 1988 ss 93C and 149(zb).

inequitable merely because it is made in a single payment, or at the time of the transfer of the rental right.

A remuneration is not equitable if it is calculated solely on the basis of the number of subscribers to a library. The Court of Justice so held in Case C-271/10 *Vereniging van Educatieve en Wetenschappelijke Auteurs (VEWA) v Belgische Staat*.[147] The remuneration should be based on the number of works made available to the public. A further factor is that borrowers may be registered with one library but may be able to borrow books from other libraries by means of reciprocal agreements between libraries. The mechanism for calculating authors' and other rightholders' remuneration from the public lending of their works was prejudicial to their right under the rental right and lending right Directive. The Court did accept that the number of subscribers might be one of the factors that could be taken into account but an important consideration was that the remuneration was intended to address the harm caused to authors by the lending of their works to the public without their authorisation. The greater the number of times their works were made available in this way, the greater the prejudice.

Arguments that the rental right distorted competition and was contrary to the fundamental right to pursue a trade or profession were rejected by the European Court of Justice in Case C-200/96 *Metronome Musik GmbH v Music Point Hokamp GmbH*.[148] Sale or other distribution did not exhaust rental rights which reflect that rental is a further form of commercial exploitation and recognised that authors and performers should be better able to recoup the substantial investment in the creation of new works. Rental right was held to be in accordance with the Community (now European Union) objectives of general interest and the right to pursue a trade or profession was not absolute and restrictions were acceptable providing they fell within the scope of general Community objectives and were not disproportionate. In the *Metronome* case, the claimant had released for sale a music CD called 'Planet Punk'. The defendant had offered copies of the CD for rental. Clearly, such rental, without the licence of the copyright owner, could seriously prejudice the economic rights under copyright law. However, the defendant's argument was not entirely without merit. Whilst copyright owners may choose to grant licences to traders desiring to rent copies to the public, they may decide not to do so, forcing persons wishing to have access to the work to buy a copy. Of course, that will be an economic decision and many copyright owners will be happy to licence their rental rights. This is very common in respect of films made available for hire on video tape or DVD.

Public performance, showing or playing a work in public

Public performances and the public playing or showing of certain types of works infringe copyright unless done with the permission of the copyright owner. These performing rights are, in a great many cases, administered by the Performing Right Society which grants 'blanket' licences in respect of music and broadcasts to be played or shown in public. The performance of a work in public is an act restricted by the copyright in literary, dramatic and musical works. It does not apply to other forms of works. Section 19(2) expands upon the meaning of performance and states that it includes delivery of lectures, addresses, speeches and sermons and, in line with modern technology, it includes in general any mode of visual or acoustic presentation, including by means of a sound recording, film or broadcast. Under s 19(3), playing or showing a sound recording, film or broadcast in public is an act restricted by the copyright in the work. Therefore, playing music to members of the public, for example background music in a café or restaurant to which the public have access, is a restricted act.

An important element is that the performance, showing or playing must be in 'public', a word which has been responsible for much judicial consideration. A consistent strand in the courts' interpretation has been the question of whether the copyright owner's

147 30 June 2011.

148 [1998] ECR I-1953.

interests have been harmed by the performance complained of. For example, would the copyright owner expect to be paid a royalty for the performance? Does the performance satisfy part of the public demand for the work and thereby reduce the copyright owner's potential income? In *Duck* v *Bates*,[149] the defendant performed a dramatic piece in a room in a hospital for the entertainment of nurses, attendants and other hospital workers without the consent of the copyright owner. No admission charge was made, but approximately 170 persons attended each performance. It was held that the room where the drama was presented was not a place of public entertainment and that, consequently, the defendant was not liable to the copyright owner in damages. Lord Brett MR said that such a private representation of the drama would not harm the copyright owner, although a public representation in any place where the public were freely admitted with or without payment would.

149 (1884) 13 QBD 843.

However, any distinction which might be drawn in this case between the public at large and an audience limited by vocation or membership does not provide a workable formula as there have been several cases involving an audience limited in such a way in which the performance has been deemed to be a performance in public. For example, in *Ernest Turner Electrical Instruments Ltd* v *Performing Right Society Ltd*,[150] the owner of a factory relayed music broadcast by the British Broadcasting Corporation and from gramophone records to his 600 employees. Strangers were not allowed access to the factory. Nevertheless, it was held that the performance was a performance in public for the purposes of the Copyright Act 1911 s 1(2). Lord Greene MR suggested that it was important to consider the relationship between the audience and the copyright owner rather than the relationship between the audience and the person arranging the performance, that is the employer. Economic considerations were also important in that the 'statutory monopoly' granted by the Copyright Act would be, in Lord Greene's opinion, largely destroyed if performances to such groups of persons were permitted.

150 [1943] 1 Ch 167. *See* also *Jennings* v *Stephens* [1936] Ch 469 concerning the performance of a play in which the audience was limited to members of a Women's Institute.

Some performances can be said to be in the copyright owner's best interests because they publicise his work and whet the public appetite and, as a result, increase ultimate sales of the work. Such an argument can be raised in terms of radio and television broadcasts of pop music. For example, *Top of the Pops* and similar programmes can influence sales of particular pieces of music. Nevertheless, broadcasters have to pay for such broadcasts. Since 1976, as a result of a change in policy, even record shops have to pay fees for playing recordings of works written by members of the Performing Right Society over loudspeakers in the shops. In *Performing Right Society Ltd* v *Harlequin Record Shops Ltd*,[151] the owner of some record shops refused to pay the requisite fee, arguing that playing the records over loudspeakers in the shops promoted sales and increased the composer's royalties and that this playing of recordings did not constitute a performance in public and, consequently, was not an infringement of copyright. However, injunctive relief was granted to the claimant and it was held that the performances were in public. The audience comprised members of the public present in shops to which the public at large were permitted and encouraged to enter. Furthermore, it was shown that a prudent record shop owner would pay the society's fee rather than discontinue playing the recordings.

151 [1979] 2 All ER 828.

For a performance not to be deemed to be a public performance, it must be to an audience of a domestic nature. It is clear that playing a video film to a group of friends or relatives will not be 'playing the work in public' and enacting a play in the presence of a few friends will not be a performance of the play in public, but the habitual playing of recordings to employees in a factory will be in public even though the employees are not charged anything for this benefit. There are, however, some instances where it is more difficult to draw a line. For example, a private hospital may transmit video films to its patients from a central machine to television monitors in individual rooms. A hotel may provide a similar service for its guests. It is probable, in these circumstances, that the performance or playing will be in public if the service is provided for all the guests or patients and, taken together, they can be said to form part of the public at large, even though only a proportion of them take advantage of the service. If a charge is made, then the question is beyond doubt.

Section 19(4) limits the personalities who can be liable for infringement by performance, showing or playing a work in public. The performers taking part in a public performance are not themselves to be regarded as being responsible for the infringement. In the case of the performance, playing or showing of the work in question by means of apparatus for receiving visual images or sounds conveyed by electronic means, the person by whom the visual images or sounds are sent is not to be regarded as responsible for the infringement. Therefore, a disc jockey at an unlicensed disco will not be liable to be sued for infringement of the public performance right. The language of the subsection appears to be difficult and inconsistent with s 19(2)(b), which is expressed in terms of 'any mode of visual or acoustic presentation', whereas s 19(4) deals only with presentation by electronic means and uses the word 'sound' rather than 'acoustic'. Taking a strictly literal interpretation of s 19(4) could produce absurd results. For example, what is the position where the performers have also arranged the infringing public performance? Section 19(4) appears to excuse their infringement, as it clearly states that the performers shall not be regarded as responsible for the infringement. It is unlikely that the courts will take this interpretation, as it plainly runs counter to the spirit of the Act.

It is inevitable that, given the size and complexity of the Act, there will be interpretational difficulties and it would have been better if, towards the end of s 19(4), the words 'to the extent that the infringement relates to their activity as performer' were added to put the matter beyond doubt.

Communication to the public

Section 20 was substituted by the Copyright and Related Rights Regulations 2003 which replaced the previous restricted act of broadcasting or inclusion in a cable programme service. New s 20 sets out the meaning of the act of communication to the public. It covers not only broadcasts (redefined to include what were formerly classed separately as cable programmes) but also making material available to the public, for example, by placing it on internet websites. Of course, all the individual rights are separate from each other and this right is no exception. A licence which covers one right will not extend to other rights. For example, a licence which grants the publication of a work in hard copy does not mean the licensee can place the work in an archive available via a website.[152]

Under s 20(1), the communication to the public is a restricted act in relation to:

(a) a literary, musical, dramatic or artistic work;
(b) a sound recording or film; or
(c) a broadcast.

Communication to the public means communication by electronic transmission and, under s 20(2), this includes:

(a) the broadcasting of the work;
(b) the making available to the public of the work by electronic transmission in such a way that members of the public may access it from a place and at a time individually chosen by them.

Guests staying in hotel bedrooms are considered to be part of the public and broadcasts received by them on television sets provided by the hotel fall within the restricted Act. So it was held in Case C-306/05 *Sociedad General de Autores y Editores de España (SGAE)* v *Rafael Hoteles SA*.[153] Although the mere provision of television sets did not constitute a communication to the public, the distribution of a signal by means of television sets to

152 *MGN Ltd* v *Grisbrook* [2011] ECDR 4 (p 91).

153 [2006] ECR I-11519.

customers staying in the rooms was a communication to the public despite the private nature of hotel bedrooms. The Court of Justice took a wide view of this act in line with the Directive on copyright and related rights in the information society.[154]

The Court of Justice gave further guidance in Joined Cases C-403/08 and C-429/08 *Football Association Premier League v QC Leisure*,[155] where it ruled that the right of communication to the public covered a situation where broadcasts were transmitted via a television screen and speakers to customers present in a public house. The broadcasts were encrypted and the public houses were able to show them to customers after obtaining decoders from Greece which had been sold on behalf of the rightholders. The communication right was engaged as the publicans had an economic interest in showing live broadcasts of English Premier Division football matches as this would be likely to attract customers.

Generally, broadcasts are simultaneous transmissions to the public: for example, as in the case of terrestrial, satellite or cable transmissions of scheduled television or radio programmes. This includes such transmissions by internet. However, excluded from the meaning of broadcasts are other forms of internet transmission,[156] a major example being where material is placed on a website or made available for downloading by individuals as and when they choose. Although such transmissions are outside the definition of broadcast, they are still within the restricted act of communication to the public. The impetus for ensuring that copyright extended to making works available online came from the Directive on copyright and related rights in the information society.[157]

Therefore, placing a work on a website or facilitating its downloading from a website (for example, by providing a hypertext link to it) will infringe if the work can be and has been downloaded by any member of the public in the UK, no matter where the computer on which the website is hosted is physically located. Recital 25 to the Directive describes this form of making available as interactive on-demand transmissions and makes it clear that all holders of copyright and related rights should have an exclusive right in respect of it.

Before the changes, it appeared that the courts were prepared to consider placing material on a website for access or downloading as falling within the meaning of a cable programme service. In *Shetland Times Ltd v Dr Jonathan Wills*,[158] the defendant included headlines from the claimant's website in articles published on the internet. The headlines fell within the meaning of a cable programme, being any item included in a cable programme service. Lord Hamilton found that the defendant infringed copyright by including cable programmes in a cable programme service. As a cable programme service was defined as a '. . . service which consists wholly or mainly in sending visual images, sounds or other information . . .' this form of infringement was very wide, as the meaning of cable programme extended to information, whether or not it was a work of copyright. At least the recent changes put infringement by making available on the internet on all fours with other forms of infringement.

Making an adaptation

In terms of the Copyright, Designs and Patents Act 1988, the word 'adaptation' has some very special meanings, depending on the nature of the work concerned, and should not be taken in its usual sense. Making an adaptation does not simply mean the same as modifying a work. The restricted act of making an adaptation applies only to literary, dramatic and musical works. Of the original works, artistic works are not covered by the act of making an adaptation. Therefore, if a person represents an existing drawing by producing a list of coordinates, he is not making an adaptation of the drawing and does not infringe the copyright in the drawing unless the list of coordinates can be considered to be a copy of the drawing.[159] If the drawing contains information to be used in the

154 Directive 2001/29/EC of the European Parliament and of the Council of 22 May 2001 on the harmonisation of certain aspects of copyright and related rights in the information society, OJ L 167, 22.06.2001, p 10. Although 'communication to the public' is not defined in the Directive, recital 23 thereto makes it clear that a wide view should be taken, stating that the right should be understood in a broad sense.

155 4 October 2011.

156 Section 6(1A).

157 Directive 2001/29/EC of the European Parliament and of the Council of 22 May 2001 on the harmonisation of certain aspects of copyright and related rights in the information society, OJ L 167, 22.6.2001, p 10.

158 [1997] FSR 604

159 If the existing work is a sculpture and a person produces a set of coordinates describing its form, that will infringe because a 'dimensional shift' has occurred which brings s 17(3) into play. Note that by s 21(5) no inference is to be drawn from s 21 as to what does or does not amount to copying.

manufacture of an article, it may also be deemed to be a literary work, in which case taking a list of coordinates from the drawing will infringe: see *Anacon Corp Ltd v Environmental Research Technology Ltd*.[160]

160 [1994] FSR 659.

An adaptation is made when it is recorded in writing or otherwise, under s 21(1). 'Writing' is defined in s 178 as including any form of notation or code, whether by hand or otherwise, regardless of the method by which, or medium in or on which, it is recorded. This definition is very wide and should present no problems in the context of making an adaptation. 'Adaptation' is defined in s 21(3) and means:

(a)   in relation to a literary work other than a computer program or a database, or in relation to a dramatic work:
  (i)   a translation of the work;
  (ii) a version of a dramatic work in which it is converted into a non-dramatic work or, as the case may be, of a non-dramatic work in which it is converted into a dramatic work;
  (iii) a version of the work in which the story or action is conveyed wholly or mainly by means of pictures in a form suitable for reproduction in a book, or in a newspaper, magazine or similar periodical;

(ab) in relation to a computer program, an arrangement or altered version of the program or a translation of it;[161]

(ac) in relation to a database, an arrangement or altered version of the database or a translation of it;[162]

(b)   in relation to a musical work, an arrangement or transcription of the work.

161 Inserted by the Copyright (Computer Programs) Regulations 1992, SI 1992/3233.

162 Inserted by the Copyright and Rights in Databases Regulations 1997, SI 1997/3032.

A 'translation' would typically include a work of literature or a play that has been translated from French to English. But, as literary works include computer programs, the word takes on a special meaning in relation to computer programs, and under s 21(4):

> . . . a 'translation' includes a version of the program in which it is converted into or out of a computer language or code or into a different computer language or code [otherwise than incidentally in the course of running the program].[163]

163 The words in square brackets were repealed by the Copyright (Computer Programs) Regulations 1992, SI 1992/3233.

The significance of making an adaptation in terms of computer programs and databases is considered further in Chapter 8.

The dramatic/non-dramatic conversion covers situations such as where a biographical book or a true story is dramatised or, alternatively, where the script for a play is reworked as a novel. For example, in *Corelli v Gray*,[164] the defendant was found to have written a dramatic sketch by taking material from the claimant's novel. The third form of adaptation in relation to literary and dramatic works is where the story or action has been changed to a form which mainly comprises pictures. An example is where a story has been converted into a strip cartoon. To do the converse is not to make an adaptation, however. To change a cartoon or other graphical means of portraying a story into a written work does not fall within the meaning of making an adaptation; it may, however, fall within the meaning of copying. The rationale for this apparent inconsistency is that, presumably, to convert a story told mainly by pictures to a written work requires a great deal of skill, effort and judgment and all that is really taken is the plot or the idea underlying the pictorial work.[165] The wordsmith has many gaps to fill in. On the other hand, to draw pictures depicting a written work leaves less to the imagination of the artist in terms of the telling of the story, although, of course, he will have free rein to express that story in his preferred way. The Act presumably considers artistic licence to be more constrained than literary licence.

164 [1913] TLR 570.

165 However, *see* the discussion on the requirement for tangibility in Chapter 3.

As far as musical works are concerned, arrangements and transcriptions of existing works are adaptations and will, if copyright subsists in the existing work, infringe that copyright. An example of an arrangement is where a piece of music written for one instrument is rewritten so that it is suitable for another, or an operatic aria is rewritten as an orchestral piece. If there is a sufficient amount of skill and judgment involved in the arrangement, it too might attract its own copyright,[166] although the permission of the owner of the copyright in the first piece of music would be required before the arranged piece could be exploited.[167]

Under s 21(2), the doing of any of the other restricted acts, described in ss 17–20, in relation to an adaptation, is also an act restricted by the copyright in a literary, dramatic or musical work. This extends to s 21(1), so that making an adaptation of an adaptation also infringes copyright if done without the permission or licence of the copyright owner. For example, if Albert writes a novel in English and Barry, without Albert's permission, translates the novel into French, Barry is making an adaptation and infringes Albert's copyright. If Celia then makes copies of Barry's translation, Celia also infringes the copyright in the original novel (regardless of whether or not she has Barry's permission to do so). Finally, if Duncan translates Barry's French version of the novel into German, Duncan infringes copyright by making an adaptation of an adaptation. In addition to the economic rights, Albert's moral rights might be infringed by the above actions, for example if he is not identified as the author. Albert will have the right to object to derogatory treatment of his work only if the translations have some additions or deletions and the treatment amounts to a distortion or mutilation of the work, or is otherwise prejudicial to Albert's honour or reputation.

Authorising infringement of copyright

Copyright is infringed by a person who performs any of the acts restricted by the copyright without the licence of the copyright owner or authorises another person to perform the infringing act under s 16(2). There is nothing in the Act to require the authorisation to be given in the UK provided the infringing act itself is carried out in the UK. In *ABKCO Music & Records Inc v Music Collection International Ltd*,[168] a Danish company granted a licence to an English company to manufacture and issue to the public recordings of the claimant's sound recordings in the UK and Eire. It was held that it did not matter where the authorisation was given as long as the restricted act was carried out within the jurisdiction. The act of authorisation was not limited territorially unlike the restricted acts themselves.

Performing a restricted act and authorising its performance are separate torts.[169] However, the authorisation is a tort only if the act authorised is restricted by copyright in the UK. Thus, if a US resident authorises persons in England to place infringing material on the internet, the US resident infringes under s 16(2) and this is within the jurisdiction of the English courts.

If an Australian makes a copy in Australia of a work subject to UK copyright, that does not infringe the UK copyright (notwithstanding the effect of the Berne Copyright Convention and any proceedings brought in Australia on the basis of an equivalent Australian copyright). If that Australian then places a copy of the work on his website and invites persons in the UK to access it and make copies, then the Australian infringes the UK copyright by authorisation. The persons accessing the work also infringe copyright by performing a restricted act, bearing in mind that simply accessing the work will produce a transient copy in the computer's memory. There is no need for a hard copy print to be made or for the work to be saved to a disk as copying includes making transient copies under s 17(6).

A director of a company who is the directing mind of the company may be liable for authorising the company's infringement by the mere fact of being a director executing his normal duties and carrying out his constitutional role in the company's governance. The

166 For example, *see Wood v Boosey* (1868) LR 3 QB 223.

167 Apart from infringing the copyright owner's rights, the moral rights of the author must be considered. By the Copyright, Designs and Patents Act 1988 s 80, the author of, *inter alia*, a musical work has a right not to have his work subjected to derogatory treatment. 'Treatment' in relation to a musical work does not include an arrangement or transcription involving no more than a change of key or register.

168 [1995] RPC 657.

169 *Ash v Hutchinson & Co (Publishers) Ltd* [1936] Ch 489.

same applies to a controlling shareholder. On the other hand, a person who is not a *de jure* director but who is a *de facto* director may be liable for authorising the company's infringement.[170]

What is authorisation?

Earlier cases show that the concept of authorisation is fairly wide, being 'sanction, countenance or approve' in *Evans v Houlton*,[171] and turning a blind eye may amount to authorisation. In *Performing Right Society Ltd v Ciryl Theatrical Syndicate Ltd*[172] it was said that 'indifference, exhibited by acts of commission or omission, may reach a degree from which authorisation or permission may be inferred'. Failing to inform users of a library with photocopying facilities about copyright law and failing properly to supervise the use of the copiers was held to authorise infringement of copyright in the Australian case of *Moorhouse v University of New South Wales*.[173] Placing a notice in proximity to photocopiers but otherwise not policing their use was authorisation. However, in *Law Society of Upper Canada v CCH Canadian Ltd*,[174] the Supreme Court of Canada thought that this approach went too far and shifted the balance too far in favour of copyright owners. The Supreme Court of Canada distinguished between authorising a person to use copying equipment and authorising infringement. It could be assumed that the former, *per se*, did not mean that infringement was authorised. As a matter of law, it should be presumed that a person who authorises an activity does so only in as much as it is in accordance with the law.

In *CBS Songs Ltd v Amstrad Consumer Electronics plc*,[175] Lord Templeman agreed with Atkin LJ in *Falcon v Famous Players Film Co*[176] where he said that, in the context of copyright, authorisation means '. . . the grant or purported grant, which may be express or implied, of the right to do the act complained of'. Although *CBS v Amstrad* concerned authorisation under the Copyright Act 1956 s 1(2), that meaning should still apply under the 1988 Act. In that particular case, Amstrad was not authorising infringement of copyright by the sale of its twin cassette tape machines, it was merely facilitating unauthorised copying. In any case, the machines could be used for legitimate purposes.[177]

It is submitted that the correct approach to authorisation by making copying equipment available is that a person is liable for the infringing acts of others if that person actively encourages infringement or turns a blind eye to the fact that infringement is likely to take place where the circumstances are such that a reasonable person would be concerned that infringement might be taking place and would want to investigate and take any action appropriate to prevent it. In *Twentieth Century Fox Film Corp v Newzbin Ltd*,[178] a slightly narrower approach was taken by Kitchin J. He said (at para 90):

> . . . 'authorise' means the grant or purported grant of the right to do the act complained of. It does not extend to mere enablement, assistance or even encouragement. The grant or purported grant to do the relevant act may be express or implied from all the relevant circumstances. In a case which involves an allegation of authorisation by supply, these circumstances may include the nature of the relationship between the alleged authoriser and the primary infringer, whether the equipment or other material supplied constitutes the means used to infringe, whether it is inevitable it will be used to infringe, the degree of control which the supplier retains and whether he has taken any steps to prevent infringement.[179] These are matters to be taken into account and may or may not be determinative depending upon all the other circumstances.

Contributory infringement

The concept of contributory infringement (sometimes referred to as vicarious infringement) is well established in the US. The UK does not have such a form of infringement as a distinct concept but it could give rise there to claims of authorising infringement or

170 *MCA Records Inc v Charly Records Ltd* [2002] FSR 26 (p 401).

171 [1923–1928] MacG CC 51.

172 [1924] 1 KB 1.

173 [1976] RPC 151. Note, however, that s 101(1) of the Australian Copyright Act 1968 expressly lists matters to be taken into account in determining authorisation, including the presence of absence of any power to prevent the infringing act, the relationship between the persons involved and whether reasonable steps were taken to prevent or avoid the infringement.

174 [2004] SCC 13.

175 [1988] AC 1013.

176 [1926] 2 KB 474. *See also Monckton v Pathé Frères Pathephone Ltd* [1914] 1 KB 395 at 499.

177 Furthermore, Amstrad was not guilty of incitement to commit either a tort or a criminal offence.

178 [2010] FSR 21 (p 512).

179 Kitchen J borrowed some of these circumstances from the Australian Copyright Act 1968, s 101(1).

joint infringement. In the US a person may be liable on the basis of contributory infringement even though he does not carry out the infringing act personally. In *Religious Technology Center* v *Netcom OnLine Communication Services Inc*[180] it was said that internet service providers could be liable for contributory infringement if they had knowledge of the infringement but had not taken any steps to put a stop to it.[181] The concept of control was important. An analogy with a building lease was rejected by the court. It had been argued that a lessor of premises later used, for example, to make infringing copies of a work, would not be liable. The court considered that an internet service provider, unlike a lessor of premises, does retain a measure of control over the use of the system. In the past, Netcom had suspended accounts of subscribers who had used the system to post infringing software.

Contributory infringement can be likened to authorising infringement, but is not so extensive. For example, it appeared that contributory infringement in the US requires actual knowledge, whereas authorising infringement in the UK can be inferred, for example, where a person is indifferent as to whether infringing material is involved.

Contributory infringement or vicarious infringement in the US are based on well-settled common law principles which were set out in *Sony Corp of America* v *Universal City Studios Inc*.[182] In that case, Sony made video cassette recorders which could be used to record television programmes including films broadcast by television. These machines could be used for making unauthorised copies of television programmes and films. They could also be used to make copies that did not infringe copyright, examples being where a copy was made for time shifting[183] or where the broadcast was itself out of copyright or with the copyright owner's permission. The Supreme Court held that Sony was not liable for contributory infringement of copyright by its customers even though it knew that the machines would be used by large numbers of persons to make infringing copies of copyright works.

Peer-to-peer file-sharing software has caused the film and music industries considerable concern. This software is downloaded on to individuals' computers enabling them to share files by copying the files from one computer to another. No central computer is required. Literally billions of files are shared across peer-to-peer networks each month.

Napster was one company which facilitated the transmission of MP3 format files between and among its users through peer to peer file sharing. It provided free software which allowed its users to make MP3 music files stored on individual computer hard drives available for copying by other Napster users, search for MP3 music files stored on other users' computers and transfer exact copies of the contents of other users' MP3 files from one computer to another via the internet. Napster also provided technical support for the indexing and searching of MP3 files, as well as for its other functions, including a chat room, where users could meet to discuss music, and a directory where participating artists could provide information about their music. In *A & M Records Inc* v *Napster Inc*,[184] the Court of Appeals for the 9th circuit varied an injunction imposed by the district court, confirming that contributory liability may be imposed only to the extent that Napster received reasonable knowledge of specific infringing files, knowing that such files were available on the Napster system (or where Napster should have known this), and where it failed to act to prevent distribution of these works.

Distinguishing *Sony* v *Universal City Studios*, the Supreme Court in *Metro-Goldwyn-Meyer Studios Inc* v *Grokster Inc*,[185] the Supreme Court found that distributing peer-to-peer file-sharing software did amount to contributory infringement of copyright. There were a number of important differences between the cases, in particular that Grokster had actively encouraged copyright infringement such as by advertising the software as suitable for making copies of films or music and instructing users how to engage in infringing use. The Supreme Court held that distributing a device with the object of promoting its use to infringe copyright made one liable for contributory infringement even though the device

180 907 F Supp 1361 (ND Cal, 1995).

181 Hails R.I., Jr. 'Liability of OnLine Service Providers Resulting from Copyright Infringement Performed by their Subscribers' [1996] 5 EIPR 304.

182 464 US 417 (1984).

183 Recording a programme to watch at a more convenient time. This is acceptable under US copyright law and, in the UK, is specifically provided for under s 70 of the Copyright, Designs and Patents Act 1988.

184 239 F 3d 1004 (9th Cir 2001).

185 545 US 913 (2005). The other defendant in the case was Streamcast Networks Inc.

could be used lawfully. This was contrasted with the situation where devices are distributed with mere knowledge that they may be used to infringe copyright. It was noted that where a device is widely shared to cause infringements on a massive scale, the only practical recourse for copyright owners is to go against the distributor for contributory infringement rather than the individuals liable for direct infringement.

There has been little case law of file-sharing software in the UK but, in *Polydor Ltd* v *Brown*,[186] Collins J held that '. . . connecting a computer to the internet, where the computer is running P2P [peer-to-peer] software, and in which music files containing copies of the claimant's copyright works are placed in a shared directory' constituted primary infringement of copyright. He also confirmed that such infringement occurred regardless of the knowledge of the person responsible and innocence or ignorance is not a defence to primary infringement.[187] In that case, the identity of the defendant in question (he was one of a number of defendants) was obtained following a *Norwich Pharmacal* order[188] made against a number of internet service providers whose facilities were used by the defendants.

In the UK, in *Amstrad Consumer Electronics plc* v *British Phonograph Industry Ltd*[189] it was held that supplying machines which would be likely to be used unlawfully to copy pre-recorded cassettes subject to copyright protection was insufficient to make the manufacturer or supplier a primary infringer of copyright or a joint tortfeasor even though the reality of the situation was that Amstrad knew that the machine would be used to infringe copyright in many cases. Nor could this be seen as authorising infringement of copyright because the supplier had no control over the way the machines were used once sold. Although the advertising mentioned that users could '. . . make a copy of your favourite cassette', a small warning about copyright infringement was also present. As in the *Sony* v *Universal City Studios*, in contrast with the *MGM* v *Grokster* case, Amstrad did not actively encourage users to infringe copyright.

Joint infringers are two or more persons who act in concert pursuant to a common design to infringe.[190] In the case of twin cassette tape machines, Amstrad had no control, nor was there any common design between Amstrad and purchasers of its machines. In the context of a company, it appears that a company director who is the directing mind of the company may be liable with the company for copyright infringement as a joint tortfeasor.[191]

Secondary infringements of copyright

In addition to infringement of copyright through the acts restricted by the copyright in the work, there are certain other infringements known as secondary infringements. Some of the criminal offences provided for under the 1988 Act closely follow the equivalent secondary infringements and the same level of knowledge is required, for example, in some cases knowing or having reason to believe that the article concerned is an infringing copy. The distinction between primary infringement and secondary infringement is that the former involves making the infringing copy or making the infringing performance, etc. while the latter involves 'dealing' with infringing copies, providing the premises or apparatus for the performance or making an article for the purpose of making infringing copies. If a secondary infringement has been committed, there will almost certainly have been a corresponding infringement of one or more of the acts restricted by copyright.[192] For a secondary infringement the person responsible must have knowledge or reason to believe that the copies are infringing copies or whatever. It would seem from the wording that the person involved must have either actual knowledge or, at least, a subjective reasonable belief that the relevant activity involves a secondary infringement. Under the

186 [2005] EWHC 3191 (Ch).

187 It could, however, prevent an award of damages, though this is without prejudice to any other remedy: s 97(1).

188 An order for discovery against a person who is not a wrongdoer but who may have information identifying the wrongdoer or evidence of a wrong. The name comes from the case of *Norwich Pharmacal Co* v *Commissioners of Customs and Excise* [1974] AC 133 where the claimant sought information as to the identity of companies importing chemicals alleged to infringe the claimant's patent. An equivalent order was implemented in Scotland by the Intellectual Property (Enforcement, etc.) Regulations 2006 SI 2006/1028, reg 4.

189 [1986] FSR 159.

190 *The Koursk* [1924] P 140, per Scrutton LJ at 156, approved by Lord Templeman in *CBS* v *Amstrad*, above.

191 *MCA Records Inc* v *Charly Records Ltd* [2002] FSR 26 (p 401).

192 But, the 'primary infringement' may have been carried out by another person, hence the need for the secondary infringements. This is especially useful when the primary infringer is outside the jurisdiction of the UK courts.

Copyright Act 1956, only actual knowledge was sufficient for the corresponding secondary infringements, but nevertheless the courts tended to take a liberal view of this and in *Columbia Picture Industries v Robinson*[193] it was held that, *inter alia*, the knowledge required extended to the situation where a defendant deliberately refrained from inquiry and shut his eyes to the obvious. The phrase 'has reason to believe' in the Copyright, Designs and Patents Act 1988 ss 22–26 was new and, in *LA Gear Inc v Hi-Tec Sports plc*,[194] it was said that it could not be construed in accordance with the 1956 Act. The test must be objective in that it requires a consideration of whether the reasonable man, with knowledge of the facts known to the defendant, would have formed the belief that the item was an infringing copy. In the trial at first instance, Morritt J suggested that, once appraised of the facts, the defendant should be allowed sufficient time to evaluate those facts so as to be in a position to draw the conclusion that he is dealing with infringing copies.[195] This is not inconsistent with an objective approach – the reasonable man also may need time for the facts to 'sink in'[196] but facts from which a reasonable person *might suspect* that the copies were infringing copies alone is not enough;[197] though one would expect that, once a suspicion is raised, enquiries would be made to see if it was well-founded. Seeking an indemnity from a supplier after being warned that infringing articles were to be supplied indicates the presence of a 'reason to believe'.[198] Situations where it may be plausible for a defendant not to have 'reason to believe' include where he believes that the copyright has expired, where copyright does not subsist in the work or where the copies have been made with the copyright owner's permission.[199]

Where legal proceedings have been initiated against a defendant alleging secondary infringement of copyright, this fact alone does not necessarily mean that he has reason to believe that he is, for example, making or selling infringing copies. Nor does the fact that the defendant had put money aside for a fighting fund for the pending litigation show that he has the requisite knowledge: *Metix (UK) Ltd v GH Maughan (Plastics) Ltd.*[200] After all, the defendant may consider that he has a good chance of successfully defending the action because he does not think, and has no reason to believe, that the copies are infringing copies. Where a person is threatened with legal action and makes enquiries with the supplier of the alleged infringing copies, he may have reason to believe if those enquiries are not answered satisfactorily, being sketchy and providing no credible answers to questions put by the claimant's solicitors: *Nouveau Fabrics Ltd v Voyage Decoration Ltd.*[201] Mann J said that an allegation of infringement does not have to be accepted by a defendant but he has to consider it. He cannot ignore it but has to evaluate the claim and this would normally involve making reasonable enquiries. A second defendant who did not make any independent enquiries but simply relied upon the first defendant was also held to have reason to believe that the articles, patterned fabrics, were infringing copies.

The need to show a mental element on the part of a secondary infringer must be contrasted with the acts restricted by copyright under ss 16–21, in which the question of the infringer's mental element does not arise. If he commits or authorises one of the acts, he infringes copyright regardless of whether he knows that copyright subsists in the existing work and regardless of whether or not it is reasonable for the infringer to suspect that copyright subsists in the work. The strictness of this state of affairs is tempered by the fact that the availability of the remedy of damages is dependent upon the infringer's mental state.[202]

Secondary infringement of copyright involves any of the following activities:

1 importing an infringing copy into the UK, other than for private or domestic use (s 22);
2 possessing or 'dealing' with an infringing copy; this includes possession in the course of business, selling, letting for hire, offering or exposing for sale or hire,[203] exhibiting or distributing in the course of business or distributing (otherwise than in the course of business) to such an extent as to affect prejudicially the owner of the copyright (s 23);

---

193 [1987] 1 Ch 38. *See* also *Infabrics Ltd v Jaytex Shirt Co Ltd* [1978] FSR 457.

194 [1992] FSR 121.

195 [1992] FSR 121 at 129.

196 Where secondary infringement is planned in the future the claimant does not have to wait to see if it is actually carried out when seeking a *quia timet* injunction: *Linpac Mouldings Ltd v Eagleton Direct Export Ltd* [1994] FSR 545.

197 *Vermaat and Powell v Boncrest Ltd (No 2)* [2002] FSR 21 (p 331).

198 *Pensher Security Door Co Ltd v Sunderland City Council* [2000] RPC 249.

199 Putting a person on notice that his actions may infringe is not sufficient. The question is whether the reasonable man would believe that he was a secondary infringer: *Hutchison Personal Communications Ltd v Hook Advertising Ltd* [1995] FSR 365.

200 [1997] FSR 718.

201 [2004] EWHC 895 (Ch).

202 On the basis of the same formula: Copyright, Designs and Patents Act 1988 s 97(1).

203 Exposing an article for sale is an invitation to treat and modern statutes use this or a similar formula to overcome the problem that this does not constitute a contractual offer, as identified in cases such as *Fisher v Bell* [1961] 1 QB 394 and *Partridge v Crittenden* [1968] 2 All ER 421.

3 making, importing into the UK, possessing in the course of business or selling, letting for hire, offering or exposing for sale or hire an article specifically designed or adapted for making infringing copies of a work knowing or having reason to believe that it will be used to make infringing copies (s 24(1));

4 transmission of the work by means of a telecommunications system (otherwise than by communication to the public) without the licence of the copyright owner, knowing or having reason to believe that infringing copies of the work will be made by means of reception of the transmission in the UK or elsewhere (s 24(2));

5 permitting the use of premises, being a place of public entertainment, for an infringing performance of a literary, dramatic or musical work; a 'place of public entertainment' includes places that are only occasionally made available for hire for the purposes of public entertainment – for example, a room in a public house which is hired out from time to time for functions such as weddings (s 25);

6 where copyright is infringed by a public performance of the work, or by playing or showing the work in public, supplying the apparatus or a substantial part of it for the playing of sound recordings, the showing of films or the receiving of visual images or of sounds conveyed by electronic means; the person supplying the apparatus or a substantial part of it must know or have reason to believe that it was likely to be used to infringe copyright or, in the case of apparatus whose normal use involves a public performance, playing or showing, he did not believe on reasonable grounds that it would not be used so as to infringe copyright (s 26);

7 an occupier of premises who gives permission for the apparatus to be brought onto those premises will also be liable for the infringement if when he gave permission he knew or had reason to believe that the apparatus was likely to be so used as to infringe copyright (s 26(3));

8 supplying a copy of a sound recording or film used to infringe copyright if the person supplying it knew or had reason to believe that it, or a copy of it, would be used so as to infringe copyright (s 26(4)).[204]

In all cases, apart from those involving public performances, to be liable the person concerned must have actual knowledge or have had reason to believe, for example, that the copy is an infringing copy or that the copy supplied by him is to be used in such a way so as to infringe copyright. However, there is a subtle difference in the mental element required for the infringement under s 25 in that the person giving permission for the premises to be used for the performance will be liable unless, at the time he gave permission, he believed on reasonable grounds that the performance would not infringe copyright. A similar expression is used in s 26(2) in terms of providing apparatus the normal use of which involves a public performance. Therefore, for these two instances, the test is a blend of the subjective and the objective. It is plain from the wording that the defendant will carry the burden of proof. He will have to show that he did not believe that copyright would be infringed, and furthermore that this belief was based on reasonable grounds. This might be an onerous burden, but the activities involved give rise to civil liability only, which accounts for the difference in the mental element compared to the other secondary infringements.[205]

Some of the secondary infringements involve 'infringing copies' of the work, and the meaning of this phrase is given in s 27 as being:

(a) an article, the making of which constituted an infringement of copyright; or

(b) an article which has been or is proposed to be imported into the UK and its making in the UK would have infringed copyright or would have been a breach of an exclusive licence agreement; or

(c) copies which are infringing copies by virtue of several provisions relating to the 'acts permitted in relation to copyright works'.[206]

204 Strangely, this provision does not extend to computer programs.

205 Under s 107(3), the criminal offences relating to public performances are available only against persons who 'caused' the work to be performed, played or shown. Furthermore, the mental element is stated to be that the person knew or had reason to believe that copyright would be infringed. It is arguable whether a person providing premises or apparatus 'causes' the work to be performed.

206 The acts permitted in relation to copyright works are described and discussed in Chapter 7.

An article for the purposes of s 27 does not have to be permanent and ephemeral copies may be caught. In *Sony Computer Entertainment Inc v Ball*[207] it was confirmed that copies of copyright works loaded into transient computer memory, facilitated by the defendant's computer chip, may be infringing copies. What mattered was the time that the copy was made and there was no requirement that the copy had any form of permanence.

207 [2005] FSR 9 (p 159).

Under s 27(5), the provisions relating to imported copies are abrogated in favour of any enforceable Community right[208] within the meaning of the European Communities Act 1972 s 2(1). This provision is not really necessary and only restates the effects of the UK's obligations as a member of the European Community (now Union). These obligations are separate from and prevail over inconsistent national law.[209] Therefore, if the importation into the UK of an otherwise infringing copy is permitted by European Union law (for example, under the exhaustion of rights principle), that copy will not be deemed to be an infringing copy and the persons involved in its importation and subsequent dealings with it will not be liable for secondary infringement. However, if a person then makes copies from the imported copy once it is within the UK that person will have infringed copyright, unless this also is permitted by prevailing European Union law, an unlikely possibility.

208 Strictly speaking it should now be a European Union right.

209 *See*, for example, Case 6/64 *Costa* v *ENEL* [1964] ECR 585.

There is a presumption, under s 27(4), that an article is an infringing copy in any proceedings where the question arises. If it is shown that the article is a copy of the work and copyright subsists or has subsisted at any time in the work, it is presumed that the article was made at a time when copyright subsisted in the work unless the contrary is proved. A person copying or dealing with a copy of any type of work should not only satisfy himself that copyright in the work had expired at the time the copy was made, or that copyright did not otherwise subsist in the work at that time, but should also be able to adduce evidence to that effect to the satisfaction of the court. Bear in mind that, in this matter, regardless of whether the proceedings are civil or criminal, proof on a balance of probabilities will suffice.[210]

In *Pensher Security Door Co Ltd v Sunderland City Council*,[211] the council placed contracts for the refurbishment of blocks of flats which included the provision of new security doors. It was held the doors supplied infringed the transitional copyright in the drawings of the doors[212] and that the council had the requisite knowledge after being warned by the copyright owner that the doors supplied were infringing copies. The council argued, *inter alia*, that once the doors had been fitted to the flats, they were no longer infringing copies for the purposes of s 27. Furthermore, the council did not act in the course of business. Both of these arguments were rejected by the trial judge and the appeal to the Court of Appeal was dismissed. Aldous LJ said that even though the doors had become part of the block of flats, they remained articles for the purposes of s 23. As regards whether the council possessed the doors in the course of business, Aldous LJ saw no reason for departing from case law in other areas such as trade descriptions law and under the Unfair Contract Terms Act 1977. He said (at 281):

210 In criminal proceedings, the prosecution must prove the accused's guilt beyond reasonable doubt and the onus is usually also on the prosecution to negate any defence put up by the accused. However, in some circumstances the accused bears the burden of proving that the defence applies on the balance of probabilities. These circumstances include express or implied statutory provision.

211 [2000] RPC 249.

212 Copyright, Designs and Patents Act 1988 Sch 1, para 19(1).

> As has been made clear in such cases as *Davies v Sumner* [1984] 1 WLR 1301 and in *R & B Customs Brokers*,[213] transactions which are only incidental to a business may not be possessed in the course of that business. However, doors to flats are not incidental to the business of managing and letting flats. They are an integral part of that business.

213 Reported at [1998] 1 WLR 321.

Publication right

From 1 December 1996 a person who publishes for the first time a literary, dramatic, musical or artistic work of a film in which copyright has expired acquires a publication right, equivalent to a copyright.[214] The provisions of chapter II of the 1988 Act apply to the publication right as they do to copyright and, therefore, infringement of the publication right is the same as for any other work of copyright under ss 16–21. However, the presumptions in ss 104–106 do not apply. These are discussed later in this chapter.

214 *See* the discussion of this right in Chapter 3.

Remedies for infringement of copyright

The remedies for copyright infringement and supplemental provisions are set out in Chapter VI of the Act in ss 96–115. This chapter of the Act comprehensively covers civil infringement, criminal offences, delivery up and destruction orders.[215] Although previous copyright legislation provided for effective civil remedies, the criminal penalties available for certain types of copyright infringement have been increased very significantly. Under the 1956 Act the maximum penalty was 40 shillings (£2.00) per infringing copy but now a maximum of ten years' imprisonment is available.

To deny a copyright owner a remedy for infringement of his copyright is to be in breach of Article 1 of Protocol 1 to the Council of Europe Convention for the Protection of Human Rights and Fundamental Freedoms. Article 1 states:

> Every natural or legal person is entitled to the peaceful enjoyment of his possessions. No one shall be deprived of his possessions except in the public interest and subject to the conditions provided for by law and by the general principles of international law . . .

In *Balan* v *Moldova*,[216] Mr Balan was the author of a photograph of a castle in Moldova. He published the photograph but, without his knowledge, the State of Moldova used the photograph, amongst others, as a background for its national identity cards. After some litigation, the Moldovian Supreme Court of Justice eventually held that the identity cards were official documents which were not subject to copyright. The court did, however, accept that Mr Balan had intellectual property rights in the photograph. The European Court of Human Rights distinguished between copyright as a property right and the property right in the identity cards themselves. Having identity cards may have been in the public interest but that could have been satisfied in other ways, such as using another photograph or by seeking a licence from Mr Balan. Thus, there was a breach of Article 1 of Protocol 1 and the court awarded Mr Balan €5,000 for pecuniary and non-pecuniary loss.

Civil remedies

The Copyright, Designs and Patents Act 1988 provides an ample range of remedies for copyright infringement. Section 96 states that infringement is actionable by the copyright owner but this is not exhaustive as, under s 101, an exclusive licensee has, except as against the copyright owner, the same rights and remedies as the copyright owner which run concurrent with those of the owner.[217] Of course, an exclusive licensee will be able to take action only if the infringement concerns the subject matter of the licence agreement. For example, if an exclusive licence is granted with respect to the public performance rights in a dramatic work, the licensee will be able to sue a person who performs the dramatic work in public, but will not be able to sue a person who simply makes copies of the work. As from 31 October 2003 a non-exclusive licensee may be able to bring proceedings. Section 101A permits this if the act complained of was directly concerned with the prior licensed act, where the licence is in writing and expressly grants the licensee a right of action.[218] Such a non-exclusive licensee has the same rights and remedies as the copyright owner and the provisions concerning the exercise of concurrent rights under s 102 apply as they do to exclusive licensees. A non-exclusive licensee is one authorised by the licence to exercise a right which remains exercisable by the copyright owner.

The civil remedies available for infringement of copyright are damages, injunctions, accounts, 'or otherwise'. These are stated by s 96(2) as being available in respect of a copyright infringement as they are available in respect of any other property right

215 Conversion damages were available under the Copyright Act 1956 but appear to be no longer available on the basis that they are not specifically mentioned in the 1988 Act though the use of the phrase 'or otherwise' after listing the civil remedies available for copyright infringement in s 96(2) may have preserved this remedy. Even so, it is unlikely that a court would award conversion damages given the availability of additional damages.

216 [2009] ECDR 53.

217 The Copyright, Designs and Patents Act 1998 s 102 deals with the exercise of concurrent rights. Normally, the copyright owner or an exclusive licensee may not proceed alone without joining the other except with the leave of the court. Section 102 also deals with the matter of remedies in cases involving exclusive licensees and copyright owners having concurrent rights.

218 Section 101A was inserted by the Copyright and Related Rights Regulations 2003, SI 2003/2498.

(remembering that s 1(1) describes copyright as a property right). Although the previous legislation included conversion damages, it is conceivable that the addition of the phrase 'or otherwise' still permits the use of conversion damages, as they are available as a general rule in tort for wrongfully dealing with another person's property.[219] Nonetheless, it is HIGHLY unlikely that such a remedy would be claimed and even less likely that it would be granted.[220] The phrase will include an order for specific performance, such as an order for a written, signed assignment of copyright in a situation where a purported assignment has turned out to be defective in some way. However, it should be noted that injunctions and accounts of profits are equitable in nature and factors that might be important are whether the claimant acted promptly, whether injustice would be done to innocent third parties and whether the claimant came to the court with 'clean hands'. Other remedies available are additional damages (s 97(2)) and delivery up (s 99).

Where the alleged infringing work is a work of architecture, it may be possible to register a caution against dealing with land under the Land Registration Act 2002 s 15.[221] This may be particularly useful in the case of a house being built for sale which is alleged to infringe the copyright in an architect's drawings, as the limitation on injunctions under the Copyright Act 1956 s 17(4) (no injunction or other order shall be made to prevent a building from being completed or to require its demolition) has no equivalent under the 1988 Act. Whilst it would be extremely unlikely that an infringing building would be ordered to be demolished, registering a caution could focus the alleged infringer's mind wonderfully. However, under s 77 of the Land Registration Act 2002, a person lodging a caution must not do so without reasonable cause and is under a duty to any person who suffers damage in consequence of the breach of that duty. Nevertheless, in limited and appropriate cases, it could prove a useful alternative approach to an application for an interim injunction (previously known as an interlocutory injunction), especially where it is doubtful that the court will grant an injunction: for example, where the balance of convenience lies in favour of the defendant.

The claimant has to elect between damages and an account. At one time, the claimant would have had to make that election without knowing what profits the defendant made from the infringement. This was very unsatisfactory and explained why accounts were rarely sought. However, in *Island Records Inc v Tring International plc*,[222] Lightman J said that a claimant should not have to make such a decision in the dark. Rather, it should be an informed decision. Thus, it might be appropriate to require the defendant to supply affidavit evidence setting out sufficient information to allow the claimant to decide. The information does not have to be enormously detailed, imposing a substantial amount of work on the defendant, and, in *Brugger v Medicaid*,[223] it was held that an affidavit setting out numbers of alleged infringing articles made and sold, the sums received or receivable and an approximate estimate of costs, together with a statement as to how that estimate was made would be sufficient. This development might have resulted in an increase in the proportion of cases in which a claimant elects for an account rather than damages, though there seems little evidence of this in practice.

In appropriate cases, a claimant may be able to obtain an order for disclosure of the identities of persons to whom infringing copies have been supplied. This could assist the claimant in putting together a claim for damages or to initiate proceedings against the recipients of infringing copies. However, a court may be reluctant to grant an order for disclosure because of the potential for harming the defendant's business.[224]

There are special provisions in respect of infringements of a copyright for which a licence is available as of right under s 144 (powers exercisable in consequence of a report of the Competition Commission).[225] In such a case, no injunction shall be granted, there may be no order for delivery up under s 99 and the amount recoverable by way of damages or an account of profits shall not exceed double the amount which would have been payable under the licence as of right provided that, in proceedings, the defendant undertakes

---

219 Conversion damages were specifically provided for by the Copyright Act 1956 s 18. Section 18 did not apply after commencement of the 1988 Act unless the proceedings began before: Copyright, Designs and Patents Act 1988 Sch 1, para 31(2). Conversion damages could result in a windfall for the claimant, for example if the subject matter of the claimant's rights was incorporated in some larger material or item.

220 A judge would surely point to the fact that if Parliament intended to retain conversion damages for copyright infringement it would have mentioned them expressly. The use of 'or otherwise' might point to other remedies such as interim remedies or, for example, a declaration.

221 Arnold, R. 'A New Remedy for Copyright Infringement?' [1997] 12 EIPR 689.

222 [1995] FSR 560.

223 [1996] FSR 362.

224 *Gemco (2000) Ltd v Daniels* [2002] EWHC 2875 (Ch). Such an order was granted in this case.

225 Copyright, Designs and Patents Act 1988 s 98.

to take a licence on terms to be agreed or, failing agreement, on terms to be settled by the Copyright Tribunal under s 144.[226] The undertaking may be given at any time before the final order in the proceedings without any admission of liability. Remedies existing before licences of right were available are unaffected.

Search orders

Obtaining and preserving evidence is an important aspect of copyright litigation, as it is with other forms of intellectual property infringements. It may be possible for the copyright owner to simply purchase alleged infringing copies or access and copy material broadcast or made available online which is alleged to infringe his work. In some cases, this may not be satisfactory, for example, in determining the scale of the alleged infringement or in determining the identity of others such as suppliers or distributors or in gaining access to equipment used to make or distribute the material in question. For such cases, the courts have the power to grant a search order. As these orders are relevant to all forms of intellectual property, they are discussed at length in Chapter 24 of this book on remedies for infringement of intellectual property rights. There is, however, a limited power of seizure available to a copyright owner which is provided for by the Copyright, Designs and Patents Act 1988 and this is described below. Search warrants and related orders in respect of the criminal offences under copyright law are covered later in this chapter in the section on criminal offences.

Copyright owner's power of seizure

The copyright owner has a limited power of seizure. Bearing in mind that pirated copies of copyright works frequently are sold at 'unofficial' markets, car boot sales and the like, s 100 gives the copyright owner a right of seizure of infringing articles at such places and the right to retain those articles. Notice of the proposed seizure must be given to a local police station and the premises at which the infringing articles are located must not be a permanent or regular place of business. Additionally, the copyright owner must leave a prescribed form giving particulars of the person making the seizure and the grounds for the seizure.[227] Force may not be used in effecting the seizure. It is unlikely that this provision will be used frequently because of the limited circumstances in which it is available and because of the attendant conditions.

Damages, accounts and additional damages

Damages, coupled with an injunction to prevent further infringing activity, are the usual remedies claimed in copyright actions. Damages may be assessed on the basis of the equivalent royalty or licence fee which the infringer would have paid to the owner had he carried out his acts under a licence. But this is not the only way damages may be assessed. For example, the copyright owner may not have any desire to exploit his work commercially or his economic interests may have been harmed in other ways. A pirate may have flooded the market with poor quality reproductions of the original work.

Damages and accounts are alternative remedies and additional damages may be available where the infringement has been flagrant. Additional damages may be claimed together with a claim for ordinary damages but not with a claim for an account of profits.

Damages

The copyright owner (or exclusive licensee or non-exclusive licensee with a right to sue under s 101A) will usually ask the court for damages, which can be expected to be calculated, as with other torts, on the basis of putting the claimant in the position he would have been had the tort not been committed, that is to compensate him for the actual loss suffered in so far as it is not too remote.[228] Importantly, damages are not available if it is shown that at the time of the infringement the defendant did not know, and had no reason to believe, that copyright subsisted in the work to which the action relates: s 97(1). This is without prejudice to other remedies that might be available to the claimant, such as an injunction or an account of profits. The formula for the defendant's knowledge is the same as for secondary infringements, and what has been said in that context above should apply here also.

In *Claydon Architectural Metalwork Ltd* v *DJ Higgins & Sons*[229] it was said that the normal measure of damages for copyright infringement is the amount by which the value of the copyright as a chose in action has been depreciated.[230] Consequential damages are available in the usual way provided that they arose directly and naturally from the tort. In the *Claydon* case, secondary damages associated with cash flow problems caused to the claimant by the defendant's acts were said to be too remote. Therefore, merely showing a causal link between the act and the loss is not enough.[231]

Some forms of damages might be available in patent cases where they would not be in a copyright case. This is a result, not of the existence of different rules on remoteness for patents and copyright, but of the different nature of the rights. In *Work Model Enterprises Ltd* v *Ecosystem Ltd*,[232] the defendant copied text from the claimant's brochure for office partitions. The claimant's claim for damages for lost sales of partitions and for price depression was held to be the result of the defendant's competition rather than the copyright infringement and, as a consequence, unrecoverable. Similarly, in *Paterson Zochonis & Co Ltd* v *Merfarken Packaging Ltd*,[233] the fact that a printer infringed the copyright in the design of packaging did not make him liable for the subsequent passing off by the customer for which he had carried out the printing work. In patent cases, there may be much more of a nexus between the infringement and, for example, lost sales in non-patented products sold alongside the patented product or in the sale of spare parts for such products.[234] This is a consequence of the nature of the monopoly right granted to patent proprietors.

Damages might be assessed as the amount of royalties the copyright owner would have secured had the infringer obtained and paid for a licence to perform whatever the infringing act was.[235] This is a somewhat artificial and rough and ready exercise as the court is trying to put a value on a transaction which did not happen: it is a notional royalty.[236] Where a copyright owner grants licences but the defendant refuses to accept a licence and chooses to infringe instead, it might be reasonable to assume that the damages should be based on the royalty asked by the copyright owner. However, this approach can be criticised as it allows the copyright owner to set the level of damages. In *Ludlow Music Inc* v *Williams*,[237] a royalty of 50 per cent was asked for but the judge awarded 25 per cent as damages.

Another way of calculating the quantum of damages, depending on the circumstances, might be based on the profit the copyright owner would have derived from sales lost as a result of the infringement. If it would be reasonable for the work to have been produced for a fee, such as an architect's drawings for a building, damages could be set at what would have been a reasonable fee for the drawings.[238] It will generally depend on whether the infringement relates to an 'original' work (for example, a literary work), or to a derivative work such as a film or sound recording; calculation by reference to lost royalties is more appropriate to the former.

One problem for a copyright owner might be proving his losses in a situation where it may appear that the defendant sold more copies of the work than the claimant might have sold. This might be because the defendant has a bigger customer base or has very effective marketing. In *Blayney* v *Clogau St Davids Gold Mines Ltd*,[239] the claimant created a new design for a ring to be made in Welsh gold. He sold these to the first defendant,

228 Apart from the criminal offences, infringement of copyright is in the nature of a tort.

229 [1997] FSR 475.

230 Per Lord Wright in *Sutherland Publishing Co Ltd* v *Caxton Publishing Co Ltd* [1936] 1 All ER 177 at 180.

231 *Cambridge Water Co* v *Eastern Counties Leather plc* [1994] 2 AC 224.

232 [1996] FSR 356.

233 [1986] 3 All ER 522.

234 See *Gerber Garment Technology Inc* v *Lectra Systems Ltd* [1997] RPC 443, discussed in Chapter 14.

235 *See*, for example, *Redwood Music* v *Chappell* [1982] RPC 109.

236 *USP plc* v *London General Holdings Ltd* [2006] FSR 6 (p 65) per Laws LJ at para 43.

237 [2002] FSR 57 (p 868).

238 *Jones* v *London Borough of Tower Hamlets* [2001] RPC 23 (p 407). Damages in that case were assessed on that basis, by consent of the parties, at £1,000.

239 [2002] FSR 14 (p 233).

who sold them on. Eventually their business relationship broke down and the first defendant engaged other craftsmen to make rings to the design. The judge held that the claimant would only have sold around 10 per cent or 25 per cent of the total sold by the defendants (depending on the period and the mode of sale) and awarded damages on the basis of the lost profits on such sales. The final award was £18,492.03 plus interest. However, the Court of Appeal increased the award to £36,279.48.[240] The Court of Appeal noted that assessing damages by reference to profits of lost sales and by way of a royalty on other infringing sales was well established in patent cases and there was no reason why the same principle should not apply in copyright cases. Of course it is necessary to guard against over-compensation where a claimant is obtaining both loss of profit of sales he has foregone and a royalty on other infringing sales.

In claiming for lost profits, causation must be shown, that is, that the defendant's infringing activities were the cause of the losses claimed.[241] In *Peninsular Business Services Ltd* v *Citation plc*,[242] both parties were in the business of providing consultancy services in the field of employment law, health and safety law and related areas. The defendant commenced business in 1995 and engaged an ex-employee of the claimant who had deliberately copied some of the claimant's handbooks which were used as a basis for the defendant's handbooks. The claimant claimed damages of around £600,000 for lost profits on lost sales and additional damages. The judge held that it was not sufficient for such a claim to show that infringing material was used by the defendant in competition with the claimant's business. It also had to be shown that the use of the infringing materials was the cause of the claimant's losses. In the present case, the use of the infringing materials were ancillary to the defendant's otherwise lawful business. The judge awarded £9,000 instead on the basis that that was a fair estimate of the cost of obtaining a non-infringing set of handbooks.[243]

It is wrong to assess damages at a fictitiously high level; compensatory damages must reflect the actual loss to the claimant. The view is reinforced by the fact that the 1988 Act provides for additional damages. In *Michael O'Mara Books Ltd* v *Express Newspapers plc*,[244] the authors and publisher of *Fergie – Her Secret Life* were aggrieved when the editor of the *Daily Express* acquired two infringing copies of the book. Unknown to him, his wife offered one copy to the *Sun* newspaper for £4,000 but a trap was set and she was arrested for being in possession of an infringing copy. The claimants asked for damages of £8,000 in respect of the two infringing copies. However, the judge did not accept that the copies could have been sold for £4,000 each and he awarded damages of £125 against each of the four defendants.

Where it is not possible to prove any loss, a court may make an award a reasonable sum for the use of the claimant's materials on the basis of the benefit accruing to the wrongdoer. The Court of Appeal approved of this principle in *Experience Hendrix LLC* v *PPX Enterprises Inc*,[245] applying the restrictive covenant case of *Wrotham Park Estates Co* v *Parkside Homes Ltd*.[246]

See Chapter 24 for more material on the award and assessment of damages in relation the infringement of intellectual property rights generally. Accounts are fully dealt with in Chapter 24. Also covered in detail is the impact of the Intellectual Property (Enforcement, etc.) Regulations 2006.[247]

Additional damages

This form of damages may be claimed in appropriate cases alongside a claim for ordinary damages. They may not be claimed with an account of profits. Additional damages are also available in relation a performer's property rights[248] and the UK's unregistered design right.[249] Additional damages may be seen as a form of 'punitive' damages[250] and such an award may be fitting if the defendant has acted scandalously or deceitfully, or if ordinary damages or an account of profits is not appropriate: for example, where the defendant has

240 [2003] FSR 19 (p 360).

241 It is wrong to take account of non-infringing uses, such as where mere ideas are taken.

242 [2004] FSR 18 (p 359).

243 The judge also awarded £18,000 for additional damages: *see* later.

244 [1999] FSR 49.

245 [2003] FSR 46 (p 853).

246 [1974] 2 All ER 321.

247 SI 2006/1028. These Regulations implemented Directive 2004/48/EC of the European Parliament and of the Council of 29 April 2004 on the enforcement of intellectual property rights, OJ L 157, 30.04.2004, p 45.

248 See Chapter 9.

249 See Chapter 18.

250 They may be so described though technically they are not punitive, although they may have a punitive element about them.

published a work of a personal nature such as a diary which the copyright owner wished to keep private. The court has a discretion to award additional damages, and in exercising its discretion must have regard to all the circumstances and in particular to:

1 the flagrancy of the infringement; and
2 any benefit accruing to the defendant by reason of the infringement.[251]

Additional damages were awarded only rarely, but there is an upward trend in asking for them. In one example, *Cala Homes (South) Ltd* v *Alfred McAlpine Homes East Ltd*,[252] additional damages were awarded for infringement of an architect's drawings of houses. It was said that neither flagrancy nor benefit accruing to the defendant were precursors in the decision to award additional damages.

Following this, in *Cala Homes (South) Ltd* v *Alfred McAlpine Homes East Ltd (No 2)*,[253] Laddie J said that additional damages were quite distinct from ordinary damages, so it was possible to claim additional damages together with an account of profits. However, in the Court of Session, Inner House, Scotland, in *Redrow Homes Ltd* v *Betts Brothers plc*,[254] it was held that a claim to additional damages under s 97(2) was not a free-standing *sui generis* right and 'additional' means additional to normal damages under s 96(2). Therefore, additional damages could only be claimed if normal damages were claimed. Otherwise, it would mean that an infringer could be sued for additional damages even if ordinary damages were not available, for example, because of lack of knowledge. Although Laddie J talked of ss 96 and 97 as being distinct, s 96(3) states that s 96 has effect subject to the following provisions of this chapter, including, of course, s 97.

Additional damages may resemble, but are not, exemplary damages. Rather, they are the result of a specific statutory provision. Unlike exemplary damages, a claim for additional damages can be added in after pleadings, by way of amendment.

Flagrancy was described in terms of deceitful and treacherous conduct in order to steal a march on the claimant in *Nichols Advanced Vehicle Systems Inc* v *Reese & Oliver*,[255] in which the defendants, including the chief designer and a racing driver who had held positions of responsibility with the claimant's company, had made use of the claimant's working drawings for a Formula One racing car to build their own cars. The defendants had inflicted humiliation and loss on the claimant that was difficult to compensate and difficult to assess. In the later follow-up case it was held by Whitford J that the award of additional damages (£2,000) should take account of the damages awarded for infringement (£1,000) and conversion (£11,000).[256]

Deliberately concealing the infringing work or disguising its origins, for example, by removing copyright notices or the name of the copyright owner or otherwise modifying the work, may suggest that additional damages might be appropriate, particularly if coupled with a wilful disregard of the claimant's rights.[257] An honest belief by the defendant that what he was doing did not infringe, perhaps after taking legal advice, might not amount to flagrancy to found a claim for additional damages.[258] However, In *Harrison* v *Harrison*,[259] HH Michael Fysh QC accepted that there was no need for a defendant to have actual knowledge that the act complained of did indeed infringe copyright for an award of additional damages to be made. Section 97(2) is not stated to be restricted to cases where the defendant knew or had reason to believe that he had engaged in an infringing activity.[260] It seems odd that the defendant's state of mind does not appear to be relevant. It is submitted that this is wrong. How can the infringement be described as flagrant if the defendant did not know that, or was not reckless as to whether, he was infringing copyright.[261] This is reinforced by the view of Brightman J in *Ravenscroft* v *Herbert*,[262] were he described flagrancy as implying:

. . . the existence of scandalous conduct, deceit and such like; it includes deliberate and calculated copyright infringements.

251 Copyright, Designs and Patents Act 1988 s 97(2).

252 [1995] FSR 818.

253 [1996] FSR 36.

254 [1997] FSR 828. Affirmed, House of Lords: [1998] FSR 345.

255 [1979] RPC 127. In *Ravenscroft* v *Herbert* [1980] RPC 193, Brightman J described flagrancy thus: '. . . in my view implies the existence of scandalous conduct, deceit and such like; it includes deliberate and calculated copyright infringements'.

256 [1988] RPC 71. The Court of Appeal reduced the interest rate from 15 per cent to 10 per cent over seven years.

257 *Cantor Fitzgerald International* v *Tradition (UK) Ltd* [2000] RPC 95.

258 per Mann J, *obiter*, in *Fraser Woodward Ltd* v *British Broadcasting Corp* [2005] FSR 36 (p 762).

259 [2010] FSR 25 (p 604).

260 See, Laddie J at first instance in *Cala Homes (South) Ltd* v *Alfred McAlpine Homes East Ltd* [1995] FSR 818 at 838.

261 But see *Cala Homos (South) Ltd* v *Alfred McAlpine Homes East Ltd* [1995] FSR 818 for the opposite view.

262 [1980] RPC 193.

Additional damages may be available where an infringer has been subject to successful proceedings for contempt of court where the copyright owner has incurred expense and losses in trying to encourage the infringer to take a licence so as to comply with copyright law. In *Phonographic Performance Ltd* v *Reader*,[263] the defendant, the owner of a nightclub, refused to take a licence permitting the playing of sound recordings in public. The claimant sought to induce the defendant to take a licence and also policed his activities. Although not recoverable as costs in the action, it was held that the expenses were reasonably foreseeable and were recoverable as additional damages. Pumfrey J awarded as additional damages the cost of hiring enquiry agents and a sum equal to the unpaid licence fees. Describing the damages as additional damages seems wrong for two reasons. First, no award of ordinary damages was sought or awarded and additional damages must be additional to ordinary damages; they cannot exist in a vacuum. Secondly, although the actions of the defendant were flagrant and there was certainly some benefit accruing to him (at least in non-payment of the licence fees), the actual award could surely have been made on the basis of ordinary damages.

What has previously been said in conversation with a potential purchaser may indicate flagrancy. In *Microsoft Corp* v *Ling*,[264] a person acting for the claimant enquired about purchasing copies of the claimant's software. What was said by one of the defendants suggested that the defendants had full knowledge that they were offering for sale unlicensed copies of the software. Prices were quoted for licensed and unlicensed copies. In the light of this and other evidence, the judge concluded that the defendants had no real prospect of defending a claim for additional damages in respect of copyright infringement.

The Copyright Act 1956 required that the court also considered whether effective relief was otherwise available, but this has disappeared from the 1988 Act. This could encourage the greater use of additional damages where the defendant's behaviour has been particularly despicable or immoral in some way. An example is provided by the case of *Williams* v *Settle*,[265] in which the defendant, a professional photographer, was commissioned by the claimant to take photographs at his wedding, the copyright in the photographs vesting in the claimant. The father of the claimant's wife was later murdered and the defendant sold photographs of the wedding group, showing the murdered man, to the press. On the basis of additional damages as provided under the Copyright Act 1956 s 17(3), or alternatively because of the court's power to award punitive damages, the claimant was awarded damages of £1,000, which were far in excess of the measure of ordinary damages that would have been awarded, as the defendant received a relatively small sum from the newspaper proprietors for the photographs.

Injunctions

An injunction is an order of the court which prohibits an act or the commencement or continuance of an act. Alternatively, the injunction might order a person to perform some act.[266] For example, an injunction may be granted by the court ordering a person to cease making infringing copies of a work of copyright, or to destroy some article in his possession which is used for making infringing copies. Injunctions are equitable and therefore discretionary. They will not generally be granted if ordinary damages would be an adequate remedy. However, in terms of intellectual property rights, injunctions are very commonly asked for and frequently granted.

A particularly useful form of injunction is the interim injunction (formerly known as 'interlocutory injunction'). Where granted, this form of injunction prohibits the continuation of, or commencement of, acts alleged to infringe the intellectual property right involved. Both forms of injunction are relevant to all types of intellectual property rights and are described in more detail in Chapter 24 on remedies for infringement of intellectual property rights. There is, however, a special form of injunction provided for by the Copyright, Designs and Patents Act 1988. This is discussed below.

263 [2005] FSR 42 (p 891).

264 [2006] EWHC 1619 (Ch).

265 [1960] 1 WLR 1072.

266 Injunctions are classified as 'prohibitory injunctions' and 'mandatory injunctions'; the latter orders the person to whom it is addressed to carry out some act, such as demolishing a dangerous wall.

Injunctions against information society service providers

Under s 97A of the Copyright, Designs and Patents Act 1988, injunctions are available against service providers,[267] being anyone providing an information society service. Examples are organisations or persons providing internet access, providing a forum for selling goods or services online or hosting a website. The service provider must have actual knowledge that someone is using the service to infringe copyright.[268] In determining whether a service provider has actual knowledge, account is taken of all matters that in the circumstances appear relevant, including whether he has received a notice, for example, sent to his e-mail address under reg 6(1)(c) of the Electronic Commerce (EC Directive) Regulations 2002,[269] and the extent to which the notice includes the full name and address of the sender and the details of the alleged infringement. Failure to use the form of notice under reg 6(1)(c) is not fatal. In *Twentieth Century Fox Film Corp* v *Newzbin Ltd*,[270] the defendant website operator denied having actual notice of infringing activity carried on through its website on the ground that it had not received a reg 6(1)(c) notice. It was held that service of such a notice was not a precondition to a service provider having actual knowledge of others using its service to infringe copyright.

Newzbin facilitated access to and downloading of large numbers of films and other works to members paying a small weekly premium. It seemed that the vast majority of the material was protected by copyright and was made available without the owner's consent. Following the grant of the injunction in favour of the claimants, Newzbin was closed down but re-appeared later as Newzbin2. It appeared to have moved offshore and outside the jurisdiction of the courts in the UK. Twentieth Century Fox and others applied for an injunction under s 97A requiring BT to block access to the Newzbin2 website in *Twentieth Century Fox Film Corp* v *British Telecommunications Ltd*.[271] This was the first application against an internet service provider, as such. If successful, the claimants intended to apply for injunctions against other ISPs. BT was chosen for the first application as it was the UK's largest ISP. BT resisted the application. Arnold J granted the order in terms that BT should prevent its service being used by users and operators of the Newzbin websites. Some of key points made in the judgment were:

- Users were not just using the Newzbin website but were also using BT's service to obtain infringing copies of films.
- 'Actual knowledge' – regard must be had to the details of the infringement. The more information the service provider has, the more likely it has actual knowledge. It was relevant to consider knowledge:
  - of particular copyright works (or classes of works)
  - of particular restricted acts involved (or types of acts)
  - of particular persons (or groups of persons) involved.
  However, it was not essential to prove actual knowledge of the specific infringement of specific works by specific individuals.
- The term 'details of the infringement in question' in s 97A(2) should not be interpreted narrowly as that section states that, in determining actual knowledge, the court shall taken into account all matters which appear to it in the particular circumstances to be relevant and, amongst other things, shall have regard to . . . details of the infringement in question. Thus, whether the service provider has actual knowledge of specific details of particular infringements is not determinative of the question of actual knowledge.
- The Court of Justice ruling in Case 324/09 *L'Oréal SA* v *eBay International AG*[272] showed that an injunction in relation to an intellectual property right does not have to be limited to prevent a continuation of a proven infringement and can be wider so as to prevent future infringements.

267 The definition of service provider is given in the Electronic Commerce (EC Directive) Regulations 2002, SI 2002/2013. Unhelpfully, the definition of 'information society services' refers to a number of EU Directives.

268 Section 97A, inserted by the Copyright and Related Rights Regulations 2003, SI 2003/2498.

269 These Regulations implemented parts of Directive 2000/31/EC of the European Parliament and of the Council of 8 June 2000 on certain legal aspects of information society services, in particular electronic commerce, in the Internal Market, OJ L 178, 17.07.2000, p 1.

270 [2010] FSR 21 (p 512).

271 [2011] EWHC 1981 (Ch). Arnold J gave a long and thoughtful judgment covering numerous aspects of EU Directives (the e-commerce, information society and enforcement Directives) the Human Rights Act 1998 and the right of freedom of expression.

272 12 July 2011. This case is discussed in more detail in Chapter 22 (on trade mark rights, infringement etc.) and Chapter 24 (remedies).

Online infringement and the Digital Economy Act 2010

Injunctions are available against service providers under s 97A, as we have seen. Typically, such injunctions will require that service providers block or disable access to websites from which infringing material may be downloaded. The service provider must have 'actual knowledge' that a person is using its service to infringe copyright. As service providers are not under a general duty to monitor information they transmit where they act as a mere conduit or in respect of caching or hosting material,[273] the requirement for actual knowledge is an important one, as noted in the *Twentieth Century Fox* v *BT* case above.

Obtaining a court order to remove access to infringing material available online or to force internet service providers to block access to such material is an important remedy and, following the *BT* case, owners of copyrights in films and music are likely to apply for similar orders against other ISPs. However, it does not deal fully with all the issues. For example, it does not, *per se*, reveal the identity of persons involved in illegal file sharing or persistently downloading infringing material. In particular, copyright owners would like to identify such persons so that legal proceedings can be brought against them.[274]

The Digital Economy Act 2010 contains provisions aimed at tackling the problem of subscribers to internet services who routinely infringe copyright on a significant scale. The basic means of dealing with this problem is set out in ss 3–16 which insert ss 124A–124N into the Communications Act 2003. The fine detail will be set out in an initial obligations code which, in the absence of a code made by any person for the purpose of regulating the initial obligations approved by OFCOM, will be made by OFCOM itself.[275]

The basic mechanism envisaged by the new provisions is:

1 A copyright owner who considers a subscriber to an ISP has used the service to infringe his copyright (or has allowed another person to use his access service to infringe copyright) may submit a copyright infringement report ('CIR') to the ISP.[276] The CIR will include details and evidence of the apparent infringement, including the subscribers IP address (this alone does not give the identity of the subscriber).

2 The ISP then notifies the subscriber within one month. The notification must include information about the apparent infringement and subscriber appeals. The notification must also include information about copyright and its purpose, advice or information about how to obtain advice as to lawful access to copyright works and how to protect his service against unauthorised use. Further information may be required to be given under the initial obligations code (this may include, for example, a statement that the copyright owner may apply for a court order to discover the subscriber's identity and may bring proceedings against him). ISPs are to keep copyright infringement lists of subscribers who receive multiple unchallenged CIRs.

3 If the copyright owner so requests, the ISP must send a copyright infringement list for the period specified which sets out in relation to each subscriber which of the CIRs relate to that subscriber, without identifying the subscribers, where the CIRs have reached a threshold set out in the initial obligations code.

4 Armed with an anonymised infringement list, a copyright owner may wish to apply to the court for a *Norwich Pharmacal* order[277] to discover the identity of the infringing subscriber or subscribers. If the order is granted, the copyright owner may then decide to bring infringement proceedings against that subscriber or those subscribers. It appears from the draft initial obligations code that a 'three strikes' regime will apply before an application will be made for a court order for disclosure of the identity of the subscriber.[278]

The basic mechanism is set out in simplified form in Figure 6.1 (overleaf).

273 See Articles 12 to 15 of Directive 2000/31/EC of the European Parliament and of the Council of 8 June 2000 on certain legal aspects of information society services, in particular electronic commerce, in the Internal Market, L 178, 17.07.2000, p 1. These provisions apply to illegal information generally and not just copyright infringement. A 'cache' is a temporary electronic store.

274 Many of those involved in file sharing and other forms of online infringement are private individuals, but the publicity of successful court proceedings could have a chilling effect on others.

275 Section 124E of the Communications Act 2003 set out the criteria for the code. At the time of writing no initial obligations code has been approved or made by OFCOM. A draft code was made by OFCOM during 2010 for a consultation period which closed on 30 July 2010. The consultation document including the draft code is available at: http://stakeholders. ofcom.org.uk/binaries/ consultations/copyright-infringement/summary/condoc. pdf. The code is subject to approval of Parliament and the EU (Standards and Technical Regulations) Committee.

276 If an initial obligations code is in force and permits the submission of a CIR by the copyright owner. A number of the steps described assume that an initial obligations code is in force and permits the particular step to be taken.

277 An order for the discovery of information, for example, about the infringement and the identity of persons involved, from the House of Lords case of *Norwich Pharmacal* v *Customs and Excise Commissioners* [1974] AC 133. For Scotland, provision for discovery is made under reg 4 of the Intellectual Property (Enforcement, etc.) Regulations 2006, SI 2006/1028. The test in whether the disclosure would be just and proportionate (Article 8 of Directive 2004/48/EC of the European Parliament and of the Council of 29 April 2004 on the enforcement of intellectual property rights, OJ L 195, 02.06.2004, p 16).

278 That is, three notifications sent to the subscriber in a 12-month period.

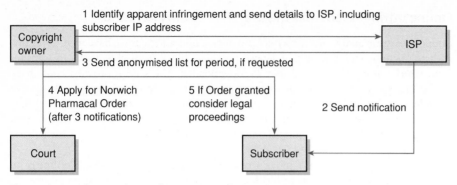

Figure 6.1 Tacking online infringement – basic procedure

The Digital Economy Act 2010 contains provisions allowing the Secretary of State to make an Order[279] setting out technical obligations to be imposed on ISPs to take technological measures against some or all relevant subscribers, being those in respect of which CIRs have reached the threshold set out in the initial obligations code. Technical measures may be needed if, for example, the basic mechanism fails to deliver a sufficient reduction in online infringement. The measures are controversial and could include action to limit the speed or capacity of the service provided to a subscriber; to prevent or limit access to particular material by that subscriber or, even, to suspend the subscriber's service or limit it in some other way. For example, the measures may include bandwidth capping or shaping, making file sharing or downloading large files difficult. Suspension of a subscriber's service is even more controversial and could be seen as being contrary to the rights of privacy and freedom of expression.

British Telecom and TalkTalk Telecom challenged the online infringement or copyright provisions of the Digital Economy Act 2010 on numerous grounds in *R (on application of British Telecom) v Secretary of State for Business, Innovation and Skills*.[280] The challenge was based on numerous EU Directives, general principles of EU law, the Human Rights Act 1998 and the Convention rights of privacy and freedom of expression. The only successful challenge was in relation to the costs provisions under which ISPs would be required to pay 25 per cent of the costs of OFCOM in the exercise of its duties under the Act. This was held to be unlawful, being contrary to Article 12 of the Authorisation Directive.[281] This means that the draft Online Infringement of Copyright (Initial Obligations)(Sharing of Costs) Order 2011 will have to be scrapped and the costs regime revisited.

Section 17 of the Digital Economy Act 2010 allows the Secretary of State to make regulations enabling the court to grant a blocking injunction, requiring an ISP to prevent its service being used to access a site from which a substantial amount of infringing material have been or is likely to be obtained or made available. This also extends to sites from which access to other sites from which a substantial amount of infringing material have been or is likely to be obtained or made available. This extends the potential use of blocking injunctions beyond that available to copyright owners under s 97A of the Copyright, Designs and Patents Act 1988.

Where a copyright owner of an ISP is in contravention of either the initial obligations code or technical obligations code (if one is made) the maximum penalty, payable to OFCOM, is £250,000.

One difficulty with the CIR and notification procedures and the use of technological measures is in respect of shared access through a single subscriber, for example, where cafés, hotels, restaurants, public houses, clubs and so on provide wi-fi internet access for customers, members or others. Some train operators also provide wi-fi internet access. Most employers have internet access, used by employees. It will prove almost impossible or at

279 After the Secretary of State directs OFCOM to report of whether technical obligations should be imposed and, if so, to take steps to prepare for such obligations including making a Technical Obligations Code.

280 [2011] EWHC 1021 (Admin).

281 Directive 2002/20/EC of the European Parliament and of the Council of 7 March 2002 on the authorisation of electronic communications networks and services OJ L 108, 24.04.2002, p 21 as amended by Directive 2009/140/EC of the European Parliament and of the Council of 25 November 2009 amending Directives 2002/21/EC on a common regulatory framework for electronic communications networks and services, 2002/19/EC on access to, and interconnection of, electronic communications networks and associated facilities, and 2002/20/EC on the authorisation of electronic communications networks and services OJ L 337, 18.12.2009, p 37.

least quite onerous for the wi-fi subscriber to police how the service is being used by individuals. Furthermore, any form of policing could be seen as intrusive and an interference with an individual's right of privacy. Even individual subscribers using wireless broadband may be vulnerable under the online infringement provisions. Other persons in the vicinity could misuse their internet access, although subscribers can at least try to ensure their security is strong and effective. However, this does not completely eliminate the risk as computer and internet security is always vulnerable to determined and skilled hackers.

Another concern about the online infringement provisions of the Digital Economy Act 2010 is that they are home grown and not the result of EU legislation. Perhaps the UK has 'jumped the gun' in this respect and it might have been better to wait for a harmonising EU Directive.[282]

At the present time, legislation in Ireland does not give a court the power to force disclosure of subscribers to ISPs who regularly download infringing material. This was noted, with some regret, by Charleton J in *EMI Records (Ireland) Ltd* v *UPC Communications Ireland Ltd*[283] in refusing to grant an injunction against the defendant ISP which had refused to block certain subscribers using peer-to-peer software to download infringing material. He also refused to grant a blocking injunction requiring the ISP to block access to the Pirate Bay website, again because Irish legislation did not provide for such a remedy.

Delivery up

Under s 99, upon application by the copyright owner, a court may order that infringing copies, or articles designed or adapted for making copies of the copyright owner's work, are delivered up to him or such other person as the court may direct.[284] Delivery up is available where a person has an infringing copy of the work in his possession, custody or control in the course of a business, or has in his possession, custody or control an article specifically designed or adapted for making copies of a particular copyright work. In relation to articles, there is an added requirement that the person knows or has reason to believe that the article has been or is to be used to make infringing copies.

There is a time limit which applies to applications for delivery up, as provided under s 113, which corresponds to limitation of actions. Under s 113(1) the time limit is six years from the time the infringing copy or article was made. However, this may be extended if the copyright owner had been under a disability (for example, a minor or person of unsound mind) as in the Limitation Act 1980.[285] Another cause for extension of the period is if the copyright owner is prevented by fraud or concealment from discovering the facts entitling him to apply for the order.

A further requirement before an order for delivery up can be made is that the court also makes, or it appears to the court that there are grounds for making, an order under the Copyright, Designs and Patents Act 1988 s 114, being an order for the disposal of the infringing copies or other articles. The order may state that the infringing copies or other articles be forfeited to the copyright owner or destroyed, or otherwise dealt with as the court thinks fit, but the court shall consider whether other available remedies would be adequate to compensate the copyright owner and protect his interests. If more than one person has an interest in the copy or other article, the court may order that the copy or other article be sold and the proceeds divided accordingly. Other persons who may have an interest include owners of performing rights or registered designs.[286] If the order under s 114 is not made immediately, the person to whom the infringing copies or other articles are delivered shall retain them pending the making of the order. If a decision is taken not to make an order under s 114, the items are to be delivered to the person who had them in his possession, custody or control immediately before being delivered up.[287] Rarely will it be necessary, or even desirable, to deliver up offending articles to the copyright owner

282 Section 97A on injunctions against service providers was, of course, a result of EU law.

283 [2011] ECC 8 (p 82).

284 The order is not based upon any notion that the property in the copies has passed to the claimants: *see Chappell & Co Ltd* v *Columbia Graphophone Co* [1914] 2 Ch 745 at 756 per Swinfen Eady LJ.

285 *See* Limitation Act 1980 s 38. In Scotland, disability means legal disability within the meaning of the Prescription and Limitation (Scotland) Act 1973 and, in Northern Ireland, has the same meaning as in the Statute of Limitations (Northern Ireland) 1958.

286 s 114(6).

287 Copyright, Designs and Patents Act 1988 s 114(5).

– he will normally be fairly compensated by the other remedies. However, an order for destruction of the offending articles under s 114 is a likely proposition, for example, in circumstances where the defendant has a stock of pirate video tapes in his possession.

Presumptions

The 1988 Act provides for certain presumptions which will apply in proceedings for copyright infringement for the purposes of facilitating those proceedings. Given that copyright can endure for a considerable period of time, some presumptions as to the identity of the author, director or publisher of the work are also helpful. Presumptions are made in terms of three classes of works:

(a) literary, dramatic, musical and artistic works (s 104);
(b) sound recordings, films and computer programs (s 105);
(c) works subject to Crown copyright (s 106).

Presumptions relating to literary, dramatic, musical and artistic works

Where a name purporting to be that of the author appeared on copies of the work as published or on the work when it was made, the person by that name shall be presumed to be the author of the work and to have been the first owner of the copyright in the work.[288] That is, the work was not made in circumstances relating to employees in the course of employment, Crown or parliamentary copyright or copyright of certain international organisations.[289] Similar presumptions apply in the case of works of joint authorship. Even where the identity of the owner is not in dispute, the identity of the author is important for establishing the duration of the copyright and, possibly, its territorial scope.

Where there is no name purporting to be that of the author on copies of the work then, under s 104(4), if the work otherwise qualifies for copyright protection by reference to the country of first publication[290] and a name purporting to be that of the publisher appeared on copies of the work as first published, then that named publisher shall be presumed to have been the owner of the copyright at the time of publication.[291] Although this deals with the question of ownership of the copyright, the identity of the author is still important and s 104(5) provides that if the author is dead, or his identity cannot be ascertained by reasonable enquiry, it shall be presumed in the absence of evidence to the contrary that the work is an original work and the claimant's allegations as to what was the first publication of the work and as to the country of first publication are correct. Therefore, in all these matters, if the defendant wishes to challenge any of them, it is he who bears the evidential burden; he must adduce evidence to the contrary. Of course, in many actions for infringement, the defendant will not wish to dispute these matters, but may base his defence on another point: for example, that he has not, in the circumstances, copied a substantial part of the work. Although the Act recognises the subsistence of copyright in literary, dramatic, musical and artistic works that are computer-generated, there are no presumptions specifically directed to such works.

Presumptions relating to sound recordings, films and computer programs

Computer programs are literary works, so the presumptions relating to literary works above apply in addition to the presumption in s 105.[292] In the case of sound recordings,

288 Copyright, Designs and Patents Act 1988 s 104(2).

289 This presumption was used in *Noah* v *Shuba* [1991] FSR 14 and the defendant was unable to adduce evidence to rebut it.

290 By virtue of the Copyright, Designs and Patents Act 1988 s 155.

291 For an example, under the 1956 Act, *see Waterlow Publishers Ltd* v *Rose* [1995] FSR 207. In that case the presumption was not rebutted.

292 Interestingly, the heading to the Copyright, Designs and Patents Act 1988 s 105 does not mention computer programs, even though they are specifically dealt with in s 105(3).

where copies are issued to the public bearing a label or other mark stating that a named person was the owner of the copyright in the recording at the date of issue of the copies, or that the recording was first published in a specified year or in a specified country, that label or mark shall be admissible as evidence of the facts stated, and shall be presumed to be correct until the contrary is proved.[293] Similar provisions apply in respect of films where copies are issued to the public bearing statements as to the director or producer of the film, the owner of the copyright in the film, and the year and country of first publication: s 105(2).

Where, under s 105(3), computer programs are issued to the public in electronic form bearing a statement that a named person was the copyright owner at the date of issue, or that the program was first published in a specified country or that copies were first issued to the public in electronic form in a specified year, that statement is also admissible as evidence of the facts stated and shall be presumed to be correct until the contrary is proved.

The utility of this presumption was seen in *Microsoft Corp v Electro-wide Ltd*.[294] The claimant applied for summary judgment under the former Rules of the Supreme Court 1965, Ord 14 in respect of an allegation that the defendant was selling computers loaded with unlicensed copies of the claimant's MS-DOS and Windows software. The defendant argued that discovery might show some hitherto defect in the claimant's title to the copyright. This argument was described by Laddie J, in granting summary judgment, as an unfounded and Micawberish hope. He said that it would be wholly improbable that a company the size of Microsoft, which was clearly alert to the importance of copyright protection, would fail to take the elementary precautions necessary to ensure that it owned the copyrights in its major assets.

All these presumptions apply equally to infringements alleged to have occurred before the date on which the copies were first issued to the public.

A final presumption in s 105 concerns the showing in public or communication to the public of a film and s 105(5) provides that if the film bears a statement:

(a)   that a named person was the director or producer of the film; or

(aa)   that a named person was the principal director of the film, the author of the screenplay, the author of the dialogue or the composer of music specifically created for and used in the film; or

(b)   that a named person was the owner of the copyright in the film immediately after it was made.

then that statement shall be admissible as evidence of the facts stated and shall be presumed to be correct until the contrary is proved.

This presumption applies equally in proceedings relating to an infringement alleged to have occurred before the date on which the film was shown in public, broadcast or included in a cable programme service. For the purposes of s 105, a statement that a person was the director of a film shall be taken, unless a contrary intention appears, as meaning that he was the principal director of the film.

Presumptions relevant to Crown copyright

The final presumption is contained in s 106 and relates to literary, dramatic and musical works in which Crown copyright subsists. Where there appears on printed copies of a work a statement of the year in which the work was first published commercially, that statement shall be admissible as evidence of that fact and presumed correct until the contrary is proven.

293 Copyright, Designs and Patents Act 1988 s 105(1). Under the Copyright Act 1956 s 12(6), sound recordings had to be date-stamped to qualify for copyright protection. This is no longer essential, but it is obviously prudent to attach a copyright notice including the year of publication as this fixes would-be infringers with knowledge of the subsistence of copyright and may be important in terms of the availability of damages.

294 [1997] FSR 580.

Criminal offences

The Copyright, Designs and Patents Act 1988, in line with the Copyright Act 1956, makes provision for certain criminal offences associated with copyright infringement. The seriousness with which certain forms of piracy are now taken, often involving organised crime and money-laundering, has been met by a substantial increase in the maximum penalties now available for the copyright offences. For many of the offences, the maximum term of imprisonment is now ten years. The changes were made by the Copyright, etc. and Trade Marks (Offences and Enforcement) Act 2002 and came into force on 20 November 2002.[295] The maximum fine for some of the offences on summary conviction was raised to £50,000 by s 42 of the Digital Economy Act 2010.[296] Curiously, the maximum term of imprisonment for summary conviction for some of the offences (though not all) has been reduced from six months to three months.[297] The Copyright Act 1956 did not provide for imprisonment at all until amended in the 1980s to provide for a maximum of two years' imprisonment and/or a fine on conviction on indictment.[298] This maximum was continued under the 1988 Act until amended by the 2002 Act.[299] It may be of some concern that the *mens rea* for the criminal offences is the same as used for secondary infringement, that is, knowing or having reason to believe. Although this could bring the provisions into conflict with the right to a fair trial under Article 6 of the Council of Europe Convention for the Protection of Human Rights and Fundamental Freedoms 1950, the House of Lords ruled otherwise in relation to the trade mark offences where the standard appears even more harsh on the defendant.[300]

Although it would be reasonable to assume that the criminal offences are suitable only for copyright pirates, there is nothing in the wording of the provisions to so limit them. In *Thames & Hudson Ltd* v *Design and Artists Copyright Society Ltd*[301] the Design and Artists Copyright Society (DACS) served summonses under s 107 of the 1988 Act on a reputable publishing company and on its directors, who now applied to have the prosecutions stayed as being vexatious and an abuse of process. The application was unsuccessful. Evans-Lombe J said (at 160):

> Parliament has elected to provide that breach of copyright can in certain circumstances constitute an offence and that where such an offence is committed by a body corporate the directors of that body corporate who connive at such commission are themselves guilty of an offence. No qualification appears in the statute limiting the types of offender capable of committing the offence to 'pirates'.

In this case, because DACS did not take an assignment of copyright from its members, there was no other way in which it could protect its members' interests.

The criminal offences reflect very closely the secondary infringements of copyright, but there are some omissions. For example, there is no equivalent criminal penalty for the secondary infringement of permitting the use of premises for an infringing performance of a literary, dramatic or musical work. Conversely, the criminal offence of making copies for sale or hire relates to the act restricted by copyright of copying and not a secondary infringement.

The offences are not of strict liability and an element of *mens rea* is required, and this mitigates the harshness of making directors of respectable companies potentially liable for infringement under criminal law. Thus, for a person to be guilty of any of the offences he must possess actual knowledge, or have reason to believe that copyright would be infringed or that he was, for example, dealing with infringing copies.

There was soon evidence that magistrates and judges were prepared to take piracy and counterfeiting of copyright works seriously. For example, in *R* v *Carter*[302] the Court of Appeal confirmed a sentence of imprisonment of nine months suspended for two years

295 The Copyright, etc. and Trade Marks (Offences and Enforcement) Act 2002 (Commencement) Order 2002, SI 2002/2749.

296 With effect from 8 June 2010.

297 Reg 5 of the Copyright, Designs and Patents Act 1988 (Amendment) Regulations 2010, SI 2010/2694.

298 By the ridiculously titled 'Copyright Act 1956 (Amendment) Act 1982' and the Copyright (Amendment) Act 1983.

299 Equivalent increases were made in relation to offences under the Trade Marks Act 1994.

300 This case, *R* v *Johnstone* [2003] FSR 42 (p 748), is discussed in Part Six of the book.

301 [1995] FSR 153.

302 [1993] FSR 303.

for a conviction of making and distributing infringing copies of video films contrary to s 107. It was observed that such an activity was really an offence of dishonesty. The offences are contained in s 107 of the 1988 Act, as amended, and are set out below.

Making, dealing, etc. (s 107(1))

A person commits an offence who, without the licence of the copyright owner:

(a) makes for sale or hire; or

(b) imports into the UK otherwise than for his private and domestic use; or

(c) possesses in the course of a business with a view to committing any act infringing the copyright; or

(d) in the course of a business –
   (i) sells or lets for hire, or
   (ii) offers or exposes for sale or hire, or
   (iii) exhibits in public, or
   (iv) distributes, or

(e) distributes otherwise than in the course of business to such an extent as to affect prejudicially the owner of the copyright;

an article which is, and which he knows or has reason to believe is, an infringing copy of a copyright work.

These activities are all commercial in nature with the exception of (e), which would apply, for example, to the situation where a private individual makes a large number of copies of a copyright work and distributes them freely, perhaps acting out of misguided social, political or moral beliefs. Some of the offences in this category are triable either way, that is they can be tried either in the Crown Court or in a magistrates' court. These are the offences relating to making, importing or distributing (whether or not in the course of a business).[303] The maximum penalty available if tried in a Crown Court is a term of imprisonment not exceeding ten years, or a fine or both.[304] There is no upper limit on the fines which can be imposed by the Crown Court. If the offence is tried in a magistrates' court, the maximum penalty is six months' imprisonment, or a fine not exceeding £50,000,[305] or both. All the other offences are triable summarily only, that is in a magistrates' court, and carry a maximum of three months' imprisonment,[306] or a fine not exceeding level 5 on the standard scale (presently £5,000) or both.[307]

For some of the offences, namely (c) and (d) above, there is a specific requirement that they were committed in the course of a business. The meaning of this might be important if the person involved has other legitimate full-time employment and is carrying out his infringing activities in his spare time or as a hobby. However, it would appear that, in terms of the Trade Descriptions Act 1968, for goods to be dealt with in the course of a trade or business, there must be a degree of regularity in such dealing as part of the normal practice of a business.[308] It would appear, therefore, that if the person involved was carrying out the offending activities on a regular basis, it would be considered that he was operating in the course of a business, even if he was doing it in his spare time. However, if the person did whatever it was, regardless of the scale, as a one-off activity, there would be no regularity, and it would appear that the relevant offences would not apply.

Articles specifically designed or adapted to make copies (s 107(2))

A person commits an offence if he makes an article specifically designed or adapted for making copies of a particular copyright work, or has such an article in his possession knowing or having reason to believe that it is to be used to make infringing copies for sale or hire or for use in the course of a business. This would include making a plate for printing

303 Section 107(1)(a), (b), (d) (iv) or (e).

304 Increased from two years by the Copyright, etc. and Trade Marks (Offences and Enforcement) Act 2002. There was a move to increase the maximum penalties to bring them in line with those already available for the trade mark offences. A Bill which would have increased the maximum term of imprisonment for copyright offences to seven years failed to complete its passage through Parliament in 2000 (Copyright and Trade Marks Bill 2000).

305 Increased form the statutory maximum by s 42 of the Digital Economy Act 2010.

306 Previously six months: reduced to three months by the Copyright, Designs and Patents Act 1988 (Amendment) Regulations 2010, SI 2010/2694.

307 The penalties are laid out in the Copyright, Designs and Patents Act 1988 s 107(4) and (5).

308 *See Davies v Sumner* [1984] 1 WLR 1301, adapting the test laid down in *Havering London Borough v Stevenson* [1970] 3 All ER 609.

artistic works, or a master copy of a sound recording from which many duplicates could be made. The offence applies only if the article is intended to be used for making copies of a particular copyright work and not for copying works generally. Therefore, the manufacture or possession of a dual cassette tape deck is not caught, as it is not intended to be used to copy a particular work but may be used to copy all sorts of works (some of which may be copied legitimately). The offence is triable summarily only and carries a maximum of three months' imprisonment, or fine not exceeding level 5 on the standard scale or both.

Communication to the public

This offence was inserted by the Copyright and Related Rights Regulations 2003. Under s 107(2A), a person commits an offence if they infringe copyright by communicating a work to the public in the course of business or otherwise than in the course of business to such an extent as to affect prejudicially the copyright owner, knowing or having reason to believe that, by doing so, he is infringing the copyright in the work. This will cover, for example, broadcasting the work or placing it on an internet website from where it may be accessed. Section 107(4A) provides that the offence is triable either way and, on conviction in a magistrates' court, the maximum penalty is a term of imprisonment not exceeding three months and/or a fine not exceeding £50,000. The maximum penalty if convicted on indictment is a term of imprisonment not exceeding two years and/or a fine. It seems strange that the opportunity was not taken to make the maximum penalty ten years' imprisonment as with the equivalent offence in s 107(1) (distributing to the public). Certainly, placing a work on a website could result in infringement on a very large scale.

Public performances, etc. (s 107(3))

This applies where copyright is infringed, otherwise than by the reception of a communication to the public, by a public performance of a literary, dramatic or musical work, or by the playing or showing in public of a sound recording or film. Any person who caused the work to be so performed, played or shown is guilty of an offence if he knew or had reason to believe that copyright would be infringed. The person who caused the work to be performed, played or shown will normally be the person who made the arrangements necessary and organised the performance. It is unlikely that a person who supplies the equipment necessary or provides the premises will be deemed to be the person 'causing'. Of course, such persons may be charged with being accomplices. An offence under this subsection carries a maximum of three months' imprisonment, or a fine not exceeding level 5 on the standard scale or both, being triable summarily only.

For all the offences in s 107, the presumptions in ss 104 to 106 do not apply to criminal proceedings but this is without prejudice to their application in proceedings for an order for delivery up under s 108.[309]

309 Section 107(6).

Liability of officers of corporate bodies

By virtue of s 110, where an offence under s 107 has been committed by a corporate body, for example a limited company, and it is proved that the offence was committed with the consent or connivance of a director, manager, secretary or other similar officer of the body, then that person is also guilty of the offence and is liable to be prosecuted.[310] This also applies to persons holding themselves out to act in such a capacity. Therefore, in the case of an offence by a corporate body, there may be two prosecutions: one against the body itself and another against a high-ranking officer of the body who has been implicated in the offending conduct. This is to prevent persons hiding behind a corporate identity in order to escape prosecution. Normally, in terms of vicarious liability in criminal law, the

310 Criminal proceedings were initiated against directors of a reputable publishing company in *Thames & Hudson Ltd v Design and Artists Copyright Society Ltd* [1995] FSR 153.

action of a high-ranking officer of the company will be deemed to be the action of the company, thereby fixing the corporate body with liability.[311] Therefore, there should be no difficulty in a finding of corporate guilt if the activity complained of has been done under the instructions or guidance of a director or company secretary, but there would be difficulty in attaching liability to the individual concerned and this provision in the Act overcomes that problem.

Search warrants, delivery up and forfeiture

Search warrants are available under s 109[312] and now extend to all types of copyright work. Search warrants can be obtained by a constable from a justice of the peace if the latter is satisfied by information given on oath by the constable that there are reasonable grounds for believing that any of the triable either-way offences under s 107 have been committed or are about to be committed and that evidence of this is on the premises to which the search warrant will apply. The warrant will authorise the constable to enter and search the premises using such reasonable force as is necessary. The warrant remains in force for three months[313] and may authorise persons to accompany the constable in his execution of the warrant. Until 31 October 2003, warrants were not available for the offences that were triable summarily only. The Copyright and Related Rights Regulations 2003 changed this and extended the availability of search warrants to all offences including the new offence under s 107(2A). Of course, evidence required to secure a conviction for any of the offences may in most circumstances be obtained in other ways, for example by simply purchasing an infringing copy which is openly on sale. In exercising his duties under the warrant, a constable may seize any article he reasonably believes to be evidence that an offence under s 107(1), (2) or (2A) has been or is about to be committed. The word 'premises' in the context of search warrants includes land, buildings, fixed or moveable structures, vehicles, vessels, aircraft and hovercraft.

Section 107A was inserted by the Criminal Justice and Public Order Act 1994, s 165 and provided that local weights and measures authorities would be given duties and powers in relation to offences under s 107 as they have under the Trade Descriptions Act 1968.[314] These would include making test purchases and powers of entry and seizure. Obstructing an authorised officer is an offence, and there are provisions for compensation for loss of goods wrongly seized. It is likely that trading standards officers will make significant use of these provisions, and the enactment of them is further evidence that Parliament now takes copyright piracy seriously. However, s 107A has not yet been brought into force.

The Copyright, Designs and Patents Act 1988 s 108 also provides for delivery up in criminal proceedings similar in nature to the civil delivery up provisions under s 99. An order for delivery up may be made by the court before which the proceedings are brought if it is satisfied at the time the accused was arrested or charged that:

1 he had in his possession, custody or control in the course of a business an infringing copy of the work; or
2 he had in his possession, custody or control an article specifically designed or adapted for making copies of a particular copyright work, knowing or having reason to believe that it had been or was to be used to make infringing copies.

The order may be made by the court on its own motion or on the application of the prosecutor, irrespective of whether the accused is convicted of the offence with which he was charged. The provisions contained in s 113 (limitation period) and s 114 (order as to disposal) also apply to delivery up in criminal proceedings. The general provisions as to forfeiture contained in the Powers of Criminal Courts (Sentencing) Act 2000 s 143 are unaffected.[315]

311 *See* the judgment of Lord Denning MR in *HL Bolton (Engineering) Co Ltd* v *TJ Graham & Sons Ltd* [1957] 1 QB 159 at 172.

312 Search warrants were first provided for by the Copyright Act 1956 s 21A, an amendment made by the Copyright (Amendment) Act 1983.

313 Increased from 28 days by para 6 Sch 16 Serious Organised Crime and Police Act 2005.

314 The relevant provisions are the Trade Descriptions Act 1968 ss 27–29 and 33.

315 Of course, there are some differences in terms of search, seizure and delivery up in Scotland and Northern Ireland, but the overall effect is generally the same.

The Act contains some controls over the importation of infringing copies along the lines of the previous Act. Section 111 extends the class of prohibited goods to infringing copies of literary, dramatic and musical works (printed copies of these three types of works) and sound recordings and films. The Commissioners of Customs and Excise must be given notice in writing by the copyright owner to the effect that he is the copyright owner. As regards literary, dramatic and musical works, the notice must also specify the period, not exceeding five years or beyond the duration of the copyright, for which the printed copies are to be treated as prohibited goods. For sound recordings and films the action is pre-emptive in nature and the notice must also specify the time and place at which the infringing copies are expected to arrive and that the copyright owner requests the Commissioners to treat the copies as prohibited goods.[316] The provisions only apply in respect of infringing copies imported from outside the EEA or from within the EEA but not having been entered for free circulation.[317]

The Copyright, etc. and Trade Marks (Offences and Enforcement) Act 2002 inserted a new s 114A which provides for forfeiture of infringing copies.[318] Where infringing copies or articles specifically designed or adapted for making copies of a particular copyright work have come into the possession of any person connected with the investigation or prosecution of a relevant offence (being one under s 107(1), (2) or (2A), under the Trade Descriptions Act 1968, the Business Protection from Misleading Marketing Regulations 2008,[319] the Consumer Protection from Unfair Trading Regulations 2008[320] or any offence involving dishonesty or deception), that person may apply for an order for forfeiture of the infringing copies or articles. A court may make such an order only if satisfied that a relevant offence has been committed in relation to the infringing copies or articles. It is acceptable if the court is satisfied that the offence has been committed in relation to copies or articles which are representative of the infringing copies or articles in question, whether they are of the same design or part of the same consignment or batch or otherwise. Any person aggrieved by an order made or refused by a magistrates' court may appeal to the Crown Court (or county court in Northern Ireland). The court may delay the coming into force of the order pending the making and determination of an appeal. Where an order for forfeiture is made, the copies or article shall be destroyed according to directions given by the court. Alternatively, the court may direct that the infringing copies or articles are forfeit to the copyright owner or dealt with in such other way as the court directs. A copyright owner may wish to obtain infringing copies of his work if the standard of the copies is high and equivalent to the standard of copies made by or authorised to be made by the copyright owner.

Other offences

A person infringing copyright (and, for that matter, infringing a trade mark or a patent) may commit criminal offences other than those contained in the part of the Copyright, Designs and Patents Act 1988 dealing with copyright. For example, there may be an offence of under the Consumer Protection from Unfair Trading Regulations 2008.[321] A trader commits an offence if he engages in a commercial practice which is a misleading action or omission. This could be where a trader falsely claims that a copy of a work is a legitimate copy.

There may be offences under s 1 of the Fraud Act 2006, for example, fraud by false representation. A person is guilty of this offence if he dishonestly makes a representation intending by doing so to make a gain for himself or another or to cause loss to another or expose another to a risk of loss.[322] A representation can be implied or express. For example, simply displaying counterfeit film DVDs in a stall at a market can fall within the offence. Possession of articles for use in frauds and making or supplying articles for use in frauds are also offences under ss 6 and 7 of the Act. Being in possession carries a

316 The Copyright, Designs and Patents Act 1988 s 112 gives power to the Commissioners of Customs and Excise to make regulations concerning the service of notices, payment of fees, providing, securing and indemnifying the Commissioners against liability or expense as regards the detention of the articles or things done to the articles in consequence of the notice.

317 Section 111(3A). Where the situation is within Article 1(1) of Council Regulation (EC) No 1383/2003 of 22 July 2003 concerning customs actions against goods suspected of infringing certain intellectual property rights and the measures to be taken against goods found to have infringed such rights, OJ L 196, 02.08.2003, p 7, s 111 does not apply. Article 1(1) covers goods entering for free circulation, export or re-export.

318 Section 114A applies to England and Wales and Northern Ireland; s 114B applies to Scotland.

319 SI 2008/1276.

320 SI 2008/1277.

321 SI 2008/1277. These Regulations implement Directive 2005/29/EC of the European Parliament and of the Council concerning unfair business-to-consumer commercial practices, OJ L 149, 11.06.2005, p 22. Numerous provisions of the Trade Descriptions Act 1968 were repealed by the Regulations which came into force on 26 May 2008.

322 Fraud Act 2006 s 2. Fraud under s 1 carries a maximum penalty of 10 years' imprisonment and/or a fine on conviction on indictment.

maximum of five years' imprisonment and/or a fine on conviction on indictment whilst making or supplying articles for use in frauds carries a maximum of 10 years' imprisonment and/or a fine on conviction on indictment. 'Article' includes any program or data held in electronic form. Thus, unauthorised copies of computer software will fall into this meaning. It is clear that pirate CDs and DVDs are also within the meaning of article as will a master copy from which pirate copies can be made.

Another offence that could be charged is forgery under the Forgery and Counterfeiting Act 1981, s 1 of which states that a person is guilty of forgery if he makes a false instrument, with the intention that he or another shall use it to induce somebody to accept it as genuine, and by reason of so accepting it, to do or not to do some act to his own or any other person's prejudice. It is also an offence to use a false instrument in such a way. Under s 8 of the 1981 Act, a false instrument includes any 'disc, tape, sound track or other device on or in which information is recorded or stored by mechanical, electronic or other means'. This definition would include sound recordings, films, computer programs and other copyright works stored in or on computer storage media, such as a copy of a computer database. Also covered would be a copy of a work such as the *Encyclopaedia Britannica* stored on CD-ROM discs. However, again there may be problems associated with whether a person would be induced to accept the article as genuine.

If legitimate copies of the original copyright work have a registered trade mark attached to them, anyone making infringing copies who also attaches a sign to his infringing copies, which is identical to, or likely to be mistaken for, the registered mark without permission of the proprietor of the trade mark, may commit an offence under the Trade Marks Act 1994 s 92. This offence is triable either way and carries a maximum penalty, if tried on indictment in the Crown Court, of imprisonment for a term not exceeding ten years, or a fine or both.

It does not appear to be possible to steal a copyright by making copies because the owner of the copyright will still have the original.[323] The copyright owner has not been permanently deprived of the copyright and can still make and license the making of copies. The fact that the copyright owner has been deprived of some of the potential income from the work is not sufficient for theft. In *R v Lloyd*,[324] a projectionist at a cinema, in league with some other persons, surreptitiously removed films from the cinema for a few hours so that they could be copied. The infringing (pirated) copies of the films were then sold, making a considerable profit for the video pirates. It was held that a charge of conspiracy to steal was inappropriate. Obviously, there was no intention to permanently deprive the owners of the films, neither was the copyright in the films stolen. Although borrowing sometimes can be regarded as theft if the period and circumstances are equivalent to an outright taking or disposal, by the Theft Act 1968 s 6(1), this would apply only if the 'goodness' or 'virtue' in the borrowed article had been exhausted by the time it was returned. An example is where a person borrows a radio battery intending to return it when its power is expended, or where a person borrows a football pass intending to return it to the rightful owner at the end of the football season. But in the case of the films, there was still virtue in them when they were returned; they were still capable of being used and shown to paying audiences, so the convictions were quashed. The fact that the owner of the copyright in the films had been deprived of potential 'sales' of the films by the circulation of pirate copies was not relevant to the offence of theft.

Whether copyright can be stolen in any circumstances is a moot point.[325] For the purposes of the offence of theft, defined as the dishonest appropriation of property belonging to another with the intention of depriving the other of it permanently,[326] 'property' is defined as including money and all other property, real or personal, including things in action and other intangible property.[327] Theoretically theft of copyright is a possibility because copyright, certainly in the context of the acts restricted by the copyright in the work, is a form of intangible property[328] and thus falls within the meaning of 'property'.

323 *See Oxford v Moss* (1978) 68 Cr App R 183.

324 [1985] 2 All ER 661.

325 It is unlikely because the owner will not usually have been deprived of the right.

326 Theft Act 1968 s 1.

327 Theft Act 1968 s 4(1).

328 It seems that copyright is not a thing in action: *see* Chapter 1.

However, the question really hinges on whether the owner has been permanently deprived of the copyright.

Summary

The owner of the copyright subsisting in a work has the exclusive right to:

- copy the work;
- issue copies of the work to the public;
- rent or lend the work to the public;
- perform, show or play the work in public;
- communicate the work to the public;
- make an adaptation of the work or do any of the above in relation to an adaptation.

The Act fleshes out the meaning of the above acts, known as the acts restricted by the copyright. For example, for the original works, copying means reproducing the work in a material form which includes storing the work in any medium by electronic means. Furthermore, copying extends to copies which are transient or incidental to some other use of the work.

Copyright is infringed by anyone who:

- does or authorises the performance of one or more of the above acts;
- directly or indirectly;
- in relation to the whole or a substantial part of the work;
- without the licence of the copyright owner.

What is a substantial part of a work is usually more a question of quality rather than quantity. In terms of the original, works of copyright (literary, dramatic, musical or artistic works) and, possibly, films, can be assessed by considering whether the part taken can be seen as an intellectual creation.

In terms of copying, particular difficulties are in relation to altered copying and non-literal (non-textual) copying.

Note that the restricted acts of copying and issuing copies to the public apply to all forms of copyright work whereas the other restricted acts are limited to only some of the works of copyright. For example, communication to the public does not apply to typographical arrangements of published editions and making an adaptation applies only to literary, dramatic and musical works.

Infringement by authorisation can apply even though the person authorising the performance of the restricted act is outside the jurisdiction of the UK, providing the act in question is carried out within the jurisdiction.

The scope of 'authorisation' is not beyond doubt but the better view is that it means (per Atkin LJ in *Falcon v Famous Players Film Co* [1926] 2 KB 474 at 499):

> . . . the grant or purported grant, which may be express or implied, of the right to do the act complained of.

Secondary infringements of copyright apply in most cases where the defendant deals with infringing copies of works for commercial purposes. Other forms of secondary infringement apply such as the provision of apparatus for making infringing copies or permitting the use of premises for an infringing performance. The test for knowledge for secondary infringement is that the defendant knew or had reason to believe that the copies were infringing copies. Having reason to believe is an objective test, based on a reasonable person aware of the facts known to the defendant at the relevant time.

Remedies for copyright infringement include:

- damages
- injunctions
- accounts
- additional damages.

A special form of injunction applies in relation to service providers. Copyright owners also have a limited right of seizure. Infringing copies and articles for making infringing copies may be ordered to be delivered up to the copyright owner.

There are a number of useful presumptions, for example, where the name of a person purporting to be the author of a work, he shall be presumed to be the author and first owner of the copyright unless the contrary is shown.

There are several criminal offences, a number of which mirror some of the forms of secondary infringement. The *mens rea* is as that for the secondary infringements, being that the defendant knew or had reason to believe that he was, for example, dealing with infringing copies. For some of the criminal offences, the maximum penalty is imprisonment for ten years and/or a fine.

Discussion questions

1 Describe and discuss the different ways in which copyright may be infringed in:
   (a) a literary work in the form of a work of literature;
   (b) an artistic work in the form of a design for a pattern used for wallpaper;
   (c) a film.

2 What does the word 'substantial' mean in relation to infringement of copyright?

3 The use of the internet for making copyright material available online has particular issues for copyright infringement. Discuss these issues and whether present copyright law has addressed these issues in a fair and balanced manner.

4 Consider and describe forms of secondary infringement of copyright and compare these to the criminal offences under copyright law. Do you agree that as (a) the economic rights under copyright are adequately protected by means of primary infringement (sections 16–21 of the Act) and (b) piracy is effectively controlled by the existence of criminal offences, there is no need for secondary infringements?

Selected further reading

Brueton, G., 'Copyright: damages for copyright infringement and infringement of performer's rights' [2010] *Chartered Institute of Patent Agents Journal*, 684 (looks at the issue of damages and additional damages).

Lim, Y. F., '"Bound to infringe": the forgotten child of the doctrine of authorisation of copyright infringement' [2011] *European Intellectual Property Review*, 91 (looks at authorisation from an Australian and UK perspective in situations where the supply of articles or services is bound, wholly or predominantly, to lead to infringement).

Massey, R., 'R. v Gilham (Christopher Paul) – pirates beware! Transient copying to RAM is sufficient for infringement of copyright' [2010] *Entertainment Law Review*, 107 (looks at the Gilham case confirming that transient copies infringe copyright).

Rizzuto, F., 'European Union telecommunications law reform and combating online non-commercial infringements of copyright: seeing through the legal fog' [2011] *Computer and Telecommunications Law Review*, 75 (looks at internet user access rights and liability for non-commercial online infringement – notes that such infringement is not recognised as a criminal offence in most EU Member States).

The ECJ cases of C-304/07 Directmedia Publishing GmbH v Albert-Ludwigs-Universität Freiburg and Case C-306/05 Sociedad General de Autores y Editores de España (SGAE) v Rafael Hoteles SA: available, respectively, at: **http://eur-lex.europa.eu/LexUriServ/LexUriServ.do?uri=CELEX:62007J0304:EN:HTML** and **http://eur-lex.europa.eu/LexUriServ/LexUriServ.do?uri=CELEX:62005J0306:EN:PDF**

Visit www.mylawchamber.co.uk/bainbridgeip to access study support resources including interactive multiple choice questions, practice exam questions with guidance, weblinks, legal updates and a legal newsfeed.

Defences to copyright infringement and the permitted acts

Introduction

The Copyright, Designs and Patents Act 1988 contains a considerable number of what are known as the acts permitted in relation to copyright works or, more simply, the 'permitted acts'. These are acts that can be performed without attracting liability for copyright infringement, but this is without prejudice to other legal rights or obligations.[1] Therefore, even though something may be done in relation to a copyright work that does not infringe by reason of being a permitted act, it may still result in a breach of confidence or in the tort of passing off, for example. There have been several reviews and reports on intellectual property law, practice and policy in the UK. Two of these, the *Gowers Review* and the *Hargreaves Report*, included recommendations relating to the permitted acts. These recommendations are briefly noted towards the end of the chapter.

Defences to copyright infringement are not restricted to the permitted acts, and there are other defences that may excuse or justify an act which at first sight infringes copyright. Of course, a person sued for infringement may claim that copyright does not subsist in the work in question,[2] that the courts in the UK do not have jurisdiction to hear the action, that the act done does not fall within the scope of the restricted acts or that the act complained of was not done in relation to a substantial part of the work. As regards the secondary infringements of copyright, some form of knowledge is required on the part of the alleged infringer, or there may be some dispute as to whether the copy dealt with is an infringing copy within the meaning assigned by s 27.

Other issues are whether the copyright owner authorised or consented to the alleged infringement, or whether the defence of public interest is relevant, or whether it is a case of non-derogation from grant. If none of the above points apply, then the defendant may attempt to justify his actions by claiming that they fall within the meaning of the permitted acts. Finally a defence based on European Union law might be applicable.[3] The flowchart in Figure 7.1 (overleaf) indicates a rational way of looking at the question of infringement and the defences.

There is no remedy in copyright law in respect of groundless threats of infringement proceedings as there are, for example, in respect of patents and trade marks. However, in appropriate circumstances, an alleged infringer may be able to mount a malicious falsehood action: for example, where letters before action are sent to persons to whom copies of alleged infringing works have been sent, such as retailers or customers. In *Creative Resins International Ltd v Glasslam Europe Ltd*,[4] the second defendant, a firm of solicitors acting for the first defendant, sent a letter to a customer of the claimant (with a copy sent to the claimant with a letter before action) alleging that the door panels manufactured by

1 Copyright, Designs and Patents Act 1988 s 28(1). To this extent, they can be classed as defences to copyright infringement. Unless otherwise indicated, in this chapter statutory references are to this Act.

2 A claim that the claimant's work itself infringes copyright is no defence if it is subject to its own copyright: *ZYX Music v King* [1995] FSR 566.

3 *See* Chapter 25.

4 [2005] EWHC 777 (QB).

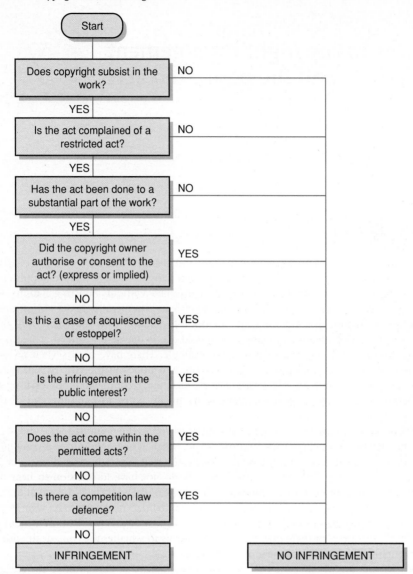

Figure 7.1 Infringement and defences

the claimant and sold by the claimant's customer infringed the first defendant's artistic copyright. The letter also stated that the first defendant had obtained an injunction against the claimant in Germany and, therefore, the claimant had a history of infringing activity. However, claims to malicious falsehood are not to be advanced lightly and proving malice is particularly difficult. On the facts before him, Tugendhat J thought both the claimant and first defendant had a real prospect of success but in the absence of further information such as the state of the German proceedings where there was some doubt that a finding of infringement had been made, he turned down the claimant's application for summary judgment.

Copyright owner authorised or consented to the act

Copyright in a work is infringed by a person who performs or authorises another person to perform one of the acts restricted by the copyright unless the licence of the copyright owner has been obtained.[5] Under s 173, in the case of a work having joint copyright owners the licence of all the joint owners is required. The meaning of 'licence' should be considered in terms of the authority of the copyright owner or his permission to carry out particular restricted acts. It would appear that the licence does not have to be formal or contractual, so that the absence of consideration, *per se*, does not affect the status of the authorisation. Of course, if the licence is not contractual, there is the problem that it may be revoked at any time subject to equitable rules and principles, such as the doctrine of estoppel.

Under normal circumstances, the licence given by the copyright owner will be formal and contractual in nature: for example, a non-exclusive licence in respect of a computer software package for a licence fee of £250. Alternatively, it may be informal and/or non-contractual. If there is no express permission or authority to carry out the restricted act concerned, it may be that the courts will be prepared to imply the copyright owner's licence. This will usually be limited to adding terms to an existing agreement. For example, if a builder commissions an architect to design and draw up plans for a new house to be built by the builder, in the absence of any express licence, there will be an implied licence that the builder may use the plans for the purposes of constructing the house. An implied licence will be restricted to the minimum necessary in the context of the intention of the parties. The builder's implied licence in the above example would not extend to constructing further houses to the plans unless this was the original intention.[6] In other circumstances, an assignment may be implied. For example, if a person obtains a licence to use a computer program, the court might imply a term in the licence agreement that the licensee will be the beneficial owner of the copyright in any reports produced by running the program. Of course, it becomes impossible or difficult to imply the copyright owner's authorisation or permission in the face of express terms to the contrary in an agreement, or if the remaining rights of the owner are prejudiced in some way. An implied licence may overcome difficulties resulting from misunderstandings about the future ownership of copyright: for example, where a person commissioning a work of copyright later discovers that he does not own the copyright and the person commissioned to create the work is trying to interfere with the subsequent use of the work.[7] Implying the copyright owner's licence may also be a way of curbing any unconscionable conduct that is proposed by the owner, such as taking advantage of an imperfect assignment or a badly drafted licence agreement.

Commercial reality must also be considered when deciding whether an implied licence is appropriate. In *Fylde Microsystems Ltd* v *Key Radio Systems Ltd*,[8] the claimant and defendant collaborated in the design of software for mobile and portable radios. The claimant was a software developer and the defendant was engaged in the manufacture and sale of mobile and portable radios. There was no contract between the parties covering the development of the software. The circumstances were such that the defendant had no ownership rights in the copyright subsisting in the software which had been written solely by the claimant. Laddie J rejected the notion that the defendant had an implied licence of a general nature allowing it to exploit the software as it thought fit. This would allow the defendant to exploit the software without making any payment to the claimant even after the claimant had spent four years developing the software. Also rejected was the argument in the alternative that the defendant had an implied licence to copy the software to replace printed circuit boards supplied by the claimant which were defective and not of merchantable quality (the current requirement is satisfactory quality). In respect of

5 Copyright, Designs and Patents Act 1988 s 16(2).

6 For example, *see Blair* v *Osborne & Tomkins* [1971] 2 WLR 503.

7 *See*, for example, *Warner* v *Gestetner Ltd* [1988] EIPR D-89 and *Blair* v *Osborne & Tomkins* [1971] 2 WLR 503, discussed in Chapter 4.

8 [1998] FSR 449.

defective printed circuit boards, the defendant would have the remedy of requiring the delivery of replacement boards or a claim in damages. The implication of a licence was, therefore, completely unnecessary.

Acquiescence, delay and estoppel

The copyright owner may be aware of activities that could infringe his copyright and yet choose to do nothing about it for a long time. Inactivity by the copyright owner in enforcing his rights may encourage the infringer to continue infringing or even scale up his activities. In other cases, the behaviour of the copyright owner may be such that an estoppel is raised against him. This might be the case where a licence might be implied where the copyright owner knows full well of what would otherwise be infringing activities and does nothing about it, leading the infringer to believe that he has the implied consent of the copyright owner. Problems may arise when the copyright owner suddenly and, perhaps, unexpectedly takes objection to the activities and commences legal proceedings.

The normal time limit for bringing proceedings for tort is, under s 2 of the Limitation Act 1980, six years from the time the cause of action arose. Where proceedings are commenced more than six years after the infringing acts started, damages only in respect of the six years immediately preceding the commencement of action can be awarded. Any delay might also affect the availability of equitable remedies such as an injunction. It is not an easy matter to lay down hard and fast rules about this and the exercise of the discretion to grant an injunction will be heavily influenced by the facts of the case and the conduct of the parties. An extreme example is given by *Cluett Peabody & Co Inc v McIntyre Hog March & Co Ltd*,[9] where it was held that a 30-year delay prevented a claim for injunctive relief in respect of an infringement of a trade mark. Until the action, it had been a case of 'live and let live'.

A considerable delay may not deprive the claimant of an injunction. In *Experience Hendrix LLC v PPX Enterprises Inc*,[10] a settlement had been reached in 1973 between the defendant and other parties including the present claimant's predecessor in title with respect to recordings made by the late Jimi Hendrix and others. At various times since the settlement, the defendant exploited a number of recordings which it was not authorised to do under the terms of the settlement. The claimant, successor in title to the estate of Jimi Hendrix now sought, *inter alia*, an injunction and an order for delivery up of the master recordings. Buckley J rejected the defendant's argument that an injunction should not be granted on the basis of the long delay in bringing the action. He said (at para 45):

> . . . it would be very difficult and probably undesirable to attempt to define categories of case in which mere delay would preclude the grant of equitable relief.

He went on to say that an example might be where there was no apparent reason for the delay other than indifference and no sufficient reason for a sudden decision to seek a remedy. Where a bare licence can be implied from the circumstances, it may be that the licence can be revoked at any time. However, if the defendant has acted to his detriment as a result of the claimant's acts (or inactivity) and the claimant knows this, he may not be able to revoke the licence at all or without giving reasonable notice on the basis of estoppel. The classic modern case on estoppel is *Taylor's Fashions Ltd v Liverpool Victoria Trustees Co Ltd*[11] where Oliver J said (at 151):

> Furthermore the more recent cases indicate, in my judgment, that the application of the *Ramsden v Dyson*L.R. 1 H.L.129 principle – whether you call it proprietary estoppel, estoppel by acquiescence or estoppel by encouragement is really immaterial – requires a very much broader approach which is directed rather at ascertaining whether, in particular individual

9 [1958] RPC 355.

10 [2003] FSR 46.

11 [1982] QB 133.

circumstances, it would be unconscionable for a party to be permitted to deny that which, knowingly, or unknowingly, he has allowed or encouraged another to assume to his detriment than to enquiring whether the circumstances can be fitted within the confines of some pre-conceived formula serving as a universal yardstick for every form of unconscionable behaviour.

Essentially, what is required for an estoppel to arise is an expectation created or encouraged by the claimant which results in the defendant incurring expenditure or some other detriment with the knowledge of the claimant and without objection from him. In such cases, the courts may compel the claimant to give effect to the expectation where it would be unconscionable for the claimant to do otherwise. The emphasis now seems to be on unconscionability. In *Confetti Records* v *Warner Music UK Ltd*[12] there was a purported agreement expressed as being subject to contract. The claimant had sent a memorandum of the deal, a copy of a cleared track of music and an invoice. This was held to be a representation that a licence had been granted in respect of the track. However, Lewinson J said that the agreement headed subject to contract could not by itself give rise to a licence but this could not prevent the sending of the track giving rise to a bare licence.[13] The question whether the claimant would be prevented from revoking the bare licence was answered in the negative by the judge who dismissed the claims in their entirety.

An important and arguably essential ingredient of estoppel and laches is the presence of detriment as a result of an expectation that the other person's behaviour encouraged an expectation that the right would not be asserted. If the other remains silent and does nothing to suggest that he will not assert his right, that is not sufficient to raise an estoppel. In *Fisher* v *Brooker*,[14] after a period of over 37 years, the claimant asserted his co-authorship of the music 'Whiter Shade of Pale'. He had written the organ solo and other organ parts for the song. If anything, the defendants had benefited by the claimant's silence as they had been paid royalties from collecting societies in respect of the song. At first instance,[15] it was held that the claimant was entitled to a 40 per cent share in the copyright in the music and a declaration was made to that effect. However, it was also held that there was an implied gratuitous revocable licence in favour of the defendants. This came to an end when the claimant began legal proceedings in 2005, after which he would be entitled to his share of the economic benefit resulting from subsequent exploitation of the work. The Court of Appeal, by a majority, whilst recognising the claimant's authorship, held that the implied licence was irrevocable because the claimant's acquiescence made it unconscionable for him now to seek to enforce his share of the copyright.[16] The House of Lords restored the decision at first instance. Acquiescence, estoppel and laches are equitable doctrines and could apply, for example, if the claimant sought to enforce his rights against the others by way of an injunction. However, copyright is a property right and a claim to copyright may be brought at any time. There is no provision for limitation of actions.[17] A declaration as to the existence of a property right is not equitable relief. Lord Neuberger said that, notwithstanding that, such a declaration might be refused on the basis of laches if it was sought solely for the purpose of obtaining equitable relief such as an injunction. He also said that in certain cases, such as the present one, estoppel and laches could be characterised as forms of acquiescence.

An estoppel might not be raised where the later commencement of proceedings can be explained by a change in the circumstances which render the earlier expectation that rights would not be enforced superseded. A copyright owner may not take action because the level of infringement is not really worth the trouble and expense of going to court. But if the defendant's use of the work suddenly takes on wholly unexpected proportions, the owner may be entitled to enforce his rights as to the future unless the newly found success of the work is the result of the defendant's work and expenditure carried on with the knowledge of the owner and without his complaint.

12 [2003] EMLR 35.

13 That an estoppel could arise where an agreement is headed 'subject to contract' was recognised in *Attorney-General for Hong Kong* v *Humphreys Estate (Queen's Gardens) Ltd* [1987] AC 114. However, the Privy Council thought that this would be unlikely in circumstances presently foreseeable.

14 [2009] FSR 25.

15 *Fisher* v *Brooker* [2007] FSR 12.

16 *Brooker* v *Fisher* [2008] FSR 26. Although recognising the claim to authorship, the Court of Appeal discharged the declaration that the claimant was entitled to a 40 per cent share in the copyright.

17 The Limitation Act 1980 does not apply to claims of ownership of copyright. Although, the position is not clear in Scotland under the Prescription and Limitation (Scotland) Act 1973.

In *Hodgens* v *Beckingham*,[18] the defendant's stage name was Bobby Valentino and he was involved in writing the violin part for a song entitled 'Young at Heart'. During 1984 it was performed by a group known as the Bluebells, the leader of which was the claimant. There had been a dispute over the authorship of the violin part but, after taking legal advice, Mr Valentino made it clear in 1984 he did not want to take it to court. The group disbanded in 1986. In 1993, their version became very popular as the background music for an advertisement for Volkswagen cars and even made it to the top of the record charts. Following this Mr Valentino asked for future royalties as being the joint author and joint owner of the copyright in the music. During 1993 Mr Hodgens assured Mr Valentino that he would 'see him right' and also said things along similar lines to Mr Valentino's girlfriend. Mr Valentino told Mr Hodgens that if he did not 'see him right' he would go to law. It was held that an implied licence existed from 1984 but that this was revoked during 1993. Mr Hodgens argued that Mr Valentino was estopped from revoking the licence. This was rejected by the judge at first instance and confirmed by the Court of Appeal. Important factors were that Mr Valentino was not claiming a share in any royalties received by Mr Hodgens before 1993, in which case Mr Hodgens' claim to have spent all the royalties he received up to 1993 was irrelevant. The fact that Mr Valentino had told Mr Hodgens in 1984 that he would take no action merely confirmed the existence of an implied licence which was revocable on giving reasonable notice. It might have been different if the second and greater success of the song had been the result of the hard work of the defendant where the claimant had known about it and stood by and done nothing.[19]

In *JHP Worldwide Ltd* v *BBC Worldwide Ltd*,[20] copyright in a number of books about the Daleks had been written by the late Terry Nation (who had created the Dalek characters). The claimant had an exclusive licence to exploit in respect of these books. The copyright passed to the estate of Terry Nation. Mr Fishman was the sole director of the claimant and contacted the BBC to see if they were interested in republishing the books in a new form which involved some re-working and the addition of new material. With the consent of Mr Fishman, two other writers worked on *The Dalek Survival Guide*. Before it was published, there was a falling out between Mr Fishman and BBC Worldwide. An attempt was made to exclude material derived from Mr Fishman and substitute it with fresh material. In the meantime, BBC Worldwide had been in negotiations with a representative of the Terry Nation estate. It was alleged that an informal agreement had been reached between them. Although the court rejected the copyright infringement claims, it went on to hold that BBC Worldwide had a licence by estoppel from the estate. In such a case, a defendant sued by an exclusive licensee has a defence under s 101(3) which states that in an action brought under s 101 by an exclusive licensee a defendant can avail himself of any defence which would have been available to him had the action been brought by the copyright owner.

Public interest

'Public interest' is a nebulous concept which can, in some cases, provide a defence for copyright infringement. Cases where the public interest is at issue often concern the publication of information, and frequently questions of confidence also will be raised.[21] Typically, a person will, without authority of the copyright owner, publish something which embarrasses the copyright owner or some other person. For example, in *Lion Laboratories Ltd* v *Evans*,[22] the defendant, a newspaper editor, wished to publish information concerning doubts about the reliability of the Lion Intoximeter 3000, a device used to measure levels of intoxication by alcohol. The device had been used to 'breathalyse' approximately 700 motorists suspected of being unfit to drive through drink. The claimant had obtained an injunction preventing the defendant from publishing the information on the basis that

18 [2003] EMLR 18.

19 *See Godfrey* v *Lees* [1995] EMLR 307.

20 [2008] FSR 29.

21 The defence of public interest in relation to copyright infringement is different to that in breach of confidence: *Hyde Park Residences Ltd* v *Yelland* [2000] RPC 604 at paras 64 and 66 per Aldous LJ.

22 [1984] 2 All ER 417.

the information was confidential, and because publication would infringe copyright. The defendant appealed against the injunction.

The defendant's appeal was allowed. The defence of public interest applied to both the confidence and the copyright issues because it was in the public interest that the information be published; further, the operation of the defence was not limited to cases where there had been any wrongdoing on the part of the claimant. The court identified matters relevant to the application of the defence of public interest as follows:

1 There was a difference between what was interesting to the public and what was in the public interest.
2 It was a fact that the media, for example newspaper proprietors, had a private interest to increase circulation by publishing what appealed to the public.
3 The public interest might be best served by giving the information to the police or some other responsible body rather than to the press.
4 The public interest did not arise only when there was an iniquity to be disclosed, and the defendant ought not to be restrained solely because what he wanted to publish did not show misconduct on the part of the claimant.

If the defence of public interest is raised, the court should weigh up the competing interests. In this particular case, it was unquestionable that it was in the public interest that the information be published. The third point above is a little worrying. Surely something either is or is not in the public interest, and this test suggests that publication for gain might injure the prospects of the defence succeeding. Surely the motive for publication should be irrelevant – it is the nature of the information that is crucial. In any case, giving the information to a 'responsible body' might lead to a 'cover-up' – if there is some matter which the public should be aware of, the press can serve a very useful function, albeit financially motivated. In *Initial Services Ltd* v *Putterill*,[23] Salmon LJ recognised that there was very little authority on the status of the person to whom documents or information were given. It was suggested by counsel for the claimant that information should have been given to the Registrar appointed under the Restrictive Trade Practices Act 1956[24] and not to the press. However, Salmon LJ said that the law should not lend assistance to anyone proposing to commit or committing a clear breach of statutory duty imposed in the public interest.

Public interest will cover situations involving the disclosure of criminal conduct, both past and contemplated,[25] or matters prejudicing the nation's security.[26] In *Attorney-General* v *Guardian Newspapers Ltd*[27] it was indicated in the House of Lords that the copyright in the Spycatcher novel would not be enforced by the courts because of the conduct of the book's author, Peter Wright, in divulging national secrets. It could be said that Peter Wright had harmed the public interest in keeping secret the activities of 'secret agents' and the like, and the nation's security could have been harmed as a result of his disclosures. As the law of confidence could provide no remedies, the book having been published elsewhere and being widely available, the House of Lords was punishing Mr Wright the only way it could. The implication was that anyone could publish the book or extracts from it without being liable for copyright infringement.

Freedom of speech can be said to lie within the public interest and as such will not be restrained by way of an interim injunction if the defence of fair dealing is likely to be raised. In *Kennard* v *Lewis*[28] the claimant had published a pamphlet entitled *30 Questions and Answers about CND* and the defendant had published a pamphlet called *30 Questions and Honest Answers about CND*, using a layout which was substantially similar. The claimant sought an interim injunction to restrain publication of the defendant's pamphlet and the defendant raised a defence of fair dealing. It was held that, as a principle, interim injunctions should not be used to restrain free speech and, *a fortiori*, should not be used to restrain political controversy.[29]

The scope of the defence of public interest came under some scrutiny in the Chancery Division and the Court of Appeal in *Hyde Park Residence Ltd* v *Yelland*.[30] Briefly, the facts

23 [1968] 1 QB 396.

24 Now repealed; replaced by the Restrictive Trade Practices Act 1976, in turn repealed by the Competition Act 1998.

25 Per Lord Denning in *Initial Services Ltd* v *Putterill* [1968] 1 QB 396. This case involved the disclosure of the operation of a price-fixing ring between laundries.

26 Per Ungoed-Thomas J in *Beloff* v *Pressdram Ltd* [1973] 1 All ER 241.

27 [1988] 3 All ER 567.

28 [1983] FSR 346.

29 *See* also *Hubbard* v *Vosper* [1972] 2 QB 84.

30 In the Chancery Division reported at [1999] RPC 655 and, in the Court of Appeal, reported at [2000] RPC 604.

were that the claimant company provided security services to Mr Mohammed Al Fayed, including the use of video surveillance at his Paris house. The day before Diana, Princess of Wales, and Mr Al Fayed's son, Dodi, were killed in a car crash, they had been recorded on video going into and out of the house. An employee of the claimant made stills from the film showing them arriving and leaving with the date and time visible. These stills found their way to the *Sun* newspaper, which published them. When sued for copyright infringement, the defendant put forward the defences of public interest and fair dealing for the purpose of reporting current events.

In the Chancery Division, both defences succeeded. After reviewing the authorities Jacob J pointed out that the public interest defence was available only in rare cases but that there were two forms of public interest. One was to deny copyright altogether in the work concerned. This could be the case where the work was grossly immoral. In other cases, it took effect as a recognised defence to copyright infringement. Most of the authorities where the defence applied were breach of confidence cases and copyright was only relied on peripherally.[31] *Lion Laboratories* was a different case in that the balance between copyright and confidence was more equal and the judges all accepted the defence as being available for copyright infringement. Furthermore, s 171(3) of the 1988 Act states that:

> . . . nothing in this Part [the Part relating to copyright] affects any rule of law preventing or otherwise restricting the enforcement of copyright, on grounds of public interest or otherwise.

The only sensible view is that Parliament was happy to accept developments in cases like *Lion Laboratories* which were decided prior to the 1988 Act. Furthermore, one can only agree with Jacob J when he said in *Hyde Park Residence*:[32]

> I think the better view is that that provision [s 171(3)] was intended to recognise a defence of public interest – either by way of refusing to recognise copyright altogether ('preventing enforcement') or by way of a defence in the particular circumstances of the case ('restricting enforcement').

The Court of Appeal overturned Jacob J's decision and gave judgment for the claimant for copyright infringement.[33] However, it accepted that, generally, there was such a defence of public interest. Noting that the circumstances in which the defence might be available were not capable of precise definition, the court pointed out that the circumstances must derive from the nature of the work itself and not those relating to the owner. The reasons for this emphasis on the work rather than the owner was because copyright is assignable and the identity of the owner may change. Aldous LJ identified some circumstances when the court might choose not to enforce copyright, being where the work:

(a) is immoral, scandalous or contrary to family life;
(b) is injurious to public life, public health and safety or the administration of justice;
(c) incites or encourages others to act in a way referred to in (a).

It was held that there was no justification for publishing the stills as there was nothing in them that could justify the court in refusing to enforce the statutory right provided for by the Act. The information of interest contained within them (the times of arrival and departure) could have been made available without publishing the stills. Even though the stills might have been of interest to the public, it did not follow that publication was in the public interest.[34]

The scope of the public interest defence may need re-visiting when it comes to the political arena. In *Unilever plc v Griffin*,[35] the British National Party made a broadcast which included an image of a large jar of Marmite together with the slogan 'Love Britain Love BNP'. An interim injunction was granted in favour of the claimant which manufactured Marmite and claimed copyright infringement and trade mark infringement. Although a defendant might run a public interest defence under copyright law, it was held that the

31 Examples being *Beloff* v *Pressdram Ltd* [1973] 1 All ER 241 and *Hubbard* v *Vosper* [1972] 2 QB 84.

32 [1999] RPC 655 at 667.

33 [2000] RPC 604.

34 The other defence, fair dealing, is considered below.

35 [2010] FSR 33.

claimant had crossed the threshold for the grant of an interim injunction.[36] However, in speaking of relatively limited scope of the public interest defence following *Hyde Park* v *Yelland* and *Ashdown* v *Telegraph (infra)*, Arnold J said (at para 18):

> I have to say that this seems to me to be an area of the law where there may be room for further development, particularly in a political context such as this.

Where public interest is at issue, it may be important to have regard to the impact of the Council of Europe Convention for the Protection of Human Rights and Fundamental Freedoms.[37] In particular, Article 10, concerning freedom of expression, may be relevant as copyright and other intellectual property rights can be seen as being a restriction on the right to exercise freedom of expression. Article 10(2) allows conditions or restrictions as prescribed by law necessary in a democratic society.[38] However, in *Ashdown* v *Telegraph Group Ltd*,[39] the Vice-Chancellor said that the Human Rights Act 1998 was not a reason for interpreting the Copyright, Designs and Patents Act 1988 any differently than before and he concluded that the Court of Appeal decision in *Hyde Park Residence* as to the scope of s 171(3) was binding on him even though the decision in that case preceded the coming into force of the Human Rights Act 1998. This was confirmed in *Imutran Ltd* v *Uncaged Campaigns Ltd*,[40] where it was accepted that the claimant was most likely to establish that publication by reproducing extracts of its documents should not be allowed. Although, by s 12(4) of the Human Rights Act 1998, the court must have particular regard to the right of freedom of expression, s 12(3) of the Act states that no relief shall be granted to restrain publication '. . . unless the court is satisfied that the applicant is likely to establish that publication should not be allowed'. Sir Andrew Morritt VC said at para 33:

> Equally, given the interaction between the law of copyright and Article 10 EHCR [the right of freedom of expression] as I consider it to be, the importance of the Convention right to freedom of expression to which s 12(4) . . . requires me to pay particular regard does not lead to the conclusion that injunctive or other relief in respect of the copyright claim should be refused.

The copyright claim concerned the publication of parts of documents belonging to the claimant, who was engaged at the time in research into xenotransplantation (the replacement of human organs by those of pigs), by the defendant which was a company having the aim of campaigning peacefully against experimentation with animals.

There is a public interest in disclosing material which may be subject to intellectual property rights such as copyright under particular legislation such as the Environmental Information Regulations 2004.[41] A public authority may refuse to disclose information in respect of which access is sought if it would adversely affect intellectual property rights. In *R (on the application of the Office of Communications)* v *Information Commissioner*,[42] the Court of Appeal considered how the balance between the public interest in disclosure and the public interest in maintaining the exception to disclosure should be applied. More than one intellectual property could be involved and, where this was the case, they should be considered in the aggregate rather than individually.[43]

Non-derogation from grant

The exercise of an intellectual property right could unduly interfere with the subsequent use of an article in which such rights subsist. We can see the way in which the law balances the rights of the intellectual property owner with those of persons using or acquiring articles in the doctrine of exhaustion of rights, or in the way in which the law has implied a 'right to repair' in relation to patented products.[44] The nature of copyright law is such that the exercise of a copyright is less likely to conflict with the subsequent use

---

36 In *Cream Holdings Ltd* v *Banerjee* [2005] 1 AC 253, the House of Lords interpreted s 12(3) of the Human Rights Act 1998, which imposes a threshold test for the grant of an interim injunction in the context of publication and freedom of expression. It was held that 'likely' does not mean 'more likely than not' in all circumstances and the court could adopt a lower threshold in appropriate cases.

37 Brought into UK law by the Human Rights Act 1998.

38 Article 8, the right to respect for private and family life, may also be relevant. This right also is subject to derogations.

39 [2001] RPC 34. The facts of the case are discussed below in relation to fair dealing.

40 [2002] FSR 2.

41 SI 2004/3391.

42 [2009] EWCA Civ 90.

43 Regulation 12(5)(c) gives an exemption for intellectual property rights and reg 12(5)(e) gives an exemption for confidential information.

44 This is on the basis of an implied licence: *see Solar Thomson Engineering Co Ltd* v *Barton* [1977] RPC 537.

or sale of articles. For example, if I wish to repair a book, I can do this without the copyright owner's permission (unless, of course, I wish to photocopy or scan into a computer an old, moth-eaten copy of a book). However, even with copyright there must be some ultimate control of the owner's rights where these could be unfairly used. In *British Leyland Motor Corp Ltd v Armstrong Patents Co Ltd*,[45] discussed in Chapter 6 (*see* p 163), the House of Lords, while accepting that there had been a technical infringement of the copyright subsisting in the claimant's drawings, refused to enforce that copyright on the basis of non-derogation from grant. That is, once an article has been sold by the rights owner, he can no longer use those rights to interfere with the purchaser's 'right' to a free market in spare parts.

The *British Leyland* case was concerned with spare exhaust pipes, and the law has changed so that design law is more appropriate to deal with such matters. Nevertheless, the non-derogation from grant principle survived the coming into force of the 1988 Act[46] and may be relevant in terms of some types of copyright work. In particular it should still be relevant for works incorporated into articles where further use or modification will involve a restricted act. One obvious example is a computer program that has errors contained within it. Although the copyright owner may be prepared to correct errors, to allow him to prohibit error correction by the licensee or a third party would be to deprive the licensee of a free market in software maintenance. This principle may also apply to more traditional types of works, such as sound recordings, photographs or films, and could allow the owner of a copy to re-record it to reduce or eliminate the presence of some defect caused by, for example, fair wear and tear.[47] Whether this would extend to enhancing the original – for example, by digitally re-recording an old scratchy vinyl sound recording or improving a photographic image by means of computer technology – is less likely, as this probably would compromise the copyright owner's interests.

It could be argued that the principle of non-derogation from grant is inconsistent with copyright law, except in the context of a licence agreement, where a term in the agreement contradicts or is inconsistent with the general rights granted by the licence. As the permitted act provisions in the Act are comprehensive, the courts should be slow to enlarge or extend defences to copyright infringement by judicial decision making only. It might be fairly thought that Parliament gave detailed consideration to defences to copyright infringement during the passage of the Bill[48] and any further development of the *British Leyland* principle should be eschewed. This was recognised in *Canon Kabushiki Kaisha v Green Cartridge Co (HK) Ltd*[49] by the Judicial Committee of the Privy Council, which said that the principle was based on overriding public policy. Nevertheless, the Committee considered it to be questionable in a constitutional and jurisprudential sense for such a policy to override a clear, express statutory right and, consequently, any prospect of extending the principle should be treated with some caution.

The permitted acts

The acts permitted in relation to copyright works are contained in the Copyright, Designs and Patents Act 1988 chapter III. The permitted acts are complex and wide-ranging in their scope and application, now occupying no less than 66 sections of the Act, but at least the Act conveniently classifies them by using appropriate sub-headings such as 'Education', 'Libraries and archives', etc. and this classification will be retained in the following description of the permitted acts. At the end of this chapter Table 7.2 shows the basic elements of the permitted acts. The rationale for the permitted acts, allowing what would otherwise be an infringement of copyright, can be seen as a way of limiting the strength of the rights associated with copyright. The justification for this restriction is that

45 [1986] 2 WLR 400.

46 *Flogates Ltd v Refco Ltd* [1996] FSR 935.

47 This is more controversial and a copyright owner would be likely to object to such copying.

48 And subsequently in relation to further forms of permitted acts inserted into the Act.

49 [1997] FSR 817.

50 *Law Society of Upper Canada v CCH Canada Ltd* [2004] SCC 13.

51 Article 10, Berne Convention for the Protection of Literary and Artistic Works 1886.

it provides a fair balance between the rights of the copyright owner and the rights of society at large.[50] The 'Berne Copyright Convention' provides for certain forms of free uses of copyright works such as in respect of quotations and teaching.[51] Generally, the permitted acts excuse activities which, although technically infringing the copyright in a work, do not unduly interfere with the copyright owner's commercial exploitation of the work. For example, a person writing an academic article is able to include attributed quotations from the writings of other authors. The permitted acts are, therefore, on the whole relatively restricted in their effect on commercial exploitation.

It should be noted that the application of some of the permitted acts depends on the amount of the first work that has been copied or otherwise used, whereas in other cases the permitted act relates to the whole work. For example, in terms of the permitted act of fair dealing for the purposes of criticism or review, it appears that it would not be fair dealing to copy the whole of an existing work of copyright, that fair dealing is limited by some measure which is based on quality or quantity, or perhaps a combination of the two. On the other hand, it is permissible to perform the whole of a dramatic work before an audience of teachers and pupils at an educational establishment.[52]

52 Copyright, Designs and Patents Act 1988 s 34.

53 HMSO 2006.

There are proposals afoot to modify some of the permitted acts and to introduce some new ones, as a result of the *Gowers Review of Intellectual Property*.[53] These are summarised at the end of this chapter.

General, including fair dealing

Making of temporary copies

54 SI 2003/2498. These Regulations implemented Directive 2001/29/EC of the European Parliament and of the Council of 22 May 2001 on the harmonisation of certain aspects of copyright and related rights in the information society, OJ L 167, 22.06.2001, p 10.

The Copyright and Related Rights Regulations 2003[54] inserted s 28A into the Act. This provides for the making of temporary copies which are transient or incidental and are an integral and essential part of a technological process, the sole purpose of which is to enable:

(a) the transmission of the work in a network between third parties by an intermediary; or

(b) a lawful use of the work;

and which has no independent economic significance.[55]

The works covered by this permitted act are:

55 In *Football Association Premier League Ltd v QC Leisure (No 2)* [2008] FSR 32, Kitchen J thought the meaning of 'independent economic significance' was not clear and he referred a question relating this, amongst a great many other questions to the Court of Justice for a preliminary ruling.

- literary works (other than computer programs and databases);
- dramatic, musical or artistic works;
- typographical arrangements of published editions; and
- sound recordings or films.

The exception is required because the restricted act of copying includes making transient and incidental copies. The types of activities covered will include the situation where a file containing one of the above-mentioned works is transmitted from one person to another as an e-mail attachment or by the use of peer-to-peer file-sharing software. In such a case, the permitted act will apply to excuse the intermediaries such as the internet service provider whose service is used to transmit the copy. This is notwithstanding that the third parties (and possibly the person supplying the peer-to-peer file-sharing software) may well infringe copyright by their activities.

56 [2009] ECR I-6569.

In Case C-5/08 *Infopaq International A/S v Danske Dagblades Forening*,[56] the Court of Justice held that printing out an extract of 11 words on paper did not fulfil the condition of being transient for the purposes of the equivalent provision in the Directive on copyright in the information society. The Court of Justice held (at para 64) that an act is transient:

. . . only if its duration is limited to what is necessary for the proper completion of the technological process in question, it being understood that that process must be automated so that it deletes that act automatically, without human intervention, once its function of enabling the completion of such a process has come to an end.

Where the destruction of the reproduction in question depends on a person destroying the paper on which it is printed, it cannot be regarded as transient.

The exception cannot be used to make lawful what would otherwise be the unlawful act of making a transient copy. An example is where a person downloads a copy of a webpage on his computer screen following an act of browsing. The copy is not part of the technological process but is generated by the deliberate act of that person. Nor can making the copy be an essential and integral part of a technological process. Rather it is the end which the process is designed to achieve. The permitted act cannot have been intended to legitimise copies made in the act of browsing.[57]

In Joined Cases C-403/08 and C-429/08 *Football Association Premier League* v *QC Leisure*,[58] the defendants sold decoders which had been lawfully acquired in Greece to publicans so that they could show broadcasts of Premier League football matches to customers in their public houses. On the provision on making temporary copies, under Article 3(1) of the Directive on copyright and related rights in the information society, the Court of Justice ruled, somewhat controversially, that all five requirements were satisfied. In particular, receiving and displaying the broadcasts in private circles was a lawful use. The decoders in question had been lawfully bought in Greece and imported into the UK. Although the importation of the decoders was against the claimant's wishes, they were not illicit devices because of the freedom to provide services under Article 56 of the Treaty on the Functioning of the EU (see Chapter 25 for this aspect of the case). Further, although the broadcasts had commercial significance, this was not independent as it did not go beyond the advantage derived from the mere reception of the broadcasts.

Fair dealing

The notion of permitting some use of a copyright work which is considered to be 'fair' is common in many jurisdictions. For example, in the USA, copyright law has its 'fair use' provisions. In the UK, 'fair dealing' is allowed in relation to a copyright work. It must be noted at once that this has nothing to do with 'dealing' in a trade sense. It can be roughly equated to 'use'. Thus, fair dealing covers research (now only non-commercial research) or private study, criticism, review and reporting current events. The fair dealing provisions allow the copying or other use of the work which would otherwise be an infringement, and in many circumstances the amount of the original work used is very relevant. It may be fair dealing to include 5 per cent of another work for the purpose of criticism or review. It would not normally be fair dealing to incorporate the whole of the other work. The proportion of work taken can be relevant to whether the second author can successfully plead the fair dealing provisions, so this immediately brings into question the relationship between fair dealing and the taking of a substantial part of a work. If the part taken is not substantial, then there is no infringement of copyright and no need to rely on the permitted acts.

It may be that, in some cases, the existence of the permitted acts is illusory. The problem lies in the determination of the relative thresholds of substantiality and the permitted act in question. In *Independent Television Publications Ltd* v *Time Out Ltd*,[59] Whitford J said:

> Indeed, once the conclusion is reached that the whole or a substantial part of the copyright work has been taken, a defence under section 6(2) or (3) [of the Copyright Act 1956, some of the fair dealing provisions] is unlikely to succeed.

57 *Newspaper Licensing Agency Ltd* v *Meltwater Holding BV* [2011] ECDR 10.

58 4 October 2011.

59 [1984] FSR 64.

If this is true, then there is no such thing as a defence of fair dealing. If the part taken is not substantial, there is no infringement and fair dealing is irrelevant, but if the part taken is substantial then, according to Whitford J, the defence will rarely excuse the defendant's use of the work. It is respectfully submitted that this is wrong and that the whole purpose of the fair dealing provisions is to permit, in appropriate circumstances, the taking of a substantial part of a copyright work. It is, however, difficult to say where the boundaries circumscribing substantiality and fair dealing lie.[60] However, in *Law Society of Upper Canada v CCH Canadian Ltd*,[61] the Supreme Court of Canada said that fair dealing should not be given a restrictive interpretation. The Court went on to say that the manner of dealing might be relevant and it might be unfair where multiple copies were widely distributed. But, where a single copy had been made and destroyed after being used for its intended purpose, this might be regarded as fair.[62]

Consider the case where an author wishes to write a learned article for an academic journal. The author wishes to discuss and critically analyse the work of an eminent professor in the appropriate field. To do this, the author will wish to include extracts from the writings of the eminent professor. But how much does fair dealing allow him to take? Lord Denning gave a good description of the scope of fair dealing for the purposes of criticism or review in *Hubbard* v *Vosper*, where he said:

> You must first consider the number and extent of the quotations . . . Then you must consider the use made of them. If they are used as a basis of comment, criticism or review, that may be fair dealing. If they are used to convey the same information as the author, for a rival purpose, they may be unfair. Next you must consider the proportions. To take long extracts and attach short comments may be unfair. But short extracts and long comments may be fair. Other considerations may come to mind also. But it must be a matter of impression.[63]

Apart from the purpose of the inclusion of copyright materials, their overall proportion to the whole must be considered. Although substantiality is determined by a qualitative test, it appears from the above quote that the scope of this particular permitted act is determined at least partly by means of a quantitative test. Hence the difficulty. Consider the following in connection with hypothetical journal articles: the author of the new article is called Aristotle and the author of the earlier article is called Plato. Aristotle uses attributed extracts from Plato's article and quotes and discusses them in his own article. Table 7.1 indicates different proportions of the total volume of the extracts used in relation both to Plato's original article and to Aristotle's new article.

For example, in the second entry in Table 7.1, Aristotle has copied 5 per cent of Plato's article and this occupies some 10 per cent of Aristotle's work. (In this case, Aristotle's

60 In the New South Wales case of *Copyright Agency Ltd* v *Haines* [1982] FSR 331 it was suggested that fair dealing does not permit as much copying as a licensing scheme permitting photocopying by educational establishments.

61 [2004] SCC 13.

62 In some countries (for example, Canada, Australia and the US), fair dealing or fair use for research purposes can cover commercial research, unlike the position now in the EU.

63 [1972] 2 QB 84 at 94.

Table 7.1 Proportions of extracts and fair dealing

Total of extracts: percentage of article written by	
Plato	Aristotle
5	5
5	10
5	20
10	5
10	10
10	20
20	5
20	10
20	20
35	5
35	20
35	50

article must be about half the length of Plato's.) It should be apparent from the table that it is not easy to decide which, if any, of these examples represents an infringement of copyright, even assuming a good motive on the part of Aristotle. In some cases, for example, where the total of the extracts represents 5 per cent of both works, it might be considered to be fair dealing, yet this might be irrelevant because a substantial part of Plato's work has not been taken. In other cases, such as the last one in the table where the extracts amount to 35 per cent of Plato's work and 50 per cent of Aristotle's work, it can be said with some certainty that a substantial amount of Plato's work has been taken and that this does not fall within the scope of the permitted act of fair dealing. However, there is a range of cases in between where it is difficult to say with any certainty. It depends on other things such as motive and the nature of the two works. In some cases it may be that the minimum percentage representing a substantial part is the same as the maximum percentage falling within the fair dealing provisions. In other words, there is coincidence in the infringement and permitted act thresholds and, thus, the permitted act is of no consequence.[64]

In some circumstances fair dealing may allow the copying of an entire work. For example, it may be fair dealing for criticism or review to publish a photograph of a painting if the purpose is to criticise the painting in terms of its style, content or composition. There is nothing in the Act to prevent fair dealing from being relied upon in respect of copying the whole work. However, such taking is unlikely to be deemed to be fair if it seriously prejudices the commercial value of the copyright work, not because of any criticism of course, but because of the widespread publication of the work.

'Fair dealing' is not defined in the Copyright, Designs and Patents Act 1988 and it is only by reference to case law that the factors that might be considered by a court can be determined. Only sometimes will the factors identified below be said to be conclusive one way or the other; in most cases it will be a matter of combining and weighting the factors. The only thing that can be said with any degree of certainty is that whether a particular act falls within the meaning of 'fair dealing' depends very much upon the circumstances surrounding that act.

1 *Purpose.* Conceivably, it might be fair dealing to take a copy of an entire work, such as a journal article, for the purposes of non-commercial research or private study. But it will not normally be fair dealing to take a large amount of another's work for the purpose of criticism or review.[65] Commercial use is acceptable for some forms of fair dealing (criticism or review and reporting current events) but not for research.

2 *Proportion.* Within a particular form of fair dealing, proportion might be important. For example, it may be fair dealing for the purposes of criticism or review to take 5 per cent of a work, but not to take 40 per cent.[66]

3 *Motive.* If the motive for the act was to compete with the other work, this is unlikely to be fair dealing.[67]

4 *Status of other work*, that is whether confidential or published. It is unlikely to be fair dealing if the work taken has not been published, or in the case of a leak to the press.[68]

5 *Extent of use*, if the work is used to an excessive extent, that might take it out of the fair dealing provisions relating to criticism or review.[69]

6 *Prejudice to the copyright owner.* Article 9(2) of the Berne Convention for the Protection of Literary and Artistic works allows countries of the Union to permit the reproduction of works in special cases provided it does not conflict with the normal exploitation of the work or unreasonably prejudice the legitimate interests of the author.

In *Hyde Park Residence Ltd* v *Yelland*,[70] Aldous LJ said that, in determining whether a defendant could fall within the fair dealing exceptions (in that case, fair dealing for the purpose of reporting current events) required a two-stage test. The first task was to ascertain whether the publication was for a purpose within the fair dealing permitted acts.

64 Of course, it is unsatisfactory to talk in terms of percentages, as substantiality is a mainly qualitative measure. This is one reason why it is so difficult to map out the start of infringement and the end of the permitted acts.

65 *See*, generally, *Hubbard* v *Vosper* [1972] 2 QB 84 and Lord Denning's judgment in particular, and the quote earlier in this chapter. *See* also *Walter* v *Steinkopff* [1892] 3 Ch 489.

66 *Walter* v *Steinkopff* [1892] 3 Ch 489. However, this may not apply to a photograph. For example, if one is critiquing a photograph, it may require the inclusion of most if not all of the work: *Fraser Woodward Ltd* v *British Broadcasting Corporation* [2005] FSR 36. The same must apply to other forms of artistic work.

67 *Weatherby* v *International Horse Agency & Exchange Ltd* [1910] 2 Ch 297. Parker J said that the issue of competition is often important and may even be a determining factor in some cases, although he did say that unfair use was wider than this.

68 *British Oxygen Co Ltd* v *Liquid Air Ltd* [1925] 1 Ch 383; *Beloff* v *Pressdram Ltd* [1973] 1 All ER 241.

69 *Hyde Park Residence Ltd* v *Yelland* [2000] RPC 604 at para 40.

70 [2000] RPC 604 at 616.

For example, could the purpose properly be described as the reporting of current events? If the court was satisfied that the purpose applied, it must ask itself whether the dealing was fair. That involved consideration of a number of factors, being the motive behind the publication,[71] the extent and purpose of use, whether the extent of the publication was necessary for the purpose in question. A final point was that, if the work had not previously been published or circulated to the public, this was an important indication that the dealing was not fair.

One thing to note is that an interim injunction will not normally be granted if the defendant is going to raise the defence of fair dealing and has at least an arguable case. This reluctance to grant interim injunctions stems from the desire of the courts to protect freedom of speech, particularly as regards the press, or in a political or quasi-political sphere.[72] However, there has to be genuine conflict and a danger that freedom of speech will be prejudiced. For example, in *Associated Newspapers Group plc* v *News Group Newspapers Ltd*,[73] an injunction was granted because there had been no interference with the press's freedom of speech, which would only be interfered with when someone was prevented from saying the truth. The principle that interim injunctions should not be granted when the defendant raises the fair dealing defence was questioned by Dillon LJ in *BBC* v *British Satellite Broadcasting Ltd*,[74] a case concerning excerpts from broadcasts of World Cup football matches made by the BBC, which BSB intended to include in its broadcasts. Nevertheless, the BBC's application for an interim injunction was refused.

There have been a number of changes over the years to the fair dealing provisions. At one time it appeared that fair dealing for the purposes of research and private study could extend to commercial research providing, of course, that it was 'fair'. Generally now fair dealing for research purposes is limited to non-commercial purposes except in the case of typographical arrangements of published editions.[75] Another change has been the introduction of a requirement for a sufficient acknowledgement for fair dealing for the purposes of research. Previously, this was required only in respect of fair dealing for the purposes of criticism, review and reporting current events.[76] The meaning of 'sufficient acknowledgement' is given in s 178 and this, together with the nature of the acknowledgement, is discussed in the section covering fair dealing for the purposes of criticism, review and reporting current events.

Fair dealing for the purposes of research or private study

The permitted act of fair dealing for research or private study is available in relation to literary, dramatic, musical or artistic works.[77] Where the purpose is research, it must be for a non-commercial purpose and there must be a sufficient acknowledgement except where this would be impossible for reasons of practicability or otherwise.[78] Commercial activity does not need to be concurrent with the research to negate the permitted act, it is sufficient if the commercial purpose is contemplated or intended to be carried out in the future at the time of the research.[79] There is no requirement for a sufficient acknowledgement where the purpose is research for private study. Under s 29(2), fair dealing with a typographical arrangement of a published edition for the purposes of research or private study does not infringe the copyright in that arrangement. In this case, fair dealing for the purpose of research is not limited to non-commercial research. It is not fair dealing to perform the acts permitted in relation to computer programs in s 50B (decompilation), removing any possible compromise of the effects of s 50B. It is not fair dealing to observe, study and test the functioning of a computer program in order to determine the ideas and principles which underlie any element of the program under s 29(4A). The reasons for this is that there is a specific permitted act covering this and, again, this removes the possibility of it being compromised by the fair dealing provisions.

---

71 Motive was also an important factor according to Robert Walker LJ in *Pro Sieben Media AG* v *Carlton UK Television Ltd* [1999] FSR 610.

72 For example, *Hubbard* v *Vosper* [1972] 2 QB 84; *Kennard* v *Lewis* [1983] FSR 346. It should be noted that *Hubbard* v *Vosper* pre-dates the *American Cyanamid* guidelines (*see* Chapter 24, p 97).

73 [1986] RPC 515.

74 Unreported, 29 June 1990 (an appeal against a decision not to grant interim relief). In the subsequent full trial, *BBC* v *British Satellite Broadcasting Ltd* [1991] 3 WLR 174, it was held by Scott J that the defence of fair dealing was available.

75 However, there may be a problem with the underlying work or works if still in copyright.

76 Though not in all cases; *see* the discussion of this permitted act later.

77 Copyright, Designs and Patents Act 1988 s 29(1).

78 Section 29(1B).

79 *Controller of Her Majesty's Stationery Office* v *Green Amps Ltd* [2007] EWHC 2755 (Ch).

Until the changes, fair dealing for the purposes of commercial or industrial research was a distinct possibility, although each case will turn on its particular facts. For example, it would not have been considered to be fair dealing to perform an act restricted by the copyright in a work for the purposes of producing a competing work. In *Independent Television Publications Ltd v Time Out Ltd*,[80] the defendant copied details of forthcoming television programmes from the *TV Times* and the *Radio Times*. The defence of fair dealing (in this case under the head of fair dealing for criticism and review) failed because the purpose was to provide a television programme listing service and had nothing to do with criticism or review.[81]

In relation to fair dealing for research or private study, factors to determine whether it is fair may be the nature of the research or study and the funds available to the researcher or student. Questions such as whether the person concerned is copying simply to save himself the expense of buying a copy of the work, or whether it is reasonable to expect a copy to be purchased, are important. Take, for example, a postgraduate research student. He will need to refer to hundreds of different journal articles and books. The student will not be able to purchase more than a handful of these; he will have to be selective. The student may decide to purchase those materials which he will need to use over and over again during the research. But many of the articles and books will be used less frequently and only small portions will be referred to. It would not be realistic to expect the student to purchase a book when he wants to refer to only a small part of it. Similarly, in the case of an article in a journal – the student would not be expected to buy the issue of the journal or have to subscribe to the journal just to have access to and refer to one particular article.[82]

It is difficult to draw the limits of fair dealing for private study; perhaps it can be suggested, partly on the basis of the permitted acts in respect of librarians, that copying the whole of one article from an academic journal would be fair dealing, or the copying of part of a book, say, no more than one chapter.[83] Any more would not be fair dealing. However, it must be noted that a great deal of copying in relation to private study is carried out by students, and it is difficult to control and monitor the use that students make of photocopying facilities in libraries. Of course, in many cases, the charges made for photocopying (usually around 10p per sheet) mean that it is not economically viable to copy a whole book – in many cases purchasing the book would be cheaper than copying it. Although photocopying immediately springs to mind, it should be remembered that copyright can be infringed by making a handwritten copy. It is less likely that a substantial part will be taken because of the effort and time required. Making handwritten notes is a selective process, and only the materials that are of direct use to the student are likely to be copied out in this way. Also, the materials are read and, usually, analysed by the student during the process. It may be that the notes taken by the student have their own copyright because of the student's expenditure of skill, effort or judgment in adding comments and supplemental notes.

The act involved in fair dealing can be done by another, such as where a librarian makes a copy of an article in a periodical for a student who requires the copy for the purposes of research or private study. However, this is limited under s 29(3), which restricts the making of copies to cases where there are not multiple copies being made or supplied to more than one person at a similar time for purposes that are substantially the same. For example, in *Sillitoe v McGraw-Hill Book Co (UK) Ltd*,[84] the defendant had published 'study notes' intended to assist students taking GCE 'O' level examinations in literature, and had reproduced a substantial part of the claimant's works in the study notes. The defendant contended, *inter alia*, that the study notes fell within the fair dealing provisions under the Copyright Act 1956 s 6(1), that is fair dealing for the purposes of research or private study. This submission failed to find favour, as the defendant was not engaged in research or private study, but was merely facilitating this for others, the students purchasing copies of the study notes.

80 [1984] FSR 64.

81 But now, as a result of the Broadcasting Act 1990 s 176, there is a duty to make information about forthcoming programmes available to other publishers. European Union law also may be appropriate here, especially Article 102 of the Treaty on the Functioning of European Union (formerly Article 82 of the EC Treaty): *see* Joined Cases C-241/91P and C-242/91P *RTE & ITP v EC Commission* [1995] ECR I-743.

82 In some cases, a blanket licence scheme will be in operation allowing more extensive copying, such as that administered by the Copyright Licensing Agency.

83 *See* Copyright, Designs and Patents Act 1988, ss 38 and 39.

84 [1983] FSR 545.

Fair dealing for the purposes of criticism, review and reporting current events

Fair dealing for the purpose of criticism or review applies to any form of work or a performance of a work and does not infringe copyright provided that is accompanied by a sufficient acknowledgement.[85] Section 30(1) makes it clear that the criticism or review may be directed towards the work in question or another work or the performance of a work. For example, it is fair dealing to include extracts from a work by T.S. Eliot in a work which is a critical analysis of the work of E.M. Forster.[86] But otherwise the work must be subjected to criticism or review. The equivalent defence under the Copyright Act 1956 was held not to apply when correspondence between the Duke and Duchess of Windsor was published without any such criticism or review.[87] This form of fair dealing may also apply where an extract from a dramatic work is used in the criticism or review of a stage play based on the dramatic work.

The requirement for the works to have been made available to the public was inserted by the Copyright and Related Rights Regulations 2003 and, under s 30(1A), this applies where the work has so been made available by any means, including:

(a) the issue of copies to the public;
(b) making the work available by means of an electronic retrieval system;
(c) the rental or lending of copies of the work to the public;
(d) the performance, exhibition, playing or showing the work in public;
(e) the communication to the public of the work;

but no account is to be taken of any unauthorised act.

Section 178 contains a definition of 'sufficient acknowledgement' and requires that it identifies both the work by its title or other description, and the author. However, if the work is published anonymously,[88] or if the work is unpublished and the author's identity cannot be ascertained by reasonable inquiry, there is no requirement for the author's name to be included in the acknowledgement. In *Sillitoe v McGraw-Hill Book Co (UK) Ltd*[89] it was held that a sufficient acknowledgement must recognise the position or claims of the author.

An acknowledgement does not have to be express and may be implied where some of a series of works used are acknowledged and a reasonably attentive person would infer that the others were by the same author. In *Fraser Woodward Ltd v British Broadcasting Corporation*,[90] of the 14 photographs used in the television programme, some were acknowledged expressly on screen (for example, by panning down to the author's name at the bottom of the photograph), for some the commentator verbally identified the author. It was held that a moderately attentive person would realise all the photographs were by the same author and, consequently, there was a sufficient acknowledgement for the purposes of s 30.

In giving a sufficient acknowledgement, it is not necessary to give the author's full name or even any name at all provided the acknowledgement is sufficient to convey to a reasonably alert member of the audience to which the work, including the copyright work, is directed. So it was held at first instance in *Pro Sieben Media AG v Carlton UK Television Ltd*,[91] where the defendant had included in its television programme a 30-second video of a woman who was then pregnant with eight foetuses. The extract contained the initials of the claimant's television programme, TAFF, and its logo, a pale, stylised number 7. It was also held that it is not necessary for criticism or review to be the only or the predominant purpose, provided that it was a significant purpose. The purpose itself is something to be tested subjectively from the point of view of the person relying on the permitted act.[92] However, in *Pro Sieben*, the defendant's purpose was to show that the defendant was above the cheque-book journalism allegedly carried on by the claimant. In the Court of Appeal,[93] it was accepted that transmission of a company's television logo

85 Copyright, Designs and Patents Act 1988 s 30(1). Criticism may be positive or negative: *David Geva v Walt Disney Corp* [1995] 2 EIPR D-39, Sup Ct of Israel.

86 Both authors are deceased but literary copyright still subsists in their works.

87 *Associated Newspapers Group plc* v *News Group Newspapers Ltd* [1986] RPC 515.

88 See *PCR Ltd v Dow Jones Telerate Ltd* [1998] FSR 170.

89 [1983] FSR 545.

90 [2005] FSR 36.

91 [1998] FSR 43.

92 This was doubted in the Court of Appeal, where it was said that motive was more likely to be relevant to the question of whether the dealing might be fair: *Pro Sieben Media AG v Carlton UK TV Ltd* [1999] FSR 610 at 620.

93 [1999] FSR 610.

could be a sufficient acknowledgement, especially if that was the manner in which the company tended to identify itself. Furthermore, in holding that the extract was fair dealing under s 30(1) (criticism or review) and fair dealing under s 30(2) (reporting current events), it was held that criticism need not be directed at the style of the copyright work but could go beyond that and be criticism of the ideas contained within it and the social and moral implications. Walker LJ said (at 620):

> 'Criticism or review' and 'reporting current events' are expressions of wide and indefinite scope. Any attempt to plot their precise boundaries is doomed to failure. They are expressions which should be interpreted liberally, but I derive little assistance from comparisons with other expressions such as 'current affairs' or 'news'.

If the work copied is not criticised, the criticism must be directed at another work rather than the actions of a particular person. In *Ashdown* v *Telegraph Group Ltd*,[94] Paddy Ashdown, then leader of the Liberal Democrats, attended a meeting with the Prime Minister and others. He later dictated a minute of that meeting. Substantial extracts from the minute were copied by the defendant in a newspaper article about secret plans to form a coalition with the Labour Party. In granting summary judgment for Paddy Ashdown, it was held that it was not necessary to publish the minute at all as the criticism was directed at the claimant and the Prime Minister, not at the minute itself. As the Vice-Chancellor stated (at para 24):

94 [2001] RPC 34.

> . . . I accept that it is necessary to have regard to the true purpose of the work. Is it 'a genuine piece of criticism and review or is it something else, such as an attempt to dress up the infringement of another's copyright in the guise of criticism, and so profit unfairly from another's work'.

Criticism can be scathing and can involve a substantial part of another work, and yet still be fair dealing.[95] In *Hubbard* v *Vosper*,[96] the defendant had been a member of the Church of Scientology for some 14 years. After leaving, he wrote a book which was highly critical of the cult of Scientology and used in his book substantial extracts from books, bulletins and letters, some of which were confidential, written by the claimant. The defence of fair dealing for the purposes of criticism and review was successfully raised as regards the copyright issues.

95 *See* also *Pro Sieben Media AG* v *Carlton UK TV Ltd* [1999] FSR 610. However, although a defendant may avail himself of the fair dealing defence in such a case, the claimant's remedy may lie in an action for defamation or malicious falsehood.

96 [1972] 2 QB 84.

In criticising a work other than the one reproduced under the permitted act, it seems that it must relate to a work in the copyright sense. This does not, however, prevent the criticism being levelled at the underlying ideas or philosophy manifested in the work. In *Fraser Woodward Ltd* v *British Broadcasting Corporation*,[97] the defendant screened a programme called *Tabloid Tales*: it used 14 photographs of David Beckham and his family which had been taken by Mr Fraser and published in newspapers. The purpose was to criticise or review tabloid journalism. Mann J confirmed that it was acceptable in this case to use the photographs to criticise or review the tabloid press, being the newspapers and ideas behind them. He confirmed that there was no need specifically to identify the other works and also rejected a submission that a valid test was whether the criticism or review could be carried out without using the works in question. Nor was this a case of copyright infringement dressed up to look like criticism or review. Although the use by the defendant was a commercial use as could have competed with the claimant's exploitation of the photographs, there was no evidence to show that the commercial value of the photographs was seriously diminished by their use in the programme.

97 [2005] FSR 36.

The motive behind the use of the claimant's work is an important factor. As Lord Denning confirmed in *Hubbard* v *Vosper*, it would not be fair dealing for a rival to take copyright material belonging to someone else to use as his own. In *Time Warner Entertainments Co Ltd* v *Channel 4 Television Corp plc*[98] the claimant obtained an injunction

98 [1994] EMLR 1. For a discussion of this case *see* Benson, C. 'Fair dealing in the UK' [1995] 6 EIPR 304.

to prevent the screening of a programme entitled *Forbidden Fruit* which contained extracts of scenes from the notorious film *Clockwork Orange*, which was withdrawn in the UK some 20 years earlier for fears of copycat violence. The defendant's programme was based on a criticism of the decision to continue to refuse to allow the film to be shown. The Court of Appeal lifted the injunction on the basis that the defendant could rely on the defence of fair dealing for criticism or review under s 30 of the 1988 Act. The court held that the criticism or review need not be directed primarily at the work itself, and this is confirmed in s 30(1). Although the copy of the film had been obtained, in the claimant's words, 'in an underhand manner' (it had been bought legitimately in Paris), this was not a case where it had been obtained in breach of confidence. In any case, of more relevance was how the work was treated, not how it had been obtained. An argument by the claimant for limiting review by third parties to a total of four minutes' duration failed to impress the court, which confirmed that, in order to criticise a film seriously, sufficient time must be spent showing extracts from the film.

In terms of fair dealing for reporting current events, the events in question do not have to be very recent but they must still be related to other events which are of current interest. In *Hyde Park Residence Ltd* v *Yelland*,[99] the publication was of stills taken from video footage recorded by security cameras which showed Diana, Princess of Wales, and Dodi Fayed arriving at and later leaving the Villa Windsor in Paris. The date of publication was nearly one year after. However, and for the purposes of the appeal, Aldous LJ held that the media coverage could be described as current events as the purpose of the reporting was to attempt to discredit what had been said, much more recently, by Mohammed Al Fayed.[100]

Fair dealing for the purpose of reporting current events does not apply in the case of a photograph. It is common practice for newspapers to copy extracts from stories in other newspapers. For example, one newspaper may have an 'exclusive' in its early morning issue and other newspapers carry the story in their later editions giving, of course, a sufficient acknowledgement. This they may do, provided a photograph is not copied without permission. Lightman J confirmed that the practice of newspapers of copying a photograph from another newspaper with the intention of obtaining a licence retrospectively was clearly unlawful.[101] Nor could such use of a photograph be considered to be fair dealing for criticism or review, such a proposition being described as totally unreal.

The fair dealing provisions are wider than under the previous Act because, apart from the exception of photographs, they are not limited to any particular type of work and can, therefore, apply to broadcasts. Indeed, according to Scott J in *BBC* v *British Satellite Broadcasting Ltd*,[102] this fair dealing provision is not limited to general news bulletins and could apply to a major sporting event such as the World Cup football competition. In this case, there had been an acknowledgement given by BSB as to the source of the film, but according to s 30(3) there is no need to give an acknowledgement in the case of reporting current events by means of a sound recording, film or broadcast where this would be impossible for reasons of practicality or otherwise.[103] It seems strange that an exception is made in the case of photographs but not broadcasts.

Incidental inclusion of copyright material

The use of movie and video cameras, still cameras, CCTV and live broadcasts means that, frequently and inevitably, copyright works will be included in the films, photographs or broadcasts whether by design or accident. To facilitate the making of photographs (and other artistic works), films or broadcasts, the incidental inclusion of a copyright work does not infringe the copyright subsisting in that work: s 31(1). Otherwise, it would be very difficult arranging to make a film or whatever, because it would be necessary to avoid

99 [2000] RPC 604.

100 However, the defence failed as the purpose was not to report the events shown in the stills.

101 *Banier v News Group Newspapers Ltd* [1997] FSR 812.

102 [1991] 3 WLR 174.

103 Note that, in relation to criticism or review, a sufficient acknowledgement is an absolute requirement.

the chance inclusion of copyright works. For example, in the case of a television broadcast made in the streets of a city, the copyright subsisting in buildings (artistic works) would be infringed,[104] as might be the copyright in advertising hoardings. The broadcast may also include a glimpse of the front page of a newspaper on sale and pick up the strains of a popular tune being played loudly further down the street. The inclusion must be incidental. It must be 'casual, inessential, subordinate or merely background'.[105]

The exception goes further in that the copyright in the work incidentally included is not infringed by other acts, such as issuing copies to the public, playing, showing or communicating to the public anything that was made without infringing copyright under s 31(1). However, as regards musical works and sound recordings and broadcasts including musical work, incidental inclusion does not extend to deliberate inclusion. This also applies to words spoken or sung with music: for example, the lyrics of a song.

The word 'incidental' is not restricted to unintended or accidental inclusion but there is no distinction between a situation where the work in question is an integral or incidental part of the work objected to. In *Football Association Premier League Ltd v Panini UK Ltd*,[106] the defendant published cards bearing photographs of football players wearing their club strips which bore the badges of the football clubs and, in some cases, the Premier League badge. People bought these cards to stick in albums. The Football Association Premier League ('FAPL'), 14 of the football clubs and an exclusive licensee sued for infringement of copyright in the FAPL emblem and club badges. The Court of Appeal confirmed that the defendant could not rely on the s 31 defence of incidental inclusion. Chadwick LJ said (at para 26):

> I would accept that, in principle, there is no necessary dichotomy between 'integral' and 'incidental'. Where an artistic work in which copyright subsists appears in a photograph because it is part of the setting in which the photographer finds his subject it can properly be said to be an integral part of the photograph: if it is part of the setting in which the photographer finds his subject, it will, necessarily, appear in the photograph unless edited out.

He went on to say that a consideration was the purpose for which the work was created and that it was artificial to test the 'incidentality' of the inclusion by artistic consideration where the purpose of the inclusion was commercial. The cards would not have been of such interest to buyers if the players were not pictured in their club strips.

In *Football Association Premier League Ltd v QC Leisure (No 2)*,[107] transmissions of football matches included the player line-up before the start of the match, during which the Premier League Anthem could be heard being played in the background. The case involved numerous issues relating to the use of unauthorised decoders used to receive transmissions of Premier League football matches. It was held that as regards the Anthem, the defence of incidental inclusion under s 31 applied. Kitchen J accepted that neither the broadcasters nor the viewers attached any great importance to whether the Anthem could be heard. The objective was to show the players lining up before the match so as to convey the excitement and anticipation in the stadium. The inclusion of the Anthem, in so far as it could have been heard at all, was purely incidental.

Although the inclusion does not have to be unintentional, a deliberate treatment of how the work is included may take it out of the permitted act. In *Fraser Woodward Ltd v British Broadcasting Corporation*,[108] of the 14 photographs of the Beckhams used in a television programme, an alternative defence of incidental inclusion was run in respect of two of the photographs. In one case, the photograph was shown as it appeared on the page of a newspaper and then the television picture zoomed in on the headline on that page. It was a deliberate way of showing the photograph in the context of the overall story (about a plot to kidnap Victoria Beckham and one of her children). It was held not to be incidental inclusion for the purposes of s 31 even though a defence under s 30(1), criticism or review, succeeded.

104 A work of architecture is an artistic work by the Copyright, Designs and Patents Act 1988 s 4(1)(a). Section 62 would also excuse – *see* below (p 240). As with other works except typographical arrangements, the copyright in an artistic work can be infringed communicating the work to the public (s 20).

105 *IPC Magazines Ltd v MGN Ltd* [1998] FSR 431, per Richard McCombe QC sitting as a deputy judge of the Chancery Division.

106 [2004] 1 WLR 1174.

107 [2008] FSR 32.

108 [2005] FSR 36.

Visual impairment

The Copyright (Visually Impaired Persons) Act 2002 inserted ss 31A to 31F into the Copyright, Designs and Patents Act 1988 to permit the making of accessible copies of literary, dramatic, musical or artistic works and published editions by or on behalf of visually impaired persons.[109] An accessible copy is one which gives a visually impaired person improved access to a work.[110] Examples might be where an enlarged copy of a book or television listings is made or a copy of a book is made available on a computer for reading on a computer screen where the person concerned is unable to hold a book or turn the pages or where a blind person has access to computer software capable of reading text out loud. It should already be clear that visual impairment is not limited to sight and a visually impaired person is, under s 31F(9), a person:

(a) who is blind;
(b) who has an impairment of visual function which cannot be improved, by the use of corrective lenses, to a level that would normally be acceptable for reading without a special level or kind of light;
(c) who is unable, through physical disability, to hold or manipulate a book; or
(d) who is unable, through physical disability, to focus or move his eyes to the extent that would normally be acceptable for reading.

The focus is on reading text or music but as artistic works are included in the list of works for which accessible copies may be made, the definition of a visually impaired person must be read in the context also of seeing an artistic work, such as a photograph or some other image.

Section 31A covers the making of a single accessible copy for the personal use of a visually impaired person if that person has the lawful use of a copy of the whole or part of a work (the 'master copy') which is not accessible to him because of his impairment. In such a case an accessible copy may be made without infringing copyright: s 31A(1). This does not apply if the work is a musical work, or part thereof, and the making of an accessible copy would involve recording a performance of the music or part of it. Therefore, if the music is in the form of sheet music, it is not permissible for someone to play it, say on piano, and record it on audio tape to give the visually impaired person to listen to. What is allowed is making an enlarged copy of the sheet music which will enable the visually impaired person to be able to read it sufficiently well to play the music himself. Also excluded is making an accessible copy of a database or part of a database if that would infringe the copyright in the database.[111] This appears to lead to a contradiction. Under s 31A(1) making an accessible copy of a database for the personal use of a visually impaired person does not infringe copyright (a database is a form of literary work). But s 31A(2) disapplies s 31A(1) if making the copy would infringe the copyright in the database or part of it. It seems that the intention must have been to exclude databases from the permitted act but it is notable that the exclusion refers to the copyright in the database and not that in the contents of the database. Therefore, it might be acceptable to make an accessible copy of some of the contents of a database providing this does not infringe the copyright in the database as a database. No mention is made of the *sui generis* database right which, if it subsists in the database, may be infringed even if the copyright is not because of differences in the scope of infringement between the two rights.

The permitted act does not apply if, or to the extent that, accessible copies are made commercially available by, or with the authorisation of, the copyright owner.[112] This only applies in respect of the actual form of impairment a particular individual has. For example, if the copyright owner sells large print copies of books, that is no answer to a

109 These provisions were brought into force on 31 October 2003.

110 Section 31F(3). Under s 31F(4) an accessible copy may include facilities for navigating around a version of the work but may not include changes unnecessary to overcome problems caused by visual impairment or changes that infringe the author's right to object to a derogatory treatment under s 80. Section 31F contains the definitions for ss 31A to 31E.

111 The exceptions for musical works and databases are contained in s 31A(2).

112 Section 31A(5).

person who is blind or physically unable to turn the pages of a book. A copy in a form accessible to that person may still be made.

An accessible copy must be accompanied by a statement that the copy was made under s 31A together with a sufficient acknowledgement. If a charge is made by a person making an accessible copy on behalf of a visually impaired person, that charge must not exceed the cost of making and supplying the copy. Records must be kept by the approved body in accordance with s 31C, as discussed below.

Accessible copies will be treated as infringing copies where a person holds an accessible copy when not entitled to have it made under s 31A(1) or where a person transfers an accessible copy made under s 31A(1) to another person unless the person making the transfer has reasonable grounds for believing that the person to whom he is making the transfer is the person entitled to have it made or has possession of the master copy and intends to transfer the accessible copy to the visually impaired person entitled to have the copy.[113] Subsequent dealing with accessible copies has the effect of their being treated as infringing copies and, if that dealing itself infringes copyright, they are treated as infringing copies for all subsequent purposes.[114] Dealing covers selling, letting for hire, offering or exposing for sale or hire or communication to the public.

Multiple copies of accessible copies may be made for visually impaired persons by approved bodies under s 31B. An approved body is an educational establishment[115] or a body that is not conducted for profit. Unlike the case with single copies made under s 31A, the master copy must be of a *commercially* available work or edition, but the forms of works covered are the same, being literary, dramatic, musical or artistic works and published editions. Similar provisions apply otherwise in respect of the exceptions for musical works and databases. There is a slight change where accessible copies are commercially available in that they must be accessible 'to the same or substantially the same degree' whereas, for single copies made under s 31A, they must be in a form 'that is accessible to that person'. This reflects the fact that multiple copies may be made for a group of persons with varying levels of impairment.

There are also requirements for an accompanying statement to the effect that the copies have been made under s 31B together with a sufficient acknowledgement. Any charges made by the approved body must not exceed the cost of making and supplying the copies.[116] A further requirement where the approved body is an educational establishment is that it must ensure that the copies are used only for its educational purposes.

Unlike the case with single copies made under s 31A, where the master copy is in copy-protected electronic form, any copies made must, as far as practicable, incorporate the same, or equally effective, copy-protection unless the copyright owner agrees otherwise.

There are similar provisions in respect of subsequent dealing, making the copies infringing copies[117] and, if the approved body is no longer entitled to make or supply copies under s 31B, any copies it continues to hold are treated as infringing copies.[118]

Section 31C applies to intermediate copies made under s 31B by approved bodies and records which they must keep of such copies. Under s 31C(1), an approved body may hold an intermediate copy of a master copy necessarily created during the production of accessible copies as long as the approved body continues to be entitled to make accessible copies for the purposes of production of further accessible copies. Any intermediate copy made in breach of s 31C(1) is treated as an infringing copy: s 31C(2). An example of an intermediate copy could be a version of a literary work which has been scanned into a computer where a navigation system has been incorporated into the copy which is then saved to a CD for loading on to computers used by visually impaired persons.

Intermediate copies made by approved bodies may be lent or transferred to other approved bodies providing the body lending or transferring the intermediate copy has reasonable grounds for believing that the other is also an approved body entitled to make

113 This is the combined effect of s 31A(6) to (8).

114 Section 31A(9).

115 Section 174 defines educational establishments as schools and other forms of educational establishment designated by the Secretary of State. Schools are defined in s 174(3) by reference to the relevant Act or Order as appropriate for England and Wales, Scotland and Northern Ireland. *See* the section on education (p 234) for further details.

116 'Supplying' includes lending under s 31B(13).

117 Section 31B(10).

118 Section 31B(9).

119 Section 31C(3) and (4).

accessible copies under s 31B and will not use it except for the purposes of making such copies.[119] Any charge made must not, under s 31C(5), exceed the cost of the loan or transfer. For the purposes of ss 31B and 31C, lending means making available for use, otherwise than for direct or indirect economic or commercial advantage, on terms that it will or may be returned. A charge not exceeding the cost of making and supplying the copy may be made.[120]

120 Section 31F(6) and (7).

Records must be kept by approved bodies of accessible copies made under s 31B and of the persons to whom they are supplied; intermediate copies lent or transferred under s 31C and of the persons to whom they are lent or transferred. The approved body must allow the copyright owner or person acting for him, on giving reasonable notice, to inspect the records at any reasonable time. The approved body must, within a reasonable time of making an accessible copy under s 31B or lending or transferring an intermediate copy under s 31C, notify a relevant representative body. This is a body which represents copyright owners (whether particular owners or owners of the type of copyright concerned). If no such body exists, the approved body must give notice to the copyright owner. A representative body must have given notice to the Secretary of State of the copyright owners or classes of owners represented by it otherwise the copyright owner must be notified directly. In the absence of relevant representative bodies, the requirement to notify the copyright owner directly does not apply if it is not reasonably possible for the approved body to ascertain the name and address of the copyright owner.[121]

121 The provisions relating to keeping records and notification are contained in s 31C(6) to (9).

Section 31D provides for licensing schemes and, where such a scheme is in force, s 31B does not apply. The scheme must be one operated by a licensing body granting licences permitting the making and supply of copies of the work in a particular form or accessible copy. The scheme must not be unreasonably restrictive and the scheme and any modification of it must have been notified to the Secretary of State by the licensing body. A scheme is unreasonably restrictive if it includes a term or condition which purports to prevent or limit the steps that may be taken under ss 31B or 31C or which has that effect. However, this does not apply if the copyright work is no longer published by or with the authority of the copyright owner and there are reasonable grounds for preventing or restricting the making of accessible copies of the work. Therefore, it may be acceptable for a licensing body to prohibit the making of accessible copies of previous editions of a book which have been replaced by newer editions or where the work is out of print and no longer available for sale. If ss 31B or 31C are displaced by a licensing scheme, ss 119 to 122 apply to the scheme as if it were one under s 117. These provisions include references to the Copyright Tribunal.

The Secretary of State is given the power to make Orders if it appears to him that the making of copies under s 31B or under a s 31C licence has led to infringement of a copyright work on a scale that would not, in his opinion, have occurred if s 31B had not been in force at the time or the licence had not been granted.[122] Such Orders may target one or more specific approved bodies or disapply the provision in respect of making copies of a specific description. Before making the Order, the Secretary of State must consult such bodies representing copyright owners and representing visually impaired persons as he thinks fit.

122 Section 31E(1).

Where the Order includes a prohibition, the Secretary of State must also consult the approved body or bodies concerned or, where the Order is to apply to one or more specified categories of approved bodies, any such body representing that category or categories of approved bodies. An approved body prohibited by an Order from acting under a licence may not apply to the Copyright Tribunal under s 121(1) in respect of a refusal or failure of a licensing body to grant such a licence.

The introduction of these complex provisions allowing accessible copies of copyright works to be made could be described as a sledgehammer to crack a walnut. A copyright owner who insisted on exercising his full economic rights to prevent the making of accessible copies for visually impaired people could only be described as miserly. In some cases, accessible copies of works are already made at no or little cost with the consent of copyright owners.[123]

123 The author made a copy of an earlier edition of this book available in software form for no charge to a blind solicitor who used reading software with the consent of the publisher.

Education

Education is treated as a special case by copyright law, and there are several exceptions to infringement contained in the 1988 Act.[124] Some control is retained – for example, reprographic copying is permitted only in limited circumstances, and some of the permitted acts can be done only for or at educational establishments.[125] Section 174 of the Act defines 'educational establishments' as being any school and any other establishment specified by order of the Secretary of State. By the Copyright (Educational Establishments) Order 2005,[126] other establishments include universities established by Royal Charter or Act of Parliament, most institutions for further or higher education and theological colleges. 'School' is defined by reference to the appropriate legislation – for example, in England and Wales it is as defined in the Education Act 1944.[127] The expressions 'teacher' and 'pupil' include, respectively, any person who gives and any person who receives instruction. Another control is that, in some circumstances where it is permitted to make copies of copyright works, if those copies are subsequently dealt with they are treated as infringing copies. 'Dealt with' generally means sold or let for hire, or offered or exposed for sale or hire or communicated to the public.

124 Copyright, Designs and Patents Act 1988 ss 32–36.

125 Reprographic copying has a wider meaning than simply making photocopies of a work: *see* s 178.

126 SI 2005/223.

127 *See* Copyright, Designs and Patents Act 1988 s 174(3) for the meaning of 'school' in Scotland and in Northern Ireland.

Section 32 deals with things done either for the purpose of instruction, or for examination purposes. Unusually, for the 'education permitted acts' there is no requirement for the instruction or examination to be done by or on behalf of an educational establishment. However, in some cases, the instruction may only be for a non-commercial purpose. Copying in the course of instruction or in preparation for instruction of a literary, dramatic, musical or artistic work is permitted as long as the copying is done by the person giving or receiving the instruction, for example the teacher or the pupil, and the copying is not by a reprographic process. The copy must be accompanied by a sufficient acknowledgement and the instruction may only be for a non-commercial purpose. For example, it is permissible for a teacher to ask a pupil to write out by hand a substantial extract from a work of literature. Another example is where a teacher reproduces an artistic work on a blackboard in a classroom for the purpose of instruction. Copying by making a film or a film sound track in the course of, or in preparation for, instruction in the making of films or film sound tracks does not infringe the copyright in a sound recording, film or broadcast. Again, the copying must be done by a person giving or receiving instruction, a sufficient acknowledgement is required and the instruction must be for a non-commercial purpose.

Where a literary, dramatic, musical or artistic work has been made available to the public, it is not infringed by being copied in the course of instruction or preparing for instruction providing the copying is fair dealing with the work, it is done by the person giving or receiving instruction, is not done by a reprographic process and is accompanied by a sufficient acknowledgement.[128] Under s 32(2B), making available to the public has the same meaning as set out in s 30(1A).

128 Section 32(2A) inserted by the Copyright and Related Rights Regulations 2003, SI 2003/2498.

As might be expected, examinations are also privileged in that anything may be done for the purposes of the examination by way of setting questions, communicating questions to candidates or answering the questions without infringing copyright, providing the questions are accompanied by a sufficient acknowledgement. However, there is an exception to this in the case of reprographic copies of musical works for use by an examination candidate in performing the work. Therefore, if the examination requires the candidates to play some music, authorisation to make copies must be obtained from the copyright owner or additional copies of the sheet music purchased. The requirement to give a sufficient acknowledgement under s 32 does not apply if it would be impossible for reasons of practicability or otherwise.

The Act prohibits the subsequent dealing with copies made under s 32 by considering such copies to be infringing copies. 'Dealt with' means sold or let for hire, offered or exposed for sale or hire or communicated to the public unless that communication does not infringe copyright under s 32(3), being anything done for the purposes of examination.

Anthologies are dealt with under s 33, which permits the inclusion of a short passage from a published literary or dramatic work in a collection provided that the collection is intended for use in educational establishments and consists mainly of material in which no copyright subsists. Such material would include works in which the copyright has expired.[129] The collection must be described in its title and in any advertisements as being for use in educational establishments. Furthermore, a sufficient acknowledgement is required. But how short is a short extract? If it is not substantial in copyright terms, then there can be no infringement anyway, and the requirements of the exception are meaningless. A further requirement is that no more than two excerpts from the copyright works by the same author can be included in anthologies published by the same publisher over any period of five years. It would seem that this permitted act is extremely parsimonious. Presumably, if there is some criticism or review of the extracts the fair dealing provisions would come into play and larger extracts could be used. Just to place a final and unnecessary imposition, s 33(4) limits the provision to the educational purposes of the educational establishment.

Performances of literary, dramatic and musical works are permitted provided the audience is made up of teachers and pupils at the educational establishment and other persons directly connected with the activities of the establishment.[130] A parent of a pupil is not to be taken as directly connected with the school by reason of being a parent only. Therefore, a play performed by pupils before an audience of parents will fall outside the scope of this permitted act. The performance may be by a teacher or pupil in the course of the school's activities, or by any person for the purposes of instruction. For the latter it is required that the performance takes place at the school, but as far as teacher and pupil performances are concerned, this limitation does not apply. However, the wording of s 34 seems to suggest that only sole performances fall within the section. The section is termed in the singular as regards the performers. There are similar provisions in respect of the playing or showing of a sound recording, film or broadcast for the purposes of instruction before such an audience as described above.

Under s 35(1), recordings of broadcasts and copies of such recordings can be made by or on behalf of educational establishments for their educational purposes without infringing copyright in the broadcast provided there is not an appropriate licensing scheme under s 143[131] and the recording is accompanied by a sufficient acknowledgement of the broadcast and the educational purposes are non-commercial. Under s 35(1A), it is not an infringement of the copyright where a recording of a broadcast or copy of such a recording whose making did not infringe copyright under s 35(1) for a person situated within the premises of an educational establishment to communicate it to the public provided it cannot be received by any person situated outside those premises. This would allow, for example, the playing of a recording of a broadcast to pupils, teachers and parents on an internal network of televisions within a school. There is no relaxation of the requirement to accompany the recording with a sufficient acknowledgement under s 35, the reason being, presumably, that it should always be possible to determine the identity of the work, by its title or other description, and the identity of the author. In any case,

129 It could also cover material published in a country which is not a member of the copyright conventions and fails otherwise to attract protection in the UK.

130 Copyright, Designs and Patents Act 1988 s 34. Such performances are deemed not to be public performances.

131 Copyright, Designs and Patents Act 1988 s 35. An example of a licensing scheme is that under the Copyright (Certification of Licensing Schemes for Educational Recording of Broadcasts) (Educational Recording Agency Limited) Order 2005, SI 2005/222.

the definition of sufficient acknowledgement under s 178 excuses the naming of the author if the work is published anonymously or where it is not possible by reasonable enquiry to determine the identity of the author. Subsequent dealing is not permitted.

Section 36(1) permits the reprographic copying of passages of published literary, dramatic or musical works by or on behalf of educational establishments for the purposes of instruction, provided the copies are accompanied by a sufficient acknowledgement and the instruction is for a non-commercial purpose. No acknowledgement is required where this would prove impossible by reasons of practicability or otherwise. Section 36(1B) permits the making by or on behalf of educational establishments of reprographic copies of passages from published editions, to the extent permitted under s 36 (that is, 1 per cent per quarter unless a licence scheme is in operation), for the purposes of instruction without infringing the copyright in the typographical arrangement of the edition. The amount that can be copied is extremely small, being not more than 1 per cent of any work in any quarter, and the authority to copy given by s 36 is subject to the availability of licences where the person making the copies knows or ought to have been aware of the availability of such licences. A licence may not attempt to reduce the portion that can be copied under s 36. Again, this provision must be considered in the light of what is a substantial part of a work. It is submitted that, in most cases, a substantial part of a work will exceed 1 per cent of the total quantity of a work. If this is so, s 36 has no effect whatsoever, it is just so many empty words. Of course, it is very difficult to predict how a court will decide the issue of substantiality, the test being based mainly on quality. However, it would be unlikely that a mere 1 per cent would capture the essence of a work. In *Hawkes & Sons (London) Ltd* v *Paramount Film Service Ltd*[132] around 8 per cent was adjudged to be substantial, but here the basic melody had been taken. Perhaps a better test would be to look at the effect, if any, on the copyright owner's interests. Has the extent of the copying been such that it would be reasonable to expect that copies of the original work be purchased instead? However, the rapid improvements made in recent times to copying technology perhaps account for the attempts to limit unauthorised copying to tiny amounts only.

As usual, subsequent dealing, which includes communication to the public, has the effect of treating copies made under this section as infringing copies for the purposes of that dealing. Where the dealing itself infringes copyright, the copies are treated as infringing copies for all subsequent purposes.

Section 36A was inserted by the Copyright and Related Rights Regulations 1996[133] and was needed to create a new permitted act in relation to lending by educational establishments as the 1996 Regulations created a right to prevent rental and lending of copyright works under s 18A of the Copyright, Designs and Patents Act 1988. Section 36A simply states that copyright in a work is not infringed by the lending of copies of the work by an educational establishment.

Libraries and archives

These provisions apply only to 'prescribed' libraries and archives, that is those prescribed by statutory instrument, which may also provide that, in some cases (also prescribed), a librarian or archivist may make a copy only if the person requesting the copy satisfies the librarian or archivist that he requires the copy only for non-commercial research or private study and makes a signed declaration in the prescribed form.[134] In such cases, a librarian or archivist may rely on a signed declaration by a person requesting a copy of part or whole of a work in which copyright subsists, unless he is aware that the declaration is false in a material particular. A signed declaration will usually contain a statement to the effect that the copy is required for the purposes of research or private study and that

132 [1934] Ch 593.

133 SI 1996/2967.

134 The Copyright (Librarians and Archivists) (Copying of Copyright Material) Regulations 1989, SI 1989/1212 specify prescribed libraries and archives and expand on the prescribed conditions, and also contain the forms to be used for declarations and written statements required in the Copyright, Designs and Patents Act 1988 ss 38–43. For example, the prescribed conditions generally include a requirement for a signed declaration or statement.

the person requesting the copy has not previously been supplied with a copy from the same work. If a signed declaration is false in a material particular, the copy supplied is considered to be an infringing copy and the person requesting the copy is liable for infringement of copyright as if he made the copy himself. The 1988 Act acknowledges that a librarian or archivist may delegate his duties and responsibilities to others.[135] In general, where the copying is permitted of certain types of work, there will be no infringement of accompanying illustrations or in the typographical arrangement.

Under s 38, a librarian may make and supply a copy of an article in a periodical to a person requiring the copy for the purposes of research or private study. The person supplied must pay at least the attributable cost, which includes a contribution to the general expenses of the library, that is overheads. No person may be supplied with more than one copy of the same article, or with more than one article from the same issue of the periodical. Similar provisions in s 39 permit the making and supplying of a copy of a part of a published edition of a literary, dramatic or musical work (other than an article in a periodical). The section refers to copying a part of a work without giving any guidance as to the maximum proportion that may be copied. Section 40 of the Act seeks to restrict the making or supplying of multiple copies of the same material by way of regulations made for the purposes of ss 38 and 39.[136]

Section 40A, inserted by the Copyright and Related Rights Regulations 1996, provides for the lending of books by public libraries where the book is within the public lending right scheme under s 1 of the Public Lending Right Act 1979 and the book falls within the scheme's provisions for eligibility, whether or not it is in fact eligible. Furthermore, lending of copies of a work by a prescribed library or archive, not being a public library, and which is not conducted for profit, is permitted without infringing copyright.

Provisions also exist so that one prescribed library may make and supply copies to other prescribed libraries of:

(a) articles in periodicals; or

(b) the whole or part of a published edition of a literary, dramatic or musical work.[137]

However, (b) does not apply if, at the time the copy is made, the librarian making it knows or could by reasonable enquiry ascertain the name and address of the person entitled to authorise the making of copies of the work. In the vast majority of cases this will be so – most published editions contain the name of the publisher and the author; and whichever of these is the copyright owner, the librarian should be able, without undue difficulty, to make contact in order to ask permission.

Subject to certain conditions, the making for another prescribed library or archive of replacement copies of literary, dramatic or musical works which have been lost, destroyed or damaged is permitted under s 42. Making copies in order to preserve the original is also permitted, for example, so that the copy may be displayed and the original placed in safe storage. However, such copying is not permitted if it is reasonably practicable to purchase a copy of the item. The copying of certain unpublished works for the purposes of non-commercial research or private study is also permitted,[138] as is the making of copies of articles of cultural or historical importance or interest which are to be exported from the UK, it being a legal requirement that such a copy is made.[139]

Under s 15 of the Copyright Act 1911, a copy of any book, serial or other printed publication was required to be deposited in one of six nominated libraries, being the British Library, the National Libraries of Scotland and Wales, the Universities of Oxford and Cambridge and Trinity College Dublin. These are collectively known as the Legal Deposit Libraries. However, s 15 of the 1911 Act applied only to materials in printed form and changes were needed to bring the provisions up to date to cover publication in other media such as on the internet. The Legal Deposit Libraries Act 2003[140] gives the Secretary of State the power to extend the system of legal deposit to cover online publication, such

135 These preliminary issues are contained in s 37.

136 The Copyright (Librarians and Archivists) (Copying of Copyright Material) Regulations 1989, SI 1989/1212.

137 Section 41. Copies may only be supplied to a person satisfying the librarian or archivist that he requires the copy for non-commercial research or private study and will not use the copy for any other purpose.

138 Section 43.

139 Copyright, Designs and Patents Act 1988 s 44.

140 This Act repealed s 15 of the Copyright Act 1911.

as on the internet, and offline publication, such as on CD-ROM. As a result of these provisions, it was necessary to insert a new permitted act in s 44A covering copying by or on behalf of deposit libraries. Copyright is not infringed in such cases by copying a work from the internet where the work is of a description prescribed by Regulations made under s 10(5) of the 2003 Act, where its publication on the internet or the person publishing it there is connected with the UK in a manner to be prescribed and the copying is done in the manner prescribed. The libraries, persons acting on their behalf and readers may not use the material, copy it, adapt any accompanying computer program or database, lend or transfer to a third party or dispose of the material unless authorised by Regulations. At the time of writing no Regulations, except for a commencement Order, have been made under the 2003 Act.[141]

141 The Legal Deposit Libraries Act 2003 (Commencement) Order 2004, SI 2004/130. The Act was brought into force on 1 February 2004.

Public administration

Copyright is not infringed by certain things done in connection with what might loosely be described as in the course of public administration. This includes parliamentary and judicial proceedings, Royal Commissions and statutory inquiries, and materials open to public inspection, on a statutory register or contained in a public record. Further, acts done under statutory authority do not infringe copyright, unless the relevant Act of Parliament provides otherwise, and the Crown may copy and issue copies to the public of materials communicated to the Crown in the course of public business.[142]

142 For the meaning of 'Crown' in this context, *see* s 48(6).

Thus, the copying of documents for a court trial does not infringe copyright, neither does playing a piece of music in court as part of the proceedings: for example, if the case concerns a dispute involving an alleged infringement of copyright in a piece of music. Copyright is not infringed by doing anything for the purpose of reporting parliamentary and judicial proceedings, or the proceedings of Royal Commissions or statutory inquiries that are held in public. This does not, of course, authorise the copying of published reports of such proceedings. It is permissible to make copies of entries in registers such as the Data Protection Register, the Register of Patents and the Register of Trade Marks, to make copies of information contained in electoral registers or to obtain copies of birth, marriage and death certificates, etc. without infringing copyright. The Copyright (Material Open to Public Inspection) (Marking of Copies of Plans and Drawings) Order 1990 contains the text of a statement to be applied to copies of plans and drawings supplied under s 47.[143] Further details of the public administration exceptions to copyright infringement are given in Table 7.2 at the end of this chapter.

143 SI 1990/1427. The statement is contained in art 2. A similar provision applies to copies of maps open to public inspection under art 2 of the Copyright (Material Open to Public Inspection) (Marking of Copies of Maps) Order 1989, SI 1989/1099.

Computer programs and databases

The Copyright (Computer Programs) Regulations 1992[144] inserted ss 50A–50C providing for some specific exceptions to copyright infringement. Under certain conditions, lawful users of computer programs may make back-up copies of computer programs, decompile programs to achieve interoperability and copy or adapt a computer program. There is also a non-derogation from grant exception in relation to databases in s 50D, inserted by the Copyright and Rights in Databases Regulations 1997[145] and, under s 50BA, a permitted act allowing observing, studying and testing of computer programs inserted by the Copyright and Related Rights Regulations 2003.[146] These exceptions are dealt with fully in the following chapter.

144 SI 1992/3233.

145 SI 1997/3032.

146 SI 2003/2498. This replaced the previous exception, slightly differently worded, which was buried in s 286A(1)(c).

Designs, typefaces and works in electronic form

The provisions relating to designs are discussed in Part Five which deals with design law; however, these provisions are still contained in Table 7.2 at the end of this chapter for completeness. Basically, the typeface provisions are to limit artistic copyright protection for the design of a typeface[147] which will fall within the graphic work category of artistic works. Using a typeface in the ordinary course of typing, composing text, typesetting or printing, possession of an article for such use or doing anything in relation to the material so produced does not infringe the artistic copyright subsisting in the design of a typeface even if the article is an infringing article.[148] However, s 54(2) goes on to apply certain provisions, including secondary infringement of copyright, to persons making, importing, dealing or possessing for the purpose of dealing with articles specifically designed or adapted to produce material with a particular typeface.[149] Section 55 of the Act limits the duration of copyright in an artistic work consisting of the design of a typeface to 25 years from the end of the calendar year during which articles specifically designed or adapted for producing material in that typeface have been marketed by or with the permission of the copyright owner.[150]

Many works are now made available in electronic form, which is defined in s 178 as being in a form usable only by electronic means, 'electronic' having a wide meaning. For example, computer programs, sound recordings, films, information and data are frequently made available in this form. The provision contained in s 56 raises a legal presumption that where a copy of work in electronic form is transferred, the transferee may do anything the original purchaser could do without infringing copyright. Before the provision can apply, the terms under which the copy had been purchased must have allowed, whether expressly, by implication or by operation of law, the purchaser to make copies, to adapt the work or make copies of the adaptation. Furthermore, there must be no express terms interfering with the transfer of the copy or with the transferee's rights. Any copies, whether or not adaptations or copies of adaptations, that were made by the purchaser and not transferred are treated as being infringing copies of the work. The provisions also apply to subsequent transfers of the copy of the work. As an example of the workings of s 56, imagine that a person, George, obtains a copy of a word-processing computer program to use on his computer. He may make a back-up copy if the licence agreement permits this, or if it is necessary to his lawful use. Suppose the licence allows George to assign it in the future. After a year or two, George wants to obtain a more powerful word-processor program and wants to 'sell' his old one to Robert.[151] George may then:

1 give Robert the original disk containing the word-processing program and the back-up copy (duplicate); or
2 give Robert the original disk and destroy the back-up copy.

If George retains the back-up copy, this will be treated as an infringing copy. Once Robert receives the original disk, he will be able to make his own back-up copy of the program.

Miscellaneous – literary, dramatic, musical and artistic works

Sections 57–65 contain a hotchpotch of provisions relating to various permitted acts in relation to literary, dramatic, musical and artistic works. Section 57 applies to anonymous and so-called 'pseudonymous' literary, dramatic, musical and artistic works and covers the situation where it is not possible by reasonable enquiry to trace the author, it being reasonable to assume that the copyright has expired or that the author died at least 70 years ago. In such a case, copyright is not infringed even if it is later discovered that copyright continues to subsist in the work. Notice that it is the identity of the author and not the owner of the copyright which is at issue. This provision does not apply to works of Crown copyright or in respect of designated international organisations. If a work is of joint authorship, the provision does not apply if any one of the authors could have been traced by reasonable enquiry, or if it is not reasonable to assume that all of the joint authors died at least 70 years ago.

Other permitted acts include:

1 The use or copying of a record of spoken words or material from it for the purposes of reporting current events or communicating to the public the whole or part of the work, subject to certain conditions (s 58).
2 The public reading or recitation of a reasonable extract of a published literary or dramatic work, subject to a sufficient acknowledgement (s 59).
3 Copying and issuing to the public abstracts of scientific or technical subjects published in periodicals, subject to the existence of a statutory licensing scheme (s 60).
4 Recording songs for the purpose of inclusion in an archive maintained by a designated body (s 61).[152]
5 Making graphic works, photographs, films or broadcasts of visual images of buildings and, if accessible by the public, sculptures, models for buildings and works of artistic craftsmanship (s 62).
6 Copying an artistic work and issuing copies to the public in order to advertise the forthcoming sale of the work, for example, to distribute photographs of an oil painting to be sold at an auction (s 63) – it seems that this may extend to making a copy of an architectural drawing to facilitate the sale of a house.[153]
7 The making of subsequent artistic works by the author of a previous work (permits an artist to use and develop his style and technique for future works) (s 64).[154]
8 Reconstructing buildings (s 65).

Miscellaneous – other works

A miscellany of permitted acts is provided for in ss 66–75. Previously, s 66 concerned rental of sound recordings, films and computer programs, and gave the Secretary of State power to order the rental to be treated as licensed, subject to the payment of a reasonable royalty. A more curious provision in s 66(5) was that copyright in a computer program was not infringed by rental to the public after 50 years from the end of the calendar year during which the program was first issued to the public. Section 66 conflicted with the Directive on rental and lending rights, and was replaced by a new s 66 by the Copyright and Related Rights Regulations 1996[155] with effect from 1 December 1996.

Now, s 66 gives the Secretary of State power to order, in such cases as are specified in the order, that the lending of copies of literary, dramatic, musical or artistic works, sound recordings or films are to be treated as licensed by the copyright owner, subject only to the payment of a reasonable royalty. No order will be made if, or to the extent that, there is a licensing scheme under s 143 providing for the grant of licences.

Section 66A contains a permitted act in relation to films. The copyright in a film is not infringed by an act done at a time, or in pursuance of arrangements made at a time when it was not possible by reasonable enquiry to ascertain the identity of any of the persons by which the duration of copyright in the film and it is reasonable to assume that copyright

152 A list of designated bodies is given in the Copyright (Recordings of Folksongs for Archives) (Designated Bodies) Order 1989, SI 1989/1012. The Copyright, Designs and Patents Act 1988 s 61 is headed 'Recordings of Folksongs' but the Act nowhere defines a 'folksong' except that, from reading s 61, it appears that a folksong is a song where the words are unpublished and of unknown authorship. In many cases, although they may have qualified under the 1956 Act, such songs will be too old for copyright protection under the 1988 Act.

153 *Thurgood v Coyle* [2007] EWHC 2539 (Ch), per Lewison J at para 8.

154 It would be unlikely that copyright would be infringed if the artist did not repeat or imitate the main design as required by s 64.

155 SI 1996/2967.

has expired or the last to die of those persons died 70 years or more from the beginning of the calendar year during which the act was done or the arrangements made.[156]

Until 1 January 2011, the playing of a sound recording did not infringe copyright if done for charitable, religious, educational or social welfare purposes if the organisation was not established or conducted for profit, and the proceeds of any charge for admission were applied solely for the purposes of the organisation. Section 67 contained the relevant provisions.[157]

Incidental recording for the purposes of broadcasting is permitted under certain circumstances.[158] It is possible to make a sound recording or film of a literary, dramatic or musical work, or an adaptation of such a work, or to make a photograph of an artistic work, or to make a copy of a sound recording or film. Such activities are treated as licensed by the owner where a person is authorised to broadcast the work by virtue of a licence or assignment of copyright. The recording, film, photograph or copy in question must not be used for any other purpose, and must be destroyed within 28 days of its first being used in the broadcast. Failure to adhere to either of those conditions results in the recording, film, photograph or copy being considered to be an infringing copy.

Section 69 permits the making or use of recordings of broadcasts for the purposes of supervision and control of broadcasts and other services by the BBC and OFCOM and under a number of provisions of the Broadcasting Acts of 1990 and 1996 and the Communications Act 2003.

A large number of video recorders are used domestically to record television programmes for viewing at a later time: for example, where the persons concerned are away from home or doing something else at the time the programme is broadcast. This is known as 'time-shifting' of broadcasts, and is permitted by s 70 if carried out on domestic premises and done for private and domestic use where the purpose is solely to enable it to be viewed or listened to at a more convenient time. Nor is the copyright in any work included in the broadcast infringed. There is no time limit, although one of 28 days was proposed at one stage during the passage of the Bill through Parliament, but this was finally dropped because it was totally unenforceable.

The restriction to recording on domestic premises might have been prompted by *Sony Music Entertainment (UK) Ltd* v *Easyinternetcafe Ltd*[159] in which the defendant ran an internet café and provided a CD burning service for customers in respect of music available on the internet. The defendant argued that this fell within the time-shifting provisions in s 70 and the copying was for private and domestic use. The defendant failed to adduce any evidence to support this argument, which was rejected by the judge in giving summary judgment to the claimant.

Strangely, s 71 permits the making on domestic premises, for private and domestic use, of a photograph of an image which is part of a broadcast. The copyright in the broadcast and any included film will not be infringed. Presumably, copyright in other works could still be infringed, such as taking a photograph of a television screen when it is showing a painting or some other artistic work. It is unclear why anyone would want to take photographs from screen images on a television set, although such photographs could be used in advertising and promotions. Where copies are made under ss 70 or 71, if they are subsequently dealt with, the copies will be treated for that dealing as infringing copies. If the dealing itself infringes copyright, the copies will continue to be treated as infringing copies for all subsequent purposes.

The free public showing or playing in public of broadcasts is permitted under s 72: for example, to the residents of an old people's home or to members of clubs or societies (unless this is not incidental to the main purpose of the club or society).[160] The copyright in any included sound recording or film likewise will not be infringed. However, certain sound recordings are excepted from this, being one whose author is not the author of the broadcast in which it is included where the sound recording is of music, with or without

156 This does not apply to films subject to Crown copyright or, where an Order has been made specifying a copyright period of longer than 70 years, to films in which the copyright first vested in an international organisation under s 168.

157 Section 67 was repealed by reg 3(1) of the Copyright, Designs and Patents Act 1988 (Amendment) Regulations 2010 (SI 2010/2694) with effect from 1 January 2011. See p 231 of the 8th edition of this book for more on the workings of s 67. The provision was incompatible with the Directive 2006/115/EC of the European Parliament and of the Council of 12 December 2006 on rental right and lending right and on certain rights related to copyright in the field of intellectual property, OJ L 376, 27.12.2006, p 28 (codified version).

158 Section 68.

159 [2003] FSR 48.

160 The European Commission initiated infringement proceedings on the basis that s 72 conflicted with Council Directive 92/100/EEC of 19 November 1992 on rental right and lending right and on certain rights related to copyright in the field of intellectual property, OJ L 346, 27.11.1992, p 61, but this was withdrawn after the Commission was satisfied that the UK later complied by modifying s 72 by the Copyright and Related Rights Regulations 2003, SI 2003/2498. Council Directive 92/100/EEC has since been repealed and replaced by codifying Directive 2006/115/EC of the European Parliament and of the Council of 12 December 2006 on rental right and lending right and on certain rights related to copyright in the field of intellectual property, OJ L 376, 27.12.2006, p 28.

words spoken or sung.[161] Reception and immediate re-transmission by cable of broadcasts is permissible under certain circumstances under s 73.[162] Where the re-transmission falls outside the area covered by the area for reception of the broadcast the copyright in any work included in the broadcast is treated as licensed subject to a reasonable royalty under s 73(4). An application to settle the royalty or other sums payable may be made to the Copyright Tribunal under s 73A.

Designated bodies may, under s 74, modify copies of broadcasts for persons who are hard of hearing or disabled (for example, by adding subtitles), subject to the existence of statutory licensing schemes; and, under s 75, recordings of certain broadcasts may be made by bodies such as the British Film Institute and the British Library for archival purposes.[163]

Adaptations

It is possible for the permitted acts to apply to a work which is an adaptation of another work. In these cases, the copyright in the first work (that is, the work from which the adaptation was made) is not infringed. This is the effect of s 76, which prevents infringement of the underlying work from which the adaptation (being a literary, dramatic or musical work) was made, provided the act in relation to the adaptation is permitted.

Statutory licence to use sound recordings in broadcasts

The UK ratified the Rome Convention for the Protection of Performers, Producers of Phonograms and Broadcasting Organisations in 1963. One provision of the Rome Convention was that ephemeral fixations of phonograms could be made by broadcasting organisations for their own broadcasts. This led to the Copyright, Designs and Patents Act 1988 s 68, which allows, *inter alia*, the incidental recording of sound recordings by persons authorised under a licence or assignment of copyright to broadcast a sound recording. In order to comply with the Rome Convention, a condition was that the copy was destroyed within 28 days of first being used for the broadcast.

Later, a report of the Monopolies and Mergers Commission (now the Competition Commission) was critical of the way in which licensing bodies such as Phonographic Performance Ltd (PPL) exercised the rights assigned to them by copyright owners in relation to royalty rates, common tariffs and imposing restrictions on performances. From this followed the introduction of a statutory licence scheme, allowing the use as of right of sound recordings in broadcasts, contained in ss 135A–135G of the Act.[164] The right is available where a licensing body could grant a licence or procure the grant of a licence and the person making the broadcast including the sound recording gives notice to the licensing body. A further condition is that the person does not have a licence and the licensing body refuses to grant or procure the grant of a licence on acceptable terms, or to comply with an order of the Copyright Tribunal, allowing unlimited needle-time, or that the person holds a licence which limits needletime and the licensing body refuses to substitute or procure the substitution of the term with one which does allow unlimited needletime. 'Needletime' is the time in any period that the sound can be included, whether calculated by hours or by a proportion of the period or otherwise.

Section 135C contains the conditions for the exercise of the right. The person making the broadcast must comply with any reasonable condition or notice given to him by the licensing body, providing that body with such information as it may reasonably require and making payments to the licensing body at not less than quarterly intervals in arrears.

---

161 Section 72(1A), inserted by the Copyright and Related Rights Regulations 2003, SI 2003/2498. Section 72(1B) contains an exception to this exception and it will not infringe the copyright in the sound recording if necessary for repairing broadcast equipment, demonstrating that the repair has been carried out or demonstrating such equipment for sale or hire.

162 The re-transmission by cable must be in pursuance of a relevant requirement imposed by the Communications Act 2003 or where the broadcast is part of a qualifying service, which includes BBC television and teletext, Channels 3, 4 and 5, etc.

163 The other bodies are the Music Performance Research Centre and the Scottish Film Council: Copyright (Recording for Archives of Designated Class of Broadcasts and Cable Programmes) (Designated Bodies) (No 2) Order 1989, SI 1989/2510.

164 Inserted by the Broadcasting Act 1990.

165 [1997] RPC 729.

In *Phonographic Performance Ltd* v *AEI Rediffusion Music Ltd*,[165] the defendant claimed that s 135C(1) gave him a right to keep copies longer than the 28 days under s 68. The main reason was that it was inconvenient and troublesome for the defendant to stay within the 28-day period. It was held that the purpose of s 135C(1) was to grant a right to make broadcasts of sound recordings and which did not extend to making copies. Any other construction would put the UK in breach of the Rome Convention and, in any case, it was not necessary to make a copy to make the broadcast. Lightman J said that the court should be slow to imply a term which encroached upon the rights of copyright owners beyond that which was clearly provided for by the Act.

Overview

Table 7.2 provides an overview of the permitted acts discussed in detail in this chapter.

Table 7.2 The permitted acts: outline

Permitted act	Types of works covered by permitted act	Comments
General and fair dealing		
Making temporary copies: s 28A	Literary works (other than computer programs and databases), dramatic, musical or artistic works, typographical arrangements of published editions, sound recordings or films	Applies to transient and incidental copies transmitted in a network between third parties by an intermediary or a lawful use of the work, in either case, which has no independent economic significance.
Fair dealing – research or private study: s 29	Literary, dramatic, musical or artistic works and typographical arrangements of published editions	In most cases, there must be a sufficient acknowledgement and research must be for a non-commercial purpose. Exceptions to this permitted act apply in relation to computer programs (provided for elsewhere).
Fair dealing – criticism, review and news reporting: s 30	Any work or performance of it, for criticism or review Any work (other than a photograph) for reporting current events	Must be accompanied by a sufficient acknowledgement (in most cases) and work must have been made available to the public.
Fair dealing – incidental inclusion: s 31	Any work – not infringed by inclusion in an artistic work, sound recording, film or broadcast	Extends also to issuing copies to public, playing, showing or communication to the public.
Visual impairment		
Making accessible copies for visually impaired persons: ss 31A to 31F	Literary, dramatic, musical or artistic works and published editions	Single copies may be made or multiple copies by approved bodies. A statement that the copy has been made under the relevant provision and a sufficient acknowledgement is required. There is also provision for licensing schemes and prohibitions may be ordered by the Secretary of State where the making of copies leads to infringement that would not have occurred but for the making of a copy or copies.

Table 7.2 *cont'd*

Permitted act	Types of works covered by permitted act	Comments
Education		
Copying in the course of instruction or preparation for instruction: s 32(1)	Literary, dramatic, musical or artistic work	Must be done by the person giving or receiving instruction and not by a reprographic process. There must be a sufficient acknowledgement and the instruction must be for a non-commercial purpose.
Copying by making a film or film sound track in the course of instruction or preparation for instruction in the making of films or film sound tracks: s 32(2)	Sound recording, film or broadcast	Must be done by the person giving or receiving the instruction and be accompanied by a sufficient acknowledgement and be done for a non-commercial purpose.
Copying a work which has been made available to the public for the purpose of instruction or preparation for instruction: s 32(2A)	Literary, dramatic, musical or artistic work	The copying must be fair dealing and be done by the person giving or receiving the instruction, is not done by reprographic copying and is accompanied by a sufficient acknowledgement.
Anything done for the purpose of examination by way of setting questions, communicating the questions to students and answering the questions: s 32(3)	Any work	The questions must be accompanied by a sufficient acknowledgement. Making a reprographic copy of a musical work for use by a candidate in performing the work is not permitted.
Inclusion of a short passage in a collection intended for use in educational establishments and so described in its title and advertisements. The collection must consist mainly of material in which no copyright subsists: s 33	Published literary or dramatic work	Must be accompanied by a sufficient acknowledgement and the work itself must not be intended for use in such establishments, and not more than two excerpts from copyright works of the same author may be included in collections by the same publisher published over any period of five years.
Performances before an audience of teachers and pupils at an educational establishment and other persons directly connected with the activities of the establishment: s 34(1)	Literary, dramatic or musical works (such performance is not considered to be a public performance)	Performance must be by a teacher or pupil in the course of the activities of the establishment or the performance may be by any person at the establishment for the purposes of instruction. A person is not directly connected simply because he is a parent of a pupil.
Playing or showing before an audience of teachers and pupils at an educational establishment and other persons directly connected with the activities of the establishment for the purposes of instruction: s 34(2)	Sound recording or broadcast (such playing or showing is not considered to be a playing or showing in public)	A person is not directly connected simply because he is a parent of a pupil.
Making a recording by or on behalf of an educational establishment or making a copy of such a recording for educational purposes of that establishment: s 35(1)	Broadcast (extends to any work included in a broadcast)	Must be accompanied by a sufficient acknowledgement and the educational purposes must be non-commercial. The permitted act does not apply if or to the extent there is a certified licensing scheme under s 143.
Communication to the public of a recording of a broadcast or copy made without infringing copyright under s 35(1): 35(1A)	Broadcast (extends to any work included in a broadcast)	Communication must be by a person situated in the premises of an educational establishment and cannot be received by a person situated outside the premises.
Reprographic copying of passages not exceeding 1 per cent of a work in any quarter by or on behalf of an educational establishment for the purposes of instruction: s 36	Published literary, dramatic, musical or artistic works and associated typographical arrangements	Must be accompanied by a sufficient acknowledgement and purpose must be non-commercial. The permitted act does not apply if and to the extent that licences are available and the person making the copies knows or ought to have been aware of that fact.

Table 7.2 *cont'd*

Permitted act	Types of works covered by permitted act	Comments
Libraries and archives Librarians of a prescribed library may, if the prescribed conditions are complied with, make and supply: (a) a copy of an article in a periodical: s 38 (b) a copy of part of a published edition: s 39	Literary work (text) and accompanying artistic works (illustrations) including the typographical arrangement Literary, dramatic or musical works including the typographical arrangement of such works	Prescribed conditions: (a) person supplied must satisfy the librarian that he requires the copies for non-commercial research or private study and will not use them for any other purpose (b) not more than one copy of periodical article (or copies from more than one article in the same issue) is supplied or, with respect to published literary, dramatic or musical works, not more than one copy of the same material or a copy of more than a reasonable proportion of any work is supplied (c) the person to whom the copies are supplied must pay at least the cost of making and supplying the copies.
Lending of a book by a library if the book is in the public lending right scheme: s 40A	Any work	
Librarian of a prescribed library may make and supply to another prescribed library, a copy of: (a) an article in a periodical, or (b) the whole or part of a published edition: s 41	An article in a periodical or literary, dramatic or musical works, including the typographical arrangement of such works	The prescribed conditions above must be complied with. (b) does not apply if the librarian knows or could by reasonable enquiry ascertain the name and address of the person entitled to authorise the making of the copy.
Librarian or archivist of a prescribed library or archive may, if the prescribed conditions are complied with, make a copy from any item in the permanent collection of that library or archive: (a) in order to preserve or replace the item (b) to replace a lost, destroyed or missing item in the permanent collection of another prescribed library or archive: s 42	Literary, dramatic or musical works plus accompanying illustrations (artistic works) and including the typographical arrangement	Prescribed conditions include restricting the making of such copies to cases when it is not reasonably practicable to purchase a copy of the item to fulfil the purpose.
Librarian or archivist of a prescribed library or archive may, if the prescribed conditions are complied with, make and supply a copy of the whole or part of a work from an unpublished document, provided that the copyright owner has not prohibited copying to the actual or constructive knowledge of the person making the copy: s 43	Literary, dramatic or musical works (extends also to accompanying illustrations)	Prescribed conditions: (a) person supplied must satisfy the librarian or archivist that he requires the copies for research or private study (b) no person is supplied with more than one copy of the same material (c) the person to whom the copies are supplied must pay at least the cost of making and supplying the copies.
Making a copy of an article of cultural or historical importance or interest which cannot be exported from the UK unless a copy is made and deposited in an appropriate library or archive: s 44	Any work	
Copying from the internet by a legal deposit library: s 44A	Works to be prescribed by Regulations	Regulations are to be made under the Legal Deposit Libraries Act 2003.

Table 7.2 *cont'd*

Permitted act	Types of works covered by permitted act	Comments
Public administration		
Anything done for the purposes of parliamentary or judicial proceedings or for the purposes of reporting such proceedings: s 45	Any work	Does not authorise copying a work which is itself a published report of the proceedings.
Anything done for the purposes of the proceedings of a Royal Commission or statutory inquiry or for the purpose of reporting such proceedings held in public or issuing to the public copies of the report of a Royal Commission or statutory inquiry: s 46	Any work	Does not authorise copying a work which is itself a published report of the proceedings.
Copying material open to public inspection pursuant to a statutory requirement, or on a statutory register, e.g. entries in the Data Protection Register or the Register of Trade Marks: s 47	Material as a literary work in as much as it contains factual information of any description. Any work where issued to the public to enable the material to be inspected at a more convenient time or place or where material contains information of general scientific, technical, commercial or economic interest for purposes of disseminating information	Copying must be by or with authority of appropriate person. Does not include issuing copies to the public except when material contains information about matters of general scientific, technical, commercial or economic interest or to enable the material to be inspected at a more convenient time or place. Includes EPO (European Patent Office) and WIPO (World Intellectual Property Organisation) materials.
Copying and issuing copies to the public of works which have been communicated to the Crown by or with the licence of the copyright owner and an item containing the work is in the custody or control of the Crown providing the work has not previously been published otherwise. Communication must have been in the course of public business, which includes any activity carried on by the Crown: s 48	Literary, dramatic, musical or artistic works	Applies only as regards the purpose or related purposes for which the work has been communicated.
Copying and supplying a copy of material contained in public records: s 49	Any work	Must be by or with the authority of any officer appointed under the Public Records Act 1958 or equivalent legislation for Scotland, Northern Ireland or Wales.
Acts specifically authorised by an Act of Parliament unless the Act provides otherwise: s 50	Any work	This does not exclude any defence of statutory authority otherwise available under or by any enactment.
Computer programs: lawful users		
Making back-up copy necessary for lawful use: s 50A	Computer program	Must be by a lawful user. A lawful user is a person having a right to use the program (whether under a licence or otherwise).
Decompiling a computer program by a lawful user: s 50B	Computer program	A number of conditions apply, e.g. it must be necessary to decompile to obtain the information necessary to create an independent program that can be operated with the program decompiled or another program.

Table 7.2 *cont'd*

Permitted act	Types of works covered by permitted act	Comments
Observing, studying and testing of computer programs by lawful user: s 50BA	Computer program	Must be in order to determine the ideas and principles underlying any element of the program by doing acts of loading, displaying, running, transmitting or storing the program as the lawful user is entitled to do.
Copying or adapting by a lawful user: s 50C	Computer program	For example, for the purposes of error correction. Does not apply to copying and adapting permitted under ss 50A, 50B or 50BA. Unlike the three permitted acts above, it appears that this can be restricted or prohibited by a term in a licence agreement, possibly subject to non-derogation from grant.
Databases Doing anything necessary for the purposes of access to and use of the contents of a database or part of a database by a person having a right to use the database: s 50D	Database	Any term or condition purporting to prohibit or restrict this is void.
Designs Making an article to a design or copying an article made to that design. The exception extends to issuing to the public, including in a film, or communicating to the public anything which was not an infringement of copyright under s 51(1): s 51	Design document or model recording or embodying the design for anything other than an artistic work or typeface. A design document could be a drawing, written description, photograph or data stored in a computer	Relates to articles which are protected by the unregistered design right and may also extend to some registrable designs (though by no means all).
Copying by making articles, doing anything for the purpose of making articles and doing anything in relation to articles, 25 years from end of calendar year in which articles first marketed: s 52	Certain artistic works that have been exploited by making articles by an industrial process and marketing the articles in the UK. Films are not 'articles' for s 52 See Copyright (Industrial Processes and Excluded Articles) (No 2) Order 1989 for meaning of 'exploitation'	Effectively limits copyright in certain types of artistic works (e.g. works of artistic craftsmanship) that are commercially exploited by making articles which will normally be taken to be copies of the artistic work. Marketing means selling, letting for hire or offering or exposing for sale or hire. Such designs may be registrable and the intention was to limit copyright, in effect, to no longer than the protection that was available by registration.
In respect of a design registration: (a) things done in pursuance of an assignment or licence granted by the proprietor of a corresponding design (b) things done in good faith in reliance on the registration without notice of proceedings for cancellation or invalidation of registration: s 53	Artistic work	'Corresponding design' means a design which if applied to an article would be treated as a copy of an artistic work.
Typefaces Using a typeface in typing, composing, typesetting or printing; possessing an article for such use; doing anything in relation to material produced by such use: s 54	Artistic work consisting of the design of a typeface	But making, importing, dealing with, possessing articles specifically designed or adapted for producing material in a particular typeface still infringes – see s 54(2).

Table 7.2 *cont'd*

Permitted act	Types of works covered by permitted act	Comments
Copying by making further such articles, etc. after 25 years from the end of the calendar year in which articles for producing material in a typeface have been first marketed: s 55	Artistic work consisting of the design of a typeface	Limits duration of copyright where the design has been commercially exploited anywhere.

Works in electronic form

Transferee of a work in electronic form may do anything purchaser was allowed to do if the terms of the original purchase allowed the purchaser to copy, adapt or copy adaptations and there are no express terms prohibiting transfer or otherwise interfering with the transferee's rights: s 56	Any work in electronic form	Terms of original purchase may be express, implied or by virtue of any rule of law. Copies and adaptations not transferred are treated as infringing copies.

Miscellaneous – literary, dramatic, musical and artistic works

Acts done in relation to works which are anonymous or pseudonymous where it is not possible to trace the author and it is reasonable to assume that copyright no longer subsists in the work: s 57	Literary, dramatic, musical or artistic works	Note: effects of longer duration of copyright, e.g. Crown copyright, on the assumption as to the time since the author died. Special provisions also for works of joint authorship.
Use of a record of spoken words or material from it, copying the record or material taken from it and use of that copy, subject to conditions: s 58	Literary work (recording, in writing or otherwise, of spoken words for purpose of reporting current events or communicating to the public)	Conditions: direct records only not taken from a previous record or from a broadcast, making of which is not prohibited by speaker and did not infringe copyright, use made not of a kind prohibited by speaker or copyright owner, use is by or with authority of lawful possessor of record.
Public reading or recitation of a reasonable extract and also the making of a sound recording or communicating to the public such a reading or recitation: s 59	Published literary or dramatic work	Must be accompanied by a sufficient acknowledgement.
Copy abstracts of scientific or technical subjects published in periodicals or issue copies to the public: s 60	Not limited but realistically only literary works though may include illustrations	Does not apply if and to the extent that there is a licensing scheme under s 143.
Making a sound recording of a performance of a 'folksong' for inclusion in an archive and subsequent supply of copies for research or private study: s 61	Literary works (words) and musical works (accompanying music)	Certain conditions must be met, words unpublished and of unknown authorship, no other copyright is infringed and not prohibited by any performer. Prescribed conditions include that the person supplied with a copy must satisfy the archivist that he requires it for non-commercial research or private study and will not use it for any other purpose and no person is furnished with more than one copy of the same recording.
Making a graphic work representing it, making a photograph or film of it or broadcasting a visual image of it. Also issuing copies to the public or communicating to the public anything the making of which was not an infringement under this section: s 62	Artistic works being buildings and sculptures, models for buildings and works of artistic craftsmanship if permanently sited in a public place or premises open to the public	
Copying and issuing copies to the public advertising the sale of a work: s 63	Artistic works	For example, in an auction catalogue. However, subsequent dealing excepted.

Table 7.2 *cont'd*

Permitted act	Types of works covered by permitted act	Comments
The making of another work by the author, not being the owner of the copyright in the first work, by copying the first work: s 64	Artistic works	Provided the main design of the earlier work is not repeated or imitated.
Reconstructing a building: s 65	Artistic works, that is, the building itself and drawings and plans from which building constructed	As regards the drawings and plans, the building was originally constructed in accordance with them by or with the licence of the copyright owner.
Miscellaneous – lending of works and playing of sound recordings Lending to the public of copies of works by order of the Secretary of State: s 66	Literary, dramatic, musical or artistic works, sound recordings or films	Such lending is treated as licensed subject only to payment of a reasonable royalty. This permitted act does not apply if and to the extent there is a licensing scheme under s 143.
Miscellaneous – films and sound recordings Acts done in relation to films where it is not possible by reasonable enquiry to ascertain the identity of persons referred to in s 13B(2) (e.g. principal director, etc.) and it is reasonable to assume that copyright no longer subsists in the work: s 66A	Films and sound recordings	Inserted by the Duration of Copyright and Rights in Performances Regulations 1995.
[s.67 repealed – playing sound recording as part of activities of or for the benefit of a non-profit club, etc.]		
Miscellaneous – broadcasts Incidental recording for the purposes of broadcast: (a) making a sound recording or film of the work or an adaptation	(a) Literary, dramatic or musical work or adaptation of such a work	Applies where person is authorised to broadcast by virtue of a licence or assignment of copyright.
(b) taking a photograph or making a film	(b) Artistic works	Such recording is treated as if licensed by the copyright owner.
(c) making a copy: s 68	(c) Sound recording or film	Recording, film, photograph or copy must not be used for any other purpose and shall be destroyed within 28 days of being first used.
Making or use of recordings, etc. for the purpose of maintaining supervision and control over programmes by the BBC and exercise of functions by OFCOM etc.: s 69	Any work	Extends to things done in pursuance of certain provisions under the Broadcasting Acts 1990 and 1996 and the Communications Act 2003.
Time-shifting broadcasts to view or listen to at a more convenient time: s 70	Broadcasts and included works	Only for private and domestic use and may only be made in domestic premises.
Making a photograph of the whole or any part of an image forming part of television broadcast or making a copy of such a photograph: s 71	Broadcasts and included films	Only for private and domestic use and may only be made in domestic premises.
Free showing or playing in public to a non-paying audience: s 72	Broadcasts and included sound recordings (but not excepted sound recording) and films	Section 72 gives guidance as to when an audience has or has not paid admission. An excepted sound recording is one whose author is not the author of the broadcast and which is a recording of music with or without words spoken or sung.

Table 7.2 *cont'd*

Permitted act	Types of works covered by permitted act	Comments
Reception of wireless broadcast made from a place in the UK and immediate re-transmission by cable if re-transmission is in pursuance of relevant requirement, or if and to the extent that the broadcast is made for reception in the area in which it is re-transmitted and forms part of a qualifying service: s 73	Broadcasts and included works	Copyright in included works is not infringed if and to the extent that the broadcast is made for reception in the area in which it is re-transmitted by cable (unless the making of the broadcast was an infringement of copyright). 'Relevant requirement' is one imposed under the Communications Act 2003 and qualifying service includes TV broadcasting and teletext of BBC, regional or national Channel 3 service, Channel 4, Channel 5 and S4C, etc. Any royalties payable under s 73 may be settled by the Copyright Tribunal: s 73A.
Making copies of television broadcasts, issuing copies to public if a designated body for purpose of providing people who are deaf, hard of hearing, physically or mentally handicapped in other ways with copies subtitled or modified for their special needs: s 74	Broadcasts and included works	But not if there is a licensing scheme under s 143.
Recording and making a copy of such recording for placing in an archive: s 75	Broadcasts and included works	Only with respect to designated classes and only for designated archives.
Adaptations Any of all of the above acts in respect of an adaptation: s 76	Literary, dramatic or musical works	Does not infringe copyright in the work from which the adaptation was made.
Statutory licensing Including in a broadcast a sound recording: s 135C	Sound recordings	Subject to conditions in ss 135A–135C.

Possible changes to the permitted acts proposed by the *Gowers Review* and the *Hargreaves Report*

The Gowers Review of Intellectual Property[166] was a sweeping review of intellectual property law, practice and policy in the UK and included a number of recommendations concerning the scope of some of the permitted acts under copyright law. Following this a consultation paper was published[167] which set out the relevant recommendations with some further narrative and discussing the possible implementations of these changes and their potential impact. The *Hargreaves Report*[168] also made recommendations which, *inter alia*, relate to the permitted acts. The Hargreaves Report Supporting Document A[169] noted that a number of key recommendations from the *Gowers Review* had not been implemented. Some of the recommendations of *Gowers* and *Hargreaves* are noted below.

Research and private study

Under s 29(1C) and (2) fair dealing for private study extends only to literary, dramatic, musical and artistic works and also to typographical arrangements. It does not cover sound recordings and films. *Gowers* considered that this hindered academic study and proposed that fair dealing for private study be extended to all forms of work. This would not extend to distribution. *Hargreaves* proposed that scientific and other researchers should be able to use text and data mining techniques, currently prohibited by copyright. It was claimed that the UK exceptions to infringement have failed to keep up with technological and social change.[170]

166 HMSO 2006, available at: http://www.hm-treasury.gov.uk/media/6/E/pbr06_gowers_report_755.pdf.

167 UK Intellectual Property Office, *Taking Forward the Gowers Review of Intellectual Property: Proposed Changes to Copyright Exceptions*, HMSO 2007, available at: http://www.ipo.gov.uk/consult-copyrightexceptions.pdf.

168 Hargreaves, I., *Digital Opportunity: a review of intellectual property and growth*, May 2011, available at: http://www.ipo.gov.uk/ipreview-finalreport.pdf

169 Audit of recommendations from previous reviews of intellectual property rights, available at: http://www.ipo.gov.uk/ipreview-doc-a.pdf.

170 *Hargreaves Report, op cit*, p 41.

Education

Section 35 (making recordings of broadcasts) and s 36 (limited reprographic copying) of the Copyright, Designs and Patents Act 1988 should be amended to cover distance learning and interactive whiteboards (*Gowers*). These permitted acts do not apply if, for s 35, there is a licensing scheme in operation or, for s 36, licences are available allowing the copying and the person making the copy knows or ought to be aware of this fact.

The permitted act in relation to broadcasts under s 35 only extends to showing them to students who are on the premises of the educational establishment, putting distance learners at a disadvantage. As regards s 36, the Copyright Licensing Agency provides licences so the permitted act is available in limited cases. However, at the present time, these licences do not cover electronic copying. Thus, under such a licence, it may be permissible to make paper copies of, say, one chapter of a book to distribute to students but it is not permissible to place a copy of a single page electronically in a virtual learning environment.[171] Thus far, ss 35 and 36 have not been amended.

Libraries and archives

Section 42 allows the making of a copy of work by libraries and archives for the purpose of preservation of a work. For example, a film or sound recording may be on media that is deteriorating and, if a copy is made only after the copyright has expired, it may by then be too late. The lack of any permitted act allowing 'format shifting' makes the problem worse. It is estimated that copying a single colour film back on to film costs \$40,000 whilst copying one hour of a colour film on to digital media only costs \$200.[172] In many cases, it may be expensive, difficult or even impossible to clear the rights needed to make a copy. Some works are 'orphan works' where the rightholders cannot be identified. In other cases, the technology to play old recordings may no longer be available.[173] *Gowers* proposed that s 42 should be amended to permit libraries and archives to copy the master copy of all classes of work in their permanent collections for archival purposes. Furthermore, libraries and archives should be allowed to format shift archival copies to ensure records do not become obsolete. This recommendation has not yet been implemented

Format shifting

At the present time, transferring a music track, for example, from a CD to an MP3 player (so that the music can be listened to whilst out walking or jogging) will infringe the copyright in the music unless the licence under which the music on the CD has been obtained expressly allow this. Both *Gowers* and *Hargreaves* recommended a specific exception that would allow format shifting by private individuals. As *Hargreaves* points out, it is difficult and confusing for individuals to understand why it is permissible to lend a paperback novel to a friend but not to give a friend a copy of a music CD.

Parody

A number of jurisdictions permit the making of a caricature, parody or pastiche without infringing copyright. For example, Art L 122-5 of the French Copyright Act[174] permits, once a work has been disclosed, the making of a parody, pastiche or caricature, observing the rules of the genre. Article 5(3)(k) of the Directive on copyright and related rights in the information society allows Member States to include such a permitted act and *Gowers* recommended that this should also be adopted in the UK, consigning cases such as *Schweppes Ltd* v *Wellingtons Ltd*[175] to the history book. *Hargreaves* agreed and states (at para 5.35):

> Video parody is today becoming part and parcel of the interactions of private citizens, often via social networking sites, and encourages literacy in multimedia expression in ways that are increasingly essential to the skills base of the economy. Comedy is big business.

171 Of course, the Copyright Licensing Agency's licences go beyond the 1 per cent allowed under s 36. So, if the change as proposed is made, it will only be possible to place a maximum of 1 per cent of a work in a virtual learning environment.

172 *Gowers Review, op cit* at para 4.82.

173 For example, a speech by Nelson Mandela in 1964 was recorded on Dictabelt and the hardware for this is no longer available: *Gowers Review, op cit* at para 4.83.

174 Law No 92-597 of 1 July 1992 on the Intellectual Property Code.

175 [1984] FSR 210.

One issue is that parody can impact on the right of freedom of expression. This was beyond the ambit of *Hargreaves*.

Orphan works

An 'orphan work' is one in respect of which the copyright owner cannot be traced. Assuming such a work is still in copyright, carrying out any of the acts restricted by the copyright will infringe. This carries the risk of a later copyright action if the owner discovers that his work has been used without his licence. This means that considerable numbers of works are effectively out of bounds. Both *Gowers* and *Hargreaves* suggested that provision be made to allow the use of such works. *Hargreaves* goes further and proposes the introduction of a Digital Copyright Exchange[176] – a network of interoperable databases which would contain details of works and licence arrangements, allowing users to quickly and automatically obtain copyright clearances. Such an exchange could be used to determine whether a work was indeed an orphan work. This could be used, subject perhaps, to licence fees being paid to a collecting society.

It should be remembered, however, that if a work is of unknown authorship, the duration of copyright is limited under s 12(3) of the Act and s 57 contains details of permitted acts in relation to works of unknown authorship.

176 *Hargreaves Report, op cit*, Ch 4, pp 28ff.

Limits on copyright

On the suggested limits on copyright, *Hargreaves* states (at p 8):

> Government should deliver copyright exceptions at national level to realise all the opportunities within the EU framework, including format shifting, parody, non-commercial research, and library archiving. The UK should also promote at EU level an exception to support text and data analytics. The UK should give a lead at EU level to develop a further copyright exception designed to build into the EU framework adaptability to new technologies.

Of course, the UK cannot simply go its own way on the permitted acts under copyright and it will, to a very large extent, depend of EU initiatives, some of which are already underway. In the meantime, apart from contributing to the debate at an EU level, the UK could adopt the exceptions now possible under EU law such as the exception for parodies. The setting up of a Digital Copyright Exchange is more controversial and will need careful thought, planning and cooperation by right-holders on an impressive and hitherto unknown scale.

Summary

There are numerous 'defences' to copyright infringement. Some may be properly described as defences, such as public interest, whilst the Copyright, Designs and Patents Act 1988 contains 'permitted acts', which may be performed without infringing copyright.

It will be a defence to show that the copyright owner authorised or consented to the act complained of, or he may be prevented from enforcing his copyright on the basis of acquiescence, delay or estoppel. In appropriate cases, there may be a defence under UK or EU competition law.

The existence of the public interest defence is expressly recognised in the Act under s 171(3). However, in the light of the Court of Appeal decision in *Hyde Park Residences* v *Yelland*, scope of the defence is fairly limited.

Non-derogation from grant came to the fore in *British Leyland* v *Armstrong Patents* but subsequent case law shows that this defence is unlikely to be successful, bearing in mind that *British Leyland* pre-dated the 1988 Act which contains provisions designed to overcome the perceived deficiencies in copyright law in relation to industrial and utilitarian designs.

The permitted acts are classified in the Act as:

- general (including temporary copies, fair dealing and incidental inclusion);
- visual impairment;
- education;
- libraries and archives;
- public administration;
- computer programs (lawful users);
- databases (a person having a right to use the database);
- designs;
- typefaces;
- works in electronic form;
- miscellaneous: literary, dramatic, musical and artistic works;
- miscellaneous: lending of works and playing of sound recordings;
- miscellaneous: films and sound recordings;
- miscellaneous: broadcasts;
- adaptations.

Many of the permitted acts are very technical. Note that each permitted act may only apply in relation to a particular type or types of works and in respect of particular acts only. Some are very limited in what is actually permitted.

There have been calls to modify the permitted acts to allow for parodies, format shifting and to include provisions dealing with orphan works. Further changes could be made in relation to the research, education and libraries and archives permitted acts.

Discussion questions

1 According to Aldous LJ in *Hyde Park Residence* v *Yelland*, the public interest defence can only apply in quite limited circumstances. Should the scope of the defence be extended in the light of the right of freedom of expression?

2 Describe the fair dealing provisions and discuss their application in practice and whether they should be limited further.

3 Compare and contrast fair dealing provisions in the UK with fair use provisions in the US. See the 'US Copyright Act § 107 Limitations on exclusive rights: fair use', available at: http://www.copyright.gov/title17/92chap1.html#107.

4 Consider how and to what extent the permitted acts impact on the operation of your institution's library and information facilities and the provision of copies of extracts from books or journal articles to students (a) individually and (b) as a class.

5 The exceptions to copyright infringement fail to address the issues posed by the digital age. Discuss.

Selected further reading

Commission to the European Union, Proposal for a Directive on permitted uses of orphan works, COM/2011/0289 final, available at: **http://eur-lex.europa.eu/LexUriServ/LexUriServ.do?uri=CE LEX:52011PC0289:EN:HTML**

Gowers Review of Intellectual Property, HMSO 2006, available at **http://www.hm-treasury.gov.uk/media/6/E/pbr06_gowers_report_755.pdf**.

Hargreaves, Professor I., *Digital Opportunity: A Review of Intellectual Property and Growth*, May 2011, available at: **http://www.ipo.gov.uk/ipreview-finalreport.pdf**.

Papadopoulo, M.D., 'Copyright limitations and exceptions in an e-education environment' [2010] *European Journal of Law and Technology*, Vol 1, Issue 2 (looks at copyright exceptions and limitations, designed for an analogue world and critically analyses them in the context of a digital world and e-education, though not limited to the education exceptions; the article is available at: **http://ejlt.org//article/view/38/57**).

Sims, A., 'Strangling their creation: the courts' treatment of fair dealing in copyright law since 1911' [2010] *Intellectual Property Quarterly*, 192 (considers whether the courts have taken and continue to take a narrow interpretation of fair dealing since their legislative introduction in the Copyright Act 1911).

Walsh, A., 'Parody of intellectual property: prospects for a fair use/dealing defence in the United Kingdom' [2010] *International Company and Commercial Law Review*, 386 (calls for the implementation of a parody exception to copyright in the UK, with some comparative US and Australian material).

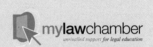

Copyright, computer software[1] and information technology

Introduction

1 For definitions relating to computers and computer software *see* the Glossary at the beginning of the book.

2 Unless otherwise stated, in this chapter statutory references are to the Copyright, Designs and Patents Act 1988.

Copyright law has a history of development that can partly be explained by reaction to technological change. Examples of advances in applied science that have in the past been addressed by copyright law include photography, sound recordings, films and broadcasting. The Copyright, Designs and Patents Act 1988[2] was an attempt to keep abreast of developments in technology coupled with an intention to enact legislation that would take future change in its stride. Of particular concern was the protection of computer programs and of other works stored or transmitted in digital forms. Two points are worth mentioning at this stage: first, computer technology is not new – universal programmable computing machines have existed for over 60 years; second, the vast majority of new technical developments involve computer technology, even if the developments themselves do not appear at first sight to be connected with such technology. Modern photocopiers and printers, facsimile transmission machines, electronic mail, cameras, mobile phones, vehicle fuel and ignition systems, even the humble automatic washing machine, all owe something to computer science.

In terms of legal protection for computer software, there are two main concerns for the copyright owners. The first is copying by out and out piracy. This has been particularly rife in relation to games software, operating system software such as Windows, popular applications software, such as word-processing software and, of course, music, films and other works in digital form, unauthorised copies of which may have been made available online. The second concern applies particularly to software that has been specially written. Typically, it might be software written for a business or other organisation to help it carry out its functions or operations. It might be software used to book holidays or flights or to control an industrial process or to run accounting functions or stock control. Two forms of copyright are relevant here, the first of which is where a duplicate is made (which may then be modified). The second is where someone undertakes to write new software to emulate the functions and operations carried out by existing software. The latter form of copying is particularly troublesome for copyright law. The new software may even have been written without access to the source code of the first software but a copy of the existing software has been used to gain a deep understanding of how it works, what it does and how it does it. This form of copying is known as non-literal or non-textual copying. As will be seen, it can be done without infringing copyright by relying on some of the specific permitted acts that apply to computer programs. But there are dangers for the person writing software to emulate the functions and operations performed by existing software, as it is possible to infringe copyright indirectly and by taking elements of computer programs not explicitly expressed in the code of the program.

There is no doubting that information technology stretches the law, which has sometimes been slow to react, and one problem has been the manner in which it has been attempted to adapt existing legal paradigms to deal with the problems posed by technological development. Nowhere can this be seen more strikingly than in the way in which copyright has been used as the main vehicle for the protection of computer programs. Whether copyright is an appropriate method of protection has been a long-running debate that still rages on and the nature of computer programs as property remains a grey area.[3] There is one great difference between computer programs and other works protected by copyright that sets them apart. Conventional works of copyright are passive. They await our attention to be read, viewed or listened to. Computer programs, on the other hand, are active – they do things – they manipulate symbols, transform, modify and retrieve digitally stored information. Even though we now have substantial experience of dealing with computer technology, it continues to cause problems, and not just in terms of substantive law. Evidence and disclosure are other areas in which problems may arise. For example, in *Dun & Bradstreet Ltd v Typesetting Facilities Ltd*,[4] an application for inspection of the defendant's computer database was held to be inappropriate as inspecting the computer disks on which a copy of the database was stored would not give the applicant what he really wanted, which was access to the information stored electronically on the disk.[5]

'Computer software' is a phrase that, like many phrases in the computer industry, is incapable of precise definition, but it is usually taken to include computer programs, databases, preparatory material and associated documentation (in printed or electronic form) such as manuals for users of the programs and for persons who have to maintain the programs. It can also include all manner of other works stored in digital form, such as conventional literary, dramatic, musical or artistic works and films, interfaces (for example, with the user or hardware or other software), programming languages and software tools to be used to develop software systems.

The lack of harmonisation in the European Union coupled with concerns about a lack of a consistent and balanced approach to the protection of computer software and copyright generally in the digital age led to a number of European Directives. In particular, the Directives on the legal protection of computer programs, the legal protection of databases and on copyright and related rights in the information society have had significant and profound influences on the protection of computer software in Europe. All were implemented in the United Kingdom by Regulations, each of which made important changes to the Copyright, Designs and Patents Act 1988. The latest significant Regulations, the Copyright and Related Rights Regulations 2003,[6] made sweeping changes across copyright law and rights in performances and these changes are discussed in appropriate places within this Part of the book where they affected works other than computer programs and databases. Of particular relevance to this chapter was the impact of the introduction of comprehensive measures to control the use of means to overcome technical measures to prevent or restrict unauthorised acts in respect of works and the introduction of specific protection of 'electronic rights management information'. These are described in detail later in this chapter.

Computer programs are considered in detail in this chapter in terms of the extent and scope of copyright protection for them and for the effects that they produce.[7] Particular issues are the 'look and feel' of computer programs in the context of non-literal copying, the decompilation of computer programs, back-up copies, and copying and adapting computer programs consistent with their lawful use. After looking at computer programs, the copyright position of programming languages, databases and other information stored in computer systems and computer-generated works is discussed. Following this, new provisions in respect of technological measures to prevent or restrict unauthorised

3 *See*, for example, Gordon, S.E. 'The Very Idea! Why Copyright is an Inappropriate Way to Protect Computer Programs' [1998] 1 EIPR 10; and Moon, K. 'The Nature of Computer Programs: Tangible? Goods? Personal Property? Intellectual Property?' [2009] 8 EIPR 396.

4 [1992] FSR 320.

5 The court allowed inspection as if the application had been made under Rules of the Supreme Court Ord 24 r 10 instead. The Rules of the Supreme Court have now been replaced by the Civil Procedure Rules 1998, SI 1998/3132, which came into force on 26 April 1999.

6 SI 2003/2498. These Regulations implemented Directive 2001/29/EC of the European Parliament and of the Council of 22 May 2001 on the harmonisation of certain aspects of copyright and related rights in the information society, OJ L 167, 22.06.2001, p 10. The Directive was implemented late and this resulted in a declaration to that effect by the European Court of Justice in Case C-88/04 *Commission of the European Communities v United Kingdom*, OJ C 45, 19.02.2005, p 11.

7 *See* Chapter 12 for the position of computer programs in patent law.

8 Preparatory design material for a computer program is also a form of literary work: Copyright, Designs and Patents Act 1988 s 3(1)(c).

9 Strictly speaking the test for originality now should be that the computer program is the result of the author's own intellectual creation, following the Directive on the legal protection of computer programs; see *infra*.

10 Application programs are designed to perform a specific task such as processing data, producing reports, word-processing, etc. They can be distinguished from operating system programs which supply the basic working environment in which the application programs operate.

11 Laddie, H., Prescott, P. and Vitoria, M. (1980) *The Modern Law of Copyright*, Butterworths, p 93.

12 For example, in *Ager* v *Peninsula & Oriental Steam Navigation Co* (1884) 26 ChD 627, a book of telegraphic codes was recognised as being suitable subject matter for literary copyright. *See also DP Anderson & Co Ltd* v *Lieber Code Co* [1917] 2 KB 469 on the same point.

13 A source code program may be written in a computer programming language, such as COBOL or BASIC, which is fairly easy for computer programmers to understand and write programs in. This source code version will usually be written down on paper or printed out. The source code will then be converted into the language of the computer, that is compiled into object code so that it can run on the computer. The object code will, if printed out in that form, be an apparently meaningless collection of numbers and letters.

14 Copyright – Copyright and Design Law, Cmnd 6732, HMSO, 1977.

15 Reform of the Law Relating to Copyright, Designs and Performers' Protection, Cmnd 8302, HMSO, 1981, cl 2.

16 The unauthorised copying and selling of computer programs including, in some cases, documentation. The USA was the first country to enact specific legislation directed towards the copyright protection of computer programs: Computer Software Copyright Act 1980, 17 USC §101, 117.

acts in relation to copyright works and the protection of electronic rights management information are described. There is a description of satellite broadcasting and the problems of unauthorised decoders and, finally, the discussion of copyright in relation to scientific discoveries, genetic sequences and formulae.

Copyright protection for computer programs

Background

It has already been seen that copyright subsists in computer programs as a form of literary work by the Copyright, Designs and Patents Act 1988 s 3(1)(b).[8] The same prerequisites of originality[9] and qualification must be present as with other forms of literary works for a computer program (or preparatory design material for a computer program) to be the subject matter of copyright. At one time it was not at all clear whether computer programs were protected by copyright. The Copyright Act 1956 made no mention of computers or computer programs. Although at the time that Act was passed computers had been around for a number of years, unauthorised copying of computer programs had not become a serious problem. There were only a few computers in existence and they were expensive and costly to operate and maintain, and there was no black market in application programs.[10] Many such application programs were specially written and maintained by the staff of computer departments for an organisation's own particular needs and would probably have been unsuitable for use by others. However, in spite of the omission of computer programs from the 1956 Act, many writers considered that they were protected as literary works. For example, Laddie *et al.* suggested that:

> . . . a computer program expressed in writing or other notation on a piece of paper is a 'literary work' within the meaning of [s 2 of the 1956 Act] . . . and if produced as a result of substantial independent skill or useful labour will be 'original' and so qualify for copyright protection.[11]

The issue may have been fairly straightforward and uncontroversial in the case of computer programs that have been printed out on paper. After all, if copyright had been extended to books of telegraphic codes as early as 1884, why should copyright be refused for computer programs printed out on paper?[12] However, if this view was accepted, it did not give any assistance in terms of computer programs that were stored in a computer, especially if those programs were in object code form having been compiled from source code programs.[13] A committee, known as the Whitford Committee, after its chairman Whitford J, was set up to examine copyright law generally, and its report was published in 1977 at a time when the problems of unauthorised copying of computer programs were beginning to be perceived.[14] The report recognised that copyright law was unsatisfactory as regards computer programs and the committee made recommendations to improve the law in this area and to put it beyond doubt that computer programs and works produced with the aid of a computer were protected by copyright. A Green Paper was published in 1981 covering copyright and related matters, and included recommendations that copyright law be amended expressly to afford protection for computer programs.[15]

Copyright law remained unchanged after the Whitford Committee report, and during the first few years of the 1980s the problem of computer software piracy[16] became a major concern for the computer industry with the loss attributable to piracy being estimated at some £150 million.[17] There were a handful of interim actions brought alleging infringement of copyright subsisting in computer programs; these actions invariably proceeded on the basis that computer programs were protected by copyright and interim relief was invariably granted. For example, in *Sega Enterprises Ltd v Richards*,[18] the claimant owned a computer game called 'FROGGER' which was effected by means of computer programs. The defendant produced a similar program, admitting that his was based on the claimant's program. The defendant argued that he had done much work on the program and that, in any case, copyright did not subsist in computer programs under English law. Goulding J said:

> . . . I am clearly of the opinion that copyright . . . subsists in the assembly code program of the game 'FROGGER'.

He went on to say that the object code derived from the assembly code program (source code) was either a reproduction or an adaptation of the assembly code version and, as a result, also protected by copyright. However, these cases were interim hearings only. Not a single case concerning the issue of the subsistence of copyright in computer programs went to full trial and the computer industry remained nervous.

The industry's fears appeared to be justified when, in 1984, the large and successful Apple Computer Corporation sued in Australia an importer of 'clones' of its computers. Appropriately enough, the clones were called 'WOMBATS'. At first instance, in *Apple Computer Inc v Computer Edge Pty Ltd*,[19] it was held that literary copyright did not subsist in the computer programs in question, being the object code programs in the ROM chips in the Apple II computer.[20] A great deal of reliance was placed by the judge on the old English case of *Hollinrake v Truswell*,[21] in which Davey LJ said that a literary work is one intended to 'afford either information and instruction, or pleasure, in the form of literary enjoyment'. Although the appeal by the claimant to the Federal Court of Australia was allowed, reversing the decision at first instance, on the basis that the object code programs were adaptations of the source code programs, the dissenting judgment by Shepherd J was the most elegant and well argued.[22] He said that an adaptation of a literary work should be capable of being seen or heard. To put the matter beyond doubt, the Australian Parliament very quickly enacted the Australian Copyright Amendment Act 1984. A further appeal restored the first instance decision on the object code point but was, of course, based on the Australian Copyright Act before amendment.[23]

The *Apple* case had serious repercussions for the UK, as Australian copyright law was, at the time, very similar to UK law. While in the USA the issue was the scope of the protection offered by copyright, in the UK doubts about whether copyright could subsist in a computer program, whatever its form, increased. Eventually, after vociferous outbursts by a worried but powerful industry, amending legislation was passed in the UK, but only by way of a Private Member's Bill. The Copyright (Computer Software) Amendment Act 1985 made it quite clear that computer programs were protected by copyright as literary works. When it was passed, this piece of legislation was seen as being a temporary measure and did not directly deal with some of the copyright issues related to computer technology, such as the ownership of works produced by or with the aid of a programmed computer.[24] One reason for the brevity and lack of consideration given to the amending legislation was that a wholesale review of copyright and design law was contemplated. That review took place and culminated in the White Paper *Intellectual Property and Innovation*, published in 1986.[25] Many of the recommendations contained in the White Paper found their way into the Copyright, Designs and Patents Act 1988, and it is to this Act and its implications that we will now turn.

17 The estimate was produced in 1984 by the Federation Against Software Theft (FAST). A later estimate, for the UK alone, was £540 million: Jervis, J. 'DTI Fires a Shot across Software Pirates' Bows', *Computing*, 1 August 1996 at p 4. There is no accurate modern figure – it must be very large, for example, in *Nintendo Co Ltd v Playables Ltd* [2010] FSR 36, no less than 165,000 devices designed to circumvent copy-protection of the claimant's games were intercepted by HM Revenue and Customs and Trading Standards on their way to the defendant.

18 [1983] FSR 73. *See also Gates* v *Swift* [1982] RPC 339; *Thrustcode Ltd* v *WW Computing Ltd* [1983] FSR 502; and *Apple Computer Inc* v *Sirtel (UK) Ltd* (unreported) 27 July 1983.

19 [1984] FSR 246.

20 A ROM chip is a read only memory integrated circuit which contains, typically, operating system programs. The defendant attacked the copyright in the Apple II programs after it was shown that the names of some of the programmers of the Apple II computer were present in the equivalent programs in the defendant's computer. This raised an almost irrefutable presumption of copying.

21 [1894] 3 Ch 420, approved in *Exxon Corporation* v *Exxon Insurance Consultants International Ltd* [1981] 3 All ER 241.

22 [1984] FSR 481.

23 *Computer Edge Pty Ltd* v *Apple Computer Inc* [1986] FSR 537.

24 HC Deb, 19 April 1985, col 558.

25 Cmnd 9712, HMSO, 1986.

Computer programs – basic position

The Copyright, Designs and Patents Act 1988 does not attempt to define 'computer program'.[26] This is probably sensible and at least allows the courts to develop the meaning of the phrase in the light of future technological change. In the Irish case of *News Datacom Ltd* v *Satellite Decoding Systems*[27] it was accepted that a 'smartcard' decoder for use with scrambled satellite television broadcasts was a computer program.

In Australia, in *Powerflex* v *Data Access Corp*[28] it was accepted, at first instance, that a single word in a computer program, being derived from the programming language used, could itself be a computer program. In a high-level language, a single statement, such as the word 'PRINT' in the BASIC programming language, is equivalent to and triggers a whole set of instructions in machine language. As such, it is arguable that it is a program. Fortunately, on appeal, the Federal Court saw the fallacy of this proposition, describing such a word as a cipher. It is not the set of instructions, merely the key to access them.[29]

It may sometimes be difficult to distinguish between 'hardware' and 'software', such as where a computer program is permanently hard-wired in a microprocessor in the form of 'microcode' or 'microprograms'. The view in the USA is that such programs or code still fall within the meaning of 'computer program' for the purpose of copyright law. In *NEC Corp* v *Intel Corp*[30] it was held that, even though the computer programs were permanently stored in 'read only memory' (ROM), the programs were still capable of copyright subsistence. The mode of storage did not change the nature of a computer program. In a later hearing between the parties in 1989,[31] an argument that the micro-code embedded within a microprocessor was a defining element of a computer and could not, therefore, also be a computer program failed to find sympathy. In the UK, it is beyond doubt that microcode will be considered to be a computer program or part of a program and will be protected by copyright.

The Copyright, Designs and Patents Act 1988 does not elaborate upon the meaning of originality in respect of computer programs. However, the European Directive on the legal protection of computer programs[32] describes originality in terms of a program being the author's own intellectual creation.[33] This approximates to the requirement under German copyright law that a work be the author's personal intellectual creation[34] and appears to be more stringent than the UK's test of originating from the author. It has been rigorously applied in Germany in the past, and in *Sudwestdeutsche Inkasso KG* v *Bappert und Burker Computer GmbH*[35] it was held that, to be protected by copyright, a computer program must result from individual creative achievement exceeding the average skills displayed in the development of computer programs.[36] However, later case law suggests that the hurdle to subsistence has been significantly lowered, as in the *Buchhaltungsprogram* case[37] in which the German Federal Supreme Court confirmed that copyright could subsist in an accounting program, taking the opportunity to signal a lowering of the standard, though, strictly speaking, this part of the decision was *obiter*.

The two most important acts restricted by copyright in relation to computer programs are those of copying and making an adaptation. Other acts may be relevant in the context of a computer program, such as issuing copies to the public, communicating to the public (for example, by making a program available for downloading from the internet) and the secondary infringements, but it is copying and making adaptations that are of particular interest as regards the scope of protection afforded by copyright. Following the uncertainty as to the copyright protection of computer programs which was finally put to rest by the Copyright (Computer Software) Amendment Act 1985, it was arguable that the pendulum had swung too far in the other direction and the protection afforded by copyright was too extensive. As a result, innovation and competition within the computer software industry could have been unjustifiably inhibited. However, the judgment of Pumfrey J in *Navitaire Inc* v *easyJet Airline Co*[38] for the first time clearly identified and

26 Nor is 'computer' defined.

27 [1995] FSR 201, Irish High Court.

28 [1997] FCA 490.

29 The copyright position of programming languages is discussed later in this chapter.

30 645 F Supp 1485 (D Minn, 1985).

31 *NEC Corp* v *Intel Corp* 10 USPQ 2d (1989).

32 Council Directive 91/250/EEC of 14 May 1991 on the legal protection of computer programs, OJ L 122, 17.05.1991, p 42 now replaced by Directive 2009/24/EC of the European Parliament and of the Council of 23 April 2009 on the legal protection of computer programs (codified version), OJ L 111, 05.05.2009, p 16.

33 Article 1(3). This also is the test for originality for databases: *see* below.

34 German Copyright Act 1965 s 2(2).

35 (1985) Case 52/83, BGHZ 94, 276.

36 For the background to the Directive, see Wilkinson, A. 'Software Protection, Trade, and Industrial Policies in the European Community' in Lehmann, M. and Tapper, C.F. (eds) (1993) *A Handbook of European Software Law*, Clarendon Press, pp 25–38 at pp 28–29.

37 BGH, 14 July 1993. *See* Günther, A. and Wuermeling, U. 'Software protection in Germany – recent court decisions in copyright law' [1995] 11 CLSR 12.

38 [2006] RPC 3.

applied the limitations on copyright protection in the Directive on the legal protection of computer programs and rejected a vague claim based on copying the 'business logic' underlying the programs at issue. This important case is discussed later in this chapter.

As with any other literary work, the copyright in a computer program is infringed by making, without the copyright owner's licence, a copy of the program or of a substantial part of it.[39] Substantiality is an issue of quality and therefore the copyright subsisting in a computer program can be infringed if the 'essence' of the program is copied, even if the part copied is relatively small quantitatively. Arguably, even a tiny part of a program could be regarded as substantial as the program probably will not function, at all or properly, without it. However, a better approach is to consider whether the part taken was the result of at least a minimal amount of skill on the part of the programmer. In other words, would the part taken, when looked at in isolation, satisfy the basic requirements for copyright subsistence?

In *Cantor Fitzgerald International v Tradition (UK) Ltd*,[40] it was suggested that every part of a computer program could be a substantial part of the program. The reasons for this were that syntactic errors will prevent the program from being compiled and semantic errors will prevent the program from running at all or will produce the wrong answer.[41] In other words, even very small parts of a computer program are important to the operation of the program. It will not run or run properly without them or if they are present but contain errors. Pumfrey J rejected this approach, pointing out that the correct approach to substantiality was determined by considering the function of copyright which is to protect the author's skill and labour used in creating the relevant work. Therefore, a person infringes the copyright in the work if he takes a part which represents a substantial part of the author's skill and labour. The closest analogy Pumfrey J came up with was the compilation cases such as *Macmillan & Co Ltd v K & J Cooper*,[42] but he warned against using the same principles that applied to literary works addressed to humans, such as a novel or poem, and applying those principles uncritically to computer programs. Unlike other forms of literary works, the purpose of computer programs is to make machines operate in a certain manner. The fact that a program will not work without a small part of it does not mean that it is a substantial part of the program, nor does the fact that a small part of a program is used frequently during the operation of the program. This might be the case, for example, where a small sub-routine within a computer program is called upon several or many times during the operation of the program.

Claimants alleging copying of parts of their programs may have difficulty in convincing a judge that a substantial part has been taken because of some judges' lack of technical knowledge. In *Total Information Processing Systems Ltd v Daman Ltd*[43] Judge Paul Baker considered that the data division of a COBOL program did not represent a substantial part of the program because it did not itself produce executable code or tell anything about the program. The data division in a COBOL program defines the nature and structure of files used by the program, and defines variables used. To many programmers, the data division is considered to be an important and essential part of the program and should certainly be considered to be worthy of protection, at the very least, as a non-literal element of the program. Fortunately, in *IBCOS Computers Ltd v Barclays Mercantile Highland Finance Ltd*,[44] Jacob J disagreed with Judge Paul Baker, and he said that there may be considerable skill involved in setting up the data division of a COBOL program such that it could be considered to be a substantial part of the program as a whole.[45] Judge Paul Baker's judgment is flawed in several other respects: for example, he said that the considerable steps taken to preserve confidentiality of the file details were suggestive that copyright did not subsist in that element of the program. This bizarre view is totally unfounded, either in legal principle or in policy, and is another aspect of the judgment in the *Total Information* case which Jacob J criticised.

Computer programs include graphical user interfaces (GUI) by which the person operating the program interacts with the program, for example, by reading a report generated

39 Copyright Designs and Patents Act 1988 s 16. In *MS Associates Ltd v Power* [1988] FSR 242, there was an arguable case that a substantial part of the original program for converting BASIC into C had been copied. The second program had 43 line similarities out of a total of 9,000 lines, although there were structural similarities and the same errors were present in both programs.

40 [2000] RPC 95.

41 The Australian case of *Autodesk Inc v Dyason* [1992] RPC 575 provides some authority for this proposition. In that case it was held that a 127-bit look-up table used with a dongle (a device plugged into a computer port and used to enable a computer program to be run) was not a computer program but was a substantial part of a computer program.

42 (1923) 93 LJPC 113.

43 [1992] FSR 171.

44 [1994] FSR 275.

45 *See also Autodesk Inc v Dyason* [1992] RPC 575, which concerned the copying of a dongle (a device plugged into a computer port and used to enable a computer program to be run). It was accepted that copying a table of codes (a 127-bit look-up table) contained in the program in the dongle infringed copyright.

by the program or inputting data to the program. In terms of protection a GUI is not part of the expression of the computer program protected under the Directive on the legal protection of computer programs but is might have separate protection if it the result of the author's own intellectual creation:[46] presumably as a literary and/or artistic work.

Judges in cases involving complex technology rely to a greater or lesser extent on the evidence of expert witnesses. That being so, it is important that expert witnesses are objective and do not act as advocates. As Pumfrey J said in *Cantor Fitzgerald*:[47]

> Where the subject matter of the action lies in a highly technical area it is of particular importance that the expert is scrupulous in putting forward all relevant considerations which occur to him or her as being relevant to the issue to be decided. The court has no points of reference other than those provided by the expert. It is reprehensible for the expert to hold back relevant information. The danger is manifest. If both experts lack objectivity the court is deprived of any proper basis to arrive at a decision.

In relation to literary works, 'copying' is defined by s 17 as a reproduction in any material form; this includes storage in any medium by electronic means and making copies which are transient or incidental to some other use of the work.[48] Thus, loading a computer program (or, for that matter, any other form of work) into a computer's volatile memory (RAM) is copying.[49] That is why a licence is required to use a computer program, in contrast to most other forms of works for which use in private does not involve an act restricted by copyright. Given the wide definition of 'electronic' in s 178 there should not be any difficulties concerning existing and future media in or on which a computer program is stored. However, Kitchen J, in *Football Association Premier League* v *QC Leisure (No 2)*,[50] suggested that a substantial part of the work in question must be held in transient storage at any given time to constitute infringement. If an entire work passes through volatile memory but only a tiny fraction of the work is in the memory at any point in time, copyright protection would be thwarted. It is submitted that he was wrong on this and 'salami slicing' a work in this way through transient memory must surely infringe. It would infringe if the work were a database protected by the database right.[51] Of course, larger parts of a work are likely to be held in computer RAM at any given time and may constitute substantial parts of the work in question. The *Football Association* case involved the showing of a film through an unauthorised decoder which only held a small number of frames of the film at any given time. In any case, Kitchen J referred numerous questions to the Court of Justice for a preliminary ruling, including a question about the scope of infringement by transient copies.

In Joined Cases C-403/08 and C-429/08 *Football Association Premier League Ltd* v *QC Leisure*,[52] the Court of Justice ruled, *inter alia*, on aspects of Directive 2001/29/EC of the European Parliament and of the Council of 22 May 2001 on the harmonisation of certain aspects of copyright and related rights in the information society.[53] In relation to the reproduction right under Article 2(a), this extends to transient fragments of a work in a satellite decoder memory and on a television screen only if those fragments contain elements which are the expression of the author's own intellectual creation. In other words, each fragment must be considered individually and not collectively. A fragment might infringe if, for example, it contains a copyright emblem. However, a live football match, *per se*, is not a copyright work.

Preparatory design material

The finished code of a computer program is the culmination of a long process involving the creation of a number of preparatory (and intermediate) works. For example, the analysts and programmers working on the development of a new program usually will produce specifications, flowcharts, diagrams, layouts for menus, screen displays, and

46 So the Court of Justice held in Case C-393/09 *Bezpečnostní softwarová asociace – Svaz softwarové ochrany* v *Ministerstvo kultury* [2011] FSR 18.

47 [2000] RPC 95 at 128.

48 In Case C-5/08 *Infopaq International A/S* v *Danske Dagblades Forening* [2009] ECR I-6569, the Court of Justice rules that printing 11 words of text on paper was an act of reproduction that was not transient. Automatic deletion without human intervention were required for the act to be transient.

49 As it is also in the US: *Advanced Computer Services of Michigan Inc* v *MIA Systems Corp* (unreported) 14 February 1994, discussed in [1994] CLSR 213.

50 [2008] FSR 32.

51 See the section on databases, *infra*.

52 4 October 2011.

53 OJ L 167, 22.06.2001, p 10.

reports and other materials. Prior to the amendments made to the Act by the Copyright (Computer Programs) Regulations 1992 in compliance with the Directive on the legal protection of computer programs, all these materials would have been protected in their own right as literary or artistic works as appropriate. In *Japan Capsules Computers (UK) Ltd v Sonic Game Sales*[54] Whitford J accepted that these and other ancillary materials, such as music generated by a program, could be protected by copyright.

The separate protection of preparatory design material as a literary work by s 3(1)(c) conflicts with the wording of the Directive, which states that the term 'computer programs' shall *include* their preparatory design material.[55] It does mean that the special exceptions for computer programs (ss 50A, 50B, 50BA and 50C) do not apply to preparatory design material. For example, it is not permissible to make a back-up copy of a computer manual unless the other permitted acts generally available for literary works allow this. Why the 1992 Regulations chose to treat preparatory design material separately is inexplicable and unforgivable, given that certainty and predictability are so important to the computer industry.[56] It could affect issues of substantiality in relation to infringement as, according to the Directive, computer programs include their preparatory design material. However, a judge would most likely go straight to the Directive and use the provisions therein. In *Nova Productions Ltd v Mazooma Games Ltd*,[57] an application was made for questions to be submitted to the Court of Justice for a preliminary ruling under Article 267 of the Treaty on the Functioning of the EU[58] on the basis that the judge at first instance[59] had erred by not considering the preparatory design material as part of the computer programs. Jacob LJ considered that a reference was unnecessary as the issues could be decided on appeal without guidance from the Court of Justice. In any case, the claimant's case could be even weaker if the computer program had been taken to include its preparatory design material.

Preparatory design material will include works that would previously have been considered to be artistic works, such as flowcharts and other diagrams.[60] These are now literary works notwithstanding the resulting implications. For example, there is no requirement for an artistic work to be recorded, and infringement and the permitted acts are not precisely the same for literary and artistic works.

Literal copying of computer programs

Copying of a computer program can be literal, where the program code itself is copied, in which case the two programs are written in the same computer programming language. Alternatively, copying can be non-literal, where elements of the program such as its structure, sequence of operations, functions, interfaces and methodologies are copied, but the program code is not directly copied.[61] The two programs may be written in the same language or in different computer programming languages. The law's recognition of non-literal copying is important because otherwise it would be too easy to defeat copyright protection of computer programs. Non-literal copying is considered later in this chapter. Literal copying occurs where a person copies an existing program by disk to disk copying (a duplicate is made on to another computer disk), or by writing out or printing the program listing, perhaps to key it into another computer at a later date. In either case, the person making the copy may make some alterations to the copy. These may be to disguise its origins or to enhance the program, for example, by including some additional functions.

Literal copying is relatively easy to test for infringement. In essence, there are three axiomatic questions for the court. First, does copyright subsist in the claimant's program? Second, has the defendant copied from the claimant's program? Finally, does the part taken by the defendant represent a substantial part of the claimant's program? If the

54 (Unreported) 16 October 1986.

55 Article 1(1) of Council Directive 91/250/EEC of 14 May 1991 on the legal protection of computer programs, OJ L 122, 17.05.1991, p 42 now replaced by Directive 2009/24/EC of the European Parliament and of the Council of 23 April 2009 on the legal protection of computer programs (codified version), OJ L 111, 05.05.2009, p 16.

56 *See* Chalton, S. 'Implementation of the Software Directive in the UK: The Effects of the Copyright (Computer Programs) Regulations 1992' [1993] 9 CLSR 115.

57 [2007] RPC 25.

58 Formerly Article 234 of the EC Treaty.

59 *Nova Productions Ltd v Mazooma Games Ltd* [2006] RPC 14.

60 An electronic circuit diagram was held to be a literary work as well as an artistic work in *Anacon Corp Ltd v Environmental Research Technology Ltd* [1994] FSR 659.

61 Alternative descriptions are 'textual' and 'non-textual' copying.

answer to these questions is in the affirmative then, unless the defendant has a defence or his actions fall within the permitted acts or some other defence, infringement is proved. In practice, the answer to the first question will seldom be negative. Even relatively small programs will be the result of the programmer's skill, experience and judgment. The following case was the first to consider seriously the issues relating to literal copying of computer programs and laid down some important precedents for software copyright law.

62 [1994] FSR 275.

In *IBCOS Computers Ltd* v *Barclays Mercantile Highland Finance Ltd*,[62] the second defendant, a computer programmer called Mr Poole, wrote a suite of programs for accounts and payroll. He owned the copyright in the programs and eventually developed a Mk 3 version. Then, with another person, he set up a firm, PK Computer Services, to provide software for agricultural machinery dealers. When Mr Poole left the company, he signed a note recognising that the company owned all the rights in the software which contained the Mk 3 suite of programs. Mr Poole was then engaged by the first defendant to write similar software. Both suites of programs were written in variants of the same programming language and there was a degree of literal similarity between them. PK Computer Services transferred its assets to the claimant which learnt of Mr Poole's activities, obtained a 'door step search order'[63] and sued for infringement of the copyright in its suite of computer programs.

63 An order requiring the defendant to deliver up relevant materials, as opposed to a search order requiring the defendant to allow the claimant to search his premises for evidence.

Jacob J held that there had been an infringement of the claimant's copyright. Not only were the individual programs protected by copyright, but also the suite of programs was protected as a compilation, being the result of sufficient skill and judgment (the claimant's computer software comprised 335 programs, 171 record layout files and 46 screen layouts). From the defendant's point of view, there were some unfortunate coincidences. Both suites of programs contained many common mistakes in the 'comment' lines (these are lines that are not executed by the computer and are inserted merely to make a program easier to understand from the programmer's perspective). Both suites of programs contained the same redundant code. In the mind of Jacob J, and in the absence of any plausible explanation from Mr Poole, this proved that there had been disk to disk copying.[64] Jacob J said that copying was a question of fact and could be proved by showing that something trivial or unimportant had been copied.

64 Mr Poole had argued that the similarities were the result of programming style, but this failed to impress the judge.

The issue of substantiality was considered and Jacob J stressed the importance of expert evidence in this respect. In the event, he decided that 28 out of 55 of the defendant's programs infringed the claimant's copyrights. He also found that a later version of the defendant's programs infringed (11 of the defendant's programs infringed and the copyright in the claimant's suite of programs as a compilation was also infringed). Furthermore, Mr Poole was in breach of confidence, the source code to the claimant's program being confidential. He had also signed a note when leaving PK Computer Services which contained a covenant in restraint of trade. However, Mr Poole was not in breach of the covenant, which was construed narrowly by Jacob J.

Jacob J made a number of other interesting points which are set out below with comments:

- Fresh copyright could be created when a program was modified. This is a question of whether sufficient skill, labour or judgment has been expended in making the modifications.
- A file record may not be a program within the Act, but it will be a compilation. Thus, the data division of a COBOL program may be protected by copyright acknowledging the work of designing the data structures used by the programs.[65]
- The inclusion of functional elements that could be expressed in only one, or a limited number of ways, does not affect the fact of copyright subsistence.
- The *British Leyland* right to repair principle did not allow copying of a file transfer program. This is a program to convert the structure of a file so that it can be used with other software. However, the decompilation permitted act may allow the necessary information to be discovered to allow the independent writing of a file transfer program.[66]

65 Now, data files may have protection as a database protected directly by copyright and/or the database right.

66 Copyright, Designs and Patents Act 1988 s 50B.

The case gave Jacob J an opportunity to make a number of criticisms of previous cases. He pointed out that UK copyright law is not the same as US copyright law and questioned the appropriateness of US precedents which Ferris J had found so helpful in *John Richardson Computers Ltd v Flanders*.[67] The judgment in *IBCOS* is comprehensive and is to be welcomed for its realistic approach. Jacob J should be congratulated for his grasp of computer technology and for his application of copyright law to the facts. Of particular importance is the recognition of the work underlying the design of computer software, including the design of the data structures used and the skill and judgment in developing the overall structure of a suite of programs. However, his comments on non-literal copying and the use of US precedents (particularly in the *John Richardson* case) should be treated with caution. *IBCOS* and *John Richardson* are distinguishable, the former being primarily concerned with literal copying. Of course, US precedents can never be binding on the courts in the UK, but they should certainly be treated with due respect in this field where the US experience of litigation is much more extensive, after making due allowances for differences compared with UK law.

Merely being in possession of a disk on which a copy of a copyright work is recorded is not a restricted act, *per se*.[68] So it was held in *Ocular Sciences Ltd v Aspect Vision Care Ltd*[69] where evidence that a reference to the predecessor of the claimant in the program in question had been changed to a reference to the defendant proved that the program must have been saved at some time in its modified form and that act of storing infringed the copyright in the program.

Indirect copying

It has already been seen that copyright law accepts the notion of indirect copying.[70] Does indirect copying apply to computer programs? Of course there must be copying, which in the *British Leyland* case was done through the medium of a finished exhaust pipe. But consider the position of a person who, having seen a computer program in operation, decides to write a new computer program to perform the same function as the original program. Does that person infringe the copyright subsisting in the original program or preparatory design material even though he has not seen a listing of the program itself or the preparatory materials? In three ways, the Act recognises that copyright can be infringed indirectly: first, by s 16(3)(b) it recognises that the acts restricted by copyright may be done indirectly; second, by s 16(3) the Act contemplates that a work may be infringed even though intervening acts do not infringe copyright; and third, by s 17(6) the Act states that copying includes the making of copies which are transient or are incidental to some other use of the work. However, the program code in the second program would most likely be significantly different from that in the original, especially if it is written using a different programming language. For this reason, the District Court in *Digital Communications Associates v Softklone Distributing Corp*[71] held that the copyright in the underlying program was not infringed by copying a screen display generated by running the program.

Non-literal copying of computer programs

With some works of copyright, it is an easy matter to distinguish between the literal and non-literal elements. For example, with a work of literature, perhaps in the form of an historical novel, the literal element comprises the words, sentences and paragraphs as expressed in print, while the non-literal element can be said to consist of the detailed plot, sequence of events, characters and scenes. In some cases, the author of the novel will produce written materials or diagrams expressing these non-literal elements, in which

67 [1993] FSR 497 *see* below.

68 It could be relevant to secondary infringement, however, such as where a person possesses an infringing copy in the course of business: s 23; or if he possesses an article specifically designed or adapted to make infringing copies: s 24(1), subject to the necessary knowledge.

69 [1997] RPC 289.

70 *See* Chapter 6, particularly the case of *British Leyland Motor Corp Ltd v Armstrong Patents Co Ltd* [1986] 2 WLR 400.

71 659 F Supp 449 (ND Ga, 1987).

case they may have their own copyright independent of the copyright subsisting in the finished novel. However, in the absence of such materials, it is clear that taking the non-literal elements can infringe.[72] One proviso is that, at a certain stage of abstraction from the literal text of the work, the non-literal elements will be no more than mere idea, though determining the threshold between the protected and the unprotected is not an easy matter. As Lord Hailsham said in *LB (Plastics) Ltd* v *Swish Products Ltd*, after remarking that it is trite law that there is no copyright in ideas,

> But, of course, as the late Professor Joad used to observe, it all depends on what you mean by 'ideas'.[73]

Non-literal copying is not a problem restricted to computer programs, and the courts in the USA also have struggled to separate unprotectable ideas from protected expression, including non-literal elements. In *Nichols* v *Universal Pictures Co*[74] Judge Learned Hand recognised the importance of protecting non-literal elements of copyright works, saying (at 121):

> It is of course essential to any protection of literary property . . . that the right cannot be limited literally to the text, else a plagiarist would escape by immaterial variations.

He then went on to discuss the various levels of abstraction, from the text to the most general statement of the play (possibly its title only), and the difficulty in determining where, along this spectrum of abstractions, the boundary between copyright and non-copyright material lay. Somewhat discouragingly, he then said, 'Nobody has ever been able to fix that boundary and nobody ever can.' In other words, it must depend on the facts of each individual case.

The same principles apply to computer programs. Copyright must not be limited to a comparison of the code of the original and alleged infringing programs. If that were so, copyright law would be easily defeated.[75] It would simply be a matter of rewriting the program in a different computer programming language or, provided changes are made to variable names, remark lines, line numbering etc., using the same programming language. In other words, it would be a simple matter to defeat copyright by making a duplicate of the original program to which a number of cosmetic alterations could be applied. The USA was the first in the field in developing tests for non-literal copying of computer programs, and before looking at the UK position it will be instructive to look at litigation in the USA. Of course, US copyright law is not exactly the same as that in the UK, though there are similarities and many of the basic principles are common. It should be noted that copyright law in both jurisdictions has a common ancestor, the Statute of Anne 1709.

Developments in the USA

If anything, the idea/expression dichotomy is even more ingrained in US copyright law, going back at least to *Baker* v *Selden*[76] where it was held that copyright subsisting in a book describing a method of book-keeping did not extend to protect the method so described and illustrated. If copyright protects expression but not idea, it is obviously important for a court to be able to distinguish between them, particularly where the law gives protection to certain non-literal elements of copyright works. However, US law goes further than that in the UK in denying protection to tangible form if it is deemed to be so closely associated with the idea underlying the work that there is no alternative way of expressing it. Hence, it is even more important in the USA to distinguish between protected expression and unprotected idea.

This issue was considered in the context of computer programs in the case of *Whelan Associates Inc* v *Jaslow Dental Laboratory Inc*,[77] the first so-called 'look and feel' case. It was said that, in relation to a computer program designed to carry out a mundane task (running dental laboratories in that case), anything that was essential to the task was 'idea' while

72 *See*, for example, *Corelli v Gray* [1913] TLR 570; *Glyn v Weston Feature Film Co* [1916] 1 Ch 261.

73 [1979] RPC 551 at 629.

74 45 F 2d 119 (2nd Cir, 1930).

75 For an argument that the law of passing off may provide some protection to computer programs, in particular screen displays, *see* Lea, G. 'Passing off and the protection of program look and feel' [1994] 10 CLSR 82.

76 101 US 99 (1880).

77 [1987] FSR 1.

anything that was not essential and could have been written in different ways was 'expression'. If these latter parts were copied, then the copyright would be infringed because the expression had been copied. If the programmer had no option but to write a part of the program the way he did because the task to be achieved dictated its form and content then that part was 'idea' and not protected by copyright. Similarly, the purpose of a utilitarian program was 'idea' and the structure of the program, if there were several different possible structures that could have been adopted, was 'expression'. Consequently, not just the actual program code but also the structure of a computer program can be protected by copyright if, because of similar structure, the 'look and feel' of the programs are similar.

Whelan was considered in numerous later cases. In *Plains Cotton Cooperative* v *Goodpasture Computer Service*,[78] an apparent rejection of the *Whelan* case can be explained by concluding that the structure of the claimant's program was 'idea' and not 'expression' because the application itself dictated the structure of the program. The program's application was to assist in the marketing of cotton and this, by its very nature, could be expressed only in computer programs exhibiting a substantially similar structure; it left no room for alternative structures.[79] Other cases have dealt with screen displays. In *Broderbund Software* v *Unison World*,[80] the court held that, as there were several means by which the screens could have been structured, sequenced and arranged, the actual way selected by the claimant was copyrightable expression.[81] The court also appears to have confirmed that copying the format, structure and sequence of screen displays infringes the copyright in the underlying programs. However, in *Digital Communications Associates* v *Softklone Distributing Corp*[82] this view was rejected on the basis that a screen display cannot be a copy of part of the program because the same screen display can be produced by various programs in different ways. Nevertheless, the court did afford protection to the screen display in its own right, and differentiated between 'idea' and 'expression' by regarding the idea of a screen display as being the concept of the screen, whereas the means used to communicate the screen's manner of operation, that is, the arrangement of terms, highlighting and capitalisation, was the expression of the screen display.[83]

Spreadsheets

A spreadsheet program is, in essence, one which comprises a grid of cells (usually two-dimensional, but 'three-dimensional' grids are now common) into which the user can enter text, numbers and/or formulae. A spreadsheet is useful for preparing an easily updated table of calculations from which graphs and barcharts can be derived. Non-literal elements of spreadsheet software include its menu system, by which the user interacts with the spreadsheet, and the system for denoting cell references, for example, C7, H21, etc.

In *Lotus Development Corp* v *Paperback Software International*[84] the defendant had developed a spreadsheet program called VP-Planner. The defendant had realised that, because of the success of the claimant's famous Lotus 1-2-3 spreadsheet program, it was desirable that VP-Planner was compatible with Lotus 1-2-3. To this end, the defendant ensured that the arrangement of commands and menus in VP-Planner conformed to those in Lotus 1-2-3, and this meant that it was possible to transfer spreadsheets from VP-Planner to Lotus 1-2-3 without losing the functionality of any macros in the spreadsheet.[85] Another reason for compatibility and similarity in screen displays and command language was that Lotus 1-2-3 users could transfer to VP-Planner without the need for any further training. When the difference in cost between the two spreadsheets is considered, it is not surprising that Lotus sued the owners of VP-Planner.[86] The defendant claimed that he had not copied the program code of Lotus 1-2-3, so this was a case of 'non-literal copying'. The central issues, therefore, were whether the non-literal elements of the claimant's program were protected by copyright, that is the overall organisation of the program (structure), the structure of the command system, the screen displays and, especially, the user interface.

78 807 F 2d 1256 (5th Cir, 1987).

79 For an argument that *Plains Cotton* is not inconsistent with *Whelan, see* Taylor, W.D. 'Copyright Protection for Computer Software after *Whelan Associates* v *Jaslow Dental Laboratory*' (1989) 54 *Missouri Law Review* 121.

80 648 F Supp 1127 (ND Cal, 1986).

81 The argument by the defendant that there was no other way to structure the screens or design the input formats was quickly overcome by the claimant who produced another competing program which performed a similar function (to design greetings cards, signs, banners and posters) but which had screen displays and screen sequences that were very different. Taylor, W.D. 'Copyright Protection for Computer Software after *Whelan Associates* v *Jaslow Dental Laboratory*' (1989) 54 *Missouri Law Review* 121 at 151.

82 659 F Supp 449 (ND Ga, 1987).

83 Some commentators argue for strong copyright protection of screen displays subject to a higher standard of originality. *See* Benson, J.R. 'Copyright Protection for Computer Screen Displays' (1988) 72 *Minnesota Law Review* 1123.

84 740 F Supp 37 (D Mass, 1990).

85 A 'macro' is a list of commands that are stored in a separate executable file. The purpose usually is to save time. For example, the user might want to combine several spreadsheets, total them, find the average and change the display format and, rather than having to enter a whole series of commands each time he wants to do this, he can store the instructions in a macro which he can call up and execute in the future at a keystroke. The command language of VP-Planner would have to be the same as that in Lotus 1-2-3 for macros to be compatible.

86 At the beginning of 1991, in the UK, Lotus 1-2-3 was available at around £200–£300 (depending on the version) while VP-Planner was available (for educational use only) at around £8. It must be noted that this version of VP-Planner had a limited overall spreadsheet size compared to Lotus 1-2-3.

Judge Keeton held that the user interface of Lotus 1-2-3, in particular the two-line moving cursor menu, was protected by copyright and that the defendant had infringed that copyright. The menu command system was said to be 'copyrightable' because it was effected in different ways in different spreadsheet programs. For example, some used a list of letters (another spreadsheet program Visicalc used 'BCDEFGIMPRSTVW-'); others used a three-line menu or pull-down menus. The two-line moving cursor menu used by Lotus 1-2-3 was said to be original and non-obvious and, thus, protected by copyright. Other features such as the rotated 'L' used to contain the grid reference letters and numbers, and the use of certain keys to call up commands and perform arithmetical functions (for example, the '+', '/', '−' and '*' keys), were held not to be protected because they were common to spreadsheets, even though they were not essential.

It was accepted by the judge that disentangling idea from expression was not an 'either/ or' or 'black and white' matter but a matter of degree, and a distinction must be made between the generality and specificity of conceptualising an idea. A legal test for copyrightability was suggested based on constructing a scale of abstraction from the most generalised conception at one end to the most particularised conception at the other end. The expression being considered was placed on this scale and a decision made based on choice and judgment, but earlier judgments by Judge Learned Hand had suggested that this could be done only in an *ad hoc* way.[87]

Useful as Judge Keeton's judgment was in terms of non-literal copying generally, it was overturned in *Lotus Development Corp* v *Borland International Inc*[88] by the First Circuit Court of Appeals. However, the reason was not so much connected with any disagreement with the way of testing for idea or expression, but a direct consequence of the US Copyright Act s 102(b) which denies copyright protection to 'any idea, procedure, process, system, *method of operation*, concept, principle or discovery . . .' (emphasis added). It was held by the First Circuit Court of Appeals that the menu system of Lotus 1-2-3 was a method of operation and, hence, not protected by copyright. This decision has serious implications for the computer industry in that it effectively puts user interfaces into the public domain. The subsequent appeal to the Supreme Court was unsatisfactory in that, whilst the decision of the Court of Appeals was affirmed, it was the result of a split decision and, in such cases, the Supreme Court gives no substantive judgment.[89] The reasoning of the Court of Appeals therefore stands.[90]

Certainly, *Lotus* v *Borland* goes much further than any case in the UK has ventured or is likely to do in the near future.[91] On the one hand, it can be said to be a liberating influence, facilitating the development of compatible interfaces, but, on the other hand, it could rob the designer of a new interface technique of any real protection from copying. The World Intellectual Property Organisation Copyright Treaty states in Article 2 that copyright protection extends to expression and not ideas, procedures, methods of operation or mathematical concepts as such.[92] Similar exceptions to protection are also present in EU Directives: for example, in Directive 2009/24/EC of the European Parliament and of the Council of 23 April 2009 on the legal protection of computer programs,[93] Article 1(2) states that ideas and principles which underlie any element of a computer program, including those which underlie its interfaces, are not protected by copyright under the Directive.

A re-formulated test for non-literal copying

Whelan and subsequent cases can be explained by the need to deal with non-literal copying of computer programs, where the first program has been unfairly used as a basis for the creation of a second program but there is no literal similarity in the actual program code because different programming languages have been used. Although the *Whelan* test proved troublesome to apply in practice, it has been superseded by a more sophisticated

87 For example, *Shipman* v *RKO Radio Pictures* 100 F 2d 533 (2d Cir, 1938).

88 [1997] FSR 61. Lotus claimed the Borland's Quattro spreadsheet infringed the copyright in the Lotus 1-2-3 menu system.

89 *See* footnote in [1997] FSR 61 and *Computing*, 25 January 1996, p 8.

90 Some earlier judgments based on *Lotus* v *Paperback*, such as *Autoskill Inc* v *National Education Support Systems Inc* 994 F 2d 1476 (10th Cir, 1993) on the use of a keying procedure using the 1, 2 and 3 keys and *Brown Bag Software* v *Symantec Corp* 960 F 2d 1465 (9th Cir, 1992), suggesting menus and keystrokes could be protected by copyright, must be viewed with some suspicion.

91 In the UK, program interfaces may be determined by decompilation, but it is at least arguable that user interfaces are protected: *see John Richardson Computers Ltd* v *Flanders* [1993] FSR 497, discussed below.

92 Geneva, 2–20 December 1996.

93 (Codified version), OJ L 111, 05.05.2009, p 16, replacing the original Directive (OJ L 122, 17.05.1991, p 42).

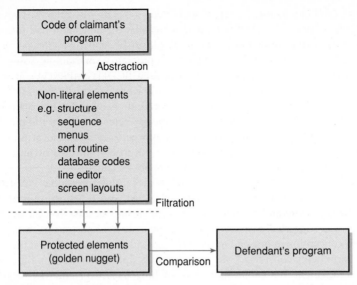

Figure 8.1 Test for non-literal copying

test which still does nothing to aid predictability. The New York Court of Appeals strongly criticised *Whelan* in *Computer Associates International Inc* v *Altai Inc*[94] as taking insufficient account of computer technology. In *Computer Associates*, the defendant had produced a program known as 'Oscar', a job scheduling program for controlling the order in which tasks were carried out by a computer. It had a common interface component allowing the use of different operating systems, and this part had been added by a former employee of the claimant which had a similar program and interface. The former employee was very familiar with the claimant's program and had even taken parts home to work on. As soon as the defendant company realised the problem, it agreed to pay $364,444 in damages and engaged other programmers to rewrite the infringing parts of its program. The claimant still sued in respect of the defendant's new version, but the judge held there was no infringement. The judgment of the court was given by Judge Walker, who laid down a three-stage test for non-literal copying as follows and as shown in Figure 8.1.

94 20 USPQ 2d 1641 (1992).

1 *Abstraction* – discovering the non-literal elements by a process akin to reverse engineering, beginning with the code of the claimant's program and ending with its ultimate function. This process retraces and maps out the designer's steps and produces, *inter alia*, structures of differing detail at varying levels of abstraction.
2 *Filtration* – the separation of protectable expression from non-protectable expression material. Some elements will not be protected being ideas, dictated by or incidental to ideas, required by external factors (*scènes a faire* doctrine) or taken from the public domain. These elements are filtered out leaving a core of protectable material – the program's 'golden nugget' or protected expression.
3 *Comparison* – a determination of whether the defendant has copied a substantial part of the protected expression – whether any aspect has been copied and, if so, whether this represents a substantial part of the claimant's program.

The judge recognised that the test would be difficult to apply, but expressed the hope that it would become less so with further case law.[95] At first sight, it seems significantly to weaken copyright protection for computer programs. Many programs contain parts taken from the public domain (such as commonly used routines to extract data from files, to perform complex arithmetical operations or to sort data into alphabetical order) and

95 It has been used subsequently. *See*, for example, *Gates Rubber Co* v *Bando Chemical Industries Ltd* (unreported) 19 October 1993, 10th Circuit Court of Appeals, discussed in [1994] 10 CLSR 101.

other parts will be significantly constrained by ideas or external factors. It would appear that, in some cases, there will be no golden nuggets left after filtration. The claimant's gold prospecting will result in bitter disappointment!

Merger of idea/expression

There may be occasions when it is impossible to separate idea from expression because of the constraints which severely limit the ways in which the ideas contained in a computer program can be expressed. In *NEC Corp v Intel Corp*,[96] such merger of idea and expression was said not to affect the copyright status of a computer program but was an issue of infringement. Even though Intel's microcode programs were declared to be 'copyrightable' material in principle, this case reinforces the look and feel approach in its practical effect because, as Intel's programs were dictated by the instruction set of the microprocessors involved and because there were no alternative ways of expressing the ideas, reverse analysis of the programs did not infringe copyright.[97]

Non-literal copying in the UK

John Richardson Computers Ltd v Flanders[98] is the first case in the UK to address fully the look and feel of computer programs and is exceptional in that the test used in the USA for non-literal copying was expressly approved of and applied, at least in part, by Ferris J in a comprehensive judgment. Both parties were in the business of developing and marketing computer programs to be used by pharmacists for the purpose of producing labels for prescriptions and for stock control. The judge found the facts of the case difficult to determine (there were a number of disputed points) and the case provides a good example of the need to document the development of copyright works carefully and to make suitable arrangements for ownership.[99]

Mr Richardson, the chairman and managing director of the claimant company, who was a pharmacist and self-taught computer programmer, developed a program written in BASIC to produce labels suitable for the Tandy computer. He was not an expert at writing programs and he, therefore, engaged a self-employed programmer to help complete the program and make it more reliable. In 1983, Mr Flanders joined the claimant company as an employee to write an equivalent program in machine code that would have the same look and feel as the original program for the BBC computer. In 1986, Mr Flanders left the employment of the claimant company, but did further work for it as a self-employed consultant, during which time he rewrote the program in assembly language, a low-level language, adding some new features. Later, Mr Flanders wrote a new version of the program (in the QuickBASIC language) for the IBM personal computer. The claimant was also working on a version for the IBM computer and sued for infringement of its copyright in the BBC version of the program and for breach of confidence.[100]

The general approach in the *Computer Associates* case attracted Ferris J, who remarked that there was nothing in any English decision which conflicted with it. However, rather than seeking the 'core of protectable expression', an English court would first decide whether the claimant's program as a whole was subject to copyright and then decide whether any similarity in the defendant's program was the result of copying a substantial part of the claimant's program. In particular, Ferris J directed his attention to the non-literal elements of the programs, finding *Computer Associates* helpful in separating idea from expression.

In the event, Ferris J held that there was a limited infringement of the copyright subsisting in the claimant's program based on the non-literal elements of the program. A literal comparison was not helpful as both programs had been written in different languages

96 10 USPQ 2d (1989).

97 This should be compared to the Australian case of *Autodesk Inc v Dyason* (unreported) 7 August 1989, Federal Court of Australia, in which the reverse analysis of a computer lock (a hardware device, sometimes called a 'dongle', which must be plugged into the computer before a particular computer program can be used) was held to infringe copyright in the computer program contained within the lock. *See* Goldblatt, M. 'Copyright Protection for Computer Programs in Australia: The Law since Autodesk' [1990] 5 EIPR 170. On appeal, the *Autodesk* decision was reversed: *see* Anon, 'Appellate Court gives Green Light to Reverse Engineering' (1991) 2 *Intellectual Property in Business Briefing* 3. However, finally in *Autodesk Inc v Dyason* [1992] RPC 575 the High Court of Australia reinstated the decision at first instance.

98 [1992] FSR 497.

99 The defendant may have been the legal owner of the copyright in parts of the program. The claimant was the owner in equity of that copyright and the difficulty beneficial owners can experience in obtaining remedies was overcome here because the legal owner was joined in the action – as defendant.

100 The breach of confidence claim was dropped.

and bore no literal similarity. He identified 17 objective similarities in the non-literal elements and then went on to consider the reasons for the similarities. The similarities and the reasons for them were classified as follows:

1 Similarities that were the result of copying a substantial part of the claimant's program, being the line editor, amendment routines and dose codes. It was in respect of these parts that copyright infringement was found.
2 Similarities that were the result of copying, but not in relation to a substantial part of the claimant's program. These were the date option, daily figures reset, operation successful message plus double bleep, data entry by quantity first, four out of eight of the pre-printing options and best day's stock control.
3 Similarities that *might* have been the result of copying but, in any case, related only to an insubstantial part of the claimant's program. These were the vertical arrangement of prompts and entries and the entry of data within the label routine.
4 Similarities that were not the result of copying, being the date entry, use of the escape key, position of label on screen, drug entry routine, secondary access to the full list of drugs on screen and label entry sequence.

The line editor, amendment routines and dose codes were deemed to have been copied and to represent a substantial part of the claimant's program. This approach affects the test of substantiality which has long been accepted as being a question of quality not quantity.[101] As adopted by Ferris J, it implies that relatively trivial elements of a program could be used in the comparison process. The manner of Ferris J's application of the test from *Computer Associates* can be criticised because he did not carry out the second stage.[102] He did not filter out those elements that might have been unprotected, such as ideas or public domain routines. Essentially, the only significant use he made of the *Computer Associates* case was in his acceptance that non-literal elements of computer programs may be protected by copyright. He did not need to rely on US precedents to do this. In the *IBCOS* case, Jacob J criticised the use of US precedents, but agreed with Ferris J that consideration must not be restricted to the actual code of the programs in question.

A concern remains with the judgment of Ferris J in that it may result in the protection of relatively trivial and mundane parts of computer programs. It should be noted that the programs in *Richardson* were by no means exceptional. They performed relatively simple functions. Additionally, both programs made substantial use of what might be termed public domain materials, or at least techniques and methods commonly used by programmers. For example, there is a limited number of ways to correct mistakes using a line editor and these are dictated to some extent by the programming language used and other features relating to the type of computer used and its operating system. It is common for standard routines to perform commonly required operations like line editing to be published in textbooks, computer journals and magazines.[103] Even if a line editor could be considered to be protectable expression, there is no doubt that, in terms of the program's function, it could never be said to form a substantial part of the program. Nevertheless, that is what the judge found.

The consideration of a program as a collection of disparate and relatively small and discrete non-literal elements could make it very difficult for ex-employees to write computer programs that perform functions similar to those performed by programs they have written for their previous employers. In this respect, copyright could now become so strong that it operates as a form of restraint of trade. It is also out of step with the law of breach of confidence which is relatively benign as regards mundane information and which generally will permit an employee to make use of what he remembers as long as he does not copy, provided the information concerned is not a trade secret.[104] Computer programs designed to perform mundane functions such as producing labels for pharmacists and handling stock control can hardly be classed as trade secrets.[105]

101 *Ladbroke (Football) Ltd* v *William Hill (Football) Ltd* [1964] 1 WLR 273.

102 In fairness to Ferris J, he did not profess to follow the *Computer Associates* test precisely.

103 However, some of the features in the claimant's program were described by Ferris J as idiosyncratic.

104 The position is best summarised by Neill LJ in *Faccenda Chicken Ltd* v *Fowler* [1986] 1 All ER 617.

105 The phrase 'trade secret' lacks precise definition but has been considered in *Lansing Linde Ltd* v *Kerr* [1991] 1 WLR 251. *See* also Coleman, A. (1992) *The Legal Protection of Trade Secrets*, Sweet & Maxwell, pp 4–28.

Abstraction in relation to conventional literary works may be a matter of considering the plot of a novel or play or the detailed and fleshed out ideas underlying the work. In some cases, it will be at that level that the author's skill and labour lies. In *Cantor Fitzgerald International v Tradition (UK) Ltd*,[106] it was said by Pumfrey J (at 134) that:

> [t]he closest analogy to a plot in a computer program lies perhaps in the algorithms or sequences of operations decided upon by the programmer to achieve his object. It seems to be generally accepted that the 'architecture' of a computer program is capable of protection if a substantial part of the programmer's skill, labour and judgment went into it. In this context, 'architecture' is a vague and ambiguous term. It may be used to refer to the overall structure of the system at a very high level of abstraction.

Although there had been no allegation of copying the architecture of the claimant's software, Pumfrey J considered this aspect of the parties' software[107] and he said (at 134):

> It is remarkable that such a similarity can be achieved with copying (so far as either party can detect) of no more than 3.3 per cent of the actual code.

A program's architecture may also be referred to as its structure.[108] Although *obiter*, what Pumfrey J had to say on the question of non-literal copying is an interesting aspect of the decision in *Cantor Fitzgerald*. He was prepared to accept that program structure can represent the programmer's skill and labour and that copying it can be an infringement of copyright. That itself is no longer controversial. However, he did not go on to explore other non-literal elements of the kind identified by Ferris J in *John Richardson Computer Ltd v Flanders*.[109] Reading between the lines, it would seem possible that Pumfrey J did not consider that anything other than structure could be protected on the basis of non-literal copying. He did not expressly say so but it is reasonable to imply, from the tenor of his judgment, that that was his view. Furthermore, he suggested that the work of individually compiling and linking modules to a small number of programs had to be seen in the context of the collection of modules as a whole. In that case, the choice of what each module contained was somewhat arbitrary and driven by considerations such as the division of labour amongst programmers and the convenience of debugging and maintenance. He thought that it would be unlikely that the skill and labour expended in making such choices would amount to a substantial part of the copyright subsisting in each module.[110]

As mentioned above, these aspects of the judgment were *obiter*. Pumfrey J found infringement of copyright by the defendant who had copied the claimant's entire software during development of its own system, in respect of two modules used for testing the defendant's software and by the defendant's copying of another module (the origin of which had been disguised) in order to save time. It is noteworthy that he did not once refer to the *John Richardson* case when considering non-literal copying. However, in *Cantor Fitzgerald*, both the claimant's and defendant's programs were written in the same programming language, BASIC, and there had been no allegation of non-literal copying. Nonetheless, the decision threw further doubt on the *John Richardson* case, especially given Jacob J's criticism of it in *IBCOS*.

Does emulating the functionality of a computer program infringe its copyright?

Mr Justice Pumfrey had the opportunity to revisit the issue of non-literal copying[111] in *Navitaire Inc v easyJet Airline Company*[112] where non-literal copying was among the allegations made by the claimant. Simply stated the facts of the case were that easyJet, the low-cost airline and the first defendant, acquired an airline booking system from Navitaire,

106 [2000] RPC 95.

107 Appendix E to the report of the case shows the overall structure of the software systems: [2000] RPC 95 at 162.

108 As per Jacob J in *IBCOS Computers Ltd v Barclays Mercantile Highland Finance Ltd* [1994] FSR 275.

109 [1993] FSR 497.

110 Compare with the finding of Jacob J in respect of copyright subsisting in a compilation of programs in *IBCOS Computers Ltd v Barclays Mercantile Highland Finance Ltd* [1994] FSR 275.

111 Described as 'non-textual' copying in the case.

112 [2006] RPC 3.

called OpenRes. EasyJet used this for some time but eventually commissioned the second defendant, Bulletproof Technologies Inc, to write a similar software system, which was called eRes. An important feature was that eRes should be virtually indistinguishable from the user's perspective (that is, that the user interfaces were to be the same) and the existing data in the databases built up using OpenRes could be migrated to eRes, that is, transferred from one to the other.

Apart from one item of software, called TakeFlight, neither defendant had access to the OpenRes source code and did not decompile or reverse engineer OpenRes to obtain the source code. In effect, what Bulletproof did was to emulate the operation and functionality of the OpenRes software by carefully studying it in use, for example, to see how it behaved, what functions and operations it could perform, how it manipulated, stored and retrieved information, etc. Navitaire sued for infringement of its copyright, *inter alia*, on the basis of non-textual copying by (i) using the look and feel of the OpenRes software, described as the business logic of OpenRes, (ii) detailed copying of the many commands entered by the user to achieve particular results and (iii) copying screen displays and reports displayed on the screen.

Pumfrey J said that if one studied software in operation so as to identify all possible responses to all possible sequences of inputs, it should be possible to create new software that would produce the same results for the same sequences of inputs. If this was done, Navitaire contended that this would infringe the copyright in the source code of the first. To the end user, the functions performed by both software systems were identical. The claimant's case was that by emulating the functions and operation of its software to produce new software that worked in the same way and produced the same outputs amounted to non-textual infringement, notwithstanding that the source code of the defendants' software must be different. The analogy of taking the plot of a literary work as a form of infringement was used by the claimant.[113] Pumfrey J described this, in effect, as a claim to copying without access to the thing copied, directly or indirectly. By emulating existing software, using it, observing what it does, how it handles inputs and what it outputs, the creator of the second software system saves himself the trouble of carrying out systems analysis and producing a functional specification. But this did not release the claimant from the need to show that the defendant had taken something not simply inherent in the nature of the business function. The claimant had to show that the defendant had taken something over and above that. A factor in this case was that the functions carried out by the software were common to flight booking systems.

Pumfrey J noted that two completely different computer programs could produce results identical at any level of abstraction. This is so even though the creator of the second program does not have access to the source code of the first. For this reason, the analogy with the plot of a literary work was not appropriate. A computer program does not really have a plot or any narrative flow. A computer program has a series of predetermined operations directed to a desired result in response to requests from the person using the program. Once the interfaces had been stripped away, all that was left was the business function performed by the software. The source code of the claimant's software was neither read nor copied by the defendants. Consequently, Pumfrey J held that there was no infringement by non-textual copying.

As to the commands, examples being the simple command 'NP' which gave access to a notepad built into the software and the complex command A13JUNLTNAMS which asked for the availability of flights from Luton to Amsterdam on 13 June, Pumfrey J held that these were not protected in their own right. The simple commands were not protected, being single words, on the basis of *Exxon Corporation* v *Exxon Insurance Consultants International Ltd*.[114] Of the complex commands, he doubted whether these could be works of copyright as they were not recorded in the program code but simply recognised by it. However, he went on to say that they were excluded as being a computer programming

113 Citing *Harman Pictures NV* v *Osborne* [1967] 1 WLR 723 and *Designers Guild Ltd* v *Russell Williams (Textiles) Ltd* [2001] FSR 11, although the latter was a case on artistic copyright.

114 [1981] 3 All ER 241.

language or user interface as the Directive on the legal protection of computer programs expressly excludes from copyright protection both computer programming languages and interfaces including user interfaces.[115] Recital 11 to the Directive on the legal protection of computer programs (codified version) states:

115 The same could be said for the set of commands as a whole.

> 11 For the avoidance of doubt, it has to be made clear that only the expression of a computer program is protected and that ideas and principles which underlie any element of a program, including those which underlie its interfaces, are not protected by copyright under this Directive. In accordance with this principle of copyright, to the extent that logic, algorithms and programming languages comprise ideas and principles, those ideas and principles are not protected under this Directive. In accordance with the legislation and case-law of the Member States and the international copyright conventions, the expression of those ideas and principles is to be protected by copyright.

Until Pumfrey J's judgment in *Navitaire*, the Directive seemed to have almost gone unnoticed by judges in software copyright cases even though it provides a clear statement of what is excluded from protection, although it excludes from protection logic, algorithms and programming languages only in as much as they comprise ideas and principles. The impact of the Directive in terms of non-literal copying means that computer programs must be treated differently to the 'plot' cases and Pumfrey J was right to reject that analogy when *Navitaire* submitted that the set of commands was akin to the plot of a novel and protected in that way. He said (at para 94):

> There is a respectable case for saying that copyright is not, in general, concerned with functional effects, and there is some advantage in a bright line rule protecting only the claimant's embodiment of the function in software and not some superset of that software. The case is not truly analogous with the plot of a novel, because the plot is part of the work itself. The user interface is not part of the work itself. One could permute all the letters and other codes in the command names, and it would still work in the same way, and all that would be lost is a modest mnemonic advantage. To approach the problem in this way may at least be consistent with the distinction between idea and expression that finds its way into the Software Directive, but, of course, it draws the line between idea and expression in a particular place which some would say lies too far on the side of expression. I think, however, that such is the independence of the particular form of the actual codes used from the overall functioning of the software that it is legitimate to separate them in this way, and not to afford them separate protection when the underlying software is not even arguably copied.

The only comfort to Navitaire in the case was that Pumfrey J found limited infringement in relation to the TakeFlight software, the databases and some of the screen displays containing graphic symbols considered to be artistic works. The symbols included icons which were accepted by Pumfrey J to be the result of sufficient skill and judgment for copyright to subsist in them.[116] Some important questions resulting from the judgment of Pumfrey J were as follows.

116 It could have been argued that designs for screen displays and reports fell within the meaning of preparatory design materials and literary works in their own right.

117 It seems reasonable to assume that the structure of a program (or its 'architecture') can be protected, especially when the Directive on the legal protection of databases expressly contemplates copyright protection covering also the structure of the database; *see* the section on databases, below.

● Is only the actual text of a computer program protected by copyright? In other words, is it no longer possible to infringe the copyright in a computer program by taking non-literal or non-textual elements? Are there any non-literal elements otherwise capable of protection that are not excluded as being ideas and principles? It is submitted that what the Directive on the legal protection of computer programs seeks to achieve is to prevent copyright protecting logic, algorithms and programming languages only to the extent that they comprise ideas and principles. To take an example, the structure of a computer program, as may be represented in a flowchart, is a form of expression.[117] What is intended is that the ideas and principles underlying it are not protected but this does not mean to say that the actual algorithm as so expressed is not protected. Say that there is a mathematical rule that is used to calculate square roots of numbers. That is an idea or principle. It may be implemented in one of a number of ways. The way chosen is potentially protectable even though not explicit in the program code and even though it may be put into effect by program codes that may be different.

- If a user interface is not protected on the basis of it being an idea, does this allow the deliberate copying of user interfaces and, if so, how does one decide what the boundaries of the interface are? Does this mean also that deliberately copying can never infringe the copyright in the computer program? Screen displays for the input of data or to display the results of processing data can properly be described as user interfaces. So too might be command sets. Why is a command set not protected but a user interface containing graphic symbols can be?

- Is a command set used to enter queries, instructions or responses a programming language? Surely a programming language is a language used to write a computer program rather than being the syntax by which the user interacts with the program? It is submitted that a command set is better classified as a user interface rather than a programming language.

Another case involving non-literal copying of computer programs in the Court of Appeal was *Nova Productions Ltd* v *Mazooma Games Ltd*.[118] This involved, *inter alia*, allegations of non-literal copying of a video game based on the game of pool. Agreeing with the judge at fist instance, Jacob LJ said that the claim could only be regarded as an allegation of copying the very general ideas such as the idea of using a 'power cue' having a pulsating power meter. There was no allegation of copying the source code of the computer programs and the claim was not sufficiently refined to cover the architecture of the programs. Jacob LJ said (at para 55):

> If protection for such general ideas as are relied on here were conferred by the law, copyright would become an instrument of oppression rather than the incentive for creation which it is intended to be. Protection would have moved to cover works merely inspired by others, to ideas themselves.

Jacob LJ, following Pumfrey J in *Navitaire*, also accepted that merely emulating another program without taking any of the source code and graphics was a legitimate exercise. This probably goes too far if it is accepted that the architecture of a computer program may be protected to the extent that it does not comprise ideas and principles. However, to date, no convincing claim of copying a program's architecture has been made in a computer program case.[119]

As the Directive on the legal protection of computer programs makes clear, ideas and principles are not protected. So, for example, if the author of the computer game had written a detailed description of the 'power cue', providing it was more than trivial, that would be protected as part of the preparatory design material (which is part of the computer program itself). But that protection would only prevent someone copying that description and would not extend to the protection of the idea of using a power cue in the game. In *Nova* v *Mazooma*, a claim that artistic copyright in the graphic images displayed to the player of the game was also rejected. Each image was undoubtedly a graphic work but the defendant's images were very different apart from sharing in common representations of a pool table with pockets, balls and a cue. Jacob LJ also rejected the idea that there was a separate artistic copyright in the series of images produced when playing the game. He said that a graphic work was a static work and there was no separate copyright in a series of still images. Support for this conclusion was the fact that there was a separate copyright in moving images as a film.[120]

The latest of the emulation cases was *SAS Institute* v *World Programming Ltd*.[121] The defendant created computer software designed to emulate the functionality of the claimant's software, comprising a suite of programs used for data processing and analysis, in particular, statistical analysis. The claimant's software had been developed over 35 years and produced a total revenue of $2.3 billion in 2009.

118 [2007] RPC 25.

119 Nor has there been a convincing case recently of copying the architecture of a conventional literary work: *see Baigent* v *The Random House Group Ltd* [2007] FSR 24, discussed in Chapter 6.

120 The claimant reserved its argument that the game had protection as a film for a possible appeal.

121 [2011] RPC 1.

Arnold J considered that a number of provisions of the Directive on the legal protection of computer programs were not clear and needed clarification by the Court of Justice of the EU. Notwithstanding this, he went on to apply case law, including *Navitaire* and *Nova* to the facts of the case. He considered that the defendant had not infringed the copyright in the SAS software except in some minor respects. In particular, he considered that the interfaces, functionality and programming language used in the SAS software were not protected by copyright. The defendant had used a 'learning edition' of the SAS software under a licence agreement which stated that it could not be used for production purposes but such restrictive terms in the agreement were null and void by reason of the observing, studying and testing permitted act under s 296A, implementing Article 5(3) of the Directive on the legal protection of computer programs.[122] However, Arnold J thought that the copyright in the SAS manuals had been infringed by the defendant in creating its own manual. There was also one minor issue in respect of the learning edition as to which Arnold J thought that the defendant may have infringed copyright (use of the learning edition to generate zip code incorporated in the defendant's software).

Arnold J decided to refer a number of questions to the Court of Justice for a preliminary ruling under Article 267 of the Treaty on the Functioning of the EU as to the scope of the following provisions of the Directive on the legal protection of computer programs. These questions included the following (in broad terms):

- whether and to what extent computer programming languages are not protected by the Directive;
- the extent to which interfaces are denied protection;
- whether the functionality of a computer program is protected under the Directive;
- the scope of the observing, studying and testing exception to the restricted acts.

At the time of writing the ruling of the Court of Justice is still awaited.[123] It will be the first significant ruling on the Directive on the legal protection of computer programs and will have very important implications for the software industry. The author's own view is that the provisional findings of Arnold J will be vindicated by the Court of Justice.

The idea/expression merger doctrine

The idea/expression merger doctrine takes on a different significance in the context of UK copyright law. In a case of suspected non-literal copying, the person who wrote the alleged copy is simply likely to deny that he copied, and both the look and feel test and the merger doctrine become important in an evidential sense. The question that falls to be resolved is whether the defendant copied a substantial part of the original computer program. If the look and feel of the two programs are similar, the fact that there are several different ways in which the program could have been written is persuasive evidence that there has been copying; while the fact that because the function dictates the program code or structure there is only one way the program could have been written, significantly weakens the claim that there has been, in fact, copying. Of course, other factors may be relevant, such as whether the defendant had access to the claimant's program. Nevertheless, as current UK copyright law declares without *caveat* that copyright subsists in original computer programs and the fact that one of the acts restricted by the copyright is copying a substantial part of a program, even copying a program or significant part of a program which is dictated by function will infringe copyright. On the other hand, two independently created programs may be similar because function dictates the program (or simply because of coincidence) and there will be no infringement of copyright. In *Total Information Processing Systems Ltd* v *Daman Ltd*[124] it was accepted that where there is only one way of expressing an idea, the idea and expression merged and were not the subject of copyright.[125] But this is to confuse the question of subsistence with evidence of

122 Any term seeking to prevent or restrict this permitted act being void in line with Article 8(2) of the Directive on the legal protection of computer programs.

123 The Opinion of an Advocate General is still awaited. It is unlikely that the Court of Justice ruling will be made until well into 2012.

124 [1992] FSR 171.

125 Disapproved by Jacob J in *IBCOS Computers Ltd* v *Barclays Mercantile Highland Finance Ltd* [1994] FSR 275.

copying. In *Kenrick* v *Lawrence*[126] it was said that a duplicate copy of a simple drawing would infringe.

126 (1890) 25 QBD 99.

Limits of look and feel

Perhaps the original program is simply altered in an attempt to disguise its origins or to improve it. Nevertheless, the question of copying still arises, as opposed to adaptation which has a precise legal meaning in terms of computer programs. In many cases, the two programs will be similar enough to raise a presumption of copying, which can shift the burden of proof, as already discussed. But if the alterations are numerous, it may be more difficult to draw this conclusion. It is a relatively simple matter to change constituent parts of a program, for example the screen displays, the names given to variables used in the program and the line numbering. If this is done, a line for line similarity between the two programs will be obscured. If the changes are merely cosmetic, it will still be possible to use a test of objective similarity based on the structure of the programs: for example, whether the flow of the program and the relative positioning of its constituent parts are similar. But even here, a determined programmer can rearrange the parts of the program to defeat this test.

Even more difficult is the situation where the new program is written using a totally different programming technique, using software tools and languages that are fundamentally different from those used to create the original program. In particular, the use of 'fourth generation' languages is relevant to this discussion as they are dissimilar to the older, more traditional programming languages, such as BASIC and COBOL, in a way that goes beyond mere syntax. A program written in a traditional programming language is written sub-routine by sub-routine and line by line. A fourth generation language is effectively a tool which automates the process of developing a computer system to a great extent. It is like a shell into which the developer specifies attributes of the required system, such as the structure of database files and the operations to be carried out by the finished system. The file-handling and other operations are then performed by the fourth generation system itself.

In *Computer-Aided Systems (UK) Ltd* v *Bolwell*,[127] some of the claimant's ex-employees devised a computer program using a fourth generation language to carry out a similar function to the programs they had written in COBOL for the claimant. The *Whelan* case was cited as authority for the notion that the structure of a computer program was a form of literary expression protected by copyright. However, Hoffmann J did not believe that a seriously triable issue was raised on the questions of copying or the misuse of confidential information. The claimant had argued that the output formats and input layouts of the two computer programs would be very similar, especially as the defendants had designed the new system so that it was compatible with the claimant's system. The defendants had refused to allow the claimant to inspect their program, but it would be highly unlikely that there would be a sufficient similarity in the programs to infer that copying had taken place because of the conceptually different nature of the languages used. Even the structure of the programs would be different.[128] The only plausible similarity might have been in the structure of the databases used by the systems because of the efforts to achieve compatibility in this respect. However, Hoffmann J expressed the opinion that the claimant's application for inspection of the defendants' program was little more than a 'fishing expedition' and he refused the application. This decision seems eminently sensible in the context of restraint of trade; after all, computer programmers and analysts should be free to exercise their skill and knowledge for other employers subject to copyright and limited confidentiality issues.[129] Although the case did not involve a detailed consideration of the issue of non-literal copying, as far as it went, the decision appears to be in line with more recent developments, as seen in the *Navitaire* case, *supra*. Hoffmann J remarked that satisfying a request to write a new program which would provide much of the information provided by the old one was not copying.

127 (Unreported) 23 August 1989, ChD.

128 It is not really appropriate to talk of computer systems developed using fourth generation languages (4GLs) as computer programs. 4GLs are more akin to system development tools. The 4GL provides a set of all-purpose computer programs and the system designer develops a set of specifications concerning file structures, calculations and reports which the programs incorporate to produce the finished system.

129 For example, in the South African case of *Northern Office Micro Computers (Pty) Ltd* v *Rosenstein* [1982] FSR 124 where it was held, *inter alia*, that an ex-employee would not have to 'wipe the slate of his mind clean'. *See also Printers and Finishers Ltd* v *Holloway* [1965] RPC 239.

Making an adaptation

The second act restricted by copyright which is highly relevant to computer programs is that of making an adaptation. An adaptation of a computer program is defined by s 21(3)(ab) of the 1988 Act as an arrangement or altered version of the program or a translation of it. For computer programs, a translation includes (by s 21(4)):

> . . . a version of the program in which it is converted into or out of a computer language or code or into a different computer language or code [otherwise than incidentally in the course of running the program].[130]

130 The words in brackets were repealed by the Copyright (Computer Programs) Regulations 1992, SI 1992/3233.

To understand fully the legal issues concerning this definition, it is important that the basic meaning of some computer terms is understood, and the definitions given in the Glossary at the beginning of the book should be referred to again. The following definitions should also be noted. *Compiling* a computer program means converting a high-level language source code program into object code, being the machine code that can be directly understood by the computer. A permanent version of the program in object code is created which can then be operated without the source code version. This must be contrasted with *interpreting*, a process by which a high-level source code computer program is temporarily converted, line by line, into object code during the operation of the program. This is not as efficient as running a compiled version of the program. *Assembling* a computer program means converting a low-level assembly language program into object code. The process of *disassembly* produces assembly language from an object code version of a computer program. Disassembly unlocks the ideas and techniques contained in the object code version of the program.

What, then, in the context of making an adaptation, does this mean? Figure 8.2 shows the relevant acts that can be done in relation to a computer program. Suppose that a computer program has been written, either in a high-level programming language such as Visual Basic or in a low-level assembly language. The legal meaning of 'making an adaptation' would certainly seem to cover the act of compiling or assembling the computer

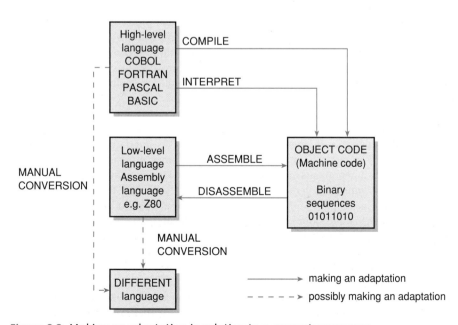

Figure 8.2 Making an adaptation in relation to a computer program

program. If the object code version of a program, produced by compiling or assembling a source code program, is later disassembled, to derive an assembly language version, that too falls within the meaning of making an adaptation.

Now that an adaptation includes an arrangement or altered version of a program, this should cover the situation where a program is manually rewritten in a different computer programming language. The meaning of 'translation' may also extend to a manual translation. There seems to be no reason why translating a computer program cannot be done manually by using a knowledge of grammatical rules and a dictionary of commands and functions. This is highly analogous to translating a work of literature from one natural language into another which is, of course, making an adaptation.

Writing a new computer program after extensively studying the operation of and output from an existing computer program in use is highly unlikely to fall within the scope of making an adaptation. This can hardly be described as 'converting' the first program. In any case, s 50BA states that it is not an infringement of copyright in a computer program for a lawful user of a copy of a computer program to observe, study or test the functioning of the program in order to determine the ideas and principles which underlie any element of the program if he does so while performing any of the acts of loading, displaying, running, transmitting or storing the program which he is entitled to do.[131]

Permitted acts in relation to computer programs

In terms of the permitted acts under copyright law, computer technology may be indirectly relevant in many cases. For example, as a computer program is a literary work, all the provisions affecting literary works apply to computer programs, unless the contrary is stated. For example, a teacher can write a listing of part of a computer program on a blackboard for the purposes of instruction. (Obtaining the listing in the first place might, however, infringe.) A design document includes data stored in a computer for the purposes of s 51 which effectively suppresses copyright in design documents where an article is made to a design.

Although the main purpose of the Directive on the legal protection of computer programs,[132] in pursuance of which the Copyright (Computer Programs) Regulations 1992[133] were passed, was the harmonisation of copyright protection for computer programs, the aspect that stimulated a most heated debate and controversy was the 'decompilation right'.[134] This is a permitted act under copyright which allows lawful users of computer programs to reverse engineer other computer programs for the purpose of achieving 'interoperability' with that or another program. In other words, it allows the act of converting a computer program (the target program) into a form easier to understand (expressed in a higher-level language) so that details of its interfaces can be discovered enabling the new program to be compatible with the target program or any other program. Prior to the amendments made by the Copyright (Computer Programs) Regulations 1992, the most important permitted act in terms of achieving the same result was undoubtedly fair dealing for the purposes of research or private study (s 29). It has been seen in Chapter 7 that the scope of this provision is difficult to predict, but it was possible that it would extend to the type of situation mentioned above. Indeed, this seems to be the case in the USA, where the equivalent act of fair use has been relied on successfully to allow reverse engineering of computer programs to discover details of interfaces.[135]

The Directive provided for other specific exceptions to copyright infringement. These have been included in the Copyright, Designs and Patents Act 1988 (amended by the 1992 Regulations) and came into force on 1 January 1993. They are all subject to conditions. Altogether, the special permitted acts for computer programs are:

131 Section 50BA was inserted by the Copyright and Related Rights Regulations 2003, SI 2003/2498, and replaced the previous imperfect statement of this permitted act in s 296A(1)(c), which has been amended accordingly.

132 Directive 2009/24/EC of the European Parliament and of the Council of 23 April 2009 on the legal protection of computer programs (codified Version), OJ L 111, 050.05.2009, p 16 (replacing the previous Directive).

133 SI 1992/3233.

134 Strictly speaking, this is not a right but an exception to infringement.

135 *Sega Enterprises Ltd* v *Accolade Inc* 977 F 2d 1510 (1992).

- decompilation of computer programs
- making back-up copies of computer programs
- making copies or adaptations of computer programs.

Sections 50A, 50B and 50C were inserted into the Copyright, Designs and Patents Act 1988 under the heading 'Computer programs: lawful users'. These exceptions to infringement apply only to acts done by lawful users of computer programs.

A further 'permitted act' was buried deep in the Act in s 296A(1)(c). This made void any term in an agreement under which a person has the use of a computer program which purports to prohibit or restrict the use of any device or means to observe, study or test the functioning of the program in order to understand the ideas and principles which underlie any element of the computer program. This was replaced by s 50BA which permits a lawful user of a copy of a computer program to observe, study or test the functioning of the program in order to determine the ideas and principles which underlie any element of the program if he does so while performing any of the acts of loading, displaying, running, transmitting or storing the program which he is entitled to do. Under s 296A, any term or condition in any agreement under which a person has use of a computer program which attempts to prohibit or restrict this, is void to that extent.

Lawful users

Although the Directive uses the terms 'licensed user', 'person having the right to use' and 'lawful acquirer', depending on the exception concerned, the Act as amended uses the term 'lawful user' for all three exceptions. Under s 50A(2), for the purposes of ss 50A, 50B, 50BA and 50C, a lawful user is:

> a person who has a right to use the program, whether under a licence to do any acts restricted by the copyright subsisting in the program or otherwise.

This will extend to licensees and, presumably, to persons acting for the licensee such as employees. Unless prohibited by the licence agreement, it should also apply to agents and independent consultants working for the licensee and to many other persons, such as students in respect of a site licence granted to an educational establishment or voluntary workers for a charity that has an institutional licence. Others, too, could fall within the definition of 'lawful user'. It may include a receiver of a company, an external auditor or anyone acting in pursuance of a legal requirement (for example, a police officer executing a search warrant or a solicitor executing a search order).

The addition of the words 'or otherwise' should cause the copyright owner to consider carefully how to exploit the program. For example, it could apply to a person who has obtained a copy of a program by rental or loan. A person who has been given a copy of a program for evaluation purposes should also fall within this category. Of course, if a copy has been made in accordance with the exceptions, at the end of the rental or loan period when the right to use the program ceases, subsequent use will infringe copyright. However, the retained copy will not be an infringing copy because s 27 was not amended to cover this possibility.[136] Selling that copy will not, therefore, be a secondary infringement of copyright.[137] This does not apply where the arrangement by which the person concerned obtained the copy falls within the meaning of s 56 (where a copy of a work in electronic form has been purchased) because any retained copies are treated as infringing copies.[138]

Decompilation of computer programs

The decompilation right[139] allows (subject to certain conditions) a lawful user of a copy of a computer program expressed in a low-level language:

136 The Copyright, Designs and Patents Act 1988 s 27(6) includes as infringing copies any copies made in pursuance of some of the permitted acts but that are subsequently dealt with. The omission of copies made in pursuance of ss 50A–50C is clearly an oversight.

137 The primary infringement of issuing to the public could apply in some cases: Copyright, Designs and Patents Act 1988 s 18.

138 It is not clear that this could apply in any case because 'purchase' is not the same as obtaining a copy under a licence. This provision may be more appropriate in terms of sound and video recordings.

139 So described in the Directive (Article 6) and in the marginal note to the Copyright, Designs and Patents Act 1988 s 50B, though it is an exception to infringement and not a right as such.

(a) to convert it into a version expressed in a higher-level language; or

(b) incidentally, in the course of so converting the program, to copy it.[140]

140 Copyright, Designs and Patents Act 1988 s 50B (inserted by the Copyright (Computer Programs) Regulations 1992 reg 8).

While it is up to the legislatures of individual Member States to choose their own form of wording to give effect to a Directive, the differences between the language of the modifications made by the Copyright (Computer Programs) Regulations 1992 and that of the Directive, which is expressed in terms of reproduction of the code and translation of its form, a much wider rubric, are unfortunate. The Directive does not use the terms 'low-level language' and 'high-level language', nor are they defined in the Act. Although someone wanting to gain access to information about the program's algorithm or its detailed workings would almost certainly want to convert from a low-level language version to a higher-level language version, the Directive is more generous, allowing translation, adaptation, arrangement or alteration. The 'decompilation right' as enacted does not expressly cover the conversion of a binary object code program into hexadecimal code, something which is commonly known as performing a 'hex dump', as there is no higher-level language involved at that stage. This would be within the exception as expressed in the Directive.[141]

141 However, this could fall within the normal fair dealing exception in the Copyright, Designs and Patents Act 1988 s 29. This is still available for acts not caught by the meaning of 'decompilation'.

The conditions that must apply for decompilation to be permitted by s 50B of the 1988 Act are stated in s 50B(2) and are that:

(a) it is necessary to decompile the program to obtain the information necessary to create an independent program which can be operated with the program decompiled or with another program ('the permitted objective'); and

(b) the information so obtained is not used for any purpose other than the permitted objective.

The purpose of decompilation is to obtain, typically, interface details. For example, Ace Software may wish to develop a new word-processing program. Ace will need to know details of various computer operating systems (these systems are a collection of computer programs) so that it can work in the computer's operating environment. Ace must determine how the operating system uses the computer's memory so that its new program can run properly. Also, to stand any chance of being successful, the new program must be compatible with existing programs. Ace's new program must be able to accept (import) word-processed files produced using other word-processing programs (and export them in the appropriate format); it would be even better if Ace's new program could accept files from other types of program such as a spreadsheet program or a graphics program. Hence the need for this interface information. Not only does the exception allow decompilation for the purpose of creating a new compatible program (for example, a new word-processing program that is compatible with an existing spreadsheet program), it also allows, in principle, the creation of new competing programs (for example, a new word-processing program that can import and export files from and to an existing word-processing program). Figure 8.3 shows the concept of interoperability.

The decompilation permitted act, in essence, gives a 'right' to information concerning interfaces so that interoperability can be achieved. It does not give a right to take the interface itself. For example, if an interface is expressed in a number of lines of computer code, that code, provided that it meets the requirements for copyright protection (and that it represents a substantial part of the program or is itself deemed to be a computer program), may not be copied because of this permitted act. Thus, taking a copy of a compression table, used to compress data so as to occupy less storage space, for the purposes of file compatibility was deemed to infringe in *Powerflex v Data Access Corp.*[142] This is confirmed by s 50B(3)(d) which states that the permitted act does not apply, *inter alia*, where the information is used to do any act restricted by copyright. Once the information is acquired by the process of decompilation, any interface code written must be done so

142 [1997] FCA 490, Federal Court of Australia, discussed in FitzSimons, J. '*Powerflex v Data Access Corporation* (Reverse Engineers Beware!)' [1998] 14 CLSR 45.

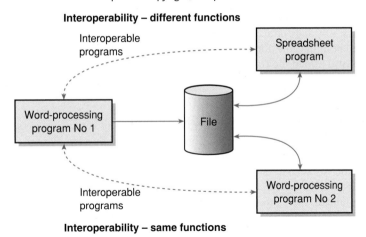

Interoperability – different functions

Figure 8.3 Interoperability of computer programs

as not to infringe copyright. This may be difficult in the extreme when the interface detail is in the form of a protocol and no design freedom is permissible.[143] It may be that in such circumstances the courts may be prepared to excuse infringement on policy grounds, otherwise the decompilation permitted act would be defeated. However, it is far from certain that the courts would so decide, given their reluctance to override a statutory provision.

The conditions cannot be met if the lawful user has readily available to him the information necessary to achieve the permitted objective, or if he does not confine the act of decompiling to that objective, if he supplies the information to any person to whom it is not necessary to supply it in order to achieve that objective, or if he uses the information to create a program which is substantially similar in its expression to the decompiled program, or to do any act restricted by copyright.[144] Most of these conditions are reasonable, and indeed the last two are probably redundant in most cases. However, it is what constitutes having the information readily available that could be difficult. Of course, the first step that a person who requires interface details of another's program should take is to ask for those details. Sometimes, the information may be freely given. In other cases, it may even be published in documentation accompanying a licensed copy of the program.

Importantly, the 'decompilation right' cannot be prohibited or restricted by any term or condition in an agreement.[145] Any term in a licence agreement purporting to do this is void, unless the agreement was entered into before 1 January 1993.[146] A considerable number of standard form software licences were amended as a result of this.

Apart from the decompilation exception, fair dealing for the purposes of research or private study still exists in relation to computer programs.[147] Therefore, it may be permissible for a person to print out and study a program in use for the purposes of understanding its operation and the techniques represented within it for non-commercial research and private study. However, the prospective author of an academic journal article cannot disassemble the computer program in order to include an extract of the program expressed in a higher-level language. That does not fall within the permitted objective of decompilation and is outside the residual fair dealing exception.

One final point about the decompilation permitted act is that, under Article 6(3) of the Directive on the legal protection of computer programs, it must not be interpreted in a way as to allow its application to be used in a manner which unreasonably prejudices the legitimate interests of the owner of the copyright subsisting in the computer program or conflicts with a normal exploitation of the computer program.[148] Although not expressly implemented by the Copyright (Computer Programs) Regulations 1992, a judge

144 Copyright, Designs and
Patents Act 1988 s 50B(3).

145 Copyright, Designs and
Patents Act 1988 s 296A (1)(b).

146 Copyright (Computer
Programs) Regulations 1992 reg
12(2).

147 Copyright, Designs and
Patents Act 1988 s 29(1) and (4).

148 This test comes from the
Berne Convention for the
Protection of Literary and Artistic
Works 1886, Article 9(2).

would have to take this into account in determining whether an act fell within what was allowed by s 50B. It is difficult to predict practical examples where this constraint on s 50B would be applicable but it would be relevant where the exercise of the 'right' under s 50B seriously harmed the commercial viability of the target program.

Back-up copies of computer programs

Section 50A of the 1988 Act permits the making of back-up copies if necessary for the purposes of the lawful use of a copy of a computer program by a lawful user. As with the decompilation right, this right cannot be taken away by any term or condition in an agreement and any such term, in so far as it purports to prohibit or restrict the exercise of this right, is void[149] provided the agreement was made on or after 1 January 1993. Prior to this amendment, there was no equivalent statutory provision, although the courts may have been prepared to imply an appropriate term into a software licence where the making of a back-up copy was necessary to the use of the program in question.[150] Of course, many software companies make express provision allowing the user to make one or more back-up copies. It is common for the installation instructions to ask the licensed user to make a copy of the program first and use this as the working copy, placing the original disks in a safe place in case the working disks become damaged or corrupted.[151]

Is each lawful user within an organisation that has a site licence or a multiple-user licence entitled under s 50A to make a back-up copy? In such a situation, it is difficult to predict just how many back-up copies would be deemed to be 'necessary'. If the program is available on a network of computers, presumably the effect of s 50A is to allow the making of one back-up copy only, to be held by the network manager. Of course, the licence agreement may make specific provision for the making of a greater number of back-up copies.

Observing, studying and testing

Computer programs are unlike other works of copyright. Ideas and principles underlying computer programs are, in most cases, not transparent. They are not readily available to a person using the program. In the case of a literary or dramatic work or an artistic work such as a painting, for example, the underlying ideas and principles are available to a person reading, watching or studying work. The plot, idea, concept or message that the author of the work intended to develop or convey is apparent, albeit in some circumstances with difficulty, for example, in the case of abstract art.

As copyright does not protect ideas (notwithstanding the difficulties associated with determining the scope of such a sweeping aphorism), it is important that they are also made available to persons who have lawful access to computer programs. Otherwise, the monopoly granted by copyright could be perceived as being too strong. In the normal run of things, ideas and principles underlying computer programs can only be gleaned by performing an act restricted by the copyright, unlike the case with traditional works of copyright. The plot underlying a play or story can be determined simply by reading it. If the copyright owner were to be allowed to use his exclusive rights to prevent access to underlying ideas and principles, this would hinder fair competition and make it considerably more difficult for a competitor to create a new computer program to perform the same function, bearing in mind that the function itself, in most cases, will not have its own protection unless it is confidential.

Directive 2009/24/EC of the European Parliament and of the Council of 23 April 2009 on the legal protection of computer programs (codified version),[152] excluded from copyright protection ideas and principles which underlie any element of a computer program, including those underlying its interfaces.[153] This was first implemented in the UK by the

149 Copyright, Designs and Patents Act 1988 s 296A(1)(a)..

150 However, s 56 recognises the possibility that back-up copies may have been made. It makes copies of works purchased in electronic form that are not transferred along with the original, in the case of it being transferred to a third party, infringing copies. However, whether it is right to speak in terms of the purchase of a computer program is uncertain.

151 It is common for the person acquiring the software to be instructed simply to copy from the supplied media to the computer's hard disk.

152 OJ L 111, 050.05.2009, p16, replacing Council Directive 91/250/EEC of 14 May 1992 on the legal protection of computer programs, OJ L 122, 17.05.1991, p 42.

153 Article 1(2).

154 SI 1992/3233.

Copyright (Computer Programs) Regulations 1992,[154] which inserted s 296A into the Copyright, Designs and Patents Act 1988. Sub-section (1)(c) made void any term in an agreement under which a person has the use of a computer program which purported to prohibit or restrict the use of any device or means to observe, study or test the functioning of the program in order to understand the ideas and principles which underlie any element of the program. This did not follow the wording of the Directive sufficiently closely and changes were made to comply more accurately by the Copyright and Related Rights Regulations 2003 which inserted s 50BA into the Act. This provides that it is not an infringement of copyright for a lawful user of a copy of a computer program to observe, study or test the functioning of the program in order to determine the ideas and principles which underlie any element of the program if he does so while performing any of the acts of loading, displaying, running, transmitting or storing the program which he is entitled to do. Section 296A still makes void any term or condition in an agreement under which a person has the use of a computer program which purports to prevent or restrict the permitted act under s 50BA.

Some examples of acts that can be performed by a lawful user of a computer program under s 50BA are where:

155 Although it is not clear whether a protocol is an idea or principle or form of expression.

- a licensee of a computer program attaches an oscilloscope or other signal detecting device to his computer to monitor the output of the computer when running to a peripheral device in order to determine the protocol used by the program to send data to the device;[155]
- a licensee of a computer program (the target program) uses another program to record the sequence of operations in the target program, for example, to determine the algorithm used in a sub-routine of the program used to sort data into alphabetic or numeric order;
- a licensee of a computer program submits a batch of carefully prepared test data to the program to determine the logic of a calculation routine.

Current examples of where the s 50BA might be particularly valuable is where a computer program is based on a new algorithm designed to evaluate bids on the futures market or to control an industrial process more efficiently than was previously possible or in relation to the first computer program to have an effective method of triangulation built into it to deal with currency conversions in respect of the euro. The permitted act could be used to try to determine the algorithms.

The denial of protection to ideas and principles is more important than the other permitted acts for computer programs in that its effect is to liberate those ideas and principles and make them, potentially, available to all. Certainly, the permitted act is very wide in scope and could be relied upon by persons writing new computer programs designed to emulate existing programs providing that such persons are lawful users. In jurisdictions outside the European Union, similar exceptions apply in respect of copyright protection of computer programs. In some cases the exceptions are wider: for example, in the US, section 102(b) of the US Copyright Act 1980 states that copyright protection does not extend to any idea, procedure, process, system, method of operation, concept, principle, or discovery, regardless of the form in which it is described, explained, illustrated, or embodied in such work. In Japan, Article 10(3) of the Japanese Copyright Act states that protection does not extend to any programming language, rule or algorithm.

156 A case number has been assigned but, of course, there is no date as yet.

157 [2011] RPC 1.

The scope of this permitted act and the extent to which it might be excluded, if at all, in particular circumstances is subject to a reference to the Court of Justice in Case C-406/10 *SAS Institute Inc* v *World Programming Ltd*.[156] The reference was submitted, on this and other issues relating to computer programs, by Arnold J in *SAS Institute Inc* v *World Programming Ltd*.[157] At the time of writing there has been no Advocate General's Opinion, let alone the Court of Justice ruling.

Copying and adapting

A licence in respect of a computer program will normally state the acts that may be done by the licensee in relation to the program. If it is silent about some particular act which is within the spirit of the agreement, then the courts will imply the appropriate terms permitting that act. Section 50C, in effect, puts this on a statutory footing by allowing a lawful user of a copy of a computer program to copy it or adapt it[158] if that is necessary for his lawful use.[159] Copying or adapting for the purpose of error correction may fall within this exception to infringement and is given as a particular example in s 50C(2).

It is common for agreements regulating the lawful use of computer programs to contain a term prohibiting modification by the client, and such terms are not controlled by the Act as amended unlike the case with the other two exceptions. However, terms seeking to prevent modification by or on behalf of the licensee might be controlled in other ways. The Court of Appeal, in *Saphena Computing* v *Allied Collection Agencies*,[160] had an opportunity to consider the position at common law with respect to modification and error correction of licensed computer programs. In that case, the licensee had been given a copy of the source code by the licensor and there was, consequentially, an implied undertaking that the licensee could use it for error correction. While the licensor was still testing and modifying the software, the agreement was determined, and it was held that the licensee could continue to use the source code for the purpose of error correction but could not use it for other modifications and improvements to the program. It was said, *obiter*, that there was not an implied duty on a licensor to supply the source code if the agreement provided only for the supply of the object code.

If the supplier is no longer able or willing to provide error correction, the principle of non-derogation from grant may be applicable, with the result that the client can maintain the program himself or approach third parties with a view to their maintaining it. Even if the supplier is prepared to maintain the program and correct errors (for example, by including an obligation to maintain the program in the licence agreement, or by offering a collateral maintenance contract), the licensee may be able to approach others for this service as the non-derogation principle could still apply. For example, in *British Leyland Motor Corp Ltd* v *Armstrong Patents Co Ltd*,[161] the House of Lords applied the principle to prevent restriction on a free market in spare parts, and extended their refusal to enforce copyright to the manufacturers of spare parts and not just to the purchaser. Their Lordships spoke in terms of articles which, by their nature, would require the fitting of replacement parts during their normal lifespan. This principle is most apposite in terms of computer programs. Virtually all computer programs contain errors, a number of which might not be discovered for some considerable time, and the lawful user of the program will require work to be done to it in order to correct those errors. The owner of the copyright subsisting in the program should not be able to use his right to prevent the lawful user asking other persons to repair the program otherwise the copyright owner could charge exorbitant prices for this work and the lawful user would have little option but to pay.[162] However, the Judicial Committee of the Privy Council has shown its reluctance to extend the *British Leyland* principle further in *Canon Kabushiki Kaisha* v *Green Cartridge Company (Hong Kong) Ltd*.[163]

Computer programming languages

Considerable research effort, investment and skill go into the development of computer languages and instruction sets. Yet, as it could be argued that these are ideas, there is some doubt about their protection by copyright. However, in the USA, an argument that a

158 'Adaptation' in relation to computer programs, by new s 21(3)(ab), means an arrangement or altered version or translation of it. 'Translation' is further defined by s 21(4) in terms of conversion into or out of a computer language or code.

159 This can be seen as a non-derogation from grant provision.

160 [1995] FSR 616.

161 [1986] 2 WLR 400.

162 In *Digital Equipment Corp* v *LCE Computer Maintenance Ltd* (unreported) 22 May 1992, it was accepted that there was an arguable case that the non-derogation from grant principle applied to maintenance of computer programs. EU and UK competition law may also be relevant to this question.

163 [1997] FSR 817.

microcode embedded in a microprocessor representing the computer's instruction set was a defining element of the computer, and therefore an idea, failed to find sympathy (*NEC Corp* v *Intel Corp*).[164] In the UK, the question of copyright protection for an instruction set was considered in *Microsense Systems Ltd* v *Control Systems Technology Ltd*.[165] The claimant made traffic control systems and a controller for pelican crossings, these being programmed using a set of *mnemonics* (a set of three-letter symbols, for example SUN for Sunday, MON for Monday),[166] and these were also used to monitor the controllers. The defendant made similar controllers and used a total of 49 of the claimant's mnemonics, arguing that there was no copyright in them because, once the functions had been decided, there was no room for skill and labour in devising the mnemonics. Aldous J thought that there was an arguable case that the list of mnemonics was protected by copyright because of the work in devising the functions and operations of the controller in the first place. He refused an injunction but ordered the defendant to pay a 2 per cent royalty into a joint bank account, this being a case where damages would be an adequate remedy for the claimant should it be determined at full trial that copyright subsisted in the list of mnemonics and that the defendant had infringed that copyright. The defendant had argued that it was important, in terms of safety, that there was some degree of standardisation in instruction sets for traffic controllers. This is an attractive argument, but is the public interest best served by denying a modest royalty to the person who devises a new and original work?

The Directive on the legal protection of computer programs recognises that programming languages (and logic and algorithms), at least to the extent that they comprise ideas and principles, are not to be protected by copyright.[167] This seems to extend also to command sets[168] and it would appear that, following the Directive, *Microsense* no longer represents the true position if the set of instructions used there could be described as a programming language. Whether it could be argued that the instruction set was a user interface rather than a programming language is debatable. After all, the instruction set was the means by which the operator programmed the desired operation of the traffic controller.

Given that programming languages are not protected by copyright, one might wonder wherein lies the incentive to create a new language. The answer lies in the fact that, usually, the program, once written, can be run in a computer only if it is converted into object code, whether temporarily, using an interpreter, or permanently, using a compiler program. The licensing of these interpreter and compiler programs, together with appropriate documentation describing the syntax, semantics and use of the language, is the method by which financial reward is usually sought. These interpreter and compiler programs are, of course, protected by copyright in their own right. The fact that the denial of protection for programming languages applies only to the extent that they comprise ideas and principles does not prevent the protection of these other materials and programs.

In *SAS Institute Inc* v *World Programming Ltd*,[169] Arnold J referred a number of questions to the Court of Justice for a preliminary ruling under Article 267 of the Treaty on the Functioning of the EU. One question sought guidance on the practical scope of the denial of protection to computer programming languages. The ruling is still awaited at the time of writing.

Databases[170]

A computer database is a collection of data stored in or on computer media usually in the form of a computer file or files. The variety and scope of databases is enormous. For example, a computer database can contain information which relates to and represents things such as:

164 10 USPQ 2d (1989).

165 (Unreported) 17 June 1991.

166 Not all the mnemonics were obvious. For example, LIT was used to determine the aspect status of the controller. The instruction set was designed so that the engineer could communicate with, monitor or modify the controller or the way it operated.

167 Recital 11 to the Directive.

168 Following Pumfrey J in *Navitaire Inc* v *easyJet Airline Company* [2006] RPC 3.

169 [2011] RPC 1.

170 For a good discussion of the problems of database protection *see* Lea, G. 'Database Law – Solutions beyond Copyright' [1993] 9 CLSR 127.

- lists of clients and their addresses
- schedules of parts or articles and their rates or prices
- lists of bibliographical references
- engineering or architectural drawings
- works of art, photographs and other images
- music and sounds
- the texts of documents
- mixed text and graphics
- films and film extracts
- computer programs or routines
- a combination of two or more of the above.

Databases are accessed, manipulated, modified, displayed and printed using computer programs and usually have associated indexes, dictionaries, format and layout files. Anything can be stored on computer media as long as it can be reduced to a digital form, and almost anything can be. In the case of text, this is done by using codes to symbolise the letters of the alphabet, for example using ASCII codes.[171] Types of storage media include magnetic disks and tape, compact discs and silicon 'chips'. In earlier times, punched card and paper tape were commonly used. There is nothing particularly unusual about computer databases compared with collections of information that are written down, typed or printed on paper or index cards. The major difference is that, in the case of a computer database, the information is not stored in its original form, but is translated into a digital representation for the purposes of storage, whereas, in the case of traditional paper files, the information is stored in its original form.[172] A rapidly growing number of computer databases are available online, that is, they are stored on a central computer and are accessible remotely. Computer programs accessing a computer database convert the digital representation to a form from which it can be displayed or printed in readable form.

Whether a computer database generated by computer can be a copyright work is not beyond doubt. In principle, there should be no problem as the Copyright, Designs and Patents Act 1988 s 9(3) contains the rule for determining the identity of the author for copyright purposes of a computer-generated literary, dramatic, musical or artistic work. A database is a form of literary work and, to complete the syllogism, it should be possible to have a computer-generated database in which copyright subsists. Until 1 January 1998, this probably would not have been an issue. However, changes made to the copyright provisions in the Act by the Copyright and Rights in Databases Regulations 1997,[173] suggest that it may no longer be possible to have a copyright database which has been computer-generated.

The test for subsistence of copyright, we have seen, has in the past been quite generous, requiring that the work originated from the author and is the result of a minimum of skill, effort or judgment. This test continues to apply to the original works of copyright, but with the exception of databases which, under s 3A(2), are original for copyright purposes if, and only if, by reason of the selection or arrangement of the contents of the database, the database constitutes the *author's own intellectual creation*. This phrase, 'author's own intellectual creation', is new to copyright in the UK and derives from the Directive on the legal protection of databases.[174] When one looks at the definition of computer-generated work in s 178, being a work generated in circumstances such that there is no human author, this strongly suggests that there can be no such thing as a computer-generated database which is, without more, protected by copyright as a database.[175] It could only be a copyright work if the skill and judgment of the computer programmer was taken into account, a form of indirect authorship. But if this is so, then the work cannot be computer-generated, adding fuel to the argument that there can be no such thing as a computer-generated work.[176] A further argument for computer-generated databases not being works of copyright is the introduction of the *sui generis* database right, discussed later.

171 ASCII stands for the American Standard Code for Information Interchange. In some cases, a form of encryption is used.

172 As an example of a digital representation of a letter, the letter 'E' is ASCII code 69 which would be represented as '01000101' using binary notation.

173 SI 1997/3032.

174 Directive 96/9/EC of the European Parliament and of the Council of 11 March 1996 on the legal protection of databases, OJ L 77, 27.03.1996, p 20. This phrase was also used in relation to computer programs in the Directive on the legal protection of computer programs, but was not included in the implementing regulations, the Copyright (Computer Programs) Regulations 1992, SI 1992/3233. *See* also the German Copyright Act s 2(2) which requires a work to be a personal intellectual creation.

175 Of course, the contents of the database may be protected by copyright, independently.

176 Computer-generated works are discussed in more detail later in this chapter.

Where a database is created by direct human skill or judgment, it may be a work of copyright even if the constituent parts are commonplace or in the public domain. Decisions as to what to include, what to exclude, what sort of information to collect and how that information will be structured and arranged may require an act of intellectual creation. In this respect, earlier judicial statements that compilations can be original even though their constituent parts are not original, such as in *Macmillan & Co Ltd v K & J Cooper*,[177] remain good law.

In general terms, it can be said that many databases are protected by copyright as literary works. A database containing, for example, selected substantial extracts from works of literature will have protection in a number of ways. Assuming it has not expired and all the other requirements are present, each extract will have its own copyright. The database as a whole will have its copyright provided it is the author's own intellectual creation. Furthermore, if the making of the database required a substantial investment, it will also be protected by the new database right, discussed later.

Before 1 January 1998, databases would fall to be protected as compilations but now, as a result of the changes made to the Act, databases are expressly excluded from compilations and are treated separately. Before looking at the changes made by the Copyright and Rights in Databases Regulations 1997, it will be helpful to look at developments in the USA in comparison to the position in the UK prior to 1 January 1998. It is highly likely that developments in the USA influenced the mechanism of protection for databases set out in the EU Directive.

Developments in the US and the UK approach before 1 January 1998

The subsistence of copyright in a database *qua* database could be questionable where its creation has not required the expenditure of skill or judgment. Some databases are the result of effort alone; once the nature of their contents has been determined, there is no room for skill or judgment in the selection of material to be entered into the database. Hence there can be no copyright in the compilation, and *GA Cramp & Sons Ltd v Frank Smythson Ltd*[178] is good authority for this proposition. An example is where a company decides to make a simple database of the names and addresses of all its clients. The 'sweat of the brow' doctrine, affording copyright protection to works which are the result of labour only, was rejected in the US Supreme Court in *Feist Publications Inc v Rural Telephone Service Co Inc*,[179] in which it was held that the 'white pages' section in a typical telephone directory was not protected by copyright because of a lack of creativity, not owing its origin to an act of authorship. The court did, however, recognise that a compilation of facts could be the subject of copyright because the author has to choose which facts to include and in what order to place them. Similarly, the 'yellow pages' section of a telephone directory could be protected because of the presence of original material.[180] In *CCC Information Services Inc v Maclean Hunter Market Reports Inc*[181] the court, in determining whether a compilation of second-hand car values was protected by copyright, considered that *Feist* did not raise a high barrier against copyright subsistence but merely required that there was some originality, although only those 'original' elements would be protected.

There were two major differences between the US and prior UK copyright law in that the UK was probably more generous in terms of originality, and the courts here would be more reluctant to break down a work into its constituent parts and consider whether certain parts were original whilst others were not.[182] However, an opportunity to examine this question was missed in *Waterlow Directories Ltd v Reed Information Services Ltd*[183] which concerned an alleged infringement of copyright in a legal directory containing names and addresses of barristers and firms of solicitors by entering extracts into a word processor.

177 (1923) 93 LJPC 113.

178 [1944] AC 329.

179 (1991) 111 S Ct 1282.

180 And the work involved in devising the classification system (a non-literal form of work?). However, in *Bell South Advertising & Publishing Corp v Donnelly Information Publishing Inc* 999 F 2d 1436 (11th Cir, 1993), the court held that taking a large amount of data from a yellow pages directory did not infringe copyright.

181 (Unreported) 5 December 1994, 2nd Circuit Court of Appeals.

182 An approach rejected by Jacob J in relation to computer programs in *IBCOS Computers Ltd v Barclays Mercantile Highland Finance Ltd* [1994] FSR 275.

183 [1992] FSR 409. The issue was whether a substantial part had been taken.

Bull argued that a single datum, for example, 'Megatron Shares – 120p', could have been protected by copyright in the UK if available as electronic text in which case it could have been considered to be a computer program.[184] Although 'computer program' is not defined in the Act, it is likely to be required to be some code that is executable by the computer's processor in a way that controls or conditions the operation of a computer. This is not the case where the datum is stored simply in ASCII code, but could be the case where it is encrypted and includes instructions so that the computer can decrypt it. Of course, a relatively small collection of such data could have qualified as a compilation under the Act before 1 January 1998.

Protection for databases from 1 January 1998[185]

The Copyright and Rights in Databases Regulations 1997[186] ('the 1997 Regulations') implemented Directive 96/9/EC of the European Parliament and of the Council of 11 March 1996 on the legal protection of databases,[187] making some changes to the copyright provisions of the Copyright, Designs and Patents Act 1988 and creating a new 'database right'. Thus, a two-tier approach to the protection of databases is taken, so that those that are the author's own intellectual creation will be protected by copyright, and databases which involve in their making a substantial investment in obtaining, verifying or presenting the contents of a database will be protected by a database right of lesser duration than copyright. The 1997 Regulations came into force on 1 January 1998, the date for compliance required in the Directive.

The desire to harmonise the protection of databases throughout the EU was an important feature of the Directive. The rationale for strong and effective protection can be seen in some of the recitals to the Directive. It is recognised that databases are vital to the development of an information market and in other fields and the exponential growth in the amount of information generated and processed in all sectors of commerce and industry requires significant investment in information systems. Identifying a great imbalance in the investment in databases as between Member States and in comparison to third countries, the creation of a stable and uniform legal protection for databases is seen as essential to ensuring that substantial investment in modern information systems is encouraged.[188] The link between legal protection and investment is seen as important, and commercially valuable databases which would otherwise fail to be protected under copyright law are given their own distinct form of protection.

Before looking separately at the changes to the copyright provisions as they apply to databases and the database right, a number of points should be made.

1 The rights provided apply to both electronic and non-electronic databases, reflecting the desire of the European Commission not to distinguish between computer databases and paper databases, so that there can be no regulatory advantage for those who do not adopt and make use of information technology.

2 The database right can be seen as a 'quasi-copyright', bearing a number of similarities with copyright. It has been referred to as a *sui generis* right.[189]

3 There is a substantial overlap between copyright and rights in databases. Thus, in most cases, a database subject to copyright may also have a database right. This has some implications: for example, the author of a database may be a different person to the maker of a database. Another factor is that the meaning of infringement and the permitted acts differ for the two rights. A given act may infringe one but not the other.

4 The structure of a copyright database may be protected as a form of expression but this does not apply in respect of the database right.

5 Copyright and the right in a database are both without prejudice to any copyright in the contents of a database. Where a database contains individual works of copyright,

184 Bull, G. 'Licensing and Distribution of Market Data' [1994] 10 CLSR 50 at 51. However, in *Powerflex* v *Data Access Corp* [1997] FCA 490, the Federal Court of Australia rejected the notion that a word in a computer program could itself be a program. Even though a single word in a high-level language program may result in a series of instructions being processed, the word is merely the cipher or trigger for the series of instructions.

185 For analysis and discussion of the new law on databases, *see*, for example, Angel, J. and Quinn, T. 'Database law' [1998] 14 CLSR 34; Lai, S. 'Database protection in the UK: The new deal and its effects on software protection' [1998] EIPR 32; and Chalton, S. 'The effect of the database directive on UK copyright law in relation to databases: a comparison of features' [1997] EIPR 278.

186 SI 1997/3032.

187 OJ L 77, 27.03.1996, p 20.

188 Recitals 5–12.

189 So described in the Directive; *see* chapter III of the Directive.

they will remain to be protected by copyright. Where a person without authorisation takes one of those works, he will infringe the copyright in the work. If he takes more than one work, he will infringe the copyright in the individual works, may infringe the copyright in the database as a whole and also may infringe the database right.

6   Authors of copyright databases have moral rights in the same way as applies to other literary works.[190] However, there are no moral rights in respect of the database right as such.

7   The new provisions as to copyright in databases and in relation to the database right do not apply to music compilations on CD-ROM.[191]

8   There are no statutory presumptions, where a database is subject to both rights, that an assignment of one right automatically carries an assignment of the other or, indeed, any rights in the works included in the database.

Copyright provisions for databases

The Copyright, Designs and Patents Act 1988 s 3(1) is amended so as to add 'database' to the growing, but clearly non-exhaustive, list of things that are literary works and to exclude databases from compilations. Thus, databases are treated separately from other forms of compilation. Though many of the copyright provisions apply identically to each, there are differences, such as in relation to the permitted act of fair dealing.

Section 3A was added to the Act, defining a 'database' as a collection of independent works, data or other materials which (a) are arranged in a systematic or methodical way, and (b) are individually accessible by electronic or other means.[192] A database is original for copyright purposes if, and only if, by reason of the selection or arrangement of its contents, the database constitutes the author's own intellectual creation. Recital 16 to the database Directive states that no other criterion should be applied, in particular, no aesthetic or qualitative criterion. This seems bound to narrow the scope of copyright protection for databases as databases in the UK with its traditional generous approach to copyright subsistence. However, pre-existing databases are not to be prejudiced. Thus, where a database was created on or before 27 March 1996 (the date the Directive was published) and was protected by copyright immediately before 1 January 1998, that copyright will continue for its full term, notwithstanding that the database would not qualify for copyright under the new test for originality.[193]

It is not beyond doubt that a database could still be protected as a compilation and it is arguable that the database Directive simply introduced two new rights for database without prejudice to pre-existing rights, if any. In *Football Dataco Ltd* v *Stan James (Abingdon) Ltd*,[194] the claimants were responsible for the annual fixture lists for the English and Scottish football leagues.

At first instance, the judge accepted that the lists were copyright databases because of the 'very significant labour and skill' used to create the lists. He also confirmed that the work involved was not mere 'sweat of the brow'. The Court of Appeal considered that there was some doubt as to the meaning and scope of the term 'author's intellectual creation' and referred questions to the Court of Justice for a preliminary ruling under Article 267 of the Treaty on the Functioning of the EU. The questions sought rulings on whether the term applied to the intellectual effort and skill in creating data (not just arranging and selecting existing data); whether selection or arrangement included adding important significance to a pre-existing item of data (for example, adding the date to a particular football match); and whether the term 'author's intellectual creation' required more than significant labour and skill.

The claimants in *Football Dataco* also claimed a copyright in the database but not as a database but as a literary work, as a compilation of data. The Court of Appeal doubted that such a right survived the implementation of the database Directive but, because of a

190   Recital 28 states that the moral rights belong to the natural person who created the database though such moral rights are outside the scope of the Directive. No moral rights are granted to makers of databases in relation to the database right.

191   Recital 19 of the Directive. Of course, protection will remain available as musical works, literary works (where there are lyrics), and sound recordings in addition to any rights in performances.

192   'Other means' indicating that the provisions apply equally to non-computer databases, confirmed in recital 14 to the Directive.

193   Recital 60. However, the effect of this derogation is confined to the territory of the Member State concerned.

194   [2011] RPC 9.

'lingering doubt' decided to refer a question on this to the Court of Justice. If such a compilation right still exists, this could circumvent the shortcomings of the database right which requires that the investment must be in terms of pre-existing data and the investment in respect of creating new data is not a relevant investment.[195]

It is arguable that a compilation of data from football matches in progress is protected by copyright. In *Football Dataco Ltd v Sportradar GmbH*,[196] at first instance the judge thought that the claimants' Football Live database was protected by copyright. The Court of Appeal did not fully consider the question as a court in Germany was first seised of the copyright action.[197] The database included details such as goals, who scored them and when, yellow and red cards and to whom they were given, substitutions and the like. The database was updated live during matches, the data being collected and submitted by ex-professional footballers who attended matches on behalf of the claimants.

We have seen that copyright protection can extend beyond the literal expression of the literal work to non-literal elements such as, in the case of a computer program, the underlying structure of the work. The same ought to apply to a database and, indeed, recital 15 to the Directive states that copyright protection should cover the structure of a database. But what is the structure of a database? Conventionally, databases are structured into records and fields. A record is simply a set of data relating to one entry in the database. For example, in the case of a database of customers, a record is all the information in the database relating to a particular customer. A record is broken down into fields. For example, in our customer database, there may be one field containing the last name of the customer, another for the first name, a field for the first line of his address, one for the second line, and so on. Figure 8.4 gives an example of a database so structured.

Fields in a database may be of different sizes and types. For example, some fields will contain alphabetic information, some may contain numeric information (integer, decimal or exponential), alphanumeric information, dates, etc. In some cases, the size of the field will be dictated by its type; in other cases, such as a field containing information relating to a person's first name, it is a matter of predetermining the longest likely name and sizing the field accordingly.[198] The work in designing the database in terms of the information it will contain and the structure of that information can be considerable. Where the design of computer software comprising computer programs and databases is concerned, the work involved in the design of the database structure can be the most difficult element in the overall design and require the greatest amount of research and development work. The fact that the Directive recognises this is to be welcomed and it is to be hoped that the courts appreciate the importance of protecting the structure of a database.[199]

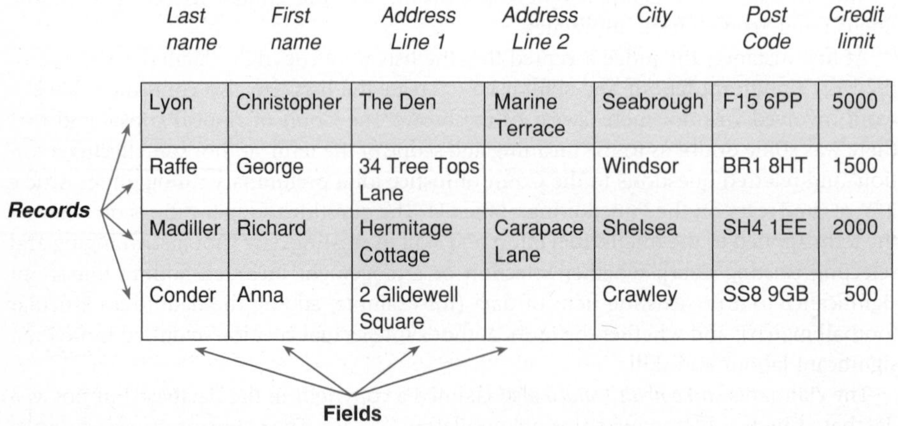

195 See the section on the database right, *infra*.

196 [2011] EWCA Civ 330.

197 The claimants allegations failed, *inter alia*, to claim that the defendants had taken what amounted to an intellectual creation. The jurisdiction aspects of the case are discussed in Chapter 26 on IPR and conflict of laws.

198 In some systems, the size of the field does not have to be specified as it is dynamic, that is, the field will grow or shrink to hold precisely the amount of information in the record in question.

199 After a shaky start, the signs are now good. *See* Jacob J in *IBCOS Computers Ltd v Barclays Mercantile Highland Finance Ltd* [1994] FSR 275 and his criticism of Judge Paul Baker in this respect in *Total Information Processing Systems Ltd v Daman Ltd* [1992] FSR 171, discussed earlier in this chapter.

	Last name	First name	Address Line 1	Address Line 2	City	Post Code	Credit limit
	Lyon	Christopher	The Den	Marine Terrace	Seabrough	F15 6PP	5000
	Raffe	George	34 Tree Tops Lane		Windsor	BR1 8HT	1500
	Madiller	Richard	Hermitage Cottage	Carapace Lane	Shelsea	SH4 1EE	2000
	Conder	Anna	2 Glidewell Square		Crawley	SS8 9GB	500

Records (bracket pointing to rows)

Fields (pointing to columns)

Figure 8.4 Structure of a database

With modern developments in computer software technology, the issue of database structure has become more complex. No longer is it appropriate to think of distinct and separate databases as in old COBOL systems. In many cases now, databases are relational, with a number of databases linked together by some common element. For example, one database may contain details of individual clients, including a reference number with another database containing transactions including customer reference numbers. By combining these databases, a list of transactions can be generated, grouped by individual customer, for example, for the purpose of sending out invoices. Further examples of database structure may be found in links in internet websites and hypertext links generally. Potentially, all such elements could be the subject of copyright protection.

The restricted act of making an adaptation has some definitions specific to particular forms of work, such as in the case of a musical work or computer program. As databases are treated individually, there is need for clarification of this restricted act for databases and, accordingly, a definition of making an adaptation of a database is inserted into the Copyright, Designs and Patents Act 1988 s 21, being an arrangement or altered version or a translation of it. Specific provision is required for making an adaptation but not for the other restricted acts in the Directive which are already covered by ss 17–20.

An arrangement of a database could be a new version in which the contents of the database have been sorted into a particular order. An altered version could be where a person has taken a partial copy of the database by omitting some of the fields. A translation of a database could occur where a person has taken a database used with a particular type of database software, such as Oracle, and imported it into a different type of database software, such as Microsoft Access.

The Directive leaves much to Member States as regards the permitted acts under copyright. The UK approach is to adopt the traditional permitted acts that apply to literary works, with the exception of fair dealing for research and private study for which specific provision is made for databases. For example, the fair dealing provisions apply to databases as they do to other literary works, apart from computer programs.[200]

Section 50D was inserted into the Copyright, Designs and Patents Act 1988, being essentially a non-derogation from grant provision for persons having a right to use a database or part of it (whether under a licence to do any of the acts restricted by the copyright in the database or otherwise). It is not an infringement of copyright in a database for such a person to do, in the exercise of that right, anything which is necessary for the purposes of access to and use of the contents of the database or of that part of the database. This provision acknowledges that a person may be restricted to using part only of a database. For example, his use may be restricted to certain records or certain fields. In the case of a database of potential customers in the UK, a person may be permitted to access and retrieve information about persons living in England, or may be permitted to access and retrieve information about all the persons in the database with the exception of credit information relating to them.

This right cannot be prohibited or restricted and s 296B makes void any term or condition in an agreement in so far as it purports to prohibit or restrict the acts permitted under s 50D or any act necessary for the exercise of the rights granted by the agreement.

The database right

The database right is intended to provide protection to databases which, although they may fail to meet the requirements for copyright protection as a database, are commercially valuable, being the result of a substantial investment. However, the right is not restricted to databases in which copyright does not subsist and many databases subject to copyright should also be subject to the database right. The overlap could be important for the owner of the database because infringement and exceptions to infringement are not

200 Initially, databases were treated differently as commercial research was not permitted and an acknowledgement of the source was required. However, these requirements now apply more generally to the original works as a result of the changes made by the Copyright and Related Rights Regulations 2003, SI 2003/2498.

identical for both rights. In particular, the repeated and systematic extraction of *insubstantial* parts may infringe the database right in circumstances where the copyright is not infringed. The first major case on the database right, *British Horseracing Board Ltd* v *William Hill Organisation Ltd*,[201] is discussed in the next section and other cases also referred to the Court of Justice for a preliminary ruling under Article 267 of the Treaty on the Functioning of the EU[202] involving football fixture lists are mentioned later.

By an Agreement with the EU signed in Brussels on 26 March 2003, the legal protection of databases by the database right was extended to the Isle of Man with effect from 1 November 2003.[203] Consequently, references to the European Economic Area ('EEA') should be taken to include, *mutatis mutandis*, the Isle of Man.

Subsistence of the database right is unaffected if the database is also a work of copyright or if the works contained in the database are themselves copyright works. Thus, a database of photographs which involved in its making the exercise of skill and judgment (or, more properly now, the author's intellectual creativity) and involved a substantial investment in its making, for example, in presenting its contents will be subject to copyright at two levels (the individual photographs and the database as a whole) and also will be subject to the database right.

The database right is set out in Part III of the Copyright and Rights in Databases Regulations 1997[204] and reg 12 contains some of the main definitions, although it should be noted that 'database' has the same meaning as for copyright.[205] The other definitions are:

- 'Extraction', in relation to any contents of a database, means the permanent or temporary transfer of those contents to another medium by any means or in any form.[206]
- 'Investment' includes any investment, whether of financial, human or technical resources.
- 'Lawful user', in relation to a database, means any person who (whether under a licence to do any of the acts restricted by any database right in the database or otherwise) has a right to use the database.
- 'Re-utilisation', in relation to any contents of a database, means making those contents available to the public by any means.[207]
- 'Substantial', in relation to any investment, extraction or re-utilisation, means substantial in terms of quantity or quality or a combination of both.

Furthermore, under reg 26, expressions used in respect of the database right under Part III of the Regulations which are defined for the purposes of Part I of the Copyright, Designs and Patents Act 1988 (the copyright provisions) have the same meaning as in that Part of the 1988 Act.

As is usual, the draftsmen of the Regulations chose to re-write the relevant parts of the Directive rather than simply copy them out. The above definitions of extraction and re-utilisation should be compared to those in the Directive, Article 7(2) of which states:

> For the purposes of this Chapter [dealing with the *sui generis* right]:
>
> (a) 'extraction' shall mean the permanent or temporary transfer of all or a substantial part of the contents of a database to another medium by any means or in any form;
> (b) 're-utilisation' shall mean any form of making available to the public all or a substantial part of the contents of a database by the distribution of copies, by renting, by on-line or other forms of transmission. The first sale of a copy of a database within the Community by the rightholder or with his consent shall exhaust the right to control resale of that copy within the Community;
>
> Public lending is not an act of extraction or re-utilisation.

An important phrase not included in the Regulations is '. . . by online or other forms of transmission'. The question is: where does a transmission take place?[208] This could be important where the work is sent from equipment located in one country to be received

---

201 [2001] RPC 31 at first instance. This case went to the Court of Appeal which referred a number of questions on the interpretation of the Directive to the Court of Justice and then, following the ruling of the Court of Justice, the Court of Appeal applied that ruling: *see infra*.

202 Formerly Article 234 of the EC Treaty.

203 The Copyright and Rights in Databases (Amendment) Regulations 2003, SI 2003/2501.

204 SI 1997/3032.

205 As given by s 3A(1).

206 This includes copying to another medium and is not confined to removal from the database to another medium: *British Horseracing Board Ltd* v *William Hill Organisation Ltd* [2001] RPC 31.

207 This is not limited to the first time the contents are made available to the public: *British Horseracing Board Ltd* v *William Hill Organisation Ltd* [2001] RPC 31.

208 The same question arises in relation to broadcasts.

209 [2011] EWCA Civ 330.

by a person in another country. In *Football Dataco Ltd* v *Sportradar GmbH*,[209] the compilations of live data about football matches alleged to infringe the claimants' database right were hosted on computers in Austria and Holland. There was evidence that persons in the UK had accessed the data. The Court of Appeal was unsure as to whether the transmission was made when it was received (in which case UK database right would be engaged) or, based on an emission theory, when it was sent. Consequently, questions were submitted to the Court of Justice for a preliminary ruling. In essence, guidance was sought in the situation where a person, X. uploads data from a protected database on a webserver in country A which is sent to a user requesting data in country B. In sending the data, does X carry out an act of extraction or re-utilisation? Does that act of extraction or re-utilisation occur in (a) country A only, or (b) country B only, or (c) both countries A and B? If the answer is (b) or (c), a defendant could be liable for authorisation infringement in the UK and by being a joint tortfeasor.

210 Copyright and Rights in Databases Regulations 1997 reg 12(2) and (3). Regulation 12(3) allows the charging of a payment, provided that it does not exceed that necessary to cover the costs of the establishment.

211 Copyright and Rights in Databases Regulations 1997 reg 12(5).

Lending a copy of a database (not for direct or indirect commercial advantage) by an establishment accessible to the public does not constitute extraction or re-utilisation of the contents of a database, but this exception does not apply to making available for on-the-spot reference use which could, therefore, fall within extraction or re-utilisation.[210] Exhaustion of rights within the EEA and the Isle of Man applies to copies sold within the EEA and the Isle of Man by or with the consent of the owner of the database right to the extent that further sale of such copies does not constitute extraction or re-utilisation of the contents of the database.[211] For example, where a copy of a database is sold on a CD-ROM, by or with the consent of the owner of the database right, a person buying that copy may resell it or import it into another Member State for resale providing that by doing so he does not make a further copy (permanent or temporary) or does not make the contents available to the public, for example, by making the CD-ROM available on a network to which the public have access. This is, of course, without prejudice to rights, if any, in the contents of the database.

212 Copyright and Rights in Databases Regulations 1997 reg 13(1).

213 Recital 40. For the database right, therefore, the 'sweat of the brow' doctrine still applies.

The database right is a property right which subsists in a database if there has been a substantial investment in obtaining, verifying or presenting the contents of the database.[212] Note that investment may be in respect of financial, human or technical resources. The Directive uses the test of an investment consisting of the deployment of financial resources and/or the expending of time, effort or energy.[213] There are also qualification requirements to be satisfied. Under reg 18, the latter are satisfied if, at the material time, the maker (or at least one of them where there are joint makers) is:

- a national of an EEA state (or habitually resident in the state);
- a body incorporated in an EEA state, having its central administration or principal place of business in an EEA state or a registered office in the EEA and the body's operations linked on an ongoing basis with the economy of an EEA state; or

214 Equivalent rules apply in respect of the Isle of Man.

- a partnership or other unincorporated body formed under the law of an EEA state, having at that time its central administration or principal place of business within the EEA.[214]

The 'material time' is the time when a database was made or, if its making extended over a period, a substantial part of that period. To give an example, say a database was partially made in Mexico by a Mexican company. The partially completed database and the rights in it were then assigned to a French company which completed the making of the database. Say that the Mexican company completed 40 per cent of the database, which took four months, and the French company completed the remaining 60 per cent, taking six months to do so. It is clear that the database was made by a company established in the EEA over a substantial part of the total period of its making.[215] If, instead of a Mexican

215 If the proportions were reversed, that is 60 per cent was made by the Mexican company, it is questionable whether 40 per cent in terms of time and quantity would be deemed to be substantial, though it would appear that it is the proportion of time that is important rather than the proportion of quantity of the database's contents.

company, the first part of the making of the database was by an English company, the whole of the making qualifies. The provisions on qualification mean that, if a database does qualify, it is protected throughout the EEA and the Isle of Man. This approach to qualification for protection is needed because, being a *sui generis* right, reciprocal protection under the Berne Convention for the Protection of Literary and Artistic Works 1886 does not apply.

The qualification requirements do not apply in the case of parliamentary database right: reg 18(3). There is no equivalent exception from the qualification requirements which has not been extended to Crown database right.[216]

The 'maker' of a database subject to the database right is defined in reg 14(1) as the person who takes the initiative in obtaining, verifying or presenting the contents of a database and assumes the risk of investing in that obtaining, verification or presentation, such acts constituting the act of making a database. Under reg 15, the maker is the first owner of the database right. There are provisions equivalent to those under copyright law for employees. Thus, where an employee makes a database in the course of his employment, it will be the employer who is the maker of the database, subject to agreement to the contrary. It is arguable whether special provision is required for this for, where a database is made by an employee, it will be the employer who normally takes the initiative in the obtaining, verification or presentation of the contents and assumes the risk of that investment. Crown and parliamentary database right are also provided for.[217] Where two or more persons act in collaboration in taking the initiative and assuming the risk of investing, they will be joint makers of the database. Unlike copyright law, there is no requirement that the contribution of each is not distinct.

The term of protection afforded by the database right is set out in reg 17 as 15 years from the end of the calendar year during which the making of the database is completed, although, if it is made available to the public before the end of that period, the right will continue to endure for 15 years from the end of the calendar year during which it was first made available.

A great many commercially exploited databases are subject to modification, either as a continual process or by subsequent releases or updates. The Directive attempted to deal with this by providing for a fresh 15-year term when the changes become substantial, including any substantial change resulting from an accumulation of successive additions, deletions or alterations, provided the database would be considered to be a substantial new investment.[218] The 1997 Regulations follow the same formula. Nevertheless, in practice, it will be extremely difficult to determine when a new database right comes into existence, especially where the database in question is subject to continual modification. Such databases are sometimes referred to as dynamic databases and may be subject to a term of protection that is continually being renewed. Databases made on or after 1 January 1983 in which database right subsists on 1 January 1998 (1 November 2003 for the Isle of Man) shall, under reg 29, qualify for 15 years beginning with 1 January 1998.[219]

Infringing acts are defined in reg 16 as the extraction or re-utilisation of all or a substantial part of the contents of the database without the consent of the owner. Bear in mind that substantiality is a question of quantity or quality or a combination of both.[220] Accepting that repeatedly taking insubstantial parts can compromise the owner's economic rights in a database, reg 16(2) provides that the repeated and systematic extraction or re-utilisation of insubstantial parts of the contents of a database *may* amount to the extraction or re-utilisation of a substantial part of those contents (emphasis added). A person could periodically and at frequent intervals extract valuable information from a very large database by searching for particular entries using keywords. It could be difficult to show that a substantial part of the database has been used. This could be particularly important as more databases will be made available online or via the internet.

In terms of 'insubstantial infringement', the Directive further requires that the repeated and systematic extraction or re-utilisation must imply acts conflicting with a normal exploitation of the database or be unreasonably prejudicial to the legitimate interests of the maker of the database. The 1997 Regulations simply state that such taking *may*

216 Both Crown copyright and parliamentary copyright are excluded from the normal qualification requirements: s 153(2).

217 Where a database is made by or under the direction or control of the Scottish Parliament, the Scottish Parliamentary Corporate Body shall be regarded as the maker of the database: reg 14A, inserted by the Scotland Act 1998 (Consequential Modifications) (No 1) Order 1999, SI 1999/1042.

218 Evaluated qualitatively or quantitatively: Article 10(3).

219 Copyright and Rights in Databases Regulations 1997 reg 30.

220 However, in *British Horseracing Board Ltd* v *William Hill Organisation Ltd* [2001] RPC 31, Laddie J suggested that both quantity and quality should be considered together. It is submitted that the correct approach is to consider each separately and then, if the part taken is not deemed to be substantial under either head, the two factors should then be considered in combination.

amount to the extraction or re-utilisation of a substantial part of the contents of the database. Certainly, prejudice to the owner's commercial exploitation should infringe, but it should be much wider than that. The owner of the database may make it available on a non-profit basis to the members of the public who satisfy certain criteria, such as being members of a club or having certain attributes.

In the event of litigation, presumably it will be for makers subject to this right to show that the accumulation of insubstantial extractions or re-utilisations has conflicted with their normal exploitation of the database or prejudiced their legitimate interests within the spirit of the Directive.

There are 'non-derogation' provisions in that a lawful user of a database which has been made available to the public has a right to extract or re-utilise insubstantial parts of the database for any purpose, and any term in an agreement, under which the right to use a database or part of a database has been granted, which purports to prevent the person having the right from extracting or re-utilising insubstantial parts of the contents of the database (or part of that database), shall be void.[221] It does not seem, however, that a wider non-derogation from grant principle, as in *British Leyland*,[222] applies. In *Mars UK Ltd* v *Teknowledge Ltd*,[223] the claimant designed and made coin-operated machines. These machines contained discriminators designed to detect whether or not a coin was genuine. A new discriminator ('Cashflow'), programmed for new coin data and which could be reprogrammed in the future was introduced by the claimant. The information contained within it had been encrypted to make it difficult for third parties to reverse engineer but the defendant managed to reverse engineer it and was then able to recalibrate other Cashflow machines.

The claimant alleged infringement of the copyright and database right in the computer programs and data, respectively, contained on the computer chips in the discriminators. There was a further claim of breach of confidence.[224] As regards copyright and the database right, the defendant accepted that it had, subject to a defence based on *British Leyland*, infringed those rights. This defence failed. Jacob J noted that there was no specific provision for such a defence in the domestic legislation and the EU Directives relating to copyright in computer programs and the database right. Where the defence applied was in respect of the public policy in maintaining a free market in spare parts. However, in the present case, persons who bought the discriminators expected that they would be repaired and maintained by the original manufacturer. Furthermore, recalibration of the discriminators so that they could test the authenticity of new coins was far removed from the concept of repair in *British Leyland*.[225]

There is a fair dealing exception to infringement. Where the database has been made available to the public, fair dealing with a substantial part of the contents is allowed if:

- the part is extracted by a person who is otherwise a lawful user;
- it is extracted for the purposes of illustration for teaching or research (but not for a commercial purpose); and
- the source is indicated.[226]

Further exceptions are set out in Sch 1 to the 1997 Regulations and cover parliamentary and judicial proceedings, Royal Commissions and statutory inquiries, material open to public inspection or on official register, material communicated to the Crown in the course of public business, public records and acts done under statutory authority. These mirror the equivalent permitted acts for copyright in ss 45–50 of the Copyright, Designs and Patents Act 1988. There is also an exception under reg 20A for the benefit of Legal Deposit Libraries which allows copying of works from the internet in accordance with Regulations made for that purpose and certain conditions without infringing the database right.[227] The purpose is to allow copies to be made by Legal Deposit Libraries of works published on the internet to be added to the collections of these libraries which have, since the Copyright Act 1911, a duty to keep copies of all published works.[228]

221 Copyright and Rights in Databases Regulations 1997 reg 19.

222 *British Leyland Motor Corp Ltd* v *Armstrong Patents Co Ltd* [1986] 2 WLR 400.

223 [2000] FSR 138.

224 For which *see* Chapter 11.

225 The courts seem increasingly reluctant to extend the principle in *British Leyland*. It is not inconceivable that, taking into account changes to copyright and design law, the defence will wither away.

226 Copyright and Rights in Databases Regulations 1997 reg 20.

227 This was inserted by the Legal Deposit Libraries Act 2003 and came into force on 1 February 2004.

228 There is also a permitted act in relation to copyright works for Legal Deposit Libraries; *see* Chapter 7.

Apart from these exceptions and others mentioned above, none of the other permitted acts that apply to literary works apply to the database right. In particular, it should be noted that fair dealing for criticism or review or for reporting current events does not apply in relation to the database right. It is questionable whether fair dealing for private study is available. It depends on whether this would fall within the meaning of research.

There is an exception to infringement of the database right which resembles one of the permitted acts for copyright works. The database right is not infringed where it is not possible by reasonable enquiry to ascertain the identity of the maker of the database and it is reasonable to assume that the database right has expired: reg 21.

There are some useful presumptions that apply to the database right, not dissimilar to some of those for copyright works. Under reg 22, where a name purporting to be that of the maker of the database appears on copies of the database as published, it is presumed that that person is the maker and the database was not made in circumstances where the employer would be the first owner or in the case of Crown or parliamentary database right. Where copies of a database as published bear a label or mark stating that a named person was the maker and that it was first published in a specified year, the label or mark shall be admissible as evidence of those facts and presumed correct until the contrary be proved.

The 1997 Regulations are silent on the burden of proof as to whether there has been a substantial change resulting in a further 15 years' protection. The recitals to the Directive state that it is the maker of the database who has the burden of proof in this respect and in terms of the date of completion of the making of the database. Nevertheless, the effect under English law is probably the same, where a defendant challenges either aspect. Perhaps it is a pity that there is not an equivalent to the presumption that applies in respect of the design right (and infringing copies of copyright works) to the effect that, if it can be shown that the right subsists or subsisted in the design, then it also subsisted at the time of the infringement unless the contrary be proved. However, this would conflict with the Directive.

The provisions for dealing, rights and remedies (including those of exclusive licensees) that apply to copyright works are declared under reg 23 to apply also in respect of the database right. Regulation 23 was substituted by the Intellectual Property (Enforcement, etc.) Regulations 2006 to include delivery up, actions by non-exclusive licensees and jurisdictional issues.

Schedule 2 to the 1997 Regulations contains provisions for licensing the database right and deals with licensing schemes and licensing bodies and referral of licensing schemes to the Copyright Tribunal. These are equivalent to the provisions in ss 116–129 and 144 of the Copyright, Designs and Patents Act 1988 that apply to copyright works with necessary changes to take account of legislation such as the Enterprise Act 2002. The jurisdiction of the Copyright Tribunal has been enlarged accordingly.

The 1997 Regulations apply to databases made before or after 1 January 1998.[229] Regulation 28 states that agreements made before 1 January 1998 are unaffected and no act done after 31 December 1997 in pursuance of an agreement made before 1 January 1998 infringes the database right. Regulation 29 provides that if a database was made on or before 27 March 1996 (the date the Directive was published in the *Official Journal*) and was a copyright database immediately before commencement, that copyright continues for the remainder of its term in accordance with s 12 of the Copyright, Designs and Patents Act 1988, that is, in most cases, life of the author plus 70 years.[230]

The database right and the *BHB* v *William Hill* case

The first significant case on the database right triggered a reference to the European Court of Justice ('Court of Justice') for a preliminary ruling as to the interpretation of a number of provisions of the Directive. In *British Horseracing Board Ltd* v *William Hill Organisation*

229 Copyright and Rights in Databases Regulations 1997 reg 27.

230 There are special provisions for the Isle of Man where the cut-off date in respect of savings is 1 November 2003.

231 [2001] RPC 31.

Ltd,[231] the British Horseracing Board ('BHB') maintained a database containing details of racehorse owners, racing colours, trainers and jockeys and pre-race information, such as the runners and riders for a given race. Nearer the date of the race, this pre-race information was updated and expanded to include, *inter alia*, the time of the race, sponsor, weights and stalls the horses start the race from.

The cost of obtaining the data, verification and presentation of the data was around £4 million per annum and fees charged by BHB came to around £1 million per annum. Third parties were allowed to use information contained in the database in return for payment of a licence fee. A declarations feed (up-to-the-minute details of races, times, declared runners and jockeys, distance of race and other details) was made available to subscribers in electronic form and to a company called Satellite Information Services Ltd ('SIS') which transmitted data from the database to its own subscribers in a form known as a raw data feed ('RDF').

The defendant, a bookmaker, established an internet site and an enhanced version went live in 1999 which allowed betting via the internet site with real time changes in odds being offered. This internet site contained information identical to that in the BHB database. BHB claimed that much of the information on the defendant's internet site came indirectly, via the SIS RDF, from the BHB database and that this was an unlicensed use. It also appeared that William Hill took some of the information from newspapers published the day before the race. This information also came, indirectly, from the BHB database. It was alleged that the database right subsisting in the database was infringed in two ways: first, by the extraction or re-utilisation of a substantial part of the database under Article 7(1) of the Directive and, second, by the repeated and systematic extraction of insubstantial parts of the contents of the database under Article 7(5).[232]

232 It is interesting to note that counsels' arguments and the judgment all refer to the Directive rather than to the Copyright and Rights in Databases Regulations 1997.

233 [2002] ECDR 4.

234 *Fixtures Marketing Ltd* v *Svenska Sp l AB* (unreported) 3 May 2001, Swedish Court of Appeal, and *NV Holdingmaatschappij de Telegraaf* v *Nederlandse Omroep Stichting* (unreported) 30 January 2001, Court of Appeal of The Hague.

235 [2004] ECR I-10415.

236 *See*, in particular, recitals 7 to 12 of the Directive.

Laddie J accepted both allegations and found that the defendant had infringed the database right in both ways. The defendant appealed to the Court of Appeal which decided to refer some questions on the interpretation of the Directive to the Court of Justice.[233] It had been pointed out that a somewhat narrower interpretation of the database right had been taken in Sweden and the Netherlands.[234] In the meantime, the injunction imposed by Laddie J was discharged.

The ruling by the Court of Justice in Case C-203/02 *British Horseracing Board Ltd* v *William Hill Organisation Ltd*[235] imposed a substantial restriction on the potential for subsistence of the database right, which seems to contradict the reason for its introduction (being to protect the investment in making databases).[236] The Court of Justice grouped together some of the questions referred by the Court of Appeal and looked at the meaning and scope of four aspects of the Directive, being 'investment', 'extraction and re-utilisation', 'substantial and insubstantial' and 'repeated and systematic extraction and re-utilisation'.

Investment

Investment relates to the creation of the database itself and not to the investment in *creating* the works or materials to be included in the database. The Court of Justice stressed that the recitals to the Directive emphasise the purpose of the *sui generis* database right is to protect the investment in seeking out existing independent materials and collecting them together in a database. However, this is a moot point. It is clear that the Directive uses the word 'obtaining' throughout but does not one obtain that which he creates? On the other hand, it may seem reasonable to assume that the Directive would have been much more explicit if it was the intention to include an investment in the creation of the contents of a database.

The Court of Justice went on to say that the investment in question involved in drawing up a list of runners for a race and associated prior checks, for example, as to the identity of the person making up the entry, is not an investment in the obtaining or verification of the contents of the database. The checking was carried out in the process of creating a list of runners for a race and, thus, was in relation to the creation of data (that is, the list of runners) and not in relation to the verification of the contents of the BHB database.

The limitation on the meaning of obtaining significantly reduces the scope of what investment covers. It does seem inconsistent that a person who makes a database but creates the data therein will not get a database right whereas a person who collects together pre-existing materials can, if the other requirements are satisfied.

Extraction and re-utilisation

Referring once more to the recitals in the Directive, the Court of Justice considered that the purpose of the right was to protect the investment of the maker of the database by giving him the right to control access to, and re-utilisation of, the contents of the database in order to guarantee the maker a return on his investment.[237] The scope of protection was, therefore, not limited to parasitic acts of making competing products but covered anything which could cause, quantitatively or qualitatively, detriment to the maker's investment. Even where the maker of a database has made access to that database available to the public, whether directly or otherwise, he still has the right to prevent access to, and further publication of, substantial parts of the contents of the database as this still requires the authorisation of the maker. This is supported by Article 8(1), setting out the rights of lawful users which allows a lawful user of a database made available to the public to extract and re-utilise insubstantial parts, not substantial parts. Of course, the particular agreement covering access may go further than this but it would have to do so expressly.

Indirect extraction or re-utilisation is also within the maker's rights as the acid test is whether his investment is prejudiced and, as such, acts of extraction and re-utilisation are not limited to acts involving direct access to the database. This could cover the situation where, for example, the maker of the database licences its use to a third party for publication by a printed newspaper and another person takes extracts from the newspaper to include in his database which is then made available to the public.

Substantial and insubstantial

Copyright law in the UK has tended to emphasise quality rather than quantity in determining whether a part of a work taken is or is not a substantial part. The Directive, however, expresses substantiality in terms of quantity or quality or both. Apart from infringement based on extracting and/or re-utilising a substantial part, there is another form of infringement based on the repeated and systematic extraction and/or re-utilisation of insubstantial parts. Consequently, the dividing line between what is substantial and what is insubstantial is very important. Extracting or re-utilising a substantial part infringes *per se*. Where there is a repeated and systematic extraction or re-utilisation of insubstantial parts, for infringement, this must conflict with the normal exploitation of the database or unreasonably prejudice the legitimate interests of the maker of the database.

A simplistic view is that what is not substantial must, by definition, be insubstantial. The Directive does not appear to admit any notion of an accumulation of insubstantial takings being viewed as a substantial part of the database. Article 7(5) is not to that effect and a literal interpretation of it suggests that an accumulation of insubstantial takings may infringe even if, collectively, they do not add up to a substantial part. The question is whether this conflicts with the normal exploitation of that database or unreasonably prejudices the legitimate interests of its maker. However, the ruling of the Court of Justice on the scope of Article 7(5) (*see* below) stresses that what is intended is to prevent anyone overcoming the prohibition in Article 7(1) by an accumulation of insubstantial extractions or re-utilisations such that at least a substantial part of the database ends up being extracted or re-utilised.

237 *See* recitals 41 and 42 to the Directive.

The UK's Copyright and Rights in Databases Regulations 1997 fail to express Article 7(5) accurately. Regulation 16(2) states that '... the repeated and systematic extraction or re-utilisation of insubstantial parts of the contents of a database may amount to the extraction or re-utilisation of a substantial part of those contents'. No mention is made of acts '... which conflict with a normal exploitation of that database or which unreasonably prejudice the legitimate interests of the maker of the database'. Nevertheless, the wording of the Directive must prevail.

The Court of Justice held that the answer is to the effect that an insubstantial part is a part that is not substantial in terms of quality and is not substantial in terms of quantity. Substantiality in terms of quality is measured by consideration of the scale of investment in relation to the contents extracted and/or re-utilised. A part of the contents of a database, even if negligible, evaluated quantitatively may still be the result of a significant investment in human, technical or financial resources in obtaining, verification or presentation.

A substantial part, evaluated quantitatively, refers to the volume of the data extracted and/or re-utilised compared with the volume of the contents of the whole database. As the Directive does not give rise to any new right in the works, data or other materials in the database, the intrinsic value of the part of the contents taken is not relevant to determining whether the part taken is substantial.

Thus, a possible approach to the question of substantiality in relation to part of the contents of a database is as follows, assuming the database as a whole is the result of a substantial investment.

1 Is the part quantitatively significant such that it can be considered to be, in proportion to the entire database, a substantial part of it? If the answer is yes, then it is substantial.
2 Is the part the result of a significant investment? If yes, it is substantial even if it is not substantial in a quantitative sense. It may be a relatively small proportion providing it is the result of a significant investment.
3 Considering the part in terms of its proportion to the whole database AND in terms of whether it is the result of a substantial investment, is it nevertheless still substantial viewed from a combination of quantitative and qualitative factors? This possibility was not mentioned by the Court of Justice but Article 7(1) of the Directive states the right is to '... prevent extraction and/or re-utilisation of the whole or of a substantial part, evaluated *qualitatively and/or quantitatively*, of the contents of that database' (emphasis added).
4 If none of the above applies, the part is an insubstantial part.

Taking an insubstantial part and rearranging it or modifying its accessibility does not change it into a substantial part.

Repeated and systematic extraction and re-utilisation

The scheme in the Directive is to allow lawful users to extract and/or re-utilise insubstantial parts of a database. Where a database has been made available to the public, any person, whether a lawful user or otherwise, may extract and/or re-utilise insubstantial parts except as provided for by Article 7(5).

The Court of Justice said that the provision was intended to prevent persons circumventing the prohibition on extraction and/or re-utilisation under Article 7(1) by carrying out repeated and systematic acts that would lead to the reconstitution of the database as a whole or, at the very least, a substantial part of it or by making insubstantial parts available to the public in a repeated and systematic manner.

The phrase 'acts which conflict with the normal exploitation of [a] database or which unreasonably prejudice the legitimate interests of the maker of the database' refer to unauthorised acts the purpose of which are to:

(a) reconstitute the whole or a substantial part of the database through the cumulative acts of extraction, or

(b) make the whole or a substantial part of the database available to the public through the cumulative effect of acts of re-utilisation,

which thus seriously prejudices the investment made by the maker of the database.

Thus, the possibility of the accumulation of extractions or re-utilisations infringing if, collectively, they do not amount to a substantial part of the database has been rejected by the Court of Justice. The actions of William Hill, although repeated and systematic, could not result in the reconstitution of, or the making available to the public of, the whole or a substantial part of the BHB database so as unreasonably to prejudice the legitimate interests of BHB.

Application of the Court of Justice ruling by the Court of Appeal

The Court of Appeal, which referred the questions in the BHB case had the task of applying that ruling to the facts of the case. This it did in *British Horseracing Board Ltd* v *William Hill Organisation Ltd*,[238] where it was held that, to the extent that the BHB database consisted of officially identified names of runners and riders, it was not subject to the database right.

BHB submitted that the Court of Justice misunderstood the facts and, applying that part of the ruling relating to investment, its database was not one made by creation but by gathering and checking independent materials as required by Article 7(1). Jacob LJ did not accept this and he said that the Court of Justice did not misunderstand the primary facts put to it in the reference from the Court of Appeal, nor had it indulged in an illegitimate fact-finding exercise. Counsel for BHB quoted a passage from the ruling where the Court said (at para 80):

> The resources deployed by BHB to establish, for the purposes of organising horse races, the date, the time, the place and/or name of the race, and the horses running in it, represent an investment in the creation of materials contained in the BHB database. Consequently, *and if, as the order for reference appears to indicate, the materials extracted and re-utilised by William Hill did not require BHB and Others to put in investment independent of the resources required for their creation*, it must be held that those materials do not represent a substantial part, in qualitative terms, of the BHB database.

It was argued that the emphasised words indicated that the Court of Justice was unsure of its understanding of the facts. But Jacob LJ said that the passage did not set out primary facts at all and was based on the material in the order for reference. Furthermore, there was nothing relevantly wrong in the facts set out in the ruling. He went on to say that much more would be needed to show that the Court of Justice had made what could only be seen as an enormous blunder.

According to Jacob LJ, counsel for BHB had come to a conclusion that the database was protected by the database right by a process of deconstruction. But what mattered was the database in its final form as published. It was the official BHB list which could only be provided by BHB. No one else could generate the database by going through a similar process. BHB was the governing body of the British horseracing industry and, therefore, the only organisation able to produce the official list. The only answer to the question whether the published database was a collection of existing independent materials was an emphatic 'NO'. The database contained unique information, the 'official list of riders and runners'. The stamp of official approval meant that the database was different to a mere database of existing material.

This approach made the ruling of the Court of Justice easier to understand. It said that the investment in selecting, for the purposes of organising horse racing, the horses admitted to run in the race concerned related to the creation of data and did not constitute

238 [2005] RPC 35.

investment in obtaining the contents of the database. The prior checking was at the stage of creating the list for the race in question and constituted investment in the creation of the data and not in obtaining them.

Jacob LJ also said that the same reasoning applied in the case of provisional lists of runners and riders which BHB published in advance of the final declarations in the case of races with a large number of runners.

Pill LJ agreed with Jacob LJ's judgment but made some points of his own. In particular, he said that the Court of Justice was making a distinction between a database as such and the contents of the database on the one hand and, on the other hand, the creation of lists of entries which are independent materials created subsequently. He referred to para 31 of the Court of Justice's ruling:

> Against that background, the expression 'investment in . . . the obtaining . . . of the contents' of a database must, as William Hill and the Belgian, German and Portuguese Governments point out, be understood to refer to the resources used to seek out existing independent materials and collect them in the database, and not to the resources used for the creation as such of independent materials. The purpose of the protection by the *sui generis* right provided for by the directive is to promote the establishment of storage and processing systems for existing information and not the creation of materials capable of being collected subsequently in a database.

Clarke LJ agreed with both Jacob and Pill LJJ although he said that this meant allowing an appeal against a decision he first thought was correct.

Of course, the work that goes into the creation of information to be placed in a database may be rewarded in other ways. It may be held that there is sufficient skill and judgment to be classed as an intellectual creation for the database to be a work of copyright or the works created may themselves be works of copyright, for example, where an artist decides to create a database of his own paintings or drawings. In a case such as the *BHB* case, the creator of the database who exploits it by licensing may try to control its use by contractual means although a lawful user cannot be deprived of the right to extract and/ or re-utilise insubstantial parts of the database for any purpose where the database has been made available to the public.

The *BHB* case demonstrates that the objectives stated in the recitals to the Directive have not adequately been met. No one would question that both the BHB database and the football fixture lists were the result of a substantial and ongoing investment. Yet neither form of database is protected from activities such as those carried out by the defendants. Where, as in the case of the BHB database, the maker has an effective monopoly in being able to create the database and the database is made available to the public by one way or another, surely a better approach would be to make the extraction and/or re-utilisation of insubstantial parts of the contents of the database subject to licensing schemes or licences of right on payment of a reasonable royalty to be set by the Copyright Tribunal if the parties cannot agree on the rate.

Football fixture lists

On the same day that the ruling was handed down in the *BHB* case, the Court of Justice also handed down rulings in three cases involving football fixture lists. In all three cases, the claimant was the same, being Fixtures Marketing Ltd, which exploited football fixture lists outside the UK by granting licences on behalf of the organisers of football matches in the English and Scottish football leagues. Separate defendants in Finland, Greece and Sweden which controlled or organised gambling activities in their respective countries made use of information from the fixture lists. Courts in each of the three countries submitted questions to the Court of Justice for a preliminary ruling on the interpretation of certain provisions in the Directive. There was some duplication between the cases and the three sets of rulings and, to some extent, with the *BHB* case. The most informative case was Case C-440/02 *Fixtures Marketing Ltd* v *Organisation Prognostikon Agonon Podosfairos*,[239] where the Court of Justice ruled that the term 'database' referred to any collection of works, data or other materials, separable from one another without the value of their contents being affected, including a method or system of some sort for the retrieval of each of its constituent materials. The Court said, on that basis, a fixture list for a football league such as that exploited by Fixtures Marketing Ltd was a database within the meaning of the Directive.

The Court also confirmed that the investment in obtaining the contents of a database referred to the resources used to seek out existing independent materials and collect them in the database and did not extend to the resources used to create the contents. In relation to the football fixture lists it did not cover the resources used to establish the dates, times and the team pairings for the various matches in the league.[240]

In all these cases, including the *BHB* case, the Court of Justice came dangerously close to making findings of fact, something outside its jurisdiction. The basis for making preliminary rulings under Article 267 of the Treaty on the Functioning of the EU,[241] *inter alia*, is to give rulings on the interpretation of EU legislation. That provision does not permit the Court of Justice to make findings of fact.

In *Football Dataco Ltd* v *Stan James (Abingdon) Ltd*,[242] the Court of Appeal declined to submit questions on the subsistence of database right in football fixture lists and the scope of 'investment', holding the matter to be *acte claire*. Jacob LJ said (at para 12)

> . . . we see no point in referring questions about Art. 7 [the provision in the database Directive which sets out the *sui generis* right], as was proposed by the claimants. Behind the proposed questions was their hope that the Court would reconsider its earlier rulings. It was suggested these caused some consternation when they were made and so the court might be open to re-consideration. But given that the rulings were of the Grand Chamber (not merely a chamber) and were comparatively recent, it is inherently improbable that the Court would change its mind. So there is no point in asking it to reconsider the position. If there is to be a change in the law it will be a matter for the legislator.

Subsequent Court of Justice rulings on the database right

In Case C-304/07 *Directmedia Publishing GmbH* v *Albert-Ludwigs-Universität Freiburg*,[243] one Mr Knoop at the University drew up a list of titles of German verse (the 1,100 most important poems in German literature between 1730 and 1900). The list was published on the internet. Directmedia published a CD-ROM containing many of the poems listed in Mr Knoop's database. It had selected the poems by consulting Mr Knoop's internet list but obtained the texts of the poems from its own sources. It was claimed, *inter alia*, that Directmedia had infringed the University's database right in the internet list of titles. The German Federal Court of Justice referred a question as to the scope of extraction and whether it required physical copying of data.

The Court of Justice ruled that a transfer of data following an on-screen consultation of the protected database could constitute an extraction within the meaning of the Directive. This would infringe the database right if it involved a substantial part of the contents, evaluated qualitatively or quantitatively, of the contents of the protected database or if the operation in question amounted to transfers of insubstantial parts which, by their repeated and systematic nature, resulted in the reconstruction of a substantial part of those contents. In its judgment, the Court of Justice made some interesting points:

- The concept of extraction does not require that the contents of the database extracted should disappear from the original medium.
- The use of the phrase 'by any means and in any form in Article 7(2)(a) indicate that a wide definition of extraction was intended (here the Court referred to its *British*

239 [2004] ECR I-10549.

240 The European Court of Justice also came to this conclusion in Case C-46/02 *Fixtures Marketing Ltd* v *Oy Veikkaus AB* [2004] ECR I-10365 and in Case C-338/02 *Fixtures Marketing Ltd* v *Svenska Spel AB* [2004] ECR I-10497.

241 Formerly Article 234 of the EC Treaty.

242 [2011] RPC 9.

243 [2008] ECR I-7565; [2009] 1 CMLR 7.

Horseracing Board judgment) – it is not limited to mechanical reproduction, without adaptation, such as by a 'cut and paste' operation.

- The scope of extraction refers to any unauthorised act of appropriation of the whole or a part of the contents of the database and it is apparent from the wording of Article 7(2)(a) that the concept of extraction is not dependent upon the nature and form of the mode of operation used.
- 'Transfer' occurs when all or part of the contents of the database are to be found in a medium other than that of the original database.
- The objective of the person making the transfer (or series of transfers) is irrelevant – in line with the *British Horseracing Board* judgment, it matters not whether the objective is to create another database, whether it will compete with the original database or not, whether it is of a different size or not and whether it is part of an activity, whether commercial or not, other than the creation of a database.
- Displaying all or a substantial part of the contents of a database on another medium so as to allow simple on-screen display of those contents falls within the meaning of extraction. Where the maker of the database makes those contents available for access by third parties (whether or not on a paid basis) his database right does not allow him to prevent those third parties from consulting the database. It is only when the consultation involves the permanent or temporary transfer to another medium that the database maker's authorisation may be required.

The final point is of particular interest as the Court of Justice accepted that displaying the whole or part of the contents of a database on-screen involves an act of extraction as it involves a transfer of those contents to another medium by any means and in any form. The judgment was silent as to whether the medium in such a case is the computer's volatile memory or the screen itself. It could be either or even both. Where a database is made freely available to the public, such by means of the internet, it is implied that persons accessing the database and viewing the contents on their computer screens have the authorisation of the database owner.[244] Where the database is made available on a paid basis, for example, by subscription, those who have subscribed to access the database are likewise taken to have the implied authorisation of the owner to access the contents.[245]

The *Directmedia* case shows that even where consultation to the contents of a database is impliedly authorised, copying parts of those contents whether by writing them out by hand or simply entering them into another computer[246] will, potentially infringe the database right.[247]

A reference from a Bulgarian court involved a number of questions concerning the database right in relation to a legal information system which contained legislation and case law. Case C-545/07 *Apis-Hristovich EOOD* v *Lakorda AD*[248] involved a claim by Apis-Hristovich, the maker of the database, that persons who had previously worked in its software department left and set up Lakorda which began to market a rival legal database which included modules on Bulgarian legislation and case law. Apis-Hristovich alleged that this involved the unlawful extraction and re-utilisation of substantial parts of its database modules. Some of the case law in the Apis-Hristovich case law module was previously unpublished and not generally accessible to the public. The Court of Justice ruled:

- *Extraction – whether permanent or temporary* – the difference between a permanent transfer of the contents of a database and a temporary transfer is based on the length of time the contents are stored in another medium – a permanent transfer means the contents are stored in a permanent manner in a medium other than the original and a temporary transfer is where the contents are stored for a limited period in other medium, such as in the operating memory of a computer. There is no legal significance in the distinction between whether the transfer is permanent or temporary though is may be relevant in assessing the gravity of the unauthorised act of extraction.

244 This must also apply to copyright works, including database subject to copyright.

245 Such access is likely to be subject to terms in the agreement under which access is granted. For example, it may be restricted to parts of the database and may allow transfers of the contents to other media, such as by saving in a file or printing on paper.

246 Whether or not saved permanently in a computer file, whether it be a database or not.

247 Providing it represents a substantial part of the first database (qualitatively or quantitatively) or is a repeated and systematic extraction of insubstantial parts which cumulatively amount to a substantial part of the contents.

248 [2009] ECR I-1627; [2009] 3 CMLR 2.

- *Time of extraction* – the time an extraction occurs is when the contents are stored in another medium other than the original.
- *Other aspects of extraction* – the concept of extraction is independent of the objective pursued by the perpetrator of the act, of any modification made to the contents of the materials transferred and any differences in the structural organisation of the databases concerned.
- *Computer program* – the nature of the computer programs used to manage the two databases is not relevant to the existence of extraction although it certainly could be factor in the light of the Directive on the legal protection of computer programs.
- *Impact of modular design* – where a module of a database on its own is protected by the database right, infringement by extraction and/or re-utilisation of all or part of the contents of that module can be assessed in relation to that database. Where modules of a database are not protected in their own right, it is a question of comparing the contents of those modules extracted and/or re-utilised with the contents of the database as a whole.[249]
- *Substantiality* – where this is measured qualitatively, it is a question of considering the scale of the investment in obtaining, verifying or presenting the contents alleged to have been extracted and/or re-utilised, regardless of whether those contents represent a substantial part of the contents measured quantitatively. A quantitatively negligible part may, nonetheless, represent a significant human, technical or financial investment in the obtaining, verifying or presenting those contents. The intrinsic value of the contents is not a relevant factor as the database right does not give rise to a new right in the contents themselves.
- *Issue of whether contents are protected by copyright* – the legislative materials were not protected by copyright because of their official nature. This does not prevent the database right from subsisting as that right applies independently to copyright.
- *Materials not available from public sources* – some of the materials in the databases were obtained from sources not accessible to the public. That might affect the assessment of whether there has been a substantial investment in obtaining those materials and, accordingly, that might affect the classification of those materials as a substantial part of the database, evaluated qualitatively.
- *Evidence* – the fact that the physical and technical characteristics present in the contents of the protected database made by a particular person are also present in the contents of a database made by another person may be evidence of extraction unless that coincidence can be explained by factors other than a transfer between the two databases. In other words, in such a case it would be for the defendant to show that the presence of the same materials did not come about by extracting those materials from the protected database. For example, this could be where the makers of both databases independently obtained the materials from publicly accessible sources. The Court of Justice went on to say that the presence of materials not available from public sources which are contained in the protected database and also appear in the second database is not sufficient, *per se*, to prove that there had been an extraction from the protected database. It could, however, provide circumstantial evidence of extraction.

The two cases above build upon the judgments in the *British Horseracing Board* case and the *Football Fixtures* cases and further fleshes out the meaning of extraction. It has to be said that parts of the ruling in the *Apis-Hristovich* judgment state the obvious given the wording of the database Directive.[250] However, some parts of the judgment are helpful, such as the discussion of the distinction between a permanent and temporary transfer and the evidential aspects. Also useful is the discussion of substantiality and the impact of modularisation.

249 The Court of Justice did not consider the position where the database right subsisted in some modules of a modular database but did not subsist in other modules. Presumably, this would require consideration of the issue of infringement in relation to each protected module and then consideration of the database as a whole.

250 For example, that the nature of the computer programs used to access the contents is irrelevant as is the copyright status of the contents of the protected database.

Computer-generated works

The Copyright, Designs and Patents Act 1988 has a curious provision in that it recognises computer-generated works as a separate species of work with different rules for authorship and duration of copyright. These provisions apply only to literary, dramatic, musical or artistic works.[251] While it is important that works produced using a computer should not be denied the protection of copyright on the basis that the direct human contribution required to make the work is small or negligible, it may be difficult to differentiate between a computer-generated work and other works that have been created with the aid of a computer system.

Section 178 of the Act defines a 'computer-generated work' as being a work that is 'generated by computer in circumstances such that there is no human author'. It is not an easy task to determine the meaning of this definition, nor is it easy to think of examples of such works. All works generated by computer owe their creation to a human being, although the human element may be indirect, such as where a computer program contains all the instructions necessary for the creation of the work and the direct human involvement consists of nothing more than switching on the computer and starting up the program. For example, take the artistic work represented in Figure 8.5. It was produced by the author of this book using a computer program containing formulae to generate fractal geometry based on the work of French mathematician Dr Mandelbrot. The only skill used by the author was to zoom in on an interesting looking part of the main figure. Is this a computer-generated work, or has the skill used in selecting an area to be enlarged prevented this result? If, incredibly, the work becomes popular and prints are made of it and sold, to whom should the royalties be paid – to the author of this book, to Dr Mandelbrot or to the person who wrote the program?[252]

The question of whether a work created using a programmed computer is or is not a computer-generated work is significant because it affects the determination of the authorship and, consequently, the ownership of the copyright subsisting in the work. Of lesser import is the fact that the copyright subsisting in computer-generated works runs from the end of the calendar year in which the work was made and not by reference to the year in which the author dies.[253] Therefore, the duration of copyright in computer-generated works will be shorter than for other original works.

251 *See* Copyright, Designs and Patents Act 1988 s 9(3).

252 And what is the position if the author did not zoom in selectively and had simply printed the first diagram produced by the programmed computer?

253 Copyright, Designs and Patents Act 1988 s 12(7).

Figure 8.5 A computer-generated work?

Indirect human authorship had been recognised by the courts prior to the 1988 Act, even in the case of a programmed computer intended to select random letters for a competition. In *Express Newspapers plc v Liverpool Daily Post & Echo plc*,[254] the defendant claimed that grids of letters produced by computer for a newspaper competition could not be protected by copyright because the grids had no human author.[255] This was rejected by Whitford J, who said that the computer was no more than a tool with which the winning sequences of letters were produced using the instructions of a programmer. He said that the defence submission that there was no human author was as unrealistic as saying that a pen was the author of a work of literature.

There are two possibilities: first that the provisions in the Act concerning computer-generated works are something of a red herring, that there can never be such a thing, or, second, that the Act overrules the *Express Newspapers* case because it is inconsistent with the Act. If the idea of human authorship can be reconciled with lists of letters drawn randomly by a programmed computer, there seems to be little possibility of a work being considered to be 'computer-generated' within the meaning of the Act, because it is difficult to think of a work where the direct human contribution is less. On the other hand, if the concept of a computer-generated work within the meaning assigned to it by the Act is accepted then, as regards works produced with the aid of a computer, it still does not help to draw the line between works that are computer-generated and those that are not.[256] However, at first instance in *Nova Productions Ltd v Mazooma Games Ltd*,[257] Kitchin J accepted that the composite frames making up the visual aspects of a computer game were either created by the programmer, who created them using computer tools such as a mouse and on-screen tools such as notional brushes and pencils and the screen colour palette, or they were computer-generated works. If the latter were correct, the programmer was the author of the computer-generated works as he had made the arrangements necessary for their creation.

Circumvention of protection measures

Many works are made available in a form to which technical measures have been applied to prevent or restrict the use that may be made of the work. In the UK this was seen as something that needed controlling, especially when unauthorised copies of computer programs and computer games, video and sound recordings were being made. The response of many copyright owners whose works were issued to the public was to apply some form of encryption or copy-protection to prevent unauthorised copying. Soon after, others were making devices or software to be used to overcome this protection. Others were publishing information advising on how copy-protection could be overcome or bypassed. The reaction of the UK government was to include provisions in the Copyright, Designs and Patents Act 1988, as originally enacted, to give persons authorised to issue copies of copyright works in electronic form a civil right to bring proceedings against persons dealing with devices (or publishing information) to circumvent copy-protection applied to such copies.[258] It was treated as an infringement of the copyright subsisting in the work. There were a number of deficiencies in that legislation as it gave no remedy against a private individual using such devices or information to overcome copy-protection and there were no criminal penalties available against persons commercialising such devices. The provisions were also targeted at a situation where copies were made available on a physical medium and did not deal effectively where works were made available on the internet or by electronic transmission.

The European Community (now EU) saw the need to give more effective protection of wider scope, particularly in relation to works made available online. Directive 2001/29/

254 [1985] 1 WLR 1089. A similar example, concerning the making by programmed computer of lists of runners and riders for horse races, is the unreported case of *The Jockey Club v Rahim* (unreported) 22 July 1983.

255 A similar example, concerning the making by programmed computer of lists of runners and riders for horse races, is the unreported case of *The Jockey Club v Rahim* (unreported) 22 July 1983.

256 Tapper argues that the computer-generated works provisions are ill-conceived and should be abolished. Tapper, C. 'The Software Directive: A UK Perspective' in Lehmann, M. and Tapper, C. (eds) (1993) *A Handbook of European Software Law*, Clarendon Press, pp 143–161, at p 150.

257 [2006] RPC 14.

258 Section 296.

259 OJ L 167, 22.06.2001, p 10.

EC of the European Parliament and of the Council of 22 May 2001 on the harmonisation of certain aspects of copyright and related rights in the information society[259] required Member States to give adequate legal protection against the circumvention of effective technological measures designed to prevent or restrict unauthorised acts (Article 6). This was implemented in the UK, *inter alia*, by the Copyright and Related Rights Regulations 2003 which modified s 296 so as only to apply to computer programs and inserted new ss 296ZA to 296ZF to deal with other works and other subject matter which include rights in performances, the database right and the publication right. The reason for treating computer programs differently is that they were dealt with by the Directive on the legal protection of computer programs which is unaffected by the information society Directive, except in one respect not relevant here.

Briefly stated, the main provisions relating to the circumvention of technological measures apply to computer programs differently than to other works, potentially give a number of persons involved in the issuing of copies to the public or communication of the work to the public concurrent rights with the copyright owner or exclusive licensee. The act of circumvention is prohibited (with the exception of cryptography research). Dealing with devices and providing services to enable or facilitate over-coming technological measures are now criminal offences and there are also civil remedies for these activities and there is provision for protecting the permitted acts if the technological measures prejudice these. It is also notable that the provisions apply also to other rights related to copyright such as rights in performances, the database right and the publication right.

Computer programs

Section 296 now applies only in relation to computer programs to which a technical device has been applied, intended to prevent or restrict unauthorised acts that would otherwise infringe the copyright. This is clearly a wide meaning though not as explicit as the definition of 'effective' in relation technological measures applied to works other than computer programs.

The imposition of liability under the section is similar to that before but there are some differences. Being in possession for commercial purposes of '. . . any means the sole intended purpose of which is to facilitate the unauthorised removal or circumvention of the technical device' has been added to the acts of making for sale or hire, importing, distributing, selling, hiring, offering, exposing or advertising for sale or hire such means. As before, liability also extends to persons publishing information intended to enable or assist persons to remove or circumvent the technical device. Liability is, however, dependent upon the person concerned knowing or having reason to believe that means or information will be used to make infringing copies, as was previously the case.

Section 296 was designed to implement Article 7(1)(c) of the Directive on the legal protection of computer programs which requires Member States to provide appropriate remedies against persons who commit any act of:

> . . . putting into circulation, or the possession for commercial purposes of, any means the sole intended purpose of which is to facilitate the unauthorised removal or circumvention of any technical device which may have been applied to protect a computer program.

260 Contrast the provisions under Article 7(1)(a) and (b) of the Directive – prohibited acts of putting a copy into circulation or possession of a copy for commercial purposes both require the defendant to know or have reason to believe that the copy is an infringing copy.

261 [2010] FSR 36.

There is no reference to knowledge, unlike s 296.[260] This difference was noted in *Nintendo Co Ltd v Playables Ltd*.[261] However, applying the test under s 296, which is more favourable to a defendant, the judge did not think that the defendant had any realistic prospect of showing that he lacked knowledge, given the publicity surrounding devices to circumvent copy-protection. Part of Nintendo's protection system was the NLDF (Nintendo Logo

Data File) stored on Nintendo's game cards. This was a digitised version of the Nintendo logo made by an employee of the claimant in the course of his employment. In *Nintendo Co Ltd v Console PC Com Ltd*,[262] the defendant's devices contained copies of the NLDF. in addition to finding the defendant liable under s 296 (and s 296ZD in respect of works other than computer programs, such as graphic works), the judge accepted that the work in the process of creating the NLDF was sufficient to make it a work of copyright which had been infringed by the defendant.

The persons who have the right to bring an action have the same rights against the person making, etc. the means or publishing the information as does the copyright owner in respect of an infringement of the copyright. The identity of the persons having the right to bring an action are:

(a) a person issuing to the public copies of, or communicating to the public, the computer program to which the technical device has been applied;
(b) the copyright owner or his exclusive licensee, if he is not the person specified in (a);
(c) the owner or exclusive licensee of any intellectual property right in the technical device applied to the computer program.

The rights are concurrent and all have the same rights as regards delivery up or seizure as regards any means intended to remove or circumvent the technical device. As previously, the presumptions under ss 104 to 106 of the Act apply, as does the withdrawal of the privilege against self-incrimination in intellectual property matters.[263]

Other works – effective technological measures

Sections 296ZA to 296ZF apply where effective technological measures have been applied to a copyright work other than a computer program and, with necessary modifications, rights in performances, database right and publication right. The interpretation section for the purposes of ss 296ZA to 296ZE is section 296ZF. This defines 'technological measures' as 'any technology, device or component which is designed, in the normal course of its operation, to protect a copyright work other than a computer program'. Such measures are 'effective' if the use of the work is controlled by the copyright owner through:

(a) an access control or protection process such as encryption, scrambling or other transformation of the work, or
(b) a copy control mechanism,

which achieves the intended protection.

The measure is one which physically prevented copying but it did not have to be completely effective, per Floyd J in *Nintendo Co Ltd v Playables Ltd*,[264] but it must be more than a mere hindrance.[265]

Reference to protection of a work is to the prevention or restriction of acts not authorised by the copyright owner that are restricted by copyright and reference to use of a work does not extend to any use outside the scope of the acts restricted by copyright.

Under s 296ZA, a person who circumvents effective technological measures applied to a copyright work other than a computer program, knowing, or with reasonable grounds to know, that he is pursuing the objective of circumventing the measures is liable as if he had infringed copyright. The persons having the right to bring an action are as in the case of computer programs above and the presumptions apply also, as does the withdrawal of privilege against self-incrimination. These provisions also apply, with necessary changes, to rights in performances, the publication right and the database right.

An important exception is in s 296ZA(2) and applies where a person does anything circumventing effective technological measures for the purposes of research into cryptography.

262 [2011] EWHC 1458 (Ch).

263 Senior Courts Act 1981, s 72 and equivalent legislation for Scotland and Northern Ireland.

264 [2010] FSR 36.

265 Per Jacob LJ in *R v Higgs* [2008] FSR 34.

This does not give rise to a cause of action under s 296ZA unless by doing so, or in issuing information from that research, the rights of the copyright owner are prejudicially affected. This is not expressly limited to non-commercial research and there is no requirement that the act itself is fair dealing.

Criminal offences associated with technological measures

The act of circumventing technological measures does not, *per se*, give rise to criminal liability. However, under s 296ZB, a number of activities give rise to offences being committed. This states that a person commits an offence if he:

(a) manufactures for sale or hire, or
(b) imports otherwise than for his private and domestic use, or
(c) in the course of a business –
    (i) sells or lets for hire, or
    (ii) offers or exposes for sale or hire, or
    (iii) advertises for sale or hire, or
    (iv) possesses, or
    (v) distributes, or
(d) distributes otherwise than in the course of a business to such an extent as to affect prejudicially the copyright owner,

any device, product or component which is primarily designed, produced, or adapted for the purpose of enabling or facilitating the circumvention of effective technological measures.

A person also commits an offence if he provides, promotes, advertises or markets:

(a) in the course of a business, or
(b) otherwise than in the course of a business to such an extent as to affect prejudicially the copyright owner,

a service the purpose of which is to enable or facilitate the circumvention of effective technological measures.

The offences are triable either way and the maximum penalty, if tried summarily, is a fine not exceeding the statutory maximum and/or imprisonment for a period not exceeding three months. On conviction on indictment, the maximum penalty is a fine and/or imprisonment not exceeding two years. There is no requirement for *mens rea* but it is a defence for the accused to show that he did not know and had no reasonable grounds for believing that the device, product, component or service enabled or facilitated the circumvention of effective technological measures. When one considers that the maximum penalties for the criminal offences under s 107 have been increased to a maximum of ten years' imprisonment and/or a fine, it is strange to think that the penalties under s 296ZB are significantly less. Presumably, in appropriate situations, a person committing offences under s 296ZB could be charged with inciting or aiding and abetting someone to carry out an offence under s 107 if such offences flow from the circumvention of technological measures.

It should be noted that there is no equivalent offence in relation to the circumvention of copy-protection of computer programs and in respect of the database right, publication right and rights in performances.

Activities of the law enforcement agencies and intelligence services in the interests of national security or for the prevention or detection of crime, the investigation of offences or the conduct of prosecutions are excluded from criminal liability. There are provisions for search warrants and forfeiture under s 296ZC as apply to unauthorised decoders under ss 297B to 297D.

The scope of these provisions was considered by the Court of Appeal in *R v Higgs*.[266] Mr Higgs, had been convicted of 26 offences under section 296ZB for selling 'modchips', installing them into computer games consoles and selling games consoles to which these modchips had been fitted. Manufacturers of computer games consoles, such as the Sony Playstation, Nintendo Gamecube and the Microsoft X-Box, embed with the consoles codes that will only allow a game on CD-ROM to be played if it contains a corresponding code. Normally, these codes are not copied if copies are made of the genuine CD-ROMs. The modchips overcame this protection and allowed 'pirate' copies of games on CD-ROMs to be played on the games consoles.

The prosecution had alleged that, by selling modchips and modified consoles, Mr Higgs was encouraging and exploiting a market for pirate games. No attempt had been made to prove that by using the modified consoles to play a game from a pirate CD-ROM itself involved any infringement of copyright.

The Court of Appeal confirmed that the 'technological measures' under section 296ZF should be narrowly construed and applied to measures which denied access to a copyright work or restricted a person's ability to make copies where access to the work had been granted. Merely having a general deterrent or discouraging effect was not enough. Infringing copies could be made without circumventing the technological measures but those copies could not be used without such circumvention. The Court of Appeal accepted that playing pirate games involved making transient copies of the works (such as images and sounds) and this infringed copyright. Had the prosecution case been that using a console to which a modchip had been fitted itself involved an infringement of copyright the convictions would have been likely to be upheld. The Court of Appeal did not give leave to the prosecution to appeal to the House of Lords but did certify a question of law of general public importance, being:

> Do the provisions of section 296ZF of the Copyright, Designs and Patents Act 1988 in relation to 'effective technological measures' apply to devices incorporated into computer games consoles and computer games which do not prevent counterfeit copies being made of such games but which do prevent the counterfeit copies from being played on games consoles?

It is important to understand that the appeal succeeded because the prosecution case was flawed rather than being a reflection of any deficiency in the scope of the offences under section 296ZB and the meaning of effective technological measures under section 296ZF.

Subsequently, in *R v Gilham*,[267] the Court of Appeal had the opportunity to reconsider the question as to whether playing a game on DVD or CD-ROM involved copying a substantial part of the game. In that case, the defendant supplied 'modchips' which, when installed on games consoles allowed pirate copies of games on DVD or CD-ROM to be played. This overcame the technological measures designed to prevent the playing of pirate copies of games. Consoles for games usually contained a code and the game on DVD or CD-ROM also contained a corresponding code which would not be copied if a duplicate copy of the game was made, thus preventing the use of pirate copies in the normal run of things. The modchips overcame this protection. As, at any given time, only a small amount of the data on a DVD or CD-ROM was loaded into the console's RAM (random access memory) it was argued that there was no infringement as a substantial part of the game as a whole was never in the RAM at the same time.[268]

The Court of Appeal rejected this 'little and often' approach, pointing out that s 17 of the Act extends to transient copying, preferring the views of Jacob LJ in *Higgs* (obiter) and Laddie J in *Sony Computer Entertainment Inc v Ball*.[269] The fact that only a small part is in the RAM at a given time makes no difference as a substantial part of the game is copied during the period of time the game is being played.[270] In any event, however, the Court of Appeal in *Gilham* found copying of artistic works such as drawings of characters such as Lara Croft.

266 [2008] FSR 34.

267 [2010] ECDR 5.

268 Typically, the RAM would only hold around 3 per cent of the whole game at a moment in time.

269 [2005] FSR 9.

270 The judgment casts even more doubt on Kitchen J's views on the equivalent point in relation to transmissions of live football matches in *Football Association Premier League* v QC *Leisure (No 2)* [2008] FSR 32.

Separate civil remedy in respect of making, importing, etc.

In some cases, acts that fall within the criminal offences under s 296ZB may also attract civil liability. Civil liability under s 296ZD applies where:

(a) effective technological measures have been applied to a copyright work other than a computer program; and
(b) a person . . . manufactures, imports, distributes, sells or lets for hire, offers or exposes for sale or hire, advertises for sale or hire, or has in his possession for commercial purposes any device, product or component, or provides services which –
   (i) are promoted, advertised or marketed for the purpose of the circumvention of, or
   (ii) have only a limited commercially significant purpose or use other than to circumvent, or
   (iii) are primarily designed, produced, adapted or performed for the purpose of enabling or facilitating the circumvention of,

those measures.

As with ss 296 and 296ZA, concurrent rights are provided for as are rights of delivery up or seizure and the presumptions apply. Liability under s 296ZD also extends to rights in performances, the publication right and the database right. The privilege against self-incrimination is withdrawn as is usual with certain intellectual property proceedings. One difference to the other civil remedies in relation to overcoming protection measures is that the test for the unavailability of damages for innocent infringement is slightly changed and the test is whether the defendant knew or had reason to believe that his acts enabled or facilitated an infringement of copyright.

271 [2010] FSR 36.

In *Nintendo Co Ltd* v *Playables Ltd*,[271] the judge, Floyd J, noted that breach of s 296ZD was a tort of strict liability, subject only to a partial defence as to remedies, as noted above. Floyd J also held that the fact that a device which has the purpose of circumventing effective technological measures also has possible non-infringing uses, such as playing home made games, is not a defence. Although he accepted that the claimant's games were computer programs, Floyd J held that s 296ZD still applied (in addition to s 296) because the games contained other works including graphic works, which were also protected by the effective technological measures. He granted summary judgment under s 296ZD (and s 296) to the claimant.

Remedy where effective technological measures prevent permitted acts

If copyright owners prevent access to their works by, for example, encryption, scrambling or password systems, this could have the effect of prejudicing the permitted acts. For example, a copyright owner could make his work available to the public by subscription on terms where copying for the purposes of fair dealing for private study or certain educational uses are prohibited. To overcome potential conflicts, s 296ZE provides for voluntary measures or agreements enabling a person to carry out a permitted act. Where a person is prevented from carrying out a permitted act he, or a representative of a class of such persons, may issue a notice of complaint to the Secretary of State who may give directions to the copyright owner or exclusive licensee.

The purpose of the directions may be to establish whether a relevant voluntary measure or agreement exists or where an appropriate measure or agreement does not exist, requiring the copyright owner or exclusive licensee to make available the means of carrying out the permitted act that is the subject of the complaint. This imposes a duty owed to the complainant and failure to act is treated as a breach of statutory duty. Directions must be in writing and may be varied or revoked by subsequent directions.

These provisions do not apply where a copyright work is made available to the public on agreed contractual terms such that members of the public can access the work at a place and time individually chosen by them. They also apply, with necessary changes, to rights in performances, the publication right and the database right but do not apply to computer programs.

A new Schedule 5A lists the permitted acts covered by s 296ZE. Significantly, permitted acts not included are fair dealing for criticism or review and fair dealing for reporting current events and the permitted act of incidental inclusion.

Electronic rights management information

A particular concern where works are made available in digital form and may, for example, be downloaded from a website or network, is that any information such as the identity of the copyright owner and what acts are authorised in respect of the work may be removed and the work then circulated or communicated to the public in that modified form. Of course, this does not prevent copyright being infringed but the danger is that third parties who access the work subsequently without such information may believe that they can copy it freely or deal with it how they wish.

Where a work is placed on the internet by or on behalf of the copyright owner and is freely available for others to access, to take an example, it is safe to assume, in the absence of any notice to the contrary, that accessing it online does not infringe copyright on the basis that the copyright owner has impliedly licensed this by his act of making it available in this way. It is not safe to assume, however, that a permanent copy of the work may be made whether by saving it onto a disk or printing it out without infringing copyright. A prudent copyright owner who wants to make his works freely available online would do well to place a prominent notice on the work stating that he is the copyright owner, when the work was first created and, where relevant, the identity of the author of the work.[272] He may also want to state what may and may not be done in respect of the work: for example, to state that private individuals may make copies for their own personal use only and must not modify the work nor remove the notice.

Recital 57 to Directive 2001/29 of the European Parliament and of the Council of 22 May 2001 on the harmonisation of certain aspects of copyright and related rights in the information society states that there is a:

> . . . danger that illegal activities might be carried out in order to remove or alter the electronic copyright-management information attached to [a work or other subject-matter], or otherwise to distribute, import for distribution, broadcast, communicate to the public or make available to the public works or other protected subject-matter from which such information has been removed without authority.

Article 7 of the Directive therefore required Member States to provide adequate legal protection for electronic rights management information. Rights management information was described in Article 7 as any information provided by rightholders which identifies the work or other subject matter, the author or any other rightholder, or information about the terms and conditions of use of the work or other subject matter, and any numbers or codes that represent such information.

The Directive was implemented in the UK by the Copyright and Related Rights Regulations 2003,[273] s 296ZG of which contains the provisions equivalent to Article 7 of the Directive. 'Rights management information' is defined in similar though not identical

272 The moral right to be identified as author (or director of a film) might be engaged.

273 SI 2003/2498.

terms to the Directive, although any differences should be of no consequence. Section 296ZG(7)(b) uses the following definition:

> . . . any information provided by the copyright owner or the holder of any right under copyright which identifies the work, the author, the copyright owner or the holder of any intellectual property rights, or information about the terms and conditions of use of the work, and any numbers or codes that represent such information.

Section 296ZG(8) states that the relevant provisions of s 296ZG apply also, with necessary changes, to rights in performances, the database right and publication right. There is no definition of the entire phrase 'electronic rights management information' but this can be taken to mean rights management information applied to electronic copies of a work. This might be where the copy is on a computer disk, including on a server computer linked to the internet, CD-ROM or DVD, etc.

A person who knowingly and without authority removes or alters electronic rights management information knowing or having reason to believe that by doing so he or she is enabling, facilitating or concealing an infringement of copyright is liable as if that person had infringed the copyright subsisting in the work. That liability is owed to the person issuing copies to the public or communicating the work to the public or the copyright owner or his exclusive licensee, all of whom have concurrent rights. For these purposes 'electronic' has the same wide meaning as in s 178.

Furthermore, a person will similarly be liable if he knowingly and without authority distributes, imports for distribution or communicates to the public copies of a copyright work from which such information, associated with the copies or appearing in connection with the communication to the public of the work, has been removed or altered without authority. The form of knowledge required is that the person knows or has reason to believe that by so doing he is inducing, facilitating or concealing an infringement of copyright. The usual presumptions apply and the privilege against self-incrimination in intellectual property proceedings is withdrawn.

Satellite broadcasting

The wireless broadcasting of television, films and the like by satellite raises fundamental issues of copyright, such as where the broadcast is made from. For example, is it made from the earth station or from the satellite? This will affect the identity of the national rules of copyright law that will apply. How does the broadcaster control the reception of his broadcast in other countries? According to the 'Bogsch' theory, the broadcaster would need to obtain the necessary right in each of the countries within the area of reception of the broadcast (its 'footprint').[274] Another difficulty is controlling the capture and re-transmission of a wireless broadcast without permission. A further problem relates to the sale of unauthorised decoders used to receive encrypted broadcasts and 'smartcards' for use with decoders.

A satellite broadcast is taken to be made from the place where, under the control and responsibility of the person making the wireless broadcast, the programme-carrying signals are introduced into an uninterrupted chain of communication (including, in the case of a satellite transmission, the chain leading to the satellite and down towards the earth).[275] Subsequently communication to the public, for example, by re-broadcasting, is a restricted act and will infringe without the licence of the copyright owner.[276] There are special provisions for determining the place of making broadcasts in the case of satellite broadcasts originating from a country outside the EEA not providing an adequate level of protection and for determining the maker of such broadcasts.[277]

274 Accepted by the Austrian Supreme Court in *Re Satellite Television Broadcasting* [1995] FSR 73. This case pre-dated Austria's accession to the EU.

275 Copyright, Designs and Patents Act 1988 s 6(4) as modified by the Copyright and Related Rights Regulations 1996, SI 1996/2967 and the Copyright and Related Rights Regulations 2003, SI 2003/2498. The former regulations implemented, *inter alia*, the Council Directive 93/83/EEC of 27 September 1993 on the coordination of certain rules concerning copyright and rights related to copyright applicable to satellite broadcasting and cable re-transmission, OJ L 248, 06.10.1993, p 15.

276 Copyright, Designs and Patents Act 1988 s 20.

277 Copyright, Designs and Patents Act 1988 s 6A, inserted by the Copyright and Related Rights Regulations 1996, discussed in more detail in Chapter 3.

Some organisations make encrypted transmissions which require a decoder to view the programme. It is an offence to make, import, sell or let for hire or offer or expose for sale or hire any unauthorised decoder; to be in possession of, for commercial purposes, an unauthorised decoder; to install, maintain or replace for commercial purposes or to advertise or otherwise promote for sale or hire an unauthorised decoder for commercial purposes under s 297A.[278] A transmission is any programme included in a broadcasting service provided from a place in the UK or other Member State or an information society service provided from a place in the UK or other Member State (the latter would cover, for example, a subscription service information made available online and accessed only by identification number and password). The maximum penalty on conviction on indictment is now a maximum of ten years' imprisonment and/or a fine.[279] It is a defence to show that the person charged did not know and had no reasonable ground for believing that the decoder was unauthorised. A 'decoder' is defined as any apparatus designed or adapted to enable (on its own or with other apparatus) an encrypted transmission to be decoded. Apparatus is defined widely as including any device, component or electronic data (including software).[280] A decoder is unauthorised if it is designed or adapted to enable an encrypted transmission, or any service of which it forms part, to be accessed in an intelligible form without payment of the fee (however imposed) which the person making the transmission, or on whose behalf it is made, charges for accessing the transmission or service (whether by the circumvention of any conditional access technology related to the transmission or service or by any other means). Conditional access technology is any technical measure or arrangement whereby access to encrypted transmissions in an intelligible form is made conditional on prior individual authorisation. There are provisions for search warrants and forfeiture under ss 297B to 297D.

Directive 98/84/EC of the European Parliament and of the Council on the legal protection of services based on, or consisting of, conditional access[281] uses the term 'illicit device' meaning '. . . any equipment or software designed or adapted to give access to a protected service in an intelligible form without the authorisation of the service provider'.[282]

In *Football Association Premier League Ltd* v *QC Leisure (No 2)*,[283] a host of issues were raised by the importation and use in the UK of decoders that had been provided to licensees in other countries to enable subscribers to watch Premier League football matches. The decoders were delivered to the licensees on the understanding that they were not to be used by persons outside the licensed territories. Some of these 'non-UK' decoders found their way into the UK where they were used, typically in bars and public houses. A question arose where the decoders were illicit devices under the Directive as they originated from the claimants. Kitchen J thought that they were not but referred a question to the Court of Justice for a preliminary ruling on this and many other matters.

Before the insertion of s 297A, although the dishonest reception of a programme included in a broadcasting service carried criminal penalties under s 297, there were only civil remedies against any person responsible for making, importing, selling or letting for hire, etc. unauthorised decoders and this provision had caused considerable problems of interpretation. In *BBC Enterprises Ltd* v *Hi-Tech Xtravision Ltd*,[284] the claimant provided a satellite television service known as 'BBC TV Europe'. The defendant sold decoders at a price considerably lower than that charged by the distributors authorised by the claimant. The offence of fraudulently receiving a programme included in a broadcast or cable programme service in s 297 of the Copyright, Designs and Patents Act 1988, was held to be inapplicable for reasons of jurisdiction. The claimant therefore based his claim on s 298 of the Act, which controls apparatus, devices or information to assist persons to receive programmes or other transmissions when they are not entitled to do so.[285] In the Chancery Division, it was held that the unauthorised reception of waves in the ether caused by wireless telegraphic transmission did not represent an interference with property rights at common law and that no one had rights of property in those wireless transmission waves.

278 Inserted by the Broadcasting Act 1990 s 179 but substituted by the Conditional Access (Unauthorised Decoders) Regulations 2000, SI 2000/1175. These Regulations implement Directive 98/84/EC of the European Parliament and of the Council of 20 November 1998 on the legal protection of services based on, or consisting of, conditional access, OJ L 320, 28.11.1998, p 54.

279 Increased from a maximum of a fine not exceeding level 5 on the standard scale by the Copyright, etc. and Trade Marks (Offences and Enforcement) Act 2002.

280 Copyright, Designs and Patents Act 1988 s 297A(4) contains definitions.

281 OJ L 320, 28.11.1998, p 54.

282 Article 2(e).

283 [2008] FSR 32.

284 [1990] Ch 609.

285 This section was substituted by the Conditional Access (Unauthorised Decoders) Regulations 2000, SI 2000/1175 to bring it in line with the changes to s 297A.

Scott J suggested that a right to prohibit reception had to be found outside s 298 before it was possible to say that persons were not entitled to receive programmes and it is not an infringement of copyright to receive a broadcast. Therefore, the foreign viewers of 'BBC TV Europe' could not be described as persons who were 'not entitled to do so' within s 298.[286] Scott J was of the opinion that s 298 was inept legislation and that the legislature was under a misapprehension as to the law.

The Court of Appeal reversed the decision in the Chancery Division. While the court accepted that the right involved was probably not a proprietary right, it was held that the claimant's claim disclosed a good cause of action, rejecting the interpretation of s 298 suggested by Scott J.[287] Staughton LJ said that s 298 contained both the right and the remedy. The person who seeks to charge for encrypted transmissions has the right not to have others making apparatus designed for use by persons not authorised by him to receive the programmes. The defendant's appeal was dismissed by the House of Lords, which held that providers of satellite programmes broadcast from the UK are protected by s 298[288] and are thus entitled to collect charges for the reception of these programmes, and this covered, indirectly, persons receiving the transmissions in other countries that lie within the 'footprint' of the transmissions.[289]

As amended, s 298 gives rights and remedies to a person who makes charges for reception of programmes included in a broadcasting service, sends encrypted transmissions of any other description or provides conditional access services, where the place from which the service is provided from (or transmitted from in the case of encrypted transmissions) is the UK or any other Member State. That person has the same rights and remedies as a copyright owner in respect of infringement of copyright against any person who (i) makes, imports, distributes, sells or lets for hire, offers or exposes for sale or hire, or advertises for sale or hire, (ii) has in his possession for commercial purposes, or (iii) installs, maintains or replaces for commercial purposes, any apparatus designed or adapted to enable or assist persons to access the programmes or other transmissions or circumvent conditional access technology related to the programmes or other transmissions when they are not entitled to do so. The same applies in respect of a person who publishes or otherwise promotes by means of commercial communications any information which is calculated to enable or assist persons to access the programmes or other transmissions or circumvent conditional access technology related to the programmes or other transmissions when they are not entitled to do so.

Where s 97(1) applies (damages not available where infringement innocent) but the reference to the defendant not knowing or having reason to believe that copyright subsisted in the work shall be construed as a reference to his not knowing or having reason to believe that his acts infringed the rights conferred by this section. The right against self-incrimination is withdrawn (as it generally is for intellectual property) and other relevant provisions apply as they do to copyright infringement.

The definitions for the purposes of s 298 are generally as those given in s 297A and conditional access service means services comprising the provision of conditional access technology.

The general reference to the UK and other Member States extends to protection to broadcasters and information society service providers throughout the European Union. A potential problem that the provisions before amendment were limited to and thereby favoured UK organisations was highlighted in *British Sky Broadcasting Group Ltd v Lyons*[290] where the defendant imported from Germany and sold in the UK unauthorised smartcards[291] (cards containing algorithms to allow a decoder to unscramble encrypted signals). He raised a number of interesting defences, all of which were rejected by Aldous J, who described him as a parasite.

Persons selling unauthorised decoders may commit other offences. For example, in *R v Maxwell-King*,[292] the accused sold devices which, when fitted to 'set-top boxes' allowed

---

286 *The Times*, 28 November 1989.

287 [1990] Ch 609.

288 This was before the changes made to s 298 by the Conditional Access (Unauthorised Decoders) Regulations 2000, SI 2000/1175

289 [1991] 3 WLR 1.

290 [1995] FSR 357.

291 The Irish High Court considered that a smartcard was a computer program in *News Datacom Ltd v Satellite Decoding Systems* [1995] FSR 201.

292 [2001] 2 Cr App Rep (S) 28.

persons to receive all services provided without paying for some of them. He was convicted of offences of incitement to commit an offence under s 3 of the Computer Misuse Act 1990, the unauthorised modification offence. Now, it is unlikely that this Act would be used, especially as the criminal offences under s 297A carry a maximum of ten years' imprisonment and/or a fine. In *Maxwell-King*, the offender was sentenced to four months' imprisonment but the Court of Appeal considered that a custodial sentence was not justified for someone of previous good character.[293] However, subsequently, the US applied for extradition of Maxwell-King on the basis of allegations involving the importation into the US of unauthorised decoders. A judge sent his case to the Secretary of State for a decision as to whether he should be extradited and Maxwell-King appealed to the Divisional Court under s 103 of the Extradition Act 2003.[294] His appeal on the basis of double jeopardy and the passage of time was unsuccessful.[295]

Scientific discoveries, genetic sequences and formulae

In this increasingly technological world, where the means of production and dissemination are more widely available than ever before, freeing authors from the control of publishers, there may be more emphasis on invention, innovation and original thought than the means of expression and commercial reproduction. An important factor is that copyright has now moved into the technological field and the shift of power from publishers to authors may serve as a catalyst for change in emphasis. Take, for example, a person who devises an original mathematical formula. It can be used to generate valuable information such as the chances of a particular horse winning a race. Or perhaps a scientist has by careful experimentation discovered a new aerodynamic model for turbulent flow of fluid over a surface which can be expressed mathematically. A geneticist determines the genetic sequence of a viral infection. Are such things the subject of copyright protection, and should they be?

We will see in Part Four of this book that certain things are expressly excluded from the grant of a patent, as such. These include a discovery, scientific theory or mathematical method, a scheme, rule or method for performing a mental act, playing a game, or doing business, or a program for a computer.[296] Practical applications of such things may, however, be patentable. For example, a scientific discovery cannot form the basis of a patent, but a new industrial process based on that theory can be patented. What the patent system cannot protect is the theory itself. Apart from anything else, the protection of theories and the like by patents would give the proprietor far too strong a monopoly position. In the light of this, should copyright protect something that the patent system does not?

Consider the case of a new formula used to calculate the size of a timber beam to support a roof over a building. Variables used by the formula might include the span (s), the horizontal spacing between beams (h), the maximum roof load (including wind and snow loads) (w), the strength of timber (t), the slenderness ratio (the ratio of the depth of the beam compared to its height) (r), the factor of safety (F) and so forth. The formula[297] might look something like this:

$$d = F \times \int (f(s) + f(h)) \div f(t) + 0.235 \times F\sum \partial w \div r$$

where $f()$ denotes some function of the variable enclosed in brackets.

The formula is likely to be the result of a significant amount of theoretical work supported by empirical research. Once it has been developed and tested, its application to practical situations will probably be a fairly simple matter, though requiring mathematical skills. Imagine that a person other than the devisor of the equation decides to use the formula in a computer program to design timber beams. The program is used to create a

---

293 The devices were not very successful.

294 *Maxwell-King* v *Government of the United States of America* [2006] EWHC 3033 (Admin).

295 On the double jeopardy point, it was accepted that the acts complained of by the US were not the same as those for which he had been convicted in the UK. Extradition was not unjust or oppressive by reason of the passage of time. He had known for some time that extradition was being sought. It appears that, along with an employee, he was convicted in a Florida court of importing devices primarily intended to be used for unauthorised decryption of satellite television services under §605(e)(4) of 47 USC (Telegraphs, Telephones and Radiotelegraphs). Maxwell-King was sentenced to time already served in custody awaiting trial, three years' probation, community service and ordered to pay over $4 million restitution.

296 Patents Act 1977 s 1(2).

297 This formula is completely fictional.

whole set of tables by which a person wishing to determine an appropriate size for timber beams to span a roof can quickly and easily do so.

Several questions fall to be considered. Is the formula a work of copyright in its own right? Is the set of tables a work of copyright? If so, does the deviser of the formula have any rights in the tables? Taking those questions *seriatim*:

1 Is the formula a work of copyright? If it is accepted that skill and judgment have been expended in the creation of the formula, there seems to be no doubt that the formula is a work of copyright, being an original literary work. Aldous J considered that there was no reason why this should not be so in *Bookmakers' Afternoon Greyhound Services Ltd v Wilf Gilbert (Staffordshire) Ltd*[298] in the context of a formula for calculating forecast dividends for greyhound races. There are authorities which suggest other-wise. In *Exxon Corp v Exxon Insurance Consultants International Ltd*,[299] the single word 'EXXON' was held not to be an original literary work, even though significant market research had been undertaken in deciding a new corporate name. In that case, great reliance was placed on the quote by Davey LJ in *Hollinrake v Truswell*[300] to the effect that a literary work should 'afford either information or instruction, or pleasure, in the form of literary enjoyment'. It is submitted that that approach is no longer valid, primarily because of the extension of literary copyright to computer programs. An object code program installed in a silicon chip and invisible to the naked eye would surely fail Davey LJ's test, yet such a program is undoubtedly protected by copyright.[301] The better view, therefore, is that a formula that is a result of skill and judgment is a work of copyright. This accords also with the approach taken by Aldous J in *Microsense Systems Ltd v Control Systems Technology Ltd*[302] where he accepted that there was an arguable case that a list of mnemonics was protected by copyright, at least by virtue of the skill and judgment in devising the functions to be represented by the mnemonics. However, this case was before the Directive on the legal protection of computer programs which states that programming languages, in as much as they consist of ideas and principles, are not protected by copyright.

2 Is the set of tables a work of copyright? Returning again to the *Bookmakers' Afternoon Greyhound Services* case, the claimant submitted that, in determining whether forecasts such as 'BAGS Forecast £2.25' derived using a formula were themselves works of copyright, the skill and judgment in devising the formula should be taken into account. Aldous J did not accept that proposition. He said:

> A person who takes a work, whether it be a formula, a book or a poem, and uses it to produce another work, will only obtain copyright in that other work, if the skill, labour and judgment used to produce that other work are sufficient.[303]

Therefore, the creation of the derivative work must itself require skill and judgment, independent from that of the first work. Making calculations using a formula might require little skill beyond a basic understanding of arithmetic, such as working out a percentage of a number, or it may require advanced mathematical skills: for example, requiring proficiency in differential calculus.[304] One problem with this approach is where the formula has been incorporated in a computer program. Here it may be a question of considering the skill and judgment of the person using the program. If he simply enters factual data the resultant output may not be protected by copyright as in the *Bookmakers'* case, *a fortiori* where only a single or small number of calculations are performed. A table is itself a work of copyright and protected as such, provided that there is skill and judgment in its making. This will be so in deriving a set of tables to design timber beams. The person setting about the task will have to decide on the ranges of parameters, the increments in those parameters, how to design the layout of the tables for ease of use, etc. A table or set of tables could also be viewed as a database,

298 [1994] FSR 723. Unfortunately, the formula is not reproduced in the law report.

299 [1981] 3 All ER 241.

300 [1894] 3 Ch 420.

301 Either in its own right or as an adaptation of the source code program.

302 (Unreported) 17 July 1991.

303 [1994] FSR 723 at 735.

304 Aldous J did not consider the fact that performing the calculations in the *Bookmakers'* case required 'a certain amount of education', meaning that the results were protected by copyright.

subject to copyright and/or the database right, whether the table resides in software form or is printed out on paper. The database right may be particularly useful as it overcomes the need for skill and judgment by requiring a substantial investment only.[305]

3 Does the deviser of a formula have any rights in the result of using it? If the formula is a work of copyright and the person using it performs any of the restricted acts without the licence of the owner of the copyright in the formula, there will be an infringement of its copyright. This would be so if the formula were expressed in a computer program, and it would seem to be sensible to hold the same if the formula is not directly expressed but is broken down into a number of individual calculations on the basis of non-literal copying. However, if a person simply uses the formula without reproducing it, there can be no infringement. The formula simply is the tool by which the calculated results are obtained in the same way as a pen or paintbrush is used to create a new work. In this respect the situation is analogous to the creation of random numbers by a programmed computer in *Express Newspapers plc v Liverpool Daily Post and Echo plc*.[306]

Similar considerations ought to apply to other technical discoveries such as a hitherto unknown chemical reaction[307] or a genetic sequence.[308] Provided that there is skill and judgment in their discovery or creation, and they have been expressed in an appropriate manner (for example, by being written down), there is no reason why they should not be protected by copyright. Copyright will not, however, prevent the use of such things by others. All that is controlled are the specific acts restricted by copyright. Nor does copyright prevent the independent creation of the same or a similar work. If the discovery or whatever is published, perhaps in an academic journal, a limited amount of copying may be permitted in the course of developing a practical application of the discovery, on the basis of the fair dealing provisions or by virtue of an implied licence. Public interest may also be an issue. Of course, where the discovery has not been published, it may be protected by the law of breach of confidence.

305 *See* the section on Databases, earlier in this chapter.

306 [1985] 1 WLR 1089.

307 Such as in *Merrell Dow Pharmaceuticals Inc v HN Norton & Co Ltd* [1996] RPC 76, where a patent for a chemical reaction in the human liver was held invalid.

308 It has been suggested that DNA sequences are protected by copyright provided they are sufficiently long: Laddie *et al.* (1995) *The Modern Law of Copyright* (2nd edn) Butterworths, p 859.

Summary

Computer programs are protected by copyright as literary works. Preparatory design material is also a form of literary work but, according to the Directive, preparatory design material is part of a computer program.

Computer programs are protected by copyright:

- provided they are original in the sense that they are the author's own intellectual creation;
- whether they are in object code or source code;
- whether copying is literal or non-literal.

Non-literal copying is a difficult concept to apply in practice. The US focuses on idea/ expression and has a three stage test (abstraction, filtration and comparison).

In the UK, it seems the architecture of a computer program is protected; it appears that writing new software to emulate the operation and functions of an existing program does not, without more, infringe. The observing, studying and testing exception to infringement is important in this respect as is the denial of protection for underlying ideas and principles.

In addition to the usual restricted acts, copying and making an adaptation are particularly important for computer programs.

The specific permitted acts that apply in relation to lawful users of computer programs are:

- decompilation;
- making back-up copies;

- observing, studying and testing;
- copying or adapting necessary for lawful use.

Databases, whether electronic or otherwise, may be protected in two ways, by copyright and by the *sui generis* database right. The definition of database is important and is the same for both rights. Both copyright in a database and the database right are without prejudice to any rights, if any, in the contents of the database:

- Copyright databases must be the author's intellectual creation (the protection extends, potentially or perhaps even exclusively, to the structure of the database).
- The database right is intended to protect a substantial investment:
  - in obtaining, verifying or presenting the contents of the database
  - in terms of human, technical or financial resources.

The investment in creating the contents of the database does not fall within the meaning of 'obtaining' – instead, this refers to the investment in seeking out pre-existing materials. Thus football fixture lists, for example, do not appear to be protected by the database right. It is possible that such lists may be protected by database copyright though this point has not been finally decided.

Literary, dramatic, musical or artistic computer-generated works, generated in circumstances such that there is no human author, are protected by copyright but for a shorter duration. The concept of a computer-generated work is a difficult one to apply in practice.

Remedies are available in respect of the circumvention of copy-protection measures in respect of:

- computer programs, which have their own separate provisions as to the circumvention of technical devices designed to prevent or restrict unauthorised infringing acts;
- other forms of works, for which criminal penalties are also available in some circumstances;
- making, importing, distributing, etc. devices or providing services to overcome effective technological measures is a tort of strict liability.

There is a remedy where effective technological measures prevent the permitted acts.

Electronic rights management information is protected. This information may include details of the copyright author and owner, or holder of other IPR, and terms and conditions on the use of the work.

Remedies exist in relation to devices designed to overcome protection of pay to view broadcast services. These include criminal penalties.

Discussion questions

1 What is the scope of protection for computer programs in the UK? Discuss the extent to which a person may go in writing a new computer program designed to emulate the operation and functions of an existing program without infringing copyright.

2 Describe the permitted acts which apply expressly to computer programs. Consider, in particular, what is and is not permitted by the 'decompilation right'.

3 Think of examples of databases which may be protected: (a) by copyright; (b) by the database right; (c) by both copyright and the database right; (d) neither copyright nor the database right. Ignore any rights subsisting in the contents of the databases.

4 The Court of Justice rulings in the *British Horseracing* case and the football fixture list cases fail to give effect to the objectives of the Directive on the legal protection of databases in

that valuable databases which resulted from substantial investment are left without protection under the *sui generis* database right. Discuss.

5   Do you think the provisions on circumvention of effective technological measures and illicit decoders are over-complex and little understood by counsel and judges?

Selected further reading

Borghi, M., 'Chasing copyright infringement in the streaming landscape', [2011] *International Review of Intellectual Property and Competition Law*, 316 (considers streaming technology and the temporary reproduction right).

Griffin, J., 'An historical solution to the legal challenges posed by peer-to-peer file-sharing and digital rights management information' [2010] *Communications Law*, 78 (an interesting discussion of the way in which UK and US copyright law moved in favour of the rightholder and calls for a system whereby the merit of the alleged infringing work should be an important issue rather than just the economic loss to the rightholder).

Perry, M. and Margoni, T., 'From music tracks to Google maps: who owns computer-generated works?' [2010] *Computer Law and Security Review*, 621 (looks at ownership of computer-generated works and compares the common law approach in Canada with the statutory approach in the UK and considers who should be rewarded for computer-generated works).

Samartzi, V., 'Optimal vs sub-optimal use of DRM protected works' [2011] *European Intellectual Property Review*, 517 (looks at private copying, DRMs and the circumvention of technological measures).

Tan, C., 'Revisiting the database Directive' [2011] *Entertainment Law Review*, 127 (a case comment on the *Football Dataco* v *Britten* case and the questions referred to the Court of justice).

Rights in performances 9

Introduction

A well-known soprano gives a live performance of an operatic aria by Mozart. Unknown to the soprano, a member of the audience makes a recording of the performance on a magnetic tape and then later makes copies which he sells to the public without the singer's permission. Under copyright law, there is nothing that can be done to prevent the sale of the recordings of the performance. The music and lyrics are out of copyright, so there is no infringement of the musical or literary work. Indeed, the only relevance of copyright law is that the person who made the recording without permission owns the copyright in it as a sound recording. Had the singer agreed a recording contract with a publisher, the publisher would be unable to use copyright law to prevent the sale of the unauthorised recordings, which have a separate and independent copyright to the publisher's recording. The authorised and unauthorised master recordings are coterminous, and there is no link between them associated with the acts restricted by the copyright in the publisher's sound recording. There may still be problems even if the music is protected by copyright, because the owner of that copyright may be reluctant to pursue a claim for infringement with respect to one performance.

This state of affairs was clearly untenable and this 'loophole' in copyright law was closed by the law relating to performances. However, this area of law only gained the status of a fully-fledged intellectual property right under the Copyright, Designs and Patents Act 1988. The first law on the subject was the Dramatic and Musical Performers' Protection Act 1925, which provided criminal penalties in respect of the making of recordings of dramatic and musical performances without consent. This Act was basically re-enacted in 1958, and by the Performers' Protection Act 1963 the provisions were extended to all the original works of copyright, that is literary, dramatic, musical and artistic works.[1] The Performers' Protection Act 1972 increased the maximum penalties available. However, these Acts appeared to give rise to criminal liability only, and did not seem to give any civil remedies to performers or to those with whom the performers may have had recording contracts. The offences related to recording a live performance, broadcasting it, transmitting it via a cable distribution system or performing it in public without the consent of the original performers. The use of an unauthorised audio or audio-visual recording for the purpose of broadcasting, inclusion in a cable system or public performance, and dealing with such unauthorised recordings, were also offences.

The question as to whether the law gave a right to civil actions was considered both in respect of performers and recording companies. In *Rickless* v *United Artists Corp*,[2] the defendant made a new film by using clips and out-takes (discarded excerpts) from previous *Pink Panther* films starring the late Peter Sellers. The claimant, who owned the

1 The purpose of the 1963 Act was to achieve compliance with the Convention for the Protection of Performers, Producers of Phonograms and Broadcasting Organisations (the Rome Convention), 26 October 1961.

2 [1988] 1 QB 40.

rights of Peter Sellers' services as an actor, sued for, *inter alia*, breach of the Dramatic and Musical Performers' Protection Act 1958 s 2 because the defendant failed to obtain the permission of the actor's executors. The trial judge awarded damages of US $1 million and the defendant appealed to the Court of Appeal, arguing that s 2 did not give rise to a private cause of action. The Court of Appeal dismissed the appeal confirming that s 2 of the Act conferred a right to civil remedies to the performer whose performance had been exploited without written consent in addition to imposing criminal penalties.[3] The basis for this decision was that, by imposing the criminal penalties, the Act imposed an obligation or prohibition for the benefit of a class of persons, in this case performers, and consequently this gave a cause of action to any aggrieved performer. However, in *RCA Corp v Pollard*,[4] the Court of Appeal reluctantly found that the Acts did not give civil remedies to recording companies. This highlighted the problem that recording companies were having with 'bootleg' recordings and the regrettable lack of civil remedies under the 1958–1972 Acts.[5] The ease of making good quality bootleg recordings because of technological advances was of particular concern.

These problems were identified in the White Paper preceding the Copyright, Designs and Patents Act 1988.[6] That Act repealed the previous Acts in their entirety and replaced them with new provisions contained in Part II of the Act. In addition to giving a civil right of action to recording companies having an exclusive licence with the performer and confirming civil remedies for performers, the new provisions extend to live performances by a variety of artistes such as jugglers and acrobats, and bring the criminal penalties and powers of search and seizure more in line with those available in copyright law.

The remainder of this chapter looks first at rights in performances briefly as set out in the Copyright, Designs and Patents Act 1988 as originally enacted. It then goes on to look at the current position. Rights in performances were substantially changed (and enhanced) by the Copyright and Related Rights Regulations 1996,[7] which implemented the Directive on rental and lending right[8] and there have been further modifications, primarily resulting from the Copyright and Related Rights Regulations 2003[9] which implemented the Directive on certain aspects of copyright and related rights in the information society.[10]

Rights granted by the Copyright, Designs and Patents Act 1988 as enacted

The Copyright, Designs and Patents Act 1988 Part II came into force on 1 August 1989. Rights in performances were considerably expanded in comparison with previous law. The provisions were retrospective in that live performances that were made prior to the coming into force of the new law were protected, but a right of action did not accrue in respect of acts carried out before that date.[11] In other words, new rights were retrospectively granted, but new liabilities had not been retrospectively imposed. For example, a live performance by a team of acrobats made in 1987 was protected. If a bootleg film was made of the performance, the making of the film did not infringe any intellectual property rights and there could be no legal action in respect of it. However, if the person who made the film decided to make and sell copies to the public, the acrobats could sue for infringement of their performers' right.[12]

Two separate and distinct rights were created by the 1988 Act: a performer's right and a recording right. The nature of the rights was somewhat peculiar as the rights were not transmissible, except that a performer's right would pass on the death of the performer concerned.[13] However, by s 185(2)(b), the benefit of an exclusive recording licence could be assigned, and by s 185(3)(b) a person could assign the benefit of a licence to make recordings for commercial exploitation. Either the person having recording rights or the

3 Applying the *dictum* of Lord Diplock in *Lonrho Ltd v Shell Petroleum Co Ltd* [1982] AC 173.

4 [1983] Ch 135.

5 In this context, a 'bootleg' recording is one made without the permission of either the performer or the authorised recording company, if any.

6 *Intellectual Property and Innovation*, Cmnd 9712, HMSO, 1986. The problems had also been discussed earlier in the Whitford Committee Report, *Copyright and Designs Law*, Cmnd 6732, HMSO, 1977 and in the Green Paper, *Reform of the Law Relating to Copyright, Designs and Performers' Protection*, Cmnd 8302, HMSO, 1981.

7 SI 1996/2967.

8 Council Directive 92/100/EEC of 19 November 1992 on rental right and lending right and on certain rights related to copyright in the field of intellectual property, OJ L 346, 27.11.1992, p 61, replaced by codifying Directive 2006/115/EC of the European Parliament and of the Council of 12 December 2006 on rental right and lending right and on certain rights related to copyright in the field of intellectual property, OJ L 376, 27.12.2006, p 28; hereinafter referred to as the 'Directive on rental right and lending right'.

9 SI 2003/2498.

10 Directive 2001/29/EC of the European Parliament and of the Council of 22 May 2001 on the harmonisation of certain aspects of copyright and related rights in the information society, OJ L 167, 22.06.2001, p 10, hereinafter referred to as the 'Directive on copyright and related rights in the information society'.

11 Copyright, Designs and Patents Act 1988 s 180(3). Unless otherwise stated, in this chapter, statutory references are to the Copyright, Designs and Patents Act 1988.

12 Assuming the making of the copies was not in pursuance of arrangements made before the commencement of the new provisions. A person having an exclusive recording contract with the acrobats in relation to the performance could also sue because his recording rights had been infringed.

13 Copyright, Designs and Patents Act 1988 s 192.

person granting the licence had to be a qualifying person. As a result of these limitations on transmissibility, rights in performances were not true property rights. The performer's right, in particular, had some features in common with the author's moral rights under copyright law.[14] However, in other respects, the rights were very similar to copyright. Rights in performances subsist alongside and were independent of copyright, both the economic and moral rights. A fairly complex mosaic of rights could be involved. For example, a live performance might take place of a piece of music by a singer (Cynthia) and orchestra (Harvey and the Syncopators). The music was recently written by Filbert and the lyrics by Hamstein, who have assigned their copyrights to the Palm Beach Music Publishing Company. A television company (SKB TV) may have had an exclusive recording contract with the singer and orchestra. If a person, John Silver, was in the audience and made a bootleg recording with the intention of making copies for sale, then John infringed the following rights:

1 Palm Beach's copyright in the musical and literary work;
2 the performance right belonging to Cynthia and to each and every member of the orchestra;
3 SKB TV's recording right.

In addition, if John had made copies that were issued to the public, but which did not mention the fact that the music was written by Filbert and Hamstein, they would have had an action against John for infringement of their moral right to be identified as the authors of the music and lyrics. If he sold or rented copies to the public, John would further infringe the copyrights.[15] The situation could be even more complex if the music was subject to an agreement with a collecting society, or if SKB TV had assigned the benefit of the exclusive recording contract to another. John was, therefore, exposed to a veritable battery of civil actions, but he was also liable to be prosecuted for offences under copyright law[16] and for dealing with illicit recordings.[17]

The meaning of recording was accepted to apply to both the recording and a record made from that recording in *Bassey* v *Icon Entertainment plc*.[18] In that case, a recording was made of a live performance by Shirley Bassey. She had the right to veto the release of records made from the recording if she was not satisfied with its quality and she exercised that veto. Together with David Bainbridge, who owned the copyright in the recording, she brought a successful action to prevent the release of those records. The court held that making records of the recording infringed those rights in the absence of express or implied consent.

Rights in performances – present position

Rights in performances were significantly strengthened as a result of the Copyright and Related Rights Regulations 1996[19] which implemented, *inter alia*, the Directive on rental right and lending right.[20] Further changes have been made, including by the Copyright and Related Rights Regulations 2003.[21] The rights of a person having recording rights were not radically changed, but the rights of performers were transformed by the 1996 Regulations and a further right (the 'making available right') was added by the 2003 Regulations. As mentioned earlier, performers' rights were analogous to moral rights under copyright law. These rights continue and new ones have been added. Performers now have full property rights which can be exploited and dealt with just as a copyright. More recently, performers have also been given moral rights: being the right of being identified as a performer and the right of objecting to a derogatory treatment of their performance. A performer now has 'property rights', 'non-property rights' and moral rights, as

14 Performers now have a separate moral right in addition to their property rights and non-property rights.

15 He could have had further liabilities arising from rental and lending rights provided for in pursuance of the rental and lending rights Directive.

16 Copyright, Designs and Patents Act 1988 s 107(1).

17 Copyright, Designs and Patents Act 1988 s 198(1).

18 [1995] EMLR 596.

19 SI 1996/2967. The new provisions came into force on 1 December 1996.

20 OJ L 346, 27.11.92, p 61 Replaced by codifying Directive 2006/115/EC of the European Parliament and of the Council of 12 December 2006 on rental right and lending right and on certain rights related to copyright in the field of intellectual property, OJ L 376, 27.12.2006, p 28

21 SI 2003/2498.

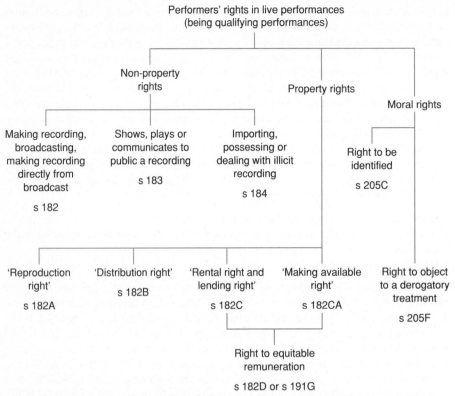

Note: If a performer transfers his rental right in relation to a sound recording or film to its producer, this is replaced by a right to equitable remuneration for the rental (s 191G(1)). There is also a right to equitable remuneration where a commercially published sound recording is played in public or broadcast to the public under s 182D.

Figure 9.1 Performers' rights

indicated in Figure 9.1. It should be noted that, in some cases, there is some relationship between the property rights, the non-property rights and also the performers' moral rights. For example, a performer's non-property rights are infringed by a person making without the performer's consent a recording of the whole or any substantial part of a qualifying performance directly from the live performance.[22] If that person then makes copies of the recording, directly or indirectly, that will infringe the performer's property right of reproduction.[23] If the copies do not bear a notice identifying the performer and are subsequently issued to the public there will be an infringement of his moral right to be identified as such as well as an infringement of the performer's property right of issuing copies to the public.

Before these important changes, the duration of rights in performances had been modified to bring them more in line with the rules applying to copyright sound recordings. Until 1 January 1996, the duration of rights in performances was simply 50 years from the end of the calendar year during which the performance took place. As a result of the Duration of Copyright and Rights in Performances Regulations 1995,[24] a new s 191 was substituted into the Act.[25] The basic rule on the duration of rights in performances is now as follows:

22 Copyright, Designs and Patents Act 1988 s 182(1)(a).

23 Copyright, Designs and Patents Act 1988 s 182A.

24 SI 1995/3297, implementing Council Directive 93/98/EEC of 29 October 1993 harmonising the term of copyright and certain related rights, OJ L 290, 24.11.1993, p 9 This Directive was repealed and replaced by a codified version, Directive 2006/116/EC of the European Parliament and of the Council of 12 December 2006 on the term of copyright and certain related rights, OJ L372, 27.12.2006, p 12.

25 Duration of Copyright and Rights in Performances Regulations 1995, SI 1995/3297, reg 13.

(a) 50 years from the end of the calendar year in which the performance takes place, or

(b) if during that period a recording of the performance is released, 50 years from the end of the calendar year in which it was released.

26 Under s 191(5), if this would be at variance with an international obligation of which the UK became subject before 29 October 1993, the duration is as specified by the basic rules on duration.

This is similar to that applying to sound recordings. Where the performer is not a national of a European Economic Area (EEA) state, the term of protection is as in the country of which the performer is a national provided it is not longer than that available under s 191 as substituted.[26]

The definition of 'released' is when the recording is first published, played or shown in public or communicated to the public. As with copyright, 'communication to the public' means broadcasting or making available to the public by electronic transmission in such a way that members of the public can access the work (in this case recoding) from a place and at a time individually chosen by them. As is general in the 1988 Act, no account is taken of any unauthorised act.

The Duration of Copyright and Rights in Performances Regulations 1995 contained a number of transitional provisions, particularly dealing with extended rights and revived rights. In principle, these are similar to those applying to extended and revived copyright, for which *see* Chapter 3 (p 83).

27 Section 180(4) states that the rights conferred are independent of 'any other right or obligation arising otherwise than under this Part'.

It is possible that a recording made without the performer's consent may be shown in public or broadcast when the performer is still alive, if the performance was more than 50 years ago and it was released soon after. However, the decision in the *Rickless* case may still give rise to a separate civil right of action based on the offences which have no time limit.[27]

In the remainder of this chapter some common ground is covered, then the performers' non-property rights as modified by the Copyright and Related Rights Regulations 1996 will be described. This will be followed by the performers' property rights and moral rights. The rights of persons having an exclusive recording contract with the performer, or the benefit of such a contract, are then considered, followed by the permitted acts, the transitional provisions and the criminal offences, which have been modified by the Copyright, etc. and Trade Marks (Offences and Enforcement) Act 2002 and added to by the Copyright and Related Rights Regulations 2003.[28]

28 SI 2003/2498.

29 *Barrett v Universal-Island Records Ltd* [2006] EMLR 21, concerning rights in performances by Bob Marley and The Wailers.

It should be noted that the performers' property rights are 'new rights' and distinct from the performers' non-property rights. The former can be dealt with as any other form of property rights whilst the latter are personal rights which are not assignable, as discussed later.[29]

Proposed extension of rights

Some performers, notably including Cliff Richard, have called for an extension to the term of protection for rights in performances. Many performers start young and, in their later years, see their income dwindling as rights in their performances expire.

30 Term of copyright and related rights (European Parliament legislative resolution), OJ, C 184, 08.07.2010, p E 331. The original Commission proposal was to extend the term to 95 years.

There is a proposal to increase the term of protection for rights in performances from 50 to 70 years. This would require amendment to the term of copyright Directive.[30] It is also proposed that, during the extended term, producers would pay 20 per cent of their revenues to a collecting society for the benefit of session musicians. Other provisions include a 'use it or lose it' system whereby rights would revert to performers if the producer does not exploit the work during the 50-year period and there would be a 'clean slate' for contracts with record producers. This would apply, for example, where a performer has assigned his exclusive rights to a producer for a single lump sum and would mean that the performer would receive unencumbered royalties or remuneration for the extended period of protection.

Common ground

The rights are given to performers and persons having recording rights, and their consent is required for the exploitation of the performance or the making of recordings.[31] Rights in performances should not be confused with 'performing rights'. This term is usually used to signify rights under copyright in relation to the acts of performing, showing or playing a work, in which copyright subsists, in public. For example, where a retail store wishes to play background music, it will require the permission of the relevant copyright owners. The copyright performing rights are usually administered by collecting societies such as the Performing Right Society (in the UK).

A performance is a live performance given by one or more individuals which is a dramatic performance (including dance and mime), a musical performance, a reading or recitation of a literary work, or a performance of a variety act or any similar presentation which is, or so far as it is, a live performance given by one or more individuals.[32] If a person sings live to a recorded backing track, for example in a 'karaoke bar', the live performance relates to the live singing only.[33] The meaning of 'recording' is important in terms of recording rights and infringement and is defined in s 180(2) as being a film or sound recording made directly from a live performance, or made from a broadcast of the performance made, directly or indirectly, from another recording of the performance. Therefore, copies made from a master recording that was made during the performance count as being recordings.

For the rights to exist, certain qualification requirements must be satisfied. The performers' rights subsist only if the performance is a qualifying performance which, by s 181, means that it must be given by a qualifying individual or take place in a qualifying country. Section 206 defines a qualifying individual as being a citizen or subject of a qualifying country or a person who is resident in such a country. 'Qualifying country' means the UK and any other Member State of the European Economic Community[34] and any other country designated by Order in Council under s 208, that is, to countries enjoying reciprocal protection.[35] The current order is the Copyright and Performances (Application to Other Countries) Order 2008.[36] This applies to countries which are parties to the Rome Convention for the Protection of Performers, Producers of Phonograms and Broadcasting Organisations 1961 and, granting limited protection to performers, to other countries party to the Agreement of Trade Related Aspects of Intellectual Property Rights.

For the recording right, by s 185, the person having recording rights who is a party to an exclusive recording contract with the performer or the assignee of the benefit of such a contract must be a qualifying person.[37] If not, then the right might still arise where a person who has been licensed to make recordings or to whom the benefit of such a licence has been assigned is a qualifying person. A qualifying person can be a qualifying individual or a body corporate or other body having legal personality formed under the law of the UK or of another qualifying country which carries on a substantial business activity in any qualifying country: s 206. It should be noted that the recording right can arise even though the performance is not a qualifying performance, so that an Italian film company having an exclusive recording contract to record the live performance of a juggler from North Korea which takes place in Jordan will have recording rights which are enforceable in the UK, even though the juggler himself has no rights in relation to his own performance subject to UK law. The performance is not a qualifying performance because the juggler fails to meet the requirements for a qualifying individual and the performance does not take place in a qualifying country.[38]

Rights in performances are conferred retrospectively by s 180(3) but there may be a problem where the performance took place in a country which was not granted reciprocal protection prior to the commencement of the 1988 Act or the 1996 Regulations as the

31 The performer's consent is required in relation to the performers' rights, but the consent of either the performer or the person having the recording right is required in relation to the recording right.

32 Copyright, Designs and Patents Act 1988 s 180(2).

33 However, there is also a public performance of the backing track and there will be an infringement of this unless permission to play the track has been obtained or a licence scheme is in operation and covers the playing of the particular backing track in question.

34 The reference to the European Economic Community remains and has not been changed to the EU.

35 This includes countries that are members of the Rome Convention for the Protection of Performers, Producers of Phonograms and Broadcasting Organisations 1961.

36 SI 2008/677.

37 An exclusive recording contract is a contract between the performer and another person under which that other person is entitled to the exclusion of all others, including the performer, to make recordings of one or more of his performances with a view to their commercial exploitation: s 185(1).

38 North Korea and Jordan are not members of the Rome Convention.

39 [2005] EMLR 18.

case may be. For example, in *Experience Hendrix LLC v Purple Haze Records Ltd*,[39] the late Jimi Hendrix gave, with others, live performances in Stockholm in 1969. Sweden did not join the European Community until 1 January 1995 and was not a qualifying country until then although reciprocal protection was granted in 1989 by an Order in Council made under s 208. It had been argued that, as there were no express transitional provisions dealing with this situation, the Stockholm performance was not a qualifying performance as Sweden was not a qualifying country at the time of the performance. This was rejected by Hart J: as a performance given in the UK before 1 August 1989 was a qualifying performance, there was nothing to suggest that a performance made before that date in another Member State of the EU could not also be a qualifying performance. Later, the Court of Appeal rejected a claim that the rights did not apply to persons who died before commencement of the Copyright, Designs and Patents Act 1988 in *Experience Hendrix LLC v Purple Haze Records Ltd (No 2)*.[40] This was so even though some of the language of the Part of the Act dealing with performance was expressed in the present tense. The argument that the rights did not apply to performers who died before commencement was only viable had the Act been construed in isolation, not talking account of international obligations and pre-existing law, including the so-called 'Rickless rights'.[41]

40 [2007] FSR 31. Jimi Hendrix died in 1970.

41 After *Rickless v United Artists Corp* [1988] 1 QB 40, *supra*.

Illicit recording

The meaning of 'illicit recording' is important in terms of some forms of infringement of the rights and for the offences. It is the equivalent of an infringing copy of a work in which copyright subsists, but there are some differences.

By s 197, an illicit recording is:

(a) for the purpose of a performer's rights, a recording of the whole or any substantial part of a performance made, otherwise than for private purposes, without the performer's consent;

(b) for the recording rights, a recording of the whole or any substantial part of a performance subject to an exclusive recording contract made, otherwise than for private purposes, without the consent of either the performer or the person entitled to the recording rights;

(c) for the purposes of ss 198 and 199 (offences and delivery up in criminal proceedings) it is an illicit recording if it falls within (a) or (b) above;

(d) a recording which is an illicit recording under the provisions of Sch 2 to the Copyright, Designs and Patents Act 1988 (the permitted acts in relation to performances). This covers recordings, the making of which did not infringe the rights in performances because they were made for a permitted act, but which have been used subsequently outside the terms of the exception: for example, where a recording made for educational purposes has been sold.[42]

42 *See* Copyright, Designs and Patents Act 1988 Sch 2, para 6(2).

The place where the recording was made is immaterial and there is no reason to believe that the question of substantiality will be construed otherwise than it is for copyright purposes.

Consent

The issue of consent is central to the infringement of the rights. There is no requirement for the consent to be in writing and, by s 193(1), consent may relate to a single specific performance, a specified description of performances or performances generally. Future and past performances are included, so that consent can be given retrospectively. Persons having any of the rights devolved to them are bound by consents given by previous right-holders. This is strict and there are no statutory exceptions for 'equity's darling'.

In the absence of express consent, it seems reasonable to suppose that it may be implied, and it will be so implied if it is necessary and reasonable to do so. The same applies to the need to obtain consent if the intended use of a recording of a performance appears to exceed the terms of the original consent. However, consent given in respect of a particular use does not necessarily prohibit, by implication, other uses; something else must be shown: for example, that the new intended use raises an implication that further consent is required. In *Grower v British Broadcasting Corporation*[43] the BBC had made a recording of a performance of 'Hoochie Coochie Man' by the Jimi Hendrix Experience for the immediate purpose of broadcasting on a radio programme hosted by Alexis Korner who had, at the invitation of Hendrix, joined in the performance, playing a guitar. It appeared that Korner had consented to the making of the recording and the broadcasting of that recording. In an agreement made in 1988, the BBC granted a licence to a Californian company in respect of the sound recording. The licence included a term that the Californian company obtained the consent of any artists who had contributed to the recording before exploiting the recording. The claimants, the executors of Korner's estate, sued the BBC (as joint tortfeasor) on the basis that the Californian company had exploited the sound recording without their consent and that this was a breach of the performer's rights under the Copyright, Designs and Patents Act 1988 Part II. It was held, *inter alia*, that the claimant would have to establish that there was an implied term that the BBC either obtain the claimants' consent to exploit the sound recording or that the BBC would guarantee that a licensee or assignee of the copyright in the sound recording would obtain the consent of all the performers, and neither implication was necessary nor reasonable in the circumstances.[44]

43 [1990] FSR 595.

44 Of course, the BBC owned the copyright in the sound recording. Nor was the BBC liable as joint tortfeasor as, although the BBC may have facilitated the infringement by the Californian company, it had not participated in it. It was, however, arguable that the making of a back-up copy of the recording was a breach of the Dramatic and Musical Performers' Protection Act 1958, and a breach of the agreement between Korner and the BBC.

Performers' non-property rights

These rights are set out in the Copyright, Designs and Patents Act 1988 s 182 (which was substituted by the Copyright and Related Rights Regulations 1996) and ss 183 and 184, which are unchanged except that the phrase 'broadcasts or includes in a cable programme service' was substituted with 'communicates to the public' by the Copyright and Related Rights Regulations 2003. A performer's rights in a qualifying performance are infringed by any person who, without the performer's consent, does any of the following acts in relation to the whole or any substantial part of a qualifying performance:

(a) makes a recording of the whole or any substantial part of a qualifying performance directly from the live performance (s 182(1)(a));

(b) broadcasts live the whole or any substantial part of a qualifying performance (s 182(1)(b));

(c) makes a recording of the whole or any substantial part of a qualifying performance directly from a broadcast of the live performance (s 182(1)(c));

(d) by means of a recording which was, and which that person knows or has reason to believe was, made without the performer's consent, shows, plays in public or communicates to the public the whole or any substantial part of a qualifying performance (s 183);

(e) imports into the UK, otherwise than for his own private and domestic purposes, or, in the course of a business, possesses, sells, lets for hire, offers or exposes for sale or hire or distributes an illicit recording, which he knows is or has reason to believe is an illicit recording (s 184).[45]

45 There is a defence to this form of infringement under s 184(2) where the defendant shows that the illicit recording was innocently acquired either by him or a predecessor in title. Innocence in this case means that the person did not know and had no reason to believe that it was an illicit recording: s 184(3). This is not a complete defence but serves to limit damages to a reasonable payment in respect of the act complained of.

Infringement is actionable as a breach of statutory duty.[46] For the infringements under s 182, damages are not available as against a defendant who can show that, at the time of the infringement, he had reasonable grounds for believing that consent had been given.

46 Copyright, Designs and Patents Act 1988 s 194.

The performer's non-property rights are not assignable or transmissible except as set out in s 192A.[47] The performer may provide for the rights to pass under his will to a specific person or persons; otherwise, on his death, the rights become exercisable by his personal representatives.[48] Should the performer bequeath his non-property rights to more than one person, the rights are exercisable by each independently of the other or others.

There are provisions for delivery up of illicit recordings following application to the court by the performer or person having the recording rights, as appropriate.[49] Performers and persons having recording rights have a limited right of seizure in respect of illicit recordings under s 196. This right is similar to that applying to infringing works of copyright under s 100. It is not to be exercised at permanent or regular places of business and notice must first be given to the police. It is intended to be used, for example, at car boot sales and the like.

Performers' property rights

These full property rights can be described as the 'reproduction right', 'distribution right', 'rental and lending right' and the 'making available right'. If the performer transfers his rental right, this is then replaced by a right to equitable remuneration in the case of the rental of a sound recording or film containing the performance. A right to equitable remuneration also applies where a commercially published sound recording of the whole or any substantial part of a qualifying performance is played in public or communicated to the public otherwise than by being made available by way of the 'making available right'.

Reproduction right

This is a right which, under s 182A, is infringed by the making of a copy of a recording of the whole or any substantial part of a qualifying performance without the consent of the performer. Making a copy includes making a transient copy or one incidental to some other use of the original recording. It matters not whether the copy is made directly or indirectly. Making the recording in the first place will infringe the performer's non-property right. The right is to authorise or prohibit the making of such copies.

All the four performers' property rights refer to the consent of the performer. As the rights are full property rights and assignable as such, the consent referred to should be that of the contemporary owner of the right. The rental right and lending right Directive is better as it speaks of the 'rightholder'.

Distribution right

Under s 182B(1), the right is infringed by a person who issues to the public copies of a recording of the whole or a substantial part of a qualifying performance without the performer's consent. Issuing to the public means putting into circulation copies not previously put into circulation in the EEA by or with the consent of the performer, or putting into circulation outside the EEA copies not previously put into circulation in the EEA or elsewhere. However, the doctrine of exhaustion of rights applies and this does not extend to subsequent distribution (without prejudice to the consent required for rental or lending) or subsequent importation into the UK or another EEA state,[50] except so far as putting into circulation in the EEA by or with the consent of the performer applies to putting into circulation into the EEA copies previously put into circulation outside the EEA.

What this contrived set of rules is probably trying to achieve is that the performer's distribution right will be infringed if a person puts copies into circulation anywhere without the consent of the performer, or imports into an EEA state copies from outside the EEA without the performer's consent, whether or not those copies were put into circulation by or with the consent of the performer. The rental right and lending right Directive is much simpler on this point, merely stating that the rightholder's distribution right is exhausted by first sale within the European Community (the reference now should be to the EEA) made by the rightholder or with his consent.[51] Of course, sale of a copy of a recording does not, by itself, exhaust any rental or lending right.[52]

Issuing copies of a recording also covers the situation where the original recording is issued to the public.

Rental right and lending right

The right here is to authorise or prohibit rental and lending of copies of the performance to the public. The right is infringed, under s 182C, by a person who, without the performer's consent, rents or lends to the public copies of a recording of the whole or any substantial part of a qualifying performance.

The meanings of 'rental' and 'lending' are equivalent to those for copyright works as set out in s 18A. Thus, rental is making available for use, on terms that the copy will or may be returned, for direct or indirect economic or commercial advantage. Lending is making a copy available, on terms that it will or may be returned, otherwise than for direct or indirect economic or commercial advantage through an establishment accessible to the public. The expressions 'rental' and 'lending' do not include making available for the purpose of public performance, playing or showing in public or communication to the public, making available for the purpose of exhibition in public or making available for on-the-spot reference use. The provisions apply equally to the original recording as they do to copies.

Making available right

The 'making available right' was introduced by the Copyright and Related Rights Regulations 2003 and was intended to cover a situation where a recording of a qualifying performance was made available electronically for access or downloading as and when a person chooses to do so. An obvious example is where a recording performance is accessible from an internet website so that a person entering the website can play the recording or download it for later playing. Another example is the access and downloading of ring tones for mobile telephones. It does not cover the position where a recording is broadcast or transmitted by cable as part of a scheduled and timetabled service.

The making available right is infringed where a person, without the performer's consent, makes available to the public a recording of the whole or any substantial part of a qualifying performance by electronic transmission in such a way that members of the public may access the recording from a place and at a time individually chosen by them: s 182CA. Thus, a person making a 'bootleg' recording of a live performance and making it available online, for example, by allowing visitors to the website to play the recording or download it, will infringe the right. Making the bootleg recording would also infringe the right under s 182 (making recording of qualifying performance without consent).

Right to equitable remuneration – exploitation of sound recording

Under s 182D, a performer is entitled to equitable remuneration from the owner of the copyright in a commercially published sound recording of the whole or any substantial

51 Article 9(2).

52 See Case C-200/96 *Metronome Musik GmbH* v *Music Point Hokamp GmbH* [1998] ECR I-1953.

part of a qualifying performance if it is played in public or communicated to the public, otherwise than by way of the 'making available right'. This latter act means broadcasting which is what is left of the meaning of communication to the public when the making available right is subtracted from it. However, s 182D(1A) was inserted to include, in the meaning of publication of a sound recording for the purposes of s 182D(1), making available by electronic transmission in such as way that members of the public may access the recording from a place and at a time individually chosen by them.[53] This right may not be assigned except to a collecting society, though it may pass under a will or by operation of law and, from then on, it may be further assigned or transferred.

The amount payable by way of equitable remuneration is to be agreed, with the possibility of application to the Copyright Tribunal in the absence of agreement.[54] An agreement purporting to exclude or restrict the right to equitable remuneration or prevent a person questioning the amount of equitable remuneration or restrict the powers of the Copyright Tribunal in respect of this right to equitable remuneration is of no effect to that extent.

Right to equitable remuneration where rental right transferred

There is a right to an equitable remuneration in respect of rental under s 191G, where the performer has transferred his rental rights in relation to a sound recording or film to the producer of the sound recording or film. The right may not be assigned by the performer except to a collecting society, defined for the purposes of s 191G as a society or other organisation having as its main object, or one of its main objects, the exercise of the right to equitable remuneration on behalf of more than one performer. The right does, however, pass under testamentary disposition or operation of law and, subsequently, can be assigned or further transmitted. The amount payable is that to be agreed by persons by or on whose behalf it is to be paid and is payable subject to a reference to the Copyright Tribunal. The right cannot be excluded or restricted by agreement and any agreement purporting to do this is of no effect to that extent.

Section 191F provides for presumed transfer of the rental right, to be replaced by a right to an equitable remuneration, in the case of an agreement concerning film production being concluded between the performer and the film producer. The absence of the signature of the performer or person acting on his behalf does not exclude the operation of s 191C which deals with prospective ownership of performers' property rights.

Dealing with performers' property rights and infringement

The provisions for assignment, licensing (including exclusive licences) and prospective ownership are similar to those applying to copyright works. Thus, the assignments must be in writing and signed by or on behalf of the assignor and assignments may be partial.[55] Exclusive licensees may sue for infringement and the provisions for the exercise of concurrent rights are equivalent to those for copyright. Remedies are damages, injunctions, accounts or otherwise[56] (as for copyright) and there is also provision for additional damages under s 191J. Also, there is provision, where licences are available as of right, for a defendant to undertake to take such a licence thereby limiting remedies to damages of twice the amount payable under such a licence.[57]

As with other intellectual property rights, the assessment of damages, including additional damages, must take account of reg 3 of the Enforcement of Intellectual Property (Enforcement, etc.) Regulations 2006.[58] As is often the case, the assessment of damages can be a difficult exercise. In *Experience Hendrix LLC* v *Times Newspapers Ltd*,[59] the defendant published a CD of Jimi Hendrix recordings which it issued free to persons buying a copy of *The Sunday Times*. The CD, known as the covermount, contained recordings from

53 Inserted by the Performances (Moral Rights, etc.) Regulations 2006, SI 2006/18 with effect from 1 February 2006.

54 The powers of the Copyright Tribunal are extended accordingly.

55 Copyright, Designs and Patents Act 1988 s 191B.

56 Copyright, Designs and Patents Act 1988 s 191I. The assessment of damages must now be made under the formula in reg 3 of the Intellectual Property (Enforcement, etc.) Regulations 2006, SI 2006/1028.

57 Section 191K.

58 SI 2006/1028.

59 [2010] EWHC 1986 (Ch).

a live concert given by Jimi Hendrix in 1969. Well in excess of 1 million copies were distributed in the UK and Ireland in September 2006. At the time the covermount was distributed, the claimants had plans to show a film of the 1969 concert together with sales of DVDs and CDs and other merchandise associated with the 1969 concert.

The judge had to decide whether to compensate on the basis of a notional licence fee or to use the losses made by the claimants as a result of the publication of the covermount, causing a significant delay in the launch of their plans. The difference between the two forms of assessment was substantial.[60] Regulation 3 of the Regulations requires the court to assess damages appropriate to the actual prejudice suffered by the claimant as a result of the infringement. Of course, where the owner of an intellectual property right grants licences, it is proper to assess damages on the basis of a notional licence. But that was not the case here and the judge considered that the 'loss sustained' approach was the correct one. The 'notional licence' approach presented insurmountable problems. The claimants would never have granted a licence to make and distribute poor quality, illicitly obtained copies of the performance, especially as they were planning to launch their own project to exploit the concert. Looking at reg 3, the emphasis must be on the negative economic consequences, including any lost profits suffered by the claimant and any unfair profits made by the defendant, subject, of course, to showing causation. The judge awarded $5.8 million plus interest to be agreed by counsel.

Under s 191JA an injunction may be granted, by the High Court or Court of Session in Scotland, against a service provider having actual knowledge that another person is using the service to infringe a performer's property right.[61] In determining whether a service provider has actual knowledge, a court must take into account all matters which appear to it in the particular circumstances to be relevant. This includes whether the service provider has received a notice, for example, sent to his e-mail address under reg 6(1)(c) of the Electronic Commerce (EC Directive) Regulations 2002, and the extent to which the notice includes the full name and address of the sender and the details of the infringement in question. These provisions on injunctions on service providers are particularly relevant in relation to online services such as providing internet access and bulletin boards.

Where a person is entitled under a bequest (general or specific) to any material thing containing an original recording of a performance which was not published before the death of the testator, the bequest shall be construed as including any performers' rights in relation to the recording to which the testator was entitled immediately before his death.[62] This is subject to any contrary intention in the will or a codicil to it. Again, this is similar to the equivalent provision under copyright law.

Performers' moral rights

The WIPO Performers and Phonograms Treaty 1996 provided for moral rights for performers and, as that Treaty and the WIPO Copyright Treaty 1996 have been specified as EU Treaties, the UK was required to make amendments to the Copyright, Designs and Patents Act 1988 to include performers' moral rights, which it did by virtue of the Performances (Moral Rights, etc.) Regulations 2006[63] which came into force on 1 February 2006.

The moral rights granted to performers of qualifying performances are the right to be identified as the performer and the right to object to a derogatory treatment of a performance. Part II of the Copyright, Designs and Patents Act 1988, dealing with rights in performances, has been restructured and chapter numbers inserted. The new moral rights for performers are contained in new ss 205C to 205N of the Act.

60 The first claimant argued that its losses were $8.94 million and the second claimant asked for £17.4 million. The defendant said that a notional licence fee would have been in the order of £100,000 at the most. Apart from performance rights, the claims including a claim in respect of copyright in the original sound recording of the concert.

61 Section 191JA was inserted by the Copyright and Related Rights Regulations 2003, SI 2003/2498.

62 Copyright, Designs and Patents Act 1988 s 191E.

63 SI 2006/18.

Right to be identified as performer

New s 205C provides for the right to be identified as performer and applies to qualifying performances given in public, broadcast live, communicated to the public in the form of a sound recording or where copies of such a sound recording are issued to the public. The meaning of a qualifying performance is as already provided for under s 206 of the Act. The right to be identified applies in relation to the whole or any substantial part of a performance.

The identification should be in such a manner which is likely to bring the performer's identity to the notice of the person hearing or seeing the performance, communication or acquiring a copy of a sound recording, as the case may be. Where the performance is given in public, identification may be given in any programme accompanying the performance or in some other manner. As an alternative, the manner of identifying the performer may be according to an agreement between the performer and person producing the performance in public, broadcasting it, communicating the sound recording of the performance or issuing copies of the sound recording to the public, as appropriate.

Where the performance is by a group, being two or more persons with a name by which they are collectively identified, they may be identified by the name of the group. One proviso is where copies of sound recordings of qualifying performances are issued to the public. In this case, the right is satisfied by naming the group solely by group name if it is not reasonably practicable to identify each member of the group separately.

As with the right to be identified in relation to original works of copyright and principal directors of films, the right must be asserted. The provisions on assertion are contained in s 205D and are similar to those for copyright works, *mutatis mutandis*. For example, an assertion may be made generally or in relation to a specific act or description of acts by written instrument signed by or on behalf of the performer or on an assignment of a performer's property rights. In the former case, anyone to whom notice of the assertion is brought is bound by it and, in the latter case, the assignee is bound as is anyone claiming through him, whether or not he has notice of the assertion. However, again like copyright, a court can take into account, in determining remedies, any delay in asserting the right. Where an assertion specifies a pseudonym, initials or some other form of identification, that form must be used; otherwise any reasonable form of identification must be used.

There are exceptions to the right to be identified, set out in s 205E, but these do not follow those relating to moral rights under copyright but primarily take into account some of the permitted acts in relation to performances in Sch 2 to the Act. The first exception is where it is not reasonably practicable to identify the performer or group where this is permitted. The right does not apply in relation to a performance given for the purposes of reporting current events or to a performance for the purposes of advertising any goods or services. The Sch 2 exceptions are in relation to news reporting, incidental inclusion, things done for the purposes of examination, parliamentary and judicial proceedings or in relation to Royal Commissions and statutory bodies. Importantly, the exceptions relating to employees for moral rights under copyright do not apply to performances.

Derogatory treatment

This also applies in relation to qualifying performances. The performer's right to object to a derogatory performance, under s 205F, is infringed in the case of a live broadcast of it or where, by means of a sound recording, it is played in public or communicated to the public with any distortion, mutilation or other modification that is prejudicial to the reputation of the performer.

A derogatory treatment for the equivalent moral right under copyright law is differently defined and is one which amounts to '. . . a distortion or mutilation of the work *or is otherwise* prejudicial to the *honour* or reputation of the author or director' (emphasis added): s 80(2)(b). For the performer's right, there is no mention of honour but, for copyright, a distortion or mutilation appears to be a derogatory treatment as being prejudicial to the honour or reputation of the author or director, *per se*. Furthermore, for the performer's right, a modification may trigger the right if it is prejudicial. The modification may be one other than a distortion or mutilation. The right would appear to apply in relation to the whole or any part of a performance and there is no requirement for the part to be a substantial part of the performance.

The right to object to a derogatory treatment is subject to the exceptions in s 205G which relate to:

- performances for the purposes of reporting current events (to which the right does not apply);
- modifications to a performance consistent with normal editorial or production practice (in this case the right applies but is not infringed);
- anything done for the purposes of avoiding the commission of any offence, complying with any duty imposed by or under an enactment or, in the case of the BBC, avoiding in any programme broadcast by the BBC anything which offends against good taste or decency or which is likely to encourage or incite crime or lead to disorder or be offensive to public feeling (again, the right is not infringed).

This last list of exceptions is subject to s 205G(5) which states that the exceptions apply only if there is a sufficient disclaimer where a performer is identified in a manner likely to bring his identity to the notice of a person seeing or hearing the performance as modified or where he has previously been identified in or on copies of a sound recording issued to the public.

A sufficient disclaimer is, under s 205G(6), in relation to an act capable of infringing the right, a clear and reasonably prominent indication that the modifications were made without the performer's consent given in a manner likely to bring it to the notice of a person seeing or hearing the performance or, if the performer was identified at the time of the act, appearing along with that identification.

A person who possesses in the course of business or sells or lets for hire, or offers or exposes for sale or hire, or distributes an article which he knows or has reason to believe is an infringing article also infringes the right to object to a derogatory treatment. An 'infringing article' is a sound recording of a qualifying performance with any distortion, mutilation or other modification that is prejudicial to the reputation of the performer.

Supplementary provisions

Performers' moral rights will endure for the same time as the performers' property and non-property rights, being 50 years from the end of the calendar year during which the performance was made or, if during that period it was released, 50 years from the end of the calendar year during which it was released.

The rights are not infringed where consent has been given by or on behalf of the performer and the rights may be waived by written instrument, signed by or on behalf of the performer, either generally or specifically: s 205J. A waiver may be conditional or unconditional and may be expressed as subject to revocation.

Moral rights of performers, like the equivalent one for copyright authors and principal directors of films, cannot be assigned but, as with copyright, there are provisions for the transmission of the rights on the death of the performer. For example, the performer may have expressed in a will that the rights devolve to a specific person or persons. Where there is no such direction, the rights devolve to the person to whom the performer's property rights devolve where they are part of the performer's estate. If neither applies, the rights are exercisable by the performer's personal representatives. There are provisions to deal with consents and waivers where more than one person is entitled to the rights.

An infringement of the right to be identified as performer or to object to a derogatory treatment is actionable as a breach of statutory duty under s 205N. Unlike the case with copyright the Regulations deal with a situation where a person falsely claims to act on behalf of a performer and purports to give consent to the relevant conduct or to waive the right. Where this causes an infringement of the right, that person will be liable, jointly and severally, with any person liable for that infringement as if he himself had infringed the right. However, it is a defence to show that a person infringing one of the rights reasonably believed that the person claiming to act on behalf of the performer and giving consent or purporting to waive the rights was indeed acting on the performer's behalf.

In relation to the right to object to a derogatory treatment, apart from the usual remedy of an injunction for a breach of statutory duty, a specific form of injunction may be granted on terms that an act is prohibited unless a disclaimer is made dissociating the performer from the broadcast or sound recording. This is possible if the court thinks it an adequate remedy in the circumstances. The terms and manner of the disclaimer dissociating the performer from the broadcast or sound recording of the performance will be as the court approves.

The new performers' moral rights are not retrospective and do not apply to performances which took place before 1 February 2006, the date these provisions came into force.

Recording rights

Recording rights are given to a person having an exclusive recording contract with a performer, being one under which that person is entitled to the exclusion of all others, including the performer, to make recordings of one or more of his performances with a view to their commercial exploitation.[64] That person must be a party to the contract and have the benefit of the contract, or be a person to whom the benefit of the contract has been assigned. He must also be a qualifying person. Apart from being able to assign the benefit of the contract, under s 192B, the right is not assignable or transmissible.

If the person who would otherwise be entitled to the right is not a qualifying person, references are instead to a person licensed by such a person to make recordings for commercial exploitation, or to a person to whom the benefit of such a licence has been assigned if that person is a qualifying person. Thus, for example, if an American company having an exclusive recording contract with a performer to record a live performance to take place in the UK grants a licence to an English company actually to make the recording, it will be the English company which is entitled to the recording right.[65]

Making a recording 'with a view to commercial exploitation' simply means, under s 185(4), with a view to recordings being sold or let for hire, shown or played in public.

A person infringes the rights of a person having recording rights by making a recording of the whole or any substantial part of the performance without the consent of the person having the recording rights or the performer under s 186. Damages are not available if the defendant shows that, at the time of the infringement, he believed on reasonable grounds that consent had been given.

Subsequent use of a recording made without consent under s 187 infringes. In this case, the use covers showing or playing the whole or any substantial part of the performance or the communication of it to the public. The consent required is that of the person having recording rights in relation to a performance or, in the case of a qualifying performance, that of the performer. Furthermore, for infringement, the person concerned

64 Copyright, Designs and Patents Act 1988 s 185.

65 The US enjoys only partial reciprocal protection as yet: Copyright and Performances (Application to Other Countries) Order 2008, SI 2008/677, as amended.

must know or have reason to believe that the recording was made without the appropriate consent, being under s 187(2) that of the performer or the person who at the time the consent was given had recording rights in relation to the performance. If there was more than one such person, the consent of all is required. Section 187(2) is curiously worded in that the second limb is stated in terms of the consent having been given.

Importing, possessing and dealing with illicit recordings, if done without consent, will infringe the recording right if the person concerned knows or has reason to believe that the recording of the performance is an illicit recording. The consent is that of the person having recording rights or, in the case of a qualifying performance, that of the performer. As usual, having reason to believe is an objective test. Section 188(2) limits remedies against a person where he, or a predecessor in title, innocently acquired the illicit recording to damages not exceeding a reasonable payment in respect of the act complained of. 'Innocently acquired' means the person acquiring the recording did not know and had no reason to believe that the recording was an illicit recording.

Infringement of recording rights is actionable as a breach of statutory duty under s 194 as is the case with performers' non-property rights.

Exceptions

The *Rickless* case was criticised in that it gave civil rights in a way that was probably not intended by Parliament and this meant that such civil rights were without the comprehensive exceptions that apply to copyright and moderate its strength. The fine balance usually maintained between the interests of the owners of intellectual property rights and the public was missing. The 1988 provisions remedied this in an extensive manner and a whole range of exceptions are made which, on the whole, are very similar to those available in copyright law. There are many cross-references to the copyright provisions for definitions. The exceptions are contained in Sch 2 to the Copyright, Designs and Patents Act 1988 and, although there is not room to discuss them here in detail, Table 9.1 should give some indication of their scope.[66] Where reference is made to exceptions to infringing, it is in relation to infringing the rights in performance set out in Part II of the Act. Other rights may be infringed nonetheless.

66 For general principles, reference should be made to Chapter 7.

The Copyright Tribunal is, by s 190, given limited powers in respect of performances, and a person who wishes to make a recording of a performance may ask the Tribunal to give consent where the identity or whereabouts of the performer cannot be ascertained by reasonable enquiry or where the performer unreasonably withholds his consent. This could prove useful in dealing with the problem of the 'Tenth Spear Carrier', that is, where an extra in a film refuses to consent.[67] In exercising this power, the Tribunal shall take into account:

67 Prime, T. (1992) *The Law of Copyright*, Fourmat, p 284.

(a) whether the recording was made with the performer's consent and is lawfully in the possession and control of the person proposing to make the new recording, and
(b) whether the making of the further recording is consistent with the obligations of the parties to the arrangements under which, or is otherwise consistent with the purposes for which, the original recording was made.

Where the performer unreasonably withholds consent, the Tribunal may give consent only if satisfied that the performer's reasons do not include the protection of any of his legitimate interests, but it is for the performer to show what his reasons are and, in default, the Tribunal may make any such inference as it thinks fit. Where the Tribunal gives consent to the making of the further recording(s), it may make such order for payment as it thinks fit as being the appropriate consideration for the consent, unless the parties have agreed payment in the meantime. Of course, in most cases, the recording company will have obtained all the necessary consents.

Table 9.1 Exceptions to infringement of rights in performances

Exception	Comment
Making temporary copies (para 1A)	Transient or incidental copies or recordings of performances may be made if an integral and essential part of a technological process, the sole purpose of which is transmitting in a network between third parties by intermediaries or a lawful use of the recording. There must be no independent economic significance.
Criticism, reviews and news reporting (para 2)	Fair dealing with performance or recording for criticism or review of that or another performance or recording of a work does not infringe providing the performance or recording has been made available to the public. Fair dealing with performance or recording for the purpose of reporting current events does not infringe.
Incidental inclusion of performance or recording in a sound recording, film or broadcast (para 3)	Extends to anything done in relation to copies of, or playing, showing or communication to public in respect of such performance or recording. As with copyright, deliberate inclusion is outside the exception.
'Educational purposes' (paras 4–6)	Similar exceptions to those for copyright but less extensive.
Lending copies of recording of a performance (paras 6A and 6B)	Lending is by educational establishment or libraries or archives.
Copy required as a condition of export e.g. article of cultural or historical importance or interest (para 7)	
Public administration (paras 8–11)	Similar to copyright exceptions but not as many.
Transfer of copies in electronic form (para 12)	Allows the making of a back-up copy in some cases.
Miscellaneous (paras 13–21)[68] Recordings of spoken words Recordings of folksongs Lending of certain recordings *Broadcasts* Incidental recording Supervision and control Time shifting Photographs of broadcasts Free public showing/playing Reception/re-transmission Subtitled copies for hard of hearing, etc. Recording for archival purposes	Most are very similar to the copyright exceptions.

68 Paragraph 15 (playing sound recordings for benefit of club etc) and para 18(1A)(a) (playing of excepted sound recording does not infringe any included performance right in relation to not-for-profit organisations) repealed by the Copyright, Designs and Patents Act 1988 (Amendment) Regulations 2010, SI 2010/2694, reg 4(2) as from 1 January 2011.

Transitional provisions and savings

The Copyright and Related Rights Regulations 1996 apply to performances given before or after commencement (1 December 1996), but no act done prior to commencement will infringe or give rise to a right to equitable remuneration.[69] Further, unless expressly agreed, an agreement made before 19 November 1992 (the date of adoption of the rental right and lending right Directive) is not affected, nor is any act done after commencement an infringement of any new right in pursuance of such an agreement.[70]

Any new right relating to a qualifying performance may be exercised from commencement and where, before commencement, the owner or prospective owner of one of the performers' rights authorised the making of a copy of a recording of a performance, any new right relating to that copy will vest on commencement in the person so authorised, in the absence of any agreement to the contrary.[71]

69 Copyright and Related Rights Regulations 1996 reg 26.

70 Copyright and Related Rights Regulations 1996 reg 27.

71 Copyright and Related Rights Regulations 1996 regs 30 and 31.

No right to an equitable remuneration arises in respect of any rental of a film or sound recording before 1 April 1997 nor in respect of any rental after that date but made in pursuance of an agreement entered into before 1 July 1994 unless, before 1 January 1997, the performer or successor in title notified the person by whom the remuneration would be payable that he intends to exercise that right. Because of the timing of the 1996 Regulations, this left just a few short weeks for performers (and relevant copyright authors) to make their notification. The significance of the dates 1 July 1994 and 1 January 1997 is that they are set out in the Directive's provisions in Article 13 (application in time).[72]

Further transitional provisions and savings were made as a result of the changes made by the Copyright and Related Rights Regulations 2003.[73]

Directive 2006/116/EC of the European Parliament and of the Council of 12 December 2006 on the term of protection of copyright and certain related rights,[74] replaced the earlier Council Directive 93/98/EEC of 29 October 1993 harmonising the term of copyright and certain related rights.[75] Article 10 of the 2006 Directive contained transitional provisions which, when implemented in Germany, denied protection in relation to recordings that had at no time been protected in Germany. In Case C-240/07 *Sony Music Entertainment (Germany) GmbH v Falcon Neue Medien Vertrieb GmbH*,[76] Falcon distributed CDs in Germany which contained recordings of Bob Dylan songs which had been recorded before 1 January 1996 (the cut-off date for protection of recordings made by foreign nationals). However, these recordings were protected in the UK. The Court of Justice held that the transitional provisions applied even though the recordings in question had never been protected in the Member State for which protection was sought. Where a national of a non-Member State benefited from protection in at least one Member State, the transitional provisions applied. Thus, the Bob Dylan recordings would be entitled to protection under German law on copyright and related rights.

Offences

The criminal offences are detailed in s 198. They apply in respect of illicit recordings, recordings shown, played or communicated to the public and in respect of the making available right. A person commits an offence if, without sufficient consent, he:

(a) makes for sale or hire, or
(b) imports into the United Kingdom, otherwise than for his private and domestic use, or
(c) possesses in the course of business with a view to committing an act infringing any of the rights in performances, or
(d) in the course of business –
    (i)   sells or lets for hire, or
    (ii)   offers or exposes for sale or hire, or
    (iii) distributes,

a recording which he knows, or has reason to believe, is an illicit recording.

The offences under (a), (b) and (d) (iii) are triable either way, carrying a maximum of ten years' imprisonment and/or a fine on conviction on indictment[77] or, on summary conviction, imprisonment for a term not exceeding six months and/or a fine not exceeding £50,000.[78] Under s 198(1A), a person who infringes a performer's making available right in the course of business or otherwise to such an extent as to prejudicially affect the owner of the right commits an offence if he knows or has reason to believe that, by doing so,

---

72 Now Article 11 of Directive 2006/115/EC of the European Parliament and of the Council of 12 December 2006 on rental right and lending right and on certain rights related to copyright in the field of intellectual property, OJ L 376, 27.12.2006, p 28. This Directive replaced the original Directive.

73 SI 2003/2498.

74 OJ L 372, 27.12.2006, p 12.

75 OJ L 290, 24.11.1993, p 9.

76 [2009] ECR I-263.

77 This was increased from two years' imprisonment and/or a fine by the Copyright, etc. and Trade Marks (Offences and Enforcement) Act 2002.

78 The maximum fine was increased by the Digital Economy Act 2010, s 42(3).

he is infringing that right. This carries a maximum penalty on conviction on indictment of two years' imprisonment and/or a fine. On summary conviction, the maximum penalty is imprisonment for a term not exceeding three months and/or a fine not exceeding £50,000.

Section 198(2) makes it an offence, without sufficient consent, to cause a recording to be shown or played in public or communicated to the public. It is required that the person concerned knows or has reason to believe that any of the rights in performances will be infringed as a result of his actions. This offence and offences under s 198(1)(c), (d)(i) and (ii) are triable summarily only and carry a maximum penalty of six months' imprisonment and/or a fine not exceeding level 5 on the standard scale.

The meaning of 'sufficient consent' depends on whether the performance is a qualifying performance.[79] If it is, then it is the consent of the performer. Otherwise, and for the purposes of the 'making' offence, it is the consent of the performer or the person having the recording rights. For all the other offences where sufficient consent is required involving a non-qualifying performance, it is the consent of the person having the recording rights.[80] There are provisions for orders for delivery up in criminal proceedings (s 199) and for search warrants (s 200), and orders may be made for the disposal of illicit recordings (s 204).

Directors, managers, secretaries, and other similar officers of corporate bodies may also be liable where the offence is committed by a corporate body with their consent or connivance.[81] It is an offence for a person falsely to represent that he is authorised by any person to give the necessary consent in relation to a performance unless he believes, on reasonable grounds, that he is so authorised. This offence is triable summarily only and carries a maximum sentence of imprisonment for a period not exceeding six months and/or a fine not exceeding level 5 on the standard scale.

Overview

The statutory extension of performers' protection to give civil rights not only to performers but also to persons having exclusive recording contracts with those performers was a welcome and direct response to the growing problem of bootleg recordings. The subsequent development of performers' property rights is further recognition of the importance of such rights, as is the recent introduction of performers' moral rights. The inclusion of variety acts, extending the scope beyond performances of the 'original works' category of copyright, is sensible as such performances are no less deserving of protection. The law on rights in performances now makes it all the more important to ascertain the consent of *all* those taking part in a performance before making a recording, and it could hinder the future use of old recordings to make new recordings, for example by making a compilation of old recordings. The spectre of 'bit-part' actors withholding consent and preventing this future exploitation will be ever present in the minds of film and record companies.[82] This could have serious consequences for the BBC which has a large number of recordings of television comedy and drama, much of which was broadcast live. However, the Copyright Tribunal is there as a last resort should the performer unreasonably withhold his consent.

Some measure of international protection is afforded through the Rome Convention for the Protection of Performers, Producers of Phonograms and Broadcasting Organisations 1961, which has been ratified by 91 countries, including the UK.[83]

Finally, it should be noted that the provisions on the circumvention of technological measures under ss 296ZA to 296ZF and the provisions on electronic rights management information under s 296ZG also apply to rights in performances.

79 Copyright, Designs and Patents Act 1988 s 198(3).

80 If more than one person has the rights, the consent of all is required.

81 Copyright, Designs and Patents Act 1988 s 202. Both the officer and the corporate body are criminally liable.

82 Of course, employment and service contracts should provide for these rights in a way that facilitates the future exploitation of the work.

83 As at 1 February 2012. The Convention has not yet been ratified by the US.

Summary

Rights in performances are rights related to copyright, sometimes described as neighbouring rights to copyright. Performers have rights in relation to live performances as do persons having exclusive recording rights; that is, the exclusive right to make recordings of live performances with a view to their commercial exploitation.

Performers have the following rights:

- property rights:
  - reproduction
  - distribution
  - rental and lending
  - making available (for this and the former, there is a right to equitable remuneration);
- non-property rights:
  - making recordings, broadcasting, making recording from broadcast
  - showing, playing communication a recording to the public
  - in respect of importing, possessing or dealing with illicit recording;
- moral rights;
  - right to be identified as performer
  - right to object to a derogatory treatment.

An illicit recording is:

- (performer's rights) a recording of the whole or a substantial part of a performance made other than for private purposes without the performer's consent;
- (recording rights) as above but with respect to a performance subject to an exclusive recording contract without consent of either the performer or person entitled to the recording right;
- recordings made for the permitted acts but subsequently used beyond the scope of the permitted act.

Remedies for infringement of the performers' property rights are very similar to those for copyright infringement. Breaches of performers' non-property rights, performers' moral rights and in respect of recording rights are actionable as a breach of statutory duty.

There are a number of criminal offences, some of which carry a maximum penalty of ten years' imprisonment.

The EU has proposed extending the duration of the rights in performances from the present 50-year rule to 70 years. Further provisions are contemplated for the extended period such as 'use it or lose it', clean breaks in contracts between performers and recording companies and a contribution to payments to session musicians.

Discussion questions

1 Discuss the proposed Directive on the term of copyright and related rights and the impact on duration and other aspects of rights in performances. Should longer protection be afforded to performers as opposed to copyright authors? Are other measures, such as 'use it or lose it', 'clean break' and the payment of 20 per cent recording companies' revenues to be distributed to session musicians, justified economically or morally?

2 Describe the development of performers' rights in performances from the introduction in 1925 of criminal penalties for making illicit recordings of live performances to the present three-way protection by way of property rights, non-property rights and moral rights. Compare and contrast these rights with the rights of authors of original literary and musical works of copyright.

Selected further reading

European Parliament legislative resolution on the proposal for a Directive amending the term of copyright and related rights Directive, OJ C 184 E, 08.07.2010, p 331, available at: **http://eur-lex. europa.eu/LexUriServ/LexUriServ.do?uri=OJ:C:2010:184E:0331:0337:EN:PDF**

Gowers, A., *Gowers Review of Intellectual Property*, HMSO, December 2006, paras 4.20 to 4.47. Available at: **http://www.official-documents.gov.uk/document/other/0118404830/0118404830. pdf**.

Way, E. and Taylor, R., 'Featured Artists' Coalition: a strong voice in shaping the music industry of the future' [2009] *Entertainment Law Review*, 149 (looks at the call for increased rights made by the Featured Artists' Coalition and the EU proposal to extend the term or protection for performance rights and make other provisions including the 'use it or lose it' scheme).

Visit www.mylawchamber.co.uk/bainbridgeip to access study support resources including interactive multiple choice questions, practice exam questions with guidance, weblinks, legal updates and a legal newsfeed.

Part Three

THE LAW OF BREACH OF CONFIDENCE

Law of breach of confidence 10

Introduction

This area of law is concerned with secrets of all kinds. They may be of a personal, commercial or industrial nature, or concern the state and its administration. State secrets received a great deal of publicity some years ago as a result of the publication of *Spycatcher*, written by Peter Wright, a former assistant director of MI5, but it is in relation to trade secrets and business information that the law of confidence is of everyday importance. An obligation of confidence may arise in contract or be imposed by equity. The vast majority of persons owe an obligation of confidence to others: all employees have a duty of confidence or fidelity to their employers, consultants owe a duty to their clients, doctors have a duty of confidence in respect of their patients, and solicitors are bound by a duty of confidence to their clients. The law of confidence also covers business transactions and negotiations, and an obligation of confidence will be implied in a great many situations where there is no express agreement as to confidentiality.

Breach of confidence lies in the domain of equity and is almost entirely based on case law. In *Kitechnology BV v Unicor GmbH Plastmaschinen*[1] it was said that claims for breach of confidence did not arise in tort, were certainly non-contractual but were part of the equitable jurisdiction of the court. However, there is statutory recognition of the law of breach of confidence. For example, the Copyright, Designs and Patents Act 1988 s 171(1) states that:

> Nothing in this Part [the part of the Act dealing with copyright law] affects . . . the operation of any rule of equity relating to breaches of trust or confidence.

The notoriously widely drafted Official Secrets Act 1911 s 2 (replaced and narrowed by the Official Secrets Act 1989 s 1),[2] provided for a number of offences relating to the disclosure of confidential information to unauthorised persons.[3] Otherwise, disclosure of confidential information lies within the scope of the civil law and, being equitable, the law of confidence has proven to be reasonably flexible and a particularly useful adjunct to other intellectual property rights.

Whereas other rights such as copyright and patents are particularly useful when the subject matter is made public by exploitation by the right owner, the law of breach of confidence gives protection to things not released to the public or part of the public domain. Indeed, this is the whole point of the law of confidence, and its most useful feature is that, in appropriate cases, an injunction can be obtained preventing an anticipated wrongful release or use of the information that is the subject matter of the confidence. In terms of patent law, confidence is vital to the grant of a patent as it is essential that details of the invention do not fall into the public domain before the filing

1 [1995] FSR 765.

2 *See Lord Advocate v Scotsman Publications Ltd* [1990] AC 812 for a discussion of the Official Secrets Act 1989.

3 Section 2 of the 1911 Act became so infamous that juries had become inclined to acquit regardless of the evidence – for example, the trial and acquittal of the senior civil servant Clive Ponting for disclosure of Cabinet minutes relating to the sinking of the *General Belgrano: see R v Ponting* [1985] Crim LR 318.

of the patent application, otherwise the patent will be refused.[4] Confidence protects the invention and its detail. In some circumstances, the inventor may decide to keep his invention secret in preference to obtaining a patent, as the latter gives a maximum of 20 years' protection only. It depends on whether the information can be kept secret. As regards copyright, it has been seen that, as a matter of principle, copyright does not protect ideas, only the expression of ideas. However, confidence can and does protect ideas, but only until such time as those ideas are published in some way.

The Copyright, Designs and Patents Act 1988 gives a limited right to privacy in respect of certain photographs and films.[5] The law of breach of confidence may protect privacy if, for example, materials of a private nature have been shown or given to another to whom a duty of confidence attaches. Breach of confidence has developed to incorporate the English approach to the rights of privacy and freedom of expression under Articles 8 and 10 of the Council of Europe Convention for the Protection of Human Rights and Fundamental Freedoms 1950.[6] The basic requirement for confidence is the existence of a duty which may be expressed or imputed from the circumstances.

Development of the law of breach of confidence

The law of breach of confidence has had an erratic history. From earlier beginnings, it largely developed in a spurt in the early to middle of the nineteenth century, and then lay relatively dormant until the late 1940s when it was realised that this was an extremely useful area of law. Some of the early cases involved 'patent medicines'. There was obviously a lot of money to be made from these magic cures, bearing in mind that conventional medicine was still fairly primitive at this time and that the public at large was relatively ignorant and uneducated. In *Morison* v *Moat*,[7] such a medicine was made known as 'Morison's Vegetable Universal Medicine'. There was a dispute between the son of the person who originally devised the recipe and the partner, Thomas Moat, who had improperly told his own son of the recipe. It was held that there was an equity against the defendant. It was a breach of faith and of contract by the partner, Thomas Moat, to tell his son of the secret who, therefore, derived his knowledge under a breach of faith and of contract and could not claim a title to the recipe. Although the term 'breach of confidence' was not used at this stage, it was clear that the breach of faith was actionable *per se* and was not dependent upon the existence of a contract. There was no contractual relationship between the son of the originator of the recipe and the son of the defendant.

Another important case which helped establish this area of law concerned etchings made by Queen Victoria and Prince Albert. The case is *Prince Albert* v *Strange*.[8] The Queen and Prince Albert made etchings for their own amusement, intended only for their own private entertainment, although they sometimes had prints made to give to friends. Some of the etchings were sent to a printer for impressions (prints) to be made from them. While at the printers, someone surreptitiously made some additional prints from the etchings, which came into the hands of the defendant, who intended to display the prints in an exhibition to which the public could go on payment of an admission charge. The defendant advertised his intention to hold the exhibition and was sued by the Queen's Consort. It was held that relief would be given against the defendant even though he was a third party. The defendant had argued that the prints were not improperly taken, but it was said that his possession must have originated in a breach of trust, a breach of confidence or a breach of contract, and therefore an injunction was granted preventing the exhibition. Again, it was clear that relief was available without having to rely on a contractual relationship.

4 An exception is made where the information has been released by a person acting in breach of confidence in the previous six months: Patents Act 1977 s 2(4).

5 Copyright, Designs and Patents Act 1988 s 85.

6 Implemented by the Human Rights Act 1998.

7 (1851) 9 Hare 241.

8 (1849) 1 Mac & G 25.

The law of confidence and privacy

There was no fundamental right to privacy at English law. Occasionally, invasions of privacy may have been dealt with under the law of breach of confidence but this area of law did not provide a comprehensive and seamless law of privacy. This was changed by the Human Rights Act 1998 which gives effect, *inter alia*, to the rights and freedoms guaranteed under the Council of Europe Convention for the Protection of Human Rights and Fundamental Freedoms 1950 (the 'Human Rights Convention'). Article 8(1) of the Convention states that: '[e]veryone has the right to respect for his private and family life, his home and his correspondence'.[9] This is subject to possible derogation for a number of purposes including national security, the prevention of crime or the protection of the rights or freedoms of others. The weakness of the law of confidence in providing a remedy for invasions of privacy before the Human Rights Act 1998 was highlighted by the case of *Kaye* v *Robertson*,[10] in which a journalist and a photographer gained access to Mr Gordon Kaye's private hospital room and took photographs and conducted an interview when Mr Kaye was in no fit state to be interviewed or to give consent. Mr Kaye, the actor from the television comedy series *'Allo 'Allo*, had, while driving, been struck by a piece of wood and suffered severe head and brain injuries. In allowing in part the appeal against an injunction imposed by Potter J, the Court of Appeal judges were unanimous in their call for a legal right to privacy.[11] Of course, since the Human Rights Act 1998, it is unlikely that *Kaye* v *Robertson* would today be decided the same way on the issue of privacy.

Since the assimilation of human rights law into the laws of the UK, there have been some important developments in the courts here, building on and supplemented by decisions of the European Court of Human Rights. It is now clear that the Convention Rights apply not only to protect individuals against arbitrary interference with the rights by public authorities but also, in relation to the right of respect for private and family life, to impose obligations on states to secure respect for private or family life even in the context of relations between individuals. This was made clear in *von Hannover* v *Germany*[12] in which photographs were taken by the press of Princess Caroline of Monaco in public places. It was held by the European Court of Human Rights that her right of privacy had been breached. The photographs did not relate to her duties, obligations or suchlike as a Princess but showed her, for example, in a restaurant with a friend, on horseback, on a skiing holiday and with her children.

This seems to go a little further than *Campbell* v *Mirror Group Newspapers*, *infra*, which English courts below the House of Lords are bound to apply. In *Murray* v *Express Newspapers plc*,[13] a photographer with a camera with a long-range lens took a photograph of J.K. Rowling's son, then under two years old, in a pushchair on a public street accompanied by J.K. Rowling and her husband. The photograph was taken without their knowledge or consent. Taking and publishing photographs of innocuous acts, such a taking a bus or walking down a street should not give rise to an action for breach of confidence or invasion of privacy. Such activities do not raise an expectation of privacy. According to Lightman J (at para 65) 'If a simple walk down the street qualifies for protection then it is difficult to see what would not.' Although he expressed sympathy for persons wishing to shield their children from intrusive media attention, as it stands, the law does not allow them '. . . to carve out a press-free zone for their children in respect of absolutely everything they choose to do'.[14] However, the Court of Appeal disagreed with Lightman J and ordered a trial.[15] Following *Campbell* v *Mirror Group Newspapers*, the Court of Appeal held that the test to be applied was whether the claimant had a reasonable expectation of privacy so as to engage his Article 8 right to privacy viewed from the perspective of how a reasonable person of ordinary sensibilities would feel if placed in the same position as the claimant and subject to the same publicity. In the circumstances of the case involving the clandestine taking of

9 Data protection law, which itself finds its roots in the Human Rights Convention, may also have an impact.

10 [1991] FSR 62.

11 Although the libel claim failed, the action for malicious falsehood succeeded, but only in as much as the defendant could not claim that the interview had taken place with Mr Kaye's consent. For contemporary articles on the then perceived need for a law of privacy, *see* Markesinis, B.S.I. 'Our patchy law of privacy – time to do something about it' (1990) 53 MLR 802; and Prescott, P. '*Kaye* v *Robertson* – a reply' (1991) 53 MLR 451. *See* also the Calcutt Committee Report, *On Privacy and Related Matters*, Cm 1102, HMSO, 1990.

12 (2005) 40 EHRR 1.

13 [2007] ECDR 20.

14 At para 66. Of course, if the media attention causes alarm or distress, there may be remedies under the Protection from Harassment Act 1997 which includes criminal penalties and civil remedies.

15 *Murray* v *Express Newspapers plc* [2009] Ch 481.

a photograph and its subsequent publication, it was at least arguable that the claimant had a reasonable expectation of privacy as a child.

The decision in *von Hannover* is wider than that in *Campbell v Mirror Group Newspapers*. In the former case, it was even held to be a breach of Princess Caroline's right to privacy to publish photographs of her in public places going about her normal business without being engaged in embarrassing, intimate or private activities. However, taking and publishing the photographs could be seen as part of a campaign of harassment conducted against her by the media. On the other hand taking and publishing a photograph of a famous person popping out for a bottle of milk would not engage the right to privacy.[16]

Article 10 of the Human Rights Convention provides for the right of freedom of expression. This right is also subject to derogations but there is ample opportunity for this right to conflict with the 'right of privacy'. In some respects, it could be claimed that the law of confidence has developed to provide a balance, for example, by protecting the right of privacy subject to disclosure in the public interest. Lord Nicholls in the House of Lords in *Campbell v Mirror Group Newspapers Ltd*[17] went so far as to say that the law of breach of confidence had developed to such a stage that it represented the UK's implementation of the Convention rights of privacy and freedom of expression. He said (at para 17):

> The time has come to recognise that the values enshrined in arts 8 and 10 are now part of the cause of action for breach of confidence. As Lord Woolf CJ has said, the courts have been able to achieve this result by absorbing the rights protected by arts 8 and 10 into this cause of action: see A v B (*a company*) [2002] EWCA Civ 337 at [4], [2002] 2 All ER 545 at [4], [2003] QB 195. Further, it should now be recognised that for this purpose these values are of general application. The values embodied in arts 8 and 10 are as much applicable in disputes between individuals or between an individual and a non-governmental body such as a newspaper as they are in disputes between individuals and a public authority.

Later, in the Court of Appeal in *Douglas v Hello! Ltd (No 6)*,[18] Lord Phillips of Worth Matravers MR said that the courts should develop, as far as they can, the action for breach of confidence so as to give effect to the Convention rights under Articles 8 and 10.[19] In that case, photographs were taken surreptitiously at the wedding of Michael Douglas and Catherine Zeta-Jones, who had 'sold' the exclusive rights to take photographs to *OK! Magazine* for £500,000 each. The unauthorised photographs were published in the defendant's magazine. The Court of Appeal confirmed that there had been a breach of the Douglases right of privacy and a breach of what was described as their commercial confidence. It was accepted that persons in the public eye who seek publicity have a right in their image as a commodity which can be dealt with as with any trade secret. In the circumstances of the case, the official photographs were such a commodity that the Douglases had a right to keep secret until the time they chose to make them public. Ordinary individuals with no 'celebrity' status would not necessarily have a commercial confidence though they do have a right of privacy. However, the Court of Appeal held that *OK! Magazine* had no right of commercial confidence it could invoke against *Hello! Magazine*, that the obligation of confidence owed to *OK! Magazine* only covered the photographs taken on its behalf and no others.

The House of Lords, by a 3:2 majority in co-joined cases known as *OBG Ltd v Allan*,[20] reversed the Court of Appeal decision in *Douglas v Hello!* to the extent that it had held that *OK! Magazine* had no right of commercial confidence. Photographs of the wedding were confidential in the sense that none was available publicly.[21] It had been made clear to everyone attending that no one other than the authorised photographer was to take photographs of the wedding. That imposed an obligation of confidence for the benefit of *OK! Magazine* as well as the Douglases. Publishing the unauthorised photographs clearly caused a detriment to *OK! Magazine* and, consequently, all the ingredients of a breach of confidence action set out by Megarry J in *Coco v Clark, infra*, were present. There was no public policy reason why the law would not protect information of a particular sort only,

16 Per Baroness Hale in *Campbell v Mirror Group Newspapers Ltd* [2004] 2 AC 457 at para 154. Of course, whilst the lower courts may have regard to decisions of the European Court of Human Rights, they are bound by previous House of Lords (now Supreme Court) decisions.

17 [2004] 2 AC 457.

18 [2005] 3 WLR 881.

19 *See* also *McKennitt v Ash* [2007] 3 WLR 194 where Buxton LJ said (at para 11) '. . . in order to find the rules of the English law of breach of confidence we now have to look at the jurisprudence of Articles 8 and 10'.

20 [2007] 2 WLR 920. This involved appeals in three cases on the tort of inducing a breach of contract or causing loss by unlawful means and, in the appeal by *OK! Magazine*, also an appeal against the finding of the Court of Appeal on whether *OK! Magazine* had a commercial confidence which it could enforce against Hello! Ltd.

21 Of course, the confidential quality in relation to the authorised photographs was lost once they were published but this did not affect the confidential nature of any other photographs.

photographic images as distinct to information about the wedding generally. Photographic images were commercially valuable and the Douglases had exercised sufficient control to impose an obligation of confidence.

The public interest defence, described in more detail later, was narrowly construed in the *Campbell* case. The supermodel Naomi Campbell had previously claimed that she did not have a drug addiction. The defendant newspaper published articles showing that she had been undergoing treatment at Narcotics Anonymous. The articles included details about the treatment she was undergoing and photographs showing her leaving meetings of Narcotics Anonymous with others undergoing treatment. The House of Lords, by a 3:2 majority, held that this was a breach of confidence. Whilst it was acceptable to publish a story about her having lied about taking drugs and her addiction and the fact that she was receiving therapy, publishing the additional information about the treatment with Narcotics Anonymous together with details of the treatment and the photograph went too far. Of course, publishing any of the information would have been a breach of confidence apart from the fact that Naomi Campbell was someone who sought publicity and was a role model.

22 [1977] 2 All ER 751.

This decision puts into doubt the correctness of some earlier cases, especially *Woodward v Hutchins*,[22] described later, in the level of detail of information that can be published on the basis of public interest where publicity-seeking celebrities are concerned. However, an important point made in *Campbell* in the Court of Appeal was that publishing the additional information and photograph was important to give credibility to the story. In the House of Lords one of the dissenting judges, Lord Hoffmann, said that some editorial latitude should be allowed. Given the exigencies of newspaper publishing, it is not always possible to judge to a nicety what should and should not be published. This is particularly so in relation to photographs which readers have come to expect. Lord Nicholls, also dissenting, said of the balance between privacy and freedom of expression (at para 28):

> The balance ought not to be held at a point which would preclude, in this case, a degree of journalistic latitude in respect of information published for this purpose.

Where the balance between privacy and freedom of expression lies may depend on the context and it may lie more towards the freedom of expression end of the spectrum where the information relates to politics rather than in the case of film and television celebrities. What these cases show is that even celebrities have a right of privacy and, whilst it might be acceptable to publish a photograph of a famous person walking down a public street, it would not necessarily be acceptable, *per se*, to publish a photograph of such a person engaged in a private meeting even if it takes place in a public place.

Of course, a right to privacy is not central to the law of breach of confidence in an industrial or commercial context and the following discussion of the modern law of breach of confidence focuses on the impact and development of this useful area of law in relation to industrial and commercial information including 'trade secrets'.

The modern law of breach of confidence

The law of breach of confidence began its renaissance about 60 years ago. It became apparent that this area of law was extremely well suited to protecting 'industrial property' during the development stages before other legal rights were able to afford protection.[23] Indeed, some industrialists had come to the conclusion that it was better to keep some details of their processes secret rather than obtain a patent which would mean that, eventually, the invention would fall into the public domain. However, it seems as if the significance of this area of law was not fully appreciated by law reporters. A number of

23 'Industrial property' can be considered to include patents, trade marks and industrial designs.

important cases were reported in some series of law reports retrospectively, several years after the judgments were handed down.

The first major case on the law of breach of confidence that laid the foundations for its modern form was *Saltman Engineering Co Ltd v Campbell Engineering Co Ltd*.[24] The claimant owned the copyright in drawings of tools for use in the manufacture of leather punches. The defendant was given the drawings and instructed to make 5,000 of the tools at 3*s* 6*d* each. After completing the order, the defendant retained the drawings and made use of them for its own purposes. In finding for the claimant, holding that there was an implied condition that the defendant should treat the drawings as confidential, not make other use of them, and should deliver up the drawings with the tools made pursuant to the agreement,[25] Lord Greene MR described the nature of confidential information thus:

> The information, to be confidential, must, I apprehend, apart from contract, have the necessary quality of confidence about it, namely, it must not be something which is public property and public knowledge. On the other hand, it is perfectly possible to have a confidential document, be it a formula, a plan, a sketch, or something of that kind, which is the result of work done by the maker upon materials which may be available for the use of anybody; but what makes it confidential is the fact that the maker of the document has used his brain and thus produced a result which can only be produced by somebody who goes through the same process.[26]

Lord Greene also emphasised that an obligation of confidence is not limited to cases where the parties are in a contractual relationship; that the law will prevent an abuse of position by the recipient of confidential information. He also indicated that there need be nothing special about the information concerned and that others may be able to derive the information for themselves but will need to invest some effort to obtain that information. In other words, the recipient of confidential information will be prevented from making unfair use of the information outside that contemplated by the person giving it. It can be said that a person fixed with a duty of confidence is in an analogous position to that of a trustee; however, in the case of a person fixed with an obligation of confidence, the nature of that duty is always negative, that is he must not use or divulge the information outside the authority given to him by his confider.

Megarry J further developed the action of breach of confidence and laid down a good working formula for the application of this area of law in the case of *Coco v AN Clark (Engineers) Ltd*.[27] The claimant, one Marco Paolo Coco, designed a moped engine and had entered into informal negotiations with the defendant with a view to the latter manufacturing the engine. In the end the negotiations broke down and no contract was executed between the claimant and the defendant. The claimant suggested that the defendant had deliberately caused the breakdown in negotiations with a view to making the engine without paying the claimant. When the defendant decided to manufacture its own engine to a design which closely resembled the claimant's design, the claimant sought an interim injunction to prevent the defendant using confidential information given by the claimant for the purposes of a proposed joint venture.

Megarry J stated that the doctrine of confidence required three elements as follows:

1 The information must have the necessary quality of confidence about it (using Lord Greene's definition in *Saltman*).
2 The information must have been imparted in circumstances importing an obligation of confidence.
3 There must be an unauthorised use of that information to the detriment of the party communicating it.

However, in the event, the claimant was not granted an injunction and had, at best, a weak case. Where information was communicated in the expectation that the claimant would be paid, it was doubtful whether an injunction was an appropriate remedy if there

24 [1963] 3 All ER 413, also reported in (1948) 65 RPC 203.

25 There was no contract between the claimant and the defendant who had been subcontracted to make the tools. The defendant was instructed to deliver up the drawings and an inquiry into damages was ordered.

26 [1963] 3 All ER 413 at 415.

27 [1969] RPC 41.

was subsequently a dispute. Megarry J ordered that the defendant give an undertaking to pay a royalty of 5s per engine made into a special joint bank account on trusts, should he manufacture the engines, pending the full trial. The formula used by Megarry J forms a useful basis for exploring the nature and scope of the law of breach of confidence and is used as a framework for the discussion later.

The equitable nature of the law of breach of confidence was stressed by Ungoed-Thomas J in *Duchess of Argyll* v *Duke of Argyll*[28] where he said:

28 [1967] Ch 303 at 322.

> These cases [*Prince Albert* v *Strange*, etc.] in my view indicate (1) that a contract or obligation of confidence need not be expressed but can be implied . . . (2) that a breach of confidence or trust or faith can arise independently of any right of property or contract other, of course, than any contract which the imparting of the confidence in the relevant circumstances may itself create; (3) that the court in the exercise of its equitable jurisdiction will restrain a breach of confidence independently of any right at law.

It is clear an obligation will be implied in many situations but, as Ungoed-Thomas J acknowledged, the obligation may be created expressly by way of a contract (an express contractual obligation may run alongside or replace an obligation that would otherwise be imposed by equity). For example, a contract of employment or service may include terms imposing an obligation of confidence on one or both parties. Further, in some contracts, the subject matter may be the confidential information itself, for example where a designer gives details of his design to a manufacturer in return for royalties.

Being rooted in equity, the law of confidence retains a useful flexibility and it has been developed at an extraordinary rate by the courts over the last three or four decades. Nevertheless, the Law Commission recommended that this area of law be codified and a draft Bill was produced in 1981.[29] A major advantage of the law of breach of confidence has been its flexibility and the way in which it has been developed by the courts, freed from the straightjacket of statutory interpretation. It might be wondered, therefore, what would be gained by codifying this area of law, which works reasonably effectively, to replace it with sterile legislation. The Law Commission must have appreciated this as much of the draft Bill is couched in general terms, and indeed the Law Commission stated:

29 Law Commission Report No. 110, *Breach of Confidence*, Cmnd 8388, HMSO, 1981.

> . . . we should emphasise that the legislative framework which we envisage would allow the Courts wide scope in applying its principles to differing situations and changing social circumstances.[30]

30 Ibid., para 6.1.

If this is the basis upon which the legislation would be founded it is difficult to see what advantage would be gained by its promulgation. Widely drafted legislation might have some unfortunate and unpredictable effects, while the track record of the courts in developing this area of equity has been good and there is no reason to believe that judicial common sense cannot provide for the future satisfactory development of the law of confidence. Such considerations may account for the fact that no moves have been made to codify the law of confidence and it would seem that codification is extremely unlikely in the foreseeable future.[31]

31 For a brief overview of the Law Commission's draft Bill, *see* Reid, B.C. (1986) *Confidentiality and the Law*, Waterlow, p 190.

One area the draft Bill addressed that was unclear and in need of development was the position of persons improperly acquiring information, for example by industrial espionage or surreptitiously. In many cases, the information concerned has been divulged willingly by the person who 'owns' the information. However, where a person acquires information by eavesdropping, or by other means such as computer hacking or other unauthorised taking or copying of information, it was not certain whether an obligation of confidence exists. Perhaps the difficulty stems from one of the guidelines laid down by Megarry J in *Coco* v *AN Clark (Engineers) Ltd*,[32] that is that the information must have been imparted in circumstances importing an obligation of confidence. This is an important point as, because of developments and improvements in areas of technology such as telecommunications, it is much easier for determined people to gain access to confidential

32 [1969] RPC 41.

information on a worldwide basis. In the case of *Prince Albert* v *Strange*,[33] the court did not know how the prints came into the defendant's possession, only that the prints must have been made surreptitiously. Nevertheless, the court was willing to give relief. It seems plausible that the principle as associated with this case can be applied to persons gaining access to confidential material without permission, that is in respect to the improper acquisition of information, and that Megarry J's test is unduly restrictive on this point. Indeed, in *Douglas* v *Hello! Ltd (No 6)*,[34] it was accepted that taking photographs surreptitiously was a breach of the right of privacy and a breach of 'commercial confidence'. The protection afforded extended to the magazine contracted to publish the authorised photographs as confirmed in the House of Lords.[35]

To determine whether information should be treated as confidential by its recipient, a reasonable person approach is helpful. In *Napier* v *Pressdram Ltd*,[36] Toulson LJ said (at para 42):

> For a duty of confidentiality to be owed . . . the information in question must be of a nature and obtained in circumstances such that any reasonable person in the position of the recipient ought to recognise that it should be treated as confidential. As Cross J observed in Printers & Finishers Ltd v Holloway (No.2) [1965] RPC 239 at 256, the law would defeat its own object if it seeks to enforce in this field standards which would be rejected by the ordinary person. Freedom to report the truth is a precious thing both for the liberty of the individual (the libertarian principle) and for the sake of wider society (the democratic principle), and it would be unduly eroded if the law of confidentiality were to prevent a person from reporting facts which a reasonable person in his position would not perceive to be confidential.

Although this case did not involve trade secrets as such (*Napier* was concerned with information about a Law Society investigation following a complaint of a conflict of interest by a solicitor and his firm), the same considerations must also apply to trade secrets.

Returning to Megarry J's formula for breach of confidence, the nature of this useful area of law is now examined in more detail commencing with the necessary quality of confidence.

Confidential quality

Nature of confidential quality

The sort of material protected may be technical, commercial or personal. In *R* v *Department of Health, ex parte Source Informatics Ltd*,[37] Simon Brown LJ accepted the proposition that there are four main classes of information traditionally regarded as confidential, being trade secrets, personal confidences, government information and artistic and literary confidences.[38] In that case, use of information about patients' prescriptions which had been converted into an anonymous form was acceptable. The purpose of the law of confidence in such circumstances was to protect personal confidences and this did not give the patients a property right in the information.

In the context of this book, the information usually will be a trade secret, related to business, commercial or industrial activity or enterprise such as in the *Coco* case. The value of such information should not be taken for granted and it can be surprising how important some secrets are even though they may seem mundane at first sight. For example, there was a dispute about a cockle bottling secret in which the cockle bottlers' greatest problem was discussed, being to achieve the right acidity level, that is, strong enough to preserve the cockles without being too strong so as to be unpleasant to taste.[39] Secrets of a personal nature are also protected, even if relating to sexual conduct of a lurid nature. It was held in *Stephens* v *Avery*[40] that there was no reason why such information,

33 (1849) 1 Mac & G 25.

34 [2005] 3 WLR 881.

35 *OBG Ltd* v *Allan* [2007] 2 WLR 920.

36 [2009] EMLR 21.

37 [2001] FSR 8.

38 See also *Electro Cad Australia Pty Ltd* v *Mejati Rcs Sdn Bhd* [1999] FSR 291, High Court of Malaysia.

39 *The Times*, 24 June 1986. In an earlier dispute which involved the same claimant who was a bottler of cockles and mussels, the founder of the claimant company had obtained £530,000 in damages in respect of the copying of an onion peeling machine.

40 [1988] 1 Ch 457. Followed in *Michael Barrymore* v *News Group Newspapers Ltd* [1997] FSR 600.

expressly communicated in confidence, could not be subject to an enforceable duty of confidence. The background to that case was the killing of Mrs Telling by her husband. Details of a sexual relationship between Mrs Stephens, the claimant, and Mrs Telling were disclosed in confidence to a friend, Mrs Avery, the defendant, who had published the information in a newspaper. While a court would not protect information of a grossly immoral nature, on the basis of *Glyn v Weston Feature Film Co Ltd*,[41] the difficulty in this instance was identifying what was grossly immoral. A general code of sexual morals accepted by the overwhelming majority of the public no longer existed and there was no common view that sexual conduct between consenting adults, two females in this case, was grossly immoral.[42] After all, the story was not so shocking as to prevent the editor spreading the story across the pages of a major national newspaper for personal profit, and it lay ill in the mouth of the defendant to claim that the law did not protect the confidentiality of information of this sort.

Confidential information is not restricted to the written or printed word and an image may properly be regarded as confidential information. In *Douglas v Hello! Ltd*,[43] an unknown person took photographs without authorisation at the wedding of the actors Michael Douglas and Catherine Zeta-Jones. These photographs were to be published by the defendant in its magazine but the actors obtained an interim injunction. The actors had carefully controlled photography at their wedding and had granted exclusive rights to publish photographs of the wedding to another publisher (the proprietor of *OK! Magazine*). Stringent security measures were in place to prevent the taking of photographs by anyone other than the official photographer engaged by the actors. The defendant knew of the measures taken and the Court of Appeal accepted that the Douglases had a right to privacy and a right to a commercial confidence which had been breached by the defendant.[44]

An objective test should be applied to determine whether information is truly confidential. Simply marking a document with the words 'PRIVATE AND CONFIDENTIAL' will not suffice if the contents are commonplace and lie within the public domain, such as a simple, straightforward recipe for bread which contains nothing unusual in terms of the ingredients or the methods to be employed in the mixing and baking of the dough. In *Dalrymple's Application*[45] a manufacturer distributed over 1,000 technical bulletins to members of a trade association, marking them 'CONFIDENTIAL' and including a statement on the front of the documents to the effect that the contents were not to be divulged to non-members. The material in the bulletins could not be regarded as confidential. Even distribution of a report marked 'PRIVATE AND CONFIDENTIAL' to only ten out of 350 members of the British Cast Iron Research Association was fatal to confidentiality.[46] On the other hand, lack of a notice that something is confidential does not mean that the information will not be protected by the law of confidence. In *Collag Corp v Merck & Co Inc*,[47] it was said that operators of manufacturing processes often consider their process to be confidential and take steps to keep it secret, imposing obligations on suppliers and the like. They would strongly resist any suggestion that their competitors be allowed to look around their manufacturing plant. However, that does not mean to say that the process is confidential and all three elements identified in *Coco v Clark* must be present for an action in breach of confidence. On the other hand, failing to mark a document as 'confidential' does not, *per se*, deprive it of any confidential nature it may possess.

Trade practice may give an indication of whether a form of information will be regarded as confidential by the courts. For example, in *IBCOS Computers Ltd v Barclays Mercantile Highland Finance Ltd*,[48] Jacob J said that the source code for a computer program was confidential because it was not usually given to clients by software developers who regarded it as confidential. Even if a source code is made available to a client under a licence agreement, the licence will most likely contain terms imposing an obligation of confidence on the licensee in respect of the source code.[49]

41 [1916] 1 Ch 261.

42 The analogy with copyright law in respect of works of a grossly immoral nature failed to find sympathy, so the modern relevance of cases like *Glyn v Weston Feature Film Co Ltd* [1916] 1 Ch 261 must be doubted.

43 [2001] FSR 40. An early example of a breach of confidence involving a photograph was *Pollard v Photographic Company* (1889) 40 Ch D 345. A photograph of a woman taken for private purposes had been incorporated in a Christmas card without permission.

44 *Douglas v Hello! Ltd (No 6)* [2005] 3 WLR 881, discussed *supra*.

45 [1957] RPC 449.

46 *Young's Patents* (1943) 60 RPC 51.

47 [2003] FSR 16.

48 [1994] FSR 275.

49 Jacob J went on to find that one of the defendants had access to the claimant's source code while writing his software and was, consequently, in breach of confidence in addition to infringing copyright.

The information does not have to be particularly special in any way and a compilation of already known information such as a list of customers can, when taken as a whole, be regarded as confidential.[50] What makes such information worth protecting by confidence is the fact that time and effort has been expended in gathering, selecting and arranging the information.[51] In other words, a competitor should not be permitted to take a short cut by 'stealing' information belonging to someone else – he should have to go through a similar process and discover the information for himself by his own labours.[52]

A combination of information taken together may be confidential even though it is doubtful that each item of information, taken separately, is confidential. In *Indata Equipment Supplies Ltd* v *ACL Ltd*,[53] the information disclosed by the claimant to the defendant concerned the provision of a fleet of cars to a potential client of the claimant, being information relating to the price of cars, full details of the client's requirements, the sums it was prepared to pay, its preferred payment scheme and its time constraints. The defendant used this information to offer the client a lower 'on the road' price for the cars. In finding the profit margin and, to a lesser degree, the invoice price to be confidential information, Otton LJ said (at 259):

> The information for which confidence is claimed must not be considered in isolation but in the context of other information where it is doubtful that any confidence arose.

Simon Brown LJ expressed some doubt about whether the invoiced prices were protected by confidence as he thought it difficult to think of circumstances in which a buyer would need the seller's authority to disclose the price of goods he had bought to another.

In *Burrows* v *Smith*,[54] the claimant had an idea for a computer game some time before entering into an employment contract. There was nothing novel about the features and elements of the game as envisaged by the claimant but, nevertheless, Norris J held that, although no single element of the game was novel, the combination of elements was original and had the necessary quality of confidence.[55]

In *Thomas Marshall (Exports)* v *Guinle*,[56] the defendant was appointed as the managing director of the claimant company for ten years. The company's business largely concerned the purchase of clothing from Eastern Europe and the Far East and the sale of such clothing to retail outlets. The defendant's service agreement stated that he was not to engage in any other business without the company's consent and that he must not disclose confidential information. Further, after ceasing to be the managing director, he was not to use or disclose confidential information about the suppliers and customers of the claimant company. The defendant began to trade on his own account and on behalf of two companies in competition with the claimant company. When his service contract had another four-and-a-half years left to run, he purported to resign. It was held that the court would restrain the defendant from committing further breaches of his employment contract and that an interim injunction would be granted in respect of the defendant's breach of the obligations of fidelity and good faith to his employer. Sir Robert Megarry V-C suggested that four elements were important when testing for confidential quality:

1 The information must be such that the owner believes that its release would be injurious to him, or would be advantageous to his rivals or to others.
2 The owner of the information must believe it to be confidential or secret and not already in the public domain.
3 The owner's belief in 1 and 2 above must be reasonable.
4 The information must be judged in the light of usages and practices of the particular trade or industry concerned.

According to this test, a certain amount of subjectivity is allowed on the part of the owner of the information, but this is restricted by the requirement that the owner's beliefs must be reasonable. On this basis, it is possible that a duty of confidence could arise and attract

50 *Inline Logistics Ltd* v *UCI Logistics Ltd* [2002] RPC 32.

51 Such a collection of data could also have protection under the database right provided for by the Copyright and Rights in Databases Regulations 1997, SI 1997/3032.

52 In *Oxford* v *Moss* (1978) 68 Cr App R 183 it was held that information is not property for the purposes of theft.

53 [1998] FSR 248.

54 [2010] EWHC 22 (Ch).

55 However, the information had not been imparted in circumstances imposing an obligation of confidence.

56 [1979] FSR 208.

legal remedies even if the information was actually in the public domain if the owner's contrary belief was reasonable. This seems to go too far. Surely, the test of whether information is confidential is objective. In *Lancashire Fires Ltd* v *SA Lyons & Co Ltd*,[57] Carnwath J, at first instance, noted this subjective emphasis in *Thomas Marshall*, saying that it does not appear in earlier authorities and explaining its presence by the context of *Thomas Marshall*, which was concerned with the construction of a specific provision in a contract. Conversely, as an actionable breach of confidence is based, at least partly, on an equity being fastened on the conscience of the defendant, the behaviour of the defendant may be a factor.[58] In *R* v *Department of Health, ex parte Source Informatics Ltd*,[59] the Court of Appeal accepted that the confidant's own conscience was the touchstone used to determine the scope of the duty and whether it had been breached.

The law of breach of confidence cannot protect information that is unmistakably in the public domain,[60] notwithstanding that a compilation of materials taken from the public domain may be protected. In some cases, the information concerned will be a mixture of confidential information and matter already in the public domain. In such cases, the onus will be on the claimant to identify what is confidential and what is not. This is important at an interim hearing as well as at a full trial. For example, if an interim injunction is granted preventing the further use or disclosure of the information, the defendant must be able to distinguish between information he must not use and that which he is free to. Where the information can be disentangled and the confidential information identified and classified as such, then the claimant must do that, even at an interim stage.[61] This is important also in determining whether confidential information had been communicated under an obligation of confidence and whether there had been an unauthorised use of confidential information.[62]

Similar principles apply to applications for search orders. In *Gadget Shop Ltd* v *Bug.Com Ltd*[63] it was held that the confidential information that was alleged to have been misused must be clearly identified at the interim stage and the claimant had failed to exercise the care required to ensure that its evidence in this respect was true. A significant amount of the information alleged to be confidential had been put into the public domain by the claimant by publication on its website.

If the claimant himself has placed information in the public domain, that does not necessarily deprive a more detailed version of that information of its confidential nature. In Ashworth *Security Hospital* v *MGN Ltd*,[64] the *Daily Mirror* published an article about Ian Brady who had been convicted with Myra Hindley of 'the Moors Murders'. During a hunger strike in 1999, Ian Brady launched a media campaign and wrote to the BBC and published information through his solicitor. The newspaper article included detailed observations taken from Ian Brady's file in a database by a person unknown who had passed on the information to a journalist. In the Court of Appeal, Lord Philips MR said:

> I do not consider the publicity generated by Ian Brady himself in the period before publication of the *Mirror* article had the effect of stripping the cloak of confidentiality from the more detailed records about Brady on the PACIS database.

The defendant's appeal against an order disclosing its source of the information as published was dismissed by the House of Lords, which agreed with the Court of Appeal decision and said that Article 10 of the Human Rights Convention required that the courts should carefully scrutinise any request for relief, including disclosure of a journalist's sources, which interfered with freedom of expression. In this particular case, it was said to be important that the source be identified and punished to act as a deterrent to such wrongdoing in future. The order for disclosure was, therefore, necessary, proportionate and justified.[65]

It is important to distinguish material alleged to be confidential from other material that can be used lawfully. In *Vestergaard Frandsen A/S* v *Bestnet Europe Ltd*,[66] an application

57 [1996] FSR 629.

58 The behaviour of the defendant in *Indata Equipment Supplies Ltd* v *ACL Ltd* [1998] FSR 248 seemed to colour the judgments of Simon Brown and Otton LJJ.

59 [2001] FSR 8.

60 Lord Goff described the public domain as information which is so generally accessible that, in all the circumstances, it cannot be regarded as confidential in *Attorney-General* v *Guardian Newspapers (No. 2)* [1990] 1 AC 109. He also said that a duty of confidence would not apply to useless information or trivia.

61 *CMI-Centers for Medical Innovation GmbH* v *Phytopharm plc* [1999] FSR 235.

62 *Inline Logistics Ltd* v *UCI Logistics Ltd* [2002] RPC 32.

63 [2001] FSR 26.

64 [2001] FSR 32.

65 [2002] 1 WLR 2033.

66 [2007] EWHC 2455 (Ch).

to strike out an action for breach of confidence failed. The confidential information related to a mosquito net. The defendants claimed that some of the information was in the public domain, being contained in a published patent specification. However, that information did not seem to be the same as the information claimed to be confidential. Furthermore, the defendants submitted an expert report which did not clearly distinguish between information claimed to be confidential and information which ex-employees could be expected to remember following termination of their employment.

Trade secret

The term 'trade secret' is often used in relation to confidential information associated with industrial and commercial activity. The classification of some forms of confidential information as trade secrets is important because the protection afforded by the law may depend upon it. Unfortunately, there is no satisfactory legal definition of the term.

In *Herbert Morris Ltd* v *Saxelby*,[67] Lord Atkinson spoke of trade secrets thus (at 705):

67 [1916] 1 AC 688.

> . . . trade secrets, such as prices, &c. or any secret process or things of a nature which the man [the defendant] was not entitled to reveal.

In that case, Lord Parker suggested a test based on the detailed nature of the information. Information that was far too detailed to be carried away in the head was a trade secret, whereas a general method or scheme that could easily be remembered could not be regarded as a trade secret. At first instance, in *Faccenda Chicken Ltd* v *Fowler*,[68] Goulding J defined three classes of information, being:

68 [1985] 1 All ER 724.

1 Information which, because of its trivial character or its easy accessibility from public sources, cannot be regarded as confidential.
2 Information which an employee must treat as confidential, but which, once learned, reasonably remains in the employee's head and becomes part of his skill and experience.
3 Specific trade secrets so confidential that a continuing duty of confidence applies even beyond the termination of employment or the service contract.

This classification provides little guidance as to what precisely distinguishes a trade secret from information in the second category, but it does show that such information will be given less protection. In *Lancashire Fires Ltd* v *SA Lyons & Co Ltd*,[69] Sir Thomas Bingham MR said that the distinction between Class 2 and Class 3 may, on the facts, be very hard to draw but the Court of Appeal did apply Goulding J's classification. There may be a problem with Goulding J's 2nd class, and in *Ocular Sciences Ltd* v *Aspect Vision Care Ltd*,[70] Laddie J admitted difficulty with it, arguing that it had little to do with confidence. Perhaps it is more a question of the employee's duty of fidelity to his present employer. This duty would prevent him, whilst still employed, putting his skill and expertise at the disposal of another employer whether or not that involved confidential information. As Laddie J said, '. . . he is expected to work for his employer not for his employer's competitors'.

69 [1996] FSR 629.

70 [1997] RPC 289.

Of trade secrets, in a restraint of trade case, *Lansing Linde Ltd* v *Kerr*,[71] Staughton LJ spoke in terms of information that would be liable to cause real harm if it was disclosed to a competitor, provided it was used in a trade or business and the owner had either limited the dissemination of the information, or at least not encouraged or permitted widespread publication. Butler-Sloss LJ stressed the need to take account of the changing nature of business and the need to take account of '. . . the wider context of highly confidential information of a non-technical or non-scientific nature'.[72]

71 [1991] 1 WLR 251.

72 [1991] 1 WLR 251 at 270.

While it is clear that a secret industrial process containing an inventive step is capable of being a trade secret, the position is less predictable in terms of confidential price lists, databases containing customer names and addresses and clients' accounts. The test of what can be remembered by an ex-employee does not help, as many new inventions may easily be remembered. Neither would it be realistic to limit trade secrets to inventions that are potentially patentable. Information relating to clients' credit ratings and the types of goods that they buy may be very valuable and, in the right circumstances, fall to be considered a trade secret. In *PSM International plc* v *Whitehouse & Willenhall Automation Ltd*[73] drawings, quotations, price costing and business strategies were considered to rank as trade secrets. On the other hand, the mere application of obvious principles to an industrial process does not, *per se*, give rise to a trade secret. Furthermore, it is unlikely, though not impossible, that the aggregation of a number of well-known or obvious features would amount to a trade secret.[74] In *Inline Logistics Ltd* v *UCI Logistics Ltd*,[75] it was held that a particular combination of non-confidential design features could be protected as confidential information. But, in *Cantor Fitzgerald International* v *Tradition (UK) Ltd*,[76] it was held that a technique used for testing computer software which was readily derivable by a skilled man from public sources is not a trade secret. It amounts to no more than a useful technique or 'wrinkle' which an ex-employee may use after cessation of his employment. However, use of the claimant's computer program source code, even if only for debugging purposes, was a breach of confidence. Thus, as a general rule, it can be said that source code programs are trade secrets unless published by the owner of the program.

Where a person carried out work which could result in inventions being made, then it is obviously falls to be classed as a trade secret. This also applies to carrying out experiments and making deductions on the basis of those experiments. In *Vestergaard Frandsen A/S* v *Bestnet Europe Ltd*,[77] the information concerned the process of discovering the most effective treatment of mosquito nets.

Publication

If the information has been published or disclosed to third parties on a reasonable scale in the absence of an obligation of confidence, it falls into the public domain and the law of confidence cannot prevent its subsequent use and further disclosure. Unless his conscience is fixed by equity, a person who has received the information in circumstances such that he was not, or could not reasonably have been, aware of the confidential nature is free to make use of that information or to pass it on to others. However, even if the information has fallen into the hands of innocent third parties because of a breach of confidence, there will be remedies available against the person in breach. When a patent is applied for, the specification of the invention is available for public inspection 18 months after the priority date. The protection afforded by the law of confidence is then lost, to be replaced by the patent, once granted.[78] The information is in the public domain even though it may be available only after a search at the Patent Office. In *Mustad & Son* v *Dosen*,[79] a case concerning information about a machine for the manufacture of fish hooks for anglers, it was held that publication through the master by obtaining a patent effectively destroys the servant's duty of confidence in respect of the subject matter of the patent grant. However, this principle has been distinguished as regards a patent obtained by a third party.

In *Cranleigh Precision Engineering Ltd* v *Bryant*,[80] Bryant was the managing director of the claimant company which manufactured above-ground swimming pools invented by Bryant. No patent had been granted in respect of the claimant's swimming pools. Patent agents, acting on behalf of the claimant, informed Bryant of a patent belonging to a rival company (known as the Bischoff patent) which concerned a similar swimming pool but which lacked two special features which the claimant's design incorporated.[81] Bryant did not inform his co-directors of the Bischoff patent. Later, Bryant left and set up his own company and obtained an assignment of the Bischoff patent. He was sued, *inter alia*, for injunctions to restrain him and his company from making use of or disclosing information relating to the claimant's swimming pools.

73 [1992] FSR 489.

74 *AT Poeton (Gloucester Plating) Ltd* v *Michael Ikem Horton* [2001] FSR 14.

75 [2002] RPC 32.

76 [2000] RPC 95.

77 [2009] EWHC 657 (Ch).

78 Once the patent has been granted, the proprietor can sue for infringement in relation to acts done after the date of publication of the patent.

79 [1964] 1 WLR 109. This case was actually decided in 1928.

80 [1965] 1 WLR 1293.

81 The special features were a plastic strip clamping the inner and outer walls together and an overlapping interfit of the metal plates forming the outside wall of the swimming pool.

It was argued on behalf of the defendant that, because knowledge of the Bischoff patent was in the public domain, there could be no breach of confidence. However, although details of the Bischoff patent could be inspected by anyone, it was especially relevant to the claimant because of the possible effect of the Bischoff patent on the claimant's swimming pools and the possibility of a conflict over rights. Bryant had acted in breach of confidence in making use, as soon as he left the claimant's employ, of the information concerning the Bischoff patent and in terms of the *various effects on the claimant's position* of that information. The case of *Mustad & Son v Dosen* was distinguished on the grounds that, in that case, the patent was granted to the master (employer), that is, publication was by the master of the person alleged to have committed the breach of confidence. In *Cranleigh Precision Engineering Ltd v Bryant*, the publication was by another; Bryant's 'master' (the claimant) had never published anything, not even the specification for its own swimming pool.

Where information is in the public domain in a particular form, such as in a published patent, it might be argued that obtaining and using that information which has been acquired by other means is a breach of confidence. In *EPI Environmental Technologies Inc v Symphony Plastic Technologies plc*,[82] the defendant had the use of the claimant's additives under a contract. These products contained material which was part of the public domain in a patent and part secret. The defendant did not consult the patent, and only discovered it later, but analysed the products. It was held that the defendant was free to use the public domain materials providing the contract did not impose any obligation not to analyse the products. If it were otherwise, the defendant would be the only organisation not able to make use of the public domain materials. The appeal to the Court of Appeal was dismissed.[83] Although proof of a sufficient similarity may 'shift' the burden of proof in as much as the evidential burden shifted to the defendant who was then obliged to give an explanation for the similarity. However, although being described as shifting the burden of proof, the burden of proof remains with the claimant. In this particular case, comparing the substances in question did not raise an inference of copying and there was nothing to suggest that the judge at first instance had misdirected himself.

If the information has found its way to the public domain, the person who owed another an obligation of confidence in respect of that information may be prevented from making use of the information himself for a period of time. This is known as the 'springboard' doctrine. The person who was under an obligation of confidence is not allowed to use it as a springboard from which to launch his own project if to do so would be harmful to the person to whom the obligation was owed. In *Terrapin v Builders Supply Co (Hayes) Ltd*[84] it was said by Roxburgh J that:

> . . . a person who has obtained information in confidence is not allowed to use it as a springboard for activities detrimental to [the owner] and springboard it remains even when all the features have been published . . .[85]

However, the springboard effect does not last indefinitely. After all, if the information has been published others are free to use it, so why should the person who originally owed an obligation of confidence be restricted? Of course, one justification is that the information has been published because of a breach of that obligation. In *Roger Bullivant Ltd v Ellis*,[86] the claimants specialised in a type of construction work known as underpinning. This is a means of replacing defective foundations. The defendant, who had been an employee of the claimants, with others, set up a rival business. It was discovered that the defendant had taken a copy of a card index of customers which had been compiled by the claimants. The defendant had deliberately made use of the card index and could not complain if the court restrained him from using it, even though his obligation of confidence as an ex-employee was weaker and he would have been free to use information that he simply had remembered. It was said that the springboard doctrine would not normally

82 [2005] FSR 22.

83 *EPI Environmental Technologies Inc v Symphony Plastic Technologies plc* [2006] EWCA Civ 3.

84 [1967] RPC 375, actually decided in 1959.

85 [1967] RPC 375 at 392.

86 [1987] FSR 172. This case was distinguished in *Nottingham University v Fishel* [2001] RPC 367 in which an application for springboard damages was refused. The defendant employee, who was not in breach of a fiduciary duty, worked for foreign clinics but this caused no damage to his employer whose clinic in England was not affected by the defendant's activities abroad.

extend beyond the period for which the unfair advantage gained would reasonably be expected to remain, and the purpose of an injunction in such circumstances was not to punish the defendant but to protect the claimant. It was argued that the information was freely available elsewhere but, on the basis of *Robb* v *Green*,[87] it was said that the defendant could not complain if the law was unable to distinguish between the information he was able to use and that which he could not.[88]

The springboard doctrine is used to deprive the defendant of that unfair advantage he might have as a result of his breach of confidence. Where the information has entered the public domain, we have seen, in *Bullivant* v *Ellis*, that any injunction imposed will be of limited duration. One justification is that the court ought to restrict the use of the information for the time it would have taken the defendant to derive the same information using his own skill and labour, where it is possible for the defendant to do this. However, if it is not possible for the defendant to derive the same information independently, then the springboard cannot apply and any injunction granted ought to be permanent. This was the case in *Electro Cad Australia Pty Ltd* v *Mejati Rcs Sdn Bhd*[89] in which the judge accepted evidence that it was impossible to reverse engineer a computer chip containing the relevant information. Thus, apart from his misuse of information learned whilst in the employ of the claimant, the defendant had no other way in which he could derive the information, used in car immobilisation devices.

Where the information has entered the public domain, it can no longer be regarded as confidential and the obligation of confidence owed by the defendant cannot continue. If everyone else is free to further publish or use the information why should the defendant be prevented from doing so? In such cases, the only justification for the springboard doctrine is to prevent the defendant having a head start over others who are free to use the information because of his breach of confidence, or to ensure that the claimant has a head start over the defendant.[90] He would be able to enter the marketplace before any other who is free to use the information. Where this is not so – for example, where the information can be put to use immediately – it would seem that the remedy ought to lie in damages only as the sole purpose of the injunction would be to punish the defendant further rather than to protect the interests of the claimant. Springboard relief will not be granted simply because the defendant has made an unauthorised use of the claimant's confidential information. The defendant must have gained an unfair competitive advantage over the claimant which still existed at the time of the action.[91]

In *Clowson Fabrics Ltd* v *Rider*,[92] the judge refused to grant a springboard injunction, pointing to the difficulty in separating what the defendants were and were not allowed to do as well as the problem of policing an injunction, which in this case, would be a fairly short duration. However, the claimant failed to demonstrate that the information was confidential, although both defendants were in breach of their duty of fidelity and had infringed the database right by taking extracts of the employer's database. One defendant was also in breach of a fiduciary duty.

In *Attorney-General* v *Guardian Newspapers (No 2)*,[93] one of the *Spycatcher* cases, Lord Goff said that it was difficult to see how a confidant who publishes information to the whole world could be prevented from further disclosing it. This would mean the confidant could not mention in public what was now common knowledge. Laddie J was attracted to this conclusion in *Ocular Sciences Ltd* v *Aspect Vision Care Ltd*,[94] thereby casting some doubt on the springboard doctrine. He said that the court counters any unfair benefit to the defendant by imposing financial penalties or imposing a constructive trust. However, the *Attorney-General* v *Guardian* case was concerned with publication rather than other forms of use. What, for example, of the situation where the defendant has published the information but can put it to practical use some time before anyone else because of his particular training and experience of using the information? Perhaps the information concerns a new technique that has to be learnt and practised before it can be applied

87 [1895] 2 QB 315.

88 But a claimant has a duty to make such a distinction if it can be made: *see CMI-Centers for Medical Innovation GmbH* v *Phytopharm plc* [1999] FSR 235, discussed above.

89 [1999] FSR 291, High Court of Malaysia.

90 *Gupta* v *Dasgupta* [2003] FSR 18, High Court of Delhi.

91 *Sun Valley Foods Ltd* v *John Philip Vincent* [2000] FSR 825.

92 [2008] FSR 18.

93 [1990] 1 AC 109.

94 [1997] RPC 289.

successfully. In such cases, there may yet be a place for the springboard doctrine. Alternatively, it may be technical information relating to a new industrial process and the defendant, because of his knowledge of specialist component manufacturers and potential customers, can realise a commercial reward long before anyone else. On the other hand, if the information can be put to immediate use – for example, if it relates to a planned takeover bid for a company quoted on the stock market – there seems little point in injuncting the defendant.

Further consideration of the springboard doctrine was given in *Vestergaard Frandsen A/S v Bestnet Europe Ltd*.[95] Arnold J doubted that *Terrapin* was authority for the proposition that an injunction could be granted once the information had ceased to be confidential. He gave a possible interpretation of the springboard doctrine expressed in *Terrapin*. If it meant that information could have a limited degree of confidentiality even though it could be ascertained by reverse engineering or by compilation from public domain sources, then the doctrine was sound. An injunction for a limited period could be granted in relation to such information. The purpose of the injunction would be to prevent the defendant from benefiting or continuing to benefit from past misuse. However, an injunction was not appropriate where the defendant had misused the information but was no longer doing so.

Public interest

As with copyright, a defence of public interest is available in an action for breach of confidence. Of course, in many cases where this is relevant, there will be issues of both confidence and copyright, such as where someone publishes a confidential document.[96] The courts will not respect an obligation of confidence if it is in the public interest that the confidential information is made known to the public at large or to a restricted class of the public, such as an official body. Public interest is relevant where it concerns the administration of justice: for example, the law of confidence cannot be used as a means of suppressing information concerning criminal conduct. But it is wider than that and can cover matters about [97]religion,[98] price-fixing,[99] experiments on animals[100] and about persons in the public eye. It can extend to 'mug-shots' (photographs taken by the police of persons suspected of having committed a criminal offence) in pursuance of the Police and Criminal Evidence Act 1984. In *Hellewell v Chief Constable of Derbyshire*[101] the claimant complained that the police had given copies of a photograph of him to local shopkeepers involved in a shop watch scheme and who were concerned at the level of shoplifting. At the time the claimant had been charged with theft, though not convicted.[102] The judge said that the police were not free to use the photograph in whatever way they wished and that it might be described as a piece of confidential information. However, the judge, referring to the claimant's long list of convictions and the fact that the dissemination of the photograph was limited to shopkeepers and their staff, held that the actions of the police were obviously and unarguably in the public interest.[103] The police had acted in good faith for the prevention or detection of crime. The provision of information to the police by a person under caution accused of a criminal offence is subject to an obligation of confidence and must not be used for any purpose other than criminal proceedings. This is a matter of public interest, being that such a person should be able to make a full disclosure without fear of it being used for extraneous purposes.[104]

Public interest must now be viewed in the context of the Human Rights Act 1998 which incorporates the Human Rights Convention into UK law. Of particular interest are Articles 8 and 10 of the Convention, the former providing a right to privacy and the latter providing a right to freedom of expression. However, both rights are subject to potential interference or derogation: for example, in the interests of national security or public safety or for the protection of the rights of others. In *R v Ashworth Special Hospital*

95 [2009] EWHC 657 (Ch).

96 For example, *Lion Laboratories Ltd v Evans* [1984] 2 All ER 417, discussed in Chapter 7.

97 *See Gartside v Outram* (1857) 26 LJ Ch (NS) 113. However, in *Re Barlow Clowes Gilt Managers Ltd* [1992] Ch 208, it was said that information received by liquidators in confidence for the purposes of liquidation should not be disclosed to defendants in collateral criminal proceedings unless there was a compelling reason to divulge the information such as a court order.

98 For example, in *Hubbard v Vosper* [1972] 2 QB 84, it was held, *inter alia*, that it was in the public interest that details about the Church of Scientology be made known to the public.

99 *Initial Services Ltd v Putterill* [1968] 1 QB 396.

100 *Imutran Ltd v Uncaged Campaigns Ltd* [2002] FSR 2.

101 [1995] 1 WLR 804.

102 He was subsequently convicted.

103 Data protection law may also be engaged. There is provision in the Data Protection Act 1998 for disclosures of personal data, which includes photographs, for the prevention or detection of crime: s 29.

104 *Robert Bunn v BBC* [1999] FSR 70.

105 *The Times*, 26 June 2001.

106 For a case involving Article 10, see *Ashworth Security Hospital v MGN Ltd* [2001] FSR 33, discussed below.

107 [2009] EMLR 22.

108 A 'blog' is a publicly accessible internet-based diary.

109 In relation to the latter, it was argued that revealing his identity would inhibit his right to impart information to the general public.

110 Per Simon Brown LJ in *R v Department of Health, ex parte Source Informatics Ltd* [2001] FSR 8, approving the dictum to that effect of Gummow J in the Australian case of *Smith Kline and French Laboratories (Australia) Ltd v Secretary, Department of Community Services and Health* [1990] FSR 617 at 663.

111 *Bonnard v Perryman* [1891] 2 Ch 269.

112 *The Times*, 20 December 1997.

Authority,[105] the Authority monitored telephone calls made by high-risk patients having violent or dangerous predilections. The monitoring was random and involved about 10 per cent of calls but excluded privileged calls, for example, made to patients' legal advisers. It was held that this was not a breach of the right to privacy in Article 8(1) of the Convention as it fell within Article 8(2) which allows interference with the right in accordance with law where necessary in a democratic society in the interests of, *inter alia*, national security, public safety, the prevention of disorder or crime or the protection of the rights and freedoms of others.[106]

In *Author of a Blog* v *Times Newspapers Ltd*,[107] the claimant was a serving police officer who was also a 'blogger'[108] and he placed information indicating his strong views of police and administration of justice matters. He wished to remain anonymous but, by detective work, the defendant discovered his identity. He sought to restrain the defendant from publishing details of his identity, arguing that there was a public interest in preserving the anonymity of bloggers and would infringe his Article 8 and Article 10 rights.[109] The claimant's application for an injunction was dismissed. It was held that the information did not have the necessary quality of confidence about it nor did it qualify as information about which the claimant had a reasonable expectation of privacy because blogging is a public activity, analogous to journalism. Furthermore, even if that was wrong, at full trial it would be likely to be held that there was a greater public interest is informing the public that a particular serving police officer was responsible for the blogs.

The scope of breach of confidence should not be drawn too widely in the first place and the scope of the public interest defence should be kept within strict limits, otherwise there is a danger that the public interest defence becomes less of a rule of law but provides ammunition to judges to allow them to decide cases on an extempore basis, depending on their subjective view as to whether the obligation of confidence in a particular case should be respected or overruled.[110]

Three points about public interest are considered below, namely where the proposed publication is potentially defamatory, where there is a conflict in public interests and, finally, as regards the scope and nature of the disclosure.

Potentially defamatory publication

It is recognised that the public has an interest in the truth. If a person intends to publish material which is clearly untrue and defamatory, there is little doubt that the courts would, if asked, grant an injunction preventing publication unless the defendant pleads justification. However, if a person has obtained information in confidence which might injure the reputation of another, he may be free to publish it if such publication can be said to lie within the public interest. This will apply particularly to information concerning the character of persons in the public limelight, such as politicians and show-business personalities who actively seek publicity. Of course, public interest can only be realised if the information is true, and the courts will not usually restrain publication if the person intending to publish the information is likely to raise the defences of justification or fair comment if sued for defamation. In this respect, there is something to be said for the 'publish and be damned' attitude of the Duke of Wellington. After all, the aggrieved party has, if the information is untrue, remedies under the tort of defamation which can be quite effective bearing in mind the burden of proof in such an action.

There are two reasons why the courts are reluctant to restrain publication of information even if claimed to be defamatory. First, the defences of justification or fair comment in a defamation action are for a jury to decide, not the court asked for injunctive relief. Second, the courts have to take account of freedom of speech.[111] The motive behind the threatened publication may not be particularly relevant to the issue, even if the defendant intended to be paid for his silence. In *Holley v Smyth*,[112] the defendant was the sole beneficiary of a trust. He threatened to send press releases to the media alleging fraud on the part of the trustees unless they paid him £200,000, being the amount by which the defendant claimed the trust had been defrauded. The Court of Appeal, by a majority, discharged an injunction restraining publication on the basis that the claimants were not entitled to interim injunctions unless the information was manifestly untrue.

In *Woodward* v *Hutchins*,[113] the defendant was a public relations officer who worked for the claimants, who were pop singers including Tom Jones, Englebert Humperdinck and Gilbert O'Sullivan. The singers wanted to be presented to the public in the best possible light in order to encourage large audiences to attend their concerts. The defendant went on tour with the singers and saw their 'goings on'. Later, when no longer engaged by the claimants, he wrote a series of articles about the claimants' discreditable conduct, including a case of adultery; it was a typical 'Sunday paper' story with headings such as 'Why Mrs Tom Jones threw her jewellery from a car window and Tom got high in a jumbo jet' and 'Tom Jones is Superstud'. The first article was published and the singers applied for an injunction to prevent further articles being published on the grounds that they were defamatory and had been written in breach of confidence. Lord Denning MR said that the public interest in the truth outweighed the public interest in protecting confidential information in this case. The remaining articles could be published, leaving the claimants free to pursue a claim for damages in libel. The defendant had made it clear that he would plead justification if sued for defamation. An important factor in the decision is that the claimants had sought publicity which was favourable to them, and they could not therefore complain if the public were given true information showing them in a less favourable light.

This case must now be read in the light of *Campbell* v *Mirror Group Newspapers Ltd*.[114] As the singers in *Woodward* v *Hutchins* had sought publicity and, to some extent, to control it to their advantage, it was right that the public should be told the truth if the public image they hoped to promote was false or a distortion of the truth. However, disabusing the public of the image the claimants had attempted to put across may not extend to publishing all the salacious details of behaviour falling short of that image. The balance between the rights to privacy and freedom of expression require some careful consideration that may not be possible in the reality of newspaper and other media publishing, working to tight deadlines. It remains to be seen whether the courts are prepared to allow some judgmental latitude to editors. The majority decision in *Campbell* suggests that latitude might be quite narrow although the majority of judges could be accused of balancing privacy and freedom of expression with the benefit of hindsight, not sufficiently taking account of the pressures on editors of newspapers and other news media to take quick, 'on-the-hoof' decisions.

Conflict of differing public interests

There may be more than one type of public interest involved where confidential information is concerned. Public interest can be served by the disclosure of certain types of information to a limited section of the public or to the public at large, depending on the nature of the information. However, the public interest can be best served by maintaining confidences generally, that is by discouraging potential breaches of confidences by a strong and certain law. For example, the public interest in maintaining confidences between doctors and their patients is extremely high. Sometimes there will be a conflict between these forms of public interest, and the court must balance one against the other in coming to its decision.

In *W* v *Edgell*,[115] W had killed five people and had been diagnosed as suffering from paranoid schizophrenia. At his trial, his plea of diminished responsibility was accepted and he was detained without time limit under the Mental Health Act 1959 ss 60 and 65.[116] Later, W's condition improved and his doctor recommended transfer to a regional secure unit. The doctor said that the illness was under control and W was no longer a

113 [1977] 2 All ER 751.

114 [2004] 2 AC 457. Further doubt was placed on the correctness of *Woodward* v *Hutchins* in *McKennitt* v *Ash* [2007] 3 WLR 194. The case did, of course, precede the implementation of the Convention rights in English law.

115 [1990] Ch 359.

116 Now the Mental Health Act 1983 ss 37 and 41.

danger provided he stayed on medication. The Home Secretary refused his consent to the transfer. W applied to a mental health review tribunal for discharge or transfer. Dr E was instructed to examine W and make out a report. The report was unfavourable to W and Dr E sent a copy to W's solicitor in the belief that it would be placed before the tribunal, but W's solicitor withdrew the application. Dr E heard of this and realised that there would not be a copy of his report on W's file for future reference. Being concerned at this, Dr E sent a copy of his report to the Home Secretary. W complained that this was a breach of the confidential relationship between a patient and a doctor.

In the High Court, it was said that Dr E owed a duty of confidence to W which was created and circumscribed by the particular circumstances of the case. Dr E considered that W had a psychopathic personality and thought that W's solicitors intended to suppress the report. Therefore Scott J considered that Dr E also owed a duty to the public which required him to place before the proper authorities the results of his examination of W, who was not an ordinary member of the public. W unsuccessfully appealed to the Court of Appeal. It was held that although W had a personal interest to see that the confidence he had reposed in Dr E was not breached, the maintenance of a duty of confidence by a doctor to his patient was not a matter of private but of public interest. The public interest in maintaining confidence had to be balanced against the public interest in protecting others from possible violence. In this case, the public interest in restrictive disclosure outweighed the public interest that a patient's confidences should be respected. Bingham LJ said:

> Only the most compelling circumstances could justify a doctor in acting in a way which would injure the immediate interests of his patient, as the patient perceived them, without obtaining his consent.[117]

On the facts Dr E acted very responsibly and, it would appear, under a sense of public duty. It is clear that breach of confidence in a relationship as sensitive as doctor and patient would be legally permissible only under the most compelling and narrow circumstances.[118]

It is contrary to the public interest to order disclosure of the identity of a press source but, in exceptional circumstances, there may be an overriding public interest equivalent to a pressing social need. In *Ashworth Security Hospital* v *MGN Ltd*,[119] the Court of Appeal confirmed an order for disclosure of the identity of the person who had provided the defendant newspaper with detailed medical records pertaining to Ian Brady. Lord Philips MR said that disclosure of the medical records to the press was serious misconduct that went beyond matters of concern to the individual. It was an attack on an area of confidentiality that required safeguarding in a democratic society. The order for disclosure involved interpretation of the Contempt of Court Act 1981 s 10 and Article 10 of the Human Rights Convention. The former provides a defence to contempt of court where a person refuses to disclose a source of information unless disclosure is necessary in the interests of justice or national security or for the prevention or detection of crime. The latter provides for a right to freedom of expression but this may be subject to formalities, conditions, restrictions or penalties:

> . . . necessary in a democratic society, in the interests of national security, territorial integrity or public safety, for the prevention of disorder or crime, for the protection of health or morals, for the protection of the reputation or rights of others, for preventing the disclosure of information received in confidence, or for maintaining authority and impartiality of the judiciary.

Although the interests of justice are not expressly mentioned in Article 10, Lord Philips was of the view that, in the present case, the claimant could argue that its claim for identification of the source of the information fell within the interests of the protection of health, the protection of rights of others and preventing the disclosure of information received in confidence. In determining whether the disclosure of the source is 'necessary', a three-stage test formulated by counsel was accepted by Lord Philips. The test is:

117 [1990] Ch 359 at 423.

118 Presumably, now the interference to the patient's right to privacy would be justified under Article 8(2) of the European Convention on Human Rights on the basis that it was necessary for public safety, the prevention of disorder or crime or to protect the rights and freedoms of others.

119 [2001] FSR 559, confirmed in the House of Lords at [2002] 1 WLR 2033.

1 Are the interests of justice engaged?
2 If so, the court then has to consider whether disclosure is necessary to achieve the relevant ends of justice.
3 As a matter of discretion, the court then has to weigh the specific interests of the claimant against the public interest in the protection of journalistic sources.

Finally, Lord Philips noted that the European approach seemed more inclined to emphasise freedom of expression and give more protection to journalistic sources than was the case in the UK. Nevertheless, the European Court of Human Rights, in *Goodwin* v *United Kingdom*,[120] recognised that, in exceptional circumstances where vital public or individual interests are at stake, an order requiring disclosure of journalistic sources can be justified. *Ashworth* v *MGN* was such a case.

120 (1996) 22 EHRR 123.

Scope and nature of the disclosure

It is clear that, in some circumstances, whether the public interest defence applies depends on the scope and nature of the disclosure. Sometimes, a very restrictive disclosure will be appropriate such as in *W* v *Edgell*, but, had that particular disclosure been made to a newspaper, the defendant probably would not have been successful in his public interest defence. In *Imutran Ltd* v *Uncaged Campaigns Ltd*[121] it was said that the public interest may be served by a limited disclosure rather than disclosure to the world but the court, as a public authority, must take into account the right of freedom of expression under Article 10 of the Human Rights Convention. If there is a public interest in the disclosure, the judges will take into account the persons to whom the confidential information is communicated. For example, the public interest might be best served by disclosure to a responsible body rather than to the media.[122] Another, often related, factor might be whether the disclosure was done for gain or reward, although this is not decisive.[123]

121 [2002] FSR 2.

122 This was identified as a factor in *Lion Laboratories Ltd* v *Evans* [1984] 2 All ER 417.

123 Profit was obviously a motive for publication in *Woodward* v *Hutchins, see* p 362.

Simply because the confidentiality of information is breached for one particular purpose does not mean that it can be used for other purposes. Certain documents were seized legally by the police investigating a fraud case in *Marcel* v *Commissioner of Police of the Metropolis*.[124] It was held that the police were not entitled to disclose those documents to a third party to use in civil proceedings, because the public interest in ensuring that the documents were used solely for public purposes appropriate to the powers of seizure conferred on the police outweighed the public interest in ensuring that all relevant information was available in civil proceedings. The police had a duty not to disclose such documents to third parties except by the order of the court. This case also provides another example of a conflict between two competing public interests.

124 [1991] 1 All ER 845. The documents were seized under the provisions in the Police and Criminal Evidence Act 1984 Part II.

In *Robert Bunn* v *BBC*,[125] the claimant had made a statement to the police under caution after being suspected of defrauding a number of banks. The statement was read in open court by the judge, but the claimant was not convicted.[126] Whilst accepting that a statement made to the police was subject to an obligation of confidence, it was held that once it had been read in open court by the judge that obligation had come to an end. The defendant was allowed to continue with its plans to broadcast a programme which made reference to the statement.[127]

125 [1999] FSR 70.

126 The judge directed the jury to acquit on one charge and let the other lie on the file. The claimant had suffered a heart attack.

127 The second defendant was allowed to continue to sell copies of a book containing a report of the claimant's statement.

Obligation of confidence

The second requirement for an action in breach of confidence is that there must be an obligation of confidence which arises from the circumstances in which the information was imparted.[128] This obligation may arise by express agreement or prior notice, or it may be implied by law: for example, in a fiduciary relationship or by general equitable principles.[129] Commonly, an obligation of confidence will be established and delineated

128 *Coco* v *AN Clark (Engineers) Ltd* [1969] RPC 41 per Megarry J.

129 It is not clear whether confidential information can be trust property under a constructive trust: *see Satnam Investments Ltd* v *Dunlop Heywood & Co* [1999] FSR 722.

by a contract which has express terms dealing with confidence or, in the absence of such express terms, by implied terms depending on the nature of the contract. For example, the contract may prohibit performing an analysis of a compound supplied under the contract. The obligation of confidence may extend beyond the termination of the contract. However, a contract is not essential and frequently the obligation will arise in preliminary negotiations for a contract, even though the contract is never executed. It is axiomatic that an obligation of confidence will apply where there is a duty of good faith: for example, between doctor and patient or between solicitor and client. Nevertheless, the circumstances where the obligation will be appropriate are much wider than this and include business transactions, commercial negotiations, the relationship between husband and wife and, sometimes, disclosures to third parties.

There are limits to the occasions when a duty of confidence will be implied. The defendant in *Carflow Products (UK) Ltd v Linwood Securities (Birmingham) Ltd*[130] was sued for infringement of a registered design and an unregistered design right in respect of a design for a steering wheel lock for cars. The defendant had made a prototype steering wheel lock of its own and Jacob J held that there was no evidence of copying and, as a result, the unregistered design right claim failed. As regards the registered design claim, the defendant argued that, as the prototype had been shown to a potential buyer before the filing date of the registered design, that buyer was not under a duty of confidence, being free in equity and law to use or disclose it. If that was the case, then the registered design would be invalid for lack of novelty.[131]

In deciding whether the disclosure was in confidence, Jacob J said there were two approaches: a subjective one (what the parties thought they were doing by way of imposing or accepting obligations of confidence) and an objective approach. As to the former, on the evidence Jacob J held that neither party thought an obligation of confidence was being imposed or accepted. As to the objective approach, the reasonable man (officious bystander)[132] would know that what was being shown was a prototype and that the law provides a number of ways in which it could be protected: for example, by registration as a design, by application for a patent or by the unregistered design right. Therefore, he would not expect that an obligation of confidence arose merely by showing a prototype for something which was being offered for sale. Obviously, in circumstances where there is any doubt as to whether an obligation of confidence will be imposed by the courts, it would be better to impose an express duty.

The fact that confidential information is made difficult to access, for example, by releasing it in encrypted form only, is not enough, *per se*, to impose an obligation of confidence. In *Mars (UK) Ltd v Teknowledge Ltd*,[133] the defendant managed to reverse engineer an EEPROM[134] computer chip to access information which it then used to recalibrate discriminators used in coin receiving and changing machines supplied to third parties by the claimant. Jacob J rejected the claimant's argument that the fact of encryption meant 'confidential – you may not de-encrypt'.[135] He said (at 151):

> The [customer] is an intended recipient of the article containing the information . . . There is nothing obviously confidential about the machine he gets. There is no marking 'confidential' and indeed there is not even any indication of encryption. By the time one gets to find out about the encryption it is, in my judgment, far too late to impose a duty of confidence.[136]

Jacob J said that the message that comes across by encrypting information is that the owner does not want another person to gain access to it. Without more, that cannot impose an obligation of confidence.

Where information contains or comprises personal data (information relating to living individuals), there is an inevitable overlap between the law of breach of confidence and data protection law. The law of confidence often imposes a duty not to disclose information and data protection law prohibits disclosures of personal data in some circumstances,

130 [1996] FSR 424.

131 Alternatively, the defendant's lock was outside the scope of the registration.

132 The reasonable man must be someone with some knowledge of the industry and the importance of securing protection of some form. The man on the Clapham omnibus knows little of intellectual property rights.

133 [2000] FSR 138.

134 Electronically Erasable Programmable Read Only Memory.

135 An obligation not to de-encrypt could have been imposed by contract, subject to the permitted acts under copyright law relating to computer programs.

136 Jacob J distinguished *Attorney-General v Guardian Newspapers (No 2)* [1990] 1 AC 109 where Lord Goff spoke of an obviously confidential document wafted by an electric fan out of a window into a crowded street.

such as where disclosure to a third party would cause them substantial damage or distress. Indeed, the Data Protection Act 1998 permits disclosures of personal data in tightly drawn circumstances only. However, if the data have been rendered truly anonymous, they will be outside the provisions of data protection law as in *R v Department of Health, ex parte Source Informatics Ltd*[137] where data relating to patients' prescriptions had been rendered anonymous before disclosure to a company processing the data for the purpose of providing pharmaceutical companies with information concerning prescribing habits and trends. Disclosures of personal data to third parties may be allowed, *inter alia*, if necessary for the legitimate interests pursued by the third party providing the disclosure is not unwarranted by reason of prejudice to the rights and freedoms or legitimate interests of the data subject.[138] In Case C-369/98 *R v Minister of Agriculture, Fisheries and Food, ex parte Fisher*,[139] the Ministry refused to provide information about crops grown in previous years on farms newly acquired by a number of farmers, claiming it would breach data protection law by disclosing personal data relating to the farmers who had previously occupied the farms in question. The European Court of Justice disagreed, noting that the test required a balancing between the legitimate interests of the third party with those of the persons to whom the personal data related.

Furnishing individuals with copies of their personal data under s 7 of the Data Protection Act 1998 might disclose information relating to third parties. In such cases, it may be necessary to obliterate or remove that information which might identify third parties. This process is known as redaction and an example is given by *Durant v Financial Services Authority*[140] where personal data were provided to the individual requesting subject access in redacted form.[141]

Four particular issues are considered below: express contractual terms imposing a duty of confidence, the employer/employee relationship, covenants in restraint of trade, and the position of third party recipients.

Express contractual term

It is quite common for formal contracts to contain terms dealing with matters of confidence and imposing a duty on one or both parties not to use or disclose certain types of information. A computer software company engaged to write and install computer programs for a client will be expected not to divulge any details of the client's business to competitors. An advertising agency asked by a drinks manufacturer to mount an advertising campaign for a new brand of lager will be under a duty not to disclose information about the new product until after its launch. A duty of confidence will exist between two companies submitting a joint tender for a contract where preparation of the tender involves an exchange of confidential information.[142] Of course there will be an equitable duty, but expressly providing for the duty in a contract means that it can be more stringent and focused in its scope. Breach of confidence will then constitute a breach of contract, giving contractual remedies to the aggrieved party. Terms dealing with confidence, often imposing a reciprocal duty, are common in contracts between business organisations, between consultants and businesses engaging them, and between employers and their employees, as discussed later.

As with any contractual term, care must be taken in the drafting. The courts will not impose a duty of confidence to benefit a person other than the person intended. In *Fraser v Evans*,[143] the claimant was a public relations consultant who had been engaged by the Greek government to prepare a report. The contract included an express term stating that the claimant must not divulge any of the information contained in the report during or after the currency of the contract. A copy of the report had been surreptitiously obtained and came into the hands of *The Sunday Times*. The claimant was granted an *ex parte* order restraining publication of the report or parts of it in the newspaper on the grounds that

---

137 [2001] FSR 8.

138 Data Protection Act 1998 Sch 2 para 6.

139 [2000] ECR I-6751.

140 [2004] FSR 28.

141 See Bainbridge, D.I. (2005) *Data Protection Law* (2nd edn) xpl publishing.

142 An interim injunction was granted to enforce or restrain derogation from agreed terms in relation to a defence contract in *Simtech Advanced Training & Simulation Systems Ltd v Jasmin Simtec Ltd* [1995] FSR 475.

143 [1969] 1 QB 349.

it would be defamatory and would be a breach of confidence. The claimant considered that an article based on the report would show him in a bad light. On the defendant's appeal, it was held that the claimant was not entitled to an injunction. Although the claimant owed a duty to the Greek government, no reciprocal duty was imposed by the contract, neither could such a duty be implied. The courts can give effect to an obligation of confidence only at the instance of the party to whom such obligation is owed. It was also held, *obiter*, that although the claimant owned the copyright in the report, this did not extend to preventing the use of the information contained within it, once again illustrating the distinction between idea and expression in copyright.

When items are distributed to the public or to a limited section of the public, it can be assumed that confidential information embodied within those items will automatically lose its confidential quality and a person obtaining one of the items will not owe an obligation of confidence to its manufacturer. Other branches of intellectual property law are more appropriate, such as patent law and copyright law. However, if the distribution occurs by way of a contract, the contract may include terms attempting to impose a continuing duty of confidence, for example by prohibiting dismantling or reverse engineering. In *KS Paul (Printing Machinery) Ltd* v *Southern Instruments Ltd*,[144] there were two defendants. The second defendant hired from the claimant a telephone answering machine which was enclosed in a box which concealed the workings of the machine. The contract of hire included a condition that the machine should not be removed from its installation position or interfered with. The machines were not available except under such conditions. The second defendant allowed the first defendant to remove the machine, dismantle it and examine it. Access to the confidential information concerning the workings of the machine was thus obtained. An injunction was granted to the claimant restraining the use of confidential information obtained from the 'machines of the type hired by the claimants . . . from any unlawful inspection of any such machines'. The contract of hire had effectively prolonged the effectiveness of confidence and applied to a third party who had been allowed by the hirer to dismantle the machine.

It is arguable that sales to the general public may not destroy the application of the law of breach of confidence if, by the very nature of the product, the secret information is not accessible or is accessible only after doing something which infringes some right or duty.[145] For example, if a computer program is licensed in object code form, the licensee, or any other person for that matter, will not be able to gain access to the ideas locked away in the program without carrying out reverse analysis of the program, an operation that will normally infringe the copyright subsisting in the program, unless falling within the scope of the permitted acts under copyright law. However, by the Copyright, Designs and Patents Act 1988 s 296A(1)(c), any term or condition in an agreement relating to the use of a computer program shall be void in so far as it purports to prohibit or restrict the observing, studying or testing of the functioning of a computer program in accordance with s 50BA.

Employer/employee relationship

An employee owes a duty of confidence to his employer and this duty may be expressly stated in the contract of employment, and in any case will be implied by law. It can be said that an employee always has a duty to act in his employer's best interests together with a duty of good faith, and this will obviously include a duty not to divulge confidential information about his employer's business to others without the consent of the employer. The sort of information concerned may be rather special, a 'trade secret' such as details of a technique to improve the strength or durability of a type of plastic, or it may be ordinary and mundane, such as details of the customers of the employer. There may be exceptions to this duty, for example, if the information pertains to a criminal offence, or if it is in the public interest that the information is disclosed.

144 [1964] RPC 118.

145 For an American view of this possibility, see Davidson, D.M. 'Protecting computer software: a comprehensive analysis' (1983) 23(4) *Jurimetrics Journal* 337 at 358. But *cf Mars (UK) Ltd* v *Teknowledge Ltd* [2000] FSR 138, discussed above (*see* p 365). Simply making access difficult is not enough, *per se*, to impose an obligation of confidence.

There is seldom any doubt about the duty owed by a present employee. Although the law will be quick to imply a duty of fidelity,[146] inclusion of terms dealing with this in a contract of employment at least have the effect of focusing the employee's attention on the importance of not misusing confidential information. If there are express terms in the contract of employment which attempt to strengthen this duty they must, of course, be clear and unambiguous.

Where the information would be likely to be regarded by employees as a trade secret, it is not essential that the employer specifically points this out. In *Lancashire Fires Ltd* v *SA Lyons & Co Ltd*,[147] Lord Bingham MR said (at 674):

> We do not accept that it is incumbent on an employer to point out to his employee the precise limits of that which he seeks to protect as confidential, particularly where, as here, what is new is an integral part of a process.

Although the employer does not have to spell out the precise limits of what he regarded as confidential, this does not mean that an employer can expect the employee to infer the confidential nature of a small part of extravagant claims made by the employer.[148] In any case, and for the avoidance of doubt, an employer would be advised to make explicit the extent of the confidential material keeping some sense of reality without making exaggerated claims.

Ex-employees

Many problems arise through the use or disclosure of confidential information by ex-employees, and here the law is faced with a dilemma, for not only does the employer have an interest in maintaining confidence, but the employee also has a competing interest in that he should be free to use his skill and knowledge to earn a living elsewhere.

After confirming that the law will restrain unauthorised disclosure or use of information which is confidential in the *Coco* v *Clark* sense, Laddie J discussed the public policy in respect of the employee's skill and knowledge in *Ocular Sciences Ltd* v *Aspect Vision Care Ltd*.[149] He said (at 370), presumably in the context of information within Goulding J's second category in *Faccenda Chicken*:

> On the other hand, for public policy reasons, an employee is entitled to use and put at the disposal of new employers all his acquired skill and knowledge. That is so, no matter where he acquired that skill and knowledge and whether it is secret or was so at the time he acquired it. Where an employer's right to restrain misuse of his confidential information collides with the public policy, it is the latter which prevails.

This goes further than other cases, and probably further than Laddie J intended, as he then went on to say the difficulty was in distinguishing between information in Goulding J's second and third categories. Certainly public policy should require that an ex-employee should be able to make use of his learned skill and knowledge as a general principle. This should not, however, extend to information in Goulding J's third category, specific trade secrets so confidential that there is a continuing duty of confidence after employment. In *Printers & Finishers Ltd* v *Holloway*,[150] Cross J referred to information regarded as a separate part of the employee's stock of knowledge which '. . . a man of ordinary honesty and intelligence would recognise to be the property of his old employer, and not his to do as he likes with . . .' adding that the court would restrain the use of such information by injunction.

Much of the attractiveness of a potential employee to other employers will be the fact that he has built up skill and experience in his previous employments, and it may be difficult to separate this from a previous employer's confidential information. As a further complication, in some cases the employment contract may contain terms trying to restrict an employee's use of confidential materials after the termination of employment. When there are no express terms, the employer will not be protected to any great extent. For

146 However, the existence of a contract of employment does not, *per se*, impose a fiduciary duty although fiduciary duties could arise out of the relationship of employer and employee. It is a matter of identifying the duties undertaken by the employee and asking whether he had to act solely in the interests of his employer: *Nottingham University* v *Fishel* [2001] RPC 22.

147 [1996] FSR 629.

148 *AT Poeton (Gloucester Plating) Ltd* v *Michael Ikem Horton* [2001] FSR 14.

149 [1997] RPC 289.

150 [1965] RPC 239.

example, if an ex-employee simply remembers some information about a few of his previous employer's customers there will be nothing to prevent the ex-employee using this information himself or putting it at the disposal of his new employer. Of course, it would be different if he deliberately memorised the customers' names or made a copy of them.[151] In the absence of an express term in the contract of employment dealing with confidentiality, it was said in *Printers and Finishers Ltd* v *Holloway*[152] that there would be nothing improper in the employee putting his memory of particular features of his previous employer's plant at the disposal of his new employer. Even if there was an express term, the previous employer would have to show that the information was over and above the employee's normal skill in the job and amounted to a trade secret.

In *Northern Office Micro Computers (Pty) Ltd* v *Rosenstein*,[153] a case from the Supreme Court of South Africa involving the laws of copyright and trade secrets relating to computer programs, the problem of where to draw the line between the conflicting interests of an employee and his previous employer was considered. It was conceded by Marais J that:

> . . . the dividing line between the use by an employee of his own skill knowledge and experience and the use by him of his employer's trade secrets is notoriously difficult to draw.[154]

In recognising that Computer programs that were not commonplace should be eligible for protection as trade secrets, Marais J said that the protection given by the law of trade secrets in the context of ex-employees should be of a limited nature only and that all that should be protected was the employer's 'lead-time', the time to develop the program. That is, the advantage the employer has in getting his product to the marketplace first should be protected and nothing more. He went on to say that, in many cases, the employer's trade secrets were no more than the result of the application by an employee of his own skill and judgment, but if the employee was engaged specifically to produce that information then it could still amount to a trade secret. However, if the material was commonplace, there would be nothing to stop the ex-employee deriving the same or similar material again as long as he did not simply copy his employer's material. The employee would not have to 'wipe the slate of his mind clean' on the termination of his employment.

Much confidential information relating to customers, suppliers, prices and costs is stored in computers. This is highly vulnerable. Employees, particularly those working their notice before setting up in competition or starting to work for a competitor, may be tempted to make copies of that information. One method is to send parts of the database to their own computer at home in the form of e-mail attachments. An employer may seek to prevent this by requiring an employee giving notice of termination to take 'garden leave' rather than work his notice. Sometimes, an employee taking parts of an employer's database may leave 'fingerprints': evidence that he has committed the acts complained of. But the use of computer technology and databases containing potentially confidential information is a growing risk. As Peter Smith J said in *First Conference Services Ltd* v *Bracchi*[155] (at para 26):

> All of this [wrongful taking of information by employees] is very easy now because of the computerisation of information. It is easily therefore transportable. In the olden days (not so long ago in reality) before the photocopier and certainly before the computerisation of material it was very difficult for employees to help themselves to material. Card indexes are not quite as accessible in a nefarious way as computers. This is one of the prices paid for modern technology. Databases cannot be made completely safe.

A test for employees' and ex-employees' obligation of confidence

An important case which clarified the principles to apply in the employer/employee relationship is *Faccenda Chicken Ltd* v *Fowler*.[156] This was about the alleged wrongful use by the defendant ex-employee (with a wonderfully appropriate surname) of his employer's

151 *Robb v Green* [1895] 2 QB 315. Making a copy of a list of customers would also be an infringement of copyright provided the list was original in copyright terms.

152 [1965] RPC 239.

153 [1982] FSR 124.

154 [1982] FSR 124 at 138.

155 [2009] EWHC 2176 (Ch).

156 [1986] 1 All ER 617.

sales information. This comprised customers' names and addresses, the most convenient routes to customers, the most suitable times for delivery, prices charged and details of customers' usual orders – information which was, by its very nature, fairly mundane and ordinary, but which was nevertheless still within the scope of the law of breach of confidence. The employer's business was supplying fresh chickens from itinerant refrigerated vans to retailers and caterers. The defendant was engaged by the claimant as a sales manager and left the claimant company to set up in business on his own account, taking eight of the claimant's employees with him. He started selling fresh chickens from refrigerated vans in the same area in which the claimant operated. The employer's action for breach of confidence failed because the information was not of the type which an employee was bound, by an implied term in his contract of employment, not to use or disclose subsequent to the termination of employment. Neill LJ, delivering the judgment of the court, stated the Court of Appeal's views on the relevant principles to apply in cases involving confidentiality between master and servant.

1 If there was a contract of employment the employee's obligations were to be determined from that contract.
2 In the absence of any express terms, the employee's obligations would be implied.
3 While still in employment, there was an implied term imposing a duty of good faith or fidelity on the employee. This duty might vary according to the nature of the contract, but would be broken if the employee copied or deliberately memorised a list of customers.
4 The implied term imposing an obligation on the employee after the termination of his employment was more restricted than that imposed by the duty of fidelity. It might cover secret processes of manufacture or designs, or special methods of construction or other information of a sufficiently high degree of confidentiality so as to be classed as a trade secret.
5 Whether information fell within this implied term to prevent its use or disclosure by an ex-employee depended on the circumstances, and attention should be given to the following:
    (a) the nature of employment – a higher obligation might be imposed where the employee regularly handled confidential material;
    (b) the nature of information – it should be an authentic trade secret, or at least highly confidential;
    (c) whether the employer stressed the confidential nature of the material; and
    (d) whether the information could be easily isolated from other material the employee was free to use, this being useful evidentially rather than being a conclusive test.

On the last point, separability of information would tend to suggest that it was more likely that the information could be classed as confidential. The court left open the question of whether it would make any difference if the ex-employee used the information himself or if he simply sold it to another. Although the decision in this case seems a trifle unfair in that the ex-employee calculatingly and deliberately took advantage of his employer's business and reputation, it can be argued that the employer should have considered using a restrictive covenant which might have prevented the employee from competing in the area for at least a year or two. However, Mr Fowler was walking a thin line, for in *Normalec v Britton*[157] the defendant decided to sell the same goods as his employer (electric bulbs and fittings) to the same customers he had been seeing on behalf of his employer. Worse still, the defendant did this while he was still in the employ of the claimant. The defendant was held to have a fiduciary duty to his employer who was entitled to the profits made by the defendant, and the court also granted an injunction preventing the defendant from selling to the claimant's customers even after the termination of his employment.[158] The one major difference between this case and the *Faccenda*

157 [1983] FSR 318.

158 In *Balston Ltd v Headline Filters Ltd* [1990] FSR 385, an intention to set up in business in competition with the company of which he was a director was held not to conflict with the director's fiduciary duty to the company even though preliminary steps had been taken while he remained a director.

Chicken case is that here the activity was commenced while the defendant was still employed and while he still was under a duty of good faith or fidelity to his employer.

The *Faccenda* test was revisited by the Court of Appeal in *AT Poeton (Gloucester Plating) Ltd* v *Michael Ikem Horton*.[159] The facts of the case were that the claimant carried on an electroplating business, specialising in the plating of the internal surfaces of cylinders of internal combustion engines. The defendant had been employed as the claimant's sales engineer and, soon after terminating his employment, he started an electroplating business. Later, the claimant commenced proceedings for breach of confidence arguing that its confidential information misused by the defendant related to:

(a) the electrolyte
(b) the apparatus used by the claimant, and
(c) a list of the claimant's customers.

At first instance, the claimant was successful in respect of the claim relating to the apparatus and an injunction was granted. The trial judge, Pumfrey J, considered that the defendant had misused confidential information in relation to the design and configuration of the plating cell contained in the apparatus, having decided that the basic idea of the cell was not protectable.

The Court of Appeal allowed the appeal.[160] As regards the design and configuration of the plating cell, the trial judge did not believe this was in the public domain but he was criticised for not considering whether it was, in whole or in part, a *trade secret*, and, if so, whether it came within Class 2 or 3 of the *Faccenda* classification, being those described by Goulding J (at first instance) in *Faccenda Chicken Ltd* v *Fowler*.[161]

To reiterate Goulding's definitions of Class 2 and 3, Class 2 is information which the servant must treat as confidential (either because he is expressly told that it is confidential or because from its character it obviously is so) but which once learned necessarily remains in the servant's head and becomes part of his own skill and knowledge applied in the course of his master's business. Class 3 comprises specific trade secrets so confidential that, even though they may necessarily have been learned by heart and even though the servant may have left the service, they cannot lawfully be used for anyone's benefit but the master's.

In the Court of Appeal in *Faccenda*, Neill LJ said that to be in Class 2 and, therefore, protectable by a restrictive covenant, the information must be a trade secret or its equivalent. In the present case the defendant's contract of employment contained no relevant restrictions on his activities after termination; therefore, to be protectable, the information must have been in Class 3.

In the present case, Morritt LJ doubted whether the aggregation of the features of the plating cell (apart from feature 'X') was indeed a trade secret but he assumed so for the purposes of applying the test of Neill LJ in *Faccenda*, to determine whether they could amount to a trade secret of such a type as to fall within Goulding J's Class 3. That test and Morritt LJ's application of it to the facts of the present case follow.

1 *Nature of employment.* The defendant was employed as a sales engineer. Although he occasionally operated the electroplating process there was nothing in his contract of employment or the work he performed to heighten his appreciation of the alleged confidentiality of the information.
2 *Nature of the information.* Although it was accepted that the plating cell was capable of being a trade secret it did not attain the degree of confidentiality required for Class 3. The concept of the process was well known and the features of the claimant's cell reproduced by the defendant were largely a consequence of using that concept.
3 *Whether the employer impressed on the employee the confidentiality of the information.* This should be to the extent that the information can be properly regarded as a trade secret.

159 [2001] FSR 14.

160 However, with respect to a feature (described as feature 'X') which the defendant apparently had become aware of only during the course of the proceedings, the Court of Appeal considered this confidential and ordered the defendant not to use it without prior leave of the court.

161 [1985] 1 All ER 724.

Although this factor was present it was clear that the claim to confidentiality was much wider than justified. Although the Court of Appeal in *Lancashire Fires Ltd* v *Lyons & Co Ltd*[162] said the employer did not have to define the 'precise limits' of what he sought to protect, that case was not one in which the employer had made 'extravagant claims'.

4 *Whether the information can be easily isolated from other information the employee is free to use or disclose.* As the relevant features were so easily seen and assimilated by the defendant during his employment, they could not easily be isolated from information the employee was free to use and could not be protected in the absence of an appropriate covenant in restraint of trade.

The last point is important and Morritt LJ said that, if employers failed to use covenants in such cases, the court should be reluctant to find information in Class 3 'tucked away in a much wider, but unjustified, claim to confidential information'. The reason was that such claims could be easily made but could be expensive and time-consuming to refute and employees should not be exposed to such risks except in clear cases. *Faccenda*, *Lancashire Fires* and *Poeton* still leave the difficulty of deciding whether information is a 'specific trade secret' within Class 3 or a 'trade secret or its equivalent' in Class 2.

Employer's obligation

The obligation of confidence arising from a contract of employment is not all one way. In many cases, the employer will owe a duty of confidence to his employees. An employer will hold information concerning the employee, such as marital status, salary and career details. This information should not be divulged to others without the employee's permission except in circumstances where disclosure is permitted by express provision (for example, in pursuance of an attachment of earnings order)[163] or is implied (for example, where salaries are calculated and paid by a third party). If the employee's details are stored on a computer, there will usually be restrictions on disclosure by virtue of the Data Protection Act 1998.[164] Prospective employers also owe a duty of confidence in respect of *curricula vitae* submitted by job applicants. Some employers operate employee suggestions schemes, usually with the possibility of rewards for suggestions having merit that will be used by the employer. By taking part in the scheme, an employee can be said to have waived his rights, if any, in the information he has disclosed in this way if his employer uses the information.[165] However, if the employer does not make use of the information it seems that a duty of confidence will arise. In *Prout* v *British Gas plc*[166] the claimant, while employed by the defendant, submitted an idea for a new design of bracket for warning lamps placed around excavations. The bracket was supposed to be vandal-proof. The claimant was given an award by the defendant on the basis of its suggestions scheme, but later the defendant said that it had no interest and agreed to allow the claimant to pursue a patent application on his own behalf. On the issue of confidence, it was held that there was a contractual or equitable duty of confidence imposed on the defendant, the employer. Although this duty would normally end once the idea was used in public for the first time without any objection from the employee, a fresh duty could arise if the employee gave notice of his intention to apply for a patent and would continue until the filing date of the application. In this particular case it was held that the employer was in breach of confidence by its subsequent use of the lamps. This extension of duty beyond the first consensual public use could apply only where long-term trade or commercial secrecy was possible, or where an application for legal protection requiring novelty was envisaged. However, public use could easily destroy novelty and would do so in many cases.

Covenants in restraint of trade

An employer must be careful not to draft terms which are too wide in a contract of employment imposing a continuing duty of confidence after the employment has been

162 [1996] FSR 629.

163 Attachment of Earnings Act 1971.

164 *See Rowley* v *Liverpool City Council, The Times,* 26 October 1989. In this case disclosure was lawful under the Data Protection Act 1984 s 34(5), being required in the course of legal proceedings. The 1984 Act has been replaced by the Data Protection Act 1998.

165 In some cases, the information will be treated as belonging to the employer by virtue of the contract of employment.

166 [1992] FSR 478.

167 The same applies to independent consultants and the like engaged to perform some work.

168 Alternatively, such a promise might be extracted from the employee on payment of a settlement at the end of the contract of employment.

169 *Berkeley Administration Inc* v *McClelland* [1990] FSR 505; *Roberts* v *Northwest Fixings* [1993] FSR 281. The courts will not lend their aid to a determined attempt to stop competition. However, a covenant in a franchise agreement has to satisfy a far less stringent test of reasonableness than is required in respect of an ex-employee: *Dyno-Rod plc* v *Reeve* [1999] FSR 148 and *Convenience Co Ltd* v *Roberts* [2001] FSR 35.

170 *Polymasc Pharmaceuticals plc* v *Stephen Alexander Charles* [1999] FSR 711.

171 It should be noted that such covenants are not always concerned with confidential information.

172 [1921] AC 158.

173 [1916] 1 AC 688.

174 Per Neill LJ in *Faccenda Chicken Ltd* v *Fowler* [1986] 1 All ER 617 at 626.

175 [1991] IRLR 214.

176 The covenant was too wide because it went beyond that necessary to protect the employer's interest.

177 [1964] 1 WLR 568.

178 [1994] FSR 52.

terminated.[167] Terms that are too wide are in danger of being struck out by a court as being in restraint of trade. On appointment, an employee may agree to sign a contract restricting his use or disclosure of information concerning his employer's business, or agreeing not to work for a competitor after the termination of the contract of employment.[168] Generally, such agreements will be enforced by the courts only if they are reasonable between the parties and not against the public interest. In particular, an employer cannot use the law of confidence to protect himself against future competition *per se*. If a term in the contract of employment is a clear attempt to prevent future competition rather than a legitimate means of protecting the employer's business interests, it will not be enforced by the courts.[169] Generally, the burden of proof is on the employer to show that the covenant is reasonable and enforceable.[170]

Restrictive terms are usually referred to as covenants in restraint of trade and are frequently expressed in terms of preventing the employee working for a competitor or setting up a business in competition within a given area and for a given period of time.[171] These two factors, time and area, define the extent of the restraint. If the covenant is too wide in terms of either factor, the courts are unlikely to enforce it, and it is clear that the two factors must be considered together. In *Fitch* v *Dewes*,[172] a solicitor's clerk was prohibited from entering into the employment of another solicitor within a seven-mile radius of Tamworth Town Hall. The restriction was indefinite in terms of time, but nevertheless, because the geographic area was small, it was held to be valid. However, in *Herbert Morris Ltd* v *Saxelby*,[173] a restriction that an engineer could not work for a competitor anywhere as an engineer for seven years was held to be void. In any case, a restrictive covenant will not be enforced:

> unless the protection sought was reasonably necessary to protect a trade secret or to prevent some personal influence over customers being abused in order to entice them away.[174]

Geographical area will not be particularly relevant if the employer's business is carried out over the telephone or by facsimile transmission: even more so if the employer is engaged in e-business, making use of the internet. A covenant prohibiting the former employee from carrying on a business as an employment agent within a 3,000-metre radius (about 1.2 miles) of the employer's place of business for a period of six months was held to be too wide in *Office Angels Ltd* v *Rainer-Thomas*.[175] It was said that, as clients' orders were placed over the telephone, the location of the business was of no concern to them. Therefore, the area restriction was inappropriate.[176] However, even a small area restriction could be unduly restrictive if the area was one where most of the relevant business was undertaken.

Covenants in restraint of trade often include non-solicitation clauses. That is, the ex-employee may not approach or do business with the employer's customers or clients. The scope of such covenants needs careful thought. In *GW Plowman & Sons Ltd* v *Ash*[177] a sales representative for the claimant, who was a corn and agricultural merchant and animal feeding stuffs manufacturer, had a service agreement which contained a covenant not to carry on a business in the same field for two years within 20 miles of Spalding after termination of employment. It also contained a non-solicitation clause as regards persons who had been customers of the claimant during the period of employment. The fact that this was not limited to customers of whom the defendant had personal experience was not fatal to the clause. It was held valid by the Court of Appeal because, in the words of Russell LJ, the sales representative would be likely to 'acquire special influence over or knowledge of the requirements of any of the employer's customers' whether or not he dealt directly with them. This was because of the nature of the employer's business and because the defendant would be well known to all the customers as representing the claimant.

There are limits to non-solicitation clauses and the above case was distinguished in *Austin Knight (UK) Ltd* v *Hinds*[178] in which the defendant, who worked for a recruitment consultancy, dealt with about one-third of the consultancy's customers. She was made redundant and her contract of employment contained a covenant preventing her from soliciting or endeavouring to entice away any person who had been a customer of the claimant during her employment. This was held to be unreasonably wide because it purported to prevent the defendant from approaching all the former customers, even though she dealt with only one-third of them. Unlike the *Plowman* case, there were no grounds to infer that she was known to the two-thirds she did not deal with. Nor was there anything to suggest that she had misused any confidential information belonging to the claimant. On this last issue it was said by Vinelott J that there was no evidence that the defendant had taken with her or misused any database or confidential documents.

If a covenant in restraint of trade is drafted too widely it will be void. The courts will not narrow it down to an acceptable level and apply that instead. In *JA Mont (UK) Ltd* v *Mills*,[179] Simon Brown LJ said:

> . . . as a matter of policy, it seems to me similarly that the court should not too urgently strive to find within restrictive covenants ex facie too wide, implicit limitations such as alone could justify their imposition.

To construe covenants otherwise would encourage employers to draft their covenants deliberately in wide terms.[180] However, in *Littlewoods Organisation Ltd* v *Harris*[181] Lord Denning MR adopted a much more relaxed approach to construction, and a covenant that an employee '. . . shall not at any time within twelve months . . . enter into a contract of service or other agreement of a like nature with GUS or any subsidiary thereto' was interpreted as being limited to the mail order side of those parts of the GUS organisation that operated in the UK. The distinction is that in this case there had been an attempt to draw up a reasonable covenant.

The Court of Appeal summarised the legal propositions that apply in the context of restrictive covenants in employment contracts in *FSS Travel and Leisure Systems Ltd* v *Johnson*.[182] This case involved a computer programmer who was required not to engage in any business that would compete with the claimant's business for a period of one year following termination of employment. The claimant specialised in the development of computer programs for the travel industry. The Court of Appeal upheld the deputy judge's decision that the covenant was unreasonable. Mummery LJ set out the following principles:

1 The court will not uphold a covenant taken by an employer merely to protect himself from competition by a former employee.
2 There must be some subject matter which an employer can legitimately protect by a restrictive covenant.
3 Protection can be legitimately claimed for identifiable objective knowledge constituting an employer's trade secrets with which the employee has become acquainted during his employment.
4 However, protection cannot legitimately be claimed in respect of the skill, experience, know-how and general knowledge acquired by an employee as part of his job, even though this may equip him as a competitor or a potential employee of a competitor.
5 The critical question is whether the employer has trade secrets which can be fairly regarded as his property, as distinct from the skill, experience, know-how and general knowledge which can fairly be regarded as the property of the employee. This requires examination of all the evidence relating to the nature of the employment, the character of the information, the restrictions placed on its dissemination, the extent of use in the public domain and the damage likely to be caused by its use and disclosure in competition to the employer.
6 The problem in making a distinction between general skill and knowledge, which every employee can take with him when he leaves, and secret or confidential information, which he may be restrained from using, is one of definition. It must be possible

179 [1993] FSR 577.

180 *See* also *Mason* v *Provident Clothing and Supply Company* Ltd [1913] AC 724.

181 [1978] 1 All ER 1026.

182 [1999] FSR 505.

to identify information used in the relevant business, the use and dissemination of which is likely to harm the employer, and establish that the employer has limited dissemination and not, for example, encouraged or permitted its widespread publication. It is a matter of examining the detailed evidence relating to the employer's claim for secrecy and deciding, as a matter of fact, on which side of the boundary line it falls. Lack of precision in pleading and absence of solid evidence in proof of trade secrets are frequently fatal to enforcement of a restrictive covenant.

183 [1965] RPC 239.

Mummery LJ then cited Cross J in *Printers & Finishers Ltd* v *Holloway (No. 2)*[183] with approval, saying that later decisions had not improved upon Cross J's approach where he said (at 244):

> If the information in question can fairly be regarded as a separate part of the employee's stock of knowledge which a man of ordinary honesty and intelligence would recognise to be the property of his old employer and not his own to do as he likes with, then the court, if it thinks that there is a danger in the information being used or disclosed by the ex-employee to the detriment of the old employer, will do what it can to prevent that result by granting an injunction.

Subject-matter of covenants

There is some judicial confusion about the proper subject matter of a covenant in restraint of trade in terms of confidential information. In *Faccenda Chicken*, Neill LJ suggested that only trade secrets or their equivalent could be protected by a restrictive covenant and that more mundane information could not. However, this was *obiter* (there was not a restrictive covenant imposed on the defendant) and it conflicts with Neill LJ's own description of the implied term imposed after termination of employment. The implied term protects trade secrets, and consequently there is no need for a restrictive covenant in respect of them. In *Balston Ltd* v *Headline Filters Ltd*,[184] Scott J declined to follow that part of Neill LJ's judgment to the effect that confidential information that could not be protected by an implied term *ipso facto* could not be protected by a suitably limited express covenant.[185] This accords with common sense as most business organisations possess information that would harm them or benefit others if divulged, even though that information is not a trade secret or associated with one. By limiting the restriction the courts are seeking to arrive at an equitable balance between the interests of employer and employee alike.

184 [1987] FSR 330, an interim hearing.

185 At first instance, in *Faccenda Chicken Ltd* v *Fowler* [1985] 1 All ER 724, Goulding J classified information available to employees into three categories. Class 2, confidential information falling short of a trade secret, was, he suggested, capable of being protected by a restrictive covenant. In the Court of Appeal, Neill LJ disagreed with this proposition.

Garden leave

Employers are often worried about the harm that can be caused to them by an employee working his notice. The employee might attempt to influence clients or remove confidential materials. It is not unknown for employees who have been given notice of termination of their employment to be told to stay at home and 'enjoy the garden' during their period of notice. This 'garden leave' may last for some time if the employee is in a senior position subject to a lengthy period of notice. If the employee attempts to work for another employer during his garden leave, the courts may act to restrain him by granting an injunction.

A 'high-flying' professional may be anxious to start work for another organisation as quickly as possible and challenge the period of notice. In *GFI Group Inc* v *Eaglestone*[186] a highly paid financial services broker challenged his 20-week period of notice. The court was tempted to hold him to this because, in his line of work, his word was his bond. However, the period was reduced to three months because of some exceptional circumstances, one of which was that some other brokers were only on four weeks' notice.

186 [1994] FSR 535.

Factors that may be relevant to the grant of an injunction include the amount and nature of confidential information the employee had access to and the seniority of the employee. However, in *Provident Financial Group* v *Hayward*[187] the Court of Appeal refused

187 [1989] 3 All ER 298.

to grant an injunction against an employee on garden leave because little of the period of notice remained, there was no evidence of a serious prospect that the employer's interests would be harmed and the employee worked in an administrative capacity, having access to very little confidential information. It could also be argued that enforced garden leave is a breach of the contract of employment, as an implied term is that the employer provides suitable work, if available.[188]

Where there is a restrictive covenant for a period of time, the time during which the employee is 'enjoying' his garden leave is not, in the normal case, deducted from the time limit in the covenant. In *Credit Suisse Asset Management Ltd* v *Armstrong*,[189] Neill LJ declined to set off the time on garden leave. In that case, the duration of the garden leave was six months and the period in the covenant was twelve months. Neill LJ did, however, add a caveat on the basis of public policy, saying that a court might decline to enforce the covenant where, for example, the length of garden leave was exceptional.

In *Crowson Fabrics Ltd* v *Rider*,[190] the defendants had been employees of the claimant and whilst working their notice, retained and took materials belonging to their employer in addition to setting up a rival company. They both lied about their future employment to avoid being sent on garden leave. Peter Smith J found the defendants liable on a number of grounds, including breaches of their duty of fidelity to their employer, soliciting agents and clients of the employer and infringement of database rights. However, the claimants failed to show that the information concerned was confidential.

Third-party recipients

The general rule is that a third party who comes by the information without knowing it to be confidential, or in circumstances where an obligation of confidence cannot be imposed, is free to use the information or to disclose it as he sees fit, especially if it entered the public domain. This is the one fundamental weakness of the law of breach of confidence – innocent third parties are largely unaffected by this area of law. They may, however, be subject to other rights, duties or liabilities. For example, the information may be in the form of a literary work and a question of infringement of copyright might be raised. Alternatively, use of the information may result in an action for passing off, or its publication may be defamatory or a breach of the right to privacy under the European Convention on Human Rights.

The position of the person who is not aware of the confidential nature of the information at the time it is disclosed to him but subsequently becomes so aware is less clear. In *Fraser* v *Evans*[191] Lord Denning MR said (at 361):

> No person is permitted to divulge to the world information he has received in confidence, unless he has just cause or excuse for doing so. Even if he comes by it innocently, nevertheless once he gets to know that it was originally given in confidence, he can be restrained from breaking that confidence.

There are *dicta* in *Prince Albert* v *Strange*,[192] *Union Carbide Corp* v *Naturin Ltd*[193] and other cases, which suggest that the power of the court to restrain use or further disclosure of confidential information could extend to cases where a person obtains information without notice of the breach. In *Lancashire Fires Ltd* v *SA Lyons & Co Ltd*,[194] the third defendant, who had been employed by the claimant as a financial manager, was given information relating to a new process for making artificial coal and logs for gas fires by the second defendant (who had also been employed by the claimant) in breach of confidence. The second and third defendants set up a company to exploit the confidential technology and the Court of Appeal confirmed that the third defendant could also be restrained from using the information. A particular factor was the public interest in the maintenance of confidences.

188 However, the contract of employment may be construed so as not to impose an obligation on the employer to provide appropriate or any work: *SBJ Stephenson Ltd* v *Mandy* [2000] FSR 286.

189 [1996] ICR 882.

190 [2008] FSR 17.

191 [1969] 1 QB 349.

192 (1849) 1 Mac & G 25.

193 [1987] FSR 538.

194 [1996] FSR 629.

It can be said that equity fastens on the person's conscience once he discovers the confidential nature of the information. However, equitable remedies are discretionary and injunctive relief may not be given where it could cause hardship to the parties. The person to whom the information has been given might have performed work or made contracts with other persons in reliance on that information before appreciating its confidential nature. This factor did not, however, prevent an Australian judge imposing injunctions on all the defendants (most of whom had unwittingly paid for the information).[195]

There will be circumstances where a third party will be bound by an obligation of confidence even though the owner of the information did not impart the information to the third party directly. The third party may receive confidential information knowing it to be confidential, or in circumstances in which a reasonable man would have suspected that it was confidential. In other cases, he may discover the confidential nature of the information subsequently. It appears that only when the recipient actually knows of the confidential nature will he be under an obligation not to use or divulge the information further. In *Fraser* v *Thames TV Ltd*,[196] three actresses formed a rock group with the assistance of a manager and developed an idea for a TV series known as *The Rock Follies*. They discussed the idea orally with Thames TV in confidence, and it was agreed that the actresses were to have first refusal should the series proceed. When Thames TV decided to proceed, one of the actresses could not get a release from another part and Thames TV replaced her with another actress. It was held that the court would prevent a person disclosing an idea in written or oral form until it became general public knowledge, provided that:

1 the circumstances imputed an obligation of confidence, and
2 the content was clearly identifiable, potentially attractive in a commercial sense and capable of being brought to fruition.

For a third party to be fixed with an obligation of confidence, they must know that the information was confidential and had been imparted in confidence. Even though it was disclosed to several people, it was disclosed to each and all of them in confidence. An argument by counsel for the defence that the idea lost its confidentiality when it was disclosed to others was rejected by Hirst J, who said that the disclosure to others was plainly also in confidence and, therefore, confidence remained intact.[197] The actress who had been replaced was awarded very substantial damages. If the information has fallen into the public domain, then there is nothing to be gained by preventing a third party from publishing it. As Lord Goff said in *Attorney-General* v *Guardian Newspapers (No 2)*[198] (at 281):

> If a person into whose possession [the confidential information] comes publishes it, and is (as he usually will be) aware of its confidential nature, he will *prima facie* be guilty of a breach of confidence and any such publication, if threatened, can therefore be restrained by injunctions as a threatened breach of confidence, subject of course to the usual limitations on the duty of confidence. One of these limitations is that information is no longer confidential once it has entered the public domain, once information relating to national security has entered the public domain, I find it difficult to see on what basis further disclosure of such information can be restrained.

The issue of the innocent third-party recipient was considered again in *Valeo Vision SA* v *Flexible Lamps Ltd*.[199] The claimant gave some drawings and other confidential information relating to rear light clusters for vehicles to a third party, the German truck manufacturer MAN. The third party later disclosed these to the defendant who took them in good faith, believing the third party had the right to disclose them. Aldous J said that the equitable rule, that a person who is a bona fide purchaser for value without notice of confidential information will escape the arm of equity, was too narrow. However, it was settled law that equity would provide relief by way of damages only where a person had his conscience

195 *Wheatley* v *Bell* [1984] FSR 16.

196 [1984] 1 QB 44.

197 *See* also *Franchi* v *Franchi* [1967] RPC 149.

198 [1990] 1 AC 109.

199 [1995] RPC 205.

fixed by equity, objectively or subjectively. Nevertheless, the court would still, in appropriate cases, grant an injunction restraining further misuse of the information. The test for whether a third party can be liable for a breach of confidence was considered further in the Court of Appeal in *Thomas* v *Pearce*.[200] The second defendant had made use of a list of clients given to her by the first defendant who had taken the list from her former employer. It was held that the correct test was whether the third party had acted honestly. Mere careless, naive or stupid behaviour is insufficient. For a third party in such circumstances to be liable for breach of confidence, the third party must have acted dishonestly, with conscious knowledge of the breach or at least deliberately closing his mind to it. This test seems narrower than the view of Aldous J in *Valeo Vision* and, in *Thomas* v *Pearce*, Buxton LJ put great store on cases on breach of trust such as *Royal Brunei Airlines* v *Tan*[201] in which Lord Nicholls said that a failure to exercise due diligence was insufficient to establish liability against a third party who procured or assisted in a breach of trust. To be liable, the third party would have to have failed to 'observe the standard which would be observed by an honest person'. However, it is arguable that it is not correct to apply principles derived from cases on breach of trust to a breach of confidence case. There was no mention in *Thomas* v *Pearce* of the cases on the position of third parties in breach of confidence cases.

The granting of an injunction would be ineffective once the information has entered the public domain and is readily available. It could also be very unfair on the innocent recipient against whom action is taken. In the above case, an injunction was held to be inappropriate as the information had already entered the public domain. Contrary to some earlier judicial statements as regards the knowledge required to bind the conscience of the third party so as to give rise to damages, Aldous J in *Valeo Vision* made it clear that constructive knowledge will suffice. That is where the third party was in the possession of such facts that would make the reasonable man suspect that the information[202] as subject to an obligation of confidence.

A discussion of third-party recipients is not complete without consideration of the position of a person who obtains the information surreptitiously, for example in circumstances involving industrial espionage. Can such a person be fixed with an obligation of confidence? At first sight it appears not, especially when the formula used in the *Coco* case is examined, as it seems to suggest that the information is given voluntarily by its owner. There is very little case law on this point, but in *Malone* v *Commissioner of Police*[203] Sir Robert Megarry V-C was of the view that an eavesdropper would not owe a duty of confidence. *Malone* involved telephone tapping, an activity which was made illegal under the Interception of Communications Act 1985 s 1, which made it an offence intentionally to intercept a communication during its transmission through a public telecommunication system.[204]

In *Malone* the telephone tap was lawful, but Sir Robert Megarry V-C spoke of unknown hearers and said that a person using a telephone to disclose confidential information must accept the risk of being overheard as that risk is inherent in the mode of communication. This case was distinguished in *Francome* v *Mirror Group Newspapers Ltd*,[205] where it was held that there was a serious issue to be tried on the basis of breach of confidence concerning information obtained by way of an illegal telephone tap. Although a person using a telephone takes the risk of being overheard because of imperfections or accidents, he does not willingly take the risk of an illegal tap. The same principle should apply to facsimile transmission or electronic mail. The sender takes the risk of the information being seen by persons other than those for whom it is intended, who have access to the room where the receiving machine is installed. Even the risk of misdirection must be accepted. It must be questionable whether confidentiality can remain intact if a number of persons, other than those directly associated with the addressee such as secretarial staff, have an opportunity to read the contents of a facsimile transmission. Likewise, the status

200 [2000] FSR 718.

201 [1995] 2 AC 378.

202 For example, Hirst J in *Fraser* v *Thames Television Ltd* [1984] 1 QB 44 at 65.

203 [1979] 2 All ER 620.

204 Now replaced by the Regulation of Investigatory Powers Act 2000 s 1 which makes it an offence intentionally to intercept a communication during its transmission through a public telecommunication system without lawful authority. The offence also applies to a public postal service and to private telecommunication systems, subject to a number of exemptions.

205 [1984] 2 All ER 408.

of a notice on the transmitted material to the effect that it is confidential and must not be read by anyone other than the addressee is doubtful. It should be noted that, in the case of *Prince Albert* v *Strange*,[206] the court found for the claimant even though it was not known how the defendant had gained possession of the subject matter, only that it must have been done surreptitiously. If the information in question contains personal data and is subsequently stored in a computer or structured manual file by the eavesdropper or spy, there may be a breach of data protection law and possibly an offence under that law.

Unauthorised use

The final ingredient for an action for breach of confidence is an unauthorised use of the information to the detriment of the party communicating it. It will usually be fairly obvious when there has been an unauthorised use of confidential material. The use or disclosure complained of must be related to the nature of the obligation of confidence. For example, in an agreement between the owner of confidential information and a manufacturing company which is going to exploit it commercially on the basis of agreed royalty payments, the company will be permitted to use the information for the purposes detailed in the agreement. In addition, other use and subsequent disclosure may be implied. For example, the company may be able to divulge the information to subcontractors while stressing its confidentiality, and to the company's own employees and to sister companies if part of a group. It is really a matter of construing the agreement.

Liability for unauthorised use may be joint, but is not restricted to cases where all joint tortfeasors have played an active role in the breach of confidence. Thus, a person embarked upon a common design with another who is solely responsible for the breach of confidence may also be injuncted.[207] However, where the confidential information is jointly owned, it appears that one joint owner cannot prevent the other joint owners making use of the information without him, in the absence of any contractual agreement to the contrary. In *Drummond Murray* v *Yorkshire Fund Managers Ltd*,[208] a team of six persons put together a package of information relating to the purchase of a company. The information was communicated to a third party by the team and the third party started to use the information with the blessing of the team bar one, the claimant, who objected and commenced proceedings to restrain the third party from using the information. Although the first two elements in *Coco* v *Clark*[209] were present, the last, an unauthorised use, was not. There was no binding agreement that all the members of the team would continue to be involved and any of them could withdraw at any time. If this was so, then some of the members of the team could decide to go ahead without one of their number, either on their own or jointly, with others. Although the information initially belonged to all the members of the team, if one could be excluded, then he could not after exclusion prevent the use of the information by the others.

If the information is a mixture of public and private materials then the recipient must be especially careful to use only that which is public, unless he has permission to use the private information. In *Seager* v *Copydex (No 1)*[210] the defendant designed a carpet grip using details from the public domain, but also incorporating some ideas it had discussed with the claimant some years before. The defendant claimed it had forgotten about the latter so it was effectively a case of subconscious copying. Nevertheless, and notwithstanding the apparent innocence of the defendant's actions, Lord Denning MR found for the claimant. It would appear, therefore, that the state of the mind of the person using the information in breach of confidence does not affect liability, although it could be relevant when it comes to determining damages. The Court of Appeal gave further support for the view that liability for breach of confidence did not require an awareness on the part of the

206 (1849) 1 Mac & G 25.

207 *Lancashire Fires Ltd* v *SA Lyons & Co Ltd* [1996] FSR 629, applying *Unilever plc* v *Gillette (UK) Ltd* [1989] RPC 583, a patent case.

208 [1998] FSR 372.

209 [1969] RPC 41, discussed at p 350 above.

210 [1967] RPC 349.

defendant that he was committing a breach of confidence: *Vestergaard Frandsen A/S* v *Bestnet Europe Ltd*.[211]

211 [2011] EWCA Civ 424.

That there should be some detriment to the party communicating the information is doubtful. Although, in *Coco* v *Clark*, Megarry J spoke of detriment as being an ingredient for an action in breach of confidence, other parts of his judgment suggest that it need not be an essential element. In *Attorney-General* v *Guardian Newspapers (No 2)*,[212] Lord Goff said that, like Megarry J in *Coco* v *Clark*, he would like to keep the point open although accepting that it will almost always be present. In many cases, the justification for protecting confidences is that they are tied up with commercial activity, investment and marketing and industrial manufacture. In other words, confidence has an economic value to its owner who will have a vested interest to see that his competitors do not have access to the information, at least not without paying for it. But the law of breach of confidence has a tremendously wide scope, and in some cases economic considerations are largely irrelevant: for example, where the disclosure of the information is likely to harm a person's public standing.

212 [1990] 1 AC 109.

Where the information has economic value, it is easily understandable why the owner of the information would not want to see his competitors have some advantage from it. In *R* v *Licensing Authority, ex parte Smith Kline & French Laboratories Ltd*,[213] SKF[214] originated a drug (Cimetidine) to control gastric acid secretion and heal peptic ulcers. SKF marketed the drug under the name 'Tagamet' and obtained patents in respect of it in 1972, which were extended to 1992 on the basis that during the last four years the patents would be endorsed 'licences of right'.[215] SKF and others wishing to sell the drug had to obtain a product licence from the licensing authority. SKF objected to the licensing authority using confidential information submitted by SKF in support of its own application in order to consider other companies' applications for product licences. The High Court held that this was a breach of confidence, but this was reversed in the Court of Appeal. The House of Lords upheld the Court of Appeal saying that the licensing authority, at its discretion and in the performance of its duties under the Medicines Act 1968 and Community law, had a right to make use of all the information provided by applicants for product licences in determining whether to grant other applications. Two important factors were the protection of public health and the harmonisation of the national laws throughout Member States.

213 [1989] 1 All ER 175.

214 Smith Kline & French Laboratories Ltd.

215 The extension was by virtue of the Patents Act 1977 Sch 1. Under the Patents Act 1949 the maximum duration of a patent was 16 years.

Of course, this case has tremendous significance for originators of medicines and generic manufacturers. The originator has all the expense of research, development and, in particular, testing new drugs and medicines. If the drug or medicine was covered by patents then, theoretically, all the competitor would have to do would be to look up the patent specifications (being documents available for public inspection) and then, at the appropriate time, apply for a compulsory licence in respect of the patents or to have the patents endorsed 'licences of right'. However, the patent owner's mono-poly will not be easily disturbed unless there is some evidence that the patent is not being worked or is being unfairly exploited in some way.[216] This reluctance to interfere with the monopoly provided by patents is justifiable in the context of something like a drug, where a potential competitor could seriously undercut the originator because the former has not spent large sums of money on research and development.

216 *See* Chapter 13 for licences of right and compulsory licences.

Remedies

The whole rationale and justification for the law of breach of confidence is that it can and should be used to preserve secrets and confidences. As a result of this the most appropriate remedy is the *quia timet* injunction, which will be granted to prevent general publication or other disclosure of the subject matter of the confidence. However, as previously noted, an injunction will not normally be granted if the aggrieved party complains that publication would be defamatory and the defendant is likely to raise a defence of justification or fair comment. In such a case, the courts will usually allow the defendant to publish and take the risk of paying damages, which could be considerable, should his defence in a defamation action fail. However, this rule of thumb has been significantly modified recently by the granting of super-injunctions, obtained typically by celebrities to prevent publication of material, often of a private nature. These injunctions are called 'super-injunctions' because the media is not even allowed to publish that a certain person has obtained an injunction. The increasing use of super-injunctions to protect privacy may be in conflict with the right of freedom of expression under the Human Rights Convention as the courts are unable, at that stage, to determine whether the information for which publication is being restrained is true.

In some cases, an injunction may be granted to prevent the defendant making use of the information himself, even though innocent third parties may be free to use it (the so-called springboard doctrine discussed earlier in this chapter). However, normally, once the information has fallen into the public domain, an injunction will not be granted because it is ineffective: for example, as in one of the *Spycatcher* cases, *Attorney-General* v *The Observer Ltd*.[217] In the House of Lords it was held that injunctions would not be granted against the *Observer* and the *Guardian* preventing them from reporting on the contents of *Spycatcher* because publication abroad had effectively destroyed the secrecy of the book's contents.[218]

Being equitable, injunctions are discretionary, and the decision to grant an injunction will be influenced by factors such as the innocence of the defendant – for example, in the case of non-deliberate use of information as in *Seager* v *Copydex (No 1)*,[219] and whether an injunction is really necessary. In *Coco* v *AN Clark (Engineers) Ltd*,[220] the court decided that payment of damages in the form of royalties would be an appropriate alternative pending full trial. Other considerations might be whether the claimant delayed in taking legal action (the doctrine of laches applies), whether he was careless with the information or whether he should have sought other legal means of protecting the information, for example by obtaining a patent.

Section 12 of the Human Rights Act 1998 applies where restraining publication might affect the Convention right of freedom of expression. Section 12(3) states that, where freedom of expression is an issue, no relief as to restrain publication before trial shall be granted unless the court '. . . is satisfied that the applicant is *likely* to establish that publication should not be allowed' (emphasis added). The *American Cyanamid* guidelines[221] used a test based on whether the applicant for an interim injunction established that there was a serious issue to be tried or that he had a real prospect of success at trial. The s 12 of the Human Rights Act 1998 brought a change in cases were freedom of expression possibly was involved. In particular, the meaning of the word 'likely' in s 12(3) was problematic. Did it mean 'more likely than not' or did it mean that the applicant simply had to show that it was possible that he might obtain an injunction at full trial?

In *Cream Holdings Ltd* v *Banerjee*,[222] the defendant was a chartered account who worked for the claimant. After termination of her employment she gave confidential information to a local newspaper investigating financial irregularities including an allegation of corruption against a director of the claimant and a local government official. After publication of two articles about the matter, the claimant sought an order restraining publication of any more of the confidential information given to the newspaper by the defendant. An interim injunction was granted at first instance and this was upheld in the Court of Appeal. The defendant's appeal to the House of Lords was successful and the injunction was lifted. The House of Lords held that Parliament had intended that some flexibility should be read into s 12(3). As a basic rule, the word 'likely' meant 'more likely than not'.

217 [1989] AC 109.

218 The *Sunday Times* was in breach of confidence when it published an extract before copies of the book had become readily available in the UK and the newspaper was liable to account for the resulting profits. However, the *Sunday Times* could now continue with its further serialisation of *Spycatcher*.

219 [1967] RPC 349.

220 [1969] RPC 41.

221 *See* Chapter 24 on remedies.

222 [2005] 1 AC 253.

However, that was not a hard and fast rule and it would depend on the circumstances. For example, it might be appropriate for a court to use a lesser standard where the disclosure may cause serious harm or where a short-lived injunction is needed to enable the court to hear and give proper consideration to the application for interim relief pending the full trial.

In terms of confidential information, an injunction may be for either or both of two purposes. The first is to restrain the continued use of the information and the second is to restrain publication. The latter will not normally be appropriate where the information has already entered the public domain, subject to what has been said earlier in this chapter in relation to the springboard doctrine. In *Ocular Sciences Ltd* v *Aspect Vision Care Ltd*,[223] Laddie J clearly distinguishes between the two purposes and when they are appropriate. In that case, he applied the guidelines in *Shelfer* v *City of London Electric Lighting Co*[224] to the effect that the court should grant damages in substitution for an injunction where the injury to the claimant's legal rights is small, is capable of being estimated in money, is adequately compensated by a small money payment and the case is such that it would be oppressive to the defendant to grant the injunction. On the facts, the information relating to contact lenses was not substantial, the damage to the claimants, if any, was small and the granting of an injunction would be oppressive. The claimants' proceedings had been vexatious in a number of respects and some reckless claims to confidentiality had been put forward. Therefore, Laddie J refused to grant this form of injunction.

If the information has been disclosed or used in some way in breach of confidence then it will usually be too late for an injunction, but damages may be available.[225] Damages may be calculated on the basis of conversion, breach of confidence being in the nature of an equitable tort. The most thorough and comprehensive discussion of the relevant principles is to be found in *Seager* v *Copydex Ltd (No 2)*,[226] where it was said that the value of confidential information depends upon its nature, and one of the following two formulae would be appropriate:

1 If there is nothing very special about the information, and it could have been obtained by employing a competent consultant, then the value (for the purpose of damages) is the fee that consultant would charge.
2 If the information is something special involving an inventive step, then the value is the price a willing buyer would pay for it.

If the information is commercial in nature and used in the manufacture of an object which is sold or hired, then it would seem that damages should be assessed on the basis of the fee the owner of the information reasonably might have expected had the information been used with his licence. Assessing damages for future infringement would be difficult using the second formula in *Seager* above. One might also question why a patent had not been applied for if there was an inventive step. A better approach would be that used in the *Coco* case, where an order was granted to the effect that the defendant should pay into a trust account a royalty on engines made in the future.

The Intellectual Property (Enforcement, etc.) Regulations 2006[227] provide a formula for the assessment of damages for the infringement of intellectual property rights. It may seem debatable whether the ownership of confidential information, *per se*, gives rise to an intellectual property right. However, the Directive on the enforcement of intellectual property rights suggests that a wide interpretation should be given to the term 'intellectual property' and goes on to state that Member States may apply the Directive to acts involving unfair competition.[228] Furthermore, the protection of intellectual property rights under the TRIPs Agreement extends to the protection of 'undisclosed information'.[229] The Directive on the enforcement of intellectual property rights recognises that the Member States and the Community itself are bound by the TRIPs Agreement. In *Vestergaard Frandsen A/S* v *Bestnet Europe Ltd*,[230] the Court of Appeal accepted that a claim to enforce confidence in an intellectual property claim came within the enforcement Directive.

223 [1997] RPC 289.

224 [1895] 1 Ch 287.

225 Exemplary damages are not available for breach of confidence or invasion of privacy: *Mosley* v *News Group Newspapers Ltd* [2008] EWHC 2341 (QB).

226 [1969] RPC 250.

227 SI 2006/1028 reg 3. The Regulations implement, *inter alia*, Directive 2004/48/EC of the European Parliament and of the Council of 29 April 2004 on the enforcement of intellectual property rights, OJ L 157, 30.04.2004, p 45 (the 'Directive on the enforcement of intellectual property rights').

228 Recital 13 to the Directive.

229 Agreement on Trade-Related Aspects of Intellectual Property Rights, Annex 1C of the Marrakech Agreement Establishing the World Trade Organisation, 1994. Under Article 39 of the Agreement, protected undisclosed information is secret information of commercial value.

230 [2011] EWCA Civ 424 at para 56.

Under reg 3 of the Intellectual Property (Enforcement, etc.) Regulations 2006, in assessing damages in cases where the defendant knew or had reasonable grounds for knowing that he was engaged in infringing activity, the court must take account of all appropriate aspects including negative economic factors such as lost profits or unfair profits made by the defendant and non-economic factors such as the moral prejudice caused to the claimant by the infringement. In appropriate cases, royalties or fees payable had the defendant taken a licence may be used as a basis for the assessment exercise. It is submitted that this will have minimal impact on the assessment of damages for breach of confidence but could impact on cases such as *Peter Pan Manufacturing Corp* v *Corsets Silhouette Ltd*, discussed below.

The market value approach has no place where the claimant would not have contemplated selling or licensing the confidential information to others. In *Cadbury Schweppes Inc* v *FBI Foods Ltd*,[231] the claimant acquired a company making a drink comprising tomato juice and clam broth, sold under the name 'Clamato'. An ex-licensee made a new drink after termination of the licence, called Caesar Cocktail. The claimant obtained some and discovered the formula and claimed that it had been made in breach of confidence. It was held, in the Supreme Court of Canada, that damages for the breach of confidence should be calculated on a 'but-for' basis as is usual with a tort. The claimant's lost opportunity was that the defendant had entered the marketplace some 12 months earlier than it would have otherwise done. However, the court would not unjustly enrich a confider by overcompensating for 'nothing very special' information.

In *Gorne* v *Scales*[232] a willing seller and willing buyer approach was taken in assessing the value of confidential information relating to a farm seed processing business. The information was in the form of a card index containing information such as customers (farmers), contact details, quantities and types of seed processed for these customers and amounts charged. In assessing damages for breach of confidence, the Court of Appeal held by a majority, that where the confidential information is a business asset, regard should be had to the market value of that information in the context of a sale between a willing seller and a willing buyer.

As regards innocent third parties, damages will be available, as a general rule, only if the third party's conscience is fixed by equity, that is, if they knew or ought to have known that the information was subject to an obligation of confidence. Injunctions may be available, if appropriate, notwithstanding the innocence or *bona fides* of the third party. Each case must be treated on its own merits and it is, effectively, a matter of satisfying the equity raised by the third party's intentions in relation to the information. Basic equitable principles should guide the courts in the exercise of their discretion in such matters and the interests of a third party purchaser without knowledge, actual or constructive, should be paramount.

If the information has been exploited commercially in breach of confidence, an account of profits may be more beneficial to the claimant. An account is an alternative to damages, and being an equitable remedy is discretionary. In *Peter Pan Manufacturing Corp* v *Corsets Silhouette Ltd*[233] a manufacturer of brassieres made use of confidential information under a licence agreement. After the expiry of a licence agreement, the manufacturer continued to use the information, clearly in breach of confidence. In an action for breach of confidence, the claimant asked for an account of profits based on the whole of the profits accruing from the brassieres, but the defendant claimed that the account of profits should be based only on the profit resulting from the wrongful use of the confidential information, that is, the profit relating to the parts of the brassieres incorporating the confidential information. The difference between the two sums was substantial and the claimant was awarded the higher sum because it was accepted by the court that the defendant would not have been able to make the brassieres at all without the use of the confidential information.

231 [2000] FSR 491.

232 [2006] EWCA Civ 311.

233 [1963] RPC 45.

Finally, another equitable remedy which might be available, depending upon the circumstances, is an order for the destruction of articles that have been made by using the confidential information, or which incorporate the tangible expression of such information. For example, an order for destruction of any of the brassieres still held in stock by the defendant in the above case might have been appropriate. Such an order would not be granted as regards articles lawfully in the possession of third parties, unless somehow implicated in the breach of confidence.

Summary

The law of breach of confidence protects trade secrets and information of all types which is not in the public domain where the secret or information:

- has the necessary quality of confidence;
- has been disclosed in circumstances imposing a duty of confidence; and
- there has been or will be an unauthorised use of the secret or information.

A secret industrial process known only to one company clearly has the necessary quality of confidence. Relatively mundane information such as a list of customers and suppliers may also be protected by the law of breach of confidence. A photograph of a person taken in a private place may also be protected as will be other information concerning an individual's private life.

The duty of confidence may be imposed expressly or it may be implied from the circumstances or the status of the person disclosing the information and the recipient, such as between a person and their legal advisor.

Unauthorised use includes a situation where the person under the duty of confidence makes use of the secret or information for their own purposes or discloses it to a third party or publishes it.

The law of breach of confidence has developed to such an extent as to reflect the rights of privacy and freedom of expression enshrined in the Council of Europe Convention for the Protection of Human Rights and Fundamental Freedoms. It may also overlap with data protection law, where the information contains personal data.

In terms of industry, business and commerce, the law of breach of confidence is very important in relation to employees and consultants. In the absence of express terms in the contract of employment, a duty of confidence will be implied but will not prevent an ex-employee making use of what they have learnt and which has become part of their skill and experience. An employer may consider using a reasonable covenant in restraint of trade to better protect his confidential information.

Although information may be secret, in some cases it may be published in the public interest, which is the main defence to a breach of confidence action, for example, where the information discloses illegal conduct or improper conduct by someone in the public arena such as a politician or celebrity.

The most important remedy for a breach of confidence is an injunction to prevent unauthorised use, whether actually occurring or anticipated. There are two purposes of injunctions in this context, being:

- to prevent the person under the obligation of confidence using the information for himself;
- to prevent the person under the obligation of confidence disclosing the information to others.

Where the person under an obligation of confidence puts the information in the public domain, he may be prevented from using it for himself for a fixed period of time even though others may be free to use the information. This is termed a springboard injunction but is without prejudice to any damages that may be awarded. However, the rationale for such springboard relief has been doubted. It may be appropriate to prevent a person benefiting from a past misuse of confidential information.

The status of third parties who acquire confidential information is not absolutely clear, but it appears that:

- where the circumstances are such that they should have realised the information was confidential they may be prevented from using it and if they have made use of it they may be required to pay damages or account for the resultant profit;
- where a third party has acquired the information unaware that it was confidential and the circumstances are not such as to objectively suggest that it was confidential, it seems that the third party will be free to make use of it.

Discussion questions

1 Discuss the extent to which the law of breach of confidence reflects the rights of privacy and freedom of expression under the Human Rights Convention.

2 An employee is employed to write computer programs and to create and maintain a customer database for his employer. In writing the programs, he makes use of a special technique known only to his employer. It appears that the programs and database have the necessary quality of confidence. After termination of his employment, he sets himself up in business as a sole trader and wishes to create similar computer programs using the special technique and a similar database containing what customer details he can remember from his previous employer's database. He has not taken away any copies of his previous employer's programs or database. The contract of employment was silent on the issue of confidentiality and contained no covenants in restraint of trade. Discuss the application of the principles in the *Faccenda Chicken* cases (Goulding J at first instance and Neill LJ on appeal) to this situation.

3 Consider the public interest defence in the context of a company which makes goods for sale. Discuss the sort of confidential information that such a company may have which, if published without the company's permission (for example, published by a whistleblower), could be subject to a public interest defence.

4 Is the springboard doctrine logically flawed? If the information in question has entered the public domain, surely the only remedy lies in monetary compensation. Discuss.

Selected further reading

Carty, H., 'An analysis of the modern action for breach of commercial confidence: when is protection merited?' [2008] *Intellectual Property Quarterly* 416 (looks at the action of breach of confidence in the light of the Human Rights Convention, particularly in relation to commercial confidences and calls for a new formulation for the action to replace *Coco v Clark*, now seen as not relevant to personal confidences).

De Werra, J., 'How to protect trade secrets in high tech sports? An intellectual property analysis based on the experiences at the America's Cup and in the Formula One Championship' [2010] *European Intellectual Property Review*, 155 (from an intellectual property perspective and in the light of Article 39 of the TRIPs Agreement, examines unfair behaviour in the field of professional sports).

Hunt, C.D.L., 'Rethinking surreptitious takings in the law of confidence' [2011] *Intellectual Property Quarterly*, 66 (controversially argues for a reversal of the recent trend in finding liability where information has been taken surreptitiously, such as the House of Lords decisions in *OBG* v *Allen* and *Campbell* v *Mirror Group Newspapers*).

Visit www.mylawchamber.co.uk/bainbridgeip to access study support resources including interactive multiple choice questions, practice exam questions with guidance, weblinks, legal updates and a legal newsfeed.

Part Four

PATENT LAW

Patent law – background, basic principles and practical aspects 11

Introduction

Patent law concerns new, industrially applicable inventions. It is perhaps fitting that intellectual property law reserves a very special and powerful mode of protection for inventions that meet exacting standards. The grant of a patent effectively gives the inventor, or more commonly his employer, a monopoly to work the invention to the exclusion of others for a period of time, not exceeding 20 years. However, the monopoly is not absolute and there are a number of checks and balances to curb its abuse. The invention might concern a new or an improved product: for example, a new type of window lock or an improvement to the design of scaffolding clamps. Alternatively, the invention may concern some industrial process, such as a new method of rust proofing motor car bodies or an improved method of making printed circuit boards for electronic equipment. Due to the strength of this form of property right, high standards are required – the invention must be new and it must involve an inventive step, that is, it must be more than merely an obvious application of technology. Furthermore, the invention must be capable of industrial application and must not fall within certain stated exclusions. These requirements are explored in detail in the next chapter; suffice it to say for now that patents are not granted lightly and an application is subjected to a thorough examination process.

In common with other intellectual property rights, a patent is a form of personal property that may be assigned, licensed or charged by way of a mortgage. However, it is declared by the Patents Act 1977 s 30(1) that a patent is not a thing in action.[1] Patent law grants a monopoly for a limited period of time in respect of an invention in return for disclosure of the details concerning the invention. These details are available for public inspection and are sufficiently comprehensive so that a person skilled in the particular art would be able to make practical use of the invention; in other words, he would be able to work the invention.[2]

Disclosure is a central prerequisite for the grant of a patent and it must be total, with nothing of substance withheld, otherwise it might be difficult for others to make use of the invention once the patent has expired.[3] In *Young* v *Rosenthal*,[4] Grove J said (at 31):

> Then he [the applicant] is bound so to describe it in his specification as that any workman acquainted with the subject . . . would know how to make it; and the reason of that is this, that if he did not do so, when the patent expired he might have some trade mystery which people would not be able actually to use in accordance with his invention (although they had a right to use it after his invention had expired), because they would not know how to make it.

Although full disclosure is required so that a person skilled in the art will be able to work the invention, that person does not necessarily need to be taught how it works by the

1 There is some doubt as to whether a copyright is a chose in action: *see* Chapter 1.

2 Patent legislation uses the term 'a person skilled in the art'. This means a person (or team of persons) having knowledge and experience of the science or technology concerned.

3 An early example of a patent being declared invalid because of a failure fully to disclose how to work it is *The King* v *Arkwright* (1785) 1 WPC 64.

4 (1884) 1 RPC 29.

Table 11.1 Patent consideration

Patent – concept of contract – consideration

Patentee's consideration	State's consideration
1 Details available for public inspection.	1 Examination and search by UK Intellectual Property Office (UK IPO) may assist in the drawing up or amendment of the application.
2 Invention falls into the public domain on expiry.	2 Wealth of information available at UK IPO will help in deciding whether to apply for a patent and in the framing of patent application.
3 Some things can be done during the life of the patent (non-infringing acts) by others.	3 The granting of a limited monopoly.
4 The invention may be vulnerable to a compulsory licence or licence of right.	4 A priority date will be given assisting in applications in other countries.
5 UK and EU Competition law may impose restrictions on the exploitation of the patent.	5 Useful evidential materials available, presumptions.
6 Fees have to be paid.	6 Inexpensive opinions available from the Comptroller of Patents as to validity and infringement.
7 The risk that the invention may be appropriated by the Crown (although payment may be made).	

disclosure. However, the holding back of part of the invention runs counter to the whole rationale of patent law and such applications will be rejected, or the applicant will be asked to modify and enlarge his disclosure accordingly.

After the expiry of the patent, the invention falls into the public domain and anyone is free to make use of it. One might wonder what the state or the general public get in return for this grant of privilege. The fact that the details of the invention are published means that competitors, researchers and the like have immediate access to this information which they may study and use subject to the scope of the infringing acts. The system benefits everyone by this because the wider availability of such information helps to spread and widen technical knowledge and, importantly, because investment is encouraged, wealth and employment are created and maintained. The whole patent transaction can be thought of as a bargain or contract between the inventor (or his employer) and the state, both parties bringing consideration to that contract[5] (*see* Table 11.1).

Without a patent system, inventors and their employers would attempt to keep the details of the invention secret, relying on the law of confidence for protection. In some cases, it would be impossible to keep the details of the invention secret. For example, if it concerned a new type of gearing arrangement for a bicycle, anyone purchasing a bicycle with the new system fitted would be able to discover the inventive step by an examination of the gears, perhaps after dismantling them. However, if the invention concerned some new industrial process used for making bicycle gears, it might be possible to maintain secrecy because an inspection of the finished product would not necessarily disclose the manufacturing process.

In the first case, obtaining a patent is the most effective way of protecting the invention and the investment incurred in developing it. Other ways do exist but are not usually as attractive. For example, the inventor will be first to the marketplace with his gear system, and it could be several months or years before competitors can equip their factories and organise their production and marketing of a similar system. The duration of this

5 The person applying for the patent brings consideration in terms of fees and by adding his invention to the store of public information, ultimately giving up his monopoly in his invention.

lead-time is often proportional to the complexity of the technology required to put the invention into practice, although this lead-time might be dramatically reduced where the first product has to undergo rigorous safety testing and the competitor's product can largely avoid this by reliance on the testing of the first product. For example, in *R v Licensing Authority, ex parte Smith Kline & French Laboratories Ltd*,[6] information given by a drug manufacturer to a licensing authority, in order to obtain a product licence in respect of a drug, was used by the authority in determining whether to grant a product licence to a second manufacturer.

In the second case, where the invention relates to a process, the owner might be well advised to seek patent protection because of the uncertainty of the law of confidence. This flawed form of legal protection is little better than useless if details of the invention fall into the hands of third parties who have acquired the information in good faith. Depending on how tight security measures can be made, a patent will usually be an attractive alternative to the law of breach of confidence. However, where secrecy can be assured, there is no need to obtain a patent, and indeed the grant of a patent is a poor alternative as competitors will be able to find out about the process and gain a valuable insight into the way the patentee's business is likely to develop in the future. The invention will be available for anyone to use after expiry of the patent and compulsory licences might be available during its existence. If the secret can be maintained indefinitely, this will be preferable on all counts.

If the invention relates to a product rather than to a process, it may be possible to register some aspects of the shape of the product as a design or it may fall within the unregistered design right.[7] Additionally, there will be copyright in the drawings and written descriptions of the invention. However, copyright protection is a poor substitute for a patent as, in principle, copyright protects only the expression of an idea, whereas a patent can protect from exploitation by others the idea that is encapsulated in the invention. The nature of patent protection was described by Buckley LJ in *Hickton's Patent Syndicate v Patents and Machine Improvements Co Ltd*[8] in the following terms:

> Every invention to support a patent must . . . either suggest a new way of making something . . . or it may mean the way of producing a new article altogether; but I think you are losing the grasp of the substance and seizing the shadow when you say that the invention is the manufacture as distinguished from the idea. It is much more true to say that the patent is for the idea as distinguished from the thing manufactured. No doubt you cannot patent an idea, which you have simply conceived, and have suggested no way of carrying out, but the invention consists in thinking of or conceiving something and suggesting a way of doing it.

The strength of protection afforded to inventions through the patent system is one reason why patent protection is of a shorter duration than that available for works of copyright.

Patent litigation is usually complex, lengthy and very expensive. This has been the case for some time and, in 1892 in the case of *Ungar v Sugg*,[9] Lord Esher MR said (at 117):

> A man had better have his patent infringed, or have anything happen to him in this world, short of losing all his family by influenza, than have a dispute about a patent. His patent is swallowed up, and he is ruined. Whose fault is it? It is really not the fault of the law: it is the fault of the mode of conducting the law in a patent case. That is what causes all this mischief.

This quote is often used even nowadays by judges in patent cases. Some moves have been made to try to reduce costs, for example, by giving the Comptroller-General the power to deliver non-binding opinions as to validity and infringement under s 74A. The UK Intellectual Property Office now also provides a mediation service as a form of alternative dispute resolution.

Subject to provisions on entitlement to a patent, the general rule is that the person who is first to file an application to patent an invention will be the person to whom it will

6 [1989] 1 All ER 175. For a fuller discussion of this case in terms of the law of confidence, *see* Chapter 10.

7 Either the UK's unregistered design right or the unregistered Community (EU) design or both.

8 (1909) 26 RPC 339 at 348.

9 (1892) 9 RPC 113.

be granted. There is a presumption to this effect in s 7. Patent law in the US is presently based on the person who is the first to invent being the person entitled to the patent. In the UK and elsewhere, if a person A makes an invention and the same invention is made by person B later, but B is the first to file an application for a patent then he will be entitled to it, providing novelty has not been compromised by A.[10] However, the US is now moving to a first to file system in order to align the US system to the rest of the world.

10 The Patents Act 1977 s 64 would give A the right to continue to work the invention if he carried out acts that would otherwise infringe the patent or had made effective and serious preparations to do so before the priority date of the patent.

Brief historical perspective

As with the origins and development of other intellectual property rights, England has a prime place in world history and has set the mould for patent rights internationally. It is no coincidence that England was the country where the first major steps towards an industrial society were taken. Whether this was a direct result of the patent system is arguable, but it is without doubt that patents had an important role to play in the Industrial Revolution. Before this, the origins of patent law can be seen emerging in late medieval times. *Letters patent* were open letters with the King's Great Seal on the bottom granting rights, often to foreign weavers and other craftsmen, allowing them to practise their trade and overcoming guild regulations which suppressed competition. The first such letters patent were granted in 1311 to John Kempe, a Flemish weaver who wanted to practise his trade in England, one of the earliest recorded instances of a patent.[11] The regulation of trade was deemed to fall within the provenance of the Crown and letters patent proved to be a useful method of encouraging the establishment of new forms of industry and commerce, giving the Crown powerful control over trade. In this early form, there was no need for anything inventive; it had more to do with the practice of a trade and the granting of favours by the Crown. However, some letters patent were granted for inventions: for example, a patent was granted to John of Utyman in 1449 for his new method of making stained glass. Eventually, there was a strong need for an effective system that prevented unfair competition where, for example, one person had made some novel invention and wanted to stop others from simply copying it. A monopoly system developed in the reign of Elizabeth I and many letters patent were granted.

11 For an early historical perspective, *see* Davenport, N. (1979) *The United Kingdom Patent System: A Brief History,* Mason; and Thorley, S. *et al.* (2005) *Terrell on the Law of Patents* (16th edn) Sweet & Maxwell.

Monopolies are controversial. There are many dangers associated with monopolies, such as overcharging, manipulation of markets or a refusal to make the product available. In particular, the Tudor monarchs saw the system of monopolies as a good way of raising revenue. However, unease was growing at how the system was open to abuse and the law began to curb such excesses. *Darcy* v *Allin*[12] is an example of an early patent case which involved a monopoly for making, importation and selling of playing cards. The patent was held to be invalid as being, *inter alia*, a common law monopoly. James I issued a number of proclamations against monopolies, including the 'Book of Bounty' which generally prohibited monopolies but excepted inventions provided they were not contrary to law, hurtful to the state or trade, or generally inconvenient. In the slightly later *Clothworkers of Ipswich Case*[13] patents of a limited duration were recognised by the courts. The Statute of Monopolies 1623 s 6[14] gave recognition to patents as an exception to the general rule against monopolies:

12 (1602) Co Rep 84b.

13 (1614) Godbolt 252.

14 21 Jac 1 c 3. It seems that the world's first patents statute was passed in Venice in 1474: *see* Reid, B.C. (1998) *A Practical Guide to Patent Law* (3rd edn) Sweet & Maxwell, p 1.

> Provided . . . that any declaration before mentioned shall not extend to any letters patent and grants of privilege for the term of fourteen years or under . . . of the sole working or making of any manner of new manufactures within this Realme, to the true and first inventor and inventors of such manufactures which others at the time of making such letters patent and grants shall not use, so as also they be not contrary to the law, or mischievous to the State, by raising prices of commodities at home, or hurt of trade, or generally inconvenient . . .

15 For example, *Buck's Invention* (1651) 1 WPC 35.

16 (1773) 1 WPC 52.

17 Between 1853 and 1857, nearly all the patents granted since 1671 were published: *see* Davenport, N. (1979) *The United Kingdom Patent System*, Mason, p 53.

18 *The King* v *Arkwright* (1785) 1 WPC 64. Arkwright was a barber from Bolton who left his business and nagging wife to pursue his interest in inventing.

19 Dickens, C. *A Poor Man's Tale of a Patent*, reprinted in Phillips, J. (1984) *Charles Dickens and the 'Poor Man's Tale of a Patent'*, ESC Publishing. In a plea to end the considerable bureaucracy involved, the closing sentence ends with the sentiment '. . . England has been chaffed and waxed sufficient'. (One of the officials involved in the process was the Deputy Chaff-wax who appears to have been responsible for preparing the wax for the Sealer.)

20 Now renamed the UK Intellectual Property Office (as its operating name).

21 In 1855. Now part of the British Library.

22 For a description of the period leading up to the 1852 Act, *see* Dutton, H.I. (1984) *The Patent System and Inventive Activity during the Industrial Revolution, 1750–1852*, Manchester University Press.

23 The Convention for the European Patent for the Common Market ('Community Patent Convention') 76/76/EEC, OJ L 17, 26.01.1976, p 1, first promulgated in 1976. Even after all this time, there remain significant problems standing in the way of a unitary European patent system.

So, the true and first inventor was given 14 years in which he could exploit his invention to the exclusion of others. The section also makes it clear that the monopoly granted is not to be abused. Although there was a long way to go, the seeds of the modern patent system were sown. The basis of the 14-year period was that the duration of apprenticeship was seven years and, at the end of the first seven years, the proprietor was expected to take on an apprentice and teach him how to work the invention. Thus, at the end of 14 years, there would be at least one other person who was free in law to work the invention.[15] In some cases, a longer term was granted. In *Lairdet's Patent*[16] a patent was granted for 18 years by private Act because it was accepted that a longer term was needed to allow the proprietor to receive adequate recompense and to encourage him to make it available to the public. However, the proprietor was constrained as to the price he could charge for his cement, the subject matter of his patent.

Initially there was no requirement for a written description of the invention to be provided by the applicant, but this gradually became common practice. At first, however, descriptions were not made publicly available. They became known, as they still are, as specifications.[17] By 1718, the provision of a specification was often a requirement. The drafting of them could be quite important, as Arkwright discovered to his chagrin when his main patent for a water-powered spinning machine was held to be invalid through want of detail in 1785.[18] Applications were still made to the Monarch, or later to the law officers of the Crown, and the system became difficult, long-winded and expensive. James Watt was critical of the system and submitted proposals for reform in 1790. Charles Dickens wrote a critical exposé of it[19] and the system was overhauled by the Patent Law Amendment Act 1852. This saw the beginnings of the Patent Office[20] and the opening of the Patent Office Library soon followed,[21] as did a system for classifying patents.[22] The Patents, Designs and Trade Marks Act 1883 gave effect to the provisions in the Paris Convention for the Protection of Industrial Property 1883. The 1883 Act also substituted the Seal of the Patent Office for the Monarch's Great Seal.

Until the early part of the twentieth century, patent applications were not searched for novelty. It was basically a deposit system, with applications simply being checked for satisfactory completion. However, as a result of the Patents Act 1902, novelty searches were commenced and the granting of patents became a much more exacting process. There were other Acts, culminating in the Patents Act 1949, all of which can be seen as being developments based on the same traditions. However, the current Act, the Patents Act 1977, is different in that it was designed to take account of the European Patent Convention, which established the European Patent Office, and the Community patent system.[23] Since the coming into force of the 1977 Act, letters patent are no longer issued, but instead a certificate from the Comptroller-General of Patents, Designs and Trade Marks is provided. The maximum term of a patent was extended from 16 years to 20 years.

Justification for patent rights

An inventor owns a property right in his invention. This is a natural right and accords with the views on property rights of philosophers such as Locke. Furthermore, there is no substantial principle of classic jurisprudence that requires that property rights be limited temporarily. Neither need they be so limited if the inventor and his successors in title choose to keep secret details of the invention or how it works. However, such a property right, protected only by the law of confidence, is very vulnerable. Details of the invention might be disclosed in breach of confidence and eventually there may be those who, having acquired the details in good faith unaware of their confidential nature, are free in law and equity to put the invention to work.

What the patent system does is to guarantee a limited term of protection in return for the inventor's agreement to disclose details of his invention and, ultimately, to abandon his property right in it. This accords with the contract view of patents discussed earlier. Inventors are offered a stronger and more effective property right than under their natural right on condition that they will lose all rights in the invention when the patent expires.

The conventional justification for a patent system is that inventors and investors are rewarded for their time, work and risk of capital by the grant of a limited, though strong, monopoly. This benefits society by stimulating investment and employment and because details of the invention are added to the store of available knowledge. Eventually, after a period of time, depending on how long the patent is renewed (subject to a maximum of 20 years),[24] anyone will be free to put the invention to use. This utilitarian approach found favour with great English philosophers such as Jeremy Bentham, who argued that, because an invention involved a great deal of time, money and effort and also included a large element of risk, the exclusive use of the invention must be reserved for a period of time so that it could be exploited and thereafter used for the general increase of knowledge and wealth. He said that such exclusive use cannot:

> . . . otherwise be put upon any body but by the head of law: and hence the necessity and the use of the interposition of law to secure to an inventor the benefit of his invention.[25]

Of course, the proprietor of a patent is likely to use this economic privilege to his advantage and the resulting product will be priced accordingly, subject to market forces. The mere fact that competition can be restrained by way of injunction will tend to maintain prices. However, that does not, by itself, indicate that patents are against the public interest. Indeed, it is in the public interest that patent monopolies are enforced.[26] The proprietor may demand a high price reflecting two factors: the cost of research and development required to bring the invention to fruition and the natural commercial desire to obtain a large profit. Another factor is the marketing effort required to establish a demand for the product or process. However, the owner of the patent (the proprietor) does not have carte blanche in fixing his prices for the following reasons:

1 Consumers have managed thus far without the invention and may continue to do so by refusing to pay high prices.
2 The equation between volume of sales and profit margin must be considered. Sometimes a cheaper price will make more money for the owner of the patent by increasing sales disproportionately.
3 The consuming public may not have a need for the invention and it may be difficult to attract sales at any price. The sad fact is that a great many inventions fail to be commercially viable.
4 There are various safeguards and controls to prevent abuse of patents both in terms of domestic law (that is, UK law) and EU law.

On the first point, John Stuart Mill, who strongly supported the patent system, was considered by Smit to have:

> . . . adopted the rhetoric of the free market economy by suggesting that the reward depended on the invention proving to have economic value and that, in any event, only the users of the commodity created were paying for the increased price caused by the patent monopoly.[27]

A patent, therefore, is not necessarily a licence to print money, and a great deal of market research and economic judgment is essential before embarking upon the development of inventions. Bearing in mind that most important patents are granted to corporate organisations, this is a highly significant factor. The days of eccentric inventors are by no means gone, and simple and easily developed inventions are still a possibility, such as the

24 Pharmaceutical patents can be renewed up to a maximum of 25 years: Council Regulation (EEC) No 1768/92 of 18 June 1992 concerning the creation of a supplementary protection certificate for medicinal products, OJ L 182, 02.07.1992, p 1 now implemented, *inter alia*, by the Patents (Compulsory Licensing and Supplementary Protection Certificates) Regulations 2007, SI 2007/3293.

25 Bentham, J., *Manual of Political Economy*, reprinted in Stark, W. (ed) (1952) *Jeremy Bentham's Economic Writings*, Vol. 1, Allen & Unwin, p 263.

26 Per Aldous J in *Chiron Corporation v Organon Teknika Ltd (No 10)* [1995] FSR 325 at 333.

27 Smit, D. van Zyl, 'The social creation of a legal reality: a study of the emergence and acceptance of the British patent system as a legal instrument for the control of new technology', unpublished PhD thesis, University of Edinburgh, 1980.

Biro ballpoint pen or reflecting roadstuds ('cats' eyes'). But in most cases the advent of technology and its increasing complexity have necessitated substantial capital investment. The pharmaceutical industry is a good example of this; the cost of developing and testing new drugs requires large and long-term investment well before any rewards can be secured. Cursorily examined, the price charged for the finished product may seem exorbitant but could be the result of all sorts of preliminary and hidden costs associated with the invention. Speaking of the once popular exaggeration that drugs cost 'twopence a bucket to make and sell at £10 per pill', Walton points out that:

> What at first sight looks like profiteering, on examination turns out to be not so. What the drug houses sell is not a substance (whose manufacturing cost is commonly negligible) but a service. The cost of research – including the cost of all the abortive investigations – the clinical trials – the creation and maintenance of the market by initial and continuing promotion – the back-up servicing by the originating drug house which has at all times to deal with any slow to emerge problems caused by use of the drug – all this has to be paid for.[28]

These costs, which can be disproportionately large in comparison with the cost of manufacturing, will be incurred only by companies and organisations that can foresee a profitable return on them, and the only way this can be guaranteed is to secure some form of legal protection that will ensure that this is a practical possibility. Without such protection another manufacturer would be able to come along, steal the idea and sell the product for far less than the originator could ever hope to. The other manufacturer would have the considerable advantage of not having to pay any of the costs identified by Walton, except, perhaps, some minimal marketing costs. Of course, the high cost of pharmaceutical products is a matter of some controversy in poorer 'third world' countries which can ill-afford the cost of buying expensive drugs to meet particular health problems. Pharmaceutical companies are being faced with the option of considerably reducing prices in poorer countries or being deprived of any form of protection in some of these countries.

The Industrial Revolution brought a great many pressures upon the patent system, eventually leading to major reforms starting with the Patent Law Amendment Act 1852. During the preceding period there had been much debate about whether inventions should be afforded legal protection by the grant of patents, and indeed in Switzerland and the Netherlands patent law was dismantled to be reintroduced later in the nineteenth century. The fact that this could happen and that the whole rationale for the granting of patents could be challenged in England now seems incredible. Nevertheless, the demise of the patent system was anticipated in the press, including *The Times* and *The Economist*.[29] Arguments for the abolition of the system centred around the detrimental effect of patents on competition and free trade.[30] Some commentators considered that patents had served their purpose and were no longer needed in a developed industrial society, while others saw patents as insidious and positively harmful, *The Economist* in 1851 noting that the granting of patents:

> . . . inflames cupidity, excites fraud . . . begets disputes and quarrels betwixt inventors, provokes endless lawsuits, makes men ruin themselves for the sake of getting the privilege of a patent, which merely fosters a delusion of greediness.[31]

Convincing arguments had to be developed by those keen to see the patent system retained and improved. As Dutton suggests, those arguments are still valid today and include:[32]

1 *The contract theory.* Temporary protection granted in reward for knowledge of new inventions.
2 *The reward theory.* Inventors should be rewarded for making useful inventions and the law must be used to guarantee this reward so that inventors can receive sufficient recompense for their ingenuity.

28 Walton, A. 'The Copyright, Designs and Patents Act 1988 (1)' (1989) 133 *Solicitors Journal* 646 at 650. Walton's comment was made in the context of compulsory licences, discussed in Chapter 13.

29 *The Times*, 29 May 1869; *The Economist*, 5 June 1869.

30 For a comprehensive description of the arguments for and against a patent system that were raging in the mid-nineteenth century, *see* Dutton, H.I. (1984) *The Patent System and Inventive Activity during the Industrial Revolution, 1750–1852*, Manchester University Press, Chapter 1.

31 *The Economist*, 26 July 1851.

32 Dutton, H.I., note 30 above.

3 *The incentive theory.* By constructing a framework whereby invention is rewarded, this will act as an incentive to make new inventions and to invest the necessary time and capital. This is a forward-looking approach in contrast to the latter which is retrospective.

4 *The natural law/moral rights theory.* Individuals have a right of property in their own ideas and this right should be protected from being usurped or stolen by others. (This is similar to moral rights in copyright law.)

In *Chiron Corporation* v *Organon Teknika Ltd (No 10)*[33] Aldous J put the justification for the patent system in very pragmatic terms, saying that nearly every country had chosen to adopt a patent system because:

> ... it is generally accepted that the opportunity of acquiring monopoly rights in an invention stimulates technical progress in at least four ways. First it encourages research and invention; secondly, it induces an inventor to disclose his discoveries instead of keeping them a secret; thirdly, it offers a reward for the expense of developing inventions to the state at which they are commercially practical and, fourthly, it provides an inducement to invest capital in new lines of production which might not appear profitable if many competing producers embarked on them simultaneously ... It is inherent in any patent system that a patentee will acquire a monopoly giving him a right to restrict competition and also enabling him to put up or at least maintain prices. That affects the public and is contrary to the public interest, but it is the recognised price that has been accepted to be necessary to secure the advantages to which I have referred.[34]

Encouragement, inducement and reward are the main factors underlying the patent system. The public interest, although apparently jeopardised by the grant of a monopoly, is secured by increased industrial activity, developing new technologies and disclosure of new and useful inventions. Furthermore, patent law contains a number of safeguards, such as compulsory licensing and Crown use, to curb any significant abuse of the patent monopoly.

Much of the dissatisfaction with the patent system until the middle of the nineteenth century could be explained by the parlous state of patent law at the time. It was clear that something had to be done – either the patent system should be abandoned, or it should be reformed and streamlined to meet the needs of a heavily industrialised society that depended on invention and innovation for future growth and prosperity. The arguments of the supporters of a strong patent system won the day and the latter course was taken. However, it should be appreciated that having a strong system of patent law is not a foregone conclusion and that there are some good reasons to the contrary. If patent law were to be abolished tomorrow, inventive activity would not cease altogether – other factors would come to the fore, such as the inventor's lead-time, that halcyon period before competitors can equip their factories and commence manufacture, when he has no competition. Depending upon the nature of the invention, that period may be long enough to justify the initial expense associated with putting the invention to use. However, in many cases, the lead-time would be insufficient and the inventor would have to look to factors such as quality and value for money as a way of making the whole undertaking profitable and worthwhile. Trade marks and business goodwill are other ways in which the invention could be successfully exploited by the inventor or the owner of the patent. In spite of the arguments for and against patents, it is now unthinkable that the patent system would be abolished. Over the last 100 or so years, patents have become established on a worldwide basis, with almost all the countries with developed industries having some form of patent protection for inventions.[35] Some industries, such as pharmaceuticals and electronics, could become stagnant without patent protection through lack of investment.

As noted above, the presence of a strong and effective patent system may bring numerous benefits such as the dissemination of information and providing an incentive to invest in the development of new products and processes which will eventually fall

33 [1995] FSR 325.

34 Ibid. at 332.

35 Even the former USSR had patent laws: Mamiofa, I.E. 'The draft of a new Soviet patent law' [1990] 1 EIPR 21.

into the public domain. However, the patent system does not always stand up well to close scrutiny as many inventors who have had to deal with the system will testify. Obtaining a patent is expensive and takes a long time. It may be several years before action can be taken against an infringer. It could be said that the system favours large wealthy corporations which have the deep pockets required to acquire patents and defend them on a global scale. Unless the sole inventor can find a 'product champion', that is, an investor prepared to put up substantial funds, he will be seriously disadvantaged. One critic of the system is James Dyson, the inventor of the wheelbarrow with a ball for a wheel and the bagless vacuum cleaner. He considered bringing a case before the European Court of Human Rights, arguing that patent renewal fees are illegal as the inventor gets nothing in return,[36] although proponents of the patent system would disagree, pointing to the continued protection afforded by payment of the renewal fees.

Another, perhaps more worrying, concern is that a system which was designed around technology from a simpler era is unable to provide an appropriate level of protection, taking account of all the checks and balances, in the context of new and emerging technologies. Information technology and genetic engineering are two important examples. We will see the difficulty patent law has in addressing the protection of software inventions in the following chapter. Consider the situation whereby a commercial organisation has economic rights in genetic material, rights which can last for up to 20 years. Thurow claims that tweaking the existing system will not provide a solution, and he argues for a new system which strikes a balance between the production and distribution of new ideas.[37] He is also critical of judge-made law in this area, saying that judges do not consider what is appropriate in terms of accelerating technological and economic progress. Rather, they are concerned with how to fit new technology into the existing legal framework with minimum disruption to established principles. In particular, Thurow suggests an optimal patent system would differentiate between different industries, types of knowledge and types of inventors. For example, the electronics industry wants speed and short-term protection, whilst the pharmaceutical industry wants long-term protection because it takes a number of years before a new drug can be sold to the public. For the most part, in the latter case the companies involved can well afford the expense of acquiring, maintaining and defending their intellectual property rights. Small, innovative electronics companies are less able to afford this expense, or even to understand such a complex system.

Patent law has undergone a number of changes in recent years and the *Gowers Review of Intellectual Property*[38] proposes some more changes. These will be set out and discussed briefly in the following chapters where appropriate. At this stage it is worth mentioning that the *Gowers Review* recommends that further support for the Community Patent Convention (now referred to as an EU patent) should be given and its introduction expedited by negotiations throughout Europe.[39] The introduction of a single unitary European patent would have significant benefits. At the present time patents, including those obtained through the European Patent Convention, have effect as national patents effective only in the relevant States.

36 *Sunday Times*, 1 March 1998.

37 Thurow, L.C. 'Needed: a new system of intellectual property rights', *Harvard Business Review*, September–October 1997, p 95.

38 HMSO, 2006.

39 *Gowers Review of Intellectual Property*, HMSO, 2006, p 81.

Patent trolls

One would normally expect a proprietor of a patent to exploit it either by working the invention himself or licensing another or others to do so in return for a royalty or licence fee. One practice that has sprung up, particularly in the US, is that of obtaining the grant of a patent and then sitting on it, waiting for an unsuspecting third party to make something or do something which might fall within the scope of the patent. The third party will then usually receive a letter before action threatening patent litigation unless a licence is taken out. This may include a claim for payment for past infringement. As patent litigation is notoriously expensive, the third party may choose to pay up, particularly if an application for an interim injunction is likely to be made. Patent proprietors who behave in this manner are often termed patent trolls.[40] They are particularly prevalent in relation to software and 'hi-tech' inventions and business methods. The ease with which patents have been granted for such inventions in the past in the US has compounded the problem.

In *eBay Inc* v *MercExchange LLC*,[41] MercExchange was the proprietor of a number of business method patents. One was for an invention being an electronic market to facilitate the sale of goods between private individuals by the establishment of a central authority to promote trust amongst participants. eBay's website allowed sellers to list goods they wish to sell either by auction or by fixed price (Buy It Now). MercExchange attempted to licence its patent to eBay but the parties failed to reach an agreement and MercExchange sued eBay for infringement of its patent.

At first instance, it was held that the patent was valid and eBay had infringed it. Although damages would be awarded, the court refused to grant a permanent injunction. On appeal, the Court of Appeals reversed the part of the decision relating to an injunction and eBay appealed to the Supreme Court which remitted the case to the first instance court to apply the proper principles in determining whether to grant an injunction. The Supreme Court criticised the test used by the Court of Appeals in deciding it was appropriate to grant an injunction. In the Supreme Court, Kennedy J said:

> An industry has developed in which firms use patents not as a basis for producing and selling goods but, instead, primarily for obtaining licensing fees . . . For these firms, an injunction, and the potentially serious sanctions arising from its violation, can be employed as a bargaining tool to charge exorbitant fees to companies that seek to buy licenses to practice the patent.

As noted in *eBay* v *MercExchange*, many of the patents filed of business methods are vague and of suspect validity. The response of large wealthy companies to such a threat is normally to challenge the validity of the patent or defend an infringement action. Small and medium-sized enterprises, and particularly start-up companies, may feel less inclined to do so. As legal costs in taking a patent to court in the US is typically around $1 million, one can understand the difficulty this places smaller companies in when faced with such threats. One advantage in the UK is the availability of a groundless threats action though this is not available in all circumstances and, if the 'threat' is carefully made, a groundless threats action may not be triggered.[42]

In England and Wales, in *Aerotel Ltd* v *Wavecrest Group Enterprises Ltd*,[43] the claimant was an Israeli company with a patent for a method of making telephone calls and a telephone system. The company did not make or sell anything but exploited the present and other patents by litigation and the threat of litigation against others, principally in the United States. Jacob LJ said of this strategy (at para 32):

> That is unimpressive, for it is notorious that at least from the middle-90s the US patent litigation scene had become immensely pro-plaintiff. A defendant faced with the possibility of litigation had to take into account all of the following matters: (1) the right of the patentee to insist upon jury trial (juries are apt to be pro-plaintiff); (2) the general level of damages awarded in the US – by juries; (3) the real possibility of triple damages for wilful infringement; (4) the fact that even if a defendant won he would have to pay his own, very considerable, legal costs; and (5) the fact that until the decision of the Supreme Court in eBay v MerckExchange U.S. No. 05–131 (2006) there was a strong view that even a non-exploiting patentee who won would get an injunction as of right.

The Court of Appeal dismissed Aerotel's appeal against the finding of HHJ Fysh QC (sitting as a Deputy High Court Judge) that the patent was invalid, mainly on the ground of obviousness. Although commercial success can be a factor (though not conclusive) in determining whether the alleged invention is or is not obvious, as Jacob LJ said (at para 30), '[t]he world beat a path to the door of Ralph Waldo Emerson's inventor of a better mousetrap, but the path to Aerotel's door remained untrodden'.

40 Presumably, so named after the *Three Billy Goats Gruff* fairy story. In *Nokia GmbH* v *IPCOM Gmbh & Co KG* [2011] FSR 15, the Court of Appeal described such a proprietor as a 'non-practising entity'.

41 547 US 388 (2006).

42 *See* the section on groundless threats of infringement proceedings in Chapter 15.

43 [2009] EWCA Civ 408.

Patent strategy

44 Rahn, G. 'Japanese patent strategy', in The European Patent Office, *Annual Report 1995*, p 9.

Intellectual property rights are considered to be of the utmost importance in Japan and companies there have developed efficient strategies for exploiting their patents to the fullest extent.[44] An 'attacking' strategy is at the forefront, an important goal being to use the patents in a way which excludes competitors and secures a large market for the proprietor. Licences are often subject to an obligation to grant back, for no fee, rights in improvements on the original invention. Of course, in the context of Europe this may well offend against domestic or EU competition law but, otherwise, there is no absolute principle of public policy against a commercial agreement whereby one party agrees that the benefit of any improvement he brings about in relation to a past invention will belong to another.[45]

45 *Buchanan* v *Alba Diagnostics Ltd* [2004] RPC 34.

An ideal outcome is where the invention for which the patent has been granted is combined with an industry standard: for example, the Japan Victor Company's VHS technology which became the industry standard for video recorders.

The Japanese also widely use patents defensively to avoid needless conflicts and litigation by 'blanketing' the invention with a close network of patent filings, trying to predict future applications and improvements on the basic invention for the purpose of pre-empting competitors and covering any possible future applications. If successful, this ties a competitor's hands together and deprives him of technical mobility and flexibility. This approach is also known as 'ring-fencing' the invention.

An important source of inventions is the employee. In many organisations employees, who are not directly employed in the search for new inventions, are encouraged to submit ideas through a company suggestions scheme. However, in the UK it is a sad fact that many suggestions, whether made as a result of a formal scheme or otherwise, are not taken up. In any case, if an employee has an idea for a new invention in a situation where he may be entitled to be the proprietor of the invention, he would be well advised to seek professional advice rather than to submit it to his employer. The rewards offered by employers for useful suggestions are likely to be minuscule compared with the income which may be derived from a successful patent.

Nevertheless, the Japanese approach is to provide an incentive to employees to be patent-minded, thinking of new inventions and ways to improve or create policies in respect of patents within the company. This is known as the 'motivation' strategy. If handled properly, it can encourage suggestions from a company's human resources at all levels, even from the humblest shop-floor worker. This in turn should engender a feeling of worth, motivation and loyalty from amongst employees.

A desideratum for many Japanese companies is to build a strong patent portfolio. This will enhance a company's technological reputation and in the area of research and development generally. This can improve investors' confidence in the company and facilitate the raising of new capital. Coupled with effective and well-known trade marks, this will be a powerful combination and will encourage other companies to seek licences to work the company's technology. A strong portfolio of intellectual property rights is central to a 'patent licensing' strategy.

With strategies such as those outlined above, Japanese companies have been extremely successful in the protection and exploitation of intellectual property. Over 80 per cent of the world's patents are granted by the European Patent Office, the US Patent and Trademark Office and the Japanese Patent Office. Japanese companies are amongst the world's most vigorous patent applicants, especially in the USA and Europe. As the Japanese economy is largely based on high-tech industry, this leads to reliance on intellectual property rights. It is widely recognised in Japan that, if it intends to keep its place as a very effective and successful high-technology industrial country, it must take intellectual property rights very seriously as the key to protecting and exploiting intellectual property.

Patent Law Treaty

The World Intellectual Property Office Patent Law Treaty 2000 sought to harmonise and streamline formal procedures in relation to patent applications. Particular issues dealt with by the Treaty were:

- Standardisation of the requirement for obtaining a filing date to minimise loss of filing date by applicants. The filing date is of the utmost importance. Three simple requirements are required:
  - an indication that the elements received by the patent office are intended to be an application for a patent for an invention;
  - indications allowing the patent office to identify or contact the applicant (both may be required);
  - material which appears to be a description of the invention (in particular, a patent office cannot require the submission of a claim or claims to be a prerequisite of granting a filing date).
- The elimination or reduction of procedural gaps between national, regional and international patent systems.
- The standardisation of model international forms to be accepted by patent offices of Contracting Parties.
- The simplification of certain procedures before patent offices to reduce costs.
- The introduction of procedures to avoid the unintentional loss of substantive rights resulting from a failure to comply with formality requirements or time limits (for example, requirements to notify applicants, extensions of time limits, reinstatement of rights and restrictions on revocation or invalidity resulting from a formal defect not notice by the office during the application stage).
- The implementation of electronic filing alongside paper communications, with the possibility of some patent offices moving entirely to electronic communications save for the purpose of obtaining a filing date and meeting the time limit for this.

The Patent Law Treaty came into force on 28 April 2005. The UK became a Contracting Party on 22 March 2006, the date the Treaty came into force in the UK. At the present time there are 31 Contracting Parties but there are some notable exceptions including some EU countries (including Germany) and the United States though they are signatories.

In the UK, the procedural requirements of the Patent Law Treaty had already been implemented by the Regulatory Reform (Patents) Order 2004[46] and the Patent (Amendment) Rules 2004.[47] The description of procedural aspects in this and subsequent chapters take account of the changes made to the Patents Act 1977 and the Patents Rules 2007 in compliance with the Treaty and in relation to other amendments made to them.

46 SI 2004/2357.

47 SI 2004/2358. These rules have been replaced by the Patents Rules 2007, SI 2007/3291.

A unitary European patent?

At the present time, in the UK it is possible to apply for a UK patent and/or apply for patents through the European Patent Convention (EPC) and/or the Patent Cooperation Treaty. The Convention and the Treaty result in a bundle of national patents, having validity in each country for which application has been made. This can cause inconsistencies and serious jurisdictional difficulties. For example, a patentee may hold UK, French and German patents obtained through the EPC. The patents are litigated in each of these countries. In France the patent is held valid and infringed, in Germany it is held valid but not infringed and in the UK it is held to be invalid. As an example of the jurisdictional difficulties,[48] say that

48 For which, see more in Chapter 26 on IPR and conflict of laws.

the patents are alleged to be infringed by a group of related companies in each of the three countries. If sued, the defendant companies would be likely to claim that the patents are invalid. The patentee would have to bring separate actions in each of the countries.[49]

How much better it would be if a patentee could seek protection for his invention throughout Europe by a single patent. Infringement and validity could be heard before a single court without the need to bring separate actions in each country. Furthermore, there would be a single process governing application, search, examination and grant and subsequent amendment and a single opposition process.[50] Fees are likely to be significantly less where protection is sought in more than a few Member States. Many of the advantages of the EU's Community trade mark and Community registered design systems would also be available.

Plans for a unitary patent for Europe have been around since 1976.[51] It would have unitary effect, that is, the requirements for patentability would have to be satisfied across Europe and would have equal effect throughout Europe. It could only be transferred or revoked in respect of all the participating States. However, this would not prevent licensing the patent separately in different parts of Europe. It would be litigated in a single unitary patent court, which would include an appellate court. One problem is that such a system might include countries outside the EU, such as Switzerland and Norway. This calls into question whether a unitary patent office and court system would be beyond the scope of the EU Treaties. The Court of Justice confirmed this obstacle in Opinion 1/09.[52] A draft Agreement on a Unified Patents Court has been published.[53] This court will have jurisdiction over unitary European patents and EPC patents. The EPC would be responsible for granting patents under the EPC and the proposed unitary system. The draft Agreement seeks to overcome the objections of the Court of Justice.

Current proposals for enhanced cooperation have been published.[54] Even if the difficulties with a unitary patent can be overcome, it still seems like it will be some time before the long overdue changes to the patent system in Europe can be made to accommodate the single European patent. This is a great pity and can only reinforce divisions in the single market and prejudice patentees in Europe.

Practical considerations

Three possibilities present themselves to an inventor who is resolved on securing a patent for his invention. An application may be made for a UK patent, for a 'European' patent designating a number of Member States of the European Patent Convention (EPC) or under the Patent Cooperation Treaty (PCT) designating some or all of the Contracting States. Applications through the EPC and PCT have additional costs in relation to translations though, in relation to the former, an Agreement concluded in London in 2000 came into force on 1 May 2008.[55] Under this Agreement, the Member States party to it waive or reduce their requirements for translations of European patents to be filed in their own national language. In many cases, this will significantly reduce the costs of obtaining patents through the EPC. At the time of writing, 15 EPO Member States have acceded to or ratified the London Agreement, including the UK.

In all cases, applications can be handled initially by the UK Intellectual Property Office (UK IPO)[56] in London. Where an application for a patent contains information relating to military technology or publication of the information is otherwise prejudicial to national security or public safety, it is an offence for a UK resident to file an application elsewhere before six weeks have elapsed from filing at the UK IPO and no directions prohibiting or restricting publication or communication of the information have been given under s 22.[57] The procedure for obtaining a UK patent will be described below, but first some definitions are given relating to the terms used and documents submitted.[58]

49 The validity of a formal national right registered in a particular country can only be challenged in that country.

50 This applies already in relation to the EPC except for post-grant amendment. Of course, once granted by the EPO, the patents devolves to a number of national patents justiciable only in each of those Member States.

51 Convention for the European Patent for the Common Market ('Community Patent Convention') 76/76/EEC, OJ L 17, 26.01.1976, p 1, first promulgated in 1976.

52 8 March 2011. The Council of the European Council sought the Opinion.

53 14 June 2011.

54 23 June 2011, available at: http://register.consilium.europa.eu/pdf/en/11/st11/st11328.en11.pdf. Also worth looking at is accompanying Staff Commission Impact Assessment Working Paper, available at: http://eur-lex.europa.eu/LexUriServ/LexUriServ.do?uri=SEC:2011:0482:FIN:EN:PDF.

55 European Patent Office, The London Agreement: European patents and the costs of translations, 2006.

56 Formerly known as the Patent Office.

57 Patents Act 1977 s 23, as amended by the Patents Act 2004 s 7. An alternative would be to seek the written permission of the Comptroller to file abroad rather than first filing at the UK IPO.

58 The procedure for a patent under the European Patent Convention is broadly similar but there are some differences: for example, opposition is decided post-grant. Patent Cooperation Treaty patents are somewhat different in that, after search and publication, applications must be made to the individual countries; this is known as entering the national phase and can be quite complex. The procedure for a UK patent is laid out in detail in the Patents Act 1977 and the Patents Rules 2007, SI 2007/3291.

Filing date

This is the date when the application is received by the UK IPO. The application must indicate that a patent is being sought, identify the person applying for the patent or contain sufficient information so that he may be contacted by the UK IPO, contain something that appears to be a description of the invention for which the patent is sought or a reference to an earlier relevant application made by the applicant or predecessor of his. This is somewhat of a relaxation of what was previously required and makes it easier to correct possible deficiencies in the application such as by filing missing parts later.[59] The applicant then has a period of 12 months of the filing date (or earlier priority date) during which he must file one or more claims and an abstract, pay the application fee and request a search and pay the search fee. Where the application refers to an earlier relevant application, the applicant must also file a description of the invention and furnish a copy of that earlier application during that same period. The filing date is important because it is the date used to determine the duration of the patent. That is, the 20 years' maximum period available starts to run from the filing date.

59 The Regulatory Reform (Patents) Order 2004 (SI 2004/2357) inserted a new s 15 into the Patents Act 1977 with effect from 1 January 2005.

Priority date

Section 5(2) of the Patents Act 1977 allows an application to claim the priority of an earlier application filed within the preceding 12 months if the later application is supported by matter disclosed in the earlier application. The priority claim must be by the applicant for the earlier patent or his successor in title.[60] For example, an inventor may apply for a UK patent for his invention and then, within 12 months, apply to the European Patent Office, designating a number of Member States, and the priority date of the resulting European patents will be that of the original UK patent, assuming that it supports the invention as claimed in the application to the European Patent Office. The consequences of a failure to support the later application can be severe. In *Biogen Inc* v *Medeva plc*[61] the House of Lords confirmed the Court of Appeal decision that the patent in suit was invalid. It relied on the priority of an earlier application. The problem was that, contrary to s 5(2), the invention claimed in the later application was not supported by matter disclosed in the earlier application. The technology in the relevant field (genetic engineering) had moved very rapidly and, without being able to rely on the priority of the earlier application, it was conceded that the second application was obvious.

60 Where, for example, the earlier application was made by two joint inventors, A and B, but only A submits a later application seeking the priority of the earlier application, the claim to priority will fail. This is so even if A subsequently acquires B's rights to the earlier application: *see Edwards Lifesciences AG* v *Cook Biotech Inc* [2009] FSR 27.

61 [1997] RPC 1.

Applications for late declarations of priority may be made under s 5(2B) and, if the request complies with the relevant rules and the Comptroller is satisfied that the failure to file within the prescribed period was unintentional, he shall grant the request under s 5(2C). In *re Abaco Machines (Australasia) Pty Ltd*,[62] an Australian company filed an application for a Vietnamese patent, intending to file an application under the Patent Cooperation Treaty and following this, in relation to the UK, file an application under the European Patent Convention. Due to an error the company missed the 12-month deadline to file the PCT application. An application was then filed for a UK national patent and an application was then made for a late declaration of priority based on the Vietnamese patent. Section 5(2) permits declarations of priority in relation to the 'application in suit'. It was held that this meant the UK national patent and the failure to file was not unintentional as the company had intended to file an application under the PCT rather than file a national application.

62 [2007] EWHC 347 (Pat).

The priority date is important because it is the state of the art at that date that is considered when judging the invention for novelty. It is also relevant in terms of infringement in that persons who in good faith, before the priority date, either have done an act that would constitute infringement or have made effective and serious preparations for such an act, may continue to do so after the grant of the patent.[63]

63 Patents Act 1977 s 64.

Specification

This is a very important document, probably the most important thing submitted by the applicant. The specification must contain a description of the invention, one or more claims together with any drawings required to illustrate the invention. The specification should fully describe the invention – anything omitted at this stage could have the effect of jeopardising the application or cutting down the usefulness and scope of the patent should it be granted. The specification should also be sufficiently detailed so that a person skilled in the art can work the invention, that is, put it into effect. For example, if the invention concerns a new type of tow bar for a vehicle, the specification should be such that a skilled vehicle engineer would be able to make it, fit it and use it.

Specifications usually contain a number of drawings. Judges by their training are better equipped to interpret the written word than drawings. In *Van der Lely NV v Bamfords Ltd*,[64] Lord Reid said that judges were not expert at interpreting visual evidence (photographs in this case) and the question to be asked is what the eye of a person with appropriate skill and experience would see in the photograph. Where the evidence was contradictory, the judge must decide which interpretation to accept, not by reading or construing the photograph, but by looking at it to see which explanation is the most plausible.

An example of a patent specification is given at the end of this chapter and should be referred to. It contains on the front page, the application number, date of filing,[65] the name and address of the applicant, inventors,[66] agent and address for service, the classifications for the invention, a document cited by the examiner which may have a bearing on the novelty of the invention, field of search, title, abstract and, usually as here, a drawing. The little numbers in brackets alongside the entries are known as INID numbers and are used to standardise the layout of the page to help with processing of the information contained on the page.[67] For example, on the front page of the sample application at the end of this chapter, (71) is the name of the applicant, (54) is the title of the invention, (57) is the abstract and (51) is the International Patent Classification. The remainder of the specification contains a detailed description of the invention and the claims. Sometimes there will be further drawings and there may be amendments to the claims.

The specification does not have to demonstrate that the claimed invention actually worked or why it worked. So it was held in the House of Lords in *Conor Medsystems Inc v Angiotech Pharmaceuticals Inc*.[68] The House of Lords held that the Court of Appeal had erred by deciding that a patent which claimed the treatment of stents with taxol to prevent restenosis was invalid because the patent merely taught that taxol was worth trying but failed to show that it actually worked in practice.[69] The House of Lords held that there was no requirement in either the EPC or the 1977 Act to the effect that the patentee had to demonstrate by experiment that the invention worked or why it worked. The question the Court of Appeal failed to address was whether it was obvious to use a taxol-coated stent to prevent restenosis. By its decision, the House of Lords agreed with a Dutch court before which parallel proceedings had taken place. The Dutch court held that it was sufficient if the patent indicated that taxol would work.

Claims

The application will include a statement of the claims defining the invention for which protection is required. There will usually be several claims, some of which may be alternatives. Often, the first claim will be developed and expanded upon by subsequent claims which may enlarge the first claim, particularise it or give specific embodiments of it. The purpose of the claims is to define the limit of the monopoly and, therefore, they must be very carefully drawn up. According to Lord Russell in *Electric & Musical Industries Ltd v Lissen Ltd*,[70] the function of the claims is to define clearly and with precision the monopoly

64 [1963] RPC 61.

65 This particular example does not have a priority date. Where the priority of an earlier application is claimed, a reference to the date and country of the earlier application will all be noted on the front page.

66 An inventor may now choose to waive their right to be named as inventor and/or to have their address published on the patent by applying in writing and giving reasons that satisfy the Comptroller of Patents: the Patents Rules 2007 r 11, SI 2007/3291.

67 This system was devised by ICIREPAT, the International Committee for Information Retrieval by Examining Patent Offices.

68 [2008] RPC 28.

69 A stent is a tubular metal device which is inserted into an artery which has become restricted to keep it open. Stents are used in angioplasty for treating sclerosis of the coronary arteries. A problem had been the injury caused to the inner wall of an artery by inserting the stent often triggered a healing response which involved the proliferation of smooth muscle cells which again restricted the artery. This is known as restenosis.

70 (1939) 56 RPC 23; *see* also *Glaverbel SA v British Coal Corp* [1995] RPC 255.

claimed so that others may know the exact boundaries of the area in which, if they venture therein, they will be trespassers. The ideal situation from the applicant's point of view is a set of valid claims which give the widest scope to the invention. The claims in the example should be carefully studied with this in mind. They provide a good example of the care and thoroughness that a patent agent employs in the drafting of claims.

Under the Patents Act 1977 s 14(5), the claims shall:

(a) define the matter for which the applicant seeks protection;
(b) be clear and concise;
(c) be supported by the description; and
(d) relate to one invention or to a group of inventions which are so linked as to form a single inventive concept.

Claims (and the same applies to amended claims) are required to be clear and concise. But, otherwise, a patentee is not restricted by the Patents Act 1977 or the EPC as to the way he defines his monopoly. However, it is also important to bear in mind that the claim defines the scope of the monopoly and everything within it is monopolised and everything without it is disclaimed.[71] In *IGT/Acres Gaming Inc*,[72] the application used terms such as 'encrypted' in relation for an electronic system for giving punters in casinos bonus rewards without having to issue loyalty cards. The system worked by a card reader which could read the required information from other cards, including driving licences, credit cards and debit cards. However, some of the cards, such as US driving licences contained open-access information and this meant that the relevant claim was not sufficiently clear.[73]

In *Strix Ltd* v *Otter Controls Ltd*,[74] a case involving a patent for a back-up control to switch off an electric kettle where there had been a failure of the kettle's 'dry-boil' protector, it was accepted that, although something clearer and more concise could have been drafted, the test was whether a person skilled in the art would have difficulty in understanding the language used in the claim. However, a failure by the UK IPO to ensure that obscure claims are not allowed could be described as an infringement of the fundamental right of the public to know precisely the scope of the monopoly claimed. Others have a right to know what they are prevented from doing by the monopoly but lack of clarity in framing the patent claims could result in the proprietor having difficulty in establishing infringement.[75]

Where a claim is unjustifiably wide, it could lead to a claim that it is bad for covetousness. The omission of a feature essential to the invention could lead to such width. In *Kimberly-Clark Worldwide Inc* v *Procter & Gamble Ltd (No 2)*,[76] the defendant argued that an amendment sought by the proprietor of a patent for nappies should be refused on the ground that the claims were covetous as they omitted a feature which went to the essence of the invention. The defendant cited *Donaldson Co Inc's Patent*,[77] in which Falconer J refused to exercise his discretion to allow an amendment to a claim that had omitted the inventive feature on the basis that the claim before amendment was covetous; the reason being that the court will not assist someone who, by omitting an essential feature of the invention, knows that his claim is invalid and who now wants to limit it. In *Kimberly-Clark*, Pumfrey J said that, for a claim of covetousness to be made out, the draftsman of the specification must have sought to obtain a claim of unjustifiable width on the basis of the material available to him, such material including the description of the invention and information as to the prior art. An amendment should not be refused on the basis of *ex post facto* knowledge of the prior art which the draftsman of the specification was either unaware of or in respect of which he failed to appreciate the significance.

The use of the word 'for' in a claim describes a purpose of the invention. This is taken to mean that the invention is suitable for that purpose but not that it is necessarily intended for that purpose or even that it is actually used for it.[78] This can leave the patent

---

71 *Kirin-Amgen Inc* v *Transkaryotic Therapies Inc* [2003] RPC 3 at para 27.

72 [2008] EWHC 568 (Ch).

73 References to encryption may have caused the patent examiner to miss some relevant prior art such as card readers which read from non-encrypted cards.

74 [1995] RPC 607.

75 *Scanvaegt International A/S* v *Pelcombe Ltd* [1998] FSR 786 at 797 per Aldous LJ. It was doubted that the *contra proferentum* rule of interpretation applied where the manner of construction was laid down by a statute.

76 [2001] FSR 22.

77 [1986] RPC 1.

78 Peter Prescott QC in *Corevale Inc* v *Edwards Lifesciences AG* [2009] FSR 8.

79 (1910) 27 RPC 341.

80 [2011] EWCA Civ 162.

81 SI 2007/3291.

82 *American Home Products Corp v Novartis Pharmaceuticals UK Ltd* [2001] RPC 8. For Article 69 and the Protocol, *see* Chapter 12.

83 *PCME Ltd v Goyden Controls UK Ltd* [1999] FSR 801.

84 *Lubrizol Corp v Esso Petroleum Co Ltd* [1998] RPC 727. In *Cartonneries de Thulin SA v CTP White Knight Ltd* [2001] RPC 6, the Court of Appeal held that a court had to do its best to reconcile the literal meaning of claims with the context provided by the rest of the specification, as read by an ordinary skilled person.

85 *Mabuchi Motor KK's Patents* [1996] RPC 387.

86 [1997] RPC 649.

87 *Catnic Components Ltd v Hill & Smith Ltd* [1982] RPC 183, discussed in detail in Chapter 14. For a description of the approach of the European Patent Office in terms of ranges of numbers *see* Ashley, G. and Björk, P. 'Patentability of alloys at the European Patent Office' (1997) 2(3) *Intellectual Property* 3.

88 [1997] FSR 547.

vulnerable to anticipation by prior art which, in practical terms, is capable of being used for that purpose even though it had not occurred to anyone to so use it. In *Adhesive Dry Mounting v Trapp*,[79] the invention was for a method of dry mounting photographs with a sheet placed between a photograph and a mount which became tacky when heated would cause the photograph to stick to the mount. An earlier sheet had the same physical properties but it had never been suggested that it could be used for the purpose of sticking photographs to mounting boards. In *Virgin Atlantic Airways Ltd v Delta Air Lines Inc*,[80] Jacob LJ noted that there was at least a very strong presumption on the basis of considerable case law and guidance at the European Patent Office that 'for' means 'suitable for'. However, in some cases, it can mean 'intended for', such as in relation to a second medical use of a known medicine. But even then, it would really mean 'intended and suitable for'. The EPO guidelines include an example of a 'mold for molten steel'. This would imply certain limitations. For example, a plastic tray with a melting point much lower that steel could not be within the claim. It would not be suitable for such a use.

The example at the end of the chapter is a good example of a group of inventions forming a single inventive concept in accordance with s 14(5)(d). Claims 1, 20 and 39 relate to three different aspects – a beverage package, a method of packaging a beverage, and a beverage when so packaged. Rule 16 of the Patent Rules 2007[81] states that where two or more inventions are claimed (whether in a single claim or in separate claims), and there exists between or among those inventions a technical relationship which involves one or more of the same or corresponding special technical features, then those inventions shall be treated as being so linked as to form a single inventive concept for the purposes of the Act. 'Special technical features' are defined as those technical features which define a contribution which each of the claimed inventions, considered as a whole, makes over the prior art.

Sometimes, an omnibus claim will be included, usually as the final claim, for example:

the widget as substantially described hereinbefore with reference to the accompanying drawings.

The way claims are interpreted is important. By s 125(1) of the 1977 Act, interpreted according to the principles set down in the Protocol on Article 69 of the European Patent Convention, the invention shall be taken to be that specified in a claim as interpreted by the description and any drawings contained in the specification.[82] The extent of protection afforded by the grant of the patent is to be determined accordingly. Any ambiguities must be resolved by reference to the specification.[83] But the specification should not be used to place a gloss upon the words of a claim that have a clear meaning.[84] However, interpretation of claims can be wider than this and a purposive approach to interpretation is taken, rather than a strict literal approach, in accordance with the European Patent Convention. This feature is discussed in depth in Chapter 14.

Patent agents use language designed to maximise the protection afforded by the patent when granted. It can, at first sight, seem curious. For example, if a person invents something that has three components, such as three legs, a patent agent will draft the claim in terms of a 'plurality' of components where it might be possible to use two or four components. However, using this term excludes the singular.[85] If the invention can be worked with one or more components, a better expression would be 'a single or plurality of . . .' or 'one or more . . .'

Often claims will contain numeric data. For example, where a range of numbers is claimed, it was held in *Auchincloss v Agricultural & Veterinary Supplies Ltd*,[86] that anything outside that range is outside the monopoly and is not a variant in the sense used in *Catnic*.[87] In *Hoechst Celanese Corp v BP Chemicals Ltd*,[88] a reference in a claim to '50 per cent of its dry physical dimension' was held to be a reference to a linear dimension (radius) of the particle concerned rather than the volume, as the defendant contended. The Court of Appeal agreed, stating that the construction put forward by the defendant would defeat the purpose of the claim, which was to include only inherently stable resins.

If the dimension was taken to refer to volume, resins which were unstable would have been included.[89]

Sometimes, patent agents and others drafting patent claims may come down with a sad case of 'parametritis'. This term has been used by judges in relation to an attempt to repatent the prior art by placing new limits on claims by using a series of parameters which were not mentioned in the prior art: for example, because the equipment to measure them did not exist at the time. Another practice is to draft claims in an unnecessarily complicated manner. As the claims of a granted patent are *prima facie* valid, this may make it difficult for an opponent to challenge the claim. However, using obscure, difficult or complex language is not, by itself, a ground for invalidity and, within wide limits and notwithstanding the requirement that the claims must be clear and concise, an applicant for a patent can use what language he wishes to define the scope of his invention. Of course, the court must be on guard not to be impressed with obfuscatory language.[90]

In the next chapter, we will see that patents are available for second uses of known substances or compositions for medicinal use. However, great care must be taken to draft the claims in such cases, and a certain form of claim has become widely acceptable, known as a 'Swiss-type claim'. In *Eisai*,[91] the enlarged board of appeal of the European Patent Office approved such a type of claim, which normally takes the form:

> Use of a substance or composition X for the manufacture of a medicament for a specified new and inventive therapeutic application.

A typical claim for a first medical use of a known product might take the form:

> Substance or composition X . . .
>   . . . for use as a medicament
>   . . . for use as an antibiotic; or
>   . . . for use in treating disease Y.

In a Swiss-type claim for a second medical use of a known substance or compound, the second use had to be inventive and new. The novelty must lie not in the method of use but in the new therapeutic purpose for which the substance or compound was used.[92] In *Hoerrmann's Application*,[93] the court held that, when making a claim to a further medical use, the claims must be supported by the description (as per s 14(5)) and, in such a case, this would require a clear indication that the treatment had been tried and tested – it must come over as a reality and not merely a possibility. Nonetheless, the tests actually used might be fairly rudimentary and it was not necessary to demonstrate that fully rigorous, detailed and conclusive tests had been carried out.[94]

Abstract

The abstract is simply a concise summary of the matter contained in the specification.[95] It must start with a title for the invention. The abstract must indicate the technical field to which the invention belongs, a technical explanation of the invention and the principal use of the invention. The abstract must not contain any statement on the merits or value of the invention or its speculative application. The abstract provides useful information to help in the searching process: for example, when searching for anticipatory materials. Indeed it is a requirement that the abstract be drafted accordingly. By reading the abstract, it should be possible to determine whether it is necessary to consult the specification itself. Abstracts are included with other information in online and printed searching services.

Procedure for a UK patent[96]

The procedure described below applies where there has not been a declaration of priority from an earlier application. If there has been such a declaration, step 2 is different in that

89 [1999] FSR 319.

90 *Raychem Corp's Patents* [1998] RPC 31 per Laddie J.

91 [1985] OJ EPO 64.

92 *Bristol-Myers Squibb Co v Baker Norton Pharmaceuticals Inc* [2001] RPC 1.

93 [1996] RPC 341.

94 *Prendergast's Applications* [2000] RPC 446.

95 Patents Rules 2007 r 15, SI 2007/3291.

96 The UK IPO website is a rich source of information and guidance about intellectual property generally and patents. For information about applying for a patent see the UK IPO publications available from its website at www.ipo.gov.uk.

the claims and abstract must be filed within 12 months of the earliest priority date or within one month of the date of filing the application whichever is the later, but the form and search fee must be submitted within 12 months of the earliest declared priority date. In simple terms, the application procedure is as follows.[97]

1 *File application*: submit application including, usually at this stage, a request for grant of a patent, identification of the applicant (full name and address), description of the patent and the application fee.[98]

2 *File claims, etc.*: within 12 months, file the claims, abstract, form requesting preliminary examination and search together with the fee.

3 *Preliminary examination and search*: the application will then be checked to ensure all necessary documents and forms have been filed and fees paid. The application will then go to a UK IPO examiner who will make a search, mainly amongst patent specifications to check for novelty and obviousness. After this a search report will be issued. This report helps the applicant to decide whether his invention is new and not obvious. In some cases, amendments may have to be made to the claims or description. Any amendment to the claims must not cover something not already disclosed in the specification as first filed. However, this does not prevent the applicant widening the scope of his claims.[99] The prohibition on amendment extending the protection afforded by the patent under s 76(3) only applies to amendments post-grant. In the light of materials identified by the search, or for other reasons, the applicant might decide to withdraw the application before early publication thereby keeping his invention secret, in as much as it is not anticipated by the prior art.

4 *Early publication*: the application will be published together with the search report and any amended claims received before date of publication. Normally, this takes place 18 months after the date of filing if there is no priority date or 18 months after the priority date, as the case may be.[100] The contents of the specification are no longer confidential and become part of the state of the art. The date of early publication is important because it is the date from which damages for infringement ultimately can be claimed. For example, if there is an infringement of the patent between the early publication and grant, assuming it is finally granted, an action in respect of that infringement can be commenced *after* the patent has been granted. Early publication is known as 'A' publication. The example at the end of the chapter is an 'A' publication.

5 *Substantive examination*: this is the final stage before the grant of the patent. Within six months of the date of early publication, yet another form and fee has to be submitted to the UK IPO. The application will lapse if the form and fee are not received within those six months.[101] Once the patent application has been published and before grant any person may make written observations on the patentability of the invention. Reasons for the observations must be given and the Comptroller must consider the observations.[102] The specification is examined to see whether it complies with the requirements of the Patents Act 1977, especially whether the invention claimed is new and non-obvious, whether the description is adequate so that it can be carried out by a person skilled in the art concerned and whether the claims are clear and consistent with the description. It is common for the specification or claims or both to require amendment in the light of objections raised by the examiner. Once all the examiner's objections have been met, assuming they can be, the patent is granted. The patent as granted is published. This is known as 'B' publication.

Figure 11.1 illustrates a simplified flowchart for the UK patent application process. The period allowed for putting an application in order so that it complies with the Act is four years six months from the date of filing or priority date, if there is one, or 12 months from the date the first report under the substantive examination provisions is sent to the applicant, whichever expires the later.[103] Under the usual procedure, it can be seen that

97 This description is necessarily simplified and takes no account of, for example, the later filing of missing parts such as a description of the invention and copy of an earlier application where the priority of an earlier application is sought.

98 The application fee may be deferred until the request for a grant of a patent is filed, if later.

99 *Spring Form Inc* v *Playhut Inc* [2000] FSR 327.

100 Patents Rules 2007 r 26, SI 2007/3291.

101 Under s 20A, the Comptroller has a discretion to reinstate an application which is refused or taken to have been refused because of a failure of the applicant, for example, failing to respond to a substantive examination report within the time limit if, *inter alia*, satisfied that the failure was unintentional. A mistaken intention to put the application on hold does not count: *Anning's Patent Application* [2007] EWHC 2770 (Pat).

102 The person making the observations does not, as a result, become a party in any proceedings under the Act before the Comptroller: Patents Act 1977 s 21. Under this provision, a person may claim that the invention is not new because he was working the invention before the priority date.

103 Patents Act 1977 s 18; Patents Rules 2007 r 30, SI 2007/3291.

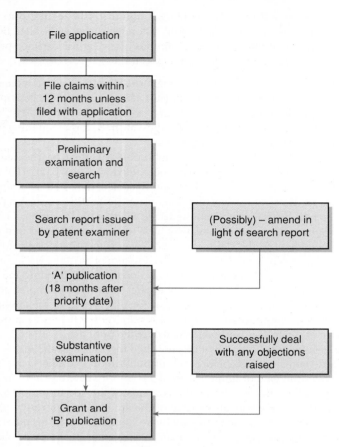

Figure 11.1 Flowchart of a UK patent application (simplified)

the shortest period is theoretically a little over 18 months, but a period of between two and three years is more realistic. However, the UK IPO will consider shortening the publication period and the time between publication and full examination if the applicant can make out a good case. The initial grant is for four years. Thereafter the patent may be renewed annually up to a maximum of 20 years from the date of filing.

On account of the difficulties faced by small and medium-sized undertakings which may need to exercise their rights much sooner than the traditional period of two to three years, bearing in mind that a patent cannot be enforced until it has been granted, the UK IPO now offers a speedier service. Patent procedure is accelerated by combining the search and examination stages and, by so doing, the time taken to obtain the grant of a patent may be as little as one year.[104]

The combined search and examination procedure, which is an alternative to the traditional procedure, is initiated by filing a request for search together with a request for examination at the same time. A request for early publication and early grant must also be made by the applicant. Combined search and examination is not likely to be appropriate in all cases. The applicant may have insufficient time fully to assess the prior art and make modifications to his application and, by the time the patent has been granted, the search and examination may not be complete. It would be likely to be useful, however, where the invention is 'clear cut' in terms of the requirements of the Act: for example, where it is clear that the invention is new, involves an inventive step, is capable of industrial application

104 *See* the Patents Application Guide available at the UK IPO website, www.ipo.gov.uk.

and not excepted. The combined search and examination procedure, which was available from 3 July 1995, is unlikely to be appropriate where the distinction between the invention and the prior art is imprecise, or where there is an issue concerning the exceptions or where the technology involved is particularly complex. Nevertheless, the fact that the UK IPO went some way to meeting the wishes of users of the patent system was generally welcomed.

Patents after grant

On the fourth anniversary of the date of filing, a patent must be renewed and then renewed annually on subsequent anniversaries. Renewal may be applied for within the three-month period ending with the end of the month during which the anniversary falls. Renewal is effected by submitting a form and the appropriate renewal fee. The renewal fees increase with each renewal.[105] Late renewal can be made up to six months after the end of the renewal period.[106] If this is not done, the patent will cease to have effect. However, during the following 13 months (that is 19 months in total from the end of the relevant renewal period) an application may be made to have the patent restored. If the restoration fee is paid and the Comptroller is satisfied that the failure of the proprietor to renew the patent was unintentional, he will restore the patent. Section 25(3) of the Patents Act 1977 reads:

> Where any renewal fee in respect of a patent is not paid by the end of the period prescribed for payment (the 'prescribed period') the patent shall cease to have effect at the end of such day, in the final month of that period, as may be prescribed.

The Patents Rules 2007[107] provide for the prescribed periods in three different situations, being as follows:

- The basic rule, not within the two other cases below.
- The case where a patent is granted on or after three years and nine months of the filing date.
- The case where the grant of a patent is mentioned in the European Patents Bulletin on or after three years and nine months of the date of filing (there are two possibilities here).[108]

Under the basic rule, the renewal date is the fourth or subsequent anniversaries of the filing date and the renewal period is the period of three months ending with the last day of the month during which the renewal date falls. Thus, if a patent has a date of filing of 6 September 2007, the first renewal date is 6 September 2011 and the renewal period runs from 1 July 2011 to 30 September 2011. The next renewal date is 6 September 2012 and the renewal period runs from 1 July 2012 to 30 September 2012, and so on.

Under s 25(4), if the renewal fee and any additional fee are paid during the period of six months after the end of the renewal period, the patent shall be treated as if it never expired and anything done during that period shall be treated as valid and any act which would have constituted an infringement of the patent had it not expired shall constitute an infringement of it. Thus, using the example dates above, late renewal can be made up to the end of March 2012 in relation to the first renewal of the patent. If the patent is not renewed during that period, an application can be made for restoration of the patent under s 28. The period during which restoration can be applied for is 13 months from the end of the period during which late renewal can be made, that is 19 months from the end of the renewal period. In our example, this would be the end of April 2013 in relation to the first renewal date. Under s 28(3), restoration will only be allowed if the relevant fees are paid, including a restoration fee,[109] and the Comptroller is satisfied that the failure of the proprietor to renew was unintentional.[110] These dates are set out in Table 11.2.

The present version of s 28(3) was substituted by the Regulatory Reform (Patents) Order 2004.[111] Previously, rather than consider whether the failure to renew was unintentional,

105 At the time of writing, the fee for the fifth year is £70, increasing to £600 for the twentieth and final year.

106 There is an additional late renewal fee, apart from the first month, of £24 per month.

107 SI 2007/3291.

108 Rule 37(2) to (4).

109 Presently £135.

110 Further renewal fees and additional fees may also be due.

111 SI 2004/2357. The Order came into force on 1 January 2005.

Table 11.2 Patent renewal and restoration dates

Filing date	6 September 2007
4th anniversary and 1st renewal date	6 September 2011
Renewal period	1 July 2011 to 30 September 2011
Late renewal period ends	31 March 2012
Restoration period (failure to renew on 4th anniversary)	1 April 2012 to 30 April 2013

a test of reasonable care was used. This was considered in *Textron Inc's Patents*,[112] where Lords Oliver and Goff said that where the renewal had been delegated to a director or an officer of a company that was the proprietor of a patent, it might be necessary to decide whether or not that person was a directing mind of the company such that the fault was the company's fault and not that of an agent or servant along the lines of *Tesco Supermarkets Ltd* v *Nattrass*.[113] In *Textron*, the failure to renew was the fault of a contractor specialised in renewing patents and to which the proprietor had entrusted the task of renewals. The new test should be fairly easy to satisfy though would not extend to a deliberate decision not to renew even though the proprietor later has second thoughts about this. Whether it will extend to negligence or mere carelessness is uncertain although it would be reasonable to expect the proprietor to show that he did intend to renew the patent and that the failure to renew was caused, for example, by a procedural error or malfunction. Before amendment of s 28(3), if a patentee could not afford to pay the renewal fee, this was a factor to be taken into account. It did not necessarily mean that he failed to exercise reasonable care but he would have to go further and show that his impecuniosity was not due to any lack of care. In *Ament's Application*,[114] the patentee was prohibited by US bankruptcy laws from applying his funds to renew the patent. Nevertheless, it was held that the patentee failed in the heavy onus to show that he had taken reasonable care. In *Bending Light Ltd's Application*,[115] the executive chairman of the patentee company, which was in financial difficulties, used company funds to meet liabilities as and when they became due to keep the company solvent. Unfortunately, he did not follow the same practice with regard to patent renewal fees. His application to restore the patent failed as it was held that reasonable care had not been taken. In particular, it was not shown that the company was not in a position to pay the necessary fees. The new test of unintentional failure seems more generous than previously but must make it harder if not impossible for impecunious patentees to secure restoration of a lapsed patent. Failing to pay for lack of money cannot be described as unintentional. A person cannot intend to pay if he has no money with which to pay.[116]

In *Atlas Powder Co's Patent*,[117] Atlas was taken over by ICI and decided not to renew its UK patent. An unforeseen consequence was that a Malaysian patent belonging to Atlas in respect of the same invention lapsed because the UK patent ceased to have effect. In terms of what was required by the first limb of old s 28(3) (reasonable care to see that the renewal fee is paid), the Court of Appeal decided that this required an intention to ensure that the fee was paid, or at least that the proprietor had taken some steps towards that. A deliberate decision not to renew is not consistent with the statutory requirement and restoration was not permitted. This case must now be read with the relaxed test to the effect that the failure to renew was unintentional.

After a patent has been granted it may still be amended under s 27 subject to s 76. Any such amendment is treated as having effect from the date of grant and there is provision for opposition. A failure to respond to any opposition will result in the application for amendment being treated as withdrawn.[118] The Comptroller may amend a specification on his own initiative to recognise a registered trade mark. Amendment under s 27 is not permitted where proceedings in which the validity of the patent has been put in issue are pending.[119]

112 [1989] RPC 411.

113 [1972] AC 153.

114 [1994] RPC 647.

115 [2009] EWHC 59 (Pat).

116 See, also, *Betson Medical (Ireland) Ltd* v *Comptroller General of Patents* [2010] EWHC 687 (Pat).

117 [1995] RPC 666.

118 *Norsk Hydro AS's Patent* [1997] RPC 89.

119 However, s 75 does permit amendment where the validity of the patent is or may be in issue in live proceedings.

120 Substituted by the Copyright, Designs and Patents Act 1988 s 295 and Sch 5, para 20.

121 Amendment under s 37(4), where an application for revocation is made in a case where the person registered as proprietor was not entitled to the patent but the person who was entitled makes a new application, is subject to not disclosing additional matter only.

122 [1996] RPC 387.

123 The 'Gillette' defence is discussed in Chapter 15.

124 Vector Corp v Glatt Air Techniques Ltd [2008] RPC 10.

125 [2007] EWHC 1367 (Pat).

126 [1991] RPC 553.

127 Nutrinova Nutrition Specialities & Food Ingredients GmbH v Scanchem UK Ltd (No 2) [2001] FSR 43.

128 Siegfried Demel (t/a as Demotec Siegfried Demel) v C & H Jefferson [1999] FSR 204.

129 Kimberly-Clark Worldwide Inc v Procter & Gamble Ltd (No 2) [2001] FSR 22. However, in this case, an argument by the defendant that the claims were covetous failed.

130 [2001] RPC 18.

Section 76[120] deals with amendment generally. The basic rule is that additional matter must not be disclosed. In terms of amendment after grant, s 76(3) requires that any amendment does not result in additional matter being disclosed in the specification or which extends the protection conferred by the patent.[121] In *Mabuchi Motor KK's Patents*,[122] it was held that an amendment to cut down the claims in a patent specification does not offend s 76. Under s 75, amendment may be allowed in infringement or revocation proceedings, subject to s 76, but this is discretionary. In *Mabuchi,* in relation to amendment under s 75, the Patents Court held that an amendment should be refused only on very compelling grounds. The proprietor's requested amendment was designed to catch infringement and to avoid the prior art, but it was accepted by the court that this was not to be equated with acting in a blameworthy manner. Although the amendment was allowed, the defendant's '*Gillette*' defence succeeded.[123]

Taking features in a specification described only in a particular context and without inventive significance and then seeking to amend by introducing them in a claim deprived of that context is sometimes referred to as an intermediate generalisation and will not normally be allowable as extending the subject matter of the patent.[124]

Article 123 of the European Patent Convention requires that amendments must not extend the subject matter beyond the patent as filed whereas the Patents Act 1977 s 76(3)(a) does not permit amendment resulting in the specification disclosing additional matter. In *Triumph Actuation Systems LLC v Aeroquip-Vickers Ltd*,[125] a question arose as to whether s 76 required a comparison with the specification of a granted patent before amendment or with the patent as filed. In the particular case, amendments during the patent application process had resulted in the deletion of matter in the specification as filed. Pumfrey J held that consistency with the European Patent Convention meant that the comparison should be with the patent as filed. Such consistency was desirable even though s 76 is not one of those provisions in the Act stated by s 130(7) to have, as nearly as practicable, the same effects in the UK as, *inter alia*, the European Patent Convention.

The correct test for added matter was set out by Aldous J in *Bonzel v Intervention Ltd (No 3)*[126] where it was held that, in deciding whether there is an extension of disclosure, the task of the court is:

1 To ascertain through the eyes of the skilled addressee what is disclosed both explicitly and implicitly in the application.
2 To do the same in respect of the patent as granted.
3 To compare the two disclosures and decide whether any subject matter relevant to the invention has been added, whether by deletion or addition.

The comparison is strict in the sense that that subject matter will be added unless such matter is clearly and unambiguously disclosed in the application either explicitly or implicitly. A deletion may add matter if what is deleted limits the scope of the subject matter: for example, if a statement in the application claims a product invention made of metal is modified to remove any reference to metal.

Amendment may be by way of deletion of invalid claims, in which case the court will refuse to exercise its discretion to allow amendment only in exceptional circumstances.[127] Furthermore, an amendment may be permitted which widens the scope of the protection conferred by a single claim provided it does not extend the protection conferred by the patent overall.[128] An example where a court may refuse to exercise its discretion to accept an amendment is where the claims in the patent as granted were covetous, that is, the draftsman deliberately sought to protect matter going beyond the scope of the invention and, consequently, the claims were unjustifiably wide.[129]

Post-grant amendment was not provided for by the European Patent Convention as patents granted under that Convention are treated as if they had been granted under the UK's Patents Act 1977: *see* s 77. In *Oxford Gene Technology Ltd v Affymetrix Inc (No 2)*,[130] it was argued that the discretion to allow amendment under s 75 was constrained by Article 138 of the European Patent Convention[131] and, consequently, the court had no option but to allow amendment under s 75 if the outcome would be a partially valid patent. This is because Article 138(2) provides that a patent *shall* be limited appropriately if the grounds of revocation are made out in part only. However, Aldous LJ pointed out that s 75 is not one of the provisions which are required by s 130(7) to be framed so as to have as nearly as practicable the same effect in the UK as the corresponding provision of the European Patent Convention, as the latter does not provide for post-grant amendment as such. Aldous LJ made the distinction that Article 138, as s 63(1), is concerned with a patent that is partially valid, whereas s 75 allows amendment to validate a patent that would otherwise be invalid. Article 138(2) and (3) of the European Patent Convention[132] now provides for amendment of the claims to limit the patent. This change was made so that national courts in invalidity proceedings to allow the proprietor to limit the patent claims. This possibility already existing in the UK but not all Member States provided for amendment where the validity of the patent was put in issue in court proceedings.

Where a court has declared a patent invalid during a trial where the patent proprietor has not taken the opportunity to propose amendment to the claims to limit that patent, the proprietor would normally be guilty of an abuse of process if he subsequently goes to court asking for amendments to be made to the claims. Jacob LJ so held in *Nokia GmbH v IPCOM GmbH & Co KG*.[133] In that case, IPCOM made a post-trial application to amend only after it had lost. To allow that would be to vex the other party with the same patent again and that would be an abuse of process.

Divisional applications

Once a patent application has been submitted, but before grant, a divisional application may be made in relation to it.[134] This is where the applicant divides out one or more claims from the original application (the 'parent' application) and makes them subject to a separate application for a patent. Typically, one or more divisional applications may be made where the patent examiner has objected on the ground that the parent application contains more than one invention or a number of inventions not having a single inventive concept.[135] However, the applicant may elect himself to make a divisional application. The advantage about making a divisional application is that, providing the Act and the Rules are complied with, it will have the same priority date as the parent application.

A divisional application can only be made in respect of subject matter which does not extend beyond the content from the application it was divided from. This is a general rule: see Article 123(2) EPC and Patents Act 1977 s 76. Although s 76 is not one of those provisions stated under s 130(7) to have as near as is practicable the same effect as the corresponding provision in the EPC and although it is differently worded compared with Article 123(2), it has been accepted that it was intended to have the same meaning in the Court of Appeal in *Napp Pharmaceutical Holdings Ltd v ratiopharm GmbH*.[136]

An example of a divisional application is where an application may be made for a patent but the application claims two inventions (X and Y) which are not so linked as to form a single inventive concept. The applicant may then make a divisional application in respect of invention X and another in respect of invention Y. The applicant may later decide to withdraw the parent application.[137] Alternatively, a divisional application may be made in relation to invention X and the parent application may be amended to exclude invention X.

The reason that it is not permissible to add subject matter in a divisional application, as is the case with a straightforward amendment, was explained by the Enlarged Board of Appeal of the EPO in Case G1/93 *ADVANCED SEMICONDUCTOR PRODUCTS/Limiting feature*[138] (at para 9) in the following terms:

131 Article 138(1) is equivalent to the grounds of revocation set out in s 72 of the Patents Act 1977 and Article 138(2) equates to s 63(1), which allows a court to grant relief to the extent that a patent is partially valid.

132 EPC 1973.

133 [2011] FSR 15. Though not described as such in the case, IPCOM appeared to be a patent troll in that it did not exploit the patents itself. Rather, it sought to persuade manufacturers to pay licence fees in relation to the patents. Jacob LJ described it as a 'non-practising entity'.

134 Article 76 of the EPC and the Patents Act 1977 s 15(9).

135 Under s 14(5)(d) the claim or claims must relate to a single invention or a group of inventions which are so linked as to form a single inventive concept.

136 [2009] RPC 18.

137 A divisional application may not be made in a number of cases. These include where the parent application has already been withdrawn or refused or where a patent has been granted in respect of it.

138 [1995] EPOR 97.

With regard to Article 123(2) EPC, the underlying idea is clearly that an applicant shall not be allowed to improve his position by adding subject-matter not disclosed in the application as filed, which would give him an unwarranted advantage and could be damaging to the legal security of third parties relying on the content of the original application. Article 123(3) EPC is directly aimed at protecting the interests of third parties by prohibiting any broadening of the claims of a granted patent, even if there should be a basis for such broadening in the application as filed.

At first sight, a previously undisclosed disclaimer of part of the subject matter of a patent application cannot add matter and should be unobjectionable. However, as the Enlarged Board of Appeal stated in *ADVANCED SEMICONDUCTOR PRODUCTS/Limiting feature*, it may add subject matter if it provided a technical contribution to the subject matter of the claimed invention. However, this would not be so if it simply narrowed the protection sought. Adding such a disclaimer cannot be viewed as giving an unwarranted advantage to the applicant. In *Napp Pharmaceutical Holdings Ltd* v *ratiopharm GmbH*,[139] the Court of Appeal agreed with Kitchen J's understanding of the position at first instance, where he said (at para 122):

139 [2009] RPC 18.

> Nevertheless, the test for added subject matter remains that set out in the Convention and the Act. The reason that disclaimers of accidental and deemed anticipations do not offend is that they do not add subject-matter relevant to the invention. If a disclaimer introduced by a divisional application does not add subject matter relevant to the invention, but merely excludes subject matter from protection, then it too will not offend against the provision.

A situation where an undisclosed disclaimer may be made is where a patent application ('A') having an earlier priority date than the one in question ('B') is published and contains subject matter also in application B. The applicant in respect of B may wish to cut his application down by excluding that subject matter from his application and limiting his claims accordingly.

Cost of applying for a patent

140 Patents (Fees) Rules 2007, SI 2007/3292, as amended by the Trade Marks and Trade Marks and Patents (Fees) (Amendment) Rules 2009, SI 2009/2089 and the Patents and Patents and Trade Marks (Fees) (Amendment) Rules 2010, SI 2010/33.

The cost of applying for a patent can be quite high; apart from paying the appropriate fees to the UK IPO, the drawing up of the necessary documents and drafting of claims will usually take a considerable amount of time. Additionally, in most cases, the services of a patent agent will be required. Some of the main fees payable to the UK IPO in respect of a UK patent, at the time of writing, are as follow:[140]

	Paper filing	Electronic or web-filing
(Application fee) for preliminary examination	£30	£20
Search fee	£150	£130
Substantive examination	£100	£80
Total fees	**£280**	**£230**

141 Further details of fees and the forms to be used are available at the Intellectual Property Office website at www.ipo.gov.uk.

There is no filing fee as such and no fee for a request for the grant of a patent. The above fees reflect an ideal situation. There are other fees which may be applicable in certain cases. Renewal fees range from £70 for the 5th year to £600 for the 20th and final year. Late renewal fees are £24 per month after the first month up to five months. If the patent is not renewed within six months application can be made for restoration. The fee for this is £135. The fee for requesting an opinion on validity or infringement is £200. Other fees apply for making an opposition, amendment, assignment, in respect of supplementary protection certificates, etc.[141]

Classification system

Current and old patents have to be consulted for several reasons, the obvious one being to determine whether a 'new' invention has been anticipated and is, therefore, likely to be refused a patent on the ground of lack of novelty. Other reasons relate to patent documents as a valuable source of information in terms of gaining information about competitors and a particular field of technology, seeing how certain problems have been tackled in the past, as a way of gaining inspiration and as a research tool. The UK IPO presently holds specifications and abstracts for every British patent dating from 1617 in addition to patents published by the USA and European Patent Offices. Additionally, computer databases hold details of many more millions of patents. It will come as no surprise that some sort of classification scheme is needed to assist in searching for relevant documents. Patent abstracts and specifications are classified and indexed to make the task of searching easier. For example, for specifications, the system used is based on three elements: a section, a division, and a heading. There are eight sections lettered from A to H as follows:

A   Human necessities
B   Performing operations
C   Chemistry and metallurgy
D   Textiles and paper
E   Civil engineering and building accessories
F   Mechanics, heating and lighting
G   Instrumentation
H   Electricity.

In addition there is a 'division not specified'. Each section is divided into between two and eight divisions, which are further divided into between two and 24 headings. As an example, the classification for toys is A6S (A6 being entertainments). Further subdivisions are used below the headings level and are known as 'terms', which are developed and expanded pragmatically in response to volume of applications.

There is also a Universal Indexing Schedule and an International Patent Classification (IPC), the latter being used by the European Patent Office. The IPC is arranged in eight sections in a way similar to the UK classification. In practice, UK patent specifications will carry all three classifications. The UK IPO and the British Library have access to several computer databases. There are now millions of applications for patents worldwide each year.

Patent agents

Persons wishing to apply for a patent normally use the services of a patent agent because of the complexity and technicality associated with patent applications and the importance of correctly defining the scope of the patent and extent of the claims. Although anyone can act for another in an agency capacity in respect of a patent application,[142] under the Copyright, Designs and Patents Act 1988 s 276, only registered patent agents may describe themselves as patent agents or patent attorneys.[143] Communications between a client and his patent agent are privileged provided the agent is registered.[144] There is a professional body for patent agents, the Chartered Institute of Patent Agents. Chartered patent agents have a right of audience in the Patents County Court.

Example patent application and specification

There follows a reproduction of a patent application made to the UK IPO (No. GB 2183592A). This is reproduced by permission of Guinness Brewing Worldwide Ltd and their patent attorneys, Urquhart-Dykes & Lord. The application should be studied in the

142 Subject to restrictions under the European Patent Convention in relation to European patents: Copyright, Designs and Patents Act 1988 s 274.

143 Solicitors may also use the description patent attorney.

144 Copyright, Designs and Patents Act 1988 s 280.

light of the description of the constituent parts of a patent specification given earlier in this chapter. The format of the specification and the high standard of draftsmanship particularly should be noted.

---

(12) **UK Patent Application** (19) **GB** (11) **2 183 592** (13) **A**

(43) Application published **10 Jun 1987**

(21) Application No **8529441**

(22) Date of filing **29 Nov 1985**

(71) Applicant
Arthur Guinness Son & Company (Dublin) Limited,

(Incorporated in Irish Republic),

St. James's Gate, Dublin 8, Republic of Ireland

(72) Inventors
Alan James Forage,
William John Byrne

(74) Agent and/or Address for Service
Urquhart-Dykes & Lord, 47 Marylebone Lane,
London W1M 6DL

(51) INT CL⁴
B65D 25/00 5/40

(52) Domestic classification (Edition I)
B8D 12 13 19 7C 7G 7M 7P1 7PY SC1
B8P AX
U1S 1106 1110 1111 B8D B8P

(56) Documents cited
GB 1266351

(58) Field of search
B8D
B8P
Selected US specifications from IPC sub-class B65D

(54) **Carbonated beverage container**

(57) A container for a beverage having gas (preferably at least one of carbon dioxide and inert (nitrogen) gases) in solution consists of a non-resealable container 1 within which is located a hollow secondary chamber 4, eg a polypropylene envelope, having a restricted aperture 7 in a side wall. The container is charged with the beverage 8 and sealed. Beverage from the main chamber of the container enters the chamber 4 (shown at 8a) by way of the aperture 7 to provide headspaces 1a in the container and 4a in the pod 4. Gas within the headspaces 1a and 4a is at greater than atmospheric pressure. Preferably the beverage is drawn into the chamber 4 by subjecting the package to a heating and cooling cycle. Upon opening the container 1, eg by draw ring/region 13, the headspace 1a is vented to atmosphere and the pressure differential resulting from the pressure in the chamber headspace 4a causes gas/beverage to be ejected from the chamber 4 (by way of the aperture 7) into the beverage 8. Said ejection causes gas to be evolved from solution in the beverage in the main container chamber to form a head of froth on the beverage. The chamber 4 is preferably formed by blow moulding and located below beverage level by weighting it or as a press fit within the container 1 by lugs 6 engaging the container walls, the container being preferably a can, carton or bottle. The chamber 4 may initially be filled with gas, eg nitrogen, at or slightly above atmospheric pressure, the orifice being formed by laser boring, drilling or punching immediately prior to locating the chamber 4 in the container 1.

The drawings originally filed were informal and the print here reproduced is taken from a later filed formal copy.

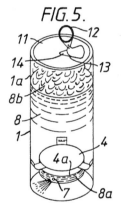

FIG. 5.

Reference to UK Patent Application 2, 183,592A is made with kind permission of Guinness Brewing Worldwide Limited and their Patent Attorneys, Urquhart-Dykes & Lord.

29 NOV 8529441

1/2

2183592

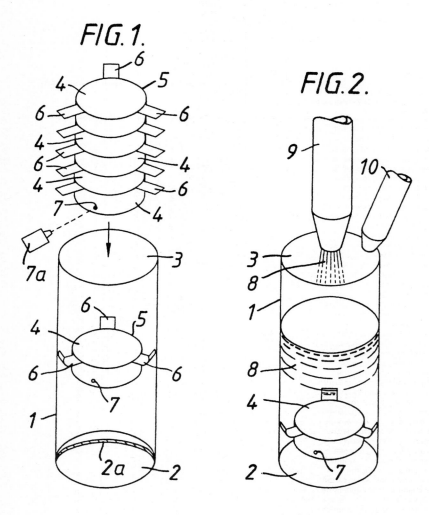

FIG.1.

FIG.2.

29   Nov 85 29441

2/2   2183592

FIG. 3.

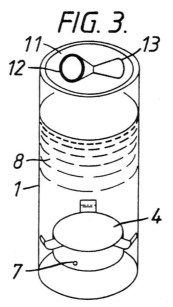

FIG. 4.

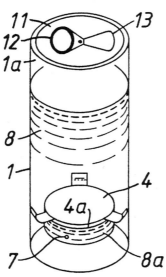

FIG. 5.

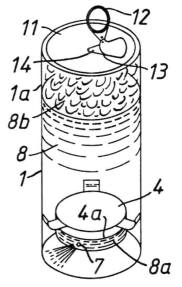

SPECIFICATION

A beverage package and a method of packaging a beverage containing gas in solution

5

Technical field and background art

This invention relates to a beverage package and a method of packaging a beverage containing gas in solution. The invention more particularly concerns
10 beverages containing gas in solution and packaged in a sealed, non-resealable, container which, when opened for dispensing or consumption, permits gas to be evolved or liberated from the beverage to form, or assist in the formation of, a head or froth on the
15 beverage. The beverages to which the invention relates may be alcoholic or non-alcoholic; primarily the invention was developed for fermented beverages such as beer, stout, ale, lager and cider but may be applied with advantage to so-called soft drinks
20 and beverages (for example fruit juices, squashes, colas, lemonades, milk and milk based drinks and similar type drinks) and to alcoholic drinks (for example spirits, liquers, wine or wine based drinks and similar).
25 It is recognised in the beverage dispensing and packaging art that the characteristics of the head of froth which is provided on the beverage by the liberation of gas from the beverage immediately prior to consumption are an important consideration to the
30 consumers enjoyment of the product and are therefore of commercial importance. Conventionally beverages of the type discussed above containing gas in solution and packaged in a non-resealable container (such as a can, bottle or carton) provide a
35 headspace in the container within which gas is maintained under pressure. Upon opening of the package, the headspace gas is vented to atmosphere and the beverage is usually poured into a drinking vessel. During such dispensing of the beverage it is
40 usual for gas in solution to be liberated to create the froth or head. It is generally recognised that when dispensing a beverage as aforementioned, the gas is liberated as a result of the movement of the beverage over a surface having so-called gas nucleation or ac-
45 tive sites which may be the wall of the drinking vessel into which the beverage is poured. There is therefore a distinct possibility with conventional beverage packages that upon opening of the container after storage and until the beverage is poured there-
50 from, the beverage will have little or no froth or head - such a headless beverage is usually regarded by the consumer as somewhat unattractive and unappealing especially where the beverage is to be drunk directly from the container. Admittedly it may be pos-
55 sible to develop a head or froth within the container by agitating or shaking the package (so that the movement of the beverage over the interior surface of the container causes the liberation of the gas in solution) but this is clearly inconvenient once the
60 container is opened and is inadvisable if the package is shaken immediately prior to opening as the contents tend to spray or spurt on opening.

There is therefore a need for a beverage package and a method of packaging a beverage containing
65 gas in solution by which the beverage is packaged in a non-resealable container so that when the container is opened gas is liberated from the beverage to form or assist in the formation of a head or froth without the necessity of an external influence being
70 applied to the package; it is an object of the present invention to satisfy this need in a simple, economic and commercially viable manner.

Statements of invention and advantages
75 According to the present invention there is provided a beverage package comprising a sealed, nonresealable, container having a primary chamber containing beverage having gas in solution therewith and forming a primary headspace comprising gas at
80 a pressure greater than atmospheric; a secondary chamber having a volume less than said primary chamber and which communicates with the beverage in said primary chamber through a restricted orifice, said secondary chamber containing beverage
85 derived from the primary chamber and having a secondary headspace therein comprising gas at a pressure greater than atmospheric so that the pressures within the primary and secondary chambers are substantially at equilibrium, and wherein said package is
90 openable, to open the primary headspace to atmospheric pressure and the secondary chamber is arranged so that on said opening the pressure differential caused by the decrease in pressure at the primary headspace causes at least one of the beverage and
95 gas in the secondary chamber to be ejected by way of the restricted orifice into the beverage of the primary chamber and said ejection causes gas in the solution to be evolved and form, or assist in the formation of, a head of froth on the beverage.
100 Further according to the present invention there is provided a method of packaging a beverage having gas in solution therewith which comprises providing a container with a primary chamber and a secondary chamber of which the volume of the secondary
105 chamber is less than that of the primary chamber and with a restricted orifice through which the secondary chamber communicates with the primary chamber, and charging and sealing the primary chamber with the beverage to contain the gas in solution and to
110 form a primary headspace in the primary chamber, and charging the secondary chamber with beverage derived from the primary chamber by way of said restricted orifice to form a secondary headspace in the secondary chamber whereby the pressures in both
115 the primary and secondary chambers are at equilibrium and gaseous pressures in both the primary and secondary headspaces are at a pressure greater than atmospheric so that, when the container is broached to open the primary headspace to atmos-
120 pheric pressure, the pressure differential caused by the decrease in pressure at the primary headspace causes at least one of the beverage and gas in the secondary chamber to be ejected into the beverage of the primary chamber by way of said restricted ori-
125 fice and the said ejection causes gas to be evolved from solution in the beverage in the primary chamber to form, or assist in the formation of, a head of froth on the beverage.

The present invention is applicable to a wide range
130 of beverages of the type as previously discussed and

where those beverages contain gas in solution which gas is intended to be liberated to form or assist in the formation of the head or froth on the beverage. Understandably the gas in solution must not detract
5 from, and should preferably enhance the characteristics required of the beverage and be acceptable for use with food products; preferably therefore the gas is at least one of carbon dioxide and inert gases (by which latter term is included nitrogen)
10 although it is to be realised that other gases may be appropriate.

The present invention was primarily developed for the packaging of fermented beverages such as beer, ale, stout, lager and cider where among the desirable
15 qualities sought in a head are a consistent and regular, relatively fine, bubble size; a bubble structure which is substantially homogeneous so that the head is not formed with large irregularly shaped and random gaps; the ability for the head or bubble
20 structure to endure during a reasonable period over which it is likely to be consumed, and a so-called "mouth-feel" and flavour whcih may improve the enjoyment of the beverage during consumption and not detract from the desirable flavour characteristics
25 required of the beverage. These desirable qualities are of course equally applicable to non-fermented beverages, for example with so-called soft drinks. Conventionally, beverages of the type to which the invention relates are packaged in a non-resealable
30 container which when opened totally vents the headspace to atmosphere, contain carbon dioxide in solution and it is the liberation of the carbon dioxide on opening of the package and dispensing of the beverage into a drinking vessel which creates the froth or
35 head; however, the head so formed has very few of the aforementioned desirable qualities - in particular it is usually irregular, lacks homogeneity and has very little endurance so that there is a tendency for it to collapse after a short period. It has been known for
40 approximately 25 years and as discussed in our G.B. Patent No. 876,628, that beverages having in solution a mixture of carbon dioxide gas and inert gas (such as nitrogen or argon) will, when dispensed in a manner whereby the mixed gases are caused to
45 evolve to develop the head or foam from small bubbles containing the mixture of carbon dioxide and, say, nitrogen gases, provide the desirable qualities for the head as previously discussed. Commericially the formation of the head by the use of mixed
50 gases as aforementioned has been widely employed in the dispensing of beverage in a draught system and on demand from a bulk container (such as a keg or barrel) where the gases are caused to evolve by subjecting the beverage to intense shear forces in
55 passing it under pressure through a set of small holes. Beverages, particularly stout, having a mixture of carbon dioxide and nitrogen gases in solution and dispensed in draught using the aforementioned technique have met with considerable commercial
60 success and it was soon realised that there was a need to make available for consumption a similar beverage derived from a small non-resealable container suitable for shelf storage and retail purposes.

Research has indicated that to achieve the initia-
65 tion of a head on a beverage containing carbon

dioxide and inert gas such as nitrogen in solution it is necessary to provide so-called "active sites" which are regions where the beverage is subjected to a high local strain (such a strain being higher than the
70 cohesive force of the beverage). In these conditions the beverage prefers to generate a bubble of mixed gases instead of "bending around" the active site. It was found that an active site could be solid, liquid or gas such as granules, restrictor holes, rapid streams
75 of liquid or bubbles and the like. It was also found that ultrasonics could produce a "ghost" active site by the formation of extreme pressure gradients. There has however been a problem in providing an "active site" in a beverage packaged in a non-
80 resealable small container in a manner which is commercially and economically acceptable. During the past 25 years considerable expenditure has been devoted to research and development in an attempt to overcome the aforementioned problem. For ex-
85 ample, our G.B. Patent No. 1,588,624 proposes initiating the evolution of mixed carbon dioxide and nitrogen gases from a beverage by subjecting the beverage to ultrasonic excitement, by injecting a gas, liquid and/or foam into the beverage by use of a
90 syringe-type device, or by pouring the beverage over an excitation surface such as polystyrene granules. Although these latter proposals were successful in achieving the desired head formation, the necessity to use ancilliary apparatus had commercial dis-
95 advantages (for example, it is unreasonable to expect a retail customer to have available an ultrasonic signal generator; also the steps required to effect initiation of the head following opening of the beverage package involved an inconvenient discipline and
100 time factor). In a further example our G.B. Patent No. 1,266,351 relates to a non-resealable package containing beverage having mixed carbon dioxide and inert gases in solution; in this disclosure a can or bottle has two chambers of which a larger chamber
105 contains the beverage while the smaller chamber is charged under pressure with the mixed gases. On opening of the can or bottle to expose the larger chamber to atmosphere, its internal pressure falls to atmospheric permitting the pressurised gas in the
110 small chamber to jet into the beverage by way of a small orifice between the two chambers. This jet of gas provides sufficient energy to initiate the formation of minute bubbles and thereby the head from the evolution of the mixed gases in the beverage
115 coming out of solution. By this proposal the small gas chamber is initially pressurised with the mixed gases to a pressure greater than atmospheric and from a source remote from the beverage; as a consequence it was found necessary, particularly in the
120 case of cans, to provide a special design of two chambered container and an appropriate means for sealing the smaller chamber following the charging of that chamber with the mixed gases (such charging usually being effected, in the case of cans, by injec-
125 ting the mixed gases into the small chamber through a wall of the can which then had to be sealed). Because of the inconvenience and high costs involved in the development of an appropriate two chambered container and the special facilities required for
130 charging the mixed gases and sealing the container,

the proposal proved commercially unacceptable.

The container employed in the present invention will usually be in the form of a can, bottle or carton capable of withstanding the internal pressures of the
5 primary and secondary chambers and of a size suitable for conventional shelf storage by the retail trade so that, the overall volume of the container may be, typically, 0.5 litres but is unlikely to be greater than 3 litres.
10 By the present invention a two chambered container is employed as broadly proposed in G.B. Patent No. 1,266,351; however, unlike the prior proposal the secondary chamber is partly filled with beverage containing gases in solution and the bever-
15 age in the secondary chamber is derived wholly from the beverage in the primary chamber so that when the contents of the primary and secondary chambers are in equilibrium (and the primary and secondary headspaces are at a pressure greater than atmosphe-
20 ric) immediately prior to broaching the container to open the primary headspace to atmosphere, the pressure differential between that in the secondary headspace and atmospheric pressure causes at least one of the beverage and the headspace gas in the
25 secondary chamber to be ejected by way of the restricted orifice into the beverage in the primary chamber to promote the formation of the head of froth without the necessity of any external influence being applied to the package. The pressurisation of
30 the headspace gas in the secondary chamber is intended to result from the evolution of gas in the sealed container as the contents of the container come into equilibrium at ambient or dispensing temperature (which should be greater than the tem-
35 perature at which the container is charged and sealed). Consequently the present invention alleviates the necessity for pressurising the secondary chamber from a source externally of the container so that the secondary chamber can be formed as a
40 simple envelope or hollow pod of any convenient shape (such as cylindrical or spherical) which is located as a discrete insert within a conventional form of can, bottle or carton (thereby alleviating the requirement for a special structure of can or bottle as
45 envisaged in G.B. Patent No. 1,266,351).

Although the head or froth formed by pouring wholly carbonated beverages tends to lack many of the desirable qualities required of a head as previously discussed; our tests have indicated that by
50 use of the present invention with wholly carbonated beverages (where the head is formed by injection of gas or beverage from the secondary chamber into the primary chamber) the resultant head is considerably tighter or denser than that achieved solely by
55 pouring and as such will normally have a greater life expectancy.

The beverage is preferably saturated or supersaturated with the gas (especially if mixed carbon dioxide and inert gases are employed) and the
60 primary chamber charged with the beverage under a counterpressure and at a low temperature (to alleviate gas losses and, say, at a slightly higher temperature than that at which the beverage freezes) so that when the container is sealed (which may be
65 achieved under atmospheric pressure using con-

ventional systems such as a canning or bottling line), the pressurisation of the primary and secondary headspaces is achieved by the evolution of gas from the beverage within the primary and secondary
70 chambers as the package is handled or stored at an ambient or dispensing temperature (greater than the charging temperature) and the contents of the container adopt a state of equilibrium. As an optional but preferred feature of the present invention, following
75 the sealing of the container, the package may be subjected to a heating and cooling cycle, conveniently during pasteurisation of the beverage. During such a cycle the gas within the secondary chamber is caused to expand and eject into the primary
80 chamber; during subsequent cooling of the package, the gas in the secondary chamber contracts and creates a low pressure or vacuum effect relative to the pressure in the primary chamber so that beverage from the primary chamber is drawn into the sec-
85 ondary chamber by way of the restricted orifice. By use of this preferred technique it is possible to ensure that the secondary chamber is efficiently and adequately charged with beverage and has the desired secondary headspace.
90 The restricted orifice through which the primary and secondary chambers communicate is conveniently formed by a single aperture in a side wall of the secondary chamber and such an aperture should have a size which is sufficiently great to alleviate
95 "clogging" or its obturation by particles which may normally be expected to occur within the beverage and yet be restricted in its dimensions to ensure that there is an adequate jetting effect in the ejection of the gas and/or beverage therethrough from the sec-
100 ondary chamber into the primary chamber to promote the head formation upon opening of the container. The restricted orifice may be of any profile (such as a slit or a star shape) but will usually be circular; experiments have indicated that a restricted
105 orifice having a diameter in the range of 0.02 to 0.25 centimeters is likely to be appropriate for fermented beverages (the preferred diameter being 0.061 centimetres). It is also preferred that when the package is positioned in an upstanding condition in which it is
110 likely to be transported, shelf stored or opened, the restricted orifice is located in an upwardly extending side wall or in a bottom wall of the secondary chamber and preferably at a position slightly spaced from the bottom of the primary chamber. It is also
115 preferred, particularly for fermented beverages, that when the contents of the sealed package are in equilibrium and the package is in an upstanding condition as aforementioned, the restricted orifice is located below the depth of the beverage in the
120 secondary chamber so that on opening of the container the pressure of gas in the secondary headspace initially ejects beverage from that chamber into the beverage in the primary chamber to promote the head formation. It is believed that such ejection
125 of beverage through the restricted orifice is likely to provide a greater efficiency in the development of the head in a liquid supersaturated with gas than will the ejection of gas alone through the restricted orifice; the reason for this is that the restricted orifice
130 provides a very active site which causes the bever-

age to "rip itself apart" generating extremely minute bubbles which themselves act as active sites for the beverage in the primary chamber, these extremely minute bubbles leave "vapour trails" of larger initia-
5 ted bubbles which in turn produce the head. Since the extremely minute bubbles are travelling at re- latively high speed during their injection into the be- verage in the primary chamber, they not only gene- rate shear forces on the beverage in that chamber
10 but the effect of each such bubble is distributed over a volume of beverage much larger than the im- mediate surroundings of an otherwise stationary bubble.
    A particular advantage of the present invention is
15 that prior to the container being charged with bever- age both the primary and secondary chambers can be at atmospheric pressure and indeed may contain air. However, it is recognised that for many bever- ages, particularly a fermented beverage, prolonged
20 storage of the beverage in contact with air, especially oxygen, is undesirable as adversely affecting the characteristics of the beverage. To alleviate this pos- sibility the secondary chamber may initially be filled with a "non-contaminant" gas such as nitrogen (or
25 other inert gas or carbon dioxide) which does not adversely affect the characteristics of the beverage during prolonged contact therewith. The secondary chamber may be filled with the non-contaminant gas at atmospheric pressure or slightly greater (to allev-
30 iate the inadvertent intake of air) so that when the container is charged with the beverage, the non- contaminant gas will form part of the pressurised headspace in the secondary chamber. As previously mentioned, the secondary chamber may be formed
35 by an envelope or hollow pod which is located as a discrete insert within a conventional form of can, bottle or carton and such a discrete insert permits the secondary chamber to be filled with the non- contaminant gas prior to the envelope or pod being
40 located within the can, bottle or carton. A convenient means of achieving this latter effect is by blow moulding the envelope or pod in a food grade plas- tics material using the non-contaminant gas as the blowing medium and thereafter sealing the envelope
45 or pod to retain the non-contaminant gas therein; immediately prior to the pod or envelope being in- serted into the can, bottle or carton, the restricted ori- fice can be formed in a side wall of the pod or en- velope (for example, by laser boring). Immediately
50 prior to the container being sealed it is also prefer- able to remove air from the primary headspace and this may be achieved using conventional techniques such as filling the headspace with froth or fob dev- eloped from a source remote from the container and
55 having characteristics similar to those of the head which is to be formed from the beverage in the con- tainer; charging the primary chamber with the be- verage in a nitrogen or other inert gas atmosphere so that the headspace is filled with that inert gas or nit-
60 rogen; dosing the headspace with liquid nitrogen so that the gas evolved therefrom expels the air from the headspace, or by use of undercover gassing or water jetting techniques to exclude air.
    Although the secondary chamber may be con-
65 structed as an integral part of the container, for the

reasons discussed above and also convenience of manufacture, it is preferred that the secondary chamber is formed as a discrete insert which is simply deposited or pushed into a conventional form
70 of can, bottle or carton. With cans or cartons such an insert will not be visible to the end user and many bottled beverages are traditionally marketed in dark coloured glass or plastics so that the insert is unlikely to adversely affect the aesthetics of the package. The
75 discrete insert may be suspended or float in the be- verage in the primary chamber provided that the re- stricted orifice is maintained below the surface of the beverage in the primary chamber on opening of the container; for example the insert may be loaded or
80 weighted to appropriately orientate the position of the restricted orifice. Desirably however the insert is restrained from displacement within the outer con- tainer of the package and may be retained in posi- tion, for example at the bottom of the outer con-
85 tainer, by an appropriate adhesive or by mechanical means such as projections on the package which may flex to abut and grip a side wall of the outer con- tainer or which may engage beneath an internal abutment on the side wall of the outer container.
90
    Drawings
    One embodiment of the present invention as app- lied to the packaging of a fermented beverage such as stout in a can will now be described, by way of
95 example only, with reference to the accompanying illustrative drawings, in which:-
    Figures 1 to 4 diagrammatically illustrate the pro- gressive stages in the formation of the beverage package in a canning line, and
100 *Figure 5* diagrammatically illustrates the effect on opening the beverage package prior to consumption of the beverage and the development of the head of froth on the beverage.

105 *Detailed description of drawings*
    The present embodiment will be considered in re- lation to the preparation of a sealed can containing stout having in solution a mixture of nitrogen and carbon dioxide gases, the former preferably being
110 present to the extent of at least 1.5% vols/vol and typically in the range 1.5% to 3.5% vols/vol and the carbon dioxide being present at a considerably lower level than the amount of carbon dioxide which would normally be present in conventional, wholly car-
115 bonated, bottled or canned stout and typically in the range 0.8 to 1.8 vols/vol (1.46 to 3.29 grams/litre). For the avoidance of doubt, a definition of the term "vols/ vol" is to be found in our G.B. Patent No. 1,588,624.
    The stout is to be packaged in a conventional form
120 of cylindrical can (typically of aluminium alloy) which, in the present example, will be regarded as having a capacity of 500 millilitres and by use of a conventional form of filling and canning line app- ropriately modified as will hereinafter be described.
125 A cylindrical shell for the can 1 having a sealed base 2 and an open top 3 is passed in an upstanding condi- tion along the line to a station shown in Figure 1 to present its open top beneath a stack of hollow pods 4. Each pod 4 is moulded in a food grade plastics
130 material such as polypropylene to have a short (say 5

millimetres) hollow cylindrical housing part 5 and a circumferentially spaced array of radially outwardly extending flexible tabs or lugs 6. The pods 4 are placed in the stack with the chamber formed by the
5 housing part 5 sealed and containing nitrogen gas at atmospheric pressure (or at pressure slightly above atmospheric); conveniently this is achieved by blow moulding the housing part 5 using nitrogen gas. The volume within the housing part 5 is approximately 15
10 millilitres. At the station shown in Figure 1 the bottom pod 4 of the stack is displaced by suitable means (not shown) into the open topped can 1 as shown. However, immediately prior to the pod 4 being moved into the can 1 a small (restricted) hole 7
15 is bored in the cylindrical side wall of the housing part 5. In the present example, the hole 7 has a diameter in the order of 0.61 millimetres and is conveniently bored by a laser beam generated by device 7a (although the hole could be formed by punching or
20 drilling). The hole 7 is located towards the bottom of the cylindrical chamber within the housing part 5. Since the hollow pod 4 contains nitrogen gas at atmospheric pressure (or slightly higher) it is unlikely that air will enter the hollow pod through the
25 hole 7 during the period between boring the hole 7 and charging of the can 1 with stout (thereby alleviating contamination of the stout by an oxygen content within the hollow pod 4).
    The hollow pod 4 is pressed into the can 1 to be
30 seated on the base 2. Conventional cans 1 have a domed base 2 (shown by the section 2a) which presents a convex internal face so that when the pod 4 abuts this face a clearance is provided between the hole 7 and the underlying bottom of the chamber
35 within the can 1. It will be seen from Figure 1 that the diameter of the housing part 5 of the pod 4 is less than the internal diameter of the can 1 while the diameter of the outermost edges of the lugs 6 is greater than the diameter of the can 1 so that as the pod 4 is
40 pressed downwardly into the can, the lugs 6 abut the side wall of the can and flex upwardly as shown to grip the can side wall and thereby restrain the hollow pod from displacement away from the base 2.
    The open topped can with its pod 4 is now displa-
45 ced along the canning line to the station shown in Figure 2 where the can is charged with approximately 440 millilitres of stout 8 from an appropriate source 9. The stout 8 is supersaturated with the mixed carbon dioxide and nitrogen gases, typic-
50 ally the carbon dioxide gas being present at 1.5 vols/vol (2.74 grams/litre) and the nitrogen gas being present at 2% vols/vol. The charging of the can 1 with the stout may be achieved in conventional manner, that is under a counterpressure and at a temperature of
55 approximately 0°C. When the can 1 is charged with the appropriate quantity of stout 8, the headspace above the stout is purged of air, for example by use of liquid nitrogen dosing or with nitrogen gas delivered by means indicated at 10 to alleviate contamina-
60 tion of the stout from oxygen in the headspace.
    Following charging of the can 1 with stout and purging of the headspace, the can moves to the station shown in Figure 3 where it is closed and sealed under atmospheric pressure and in conventional manner
65 by a lid 11 seamed to the cylindrical side wall of the

can. The lid 11 has a pull-ring 12 attached to a weakened tear-out region 13 by which the can is intended to be broached in conventional manner for dispensing of the contents.
70   Following sealing, the packaged stout is subjected to a pasteurisation process whereby the package is heated to approximately 60°C for 15-20 minutes and is thereafter cooled to ambient temperature. During this process the nitrogen gas in the hollow pod 4a
75 initially expands and a proportion of that gas passes by way of the hole 7 into the stout 8 in the main chamber of the can. During cooling of the package in the pasteurisation cycle, the nitrogen gas in the hollow pod 4 contracts to create a vacuum effect
80 within the hollow pod causing stout 8 to be drawn, by way of the hole 7, from the chamber of the can into the chamber of the pod so that when the package is at ambient temperature the hole 7 is located below the depth of stout 8a within the hollow
85 pod 4.
    Following the pasteurisation process the contents of the can 1 will stabilise in a condition of equilibrium with a headspace 1a over the stout 8 in the primary chamber of the can and a headspace 4a over the
90 stout 8a in the secondary chamber formed by the hollow pod 4 and in the equilibrium condition. With the sealed can at ambient temperature (or a typical storage or dispensing temperature which may be, say, 8°C) the pressure of mixed gases carbon dioxide
95 and nitrogen (which largely results from the evolution of such gases from the stout) is substantially the same in the headspaces 1a and 4a and this pressure will be greater than atmospheric pressure, typically in the order of 25lbs per square inch (1.72
100 bars).
    The package in the condition shown in Figure 4 is typically that which would be made available for storage and retail purposes. During handling it is realised that the package may be tipped from its up-
105 right condition; in practice however this is unlikely to adversely affect the contents of the hollow pod 4 because of the condition of equilibrium within the can.
    When the stout is to be made available for consumption, the can 1 is opened by ripping out the re-
110 gion 13 with the pull-ring 12. On broaching the lid 11 as indicated at 14 the headspace 1a rapidly depressurises to atmospheric pressure. As a consequence the pressure within the headspace 4a of the secondary chamber in the pod 4 exceeds that in the
115 headspace 1a and causes stout 8a in the hollow pod to be ejected by way of the hole 7 into the stout 8 in the primary chamber of the can. The restrictor hole 7 acts as a very "active site" to the supersaturated stout 8a which passes therethrough to be injected
120 into the stout 8 and that stout is effectively "ripped apart" to generate extremely minute bubbles which themselves act as active sites for the stout 8 into which they are injected. These minute bubbles leave "vapour trails" of larger initiated bubbles which dev-
125 elop within the headspace 1a a head 8b having the previously discussed desirable characteristics.
    It is appreciated that the headspace 1a occupies a larger proportion of the volume of the can 1 than that which would normally be expected in a 500 millilitre
130 capacity can; the reason for this is to ensure that

there is adequate volume in the headspace 1*a* for the head of froth 8*b* to develop efficiently in the event, for example, that the stout is to be consumed directly from the can when the tear-out region 13 is removed.
5   Normally however the stout 8 will first be poured from the can into an open topped drinking vessel prior to consumption but this pouring should not adversely affect the desirable characteristics of the head of froth which will eventually be presented in
10   the drinking vessel.

In the aforegoing embodiment the can 1 is charged with stout 8 (from the source 9) having in solution the required respective volumes of the carbon dioxide and the nitrogen gases. In a modification the can 1 is
15   charged with stout (from source 9) having the carbon dioxide gas only in solution to the required volume; the 2% vols/vol nitrogen gas necessary to achieve the required solution of mixed gas in the packaged stout is derived from the liquid nitrogen dosing of
20   the headspace in the can.

CLAIMS

1.   A beverage package comprising a sealed, non-
25   resealable, container having a primary chamber containing beverage having gas in solution therewith and forming a primary headspace comprising gas at a pressure greater than atmospheric; a secondary chamber having a volume less than said primary
30   chamber and which communicates with the beverage in said primary chamber through a restricted orifice, said secondary chamber containing beverage derived from the primary chamber and having a secondary headspace therein comprising gas at a pres-
35   sure greater than atmospheric so that the pressure within the primary and secondary chambers are substantially at equilibrium, and wherein said package is openable, to open the primary headspace to atmospheric pressure and the secondary chamber is arran-
40   ged so that on said opening the pressure differential caused by the decrease in pressure at the primary headspace causes at least one of the beverage and gas in the secondary chamber to be ejected by way of the restricted orifice into the beverage of the primary
45   chamber and said ejection causes gas in the solution to be evolved and form, or assist in the formation of, a head of froth on the beverage.

2.   A package as claimed in claim 1 in which the container has a normal upstanding condition with an
50   openable top and said secondary chamber has an upwardly extending side wall or a bottom wall within which said restricted orifice is located.

3.   A packaged as claimed in either claim 1 or claim 2 in which with the pressures within the
55   primary and secondary chambers substantially at equilibrium the restricted orifice is located below the depth of the beverage within the secondary chamber.

4.   A package as claimed in any one of the preced-
60   ing claims wherein the secondary chamber comprises a hollow and discrete insert within the container.

5.   A package as claimed in claim 4 in which the insert floats or is suspended in the beverage in the
65   primary chamber and means is provided for locating

the restricted orifice below the surface of the beverage in the primary chamber.

6.   A package as claimed in claim 5 in which the insert is weighted or loaded to locate the restricted
70   orifice below the surface of the beverage in the primary chamber.

7.   A package as claimed in claim 4 wherein means is provided for retaining the insert at a predetermined position within the container.
75   8.   A package as claimed in claim 7 wherein the container has a normal upstanding condition with an openable top and said insert is located at or towards the bottom of said container.

9.   A package as claimed in either claim 7 or claim
80   8 wherein the insert comprises a hollow pod or envelope having means thereon for retaining it in position within the container.

10.   A package as claimed in claim 9 wherein the retaining means comprise flexible tab means which
85   engage a side wall of the container to retain the insert.

11.   A package as claimed in any one of claims 4 to 10 wherein the insert comprises a hollow moulding.

12.   A package as claimed in claim 11 when
90   appendant to claim 10 in which the container has a side wall and the moulding is substantially cylindrical with radially extending tabs engaging the wall of the container.

13.   A package as claimed in any one of claims 4 to
95   12 in which the container has a base on which the insert is located and said restricted orifice is located in an upwardly extending side wall of the insert spaced from said base.

14.   A package as claimed in any one of the pre-
100   ceding claims in which the beverage has in solution therewith at least one of carbon dioxide gas and inert gas (which latter term includes nitrogen).

15.   A package as claimed in claim 14 in which the beverage is saturated or supersaturated with said
105   gas or gases.

16.   A package as claimed in any one of the preceding claims in which the container is in the form of a can, bottle or carton.

17.   A package as claimed in any one of the pre-
110   ceding claims in which the restricted orifice comprises a circular aperture having a diameter in the range of 0.02 to 0.25 centimetres.

18.   A package as claimed in any one of the preceding claims and comprising a fermented beverage
115   having in solution therewith carbon dioxide in the range 0.8 to 1.8 vols/vol (1.46 to 3.29 grams/litre) and nitrogen in the range 1.5% to 3.5% vols/vol.

19.   A beverage package substantially as herein described with reference to the accompanying illust-
120   rative drawings.

20.   A method of packaging a beverage having gas in solution therewith which comprises providing a container with a primary chamber and a secondary chamber of which the volume of the secondary
125   chamber is less than that of the primary chamber and with a restricted orifice through which the secondary chamber communicates with the primary chamber, and charging and sealing the primary chamber with the beverage to contain the gas in solution and to
130   form a primary headspace in the primary chamber,

and charging the secondary chamber with beverage derived from the primary chamber by way of said restricted orifice to form a secondary headspace in the secondary chamber whereby the pressures in both
5 the primary and secondary chambers are at equilibrium and gaseous pressures in both the primary and secondary headspaces are at a pressure greater than atmospheric so that, when the container is broached to open the primary headspace to atmos-
10 pheric pressure, the pressure differential caused by the decrease in pressure at the primary headspace causes at least one of the beverage and gas in the secondary chamber to be ejected into the beverage of the primary chamber by way of said restricted ori-
15 fice and the said ejection causes gas to be evolved from solution in the beverage in the primary chamber to form, or assist in the formation of, a head of froth on the beverage.
    21.   A method as claimed in claim 20 which com-
20 prises subjecting the sealed container to a heating and cooling cycle whereby gas within the secondary chamber is caused to expand and eject by way of the restricted orifice into the primary chamber and subsequently to contract and create a low pressure ef-
25 fect in the secondary chamber relative to the primary chamber to draw beverage from the primary chamber into the secondary chamber by way of said restricted orifice.
    22.   A method as claimed in claim 21 in which the
30 heating and cooling cycle comprises pasteurisation of the beverage.
    23.   A method as claimed in any one of claims 20 to 22 in which the container has an upstanding condition with an openable top and which comprises
35 locating the restricted orifice within an upwardly extending side wall or bottom wall of the secondary chamber.
    24.   A method as claimed in any one of claims 20 to 23 which comprises charging the secondary
40 chamber with beverage from the primary chamber to the extent that the restricted orifice is located below the depth of beverage in the secondary chamber.
    25.   A method as claimed in any one of claims 20
45 to 23 which comprises forming the secondary chamber by a discrete hollow insert located within the primary chamber of the container.
    26.   A method as claimed in claim 25 in which the hollow insert is to float or be suspended in the bever-
50 age in the primary chamber and which comprises loading or weighting the insert to locate the restricted orifice below the surface of the beverage in the primary chamber.
    27.   A method as claimed in claim 25 which com-
55 prises retaining the insert at a predetermined position within the container.
    28.   A method as claimed in any one of claims 25 to 27 which comprises forming the hollow insert having the restricted orifice in a wall thereof and loc-
60 ating the insert within the primary chamber prior to the charging and sealing of the primary chamber.
    29.   A method as claimed in any one of claims 25 to 28 which comprises forming the hollow insert by blow moulding.
65   30.   A method as claimed in claim 29 which com-

prises blow moulding the hollow insert with gas for dissolution in the beverage so that said gas is sealed within the secondary chamber, and forming said restricted orifice in the wall of the insert immediately
70 prior to locating the insert in the primary chamber.
    31.   A method as claimed in claim 30 which comprises sealing said gas in the secondary chamber at atmospheric pressure or at a pressure slightly greater than atmospheric.
75   32.   A method as claimed in any one of claims 25 to 31 which comprises forming the restricted orifice in the hollow insert by laser boring, drilling or punching.
    33.   A method as claimed in any one of claims 25
80 to 32 in which, prior to it being sealed, the container has an upstanding condition with an open top through which the primary chamber is charged with beverage and which comprises locating the insert through said open top to provide the secondary
85 chamber within the container.
    34.   A method as claimed in claim 33 when appendant to claim 27 which comprises press fitting the insert within the container so that during its location the insert engages with a side wall of the container to
90 be retained in position.
    35.   A method as claimed in any one of claims 20 to 34 which comprises, prior to sealing the primary chamber, purging the primary head space to exclude air.
95   36.   A method as claimed in any one of claims 20 to 35 in which the gas comprises at least one of carbon dioxide gas and inert gas (which latter term includes nitrogen).
    37.   A method as claimed in claim 36 in which the
100 beverage is fermented and has in solution carbon dioxide in the range 0.8 to 1.8 vols/vol (1.46 to 3.29 grams/litre) and nitrogen in the range 1.5% to 3.5% vols/vol.
    38.   A method of packaging a beverage as
105 claimed in claim 20 and substantially as herein described.
    39.   A beverage when packaged by the method as claimed in any one of claims 20 to 38.

110

Printed for Her Majesty's Stationery Office by
Croydon Printing Company (UK) Ltd, 4/87, D8991685.
Published by The Patent Office, 25 Southampton Buildings, London, WC2A 1AY,
from which copies may be obtained.

Summary

The grant of a patent brings a limited monopoly which can be justified on a number of grounds, such as a reward for ingenuity or to provide an incentive to bring new products to the marketplace. It could also be said that an inventor should have a property right in relation to his invention.

The monopoly rights under patents may be abused by anti-competitive practices or by the too liberal grant of patents being used by patent trolls whose only form of exploiting their patents is to threaten others with litigation unless substantial payment is made. This takes advantage of the fact that patent litigation is notoriously expensive.

Patent and IP strategies are used by major companies to maximise their protection and the advantage derived from their patents and IP rights.

Obtaining a patent can be a fairly complex process especially in determining the state of the art and in terms of drafting the specification and the patent claims. The latter, when interpreted by reference to the description and any drawings contained in the specification, define the monopoly afforded by the patent. Patent claims must:

● define the matter for which protection is sought;
● be clear and concise;
● be supported by the description;
● relate to a single invention or a group of inventions having a single inventive concept.

Patent agents are skilled at drafting patent claims and specifications. Great care must be taken so as not to limit the monopoly by the language used nor to claim too widely as to include material which is already part of the state of the art. Another important factor is that there must be full disclosure such that a person skilled in the relevant art could, on reading the specification and claims, put the invention into effect.

Basic patent procedure is as follows:

● file the application (there may be a claim to the priority of an earlier application);
● file claims (if not filed with the application);
● preliminary examination and search after which a search report is issued;
● 'A' publication;
● substantive examination;
● grant and 'B' publication.

Patents may be renewed annually after the first four years to a maximum of 20 years. A proprietor may apply for restoration of a lapsed patent (failure to renew within six months of the renewal date).

Amendments may be made post-grant but must not disclose added matter. An amendment may cut down the scope of the patent but must not extend it.

Before grant of a patent, a divisional application may be made by dividing out one or more claims and making a separate application in respect of them.

Discussion questions

1 If the patent system was abolished throughout Europe, without prejudice to other forms of intellectual property rights, what do you think the effects would be (a) in the short term and (b) in the longer term? Consider this from the perspective of large manufacturing companies, SMEs and start-up companies, investors, inventors and the public at large.

2 Discuss the pros and cons of a unified European patent system compared to the current national and EPC systems.

Selected further reading

Fisher, M., 'The case that launched a thousand writs, or all that is dross? Re-Darcy v Allen: the case of monopolies' [2010] *Intellectual Property Quarterly*, 356 (a detailed and authoritative look at this landmark case on monopolies).

Intellectual Property Office, *Patents: Basic Facts*, 2011 Revision (useful overview of patents including information about the application process). Available at: **http://www.ipo.gov.uk/p-basicfacts.pdf**. The UK IPO website has more information about patents and is worth browsing.

Poore, A., 'The European Union patent system: off course or on the rocks?', [2011] *European Intellectual Property Review*, 409 (comments on a recent decision by the EU Court of Justice holding that a European patent systems is incompatible with the EU Treaties and looks at the problems a unitary patent system has faced and will face in the future and questions whether a unitary system is feasible).

Requirements for patentability   12

Introduction

The long title to the Patents Act 1977 includes the aim of giving effect to certain international conventions on patents. The influence of the European Patent Convention ('EPC'), signed in Munich in 1973, is evident in the basic requirement for patentability. Article 52(1) EPC states:

> European patents shall be granted for any new inventions, in all fields of technology, which are susceptible of industrial application, which are new and which involve an inventive step.[1]

The Patents Act 1977 s 1(1) requires the following conditions to be satisfied for a patent to be granted for an invention:

(a) the invention is new;
(b) it involves an inventive step;
(c) it is capable of industrial application; and
(d) the grant of a patent for it is not excluded by subsections (2) and (3) or section 4A below.[2]

Further provisions apply in relation to biotechnological inventions under Schedules A1 and A2. For example, para 3 of Schedule A2 gives a list of things which are not patentable inventions including the human body, gene sequences and processes for cloning humans. It is strange that section 1(1) which sets out the conditions for the grant of a patent contains no reference to Schedule A2.

The similarities are even more pronounced when the exceptions in s 1(2) and (3) are compared to the equivalent provisions in the EPC. Given the influence of the EPC on UK patent law, where appropriate, references will be made to the Convention and to judgments of the Boards of Appeal of the European Patent Office ('EPO') in Munich. The judgments are of persuasive authority and will normally be followed by UK judges.[3] Congruity in the international development of patent law is seen as being of great importance. Indeed, the Patents Act 1977 s 130(7) states that a number of important provisions of the Act are declared to have, as nearly as practicable, the same effect in the UK as the corresponding provisions of the EPC, the Community Patent Convention ('CPC', now better described as a unitary European patent system) and the Patent Cooperation Treaty ('PCT').[4] In a case prior to the 1977 Act, Lord Parker CJ said, in terms of Australian and New Zealand decisions:

> Finally one cannot shut from one's mind the desirability of having a homogeneous development of the law in all countries which have adopted our system of patent legislation.

---

1 The reference to 'all fields of technology' was inserted into the 13th edition of the Convention, 1 July 2007.

2 The Patent Regulations 2000, SI 2000/2037 modified s 1(3). Part of the previous exception is restated in modified form in new s 1(3) (prohibiting the patenting of inventions contrary to public policy or morality) whilst old s 1(3)(b) (preventing the patenting of animal or plant varieties) has been replaced by substantially modified provisions in new Sch A2 to the Act. Section 4A (methods of treatment or diagnosis) was inserted by the Patents Act 2004.

3 And sometimes distinguished!

4 Those provisions deal with, *inter alia*, patentability, infringement, burdens of proof and extent of invention. Other provisions should, if possible and appropriate, also be construed so as to conform to the European Patent Convention.

That desirability must result in a tendency of our Court to follow those decisions if it is possible to do so.[5]

In the light of the UK's membership of the EPC, the same now holds true in respect of decisions of the EPO. The same applies as regards the PCT and, if it ever sees the light of day, decisions relating to the CPC.[6] The desirability of other provisions of the Patents Act 1977, in addition to those expressly mentioned in s 130(7), also being construed in line with the EPC and the PCT where they may properly be so construed was highlighted by Neuberger J in *Kirin-Amgen Inc's Patent*.[7]

In *Grimme Landmaschinenfabrik GmbH & Co KG v Scott*,[8] Jacobs and Etherton LJJ stressed the importance of looking at, and where possible following, important decisions in other countries which are Contracting Parties of the EPO. In their joint judgment, they said (at para 80):

> Broadly we think the principle in our courts – and indeed that in the courts of other member states – should be to try to follow the reasoning of an important decision in another country. Only if the court of one state is convinced that the reasoning of a court in another member state is erroneous should it depart from a point that has been authoritatively decided there. Increasingly that has become the practice in a number of countries, particularly in the important patent countries of France, Germany, Holland and England and Wales. Nowadays we refer to each other's decisions with a frequency which would have been hardly imaginable even 20 years ago. And we do try to be consistent where possible.

The importance of the decisions of the Boards of Appeal at the EPO is now well established in assisting judges in domestic courts interpreting national patent laws. However, it must be noted that there is no doctrine of *stare decisis* at the EPO and a submission by counsel that a statement made in a Board of Appeal is *obiter* does not necessarily carry the same weight as it would do in relation to an earlier English case.[9] Indeed, however persuasive a decision of the Boards of Appeal at the EPO, it can never be binding on an English court which may be bound by a previous decision of an English court which conflicts with that decision. In *Aerotel Ltd v Telco Holdings Ltd and Macrossan's Patent Application*[10] the Court of Appeal was bound by previous decisions of that court and was unable to follow conflicting decisions of the EPO Boards of Appeal, leading to an unfortunate disparity between case law in England and at the EPO. These developments are discussed later in this chapter in the section on computer programs.

Sufficiency

Before looking at the basic requirements for the grant of a patent, an application will be refused if the specification does not disclose the invention in a manner which is clear enough and complete enough for the invention to be performed by a person skilled in the art. This is a requirement of s 14(3) and failure to comply means that the invention is insufficiently described. This is to prevent applicants holding back some vital information needed to put the invention into effect, as alluded to in the previous chapter. Insufficiency is also a ground for invalidity of a patent.[11] Section 14(3) is the equivalent of Article 83 EPC which states that, 'The European patent application shall disclose the invention in a manner sufficiently clear and complete for it to be carried out by a person skilled in the art'.

Case law of the EPO Boards of Appeal shows that Article 83 requires that a person skilled in the art must be able to put the claimed invention into effect. In Case T422/99 *NYCOMED IMAGING AS/Method of terminal steam sterilisaton*,[12] the Board of Appeal held (at para 3.2) that Article 83 can only be satisfied:

5 *Swift's Application* [1962] RPC 37. In *Pharmaceutical Management Agency Ltd v The Commissioner of Patents* [1999] RPC 752, the High Court of New Zealand followed the European approach to Swiss-type claims (*see* Chapter 11, p 406), commenting on the desirability of following patent law in other jurisdictions providing it was not inconsistent with New Zealand patent law.

6 Although the CPC has never been brought into force, it is still relevant when construing certain provisions of the Patents Act 1977 because of s 130(7). Eventually, if it ever comes to fruition, it may be known as the unitary European patent.

7 [2002] RPC 43 at para 47 per Neuberger J. In *Unilin Beheer NV v Berry Floor NV* [2005] FSR 6, Jacob LJ said where a provision in the Patents Act 1977 was to be interpreted to mean the same as in the EPC, it was best to work from the Convention itself. The manner in which these provisions had been set out in the Act had been by way of an unhelpful rewrite rather than a copy-out.

8 [2011] FSR 7.

9 See Laddie J in *Woolard's Application* [2002] RPC 39.

10 [2007] RPC 7.

11 Section 72(1)(c).

12 26 January 2005.

(i) if at least one way is clearly indicated in the patent specification enabling the skilled person to carry out the invention, and

(ii) if the disclosure allows the invention to be performed in the whole area claimed, and

(iii) without undue burden, applying common general knowledge.

A claimed invention may be sufficiently disclosed even if some degree of trial and error experimentation is required to put it into effect in Case T1743/06 *INEOS/amorphous silicas and oral compositions*,[13] provided it is not undue experimentation. An example of undue experimentation is where a range of substances is claimed and trial and error experimentation is needed to make each and every substance claimed.

In *Novartis AG* v *Johnson & Johnson Medical Ltd*,[14] the Court of Appeal confirmed that a patent for extended wear contact lenses should be revoked for insufficiency. Jacob LJ said that the instructions contained in the patent did not enable the skilled person, lacking inventive skill, to perform the invention over the whole area claimed. He also said that the fact that the defendant had not carried out experiments to test to see if the invention could be put into effect was irrelevant. He was somewhat scathing of the patent, saying (at para 92):

> It is no more than a 'if you can find it, we claim it' patent. Its avaricious ambit coupled with its failure to provide any help makes it nothing but a hazard to those conducting research into extended wear contact lenses. It should be revoked in its entirety.

Determining sufficiency requires a two-step approach.[15] First, the invention must be identified, along with what it is claimed that the skilled person is enabled to do. Second, the specification must be examined to see whether it does enable the skilled person to carry it out. Where a principle of general application is disclosed elements of a claim may be stated in general terms and this may be sufficiently enabled if it can be expected that the invention will work with anything that falls within that general principle. The example given by Lord Hoffmann in *Kirin-Amgen Inc* v *Hoechst Marion Roussel Ltd*[16] was a reference to a requirement of 'connecting means'. This would be enabled (and not lacking for insufficiency) '. . . if the invention can reasonably be expected to work with any means of connection'. The applicant does not have to show that he has experimented with all possible means of connection. Where a claim is broad enough to cover two methods, if the skilled person would quickly realise that one would work and the other would not, the disclosure would still meet the requirement of sufficiency. In *Kirin-Amgen*, it was held that the specification did not tell the skilled person whether any given urinary erythropoietin would bring his recombinant erythropoietin within the claim – all he could do was guess and, if the specification did not tell him, it was insufficient.

A patent specification must not merely disclose a novel product or process but it must be an enabling disclosure and should support that which the teaching in the specification promises to deliver, as indicated by Lord Hoffmann *supra*. Where a claim is to a class of compounds, it must enable the invention to be performed to the full extent of the monopoly which is claimed[17] and, if the invention is to a selection of certain compounds claimed to secure some advantage or avoid some disadvantage, it must contain sufficient information to make the compounds as well as describing the advantage or how the disadvantage is to be avoided.[18]

The amount of work performed by a skilled person who attempts to carry out the invention is not irrelevant and, where it is considerable, this might suggest that the claim in question is insufficient. In *Halliburton Energy Services Inc* v *Smith International (North Sea) Ltd*[19] the alleged invention was for a method of computer simulation for the design of drill bits. Working from the specification, an extraordinary amount of work would be required to put the invention into effect. Furthermore, the basic equation underlying

13 27 November 2009.

14 [2011] ECC 10.

15 Per Lord Hoffmann in *Kirin-Amgen Inc* v *Hoechst Marion Roussel Ltd* [2005] RPC 9 at para 103.

16 [2005] RPC 9 at paras 112–113.

17 *Biogen Inc* v *Medeva plc* [1997] RPC 1 per Lord Hoffmann at page 48, overruling some previous decisions in the Patents Court where it was held that, where a range of compounds is claimed, the invention was sufficiently disclosed if the skilled person could make one embodiment.

18 *Pharmacia Corp* v *Merck & Co Inc* [2002] RPC 41 per Aldous LJ at paras 50 and 56.

19 [2006] EWCA Civ 1715.

the proposed computer model was shown to be wrong. If it is not possible for a skilled person to determine a vital parameter, such as the quantity of a compound to be used in making the invention, then the disclosure cannot be described as an enabling disclosure.[20]

Sometimes, where a range of compounds is claimed or an ambiguous word is used in a claim, there may be what is termed a 'puzzle at the edge of the claim';[21] that is, where there may be examples within the claim where the invention does not do what it promises to deliver or where the limits of the claim are imprecise. For example, in *Unilin Beheer NV v Berry Floor NV*,[22] in attacking one of the claims, it was argued that if the claim in question, relating to a snap-together flooring system, typically made of MDF, provided for a little bit of play between the floor units, this made it impossible to know how much play took one outside the claim. Jacob LJ rejected this, saying that, whatever the language, it is almost always possible to set a puzzle at the edge of the claim. In *British Thomson-Houston Company Ltd v Corona Lamp Works Ltd*,[23] the claim was to a tungsten filament lamp which required it to be of 'large diameter'. The House of Lords rejected an argument that the claim was ambiguous to such an extent that it was impossible for the skilled person to decide when the claim had been infringed. Although it might have been possible to carry out experiments using different diameters of filament so that, in some cases at the outer edges, the advantage taught by the specification evaporated, Lord Shaw said (at page 92):

> . . . in applying an invention within its successful ambit it is expected that those operating the manufacture will be honestly looking, not to failure, but for success in the range for which the principle is applied.

Therefore, the question of sufficiency has to be seen through the eyes of the skilled person who is seeking success rather than failure and, although lawyers can think of puzzles at the edge of a claim, skilled persons are interested in practicalities, not puzzles.[24] To this extent, the requirement that an invention must be capable of being performed across the entire range of what is claimed is mitigated. Where there is uncertainty at the 'edge of the claim', it might be unrealistic and disproportionate to hold a claim invalid for insufficiency but if an alleged infringement fell within the fuzzy edge, the need for certainty for third parties would require a conclusion of non-infringement.[25]

Whether one product in a class or all products in a class can be claimed depends on how the applicant for a patent is able to describe that product or products. Lord Hoffmann summed this up in *Biogen Inc v Medeva plc*[26] where he said (at p 49):

> . . . if the patentee has hit upon a new product which has a beneficial effect but cannot demonstrate that there is a common principle by which that effect will be shared by other products of the same class, he will be entitled to a patent for that product and not for the class, even though some may subsequently turn out to have the same beneficial effect . . . on the other hand, if he has disclosed a beneficial property which is common to a class, he will be entitled to a patent for all products of that class (assuming them to be new) even though he has not himself made more than one or two of them.

The manufacture of a known product by a new method of manufacture does not make the product so obtained new, although a patent may be obtained for the new manufacturing process. The fact that a product identical to an existing product made by a new process is not novel is not just a rule of practice, it is a proposition of law.[27] Where a new product cannot be satisfactorily defined by reference to its composition, it may be adequately defined by describing its process of manufacture. However, where a compound is know to exist but has not been isolated, a claim to a method of isolating the compound gives a monopoly to the compound even though other ways of making it are discovered subsequently.

In *Generics (UK) Ltd v H Lundbeck A/S*,[28] Lundbeck had a patent for the anti-depressant drug citalopram. The patent expired some years ago. Citalopram is an organic compound of a type known as a racemate, being a combination of two types of molecules in equal

20 *Mayne Pharma Ltd v Debiopharm SA* [2006] EWHC 1123 (Pat).

21 The phrase used by Sachs LJ in *General Tire & Rubber Co v Firestone Tyre & Rubber Co Ltd* [1972] RPC 457 at 511.

22 [2005] FSR 6 at para 32.

23 (1922) 39 RPC 49.

24 *Kirin-Amgen Inc v Transkaryotic Therapies Inc* [2003] RPC 3 at para 96.

25 Per Neuberger J in *Kirin-Amgen Inc v Roche Diagnostics GmbH* [2002] RPC 1 at paras 444–452.

26 [1997] RPC 1.

27 Per Lord Hoffmann in *Kirin-Amgen Inc v Hoechst Marion Roussel Ltd* [2005] RPC 9 at para 98. Aldous LJ had suggested this was a rule of practice in *Kirin-Amgen Inc v Transkaryotic Therapies Inc* [2003] RPC 3 at para 30.

28 [2009] RPC 13.

proportions. These molecules have exactly the same chemical formula and structure but are mirror images of each other. These types of molecules are known as enantiomers and are distinguished from each other by different conventions, one of which is to prefix them with a (+) or (–). It has long since been known that the two enantiomers can have different properties and one may have a therapeutic effect whilst the other has some undesirable side-effect[29] or may inhibit the therapeutic effect of the first enantiomer, as was found to be the case with citalopram. Almost the whole of the therapeutic effect of citalopram resulted from the (+)-enantiomer and the (–)-enantiomer inhibited this effect. Therefore, a drug made from the (+)-enantiomer alone was more effective.

Having found a process by which the (+)-enantiomer could be isolated and established that it was much more effective than citalopram, Lundbeck obtained a patent in respect of it. The patent claimed the (+)-enantiomer, known as escitalopram, a compound comprising it as an active ingredient and a method for making it. Generics applied for revocation of the patent on a number of grounds. The only ground relied on in the House of Lords was that of insufficiency. Section 72(1)(c) of the Patents Act 1977 states that a patent may be revoked if:

> the specification of the patent does not disclose the invention clearly enough and completely enough for it to be performed by a person skilled in the art.

This mirrors s 14(3) which requires that the specification must disclose the invention in a manner which is clear enough and complete enough for the invention to be performed by a person skilled in the art.[30] (It is worth considering the EPC provisions on sufficiency under Articles 83 and 84.) At first instance[31], Kitchen J said that the inventive step was finding how to separate the enantiomers and the technical contribution was not to find a new product but to find a way of making the product. He thought that obtaining the purified enantiomers was an obviously desirable goal. As the patent specification only described one way of making the product, if the patent effectively covered all ways of making it, that would give a monopoly disproportionate to the technical contribution. Relying on *Biogen Inc* v *Medeva plc*, he said (at para 267):

> The first person to find a way of achieving an obviously desirable goal is not permitted to monopolise every other way of doing so. Claims 1 and 3 are too broad. They extend beyond any technical contribution made by Lundbeck.

The Court of Appeal, with Lord Hoffmann sitting in that court, reversed the finding that the product claims should be revoked as lacking sufficiency.[32]

In the House of Lords, Lord Neuberger decided to consider whether Kitchen J's conclusion was justified on the basis of any principle or authority apart from *Biogen Inc* v *Medeva* and then to consider if it was justified on the basis of *Biogen*. Lord Neuberger said that he could not discern any statutory provision (including in the EPC) which supported a proposition that, once it is established that a product is novel and non-obvious, and the specification sufficiently explains to a person skilled in the art how to make it, the claim is nevertheless bad because there may be other ways of making it which are not taught by the patent. As Lord Oliver explained in *Asahi* a claim would not be supported by the description for the purposes of s 14(5)(c) unless it contained sufficient material to enable the specification to constitute the enabling disclosure as required by s 14(3). In the present case, the description clearly set out a method of making the (+)-enantiomer and clearly satisfied s 14(3).

Although 'technical contribution' is not a term from the statute, the monopoly should be assessed by the technical contribution taught by the patent. In this case, the technical contribution was to make available for the first time a product which had not previously been made available. Thus, Lundbeck was entitled to claim the product as such. This is in line with the thinking at the EPO and, in T595/90 *KAWASAKI/grain-orientated silicon sheet*[33] (at 43), the Technical Board of Appeal said:

29 Thalidomide is a notorious example.

30 The requirement in s 14(5)(c) that the claim or claims must be supported by the description is not mentioned in s 72 on revocation which sets exhaustively the grounds for revocation. However, it seems to have been accepted in the House of Lords that the requirements of s 14(3) include those of s 14(5) (c) – see *Asahi Kasei Kogyo KK's Application* [1991] RPC 485 and *Biogen Inc* v *Medeva plc* [1997] RPC 1.

31 *Generics (UK) Ltd* v *H Lundbeck A/S* [2007] RPC 32.

32 *H Lundbeck A/S* v *Generics (UK) Ltd* [2008] RPC 19.

33 [1995] EPOR 36.

. . . it is the view of the Board that a product which can be envisaged as such with all characteristics determining its identity together with its properties in use, that is, an otherwise obvious entity, may become nevertheless non-obvious and claimable as such, if there is no known way or applicable (analogy) method in the art to make it and the claimed methods for its preparation are therefore the first to achieve this in an inventive manner.

Apart from *Biogen*, Lord Neuberger accepted that, by finding one way of making a new product, a person can obtain a monopoly for that product. Furthermore, he said (at para 90):

Further, where (as here) the product is a known *desideratum*, it can be said (as Lord Walker pointed out) that the invention is all the more creditable, as it is likely that there has been more competition than where the product has not been thought of. The role of fortuity in patent law cannot be doubted: it is inevitable, as in almost any area of life. Luck as well as skill often determines, for instance, who is first to file, whether a better product or process is soon discovered, or whether an invention turns out to be valuable. Further, while the law must be principled, it must also be clear and consistent.

At first instance, Kitchen J based his finding of insufficiency largely on Lord Hoffmann's judgment in *Biogen*. However, *Biogen* was distinguishable from the present case as it concerned a product-by-process claim but related to a wide class of products. In the Court of Appeal, Jacob LJ thought that Kitchen J had extracted too broad a principle from *Biogen*. Counsel for Generics based his challenge on sufficiency mainly on a number of passages from Lord Hoffmann's judgment in *Biogen*. Lord Neuberger dealt with three of them (he said his observations applied equally to the others). They were as follows:

1 If the claims include a number of discrete methods or products, the patentee must enable the invention to be performed in respect of each of them. However, in the present case, the claim is to a single product and the product is clearly enabled by the teaching in the patent.
2 The issue is not whether the claimed invention could deliver the goods, but whether the claims cover other ways in which they might be delivered: ways which owe nothing to the teaching of the patent or any principle which it disclosed. But in *Biogen*, the patent disclosed one way in which the products might be delivered but the claim covered other ways in which they might be delivered. The claim was very different to the claim in the present case which was a claim to a 'simple' product.
3 The extent of the monopoly should not exceed the technical contribution to the art made by the invention as described in the specification. In the context of a simple product claim, especially where the claim is to a single chemical product, the technical contribution is the product itself (at least in the absence of special factors). Lord Neuberger went on to say that '. . . technical contribution can often be equated with non-obvious novelty – what is new to the art and not obvious is really another way of identifying the technical contribution' (at para 95).

It may be possible to overcome objections based on insufficiency by amendment but, assuming the specification does adequately disclose the invention, the basic requirements set out in ss 1 to 4 must then be satisfied.

Basic requirements

The basic statement of the requirements for patentability – that is novelty, inventive step and industrial application – followed by the exclusions from patentability, provides a good framework in which to explore the legal consequences and meaning of these words and phrases. The first point which must be made, however, is that the Patents Act 1977 contains no definition of what an invention is. This is perhaps because those responsible for drafting the Act felt either that the task was too daunting, or that a definition might be later seen as sterile and a fetter on the development of the law in tune with technological development. Another explanation is that they did not really know with any certainty. Many other common words from the world of technology cause similar problems: for example, 'computer' or 'computer program'. A dictionary definition of 'invention' might talk in terms of an imaginative design, or product or innovation or something produced for the first time. Schmookler gives a more rigorous definition and subdivides inventions into process inventions and product inventions.[34] The former are new ways of producing something old and the latter are old ways of producing something new. Every invention can thus be considered to be a 'new combination of pre-existing knowledge which satisfies some want'.[35] On the other hand, innovation can be said to be the first use of an invention.[36] In practice, the lack of definition causes few problems because the basic requirements of novelty, inventive step and industrial application, as defined in the statute and as interpreted by the courts, in most cases produce an effective and practical explanation of 'invention' for the purposes of patent law. Nevertheless, there may be a number of occasions when the meaning of 'invention' may be important, for example, in deciding who is the inventor and, prima facie, entitled to a patent.

The meaning of the word 'invention' in a particular patent may be determined from interpreting the claims. However, in the case of an application for a patent, there may be no claims submitted initially and the invention may be determined from an objective consideration of the inventive concept as understood from a reading of the application as a whole. Even where claims are submitted with the application as first filed, they may be over-broad and misleading.[37] It is clear that 'invention' is a term of art in patent law and is used in a special way which may vary according to the particular context. For example, it may not be what the applicant claims it to be (which may turn out not to be patentable at all) or it may be excluded from the grant of a patent, however new and non-obvious it may be, such as a method of doing business, or it may be an idea that cannot be brought to fruition in practical terms, such as a perpetual motion machine. It may be that the context requires consideration of the person or persons who devised the invention or whether it involves an inventive step. It is tempting to describe an invention as a non-obvious advance in technology but this replaces one imprecise test with one even more imprecise.[38]

The word 'invention' may be equated, to some extent, with the requirement for industrial application. In Case T854/90 *IBM/Card Reader*[39] the applicant had claimed a method of allowing any machine-readable bank card or credit card to be used by any card-reading machine to carry out any transactions. The Technical Board of Appeal of the EPO held that the method was not patentable as the use of the word 'inventions' in Article 52 of the EPC required that the claimed subject matter had a technical character and, in principle, was industrially applicable. The card was, in effect, equivalent to an application form, and the method involved (the user presenting the card to the machine) was part of a business operation as such. The Board further confirmed that the presence of technical means to carry out a business activity does not mean that the business activity has a technical character and therefore is an invention.[40]

The scope and nature of the invention as claimed must be determined from the claims as interpreted by the description. This is made clear by s 125(1) and the Protocol on Article 69 of the EPC (which concerns the interpretation of patent claims).[41]

Section 1 of the 1977 Act requires that there must be an invention, and the exclusions to patentability in s 1(2) and (3) of the Act do not limit things that are not inventions to the particular exclusions specified.[42] In *Genentech Inc's Patent*[43] Mustill LJ said (at 262):

> . . . the question whether the claim discloses anything which can be described as an invention must be answered in the affirmative before compliance with paragraphs (a)–(d) becomes relevant [s 1(1)(a)–(d)].

34 This is, indeed, the approach taken by the Patents Act 1977. The distinction is quite clearly seen in s 60, on infringement. Unless otherwise stated, in this chapter, statutory references are to the Patents Act 1977.

35 Schmookler, J. (1986) *Invention and Economic Growth*, Harvard University Press, Chapter 1.

36 Dutton, H.I. (1984) *The Patent System and Inventive Activity During the Industrial Revolution, 1750–1852*, Manchester University Press, p 9.

37 *Markem Corporation v Zipher Ltd (No 1)* [2004] RPC 10 at para 64 per Judge Fysh QC, sitting as a judge of the High Court.

38 *See*, for example, Peter Prescott QC's discussion of the problem in *CFPH LLC's Application* [2006] RPC 5.

39 [1994] EPOR 89.

40 Furthermore, the claimed invention lacked inventive step.

41 Per Hobhouse LJ in *Biogen Inc v Medeva plc* [1995] RPC 25 at 87, disapproving the suggestion of Aldous J that the invention was to be determined by the wording of the claim independently of the description in *Chiron Corporation v Organon Teknika Ltd (No 3)* [1994] FSR 202.

42 *See Lux Traffic Controls Ltd v Pike Signals Ltd* [1993] RPC 107, where it was held, *inter alia*, that the Patents Act 1977 s 1(2) comprised a non-exhaustive list of non-patentable things and a method of controlling traffic as such was not patentable.

43 [1989] RPC 147.

He went on to confirm that there will often be a substantial overlap between an objection on the basis that the thing claimed is not an invention and other objections, being lack of novelty, lack of inventive step, being incapable of industrial application or excluded by s 1(2) and (3).[44]

It is possible to apply for a single patent in relation to more than one invention if they are so linked as to form a single inventive concept.[45] This might be particularly relevant where the inventions concern a process and the product which results from putting the process into effect. In practice, this would normally cause little difficulty. However, if a claim is to a class of products, the claim might be invalid if some of the products cannot be made. In *May & Baker Ltd* v *Boots Pure Drug Co Ltd*[46] a claim to a class of 'sulpha-thiazole' products was amended to cover two specific products only as it was unlikely that all the class would have had the therapeutic properties claimed.

In *Biogen Inc* v *Medeva plc*[47] patents were granted in the EPO (designating the UK and other countries) concerning a vaccine for hepatitis B which had been genetically engineered. In an action for infringement, the defendant counterclaimed successfully for revocation on a number of grounds. The problem facing an applicant for a patent in respect of a range of products rather than a process was well stated by Hobhouse LJ (at 94):

> . . . [the claimants] could not make any claim to a process . . . if they had invented a process, they could also have claimed a monopoly over anything produced by that process. But they could not do this and had simply to claim the invention of products independently of the process by which they were produced. They wished to make the claim as wide as possible.[48]

However, the difficulty for the applicant is to take care not to claim more products than would actually display the claimed properties. It is no use claiming a vast range of products hoping to be able to show, later, that some or all of them conform. The applicant has a choice and if he wishes to claim a wide range of products of a class he must make a sufficiently wide disclosure. If he cannot make the appropriate disclosure, he is trying to claim more than he is entitled to.

Novelty

The invention must be new. It must not already have been available to the public. The question of novelty (whether the invention is new) has a special meaning assigned to it under the Patents Act 1977 s 2(1), which states that an invention is new if it 'does not form part of the state of the art'. Section 2(2) continues and describes the 'state of the art' as comprising all matter[49] made available to the public before the priority date of the invention whether by written or oral description, by use or in any other way.[50] At least one member of the public should be free in law and equity to use the invention. Disclosure to a person or persons in confidence does not invalidate a patent but disclosure to a single person in the absence of an express or implied obligation of confidence will destroy novelty even if that person chooses autonomously to keep it secret. *De facto* secrecy is not enough to preserve novelty.[51] In an unusual case, *Folding Attic Stairs Ltd* v *The Loft Stairs Company Ltd*,[52] a photographer and government Minister were invited into a factory to see a prototype of a folding loft stair. They were not under any obligation of confidence. Peter Prescott QC, sitting as a deputy judge of the High Court, held that there was no irrebuttable presumption of law that information that is capable of being perceived by persons who are on private premises is in fact perceived by them, if the circumstances are such as to make it unlikely that those persons were interested in the subject matter. This must be contrasted with a situation where the prototype was left in a public place.

44 Old s 1(3) excluded methods of treatment or diagnosis now restated with modification in s 4A. New s 1(3) excludes inventions, the commercial exploitation of which would be contrary to public policy or morality.

45 Patents Act 1977 s 14(5).

46 (1950) 67 RPC 23.

47 [1995] RPC 25.

48 For a criticism of this case and its apparent contradiction of the decision of the European Patent Office which found the patent valid, *see* Reid, B.C. 'Biogen in the EPO: the advantage of scientific understanding' [1995] 2 EIPR 98. The House of Lords confirmed the Court of Appeal decision that the patent was invalid: [1997] RPC 1, discussed below, *see* pp 446–447.

49 Whether a product, a process, information about either, or anything else (in other words, anything!).

50 The phrase 'made available to the public' was used in the definition of 'published' in the Patents Act 1949 s 101 and should be given the same meaning: *PLG Research Ltd* v *Ardon International Ltd* [1993] FSR 197.

51 Per Floyd J in *MMI Research Ltd* v *Cellxion Ltd* [2009] EWHC 418 (Pat) citing with approval Case T1022/99 *Van Wonterghem/Dispositif de transmission*, 10 April 2001 before the Board of Appeal at the EPO.

52 [2009] FSR 24.

This would be novelty-destroying without actual evidence that an interested person actually examined it to see how it worked.

The state of the art includes matter contained in other patent applications having an earlier priority date. Therefore, novelty is really a question of whether the invention has been 'anticipated': for example, by a previous patent, or by publication or use. The anticipating patent, or publication could have occurred anywhere in the world as s 2(2) refers to public availability in 'the UK or elsewhere'. Whether publication in a limited circulation journal published in a remote part of some far off country would count is a moot point. Some sense of realism must be preserved and, under the 1949 Act, anticipatory matter did not include that which would not have been discovered during the course of a diligent search.[53]

A claim in a patent may be anticipated in two ways by the prior art: either where the prior art describes something that is within the scope of the claim such that it enables the invention as claimed to be worked, or where the inevitable result of carrying out what is described in the prior art falls within the claim.[54] An example of the former is where the prior art describes an industrial process, which is at the heart of what is claimed, and an example of the latter is where carrying out that prior art process necessarily results in a product or technical effect which is now claimed.

Anticipation requires an 'enabling disclosure' such that the prior art enables a person skilled in the art to put the invention into effect. However, disclosure and enablement are two separate concepts, both of which must be satisfied and each of which has its own separate rules, as confirmed by the House of Lords in *Synthon BV* v *SmithKline Beecham plc*.[55] Of course, in many cases, the two concepts merge, such as where the specification spells out what the invention is and how it may be put into effect. Problems occur in some fields of technology, particularly in relation to chemicals and pharmaceuticals. For example, the patent may claim an invention (disclosure) but inadequately describe how it is to be made or performed (a question of enablement). In *Synthon* v *SmithKline Beecham*, Lord Hoffmann said that it was important to distinguish between disclosure and enablement, something he claimed the Court of Appeal failed properly so to do, in reinstating the decision of Jacob J in the Patents Court where he held that the patent in suit ('Synthon') was invalid having been anticipated by an earlier application that had not been published until after the priority date.[56] Lord Hoffmann summarised two important cases on the subject of disclosure[57] by saying that the '. . . prior art must disclose subject-matter which, if performed, would necessarily result in an infringement of the patent'. It may be that the prior art expressly discloses the same invention so that there will be no question that the performance of the earlier invention would infringe but patent infringement does not require awareness of infringement. Lord Hoffmann referred to *Merrell Dow Pharmaceuticals Inc* v *H N Norton & Co Ltd*[58] where taking terfenadine by hay-fever sufferers inevitably entailed the making of the acid metabolite, the subject matter of the patent in suit, in their livers even though the author of the terfenadine patent was unaware of the production of the acid metabolite. Lord Hoffmann also stressed that prior disclosure must be construed as it would have been understood by the skilled person at the date of the disclosure and not in the light of the subsequent patent.

On the question of enablement, this must be viewed from the perspective of the ordinary skilled person, not someone of exceptional skill and knowledge or, in the words of Jacob J at first instance, a world champion.[59] Lord Hoffmann said that, once the subject matter of the invention has been disclosed, the question of whether it was enabled is to be answered by assuming that the person skilled in the art is prepared to carry out trial and error experiments to get the invention to work. Whether experimentation is assumed is a question of enablement not disclosure.

In determining whether an invention is enabled, it is reasonable to read the specification from the perspective of addressee of the specification, that is, a person skilled in the

53 *General Tire & Rubber Co* v *Firestone Tyre & Rubber Co Ltd* [1972] RPC 457 per Sachs LJ. Section 130(1) defines 'published' as being made available to the public (in the UK or elsewhere) and a document shall be taken to be published if it can be inspected as of right at any place in the UK by members of the public, whether on payment of a fee or not.

54 *Inhale Therapeutic Systems Inc* v *Quadrant Healthcare plc* [2002] RPC 21 per Laddie J at para 43.

55 [2006] RPC 10.

56 This was an example of the operation of s 2(3), anticipation by an earlier patent application which had not been published as at the priority date of the patent in suit.

57 Lord Westbury LC in *Hill* v *Evans* (1862) 31 LJ (NS) 457 and Sachs LJ in *General Tire & Rubber Co* v *Firestone Tyre & Rubber Co Ltd* [1972] RPC 457, in particular where he spoke of planting a flag at the precise destination before the patentee got there (at 486).

58 [1996] RPC 76.

59 *Synthon BV* v *Smithkline Beecham plc* [2003] RPC 33 at para 57.

art, who has common general knowledge which he may use to get the invention to work and even to recognise and rectify errors in the description of the invention. However, in applying this test, the skilled person does not make undue efforts in experimentation and certainly does not have inventive skills, nor does he have an awareness of the whole state of the art: Case T206/83 *ICI/Pyridine Herbicides*.[60]

If the prior disclosure enables the skilled person to perform the patented invention it does not matter if he does not know that he is working it. Lord Hoffmann again referred to *Merrell Dow* v *Norton* where the question of enablement '. . . turned on whether the disclosure enabled the skilled man to make terfenadine and feed it to hay-fever sufferers, not on whether it enabled him to make the acid metabolite' (being the inevitable result of treating hay-fever sufferers with terfenadine).

In *Synthon BV* v *SmithKline Beecham*, Lord Hoffmann found that the earlier application disclosed the invention in Synthon. As regards enablement, he said that there was no reason for disturbing the decision of Jacob J at first instance where he said that, although the earlier application specified an unsuitable solvent, the skilled person would have tried other solvents and produced the paroxetine methanesulfate crystals (the subject matter of claim 1 of Synthon, on which the remaining claims were dependent) within a reasonable time. The Synthon patent was, therefore, invalid having been anticipated by the earlier application. Finally, Lord Hoffmann confirmed that the test for enablement in s 2(2) and (3) is the same as the test for sufficiency in s 72(1)(c).[61]

Where a prior art document claims a combination of features, say A+B+C, whether there is also disclosure of A or B or C independently depends on substance not a formula. So held Jacob LJ in *Unilin Beheer NV* v *Berry Floor NV*[62] where he said that much depended on what the features actually are. In some cases, the invention is the idea of putting those features together but in other cases they are independent. However, in that case the relevant issue was not novelty, rather whether the patent in suit could claim priority from an earlier patent, although the principle should be the same for determining whether an invention is novel over the prior art.

Oral disclosures will anticipate a patent if they are in confidence, whether express or implied. In *Visx Inc* v *Nidek Co Ltd*,[63] the patents in suit related to laser apparatus used to alter the shape of the cornea to correct myopia, hyperopia and astigmatism. The defendant counterclaimed for revocation of the patents on the basis, *inter alia*, of a number of oral disclosures, including one alleged to have been made on a train journey. Neuberger J said that the burden of proof lies with the person alleging prior disclosure[64] but, in this case, the numerous alleged oral disclosures were either insufficient to anticipate the patents or the defendant had failed to show that they were not made in confidence.

The act or series of acts that make the invention available to the public does not have to be on a particularly wide scale.[65] Using an invention in public in one locality only will suffice to anticipate a patent. In *Windsurfing International Inc* v *Tabur Marine (Great Britain) Ltd*,[66] the Court of Appeal held that a 12-year-old boy, who built a sailboard and used it in public for a few weekends at a caravan site at Hayling Island in Hampshire, had effectively anticipated a later patent for a sailboard which was declared invalid for want of novelty (and also because it lacked an inventive step).

Under s 2(3), the state of the art includes matter in other patent applications published on or after the priority date of the invention being tested against the state of the art, provided the priority dates of those other applications are earlier. Patent applications are published 18 months after their priority dates, unless withdrawn, and this provision simply includes in the state of the art all those unpublished applications that have an earlier priority date. Thus, it is possible for a patent application to be pre-empted by material that cannot, at the time of making the application, be discovered or inspected by the applicant. In *Ranbaxy UK Ltd* v *Warner-Lambert Co*,[67] carrying out the invention described in a s 2(3) prior unpublished patent application would clearly fall within a claim of the patent application

60 [1986] EPOR 232. The Technical Board of Appeal of the EPO also made it clear that, normally, patent specifications are not part of the common general knowledge for the purposes of anticipation.

61 Citing two decisions of the EPO, Case T206/83 *ICI/Pyridine Herbicides* [1986] EPOR 232 and Case No T81/87 *Collaborative/Preprorennin* [1990] EPOR 361 in which it was confirmed that the test in Article 54(2) and (3) was the same as that in Article 83 (the equivalent provisions in the EPC).

62 [2005] FSR 6 at para 61.

63 [1999] FSR 405.

64 However, as opposed to the legal burden, the 'evidential burden may shift according to the state of the evidence from time to time': *Dunlop Holding Ltd's Application* [1979] RPC 523 at 542 per Buckley LJ.

65 In *Uni-Continental Holdings Ltd* v *Eurobond Adhesives Ltd* [1999] FSR 263, the sale of two cartridges with nozzles for dispensing acrylic adhesives before the priority date was sufficient to invalidate the patent for the nozzle.

66 [1985] RPC 59.

67 [2007] RPC 4.

in question and, consequently, that claim was invalid for lack of novelty. However, prior unpublished patent applications are not taken into account in determining whether there is an inventive step. The application of s 2(3) is the same as s 2(2) and it is not correct to restrict the enquiry under s 2(3) to the contents only of the prior application but consideration should extend to what is taught by it and it is permissible to take into account experiments made on the basis of it.[68]

An applicant for a patent may decide to withdraw his patent application before it is published. This would allow him to prevent the invention becoming part of the state of the art and would enable him to later make a fresh application for the same invention. He would of course lose the priority of the earlier application. There was some doubt as to the position where the application is withdrawn but it is still published, for example, because it is withdrawn too late to prevent publication. Section 16 of the Patents Act 1977 states that the application shall be published as soon as possible after the end of the prescribed period (18 months) unless it is withdrawn or refused before preparations for its publication have been completed by the Patent Office. There is, therefore, a point of no return beyond which an application will be published even though it has been withdrawn. The question in such cases is whether the published, though withdrawn, application is part of the state of the art in determining novelty of later applications.

In *Zbinden's Application*,[69] the first application was withdrawn on 12 December 1996 but published on 18 December 1996. The second application for the same invention was filed on 16 December 1996. The examiner decided that the second application lacked novelty because of the earlier published application. The Hearing Officer agreed that the effect of s 2(3) was that the earlier withdrawn application was part of the state of the art even though this appeared to be contrary to the effect of Article 54(3) of the EPC, the equivalent provision to s 2(3). However, soon after, in *Woolard's Application*,[70] Laddie J rejected this approach and said that s 2(3) had to be interpreted in a way consistent with Article 54(3) EPC as applied at the EPO and the prior publication had to relate to an application that was still in existence. The purpose underlying Article 54(3) was to prevent double-patenting: for example, where two persons (or even the same person) obtain two patents for the same invention in the same country. As s 2 is one of the provisions of the Patents Act 1977 framed to have the same effect, in so far as is practicable, with the equivalent provisions of the EPC, CPC and PCT, Laddie J in *Woolward* must be right and does not conflict with the goal of preventing double-patenting.

Inventors may wish to demonstrate their invention to others: for example, to secure investment or to show to potential licensees. If such demonstrations are held before the priority date the inventor runs a grave risk of jeopardising his application by compromising the novelty of his invention. The inventor must be very careful not to disclose details of the invention, but it may be safe to allow third parties to see a demonstration if this is held in private and the confidentiality of the event is stressed. In *Pall Corp* v *Commercial Hydraulics (Bedford) Ltd*,[71] the claimant sent samples of his claimed product (hydrophilic microporous membranes) to a potential customer for testing in comparison with other membranes. Other suppliers were present at the test which had been arranged. However, details of the nature and construction of the membrane were not disclosed and it was not possible to determine these details from a visual inspection of the membrane. After the patent had been granted, it was challenged on the basis that it had been made available to the public before the priority date. It was held, *inter alia*, that delivering samples in confidence to persons who knew that they were experimental and secret did not make the invention available to the public for the purposes of s 2(1) and did not, therefore, prejudice the novelty of the invention.[72]

It should be mentioned that, on the issue of novelty, cases under the Patents Act 1949 must be treated with caution as, under that Act, reasons for invalidity on the grounds of lack of novelty were somewhat different and prior secret use could invalidate a patent or

---

68 *Synthon BV* v *SmithKline Beecham plc* [2003] RPC 6 per Aldous LJ.

69 [2002] RPC 13.

70 [2002] RPC 39.

71 [1990] FSR 329.

72 *See* also *Vax Appliances Ltd* v *Hoover plc* [1991] FSR 307, decided along similar lines on the issue of prior use under the Patents Act 1949 s 32.

be a reason for rejecting an application for a patent. In the 1949 Act a patent would be invalid if the invention was 'used in the United Kingdom before the priority date of the claim',[73] or if the invention 'is not new having regard to what was known or used before the priority date of the claim, in the United Kingdom'.[74] In *Quantel Ltd* v *Spaceward Microsystems Ltd*,[75] Falconer J made the point (at 108):

> [under the 1949 Act] there was no requirement that the prior dated use had to make the invention available to the public. Accordingly, cases of prior use decided under the 1949 Act not decided upon the criterion of whether the prior use made the patented invention available to the public, may no longer be good law. (original emphasis)

Under the 1977 Act, secret prior use, for example of a new industrial process by an employer whose employees are subject to a duty of confidence, cannot anticipate the patent because it is not made available to the public. However, this runs counter to the basic notion, underlying the Statute of Monopolies 1623, that monopolies ought to be limited in time.

There was a general lack of authority on the meaning of prior experimental use in the context of anticipation. Under the 1949 Act, even secret experimental use would constitute disclosure to the public unless it was reasonably necessary, by or with the consent of the proprietor, and took place within one year before the priority date.[76] There is no equivalent provision in the 1977 Act, and in *Prout* v *British Gas plc*[77] it was argued that a patent for an anti-vandal mounting bracket for a warning lamp was invalid because it had been used experimentally at a location on a public highway notorious for vandalism. However, Judge Ford held that the patent was valid nonetheless. There was some persuasive German authority that anticipatory use had to be more than mere trials in public and that the use of the finished invention was required. He also accepted that the repeal of the 1949 Act, particularly s 51(3) on trial use, revived the previous common law on the subject to the effect that experimental use to test the invention does not destroy the invention's novelty.

Field trials of a traffic light control system were carried out before the relevant filing in *Lux Traffic Controls Ltd* v *Pike Signals Ltd*.[78] The defendant argued that the invention had been made available to the public because a prototype had been used in public and it did not matter whether anyone, in fact, observed the particular feature claimed by the patentee. Aldous J confirmed that anticipation of a patent required an enabling disclosure such that the public were enabled to make or obtain the invention. He went on (at 133):

> Further it is settled law that there is no need to prove that anybody actually saw the disclosure provided the relevant disclosure was in public. Thus an anticipating description in a book will invalidate a patent if the book is on the shelf of a library open to the public, whether or not anybody read the book and whether or not it was situated in a dark and dusty corner of the library.

In the present case a prototype controller was made available to a contractor and, had a skilled man examined it, he would have seen how it worked. Whether such a person did examine it was of no consequence. The fact remained that the contractor was free in law and equity to examine the controller. If the invention has been communicated to a single member of the public without inhibiting fetter, that is enough to make it available to the public.[79] In *Lux* v *Pike*, the relevant claim in the patent was held to be invalid on the ground of lack of novelty.[80]

On the issue of prior experimental use *Lux* v *Pike* is difficult to reconcile with *Prout* v *British Gas*, and although the latter was not mentioned by Aldous J in the former case, both judges referred to the lack of English authority. In *Lux* v *Pike*, Aldous J cited three cases heard in the EPO.[81] The upshot of these three cases appears to be that if the public have an opportunity to discover the relevant features of the invention without being under any obligation of confidence then the invention is made available to the public for

73 Patents Act 1949 s 14(1)(d).

74 Patents Act 1949 s 32(1)(e).

75 [1990] RPC 83.

76 Patents Act 1949 ss 32(2) and 51(3).

77 [1992] FSR 478.

78 [1993] RPC 107.

79 Per Lord Parker CJ in *Bristol Myers Co's Application* [1969] RPC 146.

80 Arguments based on obviousness and not being an invention failed. A second patent for another controller was held valid and infringed by the defendant.

81 Case T/84/83 *Luchtenbenberg/Rear-view mirror* [1979–85] EPOR 796, Case T482/89 *Telemacanique/Power supply unit* [1993] EPOR 259 and Case T245/88 *Union Carbide/Atmospheric vaporizer* [1991] EPOR 373.

the purposes of determining the state of the art. Of course, in *Lux* v *Pike* independent contractors had been given the controllers, whereas in *Prout* v *British Gas* the prior use was by employees. However, in the latter case any member of the public, including vandals, might have taken the opportunity to examine the product to discover how it worked, though presumably, as this would probably have amounted to trespass to goods, they would not have been free in law to do so. The advice to anyone contemplating field trials in respect of a new invention must be, in the light of the uncertainty still surrounding this aspect of prior use, file the patent application first.

The enlarged Board of Appeal of the EPO addressed the question of whether something has been made available to the public in the context of the chemical composition of a substance in Case G01/92 *Availability to the Public*.[82] The President of the EPO referred the following points to the enlarged board of appeal for its determination.

82 [1993] EPOR 241.

1   Is the chemical composition of a product made available to the public by virtue of the publication of that product irrespective of whether particular reasons can be identified to cause the skilled person to analyse the composition? And, if the answer to this is in the affirmative:
2   Does the principle extend to the more general case whereby all information which can be obtained from a product is made available to the public by virtue of the availability of that product, irrespective of whether particular reasons exist to cause the skilled person to search for that information?

The Board responded by saying that the chemical composition of a substance is part of the state of the art when the substance as such is available to the public and can be analysed and reproduced by the skilled person, irrespective of whether or not particular reasons can be identified for analysing the composition. The same principles apply *mutatis mutandis* to any other product. Article 54(2) of the EPC makes no distinction between the different means by which any information is made available to the public. Where it is possible for the skilled person to discover the composition of a substance or the internal structure of the product and to reproduce it *without undue burden*, then both the product and the composition or internal structure become part of the state of the art.

83 [1996] FSR 292.

In *Milliken Denmark AS* v *Walk Off Mats Ltd*,[83] the patent for washable floor mats with a rubber or plastic backing having perforations so as to allow machine washing without the risk of the backing bursting was ordered to be revoked. There had been non-confidential prior use by an American company which was a part owner of the defendant company. The US company had previously supplied customers with mats with perforations and mere knowledge of the perforations would enable the skilled man to work the invention and the fact that he might not realise the advantage of having perforations was irrelevant. Jacob J, referring to the approach in *Lux* and *Availability to the Public*, to the effect that an invention will become part of the state of the art if the product is made available to the public even if no person in fact examines or inspects it to acquire knowledge of the invention, said (at 311):

> The rule . . . seems harsh when prior use is by the patentee. Likewise it seems harsh when the publication is in written form but is in an obscure language and a document placed in an obscure library: a leaf in a forest is available to the public even if the wise man hid it there. But the rule provides a 'brightline' test – avoiding subjectivity and most questions of degree ('undue burden' remains). Nor does it seem harsh when one considers that the patentee can protect himself by applying for a patent before making the product available to the third parties . . .

In speaking of 'undue burden', Jacob J was referring to the enlarged Board of Appeal's requirement that the skilled man must be able to discover the composition or internal structure and reproduce it without undue burden. It is clear from these cases that anticipation may occur even if the skilled person would not have appreciated the benefit or purpose of the invention. Obviously the safest course is to file the patent application first, before allowing persons not under a duty of confidence the potential of access to the invention.

Determined efforts to prevent access to details about how a product invention operates may be made such as in *PCME Ltd* v *Goyen Controls Co UK Ltd*[84] in which the electronic circuitry in a dust emission monitoring device had been embedded in resin to prevent anyone physically dismantling the device without destroying it. Nevertheless, it was held that prior use of the device by customers anticipated the patent because obvious and simple testing techniques would make the necessary disclosures. The claims in the patent were directed to the broad features that would have been disclosed by such testing.

It is only one short step from the position that an invention is made available to the public if it is made available to a person who does not in fact examine it, though he is free to do so, to the proposition that an invention is made available to the public even though the public does not know and cannot know it has been made so available. In *Merrell Dow Pharmaceuticals Inc* v *HN Norton & Co Ltd*[85] the claimant had a patent for a drug 'terfenadine' which had expired. The drug was used as an antihistamine treatment and, unknown at the time, its use caused an acid metabolite to be made in the human liver. The claimant, upon discovering this, applied for a patent in respect of the acid metabolite. The defendant started selling terfenadine after the first patent had expired and was sued for infringement of the second patent on the ground that the defendant was supplying the means to put the invention into effect.[86] The second patent was revoked in the Patents Court and the Court of Appeal dismissed the appeal of the claimant. It was held that the disclosure of a process made available to the public made available everything which inevitably took place as part of that process, whether appreciated or not. Lord Nicholls V-C said (at 238):

> Any other conclusion would run counter to one of the golden threads of jurisprudence relating to patents. Patents exist today to reward and thereby encourage inventors; they are not intended to make it possible to take out of public use processes or products already made available to the public.

The House of Lords confirmed that the patent was invalid for want of novelty.[87] The invention had been made available to the public by virtue of the specification for the terfenadine patent which included in the description of the invention the phrase '. . . a part of the chemical reaction in the human body produced by the ingestion of terfenadine and having an anti-histamine effect'. The invention was being worked before the priority date because the public were able to take terfenadine and, by doing so, necessarily they were working the invention disclosed in the second patent. The chemical reaction described was taking place in their livers even though they did not know. Lord Hoffmann said (at 90):

> It enabled the public to work the invention by making the acid metabolite in their livers. The fact that they would not have been able to describe the chemical reaction in these terms does [not] mean that they were not working the invention. Whether or not a person is working a product invention is an objective fact independent of what he knows or thinks about what he is doing.

In particular, Lord Hoffmann cited two decisions of the EPO Boards of Appeal: Case T12/81 *BAYER/Diastereomers*,[88] and Case T303/86 *CPC/Flavour Concentrates*.[89] The latter concerned an application for a patent in respect of a process for making flavour concentrates from vegetable or animal substances by extraction with fat solvents in pressure cookers. Pre-existing recipes for pressure-frying chickens disclosed processes having the same effect although they were couched in non-technical language. The Technical Board of Appeal stated (at 98):

84 [1999] FSR 801.

85 [1995] RPC 233. Affirmed in the House of Lords [1996] RPC 76.

86 An infringement under the Patents Act 1977 s 60(2).

87 *Merrell Dow Pharmaceuticals Inc* v *HN Norton & Co Ltd* [1996] RPC 76.

88 [1979–85] EPOR 308.

89 [1989] EPOR 95.

It is sufficient to destroy the novelty of the claimed process that this process and the known process are identical with respect to starting material and reaction conditions since processes identical in these features must inevitably yield identical products.

The House of Lords' avoidance of the unfortunate consequence of allowing what was, essentially, continuing protection for an expired patent accords with common sense and the views of the EPO that the effect of Article 54 (the equivalent to s 2 of the 1977 Act) is to prevent the state of the art being patented again.[90] Perhaps, however, the manner in which the Patents Court and the Court of Appeal dealt with the problem is to be preferred. Had the second 'invention' not been disclosed in the specification for the first patent, the outcome in the House of Lords might well have been different; although, if there had not been disclosure in the specification of the first patent, that could have been invalid for lack of sufficiency. Whilst there are good policy reasons for not granting protection beyond the normal 20-year period, the more technical approach of the House of Lords conforms better with patent law as it has developed. The fact that persons taking terfenadine were producing the acid metabolite should not, on the basis of *Lux* and *Availability to the Public*, be a sufficient ground without more for adding the acid metabolite to the state of the art. It could, after all, probably require an 'undue burden' to discover the composition of the metabolite. Would even the skilled man realise that it was being produced in the human liver if there was no mention of the chemical reaction in the specification for terfenadine?

In the US and in Germany, the equivalent patents for the acid metabolite produced by taking terfenadine were held not to be infringed by a defendant selling the drug after expiry of the patents. In each case, the court held that the second patent would be limited to the production of the acid metabolite *outside* the human body.[91]

If published material does not adequately describe what is claimed there can be no loss of novelty. If someone else thought of the idea underlying the invention before the priority date, that alone would not be sufficient to invalidate the patent unless it was made available to the public. For example, in *Catnic Components Ltd* v *C Evans & Co (Builders Merchants) Ltd*[92] a challenge on the ground of lack of novelty by way of another person having a similar idea and making a model of a lintel failed even though the model had been shown to a number of people. The model was not the lintel (it was in fact too short to be used as a lintel) and therefore the claimant's patent for a new lintel was valid.

A prior publication which deals with a different problem to the one dealt with in the patent application could still amount to anticipation under old UK law. In *Molins* v *Industrial Machinery Co Ltd*,[93] an application was made in respect of a method of distributing tobacco evenly in the manufacture of cigarettes on a high-speed machine. The method involved pushing the tobacco in the same direction as the paper in which it would be wrapped. But this was held to have been anticipated by an earlier patent which used the same movement but in a slow-speed machine. This was so even though the movement in the older machine was not intended to cure the problem of uneven tobacco distribution. However, a carefully drafted application that is directed to a new purpose, not previously disclosed, might now succeed.[94] It has been accepted that the nature of novelty has been changed under Article 54 of the EPC and new purposes may be patentable and not anticipated by inherent prior disclosure.[95]

Having a similar use to prior art will not necessarily anticipate a patent, especially if the purpose is somewhat different. In *Haberman* v *Jackel International Ltd*,[96] prior art consisting of two patents for feeding bottles did not anticipate a patent for a training cup. These cups were intended to be used by young children in the transitional stage between suckling from the mother's nipple or from a feeding bottle with a teat to the stage where the child could use an ordinary cup. The present invention had a spout with a self-sealing valve to prevent leakage if the cup was tipped over or lay on its side.

90 Case T12/81 *BAYER/ Diastereomers Decision* [1979–85] EPOR 308.

91 *Terfenadine* [1998] FSR 145 and *Marion Merrell Dow Inc* v *Baker Norton Pharmaceuticals Inc* [1998] FSR 158.

92 [1983] FSR 401.

93 (1938) 55 RPC 31.

94 *See* the European Patent Office case of Case G02/88 *Mobil/ Friction reducing additive* [1990] EPOR 73, discussed below.

95 Falconer J recognised the changed nature of novelty in *Quantel Ltd* v *Spaceward Microsystems Ltd* [1990] RPC 83 at 108.

96 [1999] FSR 683.

Anticipation is judged by considering how a prior publication, for example, would be construed by a person skilled in the art. This extension of the reasonable man test is essential as many technical publications are incomprehensible to the layperson. It is acknowledged that if the art is in a highly developed technology, it might be a matter of how it can be construed by a team of persons skilled in the particular art. This was accepted in *General Tire & Rubber Co* v *Firestone Tyre & Rubber Co Ltd*,[97] in which the validity of Firestone's patent for making oil-extended rubber for tyres was challenged by an alleged infringer. Attacks on the validity of patents frequently come from defendants in infringement actions, where it is often the best form of defence and certainly puts the claimant to a great deal of additional trouble. As regards the rubber patent and the issue of anticipation, there had been a prior publication, but whether it related to Firestone's patent was ambiguous. It was said that if a prior publication contained a direction that was capable of being carried out in a manner which would infringe but would be at least as likely to be carried out in a way that would not do so, the patentee's claim would not be judged to be anticipated.[98] To anticipate the claim, the prior publication must contain a clear and unmistakable direction to do what the patentee claimed to have invented. The same test that applies to infringement also applies to anticipation: that is, does the prior art fall within the claims of the patent in suit?[99] There may be a clear and unmistakable disclosure if the prior art discloses a number of alternatives, one of which is within the claim.[100]

General Tire has been used on numerous occasions as authority for the 'clear and unmistakable direction' approach to anticipatory material. An example, which adds something of a gloss to this principle, is *Union Carbide Corp* v *BP Chemicals Ltd*[101] in which Jacob J in the Patents Court said that a direction in a prior publication not to do something because it would have adverse consequences was not a direction to do that same thing because it had beneficial consequences. In such a case, the invention lies in finding that those in the art at the time of the prior publication had been wrong. Jacob J also confirmed that disclosure of a range of values, for example, 15 to 70 per cent, discloses each and every part of the range. However, there may still be room for invention if a part of the range is claimed later if there is something special (that is, inventive) about that later claimed range.

The 'clear and unmistakable directions' rule can be carried too far and result in a 'photographic approach' which ignores implicit knowledge of the skilled person. Any reader brings his own knowledge of supplementary detail which could be said to be self-evident. Of course, the prior document has to be seen through the eyes of the skilled person but there is a danger of inferring too much which would have the result of blurring the distinction between lack of novelty and obviousness. In *Hoechst Celanese Corp* v *BP Chemicals Ltd*[102] Jacob J said (at 601):

> . . . it must be right to read the prior document with the eyes of the skilled man. So if he would find a teaching implicit, it is indeed taught. The prior document is novelty destroying if it explicitly teaches something within the claim or, as a practical matter, that is what the skilled man would see it is teaching him.

The disclosure of an allegedly anticipating document must be an enabling disclosure. In *Asahi Kasei Kogyo KK's Application*,[103] Lord Jauncey said in relation to whether a patent was supported by matter in an earlier patent for the purposes of priority[104] (at 547):

> An invention is only supported by prior matter . . . if the earlier relevant application not only describes the invention but also contains an enabling disclosure thereanent [relating thereto].

Thus, the disclosure must enable the skilled person to work the invention. If the invention is a product, this does mean that the prior disclosure is such that the skilled person can

97 [1972] RPC 457.

98 It might, however, fail on the grounds of obviousness.

99 *Horne Engineering Co Ltd* v *Reliance Water Controls Ltd* [2000] FSR 90 at 109 per Pumfrey J.

100 *Ranbaxy UK Ltd* v *Warner-Lambert Co* [2007] RPC 4. See also *Laboratorios Almirall SA* v *Boehringer Ingleheim International GmbH* [2009] FSR 12.

101 [1998] RPC 1.

102 [1998] FSR 586.

103 [1991] RPC 485.

104 The same considerations apply in terms of anticipation by a patent with an earlier priority date as apply in respect of whether a later patent can rely on an earlier one for priority.

105 Per Pumfrey J in *Minnesota Mining & Manufacturing Co's (Suspension Aerosol Formulation) Patent* [1999] RPC 135 at 146, citing the House of Lords in *Merrell Dow Pharmaceuticals Inc* v *HN Norton & Co Ltd* [1996] RPC 76, discussed above.

106 [1998] RPC 517.

107 Case T303/86 *CPC/Flavour Concentrates* [1989] EPOR 95.

108 Ferris J did not accept a distinction between 'business ethics' and confidence in *Strix Ltd* v *Otter Controls Ltd* [1995] RPC 607 at 634.

109 Patents Act 1977 s 2(4). Unlawfully obtained matter would include, for example, a stolen model of something incorporating the invention or manufactured using the invention. Whether it applies to stolen information is less clear because of the difficulty with respect to theft of information: for example, *Oxford* v *Moss* (1978) 68 Cr App R 183. However, details of the invention stored on a computer would be covered, as to gain access to them without authorisation will usually be an offence under the Computer Misuse Act 1990 s 1. Of course, 'unlawfully' includes civil wrongs as well as criminal offences and could cover trespass (to land and goods) and conversion.

110 Patents Act 1977 s 2(4). The Patents Rules 2007, SI 2007/3291 r 5 sets out the detailed provisions.

111 *Lux Traffic Controls Ltd* v *Pike Signals Ltd* [1993] RPC 107. In that case a published paper did not describe the invention sufficiently clearly so as to make it known to the public.

112 *See* the discussion below on *Parks-Cramer Co* v *GW Thornton & Sons Ltd* [1966] RPC 407 (p 454). Prior to the 1977 Act, there had to be novelty in the mode of using the old product as distinguished from novelty of purpose: *Lane-Fox* v *Kensington and Knightsbridge Electric Lighting Co Ltd* (1892) 9 RPC 413.

113 Note s 2(6) was repealed and incorporated in a new s 4A which also extends to new specific uses as well as methods of treatment. The changes were made by the Patents Act 2004: the relevant provisions were brought into effect on 31 December 2007.

114 In fact, Article 54(5) of the European Patent Convention, the equivalent provision to the Patents Act 1977 s 4A(3), also includes the word 'any'.

115 [1985] RPC 545.

work the invention; it is not necessary that he knows what it is he is working.[105] As Laddie J said in relation to anticipation in *Evans Medical Ltd's Patent*[106] (at 576):

> First one must identify what the alleged invention is, that is to say what is covered by the claims in the patent, and then one must decide whether or not that invention, or any part of it, would be made inevitable by following the instructions in the prior art. If it would be, then it does not matter whether the skilled reader of the prior art would realise that he was working within the area claimed by the subsequent patent.

If a product is necessarily made as a result of a known process even though the existence of the product is not known and its manufacture is not desired by a person working the process, then the product must be part of the state of the art, nonetheless.[107] If the process is worked in public or published then the product must inevitably be part of the state of the art. To hold otherwise would allow someone to re-patent something which is already part of the state of the art.

Matter that has been obtained unlawfully or in breach of confidence,[108] or which has been divulged in breach of confidence, is to be disregarded when considering the novelty of an invention.[109] In the case of a patent application, this covers the period of six months preceding the date of filing of the patent so that, effectively, if there has been a disclosure of the invention because of a breach of confidence – for example, by a potential manufacturer of products made in accordance with the invention who has been in negotiations with the inventor – there is a six-month time limit during which that disclosure will be ignored in the determination of novelty. There is provision for the inventor to display the invention at an international exhibition without this destroying the novelty of the invention, subject to the inventor making a declaration and filing written evidence. The six-month time limit applies and the patent application must be filed within six months of the act of displaying the invention at the exhibition.[110]

One thing an inventor must be careful to avoid is anticipating his own invention: for example, by publishing details of it in an academic or trade journal before the priority date (normally the date of filing the application). However, to anticipate the invention, the publication must clearly describe the invention as claimed.[111] Tempting as it might be to publicise his ingenuity, the inventor would be advised to restrain his ego and keep the details of his invention secret, and, in any dealings with advisers, potential manufacturers, assignees or licensees, to make it clear that discussion of the invention is in the strictest confidence.

New uses for old inventions

Old inventions may be patentable if the claims are directed to a new use. If sufficiently different, the new use will not be considered to be part of the state of the art. For inventions other than drugs for the treatment of humans and animals, new uses for old inventions may be patentable up to a point if there is some new technical effect: for example, by combining two previous inventions in a new and non-obvious way.[112] In the case of drugs for the treatment of humans or animals, at first sight it appears that only the first use is patentable. Section 4A(3) states that the fact that the drug (substance or composition) already forms part of the state of the art does not prevent the new method of use from being patentable if 'the use of the substance or composition *in any such method* does not form part of the state of the art' (emphasis added).[113] The key words are 'any such method', which seems to include the first use, at least on a strict literal interpretation. The omission of the word 'any' would clearly permit 'second use patents', and the only conclusion that can be reached is that the inclusion of the word 'any' was quite deliberate.[114]

The literal approach, denying second use patents for drugs, found some support in the English case of *John Wyeth & Brothers Ltd's Application: Schering AG's Application*,[115] although, in the end, the court decided to follow the enlarged Board of Appeal of the EPO[116] which held that second and subsequent new uses of known substances or compounds were patentable. Either interpretation was possible but it was important to achieve conformity with the EPC. In Case G05/83 *Eisai*,[117] the enlarged Board of Appeal held that:

1 claims directed to the use of a product for the treatment of an illness in a human or animal body (when such use was the second or subsequent medical use) were equivalent to claims for a method of treatment of the human or animal body and therefore excluded from patentability;[118]
2 claims directed to the use of a product for the manufacture of a medicament for a specified new therapeutic use were not lacking in novelty.[119]

A second medical use must be effective to achieve the new treatment. It is not sufficient if it simply has a placebo effect. So it was held in *Lily ICOS Ltd* v *Pfizer Ltd*[120] by Laddie J. The patent was for the drug Viagra used for treating male erectile dysfunction and was a combination of a number of compounds. Laddie J also accepted the view that if a combination of compounds is used to treat a disease, then each is used for the treatment of the disease. He gave an example where a compound was used which did not produce full erections in a patient but did if it was used with another compound. In such a case he said it was fanciful to suggest that the first compound was not being used in the treatment.

Thus, second uses of known substances or compounds for new medicinal purposes may be patentable. This seems to be a restrictive interpretation which should not apply to 'non-medical' inventions, that is, those falling outside the scope of s 4A(3) where the question of novelty depends on whether the new use for a new purpose had previously been made available to the public. Secret or hidden uses will not be considered to be grounds of objection.[121] In *Mobil Oil*, which concerned a claim based on the discovery that an existing compound used for preventing rust was also effective as a lubricant, the example of a compound that had been previously known and used as a plant growth regulator was discussed. Imagine that it was later discovered that this same compound was effective also as a fungicide and the patent claim is for the use of the compound as a fungicide. The method of use is the same for both purposes, that is application to plants, and so the only novelty that can be claimed is in the use of the compound as a fungicide rather than as a growth regulator, that is in *the purpose of the use*. In such a case, the question of novelty has to be determined along basic principles: that is, has that functional technical feature previously been made available to the public?

In *Mobil Oil*, the enlarged Board of Appeal in the EPO suggested that a new use of a known compound may reflect a newly discovered technical effect which could be considered as a functional technical feature of the relevant claim. If that technical feature had not previously been made available to the public the claim would be novel even though it had inherently taken place in the course of carrying out what previously had been made available to the public.[122] However, this contradicts the view on novelty taken in *Merrell Dow Pharmaceuticals Inc* v *HN Norton & Co Ltd*[123] and was doubted as being correct in the Patents Court hearing of that same case by Aldous J.[124]

In the appeal to the House of Lords in *Merrell Dow*,[125] although their Lordships approved *Mobil Oil*, Lord Hoffmann cast some doubt on that decision. Considering the UK's provisions on infringement, he said it would be difficult to tell, for a second invention such as that in *Mobil Oil*, whether the alleged infringer was using it for the forbidden purpose. That is, how can you tell whether a person is using the oil additive as a lubricant (lawful after the expiry of the first patent) or to reduce friction (which would infringe the second patent)? However, whichever purpose the person alleged to have infringed had in mind is irrelevant to the existence of infringement. It may, at best, reduce the exposure to

116 Case G05/83 *Eisai* [1985] OJ EPO 64. *See* Paterson, G.D. 'The patentability of further uses of a known product under the European Patent Convention' [1991] 1 EIPR 16.

117 [1979–85] EPOR B241.

118 European Patent Convention Article 53(c); see also the Patents Act 1977 s 4A(1) which denies patentability to methods of treatment of the human or animal body by surgery or therapy or of diagnosis practised on the human or animal body.

119 European Patent Convention Article 54; Patents Act 1977 s 2. *See* the discussion of 'Swiss-type' claims in Chapter 11 (p 406).

120 [2001] FSR 16. The patent was ordered to be revoked on the grounds of lack of inventive step. The Court of appeal confirmed that the invention was obvious: *Lily ICOS Ltd* v *Pfizer Ltd* [2002] EWCA Civ 1.

121 Case G02/88 *Mobil/Friction reducing additive* [1990] EPOR 73.

122 The enlarged Board of Appeal said that 'making available to the public' means that the invention must have been communicated to the public or laid open for inspection. It said that the question of inherency does not arise under Article 54(2) of the European Patent Convention: [1990] EPOR 73 at 88.

123 [1995] RPC 233.

124 [1994] RPC 1 at 12.

125 [1996] RPC 76.

damages. If a person used the additive for the purpose of lubrication, it would also reduce friction, whether or not he knew this. The danger, similar to that perceived in the Court of Appeal in *Merrell Dow*, discussed earlier, is that the patent monopoly can be extended beyond its normal life if a new hitherto unknown effect can be discovered by the patentee. This might be acceptable if it involves a *new use not previously carried out* (not being a previous unknown and inherent use), but not if it involves a *known use* but for a *new purpose*. However, this approach is not in conformity with the decision in *Mobil Oil*.

The Court of Appeal had an opportunity to revisit second uses of known substances or compounds for new therapeutic uses in *Bristol-Myers Squibb Co v Baker Norton Pharmaceuticals Inc*[126] and the court also took the opportunity to give further explanation of the *Mobil Oil* case. In *Bristol-Myers Squibb*, the patent in suit was for the use of taxol for making a medication for treating cancer by administering the drug over a period of three hours, thereby reducing neutropenia (the side effect of suppression of the production of white blood cells which led to severe allergic reactions). It was already known that administering the drug over three hours was as effective as doing this over 24 hours, which had been the period previously used to minimise side effects, but it was not previously known that neutropenia was less under the three-hour regime than the 24-hour regime.

The Court of Appeal accepted the correctness of *Eisai* and confirmed that the novelty in a Swiss-type claim lay in the new subsequent therapeutic use. However, in the present case, the claim was not a claim to a second therapeutic use. The reduction of neutropenia was a discovery not a second therapeutic use. The rest of the three-hour regime, relating to the drug, the method of administering the drug and the therapeutic purpose were all the same as in the 24-hour regime. Swiss-type claims must be directed at new therapeutic uses or purposes.

As regards the *Mobil Oil* case, Aldous LJ said that it differed from *Eisai* which was concerned with the interaction between Articles 52(4) and 54(5) of the EPC. Article 52(4) denies patents for methods of treating the human or animal body whilst Article 54(5) allows patents for new uses of known substances or compositions used in such methods of treatment.[127] On the other hand, *Mobil Oil* was concerned with the purposive construction of claims on the basis of the Protocol on Article 69 such that the claim was interpreted as being limited to the technical effect, that is, the physical activity. Thus, in *Mobil Oil*, the claim to an additive in lubricating oil for reducing friction should be interpreted as a claim to a product when used for reducing friction. Aldous LJ said in *Bristol-Myers Squibb* (at 17):

> Such a claim [as in Mobil Oil] would be novel if the use had not previously been made available to the public. However, it is relevant to note that similar reasoning cannot be applied in relation to a Swiss-type claim, as such a claim cannot be interpreted as relating to a product when used because that would constitute a method of treatment which is prohibited under the EPC.

Bristol-Myers Squibb does little to resolve the problems with *Mobil Oil* pointed out by Lord Hoffmann in *Merrell Dow*. However, when one considers the basic requirement for novelty, that the invention has not been made available to the public, it is hard to fault *Mobil Oil* as a secret inherent use that is not known to the public cannot sensibly be said to be made available to the public. Indeed, in *Merrell Dow* the House of Lords recognised that previous secret and uninformative uses would, subject to s 64, infringe a patent once granted and even though they would count as infringements post-grant, they would not anticipate the patent. The difficulty in making illegal an activity that was formerly lawful by the grant of a patent is mollified by s 64 which allows the continuance of acts done in good faith before the priority date of the patent. Though one could ask, how can a person do an act in *good faith* if he does not know he is doing it?

The correctness of *Bristol-Myers Squibb* was doubted in so far as it held that a change in a dosing regime could not be a new therapeutic use in *Merck & Co Inc's Patent*[128] where

126 [2001] RPC 1.

127 Article 53(c) is equivalent to s 4A(1) and Article 54(4) and (5) is equivalent to s 4A(2) and (3).

128 [2003] FSR 29 at para 80.

the essence of the invention was using a single dose of alendronate of 70mg per week rather than a daily dose of 10mg. The former was shown to be a more effective dose for treating osteoporosis. This was objected to on the basis that it was a method of treatment of the human body by therapy and, therefore, excluded under s 4A(1),[129] as it was not a case of a second or subsequent medical use. Of course, in the Patents Court, Jacob J was bound to follow *Bristol-Myers Squibb*, being a Court of Appeal decision though he did express his regret at having to do so as this construction would act as a disincentive to research to find such improved dosage regimes. On the subsequent appeal,[130] the Court of Appeal itself was also bound by its own earlier decision in *Bristol-Myers Squibb*, although the court did indicate that the patentee could consider appealing elsewhere (the House of Lords) as it thought that *Bristol-Myers Squibb* was wrongly decided. However, when one looks at the wording of s 4A(1) and (2) (and their predecessors ss 2(6) and 4(2) and (3)) the matter seems beyond doubt, especially as s 4A(2) states that subsection (1) '. . . does not apply to an invention consisting of a substance or composition for use in any such method'. Changing a dosage regime is not the same as inventing a product for use in the treatment of the human body. It is not a new use such as where it is found that a known drug used for regulating the number of red blood cells can also be used to treat skin diseases. In *Merck* and *Bristol-Myers Squibb* the purpose of the changed regime was to treat the same condition.

Inventive step

The Patents Act 1977 does not define the term 'invention', but Lord Hoffmann usefully described different forms of invention in *Biogen Inc* v *Medeva plc*.[131] He said that it is the addition of a new idea to the existing stock of knowledge and that (at 34):

> Sometimes, it is the idea of using established techniques to do something which no one had previously thought of doing. In that case, the inventive step will be doing the new thing. Sometimes, it is finding a way of doing something which people had wanted to do but could not think how. The inventive idea would be the way of achieving the goal. In yet other cases, many people may have a general idea of how they might achieve a goal but not know how to solve a particular problem which stands in their way. If someone devises a way of solving the problem, his inventive step will be that solution but not the goal itself or the general method of achieving it.

These three forms of invention can be classified as (a) the goal itself, (b) the general method of achieving the goal, and (c) the solution to a problem. The last two forms of invention, in their different ways, can be thought of fulfilling a 'long-felt want', a phrase often used in patent law. Its presence is sometimes useful in determining whether an inventive step is present. It is not, of course, conclusive.

The invention must involve an inventive step. Under s 3, this applies when the invention is not obvious to a person skilled in the art having regard to all matter forming part of the state of the art, but not including matter from patent applications with earlier priority dates which is published later than the priority date of the invention. This is different to the position concerning novelty as, normally, matter in earlier applications that has not yet been published is taken to be a part of the state of the art.[132] This material is used to test for novelty but not for inventive step.

The word 'obvious' does not have any special legal meaning and it has been said that it is not necessary to go beyond the dictionary definition but to take it to mean 'very plain'.[133] It is manifestly evident that the notional skilled worker cannot be endowed with inventive faculties himself, however technical the art, otherwise all inventions could be considered to be obvious. The person skilled in the art is simply someone with a wide

129 This provision prevents the patenting of methods of treatment of the human or animal body by surgery or therapy or a method of diagnosis practised on the human or animal body. Under s 4A(2), this exclusion does not extend to substances or compositions for use in any such method. *Bristol-Myers Squibb* was decided under s 4(2) and (3) which were repealed and replaced by new s 4A, discussed in further detail at the end of this chapter.

130 *Merck & Co Inc's Patent* [2004] FSR 16.

131 [1997] RPC 1.

132 *See* Patents Act 1977 s 2(3).

133 *General Tire & Rubber Co* v *Firestone Tyre & Rubber Co Ltd* [1972] RPC 457.

knowledge of the technology within which the invention lies (or a team of persons so skilled). The question becomes, would the invention be obvious to such a person or persons?[134] In some fields, a person skilled in the art who does not possess inventive faculties may be a contradiction: for example, in the engineering professions where engineers are trained in problem-solving by the application of ingenuity, the very word 'engineer' sharing a common origin with the word 'ingenuity'.

134 Conversely, if the invention is not obvious to skilled and inventive persons it must involve an inventive step: *Intalite International NV v Cellular Ceilings Ltd (No 2)* [1987] RPC 537.

135 [2004] RPC 46.

In *Technip France SA's Patent*,[135] Jacob LJ described the notional skilled worker as a nerd. He would be very boring and also forgetful, for after he has read one piece of prior art, unless it forms part of his background technical knowledge, he would instantly forget it before reading the next piece of prior art unless it forms part of an uninventive mosaic or there is sufficient cross-reference between the items of prior art. Where it is appropriate to consider a team of skilled works, Jacob LJ described these as an assembly of nerds with different basic skills, all unimaginative. However, he did say that the notional skilled worker was not a complete android and will share the prevailing prejudices or conservatism in the art. Pill LJ preferred Lord Reid's description of the notional skilled worker in *Technograph Printed Circuits Ltd v Mills & Rockley (Electronics) Ltd*[136] (at 355) as:

136 [1972] RPC 346.

> . . . a skilled technician who is well acquainted with workshop technique and who has carefully read the relevant literature. He is supposed to have an unlimited capacity to assimilate the contents of . . . scores of specifications but to be incapable of a scintilla of invention. When dealing with obviousness, unlike novelty, it is permissible to make a 'mosaic' out of the relevant documents, but it must be a mosaic which can be put together by an unimaginative man with no inventive capacity.

Pill LJ said that the skilled worker must be taken to read documents assiduously, however boring, with reference to both novelty and inventive step. He may well be boring but he is never bored.

137 [2004] RPC 43.

In *Glaxo Group Ltd's Patent*,[137] Pumfrey J noted that the skilled person does not represent some sort of lowest common denominator of persons actually engaged in the field, possessed by the knowledges and prejudices all of them can be said to possess. It is also unlikely that an expert witness can be truly representative of the notional skilled person as he may be too well qualified and be subject to personal prejudices and preferences. Of course, an expert witness is not usually an unimaginative person and would find it difficult to be completely objective when it comes to giving evidence as to inventive step. Persons newly entering the relevant technical field cannot be taken into account in determining the skilled address who must represent the attainments of those already in the field, in particular, those most closely associated with that field.[138]

138 *Mayne Pharma Ltd v Debiopharm SA* [2006] EWHC 1123 (Pat), per Pumfrey J at paras 4 and 5.

139 [2002] EWCA Civ 466.

Invention may lie in the idea of taking a step from the prior art but to argue that an invention is not obvious unless there is some motivation to take that step is not necessarily relevant. As Aldous LJ said in *Asahi Medical Co Ltd v Macopharma (UK) Ltd*[139] (at para 23), 'the fact that nobody would dream of making a plate one inch bigger than the standard size does not mean that there would be invention in making one'. It may be argued that, given the prior art, it would be obvious to try to do what is now claimed. For example, in *Saint-Gobain PAM SA v Fusion Provida Ltd*,[140] the invention was for a means of protecting buried pipes (typically of iron) from corrosion by coating them with a layer of zinc/aluminium alloy. A paper published two months before the priority date of the patent suggested that it *might* be worth trying an alloy of zinc and aluminium. However, Jacob LJ said that this suggestion for further research was far from showing that the patent lacked inventive step. He said (at para 35):

140 [2005] EWCA Civ 177.

> Mere possible inclusion of something in a research programme on the basis that you will find out more and something might turn up is not enough. If it were otherwise there would be few inventions that were patentable . . . The 'obvious to try' test really only works where it is more or less self evident that what is being tested ought to work.

If it was enough to try something in case something turns up, the only research worth doing, if patent protection was desired, would be research which had little prospect of success.[141]

The 'obvious to try' test for inventive step finds its origin in the judgment of Diplock LJ in *Johns-Manville Corporation's Patent*.[142] That case involved a fairly 'low-tech' invention but the continuing value of the test was severely doubted in *Conor Medsystems Inc* v *Angiotech Pharmaceuticals Inc*,[143] particularly in the field of pharmaceuticals. It was noted by Lord Walker of Gestinthorpe that the volume of hi-tech research has increased enormously since *Johns-Manville* and, especially in the field of pharmaceuticals, enormous resources are committed to research because the rewards are so great. That being so, companies may engage in experiments which have a lower expectation of success than would have been the case in the past.

Where a granted patent is challenged on the ground of lack of inventive step, it is important that this is judged at the priority date of the patent rather than using the benefit of hindsight. This is especially so where the invention comprises a number of previously known integers. The danger of applying an *ex post facto* analysis to the question of obviousness was noted by Moulton LJ in *British Westinghouse Electric & Manufacturing Co Ltd* v *Braulik*[144] where he said (at 230):

> . . . I view with suspicion arguments to the effect that a new combination, bringing with it new and important consequences in the shape of practical machines, is not an invention, because, when it has once been established, it is easy to show how it might be arrived at by starting with something known, and taking a series of apparently easy steps. This *ex post facto* analysis of invention is unfair to inventors, and, in my opinion, it is not countenanced in English patent law.[145]

In *Davina Wheatley* v *Drillsafe Ltd*,[146] Aldous LJ suggested that a failure by the trial judge to use the structured approach to determining obviousness, proposed by Oliver LJ in *Windsurfing International Inc* v *Tabur Marine (Great Britain) Ltd*,[147] led the judge to fall into the trap of hindsight reasoning or 'being wise after the event'.[148] In *Minnesota Mining & Manufacturing Co* v *ATI Atlas Ltd*,[149] Pumfrey J said that allegations of obviousness in the light of common general knowledge are particularly prone to be tainted by hindsight. The danger of hindsight is heightened where the challenge to obviousness is based upon the common general knowledge. On a number of prior publications. As Kitchen J said in *Abbott Laboratories Ltd* v *Evysio Medical Devices ULC*[150] (at para 180):

> It is all too easy after the event to identify aspects of the common general knowledge which can be combined together in such a way as to lead to the claimed invention. But once again this has the potential to lead the court astray. The question is whether it would have been obvious to the skilled but uninventive person to take those features, extract them from the context in which they appear and combine them together to produce the invention.

Notional skilled worker and common general knowledge

The notional skilled worker does not have inventive ability, but he does have knowledge common to the particular art. That is known as common general knowledge and is the basis for determining whether, in the light of that knowledge, an invention is obvious. Common general knowledge does not include every published patent specification in a particular art, but is restricted to those which are generally known to those who engage in that particular art.[151] In *Beloit Technologies Inc* v *Valmet Paper Machinery Inc*,[152] Aldous LJ accepted that the notional skilled man may not have the advantage of the facilities available in some large corporations with extensive library facilities and patent departments. He said (at 494):

141 The 'Saint-Gobain test' will not always be appropriate: per Warren J in *Actavis UK Ltd* v *Novartis AG* [2009] EWHC 41 (Ch) at (para 163).

142 [1967] RPC 479.

143 [2008] RPC 28.

144 (1910) 27 RPC 209.

145 *This was approved by Lord Russell in Non-Drip Measure Co Ltd* v *Strangers Ltd* (1943) 60 RPC 135.

146 [2001] RPC 7.

147 [1985] RPC 59, discussed below (*see* pp 456–460).

148 However, later, in *David J Instance Ltd* v *Denny Bros Printing Ltd* [2002] RPC 14, Aldous LJ said that, although the '*Windsurfing* test' was useful, there was no precedent to the effect that it was essential that it was used and a judge could go straight to the question posed by the Act, providing he adopted the mantle of the skilled person.

149 [2001] FSR 31.

150 [2008] RPC 23.

151 *British Acoustic Films Ltd* v *Nettlefold Productions Ltd* (1936) 53 RPC 221 at 250 per Luxmore J, approved by the Court of Appeal in *General Tire & Rubber Co* v *Firestone Tyre & Rubber Co Ltd* [1972] RPC 457. Unlike the case with enablement for the purposes of anticipation, knowledge of patent specifications is included in the common general knowledge when it comes to considering inventive step.

152 [1997] RPC 489.

The notional skilled addressee is the ordinary man who may not have the advantages that some employees of large companies may have.

Therefore, the person skilled in the art does not know everything. He simply knows that which is known to a large proportion of those working in the relevant art. Knowledge which is known by some, perhaps a few only, can be described as public knowledge and this must be distinguished from common general knowledge.[153]

To test for obviousness, the person skilled in the art will normally be the same notional person or team used to determine sufficiency.[154] It has been held that this is not a hard and fast rule, particularly where the invention marries together two separate arts. In *Schlumberger Ltd* v *Electromagnetic Geoservices AS*,[155] the invention was for source electro-magnetic technology used in oil explorations. The two arts were source electron-magnetic technology and geophysics. It may be a matter of viewing obviousness from the perspective of two skilled persons or teams working together. Would it be obvious to a skilled person in either of the fields of technology? If so, the invention lacks inventive step. Or, would it be obvious for a person skilled in one of the arts concerned to call in a person skilled in the other art? In *Schlumberger*, Jacob LJ said (at para 65):

> In the case of obviousness in view of the state of the art, a key question is generally 'what problem was the patentee trying to solve?' That leads one in turn to consider the art in which the problem in fact lay. It is the notional team in that art which is the relevant team making up the person skilled in the art. If it would be obvious to that team to bring in different expertise, then the invention will nonetheless be obvious. Likewise if the possessor of the 'extra expertise' would himself know of the other team's problem. But if it would not be obvious to either of the notional persons or teams alone and not obvious to either sort of team to bring in the other, then the invention cannot fairly be said to be obvious. As it was put in argument before us the possessors of the different skills need to be in the same room and the team with the problem must have some reason for telling the team who could solve it what the problem is.

The fact that a particular piece of knowledge is well known to an expert witness does not necessarily mean that it forms part of the common general knowledge. It may be known to only a small number of workers in the field. However, it should be noted that the exercise of endowing the notional skilled worker with the common general knowledge at the relevant time is not something derived from either the UK legislation or the EPC. If one considers that the purpose of requiring an inventive step is to prevent a person monopolising something that is an obvious extension of material in the public domain, this approach is suspect. The state of the art includes a document in a dusty corner of a library that has been read by only one person. Therefore, an invention should lack inventive step if, when viewed objectively from that document, it would be obvious to the notional skilled man. The use of common general knowledge pre-dates the 1977 Act (and the 1949 Act) and it is arguable that it is no longer relevant. Apart from unpublished patent applications having earlier priority dates, the state of the art should be used for the purposes of determining both novelty and inventive step. Conversely, the fact that there is evidence that a number of others thought about taking the route taken by the inventor does not necessarily mean that the invention is obvious. Such persons may, after all, have had inventive faculties.

In *Pfizer Ltd's Patent*,[156] Laddie J discussed the nature of the skilled but non-inventive man in the art which suggests the notional skilled worker has more extensive knowledge of the prior art. He said (at para 64):

> This is not a real person. He is a legal creation. He is supposed to offer an objective test . . . He is deemed to have looked at and read publicly available documents and to know of public uses in the prior art. He understands all languages and dialects. He never misses the obvious nor stumbles on the inventive. He has no private idiosyncratic preferences or dislikes.

153 *Richardson-Vicks Inc's Patent* [1997] RPC 888, where it was said that a person skilled in the art of obtaining regulatory approval for new drugs was not a person skilled in the art of producing new combination drugs.

154 The test for sufficiency is whether a person skilled in the art can, without undue burden, put the invention into effect.

155 [2010] RPC 33.

156 [2001] FSR 16.

He never thinks laterally. He differs from all real people in one or more of these characteristics. A real worker in the field may never look at a piece of prior art – for example he may never look at the contents of a particular public library – or he may be put off because it is in a language he does not know. But the notional addressee is taken to have done so.

Laddie J went on to point out that anything which is obvious over the prior art cannot be subject to a valid patent application even if, in practice, few would have found it or have bothered to look at it. Whilst the real worker might miss some of the prior art, the notional skilled man never does. The rationale is that a person should not be able to obtain a monopoly over the prior art and anything obvious over it. In *Pfizer Ltd's Patent*, the patent related to the drug Viagra, used to treat impotence in men, Laddie J held that it lacked inventive step, *inter alia*, on the ground that it was obvious to attempt to administer known inhibitors used to treat male impotence in a more desirable way, that is, orally.

If one accepts that the common general knowledge approach is still correct, then it is not simply a matter of imbuing the notional skilled addressee with positive aspects of that knowledge. Negative aspects also must be considered. In *Dyson Appliances Ltd* v *Hoover Ltd*,[157] the judge accepted that the vacuum cleaner industry had a mindset which precluded the use of bagless vacuum cleaners. This prejudice would have cause the skilled addressee to treat the modification of prior art which included a cyclone to remove particles from the air to come up with a bagless vacuum cleaner with 'considerable reserve if not overt scepticism'. Furthermore, there was no long-felt want, there being no evidence that there was any technical problem at the relevant time in using bags in vacuum cleaners. This itself made it difficult to maintain an attack based on obviousness. Another example of mindset being a critical factor in determining obviousness was given by *Panduit Corp* v *Band-It Co Ltd*[158] where the mindset was in relation to coating metal ties fully with plastic coating to avoid problems handling the ties in cold weather and preventing corrosion. The invention was for a partially coated tie which increased the efficiency of the locking mechanism. The Court of Appeal held that the invention was not obvious. In *Buhler AG* v *FP Spomax SP*,[159] the prejudice was against the use of double-grinding. It was shown to exist in a similar technical field (grinding grain for bread flour) but there was no evidence to show that such prejudice existed in the field in question (grinding grain for starch).

The fact that a document which appears to bear upon the question of obviousness has been published does not mean that it is a realistic starting point for an obviousness attack.[160] Although the skilled person is deemed to have considered it with interest he is not taken to necessarily take it forward. He might read it and decide that it is not a worthwhile starting point and put it to one side.[161]

Invention requires something more than simply showing that something can be done. It must show how it can be done – a particular way in which the underlying idea can be translated into a practical method of implementation. Otherwise, the patent could extend to all possible ways of achieving the end result. A patent must be for more than an end result and must relate to the means utilised to realise that end. In *Biogen Inc* v *Medeva plc*[162] a patent in respect of a vaccine for hepatitis B which had been genetically engineered was declared invalid. Lord Hoffmann said (at 52):

> It is said that what Professor Murray showed by his invention was that it could be done . . . Those who followed, even by different routes, could have greater confidence by reason of his success. I do not think that this is enough to justify a monopoly in the whole field . . . The Wright Brothers showed that heavier-than-air flight was possible, but that did not entitle them to a monopoly in heavier-than-air flying machines . . . care is needed not to stifle further research and healthy competition by allowing the first person who has found a way of achieving an obviously desirable goal to monopolise every other way of doing so.

Obviousness is judged by looking at the invention as a whole and considering the entire state of the art at the relevant time. A process known as 'mosaicing' has occasionally been

157 [2001] RPC 26.

158 [2003] FSR 8.

159 [2008] FSR 27.

160 *Ratiopharm (UK) Ltd* v *Alza Corporation* [2009] EWHC 213 (Pat).

161 *Eli Lily & Co* v *Human Genome Sciences Inc* [2008] RPC 29.

162 [1997] RPC 1.

used to attack the validity of a patent by showing that it is obvious. This process consists of piecing together several unrelated bits of information in different documents which, when combined, are capable of showing obviousness. But the use of such a technique is theoretically very unsound because, if this is the first time the mosaic has been constructed, that in itself is indicative of non-obviousness. If it were otherwise someone else would have pieced the bits together previously. In practice, mosaicing is unlikely to find favour in the courts, although there are exceptions – for example, where it would be reasonable for the notional uninventive skilled worker to fit the pieces together, an unlikely phenomenon as the very act of mosaicing implies both detective and inventive skills. Accepting that the skilled man has no inventive faculties ('incapable of a scintilla of invention'), Lord Reid said of mosaicing:

> When dealing with obviousness, unlike novelty, it is permissible to make a 'mosaic' out of the relevant documents, but it must be a mosaic which can be put together by an unimaginative man with no inventive capacity.[163]

Whether the invention is obvious is a question of fact. For example, in *Lux Traffic Controls Ltd* v *Pike Signals Ltd*,[164] the defendant claimed that the claimant's two patents in relation to traffic signal control systems were invalid on a number of grounds. The second patent was for a means of varying the 'intergreen' period, the safety period between the lights in one direction changing to red and before the lights in the other direction changed to green. It was argued that it was obvious. However, being unsupported by evidence, the court expressed surprise that the invention had not been proposed before if that was the case. The invention may have been simple, but it represented an advance and a technical contribution to the art.[165] The simplicity of an invention must not be confused with obviousness.[166] The problem for the court when it comes to a simple invention is that once it was known it could be extremely easy to understand. This also brought the danger of looking at inventive step with the benefit of hindsight.

Commercial success

When obviousness has to be determined retrospectively (for example, where the validity of a patent is in issue), commercial success is an important and telling factor that can be taken into account. If the invention fulfils a 'long-felt want', this is good evidence of non-obviousness. However, commercial success can never be decisive and, if it is taken as a yardstick of non-obviousness, consideration must also be given to other factors such as market forces and nature of the advertising used to promote the product. There may be many commercial and social reasons for success but what matters for patent purposes is whether technical reasons exist.[167] In *Technograph Printed Circuits Ltd* v *Mills & Rockley (Electronics) Ltd*,[168] the defendant alleged that the claim-ant's method of making printed circuit boards using a silk screen printing method was invalid because of obviousness and lack of novelty, relying on a prior US patent relating to the manufacture of electrostatic shields and aerials. It was held that the claimant's patent was valid because the adaptation of the method described in the US patent, where it was used in relation to three-dimensional objects, to printing a pattern on a flat circuit board was not an obvious step. Although the invention turned out to be an enormous commercial success, this was some years later and the invention was not widely used for some years. At first instance, Harman J said:

> It was objected that in fact it was not until ten years after the invention was published that it was commercially adopted . . . and it was argued from this that it was not a case of filling a long felt want. I do not accept this argument. In the years immediately following the war, manufacturers could sell all the machines they wanted using the old point-to-point wiring and had no need to trouble themselves with anything better.[169]

163 *Technograph Printed Circuits Ltd* v *Mills & Rockley (Electronics) Ltd* [1972] RPC 346 at 355.

164 [1993] RPC 107.

165 The first patent was held to be invalid through lack of novelty because prototypes had been made available to contractors who were able to examine them, and such examination would have been sufficient to disclose the invention.

166 *Armour Group plc* v *LeisureTech Electronics Pty Ltd* [2008] EWHC 2797 (Pat).

167 Per Peter Gibson LJ in *Seb SA* v *Société De'Longhi SpA* [2003] EWCA Civ 952 at para 50. If an invention is technically obvious, it does not matter if the step would not have been taken for commercial reasons, that is, that the alleged invention was not commercially obvious: *Hallen Co* v *Brabantia (UK) Ltd* [1990] FSR 134.

168 [1969] RPC 395.

169 The House of Lords confirmed that the invention was non-obvious: [1972] RPC 346.

Therefore, commercial success as an indicator of obviousness must be treated cautiously. Lack of immediate commercial success, as in the above case, might be explained by factors that have nothing to do with the obviousness of the invention. The correlation that the proprietor hopes will be confirmed by commercial success is that the invention cannot have been obvious because it clearly satisfies a demand, and that demand would have been long since satisfied had the invention been obvious. While this might be a reasonable assumption, the opposite is not tenable: lack of success does not necessarily directly equate to obviousness. Something might be highly inventive but fail to sell because, put simply, consumers have no desire for it. That commercial success as a measure of non-obviousness should be treated cautiously was confirmed by Mummery J in the Patents Court in *Mölnlycke AB v Procter & Gamble Ltd (No 3)*,[170] a case involving a patent for disposable nappies, where he said that whether an invention was obvious was something which must be considered technically or practically rather than commercially. Commercial success might be relevant if it was due to the precise improvement which satisfied the long-felt want, but not if it was due to things such as appearance, get-up, price, marketing strategies or advertising campaigns. This was confirmed by Lord Nicholls V-C in *Mölnlycke AB v Procter & Gamble Ltd (No 5)*,[171] where he said that secondary evidence such as that relating to commercial success had a place, but its importance or weight would vary from case to case. The complexity and routine of such evidence must not allow it to obscure the fact that it is no more than an aid in assessing the primary evidence.

Laddie J cast further doubt on the utility of commercial success being used to suggest inventiveness in *Raychem Corp's Patents*,[172] at first instance, in which he said that commercial success was rarely an indicator of non-obviousness. It would, in many cases, be very difficult to demonstrate the necessary causal link and it may be the result of other factors such as improved marketing. He then criticised the practice of pleading commercial success saying that normally it only adds time and expense to the proceedings and serves no useful purpose. However, in that case, the evidence that commercial success resulted from non-obviousness was very weak. Of course, the court should always be wary of being seduced by evidence that the invention has been very successful but it can be useful if it is accompanied by evidence of a long-felt want.[173] But, even then, other factors such as marketing effort must also be considered. Nevertheless, if a patentee, whose patent is under attack for lack of inventive step, is confident that he can show at least an arguable case that commercial success is the result of the invention being non-obvious, he would be foolish not to put in such evidence. As the consequences of a finding of invalidity can be dire for the patentee, the court should be slow to criticise a patentee for doing what he can to protect his patent from attack.

Laddie J gave further thought to the utility of commercial success as an indicator of non-obviousness in *Haberman v Jackel International Ltd*.[174] The invention was for a spill-proof training cup for young children. It was very successful, annual sales reaching a peak of nearly 2 million. Although it is possible to make large profits by using effective marketing to sell a non-inventive product, Laddie J set out a list of nine factors, which he admitted was not an exhaustive list. These factors pointed one way or another in determining whether there was an inventive step and included:

1 The problem addressed by the claimed invention.
2 The period of time that problem had existed.
3 The significance of the problem.
4 How widely known the problem was and how many were likely to have been seeking a solution.
5 The prior art known to those seeking a solution.
6 Alternative solutions put forward before the publication of the patent.
7 What, if any, factors may have held back exploitation of the solution even if it was technically obvious?

170 [1990] RPC 498.

171 [1994] RPC 49.

172 [1998] RPC 31. The patents were held to be invalid. The proprietor's appeal to the Court of Appeal was dismissed: *Raychem Corp's Patents* [1999] RPC 497.

173 Where the prior art is available only a short time before the priority date of the patent, commercial success is not applicable: *BSH Industries Ltd's Patents* [1995] RPC 183. Presumably, this is because of an absence in such circumstances of a long-felt want.

174 [1999] FSR 683.

8 How well was the patentee's development received?
9 The extent to which it could be shown that the commercial success was due to the technical merits of the development because it solves a problem.

Success should not be taken into account if due to other factors such as the commercial power of the patentee or licensee, extensive advertising directed at features which had nothing to do with the development, branding and other technical features. In the present case, Laddie J considered the remarkable commercial success of the invention helpful. There had been a long-felt want as the problem had existed for a long time and there had been many attempts to make spill-proof training cups. The present invention was a simple but very effective solution and represented a step that anyone in the industry could have made in the preceding ten years. Against that background, there was an inventive step. Where there are numerous attempts to find a solution to a known problem and those developed before the claimed invention are significantly inferior to it as a solution to the problem, this fact is almost conclusive of non-obviousness.[175] If the claimed invention is a significant commercial success, this reinforces that view. Of course, the emphasis must be on whether the claimed invention was technically obvious rather than whether it was a commercial success, but the latter can be a good pointer to the former if analysed sensibly and in context in the manner suggested by Laddie J.

The words of the statutory provision are what are important and it is too easy to become influenced by paraphrases and linguistics. Sometimes commercial success may be a helpful pointer to inventiveness. In other cases, it may be obvious to try to make the invention. Such formulae on their own rarely provide the answer. At the end of the day, it is the nature of the alleged invention that is important.[176]

Experimentation

The fact that it would be relatively inexpensive to experiment and to make prototypes is another point in favour of a finding of non-obviousness, especially when the problem that the invention sought to solve had existed for some time. So it was held in *Mölnlycke AB v Procter & Gamble Ltd*.[177] It was argued that the claimant's dedicated fastening surface used for refastenable disposable nappies was obvious. The court disagreed because there had been an increasing need for multiple taping over a number of years and, had the idea been obvious, it would have occurred to someone much sooner, especially as it would cost very little to make prototypes. The invention was not obvious even though some of the defendant's employees had the same idea before or at around the same time. The fact that a competitor has had the same idea does not affect the state of the art unless the competitor makes it available to the public or files a patent application in respect of it.

If an invention takes a long time to conceive, that itself suggests that it is non-obvious.[178] Again, however, evidence of the length of time to find a solution can never be conclusive because researchers may work for years and still miss the obvious.[179] Neither does taking a commercial decision to pursue a series of experiments in the hope of finding a solution to a problem constitute an inventive step. In *Biogen Inc v Medeva plc*[180] the claimant embarked upon a series of experiments using known methods to find recombinant DNA molecules. Others knew that this approach might have worked, but had dismissed it as too unlikely to succeed to have been worthwhile. Hobhouse LJ made a useful analogy with placing a bet on a horse that appears to most to have little chance of winning a race. If the horse then wins, the gambler cannot be said to have invented a way of picking winners.[181]

It is not clear whether, if the notional skilled worker would perceive a significant risk of failure in pursuing a line of research, this implies that it is non-obvious to pursue that line of research. In *Pfizer Ltd's Patent*,[182] the proprietor suggested that other workers in the

175 *See* also Laddie J in *Pfizer Ltd's Patent* [2001] FSR 16 at para 115 and *Parks-Cramer Co v GW Thornton & Sons Ltd* [1966] RPC 407, discussed below.

176 Per Jacob LJ in *Angiotech Pharmaceuticals Inc v Conor Medsystems Inc* [2007] RPC 20 at para 45. An appeal to the House of Lords against the Court of Appeal decision that the specification must demonstrate that the invention worked and why it worked was successful: *Conor Medsystems Inc v Angiotech Pharmaceuticals Inc* [2008] RPC 28.

177 [1992] FSR 549; appeal dismissed: *see* [1994] RPC 49.

178 Despite *dicta* suggesting the contrary per Tomlin J in *Samuel Parks & Co Ltd v Cocker Brothers Ltd* (1929) 46 RPC 24 at 248.

179 Per Aldous J in *Chiron Corp v Organon Teknika Ltd (No 3)* [1994] FSR 202 at 224.

180 [1995] RPC 25.

181 The House of Lords found the claimed invention to be too broad and to be invalid for insufficiency: *Biogen Inc v Medeva plc* [1997] RPC 1.

182 [2001] FSR 16.

field would have been put off trying to develop an oral treatment for male impotency because of fears that any such treatment could be life-threatening. This was described by Laddie J as a lurid fear likely to obscure the issues. He said that the risk was one of failing to get the drug through the extensive and careful testing and clinical trials needed before a licence would be granted to administer the drug to patients rather than one of killing patients. Therefore, the notional skilled worker would not be deterred from finding a solution involving an oral treatment and this pointed to obviousness.

Problem solving

Some claimed inventions could be described as being no more than a general desideratum which skilled persons would aspire to. For example, in Case T389/99 *HITACHI/Electrostatic recorder and electrostatic latent image measuring instrument*,[183] the Technical Board of Appeal of the EPO held that higher accuracy in printing process control was such a general desideratum which did not imply an inventive step, *per se*. Furthermore, in Case T455/91 *GENENTECH/Expression in yeast*,[184] the Technical Board of Appeal said that it is the normal task of the skilled person to be constantly seeking the elimination of deficiencies, overcoming drawbacks and achieving improvements to known devices. Such matters can be described as 'workshop variations' generally regarded as unpatentable in the UK.

The invention may be the application of well-known technology to a particular problem, usually a new problem or an old one that has escaped attempts to solve it. Although novelty may be in issue, a second use of existing technology for a new purpose may still be acceptable on this point; but more importantly the question of obviousness will be raised. Consideration of the magnitude of the problem and whether there have been many attempts to find a solution in the past, all of which have proved to be unsuccessful, will provide a useful rule of thumb. If such is the case, it can be presumed that the invention is not obvious, and again the commercial success of the invention can prove to be a helpful factor in deciding obviousness. In *Parks-Cramer Co v GW Thornton & Sons Ltd*,[185] the invention was for a method of cleaning floors between rows of textile machines. There had been many attempts to find a satisfactory solution but none of them, unlike the present invention, actually worked. All the invention consisted of was an overhead vacuum cleaner which moved automatically up and down the rows between the machines. But attached to the cleaners were long vertical tubes, reaching almost to the floor. In the High Court, the trial judge considered that the patent was invalid because it was obvious. He said that it was common knowledge to every competent housewife that dust could be removed from a floor by the passage of a vacuum cleaner.[186] However, the Court of Appeal held that the patent was valid. The many unsuccessful attempts by inventors to find a solution and the immediate commercial success of the invention denied the possibility of a finding of obviousness. Diplock LJ said:

> As in all other cases of obviousness, the question is one of degree. There may be an inventive step in recognising that a problem exists at all; but given a problem which is known to exist which it is the object of the invention to solve, the question always is: 'Is the solution claimed by the patentee one which would have occurred to everyone of ordinary intelligence and acquaintance with the subject matter of the patent who gave his mind to the problem?'[187]

The claimant was granted an injunction and an order was made for the delivery up or destruction of the infringing articles.

Combination of known technologies

The courts have to draw a line somewhere when it comes to new uses of old technology and the question of obviousness. There must be a sufficient inventive step. Merely taking

183 6 December 2000.

184 [1996] EPOR 85.

185 [1966] RPC 407.

186 Perhaps the judge should have used the term 'houseperson' instead.

187 [1966] RPC 407 at 418.

two older inventions and sticking them together will not necessarily be regarded as an inventive step. It is all a question of degree, and it is difficult to lay down hard and fast rules. For example, in *Williams* v *Nye*,[188] Williams took out a patent for an improved mincing machine made up from a combination of two old machines: a mincing machine and a filling machine. What he did was to take the cutter from one machine and simply replace it with the cutter from the other machine. When the claimant sued the defendant for infringement of the patent, the defendant claimed that the patent was invalid, and this claim was successful because it was held that there was insufficient invention. However, the court accepted that a slight alteration might produce important results and be the result of great ingenuity. Cotton LJ said:

> . . . in order to maintain a patent there must be a substantial exercise of the inventive power or inventive faculty. Sometimes very slight alterations will produce very important results, and there may be in those very slight alterations very great ingenuity exercised or shown to be exercised by the Patentee.

Therefore, there seems to be a fine line drawn between what does and what does not constitute an inventive step. Even if the inventiveness appears at first sight trivial, the utility of the new invention and whether it is a significant improvement in the state of the art should be considered. Also one has to ask the obvious question: Why did nobody else do it before? After all, many of the most successful inventions seem, in retrospect, to be very simple, but simplicity should not be confused with obviousness.

It may be well known that you could combine two things, but nobody has thought to do it, perhaps because of technical prejudice. In *Petra Fischer's Application*,[189] the alleged invention was putting a diesel engine into a cabriolet car. The fact that those skilled in the art have been prejudiced against doing that does not mean that it is inventive. The alleged invention taught nothing new as the skilled man knew it was possible to put a diesel engine into a cabriolet car even though he did not think it was worth doing, for example, because of the problem of vibration of such an engine in a less rigid body shell or because he did not think it would sell. Reasons such as these were why it had not been done before – it had nothing to do with inventiveness.

Scientific prejudice may also be a factor. In *Ancare New Zealand Ltd's Patent*,[190] the patent in question was for a combination of two compounds, one for treating animals against tapeworm, the other for treating animals against roundworm. At the time of the application, a leading expert had written a paper to the effect that treating lambs for tapeworm was not worth doing as no harm was caused and, eventually, sheep develop a natural immunity to tapeworm. Nevertheless, many farmers did treat lambs for tapeworm. It was claimed that the inventive step was to stand out against the then received scientific wisdom to show that it was sensible to treat lambs for both tapeworm and roundworm: having the idea of combining treatment for both tapeworm and roundworm. Research carried out after the priority date of the patent did indeed show that tapeworm were deleterious to the health of lambs. The Privy Council confirmed that the patent was invalid for lack of inventive step otherwise '. . . anyone who adopted an obvious method of doing something which was widely practised but which best scientific opinion thought was pointless could obtain a patent'.[191] However, overcoming an existing prejudice can, in the right circumstances, involve an inventive step.[192] The issue is whether the prejudice is so great that overcoming it is inventive. In some cases the idea underlying the invention may be part of the state of the art as will be the prejudice that it will not work or would not be practicable. As Jacob LJ said in *Pozzoli SpA* v *BDMO SA*:[193]

> A patentee who contributes something new by showing that, contrary to the mistaken prejudice, the idea will work or is practical has shown something new. He has shown that an apparent 'lion in the path' is merely a paper tiger. Then his contribution is novel and non-obvious and he deserves his patent.

188 (1890) 7 RPC 62.

189 [1997] RPC 899.

190 [2003] RPC 8, on appeal from the Court of Appeal of New Zealand.

191 Per Lord Hoffmann at para 16.

192 *Ivax Pharmaceuticals UK Ltd* v *Akzo Nobel BV* [2007] RPC 3.

193 [2007] FSR 37 at para 27.

If an invention turns out to possess some advantage unforeseen before the priority date of a patent, that might not displace a finding of obviousness based on the prior art. In *Degussa-Huls SA* v *Comptroller-General of Patents*,[194] the prior art included a method of compressing materials for ease of packaging. It was later found that advantageous and surprising results were achieved using a different compound. Pumfrey J confirmed the hearing officer's view that the invention lacked inventive step, saying (at para 29):

> Evidence of unforeseeable advantage cannot displace a finding of obviousness if the finding of obviousness proceeds upon the suggestion that the invention is obvious for reasons which have nothing to do with the unforeseeable advantages which are said to have been obtained.

Putting two inventions together to create a new inventive concept is sometimes described as a collocation, which comes from the judgment of Lord Tomlin in *British Celanese Ltd* v *Courtaulds Ltd*[195] where he said (at p 193):

> . . . a mere placing side by side of old integers so that each performs its own proper function independently of any of the others is not a patentable combination, but that where the old integers when placed together have some working interrelation producing a new or improved result then there is patentable subject-matter in the idea of a working interrelation brought about by the collocation of those integers.

In *Sabaf SpA* v *MFI Furniture Centres Ltd*,[196] the alleged invention was to combine a low profile burner for a gas hob which drew air from above which was mixed with gas in a lower radial chamber by means of a venturi effect. This made it possible to manufacture shallow gas hobs, considered to be very desirable in modern kitchens. At first instance, Laddie J referred to an approach based on collocation but said that he was dealing with two inventions as each had no real effect upon the other. The Court of Appeal overturned his decision on the basis that Laddie J did not fully apply the *Windsurfing* test and that he applied what was described as the law of collocation; and the Court of Appeal held that the patent was valid.

The House of Lords disagreed with the Court of Appeal and agreed with Laddie J, though their Lordships confirmed that there was no law of collocation '. . . in the sense of a qualification of, or gloss upon, or exception to, the test of obviousness in s 3'. Lord Hoffmann said that, before you could apply s 3, you had to determine what the invention was and, in particular in such cases, whether you are dealing with one invention or two inventions and that two inventions do not become one simply because they are included in the same hardware. An example was given of a car made up of numerous parts, many of which could be described as inventions but operating independently of each other. This would not make the car itself a single invention. Support for Lord Hoffmann's view was provided by s 14(5)(d) which requires that a claim relate to an invention or a group of inventions so linked as to form a single inventive concept. This suggests that references to an invention are to a single inventive concept and not to a collocation of separate inventions.

Tests for inventive step

Oliver LJ postulated a test for obviousness in *Windsurfing International Inc* v *Tabur Marine (Great Britain) Ltd*,[197] being:

1 Identify the inventive concept embodied in the patent in suit.[198]
2 The court then assumes the mantle of the normally skilled but unimaginative addressee in the art at the priority date, imputing to him what was, at that date, common general knowledge in the art in question.

194 [2005] RPC 29.

195 (1935) 52 RPC 171.

196 [2005] RPC 10.

197 [1985] RPC 59 at 73.
198 This does not require the court to substitute its own language for that of the patentee, where the latter is clear. In many cases, a claim will state the inventive concept concisely: *Union Carbide Corp* v *BP Chemicals Ltd* [1999] RPC 409 at 424 per Aldous LJ.

3 Identify what, if any, differences exist between the matter cited as being 'known and used' and the alleged invention.

4 The court then asks itself the question whether, viewed without any knowledge of the alleged invention, those differences constitute steps which would have been obvious to the skilled man or whether they require any degree of invention.

199 See *Mölnlycke AB v Procter & Gamble Ltd (No 5)* [1994] RPC 49. For a good example of the test in use, see Balcombe LJ in *Optical Coating Laboratories Inc v Pilkington PE Ltd* [1995] RPC 145 at 163. In *Palmaz's European Patents (UK)* [2000] RPC 631, Aldous LJ said that he remained of the view that the best way to arrive at the right conclusion as to inventive step was to adopt the structured approach in *Windsurfing*.

200 [2001] RPC 7.

201 [1999] RPC 497.

Although *Windsurfing* involved a patent under the 1949 Act, the above test has been approved and applied on numerous occasions ever since.[199] The test has become so ingrained that failure of the judge to apply it to the question of obviousness was seen as a ground of appeal. For example, in *Davina Wheatley v Drillsafe Ltd*,[200] the patent related to a machine and method for cutting threaded holes in tanks containing liquids such as petrol. Ferris J, at first instance, decided that the invention was obvious without using the *Windsurfing* test. In the Court of Appeal, Aldous LJ accepted that the judge failed to distinguish between what was known and what formed part of the common general knowledge and he said that he suspected that this was because he failed to adopt the structured approach in *Windsurfing*. The Court of Appeal found that the patent was valid. In *Raychem Corp's Patents*,[201] Laddie J found that the inventions relating to positive temperature coefficient material were obvious without using the *Windsurfing* approach. On appeal, Aldous LJ disagreed with counsel's submission that Laddie J was wrong and, for the avoidance of similar criticism and applying the *Windsurfing* test, confirmed that the patents were invalid for lack of inventive step.

The *Windsurfing* test does not modify or supplement the statutory provision; it merely affords a structured way of assessing whether the requirement of inventive step has been satisfied. In *PLG Research Ltd v Ardon International Ltd*[202] the Court of Appeal confirmed that patents for heavy-duty plastic netting made by stretching sheets of perforated plastic were non-obvious, reversing the decision of Aldous J in the Patents Court on this point. Millett LJ neatly summarised the principles to be adopted in terms of obviousness:[203]

202 [1995] RPC 287. *See also* [1995] FSR 116 in which the judgment of the court is reported as being given by Neill LJ rather than Millett LJ.

203 The principles were first enunciated in *Mölnlycke AB v Procter & Gamble Ltd (No 5)* [1994] RPC 49, but Millett LJ's description is clearer.

204 Excluding the *Windsurfing* test, presumably.

1 The criterion for determining whether the claimed invention involves an inventive step is wholly objective and is defined in s 3 of the 1977 Act.

2 The test is qualitative, not quantitative, and paraphrasing the statutory test in other cases does not assist.[204]

3 The court must make findings of fact as to the state of the art at the priority date and, in the light of that, decide whether the invention was obvious to the skilled person.

4 Assessment of obviousness with hindsight must be avoided.

5 Where the validity of a patent is being attacked on the basis of lack of inventive step the burden of proof lies on the person making the attack to show that the invention did not involve an inventive step.

6 The *Windsurfing* test continues to be of assistance.

Millett LJ went on (at 313):

> The value of [the *Windsurfing*] analysis is not that it alters the critical question; it remains the question posed by the Act. But it enables the fact-finding tribunal to approach the question in a structured way.

205 [1999] FSR 683.

The danger of falling into the trap of applying hindsight is particularly present where the invention is already known to the court, especially where the invention operates in accordance with some simple principles of physics, chemistry or other sciences. This was pointed out by Laddie J in *Haberman v Jackel International Ltd*,[205] where he said of such inventions (at 698):

> It is normally easy to understand how they work. From this it is but a short step to thinking that a competent technician in the art would have realised, starting from the same simple principles, why the solution proposed by the patentee should have worked . . . the simpler

the solution, the easier it is to explain. The easier it is to explain, the more obvious it can appear. This is not always fair to inventors.

Almost invariably a court, faced with the task of deciding whether an invention involves an inventive step, will adopt the *Windsurfing* test.[206] It is not essential that it is used.[207] It is helpful rather than essential but may help avoid the danger of hindsight.[208] However, in spite of the popularity of the test amongst judges, there is at least an arguable case as to whether it ought to be used at all. The statutory provision seems straightforward and requires a one-step test only: that is, whether the invention is not obvious to a person skilled in the art.[209] There is a danger, in breaking this down, that artificiality will be introduced which might distort the test. A simpler formulation is to ask whether, from the point of view of a person who had total knowledge of the state of the art, the invention was obvious at its priority date. It goes without saying that the person concerned cannot be endowed with inventive faculties, otherwise not a single patent would ever be granted again. It is notable that the Boards of Appeal in the EPO do not appear to have adopted a structured approach to determining whether an inventive step is present as have the UK courts. The approach there to Article 56 of the EPC, the provision equivalent to that under the UK Act, seems to be a more straightforward application of the accepted state of the art to the statutory test, being whether, having regard to the state of the art, the invention is not obvious to a person skilled in the art. For these purposes, the closest prior art for the purpose of objectively assessing inventive step is generally that which corresponds to the same or a similar use as the claimed invention and, at the same time, that which requires the minimum of structural and functional modifications to arrive at the claimed invention.[210] Workshop improvements, increases in speed, accuracy or definition do not generally result from an inventive step as even unimaginative persons skilled in the art seek such goals. This does not mean, however, that such improvements can never be the subject of a patent as it may be that those skilled in the art had attempted for some time to make such improvements but had met with little or no success.

Perhaps English judges feel that the *Windsurfing* test prevents subjectivity, being too easily influenced by the evidence and applying hindsight. As Neuberger J said in *DSM NV's Patent*[211] (at para 58):

> I suppose that it can be said that this fourth stage approach really involves ending back up where one started, namely with the original issue, embodied in the fourth question. However, I believe that it is appropriate to apply this four stage approach . . . it ensures that one does not go straight to the question of obviousness by reference to a general impression as to the evidence as a whole. By adopting the structured approach, one ensures that there is a measure of discipline, reasoning and method in one's approach.

The structured approach in the *Windsurfing* test appears to be here to stay, although failure to use it is not fatal, providing the judge applies the statutory test correctly.[212] What can be said is that use of the test helps overcome subjectivity and falling into the error of using hindsight. It has to be said, however, that there are very few examples of judges not referring to the test and those that fail to apply the test may be guilty of leaving a hostage to fortune. The main danger in using the test is that it may put a gloss upon the statutory test that could cause a judge to lose sight of the question posed by s 3. Another difficulty is that, in a case where a judge has already decided that an invention is anticipated by the prior art, the application of step 3 of *Windsurfing* results in no differences and results in a premature conclusion of obviousness.[213] But novelty and inventive step are two independent tests and a finding of lack of novelty by the judge, which will often be based on his view of the scope and extent of the prior art coloured by the evidence of expert witnesses, should not automatically determine obviousness.

Incredibly, the House of Lords has not had an opportunity to confirm whether or not the *Windsurfing* test is appropriate and should be used. The author's view is that a stepwise

206 Even then, a judge might fail to adopt the mantle of the skilled person and also fall into the danger of adopting a classic *ex post facto* analysis in applying the fourth part of *Windsurfing: see*, for example, *Panduit Corp v Band-It Co Ltd* [2003] FSR 8 where this criticism was made by the Court of Appeal of the trial judge's application of *Windsurfing*.

207 See, for example, *David J Instance Ltd v Denny Bros Printing* [2002] RPC 14 and *Merck & Co Inc's Patent* [2004] FSR 16.

208 *Research in Motion UK Ltd v Inpro Licensing Sarl* [2007] EWCA Civ 51.

209 The Patents Act 1977 s 3 goes on to define what matter is to be taken as part of the state of the art.

210 Case T922/98 *MERCK/ Antihypertensive combination*, 16 March 2001.

211 [2001] RPC 35.

212 *David J Instance Ltd v Denny Bros Printing Ltd* [2002] RPC 14. *See* also *Sabaf SpA v MFI Furniture Centres Ltd* [2005] RPC 10 where Lord Hoffmann referred to the Court of Appeal being upset by the fact that the trial judge failed to apply *Windsurfing*.

213 This was a criticism of Laddie J at first instance by the Court of Appeal in *Technip France SA's Patent* [2004] RPC 46 at para 114.

approach to what is, in essence, a single question can increase the danger of misconstruing what s 3 requires as is evidenced by the numerous appeals based on inventive step.

One exception where the structured approach of Oliver LJ in *Windsurfing* might not be appropriate is in relation to a selection patent. This is implicit in the judgment of Aldous LJ in *Lubrizol Corp v Esso Petroleum Co Ltd*,[214] although in that case, after deciding that the patent was not a selection patent, he went on to apply the *Windsurfing* test. A selection patent is one where 'the inventive step lies in the discovery that one or more members of a previously known class of products possesses some special advantage for a particular purpose, which could not be predicted before the discovery was made'.[215] Another possible exception to the usefulness of the *Windsurfing* test is where the issue lies on the boundary of anticipation and obviousness.[216]

Finally, it is important to bear in mind the philosophy behind the doctrine of obviousness, which is, according to Millett LJ in *PLG Research* (at 313):

> ... that the public should not be prevented from doing anything which was merely an obvious extension or workshop variation of what was already known at the priority date.

Simple variants of existing inventions will be unlikely to be patentable. Something else is needed, and this could be described as the inventor's genius in thinking of something which others have not yet been able to conceptualise.

In *Pozzoli SpA v BDMO SA*,[217] Jacob LJ suggested that the *Windsurfing* test would be better restated as follows:

1 (a) Identify the notional 'person skilled in the art'.
   (b) Identify the relevant common general knowledge of that person.
2 Identify the inventive concept of the claim in question or, if that cannot readily be done, construe it.
3 Identify what, if any, differences exist between the matter cited as forming part of the 'state of the art' and the inventive concept of the claim or the claim as construed.
4 Viewed without any knowledge of the alleged invention as claimed, do those differences constitute steps which would have been obvious to the person skilled in the art or do they require a degree of invention?

This is a useful reformulation which makes the test easier to understand and apply. Some of the wording in the test as set out by Oliver LJ derives from the Patents Act 1949, for example, 'known and used' whereas the 1977 Act uses 'state of the art'. It is also preferable to change the order of the first two steps considering 'mantle first then concept'. The reformulation is welcome yet does not alter the essence of the test. Jacob LJ's version seems to have quickly established itself: see, for example, *Aerotel Ltd v Wavecrest Group Enterprises Ltd*,[218] *Dyson Technology Ltd v Samsung Gwangju Electronics Co Ltd*[219] and *Cook Biotech Inc v Edwards Lifesciences AG*.[220] However, although the test is relatively easy to describe, it can be difficult to apply. In *Virgin Atlantic Airways Ltd v Premium Aircraft Interiors Group Ltd*,[221] Lewison J said (at para 271) that one reason for this was that:

> ... at the third stage ... it is necessary to focus on the differences between the prior art and the patent in suit; but at the immediately succeeding fourth stage it is necessary to erase all knowledge of the alleged invention from the mind. That is not an easy task. Another [reason] is that where the skilled addressee is (or is a team that includes) a designer, to approach the prior art through the mind of an unimaginative designer is unreal. An unimaginative designer would soon be out of a job.

Lewison J held that the patent was valid but not infringed by the defendant. The Court of Appeal confirmed that the patent was valid but held that it was infringed by the defendant.[222] The patent concerned aircraft seating systems where the seats convert into beds. Jacob LJ said that the first three steps of the *Pozzoli* test merely orientate the

214 [1998] RPC 727 at 758.

215 Per Lord Diplock in *Beecham Group Ltd v Bristol Laboratories International SA* [1978] RPC 521 at 579.

216 Per Pumfrey J in *SmithKline Beecham plc v Apotex Europe Ltd* [2004] FSR 27 at para 64.

217 [2007] FSR 37.

218 [2009] EWCA Civ 408.
219 [2009] FSR 15.
220 [2010] EWCA Civ 718.
221 [2009] ECDR 11.

222 *Virgin Atlantic Airways Ltd v Premium Aircraft Interiors UK Ltd* [2010] RPC 8.

court properly. Step 4 is the key, statutory step. The word 'obvious' in step 4 means technically obvious rather than commercially obvious. The inventive concept in step one was the idea of making more efficient use of spare space in that part of the cabin where seats converting into beds were located. As to the application of step 4, Jacob LJ said (at para 119):

> . . . as the judge recognised, the court's assessment of obviousness at step 4 has to be made on an historical basis as at the priority date without taking into account its knowledge of the invention. Since expert witnesses are as much in danger of being affected by hindsight as the court itself, the fact that the invention was new and untried is likely to provide strong prima facie evidence that the inventive concept was not obvious to those skilled in the art absent some other explanation for their failure to adopt it.

The difficulty for judges in applying tests for obviousness, as Lewison J pointed out at first instance, is that, after identifying the inventive concept, trying to forget everything else about the patent. This reduces the danger of hindsight but cannot completely eliminate it as the state of the art will have moved on from the priority date of the patent.

Step 2 of *Pozzoli*, identifying the inventive concept, comes from the *Windsurfing* test. As Lord Hoffmann pointed out in *Conor Medsystems Inc* v *Angiotech Pharmaceuticals Inc*,[223] what matters is what is claimed. At para 19, he said:

> The patentee is entitled to have the question of obviousness determined by reference to his claim and not to some vague paraphrase based upon the extent of his disclosure in the description

In *Actavis UK Ltd* v *Novartis AG*,[224] Jacob LJ gave more consideration to the *Pozzoli/ Windsurfing* test. He noted that the inventive concept in step 2 could be a distraction or be helpful, whether or not the parties agreed on what it is. Step 4 provides no structured approach itself but a number of approaches may be helpful such as the 'obvious to try' or 'problem and solution' approaches. The latter is set out in the EPO's Guidelines for Substantive Examination and sets out three main stages:

(i) determining the 'closest prior art',
(ii) establishing the 'objective technical problem' to be solved, and
(iii) considering whether or not the claimed invention, starting from the closest prior art and the objective technical problem, would have been obvious to the skilled person.[225]

Jacob LJ accepted that the guidelines might be useful to provide a structured approach for patent examiners. But a national court may need to apply a multi-factorial analysis, including secondary indicia such as commercial success. In any case, step (i) of the guidelines is not really applicable to cases before the courts in the UK where counsel will have limited their attacks on inventive step on one or just a few citations from the prior art. There may also be problems where it is difficult to establish the objective technical problem. Jacob LJ goes on to further critique the guidelines by reference to the 'anyway up cup' in *Haberman* v *Jackel* (appreciating that a problem, tolerated for many years, can be solved) of the 'five and a quarter inch plate' paradox.[226]

223 [2008] RPC 28.

224 [2010] FSR 18.

225 This might invite the 'could/ would' question. It is not enough to show that the skilled person could have arrived at the alleged invention from the prior art, it must be shown that he would have done so.

226 A patent claims a five-and-a-quarter-inch diameter plate. No plate of such a diameter can be found. Is it therefore novel and non-obvious? But, the five-and-a-quarter-inch limitation is purely arbitrary and solves no technical problem. Trivial limitations such as choosing a particular plate diameter for no good reason are obvious because they are not inventive.

Industrial application

Another requirement is that the invention is capable of industrial application. This requirement demonstrates the practical nature of patent law, which requires that the invention should be something which can be made industrially or relate to an industrial

227 Under the Patents Act 1977 s 4(1) 'industry' includes agriculture.

228 Under the Patents Act 1949, a patent could be invalidated on the grounds of inutility: s 32(1) (g).

229 [2006] EPOR 14.

230 [2008] RPC 29. The finding of Kitchen J that the invention lacked industrial application was upheld by the Court of Appeal but reversed by the Supreme Court (see *infra*).

231 Almost identical to the requirement in Article 57 of the European Patent Convention.

232 For example, Patents Act 1949 s 101(1).

233 However, the exception of surgery, therapy and diagnosis from industrial application is important.

234 Patents Act 1949 s 32(1)(g).

235 For a more recent example, where it was argued, unsuccessfully, that not all the products claimed had a use, *see Chiron Corp v Organon Teknika Ltd (No 3)* [1994] FSR 202. The defendant also raised a number of other defences, including the s 44 defence which was successful. (Note that s 44 was repealed by the Competition Act 1998.)

236 [1969] RPC 267.

237 (1920) 37 RPC 247.

238 [1969] RPC 646.

process.[227] An application for a patent that depends upon the use of hitherto undiscovered materials in its manufacture would be refused.[228] The invention has to be something that can be worked industrially, and to some extent this requirement distinguishes patents from other forms of intellectual property such as original works of copyright. It confirms the difference between 'industrial property' and copyright.

The notion of 'industry' must be construed broadly. The Board of Appeal at the EPO so held in Case T870/04 *MAX-PLANCK/BDP1 Phosphatase*,[229] in which it said would include all manufacturing, extracting and processing activities of enterprises that are carried out continually, independently and for financial (commercial) gains. In *Eli Lilly & Co v Human Genome Sciences Inc*,[230] at first instance, Kitchen J added a proviso to this (at para 226) by saying that:

> . . . it need not necessarily be conducted for profit . . . and a product which is shown to be useful to cure a rare or orphan disease may be considered capable of industrial application even if it is not intended for use in any trade at all . . . Conversely, the requirement will not be satisfied if what is described is merely an interesting research result that might yield a yet to be identified industrial application.

The fact that an invention is not to be exploited for profit should not mean that it is not susceptible of industrial application but it is not easy to think of an example. Even if free licences are available under the patent, someone will be making financial gains.

Under s 4(1) an invention is capable of industrial application if it can be made or used in any kind of industry, including agriculture.[231] Before the 1977 Act, the requirement equivalent to industrial application came from the phrase 'manner of new manufacture',[232] but it is no easy task to tell whether the change in phraseology makes any difference when it can strongly be argued that the requirement that the invention is capable of industrial application is totally unnecessary, especially when the exceptions contained in s 1(2) (discussed below, *see* pp 464–68) are considered, as these exceptions probably account for anything which might not have industrial application.[233] Otherwise, lack of industrial application may be relevant if the invention as claimed simply does not work. This may be analogous to the provisions relating to inutility in the 1949 Act.[234]

There have been relatively few cases where the question of industrial application was at issue.[235] One example under the 1949 Act, where the phrase used was 'manner of manufacture', was *Hiller's Application*.[236] An application for a patent for an improved plan for underground service distribution schemes for housing estates was turned down. The scheme involved the location of gas and water mains, electricity cables and storm and foul water drains. The alleged novelty lay in the idea of locating the main supply route alongside the road rather than underneath it, with branches passing under the road at intervals serving adjacent houses. The appeal to the Patent Appeal Tribunal was turned down by Lloyd-Jacob J who said that the scheme could not constitute a 'manner of manufacture'. He did not need to trouble himself to go on to consider another possibly fatal objection to the application on the ground of lack of novelty. There were other good grounds why the application should have been refused which were not really considered in the judgment, not the least being that it would give a disproportionate monopoly which would be certain to restrict the freedom of providers of public utilities. Finally, the scheme lacked an inventive step, being obvious and representing no more than good practice in the construction industry.

Another example of a refusal because the invention did not represent a new manner of manufacture was *C's Application*,[237] in which an application in respect of an invention comprising a musical notation, in which sharps and flats were printed in different colours and sizes compared to natural notes, was refused. However, in *Pitman's Application*,[238] an application for a patent for an improved method of teaching pronunciation was allowed. The method involved visually conveying inflection and stress by using upper and lower case print and by the vertical displacement of the letters in relation to a median line. The arrangement was in the form of a printed sheet, but the patent specification referred to the use of the sheet in conjunction with a reading machine. The invention possessed a definite mechanical purpose when considered together with the reading machine and was not simply a literary or intellectual arrangement of matter. In this way, the case is distinguishable from *C's Application*.

Industrial application may be in issue where a range of substances is claimed and it is argued that some do not do what is claimed. In *Chiron Corp* v *Murex Diagnostics Ltd*,[239] a range of polypeptides encoded by a genome of hepatitis C virus was claimed. The defendant in an infringement action challenged the validity of the patent on the basis, *inter alia*, that the invention was not capable of industrial application because the claim included polypeptides unconnected with hepatitis C virus. These polypeptides had no conceivable use. At first instance, Aldous J held that the patent was capable of industrial application. He said (at 575):

> Although the range of polypeptides falling within the claims . . . may be large, there is no evidence to suggest that once the sequence is known they could not be made by industry.

The defendant appealed, claiming that Aldous J was wrong to substitute the word 'by' for 'in', arguing that the correct question was whether the invention could be made or used *in* industry not *by* industry. The defendant submitted that there was no industry in making the useless. The claimant argued that the defendant's objection was merely 'a puzzle at the edge of the claim'.[240] Whilst what was claimed must have some practical use, a claim in respect of practical things is not invalidated by the inclusion at the edge of the claim of something for which there is no present or foreseeable use. The Court of Appeal was unimpressed by that argument and Morritt LJ said (at 607):

> We accept that the polypeptides claimed . . . can be made . . . [but it is required] that the invention can be made or used 'in any kind of industry' so as to be 'capable' or 'susceptible of industrial application' . . . the manifest intention of the Patents Act 1977 and the European Patent Convention [is] that monopoly rights should be confined to that which has some useful purpose . . . the judge fell into error by giving the sections too literal a construction and in considering what can be made and used by industry rather than what can be made and used in any kind of industry.[241]

As a result, the court held that part of the relevant claim was invalid. Of course, in such a case where a range or class of products is claimed, it may be possible to amend the specification to eliminate those incapable of being made or not having the claimed effect.[242]

Industrial application can be equated with *technical effect*,[243] and if there is some technical effect, that is if the use or working of the invention produces some tangible and physical consequences or if the invention is itself a physical entity (as opposed to information), then the requirement should be met. Technical effect is important when considering the scope of the exceptions to patent protection contained in s 1(2) of the 1977 Act which is discussed below.

Section 4 of the Patents Act 1977 differs slightly to Article 57 EPC, although s 4 is one of those provisions stated in s 130(7) to be framed as to have, as nearly as practicable, the same effects in the UK as the corresponding provisions in the EPC, etc. Section 4 speaks of the invention being '. . . taken to be *capable* of industrial application if it can be made or used in any kind of industry, including agriculture' whereas Article 57 states that 'An invention shall be considered as *susceptible* of industrial application if it can be made or used in any kind of industry, including agriculture'. The use of 'capable' suggests something more concrete that 'susceptible' in the EPC. Perhaps nothing turns on this difference in terminology.

239 [1996] RPC 535.

240 A phrase used by Lord Shaw of Dunfermline in *British Thomson-Houston Co Ltd* v *Corona Lamp Works Ltd* (1922) 39 RPC 49 at 89.

241 However, Morritt LJ used the phrase 'made *and* used in any kind of industry' when the statutory test uses the phrase 'made *or* used in any kind of industry' (emphasis added).

242 See, for example, *May & Baker Ltd* v *Boots Pure Drug Co Ltd* (1950) 67 RPC 23.

243 The phrase 'technical effect' derives from case law; it is not taken from the Patents Act 1977.

Industrial application and bioscience patents

244 [2010] RPC 14. This case is under appeal to the Supreme Court.

245 21 October 2009.

In *Eli Lilly & Co v Human Genome Sciences Inc*,[244] the Court of Appeal, agreeing with the judge at first instance, held that industrial application required that the patent must claim something of immediate concrete benefit and mere speculation was not enough. In so holding, the Court of Appeal differed from the decision of the Technical Board of Appeal in relation to the same patent: Case T18/09 *HUMAN GENOME SCIENCES/neutrokine*.[245] The Technical Board of Appeal accepted that the patent claims lacked specific information about uses of the subject-matter but this did not preclude its possible use as an imaging, diagnostic or therapeutic agent. Jacob LJ in the Court of Appeal noted that the Board of Appeal had made different findings of fact to Kitchen J at first instance. He had the advantage of listening to and evaluating a substantial amount of evidence. Furthermore, of course, decisions of the Boards of Appeal are not binding on national courts. Indeed, decisions of the Boards of Appeal are not binding except in so far as a case is remitted back to the department of first instance.[246]

246 Case J27/94 *Université Laval/ Divisional Application* [1996] EPOR 319.

247 [2011] UKSC 51.

The Supreme Court disagreed with the Court of Appeal and reversed the finding of Kitchen J. In *Human Genome Sciences Inc v Eli Lilly & Co*,[247] the Supreme Court held that the invention, being for a nucleotide sequence of a gene (called Neutrokine-α), was capable of industrial application. The Supreme Court held that the reason the courts below differed from the Board of Appeal was not due to differences in evidence and argument before the courts and the Board of Appeal at the EPO, but was the result of an error in principle.[248]

248 Kitchen J's judgment pre-dated that of the Board of Appeal by nearly one year.

In relation to 'biotech' inventions, a distinction can be drawn between a new substance or protein which, although identified, merely indicates that a programme of research should be embarked upon to discover whether it has a particular effect and one which, in the light of the common general knowledge, has a plausible claimed use. The latter might be the case where a newly discovered protein is part of a known 'superfamily' which exhibit certain characteristics. Lord Neuberger summarised the general principles derived from the jurisprudence of the EPO Boards of Appeal in such cases as (at para 107):[249]

249 References to EPO cases removed for clarity.

(i)   The patent must disclose 'a practical application' and 'some profitable use' for the claimed substance, so that the ensuing monopoly 'can be expected [to lead to] some . . . commercial benefit'.

(ii) A 'concrete benefit', namely the invention's 'use . . . in industrial practice' must be 'derivable directly from the description', coupled with common general knowledge.

(iii) A merely 'speculative' use will not suffice, so 'a vague and speculative indication of possible objectives that might or might not be achievable' will not do.

(iv) The patent and common general knowledge must enable the skilled person 'to reproduce' or 'exploit' the claimed invention without 'undue burden', or having to carry out 'a research programme'.

Where a patent discloses a new protein and its encoding gene:

(v)   The patent, when taken with common general knowledge, must demonstrate 'a real as opposed to a purely theoretical possibility of exploitation'.

(vi) Merely identifying the structure of a protein, without attributing to it a 'clear role', or 'suggest[ing]' any 'practical use' for it, or suggesting 'a vague and speculative indication of possible objectives that might be achieved', is not enough.

(vii) The absence of any experimental or wet lab evidence of activity of the claimed protein is not fatal.

(viii) A 'plausible' or 'reasonably credible' claimed use, or an 'educated guess', can suffice.

(ix) Such plausibility can be assisted by being confirmed by 'later evidence', although later evidence on its own will not do.

(x)   The requirements of a plausible and specific possibility of exploitation can be at the biochemical, the cellular or the biological level.

Where the protein is said to be a family or superfamily member:

(xi)   If all known members have a 'role in the proliferation, differentiation and/or activation of immune cells' or 'function in controlling physiology, development and differentiation of mammalian cells', assigning a similar role to the protein may suffice.

(xii) So 'the problem to be solved' in such a case can be 'isolating a further member of the [family]'.

(xiii) If the disclosure is 'important to the pharmaceutical industry', the disclosure of the sequences of the protein and its gene may suffice, even though its role has not 'been clearly defined'.

(xiv) The position may be different if there is evidence, either in the patent or elsewhere, which calls the claimed role or membership of the family into question.

(xv)   The position may also be different if the known members have different activities, although they need not always be 'precisely interchangeable in terms of their biological action', and it may be acceptable if 'most' of them have a common role.

By its decision, the Supreme Court has aligned UK law with that of the Boards of Appeal. This decision is extremely important to the biotech industry. For most pharmaceutical companies, intellectual property is their greatest asset and they depend on their patent portfolios to attract much-needed investment for research and development. In knowing where to draw the line on the question of industrial application, care must be taken not to grant a patent too early otherwise it risks closing down competition. On the other hand, setting the hurdle too high brings the risk that a competitor will have already filed an application which may bring to an end a lengthy and costly research and development project.

Perpetual motion

The UKIPO routinely refuses claims to perpetual motion machines on the basis of lack of industrial application. The same principles apply to inventions based on theories which may appear to fly in the face of accepted science. However, the correct test is whether the evidence adduced by the applicant gives rise to any reasonable prospect that the theory in question might turn out to be correct.[250] Many theories, when first postulated, might seem improbable if not impossible, in terms of the contemporary scientific beliefs and accepted standards and theories.

250 *Blacklight Power Inc* v *Comptroller General of Patents* [2008] EWHC 2763.

Exclusions from patentability

One form of exclusion has already been described. The treatment, by surgery or therapy, or diagnosis in relation to human and animal bodies is excluded, previously on the basis that such forms of treatment were not considered to be capable of an industrial application.[251] Section 1(2) and (3) of the 1977 Act contains a range of things that are excluded from patentability. While in many cases these exclusions can be justified on the grounds of lack of technical effect or technical contribution, in some cases the exclusions are more controversial: for example, in the case of computer programs. The exclusions in s 1(2) can be classified as those necessary because of the nature of the subject matter, either being information orientated, and therefore more appropriately protected by copyright, or being too abstract and removed from immediate industrial application or manufacture. The exclusions in s 1(3) are based on public policy and morality. Further provisions prohibiting the patenting of animal or plant varieties used to be contained in old s 1(3)(b). These have been replaced and significantly modified and are now found in Sch A2 to the 1977 Act which confirms the scope of patentability of biotechnological inventions. These provisions are discussed in the section on biotechnological inventions below.

251 Now excluded simply on the basis of not being a patentable invention rather than lacking industrial application under new s 4A.

Exclusions in s 1(2)

The Patents Act 1977 s 1(2) states that anything which consists of the following (amongst other things – the list is not exhaustive) is not an invention for the purposes of the Act:

(a) a discovery, scientific theory or mathematical method;
(b) a literary, dramatic, musical or artistic work, or any other aesthetic creation whatsoever;
(c) a scheme, rule or method for performing any mental act, playing a game or doing business, or a program for a computer;
(d) the presentation of information.[252]

However, the section goes on to say that 'the foregoing provision shall prevent anything from being treated as an invention . . . only to the extent that a patent or application for a patent relates to that thing *as such*' (emphasis added). Herein lies the problem: things in the list are not excluded totally and unequivocally, but only if the patent application is directed towards the excluded thing itself.[253] This has caused some judicial differences in the way s 1(2) has been interpreted, especially in the context of computer programs. Before this is examined in detail, the nature of the other exclusions will be discussed briefly.[254]

That the list of excluded things is not exhaustive does not mean that a whole range of other things can be excluded by adding copiously to the list.[255] It is likely that any additions to the list will be, at least, analogous to those specified in the Act. One example of something added to the list was a method of controlling traffic in *Lux Traffic Controls Ltd* v *Pike Signals Ltd*.[256]

A discovery, scientific theory or mathematical method

The things excepted in this category are the raw materials which are part of the stock-in-trade of scientists, and if previously unknown ones are discovered they should be available to all. But there is another reason why they cannot be patented and that is that, by themselves, they have no technical effect. They have to be applied before there can be a technical effect and therefore an industrial application. But in common with the other exclusions in s 1(2), these exclusions relate to patent applications for the stated things as such. If a mathematical formula is embodied into a measuring device then that device itself may well be patentable.

In *Chiron Corp* v *Organon Teknika Ltd (No 3)*[257] the defendant argued that the claimant's patent sought to monopolise methods of testing blood, based on its discovery of the sequence of hepatitis C virus. However, this was rejected by Aldous J, who confirmed that a claim directed to the technical effect of a discovery may well be patentable. He said (at 239):

> Many inventions that are patented arise out of a discovery. However, the section [s 1(2) of the 1977 Act] makes it clear that something further is needed to make that discovery patentable . . . In the present case, the claims are concerned with a technical aspect of the discovery. They are limited to products, kits, methods of testing, vaccines and cell cultures.

The fact that mathematical theories cannot be patented is not new. In *Young* v *Rosenthal*,[258] there was an alleged infringement of a patent for improvements in the manufacture of corsets using seams arranged in diagonal patterns in accordance with a mathematical formula. In addressing the jury, Grove J said (at 31):

> An invention of an idea or mathematical principle alone, mathematical formula or any-thing of that sort could not be the subject of a patent. It must be a manufacture, and it must be a manufacture which is new in this realm.

252 These exclusions are derived from the European Patent Convention (*see* Article 52(2) and (3)), but the position is not far removed from earlier UK law because of the requirement that the invention was a 'manner of manufacture'. This would automatically exclude most of these things anyway.

253 Thus, theoretically it should be possible to obtain a patent on an industrial application of a scientific theory though not for the theory itself.

254 The basic principles which have been developed in respect of the patentability of computer programs should also apply to the other excluded materials mentioned in the Patents Act 1977 s 1(2).

255 *Chiron Corp* v *Murex Diagnostics Ltd* [1996] RPC 535.

256 [1993] RPC 107.

257 [1994] FSR 202.

258 (1884) 1 RPC 29.

The jury found that the claimant's invention had been copied by the defendant, but that the patent was invalid because it was neither novel nor useful. However, it is arguable that there is a technical effect.[259] The quote from Grove J confirms the view that there is a large overlap between s 1(2) and (1)(c) (the industrial application requirement) and that one or other is unnecessary.

The practical application of a discovery might be perfectly obvious once the discovery has been made yet it might still be patentable. In *Genentech Inc's Patent*,[260] involving recombinant DNA technology, Whitford J said at first instance (at 566):

> It is trite law that you cannot patent a discovery, but if on the basis of that discovery you can tell people how it can be usefully employed then a patent of invention may result. This in my view would be the case even though once you have made the discovery the way in which it can be usefully employed is obvious enough . . . The language of section 1(2) . . . is apt as an embodiment of this principle of United Kingdom patent law.

In the subsequent appeal, the Court of Appeal agreed with Whitford J.[261] Dillon LJ said (at 240):

> In so far as a patent claims as an invention the practical application of a discovery, the patent does not, in my judgment, relate only to the discovery as such, even if the practical application may be obvious once the discovery has been made, even though unachievable in the absence of discovery.[262]

Similarly, in *DSM NV's Patent*,[263] Neuberger J found that getting from the protein activity of a fungus to a point where the protein gene could be isolated, copied, multiplied and reproduced involved an inventive step and was not an application to obtain a patent on a discovery as such.

Proprietors of patents do not engage in research aimed at making discoveries simply for the acclaim resulting from their discovery. They do so with a view to developing a practical application of the discovery so that they may exploit it commercially. The scope of the exclusion of discoveries as such from the grant of a patent was reviewed again in *Chiron Corp v Murex Diagnostics Ltd*.[264] The Court of Appeal accepted that *Genentech* and *Gale* represented good law in this respect and yet again approved Whitford J's statement above. The above principles relating to the patentability of discoveries are very important in the context of genetic engineering where much research is undertaken to discover and isolate genetic sequences and to discover genetic defects causing diseases. As mentioned earlier, the rationale for allowing patents in such areas is to encourage investment in such research and reward the achievement of being able to make something useful that could not be made before.

A literary, dramatic, musical or artistic work, or any other aesthetic creation whatsoever

These works and creations are plainly the subject matter of copyright law or design law, hence the exclusion. In most cases, these works will not be capable of industrial application and are thus excluded twice over. Copyright law is more suited to these types of works because a patent would give a protection that is too strong. Copyright does not provide a monopoly and the independent creation of similar works is permissible.[265] However, such works could be indirectly patented if they were part of some machine or process: for example, as in *Pitman's Application* discussed above in relation to industrial application.

A scheme, rule or method for performing any mental act, playing a game or doing business, or a program for a computer

(Computer programs are discussed separately later in this chapter.) It is not possible to stop people thinking or doing mental arithmetic. If a patent were to be granted, say, for

259 Of course, this case long predates the specific exception in the Patents Act 1977 s 1(2).

260 [1987] RPC 553.

261 [1989] RPC 147.

262 The Court of Appeal again confirmed this approach as being correct in *Re Gale's Patent Application* [1991] RPC 305.

263 [2001] RPC 35.

264 [1996] RPC 535.

265 But a registered design enjoys a monopoly during its life. Furthermore, copyright can confer a monopoly if the owner of the copyright is the only source of the information contained within the work.

a method of mental arithmetic, it would be unenforceable anyway. As far as methods of playing games and doing business are concerned, this means that it is not possible to patent, for example, a new chess opening or a new method of assessing bids for large construction schemes.[266] However, copyright law may protect the expression of the scheme, rule or method and, depending upon the circumstances, the law of confidence could give some protection. The exclusion of methods of doing business is particularly important and there have been a number of examples of patents being refused for inventions caught under this head. For example, in Case T854/90 *IBM/Card reader*,[267] a method whereby a person could use any machine-readable card to perform transactions on automatic self-service machines was refused on the basis that it was a method of doing business, the card being analogous to an application form. The fact that the business activity was effected by technical means did not overcome the objection. Furthermore, it was held that the claimed invention lacked inventive step. However, in Case T1002/92 *PETTERSSON/Queuing system*,[268] a system for handling the queuing of customers at service points in a system incorporating a turn-number allocation unit, a selection unit, terminals, an information unit and computing means was held to be patentable. The relevant claim was directed to the functional aspects of the invention and the only function which was arguably a method of doing business was that of the claimed computing means to decide which turn-number was to be served at a particular free service point on the basis of a given rule. However, taking the claim as a whole, this function was inseparably linked to the remaining technical features.

Some of the things under this particular exception will not be capable of industrial application anyway (in a direct sense). Unlike most of the other items in this subcategory, computer programs are capable of being applied industrially and are often so used, for example, in controlling industrial processes such as an electronically controlled furnace, in telecommunications, in robotics, in imaging and even to control the operation of the humble washing machine.

A claim to a lottery game played through the internet was rejected in *Shoppalotto.com Ltd's Patent Application*.[269] The hearing officer at the Patent Office (now UK Intellectual Property Office) held that the application was for a scheme, rule or method of performing a mental act, playing a game or doing business, or a program for a computer or the presentation of information. The appeal was dismissed. Pumfrey J said that the correct approach was to ask whether there was a relevant technical effect, being one over and above 'that to be expected from the mere loading of a program into a computer'. What did the claimed programmed computer invention contribute over and above the fact that it involved a computer program? It would be patentable if there was a contribution not within the subject matter and activities declared to be 'non-inventions' as then it would not be an application for the excluded matter *as such*. He also noted that the list of things or activities excluded from the meaning of invention formed a heterogeneous collection and it was difficult to discern any underlying policy for their inclusion in the list.[270]

In *Crawford's Patent Application*,[271] a display system designed to prevent bus grouping was also held to be not an invention as it was, *inter alia*, a method of doing business. Kitchen J said that there was a consistent principle that an inventor had to make a contribution to the art, that contribution had to have a technical nature, being susceptible to industrial application and not within one of the areas excluded by Article 52(2) of the EPC. But this ignores the fact that most of the exclusions are there because they are, by their very nature, abstract and lacking industrial application in their pure form. It is the technical application of the excluded matter that overcomes the effect of Article 52(2). It is submitted that the invention in question did overcome a technical problem by technical means and would, in principle, be patentable at the EPO.

It now seems clear that the mental acts exclusion should be narrowly construed. So held Floyd J in *Kapur v Comptroller General of Patents*,[272] where he accepted that the physical

266 On arithmetic, *see Re Gale's Patent Application* [1991] RPC 305, and on methods of doing business *see Re Merrill Lynch, Pierce Fenner and Smith Inc's Application* [1988] RPC 1 and [1989] RPC 561. Both of these cases are discussed in the section on computer programs below.

267 [1994] EPOR 89.

268 [1996] EPOR 1.

269 [2006] RPC 7.

270 In *CFPH LLC's Application* [2006] RPC 5 (at para 21), Peter Prescott QC described the list of excepted matter as a 'miscellaneous rag-bag'. Although excluded for policy reasons, they were not all excluded for the same reasons.

271 [2006] RPC 11.

272 [2008] EWHC 649 (Pat).

handling and indexing of documents was not a mental act. However, as regards the exclusion, it covered clever mental acts as well as obvious ones.[273]

273 Per Floyd J in *Kapur* at para 35.

The presentation of information

This is another exception that can be best explained on the ground that it is properly within the scope of copyright or other forms of protection. Information may be presented in numerous ways: for example, by newspapers, television, slide presentation at a conference or by means of internet web pages. In many cases, the information will be protected by copyright or by the database right. In some cases, the information may be imparted in confidence giving rise to an obligation of confidence. What this exemption prevents is the presentation of information, *per se*. A particular means or method of presenting information may be subject to a patent if it otherwise complies with the requirements for patent: for example, a new and inventive visual display system.

In *Townsend's Patent Application*,[274] the application was in respect of an advent calendar having additional indicia applied to the doors of the calendar so that the 'treats' exposed when opening the doors could be fairly shared out in cases where two or more persons shared the calendar. For example, half the doors could have a male symbol printed on them with the other half having a female symbol so a sister and brother would know when it was their turn to open the door and retrieve the treat behind, such as a chocolate. It was argued that the term 'presentation of information' could mean either the expression of information or the provision of information. The applicant accepted that the exclusion would apply if it meant the provision of information as the purpose of the additional indicia was to provide information, being the identity of the person entitled to open a particular door on the advent calendar. However, he argued that the term actually meant the expression of information and concerned how the information was provided. Laddie J gave an example of the difference between the two meanings. Marking a door on an advent calendar with 'only three more shopping days to Christmas' was the provision of information. Requiring the words to be in a particular font is to stipulate the expression of the information.

274 [2004] EWHC 482 (Pat).

Laddie J considered that the answer was simple and that the presentation of information clearly meant providing information. He said that the term used ordinary English words and was unambiguous. Further, it should be construed in the light of the other exclusions in s 1(2) and he noted that in *Fujitsu Limited's Application*,[275] the Court of Appeal said that the reason for the exclusion of computer programs *as such* was to prevent the patenting of giving instructions or conveying information, *per se*.

275 [1997] RPC 608.

Computer programs

The granting of patents for software inventions has long been a matter of some controversy. An example of this was the rejection by the European Parliament of the proposed Directive on the patentability of computer-implemented inventions on 6 July 2005.[276] This proposal would have allowed the patenting of computer-implemented inventions, defined as any invention '. . . the performance of which involves the use of a computer, a computer network or other programmable apparatus and having one or more *prima facie* novel features which are realised wholly or partly by means of a computer program or computer programs'. The conditions for patentability would have been that the computer-implemented invention was susceptible of industrial application, novel and involved an inventive step by making a technical contribution not obvious to a person skilled in the art. The technical contribution would have been assessed by looking at the difference

276 COM (2002) 92 final, 20.02.2002.

between the scope of the claim as a whole, which may comprise both technical and non-technical features, and the state of the art.

Had the proposal been accepted, it could have made it easier to obtain patents for certain software inventions, particularly where the technical contribution was itself something excluded from the grant of a patent, *per se*, such as a method of doing business. One of the reasons for the proposal was that the current provisions relating to the patenting of computer programs are ambiguous and there have been differences between the way the provisions are interpreted, particularly by the Boards of Appeal of the EPO and Member States and between Member States. This is unsatisfactory and can only distort the internal market but it appears that no further action will be taken in the foreseeable future. As the Agreement on Trade Related Aspects of Intellectual Property Rights ('TRIPs Agreement') contains no express exception for computer programs from the grant of a patent this is a regrettable state of affairs, particularly when one considers that the US and Japan also have no specific exclusion for computer-implemented inventions and patents for such inventions appear to be much easier to obtain in those countries.

Proponents of open-source software were particularly concerned about the prospects of computer software being tied up by patents owned by large corporations. Copyright protection is, in the views of many, a more appropriate form of protection and does not prevent creation of new software that emulates existing software especially in terms of its underlying logic, objectives and functionality providing none of the acts restricted by copyright are performed. Numerous exceptions to copyright protection for computer programs have prevented copyright becoming the tool by which over-strong monopolistic protection for software lies in the hands of powerful corporations. Nevertheless, and in spite of the exception from patenting computer programs as such, there are tens of thousands of patents in Europe for software inventions and, as will be seen, the exception can be overcome in many cases, where there is a technical contribution to the state of the art.

Whilst differences in interpretation are almost inevitable given the way in which the EPC is drafted and where the meaning of 'invention' is given only by stating what is not an invention in a manner that could not be more imprecise, the UK courts and the Patent Office have striven to be at one with the Boards of Appeal at the EPO when considering how to determine whether an invention incorporating a computer program is patentable.

Copyright and patents as a means of protecting computer programs each have their own advantages and disadvantages from the perspective of the rightholder.[277] These are set out in Table 12.1.

Drawing a distinction between computer technology and other forms of technology in their relative patentability cannot be maintained on purely logical grounds. Why should using computer technology to solve technical problems be treated less favourably than other forms of technology? Indeed, the current version of the European Patent Convention states that patents are available for inventions 'in all fields of technology'.[278] There are, however, some practical reasons why a cautious approach to patenting computer-implemented inventions might be called for. Determining the state of the art to test novelty for computer programs is an impossible task, given the widespread use of computers in all fields of technology. This is compounded by the fact that innovation in computer software is poorly documented compared to other forms of technology, such as pharmaceuticals where there is a wealth of published information in published patent specification and learned journals. Many patents for computer-implemented inventions are very vulnerable to challenges for lack of novelty.[279]

Inventive step is another issue. For example, does one take into account what is known and used in one type of software application in other, perhaps totally unrelated, software applications? Clearly it is not inventive to take a known manual process and install it in a computer[280] but where does one draw the line?

277 Even then, the scope of copyright protection for computer programs has only recently been clarified by Pumfrey J in his excellent analysis in *Navitaire Inc v easyJet Airline Co* [2006] RPC 3, discussed in Chapter 8.

278 Article 52(1) EPC 13th edition, 1 July 2007. This suggests that the EPO will look more favourably on software inventions and seems to align the EPC better with case law at the Boards of Appeal, discussed later.

279 This has been the experience in the US where many software patents have been challenged.

280 For example, Case T258/03 *Hitachi/Auction method* [2004] EPOR 55 where a computer system used a Dutch auction to overcome potential delays in transmission of bids.

Table 12.1 Advantages and disadvantages of copyright and patents

Copyright		Patents	
Advantages	Disadvantages	Advantages	Disadvantages
Copyright is free and protection is automatic. There are no formalities.	Copyright does not normally provide a true monopoly form of protection.	Patents give strong monopolistic protection.	It is expensive to apply for and maintain patents.
The threshold for protection is much lower than that for patents.	It is possible to write programs to emulate existing programs without infringing copyright.	Publication of the specification and claims *should* make it easy to determine the scope of a patent.	The invention falls into the public domain on expiry of the patent and, in the meantime, competitors can see how the invention works – this may help them to design around it.
Copyright also protects items of software other than computer programs, such as databases, and so protects the 'whole package'.	Ideas, principles and interfaces are not protected.	The patent system increases the stock of knowledge through publication.	Infringement proceedings cannot be commenced until after the patent has been granted.
Copyright does not prevent the creation of competing software. This stimulates the market and encourages start-up companies and small and medium enterprises (SMEs).	Due to the lack of formalities, there may be evidential difficulties if proper records have not been kept.	Controls over abuses of patent monopolies.	Litigation tends to be very expensive and parallel actions may have to be brought in a number of countries.
Infringement proceedings can be commenced immediately.		In some technologies it may be possible reasonably to determine the state of the art on the basis of prior published patents and learned journal articles (though this is much more difficult in relation to computer programs).	
The state of the art is irrelevant. Copyright infringement requires acts to be performed in relation to the protected work. Independent creation cannot infringe.			
Litigation tends to be significantly less expensive than in the case of patent litigation, where validity is often an issue.			
If software is subsequently modified, new copyrights may be automatically generated.			

Finally, as confirmed by the European Commission in its consultation on the proposed Directive on the patentability of computer-implemented inventions, patents are not generally perceived as the optimum cost-effective route to protection for start-up companies and SMEs in the software industry. The 'frontier' style of innovation in software has been in sharp contrast to the substantial investment in research and development funded by large powerful corporations in many other fields. Patent protection has not been seen as a *desideratum* for the smaller software companies because of the time and expense involved in what has been a very fast-moving industry. Indeed many small software companies express concern at the danger of large powerful companies tying up vast areas of software applications by the use of patents. The fact of the matter is that start-up companies and SMEs have been responsible for substantial advances in computer software but most do not have the resources to initiate or defend patent infringement actions.

Developments at the EPO

It is perhaps with all the above issues and aspects in mind that the framers of the EPC, original version, sought to provide a compromise that would allow patents for computer-implemented inventions in certain special and deserving cases. The way in which they did it not only compounded the problems of determining what type of computer-implemented invention could be patented but also did nothing to ease the position of SMEs and individuals whose contribution to software innovation has been so vital to its growth. They could not have made the position more opaque and unpredictable even if that had been their goal. Incredibly, at the end of the day, it all comes down to ascertaining the effect of two short words: 'as such'.

The EPC lays down the basic requirements for patentability, being inventions, in all fields of technology, that are susceptible of industrial application, which are new and which involve an inventive step: Article 52(1).[281] It then goes on under Article 52(2) to state that a number of things are not to be regarded as inventions. These include, *inter alia*, discoveries, aesthetic creations and schemes, rules and methods for performing mental acts, playing games or doing business, and programs for computers. Presentations of information are also excluded.[282] There is no pattern in this and the diversity of such things is breathtaking. However, as with the UK Patents Act 1977, these things are excluded only to the extent that the application for a patent or patents relates to that thing 'as such'.

The diversity of matter excluded from the grant of a patent indicates that there is no single underlying logical thread as noted by Peter Prescott QC in *CFPH LLC's Patent Application*.[283] For example, discoveries 'as such' are excluded because this could result in far-reaching monopolies being created. Sir Isaac Newton would have become a very rich man on the basis of his theory of gravity! On the other hand, applications of discoveries in technical fields are patentable: *see*, for example, *Genentech Inc's Patent*.[284] As noted earlier, aesthetic creations and presentations of information as such are normally protected by other intellectual property rights which are not monopolistic in nature. The latter exclusion does not prevent the patenting of board games as this is a 'technical' application. Of course, the fact that a type of subject matter is protected in other ways does not mean that it cannot be protected by a patent. There is no general rule to say that a particular thing can only be protected by one intellectual property right, notwithstanding an attempt to do this in relation to copyright and the unregistered design right.[285]

The leading case on the patentability of computer programs before the EPO was Case T208/84 *VICOM/Computer-related invention*[286] in which the Technical Board of Appeal emphasised the technical contribution of the alleged invention to determine whether it was an invention for the purposes of the EPC. In that case, the claims were directed at a computer operating in accordance with instructions in a computer program to produce a

281 The reference to 'all fields of technology' was inserted in Article 52(1) in the 13th edition of the European Patent Convention, 1 July 2007. This edition came into force on 13 December 2007.

282 These provisions are mirrored in s 1(1) and (2) of the Patents Act 1977.

283 [2006] RPC 5, discussed below.

284 [1989] RPC 147.

285 See s 236 of the Copyright, Designs and Patents Act 1988.

286 [1987] EPOR 74.

technical effect (enhancing digital images on the basis of a mathematical method). This could not be said to be a claim to a computer program 'as such'. The Board of Appeal said (at 80):

> . . . a claim directed to a technical process which process is carried out under the control of a program (be this implemented in hardware or in software), cannot be regarded as relating to a computer program as such within the meaning of Article 52(3) EPC, as it is the application of the program for determining the sequence of steps in the process for which in effect protection is sought. Consequently, such a claim is allowable under Article 52(2)(c) and (3) EPC. (original emphasis)

Furthermore, although the invention used a mathematical method, it was not a claim to a mathematical method 'as such' as what was claimed was a technical process in which the method was used. However, the technical contribution test did not tell us whether the subject matter was itself an invention.

The Technical Board of Appeal at the EPO does not subscribe to a rigid doctrine of binding precedent although it is sometimes possible to tease out general principles that can be applied in domestic courts applying the equivalent provisions to those in the EPC. Often, a difficult or compromising earlier decision is sidestepped and the jurisprudence of the Boards of Appeal at the EPO is not necessarily a reflection of consistent and rational development. This means that a principle discernible from an earlier judgment, which may have been followed and applied in numerous cases in domestic courts, may be subject to subtle or even sudden change or modification. This happened in relation to the exclusion of computer programs, as such, from the meaning of invention for the purposes of Article 52 of the EPC.

In a step-by-step fashion, the Technical Boards of Appeal at the EPO have distanced themselves from the *VICOM/Computer-related invention* approach as to what constituted an invention, without expressly stating that it was wrong. It began to consider a programmed computer as an invention and the impact of the exclusions in Article 52(2) as being relevant to questions of novelty and inventive step rather than considering whether the technical contribution, as in *VICOM/Computer-related invention*, took the subject matter beyond the exclusions.

In Case T1173/97 *IBM/Computer programs*[287] it was said that determining the technical contribution of an invention was more relevant to the questions of novelty and inventive step than deciding on possible exclusion from the meaning of invention under Article 52(2) or (3). This approach was confirmed in Case T931/95 *PBS Partnership/Controlling pension benefits systems*[288] where it was held that there was no basis for applying the technical contribution approach in deciding whether the subject matter comprised an invention.

The clearest indication of the present approach was given by Case T258/03 *Hitachi/ Auction method*[289] in which the Technical Board of Appeal held that a method involving technical means is an invention within Article 52. What is important is whether the subject matter has a technical character. That technical character can be implied from the physical features of an entity, or the nature of an activity, or conferred on a non-technical activity by use of technical means.

Subject matter caught by Article 52(2), being a 'non-invention' as such, would be something which was a purely abstract concept devoid of any technical implications. The result of all this is anything carried out by a programmed computer (whether it is claimed in that way, as an entity, or the activity performed by the programmed computer) that has a technical character is, consequently, an invention and not excluded by Article 52(2). The Board of Appeal accepted that this was a very broad interpretation of 'invention' and said (at para 4.6):

> [this] will include activities which are so familiar that their technical character tends to be overlooked, such as the act of writing, using pen and paper.

287 [2000] EPOR 219.

288 [2002] EPOR 52.

289 [2004] EPOR 55.

Of course, and as the Board of Appeal pointed out, this does not mean that all methods using technical means are patentable. They still have to satisfy the other requirements of novelty, inventive step and being capable of industrial application.

The subject matter in *Hitachi* was a computer-implemented method of holding auctions. The problem to be overcome was that of delays in bidders submitting their bids due to the vagaries and nature of electronic transmission. The solution was to use a Dutch auction method where bidders submitted two bids: their desired bid and maximum bid. After bidding is finished, the result is calculated by setting a price and successively lowering it until the highest desired bid is reached. If there is more than one at the same highest desired bid, the price is automatically increased until the highest maximum price is left from those tying with the same highest desired bids.

The Technical Board of Appeal held that this did not solve the known problem (fundamentally being delays in online auctions) by technical means; it simply circumvented the problem by adapting the Dutch auction system for use on a computer. It did not, therefore, involve an inventive step. The system as adapted could just as easily be conducted using a system of postal bids. The invention was also no more than the mere automation of a non-technical activity. However, it went on to say that if a step in such a method was designed so as to be particularly suitable for being performed on a computer then, arguably, it had a technical character.

290 [2006] EPOR 414.

291 [2006] EPOR 423.

292 The Boards had the same panel and the same Chair, S V Steinbrener, as in *HITACHI/ Auction method*.

Later decisions by the Boards of Appeal involved applications by the Microsoft Corporation for patents concerning the use of clipboard formats to transfer non-file data between software applications in Case T424/03 *MICROSOFT/Clipboard format I*[290] and Case T411/03 *MICROSOFT/Clipboard format II*.[291] The decision of the Boards of Appeal[292] followed *Hitachi/Auction method* and held that a method using technical means was an invention and a computer system including a memory was a technical means. A method implemented in a computer system represents a sequence of steps actually performed and achieving an effect, and not a sequence of computer-executable instructions (that is, a computer program) which only has the potential of achieving such an effect when loaded into, and run on, a computer. The claims in the application were not, therefore, claims to a computer program as such. Even though a method of operating a computer may be put into effect by means of a computer program, a claim to such a method does not claim the computer program as such.

The Board of Appeal went on to say that the steps in the claimed method solved a technical problem by technical means as functional data structures (clipboard formats) were used independently of any cognitive content in order to enhance the internal operation of a computer system with a view to facilitating the exchange of data among various application programs. The claimed steps provided a general-purpose computer with a further functionality. The computer thus programmed assisted the user in transferring non-file data into files. Finally, a computer program on a technical carrier is not a computer program as such and may contribute to the technical character of the subject matter of what is claimed to be a patentable invention. Both Microsoft applications were held to be patentable, being new and inventive over the prior art.[293] However, the *MICROSOFT/ Clipboard format* cases are distinguishable from both *Hitachi/Auction method* and *PBS Partnership/Controlling pension benefits systems* as in the latter two cases the technical character was in relation to other matter declared to be non-inventions.

293 The closest prior art was Windows 3.1.

294 [2007] EPOR 312.

Subsequently, in Case T1023/06 *IGT/Computer implemented game process*,[294] involving an application for a patent for a method of operating an electronic video poker machine, following *Hitachi/Auction method*, the Board of Appeal held that the implementation of a card game in an electronic video poker machine involved steps implying the use of an appropriate display and control means. This bestowed a technical character on the claimed method as a whole. Where an invention consists of a mixture of technical and non-technical features, consideration must be directed to the actual contribution of each feature to the technical character by:

(a) determining the difference between the claimed subject matter and the prior art, so as to allow:

(b) the effect of each difference in relation to the prior art to be established, from which:

(c) the extent to which the respective differences contributed to the technical nature (that is, its technical 'residue') could be inferred.

In the present case, the differences addressed the technical problem of enabling a machine to play more than one game with improved readability. However, their implementation was straightforward and obvious, being non-technical modification of game rules which did not contribute to inventive step. The implementation of the changed rules within a machine in an obvious manner lacked inventive step.

In Case T49/04 *Walker/Text processing*,[295] the application was for a method for enhancing text presentation from a machine-readable natural language text based on reader-specific parameters including at least the viewing field of dimensions including parsing and folding rules. The Board of Appeal held that the mere fact that mental activities were involved did not necessarily render the subject matter non-technical as the technical solution was in providing a tool serving to assist or replace human activities, including mental ones. Technical aspects could be present in the design and use of a graphic interface. Therefore, means for analysing text, dividing it into segments related to the physical arrangement of the overall image structure of the displayed text with a view to solving the technical problem of improving text presentation, specifically readability on a display, was not excluded by Article 52(2) EPC as such.

Probably the most important aspect of the above line of authorities is the fact that the technical contribution lies within one of the other things excluded from the meaning of invention as such is not fatal to the application. This is in direct conflict with the present case law at the Court of Appeal, as will be seen later. That is not to say that a business method, for example, performed by a programmed computer is patentable. There is a still a requirement for a technical problem to be solved by a technical means.[296]

To summarise the current position at the Boards of Appeal of the EPO, the following approach in relation to computer-implemented inventions seems to be as follows:

1. Determine the technical problem which the invention seeks to overcome.
2. Look at the solution to that problem encapsulated in the invention.
3. If it solves the problem by technical means it is patentable if those means are new, inventive and capable of industrial application.
4. If it does not solve the problem by technical means it is not patentable. For example, it may use or modify matter excluded under Article 52(2), being no more than an automation of non-technical activity. However, the use of such matter designed to be particularly suitable for computer implementation may, arguably, possess a technical character and, if so, the other requirements for patentability should be tested.

It is unlikely that *Hitachi* and subsequent cases mark an end to further development of the jurisprudence on the patentability of software inventions at the EPO Boards of Appeal. Given the failure of the proposed Directive on the patentability of computer-implemented inventions, this is an important task and it may be that we end up with something not too far removed from what was proposed. The meaning of 'technical means' needs further consideration and explanation as does the position covered by the proviso in point 4 above. The author's view is that inventions implemented by programmed computers involve technical means, *per se*, and computer programs in operation are necessarily technical. That being so, it could be argued that computer programs should not be treated as 'non-inventions' as a starting point only to overcome the artificial construct of finding technical means which are not themselves excluded. If we applied the basic requirements of novelty, inventive step and industrial application,

295 [2007] EPOR 293.

296 Case T154/04 *Duns Licensing Associates/Estimating sales activity* [2007] EPOR 349. The use of mathematical and statistical methods to evaluate data about sales activity was a method of business research as such.

that should be sufficient, bearing in mind that simply automating an existing manual system, without more, can never be inventive, in line with the outcome in *Hitachi*.

Patenting computer programs in the UK before 2005

Before the 1977 Act, patents were rarely granted for computer programs as it was required that an invention had to be a manner of manufacture. This implied that a computer program operating in a computer with no external effects could not be patentable. There were some exceptions, however, such as in *Gever's Application*[297] where the program was coded on punched cards. This was said to be analogous to a CAM for controlling the cutting path of a lathe and, therefore, was a manner of manufacture. In another case, *Burrough's Corporation (Perkin's) Application*,[298] computer programs controlling the transmission of data to terminals from a central computer were held to be the proper subject matter of a patent as the programs were embodied in physical form in the electronic circuits of the computer equipment. This distinction, based on whether the program in question had a physical form, was laid to rest after the 1977 Act came into force in *Re Gale's Patent Application*,[299] where the Court of Appeal held that installing an algorithm to calculate square roots on a ROM chip did not, of itself, give it a technical character required for patentability.[300]

Following *VICOM/Computer-related invention*, the courts started to look for the presence of some technical effect. For example, in the UK, an application for a patent for an expert system shell[301] was refused in *Re Wang Laboratories Inc's Application*[302] because it was for nothing more than a computer program. When the system had been developed it did not form with the computer a new machine. Similarly, a claim in relation to a compiler program[303] was no more than a claim for the compiler program itself.[304] In Germany it has been confirmed that a similar approach applies, and in *Re the Computer Generation of Chinese Characters*[305] a word-processing program using Chinese characters was not patentable because it did not solve a technical problem by a technical method and did not make a technical contribution to the state of the art. It was mainly intellectual in nature and did not make use of methods beyond human intellectual activity.

An important case before the Technical Board of Appeal at the EPO on the subject of the patentability of computer programs was Case T935/97 *IBM/Computer programs*[306] which led to a change in practice at the UK Patent Office.[307] The Board of Appeal took the opportunity to review its previous case law relating to the patentability of computer programs and it set out comprehensively the principles that should apply. IBM had applied for a patent for a data processing system used to display information in windows such that any information displayed in one window obscured by a second window is moved automatically to a new unobscured position. The first six claims in the application related to the process and had been accepted as patentable by the examiners in the EPO but claims 7 to 10 had been rejected. These were directed, *inter alia*, to a computer program product (a medium having program code on it which caused the computer to execute the process). The Board of Appeal decision confirmed that computer programs must have a technical character to be patentable and that what can be claimed in such a case is not just the programmed computer as the means of obtaining a technical effect but also the computer program from which, when run in a computer, the technical effect is obtained and a computer program product (for example, a computer chip on which the program is stored) from which the technical effect is obtained when the program so stored is run on a computer. One could be excused for thinking that this approach promotes form over substance and this was noted by the Hearing Officer in the Patent Office in *Hutchin's Application*[308] where it was held that the Comptroller General of Patents was bound to follow decisions of the UK courts, expressing some reservation about the *PBS Partnership/ Controlling pension benefits systems* case.[309]

297 [1970] RPC 9.

298 [1974] RPC 147.

299 [1991] RPC 305.

300 At first instance, Aldous J distinguished between a program installed on a computer chip and one stored on a floppy disk: *Re Gale's Patent Application* [1991] RPC 305.

301 An expert system shell is a program or suite of programs that allows a system developer to enter rules and facts to form an expert system directed towards providing solutions in particular knowledge domains: for example, a computer system that gives medical advice on stomach pains.

302 [1991] RPC 463.

303 A program used to create an object code version of a source code program.

304 *Re Hitachi Ltd's Application* [1991] RPC 415.

305 [1993] FSR 315.

306 [1999] EPOR 301.

307 *See Patent Office Practice Note* [1999] RPC 563.

308 [2002] RPC 8.

309 Above.

The UK Patent Office changed its practice to come into line with that in the EPO with respect to claims to computer program inventions. At this stage in the development of the jurisprudence relating to computer programs, a patent would not be granted if the technical effect it produced or had the potential to produce is, exclusively, within the other exceptions in Article 52(2) EPC (together with Article 52(3) equivalent to s 1(2) of the 1977 Act). In the UK, that doctrine developed particularly in terms of technical effects which are methods of performing a mental act, the 'mental steps' doctrine.

Mental steps doctrine

Many computer programs perform operations that were or could have been performed by the human mind. As such, methods of performing mental acts are excluded by s 1(2). However, even if such a method is incorporated in a computer in a way which is different to the way a human would perform the mental act, this does not make the invention patentable. In *Re Wang Laboratories Inc's Application*,[310] Aldous J said (at 472):

> The fact that the scheme, rule or method is part of a computer program and is therefore converted into steps which are suitable for use by a person operating the computer does not matter . . . The method remains a method for performing a mental act, whether a computer is used or not . . . The method may well be different when a computer is used, but to my mind it still remains a method for performing a mental act, whether or not the computer adopts steps that would not ordinarily be used by the human mind.

One of the exceptions in s 1(2) and Article 52(2) EPC is a method of performing a mental act. In the Chancery Division, it was held that an application to patent a computer-implemented system for identifying ships was caught by the equivalent exception in s 1(2)(c) of the Patents Act 1977, *inter alia*, as being a method for performing a mental act: *Raytheon Co's Application*.[311] The system was such that it was particularly suitable for carrying out by computer, where silhouettes of ships on the horizon were captured by digital imaging and matched with a database containing data as to the shapes of known ships. This would seem to be an application particularly suitable for computer implementation as it would be likely significantly to outperform the same task carried out by a human being, armed with a book containing silhouettes of ships, both in terms of time and, probably, accuracy.

In *Fujitsu Ltd's Application*,[312] the applicant developed software to produce computer-generated images of any two chosen crystal structures of inorganic material, parts of which could be selected. This data was then converted into data containing a combination of the two chosen crystal structures producing an image of the resulting combined structure for the purpose of research. The intention was to replace the traditional, manual method of constructing a crystal structure by assembling three-dimensional plastic models. The Patent Office rejected the application, objecting that it was the performing of a mental act under s 1(2)(c). Laddie J, in the Patents Court, agreed.[313] The Court of Appeal confirmed that the application was caught by s 1(2)(c), being either an application for a computer program as such or a method of performing a mental act as such.

As the operation relied on the operator's selection of data and exercise of skill and judgment, the application was in substance for a scheme or method for performing a mental act. Originally, the traditional method was to assemble plastic models by hand and all the computer program did was to automate this operation. The images were simply substitutes of a manually assembled plastic model previously produced which did not provide a technical advantage and therefore were excluded by s 1(2)(c) as being a program for a computer. Aldous LJ rejected the appellant's argument that that exclusion should be construed narrowly, requiring that the mental act should be as performed in the human mind. He said that the question should be determined without recourse

310 [1991] RPC 463.

311 [1993] RPC 427.

312 [1997] RPC 608.

313 *Fujitsu Ltd's Application* [1996] RPC 511. Laddie J set out the principles to apply in a useful manner.

to evidence as to how the human mind actually works. Nor was there any room for reading into the test that the act had to be one that had previously been performed by the human mind.

The difficulty for the applicant was that the practical application or technical effect produced by means of the computer program was, itself, excluded material, being a scheme or method of performing a mental act. The result of all the case law in relation to s 1(2) would appear to be that a practical application of any of the things listed in the subsection is patentable in principle, provided it is not itself within the list.[314] Thus, a new software-driven process for making metal castings should be patentable, but not a new computer program to present information in a new manner even though it could be argued that such an application is neither for a computer program *as such* nor for the presentation of information *as such*.[315]

In 2002, it was noted that Aldous LJ in *Fujitsu* had said that patents were not available for discoveries or ideas *per se* '. . . but those that have a technical aspect or technical contribution are'. This was later referred to by Neuberger J in *Kirin-Amgen Inc* v *Roche Diagnostics GmbH*[316] without qualification. If this applies to discoveries and ideas, then it should follow that the same principle applies to other excluded matter. Therefore business methods and the like have a technical aspect or making a technical contribution ought also in principle to be patentable. That being so, the Patent Office issued another Practice Notice to the effect that inventions which involve a technical contribution will not be refused merely because they relate to business methods or mental acts.[317] However, it was noted that this did not affect the approach to patent applications, such as pure business method application, that had no prospect of maturing into valid patents.

Recent developments in the UK – the Court of Appeal and *stare decisis*[318]

The courts in the UK have tended to refer to *VICOM/Computer-related invention*, sometimes expressly approving of it, sometimes distinguishing it. Section 91 of the Patents Act 1977 requires judicial notice to be taken of decisions of the Boards of Appeal at the EPO.[319] In *Genentech Inc's Patent*,[320] Purchas LJ approved *VICOM/Computer-related invention* although Mustill LJ said that the report of the case was so compressed as to be 'almost incomprehensible'. In *Merrill Lynch's Application*[321] and *Gale's Application*,[322] some members of the Court of Appeal appeared to distinguish *VICOM/Computer-related invention*. But, in *Fujitsu Limited's Application*,[323] Aldous LJ said (at 614):

> However it is and always has been a principle of patent law that mere discoveries or ideas are not patentable, but those discoveries and ideas which have a technical aspect or make a technical contribution are. Thus the concept that what is needed to make an excluded thing patentable is a technical contribution is not surprising. That was the basis for the decision of the Board in *Vicom*. It has been accepted by this court and by the EPO and has been applied since 1987. It is a concept at the heart of patent law.

The apparent move away from *VICOM/Computer-related invention* at the EPO was first noticed judicially by Peter Prescott QC, as deputy judge of the High Court, in *CFPH LLC's Application*.[324] He concluded that the interpretation set out in *Hitachi/Auction method* was the correct approach. The mere fact that the claimed invention contained or used a computer program did not mean that a patent would foreclose the use of a computer program. He used an analogy, saying (at para 104), in the context of automatic pilots and computer-driven processes for making canned soup:

> The question to ask should be: is it (the artefact or process) new and non-obvious merely *because* there is a computer program? Or would it still be new and non-obvious in principle even if the same decisions and commands could somehow be taken and issued by a little

314 Assuming that all the other requirements such as novelty and inventive step are present.

315 The equivalent application by Fujitsu in Japan was granted a patent.

316 [2002] RPC 1.

317 *Patent Office Practice Notice: Patents Act 1977: Interpreting section 1(2)* [2002] RPC 40.

318 This section is based on Bainbridge, D.I., 'Court of Appeal parts company with the EPO on software patents' [2007] 23 *CLSR* 119.

319 This is not to say that such decisions are binding on the courts in the UK.

320 [1989] RPC 147.

321 [1989] RPC 561.

322 [1991] RPC 305.

323 [1997] RPC 608.

324 [2006] RPC 5.

man at a control panel, operating under the same rules? For if the answer to the latter question is 'Yes' it becomes apparent that the computer program is merely a tool, and the invention is not about computer programming at all. It is about better rules for governing an automatic pilot or better rules for conducting the manufacture of canned soup.[325]

Following these developments, the UK Patent Office again decided to change the manner in which it examined computer-implemented inventions as suggested in *CFPH LLC*. At this stage, it seemed that the UK Patent Office and the courts were attempting to reflect the current thinking of the Boards of Appeal. However, this desire for uniformity with the decisions of the Boards of Appeal at the EPO came to a shuddering halt with *Aerotel Ltd* v *Telco Holdings Ltd and Macrossan's Patent Application*.[326] *Aerotel* concerned two separate appeals heard together. One was to a telephone system allowing pre-payment from any available telephone (the Aerotel patent). The other was to a method of automatically acquiring the documents required for the formation of a company (the Macrossan application).

After reviewing the decisions of the Boards of Appeal of the EPO and of the Court of Appeal, Jacob LJ identified three different approaches, one of which had itself three variations. The approaches were as follows.

1 *The contribution approach.* Does the inventive step reside *only* in the contribution of excluded matter? If YES, the subject matter is not an invention under Article 52(2). This was the approach adopted by Falconer J at first instance in *Merrill Lynch* but expressly rejected by the Court of Appeal.

2 *The technical effect approach.* Does the invention as defined in the claim make a technical contribution to the known art? If NO, Article 52(2) applies. A possible clarification (at least by way of exclusion) of this approach is to add the rider that novel or inventive purely excluded matter does not count as a 'technical contribution'. This is the approach (with the rider) adopted by the Court of Appeal in *Merrill Lynch* and subsequently followed by the Court of Appeal in *Gale* and *Fujitsu*. The approach (without the rider as an express caution) was that first adopted by the EPO Boards of Appeal in *VICOM/Computer-related invention* and other cases in the following few years.

3 *The 'any hardware' approach.* Does the claim involve the use of, or is it to, a piece of physical hardware, however mundane (whether a computer or a pencil and paper)? If YES, Article 52(2) does not apply. This was the approach in *PBS Partnership*, *Hitachi* and *Microsoft*. It was specifically rejected by the Court of Appeal in *Gale*. However, Jacob LJ noted that there were three variants of this approach:

(i) Where a claim is to a method which consists of an excluded category, it is excluded by Article 52(2) even if hardware is used to carry out the method. But a claim to the apparatus itself, being 'concrete' is not so excluded. The apparatus claim is nonetheless bad for obviousness because the notional skilled man must be taken to know about the improved, excluded, method. This was the specific approach taken in *PBS Partnership*.

(ii) A claim to hardware necessarily is not caught by Article 52(2). A claim to a method of using that hardware is likewise not excluded even if that method as such is excluded matter. Either type of claim is nonetheless bad for obviousness for the same reason as above. This is the approach in *Hitachi*, disagreeing with *PBS Pensions* about method claims.

(iii) Simply ask whether there is a claim to something 'concrete' e.g. an apparatus. If YES, Article 52(2) does not apply. Then examine for patentability on conventional grounds – do not treat the notional skilled man as knowing about any improved excluded method. This is the *Microsoft* approach.

Instead of applying the current thinking at the EPO (*HITACHI* and *Microsoft*), Jacob LJ said that he had no choice but to follow the previous Court of Appeal decisions

325 In *Halliburton Energy Services Inc* v *Smith International (North Sea) Ltd* [2006] RPC 2, at first instance, Pumfrey J said that contribution must lie in a technical effect and not merely in excluded matter. He noted that, in Case T453/91 *IBM/Method for physical VLSI-chip design*, 31 May 1994, the Board of Appeal felt unease with *VICOM/Computer-related invention*. The Board explained *VICOM*, saying that it equated the image in question with a material object as it was an image of a material object.

326 [2007] RPC 7. Jacob LJ gave the judgment of the court. Unusually, the judgment has an Appendix setting out the case law at the EPO, in the UK and Germany on software patents.

327 None of the exceptions in *Young* v *Bristol Aeroplane Co Ltd* [1944] KB 718 applied. The House of Lords has consistently said that the Court of Appeal cannot add to the exceptions in *Young* v *Bristol Aeroplane*; *see*, for example, *Davis* v *Johnson* [1979] AC 264. However, more recently, Baroness Hale of Richmond did not rule out the possibility of a very limited extension of the exceptions in relation to conflicting Privy Council decisions in *In re Spectrum Plus Ltd (in liquidation)* [2005] 2 AC 680.

328 Applying this Jacob LJ held that the Aerotel patent was valid. It used a new combination of existing apparatus and was not a business method as such. In *Macrossan*, the alleged invention was to an interactive system to do the work normally done by a solicitor or company formation agent. This was a business method as such and also a claim to a computer program as such.

329 *Jesco Schwarzer*, 28 September 2004, 17 W (pat) 31/03.

330 This is now the basis of the test adopted by the UK Patent Office in the light of *Aerotel*, recognising that this case must now be followed.

331 [2008] EWHC 335 (Pat).

332 *Patent Office Practice Notice: Patentable subject matter*, 2 November 2006. This should be read with *Practice Notice (Patents Act 1977: patentability of computer programs)*, 8 December 2008. Cases such as *Raytheon Co's Application, op. cit.*, must now be doubted.

333 [2007] EWHC 954 (Pat).

334 [2007] FSR 26.

because of the doctrine of *stare decisis*.[327] On the basis of those decisions, there must be a technical contribution which is not itself within the matter excluded from the meaning of 'invention'. This is the second approach with the 'rider'.[328] Perhaps he drew some comfort from the fact that the German Bundesgerichtshof declined to follow *HITACHI* on one occasion.[329]

Mr Birss, on behalf of the Comptroller, suggested the following structured approach to applying the Court of Appeal decisions in *Merrill Lynch*, *Gale* and *Fujitsu*.

1 Properly construe the claim.
2 Identify the actual contribution.
3 Ask whether it falls solely within the excluded subject matter.
4 Check whether the actual or alleged contribution is actually technical in nature.[330]

Jacob LJ thought this useful and applied it to the Aerotel patent and the Macrossan application. He did say that the fourth step should have been covered by the third step though it was useful as a final check to ensure that the contribution was technical and the Court of Appeal decision in *Merrill Lynch* was being followed. In *Research in Motion UK Ltd* v *Visto Corp*,[331] Floyd J held that claim 1 of the patent in suit did not have '. . . enough of a technical effect to render the invention patentable'. But an invention either has a technical effect or it does not. What Floyd J really meant was that the technical effect did not go beyond the ordinary effects of running a computer program.

The Court of Appeal in *Aerotel* expressed some doubt, *obiter*, as to whether the exclusion for a scheme, rule or method of performing a mental act, as such, extended to electronic means of carrying out mental acts. This was in contrast with the view, also *obiter*, in *Fujitsu*. This leaves the lower courts and the UK Patent Office in the un-enviable position of having to decide which to follow. In the end the Patent Office has decided to follow the view in *Aerotel*.[332]

There have been a number of cases on software inventions following *Aerotel*. In *Oneida Indian Nation's Application*,[333] the applicant was an Indian Nation based in New York and the application was in respect of a 'system, method and article of manufacture for gaming from an off-site location'. The judge, Mr Christopher Floyd QC, sitting as deputy judge of the Patents Court in the High Court, followed *Aerotel* and the four-step test set out in that case. In *Oneida*, the contribution was a computerised two-stage gaming apparatus providing advantages such as a reduction in the number of processing steps and the data transmission steps; dispensing with the need to make an account check for every bet placed and, as a result, making the system more secure and robust. As regards the fourth step in *Aerotel*, Mr Christopher Floyd QC said (at para 10):

. . . if the invention fails to overcome that test [the third step], any technical contribution must have been one of purely excluded matter . . . The 4th step is intended merely to make sure that inventions that have *passed at step 3* are technical in nature. (original emphasis)

The claimed advantages were to a new method of doing business and fell completely within the exclusion. Although they could be described as 'technical' they did not count as such because they were not a *relevant technical effect*. They were merely the consequence of putting the new business method into effect. Furthermore, the hardware involved was standard and formed no part of the contribution.

Cappellini's Application and Bloomberg LLP's Application[334] involved two separate 'inventions'. In Bloomberg, the invention was for a method of distributing data in which the data transmitted to a user was mapped to a form suitable for the application to be used by the user. The method was to be performed in software only. The Cappellini invention was a new algorithm for planning a delivery route for a package using a network of carriers. Pumfrey J made a number of general points. First, the question of patentable subject matter was essentially a question of the scope of the claim. If the claim covered a method of arriving at a particular result by the exercise of rational processes alone, then it was a claim to a 'scheme, rule or method of performing a mental act'. Second, if a physical article resulting from the performance of a mental act, such as mathematical calculations, became a feature of the claim, the claim would not be objectionable. But it was objectionable unless 'tethered' to the claim. Pumfrey J said (at para 8) 'I do not, of course, say that every result must be a physical article before the claim is allowable'. Finally, a claim to a programmed computer as a matter of substance was just a claim to the program on a kind of carrier. If the result of running the program was no more than the performance of a business method added, this added nothing to the art that did not lie in the excluded matter.

With respect to *Bloomberg*, Pumfrey J held that the application was for a computer program as such. There was no question of matching the form of the data to any deficiency or advantageous feature of hardware. It was purely formatted to render it suitable to cooperate with particular software. As regards *Cappellini*, Pumfrey J said that this was both the presentation of information and a mathematical method. Although there was a physical effect, being the movement of known items (vehicles) over known and existing routes, this was a method of doing business (moving vehicles according to a routing algorithm). Pumfrey J criticised *PBS Partnership/Pensions*, saying that it reached the correct result by incorrect reasoning. He said he preferred *Aerotel*, an important question being what the claimed invention was as a matter of substance.[335]

A new method of inventory management, implemented by software, involving two databases, one defining the layout of a facility, the other the items in it, was the subject of the application in *Raytheon Co v Comptroller General of Patents, Trade Marks and Designs*.[336] The claimed contributions to the art were the use of visual representation, the synthesis of individual images and the navigability of the system. Kitchen J said that if the technical contribution did not wholly fall within any one of the exclusions but did fall wholly within two or more, the invention would nonetheless be excluded. The second and third aspects of the contribution were simply matters of program design and related to a computer program as such. The first aspect was a method of doing business and also no more than a method of presenting information.

Aerotel and the four-step test is now treated with the utmost respect in the Chancery Division and has been applied in the above cases and more recent cases such as *Astron Clinica Ltd v Comptroller General of Patents, Designs and Trade Marks*.[337] In *Autonomy Corp v Comptroller General of Patents, Designs and Trade Marks*,[338] Lewison J summarised the present position in England as follows (at para 29):

1 A computer program is not merely a set of instructions to a computer, but can include the medium (e.g. floppy disc or CD ROM) which causes the computer to execute the program (*Aerotel*) or a programmed computer (*Cappellini*).
2 However what is excluded from patentability is not a computer program but a computer program 'as such'. Accordingly the mere fact that a claim relates to a computer program does not necessarily disqualify it from patentability (*Astron Clinica*).
3 In order to decide whether a computer program is excluded from patentability because it is a computer program 'as such' one must consider the substance of the claimed invention (*Cappellini*).
4 If the claimed contribution exists independently of whether it is implemented by a computer, in the sense of embodying a technical process lying outside the computer, then the contribution will not be a computer program as such (*Gale; Raytheon*).
5 This will be the case even though the only practicable way of implementing the contribution is by means of a computer (*Raytheon*).
6 If the contribution requires new hardware or a new combination of hardware, or consists of a better computer or solves a technical problem in the functionality of a computer it is unlikely to be a computer program as such (*Aerotel; Raytheon*).

335 Of course, Pumfrey J had no option but to follow *Aerotel*.

336 [2008] RPC 3.

337 [2008] RPC 14.
338 [2008] RPC 16.

7 On the other hand, a mere new hardware test is not enough if the newness consists of a computer program on a known medium (*Aerotel* commenting on *Gale*).

8 The mere fact that a computer program reduces the load on the processor or makes economical use of the computer's memory or makes more efficient use of the computer's resources does not amount to making a better computer, and thus does not take it outside the category of computer program as such (*Aerotel* commenting on *Gale*; *Raytheon*).

9 An effect caused merely by the running of the program will not take a program outside the exclusion (*Aerotel*).

10 The manipulation of data stored on a computer (whether on the computer in use or on a remote computer) is unlikely to give rise to a contribution that exists independently of whether it is implemented by a computer (*Bloomberg*).

11 Even if the claimed invention is not a computer program as such, it is still necessary to ask whether the contribution lies solely in some other field of excluded matter. If it does, then the contribution will not be patentable (*Oneida*).

12 In such a case, although the contribution may well be described as having a technical effect, it is not the right kind of technical effect, and so does not count (*Shoppalotto*; *Aerotel*; *Oneida*).

This can hardly be described as bringing clarity to the question of the patentability of computer-implemented inventions. The present position in England and the disparity between that and the position at the EPO is untenable. It can rightly be described as a mess of Herculean proportions and something should be done about it soon. By narrowing the scope of the exceptions to the meaning of 'invention', the Boards of Appeal at the EPO have brought the focus of the enquiry more on whether a software invention satisfies the requirements of novelty and inventive step. This is preferable to getting involved in an over-elaborate analysis as to whether the subject matter makes the right sort of technical contribution so as to bring it within the meaning of invention. There should be no objection to this approach as many software 'inventions' will fail to meet these stringent requirements.

One could argue that the exception of computer programs 'as such' from the meaning of invention ought to be repealed. This would bring the EPC more in line with patent law elsewhere. Indeed, the Agreement on the Trade Related Aspects of Intellectual Property Rights does not have an equivalent exclusion for computer programs or, for that matter, business methods.

The decision in *Aerotel* is regrettable in two ways. It confirms that the law on the patentability of software inventions in England harks back to the position over 15 years ago. All the refinement at the EPO is ignored. Perhaps more seriously, patent law in England relating to the exceptions to the meaning of invention is now at odds to the position at the EPO. This can only result in conflicting decisions with software patents being more readily available at the EPO. Applicants may now get a UK(EP) patent from the EPO more easily than by direct application for a UK patent. Worse still, a UK software patent obtained through the EPO will be subject to challenges in the UK based on different criteria than those used at the EPO to determine whether the application was patentable in the first place. We could even end up with inconsistency within the UK as the Scots courts are not bound by the English Court of Appeal and could decide to follow the most recent case law at the EPO Boards of Appeal.

In *Aerotel*, Jacob LJ must have been very frustrated at being bound by older Court of Appeal decisions. He noted that the present position was very unsatisfactory and he even went so far as to formulate questions for the enlarged Boards of Appeal at the EPO. Of course, the position is not the same as that concerning European Union legislation with the possibility of seeking preliminary rulings from the Court of Justice and there is no requirement for the enlarged Board to look at questions offered for its consideration. The EPO may even think it presumptuous for such questions to be suggested. Nevertheless, there is force in what Jacob LJ feels about the issue and it would be timely for a decision of the enlarged Board which can be convened to consider particular points of interpretation without a case where the point has been raised *in vacuo*. However, even then the High Court and Court of Appeal could not apply such a ruling because of *stare decisis*. It would take legislative action or a House of Lords judgment to free the lower courts and the UK Patent Office from the difficult position they are now in. Perhaps in a future case on software patents the leapfrog procedure could be used to fast track an appeal from the High Court to the Supreme Court.

Subsequent developments as to the patentability of computer-implemented inventions

In *Symbian Ltd* v *Comptroller General of Patents*,[339] the invention in issue was for a method of accessing data in a dynamic link library in a computing device (a dynamic link library is one containing functions common to a number of different applications). This had the advantage of making such devices faster and more reliable in operation. The application was refused by the hearing officer as being an application to patent a computer program as such. On appeal, Patten J held the invention to be patentable. The Comptroller General appealed to the Court of Appeal. Lord Neuberger of Abbotsbury gave the judgment of the court.

That there was previously some conflict between the Court of Appeal and the EPO Boards of Appeal was highlighted in *Aerotel* by Jacob LJ who pointed out that some decisions of the Boards of Appeal were mutually contradictory and by the Board of Appeal in Case T154/04 *Duns Licensing Associates/Estimating sales activity*[340] where the Board (at para 12) described the 'technical effect approach' adopted by Jacob LJ in *Aerotel* as not being:

> . . . consistent with a good-faith interpretation of the European Patent Convention in accordance with Article 31 of the Vienna Convention on the Law of Treaties of 1969.[341]

In relation to *stare decisis*, the Court of Appeal recognised that there was a new exception to the rule in *Young* v *Bristol Aeroplane*.[342] The Court could depart (but was not bound to do so) from previous Court of Appeal decisions where they were inconsistent with clear guidance from the EPO Boards of Appeal unless satisfied that it was wrong.[343] Nevertheless, the Court of Appeal in the present case decided to follow *Aerotel*. The reason being that there have been some conflicting decisions of the Boards of Appeal after *Aerotel* which shows that the law before the Boards of Appeal is not yet settled[344] and there has not yet been a decision at the Enlarged Board of Appeal.

Although following *Aerotel* and the previous Court of Appeal decisions, Lord Neuberger cast some doubt on the approach in the decision in that court in *Fujitsu Limited's Application*.[345] Although ostensibly consistent with *Vicom* and *Gale*, it was hard to reconcile with those two cases as to what constitutes a technical contribution, the alternative ground for refusal (that the alleged invention was a method of performing a mental act) could not be faulted.

Lord Neuberger noted a major difficulty in the past was the dividing line between what was and was not 'technical'.[346] Nonetheless, he accepted that there was a need for a technical effect but it was not limited to an effect outside the computer. In the present case, the invention made a better computer in that it increased speed and reliability. The invention could also be applied to other devices such as cameras and mobile phones so any distinction between whether the technical effect lies within or outside the computer is an artificial one. In applying the law as expressed in *Aerotel* and explained in *Symbian*, it was held that the invention was not caught by the exclusion. He applied *Aerotel* thus:

339 [2009] RPC 1. After this case, the Patent Office issued a new notice: *Practice Notice (Patents Act 1977: patentability of computer programs)*, 8 December 2008.

340 15 November 2006.

341 Article 31(1) of the Treaty states: 1.A treaty shall be interpreted in good faith in accordance with the ordinary meaning to be given to the terms of the treaty in their context and in the light of its object and purpose.

342 Encouraged by Lord Hoffmann in *Merrell Dow Pharmaceuticals Inc* v *H N Norton & Co Ltd* [1996] RPC 76 and *Conor Medsystems Inc* v *Angiotech Pharmaceuticals Inc* [2008] RPC 28 where he emphasised that it was desirable for English courts to adopt the same principles as the Boards of Appeal when assessing obviousness.

343 See also Jacob LJ in *Actavis UK Ltd* v *Merck & Co Inc* [2008] RPC 26.

344 For example, in T1351/04 *FUJITSU/File search method*, 18 April 2007, the Board held that '[t]he claimed method requires the use of a computer. It has therefore technical character and constitutes an invention within the meaning of Article 52(1) EPC . . .'.

345 [1997] RPC 608.

346 The word does not appear in either s 1(2) of the Patents Act 1977 or Article 52 of the EPC.

Stage 1 of the *Aerotel* guidance was not in issue.

Stage 2 – the contribution was a program which makes a computer operate on other programs faster than prior art operating programs enabled it to do by virtue of the claimed features.

Stage 3 – the contribution was not solely excluded matter as it had the knock-on effect of the computer working better as a matter of practical reality.

Stage 4 – the contribution was technical on any view as to the meaning of 'technical'.

Put simply, a computer program invention is caught by the exception if it does not produce a technical effect at all, or if it does, that effect itself lies within the other exclusions from the meaning of invention. This accords with some, but by no means all, decisions of the Boards of Appeal. Following *Symbian*, the UK Intellectual Property Office issued a Practice Notice.[347] Extracts from paras 6 to 8 of the Notice state:

347 *Practice Notice (Patents Act 1977: Patentability of computer programs)*, 8 December 2008.

6   . . . whilst an invention involving a computer is undoubtedly 'technical', in law the mere presence of conventional computing hardware does not of itself mean an invention makes a technical contribution and so avoids the computer program exclusion. This is in contrast to the practice of the European Patent Office, which the Court of Appeal rejected in the *Symbian* case.

7   . . . one effect of the computer program exclusion is to prevent other excluded material becoming patentable merely by use of a computer in its implementation. Thus, a business method, mental act, mathematical method or presentation of information implemented on a conventional computer system or network would still be excluded.

8   . . . examiners will object to the computerisation of what would be a pure mental act if done without the aid of a computer as both a mental act and a computer program as such. A similar logic applies to the other exclusions.

348 [2009] FSR 19.

In *AT & T Knowledge Ventures LP* v *Comptroller General of Patents*,[348] Lewison J explained that *Aerotel* and *Symbian*, taken together, meant that the four-stage test in *Aerotel* was still good law but should not be followed blindly and that the question of whether the contribution is technical must be asked and answered in the course of the inquiry but it does not matter whether it is asked at stage 3 or 4. Although it is impossible to define 'technical effect' in the context of the excluded matter but Lewison J thought the following were useful 'signposts' (at para 40 and 41):

40   . . .
  i)   whether the claimed technical effect has a technical effect on a process which is carried on outside the computer;
  ii) whether the claimed technical effect operates at the level of the architecture of the computer; that is to say whether the effect is produced irrespective of the data being processed or the applications being run;
  iii) whether the claimed technical effect results in the computer being made to operate in a new way;
  iv) whether there is an increase in the speed or reliability of the computer;
  v)   whether the perceived problem is overcome by the claimed invention as opposed to merely being circumvented.

41   If there is a technical effect in this sense, it is still necessary to consider whether the claimed technical effect lies solely in excluded matter.

As regards the second question in the *Aerotel* test, identifying the actual contribution, Jacob LJ said it was a question of asking what the inventor had really added to human knowledge. In *AT & T Knowledge Ventures LP*, Lewison J said that this question requires the questioner to have some knowledge of the state of the art. In a case where novelty is also at issue, this is a good reason for considering novelty before the issue of whether the alleged invention is excluded. In *Cranway Ltd* v *Playtech Ltd*,[349] Lewison J applied the *Aerotel* test and his own 'signposts' in *AT & T* and concluded that the application to patent

349 [2010] FSR 3.

a method of online gambling fell wholly within the exclusion. The whole process was carried out on a computer and/or server, the computer architecture was standard, the computer did not operate in a new way, there was no increase in speed or reliability of the computer and the perceived problem was a business problem not a computer problem. To the extent that the alleged invention solved a problem, it was a method of doing business.

The Boards of Appeal of the EPO have recently distinguished between excluded matter and non-excluded matter where an alleged invention comprises both. In Case T1793/07 *Konami/Video game device*,[350] the claims were directed at a computer game device. The alleged invention was directed at the technical implementation of rules for playing a game.[351] It was held that only those features which contributed to technical character were to be taken into account when testing for inventive step.[352] This seems to contradict the decision in Case T208/84 *VICOM/Computer-related invention*,[353] where the Board of Appeal held, *inter alia*, that (at 79):

> . . . even if the idea underlying an invention may be considered to reside in a mathematical method a claim directed to a technical process in which the method is used does not seek protection for the mathematical method *as such*. (original emphasis.)

At long last, the President of the EPO has made a reference to the enlarged Board of Appeal to resolve the issue of the scope of the exceptions in relation to computer programs under Article 52(2) and (3) EPC.[354] The questions referred are:

1 Can a computer program only be excluded as a computer program as such if it is explicitly claimed as a computer program?
2 (a) Can a claim in the area of computer programs avoid exclusion under art. 52(2)(c) and (3) merely by explicitly mentioning the use of a computer or a computer readable storage medium?
  (b) If question 2(a) is answered in the negative, is a further technical effect necessary to avoid exclusion, said effect going beyond those effects inherent in the use of a computer or data storage medium to respectively execute or store a computer program?
3 (a) Must a claimed feature cause a technical effect on a physical entity in the real world in order to contribute to the technical character of the claim?
  (b) If question 3(a) is answered in the positive, is it sufficient that the physical entity be an unspecified computer?
  (c) If question 3(a) is answered in the negative, can features contribute to the technical character of the claim if the only effects to which they contribute are independent of any particular hardware that may be used?
4 (a) Does the activity of programming a computer necessarily involve technical considerations?
  (b) If question 4(a) is answered in the positive, do all features resulting from programming thus contribute to the technical character of a claim?
  (c) If question 4(a) is answered in the negative, can features resulting from programming contribute to the technical character of a claim only when they contribute to a further technical effect when the program is executed?

Sadly, the Enlarged Board of Appeal declared that the reference was inadmissible in Case G3/08 *Programs for computers*.[355] Under Article 112(1)(b), the President may refer questions to the Enlarged Board of Appeal in order to ensure uniform application of the law or if a point of law of fundamental importance arises or where two Boards of Appeal have given different decisions on the question referred. As to question 1, the Enlarged Board of Appeal stated that Case T154/04 *Duns Licensing Associates/estimating sales activity*[356] had created a practical system for delimiting innovations for which a patent could be granted.

350 [2009] EPOR 103.

351 The close-marking of an opponent's player in a video football game.

352 See also, to similar effect, Case T336/07 *IGT/Electronic multi-play poker* [2008] EPOR 227.

353 [1987] EPOR 74.

354 *President's reference/Computer program exclusion* [2009] EPOR 63.

355 [2010] EPOR 36.

356 [2007] EPOR 349.

As to question 2, there was no divergence identified by the referral and the question was, therefore, inadmissible. As to questions 3 and 4, there was no divergence sufficient to support the referral and, consequently, these questions were inadmissible. The Enlarged Board of Appeal made some important points, including:

- The word 'different' in Article 112(1)(b), based on the French and German versions of the EPC, was better interpreted as meaning 'divergent'.[357]
- The development of jurisprudence over time might mean that the decisions in some cases are different to decisions in others but that alone cannot justify referral to the Enlarged Board.
- Changes in direction in legal development are a normal part of judicial activity and it is wrong to speak of divergent decisions simply because departures from earlier practice are deemed necessary when homing in on the right solution to a specific case.
- Even a radical drift in jurisprudence need not fall within Article 112(1)(b) provided the Board of Appeal corrects itself, preferably in an explicit fashion, declaring the earlier practice to be no longer relevant.
- There was a clear difference between the decisions in Case T1173/97 *IBM/computer programs*[358] and Case T424/03 *MICROSOFT/clipboard format I*[359] and, although the seven years between the cases was not long in legal terms, the cases were, nonetheless, compatible with the notion of the development of case law.

As for greater harmonisation across Europe, the Enlarged Board of Appeal said (at para 29):

> Even the essentially commendable desire for harmonisation expressed by Jacob L.J. in the Aerotel Ltd v Telco Holdings Ltd judgment can be taken up by the Enlarged Board only to the extent possible under the EPC, even if his suggestion might significantly advance the cause of legal uniformity in Europe. When judiciary-driven legal development meets its limits, it is time for the legislator to take over.

The lack of any form of binding precedent, so central to Anglo-Saxon law, is lacking in continental Europe. In terms of the application of the EPC requirements for patentability to actual cases, this results in some considerable uncertainty, particularly in relation to the exclusions from the meaning of invention. Applicants for patents involving the exclusions must hope that, if they have to appeal a decision of the examination division to the Board of Appeal, it does not decide to 'create' new law to deprive their invention of patentability. A further consequence of this moveable feast of 'legitimate development' is that appellate courts in the UK (and the Republic or Ireland) should be very wary of using decisions at the EPO to support their judgments as these EPO cases might get locked into their rules of precedent whilst the EPO radically shifts its jurisprudence under the auspices of further development of the law.[360]

The President of the EPO's failed reference did not seek guidance on an important question, being what the scope of the exclusion should be if the effect of executing the computer program in question is itself amongst the exclusions under Article 52(2) and (3), for example, if the computer program when run performs a business method. There are two approaches. As held in the English courts, this would be within the exclusion but there are some Boards of Appeal decisions that seem to point the other way, such as Case T258/03 *Hitachi/Auction method*.[361] Surely, implementing a business method by technical means is not a claim to a business method *as such*. Granting a patent in such a case would not lock away the business method itself, only that method of implementation.[362] Further support for that view is given by Case T494/07 *MEI/currency validator*[363] which concerned a currency tester. One of the claims objected to in the examining division of the EPO was a method of programming a currency tester comprising storing data for executing a method as claimed in the preceding claims. The Technical Board of Appeal, citing *Hitachi/auction method*, held that the claim involved a technical means, being a currency tester,

357 The official languages of the EPC are English, French and German. All have the same status.

358 [2000] EPOR 414.

359 [2006] EPOR 39.

360 As happened in *Aerotel* v *Telco*.

361 [2004] EPOR 55.

362 Potentially answering the argument that some (though by no means all) of the exclusions are based on a desire to avoid monopolies that are too extensive.

363 [2011] EPOR 36.

and therefore, had a technical character. In particular, the claim involved the storage of data, with the effect that data are in fact stored in the currency tester after the step is executed. This must be contrasted with a sequence of computer-executable instructions (a computer program) which merely have the potential of achieving an effect when loaded in and executed by the computer. For that reason the claim was distinguishable from a computer program. There was no discussion as to whether the method of testing currency was itself excluded as being a business method.

Another ground of appeal in *MEI/currency tester* was that one claim was said to lack clarity by the examining division.[364] This was in sharp contrast with the decision in Case T410/96 *IBM/Computer-related claims*.[365] However, the Technical Board confirmed that the obligation to follow the *ratio decidendi* of a decision of the Board was limited to the same case remitted back to the examining division for further prosecution. Otherwise, no matter how alike cases were, a decision by the Board of Appeal in one was not binding on the other. If two very similar cases are decided differently, that can only be classed as an error of judgment.

Exclusions in s 1(3) – contrary to public policy or morality

Further exclusions are contained in the Patents Act 1977 s 1(3). This subsection was significantly modified by the Patents Regulations 2000.[366] Previously, s 1(3)(a) excluded inventions, the publication or exploitation of which would generally be expected to encourage offensive, immoral or anti-social behaviour.[367] Section 1(4) stated that behaviour should not be regarded as offensive, immoral or anti-social only because it is prohibited by law in the UK or any part of it. Old s 1(3)(b) excluded the patenting of any variety of animal or plant or any essentially biological process for the production of animals or plants, not being a micro-biological process or the product of such a process. This provision is now restated in Sch A2 to the 1977 Act which modifies and clarifies the position in relation to biotechnological inventions, discussed later in this chapter.

Now, s 1(3) states that a patent shall not be granted for an invention the commercial exploitation of which would be contrary to public policy or morality. This requires something more than illegality as s 1(4) states that the exploitation referred to shall not be regarded as contrary to public policy or morality only because it is prohibited by any law in force in the UK or any part of it. These provisions are equivalent to Article 53(a) EPC. However, this refers to publication or exploitation and to the law in some or all of the Contracting States. Thus, something which may be illegal in one Contracting State does not automatically mean that the publication or exploitation is automatically deemed to be contrary to public policy or morality. The purpose behind the provision in the EPC would seem to be to overcome disparities in national laws that would otherwise prevent the grant of a patent which could be exploited in other countries. For example, use of a device to give advance warning of speed traps on roads might be illegal in some countries but this should not prevent the patenting of such a device and the sale of it in other countries.

The transposition of Article 53(a) into the Patents Act 1977 makes sense as regards illegality where differences in laws in parts of the UK may occur. If, for example, the commercial exploitation of the invention is illegal in Scotland, that does not necessarily mean that a UK patent cannot be granted for it providing, of course, notwithstanding that illegality, it is not regarded as contrary to public policy or morality. The invention could be commercially exploited in the rest of the UK without difficulty. It has to be said, however, that the exploitation of an invention being illegal in only part of the UK is highly unlikely. Furthermore, the effect of s 1(3) and (4) is that it is a remote possibility (or at least not impossible) for an invention, the commercial exploitation of which is illegal in

364 The claim was to 'a currency tester comprising means for executing a method as claimed in any one of claims 1–19'.

365 [1999] EPOR 318.

366 SI 2000/2037. These Regulations came into force on 28 July 2000.

367 Article 53(a) of the European Patent Convention is the equivalent of s 1(3)(a).

the whole of the UK, to be granted a patent nonetheless, even though it cannot lawfully be exploited commercially.

Examples of things which may be excluded from the grant of a patent by these provisions could be a method of making explosives or a self-administered abortion kit.

Surgery, therapy and diagnosis of the human or animal body

Previously, methods of treatment of the human or animal body by surgery or therapy or diagnosis practised on the human or animal body were stated under s 4(2) as being incapable of industrial application and, hence, excluded from the grant of a patent. This did not prevent the patenting of substances or compounds for use in such methods of treatment or diagnosis even if they were part of the state of the art providing the use in question was not itself part of the state of the art under s 2(6) and s 4(3). These provisions were repealed and replaced by a new s 4A which came into force on 13 December 2007. This was to comply with changes to the EPC and the new mechanism is much clearer and more logical than before. Section 4A(1) states that methods of treatment by surgery or therapy of the human or animal body or diagnosis practised on the human or animal body are simply not patentable. However, s 4A(2) confirms that the exception does not apply to inventions consisting of substances or compositions for use in such methods. These are patentable even if the substance or composition itself is part of the state of the art in two cases, the distinction being that the first relates to 'use in any such method' whilst the second relates to 'a specific use in any such method'.[368] The use of the substance or compound in any such method or the specific use, as they case may be, must itself not form part of the state of the art. These provisions closely follow the equivalent provisions in the EPC.[369] Thus, the use of known substance X to treat a virus or infection Y generally or specifically is patentable providing that general or specific use is not itself part of the state of the art.

The reason for the basic exclusion under s 4A(1) is to ensure that medical practitioners (and veterinary surgeons) are not subjected to restraint by a patent when tending patients: *John Wyeth & Brother Ltd's Application: Schering AG's Application*.[370] The exclusion does not extend to products consisting of substances or compositions used in any such methods under s 4A(2) and, therefore, drugs are capable of industrial application and are patentable in principle. The words 'treatment' and 'diagnosis' imply an illness or disease of some kind which does not include conception or pregnancy, neither of which is considered to be an illness.[371] Further, as treatment of the human or animal body is excluded, treatment to rid a person or animal of, for example, an infestation of lice may be patentable if it is accepted that such treatment is directed towards ridding the human of lice and not directed to treating the human or animal body as such: *Stafford-Miller's Application*.[372] However, in Case T116/85 *WELLCOME/Pigs I*,[373] the Board of Appeal in the EPO considered an invention comprising a method of treating mange in pigs by the application of a pesticidal composition to the surface of a pig's body to be a method of treating an animal body and excluded from patentability under the equivalent provision in the EPC.[374] *Stafford-Miller* must now be doubted, especially as it was decided under the 1949 Act which had no equivalent express exclusion. However, in *WELLCOME/Pigs I*, the Board of Appeal did say that treating pigs infected by mange was a therapeutic treatment of a disease on the evidence before the Board whereas, in *Stafford-Miller*, the court decided on different evidence that an infestation of lice on human beings is not a disease.

368 Section 4(3) and (4) respectively.

369 Article 53(c) and Article 54(4) and (5).

370 [1985] RPC 545.

371 *See Schering AG's Application* [1971] RPC 337, where a patent was granted to a method of contraception involving doses of gestagen. However, in 1936, an application in respect of 'improvements in pessaries' (contraceptive devices) was refused by exercise of the Royal Prerogative: *Riddlesbarger's Application* (1936) 53 RPC 57.

372 [1984] FSR 258.

373 [1998] EPOR 1.

374 Article 52(4).

The reason for the exclusion of surgery, therapy or diagnosis is probably a policy decision to prevent restrictions on the spread and adoption of new and improved methods of treatment. For example, if a surgeon develops a new and improved way to perform back surgery, it is in the public interest that such a method be available to all surgeons. Nevertheless, this does not sit comfortably with the fact that drugs can be, and often are, patented. One difference between the surgeon and the drug company is that the former is in a profession where he is expected to pass on his knowledge to others (he will probably be very keen to publish his new technique) and will not expect financial recompense for his idea but will hope for kudos and the respect of colleagues; whereas the drug company, operating in a competitive industry, needs a patent to justify investment in research and development.

As previously, known compounds and substances for use in new methods of treatment or diagnosis are patentable as are second and subsequent uses for new methods. Additionally, new specific uses as well as methods are patentable in principle under s 4A(4). This could cover the situation where a new regime for dosing a patient is found to be more effective than known regimes and would remove Jacob LJ's regret at how the Court of Appeal interpreted the previous version of the exception for known compounds and substances used for new methods of treatment.[375]

375 In *Merck & Co Inc's Patent* [2003] FSR 29 at para 80.

Biotechnological patents

It is possible to obtain a patent in some countries for a new breed of animal (for example, in the USA), but the scope of the exclusion in old s 1(3)(b), and the corresponding provision of the EPC, Article 53(b), was unclear. The Board of Appeal of the EPO granted a patent for a laboratory mouse that had been genetically altered (a transgenic animal) so as to be more likely to develop cancerous cells in a short period of time.[376] It was accepted that this mouse was not a new variety of animal and, as a result, not excepted from the grant of a patent. Obviously, this is a very sensitive, ethical issue and decisions in this area require careful consideration of animal rights and the potential benefits to man and animal alike.

376 Case T19/90 *Onco-Mouse/Harvard* [1990] EPOR 501.

Granting patents for biotechnological inventions is an area which raises much controversy, especially where such inventions involve genetic modification of animals or plants or research carried out on embryos. There has been some criticism of the role of the EPO in this field and, in an address at the annual press conference at the EPO on 27 June 2000, the President, Mr Ingo Kober, answered these criticisms by saying that:

- the patent system is based on transparency through disclosure;
- certain technological developments are not prevented simply by denying patents for them;
- there are legal obstacles (for example, the prohibition on patenting varieties of animals and plants, *per se*) and safety precautions (such as the examination system and the awareness of patent examiners to ethical issues) built into the patent system;
- patents are not a measure of what is permissible; this responsibility lies in other areas of law, such as licensing controls.

The President dismissed claims that the EPO is lining its own pockets by encouraging applications for biotechnological patents and he pointed out that there had been two fee reductions in the preceding four years. With that background and the fact that there are some 25,000 genetic patents at the EPO, the Patents Regulations 2000 make interesting reading.

For some time, there were moves to adopt a Directive on the legal protection of biotechnological inventions. After rejecting the first proposal in 1995, the European

377 OJ C286, 22.09.1997, p 87.

378 The *Official Journal* reference of the common position text is OJ C100, 08.04.1998, p 17.

379 OJ L 213, 30.07.1998, p 13.

380 Rules 23b, 23c and 23d.

381 SI 2000/2037. The Regulations came into force on 28 July 2000. They give effect to the Directive and to Article 27(2) of the TRIPs Agreement which permits the exclusion from patentability, inventions the commercial exploitation of which would be contrary to the *ordre public* or morality and has equivalent effect to new s 1(3) and (4) of the Patents Act 1977.

382 These new definitions are inserted into s 130 of the Patents Act 1977, the interpretation section.

Parliament rejected an amended proposed Directive on 16 July 1997.[377] However, it was still accepted that this was an area in need of clarification and a further revised proposal was prepared by the Commission and was adopted by the Council on 26 February 1998. Following this, on 12 May 1998, the European Parliament voted to accept the common position text of the Directive on the legal protection of biotechnological inventions.[378] The final outcome was Directive 98/44/EC of European Parliament and of the Council of 6 July 1998 on the legal protection of biotechnological inventions.[379]

The recitals to the Directive give important information as to its *raison d'être*. It is seen as important because of the increasing role in a broad range of industries being played by biotechnology and genetic engineering. This is a matter of some importance in the future industrial development of the Community. Adequate legal protection is needed to encourage the high-risk investment involved in research and development in biotechnology, in particular in genetic engineering. Advantages of protecting bio-technology and genetic engineering identified in the recitals include the development of less polluting and more economical methods of cultivation and improvements in combating major epidemics, endemic diseases and hunger in the world. It is noted that the TRIPs Agreement requires that patent protection must be provided for products and processes in all areas of technology.

The EPC was modified to incorporate the effects of the Directive. Article 53(b) remained as before, with the general prohibition on patents for varieties of animals or plants or essentially biological processes for the production of such varieties though not extending to micro-biological processes or the products thereof. New rules were added to the Implementing Regulations to the Convention on the Grant of European Patents.[380] The overall effect follows the Directive closely as does Sch A2 to the Patents Act 1977, inserted by the Patent Regulations 2000.[381] The following description of the new regime on the patentability of biotechnological inventions is based on the changes made by the Regulations.

First, s 76A, as inserted by the 2000 Regulations, states that any provision of or made under the 1977 Act is to have effect in relation to biotechnological inventions subject to Sch A2. Provisions relating to other kinds of patents or applications for patents are unaffected. The Regulations amend the Act to allow the patenting of biotechnological inventions, which are defined as inventions concerning products consisting of or containing biological material or processes by means of which biological material is produced, processed or used. Biological material is defined as any material containing genetic information and which is capable of reproducing itself or being reproduced in a biological system.[382]

Schedule A2 para 1 states that inventions are not to be considered unpatentable solely on the ground that they concern a product consisting of or containing biological material or a process by which biological material is produced, processed or used. Provision is made for the patenting of inventions even though the biological subject matter previously occurred in nature or if the invention comprises an element isolated from the human body or otherwise produced by a technical process even if the structure of the element is identical to a natural element. This includes the sequence or partial sequence of a gene. A possible example is in respect of people living in a part of northern Italy who have a genetic make-up that appears to make them particularly resistant to a build-up of cholesterol. If a new process is made for mass-producing the relevant genetic sequence so that it may be administered to patients having high cholesterol levels, this may be patentable. Inventions may be patentable even if the technical feasibility is not confined to a particular type of animal: for example, a new gene therapy that works effectively when applied to different varieties. Thus, a new gene therapy that works for both sheep and goats may be patentable.

Schedule A2 para 3 lists inventions that are not patentable. They are:

1 the human body, at the various stages of its formation and development, and the simple discovery of one of its elements, including the sequence or partial sequence of a gene – thus, there must be some technical application of the discovery to be patentable as in *Genentech Inc's Patent*;[383]

2 processes for cloning human beings;

3 processes for modifying the germ line genetic identity of human beings;

4 uses of human embryos for industrial or commercial purposes;

5 processes for modifying the genetic identity of animals which are likely to cause them suffering without any substantial medical benefit to man or animal, and also animals resulting from such processes;

6 any variety of animal or plant or any essentially biological process for the production of animals or plants, not being a micro-biological[384] or other technical process or the product of such a process.

The latter exception is subtly changed from the previous exclusion in old s 1(3)(b) of the 1977 Act. The words 'other technical process' are inserted. Furthermore, new definitions are given and 'essentially biological process' is now defined as any process for the production of animals and plants which consists entirely of natural phenomena such as crossing and selection and 'micro-biological process' is defined as any process involving or performed upon or resulting in micro-biological material.[385]

The scope of the extent of protection afforded by patents on biotechnological inventions is set out in Sch A2 paras 7–10 as follows:

- *Biological material possessing specific characteristics* – the protection extends to any biological material derived from that biological material through propagation or multiplication in an identical or divergent form and possessing those same characteristics (para 7).

- *A process that enables biological material to be produced possessing specific characteristics as a result of the invention* – the protection extends to biological material directly obtained through that process and any other biological material derived from the directly obtained biological material through propagation or multiplication in an identical or divergent form and possessing those same characteristics (para 8).

- *A product containing or consisting of genetic information* – the protection extends to all material in which the product is incorporated and in which the genetic information is contained and performs its function, save as provided for in para 3(a) (the exclusion in relation to the human body and the simple discovery of one of the elements of the human body, including the sequence or partial sequence of a gene) (para 9).

- *Limitation* – the above protection does not extend to biological material obtained from the propagation or multiplication of biological material placed on the market by the proprietor of the patent or with his consent, where the multiplication or propagation necessarily results from the application for which the biological material was marketed, provided that the material obtained is not subsequently used for other propagation or multiplication (para 10).

Paragraph 9 above is equivalent to Article 9 on the Directive on the legal protection of biotechnological inventions. Its scope came up for a ruling before the Court of Justice in Case C-428/08 *Monsanto Technology LLC* v *Cefetra BV*.[386] The claimant had European patents for soybeans plants genetically modified to be resistant to a herbicide known as 'Roundup'. The defendants imported into the Netherlands large quantities of soy meal from Argentina.[387] Tests showed that the meal had originated from soybean plants genetically modified according to the patent. However, the soy meal was dead material. The claimants sued for infringement of its patent. The Dutch court referred questions to the Court of Justice of the EU for a preliminary ruling. The Court of Justice ruled that Article 9 does not confer protection under a patent where the product in question is contained in soy

383 [1989] RPC 147.

384 Brewer's yeast is the product of a micro-biological process. Louis Pasteur obtained a patent for purified brewer's yeast in the USA in 1873; Eisenschitz, T.S. (1987) *Patents, Trade Marks and Designs in Information Work*, Croom Helm, p 54. In *American Cyanamid Co (Dann's) Patent* [1971] RPC 425, a method of producing antibiotics using micro-organisms was held to be patentable.

385 Patents Act 1977 Sch A2, para 11.

386 [2011] FSR 6.

387 The claimant did not have any equivalent patents in Argentina.

meal but does not perform the function for which it was patented although it did perform that function previously and, if extracted from the soy meal and inserted into a living organism, might perform the function in the future.

The claimant had also argued that Article 9 was incompatible with the TRIPs Agreement but this was rejected by the Court of Justice. Article 30 of TRIPs allows limited exceptions to the rights conferred by a patent, providing they do not unreasonably conflict with the normal exploitation of the patent and do not unreasonably prejudice the legitimate rights of the patent owner, taking account of the legitimate interests of third parties. The Court of Justice considered that 'limited exceptions' might include limitations on rights, not just the exclusion of rights, and this was consistent with Article 30 TRIPs.

The principle of exhaustion of rights applies to a limited extent and the above protection does not extend to biological material obtained from the propagation or multiplication of biological material placed on the market by the proprietor of the patent or with his consent, where such propagation or multiplication necessarily results from the application for which the biological material was marketed, provided that the material obtained is not subsequently used for other propagation or multiplication.

The industrial application of a genetic sequence must be disclosed in the patent application as filed (Sch A2 para 6). Section 125A of the 1977 Act, which deals with the disclosure of inventions by their specifications in terms of the availability of samples of micro-organisms, is amended. Basically, the term 'biological material' substitutes micro-organism. Schedule 1 to the Patent Rules 2007[388] contains provisions for the deposit, access and re-deposit of biological material.

The Patents Regulations 2000 insert specific defences for farmers in relation to the use of animal or animal reproductive stock and these provisions are discussed in the following chapter in the section on defences.

As regards varieties of plants, the exclusion from patentability is of relatively little consequence as plants may be protected under the Plant Varieties Act 1997.[389] Under this Act, proprietary rights are granted to the breeders or discoverers (or their successors in title) of new, distinctive, uniform and stable plant varieties. The duration of protection is 25 years or, for potatoes, trees and vines, 30 years from date of the grant of right. These periods may be extended to 30 and 35 years respectively by the relevant National Authorities, including the Secretary of State for Environment, Food and Rural Affairs. The rights are monopolistic in nature and are to prevent production or reproduction, conditioning for the purpose of propagation, offering for sale, selling or other marketing, exporting or importing, stocking for the above purposes and any other prescribed purpose. The scheme is administered by the Plant Variety Rights Office under the control of the Controller of Plant Variety Rights, appointed by the relevant Ministers. A specific defence for farmers in relation to the product of his harvest for propagation purposes is inserted into the Patents Act 1977 (s 60(5)(g)) together with new Sch A1 limiting the circumstances in which the defence applies.

388 SI 2007/3291.

389 Since 27 May 1995 there has been a Council Regulation (EC) No 2100/94 of 27 July 1994 on Community plant variety rights, OJ L 227, 01.09.1994, p 1.

Summary

Under section 14(3) of the Patents Act 1977, the specification must disclose the invention in a manner which is clear enough and complete enough for the invention to be performed by a person skilled in the art. Failure to comply will mean that the invention lacks sufficiency and a patent should not be granted for the invention.

The requirements for the grant of a patent are that the invention:

● is new;
● involves an inventive step;

- is capable of industrial application; and
- the subject-matter is not excluded under section 1(2) or (3) or section 4A.

Novelty is determined by whether the invention forms part of the state of the art, being all matter which at any time before the priority date of the invention has been made available to the public in the UK or elsewhere by written or oral description by use or in any other way. Patent applications published on or after the priority date of the patent which have an earlier priority date are taken to be part of the state of the art. There is a six-month period during which disclosures made in breach of confidence are ignored. Disclosures at international exhibitions are not part of the state of the art under certain conditions.

The state of the art used to challenge a patent often includes prior patents and learned journal articles. If the invention in question is not new, it is said to be anticipated by the prior art.

An invention involves an inventive step if is not obvious to a person skilled in the art having regard to the state of the art. However, patent applications having an earlier priority date which are published on or after the priority date of the patent are not part of the state of the art for the purpose of determining whether the invention involves an inventive step.

The person skilled in the art is a person (or team or persons if appropriate) having no inventive ability. He has the 'common general knowledge' relevant to the art in question. A test has evolved for checking for obviousness. This is the *Windsurfing* test, as restated in *Pozzoli* (and usually now referred to as the *Pozzoli* test).

Commercial success may indicate that an invention is not obvious, particularly if there have been numerous attempts to find a solution. However, commercial success is not conclusive and it may be explained by other factors, such as marketing effort.

An invention is capable of industrial application if it can be made or used in any kind of industry, including agriculture. Rarely do inventions fail to be granted patents on the basis that they are not capable of industrial application. However, what is claimed must be of immediate concrete benefit and not merely speculative.

The exclusions in section 1(2) are very difficult to apply in practice. A major problem is that the things listed are not inventions for the purposes of the Act, *as such*. Therefore, for example, claiming a computer program is not patentable but claiming the technical effect produced by running the program may be patentable.

If the effect of executing a computer program is itself caught by section 1(2), for example, if it is a method of doing business, this will be excluded even though the invention may have a technical character.

Jurisprudence in the European Patent Office appears to be more liberal in relation to computer programs than the position in the UK. The Enlarged Board of Appeal at the EPO declined to clarify the position following a reference from the President of the EPO on the grounds that the questions asked were inadmissible. Further development in the UK is unlikely because of binding precedent although the Court of Appeal may no longer be bound by a previous decision of that court if it is in conflict with the EPO Boards of Appeal.

A patent will not be granted if the commercial exploitation of the invention would be contrary to public policy or morality.

Biotechnological inventions are patentable subject to a list of exceptions, such as the human body, animal or plant varieties or biological processes for the production of animals or plants (but not microbiological processes).

Methods of treatment of the human or animal body by surgery or therapy or a method of diagnosis practised on the human or animal body are not patentable. This does not prevent the patenting of pharmaceutical products. Even new uses for known medicines or compounds may be patentable.

Discussion questions

1 What is an enabling disclosure and it what way is it relevant to questions of sufficiency and novelty?

2 An invention has an inventive step if it is not obvious to a person skilled in the art. In the UK, the *Windsurfing* test as reformulated and restated in *Pozzoli* is used in most cases. Discuss the application of the test in practice and the extent to which, if any, it may distort or obfuscate the statutory test.

3 The list of 'non-inventions' in section 1(2) of the Patents Act 1977 has no single underlying rationale. What justification is there to exclude each of the things listed in section 1(2)?

4 What is meant by 'industrial application' in the field of biotech patents?

5 If a computer program, as such, is not an invention and a method of doing business, as such, is not an invention, why is a novel and inventive method of doing business put into effect using a computer programmed with a novel and inventive computer program excluded from protection? It is unarguable that a program whilst being executed in a computer has a technical character, so why should a novel and inventive computer program be excluded from protection (a) at law and (b) by policy?

6 Discuss the decision of the Enlarged Board of Appeal of the EPO in Case G3/08 *Programs for computers* available at: http://www.epo.org/law-practice/case-law-appeals/pdf/g080003ex1.pdf

Selected further reading

Deschamps, C., 'Patenting computer-related inventions in the US and in Europe: the need for domestic and international legal harmony' [2011] *European Intellectual Property Review*, 103 (gives a critical review of the current position as regards computer programs and conflicting decisions and developments and the impacts of diverging laws and practices and calls for a more harmonised, balanced and effective regime for computer programs).

England, P., 'Novelty and sufficiency in a single, pan-European standard' [2010] *European Intellectual Property Review*, 467 (looks at the possible development of a pan-European model, developments at the EPO and elsewhere and the Protocol on Article 69 of the EPC).

Human Genome Sciences Inc v *Eli Lilly & Co* [2011] UKSC 51, available at: **http://www.bailii.org/uk/cases/UKSC/2011/51.html**

Macleod, R., 'What does "for" mean in "means for"? The role of functional limitations in apparatus claims' [2011] *European Intellectual Property Review*, 499 (this article investigates how the EPO and the UK and US patent offices consider functional limitations and the extent to which a single functional limitation can be used to gain broad protection).

Pila, J., 'Software patents, separation of powers and failed syllogisms: a cornucopia from the Enlarged Board of Appeal of the European Patent Office' [2011] *Cambridge Law Journal*, 203 (looks at the Enlarged Board of Appeal decision on the President's reference with respect to the patentability of computer programs and related case law and the desirability or otherwise of a European Patents Court).

13 Ownership, dealing with patents, safety and security, and Crown use

Introduction

Disputes as to entitlement to patents are common. This is not surprising given the value of many patent rights. The Patents Act 1977 contains numerous provisions setting out the basic rules on entitlement and procedures for determining who is entitled in a particular case. Prime examples of issues of entitlement concern situations where two or more persons have made contributions to an invention, or where an employee makes an invention. In some circumstances, employee inventors may be entitled to compensation where the invention belongs to the employer; there have been recent changes to these provisions to make this more than a mere theoretical possibility as, until 2009, there was not one single example of an employee being successful in an application for compensation.

As is usual with intellectual property rights, patents can be dealt with in a number of ways, such as by assignment, licensing or by way of a mortgage. Certain transactions have to be registered; otherwise there may be problems with obtaining costs in infringement actions. Where a patent is owned by two or more persons jointly, each can exploit the patent by themselves or through their agents under s 36(2), but the consent of all is required in respect of certain transactions under s 36(3), notably licensing. However, the Comptroller has a discretion to order the grant of a licence under a patent. This might be important where co-proprietors cannot agree and a deadlock has been reached such that the patent is not being exploited.[1]

The Act also contains provisions for the grant of compulsory licences and for licences of right. The former are quite rare and the provisions are intended to deal with a situation where the patent monopoly is being abused although, if that is so, competition law may be triggered also. Most licences of right result from the proprietor of a patent agreeing to this as a way of reducing the renewal fees.

There are provisions relating to 'safety and security' which may result in restrictions or prohibitions on the publication of information or its communication to any specified person. There are also restrictions on applications abroad by UK residents in respect of certain types of inventions. Basically, an application must be filed first at the UK Patent Office or the Comptroller must give written authority. Finally, the provisions relating to Crown use are described in this chapter.

1 Section 37(2). *See Hughes* v *Paxman* [2007] RPC 2.

Ownership of patents

The owner of a patent is referred to as its proprietor in the Patents Act 1977 which contains a number of provisions concerning the ownership of patents not noted for their clarity. At the outset, a distinction has to be made between the inventor and the proprietor of a patent, although in some cases the inventor will be the proprietor of the patent. The inventor of an invention is, by s 7(3), the actual devisor of the invention. Where the invention is the result of the combined efforts of two or more persons, they are the joint inventors of the invention. Where there are joint inventors, it is inappropriate to divide up the claims to see which has contributed which element.[2] It is important to identify who in substance was responsible for the invention, and if that is two or more persons then they are the joint inventors. Where more than one person is involved, to determine which is or are the inventors, the first step is to identify the inventive concept.[3]

The proprietor is the person to whom the patent is granted and who, therefore, has the right to work the patent. If the inventor is not the proprietor of the patent, he has a right to be mentioned as being the inventor in any patent granted and in any published application.[4] Failure to identify the inventor will prevent an application from proceeding. However, the inventor may waive his right to be identified as such (or have his address suppressed) in a published notice or specification for the patent under s 24(4).[5] This is not an absolute right except in relation to the inventor's address and the inventor must give reasons in writing, as to why he does not want his name published, to the Comptroller who will comply if satisfied of those reasons.[6] The rationale is to protect the identity or address of inventors who may be responsible for making inventions of a controversial nature which could attract the attention of protesters.

A patent is a form of personal property,[7] but not a thing in action, and may be transferred, created or granted only in accordance with s 30(2)–(7). The availability of compulsory licences in certain circumstances prevents the abuse of the monopoly granted to the proprietor of the patent.

The proprietor of a patent may offer to surrender it at any time by giving notice to the Comptroller under s 29. A person may give notice of opposition, in which case, the Comptroller will notify the proprietor and determine the question. This could be the case where a licensee objects to the surrender of the patent. The patent ceases to have effect when notice of the Comptroller's acceptance of the offer to surrender is published in the *Patents Journal*. In *Connaught Laboratories Inc's Patent*,[8] it was held that where an offer to surrender a patent was made in revocation proceedings, the patent remained in existence until such time as the Comptroller decided to accept that offer but, until that time, a court could revoke the patent.

Entitlement to a patent

While any person can apply for a patent either on his own or jointly, it will be granted only to persons identified in s 7. Under s 7(2)(a), primarily, the patent will be granted to the inventor, or joint inventors, except where someone else has a better entitlement to it under s 7(2)(b). This is where another person or persons are entitled by virtue of ' . . . any enactment or rule of law, any foreign law or treaty or international convention, or by any enforceable term in an agreement with the inventor that was entered into prior to the making of the invention . . .'. An example might be where an inventor is commissioned to produce an invention to overcome a particular problem. Equitable interests are not effective to make any other person entitled to the patent as far as the Act is concerned. The patent will be granted to the legal owner only, although any equitable owner may have a claim to the benefit accruing from the patent under a trust.[9] Additionally, an invention made by an employee shall be taken to belong to his employer.[10] This situation might, in any case, be covered expressly by the contract of employment. Section 7(2)(c) also provides for the grant of a patent to a successor or successors in title to the person or persons who would otherwise have been entitled to the patent. The words 'and to no other person' round off s 7(2) indicating that no other rules apply to determine entitle-

2 *Henry Brothers (Margherafelt) Ltd* v *Ministry of Defence and Northern Ireland Office* [1997] RPC 693. See also *Hughes and Paxman's Patent* [2005] EWHC 2240 (Pat) where an argument that this was the reason for s 37(2), giving the Comptroller a discretion to grant a licence, was rejected. The discretion was not so limited.

3 *Henry Brothers (Margherafelt) Ltd* v *Ministry of Defence and Northern Ireland Office* [1999] RPC 442, dismissing the appeal from the Patents Court.

4 Patents Act 1977 s 13(1).

5 Inserted by the Patents Act 2004, effective from 1 October 2005.

6 Patent Rules 2007, SI 2007/3291, r 10.

7 Patents Act 1977 s 30(1).

8 [1999] FSR 284.

9 As the question of ownership of an invention had to be considered as of the date the invention was made, any constructive trust must have arisen at this time: *Christopher S French* v *Paul J Mason* [1999] FSR 597.

10 Patents Act 1977 s 39, *see* below.

ment. The most common example of someone other than the inventor being entitled is the right of an employer in the case of an invention made by an employee which is provided for by s 39, discussed later.

To facilitate patent applications there is a rebuttable presumption that the person making the application is entitled to the grant of the patent. Anyone challenging entitlement has, therefore, the burden of proof. For example, a person claiming to be entitled as or by virtue of a joint inventor has the burden of proving he was indeed a joint inventor. Furthermore, if a person is claiming to be solely entitled has the additional burden of proving that the person named as inventor was not in fact the inventor.[11]

Lord Hoffmann in *Yeda Research & Development Co Ltd* v *Rhone-Poulenc Rorer International Holdings Inc*[12] considered that s 7(2) and (3) provided an exhaustive code for determining entitlement to the grant of a patent. It was wrong to require that a person claiming to be an inventor had to rely on some other rule of law, such as a breach of contract or breach of confidence as had been suggested in *Markem Corp v Zipher Ltd*.[13] To show entitlement all that was needed was to show that the proprietor was the inventor, being the actual devisor of the invention, or was entitled under s 7(2) or (3). Lord Hoffmann considered that the Court of Appeal in *Markem* confused the rules about entitlement and validity (novelty). The latter relates to the principle that the first to file is entitled to the patent where two persons independently make the same invention.[14] But this is a rule about novelty, not entitlement. Lord Hoffmann gave an example. Where A claims that his inventive concept has been patented by B, three things might have happened as follows:

(a) B made the same invention independently and, therefore, B is entitled to the patent. A cannot patent the same invention later.

(b) A described his invention to B without imposing a duty of confidence (and no such duty could be implied in the circumstances). In that case, information about the invention has been communicated to the public and B's patent will be invalid for lack of novelty.

(c) A described his invention to B and imposed a duty of confidence. The patent will be valid and A is entitled, not because B applied for his patent in breach of confidence but because A was the inventor. The duty of confidence relates to the question of novelty under s 2 and not to entitlement under s 7.

At any time before a patent has been granted, or even before an application for a patent has been made, a reference may be made under s 8(1) to the Comptroller to determine whether the person making the reference (alone or with any other persons) is entitled to be granted the patent, or has or would have any right in or under the patent or application for the patent.[15] A reference may also be brought by any of two or more co-proprietors of an application to determine whether any right in or under the application should be transferred or granted to any other person. Where the Comptroller considers the question arising would be more properly dealt with by the court, he may decline to deal with it under s 8(7), effectively handing it over to the court. The Comptroller (or court) may order, *inter alia*, that the application may proceed in the name of the person making the reference, solely or jointly with any other applicant, or refuse to grant the patent, or order the application to be amended so as to exclude matter in respect of which the question was referred or order the transfer or grant of any licence or other right in or under the application and give direction to any person for carrying out the provisions of the order.

There are two possible situations where s 8(1) is engaged. One is where the question of entitlement arises before an application has been made. In this case, the Comptroller may have to decide, for example, which of two persons is entitled to be granted a patent for the invention.[16] The other case is where the application has been filed. In this case, the Comptroller must first determine whether the invention identified by the person referring

---

11 *Rhone-Poulenc Rorer International Holdings Inc v Yeda Research & Development Co Ltd* [2008] 1 All ER 425.

12 [2008] RPC 1 at para 18.

13 [2005] RPC 31.

14 The US patent system is based on a 'first to invent' principle but this is likely to change to a 'first to file' system to align the US system more closely with most other countries.

15 Post-grant references are brought under s 37 and should be made within two years of the date of grant: s 37(5).

16 The Comptroller has wide powers under s 8. In the example of two inventors claiming entitled, he may hold that either, both or neither is entitled to be granted a patent for the invention.

the question is one which he is entitled to as actual devisor or a successor in title. Then, the Comptroller has to decide the consequences and, at this stage, he must compare the invention which is the subject of the reference with the matter in the patent application and decide whether the person making the referral is the inventor of the invention set out in the patent application.

In *Welland Medical Ltd* v *Hadley*,[17] Welland was in the business of manufacturing ostomy pouches. These are bags for collecting bodily waste through an artificial hole in wall of the body (stoma). Welland engaged a Dr Smith to carry out research into the design of a pouch which was water soluble and could be fully flushed down a toilet. The terms of engagement of Dr Smith were such that Welland would be entitled to any resulting intellectual property rights. Dr Smith arranged to meet Mr Hadley under a confidentiality agreement. Mr Hadley owned his own company which manufactured laundry bags with a soluble seam allowing a bag of full of laundry to be washed to be placed in a washing machine without having to take the laundry out of the bag as the seam would dissolve on contact with water. Mr Hadley was shown a drawing entitled 'Fully Flushable Pouch – Concept' by Dr Smith and Mr Hadley produced a sample of material. Before the next meeting, Mr Hadley filed an application for a patent in his own name. Welland commenced proceedings under s 8.

The Comptroller held that Mr Hadley was entitled to be granted the patent. He accepted that Dr Smith's idea was to use a soluble inner bag with a very thin outer non-soluble bag and with an air gap between the two bags. On contact with water, the inner bag would rapidly dissolve; what remained of the outer bag was thin enough to be flushed away. Mr Hadley's pouch, subject to the application, was a multi-layered single bag made from soluble material, unlike the inner and outer bag idea of Dr Smith. Each had found different solutions to the problem of a flushable ostomy pouch.

On appeal to the Patents Court, Floyd J held that the hearing officer had focused too much on construing the claims in the application. Rather he should have concentrated on the information in the application to determine the inventive concept. Jacob LJ noted in *Markem Corp* v *Zipher Ltd*[18] that what is important is that s 8 calls for an identification of information and the rights in it. Who contributed what and what rights they have in it is central to the inquiry, not what monopolies were actually claimed. Furthermore, as Lord Hoffmann said in *Yeda* v *Rhone-Poulenc*, the effect of s 7(4) (presumption that the applicant is the person entitled to be granted the patent) was that a person seeking to be entitled as joint inventor has the burden of showing that he contributed to the inventive concept. Where he seeks to be substituted as sole inventor, he has the additional burden of showing that the person mentioned as inventor in the patent did not contribute to the inventive concept.[19]

In *Welland* v *Hadley*, Floyd J still accepted that Mr Hadley was entitled to the patent. Welland failed to establish what it had claimed, that Dr Smith was the sole inventor. There was no evidence to show that Dr Smith had the idea of the material from which the bag was made or of a bag made from that material. Even if he did have the idea, there was no evidence to show that he had communicated it to Mr Hadley.

A person may be entitled to a patent even though the inventor is not familiar with the applicable technology. The important thing is whether the inventor was the actual devisor of the invention, the person who came up with the inventive concept. In a case involving a patent for an insect trap, *IDA Ltd* v *University of Southampton*,[20] the inventive concept was using magnetic particles to adhere to the legs of insects such as cockroaches so that they could not grip a sloping surface that they alighted onto and would slide into the trap. This was suggested by a consultant working for the claimant company to one Professor Howse at the defendant university, which already had patents for insect traps using electrostatic powders. The consultant did not know whether his idea would work. It was held that the claimant was entitled to the patent. All that Professor Howse, his colleague and the patent

17 [2011] EWHC 1994 (Pat).

18 [2005] RPC 31 at para 101.

19 [2008] RPC 1 at para 21.

20 [2006] RPC 21.

agent drafting the application contributed was common general knowledge.[21] Jacob LJ suggested that cases such as the present one were ripe for mediation. The invention had not been exploited since the original application some eight years ago. Its exploitation was '. . . stultified by the dead hand of litigation'. He pointed out that a small share of a large exploitation was better than a large share of none or little exploitation.

In *Goddin and Rennie's Application*,[22] Rennie made contributions to Goddin's design for covers for circular fish tanks. Rennie had visited the site at which Goddin had erected a tank, under an obligation of confidence, and later it was agreed that Rennie would make the net covers for the tank to be fixed to the frame of the cover. The patent was applied for in the name of Goddin's company, Woodwick Fish Farms Ltd, and mentioned both Goddin and Rennie as inventors. Later, Goddin made an application under s 8(1). The patent application had been assigned to Goddin.

The Court of Session, Outer House, in Scotland held that there was an implied term in the agreement between Rennie and Goddin to the effect that any improvement thought of by Rennie would belong to Goddin's company. However, Rennie had made a suggestion for an elliptical frame before the contractual arrangement and separate from it. He was, therefore, entitled to the benefit of the relevant parts of the claims involving that suggestion.[23] The patent was granted in Goddin's name only, subject to Rennie having an irrevocable exclusive licence in respect of those parts of the claims relating to the feature of the elliptical frame with a power to sub-licence. The royalty was set at 2.5 per cent of the ex-works sale price of products made under those claims and Goddin was to be solely responsible for the cost of maintaining the patent.

Under s 12, provisions not unlike those in s 8 apply in relation to an application made under the law of a country other than the UK or under any treaty or in a convention country.[24] This is subject to provisions concerning jurisdiction and stays under s 82, for example, where proceedings are before the competent authority in respect of the foreign, treaty or convention application.

Where there are two or more proprietors of a patent, their ownership is equivalent to ownership as tenants in common, that is they are each entitled to an undivided share in the patent,[25] and if one of the owners dies his share passes under his will or by intestacy and does not automatically pass to the remaining owners. Where a co-proprietor is a company or other organisation the undivided share will be a company asset which, for example, can be assigned or dealt with by a receiver on insolvency.

Under s 36(2) where two or more persons are proprietors, each may 'by himself or his agents' do for his own benefit without the consent of the other or others any act which would otherwise infringe the patent. This is subject to any agreement to the contrary. The term 'agent' is used in a loose sense and would cover, for example, an independent contractor working the invention for the benefit of the joint proprietor. The question is whether the act is, in substance, an act under a licence or use by the proprietor. In *Henry Brothers (Margherafelt) Ltd* v *Ministry of Defence and Northern Ireland Office*,[26] the Crown, being a joint proprietor, engaged an independent contractor to construct a building incorporating the invention. It was held that this was use by the Crown; the contractor was the means by which the Crown obtained construction of its building. There are, however, some limits to what a joint proprietor can do without the consent of the other or others. Under s 36(3) the consent of the others is required to grant a licence under the patent, or to assign or mortgage a share in the patent, subject to any agreement in force at the time. This now also applies to an amendment to, or application to amend, the specification and an application for revocation of a patent.[27]

The Court of Appeal in *Henry Bros (Margherafelt) Ltd* v *Ministry of Defence and Northern Ireland Office*[28] considered the effect of s 36(2) and (3) and confirmed that, subject to any agreement to the contrary, one co-proprietor may, without the consent of the other co-proprietors:

---

21 Of course, without their contribution the disclosure may not have been an enabling disclosure but performing experiments to confirm the efficacy of the idea and providing technical knowledge to draft the application did not contribute to the inventive concept.

22 [1996] RPC 141.

23 However, this appears to contradict *Henry Bros (Margherafelt) Ltd* v *Ministry of Defence and Northern Ireland Office* [1997] RPC 693, at first instance, above. Unless the claims cover a group of inventions which are so linked to cover a single inventive concept, it seems logically unrealistic to separate out the claims and assign them individually to different persons.

24 An example is *Ladney and Hendry's International Application* [1998] RPC 319 where a reference was made in respect of an application under the PCT. The Court of Appeal reinstated the Hearing Officer's decision that the reference failed.

25 Patents Act 1977 s 36(1).

26 [1997] RPC 693. The proprietor's appeal was dismissed by the Court of Appeal in [1999] RPC 442.

27 Patents Act s 36(3), as substituted by the Patents Act 2004, from 1 October 2005.

28 [1999] RPC 442.

- do by himself or his agents for his own benefit what would otherwise (and apart from Crown use) be an infringing act, but
- he may not grant a licence under the patent or assign or mortgage his share in it.[29]

29 Nor amend, apply to amend or revoke the patent without the consent of the others, from 1 October 2005.

The purpose of s 36(2) is to allow what has been referred to as domestic enjoyment or 'home use'. It does not allow large-scale commercial exploitation through the grant of licences. Robert Walker LJ said that the provisions of s 36(2) will rarely be in issue as, in the vast majority of cases, there will be at least a relevant informal agreement between the co-proprietors as to the use each can make of the invention without the consent of the others. Robert Walker LJ remarked that there appeared to be almost no authority on s 36(2).

The Comptroller has a discretion to order that a licence be granted under s 37(2). After grant, on application by a person claiming a proprietary right in the patent, *inter alia*, he may determine the question and make such order as he thinks fit under s 37(1). This discretion is not prejudiced by s 36(2) as s 36 is expressed as being subject to a number of provisions including s 37.[30]

30 *Hughes v Paxman* [2007] RPC 2.

An agreement between joint owners to the effect that one will forfeit his rights under certain circumstances, for example, after failing to pay a share in the expenses related to renewing the patent, will not necessarily be considered to be void as a penalty clause. However, the court has an equitable jurisdiction to grant relief against forfeiture. It was held thus in *BICC plc v Burndy Corp*,[31] where the court granted an extension of time for payment of the agreed expenses associated with the upkeep of the patent.

31 [1985] RPC 273.

Employee inventors

The Patents Act 1977 deals with employee inventors in far more detail than is the case, for example, in copyright law. The relevant provisions are of great import because a very large number of applications for the grant of a patent will concern inventions made by employees. 'Employee' is defined in s 130(1) as being a person who works or worked under a contract of employment, or in employment under or for the purposes of a government department or a person who serves or who has served in the naval, military or air forces of the Crown. By s 39, an employee invention belongs to the employer in either of the following circumstances:

1 The invention was made in the course of the employee's normal[32] duties as an employee or, if not, in the course of duties specifically assigned to the employee, provided that, in both cases, the circumstances are such that the invention might reasonably be expected to result from the carrying out of those duties (s 39(1)(a)).

2 The invention was made in the course of the employee's duties which, at the time of making the invention, were such that the employee had a special obligation to further the interests of the employer's undertaking (s 39(1)(b)).

32 It was not acceptable to ascertain the meaning of 'normal' by reference to some other standard such as 'ordinary', 'day-to-day' or 'primary': *LIFFE Administration and Management* v *Pavel Pinkava* [2007] RPC 30.

In all other circumstances, the invention belongs to the employee rather than to the employer. Where the employee is entitled to the patent, to prevent an employer interfering with the employee's right to exploit the patent, s 39(3) provides that nothing done by or on behalf of the employee or anyone claiming under him for the purposes of pursuing an application for a patent, and nothing done by any person for the purposes of performing the invention, will infringe any copyright or design right in any model or document which as between the employee and employer belongs to the employer. It is difficult to think of examples where this provision would be needed. If there was an issue in relation to an employer's copyright or design right, a court would be likely to grant a royalty-free non-exclusive licence. However, there may be a situation where an employee has created a document or drawing for his employer in the course of employment where this represents a preliminary, though perhaps not essential, step to an invention made later to which the employee is entitled.

These provisions apply as between the employee and the employer and would not, for example, affect any third party rights. They will apply where an employee's duties include making inventions in the normal course of his duties: for example, where an employee is engaged in a research and development capacity. They would also apply where a workshop manager was given the task of trying to solve a particular problem with the employer's equipment or using his employer's working practices, and the manager makes the invention in the course of carrying out that task. They would not normally apply where, say, a clerical worker working for a manufacturing company devised an invention which improved his employer's assembly line and which had nothing to do with the employee's normal duties and in respect of which he had not been assigned any relevant specific duties.

Where the employee is engaged at a high level, such as a director of a company, the employee will face an uphill task in convincing a court that he is entitled to a patent for an invention relating to the company's business. This is because it is almost inevitable that a company director would be held to have a special obligation to further the interests of his employer's obligation. This point was made by Pumfrey J in *Christopher S French* v *Paul J Mason*,[33] in which he pointed out that, nevertheless, it does not mean to say that a director can never succeed.

Especially in the case of employees below the level of company director, the terms of the contract of employment, express or implied, will assist the court in determining whether the circumstances in which the invention was made fall into either of the above two categories. In *Electrolux Ltd* v *Hudson*,[34] an employee of the claimant (a company making electrical appliances) invented, with his wife at home one evening, an adapter for a vacuum cleaner that would allow the use of any type of disposable bag in any make of vacuum cleaner taking disposable bags. At the time the defendant was employed as a senior storekeeper. The claimant claimed entitlement to the patent for the invention on the basis of the defendant's contract of employment. However, it was held that the relevant term in the contract was too wide (it was probably too wide even for a person employed in a research capacity) and the court refused to imply an appropriate term because the employee was not employed to invent; he was employed as a storekeeper.

A reference under s 37 (determination of the right to a patent after grant) was made in *Greater Glasgow Health Board's Application*[35] to see whether an employed hospital doctor was entitled to be the proprietor of a patent for the invention of a spacing device for an ophthalmoscope. The doctor, a registrar, had a very wide job description which referred to research facilities of which the doctor was encouraged to avail himself for basic clinical research. The contract did not, however, express this as a duty and the court held that his duty to treat patients did not extend to devising new ways of diagnosing and treating patients. The doctor was entitled to be the proprietor of the patent. He had made the invention in his own time, during a period when he was working over 80 hours a week.

Some further indication of the circumstances in which an employee invention will or will not belong to the employer was given in the Patents Court *in Harris's Patent*.[36] The invention was for a slide valve for controlling the flow of material such as coal dust and was an improvement over the 'Wey' valve. Harris made the invention while he was a manager of the Wey valve department of R company, who were licensees of S, a Swiss company. Harris made the invention during the period after he was informed that he was to be made redundant and before he left the employ of R company. The patent was granted and the question of who was entitled to the patent was referred to the Comptroller under s 37. Harris's primary duty had been to sell Wey valves, and R company had no research facilities and did not undertake any creative design. Major problems were referred to the Swiss company. It was held that the rights between an employee and employer were governed only by s 39. The employee's normal duties were the actual duties he was employed to perform. Any duty of fidelity owed to the employer did not assist in formulating those normal duties. R company never solved design problems so it could not have been part

33 [1999] FSR 597.

34 [1977] FSR 312.

35 [1996] RPC 207.

36 [1985] RPC 19.

of Harris's duties to provide solutions to problems and his duty in respect of problems was to report them for transmission to the Swiss company. Neither was the invention made in circumstances such that an invention might reasonably be expected to have resulted from the carrying out of the employee's normal duties. The invention did not fall within s 39(1)(b) – the employee's obligation was to sell Wey valves.

Staeng Ltd's Patents[37] is a good example of factors that favour the employer. Staeng Ltd was the proprietor of the patents in suit and Mr Robertson, an employee of Staeng, was named as inventor. There was no dispute between Staeng and Mr Robertson. Mr Neely was employed by another company, Hellerman, which had cooperated with Staeng in the development of electrical connector kits, and there had been a number of meetings between Mr Robertson and Mr Neely. At one of these meetings, Mr Neely, after being asked by Mr Robertson whether he could think of an alternative way of holding the cable screen, suggested a constant tension spring which turned out to be an important aspect of the patents. Mr Neely later claimed that he was entitled to be named as inventor under s 13(3), and that he was also entitled to be the proprietor of the patents on the basis that his duties did not require him to invent. Nor was he under a special obligation to further his employer's interests.

The Patent Office held that Mr Neely failed to show that he was the sole inventor. He was not skilled in the relevant art and only came up with the idea after prompting by Mr Robertson. Both Mr Neely and Mr Robertson were joint inventors. On the question of Mr Neely's employer's entitlement, as between Mr Neely and his employer, it was held that the employer was entitled. Mr Neely made the invention in the course of his normal duties in circumstances such that invention could reasonably be expected to result. Although his role was primarily one of marketing, he had a wide-ranging brief to generate new ideas for new products. Furthermore, Mr Neely was a senior executive. He knew that his employer was contemplating acquiring Staeng Ltd and, that being so, the invention might be of advantage to his employer. Therefore, he was under a special obligation to further the interests of his employer's undertaking.

Further guidance on the operation of s 39 was given in *LIFFE Administration and Management v Pavel Pinkava*.[38] LIFFE operated the London Futures Market and Dr Pinkava was employed by LIFFE as its interest rate product manager. Whilst working for LIFFE he invented a system of electronic trading for financial instruments not previously traded. He applied for US patents after being advised that patents were not available in the UK because of the exclusions to the meaning of invention under s 1(2)(c) of the Patents Act 1977.[39] The source of an employee's duties was primarily contractual but some terms were implied by law. However, because it was usual for employment contracts to evolve over time, regard must be had to how the contractual duties evolved over time by a process of continual variation. Such extra or additional duties arising in this way were not specifically assigned duties but, in the course of time, became part of the employee's normal duties. Section 39(1)(a) is in terms of circumstances such that '. . . an invention might reasonably be expected to result from the carrying out . . .' of the employee's duties, whether normal duties or specifically assigned duties. This did not mean that the particular invention in question had to be envisaged from the performance of the duties, simply that any invention might be reasonably expected. If the words were limited to the invention in question then, if it could reasonably be expected to be the result, it would probably lack either novelty or inventive step. Nor was there any room for implying a further condition or qualification that the invention was similar to what might have been expected or that it provided a solution to a pre-identified problem or that it realised or contributed to the achievement of the aim or object of the employee's duties.

The test under s 39(1)(a) was purely objective. However, the majority in the Court of Appeal in LIFFE considered that it was correct to consider the particular employee's abilities and it would not be consistent to consider some notional employee of reasonable or

37 [1996] RPC 183.

38 [2007] RPC 30.

39 Presumably on the basis that the invention was a computer program and/or business method as such. The US has no equivalent exclusion.

average ability. Jacob LJ dissented from this view, probably rightly so, and he thought that the reference to the circumstance of either case (normal or specific duties) meant that the question was whether the employee was in a situation were one could objectively expect him to make the invention. He said (at para 103):

> I cannot accept that, given all other factors being equal (contract terms, nature of the job and so on), there can be a difference as to ownership depending on whether the individual employee is thick or brilliant.

This must be right. Otherwise, the test becomes fraught with subjectivity and the almost impossible task of determining the abilities of a particular individual. After all, a 'thick' employee might have a flash of inspiration that could elude a more 'clever' person who is so knowledgeable about the technology that he fails to see the wood for the trees.

Employee compensation

An employee might devise an invention which is of outstanding benefit to his employer in circumstances such that the employer will be taken as being entitled to the patent. This might seem unfair because the benefit of the invention may far exceed the employee's salary for the period of time he has been involved with making and developing the invention. However, the employee has been given consideration for his work, that is his salary, and the employer may have been prepared to pay the employee his salary even if no useful invention resulted, simply as a speculative investment in the hope that a valuable invention would result. Even so, the employee may apply for compensation under s 40, which allows the Comptroller or a court to award compensation where, having regard to the size and nature of the employer's undertaking, the invention or patent for it (or a combination of the two) is of outstanding benefit to the employer and it is just that the employee should be awarded compensation by the employer.[40] Prior to the changes to include a reference to the invention as well as the patent, there was little case law on the provisions, but it was clear that the benefit must be extraordinary and not such as might be expected to result from the employee's normal duties.[41] In fact, the use of the word 'outstanding' suggests that compensation will be awarded under these provisions only in exceptional circumstances.[42]

Section 41 lays down the basic principles for the calculation of the amount of the compensation, being an award that gives the employee a fair share in the benefit derived or expected to be derived. These provisions also apply where the invention initially belonged to the employee and he has subsequently assigned it to the employer or granted an exclusive licence to him. This might apply where, because of the employee/employer relationship, the employer is able to bring pressure to bear upon the employee. Of course, one way that the employer can avoid the compensation provisions where the employer is the person entitled to the patent is not to apply for a patent and to rely on the law of confidence. There have been very few reported cases on applications for compensation under s 40. Until recently, none had been successful. In *British Steel plc's Patent*,[43] the employee had received an *ex gratia* payment and had been honoured by the award of an MBE in addition to a licence agreement. The proven benefit was only 0.08 per cent of the employer's profits. The employee's application for compensation was refused.[44] Whether the change brought about by the Patents Act 2004 will lead to successful applications for employee compensation remains to be seen. The most significant difference is that, if an employee works the invention himself rather than granting rights under it, the benefit can be said to flow from the invention rather than the patent for it. It may be that the combination of invention and patent assists an employee in an award of compensation, say, where the employer exploits the invention himself (for example, by making and selling widgets that are the subject matter of the invention) and uses the patent rights to obtain injunctions and/or awards of damages against infringers.

40 New s 40(1) was inserted by the Patents Act 2004 to include not just the patent but the invention (or a combination of both) to be taken into account. The reference to invention may make it easier for an employee to be awarded compensation.

41 *GEC Avionics Patent* [1992] RPC 107.

42 *British Steel's Patent* [1992] RPC 117.

43 [1992] RPC 117.

44 At the time, the annual turnover of British Steel was in the region of £4.9 billion.

45 [2009] RPC 12.

The first reported case in which an application for employee compensation succeeded is *Kelly* v *GE Healthcare*[45] in which two research scientists were awarded £1 million and £500,000 respectively. They were involved in the synthesis of a compound used in a patented radioactive imaging agent which turned out to be very successful. The application for compensation fell to be determined under ss 40 and 41 before amendment by the Patents Act 2004. Floyd J set out the principles to apply, as follows:

(i)   Section 40 is available to an inventor in the sense of the 'actual deviser' of the invention, but not to those who merely contribute to the invention without being joint inventors.

(ii)   Section 40 is available to an employee who makes an invention (which is subsequently patented by the employer) in the ordinary course of his employment or in the course of duties specifically assigned to him.

(iii)   Under the section prior to its amendment, it is the patent (as opposed to the invention) which must be of outstanding benefit to the employer, having regard to the size and nature of the employer's undertaking.

(iv)   'Outstanding' means 'something special' or 'out of the ordinary' and more than 'substantial', 'significant' or 'good'. The benefit must be something more than one would normally expect to arise from the duties for which the employee is paid.

(v)   On the other hand it is not necessary to show that the benefit from the patent could not have been exceeded.

(vi)   Section 40 is not concerned with whether the invention is outstanding, although the nature of the employee's contribution may fall to be considered at the section 41 stage, if it is reached.

(vii)   It will normally be useful to consider what would have been the position of the company if a patent had not been granted, and compare this with the company's position with the benefit of the patent.

(viii) The patent must have been a cause of the benefit, although it does not have to be the only cause. The existence of multiple causes for a benefit does not exclude the benefit from consideration, although the benefit may have to be apportioned to isolate the benefit derived from the patent.

(ix)   'Patent' in section 40 does not include regulatory data exclusivity. Thus the scenario without patent protection is one where [it] nevertheless exists.[46]

(x)   It must be 'just' to make an award: the consideration of what is just is not limited to the facts set out in section 40.

(xi)   It is not a requirement of obtaining compensation that the employee can prove a loss (for example by reference to inadequate remuneration for his employment) or by the expenditure of effort and skill beyond the call of duty. These are nevertheless factors to take into account under section 41.

(xii)   The valuation of any benefit is to be performed *ex-post* and in the light of all the available evidence as to benefit derived from the patent: not '*ex-ante*'.

(xiii) Where the employee shows that the invention has been of outstanding benefit, the amount of compensation is to be determined in the light of all the available evidence in accordance with section 41 so as to secure a just and fair reward to the employee, neither limiting him to compensation for loss or damage, nor placing him in as strong a position as an external patentee or licensor.

46 In relation to medical inventions, safety and efficacy data must be generated and supplied to the regulator for approval. This data can be costly and time-consuming to generate but is not available to others for a period of time. Generic companies usually do not go through the data generation process themselves but wait until the data is made available. Until such time, the inventor or his employer has exclusivity even without the benefit of the patent. The total benefit of the patent may be reduced to allow for this exclusivity.

Floyd J held that the benefit of the patents was outstanding and conservatively valued that benefit at £50 million. He also held that it was just that the employees received a fair share of the benefit. The fact that Dr Kelly had waited until he had retired to make his claim was not a relevant factor and s 40 did not require a claim for employee compensation to be made whilst the patent in question was still in force.

The employee must take his employer as he finds him. The employer may not work the invention at all or effectively. It is no answer to show that the employer could have made substantial sums had he been better at exploiting the invention.

Difficult questions may arise where a patent is assigned to another person connected with the employer. Under s 43(8), a 'connected person' is one under s 533 of the Income and Corporations Tax Act 1970 for the purposes of the Tax Acts.[47] This would apply in relation to a group of companies. In *Shanks* v *Unilever plc*,[48] the employee, Professor Shanks, worked for Unilever UK Central Resources Ltd, and devised a means of measuring used in diabetes blood test kits. Soon after the company assigned the benefit of the invention to the parent company in the group, Unilever plc, for a nominal sum. The patent was not exploited for a number of years, but eventually, royalty income of £23 million was generated. The issue for the Court of Appeal was the meaning of 'that person' in s 41(2) in relation to an assignment, etc '. . . to a person connected with him [the employer] shall be taken to be the amount which could reasonably be expected to be so derived by the employer if *that person* had not been connected with him' (emphasis added).

Jacob LJ said that it was necessary first to consider ss 40–44.[49] The whole scheme was based around the paradigm case where the employee worked for the same company that received all the benefit of the invention. Section 41(3), which applies in relation to an inventor working for the Crown or a Research Council, should be construed in the same way as in the paradigm case. It was unlikely, therefore, that Parliament intended that an inventor should be treated differently to the paradigm case where there had been an in-house assignment of the benefit of the invention. Jacob LJ also held:

- The actual assignment from the employer to the actual connected person must be considered (in this case from Unilever UK Central Resources Ltd to Unilever plc).
- Section 41(2) requires an assessment of what the assignor 'could reasonably expect to be so derived' if the assignee was not a connected person – the use of the phrase 'so derived' refers to the beginning of the s 41(2) 'any benefit derived or expected to be derived', the same phrase as in s 41(1), the paradigm case – the amount of any benefit the employer actually got in the past and which that particular employer would get in the future.
- The benefit derived or expected to be derived from the assignment is the amount the employer could reasonably expect to derive if the assignee was not a connected person, knowing what benefit had actually been derived by the assignee; in this case £23 million.
- Consequently, 'that person' in s 41(2) means the actual assignee with its actual attributes.

Jacob LJ rejected the argument that the benefit was the putative benefit, the benefit that might have been achieved had the invention been fully exploited (a figure of £1 billion was suggested on behalf of Professor Shanks). He also rejected a suggestion that s 41(2) in referring 'to the amount which could reasonably be expected to be so derived' did not allow consideration of what actually happened. Jacob LJ said that this would end up looking at what would have happened in a notional auction of the invention at the time of the assignment. This could lead to some serious absurdities. It was left to the parties to agree what a 'fair share' should be for Professor Shanks. Section 41 is badly drafted, but what s 41(2) seems to attempt to do is to ensure that an employee is not deprived of compensation where his employer assigns the invention and any rights in it to another company within the same group of companies for a nominal sum but the other company then goes on to derive substantial financial rewards from the invention. In a case such as the present one, where the claim for employee compensation was not made until the relevant patents had all but expired, it is easy to work out what the total benefit is. But, in effect, the Court of Appeal is saying that Unilever UK Central Resources Ltd would have sold the rights in the invention to an unconnected person for £23 million. For a group of companies the size of Unilever plc, £23m does not seem to suggest that the invention was of outstanding benefit to it.

It is not uncommon for a group of companies to have amongst the group a company that concentrates on research and development with provision for assignment of any intellectual property rights arising to other companies in the group for them to exploit any subject-matter. It is common sense that, for in-house assignments, the benefit, whether actual or expected should be that derived or expected to be derived by the

47 This Act was repealed in its entirety in 1992. The present definition of connected persons is contained in s 839 of the Income and Corporation Taxes Act 1988. Curiously the Patents Act 1977 has not been amended to reflect this.

48 [2011] RPC 12.

49 Section 44 was repealed in 2000.

assignee company. This is the result achieved in *Shanks* v *Unilever*. Employee inventors considering applying for compensation should consider carefully the timing of their application. If they apply at an early stage they might receive more if, subsequently, the employer (or assignee) fails to exploit the invention to the fullest extent. But at that stage, the employee might find it hard to surmount the first hurdle, being to show that the invention is of outstanding benefit. Of course, the employee inventor seeking compensation has to show:

- that, having regard among other things to the size and nature of the employer's undertaking that the invention or patent for it was of outstanding benefit;
- that it is just that the employee is paid compensation by his employer.

If these two requirements are satisfied the court or Comptroller then has to award such compensation so as to secure a fair share for the employee. What is a fair share is difficult to predict. It might be influenced by the size of the company in terms of its turnover. A small company may be less able to pay compensation than a very large company. Both the size and nature of the employer's undertaking are to be taken into account in determining whether the invention or patent for it are of outstanding benefit. However, s 40(1) makes it clear that other factors might be relevant, such as whether the employer is a manufacturer or derives most of its income by licensing technology, whether it uses inhouse staff or sub-contracts most of its work or whether the new invention allows the employer to expand its operations, opening new branches and employing significantly more staff. Another possible issue is the amount of the benefit which the employer re-invests in its undertaking, perhaps increasing its research and development efforts or marketing efforts. Another issue may be trying to isolate the benefit resulting from the invention or patent for it from other factors such as parallel assignments or licences for other intellectual property rights, such as design rights, trade mark rights, know-how, etc.

The Court of Appeal in *Shanks* v *Unilever* seemed to accept the benefit was outstanding even though £23 million is a small sum when compared with Unilever's annual turnover, amounting, according to the Unilever's accounts for 2010, to less than 0.1 per cent.

Contracts relating to employee inventions

It is conceivable that in some circumstances where the patent initially belongs to the employee, the equitable doctrine of undue influence might apply: for instance, where an employee has been pressurised by his employer to assign the patent to his employer or to grant an exclusive licence in favour of his employer, and where the terms of the agreement are grossly unfavourable to the employee. However, the employee/employer relationship does not automatically give rise to a presumption of undue influence and the employee would have to prove the nature of the pressure. If the doctrine of undue influence does apply, the effect is to make the agreement voidable. Section 42 has a similar effect as it makes terms in contracts between an employee and his employer (or some other person at the request of the employer or through the employee's contract of employment) unenforceable if and to the extent that those terms attempt to diminish the employee's rights in inventions.

Dealing in patents

As with other forms of intellectual property, patents may be dealt with by way of assignment or licensing, either exclusive or otherwise. They may also be mortgaged or vest by operation of law as other personal property. For example, if the proprietor dies the patent will vest in the proprietor's personal representatives. Patent applications may also be dealt with, which is understandable considering the length of time that may pass before the patent is finally granted. Where there are two or more proprietors of a patent or application for a patent, the consent of all of them is required for a licence, assignment or mortgage.[50] Under s 30(6), any purported assignment or mortgage of a patent or patent application is void unless it is in writing and signed by or on behalf of the assignor or mortgagor.[51] An assent by a personal representative must be signed by or on behalf of the personal representative.

If the requisite formalities are not complied with, the agreement is likely to operate as an agreement to assign in equity. The assignee will be the beneficial owner and the assignor will remain the legal owner of the patent. The beneficial owner will be able to sue for infringement of the patent provided at some stage the legal owner is made a party to the proceedings. An example is *Baxter International Inc* v *Nederlands Produktielaboratorium voor Bloedtransfusiapparatuur BV*,[52] where the defendant applied to strike out the claimant's action on the ground that the assignments in question had been signed only by the assignor.[53] In that case, both assignments contained a covenant of further assurance common in agreements to assign. It stated:

> We agree to execute all documents required in connection with the patent applications and patents and to execute all further documents necessary to vest title in said patents and applications to the Assignee.

Agreements to assign are very common especially where the patents are part of a much larger transaction involving other forms of property rights. It is common for a short form assignment to follow an agreement to assign.[54] Transactions creating equitable interests are not registrable transactions under s 33 (see below) and are not, therefore, subject to the limitation of the availability of costs (or in Scotland, expenses) for a failure to register the transaction under s 68.[55]

In *Insituform Technical Services Ltd* v *Inliner UK plc*[56] it was held that an assignment of an exclusive licence was not a right in a patent but a right *under* a patent and therefore was not caught by s 30(6). The defendant had argued that the second claimant, an exclusive licensee, was not entitled to relief on the basis of s 30(6).[57]

A licence for the working of the invention may be granted under a patent or application for a patent by s 30(4). The licence may permit the making of sub-licences and, unless the licence or sub-licence provides otherwise, a licence or sub-licence may be assigned or mortgaged. An exclusive licence is one conferring, to the exclusion of all others (including the proprietor or applicant), any right in respect of the invention to which the patent or the application relates.[58] An exclusive licensee has the same right as the proprietor to bring proceedings in respect of any infringement of the patent after the date of the licence agreement.[59]

Certain types of transaction must be registered. They are listed in s 33(3) and are:

(a) an assignment of the patent or application for a patent;
(b) a mortgage of the patent or application or the grant of a security over it;
(c) the grant or assignment of a licence or sub-licence or mortgage of a licence or sub-licence, under the patent or application;
(d) the death of the proprietor or one of the proprietors of the patent or application or any person having a right in or under the patent or application and the vesting by an assent of personal representatives of a patent or application or any such right;
(e) any order or directions of a court or other competent authority transferring a patent or application or any right in or under it to any person, or that an application should proceed in the name of any person together with registration of the event under which the court or authority had the power to make the order or give the directions.

The scope of the term 'assignment' was considered in *Siemens Schweiz AG* v *Thorn Security Ltd*.[60] It was held in the Court of Appeal that a purposive meaning should be given and

---

50 Patents Act 1977 s 36(3). This now also extends to amendment of the specification, applications to amend and to applications for revocation.

51 In the case of a body corporate, the requirement for signing is satisfied if the transaction is done under the seal of the body: Patents Act 1977 s 30(6A), inserted by the Regulatory Reform (Patents) Order 2004, SI 2004/2357 Article 10(3) with effect from 1 January 2005. Previously, an assignment or mortgage had to be signed by or on behalf of both parties to the transaction.

52 [1998] RPC 250.

53 At that time, both parties were required to sign.

54 See, for example, *Coflexip Stena Offshore Ltd's Patent* [1997] RPC 179.

55 This section was modified by the Intellectual Property (Enforcement, etc.) Regulations 2006, SI 2006/1028. Previously the limitation was in respect of the availability of damages or accounts.

56 [1992] RPC 83.

57 In the event, the relevant patent, relating to the coating of a fibrous sheet used for lining pipes, was held to be invalid for lack of inventive step.

58 Patents Act 1977 s 130, the interpretation section.

59 Patents Act 1977 s 67. The proprietor shall be made a party to the proceedings.

60 [2009] RPC 3, overruling *Tamglass Ltd Oy* v *Luoyang North Glass Technology Co Ltd* [2006] FSR 34 on the scope of assignment under s 33(3).

the judge at trial was wrong to hold that it did not cover a series of mergers under the Swiss law of succession. In this context an assignment was not limited to an express consensual bilateral document and could include an assignment by operation of law.

It is essential that such transactions are registered for two reasons: first, the result of s 33(1) is that registration of acquisition of property in a patent or an application defeats earlier transactions, instruments or events that have not been registered; and, second, the subsequent proprietor of the patent or an exclusive licensee may be unable to obtain costs or expenses in respect of any infringement proceedings.[61]

Licences as of right

The proprietor may, at any time after the grant of the patent, apply to the Comptroller to indicate that licences as of right are available in respect of the patent.[62] The Comptroller must give notice to any person registered as having a right in or under the patent and shall make the entry provided he is satisfied that the proprietor is not precluded by contract from granting licences (s 46(2)). These provisions might be used by a proprietor who has been unable to exploit his patent to good effect and wants to reduce his renewal fees as they are reduced to half the normal rate. Whether making an entry in the register that licences are available as of right makes any difference is doubtful because, if the invention was commercially attractive in the first place, the proprietor should have had no difficulty in finding an organisation willing to exploit the patent under an assignment or exclusive licence. If any person desires to take up the offer, the licence terms shall be as agreed between the parties or, failing agreement, upon such terms as may be settled by the Comptroller on the application of either party. The entry on the register to the effect that licences are available as of right may be later cancelled by application of the proprietor (s 47).

Supplementary protection certificates (SPCs) are available for medicinal products by virtue of Council Regulation (EEC) No 1768/92 of 18 June 1992 concerning the creation of a supplementary protection certificate for medicinal products.[63] SPCs give an additional five years' protection following expiry of the basic patent. Article 5 of the Regulation confirms that the SPC confers the same rights and is subject to the same limitations and obligations as those conferred or existing under the basic patent. Thus, if licences as of right were available at the expiry of the basic patent, they will remain available under the SPC.[64] In the Patents Court, Aldous J said that an SPC gives no more or less rights than those that existed under the basic patent. An argument that s 46(3)(a), entitling any person as of right to a licence where an entry is made by the proprietor that licences are available as of right, allowed a person to have only one licence (that is, that under the basic patent) was rejected. Aldous J said (at 674):

> I cannot accept that submission. A person may only have one licence at a time, but a person can apply at any time for a licence providing he is not a licensee at the time his application is made.

Therefore, if the licence of right expires at the time of the basic patent, a new right to licence accrues with the grant of the SPC and, consequently, the Comptroller has the jurisdiction to grant such licence in appropriate terms.

An entry on the register in respect of licences as of right may also come about from the operation of s 51, which concerns references to the Competition Commission (previously the Monopolies and Mergers Commission). This applies to a competition reference that a person was engaged in anti-competitive practices which operated or are expected to operate against the public interest or, on a reference under s 11 of the Competition Act 1980, where a person is pursuing a course of conduct which operates against the public

61 Patents Act 1977 s 68. Before amendment by the Intellectual Property (Enforcement, etc.) Regulations 2006 SI 2006/1028, s 68 could operate to deprive the proprietor of damages or an account of profits.

62 Patents Act 1977 s 46. There were 1,060 applications during 2010.

63 OJ L 182, 02.07.1992, p 1.

64 *Research Corp's Supplementary Protection Certificate* [1994] RPC 387 (Patent Office) and [1994] RPC 667 (Patents Court).

interest. Following a report laid before Parliament by the Competition Commission, on application by the appropriate Minister or Ministers,[65] the Comptroller may, by order, cancel or vary conditions in licence agreements or may, instead or in addition, make an entry in the register to the effect that licences are available as of right. There are similar provisions in relation to powers under a number of provisions of the Enterprise Act 2002 to take remedial action following merger or market investigation where the matter concerns conditions in patent licence agreements or a refusal to grant licences under a patent on reasonable terms.[66]

In settling the terms of a licence of right (and a compulsory licence), the Comptroller must have regard to European Community competition law. It had been the practice in the UK to allow a licensee of right to import the patented product from outside the European Community if the proprietor of the patent worked the patent by importing the product to the UK. However, if the proprietor manufactured the product within the UK, the licence of right would not allow the licensee to import the product from outside the European Community.[67] This was held by the European Court of Justice, in Case C-191/90 *Generics (UK) Ltd* v *Smith Kline and French Laboratories Ltd*,[68] to be discriminatory because it encouraged proprietors of patents to manufacture the patented product in their national territory rather than importing the product from other Member States.

Under the Patents Act 1949, the maximum term of a patent was 16 years, but existing patents that were less than 11 years old when the 1977 Act came into force (on 1 June 1978) were extended to a maximum of 20 years subject to their being treated as endorsed 'licences of right' for the last four years of their life. However, because of the special problems with pharmaceutical products, where the exploitation period is reduced because of the time taken to test and obtain a licence under the Medicines Act 1968, the proprietor of a patent for a product was allowed to file a declaration preventing licences as of right extending to pharmaceutical use.[69]

Compulsory licences

There has always been a danger that the proprietor of a patent will abuse the monopoly granted to him. For example, an inventor, Mary, develops an everlasting light bulb and obtains a patent for it. Brightlight Ltd, a manufacturer of conventional light bulbs, offers a large sum of money to Mary for an assignment of the patent, to which she agrees. Brightlight then suppresses the invention and does not put it to use, preferring to continue making conventional light bulbs. This state of affairs cannot exist as far as a patented invention is concerned because of the availability of compulsory licences under which others may work the invention against the wishes of the proprietor of the patent. Compulsory licences not only cover situations where a patent is not being worked, but also are available in other circumstances such as where demand for a product is not being met on reasonable terms.

Compulsory licences cannot be granted until after three years from the date of the grant of the patent, after which any person may apply for a licence under the patent and/ or for an entry to be made on the register to the effect that licences are available as of right.[70] Additionally, where the applicant is a government department, an application may be made for the grant of a licence to any person specified in the application. The grounds on which such applications may be made are set out in ss 48A and 48B.[71] The former apply where the proprietor is a World Trade Organisation (WTO) proprietor and the latter apply in the case of a non-WTO proprietor. A WTO proprietor is a national of, or is domiciled in a country which is a member of, the World Trade Organisation, or has a real and effective industrial or commercial establishment in such a country.

65 Representations may be made by persons whose interests appear to be affected.

66 Patents Act 1977 s 50A, inserted by the Enterprise Act 2002.

67 This was the Comptroller's view of the provisions in the Patents Act 1977 ss 48(3) and 50(1) when the patent was not being worked in the UK. However, in Case C-30/90 *Commission of the European Communities* v *United Kingdom* [1992] ECR I-829, it was held that s 48 offends against Article 28 (formerly Article 30) of the EC Treaty: *see* below.

68 [1992] ECR I-5335.

69 Patents Act 1977 Sch 1 para 4A, inserted by Copyright, Designs and Patents Act 1988 s 293. Patents for medicinal products may now be extended to a maximum of 25 years (Patents (Supplementary Protection Certificates) Rules 1997, SI 1997/64).

70 Patents Act 1977 48(1). Note, it is three years from the date of grant, not the priority date.

71 Section 48 of the Patents Act 1977 was substituted and ss 48A and 48B were inserted by the Patents and Trade Marks (World Trade Organisation) Regulations 1999, SI 1999/1899. This was to give effect to the TRIPs Agreement.

In the case of a WTO proprietor, the grounds for the grant of a compulsory licence or entry in the register to the effect that licences are available as of right are:

(a) where the patented invention is a product, that a demand in the UK for that product is not being met on reasonable terms;

(b) that by reason of the refusal of the proprietor of the patent concerned to grant a licence or licences on reasonable terms –
  (i) the exploitation in the UK of any other patented invention which involves an important technical advance of considerable economic significance in relation to the invention for which the patent concerned was granted is prevented or hindered (in this case, the Comptroller must be satisfied that the proprietor of that other patent is able and willing to grant the proprietor of the patent concerned and his licensees a licence in respect of that other invention on reasonable terms), or
  (ii) the establishment or development of commercial or industrial activities in the UK is unfairly prejudiced;

(c) that by reason of conditions imposed by the proprietor of the patent concerned on the grant of licences under the patent, or on the disposal or use of the patented product or on the use of the patented process, the manufacture, use or disposal of materials not protected by the patent, or the establishment or development of commercial or industrial activities in the UK, is unfairly prejudiced.

No order for a compulsory licence or entry to the effect that licences are available as of right shall be made unless the applicant has made efforts to obtain a licence on reasonable commercial terms and conditions and those efforts have not been successful within a reasonable period.[72] There is an exception and these provisions do not apply to patented inventions in the field of semiconductor technology as regards WTO proprietors.

Licences granted under s 48 in respect of WTO proprietors are not exclusive and not assignable except with that part of the enterprise that enjoys the use of the patented invention, or the part of the goodwill that belongs to that part. Such licences shall be predominantly for the supply of the market in the UK and include conditions entitling the proprietor to adequate remuneration. Such licences shall be limited in scope and duration to the purpose for which the licence was granted.

Where the proprietor is not a WTO proprietor s 48B applies and contains the following grounds, which are generally more extensive:

(a) where the patented invention is capable of being commercially worked in the UK, that it is not being so worked or is not being so worked to the fullest extent that is reasonably practicable;

(b) where the patented invention is a product, that a demand for the product in the UK –
  (i) is not being met on reasonable terms, or
  (ii) is being met to a substantial extent by importation from a country which is not a Member State;

(c) where the patented invention is capable of being commercially worked in the UK, that it is being prevented or hindered from being so worked –
  (i) where the invention is a product, by the importation of the product from a country which is not a Member State,
  (ii) where the invention is a process, by the importation from such a country of a product obtained directly by means of the process or to which the process has been applied;

(d) that by reason of the refusal of the proprietor of the patent to grant a licence or licences on reasonable terms –

72 Patents Act 1977 s 48A(2).

(i)   a market for the export of any patented product made in the UK is not being supplied, or

(ii) the working or efficient working in the UK of any other patented invention which makes a substantial contribution to the art is prevented or hindered, or

(iii) the establishment or development of commercial or industrial activities in the UK is unfairly prejudiced;

(e)   that by reason of conditions imposed by the proprietor of the patent on the grant of licences under the patent, or on the disposal or use of the patented product or on the use of the patented process, the manufacture, use or disposal of materials not protected by the patent, or the establishment or development of commercial or industrial activities in the UK, is unfairly prejudiced.

The Comptroller has a discretion to adjourn an application based on a failure to work the invention commercially in the UK at all or to the fullest extent reasonably practicable if it appears that the time elapsed since the publication of notice of grant of the patent has been insufficient for the invention to be so worked.

The first of these grounds, a failure to work in the UK at all or to the fullest extent reasonably practicable, does not apply where the invention is being commercially worked in a Member State and demand in the UK is being met by importation from that Member State.

In relation to licences under s 48, where the Comptroller is satisfied that the manufacture, use or disposal of material not protected by the patent is unfairly prejudiced by reasons of conditions imposed by the proprietor on the grant of licences under the patent, the Comptroller may order the grant of licences to such customers of the applicant as he thinks fit in addition to the applicant. Where the applicant himself already holds a licence in respect of the patent, the Comptroller may order a new licence and cancel the existing one or modify the existing licence.

Guidelines for the exercise of the Comptroller's powers with respect to applications under s 48 are contained in s 50. The Comptroller shall take into account the following general purposes by s 50(1):

1 the working of the invention to the fullest extent that is reasonably practicable in the UK without undue delay if it is in the public interest for the invention to be worked on a commercial scale;

2 having regard to the nature of the invention, the inventor or other person entitled to the patent shall receive a reasonable remuneration;

3 the interests of any person currently working or developing a patented invention in the UK shall not be unfairly prejudiced.

Subject to s 50(1), in determining whether to order a compulsory licence the Comptroller must take account of a number of factors contained in s 50(2), being:

(a)   the nature of the invention, the time since publication of the grant of the patent and measures taken by the proprietor or any licensee to make full use of the invention;

(b)   the ability of any person to whom the licence would be granted to work the invention to the public advantage; and

(c)   the risks to be undertaken by that person in providing capital and working the invention if the order is granted.

No account is taken of matters occurring subsequent to the application for a compulsory licence. The fact that one of the grounds for a compulsory licence is present is not sufficient, *per se*, for the grant of the licence. In *Therma-Tru Corp's Patent*,[73] the Patents Court said that there was no reason why a compulsory licence could not include a right to sub-licence but this would be exceptional. The application was refused because both the applicant and its proposed sub-licensee were financially stretched and there was a substantial risk that the sub-licensee would not be able to work the invention.

73 [1997] RPC 777.

74 [1990] RPC 663. But this decision is now very questionable in the light of Case C-30/90 *Commission of the European Communities* v *United Kingdom* [1992] ECR I-829, discussed above.

75 [1989] RPC 722.

76 There were no applications from 1991 to 1994. There were three in 1995 and three in 1996. In the latest year for which statistics are available, 1999, there were no applications. More recent Patent Office Annual Reports do not separate out applications for compulsory licences.

If the patent is being worked in the UK, it was held in *Research Corporation's (Carboplatin) Patent*[74] that it would normally run counter to policy to grant a licence of right (or compulsory licence) which permitted importation. Furthermore, if the price of the product was reasonable and demand at that price was being fully met, it was irrelevant to say that demand would be greater if the price was lower. The question is whether, in all the circumstances, the price being charged was reasonable.

The applicant for a compulsory licence must establish a prima facie case that the grounds relied upon apply. A mere suspicion will not be sufficient and an order for discovery will not be granted unless a prima facie case is raised by the applicant. In *Richco Plastic Co's Patent*[75] the only evidence that the applicant had was that the patentee had an associated company in the UK and an investigation at the UK Companies Registry which showed an entry for the company which did not refer to manufacturing costs but only to the costs of purchasing and importing. The application was dismissed as being an abuse of process. In practice, applications for compulsory licences are very rare.[76]

Terms of licence as of right or compulsory licence

77 [1987] RPC 327.

78 The Patents Act 1949 s 41 allowed the Comptroller to grant compulsory licences, *inter alia*, for medical patents. He was obliged to secure that medicines would be available to the public at the lowest prices consistent with the patentee deriving a reasonable advantage for his patent rights. For a discussion of the effects of s 41 of the Patents Act 1949 and its demise in respect of pharmaceutical products, *see* Walton, A. 'The Copyright, Designs and Patents Act 1988 (1)' (1989) 133 *Solicitors Journal* 646 at 650–851.

79 Although many of the provisions of the 1949 Act continue to apply to patents and applications existing on 1 June 1978 by virtue of the transitional provisions, s 41 does not. However, the courts still seek guidance from s 41: *see Shiley Inc's Patent* [1988] RPC 97.

80 [1964] RPC 391, approved by the Court of Appeal in *Allen & Hanburys Ltd's (Salbutamol) Patent* [1987] RPC 327.

81 *Knutsson's and Bjork's Patents* [1996] RPC 461.

82 [1990] RPC 203.

83 *Research Corporation's (Carboplatin) Patent* [1990] RPC 663.

If the Comptroller has to settle the terms for a licence as of right or a compulsory licence he should do so with a view to securing, *inter alia*, that the proprietor of the patent receives a reasonable remuneration having regard to the nature of the invention. This can be done only by considering what a willing licensor and a willing licensee would have agreed upon as a reasonable royalty to be paid for the rights granted under the licence as of right. So it was held in the Court of Appeal in *Allen & Hanburys Ltd's (Salbutamol) Patent*.[77] This would include taking account of the research and development costs and promotional costs incurred in creating and maintaining a market for the product. Regard should also be had to the reward deserved by the proprietor for his contribution to the art, secured by an appropriate measure of profit upon the capital invested. It was suggested that this position is not unlike that pertaining under the compulsory licensing provisions in the Patents Act 1949 s 41 which caused much concern in the drug industry.[78] The s 41 approach did not altogether die with the revocation of the 1949 Act.[79] It was held in *Geigy SA's Patent*[80] that three elements should be taken into account in calculating the licence fee: an allowance for research and development costs, an allowance for promotional costs and an appropriate uplift. The first two are the compensation element and the third is the reward element. However, the applicability of this test now seems in doubt, as discussed below.

The best way of determining what willing parties would agree upon is to look at comparable licences where these exist; though even here consideration must be given to the scope of the licence and the other terms in the agreement.[81] In *Smith Kline & French Laboratories Ltd's (Cimetidine) Patents*,[82] Lloyd LJ said (at 236):

> For my part I have no doubt that where close comparables exist, they provide by far the best and surest approach. There is no better guide to what a willing licensor and a willing licensee would agree than what other licensors and licensees have in fact agreed in comparable cases.

The presumption of willing parties to a licence could be extended to contemplate that they had a common understanding about future pricing policy, and if price cutting was likely to ensue the court should decide where the floor should be and what profits should be available calculated on that basis.[83]

Another possible method of calculating the terms is the 'profits available' approach in which the exercise is to determine what the available profits are and to divide these between the licensor and licensee. However, this is difficult to apply in practice and should be considered to be a last resort where there is nothing else to go on. It is accepted by the court that there are particular 'going rates' in specific industries. For example, in *Shiley Inc's*

Patent,[84] which involved the settlement of terms for a licence of right in relation to a heart valve prosthesis, it was said the range of royalty in the mechanical engineering field was 5 to 7 per cent, but the norm in the pharmaceutical industry was between 25 and 30 per cent. However, even though the patent was in the mechanical engineering field, being a mechanical surgical device, the royalty payable was set at 15 per cent because of factors such as the proprietor's pioneering work and the high profit margins in the particular technology.

The difference between the comparable licence and the s 41 approach can be quite large. In *American Cyanamid Co's (Fenbufen) Patent*,[85] Aldous J applied both of the methods (he considered the profits available method of no assistance because there was no clear evidence of how the profits should be split). He calculated that the royalty to produce a reasonable remuneration based on comparable licences was 27 per cent, but that the application of the s 41 test gave between 45 and 54 per cent. He said that the s 41 royalty was not correct and the final figure awarded was 27 per cent uplifted to 32 per cent to take account of exceptional promotional costs.

The calculation of royalties in respect of compulsory licences and licences of right will continue to be a source of difficulty. It is not possible to lay down a strict percentage to be applied universally because of variations in development and promotional costs, and there is a danger that the patentee will be robbed of his reward if the rate is set too low. While it is essential that the incentive to invent is maintained, it is important that certain inventions, especially those related to drugs, are readily available at reasonable prices. The willing parties approach is by far the most satisfactory, but sometimes there will be nothing to compare the licence with. In such circumstances, the old s 41 approach may still be of some assistance as the profits available approach is deeply flawed. For example, what happens if there are subsequent applications for licences of right? The patentee's remaining share of the available profit will be diluted still further.

Safety and security

Where an application for a patent is filed in the UK Patent Office and it appears to the Comptroller that it contains information of a description notified to him by the Secretary of State as being information the publication of which might be prejudicial to national security, the Comptroller may give directions prohibiting or restricting the publication of that information or its communication to any specified person or group of persons.[86] The Comptroller may also issue like directions in relation to information which appears to him to be such as to be prejudicial to public safety. This can be done on the Comptroller's own initiative, without prior notification by the Secretary of State. The prohibition or restriction can endure until three months from the end of the period for publication of the application, normally 18 months from its filing date or earlier priority date if the priority of an application elsewhere is sought.

While directions under s 22 are in force, the application may proceed to the point where it is in order for the grant of a patent but it shall not be published or communicated and no patent shall be granted. If the application is for a patent under either the European Patent Convention or the Patent Cooperation Treaty, it will not be forwarded to the European Patent Office or International Bureau as appropriate. However, this does not prevent the Comptroller from forwarding information to the European Patent Office which it is his duty to send.

If directions are given under s 22, the Comptroller must give notice of the application and the directions to the Secretary of State who will then consider whether national security or public safety would be prejudiced. If he decides that either case applies, he

84 [1988] RPC 97.

85 [1990] RPC 309.

86 Patents Act 1977 s 22.

must reconsider within nine months of the date of filing the application and reconsider at least during each subsequent 12 months. If the Secretary of State is of the opinion that the publication or communication of the information would no longer be prejudicial to national security or public safety, he will then give notice to the Comptroller who will revoke the directions and is given discretion to extend any time limits.[87] Further provisions include the possibility of compensation for any hardship suffered by the applicant. Failure to comply with directions given under s 22 is a criminal offence carrying a maximum penalty on conviction on indictment of two years' imprisonment and/or a fine or, on summary conviction, a fine not exceeding £1,000.

Under s 23, where the invention relates to military technology or for some other reason publication of the information might be prejudicial to national security or the application contains information the publication of which might be prejudicial to the safety of the public,[88] a person resident in the UK cannot apply for a patent[89] in a country outside the UK unless he has written authority from the Comptroller or has already filed an application for a UK patent at least six weeks beforehand and no directions have been given under s 22 or, if they have, they have since been revoked. The penalties for not complying with these requirements are as for s 22 but the criminal offence under s 23 applies only if the person concerned knows of, or is reckless as to, the contravention.[90]

Crown use

A patent is a right granted by the Crown and there are detailed provisions in the Act for Crown use. The forms of use covered are listed in s 55 and are declared not to be an infringement of the patent.[91] They are:

1. *Product inventions*. To make, use, import, keep or sell or offer to sell it. Sale and offers to sell must be incidental or ancillary to the previously mentioned activities. To sell or offer to sell it for foreign defence purposes. For the production or supply of specified drugs and medicines, to dispose or offer to dispose of it otherwise than by selling it for any purposes.
2. *Process inventions*. To use it or to do any of the above in relation to a product obtained directly by means of the process.
3. *Specified drugs or medicines* (product inventions or the product of a process invention). To sell or offer to sell the drug or medicine.
4. *Any type of invention*. To supply or offer to supply to any person the means, relating to an essential element of the invention, for putting the invention into effect. To dispose or offer to dispose of anything made, used, imported or kept which is no longer required for that purpose.

Crown use is subject to a royalty being paid to the proprietor of the patent, but not in relation to things done before the priority date unless done as a result of a confidential relevant communication.[92] The use must be for the services of the Crown and by any government department or any person authorised in writing by a government department. A health authority is, for the purposes of s 55, a government department. In *Dory v Sheffield Health Authority*,[93] the proprietor of a patent for machines for treating kidney stones sued the health authority for patent infringement. It was held that the use of the machines by the health authority was Crown use and that the authority exercised the functions of the Secretary of State which were devolved to the authority by the National Health Service Act 1977 and regulations made under that Act.

87 Special provisions apply in relation to atomic energy under s 22(6).

88 Section 23(1A) was inserted by the Patents Act 2004 which limited the scope of s 23 to military technology, national security and the safety of the public. Previously, the restriction applied to all patent applications. This limitation came into effect on 1 January 2005.

89 Applications for protection for inventions other than patents are included under s 23(4). This could include, for example, an application for utility model protection for the invention.

90 The requirement for *mens rea* was introduced as from 1 January 2005 by insertion of s 23(3A) by the Patents Act 2004.

91 *See* also the Patents Act 1977 s 56 which expands upon the meaning of some of the provisions and terms.

92 'Relevant communication' means, by s 55(9), a direct or indirect communication of the invention by the proprietor of the patent or any person from whom he derives title.

93 [1991] FSR 221.

Section 57 deals with the rights of third parties that are affected by the Crown use and fundamentally prevents third-party rights interfering with the Crown use and apportions certain expenditure and royalty payments between the then proprietor and an assignee of the patent, or between the proprietor and an exclusive licensee. If the proprietor of the patent or an exclusive licensee suffers loss from not being awarded a contract in relation to the invention where the invention is used for the services of the Crown, the government department concerned is under a duty to pay compensation.[94] Compensation is payable only to the extent that the contract could have been fulfilled from existing capacity, and factors relevant to determining the loss are the profit that would have resulted from the contract and the extent to which manufacturing or other capacity was underused.[95] The compensation is calculable on the contract lost as a result of the Crown use only and not for other contracts. The amount payable by way of royalties in respect of Crown use or the amount of compensation is to be agreed between the relevant government department and the proprietor with the approval of the Treasury but, in the absence of agreement, may be referred to the High Court,[96] as may other disputes regarding Crown use, under s 58.

There are extended provisions for Crown use during a period of emergency, which is a period declared to be so by Order in Council.[97] During a period of emergency, the powers exercisable by any government department or person authorised by a government department include the power to use the invention for any purpose that appears to the department to be necessary or expedient for one or more stated reasons, including the efficient prosecution of any war in which Her Majesty may be engaged, the maintenance of supplies and services essential to the life or well-being of the community and for assisting in the relief of suffering in any country outside the UK that is in grave distress as a result of war. However, to these are added some reasons which extend the meaning of 'emergency' somewhat: for example, promoting the productivity of industry, commerce and agriculture and also for redressing the balance of trade, that is, increasing exports and reducing imports.

Where the Crown happens to be a co-proprietor, the provisions of s 55 still apply, irrespective of other provisions of the Act such as the rules on what a co-proprietor may do without the consent of the other co-proprietors in s 36. In *Henry Bros (Margherafelt) Ltd v Ministry of Defence and Northern Ireland Office*,[98] Robert Walker LJ accepted that 'home use' (use by one co-proprietor without the consent of the others) in relation to Crown use has an 'extraordinarily wide scope, far wider than it has for an ordinary individual'. He had no hesitation in holding that use of the invention in question by contractors working for the Crown was within the Crown use provisions and did not involve the grant of a licence within the meaning of s 36(3).

Crown use may be involved where the invention concerns national security, and directions may have been given under s 22 prohibiting or restricting the publication or communication of information contained in the patent application. Failure to comply with such directions is an offence triable either way.[99] The wide powers under s 22 apply where the information is prejudicial to national security or the safety of the public. It could mean that an invention is kept secret and the exploitation of it by the proprietor is hindered or even prevented, although the Secretary of State must keep the position under review from time to time (at least once a year). For example, in the early 1980s, an inventor devised a method of cryptography that was intended to be used for combating piracy of audio and videotapes and computer programs. However, and unfortunately for the inventor, it also had military uses and was subject to a s 22 direction.[100] As the apparent intention of the Ministry of Defence was not to use the invention but to keep it secret and prevent others from being able to use it, the unlucky inventor may have not received any income from his invention[101] unless some *ex gratia* payment was made. Had the inventor not tried to patent his invention he might have been able to exploit it relying on the law of confidence to protect his ideas.

94 Patents Act 1977 s 57A (added by the Copyright, Designs and Patents Act 1988 Sch 5 para 16(1)).

95 Patents Act 1977 s 57A(2) and (3).

96 In Scotland, the Court of Session, and, in Northern Ireland, the High Court of Northern Ireland: Patents Act 1977 s 130.

97 Patents Act 1977 s 59.

98 [1999] RPC 442.

99 The maximum penalty on indictment is imprisonment for a period not exceeding two years and/or a fine. On summary conviction, the maximum penalty is a fine of £1,000: Patents Act 1977 s 22(9).

100 *The Times*, 17 February 1984.

101 If it is used then, under the Patents Act 1977 s 55, royalties will be payable.

Summary

The person entitled to the grant of a patent for an invention is, primarily, the inventor, or joint inventors, unless someone else has a better entitlement as defined in s 7(2) or, in either case, to their successor or successor in title.

The inventor is the person, or persons in the case of joint inventorship, who is the actual deviser of the invention.

References may be made to the Comptroller as to entitlement before grant, whether or not an application for the grant of a patent has been made, under s 8. For example, any person may refer the question whether he alone or with others is entitled to the grant of a patent for the invention. Where there are two or more co-proprietors of a patent application, any of them may refer the question whether any right in or under the application should be transferred to any other person. References as to entitlement after grant may be made to the Comptroller under s 37.

Entitlement as to employee inventors is determined under s 39. The invention belongs to the employer where:

- the invention was made in the course of the employee's normal duties or in the course of duties specifically assigned to him – in either case, where the circumstances are such that the invention might reasonably be expected to result from the carrying out of those duties;
- the invention was made in the normal course of the employee's duties, which at the time, were such that the employee had a special obligation to further the interests of the employer's undertaking.

Where an employee's invention is made in circumstances such that the employer is entitled to the grant of the patent, if the invention or patent for it turns out to be of outstanding benefit to the employer, the employee may be entitled to compensation if it is just the employee to be awarded compensation to be paid by the employer. In such a case, the Comptroller (or court) must assess compensation based on a fair share for the employee. Special provisions apply where the employer assigns the rights in the invention to a connected person, such as another company within the same group of companies as the employer.

Patents and patent applications may be dealt with by means of assignment, licensing or mortgaging. They may vest by operation of law. Certain formalities are required and certain forms of transaction must be registered. Failure to register a registrable transaction may result in the transaction being defeated by a later registered transaction or, in proceedings, the loss of any right to obtain costs or expenses.

Licences of right may be available, especially where the proprietor has so indicated, as a way of reducing renewal fees. Compulsory licences may be available under certain circumstances.

There are provisions for safety and security in addition to provisions for Crown use.

Discussion questions

1   Discuss how the Comptroller should decide who is entitled to be granted a patent on a reference by (a) a person claiming to be a joint inventor; or (b) a person claiming to be the sole actual deviser of the invention where (i) no application for the grant of a patent has yet been made, or (ii) an application for the grant of a patent has been made.

2 Consider the provisions on employee compensation for inventions of outstanding benefit to the employer. Discuss, in particular: (a) what outstanding benefit means; (b) how a fair share for the employee is worked out; (c) how the provisions work in relation to assignments to persons connected with the employer.

Selected further reading

Wakely, J., 'Compulsory licensing under TRIPs: and effective tool to increase access to medicines in developing and least developed countries?' [2011] *European Intellectual Property Review*, 299 (looks at compulsory licensing under Article 31 of TRIPs – other use of a patent without authorisation – to determine its utility in relation to increasing access to medicines in developing countries and how Article 31, particularly Article 31(f) in practice restricts compulsory licensing).

Wolk, S., 'Remuneration of employee inventors – is there a common European ground? A comparison of national laws on compensation of inventors in Germany, France, Spain, Sweden and the United Kingdom' [2011] *International Review of Intellectual Property and Competition Law*, 272 (looks at the disparate laws in Europe as to employee compensation and implications for cross-border trade and questions whether the time is right to adopt uniform European laws on employee compensation).

Patents – infringement, remedies and criminal offences

14

Introduction

The strength of the rights granted by patent law is such that infringements of patents and defences to infringement have to be carefully drawn out. Patent infringement is not measured in terms of whether a substantial part has been taken, as is infringement of a work of copyright, but there are difficulties where the invention has not been taken in its entirety by an alleged infringer, or where some feature of the invention has been changed. Where the alleged infringement is not a direct copy but a variant, the courts may have some difficulty in determining whether the variant does indeed infringe the patent. It is in the light of subsequent variants of an invention that the value of a precise and appropriate specification can be seen; not too wide as to cause rejection of the application and not so narrow as to permit slight variations being made lawfully.

The scope of the infringing acts and the stated exceptions to infringement strive to achieve a balance between the interests of the proprietor and those of others, including competitors. Reverse engineering is permitted *per se*, but is hardly necessary as a study of the patent specification, a document available to the public, should be sufficient to determine how the invention works and what it does. Patent actions often involve challenges to the validity of the patent concerned and proprietors (or exclusive licensees) must be prepared to defend their patent. Commonly, challenges will be made on the grounds of anticipation or lack of inventive step. Partly because of this, but mainly as a result of the technical nature of patents, litigation in this field tends to be expensive and time-consuming. Trials lasting several weeks and costs running to millions of pounds are not unheard of. In *Chiron Corp* v *Organon Teknika Ltd (No 3)*[1] the defendant argued that the patent in suit was obvious, that it was invalid for insufficiency, that it was a patent for a discovery as such, that it was not capable of industrial application and that some claims were invalid, being methods of treatment. The defendant further claimed, successfully, that it could rely on the s 44 defence.[2]

As with other statute-based forms of intellectual property rights, with the single exception of registered trade marks, the culpability of the infringer is relevant in determining whether damages are available in a particular case. In some cases the defendant's knowledge is also the key to the question of infringement. Like design law and the new trade mark law, there is a remedy for groundless threats of infringement proceedings and, as is the case with registered designs and registered trade marks, certificates of contested validity are available. There are also some criminal penalties associated with patents.

This chapter concentrates on infringement, remedies and the criminal offences under patent law. The following chapter looks at defences to infringement, groundless threats actions and revocation of patents. The validity of patents is frequently an issue in infringement actions and it could be said in this context that attack is the best form of defence.

1 [1994] FSR 202.

2 This defence was repealed by the Competition Act 1998 s 70 with effect from 1 March 2000 (Competition Act 1998 (Commencement No 5) Order 2000, SI 2000/344). The s 44 defence, remained available in respect of contracts entered into before 1 March 2000, and could be used where the proprietor of a patent imposed certain forms of onerous terms on licensees and other parties to contracts with the proprietor.

Choice of court

Before looking in detail at infringement, defences and remedies, a brief word or two should be given on the choice of court for the hearing of a patent action.[3] In the past, litigants were faced with little option but the inevitable expense associated with an action in the Patents Court, part of the Chancery Division of the High Court. Some years ago, average costs in that court had been estimated at £500,000.[4] The Patent Office itself has limited jurisdiction to hear certain matters, as governed by the Patents Act 1977: for example, to grant compulsory licences and settle the terms of licences of right, to revoke patents, to award compensation to employees in respect of inventions of outstanding benefit to their employers, etc. Under s 61(3), with the agreement of the parties the Comptroller may hear infringement actions, in which case the remedies are limited to damages and a declaration that the patent is valid and infringed. The Patents Rules 2007 lay down the procedural aspects.[5] Now, the Comptroller may give non-binding opinions about validity (in relation to novelty and inventive step) and infringement under the Patents Act 1977, s 74A.

Following some speculation that the Patent Office should be given wider powers and a subsequent recommendation that a special county court to hear patents cases be set up,[6] the Patents County Court was established by virtue of the Copyright, Designs and Patents Act 1988 Part VI.[7] The procedure is governed by normal county court procedures with some modification.[8]

The subject matter of the jurisdiction of the Patents County Court is to hear proceedings relating to patents or designs and ancillary matters. The normal county court limits as to the damages that can be awarded do not apply and parties can be represented by a patent agent. Registered patent agents now have a right of audience in the Patents County Court.[9] The Patents County Court should result in speedier, less expensive hearings – and as might be expected has been the target of brickbats and bouquets. In *Prout* v *British Gas plc*,[10] Sir Thomas Bingham MR said:

> [the Patents County Court] has not been in operation for very long and during the period that it has been in operation it has been conspicuously successful. Part of the source of that success has been that it has set out to be as economical of time and expense and as innovative in terms of procedure as possible, consistent always of course with the requirements of justice and the entitlement of the parties to a fair hearing.[11]

A number of criticisms have been levelled at the court and its first judge, Peter Ford, and reported by Conn.[12] They include indecision and lack of firmness on the part of the judge. However, much of the trouble seems to stem from procedural difficulties to which Judge Ford addressed himself, strengthening the court's *raison d'être* of providing easy access to litigation for persons and companies without large resources. The present judge is HH Judge Birss QC. Judges of the Patents Court in the High Court may also sit as judges of the Patents County Court when the need arises.

In relation to transfers of proceedings to or from the High Court, the Patents County Court has a discretion under s 289(2) of the Copyright, Designs and Patents Act 1988 which states that the court shall 'have regard to the financial position of the parties and may order the transfer to a patents county court or, as the case may be, refrain from ordering their transfer to the High Court notwithstanding that the proceedings are likely to raise an important question of fact or law'. In *Chaplin Patents Co plc* v *Group Lotus plc*,[13] the Court of Appeal accepted the existence of that discretion, although the Master of the Rolls said that he would have ordered transfer had it been up to him, in view of the substantial nature of the action in that case.

Subsequently, in *Pavel* v *Sony Corporation*,[14] the Court of Appeal cast doubt on whether the present provisions relating to transfer of trial are satisfactory. The parties in that case

3 For a fuller description, *see* Reid, B.C. (1998) *A Practical Guide to Patent Law* (3rd edn) Sweet & Maxwell, Chapters 7, 8 and 11.

4 Conn, D. 'Cut-price Court in Spin', *The Times*, 23 November 1993.

5 The procedure for the Patents Act 1977 s 61(3) reference is stated in the Patents Rules 2007, SI 2007/3291 Part VI.

6 *Intellectual Property and Innovation*, Cmd 9712, HMSO, 1986 and the Oulton Committee Report (1987).

7 *See* also Patents County Court (Designation and Jurisdiction) Order 1990, SI 1990/1946.

8 For example, the Patents County Court may grant search orders and freezing injunctions: County Court Remedies Regulations 1991, SI 1991/1222, regs 2 and 3.

9 Copyright, Designs and Patents Act 1988 s 292.

10 [1994] FSR 160.

11 This case was an appeal from the judgment of Judge Ford in the Patents County Court [1992] FSR 478, on the question of costs.

12 Conn D. 'Cut-price Court in Spin', *The Times*, 23 November 1993.

13 *The Times*, 12 January 1994.

14 *The Times*, 22 March 1996.

were criticised for over-elaboration of the issues in what should have been a relatively simple case. The specification of the patent in issue ran to two-and-a-half pages and should have been easily understood without the need for scientific help. Altogether, there were nearly eight days of interim hearings and the trial lasted nearly four weeks, resulting in costs in the order of £2.2 million with the claimant ending up on legal aid.[15] Aldous LJ said:

> . . . whether the fault for those lamentable events was that of the procedure or something else was not for his Lordship to decide. However, some alteration was necessary if the purposes of the Patents County Court were to be achieved.

In *Halliburton Energy Services Inc* v *Smith International (North Sea) Ltd*,[16] at first instance, Pumfrey J noted that the case, which lasted 13 days with considerable pre-reading in the Patents Court, and which had started life in the Patents County Court, was not suitable for that court and should not have been commenced there.

The manner in which some litigants behave in the Patents County Court compromises its fundamental purpose of providing fast and inexpensive relief for patent proprietors who do not have deep pockets where the nature of the case is relatively straightforward. The difficulty of fixing a ceiling of, say, £50,000 is that often larger sums are at stake, even in relatively simple cases.

Inevitably, any new court must undergo its teething problems. It is reputed that the first seven decisions of the Patents County Court, tested in the Court of Appeal, were overturned.[17] The need for an inexpensive forum to hear patent disputes is, however, unquestionable, and it seems that the Patents County Court is capable of being a worthwhile and valued alternative to the Patents Court in the Chancery Division. In some ways, the deficiencies of the Patents County Court result from the behaviour and tactics of litigants, many of whom seem unwilling to avail themselves of alternative dispute resolution and who submit vast numbers of documents and often conduct expensive experiments, particularly in the field of pharmaceuticals.

Costs remain a thorny issue at the Patents County Court. In *Warheit* v *Olympia Tools Ltd*,[18] Aldous LJ considered costs approaching £250,000 claimed by the patentee in respect of a two-day trial in the Patents County Court to be excessive and not a reflection of what the Lord Chancellor envisaged when that court was set up. However, granting leave to appeal from the Patents County Court because the 'whole issue of costs in the Patents County Court is of interest to practitioners' is not, *per se*, a sufficient reason to grant leave to appeal. As a matter of principle, it is not right that the practice in relation to costs should differ in patent cases as between the County Court and the High Court.[19]

The Patents County Court has been criticised for failing to provide an affordable forum for intellectual property litigation for SMEs. A working group of the Judiciary of England and Wales has proposed some changes to improve matters.[20] First it noted that the above failure was due to two main reasons. First was the fear of meeting substantial and unpredictable costs awards if unsuccessful. Second, the procedures before the Patents County Court were costly, being the same as those of the High Court. To answer these criticisms and improve the operation of the court, the Working Group proposed, *inter alia*:

- a requirement for parties to present cases by sequential written arguments;
- the imposition of robust case management;
- to permit or require disclosures, experiments, factual and expert evidence and cross-examination only when a cost-benefit test is satisfied;
- to limit trials to one or, at the most, two days;
- to restrict costs to a scale basis similar to that (though more generous) used in the UK IPO, except where the conduct of a party has been unreasonable;
- to set a financial limit of £500,000 and to limit costs awards to £50,000;
- to rename the court as the Intellectual Property County Court and to widen its jurisdiction to cover all forms of intellectual property;

15 *The Times*, 22 March 1996, p 37.

16 [2006] RPC 2.

17 Conn, D. 'Cut-price court in spin', *The Times*, 23 November 1993.

18 [2003] FSR 6.

19 *Kavanagh Balloons Pty Ltd* v *Cameron Balloons Ltd* [2004] FSR 33.

20 Judiciary of England and Wales Intellectual Property Committee, Working Group's Final Report on Proposals for the Reform of the Patents County Court, 31 July 2009.

- to provide appropriate guidance in the Guide to the court as to the contents of statements of case and as to which sort of case is suitable for the court and criteria for transfer to the High Court.

As from 1 October 2010, some procedural changes were implemented. In particular:

- the parties are to set out their cases fully and concisely at the beginning and no further evidence, written argument or specific disclosure is allowed except by leave of the judge;
- the trial is limited to one or two days;
- costs are capped at a maximum of £50,000;
- procedures for transfers have been modified accordingly.

A limit on the total maximum award of damages or an account of profits has been raised to £500,000 by virtue of the Patents County Court (Financial Limits) Order 2011,[21] as from 14 June 2011. Awards of interest and costs are disregarded from the total figure of £500,000. There are some transitional provisions allowing the maximum to exceed £500,000, for example, where before the Order came into force, the High Court ordered a transfer of proceedings to the Patents County Court.

21 SI 2011/1402.

Non-binding opinions

There has been a trend in recent years towards mediation and other forms of dispute resolution as a quicker and cheaper alternative to full-blown litigation which, in the case of patents in particular, can be extremely expensive. In *IDA Ltd* v *University of Southampton*,[22] discussed in the previous chapter, Jacob LJ said that the case was one ripe for mediation and that a small share in a large exploitation was better than a large share of none or little. There was no evidence that the patent in question, which had been hailed as a 'cockroach trap to beat the world', had been exploited at all during the eight years since the first application for a patent had been filed. With the aim of providing a quicker and cheaper way to resolve issues of validity and infringement, the Comptroller General of Patents, Designs and Trade Marks was given the power to issue opinions about infringement and validity (novelty and inventive step only). The necessary provisions in ss 74A and 74B of the Act were inserted by the Patents Act 2004.[23]

22 [2006] RPC 21.

Under s 74A(1), the proprietor or any other person may request an opinion as to whether a particular act constitutes or would constitute an infringement of the patent in question or as to whether or to what extent the invention is not patentable for lack of novelty or inventive step.[24] It seems strange that the Comptroller can give an opinion to the effect that a patent which has been granted by him is not valid after all. Opinions are non-binding and are prepared by patent examiners. The Comptroller may refuse the request in prescribed circumstances[25] or if he considers it inappropriate. In relation to a decision as to whether to refuse the request, only the party making the request can be a party to proceedings before the Comptroller. Thus, where the applicant's request is refused, only he can challenge that decision.

23 The fine detail is contained in rr 92–100 of the Patents Rules 2007, SI 2007/3291.

24 The request is made on Patents Form 17 and the fee is £200.

25 If he considers it frivolous or vexatious or where it appears to him that the question has been sufficiently considered in any relevant proceedings: r 94 Patents Rules 2007. Relevant proceedings are those, whether pending or concluded, before the Comptroller, the court or the EPO.

Within four weeks of advertising the request, any person may submit observations, a copy of which is sent to the person making the request and, if not that person, the patent holder. Observations may then be submitted, strictly limited to matters in reply, and a copy of these is sent within two weeks to the requester or patent holder as the case may be. Observations should be sent by electronic communication. The request is then referred to an examiner and, when the opinion has been prepared, copies are sent to the patent holder, the requester (if different) and any person making observations.

Section 74B provides for reviews of opinions. Under r 98, the patent holder may apply for a review of the opinion unless the issues raised have been decided in other relevant proceedings. An application for review may only be made on the grounds that the opinion wrongly concluded that the patent was invalid wholly or partly or, by reason of its interpretation of the specification, that a particular act did not or would not infringe the patent. Rule 99 of the Patents Rules 2007 contains the procedure for reviews and, under r 100, after the completion of that procedure, the Comptroller shall either set aside the opinion in whole or in part or decide that no reason has been shown for the opinion to be set aside. Any such decision does not prevent a party to any proceedings from raising an issue regarding the validity or infringement of the patent. No appeal under s 97 (appeals from the Comptroller) lies against a decision to set aside the opinion except where it relates to a part of the opinion not set aside. Where parties are contemplating litigation, once the opinion has been issued, they might be encouraged to settle rather than proceed to lengthy and expensive litigation. There have been around 70 applications for opinions at the time of writing. It remains to be seen how effective the provisions are in terms of encouraging settlement of disputes about validity or infringement.

The question arose in *DLP Ltd* v *Comptroller-General of Patents, Designs and Trade Marks*[26] as to whether there was a right to appeal against a Hearing Officer's review of an opinion. The Patents Court in the Chancery Division held that there was such a right of appeal. Although opinions and reviews of opinions were non-binding, the court should not refuse to hear an appeal on the basis that the result would be a non-binding opinion or review. The system was of great value to those concerned and related to a living issue and it would be wrong for the court to decline to exercise its discretion to hear an appeal. However, the court should only reverse a Hearing Officer's review of an opinion if he failed to recognise that the examiner had made an error of principle or reached a conclusion that was clearly wrong. On the evidence, neither the examiner nor the Hearing Officer had made an error in law and the opinion was a reasonable one in the circumstances.

Requesting non-binding opinions has been moderately popular and, during 2010, a total of 21 opinions were issued with a further two being withdrawn.[27]

Infringement

A patent may relate to a product or a process. If the invention is a process, it may be used to make a product. An example of a product invention is a new type of golf ball, and an example of a process invention is a new process for making ordinary golf balls. Under s 130[28] a patented product is a product which is a patented invention or, in relation to a patented process, a product obtained directly by means of the process or to which the process has been applied. Article 64(3) of the European Patent Convention leaves infringement of European patents to be dealt with by national law. Under the 1949 Act there was no definition of 'infringement' in the Act. The letters patent commanded the public not to make use of the patent directly or indirectly, or put it into practice or in any way imitate the same. Thus, the 1977 Act appears to afford a more limited monopoly as regards the scope of infringement.

Section 60 defines an infringement of a patent as the doing of any of the following things in the UK in relation to the invention[29] without the proprietor's consent:

1 *Product invention*. To make, dispose of, offer to dispose of, to use or import the product or to keep it, whether for disposal or otherwise (s 60(1)(a)).[30]
2 *Process invention*. To use the process[31] or offer it for use in the UK when the person concerned does so knowing, or where in the circumstances it would be obvious to a

26 [2008] RPC 11.

27 The Opinions are published on the UK Intellectual Property website.

28 Unless otherwise stated, in this chapter, statutory references are to the Patents Act 1977.

29 The invention is, under s 125, taken to be that specified in the claim as interpreted by the description and any drawings.

30 Where an invention is a product, it does not matter whether or not it was produced by the methods described in the specification; the monopoly is in any goods fitting the description of the invention: *Raychem Corp's Patents* [1999] RPC 497 at 517 per Buxton LJ.

31 Using the process badly is still using the process for the purposes of infringement: *Union Carbide Corp* v *BP Chemicals Ltd* [1999] RPC 409.

reasonable man, that such use would be without the consent of the proprietor and would be an infringement of the patent (s 60(1)(b)).

3 *Process invention.* To dispose of or offer to dispose of, to use or import or to keep (whether for disposal or otherwise) any product obtained directly by means of the process (s 60(1)(c)).

4 *All inventions.* To supply or offer to supply in the UK a person (other than a licensee or other person entitled to work the invention) with any of the means, relating to an essential element of the invention, for putting the invention into effect (s 60(2)). The alleged infringer must know, or it must be obvious to a reasonable man in the circumstances, that those means are suitable for putting, and are intended to put, the invention into effect in the UK.[32]

Section 60(1) infringement

In terms of proving infringement, the burden of proof lies with the claimant and it is the claims in the specification that are important rather than the products actually made by the claimant. In the case of a product invention, those claims must be compared to the defendant's product.[33] In relation to the s 60(1)(a) infringement, it has been held that negotiating with a customer, during the currency of a patent, to supply a product after the relevant patent had expired did not infringe.[34]

It is no answer to an infringement action to argue that the alleged infringing product is inefficient compared with the patented product though sufficient for commercial purposes. In *Henriksen* v *Tallon Ltd (No 2)*,[35] the patent was for a ballpoint pen which had a plug of grease at the top of and in contact with the ink in the tube. This was to prevent contact between the ink and air which would cause the ink to dry. The defendant's pen had a narrower tube not needing a grease plug but one was inserted anyway. This was held to infringe. However, in *Novartis AG* v *Ivax Pharmaceuticals UK Ltd*,[36] the patent was for a formulation of an immuno-suppressant drug 'cyclosporing' aimed at overcoming the problem with the drug's almost insolubility in water. The defendant's version of the drug did not infringe. This was not a case of an inefficient product but sufficient for commercial purposes as in *Henriksen* but the defendant's formulation was nearly all that the patentee had tried to avoid.

A product obtained directly from a patented process must be obtained directly without any intermediate steps to be within s 60(1)(c). In *Pioneer Electronics Capital Inc* v *Warner Manufacturing Europe GmbH*[37] the claimant had a patent for a process for making optical discs. There were some intermediate steps, including making stampers from which the discs could be mass-produced. It was held that the defendant had not infringed the patent because none of his discs was a direct product of the patented process and that a causal link, however important, was not sufficient. Aldous J looked at the German and French versions of the European Patent Convention,[38] because, under s 130(7), a number of provisions of the Patents Act 1977, including s 60, are framed to have, as nearly as practicable, the same effects in the UK as the corresponding provisions of the European Patent Convention and the Community Patent Convention. In particular, the German word *unmittelbar* suggested that no intermediate points would be allowed between the process and the product. The Court of Appeal dismissed the claimant's appeal, agreeing with Aldous J's views on the meaning of *unmittelbar*.[39] The court also held that the product in question did not cease to be the product if it was subjected to further processing, provided that it did not lose its identity and that it retained its essential characteristics. Whether this was so was a question of fact and degree, a test which would often be difficult to apply. However, in the present case, the finished disc was not an identical copy of the master disc and different in a material way from it as a result of three further stages of production. For example, the master was not capable of being played in a compact disc player.

32 This provision does not apply to the proprietor of the patent. So, for example, if the proprietor grants an exclusive licence to one person he does not infringe by supplying the means suitable for putting the invention into effect to another person. The proprietor will probably be in breach of his licence agreement with the first person.

33 *Buchanan* v *Alba Diagnostics Ltd* [2004] RPC 34.

34 *Gerber Garment Technology Inc* v *Lectra Systems Ltd* [1995] RPC 383; appeal against damages allowed in part in the Court of Appeal: [1997] RPC 443.

35 [1965] RPC 434.

36 [2007] EWCA Civ 971.

37 [1995] RPC 487.

38 Article 24(2).

39 *Pioneer Electronics Capital Inc* v *Warner Music Manufacturing Europe GmbH* [1997] RPC 757.

Infringement by importing a product is not made out by a person in another country who simply arranges for transportation of the goods to the UK. So it was held by the House of Lords in *Sabaf SpA* v *MFI Furniture Centres Ltd*[40] in which gas hobs alleged to infringe a UK patent were transported from Italy to the UK. An Italian company had made and sold the hobs in question to MFI, the first defendant, and had arranged transportation at MFI's request. The property in the hobs passed to MFI in Italy. A trade mark case, *Waterford Wedgwood plc* v *David Nagli Ltd*,[41] was distinguished as, in that case, the seller had imported the infringing goods into the UK for transhipment to the buyer in the USA. The USA buyer could be said to have imported the goods into the USA but not the UK.

The mere sale of goods to a person outside jurisdiction who later sells those goods within jurisdiction does not, *per se*, make the seller a joint tortfeasor with the person selling them within jurisdiction. In *Generics (UK) Ltd* v *H Lundbeck A/S*,[42] an Indian company supplied a drug to Generics which had, on a counterclaim for revocation of the patent, been accused of infringement. It was later sought to join the Indian company as joint tortfeasor. This application for amendment was rejected. It made no difference that the Indian company had supplied information to the regulatory authority in the UK before its drugs could be sold in the UK by Generics. Under s 100(1), there is a presumption that, where a product produced by a patented process is new, unless the contrary is proved, the same product made by another person is taken to have been made by the same process. However, this presumption was displaced because of the provision of information required by law to the regulatory authority and there was no reason that it would mislead that authority. Indeed, providing false information is a criminal offence. The Indian company had good legal and commercial reasons not to mislead the regulatory authority.

For persons to be liable for patent infringement as joint tortfeasors, they must combine to secure the performance of acts which turn out to be infringements.[43] In *Fabio Perini SpA* v *LPC Group plc*[44], Lord Neuberger MR held that merely exporting a machine into the UK, even helping to set up the machine in the UK, was not enough, *per se*, to make a person a joint tortfeasor as it is the use of the machine which infringes. However, in this case, employees of a company supplying the machinery went further by supervising the assembly of the machines in the UK, supervising the starting up of the machinery for more than a day or two and spending some time training the first defendant's employees. These services, performed in the UK, were clearly intended to enable, assist and even join in with the use of the machines.

Where the invention is a process, it may be infringed by the use of another process which occasionally extends into the parameters covered by the patent. In *Hoechst Celanese Corp* v *BP Chemicals Ltd*,[45] the patent related to a process for making acetic acid. The defendant argued that it would only infringe the patent if its process was within the parameters of the patent for a significant period of time and that short-term fluctuation, moving into the parameters, did not infringe. This was rejected, on the facts, by Jacob J. He accepted that a patentee would not be interested in transient 'spikes' coming within the patent's parameters but would not want to exclude significant commercial production. It was pointed out that one day's production amounted to 800 tonnes.

Section 60(2) infringement – supplying or offering to supply the means

The final type of infringement ('supplying or offering to supply the means') could occur where one person supplies another with a kit of parts for the latter to assemble. This was not an infringement before the 1977 Act came into force.[46] By virtue of s 60(6), the 'supplying the means' infringement in s 60(2) does not apply in respect of a person:

40 [2005] RPC 10. The patent was held to be invalid in any case.

41 [1998] FSR 92.

42 [2006] EWCA Civ 1261.

43 *Unilever plc* v *Gillette (UK) Ltd* [1989] RPC 583 per Mustill LJ at 608–609.

44 [2009] EWHC 1929 (Pat).

45 [1998] FSR 586.

46 The Patents Act 1977 came into force on 1 June 1978.

- entitled to work the invention under the Crown use provisions in s 55;
- entitled to continue to do an act begun in good faith before the priority date of the patent (or where that person had made in good faith effective and serious preparations to do such an act before that date) under s 64; or
- entitled to work the invention because of acts done in good faith or where that person made in good faith effective and serious preparations to do such an act after it was no longer possible to renew the patent but before publication of a notice of an application to restore the patent under s 28A(4) and (5).

Furthermore, under s 60(3), infringement under s 60(2) does not extend to the supply or offer to supply a staple commercial product unless for the purpose of inducing the person supplied or to whom the offer is made do an infringing act within s 60(1).

Section 60(2) can catch a person who sells or offers to sell a product which, in the state it is sold, is only capable of infringing use if it can be readily adapted to infringe. In *Grimme Landmaschinenfabrik GmbH & Co KG v Scott*,[47] the claimant made patented machines containing rubber rollers for the separation of potatoes from weeds, stones, clods of earth and haulm (stems). The defendant made a similar machine but one which had stainless steel rollers. In that condition it did not infringe the claimant's patent. However, the steel rollers could be easily substituted by rubber rollers. The defendant sold his machines to 'middlemen' who supplied them to the end users. The defendant had stressed a selling feature of the machines being the ability to use either rubber or steel rollers. It was held that the machines in this altered state infringed the patent. The defendant infringed the patent under s 60(2) by supplying the means, relating to an essential element of the invention, of putting the invention into effect, knowing or where it would be obvious in the circumstances that the means were suitable for putting and intended to put the invention into effect. The Court of Appeal confirmed infringement under s 60(2).[48] A number of points relating to this form of infringement were made in the Court of Appeal,[49] in particular:

- Section 60(2) is a statutory tort, being actionable:
  - even though what is supplied is capable of lawful, non-infringing use;
  - even though what is supplied never has and may never be used in a way which infringes the patent;
  - without any damage being suffered by the patentee; and
  - at the moment of supply, irrespective of anything that may or may not occur afterwards.
- Infringement can occur without any actual direct infringement because the tort can be committed by offering to supply as well as by supplying.
- It makes no difference whether a machine is supplied which readily can be put into an infringing state by the addition of a part and a machine in which a part readily can be removed and replaced.
- As to the intention to put the invention into effect:
  - the intention is not that of the person supplying the means;
  - the requisite intention is not limited to that of the direct supply to an infringer but must be that of the ultimate users, otherwise the supply to 'middlemen' would escape;[50]
  - the intention does not have to be formed at the time of the supply, as with an offer to supply, at the time of the offer, the offeree cannot have formed a settled intention to put the invention into effect;
  - it is sufficient if some users will put the invention into effect, ignoring freak, maverick or unlikely uses;
  - the intention of the ultimate user need not be known to the supplier at the time of infringement;

47 [2011] FSR 7.

48 The Court of Appeal reversed the judgment at first instance to the effect that the patent was invalid.

49 The judgment was a joint one by Jacob and Etherton LJJ with whom Sir David Keene agreed.

50 Overruling Lewison J on this point in *Cranway Ltd* v *Playtech Ltd* [2010] FSR 3.

- the future intention of a future ultimate user is sufficient if that is what one would expect in all the circumstances;
- s 60(2) is aimed at persons who supply (or offer to supply) things which they know or ought to know that the 'means essential' they put or will put into circulation will infringe because ultimate users will intend to do acts amounting to infringement.

Reference was made in the judgment to the Community Patent Convention, particularly Article 26 which deals with this form of infringement. Section 60 is one of those provisions required to have the same effect as the equivalent provisions in the EPC, CPC and PCT. Although the CPC has not come into effect, it is still valid to determine the scope of infringement.[51] The Court of Appeal used the latest version of the CPC, the 1989 version.[52] However, s 60(2), although differently worded was in accordance with it.

The Court of Appeal usefully interpreted the scope of s 60(2). It was applied soon after in that court in *KCI Licensing Inc* v *Smith & Nephew plc*[53] in which the judge at first instance erred (in a retrospective sense) by distinguishing between the persons supplied and the actual users, medical institutions and medical personnel respectively in that case.

As to whether infringement by a 'kit of parts' was possible, Laddie J was referred to the judgment of Graham J in *Rotocrop International Ltd* v *Genbourne Ltd*[54] where it was held that there was direct infringement by a kit of parts for a bin for making compost of a patent which claimed a fully assembled bin. Graham J considered the kit, in the circumstances, to be the 'bin'. Laddie J thought it inappropriate to depart from that decision.[55]

Cases prior to the 1977 Act and Canadian authorities indicating infringement by a kit of parts were discounted by Laddie J who said that the 1977 Act marked a sea change in patent law. Terrell suggests that a kit of parts might infringe as it could amount to the completed article.[56] Also, unless the kit is made for export, liability for indirect infringement is also likely to arise by virtue of s 60(2). The manufacturer of a kit of parts may also be considered to be a joint tortfeasor with the person who assembles the parts. Nevertheless, doubt remains as to whether making a kit of parts for assembly outside jurisdiction infringes a patent which claims the assembled product. It is surprising that this point has not been litigated more often, and even more surprising that the 1977 Act does not directly deal with it.

Territorial scope of infringement

The infringing acts under s 60 must be done in the UK to infringe. This reflects the territorial nature of a patent. In *Lacroix Duarib SA* v *Kwikform (UK) Ltd*,[57] the claimant claimed that the defendant had infringed his patent for scaffolding to be used inside large hollow structures, such as the hulls of large ships during their construction. The defendant made its scaffolding in 'collapsed' form and it was to be assembled or erected in Korea by Daewoo in its shipbuilding operations. The defendant's argument was that, since its scaffolding was only in collapsed form in the UK, there was no infringement of the patent as claim 1 of the specification referred to the complete assembly only.

Given the territorial nature of patents, the requirement that the infringing act must take place in the UK seems simple enough. But what if the invention includes apparatus, some of which is located in the UK but part is outside the UK? The important test is where the invention is being used. In *Menashe Business Mercantile Ltd* v *William Hill Organisation Ltd*,[58] the patent was for a gaming system comprising a host computer, terminal computers which could communicate with the host computer, and computer programs. The defendant, a bookmaker, introduced a gambling system and supplied persons in the UK with computer programs on CD-ROM that could be loaded on to their computers, which could then act as terminals and communicate with the defendant's host computer, which was situated in the Netherlands Antilles. It was alleged that the defendant infringed the

51 The EPC and PCT leave it to national law.

52 There is currently a proposal for a new unitary European patent.

53 [2011] FSR 8.

54 [1982] FSR 241.

55 Laddie J considered that, if the narrower construction of s 60(1)(a) advanced by the defendant was to be taken, it would be better left to a higher court, especially as there was no authority on this issue.

56 Thorley, S. *et al* (2005) *Terrell on the Law of Patents* (16th edn) Sweet & Maxwell, para 8.21.

57 [1998] FSR 493.

58 [2003] RPC 31.

patent by supplying the means to put the invention into effect in the UK. Infringement was denied on the basis that the host computer was outside jurisdiction. The Court of Appeal held that the 'supplying the means' form of infringement meant putting the invention into an infringing state. The location of the host computer was not relevant and the pertinent question was who used the gaming system. These were the punters using their computers in the UK and they also were 'using' the host computer in the UK even though it was situated elsewhere. Therefore, supplying the programs on CD-ROM in the UK was supplying the means to put the invention into effect in the UK.

Interpretation of claims

The patent is granted on the basis of the specification and the claims included in the application, perhaps after amendment. It is to these documents that a court must turn to determine whether the patent has been infringed. This is confirmed by s 125(1) which states that a patent shall, unless the context otherwise requires, be taken to be that specified in a claim of the specification as interpreted by the description and any drawings in the specification. The extent of the protection conferred by the patent is to be determined accordingly. Hence the importance of the claims.

If the alleged infringer has simply duplicated the product or process patented as described in the specification then, subject to the defences or a challenge on the validity of the patent, there should be no hesitation in finding that an infringement has occurred. But what if the alleged infringer has not simply duplicated the invention but has introduced some changes, producing a variant? If this has happened, it is then a matter of construing the patent specification and claims to find out whether the grant extends to the variant. The alleged infringer is likely to suggest that his variant lies outside the invention claimed by the patent, while the proprietor will argue that the variant falls within the patent as granted. If the former is true, then no matter how close to that dividing line the variant lies, there is no infringement of the patent.

The claims are to be interpreted by the description and any drawings contained in the specification and the extent of the protection is to be determined accordingly.[59] The notional addressee is the person skilled in the art with the common general knowledge of that art.[60] The skilled reader is taken to know something about patent law and would not expect the patentee to use language which covered something he expressly acknowledged was old.[61] There is no rule that because prior art is referred to as such in the specification it cannot be found to anticipate the patent as claimed.[62] Of course, when drafting a patent specification, the patentee will usually have chosen words following skilled advice. As Lord Hoffmann said in *Kirin-Amgen*[63] (at para 34):

> The words will usually have been chosen on skilled advice. The specification is not a document *inter rusticos* for which broad allowances must be made.

As noted by Jacob LJ in *Virgin Atlantic Airways Ltd* v *Premium Aircraft Interiors UK Ltd*[64] it would be unrealistic to say that the notional skilled worker, probably with the benefit of skilled advice, would not know and take into account explicit drafting conventions by which a patent and its claims were drafted. Where the patent was the result of a divisional application, the skilled person would probably ask a man who knew what that meant – a patent agent. In that case, Jacob LJ also held that the inclusion of reference numerals, as found in drawings in the specification, in a claim should not influence the construction of the claim. The implementing regulations of the EPC make this clear.

Following these basic principles, the development of the approach to claim construction may now be described.

59 Section 125(1) of the Patents Act 1977. *See also* Article 69 of the European Patent Convention.

60 Per Lord Hoffmann in *Kirin-Amgen Inc* v *Hoechst Marion Roussel Ltd* [2005] RPC 9 at para 33.

61 Per Jacob LJ in *Virgin Atlantic Airways Ltd* v *Premium Aircraft Interiors UK Ltd* [2010] RPC 8 at para 13.

62 Per Lloyd LJ in *Tate & Lyle Technology Ltd* v *Roquette Frères* [2011] FSR 3.

63 *Kirin-Amgen Inc* v *Hoechst Marion Roussel Ltd* [2005] RPC 9.

64 [2010] RPC 8.

As a result of their training, lawyers are used to construing legal documents literally. There are exceptions, such as where legislation is ambiguous and a strict literal interpretation would clearly defeat the intention of Parliament to remedy some perceived defect in the law. Nevertheless, a literal approach to interpretation does not sit comfortably with the knowledge that patent specifications are written for scientists, engineers and technologists rather than for lawyers. One of the main purposes is to indicate the scope of what the invention is claimed to be. A rigid approach to interpretation could deprive a patentee of effective protection, bearing in mind that inventions are new and inventive and it is not always possible to describe them in a manner that may be robust enough to stand up to a narrow literal interpretation. After all, the patentee, although usually advised and assisted by experienced patent agents, is trying to describe something new and, in some cases, unlike anything else that has preceded the invention in question. But providing effective protection for a patentee has to be balanced by the interests of third parties who need to be able to see, from the patent specification, the extent of the monopoly granted so that they can be reasonably certain that any activities they are contemplating do not fall foul of patent law.

For some time, the courts have eschewed a strict literal approach to the construction of patent specifications and claims and in *Rodi & Wienenberger AG v Henry Showell Ltd*,[65] Lord Reid said (at 378):

> . . . claims are not addressed to conveyancers: they are addressed to practical men skilled in the prior art, and I do not think that they ought to be construed with that meticulousness which was once thought appropriate for conveyancing documents.

A claim is not bad for ambiguity because it is capable of more than one construction or because it is difficult to construe. The court should prefer the most sensible construction and not one leading to an absurd result. So it was held by a majority in the House of Lords in *Henriksen v Tallon Ltd (No 2)*.[66] In *LG Philips LCD Co Ltd v Tatung (UK) Ltd*,[67] the Court of Appeal held that the mere fact that a word or phrase in a patent claim is not wholly clear does not automatically lead to the conclusion that the claim is bad as that would set too high a standard of drafting in a technical field. Drafting patents was a particularly difficult exercise and the claim should be as clear as the subject-matter reasonably admitted.

One problem of course is where the alleged infringing product or process is not the same as the invention but is a variant of it. It used to be the case that the differences between the variant and the invention were important and the question was whether they differed in essential or inessential respects. The invention claimed was considered as comprising essential and non-essential integers (components), those that are fundamental to the invention and those that are not. If the alleged infringer has taken all of the essential integers then there was an infringement even if there were substantial differences in respect of the non-essential integers. This was described by various judges as taking the 'pith and marrow' of the invention. However, when applying this principle, the scope of the patent claims was of vital importance. Viscount Radcliffe said in *Van der Lely NV v Bamfords Ltd*[68] (at 78):

> When, therefore, one speaks of theft or piracy of another's invention . . . and this 'pith and marrow' principle is invoked to support the accusation, I think that one must be very careful to see that the inventor has not by the actual form of his claim left open to the world the appropriation of just that property that he says has been filched from him . . .

In other words, the inventor had to be very careful when drafting his claims to make sure that they were not framed too narrowly so that some slight and insignificant modification could be effected without infringing the patent. On the other hand, care has to be taken not to make the claims wide enough to cover matter already part of the state of the art.

65 [1969] RPC 367.

66 [1965] RPC 434.
67 [2007] RPC 21.

68 [1963] RPC 61.

The essential integers claimed in *Van der Lely* were those very parts which the proprietor wished to protect. There was a flaw in the application of the 'pith and marrow' test as, arguably, it could extend the monopoly claimed by the patentee beyond that encompassed in the claims as interpreted in the light of the specification. To that extent, the looser the language of the claims, the greater the monopoly afforded and the greater the range of equivalents that may have been caught. This was an unsatisfactory state of affairs and resulted in some inconsistencies. For example, in *Rodi & Wienenberger AG v Henry Showell Ltd*[69] it was held that replacing two 'U-shaped' bows in a flexible watch strap with a single large 'C-shaped' bow was not an infringement because the 'U-shaped' bow was an essential integer. Conversely, in *Marconi v British Radio Telegraph & Telephone*[70] the replacement of an auto-transformer with a two-coil transformer did not prevent a finding of infringement because it was held that the auto-transformer was not an essential integer.

Things changed with the European Patent Convention, which resulted in significant changes to patent law in the UK and the implementation of the Patents Act 1977. But even before this, the House of Lords had the opportunity to reflect on the interpretation of patent claims in the *Catnic* case.

Catnic and purposive construction

The 'pith and marrow' test failed satisfactorily to resolve the problem of interpretation, and the question of construction of patent claims in the context of variants came to a head in the case of *Catnic Components Ltd v Hill & Smith Ltd*[71] which involved several variants of steel lintels.[72] The claimant was the proprietor of a patent for steel lintels that had a rear support member which was vertical and so described in claim 1 of the specification by the phrase 'second rigid support member extending *vertically* from or from near the rear edge of the first horizontal plate or part adjacent its rear edge' (emphasis added).[73] The defendant made a similar lintel, but with the rear support member inclined between six and eight degrees (depending on the particular model of lintel) from the vertical. Figure 14.1 gives an approximate representation in cross-section of one of the claimant's lintels and one of the defendant's lintels.

The strength of a steel lintel in this form of construction derives to some extent from the verticality of the rear member, and the defendant's lintel had a reduced load-bearing capacity compared to the claimant's lintel, but because of the small inclination from the vertical this reduction was small.[74] The House of Lords found that the claimant's patent had been infringed and the defendant's argument that the verticality of the claimant's lintel was essential to its function and that, therefore, there was no 'pith and marrow' infringement was rejected. It was confirmed that a purposive approach[75] should be adopted in the construction of patent specifications, Lord Diplock saying (at 243):

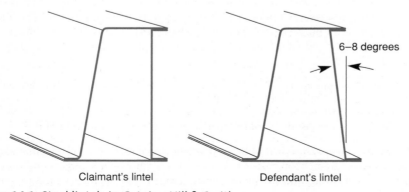

Claimant's lintel   Defendant's lintel

Figure 14.1 Steel lintels in *Catnic v Hill & Smith*

69 [1969] RPC 367.

70 (1911) 28 RPC 181.

71 [1982] RPC 183. This case concerned a patent granted under the 1949 Act, but it has been accepted as being applicable to 1977 Act patents.

72 A lintel is a beam used to support some load, such as a wall, above an opening. For example, lintels are used above windows and doors to support the wall above and any transmitted loads.

73 Patent Specification No 1298798 (GB).

74 For a six-degree inclination from the vertical the reduction was only 0.6 per cent and for an eight-degree inclination the reduction was 1.2 per cent.

75 This could be seen as a modern equivalent of the 'mischief rule', that is the rule in *Heydon's Case* (1584) 3 Co Rep 7a. In other words, the word 'vertically' did not mean 'vertically' but 'vertically or nearly so'.

> A patent specification should be given a purposive construction rather than a purely literal one derived from applying to it the kind of meticulous verbal analysis in which lawyers are too often tempted by their training to indulge.

This can be described as the *Catnic* principle, to distinguish it from a structured test to determine whether a variant infringes first set out in *Catnic* by Lord Diplock, now reformulated and usually described as the Protocol questions (see below). The *Catnic* principle still holds true and properly gives effect to the Protocol. On the other hand the Protocol questions are merely guidelines in determining what the skilled person would think the patentee meant.[76]

76 *Kirin-Amgen Inc* v *Hoechst Marion Roussel Ltd* [2005] RPC 9, per Lord Hoffmann at para 52.

The *Catnic* principle pre-dated the European Patent Convention though it could be claimed to be prophetic of it. Article 69(1) of the Convention states that the extent of protection for a European patent or European patent application shall be determined by the claims. Nevertheless, the description and drawings shall be used to interpret the claims. The Protocol on Article 69 states:

> Article 69 should not be interpreted as meaning that the extent of the protection conferred by a European patent is to be understood as that defined by the strict, literal meaning of the wording used in the claims, the description and drawings being employed only for the purpose of resolving an ambiguity found in the claims. Nor should it be taken to mean that the claims serve only as a guideline and that the actual protection conferred may extend to what, from a consideration of the description and drawings by a person skilled in the art, the patent proprietor has contemplated. On the contrary, it is to be interpreted as defining a position between these extremes which combines a fair protection for the patent proprietor with a reasonable degree of legal certainty for third parties.[77]

77 The wording of the Protocol was slightly changed for the 2000 version of the EPC (EPC 2000), which came into force on 13 December 2007.

Section 125(3) of the Patents Act 1977 provides that the Protocol shall apply for the purpose of s 125(1), which is the equivalent to Article 69(1), requiring the extent of the protection to be determined from the claims as interpreted by the description and any drawings contained in the specification.

A purposive interpretation is not always possible, for example, where the purpose of the claims could not be ascertained objectively from the language of the claims and the drawings and description. In *Rohm and Haas Co* v *Collag Ltd*,[78] the specification of the patent in suit lacked precision in the use of words and also failed to make clear the main thrust of the inventive purpose. It identified the problem but did not appear to provide any inventive solution to it.

78 [2002] FSR 28.

The *Catnic* principle remains useful in determining the scope of the monopoly claimed and whether variants infringe and can be said to be entirely consistent with Article 69 and the Protocol. Indeed, in *Kirin-Amgen Inc* v *Hoechst Marion Roussel Ltd*,[79] Lord Hoffmann said (at para 48):

79 [2005] RPC 9.

> [t]he Catnic principle of construction is, therefore, in my opinion, precisely in accordance with the Protocol. It is intended to give the patentee the full extent, but no more than the full extent, of the monopoly which a reasonable person skilled in the art, reading the claims in context, would think he was intending to claim.

The key question in interpreting patent claims to see whether an alleged infringement falls within the claims is to consider what a person skilled in the art would think the patentee was using the language of his claim to mean.

Although the *Catnic* approach has been readily accepted under the 1977 Act,[80] it was challenged in the Court of Appeal and questioned as to whether it truly accords with s 125(1) and the Protocol.[81] In *PLG Research Ltd* v *Ardon International Ltd*,[82] in an infringement action in respect of patents for making plastic nets used in civil engineering, Neill LJ seriously doubted the relevance of the *Catnic* test to the 1977 Act, confirming that claims should be construed in accordance with the Protocol on Article 69. He said (at 133):

80 For example, in *Anchor Building Products Ltd* v *Redland Roof Tiles Ltd* [1990] RPC 283, it was held that the *Catnic* test was the same as that in the 1977 Act and the Protocol.

81 For a description of the impact of the Protocol, *see* Sherman, B. 'Patent Claim Interpretation: The Impact of the Protocol on Interpretation' (1991) 54 MLR 499.

82 [1995] FSR 116. This case is also reported at [1995] RPC 287 where the judgment is stated to have been handed down by Millett LJ.

... The expression to be construed is 'substantially uniplanar.' The word 'substantially' imports a degree of flexibility which precludes an exact and literal construction, and makes it unnecessary to consider whether Lord Diplock's purposive construction was an accurate if proleptic application of the Protocol ... [the precise meaning of Lord Diplock's words are] a matter which should now be left to legal historians.

This extreme attack on *Catnic* left patent lawyers reeling. Neill LJ suggested that if the two tests were the same, reference to *Catnic* was unnecessary; while if they were different *Catnic* should not be used in any case.[83] In *Kirin-Amgen*, Lord Hoffmann said that this echoed the famous justification said to have been given by the Caliph Omar for burning the library of Alexandria, being:

> If these writings of the Greeks agree with the Book of God, they are useless and need not be preserved: if they disagree, they are pernicious and ought to be destroyed.

The attack on *Catnic* did not last long. The comments were *obiter* and Aldous J noted this in *Assidoman Multipack Ltd* v *Mead Corp*[84] where he distinguished *PLG Research* and, after reviewing the history and background of the construction of patent claims, held that the *Catnic* test was still relevant and was entirely consistent with the Protocol.[85] Aldous J said (at 236):

> I would be loathe to discard 14 years of case law ... The middle ground referred to in the Protocol is not clearly defined and every court within the Community has adopted a method of interpretation which it believes to be consistent with the Protocol ... I have been unable to think of any better guidance [than the Catnic principle] which hopefully will result in consistent decisions between the courts of this country and those of other parties to the Convention.

Aldous (by now LJ) had the opportunity soon after to reinforce his views in the Court of Appeal in *Kastner* v *Rizla Ltd*,[86] approving the *Assidoman* decision and confirming the continuing value of the *Catnic* principle as representing the *via media* called for by the Protocol. He was soon followed by Jacob J in *Beloit Technologies Inc* v *Valmet Paper Machinery Inc*[87] and all courts from the Patents County Court through to the House of Lords (now Supreme Court) now accept that the *Catnic* principle is an appropriate means of applying the spirit of the Protocol to Article 69.

Sometimes, in construing a claim, it may be important to emphasise the essential purpose of the invention rather than to look at it with mathematical precision. In *Impro Ltd's Patent*,[88] the patent was granted for apparatus designed to facilitate the lifting of disabled patients by a single nurse where formerly two nurses would be required. The Patent Office granted a declaration of non-infringement in favour of the applicant who wished to make rival apparatus. The patentee's appeal to the Patents Court was allowed. The respondent's proposed apparatus had a lifting arm 80 per cent longer than the average human thigh bone whereas the appellant's patented apparatus was claimed in terms of lifting the patient in an arc having an 'effective radius comparable to the length of the thigh bone' of the patient.

In constructing the claims, Jacob J said that the essential purpose of the invention should be taken into account, being to emulate the way nurses lifted a patient from a sitting to a standing position. He thought that the arc through which a patient would be lifted, whilst being generally arcuate, was not a precise path. Furthermore, he considered that the word 'effective' was in the context of what was effective to raise the patient and the description of the radius being comparable to the human thigh bone would be not so much a mathematical comparison but what would be comparable for the purpose of getting the patient in a standing position.

The Impro invention was litigated in Australia in *Nesbit Evans Group Australia Pty Ltd* v *Impro Ltd*,[89] where the Federal Court followed Jacob J and also held the patent infringed (Wilcox J dissenting). The court agreed that the term 'average length of the human thigh bone' should not be calculated statistically but by reference to functional considerations.

83 For a discussion of *PLG Research* v *Ardon, see* Cole, P. 'Purposive construction and inventive step' [1995] 3 EIPR 147.

84 [1995] FSR 225.

85 Aldous J's judgment was described as masterly by Lord Hoffmann in *Kirin-Amgen Inc* v *Hoechst Marion Roussel* [2005] RPC 9 at para 46.

86 [1995] RPC 585.

87 [1995] RPC 705. *See also* the Court of Appeal decision: [1997] RPC 489. The test has also been approved by the Federal Court of Canada in *Eli Lilly & Co* v *Novopharm Ltd* [1996] RPC 1.

88 [1998] FSR 299.

89 [1998] FSR 306.

Sometimes, a patentee will use a geometric term but without intending it to have mathematical precision (as with the word 'vertical' in *Catnic*). It is, however, another thing to construe a claim so as to strike out the limitation altogether which would have been the result of counsel's argument about the meaning of cylindrical, being approximately geometrically cylindrical, in relation to a stent for an aorta. The bottom part of the stent was of a fixed diameter but the upper part ballooned out to a larger diameter.[90]

The scope of the exceptions to patentability may have a bearing on the interpretation of claims. They can only be interpreted in such a way so as not to be caught by the exclusions to patentability. So it was held in *Visx Inc v Nidek Co Ltd*,[91] where the patents in suit related to laser apparatus for changing the shape of the cornea to correct defects such as short-sightedness. Section 4(2) of the Patents Act 1977 excludes from patentability methods of treatment of the human or animal body by surgery or therapy or of diagnosis practised on the human or animal body but this is subject to s 4(3) which nonetheless allows patents for substances or compositions for use in such methods. Consequently, in interpreting the claims in the patent, they had to be considered as claims to the apparatus rather than the method of treatment.

In *Horne Engineering Co Ltd v Reliance Water Controls Ltd*,[92] Pumfrey J said that the principle of applying a purposive construction to a claim is (at 100):

> Not to extract some general principle or inventive concept from a patent specification and discard those features of the claim which are inconsistent with, or unnecessary for the implementation of that principle. It must always be assumed that claims are in the form they are for good reasons.

He quoted Hoffmann LJ in *Société Technique de Pulverisation STEP v Emson*,[93] where he said that to give a purposive construction does not mean that an integer can be treated as struck out if it does not appear to make any difference to the inventive concept.

Where a claim is ambiguous, it does not seem likely that the *contra proferentum* rule applies, especially as the method of construction is laid down by the legislation in s 125(1). Aldous LJ declined an invitation to apply the *contra proferentum* rule in *Scanvaegt International A/S v Pelcombe Ltd*.[94] He expressed doubts about the applicability of the rule, having deduced the only possible meaning of the claim in question.

In *Ancon Ltd v ACS Stainless Steel Fixings Ltd*,[95] the patent was for a channel assembly of the type used in the construction industry comprising a metal channel with lugs or restraining anchors so that the channel can be fixed in concrete. The exposed side of the channel was open and allowed the insertion of bolts which could be moved along the channel to its desired position and then turned to lock it in position against the internal walls of the channel. This allowed the fixing of brackets used to support heavy loads such as external cladding. The heads of the bolts usually had a profile that prevented them from rotating when a bracket is fixed in place. In the patent the fixing bolt was described as having a 'generally elliptical cone shape'. Apart from locking the bolt so that it did not turn when the fixing nut was tightened, its shape meant that it was forced to the inside of the channel. Jacob LJ said that the skilled person would have regard to the purpose of the bolt head, being to achieve a 'camming' action into the corners of the channel. He said (at para 17) that the skilled person would reason that:

> . . . the important aspects of the 'generally elliptical cone shape' are those parts of the bolt which co-operate with the channel in the whole assembly – the sides of the bolt not the top. The 'business' bits of the bolt are the sides. This forces his attention on the cross-sections throughout the bolt – that is what the patentee is trying to convey by his words 'generally elliptical'. And considering particularly fig.13 the skilled reader would see that the phrase has a very loose meaning – it is enough that there are what might be called 'vestiges' of a true ellipse to do the necessary camming.

90 *Medtronic Corevalve LLC v Edwards Lifesciences AG* [2010] FSR 34.

91 [1999] FSR 405.

92 [2000] FSR 90.

93 [1993] RPC 513.

94 [1998] FSR 786.

95 [2009] EWCA Civ 498.

In this case, the skilled reader would know about channels and bolt fixings and the fact that rectangular headed bolts had been used. He would also know that rounded corners had been tried to make it easier to slide the bolts along the channels to the desired position. The skilled reader would see that the bolt head was a completely novel shape and because of its shape, as it was tightened, the bolt head would be forced to the inside of the channel. Jacob LJ noted that the term 'elliptical cone shape' was a geometric nonsense. In particular, an ellipse is two-dimensional whereas a cone is three-dimensional. However, the difficulty for the draftsman of the patent was how to describe a novel shape which has not existed before and for which there was no generally accepted definition.

The Protocol questions

In *Catnic*, Lord Diplock identified the real crux of the matter as being whether practical persons, skilled in the art, would understand that strict compliance with a particular word or phrase was intended by the patentee to be an essential requirement of the invention. If so, any variant that did not comply would fall outside the claim regardless of whether it had any effect. If the variant did have a material effect, there would be no infringement. Lord Diplock went on to suggest (and apply) a structured test that has become that favoured for deciding whether variants infringe, though it has since been restated.[96]

The *Catnic* test was usefully reformulated into a three-part test by Hoffmann J, as he then was, in *Improver Corp* v *Remington Consumer Products Ltd*,[97] and is as follows.

> If the issue was whether a feature embodied in an alleged infringement which fell outside the primary, literal or acontextual meaning of a descriptive word or phrase in the claim ('a variant') was nevertheless within its language as properly interpreted, the court should ask itself the following three questions:
>
> 1 Does the variant have a material effect on the way the invention works? If yes, the variant is outside the claim (and does not infringe). If no?
> 2 Would this (i.e. that the variant had no material effect) have been obvious at the date of publication of the patent to a reader skilled in the art? If no, the variant is outside the claim. If yes?
> 3 Would the reader skilled in the art nevertheless have understood from the language of the claim that the patentee intended that strict compliance with the primary meaning was an essential requirement of the invention? If yes, the variant is outside the claim.[98]
>
> On the other hand, a negative answer to the last question would lead to the conclusion that the patentee was intending the word or phrase to have not a literal but a figurative meaning (the figure being a form of synecdoche or metonymy[99]) denoting a class of things which included the variant and the literal meaning, the latter being perhaps the most perfect, best-known or striking example of the class.

Another way of expressing the third question is whether the skilled reader would understand from the language of the claim that strict compliance with the primary meaning of the claim was intended. The *Improver* questions have been applied on numerous occasions since but, whilst referring to that case, judges now tend to refer to them as the 'Protocol questions'.[100] It has been accepted that the Protocol questions assist the court to construe a claim in accordance with the Protocol on the interpretation of Article 69 of the European Patent Convention.[101] Figure 14.2 shows a flowchart approach to the *Improver* questions.

Pumfrey J suggested a technique for construction in accordance with the Protocol questions in *Consafe Engineering (UK) Ltd* v *Emtunga UK Ltd*.[102] Speaking of a claim for accommodation structures for use on oil and gas production platforms in the North Sea, he said (at 160):

96 *See*, for example, *AC Edwards Ltd* v *Acme Signs & Displays Ltd* [1990] RPC 621, concerning apparatus for displaying prices at petrol filling station forecourts; *Southco Inc* v *Dzeus Fastener Europe Ltd* [1990] RPC 587, which involved a lift and turn latch for a cabinet door; and *Improver Corp* v *Raymond Industries Ltd* [1991] FSR 223, discussed later (*see* p. 535).

97 [1990] FSR 181 at 189.

98 In *Telsonic AG's Patent* [2004] RPC 38, Laddie J thought the third Protocol question as expressed in *Improver* was the wrong way round. He said it should be whether it would have been apparent to the skilled addressee that a limitation to exclude the variant could *not* have been intended by the patentee (original emphasis). *See* also *Merck & Co Inc* v *Generics (UK) Ltd* [2004] RPC 31.

99 For an explanation of 'synecdoche' and 'metonymy', *see* note 126 below.

100 Described as the Protocol questions by the Court of Appeal in *Wheatley (Davina)* v *Drillsafe Ltd* [2001] RPC 7.

101 *See*, for example, Aldous LJ in *Davina Wheatley* v *Drillsafe Ltd* [2001] RPC 7 at paras 23–25 and in *American Home Products Corp* v *Novartis Pharmaceuticals UK Ltd* [2001] RPC 8 at para 21.

102 [1999] RPC 154 at 160 and also in *Minnesota Mining & Manufacturing Co's (Suspension Aerosol Formulation) Patent* [1999] RPC 135 at 143.

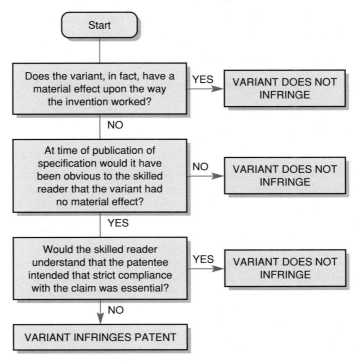

Figure 14.2 Flowchart – whether variant infringes patent

The issues which arise on construction can be satisfactorily dealt with only when the alleged infringing structure has been described. It used to be said that it was wrong to construe the claim with one eye on the alleged infringement, but it is not possible to ascertain the correct construction of the claim until a literal meaning of the claim has been arrived at, and any variants from that strict, literal meaning that are present in the alleged infringement have been identified.

There is always a danger of being unduly influenced by keeping the alleged infringement in mind when construing a claim in a patent specification. Indeed, the Protocol questions positively encourage this. It is the same sort of danger as the danger of hindsight when considering the question of anticipation. However, the first two Protocol questions are questions of fact. It is only the third question that may be influenced with knowledge of the alleged infringement and that is a matter of interpretation based on the actual words used by the patentee. The use of words such as 'substantially', as in 'substantially uni-planar', or 'vertical or nearly vertical' may catch minor variations. And, of course, there is that favourite word amongst patent agents, 'plurality', as in a 'plurality of supports'.

Where there is a range of numbers with an upper and lower limit, a departure from that range is not a variant in the *Catnic* sense. If the alleged infringement is just outside the claimed range, it does not help the proprietor to say that the departure is just a little one. So it was held in *Auchincloss* v *Agricultural & Veterinary Supplies Ltd*[103] where a patent for compositions for destroying viruses and other micro-organisms claimed ingredients within numeric ranges, for example '25 to 60 parts by weight of an oxidising agent'.[104]

A word or phrase in a claim may have a particular meaning acontextually. But it does not necessarily have the same meaning in context and the Protocol questions are particularly useful in considering the difference between the meaning out of context and in context. In *Technip France SA's Patent*,[105] Jacob LJ, at para 41, gave the example of *Catnic* itself where the word 'vertical' did not mean 'geometrically vertical' but instead meant

103 [1997] RPC 649.

104 On appeal, in *Auchincloss* v *Agricultural & Veterinary Supplies Ltd* [1999] RPC 397, the Court of Appeal allowed the claimant's appeal in part.

105 [2004] RPC 46.

'vertical enough to do the job'. However, he went on to say that to be fair to the patentee, one must use the widest purpose consistent with his teaching. Lord Hoffmann in *Kirin-Amgen Inc v Hoechst Marion Roussel Ltd*[106] thought that was to confuse the purpose of the 'utterance' with what it would be understood to mean. Lord Hoffmann said (at para 34):

> The purpose of a patent specification, as I have said, is no more nor less than to communicate the idea of an invention. An appreciation of that purpose is part of the material which one uses to ascertain the meaning. But purpose and meaning are different. If, when speaking of the widest purpose, Jacob LJ meant the widest meaning, I would respectfully disagree. There is no presumption about the width of the claims. A patent may, for one reason or another, claim less than it teaches or enables.

Nevertheless, in *Unilin Beheer NV v Berry Floor NV*,[107] Jacob LJ approached the phrase 'free from play' in a similar manner. The patent was for a flooring system made of panels of, typically, MDF (medium density fibreboard) which snap-fitted together. He said that, taking account of what would be apparent to the skilled person reading the claims and specification, the phrase meant 'free of play for practical purposes' and a little bit of play which did not matter in practice was not excluded by the claim.

In *Kirin-Amgen Inc v Hoechst Marion Roussel Ltd*,[108] Lord Hoffmann stressed that it was important to distinguish between the Protocol itself and the Protocol questions. The former is the bedrock of patent construction whilst the latter are only guidelines which may be more useful in some cases rather than others. In a case involving a patent for chemical compounds, the Court of Appeal held that the Protocol questions were not appropriate and there was no alternative but to seek the middle way as stated by the Protocol by considering the effect on the patentee and the public by reading a claim as covering a particular compound not specifically mentioned.[109]

Where the variant is not just a departure from a descriptive word in a claim, but represents the omission of whole features of the claim, the Protocol questions may have no application. In *Palmaz's European Patents (UK)*,[110] an action for a declaration of non-infringement of two patents for stents, Pumfrey J stressed that the construction of a claim, in accordance with the Protocol, must be so as to give reasonable protection for the patentee and a reasonable degree of certainty for third parties. In finding that the patents, if valid, were not infringed, Pumfrey J considered that no construction of the amended claim in suit which brought the applicant's variant within that claim could satisfy the requirement of a reasonable degree of certainty for third parties.[111]

The purposive approach to claim construction under Article 69 and the Protocol and the Protocol questions has become the basic method of determining whether variants infringe. This can be criticised because it can lead to uncertainty. If a strict literal approach were to be adopted then a potential competitor wishing to make a non-infringing variant should be able to determine just how far he can go without infringing. It would also encourage persons drafting patent claims to use greater precision which would further reduce uncertainty, or to use appropriate language such as 'generally cylindrical'.[112] Some sense of realism is called for, however, and it would be unreasonable to expect patentees to write their claims with complete precision and lacking any ambiguity in the monopoly that was being claimed. This is particularly so in complex technologies where the language to describe new inventions has not been fully developed. The Protocol and the Protocol questions attempt to strike a reasonable balance between protection for the patentee and certainty for third parties.

A doctrine of equivalents?

Sometimes the alleged infringement may contain mechanical equivalents, an alternative that works equivalently. A mechanical equivalent may be more than a mere variant as

106 [2005] RPC 9.

107 [2005] FSR 6.

108 [2005] RPC 9.

109 *Pharmacia Corp v Merck & Co Inc* [2002] RPC 41.

110 [1999] RPC 47.

111 He revoked both patents on the basis that the first patent was anticipated and obvious even if amended and that the second patent was obvious.

112 *Conoco Speciality Products (Inc) v Merpro Montassa Ltd* [1994] FSR 99.

in the *Catnic* case. In appropriate cases, it may then be a matter of applying the Protocol questions to determine whether the equivalent lies within the claims. In some cases, however, the equivalent may be further away from the invention as claimed though it may bring about the same technical effect. The doctrine of equivalents applies where there is no literal infringement, but there is equivalence between elements of the alleged infringing product or process and the claimed elements of the invention.[113] Whether the doctrine is fully within the Protocol to Article 69 of the European Patent Convention or goes beyond it is difficult to tell. If fully within the Protocol it is a danger-ous gloss upon it but if it goes further it is surely contrary to the Convention as it presently stands.[114] The existence of a general doctrine of equivalents in UK patent law has been doubted on a number of occasions, especially by Jacob LJ, a very experienced patent judge.[115]

The Court of Appeal in Hong Kong had to deal with a mechanical equivalent in *Improver Corp v Raymond Industries Ltd*.[116] The claimant's patent was for a device, called the 'Epilady', for removing hair from arms and legs. The defendant imported and distributed a device which performed the same function and was called 'Smooth & Silky'.[117] It was held, applying the *Catnic* test, that the first and second questions are questions of fact and the answers to them are not conclusive to the third question, which was one of construc-tion. Even a purposive construction might produce the conclusion that the patentee was confining his claim to the primary meaning and excluding the variant, even though the variant might make no material difference – and this would have been obvious at the time. On the evidence, there was no material difference – both devices trapped and plucked hair from the skin, and it was obvious that both worked in the same way. The answer to the first two questions in the flowchart (Figure 14.2) were therefore 'no' and 'yes' respectively, and the third question fell to be determined. It was held that it was important to look at all the essential integers in the patent specification and claim to see if all those essential integers were present in the alleged infringement.[118] The alleged infringing device could perform the same task as long as it did so differently as regards at least one essential integer, and this is so even if the difference had no material effect upon the way the invention worked.

The specification and relevant claim, therefore, must be construed to determine what the essential integers are and comparing these to the alleged infringing product or pro-cess. In the above case, the specification and claim referred to a helical spring that was rotated to pluck out hairs. It was held that this was an essential integer, and the fact the defendant used an elastomeric (rubber) rod instead (even though this had no material effect on how the invention worked) indicated that the defendant's device did not infringe the patent. The skilled man, reading the patent specification and claim, would have considered that the patentee had not intended to include such a variant. As the helical spring was rotated, its windings opened and closed up trapping and plucking out hairs. The defendant's device did the same thing but by using a rubber rod with slits in it. In a claim in the Patents Court involving the same devices, Hoffmann J applied the *Catnic* test and his answers were 'no', 'yes' and 'yes', and therefore, in his opinion, the 'Smooth & Silky' hair remover did not infringe.[119]

The 'Epilady' case is also interesting because it shows differences of approach to infringement and the effect of the Protocol on the interpretation of Article 69. In Germany, in a parallel action involving the same parties and patent, it was held, eventu-ally, that the defendant's rubber rod with slits in it infringed the 'Epilady' patent.[120] Jacob suggested that there is an approach to infringement in Germany whereby a mechanical equivalent that is obvious will infringe even though the integer it replaces is an essential one.[121] However, Lord Hoffmann in *Kirin-Amgen Inc v Hoechst Marion Roussel*[122] noted that the courts in Germany have moved closer to the Protocol questions and have even stated that the approach there is now similar to *Catnic*.[123]

113 *Graver Tank & Mfg Co v Linde Air Products Co* 339 US 605 (1950).

114 Express mention of equivalents is made in an addition to the Protocol to Article 69 in a new version of the Convention, yet to come into effect: *see* below.

115 *Mayne Pharma Pty Ltd v Pharmacia Italia SpA* [2005] EWCA Civ 137. At para 5, Jacob LJ set out a useful summary of the law on construction of claims as approved by the House of Lords in *Kirin-Amgen Inc v Hoechst Marion Roussel* [2005] RPC 9.

116 [1991] FSR 223.

117 The case was decided under the Patents Act 1977, which was then in force in Hong Kong.

118 The word 'integer' is used to describe an element of an invention, assuming that it can be broken down into elements. The number of integers can be increased by adding to the claims by use of alternatives. For example, 'an offset eccentrically mounted widget which is attached to the mounting by magnetic means (claim 1) and a widget as in claim 1 which is attached to its mounting by plastic friction clips (claim 2)'.

119 *Improver Corp v Remington Consumer Products Ltd* [1990] FSR 181.

120 [1991] RPC 597.

121 Jacob, R. 'The Herchel Smith Lecture 1993' [1993] 9 EIPR 312 at 313. According to Jacob J in *Beloit Technologies Inc v Valmet Paper Machinery Inc* [1995] RPC 705, the Epilady cases make 'an excellent discussion basis for law students'.

122 [2005] RPC 9 at para 75.

123 *Kunstoffrohrteil* [2002] GRUR 511 and *Scheidemesser I* [2003] ENPR 12 309.

The law on infringement by equivalents is not settled. It is even debatable whether there is a distinct doctrine of equivalents. Article 69 and the Protocol should provide the only means of construing patent claims. However, the 13th edition of the European Patent Convention, which came into force on 13 December 2007, includes a second Article to the Protocol on Article 69 which states:

> For the purpose of determining the extent of protection conferred by a European patent, due account shall be taken of any element which is equivalent to an element specified in the claims.

The doctrine of equivalents will be firmly back on the agenda though, like the 'pith and marrow' approach, the doctrine of equivalents in the US was described by Lord Hoffmann as being born of despair.[124] The US Supreme Court, in *Festo Corp v Shoketsu Kogyo Kabushiki Co Ltd*,[125] held that, by amending a claim, a patentee did not necessarily abandon any claim to equivalents. Kennedy J, giving the judgment of the court, said (at para 15):

> It is true that the doctrine of equivalents renders the scope of patents less certain. It may be difficult to determine what is, or is not, an equivalent to a particular element of an invention. If competitors cannot be certain about a patent's extent, they may be deterred from engaging in legitimate manufactures outside its limits, or they may invest by mistake in competing products that the patent secures. In addition the uncertainty may lead to wasteful litigation between competitors, suits that a rule of literalism might avoid . . . Each time the Court has considered the doctrine, it has acknowledged this uncertainty is the price of ensuring the appropriate incentives for innovation, and it has affirmed the doctrine over dissents that urged a more certain rule.

The balance between fair protection and a reasonable degree of certainty is difficult to achieve consistently and is often a matter of deciding where to draw the line. It would be unfair to a patentee if others were to escape infringement by making minor changes,[126] yet the need for certainty is also important. Diligent companies embarking on the manufacture of some new product or installing a new industrial process will usually consult the prior art, especially patent specifications, and it is important that they can determine with some confidence whether or not their planned activities will infringe someone else's patent rights. At the end of the day, it may simply be a matter of deciding what the skilled reader would think the patentee had intended to claim from the language with which he had expressed himself, taking account of the drawings and description.

In the light of the above, it is suggested that the following tests should be used:

1 Where the critical aspect of the alleged infringement is a minor variant, that is, it does the same thing in the same way (as in the *Catnic* case), it should not escape an infringement action merely because of an inappropriately narrow or restrictive choice of words.
2 Where the aspect of the alleged infringement under consideration is a mechanical equivalent, that is it performs the same function but by different means (as in the *Improver* case) then the issue is whether, interpreting the last *Catnic* question, the patentee intended strict compliance with the primary meaning of the language of the claim or whether he used the word or phrase under consideration as having a figurative meaning, denoting a class of things which include the variant and the literal meaning, the latter being perhaps the most perfect or best-known example of the class.[127]

The application of the purposive approach may operate harshly on a defendant, because in an interim hearing it is likely to be used even more generously. The slightest hint of infringement might be sufficient to convince a judge that there is a serious issue to be tried. In *Beecham Group plc v J & W Sanderson Ltd*, Aldous J said:

124 *Kirin-Amgen Inc v Hoechst Marion Roussel Ltd* [2005] RPC 9 at para 41.

125 535 US 722 (2002).

126 The doctrine of equivalents appears to have its origin in *Winans v Denmead* 56 US 330 (1856) per Curtis J who said (at 343), 'The exclusive right to the thing patented is not secured, if the public are at liberty to make substantial copies of it, varying its form or proportions.' The patent was for a conical-shaped car for carrying coal whilst the defendant's was an octagonal shape.

127 *Improver Corp v Remington Consumer Products Ltd* [1990] FSR 181 per Hoffmann J. He described the figure in the figurative meaning being a form of synecdoche (where a part is made to represent the whole) or metonymy (substitution of the name of an attribute or adjunct for that of the thing meant).

Patent claims are difficult to construe after a trial, and are even more difficult on motion without proper education as to the background and the technical effect of differences. This case is no exception, and I conclude that there is a serious issue to be tried as to whether the defendant's toothbrushes infringe claim 1.[128]

128 (Unreported) 18 June 1993.

Could it be that claimants are given the benefit of doubt because of the purposive approach? This particular case concerned a patent for a toothbrush having a flexible handle by virtue of 'V-shaped' folds transverse to the handle. The defendant's toothbrush achieved flexibility by means of a helical spring or auger construction, having coils connected to a central core. However, although Aldous J decided there was a serious issue to be tried, he refused an injunction after consideration of the balance of convenience, although he did order the defendant to pay 15 pence into a joint bank account for each toothbrush it sold.

If the mechanical equivalent lacks one or more of the important advantages of the patented product, that fact is suggestive that there is no infringement. In *Consafe Engineering (UK) Ltd v Emtunga UK Ltd*,[129] the patent was a moveable structure used for accommodation on oil and gas platforms in the North Sea. It had two important advantages lacking in the alleged infringement, namely, a uniform modular structure and the ability to be lifted safely without a substantial base-frame. However, Pumfrey J held that the patent was invalid because of obviousness and, had it been valid, it would not have been infringed by the defendant's structures.

129 [1999] RPC 154.

Where a variant has differences that are cosmetic and which have no effect on how the invention works, it is likely to be regarded as within the patent claims unless there was a good reason why the patentee had chosen to restrict himself to the precise literal meaning of the words he had used. In *Dyson Appliances Ltd v Hoover Ltd*,[130] claim 1 of the famous Dyson bagless vacuum cleaner described the cyclone as having a frusto-conical[131] part tapered away from its entry. The defendant alleged, *inter alia*, that there was no infringement as the equivalent part of its bagless vacuum cleaner was of a trumpet shape. In finding the patent valid and infringed, Michael Fysh QC, sitting as deputy judge of the High Court in the Patents Court, said that the skilled reader would still regard the shape as frusto-conical even though there were slight differences in the top and bottom angles from a true geometric frusto-conical shape. Furthermore, even if it was accepted that the trumpet shape was a variant, it had no effect on how the invention worked in practice and there was no reason why the patentee would have considered that strict compliance with the geometric meaning of frusto-conical was required. The Court of Appeal confirmed the decision in the Patents Court.[132]

130 [2001] RPC 26.

131 Frusto-conical means a cone with the top cut off in a plane parallel to the base of the cone.

132 *Dyson Appliances Ltd v Hoover Ltd* [2002] RPC 22.

Declaration of non-infringement

Section 71 of the Patents Act 1977 provides for applications to be made to the court or Comptroller for a declaration of non-infringement, without prejudice to the court's jurisdiction to make such a declaration otherwise, in the absence of any allegation of infringement made by the proprietor if the applicant has made a request in writing asking for a written acknowledgement for such declaration and has furnished full particulars in writing of the act in question and the proprietor has refused or failed to give any such declaration. Of course, the burden of proof lies on the applicant to show that the act or acts in question do not infringe the patent.

133 [2004] FSR 20.

In *Niche Generics Ltd v Lundbeck A/S*,[133] the claimant wrote to the defendant seeking an acknowledgement that a pharmaceutical product made in India on behalf of the claimant did not infringe the defendant's patent. When no acknowledgement was received, the claimant brought proceedings for a declaration of non-infringement but, just before, made an offer to allow the defendant to inspect the process in India to be attended also by the claimant's experts. Later, the defendant accepted that a declaration could be made in substantially the form sought but objected to paying the costs of the claimant's experts resulting from the inspection. Pumfrey J held that the defendant should pay the claimant's costs associated with the inspection.

The court has a general jurisdiction to grant declarations of non-infringement and it is not uncommon for an application for a declaration to be made at the same time as an application for revocation. In considering whether to grant a declaration of non-infringement, a court will often be faced with applying the Protocol questions to determine the scope of the monopoly claimed and whether the applicant's acts or proposed acts fall within it. In the United States, it is usual practice to use documentation in the US Patent and Trademark Office file as an aid to construing the claims of a patent. The proprietor will be estopped from denying any statement or concession made therein. This is known as 'file wrapper estoppel'.[134] In *Telsonic AG's Patent*,[135] it was held that the prosecution history of a patent should not be used to construe a patent and its claims as these were statements made by the patentee to the relevant public and their meaning and effect should be plain from the face of the published patent.

134 The Patents Court and Court of Appeal had to apply file wrapper estoppel in *Celltech (Adair's) US Patent* [2004] FSR 3. This case concerned a licence for a US patent subject to English law and the jurisdiction of the English courts.

135 [2004] RPC 38.

Evidence

Of course, in a patent infringement action, the claimant carries the burden of proof.[136] He has to adduce evidence of the infringement and convince the court, on a balance of probabilities, that the defendant has infringed his patent. However, and in exceptional cases, a judge may come to a conclusion that he just does not know on which side of the line the decision ought to be (in which case, the claimant has failed to discharge his legal burden of proof). In *Morris* v *London Iron & Steel Co*[137] May LJ accepted that this could happen. He said (at 501):

> In the exceptional case, however, a judge conscientiously seeking to decide the matter before him may be forced to say, 'I just do not know'; indeed to say anything else might be in breach of his judicial duty.

136 In a declaration for non-infringement, the burden of proof was on the defendant to prove non-infringement: *Rohm & Haas Co* v *Collag Ltd* [2002] FSR 28.

137 [1987] 2 All ER 496.

Such indecision might be caused by a real and irreconcilable conflict between rival scientific theories. It does not, however, allow the claimant the opportunity to adduce fresh evidence in the hope of tipping the balance in his favour. Under rule 52.11(2) of the Civil Procedure Rules 1998, an appeal court will not receive fresh evidence unless it orders otherwise. Previously, fresh evidence would be admitted only if special grounds existed and the courts used a three-part test set out by Denning LJ in *Ladd* v *Marshall*.[138] All three parts had to be satisfied. They were:

138 [1954] 1 WLR 1489.

1. if it is shown that the evidence could not have been obtained with reasonable diligence for use at the trial;
2. if the further evidence is such that, if given, it would probably have an important influence on the result of the case, though it need not be decisive; and
3. if the evidence is such as presumably to be believed in.

Ladd v *Marshall* remains a powerful persuasive authority and the principles are still very helpful in determining whether fresh evidence ought to be admitted. As Christopher Floyd QC, sitting as deputy judge of the High Court, said in *Stanelco Fibre Optics Ltd* v *Bioprogress Technology Ltd*[139] (at para 8):

139 [2005] RPC 16.

> The three conditions in *Ladd* v *Marshall* no longer have effect as binding precedent, but are relevant principles for the court to consider in the exercise of the discretion: see the passage

from the judgment of *Morritt LJ in Banks v Cox* cited in *Hertfordshire Investments v Bubb* [2000] 1 WLR 2318 at 2325. As Hale LJ went on to say in that case, the *Ladd v Marshall* criteria should still be 'looked at with considerable care'. It will therefore still be a very exceptional case in which an applicant who fails on one or more of the *Ladd v Marshall* criteria succeeds on an application to adduce further evidence.

In that case, the application to adduce further evidence was refused as the evidence in question could probably have been found by exercising due diligence and, furthermore, it was not certain that it would have been adduced had it been found.

140 [1995] RPC 449.

In *Imperial Chemical Industries v Montedison (UK) Ltd*,[140] the claimant failed to meet condition 1. Stuart-Smith LJ said (at 468):

> It is incumbent upon a party to adduce such evidence as he considers relevant and persuasive relating to the findings of fact which the judge may make. He cannot wait for the findings and then say 'Oh well, I could have called more evidence on that point.'

There is no exception to the rule in *Ladd v Marshall* should the judge fail to find the burden of proof discharged. The trial judge failed to make a positive finding in the *ICI* case and considered that he did not have to decide between the conflicting theories. Essentially, what he was saying was that the case was not proved to his satisfaction beyond the balance of probability.

There is no duty to keep records of non-infringement although presumptions may be drawn from the fact that a defendant had deliberately destroyed relevant records or, in particular circumstances, failed to keep records. In *Hoechst Celanese Corp v BP Chemicals Ltd*,[141] it was argued that, once some infringement had been found, the onus was on the defendant to prove non-infringement on other occasions.[142] This was rejected by Jacob J, referring to Russell LJ in *General Tire & Rubber Co v Firestone Tyre & Rubber Co Ltd*,[143] where he said (at 267) that the doctrine of *omnia praesumuntur contra spoliatorem*[144] as found in *Armory v Delamirie*[145] might be relevant in determining damages but not to prove the wrongful act itself. In *Hoechst*, Jacob J said that there was no suggestion that records had been destroyed or that *BP* had been guilty of any dishonesty or sharp practice or had turned a blind eye to what was going on.

141 [1998] FSR 586.

142 The defendant's process was proved to infringe the patent on some days only.

143 [1975] RPC 203.

144 All things are presumed against a wrongdoer.

145 (1722) 1 Stra 504. In that case the defendant, a goldsmith, was found to have converted a jewel from a ring brought into his shop by a chimney sweep who had found it. The judge directed the jury that, unless the defendant produced the jewel and showed it not to be of the finest water, they should presume the strongest against him and adopt the value of the best jewels as the measure of damages.

146 [2001] FSR 28. In the Court of Appeal, it was accepted that the court could use clarifying information in the public file relating to a patent only when, after considering the description and drawings, it was of the view that the interpretation of the claims was still open to question: *Rohm and Haas Co v Collag Ltd* [2002] FSR 28.

147 Per Lewison J in *Ultraframe (UK) Ltd v Eurocell Building Plastics Ltd* [2005] RPC 7.

148 [2005] FSR 23 at para 78.

Where a word in a claim has a technical meaning, expert evidence is admissible, of course. However, where a court is faced with conflicting evidence from two apparently credible expert witnesses, the court has the additional problem in resolving that conflict as well as resolving the centrally relevant issue, being the meaning of the word in question in the context of the document in which it is found: *Rohm & Haas Co v Collag Ltd*.[146]

It is very common to call experts to give evidence in patent cases, for example, to give evidence concerning obviousness. Expert evidence may also be important in interpreting the claims and applying the Protocol questions. For the purpose of donning the mantle of the person skilled in the art, expert evidence is not only helpful, but often essential.[147] Carrying out experiments is common in patent litigation involving claims to chemical or pharmaceutical compounds. Both sides often appoint experts. Jacob LJ thought that there was a danger of 'litigation chemistry' with experiments becoming contrived to achieve the desired result. He said it would be better if experts carrying out experiments were just given the unembellished disclosure to work from and, in *SmithKline Beecham plc v Apotex Europe Ltd*,[148] he went so far as to suggest that it would be better, in order to prove that a skilled person carrying out a recipe using his ordinary skills would be able to work the invention, simply to ask him to try. The court could appoint a single joint expert to carry out the experiments, though Jacob LJ did note that lawyers do not like that sort of approach as they lose control and fear that the expert might fail.

As to the role of expert witnesses, in *SmithKline Beecham v Apotex*, Jacob LJ said (at paras 51 and 52):

Before I go further, however, it is as well to remember what the key function of an expert witness in a patent action is – as I said in Rockwater[149] (para. 12):

> Their primary function is to educate the court in the technology – they come as teachers, as makers of the mantle [i.e. of the person skilled in the art] for the court to don. For that purpose it does not matter whether they do or do not approximate to the skilled man. What matters is how good they are at explaining things.

To that I would add this: although it is inevitable that when an expert is asked what he would understand from a prior document's teaching he will give an answer as an individual, that answer is not as such all that helpful. What matters is what the notional skilled man would understand from the document. So it is not so much the expert's personal view but his reasons for that view – these the court can examine against the standard of the notional unimaginative skilled man.

Bearing these sentiments in mind, Mr Peter Prescott QC, sitting as a Deputy Judge of the High Court in *Corevale Inc* v *Edwards Lifesciences AG*,[150] allowed for the fact that one expert witness was 'an enthusiast by temperament, very alive to the latest innovations' and the other expert witness had been '"on the road" for a long time now, having given evidence in many patent cases'.

There is a danger of repetitious evidence and calling too many expert witnesses who essentially say the same thing. The court does not decide a case by counting how many experts each party can get to say the same thing.[151] Of course, expert evidence is unnecessary to construe the meaning of words not having a technical meaning. In such cases, the construction of a claim containing non-technical words was a matter for the court. In *British Celanese Ltd* v *Courtaulds Ltd*,[152] Lord Tomlin said of expert witnesses (at 195):

> He [the expert witness] is entitled to give evidence as to the state of the art at any given time. He is entitled to explain the meaning of any technical terms used in the art. He is entitled to say whether in his opinion that which is described in the specification on a given hypothesis as to its meaning is capable of being carried into effect by a skilled worker. He is entitled to say what at a given time to him as skilled in the art a given piece of apparatus or a given sentence on any given hypothesis as to its meaning would have taught or suggested to him. He is entitled to say whether in his opinion a particular operation in connection with the art could be carried out and generally to give any explanation required as to facts of a scientific kind. He is not entitled to say nor is Counsel entitled to ask him what the specification means, nor does the question become any more admissible if it takes the form of asking him what it means to him as an engineer or as a chemist. Nor is he entitled to say whether any given step or alteration is obvious, that being a question for the Court.

Aldous LJ said that the above is particularly applicable where the evidence is contained in a witness statement and any inadmissible evidence included may be taken into account when deciding who should pay costs.[153]

Title to sue for infringement

The proprietor or exclusive licensee has title to sue for infringement of a patent. However, if the relevant interest has not been registered under s 32 the owner of the interest will not be entitled to costs or expenses in respect of infringements occurring before registration, unless registration takes place within six months: s 68.[154] The court (or Comptroller) has discretion to extend that period if satisfied that the interest was registered as soon as possible after, provided it was not practicable to register sooner. Under s 33, later transactions, instruments or events which are registered are not prejudiced by earlier unregistered transactions, providing the person having the property or other right in or under the patent was not aware of the earlier transaction.

---

149 *Rockwater Ltd* v *Technip France SA* [2004] RPC 46.

150 [2009] FSR 8.

151 *Hoechst Celanese Corp* v *BP Chemicals Ltd* [1998] FSR 586 at 590 per Jacob J.

152 (1935) 52 RPC 171.

153 *Scanvaegt International A/S* v *Pelcombe Ltd* [1998] FSR 786 at 796.

154 Until amendment by the Intellectual Property (Enforcement, etc.) Regulations 2006, SI 2006/1028, s 68 operated to deprive the proprietor or exclusive licensee of damages or an account of profits.

155 [1993] FSR 162.

If a party to proceedings is found not to have title to sue he will be struck from the action, as in *Bondax Carpets Ltd* v *Advance Carpet Tiles*[155] where the third claimant was struck from the action. His contract with the second claimant had nothing to do with the rights under the patent.

Where a registered proprietor is entitled to a patent by way of assignment including an assignment of the right to sue for past infringement, he may not be able to sue for past infringements which took place at a time when the then proprietor was not registered as such. This could happen where there is a series of assignments which had not been entered on the register. In *LG Electronics Inc* v *NCR Financial Solutions Group Ltd*,[156] the present assignee and claimant derived its title to the patent through a series of assignments, none of which had been registered. It was held that the claimant was not entitled to damages for the periods of infringement when the patent was owned by its unregistered predecessors in title.

156 [2003] FSR 24.

One or more joint proprietors of a patent may bring an action for infringement without the concurrence of the others, but they must be made parties to the proceedings.[157] The infringing acts are to be construed in the context of one or more joint proprietors of the patent subject to s 36. This means that the consent of the proprietor referred to in s 60 will usually require the consent of each and every one of the proprietors of the patent. Under s 67, the exclusive licensee of a patent has the same rights as the proprietor to bring an action for infringement committed after the date of the licence. In any action by an exclusive licensee, the proprietor shall be made a party to the proceedings.

157 Patents Act 1977 s 66(2).

Remedies

For general material on remedies and the impact of the Intellectual Property (Enforcement, etc.) Regulations 2006, *see* Chapter 24. This part of the chapter focuses primarily on remedies in relation to patent infringement.

The remedies available for infringement of a patent are an injunction,[158] damages, an account of profits, an order for delivery up[159] or destruction and a declaration that the patent is valid and has been infringed by the defendant.[160] However, damages and an account of profits are alternatives and may not, by s 61(2), both be awarded or ordered in respect of the same infringement. The question of infringement may be referred to the Comptroller if both parties (the proprietor and any other person who has allegedly infringed the patent) are willing, in which case remedies are limited to damages and/or a declaration.[161] Assessment of damages is discussed later.

The remedies in the Patents Act 1977 are not necessarily exhaustive as s 61(1) states that the remedies stated in that subsection are without prejudice to any other jurisdiction of the court. One issue is whether the courts can impose post-expiry injunctions, sometimes known in this context as 'springboard relief'. In *Crossley* v *Derby Gas Light Co*,[162] the Lord Chancellor accepted that the court could grant an injunction to prevent a person selling, after expiry of a patent, an article made during the subsistence of the patent.[163] This possibility has been confirmed under the 1977 Act in *Dyson Appliances Ltd* v *Hoover Ltd (No 2)*.[164] It had been shown that the defendant had infringed the claimant's patent in respect of its bagless vacuum cleaner. The patent was due to expire within one year of the date of the judgment and the defendant had a large quantity of its infringing vacuum cleaners in stock. The defendant had not offered an undertaking not to resume sales immediately after expiry of the patent and the claimant sought two post-expiry injunctions. The first post-expiry injunction was granted. Michael Fysh QC, sitting as deputy judge of the High Court in the Patents Court, accepted that s 61 was not exhaustive as to remedies. He concluded that s 37 of the Senior Courts Act 1981 gave the court the

158 Interdict in Scotland.

159 Section 61(1)(b) provides that a court can order delivery up not just of any patented product but also any article in which it is inextricably comprised: in *Kirin-Amgen Inc* v *Transkaryotic Therapies Inc (No 3)* [2005] FSR 41, cells containing very small quantities of a protein covered by the claimant's patent.

160 Patents Act 1977 s 61.

161 Patents Act 1977 s 61(3). Any award made by the Comptroller can be enforced by court order, decree arbitral (in Scotland) or money judgment in Northern Ireland: s 61(7), inserted by the Patents Act 2004.

162 (1834) 4 LT Ch 25.

163 The European Court of Justice upheld a decision of a Dutch court to impose a temporary injunction of 14 months after expiry of a patent. This period was the average time taken to obtain marketing approval. A third party had applied for authorisation and included a sample of the patented drug before the patent had expired: Case C-316/95 *Generics BV* v *Smith Kline & French Laboratories Ltd* [1997] ECR I-3929.

164 [2001] RPC 27.

jurisdiction (probably in addition to any inherent equitable jurisdiction) to make, *inter alia*, post-expiry injunctions.[165] The development of the defendant's vacuum cleaner up to the time of the expiry of the patent put it at an advantage in time over its competitors. The judge thought that, as Dyson would probably be able to recover secondary damages by reasons of the antecedent infringement, it was right to 'handicap' Hoover for a further 12 months to put Dyson in the position it would have been in had its patent rights been respected.[166]

In *Kirin-Amgen Inc v Transkaryotic Therapies Inc (No 2)*,[167] it was held that the claimant could pursue a claim for springboard relief as it was thought that the claimant may not be able to claim damages for the post-expiry period and would be left without a remedy. However, there was still over three years for the patent to run whereas, in *Dyson*, expiry was imminent. Although Neuberger J allowed the claimant to pursue its claim for springboard relief, on the facts it seemed unlikely that it would be successful.

Even though post-expiry injunctions may be available in appropriate circumstances, there are, however, limits to what other remedies are available and, in *Union Carbide Corp v BP Chemicals Ltd*,[168] it was held that the law of restitution did not apply so as to give a cause of action of unjust enrichment.

The purpose of an account of profits is not to punish the defendant but to prevent his unjust enrichment. An account is limited to the profits actually made and attributable to the infringement and the claimant must take the defendant's business as it is.[169] The fact that the defendant could have made more profit if he had been more efficient is of no consequence. Accounts are rarely asked for in patent cases because of the complexity in quantifying them though, in principle, they are available during the period between publication and grant, as are damages.[170] This is so even though s 69, which provides for an award of damages for the period between publication and grant, does not mention an account of profits.

Some of the principles applicable to an account of profits were set out by Laddie J in *Celanese International Corp v BP Chemicals Ltd*[171] as follows (at 220ff):

- Although an account of profits may produce a figure very different to an assessment of damages, both proceeded on the basis of legal causation.
- Where the defendant carries on several businesses or sells different products and only one infringes, he has to account only for the profits made by the infringements.
- There can be no reduction if the defendant could have made some of the profits by non-infringing means if he actually used infringing means.
- The claimant must take the defendant as he finds him and the claimant cannot ask for an increase in the amount awarded on the basis that the defendant should have generated higher profits.
- Where only part of a product infringes, the claimant is entitled only to the profit earned by virtue of the use of his invention.
- An apportionment approach is suitable where, for example, there are three stages to making a product, each of which is protected by a patent. The total profit has to be divided between the three stages.[172]
- The court should not engage in a substantial rounding up as a way of making the defendant pay punitive damages and, if insufficient information was available, it was not justifiable to pluck a figure out of the air that bore little relationship to any of the relevant facts.
- Accounting principles afforded a useful guide and it was reasonable to assume, unless there was some special reason otherwise, that the profits made on different stages of a project were in proportion to the costs and expenses attributable to those proportions.
- Acceptable deductions from the total figure were allowable costs, costs of research and development (unless there was a massive imbalance), financing costs, taxes paid.[173]

165 Section 37 of the Senior Courts Act 1981 (previously known as the Supreme Court Act 1981) allows the High Court to grant an injunction (whether interim or final) in cases in which it appears just and convenient to do so.

166 It could be argued that, if secondary damages were recoverable, an injunction was unnecessary, providing those damages could be assessed.

167 [2002] RPC 3.

168 [1998] FSR 1.

169 *Potton Ltd v Yorkclose Ltd* [1994] FSR 567.

170 *Spring Form Inc v Toy Brokers Ltd* [2002] FSR 17.

171 [1999] RPC 203.

172 Laddie J distinguished *Peter Pan Manufacturing Corp v Corsets Silhouette Ltd* [1963] RPC 45, where no apportionment was appropriate as the brassieres made by the defendant could not have been made at all without the use of confidential information.

173 The defendant would also have to account for a subsequent tax credit on any overpayment of tax.

After taking these and other factors into account, Laddie J awarded £567,840 to the claimant. The total gross profit attributable to the process for manufacturing acetic acid using a process, part of which was attributable to the claimant's patented process, was £94.64 million. However, only 0.6 per cent of the entire process was attributable to the claimant's process.[174]

In *Spring Form Inc v Toy Brokers Ltd*,[175] the claimants were the proprietors of a patent for tent-like structures and its exclusive licensee. Two of the defendants, Toy Brokers and its controlling mind, submitted to an order for an account of profits. The claimants then considered electing for an account against the remaining defendants, Worlds Apart Ltd, Argos Ltd and Woolworths plc. The tents had been sold with merchandising embellishments (Teletubbies, Barbie, Winnie the Pooh and Thomas the Tank Engine). Pumfrey J thought that it might be appropriate to take into account the licence fees in respect of the merchandising and an apportionment of net profit resulting from the use of the merchandising, though he expressed no concluded view on this. For part of the period of infringement, the second claimant's exclusive licence, having replaced an earlier registered exclusive licence, had not been registered for nearly two years. During the period of disablement from damages or an account of profits under s 68, only the first claimant was entitled to recover.[176] Both could recover for the period from registration of the first licence up to the date the second licence was entered into and for the period after registration of the second licence. Pumfrey J also confirmed that where there are two claimants – the proprietor and exclusive licensee – both have to make the same election as to damages or an account.

Pumfrey J also had to consider the case where a claimant makes a claim against an infringer, D1, who sells infringing products to D2 who also makes a profit by selling the products or using them. This could be important because, in most cases, D1 will have to indemnify D2 in respect of any claims made by the claimant. If the claimant elects to take damages, the total exposure of a defendant to indemnify the other defendants is limited to the claimant's damage. However, if he elects to take an account of profits D1 could end up losing more than his own profit. Pumfrey J said that where there was a chain of defendants, a claimant electing an account of profits should undertake not to make a claim in respect of infringing articles against any other defendant. Otherwise, the account would become 'hopelessly complicated'.

'Innocent' infringers may escape some of the remedies. Under s 62(1), neither damages nor an account of profits is available if the defendant can prove that, at the time of the infringement, he was not aware and had no reasonable grounds for supposing that the patent existed, the latter being a form of constructive notice. The application of the word 'patent' or 'patented' or words expressing or implying that a patent has been obtained for the product does not necessarily fix the defendant with notice unless accompanied by the number of the patent or application. It would, however, be difficult for a defendant to prove to the court that he did not know of the existence of the patent if he copied a product to which the word 'Patented' was applied. The burden of proof in this matter lies with the defendant.

Under s 25(4) there is, in effect, a period of six months' grace following the period for payment of a renewal fee for a patent but, by s 62(2), in respect of any infringement done during this period, the court or the Comptroller has a discretion as to whether to award damages or make an order for damages. Another provision relates to the situation where the infringement occurred before an amendment to the specification was allowed. In this case, the court or the Comptroller, when awarding damages or making an order for an account of profits must take into account:

(a) whether at the date of infringement the defendant knew or had reasonable grounds to know he was infringing the patent;

---

174 The claimant originally claimed £180 million including interest. The defendant had made a loss of £89.1 million on the other of the two alleged infringing processes. The total award was less than that calculated by the defendant but his figure was disregarded as it had been arrived at on a flawed basis.

175 [2002] FSR 17.

176 Now, s 68 only operates to deprive a proprietor or exclusive licensee of costs or, in Scotland, expenses.

(b) whether the specification as published was framed in good faith and with reasonable skill and knowledge;

(c) whether the proceedings were brought in good faith.[177]

In either case, there is no restriction on a court granting an injunction even if no damages are awarded.[178] It would be only in exceptional circumstances that an injunction would not be granted.

The meaning of the phrase 'framed in good faith and with reasonable skill and knowledge' was considered in *Hoechst Celanese Corp* v *BP Chemicals Ltd*.[179] Following Aldous J in *Hallen Co* v *Brabantia (UK) Ltd*,[180] Laddie J said that the test for 'good faith' was one of honesty, based on what the proprietor or his agent actually knew. That is a subjective test. As for 'reasonable skill and knowledge', Laddie J said that it was whether, in the circumstances pertaining at the time, including what was known of the prior art, a competent patentee (or, in many cases, the patent agent drafting the specification) would or could have been expected to frame the specification in the way it was framed. That is an objective test. In the present case, although the patentee had not bothered to examine the documents cited in the search report, it was held that the specification was framed in good faith and with reasonable skill and knowledge.[181]

By s 69, the applicant for a patent is able to sue for infringements which occurred between the publication of the application and the grant of the patent. It is also required that the act, if the patent had been granted at the date of publication, would have infringed the patent and the claims as published. The claims have to be interpreted by reference to the description and any drawings referred to in the description or claims.[182]

Damages may not be available or may be limited if the patent is found to be partially valid only by s 63. Damages and costs will not be available at all unless the court (or the Comptroller as the case may be) is satisfied that the claimant has proved that the specification was framed in good faith and with reasonable skill and knowledge. Even then, the court or the Comptroller has a discretion as to costs and as to the date from which damages should be calculated. The scope of s 63 was considered by Aldous LJ in *Lubrizol Corp* v *Esso Petroleum Co Ltd*.[183] He said that the provision applies only if the patent is partially invalid and partially valid. He said (at 790):

> Thus, if a claim specifies more than one invention, [the court or Comptroller] may grant relief in respect of one of those inventions even though the other is invalid.

Where the claims specify only one invention rather than an inventive combination, it would seem that there is little place for s 63. However, in comparison with the equivalent provision in the Patents Act 1949, there is no requirement to find a valid claim. Section 63 allows relief for infringement of a partially valid patent with or without requiring amendment.

If the validity of a patent is challenged and it is found to be wholly or partially valid, the court (or the Comptroller if the hearing is before him) may certify the finding and the fact that the validity was so contested (s 65(2)). In any subsequent proceedings, including proceedings in the same action,[184] the proprietor can obtain his costs of the further proceedings on an indemnity basis if the judgment is made in his favour. A further certificate of contested validity may be granted.

There is a limitation on the award of costs or expenses if a transaction, instrument or event by which a subsequent proprietor (or co-proprietor) or exclusive licensee acquired his rights in the patent has not been registered promptly. Section 68 so provides where the transaction, instrument or event was not registered within six months or, if it was not practicable to register in that time, it was not registered as soon as practicable after that six-month period.[185] A number of transactions, instruments and events are registrable under s 33 including assignments, mortgages, licences and sub-licences,[186] the death of a

177 Patents Act 1977 s 62(3) as amended by the Intellectual Property (Enforcement, etc.) Regulations 2006, SI2006/1028, with effect from 29 April 2006.

178 *SmithKline Beecham plc* v *Apotex Europe Ltd* [2003] FSR 31.

179 [1997] FSR 547.

180 [1990] FSR 134.

181 Although the documents had been cited by the European Patent Office, in the end the application was accepted and the documents ignored in examination. The patentee later amended his patent to take account of the prior art.

182 Section 62(2) and (3) do not apply (discretion to refuse damages in relation to the further period for renewal or with respect to an amendment to the specification). There is, however, some discretion left to reduce damages if it would have been reasonable to expect that the patent would not have been granted or the act would not have infringed (s 69(3)). This defence was first raised in *Unilever plc* v *Chefaro Proprietaries Ltd* [1994] RPC 567, where it was held to require an objective test and to be of very limited scope.

183 [1998] RPC 727.

184 *Mölnlycke AB* v *Procter & Gamble Ltd* [1992] FSR 549.

185 Previously, s 68 operated to deprive the proprietor or exclusive licensee of damages or an account of profits.

186 Assignments of mortgages, licences and sub-licences must also be registered.

proprietor and orders of the court or competent authority transferring the patent or application or any right in or under it to any person. But, as only the proprietor or exclusive licensee has a right to sue, the limitation on remedies only applies to these persons. A further incentive for registration of these and other registrable transactions, instruments and events is that, failing registration, they may be vulnerable to a subsequent change in proprietorship of the patent or application.[187] The purpose of these provisions is to ensure that the register reflects accurately the fact of proprietorship and subsisting rights in respect of a patent or an application for a patent rather than to provide a fortuitous defence.[188] However, as s 68 now only applies to deprive the proprietor or exclusive licensee of costs or expenses, the draconian nature of the provision is significantly compromised.

The working of s 68 before and after amendment was considered by the Court of Appeal in *Schütz (UK) Ltd* v *Werit UK Ltd*.[189] Protechna, a Swiss company and the patent proprietor, granted the claimant an exclusive licence in 1994. This transaction was not registered until July 2008 a few weeks before infringement proceedings were brought against the defendant.[190] Section 68 was amended by the Intellectual Property (Infringement, etc.) Regulations 2006 with effect from 29 April 2006. Previously, failure to register a registrable transaction would deprive a successful claimant of damages or an account of profits.[191] After amendment, instead of damages or accounts, costs or expenses were at risk from a failure to register. The Court of Appeal held[192] that for the period up to 29 April 2006, neither damages (or an account, as an alternative to damages) were available. This was not discretionary as the language of the section was that '. . . the court or the comptroller shall not award . . .'.[193] From 29 April to 17 July 2008 (the date of registration) damages or an account was available to the claimant but not costs. From the date of registration, both damages (or an account) and costs were available. See the timeline in Figure 14.3. However, this was subject to an additional complication in that a new exclusive licence agreement replacing the old one was made on 26 November 2009. Needless to say, that transaction had not been registered. There was no alternative but to grant an adjournment for further argument as to costs after 26 November 2009. The issue being whether s 68 operated to deprive the claimant of costs from that date or whether it did not as the register still correctly reflected the fact that the claimant was the exclusive licensee even though the new licence had not been registered.

In practical terms, the effect of s 68, before and after amendment, is limited in most cases. Patent proprietors or exclusive licensees usually commence legal proceedings soon after they suspect the patent is being infringed and quickly register any relevant transactions that they had failed to register on time. Most costs, of course, accrue after commencement of litigation. In *Schütz* the transaction was registered just before commencement of proceedings. Consequently, by the time of registration, *Schütz*'s costs would be minimal.

187 Patents Act 1977 s 33(1).

188 *Coflexip Stena Offshore Ltd's Patent* [1997] RPC 179 per Jacob J.

189 [2011] EWCA Civ 927.

190 The Court of Appeal held that the patent was valid and infringed in *Schütz (UK) Ltd* v *Werit UK Ltd* [2011] EWCA Civ 303.

191 This was without prejudice to the possibility of the grant of an injunction.

192 Sir Robin Jacob (previously Jacob LJ) gave the judgment of the court with whom the other Court of Appeal judges agreed. Sir Robin retired officially in May 2011.

193 The same applies to the amended form of s 68.

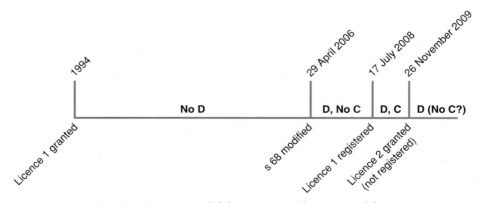

Figure 14.3 Availability of damages (D) (or an account) and costs (C) in *Schütz* v *Werit*

In many cases, the most important remedy is an injunction, unless infringement has been going on for some time.

An injunction will be granted as a general rule where the validity of the patent and the infringement are conclusively established but, of course, the grant of an injunction is discretionary. The High Court has a wide discretion to grant injunctions under s 37(1) of the Senior Courts Act 1981[194] and an injunction may be important where use of a property right is in issue, where damages may not be the main consideration.[195] Although discretionary, the normal form of an injunction is a general and unqualified one. It is for the defendant to justify departure from the norm. In *Kirin-Amgen Inc v Transkaryotic Therapies Inc (No 3)*,[196] the defendant unsuccessfully argued that the injunction be qualified to allow it to continue the infringing activity pending the appeal to the Court of Appeal.

Where an injunction is granted, it is important to limit the scope of the injunction to prohibit acts which, if carried out, would infringe the patent. The simplest formula then is to restrain the defendant from carrying out acts that infringe the patent, limited to the term of the patent.[197] Thus, the injunction is limited to the rights under s 60(1) and (2) but excludes acts which are excluded from infringement, such as the acts set out in s 60(5). The purpose of the injunction is to prevent apprehended use of the patentee's statutory monopoly, as defined in his claim.[198] In *Coflexip SA v Stolt Comex Seaway MS Ltd*,[199] the judge at first instance granted an injunction[200] which, according to Aldous LJ in the Court of Appeal, suffered from three deficiencies. It was not linked to the term during which the patent would be in existence, it exceeded the rights under s 60(1) and (2) and failed to exclude acts which are, under the Act, excepted from the right. It also raised difficult issues of construction.

An injunction granted on narrower grounds than covered by the claims at the claimant's request may not be remedied later by an application to widen its terms. In *Building Product Design Ltd v Sandtoft Roof Tiles Ltd (No 2)*,[201] the claimant sought and obtained an order restraining the defendant from making 'clay half-round ridge vent roof tiles' rather than an order in wider terms restraining the defendant from infringing the patent. The claimant later brought a second action in relation to angled tiles (the existence of these was known to the claimant at the time of the first action but it did not seek to include them in its pleadings). The second action was struck out as an abuse of process, being *res judicata*.

Exceptionally, a court may refuse an injunction to restrain the defendant from further infringement. Aldous J refused an injunction in *Biogen Inc v Medeva plc*.[202] The defendant claimed that the grant of an injunction would lead to loss of human life and/or avoidable damage to human health. The patent related to a vaccine for hepatitis B. However, the background facts were likely to change – the defendant's own vaccine might soon be approved or it might obtain a compulsory licence for the claimant's patent. In a previous case, Graham J said:

> A life-saving drug is in an exceptional position . . . it is at the least very doubtful if the court in its discretion even ought to grant an injunction . . .[203]

Of course, it must be recalled that, as an equitable remedy, the grant of an injunction is always discretionary. That is not to say that damages would not be appropriate in such cases.

Where there is an entry on the register to the effect that licences of right are available in respect of the patent and the defendant undertakes to take a licence, an injunction will not be granted against him. Also, the amount recoverable against him is limited to a maximum of double the amount that he would have paid had the infringing acts all been done under the licence.[204] It therefore makes sense for a person who is about to be sued for infringement to check whether licences of right are available for the patent concerned

---

194 Which states that the High Court may order an injunction (interim or final) where it appears to the court to be just and convenient to do so.

195 *SmithKline Beecham plc v Apotex Europe Ltd* [2003] FSR 31, per Aldous LJ at para 13.

196 [2005] FSR 41.

197 Subject, in rare cases, to an injunction that may apply for a specified period beyond the expiry of the patent.

198 *Coflexip SA v Stolt Comex Seaway MS Ltd* [2001] RPC 9 at para 18 per Aldous LJ.

199 [2001] RPC 9.

200 *Coflexip SA v Stolt Comex Seaway MS Ltd* [1999] FSR 473.

201 [2004] FSR 41. At the first trial, the claimant had sought unsuccessfully to introduce claims for damages for other shapes of tiles and tiles made of concrete into the inquiry as to damages: *Building Product Design Ltd v Sandtoft Roof Tiles Ltd* [2004] FSR 40. The judge was unaware of the defendant's other products at trial.

202 [1995] RPC 25. The patent was found to be invalid in the Court of Appeal and this was confirmed in the House of Lords: *see* [1997] RPC 1.

203 *Roussel-Uclaf v GD Searle & Co Ltd* [1977] FSR 125 at 131.

204 Patents Act 1977 s 46(3)(c). The defendant's undertaking can be made at any time before the final order in the proceedings without admission of liability: s 46(3A).

where there is any likelihood that damages will be assessed otherwise than on the basis of lost royalties and will be substantially more than the royalty payments under the licence of right. However, if the infringer did not have a licence and failed to undertake to apply for a licence of right an injunction could be imposed and damages would not be limited: they would be assessed at the damage actually caused to the claimant.[205]

205 *Gerber Garment Technology Ltd v Lectra Systems Ltd* [1995] RPC 383.

The grant of an injunction is discretionary and may not be granted where the patent in question is owned by a company which puts together a portfolio of patents, typically in the field of software or business method patents, but does not work the inventions itself. Rather, the company watches out for potential infringements and threatens the alleged infringer with legal action if it does not agree to take a licence from the proprietor. Bearing in mind the apparent ease with which the US Patent and Trademark Office grants patents for software and business method patents, coupled with the expense of defending a patent action, the courts may be less willing to grant an injunction, particularly where the defendant has the means to pay damages should it lose at full trial.

Assessment of damages

The calculation of damages can give rise to complex considerations. The test is whether an award of damages is an adequate remedy, not a perfect remedy.[206] The exercise has been somewhat modified by the Intellectual Property (Enforcement, etc.) Regulations 2006, discussed later.[207] Previously, the basic principle was stated by Lord Wilberforce in *General Tire & Rubber Co v Firestone Tyre & Rubber Co Ltd*[208] in the following terms (at 185):

206 Per Walker J in *Peaudouce SA v Kimberley-Clark Ltd* [1996] FSR 680 at 699.

207 SI 2006/1028. The Regulations implement, *inter alia*, Directive 2004/48/EC of the European Parliament and of the Council of 29 April 2004 on the enforcement of intellectual property rights, OJ L 157, 30.04.2004, p 45. It remains to be seen what effect the new provisions will have. It is unlikely that the previous method of calculating damages will be much altered.

208 [1975] RPC 203.

> As in the case of any other tort . . . the object of damages is to compensate for loss or injury. The general rule at any rate in relation to 'economic' torts is that the measure of damages is to be, so far as possible, that sum of money which will put the injured party in the same position as he would have been in if he had not sustained the wrong.

If the proprietor has been exploiting the patent by granting licences to others in return for royalties, then his loss is the capitalised value of the royalties that the infringer would have paid had he taken a licence. For example, if the infringer had made 500 articles that were covered by the patent and the proprietor had granted others a licence to make such articles in return for a royalty of £30 per article, then the damages should be assessed at £15,000. (This convenient method becomes less easy to use if the proprietor has granted licences in respect of the patent to different persons at different royalty rates.) Alternatively, the royalty may be calculated as a percentage of the net sale price of the articles where the infringer has been selling them at a lower price than legitimate licensees. Although a royalty basis is appropriate where the patentee is not a manufacturer but grants licences to work the invention, there may be losses exceeding a reasonable royalty and the measure of damages will be based on normal considerations of causation and remoteness.[209]

209 *SmithKline Beecham plc v Apotex Europe Ltd* [2003] FSR 31.

The royalty method of calculation falls down altogether if the proprietor does not grant licences but works the patent himself. In this case it is a question of the profits lost as a result of the infringer's activities. Here, many factors may be relevant, including the effect on the marketplace of the infringement. Particular issues include:

- whether every sale of an infringing article represents a lost sale for the proprietor;
- whether the proprietor would have sold other articles along with those lost sales (for example, the buyer may have also purchased non-patented articles in addition to the patented article) – these damages are often referred to as parasitic damages;
- whether the infringer had generated additional interest in the patented article through his marketing efforts;

- what the effect on the market was by changing a monopoly into a duopoly (for example, did the proprietor have to reduce his prices to compete with the infringer);
- typical profit margins for the category of article concerned;
- whether the infringer had deliberately undercut the proprietor's sale price.

The mere fact that a defendant could have made and sold as many products that did not infringe is no reason for reducing damages to a nominal sum. So it was held in an old Scots case, *United Horse Shoe and Nail Co Ltd* v *Stewart*,[210] in which the defender made and sold nails which infringed the pursuer's patent. The pursuer was entitled to damages based on the amount of profit it would have made had it made those sales itself, with a deduction to reflect the sales due to the particular exertions of the defendant. This case was still arguably good law and it was arguable that the reasoning in *United Horse Shoe* applied to contracts won by the defendant before an infringing process was used.[211]

An instructive case on the issue of damages where the proprietor had no intention of licensing the patent is *Catnic Components Ltd* v *Hill & Smith Ltd*,[212] which was a follow-up to the House of Lords case on infringement of lintels by a variant.[213] The claimant's claim for damages was under the following heads:

1 Loss of profits on each sale made by the defendant of infringing lintels – on the basis that every sale of the defendant's represented a lost sale to the claimant.
2 Loss of profits on the sale of non-patented lintels that the claimant would have sold alongside the patented lintels – parasitic damages.
3 A notional royalty of 20 per cent for any infringing lintels not subject to an award under 1 and 2 above.
4 Compound interest at 2 per cent above clearing bank base rate.
5 Exemplary damages on the sale at a large discount of infringing lintels by the defendant between the hearing in the House of Lords in the main action and the delivery of the judgment.

The defendant disputed these claims arguing that the claimant's lost sales, if any, were less than the defendant's sales of infringing lintels; that the claimant was not, in law, entitled to parasitic damages or exemplary damages and that interest payable should be simple interest at clearing bank rate *less* 2 per cent. The defendant conceded that the claimant was entitled to a royalty of 2 per cent on gross sales values.

It was held that it was proper to assume that each sale made by the defendant represented a lost sale unless the defendant could prove otherwise. A proper notional royalty rate was that which a potential licensee who had not yet entered the market would pay. No regard would be had to the fact that such a person could, instead, sell non-infringing lintels. On that basis, the appropriate royalty rate was 7 per cent net of tax. Parasitic sales were not allowable as not being a direct and natural consequence of the infringement. Although the defendant's discounted sales made shortly before the House of Lords judgment fell within the second category of acts for which exemplary damages might be awarded (benefit to defendant far outweighed the potential loss) in *Rookes* v *Barnard*,[214] they could not be awarded because there was no authority for it.[215] Neither was there any authority for compound interest, and the claimant was entitled only to simple interest calculated at clearing bank base rate plus 2 per cent.

Jacob J chose not to follow *Catnic* v *Hill & Smith* as regards 'parasitic damages'. In *Gerber Garment Technology Inc* v *Lectra Systems Ltd*[216] it was held that patent infringement is a matter where secondary loss, provided it was reasonably foreseeable, should be recoverable on basic tortious principles. Such secondary loss may consist of the sale of unpatented articles which go with the patented article as a commercial matter (in the present case, the sale of machines to be used with the patented machines, servicing the machines and the sale of spare parts). The secondary loss would even extend to loss caused by the

210 (1888) 13 App Cas 401.

211 *Coflexip SA* v *Stolt Offshore Ltd* [2003] FSR 41.

212 [1983] FSR 512.
213 [1982] RPC 183.

214 [1964] AC 1129.
215 *Broome* v *Cassell & Co* [1972] AC 1027.

216 [1995] RPC 383.

infringer establishing a 'bridgehead' or 'springboard' (for example, by negotiating with clients) before the expiry of the relevant patents.[217] A further head of damages was for price depression. More controversially, part of the overall award of $5.9 million included losses suffered by subsidiary companies. The claimant held all the shares in a number of subsidiaries and the resulting losses to these companies were taken into account on the basis that every dollar lost by a wholly owned subsidiary was a dollar lost to the parent company.[218]

In the appeal from Jacob J's award of damages, the Court of Appeal accepted that where a shareholder in a company had a cause of action but the company had none, the shareholder could, in principle, sue in respect of loss caused to the company.[219] However, in the present case, the claimant had failed to prove he had both a personal cause of action and a personal loss.[220] In this case, the companies, including the claimant and its subsidiaries, were all part of a larger group. The claimant was not the holding company but an intermediate company. Hobhouse LJ said of the 'one dollar lost' rule (at 479):

> The position of parent companies and their subsidiaries vary widely . . . there is no 'self-evident' truth. It all depends on the circumstances. Where, as here, the relevant companies are carrying on business in different countries, the starting point must be that an income loss suffered by one company will normally not translate directly into an equal monetary loss to the other company.

Hobhouse LJ compared simple groups of companies operating in the same country with groups with subsidiaries operating in different countries which may be subject to different tax regimes and exchange controls and an inflating local currency.

As an infringement of a patent is a statutory tort, it can be expected that normal tortious rules concerning damages apply as they apply to other torts. The basic rule is that the injured party should be restored to the position he would have been in had the tort not been committed. Recoverable losses are those that are foreseeable, caused by the tort and not excluded by public or social policy. In *South Australia Asset Management Corp* v *York Montague Ltd*,[221] Lord Hoffmann said that liability is normally limited to consequences which are attributable to that which made the act wrongful. Staughton LJ in *Gerber Garment* said (at 453):

> . . . at first impression the Patents Act is aimed at protecting patentees from commercial loss resulting from the wrongful infringement of their rights. That is only a slight gloss upon the wording of the statute itself. In my judgment, again as a matter of first impression, it does not distinguish between profit on the sale of patented articles and profit on the sale of convoyed goods [meaning goods sold alongside the patented articles].[222]

Gerber Garment is not inconsistent with *Catnic* v *Hill & Smith* as, in that case, it was held that the loss of sales of lintels other than those subject to the patent was not a natural and direct consequence of the acts of infringement. As a principle, losses of sales of non-patented goods sold alongside the patented goods are recoverable provided the basic test for recoverability in tort is satisfied. The same applies to the sale of spare parts and the work of servicing the patented goods. It is arguable that this basic principle goes further than now appears to be the case in the US where, in *Rite-Hite Corp* v *Kelly Co Inc*,[223] it was held that for recovery for lost sales of unpatented goods sold with patented goods, they must function together so as to produce a desired end-product or result, for example, as being components of a single assembly or which operate as a functional unit. Damages in respect of goods sold alongside the infringing goods and bought only as a matter of 'convenience or business advantage' are not recoverable. If that is so, this case is not irreconcilable with the English cases and can be said simply to point to a lack of causation in respect of such losses. In *Catnic* v *Hill & Smith*, it was accepted that, as a common practice, builders obtain from one supplier all their requirements for lintels for the erection of a

217 Jacob J claimed that the provisional opinions in *Polaroid Corp* v *Eastman Kodak Co* [1977] RPC 379 were adopted by Falconer J in *Catnic Components Ltd* v *Hill & Smith Ltd* [1983] FSR 512 as part of the *ratio* of the case. Jacob J held that he was wrong to do so!

218 This was accepted in *George Fischer (Great Britain) Ltd* v *Multi-Construction Ltd* [1995] 1 BCLC 260. In that case, the group of companies were all operating in the same country under the same tax system.

219 *Gerber Garment Technology Inc* v *Lectra Systems Ltd* [1997] RPC 443.

220 Staughton LJ dissenting on this point.

221 [1996] 3 WLR 87.

222 After reviewing the case law, Staughton LJ concluded that there was no rule of law contradicting his first impression.

223 [1996] FSR 469.

particular building, and in *Gerber Garment* the articles sold with the patented articles (automated fabric-cutting machines) were computer-aided design machines for designing cutting patterns.

Damages are available for loss of opportunity. For example, in *Les Laboratoires Servier* v *Apotex Inc*,[224] an injunction had been granted to the claimant preventing the defendant entering the market for perindopril, an anti-hypertension drug, in respect of which the claimant had a patent. The defendant had taken the view that the patent was invalid as, basically, all it claimed was the product of an earlier though expired patent. Eventually, the patent was held to be invalid but, in the meantime, the defendant had been prevented from entering the new generic market for the drug, during the 'at-risk' period.[225] Damages for this loss of opportunity were assessed at £17.5m. Norris J said that the award in such a case was one of equitable compensation, rather than damages strictly so-called.

Criminal offences

Infringements of patents associated with selling, distributing and importing products that are subject to a patent are dealt with as civil wrongs and there are no criminal penalties for such dealings, although, depending on the circumstances, trade description, forgery, copyright or trade mark offences may be committed. There are a number of offences provided for by the Patents Act 1977, but these do not directly relate to unauthorised dealing. Section 109 makes it an offence, triable either way, to make, or cause to be made, a false entry on the patents register. This also extends to writings purporting to be copies of such entries and to the use of such writings in evidence. The maximum penalty on indictment is imprisonment for a term not exceeding two years and/or a fine. On summary conviction, the maximum penalty is a fine not exceeding the prescribed maximum.

Two offences deal with unauthorised claims with respect to patents. The first, under s 110, covers false representations that anything disposed of for value is a patented product: for example, where the product has the words 'patented in the UK' or just simply the word 'patent' applied to it and there is no such patent. The second offence, under s 111, covers representations that a patent has been applied for in respect of any article disposed of for value when this is not true, or if the patent application has been withdrawn or refused. For both offences, a reasonable period of grace is allowed after the expiry or revocation of a patent, or the refusal or withdrawal of an application, to allow sufficient time to prevent the making or continuance of the representation. An example that would probably be deemed to fall within this period of grace is where an article to which a patent relates is being manufactured and has the word 'patented' embossed on it. Later, the patent is revoked. It would be expected that the person concerned would take immediate steps to prevent continuing application of the word 'patented' to new articles and that he would remove the word from his existing stock (if this is practicable), but he would not be expected to take action to remove the word from articles that he has sold to retailers. A further defence to these two offences is that the accused person had used due diligence to prevent the commission of the offence. The penalty for an offence under s 110 or 111 is a fine not exceeding level 3 on the standard scale. These offences are triable summarily only.

Any person who uses on his place of business or on any document the words 'Patent Office' or any other words suggesting a connection between his place of business and the Patent Office, or indeed that his place of business is the Patent Office, is guilty of an offence and will be liable on summary conviction to a fine not exceeding level 4 on the standard scale.[226] An appropriate officer of a body corporate who consents or connives in the commission of any offence under the Act by that body corporate is also guilty of the

224 [2009] FSR 3.

225 This is the period before the patent has expired but where the generic manufacturer takes a view on the validity of the patent and decides to market the drug anyway. Norris J's discussion of this and 'transition' periods (one or more new entrants) and 'plateau' periods (numerous generic makers) and the impact on price is very instructive. A generic entrant during the at-risk period, if his view on validity is wrong, may be faced with paying damages several times the profit he makes as the patentee will usually have been making much greater profits.

226 Patents Act 1977 s 112.

227 Patents Act 1977 s 113(1).

228 Notice the difference between this provision and the equivalent provision for registered designs, where only consent and connivance bring criminal liability on the shoulders of the officer, mere negligence being insufficient (Registered Designs Act 1949 s 35A). Neither is neglect sufficient for criminal liability of officers of corporations in respect of the offence of fraudulent application of a trade mark under the Trade Marks Act 1994.

relevant offence.[227] This also applies in the case of offences attributable to the neglect of the officer.[228] Appropriate officers are directors, managers, secretaries or other similar officers, or any person purporting to act in such a capacity. Where the affairs of the corporation are managed by its members, then those members may be liable as if they were directors.

Summary

The Patents County Court should provide a less expensive and time-consuming means of resolving IP disputes, especially as some improvements have been implemented. The availability of non-binding opinions from the Comptroller is a further useful step in avoiding expensive litigation.

There are several forms of infringement of a patent. They are:

- making, importing, keeping, disposing of or offering to dispose of a patented product;
- using or offering for use a patented process (having actual or objective knowledge that the use would infringe);
- importing, keeping, disposing of or offering to dispose of a product obtained directly from a patented process;
- supplying or offering to supply the 'essential means' to put an invention into effect knowing (actual or objective) that the means are suitable for putting the invention into effect and are intended to do so (the intention is that of the ultimate user).

The claims in a patent specification are key in determining whether there has been an infringement. The claims must interpreted by reference to the description and any drawings in the specification.

The *Catnic* principle of using a purposive construction remains valid and is in accordance with the Protocol on Article 69 of the EPC.

In relation to variants, the Protocol questions (derived from *Catnic* as restated in *Improver*) provide a useful structured approach to the question as to whether a variant infringes. However, they may not be appropriate in all cases.

Remedies for patent infringement are:

- injunctions (interdicts in Scotland);
- orders for delivery up or destruction;
- damages;
- accounts of profits (an alternative to damages);
- a declaration (declarator in Scotland) that the patent is valid and has been infringed by the defendant (defender in Scotland).

This is without prejudice to any other jurisdiction of the court.

Damages (or accounts) are not available against an 'innocent infringer' (someone who was not aware and had no reasonable grounds for supposing that the patent existed at the time of the infringement).

The assessment of damages in patent infringement actions is a complicated subject and in some cases, parasitic damages, based on the sale of non-infringing products alongside infringing products may be allowed. Basic tortious principles prevail, however.

Under certain circumstances, post-expiry injunctions may be granted for a limited period of time.

Proprietors of patents or exclusive licensees may commence proceedings for patent infringement. Usually, the other will be joined in the action as co-claimant but, in practice, may take no actual part in the proceedings.

Costs (or expenses) are not available where a registrable transaction, such as an exclusive licence, has not been registered.

There are some criminal offences but nothing equivalent to those available under copyright and trade mark law in relation to counterfeit copies.

Discussion questions

1 Discuss approaches to determining infringement of a patent in terms of deciding (a) whether an alleged infringement falls within the scope of the patent claim, and (b) whether a variant infringes or (c) whether something is alleged to infringe where it does the same thing as that which is claimed but in a different way, such as where a component made of metal is claimed in a patented product but the equivalent component in the alleged infringement is made from a different material such as wood or rubber.

2 Discuss the potential liability of a manufacturer of infringing products of being a joint tortfeasor in relation to infringement under s 60(2) (supplying or offering to supply the means essential to put the invention into effect).

3 Discuss the evidential difficulties often associated with expert evidence.

4 What are post-expiry injunctions and parasitic damages? What arguments can you raise in support of or against their continued use?

5 The impact of s 68 in its present form is limited as the failure to register a transaction such as an exclusive licence can be remedied (upon payment of the necessary fees at the UK IPO) before issuing proceedings and incurring substantial legal costs. Discuss.

Selected further reading

Grimme Landmaschinenfabrik GmbH & Co KG v *Scott*, Court of Appeal (an important case on the scope of s 60(2)), available at: **http://www.bailii.org/ew/cases/EWCA/Civ/2010/1110.html**

Laddie, H. (the late Sir Hugh Laddie), 'Kirin Amgen – the end of equivalents in England?' [2009] *International Review of Industrial Property and Copyright Law* 3 (criticises the House of Lords decision in *Kirin-Amgen* v *Hoechst Marion Roussel* as not being consistent with the legislative intent of the Protocol to Article 69 EPC).

Virgin Atlantic Airways Ltd v *Premium Aircraft Interiors UK Ltd*, Court of Appeal (particularly paras 5 to 22 on construction of patent claims), available at: **http://www.bailii.org/ew/cases/EWCA/Civ/2009/1062.html**

Wadlow, C., 'Requiem for a noun: the "terms of the claims" (1953–2007)' [2011] *European Intellectual Property Review*, 146 (considers the background to and implications of the change to Article 69 of the EPC where the 'terms of the claims' was replaced by 'claims' alone in EPC 2000).

Visit www.mylawchamber.co.uk/bainbridgeip to access study support resources including interactive multiple choice questions, practice exam questions with guidance, weblinks, legal updates and a legal newsfeed.

Patents – defences, groundless threats and revocation   15

Introduction

Being such a strong monopoly right, it is not surprising that patent rights are tempered by numerous exceptions to infringement in the form of defences. Apart from defences set out in s 60, described below, there is also a defence available to a person who has worked the invention before its priority date, or made effective and serious preparations to do so. Strictly speaking, this is not a defence and grants a right to the prior user to continue that prior use. Other defences may be available as are generally brought in relation to intellectual property rights, such as defences based on competition law, whether under domestic or EU law.

Being the owner of a monopoly right brings with it the temptation to use the right to threaten potential infringers with legal proceedings. As patent litigation is generally expensive, this might be enough to frighten off small and medium-sized enterprises which may well fear the consequences of losing a patent action. Sometimes it will be a third party who is threatened with litigation, such as a retailer or distributor of a product made by the alleged primary infringer, and the threats may be sufficient to deter the third party from placing further orders for the products in question, rather than submit to the vagaries of patent litigation. To deal with such abuses, in some circumstances, it is possible to bring an action against a person making groundless threats of infringement actions. This action is available to 'a person aggrieved' which can include the primary infringer, for example, if orders have dried up because his customers have been threatened. However, certain things can be threatened without triggering the action, which has also been watered down significantly by changes made by the Patents Act 2004.

In many cases where an infringement action is brought, the defendant will attack the validity of the patent, arguing that it ought to be revoked, typically on the grounds that the invention was not new or lacked an inventive step. Such attacks are usually costly to overcome and frequently involve lengthy and complex expert evidence, increasing the expense of patent litigation significantly. This chapter looks at the defences to patent infringement actions, groundless threats and revocation of patents. European Union competition law and the doctrine of freedom of movement of goods, both of which may be important in relation to patents, are described in Part Eight which looks at European and International aspects of intellectual property rights.

Defences

A person sued for an alleged infringement of a patent has several and varied escape routes. He might challenge the validity of the patent, claiming that it should be revoked because it has been anticipated or that it is obvious or, more rarely, that the invention is for excluded matter as such or that it lacks industrial application or is invalid for lack of sufficiency. Section 74 permits the defendant in an infringement action to put the validity of the patent in issue. Once the validity of a patent has been put in issue and evidence has been given in court, the court must rule on it even if the parties are no longer interested. The reason is that third parties may be affected.[1] Putting validity in issue may also be done under certain other circumstances.[2] The defendant may claim that the patent has lapsed or expired, or he may challenge the claimant's title to it or his right to sue. On the other hand, the defendant might be able to reduce his liability by showing that the patent is only partially valid. If the patent is only partially valid, the defendant will escape damages and costs in respect of the invalid part. In the case of a partially valid patent, under s 63, the claimant must show that the specification was framed in good faith and with reasonable skill and knowledge; but, even if he does, the court or Comptroller still has a discretion as to the date from which damages should be calculated and in respect of costs and expenses. This is an unfettered discretion though the conduct of the parties and the position of the general public may be influential.[3] Section 63 now also includes a requirement that the proceedings were brought in good faith and account must also be taken as to whether the defendant knew or had reasonable grounds for knowing he was infringing the patent at the time of the infringement.

Section 46 concerns licences of right. Where a patent has such an entry against it, in infringement proceedings (except where it relates to the importation of any article from a country outside the EU), if the defendant undertakes to take a licence on terms to be agreed (or, failing agreement, to be settled by the Comptroller) then no injunction will be granted against him and the maximum award of damages against him is double the amount payable under the licence had the licence, on those terms, been granted before the earliest infringement. This provision could be seen as encouraging infringement of patents endorsed licences of right as, if sued, all the defendant has to do is to make the necessary undertaking. If he does this, the most he risks is twice what he would have paid under the licence.[4]

Under s 60(3), the supplying the means form of infringement does not apply to the supply or offer to supply a staple commercial product unless made for the purpose of inducing the other person to do an act that would infringe under s 60(1) (making, etc. a patented product or a product obtained directly from a patented process or using, etc. a patented process).

Apart from these points, other defences to an infringement action are:

1 The act was done privately and for purposes which are not commercial: s 60(5)(a) – note the use of the conjunctive, the act must be both private and non-commercial.
2 The act was done for experimental purposes relating to the subject matter of the invention: s 60(5)(b) – this might permit making the subject matter of the invention to see more clearly how it works. However, making or experimenting with a patented product for the purposes of obtaining official approval from the Ministry of Agriculture, Fisheries and Food was held not to be within s 60(5)(b) in *Auchincloss* v *Agricultural & Veterinary Supplies Ltd*.[5] There, the act complained of was done in order to obtain official approval and not to discover something unknown or to test some hypothesis. However, such experiments might be done with a commercial outcome in mind.[6]
3 The act consists of the extemporaneous preparation in a pharmacy of a medicine for an individual in accordance with a registered medical or dental practitioner's prescription, or consists of dealing with a medicine so prepared: s 60(5)(c). Under s 60(6) a person who does not infringe under s 60(5)(a) to (c) does not become a person entitled to work the invention.
4 Use in relation to certain ships, aircraft, hovercraft or vehicles temporarily or accidentally in the UK or lawfully entering or crossing the UK: s 60(5)(d)–(f).[7] In *Stena Rederi*

---

1 *Ocular Sciences Ltd* v *Aspect Vision Care Ltd* [1997] RPC 289.

2 For example, on the application by any person that the invention is not a patentable invention, or the person to whom the patent was granted was not entitled to it or that the specification does not disclose the invention clearly and completely enough, etc. (s 72), in proceedings in connection with alleged groundless threats of infringement proceedings (s 70), proceedings in respect of a declaration under s 71 and in disputes relating to Crown use (s 58). The Patents Act 1949 contained some other specific grounds which no longer apply, for example, false suggestion under s 32(1)(j): *see Intalite International NV* v *Cellular Ceilings Ltd (No 2)* [1987] RPC 537.

3 *Gerber Garment Technology Inc* v *Lectra Systems Ltd* [1995] FSR 492 at first instance.

4 Apart from any order as to costs.

5 [1997] RPC 649, following *Monsanto Co* v *Stauffer Chemical Co* [1985] RPC 515. This was confirmed in the Court of Appeal in *Auchincloss* v *Agricultural & Veterinary Supplies Ltd* [1999] RPC 397. In *Kirin-Amgen Inc* v *Transkaryotic Therapies Inc (No 3)* [2005] FSR 41, the defence was raised initially though not pressed subsequently.

6 *See Klinische Versuche (Clinical Trials) II* [1998] RPC 423, in the Federal Supreme Court of Germany.

7 Including air space, internal and territorial waters, as appropriate. These exceptions apply to 'relevant' ships, aircraft, hovercraft and vehicles registered in or belonging to countries which are a party to the Paris Convention or are members of the World Trade Organisation, other than the UK. The provisions also apply to exempted aircraft under the Civil Aviation Act 1982 s 89.

8 [2003] RPC 36.

9 The Court of Appeal cited with approval the US case of *Cali v Japan Airlines Inc* (1974) 380 F Supp 1120, to similar effect in relation to scheduled air freight and passenger services.

10 Inserted by reg 4 of the Patents Regulations 2000, SI 2000/2037 which came into force on 28 July 2000. The 2000 Regulations also inserted Sch A1 into the 1977 Act which contains restrictions on the applicability of s 60(5)(g). Schedule A2, also inserted by the 2000 Regulations, defines *inter alia* the scope of protection afforded by biotechnological patents.

11 Under Article 13(1) to (5) of Directive 2001/82/EC of the European Parliament and of the Council of 6 November 2001 on the Community code relating to veterinary medicinal products, OJ L 311, 28.11.2001,p 1.

12 Under Article 10(1) to (4) of Directive 2001/83/EC of the European Parliament and of the Council of 6 November 2001 on the Community code relating to medicinal products for human use, OJ L 311, 28.11.2001, p 67.

13 Under s 60(6), persons who can rely on these defences are deemed to be persons entitled to work the invention for the purposes of s 60(2) – infringement by supplying or offering to supply the means to put the invention into effect. This also applies in respect of Crown use under s 55.

14 (1913) 30 RPC 465.

15 [1996] RPC 387.

16 *Solar Thomson Engineering Co Ltd v Barton* [1997] RPC 537. It is doubtful whether this can be described as a right or an implied licence: *see* the House of Lords in *United Wire*, below.

17 Previously Articles 28 to 30 of the EC Treaty.

18 Previously Articles 81 and 82 of the EC Treaty. In *Intel Corp v Via Technologies Inc* [2003] FSR 33, it was said that cases involving Articles 81 and 82 often raised mixed questions of law and fact and were generally unsuitable for summary judgment.

19 [1993] RPC 107.

20 [1983] RPC 92. Otherwise the normal limitation period of six years applies under the Limitation Act 1980.

AB v *Irish Ferries Ltd*,[8] the Court of Appeal held that the word 'temporarily' meant 'transient' or 'for a limited time' and the question whether a vessel visited temporarily could not depend on frequency. In this case, a ferry, registered in the Irish Republic and which crossed between Dublin and Holyhead up to three or four times daily was held to be within the defence.[9]

5 Certain uses by farmers of the product of their harvest or uses of animals or animal reproductive material following sale of plant propagating material or breeding stock or animal reproductive material by the proprietor of the relevant patent or with his consent: s 60(5)(g) and (h).[10]

6 Certain acts done in conducting a study, test or trial necessary for and con-ducted with a view to complying marketing authorisation in relation to veterinary medicinal products[11] and in relation to medicinal products for human use:[12] s 60(5)(i).

7 The act was done in good faith by the defendant before the priority date of the inven-tion, or he made in good faith effective and serious preparations to do such an act and, under s 64, the defendant has the right to do the act or to continue to do the act. Alternatively the defendant may claim that he has obtained this right as being a partner of such a person, or that he has acquired it with the relevant part of that person's business. Under s 28A similar provisions apply in respect of acts and preparations to do acts in relation to a patent after expiry of the renewal period and before publica-tion of an application for restoration (of course, if the application for restoration is unsuccessful, there is no question of infringement).[13]

8 The act complained of is not an infringing act; it does not fall within the meaning of infringement in s 60.

9 The alleged infringing product or process lacks novelty or is obvious. Therefore, the patent claims are invalid if they cover the alleged infringement or, if valid, they cannot cover the alleged infringement. This is the 'Gillette' defence, from *Gillette Safety Razor Co* v *Anglo-American Trading Co Ltd*.[14] This defence is not uncommon: see, for example, *Mabuchi Motor KK's Patents*[15] where the patent was held to be valid but not infringed.

10 The defendant has not made the patented product but has merely repaired it. Wrongly described as a right to repair or an implied licence.[16] The principle of non-derogation from grant may also be available but in very limited circumstances.

11 The claimant's rights have been exhausted under EU law on the basis of Articles 34 to 36 of the Treaty on the Functioning of the European Union.[17] This might apply in the case of patented products placed on the European market by or with the consent of the proprietor of the patent which are subsequently further commercialised, for example, by being bought and resold by a third party, often after exporting the products to another Member State where the products sell at higher prices. Exhaustion of rights is discussed further in Chapter 25.

12 A defence based on competition law under Articles 101 or 102 of the Treaty on the Functioning of the European Union,[18] which apply to restrictive agreements and abuses of dominant positions, discussed in Chapter 25. The equivalent pro-visions under the Competition Act 1998 may also be relevant in appropriate circumstances.

13 The doctrines of estoppel and laches may apply. However, estoppel does not place a positive duty on a proprietor of a patent to publicise the patent or make inquiries: *Lux Traffic Controls Ltd* v *Pike Signals Ltd*.[19] Inactivity on the part of the proprietor or exclusive licensee may bar him from the equitable remedies, in particular an interim injunction. A warning may suffice to prevent the claimant's claim being barred by laches: *TJ Smith & Nephew Ltd* v *3M United Kingdom plc*.[20]

14 The old section 44 defence. This is no longer available except as regards contracts made before 1 March 2000. At the time of the infringement there was in force a contract or

licence containing a condition or term void by virtue of s 44. This covered terms requiring the other party to purchase anything other than the patented product, or prohibiting the acquisition of anything other than the patented product from a specified third party. It made no difference if the contract or licence was not itself subject to the laws of the UK.[21] Section 44 was repealed by the Competition Act 1998 s 70.[22] There can be few such contracts in force now.

15 The old section 45 defence. Again this is no longer available, having also been repealed by the Competition Act 1998 s 70. However, it still may be relevant in connection with contracts entered into prior to 1 March 2000. The defence applied to licences or contracts relating to the patents that contained obligations on the licensee or other party to a contract which survived the patent: for example, where a licence included an obligation to pay royalties in respect of the manufacture of a product by the licensee after the patent had expired. Under s 45, either party could terminate the agreement to the extent that it related to the subject matter of the patent by giving three months' notice in writing to the other party. The repeal of both s 44 and s 45 must be seen in the context of the introduction of provisions in the Competition Act 1998 equivalent to Articles 101 and 102 of the Treaty on the Functioning of the European Union but set in the context of trade within the UK.

The claims may be central to the issue of infringement and validity. Where there is an application to revoke a patent under s 72(1) on the grounds of alleged invalidity, it would seem, in as much as the challenge concerns the claims, that the *Catnic* principle and Protocol questions may equally be valid as in infringement proceedings.[23] On the one hand, the defendant will want to show that the claims are too narrow and do not extend to the alleged infringement. On the other hand, the defendant will argue that the claims are too wide, and hence the patent is invalid, or only partially valid, because the claims embrace some material that lacks novelty or is obvious to the notional skilled worker. This may be particularly relevant in terms of the *Gillette* defence mentioned above, where the defendant argues that his product lacks either novelty or an inventive step or, better still, both.

Right to repair

The existence and scope of the right to repair defence was questioned in the House of Lords in *United Wire Ltd* v *Screen Repair Services (Scotland) Ltd*.[24] The claimant was the proprietor of two patents in relation to sifting screens used to recycle drilling fluid in the offshore oil-drilling industry. The screens were made from two mesh screens of different mesh sizes fixed, at differential tensions, in a metal frame. In use, the screens quickly became torn and required replacement. The defendant acquired worn out screens and reconditioned them by removing the mesh screens, cleaning the frames and fitting new mesh screens. Customers who bought the screens were given a credit for supplying old frames. The claimant sued for infringement of its patents in that the defendant made the protected product without the consent of the proprietor under s 60(1)(a).

At first instance, the judge accepted that there was an implied licence to repair a patented product. On the facts, he was narrowly persuaded that the defendant's activities could rightly be regarded as repair. The Court of Appeal disagreed and held that the defendant had made the patented product. The defendant appealed to the House of Lords on the basis that, in repairing the screens, it had not infringed the patents because:

(a) by marketing the screens, the proprietor had implicitly licensed persons acquiring them to repair them so as to prolong their useful life
(b) the doctrine of exhaustion of rights applied, and
(c) a person repairing a screen did not 'make' a screen within the meaning of s 60(1)(a).

21 *Chiron Corp* v *Organon Teknika Ltd* [1993] FSR 567.

22 Section 70 of the Competition Act 1998 was brought into force by the Competition Act (Commencement No 5) Order 2000, SI 2000/344. The transitional provisions leaving the defence for contracts made before 1 March 2000 are contained in the Competition Act 1998 (Transitional, Consequential and Supplemental Provisions) Order 2000, SI 2000/311.

23 *Conoco Speciality Products (Inc)* v *Merpo Montassa Ltd* [1994] FSR 99.

24 [2001] RPC 24.

The leading judgment was given by Lord Hoffmann who agreed with the Court of Appeal and said that neither the concept of an implied licence nor the doctrine of exhaustion of rights were relevant where it was alleged that the defendant had infringed the patent by making the patented product. The sale of a patented product did not confer a licence to make it. Lord Hoffmann agreed with Lord Halsbury LC in *Sirdar Rubber Co Ltd* v *Wallington, Weston & Co*,[25] where he said (at 543):

> . . . you may prolong the life of a licensed article but you must not make a new one under the cover of repair.

'Repair' is a concept that shares a boundary with 'making' but does not trespass on its boundary, according to Lord Hoffmann. What mattered was whether the defendant had made the patented product. He said that the Court of Appeal was right to substitute its own evaluation of whether the defendant had made the patented product as the trial judge failed to identify the patented product correctly. The defendant had prolonged the useful life of the frame which otherwise would have to be scrapped. But the screen was the combination of the frame and meshes and that ceased to exist when the meshes were removed and the frame cleaned down to bare metal. What was left was merely an important component or chassis from which a new screen could be made. Consequently, the defendant had infringed the patents by making new screens. Lord Hoffmann explained the Court of Appeal's decision in *Solar Thomson Engineering* v *Barton* to the effect that there was a 'licence to repair' a patented product, confirming that the issue was not the juridical nature of the right to repair but simply whether or not the defendant had made the patented product.

The decision in *United Wire* is significant in that it distinguishes between repair and manufacture. However, in any particular case, the question must be a matter of fact and degree. In the present case, had the defendant simply cleaned up the existing mesh screens and placed patches over damaged areas that would surely be deemed to be non-infringing repair. He would not then have 'made' the patented product.

The Court of Appeal confirmed the 'making' test in terms of repair in *Schütz (UK) Ltd* v *Werit UK Ltd*.[26] In that case, the claimant had a patent for intermediate bulk containers (IBCs), comprising a cage made from tubular metal into which close fitting removable plastic bottles with a capacity of 1,000 litres were fitted. Such bottles were part of the prior art and they tended to wear out sooner than the cages. The defendants supplied its own plastic bottles to be fitted by third parties when the bottles in the claimant's IBCs needed replacement. The patent was held to be valid and the defendant raised a defence based on the 'right to repair'. An argument that the House of Lords in *United Wire* had postulated a 'whole inventive concept' test was rejected by the Court of Appeal. Such a test would mean that the defendant's acts would have to fall within the whole of the claimed inventive concept. As Lord Hoffmann said in *United Wire*, removing the meshes meant that the whole patented product ceased to exist. Cleaning the frame and adding a new mesh amounted to making the patented product. Jacob LJ said that the same applied in the present case. The IBCs ceased to exist when the bottles were removed and what remained was merely a component from which a new IBC could be made. Therefore by supplying new plastic bottles, the defendant was facilitating the making of the patented product and was liable as a joint tortfeasor under s 60(2), the supplying the means form of infringement.

Jacob LJ also held that, although the result would mean that the claimant had a monopoly in unpatented replacement bottles, that was a concern of an economic nature and was not a matter for patent law, which had no provision to prevent this. Other areas of law might be relevant such as competition law.

Under the Patents Act 1977, there is, of course, no 'right to repair'. It is simply a matter of whether the product which is the subject-matter of the patent has been made by the

25 (1907) 24 RPC 539.

26 [2011] FSR 19.

defendant. Whether there is an implied licence to repair is again a question of whether the defendant has made the patented product.

Good faith serious and effective preparations

The s 64 defence (act done, or effective and serious preparations to do such an act, in good faith before the priority date) is an important one as, in a particular industry, many organisations may be working towards the same goal at the same time. Some important points to note about s 64 are as follows.

1   The act must be such as would be an infringement of the patent were it in force. If the prior act was not an infringement (for example, if it fell within one of the defences in s 60(5)), s 64 does not apply. There is no need to rely on it as the act does not infringe.
2   'Continue to do the act' means 'that act'. This would appear to cover the continuance of a single infringing act carried on over a period of time (for example, building an infringing radio mast). However, it would seem to allow repeating a single infringing act such as continuing to make infringing products.[27]
3   It is difficult to determine whether there are any qualitative restrictions. That is, can the person relying on s 64 in respect of an act falling within one claim work any of the other claims, including the most favoured embodiment? For example, can a prior user who made brass widgets now make plastic widgets which are covered by another claim? There were two contradictory cases on this point[28] but the better view, which has been reinforced by a subsequent case to decide the issue,[29] is that s 64 does not give a general licence to other infringing acts beyond those done before the priority date or in respect of which serious and effective preparations were made before the priority date. 'Effective' qualifies preparations and there must be something more than preparations to do the act which would otherwise infringe. It was suggested by Aldous LJ in *Lubrizol Corp v Esso Petroleum Co Ltd*,[30] that the preparations must be so advanced as to be about to result in the infringing act being done.
4   The proprietor will find that his monopoly has turned into a duopoly. However, this is not as bad as it might seem. No one else except the prior user or his assignee can do the act, and he may not be allowed to use the best embodiment unless his prior user extended to that.
5   The prior user may assign his right to continue to do the act. (Note it is a right and not just a defence.) However, he is not allowed to grant licences in relation to the act.
6   If the patent relates to a product, there may be other rights, such as a design right. Would the right under s 64 overrule these other rights?

There is a period of limbo that can apply where the prior act, or preparations for the act, comes between the priority date and the date of publication of the specification. This may be relevant where a person suspects that a patent application has been filed that may cover the act by its claims. Although no damages can be awarded for acts done before publication, they may be awarded if continued thereafter.[31] The person applying for the patent is unlikely to volunteer information concerning his patent at this stage, and the person intending to do the act has either to take a chance or wait until publication. This may be unsatisfactory, particularly where some considerable initial expense is involved such as constructing a new factory or installing a new production line.

To take an example, say that Deuce Developments Ltd commenced making and selling extendible pruning shears for reaching high branches of fruit trees in November 2008. The shears incorporated a novel design of hinge, but Deuce did not apply for a patent in respect of it. During April 2008, Metal Modes Ltd filed an application for a patent in relation to a hinge. Deuce was not aware of this and Deuce did not start making serious and effective preparations to produce its shears until June 2008. When the patent specification

27 *See* Thorley, S. *et al.* (2005) *Terrell on the Law of Patents* (16th edn) Sweet & Maxwell, para 8.59.

28 *Helitune* v *Stewart Hughes* [1991] RPC 78, taking a wide view, and *Lubrizol Corp* v *Exxon* [1992] RPC 281, taking a narrow view. Both of these cases were in the Patents Court.

29 *Lubrizol Corp* v *Esso Petroleum Co Ltd* [1997] RPC 195. On appeal, Aldous LJ said that s 64 does not give a right to manufacture any product or expand into other products. However, the protected act does not have to be exactly the same; s 64 is designed to give 'practical protection to enable a man to continue doing what in substance he was doing before': *Lubrizol Corp* v *Esso Petroleum Co Ltd* [1998] RPC 727.

30 [1998] RPC 727 at 770.

31 Patents Act 1977 s 69. Proceedings may not be brought until after the patent has been granted.

was published, Deuce decided to change the design of its hinge so as not to infringe the patent, should it be granted. When the patent is granted to Metal Modes, it can do nothing about Deuce having made the shears prior to publication (it could have sued for damages as from the publication date had Deuce continued to make shears with the hinge as covered in the claims) but it can take action against persons who acquired the early shears with the infringing hinge if those persons are using them. This is an infringement under s 60. However, those persons will be able to sue Deuce on the basis of a breach of the Sale of Goods Act 1979 s 12(2), the implied warranty of quiet possession of goods. The case of *Microbeads AC v Vinhurst Road Markings Ltd*[32] gives an excellent example of the consequences of acts done between filing and publication of a patent that infringe, which, as they were not a continuance of acts or the result of serious and effective preparations done before the priority date, are not saved by s 64. In the *Microbeads* case road-marking machines were made and sold after the priority date of the patent application made by a third party who later obtained a patent in respect of the machines.

Other points may be relevant, for example whether there is an express licence and, if so, whether it permits the acts complained of. Another way to escape liability is for the defendant to show that the claimant, if he claims to be an exclusive licensee, is indeed not an exclusive licensee, or even if he is that the acts complained of were performed before the licence took effect.[33] There is a presumption in favour of the proprietor under s 100 which states that if the patent in question has been granted for a process for obtaining a new product, the same product produced by anyone other than the proprietor or his licensee shall be taken to have been obtained by means of that patented process. This presumption is rebuttable on proof to the contrary and is relevant to infringement actions under s 60(1)(c), that is infringement of a process patent by disposing of, offering to dispose of, using, importing or keeping any product obtained directly by means of the process. In *Generics (UK) Ltd v H Lundbeck A/S*,[34] it was held that the presumption was displaced by the fact that the evidence showed that the company producing the new product had applied for permission to market the product to the regulatory authority and there were clear legal and commercial reasons why the company would not have misled the authority about its process as had been alleged. Supplying false information to the regulatory authority is a criminal offence.

Groundless threats of infringement proceedings

There is a remedy for groundless threats of infringement proceedings and a person aggrieved can bring an action for a declaration that the threats are unjustifiable, for an injunction against the continuation of those threats and for damages for any losses sustained as a result of the threats.[35] The threats may be made by 'circulars, advertising or otherwise' and need not be directed against the person aggrieved. Under s 70(2), the person bringing a groundless threats action is entitled to relief if he can show that the threats were made and that he is a person aggrieved. Where the defendant proves that the acts complained of constitute or would constitute an infringement of the patent, entitlement to relief is subject to the claimant showing that the patent is invalid in a relevant respect and, even then, relief is not available if the defendant shows that, at the time of making the threats, he did not know and had no reason to suspect that the patent was invalid in that respect under s 72(2A).[36] Having reason to suspect calls for an objective assessment based upon what the proprietor knew at the time the threat was made which includes information brought to his attention.[37] Assertions that the patent in suit is invalid are not sufficient unless substantiated.

32 [1975] 1 All ER 529.

33 The Patents Act 1977 s 130(1) defines 'exclusive licence' as a licence from the proprietor (or applicant for a patent) conferring on the licensee (including persons authorised by the licensee) and to the exclusion of all others (including the proprietor or applicant) any right in respect of the invention to which the patent or application relates.

34 [2006] EWCA Civ 1261.

35 Patents Act 1977 s 70.

36 This subsection was inserted by the Patents Act 2004.

37 *FNM Corporation Ltd* v *Drammock International Ltd* [2009] EWHC 1294 (Pat) per Arnold J at para 227. This should be compared with the meaning of the phrase 'reason to believe' in copyright law.

The provisions on groundless threats actions seem fairly straightforward at first sight, though they have generated some case law. Particular issues are: what constitutes an actionable threat, who can be a person aggrieved and what is the scope of the defences in s 70(2) and (4)?[38] A series of cases (*Brain v Ingledew* and others) have been very instructive. The issues are examined in turn below.

38 There is, of course, no case law as yet on the defence under s 70(6) which was inserted by the Patents Act 2004.

The threats

To be considered a threat of infringement proceedings, the nature of the statement depends on how it would be understood by the ordinary reader in the position of the actual recipient.[39] It is also clear from a trade mark case on groundless threats that the threat may be implicit.[40] In *FNM Corporation Ltd v Drammock International Ltd*,[41] the threats were made in a number of letters and an e-mail. The email, sent to the retailer Superdrug, pointed out that there was a current dispute with its supplier of cooling spray aerosols in relation to the patent at issue. Arnold J approved the view of Aldous J in *Bowden Controls Ltd v Acco Cable Controls Ltd*[42] where he said (at 432):

39 *Bowden Controls Ltd v Acco Cable Controls Ltd* [1990] RPC 427.

40 *L'Oréal (UK) Ltd v Johnson & Johnson* [2000] FSR 686.

41 [2009] EWHC 1294 (Pat).

42 [1990] RPC 427.

> . . . believe the recipient would consider what was the purpose of the letter. He would conclude that the purpose of the letter was to give him information and a warning. That requires the answer: a warning as to what?

Arnold J said that this was supported by the reaction of Superdrug to the e-mail which said that the owners of the patent believed the supplier was infringing the patent and then reminded the supplier that it would be liable for any incurred costs in relation to the patent dispute under Superdrug's standard terms and conditions. Consequently, Arnold J held that the e-mail constituted a threat of patent infringement proceedings.

Providing factual information about the patent or making enquiries to discover the identity of the person who made or imported a product does not, *per se*, constitute an actionable threat under s 70(5). Therefore, a timely letter pointing out that a certain invention is subject to a patent is not an actionable threat, nor is sending a letter to a retailer asking for disclosure of the identity of the person who made the alleged infringing products together with an appropriate assertion. However, if the letter is ambiguous the benefit of the doubt will not be given to the author of it. A threatening letter should be read through the eyes of the reasonable and normal person and any vagueness should be construed against the threatener. Jacob J suggested so in *Patrick John Brain v Ingledew Brown Bennison & Garrett*[43] in which he said, in relation to the s 70(4) defence, discussed later (at 597):

43 [1995] FSR 552.

> . . . to read the letter narrowly would be to give the benefit of the doubt to the threatener because he had written a woolly but ferocious letter. That cannot be right.

That case, the first in the series, *Brain v Ingledew*, involved an application under RSC Ord 14A[44] which allowed a judge to determine questions of law or the construction of a document. In finding that a threats action could be brought in respect of threats issued before a patent is granted, in respect of rights under s 69 (the right to sue for infringement between the date of publication and date of grant of the patent, subject to proceedings not being brought until after grant), Jacob J went further and made further declarations. He said that the letter did amount to a threat of proceedings within s 70; that the claimant (who had set up and managed the company threatened) was a person aggrieved and that the threats in the letter sent by the defendant went further than simply threatening to bring proceedings in respect of using a process.[45]

44 Now replaced by the Civil Procedure Rules 1998.

The Court of Appeal allowed the defendant's appeal as far as these further declarations.[46] The court held that these were matters of fact and it was not open to the judge to decide such matters under RSC Ord 14A. However, the first declaration to the effect that

45 This particular form of threat is within the defence to a threats action in s 70(4): *see* later.

46 *Patrick John Brain v Ingledew Brown Bennison & Garrett* [1996] FSR 341.

47 Section 70(2) provides that relief is not available to the person aggrieved by the threats if the defendant proves the alleged infringing acts are infringing or would infringe the patent. This is discussed below.

a threats action could be brought in respect of threats made before the patent was granted was accepted as being correct in principle. This provides the court with quite a dilemma. How does the court determine whether the act complained of infringes a patent which has not yet been granted?[47]

Person aggrieved

48 This additional defence was inserted by the Patents Act 2004.

49 *Cavity Trays Ltd v RMC Panel Products Ltd* [1996] RPC 361.

50 [1990] RPC 427.

51 [1996] FSR 622.

52 [1965] RPC 102.

'A person aggrieved' may bring a threats action. The defence to an action in s 70(4), that is, that proceedings may not be brought if the threat relates to the making or importing of a product for disposal or the use of a process, suggests that the remedy is designed to protect secondary infringers such as retailers or distributors. (This now extends to other acts of infringement made against the person who has made or imported a product or used a process.)[48] However, the action is not limited to secondary infringers and the question of whether proceedings may be brought depends on whether the threats relate to certain types of acts rather than on the type of person involved.[49] In *Bowden Controls Ltd* v *Acco Cable Controls Ltd*[50] and in *Dimplex (UK) Ltd v De'Longhi Ltd*,[51] the claimant brought an action in respect of threats made to its customers.

To bring an action, the claimant will have to show that he has been caused damage by the threats, or that it is likely that he will be damaged by them. In *Reymes-Cole v Elite Hosiery Co Ltd*,[52] it was held that the person aggrieved must establish that the threats have caused or are likely to cause damage which is more than minimal. However, customers (for example, retailers) who have been threatened with infringement proceedings may simply not want to get involved and prefer to leave it to the person supplying them to fight the threatener. That being so, it may be difficult to obtain evidence of damage. In

53 [1996] FSR 622.

Dimplex (UK) Ltd v De'Longhi Ltd,[53] there was no evidence from customers in the UK but a French customer, who had also received a letter from the defendant threatening proceedings for infringement of its patent, sought an indemnity from the claimant otherwise it would no longer sell the claimant's product. The court was prepared to accept this as evidence of how the English customers were likely to react; the fact that the customer seeking the indemnity was in France did not matter. The claimant was likely to suffer damage which was more than minimal.

54 [1997] FSR 511.

The need to prove damage has been put into some doubt by Laddie J in *Brain* v *Ingledew Brown Bennison & Garrett (No 3)*[54] where he suggested that, regardless of whether a person had been threatened directly or indirectly, he did not need to prove damage. However, he then made it clear that there must be a recognisable grievance. He said that the fact that a trader bringing the action is able to assuage the fears of potential customers who had been threatened so that the threats did not cause a recoverable loss did not mean that he was not a person aggrieved. He was a person with a real commercial interest which had been interfered with by the defendant and, consequently, his was a grievance which the court recognised.

55 [1997] FSR 511.

It has been noted that the person bringing the proceedings for a threats action need not be the person threatened and the provisions may, depending on the circumstances, extend to persons having an interest in the person actually threatened. For example, in *Brain* v *Ingledew Brown Bennison & Garrett (No 3)*,[55] the claimant had set up and was managing the company which had been threatened. The court held that a director, executive or shareholder of a company threatened could be a person aggrieved. It would be a matter of looking at the circumstances. For example, if the threats were such as to disrupt severely the sales of products made by a company so as to jeopardise the company's future viability, this could in turn have a serious impact on shareholders and directors sufficient to give them a cause of action in relation to the threats.

A real difficulty for the patentee is where the patent has not been granted. The threats are issued in that period between publication and grant. The specification, including the claims of the patent, may be amended before grant. Indeed, the patent may not be granted at all, for example, where the applicant is unable to deal with objections raised during examination. There was some judicial diversity of opinion over this point in the Court of Appeal in *Patrick John Brain* v *Ingledew Brown Bennison & Garrett*.[56] Aldous LJ said that it would be desirable for the patent to be granted before trial of the threats action, but if there was an 'extraordinary delay' in grant the court could look at the published specification and decide on a balance of probabilities whether the acts complained of would infringe the patent when granted. Hobhouse LJ was unsure of this approach, saying that he would want further evidence before concluding that the matter could be decided on a balance of probabilities. Unfortunately, the third judge, Beldam LJ, agreed with both judgments! However, in *Brain* v *Ingledew Brown Bennison & Garrett (No 2)*,[57] Laddie J said that, absent a granted patent at the time of the trial, the s 70(2) defence to a threats action could not be determined and the patentee who had issued the threats had to take the risk that the patent might not be granted by the time of trial.

Where the grant is likely to be made in the near future at the time of the trial, it may be that the court will grant a short stay in the threats proceedings. Otherwise, the applicant for a patent would be very foolish to issue threats not saved by s 70(4) or (6) until his patent is granted. The wording of s 70(2) reinforces the view of Laddie J, which is to be preferred. It states that the acts complained of must constitute or, if done, would constitute an *infringement of the patent*.

There are some forms of infringement in respect of which a patentee can threaten to bring an action without risking falling foul of a threats action. Of course, the patentee must be very careful to ensure that his 'threat' does not extend outside the bounds of 'permitted' allegations. Under s 70(4), the right to bring proceedings for groundless threats of infringement proceedings does not arise where the allegation consists of making or importing a product for disposal or of using a process or any other form of infringement by a person making or importing a product or using a process. In *Therm-A-Stor Ltd* v *Weathershield Windows Ltd*,[58] the Court of Appeal held that this extended to the 'supplying the means' infringement under s 60(2). This would require a purposive construction of the subsection which the Court of Appeal later in *Cavity Trays Ltd* v *RMC Panel Products Ltd*[59] was unable to accept in view of its clear and unambiguous wording. In that case, there was some discussion of *Therm-A-Stor* in which the judgment was regarded as difficult to follow in places and which was not taken to require a court to depart from the clear and express words of the statute.

Laddie J, in *Brain* v *Ingledew Brown Bennison & Garrett (No 3)*,[60] admitted some difficulty in understanding the legislative philosophy underlying the exceptions in s 70(4), before amendment by the Patents Act 2004. He considered that s 70(4) did not permit threats in respect of offering a process for use.[61] This is a separate form of infringement and only using a process is included in the subsection.

The threats must relate to the patent and, in *Easycare Inc* v *Bryan Lawrence & Co*,[62] although a patent for a hoof protector for horses was mentioned by the threatener who was the proprietor of the patent, the threats were clearly stated as being to protect the 'name and reputation' of the threatener. Accordingly, an application for interim relief was refused as, *inter alia*, there was no serious issue to be tried as regards the threats.

'Without prejudice' threats

Where a threat is made in a letter headed 'without prejudice', it will not normally be admissible in evidence. In *Unilever plc* v *Procter & Gamble Co*,[63] threats made at a 'without prejudice' meeting between the parties were held to be inadmissible. However, in some cases, such evidence will be admissible notwithstanding the letter or meeting is stated to be without prejudice. The privilege will be lost, for example, in cases where any agreement

56 [1996] FSR 341.

57 [1997] FSR 271.

58 [1981] FSR 579.

59 [1996] RPC 361.

60 [1997] FSR 511.

61 Such an offer would now be within s 70(4), as substituted by the Patents Act 2004, where the person threatened had been using the process.

62 [1995] FSR 597.

63 [2000] FSR 344.

between the parties should be set aside because of misrepresentation, fraud or undue influence or in cases of estoppel, where the exclusion of such evidence would be a cloak for perjury, blackmail or other unambiguous impropriety or where it is admissible as being an offer made without prejudice save as to costs. Another situation is in the context of an alleged infringement of a patent where, at the material time, there were no relevant negotiations for a settlement. In *Kooltrade Ltd v XTS Ltd*,[64] both parties imported different makes of three-wheel buggies for children. The defendant sent a letter headed 'without prejudice' to Tesco Home Shopping which had been supplied by the alleged infringer.[65] Tesco stopped marketing the buggies. This letter specifically alleged that marketing the claimant's buggy was an infringement of patent rights and was held to be an actionable threat. Although it was marked 'without prejudice', no privilege attached to the letters as, at the time, there were no relevant negotiations for settlement between the parties.[66]

Although not involving a groundless threats action as such, a 'without prejudice' letter from an Indian company to the proprietor of a UK pharmaceutical patent alleging that the patent was invalid but adding that there was no wish to embark 'on the confrontational path of revocation if there is an alternative commercial solution acceptable to both parties' was held to be privileged in *Schering Corp v Cipla Ltd*.[67] The overall message in the letter was one of wishing to negotiate.

Where an action for groundless threats has been made under s 70, it may be that a settlement is reached between the parties which may take the form of a contract. Threats of infringement proceedings made later may be dealt with as a breach of contract. In *Kenburn Waste Management Ltd v Heinz Bergmann*,[68] the action was settled on the basis of undertakings by the defendant not to communicate with individuals or companies in the UK claiming that the defendant's patent rights were being infringed by the claimant. Following allegations that the threats were repeated subsequently, the claimant brought an action for breach of contract. The defendant's application for a declaration that the court had no jurisdiction to hear the action was struck out.[69]

Declaration of non-infringement

Under s 71, any person may apply to the court for a declaration that a certain act does not constitute an infringement of the patent, provided that a written application has been submitted to the proprietor accompanied by full details and the proprietor has refused or failed to give the acknowledgement requested. This enables a person to seek clarification as to whether his intended actions will infringe where the proprietor has been unhelpful on this question. Of course, the onus lies on the applicant for a declaration to show that he is entitled to it. There is no provision to apply for declarations of non-infringement in respect of patent applications. Obviously, it would be impossible to decide the point as the claims might be subject to amendment before the patent is granted. An added difficulty is that the application might fail. To apply for a declaration there must be proceedings between the parties, that is, there must be an admissible claim of right by the proprietor of the patent.[70]

Where an action involves an application for a declaration of non-infringement coupled with a claim of groundless threats and a counterclaim for infringement, it might be preferable to separate out the groundless threats action as, if the application for a declaration of non-infringement fails and the infringement claim succeeds, this would dispose of the groundless threats action. In *LB Europe Ltd v Smurfit Bag in Box SA*,[71] a case involving a patent for a tamper-proof tap for the bag in box wine market, the judge separated out the groundless threats action. In the subsequent trial, it was held that the patent was valid but not infringed.[72] The only issue in the groundless threats action was the assessment of damages, as the patent had been held not to have been infringed by the defendant.[73]

64 [2001] FSR 13.

65 An earlier letter sent to the alleged infringer together with a copy sent to Tesco was held not to contain an actionable threat of infringement proceedings.

66 A few weeks after the date of the letter, the defendant applied for a UK patent in respect of the buggy. As the buggy had been freely on sale for some time in the UK, the patent application would almost certainly fail or, if not, result in an invalid patent.

67 [2005] FSR 25.

68 [2002] FSR 44.

69 The appeal to the Court of Appeal was dismissed. The place for performance of the contract was the UK and it was 'exceedingly strongly connected' with the UK: *Kenburn Waste Management Ltd v Heinz Bergmann* [2002] FSR 45.

70 *Unilever plc v Procter & Gamble Co* [2000] FSR 344.

71 [2006] EWHC 2963 (Pat).

72 *LB Europe Ltd v Smurfit Bag in Box SA* [2007] EWHC 510 (Pat).

73 *LB Europe Ltd v Smurfit Bag in a Box SA* [2008] EWHC 1231 (Ch). The threats had been made, *inter alia*, by e-mail. The claimant manufacturer suffered damage as its customer delayed using the product in question because of the threats.

Relief for groundless threats

The relief for a groundless threats action is, under s 70(3), a declaration to the effect that the threats are unjustified, an injunction against continuance of the threats and damages for any loss sustained by reason of the threats. Where a groundless threats action is mounted quickly, the person aggrieved may not suffer any quantifiable losses, in which case it seems reasonable to assume that a declaration and injunction may be available in the absence of any award in damages although, without an injunction, losses would be likely to ensue. As the provisions on groundless threats actions are among those that may result in a challenge to the validity of a patent, apart from requiring the proprietor to show that the acts complained of constitute, or would constitute, an infringement, proprietors should take care not to precipitate such an action.

Permissible acts and defences to a groundless threats action

The acts for which threats can be made without giving rise to a groundless threats action are set out in s 70(4) and are allegations of infringement by making or importing a product for disposal or using a process or, in relation to a person who has made or imported a product for disposal or used a process, a threat to bring proceedings for an infringement alleged to consist of anything else.[74] This could apply, for example, where a primary infringer is threatened with proceedings for selling or offering to sell a product alleged to infringe the patent in question. Further, an actionable threat is not made by providing factual information as to a patent, making enquiries for the sole purpose of discovering whether, or by whom, the patent has been infringed by making or importing a product or using a process or by making an assertion in relation to the patent for the purpose of such enquiries: s 70(5).

Notwithstanding the exceptions to groundless threats actions above, s 70(6), inserted by the Patents Act 2004, provides a defence against a groundless threats action to a person making such a threat to another if he proves that he used his best endeavours to discover, without success:

- in the case of a product, the identity of the person who made or imported it;
- in the case of a process–
  - where the alleged infringement is offering it for use, the identity of the person who used it;
  - where the alleged infringement is an act falling within s 60(1)(c) (disposing, offering to dispose of, etc. a product made directly from the process), the identity of the person who used the process to produce the product in question;

provided he notifies the person threatened accordingly before or at the time of making the threats identifying the endeavours used.

The 'best endeavours' defence for a person making threats to bring infringement proceedings is an important change and helps a patent proprietor (or exclusive licensee) in most cases where the primary infringer cannot be identified by the proprietor. In such a case, any threat made against, for example, a secondary infringer, could trigger a groundless threats action. If the identity of the primary infringer (for example, a person making or importing products alleged to infringe) could be discovered by the proprietor, he could threaten proceedings for making or importing the products without exposing himself to a groundless threats action. Section 70(6) allows the proprietor to threaten proceedings against a secondary infringer after failing to identify the primary infringer after using his best endeavours to discover the identity of the primary infringer without success. This will provide the proprietor with a defence to a groundless threats action as against the secondary infringer.

74 Section 70(4) was substituted by the Patents Act 2004 to provide for this second form of defence. However, it is only available in relation to someone who has made or imported the product, etc. It is not available to someone wrongfully alleged to have made or imported the product: *FNM Corporation Ltd* v *Drammock International Ltd* [2009] EWHC 1294 (Pat).

Revocation of patents

75 Express reference to the proprietor was inserted by the Patents Act 2004. However, where there are joint proprietors, under s 36(3)(a), all must consent to the application for revocation.

76 This is only available where the invention formed part of the state of the art under s 2(3) or in the case of dual UK and European patents designating the UK.

77 [2002] FSR 35.

In many infringement actions, the defendant will seek to challenge the validity of the patent. This may be done by an application (by any person including the proprietor)[75] to revoke the patent under s 72 or by putting the validity of the patent in issue under s 74. Furthermore, the Comptroller has limited powers to revoke a patent on his own initiative under s 73.[76] Under the Patents Act 1949 s 32(1), only 'any person interested' could apply for revocation compared with 'any person' under the 1977 Act. This means that anyone, whether with an interest under the patent or not, may make an application for revocation.

In *Cairnstores Ltd* v *Aktiebolaget Hässle*,[77] it was confirmed that any person could apply for revocation although there may be circumstances where a court might strike out an application as an abuse of process where the purpose was improper or collateral and for which the procedure was not intended. In that case, which concerned an application for revocation of a pharmaceutical patent, the applicant for revocation was an off-the-shelf company with no assets and no objects clause relating to pharmaceuticals. It refused to state what interest, if any, it had in the revocation proceedings. However, there was nothing to suggest an improper or collateral purpose. In 'straw man' cases, Pumfrey J said that security for costs would be appropriate to protect the proprietor adequately as to costs.[78]

78 Eventually, the patents in question were revoked and the appeal was dismissed. Another applicant for revocation turned up, Generics (UK) Ltd, a substantial company: *Cairnstores Ltd* v *Aktiebolaget Hässle (No 2)* [2003] FSR 23.

79 [2003] RPC 29.

The principle that any person can apply for revocation is founded on the basis that it is in the public interest to keep invalid monopolies off the patent register. Even if it appears that the applicant for revocation is an agent acting for an undisclosed principal, the court will not order disclosure of the principal. A claim that such a person would not be caught by the principle of *res judicata* and a number of other reasons put forward for disclosure of the principal were not accepted by the court in *Oystertec plc's Patent*.[79]

The grounds for revocation under s 72 are that:

80 This can only be invoked by a person found, by declaration or under s 37, to be entitled to the patent: s 72(2). There is a two-year deadline from the date of grant of the patent unless the proprietor knew he was not entitled to the patent.

(a) the invention is not a patentable invention (that is, it does not comply with s 1);

(b) the patent was granted to a person who was not entitled to be granted that patent;[80]

(c) the specification of the patent does not disclose the invention clearly enough and completely enough for it to be performed by a person skilled in the art (that is, insufficiency);

(d) the matter disclosed in the specification of the patent extends beyond that disclosed in the application for the patent, as filed, or, if the patent was granted on a new application filed under ss 8(3), 12 or 37(4) or as mentioned in s 15(9), in the earlier application, as filed (added matter);[81]

(e) the protection conferred by the patent has been extended by an amendment which should not have been allowed.

81 *See*, for example, *European Central Bank* v *Document Security Systems Inc* [2007] EWHC 600 (Pat), where an argument that the specification as originally filed implicitly disclosed what had been expressly added in a later amendment failed. The skilled addressee would not have seen any gap in the express disclosure in the original specification and, furthermore, had not experience of what had been added. The appeal to the Court of Appeal was dismissed: [2008] EWCA Civ 192.

An order made under s 72 may be for the unconditional revocation of the patent or, where one of the grounds in s 72(1) applies but only so as to invalidate the patent to a limited extent, the order may be for revocation unless the specification is amended to the satisfaction of the court or Comptroller, as the case may be: s 70(4). A person whose application for revocation has been refused by the Comptroller may apply to the court for revocation only with the leave of the court: s 70(5). Where the Comptroller has not disposed of an application for revocation, the applicant may only apply to the court either with the consent of the proprietor or where the Comptroller has certified in writing that the question is one which would more properly be dealt with by the court: s 70(6).

82 [2002] RPC 46.

Where revocation proceedings have been commenced but there is subsequently a settlement and the proceedings are withdrawn, it appears that the Comptroller still has the power to continue considering the matter by refusing to accept the withdrawal. In *R (on application of Ash & Lacey Building Products Ltd)* v *Comptroller-General of Patents, Designs and Trade Marks*,[82] the hearing officer decided to continue after withdrawal of revocation proceedings. It was decided that the patent was valid but the hearing officer put a different construction on the claims of the patent which the proprietor claimed was unfavourable to it. Laddie J, in the Administrative Court, dismissed the application for judicial review to have the decision quashed. Although the Act is silent on this matter (as it is on withdrawal) he thought that the Comptroller could refuse to accept a withdrawal on rational, non-capricious grounds. Public interest was engaged as, otherwise, a proprietor might settle revocation proceedings to keep a hopelessly invalid patent on the register. The situation is different in the courts as CPR 38.2 allows a claimant to withdraw at any time and this would also apply to revocation proceedings, such withdrawal being effective no matter what the court thought about it.

The proceedings in which the validity of a patent may be put in issue under s 74 are:

(a) by way of defence, in proceedings for infringement of the patent under s 61 or proceedings under s 69 for infringement of rights conferred by the publication of an application (rights from publication to grant);

(b) in proceedings under s 70 (remedy for groundless threats of infringement proceedings);

(c) in proceedings in which a declaration of non-infringement is sought under s 71;

(d) in proceedings for revocation under s 72;

(e) in proceedings under s 58 (relating to Crown use).

Validity may not be put in issue in any other proceedings and, in particular, no proceedings may be instituted seeking only a declaration of validity or invalidity: s 74(2). The only grounds on which the validity of a patent may be put in issue (whether in proceedings for revocation under s 72 or otherwise) are the grounds on which the patent may be revoked under s 72. Where an application for revocation is based on s 72(1)(b) (entitlement), no determination shall be made in invalidity proceedings unless it has been determined in entitlement proceedings under s 37(1) that the applicant is entitled to the patent and proceedings where validity was put in issue were commenced no more than two years from the date of grant of the patent unless it is shown that the proprietor knew at the time of grant (or transfer of the patent to him) that he was not entitled to the patent: s 74(4). Where validity is put in issue by way of defence or counterclaim, the court or Comptroller, if it or he thinks it just to do so, shall give the defendant the opportunity to claim that the patent ought to have been granted to him: s 74(5).

The validity of a patent is not put in issue merely because the Comptroller is considering its validity in order to revoke it under s 73 or its validity is being considered under an application for a Comptroller's opinion as to validity under s 74A. These non-binding opinions in respect of validity and/or infringement were provided for by the Patents Act 2004 which inserted ss 74A and 74B into the 1977 Act.

Where validity has been put in issue, the court or the Comptroller, as the case may be, may allow the proprietor to amend the specification as the court or the Comptroller thinks fit: s 75. This is subject to the court or the Comptroller's discretion as to the manner of advertising the proposed amendment and as regards costs, expenses or otherwise. Also, the amendment is subject to s 76 and must not include added matter. This includes matter additional to that in earlier priority applications under s 76(1A).[83]

An example of the workings of these provisions is *Cartonneries de Thulin SA v CTP White Knight Ltd*[84] in which the defendant successfully argued that the claimant's patent for boxes designed to hold two compact discs was invalid under s 72(1)(d) on the grounds of added matter. Another example is *Haberman v Jackel International Ltd*,[85] in which the defendant attacked the patent for training cups for children on a number of grounds including insufficiency and added matter. Allowing amendment under s 76, the court held that the patent was valid.

A proprietor of a patent can offer to surrender it at any time under s 29. Surrender may be opposed and, if so, the Comptroller shall determine the question. However, it may be

83 Inserted by the Regulatory Reform (Patents) Order 2004, SI 2004/2357.

84 [2001] RPC 6.

85 [1999] FSR 683.

86 [2003] RPC 24.

difficult to decide what to do if an offer to surrender a patent is made whilst revocation proceedings are pending. In *Dyson Ltd's Patent*,[86] the proprietor gave notice of surrender to the Comptroller but stated that revocation proceedings were pending in the High Court. Although there was no opposition to surrender, the hearing officer decided on a stay until the revocation proceedings were completed. However, later, following satisfactory reasons submitted by the proprietor, the surrender was accepted.[87] There may be an important difference between surrender and revocation in terms of royalty payments made by licensees.

87 *Dyson Ltd's Patent (No 2)* [2003] RPC 48.

88 [2002] FSR 24.

In the High Court in Ireland, in *GD Searle & Co's and Monsanto Co's Patent*[88] an application for revocation was stayed pending the outcome of opposition proceedings at the European Patent Office (note, the EPC provides for post-grant opposition unlike the position with the UK Patents Act 1977). In parallel proceedings in the UK, no application for stay was made and the patent was revoked. However, in *Glaxo Group Ltd v Genentech Inc*,[89] the Court of Appeal confirmed that the judge in the High Court had been right to refuse to stay proceedings for revocation even though there were parallel proceedings (opposition proceedings) at the European Patent Office. In spite of the problem of potential conflicting decisions, bearing in mind the length of time before the EPO would decide the case, commercial certainty in the UK required that the hearing in the UK went ahead.

89 [2008] FSR 18.

It is possible for a patent to be granted for an invention which is, in the light of expert evidence, clearly lacking in merit for want of novelty or inventive step. In *Les Laboratoires Servier v Apotex Inc*,[90] Jacob LJ said that simply comparing the patent specification with the prior art would not have revealed its lack of novelty or obviousness. To understand the patent specification, technical expertise in both chemistry and powder X-ray diffraction was needed as well as some experimentation 'in order to see just how specious the application for the patent was'. In observing that the applicant for the patent had done nothing wrong, Jacob LJ said that it was important that there was a speedy and efficient way of obtaining revocation of such a patent before it did too much harm to the public interest. Had the patent been held to be valid, Servier's monopoly of a particular salt of perindopril could have lasted, in effect, from 1980 to 2020. Jacob LJ said (at para 10):

90 [2008] EWCA Civ 445.

> It is the court's job to see that try-ons such as the present patent get nowhere. The only sanction (apart, perhaps, from competition law which thus far has had nothing or virtually nothing to say about unmeritorious patents) may, under the English litigation system, lie in an award of costs on the higher (indemnity) scale if the patent is defended unreasonably.

In such cases, it is difficult to quantify the detriment to the public before revocation. It may be several years before the patent is challenged in revocation proceedings. During all or part of this time, the proprietor may have had a monopoly and enjoyed inflated receipts. In any case, it would be extremely difficult to decide whether the applicant for an unmeritorious patent was deliberately trying to play the system or whether he honestly believed that his invention was probably or possibly patentable. As technology in fields such as pharmaceuticals is so complex, it would be next to impossible to distinguish between a 'try-on' and a bona fide application.

Summary

There are a number of defences to a patent infringement action. They include:

- acts done for private and non-commercial purposes;
- acts done for experimental purposes;
- preparation of medicines to a prescription in a pharmacy;
- acts in relation to ships, aircraft, hovercraft or vehicles entering, crossing or temporarily in the UK.

Further defences may be relevant, for example, on the basis of exhaustion of rights or competition law. A particular form of defence is the 'Gillette defence':

- At the relevant date of the patent, the alleged infringement was neither new nor inventive and consequently:
  - the alleged infringement is outside the patent claims or, if not,
  - the patent is invalid for lack of novelty or inventive step.

A further 'defence' is to the effect that the defendant simply repaired the patented product and did not make it. The test is one of 'making' rather than looking at the 'whole inventive concept'.

One defence that actually gives a right under a patent is where a person carried out an act in good faith before the priority date of the patent or made effective and serious preparations to do so. In such a case, that person has a right to continue or start the act as the case may be.

There is a limited remedy in relation to groundless threats of infringement proceedings. A person aggrieved can bring proceedings. This could be the person threatened, for example, or the person supplying such a person with alleged infringing products. Remedies are a declaration that the threats are unjustified, an injunction against the continuation of those threats, and damages to compensate for losses resulting from the threats.

There are several grounds for revocation of a patent, such as:

- the invention is not patentable;
- the patent was not granted to the person entitled to it;
- insufficiency;
- added matter;
- an amendment has extended the subject-matter.

Validity of a patent may be put in issue in the following proceedings:

- by the defence in an infringement action;
- groundless threats actions;
- an action for a declaration of non-infringement;
- revocation proceedings;
- in relation to disputes as to Crown use.

Discussion questions

1 The EPC leaves infringement (and, hence, defences) to national courts (see Article 64). On the other hand, Article 30 of the TRIPs Agreement states that:

> Members may provide limited exceptions to the exclusive rights conferred by a patent, provided that such exceptions do not unreasonably conflict with a normal exploitation of the patent and do not unreasonably prejudice the legitimate interests of the patent owner, taking account of the legitimate interests of third parties.

To what extent do the defences to patent infringement in the UK comply with Article 30?

2 Discuss the 'right to repair' in relation to (a) whether such a right exists under patent law, and (b) whether an unpatented component which is part of a patented product should be protected by patent law.

3 The provisions relating to acts done, or serious and effective preparations made, before the priority date of the patent seriously undermine the patent monopoly. In a first to invent (rather than a first to file) system, the patent would be vulnerable even if such acts or preparations were not made available to the public. Discuss.

4 Do you think the changes to the provisions relating to groundless threats actions made by the Patents Act 2004 have emasculated the action to vanishing point?

5 Discuss the situations under which the validity of a patent may be put in issue in legal proceedings.

Selected further reading

Cook, T., 'Responding to concerns about the scope of the defence from patent infringement for acts done for experimental purposes relating to the subject matter of the invention' [2011] *Intellectual Property Quarterly*, 193 (considers the experimental use defence, its scope and flexibility and proposes changes to the UK version of the defence).

Schütz (UK) Ltd v *Werit UK Ltd* in the Court of Appeal, where Jacob LJ addresses the issue of the scope of the 'right to repair', available at: **http://www.bailii.org/ew/cases/EWCA/Civ/2011/303.html**

Visit www.mylawchamber.co.uk/bainbridgeip to access study support resources including interactive multiple choice questions, practice exam questions with guidance, weblinks, legal updates and a legal newsfeed.

mylawchamber
unrivalled support for legal education

Part Five

DESIGN LAW

What is a design? 16

Introduction

Design law has undergone many changes over the past 20 or so years. Before the Copyright, Designs and Patents Act 1988, aesthetic designs were protected by registration under the Registered Designs Act 1949. Functional designs could be protected by way of copyright in drawings of designs though this led to some unfortunate consequences in that functional designs appeared to be protected for much longer than designs registrable under the Registered Designs Act 1949.[1] The House of Lords attempted to address this disparity by refusing to enforce copyright in drawings of exhaust pipes for motor cars, in *British Leyland Motor Corp Ltd* v *Armstrong Patents Co Ltd*,[2] on the basis of non-derogation from grant. This was a limited attack on copyright protection for functional designs and applied only in relation to spare parts.

The Copyright, Designs and Patents Act 1988 made some very significant changes to design law. It introduced a new form of design protection, known as the unregistered design right. It was aimed primarily, though not exclusively, at functional designs and was informal, like copyright, but of a much shorter duration, being effectively no more than ten years of commercial exploitation with licences of right being available in the last five years. The Registered Designs Act 1949 was also substantially modified including changes to the criteria for registrability and in terms of the maximum duration which was increased to 25 years.

On 9 December 2001, the law relating to registered designs was again changed (almost out of recognition compared with the previous law) as a result of implementing a Directive harmonising registered design law throughout the European Community (now European Union).[3] The UK's unregistered design right was left untouched by this. However, a further major change was made in 2002 by the introduction of the Community design.[4] This provides for a two-track approach – protection through registration for a maximum period of 25 years in five year blocks and an informal protection for three years, not subject to registration.[5] The Community design, like the Community trade mark, has a unitary nature, is effective throughout the Community and is administered by the Office for the Harmonisation of the Internal Market (Trade Marks and Designs) ('OHIM') based at Alicante in Spain. OHIM commenced accepting registrations for the Community design from January 2003 (first designs registered as from 1 April 2003) and the unregistered Community design came into force on 6 March 2002. Further significant changes to the UK registered design were made during 2006,[6] though these changes did not modify its basic nature. For example, there are no longer substantive grounds for refusal of registration. However, interested persons may raise the equivalent grounds in invalidity proceedings.

1 In those days, design registration lasted up to a maximum of 15 years whereas copyright lasted for the life of the author plus 50 years.

2 [1986] 2 WLR 400.

3 Directive 98/71/EC of the European Parliament and of the Council of 13 October 1998 on the legal protection of designs, OJ L 289, 28.10.1998, p 28. The Directive should have been implemented by 28 October 2001. The changes were made by the Registered Designs Regulations 2001, SI 2001/3949.

4 Council Regulation (EC) No 6/2002 on Community designs, OJ L 3, 05.01.2002, p 1.

5 The registered Community design gives a monopoly form of protection whereas the unregistered Community design gives protection against copying.

6 By the Intellectual Property (Enforcement, etc.) Regulations 2006, SI 2006/1028, and the Regulatory Reform (Registered Designs) Order 2006, SI 2006/1974.

The present position is that a design may be protected by one or more of four ways in the United Kingdom by virtue of:

- registration as a UK design under the much amended Registered Designs Act 1949;
- the UK's unregistered design;
- registration as a Community design at OHIM;
- the unregistered Community design.

Other intellectual property rights may also protect some designs, such as artistic copyright and trade marks.

From the outset, it should be pointed out that the UK unregistered design is quite unlike the other three forms of protection which are very similar in some respects. Another thing to bear in mind is that there are some differences between the rights and, whilst it is possible that a particular design can be protected by all four, an important feature of registration is that it provides a monopoly right whilst the unregistered design rights require proof of copying. That is one reason why registration is to be preferred. Another feature of the UK's registered design and the Community registered design is that a one-year period of grace is allowed so that the applicant for registration may, for example, market products to the design for up to one year prior to filing the application without compromising novelty. As regards the UK registered design, this was completely new and caused some difficulty in respect of the transitional provisions in the 2001 Regulations.[7]

A 'design' is aspects of or features applied to an article or product; it is not the article or product itself[8] and it should be noted that, in intellectual property law, the word 'design' has a restricted meaning. In normal usage the word 'design' can be taken to mean a plan or a scheme, which may be written or drawn, showing how something is to be constructed, or how the elements of an item or article are arranged. Alternatively, a design may be a decorative pattern. In legal terms, a design is defined by reference to the provisions applicable to the Community design, the UK registered design or the UK unregistered design right. It should be noted that the Community design and the UK registered design have almost identical requirements for registration, which are very similar to the requirements for subsistence of the unregistered Community design.

Designs may be for functional articles, such as a can opener, a tool box, a container for frozen food or an exhaust pipe for a car. Articles which are functional in nature are generally, but by no means exclusively, in the province of the UK's unregistered design right.[9] These designs are those that are original, though not commonplace, and relate to features of shape or configuration of an article. A design for which the appearance of a product to which it has been applied is new and where the design has individual character are within the scope of the Community design and the UK's registered designs.

The changes to design law over the last few years have been very welcome and have gone some way to bringing design law into the twenty-first century. The UK's unregistered design has been unaffected by the changes and there have been very few legislative changes to the right since its inception. It remains quite different to the other forms of rights in designs and it could be argued, especially with the introduction of the unregistered Community design, that it ought to be repealed. Nevertheless, it remains a useful right and infringement of the UK's unregistered design is still an issue whether in proceedings based solely on that right or together with other rights. A good example of its continuing utility was shown in the case of *Dyson Ltd* v *Qualtex (UK) Ltd*[10] where it was held that the right was infringed by a 'pattern' manufacturer of spare parts for the famous Dyson bagless vacuum cleaners.[11]

There is inevitably some overlap between the unregistered design right and the other rights in designs. There may also be some overlap between rights in designs and other intellectual property rights such as trade marks and copyright. In particular, the Trade Marks Act 1994 and the Community trade mark system allow for the registration of

7 *See Oakley Inc* v *Animal Ltd* [2006] Ch 337, discussed in Chapter 17.

8 *Clarke's Design* (1896) 13 RPC 351 per Lindley LJ.

9 Many functional articles have also been designed to make them more attractive to potential purchasers and, in a good number of cases, they may also be registrable under the UK registered design and the Community design.

10 [2005] RPC 19.

11 A pattern spare part is one which duplicates the shape and appearance of the original. This important case is discussed in more detail in Chapter 18.

12 [2011] FSR 19. This case is discussed in the patents section of the book (see p 000). Although the patented invention is not registered as a design, some of the company's other liquid containers are registered as Community designs.

shapes and containers as trade marks, subject to exceptions: for example, where a shape gives substantial value to the goods in question. This could be where the shape is that of an ornament such as a porcelain figurine. Some designs, such as the metal cage used in bulk liquid containers in *Schütz (UK) Ltd v Werit UK Ltd*,[12] may even be patentable inventions though they may not be registrable as designs if the design is dictated by technical function.

Brief history of design law up to 2001

13 27 Geo III c 38.

14 2 Vict c 13.

The law of designs has a reasonably long history dating back to the latter part of the eighteenth century. In 1787, the first Designs Act protecting designs was passed[13] which gave a two-month protection to designs applied to linens, cotton, calicoes and muslins. The origins of design law spring from this area. The Copyright in Designs Act 1839[14] set up a system of registration and also extended design laws to designs applied to articles, either as 'surface design' or 'shape designs'. Several other Acts were passed over the next few years and, eventually, these were repealed and replaced by the Patents, Designs and Trade Marks Act 1883. A previous distinction between ornamental and useful designs was removed and the duration of protection was set at five years. The Patents and Designs Act 1907 increased the maximum term of protection to 15 years, a remedy for groundless threats of infringement proceedings was introduced and provisions requiring articles to be marked was relaxed. Following further Acts in 1919 and 1932, the current statute, the Registered Designs Act 1949, was enacted. However, the 1949 Act has been transformed on two occasions, first by the Copyright, Designs and Patents Act 1988 and then by the Registered Designs Regulations 2001.[15] The result is that the Act bears little resemblance to its original form.

15 SI 2001/3949.

With the development of artistic copyright came problems of duplication of rights and the Copyright Act 1911, followed by the Copyright Act 1956, attempted to remove the overlap between a registrable design and artistic copyright. This was modified by the Design Copyright Act 1968 which permitted dual protection to a design both as a registered design and under artistic copyright, but reduced the term of copyright to 15 years.[16] If this was not bad enough, following the distinction between registrable and unregistrable designs highlighted in *Dorling v Honnor Marine Ltd*,[17] a regrettable state of affairs arose.

16 The Design Copyright Act 1968 and the Copyright Act 1956 were repealed in their entirety by the Copyright, Designs and Patents Act 1988.

17 [1965] Ch 1.

The claimant in *Dorling v Honnor Marine* designed a sailing dinghy and granted a licence to the second defendant to build dinghies to the design and to make kits of parts on his behalf, all in accordance with the claimant's drawings. The relationship between the claimant and the second defendant broke down and the latter formed a limited company, the first defendant, to which he purported to assign his licence to build the dinghies. The design of the dinghy as a whole was registrable under the Registered Designs Act 1949, but it had not been registered. The individual parts, being purely functional, were not registrable.[18] By making a three-dimensional representation of the drawings in the form of parts for a boat, the defendants had infringed the copyright in the drawings. A defence based on the Copyright Act 1956 s 10, which removed copyright protection from designs registrable under the Registered Designs Act 1949, failed because the parts, as opposed to the dinghy as an entirety, were not registrable. Thus, the outcome of the case was that if a design was aesthetic it was, subject to some other requirements, registrable under the Registered Designs Act 1949 and could be protected for 15 years.[19] If the design was purely functional it was not registrable but could attract artistic copyright through its drawings, which would last for the remainder of the life of the author plus 50 years.[20] Functional designs appeared to be far better protected than aesthetic designs (not being works of copyright), an extremely anomalous situation.

18 The Registered Designs Act 1949, at the time of this case, required that a registered design had eye-appeal. Now it is the appearance resulting from particular features of the whole or part of a product that is registrable.

19 This has now been extended to 25 years.

20 The basic term for copyright in artistic works is now 'life plus 70 years'.

The above unsatisfactory position can partly explain the House of Lords (now Supreme Court) decision in *British Leyland Motor Corp Ltd v Armstrong Patents Co Ltd*[21] concerning the reverse engineering of exhaust pipes which infringed indirectly the copyright in the drawings of the exhaust pipes. Their Lordships took the opportunity partly to redress the apparent imbalance between the protection for articles with eye-appeal and purely functional articles by using the principle of non-derogation from grant. Even if a design was registrable there was little incentive for registration as copyright in the drawings could still be enjoyed for 15 years, free of charge.[22] In 1988, the last full year before the main provisions of the Copyright, Designs and Patents Act 1988 came into force, there were only 8,748 applications for registered designs received by the Design Registry.[23]

The law of designs was radically altered by the Copyright, Designs and Patents Act 1988, both in terms of changes to the Registered Designs Act 1949[24] and the introduction of the new unregistered design right. The law prior to the coming into force of this Act remained relevant for designs which were created or recorded before 1 August 1989. Designs that were created or recorded before 1 August 1989 and which were not registrable under the Registered Designs Act 1949 continued to rely on copyright for protection although only effectively until 1 August 1999[25] (unless the copyright expired earlier in any case). Indeed, in *Valeo Vision SA v Flexible Lamps Ltd*,[26] the claimant successfully relied on copyright protection through its drawings of rear lamp clusters for vehicles even though its registered designs were held to be invalid through want of novelty.

Before looking at the rights in overview, it is important to realise that, whilst there are inevitably some similarities between the UK's unregistered design right and the other rights in designs, they are different and have different legislative origins. For example, the UK's registered design provides a monopoly right whilst the UK's unregistered design right is more like a copyright.[27] Therefore, the meaning of a word or phrase used for both rights will not necessarily be the same for both.

Although there seems to be no logical scheme underlying the protection of designs, Lords Walker and Collins described the scheme in their joint judgment in the UK Supreme Court case of *Lucasfilm Ltd v Ainsworth*.[28] It is worth setting out para 48 of their judgment almost fully:

> It is a general point as to the policy considerations underlying Parliament's development of the law in order to protect the designers and makers of three-dimensional artefacts from unfair competition . . . the Court of Appeal took the view . . . that there was no assistance to be obtained from the relationship between copyright and registered design right. We respectfully disagree, especially if the relatively new unregistered design right is also taken into account. It is possible to recognise an emerging legislative purpose (though the process has been slow and laborious) of protecting three-dimensional objects in a graduated way, quite unlike the protection afforded by the indiscriminate protection of literary copyright. Different periods of protection are accorded to different classes of work. Artistic works of art (sculpture and works of artistic craftsmanship) have the fullest protection; then come works with 'eye appeal' (*AMP Inc v Utilux Pty Ltd* [1971] FSR 572); and under Part III of the 1988 Act a modest level of protection has been extended to purely functional objects (the exhaust system of a motor car being the familiar example). Although the periods of protection accorded to the less privileged types have been progressively extended, copyright protection has always been much more generous. There are good policy reasons for the differences in the periods of protection, and the Court should not, in our view, encourage the boundaries of full copyright protection to creep outwards.

There remains some elitism which favours the work of authors over that of designers. Why should a terrible work of fiction enjoy much longer protection that the design for (a) a novel household item, or (b) a new piece of machinery or equipment which is the result of careful and thoughtful work by a qualified engineer or skilled designer and which has undergone significant materials research and testing and market research by other skilled persons?

21 [1986] 2 WLR 400.

22 Apart from the fact that registration gave a monopoly protection.

23 This compares with 30,471 patent applications received by the Patent Office in 1988 and 38,006 trade and service mark applications received by the Trade Marks Registry in the same year: *Patents, Designs and Trade Marks 1990*, 108th Annual Report of the Comptroller-General of Patents, Designs and Trade Marks, HMSO, 1990. The latest available statistics for applications (2010) are: registered designs (3,705), patents (21,929) and trade marks (26,792).

24 Prior to these changes, design registration was limited to a maximum of 15 years' protection.

25 Copyright, Designs and Patents Act 1988 Sch 1 para 19(1) prevented the operation of s 51 of that Act for ten years from commencement. Section 51 states that making an article or copying an article represented in a design document or model does not infringe the copyright in the design document or model except where the design is for an artistic work or typeface.

26 [1995] RPC 205.

27 The design right owes its origins to the Council Directive 87/54/EEC of 16 December 1986 on the legal protection of topographies of semiconductor products, OJ L 24, 27.01.1987, p 36. *See Ocular Sciences Ltd v Aspect Vision Care Ltd* [1997] RPC 289 at 421 per Laddie J. Semiconductor products are now protected by a variant of the UK's unregistered design right, described in Chapter 18.

28 [2011] UKSC 39.

Community design and the UK registered design

The registered Community design has proved very popular, with 81,737 applications during 2010. This must be compared to the applications for a UK registered design which stood at a mere 3,705 for the same year. Consequently, the focus in this and the following chapter will be on the Community design. Although it should be noted that the UK registered design is virtually identical when it come to the requirements for registrability, rights and limitations, there are some differences, such as the rules for ownership. Furthermore, some aspects of the Community design in respect of the UK are governed by UK law, such as assignment and, in the UK, there is a remedy for groundless threats of infringement proceedings in relation to the Community design.

29 Council Regulation (EC) No 6/2002 on Community designs, OJ L 3, 05.01.2002, p 1.

30 Directive 98/71/EC of the European Parliament and of the Council of 13 October 1998 on the legal protection of designs, OJ L 289, 28.10.1998, p 28.

The Community design is governed by the Community Design Regulation[29] whereas the UK registered design is subject to the Registered Designs Act 1949 which was substantially amended to comply with a Directive harmonising design law throughout Europe.[30] This explains the similarities between the registered Community design and the UK registered design.

Attempts were made to encourage greater use of the UK's registered design. Substantive examination has been ended and attempts made to ease the administrative burden for applicants, for example, in relation to applications to register multiple designs. Nevertheless, applications remain disappointingly low, even lower than a few years ago.

Community design

There are two forms of Community design, registered and unregistered. There are some differences between them but they are very similar. There are, for example, differences in the time at which novelty and individual character are judged and there are differences in infringement. For the unregistered design, proof of copying is required but this is not so for the registered Community design as this is a monopoly right. There are also differences in the duration of the rights. Initial registration gives five years protection, which may be renewed up to a maximum of 25 years in five year blocks. For the unregistered Community design, the duration is only three years from the date it was first made available to the public.

For both forms of Community design, there is no requirement for eye-appeal as such; however, the definition of design in Article 3(a) of the Community Design Regulation states that it means:

> the appearance of the whole or a part of a product resulting from the features of, in particular, the lines, contours, colours, shape, texture and/or materials of the product and/or its ornamentation.

A design must be new and have an individual character. Appearance is still a factor and it is the visual significance of the design which is important when testing for novelty and individual character. A design is new if no identical design, or one whose features differ only in immaterial details, has been made available to the public, either before the date of filing (or priority date, if relevant) for a registered Community design or, in the case of the unregistered Community design, before the date the design was made available to the public. Individual character is tested by the overall impression it produces on the informed user compared with designs already made available to the public.

A period of grace of 12 months is allowed without destroying novelty where the disclosure in question is by or through the designer or in breach of confidence; also excluded from the question of novelty are disclosures which could not reasonably become known in the normal course of business to the circles specialised in the sector concerned in the Community.

A design must be applied to a product which is defined as an industrial or handicraft item including, *inter alia*, parts intended to be assembled into a complex product, packaging, get-up, graphic symbols and typographic typefaces but excluding computer programs. A complex product is one which is composed of multiple components which can be replaced, permitting disassembly and reassembly of the product. Thus modular components may be registered as designs.[31]

There are a number of exceptions to registration, for example, where the features of appearance of a product are solely dictated by the product's technical function and there is a 'must-fit' exception (but this does not extend to modular units). Designs contrary to public policy or accepted principles of morality are likewise excluded.

The right to a Community design vests in the designer or successor in title unless the designer is an employee creating the design in the execution of his duties, in which case the right vests in his employer, subject to agreement otherwise or as specified in national law. Unless assigned, rights in designs created under a commission do not automatically vest in the commissioner.[32] Infringement of a registered Community design occurs by making, importing, using or by various forms of commercialising a product incorporating the design or to which the design has been applied without the consent of the proprietor. The unregistered Community design is infringed in similar circumstances but only if the acts in question are the result of copying the design. There are exceptions to infringement such as where the design is used for private and non-commercial purposes, experimentation or teaching and in respect of ships and aircraft registered elsewhere temporarily within the territory of the Community.

A controversial issue is the protection afforded to 'must-match' parts, being parts that must be a particular shape to match the rest of a complex product of which it is a part to restore its original appearance. An example is a replacement wing for a motor vehicle or a replacement headlamp for a vehicle. Such spare parts are not protected by the Community design[33] but the Directive harmonising design protection throughout the Community allowed Member States to retain their previous position on the protection of such parts provided that, if they made any changes, they could only liberalise the market. The main market affected was the aftermarket in spare parts for motor vehicles, estimated at €7.5 billion annually.[34] Nine Member States, including the UK, denied protection for 'must-match' spare parts but the remaining 16 Member States have protection for such parts.[35] The Commission to the European Communities was required to review the position three years after implementation of the designs Directive and it has produced a proposal to remove protection for spare parts to repair a complex product so as to restore its original appearance providing consumers are informed as to the origin of the parts so that they can make an informed choice.[36]

Figure 16.1 shows a representation of the requirements for and exceptions to the Community design (it also represents the UK's registered design).

UK registered design

The UK's registered design is very much like the registered version of the Community design though there are some differences which will be considered in more depth in the following chapter. At this stage it is worth noting that the Community Design Regulations 2005[37] have brought the two systems closer by providing a remedy for groundless threats of infringement proceedings for Community designs in the UK and by extending Crown use to Community designs. The offence of falsely representing a design as being registered also now applies to the registered Community design. The rules on entitlement are not exactly the same and there are no express provisions for commissioned designs under the Community design. Both the UK's registered design and the registered Community design

31 The definitions of 'design', 'product' and 'complex product' in Article 3 of the Regulation are identical to those in the harmonising Directive: Article 1. The definitions in the Registered Designs Act 1949 as amended are not quite verbatim though they probably have an identical effect, as they should do.

32 This was confirmed by the Court of Justice of the EU in Case C-32/08 *Fundación Española para la Innovación de la Artesanía (FEIA)* v *Cul de Sac Espacio Creativo SL* [2009] ECR I-5611. Contrast this with the position under the UK registered design and the UK unregistered design right.

33 Article 110(1) of the Community Design Regulation.

34 Proposal for a Directive of the European Parliament and of the Council amending Directive 98/71/EC on the legal protection of designs COM (2004) 582 final, SEC (2004) 1097, 14.09.2004, p 5. Of course, this proposal preceded enlargement of the Community.

35 Although Greece has a short-term protection of five years during which spare parts can be copied in return for a fair remuneration.

36 Proposal for a Directive of the European Parliament and of the Council amending Directive 98/71/EC on the legal protection of designs COM (2004) 582 final, SEC (2004) 1097, 14.09.2004. This has not been adopted at the time of writing.

37 SI 2005/2339. These Regulations came into force on 1 October 2005.

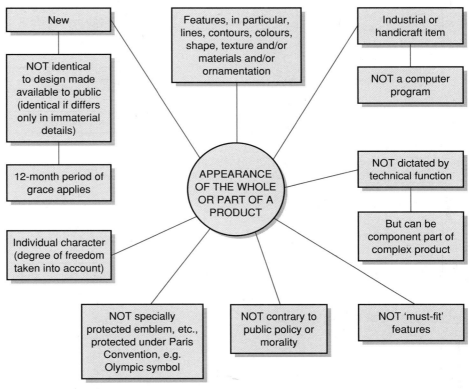

Figure 16.1 Community design

are of five years' duration, which may be renewed up to a maximum of 25 years in five-year blocks. There is no facility for deferring publication of a UK registered design unlike the case with the registered Community design.[38]

There are, of course, procedural differences between the UK registered design and the registered Community design. These will be described in the following chapter where appropriate.

38 However, designs can be prevented from publication if relevant to defence and notified by the Secretary of State as such.

Design right

A design right is declared by the Copyright, Designs and Patents Act 1988 s 213(1) to be a property right which subsists in an original design. Section 213(2) defines a 'design' as 'the design of any aspect of the shape or configuration (whether internal or external) of the whole or part of an article'. 'Article' is not defined for the purposes of the design right. The remainder of s 213 describes the requirements for a design. There are several similarities between the design right and copyright and, like copyright, the design right is automatic and does not depend on registration but requires some form of tangible expression. There are qualification requirements and the design must be 'original' for the right to subsist. Needless to say, there are differences. A design is not original if it is commonplace in the design field in question at the time of its creation. This is probably

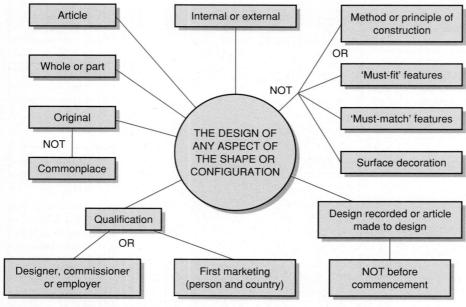

Figure 16.2 The design right

a more stringent test than is the case with copyright. Figure 16.2 shows the basic requirements for the design right.

Note that the design right applies to any aspect of the shape or configuration of the whole or part of an article; it does not apply to the article itself. Basically, for the design right to apply to a shape or configuration, it must be original (not commonplace) and it must be in some tangible form, that is, recorded in a design document (alternatively, an article must have been made to the design), and the qualification requirements must be satisfied. Some of the exceptions are similar, but not identical, to those that apply to registered designs and can be justified on the basis that they prevent the right from becoming too strong or from working to the disadvantage of consumers requiring spare parts. A further exception is surface decoration, which lies firmly within the scope of the Community design and the UK's registered design. The qualification requirements may be satisfied in one of three ways:

1 by reference to the designer,[39] or
2 if the design is created under a commission or in the course of employment, by reference to the commissioner or employer, and
3 by reference to the person by whom and country in which articles made to the design are first marketed.

The design right was a new departure for intellectual property law in the UK and there was no equivalent right before the 1988 Act, although certain features of shape and configuration may have had copyright protection. For example, a drawing of an article of a particular shape or configuration would have been an artistic work for copyright purposes. The design right provisions were not retrospective; and anything which would have qualified and which was recorded in a design document, or if an article had been made to the design, before the commencement of the design right provisions[40] was excluded.

39 The term 'designer' is used here rather than 'author': basically, the two terms are equivalent.

40 1 August 1989.

Community design, the UK registered design and the UK unregistered design right

41 A product to which a design is to be applied has to be an industrial or handicraft item. Before amendment, the Registered Designs Act 1949 required that a design was applied by an industrial process. However, this did not appear to be a limiting factor and there was no reason why designs applied to hand-crafted articles would have been denied registration on that ground alone.

42 A maximum of 25 years' protection is available for a registered design, whereas the maximum duration of the design right is 15 years, or 10 years during which it is exploited commercially.

43 If the outer surface of the article is transparent and the feature can be seen, the design may be registrable after all.

44 There is a reciprocal presumption in the Registered Designs Act 1949 s 19(3B). Further, s 19(3A) of that Act requires that the registration of an interest under a registered design will not be made unless the Registrar is satisfied that the person entitled to the interest is also entitled to the corresponding interest in the design right, if it subsists. As amended, the design right is now referred to in the Registered Designs Act 1949 as the national unregistered design right.

The UK's unregistered design right has often been described as applying to functional designs. However, that is not necessarily the sole domain of the design right. There is no reason why a new aesthetic design or a new design having individual character cannot also be subject to the design right if it relates to the shape or configuration of some article, even though it would be expected that it should be registered as a Community or UK design (or protected as an unregistered Community design). An example might be a design for a drinking tankard which is a new and unusual shape or which has a new or unusual shape of handle, made industrially or hand-made[41] and which, its maker hopes, people will buy for the visual attractiveness of its shape. This should qualify for all forms of rights in designs. One advantage of seeking registration, whether as a Community design or UK registered design, is that the period of protection is potentially longer.[42] The protection afforded by registration also is stronger, infringement not requiring proof of copying. However, the overlap between the UK's unregistered design right and the other rights in designs is not complete. The design right cannot apply to surface decoration which is specifically excluded, although this is clearly within the scope of the Community design and the UK registered design because of the definition of design (and, to a lesser extent, product) which is clearly not exhaustive and includes, for example, lines, colours, contours, texture or ornamentation. As a result of registered designs having a requirement of appearance and individual character, also excluded from registration are component parts that are hidden from view in normal use, such as 'under the bonnet' parts of vehicles. These may, however, be subject to the UK's unregistered design right.[43] Nevertheless, in many cases a design will be registrable under both the Community and UK registered design systems and yet still be subject to the UK unregistered design right where the design relates to shape or configuration. There are no provisions for abrogating one of these rights in favour of the others providing the requirements for registrability are satisfied. Indeed, in the UK, the Copyright, Designs and Patents Act 1988 explicitly recognises the dual existence of the unregistered design right and the UK registered design: s 224 of the Act raises a presumption that an assignment of a registered design automatically carries with it an assignment of the unregistered design right where the proprietor of the registered design and the owner of the unregistered design right are one and the same person.[44]

UK unregistered design right and copyright

45 For example, see LB (Plastics) Ltd v Swish Products Ltd [1979] RPC 551 and, of course, British Leyland Motor Corp Ltd v Armstrong Patents Co Ltd [1986] 2 WLR 400.

46 The so-called lay recognition test provided for by the Copyright Act 1956 s 9(8).

47 [1976] AC 64.

Design law may overlap with copyright protection. Between 1969 and 1 August 1989, an extremely powerful and wide-ranging form of protection for functional designs was to have a drawing from which the article was made. If a person copied the article, he would infringe the copyright in the drawing even though he had never seen it, no matter how mundane the article was.[45] The only provisos were that the drawing should meet the originality requirements for copyright (not an onerous standard by any means) and that a person who was not an expert in that field could recognise the article as being reproduced from the drawing.[46] Even the mass-produced – and, in the judges' opinions, vulgar – furniture in George Hensher Ltd v Restawhile Upholstery (Lancs) Ltd[47] would have been protected by copyright, indirectly, had some drawings been made which bore a two-dimensional resemblance to the furniture. Additionally, a design may overlap with other forms of copyright works such as sculptures and works of artistic craftsmanship. The design may be recorded in a document in which copyright subsists as a literary work, including computer data, or the design document may be a photograph.

To reduce this overlap, the Copyright, Designs and Patents Act 1988 contains two provisions, ss 236 and 51(1) respectively. The first is that where a work consisting of or including a design, in which the unregistered design right subsists, is protected by copyright, the design right is suppressed in favour of the copyright.[48] If what is done is an infringement of the copyright in the work, then an action lies under copyright law and not for infringement of the design right. That is, if the articles made to the design are themselves works of copyright, they will be protected by copyright rather than by the design right. This could be so if the articles were works of artistic craftsmanship: for example, a hand-made wooden toy or an item of jewellery.[49] The second exception applies to cancel out the possibility of indirect copyright infringement by copying the article embodying the design. If an article is made to the design or a copy of such an article is made, this does not infringe the copyright in a design document or model recording or embodying the design.[50] A design document is any record of the design and includes drawings, written descriptions, photographs and computer data.[51] Therefore, if the design is recorded in a drawing and a person makes an article using that drawing, he does not infringe the copyright in the drawing although he does, of course, infringe the design right. However, if the person makes a photocopy of the drawing instead, then the copyright in the drawing will be infringed in that instance, but any subsequent making of articles from the copy of the drawing will infringe the design right only.

Making a copy of garments worn by the Teletubbies indirectly through the medium of television fell within the s 51 defence, so held Laddie J in *BBC Worldwide Ltd* v *Pally Screen Printing Ltd*.[52] He accepted that it was at least arguable that the design documents showing the original designs of the Teletubbie puppets fell within s 51 and that they had been intended to decide the shape and appearance of the puppets. The purpose of s 51 is to deny copyright protection to 'ordinary functional commercial articles'. The effect of the section is to relate to any act of copying, whatever the result. In *Mackie Designs Inc* v *Berhinger Specialised Studio Equipment (UK) Ltd*,[53] the defence under s 51 was available even though the defendant had made a net list of components and interconnections in the claimant's electrical mixer by reverse analysis. From this information the defendant made circuit layouts and circuit boards.

As another example, consider a design recorded as computer data, for example as a series of numbers describing the three-dimensional coordinates of the design. Without permission, a person copies the computer data on to a magnetic disk and takes the copy away. Later, he prints out the computer data and uses the information to make articles, or he may, for example, enter the computer data into a computer-controlled lathe so that it can be used to make articles to the design. There are two infringements here. First, the copyright in the computer data (as a literary work, being a table or compilation or, possibly, a database) has been infringed by making a copy of it. This infringement is not suppressed by the design right. Secondly, by making articles, the design right is infringed. In this case, the copyright in the computer data is not infringed because it is not an infringement of a literary work to make three-dimensional work of it;[54] but even if the copyright had been infringed, say in the case of a drawing, the Copyright, Designs and Patents Act 1988 s 51 would operate to suppress that copyright. The effect of s 51 can be seen diagrammatically in Figure 16.3.

In Figure 16.3, a design is recorded in a drawing. Articles have been made to the design. It is assumed that copyright does not subsist in the articles *per se*, for example as works of artistic craftsmanship. A person obtains a drawing and one original article and does one of the following things without the permission of the rights owner:

(a) copies the drawing (directly);
(b) makes articles from the drawings;

---

48 Copyright, Designs and Patents Act 1988 s 236.

49 Copyright, Designs and Patents Act 1988 s 52 might apply, reducing the term of copyright to 25 years if the articles are not hand-made or more than 50 are made: *see* Copyright (Industrial Processes and Excluded Articles) (No 2) Order 1989, SI 1989/1070. Such a design could also be registrable.

50 Copyright, Designs and Patents Act 1988 s 51. The definition of design for the purposes of s 51 is as for the design right except that the exceptions are not mentioned apart from surface decoration. Therefore, copyright in a design document will not be infringed by copying an article made to a design even though it is not subject to the design right if it is a principle or method of construction or caught by the 'must-fit' and 'must-match' exceptions.

51 Copyright, Designs and Patents Act 1988 s 263.

52 [1998] FSR 665.

53 [1999] RPC 717.

54 *Brigid Foley Ltd* v *Ellot* [1982] RPC 433. But see *Anacon Corp Ltd* v *Environmental Research Technology Ltd* [1994] FSR 659, discussed in Chapter 6.

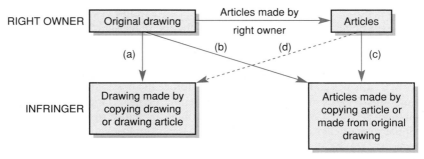

Figure 16.3 Design right and copyright

(c) makes articles from the original article; or

(d) makes a drawing from the original article.

55 Such an infringement was found in respect of drawings showing designs for rear lamps for vehicles: *see Valeo Vision SA* v *Flexible Lamps Ltd* [1995] RPC 205.

By doing act (a) the person will infringe the copyright in the drawing.[55] Both acts (b) and (c) will infringe the design right, and act (d) may infringe the copyright or the design right (this is discussed below).

An exercise in mental gymnastics may be indulged in by considering the interaction between the Copyright, Designs and Patents Act 1988 ss 51(1), 226(1)(b) and 236. Add to this the question: does making a copy of an article made to a design (as stated in s 51(1)) include making a copy in two dimensions? If the answer to this question is in the affirmative,[56] there is only an action for infringement of design right based on s 226(1)(b), which gives the design right owner the exclusive right to make a design document for the purposes of enabling articles to be made to the design. However, if the answer to the question is 'no', there potentially is an infringement of copyright and the design right because s 51(1) fails to operate, and by s 236 an action will lie in copyright only under s 17 (copying). One speculative consideration is that if s 51(1) does apply to the making of a two-dimensional copy of an article made to a design by copying the drawing, and the drawing is copied for purposes other than making articles to the design, for example to study the technology used in the manufacture of the articles, then copying the drawing may escape both copyright and design right liability. Section 51(1) removes copyright protection from the drawing because the copy of the drawing is a copy of the article made to the design and s 226(1) does not extend to making a design document for other purposes.[57]

56 In the few cases on s 51(1), judges have taken a wide approach, based on the perceived purpose of the provision, being the denial of copyright protection to functional articles: *see BBC Worldwide Ltd* v *Pally Screen Printing Ltd* [1998] FSR 665 and *Mackie Designs Inc* v *Berhinger Specialised Studio Equipment (UK) Ltd* [1999] RPC 717.

57 Note that copying in terms of both copyright and the design right may be indirect.

Particular examples

The following articles are considered in the light of the Community design (taken as including the UK registered design for these purposes), the UK's unregistered design right and artistic copyright in relation to the design of the article. The purpose of the examples is to highlight the differences between the rights, their similarities and interrelationship. Where referred to, legislation is abbreviated thus: Copyright, Designs and Patents Act 1988 (CDPA) and Community Design Regulation (CDR).

Porcelain figurine

58 Under the Copyright, Designs and Patents Act 1988 s 52 and pursuant regulations, if more than 50 figurines are made by an industrial process and marketed, the term of copyright is reduced to 25 years. It would appear from the wording of s 52 that this would apply to the original model, the cast(s) and any drawings, the figurines being three-dimensional copies of the drawings.

Artistic copyright: The figurine could be considered to be a sculpture. The original model and the cast (mould) could also be sculptures (CDPA s 4(2)) as long as they are 'original' (CDPA s 1(1)(a)), irrespective of artistic quality (CDPA s 4(1)). Drawings and preliminary sketches could also be protected by copyright.[58]

Community design: If the appearance of the figurine is new and has individual character, then it will be registrable and also protected by the unregistered Community design (CDR Articles 3 and 4). The vast majority of such designs will be protectable unless they are slavish copies of previous designs, or differing from previous designs only in immaterial details. The amount of design freedom is a factor to be taken into account. If there is little design freedom, this should improve the possibility of protection even though the design somewhat resembles an earlier design. There is no exception for sculptures and the Community design is without prejudice to other rights such as national unregistered designs and trade marks and the Regulation recognises that a design may also be eligible for copyright protection (CDR Article 96).

UK unregistered design right: If the shape or configuration is 'original' (CDPA s 213(1)), and not commonplace, then the design right applies, unless otherwise excepted (for example, under the 'must-match' and 'must-fit' exceptions).

It appears that all three rights apply. Copyright is not suppressed because the article is itself an artistic work (CDPA s 51(1)). An advantage of registering the design is that no causal link is required for infringement to be proved (CDR Article 19).[59] However, copyright is wider in terms of the types of infringement: for example, if the figurine is rented or loaned to the public without the copyright owner's licence.[60] But copyright does not prevent similar works being created by independent effort. The existence of the design right is illusory, because if the act complained of infringes copyright the design right is suppressed (CDPA s 236). Finally, it should be noted that the rights could be owned by different persons. For example, if a self-employed sculptor is commissioned to make the original model, in the absence of any agreement otherwise, he will own the copyright and be entitled to the Community design rights but, provided he has paid money or money's worth, the commissioner will be entitled to the UK registered design.

Mass-produced furniture

Artistic copyright: It is unlikely that the furniture itself will be a work of artistic craftsmanship.[61] In principle, any drawings may be protected, as will be other materials such as computer data defining the three-dimensional shape of the furniture. But this protection will be limited by the CDPA s 51, if the design falls within the basic definition of design in that section, to direct copying only: for example, photocopying the original drawing. Copyright might subsist in any document, such as a drawing, recording the design of a pattern or other surface decoration to be applied to the covers to be fitted to the furniture.

Community design: Clearly if the furniture is new and has individual character, it will be protectable as a Community design, even if it had been placed on the market by the proprietor during the 12-month period before the date the application is treated as having been made. Individual character is judged in accordance with design freedom (CDR Article 6(2)) so it is likely that similar designs will be registrable providing the differences are not in immaterial details. The exception that a design is not protected to the extent that the features of appearance are solely dictated by technical function is unlikely to apply (CDR Article 8(1)). Two identical-shape designs for furniture should be registrable if they have different ornamentation or texture, providing such designs are new and have an individual character.

UK unregistered design right: This will apply if the shape or configuration applied to the furniture is 'original' (CDPA s 213(1)). The furniture is not itself an artistic work, so the design right is not suppressed and runs alongside any registrations in respect of the design. Patterned covers and the like will not, however, be subject to the design right as these are features of surface decoration.

59 For example, in copyright, for infringement by copying, the original thing (or copy of it) must have been copied from directly or indirectly. However, damages are not available against innocent infringers: Registered Designs Act 1949 s 24B. This is not explicit in CDR but Article 89(1)(d) states that sanctions other than injunctions and seizure orders appropriate to the circumstances may be ordered as provided by the law of the Member State.

60 But the number of restricted acts is less for artistic works than it is for other original works. For example, by the Copyright, Designs and Patents Act 1988, the making of an adaptation is not an act restricted by the copyright in an artistic work (s 21), neither is it an infringement to show an artistic work in public (s 19).

61 *See George Hensher Ltd v Restawhile Upholstery (Lancs) Ltd* [1976] AC 64. In some cases, where the furniture has some particular artistic quality, it may be the subject of artistic copyright as a work of artistic craftsmanship. Past examples would include art deco or art nouveau furniture. It might also apply to hand-crafted furniture.

Some of the differences between registering the design and failing to do so may be important in this case. For example, duration is potentially longer for a registered design. For the UK unregistered design right the maximum effective protection is no more than ten years[62] and the unregistered Community design only lasts for three years from the date it was first made available to the public (CDR Article 11). Also, the exceptions are not quite the same for the UK unregistered design as for the other forms of design right. For the design right, features of shape and configuration which relate to the function of the article may be protected if not covered by the 'must-fit' and 'must-match' exceptions. Surface decoration and methods and principles of construction are excepted from the design right. These are not identical to the exceptions for the other design rights. There is also a special rule for ownership of the UK unregistered design right where a design originates from outside Europe. Where this is so, the person first marketing the design in Europe may be the first owner of the design right.

Copyright in any drawing or painting showing the design of any ornamentation could run alongside a design registration. At first sight, the advantage of registering a design can be doubted. However, there are important differences in terms of infringement and ownership which can make registration as a design a more attractive proposition.

Can opener

Artistic copyright: Following the UK Supreme Court decision in *Lucasfilm Ltd* v *Ainsworth*[63] there is now no doubt that a can opener cannot be a sculpture even though it is three-dimensional and even if it is cast from a mould. Copyright, in principle, will subsist in any drawings subject to the CDPA s 51(1).

Community design: There is no express requirement for eye-appeal although it is in respect of appearance that a design is registrable. In particular, in this case, the relevant aspects of design could be the contours and shape of the body and handle, its colour and, possibly, also texture. A can opener is obviously a product, being an industrial or handicraft item. Providing the design is new and has individual character, it will be registrable. Protection will not extend to the cutting mechanism itself as this is solely dictated by the can opener's technical function (CDR Article 8(1)).

UK unregistered design right: If the shape of the can opener is not commonplace, the design right may apply in so far as the design does not encompass a method or principle of construction, or is not dictated by the shape of the cans it has to be placed against so that it may be used to open them.

The UK unregistered design right and the Community design rights (and the UK registered design rights) can subsist concurrently in the design, but copyright is not relevant (unless someone copies the drawing). If the handle has a pretty pattern printed or embossed on it the rights under the Community design and UK registered design will extend also to that, if that also is new and has individual character. The pattern will not be within the UK unregistered design right as it is excluded, being surface decoration.

Moulded plastic tray for processed food

Artistic copyright: Although the moulded tray has shape, again, this cannot be considered to be a sculpture.[64] Any copyright in drawings for the tray is likely to be suppressed by the CDPA s 51(1).

Community design: The definition of a product expressly includes packaging and get-up and providing the design is new and has an individual character it ought to be protectable as a Community design (CDR Articles 3 and 4). As items of food are not usually exactly the same shape, there should be no place for the 'must-fit' exception (CDR Article 8(2)).

62 Although the maximum duration is 15 years, it cannot extend for more than ten years from when it was first commercially exploited.

63 [2011] UKSC 39.

64 Cases such as the New Zealand case of *Wham-O Manufacturing Co* v *Lincoln Industries Ltd* [1985] RPC 127, where it was held that a wooden model from which the moulds for 'Frisbees' were made was a sculpture and the moulds and Frisbees were engraving, and *Breville Europe plc* v *Thorn EMI Domestic Appliances Ltd* [1995] FSR 77 must now be considered to be wrong on the sculpture point. *See* Chapter 3.

Design right: If original, the shape of the tray will be protected by the design right. Registration of the design of food containers was very common under the old law in spite of any misgivings over the requirement for eye-appeal. It was a common-sense approach, rewarding the effort expended in the creation of designs intended to show off the food to best commercial effect. It should be even easier to register food packaging now. Although the informal rights are likely to apply providing the other requirements for subsistence are satisfied, registration is preferable given the longer term of protection available and the fact that there is no need to show copying in an infringement action.

Ownership – differences between rights

Some of the differences in the ownership provisions between artistic copyright, the Community design, the UK registered design and unregistered design right have already been alluded to. Before proceeding over the next two chapters to consider these differences in more detail, it will be useful to look briefly at these provisions comparatively. The fact that there are differences could be very inconvenient where a particular design attracts two or more forms of protection. The special provisions that apply, for example, in respect of Crown copyright are omitted for the sake of clarity. There are some differences in terminology. The person creating a work of copyright or a UK registered design is known as the 'author', whereas the creator of a design in which the Community design (registered or unregistered) and the UK's unregistered design right is known as its 'designer'.[65] A copyright, Community design and the UK's unregistered design right is owned by its 'owner', but for the UK's registered design the owner is known as the 'proprietor' of the design.

Artistic copyright: The author is the first owner of an artistic copyright unless he is an employee creating the work in the course of his employment, in which case his employer is the first owner (CDPA s 11(1) and (2)).

Community design: The right in a Community design vests in the designer or successor in title unless the design is developed by an employee in the execution of his duties or following instructions given by his employer, in which case the design belongs to the employer subject to contrary agreement or as otherwise specified by national law (CDR Article 14).[66] A design developed jointly by two or more designers vests in all of the designers jointly.

UK registered design: The basic rule is that the author of the design is treated as the original proprietor. This is subject to two exceptions. Where the design is created in pursuance of a commission, for money or money's worth, the person commissioning the design is treated as the original proprietor. The second exception is where the design is not created in pursuance of a commission for money or money's worth but is created by an employee in the course of his employment: the employer is treated as the original proprietor of the design. There is no specific provision for joint authors of designs but the usual rules should apply. However, where a design is computer-generated in circumstances such that there is no human author, the person making the arrangements necessary for its creation is considered to be the author of the design (Registered Designs Act 1949 s 2).

UK unregistered design right: The designer is the first owner, subject to exceptions relating to employees and commissioned designs. A 'commission' means a commission for money or money's worth.[67] A further provision applies to designs which qualify for the right by reference to the first marketing of articles made to the design. In this case, the person marketing the articles is the first owner of the right.

65 Statutory recognition is given to the fact that all these rights can be brought about by computer generation and the provisions are equivalent for each of the rights.

66 The reference to national law allows the concept of beneficial ownership to be used in the UK to deal with the problem of a Community design developed in the UK under a commission rather than by an employee.

67 Copyright, Designs and Patents Act 1988 s 263(1).

Table 16.1 Potential first owners of rights in designs

Type of right	Creator of right known as	Owner of right known as	Creator	Employer	Commissioner	Marketer
Potential identity of first owner from amongst						
Artistic copyright	Author	Owner	YES	YES	no	no
Community design	Designer	Owner	YES	YES	no	no
UK registered design	Author	Proprietor	YES	YES	YES*	no
UK unregistered design right	Designer	Owner	YES	YES	YES*	YES

* Only if the commission is undertaken for money or money's worth.

68 Ignoring the Copyright, Designs and Patents Act 1988 s 11(3) which caters for Crown and parliamentary copyright and copyright belonging to certain international organisations.

Table 16.1 shows the identity of potential first owners of the different rights. Which one it is will depend on the circumstances. For example, the first owner of a UK unregistered design right might be the designer, his employer or commissioner, or the person responsible for the first marketing. For artistic copyright, the first owner can only be either the author or his employer.[68] Of course, the first owner may assign the right to another immediately upon its coming into existence, or may agree to do so in respect of a future copyright or design.

International aspects

The Directive on the legal protection of designs achieved limited harmonisation of design law throughout Europe. The advent of the Community design has made a significant impact on the protection of designs in Europe and has proved popular and attracted large numbers of applications from within Europe and elsewhere. Both the Paris Convention for the Protection of Industrial Property and the Agreement on Trade Related Aspects of Intellectual Property Rights (TRIPs Agreement) require all participating countries to protect industrial designs but they give relatively little guidance as to the form of the protection. For example, the TRIPs Agreement goes little further than requiring protection for industrial designs that are new or original and the right extends to control making, selling or importing for commercial purposes articles that are copies of the design or substantially to the design. Member States are to give at least ten years' protection.[69]

69 Articles 25 and 26 of the TRIPs Agreement.

The World Intellectual Property Organisation includes designs within its brief and there have been moves towards international protection, but little has been achieved compared to the cooperation realised as regards copyright and patents. One reason for this is that design protection is effected in many different ways in different States. However, 48 States now belong to the Hague Agreement 1925[70] which does go some way towards a unified system for registering designs by deposit without search.[71] Application for registration is made by deposit of the design at the International Bureau of Industrial Property at Berne. Either articles to the design or representations such as drawings or photographs are submitted with details in French. The deposit takes effect as if the design was deposited in the appropriate industrial property offices in each Member State. Protection is for 15 years (divided into a five-year and a ten-year period). Individual Member States can refuse registration within a certain period of time.

70 As at 21 March 2012, there were 60 members to the Hague Agreement Concerning the International Deposit of Industrial Designs 1925. The UK is still not a party to this Agreement.

71 States which are signatories to the Hague Agreement include France, Germany, Greece, the Benelux countries, Italy and Spain. The European Community has also become a member (as from 1 January 2008).

72 However, searching for novelty is no longer carried out as a rule and it is expected that searches will be eliminated altogether before long.

Registration in the UK is subject to a search to ensure that the design is new, whereas some countries operate a simple deposit system.[72] The UK's unregistered design right is unusual in that, apart from semiconductor protection in Europe, few other countries have taken a similar approach. However, there are some reciprocal provisions for protection of design right.

International protection of UK registered designs is automatically afforded in some countries which consider the UK registration equivalent to their registered designs. These are mainly Commonwealth countries and include Bermuda, British Virgin Islands, Falkland Islands, Fiji, Gibraltar, Swaziland, Tanzania and Uganda. Others extend protection by local re-registration of a UK design: these include Guernsey, Jersey, Malta and Tuvalu. In some cases there is a time limit. Some countries no longer offer automatic re-registration. They are Hong Kong, Malaysia and Singapore.

In other cases, if international protection is required for a design, it must be obtained by application to the appropriate countries under their registered designs or utility model (sometimes referred to as a petty patent) systems.[73] There is at least the advantage of a six-month priority arrangement for designs under the Paris Convention for the Protection of Industrial Property 1883. Some countries operate a law of unfair competition which could be useful in some cases. Of course, because of the much better position under copyright laws, it may be possible to pursue actions for infringement of copyright in drawings in some foreign states which allow this possibility.

73 A petty patent (called utility models in some countries) is a weaker variety of patent which is used in countries such as Germany, Italy, Spain and Malaysia. There was a proposal for a harmonising Directive on utility models which would require the UK to introduce such a right. Subsequently, it was proposed to introduce a Community utility model. Both proposals failed to see the light of day.

Summary

Designs may be protected in a number of ways, some of which require formal registration. Specific forms of design protection are:

- the Community design, registered and unregistered;
- the UK registered design; and
- the UK unregistered design right.

Other forms of protection may be available such as copyright and trade marks.

For the Community design, registered and unregistered, and the UK registered design, the appearance of the features or the whole or a part of a product to which the design has been applied must be novel and have individual character.

The UK unregistered design right is quite different and applies to any aspect of the shape or configuration (but not surface decoration) of the whole or part of an article (internal or external) where the aspect(s) in question is not commonplace in the relevant design field at the time of its creation.

Registered designs last for five years initially and may be renewed for a further five years up to a maximum of 25 years' protection.

The unregistered Community design lasts for three years only, while the UK unregistered design right lasts for a maximum of 15 years but this may be shorter if it is exploited commercially within the first five years.

Licences of right are available during the last five years of the UK unregistered design right (this does not apply to the modified version of the right as it applies to semiconductor topographies – *see* Chapter 18).

There are exceptions to all the design rights which, according to the particular right, may be related to: principles or methods of construction; technical function; fitting or matching other articles or products; or based on public policy or morality.

Discussion questions

1   What are the justifications, if any, for differing terms of protection for works of copyright, registered designs and unregistered designs? Should the terms of protection be improved for designs?

2 Discuss the rights which may exist in respect of the shape or appearance of different types of mass-produced household and industrial items.

3 Should the various forms of design protection be replaced by a single new design right and, if so, what form should the new right take?

Selected further reading

Hargreaves, Professor I., *Digital Opportunity: A Review of Intellectual Property and Growth*, May 2011 (especially Chapter 7 on Designs). Available at: **http://www.ipo.gov.uk/ipreview-finalreport.pdf**.

Intellectual Property Office, *Designs: Basic Facts*, July 2009 (useful brief overview of design rights) available at: **http://www.ipo.gov.uk/d-basicfacts.pdf**

Office for the Harmonisation of the Internal Market (Trade Marks and Designs), *The Quick Guide to Designs*, 2011 (information about the Community Design) available at: **http://oami.europa.eu/ows/rw/resource/documents/OHIM/multimedia/quickGuide/en/designs.html**

Visit **www.mylawchamber.co.uk/bainbridgeip** to access study support resources including interactive multiple choice questions, practice exam questions with guidance, weblinks, legal updates and a legal newsfeed.

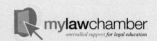

Community design and the UK registered design

Introduction

Directive 98/71/EC of the European Parliament and of the Council of 13 October 1998 on the legal protection of designs[1] was one of two main thrusts to reform design law in Europe. It resulted in limited harmonisation throughout Europe. In particular, there was no agreement as to the protection of 'must-match' spare parts and Member States were left to continue to protect them if they already did so. Any subsequent change in those Member States that chose to continue to protect designs of spare parts could only be made if they liberalised the market in must-match spare parts. In implementing the Directive, the UK decided to continue its existing exclusion of protection of must-match spare parts, being those that had to be of a particular design so as to restore a complex product to its original appearance ('must-match').[2] The most-used example of must-match spare parts are those applied to replacement body parts and panels for motor vehicles and it is in this design field that the exception has most impact by far. In line with the Directive, the Commission has reviewed the position and has proposed a modification to the Directive to exclude protection to such spare parts in all Member States as the lack of harmonisation in this respect distorts the single market and competition.[3] The only proviso would be that it would be necessary to ensure that consumers are made aware of the origin of the parts in question so that they can make an informed choice.

Although the Directive did not seek to achieve complete harmonisation and although it preceded the Community Design Regulation, it was drafted with an eye on the Community design and features that were harmonised were those dealing with registrability and protection which were to be the same as for the Community design as were the provisions on the exclusions from registrability with the exception of must-match spare parts.[4] Enforcement, remedies and procedural aspects, including renewal and invalidity, were left to Member States.

As a result of the limited harmonisation that took place not long before the introduction of the Community design, many provisions of the latter are identical or, to all intents and purposes identical to, features of the UK registered design as it now stands. One major difference is that the Community design contains two forms of protection: one through registration, the other being an informal short-term right not subject to registration. However, the basic requirements for protection by the unregistered Community design are the same, in most respects, to those applicable to the registered Community design. That being so, this chapter is structured so as to look at the Community design first (registered and unregistered) followed by the UK registered design, concentrating on those features that are additional to or different to the Community design. The following abbreviations are used in this chapter:

1 OJ L 289, 28.10.1998, p 28.

2 Registered Designs Act 1949 s 7A(5). The Act does not exclude such designs from registration but provides that using the design to restore the original appearance of a complex product does not infringe the design.

3 Proposal for a Directive of the European Parliament and of the Council amending Directive 98/71/EC on the legal protection of designs COM (2004) 582 final, SEC (2004) 1097, 14.09.2004, p 5. If adopted, Member States would have to implement it no later than two years after its adoption.

4 Although the UK and eight other Member States chose to follow the position in the Community Design Regulation on this issue.

- RCD – registered Community design
- UCD – unregistered Community design
- UKRD – UK registered design
- CDR – Community Design Regulation
- RDA – Registered Designs Act 1949, as amended.

Community design

5 OJ L 3, 05.01.2002, p 1.

The Community design is stated in Article 1(3) of Council Regulation (EC) No 6/2002 of 12 December 2001 on Community designs[5] to have a unitary character having equal effect throughout the Community. It shall not be registered, transferred, surrendered, declared invalid or the use of it prohibited save in respect of the whole Community unless as otherwise provided for by the Regulation. The recitals to the Regulation confirm that it is important that the needs of all sectors of industry in the Community should be served by the Community design and, as some sectors produce large numbers of articles which have a short market life, there should be an informal short-term protection to suit these sectors. Other sectors create designs having a longer market life and, for those sectors, the advantages given by registration (greater legal certainty and longer duration) outweigh the burdens of the registration process. A short-term informal protection might be important in the context of fashion clothing, for example, with longer-term protection by registration being more attractive to manufacturers of furniture and toys, for example.

The recitals to the Regulation also make it clear that it is not a requirement that designs have an aesthetic quality to be protected though there are a number of exceptions: for example, a technical function and a 'must-fit' exception. However, design is defined in terms of appearance, and protection is denied to the design of 'under the bonnet' parts of complex products not normally visible during normal use, but the appearance clearly does not have to be an aesthetic one.

6 By Article 8 such disclosure being deemed non-prejudicial.

There is also a 12-month period of grace which allows the owner of a design to test the market, for example, by selling products made to the design to see whether it is worthwhile applying for registration without prejudicing the novelty or individual character of the design.[6] In the meantime, the design will be protected by the unregistered right and will continue to be so protected for a maximum of three years from the date products made to the design were first made available to the public.

7 With effect from 1 January 2008.

8 Council Regulation (EC) No 1891/2006 of 18 December 2006 amending Regulations (EC) No 6/2002 and (EC) No 40/94 to give effect to the accession of the European Community to the Geneva Act of the Hague Agreement concerning the international registration of industrial designs, OJ L 386, 29.12.2006, p 14.

The RCD is administered by the Office for the Harmonisation of the Internal Market (Trade Marks and Designs) ('OHIM'). It has its own examiners, legal division and invalidity divisions and a Board of Appeal. Appeals from the Board of Appeal go to the General Court of the EU and from there to the Court of Justice of the EU. At the time of writing there have only been two cases before the Court of Justice of the EU concerning Community design. Certain national courts are designated Community Design Courts and have jurisdiction to hear cases involving the Community design. In the UK those courts are the High Court, the Patents County Court, the Court of Session in Scotland and the Court of Appeal. As the European Community (now European Union) acceded to the Geneva Act (1999) of the Hague Agreement Concerning the International Registration of Industrial Designs,[7] the CDR was amended to provide a further ground of invalidity on the basis of prior designs registered outside the Community.[8] Procedural changes were also made to the CDR to take account of designs registered under the Hague Agreement. It is now possible for an application through the Hague Agreement to include an application for a Community design.

Requirements for protection (RCD and UCD)

The basic requirements for the rights, whether registered or not, are virtually the same.[9] A design must fall within the meaning of 'design' (for which the meanings of 'product' and/ or 'complex product' are also relevant) and the design must be new and have individual character. The definition of 'design' is given by Article 3(a) as:

> . . . the appearance of the whole or a part of a product resulting from the features of, and in particular the lines, contours, colours, shape, texture and/or materials of the product itself and/or its ornamentation.

A 'product' is, by Article 3(b):

> . . . any industrial or handicraft item, including *inter alia* parts intended to be assembled into a complex product, packaging, get-up, graphic symbols and typographic typefaces, but excluding computer programs.

And a 'complex product' is, by Article 3(c):

> . . . a product which is composed of multiple components which can be replaced permitting disassembly and re-assembly of the product.

As can be seen from the definitions, the scope of designs that can be subject to protection is very wide. For example, the definition of 'product' is non-exhaustive and includes typefaces, packaging and get-up. Typefaces are protected by copyright as a form of artistic works, providing they are original and qualify for protection.[10] Packaging and get-up could also have copyright protection and be protected by the law of passing off in the UK and Ireland or unfair competition law elsewhere. Trade mark law may also be applicable in a good proportion of cases, particularly in relation to the shape of a product, graphic symbols, get-up or packaging.

It seems that graphic symbols and icons displayed on computer screens and mobile phones could be subject to the Community design because of the inclusion of graphic symbols in the definition of 'product'. It would appear that such symbols are deemed to be industrial or handicraft items and logos, screen displays and icons have been accepted for registration as Community designs.

Apart from falling within the definitions, the basic requirement for protection is that the design is new and has individual character (Article 4). Where the design is applied to a product which is a component part of a complex product, it will be protected only if it remains visible in normal use and the visible features are new and have individual character. Therefore, the design of 'under the bonnet' parts such as a car radiator or engine cowling are not protected. 'Normal use' is couched in terms of use by the end-user and excludes use for the purposes of maintenance, servicing and repair.

Article 5 states that a design shall be considered to be new if no identical design has been made available to the public. In the case of the UCD, the relevant date is the date on which products to that design were first made available to the public. For the RCD, it is the date of filing of the application for registration (allowing for priority from earlier applications elsewhere under the Paris Convention). In determining the 'prior art' for designs, that is whether a conflicting design has been made available to the public, under Article 7(1) this may be by its being published following registration or otherwise, exhibited, used in trade or otherwise disclosed before the date at which novelty is tested (and individual character: *see* later). However, such a design will not be taken into account if the event or events in question could not reasonably have become known in the normal course of business to the circles specialised in the sector concerned operating in the Community. In *Green Lane Products Ltd* v *PMS International Group Ltd*,[11] it was held that

9 There is a difference in the time novelty and individual character is tested. For the UCD it is the time the design was first made available to the public whereas, for the RCD, it is the time of filing the application or the priority date if the priority of an earlier filing is claimed.

10 The Regulation recognises that designs may also be protected under copyright law and the Regulation is without prejudice to other rights including national unregistered design rights, trade marks and patents: Article 96.

11 [2008] FSR 1.

the relevant sector was that relating to the prior art and not limited to those persons specialising in the sector specified in the application for registration. An application to register a Community design is required to identify the classification of products under the Locarno classification of designs. In the present case, that was 'Flatirons and washing, cleaning and drying equipment'. The design had been applied to spiky laundry balls. It was held that the prior art also included spiky balls used for massaging the human body. The importance of this decision is that it takes account of the scope of protection under Article 10 which is not limited to any particular product. If design fields are discrete and persons working in one field are not aware of designs in other fields, then registering in one field could give protection across all the other fields. The Court of Appeal upheld the decision at first instance in *Green Lane Products Ltd* v *PSM International Group plc*.[12] Jacob LJ considered the *travaux préparatoires* for the Community Design Regulation. Although novelty could have been decided along similar lines to that under the patent system, textile manufacturers were concerned that counterfeiters based outside Europe, for example, in the Far East, could claim some obscure prior art to defeat a Community design. Hence, the proviso to having been made available to the public such that the use, etc. under Article 7(1), '. . . could not reasonably have become known in the normal course of business to the circles specialised in the sector concerned, operating within the Community'. With that proviso, a design was made available to the public if it was part of the prior art, not limited by the description of the products or class of products to which it was intended to apply the design in question.

Under Article 7(1), disclosure to a third party under an express or implied obligation of confidence is not taken into account in determining whether a design has been made available to the public.

A design is considered to be identical if its features differ only in immaterial details. In *Crown Confectionery Co Ltd's Design*,[13] a design to be applied to pretzel-shaped biscuits was held to be invalid as it did not differ from the familiar and well-known shape of pretzels except in immaterial details. The design had some lines across the surface of the pretzel. A design may be judged to be identical to another design if, on close inspection, no apparent differences are shown.[14] In *3M Innovative Properties Co's Designs*,[15] the design in question was for a swab having a wedge-shaped head mounted on a handle. An earlier Spanish utility model for a swab had a cylindrical stem with a cylindrical head of larger diameter than the stem but the claim to the utility model said that the head could be any size, form or texture. The Invalidity Division at OHIM said that this did not disclose the specific form of the designs and did not compromise their novelty.

Article 6 states that a design has an individual character if 'the overall impression which it produces on the informed user differs from the overall impression produced on such a user by any design which has been made available to the public'.[16] The informed user would be someone who is familiar with the design field in question.

The Invalidity Division of OHIM has interpreted the informed user as being someone who is familiar with the basic features of products in question and, when assessing the overall impression of the design, will take into account whether there are any limitations on the freedom of the designer and will weigh the various features consequently. More attention will be paid to similarities of non-necessary features and dissimilarities of necessary ones. The informed user is aware of the prior art known in the normal course of business to the circles specialised in the sector concerned. Article 6(1) of the CD Regulation requires the assessment of the overall impression produced by the prior designs and the Community design on the informed user, respectively. To assess the overall impression, the designs must be compared both on their various features taken individually and on the weight of the various features according to their influence.[17]

In *Procter & Gamble Co* v *Reckitt Benckiser (UK) Ltd*,[18] the registered Community design was for a sprayer used for air fresheners. The Court of Appeal held that the 'informed user'

12 [2008] FSR 28.

13 A decision of the Invalidity Division of OHIM, No ICD000000388, 20 September 2005.

14 *Homeland Housewares LLC's Design*, Invalidity Division OHIM, No ICD000000552, 15 September 2005. The design in question was for a transparent cup used in a food mixer.

15 No ICD000000040, 12 June 2004.

16 Conflicting designs do not need to be protected as such and may be protected by other rights, such as trade mark rights and copyright. A three-dimensional trade mark may still be a design for the purposes of novelty and individual character: *see* Case No 000000222, *Mafin SpA's Design* [2005] ECDR 29.

In *Dyson Ltd* v *Vax Ltd* [2011] EWCA Civ 1206, Sir Robin Jacob pointed out that recital 14 uses the expression 'the design clearly differs' whereas Article 6 simply uses 'differs'. This difference in wording is merely the result of sloppy drafting. The same applies to the Directive on the legal protection of designs (recital 13 and Article 9 of the Directive).

17 *See*, for example, Case No 000000222, *Mafin SpA's Design* [2005] ECDR 29, at paras 26–28; and Case No 000000024, *Arrmet Srl's Design Application* [2004] ECDR 24, at paras 17 and 18.

18 [2008] FSR 8.

was not the 'average consumer' of trade mark law. The informed user would be more discriminating and what mattered was what stuck in the mind when looking at the design, not what stuck in the mind after it had been looked at. The role of imperfect recollection was, therefore, a limited one. The informed user would also know that some designs were the way they were because of limitations on design freedom. Where this was the case, smaller differences might be sufficient to create a different overall impression.

The cut-off date for designs made available to the public is the same as for novelty for the UCD or RCD as appropriate. For example, for the UCD individual character is assessed in the light of designs made available to the public before the design in question was itself made available to the public. One advantage of registration is that an application may be filed before the design is made available to the public, freezing the 'state of the art' at that date. It is also possible to defer publication of the design, for example, to prevent competitors seeing the design prematurely.

In determining whether a design has individual character, the degree of freedom the designer has in developing the design is taken into consideration. Therefore, the less the design freedom, the more likely that a design, not substantially different from existing designs, will be protected,[19] though novelty may still be an issue if the design does not differ except in immaterial details from existing designs. Design freedom was an issue in *Pepsico Inc's Design*[20] which involved a design for a disk having annular rings or corrugations to be applied to a promotional item for games. There was a prior similar design which belonged to the applicant for invalidity, Gruper Promer Mon Graphic SA. The Invalidity Division of OHIM noted that the degree of design freedom was limited only in certain respects, such as cost and child safety. Otherwise there was ample design freedom. It was said that the informed user would be familiar with promotional items for games and would know that their surfaces often have graphical elements added and would be aware that targeted consumers would pay more attention to the graphical elements than minor variations in shape. Consequently, it was held that the design was invalid as it did not produce a different impression on the informed user compared with the earlier design. The Board of Appeal at OHIM reversed the decision of the Invalidity Division on the basis that the degree of design freedom of promotional items such as 'tazos' or 'rapper' was severely restricted and the differences in the profile of the designs in issue was sufficient to conclude that they produced a different overall impression on the informed user.

There was a further appeal to the General Court of the EU[21] which annulled the decision of the Board of Appeal. In Case T-9/07 *Gruper Promer Mon Graphic SA v OHIM*,[22] the General Court noted that Article 25(1)(d) of the Community Design Regulation states that a design may be declared invalid if it is in conflict with an earlier design. Although 'conflict' is not defined in the Regulation, the Court held that this must be interpreted as meaning that a Community design is in conflict with a prior design if, when taking account of the freedom of the designer in developing the design, that design does not produce on the informed user a different overall impression from that produced by the prior design.[23] As to the informed user, the Court held that he is particularly observant and has some knowledge of the state of the prior art but is not a manufacturer or seller of the products incorporating the design. In the present case, the informed user could be a child aged five to ten years or the marketing manager of a company manufacturing products that are given away such as 'pogs', 'tazos' or 'rappers'.

This meaning of informed user was also considered by the General Court of the EU in Case T-153/08 *Shenzhen Taiden Industrial Co Ltd v OHIM*.[24] The Court held that the informed user was a person who uses the product to which the design has been applied according to its intended purpose. He is not a designer or technical expert but knows the various designs in the sector concerned, and possesses a certain degree of knowledge of the features which such designs normally include. However, the informed user is not able

19 *Procter & Gamble Co v Reckitt Benckiser (UK) Ltd* [2008] FSR 8.

20 No ICD000000172, 20 June 2005.

21 Previously known as the Court of First Instance.

22 18 March 2010.

23 Agreeing with the Board of Appeal on this interpretation.

24 22 June 2010.

to distinguish, beyond the experience gained by using the product concerned, or the aspects of the appearance of the product which are dictated by the product's technical function from those which are arbitrary. Sir Robin Jacon cited both the above General Court cases in *Dyson Ltd v Vax Ltd*,[25] noting that the informed user was not the same as the average consumer of trade mark law.

On the question of design freedom, the General Court in *Gruper Promer* said that the more the designer's freedom in developing the design is restricted, the more likely minor differences between the designs at issue will be sufficient to produce a different overall impression on the informed user. Nevertheless, applying those principles and notwithstanding the limited design freedom, the Count went on to hold that the differences compared with the prior design were insufficient to produce a different overall impression on the informed user.

Pepsico subsequently appealed to the Court of Justice of the European Union (the first case to come before that court on the Community design). In dismissing the appeal in Case C-281/10 P *Pepsico Inc v Gruper Promer Mon Graphic SA*,[26] the Court of Justice held that the concept of the informed user was somewhere between the average consumer of trade mark law and an expert with detailed technical expertise. The informed user was a particular observant user because of his personal experience or extensive knowledge of the sector in question.

In relation to the RCD, there is a 12-month period of grace and certain disclosures do not prejudice novelty nor individual character, being where the design is made available to the public by the designer, successor in title or third person as a result of information provided by, or action taken by, the designer or successor in title (Article 7(2)). The period starts 12 months prior to the date of filing the application or priority date if applicable. Note that the reference is to the designer and not the owner. This is surely wrong and should be a reference to the owner or successor in title to cover the situation where the design is developed by an employee in the execution of his duties or following instructions given by his employer. The 12-month period of grace also applies to disclosures to the public made in breach of confidence, described in Article 7(3) as an abuse in relation to the designer or successor in title.

Exclusions from the Community design

Article 8 contains a number of exclusions from Community design. Features of appearance that are dictated solely by technical function are excluded (it may still be possible to claim protection for other features, if any). In *3M Innovative Properties Co's Designs*,[27] the Invalidity Division said that the informed user would concentrate on features not necessarily dictated by function in determining whether a design had an individual character. Together with the wording of the exception, this suggests that other features may be protectable. This would accord with previous practice in the courts in the UK which accepted that only if *all* the features were dictated by function was a design excluded from protection on this basis.[28] A similar approach was accepted as correct in the Court of Appeal in *Landor & Hawa International Ltd v Azure Designs Ltd*.[29] The exception for designs dictated solely by function was a narrow one and would apply only if that design and no other could perform the function in question. The Court of Appeal thought that old tests under the Registered Designs Act 1949 before amendment by the Directive on the legal protection of designs were no longer helpful.[30] However, after the Board of Appeal at the OHIM's decision in *Lindner Recyclingtech GmbH v Franssons Verkstäder AB*[31] and the judgment of Arnold J, at first instance, in *Dyson Ltd v Vax Ltd*,[32] this is now in doubt. If the narrow approach is correct, this would mean that the exclusion would apply only in rare cases.

25 [2011] EWCA Civ 1206.

26 20 October 2011.

27 No ICD000000040, 12 June 2004.

28 *See*, for example, *Interlego AG v Tyco Industries Inc* [1989] 1 AC 217 per Lord Oliver. This aspect of the case, under an old version of the Registered Designs Act 1949 which required eye-appeal, should still be good law to the extent of the proposition above. Of course, those aspects not dictated by function should be novel and have individual character and, it is submitted, not be *de minimis*.

29 [2007] FSR 9. *See* also *Bailey v Haynes* [2007] FSR 10 in the Patents County Court.

30 In particular, the House of Lords decision in *Amp Incorporated v Utilux Pty Ltd* [1972] RPC 103, taking a wide view of the equivalent exception in the Registered Designs Act 1949 as it then was, could not be applied to Article 8(1) of the CDR.

31 [2010] ECDR 1.

32 [2010] FSR 39.

The distinction is between whether more than one designs can perform the technical function or only one design and no other. Perhaps the House of Lords in *AMP Incorporated v Utilux Pty Ltd*[33] were right in holding that the latter interpretation would reduce the equivalent exclusion in the Registered Designs Act 1949, prior to amendment, almost to vanishing point.

Article 8(2) provides for a 'must-fit' exclusion, where features have to be reproduced identically to fit another product so that either can perform its function. This applies to features of mechanical connections or other interconnections, including where two products abut each other. This exception is broadly equivalent to that for the UK unregistered design right, discussed in the following chapter. The exception will apply to features such as the pins on an electrical plug, the electrical contacts and bayonet fitting on an electric light bulb, the runners on a drawer, all manner of interfaces such as that between a teapot and its lid, screw, push-fit and other connections, even where the features are those permitting two products to be simply placed against each other so that either may perform its function.

As a result of the definition of product, the exception will not apply to features of a product designed to fit the human hand,[34] such as a computer mouse or the handle of various tools, such as a pair of scissors, or the brake levers on a bicycle (although the connections between the lever and the handlebar and the brake cable will be excluded).

Modular systems are excepted from the exclusion in Article 8(2) to the extent that designs which permit the multiple assembly or connection of mutually interchangeable products within a modular system may be protected if new and having individual character. This could apply to an interconnection such as a snap-fit connection allowing the assembly of flooring units such as those in issue in the patent case of *Unilin Beheer NV v Berry Floor NV*,[35] discussed in Chapter 12. Recital 11 to the Regulation provides the rationale for the potential protection of such interconnections and says that the mechanical fittings of modular products:

> . . . constitute an important element of the innovative characteristics of modular products and present a major marketing asset, and therefore should be eligible for protection.

Under Article 9, a Community design shall not subsist in a design which is contrary to public policy or to accepted principles of morality. There is no further guidance as to the scope of this exception. These are somewhat vague concepts and there is the added problem that they vary from Member State to Member State. They are also likely to be concepts that will shift with time, especially in relation to accepted principles of morality.[36]

It is notable that the exclusions from the Community design are not as wide as the grounds for invalidity. It would seem possible to claim a right in an unregistered Community design or register a design that would be held invalid if challenged.[37] This may be a consequence of the examiners at OHIM not carrying out searches for novelty and individual character when considering registrability.

Duration

The registered Community design lasts initially for five years from the date of filing the application to register the design: Article 12 of the CDR. This period is not reduced where the design has a priority date. Thereafter, the registration may be renewed for further five-year periods up to a maximum of 25 years.

Under Article 11(1) of the CDR, the unregistered Community design lasts for three years from the date the design was first made available to the public within the Community. Duration is not based on the end of the relevant calendar year so, if the design was first made available to the public on 1 July 2007, it will expire on midnight 30 June 2010. A design is made available to the public when it is published, exhibited,

33 [1972] RPC 103.

34 In a UK unregistered design case, *Ocular Sciences Ltd v Aspect Vision Care Ltd* [1997] RPC 289, Laddie held that the human eye could be an article for the purposes of the equivalent exception. However, the definition of 'product' clearly does not apply to parts of the human or animal body.

35 [2005] FSR 6.

36 Under the Registered Designs Act 1949, before amendment, there was an exception where a design was contrary to law or morality. Two cases could be contrasted to show how the test of morality changed over the years, being *La Marquise Footwear's Application* (1947) 64 RPC 27 and *Re Masterman's Application* [1991] RPC 89. Both designs incorporated representation of male genitalia.

37 Invalidity proceedings for a registered Community design may be brought before OHIM or at a Community design court on a counterclaim in infringement proceedings. An unregistered Community design may be declared invalid only in a Community design court either on application for such or on a counterclaim in infringement proceedings. In the UK, the Community design courts are the High Court, Patents County Court and Court of Appeal (in Scotland, the Court of Session).

used in trade or otherwise disclosed in such a way that, in the normal course of business, these events could reasonably have become known to the circles specialised in the sector concerned, operating within the Community. No account is taken of any making available to the public for the sole reason that it has been disclosed to a person under an explicit or implicit obligation of confidence.

Entitlement to a Community design

The basic rule is given in Article 14(1) and is that a Community design vests in the designer or his successor in title. Where a design is jointly developed by two or more persons, the Community design vests in them jointly. Where a design is developed by an employee in the execution of his duties or following instructions given by his employer then, unless otherwise agreed or specified under national law, the Community design vests in the employer under Article 14(3). In the case of a registered Community design, the person in whose name it is registered is presumed to be the person entitled to it in proceedings before OHIM or in any other proceedings. An equivalent presumption is made in relation to applications so that the person filing the application is deemed to be the person entitled.

There are no specific provisions for entitlement of designs developed under a commission by a designer who is not employed by the person commissioning the development of the design. This is in contrast to the position under the UK registered design where the person commissioning the development of a design for money or money's worth will be entitled to be the proprietor of it.[38] This could mean that the person entitled to be the owner of a Community design could be someone other than the person entitled to be the proprietor of a UK registered design. Say that Sarah is a self-employed freelance designer who has been asked to develop a new design for a toaster for Acme Household Products Ltd. Her contract with Acme makes no mention of ownership and contains no assignment of the rights in the design. Sarah was paid handsomely for the design. Acme will be entitled to be the proprietor of the UK registered design by virtue of s 2(1A) of the Registered Designs Act 1949 (and will be the owner of the UK unregistered design right, if it subsists in the design, under s 215(2) of the Copyright, Designs and Patents Act 1988). However, Sarah would appear to be entitled to the Community design. In court proceedings in the UK, this anomaly could be dealt with by holding that Acme was the beneficial owner of the Community design (or by an implied licence on its behalf). It is far from clear how the OHIM or other Member States would deal with this problem.

The fact that, without a specific assignment of the right to a Community design created under a commission, the person commissioning the creation of the design will not be entitled to it was confirmed in the Court of Justice in Case C-32/08 *Fundación Española para la Innovación de la Artesanía (FEIA)* v *Cul de Sac Espacio Creativo SL*.[39] FEIA set up a design project which included, *inter alia*, the commissioning of a design of cuckoo clock from Cul de Sac. The Court of Justice ruled that the terms 'employee' and 'employer' in Article 14(3) were not to be interpreted widely so as to include persons creating a design under a commission, even though such persons were paid contractually and under the direction of the commissioner. The court noted that the language of Article 14(3) referred to an employee in the execution of his duties or following instructions given by his employer. Neither the term 'agent' nor 'principal' were used. Indeed, although an earlier proposal provided for the right to commissioned designs to vest in the commissioner, that proposal was not retained in the Regulation. Furthermore, the court confirmed that Article 14(1) must be interpreted as meaning that the right to a Community design vests in the designer, unless it has been assigned by way of contract to his successor in title.

38 Registered Designs Act 1949 s 2(1A).

39 [2009] ECR I-5611.

There appears to be no place for the right to a Community design to be subject to equity and in the absence of provision for commissioned designs under the Community Design Regulation, contrary to the position under the UK registered design and the UK unregistered design, it is vital that express contractual provision is made as to the rights in commissioned designs.

As regards employee designs, an agreement between employee and employer as to entitlement, such that the employee is entitled, could take the form of an express or implied agreement. As in the copyright case of *Noah* v *Shuba*,[40] it would be reasonable that previous conduct could form the basis of an implied agreement that the employee was entitled to the Community design.

Challenges to entitlement can be made under Article 14 in respect of either the UCD or RCD. If a UCD is disclosed or claimed by, or an RCD is applied for or registered in the name of a person not entitled under Article 14, the person entitled may claim to be recognised as the legitimate holder of the design. This is without prejudice to any other remedy open to that person. Similarly, a challenge may be made by someone claiming to be a joint proprietor. However, under Article 15(3) challenges may not be brought more than three years from the date of publication of an RCD or, in the case of the UCD, more than three years from the date it was disclosed to the public. Presumably this means made available to the public under the provisions of Article 7 on disclosure. The time bar on challenges to entitlement does not apply where a person not entitled to the design was acting in bad faith at the time the design was applied for or disclosed or assigned to him. As an example, say that Andrew developed a design in circumstances that he was entitled to the rights in the design. He disclosed it to a potential licensee, Dodgy Dealers. The licence was executed and Dodgy Dealers honestly thought, having agreed to pay Andrew a royalty on products incorporating the design, that it was entitled to register the design, which it duly did. The licence was silent on ownership. Four years after the design was published, Dodgy Dealers assigned the RCD to Williams & Co, which was well aware that Dodgy Dealers was not entitled to the RCD, nor did it have the right to assign it. Soon after, Andrew discovers that he is entitled to the RCD and he may now apply to be recognised as the legitimate holder of it even though more than three years have elapsed since the design was published.

Where there is a challenge to entitlement of an RCD, the fact that proceedings have been instituted, together with the final decision or other termination of the proceedings (for example, where the challenge is withdrawn) and any resulting change of ownership, will be entered on the register of designs.

The effect of a complete change of ownership as a result of proceedings under Article 15(1) is that all licences and other rights lapse on such entry on the register (Article 16(1)). However, where a person in good faith, before the institution of such proceedings, was entered on the register and the holder of a Community design has exploited it within the Community (now European Union) or made serious and effective preparations to do so, he may continue to exploit it providing that he requests from the new holder a non-exclusive licence to be granted for a reasonable period and on reasonable terms providing he makes such request within three months of the date of entry on the register of the new holder.[41]

Under Article 18, the designer has the right to be cited as such and, where the design is the result of teamwork, the citation may be that of the team itself rather than the individual designers. Although Article 18 is silent on the point, Article 36, on the information to be provided in an application to register a Community design, makes it clear that the right to be cited may be waived.

As the Community design is declared to have a unitary character, it should not be possible for the UCD and RCD to be owned by different persons. However, the CDR does not require the applicant for an RCD to declare that he is also entitled to the UCD. A

40 [1991] FSR 14. This case is discussed in Chapter 4.

41 The period of three months is set out in Article 24(5) of Commission Regulation (EC) No 2245/2002 of 21 October 2002 implementing Council Regulation (EC) No 6/2002 on Community designs, OJ L 341, 17.12.2002, p 28 (the 'Implementing Regulation').

problem could occur where, for example, a designer assigns the UCD and then, later, applies for the RCD in his own name. What, in such a situation, would a court do if the designer claims that he intended the assignee to have rights only until the time the UCD expired?

Dealing with the Community design

A Community design is an object of property to be dealt with in its entirety (reflecting its unitary nature) and for the whole area of the Community as a national design right (Article 27). This is subject to some of the provisions of the CDR mentioned below. In respect of the national law governing dealing with a Community design, the relevant Member State is that in which on the relevant date:

(a) the holder has his seat or domicile, or
(b) in other cases, the holder has an establishment.

Where there are joint holders of a Community design, and two or more of them fall within (a) or (b), in the case of the UCD, the Member State is that of the joint holder designated by the common agreement between those joint holders. In the case of the RCD it is the first such joint holder to be mentioned in the register.

Where none of these provisions apply, that is where the holder or none of the joint holders, as the case may be, fall in neither (a) nor (b) above, the relevant Member State is that in which the OHIM is situated, presently Spain. Therefore, if the holder is a Canadian company, the law relating to dealing with design is Spanish law, subject to the other provisions of the CDR mentioned below.

There is no definition of 'relevant date' and one can only assume that it must be the date of the dealing in question. So, for example, if the holder of a Community design is a company established in France then, subject to the other provisions of the CDR mentioned below, French law relating to designs will govern dealing with it, including assignment and licensing. Thus, if the rights are assigned to an English company, the assignment will be subject to French law. If the English company then later assigns the design to a German company, that assignment will be subject to English law.

The forms of dealing with a Community design are assignment (referred to as transfer in the CDR)[42] and licensing. Furthermore, an RCD may be given as security or subject to rights *in rem* and may be levied in execution.[43] In all cases where an RCD is involved, the transfer, grant, rights, etc. shall, at the request of one of the parties, be entered on the register.[44] Certain formalities must be complied with for the transaction to be registered. For example, registration of a transfer requires, *inter alia*, proof of transfer. This can be satisfied where the application is signed both by the rightholder and successor in title (or their representatives) or, where the successor in title submits the application, a declaration made by the rightholder or by his representative agreeing to the transfer or by submitting the completed transfer form or document signed by both parties or their representatives.[45]

Under Article 31, insolvency proceedings in which a Community design is involved may only be brought in the Member State within the territory of which the centre of the debtor's main interests is situated. This applies also to the share of a joint proprietor. This indicates that joint proprietorship is on the basis of tenants in common.

Where an RCD is transferred, a successor in title may not invoke the rights arising from registration until such time as the transfer has been entered on the register. Licences may be in relation to the whole or part of the Community (now European Union) and may be exclusive or non-exclusive. The holder of the rights conferred by a Community design

42 Note that, because of its unitary nature, a Community design may only be transferred in respect of the whole Community: Article 1(3) of the CDR.

43 The courts and authorities of the Member State determined in accordance with Article 27 have exclusive jurisdiction in relation to levy of execution: Article 30(2).

44 These provisions are in Articles 28, 29, 30 and 32.

45 Article 23(4) of the Implementing Regulation.

may invoke those rights against a licensee who is in breach of the terms of the licence on duration, the form in which the design may be used or the range and quality of products, notwithstanding legal proceedings based on contract law (Article 32(2)).

A licensee can bring legal proceedings for infringement if the holder consents, although proceedings may also be brought by a licensee if the holder, having been given notice to bring proceedings, fails to do so within an appropriate period. A licensee may also intervene in an action brought by the holder so as to obtain compensation for any loss suffered by him.

Under Article 33, the effects on third parties of the legal acts referred to in relation to transfer, security, rights *in rem*, levy of execution and licensing shall be as provided by the law of the Member State determined in accordance with Article 27. However, as regards transfers, security, rights *in rem* and licences, these do not have effect on third parties in all Member States until after entry on the register. There are some exceptions to this, the first being where a third party acquired rights in an RCD after the date of the legal act in question but who knew of that act at the time he acquired the rights. This means, for example, that a third party who obtained a transfer of an RCD and knew of a licence granted earlier will be bound by the licence even though it had not been entered on the register at the time the RCD was transferred to him. Nor does a failure to register the legal acts mentioned apply to a person who acquires an RCD or right concerning an RCD in relation to a transfer of the whole of an undertaking or by way of other universal succession. Effects on third parties of insolvency proceedings are governed by the law of the Member State in which such proceedings are first brought under applicable national law or regulations.

Article 34 confirms that the above provisions on dealing also apply, *mutatis mutandis*, to applications for an RCD. Where the effect of a provision in Article 28 to 33 is conditional upon an entry in the register, that formality shall be performed upon registration of the resulting RCD.

The formalities as to assignment and licensing, for example, are left to national law. Thus, an assignment of a Community design, whether a UCD or RCD, if subject to English law, should be made with full title guarantee to take advantage of the implied covenants under the Law of Property (Miscellaneous Provisions) Act 1994. Provisions as to beneficial ownership and implied licences also ought to apply to the Community design where it is subject to the English law on dealing with design rights under Article 27 of the CDR.

Rights and infringement

The rights of the holder of a Community design are the same whether or not it is registered but with one difference. If unregistered, the right is limited to prevent the infringing acts only if they result from copying the protected design. Independent creation by a person not reasonably thought to be familiar with the design made available to the public does not infringe.[46] The right conferred is to use the design and to prevent third parties from using it without the holder's consent. Infringing acts are, if carried out by a third party not having the rightholder's consent, in particular making, offering, putting on the market, importing, exporting or using a product in which the design is incorporated or to which it is applied or stocking a product for those purposes. Note the use of the phrase 'in particular'. This suggests that the list of infringing acts is not exhaustive. Article 10(1) of the CDR also states that the scope of protection includes any design which does not produce on the informed user a different overall impression. Under Article 10(2) design freedom is taken into account, therefore the less the design freedom, the smaller the

46 Contrary to the test with copyright, it would appear that the burden of proof may rest with the alleged infringer to show that he was not familiar with the design and ought not to have been familiar on reasonable grounds.

differences which may produce a different overall impression. Issues of infringement will, of course, be determined by national Community design courts, not the OHIM.

47 [2008] FSR 8.

48 Recital 14 to the CDR.

In *Procter & Gamble Corp v Reckitt Benckiser (UK) Ltd*[47] the Court of Appeal held that in relation to infringement, the notional informed user, as in the case of individual character for registrability, was taken to be familiar with the 'existing design corpus'.[48] What mattered was whether the alleged infringing design created a different overall impression. It was not correct to say that it had to create a *clearly* different overall impression. Furthermore, the informed user would be familiar to design issues and would be fairly familiar with them. Jacob LJ (at para 35) made a number of additional observations on the application of the statutory test for infringement. The court should 'don the spectacle of the informed user' and compare the designs with a reasonable degree of care. Identify the overall impression produced by the registered design with care. The court must take care not to descend to too general a level of generality. The appropriate level is that which would be taken by the informed user. Do the same for the alleged infringement. The final step of the exercise is to ask whether the overall impression of each design is different. Jacob LJ said that this is almost the equivalent to asking whether they are the *same*, adding that the difference is nuanced, probably, involving a question of onus and no more.

The limitation on the rights of the holder of a UCD apply also in respect of an RCD where the holder has applied for deferment of publication until such time as the relevant entries in the register and the file have been made available to the public. This is the *quid pro quo* for keeping the design secret by deferring publication. However, the right to continue use begun, or commence use following serious and effective preparations made, before the filing date (or priority date) of an application for an RCD is not affected by deferred publication. Deferring publication does not extend the deadline for the right of prior use which remains the filing date or earlier priority date, if appropriate.

If legal proceedings are commenced during the period of deferred publication, it is a condition that the holder communicates to the defendant the information contained in the register and the file (Article 50(6)). If it were otherwise, of course, the defendant might not know precisely what the design in question was and whether the claimant was indeed the registered holder of the RCD.

Limitations and defences

A number of limitations are specified in Article 20. The rights in a Community design are not infringed by:

- acts done privately and for non-commercial purposes;
- acts done for experimental purposes;
- acts of reproduction for the purposes of making citations or teaching if they are compatible with fair trade practice, do not unduly prejudice the normal exploitation of the design and mention is made of the source.

As regards mention of the source of a design, the CDR gives no further guidance. It would seem reasonable to assume that the obligation would be fulfilled by a brief statement giving the identity of the holder of the right and, if an RCD, the registration number.

The rights in a Community design may also not be exercised in relation to equipment on ships and aircraft registered in a third country temporarily in the territory of the Community, importing spare parts into the Community to repair such craft and executing repairs on such craft.

The doctrine of exhaustion of rights applies under Article 21 so that the Community design rights cannot be used to prevent further commercialisation of any products, in which the design is incorporated or to which it has been applied, which have been put on the market in the Community by or with the consent of the holder of the Community design.

For the RCD only, there is a right to continue use of a design commenced before the filing date, or priority date if there is one, or to use a design where serious and effective preparations had been made before the filing date or priority date, if appropriate.[49] This is similar to the equivalent provision for patents though there is no such right in respect of the UK registered design, except in relation to the restoration of a lapsed registration. As with patents, this is not just a defence but is a right although licences may not be granted by the person taking advantage of the prior user provisions. The right is limited to the purposes to which the design was put, or in respect of which serious and effective preparations were made. This means that if the prior use related to applying the design to a particular type of product, it does not appear that it can be later applied to a different type of product by the prior user. Where the prior use related to a range of products, that use may continue in relation to that range of products. It is not clear what the position would be if the prior use and a subsequent use were in respect of closely related products, such as a teapot and coffee pot. It would seem sensible to allow subsequent uses in similar products where they are normally sold in a set of like products, such as a dinner service.

The right of prior use can be transferred but only in respect of the business or part of a business for which the act was done or preparations made provided that the business or part of it is also transferred. This allows the right to be transferred to a business successor, such as where a trader sells his business to another trader as a going concern along with the right to continue to apply the design to the products in question.

As the right to prior use applies only to the RCD and not to the UCD and it does not apply in respect of the UK registered design (except where a lapsed registration is restored),[50] this could have some strange consequences, as noted in the following examples. (Assume that the designs are identical or do not differ except in immaterial details and that the Community design and the UK registered design are capable of subsisting in them.)

49 Article 22 CDR.

50 The Directive on the legal protection of designs does not have any provisions on prior use.

Example 1

Acme Designs Ltd ('Acme'), a company established in the UK, owns a new design for an electric toaster which was created during March 2010. Acme first placed toasters to the design on the market in the UK on 7 June 2010. Taking advantage of the period of grace, Acme delayed filing an application at OHIM to register the design until 8 November 2010.

On 9 August 2010, Electrix Consumer Products ('Electrix'), placed electric toasters on the market which incorporated Acme's design.

Electrix has a right of prior use as far as the RCD is concerned but can be sued for infringing the UCD if it has copied Acme's design (and the UK unregistered design right, if it subsists in the design). The right of prior use for the RCD is of use to Electrix only if it did not copy Acme's design.

Example 2

As above, but Electrix first marketed its toaster during April 2010 (having recorded its design in a design document during that month).

Electrix will have its own UCD. Acme does not infringe that right as it could not have copied, having created its design first. Electrix may be able to challenge Acme's RCD, once granted, on the grounds that it is invalid for lack of novelty and individual character. Electrix may even claim that it is entitled to the RCD. However, Acme may have a UK unregistered design right in the design but could only enforce that right on proof of copying.

If Electrix copied Acme's design (perhaps because an employee of Acme gave a copy of the design document to Electrix in April 2010 in breach of confidence) the fact that Electrix made the design available to the public will be ignored as being an abuse in relation to the designer under Article 7(3). Acme will be the holder of both the UCD and RCD and may also sue for infringement of the UK unregistered design right if it subsists in the design. There may also be an action for breach of confidence.

Example 3

As example 1 (Acme created the design in March 2010 and first marketed toasters on 7 June 2010) but Acme applied for a UK registered design on 8 November 2010 and applied for an RCD on 5 May 2011, claiming the priority of the UK application.

Electrix first marketed its toasters to the design on 9 August 2010.

Electrix has a right of prior use in relation to the RCD though not in relation to the UK registered design (as there is no such right except for restoration of a lapsed design). Electrix can be sued for infringing the UK registered design though it has a prior use defence in relation to the RCD. Electrix may be sued for infringing the UCD (and the UK unregistered design right if it subsists) if there is proof of copying.

Example 4

As for example 3 above but Electrix first marketed its toasters to the design on 20 December 2010.

Electrix has no right of prior use under the RCD as the act was done after the priority date of the RCD and also infringes the UK registered design. On proof of copying, Electrix may also be sued for infringing the UCD and, if it subsists, the UK unregistered design right.

The right of prior use is one reason why it is not necessarily wise to take advantage of the period of grace. Even though it might be possible to rely on the UCD, proof of copying may not always be easy to obtain. Although deferring publication of the RCD does not change the situation with the right of prior use, it also limits infringement to acts of copying.

There are further 'exceptions' to the Community design which are found in the provisions on invalidity under Article 25, discussed later. Thus, apart from looking at the limitations on the Community design, a defendant may choose to challenge the validity of the design on the basis of one or more of the grounds for invalidity. Apart from failing to meet the basic requirements for protection, including conflicts with earlier designs, challenges to entitlement, specially protected emblems, etc. and works protected by copyright, there is also a 'must-match' exception under Article 110.[51] Although it does not appear that the OHIM will reject an application to register a design on this basis, it certainly is available as a defence.

Article 23 of the CDR provides for government use of Community designs but only to the extent that the use is necessary for defence or security needs. In the UK, specific provision for Crown use is made by the Community Design Regulations 2005,[52] the Schedule to which contains the detailed provisions. These are narrower than the Crown use provisions for the UK registered design (and the UK unregistered design right) and are, in line with the CDR, limited to service of the Crown necessary for essential defence and security needs. The Schedule contains all the provisions relating to settlement of terms, the impact on third parties including licensees and assignees, payment of compensation to the holder or exclusive licensee where a contract is not awarded to either of them because of Crown use and reference of disputes to the court.[53]

51 This is a transitional provision and applies until such time as the Regulation is amended with respect to 'must-match' spare parts. However, as the Commission is proposing to remove Member States' ability to retain protection for such parts if they choose, it seems unlikely that the exception for such parts under Article 110 will be repealed.

52 SI 2005/2339. These Regulations came into force on 1 October 2005.

53 The Patents County Court or High Court in England and Wales, the Court of Session in Scotland and the High Court in Northern Ireland.

Finally, a potential defendant may decide to pre-empt matters and apply to a Community design court for a declaration of non-infringement. However, under Article 84(4), the validity of a Community design may not be put in issue in such proceedings.

Remedies

The remedies available in an action for infringement or threatened infringement are set out in Article 89 and are: an order prohibiting the acts (an injunction in England and Wales); an order to seize infringing products and materials and implements predominantly used to manufacture infringing goods (providing their owner knew the effect of the intended use or where it would be obvious in the circumstances); and other appropriate sanctions provided by the law of the Member State in which the acts are committed or threatened, including its private international law. As regards the UK this would mean damages or an account of profits as an alternative.

Under Article 90, where the law of a Member State allows, provisional, including protective, measures may be granted.[54] This would permit the grant of interim injunctions. In such actions, a plea otherwise than by way of counterclaim for invalidity shall be admissible.[55] A court only having jurisdiction on the basis of Article 82(5) (place where infringement alleged) may not grant provisional measures, including protective measures, and may only find infringement within that Member State in which it is situated. Provisional, including protective, measures can be granted only by courts having jurisdiction on the basis of the domicile of the defendant or claimant, as appropriate, or Spain where neither is domiciled or has an establishment in any Member State, or where the parties agree that a particular Community design court has jurisdiction.

Groundless threats

There is a remedy of groundless threats of infringement proceedings in the UK which was provided for by the Community Design Regulations 2005[56] and which came into force on 1 October 2005. In terms of the registered Community design, the provisions are equivalent to those applicable to the UK Registered Design. In relation to the unregistered Community design, the provisions are equivalent to those for the UK unregistered design right.[57] Regulation 2 provides that where a person makes a threat of infringement proceedings, whether by circulars, advertisements or otherwise and whether or not entitled to or having an interest in a Community design, any person aggrieved may bring an action for groundless threats. Note that the action may be brought by any person aggrieved. It does not have to be the person receiving the threats. The action may be brought by a person manufacturing alleged infringing products where the threats have been directed at a retailer supplied by the manufacturer where the threat to the retailer relates to him stocking, selling or offering for sale the alleged infringing products.

The remedies are a declaration that the threats are unjustified, an injunction against a continuation of the threats and damages for any loss sustained as a result of the threats. However, the action is not available if the threats relate only to the making or importing of anything and the defendant has a defence if:

- in the case of the RCD, he shows that the acts complained of infringe the right and the claimant has not shown that the registration is invalid, or
- in the case of the UCD, the defendant shows that the right is infringed.

Mere notification that a design is an RCD or is protected by the UCD does not constitute a groundless threat of infringement proceedings.

---

54 A plea other than by way of a counterclaim relating to invalidity shall be admissible though Article 85(2) applies *mutatis mutandis* (presumption of validity of UCD on proof that Article 11 is complied with and indication of individual character made).

55 Article 85(2) applies *mutatis mutandis*. This is the presumption of validity for a UCD where the rightholder proves that the UCD is still current and indicates what constitutes its individual character. The defendant may contest validity by way of plea or counterclaim for invalidity.

56 SI 2005/2339.

57 This is so even though the unregistered Community design otherwise bears little resemblance to the UK unregistered design right, discussed in the following chapter.

A registered Community design which has not been published because the applicant requested that publication be deferred may be used as a basis for threats of litigation. In such a case, the person threatened may not be able to see the design alleged to have been infringed unless the proprietor is prepared to let him have sight of it. In *Quad 4 Kids* v *Dr Colin Campbell*,[58] the defendant was the proprietor of a number of registered Community designs subject to deferred publication. He informed eBay, using the formal VeRO notification procedure, that a number of quad bikes listed by the claim-ant on eBay infringed his Community designs. After receiving the notification, eBay removed the listings forthwith and informed the claimant accordingly in 'not entirely friendly terms'. The claimant brought a groundless threats action.

It is a defence to a groundless threats action to show that the design is or would be infringed by the acts complained of unless the claimant can show that the registration is invalid. However, validity of a registered Community design can only be raised in an application for invalidity before the Office for the Harmonisation of the Internal Market (Trade Marks and Designs) (OHIM) or by way of a counterclaim in infringement proceedings before a Community design court. It does not appear to be possible to challenge the validity of a Community design in a groundless threats action.[59] Where an action is brought concerning a registered Community design subject to deferred publication, Article 50(6) of the Regulation requires that the information in the register and in the file relating to the application has been communicated to the *person against whom the action is brought* (emphasis added). This clearly applies to infringement actions and not groundless threats actions.

In *Quads 4 Kids*, eBay, in line with its usual policy when informed of potential infringements, removed the alleged infringing listings. It was said by counsel for the claimant that eBay's approach could be described as an institutionalised avoidance of litigation when faced with a threat.[60] Pumfrey J, said it was remarkably difficult to say whether the notification to eBay amounted to a groundless threat. On the one hand, if there were not an implicit threat of proceedings against eBay, why would it withdraw the listing? On the other hand, eBay would probably have been surprised if it was sued on the basis of the alleged offending listing. Nevertheless, Pumfrey J came to the conclusion that there was a seriously triable issue as to whether the notification to eBay was a threat of proceedings. He said (at para 28):

> It may well be that we have to take a very slightly wider view of what amounts to an actionable threat than has previously been taken in the case, but the nature of the potential abuse in this case is quite clear.

He went on to say that unsupported and unchallengeable allegations of infringement of registered design rights are, potentially, an exceptionally damaging abuse of those rights. He was satisfied that there was, at least arguably, a threat of infringement proceedings in the notification to eBay. Had eBay not adopted its VeRO system and policy of removing material alleged to infringe, it would most likely have considered itself at risk of infringement proceedings. In the light of his finding, Pumfrey J then had to decide whether to grant an injunction restraining the issue of further threats. He thought the test in *American Cyanamid Co* v *Ethicon Ltd*[61] favoured the grant of an injunction. If the owner of an intellectual property right thinks that right is being infringed, he can commence infringement proceedings. He does not have to issue threats first. In the present case, there was potential damage caused by making the threat as the claimant would lose sales as a result of the listings being removed. Moreover, it was far from clear whether Dr Campbell would be in a position to pay damages should an injunction be refused. He seemed to have been reluctant to bring infringement proceedings. This may have been because of the potential financial risks involved. A further factor was that the claimant had alleged that the designs were likely to be shown to be invalid on the basis of lack of novelty. The claimant had

58 [2006] EWHC 2482 (Ch).

59 The Community Design Regulation makes no provision for this possibility whatsoever. This may have been something those drafting the UK Community Design Regulations 2005 did not appreciate.

60 Although Dr Campbell claimed to have sent representations of his designs along with his notification by email to eBay there was no evidence of that and, in the meantime, it appeared that Dr Campbell's e-mail system had been destroyed.

61 [1975] AC 396.

been selling its bikes before Dr Campbell applied to register his designs.[62] Pumfrey J said (at para 16):

> . . . it will be seen immediately that what has in fact happened is that a removal and possible consequential commercial damage has been achieved by reference to a registered design, publication of which has been deferred, and which could only therefore be sued on in court if Dr Campbell was both willing to reveal the file of the applications, and also, to make an allegation of copying . . .

Offences

As for the UK registered design, there are offences associated with falsely representing that a design is protected as a Community Design. The Community Design Regulations 2005 reg 3 makes it an offence for a person falsely to represent that a design applied to, or incorporated in, a product sold by him is a RCD. The offence is triable summarily only and the maximum penalty on conviction is a fine on level 3 of the standard scale.

It is also an offence, after expiry of a RCD, to represent, expressly or by implication, that a design applied to, or incorporated in, a product sold is still an RCD. This offence is also triable only summarily and the maximum penalty on conviction is a fine not exceeding level 1 on the standard scale.

Registration of Community design

Under Article 35 of the CDR, an application for registering a Community design must be filed at the OHIM or, to be forwarded to the OHIM, at the Member State's central industrial property office (Patent Office in the UK) or, in the Benelux countries, at the Benelux Design Office. The OHIM will inform the applicant indicating the date of receipt.[63]

The application must comply with a number of conditions under Article 36.[64] It must contain:

- request for registration;
- information identifying the applicant;
- a representation of the design suitable for reproduction (but if the design is two-dimensional and the application contains a request for deferment of publication, it may be replaced by a specimen);[65]
- an indication of the products in which the design is intended to be incorporated or to which it is intended to be applied.

Furthermore, other information may be required, depending on the circumstances, being:

- a description explaining the representation or specimen;
- a request for deferment of publication under Article 50;
- information identifying a representative, if appointed;
- the relevant classification of products under the Locarno classification;[66]
- the citation of the designer or team of designers unless the right to be cited has been waived.

The application must also be accompanied by the fees, being the registration fee and publication fee or deferment fee, if appropriate. The current fees (all in euros) at the time of writing are as follows (the additional fees are calculated per each additional design):

Registration fee	230
Additional registration fee for 2–10 designs	115
Additional registration fee for more than 11 designs	50
Publication fee	120
Additional publication fee for 2–10 designs	60
Additional publication fee for more than 11 designs	30
Deferred publication fee	40
Additional deferment fee for 2–10 designs	20
Additional deferment fee for more than 11 designs	10

Therefore, if an application is to register five designs, all of which are to be published, the total fee will be euro1,050. If applications are filed at a national central industrial property office of the Benelux Design Office for forwarding to OHIM, there will be an additional handling fee. At present the UK Intellectual Property Office (formerly known as the Patent Office) charges £15.[67]

67 Community Designs (Fees) Regulations 2002, SI 2002/2942 which came into force on 1 January 2003.

The information to be provided is, in relation to an indication of the relevant products, a description of the representation or specimen and the Locarno classification does not affect the scope of protection afforded by registration. The right given is to prevent third parties using the design without permission without being specific as to the type of product to which it is applied or in which it is incorporated.

The application may be made in any one of the official EU languages but a second language must also be used from among English, French, German, Italian or Spanish.

Several designs may be included in an application but, with the exception of ornamentation, must be in the same Locarno class. Each design in a multiple application may be dealt with separately, including being renewed, assigned or licensed separately (Article 37).

The date of filing is the date the application was filed at the OHIM, national central industrial property office or the Benelux Design Office, as appropriate. However, under Article 38, if the application is not forwarded within two months, the date of its receipt at the OHIM will be treated as the date of filing.

The priority of an earlier application in a State party to the Paris Convention for the Protection of Industrial Property or the World Trade Organisation may be claimed up to six months from filing that first application. The provisions also extend to countries giving a right of priority under bilateral or multilateral agreements. The rules on priority are contained in Article 41. Where a subsequent application has been made in a priority State but an earlier application to register that design in that State has been withdrawn, abandoned or refused without being published and without leaving any rights outstanding, not having been used for priority purposes, the subsequent application is the relevant one for the purposes of priority. That is, the earlier abortive application is of no consequence.

If priority is being claimed, a declaration to that effect must be made on the application form and a copy of the earlier application relied upon must be submitted, with a translation if required into one of the languages of the OHIM (Article 42). Priority may also be claimed under Article 44 for up to six months in relation to official or officially recognised international exhibitions within the terms of the Convention on International Exhibitions, signed at Paris 1928 as revised. The applicant must file evidence in the form of a certificate issued by the appropriate authority.

The effect of priority is that the priority date counts as the date of filing for the purposes of novelty, individual character, disclosure, right of prior use, conflicts with earlier RCD or national registered designs and the period of deferment.

Deferment of publication may be useful where the owner of a design does not want to give competitors advance notice of its appearance. Deferment may be useful, for example, in the fashion industry and give the owner time to have products made incorporating the design or to which it has been applied in advance of publication. Under Article 50, deferment of publication of an RCD will be 30 months from the date of filing or priority date,

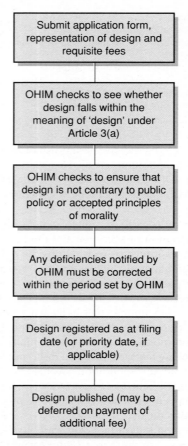

Figure 17.1 Registration of a Community design

if there is one. At the end of the 30-month period, or earlier if the rightholder requests, the file and representation will be published in the Community Designs Bulletin provided that the publication fee is paid and, where the applicant has submitted a specimen instead of a representation (where the design is two-dimensional) a representation of the design is filed. Failure to comply with these requirements will have the effect of the design being treated as never having the effects specified in the CDR, that is, it will be as if it never existed.

The registration procedure is set out in Articles 45 to 48 and is fairly straightforward, being basically a check that the necessary information has been provided and formal requirements met in accordance with the CDR and Implementing Regulation. There is no substantive examination for novelty or inventive character or for whether the exceptions apply apart from checking that the design falls within the meaning of design in Article 3(a) and it is not contrary to public policy or accepted principles of morality (Article 47). The OHIM may request that the applicant remedies deficiencies that are correctable with a period set by the OHIM (Article 46). Once everything is in order and the requirements have been satisfied, the application will be registered as an RCD, bearing the date of filing of the application in accordance with Article 38. The basic procedure for registration is shown in Figure 17.1.

Renewal of registration is covered by Article 13 and the Implementing Regulation and takes effect on the day following the day on which the registration expires. Renewal may be made up to four times, giving a maximum period of protection of 25 years. The renewal fee must be paid. The current renewal fees, in euros, are as follows.

1st renewal	90
2nd renewal	120
3rd renewal	150
4th renewal	180

Although the OHIM has to inform the rightholder and persons having a right under the RCD entered in the register of the forthcoming expiry of a registration in good time, it is under no legal duty to do so. Renewal may be made within a period of six months following the day the registration expires or within a further six months. The additional fees for late renewal are 25 per cent of the relevant renewal fee. If the design has not been renewed within the periods for late renewal, it may be restored on payment of a fee of €200 during the following six months but only if due care was taken to renew.[68] There must be a statement of grounds but restitution is discretionary. If, in the period between the loss of rights and restitution, a third party, in good faith, puts on the market products to the design, the rightholder may not invoke his rights against that third party who, in the two months following publication of the mention of re-establishment of the rights, may bring third party proceedings against the decision re-establishing the rights.

68 Article 67. The provisions for *restitutio in integrum* are not limited to late renewal and also apply to other time limits.

Invalidity and surrender

Unlike the position with the Community trade mark, there are no provisions for opposition to the registration of a Community design. As a result of this and the absence of a substantive examination of designs for novelty, individual character and some other requirements, the procedures for invalidity take on some importance. In some cases, ensuring that the register does not contain a substantial proportion of designs that are potentially invalid depends on the vigilance of others, in particular, those having conflicting rights, including designs that are similar to designs registered subsequently. Often invalidity will be brought up by way of a counterclaim in an action for infringement of a Community design.

The validity of a Community design may be brought up by way of counterclaim in an infringement action or, in the case of an RCD, by application to the OHIM. An application for invalidity of an UCD may only be brought before a Community design court, either on an application for invalidity or by way of a counterclaim in an infringement action. A further possibility is that a plea of invalidity of an RCD can be brought up in a Community design court in the absence of an infringement action if based on Article 25(1)(d) where the applicant claims it is invalid on the basis of an earlier national registered design right.

There is a presumption of validity of an RCD under Article 85(1) and also such a presumption in relation to the UCD where the holder proves the right still subsists and indicates its individual character. The defendant may challenge the validity of the UCD by way of a plea or counterclaim.

In the case of an action for a declaration of non-infringement, the validity of a Community design may not be put in issue (Article 84(4)).

Article 24 sets out the circumstances when an RCD or a UCD may be declared invalid. These provisions do not exactly tie up with the provisions of Articles 84 and 85 on actions before the Community design courts on invalidity and presumptions as to validity. In particular, Article 24 does not encompass a plea of invalidity in the absence of a counterclaim to an infringement action where the challenge is based on an earlier national registered design and is made by its owner as stated in Article 85(1).

The grounds of invalidity are set out in Article 25(1) and there are some restrictions as to the identity of the person who may invoke particular grounds. The grounds and, where applicable, limitations on persons who may invoke them are as follows:

(a) The design does not fall within the meaning of 'design' in Article 3(a).

(b) The design does not fulfil the requirements of Articles 4–9 (requirements including novelty, individual character, disclosure, technical function and interconnections exceptions, and exceptions based on public policy and accepted principles of morality).

(c) By virtue of a court decision, the rightholder is not entitled (under the provisions as to entitlement in Article 14) – *this ground may only be invoked by the person who is entitled*.

(d) Conflict with earlier design[69] made available to the public after the filing date or priority date, if there is one, but which is protected earlier. This applies to earlier RCDs or national registered designs having earlier filing dates (or priority dates, if applicable) but which had not yet been published when the application for the design in question had been filed (or at its priority date if relevant). Also included now are international registrations under the Geneva Act of the Hague Agreement which have effect in the Community – *this ground may be invoked either by the applicant for or holder of the earlier right or by the appropriate authority in the Member State concerned if national law permits this*.[70]

(e) Where a distinctive sign is used in a subsequent design and Community law or the law of a Member States gives the rightholder the right to prohibit such use (this could apply where the sign is a Community trade mark, a national trade mark or a sign protected by the law of passing off) – *this ground may only be invoked by the holder of that earlier right*.

(f) Where the design constitutes the unauthorised use of a work of copyright protected under the law of a Member State – *this ground may only be invoked by the copyright owner*.

(g) Where the design constitutes the improper use of badges, emblems, etc. protected under Article 6[ter] of the Paris Convention for the Protection of Industrial Property or other badges, emblems, etc. of particular public interest in a Member State – *this ground may be invoked either by the person or entity concerned by such use or the appropriate authority in the Member State concerned if national law permits this*.

Where an RCD has been declared invalid under grounds (b), (e), (f) or (g) it may be maintained in amended form provided it complies with the requirements for protection and the identity of the design is retained (Article 25(6)). This may require registration of a partial disclaimer.

The operation of Article 25(1)(e) was considered by the General Court of the European Union in Case T-148/08 *Beifa Group Co Ltd* v *OHIM*.[71] The designs in question were for writing instruments. They had a similar shape to well-known highlight marker pens made by Stabilo, which brought invalidity proceedings based on its earlier German registered trade mark. The designs were declared to be invalid and the Board of Appeal at the OHIM dismissed the appeal. However, the General Court annulled that decision. There had been a failure to note that the designs were for three-dimensional products whereas the registered trade mark was for a figurative trade mark (that is, two-dimensional). Of course, where a challenge is raised on the basis of an earlier trade mark, it must be shown that the design would infringe the trade mark. In the present case, the designs appeared similar but the goods were identical. The issue was whether there was a likelihood of confusion on the part of the relevant public (German consumers in this case). It was fatal, however, not to take account of the fact the trade mark was a figurative one whilst the designs were for three-dimensional products. As the General Court noted, a three-dimensional design can be viewed from different angles, creating different impressions, whilst a figurative mark can only be seen in two dimensions.

69 'Conflict' is not defined in the Regulation but the General Court has accepted, in Case T-9/07 *Gruper Promer Mon Graphic SA*, 18 March 2010, as meaning that a Community design is in conflict with a prior design if, when taking account of the freedom of the designer in developing the design, it does not produce on the informed user a different overall impression from that produced by the prior design.

70 This is equivalent to anticipation of a patent application by a patent having an earlier priority date but which had not been published at the time the application was filed under the Patents Act 1977 s 2(3).

71 [2010] ECDR 9.

Under Article 26, if a Community design is declared invalid, it is deemed to be invalid from the outset. In other words, it is as if it never existed. If partially invalid, that takes effect from the outset to the extent that it is declared invalid. However, invalidity does not affect any final decision on infringement which has been enforced before the invalidity decision nor any contract concluded prior to the invalidity decision in so far as it has been performed before that decision. Repayment of any sums paid under the contract may be claimed on the grounds of equity.

Under Article 52, an application for a declaration of invalidity before the OHIM must include a written reasoned statement and the fee for a declaration of invalidity (currently €350). The application will not be admissible if the matter has been finally decided in a Community design court. Any third party involved in current relevant infringement proceedings may be joined as a party to invalidity proceedings within three months of the commencement of the infringement proceedings, providing a written reasoned statement and the invalidity fee are paid (Article 54). Figure 17.2 shows the basic procedure for invalidity proceedings.

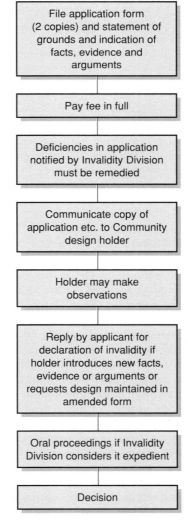

Figure 17.2 Invalidity procedure before OHIM

Where, in proceedings before a Community design court, validity is put in issue by way of a counterclaim for a declaration of invalidity, and any of the grounds in Article 25 are found to prejudice the maintenance of a Community design, the court shall declare it invalid (Article 86). Where a counterclaim for invalidity of an RCD has been filed before a Community design court, it must inform the OHIM of the date it was filed and this fact will be entered on the register. The court may, on application of the rightholder of an RCD and after hearing the other parties, stay proceedings and ask the defendant to submit an application for a declaration of invalidity to the OHIM within a specified time limit. Failure to submit within the time limit has the effect of the counterclaim being withdrawn and the proceedings will continue without considering invalidity. Where a court has made a final ruling on a counterclaim for invalidity of an RCD, it will send a copy of the judgment to the OHIM, mention of which will be made in the register. A counterclaim for invalidity of an RCD may not be made if an application relating to the same subject matter and involving the same parties has already been determined by the OHIM in a decision that has become final.

When a judgment on invalidity of a Community design court has become final and it has found the design invalid, it is treated as having the consequences of invalidity specified in Article 26 in all the Member States,[72] as is the case on a finding of invalidity by the Invalidity Division of the OHIM.

An RCD may be surrendered by written declaration submitted to the OHIM by the rightholder but shall not have effect until entered in the register (Article 51(1)). If subject to deferred publication at the time, it shall be treated as never having had the effects specified in the CDR, that is, it will be as if it never existed. Partial surrender is possible providing its amended form complies with the requirements for protection and the identity of the design is retained. Surrender shall only be with the agreement of the proprietor of a right entered in the register. If a licence has been registered, the rightholder must prove that the licensee has been informed first of the intention to surrender. Where an action has been brought as to entitlement under Article 14 before a Community design court, the fact of surrender will only be registered if the claimant agrees.

72 Article 87.

Appeals from decisions at the OHIM

Provisions for appeals from decisions of the OHIM in respect of the RCD are similar to those applicable to the Community trade mark. Article 55 gives a right of appeal against decisions of the examiners, the Administration of Trade Marks and Designs and Legal Division and Invalidity Divisions. An appeal has suspensive effect.[73] Any party to proceedings adversely affected by the decision may appeal with the other parties to the proceedings being parties to the appeal proceedings as of right (Article 56).

Notice of appeal must be filed in writing at the OHIM within two months of the date of notification of the decision being appealed but will only be deemed to be filed when the fee is paid, currently €800. Within a further four months after the date of the decision, a written statement setting out the grounds of appeal must be filed (Article 67).

The department whose decision is contested may, under Article 68, decide to rectify its decision if it thinks the appeal is admissible and well-founded, provided the appellant is not opposed by another party to the proceedings. If not rectified, the appeal must be remitted to the Board of Appeal without delay and without comment as to its merits.

If the appeal is admissible, under Article 59, the Board of Appeal shall examine whether the appeal should be allowed, inviting the parties, as often as necessary, to file observations, within a period fixed by the Board of Appeal, on communications from the other parties or issued by itself. The Board of Appeal then decides the appeal and may

73 A decision that does not terminate proceedings as regards one of the parties can only be appealed together with the final decision unless the decision allows separate appeal: Article 55(2).

exercise any power within the competence of the department responsible for the decision or remit the case to that department for further prosecution, in which case the department will be bound by the *ratio decidendi* of the Board of Appeal in as much as the facts are the same (Article 60).

Decisions of the Boards of Appeal take effect only after the period of two months after notification of its decision (the time limit for bringing a further appeal to the Court of Justice) or where an action has been brought before the Court of Justice, from the date such action was rejected, if that was the decision of the Court of Justice.

Appeals against decisions of the Boards of Appeals go to the Court of Justice on grounds of lack of competence, infringement of an essential procedural requirement, infringement of the EC Treaty (now the Treaty on the Functioning of the European Union), the CDR or any rule of law relating to their application or abuse of power (Article 61). The Court of Justice may annul or alter the contested decision and the action shall be open to any party before the Board of Appeal adversely affected by its decision. The OHIM shall take necessary measures to comply with the judgment of the Court of Justice.

Jurisdiction

Each Member State is required to designate as limited a number as possible of national courts and tribunals as Community design courts under Article 80 which have to be communicated to the Commission no later than 5 March 2005. In the UK, the designated courts are the Patents County Court, the High Court, the Court of Appeal and the Court of Session in Scotland.

Community design courts have exclusive jurisdiction on actions for infringement of Community designs, actions for invalidity of the UCD and counterclaims for declarations of invalidity for the RCD connected with infringement actions. Where the national law permits (as it does in the UK) the courts also have jurisdiction for declarations of non-infringement of Community designs. Community design courts also appear to have jurisdiction to hear actions relating to entitlement. This is not explicit in the main provisions governing the jurisdiction of Community design courts but Article 51(5) makes it clear that they do have such jurisdiction; although Article 51 deals with surrender, it refers to actions in Community design courts pursuant to Article 14 which covers entitlement.[74]

Under Article 82, the international jurisdiction of Community design courts is established for claims referred to in Article 81[75] subject to applicable provisions of the Convention on Jurisdiction and the Enforcement (the 'Brussels Convention') according to Article 79[76] (*see* below). There are three main rules for determining jurisdiction, only one of which will apply in a particular case. They are:

- the Member State in which the defendant is domiciled or, if not domiciled in any Member State, any Member State in which he has an establishment;[77]
- where the defendant is neither domiciled nor has an establishment in any Member State, the action shall be brought before the courts in the Member State in which the claimant is domiciled or has an establishment, as appropriate;
- if neither the defendant nor claimant are domiciled or have an establishment in any Member State, proceedings shall be brought in the Member State in which the OHIM is based, being Spain.

There remain some alternative ways of determining in which Member State the Community design courts have jurisdiction. Articles 17 and 18 of the Brussels Convention apply, which allow the parties to agree that a different Community design court shall

74 Article 15, which covers claims relating to entitlement, makes no mention of the forum for such claims.

75 These are infringement actions, declarations of non-infringement, declarations for invalidity of the UCD and counterclaims for invalidity of a Community design raised in infringement actions.

76 Convention on Jurisdiction and Enforcement of Judgments in Civil and Commercial Matters signed in Brussels on 27 September 1968, OJ L299, 31.12.1972, p 32. For most purposes and for most Member States, this has been replaced by Council Regulation (EC) No 44/2001 of 22 December 2000 on jurisdiction and the recognition and enforcement of judgments in civil and commercial matters, OJ L12, 16.01.2001, p 1 (the 'Brussels Regulation'). Article 79 of the CD Regulation disapplies certain provisions of the Brussels Convention, in particular Articles 2, 4, 5(1), (3), (4) and (5), 16(4) and 24 in relation to actions and claims referred to in Article 85 of the CD Regulation.

77 Article 82. This is subject to those parts of the Brussels Convention applicable by virtue of Article 79 of the CD Regulation.

have jurisdiction and a different court may have jurisdiction if the defendant enters an appearance there, otherwise than solely to challenge jurisdiction.

Where proceedings relate to infringement (and a declaration of invalidity, if raised, in an infringement action), under Article 82(5) the Community design courts in the Member States in which the infringement has been committed or threatened also have jurisdiction though, in this case, under Article 83(2), the court will have jurisdiction only in respect of acts of infringement committed or threatened without the territory of the Member State in which the court is situated. In the other cases above, the court has jurisdiction in relation to acts of infringement committed or threatened within the territory of any Member State. It can be seen that a defendant may prefer to enter an appearance in a court in a jurisdiction most suitable for him in accordance with Article 18 of the Brussels Convention, though this is not available where the sole purpose is to contest the court's jurisdiction. A defendant cannot go forum shopping by virtue of Article 82(5) to take advantage of jurisdiction limited to infringement in the Member State in which the court is situated because such an action may only be commenced by the person alleging infringement. Where the alleged infringement is taking place in a number of jurisdictions, a claimant would select a court on the basis of the other provisions.[78]

The provisions in the Brussels Convention that are disapplied in the case of actions and claims in Article 85 (proceedings for infringement and presumption of validity) are:

- Article 2 – persons domiciled in a Contracting State shall be sued in that State.
- Article 4 – if a person is not domiciled in a Contracting State, the jurisdiction of the courts in each Contracting State shall, subject to Article 16 of the Convention, be governed by the laws of that State.
- Article 5(1), (3), (4) and (5) – supplementary rules on jurisdiction applying to contract, tort, damages or restitution based on criminal liability and in respect of disputes concerning a branch, agency or establishment.[79]
- Article 16(4) – where registration or validity of a patent, trade mark, design or similar right subject to formalities such as registration or deposit is involved.[80]
- Article 24 – applications for provisional, including protective, measures may be made in a Contracting State other than the one having jurisdiction as to the substance of the matter.

Invalidity actions may only be brought before the Community design courts on the same grounds as apply to applications for invalidity before the OHIM and may only be brought by the persons entitled to make such applications before the OHIM (Article 84). If a counterclaim for invalidity is an action in which the rightholder is not already a party, he shall be informed and may be joined as a party.

The applicable law in cases before the Community design courts is stated in Article 88 as that set out in the CD Regulation except where not covered by the Regulation, in which case it will be the law of the Member State in which the court is situated, including its private international law. In terms of procedure a Community design court will apply the rules governing the same type of action relating to a national design right in its Member State.

A Community design court must stay an action, other than one for a declaration of non-infringement, where the validity of a Community design is already in issue as a result of a counterclaim or, in the case of an RCD, where an application for invalidity has been filed at the OHIM.[81]

Where a national court is dealing with an action other than one under Article 81, it must treat a Community design as valid.[82] The presumption as to validity applies under Article 85(2) providing the rightholder proves that the conditions in Article 11 apply and indicates what the individual character is (Article 94).

78 A further rule for determining jurisdiction for actions outside Article 81 is given in Article 93 on the basis of *ratione loci* and *ratione materiae* (jurisdiction based by reason of location or the subject matter respectively).

79 Under Article 5(1), where a breach of contract is alleged, the action may be brought in the State in which the obligation in question was to be performed.

80 In such cases, the courts in the State in which the right was secured by registration or deposit have sole jurisdiction.

81 Article 91. Where the OHIM has an application for invalidity and it is in issue in a Community design court, the OHIM must stay proceedings; although one of the parties at a Community design court may ask the court to stay proceedings, in which case the OHIM will continue with the proceedings. Whichever case applies, the court or the OHIM may continue regardless if there are special grounds to continue the hearing. Even if staying the action, a Community design court may still grant provisional measures including protective measures for the duration of the stay.

82 An example is where entitlement is in issue.

Finally, there are provisions to deal with parallel actions under Article 95. Where actions are brought before the courts of different Member States, one on the basis of a Community design and the other on the basis of a national design right providing simultaneous protection, the court other than the one first seized must decline jurisdiction on its own motion. It may instead stay the action if the jurisdiction of the other court is contested. What must be meant here is that there is a Community design and a registered national design for the same (that is, identical) design. The national design right cannot be an unregistered design right, as in the UK, as Article 96 states that the Regulation is without prejudice to the law of Member States relating to, *inter alia*, unregistered designs.

Where a Community design court is hearing an action for infringement or threatened infringement on the basis of a Community design, it shall reject the action if a final decision on the merits has been given on the same cause of action between the same parties on the basis of a design right providing simultaneous protection and vice versa. This prevents parties re-litigating what is essentially the same issue. This is all without prejudice to provisional measures including protective measures.

Appeals from Community design courts of first instance to 'second instance' courts are permissible in respect of Article 81 proceedings subject to the conditions for appeal determined by national law in a Member State. National rules governing further appeal shall be applicable in respect of judgments of Community design courts of second instance (Article 92). In the UK, the Patents County Court and High Court are courts of first instance, the Court of Appeal is the court of second instance and final appeal to the House of Lords (now the Supreme Court) is possible.[83]

83 Although, given the lack of jurisprudence on the CD Regulation, it is likely that a reference to the Court of Justice under Article 267 of the Treaty on the Functioning of the European Union would be made before it got that far.

UK registered design

The UK's registered design system goes back quite a long way and has undergone many changes, perhaps the most radical being as a result of implementing Directive 98/71/EC of the European Parliament and of the Council of 13 October 1998 on the legal protection of designs.[84] This Directive, intended partially to harmonise registered design law throughout the European Community, made significant changes to the UK law on registered designs and also brought it into conformity with the CD Regulation in many respects.[85] Whilst the CD Regulation left a number of aspects to be determined largely by national laws (such as dealing with a Community design), many of the important provisions of design law, particularly in relation to the criteria for protectability and invalidity, are essentially the same; although there are some differences.

84 OJ L 289, 28.10.1998, p 28.

85 The Community design came later than harmonisation of national registered designs but the latter was clearly influenced by the plans to create a unitary Community design.

86 There is bound to be some repetition as some of the provisions are the same, equivalent or very nearly the same as for the Community design. It must be remembered, however, that the Community design is completely separate to the national registered design systems and decisions in one system are not binding on the other system. This has been stated on a number of occasions by the European Court of Justice in respect of the Community trade mark and the harmonised national trade mark systems and there is no reason to believe the same will not apply to designs.

87 The UK unregistered design is the subject matter of the following chapter.

This part of the chapter looks at the UK registered design system as modified by the Directive and subsequently. It concentrates on those features that are additional to or different to those under the Community design,[86] though it is worth recalling that the Community design has a unitary nature and applies throughout the Community and cannot be registered, assigned, surrendered or found to be invalid or its use prohibited except in relation to the whole Community unless provided for in the CD Regulation. The UK national registered design, of course, applies only within the territory of the UK and other countries to which it has been extended. Another significant difference is that the Community design provides for an informal unregistered right of three years in addition to a registrable right (equivalent to the UK registered design but on a Community-wide scale). The UK's Registered Designs Act 1949 does not extend to an informal right and the UK's unregistered design right, provided for by Part III of the Copyright, Designs and Patents Act 1988, bears little resemblance to either the Community design and the UK registered design although, in a good proportion of cases, a design may be protected by the RCD, the UCD, the UK registered design and the UK unregistered design.[87]

Brief history of the UK registered design

A system of registration for designs has been around since the early part of the nineteenth century. The initial demand for a system of registration came from the textile industry, but now all manner of designs are registered, some of the most common kinds of designs for which registration is applied for in the classes of packaging and containers, recording, communications and information retrieval equipment and furnishing. Initially dealt with separately, for example, by the Copyright in Designs Act 1839, registered designs were for some time governed by the same statute as patents and, for a time, trade marks.[88] Eventually, in 1949, patents and designs legislation were separated and the present statute dealing with registered designs is the Registered Designs Act 1949 which was amended by the Copyright, Designs and Patents Act 1988.[89] That amended version of the 1949 Act came into force on 1 August 1989.

The 1949 Act was amended yet again by the Registered Designs Regulations 2001 as from 9 December 2001. The changes were made so as to comply with Directive 98/71/EC of the European Parliament and of the Council of 13 October 1998 on the legal protection of designs[90] which was intended to harmonise some aspects of the registered designs system in Europe and, in some respects, the UK law on registered designs has been very significantly altered. In particular, the new law differs in terms of subsistence, rights of the proprietor, infringement, exceptions and invalidity. Consequently, a good proportion of the case law that was applicable under previous versions of registered design law is of little or no relevance under the law as it now stands. The old law prior to 2001 is largely of academic interest now though may give some insight into the rationale of design law and why it has changed. Further significant modification and clarification has been introduced by virtue of the Intellectual Property (Enforcement, etc.) Regulations 2006[91] and the Regulatory Reform (Registered Designs) Order 2006.[92] The following description of the UK Registered Designs Act 1949 takes account of these changes.

88 For example, the Patents, Designs and Trade Marks Act 1883 and the Patents and Designs Act 1907.

89 Prior to this amendment, the right was referred to as the 'copyright in the registered design' under the old Registered Designs Act 1949 s 7(1).

90 OJ L 289, 28.10.1998, p 28.

91 SI 2006/1028, in force 29 April 2006.

92 SI 2006/1974, in force 1 October 2006.

Implementation of the Directive

As mentioned earlier, Directive 98/71/EC on the legal protection of designs was not intended to harmonise design law fully but was aimed at harmonising, in particular, those aspects of registered designs that could otherwise affect trade between Member States. Essential to this purpose was the creation of a level playing field in terms of the requirements for registrability and exceptions thereto and provision throughout the Community for the same scope of protection, being the rights of the proprietor, acts of infringement and defences to infringement. Provisions relating to sanctions, remedies and enforcement were left to national law and Member States are free to determine procedural provisions concerning registration, renewal and invalidation; but the grounds of invalidity are set out in the Directive. Even then, the Directive left some discretion to Member States, for example, in respect of some of the grounds for invalidity.

A more controversial aspect of the Directive was that it allowed Member States to continue to protect 'must-match' spare parts such as replacement panels for vehicles. The only proviso was that any changes to the protection could only be to liberalise the market. Some Member States, such as the UK, chose to deny protection for such parts whilst others, such as France, continued to protect them. As mentioned at the beginning of this chapter, moves are now afoot to modify the Directive to deny protection through design law of such parts, bringing the Directive and CD Regulation together on this issue.

The latest date for compliance with the Directive was 28 October 2001. The UK was late implementing it and the new law came into force on 9 December 2001 as a result of the Registered Designs Regulations 2001 which contain a number of transitional provisions dealing with other matters.

The late implementation of the Directive was subject to a challenge on the basis that the Regulations, or part of them, were *ultra vires*. The problem was that Article 11(8) of the Directive allowed Member States to retain their old law in relation to invalidity in respect of designs for which registration was applied for before the last date for compliance with the Directive, being 28 October 2001, which is what the UK purported to do. This meant that, where registration of a design was applied for before that date, the benefit of the 12-month period of grace did not apply. As the new law was not implemented until 9 December 2001, that meant that there would be some applications (filed between 28 October 2001 and 9 December 2001) which should have the advantage of the period of grace but did not in the UK.[93] Regulation 12(2) and (3) of the Registered Designs Regulations 2001 provided that registrations resulting from applications made on or after 1 August 1989 and before the coming into force of the 2001 Regulations should continue to be subject to the old provisions on cancellation and invalidity.

In *Oakley Inc v Animal Ltd*[94] (with the Secretary of State for Trade and Industry as intervener), the claimant filed its application to register a design for sunglasses on 27 September 1996, claiming the priority of an earlier application elsewhere. The priority date was 10 June 1996. However, exactly one month before the priority date, the claimant commenced importing sunglasses to the design into the UK. Therefore, if the old law applied, the design would be invalid for lack of novelty,[95] but, if the new law applied, the design would meet the requirements for novelty because of the period of grace. Even if the provision could have been rewritten to make the relevant cut-off date for the old law on validity as 28 October 2001, this would not help Oakley. However, it was submitted that, as the provision in the Directive allowing Member States to choose whether or not to retain their old law on validity to pre-existing applications was a derogation, this required a policy choice which could only be taken by Parliament. That being so, reg 12(2) and (3) should be excised from the Regulations, leaving the period of grace available for all earlier applications to register.

At first instance,[96] Peter Prescott QC sitting as deputy judge of the High Court agreed that the transitional provisions retaining the old law were *ultra vires* as the Secretary of State did not have the power to implement a derogation under s 2(2) of the European Communities Act 1972. However, rather than strike the offending provisions out he held that he could rewrite them so that the effective date was 28 October 2001. Oakley appealed to the Court of Appeal where all three judges held that the Regulations were validly made by the Secretary of State whose powers to make such Regulations extended to implementing derogations from Directives. The consequences of a decision to the contrary would have had profound implications in all fields of law where Directives containing derogations, as many do, had been implemented. In the Court of Appeal, Jacob LJ said (at para 48):

> Who would have guessed that a pair of fashion sunglasses could lead to a case of such constitutional importance that the Government found it necessary to intervene by its chief law officer, the Attorney General?

Article 288 of the Treaty on the Functioning of the European Union[97] states that Directives '. . . shall be binding, as to the result to be achieved, upon each Member State to which it is addressed, but shall leave to the national authorities the choice of forms and methods'. Jacob LJ said that this gave Member States some discretion as to how a Directive is implemented. As a result, it was common for Directives to be couched in general terms and to provide for alternatives. He said that there were three types of provision in a Directive, being those which:

- may be implemented only in one way;
- allow a choice of alternatives;
- allow Member States to fill in the details.

He also said that there was no rational basis for distinguishing between an option to derogate and an option to achieve one of a number of alternatives. In relation to the Directive on the legal protection of designs, Jacob LJ noted that it contained an option (refusal of registration or invalidity of certain badges and emblems, etc.) and a derogation allowing Member States to apply the old law on invalidity for pre-existing design registrations. He saw no reason to differentiate between the two.

Section 2(2) of the European Communities Act 1972 states:

(2) Subject to Schedule 2 to this Act, at any time after its passing Her Majesty may by Order in Council, and any designated Minister or department may by regulations, make provision –

(a) for the purpose of implementing any Community obligation of the United Kingdom, or enabling any such obligation to be implemented, or of enabling any rights enjoyed or to be enjoyed by the United Kingdom under or by virtue of the Treaties to be exercised; or

(b) for the purpose of dealing with matters arising out of or related to any such obligation or rights or the coming into force, or the operation from time to time, of subsection (1) above;

and in the exercise of any statutory power or duty, including any power to give directions or to legislate by means of orders, rules, regulations or other subordinate instrument, the person entrusted with the power or duty may have regard to the objects of the Communities and to any such obligation or rights as aforesaid.

Section 2(2) contemplates Directives being implemented by statutory instrument but certain things, including taxation, mentioned in Sch 2, can only be implemented by an Act of Parliament. Jacob LJ said that he found startling the conclusion of the deputy judge that derogations in Directives, not being within Sch 2, can only be implemented by Acts of Parliament.

In relation to s 2(2)(a), Jacob LJ said that the test of whether it allows the transposition of a Directive by statutory instrument is whether there is anything in it which is not explicitly contemplated in the Directive. If there is not, then it falls within s 2(2)(a) as it is made for the sole purpose of implementing the Directive. He said that the Registered Designs Regulations 2001 was such a case, rejecting the deputy judge's view that the section applied only to those parts of Directives which were essential and non-optional. The result would be that anything involving any sort of policy decision would have to be implemented by Act of Parliament, which would mean that almost all Directives would have to be complied with, at least in part, by Act of Parliament. This, as Jacob LJ pointed out, could hardly be what Parliament had intended when it passed the European Communities Act 1972.

Although not strictly relevant because of the finding in relation to s 2(2)(a), Jacob LJ went on to look at s 2(2)(b) which allows implementation by statutory instrument, matters arising out of or relating to Community obligations or Treaty rights. The deputy judge considered that a narrow construction should be taken, as this was what he described as a 'King Henry VIII' clause.[98] Another factor was that monopolies were to be tolerated only when good reason could be shown.

These views were both rejected by the Court of Appeal. Jacob LJ said the approach to s 2 could not be different depending on whether it involved an intellectual property right granting a monopoly. He held that the approach to King Henry VIII clauses was not applicable as the European Communities Act 1972 was *sui generis* and its general purpose was to bring European Community law into the UK and this was a paramount consideration.

98 A reference to the King's supposed appetite for absolute powers.

Jacob LJ considered the difference in the ambit of s 2(2)(a) and (b). If s 2(2)(a) enabled the provision of the detail to implement a Community obligation, then s 2(2)(b) appeared to go further and allowed more to be done by delegated legislation. On the other hand, if the provision of detail is not covered by s 2(2)(a), it must be within s 2(2)(b). The wider the ambit of s 2(2)(a), the narrower that of s 2(2)(b). Section 2(2)(b) must add more to s 2(2)(a) but just how much more will depend on the circumstances, with the statutory language as a guide. Jacob LJ preferred the view that 'related to' meant not distinct, separate or divorced from the Community obligation in question.[99] However, that did not mean that the power to make subordinate legislation was virtually unlimited.[100] Waller LJ thought that s 2(2)(a) permitted the implementation of a derogation by statutory instrument as a derogation did not arise out of or relate to a Community obligation but was part of bringing the obligation into force. He also thought that s 2(2)(b) enabled further measures to be taken which naturally arise from or closely relate to the primary purpose to be achieved.

Consequently, the Court of Appeal considered that the Registered Designs Regulations 2001 were validly made and it was unnecessary to decide whether reg 12 was severable or should be rewritten. However, the deputy judge had already submitted a reference to the European Court of Justice for a preliminary ruling under Article 267 of the Treaty on the Functioning of the European Union[101] asking whether late adoption of a derogation could still be valid or whether the opportunity to adopt the derogation ceased to exist after the latest date for implementing the Directive.[102] The case was later withdrawn and removed from the register of the Court of Justice.[103] It seems we will never know which is the correct view.

Requirements for registrability

The requirements for registrability of a UK registered design closely follow those for the Community design, being that:

- the design comes within the definition of 'design';
- the design is new;
- the design has individual character;
- the right is not excluded under the provisions relating to technical function or because it is contrary to public policy or morality;
- registration is refused because the design involves the use of certain emblems, etc.

Substantive grounds for refusal of registration contained in s 1A of the Act were repealed by the Regulatory Reform (Registered Designs) Order 2006[104] with effect from 1 October 2006. Consequently, applications to register designs are no longer examined for novelty and individual character. The Registrar still examines applications for the technical function exceptions, public policy and morality and whether they involve the use of certain emblems, etc. He also has a discretion to refuse if the application does not comply with rules under the Act.[105] He must also refuse an application if it appears to him that the applicant is not entitled to apply.[106] Of course, it remains possible for the validity of a registration to be challenged in invalidity proceedings brought under s 11ZB.[107]

Meaning of 'design'

Designs are incorporated in or applied to products. Under s 1(3) of the Registered Designs Act 1949, a 'product' means:

99 Two apparently conflicting decisions on the scope of s 2(2)(b) were considered, being *R v Secretary of State for Trade & Industry ex parte Unison* [1996] ICR 1003 and *Addison v Denholm Ship Management (UK) Ltd* [1997] ICR 389. In the latter, Lord Johnson suggested that if the Directive is the parent, the child cannot be larger, wider or have greater implications than the parent allows.

100 Jacob LJ's view, *obiter*, was that s 2(2)(a) covers all forms of implementation, '. . . whether by choice of explicit options or by way of supply of detail'.

101 Formerly Article 234 of the EC Treaty.

102 Case C-267/05 *Oakley Inc v Animal Ltd*.

103 OJ C 154, 01.07.2006, p 14.

104 SI 2006/1974.

105 The current rules are the Registered Designs Rules 2006, SI 2006/1975.

106 Section 3A.

107 The grounds of invalidity are set out in s 11ZA and, *inter alia*, relate to the definition of design, novelty, individual character, designs dictated by technical function, public policy or morality and in relation to certain emblems, etc. In some cases, invalidity proceedings can be brought by any person interested.

... any industrial or handicraft item other than a computer program; and, in particular, includes packaging, get-up, graphic symbols, typographic type-faces and parts intended to be assembled into a complex product.

And a complex product is:

... a product which is composed of at least two replaceable component parts permitting disassembly and reassembly of the product.

Finally, a 'design' is, under s 1(2):

... the appearance of the whole or a part of a product resulting from the features of, in particular, the lines, contours, colours, shape, texture or materials of the product or its ornamentation.

These definitions are almost identical to the equivalent ones for the Community design and in the Directive but there are some very minor differences, none of which should have any consequence. Where these provisions are in issue, the court will simply turn to the text of the Directive. It could be questioned why, in implementing these provisions, the definitions in the Directive were not simply restated verbatim rather than rewriting them introducing very minor differences.[108] This draftsman's penchant for rewriting rather than copying out measures from the European Patent Convention was criticised by Jacob LJ as unhelpful.[109] The same sentiment should hold true in terms of implementing Directives where the provisions do not require the addition of detail.

As with the Community design, the definition of product is very wide and the examples given within it are not exhaustive. Although couched in terms of 'items', whether industrial or handicraft, the inclusion of graphic symbols does not mean that the definition is necessarily restricted to tangible items, notwithstanding the exclusion of computer programs. Graphic symbols and icons generated on the screen display of a computer or mobile phone come within the meaning and should be registrable if the other requirements are satisfied.[110] The Directive gives no guidance although the exclusion of certain protected emblems and the fact that a declaration of invalidity of a registered design can be sought, *inter alia*, by the owner of the copyright in any work used in the design without consent, adds weight to this argument.[111]

The meaning of a complex product is important in respect of the substantive grounds for refusal of registration but another point to bear in mind is that, otherwise and in principle, there is nothing to prevent registration of component parts or larger products. However, as a complex product is still a product, registration of a design applied to the whole of a complex product when assembled should be possible if the other requirements are met. For example, in the case of a chest of drawers the design of the item of furniture as a whole could be registrable. The drawers themselves may be registered if, for example, they have some decoration applied to them, notwithstanding the exceptions for designs dictated by technical function, described later.

It is possible for the product in question to have a three-dimensional shape or to be flat or to be made from a piece of wire, like a wire coat hanger. Even a product's material could be deemed a design, for example, if the product is made of gold and like products have never before been made of gold. Of course, a limiting factor will be the other requirements for registrability.

A design can relate to part of a product only. This is important where other features of the appearance of the product are not new, do not have individual character or are otherwise excluded. If part only of the overall design of the product is new, has individual character and is not otherwise excluded, that part of the design will be registrable. In such a case, registration may be subject to a disclaimer if the representations of the design submitted with the application show aspects that are not, in themselves, registrable.[112]

108 For example, the definition of design in the Directive refers to '... texture and/or materials of the product itself and/or its ornamentation' whereas the Act refers to 'texture or materials of the product or its ornamentation'.

109 *Unilin Beheer NV v Berry Floor NV* [2005] FSR 6 at para 39.

110 Of course, it is the symbol itself for which protection would be afforded, not the computer program which generates it. Before changes to the Act to comply with the Directive, icons and screen displays had been accepted as potentially registrable when inherently built into a machine such as a computer on the basis that they were inherently built into software, the inclusion of which in a computer was part of an industrial process: *see Apple Computer Inc's Design Applications* [2002] FSR 38.

111 Registered Designs Act 1949 s 11ZA(4).

112 However, under s 11ZD, any modification, including a disclaimer, must not be such that the identity of the design is not retained.

Although there is no express requirement for eye-appeal or aesthetic quality it is clear that appearance is an important requirement. The definition of 'individual character', discussed below, reinforces this. However, whilst the design has to have visual impact, this does not mean that the design has to possess any aesthetic quality. Recital 14 to the Directive makes this clear.

Novelty

Under s 1B(1), a design must be new and have individual character (that latter aspect is examined in the subsequent section of this chapter). Section 1B(2) states that a design is new if:

> . . . no identical design or no design whose features differ only in immaterial details has been made available to the public before the relevant date.

There are some differences here when compared with the Community design which also has to deal with novelty for the UCD. The provisions in the Registered Designs Act 1949, as amended, should however be equivalent to those in the Directive. However, the Act has to make specific provision for the situation where an application to register a design is subsequently modified.

The first question to consider is, how similar must a pre-existing design be to prevent a design being considered to be new? The phrase 'design whose features differ only in immaterial details' was also used in the old version of the Act to determine novelty and, as the Directive uses the same test,[113] it is reasonable to assume that prior case law can still be of assistance. Although the old law also used the test of variants commonly used in the trade, the comments of Laddie J in *Household Articles Ltd's Registered Design*[114] remain apt. In that case, he said (at 685):

> . . . if all the differences between the prior art and the design in suit are immaterial or common trade variants then the design in suit is deemed not to be novel. Immaterial details are features which make no significant visual impact on the design.[115] (original emphasis)

Laddie J also held that novelty did not have to be of a startling or groundbreaking variety. He also confirmed that novelty should be judged through the eyes of the ordinary customer for, or trader in, the relevant goods. In other words, someone familiar with goods of that type. The Act does not state this explicitly but it seems reasonable to expect novelty still to be determined in this way, especially as the test for individual character is in terms of the overall impression the design makes on the informed user.

To be new the design must not have been made available to the public before the relevant date. Under s 1B(7) the relevant date is the date on which the application for registration was made, or is treated as being made by virtue of:

- the date when an application to register has been modified such that it has altered significantly (this is at the Registrar's discretion) (s 3B(2));
- where an application has disclosed more than one design which has been modified to exclude one or more designs and these are then applied for subsequently, the Registrar may treat the date of application as the date the earlier application was made (again the Registrar has discretion) (s 3B(3));
- following refusal of registration (for failure to comply with ss 1B–1D or Sch A1 – specially protected emblems etc.), any later application modified so as to comply for effectively the same design is treated as having been made at the date of the first application (s 3B(5));
- where the application is based on the priority of an earlier application in a Convention country, the date is treated to be the date of that application (if more than one, the

113 Although the Directive expresses it in a slightly different way, stating that designs shall be deemed to be identical if their features differ only in immaterial details: Article 4.

114 [1998] FSR 676.

115 He went on to say that, on the other hand, a common trade variant may well have visual significance.

date of the earliest) but no application can be made to take advantage of this provision if the earlier or earliest application in a Convention country was made more than six months before the application in the UK (s 14).[116]

Whilst these provisions are fairly self-explanatory, in most cases, the relevant date will be the date of filing the application; the next most common will be where priority is claimed from a Convention country.

The relevant date is the date taken to determine whether a design has been made available to the public. To the basic rule there are a number of disclosures which will be ignored in determining whether a design has been made available to the public before the relevant date. Under s 1B(5), a design has been made available to the public before the relevant date if it has been published (whether following registration or otherwise), exhibited, used in trade or otherwise disclosed before that date, and the disclosure does not fall within the excepted disclosures in s 1B(6). Those are, including the 12-month period of grace:

(a) disclosures such that the design could not reasonably have become known before the relevant date in the normal course of business to persons carrying on business in the European Economic Area (EEA)[117] and specialising in the sector concerned;
(b) disclosures made to a person other than the designer, or any successor in title, under conditions of confidentiality (whether express or implied);
(c) disclosures made by the designer, or any successor in title, during the period of 12 months immediately preceding the relevant date;
(d) disclosures made by a person other than the designer, or any successor in title, during the period of 12 months immediately preceding the relevant date in consequence of information provided or other action taken by the designer or any successor in title;
(e) disclosures made during the period of 12 months immediately preceding the relevant date as a consequence of an abuse in relation to the designer or any successor in title.

Under the old law, the relevant public was the public in the UK. However, it is at least arguable that, because of (a) above, the question should be determined on the basis of the public within the EEA. The OHIM does not carry out searches for novelty (or individual character) and, since 1 October 2006, nor does the UK Design Registry. In practice, this is unlikely to cause too many problems and, although there are no provisions for opposition to registration, there are detailed provisions for declarations of invalidity on a number of grounds including lack of novelty and individual character.

A design might be in use outside the EEA but not be known within the EEA by those specialising in the particular sector. For example, products in which a design is incorporated or to which a design has been applied might have recently been placed on the market in the Sudan and there have been no trade exhibitions (anywhere in the world) where the design would have been disclosed to persons specialising in the sector in the EEA who might have attended such an exhibition. Certainly, one would not expect any marketing to have taken place in the EEA, though it might be possible, in very limited circumstances, that some products have been imported into the EEA for future sale. Very limited marketing or use in the EEA would probably attract the attention of those specialising in the trade, but whether (a) above applies must always be a question of fact, depending on the particular circumstances. The presence of exception (a) does, however, qualify the approach to novelty taken in patents cases, where very limited use in public, or a document in a library open to the public but never actually read by anyone, will anticipate a patent.

Exception (b) covers a breach of confidence by any person to whom the designer (or successor in title) has disclosed the design. The breach could be by a potential manufacturer, investor or adviser, for example. Unlike the case under the law of patents, there

116 Convention countries are specified in numerous Orders in Council made under s 13 which nominate countries with a view to fulfilling the UK's obligations under the Paris Convention for the Protection of Industrial Property 1883. The most recent is the Designs (Convention Countries) Order 2007, SI 2007/277.

117 Note that reference is made in the Act to the EEA. The Community design does not, however, extend outside the European Community to the other EEA states.

is no time limit although, as soon as a designer is aware of the breach of confidence, he would be well advised to apply to register the design.

As with the RCD, there is a 12-month period of grace during which the designer can test the market to see whether his design is likely to be successful before he applies for registration. In the exceptions in s 1B(6), (c) applies to disclosures by the designer (or successor in title) and (d) applies to disclosure by others as a result of information provided by or other action by the designer (or successor in title). This could be the result of publication of the design or displaying products to the design at a trade fair or exhibition or by way of contract with a third person to manufacture the products or as a result of licensing the design. However, this provision may have dangers. If the design is disclosed in such a way and unauthorised copies are made and sold (particularly from a number of sources), this could make it difficult for the designer to fend off an attack on his design on the grounds that it was not new unless he can clearly show that his disclosure was the first in time and that the copies were a result of some abuse, as in (e) above. In any event, it may not be safe to rely on (e) as it is not clear what its scope is. After all, how can there be an abuse in relation to the designer in respect of a right which does not yet exist, unless there is a breach of confidence or the design is protected in other ways, such as by copyright.

It is likely that, because of this period of grace, the Registered Designs Act 1949, as it now is, omits any provision for exhibitions certified by the Secretary of State being excluded from the test of novelty.[118] However, whatever disclosure is contemplated by the designer, he would be wise to ensure that they are made under an express obligation of confidence[119] or, more simply, as the application to register a design is not a particularly difficult and time-consuming business, the designer would be wise to apply to register the design before any disclosures.

As appearance is an essential aspect of the requirements for registrability of a design, protection is denied to the appearance of features not normally seen during normal use of a product which is a component part of a complex product. Section 1B(8) states that a design applied to or incorporated into a product which is a component part of a complex product shall only be considered to be new and have individual character if, once incorporated into the complex product, it remains visible during normal use of the complex product and to the extent that those visible features are new and have individual character. Normal use is defined in s 1B(9) as use by the end-user and does not include any maintenance, servicing or repair work in relation to the product. This provision is intended to exclude 'under the bonnet' spare parts from protection. Internal components have no visual significance during normal use though they may be protected by the UK unregistered design right which does not depend on the article to which the design has been applied being visible, whether during normal use or at any other time.

Internal components may be registrable if they are visible, for example, where they are encased in a transparent material such as the vortex on a bagless vacuum cleaner or visible through a transparent cover such as the internal mechanism of a watch under a clear watch face. It should not be the case that the entire component product must be visible during normal use and it should be sufficient if those parts that remain visible during normal use are themselves new and have individual character.

Individual character

Not only must a design be new but it must also have individual character to be registrable. A design has individual character, under s 1B(3), if:

> . . . the overall impression it produces on the informed user differs from the overall impression on such a user by any design which has been made available to the public before the relevant date.

118 There are, however, provisions for exhibition priority in the CD Regulation.

119 An express obligation is safer than relying on the courts to imply an obligation of confidence in respect of prototypes left with buyers for potential retailing organisation: *see Carflow Products (UK) Ltd v Linwood Securities (Birmingham) Ltd* [1996] FSR 424, discussed in Chapter 10.

The relevant date is that as for novelty, with specific provision for modified designs and priority. The degree of freedom of the author in creating the design is to be taken into consideration in determining whether a design has individual character (s 1B(4)). Thus, the less the design freedom, the smaller the differences compared to the prior art might need to be for a design to have individual character. Under the Act before amendment, it was usual for the courts to view the design through the eyes of the customer who buy products of the type in question and the differences which strike such persons as important.[120] This is probably somewhat weaker than the test of the informed user who can be considered to be a customer or other buyer, for example, a person who buys products as part of his employment duties and who takes a particular interest in the type of products concerned.

In *Dyson Ltd* v *Vax Ltd*,[121] involving an allegation of infringement of the registered design protecting the Dyson DC-02 bagless vacuum cleaner, it was held that design freedom could be constrained by technical function, by the need to incorporate features common to the type of product in question and/or by economic considerations. The degree of freedom could be tested against the relevant design corpus, which could even include designs created after the design under consideration had been registered. Arnold J held that the design corpus was cylindrical vacuum cleaners. The informed user would consider the registered design to be such a vacuum cleaner but with a particular dust-separation technology. The informed user would not think about a sub-category comprising cyclonic vacuum cleaners.

In *Dyson*, Arnold J also said that the greater the design freedom the greater the protection but where design freedom was limited, protection would be less. Presumably what he meant was that, in the latter case, the focus of attention must be on the parts of the design in respect of which the designer had some freedom in creating the design. He also said that the degree of freedom would be constrained by the technical specification of the product to which the design was incorporated in or applied to. A higher technical specification might impose greater technical constraints.

In *Woodhouse UK plc* v *Architectural Lighting Systems*,[122] a case before the Patents County Court concerned with the design of lanterns for street lights, Michael Fysh QC said (at para 48) that the 'informed user' was '. . . a debutante to the pantheon of fictional English legal characters'. He said of such a user, *obiter*, that he must be a user of articles of the type subject to the registered design in question and probably a regular user: a consumer or buyer or someone otherwise familiar with the subject matter, for example, through use at work. He is a person to whom the design is directed. He went on to say that the informed user was not a manufacturer of the products concerned nor is he the man in the street. The use of the word 'informed' suggests that he is rather more familiar with the relevant type of product than the average consumer. He would have basic knowledge of product trend and availability and technical considerations, if any. Michael Fysh QC said that he felt uncomfortable with any analogy to the person skilled in the art. He thought that appearance would be more important than function or operational or manufacturing technology. This was accepted as the correct approach by Lewison J in *Procter & Gamble Co* v *Reckitt Benckiser (UK) Ltd*,[123] at first instance. Although the appeal against Lewison J's ruling was successful in the Court of Appeal,[124] this view of the 'informed user' was not itself criticised. However, the Court of Appeal added that the informed user was not the same as the 'average consumer' of trade mark law. The informed user was more discriminating. He would be aware of the existing design corpus and would also be aware that some designs were required to be as they were, to some extent at least, because of function.

Rolawn Ltd v *Turfmech Machinery Ltd*[125] concerned allegations of infringement of the UK registered design and the UK unregistered design right in relation to wide-area grass mowers. The design in question had been created by a company engaged in growing and

120 *A Fulton Co Ltd* v *Totes Isotoner (UK) Ltd* [2003] RPC 27. As the products in question were foldaway umbrellas, Michael Fysh QC, in the Patents County Court, said nearly everyone was familiar with the design field and he had no difficulty in putting himself in the role of the typical customer for such products.

121 [2010] FSR 39.

122 [2006] RPC 1.

123 [2007] FSR 13. This was a case on Community design but the principles must surely be the same. This was the test used also in the Design Registry by the Hearing Officer in *Walton* v *Zap Ltd* [2007] ECDR 10.

124 *Procter & Gamble Co* v *Reckitt Benckiser (UK) Ltd* [2008] FSR 8.

125 [2008] RPC 27.

selling turf which had built mowers to the design for use in its business only.[126] As regards the registered design, Mann J said that the informed user was someone who uses machines in the turf-growing industry. He was not as narrow as someone familiar only with mowers or wide-area mowers but he would certainly be familiar with them. It was held that the claimant's mowers had individual character as there was a clear difference between the design and the prior art, even taking account of the considerable scope for design freedom.

The informed user is also important in relation to infringement where the alleged infringing design is not identical to the protected design. The designs in question were for lanterns for street lights. Despite what he said about technical considerations and manufacturers, Michael Fysh QC went on to hold that the informed user was a regular member of a design team primarily interested with the appearance of street furniture though he would also have a basic grasp of the product's 'technical underlay' and, perhaps, cost. This seems a contradiction of his own generalisation of what an informed user was and is not the same as appears to be used at the OHIM Invalidity Divisions.[127] He had discounted manufacturers but said that the informed user was someone to whom the design had been directed. In the case of street furniture, surely the informed user would be a person whose work involved buying street furniture including lighting or, for example, specifying a design of street light to be supplied and erected under a contract such as an employee of a local authority street lighting department.

Although the informed user is not necessarily 'nerd-like'[128] he may well be, depending on the types of products in question, something of a 'train-spotter', for example, where the products are mobile phones, motor cars, football club shirts or sports footwear such as trainers.

The requirement for individual character is completely new to UK registered design law but it could be said to be broadly equivalent to the old test for novelty in that common trade variants were excluded as not being new. Under the old law a design was not new if it differed from an earlier design only in immaterial details or in features which were variants commonly used in the trade. In *Household Articles Ltd's Registered Design*,[129] Laddie J distinguished between 'differed in immaterial details' and 'common trade variants' saying that the former made no significant visual impact on the design but the latter could be visually significant. In that case, Laddie J accepted that the design for a piston-type coffee pot was novel. Although many other designs had a family resemblance (indeed, in most cases, the glass jar was a standard size as obtained from glass manufacturers), where the designer had a free hand, virtually all those details were different to the prior art.

Although the test for individual character cannot be identical to the old test of common trade variants, it is possible that its effect will be very much the same. Under the old law, in *Valeo Vision SA v Flexible Lamps Ltd*,[130] Aldous J looked at the prior art (rear light clusters for vehicles) and held that, as the position and number of lens fixing screws varied from lamp to lamp, those in the registered designs were simply variants commonly used in the trade. It is likely that, in such a case, the designs would not have created a different overall impression on the informed user over the prior art and, consequently, they would have lacked an individual character, had they been subject to the new law.

A design might fail to be registrable on the basis of lack of individual character even though it is new. This means that individual character applies where the design differs in material details over the prior art, otherwise the question should not arise. But, as we have seen under the old law, differences over what has been made available do not have to be either numerous or significant for a design to be registrable. Perhaps the acid test is whether registration would hamper designers who create designs based on the prior art and make only changes in immaterial details or commonly used features.[131] However, that is not to say that a new combination of pre-existing features cannot be registrable.

126 The claimant did not sell these mowers: they were built solely for its own use. The mowers: they were built solely for its own use. The mowers could only be seen by third parties at a distance.

127 *See*, for example, Case No 000000222, *Mafin SpA's Design* [2005] ECDR 29, discussed earlier in the section on Community design.

128 Per Jacob LJ, describing the person skilled in the art for the purposes of patents in *Technip France SA's Patent* [2004] RPC 46.

129 [1998] FSR 676.

130 [1995] RPC 205.

131 *Household Articles Ltd's Registered Designs* [1998] FSR 676 at 685 per Laddie J.

Refusal of registration

Although the substantive grounds for refusal of registration under s 1A have been swept away, the Registrar still may refuse an application in some cases. They are set out in s 3A and are:

- The application does not comply with rules made under the Act. This is expressed as a discretion by the phrase 'he may refuse to register'.
- If it appears that the applicant is not the person entitled to register the design or designs under s 3(2) (the applicant is the person claiming to be the proprietor) or s 3(3) (where the UK unregistered design right subsists in the design or designs, the applicant is the owner of that right or rights) or s 14 (where applicable, the applicant is the person who applied to register the design or designs in a Convention country in the previous six months[132] or he is his personal representative or assignee) the Registrar must refuse to register the design or designs in question.
- The Registrar shall refuse the application if it appears to him to include:
  - something which does not fulfil the requirements of s 1(2) (the definition of 'design');
  - the design does not fulfil the requirements of s 1C (design dictated by technical function) or 1D (design contrary to public policy or morality); or
  - a ground of refusal under Sch A1 applies (certain emblems, etc.).

Otherwise, the Registrar must not refuse the application to register the design or designs in question.

Designs dictated by technical function

Features of appearance of a product which are solely dictated by the product's technical function are excluded under s 1C(1). That does not prevent registration of a design which *includes* such features; it is just that features dictated by function are not to be considered when judging the requirements for registrability. Note also the inclusion of the word 'solely'. This exclusion is worded similarly to the equivalent exclusion under the old law and but appears to be interpreted more narrowly that under the old law as in *Amp Incorporated* v *Utilux Pty Ltd*,[133] where the House of Lords rejected an argument that the equivalent exclusion applied only when a precise shape and no other was necessary to perform a particular function. The exception under s 1C(1) is equivalent to that under Article 8(1) of the CDR and, in *Landor & Hawa International Ltd* v *Azure Designs Ltd*,[134] the Court of Appeal held that the Article 8(1) exception only applied to exclude a design which was the only design by which a product could perform its function. The same must apply to the exclusion under s 1C(1). The fact that there remains a some degree of design freedom should take the design out of the exception, even if it is only a small or limited degree of freedom. For example, in a design applied to a corkscrew, there is freedom in the design of the helix of the screw itself: for example, in the overall length of the formed screw, the diameter of material used to form the coil, and the pitch and curvature of the coils of the helix. The corkscrew as a whole, if new and having individual character should be registrable. The dictated by function exception will apply in very limited circumstances. It is not easy to think of a design that is dictated solely by function such that that shape and no other can be used to perform that function. It is clear, however, that it is not to be interpreted in the same way as the equivalent exception to the registrability of shapes as trade marks.[135] One reason being that a trade mark has a different nature and serves a different purpose compared with a design subject to design rights.

Landor & Hawa was distinguished by Arnold J in the Patents Court in *Dyson Ltd* v *Vax Ltd*.[136] He accepted counsel's argument that the Court of Appeal's view above (that the

132 Or where there is more than one such prior application in a Convention country, the earliest must be no more than six months previously. Convention countries are set out in the Designs (Convention Countries) Order 2007, SI 2007/277.

133 [1972] RPC 103.

134 [2007] FSR 9. This was a case on the UK unregistered design and the unregistered Community design.

135 *See* Case C-299/99 *Koninklijke Philips Electronics NV* v *Remington Consumer Products Ltd* [2002] ECR I-5475 discussed in Chapter 20, in particular in relation to the exclusion from the registration of shapes necessary to obtain a technical result.

136 [2010] FSR 39.

technical function exclusion only applied when only the design in question and no other could perform the technical function) was, strictly speaking, *obiter*. Arnold J described the approach of the Court of Appeal as being the 'multiplicity of forms' theory. He considered it to be fundamentally flawed as it would mean that, for example, if a particular technical function could be achieved by two or more methods, then none of them could be said to be solely dictated by the function in question. Therefore, each would be protectable, subject to the other requirements being satisfied such as novelty and individual character.[137] This would accord with the view of Advocate General Ruiz-Jarabo in Case C-299/99 *Koninklijke Philips Electronics NV v Remington Consumer Products Ltd*[138] in which he contrasted the technical function exclusion in design law with the exclusion of registration of signs as trade marks where they '. . . consist exclusively of the shape of goods which is necessary to obtain a technical result'. Bearing in mind the different language used, the Advocate General concluded that the level of functionality must be greater for design law and the feature concerned must not only be '. . . necessary but essential in order to achieve a particular technical result: form follows function'. Of course, as the case was a trade mark case, the view of the Advocate General is clearly obiter on this point.

In *Dyson*, Arnold J preferred the view of the Board of Appeal in *Lindner Recyclingtech GmbH v Franssons Verkstäder AB*[139] which rejected both the analysis of the Advocate General in *Koninklijke Philips* and the obiter dictum of the Court of Appeal in *Landor & Hawa*. The Board of Appeal in Lindner rejected the 'multiplicity of forms' theory on the basis that it frustrates the purposes of Article 8(1) of the Community Design Regulation[140] which would result in the exclusion of designs solely dictated by technical function applying only in exceptional cases.

It would seem that *Amp v Utilux* rules again. However, it must be stressed that the authority for this comes only from a Board of Appeal at the OHIM. A serious concern is that there are so few cases on design law at the General Court of the EU and, so far, few at the Court of Justice of the EU, that Member States applying the Community Design Regulation or their own national and supposedly harmonised registered design law are handicapped by a paucity of authority. One might say that Arnold J was being quite bold to prefer a decision at the OHIM to a considered view of the Court of Appeal, albeit *obiter*. In respect of the transparent bin in the Dyson vacuum cleaner, Arnold J held that this was not solely dictated by function as it was chosen for both technical and aesthetic factors. This seems to contradict the Board of Appeal in Lindner which said that the question of whether a design is solely dictated by function is to be answered objectively without considering what went through the designer's mind.

Features of appearance of mechanical interconnections between products are excluded under s 1C(2), which states that a registered design:

> . . . shall not subsist in features of appearance of a product which must necessarily be reproduced in their exact form and dimensions so as to permit the product in which the design is incorporated or to which it has been applied to be mechanically connected to, or placed in, around or against, another product so that either product may perform its function.

This would apply, for example, to a bayonet or screw fitting of a light bulb or a grooved rail for a desk drawer. Another example might be the vertical edges of pieces in the jigsaw. The wording of the exception is similar to that of the 'must-fit' exception for the unregistered design right under s 213(3) of the Copyright, Designs and Patents Act 1988. It is likely that the exceptions will apply in the same cases but there are some differences in terminology. An important distinction is that the unregistered design right applies in the context of 'articles' whereas the registered design applies in connection with 'products'. A 'product' is defined in s 1(3) of the Registered Designs Act 1949 but 'article' is not defined in that part of the Copyright, Designs and Patents Act 1988 dealing with the unregistered design right.[141]

137 As in *Amp v Utilux*, this would mean that the exclusion would be reduced almost to vanishing point.

138 [2002] ECR I-5475.

139 [2010] ECDR 1. The appeal to the General Court of the EU was dismissed as being out of time: Case C-290/10 P *Franssons Verkstäder AB v OHIM*, 9 September 2010.

140 Equivalent to Article 7(1) of the Directive on the legal protection of designs, implemented in the UK by s 1C(1) of the Registered Designs Act 1949.

141 In *Ocular Sciences Ltd v Aspect Vision Care Ltd* [1997] RPC 289, Laddie J accepted that an article for the purposes of the equivalent exception to the subsistence of the unregistered design right could be a human eyeball. Before amendment by the Registered Designs Regulations 2001, the Registered Designs Act 1949 contained a definition of 'article' which no longer has any relevance for the UK registered design and, probably, neither the UK unregistered design right.

Again, the exception only excludes from the determination of registrability and protection those aspects of the overall design caught by the exception.

The Directive was careful not to prevent the registration of modular systems by the working of this exception and s 1C(3) states that s 1C(2) does not prevent the right from subsisting in a design serving the purpose of allowing multiple assembly or connection of mutually interchangeable products within a modular system. Thus, features of interconnections between tiling, paving or shelving systems may still be registrable if the other requirements are satisfied. Parts of a jigsaw are not included as the pieces are not mutually interchangeable.

Contrary to public policy or immoral designs

Section 1D states that the right in a registered design shall not subsist in a design which is contrary to public policy or to accepted principles of morality. It is the whole design

Table 17.1 Grounds for refusal of registration in relation to emblems, etc.

Emblem	Condition for registration to proceed
Royal arms, crown or flags or Royal insignia, etc. or representations of members of the Royal family, or designs suggesting Royal patronage.	If it appears to the Registrar that consent has been given by Her Majesty or, as the case may be, the relevant member of the Royal family.
Union Jack or flags of England, Wales, Scotland, Northern Ireland or the Isle of Man.	Providing it does not appear to the Registrar that the use would be misleading or grossly offensive.
Arms granted by the Crown or insignia so nearly resembling them so as to be likely to be mistaken for them.	If it appears to the Registrar that consent has been given by or on behalf of the person concerned and the use is not in any way contrary to the law of arms.
Representations controlled by the Olympic Symbol etc. (Protection) Act 1995.	Application was made by the person appointed under that Act as proprietor of the Olympics Association right.
Flags of Paris Convention countries.	Either authorisation of the competent authority of the country concerned has been given or it appears to the Registrar that the use of the flag in the manner proposed is permitted without such authorisation.
Armorial bearings or other state emblems of Paris Convention countries protected under that Convention.	If it appears to the Registrar that authorisation of the competent authorities of that country has been given.
Official signs or hallmarks adopted by Paris Convention countries indicating control and warranty where the sign of hallmark is protected under the Paris Convention and where the design could be applied to or incorporated in goods of the same or similar kind as those for which the sign or hallmark indicates control or warranty.	If it appears to the Registrar that authorisation of the competent authorities of that country has been given.
Armorial bearings, flags or other emblems and abbreviations and names of international intergovernmental organisations of which one or more Paris Convention countries are members where such emblems, abbreviations or names are protected under the Paris Convention.	Either the authorisation of the international organisation has been given or it appears to the Registrar that the use proposed is not such as to suggest to the public a connection between the organisation and the design and is not likely to mislead the public as to the existence of a connection between the user and the organisation.

(whether applied to or incorporated in the whole or part of a product) which is excluded. Previously, it was a question of whether the design was contrary to law or morality in the Registrar's opinion. Under the new provisions, in effect, the Registrar will have to take a view on whether a particular design is contrary to public policy or accepted principles of morality, a difficult task, especially considering how vague the notion of public policy is. If the Registrar considers that the exception does not apply, it will be open to any person to ask for a declaration of invalidity on the basis, *inter alia*, that the design should not have been accepted for registration because of s 1D.

Certain emblems, etc.

142 SI 1995/2912. These Rules have been repealed and replaced by the Registered Designs Rules 2006, SI 2006/1975.

Designs will be refused registration if they relate to certain emblems, etc. and one of the grounds of refusal in Sch A1 applies. This Schedule is new although r 24 of the old version of the Registered Designs Rules 1995[142] required consent in the case of designs including representations of any member of the Royal Family or reproductions of armorial bearings, insignia, orders of chivalry, decorations or flags of any country, etc. The new provisions go further than before. The provisions in Sch A1 are set out in Table 17.1 in brief summary form (reference should be made to the Schedule for full details). The grounds apply where the design involves the use of the relevant emblem.

Paris Convention countries are countries other than the UK which are parties to the Paris Convention for the Protection of Industrial Property 1883. There are notice requirements for state emblems of Paris Convention countries and emblems, abbreviations or names of international organisations. The provisions relating to national flags, state emblems, official signs or hallmarks of Paris Convention countries and emblems of international organisations apply also to anything which, from a heraldic point of view, imitates the flags, emblem, sign or hallmark. However, the provisions relating to emblems, etc. of Paris Convention countries do not prevent an application for registration by a national of a country who is authorised to make use of the state emblem, official sign or hallmark of that country even though it may be similar to that of another country.

Registration

Application for registration is made on Form DF2A by the person claiming to be the proprietor of the design or designs (s 3). Where the unregistered design right subsists in the design, the application must be made by the person claiming to be the owner of that right. The application must be accompanied by one or more representations or specimens of the design or designs. The Registrar no longer carries out searches for novelty and individual character. Where the priority of an earlier application in a convention country is claimed, the details of that application must also be given. The Form also contains a space for limitations or disclaimers to be recorded. Where the application is to register more than one design, after completing the front sheet, a second sheet, plus illustration sheets are used for each design. The Registrar will then determine whether the application should be accepted under s 3A, discussed earlier.

The Registrar may allow the applicant to make any modification to the application as the Registrar thinks fit before the application is determined under s 3B. The Registrar has discretion as to the date an application is to be treated as having been made where the design is altered significantly, or in the case of divided applications (where the original application contained more than one design). Where a design is modified so as to overcome a refusal under s 3(4)(b) or (c) (dictated by technical function, contrary to public policy or morality or provisions relating to emblems, etc.) there is no discretion and the application is deemed to have been made on the date the original application was made or treated as having been made providing the identity of the design is retained and any modifications were made in accordance with any rules made under the Act. A modification may, in particular, be effected by making a partial disclaimer. The importance of determining the date an application is treated as having been made is that it determines the date on which novelty and individual character are assessed in the case of invalidity proceedings.

The date of registration of the design is determined under s 3C. The basic rule is that a design is registered as of the date on which the application was made or treated as having been made. However, that does not apply in relation to designs registration of which had previously been applied for in a Convention country under s 14(2) within the preceding six months: that is, where the application is treated as having been made by virtue of the priority provisions. This is complicated further where the application has been modified. The outcome is as follows as regards the deemed date of registration:

- it is the date the application was made in the Convention country (if applied for in more than one Convention country, the earliest) providing not earlier than six months before the application in the UK;
- in the case of a subsequent application (where the original application disclosed more than one design which was divided out and subject to the current application), treated as having been made on a particular date by virtue of the operation of s 3B(3) by reference to s 14(2), the date on which the earlier application was made;
- in the case of a design which was modified so as to overcome grounds of refusal in s 1A(1)(b) or (c) and treated as having been made on a particular date by virtue of the operation of s 3B(5) by reference to s 14(2), the date on which the original application was made.

The effect is to apply the priority provisions to determine the date of registration to the date the application is treated as having been made where it is subject to modification by excluding one of the designs applied where multiple designs are included in an application and that excluded design is applied for subsequently or modified to overcome one of the grounds of refusal other than the first ground relating to the meaning of 'design'.

The Registered Designs Rules 2006 contain the fine detail in respect of applications and modifications.[143] Fees are set out in the Registered Designs (Fees) (No 2) Rules 2006.[144] For the first design, the application fee is £60 (or £40 if consent to publication is not given).[145] For additional designs the fees are £40 (or £20 without consent to publication). The fee for subsequent consent to publication is £40 per design. Renewal fees for subsequent five-year periods are £130, £210, £310 and, for the final five-year period, £450.

By virtue of s 3D, an appeal lies from any decision of the Registrar under s 3A or 3B of the Act (provisions for determination of applications and modification of applications for registration).

143 SI 2006/1975.

144 SI 2006/2617.

145 The applicant may choose to defer publication for a period of 12 months. If not applied for within that time, the application will be deemed to have been abandoned.

Cancellation and invalidity

The registration may be cancelled by the Registrar following a request made by the proprietor in the prescribed manner (there is a form for this) (s 11). The grounds for invalidity are set out in s 11ZA and a registration may be declared invalid:

- if the design does not conform to the definition of 'design' in s 1(2) (s 11ZA(1)(a));
- if the design lacks novelty and individual character under s 1B (s 11ZA(1)(b));

- if the design is dictated by function under s 1C (s 11ZA(1)(b));
- if the design is contrary to public policy or morality under s 1D (s 11ZA(1)(b));
- if the design lacks novelty or individual character compared with a design made available to the public before the date the application is treated as having been made where that 'earlier design' is registered or has been applied for under the Registered Designs Act 1949, the Community Design Regulation or an international registration designating the Community (s 11ZA(1A));[146]
- where the registered proprietor is not the proprietor and the proprietor objects to the registration (s 11ZA(2));
- if registration would involve the use of an earlier distinctive sign, on the ground of an objection by the holder of rights to the sign which includes a right to prohibit such use in the UK (this could apply, for example, where the earlier sign is a registered trade mark) (s 11ZA(3));
- where the design constitutes an unauthorised use of a work protected by copyright in the UK, on the ground of an objection by the copyright owner (s 11ZA(4)).

Generally, references to the registration of a design include references to a former design except one cancelled under s 11.

The identity of who can apply for an application for a declaration of invalidity differs depending on the grounds. This is set out in s 11ZB as follows:

- grounds in s 11ZA(1)(a) or (b) (not a 'design', lacking novelty or individual character, dictated by technical function, contrary to public policy or morality) – *any person interested* may apply;
- grounds relating to specially protected emblems as set out in Sch A1 – *any person concerned* by the use in question may apply (for example, relevant member of the Royal family, competent authority, etc.);
- grounds under s 11ZA(1A) (earlier design) – *the relevant person*, being registered proprietor of the earlier design or the applicant to register the earlier design, including the Community design, as the case may be;
- ground that the registered proprietor is not the proprietor of the design – *the proprietor of the design*;
- ground that the design involves the use of an earlier distinctive sign – *the holder of the right to prohibit the use of the sign in the UK*;
- ground that the design constitutes the unauthorised use of a work protected by copyright law in the UK – *the owner of that copyright*.

An application for invalidity may be made any time after the design has been registered. If the application does not appear to the Registrar to have been made in accordance with any rules made under the Act or to have been made in accordance with s 11ZB above (that is, by the person entitled to bring the application), the Registrar may refuse the application for a declaration of invalidity under s 11ZC. Subject to this, the Registrar shall make a declaration of invalidity if it appears to him that the ground specified has been established in relation to the registration. Where appropriate, the declaration may be one of partial invalidity.

Where the Registrar intends to make a declaration of invalidity under 11ZA(1)(b) or (c), (1A), (3) or (4), he shall inform the registered proprietor of this fact under s 11ZD. The proprietor may apply to modify the design, and such modification may include a partial disclaimer. If allowed, the modification shall be treated always to have had effect from the grant of registration. However, the Registrar shall refuse any modification not made in accordance with rules made under the Act or where the identity of the design is not maintained or where the modified design would be invalid under s 11ZA.

To take an example, say that the registered proprietor of a design sues someone respon-sible for applying the design or a similar design to a product and that person (now being a 'person interested') applies for a declaration of invalidity and the proprietor is successful in modifying the design so as to save it from invalidity. Whether the alleged infringing acts carried out in the past actually did infringe depends on a comparison of the scope of the design as modified with the alleged infringing articles.

Cancellation of a design takes effect from the date of the Registrar's decision or from such other date as the Registrar may direct (s 11ZE(1)). Where the registration of a design is declared invalid to any extent, the registration is treated as having been invalid to that extent from the date of registration or such other date as the Registrar shall direct (s 11ZE(2)). Thus, the Registrar has some discretion except in the case of a successful mod-ification during invalidity proceedings where the design is treated as being in its modified form from the date of registration.

An appeal lies from any decision of the Registrar in respect of applications to cancel a design or for a declaration of invalidity under s 11ZF. Of course, the validity of designs is likely to be challenged in infringement proceedings. Unlike the case with patents, the Registered Designs Act 1949 does not specifically state that validity may be contested by way of a defence.[147]

147 *See* Patents Act 1977 s 74(1).

Duration

The initial registration period is five years from the date of registration of the design under s 8(1). Registration may be renewed for a second, third, fourth and fifth period of five years. Most designs have a limited commercial life and it is unlikely that many will be renewed for a fourth or fifth period (s 8(2)). There is effectively a period of six months' grace, during which time the registration can be renewed without affecting its validity. For designs first registered on or after 1 August 1989, there is a further six-month period dur-ing which the right can be restored.[148] Application must be by the person who was the registered proprietor or by any other person who would have been entitled to the right had it not expired. Where two or more persons held the design jointly, by the leave of the Registrar, the application for restoration can be made by any one or more without joining the others. The Registrar publishes notices of applications for restoration, but it is not an automatic right, the Registrar has a discretion and must be satisfied that the failure to renew under s 8(2) or (4) was unintentional. If restoration is applied for and granted there are some effects as regards infringement of the right. Figure 17.3 applies to a design first registered on or after 1 August 1989.

148 The Registered Designs Act 1949 s 8A refers to a prescribed period during which the right can be restored. By the Registered Designs Rules 2006, SI 2006/1975 r 13, the prescribed period is 12 months from the date on which the right expired.

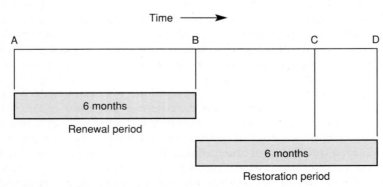

Figure 17.3 **Renewal and restoration of registered design**

Referring to Figure 17.3, during the period A to B the right may be renewed (provided it has not previously been renewed for a fifth period of five years) on payment of the appropriate renewal fee plus an additional fee (£24 per month excluding the first month). Under s 8(4), the design is treated as if it had never expired. For the sake of argument, imagine that an application to restore the right is made at time C. Then, even if the restoration is permitted, a person may acquire rights in respect of the design if, during the period B to C, he began an act in good faith or made effective and serious preparations to do such an act.[149] If the registration is restored, acts which would normally have infringed the design which were done during the period A to B are treated as infringing acts, as are continuations or repetitions of earlier infringing acts. However, an act that would have infringed, which was carried out during the period B to C, gives the proprietor no remedy unless it was a repeat of an earlier infringing act.[150] Fees for renewal are £130 for a second term, £210 for a third term, £310 for a fourth term and £450 for the fifth and final term. Restoration fees amount to £240 plus the renewal fee.[151]

Ownership and dealing with registered designs

The person creating a design is known as the author of that design and the basic rule is that the author is entitled to be the original proprietor of the design.[152] There are exceptions to this basic rule and, if the design is commissioned for money or money's worth, the person commissioning the design is, under the Registered Designs Act 1949 s 2(1A), the original proprietor.[153] Otherwise, under s 2(1B), if the design is created by an employee in the course of employment, the employer is treated as the original proprietor. The person by whom the arrangements necessary for the creation of a computer-generated design are made is taken to be the author of the design, under s 2(4). A computer-generated design (as with original works of copyright) is one which is generated by computer in circumstances such that there is no human author.

There is a difference as regards first ownership between registered designs and copyright in that the commissioners of designs are automatically given the right of ownership of a registrable design. This little inconvenience is exaggerated when the ownership of the design right is considered, because s 3(3) requires that a person making an application to register a design must also be the owner of the design right where it subsists concurrently in the design.[154] Usually, a person commissioning a design will be the proprietor of the registered design and also will be the owner of the design right. In some cases, however, a design right will be owned by the person first marketing articles made to the design in the UK, and this could be a different person claiming to be the proprietor of the design as regards the application to register.

To take an example, consider a design, which is registrable and in which the design right is capable of subsisting, created by a Chinese national resident in China under a commission for money or money's worth from a Saudi Arabian company. Articles made to the design are marketed in the European Community by an Italian company which has the consent of the Saudi Arabian company.[155] The latter would be entitled to register the design in the UK under s 3(2) but for the fact that the Italian company is the owner of the design right. The Italian company would be entitled to apply to register the design under s 3(3), being the owner of the unregistered design right in the UK but this conflicts with s 3(2). It is possible that s 3(3), requiring the applicant to be the owner of the unregistered design right, where it subsists, takes precedence over s 3(2) which requires the application to be by the person claiming to be the proprietor of the design; in which case, the Italian company would be entitled to apply to register the design. Such difficulties should not come about by assignment because, under s 19(3B), an assignment of the UK

149 The right is to do the act or to continue to do the act: Registered Designs Act 1949 s 8B(4). Section 8B(5) allows business partners and acquirers of the person's business to do the acts.

150 Registered Designs Act 1949 s 8B(3).

151 Registered Designs (Fees) (No 2) Regulations 2006, SI 2006/2617. This comprises the restoration fee of £120 and the additional fee for late renewal of £120.

152 Registered Designs Act 1949 s 2. Proprietorship is equivalent to ownership in copyright law.

153 Importers, retailers and licensees of the owner of a design are not entitled to be the proprietor: *Lazarus v Charles* (1873) 16 Eq 117; *Re Guiterman's Registered Design* (1886) 55 LJ Ch 309.

154 The present application form DF2A no longer contains a declaration to the effect that the applicant claims to own any design right subsisting in the design. The previous application form included such a declaration.

155 The Italian company would have to be exclusively licensed to place articles to the design on the market in the UK: Copyright, Designs and Patents Act 1988 ss 215(4) and 220.

unregistered design right automatically includes an assignment of the registered design if their respective owners are one and the same and a contrary intention does not appear. Similarly, an assignment of a registered design automatically carries with it an assignment of the design right, unless the latter is owned by someone other than the proprietor of the registered design.[156] If the design right is later assigned without an assignment of the registered design, the court has the power to order rectification of the register on the application of, *inter alia*, any person aggrieved (s 20(1)).[157]

The Registered Designs Act 1949 s 2(2) envisages the situation where the design is assigned, or is otherwise transmitted to another person. The transferee becomes the proprietor. Section 2(2) does not limit assignments to legal assignments and the effect of the section should be the same in relation to a beneficial assignment.[158] Joint proprietorship is expressly provided for where one of the proprietors is the original proprietor, and both are treated as being 'the proprietor'. Section 19(1) requires that where a person becomes entitled by assignment, transmission or operation of law to a registered design or to a share in a registered design, that person shall apply to the Registrar for registration of his title as proprietor or co-proprietor. Similar provisions apply where a person acquires an interest in a registered design by way of a mortgage, licence or otherwise. Alternatively, the application to register the entitlement or interest may be made by the assignor, mortgagor, licensor or other party to the instrument (s 19(2)).

The Registrar shall make the relevant entry on the register of designs if satisfied as to proof of title. A person claiming to have an interest in a registered design must also show a corresponding interest in the unregistered design right where such right subsists in the design.[159] It is important that the above transactions are noted on the register as, under s 19(5), documents in respect of which no entry has been made shall not be admitted in any court as evidence of the title of any person in respect of the design unless the court otherwise directs. This does not apply, however, in respect of applications to rectify the register. Equities in respect of the design may be enforced in the same way as with any other personal property (s 19(4)).

It is important that the register accurately reflects the true position as to proprietorship. Section 3(2) of the Registered Designs Act 1949 states that an application to register a design shall be made by the person claiming to be the proprietor of the design. If the wrong person applies, it does not matter whether he is acting in good faith or not. The entry will be wrong (as will be the entry of any subsequent dealings). In *Woodhouse UK plc* v *Architectural Lighting Systems*,[160] in the Patents County Court, it was held that an entry of the wrong person as proprietor should not be rectified and the only way forward was to cancel the registration.[161] This aspect of the case concerned the Act as it was before the changes made by the Registered Designs Regulations 2001. This was a result of the transitional provisions in the Regulations which retained the old law on cancellation for designs for which application was made on or after 1 August 1989 and before the new provisions came into force (9 December 2001). Causing a false entry to be made on the register is a criminal offence under s 34; however, knowledge that the entry is false is required for this. Therefore, someone who deliberately applies to register a design knowing that he is not entitled to be the proprietor of the design commits the offence.

A registered design and an application to register a design is, under s 15A, personal property, or in Scotland, incorporeal moveable property. A registered design or application to register a design is transmissible by assignment, testamentary disposition or by operation of law as with any other personal property or moveable property: s 15B(1). An assignment or assent is not effective unless in writing and signed by or on behalf of the assignee.[162] These provisions also apply to an assignment by way of security and a registered design or application may be subject to a charge. Any equities (rights in Scotland) are enforceable in like manner as with other personal property or moveable property.

156 Copyright, Designs and Patents Act 1988 s 224.

157 The Registrar may also cancel the registration under the Registered Designs Act 1949 s 11(2).

158 *Ifejeka* v *Ifejeka* [2010] FSR 29.

159 Registered Designs Act 1949 s 19(3A).

160 [2006] RPC 1.

161 Now, under the Act as amended, an application for invalidity could be made by the true proprietor under s 11ZB on the basis that the registered proprietor is not the true proprietor: s 11ZA(2). Rectification of the register by amending the name of the proprietor to the true proprietor is now clearly countenanced by s 20 though this is still discretionary. However, in *Re Guiterman's Registered Design* (1886) 55 LJ Ch 309 it was held that a deliberate but *bona fide* application by the wrong person could not be rectified.

162 In the case of a corporation in Scotland, this is satisfied by affixing its seal.

Under s 15B(7), the proprietor of a registered design may grant licences. Exclusive licences must be in writing and be signed by or on behalf of the proprietor: s 15C. An exclusive licensee has the same rights against a successor in title to the proprietor who is bound by the licence. An exclusive licensee may bring an infringement action, normally with the proprietor joined in the action.

Anti-competitive practices

Anti-competitive practices are dealt with under s 11A and s 11AB, powers exercisable in protection of the public interest and following mergers and markets investigations. Under s 11A, where a report of the Competition Commission has been laid before Parliament which concludes on a competition reference that a person was engaged in an anti-competitive practice which was operated or may be expected to operate against the public interest, or a reference under s 11 of the Competition Act 1980 concludes that a person is pursuing a course of conduct which operates against the public interest, the appropriate Minister may apply to the Registrar to take action.[163] The Registrar may cancel or modify any condition in a licence in respect of a registered design where that condition restricts the use of the design by the licensee or the right of the proprietor to grant further licences.

Section 11AB applies in respect of the power to take remedial action following merger and market investigations under certain provisions of the Enterprise Act 2002. The Competition Commission or the Secretary of State, as the case may be, may request that the Registrar takes action cancelling or modifying conditions in licences in respect of registered designs which restrict the use of the design by the licensee or the right of the proprietor to grant further licences.

Rights of proprietor

The registered proprietor of a design has the exclusive right to use the design and any design which does not produce on the informed user a different overall impression (s 7(1)). As the definition of individual character is in terms of producing a different overall impression on the informed user, there is little danger that the rights in two different registered designs will overlap. As with individual character, the degree of freedom of the author in creating the design is taken into consideration in determining whether a design produces a different overall impression on the informed user.[164] Under s 7(2), 'use' includes a reference to:

(a) the making, offering, putting on the market, importing, exporting or using of a product in which the design is incorporated or to which it is applied, or
(b) stocking such a product for those purposes.

This is the same as for the Community design and, similarly, the meaning of 'use' is not exhaustive.[165] The scope of the rights of the proprietor appears wider than under the old UK law on registered designs and expressly includes exporting and stocking a product, neither of which were mentioned under the Act before amendment.

The rights of the registered proprietor are subject to any limitation attaching to the registration, including any partial disclaimer or declaration of partial invalidity (s 7(4)). Where there are two or more joint proprietors, each is treated as the proprietor. Consequently, each has the full rights of proprietor. The person or persons registered as proprietor can, subject to the rights vested in others of which notice is entered on the register, assign, grant licences or otherwise deal with the design and give effectual receipts for any consideration for any such assignment, licence or dealing.[166]

163 There are provisions for publications of notices and a period of time for making representations.

164 Registered Designs Act 1949 s 7(3).

165 Although the CD Regulation and the Directive say that use '. . . shall cover, in particular . . .' whereas the Act states that use '. . . includes a reference to . . .' The different wording is unlikely to be of any consequence and, in case of any doubt, it is the wording of the Directive that should be referred to.

166 Registered Designs Act 1949 s 19(4). This is also subject to any equities in respect of the design.

Infringement and exceptions

Infringement of a registered design is actionable by the registered proprietor and there are also provisions for an exclusive licensee to bring an infringement action: s 24F. Where there is an exclusive licence, the rights of the proprietor and licensee are concurrent and, where applicable, the leave of the court is required if one brings an action without joining the other, as is normal in such cases.

Under s 7A(1), the right in a design is infringed by a person who, without the consent of the registered proprietor, does anything which falls within the exclusive rights of the registered proprietor under s 7. If a design has a number of features and not all are used in the alleged infringing product, the question is whether the latter produces a different overall impression of the informed user. The concept of 'informed user' was considered by Michael Fysh QC in the Patents County Court in *Woodhouse UK plc v Architectural Lighting Systems*,[167] where he distinguished this newcomer to English law from the average consumer, and would be someone who was familiar with the type of product in which the design was incorporated or to which it had been applied. He would be a regular user, someone who was a consumer or buyer or otherwise familiar with the type of product. Appearance was more important than function or technical considerations. In that case, which involved designs for lanterns for streetlights, Michael Fysh QC held that the informed user was a regular member of a design team primarily interested with the appearance of street furniture. He also went on to say that where a design was strikingly different to what had gone before, the scope of protection would be broader than a design surrounded by 'kindred prior art'.[168]

Arnold J in *Dyson Ltd v Vax Ltd*[169] also thought the registered design was strikingly different to the design corpus at the time of registration. However, he went on to find that there had been no infringement by the defendant's vacuum cleaner as it created a different overall impression, despite some similarities. The registered design was described as 'smooth, curvy and elegant' whilst the defendant's design was 'rugged, angular and industrial, even somewhat brutal'. Dyson's appeal to the Court of Appeal was unsuccessful. In *Dyson Ltd v Vax Ltd*,[170] Sir Robin Jacob said that he could find nothing wrong with the reasoning of Arnold J.

A number of acts are stated in s 7A(2)–(5) as not infringing a registered design. These are new to UK registered designs law, apart from s 7A(5) which is very loosely equivalent to the 'must-match' exception under the old law.

Under s 7A(2), the right in a registered design is not infringed by:

(a) an act done for private and non-commercial purposes;
(b) an act done for experimental purposes;
(c) an act of reproduction for teaching purposes or for the purpose of making citations provided the act of reproduction is compatible with fair trade practice and does not unduly prejudice the normal exploitation of the design and mention is made of the source;
(d) the use of equipment on ships or aircraft which are registered in another country but which are temporarily in the UK;
(e) the importation into the UK of spare parts or accessories for the purpose of repairing such ships or aircraft; or
(f) the carrying out of repairs on such ships or aircraft.[171]

These exceptions to infringement are almost identical to those in the CD Regulation and are similar in some respects to a number of exceptions that apply in relation to infringement of a patent. However, there is no equivalent in patent law to the teaching and citation

167 [2006] RPC 1.

168 Although the judge ordered cancellation of the design registration, he went on to consider infringement in case he was wrong on the issue of validity.

169 [2010] FSR 39.

170 [2011] EWCA Civ 1206.

171 Again, there are some very minor, inconsequential, changes to wording compared with the text of the Directive.

exception, though these exceptions do have some similarities to exceptions under copyright law and in respect of the database right.

The right in a registered design subsisting in a component part which may be used for the purpose of repair of a complex product so as to restore its original appearance is not infringed by the use for that purpose of any design protected by the registration (s 7A(5)). [172] This exception, which can be described as a 'must-match' exception, replaced the equivalent one under the old law but is different in some respects. Under the old law, registration was refused for features of shape, configuration, pattern or ornament which were dependent upon the appearance of another article of which the article was intended by the author to form an integral part. [173] The new law does not prevent the scope of registration extending to such features (bearing in mind changes in terminology) but simply states that the protection afforded by registration is not so extensive that it prevents the use of the design to use it to repair a complex product so as to restore its original appearance. The language in s 7A(5) is in terms of *any* design protected by the registration, showing that only those aspects of the design, as registered, which must be reproduced so as to restore the original appearance of the complex part can be used without infringement. If some of the other features of the design occur in an alleged infringing product, it will be a matter of comparing it with the registered design to determine whether it produces a different overall impression on the informed user, disregarding those aspects of the design which must be reproduced so as to restore the original appearance of the complex product of which the product in question is a component part.

This particular exception frees up the aftermarket in replacement parts for complex products, in particular, body panels for vehicles to replace worn or damaged parts. Harmonisation was not possible at the time the Directive was adopted as there was no consensus on this issue between Member States. In some Member States, such parts enjoy full protection under national design laws (though not under the Community design). The European Commission has proposed an amendment to the Directive to deny protection to such replacement parts in line with the Community design and the position already prevailing under some national registered designs systems including the UK.

The doctrine of exhaustion of rights is now very familiar in respect of patents, trade marks and even copyright. It has been difficult to apply in respect of registered designs in the past through lack of harmonisation but now that there is limited harmonisation of registered design law throughout the EEA, exhaustion of rights is provided for by s 7A(4). This states that the right in a registered design is not infringed by an act which relates to a product, in which any design protected by registration is incorporated or to which it is applied, that has been put on the market in the EEA by the registered proprietor or with his consent. Thus, subsequent dealings with such a product cannot infringe the right. However, there is no proviso with this form of exhaustion as there is with trade marks where, notwithstanding the doctrine, the proprietor of a registered trade mark may still object to subsequent marketing on the basis that there are legitimate reasons to oppose further commercialisation: for example, where the condition of the goods to which the mark has been applied has been changed or impaired. [174] Of course, one can see the sense of this in respect of trade marks which operate as a badge of origin or quality, particularly where the trade mark is applied to goods where safety is involved. But there are dangers for proprietors of registered designs if the product is modified subsequently in a manner which reflects badly on the proprietor. Furthermore, there are no provisions to deal with the situation where a component part is reproduced for the purposes of repair of a complex product where the purpose is not to restore the original appearance but to restore functionality apart from the exceptions based on technical function and interconnections. [175]

172 At the present time, not all Member States have this exception. Article 14 of the Directive allowed Member States to continue their previous policy on protecting such spare parts providing any changes made would be only to liberalise the market. Prior to the changes implementing the Directive, the UK already had a 'must-match' exception, though differently expressed.

173 Old s 1(1)(b)(ii). In *Ford Motor Co Ltd & Iveco Fiat SpA's Design Applications* [1993] RPC 399, it was held that this extended to main body panels, doors, bonnet and boot lids and windscreens but not to designs that could be different such as wing mirrors, wheels, seats and steering wheels. However, the House of Lords dealt with the case on the basis of the definition of 'article' instead: *Ford Motor Co Ltd's Design Applications* [1995] RPC 167.

174 Article 7(2) of First Council Directive 89/104/EEC of 21 December 1988 to approximate the laws of the Member States relating to trade marks, OJ L 40, 11.02.1989, p 1.

175 These exceptions are defined in terms of a product rather than a complex product in Article 7(1) and (2) of the Directive. However, Article 7(3), in effect, waives these exceptions in relation to complex products which fit together in modular systems.

Defences

A defendant is likely to attack the validity of the registered design on one or more of the grounds for invalidity set out in s 11ZA[176] (bearing in mind the unregistered design right may also subsist in the design and different provisions apply here in respect of subsistence and infringement). Other defences may focus on the alleged infringement producing a different overall impression on the informed user or that the features of the alleged infringing product fall within any limitation on the rights of the proprietor.

Further defences may be based on the acts which are stated as not infringing under s 7A(2)–(5), discussed above. Another possibility is that the defendant began or made serious and effective preparations to do the acts complained of during the restoration period in the case of a registration which had undergone restoration following a failure to renew within the allotted time. For the UK registered design, there is no equivalent defence in the period up to the filing date or earlier priority date of the design, unlike the case with the RCD.

176 And the RCD and UCD where these also apply to the design.

Remedies

Previously, the Registered Designs Act 1949 did not specifically state what remedies are available. Now, as a result of the Intellectual Property (Enforcement, etc.) Regulations 2006, the remedies are spelt out in s 24A(2) as being damages, injunctions, accounts or otherwise as is available in respect of an infringement of any other property right. Section 24B excuses an 'innocent' infringer from an award or damages or an account of profits.[177] This is where the defendant can show that, at the time of infringement, he was not aware and had not reasonable grounds for supposing that the design was registered. It makes good sense, therefore, for a notice to be placed upon products incorporating the design or to which the design has been applied. However, to be effective, such a notice would have to include the registration number in addition to the word 'registered' or some abbreviation. Merely affixing the words 'Registered Design' would, under s 24B(2), appear to be insufficient, but how in such a case a defendant could argue that he had no reasonable grounds for supposing that the design incorporated in or applied to the product was not a registered design is hard to imagine. However, marking a product with the word 'registered' is not conclusive that the defendant did not know and had no reasonable grounds for supposing the design was registered. It simply means that that fact alone is not sufficient to impute knowledge or reasonable grounds to suppose. Although an innocent infringer may escape an award of damages or an account, this does not prevent an injunction being granted to prevent further infringement.

Orders are now expressly available for delivery up of infringing articles and destruction of infringing articles: ss 24C and 24D. Previously, the court granted such order in any case.[178] An article is an 'infringing article' if its making to the design was an infringement of the registered design under s 24G. Also covered are articles which have been or are proposed to be imported into the UK if their making in the UK would have been an infringement of the registered design or would have been a breach of an exclusive licence. There is a presumption that where it is shown that an article was made to a design which is or has been registered, it was made at a time when the right in the registered design subsisted.

177 There is no equivalent provision under the Community Design Regulation and no possible policy reason for giving an innocent infringement defence under the national right but not under the Community right: *J Choo (Jersey) Ltd* v *Towerstone Ltd* [2008] FSR 19.

178 See, for example, *Cow (PB) & Co Ltd* v *Cannon Rubber Manufacturers Ltd* [1959] RPC 240.

Groundless threats of infringement proceedings

We have seen earlier in the chapter that there is a remedy of groundless threats of infringement proceedings in relation to the Community design, registered and unregistered. There is an equivalent provision (of older pedigree) in the Registered Designs Act 1949 with respect to groundless threats, whether by circulars, advertisement or otherwise.[179] The threats do not need to come from the proprietor of the design as the threats may be made by 'any person'. The remedies for groundless threats of infringement proceedings are:

(a) a declaration to the effect that the threats are unjustifiable;
(b) an injunction against the continuation of the threats;
(c) damages, if any have been sustained – for example, the aggrieved party's business may have been detrimentally affected by the threats, or his sales of the articles concerned may have been adversely affected.

It would seem that this provision extends to the situation where a person publicises his views that another design infringes his registration and that he will take legal action for that infringement. The burden of proof remains with the person making the threats, that is that the acts (or contemplated acts) complained of infringe the right in the registered design, although the claimant has the burden of proving the registration invalid if the acts do fall within the protection afforded by registration. The action is not available if the threats relate to making or importing anything, though the proprietor should take care to ensure that the threats cannot be constructed more widely than that. Furthermore, mere notification of the fact of registration of the design is not an actionable threat.

In *Reckitt Bensiker UK* v *Home Parfum Ltd*,[180] Laddie J noted that the groundless threats action was in conflict with the emphasis on encouraging parties to settle disputes in the Civil Procedure Rules. In that case, the claimant sued the defendant for infringing its design of air fresheners.[181] The defendant applied to join the claimant's solicitors as Part 20[182] defendants to its counterclaim based on groundless threats made by the solicitors on behalf of the claimant. The application was struck out as Laddie J considered that it was made for an illegitimate purpose, being to retaliate and make the relationship between the claimant and its solicitors as uncomfortable as possible.

Offences

There are three offences directly associated with registered designs; and if such an offence is committed by a body corporate with the consent or connivance of an officer of the body, such as a director, manager or secretary, that person in addition to the corporate body is guilty of the offence.[183] This also applies to persons purporting to act in such a capacity.

Under s 35, it is an offence for a person falsely to represent that a design applied to, or incorporated in, any product sold by him is registered.

'Represented' has a restricted meaning in that the offender must have affixed the word 'registered', or any other word(s) to the effect that the design is registered, to the product, for example by stamping, engraving or impressing such word(s). Word of mouth is not sufficient. The liability appears to be strict, albeit in a very narrow sense. For example, it is committed by a person selling the product who has impressed the word 'registered' believing that the design is subject to a valid registration and that he has the right so to mark the product.[184] This offence is triable summarily only and carries a fine not exceeding level 3 on the standard scale. It is also an offence to mark products in a like fashion after expiry of the right in a registered design (maximum fine not exceeding level 1 on the

179 Registered Designs Act 1949 s 26. It is arguable whether threats made by telephone or electronic mail direct to an alleged infringer would fall within the meaning of 'otherwise'.

180 [2004] FSR 37.

181 On the basis of the claimant's trade marks, registered designs and unregistered design right in addition to claims for passing off and breach of confidence.

182 A Part 20 claim is one made other than by the claimant against the defendant and includes a counterclaim by a defendant against the claimant and some other person: CPR 20.2. Under CPR 20.5(1) application must be made for a court order where a counterclaim is made against a party other than the claimant for that person to be made a defendant to the counterclaim.

183 Registered Designs Act 1949 s 35A(1).

184 Registered Designs Act 1949 s 35(2). Liability is strict in a narrow sense because it will not apply, for example, where the person is a dealer who sells such products which were already marked when he obtained them. The person has to do the marking himself. However, other offences might be committed, such as under the Fraud Act 2006.

standard scale). This offence could easily be committed by the proprietor of a recently expired design. However, selling products to which a design relates after expiry of the design registration is not an offence provided the products were marked before the expiry of the right.

Under s 35(3), inserted by the Community Design Regulations 2005,[185] the use of the word 'registered' or any other word or symbol importing a reference (express or implied) to registration shall be deemed to be a reference to registration under the Registered Designs Act 1949 unless it is shown that the reference is in relation to registration elsewhere and the design is in fact so registered.

Section 34 deals with the falsification of the register of designs. It is an offence, triable either way, to make or cause to be made either a false entry on the register or a counterfeit copy of a register entry. The falsification offence extends to producing, tendering or causing to be produced or tendered in evidence a counterfeit copy of an entry in the register. *Mens rea* is required for this offence, that is, the person involved must know that the entry or written copy is false. Constructive knowledge is not sufficient. If tried on indictment, the maximum punishment is a term of imprisonment not exceeding two years, or a fine or both. On summary conviction a person may be sentenced to imprisonment for a term not exceeding six months, or a fine not exceeding the statutory maximum or both. The offence is worded 'makes or causes to be made', so it could apply to the Registrar and his staff in addition to others.

The Registered Designs Act 1949 s 5 concerns requirements for secrecy in respect of designs of specified classes which are relevant for defence purposes and allows the Registrar, subject to notification by the Secretary of State, to issue instructions prohibiting or restricting the publication or communication of information pertaining to such a design. Written permission may also be required by a person resident in the UK before an application can be made outside the UK for the registration of a design of a prescribed class. Any person who fails to comply with such instructions, or who makes or causes to be made such an application, commits an offence under s 33. The offence is triable either way and carries the same maximum penalties as an offence under s 34.

Crown use and secrecy provisions

In common with patents and the design right, the Crown can make use of the subject matter of the right. As regards registered designs, the Registered Designs Act 1949 Sch 1 contains the necessary provisions.[186] Under para 1(1), any government department may use, or authorise the use of, any registered design for the services of the Crown. Terms must be agreed, either before or after use, between the government department concerned and the registered proprietor with the approval of the Treasury. If agreement cannot be reached, the terms are to be determined by reference to the High Court. 'The services of the Crown' are defined in para 1(6) and include:

(a) the supply to the government of a country outside the UK of products required for the defence of that country or of any other country, subject to an agreement or arrangement involving Her Majesty's Government

(b) the supply to the UN or any country belonging to the UN of products required for any armed forces operating in pursuance of a UN resolution, subject to an agreement or arrangement involving Her Majesty's Government.

This is not an exhaustive definition; it merely indicates that the above situations fall within the meaning of 'Crown use'. It would also extend to use for the armed forces of the UK. Given the nature of registered designs, it is unlikely that these provisions will be

185 SI 2005/2339. Regulation 3 of these Regulations also provided for equivalent offences in relation to the Community design though there is no presumption as to the use of the word 'registered' in this case.

186 Minor consequential amendments were made to Sch 1 by the Registered Designs Regulations 2001.

used to any great extent. An example could be where the design relates to an item of clothing or kit which could be used by soldiers. Alternatively, it could be that a patented product wanted for Crown use is also protected by a registered design. The only time payment will not be made is when the design has been recorded or applied by or on behalf of a government department prior to the date of registration.¹⁸⁷ This does not apply in respect of direct or indirect communications by the registered proprietor or any person through whom he derives title. The effect of this very limited provision is to allow free Crown use of a design independently and concurrently developed by a government department.

187 Registered Designs Act 1949 Sch 1 para 1(2).

Crown use is also available in respect of the Community design as discussed earlier in the chapter. However, in this case, the use is limited to services of the Crown which are necessary for essential defence or security needs, in accordance with the Directive provisions allowing government use.

Under s 5 of the Registered Designs Act 1949, the Secretary of State may give notice to the Registrar that a class of designs is relevant for defence purposes. If, in a particular case, it appears to the Registrar that the design is indeed within that class, he may give directions prohibiting or restricting the publication of information concerning the design or the communication of such information to any person or class of persons specified in the directions. Where these provisions apply, the representation of the design (or specimen, if appropriate) will not be open to public inspection while the directions remain in force. These provisions are subject to review by the Secretary of State and the directions may be revoked.

Where a design falls within a prescribed class under s 5(4), application may not be made outside the UK by any person resident there unless an application has already been made in the UK at least six weeks before and either no directions under s 5(1) have been issued or, if they have, they have been revoked. This does not apply to a non-UK resident who first filed outside the UK. There are criminal penalties for breach of the secrecy provisions.

Summary

The criteria for protection in relation to the Community design and the UK registered design are equivalent and a design must:

- fall within the definition of 'design';
- be used in relation to a 'product', which includes a 'complex product' – graphic symbols and typefaces are included in the definition of product, making it possible to protect software-generated designs; however, computer programs are excluded from the definition of 'product'.

The main criteria for protection are that, at the relevant time, the design is new and has individual character. As regards novelty, there is a one-year 'period of grace'. A design is not new if it has been made available to the public. However, this is not as stringent as the test of novelty for patents. Certain types of events which would otherwise be novelty-destroying are ignored where they could not reasonably have become known in the normal course of business to circles specialising in the sector concerned, operating within the Community.

Individual character is judged from the perspective of the informed user and the overall impression it has on such a user compared with designs which have been made available to the public. The degree of design freedom is taken into account.

There are a number of specific exclusions as to what may be protected:

- designs dictated solely by their technical function (the scope of this exclusion is not settled);

- designs of interconnections are not protected (except designs which allow the multiple assembly or connection of mutually interchangeable products within a modular system);
- designs of products which are parts of complex products not visible during normal use ('under-the-bonnet' parts);
- designs of component parts of complex products used in repair to restore the original appearance (such as a body panel for a vehicle);
- designs contrary to public policy or accepted principles of morality.

Despite the exclusions, other aspects of a design applied to or incorporated into an article may be protected if the requirements are satisfied. For example, only one part of a design may be dictated by technical function, in which case, other elements of the design may be protected.

Initial registration gives protection for five years. This may be renewed in five-year periods up to a maximum of 25 years. The unregistered Community design only lasts for three years from the date it was first made available to the public.

The scope of protection for a design includes designs which do not produce on the informed user a different overall impression, taking into account the degree of freedom the designer had when developing his design. A design which is strikingly different from the design corpus at the time of registration (or making available to the public in the case of the unregistered Community design) is likely to have greater protection.

Discussion questions

1 What do the following expressions mean in relation to the Community design (registered and unregistered) and the UK registered design: 'novelty', 'individual character' and 'solely dictated by its technical function'?

2 Discuss the extent to which spare parts are protected by the Community design and the UK registered design.

3 The lack of authoritative EU case law on the Community Design Regulation and the Directive on the legal protection of designs is contributing to uncertainty and conflicting decisions at national level. Discuss.

Selected further reading

Anon, 'OHIM wring comparison in assessing Community design' [2010] *EU Focus*, 18 (looks at the Beifa highlight marker pen case).

Farkas, T., 'Does the United Kingdom need a general law against unfair competition? A fashion industry insight: Part I' [2011] *European Intellectual Property Review*, 227 (discusses the problem of imitation of successful fashion designs and the extent to which IPR protect rightholders and contains useful material on the Community design and the UK unregistered design right).

Hartwig, H., 'Grupo Promer v OHIM and PepsiCo (T-9/07): the General Court's first decision on a Community design's validity – all's well that ends well?' [2010] *European Intellectual Property Review*, 419 (discusses the Pepsico tazo case).

Visit **www.mylawchamber.co.uk/bainbridgeip** to access study support resources including interactive multiple choice questions, practice exam questions with guidance, weblinks, legal updates and a legal newsfeed.

The UK unregistered design right 18

Introduction

The UK unregistered design right (generally referred to in this chapter as the 'design right') is quite unlike the Community design (registered and unregistered) and the UK registered design. It was brought into being primarily as a means of providing relatively short-term protection to designs applied to functional articles and to address the imbalance between the protection of functional designs and aesthetic designs, as discussed below.

The design right has more in common with copyright law than it does with the UK registered design. It subsists in original designs[1] and is an informal right which requires proof of copying for infringement. There are other similarities such as substantial copying, direct or indirect, infringes and the provisions for assignment and licensing and remedies are very similar. There are differences, however, and there is a remedy for groundless threats of infringement proceedings for the design right and licences of right are available during the last five years of the right. It is, of course, of much shorter duration than copyright.

Design right subsists in any aspect of the shape or configuration (internal or external) of the whole or part of an article. There are exceptions for methods or principles of construction and features of interconnections or dependent upon the appearance of another article. Surface decoration is also expressly excluded. These requirements should be compared with the provisions for subsistence of the Community design and the UK registered design.

Although the design right can be seen as a means of protecting designs applied to functional articles, it may also apply to aesthetic designs and there is no reason why it cannot also apply to designs protected by the Community design and the UK registered design. Although the requirements are different, a good many designs will comply with the requirements for all rights. For example, a new shape of coffee pot may be registrable as a Community design and a UK registered design in addition to the unregistered Community design and the design right subsisting in the shape.

In spite of the introduction of the Community design and the harmonisation of national registered designs, the UK's design right has proved to be a very useful right in a number of cases. Claims for infringement of design right sometimes are made in conjunction with claims for patent infringement and Community design or UK registered design infringement.

Before looking further at the design right, some background and history will help in understanding its development and rationale.

1 However, originality is not quite the same as for copyright as it requires that the design was not commonplace in the design field in question at the time of its creation.

Background

The conception of the UK's unregistered design right must be seen in the context of the history of design law prior to the enactment of the right.[2] Until the Design Copyright Act 1968, there was a gap in protection for designs which were primarily functional in nature. Copyright protected artistic works, patents were available for new inventions, and designs having eye-appeal could be protected by registration. However, a design having no eye-appeal, for example an overflow pipe for a washing machine, had no form of protection *per se*.[3] The effect of the Design Copyright Act 1968 was to extend copyright protection to designs applied industrially for a period of 15 years from the end of the calendar year during which the relevant articles were first marketed. Eventually, by way of unanticipated judicial creativity, copyright was recognised as providing protection for functional designs through the medium of drawings for 50 years after the author's death.[4] Thus, unregistrable designs were given much longer protection than the 15 years maximum then available for registered designs.[5] Later, attempts were made to redress this inequality, as in *British Leyland Motor Corp Ltd* v *Armstrong Patents Co Ltd*.[6] It was seen to be important that persons buying complex products that would need repairing during their life should be able to have access to a free market in spare parts, and that if a right in functional designs were to be established, some balance would have to be taken into account. Several options faced Parliament:

1 It could introduce a petty patent (utility model) system similar to that existing in some countries.
2 It could extend registered design law to include functional designs.
3 It could maintain the status quo, leaving protection to be gained via the medium of drawings.

The White Paper that preceded the Copyright, Designs and Patents Act 1988[7] rejected all other solutions and suggested a new right that would apply, automatically, to original designs for three-dimensional articles broadly along copyright principles. However, this was not to be an unfettered quasi-copyright. The design right is an emasculated form of artistic copyright as it applied to industrial designs.[8] A contrast can be made at once with registered designs, for which protection is along lines analogous to patent law, giving a monopoly right whereas infringement of the design right requires proof of copying.

The Patent Office (now using its operating name of the Intellectual Property Office) described the design right as:

> a new intellectual property right which applies to original, non-commonplace designs of the shape or configuration of articles . . . [It] is not a monopoly right but a right to prevent copying.[9]

Like copyright, the design right is a property right subject to qualification requirements. No formalities are required. However, the duration of the right is much less, being effectively no more than ten years. The right really applies only to designs for three-dimensional articles as surface decoration is excluded and is based on features of shape or configuration. There are some exceptions which allow the making of spare parts by others. There is an overlap between this right and the right in a registered design, whether the national registered design or the Community design and some designs that are subject to the design right may be registered and also protected by the unregistered Community design (UCD). However, there are different requirements for the UK unregistered design right compared with the other rights and this overlap is not, therefore, complete and a great many designs will be protected by the Community design or the UK registered design and not the UK unregistered design right and vice versa. One thing to stress at this

2 For a comprehensive and lively description of the background to the design right, *see* Walton, A. 'The Copyright, Designs and Patents Act 1988 (1)' (1989) 133, *Solicitors Journal*, 646.

3 Other rights could subsist such as trade marks and goodwill depending on the nature of the article.

4 Graham J in *Sifam Electrical Instrument Co Ltd* v *Sangamo Weston Ltd* [1973] RPC 899 applying *Dorling* v *Honnor Marine Ltd* [1965] Ch 1. In those days, the term of protection for the original works of copyright was generally the life of the author plus 50 years.

5 The Copyright Act 1956 s 10 effectively removed dual protection for registrable designs. The Design Copyright Act 1968 reinstated artistic copyright protection but limited it to 15 years for registrable designs.

6 [1986] 2 WLR 400.

7 Intellectual Property and Innovation, Cm 9712, HMSO, 1986.

8 Turner, B. 'A true design right: *C & H Engineering* v *Klucznik & Sons*' [1992] FSR 421.

9 The Patent Office (1992) *Designs: Basic Facts*, The Patent Office, p 6.

stage is, despite any potential overlap between different rights in designs, that the UK unregistered design right is quite different in many respects to the UK registered design and the Community design, whether registered or unregistered.

Examples of articles in which a design right is capable of subsisting include parts for motor vehicles (including under the bonnet parts), component parts of vacuum cleaners, tools, kitchen utensils, office equipment and furniture, packaging, mobile phones and folding umbrellas: in fact all manner of articles. Design right is limited so that it will not usually extend to features that must be the shape they are so that the article the design is applied to can fit or match another article. But the presence of such 'must-fit' or 'must-match' features is not fatal to the subsistence of the right as it can apply to the whole or part of an article. Compared to registered designs, the design right is weaker as it is not a monopoly right and it is of shorter maximum duration. Furthermore, in the last five years of the right, licences are available as of right.[10] However, the advantages of the design right are that it is informal, has impressive scope and has been litigated successfully on numerous occasions.

The design right came into existence on 1 August 1989 and is contained in the Copyright, Designs and Patents Act 1988 Part III. The provisions are not retrospective and designs that were expressed in a tangible form[11] prior to this date are not protected by the design right. Such designs may have been protected through their preparatory drawings as s 51 of the 1988 Act does not apply for ten years to such designs, that is until 1 August 1999.[12] The design right provisions apply to England and Wales, Scotland and Northern Ireland. This may be extended to the Channel Islands, the Isle of Man or to any colony by Her Majesty's Order in Council.[13]

As a result of compliance with an EU Directive, the UK afforded specific protection to the topographies of semiconductor products.[14] Eventually, this was done by means of the design right and the design right provisions of the Copyright, Designs and Patents Act 1988 were adapted to provide the required degree of protection. This special form of the design right is dealt with towards the end of this chapter.

The Directive on the protection of semiconductor topographies can be seen as providing the model for the design right. Thus, the design right has different origins to the registered design and, even though some of the terminology used for both rights is the same or similar, caution must be exercised; meanings applicable to one right are not necessarily directly transferable to the other right.[15] However, changes to the Registered Designs Act 1949 have removed much of the overlap in terminology between the two rights.

Subsistence of right

Section 213 of the Copyright, Designs and Patents Act 1988 sets out the basic requirements for subsistence of the unregistered design right. It is a provision not without its difficulties. As Jacob LJ said of the section in *Dyson Ltd v Qualtex (UK) Ltd*[16] (at para 14): 'It has the merit of being short. It has no other.'

Under s 213(1), the design right is a property right which subsists in . . . an original design. Furthermore, there is a requirement for qualification which must be satisfied and the design must be fixed in some tangible form by recording it in a design document or by making an article to the design. Computer-generated designs are defined in s 263(1) as designs generated by computer in circumstances such that there is no human designer. What has been said about computer-generated original works of copyright applies equally here and one can question whether there can ever be such a thing as a computer-generated design.[17]

10 This does not apply in relation to semiconductor topographies protected by a modified form of the design right.

11 Being recorded in a design document or by having an article made to the design.

12 Copyright, Designs and Patents Act 1988 Sch 1 para 19. For an example, *see Valeo Vision SA v Flexible Lamps Ltd* [1995] RPC 205. Unless otherwise stated, in this chapter statutory references are to the Copyright, Designs and Patents Act 1988.

13 Copyright, Designs and Patents Act 1988 s 255. No such Order has been made, however. Instead, the Channel Islands and the Isle of Man and a number of other countries, including New Zealand, enjoy reciprocal protection under the Design Right (Reciprocal Protection) (No 2) Order 1989, SI 1989/1294, made under s 256 of the Act.

14 Council Directive 87/54/EEC of 16 December 1986 on the legal protection of topographies of semiconductor products, OJ L 24, 27.01.1987, p 36.

15 See *Ocular Sciences Ltd v Aspect Vision Care Ltd* [1997] RPC 289 at 421 per Laddie J.

16 [2006] RPC 31.

17 *See* Chapter 8, p 305.

'Design' means the 'design of any aspect of the shape or configuration (whether external or internal) of the whole or part of an article'.[18] An aspect of shape or configuration must be such that it is readily discernible or recognisable.[19] As it can apply to a part of an article, apart from the right applying to the whole of an article, it can apply to individual aspects of its design. Subject to the requirements of originality (and not being commonplace) and the exceptions, design right is very wide and a host of design rights can subsist in respect of a single article. This is so whether it is a single article having its own separate existence or whether it is an article which is a part of a complex article comprising a number of sub-articles. Jacob LJ in *Dyson Ltd v Qualtex (UK) Ltd*[20] rejected a test of 'visual significance'. He said (at para 23) that '. . . one cannot simply forget an aspect of the design of a whole article on the grounds that it is a visually insignificant feature of the design of the whole article'.

'Configuration' is not just another way of saying shape and the word cannot have exactly the same meaning though what the difference is has long puzzled both judges and writers.[21] It is reasonable to assume that configuration means the relative arrangement of parts of an article. In *Mackie Designs Inc v Behringer Specialised Studio Equipment (UK) Ltd*,[22] Pumfrey J accepted that an electronic circuit diagram was a design document (being either a drawing or a written description) for the purposes of the design right within s 263(1). The design itself was the components and their interconnections and Pumfrey J rejected the submission that there must be only a single design recorded in a design document. Even though many circuit boards could be made from the diagram in such a way that the arrangement of the physical parts differed, the merit of the design was the selection of the components and their interconnections.

This case highlighted an anomaly. The claimant was an American company which brought an action for infringement of copyright in its drawings of circuit diagrams for electrical equipment known as a mixer. The defendant was alleged to have copied the circuitry from one of the claimant's mixers. As the circuit diagram was a design document for the purposes of the design right, s 51 applied and prevented the defendant's acts being an infringement of copyright. As the design had been created by an American citizen in America, the design did not qualify for the design right. Thus, citizens of the USA are not entitled to the design right (unless habitually resident in Europe or another qualifying country). The scope of copyright protection to which they are entitled has been limited by s 51 to prevent copyright protection for designs subject to a design right. To protect such designs, Americans must obtain patent protection or register the design under the Registered Designs Act 1949 or CD Regulation or rely on the UCD, assuming that their designs are patentable or satisfy the requirements for protection under the other forms of rights in designs.

Giving a broad meaning to configuration was rejected by David Young QC, sitting as deputy judge of the High Court in *Baby Dan AS v Brevi SRL*.[23] He said that the relative positioning of component parts of a child's safety barrier would be contrary to s 213(3)(a) which specifically excludes from protection methods or principles of construction. The deputy judge did accept, however, that configuration could be a form of arrangement of elements such as the ribbing arrangement of a hot water bottle, citing *Cow (PB) & Co Ltd v Cannon Rubber Manufacturers Ltd*,[24] a registered designs case. Unfortunately, *Baby Dan* was not referred to in *Mackie Designs* and the exception in s 213(3)(a) was not discussed in that case.[25]

In *Lambretta Clothing Co Ltd v Teddy Smith (UK) Ltd*,[26] the claimant owned a design for leisure-wear garments known as track tops. They had a blue body with red sleeves and had a white stripe down the arms. At first instance, the judge held that the juxtaposition of the colours was not an aspect of shape or configuration but were merely surface decoration, excluded from the ambit of the design right. This was confirmed in the Court of Appeal. Jacob LJ expressed some doubt as to the precise nature of 'configuration' but

18 Copyright, Designs and Patents Act 1988 s 213(2). Jacob LJ rejected counsel's submission that the use of the word 'aspect' had a limiting effect meaning a 'way of looking at' in *A Fulton Co Ltd v Totes Isotoner Ltd* [2004] RPC 16. Jacob LJ gained support from the Design Right (Semiconductor Topographies) Regulations 1989, discussed towards the end of this chapter.

19 Per Jacob LJ in *A Fulton Co Ltd v Totes Isotoner Ltd* [2004] RPC 16 at para 31.

20 [2006] RPC 31.

21 This was noted by Jacob LJ in *Lambretta Clothing Co Ltd v Teddy Smith (UK) Ltd* [2005] RPC 6. The old law of registered designs also used the term 'shape or configuration'.

22 [1999] RPC 717.

23 [1999] FSR 377.

24 [1959] RPC 240.

25 The judgment in *Baby Dan* was handed down a few months before that in *Mackie Designs*.

26 [2005] RPC 6.

noted that, for more than a century, it was never held that simply colouring an article in a novel way was a configuration for the purposes of registered design law, which also used the term 'shape or configuration'.[27] He said that this was a telling point against an argument that an arrangement of colours was a configuration. The fact that colours were configured to produce the overall finished garment did not mean that colour had anything to do with configuration.

There is no requirement for eye-appeal for the design right and, as a result, the right should be capable of subsisting in details which are not readily discernible or distinguishable by the naked eye. The subsistence of the design right in contact lenses was considered by Laddie J in *Ocular Sciences Ltd* v *Aspect Vision Care Ltd*.[28] After some initial doubt, he accepted that, as the right was intended for functional designs, the right could subsist in respect of detailed relative dimensions because the value of such designs over similar designs may be due to these tiny differences.[29] However, as we shall see, this does not square up with the test for infringement which relies on looking at the whole of the articles to which the design is applied through the eye of the interested person. In *Ocular Sciences*, Laddie J also noted that, as the design can be applied to the whole of any part of an article, a claimant can trim his claims accordingly, focusing on those aspects of the defendant's design which most closely match his. Again this is not consistent with the test for infringement given in the statute and as interpreted by the courts. It has been 'explained' subsequently. In *A Fulton Co Ltd* v *Totes Isotoner (UK) Ltd*,[30] Jacob LJ said (at para 34):

> . . . I do not fully go along with Laddie J's suggestion that what a proprietor can do is to 'trim his design right claim'. It is not really a question of 'trimming' – it is just identifying the part of his overall design which he claims has been taken exactly or substantially.[31]

Although there might be some flexibility in what is claimed under the unregistered design right, it is important that the claim as asserted in the pleadings is drafted with precision.[32] Furthermore, a claimant may wish to claim infringement of the physical embodiment of the design rather than the design drawings, which being two-dimensional, may give a distorted view of reality.[33]

It is possible for the design right to subsist in designs which are basic geometric shapes, such as a spiral, and an argument that there could be no property right in 'shapes at large' was rejected by Roger Wyand QC sitting as deputy judge of the High Court in *Sales* v *Stromberg*.[34] He said that the shape of a sphere may be a commonplace design for a ball but not for a wireless receiver. In that case, the design in question was for a spiral made from copper tubing, sealed at both ends and containing imploded water. An argument that the design document, from which articles to the design were made, was so crudely drawn and lacking dimensions that it was impossible to make an article precisely to the design found some sympathy with the judge apart from the fact that the defendant had no difficulty in producing a prototype to the design. As crudely drawn as the design documents were, they still were the result of skill and labour sufficient to pass the test of originality.

The design right provisions also apply to articles made in a kit of parts being a complete or substantially complete set of components intended to be assembled into an article, and it is possible that a design right subsists in a component as distinct from the design right in the assembled article.[35] However, as will be seen later, those features of components in the kit of parts which are shaped or configured specifically to match or fit other components are barred from design right protection.

In some respects the design right applies to a broader type of design than is the case with designs that fall within the scope of the UK registered design or the Community design. For example, the aspects of shape or configuration can be internal and may apply to an article that is not visible in normal use, such as 'under the bonnet' component parts. For a UK registered design or Community design, the requirement that the design relates

---

27 In the registered design cases of *Cow (PB) & Co Ltd* v *Cannon Rubber Manufacturers Ltd* [1959] RPC 240 the ribbing on a hot-water bottle was held to be shape and in *Sommer Allibert (UK) Ltd* v *Flair Plastics Ltd* [1987] RPC 599, it was held that grooves on plastic chairs were a feature of shape or configuration.

28 [1997] RPC 289.

29 [1997] RPC 289 at 422.

30 [2004] RPC 16.

31 Reflecting the fact that the unregistered design right can subsist in the design of part of an article.

32 Per HH Judge Fysh in the Patents County Court in *Bailey* v *Haynes* [2007] FSR 10.

33 Per Lewison J in *Virgin Atlantic Airways Ltd* v *Premium Aircraft Interiors Group Ltd* [2009] ECDR 11. This case was appealed on the basis of patent infringement but not in relation to the unregistered design right.

34 [2006] FSR 7.

35 Copyright, Designs and Patents Act 1988 s 260.

to appearance means that the features must be external unless the outside surface of the product is transparent so that the product or relevant features of it are normally visible. However, the UK registered design and the Community design can also relate to parts of articles – for example, a new design of spout for a teapot may be protectable and will not be rejected because it relates only to a part of the teapot and not to the whole pot. This is inherent in both the harmonising Directive and the CD Regulation in the definition of 'design' which is the same for both.

Originality

For a design right to subsist in a design it must be original. Whatever the meaning of original, s 213(4) states what is not original, being a design which is 'commonplace in the design field at the time of its creation'. What, then, does originality mean in the context of the design right? It is clear that it is not as high a standard as required for novelty for a registered design,[36] yet it appears to be more stringent than is usually the case in copyright which has been interpreted by judges to require simply that the work has originated from the author and has not merely been copied.[37] The statutory test suggests a two-stage approach. First, is the design original in a copyright sense (it is the author's own work) and, second, even if it is original in that sense, was it common-place in the design field in question at the time of its creation? This approach was taken by Aldous J in *C & H Engineering* v *F Klucznik & Sons Ltd*[38] where he said that the word 'original' should be given the same meaning as in respect of copyright, that is, not copied but the independent work of the designer. He went on to say that this should be contrasted with the novelty requirement for registered designs. However, Aldous J continued (at 428):

> The word 'commonplace' is not defined, but [section 213(4)] appears to introduce a consideration akin to novelty. For the design to be original it must be the work of the creator and that work must result in a design which is not commonplace in the relevant field.

There can be sufficient skill in adopting a mistake for the purposes of originality. In *Guild* v *Eskander Ltd*,[39] the design related to knitwear in the form of an ethnic dress. A mistake resulted in the garment being 100cm wide instead of the usual 88cm. This mistake was adopted and it was held that it could be the product of skill if not labour. However, the decision to adopt that width was not attributable to the claimant alone and other features, such as a cross-over collar and other details, were insufficient to confer originality on the design of the garment. The Court of Appeal said that it was important to guard against a piecemeal approach and the question was whether all, not just one or more, of the additional features gave rise to the requisite quality of originality.[40]

The design of an article might comprise a combination of old aspects or it may combine both old and new aspects. In *Dyson Ltd* v *Qualtex (UK) Ltd*,[41] the defendant made 'pattern parts' for the claimant's bagless vacuum cleaners. These are spare parts that have the same shape and appearance and the original parts. Examples being the 'wand' handle, brush bar and various tools attached to the wand handle, such as the stair tool. At first instance, Mann J found that design rights subsisted in various parts of the vacuum cleaners and these had been infringed by the defendant, whose appeal to the Court of Appeal was dismissed. Jacob LJ accepted that a combination of old aspects could involve originality but adding an old cable winder to a new handle lacked originality, being a mere collocation.

As the test for originality seems to be that as for copyright, this will be an issue only rarely and the focus will be on whether the design was commonplace in the design field in question at the time of its creation. However, before looking at what is or is not

36 In terms of being disclosed to the public, notwithstanding the period of grace.

37 For example, see the judgment of Lord Pearce in *Ladbroke (Football) Ltd* v *William Hill (Football) Ltd* [1964] 1 WLR 273.

38 [1992] FSR 421.

39 [2003] FSR 3.

40 The Court of Appeal accepted, nevertheless, that some consideration of individual features was inevitable.

41 [2006] RPC 31.

commonplace, the identification of the relevant design field is important as, without defining the design field, one cannot decide whether a design is commonplace and, consequently, denied protection.

Design field

The Copyright, Designs and Patents Act 1988 gives no guidance as to how the relevant design field should be determined.[42] A wide or narrow meaning can be taken: for example, a design field could be kitchen furniture, bathroom furniture, soft furnishings, household furniture, office furniture, garden furniture or furniture generally. The choice may be decisive and a wide approach may mean that many designs are denied protection through the design right. It may be that a particular design is commonplace in fields other than the design field to which the design under consideration belongs. This will not prevent the design right from subsisting in the design, of course.[43] The issue is subsistence and there is no test of design field for the purposes of infringement, nor is there any need for such a test. The most sensible approach is to consider who is in the best position to know what the scope of a design field is and the answer can only be determined through the eyes of designers.[44] These are the people who know what a design field is. Not only will designers be aware of, and have a familiarity with, the design of articles which they themselves design, but they can also be expected to take an interest in related design fields. A certain amount of cross-fertilisation is to be expected. In our furniture example, it is likely that someone who specialises in the design of dining room furniture will be interested in other furniture designs found in a house and even, to some extent, in relevant office furniture. He may find his inspiration from looking at designs in these other related fields. As infringement requires copying and is expressed in terms of alleged infringing designs being exactly or substantially to the design,[45] there is no need to take a particularly broad approach to the determination of the design field in a particular case. However, the present trend seems to take a less restrictive view on the breadth of the relevant design field.

The earlier cases on the unregistered design right took a fairly restricted approach to the scope of the design field.[46] In *Mark Wilkinson Furniture Ltd* v *Woodcraft Designs (Radcliffe) Ltd*,[47] it was held that the design field in question was 'fitted kitchen furniture' not 'cabinetry generally', because the former was a discrete design field with its own particular problems and characteristics. In this respect, subsistence and infringement may not mirror each other. A design right might subsist in an infringing design just as a copyright might subsist in an arrangement of music which is itself an infringement as an adaptation of the original music. In *Farmers Build Ltd* v *Carier Bulk Materials Handling Ltd*,[48] the Court of Appeal decided that the relevant design field was slurry separators not agricultural machinery generally. The design in question was for a slurry separator which separated out manure into solids and liquid.

A determination of the relevant design field from which to view whether a design is commonplace can be influenced by particular features of the article to which the design is applied: for example, the materials from which the article is made. In *Scholes Windows Ltd* v *Magnet Ltd*,[49] the decorative horns applied to windows were viewed from the perspective of a design field comprising window design in general. The judge refused to limit the design field to U-PVC windows as the horns were purely decorative features and could easily have been made in other materials. He thought the design field was window design generally. The Court of Appeal agreed, adding that the nature or purpose of an article, or its material structure, was not incorporated expressly or impliedly in the definition of 'design field in question'.[50] The Court of Appeal also confirmed that the fact that an old design had fallen into disuse did not necessarily exclude them from the design field. It was a question of whether they could fairly and reasonably be considered to be part of the design field at the relevant time. The litmus test would be whether they were still familiar to designers.

42 Nor can any guidance be gleaned from registered design law. The concept of 'informed user' cannot assist as this suggests consumers or buyers of the type of products in question whereas one would expect the design field to be something determined through the eyes of designers.

43 In *Sales* v *Stromberg* [2006] FSR 7, drawings of a spiral design were held to be common in rock art and other cultures, notably native American culture but the defendants failed to adduce any evidence that they were common in the design of articles of any kind, let alone the kind of article made by the claimant.

44 In *Lambretta Clothing Ltd* v *Teddy Smith (UK) Ltd* [2005] RPC 6, Jacob LJ referred to designs of which the notional designer of the article concerned would be familiar.

45 Copyright, Designs and Patents Act 1988 s 226.

46 The question of the scope of design field was considered in the first major case on design right, *C & H Engineering* v *F Klucznik & Sons Ltd* [1992] FSR 421 involving an allegation of infringement of design right in a pig fender by a lamb creep feeder. Although pig fenders of that type were commonplace, the one in issue had a 2-inch round tube welded to the top.

47 [1998] FSR 63.

48 [1999] RPC 461.

49 [2000] FSR 432.

50 *Scholes Windows Ltd* v *Magnet Ltd* [2002] FSR 10.

In *Christopher Tasker's Design Right References*,[51] the hearing officer selected two different design fields. One, being aluminium sliding mirror wardrobe doors, was chosen for the purpose of determining whether some of the design features were commonplace. This was because the design of those features was influenced by the choice of material.[52] However, as regards other features where the nature of the structural material was not important, the relevant design field was wardrobe doors generally. In *A Fulton Co Ltd* v *Grant Barnett & Co Ltd*,[53] Park J declined an invitation to choose between two design fields, folding umbrellas and compact folding umbrellas, saying that he would have come to the same conclusion either way.[54]

The Court of Appeal has taken a broader approach to deciding the design field in question in *Ultraframe (UK) Ltd* v *Eurocell Building Plastics Ltd*[55] which involved modular units for conservatory roofs. The court held that the design field in question was not limited to conservatory roofs but was wider and would cover windows, doors, conservatories and materials used to construct them.[56] Jacob LJ, with whom the other two judges agreed on the design right point,[57] referred to the decision of the Court of Appeal in *Lambretta Clothing Ltd* v *Teddy Smith (UK) Ltd*[58] where Jacob LJ himself, at para 45, said that '[w]hat matters are the sort of designs with which a notional designer of the article concerned would be familiar'. In *Ultraframe*, Jacob LJ developed the rationale for taking a broad approach to design field, saying (at para 54) that were it otherwise:

> . . . a designer would be able to obtain UDR in designs with which other similar designers were wholly familiar, just because the 'field' was narrowly drawn. That would be to impose too much of a fetter on freedom to use known designs . . . Suppose conservatory designers were completely familiar with a well-known design of window panel. Why should the law give a particular designer UDR protection for choosing to use in a conservatory roof a design known to all conservatory designers?

A narrower approach to design field was taken by Roger Wyand QC, sitting as deputy judge of the High Court in *Sales* v *Stromberg*,[59] which involved a design for 'personal harmonisers', pendants to a 'Celtic-type' spiral design containing imploded water and made from copper tubing. He decided that the design field was 'complementary medical devices including ornamental or decorative such devices' notwithstanding the defendant's much wider view of the relevant design field. The Court of Appeal decision in *Scholes Windows Ltd* v *Magnet Ltd*[60] was distinguished as regards the view that purpose should not be taken into account. In finding that one of the defendant's designs infringed the claimant's design right, Roger Wyand QC thought that the Court of Appeal did not intend to rule out purpose but, as the design field was window design, that itself implied purpose to some extent. It does seem difficult to divorce purpose from design field. In *Sales* v *Stromberg*, the defendants included like designs used for other purposes in their view of what the design field was, which included designs for artefacts for good luck, religious faith, ancient (especially Celtic) civilisations. However, the judge could have narrowed the design field down by looking through the eyes of the notional designer of an article of the type made by the claimant.

It is reasonable to take the approach of looking at the design field through the eyes of the notional designer. However, the scope of the design field was a matter for the court and not for expert witnesses although they could give evidence of the sort of matter that was well known to designers of the type of articles in question.[61] Once the design field has been determined, it is then a matter of considering whether the design in issue is or is not commonplace.

Commonplace

The meaning of 'commonplace' is important as a defendant is likely to argue that the claimant's design was commonplace in the design field in question at the time of its

---

51 [2001] RPC 3.

52 This case was not cited in the Court of Appeal in *Scholes Windows Ltd* v *Magnet Ltd* [2002] FSR 10 but now must be doubted on the question of whether materials are a factor to be taken into account in determining the relevant design field for the inquiry as to whether a design is commonplace.

53 [2001] RPC 16.

54 The appeal to the Court of Appeal was dismissed: *A Fulton Co Ltd* v *Totes Isotoner (UK) Ltd* [2004] RPC 16. The scope of design field was not in issue in the Court of Appeal.

55 [2005] RPC 36.

56 The reference to materials introduces something rejected earlier by the Court of Appeal in *Scholes Windows Ltd* v *Magnet Ltd* [2002] FSR 10, a decision not referred to in *Ultraframe*. However, it is likely that it was used in a different way as a feature to widen the design field rather than restricting it.

57 Neuberger LJ dissented on the patent issue in the case.

58 [2005] RPC 6.

59 [2006] FSR 7.

60 [2002] FSR 10.

61 *Ultraframe (UK) Ltd* v *Eurocell Building Plastics Ltd* [2005] RPC 36.

creation. This could be taken as meaning that, although some examples of the design may exist, they are not well known or commercialised and can only be found by a thorough search. Alternatively, it may mean that the design must differ from the existing art in the relevant design field, though not by a significant amount. In *Ultraframe (UK) Ltd v Eurocell Building Plastics Ltd*,[62] Jacob LJ said (at para 60):

> That which is commonplace in a design field will be ready to hand, not matter that has to be hunted for and found at the last minute. After all, one is trying to prove a prior design is *commonplace*, not merely (as for instance in a patent case) that it was made available to the public by use. (original emphasis)

It is self-evident that the requirement that a design not be commonplace is not the same as novelty for registered designs or patents. In *Ultraframe*, the defendant had managed to trace some products shown in catalogues of German extrusion companies. The possibility that someone in the UK might go abroad to find a maker of that sort of roof panel was, Jacob LJ said, miles away from showing that the claimant's designs were commonplace. However, if the test of whether a design is commonplace is limited to an enquiry into designs made available in the UK only, this creates a paradox for, as we shall see, a design can qualify for protection in a number of ways. One of these is where the designer is a British citizen or a citizen of another State of the European Economic Community.[63] This means, for example, that a design could be created by an Italian citizen (not being an employee or acting under a commission for money or money's worth), who created the design in Italy, which satisfies the other requirements for subsistence, and which is commercialised in Italy. No articles to the design are exported to the UK and nothing is published about the design in the UK. The design qualifies for the UK design right. A third party in the UK, not having seen the Italian design, subsequently creates a design to be applied to articles in the same design field and which is, to all intents and purposes, identical. Does that third party get his own UK design right or is it vulnerable to a challenge that it was commonplace when it was created? It would be strange if designs which qualify for the UK design right, but are created and commercialised not in the UK but within other parts of the European Economic Community, are not taken into account in determining whether a design is commonplace. If this is so, there could be several owners of what are essentially the same designs, all of which could bring infringement actions in the UK.

The Act gives no further assistance to what 'commonplace' means and it is a term of art new to English law.[64] In *Ocular Sciences Ltd v Aspect Vision Care Ltd*,[65] Laddie J remarked that the word 'commonplace' derives from the Directive on the protection of semiconductor topographies which imposed a test of intellectual creation and not being commonplace in the semiconductor industry. Although he said that it was undesirable 'to replace one ambiguous expression by another', he went on to approve counsel's submission that:

> Any design which is trite, common-or-garden, hackneyed or of the type which would excite no peculiar attention in those in the relevant art is likely to be commonplace.[66]

A design which is made up of commonplace elements may yet qualify for protection by virtue of the combination of elements provided the combination itself is not commonplace.[67]

The tests for originality and whether a design was commonplace when it was created were considered in depth in the Court of Appeal in *Farmers Build Ltd v Carier Bulk Materials Handling Ltd*.[68] In that case, the defendant designed an agricultural rotary screen slurry separator machine for the claimant. It had been agreed that the claimant would own all the intellectual property rights in the machine. Later, the defendant designed his own machine, which looked different externally, but which contained internal machinery which was almost identical to that in the claimant's machine.

Mummery LJ confirmed that the test of originality was as that for copyright. He accepted that it would be wrong to regard the requirement for a design not to be commonplace as

62 [2005] RPC 36.

63 Still expressed as such in the Act: *see* ss 206, 217 and 220.

64 Being adopted from the Directive on the legal protection of topographies of semiconductor products.

65 [1997] RPC 289.

66 [1997] RPC 289 at 429, followed by Englehart QC in *Philip Parker v Stephen Tidball* [1997] FSR 680.

67 *Farmers Build Ltd v Carier Bulk Materials Handling Ltd* [1999] RPC 461 at 467 per Mummery LJ.

68 [1999] RPC 461. This was the first case on the design right before the Court of Appeal.

the same as a requirement for novelty. He then set out a five-factor test for whether a design was commonplace, noting that the word should be interpreted narrowly rather than broadly, otherwise many designs of functional articles would be excluded from protection. Indications that this should be so could be derived from considering the short duration of the design right, the narrow scope of protection against copying and the prima facie protection given to designs of functional articles. The test is as follows:[69]

69 Some modification to the wording of the test has been made as Mummery LJ also included aspects related to an alleged infringement.

1 Compare the design with the design of other articles in the same field.
2 Has the design simply been copied from the design of an earlier article? The court must not forget that, in the field of designs of functional articles, one design may be similar, or even identical, to another design and yet not be a copy. If the design has been slavishly copied from another, then it is not original in the copyright sense and the commonplace issue does not arise.
3 If the court is satisfied that the design has not been copied from an earlier design, then it is original in the copyright sense. The court then has to decide whether it is commonplace. This requires comparison of the design for similarity with the design of similar articles in the same field of design made by persons unconnected with the parties.
4 The comparison must be conducted objectively and in the light of the evidence, including evidence from experts in the relevant field pointing out similarities and differences and explaining the significance of them. Of course, the final determination of whether a design is commonplace is for the court, being based on fact and degree. The closer the similarity of various designs to each other, the more likely it is that they are commonplace, especially if there is no causal link which accounts for the resemblance of the compared designs.
5 If there are aspects of the design in question which are not to be found in any other design in the relevant field, that is suggestive that the design is not commonplace.

Looking at point 4 above, Mummery LJ said that the fact that a number of designers working independently created very similar designs by coincidence suggested that there was only one way of designing the particular article and that such a design could be fairly described as commonplace. Furthermore, this would be a good reason for denying protection. Any such design would be bound to be substantially similar, whether or not it had been copied.

In *Farmers Build*, Mummery LJ was concerned with purely functional designs and, in *Scholes Windows Ltd* v *Magnet Ltd*,[70] Nicholas Underhill QC, sitting as deputy judge of the High Court, said that some of Mummery LJ's observations might be less relevant in the case of a design created so as to have aesthetic qualities (in particular, the observations in the preceding paragraph and point 3 of the test). *Scholes Windows* involved the design of a U-PVC window which was designed to look like a Victorian sash window and, in particular, had two projections on the bottom of the two side members of the upper casement, called horns, which were typically found on Victorian windows. It was held that the design of the horns was commonplace. The Victorian designs, although over a century old, were still current as they were to be seen *in situ* in numerous Victorian buildings all over the country. Although none of the Victorian designs were identical to the claimant's design, the latter did not differ from the Victorian designs sufficiently to 'lift it out of the ordinary run of such designs'.

70 [2000] FSR 432.

The Court of Appeal dismissed the claimant's appeal against the decision at first instance that the design was commonplace.[71] On the basis of the House of Lords decision in *Designers Guild Ltd* v *Russell Williams (Textiles) Ltd*,[72] an appellate court should not interfere with a trial judge's finding of fact unless satisfied that he had misdirected himself or erred in principle. Mummery LJ thought the trial judge used the correct approach and he rejected the submission that the issue of whether a design is commonplace should be decided from the perspective of the designer who is an expert in the design field in

71 [2002] FSR 10.
72 [2001] FSR 11.

question. Therefore, if the notional designer is used as a basis to decide what the relevant design field is, it is the viewpoint of the type of person to whom the design is marketed that is important in deciding whether a design is commonplace. Although expert evidence might help the court to perceive and appreciate the similarities and differences between designs, it is not necessary to be an expert to appreciate such similarities and differences or to form an opinion as to whether the design in issue is commonplace. Indeed, over-reliance on one side's expert witness may lead a judge to fall into error. In *Lambretta Clothing Co Ltd v Teddy Smith (UK) Ltd*,[73] the judge at first instance preferred the opinion of the claimant's expert witness as to the design field in question and this resulted in him finding that the design of the track-top was not commonplace. The Court of Appeal held that the judge had fallen into error, which enabled the court to look afresh at the issue of whether the design was commonplace. In holding that the judge at first instance had wrongly excluded retro-designs from the design field, the Court of Appeal went on to find that the design was commonplace.[74]

The addition of the test of whether a design is commonplace can be said to limit the number of designs that are subject to the design right and to prevent the right applying to designs so like earlier designs that enforcement would be difficult. But then the right is a right to prevent copying and the fact that a similar work may be independently created and have its own separate copyright does not seem to have caused any 'floodgate' problems under copyright law.

Of course, the test for whether a design is commonplace has to be judged at the time of the creation of the design and not later. As the right is informal and much of the 'prior art' that may be used to attack a design right as being commonplace may also not be subject to formal rights, establishing the design field at the time of the creation of the design may not be an easy task. This could be made even more difficult when one considers that design does not subsist until it is recorded in a design document or an article is made to the design. As neither act necessarily coincides with the time articles to the design are put on the market or otherwise made available to the public, fixing the time of creation may be difficult if the designer has not kept proper records.[75]

If the meaning of commonplace is simply that the design has been made available to the public, but not on a scale to have become well known in the design circles in the relevant design field, all manner of difficulties could arise. There would be more than one design right subsisting in the same design, or very similar design, and the test of whether a design is commonplace could be very difficult to apply. For example, consider the following situations involving two designs which are similar and have been created by two designers, Alice and Bernard. The designs are unlike any prior designs and are intended to be applied to a locking mechanism for sliding doors. They have been created independently.

1 Alice and Bernard create their designs and record them at around the same point in time.
2 Alice and Bernard create their designs and record them at around the same point in time, but there is a time difference in the marketing of articles made to the designs. Articles to which Alice's design has been applied reach the marketplace in advance of articles made to Bernard's design. In the meantime, articles to Alice's design do not sell in large numbers.
3 Again, Alice and Bernard create and record their designs at the same time and articles made to Alice's design reach the marketplace first, but this time large numbers of articles to Alice's design are sold before the appearance of articles made to Bernard's design. Generally, most designers in the same field would have seen the design before articles to Bernard's design are marketed.
4 Bernard does not create and record his design until after small numbers of articles made to Alice's design have been marketed or sold. (Bernard has not seen the articles and they are not yet generally known to designers in the field.)

73 [2003] RPC 41.

74 [2005] RPC 6. The claimant's expert witness had considered the design of the track-top as a whole, including items which should be ignored. Attention should have been directed at the red, white and blue colourways.

75 Keeping full, accurate and verifiable records is important in relation to all forms of intellectual property rights.

5 Bernard creates and records his design after large numbers of articles made to Alice's design have been marketed and sold. (Again, Bernard does not see any of the articles to Alice's design but most designers in the field will have seen Alice's design.)

6 Several other similar designs have been recorded and articles made to the designs have been marketed and sold before Bernard, in ignorance of these, creates his similar design. Again, most designers working in that field will be familiar with the design.

In 1, 2 and 3 above, both Alice and Bernard have created designs in which the design right is capable of subsisting subject, of course, to the exceptions. The design was not commonplace at the time of its creation by Alice and by Bernard because the creation of the designs was coincident in time, or nearly so.[76] The fact that numbers of articles have been sold is irrelevant to the subsistence of the design rights and reference must be made to the time when the designs were created, at which time the design or variants of it were not commonplace. Situation 6 is easily dealt with – it is clear that, at the time Bernard creates his design, the design has become commonplace in the design field. Situations 4 and 5 are less easy to distinguish, but it is clear that the test will be applied objectively, probably through the eyes of an interested person: for example, someone working in or knowledgeable about the design field in question. It is suggested that, if only small numbers of articles made to Alice's design have been sold, there is a possibility that Bernard's design can still attract the design right. This prompts another question as to whether it is sufficient that only one other example of a similar design has been created and applied to articles, or whether the design, or variants of the design, are commonly used by a majority of designers in the particular design field. Incidentally, in none of the examples above does Bernard infringe Alice's design right as he has not copied her design.

In *A Fulton Co Ltd* v *Grant Barnett & Co Ltd*,[77] it was held that prior art comprising an obscure article which looks fairly similar to the design in question would not be sufficient to make the design commonplace. In *Frayling Furniture Ltd* v *Premier Upholstery Ltd*,[78] a case involving a design applied to armchairs, Park J said:

> ... it does not disqualify the Sienna from design right if Premier [the defendant], having scoured the trade magazines, manages to come up with one or two fairly obscure items which may be said to have a close similarity.

To hold otherwise would be to impose a test of novelty not unlike that which applies in the case of a patent. If Parliament had intended to apply a test of novelty to a design subject to the design right it would have done so using clear language to that effect.

In *Dyson Ltd* v *Qualtex (UK) Ltd*,[79] Jacob LJ noted the different approaches to the meaning of commonplace in *Farmers Build, Ocular Sciences* and *Lambretta Clothing*. He said he doubted whether the differences had any significance and that it was important to focus on the context in which the questions arose.[80] He referred to Mann J at first instance where he spoke of a paradox. A very good design which became well known would lose design right because it had become commonplace. Jacob LJ thought the judge had fallen into error on this point as there was no question of this happening as the relevant time to consider whether a design was commonplace was the time of its creation. However, it is not clear whether Mann J really suggested otherwise as it appeared that he was dealing with counsel's submission to the effect that a subsequent design, having only trite differences compared with an earlier design, would be commonplace as a result of the commercial success of the earlier design upon which it was based. Nonetheless, Jacob LJ went on to consider afresh whether a later version of the wand handle was commonplace. He noted that the differences over the earlier design were significant and that the later design was the result of a redesign exercise that was no trivial operation. Similar considerations applied to another part, being the stair tool.

76 The time of the creation of a design may be of crucial importance in a case like this and the need for independent evidence as to the date of the creation of a design is a matter which should not be overlooked by designers, their employers and commissioners.

77 [2001] RPC 16.

78 (Unreported) 5 November 1998.

79 [2006] RPC 31.

80 At para 106.

Tangible form requirement

The design right springs into force when the design is recorded in a design document, or alternatively when an article has been made to the design, whichever happens first.[81] 'Design document' is defined by s 263, which contains minor definitions, as 'any record of a design, whether in the form of a drawing, a written description, a photograph, data stored in a computer or otherwise'.[82] This would appear to cover virtually any form of recording and would be likely to include data stored on a compact disc, magnetic tape or a computer disk, depending on the meaning of 'or otherwise'. Bearing in mind the wide variety of forms of storage mentioned specifically, it is certain that this will be construed very widely. The only difficulty could be with temporary storage; and on the basis of the House of Lords judgment in *R* v *Gold*,[83] temporary storage in a computer's volatile memory may not be sufficient, although as soon as the relevant data is copied on to a computer disk this will be deemed to be recorded. One question which arises is whether storage on a removable computer disk is storage *in a computer*. However, this should be caught by the scope of the phrase 'or otherwise'.

Old designs cannot be resurrected by the design right because s 213(7) declares that the right does not subsist in designs which were recorded in a design document or which have been applied to an article prior to the commencement of the Copyright, Designs and Patents Act 1988 Part III.[84]

Qualification

As with copyright law, some qualification requirements must be satisfied for the right to subsist in a design. These may be fulfilled by reference to the designer, or, where relevant, the designer's employer or the commissioner of the design. A further route to satisfying the qualification requirements is through the first person who markets articles made to the design and the country in which that first marketing took place. There are, therefore, four possible routes to qualification. However, before the provisions can be understood, three terms used have to be defined: they are 'qualifying country', 'qualifying individual' and 'qualifying person'.[85]

'Qualifying country' means the UK and other Member States of the EU.[86] Other countries may be added by Order in Council, either under s 255 or 256, the latter applying where the other country has reciprocal provisions for design rights. Bermuda, the Channel Islands, Gibraltar, the Isle of Man, New Zealand, amongst others, have been added to the list of qualifying countries by Order under s 256.[87]

'Qualifying individual' is a citizen, subject or person habitually resident in a qualifying country.[88]

'Qualifying person' means a qualifying individual or a body having legal personality, including a body corporate which has been formed under the law of a qualifying country and which has, in any qualifying country, a place of business at which substantial business activity is carried out. In determining whether substantial business is carried out, no account is to be taken of dealings with goods which are, at all material times, outside the qualifying country. References to a qualifying person include the Crown and the government of any other qualifying country.[89] Under s 263(1) 'business' includes a trade or profession.

The routes to qualification are by reference to:

1 The designer, being the person who creates the design. If the design is computer-generated, the designer is taken to be the person by whom the arrangements necessary for the

81 Copyright, Designs and Patents Act 1988 s 213(6).

82 It should be noted that it is the design that is protected, not the design document.

83 [1988] 2 WLR 984.

84 The commencement date was 1 August 1989.

85 Defined in the Copyright, Designs and Patents Act 1988 s 217.

86 Still expressed as the European Economic Community in the Act.

87 Design Right (Reciprocal Protection) (No 2) Order 1989, SI 1989/1294. Regulation 2 gives a full list of countries designated as enjoying reciprocal protection.

88 In respect of the UK, a citizen is a living person who is a British citizen or, in relation to a colony of the UK, a British Overseas Territories citizen in connection with that colony.

89 Section 217(2).

creation of the work are undertaken.[90] Under s 218(2), a design qualifies for protection if the designer is a qualifying *individual*, or, if the design is computer-generated, the designer is a qualifying person. A joint design is the result of collaboration between two or more designers such that their individual contributions are indistinct from one another.[91] A joint design qualifies if any of the designers is a qualifying individual (or a qualifying person for a computer-generated joint design). These provisions do not apply, however, if the design is created in the pursuance of a commission or in the course of employment.[92]

2   The commissioner, if the design is commissioned and the commissioner is a qualifying *person* (s 219(1)). A commissioned design is one commissioned for money or money's worth.[93]

90 Copyright, Designs and Patents Act 1988 s 214.

91 Copyright, Designs and Patents Act 1988 s 259(1).

92 Copyright, Designs and Patents Act 1988 s 218(1).

93 Copyright, Designs and Patents Act 1988 s 263(1).

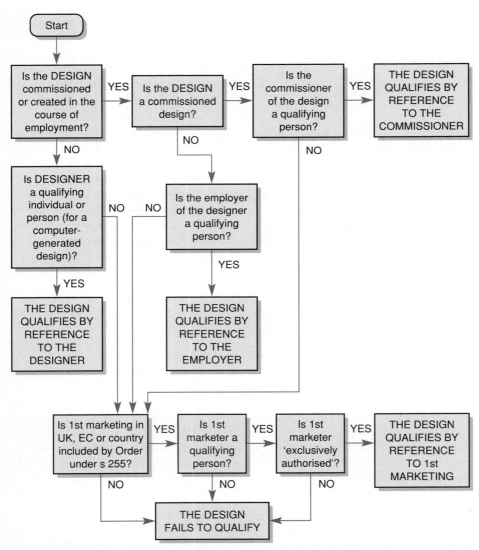

Figure 18.1 Qualification for the design right

3 The employer, if the design is created by the designer in the course of employment and the employer is a qualifying *person* (s 219(1)). Section 263(1) states that 'employee', 'employment' and 'employer' refer to employment under a contract of service or of apprenticeship. This definition is identical to that applying to copyright works.

94 Copyright, Designs and Patents Act 1988 s 220.

4 The first marketing of articles made to the design.[94] This can apply only if the other qualification requirements do not. In this case, the requirement is that the first marketing is done by a qualifying *person* exclusively authorised to put such articles on the market in the UK and it takes place in the UK, any other Member State of the European Economic Community or other country to which Part III of the Act has been extended by Order under s 255, but not to countries affording reciprocal protection included by Order under s 256. 'Exclusively authorised' refers (a) to authorisation by the person who would have been the first owner of the right as designer, commissioner or employer had he (or it) been a qualifying person, including a person lawfully claiming under him, and (b) to exclusivity capable of legal enforcement in the UK.

In the case of a joint commission, or a joint employment or joint marketing, the design qualifies if any of the commissioners, employers or marketers is a qualifying person. A design which would not otherwise qualify may so qualify for protection subject to specified requirements in an Order in Council so that an international obligation of the UK is fulfilled.[95] The flowchart in Figure 18.1 sets out the various routes to qualification and their relationship.

95 Copyright, Designs and Patents Act 1988 s 221.

Exceptions

The design right is declared under s 213(3) not to subsist in:

(a) methods or principles of construction;
(b) features of shape or configuration which:
   (i) enable the article to be connected to, placed in, around or against another article so that either article may perform its function (the 'must-fit' exception), or
   (ii) are dependent upon the appearance of another article of which the article is intended by the designer (creator of the design) to form an integral part (the 'must-match' exception);
(c) surface decoration.

A final exception which will not be examined in more detail later as it is self-explanatory is the exception from design right of a design which consists of or contains a controlled representation within the meaning of the Olympic Symbol etc. (Protection) Act 1995. This exception is provided for under s 213(5A), which was inserted into the Copyright, Designs and Patents Act 1998 by that Act of 1995. The protection is afforded to the Olympic symbol, Olympic motto (*citius, altius, fortius*) and protected words (Olympiad, Olympiads, Olympian, Olympians, Olympic and Olympics). Of course, as design right applies only in respect of shape or configuration, it is highly unlikely that it could subsist in the words; although the Olympic symbol is another matter if represented in three-dimensional form. The 1995 Act contains remedies for infringement and criminal offences, not unlike those that apply to the trade marks offences.

96 Under registered designs law as it now stands, the equivalent exception has been repealed. Features of appearance of a product which are solely dictated by the product's technical function are excluded from protection instead: Registered Designs Act 1949, s 1C(1).

97 (1936) 53 RPC 139.

Methods or principles of construction

The first exception is very similar to that which used to apply to registered designs, being identically worded, and it would seem reasonable to look to case law on registered designs for guidance.[96] In *Kestos Ltd* v *Kempat Ltd*,[97] Luxmoore J said (at 151):

A mode or principle of construction is a process or operation by which a shape is produced as opposed to the shape itself.

This was cited with approval by Park J in *A Fulton Co Ltd v Grant Barnett & Co Ltd*,[98] in which two particular methods were used to manufacture a case for a folding umbrella. One was a method by which the case retained its rectangular box-like shape; the other was a stitching technique, giving the cases outwardly pointing seams. Park J said (at para 70):

> . . . the design of the case is the shape or configuration produced by those methods or construction, not the methods by which that shape or configuration is produced. The fact that a special method or principle of construction may have been used in order to create an article with a particular shape or configuration does not mean that there is no design right in the shape or configuration.

In *Christopher Tasker's Design Right References*,[99] the Hearing Officer, again referring to *Kestos v Kempat*, said that it may be possible to obtain protection for a particular shape or configuration resulting from using a particular method or principle of construction. However, he went on to say that where the method or principle of construction leads to the manufacture of articles with a shape or configuration which may be capable of variation within very wide limits, then to allow protection for such a general conception of shape or configuration would be effectively to give protection to that method or principle of construction.[100] This must be treated with some caution and the Hearing Officer was dealing with written claims to a design right and a claim to a general shape might well be caught by the exception. However, where there is design freedom, the particular shape or configuration claimed cannot be a claim to a method or principle of construction if others using that same method or principle can manufacture articles with different shapes or configurations.

The exception must relate to techniques used to construct an article rather than the technical function the article is designed to perform. Consequently, the exception will apply only in rare cases, especially if one accepts that the presence of design freedom suggests that the shape or configuration of an article cannot be a method or principle of construction.[101] The function an article performs cannot be subject to a design right, *per se*, and features of shape or configuration resulting from technical function are likely to be caught by the 'must-fit' exception.

In *Dyson Ltd v Qualtex (UK) Ltd*,[102] at first instance, it had been argued by the defendant that a tool for the claimant's vacuum cleaner which was perforated with holes to admit air into the cleaner for the purpose of assisting in cooling the motor was within the exception. Mann J rejected this argument. The exception could apply to the idea of using holes but not to a particular design of holes. In *Landor & Hawa International Ltd v Azure Designs Ltd*,[103] Neuberger LJ considered that the exception did not preclude a design simply because it had a functional purpose. The exception was there to prevent a monopoly in articles made in a particular way. In that case, the design in question related to a suitcase with a particular arrangement of piping and a zipper. It was held that the exception would only apply if that design was the only way of achieving the functional purpose of the design. It might be hard to think of a design where this might be so but, In *Bailey v Haynes*,[104] HH Judge Ford held that the design of a micromesh used in the manufacture of textile containers to hold bait used by anglers was caught by the exception. The mesh was produced using a particular warp stitch method and, although its appearance might vary from product to product, it inevitably was a method or principle of construction.

'Must-fit'

The purpose of the 'must-fit' exception is to prevent a designer using his design right to stop others making parts which fit his article. It is often referred to as the 'interface' exception.[105]

98 [2001] RPC 16.

99 [2001] RPC 3. The references were brought under the Copyright, Designs and Patents Act 1988 s 246.

100 The Hearing Officer considered this was what Luxmoore J said in *Kestos v Kempat* and what Parker J said in *Pugh v Riley Cycle Company Ltd* (1912) 29 RPC 196 at 202.

101 That being so, the decision of Pumfrey J in *Baby Dan AS v Brevi SRL* [1999] FSR 377, to the extent that he held that the relative positioning of component parts of a child's safety barrier would be contrary to s 213(3)(a), which excludes from protection methods or principles of construction, must be viewed with some caution.

102 [2005] RPC 19. The case demonstrates the continuing usefulness of the UK unregistered design right as a means of protecting designs.

103 [2007] FSR 9.

104 [2007] FSR 10.

105 For example, in *Apps v Weldtite Products Ltd* [2001] FSR 39, it was held that the widths of slots for receiving bolts on a stabiliser to be fitted to children's bicycles were caught by the 'must-fit' exclusion.

In fact, as with the 'must-match' exception, it is not just an exception to infringement; it is an exception to subsistence of the design right in respect of the parts of the article that have to be a particular shape or configuration to fit another article so that either can perform its function. As design right can subsist in part of a design, it was important to exclude such elements of a design from subsistence of the right.[106]

106 Per Jacob LJ in *A Fulton Co Ltd* v *Totes Isotoner (UK) Ltd* [2004] RPC 16 at para 32.

107 [1997] RPC 289 at 424.

According to Laddie J in *Ocular Sciences Ltd* v *Aspect Vision Care* Ltd[107] it does not matter if those aspects excluded have other functions or if a number of different designs of interface will do. Providing the articles can be fitted together to enable either to perform its function, the exception applies. However, in *A Fulton Co Ltd* v *Grant Barnett & Co Ltd*, Park J did not accept that a case of rectangular box-like shape to fit around a folding umbrella was caught by the exception, saying (at paras 74 and 75) that, in his view, it would be:

> unacceptable to construe the provision as meaning that any article which shaped so as to cover or contain another article cannot qualify for design right . . . section 213(3)(b)(i) does not provide that design right cannot subsist in an article if it can be placed in, around or against another article. Rather it provides that design right cannot subsist in features of shape or configuration which enable the article to be so placed.

At first sight this seems to contradict Laddie J's view of the exception but it is consistent with it. The fact that certain features of a hat have to be a particular shape to fit on a head, does not mean that the other features of the shape of the hat, such as the shape of the brim or circumferential band, cannot be protected by the design right. On the other hand, the interface between the hat and the head could be circular, oval or even elliptical in plan view. Although many different alternatives exist (although perhaps only varying in small detail) they will all be caught by the 'must-fit' exception.

108 [1999] FSR 377 at 382.

This approach is consistent with that of David Young QC, sitting as deputy judge of the High Court, in *Baby Dan AS* v *Brevi SRL*[108] where he said that, where design right subsisted in component parts of a larger article, it would be circumscribed by the 'must-fit' provisions. In respect of a whole article made up of component parts, if the design right is claimed in respect of the assembled article, the 'must-fit' provisions do not apply to the shape or configuration of the various parts that enable them to be assembled. On the other hand, if what is claimed is the design rights subsisting in the component parts as individual articles, the 'must-fit' provisions apply to curtail the design rights in those parts, per se. The rationale for such an approach was that the 'must-fit' provisions were introduced to deny protection to articles such as spare parts and this required, according to David Young QC, a purposive approach to the construction of s 213(3)(b)(i). However, it should be noted that the exception applies only to those features of shape or configuration that enable the articles to be interfaced so that either can perform its function. The design right may subsist in other features of shape or configuration, if any. The provision does not deny protection to spare parts completely but it merely allows the manufacture of other articles that can be interfaced with the article in question. In the umbrella case, the object of the design right was not denied protection altogether. Although the case was designed to fit around the umbrella in its folded state, certain aspects of the design such as the outwardly facing seams were not present to enable the case to be placed around the umbrella. They were there to make the case look more attractive.

109 [2006] RPC 31.

The exception is concerned primarily with enabling function, whether that of the article in question or the other with which it connects with or is in proximity with as described in the subsection. In *Dyson Ltd* v *Qualtex (UK) Ltd*,[109] it was held that the articles did not actually have to physically touch and clearances might, theoretically, be acceptable. However, if the design of the article in question was simply to provide enough clearance to prevent it fouling the operation of the other article, that was not, *per se*, enough for the exception to apply. Enabling the function of some third article did not count. Thus, providing a vacuum cleaner nozzle with holes to prevent the cleaner's motor from overheating was not a relevant function. The nozzle was placed against a carpet, not the motor. The holes allowed the nozzle to function as a vacuum cleaner nozzle. The 'must-fit' test is an objective one and does not depend on which article was designed first. Designing an article later which fits with an earlier article can mean that some aspects of the design of the earlier article are caught by the exception. This could be the case, for example, where the first article has lugs as part of the casting and the later article is designed so that it has protuberances to fit over the lugs. It is clear that, although certain parts of an article are caught by the exception, other parts may still be subject to the design right. If one element of an article's design is constrained to enable that or the other article to enable either to perform its function, that is not to say that the remaining aspects are also excluded from protection.

The article in the 'must-fit' exception does not have to be an inanimate object. Laddie J refused to construe the exception narrowly to exclude the human eye in *Ocular Sciences Ltd* v *Aspect Vision Care Ltd*[110] in finding that some features of the design of contact lenses were caught by this exception as they adopted a particular shape to fit the human eye, so that the eye and the lens could perform their respective functions.[111] It was from the viewpoint of these functions that the features were evaluated in terms of the exception.

'Must-match'

The 'must-match' exception in s 213(3)(b)(ii) is more strongly worded than the 'must-fit' exception in that the shape or configuration has to be *dependent* upon the appearance of the other article. Furthermore, it appears that both articles are likely to have a common designer (though not essential), unlike the case with the 'must-fit' exception. The provision speaks of the intention of the designer that the article forms an integral part of the other article. An argument that the handle of the umbrella in *A Fulton Co Ltd* v *Grant Barnett & Co Ltd*[112] was caught by the exception and was of a flat, rectangular cuboid shape to match the shape of the umbrella in its case (flat and rectangular) was rejected as the designer could have used other shapes and was not constrained to use the particular shape chosen, having precisely the same aspects of shape or configuration.

Section 213(3)(b)(ii) states that the exception applies where the features of shape or configuration '. . . are *dependant* upon the appearance of another article of which the article is intended by the designer to form an integral part . . .' (emphasis added). Design dependency is, therefore, an important aspect, rather than the features of shape or configuration simply being a match. An example was given in *Dyson Ltd* v *Qualtex (UK) Ltd*[113] by Mann J, being where an obvious curved shape has to be sustained and bridged across a gap by the article in question. He also accepted that the subject article (article No 1) must be comprised in 'another article' (article No 2). That is, the subject article is part of a complex article such as a body panel for a motor car. This was the accepted approach by the Divisional Court of the High Court in *Ford Motor Co Ltd's Design Applications*, considering the then equivalent exception in relation to registered designs.[114] For example, when considering a replacement wing for a car, one had to look at the whole car including the wing, rather than the car minus the wing.

In *Dyson*, it had been suggested that dependency does not presuppose a single available design solution. For example, a boot lid could be designed for a car. Later, there is a facelift model in which the design of the boot lid is modified. In both cases, the designer created a dependency because he saw the car as an integral whole and designed the boot lid as such. Appearance is an important factor as is design dependency. The more design freedom there is, the less room there is for the exception. In respect of the Dyson vacuum cleaner, the key point about the design of the wand handle was whether it had to be to exactly the same design so as to keep the overall appearance of the vacuum cleaner the same.

110 [1997] RPC 289 at 425.

111 Laddie J considered the presumed legislative intent was to exclude all interfaces.

112 [2001] RPC 16.

113 [2005] RPC 19.

114 [1994] RPC 545.

At first instance, Mann J thought that changing one or more features of the handle would not result in the vacuum cleaner as a whole, including the handle, looking radically different. In the Court of Appeal, Jacob LJ thought this was a useful test. If the handle did not have ribbing on it, the consumer would probably not care. It would not matter if the cleaner with a replacement handle looked a bit different compared with the original. This was in contrast to replacement body panels for vehicles where it was important to consumers to restore the original appearance of the vehicle. In any case, Mann J had to make a value judgment as to dependency, and an appeal court would not interfere with his finding unless there had been an error of principle.

Implications of 'must-fit' and 'must-match'

The 'must-fit' and 'must-match' exceptions have significant implications for the manufacturers of replacement parts. These exceptions are also relevant to manufacturers of accessory parts: for example, a lamp to fit on a bicycle mounting, or a dust cover for a typewriter. As a result of the 'must-fit' exception, features that accordingly must be a certain shape or configuration can be made without infringing the design right. In the examples quoted this would extend to the connecting features of the lamp enabling it to be connected to the mounting bracket on the bicycle and the shape of the dust cover in as much as it had to be that shape to fit over the typewriter for which it was designed. Three points must be noted with respect to these exceptions:

1 *The exceptions do not extend to other features.* For example, in the case of an exhaust system for a motor car, only those parts of the design that relate to the fixing of the exhaust system to the mounting brackets on the car and to the outlet at the engine manifold are excepted from the design right. These features of shape or configuration enable the exhaust to be fitted to the car body and to the engine so that the exhaust system can perform its function, that is, the control of noise and engine emissions. Other features of the shape or configuration of the exhaust system may be subject to the right: for example, if an unusual shape is selected for a silencer box (perhaps elliptical or rectangular in cross-section rather than circular) that has nothing to do with the connection of the system to the car. A spare part manufacturer may copy the 'connecting' or interface details but nothing else, unless the other features are commonplace or any design right in them has expired. This seems to be less generous than the 'licence to copy' replacement parts granted by the House of Lords in *British Leyland Motor Corp Ltd v Armstrong Patents Co Ltd*.[115]

2 *The other article referred to in s 213(3) could be made by the same person who makes the article we are interested in.* For example, if a person manufactures something comprising two articles (or an article that can be taken apart), then the connection between the articles will not be protected by the design right irrespective of the amount of research and development which may have been expended in the design of the connection.[116] The only time this exception cannot operate is if the connection is not relevant to the performance of function by either article. However, this would be highly unlikely. With the 'must-match' exception, the article has to have been designed with the intention that it will form an integral part of another article. This means that, in many cases, the two articles will have a common designer but this is not essential, such as where a designer creates a design of an article intended to form an integral part of a pre-existing article.

3 The 'must-match' exception is effective only where there is a design dependency so that it operates only where there is no or very little design freedom. This prejudices competition by 'pattern' manufacturers of spare parts for complex articles, where the level of design dependency is missing. This is not the case with certain types of spare parts

115 [1986] 2 WLR 400.

116 'Connection' is taken in a wide sense here, covering all the situations described in the Copyright, Designs and Patents Act 1988 s 213(3)(b).

such as body panels for motor cars but the exception does not appear to extend to other articles where there is some latitude, such as in the case of vacuum cleaners and, probably also, many other household articles. The 'must-fit' exception allows competition in spare parts from manufacturers who only copy interfaces but independently design other features.

Another example of the 'must-fit' exception is where a manufacturer makes a television set and sells it together with a stand on which the set can be supported and swivelled around. The connection between the stand and the base of the television set (the mechanical interface) is not protected by the design right. All other features of the shape or configuration of both the television set and the stand are in principle (subject to the other requirements such as originality) capable of design right protection. Another manufacturer can make replacement stands for the television sets, copying details of the interface but no other details, unless they are commonplace or if the design right in relation to them has expired.

Even if there is design dependency so that the 'must-match' exception applies, it may not apply to all the design features of the article in question. Again, the motor car can provide a good example. Consider replacement doors for a car. They obviously have to be a certain profile on the outside to match the sweep of the bodywork and would look extremely odd if they did not have this profile. The replacement doors also have to be a certain shape to fit the gap left for the door in the car body and to follow the lines and contours of the outer shape of the car. All these features are excepted from the design right. There is a high level of design dependency. However, most car doors have an inner skin which is hidden from view by upholstery. The inner skin of a car door usually has holes to reduce the overall weight and stiffening ribs for strength and may also contain a side impact bar and/or airbag. The position and size of the holes and configuration of the ribs and other features are irrelevant as regards appearance and, if their design is original, they may be protected by the design right and do not fall within the scope of the exception. Spare parts manufacturers must be aware of this and be careful not to copy those aspects of shape or configuration in which a design right might subsist and only to copy those elements falling within the exceptions. It must not be forgotten that a design in which the design right subsists may relate to a part of an article and that that part may be internal. It may be difficult, in many cases, to determine where the design right does and does not apply. Also, whether a particular right has expired could be extremely difficult to ascertain as there is not the benefit of a registration system and register that can be consulted to resolve such questions.

Surface decoration

We have seen that a raised embossed or ribbed surface may be held to be a feature of shape or configuration. But is the converse true and what are the limits on surface decoration? Does it extend beyond decoration which is flat or planar? It would seem sensible to assume that the intention was the exclusion from design right protection of *decoration applied to the surface* of an article. That decoration may take many forms. It could be painted decoration or it could be a raised or embossed pattern. It could be like the dimples on a golf ball or plaster mouldings fixed to a fireplace surround or item of furniture. *Mark Wilkinson Furniture Ltd* v *Woodcraft Designs (Radcliffe) Ltd*[117] concerned an alleged infringement of design right subsisting in furniture for fitted kitchens. Noting that the Act gave no assistance, Parker J said (at 73) that 'surface decoration' includes:

117 [1998] FSR 63.

> . . . both decoration lying on the surface of the article (for example, a painted finish) and decorative features of the surface itself (for example, beading or engraving).

Parker J decided that the painted surface, the cockbeading (a chamfered edge to the line around a recess) and v-grooves (vertical grooves accentuating the curved corners of the units) were surface decoration, but not the cornice nor the recessed panels in the doors which formed part of the overall shape and configuration of the units and were themselves subject to surface decoration.[118] This latter explanation, that features are not likely to be surface decoration if they themselves are subject to surface decoration, appears attractive at first sight. However, it can be of little assistance in practice if simply applying paint is surface decoration. If a carved shallow wooden relief moulding is applied to the surface of a wooden fire surround, for example, does it cease to be surface decoration if it is painted, varnished, sandblasted or subjected to further detailed carving?

In *Mark Wilkinson*, Parker J rejected a claim by the defendant that the 'must-match' exception applied as the appearance of each unit was dependent upon the appearance of another article with which it was intended to form an integral part, that other article being the whole fitted kitchen. It was held that the fitted kitchen was made up of a number of matching units, none of which formed an integral part of another.

Whilst surface decoration can be three-dimensional, the fact that something exists only in a small third dimension does not automatically mean that it is surface decoration. In such cases, according to Park J in *A Fulton Co Ltd* v *Grant Barnett & Co Ltd*,[119] there is a value judgment for the court to make. There he held that the outwardly pointing seams of the umbrella case were significant aspects of the shape or configuration of the case and more than merely surface decoration. In *Lambretta Clothing Co Ltd* v *Teddy Smith (UK) Ltd*,[120] Jacob LJ said that a debate about whether design right is limited to three-dimensional articles does not assist. The right could subsist in what was normally considered to be a flat or two-dimensional thing such as a new design for a doily. All articles, even thin flat ones, are three-dimensional if one takes a Euclidean view of the world.

In *Lambretta*, the Court of Appeal held that the fact that colour runs through the thickness of a garment does not mean to say that it is not surface decoration. The exclusion for surface decoration still applied otherwise it would depend on how deep the colours went and Parliament could not have intended such a capricious result. Following *Mark Wilkinson*, the Court of Appeal accepted that surface decoration was not limited to something that was essentially flat.

In *Dyson Ltd* v *Qualtex (UK) Ltd*,[121] it was argued that the design right could only subsist in three-dimensional designs. Consequently, the surface decoration exclusion applied to three-dimensional shapes only. Jacob LJ rejected this and he gave an example of a two-dimensional shape, being a shape cut out from a piece of paper. He said that what was essentially two-dimensional decoration could be applied to three-dimensional objects, an example being a willow pattern applied to a plate. The reason for the exclusion of surface decoration was because it could be protected by copyright instead. This was the result of s 51 of the Copyright, Designs and Patents Act 1988. Jacob LJ considered that design law should conform with what the ordinary reasonable consumer or designer would perceive as a decorated surface. That being so, the ribbing on the wand handle was not surface decoration. Furthermore, features which had a significant function should not be classed as surface decoration. The ribbing of the wand handle of the vacuum cleaner served the purpose of providing a grip and, therefore, was not surface decoration.

Duration of design right

An important date in measuring the duration of a design right is the end of the calendar year during which the design was first either recorded in a design document or an article was made to the design. In other words, this is the end of the calendar year during which the right came into existence. In the discussion below, this date is referred to as the 'end of the creation year'. The generosity of the law with regard to the duration of protection

118 Otherwise, the design right applied to other features and was held to be infringed.

119 [2001] RPC 16.

120 [2005] RPC 6 at para 24.

121 [2006] RPC 31.

for functional designs through their drawings was severely curtailed and now the maximum length of protection for a functional design by way of the design right is 15 years from the end of the creation year. In many cases, where the design has been commercially exploited, the period will be less than that. If articles made to the design have been made available for sale or hire anywhere in the world by or with the licence of the owner of the right within five years from the end of the creation year then, by s 216(1)(b), the design right expires ten years from the end of the calendar year during which that happened (the end of the first exploitation year).

In *Dyson Ltd v Qualtex (UK) Ltd*, the meaning of making available for sale or hire was considered. It fell to be decided whether it should be construed on the basis of the date that orders for articles to the design were placed or the date when the articles which had been ordered were actually delivered. This could make a difference to the total duration of the design right, depending of the actual times of placing orders and delivery, for example, when orders were placed on 3 November 2008 but the articles were not delivered until 2 February 2009. Jacob LJ agreed with the finding of Mann J, at first instance, on this point where he said that the natural meaning of 'made available' suggests that something is actually in existence. Taking orders for articles which are not yet made is not making them available for sale or hire. In the above example, the design right will expire at the end of 2019, not 2018.[122] Similarly, licences of right will be available from the end of 2014, not the end of 2013.

The owner of the design right is given, effectively, ten years to exploit his design. However, during the last five years licences are available as of right.[123] The possible reduction in the term of protection from 15 years will not occur if articles made to the design have been offered for sale or hire by a person without the permission of the owner of the right, for example in the case of counterfeit articles, or if articles made to the design are placed in a public exhibition. However, if the owner of the design delays beyond the first five years, that will eat into the time he has in which to exploit the work. Figure 18.2

122 Assuming, of course, that the design subject to the design right was not created before the end of 2003.

123 Copyists must still beware of other areas of law which might apply to the articles such as registered design or passing off. In practice the owner will have little more than ten years depending on the time of year he commences offering articles for sale or hire.

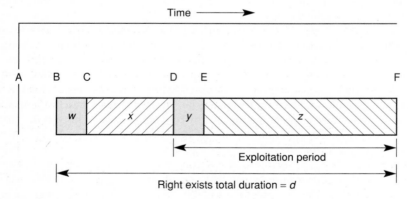

Key:
A – Designer has idea for a design
B – Design recorded in a design document or article made to design (creation)
C – End of calendar year during which creation happens (end of creation year)
D – Articles made to the design are made available for sale or hire (first exploitation)
E – End of calendar year during which articles to design are made available for sale or hire (end of first exploitation year)
F – Right expires.

Figure 18.2 **Duration of design right**

shows how the duration rules work, assuming that, at some time, articles made to the design are made available for sale or hire.

If period x is less than five years, then the total duration of the right, d, is $w + x + y + 10$ years, that is, $z = 10$ years (Date E + 10 years). However, if period x is more than five years, the total duration of the right, d, is $w + 15$ years (Date C + 15 years) and the period z is reduced accordingly. For example, if the design was created (and put in a tangible form) in April 1998, but articles made to the design were not made available for sale or hire until July 2005, the right expires at the end of year 2013. It is, therefore, important to exploit the design commercially within the first five years for maximum duration of commercial protection.

Design rights will always expire at the end of a calendar year irrespective of the actual dates of creation or first exploitation. In Figure 18.2, time interval A to B is of no relevance as regards the design right. Of course, during this period, the design right has not yet been born and there is no remedy in design law if it is reproduced, say from an oral description, although there may be a remedy under the law of breach of confidence. If the oral description is recorded on magnetic tape, with or without the permission of the designer, the right is born because the design has been recorded in a design document, and the definition of 'design document' in s 263(1) should be wide enough to include this form of storage. However, the description would have to be sufficiently precise so that the design can be appreciated for what it is. The person recording the design will have no design right in it by reason of having recorded it because rights are allocated by reference to the designer who is the person who creates the design. The designer need not be the person recording the design.[124] However, a person who records an oral description of a design will have rights under copyright law in the sound recording thus created.

Ownership

The rules for first ownership of the design right are fairly straightforward and the situation is more satisfactory than is the case with works of copyright where the concepts of an implied licence or of beneficial ownership may be called upon to do justice in the case of commissioned works where no provision has been made for ownership. Of course, first ownership is conditioned by the route to qualification and four possibilities exist, there being a one-to-one correlation between the qualifying individual or person and the first owner.

1 *Qualification by reference to the designer*, that is, in respect of a design not created either in the course of employment or in pursuance of a commission. In this case, the designer is the first owner of the design right.[125]
2 *Qualification by reference to the commissioner*. The commissioner is the first owner of the design right.
3 *Qualification by reference to the employer* (not being a design created in the pursuance of a commission). The employer is the first owner of the design right.
4 *Qualification by reference to the first marketing of articles made to the design*. The person so marketing the articles is the first owner of the design right.

The provisions as to ownership were considered in detail in *Ultraframe (UK) Ltd v Fielding*[126] in which the two parties claimed to be entitled to the design right subsisting in the design of roof panels for conservatory roofs. The designs in question had been created by a Mr Davies who operated through various companies as *de facto* controlling director.[127] Mr Davies became bankrupt and the trustee in bankruptcy purported to assign the design rights to the claimant. The defendants were directors of a company which claimed that it derived title by an assignment of the design rights from Mr Davies' companies, now

124 This point was made by Aldous J in *C & H Engineering v F Klucznik & Sons Ltd* [1992] FSR 421.

125 The basic statements of first ownership are contained in the Copyright, Designs and Patents Act 1988 s 215.

126 [2004] RPC 24.

127 At one time, he owned all the shares in some of the companies which failed and, after he was convicted of offences under s 217 of the Insolvency Act 1986, he was disqualified from acting as a company director but a new company was set up through nominees and he continued to act as director and controller of the company.

defunct. If the designs had been created by Mr Davies as an employee of his companies or under a commission for money or money's worth with his companies, those companies would have been the first owners, as appropriate, of the design rights and the defendants' company which derived title through those companies would now own the design rights. On the other hand, if Mr Davies owned the design rights, they would have passed to the claimant from his trustee in bankruptcy. The defendants further claimed that, if the designs were not created by Mr Davies in pursuance of a commission or in the course of employment, then he held the designs on trust for his companies.

At first instance, Laddie J held that Mr Davies created the designs as an employee in the course of his employment and the fact that he was a director and controlling shareholder did not prevent him from being an employee. The Court of Appeal dismissed the claimant's appeal but held that when Mr Davies created the designs he was acting as a trustee of the company. Important aspects of the case are set out below.

Employee designs

The meaning of employee has its well-understood meaning of employment acting under a contract of service or apprenticeship: s 263(1). Waller LJ said that Laddie J failed to take into account guidance by Lord Woolf CJ in *Secretary of State for Trade and Industry* v *Bottrill*[128] to the effect that factors such as the degree of control exercised by the company over the shareholder employee should be taken into account. This suggests consideration of whether there are other directors and whether the constitution of the company is such that he is answerable only to himself and is incapable of being dismissed. If he is a director, do the articles of association allow him to vote on matters in which he has a personal interest, such as termination of his contract of employment. Mutuality of obligation is also an important factor – an irreducible minimum of obligation on each side to create a contract of service: *Nethermere (St Neots) Ltd* v *Taverna*.[129]

Waller LJ said that Laddie J failed to make the distinction between Mr Davies working for the company in producing the designs because he was a 100 per cent shareholder and would benefit by virtue of that fact and creating the designs because he was under an obligation to do so under a contract of service. Although, as a 100 per cent shareholder, Mr Davies gave the orders and exercised control, albeit of himself, this may not remove the irreducible minimum of control but it must be by way of an obligation as an employee. Waller LJ said (at para 25):

> Did Mr Davies as the 100% shareholder and director of the companies place himself under an obligation to be at work a certain number of hours per week, and any obligation to produce designs in return for the £250 per week? The proper inference from the findings of fact would in my view be a clear 'no'.[130]

Commissioned designs

For a commissioned design to belong to the commissioner at first instance, it must be created *in pursuance of* the commission. Waller LJ referred to *Apple Corps Ltd* v *Cooper*,[131] concerning the position of commissioned photographs under the Copyright Act 1956. In that case, it was held that the act of commissioning must come before the creation of the work, imposing an obligation to pay for the work, prior to its creation.[132] In *Ultraframe*, Mr Davies had not placed himself under any obligation to produce the designs before he produced them, just as he did not have any equivalent obligation as an employee. If, for example, he failed to produce the designs, it was obvious that the companies would not have been entitled to sue him for breach of contract. Therefore design rights did not belong to the companies on the basis that they were created under a commission for money or money's worth.

128 [2000] 1 All ER 915.

129 [1984] IRLR 240.

130 Mr Davies drew £250 per week by way of wages.

131 [1993] FSR 286.

132 Copyright Act 1956 s 4(3). This vested copyright in a photograph made in pursuance of a commission where the person commissioning the photograph paid for it or agreed to pay for it. This should be contrasted with the position under the Copyright, Designs and Patents Act 1988 in respect of ownership of copyright works.

133 [2006] FSR 7.

In respect of commissioned designs, in *Sales* v *Stromberg*,[133] it was confirmed that an agreement to pay for a design provisional upon it being liked by the person alleging that it was created under a commission did not fall within the provisions for commissioned designs. A letter stating that, if they liked the design, the defendants would pay a royalty (of unspecified amount) to the claimant or, alternatively, manufacture articles to the design exclusively for the claimant was far from being a letter of commission.

Designer as trustee

Directors are fiduciary agents for their company and trustees of the property of the company in their hands or under their control. A transaction distributing a company's assets to shareholders other than by way of distribution of profit lawfully made or by a reduction of capital sanctioned by the court would be *ultra vires*. Waller LJ referred to Hoffmann J (as he then was) in *Aveling Barford Ltd* v *Perion Ltd*[134] where he said (at 631):

134 [1989] BCLC 626.

> A company can only lawfully deal with its assets in furtherance of its objects. The corporators may take assets out of the company by way of dividend, or, with the leave of the court, by way of reduction of capital, or in a winding up. They may of course acquire them for full consideration. They cannot take assets out of the company by way of voluntary disposition, however described, and if they attempt to do so, the disposition is ultra vires the company.

135 From *Re Duomatic Ltd* [1969] 2 Ch 365.

An argument that the 'Duomatic principle'[135] applied to the effect that all shareholders may formally or informally assent to or approve an arrangement or a transaction so that it is binding on the company was rejected because the principle cannot apply to *ultra vires* transactions. Furthermore, there was no evidence of any specific act of assent by Mr Davies nor was there any evidence of any act of ratification. Waller LJ said that to say 'the shareholders would have been happy if they had been asked' was not enough. In fact the documents suggested the opposite. There was a post-dated contract of employment produced. This indicated that it was Mr Davies' intention to ensure the rights vested in his company.[136] Later, there was a purported assignment of the design rights from that company to a new company which Mr Davies controlled through nominees. In the circumstances, therefore, Waller LJ held that Mr Davies held the design rights on trust for the company through whom he was operating his business at the time he created the designs.

136 This was produced to prevent an inference being drawn that he was a director or *de facto* director of the company.

Joint designs and joint ownership

Joint first owners are possible where there is a joint design, being one created by two or more designers acting in collaboration where the contribution of each is not distinct from the other(s).[137] A joint owner's contribution need not be in respect of recording the design but it has to be in relation to the design itself and it is not sufficient if it only relates to the manufacture of articles made to the design. For example, in *Philip Parker* v *Stephen Tidball*,[138] one of the defendants was responsible for stitching together leather cases for mobile telephones. He made suggestions and contributions but they related to the construction of the cases and not to their design. Consequently, he was not a joint owner of the designs in issue. Similarly, in *A Fulton Co Ltd* v *Grant Barnett & Co Ltd*,[139] persons making moulds for umbrella handles and sewing machinists making cases for the umbrellas were working under the instructions of an employee of the claimant and were not, subsequently, designers in respect of the design right.

137 Section 259(1).

138 [1997] FSR 680.

139 [2001] RPC 16.

140 If the designers' contributions are distinct then each will be regarded as the sole designer in respect of his own efforts: Copyright, Designs and Patents Act 1988 s 259(1). The design is thus divisible and can be regarded as a combination of separate designs which can be owned by different persons.

141 *See* Copyright, Designs and Patents Act 1988 ss 218(4), 219(3) and 220(3).

A joint design will satisfy the qualification requirements if only one individual or person meets those requirements.[140] This leaves the problem of what rights the other joint designers, commissioners, etc. have in terms of ownership, and the approach taken by the Act is that they have absolutely none; only those individuals or persons who meet the qualification requirements are entitled to the design right.[141] For example, if a design is created by three self-employed designers, one being a British citizen, one being a French citizen and the third being a Taiwanese citizen, as far as UK law is concerned, assuming the design was not created in pursuance of a commission, the joint first owners of the design will be the British citizen and the French citizen; the Taiwanese citizen will not be entitled to any ownership rights unless he qualifies by virtue of being habitually resident in a qualifying country. However, the ownership provisions are relatively generous in the scope of their reach and protection is afforded, for example, to citizens of Member States of the European Economic Community without there being any equivalent and reciprocal provisions for protection of functional designs created by British citizens in the EU unless by virtue of copyright law or individual national design laws.[142] In all cases, the place where the design was created is irrelevant.

> 142 Of course, a design might also be subject to the unregistered Community design and, if registered, Community and national registered designs.

Assignment and licensing

Design rights can be assigned but, under s 222(3), this must be done in writing and signed by or on behalf of the assignor. The right can also pass by testamentary disposition or by operation of law.[143] An assignment may be partial, limited to apply to not all the exclusive rights of the owner, or limited in terms of duration. Licences may be granted by the owner and may be exclusive or otherwise. An exclusive licence, under s 225, must be in writing signed by or on behalf of the design right owner and an exclusive licensee has the same rights and remedies, except against the owner, as if the licence had been an assignment.[144] The Act contains provisions for the exercise of concurrent rights by the owner and an exclusive licensee.[145] Although there is little practical difference between an assignment and a licence, the latter is vulnerable if the design right is assigned to a purchaser in good faith for valuable consideration and without actual or constructive notice of the licence. This also applies to persons taking the right through a *bona fide* purchaser, even if such other persons have knowledge of the licence or are made a gift of the design right.

> 143 An example of the latter would be in the case of the liquidation of a company that owns a design right.

> 144 Copyright, Designs and Patents Act 1988 s 234(1).
> 145 Copyright, Designs and Patents Act 1988 s 235.

Of course, an assignment grants a proprietary interest whereas a licence, even an exclusive licence, does not. This applies to all forms of intellectual property rights and accords with the law on licences generally.[146] An exclusive licence is, however, a right over property and a non-cash asset for the purposes of the Companies Act 2005 and previous Companies Acts.[147] This was confirmed in *Ultraframe (UK) Ltd v Fielding (No 2)*[148] in relation to an exclusive licence under unregistered design rights. It fell to be classed as a noncash asset for the Companies Act. Although assignments and exclusive licences are different and have different effects, they are both non-cash assets.[149] It would be inconsistent otherwise as assignments and exclusive licences can have very similar economic effect. It does not follow that a non-exclusive licence can be classed as a right over property. The reason is that an exclusive licence grants the right to carry out certain acts *to the exclusion of the owner* of the intellectual property right.

> 146 *See*, for example, *Thomas v Sorrell* (1671) 2 Keb 791.
> 147 A non-cash asset is defined as any property or interest in property, other than cash: s 1163 Companies Act 2005.
> 148 [2006] FSR 17.
> 149 Under s 190 of the Companies Act 2005, as with previous companies legislation, there are controls over the acquisition by directors and connected persons acquiring substantial non-cash assets from the company and vice versa. *Ultraframe* concerned the equivalent provision under the Companies Act 1985 (s 320).

A future design right, one that will or may come into existence, can be dealt with by assignment or licence just as an existing design right.[150] Prospective ownership of design right is provided for under s 223 in a like manner to copyright. Thus it is possible for the prospective owner of design right to assign that right to another by an agreement in writing and signed by or on behalf of the prospective owner. On the right coming into existence, the right will automatically vest in the assignee but will be subject to any licences granted by the prospective owner except a purchaser in good faith for valuable consideration and without actual or constructive notice or any person deriving title from him. An assignment of future design rights can apply to rights which will or might come into existence in respect of a future design or class of designs or upon the occurrence of

> 150 Copyright, Designs and Patents Act 1988 s 223.

some future event. Thus, a person who would otherwise be the first owner of a set of designs to be applied to a set of cutlery may assign those rights to a person who may reassign those rights to yet another person, and so on, before the design rights have come into existence.

In the case of a design where there is an overlap between a design right and a UK registered design, that is when both rights apply to a design, an assignment of the registered design right[151] serves also to assign the design right if the proprietor of the registered design is also the person who owns the design right, and vice versa, unless a contrary intention appears.[152] However, although it will be unusual, it is possible for the two rights to become separated, for example by an express term to the contrary in the document containing an assignment of either right. The automatic transfer of the other right is a presumption only. Of course, in such circumstances the person obtaining the one right will clearly know that the other right is not to be assigned to him and will be able to predict what he can and cannot do in relation to the design. If there is some doubt – for example, if the words expressing the contrary intention are not clear – the *contra proferentum*[153] rule of construction might be applied by the court, or a licence might be implied. At first sight, it might appear that the qualification requirements could frequently lead to separate ownership of the rights. However, under s 3(3) of the Registered Designs Act 1949, the Registrar will not entertain an application for registration of a design unless it is made by the person claiming to be the owner of the UK design right.[154]

Licences are available as of right in relation to the design right during the last five years of the subsistence of the right, under s 237. If the parties are unable to agree terms they will be settled by the Comptroller-General of Patents, Designs and Trade Marks (the 'Comptroller'). This provision significantly weakens the design right. It could be argued that, because the design right is not a monopoly right and because it is further constrained by wide-ranging exceptions, there is no need for this provision.

The would-be licensee under a licence as of right may be faced with one problem stemming from the lack of formalities for the right. That problem is how to determine the date at which the design has five years left to run. It may be difficult to determine when the design was created or first commercially exploited. In the circumstances, the owner of the right is unlikely to be particularly helpful about dates. Another difficulty for the potential licensee is that other rights may apply, such as the UK registered design and/or Community design, and licences are unlikely to be available for such other rights.

Under s 247, the licence of right takes effect from the date the application for such is made to the Comptroller or, if the application is made before licences of right are available, the earliest date such licences are available. No application can be made earlier than one year before the earliest date that licences are available as of right. Although the language of s 237(2) is in terms of the licence being settled by the Comptroller in default of agreement, it is not necessary for the parties to have entered into negotiations before an application for a licence of right can be made.[155]

Although a person applying for a licence of right might hope to limit the damages available against him in any subsequent infringement action (see later in respect to s 239), the Comptroller has no jurisdiction to take potential damages into account when settling the terms of a licence. The normal way in working out the payment to be made is to consider the right owner as right owner and not as a potential supplier. A 'willing parties' basis should be used if comparable licences exist[156] but, if not, a profits available approach could be used.[157] There is little point in including a termination for breach clause as the licensee can immediately apply for a new licence of right and, as licence is imposed on the right owner, it is inappropriate for there to be warranty to the effect that it subsists in the design and the licensor is indeed the true owner of the right. A licence of right in respect of the design right cannot affect other rights, such as copyright, trade mark rights, the UK registered design or Community design.[158]

151 Copyright, Designs and Patents Act 1988 s 224. There is no equivalent presumption in relation to the Community design.

152 Registered Designs Act 1949 s 19(3B).

153 This rule is used particularly in the context of exclusion clauses where a term that one person relies on to exclude or limit his liability (for example, under a contract where one party seeks to exclude his liability for breach of contract) is ambiguous. The court will usually take the meaning which is least favourable to the party seeking to rely on the term.

154 The Registered Designs Act 1949 s 19(3A) imposes similar requirements in respect of registration of an interest in a registered design. The applicant for registration has to sign a declaration to this effect.

155 *Stafford Engineering Services Ltd's Licence of Right (Copyright) Application* [2000] RPC 797. This case involved an application under the transitional copyright but the principles are the same.

156 This operates on the fiction that the parties are happy to negotiate a licence and licences in relation to designs applied to similar articles may provide a guideline as to the royalty rate they would be likely to agree to. Of course, in most cases, the design right owner will be very unwilling to have a licence forced upon him, often in favour of a competitor. This is made even worse when the track record of the Comptroller in settling terms is considered and royalty payments are often set at no more than a few per cent, arguably much less than if a licence was being freely negotiated.

157 *NIC Instrument Ltd's Licence of Right (Design Right) Application* [2005] RPC 1. The profits available approach looks at the overall profit likely to result from the right and to apportion this between the parties.

158 Of course, being of much shorter duration, the unregistered Community design will almost certainly have expired before application can be made for a licence of right in respect of the UK design right.

Rights of owner and infringement

Under s 226(1), the owner of a design right subsisting in a design has the exclusive right to reproduce the design for commercial purposes by making articles to the design, or by making a design document recording the design for the purpose of enabling such articles to be made. 'Commercial purposes' refers to things done with a view to the article in question being sold or hired in the course of business.[159] As the definition in s 226(2) of 'reproduction' in relation to making articles to the design uses the word 'copying', the design right will not be infringed by a person who independently produces an article made to the same design. Copying a design by making articles exactly or substantially to the design is reproduction by making articles to the design, but substantiality appears to be construed differently to its qualitative meaning in copyright law. In *Baby Dan AS* v *Brevi SRL*,[160] it was held that, where differences between the design in question and earlier designs are small, making the degree of originality small, the claimant can only succeed if the differences between the claimant's design and defendant's design are closer in comparison. The test of whether the articles are exactly, or substantially, to the same design is answered by looking through the eyes of the person to whom the designs are directed.

Apart from the above, the same general principles apply as for infringement of copyright by copying in that there must be a causal connection. That is, the infringing design must have been copied, directly or indirectly, from the first design.[161] Whilst it is rare for there to be direct evidence of copying, a close similarity coupled with an opportunity for copying will often be sufficient to change the burden of proof. This applies equally to the design right as it does copyright.[162] In *Sales* v *Stromberg*[163] the judge said that the objective similarity between the claimant's spiral copper tube design and one of the defendant's designs was such to raise an inference of copying. However, he did not need to consider that inference as there was correspondence between the parties sufficient to provide evidence of a causal connection. The requirement to show copying may be one good reason why it is preferable to register a design as a UK registered design or a registered Community design, if the design meets the requirement for registrability under those systems.

Primary infringement

The design right is infringed by any person who does anything without the licence of the right owner which is by virtue of s 226 the exclusive right of the owner. In *C & H Engineering* v *F Klucznik & Sons Ltd*,[164] in an action brought by the claimant who claimed infringement of copyright in his drawings of lamb creep feeders, the defendant counterclaimed that the claimant had infringed his design right in pig fenders.[165] The pig fender in question had a round tube attached to the top edge. Apart from this tube, the design of the pig fender was commonplace. It was held that s 226 required the owner of the design right to show copying before infringement could be proved, and in this respect the design right is similar to copyright. However, the test for infringement is different, requiring the alleged infringing article to be compared with the design document or model embodying the design to discover whether the alleged infringing article is made exactly to the design or substantially to that design. This requires an objective test, through the eyes of the person to whom the design is directed (in this case, a pig farmer), looking at the differences and similarities between the designs.[166] In this particular case, Aldous J held that there was no infringement – the claimant's pig fender was not made to the defendant's design or made substantially to that design. The objective pig farmer would consider the two designs to be different but with a similar design feature, that is a round bar or tube around the top.

159 Copyright, Designs and Patents Act 1988 s 263(3).

160 [1999] FSR 377.

161 *Mark Wilkinson Furniture Ltd* v *Woodcraft Designs (Radcliffe) Ltd* [1998] FSR 63 at 74 per Parker J.

162 *A Fulton Co Ltd* v *Grant Barnett & Co Ltd* [2001] RPC 16 at para 95. In that case, the judge found copying had taken place on this basis.

163 [2006] FSR 7.

164 [1992] FSR 421.

165 A pig fender is a device placed around the entrance to a pig shelter to allow the sow to step out into the field while retaining the piglets.

166 In *Mark Wilkinson Furniture Ltd* v *Woodcraft Designs (Radcliffe) Ltd* [1998] FSR 63 it was accepted that infringement should be looked at through the eyes of a person to whom the design was directed: for example, a person interested in buying articles made to the design.

To show infringement, two separate criteria must be present – copying and making articles exactly or substantially to the design. Mere similarity between the design and the alleged infringement is not enough. Of course, where copying is established, except in the case of an incompetent copyist, it is likely that the copy will be exactly or substantially to the design. In the absence of evidence of copying, such a level of similarity cannot infringe the unregistered design right, though a rebuttable inference of copyright may be raised.[167] The role of experts in relation to this question is to point out to the court the similarities and differences between the designs so that the court can come to a view as to whether such an inference exists. If an expert concentrates on the similarities alone or differences alone, this can lead to an unbalanced view.

The design right does not protect abstract underlying ideas and underlying concepts. In *Rolawn Ltd* v *Turfmech Machinery Ltd*,[168] Mann J said (at para 79):

> . . . the concept of 'design' (which is what is protected) which is a physical manifestation of an idea, not some underlying abstraction, and it is reinforced by the definition of the 'designer' in section 214 as: 'the person who *creates* [the design]' (my emphasis). You cannot create a design until you have actually reduced it to a particular form. It is not a design while it is a conception in the designer's head, and it becomes a design when it takes physical shape on paper or in the flesh.

It was held that Rolawn could not claim a design right in the concept of a mower having arms folding back on themselves at the mid-way point. If anything, what had been copied was methods or principles of construction which are excluded from the design right. Consequently, there was no infringement of design right.

In *Red Spider Technology* v *Omega Completions Technology*,[169] there was an allegation of copying the design of a valve. This was rejected as it was held that, at best, only basic ideas had been copied which the defendant had taken from drawings in the claimant's patent application for the valve. The representations in the drawings were not the actual design of the valve.

Where the design is for a functional article, some caution must be used when testing for infringement because functional articles may have a similar appearance without copying. As Mummery LJ said in *Farmers Build Ltd* v *Carier Bulk Materials Handling Ltd*:[170]

> Substantial similarity of design might well give rise to a suspicion and an allegation of copying in cases where substantial similarity was often not the result of copying but an inevitable consequence of the functional nature of the design . . . Copying may be inferred from proof of access to the protected work, coupled with substantial similarity. This may lead to unfounded infringement claims in the case of functional works, which are usually bound to be substantially similar to one another . . . in the field of designs of functional articles, one design may be very similar to, or even identical with, another design and yet not be a copy: it may be an original and independent shape and configuration coincidentally the same or similar.

HH Judge Birss QC referred to Mummery LJ's statement as to functional designs in the Patents County Court in *Albert Packaging Ltd* v *Nampak Cartons & Healthcare Ltd*,[171] which concerned a design for a carton with a transparent window for packaging tortilla wraps. He accepted that the claimant's carton was protected by the design right and he rejected an argument that the defendant had not copied. However, he held that the defendant's carton design had multiple identifiable sources (some of which were its own designs) and the only aspects of the claimant's design to have been copied were three dimensions. These were height of the carton to a shoulder, the height from the shoulder to the top and the depth of the carton. On this basis he held that the defendant's design was not substantially to the claimant's design.

It was accepted in *Ocular Sciences Ltd* v *Aspect Vision Care Ltd*[172] that the design right can subsist in detailed dimensions, for example, applied to a range of articles which differ

167 Per Lewison J in *Virgin Atlantic Airways Ltd* v *Premium Aircraft Interiors Group Ltd* [2009] ECDR 11.

168 [2008] RPC 27.

169 [2010] EWHC 59 (Ch).

170 [1999] RPC 461 at 481–2.

171 [2011] EWPCC 15.

172 [1997] RPC 289.

only slightly from one another, even if those differences are not readily distinguishable by the naked eye. However, where the design right subsists in relation to such detailed dimensions, for infringement to be made out the defendant's designs must be extremely close to those of the claimant. In this case, the designs were for a range of contact lenses (220 designs in total) and Laddie J found that some of the defendant's designs were extremely close to those of the claimant. However, he accepted that there had been no act of copying the claimant's designs and, consequently, there could be no infringement.

Indirect reproduction also infringes, and it is immaterial whether any intervening acts themselves infringe. Therefore, if reproduction is preceded by taking apart an article made to the design it will still be an infringement. However, if such 'reverse engineering' is done so that only non-protected elements can be copied – for example, features, that fall within the 'must-fit' or 'must-match' exceptions – then there will be no infringement of the design. Making a drawing of an article made to the design will infringe only if it is done for the purpose of enabling such articles to be made, so that making a drawing to be displayed in an exhibition of drawings will not infringe design right.[173] However, giving or selling the drawing to a manufacturer who intends to make the article would infringe if that was the purpose of making the drawing because it enables articles to be made to the design. It would appear from the language of s 226(1) that the 'purpose of enabling' should be present at the time the drawing, or other design document, was made.

In the Scottish case of *Squirewood Ltd* v *H Morris & Co Ltd*[174] the Court of Session granted an interim interdict[175] to restrain an alleged infringement of the design right subsisting in office furniture. Together with the *Mark Wilkinson* case, in which kitchen units were held to be protected, this case shows that the design right is not restricted to purely functional articles, but also applies to articles for which appearance is important in the eye of the person acquiring articles made to the design.

Copying parts of an article

It has already been noted that the design right can apply to a part of an article, but in his interpretation of the test for infringement Aldous J compared the design of the whole articles. This view is supported by the language of s 226(2), which speaks of reproduction in terms of producing articles (not parts of articles) exactly or substantially to the design.[176] This weakens the right where it is applied or limited to a part of an article only and, as in the *C & H Engineering* case, a significant design improvement may accordingly go unprotected. Turner suggests the judge was wrong to look at the whole of the article in testing for infringement;[177] but this appears to be what the statute requires.

Lewison J noted the linguistic mismatch between subsistence and infringement in *Virgin Atlantic Airways Ltd* v *Premium Aircraft Interiors Group Ltd*,[178] where he said in relation to a part of an article, being a teapot spout in his example (at para 31):

> First, although the Act allows design right to subsist in (and be claimed for) part of an article, the definition of reproduction speaks only of making 'articles'. There is, therefore, a linguistic mismatch between subsistence of design right and the right that it confers. But it must obviously have been Parliament's intention that if design right subsisted in part of an article (e.g. the teapot spout) the right would be infringed by incorporating a copy of that spout in another teapot, even if the infringing spout is not itself a whole article. Second, even if the design has been copied, the infringing article must be produced 'exactly or substantially' to the copied design. Mere similarity is not enough.

There is force in Lewison J's view that infringement must concentrate on the part on the article said to have been copied. It may be that the use of the term 'making articles to the design' in s 226(1) was an oversight in drafting. Perhaps the best view is that 'making articles to the design' should be read as 'making articles incorporating the design'. If the design right can subsist in part of an article, as a matter of logic, protection must follow

173 There may be an infringement of the copyright in the drawings in such cases.

174 (Unreported) 1 April 1993. For a description and discussion, *see* MacQueen, H.L. 'A Scottish Case on Unregistered Designs' [1994] 2 EIPR 86.

175 Equivalent to an interim injunction in England and Wales.

176 This approach was followed in *Philip Parker* v *Stephen Tidball* [1997] FSR 680.

177 Turner, B. 'A true design right: *C & H Engineering* v *Klucznik & Sons*' [1993] 1 EIPR 24 at 25.

178 [2009] ECDR 11.

subsistence. Otherwise, slavishly copying an original spout for a teapot and using it in a square teapot when the claimant's teapot is spherical might escape a claim for infringement. That cannot have been Parliament's intention.

By using the test of the eye of the interested person in *C & H Engineering*, Aldous J applied a test not dissimilar to that used for testing for infringement of registered designs. However, the design right can apply to an internal part of an article that may be concealed from view. Comparison of whole articles does not make sense in relation to internal designs and can be undertaken only when the alleged infringing article has been dismantled and the relevant part considered and compared with the equivalent part of the design document or article made to the design.

Copyright infringement requires that the alleged infringing work contains the whole or a substantial part of the original work. This is a different test to whether an article is made substantially to the same design as that alleged to have been infringed. The difference is greater if the design right subsists in the design of part of an article only where the enquiry will be directed to whether the whole design containing an element which has been copied is substantially to the same design as the protected design. The Court of Appeal confirmed this distinction between copyright infringement and design right infringement in *L Woolley Jewellers Ltd* v *A & A Jewellery Ltd*[179] concerning the alleged infringement of the design for a pendant. The judge in the Patents County Court did not direct himself as to the different test for design right compared with copyright and the Court of Appeal remitted the case back to the same judge.[180]

In *A Fulton Co Ltd* v *Totes Isotoner (UK) Ltd*,[181] counsel for the defence spoke of a design chimera[182] in the context of a design which had a missing element (a cut-away) compared with the claimant's design for folding umbrella cases. Where a design relates to parts only of an article, Jacob LJ rejected the analogy, saying that the designer of a whole article necessarily designs all its parts. Although a defendant in a design right action might not know what parts he is alleged to have infringed until the letter before action or claim form, that does not mean that he does not know where he stands. As design right infringement depends on copying, the defendant will know what part or parts he has taken exactly or substantially. Although it is for the design right owner to frame his claim properly, the subsistence of his rights does not depend on how he frames his claim.[183]

Secondary infringement

Another similarity with copyright law is the provision for secondary infringement which approximates to commercial dealing with infringing articles, but there are no equivalent criminal penalties for infringement of the design right as there are in relation to copyright. An infringing article is one the making of which to a particular design was an infringement of the design right subsisting in that design.[184] The definition of 'infringing article' extends to articles which have been or are to be imported into the UK if their making in the UK would have been an infringement or a breach of an exclusive licence in respect of the design. A design document, however, is not an infringing article. Secondary infringement occurs when a person, without the licence of the design right owner, does any of the following acts in relation to an article which is an infringing article and the person knows this or has reason to believe it to be so:

(a) imports into the UK for commercial purposes;
(b) has in his possession for commercial purposes;
(c) sells, hires or offers or exposes for sale or hire, in the course of a business.

It would seem that the knowledge requirement is the same as that for secondary infringement of copyright.[185] To determine whether a person has reason to believe involves the concept of knowledge of facts from which the reasonable man would arrive at the

179 [2003] FSR 15.

180 *L Woolley Jewellers Ltd* v *A & A Jewellery Ltd (No 2)* [2004] FSR 47. The judge confirmed, after applying the correct test, that there had still been an infringement of design right.

181 [2004] RPC 16.

182 A chimera is a mythical fire-breathing female monster with the head of a lion, the body of a goat and a serpent's tail.

183 To that extent, Jacob LJ disagreed with Laddie J's suggestion, in *Ocular Sciences*, that the claimant can trim his claim to fit the alleged infringement.

184 Copyright, Designs and Patents Act 1988 s 228.

185 *See* the discussion of the Court of Appeal decision in *LA Gear Inc* v *Hi-Tec Sports plc* [1992] FSR 121 in Chapter 6.

relevant belief. The test in *LA Gear* was applied by Park J in *A Fulton Co Ltd* v *Grant Barnett & Co Ltd*,[186] in which he held that the defendant was liable also for secondary infringement as the defendant had reason to believe it was dealing with infringing articles. However, it was held that the defendant did not have reason to believe the handle of its umbrella infringed until three weeks after service of a substituted statement of claim.[187] Under s 228(4), there is a useful presumption in favour of the claimant that when an article was made to the design in which the design right subsists or has subsisted, it was made at a time when the right subsisted unless the contrary can be proved. Bearing in mind that the claimant may be the only person with proof of the time the design right first arose, this is very favourable for the claimant.

In *Badge Sales* v *PMS International Group Ltd*,[188] the defendant imported handbags into the UK from China which were alleged to infringe three designs of handbags belonging to the claimant. The defendant asserted that he had no reason to believe that the handbags he imported into the UK were subject to UK design rights. The claimant applied for an interim injunction. Lewison J accepted that the test of knowledge for innocent acquisition was an objective test and the burden of proof was on the defend-ant to show this on a balance of probabilities. This could only be done at trial, rather than an application for interim relief but, nevertheless, s 233(2), which limits damages for innocently acquired articles in allegations of secondary infringement to no more than a reasonable royalty, did not preclude the grant of interim relief in the meantime. An interim injunction was granted pending the substantive hearing of the case, preventing the defendant from selling more handbags from its stock of around 5,500 handbags.[189]

186 [2001] RPC 16.

187 The original statement of claim was too general to put the defendant on notice.

188 [2006] FSR 1.

189 The defendant offered an undertaking not to import any more of the bags in question.

Exceptions to infringement

It is not an infringement to copy features of a design that are excluded from the scope of subsistence of design right or parts of the design of an article that are otherwise not protected, for example, because they lack originality. However, other rights may be infringed, such as registered designs (both the UK and Community registered design), the unregistered Community design, registered trade marks and, in some cases, copyright. By s 236, if copyright subsists in a work which consists of or includes a design in which design right subsists, it is not an infringement of the design right to do anything which is an infringement of the copyright in the work. The overlap of actions between the design right and copyright is removed, leaving an action in copyright only. During the last five years of a design right, licences are available as of right[190] on terms to be fixed by the Comptroller-General of Patents, Designs and Trade Marks in the absence of agreement.[191] The Secretary of State has the power, under s 237(3), to exclude by statutory instrument certain designs from the licence as of right provisions in order to comply with an international obligation, or for purposes relating to reciprocal protection for British designs in other countries.[192] Under s 245, the Secretary of State also has the power on the same basis to provide that certain acts do not infringe design right. In effect, this permits a reduction in the protection offered in respect of a foreign country if that country does not give full reciprocal protection to British designs.

190 This does not apply to the topography right, described later.

191 Licenses of right may also be available under s 238 as a result of the exercise of powers under the Enterprise Act 2002.

192 No such Orders have yet been made.

If the owner of a design right imposes restrictive conditions in a licence or refuses to grant licences, those conditions may be cancelled or modified or licences declared available as of right under certain provisions of the Competition Act 1980 and the Enterprise Act 2002. The terms of licences of right, in default of agreement, shall be settled by the Comptroller.

There are provisions for Crown use of designs subject to the design right. These apply in relation to the defence of the realm, foreign defence purposes and health service purposes, the latter being the provision of primary medical services and dental services, pharmaceutical, general medical or general dental services under relevant legislation. There are provisions for the settlement of terms and the award of compensation if the owner of the right or an exclusive licensee has suffered any loss as a result of not being awarded a contract because of Crown use.[193] It could be argued that the provisions for Crown use are inappropriate here since design right does not give rise to monopolies. However, the provisions may be important if the design is also registered under the Registered Designs Act 1949 or the Community Design Regulation (although the scope of Crown use is more limited in respect of the UK registered design and the registered Community design). It would be a nonsense if Crown use applied to one right and not the other if both rights subsisted in the same design.

193 *See* Copyright, Designs and Patents Act 1988 ss 240–244.

Defences to infringement actions

A person who has allegedly infringed a design right may plead several defences. Again, the best form of defence often is to attack the validity of the right. In the case of the design right, such an attack is almost inevitable. For example, a defendant might plead that:

1 The right is not valid because the features copied fall within the exceptions (for example, they relate to a method or principle of construction).[194]
2 The claimant's design did not originate from the designer or is commonplace and therefore not original in that sense.[195]
3 The qualification requirements are not satisfied in respect of the claimant's design.[196]
4 The design right has expired.
5 The design was recorded prior to 1 August 1989.

194 Copyright, Designs and Patents Act 1988 s 213(3).

195 Copyright, Designs and Patents Act 1988 s 213(4).

196 Copyright, Designs and Patents Act 1988 s 213(5) and ss 218–221.

Assuming that the design is valid, other defences which might be raised by the defendant include:

197 The right to bring a legal action.

(i) The claimant does not have *locus standi*,[197] for example, he is neither the owner nor the exclusive licensee.
(ii) The act does not fall within the scope of primary or secondary infringement.
(iii) The defendant's articles are neither exactly nor substantially made to the claimant's design.
(iv) The alleged infringement occurred before the right existed or after the right expired (but here the defendant has the burden of proof).
(v) In the case of an alleged secondary infringement, the defendant did not know and had no reason to believe that the article was an infringing article (this has the effect of limiting remedies to damages amounting to no more than a reasonable royalty: s 233(2)).
(vi) The act complained of falls within one of the exceptions to infringement – for example, the acts infringe copyright instead (s 236), or under the Secretary of State's powers to Order, under s 245, that specified acts do not infringe (although no such Order has yet been made).
(vii) An undertaking to take a licence of right where such a licence is available under s 239. This is not a complete defence but serves to limit remedies to an award of damages not exceeding double the amount that would have been payable under a licence of right (*see* later).

Acquiescence is always a potential defence where the circumstances are such that the claimant has made it clear by his conduct that he has assented to the infringement and will not commence proceedings in respect of it. As regards the limitation period, for a tort it is six years from the date on which the cause of action arises.[198] Where the infringement continues or is repeated, fresh causes of action will arise. However, s 36 of the Limitation Act 1980 states that nothing in the Act affects 'any equitable jurisdiction to refuse relief on the ground of acquiescence or otherwise'. For acquiescence to apply, it is not enough that the claimant merely delays bringing an action.

In *Farmers Build Ltd v Carier Bulk Materials Handling Ltd*,[199] the claimant knew that its rights were being infringed but decided to wait to see how successful the defendant's infringing machines were. This was not sufficient to count as acquiescence even when the claimant and defendant continued to have a trading relationship during the period the infringement was taking place to the knowledge of the claimant. The Court of Appeal held that the fairly modest delay by the claimant in bringing the action was not sufficient for acquiescence. None of the claimant's conduct would have led the defendant to believe that the infringement was being assented to, nor did the claimant's inactivity or other conduct cause the defendant to act to its detriment in any way.

At first instance, in *Dyson Ltd v Qualtex (UK) Ltd*,[200] a defence based on acquiescence or estoppel was rejected. It appeared that the defendant placed some articles on the market to 'test the water' and, because there had been no objection by the claimant, the defendant was encouraged to copy further designs. However, there was no evidence that the claimant knew of the defendant's activities at a high enough level for some time. There was no evidence of encouragement and there were also problems with detriment. Mann J said that the defendant's activities could be described as an attempt to establish a mutation of estoppel which he described as estoppel by entrapment. This defence was not raised on appeal.

As with the UK registered design and the Community design in relation to the UK, there is provision for a remedy against groundless threats of infringement proceedings. The remedies for groundless threats of infringement proceedings are:

(a) a declaration to the effect that the threats are unjustifiable;
(b) an injunction against the continuation of the threats;
(c) damages, if any have been sustained as a result of the threats.

The burden of proof is on the person making the threats to show that the acts to which the threats relate do, indeed, infringe or will infringe his design right. An exception to the right is in respect to threats consisting of allegations of making or importing anything and it is not a threat of proceedings merely to notify a person that a design is protected by design right.

Licences of right

A further possibility exists for an infringer to limit remedies should he be found to infringe a design right when licences are available as of right in respect of the design, as they are during the last five years of the right.[201] Under s 239, the defendant can undertake to take a licence on terms to be agreed or, failing agreement, on terms to be fixed by the Comptroller. If the defendant makes such an undertaking, an injunction will not be granted against him, no order for delivery up will be made and the amount recoverable in damages or by way of an account of profits shall not exceed double the amount which he would have paid had he obtained a licence on the terms that would have been agreed or fixed by the Comptroller before the earliest infringement.

The undertaking may be given any time before the final order in the proceedings without any admission of liability (s 239(2)). However, the position with respect to interim injunctions is more difficult, especially where the defendant makes the undertaking conditional upon losing at trial. In *Dyrlund Smith A/S v Turberville Smith Ltd*,[202] the claimant was a Danish company which made and sold office furniture. It owned unregistered design

198 Limitation Act 1980 s 2(1).

199 [1999] RPC 461.

200 [2005] RPC 19.

201 Copyright, Designs and Patents Act 1988 s 237.

202 [1998] FSR 774.

rights in three similar designs of office furniture, the design rights in two of which were in their last five years of subsistence. The claimant brought infringement proceedings against the defendants: the first defendant was a company with a paid-up share capital of £2 and the second defendant was the controlling shareholder and director of the first defendant. The defendants claimed that the designs were commonplace and the first defendant offered to undertake to take a licence of right conditional upon losing at trial. The trial judge refused to grant an interim injunction to the claimant.

The claimant's appeal to the Court of Appeal was successful and an interim injunction was granted. It was held that where there is a reasonable ground to doubt the ability of a defendant to accept and comply with the financial provisions in a licence, the defendant should put evidence before the court to show that it has a reasonable prospect of being able to enter into and discharge its obligations under the licence. The Court of Appeal said that there was nothing in the policy of s 239 that bears upon the ordinary principles used in deciding whether or not to grant an interim injunction.[203] Of course, the licence of right takes effect on the date of application and past infringements remain infringements. The only effect of s 239 in respect of such past infringements is to limit the award of damages to no more than double what would have been payable under the licence. The ability of the defendant to pay such damages was, therefore, a factor to be taken into account when considering the balance of convenience when deciding whether or not to grant an interim injunction. Further clarification of s 239 was given in *Dyrlund Smith* and the Court of Appeal said that, where it states that no injunction shall be granted against the defendant, it meant no injunction against infringing the design right. It did not preclude the grant of an injunction for other reasons: for example, to enforce compliance with the terms of a licence of right by the licensee.

Jacob LJ made some criticism of s 239 in *Ultraframe (UK) Ltd* v *Eurocell Building Plastics Ltd*,[204] where he said that the provision had not been properly thought out although he agreed with Neuberger LJ who made a distinction between an undertaking to obtain a licence of right and the general right to obtain such a licence under s 237. In the case of the former, it was a matter of limiting remedies, whereas, with the latter, it was a voluntary move to exercise a right to take such a licence. It could be said that the former was driven by damage limitation, unlike the latter which was driven by exercising a right to exploit a design belonging to another. A problem in *Ultraframe* was that the undertaking to take a licence of right under s 239 was given after the design right had expired. It was argued that it was no longer possible to exercise the right after the design right expired as s 239 spoke in terms of making such an undertaking where a licence *is available* as of right under s 237. However, this was rejected by the Court of Appeal which said that to limit s 239 in such a way would lead to arbitrary consequences depending on whether infringement proceedings were commenced before or after expiry of the design right. Neuberger LJ said that s 239 was concerned with a hypothetical licence, which may or may not lead to an actual licence, and was intended to limit remedies, including a retrospective effect in relation to damages. He said that to restrict s 239 to a situation where the design right was still in subsistence would lead to strange consequences and would be:

> . . . rather unfair on an infringer, who copied in the reasonable and honest belief that there was no design right, and against whom proceedings were brought only after the design right had expired. Such an infringer would, for quite understandable reasons, not have applied, even on a protective basis, for a licence under s 237, because of his honest belief that no design right existed . . . there does not appear to me to be any good reason for such a strict time limit in s 239(1). It is not as if there is any magic in the undertaking being given before the expiry of the design right . . . if the undertaking is given very shortly before the design right expires, it would still be effective, even though there would be wholly insufficient time for the terms of any licence to be agreed or determined pursuant to s 247.

203 As in *American Cyanamid Co* v *Ethicon Ltd* [1975] AC 396.

204 [2005] RPC 36.

There is much force in this argument as an undertaking given on the last day of the subsistence of design right would otherwise be effective to limit remedies whereas one given the day after would not and would expose the defendant to the full panoply of remedies which include additional remedies. Another consequence, not alluded to in *Ultraframe*, is that the submission that an undertaking under s 239 would be ineffective once the design right had expired would encourage claimants to delay commencing proceedings tactically to deprive the defendant of the opportunity to make such an undertaking.

The limit on damages or accounts where licences are available as of right and a defendant undertakes to take such a licence, should now be read with reg 4 of the Intellectual Property (Enforcement, etc.) Regulations 2006.[205] These Regulations implemented, *inter alia*, Directive 2004/48/EC of the European Parliament and of the Council of 29 April 2004 on the enforcement of intellectual property rights.[206] Regulation 4 provides a formula for the assessment of damages which should be appropriate to the actual prejudice suffered by the claimant where the defendant knew or had reasonable grounds for knowing that he was engaged in infringing activity. The court should take into account all appropriate aspects including, in particular, the negative economic consequences, including any lost profits, which the claimant has suffered, and any unfair profits made by the defendant; and elements other than economic factors, including the moral prejudice caused to the claimant by the infringement. Alternatively, where appropriate, damages may be awarded on the basis of the royalties or fees which would have been due had the defendant obtained a licence. It is arguable that, in some cases, such as where the infringement has been quite flagrant and deliberate and the claimant has suffered losses greater than twice the notional royalty,[207] the limit in s 239 is contrary to reg 4. However, it is clear that any such conflict must be resolved in favour of the Regulations as reg 4(3) states that the regulation does not affect the operation of any enactment or rule of law relating to remedies for the infringement of intellectual property rights *except to the extent that it is inconsistent* with the provisions of reg 4 (emphasis added).

Remedies

An infringement is actionable by the design right owner, but under s 234 an exclusive licensee has, except against the design right owner, the same rights and remedies as if he were the owner of the right. Damages, injunctions, accounts or otherwise are available to the claimant as they are in respect of the infringement of any other property right.[208] However, an award of damages is not available in the case of a primary infringement, without prejudice to other remedies, if it is shown that, at the time of the infringement, the defendant did not know and had no reason to believe that the design right subsisted in the design.[209] In the case of a secondary infringement, a defendant who shows that the infringing article was acquired innocently by him or his predecessor in title will be liable only to pay damages not exceeding a reasonable royalty.[210]

It has also been noted earlier that, under s 239, if licences are available as of right, a defendant may undertake to take such a licence at any time in proceedings until the final order and, if so, no other remedy will be available apart from an award of damages not exceeding double the amount payable under such a licence had it been taken before the earliest infringement on terms to be agreed (subject now to reg 4 of the Intellectual Property (Enforcement, etc.) Regulations 2006 as noted above). Failing agreement, the terms will be settled by the Comptroller. This is, of course, without prejudice to remedies in respect of infringements occurring before licences of right were available. Jacob LJ thought that this provision had not been properly thought out as the normal measure of

---

205 SI 2006/1028.

206 OJ L 195, 02.06.2004, p 16.

207 Or the defendant has made a profit of more than twice the notional royalty.

208 Copyright, Designs and Patents Act 1988 s 229. Bear in mind the effect of reg 4 of the Intellectual Property (Enforcement, etc.) Regulations 2006, *supra*.

209 Copyright, Designs and Patents Act 1988 s 233(1).

210 Copyright, Designs and Patents Act 1988 s 233(2). The meaning of 'innocently acquired' is given in s 233(3), being where the person did not know and had no reason to believe that the article was an infringing article.

211 *Ultraframe (UK) Ltd* v *Eurocell Building Plastics Ltd* [2005] RPC 36 at para 71.

damages in an action where licences are available as of right would be the appropriate royalty right.[211] If that is so, why set a limit of twice what would normally be payable? However, it could be that the legislature had in mind the possibility of an award for additional damages (*see* below) as well as ordinary damages or an award of an account of profits which would amount to considerably more that a notional royalty rate. It is clear that there would be no point in granting an injunction as all the defendant would have to do is apply for a licence of right. To see the workings of s 239, consider the following example.

During 1999, Folly Fabrications Ltd created a new design for a wheelbarrow which is subject to design right. Wheelbarrows to the design are put on sale the same year and sell in large numbers. Grimes Industries plc copy Folly's design and manufacture and sell wheelbarrows substantially to that design from 17 July 2003 to 31 March 2008. On 4 September 2008, Folly commenced infringement proceedings against Grimes in relation to design right. During the trial, when it becomes clear to Grimes that it will lose the action, it decides to undertake to take a licence of right. As wheelbarrows to the design were first made available in 1998, licences of right were available from 1 January 2005. Therefore, following Grimes' undertaking, the only remedy available in respect of infringement from 1 January 2005 to 31 March 2008 is an award of damages limited to no more than double what would have been payable under the licence of right. However, from 17 July 2003 to 31 December 2004, the full panoply of remedies is available to Folly, apart from an injunction, of course, which would be meaningless. It may be that Folly claims damages and additional damages for the period 17 July 2003 to 31 December 2004 as it believes Grimes' infringement was quite blatant and deliberate.

There are practical difficulties in respect of undertakings to take licences of right made during legal proceedings. For example, what if the defendant tries to unduly prolong negotiations as to the terms of the licence? Can the claimant unilaterally declare that the parties have failed to agree terms, thereby triggering a reference to the Comptroller to settle terms, if the defendant maintains that it is still prepared to negotiate? Does the court have the power to remit the settlement of terms to the Comptroller in the face of a defendant who claims that he is still prepared to negotiate? The Civil Procedure Rules probably would permit this in the interests of speedy resolution of disputes.[212] However, there are likely to be proceedings before the Comptroller with both sides making submissions as to the terms before he can settle terms. This can all take quite a long time although the court could order an interim payment to be made by the defendant to the claimant.

212 On the basis of the overriding objective and the court's case management powers: rr 1.1–1.4.

The court has a discretion to award additional damages which are provided for under s 229(3) using an identical formula to that used for copyright under s 97(2); that is, having regard to all the circumstances – in particular, the flagrancy of the infringement and the benefit accruing to the defendant. It is unlikely that additional damages will be awarded frequently in design right cases as, usually, normal damages or an account of profits will be satisfactory.

Orders for delivery up, forfeiture or disposal of infringing articles are possible and proceedings can be brought for these forms of relief in county courts in England and Wales and, subject to the county court limit for actions in tort, Northern Ireland.[213] In relation to disposal under s 231 (forfeiting articles to the design right owner, or destruction), persons having an interest in the articles in question shall be served notices and may take part in proceedings in relation to the making of orders for disposal and may appeal against such orders. Persons having an interest include persons in whose favour an order could be made under a number of provisions relating to other rights such as copyright, trade marks, UK registered designs and Community trade marks and designs.

213 Copyright, Designs and Patents Act 1988 ss 230–232.

Semiconductor topography design right

Integrated circuits are commonly known as 'silicon chips' or, quite simply, 'chips'. They are usually made from layers of materials by a process which includes etching, using various 'masks' (templates) which are made photographically. The simplest integrated circuit consists of three layers, one of which is made from semiconductor material. A semiconducting material, in terms of its ability to conduct electricity, is one which lies between a conductor, such as copper, and an insulator, such as rubber. Examples of semiconducting materials include silicon, germanium, selenium and gallium arsenide. A wafer of semiconductor material is coated with a layer of silicon oxide (an insulator) and the electronic components (for example, transistors) are formed by a process of diffusion (chemically doping the semiconductor material with impurities through holes etched through the oxide). Finally, an aluminium coating is applied which is partly evaporated using a mask, leaving behind the interconnections between components formed in the semiconductor layer.

The patterns formed by the processes of etching the layers and evaporation of the conductor make the electrical circuitry of the integrated circuit. These patterns represent the circuit design. The processes involved in the making of integrated circuits fall within the province of patent law, and the first patents for integrated circuits were filed in the late 1950s. Licences were readily available and in 1961 the first chips were available commercially. Now that the early patents have expired and much of the know-how associated with making integrated circuits lies in the public domain, it is essential that the considerable effort that goes into the design and development of new integrated circuits is protected. The feature of an integrated circuit which is specifically protected in its own right is its topography.

History

The protection of semiconductor topographies has a fairly short history, as might be expected. Before legislation was introduced, it was possible that integrated circuits were protected by copyright through drawings or photographs. Most of the masks used in the manufacture were produced photographically and would be protected as photographs. The USA was the driving force behind the development of specific protection for semiconductor topographies, and in 1984 the USA enacted the Semiconductor Chip Protection Act which gave specific protection to the circuitry contained in the layers of semiconductors. The European Economic Community felt duty bound to follow this lead on pain of loss of reciprocal protection for European designed topographies.[214] This led to the adoption of Council Directive 87/54/EEC of 16 December 1986 on the legal protection of topographies of semiconductor products,[215] and, under the authority of the European Communities Act 1972 s 2(2), the Semiconductor Products (Protection of Topography) Regulations 1987 were made and came into force on 7 November 1987.[216] The 1987 Regulations gave a right (called a 'topography right') in the layout of an integrated circuit. However, with the advent of the Copyright, Designs and Patents Act 1988, it was decided to replace these regulations with an amended version of the new design right by the Design Right (Semiconductor Topographies) Regulations 1989, which came into force on 1 August 1989.[217] The right, referred to below as the 'semiconductor design right', draws heavily on the Copyright, Designs and Patents Act 1988 Part III which deals with the unregistered design right, but with some differences as far as semiconductor topographies are concerned. The problem with this is that we now have the situation where some sections of the 1988 Act are different, depending on whether they are being applied to semiconductor designs or to designs for other articles.

214 For a discussion on the American approach and other possibilities for protection of computer programs, *see* Tapper, C. (1989) *Computer Law* (4th edn) Longman, pp 131–33.

215 OJ L 24, 27.01.1987, p 36.

216 SI 1987/1497.

217 SI 1989/1100, as amended by the Design Right (Semiconductor Topographies) (Amendment) Regulations 2006 SI 2006/1833. It is probable that the 1987 Regulations were a model for the new design right.

Design Right (Semiconductor Topographies) Regulations 1989

218 Jacob LJ referred to this provision in *A Fulton Co Ltd* v *Totes Isotoner (UK) Ltd* [2004] RPC 16 to help him reject counsel's submissions on the use of the word 'aspect' in relation to the design right in the Copyright, Designs and Patents Act 1988 s 213(2).

The 1989 Regulations are similar to the 1987 Regulations in several respects: for example, it is the topography of a semiconductor which is protected, being, by reg 2(1),[218] a design which is either:

(a) the pattern fixed, or intended to be fixed, in or upon –
   (i) a layer of a semiconductor product, or
   (ii) a layer of material in the course of and for the purpose of the manufacture of a semiconductor product, or
(b) the arrangement of the patterns fixed, or intended to be fixed, in or upon the layers of a semiconductor product in relation to one another.

'Semiconductor product' is also defined in reg 2(1) and is:

> an article the purpose, or one of the purposes, of which is the performance of an electronic function and which consists of two or more layers, at least one of which is composed of semiconducting material and in or upon one or more of which is fixed a pattern appertaining to that or another function.

219 Copyright, Designs and Patents Act 1988 s 213(4).

To be protected, the semiconductor topography must be original, and it is not original if it is commonplace in the design field in question at the time of its creation.[219] As discussed earlier in this chapter, although 'original' is liberally interpreted in copyright law, the requirement that the topography is not commonplace is likely to lead to a much narrower interpretation. The qualification requirements are very similar to those for 'normal' designs, with some minor differences.[220] In terms of the first marketing qualification rule, normally no account is to be taken of any sale or hire, or any offer or exposure for sale or hire which is subject to an obligation of confidence.[221] On the international scene, the provisions also apply to persons from member countries of the World Trade Organisation.[222]

220 For semiconductor products, the 1989 Regulations substitute different sections and parts of sections into the Copyright, Designs and Patents Act 1988: for example, a new s 217 is substituted.

221 Design Right (Semiconductor Topographies) Regulations 1989, SI 1989/1100, reg 7. This does not apply if any of these things have previously been done or in terms of a Crown obligation.

222 Design Right (Semiconductor) Regulations 1989, as amended by the Design Right (Semiconductor Topographies) (Amendment) Regulations 2006, SI 2006/1833.

223 Design Right (Semiconductor Topographies) Regulations 1989 regs 4 and 5.

224 At first sight, this seems to defeat the whole object of the Regulations, but, although reproducing the topography is permitted, reproducing by making articles is not. In some respects, this provision is similar to the decompilation right in relation to computer programs.

The ownership provisions are very similar to those for the normal design right; however, the qualification provisions are slightly changed and commissioners or employers do not have to be qualifying persons.[223] The right given is as with normal designs and on the whole infringement (primary and secondary) is similarly defined, but reproduction of the design privately for non-commercial aims is specifically excluded from the scope of the right as is an equivalent to some of the permitted acts, including fair dealing, in copyright. Section 226(1A)(b) allows reproduction for the purpose of analysing or evaluating the design, or analysing, evaluating or teaching the concepts, processes, systems or techniques embodied in it. This can be seen as paving the way for reverse analysis of existing semiconductors in the development of new, non-competing products. This is reinforced by reg 8(4), which states that it is not an infringement of the semiconductor design right to create another original topography as a result of such analysis or evaluation, or to reproduce that other topography.[224] As regards reverse analysis, a limiting factor will be the requirement for the new topography to be original and not commonplace. Regulation 8(5) retains the substantiality test for infringement. Secondary infringement does not apply if the article in question has previously been sold or hired within the UK by or with the licence of the owner of the right, or within the European Economic Community or Gibraltar by or with the consent of the person who, at the time, was entitled to import it or sell it within the appropriate territory. Thus, the doctrine of exhaustion of rights applies to semiconductor topographies.

The duration of the semiconductor design right depends on whether and when the topography is commercially exploited. A new s 216 is substituted for semiconductor products. Normally, the right endures for ten years from the end of the year in which it was first commercially exploited (anywhere in the world). However, if the right is not commercially exploited within 15 years of the creation of the topography, the right expires 15 years from the time the topography was first recorded in a design document or the time when an article was first made to the design, whichever is the earlier. Contrary to the position with other designs in which the design right subsists, licences as of right are not available during the last five years of the semiconductor design right. However, licences may be declared available as of right, as a result of a report from the Competition Commission, as with other designs. Remedies for infringement are as for the design right generally.

The topography right is a result of international pressure, especially from the USA. However, because the Copyright, Designs and Patents Act 1988 s 51 removes protection from design documents (in effect), the protection for topographies in the UK is now significantly weaker than it was before. Although copying a topography will infringe the copyright in the photographic masks and s 236 suppresses the design right in favour of copyright, it cannot apply as s 51 means that the copyright in the photographic masks is not infringed by making a semiconductor product to the same design.

Summary

The UK unregistered design is an informal right, similar in some respects to a copyright. It protects the design of the shape or configuration of the whole or part of an article, whether external or internal. The right was originally intended to protect functional designs but may also protect many attractive or aesthetic designs.

The basic requirement is that the design must be original (interpreted as being as for copyright) but it is not original if it was commonplace in the design field in question at the time of its creation. As with copyright, the design must qualify for protection.

There are a number of exceptions to the design and it does not apply:

- to methods or principles of construction;
- in the case of 'must-fit' designs;
- in the case of 'must-match' designs;
- to surface decoration.

The design right lasts for up to 15 years but this will be reduced to a maximum of ten years if commercially exploited. Licences of right are available during the last five years of its subsistence.

The rules as to the identity of the first owner basically follow those for qualification. Thus, the priority is that the designer will be the first owner, if commissioned it will be the commissioner, if not commissioned but created by an employee in the course of employment, it will be the employer. Where the design qualifies by reference to the first marketing of articles to the design, that person will be the first owner.

A design may qualify for protection by virtue of:

- (where not a commissioned design or one created in the course of employment) the designer is a qualifying individual (e.g. a citizen of the EU) or, in the case of a computer-generated design, a qualifying person (a qualifying individual or, for example, a corporate body formed under the law of a part of the UK or EU Member State);
- where the design was created under a commission for money or money's worth or created by an employee in the course of his employment, the commissioner or employer, as the case may be, being a qualifying person;
- where the design does not otherwise qualify, it may qualify by virtue of the person first marketing articles to the design in the UK or EU.

The owner of a design right has the exclusive right to reproduce the design for commercial purposes by:

- making articles to the design;
- making a design document recording the design for the purpose of enabling such articles to be made.

Reproducing a design means copying to make articles exactly or substantially to the design.

The claimant must be able to prove copying. An objective similarity may be the result of the designs being for functional articles. However, the defendant may have to explain the similarities where there is evidence of access to the protected design.

Although design right can apply to the whole or part of an article, the comparison for the purposes of infringement appears to between the claimant's and defendant's articles. However, there is a view that the focus should be on the part alleged to have been copied.

Primary infringement is by doing or authorising another to do anything within the owner's exclusive rights without the licence of the owner. For example, copying the design by making articles exactly or substantially to the design.

There are provisions for secondary infringement but no associated criminal offences under the design right.

A modified version of the unregistered design right protects semiconductor topographies.

Discussion questions

1 Discuss the provisions for ownership and qualification of the design right and compare these with the equivalent provisions for copyright.

2 Think of examples of household and industrial articles in which the design right may subsist and the effect and extent of the exceptions in s 213(3) of the Copyright, Designs and Patents Act 1988.

3 In the light of the unregistered version of the Community design, there is no longer any need for the design right. Discuss.

Selected further reading

Anti-copying in design (ACID), Submission to the Hargreaves Review, March 2011, available at: **http://www.ipo.gov.uk/ipreview-c4e-sub-acid.pdf**; see also the website of ACID at **http://acid. eu.com/** (contains many articles, news stories, etc. on protecting and copying designs – some material on design right but also covers other rights such as copyright).

The Design Council website at: **http://www.designcouncil.org.uk/resources-and-events/designers/ guides/legal-issues/** (contains information sheets on the legal protection of designs and other useful information and links).

Intellectual Property Office, 'Consultation on amendments to design legislation', November 2010, available at: **http://www.ipo.gov.uk/consult-desleg.pdf** (looks at the various design rights and makes recommendations such as the protection for innocent infringers available for the UK unregistered design right which is not available for Community design).

Visit www.mylawchamber.co.uk/bainbridgeip to access study support resources including interactive multiple choice questions, practice exam questions with guidance, weblinks, legal updates and a legal newsfeed.

Part Six

BUSINESS GOODWILL AND REPUTATION

Trade marks – introduction and background   19

Introduction

This chapter concentrates on the basic nature and development of trade mark law. The law of registered trade marks was the subject of some unsatisfactory and difficult legislation in the UK, in particular the Trade Marks Act 1938, now repealed and replaced by the Trade Marks Act 1994 which was brought in to implement the Directive on the legal protection of trade marks.[1] The result is that trade mark law in the UK has been substantially modified and reformed by the 1994 Act which very much marks a clean break with the past. Consequently, there are relatively few cases on the 1938 Act, preceding Acts and the common law before trade mark law was put on a statutory footing, that now have any authority, binding or otherwise. That is not to say that there is a lack of useful case law on our present trade mark law: quite the opposite, as the 1994 Act and interpretation of the harmonising Directive have together generated an impressive body of case law. Preliminary rulings from the Court of Justice of the EU have been particularly useful in providing guidance on those parts of the Trade Marks Act 1994 that are required to implement the Directive. The Community trade mark, which provides for trade marks that have a unitary nature and apply throughout the EC, has proved a great success and has also generated a significant amount of case law on the Community trade mark Regulation. There are numerous similarities between the Trade Marks Act 1994, the Directive and the Community trade mark Regulation.[2] After looking at the nature of and rationale for trade marks and the history of trade mark law, mention is made of the relationship between the UK trade mark and the Community trade mark and the scheme and structure of the following chapters on trade marks.

Trade marks are a diverse and familiar feature in both industrial and commercial markets. Trade marks have long been used by manufacturers and traders to identify their goods and distinguish them from goods made or sold by others. In Roman times it was common for pottery to be embossed or impressed with a mark (for example, a representation of a dolphin or the maker's initials), as a visit to the British Museum will testify. Merchants' marks were used in commerce in Britain from the thirteenth century; William Caxton used the mark W74C and gold and silver articles were hallmarked as early as the fourteenth century.[3] By the end of the sixteenth century it was very common for shopkeepers to erect signs illustrating their trade. Traders took to using cards bearing their name and address, often accompanied by a device of some sort, an early form of business card. The Industrial Revolution saw an enormous growth in the use of names and marks in advertising and the modern trade mark was born. Some of the nineteenth-century marks were glorious in their pictorial detail.[4]

Marks are a very valuable form of intellectual property because they become associated with quality and consumer expectations in a product or service. Some goods become

1 It also made provision for the Community trade mark and gave effect to the Madrid Protocol Relating to the International Registration of Trade Marks and certain provisions of the Paris Convention for the Protection of Industrial Property, as amended. The trade marks Directive (First Council Directive of 21 December 1988 to approximate the laws of the Member States relating to trade marks, OJ L 40, 11.02.1989, p 1) was repealed and replaced by the codifying Directive 2008/95/EC of the European Parliament and of the Council of 22 October 2008 to approximate the laws of the Member States relating to trade marks, OJ L 299, 08.11.2008, p 25. References to the repealed Directive should be construed as references to the new Directive, read in accordance with the correlation table in Annex II to the new Directive. Hence, references to the trade marks Directive in this part of the book apply equally to the new codified version of the Directive unless stated otherwise.

2 Of course, except in the case of derogations and options, the Trade Marks Act 1994 should accurately reflect the provisions of the Directive.

3 Hallmarking is now covered by the Hallmarking Act 1973.

4 A dated but useful practical and descriptive history of trade marks is to be found in Caplan, D. and Stewart, G. (1966) *British Trade Marks and Symbols*, Peter Owen.

almost synonymous with their trade name: for example, Hovis bread, the soft drink Coca-Cola, Mars confectionery bars, Nescafé coffee, Hamlet cigars, Domestos bleach, Cadbury's chocolate, Levi jeans, etc. Coupled with intensive advertising campaigns, the utility of marks to their owners as marketing weapons is plain to see and trade mark rights usually will be vigorously asserted and defended.

It is difficult to estimate the economic value of the power of symbolism in marketing. For example, the value of the Coca-Cola trade mark must be immense when one considers the size of worldwide sales in what could be described as a beverage based on a formula for an unexceptional syrup. Symbolism here is also reinforced by the shape of the Coca-Cola bottle (based on the shape of the coca bean), which was designed to prevent the dissipation of the company image resulting from the variety of bottles made.[5] Why else would such an expensive and impractical form of packaging be used[6]? As a matter of interest, an earlier attempt to register the Coca-Cola bottle itself as a trade mark in the UK failed.[7] Of course, the use of a similar shaped bottle by competitors would almost certainly amount to passing off. Advertising permits the creation of an image associated with a product that might have nothing at all to do with the qualities of the product itself. An old example was the advertising describing a particular brand of menthol tipped cigarettes as being 'fresh as a mountain stream', creating an image completely contrary to medical evidence of the harm that can be caused by smoking.[8]

A trade mark must be used or intended to be used in relation to certain goods or services.[9] A fundamental principle is that there is a connection between a trader and the goods or services in question, and there can be no such connection if the mark is not being used, even though it might have been so used in the past. A mark that is dormant is susceptible to challenge on the grounds of validity and may be revoked for lack of use. Another important aspect is that the mark must be distinctive in some way, and this basic fact limits the scope of signs or symbols that can be used as marks. Ownership of a mark, referred to as proprietorship, gives what can be described as a restricted monopoly in that mark, and the proprietor of a registered trade mark has a property right in the mark. The right is limited by reference to the classes of goods or services against which the mark is registered and also by way of exceptions to the rights granted to proprietors. Trade marks are afforded legal protection through a system of examination, publication and registration. Marks can be registered in one or more of the 34 classes of goods and 11 classes of services.[10]

A related area of law is called *passing off*. This can be likened to a common law version of trade mark law, and indeed both of these areas of law share a common background in the UK. Passing off, in relation to goods, can be said to be the use by a person on his own goods of a mark or get-up belonging to another person with the intention of passing off the goods as being those of that other person.[11] Quite often, a particular set of circumstances will give rise to the possibility of a cause of action in both trade mark law and passing off. Indeed, it is usual to add a claim for passing off in a trade mark action because of the risk of the registration being held invalid. The somewhat wider scope of passing off could also be important. Passing off is dealt with in Chapter 23. Another, less used, area of law is trade libel, sometimes referred to as malicious falsehood. A remedy under this might be available, for example, where one trader falsely and maliciously claims that goods of another trader are not genuine[12] or another trader is working an invalid patent.

The law relating to trade marks is substantially civil law, but there are criminal penalties associated with the unauthorised use of trade marks which could be described as draconian and which have been challenged on the basis of the right to a fair trial. Other offences apply to the falsification of the register or in relation to false copies of register entries or falsely claiming that a trade mark is registered. Other areas of criminal law may be relevant, depending on the circumstances, such as trade descriptions, theft, fraud and forgery and counterfeiting offences.

5 A great deal of this beverage is now sold in cans, but the shape of the bottle is still in evidence in the form of a curved white stripe alongside the name.

6 The bottles are not seen very often nowadays.

7 Under the 1938 Act in *Re Coca-Cola Co* [1986] 2 All ER 274. The bottle shape (with and without the stylised word Coca-Cola) was registered in 1995 under the 1994 Act (registration numbers 2000546 and 2000548).

8 Eisenschitz makes this point and emphasises the power of such advertising: *see* Eisenschitz, T.S. (1987) *Patents, Trade Marks and Designs in Information Work*, Croom Helm, pp 168–69.

9 There was an exception: defensive registration of well-known marks under the 1938 Act.

10 The classification system for trade and service marks can be seen in Appendix 1 to this book.

11 This is passing off in its traditional sense. 'Get-up' could include the appearance of goods, packaging or the general manner in which the goods are displayed, advertised or sold.

12 *Thomas* v *Williams* (1880) 14 ChD 864.

Rationale

Trade marks can be seen as serving two main purposes: first, reflecting the fact that a registered trade mark is an item of property, to protect business reputation and good-will; and, second, to protect consumers from deception, that is to prevent the buying public from purchasing inferior goods or services in the mistaken belief that they originate from or are provided by another trader. As a form of consumer protection this area of law has been an effective weapon against counterfeit and inferior goods, considerably strengthened by the introduction of draconian criminal penalties for the unauthorised use of registered trade marks. However, as far as the control of the use of marks in the civil courts is concerned, the action lies with the proprietor of the mark, enforcing his property right in the trade mark, and consumers are protected indirectly through the self-interest of those with property rights in trade marks.[13] Another way of justifying a system of trade marks is that it gives effect, to some extent, to the European notion of unfair competition.

Consumer protection, as desirable and worthy though it may be, is little more than a by-product of trade mark law. When the statutory provisions are examined, it is apparent that the overriding purpose that a trade mark serves is to distinguish the goods or services of one undertaking from those of another, to use the language of the 1994 Act. In other words, a trade mark should act as a badge of origin. According to Lord Nicholls of Birkenhead in *Scandecor Developments AB* v *Scandecor Marketing AB*:[14]

> Inherent in this definition is the notion that distinctiveness as to business source (the 'goods of one undertaking') is the essential function of a trade mark today.

Previous trade mark Acts used different language. For example, the Trade Marks Act 1905 s 3 defined a trade mark as a mark used on or in connection with goods 'for the purpose of indicating that they are the goods of the proprietor of such mark by virtue of manufacture, selection, certification, dealing with, or offering for sale'. A broader definition was in the Trade Marks Act 1938, s 68(1), which defined a trade mark as a mark 'used in relation to goods for the purpose of indicating a connection in the course of trade between the goods and some person having the right either as proprietor or as registered user to use the mark'.

The basis of trade marks being to show a connection between undertakings and their goods or services so as to distinguish them from other undertakings has important implications in terms of character merchandising and in relation to memorabilia. When a person buys a product that carries the name or image of a famous person or fictitious character, he is buying it because it carries the name or likeness and will usually be indifferent as to the source. In *ELVIS PRESLEY Trade Marks*,[15] Laddie J said (at 554):

> When a fan buys a poster or cup bearing an image of his star, he is buying a likeness, not a product from a particular source. Similarly, the purchaser of any one of the myriad of cheap souvenirs of the royal wedding bearing pictures of Prince Charles and Diana, Princess of Wales, wants mementoes with likenesses. He is likely to be indifferent as to the source.

That being so, the name, image or other mark is unlikely to serve the primary purpose of acting as a *badge of origin* and, consequently, it will not satisfy the basic requirement for registration as a trade mark. The same might apply to sports memorabilia such as football scarves carrying a football club's colours and other club logos. In such cases, and to at least some persons, the scarf could be said to act as a badge of allegiance rather than a badge of origin of the scarf itself.[16]

13 A licensee may also be able to bring an infringement action, depending on the circumstances and the terms of the licence agreement.

14 [2002] FSR 7 at para 33.

15 [1997] RPC 543.

16 This somewhat controversial argument was adopted by Laddie J in *Arsenal Football Club plc* v *Reed* [2001] RPC 46. The Court of Justice noted that even if a person buying goods sees a disclaimer as to the origin of the goods, there may be others who come across them later who will think they came from the trade mark proprietor: Case C-206/01 *Arsenal Football Club plc* v *Matthew Reed* [2002] ECR I-10273, discussed further in the following chapter.

Brief history

Although the application of distinguishing marks to goods has a long history, the law relating to trade marks is relatively young, going back to the early part of the nineteenth century.[17] However, an earlier example of an abuse of a mark is the case of *Southern* v *How*,[18] where one clothier applied another's mark to his own inferior cloth which gave rise to an action in deceit. Due to the importance of obtaining injunctions against infringers of marks, the Court of Chancery became popular for pursuing actions concerning marks, although the common law courts also began to hear such actions: for example, in *Sykes* v *Sykes*[19] where some basic principles were laid down. However, it soon became clear that this area of law needed clarifying and strengthening, and pressure grew from traders for an effective statute which would provide for a system of registration like that adopted in France. One of the problems of litigation had been that the owner of the mark might have to prove his title to the mark every time an infringer came along, and proving title depended on establishing a goodwill associated with the mark, a problem that is still present in passing off actions. This increased the expense and the uncertainty of legal proceedings.

The first statute was the Trade Marks Registration Act 1875, which established a register for trade marks and which was extremely successful judging by the number of registrations applied for. The very first mark registered was one used for beer, a label for pale ale bearing the famous Bass red triangle, the UK's No 1 trade mark which remains registered as a trade mark today and still very much in use.[20] This particular mark has been infringed on many occasions, especially in the nineteenth century and the early part of the twentieth century. The trade mark is now owned by Brandbrew SA by assignment.[21] Bass plc, the predecessor in title to the trade mark, reckoned that it had to deal with some 1,900 examples of infringement of the red triangle mark. Retrospectively, this can be seen as very flattering as a measure of perceived quality and reputation of Bass ales and beers.[22] In 1862 the Merchandise Marks Act was passed. This was a forerunner to the Trade Descriptions Act 1968 and, *inter alia*, made it a criminal offence to forge a trade mark.

After some amending legislation, trade mark law was consolidated in the Patents, Designs and Trade Marks Act 1883. A later consolidating statute, the Trade Marks Act 1905, gave a statutory definition of 'trade mark' for the first time, and a later amending statute, the Trade Marks Act 1919, divided the register into Part A and Part B marks.[23] Registration in Part A was subject to more stringent requirements but gave better protection in terms of remedies than Part B. Then came the Trade Marks Act 1938, which consolidated the 1905 and the 1919 statutes together with the Trade Marks (Amendment) Act 1937, which was instantaneously enacted and repealed on the day the 1938 Act came into force, 27 July 1938. The 1938 Act was an outstanding example of intricate and difficult draftsmanship which attracted judicial criticism on a number of occasions. In an early case of comparative advertising, *Bismag Ltd* v *Amblins (Chemists) Ltd*,[24] MacKinnon LJ found he was unable to understand s 4 (the section on infringement) saying that it was of 'fuliginous obscurity'.

The difficulty with the 1938 Act was compounded by the need to refer to earlier legislation. In *GE Trade Mark*[25] Lord Diplock said (at 325):

> My Lords it may well be a legitimate criticism of our methods of drafting legislation that in order to ascertain the meaning of an Act of Parliament passed in 1938, it should be necessary not only to consider its legislative history over the previous 63 years but also to engage in what in other systems of law might be regarded as antiquarian research, namely the state of the common law as it existed before the first Act to alter it was passed nearly 100 years ago. But, in my view, the Act of 1938 which purports to consolidate our existing law becomes intelligible only when this course . . . is adopted.

17 For a history of the legal development of trade marks and passing off, *see* Kitchin, D., Llewelyn, D., Mellor, J., Meade, R., Moody-Stuart, T., Keeling, D. and Jacob, R. (2005) *Kerly's Law of Trade Marks and Trade Names* (14th edn) Sweet & Maxwell.

18 (1618) Popham 144.

19 (1824) 3 B & C 541.

20 Bass & Co also registered two similar marks and the red triangle device on its own in the same year. The red triangle trade mark can be viewed at the Patent Office website by searching the trade mark records.

21 The Bass brewing business was sold, including its trade marks, and is now owned by Brandbrew SA, a company incorporated in Luxembourg.

22 Reputedly loved by Napoleon.

23 Fortunately, this unnecessary complexity was removed by the Trade Marks Act 1994.

24 [1940] 1 Ch 667.

25 [1973] RPC 297.

26 *The Times*, 14 February 1994.

27 Intellectual Property Rights and Innovation, Cmnd 9117, HMSO, 1983.

28 Previously service industries relied on the law of passing off.

29 The 1994 Act was supplemented by the Trade Marks Rules 1994, SI 1994/2583. The 1994 Rules were revoked and replaced by the Trade Marks Rules 2000, SI 2000/136. These rules were in turn revoked and replaced by the Trade Marks Rules 2008, SI2008/1797.

30 OJ L40, 11.02.1989, p 1.

31 The UK ratified the Protocol in 1995.

32 For example, comparative advertising was permitted providing it was in accordance with honest practices. The previous law did not allow trade marks to be registered for the purposes of licensing their use in a manner unconnected with the proprietor, something described as a complete anachronism by Lord Bridge of Harwich in *Holly Hobbie Trade Mark* [1984] FSR 199.

In comparison, the Trade Marks Act 1994 should be relatively 'free-standing' as regards previous trade marks Acts; however, Aldous J also found it necessary to delve into the provisions in earlier law, including the Acts of 1883, 1888 and 1905 and the common law before 1875, in *Loudoun Manufacturing Co Ltd* v *Courtaulds plc*.[26]

Following recommendations made in a Green Paper,[27] the Trade Marks (Amendment) Act 1984 was passed, and this made amendments to the 1938 Act and extended the scheme to service marks which can be registered in respect of services such as laundries and banking.[28] These provisions came into force on 1 October 1986 and made a bad Act even worse. The way the amendments were made required two copies of the 1938 Act to be used, and indeed the twelfth edition of *Kerly's Law of Trade Marks and Trade Names* had the two copies on facing pages. Prior to this marks could be registered only in respect of goods. Further amendments to the Act were made by the Patents, Designs and Trade Marks Act 1986 and the Copyright, Designs and Patents Act 1988. The complexity of the 1938 Act was not alleviated, only added to.

The current statute is the Trade Marks Act 1994.[29] This long-awaited legislation brought trade mark law up to date and generally was warmly welcomed. Primarily intended to implement First Council Directive 89/104/EEC of 21 December 1988 to approximate the laws of the Member States relating to trade marks,[30] the Act makes provisions for the Community trade mark and enabled the UK to give effect to the 1989 Madrid Protocol relating to the international registration of trade marks.[31] The opportunity was also taken to make some much-needed improvements to trade mark law and to bring it more in line with acceptable modern trading practices.[32] The Act came into force on 31 October 1994.

The Trade Marks Act 1994

33 First Council Directive of 21 December 1988 to approximate the laws of Member States relating to trade marks, OJ L40, 11.02.1989, p 1. A White Paper was published subsequently setting out the government's plans to conform with the Directive, *Reform of Trade Mark Law*, Cm 1203, HMSO, 1990.

34 The 1994 Act was supplemented by the Trade Mark Rules 1994, SI 1994/2583, which were revoked and replaced on 17 February 2000 by the Trade Mark Rules 2000, SI 2000/136. These rules have since been replaced by the Trade Marks Rules 2008, SI 2008/1797.

35 [1990] ECR I-4135.

36 *See* Nissen, D. and Karet, I. 'The Trade Marks Directive: can I prevail if the state has failed?' [1993] 3 EIPR 91.

The Trade Marks Act 1994 represented a milestone in trade mark law and it contains, without question, the most radical changes since the first trade mark legislation. The need for reform of trade mark law had become clear some time ago, but the opportunity to make the necessary changes was put on hold pending harmonisation of trade mark law throughout the European Community (now EU). At the end of 1988, the Council of the European Communities adopted a Directive aimed at harmonising trade mark law throughout the European Community (now European Union).[33] Although most of the basic principles of trade mark law were unaffected by the Directive there were, nevertheless, some significant and far-reaching changes required to be made to UK law.

The Directive required compliance by 1 January 1993, but the UK failed to meet this deadline. A Trade Marks Bill was introduced in the House of Lords in December 1993 for the primary purpose of implementing the regime of trade mark law contained in the Directive. It received the Royal Assent on 21 July 1994 and the Trade Marks Act 1994 came into force on 31 October 1994.[34] In the period between 1 January 1993 and 31 October 1994 the Registrar continued to apply the law in conformity with the 1938 Act and rules made in pursuance of it. But, in Case C-106/89 *Marleasing SA* v *La Comercial Internacional de Alimentación SA*,[35] it was held that national courts should interpret national laws in accordance with European Community law (now EU Law) so that, in respect of registration of marks and infringement thereto in particular, there was a conflict between the position taken by the Registrar and the position likely to have been taken by the courts in respect of provisions of the Directive that were of 'direct effect'.[36] The Registrar was placed in a difficult position because of the delay in implementing the Directive, but in the event there seem to have been no major problems. Certainly, as far as the changes to registrability were concerned, it appeared that traders were satisfied to wait until the new Act was in force before applying to register marks that would have been of doubtful registrability under the 1938 Act.

The need for reform of UK trade mark law goes back to long before the Directive, and the Trade Marks Act 1938 had been subject to much judicial criticism. But difficult and obscure though the 1938 Act was, the need for change was also a reflection of a changing advertising and commercial environment. The 1938 Act sought to protect consumers from deceptive practices by making comparative advertising unlawful but it failed to take account of character merchandising by its prohibition on trafficking in trade marks, described by Lord Bridge in *Holly Hobbie Trade Mark*[37] as a complete anachronism. In retrospect, the 1938 Act was far too restrictive in the nature of marks that could be registered and the way the legislation was altered to provide for service marks by the Trade Marks (Amendment) Act 1984 was clumsy in the extreme.

The Trade Marks Act 1994 brought a welcome breath of fresh air to trade mark law. It is fairly lengthy, comprising 110 sections and five Schedules,[38] and makes significant and substantial reforms to this important area of law. Gone is the obscure drafting of the 1938 Act. The 1994 Act, though not without difficulty, is more clearly drafted and it paved the way for improvements in both the substantive and procedural law relating to trade marks. Greater provision was made for the international aspects of trade mark law (for example, with respect to the Community trade mark), and it enabled the UK to ratify the Protocol to the Madrid Agreement on the International Registration of Marks during 1995. As was to be expected, the law of passing off is unchanged though some commentators considered that it would lessen in importance compared to trade marks law, because more marks would meet the requirements for registrability under the 1994 Act. Of course, it is difficult to tell whether this has happened to any significant extent for a number of reasons though relatively few cases have been reported recently on passing off. Many businesses fail to register their marks as trade marks due to ignorance or inertia or both. Also, even though the scope of what is registrable as a trade mark has expanded, the law of passing off remains potentially wider in scope and has demonstrated its ability to address new situations, such as in respect of internet domain names, as will be seen in Chapter 23.

The Trade Marks Act 1994 heralded the possibility of registering all manner of marks that would certainly not have been registrable before. There was much speculation and excitement surrounding the possibility of registering three-dimensional marks, containers, sound, and even smells.[39] However, a meander through the *Trade Marks Journal* (in which applications to register trade marks are published) leaves one with the impression that nothing much has changed, as the overwhelming proportion of applications are for marks distinctly lacking in frontier-expanding innovation. Even so, a few interesting examples can be found. Applications were submitted on 31 October 1994 to register the Coca-Cola bottle as a trade mark. Other registered trade marks include container marks such as the Chanel perfume bottle (No 2001783) and the Domestos bottle including wording on the bottle (No 2149830). The British School of Motoring's pyramid with L and BSM lettering has been registered (No 2000021). There are a number of sound marks including 'The sound of a dog barking' (No 2007456). Most sound marks are represented by musical notation together with a written description such as, 'The mark consists of the following notes in the key of F major: a melodic eighth note triplet, F, B Flat and G and the quarter note C . . .' (No 2105886). There are also at least two olfactory marks being 'a floral fragrance/smell reminiscent of roses as applied to tyres' (No 2001416) and 'the strong smell of bitter beer applied to flights for darts' (No 2000234). However, as will be seen, although olfactory trade marks are possible in principle, the difficulty in representing smells and odours graphically seems insurmountable at the present time, notwithstanding that some have got through the net.[40] Furthermore, s 32 of the Trade Marks Act 1994 requires that an application to register a trade mark must contain a representation of the

37 [1984] FSR 199 at 202.

38 As at Royal Assent.

39 See, for example, Lewin, R. 'A New UK Trade Marks Law – a godsend for trade mark owners or a goldmine for their lawyers?' [1994] 3 EIPR 91.

40 Those that have been registered are of very doubtful validity.

41 [2001] RPC 28.

mark. In *John Lewis of Hungerford Ltd's Trade Mark Application*,[41] it was held that the identity of a mark must be clearly and unambiguously recorded in the graphical representation filed under s 32. In that case, 'the smell, aroma or essence of cinnamon' was refused registration on the basis that it lacked precision.

It must be noted that the new law represents such a sea change in trade mark law that the utility of previous case law is questionable, particularly where the wording in the Act closely follows that in the Directive. Of course, some of the prior case law will remain helpful in interpreting the new law, but in many cases it will be inappropriate to rely on it to any great extent. In *Allied Domecq Spirits and Wines Ltd* v *Murray McDavid Ltd*,[42] Lord MacFadyen preferred the approach of Jacob J in *British Sugar plc* v *James Robertson & Sons Ltd*[43] where, in approaching the interpretation of s 11(2) from first principles rather than relying on earlier decided cases, he said (at 285):

42 [1997] FSR 864, Outer House, Court of Session.

43 [1996] RPC 281.

> The Trade Marks Act 1994, implementing an EC Directive, has swept away the old law.

44 [1996] FSR 205.

In *Bravado Merchandising Services Ltd* v *Mainstream Publishing (Edinburgh) Ltd*,[44] Lord McCluskey suggested that the use in a new statute of words and phrases used in earlier Acts which had been subject to judicial examination showed that the legislature, in deciding to use the same language, intended the same meaning as before.[45] However, in *Allied Domecq*, Lord MacFadyen said that such an approach to the construction of the new Act must be severely limited. This must be right; otherwise, if each Member State followed its own prior case law, the harmonising purpose of a Directive would be severely prejudiced. In any case, in *Allied Domecq*, the previous equivalent statutory provision used different language and concepts. Nevertheless, Lord MacFadyen felt it inappropriate to decide whether the defender's use of the pursuer's trade mark was saved by s 11(2)(b) which permits the use in the course of trade of a trade mark by a third party to indicate, *inter alia*, geographical origin provided it is in accordance with honest practices in industrial or commercial matters. The defender had obtained a quantity of the pursuer's whisky from a third party blender. The pursuer, which distilled and matured whisky at its Laphroaig Distillery on Islay, had registered 'LAPHROAIG' as a trade mark. The defender sold the whisky as being from the Laphroaig Distillery, which indeed it was. On the basis of the balance of convenience, Lord MacFadyen discharged the interim interdict which had been granted to the pursuer.

45 A provision in a Directive which is clear, unambiguous and unconditional must be implemented faithfully by national legislation. Using the old, though familiar, language of previous legislation may distort the implementation of a Directive and be invalid as Directives are binding as to the result to be achieved under Article 249 of the EC Treaty (now Article 288 of the Treaty on the Functioning of the European Union). The apparent preference of UK legislative draftsmen to rewrite rather than copy out provisions in Directives is unhelpful and, in many cases involving provisions implemented from Directives, judges will go directly to the text of the Directive rather than the Act or SI.

The Act, the Directive and the Regulation

46 Together with the Trade Marks Rules 2008, SI 2008/1797.

47 OJ L 11, 14.01.1994, p 1.

48 The operating name of the UK Patent Office.

Trade mark law in the United Kingdom is governed by the Trade Marks Act 1994,[46] interpreted in accordance with the Directive, for the UK registered trade mark, and the Council Regulation (EC) No 40/94 of 20 December 1993 on the Community trade mark[47] (the 'CTMR'), where issues relate to the Community trade mark ('CTM'). Applications to register a CTM can be made through the UK Intellectual Property Office[48] (Trade Mark Registry) and a number of forms of legal actions concerning the CTM in the UK are brought before the UK's CTM Courts, which are the High Court, the Patents County Court and a number of other County Courts (for example, Birmingham, Bristol, Cardiff and Manchester), the Court of Session in Scotland, the High Court of Northern Ireland and the Court of Appeal.

49 To which appeals from the Boards of Appeal at the Office for the Harmonisation of the Internal Market (Trade Marks and Designs) first go. From the Court of First Instance, appeals go to the Court of Justice. The Court of First Instance is now known as the General Court of the European Union.

There are a number of similarities between the Directive (and consequently also the Trade Marks Act 1994) and the CTMR. Some of the main provisions on registrability and refusal, rights and infringement, limitation of rights and revocation are the same or very similar. However, it is clear that the CTM is a distinct system which stands apart from domestic trade mark laws. The Court of First Instance[49] confirmed this in Case T-106/00

Streamserve Inc v *OHIM*.[50] An application to register STREAMSERVE, in respect of data processing equipment and such like, had been turned down by the Office for the Harmonisation of the Internal Market (Trade Marks and Designs) ('OHIM'). The appellant claimed that the mark had been accepted in Sweden, Norway, the Benelux trade mark office and France and, in the UK and Germany, had been advertised for opposition purposes without their trade mark offices raising any objections on the absolute grounds of refusal. The Court of First Instance confirmed (at para 47):

> . . . the Community trade mark regime is an autonomous system with its own set of objectives and rules peculiar to it; it is self-sufficient and applies independently of any national system (Case T-32/00 *Messe Munchen* v *OHIM (electronica)* 2000 ECR II-3289, paragraph 47). Consequently, the registrability of a sign as a Community mark must be assessed by reference only to the relevant Community rules. Accordingly, the Office and, if appropriate, the Community judicature are not bound by a decision given in a Member State, or indeed a third country, that the sign in question is registrable as a national mark. That is so even if such a decision was adopted under national legislation harmonised with Directive 89/104 or in a country belonging to the linguistic area in which the word sign in question originated.

This means that the decisions on the CTM are not binding as regards domestic trade mark law, even those parts implemented in line with provisions of the Directive which are identical to the equivalent provisions of the CTMR. The converse must also hold true, although the Court of Justice sometimes refers to previous preliminary rulings on the interpretation of the Directive in the context of CTM appeals and its own judgments in CTM appeals in cases on the Directive.[51] The Court of Justice is unlikely to depart from its own previous decisions or rulings though it cannot treat them as binding on cases involving the other system of trade marks.

The OHIM is not influenced by what has been accepted in the past as registrable as CTMs and each application is examined on its merits. In Case C-191/09P *OHIM* v *Wm Wrigley Jr Company*,[52] Wrigley's application to register the word DOUBLEMINT as a CTM had been refused by the Board of Appeal at the OHIM. The Court of First Instance (now General Court of the EU) annulled that decision and the OHIM appealed to the Court of Justice. Wrigley pointed out that a number of composite words had previously been found to be acceptable, such as Alltravel, Megatours, Transeuropean and Oilgear. Case C-383/99P *Procter & Gamble Co* v *OHIM*,[53] accepting that BABY-DRY for nappies had a distinctive character, was also cited by Wrigley. None of these impressed the Court of Justice (or were even further mentioned), which held that the Court of First Instance was wrong in suggesting that a trade mark had to be exclusively descriptive to be refused registration on the basis of Article 7(1)(c) of the CTMR.

Hierarchy of courts and trade mark offices

As regards the UK registered trade mark system, appeals against decisions of examiners refusing registration and opposition proceedings go to a Hearing Officer at the Trade Marks Registry. From there, appeals may go either to a person appointed under the Trade Marks Act 1994 or the Chancery Division of the High Court (in England). Further appeals go to the Court of Appeal and House of Lords. Where the case involves the interpretation of the First Council Directive 89/104/EEC of 21 December 1988 to approximate the laws of Member States relating to trade marks,[54] a reference may be made to the Court of Justice for a preliminary ruling under Article 267 of the Treaty on the Functioning of the European Union.[55]

In the CTM system, there are two routes to the Court of Justice. One concerns appeals originating from decisions at the OHIM whereas the other route is from national CTM

50 [2002] ECR II-723.

51 See, for example, Joined Cases C-456/01P and C-457/01P *Henkel KgaA* v *OHIM* [2004] ECR I-5089 in respect of the former and Case C-120/04 *Medion AG* v *Thomson GmbH* [2005] ECR I-8851 in respect of the latter.

52 [2003] ECR I-12447.

53 [2001] ECR I-6251.

54 OJ L 40, 11.02.1989, p 1.

55 Formerly Article 234 of the EC Treaty. A court of last resort must make such a referral where there is an issue involving the interpretation of Community legislation.

56 In addition to appeals from its Administration of Trade Marks and Legal Division.

57 Formerly known as the Court of First Instance.

courts. The OHIM has its own Board of Appeals which hears appeals from decisions of its examiners and opposition and cancellation divisions.[56] From there, appeals go to the General Court of the European Union[57] and then to the Court of Justice. There are CTM courts of first instance and second instance (in England and Wales; for example, the High Court is one of the courts of first instance and the Court of Appeal is the court of second instance). From either court, there may be references for preliminary rulings as to the interpretation of provisions in the CTMR under Article 267 of the Treaty on the Functioning of the European Union. Figure 19.1 indicates the hierarchy of the trade mark offices and the courts.

It is not impossible for references to be made from a Community trade mark court on the basis of both the CTM and a national registered trade mark. This could happen, for example, where there is an infringement action involving both the CTM and the national trade mark. Although the CTM was not in issue, the Court of Appeal, in *Société des Produits Nestlé SA v Mars UK Ltd*,[58] referred the following question to the Court of Justice for a preliminary ruling under Article 267 of the Treaty on the Functioning of the European Union:[59]

58 [2004] FSR 2.

59 Formerly Article 234 of the EC Treaty.

60 Case C-353/03 *Société des Produits Nestlé SA v Mars UK Ltd* [2005] ECR I-6135. Does this mean that, if a question arises about the interpretation of Article 7(3) of the Regulation, a national court would refer the matter to the Court of Justice or simply apply the ruling on Article 3(3) of the Directive?

> May the distinctive character of a mark referred to in Article 3(3) of [the Directive] and Article 7(3) of [the Regulation] be acquired following or in consequence of the use of that mark as part of or in conjunction with another mark?

However, as the case involved only the UK trade mark, the Court of Justice restricted its ruling to the Directive even though the relevant part of the equivalent provision in the Regulation is similarly, though not identically, worded.[60]

As far as domestic courts are concerned with their national registered trade marks, preliminary rulings from the Court of Justice on the interpretation of the Directive are

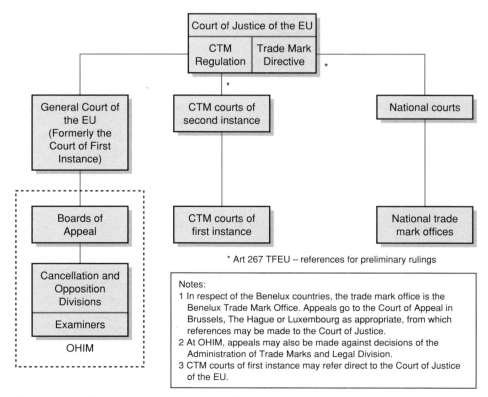

Figure 19.1 Hierarchy of trade mark offices and the courts

binding. Decisions and rulings on the CTM, although not strictly binding on cases on the harmonised national registered trade marks, will be followed in the domestic courts where the provision in question is identical to that in the Directive. Where the provisions are not identical, a domestic court may treat a decision or ruling on the CTM as persuasive (or may be able to distinguish it) in relation to a case on the national registered trade mark. Alternatively, a domestic court may feel it necessary to refer a question to the Court of Justice for a preliminary ruling on the Directive.

Community trade mark courts will be in a similar position with respect to rulings on the meaning of provisions in the Directive which may be considered to be highly persuasive or distinguishable, depending on the level of identity between the corresponding provisions of the Regulation and the Directive. If there is some doubt as to the meaning of a provision in the CTMR with no appropriate guidance from the Court of Justice, a Community trade mark court will submit a question for a preliminary ruling to the Court of Justice. The relationship between Community trade mark courts and the OHIM may be important, especially where there is a counterclaim for invalidity. In such a case, a Community trade mark court may stay proceedings and require an application for a declaration for invalidity to be made to the OHIM. Otherwise, Community trade mark courts are unlikely to regard decisions of the Boards of Appeal at the OHIM as binding or particularly persuasive and vice versa.

The jurisdiction of the Community trade mark courts and their relationship with the OHIM are described in Chapter 22.

Scheme and structure of the chapters on trade marks

Given the status of Court of Justice rulings on the interpretation of the Directive for the national registered design systems, the following chapter on registrability of trade marks under the Trade Marks Act 1994 leans heavily on those rulings. The majority of Court of Justice rulings on the Directive relate to the requirements for registration of a trade mark. A number of decisions of the Court of Justice on the CTM also have relevance where they deal with provisions which are equivalent to those in the Directive. There is a tendency for judges in the UK courts to refer directly to provisions in the Directive rather than those in the Act where the latter are supposed to be the same as the Directive. That being so, and in view of the numerous references to provisions in the Directive by the Court of Justice, Table 19.1 gives a list of some of the main provisions covered in the Trade Marks Act 1994 which are (or should be) equivalent to those in the Directive,[61] with references to the section numbers in the Act, the Article numbers in the Directive and, for completeness' sake, the equivalent provisions in the CTM Regulation.

Of course, large parts of the Trade Marks Act 1994 are outside the scope of the Directive, which left a number of features of trade mark law to be determined in accordance with national law. The Directive did not seek to achieve full harmonisation, merely an approximation of national trade mark laws. The Directive aimed to harmonise those parts of trade mark law that were most likely to affect the functioning of the internal market: in particular, the conditions for registration and renewal of trade marks, the protection afforded by a registered trade mark, exhaustion of rights, the consequences of non-use, licensing of trade marks, and acquiescence by the proprietor of an earlier trade mark depriving him from subsequently challenging a later trade mark. Other aspects, such as the registration procedure, dealing with trade marks, surrender and, of course, criminal offences, are left to Member States. The Directive also contained a number of options, allowing Member States to afford more protection to trade marks enjoying a reputation.

61 The original Directive (First Council Directive 89/104/EEC of 21 December 1988 to approximate the laws of the Member States relating to trade marks, OJ L 40, 11.02.1989, p 1) was repealed and replaced by a new codified version, Directive 2008/95/EC of the European Parliament and of the Council of 22 October 2008 to approximate the law of the Member States relating to trade marks, OJ L 299, 08.11.2008, p 25. There are no significant substantive changes but some mainly minor structural changes. In most cases, the numbering of the Articles is unchanged. References in the following chapters are to the new Directive. Usefully, the new Directive contains a correlation table in Annex II.

Table 19.1 Reference table of provisions in the Act, Directive and Regulation

Provision	Trade Marks Act 1994	Directive on the legal protection of trade marks	CTM Regulation
Basic meaning of a trade mark	S 1(1)	Art 2	Art 4
Absolute grounds for refusal			
Signs not within basic meaning	S 3(1)(a)	Art 3(1)(a)	Art 7(1)(a)
Trade marks devoid of distinctive character	S 3(1)(b)	Art 3(1)(b)	Art 7(1)(b)
'Descriptive' or 'laudatory' trade marks	S 3(1)(c)	Art 3(1)(c)	Art 7(1)(c)
Trade marks that have become customary in bona fide practices	S 3(1)(d)	Art 3(1)(d)	Art 7(1)(d)
Proviso that certain grounds can be overcome if trade mark has acquired a distinctive character	S 3(1) proviso thereto	Art 3(3)	Art 7(3)
Shapes (nature of goods, technical effect or giving substantial value to goods)	S 3(2)	Art 3(1)(e)	Art 7(1)(e)
Trade marks contrary to public policy/accepted principles of morality	S 3(3)(a)	Art 3(1)(f)	Art 7(1)(f)
Deceptive trade marks	S 3(3)(b)	Art 3(1)(g)	Art 7(1)(g)
Specially protected state emblems etc. (see Article 6ter of the Paris Convention)	S 4	Art 3(1)(h) & Art 3(2)(c)	Art 7(1)(h)(i)
Trade mark, use of which is prohibited by law	S 3(4)	Art 3(2)(a)	No direct equivalent but prohibitions on designations of origins in Art 7(1)(j) and (k)
Signs of high symbolic value, in particular, a religious symbol	No direct equivalent	Art 3(2)(b)	No direct equivalent
Bad faith	S 3(6)	Art 3(2)(d)	Missing but bad faith is a ground for invalidity: Art 51(1)(b)
Relative grounds for refusal			
Identical sign and identical goods or services compared with earlier trade mark	S 5(1)	Art 4(1)(a)	Art 8(1)(a)
Not complete identity of sign and goods or services compared with earlier trade mark but likelihood of confusion	S 5(2)	Art 4(1)(b)	Art 8(1)(b)
Identical or similar sign and unfair advantage or damage to repute to earlier trade mark having a reputation	S 5(3)	Art 4(3) & 4(4)(a)	Art 8(5)
Conflict with earlier right	S 5(4)	Art 4(4)(b) & (c)	Art 8(4) (partly)

Table 19.1 *cont'd*

Provision	Trade Marks Act 1994	Directive on the legal protection of trade marks	CTM Regulation
Infringement			
Identical sign and identical goods or services compared with earlier trade mark	S 10(1)	Art 5(1)(a)	Art 9(1)(a)
Not complete identity of sign and goods or services compared with earlier trade mark but likelihood of confusion	S 10(2)	Art 5(1)(b)	Art 9(1)(b)
Identical or similar sign and unfair advantage or damage to repute to earlier trade mark having a reputation	S 10(3)	Art 5(2)	Art 9(1)(c)
Meaning of using a sign	S 10(4)	Art 5(3)	Art 9(2)
Limits on effect of trade mark			
Own name and address	S 11(2)(a)	Art 6(1)(a)	Art 12(a)
'Descriptive', e.g. kind, quality, geographic origin	S 11(2)(b)	Art 6(1)(b)	Art 12(b)
Intended purpose, in particular accessories and spare parts	S 11(2)(c)	Art 6(1)(c)	Art 12(c)
Use of earlier right in a particular locality	S 11(3)	Art 6(2)	No equivalent
Exhaustion of rights	S 12	Art 7	Art 13
Revocation (certain grounds only)			
Non-use	S 46(1)(a) & (b)	Art 10(1) & Art 12(1)	Art 15(1) & Art 50(1)(a)
Trade mark has become a common name for goods or services because of proprietor's inactivity	S 46(1)(c)	Art 12(2)(a)	Art 50(1)(b)
Liable to mislead public as a consequence of use by proprietor	S 46(1)(d)	Art 12(2)(b)	Art 50(1)(c)

The section on registrability in the following chapter contains numerous references to Court of Justice rulings and a few to that court's decisions on the CTM. Chapter 21 covers rights, infringement, defences, remedies and criminal offences. The section on rights and infringement and, to the extent that it covers limitations on trade marks, defences also contains numerous rulings from the Court of Justice. Chapter 22 looks at the CTM in detail and includes many cases from the Court of First Instance (now known as the General Court of the European Union) and the Court of Justice on the CTM Regulation. That chapter also looks at registration of trade marks under the Madrid System, to which the European Community (now European Union) is now a Contracting Party, allowing international applications to register trade marks to include an application to register a CTM.

The CTM has proved very popular but it has not had the impact on the UK registered trade mark systems as the Community design has had on the UK registered design system which attracts less than 5,000 applications a year, almost half what it was before the Community design was available. Consequently, the UK registered trade mark remains popular for those seeking protection in the UK and, during 2004, there were nearly 28,000 applications (including applications to register in multiple classes) to register a UK trade mark. The provisions on seniority for the CTM also make the application for a national trade mark attractive as it can later be surrendered or not renewed without losing its priority in relation to a later CTM. In some cases, a CTM or an application for a CTM can be converted into an application for a national trade mark. The CTM was designed to complement national systems of trade mark registration.

The final chapter in this part of the book covers passing off in the UK. This remains a useful action to protect business goodwill which, in many cases, may involve a trade name or trade mark, whether or not registered. Passing off has been unaffected by trade mark law and this is confirmed by s 2(2) of the Trade Marks Act 1994.

Summary

Trade marks are used in relation to goods or services. Trade marks serve to indicate the origin of goods or services. They operate as 'badges of origin'.

Trade marks were transformed by the Trade Marks Act 1994 which was implemented to comply with the Directive to approximate the laws of Member States relating to trade marks. This swept away the old law which was long overdue modernisation. The Trade Marks Act 1938 was probably one of the worst drafted pieces of legislation on the statute book. The UK was late in its implementation of the Directive.

The Community trade mark regulation introduced a system of EU-wide registration of trade marks which have a unitary character. Community trade marks ('CTMs') must be valid across the EU and may only be assigned or revoked as a whole. Licences may be granted territorially.

The UK registered trade mark and the CTM have much in common, particularly in terms of registrability, rights, limitations and infringement.

To be registrable as a trade mark, a sign must be capable of being represented graphically and capable of distinguishing the goods or services of one undertaking from those of other undertakings. In particular, a trade mark may consist of words (including personal names), designs, letters, numerals or the shape of goods or their packaging.

For both the Directive and the CTM, there are 'absolute' and 'relative' grounds for refusal of registration.

The courts under the CTM Regulation and the Directive sit in a hierarchy.

The Directive and the CTM Regulation are distinct and decisions on one are not binding on the other. Nevertheless, the Court of Justice, which is the ultimate court for both systems, tends to treat decisions under system with the greatest respect in relation to decisions under the other system.

Discussion questions

1 Discuss the nature and purpose of trade marks, their power and potential value to traders. Why are trade mark proprietors vigilant in relation to the lawful uses by third parties of their trade marks?

2 Describe the hierarchy of the courts in relation to the CTM and the UK trade mark. To what extent, if any, are decisions of the courts in relation to the CTM binding or persuasive on the courts in cases on the UK trade mark?

Selected further reading

Intellectual Property Office, *Trade Marks: Basic Facts*, May 2010 (overview of trade mark law from the UK Intellectual Property Office) available at: **http://www.ipo.gov.uk/tm-basicfacts.pdf**

Office for the Harmonisation of the Internal Market (Trade Marks and Designs) ('OHIM') *The Quick Guide to Trade Marks*, (guidance on the Community trade mark) available at: **http://oami.europa. eu/ows/rw/resource/documents/OHIM/multimedia/quickGuide/en/tradeMarks.html**

Visit **www.mylawchamber.co.uk/bainbridgeip** to access study support resources including interactive multiple choice questions, practice exam questions with guidance, weblinks, legal updates and a legal newsfeed.

20

The UK trade mark – registrability, surrender, revocation and invalidity, property rights and registration

Introduction

This chapter is concerned with the requirements for registration of a sign as a trade mark, the registration process and assignment and licensing of trade marks. The basic statutory definition of a trade mark appears simple and indicates the basic function of a trade mark. If a sign can be represented graphically and can serve the function of distinguishing the goods or services of one undertaking from those of other undertakings then it is, *prima facie*, registrable. However, there are a number of grounds for refusal of a trade mark, named absolute and relative grounds for refusal.[1] Overall, the provisions on registrability have generated a substantial amount of case law, both nationally and in the Court of Justice of the European Union (the 'Court of Justice'). To some extent, this was to be expected as a result of the broadening of the scope of what is registrable as a trade mark, such as shapes, sounds and even smells. The statutory provisions on what signs are registrable as trade marks are also important in other ways: for example, persons opposing the registration of trade marks base their grounds of opposition on the statutory framework governing what is and what is not registrable. This is especially so where opposition is based on the identity or similarity of the mark for which registration is applied for with the opponent's earlier trade mark under what are known as the relative grounds for refusal. We also see the equivalent of the relative grounds for refusal cropping up again in the provisions defining infringement. Consequently, many of the cases on the relative grounds for refusal are also useful in relation to infringement and vice versa. Indeed, they are exchangeable except where infringement issues also include other aspects such as limitations on the effects of trade marks. For example, in Case C-291/00 *LTJ Diffusion SA* v *Sadas Vertbaudet SA*,[2] the Court of Justice said (at para 53):

> . . . the question submitted will be examined below solely in the light of Article 5(1)(a) of the Directive, but the interpretation adopted following that examination will also apply to Article 4(1)(a) of the Directive since that interpretation will be transposable, mutatis mutandis, to the latter provision.[3]

The relationship between the relative grounds of refusal and the provisions on infringement was also noted by Geoffrey Hobbs QC, as the Appointed Person, in *10 Royal Berkshire Polo Club*[4] where he said of the Trade Marks Act 1994 s 5(2) (part of the section on the relative grounds of refusal) and s 10(2) (the equivalent provision on infringement):

> Objections under section 5(2) are conceptually indistinguishable from actions under section 10(2). . . They serve to ensure that trade marks whose use could successfully be challenged before the courts are not registered.[5]

1 So named in the Trade Marks Act 1994. The trade marks Directive does not describe this way but lists them as grounds for refusal and further grounds for refusal.

2 [2003] ECR I-2799.

3 Article 4(1)(a) of the Directive is the relative ground for refusal where a trade mark is identical to an earlier trade mark and is to be used for identical goods or services. Article 5(1)(a) covers infringement by use of a sign identical to a trade mark in relation to identical goods or services.

4 [2001] RPC 32.

5 Echoing the same sentiment expressed in the Court of Justice in Case C-39/97 *Canon Kabushiki Kaisha* v *Metro-Goldwyn-Mayer Inc* [1998] ECR I-5507 (at para 21).

Thus, the intended scheme appears to have been that the register should only hold trade marks that could be effectively enforced against infringers and withstand attacks on their validity on the basis of earlier trade marks or other earlier rights, such as copyright or goodwill protected by the law of passing off.

In addition to looking at the basic procedure for registration, there is some discussion of the proceedings before the Trade Marks Registry and the Appointed Person and the role of the Chancery Division of the High Court. Particular attention is given to opposition proceedings, which are now very numerous. Surrender, revocation and invalidity are also discussed. Other aspects covered in this chapter include certification and collective trade marks.

As the Trade Marks Act 1994 was heavily influenced by implementing the First Council Directive 89/104/EEC of 21 December 1988 to approximate the laws of the Member States relating to trade marks,[6] full reference is made to preliminary rulings of the Court of Justice in this and the following chapter. These rulings give interpretation of the relevant provisions in the Directive.

In recent years, there have been so many rulings by the Court of Justice on the interpretation of some of the main provisions of the Directive, that it is considered better to refer to those provisions of the Directive and to other provisions where the UK has chosen to implement an option or derogation in the Directive.[7] Cross-referencing to the Act is given where appropriate but kept to a minimum to improve clarity. This approach conforms to that increasingly being used by judges in the UK, many of whom tend to go straight to the text of the Directive where the equivalent provision in the Act should be the same and have the same effect as that in the Directive. In this respect, we can do no better than follow Jacob LJ's approach as he described in *Bongrain SA's Trade Mark Application*[8] at para 7:

> In accordance with my usual practice I do not use the numbering of those provisions in the UK Trade Marks Act which enact the provisions of Directive 89/104. The language is the same and use of our local numbering merely makes our judgments less intelligible in a wider European context.

Of course, there are many provisions in the Act which have no direct parallel with the text of the Directive as certain matters are left to Member States: for example, the registration procedure, assignment, offences and the detailed provisions on licensing. For these, of course, reference must be to the provisions in the Act. Readers are encouraged to look at the Directive, which is thankfully a relatively short piece of legislation, and compare the provisions with the equivalent ones in the Trade Marks Act 1994; Table 19.1 in the previous chapter may prove helpful in this respect.[9]

Registrable trade marks

The Directive makes a basic statement of what a trade mark is in Article 2 (equivalent to s 1(1) of the Act)[10] and then sets out various grounds for refusal of registration. The grounds are set out in two categories, the first being what are known as the absolute grounds for refusal. These are a somewhat disparate set of grounds though some are concerned with signs or trade marks that are not distinctive or fail to meet the basic requirement. Others apply where the trade mark in question is excluded on grounds associated with protected emblems and the like, on policy considerations or because the application was made in bad faith. The relative grounds of refusal are based on the conflict or potential conflict between the trade mark for which registration is sought and earlier trade marks (whether or not registered) and other earlier rights: for example, a figurative sign protected by copyright belonging to a third party.

6 OJ L 40, 11.02.1989, p 1. This Directive has now been repealed and replaced by a new codified version, Directive 2008/95/EC of the European Parliament and of the Council of 22 October 2008 to approximate the law of the Member States relating to trade marks, OJ L 299, 08.11.2008, p 25. There are no significant substantive changes but some mainly minor structural changes. In most cases, the numbering of the Articles is unchanged. References in the following chapters to the 'Directive' are to the new Directive. Usefully, the new Directive contains a correlation table in Annex II.

7 An example of an option is Article 4(4) which permits Member States, *inter alia*, to give enhanced protection to trade marks of repute (which the UK has taken up). An example of a derogation is Article 15(2) which allows Member States to allow the registration of geographical names as collective and certification marks. Again, the UK has taken advantage of this.

8 [2005] RPC 14.

9 The full text of the Directive and all other Community (now EU) legislation including legislation in preparation is available at http://europa.eu.int/eur-lex/en/index.html. The full text of European Community case law is also available from that site including the European Community Reports (ECR).

10 Except the definition in Article 2 uses 'signs' whereas the UK Act, as the original Directive, uses 'sign'.

The basic definition of what constitutes a registrable mark has been significantly widened compared with the previous trade mark law in the UK and Article 2 of the Directive defines a trade mark in the following terms:

> A trade mark may consist of any signs capable of being represented graphically, particularly words, including personal names, designs, letters, numerals, the shape of goods or of their packaging, provided that such signs are capable of distinguishing the goods or services of one undertaking from those of other undertakings.[11]

The list of examples given in Article 2 is not an exhaustive one[12] but it does make it clear that shapes are registrable in principle, though shapes are subject to some specific grounds for refusal of registration, discussed later.

There are two features to Article 2 which a sign must possess before it can be considered to be a trade mark, whether or not otherwise registrable. These are that the sign must be capable of being represented graphically and also capable of distinguishing goods or services of one undertaking from those of other undertakings, that is, that it is capable of fulfilling the purpose of informing the public as to the origin of the goods or services. These two features are explored below, starting with the latter. Following this, the absolute and relative grounds for refusal are described.

Capable of distinguishing

To be capable of distinguishing goods or services of one undertaking from those of other undertakings, the sign must say, or be capable of saying,[13] on its face, that these goods or services come from X rather than from Y or Z or any other. It will still perform this function even if members of the public do not know much about who X is, provided they associate the goods or services with X and no other. It may be that the sign is an old well-known trade mark that originally belonged to a company which was long ago swallowed up by a large conglomerate that now owns and uses the trade mark.[14]

The sign must be capable of distinguishing the goods or services of one undertaking from those of other undertakings and the importance of this is borne out by the recitals to the Directive. The tenth recital states that the function of a registered trade mark is '. . . to guarantee the trade mark as an indication of origin'.[15] The mark must serve as a guarantee of trade origin: a badge of origin. If the sign cannot do this then it is not registrable, notwithstanding the grounds for refusal of registration. The sign does not get past the first hurdle. The Directive (and the Act follows in this respect) uses the terms 'sign' and 'trade mark' in the basic definition and in the absolute grounds for refusal. The two are not interchangeable and there is a distinction between them. Of course, 'sign' is not defined. It has a very wide meaning, but in this context can be said to be a mark, symbol, device or indicator (for example, an indication of quality or character). Trade marks are included within the meaning of a sign but are but a sub-species, as defined above. They are graphical representations indicating origin. When we look at the absolute grounds of refusal, some refer to signs whilst others refer to trade marks. Some trade marks are refused registration because, even though they may fall within the definition of a trade mark, there are other objections to them. Unless they are trade marks within the basic definition, signs are simply not registrable. This is confirmed in Article 3(1)(a) which states that signs which cannot constitute a trade mark shall not be registered or, if registered, shall be liable to be declared invalid.[16] The distinction between signs and trade marks is also seen in Article 3(1)(e) (equivalent to s 3(2)) which prohibits the registration of a sign consisting exclusively of certain categories of shapes. Thus, a sign that consists exclusively of the shape which results from the nature of goods is not registrable. This is not a capricious

11 This definition was implemented by s 1(1) and is considerably wider than the definitions of a 'mark' and 'trade mark' in the 1938 Act. The provision of retail services falls within the meaning of services: see Case C-418/02 *Praktiker Bau und Heimwerkermärkte AG* [2005] ECR I-5873. This is in contrast to the law under the 1938 Act where applications in relation to retail services as such were not registrable: see *Dee Corp plc* [1990] RPC 159. Note that the new version of the Directive uses 'signs' in the plural unlike the original Directive. The UK Act still is expressed in the singular.

12 For example, slogans such as 'TESCO WE SELL FOR LESS' may be registrable in principle: *Tesco Stores Ltd's Trade Mark Application* [2005] RPC 17.

13 The use of the word 'capable' presumably is intended to apply in the context of applications to register new trade marks that have not yet been put to use commercially.

14 A good example is the UK's No 1 trade mark for Bass Pale Ale, first registered in the name of Bass, Ratcliff & Gretton Ltd, now belonging to and used by Brandbrew SA, a Luxembourg company.

15 The importance of this purpose was stressed in Case C-39/97 *Canon Kabushiki Kaisha* v *Metro-Goldwyn-Mayer Inc* [1998] ECR I-5507.

16 The Trade Marks Act 1994 s 3(1)(a) states that a sign that does not satisfy the requirements of s 1(1) shall not be registered.

prohibition. It simply reflects the fact that such a sign can never act as a trade mark, as a badge of origin. Even if an undertaking[17] uses such a sign very extensively, it still cannot operate as a trade mark as it cannot distinguish that undertaking's goods from the same goods from other undertakings. As the Court of Justice said, in Case C-299/99 *Koninklijke Philips Electronics NV v Remington Consumer Products Ltd*,[18] of the exclusion of signs consisting exclusively of certain types of shapes (at para 75): '. . . a sign which is refused registration under Article 3(1)(e) of the Directive can never acquire a distinctive character for the purposes of Article 3(3) by the use made of it'.[19] However, the Court of Justice also ruled in *Philips* v *Remington* that a shape mark did not have to have some capricious addition, such as an embellishment having no functional purpose, to be capable of distinguishing. For the purposes of satisfying Article 2, a shape mark should not be treated differently to any other type of sign.

That a trade mark must act as an indicator of origin, denoting from whom goods or services come rather than what the goods or services are, is fundamental to trade mark law. The Court of Justice in Case C-39/97 *Canon Kabushiki Kaisha* v *Metro-Goldwyn-Mayer Inc* has stressed this in the following terms:

> . . . the essential function of the trade mark is to guarantee the identity of the origin of the marked product to the consumer or end user by enabling him, without any possibility of confusion, to distinguish the product or service from others that have another origin.[20]

Apart from this essential function, a trade mark has other functions, in particular, the functions of communication, investment or advertising.[21]

In *Jeryl Lynn Trade Mark*,[22] the mark was registered in relation to medicinal and pharmaceutical preparations and used for mumps vaccines. The name had been chosen in honour of Jeryl Lynn Hilleman, from whom her father isolated the original mumps virus. The mark was declared invalid, as it was the name by which the virus had become known. It served as a technical name and became overwhelmingly generic. Laddie J rejected the submission that the name had acquired a secondary function as a trade mark because the evidence simply did not show that that was the case.

The phrase 'capable of distinguishing' was also used in the Trade Marks Act 1938.[23] It was the basic test for registration in Part B of the register which afforded lesser protection than Part A. In *Davies* v *Sussex Rubber Co*[24] Sargant LJ suggested that the mark is capable in time of becoming distinctive with use or, at least, not incapable of becoming distinctive. It is arguable that this equates to the test under the 1994 Act as some of the absolute grounds for refusal can be overcome if it is shown that the trade mark has acquired a distinctive character through the use made of it.[25] However, this is retrospective in that it looks at the question at the time of applying for registration whereas Sargant LJ appears to have been looking to the future. There is nothing in the Directive, and no case law from the Court of Justice, to suggest anything other than requiring that the trade mark is already capable of distinguishing the goods or services of the applicant from those of other undertakings and that it already possesses that distinctive character.

In *AD2000 Trade Mark*[26] it was held that a sign is capable of distinguishing the goods or services of one undertaking from those of other undertakings even if it is so capable only to the limited extent of being not incapable of distinguishing. As in that case, the Court of Appeal in *1-800 FLOWERS Inc* v *Phonenames Ltd*,[27] accepted that alpha-numeric marks could be capable of distinguishing goods or services. However, the application to register 800-FLOWERS as a trade mark failed as, on the evidence, the focus was on the mark as a mnemonic for a telephone number rather than on the applicant's business.[28] In *Premier Luggage and Bags Ltd* v *Premier Company (UK) Ltd*,[29] the court held that, although 'Premier' was an ordinary laudatory word, it was capable of distinguishing the claimant's cases and bags, as it was not incapable of distinguishing them from those of other traders. Judicial examples of signs which are unregistrable on the ground that they are not capable of

---

17 'Undertaking' is the word used in the Directive and the Act to describe what used to be commonly known as a 'trader'.

18 [2002] ECR I-5475. The case involved the shape of a three-headed electric shaver.

19 Article 3(3) allows trade marks to be registered that would otherwise be refused under some, though not all, of the relative grounds of refusal (this is equivalent to the proviso to s 3(1) of the Trade Marks Act 1994).

20 [1998] ECR I-5507 at para 28.

21 Case C-87/07 *L'Oréal SA* v *Bellure NV* [2009] ECR I-5185 at para 58.

22 [1999] FSR 491.

23 Section 10. In *Messiah from Scratch Trade Mark* [2000] RPC 44, Simon Thorley QC, as the Appointed Person, accepted that there was no distinction between s 3(1)(b) of the Trade Marks Act 1994 (refusal of registration on the basis that the mark is devoid of distinctive character) and s 10 of the Trade Marks Act 1938.

24 (1927) 44 RPC 412 at 425.

25 The proviso to s 3(1).

26 [1997] RPC 168.

27 [2002] FSR 12. The Chancery Division decision is reported at [2000] FSR 697.

28 FLOWERS is equivalent to 3569377 on a telephone keypad.

29 [2001] FSR 29.

distinguishing as they describe the article to which they are applied include 'soap', 'banana', 'Bunsen burner' and 'Wellington boot'. The same could be said for marks for services such as 'window cleaning', 'car washing' or 'legal advice'.

Graphical representation

The Directive caused considerable excitement amongst trade mark proprietors and intellectual property lawyers because it seemed to be very liberal in the scope of signs that could be registrable as trade marks. Article 2 expressly mentioned the possibility of registering shapes and gave particular examples of what could be a trade mark being words (including personal names), designs, letters, numerals or the shape of goods or their packaging. The list is not an exhaustive one. There was talk of being able to register colours, sounds and, in addition to shapes, smells and fragrances. After all, the only requirement apart from possessing the ability to distinguish one undertaking's goods or services from those of other undertakings was that the sign must be capable of being represented graphically.

A limiting factor in determining whether a sign is capable of being represented graphically is the requirement for a representation of the mark to be contained in the application to register a trade mark under s 32(1). Another factor is the advertising of marks in the *Trade Marks Journal*. The application form TM3 has a square box (8cm × 8cm)[30] in which the representation must be placed. One of the main purposes of advertising is to enable other undertakings to see if newly applied for marks are identical to or very similar to their marks, or are otherwise unregistrable, which may lead them to commence opposition proceedings. This purpose could be defeated if the character of the mark was not readily apparent from an inspection of the journal and, while it may not be unreasonable to expect a person to read or play a sound mark expressed in musical notation to appreciate its character entirely, it would be unfair to expect readers of the *Trade Marks Journal* to undertake difficult, lengthy, complex or expensive procedures to be able to know the precise nature and character of the mark. The same considerations apply in relation to other national trade mark systems and the CTM system.

The Court of Justice has confirmed on numerous occasions that the requirement that a trade mark is capable of being represented graphically must:

> . . . enable the sign to be represented visually, particularly by means of images, lines or characters, so that it can be properly identified . . . [It must be] clear, precise, self-contained, easily accessible, intelligible, durable and objective.[31]

The reasons for this were set out in Case C-273/00 *Ralf Sieckmann* v *Deutsches Patentund Markenamt*[32] as being so that:

- The precise subject of the protection afforded by registration can be determined.
- Competent authorities (that is, in the UK, the Trade Marks Registry) must know what the sign is with clarity and precision so that they can fulfil their obligations: for example, in relation to examination, publication and maintaining the register.
- Economic operators must also be able, by consulting the register, to find out, with clarity and precision, about registrations and applications made by current or potential competitors and to receive information about the rights of third parties.

These considerations require that the graphical representation of a trade mark is such as to serve legal certainty. The trade mark and the nature and scope of the rights associated with it can only be determined if the representation is precise and complete on its face. A graphical representation bearing the characteristics and qualities set out in *Sieckmann* together with the description of the goods and services for which the trade mark is to be used fully defines

30 A larger image may be submitted if application is made electronically. The Community trade mark system requires that the representation must not exceed 17cm × 26.2cm but it must be suitable for reduction down to 8cm × 16cm, the size it will be reproduced at in the *Community Trade Mark Bulletin*.

31 Case C-273/00 *Ralf Sieckmann* v *Deutsches Patent-und Markenamt* [2002] ECR I-11737 at paras 46 and 55.

32 [2002] ECR I-11737.

the true extent of the monopoly as provided for in accordance with the Trade Marks Act 1994. However, the Court of Justice has held that using musical notation is an acceptable way of representing a sound mark graphically[33] even though the sign is not itself capable of being perceived visually and many persons cannot read music. In *Ty Nant Spring Water Ltd's Trade Mark Application*,[34] Geoffrey Hobbs QC, as the Appointed Person, said that:

> The degree of precision with which the sign is represented must be sufficient to permit full and effective implementation of the provisions of the Act relating to absolute unregistrability (section 3), relative unregistrability (section 5), infringement (section 10) and public inspection of the Register (section 63).

He went on to say that there may be more than one way of representing the sign with the required degree of precision and that with some signs, such as sounds or smells, the graphical representation may be acceptable even though 'interpretation or analysis may be required to detect or demonstrate use of it'.[35] It is submitted that the amount of interpretation or analysis should be minimal and easily undertaken by any reasonable person so that predictable and consistent results will be achieved. Persons consulting the register should not have to undertake detective work to find out just what the trade mark is.

Signs that comprise moving images may be represented graphically by means of drawings, perhaps supplemented by a written description. Typically, a series of drawings can effectively represent a moving computer-generated image or hologram, particularly if the description makes clear the sequence or order of the images and other information such as the speed and direction of rotation or transition. Perhaps unfortunately, it is not yet possible to submit a computer file which, when run, reproduces the moving image accurately. Nor is it possible to submit a hologram as such as a representation of the sign for which registration is sought.[36]

Bearing in mind that the vast majority of applications to register trade marks are for words (whether stylised or not) or graphical symbols (usually referred to as device or figurative marks) or a combination of these, attempts to register colours, sounds, smells and fragrances and shapes have generated a disproportionately high volume of case law both before the UK courts and the Court of Justice. In terms of whether a sign is capable of being represented graphically, it is colour marks, sound marks and smell and fragrance marks (known as *olfactory* marks) that have caused the most problems. Each of those categories is now considered in relation to the requirement for graphical representation.[37]

Colour marks

It is clear that it will not do simply to describe a colour vaguely by a verbal description such as 'red' or 'pale yellow' or even 'horizontal alternating green and purple stripes, the green stripe being 8mm wide, the purple stripe being 6mm wide'. The immediate objection is that it does not tell us enough about the colour or its shade. Such descriptions lack precision and make it difficult for others to predict whether their use of colour is likely to infringe such a trade mark if it is registered without further information about the colour.

There are two possibilities to overcome this objection. The first is to include the colour or colours either as a sample or by means of an image of the goods to which the colour is applied. The second is to use a well-known referencing systems for colours. One such system is the Pantone system.[38] One problem with providing samples of colours was that they tended to fade over time but this is no longer the problem it was as trade mark applications in the UK and for the Community trade mark ('CTM') may be filed electronically together with a digital image of the trade mark.

Applying to register as a trade mark a single colour or a colour combination in the abstract will not be easy. In Case C-104/01 *Libertel Groep BV v Benelux-Merkenbureau*,[39] an application was made to register the single colour orange in the field of telecommunications

---

33 Case C-283/01 *Shield Mark BV v Joost Kist* [2003] ECR I-14313.

34 [2000] RPC 55 at 56.

35 This is now very doubtful in the context of smells. *See* the section on olfactory marks, below.

36 Similar limitations apply in respect of sounds. Hopefully, trade mark law will catch up with technology before long. Some progress has been made, for example, by accepting e-filing but there remains an outdated desire to have representations, even if submitted in digital form, capable of being printed out on paper.

37 Shape marks have caused problems because of the specific absolute grounds of refusal that apply to shapes, discussed later.

38 Pantone Inc has what is claimed to be the most well-known standard for colour classification.

39 [2003] ECR I-3793.

and a representation was submitted in the form of a rectangle of colour with no other indication of the colour such as a reference to a colour coding system. The Court of Justice ruled that a single colour, not spatially limited, may be acceptable if an internationally recognised colour code is used but simply reproducing the colour on paper does not satisfy the requirement of being capable of graphical representation.[40]

Submitting a representation showing two colours on a piece of paper, the top half being one colour, the bottom half being the other colour may satisfy the requirement of being capable of graphical representation if the colours are referred to by an internationally recognised colour coding system. This is so even if the colours are claimed in the abstract without contours provided the representation indicates a systematic arrangement of associating the colours in a predetermined and uniform manner. The Court of Justice so ruled in Case C-49/02 *Heidelberger Bauchemie GmbH*[41] where the sign applied for was on a rectangle of paper, the top half being blue and the bottom half being yellow, with both colours referenced by codes. The applicant sold a large number of goods for the building trade and added a description to its application being 'The mark applied for constitutes the colours of the applicant's enterprise which are utilised in all conceivable forms, in particular on packaging and labels'. Of course, there could be objection to such an application on the basis of the absolute grounds of refusal and it would still have to be shown, in particular, that the sign possessed a distinctive character in relation to the goods or services for which it was to be used, taking account of the use already made of it. A further factor would be the public interest in not unduly restricting the availability of colours for other undertakings which market goods or provide services of the same type as covered by the application for registration.[42] This 'depletion' rule is not one limited to colour marks but simply a matter for consideration under Article 3(1)(b) and (c) and, possibly, other Article 3 objections.[43]

The consequence of these Court of Justice cases is that single colours and colour combinations applied for in the abstract are, in principle, capable of graphical representation if they are referred to by an internationally recognised colour coding system such as the Pantone system. The grounds of refusal may, however, prove insurmountable in many cases although there are a number of registrations for single colours and simple colour combinations.[44] Failure to use a method of defining the colour precisely and objectively is unlikely to overcome an objection that it is not capable of graphical representation.

In *Ty Nant Spring Water Ltd's Trade Mark Application*,[45] a description of a blue bottle of certain thickness and including references to spectrophotometer readings was rejected as an unsatisfactory representation. Geoffrey Hobbs QC, as the Appointed Person, said (at 59):

> unless and until [readers of the description] took such steps [tests to determine which colours fell within the readings] the actual identity of the sign put forward for registration would remain veiled by the wording of the representation. The representation did not mention the colour cobalt blue or include a graphic example of the relevant colour.

Although it is accepted that some additional information, material or benchmark (such as a Pantone colour chart) might be needed to determine the sign with precision, it would be ridiculous to expect someone consulting the register to go to such lengths as carrying out spectrophotometer tests over a range of blue bottles of all shades and tones to determine the precise shade and tone applied for, especially as using a Pantone number would have easily overcome the objection.

Sound marks

Whilst it is now the position that the use of conventional musical notation is appropriate for representing music used as trade marks,[46] confirmed by the Court of Justice in Case C-283/01 *Shield Mark BV* v *Joost Kist*,[47] how other sounds may be represented graphically

40 Applied in *Duckham & Co's Trade Mark Application* [2004] RPC 28 in respect of the colour green applied to engine oil. However, there was insufficient evidence to show that consumers relied upon the colour of the oil as indicating origin.

41 [2004] ECR I-6129.

42 The public interest in not tying up signs that other undertakings might reasonably want to use is not explicit in the Directive though could fall under the absolute ground of refusal based on public policy.

43 Per Jacob LJ in *Bongrain SA's Trade Mark Application* [2005] RPC 14 at para 23.

44 *See*, for example, the single colour orange (Pantone 151) used for, *inter alia*, telephone handsets and services (UK registration No 2007850) and the colour red (Pantone 485) applied to the surface of a passenger transport bus (UK registration No 2103551).

45 [2000] RPC 55.

46 For example, the Direct Line Insurance plc telephone jingle (UK registration Nos 2030045, 2127794 and 2127799).

47 [2003] ECR I-14313.

remains unclear. In *Shield Mark*, a whole range of sound marks were in issue, including a musical stave including the first nine notes of 'Für Elise', by Ludwig van Beethoven, descriptions of music using 'E, D#, E, D#, E, B, D, C, A', one with reference to being played on a piano, another was the denomination 'Kukelekuuuuu' (an onomatopoeia suggesting, in Dutch, a cockcrow), and, finally, a sound mark consisting of a cockcrow.

The Court of Justice ruled that Article 2 of the Directive permitted the registration of sound marks in principle, emphasising again the requirement for graphical representation in that the sign must be clear, precise, self-contained, easily accessible, intelligible, durable and objective. This could be achieved by conventional musical notation with '... a stave divided into measures and showing, in particular, a clef, musical notes and rests whose form indicates the relative value and, where necessary, accidentals'. The requirement could not be met, however, by a description in words, including a list of notes, a description of the sound (such as it being the cry of an animal) or by means of a simple onomatopoeia without more.

The ruling in *Shield Mark* casts serious doubts over some sound marks previously accepted for registration. The prime example is, 'The mark consists of the sound of a dog barking.' This is vague in the extreme and begs questions such as 'What breed of dog?' 'Is it a friendly, warning or aggressive bark?' 'How loud is it?' 'How long is the duration?' etc. The description inevitably leads to the reader's subjective interpretation and the mark must surely be invalid if challenged. It singularly fails the simple test, 'Is the graphical representation clear and unambiguous?' Apart from presenting other traders with the difficulty of not being able to know what the mark is with anything approaching precision, it would be virtually impossible to prove infringement. How could you tell whether the alleged infringing sound was similar to the trade mark?

In the future, it may become acceptable to file a sound mark in digital form[49] so that it can be played by accessing the file by computer. This should now be possible as the *Trade Marks Journal* is available electronically. However, two things stand in the way of this. It is likely that the requirement for graphical representation would have to be relaxed for digital sound and music files (unlike digital image files, they cannot be reproduced on paper in a meaningful way). The second problem is that a sound mark may not be exactly the same when played through different computer and audio systems. Until such time, if ever, that sound marks can be submitted in digital file format, it appears that conventional musical notation is the only option although, of course, the Court of Justice did not rule out other means of graphical representation in *Shield Mark*.[50] It just said what could not satisfy the requirement.

Olfactory marks

The registration of smells, odours and fragrances has met with very little success. This is not surprising, given the Court of Justice's views on what being capable of a graphical representation requires. How does one represent a smell graphically in a way which is clear, precise, self-contained, easily accessible, intelligible, durable and objective? A written description would seem out of the question as lacking precision and depending on the subjective viewpoint of the person reading the description. Nevertheless, a small number of examples of registered olfactory marks exist in the UK:

- The trade mark is a floral fragrance/smell reminiscent of roses applied to tyres (registration No 2001416).
- The mark comprises the strong smell of bitter beer applied to flights for darts (registration No 2000234).

At the Office for the Harmonisation of the Internal Market (Trade Marks and Designs) ('OHIM') an application to register 'the smell of fresh cut grass' for tennis balls was

48 The trade mark belongs to Imperial Chemical Industries plc (UK registration No 2007456). It was registered in 1995.

49 For example, as a WMA or MP3 file.

50 Would a representation of sound in wave form comply?

51 In respect of 'El olor a limon' (the smell of lemon).

52 [2005] ECR II-4705.

accepted (registration No 000428870). This is the only registered olfactory CTM though an appeal is pending in one other case.[51] An application was rejected for 'The smell of ripe strawberries' by the Board of Appeal at OHIM, and this was confirmed by the Court of First Instance in Case T-305/04 *Eden SARL* v *OHIM*.[52] The CTM Regulation has the same requirements for graphical representation as does the Directive and the 1994 Act.

Applicants hoping to register olfactory marks soon realised that a written description on its own may not be sufficient to fulfil the requirements of graphical representation and they demonstrated some not inconsiderable ingenuity.[53] In *John Lewis of Hungerford Ltd's Trade Mark Application*,[54] the trade mark was described as '. . . comprising the smell, aroma or essence of cinnamon' and was applied for in respect of furniture. In an attempt to overcome an objection that the description lacked precision (for example, it presupposed the reader was familiar with the smell of cinnamon), the applicant submitted evidence from an 'electronic nose' analysis which gave a graphical profile or 'fingerprint' of the smell of cinnamon. Geoffrey Hobbs QC, as the Appointed Person, rejected the applicant's appeal, saying (at 592):

53 What appears to be a waveform representation and a chromatograph have been used without success.

54 [2001] RPC 28.

> . . . the need to have regard to something outside the graphic representation in order to obtain a direct perception of the sign it represents does not always or necessarily indicate that the graphic representation is inadequate for the purposes of examination and registration under the Act.

He went on to point out that the accepted practice was to name colours by reference to Pantone chart numbers and to represent sound by musical notation. The 'something outside the graphic representation' alluded to by Geoffrey Hobbs QC may be some form of accessible benchmark. He gave an example of a form of description that might be acceptable in relation to olfactory marks, being 'the smell of [for example, cinnamon] as emitted by x' where the nature and condition of x, the benchmark, was clearly and unambiguously defined. In view of the Court of Justice's ruling in *Ralf Sieckmann*, below, this now probably goes too far as it still is subject to an objection that it permits too much subjectivity.

55 [2002] ECR I-11737.

Case C-273/00 *Ralf Sieckmann* v *Deutsches Patentund Markenamt*[55] is the most authoritative case on graphical representations and olfactory marks. The application was in respect of a fruity smell which included a cinnamon-like smell. Mr Sieckmann went to great lengths to try to ensure that he satisfied the requirement of a graphical representation. He described the mark thus:

> Trade mark protection is sought for the olfactory mark deposited with the Deutsches Patent und Markenamt of the pure chemical substance methyl cinnamate (= cinnamic acid methyl ester), whose structural formula is set out below. Samples of this olfactory mark can also be obtained via local laboratories listed in the Gelbe Seiten (Yellow Pages) of Deutsche Telekom AG or, for example, via the firm E. Merck in Darmstadt.

$$C_6H_5-CH=CHCOOCH_3$$

Fearing this was not enough he added the following addendum:

> The trade mark applicant hereby declares his consent to an inspection of the files relating to the deposited olfactory mark methyl cinnamate pursuant to . . . [here he refers to specific provisions of German trade mark law]

He also submitted a sample in a container which stated that the scent was usually described as 'balsamically fruity with a slight hint of cinnamon'.

The Court of Justice again confirmed that for the purposes of Article 2 of the Directive, a trade mark may consist of a sign which is not in itself capable of being perceived visually, provided that it can be represented graphically, particularly by means of images, lines or characters, and that the representation is clear, precise, self-contained, easily accessible, intelligible, durable and objective. In relation to olfactory marks, the requirement that the sign is capable of being represented graphically cannot be satisfied by a chemical formula, by a description in written words, by the deposit of a sample of the smell or by a combination of those means.

The Court of Justice did not rule out the principle that olfactory marks may be represented graphically in an acceptable manner, but it is difficult to see what form of representation can suffice. A chemical formula does nothing to inform the reader of the nature of the smell[56] and samples suffer from the disadvantage that they are likely to deteriorate and change with time. It is probably the written description that comes nearest to fulfilling the requirement, though plainly, on the basis of the ruling in *Ralf Sieckmann*, a description on its own is not good enough. It may be that the form of words suggested by Geoffrey Hobbs QC in *John Lewis of Hungerford*, 'the smell of X as emitted by Y' where 'Y' is a generally accessible and stable benchmark, might just succeed. Fresh cut grass might be such a benchmark. However, it seems that combining a description with an image of the 'benchmark' will not satisfy the requirement as in CTM case T-305/04 *Eden SARL* v *OHIM*,[57] where the description 'the smell of ripe strawberries' was accompanied by a colour image of a strawberry.

Shape marks

There should be no difficulty in providing a graphical representation of a shape mark by means of a drawing or set of drawings from different angles,[58] perhaps accompanied by a description which may include some reference to dimensions. A written description alone is unlikely to suffice unless the shape is very well known, such as a sphere or a pyramid, but then other objections based on, for example, lack of distinctive character may be raised.

The Court of Justice has made it clear that shape marks are to be treated no differently to other types of signs for the purposes of fulfilling the requirements under Article 2 of the Directive.[59]

Drawings, even coupled with written descriptions, can still suffer from the defect of lacking precision and clarity. In *Triomed (Proprietary) Ltd* v *Beecham Group plc*,[60] the South African High Court revoked a shape mark used for pharmaceuticals. One of the reasons was that, although the representation consisted of a plan and side elevation, the description was that the mark consisted of the 'shape and configuration of a tablet *substantially* as shown in the representation' (emphasis added) and, furthermore, the registration applied to all dimensions of the tablet and in all colours. The registration extended beyond the actual representation to a shape 'substantially' as depicted. An additional ground for revocation was that the mark was incapable of distinguishing the goods of the proprietor from those of other traders.[61]

In the UK, in *Swizzels Matlow Ltd's Trade Mark Application*,[62] the sign 'The trade mark consists of a chewy sweet on a stick' was held not to be capable of graphical representation as lacking precision and being ambiguous. A second application, which had a flattened version of the sweet itself attached to the application form and which indicated that the mark was a shape, had earlier wisely been withdrawn by the applicant. An application to register a mark described as 'a circular compressed tablet bearing a raised heart outline on both flat surfaces and containing within the heart outline on one side any one of several different words or phrases' (sweets sold under the trade mark 'LOVE HEARTS') also failed. This was because the description was inadequate as there was no restriction to the size, location, thickness or shape of the heart outline or to the area available for the words and phrases.[63] It was also held that the word 'graphically' extended the meaning of 'represented' and did not restrict it to a purely visual image. Thus, the graphical form used could be by writing, drawing, musical notation, written description or any combination of these. This latter point arose because a case before the Board of Appeal in the OHIM had seemingly indicated that a visual image of a mark was essential in the case of non-word marks.[64] In the present case, Simon Thorley QC, as the Appointed Person, rejected

56 Unless the reader is a chemist familiar with the odour produced by the substance represented by the formula.

57 [2005] ECR II-4705, Court of First Instance.

58 A single drawing showing a perspective view might suffice.

59 C-299/99 *Koninklijke Philips Electronics NV* v *Remington Consumer Products Ltd* [2005] FSR 17.

60 [2001] FSR 34.

61 The judge accepted that decisions on the provisions in the UK Trade Marks Act 1994 corresponding to s 10(1) of the South African Trade Marks Act 1993 were equally applicable to the South African Act. Section 10(1) prohibits registration of marks that do not constitute trade marks. Section 2 requires that marks are 'capable of distinguishing' and capable of being represented graphically.

62 [1998] RPC 244.

63 *Swizzels Matlow Ltd's Three Dimensional Trade Mark Application* [1999] RPC 879. A similar mark but having dimensions (diameter and thickness) together with a visual image has been registered (No 2153268).

64 *Antoni and Alison's Application* [1998] ETMR 460.

such a limitation. He said that he doubted that the Board of Appeal would have intended to place such a limitation on the equivalent provision in the CTM Regulation.

Some specific examples of trade marks are given in Article 2, being words (including personal names), designs, letters, numerals, or the shape of goods or their packaging.[65] This allows the registration of distinctive containers and, although there are exceptions, this could include designs registrable under the Registered Designs Act 1949 or the Community Design Regulation or protected by the unregistered Community design or the UK unregistered design right.[66] This could mean that designs which could only be protected for a maximum of 25 years under design law could be protected as registered trade marks indefinitely. However, there is an important proviso stated in Article 3(1)(e) and a sign will not be registered if it consists exclusively of the shape which gives substantial value to the goods, is necessary to obtain a technical result[67] or results from the nature of the goods themselves. Nevertheless, there remains a class of designs which may be subject to dual protection under design law and trade mark law.

A disadvantage some shape marks may have to overcome to be registrable is that the public does not necessarily regard them as trade marks.[68] This may be the case where goods of a certain shape are well known as being from a particular manufacturer, but it is the name of the manufacturer rather than the shape of the goods which is recognised as being the trade mark by the public. For example, the shape of Lego bricks, having raised circular studs which fit into tubes in the underside of the bricks, is so well known that almost everyone would instantly recognise them as Lego bricks. However, in spite of this, it was held that an application to register a brick as a trade mark must fail in *Interlego AG's Trade Mark Applications*.[69] There was no real evidence that the public recognised the bricks or the raised knobs or studs as trade marks. The Lego bricks had been subject to a patent, which had expired. Neuberger J observed that this was a factor which should be taken into account in deciding whether to register a trade mark. He rejected the existence of a rule to the effect that dual protection could not be possible,[70] but said the decision to register required balancing the very substantial benefit to the proprietor in registering a mark with the public interest against monopolies in products (as opposed to marks).

The Directive and the Act both have a ground for refusal for signs contrary to public policy but there is no express prohibition based on public interest as such. However, the Court of Justice has, on several occasions, said that the rationale of some of the grounds of refusal are based on public interest, such as the ground under Article 3(1)(c) where a trade mark consists exclusively of signs or indications describing a characteristic of goods or services, for example, in relation to kind, quality, purpose or geographical origin.[71] Other undertakings should be free to use such signs in relation to their goods or services, providing that they have not become distinctive of the goods or services of one particular undertaking. Otherwise, the common language of a particular type of business enterprise might end up being tied up in the hands of a few undertakings.

Registration will be refused if the application is made in bad faith, and it is arguable that an applicant who subsequently wishes to gain further protection for a registered design or patent, which is about to expire, could be deemed to apply in bad faith. However, bad faith requires conduct approaching dishonesty, as will be seen later.

The bad faith argument was used by the opponent in *Unilever plc's Trade Mark Applications*.[72] Unilever was the proprietor of a patent in respect of a 'layered confection product' (actually 'Vienetta' ice cream). That patent was due to expire in August 2001 and Unilever applied to register two shape marks using drawings showing the ice-cream products. The opponent claimed that the application was made in bad faith as the applications were made in order to prolong indefinitely, and to extend the scope of, the protection that had been afforded by the patent. This argument was not fully explored by the Hearing Officer, as he did not believe that registration of the marks would prevent anyone making use of the patents once they had expired.

---

65 Under the previous law, a trade mark had to be something distinct from the article marked. In *Re James Trade Mark* (1886) 33 ChD 392, an application to register a shape mark (a dome of blacklead) was refused.

66 Indeed, in *SmithKline & French Laboratories Ltd v Sterling Winthrop Group Ltd* [1976] RPC 511, Lord Diplock accepted that design registration and trade mark registration were not mutually exclusive.

67 This exception applies even if there exists more than one shape to achieve a particular technical result: *see* Case C-299/99 *Koninklijke Philips Electronics NV v Remington Consumer Products Ltd* [2002] ECR I-5475.

68 *See*, for example, Jacob LJ in *Bongrain SA's Trade Mark Application* [2005] RPC 14 at para 25. The trade mark in question was for a shape applied to cheese.

69 [1998] RPC 69.

70 Suggested by Peterson J in *Moore's Modern Methods Ltd's Application for a Trade Mark* (1919) 36 RPC 12, where an application had been made to register a trade mark, the subject matter of a patent which was about to expire.

71 Joined Cases C-108/97 and C-109/97 *Windsurfing Chiemsee v Huber and Attenberger* [1999] ECR I-2779.

72 (Unreported) 9 August 2001, Trade Marks Registry. One of the two marks (the more distinctive) was accepted for registration.

Another hurdle that stands in the way of registering shape marks results from the basic requirement that the mark must be capable of distinguishing goods or services of one undertaking from those of others. If the shape is not being generally appreciated by the public as being a trade mark, it will not be registrable, even if the public recognises or is familiar with the shape. It has to operate as a trade mark – a badge of origin.[73]

If the sign for which registration as a trade mark is sought complies with the basic requirements in Article 2, there are a number of grounds of refusal of registration, absolute and relative, and it is to these that our attention must now turn.

Unregistrable signs

Inevitably, there are some important exceptions to the types of signs that can be registered as trade marks. There are two sets of grounds for refusal of registration: absolute and relative. Generally, for the absolute grounds, marks caught are unregistrable *per se*; however, in some cases, trade marks may still be registrable if they have become distinctive through use even though they would normally be rejected (for example, a geographical name). An example is 'Yorkshire', registered for tea and which proceeded to registration on the basis of distinctiveness acquired through use.[74] For the relative grounds of refusal, the relationship between the mark for which registration is applied for and earlier trade marks or other rights is important. The relative grounds for refusal have a close parallel in terms of the ways in which registered trade marks can be infringed as a comparison between the relative grounds for refusal under Article 4(1) and (4)(a) and the forms of infringement in Article 5(1) and (2) demonstrate (the equivalent provisions in the Act are s 5(1)–(3) and s 10(1)–(3)).[75] The process of examination by the Trade Marks Registry and the fact that trade mark applications can be opposed are important features of the trade mark system.[76] As the Court of Justice stated in Case C-39/97 *Canon Kabushiki Kaisha* v *Metro-Goldwyn-Mayer Inc* (at para 21):[77]

> For reasons of legal certainty and proper administration, it is necessary to ensure that trade marks whose use could successfully be challenged before the courts are not registered.

Under Article 13 of the Directive, where the grounds for refusal exist only in respect of some of the goods or services for which registration is sought, refusal will cover those goods or services only, leaving registration possible in respect of the others applied for.[78]

The relative grounds for refusal of registration may now only be raised by the proprietor of the earlier trade mark or other earlier right in opposition proceedings as a result of the Trade Marks (Relative Grounds) Order 2007.[79] This brings the UK in line with practice at the OHIM in relation to the Community trade mark.

Absolute grounds for refusal or invalidity

The absolute grounds for refusal are set out in Article 3 (s 3 of the Act). The term 'absolute grounds for refusal' is used in the Act but not in the Directive, Article 3 of which is simply headed 'Grounds for refusal or invalidity'.[80] Apart from requiring compliance with the basic meaning of a trade mark in Article 2, the trade mark must have an inherent or acquired distinctiveness. Where the mark is a shape mark, it will be refused (or vulnerable to invalidity if registered) where the sign consists exclusively of a shape resulting from the nature of the goods, necessary to obtain a technical result or which gives substantial value to the goods. Other grounds for refusal or invalidity apply where the mark is contrary to

73 *Triomed (Proprietary) Ltd* v *Beecham Group plc* [2001] FSR 34.

74 UK Registration No 1570522.

75 Article 5 on rights and infringement (see s 10 of the Act) is less extensive than the relative grounds in Article 4 (see s 5 of the Act) as there is no need for an equivalent provision on infringement for refusal of registration based on an earlier unregistered trade mark. Article 4(4)(b) or some other earlier right in Article 4(4)(c) as an infringement action can be brought on the basis of passing off (in the UK) or, for example, copyright.

76 Observations may also be submitted by any person under s 38(3) without becoming a party to the proceedings on the application.

77 [1998] ECR I-5507.

78 This also applies to revocation and invalidity.

79 SI 2007/1976. This Order came into force on 1 October 2007.

80 One of the grounds for invalidity in the Act is if the trade mark was registered in breach of s 3: Trade Marks Act 1994 s 47(1). This is subject to a proviso that breach of s 3(1)(b), (c) or (d) will not invalidate the registration if the trade mark has become distinctive through use.

public policy or accepted principles of morality, deceptive, or if the application is made in bad faith. Further grounds apply in the context of specially protected emblems and trade marks, the use of which could be prohibited by law. The main 'absolute' grounds for refusal, under Article 3(1)(a)–(d) and (3), are set out below.[81]

Article 3 Grounds for refusal or invalidity

(1) The following shall not be registered or if registered shall be liable to be declared invalid:
   (a) signs which cannot constitute a trade mark;
   (b) trade marks which are devoid of any distinctive character;
   (c) trade marks which consist exclusively of signs or indications which may serve, in trade, to designate the kind, quality, quantity, intended purpose, value, geographical origin, or the time of production of the goods or of rendering the service, or other characteristics of goods;
   (d) trade marks which consist exclusively of signs or indications which have become customary in the current language or bona fide and established practices of the trade

   . . .

(3) A trade mark shall not be refused registration or be declared invalid in accordance with paragraph (1)(b), (c) or (d) if, before the date of application for registration and following the use which has been made of it, it has acquired a distinctive character. Any Member State may in addition provide that this provision shall also apply where the distinctive character was acquired after the date of application for registration or after the date of registration.

Before looking at the case law on these provisions, a few points can be made. Article 3(1)(a) is obviously a reference to the basic meaning of 'trade mark' in Article 2.[82] It should also be noted that acquired distinctiveness cannot rescue a sign caught by Article 3(1)(a) as Article 3(3) applies only to trade marks within Article 3(1)(b), (c) and (d).[83] Finally, the option in the final sentence of Article 3(3) has been taken up by the UK so that a challenge on the validity of a trade mark based on a breach of Article 3(1)(b), (c) or (d) can be defeated by proof of distinctiveness acquired through use.[84]

82 At the equivalent place in the Trade Marks Act 1994 (s 3(1)(a)), there is a reference back to the basic meaning in s 1(1). That Article 3(1)(a) relates directly to Article 2 was confirmed by the Court of Justice in Case C-299/99 *Koninklijke Philips Electronics NV v Remington Consumer Products Ltd* [2002] ECR I-5475.

83 Nor does it apply to shape marks within Article 3(1)(e): *see* later.

84 See the proviso to s 47(1) of the Act.

The grounds under Article 3(1)(a)–(d) (taken together with Article 3(3)) can be justified on the basis of public interest. It is not in the public interest to have signs and marks registered as trade marks which do not serve the primary function of indicating the origin of goods or services: for example, signs which are not capable of distinguishing the goods or services of one undertaking from those of other undertakings or which do not have any distinctive character. There is also a public interest in not registering trade marks which would prejudice the rights of other undertakings to use ordinary language to describe the nature and characteristics of their goods and services or which would prevent the use by others of the common stock of language generally used in a particular sector.[85] In some cases, however, a word or a term used to describe characteristics of goods or services or which was commonly used in the trade may have been used to such an extent by one undertaking that it has become synonymous with its goods or services. A mark that otherwise lacked distinctiveness may have become distinctive through continual and extensive use by one particular undertaking. In such cases, the public interest is no longer best served by denying registration. Where marks have become distinctive through use and function as indicators of origin there can be no objection, especially as the undertaking concerned may have built sufficient goodwill in the mark to be protected by the law of passing off.

85 The presence of the limitations on the rights afforded by registration in Article 6 of the Directive, such as the use by a trader of his own name or using indications describing characteristics of goods or services has no bearing on the operation of Article 3 which should be seen as the first line of protection of other traders' legitimate interests: *'Cycling . . . IS' Trade Mark Applications* [2002] RPC 37.

Relationship between the grounds under Article 3(1)(a)–(d)

It is inevitable that there will be some overlap between the four grounds under Article 3(1)(a)–(d), but each remains independent of the others. In Case C-517/99 *Merz & Krell GmbH*,[86] an application was made to register the word 'Bravo' as a trade mark for writing

86 [2001] ECR I-6959.

implements. It was objected to on the grounds that the word was within Article 3(1)(d) as it had become customary in the current language or *bona fide* and established practices in the trade and that it did not need specifically to describe the goods in question. The Court of Justice ruled that the purpose of Article 3(1)(d) was to prevent the registration of trade marks which could not distinguish the goods or services of one undertaking from those of other undertakings and it was necessary to consider the application of Article 3(1)(d) in the context of the goods or services in respect of which registration was sought. Although there was a clear overlap between Article 3(1)(c) and (d), marks covered by the latter were excluded, not because they were descriptive, but on the basis of current usage in the sectors covering trade in the goods or services for which registration was sought. The Court of Justice confirmed the independent nature of the grounds again in Case C-363/99 *Koninklijke KPN Nederland NV* v *Benelux-Merkenbureau*,[87] in which the application was for the word 'Postkantoor' (which may be translated as 'post office') for a number of classes of goods and services including paper, insurance, postage stamps, construction, telecommunications, etc. which had been refused as being exclusively descriptive. The Court said (at para 67):

> . . . it is clear from Article 3(1) of the Directive that each of the grounds for refusal listed in that provision is independent of the others and calls for a separate examination . . . That is true in particular of the grounds of refusal listed in paragraphs (b), (c) and (d) of Article 3(1), although there is a clear overlap between the scope of the respective provisions . . .

Article 3(1)(a) – not a trade mark

If a trade mark is distinctive as a matter of fact, whether through use or otherwise, it is arguable whether there is any room for testing the mark against Article 3(1)(a), at least to the extent that it is incapable of distinguishing the goods or services of one undertaking from those of other undertakings. The Court of Justice did not go quite as far as saying this in Case C-299/99 *Koninklijke Philips Electronics NV* v *Remington Consumer Products Ltd*,[88] where it ruled that there is no category of marks that are not excluded under Article 3(1)(b), (c) or (d) and Article 3(3) which is nonetheless excluded from registration by Article 3(1)(a). The case involved the shape of a three-headed shaver. However, the Court was making a generalisation in answer to the question submitted, asking whether there was a class of marks that were *de facto* distinctive which were nevertheless incapable of being distinctive *de jure* on the basis of Article 3(1)(a). Remington had sought to rely on the distinction between Article 3(1)(a) (which was based on Article 2) and the other grounds under Article 3(1)(b)–(d), arguing that signs caught by Article 3(1)(a) could never be registered, regardless of evidence of distinctiveness. This was rejected by the Court of Justice which said that there is no class of marks which are distinctive as a result of the use made of them which is not capable of distinguishing goods or services within Article 2.

Article 3(1)(b) – devoid of any distinctive character

Simple geometric shapes, single colours and descriptive or laudatory words may all fall into this ground for refusal. In some cases, such as with words such as 'Soap', 'Luxury' or 'Wholesome', there is likely to be objection also under Article 3(1)(c) and, possibly, also Article 3(1)(d). Of course, trade marks which once were devoid of any distinctive character may become distinctive through the use that is made of them.[89] Even a single colour, *per se*, may be found to be distinctive under Article 3(1)(b) and (3), as in Case C-104/01 *Libertel Groep NV* v *Benelux-Merkenbureau*[90] which concerned an application to register the colour orange in the abstract to be used in relation to telecommunications. Of course, it does not follow as a matter of inexorable logic that a mark which is not wholly descriptive must be distinctive.[91]

87 [2004] ECR I-1619.

88 [2002] ECR I-5475.

89 A triangle and diamond shape are registered trade marks dating back to 1876 in the UK (registration numbers 914 and 817).

90 [2003] ECR I-3793.

91 Per Geoffrey Hobbs QC as the Appointed Person in *'Cycling . . . IS' Trade Mark Applications* [2002] RPC 37 at paras 43 and 44, explaining the Court of Justice ruling in Case C-383/99P *Procter & Gamble Co* v *OHIM* [2001] ECR I-6251.

In assessing whether a trade mark is devoid of distinctive character under Article 3(1)(b), reference should be made to the goods or services for which registration is sought and to the perception of the relevant public, being average consumers of the goods or services in question, who are reasonably well-informed and reasonably observant and circumspect.[92]

The test for distinctiveness of a trade mark which is a surname is no different to that for any other form of trade mark and the fact that there is a limitation to the rights of a trade mark under Article 6(1)(a) so that a third party may not be prevented from using his own name and address in the course of trade is of no relevance.[93]

A question arises as to whether Article 3(1)(b) adds anything to or supplements Article 3(1)(a), especially in terms of distinctiveness.[94] One might say that it must provide an additional barrier otherwise there would be no need for the provision. In *British Sugar plc* v *James Robertson & Sons Ltd*,[95] Jacob J approached the question the other way round. He said that the requirement that the mark is 'capable of distinguishing' did not add anything to the equivalent provision to Article 3(1)(b) and (3), which 'bars the registration of a mark which is *devoid of distinctive character* unless it has *in fact acquired a distinctive character*' (original emphasis). He then went on to say that if a mark was, on its face, non-distinctive (such as a descriptive or laudatory word) but was shown to have a distinctive character in fact, then it must be capable of distinguishing.

In *British Sugar plc* v *James Robertson & Son Ltd*,[96] Jacob J considered that the phrase 'devoid of any distinctive character' required consideration of the mark on its own, assuming no use. He said (at 306):

Is it the sort of word (or other sign) which cannot do the job of distinguishing without first educating the public that it is a trade mark?

Thus, for a trade mark to be caught by the ground under Article 3(1)(b) it must be potentially capable of distinguishing the goods or services of one undertaking from those of others but, because of lack of use, it is not perceived as a badge of origin. Where the mark's inherent distinctiveness is an issue, as it is in Article 3(1)(b), the mark must perform the function of indicating origin even before the relevant public has been educated that it is to be used for that purpose.[97] Article 3(3) provides a means of escaping the prohibition by showing that the relevant public has been so educated. The distinction between a mark being inherently distinctive or having acquired distinctiveness could be described as the difference between nature and nurture as noted in *AD2000 Trade Mark*[98] by Geoffrey Hobbs QC, as the Appointed Person, where he said (at 175):

. . . a sign possesses a distinctive character if and when it is endowed by nature and/or nurture with the capacity to communicate the fact that the goods or services with reference to which it is used recurrently are those of one and the same undertaking.

The burden of proof, to show that a mark has acquired a distinctive character as a result of the use made of it, lies on the applicant to register the mark. Whether this can be satisfied without evidence of actual use is uncertain. In Case C-342/97 *Lloyd Schuhfabrik Meyer & Co GmbH* v *Klisjen Handel BV*,[99] the Court of Justice said in relation to the assessment of whether a sign had a distinctive character:

. . . account should be taken, in particular, of the inherent characteristics of the mark, including the fact that it does or does not contain an element descriptive of the goods or services for which it has been registered; the market share held by the mark, how intensive, geographically widespread and long-standing use of the mark has been; the amount invested by the undertaking in promoting the mark; the proportion of the relevant section of the public which, because of the mark, identifies the goods or services as originating from a particular undertaking; and statements from chambers of commerce and industry or other professional associations.

92 See, for example, Case C-363/99 *Koninklijke KPN Nederland NV* v *Benelux-Merkenbureau* [2004] ECR I-1619. This test is of wider application and has been used in relation to shape marks.

93 Case C-404/02 *Nichols plc* v *Registrar of Trade Marks* [2004] ECR I-8499 and *Oska's Ltd's Trade Mark Application* [2005] RPC 20.

94 Of course, there cannot be complete overlap between the provisions as Article 2, on which Article 3(1)(a) is based, requires also that the mark is a sign capable of being represented graphically. The issue is whether it automatically follows that a mark which is incapable of distinguishing must be devoid of a distinctive character and vice versa.

95 [1996] RPC 281.

96 [1996] RPC 281.

97 See *Yakult Honsha KK's Trade Mark Application* [2001] RPC 39.

98 [1997] RPC 168.

99 [1999] ECR I-3819 at para 24.

This certainly points to actual use, and probably substantial actual use, before a mark that would otherwise be caught by Article 3(1)(b)–(d) can have any chance of being shown to have acquired a distinctive character through use. However, in a number of cases, lack of evidence of use has not prevented the question from being considered, as in *AD2000 Trade Mark* above.[100] Another example is *SM Jaleel & Co Ltd's Trade Mark Application*[101] where there was only a statutory declaration from an expert in the field of resin and packaging products to the effect that the shape of a bottle having a six-fingered petaloid base was unique and distinctive. Geoffrey Hobbs QC, as the Appointed Person, disagreed. An important aspect of his decision is that he said that even if a shape mark complied with the basic meaning of trade mark and was not excluded by the grounds of refusal relating to shape marks (see below), it would still have to possess a distinctive character. It is submitted, however, that it will be highly unlikely that a mark will be saved from the grounds under Article 3(1)(b)–(d) without compelling evidence of use showing a causal link between that use and the fact that a significant proportion of the relevant public (consumers and end-users at least) perceive the trade mark as indicating the origin of the goods or services in question.

Distinctiveness in terms of shape marks is a particular issue as, in many cases, the public will not perceive them as trade marks.[102] An argument that the shapes of toasters, subject to the application, were inherently distinctive was rejected by Lloyd J in *Dualit Ltd's (Toaster Shapes) Trade Mark Applications*.[103] It is possible that the public needs educating that shapes are now generally registrable as trade marks (subject to the other grounds of refusal, in particular those specifically applying the shape marks under Article 3(1)(e)) and, even then, a particular shape mark should contain some unusual or idiosyncratic feature when compared to shapes already in use for similar articles before it is likely to have a distinctive character. Failure to educate the public that the shape of a bottle had a trade mark significance was fatal to an application in *Yakult Honsha KK's Trade Mark Application*.[104]

The Court of Justice confirmed that it may be more difficult to show that signs consisting of the shape of packaging are distinctive compared with word or figurative marks in Case C-218/01 *Henkel KGaA v Deutsches Patentund Markenamt*.[105] Average consumers are not in the habit of making assumptions about the origin of goods on the basis of the shape of their packaging, absent any graphic or word element. The test for whether the trade mark possessed a distinctive character was modified in cases where the trade mark consisted of the shape of packaging for goods packaged in the trade for purposes connected with their character (for example, in the case of a liquid or powder). The assessment was still to be based on the average consumer who was reasonably well-informed and reasonably observant and circumspect. However, additionally, such a consumer must be able to distinguish the product concerned from those of other undertakings without conducting an analytical or comparative examination and without paying particular attention.

The fact that a shape may be different may not be enough to overcome the difficulty that the public generally do not perceive shapes as trade marks. Mere use is not enough; it must be shown that the public actually perceive the shape as being a trade mark. In *Bongrain SA's Trade Mark Application*,[106] involving an application to register a three-dimensional shape for cheese, Jacob LJ said (at para 28):

> . . . an average consumer, surveying the myriad of cheeses on display in a good supermarket or on a restaurant cheese platter, would, I think, be astonished to be told that one of the shapes was a trade mark. Consumers do not expect to eat trade marks or part of them . . . without established use and recognition it cannot be said that he would, without more, regard shape alone as giving him a guarantee of origin – the essence of what a trade mark is.

The level of attention of the average consumer to trade marks is also likely to vary according to the category of goods or service in question. For example, the level of attention of consumers is not likely to be high in relation to the shape and colour of washing machine

100 See also *Ty Nant Spring Water Ltd's Trade Mark Application* [1999] RPC 392 where the Hearing Officer decided that the application was caught by s 3(1)(b) in the absence of any evidence of use.

101 [2000] RPC 471.

102 A good example of an exception to this basic premise is the Coca-Cola bottle.

103 [1999] RPC 890.

104 [2001] RPC 39.

105 [2004] ECR I-1725.

106 [2005] RPC 14.

107 Joined Cases C-468/01P to C-472/01P, *Procter & Gamble Co v OHIM* [2004] ECR I-5141 at para 11; a case on the equivalent provisions in the CTM Regulation. *See*, in respect of the Directive, Case C-342/97 *Lloyd Schuhfabrik Meyer & Co GmbH v Klisjen Handel BV* [1999] ECR I-3819 at para 26.

108 In *Colgate-Palmolive Co's Trade Mark Application* [2002] RPC 26, the sign in question was a slug of striped toothpaste which was held to lack a distinctive character. The stripes were more likely to be seen as the arrangement of the product, mere decoration or even indicating the active ingredients of the toothpaste.

109 See *Dyson Ltd's Trade Mark Application* [2003] RPC 47. Questions submitted to the Court of Justice were stayed pending resolution of the outcome of an appeal from the OHIM to the Court of First Instance in relation to the same mark, being the transparent bin used on Dyson vacuum cleaners (though not claimed to be a shape mark).

110 See, for example, Joined Cases C-53/01 to C-55/01 *Linde AG, Winward Industries Inc and Rado Uhren AG* [2003] ECR I-3161 (concerning applications to register a vehicle, torch and wrist-watch as trade marks). The Court confirmed that Article 3(1)(c) is also relevant to shape marks under Article 3(1)(e), discussed later.

111 [2002] RPC 7.

112 'Cycling . . . IS' Trade Mark Applications [2002] RPC 37.

113 [1999] ECR I-2779.

and dishwasher tablets, being everyday consumer goods.[107] The same could be said to apply to striped toothpaste and, again, the problem is that such a sign is unlikely to be taken as having a trade mark significance.[108] Even the fact that the trade mark applied for has been used by only one undertaking with a *de facto* monopoly in the mark may not overcome an objection based on lack of distinctive character.[109]

Article 3(1)(c) – descriptive of characteristics, etc. of goods or services

There are numerous cases on this ground for refusal, as might be expected. Again, the ground can be overcome by showing distinctiveness acquired through use. The public interest in allowing others freely to describe their goods or services is paramount here and subject only to acquired distinctiveness under Article 3(3).[110] For example, in *Besnier SA's Trade Mark Application*,[111] it was held that the use of the trade mark for which registration was sought, 'Day by Day', would naturally be used by other traders to describe the time of delivery for their goods and services, and the main purpose of Article 3(1)(c) was to prevent the registration of words and phrases that other undertakings would want to use in a non-trade mark sense. One would expect evidence of distinctiveness acquired through use to be convincing to overcome this public interest.

The ground for refusal requires that the signs or indications in question '. . . may serve, in trade, to designate . . .' The use of 'may' suggests a degree of foreseeability in applying the ground and it is not necessary that the trade mark already does indicate the characteristics caught by Article 3(1)(c) such as kind and purpose of geographical origin.[112]

It must be noted that the ground for refusal applies only if the trade mark consists exclusively of signs or indications of the type covered by the ground. The same applies to Article 3(1)(d). Notwithstanding the independence of the two grounds, there is clearly a large overlap between them and they serve the same public interest, being to keep free words and phrases used by or likely to be used by undertakings in relation to their goods and services by way of description or common appellation including words and phrases likely to be associated with goods and services where persons and operators in the trade can be expected to have a reasonable expectation that they are free to use them.

Speaking of signs and indications which may serve to indicate geographical origin of the goods or services for which registration is sought, the Court of Justice said in Joined Cases C-108/97 and C-109/97 *Windsurfing Chiemsee v Huber and Attenberger*[113] (at para 26):

> . . . it is in the public interest that they remain available, not least because they may be an indication of the quality and other characteristics of the categories of goods concerned, and may also, in various ways, influence consumer tastes by, for instance, associating the goods with a place that may give rise to a favourable response.

The applicant had applied to register various trade marks including the word 'Chiemsee', which is the name of the largest lake in Bavaria. The Court of Justice confirmed that the Directive did not prohibit the registration of a geographical name as trade marks where the name was associated in the minds of the relevant class of persons with the category of goods concerned. Where there is no such association currently, an assessment should be made as to whether it is reasonable to assume that such a name is capable of designating the geographical origin of the goods in question, taking into account the degree of familiarity of the relevant class of persons with the name, the characteristics of the place designated by the name and the category of goods concerned. The Court went on to say that it was not necessary for the goods to be made in a particular location to be associated with it.

The term 'relevant class of persons' is important though there is surprisingly little case law on what it means. In *Windsurfing*, the Court of Justice said that it was persons in the trade and average consumers of the category of goods in the territory for which registration is sought. It is well-settled, however, that the Court ought to take into account the presumed expectations of the average consumer who is taken to be reasonably well-informed and reasonably observant and circumspect for the purposes of determining distinctiveness.[114]

A neologism comprising two or more familiar descriptive words or abbreviations which refer to attributes of the goods or services in question may not overcome the ground under Article 3(1)(c) unless it is unusual in some way such that it does not have a meaning which is descriptive. For example, 'mildsoap', 'cleanfresh', 'easytalk' or 'quick-shine' are all likely to be unregistrable in the absence of acquired distinctiveness through use.[115] To be registrable, a neologism comprising ordinary descriptive words must be more than the sum of its parts: for example, the word 'WEBSPHERE'.[116] If it has more than one possible meaning, it may still be unregistrable if one of those meanings is descriptive of characteristics of goods or services.

In Case C-265/00 *Campina Melkunie BV* v *Benelux-Merkenbureau*,[117] the application was for 'BIOMILD' for goods which included foodstuffs and milk products. The Benelux trade mark office, which referred the case to the Court of Justice for a preliminary ruling, had initially rejected the application on the basis that its sole meaning was that the goods for which it was intended to be used were biological and mild. The Court of Justice ruled that a neologism made up of elements which were themselves descriptive of the goods or services was itself descriptive unless there was a perceptible difference between the neologism and the sum of its parts. Whilst a word such as that in issue may not have been used previously, it is sufficient for the ground of refusal to apply that it could be used to describe the qualities or other characteristics of the goods or services. A word must be refused registration, therefore, if at least one of its possible meanings designated a characteristic of the goods or services concerned. Here, the Court of Justice referred to a case under the CTM Regulation to that effect: Case C-191/01P *OHIM* v *Wm Wrigley Jr Co*,[118] which concerned a refusal to register 'DOUBLEMINT', in particular, for chewing gum. The Court of First Instance had applied a test based on whether the word was 'exclusively descriptive' of the goods or services. The Court of Justice, in referring the case back to the Court of First Instance, ruled that this was not the correct test under Article 7(1)(c) of the CTM Regulation.[119] The issue was whether it was capable of being used by others to designate characteristic of their goods or services. In Case C-383/99P *Procter & Gamble Co* v *OHIM*[120] the mark in question was 'BABY-DRY', used for disposable nappies for babies. It was held that, although the word combination alluded to the function the goods were supposed to fulfil (that is, keeping a baby dry) the syntactically unusual combination was not a familiar expression in the English language either to describe babies' nappies or their essential characteristics.[121]

The Court of Justice in *OHIM* v *Wrigley* distinguished (or clarified) the BABY-DRY case, noting that the word in question does not have to be in current use to preclude registration, but there should be a reasonable apprehension that it may be used descriptively by others in the future. Also, the fact that more than one term can be used to describe the characteristics of particular goods does not mean that those terms cease to be descriptive. It is submitted that what the Court intended in the previous sentence was in relation to the existence of more than one term used to describe a *particular* characteristic of particular goods.

In *Campina*, the Court of Justice went on to say that an unusual combination could create an impression sufficiently removed from that produced by the mere combination with the result that the word was more than the sum of its parts. The Court also confirmed, along the lines of its decision in *OHIM* v *Wrigley*, that the existence of synonyms for each component, so that competitors could use the combination of synonyms instead to describe the same properties, was not relevant. The Court of Justice, In Case C-363-99 *Koninklijke KPN Nederland NV* v *Benelux-Merkenbureau*[122] confirmed that a sign made up

114 See Case C-299/99 *Koninklijke Philips Electronics NV* v *Remington Consumer Products Ltd* [2002] ECR I-5475 at para 63 referring to Case C-210/96 *Gut Springenheide GmbH and Rudolf Tusky* [1998] ECR I-4657 at para 31, although, in the latter case, the context was whether a description including a trade mark was misleading.

115 However, there are a number of registrations for 'speakeasy'.

116 *WEBSPHERE Trade Mark* [2004] FSR 39.

117 [2004] ECR I-1699.

118 [2003] ECR I-12447.

119 This is the same ground for refusal as Article 3(1)(c) of the Directive.

120 [2001] ECR I-6251.

121 SURF UNLIMITED was unregistrable through lack of distinctive character even though it may have satisfied the BABY-DRY approach under Article 3(1)(c): *Telewest Communication plc's Trade Mark Application* [2003] RPC 26.

122 [2004] ECR I-1619.

123 [2007] ECR I-2883.

of two words, each of which is descriptive of a characteristic of goods or services remains descriptive but the combination may create an impression sufficiently removed from that produced from the simple combination of those words. Further confirmation of that approach was given, in relation to the CTM, in Case C-273/05 P *OHIM v Celltech R & D Ltd*[123] where the Court of Justice stressed that the sign must be judged as a whole and the Court of First Instance had been correct to hold that it had not been established that CELLTECH, even understood as 'cell technology', was descriptive of the goods and services for which registration was sought.[124]

124 Being 'pharmaceutical, veterinary and sanitary preparations, compounds and substances', 'surgical, medical, dental and veterinary apparatus and instruments', and 'research and development services; consultancy services; all relating to the biological, medical and chemical sciences'.

125 [1997] RPC 279.

126 [2004] ECR I-1619.

An example of an unregistrable neologism in the UK was 'EUROLAMB' and, in *EUROLAMB Trade Mark*,[125] it was held that the word for lamb meat would be understood as lamb from Europe and this was descriptive of the kind and geographical origin of the goods. The applicant cited a great many registered marks containing the word 'Euro', such as 'EUROCOOK' for cookware, 'EURO-CELL' for battery goods and 'EURODOG' for dog food. Geoffrey Hobbs QC, as the Appointed Person, said that evidence of what had previously been accepted for registration was irrelevant. The same applies generally and was confirmed by the Court of Justice in Case C-363/99 *Koninklijke KPN Nederland NV v Benelux-Merkenbureau*[126] where, at para 44, it ruled that:

> . . . the fact that a trade mark has been registered in a Member State in respect of certain goods or services has no bearing on the examination by the trade mark registration authority of another Member State on an application for registration of a similar mark in respect of goods or services similar to those in respect of which the first mark was registered.

Similar considerations apply in respect of applications to register CTMs. There are a number of reasons why evidence of registration elsewhere should not be taken into account in a pending registration (or application for invalidity). The prevailing economic and commercial circumstances may be different, as may be the relevant public's perception of trade marks and their level of education of trade marks. Socio-economic factors vary from Member State to Member State. There is also the possibility that there have been changes to social, economic and other factors since the earlier trade marks were registered. There are likely to be variations in the quality of examination of and the level of opposition to trade mark applications, not only between different Member States but also internally, as between different trade mark examiners in a particular Member State. There may also be procedural differences. All of these could have a bearing on subsequent registrability elsewhere. There are other reasons, none the least that it would over-complicate proceedings for registration and it would encourage registration first in Member States or third countries which are fairly 'soft' on accepting for registration trade marks of dubious distinctiveness.

Article 3(1)(d) – customary signs or indications

This ground excludes those trade marks consisting of signs or indications that are in common use in trade. Although not explicit in the provision, this has been interpreted as applying only in respect of the goods or services for which registration is sought. The sign or indication must designate the goods or services although this may be by association rather than in relation to the specific properties or characteristics of the goods or service. Examples of trade marks that could be caught under this provision are 'SOFA SALE', 'BARGAIN BOOZE'[127] and 'Grandma's Home Cooking'.

127 This trade mark has been registered on the basis of acquired distinctiveness.

128 [2001] ECR I-6959.

Some clarification of Article 3(1)(d) was given by the Court of Justice in Case C-517/99 *Merz & Krell GmbH*.[128] The Court ruled that for the ground for refusal to apply the sign or indication in question must designate the goods or services in respect of which registration is sought. However, it is immaterial whether the signs or indications actually describe the properties or characteristics of the goods or services. In that case, the word in question was 'Bravo', to be used for writing implements. Such a word certainly does not describe any of the properties, characteristics or other features of writing implements.

Jacob J held that the word 'TREAT' for dessert sauces and syrups probably also fell within this ground for refusal in *British Sugar plc* v *James Robertson & Sons Ltd*.[129] It was a word that had become customary in the current language as lots of people use 'Treat' in their advertisements and on their goods.[130]

Article 3(3)

Where a trade mark appears to be unregistrable because of the grounds for refusal under Article 3(1)(b), (c) or (d), it can overcome the objection if there is evidence that the trade mark has, nevertheless, acquired a distinctive character in consequence of the use that has been made of it. The logical approach would be first to consider the representation of the trade mark, on its face and in the abstract, without any consideration of any use that has been made of the trade mark. Only then should attention be turned to evidence of acquired distinctiveness to see if the relevant ground (or grounds) for refusal have been overcome. Article 3(3) is not expressed as applying to an objection under Article 3(1)(a) but it seems reasonable to assume that acquired distinctiveness means that the sign must be capable of distinguishing the goods or services of one undertaking from those of other undertakings. So, acquired distinctiveness should overcome any objection that the sign does not fulfil the second requirement under Article 2. The Court of Justice confirmed in Case C-299/99 *Koninklijke Philips Electronic NV* v *Remington Consumer Products Ltd*[131] that there is no category of signs that are not excluded by Article 3(1)(b), (c) or (d) and Article 3(3) that are nonetheless excluded by Article 3(1)(a) on the basis that the mark is incapable of distinguishing the goods or services of one undertaking from those of other undertakings. Whether a distinctive trade mark can yet be incapable of being represented graphically is another point and not a possibility specifically referred to in *Philips* v *Remington* even though this would be a problem under Article 3(1)(a) as the first limb of Article 2 would not be satisfied. However, the Court of Justice only referred to the second limb of Article 2 in terms of distinctiveness under Article 3(1)(b)–(d) and (3).

Article 3(3) does not apply to signs consisting exclusively of shapes caught by Article 3(1)(e), discussed later. However, if a shape is not excluded on the basis of Article 3(1)(e), it may still be subject to acquired distinctiveness if there are other objections based on Article 3(1)(b)–(d). This was accepted in *Philips* v *Remington* where the Court of Justice made the general finding that (at para 65):

> . . . where a trader has been the only supplier of particular goods to the market, extensive use of a sign which consists of the shape of those goods may be sufficient to give the sign a distinctive character for the purposes of Article 3(3) of the Directive in circumstances where, as a result of that use, a substantial proportion of the relevant class of persons associates that shape with that trader and no other undertaking or believes that goods of that shape come from that trader. However, it is for the national court to verify that the circumstances in which the requirement under that provision is satisfied are shown to exist on the basis of specific and reliable data, that the presumed expectations of an average consumer of the category of goods or services in question, who is reasonably well-informed and reasonably observant and circumspect, are taken into account and that the identification, by the relevant class of persons, of the product as originating from a given undertaking is as a result of the use of the mark as a trade mark.

In Joined Cases C-108/97 and C-109/97 *Windsurfing Chiemsee* v *Huber and Attenberger*[132] the Court of Justice found, in the context of the perceived importance of keeping a geographical name available for use by other undertakings, that Article 3(3) required an overall assessment of the evidence as to whether the mark has come to identify the product concerned as coming from a particular undertaking and thus to distinguish that product

129 [1996] RPC 281. On this ground, the judge said the mark probably also fell within 3(1)(d).

130 Jacob J also considered the trade mark was devoid of any distinctive character and it designated the kind, quality and intended purpose of the product.

131 [2002] ECR I-5475.

132 [1999] ECR I-2779.

from goods of other undertakings. If a significant proportion of the relevant class of persons identify goods as originating from a particular undertaking because of the trade mark, the competent authority must hold that the requirement for registering it has been satisfied. The Court of Justice even advocated the use of an opinion poll where the national trade mark authority had difficulty in making its assessment.

The acquired distinctiveness may come about even if the mark in question has not previously been used on its own but as part of a trade mark. In Case C-353/03 *Société des Produits Nestlé SA v Mars UK Ltd*,[133] the application was for 'HAVE A BREAK' for use with chocolate products and the like. The application was opposed by Mars on the basis that it was devoid of any distinctive character under Article 3(1)(b). Nestlé had earlier registrations for both 'KIT KAT' and 'Have a break . . . Have a Kit Kat' and argued that a phrase used in conjunction with and associated with a trade mark may, through repetition over time, acquire a distinctive character. The Court of Justice found that this was indeed a possibility and ruled that the distinctive character could be acquired in consequence of the use of the mark as part of or in conjunction with a registered trade mark.

The last part of Article 3(3) gives Member States the option of using acquired distinctiveness as a way of overcoming an application for invalidity based on breach of Article 3(1)(b)–(d). The UK has taken advantage of that option: see the Trade Marks Act 1994 s 47(1).

Article 3(1)(e) – shape marks

Shape marks are treated in the same way as other forms of trade marks with one important exception. There are three specific grounds for refusal of registration (or invalidity) that apply to signs which consist exclusively of one of three particular types of shape. The rationale for this could be said to be that certain types of shape can never be sufficiently distinctive to serve as indicators of origin, capable of distinguishing the goods or services of one undertaking from those of other undertakings. Another argument for denying protection as trade marks to certain types of shape is that potentially unlimited protection could otherwise be afforded to shapes that ought to be protected by design law, patent law or, in some countries though not at present the UK, utility model law. Article 3(1)(e) prevents the registration of signs which consist exclusively of:

(i)   the shape which results from the nature of the goods themselves; or
(ii) the shape of goods which is necessary to obtain a technical result; or
(iii) the shape which gives substantial value to the goods.[134]

Shapes excluded can thus be described loosely as natural, functional or ornamental. It should be noted first that the grounds in Article 3(1)(e) apply only if the sign consists *exclusively* of the type of shape mentioned. Therefore, signs which consist of shapes which are not exclusively of one of the types listed are, subject to the other grounds for refusal, potentially registrable.[135] Of course, if a shape mark is caught by Article 3(1)(e) that is the end of the matter and the mark is simply not registrable regardless of the other grounds for refusal. For shape marks, Article 3(1)(e) is preliminary to the other grounds for refusal.[136] It should also be noted that acquired distinctiveness under Article 3(3) does not apply to Article 3(1)(e). That does not mean to say, however, that Article 3(3) is of no consequence for shape marks and it may be relevant where a shape mark is not fully within one of the grounds for refusal in Article 3(1)(e). Another point is that all the grounds relate to the shape of goods. Therefore, the grounds have no application whatsoever to shapes used by providers or services where they are not also applied to goods.

Article 2 applies generally to shape marks and does not itself require that a shape mark includes some capricious addition, such as an embellishment serving no functional purpose. The question is whether the shape in question is capable of distinguishing the

133 [2005] ECR I-6135, on reference from the Court of Appeal.

134 The wording in the equivalent provision in the Trade Marks Act 1994, s 3(2) is, to all intents and purposes, identical.

135 For example, in Joined Cases C-53/01 to C-55/01 *Linde AG, Winward Industries Inc and Rado Uhren AG* [2003] ECR I-3161, it was held that Article 3(1)(c) was applicable also to shape marks, independently of Article 3(1)(e).

136 Joined Cases C-53/01 to C-55/01 *Linde AG, Winward Industries Inc and Rado Uhren AG* [2003] ECR I-3161 at para 44.

product of the trade mark proprietor from those of other under-takings, so guaranteeing the origin of the product.[137]

Shape resulting from the nature of the goods

This ground for refusal prevents the registration of a shape which results from the nature of the goods themselves, examples being the shape of an apple, potato crisp, banana or tyre for a car. However, the addition of some additional stylised feature might overcome the ground for refusal. In *Dualit Ltd's (Toaster Shapes) Trade Mark Applications*,[138] it was accepted that the shape of toasters, for which registration was applied for, possessed certain styling features which prevented them consisting exclusively of shapes resulting from the nature of goods themselves.[139]

It seems reasonable to assume that references to 'the shape' did not necessarily limit the scope of the first exception under Article 3(1)(e) to cases where the nature of the goods results in a single shape. There is something to be said for the Hearing Officer's proposition in *Dualit* that the provision should be interpreted as meaning 'a shape which results from the nature of the goods themselves'. This accords with common sense when one considers that no two bananas are exactly identical in shape and there may be some considerable variety of shapes of bananas within basic parameters. It is unclear, however, whether the exception applies only to naturally occurring shapes.[140]

In relation to determining which goods are the goods for the purposes of Article 3(1)(e)(i), one could take a wide view or a narrow view. It might depend on how the goods are described in the application. At first instance, in *Philips Electronics NV v Remington Consumer Products Ltd*,[141] Jacob J gave an example of a registration for balls compared with one for American footballs. In that case, Jacob J did not consider that the three-headed shaver was caught by the exception. He said that the answer depended on how the goods are viewed in practice as articles of commerce: how they are seen as a single type. In the present case, he said that they would be seen as 'electric shavers', which are seen as a single type of commercial article even though there exist different sorts of electric shavers. In the Court of Appeal, Aldous LJ considered that the 'goods' must be those in respect of which the mark is to be registered for rather than the particular goods for which the mark is intended to be used. There was no one shape for electric shavers, or even no one shape for three-headed electric shavers.[142] Aldous LJ considered that the exception must be read in the context of the other two grounds for refusal of shape marks and was intended to exclude registration of basic shapes which should be available for use by the public at large.[143]

Where the goods do not have an intrinsic form, such as a liquid or powder, and they are normally sold in containers or packaging, the question arises as to whether the shape of the containers or packaging can be said to result from the nature of the goods themselves. In Case C-218/01 *Henkel KgaA v Deutsches Patent-und Markenamt*,[144] an application was made to register the shape of a plastic container used for liquid detergent. The Court of Justice ruled that, for three-dimensional trade marks consisting of the packaging of goods which are packaged in the trade for reasons linked to the very nature of the goods (for example, because they are in liquid or powder form), the packaging must be assimilated with the shape of the goods so that the shape of the packaging may constitute the shape of the goods within Article 3(1)(e). The shape of packaging imposes itself on the shape of goods. This is unlike the position where the goods have their own intrinsic shape. The Court of Justice gave the example of nails. In such cases, the shape of the packaging is not assimilated with the shape of the goods themselves.

Shape necessary to obtain a technical result

The most important case on shape marks is undoubtedly Case C-299/99 *Koninklijke Philips Electronics NV v Remington Consumer Products Ltd*[145] which was a preliminary ruling following a reference to the Court of Justice from the Court of Appeal in a case involving

137 Case C-299/99 *Koninklijke Philips Electronics NV v Remington Consumer Products Ltd* [2002] ECR I-5475.

138 [1999] RPC 304.

139 Registration was refused on other grounds.

140 The better view is that artificially created shapes are outside the exception. A number of questions on this exception were referred to the Court of Justice but appear to have been withdrawn: *Unilever plc's Trade Mark Applications* [2003] RPC 35 which concerned the registrability of the shape of 'Viennetta' ice cream products.

141 [1998] RPC 283.

142 [1999] RPC 809 at 820.

143 The Court of Justice was not asked to rule on the ground for refusal for shapes resulting from the nature of the goods: Case C-299/99 *Koninklijke Philips Electronics NV v Remington Consumer Products Ltd* [2002] ECR I-5475.

144 [2004] ECR I-1725.

145 [2002] ECR I-5475.

146 The drawing can be seen in the law report in the Patents Court at *Philips Electronics NV v Remington Consumer Products Ltd* [1998] RPC 283 or by visiting the Patent Office website (registration No 1254208). Even though the trade mark was revoked eventually, the representation is still available to view.

147 *Philips Electronics NV v Remington Consumer Products Ltd* [1998] RPC 283 at 290. Jacob J found that the trade mark was not capable of distinguishing, was devoid of distinctive character and that the shape consisted exclusively from a shape necessary to obtain a technical result. The Court of Appeal agreed (*Philips Electronic NV v Remington Consumer Products Ltd* [1999] RPC 809) but referred a number of questions to the Court of Justice.

148 Other aspects of the Court of Justice ruling are discussed above.

149 *Philips Electronics NV v Remington Consumer Products Ltd* [1998] RPC 283 at 308. Jacob J noted that the majority in the Swedish court in *Ide Line AG v Philips Electronics NV* [1997] ETMR 377, involving the three-headed shaver trade mark, considered that it was not enough that the shape was functional, it also had to be necessary to achieve the result; and the exception could be defeated if it could be shown that other shapes could achieve the same technical result.

150 *Koninklijke Philips NV v Remington Consumer Products Ltd* [2005] FSR 17.

a three-headed electric shaver allegedly infringed by Remington which challenged the validity of the trade mark registration. Philips registered a drawing showing the face of its three-headed shaver under the Trade Marks Act 1938.[146] It had been transferred to the register under the 1994 Act. The registration of three-dimensional trade marks was not generally possible under the 1938 Act so the trade mark must have been the two-dimensional drawing itself. However, everyone thereafter was prepared to consider the representation as covering also a three-dimensional mark.[147]

The Court of Justice confirmed that the ground for refusal applies where the essential functional features of the shape are attributable only to the technical result. This is so even if there is more than one way of obtaining the same technical result.[148] This conformed with the view of Jacob J in the Patents Court where he said that it could not have been intended to limit the ground for refusal to an object that *must be a particular shape* to perform the function. That could make it '. . . possible to obtain permanent monopolies in matters of significant engineering design'.[149] The word 'necessary' in Article 3(1)(e)(ii), cannot be taken in a strong sense. The exception to registrability applies, therefore, where the shape is purely functional and cannot be overcome by showing that other shapes could perform the same function. The Philips shaver had its three shaving heads arranged in an equilateral triangle which had been designed on the basis of technical considerations. The fact that it was possible to arrange the three heads in an isosceles triangle did not prevent the ground for refusal applying.

In applying the ruling of the Court of Justice in the High Court, Rimer J revoked the Philips trade marks. In explaining certain aspects of the ruling, Rimer J confirmed that, if the essential features necessary to obtain a technical result also had some inherent aesthetic appeal, that would not take the sign out of the exception.[150] The word 'only' in the ruling where the Court of Justice said that '. . . the shape of a product is unregistrable by virtue [of Article 3(1)(e)(ii) – equivalent to s 3(2)(b) of the Act] if it is established that the essential functional features of that shape are attributable *only* to the technical result' (emphasis added) was, in Rimer J's view, not intended to limit the exception. Had the Court of Justice intended to limit it in this way, it would have explained this in its judgment. Furthermore, the Court of Justice's general observations about the policy underlying Article 3(1)(e) did not suggest that it had any such limitation in mind. Rimer J was also of the view that the subjective intention of the designer was not relevant. The question of functionality had to be determined objectively.

Shape giving substantial value to the goods

The obvious types of shape excluded by this ground for refusal are those applied to goods which are bought for the appearance of the goods rather than the intrinsic value of the goods themselves. Examples include ornaments such as porcelain figurines, garden statuary, fashion clothing and accessories, furniture, watches and clocks, vases and candlesticks. It may be difficult to know where to draw the line between the intrinsic value of the goods and the value added by the application of a particular shape. For example, would the shape of a design applied to jewellery made from diamonds set in gold add substantial value to the goods? What would the answer be if the same shape was used for jewellery made from base metal and paste? It would seem reasonable to interpret the provision on the basis of its supposed purpose in excluding certain types of signs from registration. That purpose (and the one based on shapes giving a technical result) was '. . . to prevent the exclusive and permanent right which a trade mark confers from serving to extend the life of other rights which the legislature has sought to make subject to limited periods. I refer, specifically, to legislation on industrial patents and designs.'[151]

That being so, it seems reasonable to set the standard of added value relatively low and ask the question – do consumers buy the goods because their primary motive is to acquire goods of that type or do they buy the particular goods from amongst other like goods because

151 Per Advocate General Ruiz-Jarabo Colomer at para 30 of his Opinion in Case C-299/99 *Koninklijke Philips Electronics NV v Remington Consumer Products Ltd* [2002] ECR I-5475.

the shape of them indicates that they come from a particular source? In other words, does the shape act as a badge of origin in the minds of the average consumers of that type of goods?

Substantial value cannot be limited to aesthetic considerations and may result from improved functional performance or other technical considerations. Again the question is whether the average consumer purchases the goods because of technical considerations or because the shape tells them the goods come from a particular undertaking. But, even if the latter is the case, the sign may still be refused registration if the shape does indeed add substantial value.

The *Philips* v *Remington* case is also important in respect of the third exception from registration in Article 3(1)(e) though the Court of Justice did not have to rule on this. At first instance, in *Philips Electronics NV* v *Remington Consumer Products Ltd*,[152] Jacob J said that the shape of the three-headed electric shaver gave substantial value to the goods, being recognised as an engineering function. He pointed out that good trade marks do add value to goods, that being one of their purposes from a trader's point of view. That being so, the exception to registrability for shapes that add substantial value must not be taken too literally. He suggested that the shape must exclusively add something of value, whether it be design or functional appearance, disregarding any value attributable to the trade mark's function of identifying the source of the goods.

152 [1998] RPC 283.

Whilst agreeing that the ground for refusal must not be taken too literally as good trade marks add value to goods, the Court of Appeal disagreed with Jacob J on the proposition that recognition of the shape as having an engineering function added substantial value to the goods.[153] Aldous LJ said that there may be some overlap between paragraphs (ii) and (iii) of Article 3(1)(e) but their purposes were different. The former was intended to exclude functional shapes whereas the latter was intended to exclude aesthetic shapes. Consideration must be given as to whether the shape gives substantial value. This requires determination of whether the value is substantial and this, in turn, requires a comparison between the shape for which registration is sought and shapes applied to equivalent articles. In the present case, Aldous LJ thought the shape applied for had no more value than other shapes which were shown to be as good and cheap to produce. He dismissed the notion that added value resulting from substantial advertising and reliability could be factors. In other words, the shape would have to be inherently better than equivalents to be excluded. This could be, for example, that it performed much more efficiently than any alternative shape or was significantly more attractive visually.

153 *Philips Electronics NV* v *Remington Consumer Products Ltd* [1999] RPC 809.

It is unfortunate that we have, as yet, no significant guidance from the Court of Justice on the scope of the ground for refusal based on shape giving substantial value. It is submitted that the Court of Appeal was wrong to suggest that functional shapes could not also add substantial value and that comparison should be made with other shapes for the same type of goods. It is submitted that the correct approach is to consider whether the goods to which the shape has been applied are bought because the shape operates as a badge of origin or because the shape is perceived as desirable *per se*, whether for aesthetic or functional reasons. One does not buy a pre-packed joint of meat on a shaped plastic tray covered in clear plastic to acquire the plastic tray. It may be that a design of plastic food tray of a particular shape and colour could become distinctive of a range of meat products and function as a trade mark. Even though this fact might help boost sales and add value from the producer's perspective, enabling him to charge a premium, it does not add substantial value to the joints of meat as joints of meat.

Article 3(1)(f) – contrary to public policy or accepted principles of morality

Trade marks cannot be registered if they are contrary to public policy or accepted principles of morality. In terms of public policy, accepting that, on this point, the Directive was confined to matters covered by the French term *ordre publique*, Jacob J did not think it extended to a situation where an applicant was attempting to extend protection afforded by other forms of intellectual property rights.[154] He soundly rejected the 'it-was-once-patented, or expired' argument, saying that there was no rule of law which generally prevented protection by parallel intellectual property rights.[155] Nor is there any public policy that a celebrity should have the exclusive right to use his own character for merchandising purposes. This possibility has been rejected on numerous occasions[156] and there appears to be a reluctance to provide such rights by legislation or to protect persons' names by the law of passing off.[157] In *JANE AUSTEN Trade Mark*,[158] the Hearing Officer said that, given this unwillingness, he would be unwise to assume that there was a public policy interest in acquisitively registering as trade marks the names of famous historical figures. However, in that case, the application was refused on the basis that the mark was devoid of any distinctive character.

Objections raised on the basis that a trade mark is contrary to accepted principles of morality are relatively rare. It is clear that the standard to be applied should be set in the context of current views and vulnerabilities. Under the 1938 Act, the equivalent test was whether the trade mark was contrary to morality.[159] In *La Marquise Footwear Inc's Application*,[160] the word 'OOMPHIES' was applied for in respect of shoes. It was rejected by the Trade Marks Registry on the ground that the word had connotations with sex appeal.[161] Evershed J allowed the applicant's appeal against that decision but said that the Registrar's duties were (at 30):

> . . . to consider not merely the general taste of the time, but also the susceptibilities of persons, by no means few in number, who still may be regarded as old-fashioned.

Essentially, the exercise of this duty is very much a matter of balance. Trade mark registries must be in touch with current standards and not locked into past values but should also be wary not to allow registration of a trade mark which would cause offence to many, even if they represent a minority of society.[162]

It is reasonable to assume that the same test applies under the Directive and the 1994 Act, though the test may vary between different Member States. There is no case law at the Court of Justice in the scope of this ground for refusal but there has been some case law in the UK.

In *Ghazilian's Trade Mark Application*,[163] the application was for 'TINY PENIS' to be used for clothing, footwear and headgear. The Hearing Officer refused registration, confirming that the mark should be judged against current views and thinking and refusal would be warranted if registration would be likely to offend persons who might be in a minority in society yet be a substantial number. She said that the words in a proper descriptive context would be unlikely to offend very many persons but, seeing the words out of context, used in advertising and displayed on goods in public, would cause offence to a substantial number of the public. Simon Thorley QC, as the Appointed Person, confirmed that there was no discretion and, if the registration was contrary to public policy or morality, it must be refused. Nor was there discretion to refuse in the opposite case. Simon Thorley QC dismissed the applicant's appeal against the refusal to register the trade mark, saying that the question was whether its use would offend the moral principles of right-thinking members of the public so that it would be wrong in law to protect it. He distinguished between offence causing distaste and offence causing outrage or to undermine current religious, family or social values. The latter would be grounds for refusal of registration if it affected an identifiable section of the public but the higher the outrage, the smaller the section of the public it affected, for refusal to be justified, and vice versa. It is noteworthy that the word 'FCUK' has been accepted for registration both under the 1994 Act and under the CTM Regulation.[164]

154 *Philips Electronics NV v Remington Consumer Products Ltd* [1998] RPC 283 at 310. The Court of Appeal did not consider this point, nor did the Court of Justice on the reference to it.

155 Although this seems to have been the basis for the second and third grounds for refusal of registration for signs consisting exclusively of certain types of shapes.

156 An example being ELVIS and ELVIS PRESLEY in *ELVIS PRESLEY Trade Marks* [1999] RPC 567.

157 See, for example, *McCullogh v Lewis A May Ltd* (1948) 65 RPC 58.

158 [2000] RPC 879.

159 Trade Marks Act 1938 s 11.

160 (1946) 64 RPC 27.

161 The word was in stylised form with the 'OO' made to look like a pair of eyes, possibly increasing the connotation of sex appeal. The mark remains on the Register.

162 See HALLELUJAH Trade Mark [1976] RPC 605.

163 [2002] RPC 33.

164 FCUK was subject to an unsuccessful application for summary judgment for infringement of the trade mark and passing off in *French Connection (UK) Ltd v Sutton* [2000] ETMR 341. The defendant has registered FCUK.com as his internet domain name.

Although there is no direct case law on this ground for refusal from the Court of Justice, in his Opinion in Case C-299/99 *Koninklijke Philips Electronics NV* v *Remington Consumer Products Ltd*,[165] Advocate General Ruiz-Jarabo Colomer gave the example which surely would be refused as being contrary to public policy, being 'Babykiller' for a pharmaceutical abortifacient (a drug that effects or encourages abortion).

In the UK, an application was made to register 'JESUS' for a range of goods in *Basic Trademark SA's Trade Mark Application*.[166] It was rejected on the basis that it was contrary to public policy or accepted principles of morality. The appeal to the Appointed Person was dismissed. He considered that, although registration for trade marks including the name 'JESUS' had been accepted by the OHIM and some national trade mark registries, this was not binding on him. The fact that there may be room for more than one view did not make the process arbitrary and Geoffrey Hobbs QC said (at para 23):

> The requirement for use of the trade mark to be seriously troubling in terms of the public interest in the 'prevention of disorder' or 'protection of morals' under Art 10 ECHR [Council of Europe Convention for the Protection of Human Rights and Fundamental Freedoms] provides . . . a proper basis for objective determination of the legal rights of persons applying for registration.

He went on to say that the view of Christians that their religious beliefs should be respected was deep-seated and widespread and the idea that the name 'JESUS' should be used for commercial exploitation would be anathema to them and to others who believed that religious beliefs generally ought to be respected. Registration would have caused greater offence than mere distaste.

If the fair and normal use of the trade mark would be likely to lead to violence, that could be sufficient to refuse registration even if the use did not amount to incitement to violence and even if that was not the intention of the applicant. Opposition by Manchester United Merchandising Ltd on the basis that the registration would be contrary to public policy was successful in *CDW Graphic Design Ltd's Trade Mark Application*,[167] in which an application was made to register 'www.standupifyouhatemanu.com' for T-shirts, baseball caps and other garments.

Article 3(1)(g) – deceptive marks

A trade mark will not be registered if it is of such a nature as to deceive the public, for instance as to the nature, quality or geographical origin of the goods or service.[168] A trade mark may be deceptive in a number of ways and the list of possibilities is not an exhaustive one and merely serves to give examples. Under the Trade Marks Act 1938, a number of examples of trade marks were held to be deceptive such as 'DAIRY GOLD' (for synthetic margarine), 'Livron' (for a medicine – there is a French town of the same name),[169] and a mark containing the words 'Forrest' and 'London' (for a watchmaker based in Coventry),[170] 'Orlwoola' (for textile clothing)[171] and 'SWISS MISS' (for preparations for making chocolate and cocoa drinks, etc.).[172]

There is no direct authority on the scope of Article 3(1)(g) from the Court of Justice but there are a number of cases where it has been mentioned or where parallels can be drawn with other legislation concerning misleading advertising or designations of origin. For example, in Case T-268/99 *Fédération nationale d'agriculture biologique des régions de France* v *Council of the European Union*,[173] the Court of First Instance noted that Article 3(1)(g) of the Directive would prevent the registration of 'Bio' for non-organic products.

Council Regulation (EEC) No 2081/92 of 14 July 1992 on the protection of geographical indications and designations of origin for agricultural products and foodstuffs[174] was in issue in Case C-87/97 *Consorzio per la tutela del formaggio Gorgonzola* v *Käiserei*

165 [2002] ECR I-5475.

166 [2005] RPC 25.

167 [2003] RPC 30.

168 The wording in the equivalent provision in the Trade Marks Act 1994, s 3(3)(b), is to the same effect.

169 *Boots Pure Drug Co's Trade Mark* (1937) 54 RPC 129.

170 *Hill's Trade Mark* (1893) 10 RPC 113.

171 *Orlwoola Trade Mark* (1906) 26 RPC 683.

172 *SWISS MISS Trade Mark* [1997] RPC 219.

173 [2000] ECR II-2893. The case concerned a challenge against a Council Regulation on the organic production of agricultural products and the like.

174 OJ L 208, 24.07.1992, p 1.

175 [1999] ECR I-1301.

Champignon Hofmeister GmbH & Co KG[175] in which objection was taken to the use of the trade mark 'Cambozola' for a creamy blue cheese, resembling Gorgonzola cheese. The defendants' cheese was made in Germany and Austria and was packaged with an indication of its origin. Article 14(1) of the Regulation prohibits the subsequent registration of trade marks which were the same, similar to or evoked a protected designation of origin but Article 14(2) contains a saving for earlier registered trade marks applied for in good faith. The use of these may continue provided the grounds under Article 3(1)(c) and (g) or 12(2)(b) of the trade marks Directive do not apply. In other words, the use of prior trade marks may continue unless they consist exclusively of signs or indications serving in trade to designate geographical origin, are deceptive as to geographical origin or have become deceptive in such a way because of the use made of them. In the present case, 'Cambozola'[176] had been registered as a trade mark before Gorgonzola because it was a protected designation of origin. The Court of Justice ruled that the word 'Cambozola' evoked the protected designation 'Gorgonzola' even though it was packaged bearing its geographical origin, but it was for the national court to determine whether the conditions under Article 14(2) of the Regulation allowed the use of the earlier registered trade mark to continue.

176 Cambozola does not refer to a real place name.

Regulation (EC) 110/2008 of the European Parliament and of the Council of 15 January 2008 on the definition, description, presentation, labelling and the protection of geographical indications of spirit drinks and repealing Council Regulation (EEC) No 1576/89,[177] is retrospective to the extent that it made trade marks which offended against the Regulation and which were registered after 1 January 1996 liable to be revoked. In Joined Cases C- 4/10 and C-27/10 *Bureau national interprofessionel du Cognac v Gust,*[178] the defendant, a Finnish company, registered two figurative marks including the word 'Cognac' in Finland. The marks were registered in 2003, after the end of the derogation period. The Court of Justice confirmed that, although the principle of legal certainty precludes an EU measure taking effect before its publication, it may do so where the purpose to be achieved so demands and the legitimate expectations of those concerned are duly respected. In respect of the latter, the Court noted that those legitimate expectations were duly respected as the previous Regulation had itself included the cut-off date of 1 January 1996.[179]

177 OJ L 39, 13.02.2008, p 16. The Regulation protects geographical indications from, *inter alia,* false or misleading indications of provenance, origin, nature or essential qualities.

178 July 2011.

179 By a subsequent amendment made by a Regulation dating from 1994.

An example of one effect of deception in advertising is given by the definition of misleading advertising. In Case C-44/01 *Pippig Augenoptik GmbH & Co KG v Hartlaeur Handelsgesellschaft mbH,*[180] reference was made to the definition of misleading advertising, being advertising that '. . . deceives or is likely to deceive the persons to whom it is addressed or whom it reaches and which, by reason of its deceptive nature, is likely to effect their economic behaviour or which, for those reasons, injures or is likely to injure a competitor'. This may be relevant in most cases under Article 3(1)(g) but may not extend to every form of deception within the provision.

180 [2003] ECR I-3095. In that case, the parties sold spectacles and lenses and the claimant objected to the defendant's comparative advertising where misleading advertising was also a feature.

There is little case law on the equivalent provision under the Trade Marks Act 1994, s 3(3)(b). Under the 1938 Act an accepted test where deception as to origin was concerned was whether a substantial proportion of the public would be misled into thinking that the goods are those of another trader.[181] This can be generalised to say that the subsection simply requires that a substantial proportion of the public would be deceived in the relevant manner. Of course, if the deception relates to the origin of goods or the identity of the service provider, this may amount to passing off and the trade mark applied for would be vulnerable to a challenge on that basis under the relative grounds for refusal or, if registered, an application for invalidity.

181 *Neutrogena Corp v Golden Ltd* [1996] RPC 473.

The wording used in the Directive and the 1994 Act is to the effect that the nature of the mark is such 'as to deceive the public' whereas s 11 of the 1938 Act was in terms of 'likely to deceive or cause confusion'. It is arguable that the absence of the word 'likely' results in a modification of the previously accepted test.

The form of deception argued in *JANE AUSTEN Trade Mark*[182] was that the public would be deceived into thinking that the goods (cosmetics and toiletry products) were approved by the trustees of the Jane Austen Memorial Trust or somehow connected with Jane Austen's literature. The trust owned Jane Austen's house and museum in Hampshire and sold souvenirs relating to the famous writer. However, the hearing officer did not think that the public would make either connection, being well aware of the nature of commercial trade in such goods. Furthermore, he considered that the ground of opposition under s 3(3)(b) was framed more like an opposition under s 5(4), one of the relative grounds of opposition. It must be noted that this was an opposition hearing and not an appeal against refusal of registration and must be treated with a little caution in relation to s 3(3)(b).

Use prohibited by law

Article 3(2) of the Directive provides Member States with the option of a ground of refusal based on the use of the trade mark being prohibited by law, other than the trade mark law of the Member State concerned or of the EU or where the trade mark covers a sign of high symbolic value, in particular a religious symbol. The UK has not expressly implemented the latter of these options although there could be other grounds that apply in such circumstances, such as public policy, morality or that the mark is deceptive. What the UK has provided for, in s 3(4), is a prohibition on registering marks to the extent that their use could be prohibited in the UK by any enactment or rule of law or by any provision of Community (now EU) law. However, that omits any exclusion of trade mark law as stated in the Directive.

If the prohibition relates to part of the mark, it will be unregistrable under this provision to this extent. As an example of the working of this provision, an application to register a word mark 'Somerset Champagne' would be refused because its use would contravene a European Council Regulation.[183] Areas of UK law that might be relevant here include the Hallmarking Act 1973 or consumer protection legislation such as the Trade Descriptions Act 1968. In fact there are numerous Acts, statutory instruments, EU Treaties, Directives and Regulations that could apply in a particular circumstance.[184] Nor is the provision limited to legislation. The prohibition may come about by civil law or criminal law. In practice, s 3(4) is likely to be an issue in very few cases.

Section 3(4) has been used as a ground of opposition in a number of unreported cases before the Trade Marks Registry. In some cases, the basis has been that the use of the mark applied for would amount to passing off or infringement of a registered trade mark. This is an unacceptable use of the provision as the text of the Trade Marks Directive states that the objection to registration applies where and to the extent that 'the use of the mark may be prohibited pursuant to provisions of law *other than trade mark law* of the Member State or of the Community'[185] (emphasis added). It is reasonable to assume that the phrase 'trade mark law' includes the law of passing off in the UK and Eire, therefore, the subsection cannot be used where passing off or trade mark infringement is alleged. In *SUREFIRE Trade Mark*,[186] the hearing officer speaking of the opponent's objections under s 3(3)(b) and (4) said that they were in fact 'relative grounds masquerading as absolute grounds'. In *Bentley's Trade Mark Applications*,[187] the Hearing Officer reiterated the view that s 3(4) is an absolute ground:

> . . . intended to prevent the registration of trade marks which would contravene the law because of some intrinsic feature of the trade mark, and is not concerned with the circular argument that the mark does not belong to the applicants or resembles someone else's trade mark and cannot therefore be distinctive of them. The question of the other party's rights in the mark is a matter to be dealt with in considering relative grounds for refusal.

182 [2000] RPC 879.

183 Council Regulation (EEC) No 823/87 of 16 March 1987 laying down special provisions relating to quality wines produced in specified regions, OJ L 84, 27.03.1987, p 59. The name would also be refused under s 3(3)(b), being deceptive as to geographical origin and use of the mark would be passing off (see *Taittinger SA v Allbev Ltd* [1993] FSR 641) which is itself a relative ground for refusing registration under s 5(4) (Article 4(4)(b) of the Directive).

184 This includes controls on protected geographical indications of products.

185 Article 3(2).

186 (Unreported) 13 July 2001, Trade Marks Registry.

187 (Unreported) 4 August 1999, Trade Marks Registry.

Specially protected emblems, etc.

Article 6[ter] of the Paris Convention for the Protection of Industrial Property 1883 requires Contracting States to prohibit the registration, without authorisation, as trade marks, of certain armorial bearings, flags and other emblems, etc. of the States and international organisations and hallmarks and other official signs indicating control and warranty under certain circumstances. Article 3(1)(h) of the Directive prohibits the registration of such trade marks unless authorised by the competent authorities. Furthermore, Member States have the option, under Article 3(2)(c), to prohibit the registration, as trade marks, of badges, emblems and escutcheons of public interest in addition to those covered by Article 6[ter] of the Paris Convention.

In the UK, s 3(5) of the Trade Marks Act prohibits the registration of specially protected emblems and the like set out in s 4. These include trade marks consisting of or containing things such as the Royal arms, flags, representations of Her Majesty or members of the Royal family, words, letters or devices likely to lead persons to think that the applicant has or recently has had Royal patronage or authorisation,[188] the UK national flag, flags of England, Wales, Scotland, Northern Ireland or the Isle of Man, national emblems of countries belonging to the Paris Convention and members of the World Trade Organisation (s 57 provides more detail) and of certain international organisations: for example, the UN (see s 58). In relation to the UK national flag and the flags of England, Wales, Scotland, Northern Ireland or the Isle of Man, consent is not a precursor to registration but trade marks including these will not be permitted if it appears to the Registrar that the use of the trade mark would be misleading or grossly offensive.

Section 99 makes it an offence, *inter alia*, without authority, to use in connection with business any device, emblem or title in such a manner as to be calculated to lead to the belief that he supplies goods or services to the Royal family. However, this provision has nothing to do with the grounds for refusal of registration and does not supplement s 3(5). There are material differences between s 99(2) and the equivalent ground of refusal provided under s 3(5), being s 4(1)(d) (things likely to lead persons to think the applicant either has or recently has had Royal patronage or authorisation). This was confirmed in *Royal Shakespeare Trade Mark*,[189] in which the Hearing Officer refused to allow an application by the opponent, the Royal Shakespeare Company, to amend one of its grounds of opposition from s 99 to s 4(1)(d).[190]

Article 3(2)(d) – application made in bad faith

Applying to register a trade mark in bad faith has long been a ground for refusal or invalidity of a trade mark and bad faith has been alleged on numerous occasions. Bad faith is a ground for refusal under Article 3(2)(d) of the Directive and finds its equivalent in s 3(6) of the Trade Marks Act 1994. There has been a great deal of litigation in the UK where bad faith has been alleged though relatively little at the Court of Justice. In a case concerning a Commission Regulation concerning marketing standards for olive oil it was accepted by the Court of Justice that applying to register a trade mark before the Regulation came into force to avoid its impact would be made in bad faith and contrary to Article 3 of the trade marks Directive.[191] Before looking further at the case law, it should be pointed out that the Trade Marks Act 1994 s 32(3) requires that an applicant to register a trade mark declares that the trade mark is being used in relation to the goods or services for which registration is sought or there is a *bona fide* intention that it will so be used. As we shall see later, lack of a *bona fide* intention can be equated to making an application in bad faith. The Directive has no equivalent in relation to the application to register. As this is a procedural aspect, Member States are left free to fix their own provisions[192] so this point does not come up for preliminary rulings at the Court of Justice. Another

188 Registration is possible with consent by or on behalf of Her Majesty or the relevant member of the Royal family.

189 (Unreported) 7 January 2000, Trade Marks Registry.

190 The application to register ROYAL SHAKESPEARE for beers and other drinks was successful.

191 Case C-99/99 *Italian Republic v Commission of the European Communities* [2000] ECR I-11535.

192 Fifth recital to the Directive.

point to note is that in the CTM Regulation bad faith crops up only in respect of invalidity and is not a ground for refusal of registration. Article 51 of the CTM Regulation states that a trade mark shall be declared invalid if, *inter alia*, the application was made in bad faith. The application to register a CTM does not have a declaration of present use or a *bona fide* intention to use the trade mark in relation to the goods or services for which registration is sought.

The main difficulty with bad faith is determining exactly what it means.[193] A number of meanings are possible. It might be restricted to cases where some dishonesty or fraud is involved on the part of the applicant or it may be relevant where the behaviour of the applicant falls below what are considered to be acceptable practices in business. Bad faith could extend to a situation where the applicant is not using the mark and has no intention of doing so: for example, where a person makes an application to register a famous name as a trade mark with the sole intention of selling it to the organisation to whom it would be expected to belong.[194] The meaning of bad faith is particularly important as it is frequently raised in opposition or revocation proceedings.

Under the 1938 Act, it was held that an application for a 'ghost mark' 'Nerit' was in bad faith: *Imperial Group Ltd* v *Philip Morris & Co Ltd*.[195] The Court of Appeal considered the application for the ghost mark was not in good faith though the court did not regard it as dishonest. The applicant sold 'Merit' cigarettes but it was thought 'Merit' was unregistrable, being a laudatory word.[196] 'Nerit' would be close enough to bring an infringement action against someone else who used 'Merit' for cigarettes.

In *Road Tech Computer Systems Ltd* v *Unison Software (UK) Ltd*,[197] Robert Walker J found difficulty in determining the meaning of 'bad faith' for the purposes of the 1994 Act. It could have the narrow meaning of dishonesty, or a wider meaning including a lack of genuine intention or purpose. Robert Walker J, whilst not deciding the point, thought it was rather easier to see an application being partly genuine and partly insincere rather than partly honest and partly dishonest.

The leading authority in the UK for what constitutes bad faith for the purposes of s 3(6) is *Gromax Plasticulture Ltd* v *Don & Low Nonwovens Ltd*.[198] In that case, the claimant sold spun-bonded non-woven polypropylene sheeting (described sometimes as 'fleece') used in agriculture, being laid in sheets over the ground or over hoops over crops. The parties had agreed to sell it under the name 'Gro-Shield'. Unknown to the claimant, the defendant had, in 1989, registered the name as a trade mark in respect of non-woven textile fabrics included in Class 24. In 1996, the relationship between the parties broke down and the claimant registered 'Gro-Shield' in Class 17, having been advised that this was the correct class for fleece. The claimant sought a declaration that the defendant's trade mark was invalid because it had been applied for in bad faith.[199] It was argued that, as it was always intended that the claimant should be the sole distributor of the fleece, it was bad faith for the defendant to register the mark. Of the meaning of bad faith, Lindsay J said (at 379):

> I shall not attempt to define bad faith in this context. Plainly it includes dishonesty and, as I would hold, includes also some dealings which fall short of the standards of acceptable commercial behaviour observed by reasonable and experienced men in the particular area being examined. Parliament has wisely not attempted to explain in detail what is or is not bad faith in this context; how far a dealing must so fall short in order to amount to bad faith is a matter best left to be adjudged not by some paraphrase by the courts (which leads to the danger of the courts then construing not the Act but the paraphrase) but by reference to the words of the Act and upon a regard to all material surrounding circumstances.

It was held that the defendant's application was not made in bad faith.[200] Lindsay J said that the fact that the claimant, as exclusive distributor, would be seen as the guarantor of quality, did not amount to bad faith on the part of the defendant. The fact that any

193 In *Tesco Stores Ltd's Trade Mark Applications* [2005] RPC 17 it was said that the scope of the provision was notoriously unclear.

194 An equivalent activity to 'cybersquatting' where someone registers a famous name as a domain name. There are a number of examples of this in the chapter on passing off.

195 [1982] FSR 72.

196 There are in fact numerous registrations for 'Merit' for a wide variety of goods and services, including cigarettes.

197 [1996] FSR 805.

198 [1999] RPC 367.

199 The defendant sought revocation of the claimant's mark. Allegations of passing off and trade mark infringement were also made.

200 It was further held that the claimant's trade mark was invalid (under s 5(1) and/or s 5(2)), the defendant was not guilty of passing off and the defendant's trade mark had been infringed by the claimant.

complaints about the quality of the fleece would be directed towards the claimant was simply one of the concomitants of an exclusive distributorship. He did say, however, that it might have been different if the defendant had abandoned all control over and regulation of the quality or origin of the fleece.

Although Lindsay J made it clear that he was not trying to lay down a universal test for bad faith under s 3(6), that seems to have been the consequence as the above quote has been used in cases on bad faith ever since. Dishonesty or at least something approaching dishonesty is required, such as reprehensible conduct. In *DAAWAT Trade Mark*[201] it was held by Geoffrey Hobbs QC, as the Appointed Person, that there was no justification for adopting a two-step approach advocated in the House of Lords in *Twinsectra Ltd* v *Yardley*,[202] a case on liability for acting as an accessory in a breach of trust case. The two-step approach is very similar to that used for dishonesty for the purposes of the Theft Acts 1968 and 1978 as in Lord Lane CJ's judgment in *R* v *Ghosh*,[203] referred to by Lord Hutton in *Twinsectra*. Effectively, the test is whether ordinary honest persons would regard what the applicant was doing as dishonest and, secondly, did the applicant know that this was the case. A purely subjective approach (called 'the Robin Hood test' by Lord Hutton) is inappropriate as the trade mark system is not there to enable dishonest persons or those with low moral standards to obtain trade mark registration in circumstances where persons abiding by reasonable standards would not. However, the two-step test in *Twinsectra* was reinstated in *Harrison's Trade Mark Application*[204] in which the applicant applied to register 'CHINAWHITE' for various alcoholic and non-alcoholic drinks. He had previously been involved in the opponent's nightclub called 'Chinawhite' and there the applicant assisted the bar manager in developing a recipe for a cocktail to be called 'Chinawhite'. In the Court of Appeal, Sir William Aldous, approving of what Lord Hutton said in Twinsectra, said (at para 26):

> The words 'bad faith' suggest a mental state. Clearly when considering the question of whether an application to register is made in bad faith all the circumstances will be relevant. However, the court must decide whether the knowledge of the applicant was such that his decision to apply for registration would be regarded as in bad faith by persons adopting proper standards.[205]

The objective part of the two-step test is that set out by Lindsay J above and does not appear to have been altered by *Harrison's Trade Mark Application*.[206] Taking legal advice and, in the light of that, applying to register a trade mark in the opinion that the applicant was doing nothing wrong does not necessarily prevent a finding of bad faith. In *Jules Rimet Cup Ltd* v *Football Association Ltd*,[207] applications were made by the claimant to register 'WORLD CUP WILLIE'[208] with a lion device as a trade mark. The defendant made it clear it would oppose the application and also informed a licensee who terminated the licence. The claimant brought proceedings for a declaration that the applications could not be successfully opposed and claimed relief for unlawful interference with its business. It was held that the claimants were aware of a residual goodwill in World Cup Willie from the 1966 football tournament and the applications were made in bad faith, notwithstanding that the claimant had made enquiries of the defendant as to whether it claimed any rights in World Cup Willie, without response and had carried out internet searches which indicated no one was using the mark. The claimant had been advised to apply to register the trade marks by its trade mark attorney.

In *Maslyukov* v *Diageo Distilling Ltd*,[209] an application was made to register as trade marks 'DALLAS DHU', 'PITTYVAICH' and 'CONVALMORE' in respect of alcoholic beverages including Scotch whisky. The names were those of Scotch Whisky distilleries which had closed in the 1980s and 1990s. The applications were limited so as not to include single malt whiskys made at the distilleries prior to their closure. It is usual practice for independent bottlers and retailed to keep stocks of vintage bottles of single malts to be

201 [2003] RPC 11.

202 [2002] 2 AC 164, in which the House referred to its own earlier judgment in *Royal Brunei Airlines Sdn Bhd* v *Tan* [1995] 2 AC 378, another breach of trust case.

203 [1982] QB 1053, a case which should be very familiar to all students of criminal law.

204 [2005] FSR 10.

205 The applicant's appeal to the Court of Appeal was dismissed. He had argued that the test for bad faith was dishonesty.

206 *Ajit Weekly Trade Mark* [2006] RPC 25, before the Appointed Person.

207 [2008] FSR 10.

208 This was the mascot for the 1966 Football World Cup.

209 [2010] RPC 21.

released in the future, sometimes up to 50 years from the date of distilling. Diageo opposed the registration of the marks on a number of grounds. The only ground to succeed was that of bad faith. The Hearing Officer held that by applying to register the names of distilleries, with which he had no connection, the applicant was attempting to appropriate the reputation of the distilleries and this fell short of the standards of acceptable commercial behaviour.

On appeal, Arnold J held that the Hearing Officer had correctly summarised the case law on bad faith and rejected the applicant's criticism of the Hearing Officer's decision, which included a submission that he had applied a presumption of bad faith as the applicant was a foreigner involving himself in the country's traditions and culture. Arnold J rejected this submission and found that the Hearing Officer had applied the law objectively and there was no evidence of prejudice against the applicant. Although the applicant claimed that he intended to carry out business honestly and had no record of dealing with counterfeit goods, Arnold J confirmed that bad faith must be viewed objectively, taking account of the applicant's knowledge and it is immaterial if the applicant sees nothing wrong in what he is doing.

It is often claimed that a lack of a *bona fide* intention to use a trade mark is equivalent to a finding that the application has been made in bad faith. The motive of the applicant might have been to prevent the use of the trade mark by another or to sell on the trade mark to an undertaking that would be interested in it or concerned about the potential of its use by a third party. In *DEMON ALE Trade Mark*,[210] an application was made to register 'DEMON ALE' (an anagram of LEMONADE) for beer and mineral water. This was subsequently restricted to beer only.[211] The owner of the trade mark 'BIERE DU DEMON', used for beer, filed an opposition. There was evidence that the applicant only intended to register the trade mark in order to prevent 'alcopop' manufacturers using it. There was no evidence that there was any *bona fide* intention that the mark would be used by the applicant or with his consent. This was a breach of statutory requirement in s 32(3) and this alone was sufficient to find that the application had been made in bad faith. It was also stressed that a finding of bad faith could be made even if the applicant saw nothing wrong with his own behaviour.

Offering to sell a trade mark application for a very high price to an organisation, which might have an interest in acquiring it, can be very suggestive of a lack of a *bona fide* intention to use the mark. In *Baywatch Trade Mark Application*,[212] the applicant, who was unconnected with the makers of the television series of that name, applied to register 'BayWatch' in respect of restaurant services in Class 42. Inevitably, there was an opposition by the production company which made the television series. The opponent's mark 'BAYWATCH' was already registered, *inter alia*, in respect of fast food items. When the opponent contacted the applicant requesting that the application be withdrawn, he responded by saying that he was willing to sell the trade mark for £15 million plus royalties. Although it was suspected that the true purpose behind the application was to sell the trade mark at an inflated price, the Hearing Officer was unconvinced that this was the original intention. Although an attempt to capture the opponent's goodwill might be a ground for refusal under s 5(3) by taking unfair advantage of the repute of the opponent's mark, this was not, *per se*, enough to amount to bad faith. However, it was accepted that, as the applicant's business plans were very sketchy and insufficiently developed at the time of the application, he had no *bona fide* intention to use the mark.

Whether an application that would otherwise be vulnerable under s 5(3) of the relative grounds for refusal[213] could be deemed to be made in bad faith seems entirely possible, given the presence of an appropriate motive on the part of the applicant. In *CA Sheimer (M) Sdn Bhd's Trade Mark Application*,[214] an application was made to register VISA for, *inter alia*, condoms and contraceptive devices. This was opposed by Visa International Service Association which operated the familiar Visa credit card. The applicant had just surrendered

210 [2000] RPC 345.

211 Presumably because its use for mineral water would have been deceptive.

212 (Unreported) 12 November 1999, Trade Marks Registry.

213 This ground applies where an identical or similar mark is used in relation to non-similar goods or services where, without due cause, it takes unfair advantage of or is detrimental to the distinctive character of a trade mark of repute: *see* below.

214 [2000] RPC 484.

215 Proceedings had been initiated by the opponent for revocation on the grounds of non-use.

an earlier registration for VISA for the same goods.[215] Geoffrey Hobbs QC, as the Appointed Person, found bad faith on the basis that the applicant's use of the mark would have been detrimental to the opponent's mark by altering perceptions of the mark negatively from the perspective of a provider of financial services. He said (at 506):

> Visa International should not have to carry the burden of advertising condoms and prophylactics at the same time as it promotes its own services.

A finding that the applicant wanted to take advantage of the repute of the opponent's trade mark was sufficient to find bad faith even if an opposition under s 5(3) was not made out.[216]

216 Geoffrey Hobbs QC also said that s 3(6) did not require an application 'to submit an open-ended assessment of its commercial morality'. He had less faith in his suggestion that 'bad faith' had moral overtones and could apply in the absence of a breach of duty, obligation or prohibition legally binding on the applicant. He thought that guidance on this matter might be required from the Court of Justice.

The wording of s 3(6) is that the trade mark shall not be registered 'if or to the extent that the application is made in bad faith'. This suggests that, in appropriate cases, particular reference should be made in relation to the specification of goods or services for which registration had been requested. Thus, where an applicant makes a statement relating to the goods or services for which the mark is to be used which is over-ambitious, including goods or services in respect of which the mark is not being or is unlikely to be used, then the application might fail partially.[217] This poses a difficult problem for applicants who may want their registration to extend to goods or services that they *might* sell or supply in the future, perhaps as a result of business expansion or diversification. Too wide a coverage may be picked up by the examiner in the Trade Marks Registry or, more likely, by an opponent. Furthermore, in the future, an over-extensive specification of goods or services may give rise to proceedings for partial revocation under s 46 based on five or more years' non-use.

217 This was a successful ground of opposition in *BETTY'S KITCHEN CORONATION STREET Trade Mark* [2000] RPC 825.

218 [2000] RPC 825.

Another form of bad faith is where there is no intention to use the trade mark in the form applied for. In *BETTY'S KITCHEN CORONATION STREET Trade Mark*,[218] the specification of goods was far too wide but there was some use in respect of hot pot meals. However, the elements of the mark 'BETTY'S KITCHEN' and 'CORONATION STREET' were placed far apart on the packaging and the two elements were depicted in completely different styles. Overall, there was nothing to suggest that a single composite mark was intended. A further factor was that the applicant, Granada Television Ltd, knew of the opponents' registrations for 'BETTY'S KITCHEN' and, it was thought, had tried to modify its mark to put just sufficient distance between its mark and that of the opponents to achieve registrability. The above factors were such as to find that the applicant's behaviour fell below 'acceptable commercial behaviour' and the application was, therefore, made in bad faith.[219] The point was made in the case that some latitude in how a trade mark may be used is permissible but must not go so far as to undermine the desirability of a person consulting the Register to determine the protection afforded by registration.

219 Another reason why the application was made in bad faith was that it was held that the applicant had no intention to use the mark over the range of goods specified. The applicant failed to show that it had made preparations to license third parties to use the mark in respect of the other goods.

220 Council Regulation (EC) No 40/94 of 20 December 1993 on the Community trade mark, OJ L 11, 14.4.94, p 1.

The above case pushes forward the boundaries of bad faith in two senses. First, it may be bad faith to use a trade mark in a form which differs significantly from the form in which it is registered. However, without more, it is hard to see how that can be. Of course, it may be relevant to revocation on the grounds of non-use or infringement. The second sense is that the decision suggests that a deliberate attempt to get as near as possible to someone else's trade mark may constitute bad faith. But is it bad faith to get as near to another trader's mark *as it is lawful to do*? The case should be treated somewhat cautiously and it is submitted that the two elements, the fact of use in a very different form and motive, taken together may be evidence of bad faith but that might not be the case if only one element is present.

221 (Unreported) 28 March 2000, OHIM, Case No C000053447/1.

222 In *Baume & Co Ltd v AH Moore* [1958] RPC 226, a case under the 1938 Act, Romer LJ said that the 'truth is that a man is either honest or dishonest in his motives; there is no such thing, so far as we are aware, as constructive dishonesty'. This casts a doubt about the term 'constructive fraud' used in *TRILLIUM*.

Bad faith in relation to the CTM Regulation[220] has been construed in a fairly narrow sense in the OHIM in *TRILLIUM Trade Mark*.[221] The First Cancellation Division said that:

> Bad faith is the opposite of good faith, generally implying or involving, though was not limited to, actual or constructive fraud, or a design to mislead or deceive another, or any other sinister motive. Conceptually, bad faith can be understood as a dishonest intention.[222]

Under the CTM Regulation, unlike the Trade Marks Act 1994, there is no requirement for a statement by the applicant that the mark is being used by him or with his consent or that he has a *bona fide* intention that it will be so used.[223] This may explain the narrower approach and it may accord more with the law in the UK under the 1938 Act but the difficulty is, if dishonesty is the key to bad faith, contemplating how an application can be made partly in good faith and partly in bad faith.[224] The CTM Regulation allows revocation in respect of only some of the goods or services for which the mark is registered, as does the UK Act.

Further guidance was given by the Court of Justice in another case involving the CTM. In Case C-29/07 *Chocoladefabriken Lindt & Sprüngli AG v Franz Hauswirth GmbH*,[225] the defendant counter-claimed for invalidity of the claimant's CTM on the ground that it had been applied for in bad faith. The trade mark was a shape mark in the form of a gold-coloured chocolate bunny, in a sitting position, wearing a red ribbon and a bell. It had been used for a number of years by the applicant but very similar chocolate bunnies wrapped in foil had been marketed by other undertakings for some time before the application was filed. The Court of Justice ruled that a determination of bad faith requires an assessment of all the factors relevant to the particular case. In a case such as the present one, this required consideration of:

- whether the applicant knows or must know that a third party was using, in at least one Member State, an identical or similar sign for identical or similar goods which was capable of being confused with the sign for which registration had been sought;
- whether the applicant's intention was to prevent a third party from using that sign;
- the degree of legal protection enjoyed by the third party's sign and the sign for which registration had been sought.

Intention is an important factor but the fact that the applicant for registration knew or must be taken to know of the existence and use of the third party sign was not, *per se*, sufficient for a finding of bad faith. The court did recognise that it might be possible that the applicant for registration had a legitimate motive, such as preventing a newcomer entering the market and using an identical or similar sign as that used for some time by the applicant for registration. A further factor in the case of shape marks is that bad faith may be more readily established where competitors are constrained from entering the market by reason of technical or commercial factors and offering comparable goods. This ruling must be treated with some caution and it is submitted that it was very much conditioned by the facts of the case. Obviously it will be bad faith to apply for a trade mark for the purpose of trying prevent a third party continuing to use a sign he has used for some time but failed to register as a trade mark.[226]

If an application has been made in bad faith, any subsequent event or transaction cannot cure it. The application must be viewed as at the time it is filed. Bad faith is judged at the time of the application but matters occurring later may be taken into account if they assist in determining the state of mind of the applicant at the time of the application.[227]

Where an application to register a trade mark was made by a person who was not entitled to the mark but the application was subsequently assigned to a person acting in good faith, the application must be refused.[228] The fact that the applicant knew he was not entitled to the mark was sufficient for a finding of bad faith even though that person claimed to be acting to protect the interests of the person rightfully entitled to the mark. It would also be bad faith to register a trade mark, having no existing title in the mark, with the intention of interfering with the rights of those who did have title to the mark and had consistently used it.[229] Where a company director registered the company name as a trade mark in his own right and for his own personal interest, without the consent of the company, this would normally amount to a breach of the director's fiduciary duties and a court would usually grant relief by ordering that the trade mark be assigned to the company and the register rectified accordingly.

223 See the discussion of this by Pumfrey J in *Decon Laboratories Ltd* v *Fred Baker Scientific Ltd* [2001] RPC 17. In respect to the Community Trade Mark, the Chancery Division was acting as a Community Trade Mark Court.

224 However, in *Knoll AG's Trade Mark* [2003] RPC 10, Neuberger J thought that *TRILLIUM* was at one with the meaning of bad faith under the 1994 Act. Dishonesty, or at least something approaching dishonesty, was required for a finding that the application had been made in bad faith.

225 [2009] ECR I-4893.

226 However, in such a case, the third party may be able to successfully oppose the application or, if the mark is registered and he is sued later for trade mark infringement, raise a counterclaim based on passing off or unfair competition and/or seek a declaration of invalidity.

227 *Ferrero SpA's Trade Marks* [2004] RPC 29.

228 *NONOGRAM Trade Mark* [2001] RPC 21.

229 *SAXON Trade Mark* [2003] FSR 39.

230 [2002] FSR 43.

In *Ball* v *The Eden Project Ltd*,[230] the defendant was an operating company through which the 'The Eden Project', the famous tourist attraction in Cornwall, operated. The claimant was a co-founder of the project and a director of the company when he registered the trade mark 'The Eden Project' in his own name. A dispute had arisen about compensation payable to the claimant for his work on the project and he sought compensation under a *quantum meruit* with a promise to assign the trade mark and other intellectual property rights to the defendant upon payment of the sums due. It was held that the claimant was in breach of his fiduciary duty to the defendant company. An argument that the application had been made in bad faith was not alleged in the counterclaim as the defendant sought assignment of the trade mark rather than a finding of invalidity. However, had the circumstances been different, an application by a company director to register the company name as a trade mark for his own benefit would surely be deemed to have been made in bad faith.

Relative grounds for refusal

The Directive contains in Article 4 a number of 'further grounds for refusal or invalidity concerning conflicts with earlier rights'. The Trade Marks Act 1994 provides for these further grounds in s 5 (supplemented by the definition of 'earlier trade marks' in s 6) under the heading 'relative grounds for refusal of registration'.[231] This is one part of trade mark law where the UK Act is generally easier to follow than the provisions in the Directive which contain a number of options for Member States. The relative grounds for refusal of registration are so described because they depend on the relationship of the trade mark subject to the application with an earlier trade mark or other earlier right, such as an unregistered trade mark or a copyright.

231 These grounds are also grounds for invalidity under s 47(2). The CTM Regulation also describes the equivalent grounds of refusal as 'relative grounds for refusal' in Article 8.

When the Trade Marks Act 1994 was enacted, it was possible for anyone to bring opposition proceedings, whether or not they were the proprietor of earlier conflicting trade marks or other rights.[232] Section 8 of the Act empowered the Secretary of State to restrict opposition applications only to those who were proprietors of earlier trade marks or other rights alleged to conflict with the mark applied for. This was to bring the UK in line with the position under the CTM Regulation where opposition can only be brought by the proprietor of the earlier trade mark or other earlier right which is the basis of opposition. The earliest time for making this change to UK law was 1 January 2006, that is, ten years after the first day for filing applications to register CTMs. With effect from 1 October 2007, by virtue of the Trade Marks (Relative Grounds) Order 2007,[233] only proprietors or earlier trade marks or other earlier rights may raise the relative grounds for refusal of registration. This must be done in opposition proceedings. Unless such opposition is raised, the Registrar shall not refuse to register a trade mark on the basis of the relative grounds for refusal under s 5. Furthermore, where opposition is based on an earlier trade mark registered for more than five years.[234] Before, these changes, in practice, the relative grounds for refusal were usually raised in opposition proceedings brought by proprietors of earlier trade marks or other earlier rights.

232 Any person can make observations without becoming a party to the proceedings on the application under s 38(3). The observations can relate to any aspect and include observations on the absolute grounds for refusal also.

233 SI 2007/1976.

234 Section 6A, described in detail later. If the earlier trade mark has not been put to use within the preceding five years it is vulnerable to revocation under s 46.

Comparison of the further (relative) grounds for refusal under Article 4 with Article 5, setting out the rights conferred by a trade mark, shows some marked similarities between some of those further grounds and acts that infringe a registered trade mark. The Trade Marks Act 1994 is even clearer and comparison between s 5 and s 10 (in particular s 5(1)–(3) and 10(1)–(3) are, in their different contexts, equivalent). This means that an application to register a sign as a trade mark, the use of which would infringe under s 10(1)–(3), should be refused on the basis of s 5(1)–(3), or the equivalent provisions in the Directive. The rationale for this is that it should limit the possibility of conflicting trade marks on the register and keep off the register trade marks which could be successfully challenged.[235]

The Court of Justice tends to treat the provisions in Article 4 and their equivalent in Article 5 the same and often rules on the pair of provisions together.[236] The Court also often notes the similarity with the equivalent provisions in the CTM Regulation.[237] Although the CTM Regulation is completely separate from national trade mark systems, as there are many similarities and, *mutatis mutandis*, identical provisions, it is sensible to adopt a common approach so that the Boards of Appeal at the OHIM and the Court of First Instance can refer to Court of Justice decisions on the Directive, even though they are not strictly binding. It is reasonable to assume that many cases on the relative grounds for refusal are helpful in interpreting the provisions on infringement and vice versa. There are numerous examples of cases on infringement and on the relative grounds being used in this way. This is particularly true in respect of whether there exists a 'likelihood of confusion' resulting from the use of the mark applied for or the use of the alleged infringing mark.

As some of the relative grounds depend on an earlier trade mark, before looking at the provisions in Article 4 in detail, it is worth looking at the definition of 'earlier trade mark' in Article 4(2) (s 6 of the Trade Marks Act 1994).

Earlier trade mark

Article 4(2) defines an earlier trade mark as one having an earlier application date, taking any priority into account, being a Community trade mark, one registered in a Member State or at the Benelux Trade Mark Office[238] or registered under international arrangements having effect in the Member State.[239] Where the earlier trade mark has not yet been registered, it will be treated as an earlier trade mark subject to its registration. Also included are CTMs having a valid claim to seniority even though the CTM has been surrendered or allowed to lapse. Seniority applies where an applicant for a CTM already holds a valid national registered trade mark for identical goods or services. The applicant for the CTM can claim the seniority of that national trade mark, preserving his prior rights even if he subsequently surrenders or does not renew the national trade mark. The reason is that the CTM system is designed to complement national systems. Of course, once a CTM has been acquired, there seems little reason to renew a national registration for an identical mark used for identical goods or services. The Trade Marks Act 1994 has been modified to include also marks having seniority converted from a CTM or international trade mark designating the EU to a national registered mark or international registration designating the UK.

The CTM may now also be acquired by application through the Madrid Protocol,[240] with effect from 1 October 2004, the date of the accession of the European Community (now EU) to the Madrid Protocol. As a result of this, the UK Trade Marks Act 1994 has been amended to include earlier international applications designating the EC.

Earlier well-known trade marks under Article 6[bis] of the Paris Convention for the Protection of Industrial Property 1883 also fall within the meaning of 'earlier trade mark'. As a result of the Agreement establishing the World Trade Organisation (the 'WTO Agreement'),[241] the UK Trade Marks Act 1994 has been modified to include also a reference to the WTO Agreement.[242] In determining whether a trade mark is well known, account is taken of the knowledge of it in the relevant sector of the public including knowledge obtained through promotion of it.[243] Section 56(1) of the Trade Marks Act 1994 defines a well-known trade mark in terms of it being well known in the UK as the mark of a person who is a national of a Convention country or is domiciled in or has a real or effective industrial or commercial establishment in a Convention country. It does not matter if the trade mark is not used in the UK or that the proprietor of the trade mark has no goodwill in the UK.[244] All this means is that an application to register a trade mark

235 However, there remains a possibility of conflicting marks through consent on the part of the proprietor of an earlier trade mark or other right (Article 4(5) or s 5(5)) or honest concurrent use (s 7).

236 See, for example, Case C-251/95 *Sabel BV v Puma AG, Rudolf Dassler Sport* [1997] ECR I-6191 and Case C-291/00 *LTJ Diffusion SA v Sadas Vertbaudet SA* [2003] ECR I-2799.

237 See, for example, Case C-353/03 *Société des Produits Nestlé SA v Mars UK Ltd* [2005] ECR I-6135.

238 In the case of Belgium, Luxembourg or the Netherlands. This Office is now known as the Benelux Intellectual Property Office.

239 For example, under the Madrid Protocol.

240 The Madrid System (the Madrid Agreement and the Protocol to the Agreement) allows for the international application for trade marks in a number of different countries. The Madrid System is described in Chapter 22.

241 Signed at Marrakesh 15 April 1994.

242 Section 6(1)(c).

243 Article 16 of the WTO Agreement on the Trade Related Aspects of Intellectual Property Rights.

244 The proprietor may also be able to obtain injunctive relief in the UK under s 56(2).

can be challenged on the basis of a well-known trade mark registered in a country outside the EC, such as the US, even though there is no registration for that trade mark in any Member State or as a CTM.

Trade marks whose registration has expired are taken into account for a period of one year after expiry, unless the Registrar is satisfied there was no *bona fide* use during the two years immediately preceding the expiry.[245] The question arises as to whether an expired mark can be taken into account if it expired between the date an application is filed and the date the final decision as to registrability is made. This can be a problem if the time between application and final decision is lengthy. Consider the following example: an application is filed in October 2005 and a similar earlier trade mark lapsed in December 2005 and has not been renewed. Opposition proceedings based on the earlier trade mark take place in April 2007. At that time the lapsed mark cannot be restored. Therefore, if the relevant time for taking into account the expired mark is the time the application is filed for the new mark, the earlier trade mark must be taken into account. However, if the relevant time is the time the decision is made (April 2007), the earlier expired trade mark cannot be taken into account. The latter view was preferred in *TRANSPAY Trade Mark*[246] where it was accepted that it was proper to take account of developments such as the lapse of an earlier trade mark between the date of filing the application and the date the decision as to registrability is taken.

Before looking in detail at the relative grounds for refusal, Table 20.1 sets them out in summary form, by reference to the provisions in the Directive and the Act. Also included are the grounds for refusal based on earlier rights other than in respect of registered trade marks.

The relative grounds for refusal will now be looked at in detail.

245 The provision in the Directive is Article 4(4)(f) which sets the period after expiry at a *maximum* of two years.

246 [2001] RPC 10.

Table 20.1 Relative grounds for refusal

Directive (Article)	Trade Marks Act 1994 (section)	Relationship with earlier mark	Relationship with goods or services for which earlier mark registered or earlier right used	Proof of likelihood of confusion	Notes
4(1)(a)	5(1)	Identical	Identical	No	Unregistrable *per se.*
4(1)(b)	5(2)	Identical	Similar	Yes	
		Similar	Identical or similar	Yes	
4(3) & 4(4)(a)	5(3)	Identical or similar to earlier trade mark having a reputation	None required*	No	
4(4)(b)	5(4)(a)	Nothing specific but use can be prohibited	Probably similar or same field of activity at least	Deception, probably	If prevented by law, in particular, passing off
4(4)(c)	5(4)(b)	Nothing specific but use can be prohibited	Depends on relevant rights and infringement	No	Other earlier right such as a copyright, design right or registered design

* Although the Directive states that the goods or services must be 'not similar', in Case C-292/00 *Davidoff & Cie SA* v *Gofkid Ltd* [2003] ECR I-389, the Court of Justice held that the provision also applied in the case of identical and similar goods or services. The UK Trade Marks Act 1994 was amended accordingly.

Article 4(1)(a) – identical trade mark, identical goods or services

There is no need to enquire into the effect of using the mark for which registration is sought for the purposes of Article 4(1)(a) as it is simply a question of whether it is identical to an earlier trade mark and is intended to be used for identical goods or services. Where there is complete identity of the sign and the trade mark and the goods or services, a likelihood of confusion is presumed.[247] Article 4(1)(a) states that a trade mark shall not be registered, or, if registered, shall be liable to be declared invalid:

> . . . if it is identical with an earlier trade mark, and the goods or services for which the trade mark is applied for or is registered are identical with the goods or services for which the earlier trade mark is protected.

As one might imagine, this ground of refusal is quite rare. Anyone applying to register a trade mark will probably have the benefit of a trade mark search and will be aware of any potential conflict under this head. It makes little sense to attempt to register a mark identical with an earlier trade mark with the intention of using it in relation to the same goods or services.

The scope of the ground for refusal depends on how much it is possible to depart from complete identity of the marks and/or goods and services and it might be expected that very slight modifications that would tend not to be noticed in practice should be ignored. At the end of the day, the question whether a sign is identical to an earlier trade mark is a question of fact for the national court to decide but the Court of Justice has given some guidance on the matter. In Case C-291/00 *LTJ Diffusion SA* v *Sadas Vertbaudet SA*,[248] the claimant argued that the defendant's trade mark infringed its trade mark. Both parties' trade marks were registered in France for clothing, the claimant's being the earlier trade mark which was the word 'Arthur' in a stylised form appearing like a signature. The defendant's trade mark was 'Arthur et Félicie' in normal type. The Court of Justice referred to the ruling in Case C-342/97 *Lloyd Schuhfabrik Meyer & Co GmbH* v *Klisjen Handel BV*[249] (at para 29) to the effect that:

> . . . the perception of identity between the sign and the trade mark must be assessed globally with respect to an average consumer who is deemed to be reasonably well informed, reasonably observant and circumspect. The sign produces an overall impression on such a consumer. That consumer only rarely has the chance to make a direct comparison between signs and trade marks and must place his trust in the imperfect picture of them that he has kept in his mind. Moreover, his level of attention is likely to vary according to the category of goods or services in question.

On that basis, the Court of Justice concluded that the marks did not have to be completely identical in all respects and '. . . a sign is identical to a trade mark where it reproduces, without any modification or addition, all the elements constituting the trade mark or where, viewed as a whole, it contains differences so insignificant that they may go unnoticed by an average consumer'. However, the Court of Justice did note that the criterion must be interpreted strictly[250] so that the absolute protection afforded by Article 5(1)(a) (the equivalent provision on infringement) should not be extended to situations that properly fell within Article 5(1)(b) where a likelihood of confusion is required.

In the UK, it has been accepted that applying to register a trade mark which is identical to an earlier trade mark but to which additional material has been added may be caught by this ground of refusal. For example, in *Decon Laboratories Ltd* v *Fred Baker Scientific Ltd*,[251] it was held that the use of an identical sign with a suffix descriptive of the nature and quality of the goods was use of an identical sign.[252] The claimant's registered trade mark was the word 'Decon' and the defendants used signs such as 'Decon-Phene', 'Decon-Phase' and 'Decon-Clean'. However, in *Compass Publishing BV* v *Compass Logistics Ltd*,[253] it

247 Case C-245/02 *Anheuser-Busch Inc* v *Budějovický Budvar* [2004] ECR I-10989 at para 8.

248 [2003] ECR I-2799.

249 [1999] ECR I-3819.

250 This seems to contradict the 'imperfect picture' test. The opacity of the judgment in this respect was noted by Jacob LJ in *Reed Executive plc* v *Reed Business Information Ltd* [2004] RPC 40 at para 25.

251 [2001] RPC 17.

252 Unlike the relative grounds, which refer to registration of a trade mark, the equivalent parts of s 10 refer to the use of a sign, for obvious reasons.

253 [2004] RPC 41.

was held that 'COMPASS LOGISTICS' was not identical to 'COMPASS' as the differences were apparent and the public would distinguish them without prior coaching. The question is what was the name that the public would perceive as being the trade mark. This might depend on the nature of the use made of the mark. That is not to say, of course, that there might be a likelihood of confusion between the two marks and objection could be taken under the grounds for refusal where there is not complete identity of the marks and goods or services. In *IDG Communications Ltd's Trade Mark Application*,[254] the hearing officer in the Trade Marks Registry held that 'DIGIT' and 'digits' were not identical though clearly very similar.[255]

Ignoring inconsequential alterations such as additions that do not affect the dominant character of a trade mark seems reasonable, especially as some persons might be likely to abbreviate the full trade mark and end up referring to the goods or services by the most distinctive part which may be identical to the earlier trade mark. It is also likely that slight changes will not be sufficient to overcome this ground of refusal, particularly if the test in *LTJ Diffusion* applies so that the average consumer, with his imperfect recollection of the marks, is likely not to notice the differences.[256] The point might seem academic because, if the sign for which registration is sought is not identical to the earlier trade mark, the next ground for refusal should apply, where a similar sign is used for identical or similar goods. However, this ground of refusal, like the equivalent form of infringement, requires a likelihood of confusion to be present. That being so, when challenging an application to register a sign as a trade mark which is very similar to, or differs only in insignificant details from, an earlier trade mark, it will be usual to base opposition on both Article 4(1)(a) and (b) (or, in the UK, on the basis of s 5(1) and (2)).

As a little leeway is possible when considering whether a sign is identical to an earlier trade mark, the same ought to apply to the description of goods and services. However, the difference should be so slight as to go unnoticed in the normal course of events, bearing in mind the ground of refusal where there is not complete identity of the sign and the earlier trade mark and the goods or services is present. In *GALILEO Trade Mark*,[257] Professor Ruth Annand, as the Appointed Person, held that overlapping specifications would satisfy the test of identical goods or services but there was no need for them to co-extend. As a likelihood of confusion is presumed where there is complete identity of the sign and the earlier trade mark and the goods or services, the ground of refusal under Article 4(1)(a) should be reserved for those cases where a significant proportion of consumers would think there was complete identity given that it has been accepted that consumers do not usually make a direct comparison between the sign and the earlier trade mark.[258]

In *Reed Executive plc v Reed Business Information Ltd*,[259] Jacob LJ did not think that 'Reed Business Information' was identical to 'Reed'. The claimants provided employment agency services and the defendants had a recruitment website, said to be the electronic analogue of job advertisements found in the job sections of numerous publications. It was held that the services were not identical. The defendants were not operating as employment agents who put potential employees in touch with employers. Whether a person consulting the website contacted an employer advertising there was unknown to the defendants and their remuneration was unaffected by whether this happened.

Article 4(1)(b) – incomplete identity of mark and goods or services

This ground for refusal is fairly common and often used in opposition or invalidity proceedings and has generated a considerable amount of case law, both in the Court of Justice and in the UK courts. It applies in circumstances as indicated in Table 20.2.

Article 4(1)(b) states that a trade mark shall not be registered or, if registered, shall be liable to be declared invalid:

254 [2002] RPC 10.

255 However, the Hearing Officer applied the decision of Simon Thorley QC, as the Appointed Person, in *Baywatch Trade Mark Application* (unreported) 12 November 1999, Trade Marks Registry, where he said that 'identical' should be given its normal English meaning. This case pre-dated the Court of Justice decision in *LTJ Diffusion* and must now be doubted on this point.

256 In *WEBSPHERE Trade Mark* [2004] FSR 39, it was held that 'WEBSPHERE' was identical to 'Websphere', applying the imperfect recollection test and also considering the aural and conceptual similarities.

257 [2005] RPC 22.

258 Case C-342/97 *Lloyd Schuhfabrik Meyer & Co GmbH v Klisjen Handel BV* [1999] ECR I-3819.

259 [2004] RPC 40.

Table 20.2 Grounds for refusal under Article 4(1)(b)

Relationship between the sign applied for and the earlier trade mark	Relationship between the goods or services for which the sign is intended to be used and those for which the earlier trade mark is used
Identical	Similar
Similar	Identical
Similar	Similar

. . . if because of its identity with, or similarity to the earlier trade mark and the identity or similarity of the goods or services covered by the trade marks, there exists a likelihood of confusion on the part of the public, which includes the likelihood of association with the earlier trade mark.

Article 4(1)(b) would seem to include the case where there is complete identity (unlike the position under the equivalent provision, s 5(2), in the Trade Marks Act 1994, which does not). This is an unnecessary possibility given the presence of Article 4(1)(a) and the Court of Justice's view that, in a case of complete identity, a likelihood of confusion is presumed. As the protection afforded by a trade mark is absolute in the case of the use of an identical sign for identical goods or services,[260] this reinforces the view that the inclusion of complete identity in Article 4(1)(b) is no more than the result of clumsy drafting.

> 260 Article 5(1)(a) and the tenth recital to the Directive.

As there is incomplete identity for Article 4(1)(b), this explains the need for showing a likelihood of confusion on the part of the public. One difficulty with this was the addition of the phrase 'which includes a likelihood of association'. Previously, under the Benelux trade mark system, it was considered that this extended to 'non-origin association': that is, where consumers are not deceived as to the origin of the goods or services but the use of the offending sign conjures up in the mind of the consumer the owner of the earlier trade mark. This might be because of some similarity between the sign applied for and an earlier trade mark, perhaps being a different word written in a similar stylised form as the earlier trade mark or having a similar semantic content: for example, if someone attempted to register a device and word mark comprising the word 'Pixie' and a drawing of a walking baby wearing a nappy, used for soaps and detergents. Even if consumers would not think it came from the same stable as Fairy washing up liquid, it would be likely to conjure that product up in their minds.

Where the similarity with an earlier trade mark results only from elements disclaimed in that earlier trade mark, there can be no similarity if no other elements are the same or similar. In *TORREMAR Trade Mark*,[261] the opponent's trade marks had been registered with the right to exclusive use of the word 'TORRES' disclaimed. There was no other similarity between the opponent's earlier trade marks and the mark now applied for.

> 261 [2003] RPC 4.

The first time the relevance of 'likelihood of association' and its impact on the scope of 'likelihood of confusion on the part of the public' was considered judicially was in the Chancery Division of the High Court *Wagamama Ltd v City Centre Restaurants plc*,[262] in which Laddie J rejected the notion that the composite phrase included non-origin association in the absence of confusion as to the origin of the goods or services. Soon after, the Court of Justice agreed in Case C-251/95 *Sabel BV v Puma AG, Rudolf Dassler Sport*,[263] ruling (at para 26) that:

> 262 [1995] FSR 713.

> 263 [1997] ECR I-6191.

> . . . the mere association which the public might make between two trade marks because of their analogous semantic content [images of bounding felines in this particular case] is not in itself a sufficient ground for concluding that there is a likelihood of confusion . . .

However, the court also said that the more distinctive the earlier mark, the greater will be the likelihood of confusion, adding (at para 24):

> . . . it is therefore not impossible that the conceptual similarity resulting from the fact that two marks use images with analogous semantic content may give rise to a likelihood of confusion where the earlier mark has a particularly distinctive character, either *per se* or because of the reputation it enjoys with the public.

Thus, we can say that likelihood of association is not sufficient by itself to give rise to a likelihood of confusion but confusion as to origin might result from the association the public makes between a very distinctive mark and the mark applied for.

In Case C-425/98 *Marca Mode CV v Adidas AG*,[264] the Court of Justice clarified the ruling in *Sabel* saying that:

264 [2000] ECR I-4861 at para 39.

> The negative formulation 'it is therefore not impossible' [used in *Sabel*] simply underlines the possibility that a likelihood may arise from the conjunction of the two factors analysed. It in no way implies a presumption of likelihood of confusion resulting from the existence of a likelihood of association in the strict sense. By such wording, the Court referred by implication to the assessment of evidence which the national court must undertake in each case pending before it. It did not excuse the national court from the necessary positive finding of the existence of a likelihood of confusion which constitutes the matter to be proved.

Having accepted that non-origin association, *per se*, is an insufficient basis for a finding of a likelihood of confusion, the precise scope of that term can be considered. There is ample guidance from the Court of Justice. Again, Case C-251/95 *Sabel BV v Puma AG, Rudolf Dassler Sport*,[265] is instructive. There it was said that the determination of whether there is a likelihood of confusion requires a global appreciation of the visual, aural or conceptual similarity of the marks based on the overall impression given by them, bearing in mind their distinctive and dominant components. In this respect, the perception of the average consumer plays a decisive role in that global appreciation and the more distinctive the mark, the greater will be the likelihood of confusion. A further point was that the court was of the opinion that the average consumer normally perceives a trade mark as a whole and does not proceed to analyse its various details.

265 [1997] ECR I-6191.

The *Sabel* case has been approved on numerous occasions. In Case C-39/97 *Canon Kabushiki Kaisha v Metro Goldwyn Mayer Inc*,[266] the Court of Justice confirmed that:

266 [1998] ECR I-5507 at para 17.

> A global assessment of the likelihood of confusion implies some interdependence between the relevant factors, and in particular a similarity between the trade marks and between these goods or services. Accordingly, a lesser degree of similarity between these goods or services may be offset by a greater degree of similarity between the marks, and *vice versa*.

This suggests a two-axis approach to determining whether there is a likelihood of confusion, as indicated in Figure 20.1 (overleaf). Where, of course, both the marks and the goods or services are very similar, there will be little doubt that a likelihood of confusion exists. Where the distinctiveness of the earlier mark is very strong, that may lessen the degree of similarity required but it does not eliminate it altogether.[267] There is, however, no minimum threshold level of similarity which has to be established before consideration of whether there existed a likelihood of confusion.[268] As Jacob LJ said in *esure Insurance Ltd v Direct Line Insurance plc*[269] (at para 71):

267 *Sihra's Trade Mark Application* [2003] RPC 44.

268 *esure Insurance Ltd v Direct Line Insurance plc* [2008] RPC 34, overturning Lindsay J on this point.

269 [2008] RPC 34.

> The Judge's attempt to analyse what is essentially a question of fact into 'a threshold', albeit low test, followed by a further consideration of the position seems to me to complicate things unnecessarily. It is all a question of fact and degree and no more.

In respect of confusion, the relevant section of the public may be confused about the place where goods are produced but, even then, there can be no likelihood of confusion if the relevant section of the public does not believe that the goods come from the same

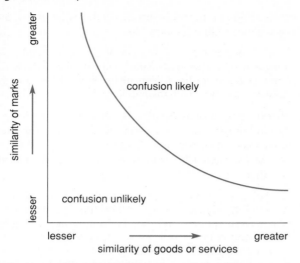

Figure 20.1 Confusion and similarity of marks and goods or services

undertaking or economically linked undertakings (for example, in the case of a subsidiary company).[270] This was held in Case C-39/97 *Canon Kabushiki Kaisha* v *Metro Goldwyn Mayer Inc.*[271] Confusion requires that the relevant section of the public believes the goods or services came from the same undertaking or economically linked undertakings. Again, the basic function of a trade mark, to operate as an indicator of origin,[272] would not be fulfilled in such a case.

The leading case before the Court of Justice which looks at the likelihood of confusion is Case C-342/97 *Lloyd Schuhfabrik Meyer & Co GmbH* v *Klisjen Handel BV.*[273] This case reinforces the *Sabel* and *Canon* cases and the 'global assessment' approach and also confirms that an aural similarity might suffice.[274] The court declined to set a percentage threshold at which a likelihood of confusion would exist. Emphasis was placed on the inherent characteristics of the mark and whether it contained descriptive elements. In Case C-120/04 *Medion AG* v *Thomson Multimedia Sales Germany & Austria GmbH*[275] the trade marks in question were 'LIFE' and 'THOMSON LIFE', both used for leisure and electronic devices. The Court of Justice ruled that, where the goods are identical, juxtaposing a company name with an earlier trade mark could result in a likelihood of confusion, where the latter still has an independent and distinctive role in the composite mark.

The use of a disclaimer displayed where goods are sold does not prevent the possibility of a finding that there is a likelihood of confusion. There may be a wider circle of consumers who do not buy the goods themselves: for example, where they are bought as presents or the goods are seen by others after sale.[276] The position is less clear where the disclaimer is part of the trade mark itself. However, trying to register a trade mark such as 'NOT CADBURY'S' to be used with confectionery would surely be caught by Article 4(1)(a) as it probably would be considered to be use of a sign identical with the Cadbury trade mark.[277]

In *BETTY'S KITCHEN CORONATION STREET Trade Mark*,[278] due to the fact that it could be shown that a sufficient number of people would be confused (because of their lack of detailed knowledge of the television soap and the character Betty Turpin), the application to register the trade mark could not be saved by showing that there was another group of people who, because of their detailed knowledge of the programme, would not be confused.

270 It seems also that a belief in the existence of a licence agreement or a joint venture is sufficient for a belief that the undertakings are economically linked: Case C-9/93 *IHT Internationale GmbH* v *Ideal Standard GmbH* [1994] ECR I-2789 and Case C-63/97 *Bayerische Motorenwerke AG* v *Ronald Karel Deenik* [1999] ECR I-905.

271 [1998] ECR I-5507 at paras 29 and 30.

272 See the tenth recital to the Directive.

273 [1999] ECR I-3819, a reference from the Landesgericht in Munich.

274 The marks in question were LLOYD'S and LOINT'S.

275 [2005] ECR I-8551.

276 Although concerned with the use of an identical sign for identical goods, this view formed part of the Court of Justice's reasoning in Case C-206/01 *Arsenal Football Club plc* v *Matthew Reed* [2002] ECR I-10273.

277 Case C-291/00 *LTJ Diffusion SA* v *Sadas Vertbaudet SA* [2003] ECR I-2799, above.

278 [2000] RPC 825.

There have been a number of cases in the UK on likelihood of confusion. Almost invariably, the above Court of Justice cases have been applied rigidly. However, in *ENER-CAP Trade Mark*,[279] having had his attention drawn to the *Sabel* case, the Appointed Person, Simon Thorley QC, thought that it gave guidelines but did not provide much assistance in identifying the criteria to be applied. For rules of comparison, he turned to the former law under the 1938 Act, citing, *inter alia*, Parker J in *Pianotist Co's Application*,[280] where he suggested the following factors should be taken into account for word marks:

- the look and sound of the words;
- the goods to which the marks were applied;
- the nature and kind of customer (for example, trade customers would be less likely to be confused as to origin than ordinary consumers);
- the surrounding circumstances;
- a consideration of what would be likely to happen if both marks were to be used.

Jacob J further developed these factors in *British Sugar plc* v *James Robertson & Sons Ltd*,[281] being:

(a) the respective uses of the respective goods;
(b) the respective users of the respective goods;
(c) the physical nature of the goods;
(d) the respective channels of trade;
(e) in the case of self-serve consumer items, where in practice they are respectively found or likely to be found in supermarkets and in particular whether they are, or are likely to be, found on the same or different shelves;
(f) the extent to which the respective goods or services are competitive; This inquiry may take into account how those in trade classify goods – for instance, whether market research companies, who of course act for industry, put the goods or services in the same or different sectors.

However, in *LIFESYSTEMS Trade Mark*,[282] the Hearing Officer said that, in the light of the *Canon* case, such factors could only be general guidance. Nevertheless, he applied those of Jacob J's factors relevant in that case. It is submitted that these factors, though of earlier pedigree, will continue to prove useful under the 1994 Act. They provide detailed criteria which may prove helpful in deciding whether there is a likelihood of confusion in fact, providing the factors are seen in the context of the Court of Justice decisions: in particular, in *Sabel*, *Canon* and *Lloyd*.

The Hearing Officer in *CODAS Trade Mark*[283] usefully summarised the test for likelihood of confusion derived from the Court of Justice cases, saying that it was clear from these cases that:

- The likelihood of confusion must be appreciated globally, taking account of all relevant factors (perhaps these could at least include the factors identified by Jacob J above).
- The matter must be judged through the eyes of the average consumer, of the goods/services in question, who is deemed to be reasonably well informed and reasonably circumspect and observant – but who rarely has the chance to make direct comparisons between marks and must instead rely upon the imperfect picture of them he has kept in his mind.
- The average consumer normally perceives a mark as a whole and does not proceed to analyse its various details.[284]
- The visual, aural and conceptual similarities of the marks must therefore be assessed by reference to the overall impression created by the marks bearing in mind their distinctive and dominant components.
- A lesser degree of similarity between the marks may be offset by a greater similarity between the goods (or services), and vice versa.

279 [1999] RPC 362.

280 (1906) 23 RPC 774 at 777.

281 [1996] RPC 281 at 296.

282 [1999] RPC 851.

283 [2001] RPC 14 at para 19.

284 Case C-251/95 *Sabel BV* v *Puma AG, Rudolf Dassler Sport* [1997] ECR I-6191 at para 23. Under the old UK law, Evershed J said in *Smith Hayden Co's Application* (1946) 63 RPC 97 at 102 that 'It is not profitable . . . to indulge in a minute analysis of letters and syllables, a process indeed notoriously productive of confusion in regards to words.'

● There is a greater likelihood of confusion where the earlier trade mark has a highly distinctive character, either *per se*, or because of the use that has been made of it.

Extensive use of a trade mark does not, *per se*, prove that it is distinctive but the less use that has been made of a trade mark, the more the protection afforded will be limited to the inherent distinctiveness of the trade mark. For use to be relevant to distinctiveness, that use must have been in a distinctive sense to have any material effect.[285] In fact, if there has been no such use in respect of a mark lacking inherent distinctiveness, it is likely to be refused under the absolute grounds of refusal.

285 Per Morritt LJ in *BACH and BACH FLOWER REMEDIES Trade Marks* [2000] RPC 513 at 530.

Where part of a word trade mark is descriptive or has a common meaning or is the same as part or all of an earlier word mark, it might be thought that this might have an impact on whether confusion is likely. However, the decision in *Sabel* shows us that, for the purposes of finding whether a likelihood of confusion exists, the marks must be compared as a whole rather than comparing similarities and differences in the detail of the marks. A mark may still possess sufficient distinctiveness notwithstanding an element which is common or the same as an element of another mark. In *POLACLIP Trade Mark*,[286] the opponent's mark was POLAROID. It was held that POLACLIP was registrable as the two words were unlikely to be confused even allowing for imperfect recollection and some slurring of speech when pronouncing the words. In the absence of evidence to the contrary, the public were more likely to take POLACLIP to mean polarising clip-on sunglasses rather than an abbreviated form of POLAROID clip-on sunglasses. Of course, when comparing two marks (as is usual in opposition proceedings) if both marks contain descriptive elements, the protection they will enjoy is limited. As the Hearing Officer said in *TRANSPAY Trade Mark*[287] when comparing TRANSPAY and TRANSCHEQ:

286 [1999] RPC 282.

287 [2001] RPC 10 at para 30.

> . . . the two trade marks, prima facie, consist of descriptive terms or at least terms which individually lack distinctiveness. The penumbra of protection each deserves is, therefore, in my view, very limited.

He went on to hold that the mark applied for 'TRANSPAY' was nevertheless registrable as, although the marks had a common prefix 'TRANS' (which might be understood as short for 'transfer'), they had different suffixes and the public was unlikely to be confused. Another example is the case of *10 Royal Berkshire Polo Club Trade Mark*[288] which was opposed by Polo Lauren Club LP, which had a registered trade mark POLO for similar goods including perfumery and shampoos. It was held that the semantic content of the marks was not such as to give rise to a belief that the opponent's goods and the applicant's goods came from the same undertaking or economically linked undertakings.[289]

288 [2001] RPC 32.

289 In the opponent's trade mark the word POLO was used as a noun whilst, in the applicant's mark, it was used adjectively. The fact that the public would be very unlikely to fail to notice the other words in the applicant's trade mark was an important factor.

The application of the test of likelihood of confusion, either in opposition or infringement proceedings, is fraught with difficulties and will depend on the circumstances of each particular case and will be heavily influenced by evidence of confusion (or lack of it) before the court. Unfortunately, the outcome will be difficult to predict in a good proportion of cases, particularly in opposition proceedings where the applicant for registration may not have had the benefit of using his trade mark previously or to any reasonable extent and this will make the task of adducing convincing evidence to the effect that there is not a likelihood of confusion considerably more difficult, especially as an opponent is likely to adduce evidence to the contrary, possibly in the form of a survey.

Article 4(3) and (4)(a) – unfair advantage of or damage to repute of trade mark having a reputation

Under the Directive, Article 4(3) provides for a ground of refusal where there is an earlier CTM having a reputation where the use of a sign (being identical or similar to the CTM) for which registration is sought without due cause would take unfair advantage of, or be detrimental to, the distinctive character or the repute of the earlier CTM. Article 4(4)(a)

290 Unlike Article 4(3), this is expressed as being a ground for refusal or invalidity to the extent that without due cause the trade mark takes unfair advantage of or is detrimental to the repute of the earlier trade mark.

291 Article 5(2).

292 The Trade Marks Act 1994 has been amended to take account of these rulings: below.

293 *CREDITMASTER Trade Mark* [2005] RPC 21.

294 *esure Insurance Ltd* v *Direct Line Insurance plc* [2008] RPC 34.

295 This accords with the CTM Regulation (*see* Article 8(5)) and also Benelux trade mark law.

296 In spite of the Lisbon Treaty, references in s 5 of the Act still refer to the EC or the Community.

297 [2003] ECR I-389.

provides that Member States may also have a ground for refusal (and invalidity) in similar circumstances where the sign for which registration is sought is identical or similar to an earlier national trade mark.[290] Both these grounds for refusal, and the equivalent provisions on infringement,[291] are based on the application to register being in respect of goods or services that are *not similar* to those for which the earlier CTM or national trade mark is registered. We shall see that the requirement that the goods or services are not similar is misleading and, as a result of Court of Justice rulings, it matters not whether the goods or services are identical, similar or not similar for these grounds of refusal (and invalidity) to apply.[292] It appears that the word 'similar' has the same meaning in this context as with Article 4(1)(b) where there is not complete identity of signs and goods or services.[293]

Where the ground under Article 4(1)(b) applies, it is almost certain that a finding under Article 4(3) will follow. For if there is a likelihood of confusion, it is just about inevitable that there will be unfair advantage of or detriment to the well-known trade mark.[294]

The UK elected to extend this ground of refusal to national trade marks as well as CTMs[295] as permitted by the Directive under Article 4(4)(a). The Trade Marks Act 1994 s 5(3), as amended applies in respect of earlier trade marks having a reputation in the UK or, in the case of CTMs or international trade marks designating the EC, within the Community.[296] The section now makes no distinction as to whether the goods or services are identical, similar or non-similar. The reason for the change was a reference for a preliminary ruling to the Court of Justice on the scope of Article 4(4)(a) and the equivalent infringement provision under Article 5(2) in Case C-292/00 *Davidoff & Cie SA* v *Gofkid Ltd*.[297] In that case, referred by the Bundesgerichtshof in Germany, the Swiss-based claimant used the trade mark 'Davidoff' in relation to high-class goods. The defendant, established in Hong Kong, used a word and device mark 'Durffee', which was alleged to be similar to the Davidoff trade mark, for a range of goods which were partly identical and partly similar to those of the claimant. It was claimed that the defendant had tried to take unfair advantage of the prestige value of the claimant and there would be damage to the reputation of its trade mark as persons do not tend to associate high-quality goods with China.

The Court of Justice ruled that Articles 4(4)(a) and 5(2) applied also in a situation where the goods and services were identical or similar to those for which the earlier trade mark was registered. The justification was that, on the basis of the overall scheme and objectives of the system of which the Directive is a part, the wording in the Articles in question should not be interpreted solely on the basis of their wording; otherwise, trade marks having a reputation would be afforded lesser protection where the goods or services were identical or similar than where they were not similar. Undoubtedly, it was the intention when the Directive was being drafted to provide additional protection (and corresponding additional grounds for refusal) for trade marks having a reputation to protect that reputation from 'blurring' (taking unfair advantage by seeking to ride on the back of the reputation) or 'tarnishing' or 'denigrating' (damaging the reputation, for example, by using a mark for inferior or distasteful goods or services).[298] It was probably also considered that the use of signs identical or similar to the earlier trade mark for identical or similar goods would be caught by the other grounds for refusal or forms of infringement, as the case might be. For some reason, those drafting the Directive did not foresee a situation, for example, where the goods or services were identical or similar and the sign was similar to the earlier trade mark, but there was no likelihood of confusion.

298 *See* Chapter 21 for examples of blurring and tarnishing.

299 [2003] ECR I-12537.

Case C-408/01 *Adidas-Salomon AG* v *Fitnessworld Trading Ltd*[299] confirmed the finding in *Davidoff* v *Gofkid* in relation to Article 5(2) that identical and similar goods or services were also caught and the provision was not limited to goods or services that are not similar, despite the express words used. The Court of Justice also confirmed in that case that, for Article 5(2), there was no need to show any likelihood of confusion and this was sufficient if the similarity between the sign and the trade mark having a reputation was such as to establish a link between the sign and the mark in the minds of the relevant public.[300] The same considerations must apply to Article 4(3) and (4)(a). Of course, without that link there can be no unfair advantage or damage to the repute of the earlier trade mark. In *Intel Corp Inc* v *CPM United Kingdom Ltd*,[301] invalidity proceedings were brought by the Intel Corp Inc (proprietor of the 'INTEL' mark for computers and the like) against the registration of 'INTELMARK' for marketing and telemarketing services. The ground relied upon was that INTELMARK took unfair advantage of and was detrimental to the distinctive character of INTEL by gradually whittling away the distinctive character of the INTEL mark, a case of dilution. The application for invalidity failed and Intel Corp Inc appealed to the Court of Appeal, which referred a number of questions to the Court of Justice for a preliminary ruling. The first question was, where:

(a) the earlier mark has a huge reputation for certain specific types of goods or services;
(b) those goods or services are dissimilar or dissimilar to a substantial degree to the goods or services of the later mark;
(c) the earlier mark is unique in respect of any goods or services; and
(d) the earlier mark would be brought to mind by the average consumer when he or she encounters the later mark used for the services of the later mark,

Are those facts sufficient in themselves to establish (i) 'a link' within the meaning of [*Adidas-Salomon*] and/or (ii) unfair advantage and/or detriment within the meaning of [Article 4(4)(a)]?

The Court of Appeal thought that the answer should be no, otherwise trade mark law would be 'oppressive and all powerful'. But, if the answer was no, further guidance was sought as to what factors should be taken into account. The Court of Appeal was also of the view that a trade mark's distinctive character or repute must be judged in relation to the goods or services for which it was registered and Article 4(4)(a) did not call for an enquiry about whether distinctiveness was affected generally. However, it is instructive to remind ourselves that the wording of Article 4(4)(a) mentions goods or services which are not similar to those for which the earlier trade mark is registered and this suggests an investigation as to whether distinctiveness is affected generally, irrespective of the goods and services. By extending the provision to identical and similar goods or services, *Davidoff* v *Gofkid* and *Adidas-Salomon* did not strike out the reference to non-similar goods and services. Cases on infringement under Article 5(2),[302] discussed in the next chapter and the other 'INTEL' case below, suggest that the Court of Appeal's preferred view is at odds with these cases and also incompatible with the law of passing off which can apply to use for non-similar goods or services where there is a danger of dilution of the claimant's goodwill.[303]

The Court of Justice ruling in Case C-252/07 *Intel Corporation Inc* v *CPM United Kingdom Ltd*,[304] confirmed that a global assessment is called for, taking into account all the factors relevant to the circumstances of the case, in order to establish whether there is a link in the *Adidas-Salomon* sense. If, for the average consumer, who is reasonably well-informed and reasonably observant and circumspect, the later mark calls into mind the mark with a reputation, this is tantamount to the existence of such a link. The same 'global assessment test' is used to determine whether the use of the later mark would be detrimental to or would take unfair advantage of the earlier mark. In a case such as the present, where it was accepted that the earlier registered trade mark was unique in respect of any goods or services and had a huge reputation for specific types of goods or services which are dissimilar or dissimilar to a substantial degree to those for which the later mark is registered, this alone does not necessarily imply such a link.

The fact that the earlier mark is unique in respect of any goods or services and has a huge reputation for specific types of goods or services which are dissimilar or dissimilar

300 The Court of Justice also said that where the sign is seen purely as an embellishment to the trade mark having a reputation, that is not sufficient to establish the required link.

301 [2007] RPC 35.

302 The equivalent provision on infringement.

303 *See*, in particular, *Taittinger SA* v *Allbev Ltd* [1993] FSR 641, discussed in Chapter 23.

304 [2008] ECR I-8823.

to a substantial degree to those for which the later mark is registered and, for the average consumer (as defined above) the later mark calls into mind the earlier mark, this is not sufficient to establish that the use of the later mark takes or would take unfair advantage of, or is or would be detrimental to, the distinctive character or repute of the earlier mark. The use of the later mark may be detrimental to the distinctive character of the earlier mark with a reputation even if that mark is not unique. However, the first use of the later mark may suffice to be detrimental to the distinctive character of the earlier mark. Furthermore, proof that the use of the later mark is or would be detrimental to the distinctive character of the earlier mark requires evidence of a change in the economic behaviour of the average consumer of the goods or services for which the earlier trade mark was registered, consequent on the use of the later mark, or a serious likelihood that such a change will occur in the future.

The ground for refusal under Article 4(3) and (4)(a) differs from the ground for refusal under Article 4(1)(b) as there is no specific requirement for showing that there is a likelihood of confusion;[305] rather the test is set in terms of taking an unfair advantage of or being detrimental to the reputation of the earlier trade. This conjures up two possibilities, the first being where some of the goodwill associated with the earlier mark is captured, diluting or blurring its distinctiveness. The sign for which registration is applied for may be used in a positive sense such that it takes unfair advantage of the earlier trade mark: for example, by drawing upon its reputation to increase the marketing impact of the applicant's goods or services. Alternatively, it may be used in a negative sense to be detrimental to the distinctive character of the earlier trade mark: for example, by causing damage to it by the cross-pollination which will occur.[306] This may be by using an identical or similar sign in relation to goods or services that are of inferior quality or have some sort of stigma attached to them. It is entirely possible for unfair advantage to be found in the absence of detriment and vice versa. In either case, the form of use which is objectionable can be described as parasitic use.[307] It seems entirely reasonable to expect that either confusion as to the origin of goods or services or non-origin association will be sufficient. A minimum is that there is a linkage between the sign and the trade mark in the eyes of the public which causes the possibility of unfair advantage or detriment.[308] This accords with the view of the Court of Justice in Case C-251/95 *Sabel BV* v *Puma AG, Rudolf Dassler Sport*,[309] to the effect that a likelihood of confusion was not necessary for this ground for refusal, as now confirmed in *Adidas-Salomon* in relation to the equivalent provision for infringement.[310] The omission of any requirement for a likelihood of confusion must have been deliberate and not the result of an oversight, especially as non-origin association appears to be a form of harm targeted by this provision and now confirmed in *Adidas-Salomon* in relation to the equivalent form of infringement. In *CORGI Trade Mark*,[311] Geoffrey Hobbs QC, as the Appointed Person, said (at 558):

> It looks to me as though the requirement for a likelihood of confusion was deliberately included in the provisions of the Directive implemented by section 5(2) and deliberately omitted from the provisions of the Directive implemented by section 5(3).

He admitted that he could see no reason why the mischief (unfair advantage or detriment) should only be objectionable where a likelihood of confusion exists. However, as he pointed out in *CA Sheimer (M) Sdn Bhd's Trade Mark Application*,[312] (the VISA condom case), the purpose of this ground for refusal is not to raise an absolute bar to the registration of a mark which is the same or similar to a mark having a reputation, nor does it make it automatically objectionable to register a mark that would, in use, remind one of another trade mark. The presence of either an unfair advantage or detriment is a requisite.

In *Sihra's Trade Mark Application*,[313] registration was sought for 'INTER-TEL' in respect of 'hand-held constructional toys being puzzles'. The famous Intel Corporation Inc, makers of the Intel computer chips, opposed registration on the basis of its registration

305 As confirmed in *Adidas-Salomon*, above, in relation to the equivalent provision under Article 5(2) on infringement.

306 See *CA Sheimer (M) Sdn Bhd's Trade Mark Application* [2000] RPC 484.

307 See *Inlima SL's Application for a 3-Dimensional Trade Mark* [2000] RPC 661.

308 *CREDITMASTER Trade Mark* [2005] RPC 21 at para 66.

309 [1997] ECR I-6191 at para 20.

310 In *Baywatch Production Co Inc* v *Home Video Channel* [1997] FSR 22 it was held that a likelihood of confusion was necessary but this is now clearly wrong.

311 [1999] RPC 549.

312 [2000] RPC 484.

313 [2003] RPC 44.

of 'INTEL' for computer games, apparatus and software. It was held, *inter alia*, that the use of the applicant's trade mark would undoubtedly dilute the strength of the 'INTEL' mark and reduce the distinctive character of it, causing detriment to it. A desire by the applicant to increase sales of its puzzle was no justification for needing to use a mark incorporating the word 'INTEL'. This seems to have been a fairly blatant case of wishing to 'cash-in' on the goodwill associated with the opponent's trade mark.[314]

The ground of opposition under the equivalent provision in the Trade Marks Act 1994, s 5(3), requires that the earlier trade mark has a reputation in the UK or, in the case of a CTM or international trade mark designating the EC, a reputation in the European Community. There is no clear guidance as to what is required before a trade mark is deemed to have a reputation in the Directive and the Trade Marks Act 1994. Nor does the Paris Convention for the Protection of Industrial Property or the WTO TRIPs Agreement assist in the meaning although 'well known' trade marks registered elsewhere are given special protection. Article 4(2)(d) of the Directive and s 6(1)(c) of the Act (part of the definition of earlier trade marks) uses the phrase 'well known' as used in Article 6[bis] of the Paris Convention for the Protection of Industrial Property. This requires that the mark is considered by the competent authority of the country of registration or use to be *well known in that country* as being already the mark of a person entitled to the benefits of the Paris Convention. In other words, the mark must be considered to be well known, in the UK, by the Registrar of Trade Marks. There is no requirement for the proprietor of the well-known mark to carry on trade in the UK. It appears that the terms 'well known' and 'having a reputation' are not synonymous as the former is viewed from the perspective of the competent authority whilst the latter is a question of the public's perception of the trade mark. In practice, this will be an evidential issue in a case where this is disputed by the applicant to register a sign as a trade mark or in an invalidity application or in an infringement action as the case may be.

Reputation has to be judged from the perspective of the UK or the European Union as appropriate. In Case C-375/97 *General Motors Corp* v *Yplon SA*,[315] the claimant was the proprietor of a Benelux[316] trade mark 'CHEVY' for motor vehicles and associated goods. Yplon was the proprietor of a Benelux trade mark 'CHEVY' registered in different classes of goods and used the mark in respect of detergents and cleaning fluids. The Court of Justice held that 'reputation' implies a certain degree of knowledge of the earlier trade mark among the public. Depending on the goods or services involved, this may mean either the public at large or a more specialised section of the public such as traders in a specific sector. The factors to be taken into account in judging reputation include, in particular:

- market share;
- the intensity, geographic extent and duration of use of the earlier trade mark; and
- the size of investment made by undertaking the promotion of the earlier trade mark.

The court also held that it is sufficient for the reputation to exist in a substantial part of the relevant territory or Member State but it did not have to exist across the entirety of the Member State or territory. This was so even though the Directive is couched in terms of the reputation 'in the Member State'.[317] The court also held that the stronger the earlier trade mark's distinctive character and reputation is, the easier it will be to find that detriment will be caused to it.

For this ground for refusal to apply, the use must be without due cause. Therefore, in some circumstances, use which takes unfair advantage of, or is detrimental to the distinctive character of, the earlier trade mark will not be a reason for refusal of registration of the later mark. It is difficult to predict examples of use not being without due cause but it could include use of a trader's own name or use of words descriptive of his goods or services, assuming the absolute ground has been overcome by use. In *PACO/PACO LIFE IN*

314 The previous trade mark used by the applicant was 'LOXOL'!

315 [1999] ECR I-5421.

316 The Benelux countries – Belgium, Luxembourg and the Netherlands – have enjoyed a unified trade mark system for some time.

317 The same sentiment ought to hold true in relation to a CTM where the reputation may exist in a substantial part of the Community but not the whole of its territory.

COLOUR Trade Marks,[318] the word 'PACO' was common to the applicant and opponent's marks. However, the applicant had chosen it because Paco was the first name of the founder of the applicant's company. It was held that this did not offend as the use was not without due cause.

Article 4(4)(b) and (c) – use may be prohibited by an earlier unregistered trade mark or other earlier right

Article 4(4)(b) and (c) is optional[319] and allows Member States to adopt grounds of refusal based on earlier unregistered trade marks and other rights, such as copyright and industrial property rights. The UK took advantage of this option and provided, under s 5(4), that a trade mark shall not be registered if, or to the extent that, its use in the UK is liable to be prevented:

(a) by virtue of any rule of law (in particular the law of passing off) protecting an unregistered trade mark or other sign used in the course of trade, or

(b) by virtue of an earlier right [other than earlier trade marks, whether or not registered, or earlier trade marks having a reputation, that is, those covered by the preceding relative grounds for refusal] . . . in particular by virtue of the law of copyright, design right or registered designs.[320]

A person so entitled to prevent the use of the trade mark for which registration is sought is known as the proprietor of the earlier right. For example, a trader may use an unregistered trade mark to which substantial goodwill is attached or may use a logo protected by artistic copyright. The purpose of this provision is, therefore, to prevent registration of a mark which would infringe one of those earlier rights. For example, in *DU PONT Trade Mark,*[321] opposition based on passing off succeeded. The opponent had a reputation in relation to fabrics in the name DU PONT. The applicant, S D Dupont, applied to register 'S D DUPONT' in stylised form as a trade mark for clothing. The Court of Appeal held that persons hearing the trade mark spoken or seeing it would think that the clothes were made from the opponent's fabric. Therefore the use of the applicant's trade mark would be liable to be prevented by the law of passing off.

The forms of intellectual property rights mentioned are not exhaustive and other forms of rights might be relevant such as the right to prevent the publication of confidential information. Although the rights mentioned are within the field of intellectual property, it is possible that the provision is more extensive and could apply in the case of data subjects' rights in relation to personal data including an image of an individual. Support for this can be found in the Directive, Article 4(4) of which lists a right to a name, a right or personal portrayal, a copyright and an industrial property right. The latter covers, in this context, patents and design rights. The prohibition is not necessarily absolute. For example, it may be possible to file a new application after suitable modification to remove the offending material.[322]

322 Amendment other than in respect of a restriction to the goods and services covered by the application is limited to the applicant's name and address, errors of wording or copying or obvious mistakes: s 30.

323 [1998] RPC 455.

324 Until such time as objection under the relative grounds of refusal will be restricted to the proprietor of the earlier trade mark or owner of the earlier right, a trade mark examiner may properly take s 5(4) into account.

325 [1999] RPC 453.

An opposition under s 5(4) must make it clear which of the paragraphs are the basis of the opposition. In some cases it may be both, such as a stylised word in which both goodwill and copyright subsist. A specific indication of which earlier right is claimed to be a reason for preventing use of the trade mark applied is required for the interests of justice and fairness. So it was held in *WILD CHILD Trade Mark.*[323] It was also said that the opponent should identify the matters claimed to prevent use and state whether the objection related to all or just some of the goods or services specified in the application.

The onus is on the opponent to demonstrate that the use of the trade mark will amount to passing off or infringement of another earlier right.[324] In *WACKERS Trade Mark,*[325] an application to register 'WACKERS' for toys and games was opposed on the grounds of passing off and bad faith. Both grounds of opposition failed. On the passing off point, the opponent had used the name in the US but had only sent two shipments of samples to the UK. Such use was *de minimis* and insufficient to establish goodwill in the UK.

In terms of copyright, the work concerned does not have to be a UK work of copyright provided it is protected in the UK by virtue of reciprocal protection as a result of the Berne Copyright Convention, the Universal Copyright Convention, the WTO TRIPs Agreement or the European Union.[326]

Other grounds for refusal under Article 4

Article 4 contains some other grounds for refusal of registration (or invalidity) which were optional. Three grounds, under Article 4(4)(d)–(f), relate to recently expired trade marks, collective marks and guarantee[327] or certification marks. If implemented, Member States had some discretion to set the maximum period since the expiry of the relevant trade mark, though limited in two of the three cases. The UK approach has been to treat all recently expired trade marks the same under s 6(3) and they may be taken into account as a basis for refusal if they had expired no more than one year previously provided that the Registrar is satisfied that there had been no *bona fide* use of the trade mark in the two years immediately preceding expiry.[328]

Article 4(4)(g) of the Directive provided a ground for refusal based on the possibility of confusion with a mark in use abroad where the applicant was acting in bad faith. The need for including this ground for refusal is doubtful as bad faith is one of the absolute grounds for refusal. Where the mark used abroad is well known or has a reputation, other grounds for refusal would also apply. The UK has made no separate provision for bad faith in relation to trade marks in use abroad.

Article 4(5) – consent

This provision is another optional one and, if adopted (as it has been in the UK in s 5(5) of the Act), none of the relative grounds of refusal prevent the registration of a trade mark where the proprietor of the earlier trade mark or earlier right consents to the registration. In practice, consent may be by virtue of a licence, whether or not a bare licence. It would appear that consent could come after the date the application to register was filed. Whether it can be implied by virtue of acquiescence coupled with a failure to oppose the applications is a moot point but does seem a reasonable interpretation, especially when one considers that acquiescence can be a reason for preventing a challenge on the validity of a registered trade mark.[329]

Honest concurrent use

The provisions governing honest concurrent use are contained in s 7 of the Trade Marks Act 1994 but, from 1 October 2007, that section no longer has effect.[330] The following description is included for interest only and should no longer be relevant. The provisions are effectively redundant now as, in the absence of opposition by the proprietor of an earlier trade mark or other earlier right, the application will proceed to registration, assuming that the other requirements, in particular the absolute grounds for refusal, were satisfied. The Directive has no specific provision covering honest concurrent use which applied where an undertaking had honestly been using a sign identical or similar to an earlier trade mark or other right for an overlapping period of time without objection having being made. The concept of honest concurrent use allowed registration of what would otherwise be a conflicting trade mark could be seen as being based on acquiescence.[331] Section 7 of the Trade Marks Act 1994 allowed an application to proceed on the basis of

---

326 See, for example, *Tom & Jerry Trade Mark Applications* (unreported) 23 May 2001, Trade Marks Registry.

327 The UK has no specific provision for guarantee marks.

328 *See* the discussion on the meaning of 'earlier trade mark', p 736.

329 *Infra.*

330 Section 7(5) states that the section does not apply once there is an order under s 8 in effect. The Trade Marks (Relative Grounds) Order 2007 was made under s 8 and limited the raising of the relative grounds of refusal to proprietors of earlier trade marks or other earlier rights.

331 The Directive does have provisions on acquiescence but these apply to invalidity and the rights afforded by registration only: Article 9.

honest concurrent use in the absence of opposition by the proprietor of an earlier trade mark or other earlier right which could have been used successfully to mount a challenge on the basis of the relative grounds. In such a case, if the applicant could satisfy the Registrar that there had been honest concurrent use, the application would proceed to registration providing it otherwise complied with the basic meaning of a trade mark within s 1(1) and was not caught by the absolute grounds for refusal under s 3.[332] Under s 7(3) 'honest concurrent use' meant such use in the UK by the applicant or with his consent which would have amounted to honest concurrent use under s 12(2) of the Trade Marks Act 1938. That provision did not say what honest concurrent use was but simply allowed registration in such a case of identical or nearly resembling trade marks in respect of the same goods or the same description of goods. The registration could be subject to conditions and limitations and the Registrar or court had a discretion whether or not to allow the application to proceed to registration.

To discover the meaning of honest concurrent use, we must turn to the case law on s 12(2) under the 1938 Act. If there was any doubt about the rights of the two proprietors, the Registrar could delay registration until after this had been resolved.[333] This might have applied where two persons had used identical or similar marks for at least five years or more in all honesty and had each built up goodwill in ignorance of the use of the mark by the other company.[334] Even though one mark was already registered, the second could be accepted for registration. There was no minimum period laid down as being acceptable.[335]

Lord Tomlin set out some criteria for deciding if the second mark should be registered in such circumstances in *Pirie's Application*[336] as follows:

1 the likelihood of confusion that may arise from the use of both marks;
2 whether the original choice and subsequent use of the second mark was honest – it could be honest even if the second company knew of the existence of the first mark if it believed there would be no confusion, this being a subjective test;
3 the length of time that the second mark has been used – five years was deemed sufficient in the *Pirie case*, but normally the Registrar might expect more;
4 whether there was evidence of confusion in actual use;
5 whether the second company's trade is larger than the first company's trade – if so, this fact could help the second company's application.

This list was not exclusive – all the surrounding circumstances would be considered in addition.

The nature and scale of the applicant's use of the trade mark had to be such as to satisfy the Registrar that it was a case of honest concurrent use.[337] The relationship between the relative grounds for refusal and the honest concurrent use provisions was explored by the Hearing Officer in *CODAS Trade Mark*.[338] Before 1 October 2007 when the relative grounds could be raised by anyone, the examiner in the Trade Marks Registry carried out a search for earlier conflicting trade marks. In the absence of any opposition, if the examiner discovered an earlier conflicting mark, he would raise an objection based upon it. The application might then have been saved if the applicant could satisfy the Registrar that there had been honest concurrent use. If there was an opposition based on one of the relative grounds for refusal, other than on the basis of complete identity of the marks and goods or services, refusal of the application was not necessarily automatic. A likelihood of confusion or the other conditions for refusal in the case of trade marks having a reputation, as the case may be, would have to be shown. In such cases, the presence of honest concurrent use would have been a factor to be taken into account.

If an application proceeded on the basis of honest concurrent use, it could be restricted in terms of the specification of goods or services in respect of which the application was made. In the *CODAS* case, the application was for the word 'CODAS' for Classes 9, 37 and 41 and covered, *inter alia*, computers, computer hardware and software, installation,

332 Section 7(4) made it clear that the absolute grounds of refusal were not affected nor were applications for invalidity under s 47(2).

333 Trade Marks Act 1938 s 12(3).

334 For example, *NUCLEUS Trade Mark* [1998] RPC 233.

335 A period of just over two years had been accepted in exceptional circumstances: *see Peddie's Applications* (1944) 61 RPC 31.

336 (1933) 50 RPC 147.

337 *REACT Trade Mark* [1999] RPC 529. A submission of honest concurrent use failed as the use was not sufficient and an argument that confusion was not likely because of the applicant's reputation failed as the trade mark could be assigned to another company at any time.

338 [2001] RPC 14.

maintenance and repair services and educational and training services relating to computers, all for use in the oil distribution industry. The opponent had used the registered trade mark 'CODA', registered against Classes 9, 41 and 42 and used, *inter alia*, in relation to computer software for financial and accounting purposes, software for composing music, and design and consultancy services relating to such software. The opponent had customers in the oil industry. It was accepted that the two marks had been able to function as trade marks for their respective owners without evidence of confusion and that this would continue to be the case if there was some restriction to the goods and services applied for. Honest concurrent use was made out even though there was an opposition. The wording of s 7(2), taken literally, was to the effect that refusal automatically followed if one of the relative grounds for refusal was raised in opposition proceedings by the proprietor of the earlier trade mark or other earlier right. It did not say that the opposition has to succeed.[339] It was, however, a matter of common sense that the ground had to be made out. Otherwise, providing that none of the absolute grounds for refusal applied, the two marks could happily coexist without the later mark infringing the other.

Proof of use

Under the CTM Regulation, as is now also the case with the UK trade mark, only proprietors of earlier trade marks or other earlier rights can oppose registration under the relative grounds for refusal.[340] Under Article 43(2) of the CTM Regulation, if the applicant so requires, an opponent basing his opposition on his earlier CTM must furnish proof of use within the preceding five years or give proper reasons for non-use, if the CTM has been registered for at least five years. The trade marks Directive also envisaged the possibility of making opposition and invalidity subject to proof of use in the Member State concerned of an earlier conflicting trade mark.[341] As regards opposition, Article 11(2) made this an option for Member States.

The UK adopted this approach in respect of opposition and invalidity. In respect of the former, s 6A[342] provides that, where opposition of registration of a trade mark under the relative grounds for refusal is based on an earlier trade mark, the Registrar will not refuse to register the trade mark by reason of the earlier trade mark unless the 'use conditions' are satisfied. These are that:

(a) within the period of five years ending with the date of publication of the application the earlier trade mark has been put to genuine use in the United Kingdom by the proprietor or with his consent in relation to the goods or services for which it was registered, or

(b) the earlier trade mark has not been so used, but there are proper reasons for non-use.

The section applies where the application has been published and there is an earlier trade mark in respect of which one of the relative grounds for refusal based on earlier trade marks applies.[343] The proof of use provisions do not apply, of course, unless the earlier trade mark has been registered for at least five years at the date of publication of the application.

Where the use conditions are satisfied only in respect of some of the goods or services for which the earlier trade mark is registered, the registration is taken to be limited accordingly. Therefore, if an application is made to register 'GORGE' for snack foods and there is an earlier trade mark 'GEORGE' registered for snack foods and also restaurant services but it has only been used by or with the consent of the proprietor for the latter during the previous five years, the opposition must fail even though the marks are similar (providing there are no proper reasons for non-use in relation to snack foods). Furthermore, the registration 'GEORGE' is vulnerable to invalidity proceedings in relation to snack foods through non-use during those five years.

339 Section 7(1) applies these provisions if 'it appears' to the Registrar that one of the grounds apply. Again there is no mention of it being successful.

340 See Article 8 of the CTM Regulation.

341 Article 11(1) and (2) together with Article 10(1)–(2) or (3) of the Directive.

342 Inserted by the Trade Marks (Proof of Use, etc.) Regulations 2004, SI 2004/946 with effect from 5 May 2004.

343 Section 5(1)–(3) of the Act, equivalent to Article 4(1), (3) and (4)(a).

344 This is the same as an equivalent provision in relation to invalidity on the basis of non-use which bears a marked resemblance to the proof of use provisions.

'Use' includes use in a form differing in elements which do not alter the distinctive character of the trade mark in the form it was registered[344] and use in the UK includes affixing the trade mark to goods or their packaging in the UK solely for export purposes. Where the earlier trade mark is a CTM, references to use are in relation to the European Community (now EU).

As the proof of use provisions require use in the UK or European Community, as appropriate, opposition cannot be based on an earlier well-known trade mark under Article 6[bis] of the Paris Convention for the Protection of Industrial Property unless it is a trade mark having effect within the UK or is a CTM or international registration designating the UK or EC. This seems to contradict the wider scope of the relative grounds for refusal set out in s 5 and supplemented by the definition of earlier trade mark in s 6.[345]

345 The Directive also limits opposition to a requirement of genuine use of an earlier trade mark in the Member State concerned: *see* the combined effect of Articles 10(1) and 11(2).

However, under s 56(2) the proprietor of a well-known trade mark may be able to obtain injunctive relief to prevent the use in the UK of an identical or similar mark used for identical or similar goods or services, providing such use is likely to cause confusion.

The proof of use provisions force a person opposing an application on the basis of an earlier trade mark to 'put up or shut up'. Proof of use is also required in invalidity proceedings where the challenge to registration is also based on an earlier trade mark. It may also be an issue in infringement proceedings where the defendant counterclaims for revocation on the basis of non-use.

Certification marks

346 A guarantee mark is one which guarantees certain characteristics of goods of undertakings. There is no provision for these in the UK or under the CTM system. The certification mark probably serves the purposes of guarantee marks in the UK.

347 References to paragraph numbers in this section of the text refer to paragraphs in Sch 2 to the Act.

Article 1 of the trade marks Directive states that it applies to individual trade marks, collective trade marks, guarantee and certification marks.[346] Certification marks were available in the UK before the 1994 Act, unlike the case with collective marks; hence certification marks will be discussed first.

The purpose of certification marks is to indicate goods or services with certain objective standards: for example, in respect to material, safety or quality. Examples are the Woolmark and the BSI Kitemark (which dates from 1921). The Trade Marks Act 1994 applies to certification marks subject to provisions set out in Sch 2 to the Act.[347] The term 'certification mark' is itself defined in s 50 as:

> . . . a mark indicating that the goods or services in connection with which it is used are certified by the proprietor of the mark in respect of origin, material, mode of manufacture of goods or performance of services, quality, accuracy or other characteristics.

The distinctiveness required by s 1(1) must be in terms of distinguishing the goods or services certified from those which are not and, unlike the usual provisions, signs denoting geographical origin may be registered.[348] The mark must not be misleading as to the character or significance of the mark, especially if it is likely to be taken as something other than a certification mark (para 5(1)), and to that end the Registrar may insist that the mark carries some indication that it is a certification mark and any application is amended accordingly.

348 Member States could allow the registration of designations of geographical origins as collective and certification marks by way of derogation: Article 15(2). An example in the UK is the STILTON certification mark. There is a word mark 'STILTON CERTIFICATION TRADE MARK' and device and word marks 'STILTON' and 'STILTON CHEESE'. The proprietor of these certification trade marks is the Chairman of the Stilton Cheese Makers Association.

An applicant for a certification mark must file regulations governing the use of the mark with the Registrar. By para 6(2), the regulations must indicate:

- who is entitled to use the mark;
- the characteristics to be certified by the mark;
- how the certifying body is to test those characteristics and supervise the use of the mark;
- what fees, if any, are to be paid in connection with the operation of the mark; and
- procedures for resolving disputes.

The mark will not be registered if the regulations do not comply with para 6(2) and further requirements imposed by rules, or are contrary to public policy or accepted principles of morality, or if the applicant is not competent to certify the goods or services for which the mark is to be registered: para 7(1). The regulations are published and may be subject to opposition or observations. The applicant must not, himself, trade in the goods or services to which the certification relates (para 4).

Assignment of a certification mark requires the consent of the Registrar. There are a number of additional grounds for revocation and invalidity of certification marks.

The grounds for revocation additional to those in s 46 are set out in para 15 and are as follows:

● The proprietor has begun to trade in the goods or services certified.
● The manner in which the mark has been used by the proprietor has caused it to become liable to mislead the public as to its character or significance – in particular, if it is likely to be taken to be something other than a certification mark.
● The proprietor has failed to observe, or to secure the observance of, the regulations governing the use of the mark.
● An amendment of the regulations has been made so that the regulations no longer comply with para 6(2), or are contrary to public policy or to accepted principles of morality.
● The proprietor is no longer competent to certify the goods or services for which the mark is registered.

The grounds for invalidity additional to s 47 are that the mark was registered in breach of the provisions of paras 4, 5(1) or 7(1).

Collective marks

Collective marks were introduced into UK trade mark law by the 1994 Act. They are defined by s 49 as:

> . . . a mark distinguishing the goods or services of members of the association which is the proprietor of the mark from those of other undertakings.

Thus, a trade association (for example, the 'Association of West Midlands Metal Bashers') may register a mark which can be used by its members on its goods or stationery. The 'Yorkshire Institute of Professional Decorators' may do likewise, as may the 'Society of Balti Restaurateurs'. At the author's former place of work, Aston Business School, there was a plaque at the front of the building denoting the collective mark 'Conference Centres of Excellence'.[349]

The Act applies to collective marks as it does to ordinary marks subject to the provisions of Sch 1 to the Act. The mark must be capable of distinguishing the goods or services of members of the association from those of other undertakings and, as with certification marks, signs indicating geographical origin may be permitted. The mark must not be misleading as to the character or significance of the mark, especially if it is likely to be taken as anything other than a collective mark (para 4(1)). The Registrar may insist on an indication that the mark is a collective mark.

Regulations governing the use of the mark must be filed with the Registrar for approval and, by para 5(2), must specify the persons authorised to use the mark, the conditions of membership and any conditions and sanctions relating to the use of the mark. The mark will not be registered if the regulations fail to comply with the requirements of para 5(2) and any rules, or are contrary to public policy or accepted principles of morality: para

349 The full text of the mark (which is a device and word mark) is 'Conference Centres of Excellence: A Consortium of Specialist Independent Conference Centres'. The registration expired during 2005. Further examples of collective trade marks are 'Association of Pharmaceutical Importers' and 'Association of Consulting Engineers'.

6(1). There are corresponding provisions to s 30 determining the rights of authorised users in cases of infringement and additional grounds of revocation and invalidity. The grounds for revocation, additional to those in s 46, are as follows:

- that because of the manner in which it has been used by the proprietor it has become liable to mislead the public as regards the character or significance of the mark, in particular if it is likely to be taken to be something other than a collective mark;
- that the proprietor has failed to observe, or to secure the observance of, the regulations governing the use of the mark; or
- that an amendment of the regulations has been made so that they no longer comply with para 5(2) or are contrary to public policy or to accepted principles of morality.

The grounds for invalidity additional to those in s 47 are that it was registered in breach of para 4(1) or 6(1).

Surrender of registered trade mark

The Directive contains provisions on revocation and invalidity of registration of trade marks but is silent on the issue of surrender of a trade mark, except in relation to the grounds for refusal based on earlier trade marks where a CTM claims seniority from an earlier national trade mark that has been surrendered or has been allowed to lapse.

The proprietor of a registered trade mark may surrender the registration in respect of some or all goods or services for which the mark is registered, by s 45. Rule 33 of the Trade Marks Rules 2008 requires that the proprietor certify that any person having an interest in the mark has been given three months' notice and either is not affected or consents. The reason for this is that surrendering a trade mark might affect the rights of a licensee of the proprietor. Following surrender, the Registrar will then make the appropriate entry in the register and publish it.

Surrender may come about as part of a settlement in an infringement action, particularly in respect of some of the goods or services for which the trade mark is registered. This may be a way of saving a registration from a counterclaim for revocation across the full extent of goods or services for which it is registered. Surrender may also be considered where an application for invalidity is made which the proprietor does not wish to fight, perhaps having lost interest in the trade mark. If the proprietor no longer wishes to use a registered trade mark, in the absence of any proceedings in respect of it, the best course otherwise would be simply to let the registration lapse when it is next due for renewal.

Revocation

350 In the following section of this chapter, references are made primarily to the Act, which sets out the grounds for revocation and invalidity in a neater manner than is the case with the Directive, unless specific reference is made to the Directive or Court of Justice cases. The relevant provisions in the Directive are Articles 10(1)–(2), 11(3), 12, 13 and 14.

Revocation of a trade mark means that it is removed from the register because it has not been used for a continuous period of five or more years without proper reasons for non-use ('non-use'), because it has become a common name for the goods and services for which it was registered, or, because of the use made of it by the proprietor, it has become likely to mislead the public ('deceptive'). Revocation may be partial where the grounds apply only in respect of some of the goods and services in respect of which the trade mark is registered. The grounds for revocation are set out in Article 12 of the Directive (see s 46 of the Trade Marks Act 1994).[350]

Revocation must be distinguished from invalidity. Revocation is a means of removing a trade mark from the register because of the presence of one or more of the above grounds. The impact of revocation is that it brings to an end the rights of the proprietor from the date of the application for revocation (or earlier, if the grounds existed at an earlier date). A trade mark may be declared invalid if any of the absolute or relative grounds for refusal of registration are found to exist, in which case the trade mark will be removed from the register on the basis that it should never have been registered. The outcome is different to revocation because, with invalidity, it is as if the trade mark never existed.[351] As with revocation, invalidity may be partial and relate only to some of the goods or services for which the trade mark is registered. Applications for revocation on the basis of non-use are fairly common.[352]

Section 46(1) of the Trade Marks Act 1994 states that a 'registration of a trade mark *may* be revoked . . .' (emphasis added) and this suggests that, notwithstanding the evidence shows that one of the grounds for revocation is satisfied, the Registrar retains a discretion as to whether or not to revoke the registration. There is an apparent conflict with the wording of the trade marks Directive, Article 12(1) of which begins, 'A trade mark shall be liable to revocation . . .' In *Zippo Trade Mark*[353] the Hearing Officer in the Trade Marks Registry accepted, given the language of the Directive, that there was no discretion. However, in *Gromax Plasticulture Ltd v Don & Low Nonwovens Ltd*,[354] Lindsay J accepted that a discretion existed as, in the circumstances, he said that this would have a been a case where the discretion to revoke should not have been used had the ground for revocation been made out. However, in *AJ & MA Levy's Trade Mark (No 2)*,[355] the Appointed Person noted that the Directive suggested by its language that there was no such discretion. The House of Lords referred the question of whether there was a discretion to revoke if one or more of the grounds for revocation applied in *Scandecor Developments AB v Scandecor Marketing AB*.[356] Unfortunately, the application for a preliminary ruling was withdrawn and there have been no further decisions on the matter or rulings from the Court of Justice. The question remains open, although the better view is that there is no discretion. The phrase in the Directive 'shall be liable' surely means that the trade mark will be revoked if any of the grounds for revocation exist subject only to someone applying for revocation.

Each of the grounds for revocation is now described in more detail.

Non-use

There are two forms of non-use being where the trade mark has been registered for five or more years and has never been used in relation to all or some of the goods or services for which it is registered or where use has been suspended for a continuous period of five years. Section 46(1) lists the grounds for revocation of a registration of a trade mark on the basis of non-use as being:

- that within five years of the date of completion of the registration procedure, [the mark] has not been put to genuine use in the United Kingdom, by the proprietor or with his consent, in relation to the goods or services for which it is registered and there are no proper reasons for non-use;
- that such use has been suspended for an uninterrupted period of five years, and there are no proper reasons for non-use.

Under s 46(2), 'use' in terms of revocation includes use in a different form provided this does not alter its distinctive character, and use in the UK includes affixing the mark to goods or packaging in the UK solely for export purposes. Genuine use does not mean the opposite of fake or sham use and advertisements in US magazines, which readers knew were from the US, and a few sales to US customers which were posted to the UK is not sufficient. Jacob J confirmed this in *Euromarket Designs Inc v Peters and Crate & Barrel*[357] where he said (at 304) '. . . "genuine use" must involve that which a trader or consumer

351 Although transactions past and closed are unaffected. It will not be possible, for example, on the basis of invalidity alone to claim reimbursement of any fees paid in respect of an assignment of a registered trade mark.

352 Revocation may also come about by reason of a counterclaim in an infringement action.

353 [1999] RPC 173.

354 [1999] RPC 367.

355 [1999] RPC 358.

356 [2002] FSR 7 at para 33.

357 [2001] FSR 20.

would regard as a real or genuine trade in this country'. The required use must be genuine use judged by commercial standards but could be established in circumstances where no actual sales of the goods had taken place.[358] This could be the case where, for example, promotional literature had been distributed.

358 *FLORIS Trade Mark* [2001] RPC 19.

359 [2003] ECR I-2439 at para 43.

The Court of Justice gave some guidance as to the meaning of 'genuine use' in Case C-40/01 *Ansul BV* v *Ajax Brandbeveiliging BV*[359] in which Ansul was the proprietor of the Benelux trade mark 'Minimax' used for various goods including fire extinguishers and associated products. Ansul's official authorisation to sell fire extinguishers ceased during 1989 but since that time it had used the trade mark in relation to component parts and substances for use in fire extinguishers. Ajax was a subsidiary of a German company Minimax GmbH and started selling fire extinguishers in the Benelux countries in 1994. When Ansul objected, Ajax applied for revocation of Ansul's trade mark and the question of what constituted genuine use was referred to the Court of Justice, which ruled that genuine use does not include token use for the sole purpose of preserving the rights conferred by a trade mark. When assessing whether use is genuine, regard should be had to all the facts and circumstances relevant to deciding whether the commercial exploitation is real, in particular:

- whether such use is viewed as warranted in the economic sector to maintain or create a market share in relation to the goods or services for which it is registered;
- the nature of the goods or services;
- the characteristics of the market and the scale and frequency of the use of the mark.

Furthermore, the Court of Justice ruled that the fact that a mark is used in relation to goods not newly available on the market but sold in the past does not mean to say that the use is not genuine if the use is in respect of component parts integral to the make-up or structure of the goods or for goods or services directly connected with goods previously sold and intended to meet the needs of customers of those goods. As regards use prior to the sale of goods or the provisions of services, such as in advertising and promotional literature, suggested as being within the scope of genuine use by Jacob J in *Euromarket* v *Peters*, the Court of Justice accepted that use could be in relation to goods or services about to be marketed for which preparations were already underway to secure customers, such as by means of an advertising campaign.[360] Internal use by the proprietor or a licensee is ignored when considering whether use is genuine. Use in relation to goods excluded from the description of goods for which a mark has been registered does not preclude its use for goods within the description. For example, in *Crocodile International Pte Ltd* v *La Chemise Lacoste*,[361] the word CROCODILE was registered for 'shirts, not including sports shirts'. Although the mark had been used on shirts sold in sports shops, there was also evidence that it had been used extensively for shirts marketed and sold as casual wear during the relevant period.

360 At para 37.

361 [2008] EWHC 2673 (Ch).

There is no qualitative or quantitative threshold which a user must satisfy before it is entitled to be taken into account when considering genuine use of a trade mark. The Court of Justice made this clear in *Ansul*. In *Galileo International Technology LLC* v *European Union (formerly European Community)*,[362] the EU applied for revocation of a number of trade marks comprising the word 'GALILEO'.[363] Counsel for the trade mark proprietor cited the General Court (then the Court of First Instance) in Case T191/07 *Anheuser-Busch Inc* v *OHIM*[364] in which it said (at para 102):

362 [2011] ETMR 22.

363 GALILEO is the name of the European satellite navigation research programme.

364 [2009] ECR II-691. A case on the Community trade mark.

> account should be taken, in particular, of the commercial volume of the overall use, as well as of the length of the period during which the mark was used and the frequency of use.

It was claimed that this and other passages from the judgment in *Anheuser-Busch* had influenced the Hearing Officer in applying a quantitative standard. Although *Anheuser-Busch* does not expressly state that there is no quantitative threshold for the requirement of relevant use, the judgment is 'littered with cross-references to Ansul' and Floyd J thought it was compatible with *Ansul* and certainly did not go as far as suggesting that there was a quantitative threshold. Had the General Court believed that such a requirement existed, it would have said so expressly. Furthermore, the Hearing Officer had not imposed such a restriction when considering genuine use in the present case.

Another point about the *Galileo* case is that it accepts that where an application for revocation covers the entire specification of goods or services for which the mark is registered, revocation in respect of some of those goods or services remains a possibility where genuine use is not found in relation to those goods or services. Of course, the proprietor has the burden of proving genuine use but can hardly be surprised, if his evidence fails to show genuine use in respect of some of the goods or services, if the registration is then revoked in relation to those goods or services. An attack on the entire specification of goods or services is an attack on each and every one of them. It is no answer to say that the applicant for revocation should have limited his application to those for which genuine use was not found.

In Case C-442/07 *Verein Radetzky-Orden* v *Bundesvereinigung Kameradschaft 'Feldmareschall Radetzky'*,[365] the Court of Justice accepted that use of a trade mark by a non-profit-making association in its relations with the public, in announcements of forthcoming activities, on business papers and on advertising materials and on badges worn by the association's members when collecting and distributing donations was genuine use. However, use of a trade mark on goods given away as free gifts to persons buying other goods was held not to be genuine use in Case C-495/07 *Silberquelle GmbH* v *Maselli-Strickmode GmbH*.[366] In that case, the trade mark 'WELLNESS' was used in relation to a non-alcoholic drink given away free to persons who bought clothes sold by the trade mark proprietor. The clothes did not bear the trade mark nor were they sold under it.

In determining whether there has been genuine use, the size of the undertaking is a factor that can be taken into account. It was important to have regard to all the relevant facts and circumstances including the size of the undertaking as this could help determine whether the commercial exploitation was real.[367]

Although token use will not suffice, minimal use or use by a single importer might where it serves a real commercial purpose. The Court of Justice so ruled in Case C-295/02 *La Mer Technology Inc* v *Laboratoires Goemar SA*,[368] in which the proprietor had sold around £800-worth of goods during the relevant five-year period. The Chancery Division of the High Court found that this was more a reflection of commercial failure than use solely for the purpose of maintaining the trade mark on the register. Shortly after the relevant period for revocation, the proprietor recruited a new sales agent to boost sales in the UK. However, applying the Court of Justice ruling, the trade mark was ordered to be revoked by the Chancery Division but the proprietor's appeal to the Court of Appeal was upheld.[369]

In *ELLE Trade Marks*,[370] the proprietor had two registrations, one for 'elle' in lower case within a circle with a cross (the female symbol) and 'ELLE' in upper case type. There was a disclaimer to any exclusive right to the use of the word 'elle'. Application had been made for the two marks to be revoked due to non-use under s 46. It was held that, although there had been some use of the word 'elle' without the device, this was not use of the trade mark as such use altered the distinctive character in a significant and substantial way.[371] Similarly, in *United Biscuits (UK) Ltd* v *Asda Stores Ltd*,[372] four pictorial marks depicting penguins, which had been used for Penguin biscuits in the past, were ordered to be revoked as there was no evidence of genuine use within the last five years either in the exact form of the marks or in a similar form so as to retain their distinctive character. Walker LJ in the Court of Appeal suggested that a two-step approach should be taken with s 46(2) in *Bud and Budweiser Budbräu Trade Marks*.[373] The first step is to determine what were the differences between the mark as used and the mark as registered. The second step then was to decide whether they altered the distinctive character of the mark as registered.

365 [2008] ECR I-9223.

366 [2009] ECR I-137.

367 *POLICE Trade Mark* [2004] RPC 35.

368 [2004] ECR I-1159.

369 *Laboratoire de la Mer Trade Mark* [2006] FSR 5.

370 [1997] FSR 529.

371 A claim that 'ELLE' had been used in advertisements in foreign magazines failed to find sympathy as there was little practical possibility of orders being placed from the UK.

372 [1997] RPC 513.

373 [2003] RPC 25.

Although the characteristics of the mark which made it striking and memorable were unlikely to be analysed by the average consumer, they were, nevertheless, capable of analysis. It was for the Registrar to analyse the visual, aural and conceptual qualities of the mark so as to make a global appreciation of the impact on the average consumer who normally perceived the mark as a whole and did not proceed to analyse its various details.

Use of a second trade mark will not save the mark under consideration if, when looking at the mark under attack with the common elements removed, it remains a distinctive mark in its own right.[374] On the other hand, use of an alternative may be considered to be use of the mark in such a form so as not to alter its distinctive character if it is the phonetic equivalent of the registered trade mark. In *SECOND SKIN Trade Mark*,[375] the registered trade mark was 'SECOND SKIN' but the proprietor had only ever used '2ND SKIN'. As the public would be likely to perceive the marks as having the same meaning, that was use for the purposes of s 46(1)(b). Whether oral use, for example, by customers ordering the product over the telephone, was sufficient was left open. The hearing officer doubted that, even if oral use alone was sufficient to defeat an application for revocation on the grounds of non-use, oral use *by customers* was probably not enough.[376] Whether or not the two marks would be accepted by the Trade Marks Registry as a series of trade marks under s 41(2) was not relevant even though that provision defines a series of trade marks in similar, though not identical, terms. Indeed, in *Digeo Broadband Inc's Trade Mark Application*,[377] in which application was made to register no less than 308 marks as a series, it was held that s 41(2) permitted less variation than s 46(2) and, in respect of the former, it was necessary also that the variations had no substantial effect on the identity of the trade mark.

There have to be proper reasons for the non-use if the proprietor is to escape an application for revocation under s 46. In *INVERMONT Trade Mark*,[378] it was argued that the non-use was due to the long and complex process of introducing a new brand into the alcoholic drinks market. It was held that the phrase 'proper reason for non-use' has to be considered in a business sense. 'Proper' means 'apt, acceptable, reasonable, justifiable in all the circumstances' and proper reasons for non-use related to abnormal situations and temporary serious disruptions affecting the proprietor's business alone. It did not cover the normal difficulties to be found in trade. The mark was ordered to be revoked; apart from failing to show that such an abnormal situation or serious disruption applied, the proprietor had failed to provide evidence as to preparations to use the mark and, therefore, the prospect of imminent future use was remote. Failure to use a mark for five years because of production difficulties outside the proprietor's control could be a proper reason for non-use. In *MAGIC BALL Trade Mark*,[379] a trade mark was registered for a new type of lollipop to be made by a new manufacturing technique. Unexpected delays were met in developing the machinery needed to make the lollipops. By the time of the application for revocation, the problems had been all but solved and the evidence was that the proprietor would soon start to use the mark. Delays caused by regulations or trade embargoes will not necessarily be proper reasons for non-use. A trade embargo imposed by the US on goods from Cuba, which at the time of the hearing had been in place for 33 years, was described as a normal condition of trade in *Cabañas Habana (Device) Trade Mark*.[380] Non-use resulting from an EU Regulation governing tar content of cigarettes was not a proper reason for non-use in *K-2 Trade Mark*[381] as the proprietor had chosen not to modify his cigarettes to comply as this would have affected their taste.

Revocation will not be ordered on grounds of non-use if the use is commenced or resumed after five years but before application for revocation is made. However, there is a three-month period prior to the application for revocation when use will be ignored unless preparations for a commencement or resumption of use were made before the proprietor became aware that an application for revocation might be made (s 46(3)).[382] This does not prevent an applicant for revocation bringing his application immediately

---

374 *Cabañas Habana (Device) Trade Mark* [2000] RPC 26. The mark under attack consisted of an elaborate device resembling a coat of arms with words and letters.

375 [2001] RPC 30.

376 In *ELLE Trade Mark*, above, the trade mark was a stylised word and, in such a case, it is the visual significance which is important.

377 [2004] RPC 32.

378 [1997] RPC 125.

379 [2000] RPC 439.

380 [2000] RPC 26. It was held that there were no proper reasons for non-use. The proprietor had failed to apply for an exemption to the embargo and there was no evidence of use prior to it.

381 [2000] RPC 413.

382 According to Jacob J in *MINERVA Trade Mark* [2000] FSR 734 at 736, the purpose of this provision is to enable the parties to negotiate. *MINERVA* and *Decon Laboratories Ltd v Fred Baker Scientific Ltd* [2001] RPC 17 provide examples of partial revocation.

the five-year period has elapsed.[383] An application for revocation may be made by anyone to the Registrar or to the court. If proceedings before the court are pending, the application must be made to the court and, in other cases, the Registrar may refer the application to the court. Revocation may be whole or partial, under s 46(5). Partial revocation may be applicable where the trade mark has been used but only in respect of some of the goods or services for which it was registered. In considering partial revocation, the court must first determine what use has been made of the trade mark, in fact. When cutting down the specification of goods, it was important not to leave a wide specification because of the possibility of infringement in relation to similar goods and services which had the effect of widening the rights under the trade mark.[384] The court should adopt the mantle of the reasonably informed consumer of the products in question and consider how he would describe such use as had been made of them. In *West (t/a Eastenders)* v *Fuller Smith & Turner plc*,[385] the trade mark 'E.S.B.', previously used as an abbreviation for 'Extra Special Bitter', was registered in respect of beers. It had never been used for any sort of beer other than bitter beer and the Court of Appeal agreed that the specification should be cut down to bitter beer only. It was held that partial revocation of the ground of non-use should be such that the restricted specification was 'a fair description which would be used by the average consumer of the products for which the mark had been used by the proprietor'.[386]

The consequences of revocation are that the proprietor's rights are deemed to cease from the date of the application for revocation, or at an earlier date if the Registrar or the court is satisfied that the grounds for revocation existed earlier: s 46(6).

Where a question arises in civil proceedings as to the use to which a trade mark has been put, it is the proprietor who has the burden of proof under s 100.[387] This is regardless of s 72 which states that registration of a person as a proprietor of a trade mark is prima facie evidence of the validity of the original registration. The proprietor also has the burden of proving that there existed proper reasons for non-use and the grant of a licence, *per se*, is not sufficient. Obstacles arising independently of the will of the proprietor might amount to proper reasons.[388]

Common name for goods or services

Successful trade marks can become so well known that they pass into the language as being the name by which a type of product is referred to rather than the name by which the product of a particular undertaking is sold. In other words, the trade mark has become a generic name for a type of product. Many trade proprietors are active in ensuring that this does not happen by always using a phrase such as 'registered trade mark', the ® symbol or some other form of words signifying the trade mark is indeed a registered trade mark. Steps often go beyond this, for example, where a trade mark has been used in a generic sense in a publication, by notifying publishers accordingly and asking them to make the trade mark's status as a registered trade mark clear in future.

Article 12(2)(a) (and s 46(1)(c) of the Act) provides for revocation if, in consequence of the acts or inactivity of the proprietor, the trade mark has become a common name for a product or service in respect of which it is registered. Note the use of the word 'product' rather than 'goods'; presumably, the word product is used in a narrow sense, being a type of or a particular species of goods. Note also that the ground applies where the trade mark has become a common name as a result of acts or inactivity on the part of the proprietor. It may be that the proprietor has engaged on an advertising campaign that causes this so that consumers ask for the product by its trade mark rather than the description of the type of product (for example, if consumers ask for a 'Hoover' rather than asking for a vacuum cleaner). Alternatively, inactivity may be failing to police and educate others using the trade mark generically that it is indeed a registered trade mark. This ground for

383 *'Philosophy di Alberta Ferretti' Trade Mark* [2003] RPC 15.

384 *Thomson Holidays Ltd* v *Norwegian Cruise Lines Ltd* [2003] RPC 32.

385 [2003] FSR 44.

386 Jacob J accepted this sentiment in *ANIMAL Trade Mark* [2004] FSR 19, in which he embarked upon an impressive pruning exercise of the specification of goods for which the mark had been registered. He also said that the notional average consumer should approach the task after being told about the scope of protection for identical and similar marks.

387 See, for example, *MINERVA Trade Mark* [2000] FSR 734 and *CORGI Trade Mark* [1999] RPC 549.

388 *'Philosophy di Alberta Ferretti' Trade Mark* [2003] RPC 15. A proprietor who does nothing for most of the five-year period and then embarks on what is known to be a lengthy procedure before the goods reach the market is unlikely to show proper reasons for non-use.

revocation will not be available, however, if the trade mark has become a common name otherwise as a result of the acts or inactivity of the proprietor.

In Case C-371/02 *Björnekulla Fruktindustrier AB* v *Procordia Food AB*[389] revocation of Procordia's trade mark 'Bostongurka' was sought as it was claimed that it had become a generic name for chopped pickled gherkins in Sweden. An issue arose as to the identity of the class of persons to whom the trade mark has become a common name. Procordia relied on a survey amongst those in the catering trade but Björnekulla's claim for revocation was based primarily on market surveys of consumers. The Swedish court was uncertain as to the class of persons to be considered under Article 12(2)(a) of the Directive and submitted a question about this to the Court of Justice for a preliminary ruling under Article 267 of the Treaty on the Functioning of the European Union.[390] The Court of Justice ruled that, where intermediaries are involved in the distribution of a product to the consumer or end user, the relevant class of persons are primarily all consumers and end users but, depending on the features of the market concerned, all those in the trade who deal with the product commercially must also be taken into account where they are in a position to influence decisions to purchase.[391]

In *Hormel Foods Corp* v *Antilles Landscape Investments NV*,[392] a claim that the trade mark 'SPAM' used for canned meats had become a common name for tinned luncheon meat because of the proprietor's inactivity was rejected. There was no evidence that it had become generic and, in any case, the proprietor had been active in policing its use in order to prevent it becoming generic. On the other hand, it was held, *obiter*, that the trade mark 'SPAMBUSTER' had become generic because of the inactivity of its proprietor. In the case of a highly descriptive trade mark, there is a heavier burden to prevent it becoming generic. It was also held that the inactivity of a proprietor did not have to be the sole cause of a trade mark becoming a common name for this ground for revocation to be made out.

Of course, if a trade mark has become a common name for a product or service, it loses its basic function of serving to indicate the origin of goods or services by distinguishing those of one undertaking from those of other undertakings. Where a trade mark has become a common name for a product or service, revocation may be partial as the registration may cover other goods and service where it still retains its distinctive character. If it has become a common name but not because of anything the proprietor has done or failed to do, an application for invalidity may be made instead on the absolute grounds: for example, on the basis that it no longer constitutes a trade mark under Article 3(1)(a), that it now lacks a distinctive character under Article 3(1)(b) or even that it has become customary in the trade.

The mark has become misleading through use

Under Article 12(2)(b) of the Directive (s 46(1)(d) of the Trade Marks Act 1994) a further ground for refusal applies where a trade mark, in consequence of the use made of it by the proprietor or with his consent in respect of the goods or services for which it is registered, is liable to mislead the public, particularly as to the nature, quality or geographical origin of those goods or services. The list of examples is illustrative only. For the purposes of this ground for revocation 'use' does not necessarily have the same meaning as for the grounds of revocation based on non-use. For the purposes of revocation for non-use, Article 10(2)(a) extends the meaning of use to use of the trade mark in a form differing in elements which do not alter the distinctive character of the trade mark in the form in which is was registered. The Trade Marks Act 1994 by s 46(2) uses this wider meaning of use for all the grounds for revocation. In practice it is unlikely to make any difference. The question is whether the trade mark, in fact, is liable to mislead the public because of the use made of it by the proprietor or with his consent. It seems beyond doubt that this could include use of a sign similar to or including the registered trade mark and not limited to the use

389 [2004] ECR I-5791.

390 Formerly Article 234 of the EC Treaty.

391 See paras 23–26.

392 [2005] RPC 28.

of the trade mark exactly as registered. In other words, it is the consequence of use that is important for this ground for revocation rather than the nature and extent of the use.

It is submitted that the relevant class of persons are consumers and end users and, where they exist, intermediaries who are in a position to influence consumers in their choices, thereby passing on any misunderstanding to which they are subject to the consumers and end users.

This ground of revocation, unlike the one relating to trade marks that have become common names, is couched in terms of use by the proprietor or with his consent. We can only assume that the difference is deliberate. On that basis, revocation on the ground that a trade mark has become a common name because of the acts or inactivity of the proprietor must be restricted to the proprietor's act or inactivity and not someone having his consent: for example, a licensee. For trade marks that have become misleading, this can clearly encompass use by the proprietor's licensee or distributor.

Invalidity

In the trade marks Directive, the grounds and further grounds for refusal of registration are also stated to apply to declarations of invalidity. The Trade Marks Act 1994 sets the grounds for invalidity out separately under s 47 which relates back to the absolute and relative grounds for refusal of registration. There is a saving where a trade mark has acquired a distinctive character after registration in cases where invalidity is alleged on the basis of s 3(1)(b), (c) or (d) (equivalent to Article 3(1)(b), (c) or (d) in the Directive).[393] Where invalidity is based on an earlier trade mark or other earlier right, it will be defeated where the proprietor of the earlier trade mark or other earlier right has consented to the registration.[394] Where a trade mark is revoked, the rights in it exist up to the date of revocation unless the Registrar was satisfied that the grounds for revocation existed earlier. That being so, it is possible to apply for a declaration of invalidity of a trade mark on the basis of an earlier trade mark which has, in the meantime, been revoked.[395]

A feature in the Act is that the Registrar may himself apply to the court for a declaration of invalidity on the ground of bad faith in the registration of a trade mark.[396] Otherwise, anyone can apply for a declaration of invalidity.

Where the relative grounds of refusal are raised as a ground for invalidity on the basis of an earlier trade mark, the person applying for a declaration of invalidity must show proof of use of that earlier trade mark where it has been registered for five or more years (or show proper reasons for non-use).[397] These provisions are the same, *mutatis mutandis*, as those for opposition based on an earlier trade mark as discussed above under s 6A in relation to the relative grounds for refusal.

Where the grounds for invalidity apply only in relation to some of the goods and services for which the trade mark is registered, the declaration of invalidity will be limited accordingly to those goods and services, leaving the registration intact for those goods and services for which it remains valid.[398]

Application may be made by anyone to the Registrar or to the court: s 47(3). If proceedings in the court are pending, the application must be made to the court and, in other cases, the Registrar may refer the application to the court. The effect of a declaration of invalidity is that the registration will be void *ab initio* (s 47(6)). However, this will not affect any transactions past and closed.

In terms of invalidity on the basis of the absolute grounds, if the proprietor claims that the mark has acquired a distinctive character through use, he will need to do more than simply show that there has been extensive use of the mark. The use must have been such that a substantial number of persons have come to recognise the sign as a trade mark.[399]

393 These relate to lack of a distinctive character, 'descriptive signs' or signs that have become customary in the trade.

394 As consent relates to the registration of the mark and not its continuing registration, it would seem that any attempt to withdraw consent after registration will be of no effect as far as the validity of the registration is concerned.

395 *RIVERIA Trade Mark* [2003] RPC 50.

396 Section 47(4).

397 Section 47(2A)–(2E).

398 Section 47(5). *See also* Article 13 of the Directive which similarly provides also for refusal of registration and revocation.

399 *British Sugar plc v James Robertson & Sons Ltd* [1996] RPC 281.

400 [1996] RPC 281.

In *British Sugar plc v James Robertson & Sons Ltd*,[400] Jacob J found that the claimant's 'TREAT' mark was invalid as being within at least some of the absolute grounds for refusal. However, he noted that, having declared the mark invalid, he did not have the power to order its revocation, as the grounds for revocation are different. This would mean that an invalid mark would remain upon the register until such time as the proprietor failed to renew the registration.

401 [1999] RPC 725.

402 Equivalent to Article 4(1)(b), (4)(a), (b) and (c) of the Directive.

An applicant for a declaration of invalidity bears the burden of proof due to the presumption of validity in s 72. In *AMAZE COLLECTION Trade Mark*,[401] the applicant for a declaration of invalidity based his challenge on the use by him of unregistered trade marks AMA ZING and AMAZING. Originally, the application was made on the basis of s 5(2)(b), (3) and (4).[402] As the applicant's marks were unregistered, only s 5(4) was relevant but, on the evidence, a passing off action was unlikely to succeed and the applicant failed to discharge the burden of proof. When the applicant chooses to object on the basis of more than one ground under s 5, it is desirable to separate them out and adduce evidence directed to each one. The reason is that the grounds in s 5 differ *inter se*. In particular, the assimilation of an objection based on an earlier registered trade mark with an objection based on some other earlier right is inappropriate.[403]

403 *CORGI Trade Mark* [1999] RPC 549.

404 [2005] RPC 28.

A person who has made one attack on the validity of a trade mark may be estopped from making subsequent attacks. In *Hormel Foods Corp v Antilles Landscape Investments NV*,[404] the applicant for a declaration for invalidity was the proprietor of the 'SPAM' trade mark for canned meats and had previously applied for a declaration of invalidity of the trade mark 'SPAMBUSTER' in stylised form for computer programming. This application failed but a new application was made. It was held that the same principles of cause of action estoppel applied as they did for patents and registered designs. A person attacking validity was under a duty to put his full case in support and he would be barred from attacking validity in subsequent proceedings even on different grounds.[405] This estoppel did not prevent a fresh attack based on revocation, however, as this was a fundamentally different claim. But now bringing an attack based on revocation was an abuse of process as nothing had happened since the Registrar's earlier decision to justify a fresh application to revoke the trade mark.

405 The first attack had been based on the absolute grounds, whereas the present attack was based on the relative grounds.

As with revocation, Article 14 of the Directive provides for establishing invalidity *a posteriori* in the case of a trade mark which has been surrendered or allowed to lapse and which was used to claim seniority in relation to a CTM. This could be important where an infringement action is brought in relation to a national trade mark which has been surrendered or allowed to lapse after the acts alleged to constitute infringement took place. The equivalent provisions in the UK are in reg 3 of the Community Trade Mark Regulations 1996[406] made under s 52 of the Trade Marks Act 1994.

406 SI 1996/1908.

The scope of protection afforded to a trade mark under Article 5 of the Directive is not relevant to the question of validity. This is different to the issue of infringement because the distinctiveness of a mark may grow over time, such as in the case of a mark accepted for registration which includes a quirky spelling of a descriptive term.[407] In *Hasbro Inc v 123 Narhmittel GmbH*,[408] Floyd J rejected a squeeze argument, familiar to patent lawyers. In a patent case, a claim has only one meaning so if a product falls within a claim for the purposes of infringement, it also falls within the claim for the purposes of invalidity. This is to prevent a patentee alleging a wide meaning of the claim for infringement but a narrow meaning for invalidity. However, such arguments have no place in relation to trade marks.

407 An example is PLAY DOH.
408 [2011] FSR 21.

Trade marks as property

The Directive has little to say as far as trade marks as property, assignment and licensing are concerned as these are primarily a matter for national law. Consequently, there is little in the Directive relevant to this part of the chapter except that Article 8(1) provides that trade marks may be licensed in respect of all or some of the goods or services for which they are registered and for the whole or part of the Member State concerned. Trade mark proprietors may also invoke their trade mark rights against licensees who contravene any provision of the licensing contract '. . . with regard to its duration, the form covered by the registration in which the trade mark may be used, the scope of the goods or services for which the licence is granted, the territory in which the trade mark may be affixed, or the quality of the goods manufactured or of the services provided by the licensee': Article 8(2). The list is exhaustive[409] but the Court of Justice accepted that 'quality of goods' covers not just the material characteristics of goods but 'the allure and prestigious image which bestows on those goods an aura of luxury'.[410] Most references in the following material on trade marks as property necessarily refer to the Trade Marks Act 1994 and case law on the Act.

The Trade Marks Act 1994 states that a registered trade mark is an item of personal property (ss 2(1) and 22, or, in Scotland, incorporeal moveable property). An application for a trade mark is also a property right under s 27 and where an applicant body was dissolved without provision for ownership of the application, it would not evaporate but vest in the Crown as *bona vacantia*.[411] Under the provisions of the Act, trade marks are easily alienable. Under s 24, trade marks can be assigned, or pass by testamentary disposition or by operation of law in the same way as other personal property with or without the goodwill of a business.

Assignments may be partial in terms of:

- some, but not all, goods or services for which the mark is registered
- use in a particular manner or in a particular locality.

This is wider than before. Under the previous law, it was possible to divide a business and assign marks with that part of the goodwill which had been divested provided that the part of the business retained was in relation to different goods.[412]

Assignments or vesting assents are not effective unless in writing and signed by or on behalf of the assignor (or personal representative) (s 24(3)). This also applies to an assignment by way of security. A registered trade mark may be subject to a charge as is other personal property. Under s 23(1), each joint proprietor is entitled to an equal, undivided share. Therefore, it would appear that they are tenants in common, unlike the position under the 1938 Act which was based on a joint tenancy. However, this is subject to any agreement to the contrary, so joint proprietors could agree on a joint tenancy. The change could reflect the desire to make the property rights in trade marks more easily alienable.

A limiting factor on split assignments will probably be the desire to retain the distinctive character of a trade mark. If the mark becomes incapable of distinguishing the goods of one undertaking from those of other undertakings, this could be a ground for invalidity or revocation if the public is liable to be misled.

There are clearer rules for joint proprietorship of trade marks. Under s 23(3), each co-proprietor may do any act for his own benefit that would otherwise infringe, but may not, under s 23(4), without the consent of the other co-proprietors, grant a licence to use the mark, or assign or charge his share in the registered trade mark.

Unlike the 1938 Act, there are detailed provisions for licensing (exclusive, non-exclusive and sub-licences). Under s 28(1), a licence may be limited – in particular in terms of the goods and services for which it is registered, or in terms of use in a particular manner or locality. A licence must be in writing and signed by or on behalf of the grantor (s 28(2)). Unless otherwise provided for, a licence is binding on the grantor's successor in title. Sub-licences are recognised as possible and, under s 28(4), references in the Act to licences include sub-licences.

409 In the absence of any phrase such as 'in particular' or 'especially': Case C-9/08 *Copad SA v Christian Dior couture SA* [2009] ECR I-3421.

410 *Copad* v *Christian Dior, op cit.*

411 *Joe Cool (Manchester) Ltd's Trade Mark Application* [2000] RPC 926. A purported assignment was void, as the assignor company had been dissolved before the date of the assignment. See also *SKYLIFT Trade Mark* (unreported) 19 July 2000, Trade Marks Registry.

412 *Sunbeam Motor Co's Application* (1916) 33 RPC 389.

413 Registered users existing at commencement were transferred to the register under the 1994 Act for transactions affecting the mark: Sch 3 para 9(2).

414 [2002] FSR 7 at para 33.
415 The reference was subsequently withdrawn.

The registered user provisions in the 1938 Act required that the proprietor must have some control over the use of the mark: for example, by exercising quality control.[413] This is not required under the 1994 Act. Licensing of trade marks has been freed from the restrictions of the old law. If the function of a trade mark is to act as a badge of origin, then even an exclusive licence which does not contain any provisions for quality control by the proprietor would seem unobjectionable. The public would perceive the goods or services as being those of the exclusive licensee. This may yet be the case where the licence is a bare exclusive licence. In *Scandecor Developments AB v Scandecor Marketing AB*,[414] Lord Nicholls of Birkenhead, referring the question to the Court of Justice,[415] suggested that a trade mark should not be regarded as liable to mislead if the origin of the goods is a bare exclusive licensee. This accords with modern business practices but the argument can be developed further.

Non-exclusive licences which are limited geographically to different regions or which are limited to different goods or services may also be possible without being vulnerable to revocation or invalidity proceedings on the basis that they are likely to be misleading or give rise to a likelihood of confusion. This is a welcome step and the inclusion of provisions for quality control by proprietors inserted into licence agreements, should no longer be required unless, of course, the proprietor actually does wish to exercise quality control. It is suspected that, in many cases, these provisions were not used but simply inserted into licence agreements to circumvent the restrictions under previous trade mark law.

The Trade Marks Act 1994 contemplates exclusive licensees and non-exclusive licensees commencing legal proceedings against infringers, although the right of a licensee to do this can be affected by the terms of the licence agreement. Under s 31(1), an exclusive licensee may, provided the licence agreement so provides, have the same rights and remedies as the proprietor. However, under s 31(4), if either the proprietor or the exclusive licensee brings an infringement action, he must join the other except by leave of the court, although this does not apply to interim remedies.

Under s 30(2), unless the licence provides otherwise, a licensee may call upon the proprietor to take action, and if the proprietor refuses or fails to take action within two months of being called on to do so, a licensee (including a sub-licensee) may bring proceedings in his own name as if he were the proprietor. Again, the proprietor would normally be joined in the action unless the court gave leave otherwise.

In terms of an exclusive licence, it is not clear whether ss 30 and 31 are mutually exclusive or complementary. There is an apparent contradiction in s 30 between s 30(1) and (7). The former suggests that s 30 does not apply where, or to the extent that, an exclusive licensee has by virtue of s 31(1) the right to bring proceedings in his own name, whereas s 30(7) states that s 30 applies in relation to an exclusive licensee if or to the extent that he has, by virtue of s 31(1), the rights and remedies of an assignee as if he were the proprietor.

In practice, the licence agreement will probably address issues dealing with rights to bring proceedings. For example, an exclusive licence may grant the licensee the same rights and remedies as if it had been an assignment. As such rights and remedies are declared by s 31(2) to be concurrent with those of the proprietor and a current proprietor with concurrent rights must be joined in the action except by leave of the court, the licence should provide for this eventuality also. The licence may state that the proprietor agrees to take part in any action as co-claimant subject to payment of his expenses by the licensee, and the licence may also provide for any apportionment of an award between the proprietor and licensee. Where the proprietor and exclusive licensee have concurrent rights, the court shall take into account the terms of the licence and any pecuniary remedy already awarded or available to either in respect of the infringement: s 31(6). In directing an account of profits, the court shall apportion the profits between the proprietor and exclusive licensee as the court considers just, subject to any agreement between them.

The following transactions affecting registered trade marks must be registered on application to the Registrar by a person claiming to be entitled to an interest in or under the mark concerned by virtue of any such transaction, under s 25(1) and (2):

- an assignment of the mark or any right in it (this could include, for example, the assignment of a licence);
- the grant of a licence under the mark;
- the grant of a security interest (fixed or floating charge) over the mark, or over any right in or under it;
- the making by personal representatives of a vesting assent in relation to the mark or any right in or under it;
- a court order (or order of other competent authority – for example, the Appointed Person or the Trade Marks Registrar) transferring the mark or any right in or under it.

Under s 25(3), until the application for registration of the transaction has been made, it is ineffective against a person acquiring a conflicting interest in or under the mark in ignorance of the transaction, and any person claiming to be a licensee because of the transaction does not have any rights and remedies for infringement.

A person becoming a proprietor or licensee has six months to register his interest (the court has discretion to extend if it was not practicable to register within six months). Failure to register within that time will mean that the new proprietor or licensee cannot obtain costs in respect of infringements occurring between the date of the transaction and the date of registration of the interest (s 25(4)).[416]

No trusts shall be entered on the register, but equities in relation to registered trade marks may be enforced as with other personal property (s 26). This permits action by beneficial owners of trade marks.

As some months may pass between application and registration, the provisions in the Act relating to assigning, licensing and registration are also effective in relation to an application to register a trade mark (s 27). Thus it is possible to grant an assignment or a licence in respect of a trade mark before it has been formally registered.

Registration

Under s 32 of the Trade Marks Act 1994, an application to register a trade mark requires the submission of the following items:

- a request for registration;
- the name and address of the applicant;
- a statement of goods or services in relation to which it is sought to register the trade mark;
- a representation of the trade mark;
- a statement that the trade mark is being used, by the applicant or with his consent, in relation to those goods or services, or that he has a *bona fide* intention of so using it;
- the prescribed fee (application plus class fees).

In the case of a three-dimensional mark, there must be a statement to the effect that such is claimed and, in respect of a colour, there must be a statement to that effect and the colour must be specified.[417] The date of filing will be the date when all the necessary documents have been furnished to the Registrar (s 33).[418] This is the date of application. Section 35 provides for priority from earlier filings from Paris Convention countries for up to six months.

416 Previously, damages or an account of profits would not be available. The change was made by the Intellectual Property (Enforcement, etc.) Regulations 2006, SI 2006/1028.

417 If the sign is a repeating pattern, that must be stated also.

418 Under r 2(3), filing means delivery to the Registrar at the Office unless a contrary intention appears.

The applicant to register a trade mark (or the proprietor of an existing mark) may disclaim the right to exclusive use of a specified element of the trade mark, or agree to a limitation (for example, a territorial limitation) under s 13. Under r 31 of the Trade Marks Rules 2008,[419] this must be by written notice, and the Registrar will make the appropriate entry in the register and publish the disclaimer or limitation. A requirement that an application include details of colour and size was not a limitation but was required so as to make the trade mark distinctive.[420]

Under s 17(1) of the 1938 Act, the applicant had to be the person claiming to be the proprietor of the trade mark.[421] There is no equivalent requirement under the 1994 Act.[422] In the absence of any ground to challenge an application on this basis, it remains possible that any other person claiming to have the right to use it may oppose the application on the basis of the relative grounds or on the ground that the application was made in bad faith under s 3(6).[423] In *Ball* v *Eden Project Ltd*,[424] in an infringement action, it was held that registration of a company name by a director of that company without that company's consent for the apparent purpose of giving the director a personal benefit was a breach of the director's fiduciary duty.

The application to register a trade mark is made on Form TM3, a copy of which can be obtained from the Patent Office website together with guidance as to completion of the form and an example application.

Registration procedure – basic steps

The registration procedure is laid out in ss 37–41. The stages are (*see* Figure 20.2, overleaf):

- *File application* – it is now possible to apply online, by electronic communication.[425]
- *Examination* – to ensure that the requirements in the Act and rules are satisfied. Although the Registrar is no longer required to carry out a search of earlier trade marks,[426] he may carry out such a search for the purpose of notifying the applicant and other persons about the existence of earlier trade marks which might be relevant to the proposed registration. Where the Registrar considers that the requirements under the relative grounds for refusal are not met, the applicant and the proprietor of the earlier trade mark are notified accordingly.[427] The opportunity will be given to the applicant to make representations and/or amend the application if the Registrar thinks that the requirements are not met (s 37).
- *Acceptance* – if it appears to the Registrar that all the requirements for registration have been met he *shall* accept the application (under the 1938 Act, the Registrar had a discretion) (s 37(5)).
- *Publication* – in the *Trade Marks Journal* (rr 16 and 81 – including particulars and such information required under the rules and any other information as the Registrar thinks fit).
- *Opposition* – under s 38(2), any person may give written notice of opposition within two months of the date of publication (r 17).[428] The grounds for opposition must be stated. Opposition based on the relative grounds for refusal may only be raised by the proprietor of the earlier trade mark or other earlier right. Where opposition is based on an earlier trade mark which has been registered for five or more years, there is a requirement that the opponent shows genuine use of that trade mark or proper reasons for non-use of it; otherwise, the Registrar shall register the trade mark. Additionally, by s 38(3), any person may make observations in writing before registration without becoming a party to the proceedings on the application. The observations will be sent to the applicant: r 22. The detailed procedure for opposition is set out in the rules and includes the possibility of a 'cooling-off' period. Where opposition is based on the relative grounds for refusal under s 5(1) to (3), licensees of the earlier

419 SI 2008/1797. The references to rules in this part of the chapter are to the Trade Marks Rules 2008.

420 *Nestlé SA's Trade Mark Application* [2005] RPC 5.

421 *AL BASSAM Trade Mark* [1995] RPC 511.

422 In *Sprints Ltd* v *Comptroller of Customs (Mauritius)* [2000] FSR 815, a challenge was mounted on the basis that the applicant did not have the right to use the mark as required by s 4 of the Mauritian Trade Marks Act 1868. The 'right' was accepted by the Privy Council to be a common law right to use the trade mark.

423 See Article 3(2)(d) of the Directive. Alternatively, if the mark has been registered, any person claiming to have a prior right to use it may apply for a declaration of invalidity. It would not seem possible that the provisions on rectification under s 64 could be used, as rectification is not possible where the validity of the registration is affected.

424 [2002] FSR 43.

425 Rule 78 of the Trade Marks Rules 2008 permit this. Unless the contrary is proved, such communication is deemed to be delivered immediately upon transmission, unless the contrary is proved: r 79.

426 Section 37(2), which required this, was repealed by the Trade Marks (Relative Grounds) Order 2007, SI 2007/1976.

427 Rule 14(1), Trade Marks Rules 2008, SI 2008/1797. Notification need not be given to proprietors who have opted out (in the case of earlier UK trade marks) or have not opted in (CTMs): r 14(2).

428 Under the old Trade Marks Rules 2000, this period was three months. It remains three months where an application for an extension of time in filing Form 7 (the form for notice of opposition) has been made.

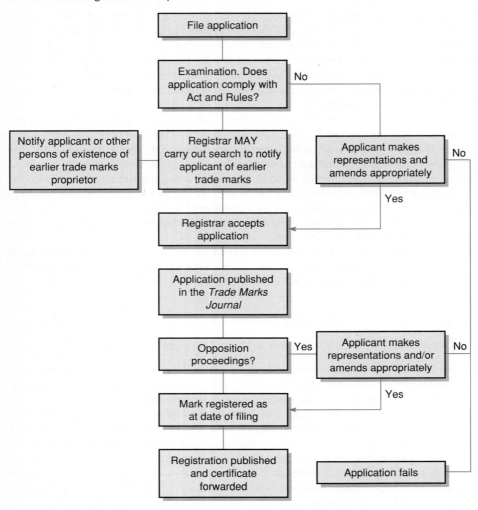

Figure 20.2 **Registration procedure**

trade mark may intervene in opposition proceedings, as may authorised users in the case of collective or certification marks.[429]

- *Registration* – where the application has been accepted and there has been no opposition (or, if there has been, the proceedings have been decided in favour of the applicant) then, unless it subsequently appears to the Registrar that the registration requirements other than those under s 5(1)–(3) were not met at the time of acceptance (s 40),[430] the trade mark shall be registered as of the date of filing, which shall be deemed to be the date of registration (s 40(3)). The registration will then be published specifying the date the mark was entered on to the register (r 23) and a certificate issued to the applicant (s 40(4)).

The wording in s 40(1), 'the registrar shall register the trade mark', appears mandatory but this is subject to the Registrar believing that, with regard to matters coming to his attention (apart from opposition under s 5(1)–(3)), the requirements for registration were met. Laddie J explained the meaning of s 40(1) in *CREOLA Trade Mark*[431] where a mark had been advertised in the *Trade Marks Journal* but the word CREOLA appeared very indistinctly.

429 Rule 21 of the Trade Marks Rules 2008 SI 2008/1797.

430 The limitation in respect of s 5(1), (2) or (3) (relative grounds of refusal on the basis of an earlier trade mark) was a result of amendment by the Trade Marks (Proof of Use, etc.) Regulations 2004, SI 2004/946.

431 [1997] RPC 507. The section has been amended subsequently but not so as to affect the decision in this case.

There had been no opposition, but the Registrar decided to re-advertise the mark printed more clearly and, on this occasion, there was an opposition. The applicant argued that the mark should automatically have been registered after the opposition period, based on the first advertisement. This was rejected by Laddie J who said that, at the end of the opposition period and in the absence of opposition, the Registrar was obliged to take steps timeously to place the mark on the register. However, until such time as the mark was placed on the register, the Registrar could take note of any material brought to his attention. Registration does not follow automatically. Had that been the intention, the statute could have provided for that in clear language.

Under s 39, the applicant may withdraw his application at any time, or restrict the goods or services covered by application. Amendment is also allowed, but only in respect of the name or address of the applicant, errors of wording or copying or obvious mistakes, provided the correction does not substantially affect the identity of the trade mark or extend the goods or services covered by the application (s 39(2)).

Applications can be divided, or merged or made in respect of a series of marks.[432] The Trade Marks Rules 2008 rr 26, 27 and 28 deal with the fine detail. The advantage of division might be that it is a way to isolate an objection while allowing the unchallenged aspects to proceed. Where an application is divided, each divisional application is to be treated as a separate application with the same filing date as the original application.[433] In *DUCATI Trade Mark*,[434] an original application (No 2055227) was divided (Nos 2055227A and 2055227B). A notice of opposition incorrectly referred to No 2055227 (it had been intended to oppose No 2055227A) and the Trade Mark Registry pointed this out and returned the fee. The mark was then registered, there being no opposition recorded against it, and the subsequent application for rectification of the register was refused. As from 1 October 2009, no more than six marks may be applied for in a series (prior to this there was no limit).[435]

A series of marks means a number of trade marks resembling each other as to their material particulars and differing only as to matters of a non-distinctive character so as not substantially to affect the identity of the mark. This is equivalent to the registration of series of marks as associated marks under the old law. However, there is no limitation on the separate assignment of such marks as there was under the old law.

The duration of registration, under s 42, is for a period of ten years from the date of registration (date of filing). It may then be renewed for further ten-year periods, *ad infinitum*.[436] Under s 43, the Registrar will send a reminder between one month and six months prior to the expiry of the last registration (r 34). Renewal shall be made on the appropriate form within six months before the expiry of the last registration. There are provisions for late renewal (if a mark has not been renewed, that fact shall be published). Renewal may take place in the six months following expiry, subject to payment of an additional fee. Otherwise the mark will be removed from the register (r 36). However, within a further six months the mark may be restored subject to an additional restoration fee if the Registrar thinks it is just to do so in the circumstances (r 37).

Generally, once registered, a trade mark may not be altered (s 44). However, an alteration may be permitted where the mark includes the proprietor's name and address – for example, where there is a change to the name or address of the proprietor – provided that the alteration does not substantially affect the identity of the mark. The alteration will be published and persons claiming to be affected by it may object.

Under s 72, registration of a person as proprietor of the mark is prima facie evidence of the validity of the original registration of a trade mark and any subsequent assignment or other transmission of it. This applies in relation to proceedings relating to a registered trade mark including proceedings for rectification.[437]

The fee to register a trade mark or series of marks is £200 plus £50 for each additional class over one. An application for an expedited examination of a single mark may be

432 Section 41. A series of marks are, under s 41(2), a number of marks which resemble each other as to their material particulars and differ only as to matters of a non-distinctive character not substantially affecting the identity of the trade mark.

433 Rule 26(2).

434 [1998] RPC 227.

435 Rule 11 of the Trade Marks and Trade Marks and Patents (Fees) (Amendment) Rules 2009, SI 2009/2089, makes the necessary amendment to r 28 of the Trade Marks Rules 2008.

436 Of course, the trade mark must be used. In the absence of proper reasons, non-use for five or more years is a ground of revocation under s 48(1).

437 Consequently, any person seeking to challenge the validity of a trade mark has the burden of proof, as is usual. He who seeks must prove: *AMAZE COLLECTION Trade Mark* [1999] RPC 725.

made under r 5(2) of the Trade Marks Rules 2008. The fee for this is £300. Renewal is also £200, plus £50 for each class renewal over one. A request to enter details of an assignment is £50 but there is no charge to record a licence or other registrable transaction or to apply for rectification. Serving notice of opposition costs £200 and this is the fee also in respect of filing applications for revocation or a declaration of invalidity.[438]

As from 1 October 2009, changes to the fee structure were introduced. There is an 'e-filing discount' of £30 if the full fees are paid with the application. A 'right-start' application system becomes available but only where the e-filing system is used. This allows the applicant to apply and pay only £100 plus £25 for each additional class of goods or services (that is, half the standard fees). An examination report is sent to the applicant. If the applicant decides to proceed, the balance of the fees must be paid within 14 days of the date of the examination report. The e-filing discount does not apply to right-start applications.

Specific procedural aspects

The basic registration procedure has been described above. In this section some specific procedural aspects are considered including hearings before the Trade Marks Registry and appeals against the Registrar's decision.

Examiners at the Trade Marks Registry check whether an application meets the requirements of the Trade Marks Act and the Trade Marks Rules: s 37. A search may be made of earlier trade marks for the purpose of notifying the applicant and any relevant proprietor about the existence of an earlier registered trade mark which may be relevant to the proposed registration.[439] Where there are potential conflicting earlier registered trade marks, the proprietor may later bring opposition proceedings. Guidance to trade mark examiners is given in a Works Manual. This is a useful tool which gives assistance on the application of the Act in practice. Subsequent editions of the Works Manual are printed to keep up with developments, particularly to reflect legal decisions. Of course, the Works Manual does not carry the force of law. The Trade Marks Registry also adopts *Practice Notes*. For example, in *Practice Note 13/00 – Change of Practice on 'Retail Services'*,[440] the practice used in relation to applications to register trade marks for certain forms of retail services was changed. Previously, applications to register services provided by department stores and supermarkets in respect of bringing together a variety of goods were refused. Such applications may now be accepted where the service is adequately defined.[441] For example, in *Land Securities plc v Registrar of Trade Marks*,[442] several applications to register trade marks for services provided by operators of retail shopping centres were refused as not being services within the meaning of the Directive and the applications also lacked sufficient clarity. The Chancery Division noted that the services had to be such as were normally provided for remuneration.[443] However, the concept of remuneration was not a narrow one and could apply to services provided by a shopping centre operator which carried on activities of a commercial nature. Such an operator could be said to be remunerated in a manner which was directly related to the custom which it attracted. The applicants were to be given an opportunity to overcome the objections raised in relation to the clarity of their applications.

If it appears that the requirements of the Act are not met, the Registrar will notify the applicant who then has an opportunity to make representations: s 37(3). If the applicant takes up this opportunity normally there will follow a 'without notice' (*ex parte*) hearing before a Hearing Officer at the Registry.

For applications that are accepted, there may be an opposition after it has been published. In respect of oppositions, there will normally be a 'with notice' (*inter partes*) hearing before a Hearing Officer at the Registry unless the opposition is withdrawn.

An appeal lies from any decision of the Registrar (including the exercise of a discretion)[444] and, under s 76, such appeal may be brought either before the Appointed Person or

438 Trade Marks (Fees) Rules 2008, SI 2008/1958.

439 This is discretionary. Notification will be given to proprietors of UK trade marks who have not opted out of notification or proprietors of CTMs or international registrations designating the EU who have requested this – for which payment of a fee of £50 is required: Trade Marks (Fees) Rules 2008, SI 2008/1958.

440 [2001] RPC 2.

441 The change was prompted by a number of factors including that the OHIM accepts such marks if adequately defined. In any case, the trade marks Directive does not expressly require that services have to be provided for remuneration. The Court of Justice also accepts that services which are paid for indirectly are acceptable.

442 [2009] RPC 5.

443 See Article 57 of the Treaty on the Functioning of the European Union, formerly Article 50 of the EC Treaty.

444 There are some exceptions where a right to appeal does not exist, for example, in respect of a decision regarding re-classification of goods or services: r 54.

before the court (in England and Wales and Northern Ireland, the High Court or the Court of Session in Scotland: s 75). The Appointed Person is provided for by s 77 and is a person appointed by the Lord Chancellor to hear and decide appeals under the Act. The Appointed Person may refer a case to the court if it appears to involve a point of general importance, if the Registrar so requests or if such a request has been made by a party to the proceedings before the Registrar: s 76(3). The power to refer to the court should be used sparingly and primarily reserved for cases where a general point of legal importance arose.[445] The *raison d'être* of the right of appeal to the Appointed Person is that this can provide a quicker and cheaper way of resolving appeals from the Registrar. This might be particularly important if one of the parties might have to discontinue the action because of the financial risks involved.

Where the Appointed Person hears and determines an appeal, his decision is final. There is no provision for appeal from it. Notwithstanding this, the Appointed Person's decision is still subject to judicial review, although he accepts that he can make a reference to the Court of Justice for a preliminary ruling under Article 234. This would be very unusual, however, and where a point of general legal importance is involved, it would be usual for the Appointed Person to refer the case to the High Court (or Court of Session, as appropriate) from which a reference to the Court of Justice could be made.[446] However, the Appointed Person retains a discretion whether or not to refer an appeal to the court even if it appears to him that the case involves a point of general legal importance.[447]

Figure 20.3 indicates the hearing and appeal system. The figure assumes that the applicant makes representations and appeals against the decision or there is an appeal from the decision in the opposition proceedings.

445 *ACADEMY Trade Mark* [2000] RPC 35.

446 For example, see *Maasland NV's Application for a 3-Dimensional Trade Mark* [2000] RPC 893.

447 *Elizabeth Emanuel Trade Mark* [2004] RPC 15.

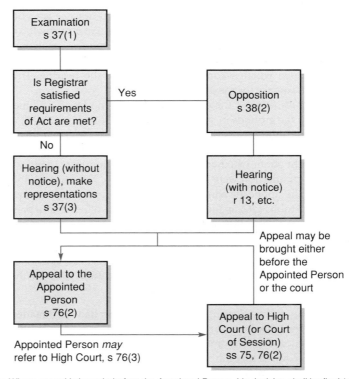

Note: Where appeal is brought before the Appointed Person, his decision shall be final (s 76(4)).

Figure 20.3 Hearing and appeal system for trade mark applications

Under r 74, the Registrar has a discretion to rectify procedural irregularities. The Registrar also has a discretion with regard to things coming to the Registrar's attention after acceptance of the application but before registration where it appears that the application was accepted in error: s 40(1). In *Andreas Stihl AG & Co's Trade Mark Application*,[448] the trade mark in question was published in the *Trade Marks Journal* with a specification of goods which was not that agreed by the applicant and the Registrar and some goods had been omitted. There was no opposition and the mark was registered. Later, the error was noticed by the proprietor and an application for rectification under s 64 was made. The issue was whether the specification could be modified by extending it to include the omitted goods. To allow the amendment would have the effect of extending the protection conferred and this did not seem possible under s 64 which prevents rectification if it affects the validity of the trade mark. In referring the matter to the High Court, the Appointed Person suggested that the Registrar had the power to correct procedurally irregular acts of registration and refusal of registration. It would be an unwanted restriction on that power if it existed only in respect of the period between the acts of accepting the application and registration.

There are usually a few hundred or so opposition proceedings each year. This is a reflection of how trade mark proprietors jealously guard their trade marks and how they try to prevent the registration of another mark which they consider might have a detrimental impact on their trade marks. The opposition procedure now provides for the possibility of a cooling-off period of 12 months if both parties agree and, in any proceedings before the Registrar, provisions for case management and a pre-trial hearing. The procedure in opposition proceedings is set out in rr 17 to 21.

It has been common for opponents to plead every ground of opposition they can think of, for example, by trying to make their arguments and evidence meet every ground under ss 3 and 5 as could possibly apply, however remotely. That practice is to be deprecated and is grossly unfair, especially when the applicant is a sole trader or small company with few resources to answer all the grounds mentioned in the opponent's statement. There are numerous examples of grounds being pleaded which have no hope of succeeding and which are often dropped when it comes to, or close to, the hearing. This may have resulted in significant expense for the applicant.

In *DEMON ALE Trade Mark*,[449] the opponent relied on no less than nine grounds of opposition. They were the grounds in ss 3(3)(b), (4), (6), 5(1), (2), (3), (4) and 56,[450] in addition to a further ground based on the Registrar's discretion. Logically, the grounds under s 5(1), (2) and (3) are mutually exclusive (though a combination could be pleaded if there was some doubt about whether the marks in question were identical or whether the goods or services in question were or were not similar). The only ground to succeed was under s 3(6) as the applicant admitted that he had no intention to use the mark applied for. Geoffrey Hobbs QC, as the Appointed Person, referred to a paper delivered by the principal Hearing Officer in which he said:

> It is a common practice in *inter partes* [with notice] proceedings before the Trade Marks Registry for the 'kitchen sink' to be pleaded . . . However, as evidence is filed, in the vast majority of cases, it becomes clear that there is no justification for the breadth of the pleadings.

The Appointed Person, whilst accepting that the application had been made in bad faith as through a lack of *bona fide* intention to use the mark, allowed the applicant's appeal against the Registrar's decision to award costs against the applicant of £300. He said that the justice of the case required that the costs of the successful opposition (though the only successful ground was not originally pleaded) be set against the costs the applicant was prima facie entitled to in the light of all the failed grounds.

448 [2001] RPC 12.

449 [2000] RPC 345.

450 Section 56 allows the proprietor of a well-known trade mark to restrain the use of an identical or similar trade mark in respect of identical or similar goods or services.

Summary

There are significant similarities between the harmonised national trade mark system and the Community trade mark.

It is increasingly usual for judges in UK trade mark cases to refer to the provisions of the trade marks Directive where the provision in question is harmonised, such as those relating to registrability, rights and infringement, limitations, exhaustion, invalidity, revocation, etc. Students are advised to study the text of the Directive (codified version of 2008) and make themselves familiar, in particular, with Articles 2 to 12.

Trade marks may be registered if they:

- are capable of being represented graphically;
- are capable of distinguishing the goods or services of one undertaking from those of other undertakings;
- do not fall within the 'absolute grounds for refusal';
- do not fall within the 'relative grounds for refusal'.

The requirement of graphical representation is difficult, if not impossible, to satisfy in the case of olfactory marks, such as perfumes and other smell marks. Other non-conventional marks, such as colour and sound marks, also present problems in terms of graphical representation.

The essential function of a trade mark is to indicate the origin of goods or services. Other functions may exist such as communication, investment and advertising.

The 'absolute' grounds for refusal (or invalidity) apply to signs which do not fulfil the function of a trade mark because they:

- cannot constitute a trade mark (for example, they are not capable of graphical representation or cannot distinguish goods or services of one undertaking from those of others);
- are devoid of distinctive character;
- indicate kind, quality, quantity, intended purpose, value, geographical origin, etc. (for example, they are descriptive);
- consist exclusively of signs or indications customary in the trade;
- consist of certain types of shape marks (shape resulting from nature of goods, necessary to obtain a technical result or give substantial value to goods).

However, apart from signs which cannot constitute a trade mark and shapes, they may still be registrable if they have acquired a distinctive character resulting from use of the sign.

The exclusion from shape marks where the shape is necessary to obtain a technical result applies even if there is more than one way of obtaining that technical result.

Other 'absolute' grounds for refusal are where:

- the mark is contrary to public policy or accepted principles of morality;
- use of the mark would deceive the public;
- use of the mark is prohibited by law;
- where the mark conflicts with specially protected emblems under the Paris Convention, such as the Olympics symbol;
- the application to register the mark is made in bad faith.

In terms of bad faith, case law suggests that this includes dishonesty but is not limited to that and also applies in cases where the dealings or behaviour of the applicant falls short of the standards of acceptable commercial behaviour. In the UK, bad faith explicitly applies where, at the time of applying to register, the mark was not being used by the applicant or with his consent and he had no *bona fide* intention that it would be used.

The 'relative' grounds for refusal (or invalidity) apply where there is a conflict with an earlier registered trade mark or other earlier right, such as a copyright or mark protected by the law of passing off. These grounds apply:

- where the trade mark in question is identical with an earlier trade mark used for identical goods or services (there is no requirement for a likelihood of confusion);
- where there is no complete identity of the trade mark with the earlier trade mark and/or the goods or services, there must be a likelihood of confusion, which includes a likelihood of association – this latter phrase does not seem to extend to 'non-origin association';
- where the trade mark is identical or similar to an earlier trade mark with a reputation where the use of the sign would, without due cause, take unfair advantage of, or be detrimental to, the distinctive character or repute of the earlier trade mark (this includes, typically, 'blurring' or 'tarnishing');
- where the use of the trade mark would conflict with an earlier right such as a right to a name, a personal portrayal, copyright or industrial property right (the UK Act mentions unregistered trade marks protected by passing off, copyright, design right or registered designs).

Other grounds apply in relation to recently expired trade marks, collective and certification marks.

The proprietor of an earlier trade mark or owner of other earlier right may consent to the registration of the trade mark in question. The provisions for honest concurrent use have been repealed.

Only the proprietors of earlier trade marks or owners of other earlier rights can oppose applications under the relative grounds for refusal. Where an earlier trade mark is concerned, if the applicant for registration so requires, the proprietor of the earlier trade mark must furnish proof of use of that trade mark.

Special provisions apply in relation to certification trade marks (indicative of standards) and collective trade marks (used by members of an association).

A registered trade mark may be surrendered by the proprietor, after giving any person having an interest three month's notice, such person either being not affected or consenting.

A registered trade mark may be revoked:

- for non-use (five years) without proper reasons;
- if it has become generic (that is, a common name for a product or service) due to the acts or inactivity of the proprietor; or
- if, because of the use of the trade mark by the proprietor or with his consent, it is liable to mislead the public.

The 'absolute' and 'relative' grounds for refusal of registration also apply to declarations of invalidity. The registration may be 'saved' if the trade mark has subsequently become distinctive through use (though not for shape marks or signs which do not constitute trade marks). There is a presumption of validity. The result of a declaration of invalidity is that the mark was void *ab initio* whereas, for revocation, the mark is valid until revoked.

The provisions as to the property rights in trade marks is left largely to Member States, except the Directive covers licensing and confirms that licences may be exclusive or non-exclusive and goes on to provide that a proprietor may invoke his trade mark rights against licensees in contravention of certain aspects of the licence agreements.

The UK Act has detailed provisions on assignment and licensing. Some transactions are registrable (assignments, licences, security interests, vesting assents and court orders transferring the mark or any right under it).

The basic registration procedure is set out under s 32 of the Act and the Trade Marks Rules. The basic steps are:

- filing
- examination
- acceptance
- publication in the *Trade Marks Journal*
- opposition (if raised)
- registration.

Discussion questions

1 Discuss the extent to which non-conventional signs, such as sounds, smells, tastes and shapes, may be registered as trade marks.

2 Discuss the meaning of bad faith as a ground for refusal of registration of a trade mark.

3 What does the phrase 'a likelihood of confusion on the part of the public...' mean? How has the Court of Justice interpreted this phrase?

4 What sort of situations can you envisage where registration of a trade mark could be said to take unfair advantage of, or be detrimental to, the distinctive character or repute of an earlier trade mark with a reputation? Give examples.

5 Discuss the meaning of 'genuine use' in the context of revocation for non-use.

Selected further reading

Ahuja, V. K., 'Non-traditional trade marks: new dimension of trade marks law' [2010] *European Intellectual Property Review*, 575 (looks at the Singapore Treaty on the Law of Trade Marks with much comparative material, including Europe, the UK and US with respect to the registration of sound marks, smell marks, taste marks, etc.).

de Almeida, A. F. R., 'Key differences between trade marks and geographical indications' [2008] *European Intellectual Property Review*, 406 (looks at the differences between trade marks and geographical indications and the implications of both systems – calls for a multilateral system for notification and registration of geographical indications).

Bainbridge, D. I., 'Smell, Sound, Colour and Shape Trade Marks: An Unhappy Flirtation?' [2004] *Journal of Business Law*, 243 (looks at the experiences of attempts to register new forms of trade marks).

Burrell, R. and Ganjee, D., 'Trade marks and freedom of expression – a call for caution' [2010] *International Review of Intellectual Property and Competition Law*, 544 (interesting exploration of the implications for freedom of expression resulting from, for example, the development of confusion and dilution tests).

Directive 2008/95/EC of the European Parliament and of the Council of 22 October 2008 to approximate the laws of the Member States relating to trade marks (codified version), OJ L 299, 08.11.2008, p 25 available at:

http://eur-lex.europa.eu/LexUriServ/LexUriServ.do?uri=OJ:L:2008:299:0025:0033:EN:PDF

Donnellan, L., 'Three dimensional trade marks: the Mars and Lindt cases' [2010] *European Intellectual Property Review*, 132 (looks at the reluctance to accept three-dimensional marks for registration and the issue of bad faith in relation to such marks).

Visit www.mylawchamber.co.uk/bainbridgeip to access study support resources including interactive multiple choice questions, practice exam questions with guidance, weblinks, legal updates and a legal newsfeed.

mylawchamber
unrivalled support for legal education

21

The UK trade mark – rights, infringement, defences, remedies and criminal offences

Introduction

This chapter focuses on the rights of the registered proprietor of a trade mark, infringement, limitations on the rights afforded by a registered trade mark and defences, remedies and criminal offences. As noted in Chapter 20, there is a great deal of similarity between the relative grounds of refusal of registration and the acts that amount to infringement. The Court of Justice of the European Union (the 'Court of Justice') recognises the equivalence between the two sets of provisions and many of the cases and rulings on the relative grounds, discussed in full detail in the previous chapter, have relevance for infringement also. Consequently, the section on infringement of registered trade marks is relatively short and focuses only on those aspects of trade mark law which are not fully dealt with in that chapter. For example, in relation to infringement based on the identity and/or similarity of the sign alleged to infringe and the registered trade mark, there is no point in repeating the same rulings of the Court of Justice which have been fully described in the previous chapter in the context of the relative grounds for refusal, apart from a brief summary. The discussion in the part of this chapter on infringement focuses on issues that may be different in the UK because of derogations, options or areas where the Directive leaves Member States some freedom in how they legislate. There is also some discussion of trade marks used on webpages and the territorial implications of such use.

There is one important difference between the relative grounds for refusal based on earlier trade marks and infringement, apart from context. An application to register a trade mark can be opposed on the basis of an earlier UK trade mark or a CTM or trade marks resulting from international applications which have effect in the UK or as a CTM. The rights and infringement under the Trade Marks Act 1994 can only relate to UK trade marks or international registrations having effect in the UK. The provisions on infringement are concerned with the use of an offending sign whereas the relative grounds for refusal are concerned with conflict with an earlier trade mark, even where the trade mark subject to opposition has never been used. Having said that, and apart from case law on use of a sign in the course of trade or use of a sign in a trade mark sense, case law on the relative grounds for refusal is exchangeable and applicable to actions on infringement.

First Council Directive 89/104/EEC of 21 December 1988 to approximate the laws of Member States relating to trade marks[1] describes in Article 5 the rights conferred by a trade mark and, in doing so, also specifies the acts that infringe a trade mark. Member States are given some discretion to give further protection for trade marks having a reputation in the Member State concerned. Article 6 limits the rights so as to allow, for example, others using their own name or address or describing certain characteristics of their own goods and services. These limitations may, typically, be used as a defence to an

1 OJ L 40, 11.02.1989, p 1. The original Directive was repealed and replaced by a new codified version, Directive 2008/95/EC of the European Parliament and of the Council of 22 October 2008 to approximate the law of the Member States relating to trade marks, OJ L 299, 08.11.2008, p 25. There are no significant substantive changes but some mainly minor structural changes. In most cases, the numbering of the Articles is unchanged. References in this chapter to the 'Directive' are to the new Directive.

infringement action along with other defences, such as the use complained of not being in the course of trade or a defence based on acquiescence. As with patents and designs, there is an action for groundless threats of infringement proceedings which also now applies in respect of the Community trade mark ('CTM').

Remedies are left to Member States though injunctions are envisaged by the Directive.[2] The Trade Marks Act 1994 also contains a number of criminal offences, some of which carry a maximum penalty of ten years' imprisonment and/or a fine. Of course, the Directive does not expressly cover criminal sanctions but the usual principle of Community law ought to apply so that penalties must be effective, proportionate and dissuasive.[3]

Although the relative grounds for refusal based on earlier trade marks and infringement of a registered trade mark are equivalent, one difference should be pointed out. The former applies in relation to applications to register a *trade mark*. On the other hand, infringement is based on the use of a *sign* identical or similar to the registered trade mark. 'Sign' is not defined but the Trade Marks Act 1994 uses the word in the same way as in the Directive. Clearly it covers the use of a trade mark, whether registered or not,[4] or some other symbol or device. Dictionary definitions of 'sign' are very wide-ranging but its natural meaning in this context is that it is placed on or around or used in relation to some thing to distinguish it from other things or another class of things in some way. The word itself does not infer use in the course of trade or even use as a trade mark but, in the context of trade mark infringement, it would seem reasonable to assume that these are required. There were, however, some doubts about whether use must be use as a trade mark.

Comparative advertising is permissible under the 1994 Act where this is in accordance with honest practices and does not take unfair advantage of or damage the repute of the other proprietor's trade mark.[5] The Directive appears to allow Member States so to provide under Article 5(5). Other laws may also be relevant where comparative advertising takes place, such as under the misleading advertising Directive (*see* later) and the Control of Misleading Advertisements Regulations 1988[6] which, as amended, has specific provisions for allowing it under specific circumstances. There is also an 'Olympic association right' which, *inter alia*, gives rights against persons using in the course of trade the Olympic symbol, motto or protected words or a representation so similar to the symbol or motto as to create in the public mind an association with it.[7]

Rights conferred by registration and infringement

Article 5 of the Directive sets out the rights conferred by a registered trade mark. These rights are exclusive and negative in nature[8] as, under the circumstances covered by the rights, the proprietor is given the right to prevent the use of a sign in the course of trade by a third party without the proprietor's consent.[9] Infringement can extend to the spoken use of words as well as to a graphic representation as, under the Trade Marks Act 1994, s 103(2), 'use' includes use otherwise than by means of a graphic representation.

The scope of the rights under a registered trade mark is subject to specific limitations by virtue of Article 6 and the doctrine of exhaustion of rights under Article 7. However, there is no general limitation based on not unduly restricting the availability of certain signs. Such an argument was rejected in Case C-102/07 *Adidas AG* v *Marca Mode CV*.[10] In that case the claimant was the proprietor of the well-known three-stripe logo applied to shoes and sports clothing. The defendants used similar logos but using two stripes. The Court of Justice confirmed that Article 6(1)(b) alone applied to the availability argument. There was no general interest form of keeping certain signs available for use by other undertakings.

2 Article 5 provides that the proprietor shall have a right *to prevent* certain uses of a sign identical or similar to the trade mark by third parties without consent.

3 Case C-326/88 *Anklagemyndigheden* v *Hansen & Soen I/S* [1990] ECR I-2911.

4 Though s 11(1) states that a registered trade mark is not infringed by the use of another registered trade mark, this applies only in connection with the goods or services for which the other is registered. In any event, the owner of the earlier mark might apply for a declaration of invalidity instead.

5 Strictly speaking, comparative advertising infringed under the Trade Marks Act 1938 but there were relatively few cases on it as it seemed to be tolerated by most trade mark proprietors.

6 SI 1988/915, as amended.

7 Olympic Symbol etc. (Protection) Act 1995.

8 The right is not to use the mark but to prevent others from using it under the circumstances set out in the legislation: *Nanjing Automobile (Group) Corp* v *MG Sports and Racing Europe Ltd* [2010] EWHC 270 (Ch) at para 121.

9 The equivalent provisions in the Act are set out in ss 9(1) and 10. Of course, for the purposes of the Act, the use to which the offending sign is put must be use in the UK.

10 [2008] ECR I-2439.

In the UK, the rights have effect from the date of registration (s 9(3)). This is the date of filing of the application in accordance with s 40(3). However, the proprietor cannot begin infringement proceedings before the date on which the mark is in fact registered, that is, the date that registration is granted. The language in the two provisions is somewhat tautologous. Section 36(3) states that the date the mark is in fact registered is the date of filing. As it is retrospective it is nonetheless a question of fact. But obviously no proceedings can be entertained until it is known that the mark has been registered.

Before looking at the individual forms of infringement, it should be noted that the use complained of, apart perhaps that for the purposes of Article 5(5), must be use in the course of trade. There is also an issue as to whether the use in question has to be use as a trade mark, that is, use in a form that indicates the origin of the goods or services.

Use in course of trade

Apart from Article 5(5) of the Directive (which in the UK is equivalent to s 10(6), which appears to permit honest, fair and non-detrimental comparative advertising),[11] the rights are infringed by using a sign in the prohibited circumstances in the course of trade. Use in the course of trade means use in the context of commercial activity with a view to economic advantage and not as a private matter.[12] In *Och-Ziff Management Europe Ltd* v *Och Capital LLP*,[13] Arnold J thought that the phrase 'and not as a private matter' imposed a separate additional criterion rather than simply clarifying the scope and meaning on the words 'in the context of commercial activity with a view to economic advantage'. He drew support for his view from Joined Cases C-236/08 to C-238/08 *Google France SARL* v *Louis Vuitton Malletier SA*[14] in which the Court of Justice ruled that an internet search engine provider did not itself use trade marks which had been allocated as keywords to advertisers. Although the search engine provider was carrying on a commercial activity, the keywords were not used by the provider as part of that commercial activity; they were used as parts of the advertisers' commercial activity. Additional support for Arnold J's view 'and not as a private matter' can be found in cases on what constitutes 'genuine use' of a trade mark. In the *Och* case, it was held that use of the trade mark in internal e-mails by the defendant was not use in the course of trade.[15]

In the Trade Marks Act 1994, the infringing acts are set out in s 10 but s 9(1) makes a basic statement of the rights given by registration, saying that the proprietor '. . . has exclusive rights in the trade mark which are infringed by use of the trade mark in the United Kingdom without his consent'. The subsection then goes on to state that the infringing acts are specified in s 10. This is quite a clumsy way to set out the rights and infringement and, because s 9(1) is not limited to use in the course of trade, it is arguable that the rights are somehow wider than the right to prevent infringement as specified in s 10 and any use of the trade mark in the UK without consent will infringe that right.

In *British Sugar plc* v *James Robertson & Sons Ltd*,[16] it was argued that s 9(1) put a gloss upon s 10, requiring that infringing use had to be use as a trade mark. Jacob J rejected this, describing s 9(1) as no more than a 'chatty introduction to the details set out in s 10', noting that s 9(1) had no equivalent in the Directive because, except as mentioned above, the Directive is quite clear that the rights are in connection with the use of a sign in the course of trade. That being so, it is safe to ignore any suggestion that s 9(1) gives more extensive rights than those set out in s 10. It is, however, arguable that use does not have to be use in the course of trade for the purposes of Article 5(5) of the Directive and s 10(6) of the Act, as discussed later.[17]

It is not clear whether 'spillover' advertising, such as where an advertisement in a magazine (or on an internet website) intended for customers in one country reaches persons in another country, is use in the course of trade. In *Euromarket Designs Inc* v *Peters and Crate & Barrel*,[18] the advertisements complained of consisted of one in a magazine

11 But see later in the section on comparative advertising.

12 See, for example, Joined Cases C-236/08 to C-238/08 *Google France SARL v Louis Vuitton Malletier SA* [2010] ECR I-2417 at para 50.

13 [2011] FSR 11.

14 [2010] ECR I-2417.

15 However, other uses by the defendant did infringe the trade mark.

16 [1996] RPC 281.

17 If that is so, this could explain the omission of any reference to the course of trade under s 9(1).

18 [2001] FSR 20.

and another on the defendant's website. The magazine was published in the UK but the advertisement was directed to trade at the defendant's shop in Dublin. The nature of the trade (sofas, tableware, beds and lighting accessories) was that of a shop and there was no evidence of mail order trade. That being so, and the same applied in respect of the website, the use of the claimant's trade mark, registered in the UK and as a CTM, was not an infringing use as it was not in the course of trade in the UK. If it were otherwise, the Directive could inadvertently have given rise to conflict in the internal market. However, this was an application for summary judgment and Jacob J rightly said that his view was provisional.

Under the Trade Marks Act 1994, s 103(1) 'trade' includes any business or profession. Article 5(3) gives some examples of what forms of use may be caught by the main forms of infringement under Article 5(1) and (2) as:

(a) affixing the sign to goods or to the packaging thereof;
(b) offering the goods, putting them on the market or stocking them for these purposes under that sign, or offering or supplying services thereunder;[19]
(c) importing or exporting goods under the sign;
(d) use of the sign on business papers and in advertising.[20]

The list is not exhaustive and other forms of use may be caught. Of course, in terms of the UK Act, the use must be in relation to goods within the UK. That being so, a person who affixes the offending sign to material in the UK to be used to package goods outside the UK does not infringe under s 10(4)(a) (Article 5(3)(a) of the Directive).[21] However, using the sign on business papers or in advertising in the UK in respect of goods packaged in the UK for sale outside the UK may infringe.

The meaning of import and export came up for determination in *Waterford Wedgwood plc v David Nagli Ltd*[22] in which the defendant had acquired through a third party a consignment of counterfeit Waterford Crystal valued at around £700,000 which was situated in Bilbao, Spain. The defendant gave instructions for the shipment of the crystal from Bilbao to New York. Unknown to the defendant, the crystal was loaded on a ship bound for Felixstowe, where it was transferred to another ship bound for New York. Although it was accepted that the property in the crystal had passed to the buyer in New York, it was held that the defendant had infringed the UK trade marks of the claimant by importing into and exporting from the UK. The shippers were acting as agents under the instructions of the defendant as principal.

The court confirmed that importation consists of bringing goods into the territorial jurisdiction of the UK and exportation consists of their removal from territorial jurisdiction. As the crystal was imported and exported in packing cases bearing the claimant's trade marks, the defendant had infringed by importing and exporting under the sign, even though the crystal was only temporarily in the UK, and even though the crystal was brought into the UK en route for New York. As regards a claim that the defendant had infringed by using the trade marks on invoices and other papers, it was held there was no infringement as the defendant, who thought the crystal was genuine, thought it was referring to genuine Waterford Crystal. The luckless defendant had challenged the validity of some of the claimant's trade marks, arguing that WATERFORD was a geographical name and LISMORE was a name for a pattern in customary use in the trade. However, this was rejected as Article 3(3) allows such marks to be registered if they have become distinctive through use, which was the case here.[23]

Where goods pass through the UK under customs control onward processing procedure from outside the EEA for trans-shipment to a destination country also outside the EEA, this does not constitute importing the goods into the UK for the purposes of trade mark infringement. So it was held in *Eli Lilly & Co v 8PM Chemists Ltd*[24] in which

---

19 Calling a car showroom 'Autodrome' did not infringe the registered mark 'AUTODROME' used for motor cars because it was not used in relation to goods under the Trade Marks Act 1938 s 4: *AUTODROME Trade Mark* [1969] RPC 564. But compare with *Cheetah Trade Mark* [1993] FSR 263 where use on an invoice was held to infringe.

20 Section 10(4) of the Trade Marks Act 1994 is expressed in very similar terms.

21 *Beautimatic International Ltd v Mitchell International Pharmaceuticals Ltd* [2000] FSR 267.

22 [1998] FSR 92.

23 The claimant's request for an account of profits was not granted as the court indicated that the defendant had not made a profit!

24 [2008] FSR 12.

pharmaceuticals were obtained in Turkey, brought to the UK and then sent to the US. Using a trade mark in the course of trade required bringing them into the EEA for the purpose of placing them on the market within the EEA. This was in accordance with the earlier Court of Justice ruling in Case C-405/03 *Class International BV* v *Colgate-Palmolive Co.*[25] The correctness of *Waterford Wedgwood* v *Nagli* must now be doubted though a distinction is that of the customs procedures under *Eli Lilly* and *Class International*. In *Class International*, the goods (Aquafresh toothpaste from South Africa intended to be shipped to the Ukraine) were brought into the Netherlands under the Community customs code of 'non-Community goods'.[26]

Use as a trade mark

The question here is whether it is required that the offending sign is being used in a trade mark sense, as an indicator of origin. There was considerable doubt as to whether the use of the sign must be use as a trade mark. In the Scottish case of *Bravado Merchandising Services Ltd* v *Mainstream Publishing (Edinburgh) Ltd*,[27] the defendant published a book about the pop group 'Wet Wet Wet' under the title *A Sweet Little Mystery – Wet Wet Wet – The Inside Story*. 'Wet Wet Wet' was registered as a trade mark and the proprietor brought an action for an interdict (injunction) against this use of the name. Lord McCluskey, *obiter*, said that use must be use as a trade mark. He said it would be bizarre if trade mark legislation, which was designed to protect indications of origin, was used to prevent publishers using a trade mark in a book about the proprietor of the trade mark or the product to which it was applied.

Jacob J disagreed with this view in *British Sugar plc* v *James Robertson & Sons Ltd*,[28] where he held that there was no such requirement in s 10(1) or (2) (equivalent to Article 5(1)(a) or (b) of the Directive). In that case, the claimant had registered 'TREAT' for dessert sauces and syrups and complained of the defendant selling a sweet spread labelled 'Robertson's Toffee Treat'. The defendant claimed that it used the word descriptively and not as a trade mark. Jacob J said there was no reason to limit s 10 in such a way and purely descriptive use would not infringe because it would be within s 11(2) which states, *inter alia*, that indications of kind, quality, quantity, intended purpose, etc. do not infringe if in accordance with honest practices in industrial or commercial matters.[29] However, Jacob J held that the trade mark was invalid and, even if it was valid, it would not have been infringed and, consequently, what he said about infringing use not being required to be use as a trade mark must not be taken too seriously.[30] In *Trebor Bassett Ltd* v *The Football Association*,[31] Rattee J felt it unnecessary to decide the point.

In *Arsenal Football Club plc* v *Reed*,[32] Laddie J thought that the scarves and other items bearing the football club's trade marks sold by a third party from a stall sited outside the Arsenal football ground and carrying a disclaimer to the effect that the goods were not official Arsenal merchandise, was not use of the trade marks as indicating origin. They operated rather as badges of support for, loyalty or affiliation to the trade mark proprietor. However, he referred the matter to the Court of Justice which ruled in Case C-206/01 *Arsenal Football Club plc* v *Matthew Reed*[33] that it made no difference that the trade marks were perceived as badges of support for, loyalty or affiliation to the trade mark proprietor. The use of the trade marks suggested that there was a material link in the course of trade between the proprietor and the goods. The use of a disclaimer did not prevent this as there would be persons who came across the goods after they had been sold and they might read the trade marks as meaning that Arsenal Football Club was the undertaking of origin of the goods.

A little earlier, in Case C-2/00 *Holterhöff* v *Freiesleben*,[34] the Court of Justice considered the position where the trade mark had been used solely to describe the characteristics of the goods and there was no danger that anyone would take it as an indication of origin.

25 [2005] ECR I-8735.

26 Article 4(7) and (8) of Council Regulation (EEC) No 2913/92 establishing the Community customs code, OJ L 302, 19.10.1992, p 1.

27 [1996] FSR 205.

28 [1996] RPC 281.

29 Article 6(1)(b) of the Directive.

30 Nor was there any need to decide this point in *Bravado Merchandising* above, as the s 11(2) defence applied there also.

31 [1997] FSR 211.

32 [2001] RPC 46.

33 [2002] ECR I-10273.

34 [2002] ECR I-4187.

Mr Freiesleben was the proprietor of two trade marks, 'Spirit Sun' and 'Context Cut', used for diamonds and other precious stones. The trade marks were associated with two particular cuts of the stones. Mr Holterhöff was a dealer in precious stones and used the names to describe stones he offered for sale. Clearly the use was in the course of trade though he claimed he had only used the trade marks to describe the type of cut of the stones offered for sale and he had not used the trade marks to indicate origin. The Court of Justice confirmed that the exclusive rights of the proprietor of a registered trade mark within Article 5(1) did not extend to a situation where a third party, in the course of commercial negotiations, reveals the origin of goods which he has produced himself and only uses the trade mark to indicate the particular characteristics of the goods he is offering for sale such that there is no question of the trade mark being perceived as a sign indicative of the undertaking of origin. In other words, provided a trade mark is not used as an indication of origin but is used to describe the goods, and this is clear in the circumstances, there can be no infringement. The trade mark has not been used in a trade mark sense. This makes sense when it is recalled that the primary function of a registered trade mark is to act as an indication of origin.[35]

In its ruling in *Holterhöff*, the Court of Justice was careful to limit the ruling to circumstances such as those in the case, being:

- where a third party refers to the trade mark in the course of commercial negotiations with a potential customer, being a professional jeweller;
- where the reference to the trade mark is made purely to describe the characteristics of the product offered for sale to the potential customer who is familiar with the characteristics of the products covered by the trade mark; and
- where the reference to the trade mark cannot be interpreted by the potential customer as indicating the origin of the product.

The Court of Justice said that, in such a case, the interests of the proprietor which Article 5(1) was intended to protect were not affected. One major distinction between *Arsenal* and *Holterhöff* is that, in the former, other persons might come across the goods later and take the trade marks as indicating origin: for example, by seeing someone wearing one of Mr Reed's scarves or being given one as a present. In *Holterhöff*, the trade mark was used descriptively to a potential customer and was not attached to the precious stones or written on associated documentation in such a way that there would be a danger that persons other than the potential customer would see the trade mark and the stones and think that they came from the trade mark proprietor. However, in *Holterhöff*, the Court of Justice did not address the possibility that a customer who is a professional jeweller might sell the precious stones to one of his customers and use the trade marks to describe the stones so that his customer, not being knowledgeable about the particular cuts, might think that the trade marks were being used to indicate origin.[36] This would prejudice the basic function of the trade marks and the interests of the proprietor protected by Article 5(1). It would, of course, be an infringement by the intermediary but would it also be an infringement by the first seller?

To say that, to infringe under Article 5(1)(a) or (b),[37] use of a sign must be use as a trade mark is not strictly accurate and the better position is to say that infringement requires that there are or may be some persons who will take the sign, which is identical or similar to the registered trade mark, to signify that the goods or services are those of a particular undertaking. In *Electrocoin Automatics Ltd* v *Coinworld Ltd*,[38] the trade marks 'BARX' and 'OXO' registered for gaming machines and the like could not be taken by reasonably well-informed and reasonably observant and circumspect consumers to be anything other than origin-neutral integers because of their past common use on fruit machines. The judge also held that the fact the claim for infringement failed did not necessarily provide justification for a finding of invalidity.

35 *See* the tenth recital to the Directive.

36 Under the Trade Marks Act 1994 s 103(2) 'use' includes use other than by graphic representation and will, therefore, include spoken use.

37 Use of an identical sign for identical goods or services or, where there is incomplete identity of the sign or the goods or services, use resulting in a likelihood of confusion.

38 [2005] FSR 7.

A company providing search engine facilities on the internet does not itself use a trade mark where persons using the search engine enter the trade mark to carry out a search. In *Wilson* v *Yahoo! UK Ltd*,[39] the claimant was the proprietor of the Community trade mark 'MR SPICY' used for certain types of food and provision of such foods. He alleged infringement of his trade mark by Yahoo! as entering Mr Spicy in the search engine would direct them to Sainsbury's and Pricegrabber's websites. It was held that the trade mark was not used by Yahoo! but was used by the browsers entering 'Mr Spicy' in the search engine.[40]

Article 5(1)(a) – identical sign, identical goods or services

The use in the course of trade, without the consent of the proprietor, of a sign which is identical to the registered trade mark in relation to goods or services identical to those for which the trade mark is registered, infringes. Nothing else is required such as proof of a likelihood of confusion or unfair advantage of or detriment to the registered trade mark. In that sense liability can be described as absolute though subject to the limitations on the effect of trade marks and other defences. The state of mind of the infringer is of no relevance to a finding of infringement and there is no statutory provision limiting an award of damages in a case of 'innocent' infringement.

In relation to infringement under Article 5(1)(a), the use should be such as to impact on the functioning of the registered trade, in particular, its essential function of guaranteeing to consumers the origin of goods. In Case C-48/05 *Adam Opel AG* v *Autec AG*,[41] the claimant was the well-known manufacturer of motor cars. It objected to the use of its Opel trade mark, registered for motor vehicles and toys, on remote control scale model cars of the claimant's Opel Astra V8 Coupe manufactured by the defendant. The Court of Justice ruled that the use in question could infringe under Article 5(1)(a) if the use affects or is likely to affect the *functions* of the trade mark[42] as a trade mark registered for toys. Although a likelihood of confusion is not expressly required for infringement under Article 5(1)(a), it is presumed under the TRIPs Agreement,[43] this decision suggests that an absence of confusion as to origin could mean that the defendant escapes. This could be the case where consumers do not think that the defendant's goods originate from the trade mark proprietor or his licensee. This could be the case in relation to scale models of motor vehicles. In other words, the use of the sign by the defendant is, at least arguably, not *use as a trade mark*.

There are issues with the Court of Justice's ruling in this and other cases. The European Commission has suggested that the Court reconsider infringement under Article 5(1)(a) as it considers that it should only apply where the function of a trade mark as an indication of origin is affected. The other functions may be relevant to infringement under Article 5(2) (unfair advantage or detriment to distinctive character or repute).

Where a sign is identical to the trade mark and the goods or services are also identical, a likelihood of confusion is presumed. This presumption is stated in Article 16(1) of the TRIPs Agreement. If it can be shown that there is no confusion, there will be no infringement, for example, because the trade mark is not being used in a trade mark sense, but to describe the characteristics of the goods or services and the customer is not deceived as to origin as he realises the sense in which the trade mark is being used. The basic function of the trade mark which Article 5 seeks to protect is not compromised.[44]

The Court of Justice has given guidance on whether a sign is identical to a registered trade mark in Case C-342/97 *Lloyd Schuhfabrik Meyer & Co GmbH* v *Klijsen Handel BV*[45] and Case C-291/00 *LTJ Diffusion SA* v *Sadas Vertbaudet SA*,[46] as discussed in the previous chapter. In summary, those cases require that the investigation is carried out from the perspective of the average consumer who is reasonably well informed, reasonably observant and circumspect. As the average consumer does not usually have an opportunity to make

39 [2008] ETMR 33.

40 There was no evidence to show that 'Mr Spicy' was a sponsored phrase although it appears that 'spicy' was.

41 [2007] ECR I-1017. The Court's ruling in relation to Article 5(2) is discussed later.

42 The primary function is that of operating as a 'badge of origin' but other functions include communication, investment and advertising: Case C-87/07 *L'Oréal SA* v *Bellure NV* [2009] ECR I-5185.

43 Article 16(1) of the TRIPs Agreement states that a likelihood of confusion is presumed in a double-identity case.

44 Case C-2/00 *Holterhöff* v *Freiesleben* [2002] ECR I-4187, discussed above.

45 [1999] ECR I-3819.

46 [2003] ECR I-2799.

a direct comparison of the sign and the trade mark and carries an imperfect picture of them in his mind, it is the overall impression that is important. Furthermore, the level of attention of the average consumer will vary depending on the category of goods or services in question.

A sign will be identical to a trade mark where it reproduces all its elements without modification or addition or where, as a whole, the differences are so insignificant as to go unnoticed by the average consumer. However, a strict interpretation must be taken, bearing in mind the protection of trade marks where the sign is similar for identical goods or services, where a likelihood of confusion exists under Article 5(1)(b).

We have seen that a stylised word may be deemed to be identical to the same word in type form and the addition of another word[47] or suffix may not prevent the sign being judged to be identical.[48] In relation to goods and services being considered identical, overlapping specifications of goods or services might be considered identical even though not coextensive[49] and the service of placing job advertisements was not identical to a recruitment agency service.[50]

Initial interest confusion occurs prior to the purchase of goods or services, typically in relation to advertisements. In *Och-Ziff Management Europe Ltd v Och Capital LLP*,[51] Arnold J held that such confusion is relevant to the question as to whether there is a likelihood of confusion. This is so even if, at the point of sale, the confusion is dispelled. This is often known as 'bait and switch'.[52] The defendant deliberately uses the claimant's registered trade mark as bait to attract a customer's attention and then uses the opportunity to switch the customer's buying intention to his own goods or services.[53] It applies particularly to 'double-identity' types of cases (identical mark/identical goods or services) but is not so limited.

Article 5(1)(b) – incomplete identity of mark and goods or services

For infringement under Article 5(1)(b), where the sign is identical or similar to the registered trade mark and is used for identical or similar goods or services, a likelihood of confusion on the part of the public, which includes a likelihood of association, is required. Consequently, the more distinctive a trade mark is, the stronger will be the protection it enjoys where a likelihood of confusion is relevant to infringement. In Case C-39/97 *Canon Kabushiki Kaisha v Metro-Goldwyn-Mayer Inc*,[54] the Court of Justice said (at para 18) that where protection depends on a likelihood of confusion:

> . . . marks with a highly distinctive character, either *per se* or because of the reputation they possess on the market, enjoy broader protection than marks with a less distinctive character.

Conversely, where the mark is weak, for example, because is contains a descriptive element, the average consumer is more likely to consider that the descriptive element was not being used to identify the goods in question.[55] Where a composite mark includes an earlier mark, there could be a likelihood of confusion if the earlier mark had an independent distinctive role but, otherwise, a likelihood of confusion would not always follow automatically.[56]

Apart from the distinctiveness of the registered trade mark, the degree of similarity will also be an issue and the greater the similarity of the sign and the trade mark and the goods or services, the easier it will be to find infringement.

As with Article 4(1)(b), the equivalent provision on infringement appears to apply also where the sign and the trade mark are identical and the goods or services are also identical. Of course, where this is the case, there is infringement under Article 5(1)(a) and there is no need to show a likelihood of confusion. If there is any doubt as to whether the sign and the trade mark are identical or the goods or services are identical, one would expect both provisions to be pleaded in an infringement action.

47 Case C-291/00 *LTJ Diffusion SA v Sadas Vertbaudet SA* [2003] ECR I-2799.

48 *Decon Laboratories Ltd v Fred Baker Scientific Ltd* [2001] RPC 17.

49 *GALILEO Trade Mark* [2005] RPC 22.

50 *Reed Executive plc v Reed Business Information Ltd* [2004] RPC 40.

51 [2011] FSR 11.

52 An example from the US is *Grotian, Helferrich, Schultz v Steinway & Sons* 523 F.2d 1331 (2nd Cir, 1975). The sale of Grotian-Steinweg pianos was objected to by Steinway & Sons. Heinrich Steinweg made pianos in Germany and, on immigrating to New York, changed his name to Steinway ('weg' in German means 'way' or 'path').

53 See the example ('Ash' and 'Birch') in the section on trade marks and the internet later in this chapter at p 800.

54 [1998] ECR I-5507.

55 *Digipos Store Solutions Group Ltd v Digi International Inc* [2008] RPC 24.

56 *Rousselon Freres et Cie v Horwood Homewares Ltd* [2008] RPC 30.

As with the equivalent ground for refusal under Article 4(1)(b), the requirement for '. . . a likelihood of confusion on the part of the public, which includes a likelihood of association between the sign and the trade mark', has been interpreted as meaning that a mere association in the minds of the public, *per se*, is not enough. There is no presumption of a likelihood of confusion resulting from a likelihood of association in a strict sense: Case C-425/98 *Marca Mode CV* v *Adidas AG*,[57] following Case C-251/95 *Sabel BV* v *Puma AG, Rudolf Dassler Sport*.[58] Non-origin association, where consumers are not mistaken about the origin of the goods to which the sign has been applied, is not sufficient on its own to give rise to a likelihood of confusion. That is not to say that it can never result in a likelihood of confusion and a likelihood of association may do this if the trade mark is particularly distinctive or because of its reputation and, as said in *Sabel*, the sign and the trade mark has a similar semantic content.

Both *Sabel* v *Puma* and *Canon* v *Metro-Goldwyn-Mayer* provide important guidance on the question of whether a likelihood of confusion exists. The average consumer, who perceives the trade mark as a whole and who does not break it down into its constituent parts, makes a global appreciation of the visual, aural or conceptual similarity of the marks based on the overall impression given by them, bearing in mind their distinctive and dominant components. The more distinctive the mark, the greater will be the likelihood of confusion. There is some interdependence between the sign and the trade mark and the goods or services so that the greater the similarity of the sign and the trade mark, the lesser the similarity of the goods or services would need to be to find infringement and *vice versa*. The type of confusion required is confusion as to origin; in other words, the average consumer would think the goods or services came from the same or economically linked undertakings.[59]

Where a trade mark had a descriptive phonetic equivalent, there was a danger in applying a principle that the mark lacked distinctive character. In *Hasbro Inc* v *123 Nahrmittel GmbH*,[60] the claimant was proprietor of the 'PLAY-DOH' trade mark. The defendant made edible dough described as 'YUMMY DOUGH'. It was described on its packaging as the 'edible play dough'. In holding that the claimant's trade mark was valid and infringed under Article 5(1)(b), Floyd J said that the aural similarity was but one factor to be taken into account in the assessment of a likelihood of confusion. The PLAY-DOH marks had achieved the status of household names and it was wrong to consider that the distinctiveness of the marks was simply due to the three letters 'DOH' or the absence of UG in the word. On seeing EDIBLE PLAY DOUGH, a significant class of consumers, with perfect or imperfect recollections, would think of the PLAY-DOH mark. That class of customers, with an imperfect recollection of the spelling, would think the defendant's sign referred to an edible version of PLAY-DOH.

It would appear that the possibility that there will be some persons who may be confused as to origin is sufficient to find a likelihood of confusion even though the persons buying goods to which a trade mark has been applied are not confused: for example, because the goods are sold under a disclaimer.[61] There may even be a likelihood of confusion without any evidence of actual confusion. It may be that confusion has not come to light. In *Julius Sämaan Ltd* v *Tetrosyl Ltd*,[62] involving an allegation of infringement of the shape of a fir tree used for air fresheners often seen hanging from car rear view mirrors, Kitchen J said that he did not consider the absence of evidence to be determinative though it may be highly material. Nevertheless, Kitchen J held that the trade mark was infringed. He considered that there was a marked similarity between the trade mark and the offending sign when stripped of their packaging.[63] In *Lewis* v *Client Connection Ltd*,[64] Norris J also noted that it is not essential that there is proof of actual confusion, the question being whether there is a likelihood of confusion. Evidence of actual confusion may simply support the conclusion that there is a likelihood of confusion.[65]

57 [2000] ECR I-4861.

58 [1997] ECR I-6191. *Sabel* was concerned with Article 4(1)(b) but the Court of Justice in *Marca Mode* accepted that the same interpretation must also apply to Article 5(1)(b).

59 Other Court of Justice cases on likelihood of confusion, discussed in Chapter 20, *see* pp. 740–2, include Case C-342/97 *Lloyd Schuhfabrik Meyer & Co GmbH* v *Klisjen Handel BV* [1999] ECR I-3819 and Case C-120/04 *Medion AG* v *Thomson Multimedia Sales Germany & Austria GmbH*, 6 October 2005.

60 [2011] FSR 21.

61 Case C-206/01 *Arsenal Football Club plc* v *Matthew Reed* [2002] ECR I-10273.

62 [2006] FSR 42.

63 *See also, D Jacobson & Sons Ltd* v *Globe Ltd* [2008] FSR 21.

64 [2011] EWHC 1627 (Ch). The claimant, Martin Lewis had the trade mark 'Money Saving Expert' for advisory services relating to financial matters provided via an internet website. The defendant carried on business under the name 'Money Claiming Expert'.

65 *Och-Ziff Management Europe Ltd* v *Och Capital LLP* [2011] FSR 11.

Bearing in mind the Court of Justice rulings above, there follows some discussion of cases in the UK where the courts have had to consider the equivalent provision under the Trade Marks Act 1994, s 10(2). These cases usefully supplement the broad principles set out in the Court of Justice rulings.

Similar sign

Account may be taken of colourable alternatives and the mark when spoken. In *Sir Terence Orby Conran* v *Mean Fiddler Holdings Ltd*[66] the claimant was registered proprietor of the trade mark 'Zinc' under the class of planning design and interior design of restaurants, cafes, bistros and wine bars, and he planned to open a series of restaurants in London and Glasgow, under the name 'Zinc Bar'. The defendant opened a wine bar in Kilburn, London calling it 'Zincbar', using the word 'ZINCBAR' on the right-hand side of the sign on the bar's fascia and 'Zn', the chemical symbol for zinc, on the left-hand side.

Walker J granted summary judgment. He considered trade mark infringement to be obvious, and the same applied to the alternatives suggested by the defendant, 'ZN', 'Sinc' or 'Sync' that were sufficiently colourably similar. Evidence of confusion included a would-be customer of the claimant who was given the number of the defendant's bar in Kilburn.

A degree of similarity is permissible provided the sign is not confusingly similar to the trade mark. After all, a likelihood of confusion is required; mere similarity is not sufficient *per se*. In *European Ltd* v *Economist Newspaper Ltd*,[67] the claimant published a weekly newspaper under the masthead incorporating the word 'European'. The masthead was a registered trade mark, but the claimant had disclaimed any monopoly in the word 'European'. The defendant's masthead included the phrase 'The European Voice'. The Court of Appeal confirmed the decision at first instance, dismissing the claimant's claim for trade mark infringement. An aural comparison was eschewed by the court. The marks were visually different but phonetically similar and any aural comparison would be to disregard the distinctive features of the claimant's mark that could be seen but not heard. The claimant's mark comprised two words in upper case though with 'THE' in a smaller font and with a dove holding a copy of the newspaper and part of the globe superimposed on the letter 'O' of 'EUROPEAN'. The defendant's masthead was in lower case type without a dove or globe, but with a star over the 'i' of 'Voice'.

The concept of imperfect recollection is recognised by the Court of Justice and may be used in determining whether there exists a likelihood of confusion and may also be relevant whether the sign is similar to the registered trade mark. In *LIFESYSTEMS Trade Mark*,[68] it was held that 'LIFESYSTEMS' was not sufficiently similar to 'LIFESTREAM' to result in confusion even allowing for imperfect recollection. This was so even taking account of the fact that the words were of similar length as they were sufficiently different, visually and phonetically.

Similar goods or services

In determining whether goods are similar, Jacob J in *British Sugar plc* v *James Robertson & Sons Ltd*[69] suggested a test derived from the old test for whether goods were of the same description used under the 1938 Act.[70] He suggested the following factors were relevant:

(a) the respective uses of the respective goods or services;
(b) the respective users of the respective goods or services;
(c) the physical nature of the goods or acts of service;
(d) the respective trade channels through which the goods or services reach the market;
(e) in the case of self-service consumer items, where in practice they are respectively found or likely to be found in supermarkets and in particular whether they are, or are likely to be, found on the same or different shelves;

66 [1997] FSR 856.

67 [1998] FSR 283.

68 [1999] RPC 851. This was an opposition case.

69 [1996] RPC 281.

70 Romer J in *Jellinek's Application* (1946) 63 RPC 59, approved by the House of Lords in *DAIQUIRI RUM Trade Mark* [1969] RPC 600.

785

(f) the extent to which the respective goods or services are competitive; this inquiry may take into account how those in trade classify goods – for example, whether market research companies, which of course act for industry, put the goods or services in the same or different sectors.

In *British Sugar* v *Robertson*, Jacob J, applying the above test, found that the defendant's sweet spread 'Robertson's Toffee Treat' was not similar to 'dessert sauces and syrups' for which the claimant's registered trade mark, 'TREAT', was registered. Jacob J's test is very useful and there is no Court of Justice ruling providing such detail. However, the Court of Justice rightly focuses upon questions of likelihood of confusion and there is a danger of becoming swamped by the detail and losing sight of the question posed by the statutory provision. This is simply whether, because of the identity or similarity of the sign and the trade mark and the identity or similarity of the goods or services, there exists a likelihood of confusion as to the origin of the goods or services on the part of the public. Is the public likely to think that the goods or services come from the same or economically linked undertakings?

A passing similarity is not enough; a mere finding of similarity does not automatically lead to a conclusion of infringement. Even if, as a matter of fact, it is held that the goods or services are similar, the claimant must still adduce evidence that such similarity is the cause of a likelihood of confusion.[71] It is submitted that it was intended that only a relatively close connection would do. Similarity and likelihood of confusion are inexorably linked and the greater the divergence between the goods or services, the more difficult it will be to prove a likelihood of confusion.[72] The only proviso to this is that the answer will also be governed by the width of the specification of goods or services for which the trade mark is registered. However, if the specification is very wide, this may leave the mark vulnerable to a counterclaim for partial revocation on the basis of non-use.

It seems that, even if there is substantial dissimilarity between the defendant's goods or services and those for which the claimant's trade mark is registered, a finding of infringement under s 10(2) may still be possible. In *Pfizer Ltd* v *Eurofood Link (UK) Ltd*[73] Simon Thorley QC, as deputy judge of the High Court, said (at para 29):

> . . . there may be substantial dissimilarity between the goods in question and yet proof of confusion. If the court is satisfied as to confusion then the relief is granted notwithstanding the measure of dissimilarity between the goods.

However, this must be treated with some caution as the wording of the Act and the Directive explicitly requires that similarity of goods and confusion are causally linked. If the goods or services are not similar then s 10(2) is not appropriate (though s 10(3), equivalent to Article 5(2) of the Directive, may well be).[74]

The makers of the popular 'Baywatch' television series were not pleased when someone started transmitting encrypted 'adult films' under the name 'Babewatch'. In *Baywatch Production Co Inc* v *Home Video Channel*,[75] it was held, *inter alia*, that the goods or services were not similar. The claimant had registrations for 'BAYWATCH' against video discs and tapes in Class 9 and had other registrations, but none that covered television programmes or broadcasting. It was also held that the signs were not similar and there was no satisfactory evidence of confusion. This must be contrasted with *NAD Electronics Inc* v *NAD Computer Systems Ltd*[76] in which the claimant had registered the trade mark 'NAD' for, *inter alia*, compact disc players. The claimant made high quality sound systems. The defendant used the word 'NAD' on his computer systems and this was held to infringe. Account was taken of the fact that computer technology has evolved and many computer systems come complete with CDROM drives and have speakers and can play music compact discs as well as read CDROM discs.

The fact that services relate to the same type of vocation or profession is not sufficient to find that they are similar. For example, providing dental services to the public is not

71 In *LIFESYSTEMS Trade Mark* [1999] RPC 851, an opposition case, Jacob J's test for similarity of goods was applied and it was held that electronic devices for attracting and killing insects were not similar to aromatherapy diffusing apparatus. In any case, the opponent to registration failed to adduce independent evidence of confusion.

72 *Pfizer Ltd* v *Eurofood Link (UK) Ltd* [2001] FSR 3. See also Case C-39/97 *Canon Kabushiki Kaisha* v *Metro Goldwyn Mayer Inc* [1998] ECR I-5507.

73 [2001] FSR 3.

74 In his judgment Simon Thorley QC did go on to say '. . . the public are not readily going to be confused between (say) ball bearings and perfumes no matter how similar the trade marks'.

75 [1997] FSR 22.

76 [1997] FSR 380.

77 *Harding* v *Smilecare Ltd* [2002] FSR 37.

similar to the provision of financial services to dentists.[77] In such cases, it would very difficult, if not impossible, to show that there was any likelihood of confusion on the part of the public even if such services were held to be similar.

Article 5(2) – unfair advantage or detriment to distinctive character or repute

Article 5(2) provides that Member States may '. . . provide that the proprietor shall be entitled to prevent third parties not having his consent from using in the course of trade any sign which is identical to, or similar to, the trade mark in relation to goods or services which are *not similar* to those for which the trade mark is registered, where the latter has a reputation in the Member State and where use of the sign without due cause takes unfair advantage of, or is detrimental to, the distinctive character or repute of the trade mark' (emphasis added). The UK has taken advantage of this optional further protection (the Trade Marks Act 1994 s 10(3)). The greater the distinctive character and repute of a trade mark, the easier it will be to find that detriment has been caused to it. This was observed by the Court of Justice in Case C-375/97 *General Motors Corp* v *Yplon SA*.[78]

78 [1999] ECR I-5421.

Infringement under Article 5(2) can be seen as being made up of three different, though possibly overlapping forms, being:

- 'free-riding on the coat tails' of the trade marks reputation (unfair advantage);
- blurring the distinctiveness of the trade mark (detriment to distinctive character); and
- tarnishing the reputation of the trade mark (detriment to reputation).[79]

79 In *Lewis* v *Client Connection Ltd* [2011] EWHC 1627 (Ch) (an application for summary judgment) although the judge did not need to make a definite finding on this matter, he thought it likely that the defendant, by cold-calling under its trading name 'Money Claiming Expert' was free-riding on the coat tails of the claimants 'Money Saving Expert' trade mark in addition to tarnishing the reputation of that mark.

80 In *Baywatch Production Co Inc* v *Home Video Channel* [1997] FSR 22 it was held, erroneously, that s 10(3) requires a likelihood of confusion.

81 [2005] FSR 30.

82 The case was overturned on appeal to the South African Constitutional Court: *South African Breweries International (Finance) BV* v *Laugh It Off Promotions CC* (unreported) 25 May 2005.

83 *Whirlpool Corp* v *Kenwood Ltd* [2010] RPC 2. The trade mark was the shape of a food mixer having a 'retro-style'. The defendant began to market a food mixer with a similar shape.

The rationale for Article 5(2) provision is that it gives protection where the use of a sign takes advantage of a trade mark with a reputation or causes damage to a trade mark, for example, by diluting or blurring its distinctive character or by tarnishing or denigrating it. The protection does not depend on any likelihood of confusion as to origin.[80] The provision could apply where another undertaking uses someone else's well-known trade mark for different goods or services, hoping to capture some of the goodwill attaching to the trade mark. It may also apply in the case of a parody of the trade mark. In *South African Breweries International (Finance) BV* v *Laugh It Off Promotions CC*,[81] the South African Supreme Court of Appeal held that not *any* detriment would do where freedom of expression is involved. This requires a balancing of the two rights, neither of which is absolute. However, a derisory parody of a trade mark will not be given protection as against the trade mark it is parodying. In that case, the defendant marketed T-shirts carrying caricatures of the claimant's trade marks used on bottles of Carling Black Label beer.[82]

The entry of a competitor into the market place is likely to have an adverse effect on the sales of goods of a particular description, especially where the trade mark proprietor had previously enjoyed a monopoly or near-monopoly. But even where the competitor uses a similar trade mark, it does not inexorably follow that there is detriment to the distinctive character of the registered trade mark.[83] Erosion of sales may be simply a result of fair competition and not due to consumers being deceived as to origin.

Another situation where this form of infringement may apply is where the trade mark was used by someone else in relation to substandard or defective goods or goods or services which some members of the public would find distasteful. The reason for limiting the provision to use of the offending sign on goods or services not similar to those for which the trade mark was registered was probably because it was felt that the use with identical or similar goods or services would be caught by Article 5(1)(a) or (b). Nobody seems to have contemplated that the forms of damage to a trade mark covered by Article 5(2) could be caused in relation to similar goods or services where persons were not likely to be confused as to the origin of the goods or services. Article 16(1) of the TRIPs Agreement is similar to Article 5(2) of the Directive and also states that the goods or services should be 'not similar'.

This unnecessary limitation to the scope of Article 5(2) came up for consideration by the Court of Justice in Case C-292/00 *Davidoff & Cie SA* v *Gofkid Ltd*,[84] where the court said that Article 5(2) should not be interpreted solely on the basis of its wording but account should be taken of the scheme and objectives of the system of which it was part. That being so, the protection afforded to trade marks having a reputation should not be less protection where used for identical or similar goods or services than where they were used for goods or services that were not similar. This case was soon followed by Case C-408/01 *Adidas-Salomon AG* v *Fitnessworld Trading Ltd*,[85] confirming that the provision also applied where the goods and services were identical or similar. Although no likelihood of confusion was necessary, there must be an association or link between the sign and the trade mark in the mind of the public.[86] For example, the use of the sign conjures up the trade mark even though consumers might not think that the goods or services came from the same or economically linked undertakings.

The Trade Marks Act 1994 was amended to remove a reference that the goods or services had to be not similar under s 10(3) by the Trade Marks (Proof of Use etc.) Regulations 2004.[87]

The test under Article 5(2) can be broken down into the separate requirements that must be satisfied as follows:

(a) The claimant's trade mark must be found to have a reputation in the UK.
(b) Identity with or similarity to the trade mark of repute must be shown.
(c) The use of the sign complained of must take an unfair advantage of or cause detriment to the distinctive character or repute of the claimant's trade mark.
(d) The use of the sign complained of must be without due cause.
(e) The public should believe that there is an association between the defendant's goods or services and the claimant.[88]

Unfair advantage may result from the use of the sign being parasitic of the trade mark of repute: that it 'rides on its back' or captures part of its goodwill. Detriment may come about in two ways, blurring or tarnishing. Blurring is where the use of the sign causes erosion or dilution of the distinctive character of the mark, making it less distinctive such as in extended passing off as in *Taittinger SA* v *Allbev Ltd*.[89] Although in *Premier Brands UK Ltd* v *Typhoon Europe Ltd*[90] Neuberger J said that dilution is a useful concept when considering s 10(3),[91] he stressed that not in every case where dilution is established will there be an infringement; nor will the absence of dilution negate a finding of infringement. Tarnishing may occur where the use of the sign is such as to imbue the trade mark of repute with negative, unpleasant or distasteful nuances, making it less attractive. An example is the use of VISA for condoms, *CA Sheimer (M) Sdn Bhd's Trade Mark Application*.[92]

In Case C-87/07 *L'Oréal SA* v *Bellure NV*,[93] the defendant sold perfumes, which were imitations of those of the claimant ('smell-alikes'), in bottles and packaging reminiscent of the claimant's trade marks but it did not appear that there was any likelihood of confusion as the defendant's perfumes were sold under quite different names to those used by the claimant. Following a reference from the Court of Appeal, the Court of Justice ruled that, for an unfair advantage to exist for the purposes of Article 5(2), there is no need to show a likelihood of confusion. Nor is it necessary to show detriment to the distinctive character or repute of the well-known mark or, indeed, to the proprietor. The court also ruled that an advantage was unfair where a defendant seeks to ride on the coat-tails of the mark to benefit from the power of attraction, reputation and prestige and to exploit, without financial compensation, the marketing effort of the proprietor in creating and maintaining the trade mark's image.

This decision generated a great deal of criticism from academic writers and also from Jacob LJ in the Court of Appeal in *L'Oréal SA* v *Bellure NV*,[94] applying the Court of Justice's

84 [2003] ECR I-389.

85 [2003] ECR I-12537.

86 The equivalent provision in the TRIPs Agreement, Article 16(3), expressly mentions the need for the use of the sign to indicate a connection between the goods or services and the owner of the registered trade mark.

87 SI 2004/946.

88 *See* Pumfrey J in *DaimlerChrysler AG* v *Javid Alavi (t/a MERC)* [2001] RPC 42 at para 88. The need for association or a link was confirmed in Case C-408/01 *Adidas-Salomon AG* v *Fitnessworld Trading Ltd* [2003] ECR I-12537.

89 [1993] FSR 641, discussed in Chapter 23.

90 [2000] FSR 767. Neither blurring nor tarnishing was found in this case.

91 US trade mark law specifically provides for dilution as a form of infringement: Lanham Act 1945 s 145.

92 [2000] RPC 484. This was an opposition case. *See* also *Lucas Bols* v *Colgate-Palmolive* (1976) 7 IIC 420 where it was held that 'CLAERYN', a registered trade mark for a Dutch gin, was infringed by the use of 'KLAREIN' for a detergent. Both words have the same pronunciation in Dutch.

93 [2009] ECR I-5185. Another aspect of this case concerned comparative advertising and is discussed *infra*.

94 [2010] RPC 23.

ruling. It means that a trader cannot say 'My product is the same as X (the trade mark) but is half the price' even if that statement is true. Jacob LJ said (at paras 6 to 9):

6   The problem, stated at its most general, is simple. Does trade mark law prevent the defendants from telling the truth? Even though their perfumes are lawful and do smell like the corresponding famous brands, does trade mark law nonetheless muzzle the defendants so that they cannot say so?

7   I have come to the conclusion that the ECJ's ruling is that the defendants are indeed muzzled. My duty as a national judge is to follow EU law as interpreted by the ECJ. I think, with regret, that the answers we have received from the ECJ require us so to hold . . . I wish to say why I regret those answers.

8   My own strong predilection, free from the opinion of the ECJ, would be to hold that trade mark law did not prevent traders from making honest statements about their products where those products are themselves lawful.

9   I have a number of reasons for that predilection. First and most generally is that I am in favour of free speech – and most particularly where someone wishes to tell the truth. There is no good reason to dilute the predilection in cases where the speaker's motive for telling the truth is his own commercial gain. Truth in the market place matters – even if it does not attract quite the strong emotions as the right of a journalist or politician to speak the truth.

There is some force in Jacob LJ's view. Indeed, the Court of Justice ruling puts all forms of comparative advertising into doubt even though it is expressly permitted if 'fair' under the misleading advertising Directive, discussed later.

The European Commission has asked the Court of Justice to reconsider a number of its previous rulings, including *L'Oréal* v *Bellure*, on the scope of Article 5(1)(a) and 5(2). The opportunity to do so arose in Case C-323/09 *Interflora Inc* v *Marks and Spencer plc* (a case of keywords used by advertisers in search engines – see later in the section on trade mark infringement and the internet). The Advocate General, in his Opinion,[95] did not address these issues as he did not consider them relevant to the particular facts of the case. He did say, however, that he thought the difficulty was with the drafting of Article 5 of the Directive.

In *Hasbro Inc* v *123 Nahrmittel GmbH*,[96] Floyd J followed the Court of Justice ruling in *L'Oréal* v *Bellure* in holding that the defendant infringed the 'PLAY-DOH' trade mark. By its use of 'edible play dough', even absent a risk of confusion, this would bring to mind the trade mark for a significant class of consumers. Although Floyd J found that there was a risk of confusion as to origin, he went on to say that, if he was wrong on that point, the defendant's use would still infringe as it took unfair advantage of the goodwill attached to the claimant's trade mark.[97]

In a case on the provision equivalent to Article 5(2) on registrability, Case C-252/07 *Intel Corporation Inc* v *CPM United Kingdom Ltd*,[98] the Court of Justice considered the case where a trade mark is unique and has a huge reputation, the trade mark in question being 'INTEL' as used for computers and computer-related goods and services. The court ruled, *inter alia*, that, even though the earlier trade mark is unique and has a huge reputation, it is still a question of fact for the trial court to decide as to whether there exists a link within the meaning of *Adidas-Salomon*. Furthermore, even if such a link is established this alone does not establish unfair advantage or detriment to the repute or distinctive character of the earlier trade mark with a reputation. On the other hand, uniqueness is not a precursor to a finding or unfair advantage or detriment and even a first use of the later mark may suffice to establish detriment to distinctive character. The court also ruled that there must be evidence of a change (or serious likelihood of a change) in economic behaviour on the part of the average consumer of the *goods or services for which the earlier mark was registered* for a finding of detriment to the distinctive character of the earlier mark. The same principles ought to apply to infringement as the court also noted that the wording of Article

95 24 March 2011.

96 [2011] FSR 21.

97 Infringement was found also under Article 5(1)(b) though not under Article 5(1)(a).

98 [2008] ECR I-8823.

4(4)(a) and Article 5(2) was essentially identical and designed to give trade marks with a reputation the same protection.

The use of the sign alleged to infringe must be 'without due cause'. This phrase governs not just the use of the sign but is also relevant in the context of unfair advantage or detriment. The defendant has to show any unfair advantage or detriment are not without due cause.[99] Examples of due cause may be where the defendant can point to an earlier right or where he is using his own name or that of a predecessor. However, under Article 6 there are specific limitations to the effects of a trade mark that might apply in such situations. The meaning and purpose of the phrase is not entirely clear and may eventually need clarification from the Court of Justice. According to Neuberger J in *Premier Brands UK Ltd v Typhoon Europe Ltd*,[100] the phrase 'without due cause' does not mean an absence of 'good faith' or that the use is contrary to 'good honest commercial reasons'. Furthermore, the test is an objective one and should not take into account either the intention of the defendant or his subconscious desires. In *Premier Brands*, Neuberger J also suggested that the burden of proving whether the use is not without due cause lies on the alleged infringer as the words act as an exception rather than an element to be proved by the claimant.

Where a trade mark is well known when used for the goods most associated with the proprietor's main business but is also registered for other goods, use by a third party of the sign may infringe. In Case C-48/05 *Adam Opel AG v Autec AG*,[101] the claimant was the well-known manufacturer of motor cars. It objected to the use of its Opel trade mark, registered for motor vehicles and toys, on remote control scale model cars manufactured by the defendant. The Court of Justice ruled that such use could constitute a use which the proprietor was entitled to prevent, providing if, without due cause, the use of the sign took unfair advantage of, or is detrimental to, the distinctive character or repute of the trade mark as registered for *motor vehicles*.[102] Of course, when the ruling is applied, the referring court may find as a matter of fact that the use is not without due cause or that it neither takes unfair advantage of nor is detrimental to the trade mark in question.

Saving under Article 5(4)

Article 5(4) contains a saving so that a sign, which would otherwise be caught under Article 5(1)(b) or (2) but could not be prohibited in a Member State before the Directive entered into force, can continue to be used without being liable to be prevented by the trade mark proprietor. This finds expression in para 4(2) of Schedule 3 to the Trade Marks Act 1994 which states that it is not an infringement of an existing registered mark[103] or a registered trade mark with the same or substantially the same distinctive elements registered for the same goods or services to continue any use which did not infringe under the old law.

Article 5(5) – protection against use other than for the purposes of distinguishing goods or services

Article 5(5) allows Member States to preserve protection against the use of a sign other than for the purposes of distinguishing goods or services in cases where the sign without due cause takes unfair advantage of, or is detrimental to, the distinctive character or the repute of the trade mark. Unlike the other forms of infringement under Article 5, there is no express requirement that the use of the sign has to be in the course of trade. It is conceivable that a sign could be used, though not in the course of trade, in such a way as it harmed the trade mark: for example, by a published claim that the goods sold under the trade mark are defective.[104] However, it could be argued that damaging use would be without due cause in any case.

99 *Premier Brands UK Ltd* v *Typhoon Europe Ltd* [2000] FSR 767 at 791.

100 [2000] FSR 767 at 790.

101 [2007] ECR I-1017. It is interesting to note that the ruling on Article 5(2) was in relation to the trade mark as registered for motor vehicles, rather than toys.

102 The Court of Justice ruled that the use in question could infringe under Article 5(1)(a) if the use affects or is likely to effect the functions of the trade mark as a trade mark registered for *toys*: *see* above in relation to Article 5(1)(a).

103 An 'existing registered mark' is one registered under the 1938 Act immediately before the commencement of the 1994 Act: para 1 Schedule 3.

104 Such a claim could result in an action for malicious falsehood: *see* Chapter 23.

105 [2002] ECR I-10913.

Article 5(5) was considered by the Court of Justice in Case C-23/01 *Robelco NV* v *Robeco Groep NV*.[105] The claimant, Robeco, had a registered trade mark 'Robeco' and complained about the defendant's use of Robelco as its company and trade name. The claimant alleged infringement, *inter alia*, of the Benelux law equivalent of Article 5(5). The Court noted that the Directive did not seek full harmonisation and Article 5(5) was one of those provisions which was left to national law as it starts 'Paragraphs 1 to 4 shall not affect provisions in any Member State . . .' Therefore, where a sign is not used for the purposes of distinguishing goods or services, it is left to national law to determine the extent and nature, if any, of the protection afforded. Member States may adopt no legislation under Article 5(5) or they may, subject to such conditions as they choose, require that the sign shall be identical or similar or that there should be some other connection between them.[106]

106 Article 5(5) is silent on whether the sign must be identical to or similar to the trade mark or whether there must be some other association between them.

In the UK, the Trade Marks Act 1994, s 10(6), allows use of a registered trade mark to identify goods or services as those of the proprietor of the trade mark. There is a proviso to this. This provision is usually associated with comparative advertising providing the use of the registered trade mark does not fall within the proviso to s 10(6). As it is for Member States to lay down the conditions which apply if they choose to implement Article 5(5), we will now consider the UK law under s 10(6) in the context of comparative advertising.

Comparative advertising

107 (1934) 51 RPC 110.

Under the 1938 Act a trade mark was infringed if it was used in comparative advertising: for example, where a trader lists his products and prices alongside those of a competitor, using the competitor's trade mark. Comparative advertising was included in the 1938 Act as a result of a failure to find infringement against a comparative advertiser in *Irving's Yeastvite Ltd* v *Horsenail*.[107] The 1994 Act allows comparative advertising to the extent that s 10(6) states that nothing in the preceding provisions of s 10 shall be construed as preventing the use of a registered trade mark by any person for the purpose of identifying goods or services as those of the proprietor. However, there is a proviso to this. The use must be in accordance with honest practices in industrial or commercial matters and, if it is not, such use will infringe if, without due cause, it takes unfair advantage of, or is detrimental to, the distinctive character or repute of the trade mark. A problem with s 10(6) is that there is no direct equivalent to it in the Directive.

108 Note that, for the purposes of s 10(6), the trade mark does not have to have a reputation in the UK, unlike s 10(3).

It should be noted that s 10(6) only applies where the use would otherwise infringe under the other provisions in s 10. This means that the trade mark may be used in identical or similar form. The language in the proviso has some similarity with that in s 10(3) but this is unlikely to be relevant in respect of comparative advertising.[108] By its very nature, such advertising usually involves use of a sign identical to the registered trade mark in relation to identical goods or services. What s 10(6) saves from infringement is use in an advertisement (within the meaning of use in s 10(4)(d)) which would, but for s 10(6), infringe under s 10(1). Exceptionally, it may prevent an infringement under s 10(2) where the sign or goods or services are not identical but sufficiently similar to make comparative advertising attractive. An example is an advertisement comparing internal air fares with rail fares to the same destination. Allowing comparative advertising within reasonable parameters is by far the most controversial aspect of s 10(6); the provision is also there to save other potential technical infringements, such as where a retailer advertises goods for sale by reference to a manufacturer's trade mark. However, there are limitations to the effects of a trade mark under Article 6 of the Directive and it is arguable that s 10(6) should be repealed, as discussed later in relation to *O2 Holdings Ltd* v *Hutchinson 3G Ltd*.[109] Before this, the case law on s 10(6) is discussed.

109 [2007] RPC 16.

The meaning of the proviso was first considered by Laddie J in *Barclays Bank plc* v *RBS Advanta*,[110] in which the claimant was the proprietor of the registered trade mark 'BARCLAYCARD'. The defendant was a joint venture between the Royal Bank of Scotland and the Advanta Corp of USA, which was about to launch a credit card called 'RBS Advanta Visa Card'. It distributed letters, leaflets and brochures. The leaflets contained a list of bullet points stating '15 ways the RBS Advanta Visa Card is a better card all round', and the brochure contained tables comparing the features of the RBS card with express reference to BARCLAYCARD and its features. The claimant applied for injunctive relief alleging that its trade mark was infringed under s 10(1) (use in the course of trade of a sign identical with the trade mark in relation to identical goods or services). The defendant argued that its advertising fell within the s 10(6) defence.

In refusing to grant an injunction, Laddie J said that the purpose of s 10(6) was to allow comparative advertising as long as it was honest. The burden was on the proprietor to show that one of the factors in the proviso to s 10(6) applied: that is, that the use was not in accordance with honest practices in industrial or commercial matters, or that it took unfair advantage of, or was detrimental to, the distinctive character or repute of the trade mark. He said that the question as to whether the use of the trade mark was in accordance with honest practices was an objective test, being whether it was considered honest by members of a reasonable audience. He also accepted that an amount of hyperbole was to be expected in much advertising copy. A reasonable audience would appreciate that an advertiser would select the most favourable features and might not show other features which showed his competitor's product to best effect. The amount of hyperbole which is acceptable will depend on the nature of the goods, and Laddie J contrasted second-hand cars with powerful medicines. In the latter case, to be in accordance with honest practices, comparative advertising should be more frank and forthright with much less scope for selecting features to show the advertiser's product in a more favourable light.

Laddie J in *Barclays*, stressed the importance of the phrase 'in accordance with honest practices' and suggested that the second part of the proviso, 'taking unfair advantage of, or being detrimental to, the distinctive character or repute of the trade mark' would add nothing of significance in the majority of cases. Jacob J agreed with this (and the basic test of whether the advertising was objectively misleading to a substantial proportion of a reasonable audience) in *Vodafone Group plc* v *Orange Personal Communications Services Ltd*.[111] In that case, which concerned an advertisement suggesting an average saving of £20 per month by switching to the defendant's mobile telephone network, Jacob J accepted that persons would generally expect some elasticity of price and usage. That is, a reasonable audience would realise that not everyone would save £20 a month and that fewer calls are generally made on a more expensive tariff.

Most cases on s 10(6) will involve comparisons of cost, specification or performance. As members of the public are far more knowledgeable and circumspect than in the past, a certain amount of 'knockabout' between competitors is to be expected and is acceptable provided it does not step beyond a particular standard. In terms of commercial or industrial activity, an honest practice is one which does not step outside accepted and common practice, bearing in mind that advertisers are not setting out to provide a balanced and objective description of their product or service. They are out to sell by making theirs look better than the rest, whether in terms of value for money, performance, ease of use, durability, etc. A certain amount of advertising puff is to be expected.

Acceptable comparative advertising can be selective. It can even skew features or prices providing sufficient information is given to make this clear or to allow readers of the advertisement the opportunity to obtain the full picture. However, what it cannot do is to present, as fact, information which the advertiser knows to be false. This probably extends to information which is false and the advertiser, whilst not having actual

110 [1996] RPC 307.

111 [1997] FSR 34.

knowledge of its falsity, has constructive knowledge: that is, that a prudent trader would have suspected that the information might be false and would have taken steps to check it. In *Cable & Wireless plc v British Telecommunications plc*,[112] it was said that a trader who made a statement knowing it to be false could not be said to be acting in accordance with honest practices. The test was an objective one and was, per Jacob J (at 391):

> . . . whether a reasonable trader could honestly have made the statements he made based on the information that he had.

Jacob J went on to say that a trader could have a defence if the information turned out to be untrue, providing he stopped once he discovered the truth. Again, however, this has to be based on an objective approach, rather than whether the trader himself could be regarded as honest. The use of misleading information which has been 'doctored' or not checked when it would be reasonable to do so is likely to infringe and will not be saved by s 10(6).[113]

In *British Airways plc v Ryanair Ltd*,[114] the defendant ran some advertisements suggesting that the claimant's fares were more expensive. The claimant's registered trade marks included 'BA' registered in respect of services including air travel services. One advertisement which contained the heading 'EXPENSIVE BA. . . . DS!' was withdrawn after a complaint to the Advertising Standards Authority. However, the fact that an advertisement was offensive did not, *per se*, mean that it was caught by the proviso to s 10(6). A second advertisement was headed 'Expensive BA' and contained price comparisons for fares, which the claimant alleged were misleading. Jacob J rejected this, saying that the average consumer would expect conditions to apply and the small print in the advertisement made this clear. One particular complaint was that like and like were not being compared in the case of flights to Frankfurt as the defendant's airplanes landed at an airport further out of Frankfurt than the claimant's airplanes. This was also rejected. Jacob J did not think this made the comparison significantly unfair.[115]

The above cases have set out useful guidance on the scope of acceptable comparative advertising within s 10(6). The decisions take a pragmatic approach and recognise that the public is knowledgeable about such advertising and realises that traders involved in such an activity will be selective in the choice of features that they use. For comparative advertising to be misleading, and therefore not in accordance with honest practices, it must amount to such a distortion that the public is deceived as to the nature of one trader's goods or services in comparison with the other trader's goods or services. Such distortion could come about because the selection of features is so unreasonable as to amount to a misrepresentation of the goods or services of either trader, or because the factual information used is inaccurate to a material extent. However, some caution is needed in respect of the above cases on comparative advertising in the light of the developments described below.[116]

It should be noted that there are controls over comparative advertising, which is allowed providing a number of conditions are satisfied. The legislation is the result of Directive 97/55/EC of the European Parliament and of the Council of 6 October 1997, amending Directive 84/450/EEC concerning misleading advertising so as to include comparative advertising.[117] The advertising (which is not limited to the use of registered trade marks) must, *inter alia*, be objective, must not be misleading, discredit or denigrate a trade mark or trade name or take unfair advantage of the reputation of a trade mark or trade name.

Section 10(6) has come in for some criticism and Jacob LJ in *O2 Holdings Ltd v Hutchinson 3G Ltd*[118] has suggested that it be repealed. He said (at para 58):

> It is a pointless provision (and could not apply to a Community TM). It should be repealed as an unnecessary distraction in an already complicated branch of law.

112 [1998] FSR 383.

113 *Emaco Ltd v Dyson Appliances Ltd* [1999] ETMR 903.

114 [2001] FSR 32.

115 Even though the defendant's airplanes landed at an airport located some 68 miles from Frankfurt city centre! However, the small print did state the airport truthfully as being Frankfurt (Hahn) Airport.

116 After completing this section, readers could consider whether the decisions in *Barclays*, *Vodafone* and *British Airways* are wrong in the light of recent Court of Justice rulings.

117 OJ L290, 23.10.1997, p 18, implemented by the Control of Misleading Advertising Regulations 1988, SI 1988/915, as amended, in particular, by the Control of Misleading Advertisements (Amendment) Regulations 2000, SI 2000/914.

118 [2007] RPC 16.

In the O2 case, described by Lewison J at first instance as a case about bubbles, the claimant complained about comparative advertising by the defendant which used images of bubbles similar to the registered trade marks. Both companies provided mobile phone services. The main thrust of the advertising was to show that the defend-ant's rates for mobile phone calls were cheaper than those of the claimant. Lewison J held that the defendant would have infringed under Article 5(1)(b) but for the defence under Article 6(1)(b) (use in the course of trade or indications concerning the kind, quality, quantity, intended purpose, value, etc. providing the use is in accordance with honest practices in industrial or commercial matters). Furthermore, he held that, since the Comparative Advertising Directive and the domestic regulations made under it, s 10(6), must be interpreted as allowing comparative advertising providing it is conducted in accordance with honest practices, as defined for the purpose of the Comparative Advertising Directive.

The Court of Justice ruled, in Case C-44/01 *Pippig Augenoptik GmbH & Co KG* v *Hartlaeur Handelsgesellschaft mbH*,[119] that price comparisons, *per se*, do not discredit a competitor under Article 3a(1)(e) of Directive 84/450/EEC. The Court also made it clear that comparative advertising was generally in the interests of consumers as it helped them to make informed choices. It also said (at para 44):

> Directive 84/450 carried out an exhaustive harmonisation of the conditions under which comparative advertising in Member States might be lawful. Such a harmonisation implies by its nature that the lawfulness of comparative advertising throughout the Community is to be assessed solely in the light of the criteria laid down by the Community legislature. Therefore, stricter national provisions on protection against misleading advertising cannot be applied to comparative advertising as regards the form and content of the comparison. (Author's emphasis)

In the light of the above, the Court of Appeal in *O2 Holdings* referred the following questions to the Court of Justice for a preliminary ruling under Article 234 of the EC Treaty (now Article 267 of the Treaty on the Functioning of the European Union):

1 Where a trader, in an advertisement for his own goods or services uses a registered trade mark owned by a competitor for the purpose of comparing the characteristics (and in particular the price) of goods or services marketed by him with the character-istics (and in particular the price) of the goods or services marketed by the competitor under that mark in such a way that it does not cause confusion or otherwise jeopardise the essential function of the trade mark as an indication of origin, does his use fall within either (a) or (b) of Art 5(1) of Directive 89/104 [the trade mark Directive]?
2 Where a trader uses, in a comparative advertisement, the registered trade mark of a competitor, in order to comply with Art 3a of Directive 84/450 as amended must that use be 'indispensable' and if so what are the criteria by which indispensability is to be judged?
3 In particular, if there is a requirement of indispensability, does the requirement pre-clude any use of a sign which is not identical to the registered trade mark but is closely similar to it?

Jacob LJ considered that using a trade mark comparatively such that the essential func-tion of the trade mark was not jeopardised did not fall within Article 5(1)(a) or (b). He also said, in the context of the case, the application of the 'global appreciation' test was such that the average reasonably well informed consumer would not be misled. Furthermore, Article 6(1)(b) covered every case of comparative advertising, providing the defendant used the indications in accordance with honest practices in industrial or commercial matters. Compliance with Article 3a of the misleading advertising Directive is essential. That states:

119 [2003] ECR I-3095. In that case, the parties sold spectacles and lenses and the claimant objected to the defendant's comparative advertising where misleading advertising was also a feature. The defendant was photographed standing 'triumphantly' outside the claimant's shop front which bore the trade mark.

Article 3a

1 Comparative advertising shall, as far as the comparison is concerned, be permitted when the following conditions are met:

   (a) it is not misleading according to Articles 2(2), 3 and 7(1);

   (b) it compares goods or services meeting the same needs or intended for the same purpose;

   (c) it objectively compares one or more material, relevant, verifiable and representative features of those goods and services, which may include price;

   (d) it does not create confusion in the market place between the advertiser and a competitor or between the advertiser's trade marks, trade names, other distinguishing marks, goods or services and those of a competitor;

   (e) it does not discredit or denigrate the trade marks, trade names, other distinguishing marks, goods, services, activities, or circumstances of a competitor;

   (f) for products with designation of origin, it relates in each case to products with the same designation;

   (g) it does not take unfair advantage of the reputation of a trade mark, trade name or other distinguishing marks of a competitor or of the designation of origin of competing products;

   (h) it does not present goods or services as imitations or replicas of goods or services bearing a protected trade mark or trade name.

2 Any comparison referring to a special offer shall indicate in a clear and unequivocal way the date on which the offer ends or, where appropriate, that the special offer is subject to the availability of the goods and services, and, where the special offer has not yet begun, the date of the start of the period during which the special price or other specific conditions shall apply.

It would appear that comparative advertising will not infringe a trade mark if it complies with Directive 84/450/EEC, as amended, with the added gloss that it must be in accordance with honest practices in industrial or commercial matters. In *O2 Holdings*, Jacob LJ suggested that a trader who is not 'Article 3a compliant' could not be regarded as so acting.[120] He also thought that even non-misleading but disparaging use would not be in accordance with honest practices in industrial or commercial matters. As he acknowledged, to that extent, his earlier decision in *British Airways* v *Ryanair* is wrong.

In its ruling, in Case C-533/06 *O2 Holdings Ltd* v *Hutchinson 3G UK Ltd*,[121] the Court of Justice confirmed that Article 5(1) and (2) does not allow a proprietor to prevent the use of a trade mark in comparative advertising where *all* the conditions in Article 3a(1) of Directive 84/450/EEC are satisfied. Of course, where there is a likelihood of con-fusion, Article 3a(1)(d) is not satisfied and the advertising will infringe. In Case C-87/07 *L'Oréal SA* v *Bellure NV*,[122] the defendant had been selling perfumes which were imitations of those sold by the claimant. The defendant published lists comparing its perfumes to those of the claimant. The Court of Justice confirmed that in such a case, Article 5(1)(a) entitles the trade mark proprietor to prevent the use of his trade mark by a third party where the comparative advertisement does not satisfy all the requirements of Article 3a(1) of Directive 84/450/EEC even where the use does not jeopardise the essential function of the trade mark (being to guarantee the trade mark as an indication of origin of goods or services) provided other functions of the trade mark are affected. These are, in particular, the functions of communication, investment and advertising. Thus, the test for whether comparative advertising is lawful under trade mark law will be a question of whether it falls within the misleading advertising Directive even if it is not essential that the competitor's trade mark is used to identify him or his goods or services.

There is now some doubt about the correctness of these decisions in terms of Article 5(1)(a) and Article 5(2). It has been argued that Article 5(1)(a) should only be engaged where the essential function of a trade mark, being as an indication of origin, is affected. The form of infringement under Article 5(2) referred to as 'free-riding on the coat-tails'

120 This was *acte claire* and did not require a reference to the Court of Justice.

121 [2008] ECR I-4231. This followed a reference from the Court of Appeal.

122 [2008] ECR I-5185. Another aspect of this case concerned Article 5(2) and is discussed *supra*.

which may be relevant in comparative advertising cases should only apply where there is confusion as to origin.[123]

123 See Jacob LJ in *L'Oréal SA* v *Bellure NV* [2010] RPC 23.

Applying mark to material, etc.

Under s 10(5), a person who applies a registered mark to material intended to be used for labelling or packaging goods, as a business paper (for example, a company letterhead, or a sheet of instructions accompanying goods), or for advertising goods or services, shall be treated as a party to any infringing use if, when he applied the mark, he knew or had reason to believe that the application of the mark was not authorised by the proprietor or a licensee.

The relevant intention in s 10(5) must be an intention that the material is used within the UK. In *Beautimatic International Ltd* v *Mitchell International Pharmaceuticals Ltd*,[124] Neuberger J held that use under s 10(4)(a) (affixing the sign to goods or packaging) must be in relation to goods in the UK and affixing a sign to material to be used as packaging for goods outside the UK could not be an infringing use. He went on to consider the relationship between s 10(4) and (5) and agreed that the two provisions must be construed so as to be consistent. Therefore, a person manufacturing packaging bearing the sign cannot be deemed to be a party to infringement if the intention is that the packaging is to be used in relation to goods outside the UK.

124 [2000] FSR 267.

Well-known marks – Paris Convention countries

Section 56(2) of the Act gives a right to relief for proprietors of marks which are well known in the UK, being a mark of a person who is a national of or is domiciled in a Paris Convention country or is entitled to protection under the World Trade Organisation,[125] whether or not that person carries on business or has any goodwill in the UK.[126] Such a person is entitled to injunctive relief against the use of an identical or similar mark used in relation to identical or similar goods or services where the use is likely to cause confusion. Thus, a foreign mark which is not used in the UK but is, nevertheless, well known in the UK, may be protected against non-consensual use there. This form of protection does not extend to use on non-similar goods or services.

A number of factors are taken into account as guidelines in determining whether a trade mark is well-known. In particular:

125 The UK is expressly excluded from the definition of 'Convention country' by s 55(1)(b).

126 This derives originally from Article 6^bis(1) of the Paris Convention for the Protection of Industrial Property 1883. The Directive is stated to be consistent with the Paris Convention: 12th recital.

1 the degree of knowledge or recognition of the mark in the relevant sector of the public;
2 the duration, extent and geographical area of any use of the mark;
3 the duration, extent and geographical area of any promotion of the mark, including advertising or publicity and the presentation, at fairs or exhibitions, of the goods and/or services to which the mark applies;
4 the duration and geographical area of any registration, and/or any applications for registration, of the mark, to the extent that they reflect use or recognition of the mark;
5 the record of successful enforcement of rights in the mark, in particular, the extent to which the mark was recognised as well known by competent authorities;
6 the value associated with the mark.[127]

127 Joint Recommendation concerning Provision on the Protection of Well-Known Marks, Assembly of the Paris Union for the Protection of Intellectual Property and the General Assembly of the World Intellectual Property Organisation (WIPO), September 1999.

128 [2009] RPC 9. The appeal to the Court of Appeal was dismissed: *Hotel Cipriani SRL* v *Cipriani (Grosvenor Street) Ltd* [2010] RPC 16.

129 The Hotel Cipriani was a famous (and very expensive) hotel in Venice.

In *Hotel Cipriani SRL* v *Cipriani (Grosvenor Street) Ltd*,[128] in granting the claimant an injunction under s 56(2), at first instance, Arnold J applied these criteria in relation to the Community trade mark CIPRIANI.[129]

There are similar provisions for injunctive relief for national and other emblems in ss 57 and 58. Furthermore, such emblems may not be registered. An example is a national flag or state armorial bearings or such devices used by international intergovernmental organisations of which one or more Paris Convention countries are members.

The internet and trade mark infringement

There are a number of issues of special interest where trade marks are used on the internet. The territorial scope of online infringement of registered trade marks is an important issue. For example, what is the reach of a trade mark placed on a website in one country? Does it infringe identical or similar registered trade marks in other jurisdictions?

Online shopping is not the same as shopping in a bricks and mortar store. This raises the possibility that the test of a likelihood of confusion is not the same as for traditional uses of trade marks. A particular issue is that of 'initial interest confusion'. The use of trade marks in keyword meta-tags, not normally seen by the person entering a query into a search engine, is another issue. A practice which has generated much case law is the use of another's trade mark in AdWords. Under what conditions does such use infringe and, if there is infringement, is the advertiser, the search engine provider or both liable for infringement.

Infringement in other jurisdictions

The internet knows nothing of territorial boundaries and material placed on the internet, say on a web page, is available, potentially, throughout the world. Traditional forms of advertising are more predictable in terms of determining and targeting the advertiser's audience. It is clear that the audience of a glossy magazine published and distributed for sale in the UK only consists of persons resident in the UK. This remains the case even if some copies of the magazine find their way to other countries, even if this is a response to orders for the magazine from persons resident in other countries. Other factors which will colour the judgment as to where an advertisement is directed include whether parallel editions are circulated in other countries and carry advertising relevant to those other countries and whether advertisers actively seek orders placed in other countries: for example, by quoting alternative prices in different countries or quoting different postal costs for orders placed in different countries or regions of the world. Even so, and to all intents and purposes, it is the advertiser who takes the decision as to where his target audience is by choosing the publications in which his advertisements appear and in selecting the content of his advertisements. If the trader's advertisements stray into a territory where he does not trade, then there can be no use in relation to goods in that territory.

The internet is a global environment and, as such, traders need to exercise greater care when using signs or trade marks that could, potentially, infringe trade marks registered in other jurisdictions. An example of the possible difficulties is provided by *Euromarket Designs Inc* v *Peters and Crate & Barrel*.[130] The defendant had a shop in Dublin and placed an advertisement on its website. Jacob J rejected the argument that the advertisement was directed at anyone in the UK. Any person carrying out a search will often pick up lots of irrelevant 'hits', many of which will be foreign. If, in this case, it could be said that the defendant was using the trade mark Crate & Barrel in the UK, this would mean that the defendant was using the trade mark in every country in the world. Jacob J distinguished the present case with Amazon.com, a company that actively seeks worldwide trade. In an earlier case, *1-800 FLOWERS Trade Mark*,[131] at first instance, Jacob J rejected the notion

130 [2001] FSR 20.

131 [2000] FSR 697.

that placing a trade mark on a website was a potential trade mark infringement all over the world as this was tantamount to use in an 'omnipresent cyberspace' and was 'putting a tentacle' into the computer of each and every user accessing the site. He gave an example of a fishmonger from Bootle (Lancashire) who advertised on his own website. Anyone accessing that website from another country would realise that it was not directed to him. In practice it will depend on the circumstances. The website owner's intention and the impact on persons accessing the website will be important, especially what a person accessing the website would understand.

The danger of accepting the proposition that placing a sign on the internet in an advertisement for goods or services is to use it in every jurisdiction has very serious consequences. Many traders have small businesses with restricted physical catchment areas with sales only to persons who visit their retail outlets and who do not engage in mail order sales or other indirect sales. An example is a small ironmongery shop with a single retail outlet in a small town, such as Pershore, Worcestershire. Say the owner decides to set up a website and advertise his business there. Clearly, the advertisement will be directed at persons within a few miles of Pershore. It would be very unfortunate if the trader decided to use a trading name that happened to be the same or similar to that used by traders selling similar goods in Rome, Melbourne or San Francisco, if placing the advertisement was considered to be use of the sign throughout the world. Whilst it may be reasonable to accept that publication on the internet is publication to the world for the purposes of defamation, this should not apply in the case of trade marks. Use within a particular jurisdiction should require evidence of actual trade or an intention to trade within that jurisdiction. On appeal, in the *1800 FLOWERS* case above, Buxton LJ said:[132]

> . . . it was a significant part of the applicant's submissions that, for instance, 'publication' of statements in a particular jurisdiction by downloading from the internet according to the rules of the law of defamation or of misrepresentation was of at least strong analogical relevance to whether a trade mark downloaded from the internet had been 'used' in the jurisdiction to which it was downloaded . . . There is something inherently unrealistic in saying that A 'uses' his mark in the United Kingdom when all that he does is to place the mark on the internet, from a location outside the United Kingdom, and simply wait in the hope that someone from the United Kingdom will download it and thereby create use on the part of A . . . the very idea of 'use' within a certain area would seem to require some active step in that area on the part of the user that goes beyond providing facilities that enable others to bring the mark into the area. Of course, if persons in the United Kingdom seek the mark on the internet in response to direct encouragement or advertisement by the owner of the mark, the position may be different; but in such a case the advertisement or encouragement in itself is likely to suffice to establish the necessary use.

132 *1-800 FLOWERS Inc* v *Phonenames Ltd* [2002] FSR 12 at paras 136–139.

Thus far, a sensible and realistic approach has been adopted in the UK. As far as traders using websites to advertise their wares are concerned, they ought to consider including statements making the geographic boundary of their prospective target audience quite clear unless they do intend to sell anywhere (in which case, they must ensure that there are no conflicting trade marks anywhere else). In the *Euromarket* case, the Irish defendant had foolishly advertised the prices of its goods in US dollars though this was later changed to Irish punts.

Confusion

Where a sign is used on a website it is arguable that the test of similarity leading to a likelihood of confusion is modified. Where the website owner does not have a physical presence in the country of a person who accesses it, there is a lack of other attributes or clues that may come into play and colour and inform the conclusion as to confusion. Where a trader has a physical presence in a particular country, those other attributes and clues include the trader's premises, including retail outlets, distribution vehicles and a rich advertising mix which might include advertisement in newspapers and magazines, on advertising hoardings and on television and radio. There may also be sponsorship of local or national activities. All of these factors may combine to negate a finding of confusion notwithstanding a passing similarity between the sign used and a registered trade mark.

In *Brookfield Communications Inc* v *West Coast Entertainment Corp*,[133] Brookfield had databases containing information about the entertainment industry and used an un-registered trade mark, 'MovieBuff'. When it tried to register moviebuff.com as its domain name, it found that it had already been taken by the defendant so it acquired 'moviebuffonline.com' and 'brookfieldcomm.com' instead. Brookfield later registered 'MovieBuff' as a trade mark in respect of software and providing access to an online database in the field of motion picture and television industries. The defendant was offering a similar database on its website and Brookfield sued for trade mark infringement.

The US Court of Appeals, Ninth Circuit, held that there was an infringement of the trade mark by the defendant. An eight-factor test is normally used for determining whether confusion exists in the US, sometimes known as the '*Sleekcraft* factors'.[134] They are:

- the similarity of the marks;
- the relatedness or proximity of the products or services;
- the marketing channels used;
- the strength of the claimant's mark;
- the defendant's intention in selecting its mark;
- evidence of actual confusion;
- likelihood of expansion into other product lines;
- the degree of care likely to be exercised by customers.

The court held that not all factors may be relevant in each case and a subset will often be sufficient to determine the question of confusion. However, the list is not necessarily exhaustive. Delivering the judgment of the court, O'Scannlain J said:

> We must be acutely aware of excessive rigidity when applying the law in the internet context: emerging technologies require a flexible approach.

He confirmed that a comparison of domain names is relevant; what mattered was a comparison between the alleged infringing sign, 'moviebuff.com', with the registered trade mark. Applying the first three factors in the *Sleekcraft* test, the court decided that the marks were very similar (almost identical even allowing for differences in capitalisation and the addition of '.com') and there was also similarity in terms of sound and meaning. The products and services were closely related, the parties were competitors and the products very similar. As regards the marketing channels used, the fact that both parties used the internet as a marketing and advertising facility was seen as exacerbating the likelihood of confusion, especially as both offered internet-based products. O'Scannlain J said:

> Web surfers are more likely to be confused as to the ownership of a website than traditional patrons of a brick-and-mortar store would be of a store's ownership.

The forms of confusion alluded to included that consumers might think that the defendant was a licensee of the claimant, that they might think that the defendant had bought out or replaced the claimant's business. Although the court accepted that there was a strong showing of confusion, it went on to consider the other factors in case they tipped the balance back in favour of the defendant. They did not. On the issue of intention, it was noted that the defendant had not adopted the domain name with an intention of selling it to the claimant.

133 174 F 3d 1036 (9th Cir, 1999).

134 *AMF Inc* v *Sleekcraft Boats*, 599 F 2d 341, 348 (9th Cir, 1979).

Brookfield was applied in *GoTo.com Inc* v *Walt Disney Corp*,[135] where it was held that the use by the defendant of a confusingly similar mark to that of the claimant infringed the latter's registered trade mark, comprising of the words 'GO' and 'TO' arranged on a green circle and usually displayed against a yellow background. Again, the fact that both parties used the internet for advertising was deemed to be a factor which exacerbated the likelihood of confusion. Furthermore, both offered search engines to the public and the defendant's logo looked very similar in terms of colouring and the font used for the lettering.

135 (Unreported) 27 January 2000.

The above cases show that the approach in the US to the use of trade marks on the internet is that a finding of confusion is more likely than is the case with traditional forms of advertising. There have, as yet, been no cases in the UK to address this possibility fully but it is likely that the outcome will be similar. The virtual world is different from the real world and there are significantly fewer clues to help users of the internet to distinguish between marks displayed on web pages. Furthermore, although a domain name is not normally regarded as a trade mark (the purpose of a domain name is entirely different, being an address to find a particular entity's website), most persons expect that a commercial enterprise's domain name will include a trade mark. That trade mark is likely to be part of the enterprise's corporate name (usually a trade mark) or its most famous product or service, again usually registered as a trade mark.

Initial interest confusion

The case of *Brookfield*, discussed above, is also instructive in relation to the use of trade marks in meta-tags. The form of confusion caused by such use was described as 'initial interest confusion'. Any person who is looking for a specific website and does not know the exact address is likely to use a search engine using words such as company names, trade marks and the like. If other sites have embedded the trade marks in meta-tags, these may also be retrieved. However, and bearing in mind that persons using search engines expect to retrieve numerous irrelevant hits, that should be where the confusion ends. At least, it is unlikely that the initial confusion will result in an order for goods or services being placed with the wrong trader through continuing confusion. However, the use of another's trade mark in meta-tags to capture initial consumer attention has usually been regarded as a potential infringement of a trade mark in the US. A nice analogy was used by the court in *Brookfield*, which is set out below, adapted to the UK:

- Trader A (Ash Ltd) and Trader B (Birch plc) both sell similar goods and both have retail outlets near junctions along the A5 Trunk Road. Both Ash and Birch are registered trade marks.
- Ash's outlet is just off the A5 along the A47 road to Nuneaton and Birch's outlet is just off the A5 along the A447 road at Hinckley (on the opposite side of the A5). (Hinckley and Nuneaton are just a few miles apart.)
- Ash places a notice on advertising hoardings along the A5 stating that customers for Birch's retail outlet should take the A47 to Nuneaton.
- A person, travelling along the A5 wanting to visit Birch's store for the first time, and seeing the advertising hoarding, would turn off the A5 at the junction with the A47 towards Nuneaton.
- Being unable to find the Birch store, that person would probably see Ash's store and might decide to shop there instead. He would not, at this stage, be confused in a narrow sense. If he decided to buy something, he would know precisely from whom he was buying.

According to the court in *Brookfield*, such an activity should infringe Birch's registered trade mark because it is a misappropriation of Birch's goodwill.

There are differences between US and UK trade mark law which mean that the US authorities do not translate particularly well in terms of similar facts in the UK (or, indeed, in Europe). The concept of *initial interest confusion* simply will not do where infringement under s 10(2) is alleged. This is because confusion for the purposes of s 10(2) has been held, on numerous occasions, to be confusion as to origin. Persons picking up the wrong website, because of its embedded meta-tags, will quickly realise that it is not the website they were seeking. Infringement by the use of meta-tags including registered trade marks may occur, however, where infringement under s 10(1) or (3) is alleged, neither of which require confusion. Thus, where the registered trade mark, being a word or phrase (not stylised), is used without modification and the goods or services offered are identical, infringement is made out, *per se*.[136] Section 10(3) may be relevant where the meta-tag includes a word or phrase identical or similar to the registered trade mark where unfair advantage or detriment is found. This might be the case where the defendant's website results in an association (though not confusion as to origin) between the claimant's and defendant's trade (blurring) or where the material available on the defendant's website tarnishes the claimant's trade mark. Nonetheless, this may be more difficult to show than in other cases given the nature of the internet, the frequency of spurious 'hits' and the fact that users of search engines are probably more likely to make distinctions between different websites.

Keyword meta-tags

Another issue in relation to the internet is whether the use in a meta-tag of a word or phrase that is similar to another's registered trade mark infringes that trade mark. A meta-tag is not visible to the user but is used by search engines to find sites matching an inquiry entered by the user. Meta-tags are embedded in HTML code.[137] There are different forms including descriptive meta-tags, containing information describing the website or keyword meta-tags containing keywords relating to the contents which are searched by search engines. Again, in the UK, there is little guidance but there is a reasonable body of case law in the US where the courts have been fairly consistent in finding that use of meta-tags which are similar to a registered trade mark will infringe if, of course, the other requirements for infringement are present. For example, in *Playboy Enterprises Inc v Calvin Designer Labels*,[138] the use of the claimant's trade marks, 'Playboy' and 'Playmate', in meta-tags on the defendant's website was held to infringe. However, in *Playboy Enterprises Inc v Welles*,[139] there was no finding of infringement. Terri Welles's website advertised the fact that she was a former Playmate of the Year, but the use of Playboy's marks was minimal and the site contained numerous disclaimers. It was held that she was not using 'Playboy' and 'Playmate' as trade marks, but as descriptive terms fairly and accurately describing her website. Her use of the trade marks in meta-tags was permissible and was an attempt, in good faith, to index the content of her website.

There are very few cases involving use of trade marks in meta-tags in the UK. In *Roadtech Computer Systems Ltd v Mandata Ltd*,[140] the defendant had used the claimant's trade mark, 'Roadrunner', and its company name, 'Roadtech', in meta-tags. However, before the hearing, the defendant removed the offending meta-tags, although it was confirmed that using the trade mark as a meta-tag was an infringement. The defendant in *Pfizer Ltd v Eurofood Link (UK) Ltd*[141] used the claimant's registered trade mark, 'Viagra', in its meta-tags. However, after finding infringement under s 10(2) or, alternatively, under s 10(3), Simon Thorley QC, sitting as deputy judge of the Chancery Division, did not expressly address the question of whether the use of a trade mark in a meta-tag infringed the trade mark. Other activities of the defendant were sufficient to decide there had been an infringement of the claimant's trade mark.[142]

The use of trade marks in meta-tags may escape if the word used in the meta-tag is not identical to the trade mark. For example, in *Brookfield*, the court said that it was acceptable

136 Providing the use is deemed to be in relation to goods or services in the UK.

137 HTML stands for Hyper-Text Mark-up Language.

138 985 F Supp 1220 (ND Cal, 1997).

139 7 F Supp 2d 1098 (SD Cal, 1998).

140 [2000] ETMR 970.

141 [2001] FSR 3.

142 It could be argued that infringement by use of meta-tags was implicitly accepted by the judge. It is a pity, however, that the opportunity was not taken to explore this further.

for the defendant to use 'Movie Buff' in a meta-tag. The space between the words was pivotal and persons trying to find the claimant's website by typing in its trade mark would be less likely to retrieve the defendant's website instead. However, in this case, the term 'Movie Buff' has an ordinary meaning and the situation might be different if both the trade mark and the word used in the meta-tag had no ordinary meaning.

The fact that a keyword meta-tag is not normally visible no longer appears to be important in the light of cases on AdWords (see *infra*) and unauthorised use of a trade mark as a keyword meta-tag may infringe if the use made of it is such as to adversely affect one of the functions of a trade mark[143] or, in appropriate circumstances, results in taking an unfair advantage of or diluting or tarnishing a trade mark with a reputation.

143 In particular, the essential function of indicating the origin of the goods or services.

Domain names

Internet domain names should be treated no differently to other marks but what is important is whether they perform as trade marks.[144] It is not enough that they function as domain names; they must have trade mark significance to be registrable. The purpose of a domain name is not the same as that of a trade mark and there must be some evidence of the public treating the domain name as a badge of origin rather than just an internet address. Adding a common internet generic or country code such as '.com', '.org' or '.co.uk' to an otherwise non-distinctive word or phrase may be sufficient to give the word or phrase a distinctiveness for trade mark purposes. There are examples of such registrations: for example, 'CAN AND WILL.COM' registered in the UK during 1998. However, the OHIM refused an application to register 'BUY.COM'. It was descriptive of an internet site at which persons could buy goods or services. It is submitted that the more knowledge the public have of domain names, the more difficult it will become to argue that simply adding an internet code as a suffix will at once transform an indistinct mark into a distinctive one.

144 *Digeo Broadband Inc's Trade Mark Application* [2004] RPC 32.

AdWords

Internet search engines, such as Google, use a system of sponsored links whereby companies and businesses pay for keywords known as 'AdWords' so that when a person enters a search which contains a particular AdWord, a list of sponsored links is retrieved in addition to other sites found during the search which may contain the searched for word, words or phrase. The sponsored list normally appears at the top or at the side of the retrieved sites and is usually described as such. In *Interflora Inc v Marks and Spencer plc*,[145] Interflora had the AdWord 'INTERFLORA'. Originally, trade marks were only permitted to be used as AdWords by their proprietors or licensees but, due to a change of policy, it became possible for other companies to 'buy' trade marks as AdWords. Marks and Spencer bought a range of keyword AdWords which comprised of or included INTERFLORA. Arnold J granted a stay pending rulings before the Court of Justice on similar matters and, also, submitted further questions for a preliminary ruling.[146] Before the ruling in *Interflora v Marks and Spencer*, the Court of Justice handed down rulings in *Google France v Vuitton* and *L'Oréal v eBay*. Those rulings are now considered before looking at the ruling in *Interflora v Marks and Spencer*.

In Joined Cases C-236/08, C-237/08 and C-238/08 *Google France SARL v Louis Vuitton Malletier SA*,[147] Google offered a paid-for referencing service called AdWords on its search engine. The advertisers using these AdWords appeared under a sponsored links list. Some advertisers chose names of rival companies, being trade marks, as their AdWords. In one of the cases, Vuitton became aware that other companies were using the Vuitton trade marks as AdWords and a search using Vuitton would trigger the retrieval in the sponsored links list of companies offering imitation products. Google was found liable for trade

145 [2009] RPC 22.

146 In the light of subsequent Court of Justice rulings, especially Joined Cases C-236/08 to C-238/08 *Google France SARL v Louis Vuitton Malletier SA* [2010] ECR I-2417 (see *infra*), Arnold J reduced the number of questions for a ruling in *Interflora Inc v Marks and Spencer plc* [2010] EWHC 925 (Ch).

147 [2010] ECR I-2417.

mark infringement at first instance. On appeal to the French *Cour de Cassation*, the court referred a number of questions to the Court of Justice for a preliminary ruling under the trade marks Directive, the Community Trade Mark Regulation and the Directive on electronic commerce.[148] The Court of Justice ruled:

148 The latter provides a defence for service providers in relation to acting as a mere conduit and caching or hosting information.

1 A trade mark proprietor may prohibit the advertising using a keyword identical with the trade mark, without the proprietor's consent, on an internet referencing service for identical goods or services in a case where the advertisement does not enable an average internet user, or enables that user only with difficulty, to ascertain whether the goods or services referred to originate from the trade mark proprietor or an economically connected undertaking or whether they originate from a third party.

2 An internet referencing service provider which stores, as a keyword, a sign identical with a trade mark and organises the display of advertisements on the basis of that keyword does not use that sign within the meaning of Article 5(1) and (2) of the trade marks Directive 89/104 or Article 9(1) of Community Trade Mark Regulation ('CTMR').

3 Article 14 of the Directive on electronic commerce[149] (the hosting defence) must be interpreted as meaning that the rule laid down therein applies to an internet referencing service provider in the case where that service provider has not played an active role of such a kind as to give it knowledge of, or control over, the data stored. If it has not played such a role, that service provider cannot be held liable for the data which it has stored at the request of an advertiser, unless, having obtained knowledge of the unlawful nature of those data or of that advertiser's activities, it failed to act expeditiously to remove or to disable access to the data concerned.

149 Directive 2000/31/EC of the European Parliament and of the Council of 8 June 2000 on certain legal aspects of information society services, in particular electronic commerce, in the Internal Market (Directive on electronic commerce), OJ L 178, 17.07.2000, p 1.

The Directive on electronic commerce provides, *inter alia*, a defence for information society service providers who store information provided by a recipient of that service providing the service provider has no actual knowledge of illegal activity or information. Once he has such knowledge, he must act expeditiously to remove or disable access to that information.

In a nutshell, the Court of Justice is saying that an advertiser using another's trade mark as an AdWord only infringes if average internet users cannot distinguish (or can do so only with difficulty) whether the goods or services come from the trade mark proprietor (or linked undertaking) or from some other undertaking. Furthermore, the service provider (Google in the present case) is not liable for storing the AdWord because (a) he does not himself use the trade for the purposes of Article 5(1) and (2) and (b) can rely on the hosting defence if he has not played an active role such as to give him knowledge or control over the relevant information subject to a duty to remove or disable access to the information should he subsequently become aware of the unlawful nature of the information or the advertiser's activities. This accords with the general principle under the Directive on electronic commerce, that service providers have no general obligation to monitor the information they store or transmit or to seek facts or circumstances indicating illegal activity.[150]

150 Article 15 of the Directive on electronic commerce.

151 [2009] RPC 21.

Further questions were submitted to the Court of Justice for a preliminary ruling in relation to internet auction sites in *L'Oréal SA v eBay International AG*.[151] L'Oréal and other cosmetics companies complained about goods being sold through eBay's via its online auction-style and fixed price sales. Submitting certain trade marked words to a search engine, such as Google, resulted in a sponsored links list which included links to products available for sale or auction on the eBay site. Evidence tendered by the claimants indicated that two test purchases were of counterfeit cosmetics whilst the remaining 15 purchases were of goods which had not been placed on the market within the EEA (or EU in the case of the Community trade mark) by the claimants, having been placed on the US and Canadian markets. There was a further claim that some goods offered for sale were unboxed or were tester products or samples not intended for resale. Arnold J considered that eBay was not jointly liable with the individual sellers as eBay was under no legal obligation to prevent third parties infringing the claimants' trade marks. Furthermore, although eBay actively encouraged the listing and sale of goods from outside the EEA, since eBay's facilities could be used in a way which did not infringe trade marks and did not inherently lead to infringement, this was insufficient to make eBay liable as joint tortfeasor. However, guidance from the Court of Justice was sought on the following:

- what the position was in relation to the sale of unboxed or tester goods;
- whether sponsoring links[152] which meant that users could access listings of infringing and non-infringing goods to be sold on eBay meant that eBay infringed the claimants' trade marks;
- whether eBay had the hosting defence under Article 14 of the Directive on electronic commerce;[153]
- the scope of the relief that Article 11 of the Directive on the enforcement of intellectual property rights[154] required national courts to grant injunctions against intermediaries such as eBay and, if so, the scope of those injunctions.

The Court of Justice handed down its ruling in Case C-324/09 *L'Oréal SA* v *eBay International AG*[155] to the following effect in relation to trade marks:

- Before considering whether the activity in question infringes, it must be determined whether it is in the course of trade – a private activity, such as a single online sale by an individual is not in the course of trade – however, where a person makes a large quantity of sales though an online marketplace, this goes beyond a private activity and is in the course of trade.
- Where goods have been put on the market by the trade mark proprietor outside the EEA or EU[156] the sale of those goods within the EEA or EU by a third party economic operator will infringe.
- As above, but where the goods have been advertised for sale, the question of infringement depends on whether the advertisement is targeted at consumers within the relevant Member State – this is an issue for national courts to determine on a case by case basis.
- By the supply to authorised distributors of testers, samples or drammers (containers from which small samples can be given to potential customers), the trade mark proprietor does not put those items on the market (consequently, the principle of exhaustion of rights cannot apply to those items).
- The proprietor may oppose the sale of goods from which the packaging, containing essential information about the identity of the manufacturer or the person marketing the goods, has been removed[157] – where the removal of packaging has not resulted in the absence of such information, the proprietor may oppose the sale if that removal has damaged the image of the product and, consequently, the reputation of the trade mark.
- As products available through eBay's online marketplace, where listed in sponsored links (which directly linked to the relevant eBay entry), meant that eBay was an advertiser (however, although eBay was using trade marks, it was not using them in relation to identical or similar goods as it was promoting its own service of making an online marketplace available), that use could be subject to examination as to whether it infringed under Article 5(2) (unfair advantage or detriment to the distinctive character or repute).
- However, in relation to the use of trade marks as keywords in search engines to promote its customer-sellers offers, that use was use of an identical sign in relation to identical goods and would infringe unless the advertising enabled reasonably well-informed and reasonably observant internet users to ascertain whether the goods referred to in the advertisement originated from the proprietor of the trade mark (or an economically linked undertaking) or from a third party.[158]
- The operator of an online marketplace does not 'use' the trade marks for the purposes of Article 5 of the trade marks Directive or Article 9 of the CTMR.

152 That is, eBay's purchase and use of trade marks as AdWords from third party search engines, as in *Interflora* v *Marks and Spencer*.

153 Directive 2000/31/EC of the European Parliament and of the Council of 8 June 2000 on certain legal aspects of information society services, in particular electronic commerce, in the Internal Market (Directive on electronic commerce), OJ L178, 17.07.2000, p 1.

154 Directive 2004/48/EC of the European Parliament and of the Council of 29 April 2004 on the enforcement of intellectual property rights, OJ L 157, 30.04.2004, p 45.

155 12 July 2011.

156 The EEA is relevant to the trade marks Directive whereas the Community trade mark applies only to the territory of the EU.

157 Certain information must be given in the case of cosmetic products such as details of the manufacturer or person marketing the product, quantity, durability, precautions and batch number under Article 6(1) of Council Directive content.

158 To the same effect on this point, *see* also Case C-278/08 *Die BergSpechte Outdoor Reisen und Alpinschule Edi Koblmüller GmbH* v *Günter Guni* [2010] ECR I-2517 and Case C-558/08 *Portakabin Ltd* v *Primakabin BV* [2010] ECR I-6959.

Thus, an online marketplace operator would not be liable for trade mark infringement apart from possibly under Article 5(2). However, an advertiser selling or offering goods for sale in the course of trade using identical trade marks for identical goods could be liable unless it is clear to average internet users that it is not the trade mark proprietor or a economically linked undertaking (such as a another company in the same group of companies or a licensee of the proprietor).

The Court of Justice went on to consider the impact of the Directive on electronic commerce on the activities of online marketplace operators such as eBay. It ruled that the operator could rely on the 'hosting defence' under Article 14(1) of that Directive unless it took an active part so as to give it knowledge or control of the relevant data. An active role includes a situation where the operator provides assistance to the advertiser, for example, by optimising the presentation of the offers for sale in question or by promoting those offers. Moreover, the operator cannot rely on the exemption in Article 14(1) from the liability to pay damages if it was aware of facts or circumstances on the basis of which a diligent economic operator should have realised that the offers were unlawful and failed to act expeditiously to remove or disable access to the relevant information.

Finally, the Court of Justice ruled that, under the Directive on the enforcement of intellectual property rights, Member States must take measures to ensure that national courts can order online marketplace operators to take measures which contribute to bringing an end to the infringement or rights by users of the marketplace and also to prevent future infringements. The measures adopted must be effective, proportionate and dissuasive.

The ruling in *L'Oréal SA* v *eBay* means that the most effective action that trade mark proprietors can take where their trade marks are used unlawfully[159] without consent on the internet is to notify the relevant service provider which, once given notice, is unlikely to be able to rely on the hosting defence under Article 14(1) of the Directive on electronic commerce. If the service provider fails to act expeditiously to remove or disable access to the offending sign, the trade mark proprietor should be able to obtain an injunction against the provider. Proceedings can also be brought against advertisers who do not make it clear that they are not the trade mark proprietor or an economically linked undertaking. The ruling does not, however, address the problem of using trade marks as keywords in sponsored links lists which are not themselves visible to the user submitting a trade mark word to a search engine.

It is notable that some similar issues in the context of copyright infringement arose in the High Court just over two weeks later than the ruling in *L'Oréal SA* v *eBay* in *Twentieth Century Fox Film Corp* v *British Telecommunications Ltd*[160] (see the discussion of this case in Chapter 6).

The problem for the proprietors of trade marks is that trade marks may be used legitimately by others in some cases, such as in lawful comparative advertising and certain descriptive uses. There is also the question as to whether such use constitutes use as a trade mark or an infringing form of use under Article 5(3) of the trade marks Directive.[161] As Advocate General Poiares Maduro said in his opinion in *Google France* v *Louis Vuitton* (at para 154):

> . . . it is important not to allow the legitimate purpose of preventing certain trade mark infringements to lead all trade mark uses to be prohibited in the context of cyberspace.

In Case C-323/09 *Interflora Inc* v *Marks and Spencer plc*,[162] the claimant had registered 'INTERFLORA' as a UK and a Community trade mark, *inter alia*, for flower delivery services. These services were operated via a network of florists. The defendant, which was not part of that network, amongst its wide variety of goods and services, also operated a flower sale and delivery service. It selected as AdWords, 'Interflora', 'Interflora Flowers', 'Interflora Delivery', 'Interflora.com', 'Interflora.co.uk' etc. When internet users entered

159 In this case, the use was alleged to be in relation to online advertising of counterfeit goods bearing the trade mark, samples and testers not intended to be sold and products intended by the trade mark proprietor to be placed on the market outside the EEA.

160 [2011] EWHC 1981 (Ch). Arnold J gave a long and thoughtful judgment covering numerous aspects of EU Directives (the e-commerce, information society and enforcement Directives) the Human Rights Act 1998 and the right of freedom of expression.

161 However, the forms of use listed in that provision are not exhaustive because of the use of the term *inter alia* before the list of prohibited activities.

162 24 March 2011.

'interflora' or any of the variants of the word in a Google search, an advertisement for Marks and Spencer came up in the sponsored links list. The advert was:

M & S Flowers Online
www.marksandspencer.com/flowers
Gorgeous fresh flowers & plants
Order by 5 pm for next day delivery

The Court of Justice summarised the generality of its previous rulings on Article 5 of the Directive and Article 9 of the CTMR[163] to the following effect:

- Where an commercial advertiser uses a sign to trigger the display of an advertisement, that use is the course of trade even if the sign is not itself displayed in the advertisement. Nevertheless the conditions in Article 5 of the Directive (or Article 9 of the CTMR) and relevant case law must still be satisfied.
- In a case of double-identity (identical sign/identical goods or services), such as the present one, the proprietor is entitled to prevent the use of the sign only if it is liable to have an adverse effect on one of the functions of the trade mark (being the essential function of guaranteeing to consumers the origin of the goods or services, the function of guaranteeing the quality of the product or service and the functions of communication, investment and advertising).[164]

The Court then considered, in the context of AdWords, the functions of guaranteeing origin, investment and advertising which it considered relevant to the present case and for which the referring court would need guidance.

Essential function of guaranteeing origin

Whether this function is adversely affected when internet users are shown, on the basis of a keyword identical with the trade mark, a third party's advertisement, such as that of a competitor of the trade mark proprietor, depends in particular on the manner in which that advertisement is presented. That function is adversely affected if the advertisement does not enable reasonably well-informed and reasonably observant internet users, or enables them only with difficulty, to ascertain whether the goods or services referred to by the advertisement originate from the proprietor of the trade mark (or an economically linked undertaking) or, on the contrary, originate from a third party.[165]

The fact that Google did not allow trade mark proprietors to prevent the selection by others of signs identical with their trade marks is irrelevant to that question. However, if an internet referencing service like Google did give trade mark proprietors this option, a proprietor that failed to take it up could be said to have given tacit consent to the use by others of its trade mark as an AdWord keyword. However, the fact that trade mark proprietors have never been asked for their consent, nor given it, merely confirms that the use of a sign identical to his trade mark is without their consent.

Advertising function

Although it may have repercussions on the advertising use of a word mark by the proprietor, it has been held that the use of a sign identical with another person's trade mark in a referencing service such as AdWords does not have an adverse effect on that function of the trade mark.[166]

Where a trade mark proprietor selects its own word trade mark as an AdWord keyword and a competitor has also registered the same word as an AdWord keyword, the proprietor may have to pay a higher price to ensure its advertisement comes higher up the list of sponsored links than that of the competitor. The fact that the proprietor may have to intensify its advertising is not, on its own, a sufficient reason for finding that the advertising function is adversely affected. It must be borne in mind that although trade marks are

163 The equivalent provision in relation to the Community trade mark.

164 Disagreeing with the European Commissions view that only the essential function of indicating origin should be relevant to infringement under Article 5(1)(a).

165 See the Court of Justice rulings in *Google France* and *Portakabin*.

166 See the Court of Justice rulings in *Google France* and *Die BergSpechte*.

an essential element in the system of undistorted competition under EU law, its purpose is not to protect proprietors against competition.

Internet advertising using trade marks belonging to others as keywords is aimed at offering consumers alternatives to the goods or services of the trade mark proprietors. Moreover, this does not deprive the proprietor from using its trade mark effectively to win over consumers.

Investment function

The investment function relates to the acquisition or preservation of a reputation capable of attracting consumers and retaining their loyalty. Although it may overlap with the advertising function it is distinct from it. In terms of acquiring or preserving a reputation, although advertising is involved, various commercial techniques are also employed.[167]

A third party's use of a trade mark adversely affects the investment function of a trade mark if it substantially interferes with the proprietor's use of the trade mark to acquire or preserve a reputation capable of attracting consumers and retaining their loyalty. Where a trade mark already enjoys a reputation, the investment function is adversely affected if a third party uses an identical mark for identical goods or services in such a way as to affect that reputation and jeopardise its maintenance.

However, in the interests of fair competition, a trade mark proprietor cannot prevent a competitor from using a sign identical with that trade mark in relation to identical goods or services, if the only consequence of that use is to oblige the proprietor of that trade mark to adapt its efforts to acquire or preserve a reputation capable of attracting consumers and retaining their loyalty. Furthermore, the fact the use complained of may result in some consumers switching from goods or services bearing that trade mark cannot be successfully relied on by the proprietor of the mark.

Unfair advantage or detriment to trade mark of repute

The Court of Justice in *Interflora* v *Marks and Spencer* also considered infringement under Article 5(2) of the trade marks Directive (and the equivalent provision, Article 9(1)(c) in the CTMR). The trade mark proprietor of a trade mark with a reputation was entitled to prevent a competitor advertising using a keyword identical to the trade mark selected in an internet referencing service where, by doing so, the competitor:

- takes unfair advantage of the distinctive character or repute of the trade mark (free-riding);
- causes detriment to the distinctive character of the trade mark (dilution, for example, by contributing to turning the trade mark into a generic term); or
- causes detriment to the repute of the trade mark (tarnishment).

However, the proprietor of a trade mark with a reputation cannot prevent the use of his trade mark as a keyword by a competitor if it puts forward alternatives to the proprietor's goods or services, not being mere imitations,[168] without causing dilution or tarnishment and without adversely affecting the functions of the trade mark. Such use falls within the meaning of fair competition and is, therefore, not without due cause. Although the competitor obtains an advantage from the distinctive character and repute of the trade mark, such advantage is not without due cause.

AdWord cases – summary and implications

The use of a trade mark by a competitor of the proprietor as a keyword used to generate a list of sponsored links is permissible under Article 5(1) of the trade marks Directive provided the advertisements displayed in those links are such as to enable reasonably well-informed and reasonably observant internet users to determine whether the goods or services in question originate from the proprietor or an economically linked undertaking

167 However, the Court did not explain what these 'commercial techniques' were.

168 As was the case in relation to some of the goods offered online in *Google France*.

or, on the contrary, originate from a third party. Notwithstanding this general rule relating to the essential function of a trade mark as an indicator of origin, the trade mark proprietor may still be able to prohibit such use of his trade mark if that use:

- *substantially* interferes with the investment function of the trade mark (the proprietor's use of the trade mark to acquire or preserve a reputation capable of attracting consumers and retaining their loyalty);[169]
- falls within Article 5(2) (dilution or tarnishment in relation to a trade mark with a reputation – though it appears that 'free-riding' is acceptable providing it falls within the meaning of 'fair competition' as such use would not be without due cause).[170]

A trade mark proprietor will be able to prohibit the use of his trade mark in an online marketplace to promote the sale of:

- counterfeit goods bearing the trade mark;
- items distributed as samples and testers not intended for sale;
- goods which he has placed on the market in the EEA but where the condition has been impaired (for example, by removal of packaging containing information about the manufacturer, conditions for use etc.);
- goods which were intended to be placed on the market outside the EEA;
- goods which are now second-hand or used but only if there is a legitimate reason to oppose the resale within Article 7(2) (for example, where the reseller has replaced the trade mark with his own or the reseller is also selling other goods of inferior quality etc. which risks seriously damaging the image the trade mark proprietor has created for his mark).

An online marketplace operator (and to that matter also an internet referencing service provider) can rely on the hosting defence under Article 14(1) of the Directive on electronic commerce provided:

- he has not played an active role in relation to the offending information (such as a word trade mark used for counterfeit goods); and
- on obtaining actual knowledge of, or becoming aware of facts which in the circumstances from which the illegal nature of the information is apparent, acts expeditiously to remove, or disable access to, that information.

An internet referencing service provider does not itself use a trade mark selected by an advertiser as its AdWord keyword.

The ruling in *Interflora* v *Marks and Spencer* shows that an online advertiser (A) using without consent the trade mark of a competitor (C) as an AdWord keyword must make it clear that it is not the competitor (C) or an undertaking economically linked to (C). Particular care must be taken not to display the trade mark in the advertisement, nor to offer goods or services which are mere imitations and not to denigrate or otherwise harm the trade mark. To this extent 'free-riding on the coat tails' is permissible as it is not without due cause as the Court of Justice recognised that such activity could, in the right circumstances, fall within the meaning of 'fair competition'.

169 In normal circumstances, it would seem that the communication function and the advertising function are not engaged even though, for example, the proprietor may have to adapt and increase its advertising budget.

170 The same applies, of course, in relation to the Community trade mark.

Evidential aspects

The proprietor bears the burden of proof as regards the use to which the mark has been put if the question arises (s 100). This will only be relevant where there is a challenge on the basis of non-use and, possibly, in connection with an application where the proprietor claims that the mark has become distinctive through use to overcome some of the absolute grounds of refusal.

Expert evidence is often submitted to show that there is a likelihood of confusion. However, such evidence is unnecessary in many cases and only prolongs the proceedings and increases costs. In *esure Insurance Ltd* v *Direct Line Insurance plc*,[171] one issue was whether there was a likelihood of confusion between esure's mouse on wheels and Direct Line's computer mouse on wheels, Maurice Kay LJ said (at para 82):

> In a case such as this, neither a hearing officer nor a judge in the Chancery Division requires the assistance of an 'expert' when evaluating the likelihood of confusion from the standpoint of the average consumer.

171 [2008] RPC 34.

The Civil Procedure Rules, r 35.1 states that expert evidence shall be restricted to that which is reasonably required to resolve the proceedings. Unfortunately, this rule does not apply to proceedings before a Hearing Officer at the Trade Marks Registry.

Under s 72, in all legal proceedings relating to a registered trade mark, the registration of a person as proprietor shall be prima facie evidence of the validity of the original registration and on any subsequent assignment or other transmission of the registered trade mark. In terms of gathering evidence of infringing use, the proprietor should be able to gain access to articles bearing infringing marks that are being offered for sale or advertisements for such articles. Where difficulties arise they are in connection with proving confusion for the purposes of Article 5(1)(b) of the Directive (s 10(2) of the Act) or association for the purposes of Article 5(2) (s 10(3) of the Act). Evidence may take many forms, including surveys of consumers, evidence from wholesalers, retailers and experts. Survey evidence is often criticised by judges and in *BACH and BACH FLOWER Remedies Trade Marks*,[172] Morritt LJ said (at 526):

172 [2000] RPC 513.

> But I do not think that the court is assisted by repetitious evidence from individuals put forward by the parties, whether expressly or not, as archetypal average consumers or end users for, by definition, no one individual is such a consumer or end user and the issue cannot be resolved by counting heads. We are told that the judges before whom cases of this sort are heard have increasingly imposed restrictions on the quantity of such evidence they are prepared to admit. In my view that practice is to be encouraged.

Even if the survey itself is properly designed, there is no guarantee that it is properly applied or that the answers are properly recorded, even if a reputable organisation is responsible for carrying out the survey.[173] Much more telling is evidence presented by witnesses who put themselves forward for cross-examination. In practice, survey evidence will be treated as hearsay and relatively little weight usually will be attached to it. In *esure Insurance Ltd* v *Direct Line Insurance plc*,[174] the Court of Appeal held that the Hearing Officer rightly rejected the survey evidence as the survey had been carried out just after an extensive advertising campaign undertaken by Direct Line.

173 See the comments of Lloyd J in *Dualit Ltd's Trade Mark Application* [1999] RPC 890 at 901.

174 [2008] RPC 34.

If the validity of a registered mark is contested and it is found to be valid, the court may give a certificate to that effect under s 73. This mirrors s 47 of the 1938 Act. Such a certificate could prove useful in any subsequent proceedings as regards an award of costs in favour of the proprietor.

Trap orders

If the proprietor of a registered trade mark believes that his mark is being infringed, it should not be necessary to apply for a search order (formerly known as an *Anton Piller* order) for the purpose of obtaining and preserving evidence of the infringement. It will usually be possible to buy examples of the product to which the alleged infringing mark has been applied. Indeed, search orders are not lightly granted and alternative means of obtaining evidence should be explored first. For example, in *Systematica Ltd* v *London Computer Centre Ltd*[175] it was pointed out that the claimant could have freely walked into the defendant's shop and purchased copies of the alleged infringing computer programs.

Several test purchases can be made to build up a pattern of infringement. It may serve a useful purpose to frame a request for goods or services in such a way as to demonstrate clearly that there is a significant chance of confusion. Such orders for goods are referred to as 'trap orders' and are commonly used as a means of obtaining evidence of infringement in relation to both trade marks and passing off actions. It is obvious that the way the order is placed is important and it should be done in a clear, unambiguous and fair way. Trap orders may indeed be essential if the trade mark infringement occurs in an advertisement, to verify that the goods or services being offered in fact are not those of the proprietor or a licensee.

One problem with trap orders is that low-level employees may be poorly trained or difficult to control, not always being aware of the dangers of supplying the wrong goods. This is particularly important where an injunction has been granted against a defendant who has infringed a trade mark or been guilty of passing off. In *Showerings Ltd* v *Entam Ltd*,[176] the claimant produced the 'Babycham' drink and sent teams of trappers into the defendant's public houses. The trappers ordered drinks including Babycham but were often supplied with a rival drink. In *British Telecommunications plc* v *Nextcall Telecom plc*,[177] some of the defendant's salespersons told lies to try to persuade consumers to change from BT to the defendant's telephone service. When the claimant complained, the defendant made appropriate undertakings but, unfortunately, the lies continued. The defendant claimed to have made attempts to prevent their salespersons telling lies. Jacob J refused to allow a qualification which would have prevented the defendant being in contempt of court if, in spite of using its best endeavours to prevent salespersons deceiving consumers, they still do so.

Trap orders can be very effective where counterfeit goods are concerned. Summary judgment is likely to follow in such cases with the only issue being the form of the injunction and the assessment of damages. In *Microsoft Corporation* v *Plato Technology Ltd*,[178] agents acting for the claimant bought five counterfeit copies of the claimant's Windows 95 operating system software from the defendant. As it was accepted that the defendant had acted honestly and had not realised the copies were counterfeit, an injunction was granted restraining the defendant from dealing in the claimant's software products which he knew, or ought upon reasonable inquiry to know, were counterfeit.

Limitations and defences

The Directive contains a number of specific limitations on the effects of a trade mark in Article 6 (see s 11 of the Act). These allow a person to use his own name and address, to use indications to describe the characteristics of his goods or services or to use the trade mark to indicate the intended purpose of a product or service, such as accessories or spare parts. There is a requirement that the use is honest in an objective sense. Earlier rights that apply only in a particular locality may also be immune from attack based on a registered trade mark if Member States so provide. The Directive also provides for a defence based on acquiescence and there may be other defences available in the circumstances, such as lack of title to sue. In many cases, a defendant will put in a defence based on lack of a likelihood of confusion or damage to the repute of a trade mark and other aspects related to the scope of the rights and infringement. It is also common for a defendant to counterclaim for revocation or invalidity.

Another form of defence may be based on the principle of exhaustion of rights, where goods put on the market within the Community[179] by or with the consent of the proprietor

175 [1983] FSR 313.

176 [1975] FSR 45.

177 [2000] FSR 679.

178 [1999] FSR 834.

179 Now the European Economic Area.

180 The Directive applies to the European Economic Area as a result of the Agreement on the European Economic Area of 2 May 1992, OJ L 1, 03.01.1994, p 3.

are further commercialised: for example, where they are bought in one Member State and imported into another Member State for resale.[180] This section of the chapter looks at the limitations in the Directive first, followed by acquiescence and exhaustion of rights.

Limitation of the effects of a trade mark

Use in accordance with honest practices in industrial or commercial matters is the test for non-infringing use in Article 6(1), which states that a trade mark shall not entitle the proprietor to prohibit a third party from using, in the course of trade:

(a) his own name or address,
(b) indications concerning the kind, quality, quantity, intended purpose, value, geographical origin, the time of production of goods or of rendering of the service, or other characteristic of goods or services,
(c) the trade mark where it is necessary to indicate the intended purpose of a product or service, in particular, as accessories or spare parts, or
(d) provided he uses them in accordance with honest practices in industrial or commercial matters.

The presence of the limitations has no bearing on the absolute grounds for refusal of trade marks. For example, the fact that a trade mark for which registration is sought is a common name or is a word or phrase that other undertakings might reasonably use to describe characteristics of their own goods or services, and could be subject to the limitations of the effects of trade marks, is not a factor to be taken into account when determining registrability. It is no answer to say that, if the trade mark is registered, any conflicts with names and descriptive words and phrases can be resolved by reference to the limitations. The limitations are there to allow the use of own names and descriptions where trade marks are registered on proof of acquired distinctiveness even though without such proof they would not be registrable.

181 Case C-558/08 *Portakabin Ltd* v *Primakabin BV* [2010] ECR I-6959. The defendant, which leased second-hand portable units made by the claimant, used 'Portakabin' and various misspellings as search engine keywords.

Where the use of trade marks as keywords in sponsored links lists (AdWords) in an internet referencing service (such as Google's search engine) can be prohibited under Article 5 of the trade marks Directive then, generally, the exception under Article 6(1) does not apply. However, it is for national courts to determine whether such use is in accordance with honest practices in industrial or commercial matters.[181]

Honest practices

Use in accordance with honest practices could be where a trader uses his own name, not having deliberately selected a trading name to capture goodwill associated with a registered trade mark. Another example is where a trader uses a geographical name to indicate the origin of his goods or the place from which he provides a service. In *NAD Electronics Inc* v *NAD Computer Systems Ltd*,[182] Ferris J considered that the test for honest practices was equivalent to *bona fide* use under s 8 of the 1938 Act, approving Lloyd Jacob J in *George Ballantine & Sons Ltd* v *Ballantine Stewart & Co Ltd*[183] in relation to the adoption of a company name similar to an existing trade mark, where he held that the relevant aspect was the use made of the company name, not the *bona fides* in selecting the name in the first place. A criticism of Ferris J's judgment on this point is that it is not clear that 'honest practices' is the direct equivalent of '*bona fides*'. Honest practices in the cut and thrust of commercial life may not necessarily be *bona fide* in a strict sense. The question should be what reasonable and honest traders consider to be acceptable.

182 [1997] FSR 380.

183 [1959] RPC 47.

It was accepted that a subjective approach to the question of *bona fide* was appropriate under the 1938 Act. However, the determination of what constitutes honest practices under the Directive is objective. In *Aktiebolaget Volvo* v *Heritage (Leicester) Ltd*,[184] the defendant had been an authorised dealer for the claimant's Volvo cars. After termination of the

184 [2000] FSR 253.

dealership, the defendant continued to use the name Volvo, but also used the words 'independent' and 'specialist' with it, as in 'Independent Volvo Specialist'. It was held by Rattee J that the continued use of the name Volvo clearly fell within the ambit of use within s 11(2)(c), but the defence was not made out as the use was not in accordance with honest practices. He said that the question was whether a reasonable motor trader would think it was in accordance with honest practices in that business. In this case, he considered that the continued use was calculated to confuse and some customers would probably believe that the defendant remained an authorised dealer for Volvo cars.[185]

The Court of Justice dealt with a not dissimilar question in Case C-63/97 *Bayerische Motorenwerke AG v Ronald Karel Deenik*,[186] in which a Dutch car dealer sold and repaired second-hand BMW cars. He advertised using statements such as 'BMW Specialist' and 'Repairs and Maintenance of BMWs'. It was held, *inter alia*, that the limitation in Article 6(1)(c)[187] applied unless the trade mark was used in such a way to create an impression that there is a commercial connection with the trade mark proprietor: for example, that the person using the mark is affiliated with the proprietor's business or there is a special relationship between the undertakings.[188] In the *Volvo* case above, the judge did think it was possible that such an impression would be gained.

In *Bayerische Motorenwerke v Deenik* the Court of Justice ruled that the condition of honest practices constitutes in practice a duty to act fairly in relation to the legitimate interests of the proprietor of the trade mark. In Case C-100/02 *Gerolsteiner Brunnen GmbH & Co v Putsch GmbH*,[189] the Court of Justice confirmed this and went further in holding that the mere fact that there is a likelihood of aural confusion between a word mark registered in one Member State and an indication of geographical origin from another Member State is not sufficient, *per se*, to conclude that the use of the indication in the course of trade is not in accordance with honest practices. In that case, Gerolsteiner made soft drinks and the like under the trade mark 'Gerri' registered in Germany. Putsch imported soft drinks bottled in County Kerry in Ireland under the name 'Kerry Spring'. The Court of Justice pointed out that, in a Community of 15 Member States with significant linguistic differences, soon due to be enlarged, the chances of a phonetic similarity between a trade mark registered in one Member State and an indication of geographical origin in another Member State was already substantial and likely to increase. Now, of course, there are 27 Member States.

Own name and address

The fact that there is an own name limitation under Article 6(1)(a) does not affect an assessment as to whether a trade mark is devoid of any distinctive character under Article 3(1)(b).[190] At the time of the adoption of the Directive, the European Council and the Commission were of the view that this limitation was restricted to the names and addresses of natural persons. However, it was accepted that the question was one for the Court of Justice and, in Case C-245/02 *Anheuser-Busch Inc v Budějovicky Budvar*,[191] the Court of Justice ruled that the limitation also applied to trade names as there was no such restriction to natural persons in the wording of the Directive.[192] In Case C-17/06 *Celine Sarl v Celine SA*,[193] the Court of Justice, referring to Anheuser-Busch, ruled (at para 34):

> . . . it must be noted that, in assessing whether the condition of honest practice is satisfied, account must be taken first of the extent to which the use of the third party's name is understood by the relevant public, or at least a significant section of that public, as indicating a link between the third party's goods or services and the trade mark proprietor or a person authorised to use the trade mark, and secondly of the extent to which the third party ought to have been aware of that. Another factor to be taken into account when making the assessment is whether the trade mark concerned enjoys a certain reputation in the Member State in which it is registered and its protection is sought, from which the third party might profit in marketing his goods or services.

185 Rattee J also found that infringement fell within s 10(1) as the sign was identical to the word mark Volvo notwithstanding the addition of other words or material.

186 [1999] ECR I-905.

187 Equivalent to the Trade Marks Act 1994 s 11(2)(c).

188 As regards the sale of second-hand BMWs the court held that the doctrine of exhaustion of rights applied as set out in the Trade Marks Directive Article 7.

189 [2004] ECR I-691.

190 Case C-404/02 *Nichols plc v Registrar of Trade Marks* [2004] ECR I-8499.

191 [2004] ECR I-10989.

192 See also Case C-17/06 *Celine Sarl v Celine SA* [2007] ECR I-7041.

193 [2007] ECR I-7041.

Previously, in the UK, there was some doubt as to whether the equivalent provision in s 11(2)(a) of the Trade Marks Act 1994 applied to company and trading names. At first sight, the language of that paragraph appears restricted to natural persons, referring as it does to 'his own name and address' (as indeed does the Directive). Under the 1938 Act, *bona fide* use by a person of his own name was assumed to apply also to artificial legal persons such as companies.[194] This issue has arisen a number of times under the 1994 Act. Although Ferris J cast some doubt on this in the *NAD Electronics* case, it was accepted by Lloyd J at first instance in *Scandecor Developments AB v Scandecor Marketing AB*.[195] He said that the use of a corporate name could be within the provision even if used with the omission of 'Limited'. The same ought to apply to 'plc' and other equivalents.[196] This conclusion seemed sensible and was followed in *Euromarket Designs Inc v Peters and Crate & Barrel*.[197] In *DaimlerChrysler AG v Javid Alavi (t/a MERC)*,[198] Pumfrey J was sympathetic to this view and, although he did not have to decide the point, he accepted that the limitation could apply also in respect of a trading name, for example, as used by the sole trader defendant in that case. However, on appeal in the *Scandecor* case,[199] the House of Lords decided to refer a number of questions for a preliminary ruling to the Court of Justice under Article 234 of the EC Treaty (now Article 267 of the Treaty on the Functioning of the European Union). One of those questions was whether a company is a person for the purposes of s 11(2)(a). Lord Nicholls of Birkenhead (at para 54) said the issue was not *acte claire*. The reference was withdrawn but has now been overtaken by the *Anheuser-Busch* ruling confirming that the limitation also applies to trade names and is not restricted to the names of natural persons.

In *Asprey and Garrard Ltd v WRA (Guns) Ltd*,[200] the claimant had a registered trade mark 'ASPREY' and the second defendant was a member of the family which had run the claimant company's predecessor in title. His name was William R Asprey and he formed the first defendant company and decided to open a shop in London which carried his name, 'William R Asprey, Esquire', across the top of the shop-front. It was held that this amounted to trade mark infringement and passing off and the 'own name' defence did not avail the defendant. The Court of Appeal confirmed that the defence could never apply to the names of new companies otherwise the route to piracy would be obvious. The same applies to a newly adopted trade name other than its own name. The Court of Appeal also held that, no matter how honest a defendant's subjective intentions were, any use of his own name which amounted to passing off could not be in accordance with honest practices in industrial or commercial matters within the s 11(2) defence. Similarly, the own name defence cannot apply to a registered company which chooses a trading name the same or very similar to a well-known trade mark. In *Hotel Cipriani SRL v Cipriani (Grosvenor Street) Ltd*,[201] the claimant owned the famous CIPRIANI trade mark registered for hotels and restaurants. The defendant opened a restaurant in London under the name CIPRIANI LONDON. It was clear that there was a likelihood of confusion as the additional word LONDON was not distinctive. As regards the own name defence, it was held that the defendant could not avail itself of the defence as it was not its own name.[202] Arnold J said that the defence could not be interpreted as applying to a company's trading name as opposed to its registered name. Otherwise, this would constitute a substantial inroad into the rights conferred by the trade mark, particularly where a company has only just commenced trading. However, in the Court of Appeal[203] Lloyd LJ said (at para 72):

> . . . the Art.12(a) defence may be available in respect of a trading name, as well as the corporate name of a company, but it will depend on (a) what the trading name is that has been adopted, (b) in what circumstances it has been adopted and (c), depending on the relevant circumstances, whether the use is in accordance with honest practices.

In *Och-Ziff Management Europe Ltd v Och Capital LLP*,[204] another case on the CTM, Arnold J held that the use of the 'Och Capital' by the first defendant, which had been set up by

194 See, for example, *Parker-Knoll Ltd v Knoll International Ltd* [1962] RPC 265.

195 [1998] FSR 500.

196 The own-name limitation will not apply in the case of a newly formed company otherwise the route to piracy would be obvious: *WEBSPHERE Trade Mark* [2004] FSR 39. However, in any case, the use has to be in accordance with honest practices.

197 [2001] FSR 20.

198 [2001] RPC 42.

199 *Scandecor Developments AB v Scandecor Marketing AB* [2002] FSR 7.

200 [2002] FSR 31.

201 [2009] RPC 9. This case involved a Community trade mark but the same principles must apply.

202 Following *Asprey*. Neither Cipriani nor Cipriani London was the name of the company even though the company name included Cipriani. Although the sole director of the company was called Giuseppi Cipriani, the company could not use this as a defence as it was the company, not he, which used the name.

203 *Hotel Cipriani Srl v Cipriani (Grosvenor Street) Ltd* [2010] RPC 16.

204 [2011] FSR 11.

the third defendant whose name was Mr Ochocki, was not in accordance with honest practices in industrial or commercial matters. Mr Ochocki had been aware of the existence of the claimant's company when he set up the first defendant company, he had not carried out a trade mark search or taken legal advice. Furthermore, the claimant had objected to the defendant company's name at an early stage when it would have been relatively easy for it to modify its name. Moreover, the first defendant had not discharged its duty to act fairly in relation to the legitimate interests of the claimant and its use of 'Och' amounted to unfair competition.

The own name defence cannot apply where an abbreviation of the name is used which appears the same or very similar to the trade mark. In *Premier Luggage and Bags Ltd* v *Premier Company (UK) Ltd*,[205] the defendant's salespersons introduced themselves as being from 'Premier', 'Premier Luggage' or 'Premier Luggage Company' rather than from 'Premier Company (UK) Ltd' and this amounted to an infringement of the claimant's trade mark 'PREMIER'.

205 [2003] FSR 5.

Indications of certain characteristics of goods or services

In Case C-100/02 *Gerolsteiner Brunnen GmbH & Co* v *Putsch GmbH*,[206] the Court of Justice confirmed that where there is a likelihood of an aural confusion between a trade mark registered in one Member State and an indication of geographic origin in another Member State, the latter may be prevented by the proprietor only if the use is not in accordance with honest practices, this being a matter for assessment of the relevant circumstances by the national court. There seems no reason to suggest that the same logic should not apply to the other indications covered by Article 6(1)(b).[207] Indeed, this should not be restricted to a likelihood of aural confusion and should apply, not only to other forms of possible confusion (for example, textual, visual and conceptual), but to indications that are identical to registered trade marks and used in relation to identical goods or services. The only issue is the question of fact – whether the use is in accordance with honest practices – this being a matter for a national court to decide. Furthermore, the Directive does not require that the indication is used in a Member State other than that in which the trade mark is registered.

206 [2004] ECR I-691.

207 Of course, the Court of Justice has to consider the questions submitted to it on a reference for a preliminary ruling and should not venture on a wholesale analysis of the relevant provisions of the legislation under hypothetical situations.

The inclusion of 'other characteristics' means that the list in Article 6(1)(b) is not exhaustive and the preceding characteristics are sufficiently diverse to suggest that almost any characteristic should be within the limitation such as the material from which goods are made, their colour and surface texture or even the manufacturing process used to make the goods.[208] However, there is no general interest rule on keeping certain signs available for use by other undertakings going beyond Article 6(1)(b).[209]

In Case C-48/05 *Adam Opel AG* v *Autec AG*,[210] the defendant made scale model cars which bore the claimant's trade mark which was registered, *inter alia*, for motor vehicles and toys. The Court of Justice confirmed that this was outside Article 6(1)(b). Applying an identical sign to the scale models so as to faithfully reproduce the claimant's vehicles, and marketing those scale models, does not constitute the use of an indication of the characteristics of the scale models within Article 6(1)(b) of the trade marks Directive. It remains possible that the use complained of does not infringe under Article 5(1)(a) on the basis that it is not use as a trade mark and does not affect the essential function of the claimant's trade mark. It may not infringe under Article 5(2) unless the use is without undue cause and takes unfair advantage of, or is detrimental to, the distinctive character or repute of the registered trade mark.[211]

208 In *O2 Holdings Ltd* v *Hutchinson 3G Ltd* [2007] RPC 16, Jacob LJ said that he could not think of any characteristic not mentioned.

209 Case C-102/07 *Adidas AG* v *Marca Mode CV* [2008] ECR I-2439.

210 [2007] ECR I-1-17.

Article 6(1)(b) (s 11(2)(b) of the Trade Marks Act 1994) has been used in the UK as a defence on a number of occasions. For example, in *British Sugar plc* v *James Robertson & Sons Ltd*[212] it was held that the defendant's use of the phrase 'Toffee Treat' was within s 11(2)(b) although, in any event, the claimant's 'TREAT' trade mark was declared to be invalid. The same result occurred in *Philips Electronics NV* v *Remington Consumer Products*

211 Assuming the registered trade mark is one having a reputation in the Member State concerned.

212 [1996] RPC 281.

213 [1998] RPC 283.

214 The Court of Appeal confirmed that the use of the sign (the defendant's three-headed rotary shaver) would be seen as an indication of its intended purpose and was within s 11(2)(b): *Philips Electronics NV v Remington Consumer Products Ltd* [1999] RPC 809. Although this case was referred to the Court of Justice, this particular aspect was not considered.

215 [1996] FSR 205.

216 [2001] FSR 32.

217 Joined Cases C-108/97 and C-109/97 *Windsurfing Chiemsee* v *Huber & Attenberger* [1999] ECR I-2779, in which the Court of Justice confirmed that Article 6(1)(b) of the Directive did not confer upon third parties a right to use the name or word as a trade mark. It only allowed them to use it descriptively, for example, as an indication of geographic origin provided the use was in accordance with honest practices.

218 [2005] ECR I-2337.

Ltd[213] (defendant's use within s 11(2)(b) but the claimant's registration was declared invalid).[214] In *Bravado Merchandising Services Ltd* v *Mainstream Publishing (Edinburgh) Ltd*,[215] the defendant published a book entitled *A Sweet Little Mystery – Wet Wet Wet – The Inside Story*. The book was about the pop group called 'Wet Wet Wet', which had been registered as a trade mark. The defendant's use of the mark fell within s 11(2)(b) because it was descriptive of the content of the book.

The relationship between s 11(2)(b) and s 10(6) came up for consideration in *British Airways plc* v *Ryanair Ltd*,[216] in which it was argued that the defence cannot apply where the trade mark is used in comparative advertising. That argument was rejected by Jacob J who gave the following two examples:

'Bisto' is as tasty as 'Oxo'
'Bisto' tastes stronger than 'Oxo'

Also alluding to the fact that traders like to compare prices in their advertising, Jacob J said that in such cases the trade mark is being used to give an indication of the characteristics of the goods.

The defence in s 11(2)(b) applies in such a way to allow traders to use a registered trade mark, or part thereof, which is descriptive or contains descriptive elements such as a geographical name, as set out in s 11(2)(b). For example, 'YORKSHIRE TEA' is a registered trade mark. This fact should not prevent another trader based in Yorkshire who sells speciality teas by mail order advertising his wares from using the phrase 'Best quality teas sent direct to you from our premises in Yorkshire'. Such descriptive use is acceptable. It may not be acceptable, however, to use the descriptive word as a trade mark for the defendant's goods such as in 'We sell only the best quality YORKSHIRE TEA and coffee'.[217]

Accessories and spare parts

Article 6(1)(c) allows third parties to use trade marks where necessary to indicate the intended purpose of their own products or services. Accessories and spare parts are mentioned as specific examples but the provision is not limited to these. The inclusion of services reinforces this. For example, services might be rendered in relation to maintenance, repair or refurbishment of products, for example. An important reason why this limitation exists is that, without it, a trade mark proprietor might be in a position to distort competition, for example, by preventing or restricting the use of the trade mark by independent spare parts manufacturers or repairers.

In Case C-228/03 *Gillette Company* v *LA-Laboratories Ltd Oy*,[218] the Gillette Company had a registration for the trade marks 'Gillette' and 'Sensor' for razors, etc. and Gillette Group Finland held an exclusive licence to use those trade marks in Finland and had been selling razors comprising handles with replaceable blades. LA-Laboratories made razors and blades sold under the trade mark Parason Flexor and sold blades with a sticker applied to their packaging which stated 'All Parason Flexor and Gillette Sensor handles are compatible with this blade'. A number of questions were referred to the Court of Justice. Particular issues were whether a replacement blade for the razor was a spare part or a product in its own right and whether the use of the trade mark to indicate the intended purpose was 'necessary', the scope of honest practices in relation to Article 6(1)(c) and whether the limitation applied where the third party not only made something which could be a spare part for the proprietor's product but also made the product itself.

The Court of Justice ruled that the use by a third party of a trade mark with an accessory or spare part may still fall within Article 6(1)(c) even if the third party also markets the product with which the accessory or spare part can be used if necessary to indicate the intended purposes and if in accordance with honest practices.

Use of the trade mark was *necessary* if it was the only way in practice to provide the public with comprehensible and complete information on that intended purpose so as to preserve the undistorted system of competition in the market for that product. This is a matter for a national court taking into account the nature of the public for whom the product is made. There is no distinction between the use of a trade mark with an accessory or spare part or other purposes to which a product may be put. Accessories and spare parts are examples of the types of products where a third party may wish to use a trade mark to indicate their intended purpose but Article 6(1)(c) is not limited to accessories and spare parts. It is, therefore, not necessary to determine whether a product is an accessory or spare part. The Court of Justice had previously held that the use of a trade mark by a third party to indicate that he specialises in the sale, repair or maintenance of a particular make of car constitutes a use to indicate intended purpose in Case C-63/97 *Bayerische Motorenwerke AG v Ronald Karel Deenik.*[219]

219 [1999] ECR I-905.

In most cases, it will be impossible to communicate the intended purpose of an accessory or spare part for a particular product or services provided in relation to a particular product without using the trade mark under which the product is sold or is known. In many cases, the name of the manufacturer of the product will be a trade mark and the main name by which the product is known, such as BMW, Ford, Kodak, Peugeot, etc. If an independent company specialises in selling second-hand BMW cars and providing servicing, maintenance and repairs for BMW cars, it would be unrealistic not to expect him to advertise his services by using the BMW name, which is a registered trade mark. If this were to be prevented, that would distort competition as only authorised dealers would be able to use the name under licence from the BMW car company.

In the *Gillette* case, the Court of Justice also set out some examples as to what would not constitute honest practices in the context of Article 6(1)(c), being where:

- the use of the trade mark gave the impression that there was a connection between the third party and the trade mark proprietor;
- the use affects the value of the trade mark by taking unfair advantage of its distinctive character or repute;
- the use entails discrediting or denigrating the trade mark; or
- the third party represents its product as an imitation or replica of the product bearing the trade mark.

The fact that a third party uses a trade mark to indicate the intended purpose of his product does not necessarily mean that it is being represented as being the same quality or having equivalent properties as the product bearing the trade mark. In *Gillette*, what the Court of Justice had to say was in the context of products, but the same considerations should also apply to services provided by third parties in relation to products.

Whilst it might be acceptable to use a trade name to advertise reconditioned goods originally made by the trade mark proprietor as suitable for use with other goods, it would be unlikely to be acceptable to fail to remove the trade mark from those reconditioned goods,[220] unless it was necessary to leave the trade mark on the reconditioned goods in order to indicate their intended purpose.

220 *PAG Ltd v Hawk-Woods Ltd* [2002] FSR 46.

Earlier right in a particular locality

The use by a third party in the course of trade of an earlier right, which applies only in a particular locality, cannot be prevented by the proprietor of the trade mark under Article 6(2). The earlier right must be one which is recognised by the laws of the Member State in question and within the limits of the territory in which it is recognised.

The Trade Marks Act 1994, s 11(3), states that an earlier right is an unregistered trade mark or other sign continuously in use in relation to goods or services by a person or predecessor in title from a time before the use or registration of the trade mark by the proprietor or predecessor in title in relation to those goods or services. In other words, the use of the earlier right must predate the first use or registration, whichever is the earlier of the registered trade mark. Furthermore, the use of the earlier right must be continuous. The earlier right must be one protected by any rule of law, particularly passing off, in the relevant locality.

To give an example, say that Andrew used the name 'Milkwood' for his homemade honey which he sold from market stalls in Devon and Cornwall from 1995 to 1998. During that time, the name became well known in that area and goodwill was established in the name but, in 1999, Andrew became ill and was unable to carry on. However, during 2001, Andrew's daughter Betty, who had returned to the UK after spending some time abroad, decided to resurrect the business and she recommenced making and selling the honey in the same locality under the 'Milkwood' name. In 2004, a French company, Miel et Cie SA, decided to start marketing its honey, jams and preserves in the UK and registered the name 'Milkwood' as a UK trade mark during that year, without any knowledge of the use of the name by Andrew or Betty. In 2005, Betty grew tired of the business and sold it to Cedric together with the goodwill of the business. Cedric took over immediately and continued to sell honey under the 'Milkwood' name in Devon and Cornwall. In 2006, Miel brought infringement proceedings against Cedric on the basis of its registered trade mark. The action will fail as the use of the name by Cedric and his predecessor in title, Betty, has been continuous since 2001, which predates the use or registration of the name as a trade mark by Miel. The conclusion would be different, of course, if Miel had started selling honey under the name during 2000 even though it did not register the name as a trade mark until after 2001, since the use of the name by Cedric's predecessors in title had been interrupted between 1999 and 2001.[221]

With the emphasis on a particular locality and the requirement for continuous use from before the use or registration of the registered trade mark, it would appear that the provision permits the continuing use of the earlier right in that locality only and does not provide a right to extend the immunity from infringement to new geographical areas. In terms of a right in goodwill the limitation will be restricted to those areas where it has already been built up and existed continuously since.

Conflict of registered trade marks

Article 9(3) of the Directive limits the right in trade marks on the basis of acquiescence for a period of five successive years. So, for example, an earlier registered trade mark or other earlier right may not be used to attack the validity of a registered trade mark or oppose its use if the conditions for acquiescence apply. In such circumstances, the later trade mark may not be used to oppose the use of the earlier trade mark or other earlier right even though they may not be invoked against the later trade mark. Acquiescence is described more fully later but the Trade Marks Act 1994 also states, under s 11(1),[222] that a registered trade mark is not infringed by the use of another registered trade mark. That does not prevent an application for a declaration of invalidity, of course. This provision makes no distinction regarding the timing of registration so will apply where there is a potential infringement of either the earlier or the later registered trade mark.

That one of two registered trade marks could otherwise be used in an infringement action against the other may seem unlikely because of the opposition process or because of the honest concurrent use provisions in s 7.[223] The situation is not, however, impossible. It may have been that an opportunity to oppose the registration of the later trade mark has been missed, through lack of vigilance, for example. In such a situation, the only way forward for the proprietor of the first mark is to apply for a declaration of invalidity in respect of the second mark. As a declaration of invalidity has the consequence that the trade mark is treated as never having been registered, in whole or to the extent that it is found to be invalid, a question arises as to whether the proprietor of the first mark, if successful in the application for invalidity, can subsequently bring an action for infringement. This would seem to be so as s 11(1) expressly draws attention to the effect

221 Even if the goodwill in the name survived the interruption and had been assigned to Betty by Andrew.

222 This appears to be a home-grown provision.

223 Under the Trade Marks Act 1994 s 7(3), honest concurrent use is declared to be as under the Trade Marks Act 1938 s 12(2). The case of *Second Sight Ltd* v *Novell UK Ltd* [1995] RPC 423 affords an example of applications for registration made under this provision. It gives a defence only as from the date of registration.

of a declaration of invalidity. In some cases, where there is a conflict between trade marks or between a trade mark and some other earlier right, a defence of acquiescence may be put forward.

Acquiescence

The proprietor's rights will be limited if he has acquiesced in the use of a later registered trade mark for a continuous period of five years, being aware of such use unless registration of the later trade mark was applied for in bad faith: Article 9(1) of the Directive. Member States may also apply this limitation in respect of some other earlier right. The UK provided for acquiescence in both cases under s 48. The proprietor of the earlier trade mark or other right will not be entitled to apply for a declaration of invalidity of the later trade mark or oppose its use. However, the limitation is reciprocal in that the proprietor of the later trade mark will not be able to oppose the use of the earlier trade mark or other earlier right even though the earlier trade mark or right can no longer be invoked against the later trade mark.

Exhaustion of rights

The principle of exhaustion of rights applies where goods are placed on the market within the Community (now applies to the European Economic Area) by or with the consent of the proprietor of any intellectual property rights subsisting in relation to the goods. The principle prevents the proprietor from using those rights to interfere with any subsequent commercialisation of the goods in question. Thus, a third party may buy goods on sale within the Community by or with the consent of the proprietor and import them into another part of the Community and resell them there. The principle is more fully explained and described in relation to intellectual property rights in general and specifically in Chapter 25. It is mentioned here briefly as it is expressly mentioned in the Directive and in the Trade Marks Act 1994.

Under Article 7(1) of the Directive, a trade mark proprietor cannot prohibit the use of the trade mark in relation to goods put on the market in the Community under that trade mark by him or with his consent. The reference to a person having his consent is, for example, to a licensee having the right to make or sell the goods or provide services under the trade mark or in relation to a distributor or agent acting for the proprietor. Thus, if a trade mark proprietor sells perfume to which his trade mark has been applied in Portugal, another person may buy a quantity of that perfume and import it into the Benelux countries and put it on sale there. There will be no infringement even though the perfume will have been exported from Portugal, imported into and put on sale in the Benelux countries.

The rationale for the principle is that, without it, undertakings would be able to control the subsequent commercialisation of their goods and this would allow them to partition or distort the market within the Community. An example would be where, taking advantage of differing economic conditions, they could charge a higher price in one Member State compared with another Member State, perhaps because consumers in one were more affluent than in others. To allow this would detract from one of the main aims underpinning the Community, being the establishment and consolidation of a single market.

A trade mark proprietor may grant licences in respect of the trade mark but may include terms in the licence agreement which seek to prevent the sale or distribution of the goods in question to certain types of wholesalers or retailers. For example, the proprietor of a trade mark used for luxury goods might want to prevent the licensee selling the goods to discount shops or selling them online. In Case C-9/08 *Copad SA* v *Christian Dior couture SA*,[224] Christian Dior was the proprietor of the Dior trade mark used in relation to luxury corsetry. The licence agreement stated that the licensee must not sell the goods to, *inter alia*, discount stores without permission from the licensor. The licensee sought permission but this was refused. In spite of this the licensee sold goods bearing the mark to a discount store. Article 8(2) of the Directive states that the proprietor of a trade mark can invoke his rights against a licensee '. . . who contravenes any provision of his licence contract with regard to its duration, the form covered by the registration in which the trade mark may be used, the scope of the goods or services for which the licence is granted, the territory in which the trade mark may be affixed, or the quality of the goods manufactured or of the services provided by the licensee'. The Court of Justice ruled that a licensee puts goods on the market without the consent of the proprietor only under one of the circumstances listed under Article 8(2). However, 'quality of the goods' can extend in the case of luxury goods the 'allure and prestigious image which bestows upon those goods an aura of luxury'.

As will be seen in Chapter 25, the rights afforded by registered trade marks have to be controlled because of the ease with which they could be used to interfere with the subsequent commercialisation of goods. At this stage it should be noted that the principle of exhaustion of rights is limited to goods put on the market in the European Economic Area ('EEA')[225] and does not apply where the goods in question are first placed on the market by the trade mark proprietor or with his consent outside the EEA.[226]

There is a proviso to the principle of exhaustion of rights under Article 7(2) which disapplies the principle in a case where there are legitimate reasons for the proprietor to oppose further commercialisation of the goods. Specific examples are mentioned, being where the condition of the goods is changed or impaired after they have been put on the market. This is particularly relevant in the case of repackaging pharmaceuticals. In some cases, this may have to be done to comply with national regulations: for example, where they require pharmaceuticals to be sold in certain quantities or where there is consumer resistance to buying pharmaceuticals in the original packaging but with labels attached.[227] In *Copad* v *Christian Dior*, the Court of Justice also ruled that, in a case where a licensee is in contravention of the licence agreement, but nonetheless a national court finds that the goods have been put on the market with the consent of the proprietor,[228] that proprietor can oppose resale under Article 7(2) only if it is established that such resale damages the reputation of the trade mark.[229] The national court will have to consider whether further commercialisation of the luxury goods bearing the trade mark by the third party, using methods which are customary in its sector of trade, damages the reputation of that trade mark.

In Case C-558/08 *Portakabin Ltd* v *Primakabin BV*,[230] the defendant sold and leased second-hand portable units (such as offices) made by the claimant. The defendant used internet search engine keywords including the Portakabin trade mark and various misspellings so as to appear in sponsored links if a person entered Portakabin or a misspelling in a search engine. In terms of Article 7, the Court of Justice ruled that the trade mark proprietor could not prevent this unless there existed a legitimate reason to oppose the advertising under Article 7(2).[231] It would be for the national court to determine whether there was a legitimate reason on the following basis:

- The court cannot find that the advertisement gives the impression that the advertiser and the trade mark proprietor are economically linked, or that the advertisement

224 [2009] ECR I-3421.

225 The Directive including the principle of exhaustion of rights applies within the EEA, which comprises the EC, Iceland, Liechtenstein and Norway: Agreement on the European Economic Area of 2 May 1992, OJ L 1, 03.01.1994, p 3. The Trade Marks Act 1994 s 12 expressly mentions the EEA.

226 See, for example, Joined Cases C-414/99 to 416/99 *Zino Davidoff SA* v *A & G Imports Ltd* [2001] ECR I-8691.

227 See, for example, Case C-143/00 *Boehringer Ingelheim KG* v *Swingward Ltd* [2002] ECR I-3759, discussed in Chapter 25.

228 For example, because the national court finds that the sale is unlikely to undermine the quality of luxury goods.

229 The examples mentioned in Article 7(2) (changed or impaired condition) are not exhaustive because of the use of the word 'especially'.

230 [2010] ECR I-6959.

231 Notwithstanding the possibility that such use might infringe under Article 5 and not be saved under Article 6 if it was not clear to the average internet user whether the advertisement was from the trade mark proprietor (or a economically linked undertaking) or from a third party.

is seriously detrimental to the trade mark, merely because of the use of the trade mark with additional wording indicating that the goods are being resold as used or second-hand.

- The court is, however, bound to find that there is a legitimate reason to oppose where the trade mark is used to advertise the resale activities where the advertiser has replaced the trade mark by his own trade mark, thereby concealing the manufacturer's trade mark.
- A specialist reseller of second-hand goods under the other's trade mark can use that trade mark to advertise its resale activities which include, in addition to the sale of second-hand goods under that mark, the sale of other second-hand goods unless, in the light of their volume, presentation or poor quality, this risks seriously damaging the image which the trade mark proprietor has created for his mark.

Article 7(2) does not prevent the repackaging of goods other than by the undertaking which then markets the goods. In Joined Cases C-400/09 and C-207/10 *Orifarm A/S v Merck, Sharp & Dohme Corp*,[232] companies (A and B), being part of a group of companies, were involved in the parallel importation and repackaging of pharmaceutical products which had been put on the market with the EEA with the consent of the trade mark proprietor. These companies had the necessary authorisations to repackage the products but the repackaging indicated the names of other companies in the group (C and D) which had the necessary authorisations to market and sell the pharmaceutical products. The Court of Justice ruled that the trade mark owner could not object on the sole ground that the packaging indicated that C and D were the repackagers even though A and B had actually repackaged the products under the instructions of C and D which assumed liability for the repackaging.

232 28 July 2011.

Groundless threats of infringement proceedings

As with patents, the UK design right and registered design and the Community Design, there is an action for groundless threats of infringement proceedings under the UK Trade Marks Act 1994: s 21. This action was not available under the Trade Marks Act 1938. It applies in the UK in respect of threats concerning a UK registered trade mark or a CTM.[233] The action under trade mark law has not been modified as it has been under patent law where the proprietor is now allowed to make enquiries to ascertain whether or by whom his patent has been infringed and the further restriction of acts in relation to the patent which may trigger a groundless threats action.[234]

233 Community Trade Marks Regulations 1996, SI 1996/1908, reg 4.

234 Patents Act 1977, s 70, as modified by the Patents Act 2004, s 12.

Under s 21(1), any person aggrieved by a threat made to bring an infringement action against another may bring an action for groundless threats except where the threat is in relation to:

(a) the application of the mark to goods or their packaging,[235]
(b) the importation of goods to which, or to the packaging of which, the mark has been applied, or
(c) the supply of services under the mark.

235 Note that use under s 10(4) mentions 'affixing' rather than 'applying'.

A groundless threats action can be brought, for example, to selling or offering to sell goods under the trade mark, using the trade mark in business papers or in advertising or stocking goods to which the trade mark has been applied for the purposes of selling them. The action is intended to prevent heavy-handed threats being made typically to secondary infringers such as retailers who may simply stop ordering further supplies of the alleged infringing goods rather than challenge the validity of the trade mark. However, the section is worded so that any person aggrieved may bring the action. For example, a manufacturer of goods to which the alleged offending sign has been applied may bring an action where a retailer is no longer willing to accept supplies of the goods because of threats made against the retailer.

Originally, there was a common law action for malicious threats similar to that for slander of title.[236] In statutory form, it first saw the light of day in the Patents, Designs and Trade Marks Act 1883. The remedy was originally used to prevent a proprietor of a patent 'from holding a sword of Damocles above another's head', particularly if they were 'willing to wound, but yet afraid to strike'.[237] The threat may be express, as in a letter or spoken, or it may be implicit.[238] The threat will typically convey the fact that the maker of the threat has a registered trade mark which he intends to enforce against the recipient. As Lightman J said in *L'Oréal (UK) Ltd* v *Johnson & Johnson*:[239]

> It matters not that the threat may be veiled or covert, conditional or future. Nor does it matter that the threat is made in response to an enquiry from the party threatened.

Relief is a declaration that threats are unjustifiable, an injunction against continuance and damages.[240] Under s 21(2), the claimant is entitled to such relief unless the defendant shows that the act in respect of which proceedings were threatened was or would be an infringement, but even then the claimant will be entitled to relief if he shows that the registration is invalid or liable to be revoked in any material respect: s 21(3). Mere notification that the mark is registered or that application for registration has been made does not constitute a threat of proceedings by s 21(4).

From the viewpoint of a proprietor of a registered trade mark, it is unwise to threaten proceedings in such a way as to precipitate a groundless threats action. He will have to show that the acts complained of infringe the trade mark and, in many cases, he will also have to withstand an attack on the validity of the mark. Even if the act complained of is one of those excepted from the action – for example, it alleges that the person threatened has applied the mark to goods or their packaging – the proprietor may not escape a groundless threats action if the claimant can show that the act does not fall within that form of infringement. For example, in *Trebor Bassett Ltd* v *Football Association Ltd*,[241] the claimant was a sweet manufacturer which sold packets of confectionery with cards inside showing photographs of famous footballers. Some were members of the English national team and had been photographed wearing shirts with the England three-lion logo which was a registered trade mark belonging to the Football Association; it complained that this was an infringement of the trade mark. The claimant filed a groundless threats action, seeking relief, *inter alia*, by way of a declaration that the threats were unjustifiable. The defendant responded by bringing a cross-action for infringement. The claimant then applied for the cross-action to be struck out as an abuse of process.

Rattee J gave summary judgment in favour of the claimant and awarded relief in the form of a declaration that the threats were unjustifiable and that the claimant's cards did not infringe the defendant's trade mark. He concluded that the claimant was not affixing or using the logo in respect of its cards within s 10(4)(a) or (b). The logo appeared on the cards only because the player was wearing the football strip with the defendant's logo on it at the time the photograph was taken and that inevitably reproduced the logo, rather as a photograph of one of the players of a team as reproduced for a newspaper. It was not even arguable that the claimant was using the logo in any real sense.

Foreign proprietors of trade marks might be surprised by a groundless threats action. For example, in *Prince plc* v *Prince Sports Group Inc*,[242] the claimant had registered 'prince. com' as its internet domain name. The defendant was an American company having registered 'Prince' as a trade mark in a number of countries including the UK. The defendant's attorneys wrote to the claimant pointing out that its use of the domain name would prevent the defendant registering that name as its own domain name and claiming

236 It appears that this action is still available: Thorley, S. *et al.* (2005) *Terrell on the Law of Patents* (16th edn) Sweet & Maxwell, at para 16.01.

237 *Day* v *Foster* (1890) 7 RPC 54 at 60. Also quoted by Lightman J in *L'Oréal (UK) Ltd* v *Johnson & Johnson* [2000] FSR 686 at 693.

238 The Court of Appeal confirmed that implicit threats are actionable in *Scandecor Developments AB* v *Scandecor Marketing AB* [1999] FSR 26.

239 [2000] FSR 686.

240 It should be noted that the court has an inherent jurisdiction to grant declaratory relief. This inherent jurisdiction may be exercised even if, on the facts, s 21 does not apply.

241 [1997] FSR 211.

242 [1998] FSR 21.

that the claimant was infringing the defendant's UK registered trade mark. Litigation was threatened if the claimant did not assign the domain name to the defendant.

The court granted a declaration that the threats were unjustified and an injunction against continuance of the threats. The basic test was held to be whether an ordinary reader would take the threat as constituting a threat of proceedings of a UK registered mark and, in the letter, reference was made to the UK registered mark. The threat was general in nature and the defendant could not take advantage of the exceptions to a threats action. A person who raised the possibility of proceedings had to take great care in expressing himself and was required to indicate precisely if he wished to rely on the exceptions. Further, where a threat was made to a person alleged to be an infringer, that person was a person aggrieved, save in exceptional circumstances.

In *L'Oréal (UK) Ltd* v *Johnson & Johnson*,[243] the defendant (the one alleged to have made groundless threats) was the proprietor of UK and Irish trade marks including 'JOHNSON'S NO MORE TEARS' and 'NO MORE TEARS'. The claimant launched in the UK and Eire similar products to those of the defendant (baby shampoos and children's hair care products) in packaging bearing the words 'No Tears! No Knots!' Solicitors acting for the defendant sent a letter to the claimant alleging infringement of the Irish trade marks. Proceedings were commenced in the High Court of Ireland but, just before, the claimant wrote to the defendant asking for confirmation that proceedings would not be brought in the UK. The defendant's English solicitor replied stating that no decision had been taken as to whether to make a claim of trade mark infringement in the UK but that third parties who had used the defendant's marks in the UK over recent years had agreed to stop using them. The letter also stated that investigations into the UK market and into English and European law were taking place and a decision would not be made immediately and that, in any case, the defendant had up to six years to make a decision.[244]

Lightman J granted the declaration sought and, of the letter, he said (at para 16):

> The Letter is the work of a master of Delphic utterances who uses his skills to say everything and nothing and to convey an enigmatic message which has the same effect on the recipient as a threat or adverse claim whilst disclaiming to be either . . . In my judgment the thrust of the Letter is a warning of the possibility in the future of proceedings for infringement, perhaps contingent on success in the proceedings in Ireland.

The basic test is how the threat would be understood by the ordinary recipient: an objective test. If a letter is sent with the intention of unnerving the recipient or influencing him so that he seriously considers refraining from an activity then, no matter how veiled the threat is or how ambiguous or indecisive it might appear, if it would tend to make an ordinary recipient fear proceedings will be initiated if he does not comply, then it is likely to constitute a threat for the purposes of s 21. This will be so even if there is no express request for the activity complained of to cease contained in the letter.

The test for whether a letter contains a threat of proceedings is to look at the offending passage through the eyes of a reasonable person in the position of the recipient of the letter, with knowledge of all the relevant circumstances at the date the letter was written, and to consider what he would have understood the writer of the letter to have intended, read in the context of the letter as a whole. Where this test is satisfied, it does not prevent it being a threat of proceedings even if it contains also a desire to see a negotiated settlement: *Best Buy Co Inc* v *Worldwide Sales Corp España SA*.[245] There was nothing to suggest that the letter in that case which contained threats and an 'invitation to treat' to negotiate a settlement was a privileged communication. Lord Neuberger MR said, *obiter*, that the 'without prejudice' rule was based on public policy and had to yield where another rule or principle applied. It was doubtful that the rule should prevail over the clear statutory policy of the threats jurisdiction in s 21 of the Act.

Remedies

Section 14(2) states that the remedies for infringement of a registered trade mark are damages, injunctions, accounts or otherwise, as are available in respect of infringement of any other property right.[246]

Orders for delivery up of infringing goods, materials or articles from a person having them in his possession, custody or control in the course of business are available under s 16(1). But under s 18, an order for delivery up is not available after the end of the period of six years from:

- (with respect to infringing goods) the date on which the registered trade mark was applied to goods or their packaging;
- (with respect to infringing material) the date on which the registered trade mark was applied to the material;
- (with respect to infringing articles) the date on which the articles were made;

unless the proprietor of the mark was suffering from a disability, or was prevented by fraud or concealment from discovering the facts entitling him to apply for the order. In these cases, the six years run from the time when the proprietor ceased to be under a disability or when he could, with reasonable diligence, have discovered the true facts.[247]

Infringing goods, materials or articles are defined in s 17. Infringing goods are those bearing (or whose packaging bears) an identical or similar mark, the application of which was an infringement of the same in respect of goods to be imported, or where the sign has otherwise been used in relation to the goods so as to infringe. This does not affect the importation of goods that can legally be imported by virtue of any enforceable Community right (s 17(3)).

Infringing material is material that bears an identical or similar mark and which is used (or is intended to be used) for labelling or packaging the goods, or as a business paper or for advertising goods or services so as to infringe (s 17(4)). Infringing articles are those specifically designed or adapted for making copies of a sign identical to or similar to a registered trade mark, and the person who has the article in his possession, custody or control knows or has reason to believe that the article has been or will be used to produce infringing goods or material (s 17(5)).

Where infringing goods, materials or articles have been delivered up in pursuance of an order made under s 16, an application can be made for an order for their destruction or forfeiture or for a decision that no such order is made. A literal interpretation suggests that an application under s 19 could only be made after the infringing goods, materials or articles had in fact been delivered up. In *Miller Brewing Company* v *Mersey Docks and Harbour Company*,[248] this was said to be wasteful of the court's time and in conflict with s 16(2) which uses the term 'also makes' in relation to an order under s 19. A strained interpretation must be given to s 19 such that it was the actual destruction or forfeiture that took place after and not the application under s 19. Persons having an interest in the goods, such as those in whose favour such an order could be made under copyright, design law etc., should be notified and can appear in the proceedings and/or appeal against any order made under these provisions.

Sections 56–58 provide for injunctive relief in favour of the proprietors of well-known marks, national emblems and the like of Convention countries, and emblems, etc. of certain international organisations. Under s 56(1), well-known marks are those entitled to protection as well-known marks under the Paris Convention for the Protection of Industrial Property or the World Trade Organisation Agreement (of which the TRIPs Agreement is an integral part), being well known in the UK as the mark of a person who is a national of, domiciled in, or who has a real and effective industrial or commercial

246 In relation to the assessment of damages, subject now to the Intellectual Property (Enforcement, etc.) Regulations 2006, SI 2006/1028, discussed previously in relation to copyright and patents and also examined in more detail in Chapter 24 on remedies.

247 Trade Marks Act 1994 s 18(2). A disability has, by s 18(3), the same meaning as under the relevant limitation legislation – in England and Wales, the Limitation Act 1980.

248 [2004] FSR 5.

establishment in, a Convention country, other than the UK.[249] There is no requirement for the proprietor to carry on business or have goodwill in the UK. With respect to emblems, there are some notification requirements to be fulfilled under s 59.

A proprietor of a trade mark which is well known in the UK may restrain by injunction the use of an identical or similar sign in the UK in respect of identical or similar goods or services where such use is likely to cause confusion: s 56(2). Thus, the proprietor of a foreign trade mark which is well known in the UK has protection equivalent to Article 5(1) of the Directive (s 10(1) and (2) of the Act) as if he had registered the trade mark in the UK.[250]

In *Philips Electronics NV v Remington Consumer Products*,[251] at first instance, Jacob J confirmed that s 56(2) puts a claimant who has a reputation but no business and, hence, no goodwill in a passing off sense, in the UK in the same position as if he did have a business and goodwill in the UK. The claimant was domiciled in the Netherlands (a Convention country) but was not able to rely on s 56(2) as there was no deceptive use. Jacob J confirmed that the provision did not extend to non-deceptive use. Section 56 is headed 'Protection of well-known trade marks: Article 6bis' and implements Article 6bis of the Paris Convention, a provision which dates from 1927. Jacob J also made the point that the claimant's shape mark was not covered by this provision as he did not consider a shape mark to be a trade mark for the purposes of the Paris Convention and that it was impossible to envisage that, in 1927, anyone would have thought the provision would cover 'engineering artefacts of this sort'. Furthermore, although certain shape marks are registrable in the European Community, they are not registrable in a great many other countries belonging to the Paris Convention. With this limitation in mind, what s 56 does is to cure the defect in the law of passing off that requires the claimant to demonstrate that he has goodwill within jurisdiction.[252]

If the application for registration of a trade mark is made by an agent of the proprietor, registration shall be refused if the proprietor opposes the application; and if the application is accepted, registration shall be refused if the proprietor applies for a declaration of the invalidity of the registration, or applies for rectification of the register so as to substitute his name as proprietor (s 60).

TRAVELPRO Trade Mark[253] provides an example of rectification under s 60. A sole distributor of an American company, which had several registrations for TRAVELPRO in other countries, applied to register the mark in the UK without informing the American company. It was held that the distributor was an agent within s 60 and had no claim to ownership of the mark. The American company's name was substituted for that of the distributor as registered proprietor.

Chapter 24 on remedies for infringement of intellectual property rights contains more material on remedies for infringement generally, much of which is also relevant to the remedies available for trade mark infringement.

Criminal offences

There are a number of offences relating to the unauthorised use of a trade mark which also cover secondary offenders who facilitate this. Other offences apply in connection to falsification of the register of trade marks and falsely representing that a trade mark is registered. As is usual, senior officers also may be found guilty of offences committed by corporate bodies.

The main offences under s 92 (unauthorised use and enforcement of s 92 by local weights and measures authorities under s 93 and forfeiture under ss 97 and 98) also apply in respect of the CTM. There is also an equivalent offence of falsely representing a trade mark as registered in respect of the CTM.

249 Well-known marks are defined in Article 6bis of the Paris Convention and Article 16(2) of the Agreement on Trade Related Aspects of Intellectual Property Rights (the TRIPs Agreement), administered by the World Trade Organisation, refers back to Article 6bis of the Paris Convention as regards the meaning of a well-known trade mark. 'Convention country' is defined in s 55(1)(b) so as to expressly exclude the UK.

250 Compare with passing off; see Anheuser-Busch Inc v Budějovicky Budvar NP [1984] FSR 413, discussed in Chapter 23.

251 [1998] RPC 283.

252 A point made in the South African case of McDonald's Corp v Joburgers Drive-In Restaurant (Pty) Ltd [1997] (1) SA 1, approved by Jacob J in Philips Electronics v Remington.

253 [1997] RPC 864.

The offences of unauthorised use are set out in s 92 and are expressed in terms of being 'with a view to gain for himself or another or, with intent to cause loss to another, and without the consent of the proprietor'. The offences under s 92 are:

- Applying a sign identical to (or likely to be mistaken as the registered trade mark of) goods or their packaging; selling, hiring, offering or exposing for sale or hire or distributing such goods; having such goods in his possession, custody or control in the course of a business with a view to selling, hiring, etc. whether by himself or another (s 92(1)).
- Applying a sign identical to (or likely to be mistaken as the registered trade mark of) material intended to be used for labelling or packaging goods, as a business paper in relation to goods, or for advertising goods; using in the course of a business such a sign for labelling or packaging goods, as a business paper in relation to goods, or for advertising goods; having such material in his possession, custody or control in the course of a business with a view to making such use of the sign, whether by himself or another (s 92(2)).
- Making an article specifically designed or adapted to make copies of a sign identical to (or likely to be mistaken for) the registered trade mark, or having such an article in his possession, custody or control in the course of a business (s 92(3)). For the offences in this subsection, a form of knowledge is required in that the person knows or has reason to believe that the sign has been, or is to be, used to produce goods or material for labelling or packaging goods, as a business paper in relation to goods or for advertising goods.

For the offences to apply, under s 92(4), the relevant goods must be those for which the mark is registered, or the trade mark must be one with a reputation and the use of the sign would take unfair advantage of, or is or would be detrimental to, the distinctive character or the repute of the trade mark. Oddly, these offences apply only in relation to goods and not to services. Therefore, providing a service under a sign that is identical to or is likely to be mistaken for a registered trade mark, in the course of trade and without consent, may bring civil liability but cannot bring criminal liability under trade mark law.

Note that the offences are committed if the sign is identical to or likely to be mistaken for a registered trade mark. This is different to the equivalent civil infringements where the sign, if not identical, must be *similar* to the registered trade mark. There are other differences, such as, where the use of the sign takes unfair advantage of or is detrimental to the repute of a well-known trade mark, there is no requirement in the criminal offence for the use to be without due cause as there is for civil infringement. It is submitted that the *actus reus* for the criminal offences cannot be more extensive than for civil infringement as this would extend the protection of registered trade marks provided for in the Directive and, apart from the possibility of granting more extensive protection in one case, registered trade marks must enjoy the same protection under the legal systems of all the Member States. The ninth recital to the Directive states that this should be so and that more extensive protection may be granted only in the case of trade marks having a reputation. It is possible that the offences in the Act were influenced to some extent by the offences under the s 58A of the Trade Marks Act 1938 although those offences required the offending mark to be identical to or nearly resembling a registered trade mark.[254]

It is a defence if the person charged can show that he believed on reasonable grounds that the use or intended use of the sign in the manner in which it was used, or was intended to be used, was not an infringement of the registered trade mark (s 92(5)).[255] There is also a defence, curiously placed in s 9(3), where the relevant act was done before the date of publication of registration, notwithstanding that, once registered, the proprietor's rights are deemed to have accrued at the filing date. The maximum penalty for all the offences in s 92 is ten years' imprisonment and/or a fine on conviction on

254 Nearly resembling was also used in relation to infringement in s 4 of the 1938 Act.

255 A civil test for a criminal offence. *See* Rawlinson, P. 'The UK Trade Marks Act 1994: It's Criminal' [1995] 1 EIPR 54.

indictment, or, if tried summarily, six months' imprisonment and/or a fine not exceeding the statutory maximum.

The phrase 'with a view to gain for himself or another, or with intent to cause loss to another', is used for all the offences and is identical to the wording in the Theft Act 1968 s 21 which contains the offence of blackmail, apart from the omission of a comma. However, there is no further clarification of this phrase in the Trade Marks Act 1994 as there is for blackmail which is limited, under the Theft Act 1968 s 34(2), to a gain or loss in money or other property.[256] It may be that gain and loss, for the purposes of trade marks, is at least as extensive as it is for the purposes of blackmail and could extend also to goodwill.[257] In *R v Zaman*,[258] the Court of Appeal held that 'with a view to' simply meant that the defendant had something in mind but not necessarily something he wanted or intended.

The offences in s 92 potentially have quite a wide scope and could apply in many cases where a trader, who is otherwise in legitimate business, deliberately uses a sign identical to or likely to be mistaken for a registered trade mark, hoping to capture some of the goodwill attached to the registered trade mark. It may be that the trader is trying to get as near as he can to the registered trade mark without infringing. Although a misjudgment on the part of the trader could leave him exposed to the possibility of criminal proceedings, it seems clear that s 92 is aimed primarily at counterfeiters and persons knowingly dealing in counterfeit goods. The presence of the defence in s 92(5) confirms this. An honest trader who misjudged how near he could get to a registered trade mark would undoubtedly argue that he did not believe what he was doing would infringe (such belief has to be on reasonable grounds though). After all, no honest trader would deliberately engage in activity which he thought would, more likely than not, infringe a registered trade mark.

The offences in s 92(1)–(3) appear to be almost strict liability and have been treated so by the courts. There is a very limited mental element, that the accused is acting with a view to gain or an intent to cause loss but, in most cases, that will not be much of a hurdle, if any, for the prosecution. Coupled with the presence of the relevant facts, the accused will be guilty unless he can rely on the defence in s 92(5) and it is he who will bear the burden of proof in respect of that. In *Torbay Council v Satnam Singh*,[259] the accused had been charged with two counts of an offence under s 92(1)(b) in that he exposed for sale two garments bearing the 'Teletubbies' logo. He argued that he did not know that the logo had been registered as a trade mark and further claimed that he checked the *Draper's Weekly* regularly for trade marks. He was acquitted and the Council appealed to the Divisional Court by way of case stated. The appeal was allowed and the court confirmed that an offence under s 92(1) was made out if it was proved:

(a) that the trade mark was registered and the sign used was identical to it or likely to be mistaken for it;

(b) that the accused was acting with a view to gain for himself or another or with intent to cause loss to another; and

(c) that his use was without the consent of the proprietor of the trade mark.

As regards the defence in s 92(5), the court said that it required a reasonable belief that the use complained of did not infringe the registered trade mark and this presupposed a knowledge of the fact of registration. It did not require an investigation into the accused's state of mind as to whether there was or was not a registered trade mark capable of being infringed. Doubts about this aspect of *Torbay v Singh* were expressed in the Court of Appeal in *R v Rhodes*[260] and it was expressly overruled by the House of Lords in *R v Johnstone*,[261] below.

The maximum penalties for the offences in s 92 seem draconian, especially when they are almost offences of strict liability and, in most cases, the accused will have to prove the

256 There is further clarification of 'gain' and 'loss' in the Theft Act 1968 s 34(2): for example, 'gain' includes keeping what one has, as well as getting what one has not.

257 The definition of 'property' in the Theft Act 1968 s 4(1) includes things in action and other intangible property. Goodwill protected by passing off has long been recognised as a form of property.

258 [2003] FSR 13.

259 [2000] FSR 158.

260 [2003] FSR 9.

261 [2003] FSR 42.

defence. Nevertheless, there can be little sympathy for counterfeiters and persons know-ingly dealing in counterfeit goods. For such cases, custodial sentences may be appropriate. In *R v Adam*,[262] the Court of Appeal (Criminal Division) said that a deterrent sentence was called for. In that case, the offender had persisted in his activities in the face of a clear warning and had been sentenced to seven months' imprisonment despite having no previous convictions. In *R v Burns*,[263] the Court of Appeal (Criminal Division) upheld a custodial sentence of 12 months. The accused had pleaded guilty to 53 offences relating to counterfeit clothing bearing well-known trade marks such as 'Adidas' and 'Calvin Klein'. He had two recent previous convictions and the case was deemed more serious than *Adam*. A court may make a confiscation order under s 71 of the Criminal Justice Act 1988, as it did in *R v Davies*[264] in a case where the offender had a turnover of about £1 million in around 18 months from selling counterfeit goods to which trade marks had been applied. Davies was also sentenced to three-and-a-half years' imprisonment. His appeal against the confiscation order was dismissed by the Court of Appeal.

Selling counterfeit goods at a car boot sale may also incur a serious punishment. In such a case, *R v Keane*,[265] two offences of offering for sale under s 92(1)(b) and five possession offences under s 92(1)(c) resulted in a sentence of 150 hours' community punishment.

The House of Lords, in *R v Johnstone*,[266] had to consider a number of issues relating to the offences under s 92, including whether the offences were in breach of the right to a fair trial under Article 6(2) of the Council of Europe Convention for the Protection of Human Rights and Fundamental Freedoms, 1950 (the 'Human Rights Convention').

Johnstone was involved with 'bootlegging' activities relating to unauthorised copies of recordings of performances of famous singers and groups. His activities were discovered when a parcel containing over 500 CDs was misdirected and received by a third party and the police were contacted. They searched his house and found more CDs there. Most of the CDs were of unauthorised recordings of performances. The CDs bore the names of the performers, such as Bon Jovi, many of which were also registered trade marks. Johnstone was charged with a number of specimen counts under the Trade Marks Act s 92(1)(c) of being in possession of goods bearing trade marks with a view to selling them.

It was argued that, before an offence could be established under s 92, it must be proved that there had been a civil infringement of the trade mark under ss 9–11 of the Act (Articles 5 and 6 of the Directive). Johnstone's defence was based on s 11(2)(b) (indica-tions of certain characteristics of goods) claiming that the names of the performers on the CDs were not indications of origin but were merely there to indicate the identity of the performers. An alternative defence was based on s 92(5) (belief on reason-able grounds that the use in question was not an infringement of the trade mark).

In the Crown Court, the judge rejected the defence submissions on the basis of previous decisions in the Crown Court. He accepted that s 92 was a 'standalone' provision and it was not necessary to prove civil infringement. The judge also accepted that, under s 92(5), infringement meant unauthorised use as defined earlier in s 92. Consequently, Johnstone changed his plea to guilty and was sentenced to six months' imprisonment concurrent on each count and a confiscation order was made for £130,181.24 together with orders for forfeiture.

Johnstone appealed to the Court of Appeal which held that, unless the defences available for a civil claim of trade mark infringement were available also for the criminal offences, behaviour which could not result in a successful civil action could result in conviction and that infringement, for the purposes of s 92(5), was as defined in ss 9(1) and (2) and 10.[267] Furthermore, the Court of Appeal held that the prosecution did not have to prove that the defendant's conduct amounted to a civil infringement unless the defendant raised a defence on the basis of ss 10–12 of the Act. As Johnstone had not been

262 [1999] 1 Cr App R (S) 403.

263 [2001] FSR 27.

264 [2004] FSR 24.

265 [2001] FSR 7.

266 [2003] FSR 42.

267 As in the index of defined expressions in s 104.

allowed to have his defence under s 11(2)(b) put to the jury, his appeal was allowed; but a question was certified for determination by the House of Lords as to whether it was a defence to a charge under s 92 if the defendant's acts did not amount to a civil infringement of the registered trade mark.

The Lords' decision covered several aspects relating to the offences under s 92. The House confirmed that it was implicit that the offending use must be use as a trade mark. Descriptive use, that is, use other than as an indication of trade origin, was not within s 92. If the offences were interpreted as extending to circumstances beyond ss 9–12, it could lead to an inconsistency with the Directive. The equivalent provisions in the Directive, Articles 5–7, are amongst those for which complete harmonisation is required. Therefore, the prosecution must prove that the use of the sign in question was use as an indication of trade origin as this was an essential element of the offences. Determination of this was a question of fact.

On the facts of the case, Johnstone would commit an offence, for example, if he sold CDs under the Bon Jovi trade mark. This would be an indication of trade origin. However, if his use would be understood to be exclusively as identifying the performer, this would be descriptive use only and not an indication of trade origin.

One difference between the terminology used for civil and criminal liability is that the former requires the use of the sign in the course of trade whereas, for some of the criminal offences, the conduct must be in the course of a business. This difference is probably not of any practical importance, especially as all the criminal offences required that the accused act with a view to gain for himself or another, or with intent to cause loss to another. Lord Nicholls said that it would be hard to think of a realistic example of conduct that would attract criminal liability, but not civil liability, because of this difference.

Previous case law suggested that lack of knowledge as to whether the trade mark in question is registered deprives the accused of the defence.[268] Lord Nicholls thought that Parliament could not have intended that a person could put forward the defence of reasonable belief only if he knew of the existence of the trade mark registration but could not if he did not know of it. Therefore, the defence is available in either case and *Torbay v Singh* must now be regarded as wrong on this point. Of course, the defendant must show his belief was on reasonable grounds. This brings us to the burden of proof.

Article 6(2) of the Human Rights Convention states that every person charged with a criminal offence shall be presumed innocent until proved guilty according to the law. Section 92(5) appears to place the burden of proof on the defendant as it states that '[i]t is a defence for a person charged with an offence under this section to show that he believed on reasonable grounds . . .'[269] Lord Nicholls thought that, unless incompatible with Article 6(2) of the Human Rights Convention, s 92(5) placed on the accused the burden of proving that he did believe on reasonable grounds that the use of the sign did not infringe the registered trade mark on a balance of probabilities. In other words, s 92(5) places a legal or persuasive burden on the accused. This appears to be in conflict with Article 6(2). However, the European Court of Human Rights has accepted that the right to a fair trial and the presumption of innocence does not necessarily prevent presumptions of fact or law but that they must be kept within reasonable limits, taking into account the importance of what is at stake and maintain the rights of the defence. A balance must be struck between the rights of the individual and the public interest and it is for the state to justify any derogation from the presumption of innocence. Lord Nicholls then considered six factors in determining whether the derogation was justified:

1 Counterfeiting is a serious problem which has severe economic consequences and has adverse effects on consumers in terms of quality and even, in some cases, health and safety. Protection of consumers and honest traders is an important policy consideration.

268 *Torbay Council* v *Satnam Singh* [2000] FSR 158 and *R* v *Keane* [2001] FSR 7. However, this was doubted in the Court of Appeal in *R* v *Rhodes* [2003] FSR 9, where it was suggested that a trader who engaged a reputable trade mark agent to carry out a search to see if a particular trade mark was registered should not be deprived of the defence if that agent made a mistake.

269 The Court of Appeal thought that this was an evidential burden only and, once the accused had adduced evidence sufficient to raise an issue, the prosecution would then have to disprove it. However, in *R* v *S (Trade mark defence)* [2003] 1 Cr App R 35, the Court of Appeal questioned this.

2 The offences in s 92 have been described as offences of near absolute liability and the prosecution does not have to prove an intention to infringe a registered trade mark.

3 The potential penalty is severe, with up to ten years' imprisonment and/or an unlimited fine together with confiscation and forfeiture orders.

4 Traders are aware of counterfeit goods and the need to be on guard against them and to deal only with reputable suppliers and keep records.

5 The s 92(5) defence relates to facts that are within the accused's own state of knowledge; his state of mind and the reasons why he held the belief in question. Furthermore, he knows his sources of supply.

6 Those who supply counterfeit goods are unlikely to be cooperative, even if traced by investigators. Therefore, if the prosecution were required to prove that the accused acted dishonestly, fewer investigations and prosecutions would take place.

Lord Nicholls considered that points 4 and 6 above were compelling reasons why the accused should have the persuasive burden placed on him and it was fair and reasonable that the accused should prove on a balance of probability why he honestly and reasonably believed that the goods in question were not counterfeit. This was not incompatible with Article 6(2) of the Human Rights Convention.

Both Lord Nicholls and Lord Walker, with whom the other judges agreed, thought that s 92 contained the complete code for the criminal offences but the test for civil infringement was not completely irrelevant. The key is s 104 which indicates that the meaning of infringement for the purposes of the Act was to be found in s 9(1) and (2) and s 10. Lord Nicholls said (at para 33) that:

> . . . the circumstances in which criminal liability arises are for the most part either the same as, or narrower than, the circumstances in which civil liability arises under sections 9 to 11.

Lord Walker appeared to accept that consideration could also be given to ss 11 and 12. Both Lord Nicholls and Lord Walker accepted that whether use of a sign is trade mark use is a question of fact of a fairly complex sort. Lord Walker said (at para 88) that trade mark use is a necessary ingredient of criminal liability under s 92 and, that being so,

> . . . there is no need to go on a circuitous route through Article 6(1)(b) [of the Directive] or section 11(2)(b) in order to arrive at that conclusion. It is adequately (if not pellucidly) expressed in the language of section 92 . . .

Lord Walker went on to say that facts such as those in *Mothercare UK Ltd* v *Penguin Books Ltd*[270] (use of Mother Care/Other Care for a book title) and Case C-2/00 *Michael Hölterhoff* v *Ulrich Freiesleben*[271] (discussed above, *see* p 781) would not fall within the offences within s 92. The use of trade marks in those cases was purely descriptive rather than as indicating origin.

Lord Nicholls and Lord Walker both referred to the Australian case of *Musidor BV* v *Tansing (t/a Apple Music House)*[272] which involved bootleg copies of recordings of the Rolling Stones. The packaging bore a photograph of the Rolling Stones and the group's name in prominent lettering. In a majority decision, it was held that there was no infringement of the Rolling Stones' trade mark as the use in question was not use as a trade mark. The dissenting judgment by Davies J was to the effect that such use will normally inform the public that the recording is of a performance by the group and that the group has authorised its release. The Court of Appeal had preferred the dissenting view but emphasised that whether the use is use as a trade mark is a question of fact in every case. However, in the House of Lords in *R* v *Johnstone*, Lord Walker thought that the minority view in *Musidor* went too far and not every bootlegging case of that kind would necessarily involve trade mark use.

270 [1988] RPC 113.
271 [2002] ECR I-4187.
272 (1994) 123 ALR 593.

In *Johnstone*, Lord Nichols said (at para 43):

> Section 92(5) is concerned to provide a defence where the person charged has a reasonable belief in the lawfulness of what he did. Those who act honestly and reasonably are not to be visited with criminal sanctions.

Although s 92(5) does not use the word 'honestly', the last sentence of the quote was picked up in the magistrates' court in *Essex Trading Standards* v *Singh*.[273] The accused had agreed to look after a market stall for a third party who was a drug addict and unwell at the time. At the trial for offences under s 92(1)(c), the magistrates concluded that the accused was not guilty. He was inexperienced in selling from a market stall and of previous good character. He had asked the third party whether the shoes were dodgy but had been assured that they were not. However, the magistrates posed some questions for the Divisional Court of the High Court, in particular, whether they were wrong in law to apply the principles set out in *Johnstone*, namely that 'those who act honestly and reasonably are not to be visited with criminal sanctions' in the instant case, when the defendant argued that he did not know the goods were counterfeit? The Divisional Court held that previous good character was relevant to the question as to whether a person acted honestly but was irrelevant as far as whether a person acted reasonably. It was held that no reasonable court could find that the accused discharged the burden of proof under s 92(5) to show that he had objectively reasonable grounds for believing the shoes were genuine. The accused had known that the selling price was low, his belief was based on the word of an unwell drug addict and he had not sought independent evidence to show that the shoes were genuine, such as documentary evidence relating to the supply of the shoes and their provenance. The Divisional Court concluded that the magistrates were wrong to apply the above-mentioned test. Although not explicit in the relatively brief judgment, honesty was not an issue, it being simply a matter of whether the accused believed on reasonable grounds that the use of the sign in the manner in which it was used, or was to be used, was not an infringement of the registered trade mark.

Guidance on the scope of s 92(1)(c) was given in the Court of Appeal in *R* v *Boulter*,[274] in which the accused pleaded guilty to 19 counts of possession of counterfeit CDs and DVDs bearing the logos of EMI and other companies which were registered trade marks. He also asked for a further 144 offences to be taken into account. His guilty plea came after the trial judge ruled that his defence, that the material bearing the trade marks was of such poor quality that no one would think it came from the trade mark owners, was ineffective. It did not matter that the quality of the counterfeiting was so poor that no one would think the trade origin was the trade mark owner.

On appeal it was argued that there could be no criminal offence under section 92 if the intended usage of the goods would not infringe the trade mark under section 10 of the Act. The defence argued that, for there to be a civil infringement, there must be a likelihood that the public would be deceived or confused. This was rejected by the Court of Appeal because it failed to draw a distinction between s 10(1) and 10(2). The former, use of a sign identical to a registered trade mark for identical goods or services infringes *per se* and requires no evidence of confusion on the part of the public. Although the trade marks had been badly copied, the usage was still within s 10(1). A further argument was that it had to be established that the use was use as a trade mark. The essential function of a trade mark is to guarantee the origin of goods bearing the trade mark. Use which is purely descriptive does not infringe. In *Johnstone*, Lord Nicholls considered a problem under the old law whereby a trader would describe his goods as 'genuine fakes', for example, and accepted that s 92 avoided this problem. In the present case, Toulson LJ said (at para 9):

273 [2009] EWHC 520 (Admin).

274 [2009] ETMR 6.

In our judgment, it is impossible to read Parliament as having intended that, where there is straightforward counterfeiting of goods and their registered trademark, it is open to a defendant to advance a defence that the quality was so poor as not to give rise to any risk of confusion, not only because that would fail to recognise the distinction drawn between section 10(1) and 10(2) but it would go a considerable way to assist the vice which Lord Nicholls at any rate thought that Parliament had attempted to combat, namely the counter-feiter who sells his wares as 'genuine fakes'.

275 [2009] 2 Cr App R 5.

The appeal was dismissed. In another Court of Appeal case, *R* v *Kousar*,[275] the appellant was convicted of a number of counts of unauthorised use of the trade mark contrary to s 92(1)(c). The appellant's husband was a market trader and was a co-defendant and had been convicted on all counts. The case against his wife was that Trading Standards Officers seized a number of counterfeit goods from the loft in her home (which she shared with her husband) and from the husband's van which was parked on the drive to the house. It was claimed that she was in joint possession of these goods as she was aware of their presence. The appellant claimed that she was did not know the goods were counterfeit. She took no part in her husband's business and was in unrelated employment. Nor did she use the van.

The Court of Appeal distinguished a number of cases on possession of drugs (for which there is a separate offence of permitting premises to be used for certain activities but for which there is no equivalent in relation to the trade mark offences). Two reasons were given for allowing the appeal:

1 Permission is not the same as possession. Generally, one is not in possession of a spouse's personal property (for example, a husband cannot be said to be in possession of his wife's cosmetics). If it is accepted that the appellant permitted the counterfeit goods to be in her house and in the van, this is not enough. Permission may be more than acquiescence. A key point is that s 92(1)(c) refers to possession, custody or con-trol. A finding that the appellant had the ability to exercise a measure of control is far from a finding that she did actually exercise control.

2 The offence requires that the possession, custody or control be in the course of a busi-ness. This element could be satisfied only if the prosecution could show that the accused was in possession of the goods in the course of a business. It had not been shown that she was involved in her husband's business, whether paid or otherwise. Even if, contrary to the view of the court, it had been shown that her 'ability' or right to control the goods was sufficient to render her in possession of them, this further element of the offence was not established.

An interpretation can be placed on s 92 which does not yet appear to have been con-sidered. Having a view to gain for himself or another or cause loss to another may simply be taken to mean an intention to make money by selling articles and depriving a competitor of sales. A different, and far more satisfactory, interpretation is possible by reading the view to gain or cause loss in context with the rest of the relevant subsection. For each of the offences the view to gain or cause loss relates to a specific act of the accused: for example, by applying the sign to goods. Therefore, it could be said that the view to gain or cause loss is formed because, when the accused applied the sign to the goods, he wanted, by that act, to gain or cause loss; not by selling what he thought were goods to which a non-infringing sign had been applied but because he realised that the sign infringed the trade mark or was likely to infringe it. All traders want to make a gain by selling more than competitors or to cause loss to competitors by diverting sales from them. This is a fact of normal honest commercial life. For the offences the gain or loss must be read in context of the use of the sign. It is as if, for the offence to be made out, the offender has said to himself: 'By using a sign on my goods that looks like the sign of a well-known and respected undertaking, I will be able to sell more of my goods because customers might think they are from that undertaking.'

If that approach is followed, it does not make the defence in s 92(5) redundant. Its purpose is to protect a trader who uses a sign similar to a registered trade mark but who believes, on reasonable grounds, that he does not infringe it, for example, because there is no likelihood of confusion. This approach would also bring the offences nearer to those under the 1938 Act where the offence required that the offender intended the goods in question should be accepted as those of the person entitled to use the registered trade mark.

Given the problems with the *mens rea* for these offences and the fact that s 92 appears not to be completely in line with the rights and infringement under ss 9–12, it would be better for s 92 to be replaced by a new section that meets the above concerns. One way would be to provide that it is an offence to carry out any of the acts infringing a registered trade mark with the intention of causing a deception on the part of the public as to the origin of the goods. This would tie in with the basic purpose of trade marks and would not detract from the reason for having trade mark offences as that intention would not be difficult to prove in the case of counterfeiters. Another issue is whether the offences should be extended to services to catch the situation where a service provider deliberately uses the name of a well-known service provider.[276]

276 Of course, in some circumstances, offences may be committed under other laws such as consumer protection laws.

Enforcement, etc. of s 92

There are provisions in s 93 for enforcement of s 92 by local weights and measures authorities and provisions for forfeiture in s 97. The equivalent provisions for forfeiture for Scotland are contained in s 98.[277] Forfeiture is available in respect of offending goods, material or articles which have come into the possession of any person in connection with the investigation or prosecution of any relevant offence (under s 92, under the Trade Descriptions Act 1968 or any offence involving dishonesty or deception). An application for an order for forfeiture must be obtained from the court where proceedings have been brought, or otherwise from a magistrates' court. The order will be granted only if the court is satisfied that the relevant offence has been committed, but the inference may be made that the offence has been committed in relation to a batch or consignment of goods from consideration of a representative sample.

277 Both ss 97 and 98 are modified in respect of the Olympic symbol, motto or protected words under the Olympic Symbol etc. (Protection) Act 1995, s 11.

The order may require the offending goods, materials or articles to be destroyed, or to be released to such person as the court may specify on condition that the offending sign is erased, removed or obliterated. An appeal from a forfeiture order lies to the Crown Court in England and Wales.[278]

278 In Northern Ireland, the County Court; in Scotland, the High Court.

The Copyright, etc. and Trade Marks (Offences and Enforcement) Act 2002 inserted s 92A into the Trade Marks Act 1994 which provides for search warrants where, on information on oath, given by a constable, there are reasonable grounds for believing that an offence under s 92 has been or is about to be committed on premises and evidence is on those premises.[279] Reasonable force may be used by the constable in executing the warrant.

279 In England and Wales, the warrant cannot extend to personal and confidential material under s 9(2) of the Police and Criminal Evidence Act 1984.

The warrant must be executed within 28 days (3 months in England and Wales) but may authorise persons to accompany the constable executing the warrant. Such persons could be, for example, the trade mark agents of the proprietor of the trade mark alleged to have been infringed, a trading standards officer or lawyer experienced in trade marks law. The constable may seize articles he reasonably believes constitute evidence that an offence under s 92 has been or is about to be committed. 'Premises' is given its usual wide definition and includes land, buildings, fixed or moveable structures, vehicles, vessels, aircraft and hovercraft. Search warrants under s 92 are additional to and separate from the powers of local weights and measures authorities, *inter alia*, to enter premises and seize goods and documents.

Other offences

The offence of falsifying the register of trade marks is set out in s 94. It applies where a person makes, or causes to be made, a false entry on the register, knowing or having reason to believe that it is false. It is also an offence to make or cause to be made anything falsely purporting to be a copy of an entry in the register or to produce or tender or cause to be produced or tendered in evidence such a false copy, knowing or having reason to believe that it is false. The maximum penalty on conviction on indictment is imprisonment for two years and/or a fine. The maximum on summary conviction is six months' imprisonment and/or a fine not exceeding the statutory maximum.

Falsely representing a trade mark as registered is triable summarily only and carries a maximum penalty of a fine not exceeding level 3 on the standard scale. Under s 95, it is an offence falsely to represent that a mark is a registered trade mark, or to make a false representation as to the goods or services for which a trade mark is registered where the person making the representation knows or has reason to believe that the representation is false. There is an equivalent offence in respect of the CTM under reg 8 of the Community Trade Marks Regulations 1996.[280]

The test of having reason to believe is an objective test. What would the reasonable trader, having knowledge of the facts known to the accused, believe? For the purposes of these offences, the use of the word 'registered' or any other word or symbol importing an express or implied reference to registration is deemed to be a representation as to registration of the trade mark. Using a phrase such as 'registered trade mark', or the familiar ® symbol for an unregistered mark, would be falsely representing a mark to be registered.

There is a defence in s 95(2) where it is shown that the reference is to registration elsewhere than in the UK and the reference is consistent with that registration and to the goods or services for which it is there registered: s 95(2).[281] In *Second Sight Ltd* v *Novell UK Ltd*[282] the defendant used its US registered mark TUXEDO in the UK with the word 'registered' and the ® symbol before it had registered the mark in the UK. Lightman J considered that s 95(2) ought to be construed so as to excuse if the reference is consistent with a registration elsewhere and such registration does, in fact, exist. It is unnecessary to refer to the foreign registration on the face of the material or article on which the trade mark is displayed.

Unauthorised use of the Royal arms or other devices, emblems or titles of Her Majesty or a member of the Royal family may constitute an offence under s 99 triable summarily only with a penalty of a fine not exceeding level 2 on the standard scale. Apart from being unauthorised, the use of the Royal arms (or arms so closely resembling the Royal arms as to be calculated to deceive) must be in connection with any business and used in a manner calculated to lead to the belief that the person using the arms is duly authorised to use them. In respect of devices, emblems and titles, again this must be in connection with any business. However, in this case, the use must be in a manner as to be calculated to lead to the belief that the person is employed by, or supplies goods or services to Her Majesty or the relevant member of the Royal family.

Contraventions may be restrained by injunction in proceedings brought by the person authorised to use the arms, device, emblem or title in question or by any person authorised by the Lord Chamberlain. These provisions do not affect the right of a proprietor of a registered trade mark containing any such arms, device, emblem or title to use that trade mark.

Finally, it should be noted that s 101(5) extends potential liability for all the criminal offences to directors, managers, secretaries or other similar officers of a corporate body where that body commits the offence. Liability also applies in respect of persons purporting to act in such a capacity. The test is that the offence was committed with the consent or connivance of the senior officer concerned. There are special provisions for offences

280 SI 1996/1908.

281 There is no equivalent defence for the CTM. There is no need for one as a claim that a mark is a CTM cannot be interpreted as a reference to a registration elsewhere.

282 [1995] RPC 423.

committed by partnerships. Under s 101(1), proceedings are to be brought against the partnership in its name and not against the partners. However, under s 101(4) every partner may also be prosecuted unless it is proved that a partner was ignorant of the offence or attempted to prevent the commission of the offence.

Summary

The rights conferred by a trade mark are negative in nature as they give the proprietor the right to prevent others using the trade mark without his consent as provided for in the trade marks Directive.

To infringe, the trade mark must be used in the course of trade and not merely be private use, such as by a private individual for non-commercial reasons or in a company's internal communications. The use must also be use as a trade mark. Thus, for example, mere descriptive use is not use as a trade mark.

A trade mark has a number of functions. The most important function is to guarantee the origin of the goods or services concerned. Other functions include those of:

- guaranteeing the quality of goods or services
- communication
- investment
- advertising.

Trade marks may be infringed in a number of ways, being:

- use of a sign identical with the mark for identical goods or services (double identity): there is no need to show a likelihood of confusion – it is presumed under the TRIPs Agreement;
- use of a sign identical or similar to the mark for identical or similar goods or services (but not double identity cases) – it must be shown that there is a likelihood of confusion which includes a likelihood of association (though not non-origin association);
- use of a sign identical or similar to the mark for identical, similar or non-similar goods or services where the mark in question has a reputation in the UK where the use in question, without due cause, takes unfair advantage of ('free-riding'), or is detrimental to, the distinctive character or the repute of the trade mark (dilution, blurring or tarnishment).

Comparative advertising is possible without infringing a trade mark if it complies with the comparative advertising Directive. If it does comply, this can be said to be acceptable on the grounds of fair competition.

A number of issues arise in relation to the use of trade marks on the internet. Particular issues include the territorial reach of infringement (depends on the location targeted), confusion and initial interest confusion, keywords and AdWords used online by advertisers and the liability of internet service providers including search engines and online sales and auction facilitators.

Where X uses, without consent, Y's trade mark as a keyword or AdWord to retrieve X's own advertisement, Y will be able to prohibit such use if the essential function of the trade mark (indicating origin) is adversely affected. This will be so if a reasonably well-informed and reasonably observant internet user is not able to identify (or only able to identify with difficulty) whether the goods or services originate from Y (or an economically linked undertaking) or, on the contrary, from a third party. Even if this essential function is not adversely affected, other functions of the trade mark may be, such as that of investment. Furthermore, there may still be infringement in the case of a trade mark with a reputation where unfair advantage is taken or the distinctiveness of the mark is diluted or its reputation is tarnished.

There are some limitations to the rights of the proprietor, such as the own name 'defence' or indications which are descriptive or relate to intended purpose (for example, as an accessory or spare part) if such use is in accordance with honest practices in industrial or commercial matters.

The doctrine of exhaustion of rights applies to goods placed on the market within the EEA by the proprietor or with his consent unless there are legitimate reasons for the proprietor to oppose further commercialisation, for example, where the condition of the goods has been changed or impaired. Where repackaging is involved, in the relevant field, it must be done in accordance with national rules. Removal of packaging of perfumes may give a reason to oppose further commercialisation where the packaging contains required information not duplicated on the perfume container.

Groundless threats actions are possible and any person aggrieved by the threats may commence proceedings.

Remedies include damages, injunctions and accounts. There are also some criminal offences under the Trade Marks Act 1994 which are almost strict liability and carry a maximum of ten years' imprisonment and/or a fine. The offences do not conflict with the right to a fair trial.

Discussion questions

1   Consider and discuss the various functions of a trade mark. To what extent are the functions, other than the essential function of guaranteeing the origin of goods or services, relevant to trade mark infringement.

2   Discuss the meaning of a likelihood of confusion including the likelihood of association.

3   What forms of activity fall within Article 5(2) of the trade marks Directive (unfair advantage or detriment to distinctive character or repute)? Give examples.

4   Discuss the Court of Justice rulings in the quartet of cases on AdWords used by search engines to generate lists of sponsored links and how to distinguish between infringing use and non-infringing use.

5   Can a letter before action alleging trade mark infringement constitute a groundless threat if the letter also contains an offer to negotiate a settlement?

6   Why are the offences under s 92 in accordance with the Convention right to a fair trial even though they are almost strict liability subject to a defence of believing on reasonable grounds that the use or intended use was not an infringement? The House of Lords in *R* v *Johnstone* considered that the offence applied if the essential function of guaranteeing origin was adversely affected. Since that case, the Court of Justice of the EU has expanded the functions of a trade mark to include guaranteeing quality, communication, investment and advertising. Does this expand the scope of the criminal offences?

Selected further reading

Fhima, I.S., 'Dilution by blurring – a conceptual roadmap' [2010] *Intellectual Property Quarterly*, 44 (looks at theories on the justification for protection against dilution by blurring).

Gangee, D., 'Trade marks and freedom of expression – a call for caution' [2010] *International Review of Intellectual Property and Competition Law*, 544 (considers whether the application of freedom of expression as a means of constraining the scope of trade mark rights is misplaced and queries why trade mark rights should be so expansive).

Google, 'What is Google's AdWords and AdSense trademark policy?' available at: **http://adwords. google.com/support/aw/bin/answer.py?hl=en&answer=6118**

Kulk, S., 'Search engines – searching for trouble?' [2011] *European Intellectual Property Review*, 607 (looks at the implications of the Court of Justice ruling in *Google France* v *Louis Vuitton*).

McMahon, B., 'Imposing an obligation to monitor on Information Society service providers' [2011] *Computer and Telecommunications Law Review*, 93 (looks at the Directive on electronic commerce in relation to internet auction sites).

Smith, J., 'Court of Appeal allows appeal in threats case – trap for the unwary: *Best Buy Co Inc* v *Worldwide Sales Corp Espana*' [2011] *European Intellectual Property Review*, 662 (examines the decision in the *Best Buy* case).

Community trade mark and the Madrid System

22

Introduction

1 This also extends to an organisation having such an establishment in, or which is domiciled in, the territory of an intergovernmental organisation which is a party to the Protocol and to nationals of a Member State of such an organisation.

2 Article 5 of the CTM Regulation (codified version).

3 OJ L 78, 24.03.2009, p 1. This codified version of the CTM Regulation repealed and replaced the original Regulation (Council Regulation (EC) No 40/94 of 20 December 1993 on the Community trade mark, OJ L 11, 14.01.1994, p 1), as amended. The Implementing Regulation, dealing with much of the fine detail, is Commission Regulation (EC) No 2868/95 of 13 December 1995 implementing Council Regulation (EC) No 40/94 on the Community trade mark, OJ L 303, 15.12.1995, p 1, as amended.

4 References in this chapter are to the codified Regulation. This Regulation contains a correlation table in Annex II.

5 OJ L 40, 11.02.1989, p 1.

6 Directive 2008/95/EC of the European Parliament and of the Council of 22 October 2008 to approximate the laws of the Member States relating to trade marks, OJ L 299, 08.11.2008, p 25.

7 There are some differences: for example, bad faith is not included in the absolute grounds for refusal in Article 7 of the Regulation although it is a ground for invalidity under Article 53.

A person seeking to gain protection for his trade mark by registration has a number of routes open to him. He may apply for a national registration, direct to the relevant national trade marks office, apply for a Community trade mark ('CTM'), which takes effect throughout the European Union and has a unitary nature, or he may apply to register the trade mark in a number of countries, which have ratified either the Madrid Agreement on the International Registration of Trade Marks or the Protocol to the Madrid Agreement (collectively known as the 'Madrid System'). Anyone may apply for a national registration, but application under the Madrid Agreement or Protocol may only be used by a natural person who, or a legal entity which, has a real and effective industrial or commercial establishment in, or is domiciled in, or is a national of, a country which is party to the Agreement or the Protocol, as appropriate.[1] In terms of the CTM, there used to be a requirement based on nationality or domicile, but this was removed so that now any natural or legal person, including authorities established under national law, may be the proprietor of a CTM.[2]

The CTM is provided for by Council Regulation (EC) No 207/2009 of 26 February 2009 on the Community trade mark[3] (the 'CTM Regulation')[4] and marked an important step forward in relation to the single market in Europe following on from the limited harmonisation achieved by the First Council Directive 89/104/EEC of 21 December 1988 to approximate the laws of the Member States relating to trade marks[5] repealed and replaced by Directive 2008/95/EC[6] (the 'Directive'). As we will see there are many similarities between the CTM Regulation and the Directive, especially in terms of the requirements for registration and grounds for refusal, the rights and limitations and surrender, revocation and invalidity. Many of these provisions are equivalent.[7] In other respects, there are similarities with the Community design, especially in relation to infringement proceedings, hearings and appeals at the Office for Harmonisation in the Internal Market (Trade Marks and Designs) (the 'OHIM') and jurisdictional issues. As with registered Community designs, the OHIM handles registration and a number of other procedural issues.

After looking at the substantive and procedural aspects of the CTM, this chapter briefly describes the Madrid System for the international registration of trade marks. This system is of increasing interest, as now it is possible to obtain registration of a trade mark as a CTM through the Madrid Protocol as the European Community (now European Union) joined the Protocol on from 1 October 2004.

Community trade mark

The CTM Regulation established the OHIM, which commenced accepting applications for registration of trade marks as CTMs on 1 January 1996.[8] The Office is situated in Alicante, Spain. As the CTM has a unitary nature, only marks which can have effect throughout the entire EU will be accepted.[9] This is one reason why existing national systems will continue to operate. For example, it may be that a trade mark for which registration as a CTM is sought is similar to an existing national registration in one or more Member States so that the relative grounds of refusal apply. To overcome practical problems of that nature, it is possible to convert an application for a CTM or a registered CTM into an application for a national trade mark, retaining the priority of the CTM or the application for the CTM or, where appropriate, any claim to seniority.[10]

Community collective marks are provided for in Articles 66–74 and require an applicant also to submit regulations governing the use of the mark. There are also additional grounds for revocation and invalidity and it is possible to register geographical names as a Community collective mark. There are no provisions for certification marks or guarantee marks.

As many of the provisions of the substantive law of the CTM are equivalent to those under the Directive, most of the decisions of the Court of Justice of the European Union (the 'Court of Justice') on the Directive are useful in determining the scope and interpretation of the CTM Regulation. However, the CTM and the national trade mark systems are separate and distinct and decisions and rulings on either are not binding upon the other.[11] Having said that, it is becoming increasingly common for the Court of Justice and the General Court (formerly the Court of First Instance),[12] which hears appeals from the OHIM, to refer to earlier cases on the other system.[13] As the Directive is of older pedigree, the 'traffic' is more one way than the other at the present time but cases on the Regulation have been cited on a number of occasions in cases on the Directive.[14] One thing that is clear is that decisions in the national courts have little, if any, persuasive authority on cases on the CTM just as decisions before the OHIM are of limited utility before the national courts looking at the Directive. Of course, there are some differences between the Directive, which carried out a limited harmonisation of national trade mark laws, and the Regulation which, with the Implementing Regulation, sets out an entire legislative framework for trade marks. One example is that the absolute grounds for refusal apply even if they obtain only in part of the EU. Another difference is that the limitation on the effect of a trade mark to prevent the proprietor prohibiting a third party using in the course of trade an earlier right which only applies in a particularly locality within a Member State does not apply to the CTM. However, under Article 111 of the CTM Regulation, the proprietor of an earlier right in a particular locality can actually oppose the use of the CTM in that locality.

The OHIM has its own Boards of Appeals to hear appeals, *inter alia*, from the examiners and Opposition or Cancellations divisions. From there, appeals go to the General Court and then, finally, to the Court of Justice. Decisions of the Boards of Appeal must be based solely on the CTM Regulation and not the practice of the OHIM in previous cases. Therefore, citing examples of trade marks registered as CTMs in the past should not influence a decision in respect of a subsequent application.[15]

In the following section on the CTM, it might be worth reflecting on Table 19.1 in Chapter 19 which gives a comparison of the references in the UK Trade Marks Act 1994, Directive and the CTM Regulation. The description of the substantive and procedural aspects of the CTM is intended, wherever possible, to avoid too much repetition of what has been discussed in the previous chapters on trade marks. Emphasis is placed on differences between the CTM Regulation and the Directive and on cases on the CTM Regulation,

8 Though the official date was 1 April 1996, the Regulation in its original form allowed applications up to three months before that date to be deemed to be made on 1 April 1996.

9 The European Community should now read European Union. However, provisions of the Community trade mark Regulation still refer to the Community.

10 Articles 112–114 of the CTM Regulation.

11 The fact that the CTM system is autonomous has been stated by the Court of First Instance (now General Court) and European Court of Justice (now the Court of Justice of the European Union) on numerous occasions. *See*, for example, Case T-281/02 *Norma Lebensmittelfilialbetrieb GmbH & Co KG v OHIM* [2004] ECR II-1915 at para 35.

12 In this chapter references to the Court of First Instance are still used for cases before that court was renamed the General Court. The European Court of Justice is now known as the Court of Justice of the European Union, referred to hereinafter simply as the Court of Justice.

13 There are many examples. In Case C-329/02 P *SAT.1 SatellitenFernsehen GmbH v OHIM* [2004] ECR I-8317, the Court of Justice cited six earlier cases before the court on the Directive as authority for issues including the basic function of a trade mark, the average consumer and whether a combination of indistinctive signs can itself be distinctive.

14 For example, in Case C-404/02 *Nichols plc v Registrar of Trade Marks* [2004] ECR I-8499 the Court of Justice cited Case C-445/02 P *Glaverbel SA v OHIM* [2004] ECR I-6267 on the fact that there is no distinction between different categories of trade marks in determining whether they have a distinctive character.

15 See, for example, Case C-51/10 P *Agencja Wydawnicza Technopol sp z oo v OHIM*, 10 March 2011.

many of which may also be instructive in relation to the Directive just as many decisions on the Directive will be helpful in the interpretation of many of the substantive law provisions of the CTM Regulation.

Nature of the CTM

16 Unless otherwise stated in this section on the CTM, statutory references are to the CTM Regulation.

17 However, under Article 111, the proprietor of an earlier right that applies in a particular locality can oppose the use of the CTM in that territory where the earlier right is protected.

18 See Articles 17 and 22.

A CTM is stated, under Article 2,[16] to have a unitary character having equal effect throughout the EU.[17] A CTM may not be registered, transferred or surrendered, or be subject to a decision revoking the proprietor's rights or be declared invalid, neither shall its use be prohibited save in respect of the whole EU. Thus the unitary character of a CTM cannot be compromised. This does not prevent the transfer of a CTM in respect of some or all the goods or services for which it is registered, and the grant of licences, exclusive or non-exclusive is expressly provided for.[18] Licences may be partial in respect of the whole or any part of the EU and in respect of some or all the goods or services for which it is registered. Assignments and licences may, of course, also be limited in time. The proprietor must be careful to avoid the danger of the mark becoming deceptive and liable to revocation proceedings by granting too many licences or by transferring the CTM in respect of some of the goods or services only, whilst retaining it and using it for the remainder of the goods or services. If the transfer is likely to mislead the public as to the nature, quality or geographic origin of the goods or services, the OHIM will not register the transfer unless the successor agrees to limit the registration to goods or services so as it is not likely to mislead.[19]

19 Article 17(4).

Where there is a transfer of the whole of an undertaking, the CTM will also be transferred in accordance with the law governing the transfer unless there is agreement to the contrary or the circumstances clearly dictate otherwise.[20]

20 Article 17(2).

Any natural or legal person, including authorities established under public law, may be the proprietor of a CTM and companies, firms and other legal bodies are to be regarded as legal persons if, under the law governing them, they have capacity in their own name and have rights or obligations of all kinds, to make contracts or accomplish other legal acts and sue or be sued: Articles 3 and 5.

Requirements for registration

Article 4 states that a CTM '…may consist of any signs capable of being represented graphically, particularly words, including personal names, designs, letters, numerals, the shape of goods or of their packaging, provided that such signs are capable of distinguishing the goods or services of one undertaking from those of other undertakings', a definition which is virtually identical to that in the Directive. As the definition of a CTM includes letters, it seems that even a single letter may be registrable if it has become distinctive of an undertaking's goods or services.[21]

21 See Case T-23/07 *BORCO-Marken-Import Matthiesen GmbH & Co KG v OHIM* [2009] ECR II-887. This case involved an application to register the Greek symbol alpha ('∝') as a trade mark.

22 [1998] ETMR 460.

23 [1999] RPC 879.

The requirement for being capable of being represented graphically was interpreted by the Board of Appeal at the OHIM, in Case R 4/97-2 *Antoni and Alison's Application*,[22] in the context of a mark other than a word mark, as requiring a drawing or a like representation. The following description was rejected: '…the vacuum-packing of an article of clothing in an envelope of plastic'. In *Swizzels Matlow Ltd Three-Dimensional Trade Mark Application*,[23] Simon Thorley QC, as the Appointed Person, said that decisions of the OHIM were persuasive but not binding. Furthermore, in upholding practice at the UK Registry, he said that the word 'graphically' serves to extend the meaning of the word 'represented' rather than to restrict it to a visual image and went on to suggest that the Board of Appeal at the OHIM probably did not intend such a restrictive approach. However, Article 4 of the CTM Regulation uses the phrase 'capable of being represented graphically'. The order of the words does, indeed, suggest a narrowing rather than an extension of the requirement that the mark be represented.

Absolute grounds for refusal

There are absolute and relative grounds for refusal of registration in Articles 7 and 8 which are very similar to those in the Directive, though there are some differences. Of the absolute grounds, those common to both the CTM Regulation and the Directive are that the sign does not meet the basic definition of a trade mark, that the mark lacks a distinctive character, that it consists exclusively of signs or indications which may serve, in trade, to designate kind, quality, quantity, etc. or have become customary in the trade, signs consisting exclusively of certain types of shape, trade marks contrary to public policy or accepted principles of morality, deceptive trade marks and trade marks not authorised by competent authorities and are to be refused in accordance with Article 6ter of the Paris Convention for the Protection of Industrial Property[24] and badges, emblems and the like other than those under Article 6ter of the Paris Convention unless the consent of the relevant authority is obtained.[25] In Joined Cases C-202/08 P and C-208/08 P *American Clothing Associates NV v OHIM*,[26] the Court of Justice confirmed that the prohibition against registering State flags and emblems, etc. applies even if the sign applied for also contains other elements. Furthermore, the Court of Justice held that there is no distinction between goods and services for signs falling within Article 6ter and other badges, etc. outside that provision. The applicant for a sign including the maple leaf, being part of the Canadian flag, argued that Article 6ter applied only to trade marks and not to service marks.

The CTM Regulation has no equivalent absolute ground for refusal of registration to the optional ones in the Directive where the use of the trade mark may be prohibited by law other than trade mark law or where the application was made in bad faith.[27]

The CTM Regulation has some additional absolute grounds for refusal of registration inserted by subsequent amendment. The first is in respect of trade marks for wines or spirits containing or consisting of geographical indications of origin when the wines or spirits do not have that origin. The second also relates to geographical origin, but in connection with agricultural products and foodstuffs.[28] An example where this ground for refusal could apply is if a Dutch producer of ham tried to register 'Parma Ham' for his products. The Directive instead has an absolute ground for refusal based on the use of the trade mark being prohibited by law, other than trade mark law, which would cover these grounds expressly mentioned in the CTM Regulation.

As with the Directive, some of the grounds for refusal can be overcome by showing that the trade mark has, in fact, acquired a distinctive character in consequence of the use that has been made of it (Article 7(3)). The grounds for which acquired distinctiveness can overcome refusal of registration are as those in the Directive. The time at which the sign in question must have acquired a distinctive character is at the time of the filing of the application to register and not after.[29]

An important proviso for the CTM is that the sign or trade mark will be unregistrable if any of the grounds apply only in respect of part of the EU (Article 7(2)). Thus, for example, if a trade mark is descriptive of the characteristics of the goods for which it is intended to be used only in German-speaking parts of the EU, it will still be caught by Article 7. That would not prevent the conversion of the application into a number of national applications in non-German-speaking countries where the mark might have no particular meaning for persons not fluent in German. In Case C-104/00 P *DKV Deutsche*

24 Article 7(1)(h). These include armorial bearings, flags and other State emblems.

25 Article 7(1)(i). This latter ground for refusal was, in the Directive, an option for Member States.

26 [2009] ECR I-6933.

27 But making an application in bad faith is a ground for invalidity of a CTM under Article 52(1)(b).

28 Council Regulation (EEC) No 2081/92 of 14 July 1992 on the protection of geographical indications and designations of origin for agricultural products and foodstuffs, OJ L 208, 24.07.1992, p 1. The ground for refusal applies to situations under Article 13 of the Regulation: for example, where the trade mark is misleading or evokes the product for which registration has been granted under that Regulation.

29 Case C-42/07 *Imagination Technologies Ltd v OHIM* [2009] ECR I-4937.

30 [2002] ECR I-7561.

31 The applicant cited numerous examples of UK registered trade marks ending in '-line', to no avail.

32 Which has exclusive jurisdiction to make such findings as between the Court of First Instance and the Court of Justice.

33 Joined Cases C-468/01P to C-472/01P *Procter & Gamble Co v OHIM* [2004] ECR I-5141.

34 [2004] ECR I-10031.

35 In English the phrase means the principle of comfort.

36 An advertising slogan may be registrable but may face an uphill task, especially if it, or something similar, is in common use such as 'REAL PEOPLE, REAL SOLUTIONS': Case T-130/01 *Sykes Enterprises Inc v OHIM* [2002] ECR II-5179. *See* also Case T-122/01 *Best Buy Concepts Inc v OHIM* [2003] ECR II-2235 ('BEST BUY') and Case T-281/02 *Norma Lebensmittelfilialbetrieb GmbH & Co KG v OHIM* [2004] ECR II-1915 ('Mehr fur Ihr Geld' meaning 'More for your money').

37 21 January 2010.

38 Registration had been sought in a wide variety of classes. In relation to vehicles, it had previously been accepted that the sign had acquired a distinctive character through use.

39 [2004] ECR I-8317.

40 Citing Case 102/77 *Hoffmann-La Roche & Co AG v Centrafarm Vertriebsgesellschaft mbH* [1978] ECR 1139 and Case C-299/99 *Koninklijke Philips NV v Remington Consumer Products Ltd* [2002] ECR I-5475.

41 Citing Case C-342/97 *Lloyd Schuhfabrik Meyer & Co GmbH v Klisjen Handel BV* [1999] ECR I-3819 and Case C-104/01 *Libertel Groep BV v Benelux Merkenbureau* [2003] ECR I-3793.

42 The Court of First Instance paid too much attention to the individual elements of the trade mark and failed to take into account aspects such as the existence of an element of imaginativeness.

43 [2011] ECR I-0000.

44 [2007] ECR I-2883.

45 Of course, it may be the case that a sign is caught by more than one of the grounds under Article 7, for example, it is both descriptive and devoid of distinctive character.

46 [2005] ECR I-7975.

Krankenversicherung AG v OHIM,[30] the Court of Justice confirmed that the Court of First Instance rightly held that the trade mark 'Companyline' was not registrable as it was not distinctive in English-speaking areas of the EU.[31]

The Court of Justice and the Court of First Instance have dealt with numerous appeals from decisions on the absolute grounds for refusal. The Court of Justice will not interfere with findings of fact before the Court of First Instance[32] unless it made a substantive inaccuracy in its findings attributable to the documentation submitted to it or where the evidence produced before the court has been distorted.[33]

There have been numerous cases on Article 7(1)(b), the ground for refusal where a sign is devoid of any distinctive character. In Case C-64/02 P *OHIM v Erpo Möbelwerk GmbH*,[34] an application was made to register 'DAS PRINZIP DER BEQUEMLICHKEIT' in relation to goods including furniture.[35] The Court of Justice confirmed, in accordance with the case law on the equivalent grounds in the Directive, that there is no distinction between different categories of trade marks when assessing whether a trade mark has a distinctive character for the purposes of Article 7(1)(b). The Court of First Instance (now the General Court) had erred in finding that, in relation to a trade mark which appears to be a slogan, it is not devoid of a distinctive character unless it is shown that it is commonly used in business communications and, in particular, in advertising. This went outside the bounds of the statutory provision.[36]

In Case C-398/08 P *Audi AG v OHIM*,[37] in relation to '*Vorsprung durch Technik*', the Court of Justice again confirmed that a sign may be registrable if the relevant public perceives it as an indication of origin even though it may also be understood, perhaps even primarily understood, as an advertising slogan.[38]

The Court of Justice relied heavily on its own case law on the Directive in Case C-329/02 P *SAT.1 SatellitenFernsehen GmbH v OHIM*.[39] The court confirmed that, in assessing distinctive character, the basic function of a trade mark must be considered, being to identify the origin of the goods or services.[40] Furthermore, in making that assessment, it is appropriate to take the viewpoint of the average consumer who is reasonably well informed and reasonably observant and circumspect.[41] The Court of Justice also held that each of the grounds for refusal of registration under Article 7 is separate and independent of the rest although there is inevitably some overlap between them. They should be examined in the light of the different considerations underlying them. Article 7(1)(b) is inexorably linked with the essential function of a trade mark. In the above case, the applicant sought to register 'SAT.2' in relation to satellite broadcasting. The Court of Justice held that, where a trade mark comprises two elements, a word and a digit in this case, the combination may possess a distinctive character even though each taken separately would not.[42] It is the overall impression of the trade mark that is important.

In Case C-92/10 P *Media-Saturn Holding GmbH v OHIM*,[43] the Court of Justice confirmed the decision of the General Court that a figurative mark with the words 'BEST BUY' lacked distinctive character. At best, the sign was an advertising slogan.

The trade mark CELLTECH might be interpreted as an abbreviation for 'cell technology' but it is the combination that is important and, in Case C-273/05 P *OHIM v Celltech R & D Ltd*,[44] the Court of Justice confirmed that it had not been shown that the trade mark was descriptive of the goods or service for which registration had been sought.

The independence of the grounds under Article 7 means that criteria used under Article 7(1)(c) (that is, where the trade mark is descriptive of certain characteristics of goods or services) cannot be used as a basis for finding that the trade mark is devoid of any distinctive character for the purposes of Article 7(1)(b).[45] A finding that a trade mark is commonly used in the trade did not justify a finding that it lacked distinctiveness in Case C-37/03 P *BioID AG v OHIM*.[46] The trade mark for which registration was sought was 'BioID.®' for software and telecommunications services and the like relating to biometric identification. Where a decision of the Court of First Instance is quashed, as it was in this case, the Court of Justice may itself give final judgment. Consequently, the Court of Justice examined the trade mark. It held that the dominant element of the mark when its overall impression is examined through the eyes of the relevant public was the abbreviation BioID, which would be understood as meaning 'biometric identification', and this lacked distinctive character.

Article 7(1)(c) prevents registration of trade marks which consist exclusively of signs or indications which may serve, in trade, to designate kind, quality, quantity, etc. or other characteristics of goods or services. Usually, an application to register a geographical name as a trade mark will be refused on this ground in the absence of distinctiveness acquired through use. However, for this ground to apply to a geographical name, it must be perceived as indicating geographical origin. If it does not it may be registrable. In Case T-379/03 *Peek & Cloppenburg KG v OHIM*,[47] an application was made to register 'Cloppenburg' for retail trade services. Cloppenburg is a small town in Saxony, Germany. It was refused on the basis of Article 7(1)(c) but the applicant's appeal to the Court of First Instance was successful.

It was held that, even if the relevant public knows of the town of Cloppenburg, it does not automatically follow that the sign may serve, in trade, to designate geographical origin. Account must be taken of all the circumstances, such as the nature of the goods or services, the greater or lesser reputation of the geographical location within that economic sector, the level of the relevant public's familiarity with it, the customs obtaining in the area of activity concerned and the question to what extent the geographical origin of the goods or services at issue may be relevant, in the view of the persons concerned, to the assessment of the quality or other characteristics of the goods or services concerned. Applying these principles, the court noted that the town was a small one, there was no evidence that it enjoyed a reputation as the place where any class of goods are produced or services rendered. Furthermore, there was nothing to suggest that it was current practice in trade to indicate the geographical origin of retail trade services and, in any case, the geographical origin of such services is not usually regarded as relevant when assessing their quality or characteristics.

As is the case with the equivalent provision in the Directive, Article 7(1)(c) serves the public interest in keeping descriptive signs and indications free for all to use.[48] However, accepting this was so, in Case T-356/00 *DaimlerChrysler AG v OHIM*,[49] the Court of First Instance held that the fact that competitors do not need to use the sign for which registration is sought is not relevant to the inquiry and there does not need to be a real, current or serious need to leave the sign free. The question is whether there is a sufficient direct or specific association between the sign and the goods or services and if one of the possible meanings of the sign identifies a feature of the goods or services that is sufficient. The descriptiveness of a sign must be assessed in the light of the goods or services for which registration is sought. The trade mark in question, 'CARCARD', was capable of designating the kind or quality of some of the services applied for such as credit cards and cards for carrying information relating to aspects of cars such as details of servicing and repairs. Although in respect of other services, such as rental and leasing of data processing equipment, the trade mark was not descriptive and did not serve to designate specific characteristics of those services. Consequently, the trade mark was registrable in relation to some though not all of the services applied for.

The same principle applies to composite marks as with the equivalent provision in the Directive and, where the individual components are descriptive, the impression created by the combination must be greater than the sum of its parts. The leading cases on this, involving the CTM, are Case C-383/99 P *Procter & Gamble Co v OHIM*[50] where it was held that 'BABY-DRY' for nappies was registrable as it was a syntactically unusual combination not familiar in the English language.[51] On the other hand, 'DOUBLEMINT' for chewing gum was not registrable as one of its possible meanings alluded to the characteristics of

47 [2005] ECR II-4633.

48 Joined Cases C-108/97 and 109/97 *Windsurfing Chiemsee v Huber and Attenberger* [1999] ECR I-2799. A similar public interest applies in respect of Article 7(1)(d).

49 [2002] ECR II-1963.

50 [2001] ECR I-6251.

51 See also Case C-408/08 P *Lancôme parfums et beauté & Cie SNC v OHIM*, 25 February 2010, in relation to 'COLOR EDITION'.

52 [2003] ECR I-12447.

the goods: Case C-191/01 P, *OHIM v Wm Wrigley Jr Co.*[52] The trade mark does not have to be exclusively descriptive for the purposes of Article 7(1)(c), nor does it need to be in current use; it is sufficient if this is a possibility in the future.

That a combination mark must not be inherently descriptive but has acquired its own distinct meaning as an indication of origin has been accepted on a number of occasions after the 'BABY-DRY' and 'DOUBLEMINT' cases by the Court of First Instance. For example, in Joined Cases T-178/03 and T-179/03 *CeWe Color AG & Co OHG v OHIM*,[53] the court cited the ruling in Case C-363/99 *Koninklijke KPN Nederland NV v Benelux-Merkenbureau*[54] on Article 3(1)(c) in the Directive, which was approved by analogy.[55] The signs applied for in *CeWe Color* were 'DigiFilm' and 'DigiFilmMaker' for a range of goods and services. Those relating to digital photography and digital image processing and the like were rejected on the basis of Article 7(1)(b) and (c). Of course, as the grounds for refusal are independent, even if there is some overlap, it is sufficient if only one ground for refusal applies.

53 [2005] ECR II-3105.
54 [2004] ECR I-1619.
55 As with many of the provisions of the CTM Regulation and the Directive, it can be said with a fair degree of certainty that their interpretation is at one.

Although numerals are mentioned in the non-exhaustive list of signs which may be registered and even though OHIM guidelines mention that numerals are generally acceptable for registration, a sign comprising of numerals may still be denied registration under the absolute grounds for refusal. In Case C-51/10 P *Agencja Wydawnicza Technopol sp z oo v OHIM*,[56] an application was made to register '1000' as a trade mark for, inter alia, periodicals, including periodicals containing crossword puzzles. The Court of Justice held that the sign was characteristic of the goods for which registration was sought. It was descriptive of quantity in that the relevant class of persons would perceive it to mean the publication contained 1000 crossword puzzles.[57] The principles of equal treatment and sound administration required that OHIM considered its own previous decisions in similar cases and it had to take special care to consider whether or not it should decide a new case in the same way. In any event, those principles must be applied with respect for legality. The guidelines of the OHIM are, of course, not legally binding.

56 10 March 2011.

57 Numerous magazines use numbers on their front page.

Acquired distinctiveness

Article 7(3) allows registration to proceed where some of the absolute grounds for refusal appear to exist if, in consequence of the use made of it, the trade mark has become distinctive as a matter of fact. It has been argued by applicants that the relevant date at which to determine whether a trade mark has any distinctive character should be the date of filing the application rather than the date the trade mark would be registered. This could make a difference where, in between those dates, more under-takings started using similar signs. In Joined Cases C-456/01 P and C-457/01 P *Henkel KGaA v OHIM*,[58] an application to register three-dimensional shapes for tablets for washing machines and dishwashers was refused as the tablets were devoid of distinctive character. It was argued that distinctiveness should be assessed at the time of filing the application as there were not many similar tablets on the market at that time, unlike the position later. The Court of Justice upheld the Court of First Instance's finding that it did not need to decide the point as the trade mark simply was not distinctive and it did not matter how many similar tablets were on the market.[59] In some cases, an applicant might argue that the later date should be used where he thinks it is more likely that there will be evidence of acquired distinctiveness by this time.

58 [2004] ECR I-5089.

59 See also Joined Cases C-468/01 P to C-472/01 P *Procter & Gamble Co v OHIM* [2004] ECR I-5141, concerning three-dimensional shapes for washing machines and dishwashers.

60 Trade Marks Act 1994, s 40(3).

61 Indeed the Court of First Instance accepted this, referring to Article 9(3) rejecting evidence of distinctiveness acquired after the date of filing in Case T-247/01 *eCopy Inc v OHIM* [2002] ECR II-5301.

The rights to a CTM relate back to the date of publication of the application under Article 9(3), although any decision on infringement cannot be made until after the date of publication of the fact of registration. As regards a UK registered trade mark, it is deemed to be registered as at the date of filing the application.[60] Consequently, the time for determining whether a trade mark has a distinctive character can only be the date of filing.[61] If other undertakings subsequently use similar signs in the period between filing and registration, rather than detracting from registrability, they potentially infringe the trade mark. Using the date of filing as the relevant date for acquired distinctiveness also avoids the unsatisfactory position that the longer the procedure to registration at the OHIM takes, the better the chances that this ground for refusal will be overcome on the basis of Article 7(3).

In Case T-16/02 *Audi AG v OHIM*,[62] the Court of First Instance held that, to satisfy the requirement for acquired distinctiveness to overcome the absolute grounds for refusal under Article 7(1)(b)–(d), the trade mark must be seen by a significant proportion of the relevant public as identifying the origin of the goods or services in respect of which the trade mark is used and that distinctive character must be shown to exist in the substantial part of the EU where it was, in the case of Article 7(1)(b), devoid of any distinctive character. Factors to be taken into account include market share, intensity, geographic scope and duration of use and the amount of promotion of the mark.[63] The court also confirmed its earlier decision in Case T-247/01 *eCopy Inc v OHIM*[64] to the effect that the relevant time for assessing distinctive character was the date of filing the application.

Relative grounds for refusal

A precondition for the relative grounds for refusal applying is that they depend upon the proprietor of an earlier trade mark opposing the application (Article 8(1)) or, in the case of objection based on an earlier unregistered trade mark or other sign used in the course of trade, opposition of the proprietor of that unregistered trade mark or sign (Article 8(4)).[65]

The relative grounds for refusal based on earlier trade marks are as those in the Directive, that is, where the mark for which registration is sought is identical and is to be used for identical goods or services or where there is not complete identity, registration will be refused if there exists a likelihood of confusion on the part of the public. The option in the Directive (which was taken up in the UK) for refusal in the case of an earlier trade mark of repute where the use of the mark would take unfair advantage of or be detrimental to the distinctive character or repute of the trade mark is included in the CTM Regulation under Article 8(5). Although it is still expressed in terms of use for goods or services that are not similar to those for which the earlier trade mark is registered, it is almost certain that, should the matter come up, the ruling in Case C-292/00 *Davidoff & Cie SA v Gofkid Ltd*,[66] confirmed in Case C-408/01 *Adidas-Salomon AG v Fitnessworld Trading Ltd*,[67] to the effect that the equivalent provision in the Directive also applies to identical or similar goods or services, would be followed, even though, strictly speaking, these cases are not binding as regards the CTM.

A further relative ground is, under Article 8(3), where an agent or representative has applied to register a trade mark in his own name without the consent of the proprietor who now opposes the registration.[68]

Unlike the Directive, the CTM Regulation does not provide for relative grounds for refusal based on, for example, copyright and other industrial property rights, although it does provide a relative ground of refusal based on earlier unregistered trade marks and other signs used in the course of trade. However, earlier copyright and industrial property rights, *inter alia*, may be used to challenge the validity of a CTM as well as earlier registered and unregistered trade marks and other signs used in the course of trade.

Under Article 8(2) earlier trade marks include CTMs, trade marks registered in Member States,[69] trade marks registered under international arrangements which have effect in Member States or the EC, applications for such trade marks and well-known marks within the meaning of Article 6bis of the Paris Convention. To be taken into consideration, the earlier trade mark must have an application date earlier than that of the application for the CTM, allowing for any priority claimed for the earlier trade mark, if appropriate.

There have been very few cases on the ground for refusal under Article 8(1)(a) – identical signs for identical goods or services. However, in Case T-317/01 *M + M Gesellschaft*

62 [2003] ECR II-5167. The mark applied for was 'TDI' for vehicles and repair and maintenance of them.

63 It is not permissible to adduce evidence of acquired distinctiveness for the first time before the Court of Justice in the absence of distortion by the Court of First Instance of the facts or evidence before it: Case C-286/04 P *Eurocermex SA v OHIM*, [2005] ECR I-5797.

64 [2002] ECR II-5301.

65 Until recently in the UK, any person could oppose an application to register a UK trade mark; however, where this was based on an earlier trade mark more than five years old, the opponent had to prove that the trade mark has been used in the last five years. Now, opposition may only be brought on the relative grounds by the proprietor of the earlier trade mark or other earlier right. Proof of use still applies.

66 [2003] ECR I-389.

67 [2003] ECR I-12537.

68 In this case the term 'proprietor' must be taken to mean the person entitled to be the proprietor once registered.

69 Or, in the case of Belgium, the Netherlands and Luxembourg, registered at the Benelux Intellectual Property Office.

70 [2004] ECR II-1817.

71 This part of the decision was not appealed to the Court of First Instance.

72 [2006] ECR I-643.

Unternehmensberatung und Informationssysteme mbH v *OHIM*[70] it was noted that the Board of Appeal considered 'EUROdATA' to be identical to 'EURODATA'.[71]

In terms of the relative grounds for refusal, where appropriate, rulings on the provisions in the Directive are followed for the CTM. The most important case thus far is Case C-316/04P *Ruiz-Picasso* v *OHIM*,[72] in which the Court of Justice, on appeal from the Court of First Instance, applied some of the leading cases on the Directive. In particular, the test for a likelihood of confusion must be assessed by a global appreciation taking account of all the circumstances and that global appreciation of the visual, aural or conceptual similarity based on the overall impression given by the marks bearing in mind, in particular, their distinctive and dominant components.[73] The interdependence of the similarity

73 Case C-251/95 *Sabel BV* v *Puma AG, Rudolf Dassler Sport* [1997] ECR I-6191.

between the signs and the similarity between the goods or services are amongst the factors to be taken into account. Again, in line with cases on the Directive, the greater the similarity of the signs, the lesser the similarity of the goods or services required to find a likelihood of confusion and vice versa.[74] The Court of First Instance applied this interdependence in Case T-162/01 *Laboratories RTB, SL* v *OHIM*,[75] holding that there was no likelihood of confusion between 'GIORGIO BEVERLEY HILLS' and earlier Spanish marks 'J GIORGI', 'Miss GIORGI' and 'GIORGI LINE' even though there was identity and similarity between the goods in question.

74 Case C-39/97 *Canon Kabushiki Kaisha* v *Metro Goldwyn Mayer Inc* [1998] ECR I-5507 and Case C-342/97 *Lloyd Schuhfabrik Meyer & Co GmbH* v *Klisjen Handel BV* [1999] ECR I-3819.

75 [2003] ECR II-2821.

In *Ruiz-Picasso* v *OHIM*, the estate of Pablo Picasso, which had a CTM for 'PICASSO' for motor vehicles, opposed an application by DaimlerChrysler AG to register the name 'PICARO' for motor vehicles.

The degree of attention an average consumer will have varies according to the category of goods or services; the attention paid in the field of motor vehicles is high. In any case, the mark 'PICASSO' would be taken by the public to refer to the painter and the name, regardless of any inherent distinctiveness, was devoid of any distinctive character vis-à-vis motor vehicles. It would not have any resonance with motor vehicles even though it had been registered for these. The Court of Justice accepted this, answering an objection that the Court of First Instance failed to take into account previous case law to the effect that the greater the reputation, the wider the protection afforded.[76] There was no likelihood of confusion and the relevant public would not think that goods bearing the two marks would come from the same or economically linked undertakings.

76 Case C-251/95 *Sabel BV* v *Puma AG, Rudolf Dassler Sport* [1997] ECR I-6191, Case C-39/97 *Canon Kabushiki Kaisha* v *Metro Goldwyn Mayer Inc* [1998] ECR I-5507 and Case C-342/97 *Lloyd Schuhfabrik Meyer & Co GmbH* v *Klisjen Handel BV* [1999] ECR I-3819.

77 [2003] ECR II-43.

The relevant public will not make an elaborate analysis to distinguish between two marks where, for example, there is a similarity of goods and an aural similarity between the mark applied for and the earlier trade mark. The Court of First Instance confirmed this in Case T-99/01 *Mystery Drinks GmbH* v *OHIM*[77] in which the mark applied for, 'MYSTERY', for non-alcoholic beverages, with the exception of non-alcoholic beers, was held to be unregistrable to that extent because of the existence of an earlier trade mark, 'Mixery', registered in Germany for beers and the like. Visually the marks were readily distinguishable ('MYSTERY' was in stylised form) but aurally they were similar. Conceptually, the marks were held to be similar as the evocative meaning of them was not so direct so as to be immediately perceived by consumers.

78 [2007] ECR I-3569.

An aural and visual similarity would suggest that the grounds for opposition might be made out. In Case C-412/05 *Alcon Inc* v *OHIM*,[78] an application was made to register 'TRAVATAN' for ophthalmic pharmaceutical products. The proprietor of the earlier trade mark 'TRAVISTAN', registered for pharmaceuticals available under prescription only, opposed the application. The relevant consumers included healthcare professionals and end users. Although the former might have some influence, an issue was whether ultimate consumers were likely to be confused as to the origin of the pharmaceuticals in question. The Court of First Instance had given inadequate reasons for its assessment of the visual and phonetic similarity of the marks, but that was not enough to invalidate its judgment that, because there was a sufficient similarity between the sign and the trade mark and the goods, there was a likelihood of confusion between them.

Although goods or services may be similar, there may be no likelihood of confusion if they are aimed at different markets. For example, in Case T-316/07 *Commercy AG v OHIM*,[79] an application for invalidity was brought in relation to the CTM easyHotel on the basis of the earlier national mark EASYHOTEL. Both were used for computer software reservation systems but the earlier national mark was used for software sold to hotels and the like whilst the latter was used by persons making bookings online. The goods and services were sold to different publics.

79 [2009] ECR II-43.

Where registration is applied for a sign that contains a word subject to an earlier registration by another, that fact alone is not conclusive that the sign is similar to the earlier trade mark. In Case C-553/09 P *Ferrerro SpA v OHIM*,[80] the sign applied for was a figurative one containing the words 'TiMi' and 'KINDERJOGHURT'. It was opposed by Ferrerro which had the very well-known word mark 'KINDER'. The Court of Justice confirmed that the sign and the mark were not similar so the question of whether it was barred registration under Article 8(1)(b) or Article 8(5) did not arise, no matter how great the reputation in the opponent's mark. Ferrerro was relentless in its objection to the registration of the sign. It brought opposition proceedings and when it lost those, appealed to the Board of Appeal which confirmed the finding of the Opposition Division. Following acceptance of the sign for registration, Ferrerro then brought invalidity proceedings before the Cancellation Division of the OHIM based on Article 8(1)(b) and 8(5). It was successful but the owner of the KINDERJOGHURT mark successfully appealed to the Board of Appeal of the OHIM. Ferrerro's subsequent appeal against that decision was rejected by the General Court and its final appeal to the Court of Justice was also dismissed.

80 24 March 2011.

Rights, infringement and remedies

Article 9 sets out the rights conferred on the proprietor of a CTM which are exclusive rights. The proprietor is entitled to prevent third parties not having his consent from using in the course of trade:

(a) an identical sign for identical goods or services;
(b) an identical or similar sign for goods or services that are identical or similar subject to a likelihood of confusion on the part of the public which includes a likelihood of association; or
(c) an identical or similar sign for goods or services that are not similar where the CTM has a reputation and the use of the sign would take unfair advantage of or be detrimental to the distinctive character or repute of the CTM.

Again, this latter right must also extend to goods or services that are identical or similar in line with the Court of Justice ruling in Case C-292/00 *Davidoff & Cie SA v Gofkid Ltd*.[81]

81 [2003] ECR I-389.

Article 9(2) states that the uses that may be prohibited include affixing the sign to goods or to their packaging, offerings goods, putting them on the market or stocking them for such purposes under the sign, offering or supplying services under the sign, importing or exporting goods under the sign or using the sign on business papers and in advertising. This list is not exhaustive.

Article 10 has no equivalent in the Directive and is designed to help proprietors to prevent their trade marks becoming generic names and, as a result, being vulnerable to revocation.[82] If the reproduction of the CTM in a dictionary, encyclopaedia or similar reference work gives the impression that the mark is a generic name, the publisher must, at the request of the proprietor, ensure that the reproduction is accompanied by an indication that it is a registered trade mark by the time of the next edition at the latest.

82 Article 51 includes as one of the grounds for revocation where the mark, as a consequence of the inactivity of the proprietor, has become a common name in the trade for the product or service in respect of which it is registered.

Article 10 does not say what should happen if the publisher fails to comply. Presumably if this happens, any evidence that a CTM has become a common name to the extent that it is the result of its use in a dictionary or other work would be disregarded if the proprietor of the CTM has requested the publisher to mention that the CTM is registered.

In a case where a CTM is registered in the name of an agent or representative of the proprietor without the proprietor's authorisation, the proprietor may oppose such use unless the agent or proprietor justifies his action (Article 11). The use of the word 'proprietor' in this sense must mean the person who should be entitled to register the trade mark as a CTM and covers a situation where, for example, his trade mark agent registers it in his own name. In cases, such as these, Article 18 allows for the assignment of the CTM from the agent or representative to the proprietor, unless the agent or representative can justify his action.

Article 14 confirms that the effects of a CTM shall be as governed by the CTM Regulation but, in other respects, infringement shall be governed by the national law relating to infringement of a national trade mark. This means that, for example, if an infringement action is brought before a UK Community trade mark court (assuming it has jurisdiction, as discussed later), such as the Chancery Division of the High Court, the usual remedies for infringement will be available as with infringement of a UK registered trade mark. An action could be brought in the national court on the basis of national law relating to civil liability and unfair competition. This would allow an action to be brought in the UK, subject to the court having jurisdiction, for passing off and, presumably, also malicious falsehood, in appropriate circumstances.

The unitary character of a CTM in having effect throughout the EU may be compromised by an earlier right which applies in a particular locality as, where such a right exists, its proprietor may oppose the use of the CTM in the territory where it is protected in so far as the law of the relevant Member State permits (Article 111). This would allow a person having business goodwill protected by the law of passing off in, for example, the north-west of England opposing the use of the CTM there. Five years' acquiescence will defeat such opposition to the use of the CTM in that locality provided the CTM was not applied for in bad faith. The proprietor of the CTM will not be able to oppose the use of the earlier right in that locality even though there has been acquiescence so that it can no longer be invoked against the CTM. The relative grounds for refusal do not permit opposition of an application for a CTM on the basis of an earlier unregistered trade mark or sign used in the course of business if the right attaching to it has merely local significance. Furthermore, the CTM Regulation does not affect claims for infringement of earlier rights under the laws of Member States.[83]

83 Article 110. Unless otherwise provided for in the CTM Regulations, laws of Member States which can be invoked against the use of national trade marks may be used against CTMs.

Limitation of the effects of a CTM

Article 12 on the limitation of the effects of a CTM mirror those in Article 6(1) of the Directive.[84] It is likely that the case law of the Court of Justice in relation to the Directive will be used as precedent though, strictly speaking, not binding.

The doctrine of exhaustion of rights applies under Article 13 in relation to goods placed on the market within the EU by or with the proprietor's consent and there is an equivalent proviso to that in the Directive allowing the proprietor, where there exist legitimate reasons, to oppose further commercialisation of the goods where their condition has been changed or impaired.

As with the harmonised national trade mark, exhaustion of rights will not apply where the goods have been placed on the market by the proprietor, or with his consent, outside the EU. However, unlike the national trade mark, where exhaustion applies to goods

84 There is no equivalent to Article 6(2) of the Directive which limits the right in respect of earlier rights which apply only in a particular locality.

placed on the market within the European Economic Area ('EEA'),[85] exhaustion for the CTM is limited to goods placed on the market within the EU.

A defence in an infringement action may be based on acquiescence under Article 54 where an allegation relates infringement of an earlier CTM, national trade mark within Article 8(2) or other earlier sign within Article 8(4) and the proprietor has acquiesced in the use of a later CTM for five successive years while being aware of its use, provided the application to register the later CTM was not made in bad faith.

Applying for and registration of a CTM

The application to register a trade mark as a CTM may be filed, at the choice of the applicant, direct at the OHIM or at the relevant national industrial property office (in the UK, the Trade Marks Registry) or the Benelux Intellectual Property Office. In the latter two cases, the application should be forwarded to the OHIM, retaining the original filing date.[86] The application must contain a request for registration as a CTM, information identifying the applicant, a list of goods or services for which registration is sought and a representation of the trade mark.[87] The application must also conform to any condition laid down in the Implementing Regulation and the fee must be paid within one month. Where the priority of a filing elsewhere is claimed, a declaration of priority must be claimed together with a copy of the previous application, including a translation if necessary.[88] A claim for seniority may also be made, including a claim made after registration of the CTM.[89]

The OHIM will examine the application to ensure that the conditions of filing are satisfied, including those in the Implementing Regulation, and that the fee has been paid within the prescribed period. There will also be examination in respect of the absolute grounds for refusal. A search is carried out of earlier CTMs and earlier applications for CTMs and a search report is produced. National trade mark offices which have indicated their willingness to carry out searches in respect of CTM applications are also required to carry out a search of their registers and produce search reports. These search reports are then sent to the applicant. The application may be withdrawn at any time or the applicant may choose to restrict the goods or services for which registration is sought. The application is then published and observations may be submitted or opposition raised. Proprietors of earlier CTMs or applications for CTM cited in search reports are notified of the act of publication. Opposition may be made only by the proprietor of an earlier trade mark or other earlier right or by licensees.[90] There have been some changes to the search provisions with effect from 10 March 2008.

Following publication, any person may make observations without becoming a party to any proceedings before the OHIM. The observations, which will be communicated to the applicant, who may comment on them, should be based particularly on the absolute grounds for refusal.

Within three months after publication, opposition may be raised on the basis of the relative grounds for refusal. Under Article 41, opposition may be raised only by the proprietors of earlier trade marks (or their licensees) on the basis of Article 8(1) or (5) (refusal based on identity or similarity with earlier trade mark) or by proprietors of trade marks where an agent or representative has applied for registration in his own name under Article 8(3) or by proprietors of earlier unregistered trade marks or other signs used in the course of trade under Article 8(4) (or persons authorised under national laws to exercise those rights under Article 8(4)).

Where the applicant so desires and the opposition is based upon an earlier trade mark which is five or more years old, the opponent must furnish proof that it has been put to genuine use in the last five years or there are proper reasons for non-use (Article 42(2)).

85 The Directive now has effect in the EEA, not just the EU.

86 If the applications reach the OHIM more than two months later, they will be accorded a filing date of the date they were received by the OHIM. The national office or Benelux Intellectual Property Office may charge a handling fee not exceeding the administrative costs.

87 Article 26.

88 Priority may also be claimed in respect of recognised international exhibitions: Article 33.

89 Articles 34 and 35.

90 In respect of opposition where the application is made by an agent or representative of the proprietor without his consent, only the proprietor may oppose.

Genuine use requires real use, not token use or artificial use merely to maintain the trade mark on the register.[91] Following opposition, the application may be rejected in whole or in part, otherwise the opposition will be rejected. There are provisions for withdrawal, restriction, amendment or division of the application. Division might be advisable where, for example, it appears that there may be objection to some of the goods or services applied for or some marks in a series of marks applied for. Dividing the application may allow the non-contentious elements to proceed to registration allowing the others to be dealt with in more detail at a later stage. Division of an application may not be made during opposition proceedings or proceedings for an application for revocation or a declaration of invalidity unless it would not prejudice those proceedings.

The duration of registration (initial and on renewal) is, under Article 46, ten years, as it is in respect of national registered trade marks. Renewal must be applied for within six months of expiry. There is a further six months for late renewal subject to an additional fee. There are no provisions allowing for restoration of a lapsed CTM as there are for the UK registered trade mark.

An applicant for a CTM may convert his application into a national trade mark application, under Article 112, to the extent that the CTM is refused, withdrawn or deemed to be withdrawn or to the extent that it ceases to have effect. Conversion is not allowed if the CTM has been revoked for non-use unless it has been put to use in the Member State for which conversion to national trade mark is sought or for the purpose of protection in a Member State when there has been a decision of the OHIM or national court that grounds for refusal, revocation or invalidity apply to the application for a CTM or a registered CTM.[92] Where conversion takes place, the application to the trade mark office in the relevant Member State will retain its priority or seniority as appropriate. The time limit for conversion is generally three months after withdrawal, surrender or refusal, otherwise priority will be lost.

Property rights in a CTM

CTMs are treated as objects of property which, in their entirety and for the whole of the EU (except as otherwise provided for under Articles 17–24 – the other provisions on property rights in CTMs), are to be dealt with as national trade marks in the Member State where the proprietor has his seat or domicile or, failing this, his establishment. If none of these apply, it is the Member State where the OHIM is situated, at the present time, being Spain.[93]

A CTM may be transferred, with or without the transfer of the undertaking, for all or some of the goods or services for which it is registered (Article 17). There is a presumption that the transfer of an undertaking also transfers the CTM[94] and, as mentioned earlier, the OHIM may insist on limiting the transfer to goods or services so as not to mislead the public. Any assignment must be in writing, signed by the parties unless the transfer is the result of a judgment; otherwise the assignment is void. This is, however, without prejudice to a presumed transfer where the undertaking has been transferred. A successor in title cannot invoke the rights under a CTM until such time as his name is entered in the register. Article 18 provides that the proprietor may demand the transfer of a CTM wrongly registered by his agent or representative unless the agent or representative justifies his claim to the CTM. The right subsisting in the CTM may be charged as security or made subject to rights *in rem* (Article 19). A CTM may be levied in execution or be subject to insolvency proceedings.[95]

Article 22 contains the provisions for licensing CTMs and licences may be exclusive or non-exclusive and may be in relation to all or some of the goods or services for which the

91 Case T-39/01 *Kabushiki Kaisha Fernandes* v *OHIM* [2002] ECR II-5233.

92 In such a case, the refusal etc. is determinative of the position at the national level. However, there is nothing to prevent an applicant making a fresh application to a national trade mark office (of course, losing any right to priority or seniority): Case T-342/02 *Metro Goldwyn Mayer Lion Corp* v *OHIM*, [2002] ECR II-3191. Of course, conversion, where available, is optional.

93 Article 16, which also has provisions to determine the Member State in the case of joint proprietors.

94 The presumption does not apply where there is agreement to the contrary or the circumstances clearly dictate otherwise.

95 Articles 20 and 21. There are provisions relating to jurisdiction for insolvency proceedings.

CTM is registered. Licences may be for the whole or part of the EU. Licensees may bring infringement proceedings if the proprietor consents, although, where the proprietor does not himself bring proceedings within a reasonable time, an exclusive licensee can bring such proceedings without consent. Where a proprietor has brought proceedings, a licensee may intervene for the purpose of obtaining compensation for damage caused to him by the infringement. Finally, at the request of one of the parties, the grant or transfer of a licence will be entered in the register and published. In almost all cases, licence agreements will contain express provision dealing with the right to bring proceedings for infringement of the CTM covered by the agreement.

Rights acquired by transfer under Article 17, rights *in rem*, etc. under Article 19 and licences under Article 22 only have effect as regards third parties after entry in the register except where the third party acquired rights in the CTM subsequently but knew of the relevant act by which the earlier rights were acquired. For example, an assignee of a CTM will take free of any mortgage granted earlier with the CTM as security unless the mortgage is registered or the assignee knew of the mortgage. However, this 'third party' rule does not apply where the CTM or right in question was acquired by way of a transfer of the whole undertaking or by way of other universal succession. However, effects on third parties in the case of bankruptcy and the like are governed by the law of the Member State where such proceedings are brought.

Finally, as is usual, the rules on CTMs as property rights also apply in respect of applications to register CTMs. For example, an application may be assigned or licences granted in respect of it.

Surrender, revocation and invalidity

A CTM may be surrendered by written declaration by the proprietor in respect of some or all the goods or services for which it is registered under Article 50. It takes effect once entered in the register. Any person registered as having a right in the CTM must have agreed to the surrender and the proprietor must prove that he has notified any registered licensees of his intention to surrender.[96]

The grounds for revocation are set out in Article 51 and closely follow those in the Directive, being based on non-use for a continuous period of five years without proper reasons for non-use, where the CTM has become a common name for a product or service for which it is registered or where it has become deceptive. Where the grounds exist only in relation to some of the goods or services for which the CTM is registered, revocation will be limited accordingly.

There are absolute and relative grounds for invalidity in Articles 52 and 53. Both can be raised on application to the OHIM or by way of a counterclaim in infringement proceedings. The absolute grounds for invalidity are based on the registration being contrary to the absolute grounds for refusal under Article 7 plus, in addition, where the applicant was acting in bad faith when he filed the application. The absolute grounds under Article 7(1)(b), (c) or (d) can be overcome by showing that the CTM has subsequently acquired a distinctive character because of the use made of it.[97] If the ground for invalidity under Article 52 applies only in respect of some of the goods or services for which it is registered, it will be declared invalid for those goods or services only. It may be bad faith to apply to register a sign as a trade mark for the intention of defeating the prior use of that sign by other undertakings which had not registered that sign as a trade mark. This may be particularly relevant where the sign in question is a shape mark and there are technical and commercial reasons why it would be difficult for competitors to offer comparable products. The Court of Justice ruled to this effect in Case C-529/07 *Chocoladefabriken Lindt*

96 Under rule 36(2) of the Implementing Regulation, where a licence has been registered, surrender takes effect three months after the proprietor has satisfied the OHIM that he has notified the licensee unless the proprietor proves the licensee consents, in which case the surrender will take effect immediately.

97 These grounds are where the trade mark is devoid of any distinctive character, 'descriptive' or customary in the current language or *bona fide* and established practices of the trade.

98 [2009] ECR I-4893.

& *Sprüngli AG* v *Franz Hauswirth*[98] in relation to an application to register as a CTM a sign depicting the shape of an Easter chocolate bunny covered in foil. Other undertakings had previously sold similar shaped chocolate bunnies for a number of years.

The relative grounds apply where there is an earlier trade mark or other earlier right and the conditions set out in the relevant parts of Article 8 are fulfilled. Article 53(1) effectively mirrors Article 8. However, Article 8(2) permits invalidity to be based on some other earlier right such as a copyright or industrial property right where the use of the CTM could be prohibited on the basis of such right under EU legislation or national law.[99] This ground for invalidity is additional to the relative grounds for refusal of registration which have no equivalent ground, unlike the case in the Directive. As with revocation, invalidity may be partial.

99 Article 53(2) gives a non-exhaustive list of rights, being a right to a name, a right of personal portrayal, a copyright and an industrial property right, as does the Directive. The reference to Community legislation was the result of an amendment to the CTM Regulation and is intended to allow invalidity on the basis of an earlier Community design.

A CTM may not be declared invalid if the proprietor of the earlier trade mark or other right has expressly consented to the registration before applying for a declaration of invalidity. Also, if such a proprietor has already sought a declaration of invalidity he may not put it in issue again on the basis of another earlier trade mark of right which he could have invoked in support of his first application or counterclaim.

Under Article 54, the proprietor of an earlier CTM may not use that to challenge the validity of a later CTM or oppose its use if he has acquiesced in the use of the later CTM, being aware of its use, for five successive years unless it was applied for in bad faith. The same applies to proprietors of earlier national trade marks within Article 8(2) and other earlier signs referred to in Article 8(4). The proprietor of the later CTM may not oppose the use of the earlier CTM or other right which, under Article 54, can no longer be invoked against that later CTM.

Where a CTM is revoked, this takes effect from the date of application (or counterclaim, as appropriate) but in the case of invalidity, the CTM is deemed not to have had the effects set out in the CTM Regulation from the outset, to the extent that it is declared invalid. Subject to national provisions relating to claims for compensation or damage caused by negligence or lack of good faith on the part of the proprietor, or to unjust enrichment, the retroactive effect of revocation or invalidity does not affect:

100 The UK Trade Marks Act 1994 expresses the effect in much simpler language stating that a finding of invalidity shall not affect transactions past and closed. The practical effect is probably the same.

- decisions on infringement which have acquired the authority of a final decision and have been enforced prior to the revocation or invalidity decision; or
- any contract concluded prior to the revocation or invalidity decision, in so far as it has been performed before that decision (subject to repayment on the grounds of equity).[100]

Articles 56 and 57 govern proceedings at the OHIM in relation to applications for revocation or invalidity. In cases covered by Articles 51 and 52 (revocation and the absolute grounds for invalidity) any natural or legal person may make the application as well as any group or body set up for representing the interests of manufacturers, producers, suppliers of services, traders or consumers, which, under the law governing such group or body, has capacity to sue and be sued in its own name. In the case of invalidity on the basis of an earlier trade mark or earlier unregistered trade mark or sign used in the course of trade – that is, where Article 53(1) applies – the application can only be brought by the proprietor of that earlier trade mark or sign. Where invalidity is based on an earlier right, such as a copyright or industrial property right under Article 53(2), only the proprietor of that earlier right may apply. Furthermore, the OHIM will declare as inadmissible if an application relating to the same subject matter, the same cause of action and involving the same parties, has been adjudicated on by a court in a Member State that has acquired the authority of a final decision.

In proceedings before the OHIM, the proprietor of the CTM being challenged may require proof of use of an earlier CTM or earlier national trade mark used as a basis for the application for revocation or invalidity, as is the case in opposition proceedings. The OHIM may, if it thinks fit, invite the parties to make a friendly settlement.

Decisions at OHIM and appeals

As well as the examiners, the OHIM has Opposition Divisions (deciding oppositions to registration) and Cancellation Divisions. The latter is responsible for deciding applications for revocation or for declarations of invalidity. An Opposition Division or Cancellation Division must consist of three members, one of whom is legally qualified. A further Division is the Administration of Trade Marks and Legal Division which is responsible for decisions under the Regulation which do not fall within the competence of an examiner, an Opposition Division or a Cancellation Division. Examples are decisions in respect of entries in the register of CTMs and keeping a list of professional representatives who may act for persons in the OHIM. Decisions of this Division may be taken by one member.

Appeals from the examiners or Divisions lie to the Boards of Appeal. Appeals have suspensive effect. The Boards sit with three members, of which at least two must be legally qualified. Appeals from the Boards of Appeal go to the Court of First Instance and, from there, to the Court of Justice.

The Board of Appeal at the OHIM considered that the Cancellation Division OHIM was bound by previous decisions of the OHIM in relation to the same case on the basis of the maxim *nemo potest venire contra factum proprium* to the effect that it must comply with its own previous acts, thus bringing the protection of acquired rights, and the principles of legal certainty and the protection of legitimate expectations. However, the General Court disagreed with this in Case T-140/08 *Ferrerro SpA* v *OHIM*,[101] saying that if this were so, subsequent applications for a declaration of invalidity in a case where there had been opposition proceedings between the same parties would be deprived of practical effect. On the subsequent appeal, the Court of Justice made no finding on this issue.[102]

101 [2009] ECR I-10533.

102 Case C-552/09 P *Ferrerro SpA* v *OHIM*, 24 March 2011.

Jurisdiction

Under Article 95, each Member State is required to designate as limited a number as possible of national courts and tribunals of first and second instance, known as Community trade mark courts. In the UK, the designated courts are the Patents County Court and a number of other county courts, the High Court, the Court of Appeal, the Court of Session in Scotland and the High Court in Northern Ireland.

Community trade mark courts have, under Article 96, exclusive jurisdiction on actions for infringement of CTMs (and, where permitted under national law, actions for threatened infringement), actions for declaration of non-infringement if permitted under national law, actions in respect of the period between publication of the application and publication of registration as under Article 9(3), and counterclaims for revocation and invalidity.

Under Article 97, the international jurisdiction of Community trade mark courts is established for claims referred to in Article 96 subject to the provisions of the CTM Regulation and to applicable provisions of Council Regulation (EC) No 44/2001 of 22 December 2000 on jurisdiction and the recognition and enforcement of judgments in civil and commercial matters (the Brussels Regulation)[103] according to Article 94 of the CTM Regulation. There are three main rules for determining jurisdiction, only one of which will apply in a particular case. They are:

- the Member State in which the defendant is domiciled or, if not domiciled in any Member State, any Member State in which he has an establishment (Article 97(1));[104]

103 OJ L 12, 16.01.2001, p 1 (see Chapter 26 for more on the Brussels Regulation). With the exception of Denmark, replacing the Convention on Jurisdiction and Enforcement of Judgments in Civil and Commercial Matters signed in Brussels on 27 September 1968, OJ L 299, 31.12.1972, p 32. Article 94 of the CTM Regulation disapplies certain provisions of the Brussels Regulation, in particular Articles 2, 4, 5(1), (3), (4) and (5) and 31 in relation to actions and claims referred to in Article 96 of the CTM Regulation. Articles 23 and 24 of the Brussels Regulation apply subject to limitations in Article 97(4) of the CTM Regulation.

104 This is subject to those parts of the Brussels Regulation applicable by virtue of Article 94 of the CTM Regulation.

- where the defendant is neither domiciled nor has an establishment in any Member State, the action shall be brought before the courts in the Member State in which the claimant is domiciled or has an establishment, as appropriate (Article 97(2));
- if neither the defendant nor the claimant are domiciled or have an establishment in any Member State, proceedings shall be brought in the Member State in which the OHIM has its seat, presently being Spain (Article 97(3)).

There remain some alternative ways of determining in which Member State the Community trade mark courts have jurisdiction. Articles 23 and 24 of the Brussels Regulation apply, which allows the parties to agree that a different Community trade mark court shall have jurisdiction and a different court may have jurisdiction if the defendant enters an appearance there, otherwise than solely to challenge jurisdiction (Article 97(4)).

Under Article 97(5), with the exception of actions for a declaration of non-infringement, actions may also be brought in the Community trade mark courts in the Member States in which the infringement has been committed or threatened or other act within Article 9(3), second sentence, being an action for compensation for acts between publication of the application for a CTM and publication of its registration.

For an example of an infringement action based upon the High Court's jurisdiction as a Community trade mark court under Article 97(1) (the defendant was a UK company), *see Pfizer Ltd v Eurofood Link (UK) Ltd.*[105] In that case, it was held that the CTM was infringed, as was the claimant's UK registered trade mark.

105 [2001] FSR 3.

Where a Community trade mark court has jurisdiction under Article 97(1)–(4) it can deal with acts of infringement committed or threatened within the territory of any of the Member States including acts within Article 9(3), second sentence. In such cases, any prohibition against further infringement or threatened infringement should, as a general rule, extend to the territory of the entire EU.[106] This is a consequence of the unitary nature of the CTM. Although this is a general rule, there may be exceptions, such as where the proprietor has limited the territorial scope of his claim or where the functions of the trade mark are not affected in some Member State, for example, because of linguistic differences.

106 Case C-235/09 *DHL Express France SAS v Chronopost SA*, 12 April 2011.

Where jurisdiction is based on Article 97(5) a Community trade mark court can only deal with acts committed or threatened within the Member State in which it is situated.[107]

107 Article 98.

Community trade mark courts must treat a CTM as valid unless validity is put in issue by way of a counterclaim for revocation or declaration of invalidity (Article 99).[108] In an action for a declaration of non-infringement, validity may not be put in issue. In actions for infringement, threatened infringement and under Article 9(3), a plea relating to revocation or invalidity other than by way of a counterclaim is admissible in so far as the defendant claims the rights could be revoked for lack of use or declared invalid because of the defendant's earlier right.

108 Where a national court is dealing with an action other than one under Article 96, it must treat the CTM as valid.

Article 100 contains provisions relating to counterclaims. In the case of revocation or invalidity, the only grounds on which the counterclaim can be based are those in the CTM Regulation but a Community trade mark court must reject the counterclaim if a decision made by the OHIM, involving the same subject matter and cause of action and the same parties has already become final. If the proprietor is not a party to an action where a counterclaim is made, he shall be informed and may be joined as a party in accordance with the conditions set out in national law. The OHIM must be informed if a counterclaim is made for revocation or invalidity and this fact will be recorded on the register. Article 57(2)–(5) applies, which includes provisions relating to proof of use where an earlier trade mark is used to challenge validity and the power of the court to encourage a friendly settlement, if it thinks fit. A copy of a judgment that has become final will be sent to the OHIM where it will be mentioned in the register. Finally, a Community trade mark court hearing a counterclaim for revocation or invalidity may stay proceedings on application by the proprietor of the CTM after hearing the other parties and may request that the defendant apply to the OHIM within a reasonable time which the court will set. If it is not submitted within that time, the proceedings will continue with the counterclaim treated as withdrawn. As with other stays, the court may make other provisional and protective measures, for example, by granting an interim injunction.

The applicable law in cases before the Community trade mark courts is stated in Article 101 as that set out in the CTM Regulation except where not covered by the Regulation, in which case it will be the law of the Member State in which the court is situated, including its private international law. In terms of procedure a Community trade mark court will apply the rules governing the same type of action relating to a national trade mark in the Member State where it has its seat.

There are other provisions to deal with stays of proceedings where there are related actions, provisional and protective measures and sanctions.[109] Disputes relating to CTMs other than those within Article 96 may be brought in other courts which have jurisdiction under the Brussels Regulation, *ratione loci* and *ratione materiae* (jurisdiction based by reason of location or the subject matter respectively) to hear national trade mark cases.

The UK Community Trade Mark Regulations

The Community Trade Mark Regulations 1996[110] contain a number of important provisions, including designating the UK's Community trade mark courts. Other provisions include:

110 SI 1996/1908.

- The extension of the provisions relating to groundless threats of infringement proceedings under the Trade Marks Act 1994 s 21 to CTMs (reg 4).
- A declaration can be sought, where the proprietor of a CTM claims the seniority of a UK registered mark which has been removed from the Register failing renewal or has been surrendered, that the registration would otherwise have been liable to revocation or invalidity (reg 3).
- Applying most of the criminal offences and provisions relating to forfeiture and treating infringing goods as prohibited goods to CTMs (regs 6–8).
- Conversion of CTMs or applications for CTMs to applications for UK registered trade marks (reg 10).

International registration of trade marks

Registration of trade marks may be achieved by single applications to each country in which registration is sought. However, this can be expensive and time-consuming and will require the application to be made in that country's language, necessitating additional costs associated with translation. Whilst the situation within Europe is much easier, either by national applications in Member States having harmonised trade mark laws or by application for a CTM, the situation elsewhere would be less satisfactory were it not for the Madrid System for the registration of trade marks. A major advantage is that, after filing an application for registration of a trade mark or following registration in the trade mark office in the applicant's country, only one application need be filed and one fee paid to that trade mark office (the Office of Origin).

The Madrid System is administered by the World Intellectual Property Organisation (WIPO) and comprises the Madrid Agreement of 1891 and the Protocol to the Madrid

Agreement, adopted 1989 and which came into force on 1 April 1996. Together, the Agreement and Protocol form the Madrid Union which is a Special Union recognised under the Paris Convention for the Protection of Industrial Property.[111]

111 Article 19.

The UK is not a member of the Madrid Agreement but is a member of the Protocol, as is the European Community (now EU). The Agreement is better suited to countries which do not have rigorous examination systems. A further issue is that French is the only official language for the purposes of the Agreement whereas English and French are the official languages of the Protocol. The advantage of the EU belonging to the Protocol is that an application may include a request to apply for a CTM. As at 15 July 2011, there were 56 States party to the Agreement and 84 States party to the Protocol. Apart from the UK, amongst the latter are Bahrain, China, Denmark, France, Germany, Iceland, Ireland, Japan, Norway, Sweden and the US. Many States are a party to both, though by no means all.

An applicant for international registration of marks must be domiciled in, be a national of or have a real and effective industrial or commercial establishment in a country which is a party to either the Agreement or the Protocol. The applicant must designate one or more Contracting Parties to the Agreement and/or Protocol as appropriate. Application is made to the Office of Origin in the Contracting Party in which the applicant is domiciled, etc. Thus, a company established in the UK will apply to the UK Trade Marks Registry which then passes the application through to the International Bureau in Geneva.

If the application complies with requirements, it will be recorded in the international register and published in the WIPO *Gazette of Trade Marks*. Each of the Contracting Parties designated are then notified. From the date of international registration, protection is granted in each Contracting Party as if the application had been deposited directly with that Contracting Party. However, each Contracting Party may refuse protection within a time limit which is generally 12 months, though some Contracting Parties may work on a time limit of 18 months or longer in the case of refusal of protection based on opposition.

International registration for the first five years is based on the mark registered or applied for in the country of origin. That may cease to have effect, for example through cancellation, a decision of the Office of Origin or by a court, or if it is surrendered. Where this happens, the international registration is no longer protected. Thus, the international registration is vulnerable to acts or decisions in the Office of Origin but, after five years, the international registration becomes independent of the basic registration or application in the country of origin. As with the UK trade mark and the CTM, the registration is subject to renewal every ten years. The Madrid System is reasonably popular and 35,925 trade marks were accepted for registration during 2009.[112]

112 WIPO Gazette of International Marks, Statistical Supplement for 2009, Table 2.

Countries with lengthy examination systems for their national trade marks tend to be members of the Protocol. This is because one of the advantages of the Protocol over the Agreement is that an application for international registration may be based on an application for a trade mark in the Office of Origin, whereas the Agreement needs an actual registration in the Office of Origin to be used as the basis for the international registration. Other advantages of the Protocol include the implications of cancellation of registration in the Office of Origin. In this case, the application may be converted into national applications in the other Contracting Parties designated and still take advantage of the priority of the initial application.

As from 1 October 2004, the European Community (now EU) became a party to the Protocol. This means that an application for international registration may be based on an application for a CTM or registration at the OHIM. Furthermore, it will be possible to designate the EU using an application for international registration under the Madrid Protocol.

Summary

The Community trade mark (CTM) has a unitary nature and has equal effect throughout the European Union. It may only be registered, transferred or surrendered or be revoked or declared invalid or its use prohibited in respect of the whole of the EU. It may, however be subject to territorially limited licences.

The CTM is administered by the Office for Harmonisation in the Internal Market (Trade Marks and Designs) (OHIM) which has its own examination, opposition, and cancellation divisions in addition to it own Boards of Appeal. Appeals from the OHIM go to the General Court of the EU and then to the Court of Justice of the EU.

The requirements for registrability and provisions for infringement and limitation of the rights in a CTM are very similar to those which apply to the harmonised national trade mark. Apart from the fact that the requirements for registrability must apply throughout the EU, there are some differences. For example, compare Article 3 and 4 of the trade marks Directive with Article 7 and 8 of the CTM Regulation (grounds for refusal of registration).

To be registrable as a CTM, a sign must be capable of being represented graphically, particularly words, including personal names, designs, letters, numerals, the shape of goods or their packaging, provided that the sign is capable of distinguishing the goods or services of one undertaking from those of other undertakings.

There are absolute and relative grounds for refusal or registration and a sign will not be registered if one the absolute grounds for refusal applies only in a part of the EU. The grounds for refusal are similar to those under the trade marks Directive though not identical. As with the Directive, some, though not all, of the absolute grounds for refusal may be overcome if, because of the use made of it, the sign has acquired a distinctive character.

For the relative grounds to be considered, there must be opposition from the proprietor of the earlier trade mark or owner of some other conflicting right, such as an unregistered trade mark or sign used in the course of trade of more than local significance.

Infringement is by certain uses (for example, applying the offending sign to goods or packaging, offering goods or services under the sign, etc.) where the sign is:

- identical to a CTM and used for identical goods or services (double identity);
- identical or similar to a CTM used for identical or similar goods or services (but not double identity) provided there is a likelihood of confusion including a likelihood of association;
- identical or similar to a CTM with a reputation in the EU where the use of the sign, without due cause, takes unfair advantage of or is detrimental to the distinctive character or repute of the CTM – although the CTM Regulation states that the sign must be used for non-similar goods or services, it must surely apply in the case of identical and similar goods or services, in line with case law on the equivalent provision in the trade marks Directive.

The limitations on the rights of the proprietor follow those in the Directive, being certain uses in accordance with honest practices in industrial or commercial matters, such as use of one's own name and address, use descriptive of characteristics of goods or services and use associated with intended purpose, in particular, as accessories or spare parts.

The exhaustion of rights principle also applies in respect of goods put on the market in the EU by the proprietor or with his consent, provided there are not legitimate reasons to oppose further commercialisation, for example, where the condition of goods has been changed or impaired. A common issue is where goods are repackaged.

CTMs give property rights which may only be assigned in relation to the whole EU. Applications for CTMs may also be assigned. CTMs may be assigned with or without the transfer of the relevant undertaking.

CTMs may be surrendered provided any person having a right under it (for example, a licensee) consents or has been given notice of the surrender. Grounds for revocation and invalidity are similar to those applying to the harmonised national trade mark.

Designated national courts may hear cases on the CTM concerning infringement, threatened infringement and declarations of non-infringement. Injunctions granted by national courts are normally effective throughout the EU, thus having cross-border effects. Detailed rules of jurisdiction apply including some of the provisions under the Regulation on jurisdiction and the enforcement of judgments (apart from Denmark which continues to use the Brussels Convention).

In the UK, the groundless threats provisions and criminal offences which apply to the UK trade mark also apply in relation to the CTM.

International registration of trade marks is provided for under the Madrid System (Agreement and Protocol). The UK is a member of the Protocol as is the EU.

Discussion questions

1 Discuss the extent to which the harmonised national trade mark under the trade marks Directive is the same as or differs from the CTM.

2 Discuss the ways in which the proprietor of a CTM can exploit the trade mark.

3 Under what circumstances may a CTM be (a) revoked and (b) invalidated? What are the practical consequences of revocation and invalidity?

4 A company alleged to have infringed a CTM is based in Greece. Where can the proprietor bring infringement proceedings where that proprietor is based in (a) the UK, (b) the United States? Would it make any difference if the alleged infringing company was based in China with no establishment in the EU but is alleged to infringe the CTM by shipping the relevant goods from China to Greece?

5 In what ways should the European trade mark system be modified (see the Study on the Overall Functioning of the European Trade Mark System noted in Further Reading below)?

Selected further reading

Anon (Case Comment), 'National ruling on CTM has effect EU-wide' [2011] EU Focus, 26 (looks at the DHL case on the scope of injunctions and other measures to protect CTMs).

Max Planck Institute, 'Study on the Overall Functioning of the European Trade Mark System', 2 May 2011, available at: **http://ec.europa.eu/internal_market/indprop/docs/tm/20110308_allensbach-study_en.pdf**

Office for Harmonisation in the Internal Market (Trade Marks and Designs) website at: **http://oami.europa.eu/ows/rw/pages/index.en.do** (see various documents, guidance and statistics on the CTM).

WIPO website materials on the Madrid System (including a video) at: **http://www.wipo.int/trademarks/en/**

Visit **www.mylawchamber.co.uk/bainbridgeip** to access study support resources including interactive multiple choice questions, practice exam questions with guidance, weblinks, legal updates and a legal newsfeed.

23 Passing off and malicious falsehood

Introduction

The law of passing off and trade mark law have common roots and therefore are, in many respects, similar. Passing off is a tort and can be described as the common law form of trade mark law. The Trade Marks Act 1994 s 2(2) makes it clear that the law of passing off is unaffected by the Act.[1] Business 'goodwill' is protected by passing off and, whilst this may be associated with a particular name or mark used in the course of trade, this area of law is wider than trade mark law in terms of the scope of marks, signs, materials and other aspects of a trader's 'get-up' that can be protected.[2] The owner of the goodwill has a property right that can be protected by an action in passing off. Buckley LJ described the nature of the proprietary right thus:

> A man who engages in commercial activities may acquire a valuable reputation in respect of the goods in which he deals, or of the services which he performs, or of his business as an entity. The law regards such a reputation as an incorporeal piece of property, the integrity of which the owner is entitled to protect.[3]

He went on to confirm that the property right is not a right in the name, mark or get-up itself but that it is a right in the reputation or goodwill of which the name, mark or get-up is the badge or vehicle. The words 'reputation' and 'goodwill' are often used interchangeably but it is really in connection with goodwill that passing off is concerned. It is possible, after all, to have a reputation without goodwill, the Russian monk Rasputin providing a good example of this. The existence of reputation (in this case a favourable one) without any associated goodwill was fatal to a claim in passing off in *Anheuser Busch Inc* v *Budějovický Budvar*.[4] The Budweiser name for beer was well known in the UK but, in the absence of a trading presence here, the claimant could not establish the necessary goodwill to sustain an action in passing off.[5]

Lord Macnaghten gave a useful definition of goodwill in *Commissioners of Inland Revenue* v *Muller & Co's Margarine Ltd*,[6] where he said (at 223):

> What is goodwill? It is a thing very easy to describe, very difficult to define. It is the benefit and advantage of the good name, reputation, and connection of a business. It is the attractive force which brings in custom. It is the one thing which distinguishes an old-established business from a new business at its first start. The goodwill of a business must emanate from a particular centre or source. However widely extended or diffused its influence may be, goodwill is worth nothing unless it has power of attraction sufficient to bring customers home to the source from which it emanates.

The description of goodwill as the attractive force bringing in custom is very apt even though the customers may not know or care of the identity of the owner of the goodwill provided that they appreciate that there is such a person and the goods or services

1 The Trade Marks Act 1994 s 2(1) also states that no action is available under the Act for the infringement of an unregistered trade mark. Passing off is a ground for refusal of registration for a trade mark: s 5(4)(a).

2 Though the recent changes to trade mark law have brought the scope of trade mark law nearer to passing off. W & G was refused registration as a trade mark (*Registrar of Trade Marks* v *W & G Du Cros Ltd* [1913] AC 624) but a passing off action succeeded (*Du Cros (W & G) Ltd* v *Gold* (1912) 30 RPC 117).

3 *HP Bulmer Ltd* v *J Bollinger SA* [1978] RPC 79 at 93.

4 [1984] FSR 413.

5 However, this case should be compared with *Maxim's Ltd* v *Dye* [1977] 1 WLR 1155; the Indian case of *Calvin Klein Inc* v *International Apparel Syndicate* [1995] FSR 515, and the Singaporean case of *Pontiac Marina Private Ltd* v *CDL Hotels International Ltd* [1998] FSR 839, all discussed below.

6 [1901] AC 217.

7 *United Biscuits (UK) Ltd* v *Asda Stores Ltd* [1997] RPC 513.

emanating from that person are of an expected standard.[7] This is particularly important in the context of corporate takeovers and mergers. If asked, many people would not be able to identify the maker of many products now available without referring to the product itself.

Quite often, passing off actions will be brought in respect of an unregistered trade mark, a mark that has not been registered through inertia on the part of the owner of the mark or as a result of ignorance of the advantages of trade mark law or because the mark fails to satisfy the requirements for registration. The great majority of cases will involve a mark in the wide sense, including containers and packaging, but business goodwill can be achieved and maintained in other ways and it is possible that business methods and get-up, marketing strategy and advertising themes can be protected by this useful area of law. Goodwill may attach to the shape and appearance of goods but it will usually be more difficult to prove it exists in such cases. In *Numatic International Ltd* v *Qualtex Ltd*,[8]

8 [2010] RPC 25.

the claimant made the famous and easily recognised Henry vacuum cleaner which was tub shaped and had a top which looked like a bowler hat. A smiley face was printed to the side of the tub with a hole for the nose into which the tube was fitted, looking like an elephant's trunk. Brand names are usually chosen to denote origin and the get-up, such as the shape and appearance of a product, are not normally chosen for this purpose. In such a case, the claimant must show that the get-up has come to denote a particular source of the product in the eyes of the relevant public. It had done so in the present case.

Passing off actions have never been limited to goods and passing off in respect of the provision of services has always been a possibility. However, it is clear that the tort applies in a business context, directly or indirectly, although in other circumstances a passing off type of activity could amount to defamation.[9]

9 For example, *Tolley* v *JS Fry & Sons Ltd* [1931] AC 333.

The main point about passing off is that goodwill has been established by one trader and another trader tries to take advantage of that goodwill, to cash in on it to the detriment of the first trader. There are two main reasons why a trader would wish to pass off his goods or services as being those of another, established trader. The first is that by doing so, a significant portion of the established trader's custom might be captured because of confusion amongst the buying public as to whom they are dealing with. The second reason is that sales might be boosted by unjustifiably imputing a quality to the second trader's goods that is widely recognised in connection with the goods of the established trader. In both cases, the established trader suffers damage by a shortfall in trade, but in the second case the damage may be even more far-reaching in that he stands to lose his goodwill and reputation for high quality goods if, because of the misrepresentation, the buying public associate inferior goods with him. Alternatively, the harm may be subtler and result in a gradual degradation or erosion of the first trader's name or get-up as an indicator of origin or quality,[10] the result being a blurring of distinctiveness of the first trader's name or mark in which his goodwill subsists.

10 This is a continuing concern for traders dealing with high-quality goods. *See* the discussion on the 'champagne' cases below, pp 881 and 895.

11 [1986] FSR 63.

The preservation of business goodwill is the prime concern of passing off but the protection of consumers from deception is an ancillary effect. The New Zealand case of *Plix Products Ltd* v *Frank M Winstone (Merchants)*[11] involved pocket packs for kiwi fruit. The claimant had a monopoly in such packs as a result of the sole approval of the claimant's design for such packs by the New Zealand Kiwifruit Authority. The case turned on copyright issues in addition to passing off and in the former it was established that copyright infringement could occur through a verbal description. On the passing off claim it was held that a cause of action in passing off depended on damage to the claimant's reputation and not upon the premise that purchasers might confuse the claimant's and the defendant's packs and obtain an inferior or different product to the one they thought they were acquiring.

Passing off may overlap with other rights, especially trade marks and copyright, and a given set of circumstances may give rise to an action involving two or more different rights. For example, in *Mothercare UK Ltd v Penguin Books Ltd*[12] the defendant published a book, first published in the USA, about bringing up children, entitled *Mother Care/Other Care*. The claimant, who operated a chain of retail shops selling various items for babies, small children and expectant mothers, sued for trade mark infringement and for passing off. It was held the defendant had not infringed the 'Mothercare' trade mark because it had not been used in a trade mark sense. On the passing off action it was said that, considering the title of the book as a whole, there had not been a misrepresentation by use of that title.[13] In *Visual Connection (TVC) Ltd v Ashworth Associates Ltd*,[14] the claimant sued for infringement of copyright in photographs and for passing off resulting from the use by the defendant of the photographs, representing his business as that of the claimant.[15]

There may be a conflict between passing off and trade marks law. Section 2(2) of the Trade Marks Act 1994 confirms that nothing in the Act affects the law relating to passing off. The general rule for determining the date at which goodwill should be assessed in a passing off action is the date that the defendant's acts, in respect of which complaint is made, commenced. Determining this date may be particularly important when the claimant is building up his goodwill around that time: for example, where he has recently started trading. The consequence of filing an application to register a trade mark is that, under s 40(3) of the Trade Marks Act 1994, it is deemed to have been registered as from the date of filing and so, the proprietor's rights date back to the filing date under s 9(3). The problem here is that one trader may be using an unregistered trade mark in which goodwill is being built up but another trader applies to register a conflicting mark but does not use it until later. At the time of filing the application, goodwill might not yet exist in an actionable sense under passing off but it might by the time the second trader actually starts using his trade mark.

This conflict came up for consideration in *Inter Lotto (UK) Ltd v Camelot Group plc*.[16] The claimant started using the unregistered trade mark 'HOTPICK' during August and September 2001. The defendant, responsible for running the national lottery under licence from the National Lottery Commission (the 'NLC'), caused the NLC to register 'HOTPICKS' as a trade mark and the application was duly filed on 17 October 2001 but it was not used by the defendant until around July 2002. The claimant opposed the trade mark application. That opposition was pending. The question was whether the date at which the claimant's goodwill should be assessed was the date of filing the application or the date the defendant actually started using the trade mark.

- If the former, the opposition might fail as the claimant opposing the trade mark application may not be able to show that it had by that time built up goodwill in the 'HOTPICK' name.
- If the latter, the opposition might succeed as, by then, the claimant might be able to show that it had a goodwill in the name.

The Court of Appeal, dismissing the defendant's appeal, held that the relevant date was the date the use of the trade mark by the defendant commenced. That was the effect of s 2(2) of the Act which defeated any claim that the relative ground for refusal under s 5(4) of the Act, and the fact that the Act treats registration as being effective as from the date of filing the application to register a trade mark, prevented reliance on any goodwill established between the date of filing the application and the date the applicant actually started using his trade mark. Section 2(2) confirms that the Act does not affect the law of passing off. Otherwise, in a case like *Inter Lotto*, on the basis of deemed registration at the date of filing, a proprietor may be able to invoke his trade mark to prevent another trader using a similar though unregistered trade mark which had not built up actionable goodwill at that date even though it did subsequently before the date that the trade mark proprietor actually started using his trade mark.

12 [1988] RPC 113.

13 Dillon LJ considered the recent fashion for conducting surveys to be unhelpful. He also deplored the proliferation of affidavits, assertions and counter-assertions common when wealthy companies are involved in passing off, copyright or trade mark cases.

14 (Unreported) 14 January 1986.

15 *See* also *Columbia Picture Industries v Robinson* [1987] 1 Ch 38 in which the claimant alleged infringement of copyright and trade marks and passing off. The defendant admitted to these and injunctive relief and an inquiry as to damages was ordered but the claimant had to pay £10,000 to the defendant because of an abuse of the search order (*Anton Piller* order).

16 [2004] RPC 9.

Classic and extended passing off

Classic passing off occurs typically where a trader misrepresents his goods or services as being those of another trader. A hypothetical example is where a trader unconnected with a supermarket chain with the name of 'Lotus', selling various foods, drinks and clothing, opens a shop selling food produce under the name 'Lotus Foods'.[17] In classic passing off consumers are fooled, by virtue of the defendant's misrepresentation, into thinking the defendant is the claimant (or connected to him) or into thinking the defendant's goods or services are those of the claimant.

Extended passing off applies where goodwill exists in the descriptive, or even generic, name of a particular type of goods or products which has achieved a significance such that persons know the goods or product to have some sort of quality or character. A feature of extended passing off is that it can apply to a group of traders making the product concerned. Examples, discussed in this chapter, include advocaat, champagne and Swiss chocolate. In these cases, the focus has switched from the name and reputation of the manufacturer to the name of the product. So, if someone sells Old English Advocaat, Spanish Champagne, Elderflower Champagne, or chocolate under the name 'Swiss Chalet', they are guilty of passing off.

The same principles apply to extended passing off as they do to classic passing off, being the presence of the claimant's goodwill, a misrepresentation by the defendant and damage (actual or potential) to the claimant as a result of that misrepresentation. One distinction between these forms of passing off is that for classic passing off the damage usually will be a loss of business, such as where the defendant has diverted some of the claimant's business to himself. In extended passing off, damage is more likely to result in erosion of the goodwill in the name which will occur even if consumers are not taken in by the misrepresentation.[18]

The word 'Whisky' is protected by extended passing off. Thus, where a trader sells as whisky a drink which has not been produced in the usual way, that will be passing off.[19]

In *Diageo North America Inc* v *Intercontinental Brands (ICB) Ltd*,[20] the claimant made Smirnoff vodka and the defendant brought out a new drink called VODKAT. It was not vodka but was a mixture of vodka and neutral fermented alcohol having an alcohol by volume strength of 22 per cent (compared with vodka which had to be at least 37.5 per cent).

At first instance,[21] the judge held that 'vodka' referred to a distinct class of goods, that it was recognised as a drink with 'recognisable qualities of appearance, taste, strength and satisfaction' and had acquired a reputation giving rise to goodwill in England. The use of the word VODKAT was calculated to deceive a substantial number of members of the public into thinking it was vodka and a further substantial number of members of the public might have concluded it was a weaker version of vodka. There was damage in terms of both lost sales and the continued use of VODKAT, without it being sufficiently differentiated from vodka, was likely to erode the distinctiveness of the word 'vodka'. The judge granted a limited injunction that would permit the defendant to continue to use the name VODKAT subject to a number of conditions which should prevent future confusion between that drink and vodka.

The defendant appealed on the ground that the judge erred by not holding that extended passing off only applied where the goods in question had some sort of 'cachet'. The defendant argued that 'vodka' did not posses such a cachet in the mind of the public. The claimant cross-appealed against the limited injunction. The Court of Appeal dismissed the appeal and the cross-appeal. It was held that products could qualify for extended passing off if they had acquired goodwill in the name by virtue of the properties or characteristics which the products possessed but that there was no need to show that the name had become a badge of quality. Nor was there any need to show that the name

17 Assuming all the requirements discussed below are present, such as goodwill, misrepresentation and damage.

18 For example, most people know that champagne is a sparking wine drink coming from the Champagne region of France and would know that 'Spanish Champagne' was not a genuine champagne drink..

19 The *Scotch Whisky Association* v *Glen Kella Distillers Ltd* [1997] ETMR 470. The defendant, based on the Isle of Man made a drink from re-distilling matured and blended whisky to render it colourless. Even though the defendant's drink was made from whisky and tasted like whisky, he was not allowed to describe it as such.

20 [2011] RPC 2.

21 [2010] RPC 12.

had achieved a cachet in the sense of the product being a superior or luxury brand. In relation to the injunction, the Court of Appeal held that whether the injunction granted would mean that the defendant could use his name for his product so as not to cause confusion was a matter for the trial judge.

Although agreeing with the other judges, Rix LJ expressed some concern that, by extension upon extension, the tort of passing off was in danger of becoming a means of preventing fair competition. After all, the defendant had made a drink which largely contained vodka. Rix LJ said (at para 77):

> The attractiveness of the product is that it is cheaper, because at the lower 22% ABV the incidence of duty is much reduced, but also, it might be said, because it is less alcoholic and thus permits the drinker to extend its use as an alcoholic mixer without early intoxication. There ought in such circumstances to be room for its manufacturer to market what might be called a vodka-type product in such a way that the consumer (barring the ignorant or foolish) knows what he or she is and is not getting, and yet the association with vodka is legitimately and not deceptively made.

However, the injunction did allow the defendant to continue to describe his drink as VODKAT provided it was made clear that it was not vodka. But one can see the sense in Rix LJ's concern. Extended passing off has developed and become wider in scope as the earlier cases related to geographically limited products, such as Champagne. Now products like Whisky and Vodka are protected even though either product can be made anywhere.[22]

Basic requirements for a passing off action

In *Perry v Truefitt*[23] it was said by Lord Langdale MR that, 'a man is not to sell his own goods under the pretence that they are the goods of another trader'; that is, the law would restrain one trader from passing off his goods as being those of another trader. The essence of the action is a misrepresentation, either express or implied.[24] This was expanded to include a situation where the origin of the goods was not at issue; rather it was the quality of the goods. In *Spalding & Bros v AW Gamage Ltd*,[25] the claimant was a dealer in footballs described for some years as 'Orb' footballs and this description and descriptions including the word 'Orb' became distinctive of the claimant's footballs. The claimant sold a quantity of defective balls to a waste rubber merchant and, eventually, they fell into the hands of the defendant who advertised them as being 'Orb' balls. An injunction was granted in favour of the claimant and Lord Parker considered the nature of passing off, saying:

> The more general opinion appears to be that the right [that is, the right to take action to prevent passing off] is a right of property . . . property in the business or goodwill likely to be injured by the misrepresentation.[26]

23 (1842) 49 ER 749.

24 Misrepresentation is one of the essential ingredients of a passing off action but its presence is a question of fact depending on the circumstances: *Harding v Smilecare Ltd* [2002] FSR 37.

25 (1915) 84 LJ Ch 449.

26 [1979] 1 CMLR 326.

An important case in which the basic requirements for success in a passing off action were described in the House of Lords was *Erven Warnink Besloten Vennootschap v J Townend & Sons (Hull) Ltd*.[27] The claimants made a liqueur called Advocaat which came to be well known.[28] It was a high-quality liqueur made from brandewijn, egg yolks and sugar which acquired a substantial reputation and sold in large quantities. The defendant decided to enter this market and made a drink called 'Keeling's Old English Advocaat' which was made from Cyprus sherry and dried egg powder, an inferior but less expensive drink compared to the claimants'. This captured a large part of the claimants' market in the UK but it could not be shown that consumers would mistake it for the claimants' drink. Nevertheless, it was held that the reputation associated with the claimants' product should be protected from deceptive use of its name by competitors even though several

27 [1979] AC 731.

28 The claimants were representative of the Dutch manufacturers of Advocaat.

traders shared the goodwill. There was a misrepresentation made by the defendant calculated to injure the claimants' business or goodwill and an injunction was granted in favour of the claimants, there being no exceptional grounds of public policy why an injunction should not be granted. Lord Diplock laid down the essentials for a passing off action, derived from the case of *Spalding & Bros* v *AW Gamage Ltd*[29] and subsequent cases, as being:

29 (1915) 84 LJ Ch 449.

- a misrepresentation;
- made by a trader in the course of trade;
- to prospective customers of his or ultimate consumers of goods or services supplied by him;
- which is calculated to injure the business or goodwill of another trader (in the sense that this is a reasonably foreseeable consequence); and
- which causes actual damage to a business or goodwill of the trader by whom the action is brought or (in a *quia timet* action) will probably do so.

Lord Oliver reduced this list to three elements in *Reckitt & Colman Products Ltd* v *Borden Inc*,[30] namely, the existence of the claimant's goodwill, a misrepresentation as to the goods or services offered by the defendant, and damage (or likely damage) to the claimant's goodwill as a result of the defendant's misrepresentation. Nevertheless, many judges still prefer Lord Diplock's authoritative test.[31] In the *Erven Warnink* case, Lord Fraser proposed a different formula to that used by Lord Diplock. Lord Fraser said:

30 [1990] 1 All ER 873.

31 *See*, for example, the judgments in *Taittinger SA* v *Allbev Ltd* [1993] FSR 641. The simpler statement of passing off is, however, preferred by some judges; *see Consorzio de Prosciutto di Parma* v *Marks and Spencer plc* [1991] RPC 351.

32 [1979] AC 731 at 755. Being able to identify the class of products is essential. In *Sweeney* v *MacMillan Publishers Ltd* [2002] RPC 651, the trustees of the estate of James Joyce who did not themselves sell products failed to identify a clearly defined class of products to which the goodwill might have attached. This was fatal to an action for passing off in relation to the publication of the bulk of Joyce's novel, *Ulysses*.

> It is essential for the claimant in a passing off action to show at least the following facts: (1) that his business consists of, or includes, selling in England a class of goods to which the particular trade name applies; (2) that the class of goods is clearly defined, and that in the minds of the public, or a section of the public, in England, the trade name distinguishes that class from other similar goods; (3) that because of the reputation of the goods, there is goodwill attached to the name; (4) that he, the plaintiff, as a member of the class of those who sell the goods, is the owner of goodwill in England which is of substantial value; (5) that he has suffered, or is really likely to suffer, substantial damage to his property in the goodwill by reason of the defendants selling goods which are falsely described by the trade name to which the goodwill is attached. Provided these conditions are satisfied . . . the claimant is entitled to protect himself by a passing off action.[32]

33 Lord Diplock later states that 'calculated to injure' does not require actual intention to injure. It is more to do with whether injury is a reasonably foreseeable consequence.

34 *See British Broadcasting Corp* v *Talbot Motor Co Ltd* [1981] FSR 228; *Bristol Conservatories Ltd* v *Conservatories Custom Built Ltd* [1989] RPC 455. In the former case, Lord Megarry VC suggested that the two tests may have been cumulative but, in the latter, it was held that they were not cumulative. In *Pete Waterman Ltd* v *CBS UK Ltd* [1993] EMLR 27, Lord Browne-Wilkinson VC suggested that the Diplock and Fraser tests should be read together as the Diplock test focuses on the defendant's activities whereas the Fraser test concentrates on what the claimant has to show to succeed.

35 [1991] RPC 351.

The definitions given by Lords Diplock and Fraser can be seen as attempts to produce a generalised, all-purpose rule, but it is probable that their Lordships were too strongly influenced by the facts of the case before them. In particular, Lord Fraser's definition is far too narrow – being restricted to goods sold in England (although recognising that trade reputation has a specific locality) – but he does specifically mention the need for a goodwill associated with the goods although this is implicit in Lord Diplock's statement. Lord Diplock talks in terms of goods and services and it is clear that a passing off action is available in respect of services. Lord Diplock, by using the phrase 'calculated to injure', seems to suggest some fraud or malice on the part of the defendant whilst Lord Fraser makes no such inference.[33] As will be seen later, relief can be given when the misrepresentation is unintentional; the action is not limited to goods; the geographical scope can extend outside the UK as far as the trade is concerned; and passing off is not limited to trade names as indicated by Lord Fraser. On the whole, Lord Diplock's definition is probably closer to the present legal position and is the one most referred to. In subsequent cases, there has been some conflict about whether the Diplock and the Fraser test should be applied together.[34] On the whole, Lord Diplock's test is of more general application than Lord Fraser's test.

As well respected as *Erven Warnink* is, another line of definitions adopting the simpler approach in *Reckitt & Colman* has the approval of a number of judges. For example, in *Consorzio de Prosciutto di Parma* v *Marks and Spencer plc*,[35] Nourse LJ identified the ingredients of a passing off action as being comprised of:

- the goodwill of the claimant;
- the misrepresentation made by the defendant; and
- consequential damage.

Jacob J approved of this formula in *Hodgkinson and Corby Ltd* v *Wards Mobility Services Ltd*,[36] stressing that the essence of passing off is deception which misleads customers. This line of authorities is not inconsistent with *Erven Warnink* and can be regarded as a clearer statement of passing off, bearing in mind that Lord Diplock's phrase 'calculated to injure' appears to be redundant. However, the simpler statement of passing off ought to have some reference to the fact that it is set in the context of trade.

In most cases, the defendant will have deliberately used some name, mark or get-up designed to capture part of the claimant's business but a fraudulent motive is not essential to the tort.[37] Even if the passing off is 'innocent', relief may be granted.[38] It depends mainly on whether the goodwill associated with the claimant's business is harmed because the nature or origin of the defendant's goods or services is misrepresented and the buying public or ultimate consumers are taken in by that misrepresentation. A statement which is true may give rise to the action. If a sole trader with a retail clothing business changes his name to Levi Strauss by deed poll, having the name sign-written above his shop, it is not a false misrepresentation but it is, nevertheless, likely to be restrained if the clothing manufacturer by that name sues for passing off.[39] Although it is generally accepted that honest use of one's own name is permitted, regardless of the fact that customers may be misled, such honest use must be done in a way so as not to exaggerate the connection. For example, in *Wright, Layman & Umney Ltd* v *Wright*[40] the claimant had a wide reputation under the name 'Wright's', as in 'Wright's Coal Tar Soap'. The defendant, trading as 'Wright's Chemical Company', had, without any dishonesty on his part, passed off his goods as those of the claimant by using the name 'Wright's' in relation to them. Lord Greene MR said:

> A man may sell goods under his own name as his own goods. If he does so, he is doing no more than telling the truth. If there happens to be already on the market another trader of that name . . . that is just his misfortune . . . provided that a man keeps within the limit of using his own name and does so honestly and *does not go beyond that*, nobody can stop him even if the result of him doing so leads to confusion.[41] (emphasis added)

It is apparent from the above case that a trader can easily go beyond the limit of using his own name honestly and the original injunction was extended to prevent the use by the defendant of the name 'Wright' or 'Wright's' in a descriptive phrase applied to his products. It is difficult to see what use of his own name the defendant was left with and the spirit of the sweeping and generous statement by Lord Greene does not appear to have been reflected in his judgment, bearing in mind the defendant's real surname was 'Wright'.

Claimant's goodwill

Merely copying the name or style of another trader is not, *per se*, sufficient for a passing off action although it could give rise to an action for infringement of copyright if what is copied is more than a simple name: for example, a logo. There must have been a goodwill associated with reputation which had been acquired by the claimant in relation to that name or style. Reputation comes about through consistent use:[42] for example, the phrase 'Camel Hair Belting' used by the claimant from 1879 to 1891 was considered by the jury in *Reddaway* v *Banham*[43] to have become distinctive of the claimant's belting even though it was entirely descriptive. In *County Sound plc* v *Ocean Sound plc*,[44] the phrase 'Gold AM'

36 [1995] FSR 169.

37 *Baume & Co Ltd* v *AH Moore Ltd* [1958] RPC 226.

38 *See*, for example, *Gillette UK Ltd* v *Edenwest Ltd* [1994] RPC 279.

39 *See Croft* v *Day* (1843) 7 Beav 84. However, a true statement that the defendant had operated the fine art department in the claimant's store was not passing off: *Harrods Ltd* v *Schwartz-Sackin & Co Ltd* [1991] FSR 209.

40 (1949) 66 RPC 149.

41 (1949) 66 RPC 149 at 151.

42 Suspension of use for a long period of time might result in the later recommencement of use being insufficient to revive any residual goodwill or raise an issue of concurrent goodwill in the face of another trader who had been using the name during the period of suspension of use: *Patience and Nicholson (NZ) Ltd* v *Cyclone Hardware Pty Ltd* [2002] FSR 40 in the Court of Appeal, New Zealand.

43 [1896] AC 199.

44 [1991] FSR 367.

used in connection with broadcasts of 'golden oldies' was held not to have acquired goodwill because it was often used in conjunction with the name 'County Sound', it was immediately descriptive of a certain type of radio programme and it did not indicate the source of such programmes. Nourse LJ acknowledged that, had the name been truly distinctive, goodwill in that name could have been acquired within a period of six months. However, the test for whether a trade has established goodwill protected by passing off is not the same as distinctiveness for trade mark purposes.[45]

If a trader has only just started in business or has only recently started using an unregistered mark or 'get-up' he may be unable to succeed in a passing off action. Passing off does not protect goodwill of a trivial extent.[46] Even where sufficient goodwill once existed, it may diminish over time and later become trivial.[47] Nor is contemplating future goodwill likely to be helpful even though passing off may be able to protect the development of a growing business.[48] Although a newly registered trade mark has immediate protection, with passing off the claimant must be able to prove that he has built up a reputation around the name, mark or 'get-up': that is, he has acquired a property in the goodwill associated with the subject matter.[49] It is not possible to lay down hard and fast rules as to the period of time taken to acquire protectable goodwill. It depends on the circumstances. If there is a great deal of commercial activity and advertising throughout the UK, goodwill could be acquired in a relatively short period of time even prior to the availability of the goods or services to which the goodwill relates. In *Stannard* v *Reay*[50] it was held that three weeks was sufficient time to build up goodwill in the name 'Mr Chippy' for a mobile fish and chip van operating on the Isle of Wight. The central question is whether a sufficient reputation has been acquired, and it is possible for the goodwill to be shared amongst a number of traders or businesses as the *Erven Warnink* case emphatically indicates.

It is generally accepted that the date at which goodwill is required to be shown to exist is the date of commencement of the defendant's acts which are the subject of the complaint.[51] However, in *Scandecor Development AB* v *Scandecor Marketing AB*,[52] it was said that:

> As a general rule, the goodwill which it is sought to protect must exist at the date of the proceedings. That is therefore the correct date on which to concentrate . . . however, in a case such as this, where the goodwill in dispute originates from a common source overseas, but then expands, spreads and is developed by different companies in different territories, it is also important to analyse the effect of the changes occurring from time to time in the control and ownership of the businesses which generate the goodwill.[53]

It is submitted that the latter approach is incorrect because, as a matter of logic, the existence of goodwill must coincide with the acts complained of. In the event that goodwill can be proved to exist no earlier than the date of proceedings, then what the defendant had been doing previously was not unlawful. Indeed, in *Cadbury Schweppes Pty Ltd* v *Pub Squash Co Pty Ltd*,[54] Lord Scarman, delivering the judgment of the Judicial Committee of the Privy Council, confirmed that the relevant date is, at law, the date that the conduct complained of commenced. The only possible proviso is that, where the claimant seeks a *quia timet* injunction, he must, at least, be able to show goodwill at the commencement of proceedings.

Goodwill can exist even if the product or service to which it relates has not yet been made available if a significant proportion of the public knew about the product or service because of a great deal of publicity. So it was held in *British Broadcasting Corp* v *Talbot Motor Co Ltd*,[55] where there was evidence that a significant part of the public recognised the name CARFAX as distinctive of the BBC's traffic information system capable of being received in vehicles by special radios. Similarly, in the Singaporean case of *Pontiac Marina Pte Ltd* v *CDL Hotels International Ltd*[56] it was held that a trader could, through extensive advertising, acquire a goodwill before he commenced trading.[57] Furthermore, goodwill

45 *Phones 4u Ltd* v *Phone4u.co.uk Internet Ltd* [2007] RPC 5.

46 *Hart* v *Relentless Records Ltd* [2003] FSR 36, per Jacob J noting that before registration of trade marks was possible, the property right in a mark could be acquired in a relatively short time simply by putting the mark to use. That did not apply now to goodwill.

47 *Knight* v *Beyond Properties Pty Ltd* [2007] FSR 34.

48 *Teleworks Ltd* v *Telework Group plc* [2002] RPC 27.

49 Just as, in the law of real property, a person may acquire property rights by continued use: for example, by prescription.

50 [1967] RPC 589.

51 *Premier Luggage and Bags Ltd* v *Premier Company (UK) Ltd* [2001] FSR 21. Confirmed on this point in the Court of Appeal in *Premier Luggage and Bags Ltd* v *Premier Company (UK) Ltd* [2003] FSR 5.

52 [1999] FSR 26.

53 [1999] FSR 26 at 42. The judgment as reported is unattributed.

54 [1981] 1 All ER 213 at 221.

55 [1981] FSR 228.

56 [1997] FSR 725, affirmed in the Singaporean Court of Appeal, [1998] FSR 839.

57 In contrast to what Lord Macnaghten suggested in *Commissioners of Inland Revenue* v *Muller & Co's Margarine Ltd* [1901] AC 217, quoted above.

is not restricted to traders which are large companies with high turnovers, and a small trader may establish goodwill in a particular locality or because he is well known in a specialist field.[58]

It is important to consider how the goodwill is associated with the product or service concerned. This may, of course, be influenced by the form of an advertising campaign. In *Whitworth Foods Ltd* v *Hunni Foods (International) Ltd*[59] the defendant deliberately copied the claimant's containers for glacé cherries. Viewed from the top, the cartons were easily distinguishable because the two companies' names were represented differently and set on different colour backgrounds. However, from the side the cartons looked very similar (both carrying the words 'Glacé Cherries') and the claimant argued that if the cartons were displayed on supermarket shelves, stacked on top of one another with the claimant's and the defendant's cartons adjacent to each other, there was a danger of confusion. In considering the association of the claimant's reputation with the features of their carton, Hoffmann J said that the claimant's goodwill was chiefly associated with their name and not the design of their containers and that this was confirmed by evidence of the claimant's advertising which was done in a general way without specific reference to their individual products.

Sometimes, the defendant may also have a goodwill associated with the name used by the claimant. If this relates to different goods or services, this may not be a problem. However, the possibility for a conflict arises if the defendant later wishes to diversify and enter the claimant's field of activity. In *Provident Financial plc* v *Halifax Building Society*,[60] the claimant had built up a substantial goodwill in the name Halifax which it used in respect of its motor insurance underwriting which it carried out through brokers. The defendant, then one of the leading building societies, widely known as 'The Halifax', decided to launch motor insurance services under its Halifax name and 'X' logo. Granting an injunction to maintain the status quo until a full trial, it was held that it was reasonably arguable that, if the defendant were allowed to move into motor insurance, it would misrepresent that it was connected with the claimant. An important factor was that the defendant's goodwill and enormous public profile (it had spent over £27 million in advertising in 1991) would have been likely to have swamped and subsumed the claimant's goodwill.

Goodwill may be built up over a considerable period of time and transferred with the sale of the business with which it is associated. The fact that a member of a family business was employed by that business before its sale does not give that family member any goodwill in his own right even if the goodwill subsists in his own name.[61]

Shared goodwill and ownership of goodwill

We have seen in *Erven Warnink Besloten Vennootschap* v *J Townend & Sons (Hull) Ltd*,[62] that goodwill can be shared by a number of traders. In that case the shared goodwill was in the name 'Advocaat', describing a particular type of alcoholic beverage, and that the goodwill was shared between the Dutch companies making the drink. The companies may also have an additional goodwill in their trading name which can reinforce and supplement the shared goodwill, such as in 'Warnink's Advocaat'.

In most cases, it will be obvious who owns the goodwill in question, even if shared. However, where more than one entity is involved in the placing of a product on the marketplace, there may be issues as to who owns the goodwill which has been generated or whether the goodwill is shared between them. This might be in the context of a group of companies or where one company acts as a distributor for another or operates as a licensee under a licence agreement.

In *Scandecor Development AB* v *Scandecor Marketing AB*,[63] two students at Uppsala University realised the potential of selling posters to students who, presumably, would be

58 *NAD Electronics Inc* v *NAD Computer Systems Ltd* [1997] FSR 380. In this case, the trader made superior 'hi-fi' systems.

59 (Unreported) 20 October 1986.

60 [1994] FSR 81.

61 *Asprey and Garrard Ltd* v *WRA (Guns) Ltd* [2002] FSR 31. The second defendant (the first defendant was his company) used his name, 'William R Asprey, Esquire', above his shop front.

62 [1979] AC 731.

63 [1998] FSR 500.

pleased to find a relatively inexpensive way of brightening up their student accommodation. They set up a company in Sweden but eventually fell out with each other. They agreed to split the business territorially and one set up a company in the UK. For a time, the English company obtained its posters from the Swedish company. At first instance, it was held that the goodwill was shared, the English company having a distributor's goodwill and the Swedish company having a publisher's goodwill.

The court went further to suggest that goodwill was shared as in a group of companies, with neither being able to restrain the other from using the *Scandecor* name in which the goodwill subsisted. Lloyd J referred to *Dent* v *Turpin*,[64] in which it was held that neither of the two stepsons of E.J. Dent could restrain the other from using the name (though either could stop a third party from using the name).

64 (1861) 2 John & H 139.

65 [1999] FSR 26.

In the Court of Appeal[65] it was held that there was no rule of law or presumption of fact that goodwill generated by trading activities of a wholly owned subsidiary belonged to the parent company or was the subject of an implied, if not express, licence in favour of the subsidiary. The Court of Appeal disapproved of Lloyd J's finding that there were two different but connected goodwills in separate, not shared, ownership. Rather it accepted that it was legally and factually possible for a business based outside the UK to acquire goodwill in the UK by means of the supply of products through a subsidiary, agent or licensee. However, on the facts before the court, it was held that the Swedish company did not have goodwill in the UK because it neither traded there nor exercised any business control over activities in the UK such as to acquire goodwill.

In *Scandecor*, the Court of Appeal did not need to explore fully the possibility of goodwill being shared but it is by no means a novel concept. For example, in *Erven Warnink* (above), the House of Lords accepted that goodwill could be shared amongst an unrelated group of producers of Advocaat. In *Gromax Plasticulture Ltd* v *Don & Low Nonwovens Ltd*,[66] the claimant marketed a plastic crop cover made by the defendant. They agreed that it should be marketed under the name 'Gro-Shield' and cooperated to promote these products. At first, it was sold in such a way to indicate the defendant as the manufacturer but later publicity linked the product only with the claimant. The court held that, at the beginning, the factors pointed both ways as to who was responsible for the character and quality of the product and, as a consequence, the goodwill was shared. The claimant was unable to discharge the burden of proving that it alone had the sole right to use the name.

66 [1999] RPC 367.

A goodwill which is shared between two businesses may have the effect of giving an impression that the businesses are bigger than they actually are. Where two companies share goodwill in their dominant trading names, care must be taken not to make changes to them which could amount to passing off. In *Sir Robert McAlpine Ltd* v *Alfred McAlpine plc*,[67] the two companies derived from a single company originally set up by Sir Robert McAlpine in the nineteenth century. During 1935, the company split, with one of Sir Robert's sons, Alfred, taking one of them. The companies agreed on a geographical split which lasted until 1983. There had been informal agreements that 'Alfred' would be used in the name of Alfred's company. The defendant was the holding company of Alfred's trading company, which changed its name in 2003 to McAlpine Capital Projects Ltd, although the holding company did not change its name. It was held that the trading company was guilty of passing off although it was accepted that the claimant and defendant had goodwill in the name 'McAlpine'. However, neither could complain of the other having that goodwill providing it took steps to use an appropriate identifier to make it clear it was not associated with the other company. By stopping using 'Alfred' in its name, this was something the defendant's trading company failed to do. Just as the sole owner's rights in goodwill should not be prejudiced, neither should joint owners be prejudiced whether at the hands of the other joint owner or a third party.

67 [2004] RPC 36.

Determining the identity of the owner of goodwill is a question of fact. Though it might be convenient to make use of a time-worn presumption, it seems the question can only be answered by looking at the facts of a particular case. For example, in *Medgen Inc v Passion for Life Products Ltd*,[68] it was held in the Chancery Division that ownership of goodwill was a question of fact and that there was no presumption that, as between a foreign manufacturer and UK distributor, goodwill belonged to the former. The facts of the case are that the claimant manufactured an anti-snoring remedy under the name 'Snorenz' which the defendant sold in the UK as the claimant's exclusive distributor. When the relationship broke down, the defendant started selling its own equivalent product under its registered trade mark 'Snoreeze'. Both claimed goodwill in 'Snorenz'. A number of factors were important in the decision that the claimant owned no goodwill in the UK. The claimant carried on no direct business in the UK, the packaging bore no reference to the claimant, all the marketing and sales activity in the UK was carried out by the defendant and all references on the packaging and advertisements related exclusively to the defendant to whom trade customers turned if there were any problems. Finally, there was no evidence that retailers or ultimate customers knew or cared that the claimant was the developer or manufacturer of the product.

In the context of a licence or distributorship agreement, where the licensor or manufacturer is based in another country which recognises the law of passing off, it may be possible that each will share goodwill but will own it on a territorial basis. For example, in *Electro Cad Australia Pty Ltd* v *Mejati RCS SDN BHD*,[69] pre-launch publicity and promotions in Malaysia established goodwill in 'Stopcard', a device which allowed the owner of a vehicle which had been stolen to dial a telephone number to bring the car to a gradual stop. It was held that the goodwill was shared between the Australian manufacturer and the Malaysian company that had been granted exclusive rights to market the product in Malaysia. However, as regards Malaysia that goodwill was owned solely by the Malaysian company.[70]

In many cases, a licence agreement or distributorship agreement will contain specific provisions dealing with the issue of goodwill and ownership of it. It clearly makes good sense to deal with this question where the goodwill subsists in a trading or product name. Often the ex-licensee or ex-distributor will be contractually barred from using the relevant name as the licensor or manufacturer, as the case may be, will be careful to prevent the continued use of the name post-agreement as this could have the effect of eroding the goodwill or causing confusion in the relevant market. This could lead to the eventual destruction of the goodwill. The same considerations apply where a subsidiary company, trading under a variation of a name used by other members of the group, falls into the hands of a third party. In *Dawnay Day & Co Ltd* v *Cantor Fitzgerald International*,[71] a subsidiary company of the claimant was known as Dawnay Day Securities Ltd. Eventually, due to a management deadlock, an administrator sold the business to the defendant for £2.5 million with the right to use the name 'Dawnay Day Securities' so far as it was lawfully able to do so.

Sir Richard Scott VC, in the Court of Appeal, said it was unnecessary to analyse the ownership of the 'Dawnay Day' name but he said that all the remaining members of the group were entitled to restrain the use of the name by the defendant. He had no hesitation in finding passing off, pointing out it was a clear misrepresentation for the defendant to use the name as that would send out a message that the defendant was associated with the group. The only way in which the defendant could continue to use the name would be if he could show that the name had ceased to be distinctive of the group of companies.

A trader might build up goodwill in his business, then sell that business as a going concern together with that goodwill. Difficulties might arise if the original trader later wishes to start up business again and use a similar name. In some cases, the name in which the goodwill exists may be the original trader's own name. One way to deal with this potential difficulty is for the buyer of the business to ask for an appropriate restrictive covenant from the seller of the business and, of course, to ensure that the sale agreement

---

68 [2001] FSR 30.

69 [1999] FSR 291.

70 The defendants were guilty of passing off by placing an equivalent product on the market in Malaysia under the name 'Stopcar'.

71 [2000] RPC 669.

72 [2006] FSR 16.

does include the assignment of the goodwill, properly defined. In *I N Newman Ltd* v *Richard T Adlem*,[72] the defendant operated a funeral undertaking business under his own name. He later sold the business to the predecessor in title of the claimant for £55,000 (comprising £54,000 for the goodwill and £1,000 for the stock in trade). He granted a lease of the Chapel of Rest to the buyer and continued to provide services to the new owner. There was a covenant in restraint of trade which prevented, *inter alia*, the defendant carrying on an undertaking business for five years within a ten-mile radius. After the covenant expired and following failure to agree a new covenant, the defendant recommenced an undertaking business on his own account and under his own name, Richard T. Adlem, and he applied to register 'Richard T. Adlem Funeral Director' as a trade mark. At first instance, the judge held that the parties both shared goodwill in the name Richard T. Adlem.

The majority of the Court of Appeal disagreed and held that the goodwill in the name had been sold with the business and validly assigned to the claimant. The defendant was, therefore, guilty of passing off. Furthermore, the trade mark, which had by now been registered, was invalid. The trial judge erred in finding that both parties had concurrent goodwill. This seems to have been based on the fact that the defendant carried on working for the business after the sale in a personal capacity. However, any goodwill he built up during that period belonged not to him but to the business.[73] Once the restrictive covenant had expired, there was nothing to prevent the defendant starting up business in his own right again and even using his own name, but he was under a duty to make it clear that his new business was nothing to do with that of the claimant. Disclaimers had been used but these were insignificant and not sufficiently 'up front'. Such disclaimers should be viewed from the perspective of all types of person who read them including those with a less than perfect memory.

73 Arden LJ dissented. She pointed out that some parts of the original business had been retained by Mr Adlem, including the headstone business and that, in any case, most of the purchase price was to be paid over a period of time out of profits made by the buyer of the business.

Descriptive words and geographical names

As the *Halifax* case shows, it is possible to acquire goodwill in a name which includes a geographical name. However, geographical names and, *a fortiori*, descriptive words are likely to lack distinctiveness in most cases such that it will be difficult, if not impossible, for a trader to demonstrate that he has a goodwill associated with the word or words in question.

74 (1946) 63 RPC 39.

In *Office Cleaning Services Ltd* v *Westminster Windows and General Cleaners Ltd*,[74] the claimant unsuccessfully tried to restrain the defendant from using the trading name 'Office Cleaning Association'. In the claimant's unsuccessful appeal to the House of Lords, Viscount Simonds said (at 42):

> . . . the courts will not readily assume that the use by a trader as part of his trade name descriptive words already used by another trader as part of his trade name is likely to cause confusion and will easily accept small differences as adequate to avoid it. It is otherwise where a fancy word has been chosen as part of the name.

75 [1981] RPC 69.
76 [1983] RPC 407.

Other examples of descriptive words denied protection by the law of passing off include 'Oven Chips' in *McCain International Ltd* v *Country Fair Foods Ltd*[75] and 'Chicago Pizza' in *My Kinda Town Ltd* v *Soll*.[76] Where such words are used, there are two issues in effect. First, because descriptive words are unlikely to be distinctive, it is difficult for a trader to show that he has established goodwill in the words. Second, a trader complaining that another trader is wrongfully using the words will find it almost impossible to prove that there is a likelihood of confusion in the minds of the buying public and, that being so, proof of damage (an essential element in passing off) will not be present.

If things were otherwise and protection was readily afforded to descriptive words, it would become very difficult for other traders to describe their activities to potential customers. As Laddie J said in *Antec International Ltd v South Western Chicks (Warren) Ltd*[77] (at 285):

> As it is sometimes put, no trader will be allowed to fence in the common of the English language. From this it flows, that in some cases where a trader has used a highly descriptive name he will find it virtually impossible to obtain protection at all by means of passing off proceedings.

He went on to say that this is not, however, an exact science, echoing Oliver LJ in *My Kinda Town Ltd v Soll* who said that there was no clear dichotomy between unprotected descriptive words and fancy names. Of course, made-up words ('fancy names'), unless very similar to already known words, are distinctive *per se* and there should be little difficulty in establishing a likelihood of confusion. In *Antec*, the phrase in issue was 'Farm Fluid' used for disinfectants used at farms, and, although Laddie J accepted that it was relatively descriptive, he nevertheless went on to grant an interim injunction to restrain passing off. It was at least arguable that persons buying under that phrase wanted the claimant's product and, furthermore, no other trader, apart from the defend-ant, was using 'Farm Fluid' to describe their disinfectant.

At the full trial of the action, Michael Hart QC accepted that the words 'farm' and 'fluid', taken together, as 'farm fluid', were not part of the common of the English language.[78] Acknowledging them separately as ordinary English words did not inexorably mean to say that the phrase is simply descriptive of the product. He pointed out that there was no evidence to support the notion that the term 'farm fluid' was in general usage amongst farmers. On the contrary, the evidence established that the term had become associated by farmers with the claimant's agricultural disinfectant.

A word may be descriptive but may also develop a secondary meaning which could be protected by goodwill. In *Knight v Beyond Properties Pty Ltd*,[79] the claimant had authored some children's books, using the word 'Mythbusters' in the titles. Although this was descrip-tive, by 1993 it had also acquired a small-scale reputation sufficient to attract attention. However, by the time the defendant had produced some television programmes under the name 'Mythbusters' (around 2002–2006) the reputation in relation to the books had diminished to the point that it had become trivial and no longer protected.

Where, generally, one trader uses descriptive words and another trader uses similar words, the court will tend to concentrate on the differences. Thus, in the *Office Cleaning* case, the court isolated 'Services' and 'Association' and held that there was a sufficient differentiation between them such that the defendant was not guilty of passing off. The opposite was held in *British Diabetic Association v Diabetic Society Ltd*,[80] in which Walker J accepted that 'Society' and 'Association' were similar in derivation and meaning and 'not wholly dissimilar in form'.[81] Therefore, there was not a sufficient differentiation to avoid passing off and a final injunction was granted.

In *S\$1.99 Pte Ltd v Lifestyle 1.99 Pte Ltd*,[82] it was confirmed that, if a name or mark was descriptive, it could only be protected if it could be shown that it had acquired a second-ary meaning. Furthermore, where descriptive words were used, a slight difference would suffice to distinguish them.

In that case, the claimant operated a retail outlet at which everything was sold for the price of \$1.99 (Singaporean dollars). It used a logo with the words 'ONE.99 Shop'. The defendant opened a similar outlet selling most of its goods for \$1.99 under a sign which included the word 'Lifestyle' under which the figure 1.99 appeared prominently. Accepting that figures could become distinctive for the purposes of a passing off action, the Singaporean Court of Appeal held that the defendant was not guilty of passing off as the defendant had used the word 'Lifestyle' and used different colours for their logos.

77 [1997] FSR 278, an interim hearing.

78 [1998] FSR 738.

79 [2007] FSR 34.

80 [1996] FSR 1.

81 The word 'British' was not considered as part of the claimant's name for the purposes of the decision.

82 [2001] FSR 10.

Consequently, there was little likelihood of deception. The court went on to say that, although it appeared that the defendant was deliberately 'cashing in' on the favourable publicity generated by the claimant, there was no such thing as a tort of unfair competition.

In *British Broadcasting Corporation* v *Talksport Ltd*,[83] the BBC had sole radio broadcasting rights in the UK for the Euro 2000 football championship. It alleged that the defendant falsely represented that it provided live coverage of the competition when, in fact, it only offered 'off-tube' broadcasts (commentaries provided by commentators who watched live TV broadcasts, rather than being at the stadium at which matches were being played). The defendant nevertheless advertised its coverage as being 'live'. The defendant gave certain undertakings including that it would not represent that it held official or live broadcasting rights and that it would make it clear that its broadcasts were 'off-tube' and that it was not the BBC. At a resumed hearing, the BBC sought an order to restrain the defendant from representing by the use of sound broadcasts that any broadcast contained live coverage of Euro 2000 matches.

As a result of the defendant's skill in dubbing ambient sound on to the commentary, Blackburne J, in deciding whether to grant a further interim injunction, thought that the ordinary listener might think the defendant's broadcast was live. However, the judge did not accept that goodwill could subsist in words which were merely descriptive of the product or service. He said it was the indicia by which an activity was known rather than the activity itself which gave rise to goodwill. Thus, there could be no goodwill in the phrase 'live sports broadcasting'. In other words, the phrase remained descriptive and had not acquired a secondary meaning in respect of the BBC's activities.

A trader using a descriptive word is more likely to acquire goodwill if the word is not generally used in the trade in which the trader is involved. For example, the word 'Millenia'[84] was held not to be descriptive in the context of offices, shops and hotels.[85] The decision was upheld on appeal.[86] The claimant had used the word 'Millenia' for a complex comprising two office towers (including one named Millenia Tower), a shopping mall named Millenia Walk and two hotels including one named Ritz-Carlton, Millenia Singapore. An argument that the name of the hotel was Ritz-Carlton and 'Millenia' only served to designate the location of the hotel was rejected. Even if it was accepted that it was a geographical description, the word was more fanciful than obviously descriptive. Therefore, goodwill subsisted in the claimant's business operations associated with the word 'Millenia'.

Whether a word is capable of supporting goodwill depends very much on its context. Descriptive words may reach the status of fancy names if they are used in an unusual or unexpected context. For example, 'Spectrum' would be descriptive in terms of optical lens manufacture, but not when used in the field of lawnmowers. The issue is distinctiveness rather than whether the word or phrase is descriptive or fancy. Similarly, with a slang term, it will be difficult to establish the presence of goodwill associated with the term. To be successful, the claimant must show that the term has acquired a secondary meaning, being indicative of the claimant's goods. Thus, in *Box Television Ltd* v *Haymarket Magazines Ltd*,[87] it was held that the claimant had failed to show that it had goodwill in 'The Box' for its cable TV channel. Parker J considered that 'The Box' was simply a colloquialism for a television set. That is not to say, however, that it is impossible to acquire goodwill in a slang term, merely that a trader will face an uphill task in convincing a court that the public associates the term with his goods or services.

A phrase such as 'Internet World' seems very descriptive at first sight, but in *Mecklermedia Corp* v *DC Congress Gesellschaft mbH*,[88] the claimant claimed extensive goodwill in the phrase as regards its activities in respect of its website and magazines. The defendant had registered the name as its trade mark in Germany and had already commenced proceedings there for trade mark infringement. Jacob J held that, although 'Internet World' was to some extent descriptive, it was not so descriptive that goodwill could not exist in

83 [2001] FSR 6.

84 The correct spelling is 'Millennia'.

85 *Pontiac Marina Pte Ltd* v *CDL Hotels International Ltd* [1997] FSR 725, High Court, Singapore.

86 [1998] FSR 839.

87 *The Times*, 3 March 1997.

88 [1997] FSR 627.

it and he accepted that the claimant had established a serious question that it had extensive goodwill in England.[89] He refused to strike out the claim, stay the action or decline jurisdiction pending the outcome in the German case. The two claims were different and there was no danger of conflicting decisions as the German case involved a trade mark whereas the English case was concerned with passing off. Jacob J considered that the English courts were the most convenient forum for hearing an English passing off case.

A geographical name used by a trader could have one of three meanings. It could indicate that:

- the trader's goods come from that place;
- the trader's goods are of a particular type associated with that place and, therefore, likely to appeal to a particular taste; or
- it is the product of a particular trader.

The third meaning has been described in the House of Lords in the 'Stone Ale' case[90] as a secondary meaning to which goodwill could attach and which could be established by evidence. However, in *Barnsley Brewery Co Ltd v RBNB*,[91] the court declined to renew an injunction against the use of 'Barnsley Bitter' by the defendant as the claimant did not have a strong case that the phrase had acquired such a secondary meaning. 'Barnsley Bitter' had been used by a third party at its Oakwell (near Barnsley) brewery from 1883 to 1976. Both the claimant and defendant were hoping to capture the historical goodwill associated with the name.

In some cases, geographical names have a special form of protection by virtue of European Union Regulations: for example, Council Regulation (EEC) 1576/89 of 29 May 1989 laying down general rules on the definition, description and presentation of spirit drinks,[92] which restricts the use of geographical names for spirits such as Scotch whisky, and Council Regulation (EEC) No 2081/92 of 14 July 1992 on the protection of geographical indications and designations of origin for agricultural products and foodstuffs.[93] In the case of the former Regulation, in *Matthew Gloag & Sons Ltd v Welsh Distillers Ltd*,[94] the defendants bought Scotch whisky and marketed it under the name Welsh whisky. It was held that the claimants had an arguable case for passing off[95] and that they also had a private right under the Regulation which allowed the use of other geographical names provided that they did not mislead customers.

As regards the latter Regulation, at first instance it was held that Asda Stores could not be prevented by virtue of the regulation from selling Parma ham which had been sliced and packaged outside the Parma region of Italy even though that was contrary to Italian law.[96] The ham itself came from the Parma region and was not misdescribed as the Regulation was concerned with designation of origin and contained no direct reference to slicing and packaging. The Parma Ham Association appealed. In *Consorzio del Prosciutto di Parma v Asda Stores Ltd*,[97] the House of Lords referred the following question to the European Court of Justice for a preliminary ruling under Article 234 of the EC Treaty (now Article 267 of the Treaty on the Functioning of the European Union):

> Whether, as a matter of Community law, Council Regulation (EEC) No. 2081/92 read with Commission Regulation (EC) No. 1107/96 and the specification for the PDO[98] 'prosciutto di Parma' create a valid Community right, directly enforceable in the court of a member state, to restrain the retail sale as 'Parma ham' of sliced and packaged ham derived from hams duly exported from Parma in compliance with the conditions of the PDO but which have not been thereafter sliced, packaged and labelled in accordance with the specification.

Although clearly contrary to Italian law,[99] concerns had been expressed in that the specification containing the description of the product (and in particular the requirements as to the packaging and labelling of sliced ham) had not been published in the *Official*

89 The defendant's claim that 'Internet World' was too descriptive for goodwill to exist in it lay ill with its claim to have a valid registered trade mark in Germany consisting of that name.

90 *Montgomery v Thompson* [1871] AC 217.

91 [1997] FSR 462.

92 OJ L 160, 12.06.1989, p 1.

93 OJ L 208, 24.07.1992, p 1.

94 [1998] FSR 718.

95 On the basis of inverse passing off, as in *Bristol Conservatories Ltd v Conservatories Custom Built Ltd* [1989] RPC 455.

96 *Consorzio del Prosciutto di Parma v Asda Stores Ltd* [1998] FSR 697.

97 [2002] FSR 3.

98 PDO means protected designation of origin.

99 Law No 26 of 13 February 1990, entitled 'Protection of denomination of origin "Prosciutto di Parma"'.

Journal, or, for that matter, anywhere else. The Court of Appeal said that it was a general principle of European law that any measures directly enforceable against the citizen should be transparent and readily accessible.

The Court of Justice ruled[100] that the Regulation did not prevent the use of a protected designation being subject to conditions such as slicing and packaging being carried out in the region of production. Although this was a quantitative restriction on exports, it could be justified under Article 29 of the EC Treaty (now Article 35 of the Treaty on the Functioning of the European Union). However, the condition in question could not be relied on against economic operators as it was not brought to their attention by adequate publicity in EU legislation.

The scope of passing off

The scope of passing off is quite wide and it can protect unregistrable business names, unregistered trade marks, advertising and general 'get-up'; in fact, anything that is distinctive of the claimant's goods, services or business. Trade mark law requires some use of the mark whereas, in passing off, no express use or mention of a trade name is required; mere implication is adequate. For example, in *Copydex Ltd* v *Noso Products Ltd*,[101] the claimant had given a demonstration of its glue on television although the name of the product was not mentioned (this was before the days of commercial television and great care was taken not to mention trade names, even to the extent of covering over manufacturers' names on items used in dramatic sketches). The defendant company also made glue and one of its salesmen gave a demonstration of its glue in a large retail store. During the demonstration a large card was displayed which bore the words: '"NOSO" here again! As shown on television "Women's Hour"'. When the claimant complained, the defendant gave the court an undertaking not to do it again; otherwise an injunction would have been granted in favour of the claimant.

The scope of passing off can be considered in terms of the meaning of 'in the course of trade', the extent of marks and 'get-up' protected and geographical range.

In the course of trade

Although some judges have talked about passing off in relation to trade in goods, it is clear that it applies equally to services as well. Before service marks could be registered, this was of exceptional importance as the use of another's name in relation to the provision of services could only be actionable as passing off. In *Harrods Ltd* v *R Harrod Ltd*,[102] the claimant was a well-known company with a banking department, but which was precluded from operating as a moneylender by the articles of association. The defendant registered a money lending company under the 'fancy name'[103] of R Harrod Ltd, that is a name having nothing to do with his own name. This fact, together with his advertising style, showed that he was acting fraudulently in an attempt to gain advantage from these similarities and the claimant was granted an injunction to restrain the defendant from using that name.

'Trade' does not have to be primarily associated with commercial enterprise and in *British Medical Association* v *Marsh*[104] the claimant, a professional body constituted as a non-profit-making unincorporated association, was able to obtain an injunction to prevent the defendant passing off his business as that of the claimant's. The Association had published analyses of 'quack medicines' because of concern that they were of no medical value and were being sold at excessive prices. The defendant started making up proprietary medicines from the Association's analyses and sold them in a drug store which had the

100 Case C-108/01 *Consorzio del Prosciutto di Parma v Asda Stores Ltd* [2003] ECR I-5121.

101 (1952) 69 RPC 38.

102 (1924) 41 RPC 74.

103 It may have been so described because the Patents, Designs and Trade Marks Act 1883 permitted the registration of 'fancy words', although the phrase 'invented word' was soon to replace it.

104 (1931) 48 RPC 565.

letters 'B.M.A.' displayed in the window together with other references to the Association. To describe the Association's operations as being in the course of trade shows a certain elasticity of thought but it was said that the claimant's 'business' would be harmed because the passing off might cause existing members to leave the Association or to discourage potential members from joining. That is, existing and potential members might think that the defendant's activities were approved of or connected with the Association.

It has been accepted that a charity, too, is capable of possessing goodwill indistinguishable from commercial goodwill which was equally entitled to legal protection through an action in passing off. In *British Diabetic Association* v *Diabetic Society*[105] the defendant charity was restrained from using its name, such use amounting to a deception calculated to injure (albeit unintentionally) the reputation and goodwill of the claimant charity. Walker J expressed his profound regret at the failure of the parties to settle the dispute, the costs of which were £750,000. He said that it was difficult even for a lawyer to comprehend how the litigation could help diabetics whose subscriptions and gifts would ultimately be the source of payment of the lawyers' bills.[106]

The fact that goodwill can attach to non-profit-making organisations was confirmed again in *Burge* v *Haycock*[107] in which a former member of the British National Party purported to stand in a council election as a candidate of the Countryside Alliance. His nomination and ballot paper describing him as such a candidate had been accepted by the returning officer but the Countryside Alliance, which campaigned and lobbied against the abolition of field sports such as hunting with dogs, sued for passing off. The court held, on the basis of a long line of authorities, that the claimant had protectable goodwill which could be injured by loss of control of its name or by association with the defendant.

Such a robust view of trade and potential harm has not readily been embraced in cases involving individuals whose names have been used without their permission. In *McCullogh* v *Lewis A May Ltd*[108] the claimant was a well-known children's broadcaster who used the name 'Uncle Mac'. The claimant had some physical infirmities. The defendant sold cereal under the name 'Uncle Mac', with indirect reference to the claimant's infirmities, without the claimant's permission. It could be argued that, in such a situation, inferences might be drawn by the public seeing the cereal which might be harmful to the claimant. For example, it could be inferred that the claimant had to resort to allowing his nickname to be used in this way to earn more money and that to soil his hands with advertising was contrary to the image he was trying to maintain. However, it was held that the facts could not give rise to passing off because the claimant was in no way involved in the making or marketing of cereals; instead, he was a broadcaster. There was no common field of activity.[109] The decision totally fails to take any account of the fact that many of the public buying and eating the cereal would assume that the claimant had given permission for his nickname to be used in such a fashion and the possibility that he might lose popularity as a broadcaster because of the lower regard in which media personalities involved with advertising were once held.

Where a personal name has been used without permission in order to promote a product or a service, there is always a possibility of an action in defamation.[110] 'Uncle Mac' may have stood a better chance had he sued in libel, as Wynn-Parry J said: 'If it were anything, it were libel, as to which I say nothing.' In *Sim* v *HJ Heinz Co Ltd*,[111] Ron Moody, the actor, was engaged to read the commentaries for advertisements for the defendant's products to be broadcast on television. In making the commentaries, he mimicked the voice of another popular actor, Alistair Sim, who took objection. However, it was held that an injunction would not be granted, whether on the basis of defamation or passing off, because there was no evidence of damage to the reputation of the claimant. Again, there is no common field of activity: the claimant was in the business of acting and not in the business of making and selling soups and baked beans. It is certainly far less likely that the claimant's business goodwill would be harmed in cases such as this compared to the 'Uncle Mac' case.

105 [1996] FSR 1.

106 *The Times*, 14 October 1995, p 6.

107 [2002] RPC 20.

108 (1948) 65 RPC 58.

109 The need for the common field of activity is discussed later in this chapter.

110 An example where the claimant successfully sued in defamation is *Tolley* v *JS Fry & Sons Ltd* [1931] AC 333 where the picture of the claimant was printed on the wrappers of chocolate bars.

111 [1959] 1 All ER 547.

Both of the above cases must now be seen in the light of *Irvine v Talksport Ltd*[112] in which it was accepted that falsely implying that a celebrity was endorsing a product is actionable under passing off. However, in *Irvine v Talksport* a doctored photograph was used rather than the use of a name or the voice of a mimic. Nevertheless, it is submitted that now a court would be more ready to find passing off in wider circumstances, given that the public is now more used to the fact that celebrities commonly endorse products in return for payment.

Registering a domain name on the internet which includes a famous person's name may be actionable as passing off, on the basis that the person registering the name has made an instrument of deceit, if there is evidence that there is a dishonest or fraudulent motive behind it.[113]

Extent of protection of marks and 'get-up'

Passing off goes beyond the type of mark that is registrable as a trade mark and can apply in respect of containers and packaging.[114] In a controversial case which went all the way to the House of Lords, *Reckitt & Colman Products Ltd v Borden Inc*,[115] it was held that the law of passing off protected the Jif lemon. The Jif lemon is a plastic lemon coloured and shaped receptacle in which the claimant's lemon juice was sold. The defendant sold lemon juice in a similar but not identical container (it was bigger, having a green cap and a flat side) and was restrained from passing off its lemon juice as that of the claimant by use of a deceptively similar 'get-up'. Lord Bridge said that the result was to give the claimant a *de facto* monopoly on the container which was just as effective as a *de jure* monopoly and he commented on the fact that a trader selling lemon juice would never be allowed to register a lemon as a trade mark but that the claimant had achieved that result indirectly.[116] However, Lord Bridge reluctantly had to agree that that was the outcome on the basis of the application of the law of passing off.[117] Lord Oliver said that all the main ingredients of a passing off action, namely goodwill, misrepresentation and damage, were present. The Jif lemon had been on sale since 1956 and a considerable goodwill had built up associated with it; it was likely that a good number of housewives would purchase the defendant's lemon juice in the belief that they were purchasing Jif lemons even though careful inspection would show that the defendant's lemons were not Jif lemons because of the different shape and the attached labels.[118] The essence of a passing off action was said to be a deceit practised on the public. Customers were to be taken as they were found, it being no answer to the claim that customers would not have been mistaken had they been 'more careful, more literate and more perspicacious'.

The decision seemed out of step with trade mark law at the time which, generally, denied registration to containers, as in the trade mark case of *Re Coca-Cola Co*[119] where the House of Lords was concerned about creating a monopoly in a container. The decision in *Reckitt & Colman v Borden* did raise the question as to whether a greengrocer could ever be accused of passing off his natural lemons as Jif lemons! Of course, the decision stops short of this. Now, with the Trade Marks Act 1994, the congruence between the law of passing off and trade mark law is much greater.

The law of passing off does not stop short at containers. Even the shape or appearance of the article itself may be protected. In *Hodgkinson and Corby Ltd v Wards Mobility Services Ltd*,[120] the claimant made a cushion for use by permanently immobile persons to prevent pressure sores. It had a distinctive appearance. The defendant was planning to sell a 'lookalike' cushion though under a different trade name. It was held that passing off could occur even when the appearance of goods had been copied and that passing off was not restricted to taking a name, mark or sign. Although copying the appearance of a product is not unlawful, *per se*, in the absence of infringing an intellectual property right, in terms of passing off, the defendant must always do enough to avoid the deception.

The ability of purchasers to make subtle distinctions was considered to be a factor in the Privy Council case of *White Hudson & Co Ltd v Asian Organisation Ltd*[121] in which the claimant had sold cough sweets wrapped in red cellophane in Singapore since 1953. The wrapper bore the word 'Hacks' and a list of ingredients. From 1958, the defendant also sold cough sweets of a similar colour and shape which were also wrapped in red cellophane but with the name 'Pecto' printed on the wrappers. It was held that the claimant had established a get-up in the red coloured wrapper that was distinctive of his cough sweets and there was a danger of confusion, especially as few purchasers could read the words 'Pecto' and it was shown that many customers asked for 'red paper cough sweets'. Although no deception was proved on the part of the defendant, the get-up of the defendant's sweets was calculated to deceive and the injunction granted to the claimant in the Court of Appeal in Singapore was confirmed. To avoid confusion the defendant could have simply used a different colour for its wrappers or used a prominent symbol on the wrapper. The use of a different colour will not always be a realistic option: for example, as in the Jif lemon case.

The protection of wrappers and containers by passing off is one example of the width of this area of law compared to trade marks, although the latter has now caught up as a result of amendments to trade mark law so as to implement the Trade Marks Directive.[122] But passing off can go even further in the subject matter protected and can protect, in principle, anything associated with goodwill such as a method of doing business or a theme used in advertising. Of course, the less tangible the subject matter is, the less likely it is that the claimant can show that there has been or will be damage to his goodwill as a result of the defendant's misrepresentation. In *Cadbury-Schweppes Pty Ltd v Pub Squash Co Pty Ltd*,[123] the claimant marketed a soft drink in Australia called 'Solo' which was sold in cans resembling beer cans bearing a medallion device. An intensive advertising campaign portrayed it as a drink associated with 'rugged masculine endeavour' and, in total contradiction of the popular image of the Australian male, it sold well. The defendant later started selling a comparable drink called 'Pub Squash' in similar cans with advertising in a similar vein. It was held that the claimant had failed to acquire an intangible property right associated with its advertising campaign because it never became a distinguishing feature of the product or generally associated with it. Although it was conceded that the defendant had deliberately taken advantage of the claimant's advertising campaign, the consuming public were not misled or deceived by this into thinking that Pub Squash was the claimant's drink. In other words, the claimant could show no damage resulting from the defendant's use of similar advertising and get-up.

The *Pub Squash* case shows that distinctiveness is important to success in a passing off action. If a name is descriptive this will reduce or even eliminate the possibility of it being distinctive of a particular trader's business. For example, in *Advance Magazine Publishing Inc v Redwood Publishing Ltd*,[124] the claimant published a food magazine entitled 'GOURMET'. The defendant planned to publish, as part of a series of magazines, a food magazine called 'BBC Gourmet Goodfood'. Harman J refused to grant interim relief to the claimant. As the word 'Gourmet' was descriptive, small differences in get-up would be sufficient to avoid confusion. Furthermore, the claimant had failed to establish an arguable case. The magazines were different when looked at alongside each other and, even though purchasers might shorten the defendant's title to 'Gourmet', magazines were not usually sold by name over the counter but from racks from which purchasers would select the magazine they wished to buy.

The use of numbers may be controlled by the law of passing off. It was recognised in *Pontiac Marina Pte Ltd v CDL Hotels International Ltd*[125] that figures such as 1.99 could be protected if they achieved a secondary meaning, being distinctive of a trader's goods. It has become very common for motor vehicle manufacturers to use numbers as model identifiers: for example, Peugeot 306, BMW 318i, Volvo 850, Mercedes C180 and so on. The use of

---

121 [1964] 1 WLR 1466.

122 Even so, the law of passing off may prove wider in this respect as there are some exceptions that affect the registrability of marks.

123 [1981] 1 All ER 213, PC.

124 [1993] FSR 449.

125 [1998] FSR 839.

one maker's number by another could raise an arguable case of passing off; depending on how well established the number is. In many cases, showing goodwill should present no problem and using another manufacturer's number certainly could be described as a misrepresentation. The difficulty lies in proving consequential damage. If Peugeot decided to sell a car under the name 850, would any potential buyer be deceived into thinking he was ordering a Volvo? It seems unlikely in the extreme unless the car became so well known by the number on its own without reference to the maker. However, as we shall see, the law of passing off has developed to accept erosion of goodwill as a form of damage. This could apply where one car maker uses a number that has become strongly associated with a particular manufacturer's car which is, itself, of high quality or performance.

126 [1995] RPC 16.

Where the use of a number is at issue, the individual circumstances may be highly relevant. In *Law Society of England and Wales* v *Griffiths*,[126] the claimant had launched a 'phone in' advice line in respect of accidents and personal injuries. The telephone number was 0500–192939. The defendant, who was not part of the claimant's scheme, set up one of his own and obtained and used the telephone number 0800–192939. It was held that there was a serious issue to be tried by the court, which granted an interim injunction in favour of the claimant. By deliberately choosing a confusingly similar number, the defendant was representing that he was the claimant either by saying so or by failing to disabuse callers. The effect would be to cause a serious loss of business to the claimant, which had built up a substantial goodwill associated with its scheme. It appeared that the defendant had deliberately selected his telephone number in order to divert business away from the claimant.

Geographical range

127 [2003] FSR 51.

128 [2008] FSR 6.

Goodwill may vary depending on the geographical area under consideration. In *Associated Newspapers Ltd* v *Express Newspapers*,[127] it was accepted that the claimant's reputation in its newspapers, especially in respect of its newspaper the *London Evening Standard*, was particularly pronounced in the south-east of England. Whilst injunctive relief may be appropriate limited to the south-east, it would be important not to grant more extensive relief. Where goodwill is local only, the area of the defendant's activities may be relevant. In *Bignell* v *Just Employment Law Ltd*,[128] the claimant was a sole principal solicitor trading under the name 'JUST EMPLOYMENT'. He was based in Guildford, Surrey. The majority of the claimant's clients came from the Guildford area. The defendant operated a business offering legal advice on employment law matters. It was based in Glasgow though did have a service office with one employee in London. Although both parties operated in the same field, it was held that none of the three requirements in *Reckitt & Colman* v *Borden* were satisfied. Although the claimant had goodwill in and around Guildford, it did not extend elsewhere.

If passing off by one trader is to damage another trader's interests in the goodwill he has acquired, it should be reasonable to assume that there should be some overlap in the geographical location and extent of the catchment area of their respective businesses. For example, it might be assumed that a baker in Leeds operating under the name 'Melwood Bakeries' would not be able to restrain another baker using the same name in Dover; but he might be able to restrain the use of the name by a baker in Bradford, which lies relatively close to Leeds. Bearing in mind the basic test for passing off stated in its barest form as being a misrepresentation that causes damage to business goodwill, there is a possibility that people in Bradford will think that the bakery there and the one in Leeds are owned by the same person and the latter may lose sales as a result. Overlapping or contiguous geographical areas would seem to be precursors for a passing off action.

The narrow view above does not take account of future growth of businesses and this may be a reason for allowing passing off an expansive geographical range. For example, the baker in the above example may be ambitious and his business may grow so that eventually he has a chain of bakeries spanning the whole of England, including Dover.[129] The goodwill may even be in relation to activities in a different country. In *Maxim's Ltd v Dye*,[130] the claimant, an English company, owned a world-famous restaurant in Paris known as 'Maxim's'. The defendant opened a restaurant in Norwich and also named it 'Maxim's'. It was held that the claimant had goodwill in England derived from the business in France which might be regarded as being prospective. The claimant might want to commence trading in England in the future and should be able to rely on the goodwill he had in connection with the name.[131] Such international extent of goodwill will not be common, but if an international reputation has been achieved, there is a danger that another person carrying out business using the same name could cause confusion and customers might think that they were dealing with the claimant's business. This is particularly so in the case of large multinational organisations such as 'McDonald's'. The above case is also an example of a remedy being available without proof of any actual or immediate damage; indeed, the damage is purely speculative as the claimant might never open a restaurant in Norwich, England or the UK. The decision can be justified on the basis that, by his choice of name, the defend-ant attempted to cash in on the claimant's goodwill. Additionally, there is always the danger that, had the defendant's food not been of a high quality, the claimant's reputation, which it enjoyed in the UK, might have been harmed as a consequence. Dilution of goodwill is also a possible factor.

Maxim's v *Dye* was followed in the Calcutta High Court in *Calvin Klein Inc v International Apparel Syndicate*,[132] where it was held that it was not necessary to have trade in India to have a reputation there. In that case, the emphasis seemed to be on reputation rather than goodwill. But we have seen that reputation without goodwill is insufficient to support an action in passing off: *Anheuser Busch Inc v Budějovický Budvar* (Budweiser beer).[133] The distinction that can be made between *Maxim's* and *Anheuser Busch* is that, in the former, the claimant was established in the UK and persons living there might go to Maxim's in Paris on a weekend break, or whatever, attracted by its reputation.

It has been suggested that the claimant, wherever located, must be able to show at least a customer or customers in England. In *Panhard et Levassor SA v Panhard Levassor Motor Co Ltd*,[134] the French car manufacturer had goodwill in the UK even though it had no established place of business there. The goodwill was based on the fact that the claimant sold cars to customers in the UK either directly from Paris or through importers. There are other contrasting cases on the subject. In *Sheraton Corp of America v Sheraton Motels Ltd*,[135] the claimant was granted an interim injunction on the basis that, although it had no hotels in the UK, it took bookings for its American hotels from an office in England whereas, in *Alain Bernadin et Cie v Pavilion Properties Ltd*,[136] an injunction was refused to the claimant, which owned the Crazy Horse Saloon in Paris, to prevent the defendant using the name for its establishment in London. The claimant did not have any place of business in the UK nor did it take bookings there. The *Alain Bernadin* case was cited with approval in the *Anheuser Busch* case, but has been criticised. One distinction between the *Alain Bernadin* and *Panhard* cases is that the former was concerned with a local activity (eating, drinking and making merry) compared with the 'rather more durable enjoyment of a Panhard car'.[137] The authorities seemed in a confused state and irreconcilable.

Recent case law, albeit foreign, tends to support the approach taken in *Maxim's*. For example, in *WHIRLPOOL Trade Mark*,[138] the Supreme Court of India held that a trader did not need to show actual sales in India to establish goodwill there. In such a case, goodwill could result from advertising in magazines which were circulated in India. In *C & A Modes v C & A (Waterford) Ltd*,[139] the defendant began trading under the name and symbol 'C & A' in Ireland and was held to be guilty of passing off by the Supreme Court of Ireland. The claimant did not have any trade outlet in Ireland, although it did in Belfast in Northern Ireland. However, many of the customers at the Belfast store had travelled

129 *See*, for example, *Brestian v Try* [1958] RPC 161 where the claimant, who had hairdressing shops in London, Wembley and Brighton, succeeded in obtaining an injunction to prevent the defendant using the same name in Tunbridge Wells.

130 [1977] 1 WLR 1155.

131 Compare with *Anheuser Busch Inc v Budějovický Budvar* [1984] FSR 413, discussed *supra*.

132 [1995] FSR 515.

133 [1984] FSR 413.

134 (1901) 18 RPC 405.

135 [1964] RPC 202.

136 [1967] RPC 581.

137 *Jian Tools for Sales Inc v Roderick Manhattan Group Ltd* [1995] FSR 924.

138 [1997] FSR 905.

139 [1978] FSR 126.

from Ireland to shop there. The Supreme Court of Ireland held that goodwill does not necessarily stop at the frontier and the defendant's activities were calculated to cause confusion in the minds of existing or potential customers. Similarly, in *McDonald's Corp v McDonald's Corp Ltd and Vincent Chang*,[140] the Court of Appeal in Jamaica accepted that the famous worldwide chain of fast-food restaurants had a goodwill in Jamaica before it started trading there because of intensive advertising.

The correctness of *Alain Bernadin* must now be doubted. The international nature of many business operations shows that this case is no longer relevant. In many cases, the reputation of large multinational organisations precedes them as they expand their activities into other countries. Reputation in that sense must equate with goodwill because, if the reputation is harmed, the consequence is that, once established in those other countries, turnover there will also be harmed. Injuring reputation prospectively injures goodwill in future trade. That being so, *Anheuser Busch* must also be doubted.

Incidentally, there is no problem with finding passing off where the activity complained of occurs in another country, provided the defendant's misrepresentation in that other country is likely to injure the claimant's goodwill.[141] What matters is whether the claimant's goodwill has been injured and this requires consideration of a supplementary question when looking at the classic trinity of goodwill, misrepresentation and damage. That question is to ask whether the claimant's goodwill has extended to the territory where the defendant's activities have taken place. If the answer to this is 'No', a further question arises, being whether knowledge of the defendant's activities would reach a substantial number of persons in the territories to which the claimant's goodwill has extended.

There may be a distinction between a foreign business with an international reputation and clientele and a foreign business which attracts customers from the UK so that it is known in the UK but whose reputation does not bring in significant business from the UK.[142] In *Hotel Cipriani SrL v Cipriani (Grosvenor Street) Ltd*,[143] the claimant owned the famous and expensive Hotel Cipriani in Venice. In 2004, the first defendant opened a restaurant in London using the Cipriani name. The second defendant's name was Cipriani, and he was the sole director of the first defendant. He was related to the Cipriani family which opened the Venice hotel. The defendants also ran Harry's Bar in Venice which was established in 1931.

In finding passing off and rejecting an argument that the defendants also had concurrent goodwill in the Cipriani name, the Court of Appeal held that the claimant had goodwill in England as many of its customers came from there and a significant amount of business was the result of bookings made in England through travel agents, tour operators and individual telephone bookings. As Lloyd LJ said (at para 118):

> On that basis [the business derived from bookings placed in England] it seems to me clear that the international reputation of Hotel Cipriani, and the use of the mark Cipriani, was something that brought in business from England – it was an attractive force that brought in English custom – and accordingly the business had goodwill in England at the relevant time.

Although the defendants had goodwill in the name Harry's Bar in England because of a significant number of customers from England, that did not extend to the Cipriani name because of a lack of association. The defendants also had Cipriani restaurants in New York but there was insufficient evidence to show that these had goodwill in England even though they had a slight reputation in England.

Of course, now with the internet and websites from which goods and services may be ordered or booked from businesses established in other countries, this is bound to have some implications for determining the presence of goodwill in the UK. The *Cipriani* case was not a suitable one to explore foreign businesses acquiring goodwill in the UK through internet bookings (either through their own websites or shared websites).

140 [1997] FSR 760. It was held that both parties could trade under the name McDonald's. The defendant had been trading under that name in Jamaica since 1971, whereas the worldwide food chain had only recently commenced trading in Jamaica.

141 In which case, for jurisdictional purposes, the tort occurs in the country where the goodwill exists: *Mecklermedia Corp v DC Congress Gesellschaft mbH* [1997] FSR 627.

142 *Hotel Cipriani SrL v Cipriani (Grosvenor Street) Ltd* [2010] RPC 16, per Lloyd LJ at para 118.

143 [2010] RPC 16. The claimant also succeeded on the trade mark action (see Chapter 21).

The nature of the misrepresentation

Misrepresentation is an essential element in the tort of passing off. It may be that the misrepresentation goes to the origin of goods or it may be that, because of the manner in which the goods are marketed, some attribute is falsely associated with the goods by a significant sector of the public.[144] Misrepresentation may come about in numerous ways such as by written or oral statements or by implication or by similarity in appearance or presentation of goods or even from the presence of some object which acts as a signpost to the owner of the goodwill, such as 'swing tags' attached to luggage, similar to those used by the claimant.[145] To be actionable, however, the misrepresentation does not have to suggest that the defendant's business is that of the claimants and it is sufficient if the misrepresentation indicates an association between the businesses of the claimant and defendant.[146]

Misrepresentation is not a question of whether there is a risk of confusion because the defendant's name was similar to that of the claimant but whether the defendant's use of his own name in connection with his goods or business could be taken to be a representation that those goods were, or his business was, those of the claimant or had some connection with the claimant so giving rise to or a risk of harm to the claimant's goodwill which the claimant was entitled to protect.[147]

The misrepresentation or deception is not necessarily limited to an exact copy of a name, mark or 'get-up'. Similarity sufficient to result in confusion will do, an important factor being whether purchasers or consumers of the product or services have been or are likely to be misled. For trade marks, except where there is identity of the mark and the goods, the litmus test is whether the use of the second mark is likely to cause confusion on the part of the public, including a likelihood of association.[148] So too with passing off but set in the wider context of 'get-up'. In deciding whether the buying public (or the ultimate consumer) is likely to be misled or confused, it is not necessary to consider whether members of the public who are knowledgeable about the particular product or service are deceived and it may be sufficient if members of the public who have relatively little knowledge of the product or service are deceived or are likely to be deceived.

There must be a misrepresentation for passing off; a likelihood of confusion will not suffice per se,[149] though it is not easy to think of examples of confusion absent a misrepresentation which may be direct or indirect, deliberate or innocent. Misrepresentation can take many forms. For example, it may confuse as to the origin of goods or services or the nature of the defendant's goods or services.[150] It may be made in words or pictorially,[151] or be implied from behaviour. It could be that a trader fails to disabuse customers about their mistaken beliefs, which may have been encouraged by the trader. Using a statement which implies that a trader is an authorised distributor may amount to passing off when this is not, or no longer is, the truth. In Musical Fidelity Ltd v Vickers,[152] the claimant had undoubted goodwill in the name 'Musical Fidelity' for hi-fi equipment and numerous internet domain names. The defendant, who had at one time been an authorised distributor, registered 'www.musicalfidelity.co.uk' as his domain name and his advertisement on the website included the phrase 'Welcome to the website of one of Musical Fidelity's oldest retailers'. The Court of Appeal confirmed that this was passing off as it indicated a continuing connection with the claimant, especially because of the use of the possessive form of its name.

A number of factors will affect whether the misrepresentation is likely to confuse, such as whether the traders operate in the same field of activity, the distinctiveness of the claimant's get-up, how well-known and familiar the get-up is and the sales outlets for the traders' goods. In NAD Electronics Inc v NAD Computer Systems Ltd,[153] important factors in finding passing off (and trade mark infringement) were the facts that the goodwill

144 For example, by naming a chocolate bar 'Swiss Chalet' it was held that the defendant was guilty of passing off: *Chocosuisse Union des Fabricants Suisses de Chocolat* v *Cadbury Ltd* [1999] RPC 826.

145 *Premier Luggage and Bags Ltd* v *Premier Co (UK) Ltd* [2001] FSR 29. However, in the Court of Appeal at [2003] FSR 69, it was held that there was no passing off in relation to the swing tags.

146 *Sir Robert McAlpine Ltd* v *Alfred McAlpine plc* [2004] RPC 36.

147 *Premier Luggage and Bags Ltd* v *Premier Company (UK) Ltd* [2003] FSR 5.

148 Trade Marks Act 1994 s 10(2).

149 *Barnsley Brewery Co Ltd* v *RBNB* [1997] FSR 462.

150 For example, in *Law Society of England and Wales* v *Society of Lawyers* [1996] FSR 739, there was a risk that members of the public might believe that the defendant's members had recognised legal qualifications or even were solicitors.

151 For example, the use of another seabird (a puffin instead of a penguin) and similar coloured get-up in *United Biscuits (UK) Ltd* v *Asda Stores Ltd* [1997] RPC 513.

152 [2003] FSR 50.

153 [1997] FSR 380.

subsisted in 'NAD', a fancy name, that the goods were advertised in similar ways (the claimant sold hi-fi systems of high quality and the defendant sold computers) and both traders' goods were sold alongside each other in retail outlets such as Dixons.

In *HFC Bank plc v Midland Bank plc*,[154] the claimant objected to the use by the defendant of the name HSBC. It was confirmed that evidence of confusion alone does not constitute passing off. What is required is that the claimant shows that it has achieved brand name recognition. Up to the time that the defendant had started using HSBC, the claimant's name had a relatively low profile. Lloyd J quoted Lord Greene MR in *Marengo v Daily Sketch & Sunday Graphic Ltd*[155] where he said (at 2):

> No one is entitled to be protected against confusion as such. Confusion may result from the collision of two independent rights or liberties, and where that is the case neither party can complain . . . The protection to which a man is entitled is protection against passing off, which is quite a different thing from mere confusion.

In the present case Lloyd J said that, now that there was an actively promoted brand somewhat similar to the claimant's, it would be more difficult for the claimant to improve its own brand recognition. However, that was a reflection that it had an easy task until the time the defendant launched its new brand name and that the claimant would now have to try harder. It did not entitle it to a *cordon sanitaire*. Finally, Lloyd J thought this was a case of non-actionable confusion.

In *Dawnay Day & Co Ltd v Cantor Fitzgerald International*,[156] the defendant was a firm involved in financial services including broking which was totally unconnected with the claimant group of companies but which had acquired one of the group of companies, known as Dawnay Day Securities Ltd. Confirming that the use of the Dawnay Day name by the defendant would be passing off, Lloyd J said that it would be impossible not to conclude that the use by the defendant of the Dawnay Day name would be a plain misrepresentation.

The public is not expected to be particularly knowledgeable about the product concerned.[157] The reasonable man is no connoisseur of fine wines and exotic foods. In *J Bollinger v Costa Bravo Wine Co Ltd (No 2)*,[158] the claimant made the famous sparkling wine known as 'champagne' in the Champagne region of France. This drink has a very high reputation and is often bought for special occasions by people who do not purchase it regularly. The defendant imported into the UK a sparkling wine called 'Spanish Champagne' which was supposed to be like the claimant's product but made in Spain. The defendant claimed that, by adding the word 'Spanish', this clearly indicated that the wine was not made in France and, because champagne was such a well-known product, only a tiny portion of ignorant, ill-educated persons would be misled. The defendant further claimed that the word 'champagne' had become a generic description. An injunction was granted preventing the use of the word 'champagne' by the defendant. It was held in the High Court that a substantial number of persons, whose life and education had not taught them much about the nature and production of wine, might want to buy champagne from time to time and these people might be misled by the description of the defendant's sparkling wine as 'Spanish Champagne'. The description 'Spanish Champagne' was intended to attract to the defendant's product the goodwill connected with the reputation of champagne and amounted to dishonest trading. Danckwerts J said, 'it seems to me that close resemblance makes the counterfeit not less but more calculated to deceive . . .' 'Champagne' had not become a generic name because corresponding wines made elsewhere were not described using that word.

A misrepresentation that is ineffective because the public see through it is not actionable in passing off because one important and fundamental requirement is missing.[159] In the absence of confusion there can be no harm to goodwill and, therefore, no damage to the claimant. In *Tamworth Herald Co Ltd v Thomson Free Newspapers Ltd*,[160] the claimant's

154 [2000] FSR 176.

155 [1992] FSR 1.

156 [2000] RPC 669.

157 However, the degree of attention paid by a consumer depends on the nature of the goods or services. In some cases, purchases are considered more carefully and opportunities for confusion are reduced accordingly: *Teleworks Ltd v Telework Group plc* [2002] RPC 27.

158 [1961] 1 All ER 561.

159 See, for example, *Ciba-Geigy plc v Parke Davis & Co Ltd* [1994] FSR 8 where it was held that a reasonable doctor, reading the defendant's advertisement for its drug, which was equivalent to the claimant's drug and which used a picture of a green apple as used by the claimant, would not think the defendant's drug was associated with the claimant's drug, business or slow release formulation.

160 [1991] FSR 337.

newspaper had been published since 1868 as the *Tamworth Herald*, a weekly newspaper selling at 23 pence at the time of the action. The defendant bought the rights in a weekly free newspaper called the *Tamworth Trader* and intended to change its name to the *Tamworth Herald & Post*. Both newspapers were circulated in the same geographical area and the claimant commenced a *quia timet* action for passing off but was refused an injunction. It was held by Aldous J that it was improbable that the recipients of the defendant's paper would believe it was published by the claimant. An example of the defendant's new 'masthead' included a reference that the paper was formerly the *Tamworth Trader*. Potential advertisers would obtain the address or telephone number from the newspapers themselves or from the Yellow Pages and would in neither case be under a misapprehension as to whom they were dealing with.[161] The possibility of confusion and subsequent damage to the claimant's goodwill was, therefore, remote.[162]

Giving a false impression that a celebrity is endorsing a product is likely to amount to passing off. In *Irvine* v *Talksport Ltd*,[163] the defendant ran the radio station 'Talk Radio'. It mounted a promotional campaign which included photographs of Eddie Irvine, the Formula One Grand Prix racing driver. The photograph had been manipulated. It originally showed Mr Irvine speaking on a mobile phone but was changed so he held a portable radio on which the words 'Talk Radio' were clearly visible. It was held that this gave the impression that he endorsed the radio station and this false representation was passing off. The Court of Appeal described as somewhat surreal the photograph, as altered, showing Mr Irvine wearing his Ferrari racing gear amid the hubbub of a Grand Prix, listening intently to Talk Radio. Product endorsement is very common and celebrities expect to be paid large sums of money for such activities.[164]

The use of a disclaimer will not necessarily take the sting out of a misrepresentation. For example, in *Westwood* v *Knights*,[165] the claimant was Dame Vivienne Westwood OBE, the famous fashion designer. The defendant sold over the internet fashion clothing and accessories using some of the claimant's names and marks. One example of the defendant's goods was a red and white gingham shoulder bag. An advertisement for the defendant's bag on eBay carried the statement 'I am not claiming it is made by Vivienne Westwood'. This was not sufficient to overcome the obvious inference of passing off by the use of the claimant's names and marks, especially as the statement ended with 'but it has her famous design', being the claimant's Too Fast To Live Too Young To Die device. There was evidence that some persons who bought these bags were annoyed to discover they were not genuine Vivienne Westwood bags. HH Judge Birss QC said (at para 226):

> Mr Knight's approach to trading involves him using versions of many of the claimant's marks. Some are identical and some are somewhat different from the original but not greatly so. These combinations all serve together to reinforce the message that the goods are connected with the claimant. In my judgment Mr Knight's business as a whole amounts to an exercise in passing off his own goods as and for those of the claimant . . .

Parodies

In terms of passing off a parody is acceptable provided that it is clear that it is a parody and not associated with the claimant. There is no misrepresentation if the source is made absolutely clear.[166] However, great care must be taken because, as mentioned above, the public is not generally expected to be particularly knowledgeable. On the same basis, the general public is not taken to be particularly careful and scrutinise the goods or services in question to determine their true origin.

Alan Clark, the famous Member of Parliament, had published his 'Diaries', which proved somewhat controversial, though very successful. The *London Evening Standard*

161 Whether two business concerns having similar names can be easily distinguished in the Yellow Pages is a nice objective test for passing off.

162 That the word 'Herald' is commonly used in the newspaper industry was a factor. The claimant was also concerned about the possibility of confusion resulting from telephone canvassing but this would not happen if the canvassers followed their instructions carefully and it was wrong to assume that they would not do so.

163 [2003] FSR 35.

164 The Court of Appeal increased the award of damages from £2,000 to £25,000.

165 [2011] EWPCC 8.

166 Even though there is no passing off, the aggrieved party may have remedies under copyright law and the law of defamation.

published a weekly spoof of Alan Clark's diaries based on what a journalist imagined Alan Clark would record in his diary. The newspaper column was headed 'Alan Clark's Secret Political Diaries' and included a photograph of Alan Clark. Below was a note identifying the journalist as the author and what the basis for the column was. In *Alan Kenneth McKenzie Clark* v *Associated Newspapers Ltd*,[167] the proprietor of the *Evening Standard* was held liable for passing off and for false attribution of authorship under copyright law. The court held that, to be actionable as passing off, the deception had to be more than momentary and inconsequential (as it might have been had the true fact of authorship been more prominent).

167 [1998] RPC 261.

In cases where there are mixed and conflicting messages, the dominant message matters and it is not sufficient to claim that a careful sensible reader would read the 'disclaimer'. The work had to be looked at as a whole to decide whether a substantial number of readers would be misled into thinking that the column was written by Alan Clark. Nor was it a defence to claim that readers of the column would not be misled had they been more careful. The court did not prevent the continuing publication of the column but insisted that, should it continue, the identity of the true author must be made sufficiently clear.

As will be seen later, for passing off there must be a common field of activity (although it is arguable that this rule has been relaxed of late). There was a common field of activity here as Alan Clark had himself written diaries. Had he not, the passing off action might not have succeeded, although this would leave the false attribution of copyright claim intact.

Acquiescence

A case with similar facts to the *J Bollinger* (Spanish Champagne) case demonstrates that acquiescence in an activity that could be passing off will defeat the claimant's claim. In *Vine Products Ltd* v *MacKenzie & Co Ltd*,[168] the Spanish producers of sherry tried to prevent the use of that word as in British Sherry, South African Sherry, Cyprus Sherry, etc. The genuine drink derives it name from the Jerez region in Spain and is a high-quality product. However, similar fortified wines have been produced in other countries, such as Australia, South Africa and Cyprus, and sold under names including the word 'sherry': for example, 'British Sherry' and 'Cyprus Sherry'. There was no evidence of confusion amongst the wine-drinking public and these other wines had been so described for a considerable period of time. It was held that the word 'Sherry', standing alone, meant a wine from Jerez and others would be prevented from using the word on its own. However, the use of other descriptions such as 'British Sherry' would not be restrained because of acquiescence on the part of the claimant. In practice, each type of sherry from different countries had achieved, over a long period of time, its own individual and distinct reputation. For example, it could be said that 'Cyprus Sherry' is a very pleasant and inexpensive form of the wine whilst the Spanish variant retains its high reputation as the wine of the highest quality. It is self-evident that the owner of an unregistered trade mark or other name or mark or get-up should not delay in taking action against any person copying that mark, name or get-up.

168 [1969] RPC 1.

Subsequent case law confirms the importance of acquiescence as a way of defeating a claim in passing off. In *Taylor's Fashions Ltd* v *Liverpool Victoria Trustees Co Ltd*,[169] Oliver J said that the approach to be entertained by the court is:

169 [1982] QB 133.

> . . . ascertaining whether, in particular individual circumstances, it would be unconscionable for a party to be permitted to deny that which, knowingly or unknowingly, he has allowed or encouraged another to assume to his detriment.[170]

170 See also *Habib Bank Ltd* v *Habib Bank AG Zurich* [1982] RPC 1; *International Business Machines Corp* v *Phoenix International (Computers) Ltd* [1994] RPC 251.

If the claimant has been given prior warning of the defendant's planned activities and fails to object, he is less likely to be granted an injunction by the court. In *Dalgety Spillers*

Foods Ltd v Food Brokers Ltd,[171] the defendant wrote to the claimant (which marketed 'Pot Noodles') indicating an intention to sell a similar product under the name 'Cup Noodles', enclosing an example of the container. When the claimant, some time later, complained and requested an injunction it was refused on the balance of convenience. An important factor was that the claimant could give no convincing explanation for its inactivity following the defendant's letter putting it on notice and, in the meantime, the defendant had spent time, trouble and expense in launching its 'Cup Noodles' product.

Inverse passing off

It has been said that passing off can be one of two types:

1 classical passing off, where B represents his goods as being those of A
2 extended passing off, where A uses a false description for his goods to impute some quality to his goods – for example, as in the Spanish Champagne case or the Advocaat case.[172]

However, passing off is not necessarily limited to these two forms and the common law should develop in such a way to reflect the higher standards of consumer protection now available. Indeed, in the Advocaat case, Lord Diplock said that passing off ought to proceed upon a parallel rather than diverging course to the trend in legislation.[173] Inverse passing off (if it exists as a separate species) occurs where the defendant falsely claims that the claimant's goods or services are actually made by, or provided by, the defendant. For example, in *Bristol Conservatories Ltd v Conservatories Custom Built Ltd*,[174] the defendant's sales representatives showed potential customers photographs of conservatories as a sample of the defendant's workmanship. The photographs were, in fact, of the claimant's conservatories. The Court of Appeal had no doubt that this constituted passing off although refusing to describe it as inverse (or reverse) passing off.[175] Nevertheless, the boundaries of passing off are not fixed and false claims as to patents or testimonials may fall within its ambit.[176]

Inverse passing off may also be committed by implicitly encouraging others to think that one is associated or responsible for material created and belonging to another. For example, in *John Robert Powers School Inc v Denyse Bernadette Tessensohn*,[177] the defendant, in her manner of leaving the claimant's study notes on shelves easily accessible to students and customers, was holding out that they were her notes and this misrepresentation amounted to inverse passing off.

In *Matthew Gloag & Sons Ltd v Welsh Distillers Ltd*,[178] the defendant obtained genuine Scotch whisky and blended it with herbs which it sold in bottles labelled 'Welsh Whisky'. This case was different to the *Bristol Conservatories* case in which the defendant was claiming that the claimant's buildings were actually those of the defendant. In the present case, the defendant was not claiming its product was that of the claimant; conversely, the defendant, by labelling it as Welsh whisky, was denying that it was Scotch whisky. The claimant alleged, *inter alia*, reverse passing off. Although the defendant's strike out application failed, as the judge did not think the allegation was bound to fail, he did say (at 725):

> The borderline between reverse passing off of the Bristol Conservatories variety and cases falling outside the tort is difficult to formulate.

Misrepresentation by imputing authorisation

Misrepresentation is not limited to the use of a name or a similar get-up and it can even extend to an act that implies that it is authorised or consented to by another person. Placing advertising leaflets inside magazines and newspapers is a fairly common activity nowadays and this may be done after the magazines and papers have been delivered to the newsagents with neither the permission nor the authority of the proprietors of the

171 [1994] FSR 504.

172 These two types of passing off are not two separate torts, they are simply convenient labels to describe the two most obvious situations: see Patten LJ in *Diageo North America Inc v Intercontinental Brands (ICB) Ltd* [2011] RPC 2 at para 23.

173 *Erven Warnink Besloten Vennootschap v J Townend & Sons (Hull) Ltd* [1979] AC 731 at 743.

174 [1989] RPC 455.

175 For a discussion of inverse passing off, *see* Carty, H. 'Inverse passing off: a suitable addition to passing off?' [1993] 10 EIPR 370.

176 For example, *Copydex Ltd v Noso Products Ltd* (1952) 69 RPC 38 ('as shown on television'); *Lawrie v Baker* (1885) 2 RPC 213 where the defendant sold, as patented, articles that were not patented but the claimant held a patent such that the consumers would think that the defendant was selling articles made to that patent.

177 [1995] FSR 947, CA, Singapore.

178 [1998] FSR 718.

magazines and newspapers. An independent advertising company may approach news-agents and ask them to insert advertising leaflets and one complication is that, at this time, the title to the magazines and newspapers will have passed to the newsagent. Although such an activity by itself will not amount to passing off, it will do so if sufficient persons are likely to believe that the leaflets were inserted with the authority of the publishers of the magazines and newspapers. So it was held in the Court of Appeal in *Associated Newspapers (Holdings) plc* v *Insert Media Ltd*.[179] The mere fact that the advertisements had been inserted in the claimant's newspapers without its permission did not establish the existence of a misrepresentation and it was necessary to consider whether a substantial number of people would think that the insertion had been authorised by the proprietor of the newspaper. It had been shown that the essence of the plan to insert the advertising was the defendant's hope that it would be associated with the newspaper concerned, the *Daily Mail*, to the effect that the advertising would appear to have the newspaper's seal of approval. The claimant might thus suffer damage to its reputation and goodwill. The Court of Appeal rejected a suggestion that a disclaimer should be printed on the inserts on the grounds that it would not be effective.

This case represents a new extension to the law of passing off because, in the High Court, it was doubted that such an activity could amount to passing off.[180] However, it does illustrate the potential width of passing off and the way that it is capable of being developed to meet new mischiefs. Nevertheless, the case is unusual on its facts and the normal way of imputing authority will involve the use of a name or mark. For example, a person might falsely claim to be a member of a professional body and the body will be able to take action to have the claim withdrawn and not repeated.

Impliedly representing that the claimant's helmets would comply with safety regulations when fitted with the defendant's lens was said to be on the outer limits of passing off in *Hodge Clemco Ltd* v *Airblast Ltd*.[181] Helmets for use with sand-blasting had to comply with the regulations and be approved by the Health and Safety Executive. It was unlawful to use helmets which did not comply. At the time of the action, the defendant was seeking the approval of its lens and it looked like such approval would be forthcoming soon but, until it was granted, using the claimant's helmets fitted with the defendant's lenses was unlawful. The claimant claimed that the defendant, by representing that its lenses were suitable for the claimant's helmets, was misrepresenting that the helmets when fitted with the lenses would comply with the regulations. Although it was arguable that advertising the lenses as suitable for the claimant's helmets suggested that customers could lawfully use them, an injunction was refused as the balance of convenience lay in the defendant's favour, especially as it was likely to obtain approval as soon as its lenses had successfully completed the required tests.

Intention

The great majority of passing off cases involve a deliberate and calculated attempt to take advantage of the goodwill owned by another trader and associated with goods manufactured or sold by him or services supplied by him. However, a fraudulent motive is not necessary to a passing off action and, indeed, innocence is no defence,[182] the main thrust of the law of passing off being the protection of goodwill. In *Taittinger SA* v *Allbev Ltd*[183] Peter Gibson LJ said:

> Lord Diplock's phrase 'calculated to injure', as he himself made plain, does not import a test of actual intention to injure: it is sufficient that this should be the reasonably foreseeable consequence of the misrepresentation.

In contrast, in some cases, a person may make a deliberate misrepresentation that is intended to boost the reputation and sales of his product or services but against which

179 [1991] 3 All ER 535.

180 *Mail Newspapers plc* v *Insert Media Ltd* [1987] RPC 521.

181 [1995] FSR 806.

182 See *Baume & Co Ltd* v *AH Moore Ltd* [1958] RPC 226. However, motive may influence the decision whether to grant an interim injunction: *see Law Society of England and Wales* v *Griffiths* [1995] RPC 16 where there was clear evidence that the defendant deliberately selected a similar telephone number to that of the claimant in order to divert business from the claimant.

183 [1993] FSR 641 at 667.

there is no legal remedy under the law of passing off.[184] Some examples of this will be seen later in the section on character merchandising. A reading of the cases does, however, give the impression that intention may be an influential factor in the court's decision-making process;[185] although a deliberate and fraudulent act of copying someone else's get-up will not amount to passing off if there is little danger of the public being deceived, as in *Whitworth Foods Ltd* v *Hunni Foods (International) Ltd*, discussed above, where the defendant had placed an order with the company making containers for the claimant for containers that were similar in shape and appearance.

In *Harrods Ltd* v *Harrodian School Ltd*,[186] one interpretation of the defendant's evidence as to why he chose that name as the name of his school (occupying the building that had formerly been a club for members of Harrods and known as the Harrodian Club) was that he had deliberately chosen the name because he thought it would be an advantage to him to indicate a connection with Harrods. However, that interpretation was rejected in the Court of Appeal in favour of one based on a selection of the name simply because the school occupied a magnificent site which had formerly been occupied by the Harrodian Club. As regards intention, Millett LJ said (at 706):

> Deception is the gist of the tort of passing off, but it is not necessary for a plaintiff to establish that the defendant consciously intended to deceive the public if that is the probable result of his conduct. Nevertheless, the question why the defendant chose to adopt a particular name or get up is always highly relevant.

One is left to wonder why motive is 'highly relevant' if it is accepted that the absence of a deliberate intention to deceive customers does not prevent the defendant's activities constituting a misrepresentation for the purposes of passing off. The test surely is whether, in fact, customers are deceived: a purely objective test.

Common fields of activity

In most cases, the rights associated with registered trade marks are restricted in terms of the classes of goods and services against which the marks are registered. Therefore, if Trader A has a trade mark consisting of a representation of a Harp registered for Class 2 goods (paints, varnishes, lacquers, etc.) and Trader B copies this mark but only uses it in respect of wines (falling within Class 33), Trader B does not infringe Trader A's trade mark unless it is a mark of some repute and such use would take unfair advantage of or be detrimental to Trader A's mark.[187] Apart from this latter exception, trade mark law, by reference to identical or similar goods or services, requires a 'common field of activity' between the claimant and defendant.

Passing off is limited in a similar way in that there must be a common field of activity between the claimant and the defendant. There must be some common ground; otherwise there can be no trespass to this form of intellectual property. The justification for this is that, if there is no common field of activity, there can be no damage to the claimant's goodwill because the public will not make a connection between the traders and their different fields of activity. For example, if Trader A uses an unregistered trade name, 'Spright', for its margarine and, later, Trader B uses the same name for its bicycles, there will be little danger of damage to Trader A's goodwill (irrespective of the quality of the bicycles) because the public are not likely to think that the bicycles are made by or with the licence of Trader A. An electric shaver called a 'Rolls Razor' would not normally be confused with the makers of 'Rolls-Royce' motor cars; at best it indicates that the razor is claimed, rightly or wrongly, to be of high quality.

A simple example of the common field of activity doctrine was the case of *Granada Group Ltd* v *Ford Motor Company Ltd*,[188] the outcome of which was that the Granada television group, famous for making the television serial *Coronation Street*, could not prevent the Ford

184 See, for example, *McCullogh* v *Lewis A May Ltd* (1948) 65 RPC 58.

185 See, for example, *Harrods Ltd* v *R Harrod Ltd* (1924) 41 RPC 74.

186 [1996] RPC 697.

187 This is an infringement under the Trade Marks Act 1994 s 10(3) where the goods or services are non-similar.

188 [1973] RPC 49. *See* also *Harrods Ltd* v *Harrodian School Ltd* [1996] RPC 697.

189 The name 'Granada' could not have been registered in Part A of the register of trade marks, being a relatively well-known geographical name: Trade Marks Act 1938 s 9. It was unlikely that it would have been accepted for Part B registration.

Motor Company naming one of its cars the 'Ford Granada'. There was no danger of confusion because of the different fields of activity (television and motor cars) and, consequently, there was little possibility of the claimant's goodwill being harmed.[189] This decision accords with common sense as it is highly unlikely that ordinary members of the public, even those knowing nothing about cars, would think that the car had anything whatsoever to do with the television company. The test of common field of activity is concerned with making an objective determination of the likelihood of damage to goodwill. This can only occur if there is, at least, a possibility of confusion. Yet, the test can be criticised because the diversification of business concerns and their fields of activity make the application of the test imperfect. Many members of the public realise that some large companies have interests that are wide and disparate in nature. With a registered trade mark that has a reputation in the UK, use in respect of non-similar goods or services may infringe.[190] However, where such trade mark infringement cannot be made out, the common field of activity rule seems coarse and arbitrary in terms of well-known names, marks and get-ups. To make the issue more difficult is the general desire amongst judges not to restrict competition unduly.

190 Trade Marks Act 1994 s 10(3). Under the previous Act, defensive registration was possible.

Where fields of activity are converging, it is easier to accept that confusion is likely. For example, developments in computer technology have resulted in most modern personal computers having a compact disk drive capable of reading CD-ROMs and stereo speakers. They can also play audio compact discs. Therefore, the fields of audio entertainment and computers are converging. So it was held in *NAD Electronics Inc* v *NAD Computers Systems Ltd*.[191]

191 [1997] FSR 380.

Showing a determined flexibility, the law of passing off has developed to embrace a situation where a name or mark is very well known, and in such cases the boundaries of the activities may be moved, dramatically enlarging the field of play. In *Lego Systems A/S v Lego M Lemelstrich Ltd*,[192] the very well-known Lego company, that makes coloured plastic construction bricks for children, was granted an injunction preventing the use of the name Lego by the defendant, which was planning to use it for its plastic irrigation and garden equipment. The defendant had used the name Lego for its equipment in various other countries such as Israel, but the claimant's children's bricks had become so well known, as had the name Lego in association with these bricks, that the House of Lords was of the opinion that confusion was extremely likely. In this case, the common field of activity was, effectively, coloured plastic.[193] If the claimant's business had not been so successful and on such a grand scale in the UK, the claimant's field of activity might have been restricted to coloured children's plastic construction bricks, a much narrower field. Note that the quality of the defendant's products was not an issue: once the danger of confusion is present, it is assumed that there is a possibility that the claimant's reputation will be harmed. Such harm can go beyond the quality of the products concerned, and in the Lego case harm could be the result of the public thinking that the company was no longer concentrating on children's construction kits and might not continue to make the kits and additional parts for them so that it might not be feasible for a child to build up a large collection of Lego bricks and materials over a long period of time. In *Teleworks Ltd v Telework Group plc*,[194] it was said that, if the strength of goodwill is such as to induce a belief that there was a connection between the defendant and the claimant, that goodwill will be protected in fields that claimant had not yet entered and may not have had the slightest intention of entering in the future.

192 [1983] FSR 155, yet another case involving a survey of the public used in support of the claimant's argument that the public would be deceived.

193 See also *Annabel's (Berkeley Square)* v *Schock* [1972] RPC 838, where it was held that there was a possibility of confusion between a nightclub and an escort agency as both could be considered to be night-time activities.

194 [2002] RPC 27.

Although *Lego* and *Teleworks* can be said to show that the requirement for a common field of activity is not as rigidly applied as before, it was still relevant in terms of whether there existed a likelihood of confusion.[195] If the claimant and defendant are engaged in the same field of activity, then confusion is all the more likely. If they operate in completely different fields, there is far less likelihood of confusion though the possibility is not entirely extinguished. Given the breathtaking diversification of many large corporations, especially from the Far East, some relaxation of the rule is appropriate.

195 *Nice and Safe Attitude Ltd* v *Piers Flook* [1997] FSR 14.

The boundaries of the claimant's field of activity appear to be directly proportional to the magnitude of his goodwill: the greater the goodwill, the greater the net of passing off will be cast and the more likely it is that the defendant will be found to have committed passing off. However, the Lego approach was distinguished in *Fortnum & Mason plc* v *Fortnam Ltd*,[196] where the defendant imported low-price goods from the Far East, mainly for export to the rest of Europe, and operated under the name Fortnam Ltd but did not apply the name to the goods. The claimant had a well-known and high-class store in Piccadilly and sued in passing off. Although the claimant was primarily known for its groceries, food and wine of high quality, it also sold fashion clothing, toys and various other articles. The defendant accepted that the claimant had an outstanding reputation associated with the name Fortnum and Mason, often abbreviated to Fortnums. However, in refusing the interim injunction sought, Harman J considered that the defendant was not guilty of passing off. It was extremely unlikely that anyone would buy the defendant's goods thinking that they were the goods of the claimant. Relevant factors were the quality of the goods and the nature of the trade. Although there was some overlap in the goods the parties sold, the defendant's were mostly cheap and plastic and not likely to be associated with the claimant's business. Furthermore, the defendant mainly exported his goods rather than selling them in the UK. Harman J distinguished the *Lego* case, which he suggested was strongly influenced by the fact that both the claimant's goods and the defendant's goods were made from the same raw material, being plastic. The ordinary person might think that the claimant had developed a further branch of its business. Thus, whilst it might be reasonable to think that Lego had diversified in such a way, it would be unreasonable to think that Fortnum and Mason had suddenly decided to sell 'cheap and nasty' goods.

196 [1994] FSR 438.

Character merchandising

A fictitious or fantastic character might be devised for a television series, a book, a film or a computer game: for example, Harry Potter, Lara Croft, the Teletubbies, Kojak, the Wombles, Thunderbirds, the Simpsons, Teenage Mutant Hero Ninja Turtles, etc. The person who devised the character or the person commissioning the design will want to maximise the financial return on the investment involved. One way of doing this is to license others to sell articles to which a representation of, or the name of, the character is applied. Examples are very common: Action Man watches, Bob the Builder figures and T-shirts, Pink Panther mugs, Postman Pat toys, etc. Using fictitious characters in order to sell ordinary items is known as character merchandising and is very popular, particularly with respect to children's toys, games and stationery. It is big business. The normal way it is done is for the merchandising organisation to obtain a licence from the creator of the character permitting the application of a representation of the character to the articles. In a few cases, the creator of the character or the owner of the rights in the character will retail the articles direct. Character merchandising is not limited to fictitious characters. Many famous sportsmen and women and television personalities allow their name to be used for promotional purposes. In this case, unauthorised appropriation of their name or nickname may not be remediable either under the law of passing off or under copyright law but it may be actionable as being defamatory.[197]

Character merchandising is not a new phenomenon. Walt Disney characters in particular have been used in this way for a long time. However, when this operation is related to intellectual property rights subsisting in such characters, some major gaps appear. Copyright can give a fair degree of protection: for example, where a representation of the character infringes the copyright in a drawing of that character. For example, if a

197 See *McCullogh* v *Lewis A May* (1948) 65 RPC 58; *Tolley* v *JS Fry & Sons Ltd* [1931] AC 333.

company wishes to sell a mug to which a picture of Mickey Mouse has been applied by transfer printing, this will infringe the copyright in the original drawings of Mickey Mouse. If a photograph is made from a Mickey Mouse cartoon or film, whether to be reproduced and sold as photographs or used as a medium from which to prepare a representation for transfer printing, the copyright in the film will be infringed. If a doll or three-dimensional figure is made, then the copyright in the drawings will be infringed, as it was in the case of Popeye dolls which were held to infringe the cartoon drawings of the Popeye character in *King Features Syndicate Inc v O and M Kleeman Ltd*.[198] But, difficulties arise where only the name of the character is used. We have seen in Chapter 3 that copyright will not be afforded to a title for a film or a book and that it was also denied to the word 'Exxon'.[199] Neither does copyright protect the name of a fictitious character. This can be seen as the working of the *de minimis* principle and a throwback to the judgment of Davey J in *Hollinrake v Truswell*[200] to the effect that a literary work should offer information, instruction or pleasure in the form of literary enjoyment.

All that is left to protect a name is the law of passing off, or, in some cases, trade mark law. With respect to the latter, until the Trade Marks Act 1994 came into force, the question hinged simply on whether the merchandiser had applied the name to the same or similar goods. However, it was not possible to use trade mark law to promote character merchandising because the Trade Marks Act 1938 s 28(6) required the Registrar to refuse an application for registration of a registered user if it appeared to him that this would tend to facilitate trafficking in the mark. The House of Lords confirmed that trade marks law was not to be used to facilitate character merchandising in confirming the Registrar's refusal to register the 'Holly Hobbie' device, including a drawing of a young girl, as a trade mark.[201] This mark had been very successfully exploited in the USA but the registered user provisions in the UK were a considerable hurdle. One way over this hurdle was to show that the proprietor of the mark was able to maintain strict quality control over the articles to which the mark was applied, so demonstrating a sufficient connection in the course of trade. However, in the *Holly Hobbie Trade Mark* case, the applicant was unable to show this, partly because of the enormous scale of the planned commercial activities. Thankfully the registered user provisions and the bar over trafficking in trade marks has been swept aside to be replaced by licensing provisions which are much more suited to modern commercial practices.

Passing off may not be very effective in the context of character merchandising because of the requirement of a common field of activity and without this there can be no harm to the owner of the name of the character. For example, if someone buys a 'Garfield' telephone, that person would not be likely to complain to the makers of the Garfield cartoons and comic strips if the telephone turns out to be faulty.[202] The general public probably have a much better understanding of character merchandising than the judges have, in the past, given them credit for.

In the South African case of *Lorimar Productions Inc v Sterling Clothing Manufacturers (Pty) Ltd*[203] the Supreme Court considered that character merchandising was not particularly well known and, in the absence of evidence to the contrary, it could not be assumed that the man in the street would have any knowledge of it. The claimant owned the rights in the television series *Dallas* and failed to show an association in the minds of the public between the goodwill in the series and clothing or restaurants owned by the defendant which used names, locations and titles from the series.

The case of *Tavener Rutledge Ltd v Trexapalm Ltd*,[204] involving the television detective character 'Kojak', demonstrates some of the deficiencies of the law as regards character merchandising. Kojak, played by Telly Savalas, was often seen in the series sucking a spherical lolly. The claimant made similar shaped lollies and used the word 'Kojakpops' as a brand name for these lollies and quickly built up a substantial trade in respect of them. The claimant had not obtained the permission of the makers of the *Kojak* television

198 [1941] AC 417. But now this may be subject to a defence under the Copyright, Designs and Patents Act 1988 s 51.

199 *Exxon Corporation v Exxon Insurance Consultants International Ltd* [1981] 3 All ER 241.

200 [1894] 3 Ch 420.

201 *Holly Hobbie Trade Mark* [1984] FSR 199. This limitation does not apply under the Trade Marks Act 1994.

202 For a discussion on trafficking in marks where this point is made, *see* Pearson, H.E. and Millar, C.G. (1990) *Commercial Exploitation of Intellectual Property*, Blackstone Press, pp 216–17

203 [1982] RPC 395.

204 [1977] RPC 275.

series to use this name or to make similar shaped lollies. Some time later, the defendant started making similar lollies called 'Kojak lollies' and claimed to have a licence agreement with the owners of the television series allowing it to do this. The claimant commenced an action for passing off[205] and applied for an interim injunction. The defendant claimed that there was a sufficient connection in the course of trade between the lollies and the owners of the Kojak name because there were provisions for quality control contained in the licence agreement between the defendant and the owner of the name, and because of this quality control arrangement there was a common field of activity. Nevertheless, the injunction was granted to restrain the defendant passing off its lollies as being those of the claimant. The claimant had built up a considerable reputation in its lollies and the introduction of a similar lolly would cause confusion. Walton J considered that the defendant's lollies were not as good value as the claimant's and, as a consequence, the claimant's reputation would be seriously harmed. The licence agreement argument failed on the basis that there was no actual or potential field of activity between the owners of the television series and the claimant's business.[206] The point had not been reached where the fact of quality control was so well known that the public would rely on the existence of the licence as a guarantee of the defendant's product. Indeed, the public, in general, were not to be taken as having any particular knowledge of character merchandising. Finally, Walton J confirmed that there is no property in a name or a word, *per se*.

A common field of activity is the key to an action in passing off and no more so than where character merchandising is involved. It is important for the parties to a licence agreement to construct a connection in the course of trade between the owner of the name, the licensor, and the goods or services to which the name is to be applied. One way to do this has been hinted at above and that is to establish a system of quality control so that the owner of the name has a part to play in the practical aspects of the marketing exercise. In this way, the reputation of the name's owner will be extended into the other fields of activity defined by the merchandising project. This approach was successful in Australia, where a licence agreement for the making of soft toys of the Muppet characters contained quality control provisions,[207] but has yet to find favour in the UK. It is submitted that the exercise of quality control must be known about by the public and that appropriate advertising, marketing and labelling of the goods can do much to spread the word, thus extending the fields of activity.

Even if the field of activity can be widened by careful licensing and advertising, there will still be cases where this will not be sufficient to provide a remedy, bearing in mind that the prospect of harm to goodwill is a fundamental requirement. If there is no obvious link, regardless of any character licences, then there is no remedy under the law of passing off although there may be copyright issues, particularly if a drawing of the character is used. *Wombles Ltd* v *Wombles Skips Ltd*[208] shows that a wide disparity in fields of activity is fatal to a claim in passing off. The Wombles are fictitious animals from a television series and are noted for cleaning up litter and putting it to good use. The claimant company owned the copyright in the books and drawings of the Wombles. Its main business was granting licences in respect of the characters; for example, it granted one such licence for wastepaper baskets for children. The defendant formed a company to lease builders' skips, containers used typically for building rubble. After considerable thought, and remembering the Wombles' reputation for clean habits, he decided to call his company Wombles Skips Ltd and registered the company name accordingly. The claimant argued that the use of the name would lead some persons to conclude that the defendant's business was connected with the claimant and that there was a common field of activity because one of the licences was for wastepaper baskets. It was held that there was no common field of activity and this was an essential ingredient in a passing off action. Without a common field of activity there is no danger of confusion and, in this case, the similarity between the making and selling of waste-paper baskets and hiring out builders'

205 There was also a trade mark issue because the claimant had applied for a trade mark but, because the passing off action succeeded, it did not require consideration.

206 *See* also *Nice and Safe Attitude Ltd* v *Piers Flook* [1997] FSR 14, where the claimant, which used a logo similar to that used by the US National Aeronautics and Space Administration (NASA), succeeded in preventing a rival organisation, having a licence from NASA, using the logo.

207 *Children's Television Workshop Inc* v *Woolworths (New South Wales) Pty Ltd* [1981] RPC 187.

208 [1977] RPC 99. This case may be difficult to reconcile with the *Lego* case. However, neither the *Wombles* case nor the *Kojak* case was mentioned in Falconer J's judgment.

skips was not strong enough. The plain fact of the matter was that it was highly improbable that ordinary members of the public would think that the skips were associated with the Wombles in any way, just as a link between Granada Television and Ford Granada cars is quite absurd. Such an association might be made, however, in the case of wastepaper baskets for children and Wombles toys and dolls.

Full legal protection of character merchandising by the law of passing off has yet to find favour in the UK courts, although there are now signs that the position is changing. There is a contradiction in the way the law has tended to dislike this form of exploitation and the way in which it has given full protection to other forms of intellectual property rights. The owner of the character has made an investment of time and money in creating and developing the character. In many cases, the character is the result of substantial flair and imagination which should be no less deserving of protection than, say, literary and artistic works. Whilst it is clear that the law gives some protection – for example, copyright subsisting in drawings of characters or in written thumbnail sketches of characters[209] and other descriptive material – there are some gaps, and it is with respect to names that the law seems to be least effective. Trade mark law will only give a remedy in respect of use of a registered mark in respect of non-similar goods or services if the mark is one having a reputation in the UK.[210]

Consider the following possibilities concerning *Coronation Street* characters. What if the name 'Rover's Return' is used for a public house in the Salford area? What if a tobacco company starts marketing 'Mike Baldwin cigars' or, for those with longer memories, a trader starts selling 'Ena Sharples hairnets'? There seems to be little that the makers of the television series can do because of a lack of a common field of activity. But, there is a possibility that some portion of the public will take the use of names to indicate that the products have some seal of approval from the television company and have achieved certain standards. This might allow the traders concerned to overcharge for sub-standard goods. In attempting to cut back the degree of protection offered to the owners of ficti-tious characters and the like (and indeed, their licensees and franchisees), the courts may indirectly be encouraging unfair and undesirable trading practices whereby unscrupulous traders still manage to cash-in on someone else's reputation in a way which transcends the artificiality of compartmentalised fields of activity.

There have been signs of a change of heart. The case of *Mirage Studios v Counter-Feat Clothing Co Ltd*[211] is a good example, Lord Browne-Wilkinson VC seeming to prefer the way in which Australian passing off law has developed compared to UK law. The facts of the case were that the claimant created the Teenage Mutant Hero Ninja Turtle characters and made and marketed cartoons, films and videos containing these characters. Part of the claimant's business involved licensing the reproduction of the characters on goods sold by licensees, that is, character merchandising. It was almost inevitable, in view of the success of the characters, that someone else would wish to take an unfair advantage of the immense goodwill built up by the claimant. The defendant, without the claimant's permission, made drawings of humanoid turtle characters that were similar in appearance to the claimant's characters. They were not exact reproductions. The defendant then began to licence these drawings to garment manufacturers for the purpose of applying them to T-shirts and the like. The defendant claimed that there were no intellectual property rights either in the name or the idea of the 'Turtles'. The Vice-Chancellor granted an interim injunction to the claimant on the basis of an arguable case in copyright and for passing off. He found passing off to have occurred by applying Lord Diplock's test in the *Erven Warnink* (Advocaat) case.[212] The misrepresentation made by the defendant was that a substantial number of the buying public would believe that the reproduction of the figures was the result of a licence between the owner of the rights in the original drawings of the turtles. The result of the defendant's action would be that, because the public associated goods bearing the defendant's drawings with the creator of the cartoons, the claimant's

209 This protection might be less effective. Obviously, an unauthorised photocopy will infringe, but will there be copyright infringement if a rival copies the nature of the character? Perhaps there might be a possibility that the restricted public performance will be relevant if the rival character faithfully follows the written description.

210 Trade Marks Act 1994 s 10(3).

211 [1991] FSR 145.

212 *Erven Warnink Besloten Vennootschap v J Townend & Sons (Hull) Ltd* [1979] AC 731.

goodwill would be harmed by fixing representations of turtles to inferior goods. The potential value of the claimant's licensing rights would be seriously harmed. Furthermore, there was a sufficient link between the claimant and the goods to found a case in passing off. At last, it seemed an English judge was prepared to accept that the public are aware of character merchandising.

Lord Browne-Wilkinson VC considered that the law as developed in Australia was sound and applied *Children's Television Workshop Inc* v *Woolworths (New South Wales) Ltd*,[213] in which it was held that the defendant, by his unlicensed use of the Muppet characters, had misrepresented that he had a connection with the owner of the copyright in drawings of the characters and was a *bona fide* licensee of rights in the Muppets. The Vice-Chancellor managed to distinguish three English cases involving the Wombles, Kojak and the pop group 'Abba',[214] although he seemed unduly cautious about doing so. The three English cases are distinguishable very easily because they only involved a name and not a drawing and are still good law. The question is whether the *Mirage Studios* (Turtles) case has modified the requirement of a common field of activity for an action in passing off to succeed. Certainly, there is now a greater awareness of character merchandising amongst the public, but it may be insufficient to found an argument that goodwill will be harmed by unlicensed use of names and representations of characters. The public may be aware that the creator of a fictitious character will licence its use in this way, but equally may be prepared to accept that other companies can use the characters without such a licence. There may be a connection between quality products and the creator of the character, but the public may simply assume that cheaper, inferior goods are made without the creator's specific permission and the link between inferior goods and the creator, essential for a passing off action to succeed, is thus absent. Put crudely, do the public really care? Many members of the public probably think that the creator of the character has made enough money through films, books and cartoons.

One major criticism of the judgment in the *Mirage Studios* (Turtles) case is that the copyright issue alone should have been sufficient to dispose of it, and this will usually be so where representations of characters are used, whether two-dimensional or three-dimensional. In the future, fictitious names may be registrable as trade marks.[215] Lord Browne-Wilkinson's views on passing off could be considered to be *obiter*. Where names are used, there must be a common field of activity for there to be a prospect of harm to goodwill. The only way a character merchandiser can establish a sufficient link is to exercise a form of control over the goods to which the character or its name is applied and this link must be such that sufficient numbers of the public are aware of it. This view is consistent with Australian law and prior UK law.

Essentially, the issue of passing off in relation to character merchandising is one of deceit. If the public is insufficiently aware of character merchandising ordinary persons will not associate the use of the character with the origin of goods. Therefore, there can be no passing off because any misrepresentation by the defendant is ineffective and, hence, causes no damage. Furthermore, these are not cases where erosion of goodwill is really an issue. In *BBC Worldwide Ltd* v *Pally Screen Printing Ltd*,[216] Laddie J dismissed an application for summary judgment by the owners of the rights in the famous fictional television characters the Teletubbies (rotund furry creatures with television screens set into their abdomens) for passing off (and copyright infringement). He considered that the defendants, who made and sold T-shirts showing representations of the Teletubbies, had an arguable defence that they were not guilty of passing off because it was possible that members of the public, seeing the T-shirts bearing representations of the characters, would see them for no more than that. They would not necessarily consider that the T-shirts were sold by or with the consent of the claimant.

In *Arsenal Football Club plc* v *Reed*,[217] the defendant had, for over 30 years, sold memorabilia bearing the football club's name and logo. In respect of passing off, Laddie J held

213 [1981] RPC 187. He also approved of a similar decision, *Fido-Dido Inc* v *Venture Stores (Retailers) Pty Ltd* (1988) ATPR 40–235.

214 *Wombles Ltd* v *Wombles Skips Ltd* [1977] RPC 99; *Tavener Rutledge Ltd* v *Trexapalm Ltd* [1977] RPC 275; *Lynstad* v *Annabast Products Ltd* [1975] FSR 488.

215 *Reform of Trade Mark Law*, Cm 1203, HMSO, 1990.

216 [1998] FSR 665.

217 [2001] RPC 46.

218 This point was also relevant to the trade mark issue in the case. Laddie J later referred the case to the European Court of Justice for a Preliminary Ruling under Article 234 of the EC Treaty on the trade mark point (now Article 267 of the Treaty on the Functioning of the European Union).

that the claimant had failed to show any evidence of confusion. It appeared that the defendant's customers bought his products as badges of allegiance to the football club and realised they neither came from nor were sanctioned by the club.[218]

Post-sale confusion

For a passing off action to succeed there must be evidence that customers or ultimate consumers have been deceived or, if the defendant's planned activity were to come to fruition, a real likelihood of confusion. The key is confusion and it might be reasonable to assume that the confusion must occur at the time the goods are purchased, not later. For example, in *Bostick Ltd* v *Sellotape GB Ltd*[219] the claimant made adhesive putty called 'Blu-tack' which was coloured blue. Apparently the colour was chosen because it might be less likely to be swallowed by children, as there are very few edible materials of that colour. The defendant launched an equivalent product called 'Sellotak' which was also coloured blue. However, the defendant's adhesive putty was not visible in the packet it was sold in and could only be seen after it had been purchased by removing it from its packaging. Nevertheless, the claimant sued for passing off. It was held that, as the defendant's product could not be seen at the point of sale, there was no danger of confusion and it was highly unlikely that the similarity in colour would lead to confusion and influence future sales to the detriment of the claimant.

219 [1994] RPC 556.

The concept of post-sale confusion, that is where the misrepresentation so essential for passing off comes after the goods have been purchased, seems, at first, difficult to accept as a possibility. Even if there is confusion post-sale, how could that lead to damage to the claimant? However, it must be stressed that it is business goodwill which is protected by passing off, not just trade or reputation. Damage extends beyond a straightforward and immediate loss of sales as a result of the defendant's misrepresentation. The more distinctive the name or mark used by the claimant, the greater the goodwill is likely to be. Even if there is no deception at the time of sale, later confusion as to the origin of the name, mark or device can still damage the goodwill by a process of dilution or erosion. So it was held in the New Zealand case of *Levi Strauss & Co* v *Kimbyr Investments Ltd*.[220] The defendant used a protruding tab on its jeans which was similar to the distinctive tab used by the claimant on its jeans. As a result of the defendant's cardboard advertising labels attached to the jeans displayed for sale, there was little likelihood of confusion at the point of sale. However, the court held, *inter alia*, that it was irrelevant that the confusion took place after sale and that the owner of goodwill in a product or get-up was entitled to have that goodwill protected throughout the life of the product. The claimant could show that the tab continued to operate as an effective badge connecting the jeans with it. The post-sale confusion would lead to a dilution of the distinctiveness of the tab and, accordingly, damage the claimant's goodwill.[221]

220 [1994] FSR 335.

221 For a discussion of this trend, see Karet, I. 'Passing off and trade marks: confusing times ahead?' [1995] 1 EIPR 3.

If post-sale confusion is accepted in the UK, which it might in view of the acceptance of the principle of erosion of goodwill as being a form of damage, then manufacturers of lookalike articles who attempt to avoid allegations of passing off by the use of distinguishing labelling or disclaimers had better tread warily. However, this would represent a further extension of passing off which could result in protecting the shape of goods even where such shapes would not be registrable as trade marks, for example, by being necessary to achieve a technical result of giving substantial value to the goods.[222] This might turn out to be as effective as the old indirect copyright infringement through drawings suppressed by the Copyright, Designs and Patents Act 1988 s 51. Shapes, colours and other aspects of appearance of articles could end up with protection where those features cannot be protected by any other intellectual property right through lack of novelty or the

222 Trade Marks Act 1994 s 3(2).

expiry of a pre-existing right such as a registered design or patent. This could be a dangerous road to take. Imagine if the Coca-Cola company could have prevented other manufacturers from producing a drink having a similar colour.

Damage to goodwill

Damage to goodwill, or at least a probability that damage will ensue, is one of the essential requirements for a passing off action.[223] Damage is not limited to the direct diversion of sales[224] and may result in a number of ways. The diminution in the claimant's goodwill may be caused by:

1 lost sales because buyers confuse the defendant's products (or services) with those of the claimant;[225]
2 the fact that the defendant's product is inferior to the claimant's product and buyers think the defendant's product is the claimant's;[226]
3 erosion, blurring or debasement of a name that is exclusive and unique and which is used by the claimant (or a number of persons entitled to use it);[227] indirect though invidious damage which prevents the claimant controlling and developing his goodwill in the future as he wished even though none would be deceived into thinking the defendant's product was from the claimant.[228]

In *National Association of Software and Service Companies* v *Ajay Sood*,[229] in the High Court of Delhi, it was suggested that the activity of 'phishing' (misrepresenting that the sender of an e-mail was a legitimate organisation to induce the disclosure of personal information) could give rise to an action in passing off. The court said that this would be passing off if it affected or tarnished the image of the organisation in question. However, there is little case law on whether 'tarnishing' goodwill would be a natural result of phishing. Certainly, the 'instrument of deceit' approach should apply in such circumstances.

A court may look to potential risk to reputation or goodwill: for example, in *Sir Robert McAlpine Ltd* v *Alfred McAlpine plc*,[230] the court held that, although the defendant currently had a good reputation, things could change, for example, if it suffered a setback or got involved in an environmentally sensitive project. Such things might not be probable though neither were they fanciful in a modern commercial context.

As the essence of passing off is deception, the basic test is whether a substantial number of persons have been deceived or are likely to be deceived by the defendant's misrepresentation.[231] If the vast majority of persons to whom the misrepresentation is addressed simply see through it and do not believe it, then there can be no damage, subject to what is said below in respect of erosion of goodwill as a form of damage. In conventional passing off cases, the *dictum* of Lord Morris in *Parker-Knoll Ltd* v *Knoll International Ltd*[232] holds true, where he said (at 281):

> the issue . . . is whether the respondent clearly established that if furniture is sold under the mark Knoll or Knoll International there will be a serious risk that substantial numbers of the purchasing public will be led to believe that they are buying Parker-Knoll furniture.

The question of whether or not there is a real likelihood of confusion is, of course, a matter for the court and not for the witnesses to decide;[233] it is a 'jury question'.

An association with an overall project or scheme does not necessarily mean that there is an association with someone who made a contribution to that project. In *Pasterfield* v *Denham*,[234] the claimant was commissioned to design leaflets and brochures for a tourist attraction, the Plymouth Dome. The defendants were later commissioned to update the leaflets and, after around one million of the new leaflets had been produced and distributed,

223 *Erven Warnink Besloten Vennootschap* v *J Townend & Sons (Hull) Ltd* [1973] AC 731 per Lords Diplock and Fraser. Lord Fraser spoke in terms of a real likelihood of suffering substantial damage to goodwill.

224 *Phones 4u Ltd* v *Phone4u. co.uk Internet Ltd* [2007] RPC 5.

225 See, for example, *Reddaway* v *Banham* [1896] AC 199.

226 For example, as in *Spalding & Bros* v *AW Gamage Ltd* (1915) 84 LJ Ch 449.

227 *Sir Robert McAlpine Ltd* v *Alfred McAlpine plc* [2004] RPC 36.

228 *Associated Newspapers Ltd* v *Express Newspapers* [2003] FSR 51.

229 [2005] FSR 38.

230 [2004] RPC 36.

231 The fact that some persons would not be confused did not, by itself, prevent a finding of misrepresentation: *Sir Robert McAlpine*.

232 [1962] RPC 265.

233 See, for example, Jacob J in *Neutrogena Corporation* v *Golden Ltd* [1996] RPC 473 at 482.

234 [1996] FSR 168.

235 As to the copyright claims, the court held that Plymouth City Council, which had commissioned the first and later leaflets, had the benefit of beneficial ownership of copyright or, alternatively, an implied licence. Nor was there a derogatory treatment as the minor changes made to the drawing did not amount to a distortion or mutilation which was prejudicial to the claimant's honour or reputation as an artist.

236 [2001] RPC 46.

237 [1993] FSR 641. The case also hinged on Council Regulation (EEC) No 823/87 of 16 March 1987 laying down special provisions relating to quality wines produced in specified regions, OJ L 84, 27.03.1987, p 59, amended by Council Regulation (EEC) No 2043/89 of 19 June 1989 amending Regulation (EEC) No 823/87 laying down special provisions relating to quality wines produced in specified regions, OJ L 202, 14.07.1989, p 1, limiting the use of names for wines which refer to specified regions.

238 Other examples are provided by the *Erven Warnink* (Advocaat) case and the *Bollinger* (Spanish Champagne) case discussed earlier.

the claimant sued for copyright infringement, derogatory treatment and passing off.[235] With respect to the passing off claim there was no actual proof of damage. The court accepted that one of the defendants, by placing the words 'Designed and Produced by Denham Design 0752 671787' on the leaflets was attempting to associate himself with the Dome project rather than the claimant's drawings on the leaflets. The judge said that there had been no suggestion of dishonesty or fraud and, if anyone had been deceived and had asked the defendant for a similar drawing, the defendant would have most likely disclaimed authorship of the drawing.

The use of a disclaimer may be an important factor in the court's determination of the question of damage to goodwill. If it is clear and effective, this would tend to suggest that substantial persons will not be confused. It was an important factor in *Arsenal Football Club plc* v *Reed*,[236] where the defendant used a disclaimer making it clear that his Arsenal memorabilia had no association with official club merchandise. However, the outcome may be different, notwithstanding the use of a disclaimer in the case of an allegation of damage in the form of erosion of goodwill or in respect of a trade mark.

The case of *Taittinger SA* v *Allbev Ltd*[237] provides an important example of erosion as a form of damage to goodwill.[238] The defendant, an English company, made a non-alcoholic drink called Elderflower Champagne. Not surprisingly, it attracted the attention of the French makers of champagne who had previously taken legal action no less than 46 times in England to protect the name 'champagne'. The High Court judge found for the defendant. He applied Lord Diplock's test and, although he found all the other elements present, he decided that there was no real likelihood of serious damage to the claimant's undoubted goodwill. Elderflower Champagne was only £2.45 for a 75 cl bottle and had wording on the label to the effect it was non-alcoholic. Davies J considered that only a small number of persons would be confused even though Elderflower Champagne was sold in bottles resembling champagne bottles. A representation of the label is shown in Figure 23.1.

The Court of Appeal allowed the claimant's appeal because use of the word 'champagne' by those not entitled to use it would inevitably diminish the goodwill associated with it. Peter Gibson LJ said (at 670):

Figure 23.1 Elderflower Champagne bottle label

. . . it seems to me no less obvious that erosion of the distinctiveness of the name champagne in this country is a form of damage to the goodwill of the business of the champagne houses.

Erosion of goodwill may be a possibility even where the second form of damage identified above is also possible (that is, where inferior goods or services provided by the defendant are taken to be those of the claimant). In *Dawnay Day & Co Ltd v Cantor Fitzgerald International*,[239] one company (Dawnay Day Securities) within a group of companies, using the name Dawnay Day in the names of the individual companies, fell into the hands of the defendant which was unconnected with the Dawnay Day group. An action was brought to restrain the defendant using the name Dawnay Day. In the Court of Appeal, Sir Richard Scott VC identified two forms of damage, the first being because the Dawnay Day group members, collectively and individually, had no control over the activities of Dawnay Day Securities and might suffer if those activities '. . . become in any way reprehensible'. The second form of damage was recognised as an erosion of the distinctiveness of the Dawnay Day name, as in the *Taittinger* v *Allbev* sense.

239 [2000] RPC 669.

In *Harrods Ltd v Harrodian School Ltd*,[240] Millett LJ found it difficult to accept that erosion of goodwill was sufficient, *per se*, to amount to damage for passing off. However, in that case, there was no danger that Harrods would become a generic term for retailing luxury goods by virtue of the defendant's activities. It is arguable that in *Taittinger*, the use of the word 'champagne' by the defendant for a drink would be the bridgehead by which other manufacturers of drinks would start using the name. In *Harrods*, the fields of activity (retailing and education) were very different.[241] This was not so in *Taittinger* where the fields were alcoholic sparkling drinks and non-alcoholic sparkling drinks. The 'insidious' form of damage that erosion of goodwill is recognised as by some judges was evidenced again in *Chocosuisse Union des Fabricants Suisses de Chocolat v Cadbury Ltd*[242] where the name 'Swiss Chalet' was given by the defendant to a new range of bars of chocolate. The damage was that the exclusivity of the designation 'Swiss Chocolate', descriptive of chocolate made in Switzerland, would suffer, even though lesser numbers of persons might wrongly think the defendant's chocolate was made in Switzerland according to Swiss food regulations compared to the number of persons who would not be confused. As not all chocolate made by Swiss companies and described as Swiss chocolate is actually produced in Switzerland, this case must stand at the very limits of passing off.

240 [1996] RPC 697.

241 In *Dawnay Day & Co Ltd v Cantor Fitzgerald International* [2000] RPC 669, at first instance, *Harrods v Harrodian School* was distinguished because in *Dawnay Day* the two businesses were in closely connected fields.

242 [1998] RPC 117.

In the Court of Appeal,[243] confirming the decision in the Chancery Division, Chadwick LJ said that the trial judge, Laddie J, accepted that the question of confusion was a difficult one in this case but that he approached it carefully and on the correct basis. Laddie J concluded that the number of persons likely to be confused would be smaller than those that would not (given the domestic significance of the name 'Cadbury') but, nevertheless, he concluded that it was still likely to be a significant number.

243 [1999] RPC 826. Although some of the Swiss manufacturers of chocolate had made chocolate outside Switzerland, there was no evidence that a substantial proportion of the public regarded such chocolate as 'Swiss Chocolate'.

Protection of goodwill from erosion by 'non-origin association' can be seen as an extension of the tort of passing off because in the *Erven Warnink* case there was also a substantial diminution in the sales of the claimant's drink.[244] However, it could be argued that the claimant acquiesced in the use of the name 'champagne' by others as it had been used in the UK and elsewhere for a number of years to describe a variety of locally made products. For example, 'rhubarb champagne' and 'greengage champagne', *inter alia*, have been used to describe home-made wines as the extracts below taken from *Peggy Hutchinson's Home Made Wine Secrets*, published around the time of the Second World War, demonstrate:[245]

244 Russell, F. 'The elderflower champagne case: is this a further expansion of the tort of passing off?' [1993] 10 EIPR 379.

245 Hutchinson, P. *Peggy Hutchinson's Home Made Wine Secrets* (undated) Foulsham & Co. The preface for the book starts 'The recipes for this book were originally compiled in the days of plenty before the Second World War. Times have changed; some of the ingredients are no longer easy to obtain . . .' I am indebted to Lorraine Keenan for finding this book. No representation is made as to the taste or quality of alcohol made in accordance with the recipe.

GREENGAGE CHAMPAGNE
Ingredients:
4 lbs greengages
20 vine leaves
1 gallon water
4 lbs sugar

1 slice toast; 1 oz yeast

Method:

1 Put the greengages and vine leaves in a bowl, cover with cold water. Take the vine leaves out in 3 days but mash and stir the plums for 8 days, then strain.

2 Then add the sugar and yeast spread on both sides of the toast and leave to ferment 14 days.

3 Skim and bottle.

A further form of damage is tarnishment of the claimant's goodwill. This does not need to relate to unsavoury or immoral behaviour but may be, for example, the association of the claimant's name with a project which is not as expensive or luxurious as the claimant's activities.[246]

Proof of damage

A claimant must be able to satisfy the court that he has, or will, suffer substantial damage to his goodwill. Mere speculation will rarely suffice. Nor will the fact that 'only a moron in a hurry would be misled'.[247] In many cases proof of damage is not only important in quantifying damages to be awarded to the claimant but also it may be essential in demonstrating that there has been a misrepresentation calculated to injure the claimant's goodwill. In the case of *Tamworth Herald Co Ltd* v *Thomson Free Newspapers Ltd*,[248] the claimant did not put in any evidence of actual confusion on the part of persons seeking to place advertisements in its newspaper. However, in some cases, particularly in interim hearings, there will be no actual damage to put before the court. The claimant must be able to convince the judge that there is a risk of confusion amongst the public. This will help to show that there is a serious issue to be tried and the judge can then move on to consider the balance of convenience and whether an interim injunction should be granted.

Where the defendant has been engaged in the activity complained of over a long period of time, the fact that the claimant fails to adduce any hard evidence of actual confusion will be fatal to his case. In *Arsenal Football Club plc* v *Reed*,[249] the defendant had been selling Arsenal football memorabilia, such as scarves carrying names 'Arsenal' and 'Gunners' and the football club logo, for over 31 years. In spite of this long period of trading, the football club failed to find sufficient evidence to persuade the judge that there had been the slightest confusion on the part of persons buying the defendant's products. It is possible that this case, and others, represents a growing recognition of the importance of intellectual property rights in areas where little attention has been paid to them in the past. It also reflects the contemporary importance of merchandising.

Where the alleged damage is of the erosion of goodwill type, the claimant will be unable to show sales have been or are likely to be diverted to the defendant. Instead, it is long-term commercial damage that will ensue from the deception. Indeed, it could be argued that, if there is a deception, damage is almost certain to follow, whether in the short or longer term, as in *Kimberley-Clark Ltd* v *Fort Sterling Ltd*,[250] where the defendant placed an offer on its packs of Nouvelle toilet tissue stating:

Softness guaranteed (or we'll exchange it for Andrex®).

There was an acknowledgement under the 'Andrex®' to the effect that this was the claimant's registered trade mark. The case proceeded on the basis of passing off and the court was satisfied that the overall impact on normal but busy customers was that the product was that of the claimant or somehow associated with the claimant.[251] The damage would come about from the defendant taking the benefit of the claimant's mark and its goodwill which would strengthen the defendant's position relative to the claimant. The court confirmed that, in such a case, the claimant would not be required to point to particular examples of sales lost to the defendant as a result of the misrepresentation.

246 *Novelty Pte Ltd* v *Amanresorts Ltd* [2009] FSR 20, Court of Appeal of Singapore.

247 Per Foster J in *Morning Star Cooperative Society Ltd* v *Express Newspapers Ltd* [1979] FSR 113 in which the proprietor of the *Morning Star* had objected to the name *Daily Star*.

248 [1991] FSR 337.

249 [2001] RPC 46.

250 [1997] FSR 877.

251 Confusion leading persons to believe that the defendant is connected to the claimant as being sufficient to prove damage was identified in *Ewing* v *Buttercup Margarine Co Ltd* (1917) 34 RPC 232 by Lord Cozens-Hardy MR.

In *Morgan-Grampian plc v Training Personnel Ltd*[252] the claimant published a series of magazines with titles beginning with the phrase 'What's New in . . .' and the defendant later changed the title of one of its publications to 'What's New in Training'. An interim injunction was granted. There was a risk of confusion and the fact that it would be difficult to quantify damage in monetary terms helped to tilt the balance of convenience in favour of the claimant.

252 [1992] FSR 267.

It may be tempting to obtain evidence of damage through surveys and trap orders. Surveys are carried out for a number of reasons but, unless they are properly carried out, they will fail to impress the court. For example, in *Imperial Group plc v Philip Morris Ltd*[253] it was held that there was no passing off by the defendant who used black and gold packets for 'Raffles' cigarettes. The claimant made John Player Specials (JPS) cigarettes in black with gold lettering and a gold monogram. The claimant had used surveys to show that there was a high degree of association between the colours black and gold and the JPS cigarette. Whitford J criticised the survey techniques used and he laid down some guidelines if a survey is to have validity, being:

253 [1984] RPC 293.

- the persons interviewed must be selected to represent a relevant cross-section of the public;
- the sample size must be statistically significant;
- the survey must be conducted fairly;
- all the surveys carried out must be disclosed fully (a 'warts and all' approach);
- all the answers given must be disclosed and made available to the defendant;
- no leading questions should be put to interviewees;
- interviewees must not be led to embark upon a field of speculation they would not otherwise have considered;
- instructions to interviewers must be disclosed;
- if the answers are to be coded for computer input, the coding instructions must also be disclosed.

In other words, good statistical methods must be used coupled with complete openness and disclosure. In many cases, fulfilling these requirements will result in the survey being prohibitively expensive.

Trap orders are often used to provide evidence of passing off. For example, an order may be placed by the claimant (or his agent) for genuine goods in the hope that the defendant will supply other goods instead. A trap order was used in *Showerings Ltd v Entam Ltd*,[254] in which the claimant made a drink called 'Babycham' and sent teams of trappers into the defendant's public houses to order a round of drinks including Babycham. Often, a rival drink was provided without the bar staff first pointing out that it was not Babycham. Where used, trap orders should be fair and, preferably, in writing where this is possible. In effect, in executing a trap order, the claimant is representing himself as a *bona fide* customer – in other words, he himself is making a misrepresentation. This he is allowed to do and his solicitor is allowed to advise him that he may do this and to make the necessary arrangements.[255] If the defendant had been 'caught' by a trap order, he should be put on notice immediately so that he can recall the facts clearly.[256]

254 [1975] FSR 45.

255 The 'clean hands' doctrine does not appear to apply to trap orders: *see Marie Claire Albums SA v Hartstone Hosiery Ltd* [1993] FSR 692.

256 *Cellular Clothing Co Ltd v G White & Co Ltd* (1952) 70 RPC 9 where a trap order was held to be unsatisfactory for want of notice.

Passing off and internet domain names

Any person may obtain an internet address (domain name) for his own web pages. There are certain naming conventions. There are generic top level domains (gTLDs) such as '.com', '.org' and '.net'[257] and country code top level domains (ccTLDs) such as '.uk' (UK), '.de' (Germany), '.fr' (France), '.jp' (Japan), '.tv' (Tuvalu), '.us' (USA), etc. Within the

257 ICANN, the Internet Corporation for Assigned Names and Numbers, has overall control.

country code domains, there is further subdivision, for example, by using '.co', '.ltd', or '.ac'. Thus, an English-based company called Acme Trading Ltd may have registered 'acme-trading.co.uk' or 'acme-trading.ltd.uk' as its domain names. An educational institution called Rutland University may have chosen to register 'rutland.ac.uk' as its domain name. These organisations may have also chosen to register some gTLDs such as 'acme-trading.com' or 'rutland.net'.

Each domain name must be distinct from every other one. One problem is, however, that computers will distinguish between names if there is only one character different. This enables the registration of very similar domain names. For example, as regards Acme Trading Ltd, the following might have been registered by third parties: 'acmetrading.co.uk', 'acme-trading.co.uk', 'acme-traders.co.uk', 'acmetraders.co.uk', and so on. Another problem is that someone might register a domain name before the person or organisation which might be expected to have an interest in the name. A person, having no connection or association whatsoever to the pop singer Madonna, the footballer Wayne Rooney or the company Burger King Ltd might choose to register these names as domain names,[258] pre-empting or blocking appropriate registrations by those persons or organisations. Such persons are sometimes referred to as 'cybersquatters'. Their activities have given rise to some litigation and have also resulted in dispute resolution systems being set up. Typically, cybersquatters register names and then try to sell them to the persons or organisations which one might expect to have a legitimate interest in them because they are their real names or trading names or registered trade marks.

In the UK, a body called Nominet UK allocates the addresses. It used to allocate names purely on a first-come-first-served basis, and made no checks to see if the applicant or any others were entitled to any rights in the name. Generally, bodies such as Nominet UK allocate names by automation without human intervention and do not assess the legality of a registration, or require a declaration of a right to use or operate an opposition system.[259] Past examples of domain names registered by persons not connected with the organisation whose name was used include 'mcdonalds.com', 'mtv.com' and 'harrods.com'.[260]

The first-come-first-served rule was shown to be unsatisfactory in *Pitman Training Ltd* v *Nominet UK*[261] in which two companies, having a common origin, Pitman Training Ltd and Pitman Publishing, now trading under the Longman name, a division of Pearson Education Ltd, clashed over the domain name 'pitman.co.uk'. Pitman Publishing, the second defendant, applied for and secured that name, but did not make use of it initially. Due to a mix up, the name was reallocated to Pitman Training Ltd, the claimant, but following complaints from Pitman Publishing, Nominet UK, the first defendant, reallocated the name to Pitman Publishing. The claimant commenced proceedings for reinstatement of the domain name, contending that its use by the second defendant amounted to passing off.[262] This was dismissed by the judge who thought it highly unlikely that the public would associate the domain name with the claimant; rather it was the second defendant which was more likely to have goodwill in that name as it had been trading under that name for nearly 150 years. Furthermore, when the Pitman companies were de-merged in 1985, there was an express agreement that Pitman Training Ltd would not use the word Pitman without the word 'training' and the use by the claimant of the domain name would probably be a breach of that agreement.

The registration of 'harrods.com' initiated the first case in the UK on domain names. It was registered to a person with no association with the famous Knightsbridge store and was registered through an American organisation, Network Solutions Inc, which provided registration services. Harrods complained to Network Solutions, which suspended the domain name pending the outcome of its dispute resolution process. In the meantime, Harrods Ltd commenced proceedings for trade mark infringement and passing off. In *Harrods Ltd* v *UK Network Services Ltd*,[263] summary judgment was granted and the defendants were ordered to release the domain name 'harrods.com'. However, this was

258 These are true examples and all three were successful in having the names transferred. The singer known as 'Sting', unfortunately, was unsuccessful.

259 Wood, N. 'The trouble with domain names' (1997) 2(3) *Intellectual Property* 7.

260 See ibid. for a discussion of these and other examples. Nominet UK has an 'Expert Determination' process to resolve disputes.

261 [1997] FSR 797.

262 There were also claims of unlawful interference with contract (the contract between the claimant and its internet service provider) and abuse of process, neither of which was deemed to be even arguable.

263 [1997] EIPR D-106.

an application for summary judgment only under the former RSC Ord 14, and the defendants were not represented so the case was not fully contested. As no use had been made of the website, it was arguable whether it was passing off.[264] Presumably, the intention of the defendants was not to use the website but to sell the domain name to Harrods Ltd.

The next case shows that, even without evidence of use of a domain name, the courts are prepared to use the law of passing off to prevent persons registering a domain name with the hope of selling it to a company that already has rights in the name as a trade mark or has established substantial goodwill in the name. In such circumstances, it was held that the domain name itself was an instrument of fraud.

In *Marks & Spencer plc v One in a Million Ltd*,[265] five actions for summary judgment were brought by well-known business organisations, having substantial goodwill, against the defendants, who were dealers in internet domain names and who registered names to sell to potential users. The defendants had registered a number of names including 'bt.org', 'sainsbury.com', 'marksandspencer.co.uk'. Jonathan Sumption QC, sitting as a deputy judge, considered that threats of passing off and trade mark infringement were made out and he granted *quia timet* injunctions which went beyond normal *quia timet* injunctions in that the defendants were ordered to take the necessary steps to assign the domain names to the claimants.

At the time of the hearing, the defendants had not made any use of the domain names but, following *Singer v Loog*,[266] it was held to be sufficient for passing off for a person to put an 'instrument of deception'[267] into the hands of another or to authorise another to do so. This would be the case should the defendants transfer the domain names to third parties which might or might not have any connection with the names concerned. For example, the name 'j.sainsbury.com' could be sold to Joe Soap & Co or to someone who, by coincidence, happened to have the name John Sainsbury. In either case, use of the domain name by the third party would be highly likely to amount to passing off.

Two further possibilities were identified. First, and most obvious, the defendants might sell the domain name to the organisation with that name or trade mark. Another option might be for the defendants simply to retain the name without using it, thereby blocking the organisation from registering its own name (at least in an identical form). Neither of these possibilities would result in or involve passing off. It was not, therefore, certain that passing off would occur. Nevertheless, the judge thought it sufficient, even for a final *quia timet* injunction, that what had been done was calculated to infringe the claimant's rights.

The defendants appealed unsuccessfully to the Court of Appeal in *British Telecom plc v One in a Million Ltd*.[268] In respect of Marks and Spencer, it was noted that any person who entered 'marksandspencer' in an internet register to find the identity of the owner would obtain details of One in a Million Ltd. As most persons would not have heard of that company otherwise, they would naturally assume it was somehow connected or associated with Marks and Spencer plc. Furthermore, erosion of goodwill would result from registration of the name as a domain name by anyone other than Marks & Spencer plc. Aldous LJ said that domain names which comprised distinctive names were instruments of fraud. In the other cases, Aldous LJ said that passing off or threatened passing off had also been demonstrated and that the domain names in those cases also were instruments of deceit. He said that the court would interfere in cases where:

- passing off was established;
- the defendant was a joint tortfeasor with another in actual or threatened passing off;
- the defendant equipped himself or intended to equip another with an instrument of fraud.

The motive of the defendants was clearly influential. They had offered to sell the domain names to the relevant organisations for large sums, usually with an express or implied threat to sell to third parties otherwise. The reason why the defendant had registered those

264 But *see* the *One in a Million* case below.

265 [1998] FSR 265.

266 (1880) 18 ChD 395.

267 The Court of Appeal preferred the term 'instrument of fraud'.

268 [1999] FSR 1. Marks and Spencer plc was also a co-respondent, along with others.

very names was, in the view of Aldous LJ, because of the value of the goodwill subsisting in them. On the point of restraining the use of an instrument of fraud, Aldous LJ said (at 18):

> . . . there can be discerned from the cases a jurisdiction to grant injunctive relief where a defendant is equipped with or is intending to equip another with an instrument of fraud. Whether any name is an instrument of fraud will depend upon all the circumstances. A name which will, by reason of its similarity to the name of another, inherently lead to passing off is such an instrument. If it would not inherently lead to passing off, it does not follow that it is not an instrument of fraud. The court should consider the similarity of the names, the intention of the defendant, the type of trade and all the surrounding circumstances.

Aldous LJ went on to say that an intention to appropriate goodwill or enable someone else to do so, allows the court to infer that it will happen even if there is a possibility that it will not take place. An injunction is appropriate in such circumstances. In that way he dealt with the problem that a threat to use a domain name or to put it into the hands of another to use may not, in fact, materialise. He appears to suggest also that a name which, if used in a particular manner, may not amount to passing off, may still be deemed to be an instrument of fraud attracting injunctive relief. However, what he is probably suggesting is that use of the name, *per se*, may not inexorably lead to passing off but it will do if used in a particular way. Injunctive relief is appropriate where a person is in possession of a name produced or adapted to enable passing off if fraudulently used, where it is likely that it will be so used.

Both *Directline Group Ltd* v *Directline Estate Agency*[269] and *Glaxo plc* v *Glaxowellcome Ltd*[270] were cited with approval in the One in a Million case. In both of those cases, injunctions were granted to restrain threatened rather than actual passing off and trade mark infringement. The companies that had been set up had not traded, but the threat of passing off was very real. In *Directline*, Laddie J accepted that the companies, which included Manchester U Ltd, Virgin Jeans Ltd, Jean Paul Gaultier Ltd and Cantona French Brandy Ltd, had been set up with the intention of trading off the claimants' reputations and there was a strong case that passing off would occur. Laddie J described the defendants' activities as a 'scam'.

In *Glaxowellcome*, the defendant was quick off the mark to register that name as a company name when it realised that there was likely to be a takeover bid by Glaxo plc for Wellcome plc, and that the new company would be known as Glaxo-Wellcome plc. When the claimant Glaxo discovered the registration, it tried to persuade the defendant to change the name of the defendant company or to sell it to the claimant at the standard price asked for by a company registration agent of £1,000 (the third defendant was a company registration agent). The defendant responded with a demand for £100,000. Lightman J granted an injunction on the basis of passing off saying that an injunction would be granted in such a case, whether or not the defendant's company had traded. The injunction was mandatory, requiring the defendant to take steps to change or facilitate a change in name of the company.

Registering a well-known company name as a trade mark may amount to passing off but the instrument of deceit concept may be more difficult to show an intention to deceive. Although he remarked that there may be differences compared with registering a well-known company name as a domain name, Patten J refused to strike out an application for passing off in *Reality Group Ltd* v *Chance*[271] where, two days after an announcement that the name Reality used by a recently acquired subsidiary company was to be used for its business, the defendants applied to register the name as a Community trade mark.

Where a third party registers another company's trading name as a domain name, there must still be proof of damage or a likelihood of damage and this will be difficult to show if the claimant has chosen a descriptive or generic name for his business. For example, in *Radio Taxicabs (London) Ltd* v *Owner Drivers Radio Taxi Services Ltd*,[272] the defendant registered 'www.radiotaxis.com' as a domain name and from there provided a link to its

269 [1997] FSR 374.
270 [1996] FSR 388.

271 [2002] FSR 13.

272 [2004] RPC 19.

previously registered domain name 'www.dialacab.co.uk' which contained its main website presence. The defendant's trading name was Dial-A-Cab. There was no real evidence to show that the defendant had registered the domain name with the intention of either taking advantage of the claimant's goodwill or diverting business from the claimant. In the absence of an intention to deceive, the claim for an order to assign the domain name to the claimant on the basis that it was an instrument of deceit could not succeed. The claimant had taken the risk of choosing a descriptive or generic name for its business. Any representation by the defendant was simply that it operated a radio taxi service.

It is possible that the look and feel of a website might amount to passing off. Even though the domain name itself has no connection with the aggrieved party, the site accessed by the domain name may look deceptively similar to another site or be similar to the get-up of another trade so as to be likely to cause confusion.[273] This possibility may be enhanced in the view of the fact that websites are often linked to other websites by a process of linking which may, in some cases, involve deep links, by-passing the front page of a particular site. The basic test of passing off applies nonetheless to the internet. Has the claimant goodwill in his product or service? Has the defendant made a misrepresentation (which may be by virtue of his domain name or the look and feel of his website)? Has there been or is there likely to be damage to the claimant's goodwill? This might be because the deception causes persons to be confused as to the origin of the product or service concerned or by erosion of the claimant's goodwill. Links from the defendant's to the claimant's website may increase the likelihood of confusion and disclaimers are less likely to be effective than in other forms of advertising as they are more likely to be missed in this context.[274] It is perhaps in terms of the internet that passing off has recently displayed its utility as a method of preventing unfair competition.

A plausible application of the law of passing off in the context of registration of a company name was given in *Compagnie Générale des Eaux* v *Compagnie Générale des Eaux Sdn Bhd*.[275] In that case, the claimant was a large company based in France and operating internationally. It had been established for 138 years and had interests in Malaysia providing training and technical services to a group of Malaysian companies. The claimant earned income and paid taxes in Malaysia. The defendant registered an identical name as a company name in 1991 and offered to negotiate favourable terms as to the future use of the company name by the claimant.

In finding that the claimant had goodwill in Malaysia and the existence of a likelihood of confusion, the High Court of Malaysia found that there was a probability of damage of one of two types. Either the claimant would suffer damage as a result of confusion, or the claimant would suffer damage by virtue of being unable to register its own name as its company name in Malaysia because of the defendant's prior registration. An important aspect of this case was that the actions of the defendant were clearly *mala fides* and he had refused to disclose the nature of the business he intended carrying on, in which case the court felt entitled to assume that it was for an improper motive. The concept of suffering damage as a result of being unable to register a name as a company name or, for that matter, as a domain name, is a very real form of damage. Otherwise, why would a person try to register names of famous organisations?

Registering a domain name very similar to that used by an established trade will almost inevitably lead to a conclusion that passing off is or will occur. In *Phones 4u Ltd* v *Phone4u.co.uk Internet Ltd*,[276] the claimant had already acquired goodwill in 'Phones 4u' used for its mobile phone business when the defendant registered 'Phone4u.co.uk' for its business. In the Court of Appeal, Jacob LJ said that there was no realistic use of the latter without causing deception and there was some evidence that potential customers of the claimant had visited the website and the defendant then sought to take advantage of the misunderstanding by trying to deal with them. At one stage, the defendant sought to sell the domain name to the claimant. The defendant said, untruthfully, that he had already

273 In *easyJet Airline Co Ltd* v *Dainty* [2002] FSR 6, the defendant had the domain name 'www.easyRealestate.co.uk' (a cut-price estate agency) but, because of the similar look and feel of his website compared to the claimant's airline website, he was held to be guilty of passing off. The defendant had informed the claimant that the domain name was to be auctioned off and that a number of persons were interested.

274 *See Yahoo! Inc* v *Akash Arora* [1999] FSR 931 in which the defendant registered Yahooindia.com. The High Court of Delhi held that this was passing off (the claimant being the registered proprietor of the trade mark YAHOO! in 69 countries and the owner of the domain name yahoo.com). The court also held that the defendant's disclaimer was ineffective as the nature of the internet meant that the use of a very similar domain name could not be rectified by the use of a disclaimer.

275 [1997] FSR 610.

276 [2007] RPC 5.

been offered £100,000 for the domain name by a third party. The Court of Appeal, reversing the judge at first instance, confirmed that the domain name was an instrument of deceit.

In view of the difficulties of registration of domain names by persons who are not otherwise entitled to use the name, dispute resolution systems have been set up. ICANN has such a process, as does the World Intellectual Property Organisation which deals with disputes over gTLD names and some ccTLD names. In the UK, Nominet is in the process of unveiling a dispute resolution system. Whilst such means of resolving disputes may be reasonably effective in relation to cybersquatting,[277] they are unlikely to be very effective with more subtle forms of passing off on the internet, such as where the look and feel of a website has been imitated. The law of passing off still has an important role to play, as indeed does the law of copyright.

Where a foreign defendant has a website, the question of jurisdiction comes into play. It would seem that the approach here is similar to that under trade mark law. For passing off to be actionable in a jurisdiction other than the one in which the website is situated, there must be some targeting of customers in that other jurisdiction.[278] For example, if a company based in Italy with a website run from a server in Italy carries on a website advertisements for goods priced in Euros and in Pounds Sterling, it can be said that the company is targeting customers in the UK. Of course, without more, this is not passing off: all the elements of which must be present for a passing off action to succeed.

Defences

Defences to a passing off action are fairly straightforward. In the case of the first (no confusion and thus no harm to goodwill), the defendant may commission a survey to demonstrate that there is no confusion although it is more likely that the claimant will commission such a survey to show the opposite. The utility of such surveys has been doubted, as mentioned above, and the main difficulty is ensuring objectivity. The defences to a passing off action include:

1 The claimant does not have *locus standi*; as discussed earlier in the chapter, in some cases there may be a real issue as to who owns the goodwill in question.
2 The defendant's activities have not harmed and are not likely to harm the claimant's goodwill associated with the name, mark or get-up. This may be because there is no common field of activity or because there is no danger of confusion as to the origin or quality of the goods or services.[279]
3 The passing off is not in the course of trade, that is, the defendant is not using the name or get-up in the course of trade.
4 The claimant has no trade interest to be harmed, that is, the claimant is not using the name or mark in the course of trade.[280]
5 The claimant has not established the existence of goodwill associated with the name, mark or get-up concerned.[281]
6 The defendant is simply making honest use of his own name or company name. Nevertheless, the actual use must be done carefully so as not to appear as passing off.[282]
7 The claimant has acquiesced in the defendant's use of the name or mark, or has expressly or impliedly granted the defendant permission to use the name or mark – for example, in a contract for the sale of a business including the goodwill.[283]
8 The claimant is estopped from enforcing his rights under passing off because he has encouraged the defendant's act.[284]

According to the judgment of Lord Diplock in *Erven Warnink Besloten Vennootschap* v *J Townend & Sons (Hull) Ltd*,[285] the misrepresentation made by the defendant must be

277 An example is *WH Smith Ltd* v *Peter Colman* [2001] FSR 9. The defendant later claimed to have transferred the domain name 'WHSmith.com' to an individual with a Bahamian address who happened to be called William Harold Smith.

278 *Banyan Tree Holdings (P) Ltd* v *Reddy* [2010] FSR 8; High Court of Delhi, India. In terms of trade marks, see the section on the internet and trademarks infringement in Chapter 21.

279 This line of defence succeeded in *Wombles Ltd* v *Wombles Skips Ltd* [1977] RPC 99.

280 *McCullogh* v *Lewis A May Ltd* (1948) 65 RPC 58.

281 *County Sound plc* v *Ocean Sound plc* [1991] FSR 367.

282 *See*, for example, *Wright, Layman & Umney Ltd* v *Wright* (1949) 66 RPC 149.

283 *Vine Products Ltd* v *MacKenzie & Co Ltd* [1969] RPC 1 is an example of acquiescence.

284 *Habib Bank Ltd* v *Habib Bank AG Zurich* [1982] RPC 1. This can be seen as a more positive form of acquiescence.

285 [1979] AC 731.

calculated to injure the claimant's business or goodwill. But, as mentioned earlier, innocence does not provide a defence to a passing off action[286] and whether the misrepresentation is intended or accidental should make no difference as to whether an injunction is available. One point about this is that, if knowledge was a factor, there might be difficulty concerning proof and, generally, other intellectual property rights are enforceable regardless of the defendant's state of knowledge although this may be relevant as to the availability of some of the remedies, especially damages.

286 *Baume & Co Ltd* v *AH Moore Ltd* [1958] RPC 226.

Remedies

Remedies available are injunctions (especially interim injunctions and *quia timet* injunctions)[287] and/or damages or, as an alternative, an account of profits. Additionally, an order may be granted for the delivery up or destruction of articles to which the name or mark has been applied or, if possible, an order for the obliteration of such names or marks. A declaration may be sufficient if the defendant has agreed not to continue the acts complained of.

287 A *quia timet* injunction is one granted to prevent a threatened act of passing off.

Where the claimant's goodwill is localised, an injunction may be limited geographically to reflect that fact. In *Redwood Tree Services Ltd* v *Apsey (t/a Redwood Tree Surgeons)*,[288] both parties operated as tree surgeons in their respective local areas. The claimant was based in Bisley, Surrey, and the defendant was based in Eversley, Hampshire. The judge thought an injunction limited to the GU, SL and, possibly, KT postcodes[289] would be appropriate. With respect to the defendant's website, looked at nationally, the judge thought that the claimant had no better right to use a website using Redwood Trees as the defendant.[290] No injunction was imposed as to the website apart from requiring the defendant to make it clear that it was not connected with the claimant and was neither based in nor operated in the areas covered by the above postcodes.

288 [2011] EWPCC 14.

289 Guildford, Slough and Kingston upon Thames.

290 There was a further Redwood Trees Services business in West Sussex.

As usual, an applicant for an interim injunction should act quickly. In *Blinkx UK Ltd* v *Blinkbox Entertainment Ltd*,[291] both parties operated internet businesses under the names Blinkx and Blinkbox respectively. Floyd J refused to grant an interim injunction to the claimant as it had failed to act quickly and could offer no good reason for the delay.

291 [2010] EWHC 1624 (Ch).

Quia timet injunctions may be possible if the defendant has not yet carried out the acts complained of but is likely to do so in the future. The problem for the claimant asking for such an injunction is that two of the requirements (misrepresentation and damage) may be somewhat theoretical at this stage. In some cases, it may be fairly obvious that the defendant, if unchecked, will be guilty of passing off but it may be much harder to show in other cases.[292] For example, it is unlikely that there will be any direct evidence of confusion. Where the potential damage relied on is the diversion of sales from the claimant's goods to that of the defendant, it must be established that this is likely to happen. It is not enough if the consumer is simply caused to wonder about the origin of the goods.

292 *Numatic International Ltd* v *Qualtex Ltd* [2010] RPC 25.

Damages will usually be based upon the actual loss attributable to the passing off, that is, resulting from the loss of sales experienced by the claimant.[293] How else can harm to goodwill be measured? However, in some cases, damages may be calculated on a royalty basis, that is, based on the amount that would have been payable by the defendant if he had sought a licence to use the name or mark from the claimant. This possibility was discussed in *Dormeuil Frères SA* v *Feraglow Ltd*[294] although it was accepted that there was no authority to that effect. However, a royalty basis could be applicable if it would yield a greater amount than that attributable to loss of sales. Of course, it will always be difficult to calculate damages resulting from a loss of sales and each sale by the defendant does not necessarily represent a sale lost by the claimant. A lost sale in a strict sense occurs where a purchaser buys the defendant's goods thinking that they are the claimant's goods.

293 But *see* now the Intellectual Property (Enforcement, etc.) Regulations 2006, SI 2006/1028, reg 3 which covers assessment of damages, discussed in more depth in chapter 24.

294 [1990] RPC 449.

However, some of the defendant's customers will not have heard of the claimant, or even if they have will realise that they are not dealing with the claimant. In the above case, the claimant reckoned that 75 per cent of the defendant's sales of cloth represented sales of which the claimant was deprived as a result of the passing off. The claimant also claimed damages on a royalty basis for the remaining 25 per cent of the defendant's sales and damages for damage to goodwill because the defendant's cloth was of an inferior quality. The claimant was awarded a total of £20,000 damages which included interest and the unrecovered costs expended in pursuing foreign manufacturers of infringing cloth.

If the passing off is of the extended variety as in *Erven Warnink*, the assessment of damages may prove very difficult. The same applies to inverse passing off. However, in many cases of this sort, the main remedy sought by the claimant will be an injunction, often at the interim stage before any actual damage to the claimant's goodwill has been caused. In an interim hearing, the fact that damages will be difficult to quantify should an injunction not be granted may be a factor, though not a conclusive one, to be taken into account.[295] In interim hearings, the judge is entitled to take account of the behaviour of the parties as well as considering the balance of convenience as in *Dalgety Spillers Foods Ltd v Food Brokers Ltd*,[296] discussed earlier.

Nominal damages will be available against a trader who commits passing off innocently (an injunction almost certainly will be granted in addition). An account of profits may be a possibility in relation to the period following the time when the innocent trader is disabused of his innocence if he continues the passing off beyond this time. The position of the innocent passer off was well put by Lord Parker in *Spalding & Bros v AW Gamage Ltd*[297] where he said:

> Nor need the representation be made fraudulently. It is enough that it has in fact been made, whether fraudulently or otherwise, and that damages may probably ensue, though the complete innocence of the party making it may be a reason for limiting the account of profits to the period subsequent to the date at which he becomes aware of the true facts. The representation is in fact treated as the invasion of a right giving rise at any rate to nominal damages, the enquiry being granted at the plaintiff's risk if he might probably have suffered more than nominal damages.[298]

Passing off resulting from a false impression that a celebrity has endorsed a product may be determined on the basis of what that celebrity would normally charge as a fee for such an endorsement. In *Irvine v Talksport Ltd*,[299] the Formula One racing driver Eddie Irvine said that he would not have 'bothered to get out of bed' for less than £25,000. He led evidence as to the sort of fee he would normally charge, but the judge at first instance awarded him only £2,000. However, the Court of Appeal held that the judge had erred in rejecting Mr Irvine's evidence, which had not been challenged, and the award was increased to £25,000.

If the defendant's actions infringe a trade or service mark as well as constituting passing off, the damages that may be awarded are not cumulative. However, if passing off (or trade mark infringement) and copyright infringement both occur in relation to the same events, then the damages for passing off and copyright infringement may well be accumulated.[300]

Malicious falsehood

A tort that is related to passing off is that known as malicious falsehood, sometimes referred to as trade libel.[301] This could occur where someone publishes information that is capable of seriously damaging a trader's position or reputation. For example, one trader might unjustifiably state that another trader's goods are of poor quality or are counterfeit.[302]

295 See *Morgan-Grampian plc v Training Personnel Ltd* [1992] FSR 267; cf *Blazer plc v Yardley & Co Ltd* [1992] FSR 501.

296 [1994] FSR 504.

297 (1915) 85 LJ Ch 449.

298 (1915) 84 LJ Ch 449 at 449.

299 [2003] FSR 35.

300 *Columbia Picture Industries v Robinson* [1987] 1 Ch 38.

301 For fuller description of this tort, *see* Jacob, R., Kitchin, D., Mellor, J. and Meade, R. (2000) *Kerly's Law of Trade Marks and Trade Names* (13th edn) Sweet & Maxwell.

302 This might also be a personal libel, depending upon the circumstances.

The tort is wide-ranging, having originated from slander of title and developed to include slander of goods and any false disparagement about a business. But it is not limited to commercial activities and has been used in respect of a false and malicious allegation that a woman was already married and, more recently, a false and malicious statement that a dismissed company director had broken into the company premises and stolen a cash box, was setting up a business of his own and was in breach of his fiduciary duty as a company director: *Sallows (Mark)* v *Griffiths (Laurie)*.[303]

303 [2001] FSR 15.

Advertising 'puff' and mere claims that one trader's goods are superior to those of another trader does not, *per se*, amount to malicious falsehood. For example, in *Hubbuck & Sons Ltd* v *Wilkinson, Heywood & Clerk Ltd*,[304] a published statement that the defendant's zinc paint had a slight advantage over the claimant's paint was held not to be a malicious falsehood, even if the statement had been made maliciously. Nor is vulgar abuse actionable as malicious falsehood. In *British Airways plc* v *Ryanair Ltd*, the defendant was involved in comparative advertising and placed advertisements comparing its prices with those of the claimant under the headings 'EXPENSIVE BA. . . . DS!' and 'Expensive BA'.[305]

304 [1899] 1 QB 86.

The statement complained of must refer to the claimant or his goods or services. If the statement exaggerates the qualities of the defendant's goods or services that is not sufficient. To hold otherwise would result in a considerable extension to the tort. So held Jacob J in *Schulke & Mayr UK Ltd* v *Alkapharm UK Ltd*.[306] The claimant had, at one time, been the defendant's distributor for a disinfectant for dentists' instruments manufactured by the defendant. Subsequently, the claimant began to manufacture its own equivalent product and, around that same time, the defendant issued an advertisement which made certain claims in relation to the defendant's disinfectant. The advertisement claimed that the defendant's disinfectant was 'The most powerful; the most stable' and also stated that these attributes had been independently confirmed. There was no reference whatsoever to the claimant's product.

305 [2001] FSR 32. Jacob J said that the malicious falsehood claim 'does not get off the ground'. However, in relation to trade marks, it has been recognised that comparative advertising must comply with the Comparative Directive: *see O2 Holdings Ltd* v *Hutchinson 3G Ltd* [2007] RPC 16, discussed in Chapter 21.

306 [1999] FSR 16.

Jacob J rejected the claimant's submission that, for a cause in action in malicious falsehood, three things must be shown, being:

- that the statements were untrue (specifically false and not a mere puff);
- that the statements were made maliciously, that is, without just cause or excuse; and
- that the claimant had suffered special damage or, as a result of the Defamation Act 1952 s 3, the words were calculated to cause pecuniary damage to the claimant.

Jacob J said of that submission (at 164):

> It is a far-reaching and bold submission. It would mean that many aspects of the law of passing off would become unnecessary . . . It would mean, and would involve, a very considerable extension by the common law into a field mainly regulated by statutes.[307]

What Jacob J was referring to was the requirement to show that the statement was untrue without necessarily being a statement expressly directed to the claimant's goods. He referred to *White* v *Mellin*,[308] discussed below, in which Lord Watson said (at 166):

307 Jacob J went on to point out that such an extension as implemented in Australia by the Trade Practices Act 1974 s 52, effectively doing away with the need to prove malice, has significantly increased litigation.

308 [1895] AC 154.

> In order to constitute disparagement which is, in the sense of law, injurious, it must be shewn that the defendant's representations were made of and concerning the plaintiff's goods; that they were in disparagement of his goods and untrue.

In *Schulke* v *Alkapharm*, a further cause of action, passing off failed because the representation, even if it was false, did not relate to the claimant's product or goodwill. A 'false representation in the air' cannot found an action in passing off.

The basis of the action is a false statement made maliciously, that is, without just cause or excuse. These two ingredients, falsity and malice, are essential if the claimant is to succeed. The claimant failed in *White* v *Mellin*[309] where the defendant sold the claimant's infants'

309 [1895] AC 154.

food after fixing labels to the wrappers stating that the defendant's food for infants was far more nutritious and healthful than any other. There was no proof that the statement was untrue or that it had caused damage to the claimant. Proof of financial loss is another requirement but this was relaxed by the Defamation Act 1952 s 3 which states that proof of special damage is not necessary if the statement was calculated to cause pecuniary damage to the claimant:

(a) and was published in writing or some other permanent form, or
(b) was made in respect of any office, profession, calling, trade or business held or carried on by him at the time of publication.

Prior to the Defamation Act 1952, proof of special damage was not always required and general damage such as a significant fall in a trader's turnover could be sufficient. In *Ratcliffe* v *Evans*,[310] the claimant carried on business under the name 'Ratcliffe & Sons'. The defendant published a weekly newspaper circulated in the area where the claimant's business was situated. One week the newspaper carried a statement implying that the claimant had ceased trading and that the firm known as 'Ratcliffe & Sons' no longer existed. Not surprisingly, this untrue statement caused the claimant to experience a fall in business activity. It was held in the Court of Appeal that an untrue statement maliciously published about a claimant's business which is intended to produce and does indeed produce a loss is actionable as a malicious falsehood. Evidence of general loss, as was the case here, as opposed to evidence of particular loss (for example, where a named customer takes his trade elsewhere as a result of the untrue statement), was admissible in evidence and was sufficient to support the action.

Other examples of trade libel include circulars suggesting that the claimant's goods were not genuine[311] and claims that the claimant was intending to make use of a patented invention the use of which had been abandoned earlier by the defendant as being inadequate.[312] Selling one class of the claimant's goods as a different class can amount to malicious falsehood and passing off. The defendant in *Wilts United Dairies Ltd* v *Thomas Robinson Sons & Co Ltd*[313] obtained large quantities of the claimant's condensed milk that had been sold off by the Ministry of Food at a very low price on condition that it should be used for animal food, manufacturing or export. The milk was old (it had been stocked during the Second World War) and it was known that it deteriorated with age. The claimant always had required that retailers sold the cans of milk within six months. The defendant offered the old milk for sale for human consumption. It was held that the defendant had passed off one class of the claimant's milk (that is, old stock not fit for human consumption) as another class (normal quality) and this amounted to a malicious falsehood calculated to injure the claimant's reputation. In many respects, the basic principles in this case are the same as those applying to the passing off case of *Spalding & Bros* v *AW Gamage Ltd*,[314] discussed earlier in this chapter, *see* p 905, where the defendant sold defective footballs made by the claimant as if they were of normal quality.

Malicious falsehood could be a possibility where a trader engages in comparative advertising in a way in which the stated facts concerning the other traders' goods are untrue or misleading. In *Compaq Computer Corp* v *Dell Computer Corp Ltd*[315] the defendant advertised using a photograph showing its computer and the claimant's computer side by side. Underneath were details of the two computers including price and performance. This information was selected so as to show off the defendant's computer as being the best value. However, the information was misleading, particularly as regards price. The defendant had indicated a heavily discounted price for its machine compared to the list price (undiscounted) of the claimant's machine. An interim injunction was granted because, although the defendant intended to justify his statement, the test was whether a jury would reasonably conclude that the statement was true.[316] However, this case should be compared with *McDonald's Hamburgers Ltd* v *Burgerking (UK) Ltd*,[317] where it was held

310 [1892] 2 QB 524.

311 *Thomas v Williams* (1880) 14 Ch D 864.

312 *London Ferro-Concrete Co Ltd v Justicz* (1951) 68 RPC 65. The statement had been made in hope that this would induce a contractor to divert a subcontract to the defendant.

313 [1958] RPC 94.

314 (1915) 84 LJ Ch 449.

315 [1992] FSR 93.

316 However, there is no entitlement to a jury in a malicious falsehood action, unlike the case with defamation. The case also involved a trade mark infringement although the judge considered that there was an arguable case that the trade mark 'Compaq' was invalid.

317 [1987] FSR 112.

that an advertising campaign for 'Whopper' burgers using the slogan 'It's Not Just Big Mac' in close proximity with the phrase 'Unlike some burgers, it's 100 per cent pure beef . . .' did not amount to a malicious falsehood. It did, however, constitute passing off.

Another comparative advertising case was *DSG Retail Ltd* v *Comet Group plc*.[318] The claimant traded under the familiar High Street name 'Currys' and the defendant was a rival company. The defendant placed advertisements, mainly by way of posters displayed at its stores claiming that its prices were lower than its competitors. A claim was also made that the defendant would beat any of its competitors' 10 per cent off and weekend £10 price-cut promotions. Fixed to some of the posters were prominent cuttings from national newspapers showing advertisements placed by the claimant. An injunction had been obtained against the defendant but there was some evidence that some of the offending posters had been displayed in defiance of the injunction. Owen J extended the injunction. He reviewed the principles in the context of the facts of the case, saying that the following questions were relevant:

- whether the defendant's advertisements were directed at the claimant;
- whether the meaning in the advertisements was false;
- whether the advertisements were intended to be taken seriously;
- whether the advertisements had been published maliciously; and
- whether there was a likelihood that the claimant would suffer actual damage.

He found that all these questions were to be answered in the affirmative though he said it was to be regretted that parties to such disputes could not resolve them without recourse to the courts.

Single meaning rule

In passing off the test is whether a substantial number of people would be deceived. Until recently, that was not the test to be used in malicious falsehood where the single meaning rule was used. The judge, as notional jury, had to decide a single and natural meaning of the defendant's statement and determine its falsity on the basis of that meaning. So held Jacob J in *Vodafone Group plc* v *Orange Personal Communications Services Ltd*,[319] where the defendant advertised with the slogan 'On average, Orange users save £20 every month'. Jacob J decided the single meaning was that if Orange users had been using Vodafone, on the basis of the same amount of usage, on an arithmetic average they would pay £20 per month more including VAT. It did not mean that every single user would save £20 by switching to Orange.

In disallowing the claimant's claim for malicious falsehood, Jacob J held that the statement was neither misleading nor made with malice.[320] As to the claimant's submission that the saving was only around £15 per month, Jacob J said that the sting in the advertisement would not have been much less if that figure had been used instead. Orange would have been happy to show a saving of £10 per month.

The single meaning rule is firmly rooted in defamation cases though it does seem to have come about as an accident of history. It was 'put beyond redemption' by Diplock LJ in *Slim* v *Daily Telegraph*.[321] The rule can cause injustice, for example, where a statement can bear two meanings, one innocuous and one damaging. The judge has to choose between them. If he takes the innocuous meaning,[322] the claimant will lose even though a substantial number of persons may take the damaging meaning.

In *Ajinomoto Sweeteners Europe SAS* v *Asda Stores Ltd*,[323] the Court of Appeal rejected the single meaning rule for malicious falsehood cases. The defendant sold health foods the packaging of which contained the phrases 'No hidden nasties' and 'No artificial flavours and no aspartame'. At first instance, after rejecting two of a possible four meanings for the wording, Tugendhat J considered that two possible meanings were:

318 [2002] FSR 58.

319 [1997] FSR 34.

320 He also dismissed a claim of trade mark infringement.

321 [1968] 2 QB 157, endorsed by the House of Lords in *Charleston* v *News Group Newspapers* [1995] 2 AC 65.

322 For example, on the grounds of freedom of expression under s 12(4) of the Human Rights Act 1998.

323 [2010] FSR 30.

- there is a risk that aspartame is harmful or unhealthy; or
- the foods in question were for persons who found aspartame objectionable.

Tugenhadt J took the single meaning rule to require him not to take one bad meaning where other non-defamatory meanings were possible. Accordingly, giving weight to the right of freedom of expression, he chose the latter of the two above meanings. The claimant's appeal to the Court of Appeal was successful. Sedley LJ said (at paras 30 to 33):

30. [defamation and malicious falsehood] are not so close as to be variants of a single tort, as libel and slander might be said to be. For historical reasons they have developed with different characteristics; they make different demands on the parties; and they offer redress for different things. This is the gap across which it is sought to make the single meaning rule jump.

31. In my judgment the powerful reasons advanced by Mr Caldecott for doing this are outweighed by one dominant fact: the rule itself is anomalous, frequently otiose and, where not otiose, unjust.

32. The anomaly is very nearly common ground. . . . we have seen how a pragmatic practice became elevated into a rule of law and has remained in place without any enduring rationale. It is frequently otiose, as counsel's own experience testifies, because in the great majority of defamation cases the choice between libel and no libel, by the time the case goes to a verdict, is an either-or choice.

33. But where it is capable of being applied, as it is in the present claim, the rule is productive of injustice. On the judge's unchallenged findings, the meanings which reasonable consumers might put on Asda's health-food packaging include both the damaging and the innocuous. Why should the law not move on to proof of malice in relation to the damaging meaning and (if malice is proved) the consequential damage without artificially pruning the facts so as to presume the very thing – a single meaning – that the judge has found not to be the case?

Consequently, all three Court of Appeal judges rejected the application of the single meaning rule in malicious falsehood cases.

Defamation and malicious falsehood

In some cases there may be an overlap between malicious falsehood and defamation and, if that is so, it may be advantageous to bring an action in malicious falsehood as legal aid is not available for defamation. To do this is not an abuse of process even if the sole aim is to facilitate an application for legal aid and in spite of the fact that the defendant will thus be deprived of a right to elect trial by jury. So it was held in *Joyce* v *Sengupta*[324] in which a former lady's maid of the Princess Royal took action in respect of an allegation by the defendant (a reporter for the *Today* newspaper) that the claimant had stolen intimate letters belonging to the Princess Royal and handed them to the newspaper. Lord Nicholls VC also confirmed that the effect of the Defamation Act 1952 s 3 was not to limit damages to nominal damages only.[325]

Local authorities may not sue in defamation because to allow defamation actions by local authorities and other bodies run on political lines would be an undesirable fetter on the freedom of speech. The House of Lords so held in *Derbyshire County Council* v *Times Newspapers Ltd*,[326] applying authorities from the USA, in particular, *New York Times Co* v *Sullivan*.[327] Although the US cases were related to the American Constitution provisions securing freedom of speech, the UK principle of public interest was just as valid. Previous UK law as expressed in *Bognor Regis UDC* v *Campion*[328] was unsatisfactory and this case was overruled by the House of Lords. In that case, the Council had been awarded £2,000 in damages after the defendant had circulated a leaflet savagely attacking the Council. Of course, a personal individual such as a councillor or an officer of the council will be able to bring a libel action if his individual reputation was wrongly harmed. Indeed, the leader

324 [1993] 1 WLR 337.

325 Proof of special damage is unnecessary in certain cases.

326 [1993] AC 534. The Court of Appeal decision to the same effect is reported in [1992] QB 770.

327 (1964) 376 US 254.

328 [1972] 2 QB 169.

of Derbyshire County Council had brought a personal action based on the same facts as in the local authority action.

At the interim stage where malicious falsehood is in issue and the defendant intends to plead justification a court will not normally grant an injunction if the statements are not obviously untrue.[329] Furthermore, where the balance of justice favours neither party an injunction should be refused on the grounds that it would interfere with the defendant's right of free speech.[330] In this respect, the courts behave in a similar manner as in breach of confidence cases where defamation is alleged by the confider.

329 *Macmillan Magazines Ltd* v *RCN Publishing Co Ltd* [1998] FSR 9.

330 *Bestobell Paints Ltd* v *Bigg* [1975] FSR 421.

Overview

The establishment and development of passing off is a typically common law method of protecting traders' rights but it does have equivalents in other forms of jurisdiction, broadly falling under the heading of unfair competition.[331] For example, in Germany, there is trade mark law-like protection for the *Ausstattung* (get-up) of goods, pack-aging, their advertising and the like.[332] For traders contemplating operations overseas, it is obviously important to take precautions such as seeking registrations of trade marks. In terms of the Treaty on the Functioning of the European Union (formerly the EC Treaty), the law of passing off does not appear to pose any particular problems and, because of differences between trade mark law and the law of passing off, the difficulties experienced in respect of parallel importing and trade marks do not seem to occur. It is apparent that passing off provides a very useful remedy where there is no trade mark and the wider scope of passing off can be important in restraining unfair practices. However, the scope can sometimes appear to be too wide, as in the Jif lemon case, and there are certainly some defects and gaps, particularly in the field of character merchandising. Nevertheless, the law of passing off is alive and kicking and prevents a great deal of unfair appropriation of business goodwill. It still proves to be a useful supplement to trade mark law. In turn, the law of malicious falsehood provides a useful supplement to passing off. It should be noted that, in a significant number of cases where passing off is an issue, criminal offences may have been committed such as making a false instrument[333] or offences under the Fraud Act 2006, in addition to offences under the Trade Descriptions Act 1968 and Consumer Protection Act 1987. A local trading standards officer is likely to take an interest in an activity where a name or mark has been used without permission in circumstances where the public are likely to be deceived, as is the trader whose name or mark it is.

331 In *Arsenal Football Club plc* v *Reed* [2003] RPC 39, Aldous LJ said that the law of passing off had developed to a considerable extent and, for example, could now take in situations where there is blurring of the distinctive character of a mark, that it might better now be described as unfair competition.

332 For an overview of German intellectual property law as it applied to the appearance of articles including get-up, see Rohnke, C. 'Protection of external product features in West Germany' [1990] 2 EIPR 41.

333 Forgery and Counterfeiting Act 1981 s 1.

Summary

The law of passing off is based around what has been described as the 'classic trinity', being:

- the existence of goodwill;
- a misrepresentation made by the defendant;
- consequential damage, actual or anticipated.

Goodwill may be built up over a period of time and may be shared by a number of traders. It is the attractive force that 'brings in customers'. Goodwill usually, though not exclusively, applies to a name, word, phrase or sign. It may also apply to other aspects of carrying out business. Where it is claimed in the shape or appearance of a product, it may be more difficult to prove goodwill as the public do not generally expect that the shape and appearance of an object to signify its origin.

There are three forms of passing off:

- Most commonly it could be such that consumers think that trader A's goods are actually those of trader B, for example, where trader A uses the same name for his goods as that used by trader B (classic passing off).
- Where the goodwill of traders in relation to the name of a product having particular characteristics, such as 'champagne', 'Swiss chocolate' or 'vodka' could be eroded by the use of the name by another trader for a product not having those characteristics, for example, by selling a sparkling soft drink as 'Elderflower chapagne' or by selling chocolate made in the UK under the name 'Swiss Chalet' (extended passing off).
- Where trader A claims that trader B's goods are actually his (inverse passing off).

All these forms of v passing off are examples of the same tort. The different descriptions are but labels by which they are known.

The misrepresentation may be implied but need not be deliberate. It often results in confusion and evidence of this is useful but it is not essential.

Usually, there must be a common field of activity between the claimant's and defendant's activities, but this is not a hard and fast rule. It may assist in determining the presence of damage.

Character merchandising is a controversial area in which passing off may be found.

Damage may involve lost sales through diversion or damage to goodwill through erosion, or claims that the other trader's goods are inferior (tarnishment). In an application for a *quia timet* injunction, apart from goodwill, the presence of the other elements may be somewhat theoretical.

Passing off has been very successful in countering 'cybersquatting' where domain names registered to speculators have been held to be instruments of deceit.

The tort of malicious falsehood is seldom used as it is difficult to prove. It requires a false statement made with malice which causes special or pecuniary damage. It could apply, for example, where an untrue claim is made that another trader's goods are inferior or defective and which is calculated to cause loss of business to that trader. Something more than mere advertising 'puff' is required.

Discussion questions

1 Discuss the essential elements for a passing off action and compare and contrast the tests for passing off set out by Lords Diplock and Fraser in the 'Advocaat' case and Lord Oliver in the 'Jif Lemon' case.

2 How and to what extent can a foreign company, which carries on no business in the UK, acquire goodwill in any part of the UK?

3 The scope of passing off was extended by the Court of Appeal in *Taittinger* v *Allbev*. Discuss whether this extension is desirable and the extent to which, if any, the law of passing off differs from trade mark law in protecting against erosion.

4 What is the single meaning rule used in defamation cases and why does it have no place in the tort of malicious falsehood?

Selected further reading

Hotel Cipriani SrL v Cipriani (Grosvenor Street) Ltd – Court of Appeal judgment available at: **http://www.bailii.org/ew/cases/EWCA/Civ/2010/110.html** – (also covers trade marks validity and infringement).

Lievens, D., 'eBay's accessory liability for counterfeiting – why joint tort liability just doesn't cut the mustard' [2011] *International Review of Intellectual Property and Competition Law*, 507 (looks at the liability of internet auction sites as joint tortfeasors, including material of the tort of passing off).

Naniwadekar, M., 'The application of the single meaning rule to cases other than defamation' [2010] *International Company and Commercial Law Review*, 408 (comments on the 'Aspartame' case on malicious falsehood).

Tumbridge, J., 'Diageo North America Inc v Intercontinental Brands (ICB) Ltd: vodka is special: the VODKAT case' [2010] *European Intellectual Property Review*, 290 (comments of the vodka case at first instance and whether extended passing off only applies where the name in question has a 'cachet'. Read this before looking at the Court of Appeal decision available at: **http://www.bailii.org/ew/cases/EWCA/Civ/2010/920.html**).

Wadlow, C., 'Passing off at the crossroads again: a review article for Hazel Carty, An analysis of the economic torts', [2011] *European Intellectual Property Review*, 447 (looks at passing off from the perspective of three intersections: consumer and producer interests; ethical and economic justifications; and misrepresentation with misappropriation; Hazel Carty's second edition of *An Analysis of Economic Torts*, (OUP, 2010) is also worth looking at).

Part Seven

REMEDIES FOR INFRINGEMENT OF INTELLECTUAL PROPERTY RIGHTS

Remedies for infringement of intellectual property rights 24

Introduction

The aim of this chapter is to provide an overview of the remedies available for intellectual property infringements. In the earlier parts of this book, some of these remedies have been fleshed out in more detail in terms of individual rights, where further explanation and discussion is appropriate. A number of the remedies are common to all forms of intellectual property rights though there are differences. For example, additional damages are available for infringements of copyright and related rights and the UK unregistered design right though this form of damages is not available for other rights, such as patents. Particular remedies available for some though not all intellectual property right infringements are discussed in fuller detail in the relevant chapters of the book.

One thing to bear in mind is that an infringement of an intellectual property right is a tort (delict in Scotland) and the general principles applicable to remedies for torts apply also in the context of intellectual property rights. Of course, contractual remedies may also be relevant, such as where the defendant has a licence from the owner of the intellectual property right but is performing acts alleged to go beyond the scope of the licence agreement.

For those intellectual property rights provided for by legislation, the remedies are set out in that legislation as interpreted and applied by a substantial body of case law. In some cases, the legislation itself provides some guidance. For example, in determining whether additional damages are available for copyright infringement, the court must have regard to all the circumstances including the flagrancy of the infringement and the benefit accruing to the defendant by reason of the infringement.[1] A European Union Directive[2] also sets out principles and measures to be applied in the granting of remedies in intellectual property cases as discussed later in this chapter.

Two important weapons in the fight against the infringement of intellectual property rights are the search order and the interim injunction. To a large extent, both of these orders have their origins in intellectual property cases. As these orders may apply to any form of intellectual property right, they are discussed more thoroughly in this chapter. First, the basic remedies are described briefly.

1 s 97(2) Copyright, Designs and Patents Act 1988.

2 Directive 2004/48/EC of the European Parliament and of the Council of 29 April 2004 on the enforcement of intellectual property rights, OJ L 157, 30.04.2004, p 45 (hereinafter, the Directive on the enforcement of intellectual property rights). Implemented in the UK by the Intellectual Property (Enforcement, etc.) Regulations 2006, SI 2006/1028.

Injunction

An injunction is usually imposed to prevent future infringements of intellectual property rights. Claimants may see the grant of an injunction as a natural and automatic right but this is not the case. First, being an equitable remedy, the court has discretion as to whether or not to grant an injunction. Secondly, an injunction may not be effective, such as where information relating to a trade secret has entered the public domain and members of the public are now free at law and equity to make use of the information.[3] Thirdly, an injunction may not be appropriate such as where the claimant is a 'patent troll' alleging infringement of his patent.[4] Even if an injunction is warranted under the circumstances of the case, there may be difficulty in framing the scope of the injunction. It must not prevent the defendant doing something which he may legally do. Nor must it be vague or ambiguous: its scope must be clear to the defendant; bearing in mind failure to comply may result in an action for contempt of court.

By s 50 of the Senior Courts Act 1981,[5] the court has discretion to award damages in lieu of, or in addition to, an injunction. In *Chiron Corp v Organon Teknika Ltd (No 10)*[6] the defendant argued that an injunction would be contrary to the public interest. The patent in question related to test kits for the hepatitis C virus, and the defendant claimed that an injunction would prevent the public having access to the kits and would hinder research and development. Aldous J said that the test in *Shelfer v City of London Electric Lighting Co*[7] laid down by Smith LJ was still appropriate. The test (or rather, working rule) is that:

1 if the injury to the claimant's legal rights is small; and
2 is one which is capable of being estimated in money; and
3 is one which can adequately be compensated by a small monetary payment; and
4 the case is one in which it would be oppressive to the defendant to grant an injunction;

then damages in substitution for an injunction may be given. However, that is a 'good working rule' and the court's discretion under the section is not limited and the interests of third parties or the public can be taken into account. Considering the general nature of the patent monopoly and controls over abuses, Aldous J refused to limit the injunctions sought. He also refused a stay of the injunctions pending appeal.

Where the loss claimed is not itself recoverable, for example, for being too remote under tortious principles, an injunction will not be granted to protect the proprietor or exclusive licensee from such loss. This was said by Goff LJ in *Polaroid Corp v Eastman Kodak Co*[8] and, in *Peaudouce SA v Kimberley-Clark Ltd*,[9] the court held that it was wrong in principle to grant an injunction to protect against an irrecoverable loss, in that case, being a loss to other members of the claimant's group of companies.

Where a case has been determined on its merits and there is an appeal, the court may decide to grant a stay of any injunction. However, in such cases, the *American Cyanamid*[10] principles (discussed later) are less relevant: they apply to interim hearings. Where there is an appeal against a decision taken at full trial, an application for a stay should be decided in accordance with the approach set out by Buckley LJ in *Minnesota Mining and Manufacturing Co v Johnson & Johnson Ltd*.[11] A major factor is that the claimant's patent has been held to be valid and infringed and, in *Minnesota Mining*, Buckley LJ said (at 676):

> The object . . . must surely be so to arrange matters that, when the appeal comes to be heard, the appellate court may be able to do justice between the parties, whatever the outcome of the appeal may be.

Important factors are whether the appeal is to be made in good faith and whether there is a genuine chance of the appeal being successful, damage caused to the parties either way and, of course, the particular facts of the case.

There are special provisions which apply in relation to injunctions against service providers (including internet service providers) under the law of copyright and rights in performances which are discussed further in Chapter 6.

A special form of injunction is the interim injunction. This prevents the alleged infringer carrying out the alleged infringing acts until the full trial of the action. Interim injunctions are discussed in more detail later in this chapter.

3 A limited injunction may be available against a wrongdoer who was responsible for publishing the information in breach of confidence.

4 A patent troll is a person holding a patent but who does not exploit it or grant licences in the normal run of things. He simply waits for a third party to carry out some act which he alleges infringes his patent and then threatens litigation unless the third party agrees payment, often in the form a lump sum and ongoing royalty payments. See the section on patent trolls in Chapter 11.

5 Previously named the Supreme Court Act 1981. It was renamed to reflect the changes to the courts resulting in the replacement of the House of Lords court by the Supreme Court.

6 [1995] FSR 325.

7 [1895] 1 Ch 287.

8 [1977] RPC 379.

9 [1996] FSR 680.

10 *American Cyanamid Co v Ethicon Ltd* [1975] AC 396.

11 [1976] RPC 672.

In relation to the special provisions that apply to injunctions against information society service providers there is also a mechanism involving internet service providers under the Digital Economy Act 2010, which inserts a new s 124H into the Communications Act 2003, in relation to online infringement of copyright. Both of these sets of provisions are discussed in Chapter 6 on rights, infringement and remedies.

Damages

The general rule is that damages should by assessed on the basis that the award is intended to place the claimant in the position he would have been in but for the wrong. As Lord Wilberforce said in *General Tire & Rubber Co* v *Firestone Tyre & Rubber Co Ltd* (at 824):[12]

12 [1975] 1 RPC 203.

> As in the case of any other tort (leaving aside cases where exemplary damages can be given) the object of damages is to compensate for loss or injury. The general rule at any rate in relation to 'economic' torts is that the measure of damages is to be, so far as possible, that sum of money which will put the injured party in the same position as he would have been in if he had not sustained the wrong.

In relation to patents, Lord Wilberforce went on to identify three types of situation:

1 Where the claimant makes and sells a product, the damages should be assessed on the basis of the profits lost by the claimant as a result of the infringement.
2 Where the claimant grants licences to others to exploit his invention, damages should be calculated on the basis of the royalties the defendant would have paid, had he acted legally.
3 Where it is not possible to prove a normal rate of profit or a normal licence royalty, damages must still be assessed. In such a case, it is for the claimant to adduce evidence to guide the court. This may include evidence of licences in the relevant or analogous trades. The court will then have to assess the relevance and comparability of such licences and apply them so far as it can to the hypothetical bargain made by the parties: on the basis of a notional licence between a willing licensor and willing licensee.

Of course, Lord Wilberforce was dealing with a patent case and the three situations are not of universal application. For example, what is the measure of damages in relation to infringement of a copyright work which its owner has no intention of exploiting economically, such as personal diary? What if the owner of a patent who makes and sells the product protected by the patent also claims to have lost sales in other non-patented products normally sold alongside the patented product? We will see how the courts deal with such issues in the relevant Parts of this book in relation to particular intellectual property rights.

The Directive on the enforcement of intellectual property rights must now be taken into account. Article 13 of the Directive deals with the assessment of damages. It is set out fully in the section on the Directive later in this chapter. It is arguable whether it adds anything to the court's previous powers and discretions in relation to the assessment of damages. However, Article 13 does specifically mention moral prejudice as being a potential factor in the assessment of damages.

Certainly, where the subject-matter is exploited by the owner of the relevant intellectual property right, damages may be assessed on the basis of lost profits or the royalty or fees he would have earned had he licensed the use complained of. Moral prejudice may be relevant in terms of damages for infringing certain works of copyright or rights of performers. An account of profits may be appropriate where the defendant did not know and did not have reasonable grounds to know that he was engaged in an infringing activity.

Account of profits

An account of profits is a remedy expressly available in legislation relating to actions for infringement of copyright and related rights, patents, designs and trade marks. It is an alternative to damages which the claimant may elect between. An account is also available for the equitable action of breach of confidence and the common law tort of passing off.

An account of profits may be a useful alternative for the claimant in that the infringer may have made a profit from his actions which exceeds in value what would be the normal award of damages. The purpose of the remedy is to prevent unjust enrichment of the defendant.[13] The quantum of an account is the profit, that is the gain, made by the defendant attributable to the infringement and not the wholesale or retail value of the offending articles or materials. Consider the following hypothetical example which, for the sake of simplicity, ignores taxes. Arthur makes 2,000 pirate copies of a popular sound recording, the copyright in which is owned by Zenith Ltd, and has sold the copies to a retailer, Nadir Music Ltd. Arthur charged Nadir £3 for each one and Nadir sells them at £5.50 each. The cost to Arthur of making the pirate copies, packaging and delivery, etc. is £3,750. If Arthur is successfully sued by Zenith for the infringement by making copies, and Zenith asks for an account of profits, Zenith should be entitled to the following sum:

Authur's income	2,000 × £3	= £6,000
Authur's expenditure		= £3,750
Profit made by Authur		= £2,250

Therefore, an account of profits should yield Zenith £2,250 (plus interest from the date or dates of infringement). This may be better than claiming damages, which will not be available in some cases[14] (although it is almost certain in the example that Arthur would have known that copyright subsisted in the original sound recording). Damages could be based on the fact that Zenith has been deprived of 2,000 sales, and if its profit margin is usually 10 per cent and the normal retail price is £7.50, damages would amount to £1,500: 2,000 × £7.50 × 10% = £1,500. Damages based on a notional lost royalty might amount to only: 12.5 per cent of 2,000 × £3 = £750, assuming a typical royalty of 12.5 per cent.

Attractive though an account of profits might appear, there are likely to be great practical difficulties in determining what the profit was in relation to the infringement, and it may be well nigh impossible to isolate this profit from the other profits made concurrently by the defendant in other, legitimate, dealings. Nevertheless, because, unlike ordinary damages, accounts are available regardless of the defendant's knowledge as to whether copyright subsisted in the work, an account of profits may be the only way in which the copyright owner can recover some monetary compensation for the infringement if the defendant's knowledge is likely to be in issue. It is clear that an account of profits is available, subject to any equitable defences, regardless of the defendant's knowledge.[15] In practice, the remedies of damages and accounts should be considered to be alternatives. Where additional damages are available,[16] they can only be claimed in addition to ordinary damages and not an account of profits.

Additional damages

Additional damages are a possibility for infringement of copyright and related rights and the UK unregistered design right. They can be thought of as a form of punitive damages

13 *Potton Ltd* v *Yorkclose Ltd* [1990] FSR 11 per Millett J.

14 Where the defendant did not know and had no reason to believe that copyright subsisted in the work in question. Similar provision is made in relation to patents and designs though not registered trade marks.

15 *Weinerworld Ltd* v *Vision Video Ltd* [1998] FSR 832. Although s 97(1) states that damages are not available if the defendant did not know and had no reason to believe that copyright subsisted in the work infringed, this is without prejudice to any other remedy.

16 As they are, in appropriate cases, in cases on copyright and related rights and the UK unregistered design right.

although, strictly speaking, they are not. Additional damages are intended to be awarded where the justice of the case so requires. In deciding whether an award for additional damages is appropriate, the court should take into account all the circumstances, in particular, the flagrancy of the infringement and the benefit accruing to the defendant by reason of the infringement.[17]

Additional damages are discussed in more detail in Chapter 6 in the context of remedies for copyright infringement.

17 See, for example, ss 97(2) and 191J(2) of the Copyright, Designs and Patents Act 1988.

Groundless threats

Where a person threatens another with litigation for the infringement of an intellectual property right, any person aggrieved by the threats, may in some circumstances bring an action for groundless threats of infringement proceedings. This remedy is particularly important in terms of monopoly rights such as patents, trade marks and registered designs. It does not apply to copyright and related rights, breach of confidence or passing off. Curiously, however, it does apply to the UK unregistered design right.

As the scope and nature of the remedy varies depending which form of right is engaged, the remedy is discussed more fully in the relevant chapters on patents, design rights and trade marks. Suffice it to say at this stage that the remedy does not apply in all cases. Some types of threat cannot give rise to a groundless threats action, such as a threat of patent infringement proceedings in relation to an allegation of making or importing a product. There are also some defences to the action. A patent proprietor faced with a groundless threats action will have a defence if he shows that the patent is valid in the relevant aspects and the acts concerned indeed do infringe the patent.

The rationale behind groundless threats actions is to discourage the owner of the right from making threats against retailers and distributors of the products or signs subject to the rights: 'secondary infringers'. Such persons might be too easily dissuaded from continuing to deal with the alleged infringing articles to the detriment of the manufacturer or importer of the articles. If this happens, the alleged primary infringer, as a person aggrieved by the threats, may bring a groundless threats action even though he is not himself the direct subject of the threats. He will be a person aggrieved by the threats because his customers may no longer stock or deal with his products.

18 Patent proprietors appear to be more generously treated than the owners of other rights subject to the groundless threats action.

Although groundless threats actions vary depending of the right,[18] the remedies available if the threats are found to be groundless are the same in all cases, being:

- a declaration to the effect that the threats are unjustifiable;
- an injunction against the continuance of the threats; and
- damages in respect of any loss which the claimant has sustained by the threats.

Other remedies

Depending on the right concerned, other remedies may be available, such as delivery up of infringing articles or disposal of them. Provision is also made for search warrants in relation to some of the rights. HM Revenue and Customs also have certain powers of search and seizure in relation to infringing articles being imported into the territory of the UK.

The Directive on the enforcement of intellectual property rights

The preamble to the Directive notes that disparities between Member States in enforcing intellectual property rights prejudice the proper functioning of the internal market and make it impossible to ensure that intellectual property rights have equivalent protection throughout the European Union. The measures to be adopted in the Member States to comply with the Directive should be effective, proportionate and dissuasive.[19]

19 Article 3(2).

We will look in more detail later at Article 13 of the Directive which deals with damages. Some of the other notable provisions of the Directive are:

- allowing legal action to be commenced by rightholders, licensees in so far as permitted by the applicable law, collecting societies and professional defence bodies regularly recognised as having a right to represent holders of intellectual property rights;
- presumptions of authorship of copyright and ownership of related rights; it being sufficient that the name of the author or owner appears on copies of the work for that person to be entitled to commence legal proceedings;
- the obtaining and preservation of evidence (as provided in UK law by search orders, described later);
- ordering the provision of information as to the origin and distribution of infringing goods or services (courts already has this power in England and Wales and Northern Ireland[20] but specific provision is made for Scotland in the Intellectual Property (Enforcement, etc.) Regulations 2006);

20 As a result of the House of Lords decision in *Norwich Pharmacal v Customs and Excise Commissioners* [1974] AC 133.

- the use of interlocutory injunctions (now known in as interim injunctions, described later) and orders for seizure and delivery up and other measures such as destruction of infringing goods;
- the use of injunctions to prevent a continuation of infringing activities, including injunctions against intermediaries, without prejudice to the Directive on copyright and related rights in the information society;[21]

21 Directive 2001/29/EC of the European Parliament and of the Council of 22 May 2001 on the harmonisation of certain aspects of copyright and related rights in the information society, L 167, 22.06.2001, p 10.

- the option for a court to award pecuniary compensation instead of any of the above measures if the infringer acted unintentionally and without negligence, if the execution of the measures in question would cause the infringer disproportionate harm and if the compensation awarded to the claimant appears reasonably satisfactory;
- if the applicant so requests, the court may order the dissemination of information about the decision; Member States may provide for additional publicity measures, as appropriate in the circumstances, including prominent advertising (specific provision is made for Scotland in the Intellectual Property (Enforcement, etc) Regulations 2006);
- Member States may apply other appropriate measures where intellectual property rights have been infringed;
- Member States shall encourage the development of codes of conduct at an EU level to contribute to the enforcement of intellectual property rights, including, for example, the use of codes on optical discs enabling the identification of the origin of their manufacture.

Most of these measures and provisions were already catered for in the UK in terms of the court's powers and discretions, existing intellectual property legislation, rules of court and Practice Directions. Some changes were necessary, such as provision for Scotland as noted above. Apart from expressly implementing the provision on damages,[22] amendments were made to the Registered Designs Act 1949, the Patents Act 1977, the Copyright, Designs and Patents Act 1988 and the Trade Marks Act 1994 and some secondary legislation. Some of these amendments implement the presumptions where they were not

22 This was probably unnecessary in the light of the judge's discretion.

23 For example, presumptions in relation to performers' right, the publication right and the database right.

24 SI 2006/1028.

25 As usual, the UK implementing legislation rewrites Article 13.

26 In practice, the calculation will often be more complex. For example, Ferric may have reduced the price of its articles in an attempt to compete with Alloys.

27 Exclusive licensees also have the right to bring an action for infringement of a patent: s 67 Patents Act 1977. For some of the other intellectual property rights, under certain circumstances, non-exclusive licensees also have a right to bring an infringement action. An example is s 101A of the Copyright, Designs and Patents Act 1988. For the meaning and implications of exclusive and non-exclusive licensees, *see* the Glossary at the start of the book and sections covering ownership and dealing with the relevant rights.

already provided for.[23] Other amendments implement provisions contained in some legislation but inexplicably missing in other legislation, such as the nature of the property right in a registered design, assignment and exclusive licences and the exemption from liability for damages of 'innocent infringers' in relation to registered designs. The discussions in the relevant sections of this book take account of these and other changes made by the Intellectual Property (Enforcement, etc.) Regulations 2006.[24]

Assessment of damages

Article 13 of the Directive states:

1   Member States shall ensure that the competent judicial authorities, on application of the injured party, order the infringer who knowingly, or with reasonable grounds to know, engaged in an infringing activity, to pay the rightholder damages appropriate to the actual prejudice suffered by him as a result of the infringement.
When the judicial authorities set the damages:

(a) they shall take into account all appropriate aspects, such as the negative economic consequences, including lost profits, which the injured party has suffered, any unfair profits made by the infringer and, in appropriate cases, elements other than economic factors, such as the moral prejudice caused to the rightholder by the infringement; or

(b) as an alternative to (a), they may, in appropriate cases, set the damages as a lump sum on the basis of elements such as at least the amount of royalties or fees which would have been due if the infringer had requested authorisation to use the intellectual property right in question.

2   Where the infringer did not knowingly, or with reasonable grounds to know, engage in infringing activity, Member States may lay down that the judicial authorities may order the recovery of profits or the payment of damages, which may be pre-established.[25]

Paragraph 1 of Article 13 applies where the defendant knew or ought to have known in the circumstances that he was infringing the intellectual property right. Two possibilities then exist. Either the court awards damages based on the claimant's actual loss taking into account any unfair profits made by the defendant and non-economic factors such as moral prejudice suffered by the claimant as a result of the infringement. In the alternative, the court will assess damages based on a hypothetical licence which would have made the defendant's acts lawful. It all depends on the circumstances. Take some examples:

● Ferric Ltd is the proprietor of a UK patent and it manufactures and sells articles made in accordance with that patent in the UK at £50 each. Ferric makes a profit of £10 on each article. Alloys Ltd has been selling in the UK equivalent articles which infringe the patent but sells them at £45. Although Alloys did not know of the patent, the circumstances are such that it ought to have known about it. Ferric has evidence that it has lost sales of some 3,500 units. Damages might be assessed at 3,500 × £10 = £35,000.[26] Ferric would also ask for an injunction to prevent a continuation of the infringement.

● As above, but rather than manufacture the articles itself, Ferric granted non-exclusive licences to companies wishing to manufacture the articles.[27] The royalty rate is set at 15 per cent of the price charged by the companies for the articles, which averages around £40. Alloys has made and sold 2,000 articles which infringe the Ferric patent. Damages based on a notional licence agreement with Alloys would be 2,000 × £40 ×15% = £12,000.

● Peter wrote a short story which he published himself. It sold at £6.00 a copy. Publishing and distribution costs worked out at £3.50 each. Linda wrote a spoof of the story which she placed on a website. Peter has evidence that, as a result or persons thinking that the spoof was a reflection of the quality of his story, he has lost sales of some 500 copies. The court also accepted his claim that the spoof was a derogatory treatment of his story. The award is 500 × £2.50 = £1,250 for lost sales and the court has also awarded £2,500 on the basis of the derogatory treatment of his story, accepting that it was prejudicial to his honour and reputation as an author.[28]

Paragraph 2 of Article 13 covers the alternative case where the defendant did not know and did not have reasonable grounds to know he was infringing the right. Typically UK law provides that 'innocent infringers' may still be liable for an account of profits.

Blackburne J applied Article 13 of the Directive in *Experience Hendrix LLC* v *Times Newspapers Ltd*[29] in his initial assessment of damages in respect of the distribution of a CD of Jimi Hendrix recordings with the *Sunday Times*. The CDs had previously been held to infringe performance rights and rights in recordings.

First, Blackburne J held that paragraph 1 applied as, at the relevant time, the defendant had reasonable grounds to know that it was engaged in an infringing activity. He then went on to identify Article 13(1)(a) as being a 'loss sustained' approach, whilst Article 13(1)(b) was a 'notional licence' approach. He decided a loss sustained approach was the correct one in the circumstances. The claimants had to suspend their exploitation of their recordings because of the distribution of the CDs by the defendant. Furthermore, the notional licence approach raised formidable difficulties as it would require the court to estimate what royalties would have been payable in respect of making and distributing poor quality illicit recordings of Jimi Hendrix's performances: something the claimant's would never have permitted. After considering the evidence, Blackburne J reckoned that the claimants had been deprived of the use of $5.8 million by virtue of delaying their exploitation of the recordings. He therefore awarded the interest this sum would have made at US bank base rate plus 1 per cent for a period of nearly two years.[30] This would be considerably less than the original claims.[31]

Publicity

At the request of the applicant (that is, claimant) in an IP infringement case and at the expense of the infringer, Article 15 of the Directive requires Member States to take appropriate measures to disseminate the decision. This includes displaying the decision and publishing it in full or in part. Furthermore, Member States may provide for additional publicity measures which are appropriate to the particular circumstances including prominent advertising.

The fact that full judgments are published in most cases will at least go some way to satisfying these requirements. Sometimes more is needed. In *Redwood Tree Services Ltd* v *Apsey (t/a Redwood Tree Surgeons)*,[32] a passing off case, the claimant sought an order for dissemination of the judgment. Although passing off was found, the injunction was in relation to a local area and the defendant could continue to use his trading name in other areas and on his website providing he made it clear that his business was not, and not connected with, the claimant's business. As far as dissemination of the judgment, HH Judge Birss QC thought it was appropriate to require that the defendant placed a reference to the judgment on his website. This was to be for a limited time only and, after hearing counsel, the judge ordered that the reference should remain on the defendant's website for six months.

EU Report on the Directive

Since the implementation of the Directive, there has been a report from the EU which notes that, following implementation, there has been an improvement in enforcement procedures.[33] However, the volume and financial value of intellectual property infringements

28 The right to object to a derogatory treatment of a work is one of the moral rights under copyright law.

29 [2010] EWHC 1986 (Ch).

30 In practice the calculation was somewhat more complicated than this.

31 The first claimant had claimed nearly $9 million and the second claimant had claimed over $17 million.

32 [2011] EWPCC 14.

33 Commission Report on the Application of Directive 2004/48/EC of the European Parliament and of the Council of 29 April 2004 on the enforcement of intellectual property rights, COM (2010) 0779 final.

is alarming. A major reason for this is the increased opportunities to infringe offered by the internet, something the Directive was not specifically designed to deal with. The Report recognises that this is the main issue requiring further attention. Clarification of some of the provisions in the Directive should also be considered in future initiatives.

There follows a discussion of two of the main weapons in the armoury of claimant in intellectual property cases, the search order and the interim injunction. Both of these have the main origins in intellectual property cases.

Search order

In terms of all the forms of intellectual property, the question of obtaining evidence is of vital importance. If the person infringing the right discovers that he is about to be sued for that infringement, he may be tempted to destroy materials and articles which would incriminate him, such as pirate copies of music and film on CDs or DVDs. If the owner of an intellectual property right believes that his rights are being infringed and there is a real danger that the person involved will dispose of the evidence before the trial, the owner can apply to the High Court for a search order (formerly known as an *Anton Piller* order) which will enable him, accompanied by his solicitor, to enter the premises where the offending materials and articles are kept and remove them, or have copies made, so they can be produced at the trial.

The *Anton Piller* order took its name from a case involving the alleged disclosure of confidential information and copyright documents relating to frequency converters for computers. In *Anton Piller KG* v *Manufacturing Processes Ltd*,[34] it was held that, in exceptional circumstances, where the claimant has an extremely strong *prima facie* case, where the actual or potential damage to the claimant is very serious, where it was clear that the defendant possessed vital evidence and where there was a real possibility that he might destroy or dispose of such material so as to defeat the ends of justice, the court had the jurisdiction to order the defendant to 'permit' the claimant's representatives to enter the defendant's premises and inspect and remove such materials.

The object of a search order in this context is the preservation of evidence. When an order is granted, the claimant has to give an undertaking in damages in case the claimant is wrong and the defendant suffers damage as a result of the execution of the order. However, before the court will grant a search order, the claimant must be able to convince the court that he has a strong case and that the order is indeed essential to the ends of justice.[35] In *Systematica Ltd* v *London Computer Centre Ltd*,[36] Whitford J said that 'too free a use is being made of the *Anton Piller* provision'. In that case, the defendant was carrying on his business quite openly and there was only a mere suspicion that he was infringing the claimant's copyright. There was nothing to stop the claimant from simply walking into the defendant's shop and buying the articles in question over the counter. Sometimes, there is a suspicion that the motives for applying for the order are not to obtain evidence, but to remove so much material that the alleged infringer is, effectively, put out of business.

It is very important that the claimant does not exceed the provisions of a search order. In *Columbia Picture Industries* v *Robinson*,[37] the claimants (there were 35 of them) alleged that the defendant was a video pirate and claimed that he had copied 104 films, infringing copyright, registered trade marks and, additionally, being guilty of the tort of passing off. The claimants sought and obtained a search order and a freezing injunction (previously known as a *Mareva* injunction), the purpose of the latter being to freeze the defendant's assets, preventing him from removing them from the jurisdiction of the court. But the claimants were excessive in their execution of the search order and they took more material than was identified in the order, virtually emptying the defendant's

34 [1976] 1 Ch 55. The first reported search order case, *EMI Ltd* v *Pandit* [1975] FSR 111, involved an action for infringement of copyright. In that case, reference was made to an application for an *ex parte* order for inspection in a much older case, *Hennessy* v *Bohmann, Osborne & Co* [1877] WN 1 – a passing off action.

35 In *Jeffrey Rogers Knitwear Productions Ltd* v *Vinola (Knitwear) Manufacturing Co* [1985] FSR 184, Whitford J, in discharging an *Anton Piller* order, said that it was improper to rely on stale evidence used in other proceedings in making application to the court for an order. The applicant must prepare his application to a very high standard, especially if it is made *ex parte* (now without notice), as will usually be the case.

36 [1983] FSR 313.

37 [1987] 1 Ch 38.

premises, apparently taking even the defendant's divorce papers and private correspondence. It appeared that the claimants' real motive in obtaining the order was to shut down the defendant's business. It was held that the method of execution was an abuse of the order. While accepting that the defendant had been infringing copyright and awarding an injunction and damages to the claimants, Scott J awarded the sum of £10,000 in compensatory and aggravated damages to the defendant under the claimants' cross-undertaking in damages.

Scott J identified five criteria essential to the execution of a search order as follows.

1 The order must be drawn so as to extend no further than the minimum extent necessary to achieve its purpose, that is the preservation of documents or articles which might otherwise be destroyed or concealed. After inspection and copying by the claimant's solicitors, the materials should be returned to the owner.
2 A detailed record should be made by the solicitors executing the order of the materials to be taken before removal from the defendant's premises.
3 Only materials clearly covered by the order should be taken.
4 If the ownership of seized material is in dispute, it should be handed over to the defendant's solicitors on their undertaking for its safe custody and production.
5 The affidavits in support ought to err on the side of excessive disclosure. In the case of material falling in the grey area of possible relevance, the judge, not the claimant's solicitor, should be the arbiter.

Search orders have been abused in their exercise in the past, so they are now granted sparingly. Further guidelines were suggested by Nicholls V-C in *Universal Thermosensors Ltd v Hibben*[38] which concerned the execution of an order at a private house at 7.15 am. The house was occupied at the time by a woman and her children. The Vice-Chancellor made the following points:

38 [1992] 3 All ER 257.

(a) The order should be executed during normal office hours so that the defendant could take immediate legal advice.
(b) If the order was to be executed at a private dwelling and there was a chance that a woman might be alone there, the solicitor executing the order should be accompanied by a woman.
(c) A list of items taken should be made, giving the defendant an opportunity to check it.
(d) If the order contained an injunction restraining the defendant from informing others (for example, co-defendants), the period should not be too long.
(e) In the absence of good reason otherwise, orders should be executed at business premises in the presence of a responsible officer or representative of the defendant's company.
(f) Provision should be made to prevent the claimant going through all the defendant's documents (for example, where the parties were competitors and the claimant could thereby gain useful and sensitive information about the defendant's business unrelated to the alleged infringement).
(g) Ideally, the order should be executed by a neutral solicitor who was experienced in the execution of search orders.

A standard form was developed for search orders.[39] A copy of the form, which should be used except where the judge hearing the application considers there is good reason for using a different form, is contained in the *Practice Direction: Mareva Injunctions and Anton Piller Orders*.[40] The order requires the addressee to allow the persons listed to enter the named premises, to hand over articles and provide information as required. It also states that the addressee may insist that, apart from the claimant's solicitor, any person who could gain commercially from what he might read or see is not present and that entry may be refused before 9.30 am or after 5.30 am, or on Saturday or Sunday.

39 Standard forms have also been made for notice of *Mareva* injunctions.

40 [1994] 1 WLR 1552. The standard forms were replaced by those in the *Practice Direction (Mareva Injunctions and Anton Piller Orders: Forms)* [1996] 1 WLR 1552.

The *Practice Direction* itself stresses the use of an independent supervising solicitor who is familiar with the operation of search orders and, *inter alia*, requires a woman to be present when the order is served if it is likely that the premises are occupied by an unaccompanied woman and, where appropriate, that items removed under the order are insured by the claimant.

Although the *Practice Direction* made the use of search orders more satisfactory, controversy about them and their execution remained. The Lord Chancellor's Department had previously issued an advisory paper suggesting, *inter alia*, that the order be placed on a statutory footing.[41] This was done and, in England and Wales, is provided for under s 7 of the Civil Procedure Act 1997. This allows the court to make an order for the purpose of securing the preservation of evidence or property that may become the subject matter of proceedings. The order will describe the steps to be taken which may include carrying out a search for or inspecting anything described in the order or the making or obtaining of a copy, photograph or sample or other record as may be described in the order. The order may also require the provision of information or articles and for the safe keeping or retention of anything described in the order. The right of an individual (or spouse or civil partner) to refuse to do anything on the grounds of self-incrimination is not affected by s 7.

Even though a defendant has behaved wrongfully the grant of a search order is not inevitable apart from any issue of the balance of convenience. For example, a person who has knowingly and wrongfully taken confidential information may still comply with a court order for delivery up. In *Lock International plc* v *Beswick*,[42] Hoffmann J said that there must be proportionality between the perceived threat to the claimant's rights and the remedy granted. Where the subject matter of a search order is in software form stored on computers in the defendant's possession and there is a serious danger that, although the defendant was likely to comply with an order for delivery up of the computers, he will first erase the software, the grant of an order might well be appropriate.[43]

Search orders and the privilege against self-incrimination

Infringing intellectual property rights, in some circumstances, may also involve criminal offences. For example, making copies of a work of copyright without permission and selling those copies, knowing or having reason to believe the copies are infringing copies is a criminal offence under the Copyright, Designs and Patents Act 1988 s 107, as well as a civil infringement of copyright under s 16 and, indeed, a secondary infringement under s 23. Making or dealing with counterfeit articles may also attract criminal liability in a number of ways, under specific intellectual property legislation, trade descriptions and related legislation or, where two or more people are involved, as common law conspiracy to defraud. In many cases, civil wrongs will also be committed, such as under the Trade Marks Act 1994.

The rule against self-incrimination is firmly rooted in English law. However, because of the overlap between the civil and criminal law in intellectual property matters, a defendant complying with a court order, such as a search order, may find that he is asked to hand over documents or other materials tending to show that he has committed criminal offences. In *Rank Film Distributors Ltd* v *Video Information Centre*,[44] the House of Lords upheld the Court of Appeal's decision to the effect that the privilege against self-incrimination could be invoked in such cases, pointing to practical difficulties including the fact that search orders are intended to take effect immediately. To overcome this decision, which could have significantly weakened if not destroyed the effectiveness of search orders, in England and Wales, the Senior Courts Act 1981[45] s 72 withdrew the privilege in civil proceedings relating to infringement of intellectual property rights and passing off. In terms of proceedings for intellectual property infringement or passing off, to obtain

41 *Anton Piller Orders: A Consultation Paper*, Lord Chancellor's Department, November 1992.

42 [1989] 1 WLR 1269 at 1281.

43 *Indicii Salus Ltd* v *Chandrasekaran* [2006] EWHC 680 (Ch).

44 [1982] AC 380.

45 Previously known as the Supreme Court Act 1981.

disclosure of information relating to intellectual property infringement or passing off or to prevent any apprehended infringement of any intellectual property right or for passing off, it states that:

> . . . a person shall not be excused, by reason that to do so would tend to expose that person, or his or her spouse or civil partner, to proceedings for a related offence or for the recovery of a related penalty –
> (a) from answering any question put to that person in the first-mentioned proceedings; or
> (b) from complying with any order made in those proceedings.

The section goes on to say that statements or admissions made in answering questions or complying with an order are not admissible in proceedings for related offences or the recovery of related penalties, except in proceedings for perjury or contempt of court.

The scope of the rule against self-incrimination and the impact of s 72 of the 1981 Act are very important in terms of intellectual property matters, particularly in terms of whether the protection in s 72 is available in respect of civil contempt. This may be relevant in terms of a failure to comply with a court order: for example, a search order or undertakings given to the court, say, in a consent order. Distinguishing civil contempt from criminal contempt, it was held in *Cobra Golf Inc* v *Rata*[46] that civil contempt was a related penalty and s 72 applied. In that case, the alleged contempt was in relation to a consent order given by the defendants in an action for trade mark infringement and passing off concerning golf clubs bearing a snake device.

Not all forms of confidential information can be considered to fall within the meaning of intellectual property. Section 72(5) defines 'intellectual property' as '. . . any patent, trade mark, copyright, design right, registered design, technical or commercial information or other intellectual property'. In *Gray* v *News Group Newspapers Ltd*,[47] involving the interception of mobile phone communications made or received by the football commentator Andy Gray and the comedian Steve Coogan, Vos J held that the type of technical or commercial information which s 72(5) was aimed at was that which was confidential and protectable by an action in breach of confidence, breach of contract or some other breach of duty.

Following the Directive on the enforcement of intellectual property rights, discussed earlier in this chapter, the European Commission issued a statement identifying those rights which it regarded as falling within the scope of intellectual property rights covered by the Directive.[48] Those rights were: copyright, rights related to copyright, the *sui generis* database right, semiconductor topography rights, trade mark rights, design rights, patent rights (including rights under supplementary protection certificates), geographical indications, utility model rights, plant variety rights and trade names where protected as exclusive property rights in Member States. The list is not exhaustive and doubts still remain, in particular, as to whether domain names and trade secrets (including know-how) are covered.

Interim injunction

In a situation where a person is selling or distributing infringing articles, it is vital that the owner of the right takes action as quickly as possible.[49] Unless the person infringing the intellectual property right concerned can be stopped quickly, the damage will be considerable, and it may be a number of years before a full civil action can be heard, after which time the person responsible for the infringement may have disappeared or dissipated his assets and be a 'man of straw'. Therefore, the availability and use of interim injunctions (formerly known as 'interlocutory injunctions') is extremely important in terms of all intellectual property rights. An interim injunction is intended to take effect pending the full trial. The claimant must undertake to pay the defendant's losses resulting from the

46 [1997] FSR 317.

47 [2011] 2 WLR 1401. In that case, no less than 20 statutory definitions of 'intellectual property' were found.

48 Statement by the Commission concerning Article 2 of Directive 2004/48/EC of the European Parliament and of the Council on the enforcement of intellectual property rights, L 94, 13.04.2005, p 37.

49 The doctrine of laches ('delay defeats equity') is relevant here.

interim injunction should the defendant succeed at the full trial. Interim injunctions are often sufficient to dispose of a case which never comes to a full trial, either because the defendant loses heart and realises he has little chance of eventual success or because the effects on his business are crippling: therefore, such injunctions are not lightly granted.

Certain criteria are used by the courts in determining whether or not to grant an interim injunction. In *American Cyanamid Co v Ethicon Ltd*,[50] a case concerning an alleged infringement of the patent relating to a surgical suture, the basis for granting an interim injunction was discussed. Lord Diplock said (at 406):

50 [1975] AC 396.

> The object of an interlocutory injunction is to protect the claimant against injury by violation of his right for which he could not be adequately compensated in damages recoverable in the action if the uncertainty were resolved in his favour at the trial; but the claimant's need for such protection must be weighed against the corresponding need of the defendant to be protected against injury resulting from his having been prevented from exercising his own legal rights for which he would not be adequately compensated under the plaintiff's undertaking in damages if the uncertainty were resolved in the defendant's favour at the trial. The court must weigh one need against another and determine where the 'balance of convenience' lies.

Obviously, the court must be satisfied that there is a serious issue to be tried. If there is, then the court must weigh the claimant's and the defendant's needs in the balance of convenience. In a wide sense, this will call for a consideration of whether damages would adequately compensate the claimant if the injunction were refused and the claimant succeeds at the trial, and whether the claimant's undertaking in damages to an injuncted defendant would be adequate to protect him should he succeed at the trial. If there is some doubt as to whether damages would adequately compensate either party, depending on the outcome at the trial, a narrow balance of convenience is used involving a variety of factors. This will usually call for a consideration of the impact of granting or refusing the injunction on each of the parties.

The test was later modified for cases where the granting or refusal of the injunction would have the effect of finally disposing of the matter (for example, where it would completely close down the defendant's entire business operation). In such cases, in *NWL Ltd v Woods*,[51] which concerned a shipping trade dispute, Lord Diplock said that the likelihood of the claimant succeeding in his claim for an injunction at the full trial was a factor that should be brought into the 'balance of convenience' by the judge in considering the risks of injustice from his deciding the application one way rather than another. The *American Cyanamid* approach is not of universal application. For example, if the complaint concerns an alleged breach of covenant in restraint of trade, an interim injunction will be appropriate if the covenant is prima facie valid.[52] To fail to grant the injunction would be to deprive the covenantee completely of the benefit of the covenant.

51 [1979] 1 WLR 1294.

52 *Office Overload Ltd v Gunn* [1977] FSR 39.

At one time, it was thought that, except in exceptional cases like *NWL v Woods*, all the claimant had to show was a serious issue before the court engaged in a consideration of the balance of convenience. Interim injunctions can be traced back to the Court of Chancery and, before *American Cyanamid*, the courts usually adopted a flexible approach. For example, in *Hubbard v Vosper*,[53] Lord Denning said (at 96):

53 [1972] 2 QB 84.

> The remedy by interlocutory injunction is so useful that it should be kept flexible and discretionary. It must not be made the subject of strict rules.

Whilst the sentiment was approved by the House of Lords in *American Cyanamid*, many thought that Lord Diplock had intended that a consideration of the relative strength of the parties' cases should not be made. Of course, one justification for this was that the court would not, in an application for an interim injunction, have the benefit of all the evidence and argument that would be present in a full trial. Nevertheless, Laddie J disagreed with this interpretation of Lord Diplock's judgment in *Series 5 Software Ltd v Philip*

Clarke.[54] After looking again at *American Cyanamid*, Laddie J said that, when deciding whether to grant interim relief, the court should bear the following matters in mind:

54 [1996] FSR 273.

(a) The grant of an interim injunction was a matter of discretion and depended on all the facts of the case.
(b) There were no fixed rules.
(c) The court should rarely attempt to resolve complex issues of disputed fact or law.
(d) Major factors to be taken into account are:
  (i) the extent to which damages would be likely to be an adequate remedy and the ability of the other party to pay
  (ii) the balance of convenience
  (iii) the maintenance of the status quo, and
  (iv) any clear view the court may reach as to the relative strength of the parties' cases.

This approach of taking the relative strength of the parties' cases into account was followed in *EMAP Publications Ltd v Security Publications Ltd*.[55] An interim injunction was granted which prohibited the defendant from using a magazine cover format bearing some similarities to that of the claimant. The grant of the injunction would have been decisive, as the defendant would not have returned to its original design of cover even if it won at full trial. In such circumstances, the court was entitled to take a view as to the strength of the respective cases of each party.

55 [1997] FSR 891.

An interim injunction will not be granted if the claimant's claim is frivolous or vexatious, or if there is some doubt about whether the claimant would be granted an injunction and substantial damages at the full trial. It was so held in *Entec Pollution Control Ltd v Abacus Mouldings*,[56] in which it was alleged that the defendant had indirectly infringed the claimant's copyright in sketches for flask-shaped septic tanks. It was doubtful that the defendant would have been able to pay substantial damages, but it was equally doubtful whether the claimant would indeed be awarded substantial damages. As the claimant did not have a strong case, the issue would have to be tried at a full trial and not pre-empted. In some cases, the public interest may be relevant, and in *Secretary of State for the Home Department v Central Broadcasting Ltd*[57] it was held that the public interest did not require an interim injunction to prevent the showing of a film, alleged to infringe copyright, which included an interview with the serial killer Denis Nilsen. The appellant's argument that the trial judge had taken too narrow a view of the balance of convenience and had failed sufficiently to consider the risk of distress to the relatives of the killer's victims was rejected by the Court of Appeal.

56 [1992] FSR 332.

57 *The Times*, 28 January 1993.

As mentioned above, an injunction, including an interim injunction, will not usually be granted by the court if it appears to the court that damages will fairly compensate the claimant. Two questions are relevant in this respect:

1 Will the loss to the claimant be adequately compensated for by damages awarded later?
2 Is the defendant likely to be able to pay such damages?

In an application for an interim injunction, the application of the *American Cyanamid* principle may come down in favour of the holder of the intellectual property right concerned where it appears to the court that the assessment of the loss caused to the rightholder is so difficult as to be almost incalculable. For example, in *Leo Pharma A/S v Sandoz Ltd*,[58] a patent was for a combination cream for the treatment of psoriasis. Jacob LJ said (at para 22):

58 [2008] EWCA Civ 850.

> The real point is that Leo currently have a monopoly price. If Sandoz come in with their considerable marketing powers, as a substantial company, and were to lower their price, the consequences of working out the financial damage to Leo go beyond merely difficult to being incalculable.

The speed with which the claimant seeks the injunction may be relevant, because if the infringement complained of has been tolerated for some time, the assumption is that the effects cannot be that serious. Additionally, failure to apply for an interim injunction may seriously prejudice the claimant's chances of obtaining a permanent injunction at the full trial.[59]

59 *Jaggard* v *Sawyer* [1995] 1 WLR 269.

60 [1999] FSR 834.

The terms of the injunction are important and should not leave the defendant in danger of contempt of court proceedings through no fault of his own. In *Microsoft Corp* v *Plato Technology Ltd*,[60] the defendant sold five copies of infringing software without realising they were counterfeit. He had bought them from an unauthorised dealer. The terms of the injunction were that the defendant undertook not to deal with the claimant's software which he knew or ought upon reasonable inquiry to have known to be counterfeit. An order not to obtain software from unauthorised dealers, whilst it would have met the claimant's concerns, was considered by the judge to be an unreasonable restraint of trade.

Interim injunctions and freedom of expression

61 Under Article 10 of the Council of Europe Convention for the Protection of Human Rights and Fundamental Freedoms.

62 [2005] 1 AC 253.

In an application for an interim injunction where the Convention right of freedom of expression[61] is an issue, s 12(3) of the Human Rights Act 1998 is engaged. This prevents relief to restrain publication before the full trial unless the court is satisfied that the applicant is '*likely* to establish that publication should not be allowed' (emphasis added).

In *Cream Holdings Ltd* v *Banerjee*,[62] the House of Lords held that the word 'likely' in this context meant 'more likely than not' as opposed to meaning that the applicant having to show that it was possible that he might obtain an injunction restraining publication at the full trial. However, the House of Lords went on to say that this was not a hard and fast rule and it would depend on the circumstances. For example, where disclosure could cause serious harm to the applicant for an interim injunction, a lesser standard would apply.

Freedom of expression is most likely to be an issue in breach of confidence cases and some cases involving copyright works. In such cases, the *American Cyanamid* test, as it has developed, is further modified where freedom of expression is an issue.

Criminal offences

For some of the intellectual property rights, forms of infringement which can be loosely described as counterfeiting or piracy, carry very severe maximum criminal penalties on conviction. These rights include copyright, rights in performances and registered trade marks. The maximum penalty for particular offences is a fine and/or a maximum of ten years imprisonment. Not that long ago, the maximum penalties were much lower,[63] but the massive increase of piracy and counterfeiting together with the involvement of organised gangs has justified the increases in penalties.

63 At one time, offences under copyright law carried a maximum penalty of £2 per infringing copy.

Some intellectual property rights do not carry equivalent offences. For example, it is not a criminal offence to work an invention covered by a patent. It is, however, an offence to make a false entry in the register of patents or to falsely claim that a product being sold is subject to a patent or to misuse the title 'Patent Office'. These offences carry lighter penalties and, in some cases, are not imprisonable offences.

One concern is that the mental element (*mens rea*) for some of the offences carrying potentially long prison sentences does not appear to be set at a high threshold. For example, the copyright offences simply require that the offender knew or had reason to believe that he was dealing with an infringing article. The latter part of the test being objective. The trade mark offences almost appear to be strict liability subject to a defence.

The criminal offences relating to intellectual property rights are described in more detail in the relevant parts of the book.

Summary

The main and most commonly claimed remedies for infringement of intellectual property rights are:

- injunctions;
- damages or, as an alternative, an account of profits.

An injunction is an equitable remedy and, as such, is discretionary. The purpose is to prevent the continuation of, or the commencement of, infringing activity. Under the Senior Courts Act 1981, a court may award damages in lieu of, or in addition to, the grant of an injunction. The purpose of damages is to place the claimant in the position he would have been in but for the wrong, as far as monetary compensation can do this.

For copyright and related rights and also the UK unregistered design right, additional damages are available in appropriate circumstances such as where the infringement has been flagrant. Additional damages are additional to ordinary damages only and may not be claimed alongside a claim for an account of profits.

There is an action for groundless threats of infringement proceedings which applies to some of the intellectual property rights, such as patents, trade marks and designs. These are intended to give a remedy where the owner of the right uses it to threaten litigation, for example, against retailers and distributors. Importantly, the action does not apply to copyright and rights in performances.

The Enforcement Directive sets out remedies, principles relevant to the grant and assessment of remedies and procedures for securing evidence and other measures. There is some doubt as to whether trade secrets and the rights to domain names fall within the meaning of intellectual property for the purpose of the Directive.

Important 'preliminary' remedies are:

- search orders (when granted, they will usually be 'without notice') – the rule against self-incrimination does not apply in relation to search orders and intellectual property offences;
- interim injunctions – the balance of convenience is often used to determine whether an interim injunction will be granted.

Other remedies may be available in relation to some rights and in some circumstances such as orders for delivery up, forfeiture and disposal of infringing articles. Bodies such as trading standards and HM Revenue and Customs have powers to seize counterfeit goods as does a constable executing a search warrant.

Discussion questions

1 Under what circumstances would it not be appropriate to grant (a) a permanent injunction or (b) an interim injunction?

2 What are the factors to be taken into account by a court in awarding damages in intellectual property infringement cases? Think of examples where the various factors mentioned in Article 13 of the Enforcement Directive might be applicable.

3 Are the safeguards associated with the grant and exercise of a search order sufficient to protect the rights and interests of the person who is the target of the order?

Selected further reading

Bonadio, E., 'Remedies and sanctions for the infringement of intellectual property rights under EC law', [2008] EIPR 320 (describes the provisions of the Enforcement Directive and a proposal for a Directive on criminal sanctions for IPR infringement).

Cohen, J., 'Entering the breach' (2009) New Law Journal 1575 (considers, *inter alia*, the remedies for breach of confidence).

Commission Report on the Application of Directive 2004/48/EC of the European Parliament and of the Council of 29 April 2004 on the enforcement of intellectual property rights, COM (2010) 0779 final, available at: **http://eur-lex.europa.eu/LexUriServ/LexUriServ.do?uri=COM:2010:0779:FIN:EN:PDF**.

Part Eight

EUROPEAN AND INTERNATIONAL PERSPECTIVES ON IPR

Freedom of movement of goods and services and EU competition law

25

Introduction

1 Replacing the EC Treaty.

The Treaty on the Functioning of the European Union (TFEU)[1] has many and varied competencies, principles and aims. These include a prohibition of discrimination on the grounds of nationality; the establishment and functioning of the internal market; and measures against anti-competitive practices. In the context of intellectual property, the following provisions are particularly important, being:

- 'freedom of movement of goods' – Articles 34 and 35 – prohibitions on quantitative restrictions on imports and exports (subject to derogations in Article 36);
- 'freedom to provide services' (Article 56);
- prohibition of agreements, decisions and concerted practices, which affect trade between Member States, and which have as their object or effect the prevention, restriction or distortion of competition within the internal market (Article 101);
- prohibition of abuses of dominant positions within the internal market (or a substantial part thereof) in so far as they affect trade between Member States (Article 102).

We have also seen in previous chapters, the impact of the EU in terms of the approximation of laws in the field of intellectual property[2] and the introduction of EU-wide intellectual property rights such as the Community trade mark. It is also worth noting at this stage that Article 17(2) of the Charter of Fundamental Rights of the European Union[3] confirms that intellectual property shall be protected.

2 By the adoption of various harmonising Directives. The approximation process is carried out under Article 114ff of the TFEU.

3 OJ C 83, 30.03.2010, p 389.

An intellectual property right places the owner in a privileged position by allowing him to prevent third parties doing certain acts in relation to the subject matter of the right. Certain of these rights are not intrinsically controversial, such as the right to prevent others making copies of a work in which copyright subsists without the owner's licence. Indeed, the owner of a copyright may decide not to place his work, or copies of it, on the market in the first place. However, intellectual property rights can and do come into conflict with some of the aims and objectives of the TFEU. Infringement of some intellectual property rights, such as patents and trade marks, extends to the import of infringing goods into the Member State where the patent or trade mark is registered. This could allow proprietors of patents or trade marks to interfere with the subsequent commercialisation of goods which they themselves have placed on the market in another Member State. This could lead to the fragmentation of the internal market. For example, a company which makes clothing bearing the company's trade mark, registered in France and the UK, could sell a quantity of the clothing in France and then use his UK trade mark to object to a third party, who bought some of the clothing legitimately in France, importing the clothing into the UK for resale. If this right to prevent importation were to be upheld without modification, it would encourage the company to sell its clothing at different prices in different parts of the EU. This would contribute to the fragmentation of the internal market, reinforce price differentials within the EU and interfere with the freedom of movement of goods.

Another way in which the owner of an intellectual property right can distort the market is by the way in which he grants rights to others to use the right: for example, by including restrictive terms in licence agreements or granting similar licences to a number of licensees, each in their own Member State, on different terms. Another potential abuse is for the proprietor of an intellectual property right to refuse to grant licences at all, whilst keeping prices high by limiting supplies of goods subject to the right. Yet another form of abuse is a campaign of buying all the rights in a particular technology to eliminate competition.

The relevant parts of the TFEU which apply to such activities and abuses are: Articles 34 to 36 which prohibit quantitative restrictions on imports and exports, and measures having equivalent effect, with some exceptions which include, *inter alia*, the protection of industrial and commercial property; Article 101 which prohibits certain types of restrictive agreements, decisions and practices; and Article 102 which controls abuses of dominant positions within the Community. The Agreement on the European Economic Area (the 'EEA Agreement') contains equivalent provisions in Articles 11–13, 53 and 54. The Contracting Parties to the EEA Agreement are the EU Member States, the EU itself and Iceland, Liechtenstein and Norway (the European Free Trade Area 'EFTA' States). Many of the harmonising Directives in the field of intellectual property apply also to the EFTA States.[4]

Another provision prevents discrimination on the grounds of nationality and has proved important where lack of harmonisation has enabled a Member State to treat nationals of other Member States differently to their own nationals, for example, by failing to give foreign nationals rights to prevent the sale of bootleg recordings made elsewhere. At one time, German law on copyright and related rights provided that non-German nationals could not rely on the provisions which prohibited the distribution of unauthorised recordings of performances given outside Germany.[5] In Joined Cases C-92/92 and C-326/92 *Collins* v *Imtrat Handelsgesellschaft mbH*,[6] Phil Collins and Cliff Richard argued that this provision offended against Article 12 of the EC Treaty (now Article 18 TFEU) in an action relating to the distribution in Germany of bootleg recordings of their performances given in the USA and the UK. The German court referred the matter to the European Court of Justice (now the Court of Justice of the European Union, or simply the 'Court of Justice') for a preliminary ruling under Article 234 of the EC Treaty,[7] where it was confirmed that copyright and related rights fell within the scope of Article 12 and the principle of non-discrimination applied to those rights.[8] Even though there was not yet full harmonisation of copyright and related rights throughout the EU, they fell within the Treaty's provisions because of their effect on trade in goods and services within the EU.

The remainder of this chapter looks at the impact of Articles 34 to 36, Article 56 and Articles 101 and 102 TFEU on the exercise of intellectual property rights. What follows is not, however, to be an exhaustive exposition or study of EU competition law and readers wanting a fuller description and analysis should turn to leading texts on this important area of law.[9]

4 References, generally, in what follows are stated in terms of the TFEU.

5 German Copyright Act 1965, ss 96(1) and 125(1).

6 [1993] ECR I-5145.

7 Now Article 267 TFEU.

8 See also Article 4 of the EEA Agreement.

9 Whish, R. (2008) *Competition Law* (6th edn) OUP.

Freedom of movement of goods

Articles 34 and 35 TFEU Treaty prohibit quantitative restrictions on imports and exports and measure having equivalent effect. Article 36 contains a saving so that prohibitions and restrictions may be justified on a number of grounds such as public morality, public policy and public safety. Other grounds include the protection of industrial and

10 It is self-evident that patents, trade marks and rights in designs fall within the meaning of industrial property and, in Joined Cases 55/80 and 57/80 *Musik-Vertrieb Membran and K-Tel International* v *GEMA* [1981] ECR 147, it was confirmed that copyright was also included. By parity of reasoning, rights related to copyright must also be included.

commercial property[10] and intellectual property rights fall within these forms of property so immediately there is a balance to be struck between restriction on imports and exports and intellectual property rights. This has led to the important principle of exhaustion of rights. The proprietor's rights further to commercialise particular goods are said to be exhausted by the first consensual sale of those goods. Of course, the exhaustion of rights is not absolute and other acts may infringe the relevant intellectual property rights, such as making copies of the goods without consent.

Exhaustion of rights means that the holder of intellectual property rights cannot use his rights to prevent the further commercialisation of goods which have been placed on the market within the EU (or, in reality, the EEA as the EEA Agreement contains provisions equivalent to Articles 34 to 36 TFEU) by him or with his consent. To this extent, his intellectual property rights have been compromised. However, this does not affect the fact that he has these intellectual property rights. There is a distinction between the *existence* of intellectual property rights and the *exercise* of those rights. Article 345 TFEU states that the Treaty shall in no way prejudice the rules in Member States governing the system of property ownership. Exhaustion of rights does not prejudice rules on ownership, nor does it prejudice the existence of those rights; it merely controls the exercise of those rights where such exercise conflicts with the principle of freedom of movement of goods. The principle is not an absolute one and will not apply under certain circumstances, such as where the further commercialisation involves acts which would be prejudicial to the holder of the intellectual property right, such as where he has repackaged the goods or altered them in an unacceptable way.

Where relevant, EU Directives and Regulations specifically provide for the working of the principle of exhaustion of rights. An example is found in Directive 2008/95/EC of 22 October 2008 to approximate the laws of the Member States relating to trade marks (codified version),[11] Article 7 of which states:

11 OJ L 299, 08.11.2008, p 25.

1 The trade mark shall not entitle the proprietor to prohibit its use in relation to goods which have been put on the market in the Community under that trade mark by the proprietor or with his consent.
2 Paragraph 1 shall not apply where there exist legitimate reasons for the proprietor to oppose further commercialisation of the goods, especially where the condition of the goods is changed or impaired after they have been put on the market.

Article 4(2) of Directive 2001/29/EC of the European Parliament and of the Council of 22 May 2001 on the harmonisation of certain aspects of copyright and related rights in the information society[12] states that the distribution right is not exhausted in relation to the original or copies of a work except where the first sale or other transfer of ownership in the Community of that object is made by the rightholder or with his consent.[13] These and other provisions on exhaustion have been implemented expressly in UK law.[14] However, the principle applies even without express legislation. The European Patent Convention and the UK Patents Act 1977 do not expressly mention the principle, but there is a wealth of case law before the Court of Justice to show that it applies to patents as it does to other intellectual property rights. Indeed, the principle of freedom of movement of goods existed to some extent in the UK prior to its membership of the EU and, in some cases, the courts were prepared to imply a licence allowing the purchaser of an article to resell it. For example, in *Betts* v *Willmott*,[15] an old patent case, the claimant sold metal capsules to the defendant in France. The claimant, who had factories in England and France, tried to prevent the capsules being resold in England. Lord Hatherley said (at 245):

12 OJ L 167, 22.06.2001, p 10.

13 In Case C-479/04 *Laserdisken ApS* v *Kulturministeriet* [2006] ECR I-8089, the Court of Justice confirmed that national rules providing for exhaustion in relation to objects placed on the market outside the EEA were not permitted and Article 4(2) was valid.

14 For example, see the Trade Marks Act 1994 s 12, the Registered Designs Act 1949 s 7A, the Copyright, Designs and Patents Act 1988 s 18 and, in respect of Community-wide rights, there are similar provisions in relation to the Community design and the Community trade mark.

15 (1871) LC 6 Ch App 239.

When a man has purchased an article he expects to have control of it, and there must be some clear and explicit agreement to the contrary to justify the vendor in saying that he has not given the purchaser his licence to sell the article, or use it wherever he pleases as against himself.

Of course, under traditional English law, such freedom to resell (and presumably also to import) was entirely vulnerable to the principle of freedom of contract. Another area of English law which could apply to ensure freedom of movement in limited circumstances is the doctrine of non-derogation from grant; however, the relevant provisions of the TFEU and other EC legislation are much stronger and of far greater application.

Article 36 TFEU overcomes Articles 34 and 35 where the protection of industrial and commercial property is at stake and this is interpreted as protecting the 'specific subject matter' of the intellectual property right in question. The definition of what constitutes the specific subject matter of a patent was given in Case 15/74 *Centrafarm BV v Sterling Drug Inc*[16] as being:

> . . . the guarantee that the patentee, to reward the creative effort of the inventor, has the exclusive right to use an invention with a view to manufacturing industrial products and putting them into circulation for the first time, either directly or by the grant of licences to third parties, as well as the right to oppose infringements.

It is essential that trade between Member States is affected or likely to be affected by the restriction or measure in question. The grant of a compulsory licence to work a patent subject to a prohibition on importation from outside the EU did not affect trade between Member States in Case C-191/90 *Generics (UK) Ltd v Smith Kline and French Laboratories (UK) Ltd.*[17] The imposition of excessive prices in the UK did not, *per se*, affect trade between Member States.[18]

The effect of Article 34 on the exercise of a patent right is often brought into question in cases involving 'parallel importing', the term used to describe the activity of buying goods in one Member State and importing them for resale in another Member State, usually undercutting the price charged by the proprietor of the intellectual property right in that destination Member State. Manufacturers of goods leave themselves wide open to this practice if they charge different prices in different Member States. They may try various ways of preventing parallel importing, for example, by their contracts with distributors or retailers imposing obligations to sell only to private individuals and to sell only limited numbers to any particular individual. Parallel importers usually still manage to get their hands on the goods, even going to such lengths as sending out dozens of persons posing as private buyers.

An example of parallel importing was Case 15/74 *Centrafarm BV v Sterling Drug Inc.*[19] Sterling Drug was the proprietor of patents in the UK and the Netherlands in respect of a pharmaceutical product. It had UK and Dutch subsidiary companies and granted licences to both of them in respect of the drug. Due to government regulations in the UK, the pharmaceutical product there cost approximately half that in the Netherlands. The UK company exported large quantities of the pharmaceutical to the Netherlands, undercutting the Dutch company. It was held that this was permissible because the pharmaceutical product had been put on the market with the parent company's consent, thereby exhausting its rights under the patent. The Dutch subsidiary had wanted the parent company to exercise its patent rights to prevent the importation into the Netherlands of the pharmaceutical made in the UK. Therefore, it is difficult for a proprietor of patents in respect of the same invention in different Member States to maintain price differentials between those Member States. Purely economic considerations affecting the marketing of a product may be distorted and it could mean that a decision is taken not to market a product in a country where a low price would be appropriate or necessary. However, for the exhaustion doctrine to apply, the first marketing must have been by or with the consent of the patentee, and in Case 24/67 *Parke, Davis & Co v Probel*[20] the doctrine did not apply and the proprietor of a Dutch patent was able to prevent the importation of quantities of a pharmaceutical product into the Netherlands from Italy where it had been made without the consent of the patentee.[21] At the time, the pharmaceutical could be lawfully made by a third party in Italy as it did not, at that time, extend patents to pharmaceuticals.

16 [1974] ECR 1147, affirmed in Case C-30/90 *Commission of the European Communities v United Kingdom* [1992] ECR I-829.

17 [1992] ECR I-5335. However, the criteria could be applied in such a way as to affect trade between Member States.

18 *Chiron Corp v Organon Teknika Ltd (No 2)* [1993] FSR 324.

19 [1974] ECR 1147.

20 [1968] ECR 55.

21 The availability of a licence in one Member State may also defeat the right to prevent imports made in another country without consent: *Allen and Hanbury v Generics (UK)* [1986] RPC 203.

22 Case 187/80 *Merck & Co Inc* v *Stephar BV* [1981] ECR 2063.

23 [1996] ECR I-6285. The defendant in the original infringement action had bought the drugs in Spain and Portugal and imported them into the UK.

24 The case was referred to the Court of Justice by Jacob J: see *Merck & Co Inc* v *Primecrown Ltd* [1995] FSR 909.

25 [2000] FSR 17.

26 [1997] ECR I-3929.

The consensual marketing of goods in a Member State lacking protection in a relevant respect still will exhaust the right to prevent further commercialisation of the goods.[22] In some cases, the principle of exhaustion of rights might be postponed when a new Member State joins the Community. In Joined Cases C-267/95 and C-268/95 *Merck & Co Inc* v *Primecrown Ltd*,[23] before Spain and Portugal joined the then European Community, patents for pharmaceutical products were not available. Under the Acts of Accession to the Community, these countries were required to grant patents for pharmaceutical products but the principle of exhaustion of rights was not to apply for three years after pharmaceutical products first became patentable in Spain and Portugal. Two issues required to be resolved by the Court of Justice. The first was to determine precisely when the three-year period postponing the application of exhaustion of rights to pharmaceutical products ended. Was it three years after such products became patentable, or three years from the end of the calendar year during which they became patentable? The second question for the court was whether the rule in *Merck* v *Stephar* needed reconsidering.

The court held that the three-year period expired three years from the precise time at which drugs became patentable in Spain and Portugal and not three years from the end of the calendar year during which they so became patentable. The Acts of Accession were ambiguous on this point but, because the three-year period was a derogation from the normal working of the EC Treaty (now replaced by the TFEU), the court said that it must be construed so as to cause the earliest application of Articles 28 and 30 (now Articles 34 to 36 TFEU). The Court of Justice confirmed that the rule in *Merck* v *Stephar* still applied. The claimant submitted a number of reasons for modifying the rule, including state controls on prices and ethical or moral obligations to supply drugs in a Member State even though they were not patentable there. However, the claimant had freely sold its pharmaceuticals in Spain and Portugal.[24] It had not been compelled to do so by any rule of law. Simply being under an ethical or moral obligation was not a reason to depart from the rule. Neither was the imposition of price controls by a Member State a reason to depart from the rule. The distortion caused by price controls was a matter to be dealt with by measures taken by the EU rather than by providing a special derogation from the principle of freedom of movement.

The Court of Justice accepted that, where a proprietor of a patent was compelled by law to sell his products in a Member State, he did not consent to the sale in any real sense and could use his rights to prevent imports. That had not been the case here. Thus, the rule in *Merck* v *Stephar* has been qualified to that limited extent only. Neuberger J applied *Merck* v *Stephar* in *Sandvik Aktiebolag* v *KR Pfiffner (UK) Ltd*,[25] where he rejected counsel's argument that the observations of the Court of Justice in *Merck* v *Stephar* should be limited. Neuberger J stressed that the consent required for the purposes of exhaustion of rights must be a consent to marketing rather than a consent under the patent. This is an important distinction especially where a product is put on the market by or with the consent of the proprietor of patents for an invention in a Member State in which he holds no patent.

Often, there will be a tension between Article 34 and Article 36. In Case C-316/95 *Generics BV* v *Smith Kline & French Laboratories Ltd* ('SKF'),[26] SKF had a Dutch patent for the drug cimetidine. Before the patent expired, a third party filed applications for marketing authorisation in respect of the drug to the Dutch assessment board for medicinal products, submitting samples of the drug as required. The authorisations were granted and were assigned to Generics shortly before the patent expired. SKF applied for and was granted a temporary injunction to take effect immediately upon the expiry of the patent, restraining Generics from offering for sale or supplying the drug. The injunction was to last 14 months after the patent expired, this being the average time it took to obtain marketing authorisation.

The Court of Justice accepted that the consequence of Dutch law was that a person other than the proprietor of the patent could not sell cimetidine as soon as the patent had expired. This was a measure having equivalent effect to a quantitative restriction on importation within Article 28 of the EC Treaty (now Article 34 TFEU). The drugs were lawfully on the market in other Member States, but the effect of the approach of the Dutch court was to prevent anyone importing them from another Member State and offering them for sale in the Netherlands.[27] However, the Court of Justice also held that such a restriction was justified under Article 30 (now Article 36 TFEU) and confirmed that the use of samples to obtain marketing authorisation was within the specific subject matter of a patent.

The outcome of the case was to place the proprietor of the patent in the same position he would have been in had his patent rights been respected whilst the patent was still in force. However, neither the Patents Act 1977 nor the European Patent Convention extend the meaning of infringement to obtaining authorisation.[28] The applicant for authorisation would only infringe if he made the product whilst the patent was still in force.[29] What if the third party lawfully purchased a quantity of the drug made by the proprietor of the patent and submitted that for marketing authorisation? In the present case, the samples submitted by Generics had not been put on the market by or with the consent of SKF.

Of course, the proprietor or his licensee might attempt to use contractual methods to prevent the subsequent resale of the products, and if it affects trade between Member States this also will be controlled. The fact of the matter is that, in the European context, the use of patents (or other intellectual property rights) to divide the market and maintain territorial boundaries is vulnerable to challenge and control. This may be a good thing: for example, where a manufacturer is deliberately operating price differentials for no other reason than to make unreasonable profit margins, a parallel importer may soon put an end to this practice. However, there may be other good reasons for selling goods at different prices in different Member States based on economic factors, though such reasons should disappear or at least diminish as the concept of the single market becomes more of a reality.

In terms of trade mark law, Article 8(2) of the trade marks Directive allows a proprietor to oppose a licensee who contravenes any provision in the licence agreement relating to, *inter alia*, the quality of the goods. Where the goods are luxury goods, this can apply to the resale of the goods to discount stores in contravention of the licence.[30]

One important exception to the principle of exhaustion of rights is that it does not apply to works and other subject matter subject to copyright or related rights which have been made available online. A distinction is made between, for example, a work of copyright released on tangible media (such as a compilation of music sold on CDs or films sold on DVDs) and the same work made available online. In the first case, the normal principle of exhaustion of rights applies but in the latter case, the owner is not to be taken to have abandoned his rights to control subsequent commercialisation. This also applies to material copies made by users of online services.[31]

Repackaging

The principle of exhaustion of rights will not apply if the effect is seriously to damage the intellectual property right in question. Where exhaustion of rights has been expressly stated in trade marks legislation it is coupled with a proviso that it will not apply where there exist legitimate reasons for the proprietor of the trade mark to oppose further commercialisation of the goods, especially where their condition has been changed or impaired after they had been put on the market.[32] An equivalent proviso must apply in other cases where the legislation does not specifically mention exhaustion of rights or contain a similar proviso as it can be explained as being an example, in the context of the derogation in Article 36 TFEU on the basis of the protection of industrial or commercial

27 The rule in Case 8/74 *Procureur du Roi* v *Benoit and Dassonville* [1974] ECR 837 applies Article 28 where the law in question is capable of hindering directly or indirectly, actually or potentially, intra-Community trade.

28 The defence of doing an act for experimental purposes would not seem to apply. Dutch patent law allows examination of the patented product, but has been held not to apply to the submission of samples of medicinal products.

29 Or performed any of the other infringing acts unless the proprietor's rights had been exhausted.

30 Case C-9/08 *Copad SA* v *Christian Dior couture SA* [2009] ECR I-3421, discussed in Chapter 21.

31 This 'derogation' from the principle of exhaustion of rights applies to services including online services: Directive 2001/29/EC of the European Parliament and of the Council of 22 May 2001 on the harmonisation of certain aspects of copyright and related rights in the information society, OJ L167, 22.06.2001, p 10, recitals 28 and 29 and Articles 3(3) and 4(2).

32 Article 7(2) of the trade marks Directive and Article 13(2) of the Community Trade Mark Regulation. Note that the examples given (changed or impaired condition) are not exhaustive.

property. Therefore, it is submitted that any subsequent commercialisation of a product subject to an intellectual property right, which has the effect of seriously prejudicing or harming that intellectual property right, should permit its proprietor to oppose that subsequent commercialisation.

The application of Article 36 TFEU in relation to intellectual property rights is usually seen in the context of trade marks and the reference to further commercialisation after the condition of the goods have been changed or impaired are only examples of situations where the proprietor may be able to oppose that later commercialisation. For example, it may be that the reputation of a trade mark used for prestige or luxurious goods is harmed by the manner in which the reseller advertises those goods using the trade mark.[33]

It is common for pharmaceutical products to undergo relabelling or repackaging by parallel importers so as to be suitable for resale in other Member States. This may be a result of compliance with national rules concerning the sale of pharmaceuticals: for example, the quantities a drug may be supplied in. There may be consumer resistance to adding labels to the outside of the trade mark proprietor's own packaging and it may be preferable to manufacture replacement packaging which will normally carry the trade mark. The extent to which, and conditions under which, repackaging is permitted has been considered on a number of occasions by the Court of Justice.

In Case C-143/00 *Boehringer Ingleheim KG* v *Swingward Ltd*,[34] a number of pharmaceutical companies brought trade mark infringement proceedings against the defendant who had bought quantities of the claimants' pharmaceutical products and imported them into the United Kingdom. The form of repackaging varied. In some cases, a label setting out critical information, such as the name of the parallel importer and its parallel import licence number, had been attached to the original package. Wording in languages other than English remained visible and the trade mark was not covered up. In other cases, boxes designed by the parallel importer and carrying the trade mark were used. In yet other cases, the product was repackaged in boxes designed by the parallel importer but which bore the generic name of the product, not the trade mark. Inside such boxes, the inner packaging bore the original trade mark, over-stickered with a label with the generic name as well as the identity of the manufacturer and of the parallel import licence holder. In all cases, the boxes contained an information leaflet for the patient written in English and bearing the trade mark.

The Chancery Division of the High Court sought a preliminary ruling from the Court of Justice, which ruled:

- A trade mark proprietor can prevent a parallel importer from repackaging pharmaceutical products unless the exercise of his trade mark rights contributes to the artificial partitioning of the markets between Member States.[35]
- However, where the repackaging is necessary for the pharmaceutical products concerned to be marketed in the importing State, for example, because of national rules or practices, the exercise of trade mark rights to prevent repackaging contributes to such artificial partitioning. But such repackaging must have regard to the legitimate interests of the proprietor.[36]
- The proprietor can oppose repackaging where it is done by a parallel importer solely to gain a commercial advantage.[37]
- Replacement packaging of pharmaceutical products, rather than simply sticking labels on those packages, is objectively necessary if, without such repackaging, effective access to the market concerned, or to a substantial part of that market, is hindered as the result of strong resistance to such re-labelling from a significant proportion of consumers for pharmaceutical products. The presence of some resistance is not necessarily such an impediment to effective market access to make repackaging necessary. The question as to whether it is necessary is a question for the national court.

33 This was noted as a possibility in Case C-337/95 *Parfums Christian Dior SA* v *Evora BV* [1997] ECR I-6013.

34 [2002] ECR I-3759.

35 Case 102/77 *Hoffmann-La Roche & Co AG* v *Centrafarm Vertriebsgesellschaft mbH* [1978] ECR 1139. In that case, the Court of Justice ruled that the repackaging must be such so as not adversely to affect the original condition of the product, the trade mark proprietor must be notified beforehand and the name of the repackager must appear on the packaging.

36 Joined Cases C-427/93, C-429/93 and C-436/93 *Bristol-Myers Squibb* v *Paranova A/S* [1996] ECR I-3457.

37 Case C-379/97 *Pharmacia & Upjohn SA* v *Paranova A/S* [1999] ECR I-6927.

- Even where a parallel importer is otherwise entitled to repackage trade-marked pharmaceutical products, he must notify the proprietor before he puts the repackaged product on sale and must, if requested to do so, provide a sample to the proprietor. This enables the proprietor to check to make sure the condition of the original product is not affected and that the reputation of the trade mark is not damaged. It also enables the proprietor to protect himself better from counterfeiters.[38]

- In the event of dispute, it is for the national court to assess, in the light of all the relevant circumstances, whether the proprietor had a reasonable time to react to the intended repackaging.

Parallel importers will be able to repackage pharmaceutical products, as opposed to sticking a label on the original packaging, where this is necessary to overcome what would otherwise amount to an artificial partitioning of the market between Member States. They have to comply with the requirements for notice and give the proprietor sufficient time to consider the proposed repackaging and its impact on the condition of the product and the trade mark. It would be reasonable to assume that the time should be such to allow for any concerns of the proprietor to be addressed and other issues to be resolved. If the consent is not forthcoming, it should be a matter of an objective assessment of whether the condition of the product or the trade mark's repute would be likely to be adversely affected. Such issues are for the national courts to determine in a particular case.

Exercising trade mark rights to prevent the removal of identification numbers applied to goods for the purposes of complying with legal obligations, product recall and to combat counterfeiting do not offend under Article 7 providing they are not also used as a means of preventing parallel importing. In Case C-349/95 *Frits Loendersloot* v *George Ballantine & Son Ltd*,[39] Ballantine brought trade mark infringement proceedings in the Netherlands against a transport and warehousing firm whose customers were engaged in the parallel importation of Ballantine's Whisky. The complaints included removing labels and replacing them with copies, removing identification numbers, removing the name 'pure' and the name of the approved importer. The Court of Justice confirmed that Article 7 of the trade marks Directive should be interpreted in the same way as Article 36 TFEU and held, *inter alia*, that a trade mark proprietor could use his rights to prevent a third party removing and reaffixing or replacing labels bearing the trade mark unless:

- it is established that the use of the trade mark rights to oppose the marketing of relabelled products under the mark would contribute to the artificial partitioning of the internal market;
- it is shown that the relabelling cannot affect the original condition of the product;
- the presentation of the relabelled product is not such as to be liable to damage the reputation of the trade mark and its owner;[40] and
- the person who relabels the products informs the trade mark owner of the relabelling before the relabelled products are put on sale – there is no duty otherwise to inform the trade mark proprietor or to provide samples on demand.

A further reference for a preliminary ruling was made in a subsequent appeal in the *Boehringer Ingleheim* v *Swingward*[41] case. The case still rumbles on. In that second reference, the Court of Justice ruled, *inter alia*, that where the criteria laid down in the *Bristol-Myers Squibb* v *Paranova* and the first *Boehringer Ingelheim* v *Swingward* case (Case C-143/00) were complied with, the trade mark proprietor would not have any reason to oppose the further commercialisation of the goods to which the trade mark had been applied.[42] However, it seems there may be a conflict between these rulings and that in *Frits Loendersloot* v *Ballantine* and the Court of Justice appears ready to reconsider the position following a reference from Austria.[43] In the latest appeal to the Court of Appeal,[44] Jacob LJ thought he had no option but to defer making a final decision pending the ruling from the Court of

38 *Bristol-Myers Squibb* v *Paranova A/S* [1996] ECR I-3457 at para 78.

39 [1997] ECR I-6227.

40 In *Glaxo Group Ltd* v *Dowelhurst Ltd (No 2)* [2000] FSR 529, Laddie J suggested that some damage was acceptable providing it was not substantial.

41 *Boehringer Ingelheim AG* v *Swingward Ltd* [2004] ETMR 65.

42 Case C-348/04 *Boehringer Ingelheim AG* v *Swingward Ltd* [2007] ECR I-3391.

43 Case C-276/05 *Wellcome* v *Paranova*.

44 *Boehringer Ingelheim AG* v *Swingward Ltd* [2008] EWCA Civ 83.

Justice. Needless to say, the law on repackaging is in a mess that can only be resolved by the Court of Justice. In the latest Court of Appeal case, Jacob LJ said (at para 2):

> Notwithstanding the two references to the ECJ and its answers, each 'side' . . . claims to have won. That is a sorry state of affairs. European trade mark law seems to have arrived at such a state of uncertainty that no one really knows what the rules are, outside the obviously core case of straightforward infringement . . . The compromises which have emerged have very fuzzy lines. So it is that in this case, notwithstanding two references (and a host of cases about relabelling parallel imports going back at least 30 years, see *Hoffmann-La Roche* v *Centrafarm*, Case 102/77 [1978] ECR 1139), there is still room for argument. There is indeed a yet further reference about the subject still pending before the ECJ . . .

Repackaging might be carried out by one company in a group of companies on behalf of another company in the group. The packaging may identify that latter company rather than the company actually repackaging the product. This is acceptable in principle as the Court of Justice ruled in Joined Cases C-400/09 and C-207/10 *Orifarm A/S* v *Merck, Sharp & Dohme Corp*,[45] provided Article 7(2) of the trade marks Directive is not in issue.

Goods placed on the market outside the EEA[46]

The doctrine of exhaustion of rights does not apply to goods that have been placed on the market outside the EEA, as the case may be.[47] In Case C-355/96 *Silhouette International Schmied GmbH & Co KG* v *Hartlauer Handelsgesellschaft mbH*,[48] the claimant made and sold spectacles in a number of countries under its Austrian registered trade mark 'Silhouette'. Large numbers of older designs had been sold by the claimant outside the EEA in Bulgaria and quantities of these had been bought by the defendant and imported into Austria where they were put on sale. Trade mark law in Austria at the time appeared to countenance international exhaustion of rights.[49] The Court of Justice ruled that national rules regarding goods put on the market outside the EEA by the proprietor or with his consent were contrary to Article 7(1) of the trade marks Directive. The reason being that, if it were left to each Member State to choose whether exhaustion should be limited to the EEA or not, barriers to trade within the EEA would thereby be erected. Consequently, Article 7(1) provided for exhaustion in respect of goods put on the market within the EEA only and a trade mark proprietor could exercise his rights to prevent the importation of goods from outside the EEA to an EEA Member State even if those goods had been placed on the non-EEA market by or with the proprietor's consent.[50] *Silhouette* was followed by the Court of Justice in Case C-173/98 *Sebago Inc* v *GB-Unic SA*.[51] That case also confirmed that exhaustion applies only in respect of *those* goods put on the market within the EEA by or with the consent of the proprietor and not that class of goods.[52]

A further challenge to the limitation of the principle of exhaustion of rights to the EEA, as the case may be, was made in Joined Cases C-414/99 to C-416/99 *Zino Davidoff AG* v *A & G Imports Ltd*,[53] in which goods were placed on the market outside the EEA by Davidoff and Levi Strauss. Davidoff's toiletries had been placed on the market in Singapore from where they had been bought by A & G Imports and imported in to the UK for sale. Quantities of Levi jeans put on the market mainly in Canada, the US and Mexico had been bought by Tesco Stores and Costco Goods and imported into the UK for sale.

The Court of Justice again confirmed that placing goods, bearing the proprietor's trade mark, on the market outside the EEA by or with the consent of the proprietor does not exhaust the rights of the proprietor to control their initial marketing in the EEA. A major issue was whether a trade mark proprietor's consent to importing the goods into the EEA from outside for resale could be inferred or whether such consent had to be express. The Court of Justice held that the concept of consent must be applied uniformly throughout the EEA. As the effect of extinguishing exclusive rights is serious, the proprietor must

45 28 July 2011.

46 The principle of freedom of movement of goods (and the other 'freedoms') also applies to the other Contracting Parties to the EEA Agreement, being Iceland, Liechtenstein and Norway.

47 For example, exhaustion as regards the harmonised national trade mark applies within the EEA but, in relation to patents and the Community trade mark, it applies to the EC.

48 [1998] ECR I-4799.

49 That is, where the goods had been sold by or with the proprietor's consent anywhere in the world.

50 However, Article 7(1) does not, *per se*, give a proprietor a right of action. This depends on the implementing legislation in Member States.

51 [1999] ECR I-4103.

52 See also Case C-479/04 *Laserdisken ApS* v *Kulturministeriet* [2006] ECR I-8089.

53 [2001] ECR I-8691.

evince an intention to renounce his rights unequivocally. This would normally be only by way of an express statement of consent. However, it may be possible to infer such consent from the facts and circumstances prior to, simultaneous with or subsequent to the placing of the goods on the market outside the EEA which, in the view of the relevant national court, unequivocally demonstrates that the pro-prietor has renounced his rights to object to their further commercialisation within the EEA.

The Court of Justice confirmed that implied consent to the marketing of goods placed on the market outside the EEA to their subsequent marketing within the EEA cannot be inferred merely from facts such that:

- the proprietor has not communicated his opposition to marketing in the EEA to all subsequent purchasers of the goods; in other words, mere silence on the part of the proprietor does not imply consent;
- the goods carry no warning of a prohibition on their being placed on the market within the EEA;
- the proprietor has transferred his ownership of products bearing the trade mark with-out imposing any contractual reservations and that, according to the law governing the contract, the property right transferred includes, in the absence of such reservations, an unlimited right to resell or, at the very least, a right to market the goods subsequently in the EEA.

The Court of Justice further held that the burden of proof lies on the person alleging consent. It is he who must prove consent and it is not for the proprietor to demonstrate its absence. In answer to further questions referred by the Patents Court in the UK, the Court of Justice ruled that, having regard to exhaustion of rights, it is not relevant that the importer of goods is unaware of the proprietor's objection to the goods being placed on the market within the EEA or being sold there by persons other than authorised traders. Nor is it relevant that authorised retailers and wholesalers have not imposed on their own purchasers contractual reservations setting out such opposition, even though they have been informed of such opposition by the trade mark proprietor.

The *Davidoff* case shows that it might be possible to find implied consent from the circumstances which will mean, in effect, that the proprietor has waived his right to object to the further commercialisation of goods, which he placed on the market outside the EEA situation, within the EEA. The practical effect of the ruling will be, of course, that proprietors of trade marks or other intellectual property rights make it clear to their dis-tributors and retailers that the goods are not for resale within the EEA, perhaps adding a note to that effect on labels or tickets attached to the goods.

One argument often used by proprietors of intellectual property rights such as trade marks is that, through their authorised retailers, they have cultivated a high-quality ex-perience for consumers which could be harmed by parallel importers selling the goods in less luxurious surroundings. The sale of expensive perfumes from department stores could be compared with the sale of the same perfumes, imported from other parts of the market, in relatively low-cost outlets, now familiar on High Streets. As far as imports from outside the EEA, sometimes the products sold there by the proprietor may be of a inferior quality to those placed on the market within the EEA by that proprietor. This may be a reflection of the differing amounts of consumer spending power in other countries. Another issue might be after-sales service where authorised retailers operate under per-formance levels set down by and monitored by the proprietor of the relevant intellectual property right.

The UK courts had the opportunity to consider parallel importing from Brazil in *Colgate-Palmolive Ltd* v *Markwell Finance Ltd*.[54] The US parent company of the UK company and the Brazilian company owned trade marks registered in the UK and similar marks registered in Brazil. The defendant imported into the UK and sold the toothpaste made

54 [1989] RPC 497.

in Brazil, which was of a poorer quality than that made in the UK. The Court of Appeal held that the UK trade marks were infringed, and the defendant's argument that the parent company had expressly or impliedly consented to the importation was rejected because it would amount to a misrepresentation to consumers as to the quality of the goods.[55]

This approach found some sympathy in the Court of Justice because of the deception as to quality operating on members of the public. For example, in Case C-10/89 *Cnl-Sucal NV SA* v *Hag GF AG*,[56] an unusual case involving the same trade mark ('Kaffee Hag' for coffee) owned by different proprietors in Belgium and Germany,[57] the current owner of the Belgian mark sought to sell its coffee in Germany. It was held that Articles 28 to 30 of the EC Treaty (now Articles 34 to 36 TFEU) did not prevent national legislation from permitting an undertaking which owned a trade mark in one Member State from restraining the importation from another Member State of similar goods bearing a similar mark. The justification was that otherwise consumers would not be able to identify with any certainty the origin of the product and the owner of the mark in one Member State might be blamed for the poor quality of goods for which he was not responsible. However, this case must now be reconsidered in the light of the harmonisation of national trade mark law in Europe and the fact that a trade mark has become deceptive is a reason for invalidation or in terms of infringement by causing detriment to the repute of a well-known trade mark.

As far as *Colgate-Palmolive* is concerned, this now is of historical interest as the rulings of the Court of Justice, in cases such as *Zino Davidoff*, show that the proprietor can object to the subsequent commercialisation in the EEA of goods he has placed on the market outside the EEA, without having to show any possibility of detriment or other adverse effect. The only time exhaustion will apply in such a case is where there is evidence that the proprietor has consented to the importation and resale of the goods in question within the EEA.

Finally, one issue is whether the fact that the principle of exhaustion of rights does not extend to goods placed on the market outside the EEA enabling the rightholder to enforce his rights to prevent importation into the EEA could, nonetheless, form the basis of an allegation of an abuse of a dominant position under Article 101 TFEU. In Case T-198/98 *Micro Leader Business* v *EC Commission*,[58] Micro Leader (a French company) imported into France copies of Microsoft software in the French language which it had purchased in Canada. Eventually, Micro Leader was unable to obtain further copies and brought an action based on a breach of Articles 81 and 82 of the EC Treaty (now Articles 101 and 102 TFEU) by Microsoft Corporation. The Court of First Instance (now the General Court), in annulling the decision of the Commission in rejecting the complaint,[59] ruled that, although it was clear from case law that the holder of a copyright could prevent the importation into the EU of goods placed on the market outside, it is not itself a breach of Article 82 of the EC Treaty but it could be in exceptional circumstances.

Exhaustion of rights and disparities between national laws

The application of the freedom of movement of goods and exhaustion of rights may be compromised where different Member States have different internal rules relating to a particular product. In Case 120/78 *Rewe-Zentral AG* v *Bundesmonopolverwaltung für Branntwein*[60] (known as the *Cassis de Dijon* case), the Court of Justice had to consider such a problem. Cassis de Dijon is an alcoholic blackcurrant liqueur. It was made in France lawfully at a strength of 15–20 per cent alcohol by volume. In Germany, the law prevented the sale of spirits of the type in which Cassis de Dijon fell unless the strength was at least 32 per cent alcohol by volume. An action was brought by an importer claiming that the German law was incompatible with Article 28 of the EC Treaty (now Article 34

55 The licence agreement between the parent company and the Brazilian subsidiary contained a clause declaring that no restrictions were to be placed on exports. This was held not to be equivalent to express consent and was narrowly interpreted because it was inserted so as to comply with Brazilian law.

56 [1990] ECR I-3711.

57 This was a result of expropriation of the Belgian mark after the Second World War.

58 [1999] ECR II-3989.

59 On the basis of a manifest error of assessment of the evidence.

60 [1979] ECR 649.

TFEU) and an Article 234 (now Article 267 TFEU) reference was made to the Court of Justice.

The court accepted that, pending harmonisation, it was for Member States to regulate the production and marketing of alcoholic drinks on their own territory, but this is subject to EU law and can only be justified if necessary to '. . . satisfy mandatory requirements relating in particular to the effectiveness of fiscal supervision, the protection of public health, the fairness of commercial transactions and the defence of the consumer'. German law did not discriminate against imports as such and applied to all liqueurs regardless of origin. However, such a law could clearly affect trade between Member States and could only be allowed to affect trade if it was justified by the Member State in accordance with the criteria above. A claim that the law helped to prevent alcohol abuse did not impress the court (banning weaker rather than stronger spirits seems an odd way of preventing alcohol abuse) and, in any case, any restriction to satisfy mandatory requirements must be proportionate and any alternative that could achieve the objective in a less onerous manner should be adopted, that being a matter for the national court following the Article 234 reference. The objective could be achieved simply by clearly labelling the drink with its alcoholic strength.

The *Cassis de Dijon* principle has been applied on a number of occasions and is of much wider application than freedom of movement of goods in relation to intellectual property rights. For example, in Case C-30/99 *Commission of the European Communities* v *Ireland*,[61] provisions in Irish law on hallmarking precious metals which resulted, *inter alia*, in the prohibition of imports lawfully made in the Member States of origin, were contrary to Article 28 of the EC Treaty (now Article 34 TFEU).

In relation to trade marks, in Case C-313/94 *Fratelli Graffione SNC* v *Ditta Fransa*,[62] the Scott Group marketed toilet paper and paper handkerchiefs under the trade mark 'Cotonelle' in Italy. In 1993, the Italian courts declared that the trade mark was invalid as it was misleading to consumers who might think the product contained cotton. The Scott Group stopped selling the products under that name in Italy. The trade mark was challenged in other countries, including France, where it was successfully defended, and the Scott Group continued to sell the products under that trade mark in France. The defendant bought quantities of the goods in France and exported them to Italy where he sold them under the 'Cotonelle' trade mark. The claimant, a distributor of Scott products, sought to prevent the sales by the defendant in Italy on the basis that the use of the 'Cotonelle' trade mark was misleading. Traders who wished to sell the goods of the proprietor of the trade mark under that trade mark could do so by importing them from other Member States but, if an injunction were to be granted prohibiting the marketing of those products in Italy, this would operate as an obstacle to intra-state trade.

The Court of Justice ruled that obstacles to intra-state trade resulting from differences in national law were acceptable provided that:

- they were applicable to domestic and imported goods without distinction, and
- they were necessary to satisfy overriding requirements relating, *inter alia*, to consumer protection or fair trading.

Applying *Cassis de Dijon*, the court held that protection against the risk of misleading consumers by the use of a misleading trade mark could justify a barrier to the free movement of goods. The court went on to say that, before making an order, the national court must be satisfied that:

- the risk of misleading consumers was sufficiently serious to justify a barrier by preventing the use of the 'Cotonelle' trade mark, and
- the prohibition was necessary to prevent consumers being misled and was proportionate to that objective such that no other measure less restrictive of intra-Community trade would be capable of preventing consumers from being misled.

61 [2001] ECR I-4619.

62 [1996] ECR I-6039.

The national court must take into account factors such as the circumstances in which the goods are sold, the information on the packaging and its clarity, the presentation and content of advertising material and the risk of error in relation to the type of consumers of that product.

Although a law aimed at preventing unfair competition could justify a barrier to trade between Member States, it was not so here where one trader bought goods in one Member State where they were lawfully on the market and imported them into another Member State under the trade mark when other traders had the same right, even if they did not choose to exercise it.

Where EU law of freedom of movement of goods conflicts with domestic laws, it is for the Member State to justify any obstacle to trade between Member States. Freedom of movement can be seen as the overriding principle and, where there is a justifiable objective to be achieved by domestic law, careful consideration should be given as to alternative ways of achieving that objective which are less restrictive of trade. An outright ban on importation will rarely succeed as clear and appropriate information in the form of labels or advertising will usually be sufficient to achieve the objective. Of course, as more intellectual property laws have become harmonised, there is less danger of conflict between domestic law and EU law as regards freedom of movement. For example, a number of cases on exhaustion of rights under copyright and rights in performances confirming that sale of a copy of a work does not exhaust the right to control rental[63] are no longer relevant as EU law has now clearly provided for rental and lending as distinct additional rights.[64]

Freedom to provide services

Article 56 of the Treaty on the Functioning of the European Union (TFEU)[65] provides that restrictions on freedom to provide services within the Union shall be prohibited in respect of nationals of one Member State proving services to a person in another Member State.[66]

The freedom to provide services usually does not involve intellectual property rights but it can in limited areas such as broadcasting by satellite or otherwise. In Joined Cases C-403/08 and C-429/08 *Football Association Premier League Ltd* v *QC Leisure*,[67] the Football Association Premier League (FAPL) granted licences of three-year duration to broadcasters to allow them to broadcast English Premier League matches to their viewers. The licences were granted through an open competitive tendering system in which broadcasters could bid on a global, regional or territorial basis. As most broadcasting organisations are based territorially, most of the licences were limited territorially. The licence agreements contained terms such that the broadcaster undertook:

● to encrypt the broadcasts;
● not to allow the public outside the licensed territory to receive those broadcasts;
● not to supply decoders and cards to operate the decoders to persons who would use them to receive the broadcasts outside the licensed territory.

By this approach, FAPL facilitated the viewing of their matches whilst maximising the revenues for their members, the Premier League football clubs. The licences in some countries, such as the UK, would be considerably more costly than in other countries, such as Greece.

Some public houses, bars and restaurants in the UK managed to obtain decoders and cards sourced from the Greek licensee broadcaster. They appear to have been obtained by some of the defendants in the first case by giving false names and addresses to the Greek

63 See, for example, Case C-61/97 *Foreningen af danske Vidoegramdistributorer* v *Laserdisken* [1998] ECR I-5171 and Case 158/86 *Warner Bros Inc* v *Christiansen* [1988] ECR 2685.

64 Council Directive 92/100/EEC of 19 November 1992 on rental right and lending right and on certain rights related to copyright in the field of intellectual property, OJ L 346, 22.11.1992, p 61. This Directive has been replaced by codifying Directive 2006/115/EC of the European Parliament and of the Council of 12 December 2006 on rental right and lending right and on certain rights related to copyright in the field of intellectual property, OJ L376, 27.12.2006, p 28.

65 Formerly Article 49 of the EC Treaty.

66 Within the framework of relevant provisions in the TFEU.

67 Court of Justice, 4 October 2011.

licensee. The defendants in the first case were sued for infringement of copyright under s 298 of the Copyright, Designs and Patents Act 1988 (importing, selling etc. apparatus designed or adapted to circumvent encrypted broadcasts). In the second case, the defendant was one Ms Murphy who was the manager of a public house[68] in which a foreign decoder was in use. She was prosecuted under s 297(1) of the Copyright, Designs and Patents Act 1988. In both cases, the English courts submitted questions to the Court of Justice for a preliminary ruling under Article 267 TFEU.

The Court of Justice held, *inter alia*, that national law making it unlawful to import, sell and use foreign decoding devices giving access to encrypted satellite broadcasts from another Member State which includes material protected in that first State, is contrary to the freedom to provide services under Article 56 TFEU. This was so even though the decoders and/or cards in question had been obtained or enabled by giving a false identity and address with the intention of circumventing the territorial limitation. Nor was it affected by the fact that the decoders or cards had been supplied for private use but had been used for commercial purposes.

Rightholders are entitled to exploit their works commercially in return for an appropriate remuneration, and payment of a premium for territorial exclusivity may be acceptable. However, in a case such as the present one, where broadcasters are effectively involved in an 'auction' for territorial broadcast rights, this results in artificial price differences in partitioned national markets. This is irreconcilable with a fundamental aim of the TFEU which is the completion of the internal market.

It should be noted that in a case such as this, where decoders were required to receive the broadcasts, it was possible to determine with some precision the total number of viewers within and outside the Member State concerned.

Competition law

Domestic laws have, for some time, attempted to prohibit anti-competitive agreements and abuses which militated against fair competition. Many European countries had laws on unfair competition and, in the UK, there were laws to prevent restrictive trade agreements and anti-competitive practices, as there still are. Many of these laws could be engaged by abuses involving intellectual property but competition law is of much wider reach and would apply, to give just one example, to price-fixing arrangements between undertakings. The common law in the UK also developed controls: for example, terms in contracts in restraint of trade.[69]

The ability of domestic laws to control abuses within a country is clearly desirable but, in the context of the EU, having control over anti-competitive practices which detract from the goal of a single market is important. The TFEU Treaty itself recognises this and has, as one of its aims, the removal of barriers to, and the promotion of, fair competition and the need to ensure competition in the internal market is not distorted. Abuses may take many forms and include setting up barriers to make it difficult or impossible for other undertakings to enter a particular market, agreements between undertakings to divide up the internal market, inserting restrictive terms in intellectual property agreements, refusing to grant licences and abusing the monopoly rights provided by, for example, a portfolio of patents.

Freedom of movement of goods can be seen as one of the means of preventing anti-competitive behaviour by preventing the partitioning of the internal market which would enable manufacturers to maintain price differentials and exploit variances in consumer spending power in different Member States. The TFEU has, however, two specific provisions attacking anti-competitive practices, being Article 101 which controls anti-competitive

68 The Red, White and Blue public house, Southsea.

69 *See*, for example, *Esso Petroleum Co Ltd v Harper's Garage (Stourport) Ltd* [1968] AC 269.

70 There are equivalent measures in the EEA Agreement.

71 [1969] ECR 295.

72 Commission notice on agreements of minor importance which do not appreciably restrict competition under Article 81(1) of the Treaty establishing the European Community (*de minimis*), OJ C 368, 22.12.2001, p 13.

73 European Commission, Guidelines on Vertical Restraints, OJ C 130, 19.05.2010, p 1 and European Commission, Guidelines on the applicability of Article 101 of the Treaty on the Functioning of the European Union to horizontal co-operation agreements, OJ C 11, 14.01.2011, p 1.

74 For which reference should be made to one of the leading texts on competition law such as Whish, R. (2008) *Competition Law* (6th edn) Oxford University Press.

agreements, etc., and Article 102 which controls abuses of dominant trading positions.[70] In both cases, it does not matter whether the prohibited behaviour is intended to affect trade between Member States; it is sufficient if that is the effect. The offending behaviour is to be determined along the lines of objectivity rather than the subjective intention of the undertaking or undertakings in question.

It should be noted that there is a *de minimis* principle that applies in relation to Articles 101 and 102. Article 101 will not apply where the effect on the market is insignificant: see Case 5/69 *Franz Völk v SPRL ets J Vervaecke*.[71] The European Commission has also issued notices setting out the threshold below which Article 101(1) will not apply, based on the size of undertakings and market share.[72] The criteria are for guidance only, however, and are not conclusive. Guidelines have also been issued as to the application of Article 101(1) to 'vertical' and 'horizontal' agreements.[73]

Both of these provisions, being Article 101 and Article 102 TFEU, in the context of intellectual property rights, are considered below. As mentioned earlier, it should be remembered that each has much wider application than just in relation to intellectual property rights and what follows is considered from the perspective of intellectual property rights and is not intended to provide a comprehensive description of EU competition law.[74]

Article 101 – restrictive agreements, etc.

Article 101 TFEU (formerly Article 81 of the EC Treaty) prohibits agreements between undertakings, decisions by associations of undertakings and concerted practices which may affect trade between Member States and which have as their object or effect the prevention, restriction or distortion of competition within the internal market, and in particular those which:

(a) directly or indirectly fix purchase or selling prices or any other trading conditions;
(b) limit or control production, markets, technical development, or investment;
(c) share markets or sources of supply;
(d) apply dissimilar conditions to equivalent transactions with other trading parties, thereby placing them at a competitive disadvantage;
(e) make the conclusion of contracts subject to acceptance by the other parties of supplementary obligations which, by their nature or according to commercial usage, have no connection with the subject of such contracts.

75 See Commission Regulation (EU) No 330/2010 of 20 April 2010 on the application of Article 101(3) of the Treaty on the Functioning of the European Union to categories of vertical agreements and concerted practices, OJ L 102, 23.04.2010, p 1.

76 See Commission Regulation (EU) No 1217/2010 of 14 December 2010 on the application of Article 101(3) of the Treaty on the Functioning of the European Union to certain categories of research and development agreements.

77 OJ L 6, 10.01.2003, p 1.

78 Some of the other fines were reduced. One company which acted as a whistleblower had its fine commuted: Joined Cases T-22/02 and T-23/02 *Sumitomo Chemical Co Ltd v Commission of the European Communities* [2005] ECR II-4065.

79 [2008] ECC 13.

80 However, it appears that exemplary damages or an account of profits is not. The former would inevitably involve an element of double counting and be contrary to the principle *non bis in idem*.

Article 101(2) makes such agreements or decisions void. This does not mean to say that the whole agreement will be void if the objectionable terms can be severed whilst leaving the agreement intact in a meaningful way. The list of agreements and the like is, as usual, non-exhaustive. In terms of intellectual property rights, Article 101 is particularly concerned with terms in licence agreements (described as vertical agreements)[75] or agreements between undertakings, for example, to pool or share rights or provide for joint research and development with the intention of creating new rights (horizontal agreements).[76] A cartel is a typical sort of agreement caught by Article 101. In the case of cartels, the goods or services may or may not be subject to intellectual property rights. An extreme example of a cartel was given by a price-fixing arrangement between suppliers of vitamins in Commission Decision 2003/2/EC of 21 November 2001 relating to a proceeding pursuant to Article 81 of the EC Treaty and Article 53 of the EEA Agreement.[77] Fines of up to €462 million were imposed.[78] In the civil follow up case before the High Court, *Devenish Nutrition Ltd v Sanofi-Aventis SA (France)*,[79] it was accepted that, despite the punitive and deterrent elements of the fines, compensatory damages might also be available.[80]

Where a body has a monopoly in relation to a particular activity, exclusive agreements made by a number of undertakings involved in that activity with a new entrant is unlikely to be caught by Article 101. In *Bookmakers' Afternoon Greyhound Services Ltd* v *Amalgamated Racing Ltd*,[81] a company owned by the leading bookmakers in the UK had exclusive media rights with racecourses and broadcast live horse races to licensed betting offices. Eventually a significant number of racecourses set up a rival service to which they granted exclusive media rights. The claimants alleged that this had the object or effect of restricting or preventing competition but, at first instance, the judge considered that the defendant's object was pro-competitive and the Court of Appeal agreed, holding that there was no breach of Article 101(1). As per Article 87 of Commission Notice, Guidelines on the applicability of Article 81 of the EC Treaty to horizontal cooperation agreements:[82]

> Cooperation between firms which compete on markets closely related to the market directly concerned by the cooperation, cannot be defined as restricting competition, if the cooperation is the only commercially justifiable possible way to enter a new market, to launch a new product or service or to carry out a specific project.

The basic prohibition in Article 101(1) does not apply in the case of any agreement or category of agreements between undertakings, any decision or categories of decisions by associations of undertakings or any concerted practice or category of concerted practices, which contributes to improving the production or distribution of goods or to promoting technical or economic progress, while allowing consumers a fair share of the resulting benefit, and which does not:

- impose on the undertakings concerned restrictions which are not indispensable to the attainment of these objectives;
- afford such undertakings the possibility of eliminating competition in respect of a substantial part of the products in question.

The purpose of Article 101(3) is to exempt from the general prohibition agreements and the like which have beneficial effects and in which consumers may participate provided they go no further than necessary and do not provide an opportunity to eliminate competition for a substantial part of the products in question.

Copyright and restrictive agreements

Although copyright is not a true monopoly right, apart from the rare example where the owner has exclusive access to the information contained within the work, copyright may be subject to the abuses sought to be prohibited under Articles 101 and 102. The Court of Justice has made it clear that it will be prepared to act against exclusive copyright licences if they offend,[83] and although intellectual property rights *per se* do not fall within the meaning of term 'agreement' within Article 101(1), the exercise of an intellectual property right might well do so.[84] Terms within licence agreements, such as export bans, may be susceptible to control. To some extent it is a matter of whether the provision is part of the specific subject matter of the right, and in *Re Ernest Benn Ltd*[85] an export ban was objected to on the basis of Article 101(1). There are no specific block exemptions directed at copyright works.

Reciprocal agreements between collecting societies protecting national interests do not fall foul of Article 101. In Case 395/87 *Ministère Public* v *Jean-Louis Tournier*[86] it was held that such collecting societies were pursuing legitimate aims where they sought to safeguard the rights and interests of their members, and contracts with users for that purpose could not be regarded as falling within the meaning of Article 101(1). However, this assumed that the practice was not excessive and did not go beyond what was necessary to achieve those legitimate aims.

81 [2009] EWCA Civ 750.

82 OJ C 3, 06.01.2001, p 2.

83 Case 262/81 *Coditel SA* v *Ciné Vog Films SA* [1982] ECR 3381.

84 Case 144/81 *Keurkoop BV* v *Nancy Kean Gifts BV* [1982] ECR 2853.

85 [1979] 3 CMLR 636.

86 [1989] ECR 2521.

In *Football Association Premier League* v *QC Leisure*[87] the Court of Justice held that territorial exclusive licence agreements permitted the licensee to broadcast within a given territory were caught by Article 101. The agreements in question contained terms obliging the licensee not to supply decoding devices enabling access to the broadcasts of English Premier League football matches by viewers outside the licensed territory. This was a restriction on competition prohibited under Article 101.

Patents and restrictive agreements

Being such a strong monopoly right, one might expect that there are ample opportunities for patent agreements to be caught by Article 101(1). The holder of a patent is placed in a strong bargaining position when it comes to negotiating with potential licensees. However, it is impossible to predict all the circumstances under which patent licences or horizontal agreements between patent proprietors are concluded and provision is made for exemption from the rigours of Article 101(1). This is because there may be circumstances in which an agreement, which appears at first sight to offend under Article 101(1), has positive effects, and can provide consumers with benefits, whilst not being unduly restrictive or abusive of competition.

Exemption from Article 101(1) is available under Article 101(3) on the basis of 'Block Exemption Regulations', where available, or on an individual basis otherwise. There is a block exemption on technology transfer agreements (relevant particularly to patent and know-how licences) but there are no block exemptions covering patent pooling agreements. Application may be made for individual exemption or negative clearance. The latter applies where the Commission does not grant exemption but is to the effect that the Commission does not consider the agreement is caught by Article 101(1), or that it is but is saved by Article 101(3). This means that the Commission can see no reason to intervene in the light of information available to the Commission at the time. An individual exemption under Article 101(3) is granted for a specific period of time which may be extended. The advantage of an Article 101(3) exemption over a negative clearance is that the former carries immunity against fines imposed by the Commission while the latter does not.

88 Subsequently Article 81 of the EC Treaty, now Article 101 TFEU.

89 OJ L32, 03.02.1990, p 19; [1991] 4 CMLR 208.

In Commission Decision 90/46/EEC of 12 January 1990 relating to a proceeding under Article 85 of the EEC Treaty[88] (*Alcatel Espace/ANT Nachrichtentechnik*)[89] there was an application to the Commission for a negative clearance or individual exemption in respect of an agreement between a French company and a German company, both involved in the manufacture of communication equipment, for the purposes of joint research and development, production and marketing activities. The agreement included a term to the effect that the relevant patents owned by each party (or to which each party was entitled) would be communicated to the other party and the parties would be free to work each other's patents on a royalty-free, non-exclusive licence basis. First of all, the Commission held that the agreement offended against Article 101(1) because it would allocate research and development so that only one party would carry this out, that the agreement provided for the procurement by one party of equipment made by the other and that decision-making processes were to be allocated to common committees. The Commission considered all of these would restrict competition. The block exemption relating to research and development agreements was not applicable as the agreement went beyond its scope. However, the Commission granted an individual exemption under Article 101(3) for a period of ten years, subject to notification of changes in the agreement. The reasons given by the Commission are instructive:

1 The planned cooperation would lead to improved technical solutions which would be discovered more rapidly and would contribute to technical progress which would benefit customers.

2 The agreement only imposed restrictions necessary to the above objective. The fact that the agreement did not prohibit either party from engaging in other activities outside the scope of the agreement was an important factor.
3 The nature of the market implied that separate marketing was not practicable.
4 The parties' market share was not high.

Agreements of the type mentioned above are sometimes described as 'horizontal agreements' because they reflect mutuality of restrictions, in contrast with a vertical agreement, a typical example being one between licensor and licensee.[90] Both types of agreements could be invalid if challenged if they affect trade between Member States. The types of terms that are likely to cause problems are those that attempt to extend the agreement or any part of it beyond the term of the patent, those which tie the licensee to the licensor (for example, where the licensee agrees to purchase goods from the licensor that are unconnected with the patent in question), and terms which state that the licensor is not to work the patent in countries other than those included in the licence agreement.[91] It is certainly the case that any licence which includes some sort of exclusive right should be drawn up very carefully and specialist advice taken where there is any possibility of exploitation in more than one Member State, or where the product is likely to be exported, with or without the consent of the parties to the agreement. However, some terms have been declared to be permissible, such as minimum royalty clauses and terms requiring minimum quantities of the product to be made by the licensee, as they are properly within the normal exploitation of the patent and go to the specific subject matter of the patent. Terms which purport to prevent the licensee from challenging the validity of the patent, or which require him to refrain from competing with the licensor, are likely to be struck out by the Commission or Court of Justice if they could affect inter-state trade.

Patents are territorial and one aspect of the European Patent Convention is that patents in respect of a particular invention may exist in some Member States but not others. This fact may encourage a proprietor to include territorial restrictions in any licence granted under the patent. Such restrictions, when viewed from that perspective, are, in principle, compatible with Article 101.[92] In Case 193/83 *Windsurfing International Inc* v *EC Commission*,[93] the Court of Justice held that the following did not fall within the specific subject matter of a patent and, as far as they restricted competition, were incompatible with Article 101:

(a) provision for quality control by the licensor either in respect of a product not covered by the patent or without being based on objective criteria set out in advance;
(b) an obligation, arbitrarily imposed, that the licensee only sell the patented product in connection with a product outside the scope of the patent;
(c) a method of calculating royalties which induced the licensee to sell the patented product together with a product not covered by the patent;
(d) a clause prohibiting manufacture of the patented product in a state where the licensor has no patent protection (note that this is in terms of manufacture, not subsequent sale or use).

An obligation in a licence agreement to pay an excessive royalty may constitute an abuse under Article 101, although charging excessive royalties might properly be expected to be relevant to abuses of dominant positions under Article 102. In *Philips Electronics NV* v *Ingman Ltd*,[94] Laddie J pointed out that fixing prices at unfair levels was accepted as being contrary to Article 82 in cases such as Case 53/87 *CICRA* v *Renault*[95] and that this principle seems to have been applied in connection with intellectual property licences in Case 262/81 *Coditel SA* v *Ciné Vog Films SA*[96] (although this was a case on a copyright licence).

A whole list of provisions in a licence agreement in respect of a patent and a trade mark were, according to the Commission in the case of *Velcro SA* v *Aplix SA*,[97] caught by Article 101(1), including:

90 Other examples include franchise and distributorship agreements.

91 The case of *AIOP* v *Beyrard* [1976] FSR 181 concerned a provision which purported to allow the unilateral extension of the licence by the licensor. *See* also Case 320/87 *Kai Ottung* v *Klee & Weilbach A/S* [1989] ECR 1177, about an obligation to pay royalties after the expiry of a patent. The Court of Justice considered that whether an agreement affected inter-state trade, and thus offended against Article 81(1), was a matter for a national court to decide from the economic and legal context in which the agreement was concluded.

92 *Sandvik Aktiebolag* v *KR Pfiffner (UK) Ltd* [2000] FSR 17.

93 [1986] ECR 611.

94 [1999] FSR 112.

95 [1988] ECR 6039.

96 [1982] ECR 3381.

97 Commission Decision 85/410/EEC of 12 July 1985 relating to a proceeding under Article 85 of the EEC Treaty (*Velcro/Aplix*), OJ L 233, 30.08.85, p 22; [1989] 4 CMLR 157.

1 exclusivity preventing the licensor exploiting the patents and trade mark in the licensed territory, or granting further licences there when the basic patents expired;
2 an export ban preventing the licensee selling outside the licensed territory;
3 the automatic extension of certain terms on the expiry of basic patents on the basis of improvement patents;
4 an obligation to obtain manufacturing equipment exclusively from a named manufacturer;
5 an obligation not to use specialised manufacturing machinery outside the licensed territory;
6 an obligation on the parties not to compete with each other;
7 an obligation to allow the licensor to acquire title to improvement patents in other Member States for improvements discovered by the licensee; and
8 a provision for the unilateral extension of the patent licence.

It cannot be disputed that the agreement in this case contained a great many provisions that were capable of affecting trade between Member States (the above list is not complete – there were other reasons why the agreement was caught by Article 101(1)). However, it is natural for commercial organisations to have their own interests at heart when drawing up licensing agreements, and too much interference by the Court of Justice can be criticised as being counter-productive and likely to restrict trade, the flow of information and collaboration by destroying the commercial viability of licences and other agreements. A comparison of the *Velcro* and *Alcatel Espace* cases indicates that the 'look and feel' of an agreement is very important – whether it prohibits certain activities, or merely discourages them. For example, a collateral term insisting that equipment is obtained only from the other party will be struck down, but a term stating that equipment should or may be obtained from the other party may survive an attack based on Article 101(1). Another factor is that, in some cases, the complaint has not come from a third party whose trade has been affected adversely by the operation of the agreement, but from one of the parties to the agreement itself, who is now trying to free himself of terms to which he had earlier expressly agreed.

The Technology Transfer Regulation

The European Commission is empowered to provide for block exemption for certain categories of agreements and concerted practices which fall within the scope of Article 101(1). It may also grant individual exemption. The first block exemption for patent licences came into force in 1984 and was intended to last for ten years.[98] There was also a block exemption for certain categories of know-how licensing agreements.[99] As know-how (generally confidential information relating to the use or application of industrial processes) is often licensed along with patents, it was considered desirable, in the interests of simplification and encouraging the dissemination of technical knowledge, to combine the two block exemptions into a single Regulation. The 1984 Regulation on patent licensing was extended beyond its normal ten years pending the Commission Regulation (EC) 240/96 on the application of Article 81(3) of the EC Treaty to certain categories of technology transfer agreements, often referred to as the Technology Transfer Regulation.[100] This Regulation came into force on 1 April 1996 and was declared to apply until 31 March 2006. Pre-existing agreements in force at 31 March 1996 which fulfilled the requirements of the previous two Regulations are unaffected by the prohibition in Article 81(1). The 1996 Regulation was prematurely repealed following an evaluation report and replaced by Commission Regulation (EC) No 772/2004 of 27 April 2004 on the application of Article 81(3) [now Article 101(3) TFEU] of the Treaty to categories of technology transfer agreements,[101] which came into force on 1 May 2004.

98 Commission Regulation (EEC) 2349/84 on the application of Article 85(3) [now Article 101 TFEU (3)] of the Treaty to certain categories of patent licensing agreements, OJ L 219, 16.08.1984, p 15.

99 Commission Regulation (EEC) No 556/89 of 30 November 1988 on the application of Article 85(3) of the Treaty to certain categories of know-how licensing agreements, OJ L 61, 04.03.1989, p 1.

100 OJ L 31, 09.02.1996, p 2.

101 OJ L 123, 27.04.2004, p 11.

The Technology Transfer Regulation moves away from an approach based on listing clauses in agreements deemed to be exempt to place greater emphasis on defining categories of agreements exempted up to a certain level of market power and specifying restrictive clauses that must not be included in such agreements. It is certainly much easier to understand than its predecessors. The Regulation applies to licensing agreements but not to pooling arrangements. The market share thresholds are 20 per cent where both parties are competitors and 30 per cent where they are not competitors. There is no presumption that the agreement automatically falls within Article 81(1) (now Article 101 (1) TFEU) if the market share thresholds are exceeded but the Commission may withdraw the benefit of the block exemption in a particular case.

'A technology transfer agreement' is a patent licensing agreement, a know-how licensing agreement, a software copyright licensing agreement or a mixed patent licensing agreement, know-how licensing agreement or software copyright licensing agreement. Certain collateral agreements are also included provided they do not detract from the primary objective of the technology transfer agreement. Also covered are assignments of rights in patents, know-how and software copyright where the assignor continues to bear some of the risk after assignment. This would include the position where the assignor is paid a royalty based on future sales. The previous Technology Transfer Regulation did not apply to software copyright and its inclusion now is perhaps a reflection of the immense market power of some software companies.

Know-how is the practical knowledge based on experience and testing which is not patented but which is secret, substantial and identifiable. It may be, for example, the knowledge to put a patented invention to best effect of a 'shop-floor' technique used by one undertaking over a period of time which has proved valuable even though it is not capable of the precise definition required for patenting.

Particular clauses, described as 'hardcore restrictions', are not permitted under Article 4(1) of the Regulation where the parties to the agreement are competitors. These include controls over prices at which products are sold to third parties, certain limitations on output and allocation of markets and certain restrictions on the use by the licensee of his own technology and any clauses restricting research and development by either party.

Examples of limitations on the allocation of markets that are acceptable are:

- obligations to produce with the licensed technology only within one or more technical fields of use or one or more product markets;
- in a non-reciprocal agreement, an obligation on either party not to produce with the licensed technology within one or more technical fields of use or one or more product markets or one or more exclusive territories reserved for the other party.

For example, it should be acceptable to impose an obligation on the licensor not to exploit the technology in the territory reserved for the licensee. That could include, in a non-reciprocal agreement, an obligation on the licensor not to sell products made with the licensed technology, actively or passively, in the territory reserved by the licensee. There may also be a restriction on the licensee not to grant other licences in respect of the licensed territory. Where licences are granted to two or more licensees operating in different territories, there may be non-reciprocal restrictions on the active sales by the licensee in the territory reserved for the other licensee, provided he is not a competitor of the licensor.

Article 4(2) sets out the restrictions which will not benefit from block exemption in agreements between non-competing parties. They include obligations in relation to prices, though not the setting of a maximum or recommended price and restrictions on the allocations of markets, though not as restrictive as in the case of parties that are competitors.

Article 5 sets out other terms that are described as excluded restrictions and these include obligations to grant-back exclusive licences in respect of severable improvements or to assign rights in such improvements and obligations not to challenge the intellectual property rights held by the licensor in the common market. However, it may be provided for that such a challenge would bring the technology transfer agreement to an end.

Article 102 – abuse of a dominant trading position

The owner of a true monopoly intellectual property right, such as a patent, can be in a dominant position. However, although copyright and rights related to copyright are not true monopoly rights as such, the owner of a copyright or related right can still be in a dominant position. This might be the case where the owner is the sole source of the information, data or other material incorporated in the work. Whilst being in a dominant position, *per se*, is not controlled by the TFEU, certain abuses of dominant positions are. Article 102 prohibits the abuse of a dominant position within the common market. It states:

> Any abuse by one or more undertakings of a dominant position within the common market or in a substantial part of it shall be prohibited as incompatible with the common market insofar as it may affect trade between Member States . . .

102 Although there may be a remedy under national law. For example, the UK Competition Act 1998 contains provisions equivalent to Articles 101 and 102 set in the context of the UK: see ss 2 and 18 of the 1998 Act. These provisions apply where trade within the UK is affected.

Again, it must be noted that the abuse must affect trade between Member States, and if it does not there is no remedy under EU law no matter how unfair the practice concerned.[102] Also, there is no need for trade actually to be affected and it is sufficient if it may be affected by the abusive behaviour. Four examples of abuse are given in Article 102:

- the imposition of unfair trading conditions or prices;
- the limitation of production, markets or technical developments to the prejudice of consumers;
- discrimination against some trading parties by applying dissimilar conditions to equivalent transactions;
- the imposition of unconnected supplementary obligations in contracts.

Examples would include the limitation of the supply of music recordings or video films in respect of some Member States, probably coupled with high prices. A supplementary obligation that would offend is where a publisher will supply only to retail outlets who agree not to buy from a rival publisher resident in another country.

103 [1979] ECR 461.

What constitutes an abuse of a dominant position is not defined as such in Article 102, but in Case 85/76 *Hoffmann-La Roche AG* v *Commission to the European Communities*[103] it was described as:

> . . . an objective concept relating to the behaviour of an undertaking in a dominant position which is such as to influence the structure of the market where, as a result of the presence of the undertaking in question, the degree of competition is weakened and which, through recourse to methods different from those which condition normal competition . . . has the effect of hindering the maintenance of the degree of competition still existing in the market or the growth of that competition.

Abuse is therefore directed at the use of methods different from normal commercial practices. Refusing to supply further goods until those already supplied have been paid for is outside Article 102.[104] This is a normal business practice.

104 See *Leyland Daf Ltd* v *Automotive Products plc* [1994] 1 BCLC 245.

105 [1987] ECR 1747.

Merely occupying a dominant position does not automatically bring Article 102 into play. For example, a collecting society occupies a dominant position in its particular country of operation, and in Case 402/85 *Basset* v *SACEM*[105] the French collecting society SACEM was occupying a dominant position but the exercise of its power was not an abuse as such. The Court of Justice will not normally interfere unless some plain abuse is present. A collecting society which uses different royalty models for commercial broadcasters compared with public broadcasters is not necessarily in breach of Article 102. In Case *C-52/07 Kanal 5 Ltd* v *Föreningen Svenska Tonsättares Internationella Musikbyrå (STIM)*,[106] the collecting society 'STIM' collected in Sweden royalties on behalf of music composers and recording companies. It had a monopoly in Sweden in relation to music played in broadcasts. With respect to commercial broadcasters, STIM based the royalty on the revenue of the broadcaster together with the amount of music played. For the public broadcaster in question, STIM charged a lump sum. The Court of Justice ruled that a model which took account of the amount of music played was not necessarily an abuse of the collecting society's dominant position. In certain circumstances, however, it could amount to an abuse, in particular, where another method of calculating the royalties payable existed which enabled the use of the music and the audience to be identified and quantified more precisely providing it did not lead to a disproportionate increase in the cost of managing and supervising the scheme. As regards the different model used for the public broadcaster, it was for the national court to determine whether:

106 [2008] ECR I-9275.

- the commercial broadcasters were placed at a competitive disadvantage;
- in fact the public broadcaster was a competitor of the commercial broadcasters; and
- the practice of having different models could be objectively justified.

A factor to be taken into account was that the public broadcaster had no revenue from advertising or subscription contracts.

In Case 238/87 *Volvo AB* v *Erik Veng (UK) Ltd*,[107] Volvo refused to grant licences to spare parts manufacturers and the Court of Justice held that the proprietor of a protected design has a right to prevent third parties from manufacturing, selling or importing spare parts incorporating the design and that this was the very subject-matter of the right. Consequently, the court would not impose a compulsory licence, because to do so would be to take away the essence of the right even though royalties would be payable. Volvo's decision to refuse to grant a licence was not, therefore, an abuse of its dominant position.[108] Lack of harmonisation in design law at the time was a significant reason for the court's reluctance to intervene. The outcome might be different now, say in relation to the Community design where there is some abuse present.

107 [1988] ECR 6211.

108 Compare this with *British Leyland Motor Corp Ltd* v *Armstrong Patents Co Ltd* [1986] 2 WLR 400.

This lack of interference with the exercise of the right to choose whether to grant licence rights is not absolute, and in Joined Cases C-241/91P and C-242/91P *RTE and ITP* v *Commission of the European Communities*,[109] the Court of Justice dismissed an appeal from a decision of the Commission and Court of First Instance finding that refusal to make available to third parties in advance listings of forthcoming television programmes was an abuse caught by Article 102. Although the court accepted that mere ownership of copyright did not confer a dominant position on its owner, the fact that the television companies had a *de facto* monopoly in relation to information concerning forthcoming programme schedules meant that they were in a dominant position. The companies could effectively prevent competition from weekly television magazines containing listings of programmes. Exercise of the property right in a work of copyright would not, on the basis of the *Volvo* v *Veng* decision, normally constitute an abuse of a dominant position. However, by withholding the information, the television companies were preventing others from marketing a competing product for which there was public demand. Such refusal to licence could not be justified on the basis of the companies' broadcasting or publishing activities. The Court of Justice confirmed that the requirement that trade between Member States be affected was satisfied by showing that the conduct concerned was capable of affecting such trade, and it was not necessary to show that trade had in fact been affected.[110]

109 [1995] ECR I-743.

110 The Court of First Instance (now General Court) had correctly found that the exclusion of all potential competitors had affected the market comprising Ireland and Northern Ireland.

A distinction can be made between the *RTE* and the *Volvo* cases in that, although it refused to grant licences, Volvo did supply spare parts; whereas in the *RTE* case, the listings were not made available in advance at all. The Broadcasting Act 1990 anticipated the outcome of the *RTE* case, as s 176 imposes a duty to provide advance information about programmes broadcast by the BBC, the Independent Television Commission, Channel 4 and the public television services of the Welsh Authority.[111]

The *RTE* and *Volvo* cases have been used numerous times. In Case C-418/01 *IMS Health GmbH & Co OHG v NDC Health GmbH & Co KG*,[112] both parties provided services in relation to data on regional pharmaceutical sales. IMS was the owner of copyright in a 'brick structure' used to represent regions and their attributes and had distributed the structure to pharmacies and doctors' surgeries free of charge, thereby building up a market prominence such that clients were reluctant to accept other structures. The defendant which was the successor to a company set up by a former manager of IMS tried to use structures very much like the claimant's. IMS sued for infringement of its copyright in the brick structures and the defendant counterclaimed, arguing that the claimant's refusal to grant it a licence was contrary to Article 102. The Court of Justice confirmed, on the basis of *RTE* and *Volvo*, that a refusal to grant a licence, *per se*, did not amount to an abuse under Article 102. However, it could do if coupled with other factors, being:

- where the undertaking requesting the licence intended to offer new products or services not offered by the copyright owner and in respect of which there was a potential consumer demand;
- where the refusal to grant the licence cannot be justified on objective considerations; and
- where the refusal is such as to reserve to the copyright owner the market for the supply of the data in question in the Member State concerned by eliminating competition in that market.

Abusive pricing

Simply charging a high price is not necessarily abusive under Article 102. The British Horseracing Board Ltd ('BHB') was the governing body of horseracing in Great Britain. It controlled and maintained a database of information including 'pre-race data' about horse races, horses, trainers, jockeys and owners. In *Attheraces Ltd v British Horseracing Board Ltd*,[113] the claimant made transmissions via websites and television providing customers with information which originally came from the BHB database. The claimant alleged that the BHB, which had a monopoly in such data, was abusing its dominant position under Article 82 of the EC Treaty (now Article 102 TFEU) and s 18 of the Competition Act 1998 by charging excessive, unfair and discriminatory prices for its pre-race data. At first instance,[114] the judge agreed. The Court of Appeal held that the trial judge had erred by calculating the economic value of the pre-race data as the cost of producing it plus a reasonable margin, described as a 'cost plus' approach. That did not take account of the value of the pre-race data to the claimant and resulted in a value too near to the cost of production. BHB's prices were neither excessive nor unfair and there was no discriminatory pricing.[115]

In another case involving the BHB database, following the Court of Justice ruling in Case C-203/02 *British Horseracing Board Ltd v William Hill Organization Ltd*,[116] which appeared to significantly prejudice any rights BHB owned in respect of the database, the defendant bookmaker in *BHB Enterprises plc v Victor Chandler (International) Ltd*[117] decided to stop paying a licence fee to the claimant for the pre-race data. The claimant threatened to withdraw the supply of the pre-race data to the defendant. This was argued to be contrary to Article 82 of the EC Treaty (now Article 102 TFEU) and s 18 of the Competition Act 1998. The cost of maintaining the BHB database was estimated at around £4m per annum. However, it was claimed that the income BHB received from exploiting it was in the region of £600m over the previous five years. The defendant had

111 It applies to the BBC's UK services, the ITC's regulated services, and, in addition, to any national service regulated by the Radio Authority. In the absence of agreement as to the payment, the Copyright Tribunal has the power to fix payments. These provisions came into force on 1 March 1991.

112 [2004] ECR I-5039.

113 [2007] ECC 7.

114 [2006] FSR 20.

115 BHB also threatened to refuse to licence the use of the pre-race data by the claimant. The Court of Appeal confirmed that such refusal did not constitute an abuse under Article 82.

116 [2004] ECR I-10415.

117 [2005] ECC 40. BHB Enterprises plc was, in effect, the trading arm of the BHB.

been paying £60,000 per month for the pre-race data, based on 10 per cent of the defendant's gross profit or 1.5 per cent of its turnover. Laddie J rejected the allegation that the price charged was unfair through lack of evidence showing this to be the case. The defendant's approach failed to consider the value of the database as an asset and concentrated on the cost of acquisition or creation instead.

Failing to provide information

The permitted act of decompilation of a computer program for the purposes of achieving interoperability with that or another program under s 50B of the Copyright, Designs and Patents Act 1988 originates from Council Directive 91/250/EEC of 14 May 1992 on the legal protection of computer programs.[118] Sometimes the permitted act may turn out to be illusory and obtaining the information necessary to achieve interoperability may be technically extremely difficult if not impossible.

118 OJ L 122, 17.05.1991, p 42, Article 6.

A number of software companies, including Sun Microsystems Inc, applied to the Microsoft Corporation asking for information which would allow them to interoperate their software systems with Microsoft's Windows client PC operating system. Failing provision of this information, Sun Microsystems lodged a complaint with the Com-mission to the European Communities. The Commission imposed a fine of Euro 497,196,304, holding that failing to make the interoperability information available to competitors was an abuse of a dominant position under Article 82 (now Article 102 TFEU).[119] The Commission required Microsoft to submit a proposal for a mechanism which included a monitoring trustee with the power of access to Microsoft's information, documentation, employees and source code without recourse to the Commission with costs to be borne by Microsoft and a right reserved to the Commission to impose such a mechanism. Microsoft's appeal failed in respect of the abuse of a dominant position and the level of the fine but it succeeded in relation to the imposition of the monitoring mechanism before the Court of First Instance in Case T-201/04 *Microsoft Corp* v *Commission to the European Communities*.[120]

119 Commission Decision 2007/53/EC of 24 March 2004 relating to a proceeding pursuant to Article 82 (EC) and Article 54 of the EEA Agreement against Microsoft Corp, OJ L 32, 06.02.2007, p 23. The fine included an amount for the objectionable tying of Windows Media Player: *see* later.

120 [2007] ECR II-3601.

There were parallel proceedings in the US against the Microsoft Corporation under US antitrust law. Eventually a settlement was reached between Microsoft and the US Department of Justice and the Attorney Generals of nine States. Microsoft agreed to draw up the specifications of the communication protocols used by the Windows server operating systems in order to 'interoperate', that is to say, to make them compatible with the Windows client PC operating systems and to grant third parties licences relating to those specifications on specific conditions. Furthermore, Microsoft was required to allow original equipment manufacturers and end users to activate or to eliminate access to its middleware which included Windows Media Player. This was intended to ensure suppliers of media software could develop and distribute products which would function properly with Windows. The settlement was affirmed by the Court of Appeals, District of Columbia, in *Commonwealth of Massachusetts* v *Microsoft Corp*.[121]

121 30 June 2004.

Sword or shield

A defendant sued for an infringement of copyright might advance a 'Euro-defence', for example under Article 102 of the Treaty. If nothing else, such a ploy might lengthen the proceedings, especially if the case is referred to the Court of Justice for a preliminary ruling under Article 267 TFEU.[122] In *Ransburg-Gema AG* v *Electrostatic Plant Systems*[123] it was alleged that the defendant had infringed the copyright subsisting in certain drawings. The defendant entered a 'Euro-defence' claiming that the claimant was guilty of a breach of Article 82 (now Article 102 TFEU). In striking out the 'Euro-defences', Aldous J held that there must be a connection between the alleged actions of the claimant and the

122 This can take about 18 months.

123 [1990] FSR 287.

alleged breach under Article 82. The existence of an exclusive right and its exercise were not per se a breach of the Treaty of Rome. Further, to show this, the Euro-defence must be sufficiently detailed. In the earlier case of *Imperial Chemical Industries Ltd* v *Berk Pharmaceuticals Ltd*,[124] Megarry V-C struck out Euro-defences because the defendant had failed to show a sufficient nexus between the alleged breach of Article 82 and the right claimed by the defendant – in that case, to imitate the claimant's get-up.[125] In *Her Majesty's Stationery Office* v *The Automobile Association Ltd*,[126] Laddie J struck out defences based on an abuse of a dominant position in relation to an infringement action involving Ordnance Survey maps. He said that the defendant had not been able to put forward a case even up to the low level required to withstand a strike out attack.

Defences under Article 102 are common but rarely, if ever, succeed in the English courts. In *Pitney-Bowes Inc* v *Francotyp-Postalia GmbH*,[127] Hoffmann J said (at 77):

> There is, as far as I know, no English case in which a defence under Article 86 [subsequently Article 82 EC Treaty, now Article 102 TFEU] to an action asserting intellectual property rights has actually succeeded.

It is clear that Articles 101(1) and 102 can be used in national courts as a sword or a shield and have a much better success rate when used as a weapon of attack. For example, in *Cutsforth* v *Mansfield Inns Ltd*,[128] the claimant succeeded in obtaining an injunction in the High Court to prevent the defendant brewery enforcing an obligation to purchase games equipment from nominated suppliers (not including the claimant), which was contained in agreements between the brewery and tenants of public houses. In *Attheraces Ltd* v *British Horse Racing Board*,[129] the claimants brought proceedings against the defendant which had a monopoly in pre-race data for horse races and which attempted to impose onerous terms and had also threatened to terminate the supply of such data. At first instance, it was held that the defendant was in breach of Article 82 of the EC Treaty (now Article 102 TFEU) and also s 18 of the Competition Act 1998, which is equivalent though in the context of trade being affected within the UK rather than as between Member States. However, the Court of Appeal reversed this decision.[130]

The occasions when the Court of Justice will interfere with the normal exploitation of copyright are quite rare, and the court seems to have achieved a fine balance between commercial exploitation and misuse of the right. The fact that copyright law is not fully harmonised throughout the EC has the effect of raising the status of, and hence the ability to rely on, national laws.

Abuse of a dominant position and patents

The ability of patents to place their proprietors in a dominant position is self-evident, especially where there are no effective alternative technologies or where the proprietor has built up a portfolio of patents in a particular technology. One might think that a refusal to licence patented technology cannot be an abuse as such as the decision to licence surely falls with the specific subject matter of a patent. In *Chiron Corp* v *Organon Teknika Ltd (No 2)*[131] Aldous J restated that a refusal to grant a licence to work an intellectual property right could not, per se, be an abuse of a dominant position. Therefore, refusal to grant a licence except on unfair or unreasonable terms also was not an abuse.[132] However, this must now be reviewed in the light of Joined Cases C-241/91P and C-242/91P *RTE and ITP* v *Commission of the European Communities*,[133] in which the Court of Justice held that the television organisations were abusing their dominant position under Article 82 (now Article 102 TFEU) by refusing to grant licences in respect of information concerning forthcoming television programmes. An important feature of this case was that the information was not available elsewhere and, furthermore, the Court of Justice made it clear that this was an exceptional case. Therefore, at least where there are comparable or equivalent

124 [1981] FSR 1.

125 See also, to similar effect, *International Business Machines Corp* v *Phoenix International (Computers) Ltd* [1994] RPC 251.

126 [2001] ECC 34.

127 [1991] FSR 72.

128 [1986] 1 WLR 558.

129 [2006] FSR 20.

130 *Attheraces Ltd* v *British Horse Racing Board* [2007] ECC 7.

131 [1993] FSR 324.

132 Following Hoffmann J in *Pitney Bowes Inc* v *Francotyp-Postalia GmbH* [1991] FSR 72, who in turn followed the Court of Justice in Case 238/87 *Volvo AB* v *Erik Veng (UK) Ltd* [1988] ECR 6211.

133 [1995] ECR I-743.

products on the market, refusal to grant a licence should not, *per se*, be an abuse of a dominant position. The issue is more unpredictable when there are not similar or equivalent products available, although in *RTE* a significant factor was that, by denying access to the information to others, the television organisations were reserving for themselves the secondary market of publishing details of forth-coming television programmes.

An argument that the decision in *RTE* was applicable to patents was rejected by Laddie J in *Philips Electronics NV v Ingman Ltd*.[134] The defendant in an action for infringement of patents in relation to the design and manufacture of compact discs raised defences under Articles 81 and 82, *inter alia*.[135] The defendant had earlier refused to take on the claimant's standard form licences on the grounds that the terms were unfair. Of the defence under Article 82, Laddie J said (at 124):

> . . . a patent entitles the proprietor to the exclusive right to prevent others from exploiting his invention. The exclusive right is the central defining characteristic of a patent. It is what gives it its legal and commercial value . . . The reward takes the form of a right to exclude competitors from using or exploiting any inventive product of such research and development. The purpose and effect of that right of exclusivity is to enable the owner of the patent to take advantage of the absence of competition so as to increase his prices and thereby increase his profits or market or both.

Laddie J then rejected the notion that the EC Treaty (now TFEU) obliges patentees to grant licences on fair and reasonable terms. Otherwise, patent rights would be emasculated, in the words of Laddie J. He accepted that Articles 81 and 82 have to live side by side with intellectual property rights which are, because of their very nature, anti-competitive. Of course, it is very much a matter of reconciling Article 345 TFEU which states that the Treaty shall in no way prejudice the rules in Member States governing the system of property ownership. Articles 101 and 102 apply to specific forms of abuse and cannot be widened out in such a way as to prejudice intellectual property rights. The drive to greater harmonisation of intellectual property rights and the introduction of Community-wide rights confirm the importance with which these rights are seen by the European Commission, Parliament and the Council, as will a reading of the recitals in Directives and Regulations relating to intellectual property rights.

In *Philips Electronics*, Laddie J also made the point that it did not follow that the same principles apply to all intellectual property rights when it came to Article 82 (or other provisions of the EC Treaty for that matter). He said (at 134):

> . . . not all intellectual property rights are equal. Some are more equal than others. It is convenient and conventional to treat copyright, designs, topography rights, moral rights, confidential information, patents and trade marks as a group. But there are substantial differences between them. They last for different periods in respect of different types of subject matter. They are infringed by different types of activity. They are subject to different types of defences or exceptions. For example, the fair use defences in copyright have no equivalent in patent law and the compulsory licence provisions in patent law have no equivalent in copyright law. In *Magill* [the RTE case] what was being considered was the rights in a subspecies of copyright. It does not follow inevitably that Magill can be applied by analogy to a patent case.

Although *RTE* involved a quasi-monopoly situation, the decision can be seen as a response to a particular form of abuse in respect of an intellectual property right that does not normally give rise to a monopoly as the independent creation of a similar work does not infringe copyright. Furthermore, as Laddie J noted above, stronger monopoly rights, such as those associated with patents, have built-in statutory controls over abuses of the monopoly, such as compulsory licensing and, in the UK, Crown use. It should also not be forgotten that Articles 101 and 102 are concerned with abuses that affect trade between Member States, being contrary to one of the basic tenets of the common market. Again,

134 [1999] FSR 112.

135 Now Articles 101 and 102 TFEU.

it must be emphasised that these provisions (and Article 34 TFEU) are there to control exploitation of rights that run counter to the effective working of the common market rather than to question the very existence of those rights.

The basic ingredients for an infringement of Article 82 were laid down in Case 24/67 *Parke, Davis & Co v Probel*[136] as:

1 the existence of a dominant position;
2 an improper exploitation of it; and
3 the possibility that, as a result, trade between Member States may be affected;

confirming that being in a dominant position is not sufficient by itself to bring Article 102 into play – something further is needed. An important factor indicating dominance is the ownership of intellectual property rights. In particular, ownership of a patent might constitute a considerable barrier to entry into the relevant market by third parties. Adopting commercial strategies to establish barriers to competitors entering the market was held to be an abuse.[137]

Neuberger J confirmed that the task faced by a defendant running a defence under Article 82 (now Article 102 TFEU) was fourfold.[138] In addition to showing the three elements in *Parke, Davis & Co*, he also had to demonstrate a nexus between those elements and his defence on the facts. Neuberger J said that he did not doubt that a breach of Article 82 could result in a court ordering the holder of an intellectual property right to grant a licence to another, though this would be exceptional.

Where it is held that there is a breach of Article 102, large fines can be imposed. In Case T-51/89 *Tetra Pak Rausing SA v Commission to the European Communities*,[139] Tetra Pak, the world leaders in cartons and filling machines for liquid foods, especially aseptic packaging for UHT milk, through the acquisition of another company, obtained the exclusivity of a patent licence for an alternative process of sterilisation.[140] Tetra Pak argued that Article 82 (now Article 102 TFEU) was inapplicable because a block exemption applied to the licence.[141] The Court of First Instance considered the implications of Article 82 and the relationship between Articles 81(1) and 82 (now Articles 101(1) and 102 TFEU), and the effect of an exemption under Article 81(3) on the operation of Article 82. It was held that Articles 81 and 82 were complementary in as much as they have a common objective in accordance with Article 3(g) of the EC Treaty (the institution of a system ensuring that competition in the common market is not distorted),[142] but the Articles constitute two independent provisions addressing different situations. Therefore, an exemption under Article 81(3) cannot be such as to render Article 82 inapplicable. The fact that a company in a dominant position becomes more dominant through the acquisition of a patent licence does not *per se* constitute an abuse within Article 82. Account must be taken of the circumstances surrounding the acquisition, such as the effect on competition within the relevant market. The Court of First Instance upheld the Commission's finding that there had been an abuse of a dominant position. The Commission imposed a fine of ECU 75 million.[143]

A tying clause is one that requires a buyer of goods or a licensee under a patent to obtain other goods or services or raw materials from the seller or licensor. For example, a company selling patented toothbrushes to retail outlets might insist that the company's toothpaste is also purchased by the outlets. The Patents Act 1977 could make such tying clauses void under certain circumstances, and the existence of contracts or licences containing them could provide a complete defence to an infringement action.[144] EU law can also control such tying clauses if they conflict with Article 82 (now Article 102 TFEU). For example, in Case T-30/89 *Hilti AG v Commission to the European Communities*,[145] users of Hilti nail-guns, used to fire nails into walls, were required to buy nails from Hilti when they bought cartridges for the guns. Other manufacturers made suitable nails. Hilti was fined ECU 6 million for this infraction of Article 82. The tying of the purchase of

136 [1968] ECR 55.

137 *Masterfoods Ltd v HB Ice Cream Ltd* [1994] FSR 1, High Court of Ireland.

138 *Sandvik Aktiebolag v KR Pfiffner (UK) Ltd* [2000] FSR 17.

139 [1990] ECR II-309.

140 Tetra Pak had 92 per cent of the European Community market in aseptic filling machines, and 89 per cent of the market for cartons.

141 Under Commission Regulation (EEC) 2349/84 of 23 July 1984 (exemption from Article 85(1)).

142 There is no direct equivalent statement in the TFEU but is has a number of measures to the same effect.

143 Tetra Pak's appeal to the Court of Justice was dismissed: Case C-333/94P *Tetra Pak International SA v Commission to the European Communities* [1996] ECR I-5951.

144 Patents Act 1977 s 44, now repealed.

145 [1991] ECR II-1439.

sailboards and rigs was also held to be an abuse of a dominant position in Case 193/83 *Windsurfing International Inc* v *Commission to the European Communities*.[146]

146 [1986] ECR 611.

The Microsoft Corporation distributed Windows Media Player bundled in with its Windows 2000 software package. The Commission to the European Communities held that this constituted an abuse of a dominant position and the Court of First Instance confirmed this in Case T-201/04 *Microsoft Corp* v *Commission to the European Communities*.[147] The court required that, in future, Microsoft must distribute its Windows software package with the Media Player being included only as an option.

147 [2007] ECR II-3601.

Compulsory licences may not be liked by proprietors of patents but, if they are uncooperative in settling the terms of such licences that might be viewed as an abuse under Article 102 if the purpose is to delay the evil day when the licence is available. Hilti were held needlessly to have protracted proceedings for the grant of a licence of right and had demanded a royalty six times that finally adopted by the Comptroller of Patents. The patent had originally been granted under the Patents Act 1949 and an additional four years were allowed subject to licences being available as of right.[148]

148 Patents Act 1977 Sch 1, para 4.

Summary

The following provisions of the Treaty on the Functioning of the European Union impact on the exploitation of intellectual property rights:

- the principle of freedom of movement of goods (Articles 34 to 36);
- the principle of freedom to provide services (Article 56);
- controls over certain anti-competitive practices such as restrictive trade agreements (Article 101(1)); and
- controls over abuses of dominant trading positions (Article 102).

Freedom of movement of goods gives rise to the doctrine of exhaustion of rights. However, the owner of an intellectual property right may still object to the further commercialisation of the relevant goods if there exist legitimate reasons for doing so. A major example is where goods have been poorly repackaged.

Freedom to provide services applies, for example, to broadcasts from one Member State which may be received by persons in another Member State.

The Technology Transfer Regulation gives block exemption from Article 101(1) in specified cases. Individual exemption is also possible.

Being in a dominant position, *per se*, does not fall foul of Article 102. There must be some sort of abuse.

Under ss 2 and 18 of the Competition Act 1998, the UK has equivalent provisions to Articles 101 and 102 of the Treaty on the Functioning of the European Union.

Discussion questions

1 Discuss the ways in which exhaustion of rights facilitates and supports the notion of the internal market and prevents partitioning of the market by owners of intellectual property rights.

2 Discuss the circumstances under which licence agreements could fall foul of Article 101(1) of the Treaty on the Functioning of the European Union.

3 Discuss possible situations where an abuse of a dominant position contrary to Article 102 of the Treaty on the Functioning of the European Union could be present in relation to the exercise of informal rights such as copyright, rights in performances and the database right.

Selected further reading

Bonadio, E., 'Parallel imports in a global market: should a generalised international exhaustion be the next step?' [2011] *European Intellectual Property Review*, 153 (looks at the doctrine of exhaustion of rights and argues that it should be imposed on all WTO countries).

Engelen, H., 'Fines under Article 102 of the Treaty on the Functioning of the European Union' [2011] *European Competition Law Review*, 86 (a critical look at the fines imposed by the European Commission for abuses of dominant positions).

France, H., 'European Union: reasons given for AstraZeneca fine for abuse of dominant position' [2007] *World Intellectual Property Report* 6 (looks at the European Commission decision and the particular abuses by AstraZeneca).

Kellaugher, J. and Weitbrecht, A., 'Developments under Articles 101 and 102 TFEU in 2010' [2011] *European Competition Law Review*, 333 (considers recent experiences in relation to Articles 101 and 102 and concludes that the competition law regime is well-developed and mature).

The Technology Transfer Regulation, available at: **http://eur-lex.europa.eu/LexUriServ/LexUriServ. do?uri=OJ:L:2004:123:0011:0017:EN:PDF**

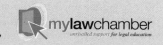

26 IPR and conflict of laws

Introduction

Conflict of laws, sometimes referred to as private international law, is an area of law which has developed to resolve three particular issues that a court may be faced with deciding in a case which has a foreign element. The issues are whether a court in a particular country has jurisdiction to hear a case, what body of law should apply to the case and the recognition and enforcement of judgments of foreign courts. These issues do not come up in every case, of course. In fact, conflict of laws comes up only in a minority of cases where there is a foreign dimension to the case, such as where the parties are domiciled in different countries. Where, for example, a British citizen resident in England owns a work of UK copyright which is infringed in the UK by another British citizen who is also resident in England, one would naturally assume that the infringement action would be commenced in the courts of England and Wales. However, even this is not always that clear cut as the UK is comprised of different jurisdictions (England and Wales, Scotland and Northern Ireland) and, furthermore, there are other jurisdictions in the British Isles such as the Isle of Man, Jersey and Guernsey. What if the infringer was a British citizen resident in Scotland?

One thing that must be made clear from the outset is that intellectual property laws are, generally, territorial. They subsist and can be infringed only in their relevant territories. This is the same with European Community-wide rights such as the CTM and Community design although here we are talking of the territory of the Community. This rule is not without exception, however, as business goodwill protected by passing off may be protected outside the geographical limits of its country. This could be the case where goodwill acquired in respect of a business in Northern Ireland could be the basis of a passing off action in neighbouring areas of Ireland.[1]

There are some other exceptions to the territorial limitation of some intellectual property rights. For example, copyright can be infringed by authorising of the acts within the exclusive rights of the owner. In such a case, a UK copyright will be infringed by carrying out one of these acts, in the UK, without the consent of the copyright owner. However, the person authorising the act will also be liable for infringing the UK copyright even if he was outside the UK when he gave his authorisation.[2] The corollary to this rule is that the courts of one jurisdiction would not be expected to accept jurisdiction over disputes relating to alleged infringements of foreign patents, copyrights or trade marks.[3] However, as we will see, this has been compromised, certainly as regards the informal rights and even formal intellectual property rights where there is no challenge to the validity of the right.

The courts in the UK and other countries developed their own rules as to whether to accept jurisdiction and which law to apply and the enforcement of foreign judgments.

1 *See*, for example, *C & A Modes v C & A (Waterford) Ltd* [1978] FSR 126, discussed in Chapter 23, p 878.

2 *ABKCO Music & Records Inc v Music Collection International Ltd* [1995] RPC 657.

3 *Tyburn Productions Ltd v Conan Doyle* [1991] Ch 75, applying *Def Lepp Music v Stuart Brown* [1986] RPC 273.

Treaties and arrangements with other countries were entered into. An important principle was *forum non conveniens*. This meant that an English court would decline jurisdiction to hear a case if the courts in another country would be more suitable to hear the case. This principle reached a high point in the House of Lords in *Spiliada Maritime Corp* v *Cansulex Ltd (The 'Spiliada')*,[4] in which guidelines for the application of the principle were set out by Lord Goff. The principle is still very important in some situations but has, in the context of conflict of laws in a European context, lost much of its relevance. In Europe there are a number of Conventions and Regulations that set out a fairly comprehensive system for determining the issues that may arise.

As with the previous chapter, this does not attempt to present a detailed view of conflict of laws and reference should be made to a suitable book on the subject.[5] Rather, this chapter examines the subject from the perspective of intellectual property rights and is focused accordingly. In particular, jurisdiction is the main area covered, with some material on applicable law.

Jurisdiction[6]

The main piece of legislation in Europe is Council Regulation (EC) No 44/2001 of 22 December 2000 on jurisdiction and the recognition and enforcement of judgments in civil and commercial matters.[7] This Regulation is referred to as the 'Brussels Regulation' and replaced the Brussels Convention 1968[8] on jurisdiction and the recognition and enforcement of judgments in civil and commercial matters which was retained only by Denmark. For our purposes, there is only one minor difference between the Regulation and the Convention in that the former expressly applies to torts which *may* occur whereas the latter does not, although the Court of Session, Outer House, in Scotland held that the Brussels Convention also applied to threatened torts (or, in Scotland, delicts).[9]

A parallel Convention to the Brussels Convention is the Lugano Convention on jurisdiction and the recognition and enforcement of judgments in civil and commercial matters, 1988 ('Lugano Convention'). This has equivalent provisions to those relevant to intellectual property rights and, in effect, extends them to the other EEA Member States.[10] The following discussion on jurisdiction is based on the Brussels Regulation, unless otherwise stated.

The basic rule in Article 2 is that defendants should be sued in the courts in the Member State in which they are domiciled, whatever their nationality. If they are not nationals of the Member State in which they are domiciled, they are governed by the rules of jurisdiction applicable to nationals of that Member State.[11] This basic rule is subject only to the possibility that such persons may be sued in the courts of another Member State only if provided for by the Regulation.

Simply put, the basic rule is that defendants 'play at home'. The Brussels Regulation contains a number of other provisions which displace that rule or even give alternatives as to the courts in which Member States have jurisdiction. Before looking at the exceptions to the basic rule, the fact that in some cases the courts of more than one Member State may have exclusive jurisdiction under the Brussels Regulation, one additional rule should be mentioned. This prevents parallel actions in a number of Member States for the same cause of action and between the same parties.

Where proceedings involving the same cause of action and the same parties are brought before the courts of different Member States, any court other than the court first seised shall stay proceedings until the jurisdiction of the court seised is established: Article 27. Where the jurisdiction of the court first seised is established, other courts must decline jurisdiction in favour of the court first seised. A simple example should help. Albert and

4 [1987] 1 AC 460.

5 The leading text is Collins *et al.* (2010) *Dicey and Morris on the Conflict of Laws* (14th edn) Sweet & Maxwell. An excellent and more accessible text (though now somewhat dated) is Collier, J.G. (2001) *Conflict of Laws* (3rd edn) Cambridge University Press. Few major texts on the subject carry much material on intellectual property rights.

6 See Dutson, S. 'Actions for infringement of a foreign intellectual property right in an English Court' (1997) 46 *International and Comparative Law Quarterly* 918.

7 OJ L 12, 16.01.2001, p 1. The Civil Jurisdiction and Judgments Order 2001, SI 2001/3929, made the necessary changes to the Civil Jurisdiction and Judgments Act 1982.

8 OJ C 27, 26.01.1968, p 1.

9 *Bonnier Media Ltd* v *Greg Lloyd Smith* [2003] SC 36.

10 The numbering of equivalent provisions in the Lugano Convention is not the same as in the Brussels Regulation. The Lugano Convention is to be replaced by the Convention on jurisdiction and the recognition and enforcement of judgments in civil and commercial matters, OJ L 339, 21.12.2007, p 3. Denmark will also join this Convention.

11 If the defendant is not domiciled in a Member State, the jurisdiction of each Member State will be determined by the law of that Member State, subject to Articles 22 and 23 which apply, *inter alia*, to land, formal intellectual property rights and agreements between the parties as to which courts should have jurisdiction. Against such a defendant, a person domiciled in a Member State may avail himself of the rules of jurisdiction as apply to nationals of that State.

Bertie are parties to a contract which is to be performed in England. Albert is domiciled in England and Bertie is domiciled in France. On 1 May 2006, Albert commences proceedings against Bertie for breach of contract in the English courts. On 8 May 2006, Bertie commences proceedings against Albert for breach of contract in France. Under the Regulation, the French court must stay the action until the English court has decided whether it has jurisdiction, which it will confirm it has, as it is possible to sue a defendant in a contract case in the courts in the Member State where the contract is to be performed. Once the English court has established that it does indeed have jurisdiction, the French court must decline jurisdiction. Even where, as in the case of Albert and Bertie, the courts of both England and France have jurisdiction, the French court must still decline jurisdiction in favour of the English court which was first seised.[12]

Notwithstanding the basic rule that a defendant should be sued in his home Member State, Article 5 of the Brussels Regulation provides that a person domiciled in a Member State may be sued in another Member State under certain circumstances. These include:

- in relation to a contract, the courts for the place of performance of the obligation in question;[13]
- in relation to a tort, delict or quasi-delict, the courts for the place where the harmful event occurred or may occur.[14]

Infringement of an intellectual property right is a tort and many intellectual property rights are exploited by means of a contractual licence. These two particular situations potentially give an alternative forum for hearing a dispute in intellectual property cases involving a foreign element. For example, suppose the contract between Albert and Bertie was a copyright licence which permitted Bertie to make and sell copies of a watercolour painting and for these purposes he is provided with a master copy of the painting. Albert owns the copyright in the painting. It is a work of UK copyright but, in accordance with Article 5 of the Berne Convention for the Protection of Literary and Artistic Works, Albert is able to enforce his copyright in other countries where he will be entitled to the relevant national copyrights. Say that, in breach of the licence agreement, Bertie makes a duplicate of the master copy which he sells to Cedric, domiciled in Germany, who makes and sells prints in Belgium. Albert can sue in France (breach of licence agreement[15] and infringement of copyright by the making of duplicates by Bertie) or Belgium (infringement of copyright there by Cedric). Albert cannot sue in England as his UK copyright has not been infringed. He has to rely on the licence agreement and his equivalent French and Belgian copyrights.

The next rule is that, under Article 6(1), where there is more than one defendant and the claims against each are so closely connected that it is expedient to hear them together to avoid the risk of irreconcilable judgments resulting from separate proceedings, the defendants may be sued in the courts in the Member State in which any one of them is domiciled.[16] In our example, if Bertie and Cedric are, in effect, joint tortfeasors in relation to the sales in Belgium,[17] on the basis of this rule, Albert can sue in France or Germany. This rule does not prevent the working of Article 5 so the potential alternatives for Albert, depending on the precise circumstances, are:

- sue Bertie in France and Cedric in Germany (Article 2);
- sue Bertie in France for breach of contract and for making an infringing copy there (Article 5);
- sue Cedric in Belgium for making and selling infringing copies there (Article 5);
- sue Bertie and Cedric in either France or Germany as being joint tortfeasors in respect of making and selling infringing copies in Belgium (Article 6(1)).

Where there is a contract, for example, a licence agreement in respect of intellectual property rights, one would expect the contract to include express provision for applicable law and

12 Being 'seised' means having the document instituting proceedings lodged with the court. Under the Brussels Convention there was no further guidance on the meaning of 'first seised', unlike the modest attempt to define the term under Article 30 of the Brussels Regulation: see *Tavoulareas v Tsavliris* [2004] 1 Lloyd's Rep 445.

13 In a sale of goods contract this is the place the goods were or should have been delivered and, in the case of a service, the place where the service was, or should have been, provided.

14 There are further circumstances under Article 5 including maintenance, agency or trusts.

15 Assuming the licence does not contain a clause giving the courts of one Member State exclusive jurisdiction.

16 The test of close connection and expediency was a result of the decision of the Court of Justice in Case 189/87 *Athanasios Kalfelis v Bankhaus Schröder, Münchmeyer, Hengst & Co* [1988] ECR 5565 in which the court interpreted the previous provision in the Brussels Convention narrowly.

17 In other words, it was a joint venture to infringe the copyright.

it may also include an agreement between the parties as to exclusive jurisdiction. Article 23 of the Brussels Regulation allows the parties, one or more of which is domiciled in a Member State, to agree that a court or the courts of a Member State are to have jurisdiction to settle disputes which have arisen or may arise out of a particular legal relationship. That jurisdiction shall be exclusive unless the parties agree otherwise. The agreement conferring jurisdiction must be in writing[18] or evidenced in writing or in a form in accordance with practices established by the parties or in a form in international trade or commerce which is widely used and regularly observed by parties to such contracts and the parties to the present contract are, or ought to be, aware of this. Such an agreement cannot oust the jurisdiction of a court which has exclusive jurisdiction under Article 22, including Article 22(4) below.[19]

The next provision of the Brussels Regulation of particular interest in relation to intellectual property rights applies where the right is formal in nature, being subject to registration, such as a patent or trade mark, and the proceedings are concerned with the registration or validity of the right in question: Article 22(4). In such cases, the courts of the Member State, in which the right, such as a patent, trade mark, design or similar right, is secured by registration or deposit, have exclusive jurisdiction. This applies also to application to register such rights and to European patents granted under the European Patent Convention.

Therefore, in an action concerning a UK patent, trade mark or registered design where registration or validity is an issue in the case, the courts of the UK have exclusive jurisdiction. Of course, if neither registration nor validity is in issue, then the usual rules apply. However, in most cases, a defendant will mount an attack on validity. The impact of Article 22(4) can be serious when dealing with parallel infringements of national registered intellectual rights covering the same subject matter, such as where a proprietor of a bundle of national patent rights acquired through the European Patent Convention could be faced with the expense of bringing parallel proceedings in a number of Member States for what might amount to the same infringing acts in relation to the same invention. The rules in Article 22 (Article 16 of the Brussels Convention) are exclusive and mandatory by nature. It is almost inevitable that validity of a patent or other registered property right will be challenged, even indirectly, in infringement proceedings. It does not matter whether validity is brought up by an action, for example, for revocation or invalidity, or by way of a defence and it does not matter at what stage in the proceedings validity is raised.[20] For example, if there is a later challenge to a patent registered in another Contracting State, the court hearing the action will have no option but to stay proceedings.

Even though validity has not yet been put in issue, if it is clear that it will be in the future, either in the current proceedings or where new proceedings alleging invalidity are likely to be commenced, no purpose is to be served by a court in a country other than that in which the patent is registered accepting jurisdiction. In *Knorr-Bremse Systems for Commercial Vehicles Ltd* v *Haldex Brake Products GmbH*,[21] Knorr-Bremse brought an action in England for a declaration of non-infringement of Haldex's patents valid in a number of European countries including the UK. Haldex sought an order for a stay of proceedings.[22] However, Knorr-Bremse had already indicated that it intended to claim that the patents were invalid and had instructed its attorneys to file a counterclaim for invalidity once Haldex had served its defence. Lewison J referred to the ECJ case of *Gesellschaft für Antriebstechnik*, noted above,[23] and Laddie J in *Coin Controls Ltd* v *Suzo International*[24] and said that where it was clear that validity 'is to be put in issue' in the future, the court should decide the application on the basis that validity is one of the issues in the case. It is not necessary for the allegation of invalidity to be formally pleaded. In such a case, if the action were to be stayed, there would be nothing to stop the relevant party starting a new action alleging invalidity as well as non-infringement. If Haldex brought proceedings before the German

18 'Writing' includes an electronic communication which provides a durable record of the agreement.

19 The Court of Justice confirmed in Case C-4/03 *Gesellschaft für Antriebstechnik mbH & Co KG* v *Lamellen und Kupplungsbau Beteiligungs KG* [2006] ECR I-6509 that parties may not derogate from Article 16 of the Brussels Convention by agreement conferring jurisdiction or by voluntarily putting in an appearance. Article 22 of the Brussels Regulation is equivalent to Article 16 of the Brussels Convention.

20 Case C-4/03 *Gesellschaft für Antriebstechnik mbH & Co KG* v *Lamellen und Kupplungsbau Beteiligungs KG* [2006] ECR I-6509.

21 [2008] FSR 30.

22 Haldex argued that an agreement between it and the German parent company of Knorr-Bremse in settlement of an earlier patent dispute conferred exclusive jurisdiction on the Landgericht Düsseldorf in Germany.

23 See note 20.

24 *Infra*.

court, that court would have to decline jurisdiction once the allegation of invalidity of the UK designations of the European patents had been raised here. Lewison J said that he could not see the point of that.

The Community trade mark and Community design both have their own rules of jurisdiction under which a number of the rules of the Brussels Regulation are suppressed or modified. Jurisdictional issues relating to these Community-wide rights, including the unregistered Community design, are specifically provided for in the relevant Regulation and are described in Chapters 17 and 22.

Before looking further at jurisdiction in particular cases, it should be plain from what has been said above that the issues can be somewhat different for the informal intellectual property rights such as copyright and the formal rights.

Copyright

A case that signified an important step in applying the then Brussels Convention to intellectual property disputes was *Gareth Pearce* v *Ove Arup Partnership Ltd*.[25] In that case, the claimant claimed that he had UK and Dutch copyright in his architectural drawings for a building, originally drawn by the claimant for a town hall in London Docklands. He alleged that the second and third defendant copied his plans and used them to construct a building called the Kunsthal in Rotterdam, built by the first defendant. The fourth defendant was the owner of the building. This, the claimant alleged, was an infringement of his Dutch copyright. He sued in England on the basis of the Brussels Convention, Article 6(1),[26] in that at least one of the defendants (civil engineers for the construction of the building) was domiciled in the UK. One of the main issues in the case was whether the action was justiciable in the English courts.[27]

On the basis of *British South Africa Co* v *Companhia de Moçambique*[28] and *Def Lepp Music* v *Stuart Brown*,[29] a claim made in respect of a breach of a foreign statutory intellectual property right would not be entertained in an English court, such a claim being regarded purely as local. Further, the *Def Lepp* case is also an example of a claim failing because of the double actionability rule. However, the *Moçambique* rule and the double actionability rule were effectively overruled by the Brussels Convention as far as necessary to give effect to that Convention.[30] Therefore, the English courts had jurisdiction to hear the claim of infringement of Dutch copyright against the first, English domiciled defendant and, by the operation of Article 6(1) of the Convention, the English courts also had jurisdiction to hear the action against the other defendants.

In the *Gareth Pearce* case, Lloyd J remarked on the possibility of 'forum shopping', where a claimant takes into account the procedures and remedies available in different states where he has a choice, and accepted that, in appropriate circumstances, an English court might not be able to refuse jurisdiction to hear cases involving, for example, infringement of the French law of privacy or the German law of unfair competition or some other action in foreign law not having a direct equivalent in English law.[31]

At first instance, in the *Gareth Pearce* case, whilst deciding that the English court had jurisdiction to hear the action based on Dutch copyright, Lloyd J struck out the action as being an abuse of process as there was insufficient similarity between the drawings submitted by the claimant and those for the building in Rotterdam. The claimant appealed to the Court of Appeal,[32] seeking to adduce further evidence. A portfolio of 18 drawings were received by the court on the basis that they did not constitute additional evidence but were an explanation of counsel's submissions on behalf of the claimant.[33] The Court of Appeal affirmed that decision that the English court was not bound to refuse to hear the claim on the basis of the *Moçambique* rule nor on the basis of the first limb of the double actionability rule. Although still relevant to the present case, following *Red Sea Insurance Co Ltd* v *Bouygues SA*,[34] the first limb of the double actionability rule (that the

25 [1997] FSR 641, approved by the Court of Appeal in *Fort Dodge Animal Health Ltd* v *Akzo Nobel NV* [1998] FSR 222, a patent case.

26 Whether the actions between the defendants were so closely connected that it would be expedient to hear them together is now a test for the application of Article 6(1) of the Brussels Regulation.

27 The other main issue was whether the action should be struck out as an abuse of process, being purely speculative. On this point the defendants succeeded.

28 [1893] AC 602, a claim involving trespass to foreign land.

29 [1986] RPC 273, followed in *Tyburn Productions Ltd* v *Doyle* [1991] Ch 75.

30 The double actionability rule required that an act done in a foreign country is a tort and actionable in England only if it was a tort had it been done in England and was also actionable according to the law of the country where it was done. This was abolished on 1 May 1996 by the Private International Law (Miscellaneous Provisions) Act 1995 s 11(1). However, the facts in the *Gareth Pearce* case occurred before that date.

31 [1997] FSR 641 at 652.

32 *Gareth Pearce* v *Ove Arup Partnership Ltd* [1999] FSR 525.

33 The Court of Appeal decided that the claimant's allegations were not so fanciful as to be regarded as wholly speculative.

34 [1995] AC 190.

act must be a tort in England had the act occurred there) is a matter of determining the choice of law rather than a matter of jurisdiction. This is an exception to the double actionability rule and it enables the English court to hear a claim involving an alleged infringement of Dutch copyright. Not only can an English court deal with issues of infringement of a foreign copyright where subsistence is not an issue, in appropriate cases, it can also deal with subsistence of a foreign copyright.

Whilst the Brussels Regulation gives exclusive jurisdiction to the courts of the country where formal rights such as patents and trade marks are registered where there is an issue of validity of the right, there is no such limitation for informal rights such as copyright. This is of course, subject to the court in the country first seised having jurisdiction under the Regulation, such as the defendant being domiciled in that country. It now appears that this also now applies where the informal right is in a territory outside the Brussels or Lugano States, such as the United States.

In *Lucasfilm Ltd* v *Ainsworth*,[35] the Supreme Court held that the courts in England had jurisdiction to entertain a claim of infringement of a United States copyright against a defendant domiciled in the UK.[36] This was so even though enforcement of United States copyright in the United States required registration of the copyright for proceedings to take place there. However, this was simply a pre-requisite of commencing legal proceedings and nothing to do with subsistence. Bringing proceedings in England did not challenge the act of a foreign state, unlike the case with the validity of a foreign patent.

Where the defendant is not domiciled in a Contracting State, he can be served with process if he is present within the jurisdiction of a part of the UK, otherwise leave of the court is required. It might be given, for example, in the case where a tort has been committed within jurisdiction and the court considers it proper for service of process out of jurisdiction.

However, even if a court within part of the UK could entertain a claim against a defendant domiciled out of jurisdiction, where there is a conflict between that part of the UK and a non-Brussels Regulation state, the court here might stay or dismiss the action on the grounds of *forum non conveniens*, that is, that the courts here are less appropriate to hear the case than the courts in that other country. For example, in *Re Harrods (Buenos Aires) Ltd*[37] the English court considered that the Argentinean courts were more appropriate to decide the issues. As will be seen later, *forum non conveniens* has no place in relation to the Brussels Regulation and Lugano Convention though may still be relevant where the foreign element is outside Europe.

Patents

Before the Brussels Convention, previous law in the UK included the *Moçambique* rule[38] to the effect that the English courts did not have jurisdiction over disputes concerning foreign land, a rule which was later applied to intellectual property on the basis that it too was an 'immoveable'. It was held by Laddie J not to apply to intellectual property in *Coin Controls Ltd* v *Suzo International (UK) Ltd.*[39] He said that patents and other intellectual property rights are not accurately described as immoveable. Indeed, a patent is described in the Patents Act 1977 as personal property or, in Scotland, as incorporeal moveable property.[40]

A further rule was that of double actionability. In *Boys* v *Chaplin*[41] it was said that, for an act done in a foreign country to be actionable in England, it must first of all be actionable as a tort according to English law (it would be a tort if committed in England) and, second, it must be actionable as a tort according to the law of the foreign country in which the act was done. However, it was pointed out in *Def Lepp Music* v *Stuart Brown*[42] that an English intellectual property right could never be infringed by an activity taking place out of jurisdiction and could not, therefore, be treated as if it had been done in

35 [2011] UKSC 39.

36 Overturning the Court of Appeal on this point and holding that *Tyburn Productions Ltd* v *Conan Doyle* [1991] Ch 75 was wrongly decided.

37 [1992] Ch 72.

38 *British South Africa Company* v *Companhia de Moçambique* [1893] AC 602.

39 [1997] FSR 660.

40 Sections 30(1) and 31(1), respectively.

41 [1971] AC 356.

42 [1986] RPC 273.

England.[43] The double actionability rule was abolished as far as it applies to a claim in tort (or delict in Scotland) by the Private International Law (Miscellaneous Provisions) Act 1995 s 10.

43 The one exception is in relation to infringing by authorising an infringing act: *ABKCO Music & Records Inc v Music Collection International Ltd* [1995] RPC 657.

The rule in relation to the court first seised also applies where there are related actions in different Member States, although this is expressed as discretionary in Article 28 which states that any court other than the court first seised *may . . .* stay its proceedings. In *Fort Dodge Animal Health Ltd* v *Akzo Nobel NV*,[44] Lord Woolf MR said (at 243) of actions involving a UK patent and a Dutch patent:

44 [1998] FSR 222.

> They are actions relating to two different national rights. True they stem from the same patent application [before the European Patent Office] and similar rules of construction will be applicable, but the rights given by those patents are national rights limited in territory to the State in which they are registered and the ambit of the monopolies will not necessarily be the same as amendment is possible . . . a judgment on infringement in the United Kingdom will depend upon a national right having effect only in the United Kingdom. The same applies to a judgment on the Dutch patent.

In *Research in Motion UK Ltd* v *Visto Corporation*,[45] the Court of Appeal held that Article 28 does not require a mechanical test unlike Article 27. Under Article 28(3), actions are related '. . . where they are so closely connected that it is expedient to hear and determine them together to avoid the risk of irreconcilable judgments resulting from separate proceedings'. This does not mean that a court must consider actions to be related if there is any possibility of inconsistent judgments. In that case, proceedings had been commenced in England on 30 October 2006 by Research in Motion (RIM – which makes the famous BlackBerry hand-held device) for revocation of Visto's patent.[46] On 5 December 2006, RIM also commenced proceedings in England for a declaration of non-infringement of the patent but this excluded the BlackBerry Mail Connector. On 27 December 2006, RIM commenced proceedings in Italy applying for revocation of Visto's equivalent Italian patent and declarations of non-infringement of the Italian patent and of the equivalent German, French, Spanish, Dutch and Belgian patents. On 2 February 2007 Visto served a defence and counterclaim to the English action which included a claim to damages under Article 96 of the Italian procedural code which provides for a separate award of damages against a losing party where it has brought or resisted a claim in bad faith or with gross negligence. RIM successfully sought an order from Lewison J declining jurisdiction or a stay of proceedings. RIM later dropped the English action for a declaration of non-infringement after Visto accepted that the BlackBerry device without the Mail Connector did not infringe its patent. Visto appealed to the Court of Appeal against the order of Lewison J. The only way in which the actions were related was the Article 96 claim. In dismissing Visto's appeal, the Court of Appeal said (at para 38):

45 [2008] FSR 20.

46 Visto's patent was granted by the EPO in May 2006 designating a number of Contracting States to the EPC. There were on-going opposition proceedings before the EPO brought by RIM (note that the EPO has a post-grant opposition procedure). Such proceedings can take five or more years to conclusion.

> The substance of the English proceedings is declaration about an English patent and a particular product [the BlackBerry without the Mail Connector]. The substance of the Italian proceedings is other designations, but not focusing on the same product [the BlackBerry with the Mail Connector]. The abuse of Italian process is a link between them, but it is the only link; it is only in relation to that point that there is a risk of inconsistent judgments. It does not seem to us that Article 28(3) requires one to find that any possibility, no matter how small the point, requires the conclusion that the actions are related. One still has to consider expediency. We consider that the area of potential conflict is not sufficiently great to lead to the conclusion that expediency would require one trial even if it were theoretically possible.

It is important to note that, even though patents may go through the European Patent Office, once the national stage is reached different rules of procedure and amendment apply in different countries. It is possible for two national patents based on the same invention to end with differing claims because of amendment. In *Coin Controls Ltd* v

47 [1997] FSR 660.

Suzo International (UK) Ltd,[47] Laddie J considered that, for Article 6(1) to apply where two or more national patents are involved, it is crucial that the patents are identical (providing, of course, there is no challenge to validity). In *Fort Dodge*, Lord Woolf MR seems to suggest that Article 6(1) would not apply even where the patents are identical in all respects.

What Lord Woolf MR is not saying, however, is that an action for infringement of a foreign patent cannot be heard before an English court. His comments are in relation to Article 6(1) and must be restricted to that provision. *Gareth Pearce* v *Ove Arup Partnership Ltd*[48] and *Coin Controls Ltd* v *Suzo International (UK) Ltd*[49] are authorities for the proposition that the Brussels Regulation can force the courts in a Member State to hear and determine foreign infringement proceedings, and both were approved by Lord Woolf MR on this point in *Fort Dodge*. The major exception is where there is an issue concerning the validity of the patent or some aspect of its registration, in which case Article 22(4) applies leaving the courts of the place where the right is registered as having exclusive jurisdiction.

48 [1997] FSR 641.
49 [1997] FSR 660.

In such a case, under Article 25 a court in any other Member State seised of a claim which is *principally concerned* with a matter in Article 22 must declare by its own motion that it has no jurisdiction. Validity is often put at issue by a defendant and the Patents Act 1977 s 74(1)(a) expressly states that validity may be put in issue as a defence in infringement proceedings. As Laddie J said in *Coin Controls*, 'we have always taken the view that you cannot infringe an invalid patent'. The *Gillette*[50] defence is quite common. The defendant submits that the patent is invalid if the alleged infringing act falls within its claims, for example, because what the defendant did was not novel or inventive at the priority date of the patent, or the defendant's acts fall outside the scope of the patent claims.

50 *Gillette Safety Razor Co* v *Anglo-American Trading Co Ltd* (1913) 30 RPC 465.

There does not appear to be any authority on the meaning of 'principally concerned', but the Jenard Report[51] suggests that preliminary or incidental matter is ignored. As Laddie J said in *Coin Controls* (at 676):

51 One of two reports, named after their authors, on the Brussels Convention and which may be referred to in determining the meaning of the provisions of the Convention: Civil Jurisdiction and Judgments Act 1982 s 3(3). The other report is the Schlosser Report.

> Something which is a major feature of the litigation is not incidental and is therefore a matter with which the action is primarily concerned.

Therefore, validity or registration does not have to be the prime issue provided it is a major issue for Articles 22(4) and 25 to apply, giving exclusive jurisdiction in the state where the patent has been applied for or granted. Of course, it is possible to have an action, for infringement or otherwise, where validity is not in issue. In such a case, Articles 22(4) and 25 do not apply and exclusive jurisdiction is not granted, by virtue of these provisions, to the state in which the patent is in force or has been applied for. This was so in *Plastus Kreativ AB* v *Minnesota Mining and Manufacturing Co*[52] where Aldous J struck out claims relating to French and German patents, though not for reasons associated with the then Brussels Convention.[53]

52 [1995] RPC 438.

53 The claimant sought a declaration of non-infringement in respect of UK, French and German patents, but the defendant (proprietor of the patents) had made no claim in respect of the French and German patents.

54 [1998] FSR 199.

55 A stent is a tubular prosthesis to be inserted into a hollow structure such as a blood vessel.

56 District Court of the Hague.

Where an action has been commenced in a country other than that in which the patent has been registered and validity has later been put in issue, the court first seised of the action does not necessarily have to decline jurisdiction. The Dutch courts have taken a less cautious approach on this point. *Julio Cesar Palmaz* v *Boston Scientific BV*[54] concerned an action for infringement of European patents for stents.[55] Of the defendants, all of which were interconnected companies, there were two Dutch, one Belgian, one English, one Swiss, one Norwegian, one French, one Spanish and one Italian. Interim injunctions were sought by the claimant in respect of all the countries with the exception of England and Germany. The Dutch court[56] accepted that it had jurisdiction on the basis of Articles 2 and 6(1).

The claims in *Julio Cesar Palmaz* concerned the same European patents. The Dutch court remarked that Article 49 of the European Patent Convention required that they should be interpreted in the same manner and, so as to avoid conflicting decisions, it was expedient that the Dutch court determine the claims. The question of infringement could not be determined without taking a decision on the validity of a patent; this produced a dilemma in respect of Article 22. There were two possibilities. First, the court first seised should divest itself of jurisdiction immediately the validity of a foreign patent is put in issue, as in *Coin Controls*. The second possibility is for the court first seised to stay proceedings until the question of validity has been determined in the other jurisdiction. The second alternative was preferred by the Dutch court as being the more satisfactory. The jurisdiction of the court was based on Articles 2 and 6(1) of the Brussels Regulation (and Brussels Convention) and the court had jurisdiction to grant cross-border injunctions.[57] The first option was deemed to be unacceptable because jurisdiction would not be established until after the defence had been pleaded and this was said to be contrary to the objects of the Brussels Regulation or Brussels Convention and the Lugano Convention.[58] Furthermore, Article 16 of the Brussels Convention (Article 22 of the Brussels Regulation) was a derogation from the main rule on jurisdiction and, as such, should be interpreted restrictively.

A consequence of the decision of the Dutch court in *Julio Cesar Palmaz*, where the validity of a patent registered in another state is put in issue, is that a court having jurisdiction under Articles 2 and 6(1) can stay proceedings pending determination of the validity of the patent in the courts of that other state. In the meantime, the court first seised can grant interim relief. Following the determination of validity, the court first seised may then apply that finding to the question of infringement before it.

Two points can be made. First, it is not clear whether the same principles would apply in respect of a court having jurisdiction under Articles 5 and 6(1). The main rule, to which Article 22 is a derogation, is that in Article 2 defendants shall be sued in the courts of the Member State in which they are domiciled. Article 5 could, itself, be seen as a derogation from Article 2. The second point is that Article 25 uses the phrase 'principally concerned' and this gives the clue that there may be other issues involved. Nevertheless, Article 22 clearly states that the court seised of a claim in respect of which the courts of another Member State have exclusive jurisdiction by virtue of Article 22 *shall* declare of its own motion that it has no jurisdiction. There is no discretion in Article 25. It does not say that the court first seised shall stay proceedings until the determination of the validity of the patent or other registered right by the court in that other Member State. It is submitted that the decision of the Dutch court was wrong, although the court did highlight ambiguities in the Jenard Report and concluded that neither that report nor the Brussels Convention foresaw that issues of infringement and validity are, in patent cases, almost inseparable. The opportunity to remedy the situation when the Brussels Regulation was formulated was not taken.

Of the approaches taken in *Coin Controls* and *Julio Cesar Palmaz*, neither is satisfactory. If the court first seised divests itself of jurisdiction this will lead to delay. It may also encourage defendants to plead invalidity (although the English courts appear to treat infringement and invalidity as a single issue). It also means that interim relief is not available until the action brought before the court in the state in which the patent is registered. The possibility of staying the action pending a decision as to validity can also be criticised as causing delay and the inconvenience of hearings before two different courts in different Contracting States. An amendment to the Brussels and Lugano Conventions to widen the scope of Article 22 to include infringement actions would be most welcome.

The rationale for the rule in Article 22[59] was described by the Court of Justice in Case C-4/03 *Gesellschaft für Antriebstechnik mbH & Co KG* v *Lamellen und Kupplungsbau Beteiligungs KG*,[60] a challenge was made to the validity of two French patents in a German court. The purpose of the rule is to ensure that jurisdiction is placed before the court most closely linked with the proceedings in fact and law. The courts in the Contracting State where a patent is registered are best placed to rule on validity or registration and rule on such matters according to their own national law on validity and the effects of registration.

57 In the event, the Dutch court came to a provisional conclusion that the patents had not been infringed.

58 Lugano Convention on Jurisdiction and the Enforcement of Judgments in Civil and Commercial Matters, 16 September 1988.

59 The Court of Justice was actually dealing with the equivalent provision in Article 16 of the Brussels Convention.

60 [2006] ECR I-6509.

This meets concerns for sound administration of justice, particularly in a specialised field such as patents also bearing in mind that a number of Contracting States have established special courts to hear patent cases. The Court of Justice confirmed that the rule in Article 22 was of an exclusive and mandatory nature and could not be derogated for by the an agreement between the parties conferring jurisdiction elsewhere or by the defendant's voluntary appearance elsewhere. The Court of Justice also noted that infringement actions almost always involve issues of validity and it did not matter whether validity was raised as a claim or a defence or at what stage in the proceedings it became an issue. The importance of Article 22 is such that any decision which fell foul of it would not benefit from the system of recognition and enforcement of judgments under the Brussels Regulation.

Patents and the European Patent Convention

61 [1999] FSR 746.

The meeting of the Brussels Regulation and the European Patent Convention is not a particularly happy one. The case of *Sepracor Inc* v *Hoechst Marrion Roussel Ltd* [61] gives a glimpse of the nightmare that lies in wait for patent proprietors who have a number of patents for the same invention in force in different Contracting States of the European Patent Convention. In that case, Sepracor was a co-proprietor of patents for an anti-histamine drug. There were 17 national patents in all, granted through the European Patent Office. Sepracor considered that its patents were being infringed in the UK and some other countries. The timing of what happened next is important. Before Sepracor commenced the English action, one of the defendants in that English action took a pre-emptive strike and commenced proceedings in Belgium for a declaration that the Belgian and German patents were invalid or not infringed. Later, Sepracor commenced proceedings in England for a declaration that its UK patent and equivalent patents in 12 other countries were valid and infringed by the defendants. Where there is choice of forum, a defendant might be tempted to commence proceedings, typically for invalidity of one of a bundle of national patents in a country perceived to be 'infringer-friendly' on the basis that the action in that country will take a long time. In Belgium, in a patent infringement case, a typical action might take five years to come to trial and any appeal might take another five years. Amongst practitioners, this practice is known as 'deploying the Belgian torpedo'.[62]

62 There is also an Italian torpedo.

63 The defendants included a German company and its subsidiary companies in the UK, Germany and the USA.

Laddie J accepted that there would never have been any proceedings in Belgium had it not been for a desire to frustrate proceedings in Germany which was most likely the source of the drugs made in Europe by the defendants.[63] The true position was that the defendants wanted all the issues resolved in Belgium whilst the claimant wanted all the issues resolved in England. Laddie J said (at 752):

> . . . it may well be that issues such as the law of patent infringement and validity in most of the foreign countries referred to in the writ . . . and the law of joint tortfeasance in each of them would never have arisen at all . . . had sensible procedures for investigating the validity and infringement of patents obtained under the EPC been in place. As it is there is a positive incentive to commence proceedings in countries where they are not likely to come to a hearing within a reasonable period of time or in countries which have no real relationship to the acts of infringement alleged or, as here, in both. A less sensible system could not have been dreamt up by Kafka.

64 According to Laddie J, the litigation in *Fort Dodge* looked likely to come to a halt and a reference from the Dutch Court of Appeal (*Boston Scientific NV* v *Cordis* [2000] ENPR 87) seemed bound to go the same way. That appears to have been the case.

In striking out those parts of the writ, statement of claim and particulars of infringement relating to foreign patents, Laddie J went on to remark that the fact that courts in some countries have differing opinions about the effect of the Brussels Convention has not caused the problem but it has exacerbated it. Although references have been made to the Court of Justice that might have clarified the matter, these appear to have fallen by the wayside.[64] This sort of problem, which could have resulted in separate actions being brought in 13 countries, with 26 teams of lawyers being instructed, can only be resolved when the Community patent becomes available. Even then, the resolution cannot be complete as national systems will run alongside the Community patent. The only alternative is for changes to be made to the Brussels Regulation or the European Patent Convention or both. One possible solution would be for domestic actions to be stayed whilst the European Patent Office determines validity, where this is likely to be an issue between the parties. A further complicating factor in the *Sepracor* case was that opposition proceedings had been commenced in the European Patent Office. There, opposition proceedings are commenced post-grant. Article 99 of the European Patent Convention allows notice of opposition to be filed within nine months of publication of the grant of the patent.

Where there are opposition proceedings underway at the European Patent Office (bearing in mind that opposition takes place post-grant at the EPO) and an application for revocation is brought before a national court, that national court is not bound to stay proceedings. The Court of Appeal so held in *Glaxo Group Ltd* v *Genentech Inc*[65] in which the defendant first brought opposition proceedings before the EPO and then initiated revocation proceedings before the Patents Court. The Court of Appeal confirmed the decision to refuse a stay. The risk of duplicate proceedings was inherent in relation to the European Patent Convention as, even if opposition failed, the national courts could still be asked to decide on validity. If the Patents Court could resolve the matter sooner than the EPO, that would be a factor for refusing a stay where the evidence indicated that the EPO would take significantly longer.

> 65 [2008] FSR 18.

Where a number of national patents for the same invention obtained through the European Patent Convention are alleged to be infringed, as in the *Sepracor* case above, there is a danger that the application of the rules in Article 22 will result in conflicting judgments even where the infringements in different Contacting States are being carried out by sister companies to a common plan. Even then, there is no place for abrogation of the rules. In Case C-539/03 *Roche Nederland BV* v *Primus*,[66] allegations were made of infringement of European patents owned by two persons domiciled in the US. The infringements were alleged to have been carried out by companies in the Roche Group in a number of countries including the Netherlands, Belgium, Germany, France, the UK, Switzerland, Austria and Sweden. The proprietors commenced proceeding in the Netherlands and the Roche Group companies not established in the Netherlands contested the jurisdiction of the court on the basis of lack of infringement and invalidity of the patents. Questions were referred to the Court of Justice for a preliminary ruling. The case concerned the Brussels Convention, Article 6(1) of which stated that a person domiciled in a Contracting State may also be sued, where he is one of a number of defendants, in the courts for the place where any one of them is domiciled. Subsequent case law required a connection between the defendants such that it was expedient to determine the actions together so as to avoid irreconcilable judgments.[67] However, the Court of Justice ruled that even if 'irreconcilable' meant 'contradictory' this did not prejudice the operation of Article 22. Although national courts ruling on infringement and validity of what was essentially the same patent could reach different conclusions, those decisions were not contradictory as such. Although the grant of European patents was in the hands of the EPO, they were subsequently subject to national laws as regards infringement and validity. Any divergence in those decisions was, therefore, the result of the application of different legal situations and could not be said to be contradictory. This meant that Article 6(1) could not apply to proceedings involving a number of companies established in different Contracting States, even if those companies were part of a group acting in an identical or similar manner in accordance with a common policy. Even if a court seised by the defendant accepted jurisdiction where there was a consolidation of patent infringement actions, there would almost certainly be at least a partial fragmentation of the

> 66 [2006] ECR I-6535.

> 67 Case 189/87 *Athanasios Kalfelis* v *Bankhaus Schröder, Münchmeyer, Hengst & Co* [1988] ECR 5565. Article 6(1) of the Brussels Regulation includes such a test.

actions as at least some would involve validity triggering the rules in Article 22 on exclusive jurisdiction.

Some criticism of the Brussels Regulation in relation to intellectual property was made by the Court of Appeal in *Research in Motion UK Ltd v Visto Corporation.*[68] The Court noted that the Regulation (as the Convention) did not specifically address the problem of parallel claims but was intended to deal with the simpler and more ordinary case of a claim for breach of contract or tort or delict. A number of complications in the context of intellectual property rights were identified by the Court of Appeal, being:

1 There is considerable scope for forum shopping as there is often a range of potential defendants ranging from the manufacturer, importer and ultimate user. Depending on the circumstances and the nature of the right, each may infringe. The rightholder may bring an action against one defendant domiciled in a country of his choosing under Article 2 and then join others domiciled elsewhere under Article 6.
2 The existence of the action for a declaration of non-infringement means that a potential defendant can commence proceedings before being sued for infringement.
3 The only courts that can rule on the validity of a registered intellectual property right are the courts in the country where the right is registered. But a range of possibilities may arise in practice in, for example, a patent infringement action. A defendant may simply say that what he is doing is outside the scope of the patent. He may say that, although he is within the scope of the patent, it is invalid in whole or to a relevant extent. Finally, he may raise the 'Gillette' defence and claim that if the scope of the patent is wide enough to cover what he does, then the patent is invalid.
4 A final complication is the existence of the 'Italian torpedo'.[69]

Finally, the potential difficulties arising from courts ruling on foreign law should not be a reason to decline jurisdiction. So the Schlosser Report stated, adding that 'where the courts of several States have jurisdiction, the claimant has deliberately been given a right of choice, which should not be weakened by application of the doctrine of *forum conveniens*'.

Forum shopping

In some cases, a potential litigant may have a number of options in deciding where to commence proceedings. It may be advantageous to bring an action in a Member State which has quick and effective protective measures such as interim injunctions and freezing injunctions and where the full trial will happen relatively quickly. On the other hand, a defendant may wish to take pre-emptive action and commence proceedings for a declaration of non-infringement, for example.

Tactical decisions are not taken into account in applying the Brussels Regulation and an argument that a particular court has been first seised by a party to a dispute to deliberately slow things down is unlikely to have any impact: for example, in Case C-116/02 *Eric Gasser GmbH v MISAT Srl*,[70] in which the defendant, an Italian company, commenced proceedings in Italy before the claimant, an Austrian company, began proceedings in Austria. The Court of Justice confirmed that Article 27[71] cannot be derogated from where, in general, the duration of proceedings before the courts of the Member State in which the court first seised is shown to be excessively long. This is because there is no provision for such a situation and the Convention (now Regulation) is based on a mutual trust as regards each Member State's legal systems and judicial institutions.

To give an example of forum shopping, consider a Scottish company which is the proprietor of a Spanish patent and the following scenario.

68 [2008] FSR 20.

69 There is also a Belgian torpedo. As the legal systems are very slow in these countries, this can have the effect of tying up litigation for a considerable time. However, it seems that both countries have made improvements in this respect.

70 [2003] ECR I-14693.

71 Actually Article 21 of the Brussels Convention, equivalent to Article 27 of the Brussels Regulation.

1   The patent is infringed in Spain by a Spanish company. The Scottish company can sue in Spain on the basis of Article 2 (basic rule – defendants play at home). This was so before the Brussels Convention or Regulation.[72]

2   The patent is infringed in Spain by a French company. The Scottish company can sue in France on the basis of Article 2 or Spain on the basis of Article 5 (the place where the tort occurred).

3   The patent is infringed in Spain by a French company and an English company, as joint tortfeasors. The Scottish company can sue in either France or England by virtue of Article 2 and Article 6(1) (the defendant is one of a number of defendants who can be sued in the courts for the place where any one is domiciled where actions are related).[73]

4   As 3 above, but the defendants claim that the patent is invalid. The Scottish company may only sue in Spain on the basis of Article 22(4) and Article 25 (exclusive jurisdiction where the case is principally concerned with validity).

In the third example, the claimant has a choice. He can go 'forum shopping' and choose the country which suits him best. It is likely that factors such as the availability of interim relief, cost, time to come to trial and interpretation of the scope of infringement will strongly influence him. If he selects England or France in which to commence legal action, the courts there may not be keen to apply foreign law, even though there is some common origin in the European Patent Convention but that is the effect of the Brussels Convention. Of course, from a defendant's point of view, he could counterclaim for revocation of the patent on the grounds of invalidity, thus taking away the claimant's choice, leaving the country in which the patent has been granted as the only forum. Of course, in the above example, it would be rare for the validity of the patent not to be challenged, even indirectly and whether at the outset or later in the proceedings. Indeed, it has been said that one cannot infringe an invalid patent and issues of infringement and validity are almost always entangled.

Where there are several discrete issues before a court where validity is raised, it may be possible to sever the issues and try some of them. However, as Laddie J pointed out in *Coin Controls*, infringement and validity are so interwoven that they should be tried together in the same court. It would be undesirable to split the issues of infringement and validity, and to do so could only result in a proliferation of court actions.

The prospect that courts in England and other parts of the UK could be forced to hear proceedings involving foreign patents is not something judges are likely to view with relish, with the exception of Jacob J who seemed to enjoy the opportunity immensely in deciding whether a licence for a US patent extended to particular acts alleged to fall within the claims, applying US patent law on file wrapper estoppel.[74] In *Plastus Kreativ AB v Minnesota Mining and Manufacturing Co*,[75] Aldous J expressed his concern at the prospect, especially as a decision could affect the prices the public have to pay for a product in another country. For example, if an English court decided that a German company was infringing a German patent belonging to the English company, that could drive up prices in Germany for the product. Aldous J suggested such decisions would carry the respect of the public better if tried in the local courts.

Nor was Laddie J happy with the impact of the Brussels Convention on intellectual property disputes. Registered and unregistered rights may be subject to different regimes. This could be particularly so in relation to passing off and registered trade marks. Actions for these two rights often go hand in hand. An English court could hear an action for passing off by an activity taking place in Germany which also results in a challenge to the validity of a German trade mark, meaning that the trade mark issue must be heard in Germany. Laddie J gives a wonderful example of the potential for complexity and confusion in *Coin Controls*. He stated (at 678):

72 As a result of Article 2 of the Paris Convention for the Protection of Industrial Property 1883.

73 As there is only one patent which is only being infringed in one State, Case C-539/03 *Roche Nederland BV* v *Primus* [2006] ECR I-6535 does not apply to negate the application of Article 6(1).

74 *Celltech Chiroscience Ltd* v *MedImmune Inc* [2003] FSR 25. The validity of the patent was not put in issue. The Court of Appeal dismissed the claimant's appeal but allowed the defendant's cross-appeal in part in allowed *Celltech Chiroscience Ltd* v *MedImmune Inc* [2004] FSR 3.

75 [1995] RPC 438.

. . . an English company might be sued in England for unfair competition in Holland or Germany by alleged use of an unregistered trade name. The court here will not only have to decide questions of Dutch and German law but also factual issues relating to the pronunciation and meaning of similar words spoken in Dutch or German . . . Similarly, the fact that what are likely to be essentially the same issues of patent validity may have to be litigated in a number of countries simultaneously is unlikely to impress the user of the EPC system, but this appears to be an inevitable consequence of Article 16(4) of the Convention [Article 22(4) of the Brussels Regulation].

Forum non conveniens

Where there is a choice of countries in whose courts a legal action may be commenced, each of which have jurisdiction, the courts of one country may decline to hear the action on the basis that the courts of another country are more suitable to hear the case. There may be a number of factors to take into account such as the applicable law, the location of the evidence and witnesses, the nationality of the would-be litigants and the enforceability of judgments and awards.

The high point of the doctrine in the UK was the case of *Spiliada Maritime Corporation v Cansulex Ltd,*[76] in which Lord Goff laid down guidelines applicable to a decision whether an English court should accept jurisdiction in a particular case or stay proceedings as follows, in summary form.

1 A stay will be granted only if the court is satisfied that there is another court available having a competent jurisdiction which is appropriate for the trial because the case may be tried there more suitably for the interests of the parties and the ends of justice.

2 The burden of proof rests with the defendant to persuade the court to exercise its discretion to stay in the defendant's favour.

3 The defendant must show that not only is England not the natural or appropriate forum but that there is another forum that is clearly or distinctly more appropriate. In any case, if the connection with the English forum is a fragile one (for example, if he is served with proceedings during a short visit to England), it will be easier for him to show that another clearly more appropriate forum exists overseas.

4 Factors which point to another forum must be considered by the court such as convenience, expense, availability of witnesses, governing law and the places of residence or business of the parties.

5 A stay will almost certainly be refused if the court decides that no such other clearly appropriate forum exists.

6 If the court decides that there is, prima facie, a more appropriate forum, it will normally grant a stay but the claimant, who now bears the evidential burden, may be able to show that circumstances additional to those in 4 above exist such that a stay should be refused. For example, the claimant may be able to show that he will not be able to obtain justice in a foreign court.

However, the Brussels Regulation makes no mention of *forum non conveniens* and makes no exceptions for it. Whilst it may be reasonable to assume that the doctrine has no place where the parties and cause of action all are within Member States of the Brussels Regulation, the position was not clear where there was a foreign element which was outside the Member States. It might have been thought the doctrine could still apply in such cases. This has proven not to be so, except as between parts of the United Kingdom, for example, as between England and Scotland.[77]

In Case C-281/02 *Owusu* v *Jackson,*[78] the claimant lived in England and was on holiday in Jamaica at a villa at Mammee Bay which was owned by the first defendant, Mr Jackson,

76 [1987] AC 460.

77 *Ivax Pharmaceuticals UK Ltd* v *Akzo Nobel BV* [2006] FSR 43 and *Vetco Gray UK Ltd* v *FMC Technologies Inc* [2007] EWHC 540 (Pat).

78 [2005] ECR I-1383.

who was domiciled in England. Mr Owusu walked into the sea up to his waist and then dived in. He struck his head on a submerged sandbank and was rendered tetraplegic. Two years earlier another English holidaymaker suffered a similar accident and was also rendered tetraplegic.

Mr Owusu commenced proceedings in England against Mr Jackson for breach of contract and the other defendants, Jamaican companies involved in one way or another with the beach at Mammee Bay, for the tort of negligence. The claim against Mr Jackson was based on an implied term to the effect that the beach would be reasonably safe and free from hidden dangers. The tort claims were based on a contention that the other defendants failed to warn swimmers of the hazard of the submerged sandbank and that they failed to heed the earlier accident.

At first instance, the judge held that the United Kingdom was the State which was the appropriate forum. An appeal to the Court of Appeal resulted in questions being referred to the Court of Justice for a preliminary ruling under Article 234 of the EC Treaty. The essential point was whether Article 2 of the Brussels Convention (now Article 2 of the Brussels Regulation) was mandatory or whether it was subject to the *forum non conveniens* rule in cases where there was a connection between a Contracting State and a non-Contracting State (in this case Jamaica).

The Court of Justice noted that one of the main purposes of the Convention was to bring about certainty and predictability so that persons who were likely to be sued could predict in which State they might be sued. Article 2 clearly has an international flavour and determines jurisdiction (subject to other provisions of the Convention) where relationships between different Contracting States are involved. However, it still applies where the issue is international involving a Contracting State and a non-Contracting State. This does not displace the general rule in Article 2. The rules of jurisdiction in the Convention are not intended to apply only to situations where there is a real and significant link with the working of the internal market.

It was argued that the Convention cannot impose obligations on States which have not agreed to be bound by it. The Court of Justice countered this by saying that designating a Contracting State, in which a defendant has a domicile, even where the proceedings are at least partly connected with a non-Contracting State, is not such as to impose an obligation on that latter State. Consequently, the Court of Justice held that Article 2 applies to circumstances involving relationships between the courts of a single Contracting State and those of a non-Contracting State.

Article 2 is mandatory in nature and there can be no derogation from it except as laid down in the Convention itself. Therefore, national rules such as the doctrine of *forum non conveniens* provide no exception. The principle of legal certainty would be undermined otherwise, as would the legal protection of persons domiciled within the European Community. The fact that there may be practical difficulties, such as logistical difficulties, enforceability of a default judgment in Jamaica and cross-claims against other defendants, was of no consequence and could not affect the mandatory nature of Article 2 of the Convention.

In respect of the UK it could now be said that the doctrine of *forum non conveniens* can apply only to a case outside the scope of the Brussels Regulation.[79] However, the scope of the *Owusu* ruling is not beyond doubt and, in *Antec International Ltd v Biosafety USA Inc*,[80] Gloster J noted that the Court of Justice did not look at the position where the parties had agreed a choice of jurisdiction under Article 23.[81]

Where the claimant is based in the UK and the defendant is based in the US and the contract (the place for the performance of which is in the US) is subject to English law, it would seem that the Brussels Regulation has no effect in the absence of a choice of jurisdiction clause. In *Sawyer v Atari Interactive Inc*,[82] Collins J[83] held that the claimant, a Scot, had established that England was the most appropriate forum to hear the case. A significant factor was that the contract was subject to English law.[84]

79 Specific exceptions are mentioned in Article 1 of the Regulation and include arbitration. Also, the Civil Jurisdiction and Judgments Act 1982, s 49, as amended, allows a court to apply *forum non conveniens*, providing it is not inconsistent with the Brussels Regulation or Lugano Convention. Furthermore, it has been accepted that the doctrine still applies as between countries in the UK, such as between England and Scotland.

80 [2006] EWHC 47 (Comm).

81 Even though the choice was for a non-exclusive jurisdiction.

82 [2005] EWHC 2351 (Ch).

83 Himself an editor of *Dicey and Morris on Conflict of Laws*.

84 The defendant's arguments included a submission that the claimant, being a Scot, had no connection with England as a forum apart from the choice of law clause.

Applicable law

Determining which system of law should apply in a particular situation is not usually difficult. Where two English persons make a contract in England, it can safely be assumed that, in the absence of any express mention of the question of applicable law, the law governing the contract will be English law. Where a UK copyright is infringed, the law will be that under the Copyright, Designs and Patents Act 1988. If a UK patent is infringed, the law governing the infringement will be that under the UK Patents Act 1977 even if the UK patent was obtained through the European Patent Convention.

In one major respect, contract law is different in that the parties to a contract can decide what law should apply to the contract. This has long been the case in the UK and would seem to be an eminently sensible way of proceeding in a business or commercial relationship. Where contracts were silent as to the applicable law, the English and other common law courts applied presumptions such as the law was that of the country where the contract was made or which had the closest connection to the contract, where the parties were domiciled in different countries.[85] More flexibility was introduced in these rules of thumb in *Brinkibon Ltd v Stahag Stahl und Stahlwarenhands-gesellschaft mbH*.[86]

The 1980 Rome Convention on the law applicable to contractual obligations[87] made the situation more consistent where a contract was involved. It retained the basic rule that the parties should be free to choose the law applying to a contract under Article 3.[88] It does not matter if the basic subject matter of the contract is an intellectual property right and, for example, it is possible, and not uncommon, to have a patent licence agreement subject to the law of a country other than that in which the patent is registered. Lack of a choice of law clause in any significant licence agreement for the exploitation of intellectual property rights would be rare and somewhat careless. It is bad enough if there is a dispute under the agreement without adding a further dimension to the dispute.

In cases where there is no choice of law clause, the Rome Convention provides some rules for determining which law applies. Under Article 4, the contract shall be governed by the law of the country with which it is most closely connected.[89] The Convention appreciates that a separable part of the contract may be more closely connected to another country and that, consequently though exceptionally, part of the contract may be governed by the law of one country whilst another part is governed by the law of another country.

A contract may be subject to legal controls over exclusion clauses, anti-competitive measures or consumer protection laws. In some cases, these cannot be overcome or side-stepped by a choice of law clause. The fact that a patent licence between an English company and a Swiss company, containing terms in breach of Article 81(1) of the EC Treaty, is expressed as being subject to the laws of Florida will not escape the application of Article 81(1) provided it affects trade between Member States and has, as its object or effect, the prevention, restriction or distortion of competition within the European Community.

With respect to Community-wide rights, the applicable law is as set out in the appropriate Regulation except where Member States are to apply their own laws. For example, in relation to the Community trade mark, the law relating to provisions on registrability, infringement, revocation and invalidity is set out in the Regulation and must be applied, in accordance with any case law of the Court of Justice interpreting those provisions. The rules on dealing with a Community trade mark and transfer fall to be determined under the law of the Member State in which the proprietor is domiciled or has his establishment.[90]

Some modification of the rules on applicable law was made by Regulation (EC) No 864/2007 of the European Parliament and of the Council of 11 July 2007 on the law

85 *Entores Ltd* v *Miles Far East Corporation* [1955] 2 QB 327.

86 [1983] 2 AC 34.

87 OJ C 27, 26.01.1998, p 34 (consolidated version); brought into UK law by the Contracts (Applicable Law) Act 1990.

88 Subject to requirements for formalities and to subsequent variation by the parties. Also some 'mandatory provisions' cannot be compromised, such as consumer rights in the EU.

89 This will usually be based on the domicile of the party responsible for the characteristic performance of the contract: for example, in a sale of goods contract, the place the seller is established.

90 If the proprietor is not domiciled nor has an establishment in any Member State, the rules are those of the Member State in which the Office for the Harmonisation of the Internal Market (Trade Marks and Designs) is situated, presently Spain.

applicable to non-contractual obligations (Rome II).[91] Article 8 of the regulation states that the law applicable to a non-contractual obligation arising from an infringement of an intellectual property right shall be the law of the country for which protection is claimed. In the case of a unitary Community intellectual property right, in a case where the applicable law is not governed by the relevant Community instrument, the applicable law shall be that of the country in which the act of infringement was committed. There can be no derogation from these rules by virtue of a choice of law agreement. Rome II clarifies that the court having jurisdiction under Regulation 44/2001 may apply the laws of other countries in appropriate cases. For example, if Luigi, based in Italy, is distributing products in Italy, France and Germany which infringe patents which protect the product in those countries, the proprietor may sue Luigi in Italy under Article 2 of the jurisdiction Regulation. The Italian court may then apply Italian, French and German patent law to the infringements occurring in those countries, provided, of course, that there is no challenge to the validity of the patents.

91 OJ L 199, 31.07.2007, p 40. The Regulation does not apply to Denmark.

Summary

In Europe, jurisdiction over civil and commercial matters is determined under the provisions of the 'Brussels Regulation' (with the exception of Denmark for which the Convention still applies).

The basic rule under the Regulation is that defendants should be sued in the Member State where they are domiciled. To this there are some important exceptions, including:

- In the case of a tort (infringement of an intellectual property right is a tort), a defendant could instead be sued in the Member State where the harmful event occurred or is threatened.
- Where there are co-defendants domiciled in different Member States inexorably involved in the same alleged wrong, the action could be brought in any of those Member States.
- Where the action involves the registration or validity of a formal right such as a patent, the action must be brought in the Member State where it is registered.

In some cases, a litigant may have a choice of Member States in which to commence the action. Any court other than the one first seised must decline jurisdiction.

There is no place for the principle of *forum non conveniens* in cases where the Brussels Regulation applies.

Discussion questions

1 Discuss the jurisdictional issues in relation to the alleged infringement of a foreign copyright in the UK. Would it make any difference if the copyright was a copyright from an EU Member State or a State outside the EU?

2 Parallel patents are held in a number of Member States and are alleged to have been infringed in each and validity is going to be challenged by the defendant(s); there is no option but to bring separate actions in each of those Member States. Discuss this unsatisfactory state of affairs and how it can be or should be remedied.

Selected further reading

Hartley, T.C., 'The European Union and the systematic dismantling of the common law of conflict of laws' (2005) 54(4) *International and Comparative Law Quarterly* 813 (discusses how private international law has developed along civil law rather than common law principles and the erosion of *forum non conveniens*).

Jandolini, V., 'Cross-border litigation again? This time the legislator intervenes', [2009] *European Intellectual Property Review*, 236 (discusses jurisdiction, the *Roche* v *Primus* ECJ case and the implications of Rome II).

Lucasfilm Ltd v *Ainsworth*, Supreme Court, 27 July 2011, particularly paragraphs 51 to 115 of the joint judgment of Lords Walker and Collins: available from: **http://www.bailii.org/uk/cases/UKSC/2011/39.html**

Torremans, P., 'The sense or nonsense of subject-matter jurisdiction over foreign copyright' [2011] *European Intellectual Property Review*, 349 (takes a critical look at the Court of Appeal decision in *Lucasfilm* v *Ainsworth* – now overtaken, of course, by the Supreme Court decision – but the article is still good reading).

Appendix 1
Trade mark classification for goods and services

Note: the classification below is based on the class headings from the Ninth Edition of the International Classification of Goods and Services (made under the Nice Agreement concerning the International Classification of Goods and Services for the purposes of the Registration of Marks of 15 June 1957). This current edition dates from 1 January 2007. The Tenth Edition will enter into force on 1 January 2012. Further detail can be obtained from the UK Intellectual Property Office and the World Intellectual Property Office.

Classification for goods (34 classes)

1 Chemicals used in industry, science and photography, as well as in agriculture, horticulture and forestry; unprocessed artificial resins, unprocessed plastics; manures; fire extinguishing compositions; tempering and soldering preparations; chemical substances for preserving foodstuffs; tanning substances; adhesives used in industry.

2 Paints, varnishes, lacquers; preservatives against rust and against deterioration of wood; colourants; mordants; raw natural resins; metals in foil and powder form for painters, decorators, printers and artists.

3 Bleaching preparations and other substances for laundry use; cleaning, polishing, scouring and abrasive preparations; soaps; perfumery, essential oils, cosmetics, hair lotions; dentifrices.

4 Industrial oils and greases; lubricants; dust absorbing, wetting and binding compositions; fuels and illuminants; candles and wicks for lighting.

5 Pharmaceutical and veterinary preparations; sanitary preparations for medical purposes; dietetic substances adapted for medical use, food for babies; plasters, materials for dressings; material for stopping teeth, dental wax; disinfectants; preparations for destroying vermin; fungicides, herbicides.

6 Common metals and their alloys; metal building materials; transportable buildings of metal; materials of metal for railway tracks; non-electric cables and wires of common metal; ironmongery, small items of metal hardware; pipes and tubes of metal; safes; goods of common metal not included in other classes; ores.

7 Machines and machine tools; motors (except for land vehicles); machine coupling and transmission components (except for land vehicles); agricultural implements other than hand-operated; incubators for eggs.

8 Hand tools and implements (hand operated); cutlery; side arms; razors.

9 Scientific, nautical, surveying, photographic, cinematographic, optical, weighing, measuring, signalling, checking (supervision), life-saving and teaching apparatus and instruments; apparatus and instruments for conducting, switching, transforming, accumulating, regulating or controlling electricity; apparatus for recording, transmission or reproduction of sound or images; magnetic data carriers, recording discs; automatic vending machines and mechanisms for coin-operated apparatus; cash registers, calculating machines, data processing equipment and computers; fire-extinguishing apparatus.

10 Surgical, medical, dental and veterinary apparatus and instruments, artificial limbs, eyes and teeth; orthopaedic articles; suture materials.

11 Apparatus for lighting, heating, steam generating, cooking, refrigerating, drying, ventilating, water supply and sanitary purposes.

12 Vehicles; apparatus for locomotion by land, air or water.

13 Firearms; ammunition and projectiles; explosives; fireworks.

14 Precious metals and their alloys and goods in precious metals or coated therewith, not included in other classes; jewellery, precious stones; horological and chronometric instruments.

15 Musical instruments.

16 Paper, cardboard and goods made from these materials, not included in other classes; printed matter; bookbinding material; photographs; stationery; adhesives for stationery or household purposes; artists' materials; paint brushes; typewriters and

office requisites (except furniture); instructional and teaching material (except apparatus); plastic materials for packaging (not included in other classes); printers' type; printing blocks.

17 Rubber, gutta-percha, gum, asbestos, mica and goods made from these materials and not included in other classes; plastics in extruded form for use in manufacture; packing, stopping and insulating materials; flexible pipes, not of metal.

18 Leather and imitations of leather, and goods made of these materials and not included in other classes; animal skins, hides; trunks and travelling bags; umbrellas, parasols and walking sticks; whips, harness and saddlery.

19 Building materials (non-metallic); non-metallic rigid pipes for building; asphalt, pitch and bitumen; non-metallic transportable buildings; monuments, not of metal.

20 Furniture, mirrors, picture frames; goods (not included in other classes) of wood, cork, reed, cane, wicker, horn, bone, ivory, whalebone, shell, amber, mother-of-pearl, meerschaum and substitutes for all these materials, or of plastics.

21 Household or kitchen utensils and containers; combs and sponges; brushes (except paint brushes); brush-making materials; articles for cleaning purposes; steelwool; unworked or semi-worked glass (except glass used in building); glassware, porcelain and earthenware not included in other classes.

22 Ropes, string, nets, tents, awnings, tarpaulins, sails, sacks and bags (not included in other classes); padding and stuffing materials (except of rubber or plastics); raw fibrous textile materials.

23 Yarns and threads, for textile use.

24 Textiles and textile goods, not included in other classes; bed and table covers.

25 Clothing, footwear, headgear.

26 Lace and embroidery, ribbons and braid; buttons, hooks and eyes, pins and needles; artificial flowers.

27 Carpets, rugs, mats and matting, linoleum and other materials for covering existing floors; wall hangings (non-textile).

28 Games and playthings; gymnastic and sporting articles not included in other classes; decorations for Christmas trees.

29 Meat, fish, poultry and game; meat extracts; preserved, frozen, dried and cooked fruits and vegetables; jellies, jams, compotes; eggs, milk and milk products; edible oils and fats.

30 Coffee, tea, cocoa, sugar, rice, tapioca, sago, artificial coffee; flour and preparations made from cereals, bread, pastry and confectionery, ices; honey, treacle; yeast, baking-powder; salt, mustard; vinegar, sauces (condiments); spices; ice.

31 Agricultural, horticultural and forestry products and grains not included in other classes; live animals; fresh fruits and vegetables; seeds, natural plants and flowers; foodstuffs for animals; malt.

32 Beers; mineral and aerated waters and other non-alcoholic drinks; fruit drinks and fruit juices; syrups and other preparations for making beverages.

33 Alcoholic beverages (except beers).

34 Tobacco; smokers' articles; matches.

Classification for services (11 classes)

35 Advertising, business management; business administration; office functions.

36 Insurance; financial affairs; monetary affairs; real estate affairs.

37 Building construction; repair; installation services.

38 Telecommunications.

39 Transport; packaging and storage of goods; travel arrangement.

40 Treatment of materials.

41 Education; providing of training; entertainment; sporting and cultural activities.

42 Scientific and technological services and research and design relating thereto; industrial analysis and research services; design and development of computer hardware and software.

43 Services for providing food and drink; temporary accommodation.

44 Medical services; veterinary services; hygienic and beauty care for human beings or animals; agriculture, horticulture and forestry services.

45 Legal services; security services for the protection of property and individuals; personal and social services rendered by others to meet the needs of individuals.

Appendix 2
Useful websites and links

Links to these and many other websites, including those listed in the chapter summaries are available on the companion website to the book.

UK and EU law reports, judgments and legislation

BAILII
http://www.bailii.org
Masses of judgments (full text) and legislation and world law resources and much more. Includes Irish cases, cases at the Court of Justice and General Court of the EU and the European Human Rights Court. Probably the most useful free resource for case law.

UK Legislation
http://www.legislation.gov.uk/
UK Legislation, managed by the National Archives. Access from here to Acts of Parliament, Statutory Instruments and draft Statutory Instruments.

Supreme Court judgments, etc.
http://www.supremecourt.gov.uk/
The Supreme Court website – full text of judgments appear within hours. Current cases, information about the court and procedures. Live televised sittings. All judgments from the first (29 October 2009). Links including biographies of the Justices. Previous House of Lords judgments can be found on the BAILII website (above).

CURIA
http://curia.europa.eu/jcms/jcms/j_6
CURIA – European Court of Justice site with case law of Court of Justice and Court of First Instance and other information and links. This link is to the English version but many other languages are available. Use case number to search – e.g. C-324/09 to retrieve *L'Oréal* v *eBay*.

EUR-LEX
http://eur-lex.europa.eu/en/index.htm
EUR-LEX – EC legislation and cases before the European Court of Justice and General Court of the EU together with the full text of Directives, Treaties and Regulations including legislation in preparation. Most useful search is by document number and year. For example to retrieve the trade marks Directive (latest codified version) which is numbered 2008/95/EC check the box for Directives and enter the year 2008 and number 95. Site also contains the Official Journal of the European Union. Very useful directory of legislation in force. Go to '17 Law relating to undertakings' and then to '17.20 Intellectual Property law'.

Intellectual property offices

UK Intellectual Property Office
http://www.ipo.gov.uk
The UK Intellectual Property Office (the operating name of the UK Patent Office) home page. Lots of useful information about intellectual property including descriptions of rights, the work of the Office and news releases and links to numerous other intellectual property related sites. Full text of cases before the Comptroller-General of Patents, Designs and Trade Marks and before the Appointed Person (Trade Marks) and much intellectual property legislation. Databases of patents, registered designs and trade marks.

European Patent Office
http://www.epo.org
European Patent Office home page with much useful information and full text of cases before the Boards of Appeal and Enlarged Board of Appeal, text of the European Patent Convention, many links to other sites including national patent offices, patent databases, etc. Subscribe to a fortnightly electronic newsletter.

Office for the Harmonisation of the Internal Market (Trade Marks and Designs)
http://oami.europa.eu/ows/rw/pages/index.en.do
General information plus decisions of the Divisions and Boards of Appeal, databases of Community Trade

Marks and Designs. Case law on trade marks and designs before the Office, ECJ case law on trade marks and designs, legal texts and decisions of the Member States' CTM courts.

World intellectual property organisation

http://wipo.org

World Intellectual Property Organisation – text of treaties including Berne, Paris, Madrid and classification systems, such as Nice and Locarno, list of Convention countries and general information. Domain name resolution decisions. Sign up for e-newsletters including the WIPO Magazine (published six times each year). There is a useful collection of laws for electronic access including main IP legislation in a great many countries. For example, the US, Malaysian and Australian Copyright Acts are available. Some foreign legislation is available translated into English, for example, the French and German Copyright Acts. Caution may be needed, as some legislation may not be fully up to date.

Reports and miscellaneous

Copyright Licensing Agency
http://www.cla.co.uk
Useful information about the organisation, licensing, news releases, copyright on the internet, links to other organisations, etc.

Gowers Review of Intellectual Property
http://www.official-documents.gov.uk/document/other/0118404830/0118404830.pdf
Critical examination of intellectual property with proposals for change.

Hargreaves Report
http://www.ipo.gov.uk/ipreview-finalreport.pdf
Subsequent to Gowers, re-iterates some of Gowers' recommendations with new suggested changes.

HM Courts and Tribunals Service
http://www.courtservice.gov.uk
Information about the courts and tribunals, etc.

ICANN
http://www.icann.org/udrp/udrp.htm
ICANN Uniform Domain Name Dispute Resolution Policy, including summaries of cases.

United States websites

US Supreme Court
http://www.supremecourtus.gov

US Patents and Trademark Office
http://www.uspto.gov
Includes access to US legislation on patents and trade marks.

Cornell Law School Legal Information Institute.
http://www.law.cornell.edu/
Impressive databases and links. US laws and cases (including full text Supreme Court from 1990) and comprehensive world law materials (even including Magna Carta).

Note: Websites and addresses may be subject to change and the information available from them and the links to other sites may change from time to time. In some cases you will need an Acrobat Reader from Adobe Systems Inc to access or download larger files. It is possible to obtain a free copy via the internet from some of the websites listed above: otherwise your IT department will be able to help or provide you with a copy. Acrobat is a registered trade mark.

The amount of useful information now available on the internet is impressive and it is growing at a phenomenal rate.

The vast majority of the information available from the above websites may be accessed and viewed free of charge. However, this is not always so. Please ensure that you abide by the terms or conditions of use. Some allow printing or downloading for your own personal use only.

Bibliography

Books

Akdeniz, Y., Walker, C., Wall, D. and Wall, D.S. (2001) *The Internet, Law and Society*, Longman.

Bainbridge, D.I. (2005) *Data Protection Law* (2nd edn) xpl publishing.

Bainbridge, D.I. (2008) *Introduction to Information Technology Law* (6th edn), Longman.

Bentham, J. *Manual of Political Economy*, reprinted in Stark, W. (ed.) (1952) *Jeremy Bentham's Economic Writings* Vol. 1, Allen & Unwin.

Bowker, R.R. (1912) *Copyright: Its History and its Law*, Houghton Mifflin.

Caplan, D. and Stewart, G. (1966) *British Trade Marks and Symbols*, Peter Owen.

Coleman, A. (1992) *The Legal Protection of Trade Secrets*, Sweet & Maxwell.

Collier, J.G. (2001) *Conflict of Laws* (3rd edn), Cambridge University Press.

Collins, L., *et al.* (2010) *Dicey and Morris on the Conflict of Laws* (14th edn), Sweet & Maxwell.

Davenport, N. (1979) *The United Kingdom Patent System: A Brief History*, Mason.

Dickens, C. *A Poor Man's Tale of a Patent*, reprinted in Phillips, J. (1984) *Charles Dickens and the 'Poor Man's Tale of a Patent'*, ESC Publishing.

Dutton, H.I. (1984) *The Patent System and Inventive Activity during the Industrial Revolution, 1750–1852*, Manchester University Press.

Drone, E.S. (1879) *A Treatise on the Law of Property in Intellectual Productions in Great Britain and the United States*, Little, Brown & Co.

Edwards, L. and Waelde, C. (2000) *Law and the Internet: a Framework for Electronic Commerce*, Hart Publishing.

Eisenschitz, T.S. (1987) *Patents, Trade Marks and Designs in Information Work*, Croom Helm.

Gallafent, R.J., Eastaway, N.A. and Dauppe, V.A.F. (2003) *Intellectual Property Law and Taxation* (6th edn) Sweet & Maxwell.

Gringras, C. (1997) *The Laws of the Internet*, Butterworths.

Groves, P. (1997) *Sourcebook on Intellectual Property Law*, Cavendish Publishing.

Hutchinson, P. (undated) *Peggy Hutchinson's Home Made Wine Secrets*, Foulsham & Co.

Jacob, R., Kitchin, D., Mellor, J. and Meade, R. (2000) *Kerly's Law of Trade Marks and Trade Names* (13th edn), Sweet & Maxwell.

Kitchin, D., Llewelyn, D., Mellor, J., Meade, R., Moody-Stuart, T., Keeling, D. and Jacob, R. (2005) *Kerly's Law of Trade Marks and Trade Names* (14th edn), Sweet & Maxwell.

Laddie, H., Prescott, P. and Vitoria, M. (1980) *The Modern Law of Copyright*, Butterworths.

Laddie, H., Prescott, P. and Vitoria, M. (1995) *The Modern Law of Copyright* (2nd edn), Butterworths.

Lehmann, M. and Tapper, C.F. (eds) (1993) *A Handbook of European Software Law*, Clarendon Press.

Merkin, R. (1989) *Copyright, Designs and Patents: The New Law*, Longman.

Pearson, H. and Miller, C.G. (1990) *Commercial Exploitation of Intellectual Property*, Blackstone Press.

Penner, J.E. (1997) *The Idea of Property in Law*, Oxford University Press.

Prime, T. (1992) *The Law of Copyright*, Format.

Reid, B.C. (1986) *Confidentiality and the Law*, Waterlow.

Reid, B.C. (1998) *A Practical Guide to Patent Law* (3rd edn), Sweet & Maxwell.

Schmookler, J. (1986) *Invention and Economic Growth*, Harvard University Press.

Tapper, C. (1989) *Computer Law* (4th edn), Longman.

Thorley, S., Miller, R., Burkill, G. and Birss, C. (2005) *Terrell on the Law of Patents* (16th edn), Sweet & Maxwell.

Whish, R. (2008) *Competition Law* (6th edn), Oxford University Press.

Reports

Anton Piller Orders: A Consultation Paper, Lord Chancellor's Department, November 1992.

The Banks Report, *Committee to Examine the Patent System and Patent Law*, Cmnd 4407 (HMSO, 1970).

The Calcutt Committee, *Report on Privacy and Related Matters*, Cm 1102 (HMSO, 1990).

European Patent Office, *The London Agreement: European patents and the costs of translations*, 2006, available at: http://www.epo.org/about-us/publications/general-information/london-agreement.html.

Gowers Review of Intellectual Property (HMSO, 2006), available at: http://www.hm-treasury.gov.uk/media/6/E/pbr06_gowers_report_755.pdf.

Hargreaves, I., *Digital Opportunity: a Review of Intellectual Property and Growth*, May 2011 available at: http://www.ipo.gov.uk/ipreview-finalreport.pdf

Intellectual Property and Innovation, Cmnd 9712 (HMSO, 1986).

Intellectual Property Rights and Innovation, Cmnd 9117 (HMSO, 1983).

Judiciary of England and Wales Intellectual Property Committee, *Working Group's Final Report on Proposals for the Reform of the Patents County Court*, 31 July 2009.

Law Commission, Law Com No 110, *Breach of Confidence*, Cmnd 8388 (HMSO, 1981).

OHIM, *Statistics of Community Designs 2010*, 11 January 2011, SSC007.

Patent Office, *Annual Report 2010–2011*, 2011.

Reform of the Law Relating to Copyright, Designs and Performers' Protection, Cmnd 8302 (HMSO, 1981).

Reform of Trade Mark Law, Cm 1203 (HMSO, 1990).

Taking Forward the Gowers Review of Intellectual Property: Proposed Changes to Copyright Exceptions (UK Intellectual Property Office, 2008) available at: http://www.ipo.gov.uk/consult-copyrightexceptions.pdf.

The Whitford Committee, *Copyright – Copyright and Design Law*, Cmnd 6732 (HMSO, 1977).

WIPO, *Gazette of International Marks, Statistical Supplement for 2009*, Table 2.

Journal articles

Note: the summary at the end of each chapter contains a section on further reading with recent journal articles not listed below.

Anderson, M. 'Applying traditional property laws to intellectual property transactions' [1995] 5 EIPR 237.

Angel, J. and Quinn, T. 'Database law' [1998] 14 CLSR 34.

Anon. 'Appellate Court gives green light to reverse engineering' (1991) 2 *Intellectual Property in Business Briefing* 3.

Arnold, R. 'A new remedy for copyright infringement' [1997] 12 EIPR 689.

Ashley, G. and Björk, P. 'Patenting of alloys at the European Patent Office' (1997) 2(3) *Intellectual Property* 3.

Bainbridge, D.I. 'Court of Appeal parts company with the EPO on software patents' [2007] 23 *CLSR* 119.

Benson, C. 'Fair dealing in the UK' [1995] 6 EIPR 304.

Benson, J.R. 'Copyright protection for computer screen displays' (1988) 72 *Minnesota Law Review* 1123.

Brown, B. 'The idea/expression dichotomy and the games that people play' [1995] 5 EIPR 259.

Bull, G. 'Licensing and distribution of market data' [1994] 10 CLSR 50.

Carty, H. 'Inverse passing-off: a suitable addition to passing-off?' [1993] 10 EIPR 370.

Chalton, S. 'Implementation of the software directive in the United Kingdom: the effects of the Copyright (Computer Programs) Regulations 1992' [1993] 9 CLSR 115.

Chalton, S. 'The effect of the Database Directive on UK Copyright Law in relation to databases: a comparison of features' [1997] 6 EIPR 278.

Cole, P. 'Purposive construction and inventive step' [1995] 3 EIPR 147.

Cornish, W.R. 'Authors in law' (1995) 58 MLR 1.

Davidson, D.M. 'Protecting computer software: a comprehensive analysis' (1983) 23(4) *Jurimetrics Journal* 337.

de Freitas, D. 'The Copyright, Designs and Patents Act 1988 (2)' (1989) 133 *Solicitors Journal* 670.

de Freitas, D. 'The Copyright, Designs and Patents Act 1988 (4)' (1989) 133 *Solicitors Journal* 733.

Dutson, S. 'Actions for infringement of a foreign intellectual property right in an English Court' (1997) 46 *International and Comparative Law Quarterly* 918.

Dworkin, G. 'Authorship of films and European Commission Proposals for harmonising the term of copyright' [1993] 5 EIPR 151.

FitzSimons, J. 'Powerflex *v* Data Access Corporation (Reverse Engineers Beware!)' [1998] 14 CLSR 45.

Goldblatt, M. 'Copyright protection for computer programs in Australia: the law since Autodesk' [1990] 5 EIPR 170.

Gordon, S.E. 'The very idea! Why copyright is an inappropriate way to protect computer programs' [1998] 1 EIPR 10.

Günther, A. and Wuermeling, U. 'Software protection in Germany – recent court decisions in copyright law' [1995] 11 CLSR 12.

Hails, R., Jr 'Liability of on-line service providers resulting from copyright infringement performed by their subscribers' [1996] 5 EIPR 304.

Hohfeld, W.N. 'Fundamental Legal Conceptions as Applied in Judicial Reasoning', 23 Yale Law Journal 16 (1913–1914).

Jacob, R. 'The Herchel Smith Lecture 1993' [1993] 9 EIPR 312.

Karet, I. 'Passing off and trade marks: confusing times ahead?' [1995] 1 EIPR 3.

Kinnier-Wilson, J. 'Criminal copyright offences under Sections 107 and 110 UK CDPA' [1995] 1 EIPR 46.

Lai, S. 'Database protection in the UK: the new deal and its effects on software protection' [1998] 1 EIPR 32.

Lea, G. 'Database law – solutions beyond copyright' [1993] 9 CLSR 127.

Lea, G. 'Expropriation of business necessity?' [1994] 10 EIPR 453.

Lea, G. 'Passing off and the protection of program look and feel' [1994] 10 CLSR 82.

Lewin, R. 'A New UK Trade Marks Law – a godsend for trade mark owners or a goldmine for their lawyers?' [1994] 3 EIPR 91.

MacQueen, H.L. 'A Scottish case on unregistered designs' [1994] 2 EIPR 86.

Mamiofa, I.E. 'The draft of a New Soviet Patent Law' [1990] 1 EIPR 21.

Markesinis, B.S. 'Our patchy law of privacy – time to do something about it' (1990) 53 MLR 802.

Monotti, A. 'The extent of copyright protection for compilations of artistic works' [1993] 5 EIPR 156.

Moon, K. 'The nature of computer programs: Tangible? Goods? Personal property? Intellectual property?' [2009] 8 EIPR 396.

Nissen, D. and Karet, I. 'The Trade Marks Directive: Can I prevail if the State has failed?' [1993] 3 EIPR 91.

Paterson, G.D. 'The patentability of further uses of a known product under the European Patent Convention' [1991] 1 EIPR 16.

Prescott, P. '*Kaye* v *Robertson* – a reply' (1991) 53 MLR 451.

Rawlinson, P. 'The UK Trade Marks Act 1994: It's criminal' [1995] 1 EIPR 54.

Reid, B.C. 'Biogen in the EPO: the advantage of scientific understanding' [1995] 2 EIPR 98.

Rohnke, C. 'Protection of external product features in West Germany' [1990] 2 EIPR 41.

Russell, F. 'The Elderflower Champagne case: is this a further expansion of the tort of passing off?' [1993] 10 EIPR 379.

Sherman, B. 'Patent claim interpretation: the impact of the Protocol on Interpretation' (1991) 54 MLR 499.

Stokes, S. 'Covenants for title in IP Dispositions' [1995] 5 EIPR D-138.

Taylor, W.D. 'Copyright protection for computer software after Whelan Associates *v* Jaslow Dental Laboratory' (1989) 54 *Missouri Law Review* 121.

Thurow, L.C. 'Needed: a new system of intellectual property rights' *Harvard Business Review*, September–October 1997 at 95.

Turner, B. 'A true design right: C & H Engineering *v* Klucznik & Sons' [1993] 1 EIPR 24.

Walton, A. 'The Copyright, Designs and Patents Act 1988 (1)' (1989) 133 *Solicitors Journal* 646.

Wood, N. 'The trouble with domain names' (1997) 2(3) *Intellectual Property* 7.

Miscellaneous

Alberge, D. 'MoD will claim copyright on SAS book if ban fails', *The Times*, 5 August 1995.

Conn, D. 'Cut-price court in a spin', *The Times*, 23 November 1993.

Gibb, F. 'Attack on copyright', *The Times*, 5 December 1995.

Jervis, J. 'DTI fires a shot across software pirates' bows', *Computing*, 1 August 1996.

OHIM, *Statistics of Community Designs to 31/10/2005*, 3 November 2005, SSC007, p 1.

Patent Office, *Facts and Figures for 2004–2005*, 2005.

Rahn, G. 'Japanese patent strategy', *European Patent Office Annual Report 1995* at 9.

Smit, D. van Zyl, 'The social creation of a legal reality: a study of the emergence and acceptance of the British patent system as a legal instrument for the control of new technology', unpublished PhD Thesis, University of Edinburgh, 1980.

Index